The Cultural
Encyclopedia
of Baseball
Second edition

The Cultural Encyclopedia of Baseball

Second edition

Jonathan Fraser Light

McFarland & Company, Inc., Publishers

Jefferson, North Carolina, and London

Front cover: Shea Stadium in Flashing, New York (Photodisc)

Credit is given to the following people and institutions: Merle A. Branner
page 266, 325, 334, 387, 450, 574, 666, 773, 824, 881, 896, 965, 1029,
1030; Ernie Carrasco 873 (bottom); Spencer and Betty Garrett 410; Paul
Kurzeka 505; Angela Rains Light 128, 235; Jonathan Fraser Light 87, 534;
Robert M. Light 837; Jeffrey Loebl 267, 409, 588; Michael W. Monk 769;
National Baseball Hall of Fame and Museum 6, 15, 28, 31 (and John
Guinozzo), 74, 95, 97, 111, 119, 122, 134, 141, 145, 154, 157, 159, 168 (and J.Y.
Bowman), 171, 174, 176, 193, 200, 207, 211, 219, 226, 243, 286, 302 (and
William C. Greene), 306, 338, 376, 378, 379, 389, 397, 400, 447, 461, 493,
497, 499, 509, 512, 529 (and Barry Halper Archives), 556, 568, 571, 580,
597, 605, 623, 628, 633, 638, 650 (and Robert Payne), 651, 670, 679, 707,
721, 722, 744, 771, 786, 803, 831 (and Chuck Youdris), 832, 840, 841, 856,
857, 873 (top), 882 (and Fred Roe), 890, 914, 915, 918, 925, 964, 960, 977,
987, 988, 991 (and Paul Thompson), 994, 1003, 1017, 1018, 1025, 1032;
Edwin Remsburg 422; Loyd Sigmon 33; *The Sporting News* 141, 142; Suzanne
and Craig Stavert 1036; Jay and Jonathan Winters 194, 598.

"Line Up for Yesterday," by Ogden Nash, reprinted by permission of
Curtis Brown, Ltd., and Little, Brown and Company. Copyright 1935
by Ogden Nash, renewed. Excerpts from *How to Watch a Baseball Game*,
by Fred Schwed, Jr., copyright 1957 by Fred Schwed, Jr. Copyright renewed 1985
by Harriet W. Schwed. Reprinted by permission of HarperCollins Publishers, Inc.,
and Russell & Volkening Literary Agents.

British Library cataloguing-in-publication data are available

Library of Congress Cataloguing-in-Publication Data

Light, Jonathan Fraser, 1957–
The cultural encyclopedia of baseball / Jonathan Fraser Light. — 2nd ed.
        p.   cm.
Includes bibliographical references and index.
ISBN 0-7864-2087-1 (illustrated case binding : 50# alkaline paper) ∞

1. Baseball — Encyclopedias.   2. Baseball — Social aspects — Encyclopedias.   I. Title.
    GV862.3.L54   2005   796.357'03 — dc22   2005001718

Manufactured in the United States of America

*McFarland & Company, Inc., Publishers
Box 611, Jefferson, North Carolina 28640
www.mcfarlandpub.com*

Contents

To my wife, Angela,
a teacher of extraordinary talent and dedication.

"In the life of every student, there's a vacuum waiting to be filled by a teacher
who can impart greater self-confidence, who can nurture undiscovered talents,
and who can direct untapped energies into some form of personal fulfillment."
— Dr. Anthony P. Witham.

Preface

"Knowin' all about baseball is about as profitable as bein' a good whittler."
— Indiana humorist Kin Hubbard.

"Here's a message from someone named Bob Costas from NBC, calling about your book. But I think it's one of your baseball buddies yanking my chain," said my secretary, Gayle Hentschel, in late 1997, shortly after the first edition of the *Encyclopedia* was published. Gayle doesn't own a television, and she wasn't quite sure who this Costas character was.

I just about had a heart attack knowing that I missed almost everyone's choice back then for commissioner of baseball. I returned the call and found Costas to be gracious and engaging. This was just one of the many terrific experiences I had as a result of my book's being published. Letters from Dodger broadcaster Vin Scully ("It certainly reads and feels like a winner") and former commissioner Peter Ueberroth ("Looking forward to digging into your tome"). A 15-minute radio segment for over a year. Television interviews, national radio interviews. Speeches around the country and to almost every service club in two counties, as well as annual appearances at my wife's and my sister's elementary school classes. The most probing question from these presentations came from one of my wife's first-graders: "Mr. Light, when is this going to be over?" And all I wanted was to see my name in print in something classy that had a binding on it (wish fulfilled!).

A few years later, I noticed copies of my book ("inscribed by the author") available on eBay and used bookstore sites. Former recipients cashing in on the book, or they simply didn't like it? In 2003 I had a nurse in my office taking blood for new life insurance, and she was excited to see my book on my credenza. "Did your dad write that?" she inquired. After I set her straight, she told me that she was so happy because she had bought my book at a local thrift store for a buck, and "I resold it on eBay for $30!" Think what it would have brought had it been inscribed.

Then McFarland sold out the fifth printing and said I'd better write a second edition. It's been a lot easier this time around using the Internet. Updating seasons beginning with 1997, and anything else I discovered along the way, was far less painful than anticipated, thanks to such unbelievable websites as BaseballAlmanac, Retrosheet, Baseball-Reference, BaseballArchive and BaseballLibrary.

I could live forever, however, without having to compile another index. Please take a moment, even if you really don't care, to thumb through the Index and get a feel for what an incredible chore it was to prepare. It's the only aspect of the book I didn't love working on. There's no foolproof way to prepare a comprehensive index without slogging through every line; a horrendous task, but one that had to be done.

"Thank you" to those who contributed several photographs to the book, including SABR member and photographer Merle A. Branner and former Sioux Falls Canaries general manager Jeffrey Loebl (whose father once owned a piece of the White Sox with Bill Veeck), former Padres minority owner Michael W. Monk (now floating on air after his beloved Red Sox won the World Series — he was in the Bosox owners' box for Games 1 and 2), photographer Edwin Remsberg, Jay Winters (son of entertainer Jonathan Winters), former minor league pitcher Ernie Carrasco, and long-time friends Suzanne and Craig Stavert. A very special thanks to SABR member and then–UC Berkeley freshman Stuart Schimler for volunteering to help update the entire 1997 season, and to SABR member Jerry Winter in New York City for preparing bios for each of the newly admitted Hall of Famers. Both men undertook time-consuming tasks that helped enormously. William C. "Bill" Burdick at the Hall of Fame identified new and interesting photos and coordinated their delivery, and Hall researcher Gabriel Schechter helped with last-minute factual research. Thanks to Doug Lyons, co-author of *Out of Left Field*, for forwarding every baseball tidbit from the wire services for five years; to Tim Wiles at the Hall for his continued support of the project; and to my best friend, David Bordeaux, for his priceless reaction to receiving the First Edition.

1

And may we all have the enthusiasm for baseball of my young friend Eric Hallett, whom I met at UCLA's summer family camp, BruinWoods. The 10-year-old had a broken arm the first summer we met, so he couldn't participate in some of the kid-friendly activities. I found in Eric an acolyte of intense dedication. At every meal, and at every moment he could find me on the grounds, his first words were, "I'm ready for more questions." And what a coincidence to find him on our two-hour fishing venture that seated only six! He was captivated, and I was a captive. Eric had managed to memorize facts from several baseball books, and his enthusiasm never waned. I could barely keep up with the trivia, getting down to the final score of the last game of the 1908 World Series (I didn't know the answer; he knew the *attendance*). Eric was in the midst of the Angels' 2002 championship run, and for two years his family vacations were visits to a series of Major League ballparks in several states, parents Bruce and Beth cheerfully in tow. I suspect that Eric will remain a fan throughout his life, though the last time I saw him, as a wordly 12-year-old, he solemnly reported, "I've developed an interest in the Beatles."

I must also mention my daughter, Katherine, who, although perhaps not a lifelong fan, had a savant-like memory of baseball facts that burned brightly during her second-grade year, before her zeal for all things baseball waned. But what a year! Baseball cards galore, books read, criticism from her teacher for weaving all writing assignments through the national pastime, and all art projects centered on baseball. And from her my favorite response to a quiz question: "How many home runs did the top three home run hitters of all time hit, and what are their names?" I wondered if she had remembered the three, and their pre–Bonds magic numbers of 755, 714 and 660. A few moments later she said, "Aaron, Ruth, Mays — 2,129." I looked at her, puzzled at her odd response, and then it hit me. She had added them up in her head. Perhaps a math whiz was born at that moment.

Another highlight of that period was spring 2000, when I experienced a softball coach's (and dad's) dream season. My identical twin daughters formed a rather formidable battery for our 8-and-under team. Elena, throwing to her sister behind the plate, was an accurate though not terribly fast pitcher, and she helped carry our underdog White Lightning club to a near-championship. Alas, ballet charmed Elena and after an All-Star stint in 10-and-unders, she retired her glove in favor of pointe shoes (and her father is now a rabid aficionado — if one can be "rabid"— of ballet). Katherine ("Kat"), however, continues her stellar catching, fearless behind the plate and accurate of arm.

My wife Angela was disappointed to learn I was working on a second edition, as would have been my law firm partners, had I not kept it to myself for as long as possible. I'm sure they expected a share of the royalties, given the time spent between 1989 and 1997 to complete the first edition. Had she, and they, learned early of my work on a new edition, I suspect I would have been drummed out of both partnerships. I'll never forget the first time Angela saw me on the Internet looking up baseball facts after a five-year hiatus: "You're working on your book again, aren't you," she said, not so much as a question. Perhaps she was more resigned to her fate than horrified by the discovery. The only saving grace, at least from her perspective, was that we now had a computer room for such work, where everyone in the family hangs out. This area replaced the "formidable clutter" on the kitchen table described in the first edition. Alas, the remodeled room is the former baseball room that had housed my beloved 1,000 or so baseball books. Only a small fraction remain indoors (*Voices of the Game, The Celebrant* and members of the Putnam series from the 1940s among them); the rest having been banished to boxes in the garage.

And I should give some note, and perhaps a sales boost, to another classic. In September 2003 I received an e-mail from a client asking if I had written another book. After I responded in the negative, he wrote, "Then you'd better check out Barnes & Noble's website." I clicked on the link he provided, and up popped "books by Jonathan Light." And there they were, now *two* books — the *Encyclopedia,* of course, and, of all things, *The Art of Porn.* Turns out there's another Jonathan [N.M.I.] Light of Lighthouse Publications in Santa Barbara (only 45 minutes away). Oh, great, I thought. This could hurt sales. Though considering the typical male baseball fan it might actually provide a boost. And my office's IT guru offered, tongue-in-cheek, to prepare, *gratis*, a photographic PowerPoint presentation for the new book. No thanks. It's not a bad book, however, depending on one's taste.

But back to *my* book (really, I didn't write that other one), a 1997 *The Sporting News*/SABR Research Book of the Year and a Booklist *Editor's Choice.* The second edition brings the *Encyclopedia* forward from the 1997 season through the 2004 postseason, and includes hundreds of new anecdotes and quotes from the years prior to 1997 based on additional research and new sources. Not bad for something I did in my "spare" time. The last eight years with my published "tome" have been fantastic.

Jonathan Fraser Light
jlight@nchc.com / *Camarillo, California* / *Spring 2005*

"Dick, I was thinking the other day how much time we've put into this game all these years. What if we'd put that time into work, making a living. We'd probably be rich."   — Richard Hugo, in "The Anxious Fields of Play" (1977).

About the Encyclopedia

The Cultural Encyclopedia of Baseball, second edition, is organized alphabetically and is patterned after comprehensive general encyclopedias. If the reader is unable to find a topic under its logical heading, then the Index might be useful to locate an anecdote or player that does not have a separate heading. Terms are used as they would be in baseball. For example, "hitting streak" is commonly used instead of "batting streak." Anecdotes about specific players are spread throughout the book. For example, Henry Aaron merits a separate biography because he is in the Hall of Fame, but he is referred to in many other sections, including *Racism, Home Runs* and *Batting Grips*. The Index exists in order to lead the reader to all such mentions.

There are quotations and biographical sketches for all Hall of Fame players, managers, owners, umpires and front office personnel. A few Ford Frick Award and Spink Award winners also have separate biographical sketches (e.g., Red Barber and Vin Scully). Biographical sketches for commissioners and league presidents, regardless of whether they are in the Hall of Fame, are found under *Commissioners* and *American League Presidents* and *National League Presidents.*

There are entries for every club that played in the National Association, National League, American Association, Union Association, Players League, American League and Federal League. There also are entries for selected Negro League clubs, 19th century amateur clubs and minor league clubs. All 20th century National League and American League club entries have the following subheadings: **Origins, First Game, Key Owners, Nicknames, Key Seasons, Key Players, Key Managers, Ballparks, Key Broadcasters** and **Books.**

Words or phrases in bold italics indicate that there is more information on that subject under that heading elsewhere in the book. For example, in the entry on *Fathers of Baseball,* there is a reference to additional information to be found under *Origins of Baseball.*

Bold words or phrases in a sentence indicate that additional information on that topic is contained elsewhere *within that entry.* For example, in the entry on *Balls,* the reference, under the subheading **Size and Weight,** to **Lively Balls** indicates that additional information on the content of the ball is found under the subheading **Lively Balls.**

These abbreviations are used throughout the book:

AA   American Association
AL   American League
HF   Hall of Fame
NL   National League
NLC Negro League Committee (Hall of Fame)
PL   Players League
UA   Union Association
VC   Veterans Committee (Hall of Fame)

References to books at the ends of entries are only to works devoted exclusively to a particular topic. Articles in magazines or sections within books (e.g., *The Greatest Catchers of All-Time,* containing a section on Johnny Bench) are not referenced because their numbers would exceed the scope of the book. Myron Smith's baseball bibliography (a second edition is forthcoming in 2005 from McFarland) is the best source for books and magazines covering all of baseball.

The *Encyclopedia* is complete through the 2004 postseason.

"What a Labour of Love, Jonathan Light! To my knowledge no one has ever looked at 'The Cultural Side [i.e., Encyclopedia] of Baseball' before — certainly not in such depth and with such intensity. After perusing such a tome I too wish you could have met Bill. He is someone who would *truly* have appreciated your work and his appraisal with you would have led to endless hours of discussion. Thank you for your *most* worthwhile work."
— February 2002 letter to the author from Bill Veeck's widow, Mary Francis Veeck, after mutual friend Jim Loebl (a co-owner of the White Sox with Veeck in the 1970s) sent her a copy of the first edition of the *Encyclopedia.*

"Dad, your book has made you a little bit famous. But just a little bit."
— Six-year-old Elena Rose Light.

The Encyclopedia

"Have you ever tried to explain baseball, on paper, starting at the beginning? Mind you, you can explain chemistry, starting at the beginning, and chemistry is a lot more complicated. But with baseball, where do you begin?" — Fred Schwed, Jr., in *How to Watch a Baseball Game* (1957).

"**A** is for Alex
The great Alexander
More goose eggs he pitched
Than a popular gander."
— First stanza of "Line-up for Yesterday," by Ogden Nash, referring here to Grover Cleveland Alexander; each of the 26 stanzas refers to one letter of the alphabet and each leads off the corresponding alphabetical section of this *Encyclopedia*.

Henry Aaron (1934–)

Hall of Fame 1982

"I came to the Braves on business, and I intended to see that business was good as long as I could."— Aaron.

"Playing in the big leagues wasn't nearly as hard as getting there." — Aaron.

"Aaron was to my time what DiMaggio was to the era when he played."— Mickey Mantle.

"While Aaron had the numbers, he didn't have much fan appeal. He was considered hard working, humble and shy, just as Joe DiMaggio was. But while those qualities made DiMaggio a hero, they made Aaron an enigma. Aaron was often overlooked as one of the game's greats until he took off on his chase of the Bambino. Racism had something to do with it, as well as his playing in the Atlanta and Milwaukee markets."— Larry Schwartz.

"I looked for the same pitch my whole career. A breaking ball. All the time. I never worried about the fastball. They couldn't throw it past me. None of 'em."— Aaron.

Aaron is the Major League's all-time home run hitter with 755 over 23 seasons beginning in 1954.

Born in Mobile, Alabama, Henry Louis Aaron (he apparently prefers Henry to Hank) began his professional career with a Negro team called the Black Bears. He signed for $200 per month with the Indianapolis Clowns of the Negro American League, for whom he played shortstop in 1952. In his first appearance for the club, he started five double plays and was 10-for-11 in a doubleheader.

Aaron moved to the Boston Braves farm system in June 1952 for $350 per month after the Braves paid the Clowns $10,000. He was one of the first black players at Jacksonville in the South Atlantic League, where he played second base.

Aaron arrived in the Major Leagues in 1954, playing in the Milwaukee Braves outfield and batting .280 with 13 home runs and 69 RBIs before breaking his ankle in early September. He validated his Major League credentials the next season, when he hit .314 with 27 home runs and 106 RBIs. After winning the batting title in 1956, he established his home run prowess when he exploded for 44 home runs and 132 RBIs in 1957 and was voted the league's MVP.

Aaron finished with a record 20 seasons of 20 or more home runs and led the league in home runs four times, with a high of 47 in 1971. He led the league in RBIs four times and drove in more than 100 runs in a season 11 times. He led the league in batting twice on his way to a .305 career average.

He was an All-Star in each of his 23 seasons and averaged 33 home runs per year. The closest he came to winning the Triple Crown was in 1963, when his .319 average was third behind Roberto Clemente at .320 and Tommy Davis at .326.

Aaron finished the 1973 season with 40 home runs, putting him one short of Babe Ruth's all-time record. He hit ***Home Runs*** number 714 and 715 in early 1974, despite numerous death threats throughout the previous season and off-season (see also ***Racism***). Aaron had hopes of managing the Braves near the end of his career, but when the offer did not materialize he moved on to the Milwaukee Brewers. He hit another 22 home runs in 1975 and 1976, finishing with 755.

After his playing career ended, Aaron moved into the Braves front office and remained an outspoken critic of racism in Baseball. Since 1989 he has served as a senior vice president and assistant to the president, but he is more active for Turner Broadcasting as a corporate vice president of community relations and a member of the TBS board of directors. He also is vice president of business development for The Airport Network, and by 2003 Aaron owned 18 restaurants and a car dealership.

Aaron may be the most underrated ballplayer in the history of Major League Baseball. His quiet style has caused almost every significant historian to leave him off any list of all-time superstars by position, though he is the all-time leader in home runs and RBIs, second in runs scored, third in hits and had a .555 slugging average. He stole 240 bases and batted .364 in two World Series.

In April 1995 WTBS in Atlanta aired "Chasing the Dream," a chronicle of Aaron's career and his quest of Ruth's home run record. Aaron was awarded the Presidential Medal of Freedom by George

With a collage of advertising as a backdrop, Negro League star Josh Gibson of the Homestead Grays rounds third in the bottom of the 2nd inning at Griffith Stadium in Washington, as Felton Snow looks on.

W. Bush in 2002. He was among 12 recipients that year, including former South African President Nelson Mandela and Fred Rogers of "Mister Rogers' Neighborhood" fame on public television.

Books. Henry Aaron and Furman Bisher, *Aaron* (1974); Henry Aaron and Lonnie Wheeler, *I Had a Hammer* (1991); Henry Aaron with Dick Schaap, *Home Run: My Life In Pictures* (1999); Stan Baldwin and Jerry Jenkins, *Bad Henry* (1974); Al Hirshberg, *The Up-to-Date Biography of Henry Aaron: Quiet Superstar* (1974); Jerry Poling, *A Summer up North: Henry Aaron and the Legend of Eau Claire Baseball* (2002); Milton Shapiro, *The Henry Aaron Story* (1961); Tom Stanton, *Hank Aaron and the Home Run that Changed America* (2004); Sandy Tolan, *Me and Hank: A Boy and His Hero, Twenty-Five Years Later* (2000).

Actors See ***Movies*** and ***Television Shows***

Admission Prices See ***Gate Receipts*** and ***Tickets***

Advertising

"Last year, Zack Wheat caught 288 flies; Tanglefoot caught 15 billion." — Flypaper advertisement on a Major League ballpark's outfield wall in the 1920s.

"We *never* make fun of the sponsors." — Fox Sports broadcast director in *Sports Illustrated* columnist Rick Reilly's earpiece, during Reilly's cameo broadcast stint in 2003. After a La Quinta hotel promotion, Reilly said "La Quinta is Spanish for 'Next to Denny's.'"

See also ***Gambling*** — **Casino Advertising.**

Early in the history of professional baseball, *The Sporting News* criticized clubs for not advertising (probably to drum up business for itself). By the 1890s Charles Ebbets of Brooklyn was typical of owners who bought advertising space in railroad and trolley cars and put players' pictures in taverns.

Outfield Walls.
"The fence signs at the ballpark are yellow, green and red,
The fierce glare queers the hitting; the batting eye goes dead.
It seems to hurt the Giants even more than other nines,
But Cobb and old Sam Crawford — they just don't believe in signs!"
— Poem (author unknown) appearing in the 1915 *Reach Guide*.

Seibert's Suits advertised on the Ebbets Field outfield wall in the 1950s: "Hit Sign, Win Suit." 1950s National League outfielder Wally Post hit the sign 11 times to augment his wardrobe.

Tradition. Ballpark outfield walls were covered with advertising for many years, a practice still prevalent in the minor leagues.

Baker Bowl. Philadelphia's Baker Bowl housed the Phillies through the first four decades of the 20th century when the Phillies were perennial doormats. One outfield sign noted that "The Phillies Use Lifebuoy" soap, prompting a fan to scribble next to it, "and they still stink."

Fenway Park. In 1947 the advertising was removed from Fenway Park's left field wall, allowing it to be painted green and called the Green Monster.

Crosley Field. The ballpark was the last old-time Major League park to have advertising on its outfield walls when it was abandoned in mid–1970. The practice was revived in 1992 when the Orioles opened old-style Oriole Park at Camden Yards and featured an oil company sign and a bank advertisement.

Beer and Alcohol.
See ***Alcoholic Beverages*** — **Advertising.**

Cereal. In 1993 Ken Griffey, Jr., did a commercial for Kellogg's Frosted Flakes in which only his silhouette was shown.

Contract Resolution. During Vida Blue's contract dispute with A's owner Charlie Finley after the 1971 season, Blue suggested making up the difference in their negotiation by making a television commercial together. Finley's wife vetoed the idea because it was "demeaning."

Fat Chance. In 2004 Steve Garvey was absolved of wrongdoing by a federal court after he had hawked a weight loss product that supposedly allowed users to eat fatty foods and still lose weight. Garvey appeared in 48,000 infomercials between 1998 and 2000, for which he earned $1.1 million.

Lame Duck. During the 1965 season, the Milwaukee Braves were a lame duck team known to be moving to Atlanta for the following season (see also *Franchise Shifts*). The club's sponsors did not want to be associated with it anymore, so the radio station aired no commercials. Instead, the broadcasters taped 60-second interviews with the players so that they could catch their breath between innings.

Negative Publicity. In 1980 the Mets were fined $5,000 after their ad agency prepared and aired a commercial suggesting that Yankee Stadium was unsafe for fans because of the bad neighborhood surrounding it.

Commercial Sponsors. In 1992 commissioner Fay Vincent vetoed a plan by the Arizona Fall Baseball League to incorporate commercial sponsors into its name and the names of the league's six clubs. The league originally intended to call itself the Safeway Arizona Fall League.

In 1995 True Value Hardware signed a $40 million deal to become the official hardware store of Major League Baseball. The key component of the deal turned Opening Day in each ballpark into "True Value Opening Day," including logos in foul territory and near the on-deck circles.

Lawsuit. Broadcaster Chuck Thompson was on the air in October 1960 when Yankee pitcher Ralph Terry gave up the Series-winning home run to Pirates second baseman Bill Mazeroski. Thompson mistakenly identified Art Ditmar as the pitcher just as the pitch was thrown and called the score as 10–0 after the ball went over the fence (the home run made it 10–9). In 1985 Budweiser aired a commercial featuring the call, but edited it so that Terry was correctly identified. Ditmar sued, contending that the verbatim republication of the erroneous broadcast would have enhanced his publicity value. The case was dismissed.

Credit Card. In late 2002 Yankee owner George Steinbrenner criticized shortstop Derek Jeter for his off-season party lifestyle. In 2003 the two appeared together in a credit card ad for Visa in which they spend the night out on the town and participate in a conga line.

In a 2004 Olympics ad, Visa featured Yankee manager Joe Torre telling the trainer that he needed his guy's right arm back in action. The "guy" was owner George Steinbrenner, to whom Torre handed a pen to enable the Ace-bandaged Steinbrenner to sign a check. The tag line, "when you've been writing too many checks, and need a break…."

Casino Advertisers. See *Gambling*—Casino Advertisers.

Strike Season. Nike staged a unique advertising campaign during the 1994 player strike. Its ads featured actor Ryan Stiles doing a series of stunts in an empty field or heckling a lone groundskeeper. There was no voiceover, just a graphic that said "Play ball. Please."

Bases. In May 2004 Major League Baseball and Columbia Pictures announced a marketing plan to put *Spider-Man 2* logos on the center of the bases during the weekend premiere of the movie. After a huge public outcry (and the desired media attention for the movie), the plan was scrapped the next day. The deal was worth $3.6 million and 14 home clubs were to participate.

Book. Historian Harold Seymour's *Baseball: The Golden Age* (1971) contains an excellent discussion of 19th century advertising efforts.

Africa

"The sport itself is a primitive instinct: a mystery in ethnology that I do not attempt to explain. All I know is that in Zululand a couple of years ago we handed a new baseball to a young induna, or chief, and the first thing he did was to 'play catch' with it. After that, he threw as far as he could and then proceeded to soak it with his war-club. He felt the seams, hooked his fingers around it like McGinnity or Chesbro, rubbed it over his cheek, and finally offered an ingénue from his harem in exchange."— Allen Sangree in a 1905 *Saturday Evening Post* article.

"I don't care if he done it in Africa, it's still .392."— Casey Stengel after Billy Martin hit .392 at minor league Phoenix.

Hall of Fame records show that there was an Algiers Baseball League formed in 1933. The Baseball Club of Africa was formed in 1921 in Tunis. The founder was C. Guyer Kelly, who reported on the event in the Johns Hopkins University alumni magazine in November 1933. Eventually there were 16 teams affiliated with the club in the form of a league.

The first game played between North Africa and North America occurred in July 1932. Members of the Tunis League played members of the crew and tourists of the ocean liner *President Johnson*.

During World War II, American soldiers staged the first African World Series.

In 1990 the African Baseball and Softball Association was formed at a meeting in Nigeria.

Agents

"When they smile, blood drips off their teeth."— Ted Turner.

"I don't need an agent. Why should I give somebody 10% when I do all the work?"— Mark Fidrych.

"They all changed. Most of them got agents, and I ceased to talk to 'em. 'Like to use this toilet paper?' 'Dunno, I gotta talk to my agent.'"— Bill Lee on modern players.

"A complete ballplayer today is one who can hit, field, run, throw and pick the right agent."— Giants owner Bob Lurie.

Early Agents. David L. Fultz organized an early players' *Union*, the Protective Association of Professional Baseball Players, established in 1900. He also acted as a player agent, advising players behind the scenes in their contract negotiations.

Joe DiMaggio once claimed that he had the first agent in Baseball, none other than Ty Cobb. Cobb frequented the DiMaggio family restaurant in San Francisco and he became friends with the family. When the Yankees bought DiMaggio's contract from the San Francisco Seals (for $25,000), the Yankees offered him a $5,000 contract. Cobb was outraged, and he wrote to Yankees general manager Ed Barrow. Barrow came up with another $500. After a second letter, Barrow added another $500. This apparently went on for seven letters, when Barrow wrote, "This is all! Tell Cobb to stop writing letters!" DiMaggio ended up with $8,500 and Cobb ate for free at the restaurant.

Bargaining with Owners. In 1946 players won the right to bargain through player representatives, though few (if any) risked the wrath of the owners by actually engaging an agent to handle negotiations. Agents were not formally recognized in a collective bargaining agreement until 1970 (there were no collective bargaining agreements until 1967).

Agents who negotiated directly with owners are a phenomenon that first appeared in the 1960s. In 1965 Jim Lefebvre asked the Dodgers if Larue Harcourt could help him as an investment counselor, but not in salary negotiations. Dodger general manager Buzzie Bavasi agreed because he knew that Harcourt was a college professor. Bavasi swore he would not negotiate with any agents, which of course was a promise that he could never fulfill. Harcourt later represented Don Sutton and Bob Forsch, among many others.

Prominent Agents.

"Didn't he get enough from Alex Rodriguez." — Gary Sheffield in 2004, after his former agent, mega-agent Scott Boras (who also represented Rodriguez in his huge deal with the Rangers), claimed that he was owed 5% of Sheffield's $39 million deal with the Yankees. Sheffield contended that he negotiated the deal himself with George Steinbrenner after he left the Braves.

Frank Scott was one of the earliest and most powerful player agents of the 1950s and early 1960s, though he acted behind the scenes and often in connection with exhibitions and other promotions, as opposed to direct salary negotiations with owners. Joe Tubiolo was another prominent agent of the 1960s, though he focused primarily on football. Among his 1960s clients was manager Dick Williams.

Bill Hayes was the agent for Don Drysdale and Sandy Koufax during their famous joint *Hold-Out* of 1966. He has been credited as the first attorney to represent a player in salary negotiations.

The most influential agent of the 1970s was Jerry Kapstein, who represented a number of the first truly free agents in 1976. He earned $700,000 for his efforts in negotiating contracts for those players. Of the 13 largest contracts negotiated among the 22 free agents that winter, Kapstein's clients received 10 of them.

Leigh Steinberg was probably the most influential agent of the 1980s and 1990s. He was respected and generally well-liked by most general managers, in contrast to Howard Slusher, who was almost universally despised.

By the 2000s, Jeff Moorad had emerged as one of the most prominent agents, representing dozens of Major Leaguers, including Raul Mondesi, Mo Vaughn and Shawn Green. In 2004, however, he moved into management (see **Switching Roles**).

Arn Tellem has been a prominent agent in the 1990s and 2000s, and because of his Japanese baseball clients, he was known as "moi-yari no aru dairinin," translated as "the compassionate agent." He was the agent for future Yankee outfielder Hideki Matsui and then future Mets shortstop Kazuo Matsui (no relation).

Earnings. Agents used to earn 10% to 20% of players' salaries and some may earn annual guaranteed payments or a percentage of all endorsements and other deals entered into by players. As contracts became so large, the agent's percentage dropped to between two and four percent. David Falk reportedly made $30 million negotiating contracts in 2001 and sold his company for about $100 million in cash and stock.

Young Clients. Although Major League Baseball prohibits its teams from signing any player younger than 16 years and 9 months, there is no such prohibition against agents signing players to representation deals. Some kids have agents by the time they are 12.

Switching Roles.

"I'm a big boy. When I got over the initial pain of it, it seemed to make sense." — Jerry Colangelo.

"They will always have a fond place in my heart ... until they come negotiating with us." — Agent Jeff Moorad, after giving up his practice to move into management.

In August 2004 Moorad was named CEO of the Diamondbacks, giving up his agent relationship with Arizona outfielder Luis Gonzalez (among others, including Manny Ramirez). He replaced Jerry Colangelo as the head of the worst team in the Major Leagues.

In February 2004 agent Dennis Gilbert interviewed for the Dodgers' general manager job and then took a special assistant position with the White Sox. He had been part of the group headed by former Mariners owner Jeff Smulyan that tried to buy the Dodgers when Frank McCourt made his successful bid. Gilbert, 55 at the time, had represented George Brett, Barry Bonds, Jose Canseco, Mike Piazza, Bret Saberhagen, Bobby Bonilla and Danny Tartabull. Gilbert sold out his interest in his agency in 1998. He played minor league ball for four years in the late 1960s and early 1970s, and once described himself as a "three-tool player": "I could hit, run and talk."

Japanese Players. Don Nomura was the first player agent in Japan, making him highly unpopular among Japanese owners. Nomura represented Hideo Nomo in his negotiations in Japan and then in the United States. His mother was Japanese and his father was a Jewish bowling-ball importer from Brooklyn. His stepfather was a Japanese league Triple Crown winner. Nomura attended college in California and became part-owner of the Class A Salinas Spurs before returning to Japan to become an agent.

Cuban Connection. Joe Cubas, known as "El Gordo," the fat man, is an agent who specializes in helping Cuban players defect to the United States. His last coup was pitcher Rolando Arrojo, who jumped his Cuban national team on July 9, 1996.

Association. Professor William Weston of the University of Baltimore Law School founded the Association of Representatives of Professional Athletes (ARPA).

Strike Agents. In 1995 the Players Association announced that it would order sanctions against any agent who represented a strike-breaking replacement player.

New Agency. In 1995 Jose Canseco announced the formation of 40–40 Sports Council, an agency created to represent professional athletes. He hoped to concentrate on the Latin American market for Baseball players, but the organization instituted plans to represent athletes in a number of sports. The company failed after a brief stint in the business.

Books. Randal A. Henrick, *Inside the Strike Zone* (1994).

Airline Travel

"The more we lose, the more Steinbrenner will fly in. And the more he flies, the better chance there will be a plane crash." — Yankee third baseman Graig Nettles during spring training in 1977.

"You mean we have to fly with people?" — Willie Wilson when told the team was flying commercial rather than charter.

Early Flying.

"Most had never flown before. A lot of us were scared. But there was a lot of joking and kidding around. In the end, the players all enjoyed it. I took it in stride, because I had flown before." — Red Sox third baseman Bill Werber on his club's 1936 flight.

It is generally believed that the 1928 Hollywood Stars were the first professional baseball team to fly. However, it has been reported that in August 1921 a club from Marysville, California, was the first to make an airplane flight. The team flew 80 miles to play a game in Woodland, California, and then made the return trip by air.

On June 7, 1934, the Reds became the first Major League club to take an airplane. It took two regularly scheduled flights to get the team to its destination. Mark Koenig and Jim Bottomley, both nearing the end of long careers, refused to fly and instead took a train to the next city.

On July 30, 1936, the Red Sox became the first club to fly to the next city on their playing schedule (the Reds were not traveling to a game). A total of 21 players, coaches and officials took the plane. Lefty Grove was booked on an earlier flight because he was scheduled to pitch in the game. The club's equipment went by train.

The Cardinals took their first airplane trip in 1938 on a mail plane from Boston to Chicago. A flood prevented them from taking the scheduled train. Owner Sam Breadon had telegraphed the team, telling them to find travel means other than an airplane, but it was too late. Nevertheless, the team and the mail arrived safely.

The Dodgers took their first flight on May 7, 1940, flying from St. Louis to Chicago.

World War II restrictions forced Major League clubs back to the rails exclusively. As the war ended and clubs were free to travel by air, United Airlines was the carrier of choice for 11 Major League teams.

In 1946 the Yankees became the first Major League club to travel extensively by air and to fly outside the United States. They first traveled with a four-engine C-54 transport plane. The club had previously traveled by air to Panama and Puerto Rico for spring training. In 1947 the club went to Havana, Caracas and San Juan before finishing spring training in St. Petersburg.

In the mid–1940s the Yankees gave their players the option of flying or traveling by train for certain regular season games. Red Ruffing was one who always took the train. In 1947 most Yankee players did not like to fly, but almost all still did it. Because of the significant number of players who did not want to fly, the club went back to trains exclusively. With the West Coast expansion in 1958, all clubs were required to do some traveling by airplane.

In May 1950 a railway strike forced five teams — Red Sox, Yankees, Dodgers, Giants, and Reds — to fly home or away to play their next scheduled games.

Team Plane. During the 1960s the Dodgers owned a team plane. It was a Boeing 720 known as the Kay O' II, in honor of Walter O'Malley's wife, Kay. The players apparently appreciated their pilots, once voting $500 World Series shares to each of the three.

Personalized. Japan Airlines passed out tiny Hideki Matsui dolls in 2003 and painted a plane with his image splashed across the fuselage. It was dubbed the "Matsui Jet."

In January 1999 Nolan Ryan became the first passenger on the "Nolan Ryan Express," a Southwest Airlines Boeing 737. He autographed the plane's nose on two specially designed decals featuring baseballs with wings. Later that year, Ryan boarded the plane to fly to the Hall of Fame induction ceremony.

Disaster Plan.

"All the time it's fasten your goddamn seatbelt. But how come every time I read about one of those plane crashes, there's 180 people on board and all 180 die? Didn't any of them have their seatbelt fastened?"— Pilots pitcher Fred Talbot.

When airplane travel was required when the Giants and Dodgers moved to the West Coast for the 1958 season, the National League created a disaster plan for the redistribution of talent in the event of a crash. A form of the plan is still in effect, although it was modified to be consistent between the leagues when the leagues were merged after the league president position was abolished.

If a National League club lost seven or more players for at least 60 days, the other clubs had to each submit a list of 12 players. The weakened club would then choose players until it had picked six fewer than it had lost, although originally the plan allowed the club to replace all players from other clubs. Later, the final six would come from the club's minor league roster.

The American League rule provided that if a club loses six or more players for at least 30 games, it could draft players from other clubs. Players with 10 years in the Major Leagues and five years with one club or with no-cut or non-assignable contracts were excluded from the plan. Clubs in the league had to submit a list of four active players to the league office: a pitcher, a catcher, an infielder and an outfielder. The team that lost players would then choose players until it had selected five fewer than it had lost, replacing the lost players with others who play the same position. The last five would come from within the club's own organization.

Under both plans a team could not have two players selected off its list until every other team has had a player selected. A form of these plans is now part of the Major League Rules (Rule 29 — Disaster Plan).

Jet Lag. It has been determined that jet lag is worse traveling from East to West, but the effect on the standings has never been analyzed.

Fly Boys. During World War II, Buddy Lewis of the Senators enlisted in the Army Air Corps and received pilot training. He once flew a military plane from a nearby base and buzzed Griffith Stadium during a game.

Pitcher and pilot Denny McLain flew a Cessna airplane to the 1969 All-Star Game. He was to have started the game, but he arrived in the 4th inning, pitched briefly, and then flew off before the game ended.

Don Sutton, Rick Monday and Reggie Smith each earned his pilot's license while playing for the Dodgers during the 1970s. Smith was one hour short of receiving an aerobatics rating in 1978.

See **Deaths** for the plane crash death of Thurman Munson and other active ballplayers.

Fear of Flying. Rusty Staub hated airline travel. According to Mets President M. Donald Grant, when Staub was with the Mets he insisted that on charter flights the runways be of a certain length.

Jackie Jensen of the Red Sox cut his 11-year career short rather than travel by airplane. He once lost $750 in salary when he refused to board a plane to California. In 1961, his last season, he refused to fly several times.

Jim Duckworth pitched for the Senators from 1963 until 1965, but went on the disabled list to overcome his fear of flying. He returned for part of the 1966 season and then was cut.

Jim "Mudcat" Grant said that Lee Maye hated to fly and during his post-baseball singing career he traveled by motorhome.

First Class. Recent collective bargaining agreements require that a player must have an open seat next to him if he does not have a first-class seat.

Contract Clause. When Kevin Brown signed a $105 million contract before the 1998 season, the Dodgers agreed to fly his family into town on a private charter for games at least six times a year.

Flight Attendant. Frank Thomas, an original New York Met, helped the flight attendant serve on a crowded flight early in the club's first season. He continued it on each flight that year.

Bad Food. On an Angels team flight, Reggie Jackson had ordered a vegetarian meal, but didn't like the food. He asked for a replacement tray of the regular meal, but the flight attendant informed him that there were no more meals available. After Jackson tossed the tray of food at the attendant, Bobby Grich punched him in the face.

Alaskan Leagues

"After a season of practice, during which there was much speculation as to the merits of the various nines and no end of chaff and banter, the first game of the series was played, and in the brief twilight of an arctic December day, with the mercury 38 below zero, the 'Roaring Gimlets' vanquished the 'Pig Stickers' by a score of 62 to 49." — Brigadier General Frederick Funston describing the Arctic Baseball League of Alaska in Albert Spalding's *Base Ball— America's National Game* (1911).

Early League. During the winter of 1894 to 1895, a fleet of 17 whaling ships became icebound above the Arctic Circle. One of the ships carried a supply of baseball equipment. The whalers broke out the equipment and formed seven clubs that competed for the Arctic Whalemen's Pennant, "a strip of drilling nailed to a broom handle."

Summer League. Alaska has for a number of years hosted a thriving short summer league that has helped produce over 600 Major League players, including Tom Seaver, Dave Kingman, Bob Boone, Dave Winfield, Kevin McReynolds, Rick Monday and Graig Nettles. Barry Bonds had 18 at-bats for the Alaska Goldpanners in 1983.

Alcoholic Beverages

"The two greatest obstacles to success of the majority of professional ball players are wine and women." — 1889 *Spalding Guide.*

"Seems like they'd be better off sponsoring the bottom of the fifth." — Tim Keown of ESPN.com after Jack Daniel's bourbon sponsored the seventh inning stretch during a game in Oakland in 2004.

"I didn't change my uniform. Everybody was telling me I should, but I can play with a little beer on my shirt." — Devil Rays outfielder Rocco Baldelli, after a White Sox fan poured beer on his head and back.

"Billy Lush, John Boozer, Ad Swigler, Dan Tipple, Jack Daniels, Highball Wilson, Alex Beam, Johnny Walker, Don Collins, Pedro Borbon, Wedo Martini, Tinsley Ginn, Sherry Robertson, Norm Sherry, Brandy Davis, Sherry Smith, Bobby Wine, Bob Vines, Dave Vineyard, Charlie Ripple, Jim Ripple, Ed Pabst, Clarence Beers, Jim Brewer, Bud Weiser, Dots Miller, Allyn Stout, Biff Schlitzer"

See also ***Alcoholism.***

19th Century.

"Any man now desirous of using his physical and mental powers to their utmost advantage, must ignore first, intemperance in eating, and second, refuse to allow a drop of alcoholic liquor, whether in the form of spirits, wine or beer, to pass down his throat." — 1870s *Beadle's Dime Base-Ball Player.*

"Puritanical Worcester is not liberal Cincinnati by a jugful, and what is sauce for Worcester is wine for the Queen City. Beer and Sunday amusements have become a popular necessity in Cincinnati." — 1880s Cincinnati newspaper.

Alcohol and baseball have been interwoven since the very earliest days of amateur baseball in the 1840s. The clearest connections came later when owners installed liquor concessions at ballparks and many teams were owned by beer barons (at first primarily in the American Association).

Alcoholic beverages became a national phenomenon in the 1860s and 1870s. There was a 700% increase in liquor business investment during those 20 years. The encroachment of liquor into the game led inevitably to heavy drinking and frequent cases of alcoholism among ballplayers.

Beer sales were especially important to certain clubs. Cincinnati was a focal point, with 27 breweries in the city in 1879. The Red Stockings sold an average of $3,000 in beer during each season of that era. Cincinnati's one concession to the National League establishment was that it stopped selling beer in the stands, forcing fans to go to a bar behind the stands. National League leader William

Hulbert tried to eliminate the sale of beer during games, and in October 1880 the league voted to expel Cincinnati after the team refused to adhere to the league rules prohibiting beer sales and ***Sunday Baseball.***

The American Association of the 1880s was backed heavily by Christopher Von der Ahe, Harry Von der Horst, John Park and John Hauck, all of whom were prominent brewers or tavern owners.

St. Louis Brown Stockings owner Christopher Von der Ahe originally owned a saloon one block south of the ballpark. He discovered that his sales rose dramatically whenever there was a ball game. Credit has been given to his bartender, Edgar Cuthbert, who had played professional baseball, for suggesting to Von der Ahe that he invest in the local ball club and sell beer to fans. Von der Ahe bought into the Brown Stockings in 1880, two years before the club became part of the new American Association.

When the four strongest American Association teams merged into the National League in 1892, beer sales were made optional. Cincinnati again sold beer in the stands and the Giants had a bar set up that was in full view of the field.

Brewers as Owners. See ***Owners.***

Anheuser-Busch.

"Where else can you consume $50-$60 worth of beer and still be under the legal limit" — Bob Lacey on the exorbitant prices at San Francisco's SBC Park.

Anheuser-Busch Brewery owned the Cardinals from 1953 through early 1996 and is reportedly the world's most frequent sponsor of sporting events. In the 1950s Busch's Budweiser beer was the number two beer behind Schlitz. By 1957 Budweiser was number one and never looked back. In 1995 Anheuser-Busch had ties to 26 of the 28 Major League clubs and spent more than $17 million on baseball-related television and radio advertising. It also ranked first in ballpark signage (Miller Brewing Company was fourth).

In August 2001 a jury ordered the company to pay $50 million to the family of Roger Maris for improperly taking away a beer distributorship

Ballplayers.

"*I Hate the Game, But I Love Drinking the Beer.*" — Proposed title of Kent Hrbek's autobiography, after he heard that teammate Kirby Puckett had titled his book, *I Love This Game!*

Indians rookie star Super Joe Charboneau often demonstrated his ability to open a beer bottle with his eye socket. He also could drink beer through a straw up his nose.

In 1993 Harmon Killebrew and Cold Spring Brewing Company began marketing "Killebrew," the slugger's home brew root beer that he learned to make as a boy in Oregon.

Commercials.

"I still don't know why they asked me to do this commercial." — Mets legend Marvelous Marv Throneberry, reflecting on his renewed notoriety after appearing in a series of 13 Miller Lite Beer commercials in the 1970s and 1980s. Numerous former players and umpires have appeared in beer commercials. Jim Honochick was a minor league player who umpired in the American League from 1949 through 1973. He later became famous as the myopic umpire in the Miller Lite commercials with Boog Powell of the Orioles.

Yankee broadcaster Mel Allen saluted all Yankee home runs as "Ballantine Blasts" in honor of 1950s sponsor Ballantine Beer.

The day after the 1962 Mets won their first game ever, against the league-leading Pirates, Mets manager Casey Stengel appeared in an ad in uniform with the voluptuous Miss Rheingold for Rheingold Extra Dry Lager. He was fined $500 by commissioner Ford Frick for the uniformed appearance.

Insurance.

"We'll be back after this word from Manufacturers *Hangover*."— Ralph Kiner.

In 1985 a Class A club in Madison, Wisconsin, had its liability insurance cancelled by its carrier because of concerns over alcohol-related incidents. Attendance plummeted and in response the minor league organization, the National Association of Professional Baseball Leagues, set up a group insurance plan that any minor league club may join.

Airline Travel/Clubhouses. In 1995 *Baseball Weekly* surveyed Major League clubs and determined that eight did not allow beer or wine in the home team locker room. Only the Dodgers did not allow alcohol in the visitor's locker room. The Giants did not allow alcohol on return flights because many players would be driving home.

Ballpark Names. One of Denver's minor league ballpark's originally was known as Coors Field (for the Colorado-based brewery) and the new Major League ballpark that opened for the 1995 season was known by the same name. In the 1960s the Cardinals planned to call their new ballpark Budweiser Stadium after their most popular beer. Major League Baseball objected and the Cardinals went with Busch Stadium, which was not only the name of one of its beers, but also the surname of the owner. The dual-use name apparently was less objectionable to Major League Baseball.

Dry Ballpark. The Blue Jays did not serve beer during their first four seasons.

On April 11, 1998, for the first time since Prohibition, there was no beer served for the first Red Sox home game. This was because the opener coincided with Good Friday and Passover. Club management thought it would be in poor taste for fans to drink on a holy day.

Semi-Dry Ballpark. In 1981 when Jerry Reinsdorf bought the White Sox from Bill Veeck, one of the first moves he made was to ban the sale of hard liquor in the stadium because of all the fights that had occurred.

Protest. In April 1997, Cubs broadcaster Harry Caray dropped the price of beer at his Chicago restaurants to 45 cents during the Cubs' horrendous 0–13 start of the season. He picked that price to honor the year in which the Cubs had last appeared in the World Series, and left it there until the Cubs won (good thing he didn't leave it at that price until the Cubs reached the World Series).

Cost. The price for a 20-ounce beer at Dodger Stadium was $7 in 2003. The most expensive beer in the country in 2003 was found in Fenway Park, where 12 ounces cost $5.

Alcoholism (and Alcohol-related incidents)

"I have found that the ones who drink milkshakes don't win many ballgames."— Yankee manager Casey Stengel defending the hard-drinking ballplayer.

"There is much less drinking now than there was before 1927, because I quit drinking on May 24, 1927."— Cardinals shortstop Rabbit Maranville in 1928.

"It depends on the length of the game."—19th century star Mike "King" Kelly when asked if he drank during games.

"I can't hit the ball until I hit the bottle."— Louisville Slugger Pete Browning.

"A keg of beer will catch for Louisville today."— Derisive headline by Cincinnati sportswriter O.P. Caylor.

"Boys, I hope you enjoy sports. But I will warn you about one thing. Don't take to drink, because look what it's done to me."— Alcoholic pitcher Grover Cleveland Alexander's entire speech to a group of eighth grade boys at a sports banquet in Springfield, Illinois. Among the schoolboys was future Phillies pitcher Robin Roberts.

"You are an applehead! I repeat, sir, you are an applehead! You are also a counterfeit and a fraud! Why don't you go down to the press room and wipe the brandy drippings off your lips so you won't look like the common, ordinary barroom bum that you are! You are an applehead, sir! But you certainly picked on a honey when you picked on me!"— Chief umpire Bill Klem to Dodger general manager Larry MacPhail during the 1942 World Series after MacPhail tormented plate umpire Al Barlick. MacPhail was a heavy drinker who routinely fired Dodger manager Leo Durocher. All would be forgiven (and apparently forgotten) the next day.

"They, whoever that is, have called me a fanatic on the liquor question, and they are right. That stuff not only destroys lives, but also it has done more to harm my business than anything of which I am aware."— Branch Rickey.

"What we have are good gray ballplayers, playing a good gray game and reading the good gray *Wall Street Journal*. They have been brainwashed, dry-cleaned and dehydrated!... Wake up the echoes at the Hall of Fame and you will find that baseball's immortals were a rowdy and raucous group of men who would climb down off their plaques and go rampaging through Cooperstown, taking spoils.... Deplore it if you will, but Grover Cleveland Alexander drunk was a better pitcher than Grover Cleveland Alexander sober."— Bill Veeck in *The Hustler's Handbook* (1966).

"Not nearly enough."— Pitcher Duane Ward, subsequently released by the Rangers in spring 1997, when asked by a police officer how much he had to drink before getting behind the wheel.

See also *Alcoholic Beverages*.

19th Century Problems.

"Larkin's [court] examination was adjourned for a week so he could get the liquor out of him."—1880s newspaper report on pitcher Terry Larkin. He was a heavy drinker who once shot his wife and then tried to commit suicide, among other brushes with the law while intoxicated.

The 1870s professional National Association had a significant problem with players who drank while playing. This continued to some degree in the National League and the American Association. Typical was a newspaper entry of May 28, 1889, in which the *Cincinnati Enquirer* reported that Leon Viau went to the mound drunk, with "a head on him the size of a brewery tub." Viau still managed to win 22 games that year for the American Association Cincinnati Red Stockings.

When National League president William Hulbert died in 1882, he had just instituted lifetime expulsions against 10 of the hardest drinkers in the league.

Nineteenth-century umpire Jack Sheridan was once suspended because of drunkenness on the field.

Contract Clause.

"I see that Sockalexis must forgo frescoing his tonsils with the cardinal brush; it is so nominated in the contract of the aborigine."— Orator Jim O'Rourke on the contract forbidding *Native American* Louis Sockalexis from using alcohol.

"It is understood that the player shall at all times during the term through the years 1922 to 1923 to 1924 and the years 1925 and 1926 refrain and abstain entirely from the use of intoxicating liquors, and that he shall not during the training and playing season in each year stay up later than 1 o'clock a.m. on any day without the permission and consent of the club's manager."—1922 letter imposing a $9,017.10 fine on Babe Ruth by the Yankees.

The members of the National Association Middletown Mansfields signed an abstinence pledge.

Ed Ruelbach was the secretary of the Players Fraternity union of the early 20th century and wanted abstinence to be a regular part of the standard player contract. This theme was renewed in 1912 when Pirates owner Barney Dreyfuss and other owners lobbied to have a total abstinence clause made a part of the standard player contract. Nothing ever came of these efforts.

In 1909 Howie Camnitz of the Pirates was to be given a $1,200 bonus if he stopped drinking and remained sober throughout the season. He was unable to earn the bonus, but still won 25 games with a 1.62 ERA. He had a poor World Series that year, prompting one writer to blame it on his alcohol-related unreliability. He pitched 3⅔ innings, giving up eight hits and compiling an ERA of 12.27.

In 1910 catcher Larry McLean of the Reds had a clause in his contract that $25 would be deducted whenever he took a drink. He survived the season with his salary relatively intact. For the 1911 season he wanted a clause providing that he would *receive* $25 whenever he refused a drink and said that he would pay for someone to monitor his conduct. The club declined the offer.

R & R. Long-time Red Sox owner Tom Yawkey's adoptive uncle, William Yawkey, owned the Tigers in the first few years of the 20th century. After a long losing streak, he decided to take the players barhopping and then to a Turkish bath. The rest and relaxation worked, as the club went on a five-game winning streak.

Commissioner. Judge Landis officially supported the 18th Amendment to the U.S. Constitution establishing Prohibition, but privately drank with friends. Ban Johnson expected Prohibition to cause a 10–15% increase in attendance because of less rowdyism, but others had mixed reactions to it. It appears to have had a negligible effect on attendance during the booming, yet dry, 1920s. Home runs and a prosperous economy appear to have had the greatest effect on baseball's popularity at that time. Prohibition was not repealed until 1933 when Franklin Roosevelt took office.

Raid. During Game 2 of the 1920 World Series at Ebbets Field, federal agents raided the press box. They were acting on a tip that the Dodgers were supplying pints of rye whiskey to the press during this Prohibition-era game. The agents found nothing.

Suspensions. Chief Bender and Rube Oldring were suspended in 1911 for excessive alcohol consumption.

Sig Jakucki pitched the Browns to the pennant on the last day of the 1944 season against the Yankees, despite a serious drinking habit. In 1945 he was suspended for heavy drinking and never again appeared in the Major Leagues.

Frequency of Abuse. When pitcher Ryne Duren drank himself out of Major League Baseball in 1965, he estimated that 35% of all Major League players had a problem with alcohol. In the late 1980s Duren was the head of Organized Baseball's rehabilitation program.

In an anonymous survey in 1993 by Major League Baseball's medical advisor, Dr. Robert B. Millman, it was estimated that 5% of the players had serious alcohol problems.

Combating the Problem. In 1987 commissioner Peter Ueberroth formed T.E.A.M., an acronym for Techniques for Effective Alcohol Management. Part of the reforms were alcohol-free seating areas in most ballparks.

Injury. Pitcher Ron Bryant of the Giants won 24 games in 1973. While drunk during the following off-season, he hurt his back in a diving board accident and was 3–15 the next season. He was

traded to the Cardinals and released after only 10 games of the 1975 season.

Rube Waddell. The eccentric A's pitcher continually drank his way into problems and once got into a fight in a saloon. To curtail such activity, Connie Mack bandaged a man and staged a mock court proceeding with a judge friend of his. Waddell was brought up on "charges" that he beat the man and the judge threatened Waddell with jail time if he drank. The ruse apparently worked for at least one season.

Phil Douglas. Douglas was barred from baseball in 1922 as a result of a letter he wrote while under the influence of alcohol. He had frequently disappeared while with various teams after arriving in the Major Leagues in 1912. During the 1922 season with the Giants, his disappearances became more frequent and long-time outfielder Jesse Burkett was assigned to be his keeper.

One night late in the season, Douglas ditched Burkett and went on a four-day binge. When he showed up to play, manager John McGraw berated him. To retaliate, the still-woozy Douglas wrote a letter to a friend on the Cardinals, Leslie Mann. Douglas's letter suggested that he might "go fishing" for the remainder of the season to prevent the Giants from winning the pennant, if the Cardinals "would make it worth my while."

A day or two later, a sober Douglas called Mann and told him to destroy the letter. It was too late, as Mann had shown it to general manager Branch Rickey, who had called Judge Landis.

After Douglas readily admitted writing the letter, though blaming his intoxicated state, Landis banned him for life. But for the then-recent epidemic of *Gambling and Fixed Games* in baseball, the event might have gone unnoticed or the punishment might have been far less severe. For a chronicle of the incident and Douglas's life, see Tom Clark, *One Last Round for the Shuffler* (1979).

Joe McCarthy. Highly successful Cubs, Yankees and Red Sox manager Joe McCarthy was a serious alcoholic who often disappeared for days at a time and would be found passed out in his own waste. He eventually lost his job with the Red Sox over this behavior, though the official reason for his departure in mid–1950 was "ill health."

Charlie Sweeney. In 1884 Old Hoss Radbourn won 60 games for the Providence Grays, but he was not the only pitcher on the team. Charlie Sweeney was the other and a conflict developed. Sweeney was a good pitcher in his own right, striking out 19 in one game and doing well otherwise, so the rivalry increased.

Sweeney pitched in Philadelphia one day while half drunk, but managed to be ahead 6–2 in the 7th inning. Manager Frank Bancroft asked him to go to right field to save his arm — or, according to one source, so that Bancroft could try out the club's new pitcher, Cyclone Joe Miller. Sweeney stormed off the field and next pitched for the St. Louis Grays of the Union Association, for whom he won 24 games that season. There is evidence that Sweeney deliberately provoked the release so that he could sign with the rival league's club (sometimes erroneously reported as the American Association club in St. Louis). Radbourn pitched full-time the rest of the season, which put a tremendous strain on his arm and helped cause his premature departure from baseball.

Larry McLean. McLean was an infielder for various clubs in the early part of the century. He had a serious drinking problem when he challenged John McGraw and his coaches to a fight. After one of McGraw's people broke a chair over his head, McLean was cut from the team. He was shot to death at age 39 during a dispute in a Boston bar.

Bugs Raymond.

"I took him out and as he reached the bench, I saw he was

bleary-eyed. He hadn't stopped at the bullpen when I sent him down to warm up but kept going, right out of the park and across the street to a gin mill, where he traded in the ball for three shots of whiskey." — Giants manager John McGraw on Raymond, who never again appeared in a game for the Giants.

"[Bugs] Raymond was a performer of near-legendary accomplishment. He could throw a spit ball at three different speeds, something not even the renowned Spittin' Ed Walsh of the Chicago White Sox could do. But as an eager consumer whenever liquid refreshment was poured from pitcher, bottle or vat, Raymond also could get himself thrown out of saloons at three different speeds." — Clem Boddington in "Bugs" (1958).

Raymond pitched six seasons, with high years of 15–25 for the Cardinals in 1908 and 18–12 for the Giants in 1909. His last season was 1911, when he was 6–4 in 17 appearances for the Giants. He was out of baseball before age 30 due to alcoholism. He died of a cerebral hemorrhage sustained from a kick to the head in a fight. He once was placed in a sanitarium by the Giants as a result of heavy drinking.

Grover Cleveland Alexander. See **Strikeouts** for the 1926 World Series confrontation between a supposedly hung-over Alexander and Tony Lazzeri.

John McGraw. On August 8, 1920, while under the influence of alcohol, the Giants manager went to the Lambs, a club featuring theatre people. His strong language in front of two scrubwomen caused an argument, leading to club member and actor William Boyd breaking a water carafe over McGraw's head, prompting this response to an investigator from McGraw: "I guess it was a case of bunched hits. First I hit the bottle and then the bottle hit me."

McGraw claimed that he never fought unless he was drunk, a claim he made after this fight. He was found not guilty of assault and carrying liquor during Prohibition at a jury trial presided over by Judge Learned Hand.

Harry Heilmann.

"How the hell can you fine a .400 hitter?" — Tiger manager Ty Cobb on Heilmann, who once showed up to a ballgame still wearing his tuxedo from the night before. Cobb ordered him to play and he promptly tripled. After Heilmann collapsed on third base, Cobb took him out of the game. Heilmann was a notoriously heavy drinker who once admitted to driving a small Austin automobile down a flight of stairs directly up to the bar of a speakeasy during Prohibition.

Paul Waner.

"Waner had to be a very graceful player because he could slide without breaking the bottle on his hip." — Casey Stengel on the legendary drinker.

"Paul Waner was always sipping from a Coke bottle in the dugout. One day, while he was batting, a new batboy snuck a long swig. The kid woke up with a crashing hangover." — Columnist Mike Royko.

Hack Wilson.

"Hack Wilson usually played in the outfield, but I'd put him at first base because he wouldn't have as far to stagger to the dugout." — Royko.

When an impoverished Wilson died of alcoholism in 1948 at age 47, the National League granted $350 for his grave. Manager Joe McCarthy once demonstrated to Wilson the evils of alcohol by dropping a worm in a glass of whiskey. Pointing to the dead worm, McCarthy asked "What does this prove, Hack?" Wilson supposedly said "It proves that if you drink, you won't get worms." The demonstration apparently made no impression on the alcoholic

McCarthy. See also Clifton Blue Parker, *Fouled Away: The Baseball Tragedy of Hack Wilson* (2004).

Mike Kreevich. Kreevich was released in 1942 by the A's because of a serious drinking problem. He signed with the Browns in 1943 and managed to hang on for their 1944 pennant-winning season. Manager Joe Sewell helped him out by introducing him to one of the Alcoholics Anonymous founders and Kreevich was fine during the season. Sewell also had him room with a non-drinking player who gave him candy bars when he wanted a drink. Sewell even arranged for regular visits from a priest. It must have worked, because Kreevich hit .301 in 105 games.

Sam McDowell.

"I was the biggest, most hopeless, and most violent drunk in baseball." — McDowell, who was a fear-inducing strikeout pitcher primarily in the 1960s whose his career was cut short by alcoholism. In 1973 the Yankees assigned someone to watch McDowell 24 hours a day, but by 1975 no club would sign him. McDowell later admitted that he regularly got his chaperon drunk. He finally sobered up in 1980 and took a job as a drug and alcohol counselor for Major League players with the **Baseball Assistance Team** and the Major League Baseball Players Alumni Association.

Milton Bradley. In 2001 outfielder Milton Bradley was taken to a hospital by medical workers after refusing to leave a restaurant because he was drunk. In February 2004 Bradley was sentenced to three days in jail for speeding away from police. In spring training that season he was suspended by the Indians after refusing to run out a pop fly that was dropped. He was then cut by the club (who had signed him for $1.73 million in November 2003) and signed with the Dodgers.

Flipped Out. In January 1998 Mo Vaughn was arrested for drunk driving when his pickup truck struck an abandoned car and flipped over.

Bar's Open. When Rod Beck played for the Class AAA Iowa Cubs in early 2003 when he was rehabilitating his arm and hoping for a Major League contract (see **Comebacks**), he was living in his 36-foot Winnebago motor home parked behind the right field stands. It was 159 steps from his locker to the clubhouse. He pitched well and had an open door — and open bar — policy. After games it was common for Beck to share a beer with fans at his RV. When the blue martini-shaped neon glass was lit, the bar was open. If it was off, Beck was closed for the night. During spring training in 2004 he left the Padres (with whom he signed in mid–2003) due to "personal problems."

Manager. Alvin Dark was a religious teetotaler who supposedly refused to manage the Cardinals because they were owned by Busch Brewery.

Clubhouse Celebration Rules.

"Can you imagine what it would be like if you were a Yankee player and you didn't like the taste of champagne?" — Steve Lyons.

"In case we win again next year and Gibby's still around." — Inscription on a football helmet presented to Sparky Anderson after Kirk Gibson drew blood from Anderson's scalp with a champagne bottle during the Tigers' 1984 World Series celebration.

Following the raucous clubhouse celebration by the Mets after winning the 1986 World Series, Commissioner Peter Ueberroth ordered that subsequent celebrations tone down and leave the champagne off-camera as much as possible. The 1987 postseason celebrations were much more subdued. In contrast, since the early 1960s, alcohol has been banned from NFL locker rooms, even after Super Bowl victories.

Punishment. In 1962 Mickey Mantle, known for his frequent carousing, was caught by manager Ralph Houk after an all-night effort with Roger Maris (not known for this type of behavior). Mantle could barely stand up and Maris was hurting, but as punishment Houk made them start the game.

In the 1st inning in the field, three infield ground balls kept outfielders Mantle and Maris out of the action. Maris struck out on a called third strike in his 1st inning at-bat. According to Tony Kubek, in Mantle's at-bat that inning, he started to swing on a change-up, stopped, and then swung again for a 500-foot home run. Houk took them out of the game before the 2nd inning.

On April 22, 1964, Warren Spahn, Phil Roof and six others were arrested for drinking after hours in a Houston bar. They each were fined $10 by the local authorities.

Nerve Problem. In 1945 Dodger manager Leo Durocher had a nervous pitcher on the team, Tom Seats. Whenever Seats pitched, Durocher gave him a shot of whiskey immediately before the game to calm him down. General Manager Branch Rickey was furious when he found out and Seats never again pitched for the club.

Hotel Bar. There is an unwritten rule that the bar located in the hotel in which the team is staying is off limits to all except the manager and his coaches.

Beer Promotions That Backfired.

See **Promotions**—Promotions That Backfired.

1980s Active Player Recoveries. Reliever Dennis Eckersley and starter Dennis Martinez both joined Alcoholics Anonymous and made tremendous comebacks during their 30s in the late 1980s and sustained them into the mid–1990s. Eckersley became the premier reliever in the Major Leagues for the A's and Martinez became the ace of the Expos staff and pitched a perfect game in 1991.

Books. Bob Welch and George Vecsey wrote a book about Welch's battle with alcoholism, *Five O'Clock Comes Early: A Young Man's Battle with Alcoholism* (1986). Once Welch's alcoholism was brought under control, he won 27 games in 1990 and finished with 211 career wins. He was described at his retirement in 1995 as "the best guy I've ever had, the model of a professional," by A's manager Tony LaRussa and "one of the most honest, best-hearted guys I've ever met," by Giants manager Dusty Baker.

Ryne Duren wrote *The Comeback*, with Robert Drury (1978), the story of his recovery from alcoholism after his 1960s career as a myopic American League fastball pitcher. See also Ryne Duren, *I Can See Clearly Now* (2004).

Pitcher Kirby Higbe's *The High Hard One* (1967) is an account of his battle with alcoholism and his descent into the minor leagues and out of baseball.

Grover Cleveland Alexander (1887–1950)

Hall of Fame 1938

"Alexander is the one player in our league who could win the pennant for any of the seven teams that were not in first place."— Umpire Bill Klem.

"I would have to say that Alexander was the most amazing pitcher in the National League. Alexander had to pitch in the little Philadelphia ball park, with that big tin fence in right field, and he pitched shutouts, which must mean he could do it. He had a fast ball, a curve, a change of pace and perfect control. He was the best I batted against in the National League."— Casey Stengel quoted in Leonard Koppett's *A Thinking Man's Guide to Baseball* (1967).

Alexander is considered by many as the greatest pitcher in National League history, winning 373 games between 1911 and 1930.

Alexander was born in Nebraska and almost had his pitching career cut short while in the minor leagues. He suffered from double vision from an on-field accident, but recovered to win 29 games for Syracuse in 1910. Although the fastball was Alexander's key pitch, he had a curveball and later developed a change-up and fadeaway.

During his best years in Philadelphia he was incredible, starting with a rookie season in which he won 28 games. He won 190 games in seven seasons from the start of his Major League career in 1911, including 30 or more in three straight years. Perhaps his best season was 1916, when he had 16 shutouts. He had a three year run beginning in 1915 in which he won 94 games, including 12 more shutouts in 1915. The Phillies were concerned that he would be drafted into the Army during World War I, so before the 1918 season the club sold him to the Cubs for $60,000 and two players. Alexander did join the Army and served in France and missed almost all of the 1918 season, but he returned to the Cubs for seven years.

Despite chronic alcoholism and epilepsy, he won 128 games for the Cubs, including 27 wins in 1920 and 22 wins in 1923, before the Cardinals bought him in 1926. This set up the famous World Series confrontation that season between Alexander and Tony Lazzeri of the Yankees (see also **Strikeouts**).

Alexander had one more very good season, winning 21 games for the Cardinals in 1927. He began to fade after that, finishing his Major League career in 1930 with the Phillies. His last victory tied him with Christy Mathewson with 373 wins, though at the time it was thought that Mathewson had only 372. Alexander finished with 90 shutouts, highest in National League history, and probably would have won 400 games had he not missed all but three appearances in 1918 due to the war.

"Old Pete" played briefly in the minor leagues in Dallas after leaving the Phillies and then hooked up with a House of David baseball team in the 1930s. He worked in a flea circus in New York after he could no longer pitch competitively. He made his way to Philadelphia for the 1950 World Series, but was barely recognized in the press box. A month later he was dead.

Alibi

"His right name was Frank X. Farrell, and I guess the X stood for 'Excuse me.' Because he never pulled a play, good or bad, on or off the field, without apologizin' for it."— First lines of Ring Lardner's "Alibi Ike."

"[Dodger pitcher Billy] Loes was a reincarnation of Lardner's Alibi Ike, and to explain away his setbacks, he crowded his professional world with bugaboos of a very special sort. Malicious puffs of wind goosed ordinary fly balls over the fence. Blinding shafts of sunlight deflected themselves unnaturally, like the planes in a Picasso painting, to transfix him at the moment of truth. Atmospheric conditions of a peculiarly sinister nature flattened out his fastball and straightened his curve. In short, his failures could be traced less to his stuff on any given day than to demonology."— Frank Graham, Jr., in *Farewell to Heroes* (1981). Loes won 80 games in 11 seasons for the Dodgers, Orioles and Giants, with a high of 14 wins in 1953 for Brooklyn.

"An alibi is sound and needed in all competition. I mean in the high-up brackets. One of the foundations of success in sport is confidence in yourself. You can't afford to admit that any opponent is better than you are. So, if you lose to him there must be a reason—a bad break. You must have an alibi to show why you lost. If you haven't one, you must fake one. Your self-confidence must be maintained."— Christy Mathewson as told to Grantland Rice, quoted in Rice's autobiography, *The Tumult and the Shouting* (1954). The postscript to Mathewson's theory, as reported by Rice: "Always have that alibi, but keep it to yourself. That's where it belongs. Don't spread it around. Lose gracefully in the open. To yourself, lose bitterly — but learn! You can learn little from victory. You can learn everything from defeat."

All-American Girls Professional Baseball League (AAGPBL) (1943–1954)

"Femininity is the keynote of our League; no pants-wearing, tough-talking female softballer will play on any of our four teams." — League president and former Major Leaguer Max Carey.

"May I take this opportunity of expressing my deepest appreciation to you for your splendid exhibition of pitching.... I realize that our team was the loser, but nevertheless that does not in any way detract from the fine exhibition of ball playing presented. Frankly, I was surprised at the talent which you girls have for the game. I can truthfully say that I enjoyed the game fully as much as any men's professional team."—Letter from a fan to Dottie Wiltse Collins in 1944. Collins was a 20-game winner four times in the league.

Origins. The league was the brainchild of Cubs owner and chewing gum magnate Phil Wrigley, who was looking for ways to boost attendance while Major Leaguers were away serving in the military during World War II. The first tryouts in Chicago in spring 1943 drew over 280 girls from across the United States and Canada. Wrigley originally envisioned a softball league, but the over 600 women who played in the league from 1943 through 1954 played hardball for most of the league's existence.

The league started with four clubs in 1943 (Rockford, Racine, South Bend and Kenosha), and expanded to eight in 1946. The league at times included the Racine Belles, Fort Wayne Daisies, South Bend Blue Sox, Minneapolis Millerettes, Kenosha Comets, Kalamazoo Lassies, Muskegon Lassies (later the Belles), Grand Rapids Chicks, Peoria Redwings, Milwaukee Chicks, Chicago Colleens, Springfield Sallies and Rockford Peaches. At its peak the league had 10 teams before folding in 1954. The only club that survived the end of the league was the Fort Wayne Daisies, who continued to play under AAGPBL rules through 1973.

Stars. One of the star players was Helen Callaghan, mother of 1990s Major Leaguer Casey Candaele, who played for the Astros. Two of the league's other stars included shortstop Dottie Schroeder, batting champion and first baseman Dorothy Kamenshek; sisters and batting champions Joanne Weaver and Betty Weaver Foss; and pitcher and AAGPBL Player of the Year Jean Faut.

Attendance. Attendance rose steadily in the 1940s from 259,000 in 1944 to 450,000 in 1945, 754,000 in 1946 and 1 million in 1948. Mirroring the diminishing attendance in the minor leagues, the AAGPBL's attendance declined after that and the league folded after the 1954 season. Television, which aired a few Major League games, contributed to the league's demise.

Black Player. At least one black female player was turned down in her bid to play in the league. In 1953 Mamie Johnson instead played for the Indianapolis Clowns of the Negro Leagues.

Rockford Peaches star Dorothy Kamenshek, one of the greatest players in the history of the league.

Major League Affiliation. Former Major Leaguers Jimmie Foxx, Bert Niehoff, Josh Billings, Max Carey and Johnny Rawlings were hired as club managers. Carey also served as president of the league.

Schedule/Salary. Teams played 120 games each season and players received salaries of generally no more than $150 per month.

Uniforms. Uniforms consisted of a one-piece dress with a short, flared skirt and satin shorts underneath, designed after the field hockey and figure skating outfits of the day. The artist who fashioned the uniforms also conceived the green pixies to advertise Wrigley's chewing gum. Helena Rubenstein of cosmetic fame was hired to conduct spring training charm school.

Pitching Style. In 1943 the women pitched underhanded and threw a 12-inch softball rather than a standard nine-inch baseball.

The mound was 40 feet from home plate. The ball was reduced to 11½ inches in 1944 and the mound moved out slightly to 42 feet in 1945. In 1946 the ball was 11 inches and the mound 43 feet. Sidearm pitching was introduced in 1946 and allowed through 1947, though some players stuck with the underhand style with great success. The league went to complete overhand pitching in 1948 with a 10⅜ inch ball and a mound 50 feet from home plate. From 1949 to 1953 the ball was 10 inches and the distance was 55 feet. In the last year of the league's existence, the ball was the same as in the Major Leagues (9 to 9¼ inches), and the mound just slightly shorter than that in the Major Leagues, at 60 feet.

Movie. The league gained notoriety in the early 1990s when two *Movies* were made, including the successful *A League of Their Own*, starring Tom Hanks, Geena Davis, Rosie O'Donnell and Madonna (with Tia Leone on the mound).

Statistics. *The Baseball Encyclopedia* added the league's statistics to its 1993 ninth edition.

Thank You. To Carolyn Trombe, who is writing a book on AAGPBL star Dottie Collins, for editing this section of the *Encyclopedia*. Collins was a star pitcher in the league, compiling an all-time league-best ERA of 1.83, four 20-win seasons, 17 shutouts in 1945, two no-hitters in 17 days, and four complete-game victories in two doubleheaders. Collins was instrumental in forming a Players Association in 1987 after more than 30 years of obscurity for the AAGPBL and its players.

Books. Patricia I. Brown, *A League of My Own: Memoir of a Pitcher for the All-American Girls Professional Baseball League* (2003); Lois Browne, *The Girls of Summer* (1992); Margot Fortunato Galt, *Up to the Plate: The All-American Girls Baseball League* (1995); Diana Star Helmer, *Belles of the Ballpark* (1993); Susan E. Johnson, *When Women Played Hardball* (1994); Sue E. Macy, *Whole New Ball Game: The Story of the All-American Girls Professional Baseball League* (1995); W. C. Madden, *Women of the All-American Girls Professional Baseball League: A Biographical Dictionary* (1997).

Mel Allen (1913–1996)

Hall of Fame (Frick Award) 1978

"I had the microphone close to my chest, as was my custom, hoping, that way, to call any play a split second before the crowd actually roared. And I was thinking, as I always did, about one solitary fan — Ralph Edwards taught me this — who I imagined sitting just a few feet away from me. In my mind, that one guy — a blank face, maybe, but one person — was my audience. I was talking to him." — Allen's philosophy of broadcasting a baseball game, quoted in Curt Smith's *Voices of the Game* (1987). "That ball is going, going, gone!"

"How about that!" — Allen's trademark calls.

"Baseball has Mel Allen dispensing weekly notes from beyond the grave on ESPN Classic — an estimable pleasure, but one that is, demographically speaking, more Preparation H than Generation Y." — Steve Rushin in 2002. Allen was the long-time voice of the Yankees and television's *This Week in Baseball*.

Allen was born in Alabama as Melvin Israel. He sold hot dogs at Navin Field in Detroit during the summer before broadcasting University of Alabama football games at age 20. Though trained as an attorney, Allen reportedly never wavered from his course of becoming a broadcaster; in fact, he headed for New York on vacation in the mid–1930s and went to CBS on a lark after broadcaster Ted Husing had reported favorably on his Alabama broadcasts. Allen moved to CBS Radio in 1936 (after finishing a teaching assignment) and his broadcast career was on its way.

Allen made it to a Major League broadcast booth with the Yankees in late 1939 after losing out on the Senators job to retired pitcher Walter Johnson. Allen remained in New York until he departed for the Army in 1943. He did not return until 1946, but thereafter was a fixture in the Yankee broadcast booth through late 1964.

Allen broadcast the World Series 20 times from the 1940s through 1963 and each All-Star Game from 1952 through 1961. During the 7th inning of Game 4 of the 1963 World Series (the Dodgers swept the Yankees), Allen lost his voice and had to be replaced to finish the game.

He returned for the 1964 season, but was fired in September of that year. He did not return to baseball until he began announcing on the Yankees' cable television station in 1976. He went national again in 1977 when he began the *"This Week in Baseball"* television series, which he continued to narrate until his death. In 1978 Allen and Red Barber were the first two broadcasters to receive the Frick Award and be inducted into the broadcasters' wing of the Hall of Fame.

Book. Mel Allen and Ed Fitzgerald, *You Can't Beat the Hours: A Long, Loving Look at Big League Baseball, Including Some Yankees I Have Known* (1964).

All-Nations Team (1912–1918)

"If Donaldson were a white man, or if the unwritten law of baseball didn't bar Negroes from the Major Leagues, I would give $50,000 for him and think I was getting a bargain." — John McGraw on All-Nations star pitcher John Donaldson (or Jose Mendez, depending on the source). Revisionist historians have indicated that this comment was made in a racist vein because Mendez and his Cuban team had thrashed McGraw's club during a tour of Cuba by the Giants.

The All-Nations Team was founded in 1912 by J.L. Wilkinson, later a white owner in the Negro National League. The club was composed of black, white, Latin, Japanese, Hawaiian and Native American players. The club also featured one woman, who was billed as Carrie Nation. It was a prominent and powerful team prior to World War I, but disbanded in 1918 when many of the players were drafted. Shortly after the war, many of the minority players regrouped as part of the Kansas City Monarchs of the Negro National League.

The All-Nations club was 3–1 in 1916 against the powerful Indianapolis ABC's (an prominent independent black team of the era) and split a series with the Chicago American Giants. Pitcher Jose Mendez was 8–7 in exhibition games against Major League teams, defeating Jack Coombs in 1908 and Eddie Plank in 1909. He also split two games with Christy Mathewson.

All Positions Played

"Back then, my idol was Bugs Bunny, because I saw a cartoon of him playing ball — you know, the one where he plays every position himself with nobody else on the field but him? Now that I think of it, Bugs is still my idol. You have to love a ballplayer like that." — Nomar Garciaparra.

Bert Campaneris.

"I didn't know how to drive." — The A's shortstop on the only problem he had when A's owner Charlie Finley rewarded him with a new Mustang convertible after playing all nine positions in a game on September 8, 1965. He left the game in the 9th inning while playing catcher; he suffered an injury during a home plate collision with runner Ed Kirkpatrick. The Angels won 5–3 in 13 innings. Campaneris had played all nine positions in a game twice in the minor leagues.

Cesar Tovar. The Twins utilityman played every position on September 22, 1968, as the Twins lost to the A's 2–1. Coincidentally, Bert Campaneris led off the game for the A's. Tovar struck out Reggie Jackson during his pitching stint.

Scott Sheldon. On September 6, 2000, the Rangers' Scott Sheldon played every position in a 13–1 loss to the White Sox, who scored 10 runs in the first two innings. Shelton had played all nine positions in a spring training game against Class AAA Oklahoma.

Dale Long. Long, famous for *Home Runs* in eight consecutive games and as the last out of Don Larsen's perfect game, and less famous for playing catcher left-handed (see also *Left-Handers*), played all nine positions in a 1954 game for the Hollywood Stars.

Martin DiHigo. The versatile Negro League star and Hall of Famer, considered by many the best all-time ballplayer of any color, often played every position during a single game.

Greg Litton. In 1991 the Giants infielder played a position an inning during the Hall of Fame Game in Cooperstown.

Career. Nineteenth century star Mike "King" Kelly played all positions in 1891, but not in the same game. Hall of Famers Roger Bresnahan and Cap Anson played all nine positions during their long careers.

The last Major Leaguer before 2000 to play all nine positions over his career was the Royals' Bill Pecota, who completed the "cycle" in 1991 by pitching the last two innings of a game against the Angels in a 9–4 win.

On July 4, 2000, the Tigers beat the Devil Rays 11–0, and Detroit's Shane Halter took over at catcher so that he then had played every position in the Major Leagues. He had pitched on July 17, 1998. Halter did it again on October 1, 2000, in the 12–11 Tigers win over the Twins. He went 4-for-5 and scored the winning run in the bottom of the 9th inning.

Negro Leagues. The following Negro Leaguers played every position at one time in their careers (primary position noted): George Britt (pitcher), Jim Brown (catcher), Mac Eggleston (catcher), Harry Jeffries (third base), Biz Mackey (catcher), William "Stack" Martin (outfield) and Quincy Trouppe (catcher).

Only Position Played. Only one player among the many non-pitchers in the Hall of Fame played only one position during his entire career. During his 18-year (1956 to 1973) Major League career, Luis Aparicio never left his full-time job, playing 2,581 games at shortstop, the most games all at one position of any Hall of Famer.

All-Star Games

"The toughest assignment a baseball reporter has is the annual major league All-Star game, because of its many added dimensions. Not only what happens on the field, but the players' team affiliations, and past All-Star records or lack of same, plus ever-changing lineup and position switches, plus the unique characteristics of the game itself—all these must be handled swiftly, completely, briefly, colorfully if possible, and with some semblance of putting first things first."—Charles Einstein in *The Fireside Book of Baseball* (1956).

Results. Through 2004 the National League leads the series 40–34–2. The American League won eight straight through 2004.

Earliest. The original "All-Star" games were played in 1858 at the Fashion Race Course near Jamaica, Long Island, New York. During a three-game series over three months, all-stars from various Brooklyn teams played all-stars from New York in front of crowds of at least 1,500 spectators (though some sources erroneously report crowds of 20,000). Admission was charged for the first time and New York won the series 2–1, with scores of 22–18, 8–29 and 29–18.

The Modern All-Star Game.

"The 1930s also saw an effort to apply the principles of business to baseball, especially in the areas of advertising and promotional techniques.... The first major breakthrough came in 1933 with the institution of the All-Star game.... [Sportswriter] Dan Daniel ... felt that it was about time baseball did something to focus attention on itself and encourage interest: 'What baseball needs is more showmanship, more innovations, in place of mental static and physical inertia which now are found in so many high places in the game.'"—Richard C. Crepeau in *Baseball: America's Diamond Mind* (1980).

Arch Ward, sports editor of the *Chicago Tribune*, supposedly conceived the idea of a modern All-Star Game in the early 1930s. However, what Ward probably conceived was having a high-profile game of some sort tied to the 1933 Chicago World's Fair, otherwise known as the Century of Progress Exposition. *Baseball* magazine had campaigned for an All-Star Game for 20 years, so the idea was nothing new.

In the depths of the Depression in 1933, attendance was slipping at the World's Fair and Ward was its sports chairman. He talked to Judge Landis, who liked the idea of the game. Club owners were not as enthusiastic because they feared injury to the players and dilution of their own gate receipts. Clark Griffith of the Senators was the most vociferous in his opposition, but the owners finally voted to hold it, but only as a one-shot event.

Fans and sportswriters were strongly supportive of the event. In an interview a few years later, American League president Will Harridge recalled how Ward had approached him about the idea and that he had supported it. Harridge said that National League president John Tener initially opposed it.

First Game. John McGraw, having resigned from the Giants the year before due to poor health, was asked to manage the National League team. Connie Mack, already 68 years old but destined to manage another 17 years, headed the American League squad. A total of 47,595 fans (or 51,000 in some sources) attended the game at Comiskey Park on July 6, 1933.

Babe Ruth and Dizzy Dean captained the two teams. The two stars used the old-fashioned method of determining the home team: they alternately gripped the bat one hand over the other to the top of the handle. Ruth hit the first home run in All-Star Game history and fouled out in his only other at-bat. The home team American League won 4–2.

The Early Years. After the first game the National League asked for and received permission to host a rematch, though a number of owners opposed the idea as an unnecessary interruption in the schedule. By the late 1930s, the National League considered abandoning the game because it was looking bad: the American League had won the first five games.

Ballot Mistake. In 1974 perennial all-star Luis Aparicio was on the All-Star ballot as an infielder for the Red Sox even though he was cut before the start of the season.

Black Players. The first black players to appear in an All-Star Game were Jackie Robinson, Larry Doby, Roy Campanella and Don Newcombe, all in 1949.

The National League's dominance in the 1960s, with an 11–1 record (with one tie and three years with two games), was attributed in part to the predominance of star black players in the National League. The American League teams were much slower to fully embrace integration.

Brothers. See *Brothers—All-Stars.*

Captain. For the first time, the 1998 All-Star team had a woman as a captain. National League president Leonard Coleman appointed Vera Clemente the position; she is the widow of Roberto Clemente.

Confusion. One source erroneously described the 1940 All-Star Game as being in Tampa on March 13 in front of 13,000 fans. The National League won the game. Whatever exhibition game this might have been, it was not the All-Star Game. The real game was played on July 10 at St. Louis, as the National League shut out the American League 4–0.

Extra Innings. The National League has won eight of nine extra-inning games, with one **Tie** (2002).

Fathers and Sons. See *Fathers and Sons—All-Stars*

Franchise Shift. When the Boston Braves left for Milwaukee at the start of the 1953 season, the All-Star Game had already been scheduled for Boston's Braves Field. The game was then awarded to Cincinnati.

Futures. In 2004 Goose Gossage and Fernando Valenzuela managed the Futures teams at the All-Star Game in Houston. Gossage managed the American minor league stars in a game that preceded the Major League game, and Valenzuela managed the World team against them.

Home Field Advantage. In 2003 Fox television tried to boost ratings in conjunction with Major League Baseball's announcement that the winner of the All-Star Game would have home field advantage for its league in the World Series. The ratings didn't materialize, as they were the same as 2002, a 9.5 rating and a 17 share.

Home Run Derby. In the early 1990s Baseball attempted to beef up the ratings for the game by adding a home run derby competition the day before. It proved to be a great success, though Barry Bonds decided not to participate in 2003, using the following logic: "Because I'm a grown man and I don't have to do it."

Injuries.

"Well Grant, it ain't what it was … but then what the hell is?"— Dizzy Dean to Grantland Rice when Rice inquired about Dean's sore arm caused by an All-Star Game injury.

Dean suffered the most famous All-Star Game injury when Earl Averill hit a line shot off his toe. The broken toe did not heal quickly and Dean altered his pitching style to accommodate it. The result was a sore shoulder and the end of Dean's enormous success.

Ted Williams suffered perhaps the second-most famous All-Star Game injury when he broke his elbow banging into the outfield wall making a catch during the 1950 game (see *Injuries and Illness—Elbow*).

See *Home Plate Collisions* for catcher Ray Fosse's collision with Pete Rose at home plate in 1970.

In 1990 Jose Canseco had not played all season due to injury, but nevertheless was elected to the All-Star Game (but did not play).

Invitation Rescinded. In 2003 Roger Clemens made what was thought to be his farewell tour of the Major Leagues and was having a first half that warranted inclusion on the American League All-Star roster. He was left off, which caused an uproar. To remedy the mistake, commissioner Bud Selig conspired with club owners to determine that previously selected pitcher Barry Zito of the A's would be left off the roster even though Zito was having a fine season and was the reigning Cy Young Award winner. The pretext was that Zito had pitched eight innings on the Sunday before the All-Star Game. Unfortunately, he wasn't informed until he arrived in Chicago for the All-Star Game.

Zito may have received the better deal, because instead he appeared on David Letterman's show to throw a baseball through a plate-glass window. Clemens braved a hurricane to get to the game, and his seven-year-old son was disappointed that the family vacation was being interrupted: "Dad, why can't they get Andy Pettitte?"

Longest/Most Hits. The July 7, 1998, All-Star game was won by the American League, 13–8, as the teams combined for a record-tying 31 hits and played for 3 hours 38 minutes, the longest nine-inning game in the 69-game run of the contest.

Managers.

"The only thing bad about winning the pennant is that you have to manage the All-Star Game the next year. I'd rather go fishing for three days."—Whitey Herzog.

After the inaugural game in 1933, the managers whose clubs won pennants the previous season managed the All-Star teams. After divisional play began in 1969, the managers of the teams which lost the previous years' League Championship Series were the coaches for the next season's All-Star Game.

Most Appearances. Stan Musial, Willie Mays and Henry Aaron each appeared 23 times in the All-Star Game. Among pitchers, Warren Span appeared 17 times, Tom Seaver 12 times, 10 times each for Juan Marichal, Steve Carlton and Don Drysdale, and nine times each for Carl Hubbell, Jim Bunning, Goose Gossage, Early Wynn and Roger Clemens.

In 1998 Cal Ripken set a record with 15 straight All-Star game starts, the previous two at third base. It broke the record that he shared with Willie Mays.

Multiple Positions. Pete Rose and Paul Molitor are the only players in All-Star Game history to be elected at five different positions. Molitor played second base, third base, center field, right field and designated hitter. Rose played left field, right field, first base, second base and third base.

No-Show.

"If I ain't startin', I ain't departin'."—Proclamation of temperamental shortstop Garry Templeton, chosen only as a reserve for the 1981 All-Star Game.

Bob Feller was a no-show for the 1948 All-Star Game. His club was in a tight pennant race and Indians manager Lou Boudreau told him to rest and not appear. Feller went hunting instead.

In 1998 Rangers outfielder Juan Gonzalez declined an appearance in the All-Star Game as a substitute after overzealous voters in Cleveland stacked the American League lineup with Indians.

Number of Players. In 2003 the number of players on each squad was increased from 30 to 32, in part due to the fiasco the previous season with the lack of pitchers forcing the extra-inning tie game to end early. The standard number had been 28 into the 1980s.

Number of Pitchers. In 1935 Lefty Gomez of the Yankees and Mel Harder of the Indians were the only American League pitchers used. They combined to hold the National League to four hits. After the game Judge Landis ruled that in the future no pitcher could go more than three innings.

At the 1942 All-Star Game each team was allowed to use only two pitchers. This ruling by Judge Landis was made because the other All-Star pitchers were needed for charity games the following day against military teams.

Pitchers. Vida Blue is the only pitcher to win All-Star Games in each league: for the American League while with the A's in 1971 and for the National League while with the Giants in 1981.

Steve Carlton is the last pitcher to get a hit in an All-Star Game, a double in the 3rd inning of the 1969 game.

Don Drysdale, Robin Roberts and Lefty Gomez each started five All-Star Games.

Rain. In 1952 the National League was declared a 3–2 winner after five innings in Philadelphia because of heavy rains.

In 1961 in Boston a tie game was rained out after the 9th inning.

In 1969 rain postponed the game in Washington from Tuesday to Wednesday afternoon.

Retirement. Mike Schmidt retired in May 1989 and then was elected as a starter for the 1989 National League All-Star team. He did not play in the game.

Strike Season/1981. When the 1981 player strike ended, the restarted second half of the season commenced with the All-Star Game. Two rules were changed to compensate for the lack of activity. Pitchers were allowed to pitch no more than two innings (instead of three), and rosters were expanded from 28 to 30 players.

Tie Game. In 2002 commissioner Bud Selig took heat for ending the game after completion of the 12th inning, but both teams had run out of pitchers. Fans got their money's worth, however, as they saw a 7–7 tie. He didn't make the decision until after consulting with both managers.

Tough to Get In. Hank Greenberg had 100 RBIs at the All-Star break in 1935 and 170 for the year, but still could not make it to the All-Star Game because Lou Gehrig and Jimmie Foxx were ahead of him at first base.

Tribute. In 1999 the game was played at Fenway Park and the start was delayed 15 minutes when Ted Williams rode out in a golf cart and the All-Stars all gathered around him spontaneously in tribute.

Two Games. From 1959 through 1962, two All-Star Games were played each season. Don Drysdale of the Dodgers started both games in 1959. The games were held two days apart in 1960; otherwise they were approximately 20 days apart. In 1961 one of the games was in Candlestick Park, when the wind knocked pitcher Stu Miller off the mound and a **Balk** was called.

Voting Procedure.

"In all-star games the players are chosen by balloting. Millions of fans vote. It is Democracy at its most transcendent. All the voters get out of it is the loss of a three-cent stamp or a two-cent postal card. Dishonesty in counting the votes has never been charged."—Fred Schwed, Jr., in *How to Watch a Baseball Game* (1957); though as noted below there were accusations of ballot stuffing in Cincinnati in 1957 shortly after Schwed's book was published.

Many sources report that in 1933 the fans elected the players to the game, as the sponsoring *Chicago Tribune* used *The Sporting News* to disseminate ballots. What is not generally known is that the balloting was advisory only, as each team's manager for the game was entitled to pick his starting line-up. This format was followed in 1934. In 1933 the top vote getter among the 500,000 votes cast was Al Simmons of the A's. He received 346,291 votes. National League outfielder Chuck Klein was second with 342,283 votes. Babe Ruth received 320,518 votes.

From 1935 through 1946, the manager picked the entire squad, which sometimes caused problems. The 1942 All-Star Game had a record nine Yankees, six of whom were in the starting line-up. In 1943 All-Star Game manager Joe McCarthy of the Yankees did not use any of the six Yankees he had selected for the game because of his resentment over accusations of favoritism. The American League won anyway, 5–3. This was in contrast to the 1939 game, in which McCarthy used five of his Yankee starters for the entire game; only pitcher Red Ruffing came out.

From 1947 through 1957 the vote was given to the fans, which created its own problems. Eight of the 1957 Reds were elected to the starting line-up by a vote of the fans. Commissioner Ford Frick nullified the voting results and gave the outfield starts to the three who were leading the balloting before a last-minute flurry of votes for the Reds players: Stan Musial was among the top three elected anyway, but Willie Mays and Henry Aaron were added in place of Gus Bell and Wally Post of the Reds.

From 1958 through 1969 the players and the managers chose the players in their own league and could not vote for anyone on their own team. The vote was returned to the fans in 1970.

As a result of the 1994 to 1995 player strike, in 1995 the number of All-Star ballots cast plummeted. The 5,808,000 votes cast were less than the 6,079,688 votes Ken Griffey, Jr., received in 1994, when more than 14 million votes were cast.

Despite the Yankees having the best record in baseball at the 1998 All-Star break, no Yankees were voted into the starting line-up. There was a suggestion that the voting was unfair, because each club was given one million ballots to pass out at its ballparks. Therefore, the attendance numbers during that period would have had an impact on how many votes were cast. According to Rich Levin, the executive director of public relations for Major League Baseball, no record was available as to how many ballots were cast in each of the various franchise areas.

In 2003 for the first time voting was allowed on the Internet. Fans could vote for one additional player to each squad, after the initial voting was completed. Also, managers and players were allowed to vote for some of the spots. Players, coaches and managers were allowed to vote for eight position players, a designed hitter, five starters and three relievers in their league.

Winning Streak.

"I think the National League has better biorhythms in July."—Orioles manager Earl Weaver in 1979 when the National League was nearing the end of a streak in which it won 19 of 20 games between 1963 and 1982. The American League won only in 1971, when Vida Blue earned the victory.

World War II.

"American League power erupted with almost sadistic violence today … [leaving] the National League humiliated, bedraggled and all but comatose under a 12–0 defeat in baseball's first All-Star game of the postwar period."—Sportswriter David J. Walsh on the 1946 game.

The All-Star Game has been held every year since 1933, except 1945, when it was cancelled due to wartime travel restrictions. The war in Europe was over by midseason (May) and prior All-Star Games had not been cancelled during the worst periods of the war. Some contend that the game was cancelled because all of baseball's stars were in the military. The actual reason was that trains were overtaxed because of the enormous number of returning servicemen and other troop movements around the country.

The game was cancelled in February when the government requested a 25% reduction in transportation. When the war ended in Europe in May, there was hope that the game would be rescheduled. Monroe Johnson, head of the Office of Defense Transportation, put an end to such speculation: "They ought to stop yapping about that sort of thing. Conditions are far worse now. Sports will be lucky to play out the regular schedules this summer and fall unless Japan quickly folds up, relieving the burden on transportation. It already has been demonstrated in redeployment following Germany's defeat that the impact on sports, like everything else, will be terrific."

The cancelled game was replaced by seven simultaneous games pitting a National League team against an American League team to raise money for war relief (one of the eight scheduled games was cancelled).

In 1942, on the day following the All-Star Game, the victorious American League All-Stars defeated "Mickey Cochrane's Service All-Stars" 5–0.

Write-in Candidates. In 1970 Rico Carty became the first write-in candidate selected for a starting position. He had a big season in 1969 but was not on the 1970 ballot. When he started fast in 1970, the fans voted him onto the squad.

In 1974 Steve Garvey became the second write-in starter and went on to win the Game's MVP award (and was the National League MVP that season). He also won the MVP Award at the 1978 All-Star Game after becoming the first player to amass four million votes.

Books. Donald Honig, *All-Star Game: A Pictorial History* (1987); Jeff Lenburg, *Baseball's All-Star Game: A Game-by-Game Guide* (1986); Robert Obojski, *All Star Baseball Since 1933* (1980); David Vincent, Lyle Spatz and David W. Smith, *The Midsummer Classic: The Complete History of Baseball's All-Star Game* (2001).

Walter Alston (1911–1984)

Hall of Fame (VC) 1983

"P.S. I nearly forgot the manager. This team [of all-time all-stars] doesn't really need one, but the union requires one be named. So I picked Walter Alston. He's the best handler of men in the game today, and this bunch requires a lot of handling."— Ford Frick in his autobiography, *Games, Asterisks, and People* (1973).

"I would be a liar if I denied that all this heat bothered me, but my philosophy is simple. I merely say that a man must do the best he can—and the hell with everything else."— Alston during the pressure of the 1962 pennant race and play-off loss by the Dodgers.

Alston managed the Dodgers for 23 seasons beginning in 1954, winning seven pennants and four World Series.

Alston had a 13-year minor league playing career beginning in 1935. Late in 1936 he played in one Major League game and struck out in his only **At-Bat**. He managed in the minor leagues beginning in 1940 and remained a player-manager until 1947, when he retired as a player. After the Dodgers promoted him from the Montreal Royals to manage in the Major Leagues for the 1954 season, the club finished second and then won pennants in 1955 and 1956. The Dodgers won their first World Series in 1955 and lost in seven games in 1956.

Alston and the Dodgers moved to Los Angeles in 1958. He led them to pennants in 1959, 1963, 1965, 1966 and 1974, winning the World Series the first three times. The Dodgers lost in a play-off to the Giants in 1962. After the club finished a distant second in 1975 and 1976, he retired gracefully under pressure. Tommy Lasorda replaced him with four games remaining in the 1976 season. Alston left after 23 seasons (signing 23 consecutive one-year contracts), finishing with 2,040 wins, now sixth all-time. He guided the Dodgers to 15 first- or second-place finishes. He was named manager of the year by the Associated Press six times and UPI five times.

Following his retirement, he lived near his hometown in Ohio before succumbing to the heart condition that plagued him in his later years.

Books. Walter Alston with Si Burick, *Alston and the Dodgers* (1966); Walter Alston with Jack Tobin, *A Year at a Time* (1976).

Altitude

"Judging a ball in that atmosphere was mere guess work. Fielder Jones, one of the greatest outfielders in the business, missed the first high fly sent in his direction by fifty feet. Frank Isbell stood under a pop-up at third base and saw it drop ten feet away from him."— G.W. Axelson in *"Commy"* (1919), describing the Chicago White Sox "training on the roof of the continent" in Mexico City in 1907.

Altitude and air pressure affect pitching even more than wind and its direction. Most ballparks in the United States are located at latitudes where the barometric pressure rarely is outside 29.7 to 30.3 inches of mercury. High pressure slows a fastball and adds curve to a pitch. Air pressure can change dramatically in a few minutes in storm areas, and pitches are equally affected.

Atlanta. Before the Colorado Rockies came into the National League, Atlanta's ballpark was the highest in the Major Leagues at 1,000 feet above sea level. Denver is about one mile (5,280 feet) above sea level.

Chicago. Most attribute the many home runs at Wrigley Field to the wind, but another factor is that the ballpark is 600 feet above sea level.

Denver.

"I'd lower Denver."— Composer Randy Newman asked in 1997 on National Public Radio how he would speed up games if he were commissioner. Newman is the writer of the song "Short People [got no reason to live]."

"They might be able to predict hurricanes and tornadoes, but meteorologists have been unable to explain why the air is thinner at Coors Field more often in the top of an inning."— Bernie Lincicome of the *Rocky Mountain News* on the weak Colorado Rockies.

When the Rockies were chosen as a National League expansion club, numerous studies were published about the effect of Denver's altitude on the game. One physicist estimated that balls would fly 10% farther, which might have been a problem considering that Mile High Stadium's left and right field outfield walls were only 335 feet from home plate. The dimensions had been changed periodically to accommodate seating for football and there was no more room to move the fences. The club moved into new Coors Field in 1995. Another study estimated that a curveball that normally breaks 14 inches will lose three inches in the light Denver air.

Tom Glavine had the first shutout at Coors Field, in 1995. He didn't pitch another shutout until April 1997, again at Coors Field.

Darryl Kile signed a three-year deal with the Rockies after the 1997 season, but his curveball flattened out in the altitude and he was a bust, going 13–17 and 8–13 in his two seasons with the club. When he got back near sea level in 1999 with the Cardinals, he won 20 games.

Altoona Pride

Union Association 1884

"Perhaps the Altoona Base Ball Association, Limited, made a mistake entering the Union Association. Maybe the organizers got themselves in over their heads. But with both the Inter-State and Eastern Leagues out of the picture, at least for a month and a half and twenty-five games, the city of Altoona had a fling with professional baseball. Major league? Maybe."— Jerry Jaye Wright in *The National Pastime.*

The Pride, also known as the Mountain Citys, was financed by the Pennsylvania Railroad because the city was a railroad hub connecting East and West. The franchise was the first casualty of the

Union Association's war with Organized Baseball. The club lasted only six weeks with a 6–19 record after losing its first 11 games. Despite four straight wins in May, the Association replaced the financially strapped club with a franchise in Kansas City.

Amateur Baseball

"What must be the contempt for those who would degrade our great 'National Game' and make it a *business*?"—An 1866 amateur player lamenting the creeping professionalism in baseball.

See also *Origins of Baseball*.

19th Century. One source cited the Rochester club of 1825 as the earliest amateur baseball club, closely followed by an 1831 club in Camden, New Jersey. These were Town Ball clubs that were reasonably well established by the mid–1830s.

The New York Nine began play in approximately 1843, prior to the New York Knickerbockers, but as Alexander Cartwright pointed out in later writings, the Nine apparently never had a formal organization. In September 1845, the younger members of the New York Nine formed the Knickerbockers. The Eagle Club of New York may have existed as early as 1840.

In addition to the Knickerbockers, other amateur teams of the early 1850s were the New York Gothams, New York Mutuals, Philadelphia Olympics and the Forest Citys club of Rockford, Illinois (for whom Albert Spalding pitched).

Possibly the best amateur team of the 1860s was the Brooklyn Atlantics, though the team paid many of its players. In 1866 the Philadelphia Athletics openly paid three players $20 a week.

By 1868 so many "amateur" teams were paying players that the existing national baseball organization, the *National Association of Baseball Players*, was forced to recognize them as a separate class of clubs. By that time the top amateur clubs were the Troy Haymakers, Chicago White Stockings, the Lansingburgh (New York) Unions, Cincinnati Buckeyes and Baltimore Marylands.

The formalized 19th century amateur game disappeared after the start of the 1871 professional National Association. Except in colleges and high schools, organized amateur baseball did not reappear until the 20th century.

Hierarchy. There was a hierarchy among early amateur teams. The lowest level clubs were known as muffins, followed by amateurs, second nines and first nines.

Social Atmosphere. The 1840s baseball clubs were social groups restricted primarily to the higher social classes and professionals, making it a "gentleman's game." Home teams would treat visitors to a dinner and, during the off-season, parties were staged. The high society gradually gave way to the common man, reflected in the amateur clubs formed by shipbuilders, firefighters and steamfitters.

20th Century. In the mid–1920s *American Legion Baseball* for boys was formed by Major John L. Griffith. The *American Baseball Congress* was formed in 1935, followed by *Little League Baseball* in 1939. After World War II, *Babe Ruth Leagues*, *Pony Leagues* and *Colt Leagues* for older boys were formed as unrelated offshoots of Little League.

By 1942 five million kids were playing amateur baseball. By the 1960s that number had increased to seven million, with an additional three million playing with no affiliation. More recently, over 30 adult amateur baseball leagues have formed around the country. These include the Roy Hobbs Baseball League for players over 35 years old. Hobbs was the fictional lead character in Bernard Malamud's *The Natural* (1952).

International Baseball. The U.S. did not play in a sanctioned world championship until 1969. The national committee for ama-

teur baseball was not formed until the 1950s after urging from commissioner Ford Frick. This was a national association of college, high school and youth baseball associations. The United States Baseball Federation (USBF) was formed in 1962 as an outgrowth of this effort. The USBF was empowered by a 1978 act of Congress to be the governing body for amateur baseball in the United States.

An international association was formed in 1976, the Association Internationale de Baseball Amateur (AINBA). The U.S. was a strong supporter of this organization and helped spearhead the effort to bring baseball to the Olympics. Over 30 countries were represented in the AINBA by the mid–1970s. In 1984 the AINBA had teams in over 50 countries.

Olympic Games. See *Olympic Games*.

Book. Melvin Adelman, *A Sporting Time* (1986), covers New York City and the rise of modern athletics from 1820 to 1870; Warren J. Goldstein, *Playing for Keeps: A History of Early Baseball* (1990); Jerry Kelly, *Bushville: Life and Times in Amateur Baseball* (2001); George B. Kirsch, *The Creation of American Team Sports: Baseball and Cricket, 1838–1872* (1989); Harry G. Santos, *Town Team: The Folklore of Town Team Baseball* (1990); Jack Selzer, *Baseball in the 19th Century: An Overview* (1986).

Ambidextrous

"Mickey Mantle can hit just as good right-handed as he can left-handed. He's just naturally amphibious."—Teammate and malapropism artist Yogi Berra.

"I'm a natural left-hander, but I bat and throw right-handed because that's the way I learned. But I eat left and drink left and write left. I'm amphibious."—Dale Murphy.

"Amphibious? What's that mean, that he can pitch underwater?"—Andy Van Slyke.

"Someday he's going to be our No. 1 starter and our No. 3 starter as well."—Harvard coach Joe Walsh on Matt Brunnig, a 6'7" pitcher for Harvard in 2003. He was nicknamed "Freak" because he could pitch about 85 mph left-handed and near 90 right-handed. Brunnig threw primarily right-handed.

See also *Switch Hitters*.

George Wright. Wright of the 1869 Cincinnati Red Stockings and an early *Shortstop* who refined that position, could throw with either hand.

Tony "The Count" Mullane. Mullane was the first well-known ambidextrous pitcher, though he normally threw left-handed. Born in Ireland in 1859, he turned pro in 1880 and by the mid–1880s was receiving a salary of $6,000, one of the highest of that period. He won 285 games over a career that lasted into the 1890s. He was extremely strong and reportedly began throwing left-handed only after he hurt his right arm throwing a ball 416' 7" in a contest. More accurate sources report that on July 18, 1882, Mullane pitched with both hands in a game. He switched to his left hand in the 4th inning and eventually lost the game 9–8. He wore no glove, so switching off was not a problem. On July 14, 1893, Mullane threw left-handed during the last inning of a game for the Baltimore Orioles against the Chicago White Stockings. He gave up three runs in a 10–2 loss. He later became a Chicago policeman and died at age 85.

Larry Corcoran. On June 16, 1884, Corcoran pitched for the Chicago White Stockings against Buffalo. He alternated both arms for four innings before switching to shortstop.

Elton "Icebox" Chamberlain. Chamberlain was the last pitcher before 1995 to throw with both hands during a Major League game. On May 9, 1888, the Louisville pitcher threw from both sides of the plate during the last two innings of an 18–6 victory over Kansas City in the American Association.

Jeremiah Denny. Denny, the last player to go his entire career without a glove (he retired in 1894), was ambidextrous. He made plays at third base with either hand as the situation dictated, which could not have been done had he worn a glove.

Tris Speaker. As a boy, Speaker broke his right arm falling off a horse and had to learn to use his left arm. After that he was generally ambidextrous, though he performed right-handed.

Paul Richards. Richards, a Major League general manager in the 1960s and 1970s, was an infielder for Muskogee of the Western Association in 1928. In a brief pitching appearance he threw both left- and right-handed to a single batter, switching gloves on each pitch.

Ray Prim. Prim, who pitched in the 1930s and 1940s, originally was a right-hander, but a bad burn damaged the tendons in his right hand and turned him into a left-hander.

Ed Head and Boo Ferriss. Pitchers Ed Head of the Dodgers and Boo Ferriss of the Red Sox pitched with both hands during exhibition games in the 1940s.

Bert Campaneris. The long-time A's shortstop pitched with both hands in a 1962 game for Daytona Beach of the Florida State League.

Korean Player. Pitcher Won Kuk Lee of Korea signed with the Giants in 1964. He pitched ambidextrously during a brief spring training tryout with the club. After his release he pitched strictly right-handed and won more than 150 games in the Mexican Leagues.

College Players. In the late 1980s, Todd Cason, a right-handed pitcher for St. Leo-Florida City College, started four times in six days by switching hands. He pitched 85 mph right-handed and 82 mph left-handed. The home plate umpire ruled that he could not change gloves during an inning and he could not switch hands during a batter's at-bat.

Jamie Irving pitched both right- and left-handed for Harvard College in the early 1990s. A natural right-hander, he began pitching left-handed as a seven-year-old.

High School Player. In 1992 Rich Brady of Holy Ghost Prep School in Philadelphia was 2–0 as the team's best left-handed pitcher. He was 5–0 with a 1.78 ERA as the team's ace right-handed pitcher. As with other ambidextrous pitchers, he was not allowed to switch hands while pitching to a single batter.

In 2003 the Twins drafted Pete Taraskevich in the 27th round out of American Heritage High in Sunrise, Florida. He was a legitimate switch-pitcher, throwing 90 mph from the right side and 85 mph from the left.

Greg Harris. The Red Sox pitcher was capable of throwing with either hand, but until 1995 did it only in batting practice. In 1993 American League president Bobby Brown circulated a memo to the league's general managers to thwart an attempt by Harris to throw with both hands during a game. Even though Harris had never thrown left-handed in a game, the rules were to "protect against unusual liberties being taken thus creating an intolerable situation on the mound and at the plate."

The rules included the following:

— The pitcher must indicate to the hitter the arm he intends to use;
— The pitcher may change arms on the next hitter but must indicate the arm to be used;
— There will be no warm-up pitches between the change of arms;
— If an arm is injured, the pitcher may change arms and the umpire is notified of the injury. The injured arm cannot be used again in that game.

The response to the memo by one American League general manager: "I threw it directly into the garbage."

On September 28, 1995, Harris finally was able to demonstrate his prowess in a regular-season game. At the time he was 39 and the oldest pitcher in the National League. He pitched the 9th inning of a game for the Expos in a 9–7 loss to the Reds. He faced four batters in the inning, two while pitching right-handed and two left-handed. He used a special six-finger glove that could be used on either hand. He first pitched right-handed and induced Reggie Sanders to ground out. Pitching left-handed, he walked Hal Morris on four pitches. While still pitching left-handed, he got Eddie Taubensee to ground out. Switching back to his right hand, Harris retired Bret Boone on a ground ball.

American Amateur Baseball Congress See *American Baseball Congress*

American Association (1882–1891)

"The Beer and Whiskey League"

The American Association, formally known as the American Association of Professional Base Ball Clubs, operated as a Major League rival to the National League from 1882 through 1891.

Clubs. The following is a list of all cities which had clubs in the American Association and the years of their existence. Dates in parentheses indicate championship seasons.

Baltimore	1882–1891
Boston	1891 (1891)
Brooklyn	1884–1890 (1889)
Cincinnati	1882–1889, 1891 (1882)
Cleveland	1887–1888
Columbus	1883–1884, 1889–1891
Indianapolis	1884
Kansas City	1888–1889
Louisville	1882–1891 (1890)
Milwaukee	1891
New York	1883–1887 (1884)
Philadelphia	1882–1891 (1883)
Pittsburgh	1882–1886
Richmond	1884
Rochester	1890
St. Louis	1882–1891 (1885–1888)
Syracuse	1890
Toledo	1884, 1890
Washington	1884, 1891

Formation. The first attempt to create a rival to the National League occurred in 1880. Groups in St. Louis, Philadelphia and Cincinnati led the initial effort after those cities had their clubs expelled from the National League.

National League president William Hulbert was successful in derailing the effort by persuading the important independent New York Metropolitan club to abandon the American Association's organizational attempts and join the *League Alliance* of clubs friendly to the National League. National League clubs also signed a number of players from the Washington club that had been expelled from the League Alliance, whose owners were considering a move to the proposed American Association.

Another attempt at formation was made in 1881, when "Hustling" Horace B. Phillips, owner of the independent Philadelphia A's and "a neglected hero of the game," wrote to Alfred H. Spink, St. Louis sportswriter and future publisher of *The Sporting News*.

Phillips suggested that they form an association of clubs in St. Louis, Cincinnati, Louisville, Pittsburgh, Baltimore and Philadelphia.

Phillips called a meeting in Pittsburgh to discuss the idea, but only two people showed up. Phillips himself forgot about the meeting. The two who showed up telegrammed others known to be interested in a league and they agreed to participate.

Meetings were held on October 10, 1881, and November 2, 1881, with Spink heavily involved by then. The group consummated efforts to form the American Association of Professional Base Ball Clubs, known as the American Association.

Harmer Dennis "Denny" McKnight of Pittsburgh was elected the first president. J. H. Park, an institution in Louisville as head of a Kentucky malting company, was elected secretary-treasurer.

First Season/Original Clubs. The original American Association clubs primarily filled a void in the Midwest. The first five were the Brooklyn Atlantics, Pittsburgh Alleghenys, Cincinnati Redstockings (owned by former *Sportswriter* O.P. Caylor), St. Louis Brown Stockings (organized by Spink), and the Louisville Eclipse. Brooklyn was dropped before the inaugural season of 1882 (pleading lack of funds) and was replaced by Baltimore, owned by brewer Harry Von der Horst. The Philadelphia Athletics joined the group to create the initial six-team league. Two Philadelphia clubs had vied to represent the city in the Association, but only one was accepted because it alone had a playing field.

Dues initially were $50 per club, which increased to $100 the second year. The American Association cities had a total population of 2,370,000, greater than the combined National League total of 1,156,000. This gave the American Association the edge in potential attendance. Cincinnati won the first pennant with a 55–25 record and attempted to play a *Championship Series* with the National League pennant winner. Each American Association home team was allowed to guarantee 65% of the gate for itself, but proceeds were divided equally on holidays.

Key Differences with the National League. There were three key differences between the American Association and the National League: the Association played Sunday ball, sold beer (some of the owners were wealthy beer barons), and the admission price was 25 cents (half the National League price). The Association also had a permanent core of umpires and was the first league to base a championship on winning percentage, rather than total wins. This was an important factor because teams often played a different number of games. Partly as a result of these differences, the Association flourished at its inception.

National League Disdain.

"The [National] League does not recognize the existence of any Association of ball clubs excepting itself and the League Alliance…. I don't care to go to the question of the League's attitude toward the so-called American Association further than to say that it is not likely the League will be awake nights bothering its head about how to protect against a body in which it has no earthly interest, and which voluntarily assumed a position of hostility toward the League."—National League president William Hulbert.

The National League supporters referred to the Association as the "Beer & Whiskey League," in part because three of the eight early owners were liquor and beer barons. The Association players also wore brighter uniform colors than the National League, prompting the derisive name "jockey silks."

By May 1882 the rift between the leagues had widened and the new Association forbade interleague play mixed in with intraleague games. Up to that point, it was customary for league clubs to schedule games with non-league clubs when the league schedule permitted. A postseason series between Cincinnati of the Association and Chicago of the National League ended after only two games. American Association President McKnight supposedly threatened Cincinnati with expulsion if the series was not stopped. However, other sources point out that the *Championship Series* was only scheduled for two games and that it was discontinued because of other postseason commitments previously scheduled by the two teams.

The Association was a strong league in 1882 and soon extended open invitations to the National League's players, prompting a series of lawsuits over club-jumping. The Association went to court to enjoin Samuel Wise from jumping to the National League's Boston Red Stockings. This was the first well-known lawsuit involving Major League Baseball. The Association then moved into New York and Columbus for the 1883 season, in which the Philadelphia Athletics won the pennant.

The 1884 Union Association Challenge. In response to the proposed 1884 Union Association, the American Association immediately expanded to a 13-team league that included Toledo, Indianapolis, Richmond, Brooklyn and Washington. This was an attempt by the Association to become a truly national league. This strategy was successful later when Ban Johnson's Western League expanded eastward and changed its name to the American League in 1900. When the Union Association folded after one season in 1884, the Association rolled back to eight teams and accepted back its few players who had defected to the Union Association. Only 27 jumped from the American Association and the National League.

Problems by Mid-Decade. By 1886 the Association was beginning to show signs of problems. The Pittsburgh owners were upset over treatment the club received from the Association over player contract disputes. As a result, the club defected to the National League after the 1886 season. Later defections included Cleveland, Cincinnati and Brooklyn. Brooklyn left in part because of a dispute with St. Louis over a *Forfeit* in September 1889. This left Christopher Von der Ahe in St. Louis as one of the few remaining strong owners. There was also increasing club jumping by players (in both directions) as the Association increased its signing of blacklisted National League players.

In the mid–1880s the National League New York Giants and American Association New York Metropolitans were owned by the same group. After the 1885 season the owners shifted the best of the Metropolitan players to the National League Giants. A weak American Association franchise in large-market New York was detrimental to the overall health of the Association.

Founding President Dennis McKnight was implicated in player manipulations involving Sam Barkley of the Pittsburgh club. McKnight had been a part-owner of the club, though the relationship was nominally severed after the 1884 season. McKnight had a business administration background but was viewed as only adequate and ultimately lost his battle to retain the presidency. However, he was the only president to last for a significant period of time, from 1882 through 1889.

McKnight was succeeded at the 1889 winter meeting by weak Wheeler Wikoff, who was chosen after an election stalemate was broken when Brooklyn and Cincinnati resigned from the Association.

1890 and the Players League. The departed Brooklyn and Cincinnati clubs had been two of the Association's stronger teams and the Association was weakened significantly even before the 1890 Players League. Brooklyn won the National League pennant that season with its leftover 1889 American Association club. Also in 1890, the Association's Louisville club became the only team in Major League history until 1991 to go from last (in 1889) to first in one year.

As part of an overall reorganization of the leagues after the tumultuous and financially devastating Players League challenge of 1890, the Association bought out its weak franchises in the smaller towns of Toledo, Rochester and Syracuse. The owners of these teams were paid a total of $24,000. That same year the Association's Philadelphia franchise was expelled for not meeting its financial obligations to the Association.

The Post-Players League Fight with the National League. Allan Thurman became president of the American Association after playing a key role in negotiating peace between the remaining leagues after the 1890 season. Nevertheless, he was faced with resolving significant differences with the National League. He wanted the Association to place a club in Philadelphia and worked with National League owner Albert Spalding to attempt a compromise that included an Association team in Chicago. The Association also proposed placing a team in Washington after the National League abandoned that city.

As the negotiations began to break down, there was talk of the American Association merging with the remnants of the Players League to counter the National League's stronger position. Ultimately the National League and American Association agreed on an Association team in Boston created out of Charles A. Prince's Players League club in that city. The Association's new Philadelphia A's club was created out of the Philadelphia Players League club. No Association club was placed in Chicago.

The two remaining leagues appeared to have worked out their differences in achieving peace through dispersal of the Players League teams in late 1890. However, the leagues began quarreling over the division of players, with two players at the center of the controversy: Harry Stovey and Louis Bierbauer. Philadelphia of the Association had failed to reserve the players and Pittsburgh of the National League signed them. This led to the "Pirates" nickname for the Pittsburgh club.

Philadelphia appealed to the National Agreement Board and lost. As a result, Allan Thurman was removed as Association president and replaced by Louis Kramer, a Cincinnati lawyer and one of the founders of the Association. Kramer then moved to withdraw from the National Agreement.

The Failure of the Association.
"Lacking in business sense, in shrewdness, in knowledge, in foresight, in strategy, in unity of purpose, in faith in each other and, finally, in a positive head — its chief constantly intimidated by aggressive owners." — Association president Dennis McKnight summing up the ultimate reasons for the downfall of the American Association.

As a result of the 1890 player reassignment dispute with the National League, the American Association withdrew from the National Agreement and tried to exist separately. In the spring of 1891, with the American Association floundering, the National League withdrew from exhibition games with the Association. This caused further financial strain on the Association, which had already endured problems during the 1890 Players League fight. Only four or five Association clubs were profitable during 1891 and the Association was pooling income in desperation, but its ownership was less cohesive than that of the National League.

After the 1891 season, the Association outlined a peace plan at a December 1891 meeting. The plan was designed to save the Association and allow it to coexist with the National League. The Association's so-called Peace Committee was thought to be making progress with the National League, but Mike "King" Kelly jumped from the Association to the National League's Boston franchise and the peace was called off.

When the peace conference reconvened, owners Stanley Robison of the Association's Cleveland club and Christopher Von der Ahe of the Association's St. Louis club orchestrated the disbanding of the Association and the creation of a 12-team National League that included their two Association teams. The meeting appears to have been a power play by these two strongest Association clubs to remain in existence and be absorbed into the National League.

Eventually four Association teams were absorbed by the National League: St. Louis, Baltimore, Washington and Louisville. The Association teams that were not absorbed into the National League threatened suit and in response the league paid them a total of $131,000. The payments were funded by each National League club withholding 10% of its gate receipts over the next few years. Association clubs Boston, Philadelphia, Columbus, Milwaukee and Chicago were bought out, with the Wagners of Philadelphia buying the stock of the National League Washington club.

Technically, there was to be a single 12-team "National League and American Association of Professional Baseball Clubs," but that entity never existed after the Association disbanded during the December 1891 negotiations. The fiction of the two leagues having merged was maintained at least through 1898. In formal resolutions through that season the National League referred to itself as the National League and American Association of Professional Base Ball Clubs.

1894 Attempt to Revive the American Association. An attempt was first made to revive the Association in 1894, but nothing came of it. The plan was to have eight teams, 25-cent admission and no reserve clause.

New American Association. Plans for a new Association were announced in 1899 and became more likely when the National League was rumored to be reducing its number of clubs from 12 to eight. It was believed that the new league could sign the players whose teams were eliminated and establish clubs in at least some of the abandoned cities.

The prime mover of the new league was George Schaefer, a 30-year-old St. Louis alderman. After attempting unsuccessfully to purchase the National League Cardinals in 1898, he met with former American Association backers A. H. Spink of *The Sporting News* and Christopher Von der Ahe, former owner of the Browns who had lost his team due to financial problems. Ban Johnson was among those invited to an organizational meeting in September 1899, but he apparently declined to participate. Another notable attendee was Cap Anson, who had left the Chicago White Stockings after 27 years with the club.

By late 1899 the fledgling league had franchises ready to play in St. Louis (backed by Von der Ahe and Spink), Chicago (with Anson) and Milwaukee. Former National League star Tommy McCarthy was ready with a team in Boston, but the important New York franchise did not materialize after early promise.

John McGraw and Wilbert Robinson were to lead a franchise in Baltimore, but could not secure a park to play in after much haggling with the owners of the National League franchise in Baltimore, Ned Hanlon and Harry Von der Horst.

The National League countered by working with the Western Association to place teams in the prospective American Association cities to provide additional competition. The older league also planned to sue the new American Association over the use of the name because the National League had acquired it with the merger of the two leagues in 1892. As a result, the proposed league officially began calling itself the New American Association.

In January 1900 the new Association's first seven cities were announced: Baltimore, Boston, Chicago, Detroit, Milwaukee, Philadelphia and Detroit. Providence and Washington were considered for the last spot. The league then met for what was anticipated to be the final preseason planning session. Play was to begin on April 16, 1900. Two days after the meeting, however, Cap Anson announced that the new league had collapsed because the well-financed Philadelphia franchise had dropped out. There was a brief effort to form the league for the 1901 season, but nothing came of it.

Resurrection as a Minor League in 1902. See *American Association* (Minor League).

Books. David Nemec, *The Beer and Whiskey League* (1994).

American Association (Minor League) (1902–1997)

Creation. When the American Association was resurrected in 1902, it did so as a minor league. In 1915 the Association again tried to become a third Major League, but its attempt was rejected by the National Commission. At the time, the Association's attendance of 1.4 million was 40% of the respective attendance of the National League and American League.

Modern Teams. In 1996 the American Association had the following teams: Nashville Sounds, Louisville Redbirds, Buffalo Bisons, Indianapolis Indians, Iowa Cubs, Omaha Royals, New Orleans Zephyrs and Oklahoma City 89ers.

Disbanded. After the 1997 season the league disbanded and its clubs were absorbed into the International League or the Pacific Coast League. The Buffalo Bisons defeated the Iowa Cubs for the last American Association title.

Book. Bill O'Neal, *The American Association: A Baseball History 1902–1991* (1992).

American Baseball Congress (1935–)

This organization was founded in 1935 in Battle Creek, Michigan, where it is still headquartered. It was created to serve adults in amateur leagues, but now has different levels of play that includes children and teenagers. The word "amateur" was added to the name in 1955 but later eliminated. By 1950 the ABC had affiliates in Argentina, Austria, Canada, Ecuador, Guatemala, India, Israel, Japan, Korea, Mexico, Netherlands Antilles, Nicaragua, Panama, Philippines, Taiwan and Venezuela. International membership expanded dramatically after 1970.

By the 1980s the organization had 3,000 teams and 75,000 players. Its divisions:

Minor Willie Mays	Ages 8 & Under
Willie Mays	Ages 10 & Under
Pee Wee Reese	Ages 12 & Under
Sandy Koufax	Ages 14 & Under
Mickey Mantle	Ages 16 & Under
Connie Mack	Ages 18 & Under
Stan Musial	Ages 19 & Over

American Baseball Guild (1946)

This was an attempt to organize a Major League players *Union* spurred primarily by the desire for a *Pension Plan*.

American League (1901–)

("American League of Professional Baseball Clubs")
Chicago, Illinois
May 8, 1901

"Dear Sir:

The clubs will please make their ten percent returns after each series of games. All transportation bills must be paid promptly. For all amounts exceeding one hundred dollars please send a New York draft or Chicago Exchange. The rule requiring the clubs to cut their players to fourteen will not be in force until May 20th. Please notify your official scorer to make his reports after each series of games. I will permit no delay in this matter.

The club Managers are requested to institute such reforms as will shorten the games. In some of the cities of the American League the games have been long drawn out, and there has been much complaint. The catchers hereafter will play up behind the bat throughout the game. This is a standing order.

CLEAN BALL is the MAIN PLANK in the American League platform, and the clubs must stand by it religiously. There must be no profanity on the ball field. The umpires are agents of the League and must be treated with respect. I will suspend any Manager or player who uses profane or vulgar language to an Umpire, and that suspension will remain in force until such time as the offender can learn to bridle his tongue. Rowdyism and profanity have worked untold injury to base ball. To permit it would blight the future of the American League. This bulletin you will please hand to your Manager so that he may impart its content to the players.

All fines must be paid within five days of the date of mailing notice. In the event of a club failing to pay a fine the player will be suspended until the fine is paid. You will please forward to me at once your contracts with the players so that they be approved and filed. I am —
Yours truly,
B. B. Johnson"

— An early 1901 directive from the American League president.

Formation.

"I have always regarded Comiskey as the father of the American League and the sponsor of the president of that organization. There never has been any doubt in my mind that it was Comiskey who made the American League what it is today — the rival of the National League. His practical knowledge of baseball was known throughout the country and when he advised men with capital to become club-owners they listened to him and heeded his advice." — Former newspaperman and Cubs owner Charles Murphy.

The American League was originally called the *Western League*. *American League President* Ban Johnson changed the name from Western League to American League in October 1899 to give it a more national flavor. This was part of his overall scheme to have the National League and Organized Baseball recognize the American League as a second Major League. The so-called "Junior Circuit" was not recognized by the National Association as a Major League until the 1901 season.

On October 14, 1900, the five-year Western League agreement expired and this gave Johnson the option of realigning the teams.

As part of his plan, Johnson, Charles Comiskey and Cleveland owner Charles Somers set out to find appropriate eastern cities in which to place American League teams. Connie Mack worked to find backing for a team to be placed in Philadelphia. A group in Boston was ready to sponsor a team in 1901, and John McGraw and Wilbert Robinson were prepared to sponsor a team in Baltimore.

See also *Western League — Statistics* for the treatment of the 1900 season statistics in relation to Major League totals for those players who were in the Western League that season.

National League Objection. Charles Hart of the Chicago Cubs initially objected to the American League's placement of a team in Chicago. After meeting with Ban Johnson, however, he rescinded his objection to avoid interleague war — but only after the National League received assurances from Johnson that the American League would: 1) abide by the National Agreement regarding player contracts; 2) pay the National League for improvements previously made to the Cleveland ballpark abandoned by the National League and to be occupied by the American League; and 3) allow Hart to take a few quality American League players (actually only one Chicago White Sox player). However, this initial effort at harmony did not prevent all-out war.

Johnson tried to achieve a compromise with the National League in late 1900, but the older league snubbed him at its December meeting. The National League had told Johnson that it was interested in discussing a merger and had invited him to address its owners. Johnson came to the meeting, but was left standing outside the meeting room as the National League abruptly changed its strategy and awarded the American League's Minnesota and Kansas City territories to a new Western League before the American League had abandoned those cities.

The National League further snubbed the American League's overtures by demanding that the American League pay its traditional minor league fee to the National League. Johnson ignored this demand and became even more aggressive.

First Player Signed. When the American League announced its realignment for 1901, Joe McGinnity signed the league's first new contract, with Baltimore.

The Original Teams and Their Owners. The last pre–American League cities in the Western League were Detroit, Buffalo, Philadelphia, Minneapolis, Indianapolis, Milwaukee, Cleveland and Kansas City. In 1901, primarily Midwest and small-market Indianapolis, Minneapolis, Kansas City and Buffalo were replaced by the primarily eastern and large-market cities of Boston, Chicago, Baltimore and Washington. This put intracity rival clubs in Chicago and Boston, joining Philadelphia with more than one Major League club.

The American League backers were Tom and Ben Shibe, Philadelphia sporting goods tycoons; Charles Somers, a Cleveland building contractor and coal baron; former sportswriter Ban Johnson; and pure baseball men Charles Comiskey, Connie Mack and Clark Griffith.

Teams: 1901–1903. The American League clubs were juggled considerably between 1900 and the start of the 1903 season. However, the 1903 group proved to be an enduring combination because there were no franchise moves until 1953. The 1901–1903 teams (championship years are in parentheses):

Baltimore	1901–1902
Boston	1901–1903 (1903)
Chicago	1901–1903 (1901)
Cleveland	1901–1903
Detroit	1901–1903
Milwaukee	1901
New York	1903
Philadelphia	1901–1903 (1902)
St. Louis	1902–1903
Washington	1901–1903

First Game. In the first American League game, Cleveland played Chicago on April 24, 1901, with Ollie Pickering as the first American League batter. This game was the only one played on that date because the other three games were rained out. Chicago won 8–2 in front of 9,000 fans in a game that took 3 hours and 35 minutes to play.

One source incorrectly identified the first American League game as played on April 26, 1901, when Baltimore defeated Boston 10–6 in front of 10,371 fans.

Last Survivor. The last surviving player of the American League's inaugural Major League season in 1901 was Paddy Livingston of Cleveland, who died in 1977 at age 97.

Player Raiding and Competition. The National League's salary cap of $2,400 made it easier for the American League to raid its players. Nevertheless, a number of National League owners circumvented the salary cap by paying bonuses. There was a large pool of available ex–National Leaguers when that league contracted from 12 to eight teams after the 1899 season.

In 1901, 111 of 182 American League players were ex–National League players, which resulted in a few lawsuits between the leagues. In three cities where both leagues competed (Chicago, St. Louis and Philadelphia), American League attendance was better in 1902.

1902–1903/A Team in New York. Ban Johnson was interested in having John McGraw manage a new Baltimore franchise in the American League after the National League eliminated its Baltimore club after the 1899 season. As a result, McGraw became the chief stockholder and manager of the new American League club in Baltimore.

Johnson and McGraw began to feud over McGraw's on-field conduct against umpires (he was suspended at least once) and McGraw eventually sandbagged Johnson and took over as manager of the National League Giants. Johnson then completed his effort to move the Baltimore franchise to New York (which apparently was always his secret plan), but held life-long animosity toward McGraw for abandoning the league.

National League historian Lee Allen had a theory, however weak, that the feud was orchestrated to place an American League team in all-important New York. Allen's theory is supported by (and maybe based on) a 1953 book by Mrs. John McGraw, *The Real McGraw*. She claimed that her husband and Ban Johnson did not feud and carefully planned the move to New York. Allen believed that the sequence of events was as follows:

1) McGraw had spent several thousand dollars on the Baltimore club's debts; the director of the club gave him his release to manage a big league club in New York (his dream) instead of reimbursing him on the debt. The club also let him take key players with him;

2) The owner of the Orioles was bought out by the American League (actually Johnson himself until he could find local backers), and Johnson's son-in-law, Baltimore star Joe Kelley, was allowed to sign as player-manager with Cincinnati in the National League. Cy Seymour was also sent to the Reds;

3) John Brush, whom Johnson did not like from his days as a sportswriter in Cincinnati, sold the Reds to brothers Max and Julius Fleischmann, as well as George Cox (political boss of the city). The Reds' operations were then turned over to Garry Herrmann, a ward politician in that city;

4) Brush then bought the New York Giants from the universally despised Andrew Freedman and peace was made with the Albert Spalding (Cubs owner) faction in the National League. Harry Pulliam was then elected National League president at the urging of Pirates owner Barney Dreyfuss;

5) The National League allowed the American League to put a club in New York in 1903, with Frank Farrell as owner. Farrell had been associated with the Fleischmanns in New York thoroughbred racing circles.

The problem with the theory is that McGraw himself acknowledged that he was at odds with Johnson, as quoted by Fred Lieb in *The Baseball Story* (1950): "I knew what Ban Johnson was up to. As far back as midseason of 1902, he made secret plans to drop Baltimore and move the franchise to New York. That was all right with me, as I expected to go along as manager, with a share in the club. But, when I learned I did not enter into Johnson's New York plans, and that he was ready to ditch me at the end of the 1902 season, I acted fast. He planned to run out on me, so I ran out on him, and beat him to New York by nearly a year."

1903/The Dispute Ends. By 1903 the National League was feeling the pinch of competition and offered a merger proposition. Johnson initially refused because there was parity between the leagues and the American League had an established team in New York. The only concession that Johnson made was not to move the financially hurting Tigers to small-market Pittsburgh to compete with the Pirates.

Because of the compromise, the leagues were able to play the first World Series in 1903. The new tradition was temporarily suspended in 1904 when the Giants won the National League pennant. Owner John Brush still held lingering animosity toward Johnson and decided to snub him and his league by refusing to play in the Series. Some said that manager John McGraw also favored the boycott, but more reliable sources blame only Brush. The Series resumed for good in 1905, ironically under a set of rules devised by Brush.

1903–1919.
"From 1901 through the First World War, [Johnson] ruled with an iron hand—not only his own league, but pretty much all baseball. He never ducked a fight. He was never neutral. He was unforgiving in his enmities, and blind to any shortcomings in his friends. He was intolerant of opposition and enraged by criticism."—Ford Frick in *Games, Asterisk and People* (1973).

This period saw the consolidation of Johnson's power and the strengthening of the American League. Johnson guided the league through the Federal League challenge of 1913–1915 and he still had considerable power through the end of World War I in 1918. However, by the end of the decade, certain American League owners were openly hostile toward Johnson, primarily over decisions involving player movement between clubs. Johnson's power began to erode, a process accelerated by the appointment of Judge Landis as commissioner in 1920.

Curbs on Johnson's Power. In 1919 the American League's board of directors consisted of Ban Johnson, Jim Dunn of Cleveland, Charles Comiskey of Chicago, Jacob Ruppert of New York and Harry Frazee of Boston.

In 1920 certain owners sought to curb much of Johnson's power, culminating in a decision in the *Carl Mays Incident*. The dispute over which team the pitcher would play for severely divided the owners. As a result, on February 10, 1920, a two-man board of review was created, which lasted for two years. Rupert of the Yankees, who feuded with Johnson over Mays, and Clark Griffith of the Senators, who sided with Johnson, made up the committee. If

they could not agree on penalties of $100 or more, or resolve other disputes, then they were to submit the dispute to a federal court judge in Chicago. That judge could have been the future commissioner, Judge Landis, who was a federal court judge sitting in Chicago at the time and didn't become commissioner until November 1920, but the facts are unclear in the available sources. From that point forward Johnson's power was significantly curtailed (see also *American League Presidents*).

After the late 1926 *Gambling* revelations involving Ty Cobb and Tris Speaker, Johnson was at odds with Judge Landis. All American League owners except Phil Ball repudiated Johnson's remarks about the incident and forced Johnson to take a leave of absence. Interim control was given to Frank Navin of the Tigers. At the start of the 1927 season, Johnson declared himself ready to resume his duties, but he was voted out at a special meeting on July 8. He hastily scribbled his resignation and presented it to Jacob Rupert of the Yankees, effective after the season. His $40,000 annual salary was payable until 1935, but reportedly he took nothing after 1927. He died in 1931.

Rifts with the National League. Over the years, there have been numerous disputes with the National League, the most recent of which was the sharing of *Expansion* fees that the National League received in 1992 and reluctantly shared with the American League.

The American League has often been perceived as the more progressive league, as evidenced by a comment about the National League owners by former Orioles owner and prominent Washington lawyer Edward Bennett Williams: "They move very, very reluctantly. I think it was a long time before any of them had inside plumbing."

Rifts were impossible after 1999, when the two leagues' presidencies were abolished and the commissioner's office melded both offices.

Club Departure. The Milwaukee Brewers left the league after the 1997 season and rejoined the National League in 1998.

Books. Lee Allen, *The American League Story* (1962); Glenn Dickey, *History of American League Baseball Since 1901* (1980); Ed Fitzgerald, ed., *The American League* (1952); Donald Honig, *American League: An Illustrated History* (1987); David Lee Poremba, *The American League: The Early Years* (2000); Joel Zoss, *The American League: A History* (1986).

American League Presidents

"All I ever wanted to be was president of the American League." — A. Bartlett Giamatti, then Yale University president and future *National* League president and commissioner of baseball.

This section contains biographical sketches of each American League president until the position was eliminated in early 2000:

1901–1927	Ban Johnson
1927–1931	Ernest Barnard
1931–1959	Will Harridge
1959–1973	Joe Cronin
1974–1983	Lee MacPhail, Jr.
1983–1994	Bobby Brown, M.D.
1994–2000	Gene Budig

Overview. Johnson was a former sportswriter. Barnard and MacPhail were front office executives. Harridge was a railroad clerk and Johnson's secretary for many years. Cronin and Brown were former players. Budig was a college president.

Byron Bancroft "Ban" Johnson (1864–1931)
Served 1901–1927
Hall of Fame 1937
"His contribution to the game ... is not closely equaled by any other single person or group of persons."—Branch Rickey.

"Johnson, a ruthless dreamer who lived and died believing that baseball was perfected in order to serve him as a gigantic chess board on which to move his living pieces..."— Bob Considine in a 1948 *Life* magazine article about Connie Mack.

"The hiring of Landis was the thing that turned Johnson into a screaming harridan. And had Ban been just a little less arrogant he might have saved himself the crushing burden of dealing with the equally arrogant Landis."— Umpire Bill Klem.

"The voice of the lion is stilled; they say the lion was getting old, that his roar had become a mumble. It may be so. But never, maybe, will be heard again such a voice — the roar that struck terror to evil doers, in high estate or low, and thrilled to new encouragement those who had ideals and the vision Ban Johnson had..."— Earl Obenshain in *The Sporting News* when Johnson retired in 1927.

Founder of the **American League**, Byron Bancroft ("Ban") Johnson was considered an unlikable autocrat, publicity hungry, a hard drinker and quick-tempered. He was known as the "Czar of Baseball" until Judge Landis was appointed commissioner in late 1920.

The son of a minister, Johnson became a college professor after playing baseball in Ohio as a catcher at Oberlin and Marietta colleges, the latter where he graduated in 1887. He made no attempt to play professionally, though he briefly tried semipro ball.

After his teaching days, Johnson was a sportswriter for the *Cincinnati Commercial-Gazette*. His first formal experience as a baseball executive was as **Western League** president, having been recommended by National League Cincinnati owner John Brush. Johnson had been critical of Brush's club, so some sources report

American League founder and autocratic long-time president, Byron Bancroft "Ban" Johnson.

that Brush helped Johnson get the Western League job to get rid of him. In 1901 Johnson orchestrated the Western League's challenge to the National League after a 1900 name change to American League.

By 1910 his salary was $25,000, plus expenses. He also held financial interests in certain of the league's clubs, often as security for loans he made to struggling franchises such as Washington. He was earning $40,000 annually by the 1920s.

Johnson and White Sox owner Charles Comiskey were friends from the days when Johnson reported on Comiskey's old American Association club. The friendship began to deteriorate in 1905, which later would lead to an erosion of Johnson's power. That year Johnson upheld the suspension of White Sox outfielder James "Ducky" Holmes after he had a dispute with an umpire. Comiskey then moved out of the office that he had shared with Johnson in Chicago. In 1907 another Chicago player was suspended and their friendship was superficial thereafter. Johnson remained firmly in control of the league until 1918, despite having the powerful and respected Comiskey as an adversary.

By 1918 the Comiskey/Johnson relationship had broken down completely over a dispute involving pitcher Jack Quinn (see **Trades and Player Sales**—Feud). In late 1919 when Johnson started his own **Black Sox Scandal** probe, he apparently believed that he could use the incident to drive Comiskey out of baseball. As a result of the increased animosity that resulted, they were bitter enemies until they died a few months apart in 1931.

In 1920 Johnson's power was eroded almost completely as a result of the **Carl Mays Incident**, requiring a decision as to which club owned rights to the pitcher. On February 10, 1920, the American League owners held a final meeting to resolve the Mays case and all other American League differences. At 2 a.m. a settlement was reached and power was taken out of Johnson's hands.

In 1925 Johnson's contract was extended another five years, though he was virtually a figurehead at that point. Another source reported that he received a 20-year contract in 1911, so either that source is wrong or the long contract was torn up as part of the restructuring of Johnson's power.

In 1926 he clashed with Judge Landis over evidence of a **Gambling** scandal involving Ty Cobb and Tris Speaker. Johnson and Landis disagreed over the proper discipline for the two stars. Landis prevailed and allowed Cobb and Speaker to remain in baseball. With the exception of Phil Ball of the Browns, American League owners sided with Landis on the issue. As a result, the owners stripped Johnson of the last bit of his power. In January 1927 he was sent on a forced vacation but returned for the season. It was publicly announced in July that he would resign effective in November.

He resigned at the end of the season on October 18, 1927. Most sources accurately report that he resigned because of the loss of power, but some earlier sources more generously claim that he retired due to poor health. He died of diabetes four years later on March 29, 1931. See also, Eugene C. Murdock, *Ban Johnson: Czar of Baseball* (1983).

Ernest Sargent Barnard (1874–1931)
Served 1927–1931

"At Otterbein in Ohio, Ernest S. Barnard ... appointed himself coach and manager of the baseball team. Once he found himself without a battery, so he borrowed pitcher John Cooney and catcher Bob Quinn from a non-college team in Columbus, collecting them himself with a horse and wagon. With these ringers in tow, Otterbein scored a series of successes..."— Harold Seymour in *Baseball: The People's Game* (1990).

Barnard attended Otterbein College in Ohio, where he organized and coached the school's first football team and the baseball team. He later coached at Army and the Ohio Medical University. After working for the Columbus Builders' Exchange he quit to become a sports editor at a newspaper in Columbus, Ohio. He was part of the group that helped organize the **National Association of Professional Baseball Leagues**, the minor league association founded during the 1901–1903 war between the American and National Leagues.

He became the road secretary for the American League franchise in Cleveland in 1903 and moved up to vice-president and general manager before owner Charles Somers was forced to sell the club in 1916. When Jim Dunn bought the Indians, Barnard became club president and remained at the helm until it was made known to him that he could become American League president if he left Cleveland.

Barnard was appointed to succeed Ban Johnson in November 1927 and served for slightly over three years. His tenure was marked by successful Major League franchises and stabilized relationships between the Major and minor leagues. After complaining of illness, he checked himself into the Mayo Clinic. He died a few days later in March 1931, only four months after receiving a five-year contract extension.

Will Harridge (1883–1971)
Served 1931–1958
Hall of Fame (VC) 1972

"William Harridge, the American League's new president, kept silent on the subject of the [lively 1930] baseball, showing the official cautiousness that would feature his twenty-seven-year tenure." — Charles Alexander in *Our Game* (1991).

Harridge was Ban Johnson's private secretary from 1911 until Johnson was forced out in 1927. He was the interim president until Ernest Barnard was chosen to succeed Johnson, and then Harridge succeeded Barnard.

Harridge became involved with baseball when he was a clerk for the Wabash Railroad in charge of routing and scheduling for American League teams. He was formally assigned to the American League office to handle those duties and eventually became Johnson's secretary.

After becoming president, Harridge saw the league through the difficulties of the Depression and World War II. He presided over the enormous popularity of the league after the war and through the 1950s. Harridge supported the All-Star Game concept in the 1930s. He initially opposed night baseball, but became a supporter during World War II.

Harridge supposedly surprised the owners at the 1958 winter meetings when he announced his retirement. He gave no reason, but many believed that he was leaving due to the pressures of the many issues facing baseball at the time. They included franchise shifts, expansion, the possibility of a third league, player demands for a portion of gate receipts and regulation of television. More accurate sources report that Harridge was forced out by the American League owners at age 75. Following his resignation, Harridge was elected as the figurehead chairman of the league, a position he held until his death in 1971.

Joe Cronin (1906–1984)
Served 1959–1973
Hall of Fame 1956

"I think Joe Cronin will probably go down as the worst president the American League ever had. I used to have all the respect in the world for him, and the umpires were tickled to death when he came in as president; but he turned out to be a horse's ass to the

umpires." — Long-time American League umpire Joe Rue quoted in *The Men in Blue*, by Larry Gerlach (1980).

Joe Cronin was a Red Sox star shortstop and player-manager who later became the first former player to head the American League. He presided over the league during the 1960s expansion and through the change to divisional play in the late 1960s. He left the position at the height of baseball's unpopularity in 1973.

Leland ("Lee") S. MacPhail, Jr. (1917–)
Served 1974–1983
Hall of Fame 1998

"In every sporting endeavor that is measurable by a clock — which baseball isn't, of course — the performances are superior with each succeeding generation. So why shouldn't baseball players be as good or better than their dads." — MacPhail.

Son of flamboyant general manager Larry MacPhail, Lee graduated from Swarthmore College in Pennsylvania and began his baseball executive career with Reading in the International League in 1941. He became director of player personnel for the Yankees for 10 years starting in 1948, then shifted to the Orioles in 1958.

In 1965 he moved to the commissioner's office to assist the inept William Eckert. In October 1966 he returned to the Yankees until 1973, when he left to take over as president of the American League. MacPhail resigned at the end of 1983, when he took over a new position as president of the Player Relations Committee.

Considered moderate and reasonable during his 10 years as president, he oversaw expansion to Toronto and Seattle in 1977, implementation of the **Designated Hitter** rule and a general resurgence of baseball's popularity. MacPhail's autobiography is *My 9 Innings* (1979).

Bobby Brown, M.D. (1924–)
Served 1983–1994

"… It's a good color combination to say the least." — Brown on being told that Bill White had been made National League president; apparently referring to their surnames and not their ethnic backgrounds (White is black).

Brown hit .460 for Stanford in 1943 and was All-Conference. When he enlisted in the Navy, he transferred to UCLA to complete his pre-med studies while in an officer training program. He hit .444 for the Bruins and led them to the conference title. He left for medical school at Tulane in 1945 and hit .500 while leading the team to a 22–6 record. He later became the only athlete enshrined in three college Halls of Fame (Stanford, UCLA and Tulane).

Brown signed with the Yankees for $52,000 in 1945 and made it to the Major Leagues briefly in 1946. He played sporadically over the next three seasons, returning each year to medical school at Tulane. After the 1950 season he reportedly became the first active player to earn his medical degree (but not true; see also **Doctors**). After an internship on the West Coast, Brown moved to Fort Worth and practiced cardiology from 1958 through 1983. His time in the practice was interrupted briefly in 1974 when he assumed the presidency of the Texas Rangers for a season.

In 1983 he was elected president of the American League. He presided over a period of stability through the 1980s. However, as player relations deteriorated in the early 1990s and salaries spiraled upward, the complications transcended the league president's office. The search for Brown's successor began in 1993 and intensified after he was found to have a malignant tumor in his prostate. Brown was considered for the commissioner's job, but when Lee MacPhail retired, Brown instead was selected as American League president.

Gene Budig (1939–)
Served 1994–2000

"There's simply no baseball for Gene Budig. Not since August

12 [1994] when the players in the American and National Leagues went on strike. For Budig, it was like being appointed as Gary Cooper's deputy at one minute past high noon, like being hired as Nero's chief violin maker after the smoke was, indeed, followed by fire."—Claire Smith in the *New York Times*.

"Everybody likes him. He's a true gentleman. He's a low key individual who doesn't cause confrontations, and keeps the league running very smoothly."—White Sox owner Jerry Reinsdorf.

Budig was a former sportswriter who became a college chancellor. In 30 years he headed three state universities—West Virginia, Illinois State and Kansas. His last position was 13 years at Kansas in Lawrenceville. He was also a major general in the Air National Guard for 29 years and had been a reporter for the *Lincoln Star and Journal* for five years. He became president of the American League on August 1, 1994. In 1999 it became clear that with Bud Selig running the show, and with the combining of several functions previously designated to the leagues, the position of league president was no longer needed. As a result, in late 1999 Major League Baseball announced that the functions of the president would be merged into the commissioner's office, and Budig formally resigned in January 2000.

During the early 2000s, Jackie Autry, widow of long-time Angels owner Gene Autry, was the honorary American League president and was allowed to present the American League Championship Series trophy.

American Legion Baseball (1925–)

"I decided not to try out for the American Legion Junior Baseball team that summer. Legion baseball was an important thing for country boys in those parts, but I was too young and skinny, and I had heard that the coach, a dirt farmer known as Gentleman Joe, made his protégés lie flat in the infield while he walked on their stomachs; he also forced them to take three-mile runs through the streets of town, talked them into going to church, and persuaded them to give up Coca-Colas."—Willie Morris in *North Toward Home* (1967).

"The Legion established Junior Baseball not as part of a boys' program but under its 'Americanism program' as a counter to the so-called Red Scare that permeated America at the time."—Harold Seymour in *Baseball: The People's Game* (1990).

Origins. Known originally as the American Legion Junior League, this organization was formed in South Dakota in 1925 for boys up to 17 years old. It became a national organization the following year. Its leagues are now for boys 15–18 years old and the season finishes with an eight-team World Series.

It was formed as a result of a survey by Major John L. Griffith, commissioner of the Big Ten college conference (then the Western Conference). The survey showed that boys were drifting away from baseball in small towns, especially to golf, softball and the movies. Some sources credit George Maines, a member of Oakley Trainer Post in Flint, Michigan, with conceiving the idea of Legion baseball.

The American Legion agreed to sponsor the league and in 1928 it asked for and received financial help from Organized Baseball. The first national competition was in 1926. In 1950 the Legion added 18 year olds and Junior was dropped from the name. By the 1970s there were 3,200 teams composed of 16–18 year olds and by the 1990s there were 90,000 youth and 4,700 teams competing in the U.S., Canada and Puerto Rico. Through 1996, 36 Major League Hall of Famers had played American Legion ball.

Awards. The winners of the American Legion tournament are invited to attend the Major League World Series. The winner of the Legion's MVP award is invited to the Hall of Fame induction ceremonies to receive his plaque.

Girls. In 1928 Margaret Gisolo played on an Indiana Legion team in a regional tournament. There were protests, but Judge Landis supported her (at least publicly). In 1929 the organization's by-laws were amended to provide for "Boys only." The rules later were relaxed and a handful of women played American Legion ball each year. Julie Croteau, who later played college ball and for the Colorado Silver Bullets (see **Women in Baseball**), played American Legion ball.

Amateur Draft. See **Drafts** for a description of the 1965 and 1966 special amateur draft of American Legion ballplayers that was quickly phased out for lack of interest.

Amputees

"They've taken the foot off Johnny Grubb. Uh, they've taken the shoe off Johnny Grubb."—Jerry Coleman.

"That 1871 opener in Washington was the first in the National League with Boston the opposition. The umpire, a veteran of the Civil War, had only one leg and hobbled around on a crutch. He was smacked painfully on his stump by a liner in the eighth but stayed in action."—*The Sporting News*.

Pete Gray.

"After making a catch, Gray places the ball against his chest and moves his left hand to the stub of his right arm. In this motion, the ball rolls out of his glove and up his wrist as if it were a ball-bearing between the arm and the body. When the glove is tucked under the stub, Gray draws his arm back across his chest until the ball rolls back into his hand, ready for a throw."—Memo to umpires from American League president Will Harridge on World War II outfielder Pete Gray's method of catching and throwing.

Gray lost his arm in a truck accident as a youth, though one source reported that he fell off a wagon and his arm caught in the spokes. He played semipro ball in 1940 and then moved to the minor leagues with Memphis in 1943, receiving nationwide attention. As an outfielder he was voted MVP of the Southern Association that year, batting .333 with five home runs and 68 RBIs. His 63 stolen bases tied a league record and he had the highest fielding percentage among outfielders in the league.

He played for the American League Browns in 1944 after the club paid Memphis $20,000. Gray batted .218 with three triples and no home runs. He was vulnerable to the change-up because he had to start his swing early to compensate for having only one arm. He was disliked by his teammates and some of them claimed that he cost them the 1945 pennant due to his poor outfield play—runners often took an extra base because of his inability to get the ball back quickly to the infield.

After the 1945 season he went on a barnstorming tour with a Negro League team that featured one-armed Jess Alexander. After Gray retired, he lived in obscurity in a small Southern town and had little interest in the 1986 television movie about his life, "A Winner Never Quits," starring Keith Carradine.

In *The Bill James Historical Baseball Abstract*, James voted Gray, "with apologies," as having the worst arm of any Major League player of the 1940s (cruel!). See William C. Kashatus, *One-Armed Wonder: Pete Gray, Wartime Baseball and the American Dream* (1995).

Jimmy Wood. This National Association player cut himself on the left leg before the 1874 season. It became infected and he lanced it with a pocket knife. The knife slipped and he cut him-

BROWN vs. MATHEWSON
GREATEST TREAT of THE YEAR for BASEBALL FANS

CINCINNATI, OHIO, SEPT. 1, 1916.

"YOU CAN POSITIVELY COUNT ON MY PITCHING AGAINST BROWN ON SEPT. 4th."

CHRISTY MATHEWSON,
MANAGER CINCINNATI REDS.

CHRISTY MATHEWSON

BROWN'S TWIRLING HAND

"THREE FINGERED" BROWN

CHICAGO, ILL.
"MORDECAI BROWN WILL BE READY TO BATTLE AGAINST MATHEWSON LABOR DAY."
JOE TINKER,
MANAGER CUBS.

— 1916 —

| First Game at 1:30 P.M. | DOUBLE HEADER LABOR DAY | First Game at 1:30 P.M. |

WEEGHMAN PARK

STARS OF MANY YEARS TO PITCH FOR CHICAGO CUBS AND CINCINNATI REDS

NORTH CLARK AND ADDISON STREETS.

THE DAILY NEWS BOYS BAND WILL RENDER MUSIC

RESERVED SEATS AT A. G. SPALDING & BROS. 28 S WABASH AVE. TEL. CEN. 448.

self on the right leg, spreading the infection. The resulting blood poisoning forced him to have the right leg amputated.

Lost Limbs. In 1883 two teams in Philadelphia, presumably comprised of Civil War veterans, scheduled a series of games. The Snorkey Club was composed of only one-armed players and the Hoppers had only one-legged players.

Hugh "One Arm" Daily. Daily pitched in 1880 for the New York Metropolitans. Most sources claim that his arm had been amputated as a boy after he was trapped during a theater fire. Other apparently more accurate sources claim that he lost only his hand after a gun accident and that he wore a pad to protect his wrist. He won 23 games for Cleveland in 1883 and a total of 28 games for three teams in 1884. He once pitched a no-hitter and supposedly played second base, shortstop and outfield in the no-glove era (though *The Baseball Encyclopedia* has no record of that claim).

Top: Flyer promoting a big 1916 National League pitching duel between Chicago's Mordecai "Three Finger" Brown and New York's Christy Mathewson. Note Brown's mangled fingers that earned him his nickname. *Right:* One-armed Pete Gray of the 1943 Memphis Chicks shows a young fan how to bat.

Charlie Bennett.

"I'm looking forward to the time I can stumble around on artificial limbs." — Bennett in a letter to *Sporting Life*.

Bennett was a catcher in the National League in the 1880s and early 1890s for Detroit and Boston. While still an active player he lost his legs in 1893 after getting off a train to speak to a friend in Wellesville, Kansas. He slipped on an icy platform and fell under a moving train. His legs were crushed and had to be amputated. Despite the seriousness of the injury he lived until 1927.

Pitcher John Clarkson, arguably the premier pitcher of the 1880s, supposedly had a delicate psyche and after witnessing the accident he was able to pitch only one more year in 1894 for Cleveland. He had won 25 games in 1892, but slipped to 16 in 1893 and finished in 1894 with an 8–9 record.

Mordecai "Three Finger" Brown.

"I don't know which fingers [he lost], but I'll tell you this. He always gave 60%." — Cardinals broadcaster Jack Buck.

"To know for sure, I'd have to throw with a normal hand, and I've never tried it." — Brown, when asked if his curve was helped by the absence of an index finger.

The Hall of Fame pitcher lost his index finger above the knuckle and part of another finger in a thresher accident as a boy. Later, chasing a hog, he broke the third and fourth fingers while still in a splint. This further mangled the hand and made his little finger useless. Despite the digit loss, he was considered one of the best pitchers of his era (1900–1920), compiling a 239–129 record over 14 seasons.

Danny Shay. Shay was a shortstop for the Cardinals in 1905 when his finger was amputated. He tried to come back in 1907, batting .190 over 35 games before retiring. He later was acquitted of shooting a black waiter over the amount of sugar in a sugar bowl.

Dave Keefe. Keefe, who played for the 1919–1922 A's, is credited by some with developing the forkball (see also **Pitches — Forkball**). It was a natural pitch for him because he lost the middle finger of his pitching hand in a childhood accident.

Red Ruffing. The Yankee pitcher lost four toes from his left foot in a mining accident that restricted his running. He also had to land on the left side of his foot to avoid the pain of landing on the toeless area.

Monte Stratton. Stratton's Major League career ended at age 26 after a hunting accident in November 1938 forced the amputation of his right leg. Stratton had other bad luck before the amputation. He suffered an appendicitis attack in 1936 and a sore arm ended his 1937 season after he started off with a 15–5 record. He still led the White Sox in wins that year and in 1938 led the club again with a 15–9 record before the accident.

In May 1939 Dizzy Dean, suffering from an admittedly sore arm, pitched in a benefit game for Stratton, which raised between $25,000 and $30,000. Though Stratton's professional career was thought to be over, fitted with a prosthetic he won 18 games in 1946 in the Class C East Texas League.

World War II Legislation. In 1945 at the end of World War II, Senator William A. "Wild Bill" Langer of North Dakota introduced legislation requiring all Major League baseball teams to have 10% of their players with lost limbs. The bill was not seriously considered by the full Senate.

After World War II teams of veterans who were amputees staged benefit games around the country.

Bert Shepard. Shepard pitched one game on an artificial leg for the Senators at Griffith Stadium on August 4, 1945. He was injured when his plane was shot down during World War II on May 21, 1944. German doctors amputated his leg and a Canadian prisoner constructed Shepard's first prosthesis. He returned to the United States in an exchange of wounded prisoners.

When Shepard returned to the States he was asked by Undersecretary of War Robert Patterson what he wanted to do. After Shepard indicated that he thought he could still play baseball, Patterson arranged a tryout with his friend Clark Griffith of the Senators.

He was never considered a Major League caliber pitcher, though he had been signed into the White Sox organization before going into the military. On one good leg he was still able to field bunts and cover first base in military games after his return to the States. He signed with the Senators and served as a coach while pitching in several exhibition games. He defeated the Brooklyn Dodgers in an exhibition on July 10, 1945.

In Shepard's only regular-season game, he pitched 5⅓ innings of relief in a 15–4 win, giving up one run, three hits, one walk and striking out two. He relieved Joe "Fire" Cleary, who made his only Major League appearance in that game. Cleary set a record for highest *Earned Run Average* in Major League history after facing nine batters and leaving with a 189.00 ERA.

After the season Shepard returned to the hospital to have more of the leg taken off. Rather than a six-week recovery period, he was in and out of the hospital for 2½ years. Nevertheless, in 1946 Shepard appeared in seven games for Chattanooga in the Class AA Southern League. After compiling a 2–2 record, he had a series of operations on his thigh. He returned as a player-manager in 1948 with Waterbury of the Class B Colonial League. The club finished 62–63 and Shepard was 5–6 as a pitcher with a .229 batting average when he appeared as the club's first baseman. He also stole five bases.

In 1949 Shepard went to work selling typewriters for IBM and in 1993 he tracked down the Austrian doctor, Ladislau Loidl, who pulled him from his plane's wreckage and prevented the locals from shooting him. The meeting was arranged by an Englishman, Jamie Brundell, who had met Loidl while on a hunting trip in Hungary.

Hughie Alexander played seven Major League games in late 1937, with one hit in 11 at-bats. He lost his hand in the gears of an oil rig in December 1937. For a description of the incident and Alexander's reaction, see page 36 of Kevin Kerrane's, *Dollar Sign on the Muscle* (1984). Alexander became a scout for almost 50 years for the Indians, White Sox, Dodgers and Phillies. Among his signees were Doyle Alexander, Allie Reynolds, Steve Garvey, Ron Cey and Bill Russell. Reynolds was recommended by long-time Oklahoma A & M basketball coach Hank Iba.

Bill Veeck, Jr. The long-time entrepreneurial Major League owner lost a leg during World War II when an antiaircraft gun recoiled into his leg.

Dave Dravecky. In 1988 the Giants pitcher began treatment for cancer in his left (pitching) shoulder. He had surgery to remove the tumors, and his arm was frozen to facilitate the surgery. Although told he could not pitch again, 10 months after the surgery, on August 10, 1989, he pitched seven shutout innings in a 4–3 win for the Giants. Five days later he was pitching a shutout in the 6th inning of what was ultimately a 3–2 victory for him. However, after a wild pitch he fell to the ground in agony, his upper left arm broken from being weakened by the freezing process. During a 1989 division-clinching on-field celebration by the Giants, Dravecky ran out from the dugout with his teammates, but was jostled and again broke the arm. He retired from baseball and was forced to have the arm amputated in June 1991.

Dravecky wrote about the positive recovery experience in *Comeback*, with Tim Stafford (1990). When things went badly, he and his wife Jan wrote *When You Can't Come Back*, with Ken Gire (1992).

Anaheim Angels

(Formerly Los Angeles Angels and California Angels)
American League 1961–
"The Angels are a different lot. While the Dodgers have a long and rich history, the Angels' is short and sour, and filled with disappointments. If they somehow make the playoffs, it's only to find a new way to lose. Usually though, they don't even get that chance." — Bob Wood in *Dodger Dogs to Fenway Franks* (1988).

Origins. In 1960 singing cowboy and movie star Gene Autry, reputedly a former semi-pro baseball outfielder, owned the Golden West Broadcasting Corporation. Its flagship radio station, KMPC in Los Angeles, had just lost the broadcast rights to the Dodgers. On December 6, 1960, the American League formally awarded a new franchise to Autry, Robert Reynolds and their associates. Two days later former Braves general manager Fred Haney was named general manager. On December 14, 1960, the original Angels were selected in the first *Expansion Draft* (see also *Expansion*).

First Games. On April 11, 1961, the Angels went on the road to defeat the Orioles 7–2 in their first game. The club's first home game was on April 26, 1961. Ty Cobb threw out the first pitch as myopic Eli Grba defeated the Orioles.

Key Owners.
Gene Autry/Jackie Autry 1961–1995.
"Grantland Rice can go to hell." — The pennant-less Autry on Rice's maxim that "it's not whether you win or lose, but how you play the game."

Gene Autry owned the club from its inception in 1961 into the 1990s after buying out his partners in 1983. In the late 1920s, Autry was offered $100 a month to play Baseball in the St. Louis Cardinals minor league system. He turned down the offer and remained as a telegraph operator. When humorist Will Rogers heard Autry strumming a guitar and singing to himself in the telegraph office (apocryphal?), he arranged for Autry to get on the radio and into show business. The rest became singing cowboy history.

In 1948 Autry bought a Phoenix radio station and began his long career as a broadcast executive. His empire included 10 radio stations and a Los Angeles television station, a flying school, a music publishing company, and a 20,000 acre cattle ranch in Arizona.

Autry met future wife Jean when she was a vice president at Security Pacific National Bank in Palm Springs in the early 1980s and handling the Autry hotel account. Autry began dating her shortly after his first wife died, and they were married a few weeks later (he had married his first wife after only three dates). He was 73 and she was 39. Jackie had played baseball as a kid and knew the game, though she was more of a football fan when they were married. She ran the club in the late 1980s and 1990s as Autry slowed down due to old age. The beloved owner of the club had his "number" 26 retired in 1982.

In early 1993 Autry announced that he would sell the club if the right offer came along, in the neighborhood of $200 million. He claimed that he lost $10 million in 1992 and he was "too old to go make a movie to make up for it." In 1994 Autry was reportedly worth $300 million after making most of his fortune in real estate.

In 1994 the Autrys announced that a minority interest in the club was for sale. Former commissioner Peter Ueberroth was to be the new minority owner with an option to buy the entire club at Autry's death, which occurred on October 2, 1998, at age 91. How-

Long-time Angels owner Gene Autry poses in full cowboy regalia during an early 1960s spring training in Palm Springs. He is with broadcast engineering pioneer Loyd Sigmon, a long-time executive with the Angels' flagship radio and television stations, KMPC and KTLA. Sigmon is credited with the SigAlert traffic accident information system in Southern California and may have been the first to televise a Major League baseball game. He was an engineer at a station in a building across from Fenway Park in the early 1930s. He set up a television camera and broadcast the game illegally to a few thousand purchasers of a kit that could be built into a 2" × 2" television screen that required a magnifying glass to watch.

ever, that deal fell through in favor of the Disney Company. See also David Rothel, *The Gene Autry Book* (1988).

The Disney Company/1995–2003.
"Exciting news from Burbank: The California Angels are being sold by the singing cowboy to the talking mouse.... Disney's venture into baseball comes as very good news, and I am particularly looking forward to their Pittsburgh Pirates of the Caribbean ride. We should be seeing some wonderful innovations, including first baseman J.T. Snow White." — Columnist Mike Downey.

In May 1995 the Disney Company paid $30 million for a 25% minority interest in the club, with an option to purchase the balance upon Gene Autry's death in October 1998. Disney ended up paying $140 million for the full interest, and then spent another $70 million to refurbish the ballpark.

Disney outbid a group represented by Peter Ueberroth. As part of the deal, Autry relinquished control of the front office to Disney. Disney had turned down an offer in 1966 to become Autry's partner when the club moved to Anaheim. The deal was not finalized until March 1996, when Disney came to terms with the city of Anaheim on a renovation of Anaheim Stadium and a renegotiation of the antiquated stadium lease. Disney's bid also was slow to be approved in part because of its holdings in casino operations on cruise ships.

Disney suffered financially during its tenure, and put the club up for sale in early 2002. The value presumably increased significantly after the Angels won their first World Series that year. It was estimated that Disney lost $50 million before selling in April 2003.

Arturo Moreno/2003– .

"A down-to-earth guy who opens his own mail, has no secretary, and is called Arte by all around him."—*Fortune* magazine.

Arte Moreno, 56 at the time, purchased the Angels for $184 million in 2003. A fourth-generation native of Arizona and a Vietnam veteran, Moreno was declared by *Sports Illustrated* in May 2003 to be the fifth most influential minority in sports. He appointed Dennis Kuhl as club president, who was Moreno's former classmate and fraternity brother at the University of Arizona. Moreno had been a minority owner in the Phoenix Suns basketball team and had held a small interest in the Arizona Diamondbacks. He was also one of 17 owners in the Salt Lake City Trappers when they won 29 straight games in 1987.

Moreno began his career as a billboard salesman for a small Phoenix-based company, and eventually moved into an ownership position. He then made a fortune in outdoor advertising while still based in Arizona, and then sold his company, Outdoor Systems, to Infinity Broadcasting for $8.7 billion in stock in 1999. In 2002 *Forbes* listed him at No. 246 on its list of 400 wealthiest Americans at $940 million, and he topped $1 billion in 2003. He made a splash before the 2004 season when he signed several high-profile free agents, most notably Vladimir Guerrero from the Expos.

Nicknames. The Angels adopted the name of the long-time Pacific Coast League entry in Los Angeles (the city's name means "angels" in Spanish). The club changed its name to the California Angels as of September 2, 1965. The Angels are sometimes referred to as the Halos because of the halo that was once on top of the players' caps. The halo was resurrected for the 1993 season. When Disney took over in late 1995, the new owner made a decision to change the club's name to Anaheim Angels for the 1997 season.

In 2004 owner Arte Moreno created a stir when he proposed to change the name back to Los Angeles Angels. The Anaheim city council opposed any name change, which became the awkward "Los Angeles Angels of Anaheim."

Key Seasons.

"HEAVEN CAN WAIT! ANGELS IN 1st on 4th"—Midseason 1962 headline in the *Los Angeles Times*; it was one of the few bright moments in the club's history.

1961. The Angels played surprisingly well in their first season, finishing in eighth place with a 70–91 record. They had five players who hit 20 or more home runs.

1962. The Angels finished a strong third. They were led by Dean Chance's 14 wins and the power hitting of Leon Wagner (37 home runs and 107 RBIs) and Lee Thomas (26 home runs and 104 RBIs).

1967. The club was in the pennant race until the last two weeks of the season. They finished eight games out in fifth place behind Don Mincher's 25 home runs. Minnie Rojas led the league with 27 saves.

1979. After more than a decade of mediocrity, the Angels won their first division title by three games over the Royals. American League MVP Don Baylor had a league-leading 139 RBIs and Nolan

Ryan won 16 games. They lost the League Championship Series to the Orioles in four games.

1982. The Angels won the division by three games over the Royals. Reggie Jackson hit a league-leading 39 home runs. In a heart-breaking play-off series with the Brewers, the Angels won the first two games before losing three straight.

1986. The club won 92 games under manager Gene Mauch, led by Wally Joyner's 100 RBIs and Mike Witt's 18 wins. They were one strike away from their first pennant in Game 5 of the Championship Series when reliever Donnie Moore gave up a two-run home run to Boston's Dave Henderson. Though the Angels tied the game in the bottom of the 9th inning, the Red Sox went on to win the game and sweep the final two games in Boston. Moore later committed *Suicide*.

1995. The Angels led their division by 11 games in August and then had two nine-game losing streaks to fall into a season-ending tie with the Mariners. The Mariners beat them in a one-game play-off. Tim Salmon hit 34 home runs and batted .330, Jim Edmonds hit 33 home runs, and Chuck Finley and Mark Langston each won 15 games.

2002. The Angels were the wild card team with a 99–63 record, four games behind the A's in the West. Remarkably, the Angels had lost 19 of 21 to end the 2001 season and 14 of 20 to start the 2002 season. Anaheim beat the Yankees in four games in the division series. In the ALCS they beat the Twins in five games, and then staged a dramatic comeback in Game 6 of the World Series against the Giants. Down 5–0 with one out in the 7th, the Angels came back to win Game 6 and then won Game 7 for their first championship. Troy Percival saved 40 games and compiled a 1.92 ERA, Jarrod Washburn was 18–6, Garret Anderson hit 29 home runs with 123 RBIs, and Troy Glaus hit 30 home runs and drove in 111 runs.

2004. The Angels stayed close all season and then beat the A's on the last weekend to win the American League West with a record of 92–70. American League MVP Vladimir Guerrero had 39 home runs and 126 RBIs to lead the club, and Jose Guillen, suspended late in the season, had 27 home runs and 104 RBIs. Bartolo Colon led the staff with an 18–12 record and John Lackey had 14 wins. Troy Percival (33) and Francisco Rodriguez (12, along with 27 holds) combined for 45 saves. In the division play-off against the Red Sox, the Angels were blown out in their first two games in Anaheim. In Game 3, Vladimir Guerrero hit a grand slam in the 7th inning to tie the game, but after the Angels had a chance to score in the 9th, David Ortiz homered in the bottom of the 12th to give Boston the series sweep.

Key Players.

Dean Chance pitched for six seasons with the Angels, with a best of 20–9 in 1964.

Jim Fregosi played 11 games for the Angels in the club's first season and went on to become the regular shortstop through the 1971 season. He was then traded to the Mets for Nolan Ryan. He hit 115 home runs for the Angels.

Clyde Wright pitched eight seasons for the Angels, with a best of 22–12 in 1970.

Nolan Ryan (HF) pitched in the prime of his long career with a number of mediocre Angels teams from 1972 through 1979. He led the league in strikeouts seven times and won 138 games for the club.

Rod Carew (HF) played the last seven years of his 19-year career with the Angels. He batted over .300 five times and played primarily at first base for the club.

Brian Downing played 13 seasons for the Angels, seeing the best and worst the club could do from 1978 through 1990. He hit

222 home runs for the Angels with a career best average of .326 in 1979.

Chuck Finley played 11 seasons for the club through 1996, with a best of 18 wins in both 1990 and 1991.

Tim Salmon. Drafted in the third round by the Angels in 1989, Salmon arrived in the Majors in 1992 and was still going strong in 2004. Through 2003 the right fielder was the team's career leader with 288 home runs and 966 RBIs.

Troy Percival. Through 2003 the hard-throwing reliever had 283 saves over nine seasons with the Angels beginning in 1995.

Garret Anderson emerged as a star for the Angels by the 2000s, and by 2003 had 10 seasons with the club and was its career hit leader with 1,633 hits. He hit .299 with 193 home runs and 872 RBIs while starring in center field.

Key Managers.

Casey Stengel. No, Stengel did not manage the Angels, but he was the club's first choice. Stengel declined the offer because of a contract he had signed with the *Saturday Evening Post* which provided that until his story was serialized and published he had to remain out of baseball. He had also just become a director of a Los Angeles bank and he was reluctant to give up the position.

Bill Rigney was the first Angels manager, lasting nine years until 39 games into the 1969 season. The club finished a surprising third in 1962, but that was the best it could do under Rigney, who otherwise never finished higher than fifth.

Jim Fregosi managed the Angels from 1978 through part of 1981, leading the club to a division title in 1979.

Gene Mauch managed the club to division titles in 1982 and 1986, but both times witnessed crushing losses in the League Championship Series. In three other seasons, his best finish was second place in 1985.

Mike Scioscia. The former Dodger catcher took over the Angels in 2000 and led them to a World Series victory over the Giants in 2002. Through 2003 he had a .514 winning percentage.

Ballparks.

"The Dodgers are doing 75% of the business and the Angels are paying for 25% of the toilet paper." — Gene Autry on his strained landlord-tenant relationship when the Angels briefly occupied Dodger Stadium. Long-time Yankee owner Del Webb arranged the club's move to Anaheim in return for the contract to build the ballpark.

Wrigley Field. Commissioner Ford Frick decided that the new rule regarding *Fence* distances prohibited the Angels from playing in the Los Angeles Coliseum in 1961 unless the Angels immediately agreed to play two years in Dodger Stadium, which was not yet built. Though the Angels initially did not agree to play in Dodger Stadium in 1962, the club eventually relented. Nevertheless, the Angels spent their first season in Wrigley Field in Los Angeles, instead of the Coliseum.

Ancient Wrigley (built in 1925) was patterned after Wrigley Field in Chicago and had dimensions from left to right field of 340–412–338. In 1961 it surrendered the most home runs in one season of any ballpark in the history of Major League Baseball, 248. It was demolished in 1966 and replaced by a mental health facility.

Dodger Stadium. After one season in 22,000-seat Wrigley Field the Angels moved over to Dodger Stadium for the next four seasons. The Angels drew 603,510 fans to Wrigley Field in their first season. They drew 1,144,063 the next season in Dodger Stadium. So that they did not have to use the Dodger name in their marketing materials, the Angels referred to Dodger Stadium as Chavez Ravine.

Anaheim Stadium/Edison International Field. The Angels moved into Anaheim Stadium in 1966. It originally held 43,250 fans, but was expanded in 1980 to accommodate the NFL Los Angeles Rams and the seating capacity has been adjusted at various times to the current 64,593. The field has always had natural grass. The dimensions from left to right field are 333–375–404–375–333; all except the foul lines have fluctuated slightly over the years.

The stadium is known as "The Big A" for its 230-foot high A-shaped scoreboard behind the left field seats. The "A" was inside the ballpark until the double-decking of the outfield area in 1980 forced it to be moved. The scoreboard crashed into the bleachers during a January 1994 earthquake that was centered in Los Angeles. Former Angels manager Buck Rogers is the only man to hit a home run in each of the three ballparks occupied by the Angels.

When Disney bought into the club, it pledged $70 million to refurbish the ballpark, along with a $30 million contribution from the city of Anaheim. Prior to the 1998 season the club eliminated the upper deck and center field bleachers after the NFL's Rams left town for St. Louis. It was also the first time the ballpark was called Edison International Field of Anaheim — Edison Field or the Big Ed for short. This was because on September 15, 1997, the club announced that electricity utility Edison had paid $50 million over 20 years for naming rights. Edison ended its affiliation with the Angels during its financial hard times in December 2003. The club indicated that it would use Angels Stadium as the new moniker and would try to go without a sponsor. The Angels are bound to the ballpark through 2030, with an escape clause in 2017.

Key Broadcasters. One of the first Angel broadcasters was ex-ballplayer Buddy Blattner, who broadcast in the Major Leagues for 26 years. The flagship station of KMPC carried the club into the 1990s, bringing to the airwaves such luminaries as Dick Enberg from 1967 through 1978 and Don Drysdale in the 1970s.

Dave Niehaus was one of the primary Angel broadcasters from 1969 until he left for the expansion Mariners in 1977. Ron Fairly broadcast for the club between 1982 and 1986. Bob Starr broadcast for the club in the 1990s and Ken Brett was with the team from 1987 through 1996. Steve Physioc has been the longest tenured recent broadcaster, beginning in 1996. Several former Major Leaguers had brief stints with the club in the broadcast booth, including Reggie Jackson (1990), Joe Garagiola (1990), Jerry Reuss (1996–1998), Sparky Anderson (1996–1998), Rex Hudler (1999–2003), and Jose Tolentino (1998–2001).

Books. Ross Newhan, *The California Angels* (1982); Ross Newhan, *The Anaheim Angels, A Complete History* (2002); Wayne Stewart, *The History of the California Angels* (2002).

Animals

"Darryl Strawberry is not a dog. A dog is loyal and runs hard after balls." — Tommy Lasorda after a cable-TV show caller referred to Strawberry as a dog after he checked himself into a drug rehab center at the start of the 1994 season.

"Ron Guidry is not very big, maybe 140 pounds, but he has an arm like a lion." — Jerry Coleman (as usual, we are fairly sure we know what he means).

"[Bob] Shirley and [Ken] Griffey get along like a rattler and a parrot." — Jerry Coleman.

"Sometimes, big trees grow out of acorns. I think I heard that from a squirrel." — More Coleman.

"Gonzo leaps like a giraffe and grabs it." — And still more Coleman.

"They tried the horse at second and short, but he was a little slow on the pivot when compared with men like Napoleon Lajoie. Then they tried him at third base, and knew that was the right, the inevitable place. He was a Great Wall of China. He was a flash of brown lightning. In fact, he covered half the shortstop's territory and two-thirds of left field, and even came behind the plate to help the catcher with foul tips. The catcher got pretty sore about it. He said that anybody who was going to steal his easy put-outs would have to wear an umpire's uniform like the other thieves."—Wilbur Schramm in "My Kingdom for Jones" (1945), about a horse that played third base.

"Charlie Fox, Chicken Wolf, Bob Moose, Moose Clabaugh, Steve Staggs, Moose Haas, Lyman Lamb, Al Doe, Goat Anderson, Possum Whitted, Hippo Vaughn, Mudcat Grant, Joe Gibbon, Bull Wagner, Snipe Hansen, Fenton Mole, Snake Henry, Snake Wiltsie, Cub Stricker, Ox Echardt, Pete Elko, Snake Deal, Old Hoss Twineham, Moose Grimshaw, Snipe Corley, Hanson Horsey, Vic Sorrell, Mule Watson, Old Hoss Radbourn, Russ Lyon, Jim Panther, Jose Tartabull, Brad Hogg, Bert Hogg, Johnnie Seale, Wilbur Coons"

See also **Birds**, **Insects**, **Mascots** and **Superstitions**.

Monkey. Cliff Carroll was a Major League outfielder in the 1880s and 1890s. He carried a monkey around the league with him that eventually died and was buried under home plate in Pittsburgh.

Several live monkeys showed up at the Anaheim Angels' ballpark in 2002, as the club's "Rally Monkey" stuffed-toy mascot spawned several live imitations.

Parrot. Shoeless Joe Jackson carried around a parrot whose vocabulary was limited to screeching, "You're out!"

Dog Day Afternoon.

"Aaron Pointer, Mutt Wilson, Jack Kibble, Doggie Miller, Charlie Bassett, Bow Wow Arft, Mutz Ens, Ray Barker"

Chicago's New Comiskey Park has an area called "Pet check," where dogs and cats can be boarded during a game. One frequent boarder was a St. Bernard named "Carlton Frisk." Catcher Carlton Fisk, who had feuded with the White Sox management near the end of his career, said that he "could tell him a lot about what it's like to be in the White Sox doghouse."

On June 7, 1997, the White Sox staged "Dog Day" at Comiskey Park, allowing owners to bring 425 canines to the park for the game. The yelping must have helped, as the White Sox beat the Orioles 1–0.

Pets. In September 2003 the Blue Jays held a promotion that allowed pets into the Skydome during a game. There were 240 dogs in attendance (not counting the "dogs" playing for the pitiful Detroit Tigers that day).

Rabbit.

"Bunny Hearn, Bunny Brief, Rabbit Maranville, Bunny Fabrique, Joe Rabbit"

In an 1897 box score there appeared a notation of "Home run — Rabbit." Long-time home run statistician John Tattersall could never find corroboration of the home run and the official records finally were modified to reflect what had happened. The official scorer for the game had watched the players chase a rabbit around the infield and across home plate before being captured. He put a tongue-in-cheek entry in the box score.

Polar Bear. For years the Dodger Stadium restaurant foyer greeted diners with an eight-foot stuffed polar bear shot by Walter O'Malley.

Iguana. In Venezuela's winter leagues, fans have been known to throw iguanas at players.

Skunk. During the 5th inning of the Milwaukee Braves' last game in County Stadium, a skunk ran across the outfield.

Elephant. On Opening Day 1997, Reds owner Marge Schott brought Princess Schottzie, an elephant, from the Cincinnati Zoo, who gave her a kiss during the opening ceremonies.

Cow. On April 1, 2002, a cow named Cinci Freedom was scheduled to participate in the Reds' opening day festivities. The cow had jumped a six-foot fence to avoid slaughter and evaded capture for 10 days before being sent to a sanctuary by artist Peter Max and his wife, Mary.

Just Ducky. In July 2001, Carlos Baerga was playing with the Long Island Ducks in the independent Atlantic League when his contract was sold to the Samsung Ducks in the Korean Baseball League.

Announcers See *Broadcasters* and *Public Address Announcers and Systems*

Cap Anson (1852–1922)

Hall of Fame 1939

"How old is Anson? When the ark
First found once more a resting place,
Old Noah, groping in the dark,
Discovered Anson on first base —
The grand old man had held it down
In spite of floods that came to drown."— Newspaperman Hyder Ali in 1897, Anson's last season.

"Anson's name was better known, it was said, than that of any statesman or soldier of his time."— Fred Lieb.

"A man who once seemed destined to play the game forever."— Lee Allen.

Anson played 27 professional seasons in the 19th century and is now credited with 2,995 Major League hits and a .329 average.

Adrian Constantine Anson was born in Marshalltown, Iowa, and was discovered in 1868 by the Rockford team which featured pitcher Al Spalding. Anson's 27 professional seasons were an early record for longevity. Five of those seasons were in the 1871–1875 professional National Association, the immediate predecessor to the National League. Primarily a first baseman, he appeared in 2,276 games over his 22-year National League career.

Anson wrote one of the first baseball autobiographies in 1900, *A Ballplayer's Career, Being the Personal Experiences and Reminiscences of Adrian C. Anson*. He also appeared in an early theater production about baseball, *A Runaway Colt*.

Anson is credited as the first manager to coordinate the positioning of his infielders and outfielders and to start **Spring Training**. He was also reportedly the first manager to **Coach** from the baselines and to institute a pitching rotation. Some modern commentators suggest that Anson was not the first to implement many of these innovations, but merely was around in the 20th century to claim that he was the first.

Anson was one of baseball's most visible and vocal racists of the 19th century, refusing to play against black players on other teams (see also **Integration**).

He was the first player acknowledged to have achieved 3,000 hits, although his official totals fluctuated after *The Baseball Encyclopedia* was first published in 1969. Errors in the original edition were discovered later and corrected in subsequent editions and *Total Baseball* now officially reports that he has 2,995 hits. He finished his Major League career in 1897 with a .329 lifetime average and 1,715 RBIs.

Anson passed his last few years working in vaudeville houses, as city clerk of Chicago and as manager of a pool hall.

Book. Howard W. Rosenberg, *Cap Anson: When Captaining a Team Meant Something: Leadership in Baseball's Early Years* (2003).

Antarctica

"Baseball is a funny thing. There is a reason that it is called our national pastime and while perhaps some of the luster has worn off after 16 decades, baseball is still growing and spreading beyond the borders of the United States. In fact, American baseball is played on at least six of the seven continents (it might be played in Antarctica too, but I am not sure about that) and in much of the world it is a growing sport."—Jonathan Leshanski.

A baseball game was played in Little America, Antarctica, on August 25, 1957. This was reported by Paul C. Dalrymple in a letter to the Hall of Fame that year. The game was played by a group of SeaBees against a collection of civilians. The SeaBees won 11–6 in two innings due to an on-field temperature of a cool –40 degrees at 2 p.m.

Antitrust

"Gentlemen, we have the only legal monopoly in the country and we're fucking it up."—Ted Turner.

"In an effort to avoid publicity, the group started by interviewing that celebrated authority on constitutional law, Mr. Ty Cobb."—Red Smith criticizing a 1952 congressional committee's motives in investigating baseball's antitrust exemption.

"Baseball is today big business that is packaged with beer, with broadcasting, and with other industries. The beneficiaries of the *Federal Baseball Club* decision are not the Babe Ruths, Ty Cobbs and Lou Gehrigs…. The owners, whose records many say reveal a proclivity for predatory practices, do not come to us with equities…. There can be no doubt 'that were we considering the question of baseball for the first time upon a clean slate' we would hold it to be subject to federal antitrust regulation."—Justice William O. Douglas in his dissent in the *Curt Flood* decision, 407 U.S. 282; 92 S.Ct. 2099 (1972) (See *Reserve Clause* for more on this decision).

See also *Franchise Shifts*, *Free Agents* and *Reserve Clause*.

The Issues. Two antitrust issues have faced baseball over the years: 1) movement of clubs from one city to another (a phenomenon primarily in issue beginning in the 1950s); and 2) movement of players from one team to another independent of a reserve clause. Various legislators, courts and arbitrators have had the opportunity to review the antitrust ramifications of both issues.

Ty Cobb.

"Baseball is a sport, never a business."—Cobb testifying in support of maintaining the reserve clause at the 1952 Congressional hearings.

In early 1912 Cobb was a holdout over his contract. The notoriety of the dispute sparked threats of antitrust legislation in Congress directed at the reserve clause, which prohibited players from bargaining freely with other clubs. During this period of rampant federal "trust busting" in other businesses, a congressional resolution was introduced that would have caused the appointment of a seven-man commission to investigate baseball as a trust. The resolution died shortly after the Cobb incident was resolved, when he signed his contract.

1922 Decision. In 1922 the U.S. Supreme Court, with Justice Oliver Wendell Holmes writing the opinion, ruled that baseball was not subject to the antitrust laws because it was a sport and not a business. As a result, the anticompetitive reserve clause was left intact. Baseball may have benefited from the fact that the Chief Justice was future U.S. President William Howard Taft. His brother was Charles P. Taft, former owner of the Cubs.

The case had been filed by the Baltimore club of the Federal League. The club had been shut out of financial benefits after the Federal League folded and some of its owners were paid settlements. Baltimore won in the lower court but the $900,000 award was overturned by the Supreme Court.

Some sources reported erroneously that the Supreme Court's opinion in this case was written in the earlier Federal League lawsuit against Organized Baseball that was presided over by Judge Landis. That case was settled without a trial and no appellate opinion was ever written.

1952 Hearings. In 1952 Congress held hearings to again consider the business of baseball and the antitrust laws. The hearings were known as the Emmanuel Celler hearings for the name of the congressman who chaired the committee. Ford Frick testified at the hearings: "Frankly, gentlemen, I don't see why all the furor about the reserve clause. Basically it is a long-term contract which is nothing unusual where distinctive personal services are contracted for. I read by the papers that Milton Berle has just signed such a contract for thirty years. The only difference in the baseball contract is that the player's salary is renegotiated annually on the basis of the services rendered the previous season—subject to a limitation in favor of the player that the maximum reduction may not exceed 25%. There is no limitation on the amount of the increase, which may be asked or paid."

The 1952 committee's conclusion: "On the other hand the overwhelming preponderance of the evidence established baseball's need for some sort of reserve clause. Baseball's history shows that chaotic conditions prevailed when there was no reserve clause. Experience points to no feasible substitute to protect the integrity of the game or to guarantee a comparatively even competitive struggle. The evidence adduced at the hearings would clearly not justify the enactment of legislation flatly condemning the reserve clause."

Toolson Decision. On November 9, 1953, in a case involving minor leaguer George Toolson, the U.S. Supreme Court ruled for the second time that baseball was a sport and therefore did not constitute interstate business. This was consistent with the Supreme Court's 1922 opinion. Nevertheless, a subsequent New York federal court ruling criticized both: "We freely acknowledge our belief that *Federal Baseball* was not one of Mr. Justice Holmes' happiest days, that the rationale of *Toolson* is extremely dubious and that, to use the Supreme Court's own adjectives, the distinction between baseball and other professional sports is 'unrealistic,' 'inconsistent' and 'illogical.' … While we should not fall out of our chairs with surprise at the news that *Federal Baseball* and *Toolson* had been overruled, we are not at all certain that the Court is ready to give them a happy dispatch."—Judge Friendly of the 2nd Circuit Court of Appeal (sitting in New York) in 1970 in *Salerno v. American League.*

1957 Ruling. In 1957 the U.S. Supreme Court ruled that professional football was subject to the antitrust laws. The court also declared that baseball's exemption was "unreasonable, illogical and inconsistent" and left the burden on Congress to make the change. As of 2004 there was no change in the law.

1958 Hearings. On July 9, 1958, the day after the All-Star Game in Baltimore, Casey Stengel, Mickey Mantle, Clark Griffith and other baseball dignitaries testified at new hearings before Congress on baseball as a business. The purpose of the hearings was to determine if the major sports should be exempt from the antitrust laws or whether a new bill should be enacted to ensure that the exemption remained for baseball and expanded to other sports. Stengel's comments made almost no sense — a classic case of Stengelese — and were used in a humorous 1990 radio advertisement. Stengel managed 7,000 words in 45 minutes, only slowing to let the laughter die down. A sampling of the questions and answers:

SENATOR ESTES KEFAUVER: Mr. Stengel, you are the manager of the New York Yankees. Will you give us very briefly your background and your views about this legislation?

STENGEL: Well, I started in professional ball in 1910. I have been in professional ball, I would say, for 48 years. I have been employed by numerous ball clubs in the Majors and in the minor leagues.

I played as low as Class D ball, which was at Shelbyville, Kentucky, and also Class C ball and Class A ball, and I have advanced in baseball as a ball player.

I had many years that I was not so successful as a ball player, as it is a game of skill.

And then I was no doubt discharged by baseball in which I had to go back to the minor leagues as a manager, and after being in the minor leagues as a manager, I became a Major League manager in several cities and was discharged, we call it discharged because there is no question I had to leave.

And I returned to the minor leagues at Milwaukee, Kansas City and Oakland, California, and then returned to the Major Leagues.

In the last 10 years, naturally, in Major League Baseball with the New York Yankees, the New York Yankees have had tremendous success and while I am not a ball player who does the work, I have no doubt worked for a ball club that is very capable in the office.

I have been up and down the ladder. I know there are some things in baseball 35 to 50 years ago that are better now than they were in those days. In those days, my goodness, you could not transfer a ball club in the minor leagues, Class D, Class C ball, Class A ball.

How could you transfer a ball club when you did not have a highway? How could you transfer a ball club when the railroads then would take you to a town you got off and then you had to wait and sit five hours to go to another ball club?

How could you run baseball then without night ball?

You had to have night ball to improve the proceeds, to pay larger salaries, and I went to work, the first year I received $135 a month.

I thought that was amazing. I had to put away enough money to go to dental college. I found out it was not better in dentistry. I stayed in baseball.

Any other questions you would like to ask me?

KEFAUVER: Mr. Stengel, are you prepared to answer particularly why baseball wants this bill passed?

STENGEL: Well, I would have to say at the present time, I think that baseball has advanced in this respect for the player help. That is an amazing statement for me to make, because you can retire with an annuity at 50 and what organization in America allows you to retire at 50 and receive money?

Now, the second thing about baseball that I think is very interesting to the public or to all of us that it is the owner's fault if he does not improve his club, along with the officials in the ball club and the players.

Now, what causes that?

If I am going to go on the road and we are a traveling ball club and you know the cost of transportation now — we travel sometimes with three Pullman coaches, the New York Yankees, and I am just a salaried man and do not own stock in the New York Yankees, I found out that in traveling with the New York Yankees on the road

and all, that it is the best, and we have broken records in Washington this year; we have broken them in every city but New York and we have lost two clubs that have gone out of the city of New York.

Of course, we have had some bad weather, I would say that they are mad at us in Chicago, we fill the parks.

They have come out to see good material. I will say they are mad at us in Kansas City, but we broke their attendance record.

Now, on the road we only get possibly 27 cents. I am not positive of these figures, as I am not an official.

If you go back 15 years or if I owned stock in the club, I would give them to you.

KEFAUVER: Mr. Stengel, I am not sure that I made my question clear.

STENGEL: Yes, sir. Well, that is all right. I am not sure I am going to answer yours perfectly, either.

SENATOR JOSEPH C. O'MAHONEY: How many minor leagues were there in baseball when you began?

STENGEL: Well, there were not so many at that time because of this fact: Anybody to go into baseball at that time with the educational schools that we had were small, while you were probably thoroughly educated at school, you had to be — we have only small cities that you could put a team in and they would go defunct.

Why, I remember the first year I was at Kankakee, Illinois, and a bank offered me $440 if I would let them have a little notice. I left there and took a uniform because they owed me two weeks' pay. But I either had to quit but I did not have enough money to go to dental college so I had to go with the manager down to Kentucky.

What happened there was if you by July, that was the big date. You did not play night ball and you did not play Sundays in half of the cities on account of a Sunday observance, so in those days when things were tough, and all of it was, I mean to say, why they just closed up July 4 and there you were sitting there in the depot.

You could go to work someplace else, but that was it.

So I got out of Kankakee, Illinois, and I just go there for the visit now.

SENATOR JOHN A. CARROLL: The question Senator Kefauver asked you was what, in your honest opinion, with your 48 years of experience, is the need for this legislation in view of the fact that baseball has not been subject to antitrust laws.

STENGEL: No.

SENATOR CARROLL: I had a conference with one of the attorneys representing not only baseball but all of the sports, and I listened to your explanation to Senator Kefauver. It seemed to me it had some clarity. I asked the attorney this question: What was the need for this legislation? I wonder if you would accept his definition. He said they didn't want to be subjected to the *ipse dixit* of the federal government because they would throw a lot of damage suits on the *ad damnum* clause. He said, in the first place, the Toolson case was *sui generis*, it was *de minimis non curat lex*. Do you call that a clear expression?

MR. STENGEL: Well, you are going to get me there for about two hours [laughter].

SENATOR KEFAUVER: Thank you, very much, Mr. Stengel. We appreciate your presence here.

Mickey Mantle testified immediately after Stengel. His comments are set forth in their entirety:

"My views are just about the same as Casey's."

After the hearings and this persuasive testimony, baseball was again spared application of the antitrust laws.

Milwaukee Moves to Atlanta. After Milwaukee lost the Braves to Atlanta in 1966, Congressman Celler repeated his 1952 view that baseball clearly was a federal monopoly and that a federal antitrust suit was "long overdue."

Curt Flood Decision. Challenges to the antitrust laws came to a head again with the June 21, 1972, opinion by the U.S. Supreme Court in the Curt Flood case, which again upheld the *Reserve Clause*. The court took a dim view of the clause but did not strike it down; instead it called on Congress to abolish it as to the players. The issue was rendered moot as to the players when arbitrator Peter Seitz struck down the reserve clause in his December 1975 *Arbitration* decision.

Between *Toolson* and *Flood* there were approximately 20 attempts to introduce and pass legislation in Congress to remove Baseball's exemption

1976 Committee Activity. In 1976 the House Select Committee on Professional Sports concluded that the antitrust exemption was unwarranted, but no significant action was taken.

1993 Antitrust Lawsuit. In August 1993 a federal judge in Philadelphia ruled that a case could go to trial in which a group of Florida businessmen were seeking damages against the Giants and Major League Baseball based on a claim that baseball's monopoly over clubs violated the antitrust laws. The plaintiffs included Vince Piazza, father of Dodger catcher Mike Piazza.

The judge ruled that the 1922 Supreme Court decision that solidified baseball's antitrust exemption referred only to player contracts and matters unique to the "business of baseball." He also ruled that the buying and selling of baseball teams is not unique to baseball. In September 1994 the case was settled by Major League Baseball paying $6 million to Piazza and his group.

1993 Proposed Legislation. In 1993 bills were again unsuccessfully introduced to eliminate baseball's antitrust exemption. Moves to eliminate the exemption were sometimes driven by sour grapes. Senator Stuart Symington of Missouri threatened it when the A's left for Oakland in the late 1960s and in 1969 the Royals replaced them. Senator Henry "Scoop" Jackson of Washington threatened it when the Seattle Pilots moved to Milwaukee and the Mariners replaced them in Seattle. Most recently, senators from Florida, disappointed at St. Petersburg's inability to obtain the San Francisco franchise, introduced legislation to allow the movement of a team without approval of the league's owners. After the hearings concluded in June 1994 the Senate again refused to rescind baseball's exemption from the antitrust laws by a 10–7 vote of the Judiciary Committee.

1995 Committee Activity. In August 1995 a Senate committee on a 9–8 vote approved a bill that would end baseball's antitrust exemption. It died in the full Senate.

1998 Senate Activity. The Senate Judiciary Committee again considered a bill that would have allowed players to challenge owners' actions in a labor dispute and alter the antitrust exemption. Surprisingly, for the first time the bill was supported by owners, players, and the minor leagues. Named the Curt Flood Act, it would not have affected the status of antitrust law with respect to the minor leagues, franchise expansion or relocation, or the amateur players' draft. It died in committee, but another version of the bill was signed by President Clinton.

Recent Efforts To Eliminate. In October 1998 Congress passed a bill to overturn the antitrust exemption, which would reverse the "aberrant" 1922 Supreme Court ruling, according to Utah Senator Orrin Hatch. It was never signed.

Calls to eliminate baseball's exemption were renewed in late 2001, after Bud Selig announced possible contraction of Major League teams from 30 to 28. As usual, nothing came of it.

Book. Warren Freedman, *Professional Sports and Antitrust* (1987).

Luis Aparicio (1934–)

Hall of Fame 1984

"I want the Aparicio type. Someone who when he gets on base, they don't know what he's gonna do."—Manager Al Lopez on who he thought would be exciting for the fans to have on his club.

Aparicio was the preeminent American League shortstop of the late 1950s and 1960s for the White Sox and Orioles.

A native of Venezuela, Aparicio spent two years in the minor leagues before arriving with the White Sox in 1956. He led the league with 21 stolen bases, the first of nine straight seasons that he did so.

He helped lead the White Sox to the American League pennant in 1959, stealing 56 bases and batting .257. His other specialty was defense, as he led American League shortstops eight straight seasons in fielding, seven times in assists, four times in putouts and twice in double plays.

In 1963 he was traded to the Orioles and made it to the World Series in 1966. He later returned to the White Sox and finished his career for the Red Sox in 1973. He finished with 506 stolen bases and a .262 average.

He made the All-Star team eight times over his 18-year career and was elected to the Hall of Fame in 1984. He named his son Nelson after his long-time double play partner with the White Sox, Nellie Fox.

Appeals

"[Kelly has taken] the decision of the Great Umpire from which there is no appeal."—Boston newspaper obituary at Mike "King" Kelly's death at age 37.

See also *Protests* and *Suspensions*.

Knickerbocker Rule. The original Knickerbocker rules (see also *Origins of Baseball*) addressed the issue of appeal: "17th.—All disputes and differences relative to the game, to be decided by the Umpire, from which there is no appeal."

Modern Rules. There are five on-field appeals that may be made to an umpire: 1) batting out of turn; 2) failing to return to first after an overrun or overslide; 3) retouching a base after a fly ball is caught; 4) missing a base; or 5) missing home plate. There is no formal appeal allowed of a judgment call.

Half Swing. Originally umpires were not required to accept an appeal to another umpire on half swings.

Rulebooks. In 1960 Senators owner Calvin Griffith ordered 25 rulebooks for his team when his first baseman did not know how to make an on-field appeal.

Luke Appling (1909–1991)

Hall of Fame 1964

"You can't let any team awe you. If you do, you'll wind up a horseshit player."—Appling quoted in *The Official New York Yankee Hater's Handbook*, by William B. Mead (1983).

Appling was a 20-season shortstop star for the White Sox between 1930 and 1950.

Lucius Benjamin Appling, later known as "Old Aches and Pains" for his hypochondria (see also *Injuries and Illness*), grew up in Georgia and attended Oglethorpe University before playing in the Southern Association. He moved up to the White Sox near the end of his first professional season in 1930. He became the club's regular shortstop in 1932 and remained in that role through 1949, with the exception of two seasons missed due to World War II. During the war Appling managed and played shortstop in 1944 for the Camp Lee Travelers.

Appling finished his career with the most games played at shortstop at that time, 2,218. He had 2,749 hits over his 20 years with the White Sox and batted .310. He never played in the World Series, but hit .444 in the All-Star Game. He won batting titles in 1936 and 1943, the first in the history of the White Sox. He finished his career as a reserve in 1950 and in 1969 was voted the greatest living White Sox player. He managed the Kansas City Athletics for 40 games in 1967, winning 10. He is one of the few Major League managers whose winning percentage is lower than his lifetime batting average.

He resurfaced as a folk hero in the 1980s when he appeared in the first Crackerjack *Oldtimers Game*. At age 75 he hit a home run over a shortened left field fence and the crowd went wild. His notoriety having been reestablished, he remained prominent until his death.

April Fool's Day See *Bats*—Aluminum and *Sidd Finch*

Arbitration (1970–)

"No problem. I was either going to wake up rich or richer."— Oakland A's pitcher Mike Norris on the $325,000 he received instead of the $450,000 he had demanded.

"Be it observed that I did not kill baseball, and for all I know, someday—I should live so long—revisionists will suggest that I should be immortalized in the pantheon in Cooperstown, New York."—Tongue-in-cheek response by Peter Seitz, the arbitrator who ruled in favor of the players in the *Reserve Clause* test cases of late 1975, which opened the floodgates to astronomical salaries for players.

"I knew I was in trouble when the arbitrator asked what we meant by such symbols as IP, BB and ERA."— Giants pitcher Greg Minton.

See also *Free Agents*.

First Required. Arbitration of disputes was first mandated in the 1970 collective bargaining agreement, though it did not cover arbitration of player salaries. It was expanded to include salaries in 1973.

First Important Decision. According to Players Association executive director Marvin Miller, the first important arbitration was over Alex Johnson's *Psychological Problems* with the Angels in 1971. The issue was whether a player could be placed on the disabled list for emotional problems as well as physical problems, and whether the club would pay for his treatment if there were only psychological problems. The union prevailed.

1976 Agreement. Following the landmark free agent arbitration decisions by Peter Seitz in late 1975 in favor of pitchers Andy Messersmith and Dave McNally, the owners agreed to a new collective bargaining agreement that allowed arbitration of a player's salary after his second year in the Major Leagues.

After the ruling, 48 players invoked the new procedure on the first date possible. The first to go to arbitration was pitcher Dick Woodson of the Twins. The arbitrator was Harry H. Platt, a Detroit lawyer and arbitrator, and the arbitration took four hours. Under the new rules, the arbitrator had 72 hours within which to pick the monetary figure offered by the player or the club. He could not pick a middle ground number. That rule still existed into the mid–1990s. Owners desperately wanted to jettison the arbitration system because of its impact on salary escalation.

1985 Agreement. In 1985 a new agreement required a player to be a three-year veteran before becoming a free agent. By the 1990s the rule was that the upper 17% of players with service between two and three years were eligible for arbitration. For example, the cutoff in 1993 was two years and 138 days.

1994 Proposal. In 1994 the owners proposed to lengthen the time for a player to be eligible for arbitration. The proposal contemplated that players called up only in September would not count toward a player's eligibility for arbitration. The owners also wanted to allow only 50% of the time on the disabled list as time toward eligibility for arbitration.

1995 Agreement. The current version of arbitration was negotiated as part of the 1995 collective bargaining agreement. Under the current agreement there are two classes of players who are eligible for salary arbitration. One is for players after their third year of service (and the top 17% of players of total service with two years of service and at least 86 days of service in the preceding season) and prior to their sixth year of service, while they are still under the reserve system. The other is certain players who are eligible for free agency.

The first group of players is still subject to the reserve clause and can only negotiate with one team. That team must tender a contract offer to the player on or before the third Friday in December. The player then has until mid-January to negotiate with his team. By mid-January the player has to choose whether or not to accept arbitration. If a player in this category has not been tendered a contract by the late-December deadline he becomes a free agent.

More experienced players who are truly free agents are eligible for arbitration under a different set of rules. Those players must be offered arbitration on or before December 7 and must accept arbitration on or before December 19. If the player accepts arbitration he is considered signed for the next year. If the player does not accept arbitration the team may not negotiate with or sign the player from January 8 through May 1.

If a team offers arbitration and the player rejects the offer to arbitrate, then the team can be compensated with draft picks from the signing team. If arbitration is not offered, the team gets nothing.

If the player declines arbitration the club has until early January to re-sign him. Arbitration figures are exchanged in January and arbitration hearings are held in February.

Arbitrators. Long-time arbitrator George Nicolau was fired at age 70 during the 1995 season. The owners' Player Relations Committee exercised its right under the collective bargaining agreement to unilaterally fire him. Nicolau had ruled in 28 disputes since 1987, the most important of which were the *Collusion* cases of the late 1980s.

Arbitrators are members of the American Arbitration Association (AAA). Any member of the AAA may volunteer to be in the "pool" of arbitrators eligible to hear baseball cases. They are selected at random for a particular arbitration. Players and owners must both approve the arbitrator, which discourages bias by the arbitrators. Cases are heard by three-person panels, with one impartial arbitrator and one arbitrator chosen by each side. This new format was phased in over the first three years of the 2002 collective bargaining agreement (CBA). Previously, only a single arbitrator was used.

Arbitration can be offered only by the team; a player cannot force his team to offer arbitration, although he can refuse an offer of arbitration if he is eligible for free agency. The player and the team submit their proposed salaries to an arbitrator, and present their cases. Team finances may not be considered in arbitration (although attendance can be). Under the 2002 CBA this rule was extended to exclude the luxury tax from consideration, so that players do not have their arbitration salaries reduced because the team's payroll causes a tax to be imposed. The arbitrator must choose one figure or the other, which tends to narrow the range of the offers by both sides. The award is always for only one year, and is to be based on the salaries of comparable players.

Standard Arbitration Clause. In addition to the unique player salary arbitration provisions contained in the CBA, both sides are entitled to arbitrate claims that either side violated a provision of the CBA.

Female Arbitrator. On February 8, 1999, Midre Cummings' arbitration case was decided by Elizabeth Neumeier, the first female to decide one of the 410 cases to that point.

Selection of Arbitrators. Each year about 20 arbitrators are chosen from the National Academy of Arbitrations. Major League Baseball does so in consultation with the Players' Association. A three-person panel is selected for each arbitration. Most arbitrations consist of each side preparing comparisons to other players making the amount of money each side would like to see the panel choose. Arbitrators find the midpoint between the two sides' numbers, and then determine whether the player is worth more or less than the midpoint.

Acrimony/Number of Arbitrations.

"Salary arbitration is the Major League equivalent of divorce court: Owners and players hate going there, and when a case ends, both sides leave with hard feelings."—Stephen Cannella.

The process is so distasteful that both sides make extraordinary effort to resolve their contract differences before getting to arbitration.

Through 2003 there were 446 arbitrations, an average of 17 a year; but there have been far fewer since the 1995–1996 labor dispute. In the early years (1974–1980) 92 of 212 went to arbitration (43%), with players winning 47.8% of the time. From 1981 to 1993 there were 1,564 players offered arbitration, with only 267 going through the hearing process (17%), which the players won 43.4% of the time. Between 1995 and 2002, 87 of 725 cases went through hearing (14%) and players won only 36.8% of them. In 2001 only 14 of 102 players who filed actually completed arbitration.

Highest Award. In February 2001 Braves outfielder Andruw Jones received a record $8.2 million in arbitration. The previous record was the $7.25 million awarded to reliever Mariano Rivera of the Yankees in 2000.

Reliever. In 2004 the Dodgers went to arbitration against star reliever and Cy Young Award winner Eric Gagne. The pitcher sought $8 million, but the club prevailed with its offer of $5 million, the second highest ever paid a reliever after Mariano Rivera's $7.25 million. The year before, Gagne was disappointed to receive only $550,000 after his breakthrough 52-save season. The Dodgers countered that he was offered $750,000 more than the $4.25 million that Rivera received in 1999.

Surprise. In early 1998 the Diamondbacks won their arbitration case against catcher Jorge Fabregas, but owner Jerry Colangelo surprised the baseball community when he offered Fabregas a two year deal worth $2.9 million that included a significant raise over what the arbitrator had awarded for the first year.

Arizona Diamondbacks

National League 1998–

"We wanted to put a little BITE into our nickname!"—Phoenix owner Jerry Colangelo on the rattlesnake theme.

Origins. The Diamondbacks were an expansion team created for the 1998 season, along with the Tampa Bay Devil Rays.

First Game. The Diamondbacks debuted on March 31, 1998, with a 9–2 loss at home against the Rockies. Darryl Kile beat Andy Benes in front of 47,484 fans (or 50,179, depending on the source). Karim Garcia and Travis Lee hit home runs for the Diamondbacks. On May 12, 1998, Mark Grace became the first player to hit a home run into the swimming pool at the ballpark.

Key Owners.

Jerry Colangelo et al./1998–2004. The club is owned by Arizona Professional Baseball Team, Inc., headed originally by Jerry Colangelo, who also owns the Phoenix Suns. Other original investors included John Teets, the chairman of the board of Dial Corp. of America; Phil Knight of Nike; comedian Billy Crystal; Phoenix Newspapers, Inc.; Bank of America; and Pulitzer Publishing. Basketball player Danny Manning was given the right to buy one share of the club, worth $5 million. The club's first general manager was Joe Garagiola's son, Joe, Jr., a successful Arizona attorney. The club paid $5.1 million to the Pacific Coast League Phoenix Firebirds for taking over their Class AAA territory. The Diamondbacks were so popular before they had played a game that they sold 35,000 season tickets, second most in the Major Leagues. After only a year of operation, *Forbes* magazine valued the club at $291 million.

Dale Jensen et al./2004– .

"We didn't get to where we are by being sheep. We like to win. We don't play for second."—Jensen.

In March 2004 the ownership was restructured to give certain of the shareholders a majority interest. The move was made to produce an infusion of cash for the financially strapped franchise. Jensen and two other new majority owners, Mike Chipman and Ken Kendrick, all living in Arizona, made their fortunes in computer software. A fourth majority owner, Canadian J.C. Royer, made his money in cable television. In 2002, Jensen, Chipman and Kendrick committed $160 million over 10 years for a larger share of ownership, and then added more in 2004 to take over the club.

Jerry Colangelo was to remain active as Chairman and CEO, but the previous ownership structure was not generating sufficient revenue to keep the franchise viable after Colangelo committed to over $250 million in deferred salaries to make the club an immediate winner. In August 2004 *Agent* Jeff Moorad was given an ownership interest and named the new CEO. Colangelo was to remain as the chairman for another year, but abruptly resigned in September 2004.

Nickname. The nickname came from the rattlesnake that is common to the area.

Key Seasons.

1998. The Diamondbacks started their existence with a 65–97 record and last place in the National League West. Four players had 20 or more home runs, Andy Benes won 14 games, and Gregg Olson saved 30 games.

1999. The Diamondbacks won 100 games and captured the West by 14 games, the fastest trip to the postseason by any expansion team. The Diamondbacks lost in the first round in four games to the Mets. Randy Johnson won 17 games and the Cy Young Award, Matt Williams had 35 home runs and 142 RBIs, and Luis Gonzalez hit .336 with 26 home runs and 111 RBIs.

2001.

"Surely the country, still grieving, would have embraced such a fairly tale, but Arizona was not a party to such karmic conspiracy. The Diamondbacks laid out their version of real life (unforgiving and unsentimental, isn't it?) and won the next two games and the Series with their own comeback. It was not storybook by any means, but who could begrudge Arizona the championship after a World Series that had been so much fun."—Richard Hoffer in *Sports Illustrated*, on the New York Yankees trying to win the World Series after the devastation of September 11, 2001.

The Diamondbacks finished first in their division with a 92–70 record. They beat the Cardinals in the bottom of the 9th inning of the division series' deciding fifth game, and then beat the Braves in five games to advance to the World Series against the Yankees. In a thrilling seven-game Series, Arizona scored two runs in the bottom of the 9th inning of Game 7 to win their first championship. Luis Gonzalez had 57 home runs and 142 RBIs. Curt Schilling won 22 games and Randy Johnson won 21, as each posted an ERA under 3.00.

2002. Arizona won the West again with a 98–64 record, but were swept in the division series by the Cardinals. Randy Johnson was 24–5 with an ERA of 2.32 and Curt Schilling was 23–7 with a 3.23 ERA. Luis Gonzalez had 28 home runs and 103 RBIs to lead the club in both categories.

Key Players.

Luis Gonzalez. Gonzalez joined the club in 1999 and exploded in 2001 with 57 home runs, 142 RBIs and a .325 average. He tailed off in 2002, but still managed to hit 28 home runs and drive in 103 runners, and repeated almost identical statistics in 2003 (26/104).

Randy Johnson. Johnson joined the club in 1999 and remained there through the 2004 season. He won two Cy Young Awards for Arizona and won 84 games for the club in four seasons beginning in 1999. 2003 was mostly lost to injury, and he won only six games, but rebounded strongly in 2004.

Curt Schilling. Schilling joined the Diamondbacks midway through the 2000 season and then posted 22- and 23-win seasons in 2001 and 2002 before injuries reduced his 2003 season to 8–9.

Key Managers.

Buck Showalter. The former Yankee manager was named the club's first manager in November 1995, over two years before the club played its first game. He was hired after Yankee owner George Steinbrenner fired him in favor of Joe Torre, and then offered him his job back after a public outcry.

Showalter came in fifth his first season, and then the club finished first in 1999. He led the Diamondbacks to a third-place finish in 2000 before being replaced.

Bob Brenley. The former Giants player left the broadcast booth in 2001 and led the club to a World Series win. He repeated in 2002 with 98 wins before fading to an 84–78 record and a third-place finish.

Ballpark. Bank One Ballpark opened on March 31, 1998, in front of 50,179 fans, though capacity officially was only 49,075. Andy Benes delivered the first pitch, but Colorado won 9–2. The $355 million facility featured the Sun Pool Party Pavilion and a retractable roof to keep out the heat. In 1989 the state legislature authorized a quarter-center sales tax to build a stadium. The new levy bypassed Phoenix voters, who had rejected a stadium referendum. The legislation raised $238 million toward the building cost, which rose more than 20 stories high. The Diamondbacks were responsible for $111 million of the cost, which was originally estimated to be $279 million. Bank One paid $66 million over 30 years for naming rights, but it quickly became known as "the BOB." The 4,500-ton retractable roof can open or close in five minutes and the air conditioning system can cool the facility by 30 degrees in three hours. Ground was broken in the fall of 1996 and the project was completed in time for opening day.

Key Broadcasters. In late 1995 the club named Thom Brennaman, son of long-time Reds broadcaster Marty Brennaman, to be its first play-by-play announcer. He was to continue with Fox television on NFL telecasts after broadcasting for the Cubs. Joe Garagiola, who lived in Arizona, also broadcast for the club beginning in 1998. Former players Jim Traber and Steve Lyons began as commentators in the 2000s.

Books. John Nichols, *The History of the Arizona Diamondbacks* (2002); Len Sherman, *Big League, Big Time: The Birth of the Arizona Diamondbacks, the Billion-Dollar Business of Sports, and the Power of the Media in America* (2002).

Arizona Fall League (1992–)

"Safeway Arizona Fall League"—The league initially planned to have the Safeway supermarket chain involved using the corporation's name as part of the league's name. The plan was vetoed (see also ***Advertising***).

Formation. This league played its first season in late 1992, featuring top minor league prospects on six clubs. Teams were the Sun Cities Solar Sox, Tempe Raptors (later the Rattlers), Scottsdale Scorpions, Tucson Javelinas, Chandler Diamondbacks and Mesa Saguaros. By 1995 the Peoria Javelinas had replaced Chandler. The league was created as a domestic alternative to the Caribbean winter leagues. Its first president was former Angels general manager Mike Port. ***Basketball*** player Michael Jordan gave a boost to the league over the 1994 winter season when he played for Scottsdale.

Art

"George Steinbrenner has compared owning the New York Yankees with owning the Mona Lisa. Well, George, thanks for spray-painting the Mona Lisa."—Letter to *The Sporting News* from Robert Morgenbesser of Coral Gables, Florida.

"Only in sports do we let our works of art and working artists fade out like light bulbs while the claque rushes off in hot pursuit of the incandescence of a new one."—Jim Murray.

"Such bastardization reached absurd proportions in Game 5 of the 1997 NLCS, when Florida's Livan Hernandez struck out 15 Braves with the assistance of umpire Eric Gregg, whose abstract rendering of the zone made [artist Willem] De Kooning look like a master of realism."—Tom Verducci in *Sports Illustrated*.

"Baseball is caring. Player and fan alike must care, or there is no game. If there's no game, there's no pennant race and no World Series. And for all any of us know there might soon be no nation at all. It is good to care—in any dimension. More Americans put their caring into baseball than into anything else I can think of—and most put at least a little of it there. Baseball can be trusted, as great art can, and bad art can't."—William Saroyan.

"I would like to be a great artist. I would quit pitching if I could paint like Monet or Rousseau. But I can't. What I can do is pitch, and I can do that very well."—Tom Seaver.

Early Baseball Art. The earliest known illustrated reference to "base-ball" was a 1744 woodcut in a children's book, *A Little Pretty Pocket Book* (See also ***Origins of Baseball***). In 1839 a Boston Commons children's book, *The Boy's Book of Sports*, was the first American book to have illustrations of children playing a form of baseball.

On September 12, 1857, *Porter's Spirit of the Times* sports tabloid newspaper was the first publication to illustrate adults playing baseball, from a game between the New York Eagles and New York Gothams.

The Currier & Ives series is probably the most famous group of baseball pictures from the 19th century. The most reprinted picture, which purports to depict the "first game" in 1846, is actually a portrait of a game in the 1860s.

The first major American artist to depict baseball was Thomas Eakins.

Norman Rockwell.

"He is what Norman Rockwell would draw for a *Saturday Evening Post* cover if he was doing a ballplayer. Pete [Rose] looks as if he should have a dog with him." — Jim Murray.

Rockwell painted numerous magazine covers depicting baseball themes. The first was a 1916 *Saturday Evening Post* cover. The most famous may be the April 23, 1949 *Post* cover featuring three umpires and two managers lamenting the onset of rain. The umpires were Beans Reardon, Lou Jorda and Larry Goetz. Jorda was behind the plate when Bobby Thomson hit his 1951 play-off home run against the Dodgers.

Exhibition. The traveling exhibition entitled "Diamonds Are Forever: Artists and Writers on Baseball," opened in Albany, New York, in 1987 and toured 19 U.S. cities through 1992. It was perhaps the most comprehensive exhibition of baseball art and was put into book form, *Diamonds Are Forever*, by Peter H. Gordon (1987).

Book. Shelly Melman Dinhofer, *The Art of Baseball* (1990), a compendium of baseball in painting, sculpture and folk art.

Artificial Turf

"If horses don't eat it, I don't want to play on it." — Future horse trainer and thoroughbred owner Dick Allen in 1972.

"We can put a man on the moon and we can't grow grass under a dome." — Pitcher Dick Radatz after the grass died in the Astrodome.

"They've played on grass and they've played on Astroturf. What they should do is put down a layer of paper in Candlestick Park. After all, the Giants always look good on paper." — Don Rose.

"Players hate artificial turf.... George Brett worries about his family jewels on the turf. That's never a problem on grass." — Royals groundskeeper George Toma quoted in Angus G. Garber III's, *The Baseball Companion* (1989).

"I don't know. I never smoked Astroturf." — Reliever Tug McGraw when asked whether he preferred grass to Astroturf.

"I count this as one of the greatest days of my life." — Royals groundskeeper George Toma on Opening Day in 1995, when the Royals unveiled real grass for the first time in 22 seasons. Toma threw out the first ball while wearing a white Tuxedo. He was escorted to the mound in a pink Cadillac.

Origins.

"The sinister, unnatural 'Plague'..." — Los Clems Baseball website.

The turf reportedly was developed in 1964 through a Ford Foundation grant study that concluded that urban youth entering the military had lower coordination levels because they had nowhere to play. The first artificial turf was installed at Moses Brown Playground in Providence, Rhode Island, and Astros owner Roy Hofheinz installed a small piece at the Astros' spring training site.

Lighting Problems. In July 1966 Houston's **Astrodome** featured the first artificial turf in a Major League ballpark, though natural grass originally was installed. A financial grant had been awarded to a team of horticulturalists to come up with a grass that would grow under the filtered roof panels that let in natural light. The grass, Tiffway Bermuda, was installed and grew well enough for awhile, but there was too much glare from the panels and fielding was a nightmare. Astros owner Roy Hofheinz considered painting the turf purple to reduce glare.

The 4,796 panes of glass that let in natural light had to be painted over, killing the grass. The grass was beginning to die anyway, so an artificial surface was installed in July 1966. A Monsanto subsidiary, ChemStrand, quoted a price of $375,000, but Hofheinz obtained it for free by allowing Monsanto to promote its product as "Astroturf." The head of the development team at ChemStrand was David Webb Chaney, who died in 2004 at age 88. Chaney was a research chemist and dean of North Carolina State's textile school from 1967 to 1981.

One source erroneously reported that the first regular season Major League game on artificial turf was played between the Astros and Dodgers on April 8, 1966. However, the source forgot that the turf was installed midseason.

First Cutouts. Riverfront Stadium in Cincinnati was the first ballpark to have infield dirt only in the cutouts surrounding the bases. Originally, any Major League field with artificial turf was required to have a dirt infield, but this rule was eliminated for Riverfront's first season.

Cost. The turf in the Minnesota Metrodome cost $1.35 million in the early 1980s (including installation). The Phillies spent $2.1 million for their most recent artificial turf in the early 1990s. Much of the cost is driven by the irrigation system, which generally is a layer of artificial turf over a perforated asphalt pad lined with gravel. This design has been criticized for being too hard. Some surfaces eliminate the crushed asphalt and use softer material.

Ballparks with Artificial Turf.

"Inorganic grass is finally going the way of the leisure suit." — Roy Blount Jr., commenting on a trend in the late 1990s to move back to real grass. Between 1970 and 1990, only one new ballpark was built without artificial turf, Arlington Stadium in Texas. Fourteen ballparks used artificial turf at some point in those 20 years. Clubs have used products known as Astroturf, Tartan Turf, NeXturf, FieldTurf and SporTurf. Ballparks with artificial turf at some point in their existence, in chronological order of first use of the product:

Astrodome (Houston) (mid-1966–1999) (Grass in 1965 and early 1966) The club moved to its new ballpark after the 1999 season.

Comiskey Park (Chicago) (1969–1975) When Bill Veeck took over the club in late 1975, he ordered removal of the artificial turf, called Sox Sod. During seven seasons the club used grass in the outfield and artificial turf in the infield.

Busch Memorial Stadium (St. Louis) (1970–1995) (Grass in 1966–1969)

Riverfront Stadium/Cinergy Field (Cincinnati) (1970–2000)

Three Rivers Stadium (Pittsburgh) (1970–2000) The club moved to its new ballpark in 2001.

Veterans Stadium (Philadelphia) (1971–2003) The club installed a more natural "NeXturf" in 2001.

Candlestick Park/3Com Park (San Francisco) (1971–1978) At least one source reported erroneously that the artificial turf was installed only for the 1972 season.

Royals/Kauffman Stadium (Kansas City) (1973–1994) Natural turf was installed for the 1995 season.

Kingdome (Seattle) (1977–1999) The club moved to its new ballpark for the 2000 season.

Olympic Stadium (Montreal) (1977–2004)

Exhibition Stadium (Toronto) (1977–1989) The Blue Jays moved into the Skydome in mid-1989.

Metrodome (Minnesota) (1982–). In 2004 the Twins installed a new playing surface that looks like plastic grass and is much softer than the old turf.

SkyDome (Toronto) (1989–)

Tropicana Field (Tampa Bay) (1998–) The club installed a more natural "FieldTurf" in 2000.

Effects of Artificial Turf.

"On artificial turf, the ball says, 'catch me.' On grass, it says, 'Look out, sucker.'"—White Sox infielder Greg Pryor.

Artificial turf means fewer rainouts and correspondingly fewer doubleheaders. This puts less strain on a pitching staff. Talents of infielders have changed, as they have become more acrobatic to accommodate the faster ground balls and stronger bounces. The prototype of the new breed is Ozzie Smith, who spent most of his career on Astroturf in Busch Stadium in St. Louis.

Hitting on artificial turf versus natural grass evens out: there are fewer bobbled balls on artificial turf because of truer bounces, but shots in the infield often go through for hits on the springier surface. In addition, the ball bounces differently off artificial turf depending on whether it is a day or night game, whether it is hot or cold, and whether it is wet or dry.

Artificial turf tends to cause more injuries, such as "turf toe" (bruised toes), and the intense heat reflected from the surface is debilitating to players. This has been well-documented in St. Louis and Kansas City, where the surface temperature can often be well over 100 degrees on hot days. The temperature on the artificial turf reached 152 degrees in Cincinnati's Riverfront Stadium on July 27, 1997, in a game the Reds lost 3–2 to the Braves. Perhaps one of the toughest places to play Major League Baseball was San Juan, Puerto Rico. In 2003, when the Expos played 22 home games there, the temperature on the artificial turf field was as high as 153 degrees.

Completely Artificial. In 1969 in Oregon the Portland Beavers' Class AAA ballpark was outfitted for one game with a totally artificial playing surface. There was no dirt on the field because the areas around the bases were sprayed with a granulated substance to simulate dirt. Unfortunately, when base runners slid in, they kept sliding right past the bags.

Aruba

"The name sounds like it belongs to a French ballet dancer, but there's nothing fancy about Sidney. In fact, he's the anti-prima donna. When the catcher throws the ball to Ponson, he does a strange and unusual thing. He pitches it. Quickly. In Aruba, apparently they don't teach young pitchers the fine art of talking to the resin bag like it's Yorick's skull [read Shakespeare's *Hamlet*]."—Scott Ostler on Aruban Sidney Ponson.

The first Aruban player was Calvin Maduro, who pitched five seasons in the Majors beginning in 1999. He played for the Phillies and Orioles while compiling a 10–19. The most famous Aruban Major Leaguer is Sidney Ponson, who emerged in the 2000s as a star pitcher primarily for the Orioles. He was knighted by Queen Beatrix of the Netherlands in April 2003 (The Dutch colonized Aruba in 1637 and then the British took it over in 1805 before returning it to the Netherlands in 1816).

Richie Ashburn (1927–1997)

Hall of Fame (VC) 1995

"You seem to be a better ballplayer after you're dead than when you were alive."—Ashburn to a reporter when his Hall of Fame selection was announced.

"He was one of the most popular men ever to play here."—Ray Kelly in the *Philadelphia Bulletin*.

"They lost one hundred and twenty times and Ashburn went

down kicking and screaming one hundred and twenty times."—George Vecsey on the 1962 Mets.

Ashburn starred in center field mostly for the Phillies during the 1950s.

Rich (NMI) Ashburn began his professional career 40 miles from Cooperstown in Utica of the Eastern League in 1945. After a military commitment in 1946 he returned to baseball in Utica and made it up to the Phillies as a regular in 1948, hitting .333 and leading the league in stolen bases. He was the only rookie elected to the All-Star Game that season.

Ashburn had over 200 hits three times and hit over .300 seven times over the next 11 seasons with the Phillies. He won two batting titles and twice led the league in triples. He was a fine defensive center fielder, leading the league nine times in outfield putouts and three times in outfield assists despite what was regarded by some as a relatively weak arm. He was durable, playing in 731 straight games in the early 1950s.

He was traded to the Cubs in 1960 for two seasons and finished out his 15-year career with a .306 average for the Mets in 1962, for whom he was the team MVP. Rather than face another year of mediocre play with the club, he retired.

Ashburn finished with a .308 average, 2,574 hits and 1,198 base on balls. He moved into the broadcast booth for the Phillies and remained there for 35 years into the mid–1990s. He died in New York in 1997.

Book. Joseph Archibald, *The Richie Ashburn Story* (1962).

Asia

See specific countries, including **China**, **Japan**, **Korea**, **Philippines** and **Taiwan**.

Book. Joseph A. Reaves, *Taking in a Game* (2004) (baseball in Asia).

Assists

"Don't tell me I don't know where to play the hitters."—Pitcher Ray Culp, after a hit ricocheted off his head and was caught by the centerfielder for an out.

"Mays threw so many base runners out he may lead the entire Giant infield in assists. He should play in handcuffs to even things up a bit."—Jim Murray.

"[Phil] Niekro struck out a hitter once and I never touched the ball. It hit me in the shinguard, bounced out to Clete Boyer at third base and he threw out the runner at first. Talk about a weird assist: 2–5–3 on a strikeout."—Catcher Bob Uecker.

See also **Triple Plays**.

Pitching Statistic. For one year only, 1885, pitchers were credited with an assist on all strikeouts.

Most Outfield Assists. A's right fielder Chuck Klein had 44 assists in 1930 in tiny Baker Bowl. Balls would carom off the short right field wall and Klein sometimes threw out batters running to first base.

Dummy Hoy (see also **Deaf Ballplayers**) is one of three players to throw out three base runners at the plate in a single game. He did it on June 19, 1889.

On April 26, 1905, Jack McCarthy of the Cubs became the only 20th century Major League outfielder to throw out three runners at the plate. He did it in a 2–1 victory over the Pirates and each out was the back end of a double play.

On May 30, 1895 in Philadelphia, Phillies right fielder Dusty Miller threw out four Cincinnati batters at first base.

Bob Meusel is one of the outfielders who holds the Major League record for outfield assists in a game, with four.

One source credits Joe Sommer with three assists in an inning for the American Association Baltimore club on August 9, 1887. However, the catcher dropped one of the three throws to the plate for an error, so Sommer rightfully should be credited with two assists that inning.

Red Sox and Indians center fielder Tris Speaker is the all-time leader among outfielders with 449 assists in 22 years.

Most Infield Assists. Turn-of-the-century infielder/catcher Lave Cross once had 15 assists at second base in a 12-inning game.

Pitcher Assists. During the 26-inning tie between the Dodgers and Braves on May 1, 1920, Dodger pitcher Leon Cadore had 12 assists, still a Major League record for pitchers.

No Assists/Team. On July 22, 1906, Bob Ewing pitched the Cincinnati Reds to a 10–3 victory over the Philadelphia Phillies without a single assist registered by his teammates.

On August 8, 1943, the Browns had no assists against the Indians. The visiting Browns lost the nine-inning game 5–2, recording 24 putouts.

On July 4, 1945, the Indians had no assists in their defeat of the Yankees at Cleveland. There were four strikeouts, eight hits, 15 flyouts and 27 putouts.

On June 25, 1989, for the first time in National League history, the Mets recorded no assists in a 5–1 win over the and Phillies.

On August 20, 1997, the Reds recorded no assists in a 5–3 loss to the Rockies at Riverfront Stadium. There were 14 fly ball outs, 12 strikeouts and one unassisted ground out.

On May 17, 2003 the Devil Rays had no assists in a 2–0 loss to the Orioles. It was the eighth time this had happened in Major League history. The last time it happened was in May 2002 … by the Devil Rays.

No Assists/First Baseman. On June 29, 1937, first baseman Rip Collins of the Cubs played an entire game without a putout or an assist.

Making a Point. Yankee catcher Thurman Munson disliked his 1970s Red Sox counterpart, Carlton Fisk. The Yankee publicist once issued a daily statistics sheet that showed Fisk leading Munson in assists, 27 to 25, primarily reflecting their ability to throw out base runners trying to steal. Munson did not think much of the statistic and did not appreciate being shown up by his own team's publicist. During the game that day, Munson uncharacteristically dropped three third strikes, picked up the ball each time and threw to first base for an assist on the putout. That gave him the lead in the category, 28 to 27.

Association of Professional Ball Players of America (1924–)

"We do not publicize our efforts, and this is by design. We have an obligation to protect the dignity and anonymity of our members who are having a difficult time of it. All of our cases are investigated with great discretion. Although major league players of today are well paid, only one of ten ballplayers ever plays even one day in the big leagues. The minor league players have needs like everyone else, but they have only the Association to help them when times are difficult."—From the APBPA website.

Anyone who earned money as a Major or minor league professional baseball player, coach, scout, umpire or clubhouse worker is entitled to be a member of this organization, which was founded in 1924 by 12 former players in Los Angeles. Among other services,

the Association arranges for the care of sick and indigent players, managers, umpires and trainers. The organization is headquartered in Garden Grove, California. By the 1990s there were 13,000 members and the organization had served 59,000 members (with $4.2 million) since being founded. The group is similar to the more high-profile *Baseball Assistance Team* ("BAT"), founded by Joe Garagiola.

Board members over the years have included Babe Ruth, Lou Gehrig, Casey Stengel and Joe DiMaggio, and the most recent additions are Orel Hershiser and Mark Grace.

Asterisks *

"A season is a season, regardless of the number of games."—American League president Joe Cronin, disagreeing with commissioner Ford Frick over the asterisk controversy surrounding the 61 home runs hit by Roger Maris over 163 games in 1961.

"Up Your Asterisk"—Yankee Stadium banner directed toward Frick during the Roger Maris home run assault on Babe Ruth.

Roger Maris. It is commonly assumed that in 1961 commissioner Ford Frick ruled that Roger Maris's home run record of 61 would have an asterisk (*) by it to denote that the record was set in a 162-game season.

Frick ruled midseason that for any records made in the "extra" games (because of expansion that year from the traditional 154-game schedule), "some distinctive mark" would be needed to designate such records. Reference to the term "asterisk" actually started in a newspaper column written by New York sportswriter Dick Young.

Frick had discussed the extra-game issue in a preseason television interview with columnist Red Smith. He expressed more worry about home run assaults by Gil Hodges and Charlie Neal than anyone else. Frick was an acknowledged supporter of Babe Ruth, having been one of Ruth's ghostwriters during his newspaper days.

Mickey Mantle supported Frick's edict (at least before Maris closed in on the record), while Al Kaline disagreed. In a poll of Baseball Writers Association members, they supported Frick by a 2-to-1 margin. Frick's mistake may have been in not announcing the plan until July 18 of that year.

As noted by New York Yankee shortstop Tony Kubek in his book *Sixty-One*, the entire controversy might have been avoided had Maris had some luck in game 154. Maris had 59 home runs going into the game in Baltimore, Ruth's hometown. He hit a ball that initially was clearly deep enough, but was pushed back into the field by a strong wind and was caught.

He hit another that was out of the park, but just foul; he hit a third that fell only 10 feet short. In the 9th inning, the Orioles brought in knuckleball specialist Hoyt Wilhelm. It was practically impossible for a home run to be hit off his extremely slow pitches. Maris finished his last at-bat that day by hitting a ground ball back to Wilhelm for the last out of the game.

It is generally considered fact that Maris hit 59 home runs in 154 games, the 60th in game 159, and the 61st in game 162. However, Maris played in 163 games—and Babe Ruth in 155 rather than 154—both due to replayed ties in which the players' individual statistics counted. Maris had 698 plate appearances to Ruth's 692. Maris had 50 more official at-bats, 590 to 540. Ruth played in 151 games with no pinch hit appearances. Maris appeared in 160 games with one pinch hit appearance.

No "asterisk" ever appeared in the record books, but Frick's ruling was adhered to by including a dual listing of both pre- and post-expansion records. Some sources note that his action later was overruled by Major League Baseball's Rules Committee before the 1990s. However, it was not until 1991 that the so-called asterisk was removed permanently. Commissioner Fay Vincent headed an eight-man committee on statistical accuracy that eliminated the dual listings.

Maury Wills. Frick also advocated use of dual listings when Maury Wills was about to break Ty Cobb's single-season stolen base record in 1962, the National League's first expansion season. Wills had stolen 95 bases by game 154 to Cobb's 96. However, it was pointed out that Cobb played in 156 games that year because of two replays due to tie games. In game 156 Wills stole two bases against the Cardinals to break the record in the same number of games needed by Cobb. Wills went on to steal 104 bases. Frick nevertheless refused to change his ruling and required dual listings.

Henry Aaron. When Aaron broke Ruth's home run record, the use of an asterisk was discussed because Aaron had so many more at-bats. Others responded sarcastically that the only asterisk that should be placed on all baseball records should be for those records established before integration in 1947.

Steroids. Some suggested that the home run records of the late 1990s and early 2000s should carry an asterisk because of the apparently rampant steroid and performance-enhancing drug use in that period.

Astrodome (1966–1999)

"The Eighth Wonder of the World"—Early nickname for baseball's first indoor ballpark.

"It will revolutionize baseball. It will open up a whole new area of alibis for the players."—General manager Gabe Paul.

See also *Artificial Turf, Houston Astros* and *Indoor Ballparks*.

Construction. The Houston Astrodome was the first indoor ballpark in the Major Leagues. First known as Harris County Domed Stadium, it was built for the 1965 season at a cost of $31.7 million. It was 18 stories high and had parking spaces for 30,000 cars. The entire project (including subsequently built, adjacent buildings and hotels) took four years to complete and was part of a $38 million construction bond issue floated by Harris County, Texas. The stadium's 53 luxury boxes, installed in the mid–1970s, rented for between $15,000 and $34,000, approximately $75,000 and $175,000 in 2000 dollars.

Dimensions and Seating. The ballpark's dimensions from left to right field originally were 340–375–406–375–340, but were reduced slightly over the years. With the lack of wind in the stadium and despite moving in the fences in the 1980s, it was the foremost pitcher's park in the Major Leagues.

Only three players hit balls to the highest level of the stands, the second deck in left field: Astros Jimmy Wynn and Doug Rader, and Expo Andre Dawson. A cannon marks the seat where Wynn's (the "Toy Cannon") ball landed. A rooster (Rader's nickname) is painted on the seat where Rader's ball landed.

Seating capacity initially was 46,217, with increases to a high of 54,816 in 1990. The Astrodome had the first theater-type seats installed in a Major League ballpark.

Air Conditioning. Early in the ballpark's history, Ed Kranepool of the Mets noticed that the air-conditioning was blowing toward the outfield during the Astros' at-bats, but was turned off when the visiting team batted. This was soon rectified. The indoor air temperature was kept at a constant 72 degrees. The air conditioning bill was $30,000 per month when the ballpark first opened.

First Game. The first exhibition game in the ballpark between Major League teams was played on April 9, 1965, when the Astros hosted the Yankees. Mickey Mantle hit the first home run.

The first regular-season game was played on April 12, 1965, as the Phillies defeated the Astros 2–0 behind pitcher Chris Short. Dick (then Richie) Allen hit the first regular season home run in the facility off Bob Bruce. Tony Taylor was the first batter in the game and shortstop Bob Lillis was the first Astros batter. Bill Giles, later president of the Phillies, arranged for 24 astronauts to open the Astrodome by having them throw 24 balls to 24 different players and coaches.

One source reported erroneously that the Dodgers' Maury Wills was the first official regular season batter in the ballpark, on April 18, 1965.

Last Game. The last regular-season game was played there on Sunday, October 3, 1999, as the Astros beat the Dodgers 9–4 behind Mike Hampton's pitching. The Astros had a brief postseason experience that year before the Braves beat them in four games.

Lighting Problem. On April 19, 1965, painters covered over many of the 4,596 (or 4,796) plastic skylights in the ballpark because the sunlight was causing a terrible glare. During early exhibition games outfielders had to wear batting helmets to avoid the danger of unseen balls.

The paint job reduced lighting by 25–40% and lights were installed. However, the lack of sunlight eventually killed the grass, the last of which made it to July 19, 1966, when installation of *Artificial Turf*, dubbed "Astroturf," was completed.

Gondola. On April 28, 1965, Mets broadcaster Lindsey Nelson called the game for the Mets in a gondola 208 feet above second base (the highest point inside the park, equivalent to 18 stories). The umpires ruled that the gondola was in play. Nelson sat in the gondola for four hours with executive producer Joel Nixon, who had a telephone hook-up to director Joe Gallagher. Nelson did play-by-play in the 7th and 8th innings. The rest of the game he did color commentary for Ralph Kiner and Bob Murphy. He took with him only a scorecard and binoculars because he was afraid that he might drop his pen on a player if he kept score. Houston won 12–9.

Entertainer Bob Hope was at the game and afterward he was invited to see Hofheinz's apartment built inside the stadium. He asked to wait a moment to see if Nelson made it down safely as the gondola was lowered. Nelson survived the descent and later broadcast from the Goodyear blimp over Shea Stadium in New York.

Multi-Purpose. The Astrodome later had separate retractable fields for football and baseball.

Speakers. See *Indoor Ballparks*—**Speaker Problems.**

Tenant.

"If the Astrodome is the Eighth Wonder of the World, then the rent is the ninth."—Owner of the NFL Houston Oilers, complaining about the high rent the club paid as a tenant of the Astrodome.

Astrology See *Superstitions*

Astroturf See *Artificial Turf* and *Astrodome*

At-Bats

"When you play the game 10 years you go to bat 7,000 times and get 2,000 hits, you know what that means—it means that you've gone 0 for 5,000."—Reggie Jackson.

No Official At-Bat. On April 17, 1890, Charlie Smith of the Boston Red Stockings became the first player in history to make six plate appearances without earning an official at-bat. He walked five times and was hit by a pitch.

Batting Leader. In 1976 George Brett led the league both in batting with a .333 average and at-bats with 645. The last American Leaguer to accomplish the rare double was Snuffy Stirnweiss, who hit .309 with 632 at-bats in 1945.

The only other American Leaguers to do so in the 20th century were Nap Lajoie (1910), Ty Cobb (1917) and George Sisler (1920).

The only National League hitters to do it in the 20th century were Jesse Burkett (1901), Joe Medwick (1937), Stan Musial (1946) and Pete Rose (1973).

Batting and Slugging Title Qualifying.
See *Batting Champions* and *Slugging Average*.

Most At-Bats/Career. The all-time leaders in at-bats (through 2004):

14,053	Pete Rose
12,364	Henry Aaron
11,988	Carl Yastrzemski
11,551	Cal Ripken
11,429	Ty Cobb
11,336	Eddie Murray
11,008	Robin Yount

Most At-Bats/Season. Willie Wilson of the 1980 Royals had 705 at-bats. The National League record is held by Juan Samuel, who had 701 at-bats for the 1984 Phillies. Dave Cash is third with 699 at-bats for the 1975 Phillies.

Most At-Bats/Season/No Home Runs. Rabbit Maranville holds the record for most at-bats in a season without a home run: 672 for the Pirates in 1922.

Most At-Bats/Inning. 1980s outfielder Jeffrey Leonard once batted four times in one inning, in the following sequence: 1) out, and the fielding team went to the dugout, but the at-bat was ordered replayed because there was a ball on the field; 2) single, but the first baseman had returned to the field slowly, and because only eight men were on the field at the time of the hit, the at-bat was ordered replayed; 3) out, but a protest regarding the earlier single was upheld so the at-bat was ordered replayed; 4) out.

One At-Bat/Career. A number of players have had only a single Major League at-bat for their career. Dodger manager Walter Alston had one at-bat in the Major Leagues only because Cardinals first baseman Johnny Mize was thrown out of a game in 1936. Alston replaced him in the 7th inning against the Cubs and struck out later in the game against Lon Warneke.

In the *Movie Field of Dreams*, Burt Lancaster played Moonlight Graham, who appeared in one Major League game for the Giants in 1905, but did not get to bat. In the movie he comes back to life to bat in a game played on the "Field of Dreams" built by Kevin Costner's character, Ray Kinsella.

Long At-Bat. See *Foul Balls*.

First At-Bat. See *First Game of Career*.

First At-Bat/Home Run. See *Home Runs — First At-Bat*.

Last Career At-Bat. See *Last At-Bat/Last Game*.

Atlanta Braves

National League 1966–
"America's Team" — Owner Ted Turner's name for his club after superstation WTBS broadcast games nationwide. The term took on international significance when the Braves played the Toronto Blue Jays in the 1992 World Series.

Origins. The club moved from Milwaukee for the 1966 season (see also *Franchise Shifts*).

First Game. The Atlanta Braves played their first regular season game on April 12, 1966, as a crowd of 50,671 watched Willie Stargell hit a 13th-inning home run to give the Pirates a 3–2 victory. The first Braves home run was by Joe Torre. The club's first home run in an exhibition game was by Henry Aaron's brother, Tommy, who had 13 in his career.

Bridging the Generations. Eddie Mathews is the only player to have played for the three Braves franchises in Boston, Milwaukee and Atlanta. Mathews also played for minor league clubs in Atlanta and Milwaukee before landing with the Major League club in Boston.

Key Owners.
Bill Bartholomay, et al./1966–1976. Bartholomay and Thomas Reynolds had purchased the *Milwaukee Braves* in the early 1960s and spearheaded the franchise shift to Atlanta in 1966. They held the club until 1976.

Ted Turner/1976– .
"One of my goals in life was to be surrounded by unpretentious, rich young men. Then I bought the Braves and I was surrounded by 25 of them." — Turner.

"There's a fine line between being colorful and being an asshole, and I hope I'm still just colorful." — Turner.

"If I only had a little humility, I would be perfect." — Turner.

Turner made his original fortune from a Miami television station, Channel 17, and later expanded his television empire to include Superstation WTBS. He purchased the club in 1976 and held it through the 1990s. Turner won the America's Cup yacht race and has held major interests in movie studios and the Atlanta Hawks basketball team. In 1991 Turner was named *Time* magazine's Man of the Year. In 1994 Turner was reported to be worth $1.9 billion and his then-wife, actress Jane Fonda, reportedly was worth $40 million. Time-Warner bought out Turner in the 1990s and the parent corporation controlled the club's finances after that. See also Robert Goldberg and Gerald Jay Goldberg, *Citizen Turner: The Wild Rise of an American Tycoon* (1995).

Nickname. The Braves nickname originated with the old *Boston Braves*. In 1991 and 1992 there were efforts to change the club's nickname because of the perceived slur against *Native Americans*. Though the name was retained, there was talk of eliminating the more offensive "Tomahawk Chop" popularized by Atlanta's fans. However, the 1992, 1995 and 1996 World Series made it apparent that the Chop was as popular as ever.

Key Seasons.
"Rose is a Red,
Morgan's one, too.
They finished first
Like we wanted to do.

But last year's behind us
We're happy to say.
Now we're tied for first,
Happy Valentine's Day" — A 1990s Valentine's Day card to the club's season ticket holders.

"The Atlanta Braves are in last place, where they have been for the last four years. I wonder if they signed a lease?" — Broadcaster Hank Greenwald.

"The Braves are as reliable as locusts." — Allen St. John in early 2004 in *Playboy*, after the Braves had won their division for more than a decade.

1969. Atlanta won the National League West crown with a 93–69 record, three games ahead of the Giants. The Braves lost to the Miracle Mets in the first year of the League Championship

Series. Phil Niekro had 23 wins and Henry Aaron had 44 home runs and 97 RBIs.

1982.

"We have no crazies or flakes or drug addicts."—Ted Turner on the reason for the success of the 1982 club.

After being a doormat for most of the 1970s, the Braves won the Western Division title by one game over the Dodgers on the last day of the season. The club finished with an 89–73 record under first-year manager Joe Torre, but were swept in three games by the Cardinals in the NLCS. Dale Murphy hit 36 home runs and led the league with 109 RBIs, and Bob Horner hit 32 home runs.

1983. The club finished second to the Dodgers, three games back after leading the league late in the season. Dale Murphy led the league with 121 RBIs and hit 36 home runs. The Braves finished a distant second in 1984 and then began a slide into mediocrity for the balance of the decade.

1991. The Braves finished last in 1990, but became one of two clubs in 1991 (along with the Twins) to go from last to first in consecutive seasons. It was the first time in the 20th century that this had been accomplished by any Major League club. The Braves won the National League pennant in seven games over the Pirates and extended the Twins in the World Series to the 10th inning of Game 7 before losing 1–0. Tom Glavine led the league with 20 wins and Terry Pendleton won the batting title with a .319 average. Ron Gant hit 32 home runs and had 105 RBIs.

1992. The club won the division title and then captured the pennant against the Pirates in a miracle bottom-of-the-9th inning finish in Game 7. The Braves lost to the Blue Jays in six games in another close World Series. Tom Glavine again led the league with 20 wins and Terry Pendleton hit 21 home runs and had 105 RBIs.

1993. The Braves made a furious comeback late in the season and overtook the Giants, but the Giants came back to tie the Braves and the season went down to the last game. The Braves beat the Rockies and the Giants lost to the Dodgers, giving the Braves their third consecutive Division championship. They lost a six-game series to the Phillies in what was widely claimed to be an upset. Greg Maddux won 20 games and the Cy Young Award.

1994. The Braves ran away with the Eastern Division title in the strike-shortened season. Greg Maddux won his third consecutive Cy Young Award.

1995. The Braves again ran away with the Eastern Division title and beat the Rockies in the new play-off round. They swept the Reds in the NLCS and won the World Series in six games over the Indians. It was the first world championship in any sport in Atlanta history. Greg Maddux won his fourth straight Cy Young Award with a 19–2 record and Fred McGriff hit 27 home runs.

1996. The Braves won the National League East by eight games over the Expos and then swept the Dodgers in the first round of the play-offs. The Braves almost went out of the postseason when they were down 3–1 in games to the Cardinals, but came back to win the pennant and then lost to the Yankees in six games in the World Series after winning the first two games. Fred McGriff, Ryan Klesko and Chipper Jones each hit 28 or more home runs and John Smoltz led the league with a 24–8 record.

1997. With a fast start of 19 wins in April (a record), the Braves went almost wire-to-wire for their sixth straight division title (not including strike-shortened 1994) and a record of 101–61. In the play-offs they swept the Astros, but lost the National league pennant to the Marlins in a six game series. Four players hit more than 20 home runs and Chipper Jones led the club with 111 RBIs. Denny Neagle was 20–5 and Greg Maddux was 19–4. Mark Wohlers had 33 saves.

1998. The Braves again ran away with the division title with a 106–56 record. In the postseason, the Braves swept the Cubs 3–0, but then lost the NLCS to the Padres in six games. Andres Galarraga had 44 home runs and 121 RBIs while batting .305, and Javy Lopez and Chipper Jones each hit 34 home runs. All five starters won at least 16 games, led by Tom Glavine at 20–6. Greg Maddux had a 2.22 ERA and Kerry Ligtenberg had 30 saves.

1999. Once again the Braves won over 100 games (103–59) to win the division title. They beat the Astros in four games in the division series, and then beat the Mets 4–2 for the National League pennant. In the World Series, they were swept by the Yankees. Chipper Jones hit 45 home runs and drove in 110, and Brian Jordan had 115 RBIs. Greg Maddux was 19–9 and Kevin Millwood was 18–7, while John Rocker recorded 38 saves.

2000. The Braves won the East again with a 95–67 record, but were swept by the Cardinals in the division series. Andres Galarraga, Chipper Jones and Andruw Jones each had 100 or more RBIs and at least 28 home runs. Tom Glavine was 21–9 and Greg Maddux won 19 games. John Rocker saved 24 games.

2001. The Braves won their 10th consecutive division title with an 88–74 record, then swept the Astros in the division play-offs to reach their ninth NLCS in 10 seasons. They ran into the hot Diamondbacks and lost to the eventual champions in five games. Chipper Jones and Andruw Jones each had at least 34 home runs and 102 RBIs, Greg Maddux was 17–11, Tom Glavine was 16–7, and John Rocker had 19 saves.

2002. The Braves won the division title again with a 101–59 record, but lost to the Giants in the deciding Game 5 of the division series after leading the series 2–1. Chipper Jones led the club with 100 RBIs and Andruw Jones led with 35 home runs. Tom Glavine and Kevin Millwood each won 18 games and John Smoltz had 55 saves.

2003. The club won its 12th straight division title with a 101–61 record, but lost in the first round of the play-offs to the Cubs in the deciding Game 5. Catcher Javy Jopez had a career year with a .328 average, 43 home runs and 109 RBIs. Gary Sheffield and Chipper Jones each had at least 36 home runs and Sheffield had 132 RBIs. Russ Ortiz was 21–7 and John Smoltz saved 45 games.

2004. The Braves won the East for the 13th straight season with a 96–66 record, although not picked to finish there after bringing in new starters on the mound. In the division series the club lost to the Astros in the deciding fifth game and failed to advance to the NLCS for the fifth straight time. Andruw Jones, Chipper Jones and J.D. Drew each hit between 29 and 31 home runs and drove in between 91 and 96 RBIs. Jaret Wright and Russ Ortiz each won 15 games and John Smoltz saved 44 games.

Key Players.

Henry Aaron (HF) continued his home run success after the club moved to Atlanta, reaching 715 home runs in 1974. He played nine seasons there and led the club to one division championship.

Dale Murphy is probably the most popular player in Atlanta history. He played 15 seasons for the Braves before moving on to the Phillies. He won back-to-back MVP Awards in 1983 and 1984 and hit over 30 home runs six times.

Phil Niekro (HF) was a knuckleballer who played 18 of his 24 seasons in Atlanta, winning 20 or more games in a season three times. He also led the league in losses four times.

Tom Glavine.

"He's like a tailor; a little off here, a little off there and you're done, take a seat."—Vin Scully.

Glavine won 20 or more games three years in a row for the Braves beginning in 1991 and helped lead the club to three division titles and three World Series appearances. He was the Series MVP in 1995 and then won 20 games in 1998 and 2000. He won 242 games over 16 seasons for the Braves before signing with the Mets for the 2003 season.

Greg Maddux.

"One thing anyone can go through is a slump. Unless you're Greg Maddux, it's going to happen to everybody."—Dodger catcher Mike Piazza.

Maddux won three straight Cy Young Awards with the Braves between 1993 and 1995. He set a Major League record with 18 straight road *Wins* between mid–1994 and early 1996. He won between 15 and 20 games each season between 1993 and 2003, including 20 in 1993, before signing with the Cubs.

Chipper Jones. In nine full seasons beginning in 1995, the third baseman hit .309 with 280 home runs. He drove in over 100 runs in all but one season. His peak year was 1999, when he hit 45 home runs, drove in 110, and batted .319 with a .633 slugging percentage.

Andruw Jones. In seven full seasons beginning in 1997, Jones anchored center field for the Braves while generally hitting over 30 home runs and, earlier in his career, stealing over 20 bases each season.

John Smoltz won 157 games for the Braves as a starter from 1988 through 1999, with a peak of 24 wins in 1996 at age 29. Shoulder problems put him in the bullpen in 2000, where he flourished with 100 saves over the 2001 and 2002 seasons.

Key Managers.

Bobby Bragan was the first Braves manager in Atlanta after having served for three years in Milwaukee before the franchise shift. Bragan lasted 111 games with a 52–69 record before he was fired. He never managed again.

Lum Harris lasted from 1968 to 104 games into the 1972 season. He managed at Houston before guiding the Braves to 5th in 1968 with an 81–81 record. The Braves hit a high-water mark with a 93–69 record and first place in 1969, but were swept by the Mets in the first National League Championship Series. After finishing fifth and third he was 47–57 and in 5th place when he was fired in 1972. He never managed again.

Eddie Mathews (HF), a longtime Braves hero, finished the 1972 season with a 23–27 record. After leading the team to a fifth-place finish in 1973, he was fired after compiling a 50–49 record and fourth-place during two-thirds of the 1974 season. He never managed again.

Ted Turner. See *Managers—Owners Who Managed.*

Joe Torre was hired to manage in 1982 and he won the division with an 89–73 record, but lost in the Championship Series to the Cardinals 3–0. He finished second the next two years before being fired.

Bobby Cox lasted four years in his first stint with the club that began in 1978. He finished last his first two seasons and then moved to fourth place in 1980 with an 81–80 record. During the 1981 strike season he finished the two halves in fourth and fifth. After being fired he became general manager, but returned to bench manager in mid–1990, guiding the club to the World Series in 1991 and 1992 and a division title in 1993. In 1994 the club was leading the division, but the strike aborted the season. He succeeded with a World Series win in 1995, but lost the Series in 1996. His clubs have come in first every season through 2004, but have managed only a single World Series appearance, in 1999. Through 2003 he had won 2,092 games.

In 2003 he had his sixth 100-win season with the same club, becoming only the second manager, with Joe McCarthy of the Yankees, to accomplish the feat.

Ballparks.

Atlanta-Fulton County Stadium.

"The Launching Pad."— The ballpark's nickname.

Atlanta–Fulton County Stadium, built for $18.5 million, was home to the Braves through 1996 and was known for the frequency with which home runs were hit. The atmospheric conditions made it a favorite among hitters. Completed in 1965, the ballpark had natural turf and was home for many years to the Atlanta Falcons football team.

The ballpark's original dimensions from left to right field were 325–385–402–385–325. Some sources report that for the 1974 season the fences were moved in 10 feet to help Henry Aaron's assault on Babe Ruth's home run record and were moved back out the following season after he broke the record. Philip Lowry's, *Green Cathedrals* (1982), does not support this claim. It reports that the power alleys were shortened by 10 feet in 1969 and moved back out in 1974.

The Braves' first regular-season game at the stadium was played April 12, 1966, against Pittsburgh. A sellout crowd saw the Braves lose 3–2 in 13 innings.

On April 8, 1974, the Braves drew 53,775 for Aaron's 715th home run, even though capacity was listed at 52,870. Capacity originally was 51,500 and fluctuated slightly over the years to a 1990 level of 52,007.

The last regular season game in the facility was on September 23, 1996, as the Braves beat the Expos 3–1. The last postseason game was the Yankees' third straight win in the World Series, a 1–0 victory that set the stage for the Yankees to win the Series in New York after losing the first two games at home.

Turner Field.

In 1997 the club moved into a new ballpark, Turner Field (originally to be called Turner Stadium), following the conclusion of the 1996 Olympic Games. The new $230 million facility was built immediately south of the existing facility, which was leveled in early 1997 and converted into a parking lot. The Braves had to contribute only $23 million in upgrades to convert it from the Olympic venue.

The new ballpark featured 62 luxury suites and seated 80,000 (85,000 in some sources) for the Olympics, but was reduced to 49,714 for use by the Braves. In their first game at the ballpark, played April 4, 1997, the Braves beat the Cubs 5–4. Home plate from Fulton-County Stadium was brought in through the center field gates by a group of neighborhood children and handed to Henry Aaron, who carried it onto the field.

The ballpark is located on Hank Aaron Drive. Monument Grove is a large, park-like area adjacent to the Braves ticket windows. The Hank Aaron, Phil Niekro and Ty Cobb statues from Atlanta-Fulton County Stadium have been relocated to Monument Grove along with the bust of Aaron. There are also statues of the Braves players who have had their numbers retired.

The Braves have a much more lucrative deal in their new ballpark. At Fulton-County Stadium, the Braves paid rent equal to 5% of the first 1.2 million paid admissions. The club received no parking or signage revenue, and gave up 10% of the concession revenue. At Turner Field the Braves receive 100% of the concessions, advertising and luxury box revenue. They keep over 90% of the parking revenue and half the money from non-baseball events.

Key Broadcasters. The first Braves broadcaster was a surprise choice. Though Mel Allen lobbied for the job after broadcasting with Milwaukee in 1965, the choice was Milo Hamilton. People in Atlanta knew his work from network radio broadcasts and he was well received at preseason luncheons. He lasted 10 years with the club. Former player Ernie Johnson, who had broadcast in Milwaukee, broadcast for many years in Milwaukee and Atlanta, between 1962 and 1999.

Skip Caray, Harry Caray's oldest son, was the voice of the Braves from 1976 through the 2004 season. Pitcher Don Sutton broadcast for the club beginning in 1989 and through the 2004 season. Skip's son, Chip, broadcast in 1991–1992, and the other stalwart of the crew was Pete Van Wieren, who started with the club in 1976 and was still going in 2004.

Books. Gary Caruso, *The Braves Encyclopedia* (1995); Robert Ashley Fields, *Take Me Out to the Crowd* (1977); Bob Klapisch and Pete Van Wieren, *The Braves: An Illustrated History of America's Team* (1995); John Thorn, Pete Palmer, Michael Gershman, David Pietrusza and Dan Schlossberg, *Total Braves* (1996).

Attendance

"When the great scorer comes to mark against your name, it's not whether you won or lost but how many paid to see the game."—Peter Bavasi.

1860s Figures.

"The trees bore human fruit."— Newspaper account of a game purportedly drawing 40,000 spectators in 1866.

Before the 1880s few teams drew over 5,000 fans per game. In 1865, 20,000 saw the Brooklyn Atlantics defeat a New York club. Another source reported that the Philadelphia Athletics played a "Grand Match" in 1864 that supposedly drew 20,000 fans and another on October 1, 1866, that drew 40,000 fans to an 8,000-seat ballpark.

These figures may be grossly exaggerated. For example, the game of October 1, 1866, has been described as having the largest 19th century crowd ever assembled to see a game for the Brooklyn Atlantics versus the Philadelphia Athletics in Philadelphia. The crowd of 40,000 was so large that the game purportedly had to be cancelled after the 1st inning when the crowd surged onto the field. This was actually a series of games between October 1 and October 5. Twelve teams met in a single-elimination tournament. *Total* attendance apparently was 20,000.

National Association. In the early days of professional baseball, owners refused to give out attendance figures and the only figures available were from newspaper accounts. Attendance during the 1871–1875 National Association seasons supposedly averaged slightly less than 3,000 per game, though the actual totals may have been substantially lower. The first-place Boston Red Stockings led all clubs in 1875 by drawing 70,000 fans in approximately 40 games (approximately half their total of 79), for an average of only about 1,750.

Early National League. In the National League's first season, pennant-winning Providence drew 42,000 fans for the entire season. In 1879 (or 1876, depending on the source) in the National League, total attendance has been reported as 343,750, an average of 1,319 per game. Another source noted that 40,000 was the total seating capacity for all National League ballparks that year.

The 1880s/Healthy Competition. The 1889 pennant-winning Giants had total attendance of 201,662, an average of approximately 3,100 per game, which was typical of that decade.

In 1889 Brooklyn of the American Association set the 19th century season record by drawing 300,000 fans. With approximately 70 home games, the club averaged 4,300 fans per game.

The 1890s/A War Year and Then No Competition. During the 1890 "war" year among the Players League, National League and

American Association, the Players League had decent attendance of 981,000, the National League had mediocre attendance of 814,000 and the American Association had poor attendance of approximately 500,000. There was intense competition among the multitude of clubs for the diluted talent, which made all clubs less appealing to fans. The owners suffered not only because of low attendance, but also because of high salaries paid by teams to prevent club-jumping prompted by the Players League war.

After the demise of both the one-year Players League following the 1890 season and the American Association after the 1891 season, average yearly National League team attendance was about 185,000 during the balance of the 1890s. This was an average of approximately 2,500 per game. This was lower than attendance during the 1880s when two Major Leagues existed to generate more competition and fan interest.

The 1900s/War Years and then Peace. 1901 and 1902 were "war" years between the National and American Leagues. The negotiated peace of 1903 resulted because the newer American League was winning at the gate: In 1902 it drew 2.23 million fans (averaging almost 4,000 per game) while the National League drew 1.68 million (averaging 3,000 per game). This was due in part to the American League having a larger population base among its cities.

From 1901 through 1907 the American League averaged 2.75 million fans and the National League averaged 2.5 million (with a high in the National League of 2.74 million in 1907 and in the American League of 3.39 million that year). In 1908 National League attendance was 3.63 million and American League attendance was 3.61 million. This was the first year that attendance for all Major League teams was over 7 million.

The highest team attendance of the decade was the New York Giants' 910,000 in 1908, an average of 13,000 for approximately 70 home games. The lowest was the Phillies' 112,066 in 1902, an average of 1,600 per home game. During this decade, attendance boomed due to high interest in the World Series, lack of rowdyism and close pennant races. Attendance for the decade was almost 50 million (49,880,718).

From 1901 to 1909 the combined leagues more than doubled their attendance, a rise that tracked the rise of urban America. In 1900, 40% of the country's population lived in cities. By 1910, the figure was 46% and by 1920 it was 50%.

The 1910s/Federal League Challenge and World War I. From 1909 through 1913 the American League averaged 3.4 million fans and the National League averaged 3 million, approximately 5,000 per game. The presence of the rival ***Federal League*** hurt attendance in 1914 and 1915, as the American and National Leagues averaged a combined 5 million, or only 4,000 per game.

The 1914 Miracle Braves led the National League with 383,000 admissions (almost 5,000 per game), but other clubs did far worse. By 1916, however, combined National and American League attendance was up again to 6.6 million (5,400 per game) and was also stronger in 1917, though still weaker than some pre–Federal League years.

It is convenient to blame low Major League attendance in 1914–1915 strictly on the Federal League challenge. However, attendance also suffered in the minor leagues and in Major League cities with no competition from the new league — areas where attendance should not have suffered. New competition for leisure time interest came from the motion picture business, among other diversions, and the general decline in the economy hurt gate receipts.

As the Federal League departed, World War I arrived to continue the depressed attendance figures. America's entry into World

War I in 1918 hurt attendance terribly. For example, American League attendance in 1918 was only 3 million, as the season was shortened by a month. According to one source, this was the lowest since 1902 (though, as reported above, the league *averaged* less than 3 million through the first eight years of the decade). The Giants drew only 256,000 in 1918, a record low for the club since 1900. In 1919 Major League attendance increased to over 6.5 million, but it took the attendance explosion of the 1920s to restore sustained profitability over a 154-game schedule.

1920s/The Golden Era. This decade saw an explosion in attendance as a result of the end of World War I, general prosperity in the country and the increased popularity of the home run — with the entire parade led by the larger-than-life Babe Ruth. The Major Leagues averaged 9 million fans per season over the decade, with steady increases through 1927. This was an average of 7,300 per game.

The American League's 1920 attendance was up 1.5 million and the league was the first to top 5 million for a season (8,100 per game). Major League attendance in 1920 was 9 million, the highest ever, up from 6.5 million only two years earlier.

Most clubs enjoyed huge increases in attendance once the war ended. The Yankees actually doubled their attendance between 1919 and 1920. In 1920 they became the first club to draw over 1 million fans (1,289,422), up from 619,194 in 1919. No other club drew over 700,000 that season. This was the American League high until after World War II. The Cubs set the then–National League standard in 1929 with 1,485,166. The Cubs and Tigers each drew one million fans at least once during the decade, the only clubs other than the Yankees to do so.

The 1930s/Depression. Baseball was, like most activities, negatively affected by the ***Depression. Night Games*** were tried in various cities to help spur attendance. It was so successful that most teams installed lights by the end of the decade.

In 1930 Major League attendance was at 10.1 million (8,200 per game), an all-time high that would remain the record until 1945. After 1930, attendance dropped steadily over the next few years. By 1934 it had bottomed out (along with the economy) to 3.2 million in the National League (5,200 per game). American League attendance plummeted from 5.44 million in 1930 to 3.17 million in 1933. This was the lowest since the World War I–related 1919 short season. Major League attendance did not reach the 1930 level again until 1940.

The Cardinals won the pennant in 1934 and drew only 325,056, an average of 4,200 per game. One source reported that the figure was 2,100 per date, forgetting that the club only played half its games at home. The Reds drew 206,773, averaging only 2,700 per date. The Browns were the worst, with only 88,000 total attendance in 1933 (an average of 1,150 per game), 82,000 in 1935 and 93,000 in 1936. In 1937 the club increased to 123,000 under new ownership (1,600 per game). The Major Leagues recovered to set a record in 1940 when attendance reached 10,281,953.

World War II and Depressed Attendance. In 1941 attendance dropped to 9.69 million as the war approached and dropped again to 8.62 million in 1942 (average attendance was down from 7,850 to 7,000) as the U.S. was participating fully in World War II. Attendance slumped further in 1943 to 7.15 million (5,800 per game), though many stars were still in baseball uniforms. By 1944 and 1945, even though virtually all the quality players were in the military, attendance was up again to 8.7 million and 10.8 million. This was in part due to the improving mood of the country as the war effort was succeeding. In 1945 the American League reached 5 million for the first time since 1930, an average of 8,100 per game.

Post–World War II Boom. The 1946 season saw the greatest single year percentage rise in attendance from the previous year. A total of 18.5 million fans attended games, an average of over 15,000 per game. This was a 70% increase from the almost 11 million that attended games in 1945, the last war year. The Yankees were the first club over 2 million in 1946 at 2,265,512, but finished third to the Red Sox. The National League was the first to go over the 10 million mark when it reached 10,388,470 in 1947.

By 1948 attendance had reached almost 21 million, an average of 17,000 per game. In 1948 the Indians set a new season record with attendance over 2.6 million. That season the American League reached 11.5 million, but dropped to 8.9 million in 1950. Major League attendance during the 1950s never reached the 1948 high of almost 21 million. In 1959 over 30 million fans attended games at all levels of Organized Baseball (see **Minor Leagues/ 1945– **).

The 1960s and Early 1970s/Continued Boom and then Bust. The 1962 season saw the Major League's highest attendance to that point, 21 million. This was primarily because of the increase in games caused by expansion of two teams in the National League (the American League had expanded by two teams in 1961).

American League attendance dropped by 1 million in 1963, steadied in 1964, but was down to 8.86 million in 1965 (10,900 per game). In 1966 National League attendance was 13.5 million (16,700 per game). American League attendance was low in part because the large-market Yankees were mediocre and their attendance declined dramatically. The Yankees historically were a huge draw on the road, but that attendance fell off dramatically when the club declined after 1964. Major League attendance also was slipping because the unwieldy 10-team leagues, with no divisional play, caused many teams to be eliminated early in the season.

Even when the Yankees were successful earlier in the decade and helped attendance on the road, they still were blamed for overall attendance problems. This was because the club's dominance of the American League from 1960 through 1964 (winning each pennant) caused fans in other cities to lose interest early in the season. This was also true in the National League because the Dodgers and Cardinals won every pennant between 1963 and 1968 despite close pennant races each season. Some sources note that attendance in the National League was better because of newer parks in the league, including Dodger Stadium, Busch Stadium, Candlestick Park, the Astrodome and Shea Stadium.

The years 1966 through 1974 were the "Dark Ages" of baseball. Attendance in 1965 was 22.44 million and increased to 25.19 million in 1966. After that, however, attendance was stagnant through the early 1970s (with appropriate adjustments for the four-team expansion in 1969, when attendance was 27,225,765).

During the early 1970s, attendance averaged 30 million per season, which was poor considering the increase in the number of teams. The sagging attendance was caused primarily by the increase in the ***Popularity*** of football. The attendance slide did not end until the exciting 1975 World Series ushered in a new era.

1975–1990/Renewed Popularity. Attendance increased steadily beginning in 1976, in part due to the American League expansion by two teams in 1977 and also because of increased popularity of the game. The landmark date for the resurgence in interest in baseball is Game 6 of the 1975 World Series, considered by many to be the most exciting baseball game ever played (though argument in favor of Game 7 of the 1960 World Series might be persuasive). Major League attendance reached 43 million in 1979 and 1980 (20,400 per game) and steadily increased throughout the decade. In 1987 attendance was 52 million.

The 1990s/Labor Strife. In 1991 the Major Leagues set an attendance record of over 54 million. In 1992 Major League attendance declined at 18 of the 26 ballparks. With expansion in the National League in 1993, the 1991 record was broken with a 23% increase. Total attendance was 70,245,327, an average of 31,332 per game.

In 1995 Major League clubs averaged only 25,000 fans per game during the strike-shortened season, though the Indians led all clubs with 40,000 per game, 61.5% above the average. The average was 26% less than the 1994 attendance, which was also skewed because of the player strike that ended play on August 12 that season.

In 1995 minor league attendance was 33.1 million, down over 200,000 from 1994. The drop was attributed to a 617,000 drop in the Mexican Leagues and a 200,000 drop in the Southern League as Michael Jordan was no longer a drawing card for the Birmingham Barons. Nevertheless, the minor leagues were extremely healthy across the country.

Average Major League club attendance rose fairly steadily for three years from a low of 2,169,949 in 1996 to 2,401,674 in 1998, and then dropped to 2,380,436 to finish out the decade. Note that 1998 was the first year for the expansion Diamondbacks and Devil Rays, and also was the year of the great home run seasons of Mark McGwire and Sammy Sosa.

2000– . Average attendance rose to about 2,480,000 in both 2000 and 2001, and in 2000 Major League Baseball had rebounded to attendance of 73 million. New ballparks were a good drawing card for clubs, but when the novelty wore off and the clubs played poorly attendance decreased to prior levels. Of the 12 teams that built new stadiums between 1992 and 2003, 10 were averaging fewer fans in 2003 than they did in the year before the new ballpark opened. Attendance decreased 6% in 2002 and was down 5% in 2003. Major League attendance in 2003 was 67.67 million, an average of 28,055 per game. The home game high was 3,465,640 by the Yankees in the American League and 3,264,628 by the Giants in the National League. The lows were 1,058,677 in Tampa Bay and 1,025,639 in Montreal/San Juan.

Attendance in 2004 was up about 13% and 22 teams were drawing better than 2003, projecting attendance at a record 70.8 million.

Effect of New Ballparks. Season attendance at Cleveland Indians games jumped from 1.9 million in 1994 to 3.4 million in 1995 after Jacobs Field opened downtown, which helped support the Flats entertainment district. The club had 455 consecutive sellouts.

The Rockies sold out 203 games when they opened Coors Field in 1996.

The Orioles had 67 consecutive sellouts when Camden Yard opened.

The Brewers drew 2.8 million in 2001 when Miller Park opened, but fell to 1.9 million 2002.

The Tigers drew 2.5 million in 2000 in Comerica Park, but were down to 1.5 million in 2002 with a lousy team.

The Pirates drew an average of 9,000 fans in 2000, a figure that rose to 17,000 in 2001 when PNC Park opened, but the club was back to 9,000 in 2002 with a mediocre team.

In 2003 the Reds became the first team in 10 years not to average 30,000 in a new ballpark.

Single Game Records/19th Century. On May 31, 1886 (Memorial Day), the New York Giants played the Detroit Wolverines in a morning/afternoon doubleheader (meaning two separate crowds attended the games). The afternoon game drew 20,709, the first time that more than 20,000 fans attended a Major League game. The club reportedly drew 30,000 to a game later in the season.

Single Game Records/20th Century. When the Yankees first played in Yankee Stadium on Opening Day in 1923, they set a single-game attendance record of approximately 60,000. The previous Major League record was approximately 42,000 at Braves Field in 1915.

The Indians set the Major League record when they drew 84,587 paid and 86,563 in the park for a game against the Yankees during the Indians' pennant-winning season on September 12, 1954. Before that the Major League high was a crowd of 81,841 that the Yankees reportedly drew on Memorial Day 1938 against the Red Sox (where did they put them all?).

The Los Angeles Dodgers drew 78,672 on April 18, 1958 in the cavernous Los Angeles Coliseum when they played the Giants in their home opener. It was the largest crowd in National League history until the Rockies began play in 1993.

On May 7, 1959, the Dodgers drew 93,103 to the Coliseum for the Roy Campanella Night fundraising exhibition game with the Yankees.

Opening Day. On April 9, 1993, the Rockies played their first home game in front of 80,277 fans, breaking the record for a Major League opener.

World Series High. The highest World Series game attendance was 92,394 for Game 3 of the 1959 World Series in the Los Angeles Coliseum between the Dodgers and White Sox. This is a Major League record for any type of game.

World Series Low. The record for lowest World Series attendance was the 6,210 fans that saw Game 5 of the 1908 Series between the Cubs and Tigers in Detroit. The Tigers trailed in the Series 3–1 and the Detroit fans had little faith that their club would come back from the deficit. They were right, as the Cubs finished out the Series with a 2–0 victory in the fastest game in Series history. It was played in 1 hour and 25 minutes.

Season Records. In 1920 the Yankees became the first club to draw over 1 million fans (1,289,422). The Cubs were the only National League club over 1 million in the 1920s. In 1946 the Yankees were the first club over 2 million with 2,265,512. In 1948 the Indians became the first club to pass 2.5 million fans (2,620,627).

The Dodgers set a new National League record in 1947 when they reached 1,807,526. The Braves topped that mark in their inaugural 1953 season in Milwaukee with 1,826,397. In 1954 they became the first National League club to reach 2 million. The Dodgers reached 3 million in 1978, the first time that milestone was topped. In 1988 the Twins became the first American League team to top 3 million. In 1982 the Dodgers drew 3,608,881, a record that stood until 1990. In 1990 the Blue Jays drew 3,885,284 fans to the club's new Skydome. In 1991 with a pennant contender that won the Eastern Division title, the Blue Jays broke the 4 million mark. They averaged just under 50,000 fans per game for the 1990 and 1991 seasons. The Blue Jays increased their record to 4,028,318 in 1992.

The Rockies played their first two seasons in Mile High Stadium in Denver, which held over 80,000. In their first year in 1993 the Rockies broke the Dodgers' 1982 National League season mark in only their 62nd home game, when they reached 3,617,863. Los Angeles set the previous record of 3,608,881 in 1982. The Rockies broke the Blue Jays' Major League record on September 17 when they reached 4,054,587. They finished the season at 4,483,350, more than the Mets and Yankees attendance combined. The club's smallest crowd was 48,768. The Rockies averaged 57,000, about 60% more than the other clubs. The Rockies had nine crowds over 70,000, 27 crowds over 60,000 and 63 crowds over 50,000. In 1995 the club moved into Coors Field, which held less than 50,000 fans, but was more baseball friendly.

In 1998 the Diamondbacks led the Major Leagues with attendance over 3.6 million.

The 2003 Angels (3,061,094) and Dodgers (3,138,626) each drew over three million fans, becoming the first time in Major League history that two teams in the same market each drew over that number.

The Dodgers hold the Major League record by topping the one million mark every season since 1945.

Road Attendance. In 1966 the Dodgers became the first club to reach two million attendance on the road. The Yankees of the 2000s drew an extra 13,000 fans on the road, an average of $1.3 million extra revenue for the home team over a three-game series.

Total Attendance. In 1993 the Rockies became the first club to be seen by 7 million fans in a single season (both home and road games). Over the first 70 years of the 20th century, attendance at Major League Baseball games was estimated to be 800 million. From 1890 through 1993, 1.7 billion fans attended Major League games.

Night Game. On August 20, 1948, the Indians drew 78,382, the highest-ever attendance at a night game. The game was Satchel Paige's second straight shutout in his rookie year at age 42.

Expansion Club. The 1993 Rockies set a new expansion season record when they pulled ahead of the Blue Jays' record of 1,701,052, set in 1977 — eventually more than doubling it (see also *Expansion*—Club Attendance).

Fastest to One Million. The 1992 Blue Jays drew over 1 million fans in only 21 home games, the fastest attendance start ever.

Fastest to Two Million. The 1993 Rockies set a Major League record when they broke the 2 million mark in only 36 games in their first season. The Blue Jays did it in 41 games in 1992.

Three-Game Series.

"When the third day's battle ended a sad and sticky throng oozed out of the ball yard. It is warm rooting these hot autumnal days and the huge crowd left no noise unturned to rattle the avenging Sox. No use were the bells, the horns, and the loud and boastful bleats."—Sportswriter Charles Dryden on the third game of a 1905 late season three-game series between the A's and White Sox that drew 64,820, including the largest White Sox crowd to that date, 25,187.

In late 1993 the Indians drew 216,904 fans for a three-game series, more than 72,000 per game. It was their last home stand at Municipal Stadium before moving into their new home for the 1994 season. The new ballpark holds only 42,000.

A few weeks earlier, the Rockies set a short-lived record by drawing 216,349 fans for a three-game series against the Giants. The Rockies reclaimed the record in June 1994 when they drew 217,009 for a three-game series against the Giants.

Four Game Series. In July 1993 the Rockies drew 251,521 for a four-game series against the Cardinals.

That Postseason Works Wonders. The 2003 Marlins drew more fans to three home playoff games against the Cubs than they did during April, May and June combined. They had no less than 65,000 fans at every play-off game against the Cubs, but averaged 16,920 for the regular season.

Minor Leagues/1945– . The minor leagues continued strong in the mid– and late 1940s until about 1950, peaking in 1949 in both size and attendance. A 1949 sampling:

Pacific Coast League	AAA	3,718,653
Southern Association	AA	1,831,236
Western League	B	780,443

Rochester's 1941 opening game at Jersey City drew 56,391, a minor league record at the time. On August 7, 1956, the largest crowd in minor league history to that time, 57,000, saw 51-year-old Satchel Paige of Miami beat Columbus in an International League game played in the Orange Bowl. Paige made his entrance by helicopter. In 1982 Denver drew 65,666 for a Fireworks Night for the minor league record.

Buffalo reached the 1 million season attendance mark seven times through 1994. Only Louisville has reached that level even once, in 1983.

In 1993 the minor leagues drew 30,022,761, the highest total since 1950 and the sixth-highest ever. It was the ninth consecutive year of minor-league attendance growth. The overall average of 3,316 per game was an all-time high. Class AAA crowds averaged between 5,000 and 7,000 in the 1990s. In 1994 the minor leagues established a new record with attendance of 33 million.

The minor leagues drew 38,639,142 among its 176 teams in 2002, the third highest total in history behind 2001 and 1949.

Worst Attendance.

"A game between the Allentown and Lancaster Clubs, scheduled May 27, 1885, was postponed on account of no one being in the grounds."—George Moreland in *Balldom* (1914).

On July 8, 2002, ace promoter Mike Veeck sponsored "Nobody Night." His Charleston RiverDogs locked the gates to Joe Riley Stadium and held a party in the parking lot during the game. Fans were not allowed in until the 6th inning, after the game became official and the team had set a record for lowest paid attendance (zero). The RiverDogs beat the Class A Columbus RedStixx 4–2. The previous mark was thought to be 12, set in 1881.

In the last game of Troy's 1881 season, it hosted Chicago on September 27. Twelve people showed up in a driving rain. This story is also attributed to 1878, but most sources note that Chicago had clinched the pennant, which it did in 1881 but not 1878.

At one 1890 game in Pittsburgh, 17 fans attended, with only six paid. The pitiful Cleveland Spiders drew only 75 fans to a game in the late 1890s.

In 1914 during the height of the Federal League's popularity, which was especially strong in Baltimore, the rival International League club in Baltimore drew only 17 fans to a game — while the club was in first place.

On July 28, 1935, the Braves drew 95 fans against the Dodgers. The Browns had total attendance in 1935 of 82,000. In one game in 1933 the Browns drew 34 fans. The last game of the 1944 season (in which they won their only pennant) was the first Browns sellout in 19 years. When the Browns won the 1944 American League pennant they still finished last in attendance.

On September 11, 1942, the Phillies drew 393 fans to a game against the Reds.

On September 19, 1956, the Indians hosted the Senators in front of 365 fans. The Cubs drew 595 fans to Wrigley Field against the expansion Mets in their second-to-last game of the season on September 29, 1962.

A symbol of the Yankees' mid–1960s decline was attendance of 413 on September 23, 1966. On September 20, 1965, shortly before Milwaukee concluded its "lame duck" season before moving to Atlanta, only 812 fans showed up for a game shortly after the team dropped out of the pennant race.

On September 8, 1975, the Braves drew 737 fans against the Astros. The Red Sox drew 409 fans against the Angels on September 29, 1965.

On April 7, 1997, during extremely cold weather, the White Sox drew 746 fans, their lowest total in 27 years. The game time temperature was 34 degrees, not including the wind chill factor. Roger Clemens suffered a pulled groin in the game due to the cold weather.

Philip J. Lowry's *Green Cathedrals* (1992) contains the best and worst attendance in most of the Major League ballparks.

Sellouts. The Orioles set a new record when they reached 60 consecutive sellouts at their new facility, Oriole Park at Camden Yards. They were topped by the Rockies, who reached 203 straight sellouts, but the streak ended on September 6, 1997, when they drew 44,288 against the Cardinals.

Spring Training Attendance. Spring training attendance now averages 1.5 million, up from 900,000 in the early 1980s.

College. On April 10, 2002, at the New Orleans Superdome, a record college game crowd of 27,673 saw LSU beat Tulane 9–5. The previous record was 24,859 for consecutive games at the College World Series in 1999, in which Miami played Alabama and Rice played Oklahoma State.

Japan Leagues. The Japanese Major Leagues draw approximately 20 million fans annually. By the early 1960s attendance in the two leagues had reached 9 million.

Calculating Attendance. Until 1993 the American and National Leagues differed in their methods of calculating game attendance. The American League calculated attendance by number of tickets sold, rather than actual attendance in the park. The National League adopted the latter approach. The American League's system created somewhat inflated attendance figures because season ticket holders who did not attend were still counted. The National League counted free admissions in its method. If the importance of the count is revenue, then the American League's is more accurate. If the important figure is how many people were actually present (a barometer of fan interest, though somewhat skewed by free admissions), then the National League system is better. In 1993 the National League changed over to the American League method of tracking attendance.

In 1995 the issue of announced versus actual attendance came to a head because of the low attendance figures following the player strike. The Atlanta newspapers decided not to list attendance in the box scores. Many other newspapers reported the paid attendance and some put the actual attendance in parentheses. Others listed the paid attendance and the ballpark capacity.

The Cardinals are the only club to count standing room only figures in their total attendance. They have SRO for about 1,500 fans.

Attendance Contract Clause See *Bonus Clauses and Incentives*

Attorneys

"Baseball is almost the only orderly thing in a very unorderly world. If you get three strikes, even the best lawyer in the world can't get you off." — Bill Veeck, Jr.

"You've heard of guys being called clubhouse lawyers. He's an entire bar association." — Columnist Bob Smizik on Kevin McReynolds.

"George Brett's pine tar almost let the plague of modern life, lawyers, into the sole redeeming facet of modern life, baseball." — George Will writing in 1984 about the George Brett *Pine Tar* incident.

"A ballplayer goes into the office now with his attorneys with him — attorneys, not one — he's got a firm behind him!" — Former Negro League star Buck Leonard.

"We're doing this whole thing backward. Attorneys should wear numbers on their backs, and box scores should have entries for writs, depositions and appeals." — Bill Veeck, Jr., during the 1970s.

"The record for continuous days worked had previously been held by Lou Gehrig who worked in the New York office from 1925 until just before his death in 1941. The cause of Gehrig's death, law firm overwork, was unknown in the legal community at the time and has since come to be known as 'Lou Gehrig's Disease.' To this day, no cure other than a substantial cut in salary has been found for the disease and it continues to attract tens of thousands of young lawyers around the world.... The streak started on November 24, 1989, when Ripken, then a rookie attorney, was called at home while enjoying Thanksgiving dinner with his family. A fellow associate at the firm had suddenly been fired for insubordination and Ripken was summoned to the office to help prepare documents. He has not missed a day of work since." — From *The Rodent*, "The Official Underground Publication for [Law Firm] Associates."

Umpire. The first known umpire in a recorded New York Knickerbocker game, played October 6, 1845, was attorney William R. Wheaton (and not Alexander Cartwright as many believe — see also *Umpires — First*).

Players.

"I don't want to be known as a ballplayer who read a book, and I don't want to be known as a lawyer with a bat on my shoulder. I practice law in the winter and I play ball in the summer, and I am careful to keep the two separate in my life." — Future *Spy* Moe Berg, who graduated from Columbia Law School in 1929 after appearing in 73 Major Leagues games in 1928. He spent the next 13 years in the Major Leagues.

John Montgomery Ward. Ward purportedly entered Penn State University at age 13. He received a law degree from Columbia University in 1885 and spoke five languages. He was an attorney during his playing days and was instrumental in the formation of the 1890 Players League. At the height of his managerial career, Ward quit baseball and began practicing law. He was an accomplished attorney who for a time was the chief counsel to the National League.

Orator Jim O'Rourke. O'Rourke graduated from Yale Law School before making the first base hit in the history of the National League.

Harry Taylor. Taylor, a Buffalo attorney and former Major League ballplayer, was one of the organizers of the Brotherhood Association *Union* of the early 20th century.

Robert Murray Gibson. Gibson pitched in four Major League games in 1890 before becoming an attorney and later a judge in western Pennsylvania.

Edward Grant. The late 19th century infielder was a practicing attorney after he retired. He is remembered primarily as the most prominent former ballplayer killed while on active duty in Europe during *World War I*.

David Fultz. The turn-of-the-century outfielder became an attorney and organized the 1912 Players Fraternity, an early *Union*. Fultz played from 1898 through 1905, batting .271, and later became president of the International League.

Muddy Ruel. The catcher, famous for describing his *Catcher's Equipment* as the "Tools of Ignorance," was a practicing attorney in the off-season.

Donn Clendenon. The Mets slugger became an attorney in South Dakota after he retired.

Owners. Larry MacPhail and Branch Rickey were law students at the University of Michigan. Long-time Tigers owner Frank Navin went to law school before going to work in the insurance business as an accountant and then moving to the Tigers. He also ran unsuccessfully for justice of the peace. Others who were attorneys were Dodger owner Walter O'Malley, Braves owner Judge

Emil Fuchs (never a judge), and Orioles owners Edward Bennett Williams and Peter Angelos. White Sox owner Eddie Einhorn was a tax attorney with the IRS who pursued Bill Veeck at one time (see also *Taxes*).

Commissioners/League Presidents. Commissioner Happy Chandler graduated from the University of Kentucky Law School (reported as Harvard in one source). Judge Kenesaw Mountain Landis had been an attorney before taking the bench, as were commissioners Bowie Kuhn and Fay Vincent.

Giants executive and National League president Chub Feeney passed the bar exam after attending Fordham Law School, but never practiced law.

Managers.

"He passed the bar exam and there were times when I hardly passed a bar." — Pirates manager Jim Leyland on A's manager Tony LaRussa.

Managers Hughie Jennings of Cornell (and the Tigers), Miller Huggins of Cincinnati (Yankees) and Tony LaRussa of Florida State (Oakland A's) held law degrees while managing. Jennings had a successful law practice in the off-season despite suffering three skull fractures as a player. Some of the fractures may have occurred in 1904 when he jumped head first into an empty swimming pool. There is no evidence that any of the others practiced law in the off-season. LaRussa received his law degree in 1978 after five years of law school, but has never practiced.

Broadcasters. Long-time Pirates broadcaster Bob Prince dropped out of Harvard Law School before becoming Pittsburgh's number two broadcaster in 1948. Russ Hodges (Giants) and Mel Allen (Yankees) each held law degrees and Hodges passed the bar exam.

Judges. See *Judges*.

Good Marketing. In 2003 the minor league Wilmington (Delaware) Blue Rocks had attorneys from a local law firm appear as color commentators during the 3rd inning. The marketing gimmick was a success, as the broadcaster would quiz the lawyer (ranging each game from a lowly associate to a senior partner) about the legal practice and personal items; in addition to having the barrister read the broadcast copyright disclaimer.

Miscellany. Attorney Clarence Darrow recounted in his autobiography that when he was a schoolteacher in the 1880s he extended the recess period to give the students more time for sports, "including, of course, baseball."

Australia

"A game had been scheduled at Freemantle, West Australia, but on arrival the tourists discovered that the local committee had forgotten to make arrangements for a playing field." — G.W. Axelson in "*Commy*" (1919), describing the Charles Comiskey–led international tour of American Major Leaguers in 1913.

Origins. Baseball was introduced to the country by American gold miners in the 1850s. The first Australian club team was the St. Kilda club of Melbourne, founded in the 1870s. After a visit by Albert Spalding's touring group in 1888, baseball's popularity increased and the Victoria Baseball League was founded in 1890. An Australian club team visited the United States in 1897, but the club ran out of money and illness incapacitated most of the squad.

Olympics. At the 1988 Olympics, the Australian national team defeated Canada, lost to South Korea and then lost to the U.S. 12–2. In 2000 Australia was 2–5 in the Sydney Games, their only wins coming against South Korea and South Africa.

Australian Baseball League. In 1992–1993 the Australian professional league, which started in 1989–1990, had the following teams: Brisbane Bandits, Sydney Blues, Waverly Reds, Canberra Bushrangers, Melbourne Monarchs, Perth Heat, Adelaide Giants and East Coast Cougars. Each Australian League club had an American Major League affiliate by the 1993–1994 season, but only the Los Angeles Dodgers and the Adelaide Giants continued their relationship for the duration of the league's 10-year existence.

In late 1993 Padres first base coach Dan Radison was hired to manage the Brisbane Bandits and former Brewers manager Tom Trebelhorn was signed to manage the Perth Heat. Each Australian team originally was allowed four American players on its roster. In 1995 each of the eight ABL clubs was still affiliated with a Major League organization, but each received only three non–Australian minor leaguers.

The Australian Baseball League (ABL) encountered financial problems for most of its 10 seasons until it was purchased by Major League player Dave Nilsson, who formed the International Baseball League of Australia (IBLA). Over 50 ABL players were either current or future American Major Leaguers. Lack of decent baseball facilities hurt attendance, and knowledgeable sources rated the leagues at about American Class A or Independent League level.

Major League Players. Craig Shipley of Sydney was a utility player for the Dodgers in 1986 and 1987. Shipley was the first native Australian to play in the Major Leagues since Joe Quinn in 1901 (born in Sydney in 1864). No Australian player was a Major League starter until catcher Dave Nilsson of the Brewers in the early 1990s. His father and brother played baseball at the club level in Australia. Nillson signed a 2000 contract with the Chunichi Dragons, which allowed him to play for Australia in the 2000 Olympics.

At the start of the 1992 season, there were 13 Aussies in Organized Baseball. In 1993 Yankee pitcher Mark Hutton became the fifth Aussie to play in the Major Leagues. Australian high school player Glen Williams was 16 years old when he signed for $960,000 with the Braves in 1993, but never made it to the Majors.

Jeff Williams pitched 23 innings for the Dodgers in 1999 and 2000, compiling a 2–0 record.

By 2004 other Australian players who had made it to the Major Leagues included Mark Gourley, Luke Prokopec, Travis Blackley, Damian Moss, Trent Durrington, Chris Snelling, Grant Balfour and Graeme Lloyd. All except earlier players Joe Quinn and Craig Shipley had played in the ABL.

Authors See *Books*

Autobiographies See *Books*

Autographs

"Kids should practice autographing baseballs. It's a skill that's often overlooked in Little League." — Tug McGraw.

"Oh, hell, who wants to collect that crap?" — Babe Ruth on autographs.

"There's no telling what that ball was worth before I signed it." — Gorman Thomas, after signing a ball autographed by Babe Ruth, Joe DiMaggio, Mickey Mantle and Henry Aaron.

"When I was a little kid, teachers used to punish me by making me sign my name 100 times." — Willie Wilson explaining why he refused to give autographs.

"[The player] scrawled his name out rapidly on a dozen grimy bits of paper, skillfully working his way along through the yelling, pushing, jumping group, and all the time keeping up a rapid fire of banter, badinage, and good natured reproof." — Writer Thomas Wolfe.

"The Senators saved money for nobody ever asked a Washington player for an autographed baseball." — Sportswriter Arthur "Bugs" Baer.

"Every time I sign a ball, and there must have been thousands, I thank my luck that I wasn't born Coveleski or Wambsganss or Peckinpaugh." — Mel Ott, whose short name enabled him to sign 500 autographs per hour.

"Hey, stop complaining. Five years from now you'll probably be an insurance agent and nobody will want your autograph." — Team official to a player complaining about signing autographs at the College World Series.

"I didn't admire these men for their penmanship." — Wilfrid Sheed on why he collected so few autographs — only Mel Ott, Eddie Stanky, Bob Johnson and Roberto Clemente.

See also **Baseball Cards** and **Memorabilia**.

Early Autographs. Some sources contend that 1880s star Mike "King" Kelly may have been the first serious object of autograph seekers.

Autographs on baseballs became popular as fans and others began collecting balls hit into the stands by Babe Ruth and keeping them for souvenirs (see also **Foul Balls**).

Prohibited.

"If you don't want anybody to talk to the Big Guy, Judge, you tell him." — Gabby Hartnett to Judge Landis about gangster Al Capone. Landis barred autographs by players while on the field after Cubs catcher Hartnett signed an autograph for Capone's son.

Autographs became a national phenomenon in the 1980s, mirroring the dramatic rise in the popularity of baseball cards. The clamor for autographs became a problem at the Hall of Fame induction ceremony. In 1990 the Hall discontinued its autograph session with the new inductees, which had been a feature since 1982. Over 2,000 fans were lining up for the event and the local townspeople were complaining. Officials cancelled the event after recognizing that many dealers and others in it strictly for profit were attempting to get autographs at the session.

Fraud.

"Signing baseballs that were to be given to big shots and their kids was an irksome chore for the players. The balls sat around in their boxes for so long that if they had been tomatoes, they would have rotted. When, after a suitable interval, large, uninked gaps remained on the balls, DiGiovanna picked them one by one from their boxes and carefully forged the appropriate signatures. Many an aging Dodger fan now preserves in his rumpus room a baseball whose stitched cover is densely scribbled all over with the various signatures of [Dodger batboy] Charlie the Brow." — Frank Graham, Jr., in *Farewell to Heroes* (1981).

Autograph values took a nose dive in the mid–1990s as the 1994 player strike, market saturation and consumer fraud took their toll. It has always been the job of batboys and clubhouse attendants to learn the signatures of players so that they can sign the dozens of baseballs in bulk.

Ryan Mania. In 1991 when Nolan Ryan was still pitching no-hitters, a sign was posted in the visiting players' clubhouse at Arlington Stadium in Texas: Ryan would sign autographs for opposing players only on the second day of a series with that team, and would provide only two autographs for each player.

No Dummy. In order to accommodate as many fans as possible, Lefty Grove had a rubber stamp made. The plan backfired on

him, because his rural Maryland hill country background and the rubber stamp led many to believe that he was illiterate.

Should Have Been a Better Saver. Broadcaster Vin Scully remembers running into Babe Ruth at the Polo Grounds. Instead of signing autographs, Ruth handed out business cards with his signature already on them.

Ice Cream Substitute. Jose Canseco was once mobbed by a group of boys seeking autographs. He counted off 33 boys (his number) and took them all out for ice cream instead of giving autographs.

Nice Guy. In 1991 a 10-year-old fan reached out over the Yankee dugout with a ball suspended from a stick and some string. A note was attached that said it was the only game he and his brother would attend that year and requested an autograph. Yankee outfielder Mel Hall saw the ball, but instead of signing it, he went into the clubhouse for a pair of scissors and cut the string.

Truly Nice Guy. When Dave Henderson signed autographs, he wrote under his signature, "Still having fun."

Signing Authority. "Shoeless" Joe Jackson was illiterate, so his wife signed all autograph requests that arrived at his house. Among his possessions when he died were two cards containing poignant attempts by him to sign his name.

Mickey Mantle. In 1992 Upper Deck signed Mantle to a three-year contract reportedly worth $9 million. The key issue with most autographs by the 1990s was authenticity. By signing Mantle to an exclusive deal, the company could help Mantle ensure the authenticity of his signature on any new memorabilia. The Mantle rookie card (though not from his rookie year) was actually worth more unsigned ($25,000) than signed by Mantle because it was considered in mint condition without the signature and there was no chance of a forgery. Mantle usually received $70,000 for a three-hour appearance at a card show to sign autographs.

No Respect.

"No autographs." — New Yankee outfielder Ruben Sierra when Hall of Famer and Yankee broadcaster Phil Rizzuto approached him in a hotel lobby and said, "Hi Ruben, I'm Phil Rizzuto."

Curfew. A few managers have used bellman or elevator operators at hotels to collect autographs on balls to screen for **Curfew** violators.

Baseball Trio. A single baseball bears the signatures of Babe Ruth, Henry Aaron and Roger Maris. Bob Woytych, who turned 80 in 1995, obtained each of the signatures between 1927 and 1974. It is believed to be the only ball of its kind and Woytych donated it to the Hall of Fame.

Star Struck. In 1994 Barry Bonds appeared in court during the player strike to have his spousal and child support payments of $15,000 per month cut in half because of the strike. Bonds' former wife, Sun, was seeking $262,000 per month, but later dropped her demand to about $130,000 per month. The judge complied with Bonds' request and then created a furor when he asked Bonds for his autograph. After a media frenzy over the incident, the judge returned the ball and took himself off the case.

Extra Effort. On August 29, 1998, a fan went to extra lengths to get Ken Griffey, Jr.'s, autograph during a game between the Mariners and Yankees. Wearing a No. 24 Griffey jersey, the fan ran from the stands into center field, as security people ran after him. Griffey didn't move, unsure what to expect. The fan handed Griffey a regulation-size football and a pen, just before being tackled by security. Griffey wrote his name on the ball and as the fan was escorted away, Griffey handed him the ball. The souvenir was later taken away by security people.

Wall. When the Phillies demolished Veteran's Stadium, at a cost of approximately $11 million, they saved a wall in the bullpen that had been signed by several Major League Baseball stars.

Checkbook. A personal check signed by Lou Gehrig using his full name was sold at a November 1998 auction for $15,306.

Writer's Cramp. On June 3, 1997, after playing in the game that night, Cal Ripken was up until 3 a.m. signing 2,200 copies of his new book. Apparently he didn't suffer from it, as he hit a home run in the next game.

In 2004 Pete Rose signed 3,350 copies of his book, *My Prison Without Bars*, in seven hours in a Cincinnati bookstore — one every 7.5 seconds.

Asset Protection. When Pete Rose, Jr., filed for bankruptcy, he listed among his assets a ball signed by his father worth $75.

Umpire Coercion. In June 2001 Major League Baseball fired umpire Al Clark. There were allegations that Clark had been asking players for a large number of autographs with implicit threats of retaliation on close calls if they didn't agree. Clark later pleaded guilty to fraud. (see also *Umpires*).

Handwriting Expert. Charlie Metro was part of the Chicago Cubs *College of Coaches* experiment in 1962. To gain an edge, in addition to trying ventriloquism (see *Signs*), he hired a California graphologist to analyze the signatures of all the other National League managers. Given that the Cubs finished ninth, ahead only of the new and pitiful Mets, the handwriting analysis probably can't be judged a success by any standard. A sampling of the analysis, by a person who was not a baseball fan and did not know the names:

"Casey Stengel(Mets): 'A pioneer, explorer, discoverer type. Goes into things with great verve and enthusiasm. Outspoken ... modest in ego.... He acts like a psychiatrist to his boys — open, receptive....'

Walter Alston (Dodgers): 'Friendly obliging and good nature. Good strategist.... Not very profound or scientific often inaccurate.... When emotional not so reliable [Walter Alston emotional??].'

Charlie Metro (Cubs): 'Objective.... A good leader in times of peace but not in times of war. He is sane and sober-minded. Best balance of all the managers.'"

Retribution. When Tommy Lasorda arrived in the minor leagues, he threw four straight pitches that almost hit Buster Maynard, an ex–Major Leaguer. After the game, Maynard asked Lasorda why he went after him, because Maynard was sure that Lasorda didn't know him. Lasorda's screamed response: "When I was a kid in the eighth grade you used to pitch for the New York Giants! I used to save up enough money to go to a game. When I got there, I asked you for an autograph and you just pushed me aside and kept walking! I wish I had hit you, you busher!"

Books. Mark A. Baker, *Baseball Autograph Handbook* (1991); James Beckett, *The American League [and National League] Baseball Autograph Book* (1987).

Automobiles

"Part of it is his timing is off. If you have a Volkswagen and the timing is off, it still runs OK. If it's a Ferrari and the timing is off, it runs like a tractor." — Giants manager Dusty Baker on slumping star Barry Bonds.

"I'm very pleased and very proud of my accomplishments, but I'm most proud of that [hitting four-hundred home runs and three-thousand hits]. Not Williams, not Gehrig, not DiMaggio did that. They were Cadillacs and I'm a Chevrolet." — Carl Yastrzemski.

"Some years ago 'auto polo' became the rage. Some of Comis-key's friends were interested in its promotion. Could they have the use of the field? Certainly, and 'use' it they did. Up in the stands sat Comiskey watching the two contesting cars chop his field into ribbons. It cost him $400 to repair the damage." — G.W. Axelson in *"Commy"* (1919).

"Look at our parking lot, and you see a lot of Hyundais and Geo Storms. You don't see a lot of Lexuses and Mercedes." — Keith Osik of the Pirates, reflecting on the fact that the 1997 payroll for the entire Pirates' roster was less than the $10 million being earned by Albert Belle.

"I don't think my insurance company would think that's a good idea." — Boston's Tim Wakefield, who pitched a complete-game six-hitter a day after being involved in a minor car accident, when it was suggested that he copy the pre-game routine before every start.

"[Watching baseball] is clearly superior to holiday motoring and is much less conducive to sudden death." — Fred Schwed, Jr., in *How to Watch a Baseball Game* (1957).

"I'm a four-wheel-drive-pickup type of guy, and so is my wife." — Mike Greenwell.

"Billy Nash, Cotton Nash, Nat Hudson, Gene Packard, George Stutz, Lew Carr, John Dodge, Dan Ford, Sam Dodge, Lerton Pinto, Jack Bentley, Joe Benz, Royce Lint"

See also *Chalmers Award*.

Umpire Gift. In 1935 *The Sporting News* ran a poll naming Dolly Stark as the most popular umpire. Near the end of the season, fans at the Polo Grounds presented him with a new automobile.

Official Car. In 1965 the official car of the Mets was a Nash Rambler and many players on the team bought one at a discount.

Contract Bonus. When Vida Blue had a tremendous start in 1971, A's owner Charlie Finley made a great show of presenting him with a powder blue Cadillac with "Blue" license plates. Blue was furious because he did not want to be perceived as a stereotypically flamboyant black man driving a Cadillac. Instead, he would have preferred that Finley tear up his near–Major League minimum contract and increase his salary.

In 1977 free agent Reggie Jackson negotiated with George Steinbrenner of the Yankees to leave the Orioles and move to New York. Steinbrenner told Jackson that as part of their negotiations a $63,000 Rolls Royce was Jackson's, no strings attached and regardless of whether he ultimately signed. The ploy may have helped, because Jackson, a vintage car buff, went on to star for the Yankees.

Shoddy Treatment. Terry Pendleton went to high school in the county in which this author lives. In 1990, the year before Pendleton won the National League MVP award, the author saw a car near his office with a license plate frame that read, "Terry Pendleton's Mother." It was a beat-up old Toyota. Presumably Pendleton eventually upgraded his mother's transportation. Others in the community reported that he bought her a beautiful house.

Bad Day At the Office. In 1956 the Phillies lost a doubleheader to the Reds, blowing a 10-run lead in the second game. Phillies center fielder Richie Ashburn was in a foul mood as he walked to his car, pushing past and ignoring pleas for autographs from young fans. He got into his Cadillac and threw it into reverse, but he slammed into a fans' car. A parent of one of the kids softly said to Ashburn, "You know, Son, what happened over there today, 30 years from now will not amount to a teaspoon of sand, but these boys will always remember their hero at his worst." Ashburn changed demeanor completely, and agreed with the him. He apologized to the man, put his arm around the boys, and then pulled two new baseballs from his trunk, signed them and gave them to the boys.

Funereal. For a number of years reliever Don Stanhouse drove a black hearse to the ballpark.

License Plates. Mets fans have purchased the following vanity license plates: METSFANS, GOMETSGO, ILUVMETS, 69–73–86 (World Series winners), and GAME6–E3 (Bill Buckner — see also *Errors*).

Nice Wheels. In 2001 Cubs reliever Jason Bere parked his $112,000 Porsche 996 Carrera convertible at a hotel in Milwaukee. A man then casually asked the valet for the keys and drove away with the car, which he returned, unharmed, an hour later.

Hummer. When Roger Clemens retired from the Yankees after the 2003 season, the club presented him with a Hummer. After teammate Andy Pettitte signed with the Astros, Pettitte persuaded a Houston auto dealer to provide Clemens with a new Hummer, painted orange to match Clemens' Texas alma mater, if he would sign with the Astros. Clemens signed; no word on the new Hummer.

Reserved. In 2004 the Braves had a Lexus-only parking lot at Turner Field.

Earl Averill (1902–1983)

Hall of Fame (VC) 1975

"If Earl Averill, the young Washington outfielder, whom Cleveland bought from San Francisco a year ago for $50,000, has a middle name, it probably is 'nonchalant.' If not, it ought to be, for a more blasé major league rookie never flashed across." — Henry P. Edwards of the Magazine Service Bureau.

Averill was a star outfielder primarily for the Indians between 1929 and 1941.

Averill grew up in Washington and played in the Pacific Coast League before the Indians purchased him for $50,000 in 1928. In his last PCL season he hit .354 with 36 home runs and 178 RBIs. In his first game for the Indians at age 26 he became the first American Leaguer to hit a home run in his first Major League at-bat.

An outfielder, Averill batted over .300 in each of his first six seasons and reached a high of .378 in 1936. That year he had 232 hits, 15 triples and 28 home runs to go with 126 RBIs and 136 runs scored.

He began to fade after that and the Indians traded him to the Tigers in 1939, for whom he had three unsuccessful at-bats in the 1940 World Series. He ended his career with eight games in 1941 for the Braves, finishing with a .318 lifetime average and 238 home runs over 13 seasons. His son played parts of seven seasons in the Major Leagues in the late 1950s and early 1960s.

Awards

"I will perish this trophy forever." — Johnny Logan.

"If you can't eat it, drink it, cash it or sleep with it, don't worry about it." — Sportscaster Keith Jackson on the importance of awards.

There have been a number of awards, many now long-abandoned, presented to ballplayers and others in baseball. There are separate entries for many of the awards listed below.

Al Somers Umpire of the Year Award. The Somers umpiring school began presenting the award in 1971. The first recipient was Hall of Famer Al Barlick.

Aqua Velva Award. After Pete Rose hit in 44 consecutive games in 1978, Aqua Velva began awarding $1,000 to charity for every game in the longest streak of the season. It has sometimes been described as the Pete Rose Streak Award.

Arby's RBI Award. This award has been presented annually since 1986 to the RBI leader in each league. The food company donates $1,000 to charity for each RBI by the league leaders. The award is actually called the Henry Aaron Trophy, because he was the first spokesman for the award.

Arch Ward Award. This award was presented by Rawlings to the MVP of the All-Star Game in honor of the man credited with creating and organizing the first game in 1933. In 1970 the award was changed to the Commissioner's Award and Ward's name was dropped.

Arthur Ashe Award for Courage. The award was presented to umpire Steve Palermo in 1994. It was created in 1993 as part of ESPN's "ESPY" telecast and is awarded to a member of the sports community who has exemplified courage, spirit and determination to help others despite hardship (Palermo was partially paralyzed by a gunman's bullet — see also *Murder*). Ashe was a professional tennis player who died of AIDS from a blood transfusion.

Associated Press Baseball Player of the Year. This award was inaugurated in 1988. In 1995 Greg Maddux became the first pitcher to receive it.

BABE Award. This award was first presented in 1979 by Major League broadcasters to the manager of the year and the most outstanding player in each league exhibiting personal qualities over and above playing ability. There was also a broadcasting award. The acronym stands for Broadcasters Annual Baseball Elections.

Babe Didrikson Award. This award was created in 1957 in memory of the great woman track star and golfer who died of cancer in the 1950s. When John Hiller won the Comeback Player Award in 1973 after a heart attack, he also won this award, presented to someone who has overcome personal injury or illness.

Babe Ruth Award. This award is presented to the World Series MVP. Joe Page was the first recipient in 1949, the year after Ruth's death.

Bart Giamatti Caring Award. The award is presented annually to a player for community and charitable work. The first recipient was Cal Ripken, Jr., in 1989.

BBWAA Awards. By the 1990s the baseball writers presented awards in each league for Manager of the Year, Rookie of the Year, Most Valuable Player, and Cy Young Award winner.

Ben Epstein Good Guy Award. The New York press annually presents this award to a player for cooperating with the press. It was first awarded in 1959 to Hank Bauer after Epstein's death in 1958. He had covered the Yankees for the *Daily Mirror*.

Big Stick Award. Adirondack bats (now owned by Rawlings) presented this award to the season home run leaders in the 1970s.

Bill Klem Award. This umpire award was presented briefly during the 1950s.

Bill Slocum Memorial Award. This award was created in 1929 by the Baseball Writers of America to honor a person who made "high contribution to baseball over a long period" (or "Long and Meritorious Service to Baseball"). The first was awarded posthumously to Miller Huggins, who had died late in the season. In 1946 it was awarded to *Clown Prince of Baseball* Al Schacht for his work with the USO during World War II.

Branch Rickey Award. This award was presented for community service by a Major League player.

Buck Canel Award. The award was named after the long-time Hispanic broadcaster from New York and is presented to a Hispanic player. The first recipient was Manny Trillo in 1980.

Casey Stengel "You Could Look It Up Award." This award

was created in 1960 by the New York press and first presented to Ty Cobb.

Chalmers Award. The Chalmers Automobile Company presented an automobile to each league's MVP between 1911 and 1914. In 1910 the award was presented to each league's batting champion, but the criteria was changed for the following season.

Comeback Player of the Year Award. This award has been presented since the 1950s to a player in each league who makes the biggest comeback from the previous year. Often it is given to a player who had a horrendous prior year, but sometimes has been presented to a player who returned from significant injury.

Commissioner's Award. This award was inaugurated in 1970 and is presented to the MVP of the All-Star Game (replacing the Arch Ward Award).

Commissioner's Historic Achievement Award. It was presented to Roger Clemens at the 2004 All-Star Game and to the Seattle Mariners in recognition of their 2001 record-setting regular season. It was presented at the end of 2004 when Ichiro Suzuki passed George Sisler on the all-time season hit list. The first recipient was Cal Ripken in 1995, in recognition of his consecutive games played streak. Others winners are Barry Bonds (2001 season), Mark McGwire (1998) and Sammy Sosa (1998), Rickey Henderson (stolen base record), and Tony Gwynn (career).

Congressional Gold Medal. In 2003 President Bush honored Jackie Robinson by signing legislation awarding Congress' highest honor, the Congressional Gold Medal, recognizing his achievements in sports, civil rights and business. At the end of his playing career, Robinson toured the country in support of the NAACP, the Anti-Defamation League and B'Nai B'rith. He also helped found the Freedom National Bank of Harlem. Robinson joined over 300 people who have received the Gold Medal since George Washington received the first one in 1776. Honorees have included Mother Teresa, Pope John Paul II, Robert Frost, Joe Louis, Rosa Parks, and Ronald and Nancy Reagan.

Consort Control Pitcher Award. This award was created in 1986 by the hair care company in conjunction with *The Sporting News* based on a computerized rating system that compared each starting pitcher's skill based on his ERA, strikeouts and hits allowed against the league average.

Cy Young Award. This award is presented to the outstanding pitcher in each league, though originally (1956–1966) it was presented only to the top pitcher in the Major Leagues.

Danny Thompson Award. This award is presented by The Baseball Chapel (see also ***Religion***) for "exemplary Christian spirit in baseball." The award honors the seven-season Major League infielder who died of leukemia at age 29 in 1976. He played the last four years knowing that he had the disease. It was first presented in 1977 to Don Kessinger.

Dauvray Cup. The cup was presented between 1887 and 1889 to the winner of the Championship Series played between the American Association and National League pennants winners.

Early Award. One of the earliest attempts at an award was by one of the 1850s amateur teams, the New York Clippers. The team tried to start a system of championship rankings by offering a gold medal to players who were best at their position and a gold ball to the winner of a best-of-three championship series. The Brooklyn Atlantics and New York Mutuals, the recognized champions when the award system was announced, refused to play and the plan apparently was never implemented.

Eraser Rate Award. This award was created in 1982 and sponsored by Major League Baseball and EraserMate, a product of Paper Mate. The award is given to the team in each league that has the best percentage of opponents caught stealing per total attempted steals.

Ernie Meld Award. The award was presented to the "figure who has contributed greatly to the overall image of professional baseball both on and of the field." Don Newcombe, Ernie Banks, Roberto Clemente and Phil Niekro are among the winners. [The award may be extinct; a search of the Internet turned up only a "Meld Award" for a pinochle tournament].

Executive of the Year. This award is presented by *The Sporting News* to the top Major League executive. There is also a minor league version of the award.

Exemplary Conduct Trophy. Pete Rose's Exemplary Conduct Trophy (a silver cup), awarded by the writers at least in the 1970s, sold for $9,775 in the early 2000s.

Fireman of the Year. This award is presented to the top reliever in each league by *The Sporting News*. It is separate from the corporate-sponsored **Rolaids Relief Award**.

Ford Frick Award. Created in 1978, this award is presented by the Hall of Fame to broadcasters who have made a "major contribution" to baseball.

Gold Glove Award. Presented by Rawlings to the best defensive player at each position.

Golden Spikes Award. USA Baseball and Topps, in conjunction with the United States Baseball Federation, present the award annually to the outstanding amateur baseball player. Former winners include Bob Horner and Will Clark.

Grantland Rice Award. This award was created after Rice's death in 1955 and was presented for "an outstanding example of sports reporting in the Grantland Rice tradition."

Greyhound Award. This bus company presented its award to the stolen base king in each league from 1975 through the early 1980s.

Henry Aaron Award. This award originally was presented to the National League's best hitter, and then the award was expanded in 1999 to include both leagues.

Hutch Award. This award was created in 1965 by friends of Reds manager Fred Hutchinson, who died of cancer that year. It recognizes a Major League player who has overcome serious adversity and best exemplifies the character and qualities of Hutchinson, including community service. Voters contribute $10 to a scholarship fund, from which comes an annual scholarship awarded to a young medical student. Early winners were Mickey Mantle, Carl Yastrzemski and Sandy Koufax. David Cone won the award in 1998 after coming back from surgery to repair an aneurysm in his shoulder.

By 2001 the award was being presented by Seattle's Cancer Research Center to a player who displays "honor, courage & dedication to baseball while overcoming adversity in their personal or professional lives."

Joan Payson Award. This award was created by the New York press and first presented in 1975 to Payson, the first owner of the Mets. John Franco was the 2003 recipient in recognition of his charity work.

Joe Cronin Award for Significant Achievement. The American League presents this award annually to a baseball personality who has made a "Significant Achievement." In 1993 Dave Winfield received it for reaching 3,000 hits.

Joe DiMaggio "Toast of the Town" Award. This award was created by the New York press in 1983 and first presented to Lou Piniella and Bobby Murcer.

John H. Johnson President's Trophy. This award is presented by the minor league National Association to a minor league club based on franchise stability, contributions to baseball in its community and promotion of the baseball industry.

King of Baseball Award. This award is presented by the National Association of Minor Leagues to the top minor league player.

Larry MacPhail Award. This award is presented to a minor league executive for top promotion efforts.

Lou Brock Award. This award was created in 1977 to honor the stolen base leader in each league.

Lou Gehrig Memorial Award. The award was created by Gehrig's fraternity at Columbia University, Phi Delta Theta. Henry Aaron received it in 1970 for achieving 3,000 hits.

Louisville Slugger Award. This award was first presented in 1971 to new Hall of Fame inductees who were batting stars.

Manager of the Year. The Baseball Writers began presenting this award in 1983.

Mel Ott Award. In the years when Mel Ott was still the National League's career home run leader (before Willie Mays overtook him), the Mel Ott Plaque was awarded to the season home run leader in the league.

Most Valuable Little Player Award. This award was presented by Volkswagen in the late 1960s and early 1970s to a player of small stature.

Most Valuable Player Award. The Baseball Writers Association presents this award to the most valuable player in each league. *The Sporting News* has also participated at various times in presenting MVP Awards over the years.

Multiple Awards. Only six players have won a Rookie of the Year Award, MVP Award, Gold Glove and were part of a World Series winner: Willie Mays, Frank Robinson, Pete Rose, Johnny Bench, Thurman Munson and Cal Ripken, Jr. (as determined by Steve Lombardi of NetShrine). Fernando Valenzuela is the only pitcher to receive each of these honors, substituting a Cy Young Award for the MVP.

Negro Baseball League Awards. These awards were inaugurated in 1994 to honor outstanding African-Americans involved in baseball. The awards include the Buck O'Neil Lifetime Achievement Award and the Josh Gibson Professional Achievement Award.

Outstanding Designated Hitter Award. This award was established in 1973 by the American League in conjunction with the *Union Leader* newspaper in Manchester, New Hampshire.

Pitcher of the Month/Week. In 1975 the National League started the Pitcher of the Month award and later added Pitcher of the Week.

Player of the Month/Week.
"That just shows you how this league has gone to hell." — Left-hander Chuck Finley, on his selection as American League Player of the Week. The Player of the Month Award was created in the late 1950s. The weekly award began in the National League in 1972.

Players Choice Award. This award is presented by the Major League Players Association to the best player in each league. Each player on a Major League roster or disabled list as of August 30 is asked to vote by secret ballot for the best player in his league.

Rae *Hickok Award.* The Hickok Belt was presented to the professional athlete of the year from 1950 through 1976.

Rawlings Woman Executive of the Year Award. This award is presented to the top woman executive in professional baseball.

Retroactive Award. This award was created in 1960 and is presented to a former star by the New York press.

Robert O. Fishel Award. This award was created by Major League Baseball in 1981 and first presented to Fishel himself. It is

awarded to the top publicist in the Major Leagues. Fishel signed *Midget* Eddie Gaedel for the Browns and was the Yankee publicist for 20 years before moving into the American League office in 1973.

Roberto Clemente Humanitarian Award. After Clemente died while taking supplies to earthquake victims in Nicaragua (see also **Deaths**), Major League Baseball renamed an existing award in his honor. The award goes to a player who best exemplifies the game both on and off the field.

Rolaids Relief Award. Rolaids began sponsoring this Relief Pitcher award as a tie-in to its product (see also Fireman of the Year).

Rookie of the Year Award. In 1947 Major League Baseball presented its first Rookie of the Year Award to Jackie Robinson. It is now known as the Jackie Robinson Rookie of the Year Award. Prior to 1947 *The Sporting News* presented a Rookie of the Year Award.

Scout of the Year. This award has been presented annually since 1984 at the winter baseball meetings. It honors active scouts with more than 25 years of experience for career excellence and professionalism.

Seagram's Seven Crowns of Sports. In 1974 Seagram's distillery created this award to honor a player from each of seven sports. Each annual winner received $10,000 and there were also monthly winners.

Sid Mercer Award. Created by the New York writers in memory of the long-time sportswriter, it is presented to the top Major League player each season. The first recipient was Bill Terry.

Silver Bat Award. This award was created in 1986 by *The Sporting News* to recognize the top batter at each position (though not necessarily with the highest average). An earlier Silver Bat Award was created in 1950.

Silver Glove Award. Rawlings presents this award to members of *The Sporting News* minor league all-star team.

Silver Shoe Award. This award was created in 1982 by Pony Sports and Leisure in conjunction with *The Sporting News* to honor the top base stealer in Major League Baseball.

Silver Slugger Award. This award, sometimes known early on as the "Silver Bat Award," is presented annually by Hillerich & Bradsby and *The Sporting News* to the top hitter at each position in each league. The Louisville Slugger silver bats that come with the award were first presented in 1946 only to the league leaders, with Mickey Vernon and Stan Musial the winners. The first three sets of winners by position received sheepskin certificates and a sum of cash. Subsequent winners received the certificates and the silver bats instead of cash.

In the spring of 1954, President Eisenhower came out to the Senator's ballpark to present the Silver Slugger Award to Mickey Vernon, which a member of the Hillerich family brought from the bat company in Louisville. It may have been the only time a President made the presentation.

Spink Award. Presented by the Hall of Fame "for meritorious contributions to baseball writing" to a current or former sportswriter almost every year since 1962. The award is named after the most prominent 20th century publisher of *The Sporting News*, J. G. Taylor Spink.

Ted Williams All-Star Game MVP. After Williams died, the All-Star Game MVP Award was named for him.

Temple Cup. Because there were 12 clubs in the National League in the 1890s, for a few seasons the first and second-place clubs played a postseason series to determine the pennant winner. Between 1894 and 1897 the winner of the postseason series received the Temple Cup, named after the Pittsburgh owner who donated it.

Tip O'Neill Award. The award is presented to the top Canadian player in the Major Leagues, named after a 19th century Canadian player who batted .326 over 10 seasons, primarily in the American Association.

Tony Conigliaro Award. The Red Sox began presenting this award in 1990 after Conigliaro died following a massive heart attack. It is presented to a player who has overcome adversity through his spirit, courage and determination in the manner that Conigliaro came back from his 1967 beaning. Winners have included Jim Eisenreich (Tourette's Syndrome), Dickie Thon (severe beaning), Jim Abbott (birth defect), Bo Jackson (hip replacement) and Scott Radinsky (Hodgkin's Disease).

Topps Organization of the Year. This award is presented to a well-run professional club in Organized Baseball.

Umpires. By the 1930s *The Sporting News* began presenting an award to the best umpire in each league (voted by the players).

Van Heusen Award. This award was created in the early 1970s to recognize singular achievements throughout a season where it was felt that the achievement would be forgotten by the end of the season.

Warren Giles Award. This award is named after the long-time National League president and is presented to the National League pennant winner. There is also a minor league version of the award presented to top executives.

Willie McCovey Award. The Giants present this award to their post inspirational player.

Big Year. In 1991 Cal Ripken became the second player in Major League history to be named the league's MVP, Major League Player of the Year (by *The Sporting News,* Associated Press, and *Baseball Digest*), All-Star Game MVP, and winner of a Gold Glove in the same season. The other was Maury Wills in 1962.

Memorabilia Sales. Mickey Mantle's 1957 American League MVP Award sold at auction in 2003 for $275,000. His 1962 MVP Award sold for $250,000 and his 1956 Silver Bat award brought $270,000. His Hall of Fame gold watch sold for $9,500.

"**B** is for Bresnahan
Back of the plate;
The Cubs were his love,
And McGraw was his hate."
—Ogden Nash on Roger Bresnahan.

Babe Ruth League (1952–)

"In fact, I was exposed to almost every sort of baseball except Little, Pony, and Babe Ruth Leagues. In my boyhood, no adult told me what position to play or made me take a three-one pitch. The kids I played with had figured out what the children of the Bad News Bears never understood—that adults were the natural enemy of kids. Perhaps I never 'got baseball out of my system' because no adult ever had a chance to drive it out."—Thomas Boswell in *How Life Imitates the World Series* (1982).

The Babe Ruth League was formed in 1952 in Trenton, New Jersey, for boys age 13–15. It was originally known as the "Little Bigger League," in deference to **Little League**, but was never affiliated with that organization. By the 1970s there were over 11,000 teams active in the United States.

Bad Ball Hitters

"He isn't much to look at, and he looks like he's doing everything wrong, but he can hit. He got a couple of hits off us on wild pitches."—Comments about notorious bad ball hitter Yogi Berra.

"How can a pitcher that wild stay in the league."—Berra after striking out swinging on three very bad pitches.

"The Curly Shuffle."—The name for the unorthodox two-step toward the ball used by Tony Pena, a notorious bad ball hitter; named for one of The Three Stooges.

"Manny Sanguillen is totally unpredictable to pitch to because he's so unpredictable."—Jerry Coleman.

"The worst thing to throw at the big fellow was a wild pitch, for Ed loved to hit wild pitches out of the park. He would stand on tiptoe, arms and elbows well away from his body, hold his bat apparently by the utmost inch of the handle, and clout an out-of-reach ball so far the fielders would lose it."—Manager Patsy Tebeau on 19th century star Ed Delahanty, quoted in *Baseball,* by Robert Smith (1970).

"Throw a fat strike right down the middle…. Lou might knock a wide, inside, or high ball out of the park, but he couldn't hit a decent pitch."—Satchel Paige on Lou Novikoff.

"If you'd think before you swing, you wouldn't be hitting at so many bad balls."—Manager Bucky Harris to Yogi Berra after striking out.

"For chrissakes, how do you expect a man to think and hit at the same time."—Berra's response to Harris. Pitcher Warren Spahn did not agree with the assessment that Berra was a bad ball hitter. He believed that Berra guessed with the pitcher about location.

Roberto Clemente. Clemente was a famous bad ball hitter, though some writers have theorized that Clemente and others were not necessarily undisciplined hitters. They contend that hitters like Clemente are more accurately characterized as guess hitters who believed that a pitch was going to be in a particular area and would swing regardless of whether or not it was in the strike zone. Others have theorized that Clemente and other Latin and black ballplayers were free swingers to avoid biased calls by umpires.

Nap Lajoie. Lajoie was a notorious bad ball hitter who hit .422 in 1901, but was known as a "careless" hitter.

2000s. The best bad ball hitters of this time frame may have been Red Sox outfielder Manny Ramirez and Rangers/Marlins catcher Ivan Rodriguez.

Bad Hops

"Has anyone ever satisfactorily explained why the bad hop is always the last one?"—Giants broadcaster Hank Greenwald.

"Do not alibi on bad hops; anybody can field the good ones."—Yankee manager Joe McCarthy.

Fred Lindstrom.

"It wasn't Freddy's fault. It could have happened to anybody. He never had a chance to get the ball. It was Fate, that's all. Fate and a pebble."—Heinie Groh on the bad hop Lindstrom suffered at third base in the last inning of Game 7 of the 1924 World Series.

"It was no big deal. Anyone could have done it."—Lindstrom.

Giants third baseman Fred Lindstrom was the victim of a bad hop during Game 7 of the 1924 World Series against the Senators. In the bottom of the 12th inning, a ground ball by Earl McNeely hit a pebble and bounced over Lindstrom's head, scoring Muddy Ruel from second base to win both the game and the Series, 4–3. Ruel had reached base on a double after a dropped foul by Giants catcher Hank Gowdy. Gowdy stepped in his mask chasing the foul ball.

What most sources do not recount is that in the 8th inning, with the Giants ahead 3–1, a ground ball by Senators manager Bucky Harris hit a dirt clod and bounced over Lindstrom's head to score the tying runs.

Tony Kubek. Yankee shortstop Tony Kubek was the victim of a bad hop that hit him in the Adam's apple during the 8th inning of Game 7 of the 1960 World Series against the Pirates. He had to come out of the game and the Pirates scored five runs to erase a 7–4 Yankee lead.

Frank "Home Run" Baker (1886–1963)

Hall of Fame (VC) 1955

"What I was about to watch and write about at age twenty-three came to be known as the Home Run Baker Series (1911). In it John Franklin Baker, the Athletics third baseman, would hit two dramatic homers and become the nation's idol, foreshadowing the popular affection that began a decade later for another home-run hero, Babe Ruth."— Fred Lieb in *Baseball as I Have Known It* (1977).

Baker was a star third baseman primarily for the A's and Yankees from 1908 through 1922.

John Franklin Baker grew up in Maryland and began his professional career with Reading of the Tri-State League. He was picked up by the A's late in the 1908 season and began seven years with the club at third base. He led the league in home runs four straight seasons beginning in 1911, with totals of 11, 10, 12 and 9. He hit two home runs in the 1911 World Series, a rare accomplishment at the time, which led to his famous nickname.

Baker had two career interruptions. The first was in 1915, when he refused to report to the A's and played outlaw ball in Pennsylvania. A's owner Connie Mack sold him to the Yankees after the season for $35,000. Baker played for the Yankees until 1922. He missed the 1920 season due to the illness and then death of his first wife.

Baker played the last two years of his career with Babe Ruth, hitting nine and seven home runs in those two seasons. He batted .363 in the six World Series in which he played. He had a lifetime .307 average and hit 96 home runs.

After his playing career he managed in the Eastern Shore League and is credited with discovering Jimmie Foxx, who signed with the A's. He then returned to his hometown in Maryland and farmed for the rest of his life. He returned periodically to Philadelphia and New York for old-timers games and other appearances until his death in 1963.

Baker Bowl (1887–1938)

"Coca Cola and Lifebuoy Health Soap Stops B. O. signs were on the high right field wall. Three sheep and a ram grazed on the outfield grass between games. Over the years, it housed various events such as donkey baseball, midget auto racing, crusades, police and fire department parades, roller skating, and ice skating."— Philip J. Lowry in *Green Cathedrals* (1992).

"We once had a great respect for high-sounding construction terms. But since we saw Baker Bowl we sneer when we hear of cantilevers, for we have read that Baker Bowl was the first ever built of steel cantilever construction and was regarded as the grandstand wonder of its age. Our recollection of that grandstand wonder is of showers of grimy rust falling in our thinning hair each time a foul hit the roof above; and that roof was just tin, with not a cantilever in an acre. Of the crowded press box, the creaky joists, the ill-smelling lemonade barrels and wonderment that the director of public safety and the health department didn't do something about the park, even if they couldn't do anything about the Phillies."— J. Roy Stockton in *The Gashouse Gang and a couple of other guys* (1945).

Named after William F. Baker, the park (or its predecessor on the same site) was home to the Philadelphia Phillies from 1887 through June 1938. The team abandoned the park in midseason to become a tenant a few blocks away at more comfortable and spacious Shibe Park, the home field of the A's. Baker Bowl's dimensions from left to right field were 341–408–281 and seating capacity reached a high of only 20,000 in 1929.

The ballpark opened as the Philadelphia Baseball Grounds in 1887 at a cost of $80,000 and was destroyed by fire in 1894. It was rebuilt into what became known as Baker Bowl. In August 1903 some of the grandstand collapsed, killing 12.

On May 14, 1927, 10 rows in the right field section collapsed and one fan was killed. The ballpark was known as The Hump because it was on an elevated area that allowed a railroad tunnel to run underneath center field.

First Game. Most sources report that the first game was played on April 30, 1887, when the facility was known as the Philadelphia Baseball Grounds. Over 14,500 fans saw the Phillies defeat the New York Giants 15–9 The first game in the rebuilt structure that became known as Baker Bowl was played on May 2, 1895. The Phillies lost to the Giants 9–4.

Last Game. The Phillies lost to the Giants 14–1 on June 30, 1938. Claude Passeau took the loss in the last game before the Phillies moved to Shibe Park. Baker Bowl was torn down in 1950.

Balks

"I never called a balk in my life. I didn't understand the rule."— Umpire Ron Luciano.

"Too much spit on it."— Dodger pitcher Bill Loes on why he committed a crucial balk during the 1952 World Series.

"I'm not going to let you win as important a game as this on a technicality."— Response of umpire Al Barlick to Dodger manager Leo Durocher during the 1941 pennant race. Dodger outfielder Pete Reiser was on third base and was an excellent threat to steal home. On an obvious balk, Barlick refused to call it.

Origin. A balk rule was enforced by Alexander Cartwright's Knickerbocker Club in the 1840s. One source reported that the rule provided that the pitcher could not fake to a base once he started his pitching motion. The formal rule, which does not specifically define a balk: "A runner cannot be put out in making one base, when a balk is made by the pitcher."

Rules. The modern balk rule was created in 1899. The rules first required a pitcher to throw to first base if he faked a throw to that bag. If a pitcher commits a balk, the runners are entitled to move up one base.

During the 1956 winter meetings it was suggested that umpires drop a handkerchief to signal a balk. This was rejected by American League president Will Harridge. Instead, the leagues continued the tradition of signaling a balk by clenched fist with the left hand.

During the winter of 1971 the Rules Committee decided that a pitcher must stop for one full second before making his delivery. Too many balks were called in the first month of the 1972 season, so the rule was amended to relax the one second rule.

In 1989 balks again were enforced more strictly, resulting in a huge rise in their numbers. By midseason the rule was again relaxed.

Japan. The balk is not well-enforced in Japan, which may explain why Hideo Nomo and Hideki Irabu had problems with it when they arrived in the Major Leagues.

Bad Start. Perhaps indicative of their first several years of futility, the Mets scored the first run of their existence on a balk.

Most/Season/Pitcher. Dave Stewart of the A's holds the record of 16 balks in a season, set in 1988.

Collusion. Third baseman and future Giants manager John McGraw and pitcher and future Senators owner Clark Griffith argued often, as did McGraw and the umpires. In one game in which Griffith was pitching, McGraw was on first base. The umpire purportedly suggested to Griffith that he pick McGraw off base, but McGraw was too close to the bag. The umpire then said that Griffith should "balk" McGraw off first. Griffith promptly balked, McGraw took off for second on the obvious balk, but the umpire refused to call a balk and Griffith threw out McGraw. McGraw was so furious that he was thrown out of the game.

Problem Child. The National League began enforcing the balk rule more tightly during the 1930s. Dizzy Dean thought the rule was stupid and would pause for two minutes or more on the mound to make his point. He once took 11 minutes to throw three pitches. Umpire George Barr called a balk after Dean's stunt and Dean took it out on National League president Ford Frick: "He's a great little president, but a pain in the neck for me."

Frick briefly suspended Dean and prepared a written retraction for him to sign, but Dean apparently never signed it.

Time Out. On June 11, 1962, with the bases loaded, Indians runner Tito Francona yelled to Red Sox pitcher Earl Wilson to "hold it, Earl" during his wind-up. Wilson froze and a balk was called. The rules provide that no player shall do anything to distract the pitcher into committing a balk, such as what Francona did by calling time out. However, the umpires claimed that they did not hear anything and let the balk stand. The shaken Wilson then gave up a three-run home run for a 4–0 deficit.

1961 All-Star Game. In July 1961 at the first All-Star Game that season (there were two each year from 1959 through 1962), 5'11" and 165-pound pitcher Stu Miller was blown off the mound during his wind-up at notoriously windy Candlestick Park in San Francisco. Umpire Stan Landes called a balk, the first of Miller's career, which advanced the runners to second and third.

National League manager Danny Murtaugh protested the balk call by claiming that it was an Act of God, but the protest was rejected. The incident occurred in the 9th inning and helped the American League tie the game. Nevertheless, Miller got the win in the 10th.

July has always been the worst month for wind in San Francisco. By the Saturday after the All-Star Game the umpires had instituted a temporary rule that if a pitcher stepped off the mound during his wind-up because of wind, a balk would not be called and the otherwise illegal move would be deemed an Act of God.

Bet. Relief pitcher Tug McGraw once bet his friends that there was no such thing as a balk with no one on base. To prove his point and win the bet, he balked wildly while on the mound, falling straight backward. He assured the trainer who came to his aid that he was okay and just needed to win the bet.

Starting Off on the Wrong Foot. Pitcher Joe Hesketh was called up to the Expos in 1984 and was called for a balk before he ever threw a pitch.

Catcher's Balk. If a catcher is not in the catcher's box at the start of the pitch, a catcher's balk is called. The runners advance only if forced and the batter is entitled to first base regardless of whether the bases are full.

On June 24, 2000, the Braves had a controversy over a catcher's balk. The club had been criticized for having an overly large catcher's box (beyond the allowed 43"-wide box), which enabled the Braves catchers to set up farther outside than allowed. This would give their pitchers an opportunity to receive more strike calls on outside pitches. Home plate umpire John Shulock ruled that Braves catcher Fernando Lunar set up outside the box, and the balk call led to Milwaukee's first run of the night. Braves manager Bobby Cox was ejected from the game, which the Braves lost 2–1.

The Braves announcers discussed the catcher's box on the air during the game, pointing out that it was a few inches smaller than it had been the previous night, when the Milwaukee manager had complained. As a result of the on-air discussion, the club barred its four broadcasters from the team charter flight. Skip Caray, Pete Van Wieren, Joe Simpson and Don Sutton were tossed off a flight to Montreal and forced to take a commercial flight. The club later backed off of the ban.

Ballparks

"Decades after a person has stopped collecting bubble gum cards, he can still discover himself collecting ballparks ... their smells, their special seasons, their moods."—Thomas Boswell.

"The future of baseball is without limit. The time is coming when there will be great amphitheaters throughout the United States in which citizens shall be able to see the teams take part in the finest athletic struggles in the world."—Albert Spalding in the 1880s.

"Several rules of stadium building should be carved on every owner's forehead. Old, if properly refurbished, is always better than new. Smaller is better than bigger. Open is better than closed. Near beats far. Silent visual effects are better than loud ones. Eye pollution hurts attendance. Inside should look as good as outside. Dome stadiums are criminal."—Thomas Boswell in How Life Imitates the World Series (1982).

"Ballparks are the most exciting buildings in America. They're trendsetters in architecture and urban renovation. Even better, baseball is played in them."—W. Blake Gray.

"As I say, I never feel more at home in America than at a ballgame be it in park or in sandlot. Beyond this I know not. And dare not."—Robert Frost in Sports Illustrated in July 1956.

See also ***Advertising, Artificial Turf, Fences, Fields and Field Dimensions, Fires, Indoor Ballparks, Infields and Dirt, Parking, Seating Capacity*** and ***Sun***.

This section contains general information primarily regarding 19th century ballparks and a brief chronology of many ballparks used by Major League teams. More detailed information about the most famous 20th century ballparks is contained in entries under specific names of the more famous ballparks (for example, ***Ebbets Field***). Histories of the less prominent ballparks are contained in subheadings for **Ballparks** within team histories.

The Earliest Ballparks. The earliest parks were built in the 1850s and were used for more than baseball. By the late 1850s there were over 60 ballparks in New York City and the immediate vicinity. An early park used for baseball was the Fashion Race Course near Jamaica, Long Island, New York. This was the site of the All-Star Challenge Series in 1858, when the first ***Admission*** was charged.

Ballparks originally were not enclosed, but efforts to enclose them and charge admission became known as the "Enclosure Movement." This allowed owners not only to charge admission, but also to create more order at games, as fans could not simply sit wherever they pleased and encroach onto the outfield areas.

William Cammeyer, prominent owner of the New York Mutuals, invested in the Union Grounds in Brooklyn (often confused with the Capitoline Grounds) by enclosing the field (the first time ever), grading the diamond and constructing a clubhouse; this all led to his regularly charging admission to the facility, which he opened on May 15, 1862. The Union Grounds held 1,500 fans on wooden benches and had a six-foot-high fence approximately 500 feet long around a portion of the six-acre park. It was home to clubs in the National Association and early National League from 1871 through 1877.

The Capitoline Grounds opened in Brooklyn in 1864 and was the less-used of the two parks. Of National Association and National League clubs, only the Brooklyn Atlantics played there in 1872.

The all-professional Cincinnati Red Stockings of 1869 played their home games at the Lincoln Park Grounds, which opened in May of that year.

Key Ballparks/Chronology.

All seating capacities are the original capacities.

Early and Mid–1870s.

South End Grounds—Boston. This was home to the Boston Red Stockings of the National Association and National League from 1871 through 1887.

Jefferson Street Grounds—Philadelphia. This was home to the National Association clubs in the city and the National League Athletics in 1876. It was used as a Major League park by the American Association club through 1890.

1875.

Grand Avenue Park—St. Louis. The original version of the park was built by Henry Lucas and seated 9,000. He was the millionaire backer of the 1884 Union Association who built this small park on his estate. The park is sometimes erroneously referred to as the original Sportsman's Park.

1877.

Lakefront Park—Chicago. This was considered by some as the premier ballpark of its era.

Late 1870s.

Sportsman's Park (first version)—St. Louis. The park originally seated 6,000, but expanded to 12,000 when it housed the American Association Browns from 1882 through 1891.

New Generation of Parks/The 1880s and 1890s. Owners were reaping greater profits in the 1880s due to a period of stability in part brought on by the introduction of the reserve clause. Owners were now less reluctant to put money into their parks and the 1880s and early 1890s saw a rash of new construction and refurbishing.

Most early parks were rectangular to accommodate the set-up of long city blocks and adjacent streetcar lines. This usually created a short right field and favored left-handers. By 1900 virtually all existing ballparks, which were always wooden, were in need of repair. This led to the construction of the group of steel and concrete ballparks that housed Major League teams through the 1950s and, in a few instances, into the 1990s and beyond.

1880.

Polo Grounds—New York. This was the original Polo Grounds, where Polo was actually played. The ballpark could accommodate 20,000 fans, though not all were seated. The National League Giants played here from 1883 through 1888.

1882.

Exposition Park—Pittsburgh. This park was built on the same site as Three Rivers Stadium.

Union Park—Baltimore. This park seated 6,000–6,500 and had an upper deck and a beer garden.

Recreation Park—Philadelphia. This park was built for a minor league team and burned down in 1889. When Alfred Reach bought the Worcester club and moved it to Philadelphia for the 1883 season, he supposedly built this park. Rather, he simply moved the club into the existing park. Most sources report that it was built in 1883, but it was built in 1882 and Major League games were first played there the following year.

1883.

Lakefront Park—Chicago (remodeled). Constant improvements were made to this ballpark. It purportedly seated 10,000 and was the largest in the country at that time. However, Philip Lowry's *Green Cathedrals* (1982) reports its capacity at only 5,000. Owner Albert Spalding built himself a private box that later had a telephone. The facility also had 18 private boxes with curtains.

Oriole Park—Baltimore. This ballpark was built for $5,000 and was home to the American Association club through 1889.

Washington Park—Brooklyn. This park seated only 2,000 and

Aerial view of Ebbets Field, one of the storied ballparks in Major League history.

was considered too small soon after it opened for minor league play, but was used by the American Association club in Brooklyn from 1884 through 1889.

1884.

Redland (League) Park—Cincinnati. Built in one month for the American Association club. It later collapsed, killing one spectator. It was renovated in 1894 with concrete and steel.

Capitol Park—Washington. Built by the Hewitt brothers, it had a capacity of 6,000 and housed the Union Association club of 1884.

1885.

West Side Grounds—Chicago. Home to the National League White Stockings/Cubs from 1893 through 1915. It seated 16,000 fans.

1887.

Philadelphia Baseball Grounds (Also known as the Huntington Grounds)—Philadelphia. After Athletics owner Alfred Reach had been in Philadelphia for a few years, he built the Huntington Grounds because Recreation Park was too small. It was considered an excellent park and seated between 15,000 and 20,000 in two decks. It burned in 1894 and was rebuilt into what was later named Baker Bowl.

1888.

(New) South End Grounds—Boston. It seated 6,800 and was home to the Red Stockings through 1894.

1890.

Manhattan Field—New York. Renamed the new Polo Grounds in 1891, it seated 16,000 and was the best new park of the era. It housed the Giants through 1910.

South Side Park—Chicago. Built adjacent to the future site of Comiskey Park, the park was in use from 1890 through 1893.

Eastern Park—Brooklyn. Home of the Trolley Dodgers from 1891 until 1897.

Exposition Park—Pittsburgh. The ballpark seated around 10,000 at its opening, but was expanded to 16,000 during the years in which it was occupied by the Pirates (1891–1909).

1891.

League Park—Cleveland. It seated 9,000, though some sources report incorrectly that the original capacity was 16,000 (which was not even the capacity of the rebuilt League Park in 1910).

Boundary Field (National Park)—Washington. It seated 6,500 and housed the American Association Washington Nationals in 1891 and National League Washington Senators from 1892 through 1899.

1893.

Sportsman's Park (second version)—St. Louis. Seated 14,500 (erroneously 10,000 in some sources). This ballpark was renamed Robison Field late in the 19th century for a few years and housed the Cardinals from 1893 through mid–1920.

1894.

Baker Bowl—Philadelphia. This 1887 park was rebuilt after it was destroyed by fire. It seated 18,000 and housed the Phillies through 1938 (with two brief exceptions).

(New) South End Grounds—Boston. Completely rebuilt for the National League Red Stockings after a fire.

League Park—Cincinnati. Rebuilt within sight of the original League Park. It burned in 1901 and was rebuilt into what was later known as Crosley Field.

1896.

Bennett Park—Detroit. Capacity originally was 5,000, but was expanded in 1901 to 8,500 when the Tigers moved in.

1901.

Huntington Avenue Grounds—Boston. The American League Red Stockings occupied this park until 1910. It originally seated 9,000.

South Side Park—Chicago. Rebuilt to seat 15,000, it housed the White Sox through mid–1910.

Columbia Park—Philadelphia. Occupied by the Philadelphia A's through 1908, it seated approximately 9,000 fans.

American League Park—Washington. The ballpark housed the Senators from 1901 through 1903.

1902.

Palace of the Fans—Cincinnati. Occupied by the Reds from 1902 through 1911.

Sportsman's Park (renovated)—St. Louis. When the American League Browns arrived, this ballpark (the old Robison Field) housed them from 1902 through 1908 and seated 18,000.

1903.

Hilltop Park—New York. Occupied by the Highlanders/Yankees through 1911, it seated 15,000.

Bennett Park—Detroit. Rebuilt after a section collapsed.

American League Park—Washington. This renovated ballpark burned down during the spring of 1911.

1909.

League Park (concrete version)—Cleveland. The original park was built in 1891. The original rebuilt capacity was 21,000.

Sportsman's Park (renovated)—St. Louis. The new version originally seated 17,600 and housed the Browns until 1953 and the Cardinals from 1920 through mid–1966. It was renamed Busch Stadium in 1953.

Shibe Park—Philadelphia. This was the first concrete and steel park in Major League history, opening in April 1909. It seated 20,000. It was renamed Connie Mack Stadium in 1953.

Forbes Field—Pittsburgh. Opened in June 1909 with a capacity of 23,000.

1910.

Comiskey Park—Chicago. Known as White Sox Park at its opening, it originally seated 28,800 and was considered the finest park of the era.

1911.

Griffith Stadium (originally National Park)—Washington. This 32,000-seat park was rebuilt after a fire and later was renamed Griffith Stadium after owner Clark Griffith.

Polo Grounds—New York. This was the largest ballpark to date, having been rebuilt after another fire and seating 34,000.

1912.

Navin Field—Detroit. Rebuilt version of Bennett Field. It later was renamed Briggs Field and then Tiger Stadium. The 1912 version originally seated 23,000.

Fenway Park **Grounds**—Boston. Seated 27,000 when first built, though a few sources erroneously cite a larger capacity, 33,379, that came only with expansion of the facility a few years later. It opened on the same day as Navin Field, April 20, 1912. *Green Cathedrals* reports an original capacity of 35,000.

Crosley Field—Cincinnati. Rebuilt after being destroyed by fire, it seated 25,000 after renovation.

1913.

Ebbets Field—Brooklyn. It seated 18,000 when it first opened.

Sick Stadium—Seattle. This ballpark eventually housed the 1969 Seattle Pilots. It seated 15,000 in its original configuration.

1914.

Wrigley Field—Chicago. Known originally as Weeghman Park, it was built to house the Federal League Chicago Whales, owned by Charles Weeghman. Its original seating capacity was 14,000, but was expanded to 38,396 in 1927. It became known as Cubs Park in 1920 and Wrigley Field in 1926.

1915.

Braves Field—Boston. This was the largest Major League ballpark up to that time, seating 40,000.

By 1915 the flurry of new ballparks ended. All Major League clubs except the Phillies had built (or rebuilt) concrete and steel parks within the previous 10 years. With the exception of Yankee Stadium in 1923 and Cleveland's Municipal Stadium in 1932, no new Major League ballparks were built until the 1950s. The innovative feature of the new steel and concrete ballparks was not the construction material itself, but the upper decks that were built to seat additional fans close to the action.

1923.

Yankee Stadium (American League Baseball Grounds) — New York. The ballpark had a seating capacity of 57,545, the largest in the Major Leagues to that time. It was also the first triple-decked stadium.

By 1923 Major League ballpark capacities ranged from 18,000 in St. Louis and Philadelphia to over 57,000 in Yankee Stadium and 54,000 in the Polo Grounds. The average size was 30,000 and the mean was 24,000.

Municipal Stadium — Kansas City. Originally seated 17,476 and housed the Athletics from 1955 through 1967 and the Royals from 1969 through 1972.

Memorial Coliseum — Los Angeles. It originally seated 74,000 for football, but when the Dodgers moved in from 1958 through 1961, capacity for baseball was 93,000 and for football was over 100,000.

1925.

Wrigley Field — Los Angeles. Original capacity was 22,000, slightly more than the 20,457 it seated when the Angels played there in 1961.

1931.

Seals Stadium — San Francisco. Originally seated 16,000 and housed the Giants in 1958 and 1959.

1932.

Municipal Stadium — Cleveland. This was a huge ballpark that seated 77,797 and housed the Indians until 1994. It was the first ballpark built with public funds.

1949.

Memorial Stadium — Baltimore. This park originally seated 31,000 and then increased to 47,855 when the Orioles moved into the park in 1954.

1953.

County Stadium — Milwaukee. The first Major League ballpark built with lights, it originally seated 35,911, but was expanded to 43,091 the following season.

1956.

Metropolitan Stadium — Minneapolis. Seated 18,200 when it opened and then housed the Twins beginning in 1961. Some sources erroneously suggest that the park was built in 1960 for the Twins.

1959.

Exhibition Stadium — Toronto. Seated 25,303 before it housed the Blue Jays from 1977 through 1989. It was renovated in 1977 to seat 43,765.

1960.

Candlestick Park — San Francisco. Originally seated 43,765. Renamed 3Com Park in 1995.

1962.

Dodger Stadium — Los Angeles. Originally seated 56,000. It was the first privately funded ballpark since Yankee Stadium in 1923.

D.C. Stadium (RFK Stadium) — Washington. Originally seated 43,500.

Colt Stadium — Houston. Originally seated 32,601.

1964.

Shea Stadium — New York. Originally seated 55,000.

1965.

Astrodome (Harris County Domed Stadium) — Houston. The first indoor ballpark originally seated 46,217.

Arlington Stadium — Arlington, Texas. Originally called Turnpike Stadium, its capacity was 35,185 when Major League ball arrived in 1972, but its capacity when it was built in 1965 was only 10,500.

1966.

Anaheim Stadium — Anaheim. Originally seated 43,500 for the Angels. Later named Edison Field before reverting to the original name.

Atlanta–Fulton County Stadium — Atlanta. Originally seated 51,500. The Braves occupied the ballpark in 1966 when they arrived from Milwaukee.

Busch Memorial Stadium — St. Louis. Originally seated 49,275.

1967.

Jack Murphy Stadium — San Diego. Originally known as San Diego Stadium and seated 50,000. It was renamed Qualcomm Park in 1997 until abandoned after the 2003 season.

1968.

Oakland Coliseum — Oakland. Originally seated 50,000. Also known as Oakland-Alameda County Stadium. Renamed Network Associates Coliseum in 2001.

1969.

Jarry Park — Montreal. Parc Jarry was known as Recreation Field and seated 3,000 before being renovated to seat 28,456 for the start of the 1969 season.

1970.

Three Rivers Stadium — Pittsburgh. Originally seated 50,500.

1971.

Riverfront Stadium — Cincinnati. Originally seated 51,050 (51,726 in some sources). Renamed Cinergy Field in 1997.

Veterans Stadium — Philadelphia. Originally seated 56,371.

1973.

Royals Stadium — Kansas City. Originally seated 40,613 (40,762 in some sources, but this was the 1974 total). Renamed Kauffman Stadium in 1994.

1976.

Olympic Stadium — Montreal. Stade Olympique seated 58,838 in 1977 for the Expos after being used for the 1976 Olympics. Some sources erroneously report capacity at 59,511 (which was the 1980 capacity).

Kingdome — Seattle. Originally seated 59,059.

1982.

Metrodome — Minneapolis. Also known as Hubert H. Humphrey Metrodome, it originally seated 54,711.

1987.

Joe Robbie Stadium. Originally used exclusively for football, the Devil Rays occupied the ballpark in 1998. It was renamed Pro Player Stadium in 1997 and seated 36,331 in 1998.

1989.

Skydome — Toronto. The Blue Jays occupied the park in June 1989, when it seated 50,516.

1991.

New Comiskey Park — Chicago. Originally seated 44,702. Renamed U.S. Cellular Field in 2003.

1992.

Oriole Park at Camden Yards — Baltimore. Originally seated 46,500.

1994.

The Ballpark — Arlington. Originally seated 48,000.

Jacobs Field — Cleveland. Originally seated 42,000 and was known as the Gateway Sports Complex before it was renamed.

1995.

Coors Field—Denver. Originally seated 45,000.

1997.

Turner Field—Atlanta. Originally seated 47,000.

1998.

Tropicana Field—Tampa Bay. Built in 1990, it was not used for Major League Baseball until 1998 when the Devil Rays started play. Originally it seated 48,000, but was reduced to 45,000 when the franchise began play.

1999.

Safeco Field—Seattle. Originally seated 47,116.

2000.

Enron Field—Houston. Originally seated 42,000. Renamed Astros Field in February 2002 after the Enron scandal surfaced, then Minute Maid Park in June 2002.

Comerica Park—Detroit. Originally seated 47,637.

SBC/PacBell Park—San Francisco. Originally seated 40,800. The name changed to SBC for the 2004 season, reflecting PacBell's corporate name change.

2001.

Miller Park—Milwaukee. Previously scheduled to open in 2000 before construction problems delayed the opening. Originally seated 43,000.

PNC Park—Pittsburgh. Originally seated 38,127.

2003.

Great American Ballpark—Cincinnati. Originally seated 42,059.

2004.

Petco Park—San Diego. Originally seated 46,000.

Other Uses. Ballparks have been used to generate other income from movies, dancing, dog races, carnivals, amateur ballgames and, more recently, concerts, religious programs and recreational vehicle shows.

Construction Problem. In 1942 when Pawtucket's McCoy Stadium was being built (site of the **Longest Game** in professional baseball history), a five-ton truck sank into the swampy outfield area, never to be seen again.

Symmetry.

"I had become as accustomed to an entirely new generation of ballparks, round as doughnuts, merry nursery rooms, and as artificial and undistinguished as the suburbs in which they nestled. They look, all of them, like gigantic tiered wedding cakes with their centers sucked out."—Stanley Cohen in *The Man in the Crowd* (1981).

"Every ballpark used to be unique. Now it's like women's breasts—if you've seen one, you've seen 'em both."—Jim Kaat.

"Let me get this straight. We're bulldozing real vintage ballparks like Tiger Stadium and Fenway Park to put up fake vintage ballparks?"—Rick Reilly in *Sports Illustrated.*

Philip Lowry has calculated that of the 16 classic Major League ballparks of the 20th century, 14 were asymmetrical. Of the 26 Major League ballparks in use in the late 1980s, only six were asymmetrical. Oriole Park at Camden Yards restored that tradition, and virtually every ballpark built after that has contained elements of the old-style ballparks, including asymmetry.

Last Wooden Structure. The last all-wood structure used in the Major Leagues was Robison Field in St. Louis, which was abandoned in 1920 for already-existing Sportsman's Park. The last Major League game was played at Robison Field on June 6, 1920.

Multi-Purpose. The first multi-purpose Major League ballpark that had retractable stands for football or baseball was RFK Stadium in Washington.

When the Minnesota Metrodome is not in use, the Stadium rents it out to rollerbladers to ride wherever they want on the artificial turf for $5, with another $4 charged for skate rental. The club made $125,000 on this endeavor in 1996. On other nights they turn the stadium over to walkers and joggers at $1 per head.

Longest in Service. Sportsman's Park in St. Louis was used for Major League games from 1876 to May 8, 1966, when Busch Memorial Stadium opened. In the minor leagues, Sulphur Dell Stadium in Nashville of the Southern Association was in service from 1866 through 1963. The ballpark had a highly irregular playing field, with hills and valleys throughout. It was named by sportswriter Grantland Rice.

Best. In a 2003 poll of 550 Major League players by *Sports Illustrated*, the best ballparks were in Southern California. Dodger Stadium was voted the best by 23.3% and Edison Field in Anaheim was second with 11.2% of the vote. The worst: Wrigley Field and Fenway Park.

According to Bob Wood in *Dodger Dogs to Fenway Franks,* ranked tied for first were Dodger Stadium, which did poorly only in its food rating, and Royals Stadium, which graded poorly only for its ball field because of artificial turf (a defect corrected for the 1994 season). Four parks tied for last with a D+: The Astrodome, with no redeeming qualities; Exhibition Stadium in Toronto (no longer in use), which received its only good grade for the overall facility (but great only for football); the Seattle Kingdome, with a D- for atmosphere; and Candlestick Park, with the worst ballpark employees.

Below-Ground. The only two Major League parks that were to be entered from above and were dug at least partially out of the ground are Dodger Stadium in Los Angeles and Arlington Stadium, until 1994 the home of the Rangers.

Toilets.

"Raise the urinals."—Darrel Chaney on how management could keep the Braves on their toes.

Before the first exhibition game at the new PNC Park in Pittsburgh in 2001, the facility's 600 toilets and 400 urinals were flushed repeatedly, and simultaneously, to ensure uninterrupted service for fans.

Escalator. In 2003 Coors Field management had to close seven escalators after one malfunctioned on July 2, throwing dozens of fans on top of each other. The three-story escalator suddenly sped up after a post-game fireworks show.

All Parks Visited. During the summer of 1993, four college students watched 28 Major League games in 28 different ballparks in 28 days. In 1985 Bob Wood made the trek almost as quickly to research *Dodger Dogs to Fenway Franks* (1989) (see also **Books**). See Brad Null and Dave Kaval, *The Summer That Saved Baseball: A 38–Day Journey To All 30 Major League Ballparks* (2001).

Minor League Ballparks. The National Association of Professional Baseball Leagues (NAPBL) has a 17-page book on guidelines which minor league ballparks were to meet by April 1, 1995. The guidelines were created in 1990 and called for Major League clubs to pull their affiliation with any club with a ballpark that was not in compliance. A few highlights:

Seating Capacity: 4,000

Home Dressing Room: 1,000 square feet

Visitors Dressing Room: 750 square feet

Home Club Showers: 8–10 shower heads

Visiting Club Showers: 6–8 shower heads

Umpires Facilities: 200 square feet

Flag Pole: All facilities shall have a flag pole in clear view of the entire seating area

Field Lighting: 70 foot-candles average in the infield, 50 foot-candles average in the outfield

Minor League Club in Major League Ballpark. In 1993 Memorial Stadium in Baltimore was used by the minor league BaySox of the Eastern League when their new park was not yet finished. They were the first minor league club since 1915 to play in the same city as their parent Major League club. The Toledo Mud Hens played in Cleveland in 1914–1915 to help block a Federal League franchise from moving in.

Books. Bob Wood wrote *Dodger Dogs to Fenway Franks* (1989), about his summer tour of every Major League park. As a junior high school teacher, he was the perfect candidate to grade each ballpark in a number of categories, including food, attendants, amenities, sightlines, seats, parking and aesthetics.

Philip J. Lowry's *Green Cathedrals* (1983), is the most comprehensive — though occasionally inaccurate — look at every ballpark used by Major League, National Association and Negro League clubs since 1871 (271 through the 1992 edition). Lawrence Ritter's *Lost Ballparks* (1992) focused on 22 of the best known parks.

See also Michael Benson, *Ballparks of North America* (1989), the most comprehensive, covering baseball fields from 1845 through the 1990s; Rick Dubroff, *How Was the Game* (1994), compares watching a game in each Major League ballpark from the perspective of a fan and a writer; Philip Bess, *City Baseball Magic — Plain Talk and Uncommon Sense about Cities and Baseball Parks* (2003); Michael Gershman *Diamonds: The Evolution of the Ballpark* (1993); Rand McNally, Inc. (ed.), *Official Baseball Atlas* (1993), a guide to all Major League ballparks, including facts and travel tips; Lowell Reidenbaugh, *Take Me Out to the Ballpark* (1987); Ira Rosen, *Blue Skies, Green Fields: A Celebration of 50 Major League Baseball Stadiums* (2001); Bill Shannon and George Kalinsky, *The Ballparks* (1975); Ron Smith, *The Ballpark Book* (2002).

Balls

"The human hand is made complete by the addition of a baseball." — Paul Dickson.

"Any baseball is beautiful. No other small package comes as close to the ideal design and utility. It is a perfect object for a man's hand. Pick it up and it instantly suggests its purpose; it is meant to be thrown a considerable distance — thrown hard and with precision." — Roger Angell.

"However views of individuals may differ as to the origin of the American national game, all must agree that the sport had as its foundation — a Ball. Without that as its basis, the superstructure of the grandest pastime ever devised by man could never have been erected." — Albert Spalding in *Baseball — America's National Game* (1911).

"Throughout history the ball has been the most common object around which games have been focused. Balls come in a variety of shapes, sizes, and compositions, and they can be thrown, kicked, carried, cradled, balanced, dribbled, racketed, wicketed, or clubbed." — Dr. Joseph A. Baldassarre.

The baseball has gone through a key transition over the years — from dead ball to lively — and historically has been the most tampered-with piece of baseball equipment.

Balata Balls. During World War II, the balata ball with a synthetic rubber center was used for a short time because of the shortage of natural rubber. Balata was the material used as the core for golf balls, a commodity not needed during the war. This short-lived wartime baseball had a granulated cork center with a double shell of balata.

Spalding Sporting Goods introduced the ball at the beginning of the 1943 season and it was a disaster from the outset because it was so dead. For example, the Cardinals started the season by losing 1–0 in 11 innings, losing 1–0, winning 2–1 and winning again 1–0. Eleven games were played before the first home run in the Major Leagues, by the Yankees' Joe Gordon. Only nine home runs were hit in the first 72 American League balata ball games. It was clear to all that the excitement of the game was gone.

The Spalding company finally admitted the obvious, that the ball was 25% less resilient. It unconvincingly blamed the problem on wartime cement made of reprocessed rubber, rather than on the balata core. The leagues found enough prewar balls to use so that the balata ball could be abandoned. In 1944 cork and rubber were again made available for baseballs and manufacturing resumed.

Broken Balls. In a game between Cascade and Buckhorn in the minor leagues a fly ball to the outfield broke in half. The outfielder purportedly caught one half of the ball and the other half flew over the fence. It was ruled an out.

Cleaner Balls. Following Ray Chapman's *Death* in 1920 after being struck by a pitched ball, umpires made a much greater effort to keep cleaner balls in play. Coupled with the 1921 ban on applying substances to the ball, the cleaner balls made it easier for hitters to see pitched balls (see also *Illegal Pitches*).

During the 1921 season pitchers complained that they could not properly grip the glossy balls, so umpires began rubbing them down before games. This led to the later practice of rubbing them with special *Mud* that reduced the gloss and slickness without dirtying the ball.

Colored Balls. In the early days of professional baseball there was limited uniformity in the type of baseballs used. For example, red balls were used by some teams in the 1870s.

In August 1928 a yellow ball was used in a minor league game between Milwaukee and Louisville.

In 1938 Dodger general manager Larry MacPhail suggested using dandelion yellow balls to determine if they could be seen more easily. The so-called "stitched lemons" were first used in the opening game of a doubleheader on August 2, 1938, when the Dodgers defeated the Cardinals 6–2 at Ebbets Field behind the pitching of Freddie Fitzsimmons. Fitzsimmons complained that the dye wore off and the balls seemed too slick, so they were not used in the second game.

In 1939 the balls were used in three games, with the Cardinals defeating the Dodgers 12–0 and 5–2, and the Dodgers beating the Cubs 10–4. That type of ball was never used again.

Phosphorescent balls were tried at night, but they were hard to pick up due to depth perception problems. Day-glo balls were tried when the White Sox and Cardinals used the "Glo-bal" before a 1956 spring exhibition game in Wichita, Kansas. The players purportedly liked the ball, but it never gained acceptance.

When the Astrodome first opened and glare was a serious problem, ten dozen baseballs were dyed in contrasting colors to counteract the all-white effect of the domed stadium. The colors were yellow, orange and cerise (cherry red).

In 1973 A's owner Charlie Finley used orange balls for a brief period during spring training. He reasoned that the color would help diminish the effect of glare. The orange balls were the brainchild of Ray Dumont, president of the National Baseball Congress semipro organization.

Composition/Construction. Construction of the modern ball starts with a one-half ounce, 2.86 to 2.94 inches diameter composition cork nucleus; two thin rubber layers, one black, one red, weighing ⅞ of an ounce; 121 yards of tightly wrapped blue-gray wool yarn, giving the ball at that point a weight of 2⅞ ounces; 45 yards of white wool yarn to bring the circumference to 8¾ inches; 53 more yards of blue gray wool yarn, bringing the weight to 3¹¹⁄₁₆ ounces and circumference to 8¾ inches; then 150 yards of fine cotton yarn, bringing the weight to 4⅝ ounces.

After these materials are machine wound under high tension, a coat of rubber cement is applied. Next is a tanned cowhide exterior held together with 216 slightly raised red cotton stitches and rubber cement on the inside. **Horsehide** was used until 1974, when it became too difficult to obtain in large quantities and was replaced by cowhide in 1975. The ball is placed in a rolling machine for 15 seconds while slightly damp to flatten the stitches on the surface and make it uniform. The final weight is required to be between 5 ounces and 5¼ ounces.

Some early balls had different centers, depending on availability of materials. Some ingredients for the center were bullets, rubber overshoe strips and cork pieces. After 1876 no more than one ounce of vulcanized rubber was allowed.

In the 19th century Ben Shibe patented the two-piece leather cover for baseballs that could be machine-stitched.

Cooking. See *Illegal Pitches*.

Cork. See **Composition** and **Lively Balls**.

Cost. In the 1890s a Major League-quality ball cost $1.50. In the 1980s Major League teams paid a bulk wholesale price of $3 per ball ($12 to retail customers) or approximately $47,500 per season. Based on that calculation, the 26 Major League teams together annually paid over $1,230,000 for baseballs.

Cowhide. See **Composition** and **Horsehide**.

Dead Ball Era. One 1871 ball manufacturer advertised "dead balls with yarn and without rubber and deadest of all." The dead ball era lasted through 1909, when a **Lively Ball** was introduced gradually to increase scoring. The dead ball originally was the preferred style, as suggested by a 19th century advertisement by Peck & Snyder for a "Professional Dead Ball."

In Wilmington, Delaware, on August 14, 1884, it was reported that the Baltimore Unions had pulled a fast one on the Wilmington club. Baltimore was using a lively ball for its turn at bat, and then replacing it with a dead ball when Wilmington came up. Upon discovery, a riot almost ensued but the 500 spectators who rushed the diamond were dissuaded by the local police and "cooler spectators."

Early Balls.

"If a base-ball was required, the boy of 1816 founded it with a bit of cork, or if he were singularly fortunate, with some shred of India rubber. Then it was wound with yarn from a raveled stocking, and some feminine member of his family covered it with patches from a soiled glove." — Reminiscence of an early 1800s gentleman, Charles Haswell, recounted in Harold Sherman's *The Man Who Invented Baseball* (1973).

The French played a game called "Katt" in the 1750s that used a very hard ball that was larger than a golf ball but smaller than a tennis ball. The ball had a core of lignum vitae (a hardwood), wrapped with tightly wound hemp. The ball was then dipped in hot tar and wrapped in white sheepskin.

A ball purportedly used by the Knickerbockers in the "first game" (see also *Origins of Baseball*) is on display at the Hall of Fame.

Foul Balls. See *Foul Balls*.

Freezing. See *Illegal Pitches*.

Horsehide.

"Some people think, absurdly, too,
That the horse's day is o'er;

Fact is, the time is nearly due
when we'll need him more and more.
We have ceased to be horse lovers,
As the term was once applied,
But to make our baseball covers,
we've got to have horsehide!" — 1910 poem by Hubert R. Kotterman.

Before World War II the horsehides used for baseballs came from Belgium and France. After that, Bolivian horsehides were used until 1974, when cowhide from Eastern Europe permanently replaced horsehide. The switch to the less expensive material reportedly saved each Major League owner approximately $2,000 per year.

Illegal Substances. See *Illegal Pitches*.

Ivory Nut. Charles Webb Murphy, obnoxious owner of the Chicago Cubs around 1915, learned about the "ivory nut" material that was used to make buttons. He predicted that it would be the new core for baseballs. A's owner Ben Shibe, who held a number of baseball-manufacturing patents, responded negatively: "I look for the leagues to adopt an 'ivory nut' baseball just as soon as they adopt a ferro concrete bat and a base studded with steel spikes."

Japanese Baseballs. Japanese baseballs are wound somewhat tighter and are smaller than their American counterparts, allowing them to carry farther. At the 1978 All-Star Game, Pete Rose arranged for his glove supplier, Mizuno, to have Japanese baseballs served up to the National League hitters during batting practice to psych out the American League pitchers. The National League won 7–3 for its seventh straight victory.

Lively Ball.

"From my observation and my judgment, the ball in use this season is livelier than any ball that has been used during all the years I have been in baseball." — Charles Ebbets in July 1921.

"A leather-covered sphere stuffed with dynamite." — Ring Lardner about the even livelier ball used in 1930.

"Coefficient of restitution." — Technical term for the liveliness of the ball.

"They already lived up the ball. It's too fast for the pitcher, he'd say, and the infielder too and there is a problem if you would like to bunt, which most do. The pitcher is liable to get hurt and the infielder too and I would say you could say there will be more hitting because the ball gets down there faster and it goes through because you can't get there to catch the ball which you would have." — Casey Stengel in 1969 on the possibility of a livelier ball being used that season.

1860–1910. The debate over the liveliness of the ball has existed since at least 1862, when noted sportswriter Henry Chadwick claimed that the ball was "overelastic." A cork center was first introduced in a cricket ball in 1883, but it would be more than 25 years before it was introduced to Major League Baseball.

1900–1913. A's owner Ben Shibe is credited with inventing the cork center for a baseball in 1909. At least one source reported that in 1900 Spalding briefly introduced a cork-center ball, but it failed because the wool yarn swelled after the ball was stitched. The 1910 version was successful because the size of the cork was reduced and covered with rubber.

The American League ball was patented by George Reach's sporting goods company based on his partner Shibe's design. The National League reportedly had its ball developed by Spalding Sporting Goods, but it was the same design because Spalding owned Reach Manufacturing and the balls came from the same factory.

Although the Major Leagues officially adopted a livelier ball in

1911 (American League) and 1912 (National League), in 1910 the leagues secretly experimented with a lively ball containing a cork center. This was done at the end of the season, and at first was known only to Ben Shibe, George Reach, Connie Mack and the league presidents. It was used in a few 1910 late-season games and possibly during the World Series before being used full-time the following season.

Batting averages rose dramatically in the American League in 1911 and in the National League in 1912. In 1913 averages dropped back somewhat and continued in that lower range until 1920. The only available explanation is that pitchers used more illegal substances on balls in the years leading up to the ban implemented in 1920.

After the change in 1910, home runs increased in the Major Leagues from 260 in 1909 to 359 in 1910 and 515 in 1911. Home runs were back down to 441 in 1912.

1920s. Before the 1920 season, the ball supposedly was juiced up again. The American League formally adopted the livelier ball in 1920 and the National League followed in 1921, though statistics suggest that the National League also began using it in 1920. Home runs in the Major Leagues increased from 384 in 1915 to 631 in 1920.

Despite these "formal" actions referenced in a number of sources, historian Bill James makes a persuasive case for the increase in home runs during the early 1920s as having no relationship to a supposedly livelier ball. He claims that manufacturers did nothing to the ball (allegedly by their own admission) and that it was simply a matter of ballplayers following Babe Ruth's example in trying to hit more home runs.

Julian Curtis of Spalding said there were no new balls introduced in the 1920s, but that the wool was better after World War I and new winding machines made for a tighter, springier ball. James and others believe that this factor had only an incidental effect on hitting. George Reach (Al's son) claimed that the manufacturers occasionally tinkered with the balls.

The Bill James theory is supported by the increase in home runs that actually began in 1918, well before the introduction of the even livelier ball. In 1918 National League players hit 138 home runs. In 1919 that total increased to 206, then to 261 in 1920. Other statistics support the 1920 livelier ball theory. In 1920 George Sisler established a record for number of hits in a season, 257. National League batting averages improved from .258 in 1919 to .270 in 1920 and the American League improved from .268 to .283.

1925. Some sources claim that there is evidence that in 1925 a livelier cork-centered ball was introduced, which may have led to the higher batting and home run totals through the end of the decade.

1930. With supposedly an even livelier ball in play in the National League for one season, no player with 400 at-bats hit less than .250 except Hod Ford of the Reds, who hit .231 in 434 at-bats. A total of 71 players who appeared in 10 or more games that year hit over .300. The National League hit for a collective .303, including pitchers.

A number of National League records were set that year: the then-rookie home run record, 38, by Wally Berger of Cincinnati; rookie batting average, .373, by George Watkins of the Cardinals; home run record, 56, by Hack Wilson; RBI record, 190, by Wilson; rookie RBI record, 119, by Berger.

The problem with these records is that no one is quite sure what action was taken to deaden the ball for the next season. There is some evidence that a less resilient cushioned cork center was introduced for the 1931 season, which may have contributed to lower home run totals that year (to 1,068 from 1,565 in 1930). The "cushioned" cork center consisted of two black cork centers surrounded by a cushion of red rubber.

After the 1933 season, the National League heavily publicized its attempt to again put more life into the ball. Although National League run production increased by almost 25% in 1934, it was still significantly below production in the more star-studded and powerful American League.

1969. At least during exhibition games in 1969 — if not the season itself — the leagues used the 1–X ball, which was 10% livelier than the ball used in 1968, the Year of the Pitcher.

1987. During the 1987 season there was a dramatic increase in home runs and corresponding claims of a livelier ball. The balls were tested but nothing significant was found. Mark McGwire shattered the rookie home run record with 49 and there were 17% more home runs over the prior year. See **Weather** for a possible explanation for the increase (due to a season-long barometric abnormality).

1994.

"Why are you asking me? Do my grounders to second look a little harder?" — Kent Hrbek of the Twins during the "juiced ball" 1994 season in which home run production was up dramatically. A number of batters were on their way to career high years and possible records before the player strike wiped out the season. Rawlings as usual denied that there was any change in the ball.

1996. In 1996 a "juiced ball" theory surfaced due to the huge number of home runs early in the season. Some contended that Major League Baseball wanted a livelier ball because it would help attract more fans after the disastrous public relations from the player strike.

2002. During the 2002 World Series, players claimed that the ball was juiced, and that it was smaller and harder than the regular season ball. Sandy Alderson in the commissioner's office denied any differences or problems with the 500 World Series balls. Reliever Al Levine, not active for the World Series by the Angels, was in the clubhouse during the Series and used a Ginsu knife to slice open two balls. He claimed that the World Series ball was harder to cut and that it was wound tighter.

Lost Ball Rule. In 1886 the "Lost Ball Rule" was eliminated. Prior to that, five minutes were allowed for players to look for a lost ball before a new one was put in play. The time limit apparently was suggested in 1877 by sportswriter Henry Chadwick. As a result of the elimination of the rule, the home club was required to give the umpire two clean baseballs to start the game.

Manufacturers.

"A heterogeneous conglomeration of odds and ends of leather piled up in the basement at the factory where baseballs are made. Tons upon tons are scattered over a space equal to an acre; 8,000 pigskins are only one item." — Description of an Ohio factory that was producing 4,000 balls per day in the 1950s.

Baseballs originally were made by hand, which was considered somewhat of an art to properly wind the sphere. As demand grew, companies began manufacturing balls by machine. The first manufactured baseball supposedly was produced in 1858 by H. (Harrison) Harwood & Sons. In 1909 A.J. Reach received a **Patent** for the machine.

When the National League was formed in 1876, it granted Albert Spalding's company, Spalding Sporting Goods, the exclusive right to supply the official ball to the league. For years Spalding gave free balls and then cash grants to Major League clubs and also sold the balls to clubs at a discount.

Reach Sporting Goods, founded by A.J. Reach in 1877, was the first manufacturer of the ball used by the Western League (the future

American League). After Spalding acquired Reach in the late 19th century, Spalding operated the company as a subsidiary, but left the Reach name on the American League ball. With the exception of a short period when the **Stitches** were slightly different, the Spalding and Reach balls were identical because after Spalding bought Reach, the balls were manufactured at the same plant.

In 1884 the Union Association's official ball was supplied by Wright & Ditson Sporting Goods, formed in 1871 by former Cincinnati Red Stockings player George Wright. The balls had names such as the "Rattler," "the Boss" and "Eureka." Spalding later bought Wright & Ditson, solidifying his monopoly of the sporting goods industry. He kept the name (as he did with Reach), and Wright & Ditson existed into the 1970s.

The Kiffe ball was manufactured starting in the 1880s. It was to be the American Association's official ball when attempts were made to resurrect the Association in 1894. The Kiffe ball remained in existence well into the 20th century, primarily as a lesser quality sand-lot ball.

There was significant infighting among National League owners in the mid–1890s. Albert Spalding, who still owned the White Stockings/Cubs, was directly involved with some of it. As a result, there was a movement among some owners to award Spalding's National League ball contract to Overman Wheel Company of Chicopee Falls, Massachusetts, which already manufactured the Victor ball. In response, Spalding bought the Overman plant to protect his contract.

One source reported that in 1901 Ben Shibe of Reach was induced to assume ownership of the Philadelphia franchise in the new American League on the promise by league president Ban Johnson that Shibe's baseball manufacturing company would receive an exclusive contract to supply the new league with balls. However, Shibe already had the contract from his Western League days.

The official 1914 Federal League ball was manufactured by what was by then known as the Victor Sporting Goods Company, located in Springfield, Massachusetts. It also was owned by Spalding.

The Goldsmith 97 was an extremely lively ball used in the minor leagues in the South in the early 20th century.

By the 1950s there were at least 28 styles of balls made.

Rawlings Sporting Goods Company started manufacturing balls in 1955 only when it was bought out by Spalding. The balls were manufactured by Rawlings in St. Louis and then shipped to Chicopee, Massachusetts, for stitching the leather cover. Both the American and National League balls were made by the same company, even though the American League balls were stamped with the Rawlings name and the National League balls were stamped with the Spalding name (consistent with earlier practice).

This cross-ownership continued until 1968 when Spalding was forced to sell Rawlings after an antitrust investigation by the government. Nevertheless, Spalding continued to contract with Rawlings for its balls until 1973. At that point Spalding moved its own operation to Haiti. In late 1976 Rawlings took over all Major League Baseball manufacturing, using Taiwan and later Haiti. Each ball was stitched and finished abroad for about 10 cents per ball. Each of the 650 seamstresses made three dozen balls per day. Rawlings later moved its stitching operations to Costa Rica, where they have been produced since December 1990. By 1994 Rawlings was supplying the Major Leagues with approximately 720,000 balls each season. The hide is from Tennessee, the yarn from Vermont and the cork from Mississippi. All pieces are then shipped to Costa Rica for assembly.

The Haitian-sewn balls sometimes were of dubious quality. In the 1975 World Series, Red Sox second baseman Denny Doyle threw a double play ball into the dugout after the Reds' Johnny Bench had almost literally torn off the cover.

In 1993 the Major Leagues, the California League and the Pacific Coast League used Rawlings baseballs. All other minor leagues used Wilson balls. In 1998 Rawlings supplied 600,000 balls to the Major Leagues at a cost of approximately $6 million.

Massachusetts Ball. The New England version of baseball was known as the *Massachusetts Game* and employed a different ball than that used in the *New York Game* of the 19th century. The Massachusetts ball was one third the weight because it had no rubber and no yarn.

Mud. See *Mud*.

Number Used Per Game.

"The game is played on dirt and grass, but if the ball gets dirty, it is replaced with a new clean ball."—"6th Reason Why Baseball is a Weird Sport," by *Encarta*.

19th Century. Only one or two balls per game were used in the early years, causing balls to soften as the game wore on. They were replaced only if the yarn was exposed. In the 1880s one ball was used unless it was lost (see also **Lost Ball Rule**). Foul balls were returned by boys in the stands in return for free admission to another game. Longer hits increased in the mid–1890s and clubs were required to keep one dozen balls on hand and put a new one in play whenever the old one was seriously scratched or dirty. In 1882 a New York newspaper expressed astonishment that three balls could be used up in a game. In the late 19th century the Spiders were criticized for spending $390 in balls in a single season.

20th Century. Senators shortstop Roger Peckinpaugh said that the same soggy ball was used throughout one game during the 1925 World Series (maybe explaining, and excusing, some of his eight errors in the Series), though this seems unlikely for that time period and a game of that importance.

During the 26-inning marathon between the Dodgers and Braves in 1920 there were only three balls used.

The 1909 Tigers used 2,460 balls. In the 1920s, 55,000 balls could last a full season for all Major League teams. Today that many new balls are used in less than a month. In 1983 the Dodgers used approximately 15,800 balls; 500 for spring training, 10 dozen for each home game and six dozen old balls for practice during road games. Major League Baseball now uses about 500,000 balls per season. The average lifespan of a Major League ball is seven pitches.

The balls are delivered to the umpires before games in sealed, tamper-proof packets, and only the umpires may unseal the packets. All balls must be obtained from the league secretary. Clubs now average about eight dozen new balls a game and go through another six to eight dozen old balls during batting practice. One dozen balls costs close to $50 including shipping. Clubs annually spend about $140,000 on balls. For the entire 1880s, five million balls of varying quality were manufactured for professional and amateur use. By the 1980s, the national figure was 20 million annually (see also **Manufacturers**).

Patents. The first baseball patent was taken out on July 7, 1868. By 1960 there were 65 patents for improving the baseball, many relating to Philadelphia owner Ben Shibe's intricate machines used to make balls for the A.J. Reach Sporting Goods Company. He first received a machine patent in 1909.

Practice Balls. On July 3, 2002, the Astros and Reds played the 1st inning in Cincinnati with non–regulation baseballs, the result of a mix–up by an attendant in the umpires' locker room. The attendant did not notice the word "practice" stenciled on the 144 balls he rubbed up for the game. Practice balls generally have defects such as irregular stitching or weight deviations. Reds pitcher Wade Miller noticed the practice ball while warming up in the bottom of the 1st inning and informed umpire Mark Hirschbeck. Hirschbeck ruled that the practice balls had to be used in the bottom of the 1st before switching, because the Astros had already seen them. Miller gave up a home run to Lance Berkman.

Price. See **Cost.**

Rejecting Balls by Pitchers. In a game between the Cleveland Spiders and New York Metropolitans at the Polo Grounds on August 7, 1882, rain had made the ball wet, soggy and lopsided. However, under the rules in effect at that time, a player was not allowed to request a new ball until after a full inning was completed.

In connection with the 1920 rule outlawing the *Spitball* and other *Illegal Pitches*, the rules for rejecting a ball were modified to make it easier to put into play a cleaner and easier-to-see ball. Some historians erroneously claimed that this rule was instituted solely because Cleveland shortstop Ray Chapman died that season after being beaned by Carl Mays. However, efforts to change the rule had begun in 1919.

Seams. See **Stitches.**

Size and Weight.

"The new Haitian baseball can't weigh more than four ounces or less than five." — Jerry Coleman.

In the early 1840s balls might have weighed as little as 3 ounces and often were randomly larger or smaller than today's balls. For example, the original Knickerbocker club ball of the late 1840s was slightly larger than today's ball, and had a rubber center bound with yarn and leather. The ball weighed 6 ounces to 6½ ounces and was 10 inches to 10½ inches in circumference (5½ ounces — 6 ounces and 11 inches in some sources). Other early balls were smaller, sometimes 8½ inches in circumference.

The ball shrank somewhat in 1860 and then the size and weight were codified in 1872: 5 ounces to 5½ ounces and 9 inches to 9½ inches in circumference (see also **Composition**).

Stitches.

"I know things — for instance, there are 108 beads in a Catholic rosary. And … there are 108 stitches in a baseball. When I learned that, I gave Jesus a chance." — Susan Sarandon's character Annie in the movie *Bull Durham.*

"The pitcher will take the ball and feel it all over, rub it up and down and sideways, roll it around between the cupped palms of his hands and even stare at it momentarily, like a scientist examining a new species of bug under a microscope.

"He doesn't indulge in this hocus-pocus out of superstition, although ballplayers are notoriously full of that. He does it in the dim hope that he'll find some slight flaw in one of the 108 stitches which hold a baseball together. If he can spot one, no matter how tiny, he'll have gained a secret advantage over the batter." — Sportswriter Duane Decker.

In 1888 Al Reach developed a seamless ball, "as smooth and even as a rubber ball." Without the seams, the pitchers wouldn't hurt their fingers on the cat gut stitching, but there would also be no stitches to pick up the air currents and help create motion on the ball. Hitters might have had a field day.

The stitches on the National League's balls were higher in the 1920s and 1930s, giving an edge to pitchers who threw curveballs and other "movement" pitches. The higher stitches (or "seams") were more susceptible to air friction, which caused greater movement on the ball. Fastball pitchers did not benefit from the higher seams, which has been used to explain why historically there were supposedly more junkball pitchers in the National League and more fast-

ball pitchers in the American League. The higher stitches only lasted a few years, so the explanation does not hold up after the 1930s.

Today red threading is used on the balls for both leagues. In the past, red and black stitches were used in the National League and red and blue in the American League.

Storage. In April 2002, the Rockies began storing their balls in a temperature-controlled room that kept the humidity at a more normal 40% — in contrast to the 10% typical in Denver. The greater moisture in the balls had an immediate impact on run production. In the previous seven Aprils, the Rockies and their opponents combined for 15.1 runs per game. In 2002, it was 9.8.

Tampering.

See *Illegal Pitches.*

Testing. Sample balls are tested by the manufacturer by shooting them from an air gun at 85 mph against a board wall eight feet away. The rebound must be 54.6% of the original velocity, within a margin of 3.2%.

Theft.

"Just let it go." — Dodger clubhouse man Nobe Kawane to early 1960s batboy Jim Reynolds, after Reynolds discovered umpires stealing baseballs; apparently it was a routine practice overlooked by Major League clubs.

Trophies. In early amateur games, the winning team kept the game ball brought by the losing team and often displayed balls as trophies with information regarding the game hand-printed on the ball.

Wiffle Ball.

"Mike Scott's scuffball. There ain't never been anything thrown as nasty as that…. It's a Wiffle Ball." — Barry Bonds on the toughest pitch he ever saw.

This ball was invented in 1953 by David Mullaney and his father. They first used packing material and tape to invent the plastic ball that makes batters "whiff" — hence the name. Incredibly, the author received a demand letter from the attorneys for the Wiffle ball people (The Wiffle Ball Inc.) demanding that the term only be referred to as: "WIFFLE®."

Okay, done. [and now it's buried in this section on balls, rather than in its owner entry in the first edition of the *Encyclopedia.* The author hopes that *Sports Illustrated* received the same letter when it did an article on the inventors and failed to include any registration notice.]

Baltimore

"The trouble with Baltimore is that it's in Baltimore." — Reggie Jackson.

"Baltimore's such a lousy town, Francis Scott Key went out in a boat to write 'The Star Spangled Banner.'" — Billy Martin in 1978 while managing the Yankees.

Baltimore has had teams in the following Major Leagues:

American Association	1882–1891
Union Association	1884
National League	1892–1899
American League	1901–1902, 1954–
Federal League	1914–1915

Baltimore also had a club in the first professional league, the National Association. The city was part of the Class AAA International League until 1954, when the St. Louis Browns moved in. Suffering from competition from the 1914–1915 Federal League club in Baltimore, owner Jack Dunn was forced to move his International League club to Richmond for one season.

Book. Ted Patterson, *The Baltimore Orioles: 40 Years of Magic from 33rd Street to Camden Yards* (1995), covers the entire history of Major League Baseball in Baltimore with focus on the modern American League Orioles.

Baltimore Lord Baltimores/Marylands

National Association 1872–1874

"The 1872 Lord Baltimores made a strong fashion statement when they took the field for the first time. Baltimore's players looked ridiculous, sporting bright yellow trousers beneath yellow and black striped silk shirts with matching hats. A viscount's cornet on the left breast completed this haberdasher's travesty. After their initial appearance, many eschewed the team's given nickname and referred to them as the Canaries."—William J. Ryczek in *Blackguards and Red Stockings* (1992).

The club joined the National Association in 1872, finishing a strong third. It repeated that showing in 1873 before finishing last in 1874 and dropping out of the league. Some sources report that the club was known as the Marylands in 1873, but that was a separate short-lived team and there were two teams from Baltimore in the Association that season.

Baltimore Marylands

National Association 1873

"By the time the Marylands realized the futility of their mission, they were 0–6 and finished for the season, or any other season."—William J. Ryczek in *Blackguards and Red Stockings* (1992).

The club was 0–6 before dropping out of the league early in the 1873 season.

Baltimore Monumentals

Union Association 1884

This 1884 club was financed by A.H. Henderson, a Baltimore mattress manufacturer, who also financed the Union Association's Chicago entry. Baltimore finished fourth with a 58–47 record, playing all but one game at Belair Field.

Baltimore Orioles

American Association 1882–1891

Beer baron Harry Von der Horst owned the Baltimore franchise in the American Association from its formation in 1882 through its entry into the National League after the 1891 season.

With Bill Barnie as manager throughout the 1880s, the team was a doormat. It was last in 1882–1883, sixth in 1884, and last in 1885 and 1886. The team moved up to third in 1887, but was back to fifth place in 1888 and 1889. In 1890 the club shifted to Brooklyn after starting the season 15–19. The club returned to Baltimore in the American Association the next season, finishing fourth.

The 1886 team featured Matthew Aloysius "Matches" Kilroy, a left-handed pitcher who struck out 513 batters in 583 innings. When the American Association folded, the team remained intact and was absorbed into the National League's new 12-team format for the 1892 season, with Von der Horst still in control.

Baltimore Orioles

National League 1892–1899

"They were mean, vicious, ready at any time to maim a rival player or an umpire, if it helped their cause. The things they would say to an umpire were unbelievably vile, and they broke the spir-

its of some fine men."—National League president and former 1890s umpire Thomas Lynch.

Origins. When the American Association folded, the Orioles were absorbed into the National League's new 12-team format.

Key Owner. Harry Von der Horst owned the club throughout the 1890s, though when the club moved from the American Association a syndicate was formed to try to take control from him. The unsuccessful group included the cigar manufacturing Mencken brothers, the father and uncle of writer H.L. Mencken, who hated baseball.

Baltimore/Brooklyn Connection. In 1899 manager Ned Hanlon and Von der Horst coveted the more lucrative New York market, so they arranged to purchase 50% of the Brooklyn Dodgers in exchange for 50% of the stock in the Baltimore franchise. Ferdinand Abel of the Dodgers had controlled the Brooklyn stock and he took 40% of each team's stock as part of the reorganization. Charles Ebbets took 10% of each. The stock was transferred in a complicated maneuver and Hanlon moved over to Brooklyn as manager (while still president of Baltimore) and won the pennant with Brooklyn with a number of Baltimore's former players.

Despite the loss of players, Baltimore finished third in 1899 with John McGraw as manager. McGraw was feuding with the league in part because of the so-called Brush Resolution, which prohibited swearing and abuse of umpires.

After the season a number of Baltimore players were sent to St. Louis, including McGraw and Wilbert Robinson, and the Baltimore franchise was eliminated as the National League cut down from 12 to eight teams.

Nicknames. The "Orioles" name came from a bird prominent in the area designated as the Maryland state bird. The often-used "Superbas" name of the 1890s apparently derived from a vaudeville act of the same name—though some sources attribute it solely to a Baltimore pool parlor of that name run by manager Ned Hanlon.

Key Seasons. The Orioles and Boston Red Stockings dominated the 1890s. The Orioles won pennants in 1894, 1895 and 1896, lost on the last day to Boston in 1897 and finished second in 1898 with a 96–53 record.

Baltimore had mixed success in the National League championship series during the decade. The play-offs were contested between the first- and second-place teams in the league, who were competing during some years for the ***Temple Cup***. The Orioles lost in 1894 to the New York Giants; lost in 1895 to the Cleveland Spiders; defeated Cleveland in 1896 and defeated Boston in 1897. That was the last year in which any postseason championship play occurred until the World Series was established in 1903.

Key Players.

John McGraw (HF) played with the club throughout its eight years in the National League. He batted .321 or better in all but his first season. He led the league in RBIs and runs scored in both 1898 and 1899.

Wilbert Robinson (HF) was the club's catcher for eight years, batting .315 or better four times.

Wee Willie Keeler (HF) starred for the club from 1894 through 1899 when he moved to Brooklyn. He batted at least .361 each season, with league highs of .424 in 1897 and .385 in 1898.

Key Manager.
Ned Hanlon (HF).
"Ask Hanlon"—Lapel button worn by Orioles owner Harry Von der Horst when he hired Ned Hanlon as his manager. Von der Horst had been criticized for second-guessing his former manager, so he had the button made.

One of the best teams of the 19th century, the 1896 Baltimore Orioles: *front row, left to right:* Jack Doyle, John McGraw, "Wee" Willie Keeler and Arlie Pond. *Middle row, left to right:* Steve Brodie, Bill Hoffer, Joe Kelley, Ned Hanlon, Wilbert Robinson, Hughie Jennings and Heinie Reitz. *Rear, left to right:* Joe Quinn, Sadie McMahon, Duke Esper, George Hemming, Frank Bowerman, Bill "Boileryard" Clark and Jimmy Donnelly.

Baltimore started the 1892 season with outfielder George Van Haltren in charge, but the team lost 14 of its first 15 games. Jack Waltz, a beer salesman at Von der Horst's brewery, was then appointed manager and lost six of eight. This lasted until May 9, 1892, when Ned Hanlon moved to the team and bought a 20% ownership interest. He managed the dynasty through the 1898 season, winning three pennants and finishing second twice.

Ballparks. After Union Park burned in 1894, Baltimore built a new ballpark on the same site. The new Orioles Park seated 15,000. The definitive *Green Cathedrals*, by Philip Lowry (1982), makes no mention of a Union Park, referring to this newly built park as Oriole Park III and making no mention of the fire.

Baltimore Orioles

American League 1901–1902
1901 Formation. When the National League Baltimore franchise was dissolved after the 1899 season, the city had no Major League team for 1900. Over the winter of 1900–1901, Harry Goldman put together a group to finance a new American League club in the city. The Baltimore Base Ball and Athletic Company was capitalized with $40,000. Sydney Frank held the largest block of the 400 issued shares and became president. Goldman became secretary and John McGraw and Wilbert Robinson bought stock in return for smaller salaries as manager and coach.

McGraw had spent the 1900 season with St. Louis in the National League after a falling out with the National League club in Baltimore. There were also several other minority shareholders,

including politician and contractor John J. McMahon, father-in-law of former outfielder Joe Kelley.

The club finished fifth under McGraw, though he was suspended during the season for feuding with umpires. Joe McGinnity won 26 games and both McGraw and Robinson hit over .300 in limited action.

1902 Problems. McGraw's problems with the umpires—and thus Ban Johnson—continued in 1902. In July, Johnson suspended McGraw indefinitely. McGraw was then involved in negotiations to move to the National League Giants, owned by John T. Brush. McGraw resigned midseason (with a 28–34 record) and immediately moved over to manage the Giants.

When McGraw made the move, the Orioles owed him $7,000. He bargained for his release by giving up his right to the money on the condition that he could take certain players with him to the Giants. Some of the players also were sent to the Reds. After having its roster decimated, Baltimore could not field a team against St. Louis on July 17, 1902. Johnson stocked the Orioles with players from other teams and appointed Wilbert Robinson as manager. Baltimore finished the season at 50–88 and in last place.

After the season Johnson revoked Baltimore's franchise and paid off the owners. Baltimore operated the rest of the season on American League funds and players from other teams. One source claimed that this "decisive action saved the league," but it is doubtful that the league would have folded over this. More important to the American League's ultimate stability and success was that Johnson, getting a measure of revenge against McGraw, sent the Baltimore franchise to New York to become the Highlanders (later the Yankees).

Baltimore Orioles

American League 1954–

"The Baltimore Orioles are in town. Which reminds me of a cartoon I once saw. It showed a little boy forlornly carrying a glove and a bat over his shoulder. 'How'd you do, son?' his father asks. 'I had a no-hitter going until the big kids got out of school,' the kid says."—Pitcher Jim Bouton in *Ball Four* (1970). His pitiful Seattle Pilots had been playing reasonably well before playing the powerful Orioles.

Origins. Baltimore did not have a Major League team from 1903 until Baltimore brewer Jerry Hoffberger became the principal owner of the St. Louis Browns. Shortly before buying the club from Bill Veeck, Jr., Hoffberger received approval from the American League on September 29, 1953, to move the club to Baltimore (see also *Franchise Shifts*).

First Game. On April 13, 1954, the Tigers shut out the Orioles 3–0 in front of 46,994 fans at Briggs Stadium in Detroit. The club's first home game was on April 15, 1954, a 3–1 win over the White Sox in front of 46,354 fans. Bob Turley was the winner.

Key Owners.

The Hoffberger Group/1954–1979. The club (still the St. Louis Browns) was sold by Bill Veeck for $2,475,000 to a group headed by Jerrold C. "Jerry" Hoffberger's National Brewery Company and Baltimore attorney Clarence W. Miles. Hoffberger once tried to buy the Tigers with Veeck. Hoffberger served in World War II and in 1946 at age 26 he was named general manager of the brewery. He became president in 1947 and remained in that position until 1975.

Hoffberger became one of the club's principal stockholders in 1960 and took financial control in 1963 when he became chairman of the board. The family owned the club through the 1960s, when Hoffberger increased his individual holdings. Hoffberger became a severe critic of Bowie Kuhn in the early 1970s and he put the club up for sale in 1974 for $12 million. In mid-1975 he took the club off the market. Hoffberger became the head of Carling Brewery that year when his brewery merged with Carling. However, the family's interest in the club remained outside the Carling structure. Hoffberger held the Orioles until August 1979, when Edward Bennett Williams bought the club.

Edward Bennett Williams/1979–1988.

"I have no partners. I am the group."—Williams stressing that he was the new sole owner of the club.

"He's become far more addicted to the sport, the team and the town than he expected. 'EBW' had plenty of jetsetter in him. However, he reformed enough so that he came to see the Orioles (as long as they don't cost him money) as a community trust, an indigenous part of the genteel, old-fashioned Baltimore ethos."—Thomas Boswell in *Why Time Begins on Opening Day* (1984).

Williams paid $12 million to Hoffberger, his long-time friend and business associate. Williams was persuaded to buy the club by former U.S. Treasury Secretary Williams Simon when the club was in danger of being moved. Long-time NFL Redskins owner Jack Kent Cooke was initially involved in the negotiations, but dropped out. When Williams died of cancer, his long-time law partner, Larry Lucchino (himself a cancer survivor), took over as president until the sale of the club in 1988. He remained as a minority owner after the sale.

Eli Jacob/1988–1993. Jacob bought the club on December 6, 1988. The other key owners were Larry Lucchino and Sargent Shriver, who had married into the Kennedy family and was the Democratic vice-presidential candidate in 1980.

Jacob bought an 87% interest in the club for $70 million and then tried to sell it for as much as $200 million in 1993. Jacobs was worth $500 million in 1991, but his fortune was declining rapidly due to failed investments. He was in financial trouble, having been accused by his creditors of defaulting on almost $44 million in loans and personal guarantees. Jacob declared personal bankruptcy in April 1993, but it did not interfere with a sale of the Orioles.

Peter Angelos, et al./1993– .

"New Baltimore Oriole part-owner Tom Clancy is hard at work on his new book: *The Hunt for Mr. October*."—Columnist Mike Downey.

Attorney Peter Angelos led a group that bought the club with Cincinnati businessman William DeWitt, whose father had owned the Browns in the 1940s. Three groups bid for the club at an auction conducted by a local judge on behalf of the bankrupt Jacob. The group that eventually succeeded in the spirited bidding included tennis star Pam Shriver, broadcaster Jim McKay, author Tom Clancy and director Barry Levinson. At the time of the purchase, DeWitt was part-owner of the Rangers, but he sold his interest to participate in the Orioles purchase. The final purchase price was a then-record $173 million.

Angelos became an attorney and was a Baltimore city councilman in 1959 at age 29. He ran for mayor on Baltimore's first interracial ticket in 1967, but was soundly defeated. He made more than $400 million representing 8,700 steelworkers and others in asbestos exposure cases. He was a maverick owner during the 1994–1995 player strike, refusing to field a spring training replacement club (in part to protect Cal Ripken, Jr.'s, streak) and repeatedly criticized interim commissioner Bud Selig for his handling of the strike.

Nickname. The Oriole is the Maryland state bird.

Key Seasons.

1950s-1960. Baltimore finished in the middle of the pack through the 1950s, but managed a second-place finish in 1960.

1966. The club finished a strong third in 1965 in a tight race and then established itself as a powerhouse in 1966, winning the pennant by nine games over the Twins. The Orioles swept the Dodgers in the World Series behind Frank Robinson's MVP and Triple Crown season. See also Gordon Beard, *Birds on the Wing* (1967).

1969. In the first season of divisional play, the Orioles won 109 games and captured the division title by 19 games over the Tigers. Baltimore swept the Twins in the first League Championship Series, but lost the World Series to the Mets in five games. Mike Cuellar and Dave McNally each won 20 or more games and Frank Robinson hit .308 with 32 home runs. Boog Powell hit 37 home runs and drove in 121 runs.

1970. The Orioles won 108 games to win the division by 15 games. They swept the Twins in the League Championship Series and beat the Reds in five games as Brooks Robinson dominated the Series. Mike Cuellar and Dave McNally tied for the league lead with 24 wins and Boog Powell had 35 home runs and 114 RBIs.

1971. The Orioles again won over 100 games (101) and again swept their opponent in the play-offs (A's). Though favored in the World Series against the Pirates, the Orioles fell in seven games after winning the first two. The club had four 20-game winners in Mike Cuellar, Jim Palmer, Pat Dobson and Dave McNally.

1973. After a third-place finish in 1972, the Orioles returned with 97 wins to claim the division title by eight games over the Red Sox. The A's beat the Orioles in five games in the ALCS as Catfish Hunter shut them out in Game 5. Jim Palmer won 22 games and led the league with a 2.40 ERA. Designated hitter Tommy Davis led the club with 89 RBIs.

1974. The Orioles won the division by two games over the Yankees, but lost again to the A's in the Championship Series, this time in four games. Mike Cuellar won 22 games and Tommy Davis again led the club with 84 RBIs.

1979. The Orioles finished second three years in a row and then won 90 games in 1978, but finished fourth. In 1979 they won 102 games, good for the division title by seven games over the Brewers. They beat the Angels in the Championship Series and then led the Pirates 3–1 in the World Series, but Pittsburgh rallied to win the title in seven games. Mike Flanagan led the league with 23 wins and Ken Singleton had 35 home runs and 111 RBIs.

1983. The Orioles won 100 games in 1980 to finish second and also finished second during one half of the 1981 strike season and second by one game in 1982. They returned to the postseason in 1983 by winning 98 games and finishing six games ahead of the Tigers. The Orioles beat the White Sox in the Championship Series in four games and defeated the Phillies in five games to win the World Series. Eddie Murray hit 33 home runs and Cal Ripken hit 27; each drove in more than 100 runs.

1989. After losing more than 100 games in 1988 and suffering through a 21-game losing streak at the start of that season, the Orioles rebounded in 1989 to finish in second place. They ended the season only two games behind the Blue Jays after leading the division for most of the season.

1996. The Orioles were the wild card club and then beat the powerful Indians in the first round of the playoffs before losing to the Yankees for the pennant. The club featured nine players with more than 20 home runs, led by lead-off batter Brady Anderson, with 50. Mike Mussina led the club with 19 wins.

1997. The Orioles went wire-to-wire to win the American League East with a 98–64 record. They beat the Mariners in four games in the division series, but lost the ALCS to the Indians in six tough games. Rafael Palmeiro led the club with 38 home runs and 110 RBIs, and Roberto Alomar batted .333. Jimmy Key, Mike Mussina and Scott Erickson each won at least 15 games and Randy Myers had 45 saves.

Key Players.

"I'm just playing between legends—Brooks and Rip."—Third baseman Doug DeCinces, who played regularly for the Orioles from late 1975 through 1981.

Frank Robinson (HF) was traded to the Orioles for the 1966 season and promptly won the Triple Crown while leading Baltimore to a World Series sweep of the Dodgers. He played another five years with the club and hit over .300 three more times while leading the Orioles to the World Series in 1969, 1970 and 1971.

Brooks Robinson (HF) played his entire 23-year career with the Orioles, from 1955 through 1977. He played in four World Series and established himself as the premier defensive third baseman of his era, if not in baseball history. In 1969 Robinson was voted the all-time greatest Oriole.

Boog Powell played 14 seasons for the Orioles, hitting more than 20 home runs eight times. One of the most popular Orioles players, he anchored first base for the club during its glory years in the 1960s and early 1970s.

Dave McNally won 20 games four years in a row for the Orioles from 1968 through 1971. He helped lead the club to four World Series during his 13 years in Baltimore from 1962 through 1974.

Jim Palmer (HF) played his entire 19-year career with the Orioles, winning 268 games, including 20 or more in a season eight times in nine years. He pitched in six World Series, winning four games.

Eddie Murray (HF) played 12 seasons for the Orioles between 1977 and 1988. He drove in more than 100 runs in five seasons and

hit 333 home runs for the club. He returned in mid–1996 to finish his quest for 500 career home runs.

Cal Ripken, Jr.

"Ripken will almost certainly finish his career without changing teams, without trash-talking an opponent, without checking into a rehab center, without cutting an album and without winding up under the 'Jurisprudence' heading in your sports section. That alone puts him in select company in these days of packaged sports stars who are long on style but short on substance."—Tom Verducci in *Sports Illustrated*.

The iron man of the late 20th century first played shortstop for the Orioles in 1981 and began his ***Consecutive Games Played*** streak the following season. He broke Lou Gehrig's record in September 1995 and later moved over to third base. He finished his career in 2001 with 431 home runs and a .276 average over 21 seasons. See also The Sporting News, *Cal: Celebrating the Career of a Baseball Legend* (2004).

Key Managers.

Paul Richards managed the club from its second season in Baltimore in 1955 through most of the 1961 season. His best finish was second place in 1960, but his primary contribution was in general management and player development for the Orioles and other clubs.

Earl Weaver (HF).

"My best game plan is to sit on the bench and call out specific instructions like 'C'mon Boog,' 'Get ahold of one, Frank,' or 'Let's go, Brooks.'"— Weaver, a proponent of the three-run homer game plan. Weaver led the Orioles from midway into the 1968 season through 1982. During that span the club won six division titles and made four World Series appearances (winning only in 1970). He also had six second-place finishes. After retiring in 1982 he returned to the Orioles for part of 1985 and the entire 1986 season (finishing fourth and seventh) before retiring permanently.

Ballparks.

"Here we are for the final game of the year and the final game at Memorial Stadium."— Ernie Harwell's first words over WJR 760 before the final game at Memorial Stadium in 1991; and his final game as a Tiger broadcaster under owner Tom Monaghan. Harwell was the first Orioles broadcaster in 1954.

Memorial Stadium. After the Federal League folded in 1916, Terrapin Park was used by the International League Baltimore entry that won the pennant each season from 1919 through 1925. It was called Oriole Park and Babe Ruth Stadium at various times until it burned down in 1944.

In 1950 Memorial Stadium was built out of the ashes of the earlier ballpark using a football-oriented layout. It was the first Major League ballpark built with lights as part of the original configuration. With an initial capacity of 47,806, its seats were so hard that it was affectionately known as Hemorrhoid Stadium. The capacity was increased when it was double-decked in 1953.

Its original dimensions from left to right field were 309–446–445–446–309. There was no fence from left center to right center, just a hedge. The dimensions were so prodigious that in 1954 Vern Stephens led the team with eight home runs and 45 RBIs. The Orioles hit only 19 home runs at home, while the visitors hit 23.

On August 10, 1957, Mickey Mantle became the first player to clear the monstrous center field hedge with a 460-foot home run off the base of the scoreboard. In 1966 Frank Robinson became the only man to hit a ball completely out of the ballpark. He did it off Luis Tiant of the Indians. The dimensions later were reduced to 309– 370–410–370–309.

At Baltimore's last game in the park, the honor of throwing out the first ball went jointly to Johnny Unitas, quarterback of the Baltimore Colts, and Brooks Robinson, stellar third baseman for the Orioles from 1955 through 1977. Mike Flanagan, who starred for the Orioles for many years, threw the last official pitch for the Orioles in the ballpark. Though they lost the last game, the Orioles won 1,706 games and lost only 1,321 in the park. Frank Tanana won the last game for the Tigers.

When Memorial Stadium was razed in 2002, 10,000 cubic yards of broken-up concrete were used to build an oyster reef in Chesapeake Bay.

Oriole Park at Camden Yards.

"Welcome to instant prepackaged, brand-new oldness. Camden Yards was baseball's first attempt to bring its past back from the dead. Evocative, nostalgic, and unleashing of a frenzy of building the newest old stadiums man could build, which now, in a total perversion of the idea of actual architectural history, threatens Fenway."—Broadcaster Keith Olbermann in August 2000.

The Orioles opened their new park for the 1992 season. The club hosted its first exhibition game in the ballpark on April 3, 1992, against the Mets. The first official game was Opening Day on April 6, 1992. The first night game was played on April 8, 1992, as Paul Sorrento of the Indians hit the park's first home run, a three-run shot.

In the tradition of older ballparks and their uneven dimensions, the dimensions from left to right field are 333–373–399–386–318. In 2001, home plate was moved approximately seven feet closer to the backstop, increasing the distances to the fences by five to 10 feet. Capacity is 46,500. The site covers 85 acres and 71 city blocks. It also contains 72 skyboxes and three large suites which lease for $55,000 to $90,000 annually. The total building cost was $100 million, with an additional $99 million to purchase the property and demolish the buildings on site. It was financed with lottery monies and bond issues. The saloon owned by Babe Ruth's father is now the site of Camden Yards' center field. See also Peter Richmond, *Ballpark: Camden Yards and the Building of the American Dream* (1993), the story of how the ballpark was created.

From 1992 through 2002 the club averaged 3.3 million fans in Camden Yards, up from 2.5 million in their final season at Memorial Stadium.

Key Broadcasters.

"George Kell, who does the play-by-play on TV ... is a pretty good game announcer. Neither he nor [Al] Kaline is a master of English grammar and diction, but I guess you can't have everything."—Art Hill in *I Don't Care If I Never Come Back* (1980).

Ernie Harwell was the team's first broadcaster, lasting six years from 1954 through 1959. Harwell was replaced by Herb Carneal for the 1960 season after leaving to become the Tigers' long-time announcer. In 1991 while with the Tigers, Harwell broadcast his last game for the Tigers and the last game in Memorial Stadium.

Former third baseman George Kell broadcast for the club in the 1950s and 1960s. Chuck Thompson covered the Orioles in 1955 and 1956 before leaving briefly for the Senators, network baseball and football. He began his career in 1949 in the International League. He called the 1960 World Series and in 1962 he became the Voice of the Orioles for the next 21 years. His long-time colleague was Bill O'Donnell from 1966 through 1982. Thompson's primary cries were "Go to war Miss Agnes!" and "Ain't the beer cold!" He was brought out of retirement in 1991, received the Ford Frick Award in 1993, and remained a part-time member of the television team through the 2004 season.

Jon Miller arrived with the Orioles in 1983 to replace Thompson. Miller came to the Orioles after stints with the A's, Rangers

and Red Sox and remained with the club until 1997. Brooks Robinson broadcast for the club from 1978 through 1993 and then Jim Palmer began a part-time broadcast stint that continued through the 2004 season, joined by former Major League player and manager Buck Martinez.

Jim Hunter began with the club in 1997 after 15 years with CBS sports and had also broadcast the Olympic Games.

Books. Rex Barney with Norman L. Macht, *Rex Barney's Orioles Memories* (1994); Louis Berney, *Tales from the Orioles Dugout* (2004); James Bready, *The Home Team* (1959); James E. Miller, *The Baseball Business: Pursuing Pennants and Profits in Baltimore* (1990); Ted Patterson and Brooks Robinson, *The Baltimore Orioles: 40 Years of Magic from 33rd Street to Camden Yards* (1994).

Baltimore Terrapins

Federal League 1914–1915

"Actually, the playing surface was hardly in first class condition and only the skeleton framework of the grandstand roof was in place. But the gala event took place with as much fanfare as ever seen for an opening baseball game.... President Gilmore, Harry Sinclair, Pat Powers and other dignitaries were grinning from ear to ear as the photographers clicked away."—Marc Okonnen in *The Federal League of 1914–1915* (1989) on the opening game in Baltimore.

The club was owned by 600 investors, including Ned Hanlon of the 1890s Baltimore Orioles. The Terrapins finished third in 1914 with an 84–70 record behind player-manager Otto Knabe. Knabe also led the club to an abysmal 47–107 record in 1915.

The club's only serious claim to fame arose when it was shut out of the settlement money paid by the National League to some of the Federal League owners. Baltimore filed suit, claiming federal **Antitrust** violations. The case reached the U.S. Supreme Court in 1922, which ruled that baseball was not subject to the antitrust laws and Baltimore was not entitled to any money.

Dave Bancroft (1891–1972)

Hall of Fame (VC) 1971

"In 1908 at the age of 17 I tried out for the Winona team in the Minnesota-Wisconsin League. On the day before the season started, the manager came into the clubhouse and laid new uniforms on a table. I kept looking and I didn't find one for me, so I knew I didn't make the team. I cried all the way home."—Bancroft, quoted in the *National Baseball Hall of Fame and Museum Yearbook*, edited by Bill Guilfoile (1989).

Bancroft played shortstop primarily for the Phillies and Giants for 16 seasons beginning in 1915.

Dave James Bancroft, known as "Beauty," arrived in the Major Leagues in 1915 from the Pacific Coast League after beginning his minor league career in 1909 in Duluth and Superior in the Wisconsin-Minnesota League. He made an immediate impact at shortstop, helping lead the Phillies to the National League pennant. His best season was 1922, when he hit .321 with 41 doubles and 117 runs scored.

He played shortstop for 16 years in the National League from 1915 through 1930, starting primarily for the Phillies (1915–1920) and Giants (1920–1923). He also played four years for the Braves, two years for the Dodgers and a few games for the Giants in 1930. He played in one World Series for the Phillies and three World Series with the Giants in 1921, 1922 and 1923, hitting a combined .172.

Bancroft hit a lifetime .279 with 2,004 hits and was considered the premier defensive shortstop of his era. He was player-manager of the Braves while hitting over .300 twice in four years. After his playing days, he managed and coached in the minor leagues before fully retiring from baseball.

Bankruptcy

"I called home and told my wife I went 0-for-2 and got hit in the back by a pitch. She said, 'Did you owe him money too?'"—Jack Clark of the Red Sox, who filed for bankruptcy in 1992, on Sam Militello's one-hit shutout.

"Sounds like the perfect guy to manage Jack Clark's finances."—Pete Gammons of the *Boston Globe* on Kenny Henderson. In 1992 Henderson turned down $650,000 from the Brewers as their first draft pick. In 1994 he turned down $350,000 from the Expos as their second draft pick. In 1995 he accepted $55,000 from the Padres and never obtained his college degree. Nor did he ever make it to the Major Leagues.

"I like my players to be married and in debt. That's the way you motivate them."—Ernie Banks, at the time a Cubs minor league instructor.

"It's possible to spend money anywhere in the world if you put your mind to it, something I proved conclusively by running up huge debts in Cincinnati."—Leo Durocher.

Ernie Banks (1931–)

Hall of Fame 1977

"It's a great day for a ballgame. Let's play two."—Banks' signature line.

"His wrists are the secret of Banks' success. Instead of taking the big Ruthian type swing of the lively ball era, he swings his bat as if it were a buggy whip, striking at the ball with the reflexive swiftness of a serpent's tongue."—Bill Furlong in *Baseball Stars of 1959.*

"And it was fine to discover that some legends and stereotypes are based on truth. At the beginning of this day, while the rest of the old-timers waited leisurely in the locker room, getting dressed and renewing old friendships, one man hurried onto the field alone and, in full uniform, paced back and forth, impatiently waiting for the others to come out and play baseball with him. Ernie Banks."—Bob Greene.

Banks starred for the Cubs at shortstop and first base for 19 seasons beginning in 1953.

A Texas native, Ernest "Mr. Cub" Banks starred in football and basketball in high school before playing for a Negro team in 1948 known as the Amarillo Colts. By 1950 Banks was with the Kansas City Monarchs. After serving in the Army, he signed with the Cubs and, with Gene Baker, became the first two black players for the club in September 1953.

Banks established himself in 1954, hitting .275 with 19 home runs in 154 games. Over the next seven years he became one of the most powerful offensive weapons in the Major Leagues while playing shortstop. He hit more than 40 home runs five times, with a high of 47 in 1958. He won back-to-back MVP Awards in 1958 and 1959 when he hit a total of 92 home runs and drove in 272 runs. Between 1955 and 1960 he hit more home runs than Mantle, Mays and Aaron.

Banks continued to star in the 1960s, with his last strong year in 1969 when he hit 23 home runs and drove in 106.. In 1962 he made the switch from shortstop to first base, where he remained for the balance of his career.

The 13-time All-Star hit his 500th home run in 1970 and finished with 512. He hit .274 lifetime and drove in over 100 runs eight times.

He was a player-coach beginning in 1967 and became a full-time coach after his retirement. He left baseball to become a full-time businessman in Chicago, but remained the all-time most popular Cubs player.

Book. Ernie Banks and Jim Enright, *Mr. Cub* (1971).

Red Barber (1908–1992)

Hall of Fame (Spink Award) 1978

"The Bases are FOB."—Barber's famous call when the bases were "Full of Brooklyns."

"Some people are disappointed when it rains at a ball game. Not me. Every time it looks like rain and I know the Yanks are playing at the Stadium, I quickly turn on Red Barber to get his breathtaking, thrilling rundown of the work of the grounds-keepers. Red never allows a little rain to change the pace of his coverage. Of course, he gives it that old 'catbird seat' drawl, but the words come out just the same."—Sportswriter Tom O'Reilly of the *New York Morning Telegram.*

Barber was a long-time broadcaster for the Reds, Dodgers and Yankees.

Mississippi native Walter Lanier "Red" Barber was studying to be an English professor at the University of Florida when he started in sports broadcasting by doing re-creations in 1934 for the Reds. He refused to make up information and gloss over facts during his re-creations. He was very straightforward in his sophisticated Southern-style presentation, unlike many others doing **Re-Creations** in that period. This remained his style for live broadcasts throughout his career.

In 1939 Reds general manager Larry MacPhail moved to the Dodgers and hired the 31-year-old Barber to be the team's broadcaster. That same year, Barber announced the first Major League game broadcast on **Television**. Barber stayed in Brooklyn until 1954, when he moved to the Yankees after Dodger owner Walter O'Malley failed to support him in his dispute over low pay for broadcasting the World Series. He finished his career in 1966 after being told by the Yankees that he would not be rehired after the season, which had three games remaining. He never broadcast for the club again because the three games were rained out. During his years with the Yankees he became a minister ordained in seven states.

On August 7, 1978, he and Mel Allen became the first broadcasters inducted into the baseball Hall of Fame. Between the two of them they broadcast for 59 years, covering 33 World Series and 29 All-Star Games. Two of the game's great broadcasters began their careers with Barber as their mentor: Vin Scully (who called him a second father) and Ernie Harwell.

Barber was resurrected as a broadcaster on December 14, 1980. Yankee catcher Elston Howard had died and National Public Radio (NPR) was looking for someone to comment on his passing. Barber was tracked down in retirement in Tallahassee, Florida, and made a favorable impression on the air. As a result, he began a weekly spot on January 1, 1981, which continued until shortly before his death at age 84 during the 1992 World Series. In 1985 he received the George Polk Award for his career in broadcasting and in 1991 he received the George Peabody Award for six decades of excellence behind the microphone.

Books. Lylah Barber (Red's wife), *Lylah* (1985); Red Barber, *The Broadcasters* (1970); Red Barber and Robert W. Creamer, *Rhubarb* *in the Catbird's Seat* (1968); Bob Edwards, *Fridays with Red: A Radio Friendship* (1993).

Al Barlick (1915–1995)

Hall of Fame (VC) 1989

"Bill Klem told me I'd meet some people in baseball I'd like. I'd meet some people I didn't like. But you help them all, because in doing that you'd be helping all baseball. And you must remember only two things — dedicate yourself to baseball and do your utmost to make the right decision on every play. It's not easy. Everybody is subject to human error. The tough part is that the players and fans only remember the ones they think you missed." — Barlick on receiving the 1971 Umpire of the Year Award from the Al Somers Umpire School.

Barlick umpired in the National League for 27 almost consecutive seasons beginning in 1940.

Originally a coal miner, Barlick began his umpiring career in the Northeast Arkansas League in 1936 for $75 a month. He moved up the minor league ranks until he was hired as the youngest umpire in modern Major League history at age 25. Barlick served as a National League umpire from 1940 through 1943 before entering the Coast Guard. He returned in 1946 and remained until 1955, when a heart condition forced him out for two years. He returned in 1958 and umpired in the National League until 1971. Barlick thought Roberto Clemente was the best player he had seen, at least in the National League.

Barlick umpired in seven World Series and seven All-Star Games. After retiring from the field, he served as a National League umpire consultant by coaching umpires and scouting minor league umpires.

Ernest S. Barnard (1874–1931)

Barnard succeeded Ban Johnson in 1927 for four years as the second *American League President*.

Barnstorming

"Last year spring training lasted two days, and I'm told that in the glory days of barnstorming the club would stay in the Deep South to scrimmage for two weeks. This year's spring training was on the lean side of ninety minutes." — Bill Heward in *Some Are Called Clowns* (1974), an account of his 1973 "season with the last of the great barnstorming baseball teams." In their heyday, the Indianapolis Clowns had Henry Aaron and previously were one of the better barnstorming Negro League clubs.

See also *Exhibitions* and *Spring Training*.

Barnstorming is a phenomenon that dates back to before the 1869 all-professional Cincinnati Red Stockings. In 1860 the Brooklyn Excelsiors went on a tour of New York state, Baltimore and Philadelphia, one of the earliest tours on record. As leagues became more organized, scheduling became more rigid and games against non-league clubs were forbidden. As a result, unsanctioned barnstorming eventually was eliminated except for pre- and postseason games.

Postseason barnstorming became the norm by the 1880s. It was even more formalized after the World Series was initiated in 1903. From 1900 until 1920, Cuba was a popular destination for both spring training and postseason barnstorming. Resistance to unofficial postseason games by Major League officials began to surface in the early part of the century. For example, in 1910 promoter

Daniel A. Fletcher offered $500–$1,000 to Major League players to appear in postseason exhibition games. The National Commission objected on the ground that it diminished the glamour and importance of the World Series. It probably did neither, but the governing National Commission was looking for ways to control the activity and collect some of the revenue.

The "no barnstorming" rule was formalized in 1914 by adding a clause to the standard player contract that prohibited non-sanctioned exhibition games. Nevertheless, the rules were not strictly enforced until Judge Landis became commissioner in 1920. He more stringently enforced the rule in part because Negro League teams were defeating Major League teams and Organized Baseball's all-white image was tarnished by the defeats (see also *Negro Leagues*).

After the 1921 World Series, Babe Ruth and Bob Meusel were suspended by Landis for defying his order not to play during a postseason barnstorming tour. Landis even impounded Ruth's World Series loser's share of $3,510. The two players were suspended until May 20 of the 1922 season, but the Yankees nevertheless were in first place when the pair rejoined the team.

In 1927 as part of a sanctioned postseason tour, Ruth and Lou Gehrig were among a group that traveled to 20 cities and played in front of 220,000 fans. In 1928 Ruth arranged to receive a percentage of the gate of a spring training barnstorming tour by the Yankees.

By the 1950s barnstorming had faded in popularity because it was too expensive and the proliferation of radio and television made baseball less of a novelty in non–Major League cities and outlying areas.

A number of *International Tours* were organized that took teams abroad, most of which were sanctioned by Organized Baseball (see also *Japanese Baseball*).

Barred from Baseball

"[Barring players] against whom the charges of general dissipation and insubordination have been repeatedly made ... no League club should play against any club employing as manager, umpire, or player any of such proscribed players." — September 1881 resolution by the National League.

See also *Alcoholism, Blacklists, Black Sox Scandal, Drug Abuse, Felons, Gambling and Fixed Games, Mexican Leagues — 1940s Raiding of American Teams* and *Suspensions*.

A number of players and owners have been barred from baseball (primarily for gambling offenses). Judge Landis banished 15 players in his first full year at the helm (1921) and at one point had made 53 players ineligible.

Horace Fogel. Fogel headed the group that bought the Phillies in 1909 and was president of the club until forced out of baseball in 1911. That year he was expelled for alleging that catcher Roger Bresnahan of the Cardinals and other former Giants stars had rigged the season to allow John McGraw's Giants to win the pennant. Fogel also told the New York writers that the season had been rigged in favor of the Giants by National League president Thomas Lynch and the umpires. He repeated this charge in a telegram to Reds owner Garry Herrmann. Fogel also wrote the same allegations in an article after being encouraged by the always annoying Cubs owner, Charles Murphy.

Fogel implicated Murphy as participating in these allegations, but the league barred only Fogel from baseball. He returned to the newspaper business and died in 1928.

Joe Harris. He was barred from the American League for two seasons (1920–1921) for playing in a league that was not part of Organized Baseball.

Ray Fisher. In 1921 the National League pitcher was barred from baseball for reneging on his contract with the Reds. At least one source contended that Judge Landis barred Fisher in order to enlist the general support of Reds owner and former National Commission member Garry Herrmann.

Dickie Kerr. The pitcher was one of the clean White Sox of the 1919 World Series. He was suspended in 1923–1925 for pitching against an outlaw team during a contract dispute. Perhaps not coincidentally the opposing team included two of the Black Sox players who had been banned for life from Major League Baseball.

Ted Turner. The Braves owner was early in his second year of ownership in 1976 when he was suspended from the day-to-day operations of his club for tampering with outfielder Gary Matthews of the Giants. Turner began negotiations to sign Matthews during the season before Matthews officially became a free agent after the season.

Mickey Mantle and Willie Mays. Bowie Kuhn barred Mantle from baseball after Mantle went to work as a greeter at the Claridge Hotel and Casino in Atlantic City. He did the same thing to Mays under similar circumstances, but both were immediately reinstated by Kuhn's successor, Peter Ueberroth.

George Steinbrenner. Commissioner Bowie Kuhn imposed a two-year suspension and $15,000 fine against the Yankees' managing general partner after Steinbrenner was convicted of making illegal campaign contributions to Richard Nixon in connection with Nixon's 1972 reelection campaign.

In 1990 Steinbrenner was "permanently" barred from baseball after it was proven that he paid $40,000 to known gambler Howard Spira, who allegedly had Mob connections. Steinbrenner paid Spira to obtain damaging information about Yankee outfielder Dave Winfield, with whom Steinbrenner had been feuding for some time. Spira was arrested in 1990 after attempting to extort money from Steinbrenner. He was convicted and served most of a 30-month sentence.

Steinbrenner originally was to receive a two-year suspension, but Steinbrenner feared that use of the word "suspension" might cause him to lose his position with the United States Olympic Committee. In further negotiations, Steinbrenner somehow managed to walk away with a more severe "permanent" bar as managing general partner of the Yankees. Nevertheless, in August 1992 Fay Vincent ruled that Steinbrenner would be reinstated at the start of the 1993 season.

Pete Rose. See *Gambling and Fixed Games*.

Marge Schott. See *Racism*.

Ed Barrow (1868–1953)

Hall of Fame (VC) 1953

"A nice guy, but one tough cookie." — Joe DiMaggio.

"He will storm and growl and curse, and he hopes you will understand the painful justification. Mr. Barrow used to be known as a very strong, truculent character. In recent years he has softened up more than somewhat, but we suspect he likes to play the old role at intervals just for the hell of it." — Sportswriter Joe Williams.

Barrow was the general manager of the Yankees in their glory years from the 1920s into the 1940s.

Edward Grant Barrow was a newspaperman in the 19th century, later hooking up with concessionaire Harry Stevens in a deal to supply the Pirates' ballpark with concessions near the end of the 1890s. He moved on to become a minor league general manager and president. He managed the Tigers in 1903–1904 before leaving baseball for a few years.

In 1910 he returned to the minor leagues and then managed the Red Sox during their strong years from 1918 through 1920. He signed with the Yankees as general manager in 1921, beginning a run of 25 years in that position. He also was club president beginning in 1939. During his tenure the club won 14 pennants and 10 World Series, including five sweeps. Barrow also was instrumental in developing the Yankee farm system. He was approached to be commissioner in the mid–1940s, but ill health forced him to decline the offer.

Book. Ed Barrow with James Kahn, *My Fifty Years in Baseball* (1951).

Base Ball Reporters Association of America (1887–1890)

"The time has come when the National game and the scorers and the base ball reporters of America look to each other for support and assistance. All sides now recognize that their interests are identical. The reporters have found in the game a thing of beauty and a source of actual employment. The game has found in the reporters its best ally and most powerful supporter. Hence the good feeling all along the line." — 1889 *Reach Guide*.

This was the short-lived 19th century predecessor to the **Baseball Writers Association of America**. Sportswriting pioneer Henry Chadwick spearheaded this first effort to form a baseball writers association.

On December 12, 1887, the Baseball Reporters Association was formed in Cincinnati, with Chadwick as vice-president. George Munson of *The Sporting News* was elected president and annual dues were set at $1. Business managers of certain teams (some of whom were also owners in those years) helped the writers organize.

In 1890 the Reporters Association officially sided with the one-year Players League. When the league collapsed, the Reporters Association followed it into extinction because the remaining Major League owners were displeased with the reporters and did their best to make life miserable for them.

Base on Balls

"Oh, those base on balls!" — 1914 Braves manager George Stallings explaining on his deathbed why his health had broken.

"What's the matter, didn't the bullpen have any home plates?" — Yankee third baseman Graig Nettles to reliever Goose Gossage, who once threw eight straight balls after he arrived on the mound.

"I'm working on a new pitch. It's called a strike." — Jim Kern after a series of wild outings.

"If I had my career to play over, one thing I'd do differently is swing more. Those 1,200 walks I got ... nobody remembers them." — Pee Wee Reese.

See also *Intentional Walks*.

Early Terminology. Balls originally were called "unfair balls."

Umpires Calling Balls. At its 1862 convention, the amateur National Association voted to have umpires call balls as well as strikes, but only to prevent delay.

Rules. In the National League's first season in 1876, nine balls were allowed. The umpire would announce every third ball as an "unfair pitch." After the third set of three, the batter was awarded first base. The number of balls needed for a base on balls was gradually reduced over 13 years:

1876	9
1880	8
1882	7
1884	6
1886	7
1887	5
1889	4

In 1887 a base on balls was scored as a hit, greatly inflating batting averages that season. After the season the Major Leagues adopted the current rule, whereby a base on balls is not charged as a time at-bat. The 1968 Joint Rules Committee nullified the short-lived 1887 rule that walks would be scored as hits and recalculated all records to eliminate this anomaly (see also *Statistics*).

Pitcher's Fielding Record. A base on balls was rare in the early years and was originally scored as an error as part of a pitcher's fielding record.

Official Statistic. In 1909 National League president John Heydler added base on balls as an official batting statistic.

Consecutive Innings/No Walks.
"The only pitcher I ever faced who had the control Mathewson had was Grover Cleveland Alexander when he was with the Phillies. Neither Mathewson or Alex ever let you have a ball in the spot where they knew you could hit."—Honus Wagner.

Christy Mathewson, noted for his amazing control, pitched 68 consecutive innings without giving up a walk in 1913. In 1976 Randy Jones of the Padres tied Mathewson's then-National League record of 68 consecutive innings without giving up a walk. He won 22 games that year to earn the Cy Young Award.

Mathewson's record streak was broken in 1962 by journeyman Bill Fischer of the A's. Fischer pitched 84⅓ consecutive innings without issuing a walk during an otherwise dismal 4–12 season.

In 1995 Greg Maddux of the Braves pitched 51 innings without giving up a base on balls. He ended the streak when he intentionally walked pitcher Joey Hamilton, a career .041 hitter. Maddux bettered the National League record in 2001 with 72⅓ innings without a walk before giving up an intentional pass.

Season and Career Walks/Pitcher. Grover Cleveland Alexander was also known for his extraordinary control, walking only 1.66 batters over nine innings during his career.

Babe Adams of the Pirates walked only 18 batters in 263 innings in 1920. Over his career, he walked only 430 batters in 2,995 innings, an average of 1.29 every nine innings.

In 1908 Christy Mathewson pitched 416 innings and walked only 42 batters. Over his career of 4,781 innings, he walked only 1.59 batters per nine innings.

More Walks Than Hits.
"I pitch like I'm sitting in an easy chair and he pitches like his hair is on fire."—Rick Sutcliffe on Mitch Williams.

"Mitch Williams has walked more people than a seeing-eye dog."—Sportswriter Frank Luksa.

When Mitch "Wild Thing" Williams was cut by the Angels in mid–1995, he finished as the only pitcher in Major League history with more than 250 innings pitched who gave up more walks than hits. After an unsuccessful comeback attempt, he surfaced at age 37 as the manager of the Atlantic City Surf of the Atlantic League. He had been serving as the club's pitching coach and pitched occasionally.

No Balls Called. Stan Coveleski supposedly once pitched seven innings using a spitter, fastball and curveball. Every pitch was either a strike, put into play by the batter, or fouled off. No balls were called.

Most/Career by Pitcher. Nolan Ryan is by far the career leader in walks with 2,795. He is the only 20th century pitcher to walk more than 200 batters in two different seasons, 1974 (202) and 1977 (204). He averaged 4.67 walks per nine innings over his career.

Start of Game. Roger Pavlik of the Rangers set the American League record when he walked the first four Toronto batters he faced on April 18, 1997. The Rangers lost, 6–5.

Most By Team/Game.
"Little League is the citadel of no-hit, 25–11 games. I think the record number of bases-on-balls was 108 in a doubleheader once. Of course these were second-line pitchers. Front-line pitchers rarely give up over 50 walks a game."—Jim Murray.

On April 30, 1944, the Dodger pitchers issued 17 walks to the Giants.

On May 24, 1995, the White Sox and Rangers split a double-header that featured 32 walks.

Season At Bats/No Walks. The record for most at-bats in a season without drawing a walk is 154, by pitcher Ed Walsh of the 1907 White Sox. Among position players, the record is held by Craig Robinson of the 1973 Phillies, with 146 at-bats.

No Control.
"Son, I think maybe we've had our workout for the day, don't you?"—Senators manager Bucky Harris to pitcher Ray Scarborough during a 1942 game after he walked the first seven Red Sox he faced. In his Major League debut one game earlier, Scarborough gave up seven runs in the 1st inning to the Yankees. He lasted until 1953 and won 80 games for five American League clubs.

On June 23, 1915 Bruno Haas of the A's walked 16 Yankees. He never again pitched in the Major Leagues after he retired the last batter of the game. Six years later he played halfback in the new National Football League.

Henry Mathewson, Christy's brother, walked 14 batters in 10 innings in his only Major League start, October 5, 1906, for the Giants against the Braves.

On August 28, 1909, Dolly Gray of the Senators walked seven consecutive batters for a total of eight in one inning.

On August 1, 1941, Lefty Grove of the Red Sox walked 11 batters in a 9–0 shutout of the Browns.

George Brunet of the A's gave up five bases loaded walks and hit another batter with the bases loaded during a one-hit, 11-run 7th inning by the White Sox on April 22, 1959. Three A's pitchers gave up 10 walks during the inning, eight with the bases loaded. The A's also made three errors in the inning. The final score was 20–6.

On April 27, 1994, Mariners pitcher Dave Fleming walked five straight Yankee batters with two outs and no one on base in the 3rd inning. Reliever Jeff Nelson came in and hit Bernie Williams with a 3–2 pitch before walking two more batters.

Most Received by Team/Season. The 1949 Red Sox drew 835 base on balls. The club's Major League record walk parade was led by Ted Williams with a league-leading 162.

Most Received by Hitter/Career. Babe Ruth was the lifetime leader with 2,056 (officially amended in June 1999 to 2,062) base on balls until Rickey Henderson broke his record in 2002 and finished in 2003 with 2,190. In July 2004 Barry Bonds received his 2,191st base on balls to pass Henderson. The next-highest active player at the time was Frank Thomas, who was 19th all-time at 1,449.

Ted Williams is a close fourth with 2,019 in almost 300 fewer games. Ruth led the league in base on balls 11 times and Williams led eight times. Henderson led only four times. Barry Bonds led the league in walks 10 times in 13 seasons between 1992 and 2004.

Most Received by Hitter/Season. Babe Ruth walked 170 times in 1923 for the American League record. Mark McGwire walked 162 times in 1998 to break the National League record temporarily. Barry Bonds topped McGwire and Ruth with 177 walks in 2001, then 198 in 2002, and a whopping 232 in 2004. Next on the list that year were three players tied at 127, including Todd Helton.

Most Received by Hitter/Game. Jimmie Foxx received six base on balls on June 16, 1938, while playing for the Red Sox against the Browns. The Red Sox won 12–8. He tied a record set by Walt Wilmont of the Chicago White Stockings on August 22, 1891.

On August 20, 1999, Jeff Bagwell walked six times. The Astros lost 6–4 in 16 innings, despite holding a 4–0 lead. The Astros struck out 17 times and left 20 runners on base.

Most/World Series. Babe Ruth walked 11 times during the 1926 World Series, a record broken by Barry Bonds in 2002, when he was walked 13 times by Angels pitchers. Mickey Mantle holds the career World Series record with 43.

Most Consecutive/Hitter. In 1992 Jose Canseco became the fourth player to walk in seven consecutive at-bats over multiple games, joining Billy Rogell (1938 Tigers), Mel Ott (1943 Giants) and Eddie Stanky (1950 Giants).

Consecutive Games. In September 2002, Barry Bonds walked in his 16th straight game to tie the National League record set by Jack Clark in 1987. Bonds set a new record of 20 a few games later. Roy Cullenbine of the Tigers walked in 22 straight games in 1947.

Fast Career Start. Roy Thomas had at least 100 base on balls in each of his first six seasons beginning in 1899. Frank Thomas of the White Sox had over 100 base on balls in each of his first full eight seasons beginning in 1991.

Ball Five. On May 5, 1978, Tug McGraw threw ball four to Lenny Randle of the Mets, but Randle did not realize it was ball four and stepped back into the batter's box. Umpire John Kibler thought that he had made the mistake, so he changed his indicator to reflect a full count. The scoreboard operator thought he had made the mistake, so he also left the count at 3–2. Only McGraw and the Phillies knew of the error and they kept silent. Randle tripled on the next pitch, but McGraw stranded him at third base.

Reward. Twins catcher A.J. Pierzynski received $5 from his mother every time he walked. In 2002 he received $75 for 15 walks in 472 regular- and postseason at-bats.

Base Running

"The runners have returned to their respectable bases."— Broadcaster Dizzy Dean.

"Base running is an art and a skill … if I'm on second, one ball on the batter, I'm going to try and get a big lead to distract the pitcher. My job is to help get ball two. Now the pitcher's got to throw a strike. Batter knows that. I know that. He's in a position to get good wood on the ball. He gets a single, I score. That's good base running."— Dick Allen in *Crash* (1989).

"I tell my fellers that there ain't no barbed wire entanglements or elephant traps on them base paths. They're as smooth as a billiard table. My fellers don't have to watch where they're placin' their feet. They should keep an eye on the ball."— Casey Stengel as related by sportswriter Arthur Daley.

See also **Home Run Trot** and **Interference**.

Rules. Base runners must touch all bases and retrace their steps if they do not, with two exceptions: on a home run, the batter must start over if he misses a base; a runner cannot retrace his steps if a runner behind him has scored or passed him on the base paths.

Until 1870 batters running to first base were not allowed to overrun the bag.

Home to First.

"Run the fucking ball out, you piece of shit."— Catcher Carlton Fisk to batter Deion Sanders, after Sanders ran about 20 feet while watching his infield pop-up.

It takes a right-handed batter about 4.3 seconds to get to first base; a left-hander takes about 4.1 or 4.2 seconds.

Fred Merkle's "Boner."

"McCormick trots home, the merry villagers flock on the field to worship the hollow where the Mathewson feet have pressed, and all of a sudden there is doings at second base."— The *New York Times* on September 24, 1908, referring to the apparent 9th inning Giants victory over the Cubs the day before in the heat of the pennant race with only a few games to play. Christy Mathewson was the apparent winning pitcher that day and the "doings" at second base became infamous.

Fred Merkle of the Giants failed to touch second base at the end of a crucial late season game against the Cubs at the Polo Grounds. He was a 19-year-old rookie playing his first full game for the Giants, starting in place of the injured Fred Toney. It was the first game Toney missed that season. One of the most scrutinized events in baseball history became known forever after as "Merkle's Boner."

In the bottom of the 9th inning with the score tied, Harry "Moose" McCormick of the Giants was on first base with two out. Merkle singled and McCormick took third. Merkle could have stretched it into a double, but did not want to take a chance on making the last out in a tie game. Al Bridwell then hit an apparent game-winning single, scoring McCormick from third. Because fans immediately ran on the field to celebrate, Merkle did what was not uncommon in that era: as he ran from first and McCormick was scoring the winning run on the hit, Merkle veered off from second base to avoid the crowd and headed for the clubhouse in center field.

Cubs infielder Johnny Evers saw that Merkle had not touched second to cancel the force play and yelled for the ball. Center fielder "Circus" Solly Hoffman, always the jokester, allegedly threw a curveball to Evers and overthrew him. Other sources reported that Giants pitcher Joe McGinnity (who was coaching third base) saw what was happening, intercepted the ball and threw it into the stands. Evers tracked down the ball (although possibly not the original ball), stepped on second and appealed to field umpire Howard Emslie. Emslie apparently did not see it (earning the nickname "Blind Bob" from manager John McGraw), but home plate umpire Hank O'Day did, and called Merkle out. Rule 59 governs the play: "One run shall be scored every time a baserunner, after having legally touched the first three bases, shall legally touch the home base before three men are put out; provided, however, that if he reach home on or during a play *in which the third man be forced out* or put out before reaching first base, a run shall not count. A force-out can be made only when a baserunner legally loses the right to the base he occupies and is thereby obliged to advance as the result of a fair hit ball not caught on the fly."

One account has it that Merkle swore he went back and touched second base when he saw what was happening. The same source reported that umpire Emslie was not paying attention because he had ducked down to avoid the line drive and was "adjusting his toupee."

Another version has it that Hoffman's throw from center field rolled onto the infield, where McGinnity, Evers and Cubs shortstop Joe Tinker wrestled for the ball. McGinnity grabbed it and threw it into the stands, where it was caught by a man wearing a bowler hat. Cubs third baseman Harry Steinfeldt and pitcher Floyd

"Rube" Kroh begged the fan for the ball, but he refused. Kroh then pulled the bowler over the man's eyes and grabbed the ball, tossing it to Tinker, who relayed it to Evers. Cubs manager Frank Chance then tracked down umpire O'Day (some say biting him to get him to come along), who saw Evers on second base holding the ball and called Merkle out.

Mathewson supposedly saw what was happening and ran to Merkle to push him back toward second base. Mathewson later claimed that Merkle touched the bag as the throw from Hemus came in high. Sportswriter Joe Vila wrote that Mathewson got to Merkle, but that he was too late. Vila also confirmed that McGinnity threw the ball into the stands and that a ball arrived back onto the field from the vicinity of the stands, but it was unclear whether it was the original ball. There was a race to the bag with a ball as police ran onto the field.

Sportswriter Fred Lieb reported that McGinnity told him that Evers never touched second base with the original ball. Rube Kroh, who was on the bench for the Cubs, supposedly threw in another ball from the dugout.

In a biography of her husband, Mrs. John (Blanche) McGraw reported that he saw Kroh pick up the ball first, but that McGinnity grabbed it from him and threw it into the right field stands.

In a 1943 account by Evers, he reported that he and Tinker raced for the ball after it was thrown in over their heads. McGinnity reached it and Tinker and Evers wrestled with him, but McGinnity threw it into the stands. A fan caught it, but Kroh and Harry Steinfeldt raced over to retrieve it. The fan would not give it up, so one of the players hit him on the head and the ball fell loose. Kroh picked it up and threw to Tinker, who threw to Evers, who stepped on the bag while O'Day watched. O'Day then immediately said, "the run does not count."

Still another account from humorist Ed Ford has it that Kroh was the pitcher tabbed to guard the bag holding the club's valuables (no safes for the club in those days). Instead of throwing in a new ball, Kroh ran to the fan and asked for the ball. When the fan refused, Kroh wrestled him to the ground and retrieved the ball for Evers. In the melee Kroh lost the sack of valuables with approximately $5,200 in cash and jewelry.

After the play ended, umpire Hank O'Day could have resumed play because there was enough sunlight available. Because of the riot atmosphere he called the game a tie due to darkness. O'Day was also involved in a critical **Foul Ball** call that prevented the Pirates from ending the season in a three-way tie with the Cubs and Giants.

O'Day had been sensitized to the force play issue because the identical problem occurred on September 4, also involving Cubs second baseman Evers. In a scoreless game in the 10th inning, Pittsburgh's Owen Wilson singled to drive in the winning run. Rookie Warren Gill was running from first base and, like Merkle, failed to touch second base as the game-ending run scored. Evers tried the same force play then, but O'Day claimed he did not see it, and either vowed to call it an out the next time or would "watch for it" in the future. Evers filed a protest over that 1–0 loss, but National League president Harry Pulliam denied it on the following grounds: "The question of whether there was a force play ... rests solely with the umpire. The umpire in this case, by allowing the winning run, ruled that there was no force at second, because if there had been the run could not have been scored."

After the Merkle game, Pulliam again supported his umpire and ruled that a doubleheader would be played the next day. Cubs owner Charles Murphy immediately filed a protest, claiming that the Giants had forfeited the game because they had not cleared the field of fans after the incident. The automatic five-day review period delayed the replay, and when it was clear that the doubleheader would not be played, Murphy supposedly withdrew the protest. To support the forfeit claim, Cubs manager Frank Chance had his players take the field the next day and make a phantom first pitch with no Giants batter on the field.

Pulliam supported his umpire's ruling despite terrible pressure in New York. The league's board of directors upheld Pulliam after hearing two days and one night of testimony, ruling that the Giants would have won but for Merkle's mistake. Pulliam then ruled that a make-up game would be played at the end of the season, if necessary. It was.

At the end of the regular season the Giants and Cubs were tied at 98–55 and a replay of the game was held on October 8, 1908. Christy Mathewson pitched for the Giants and lost 4–2 to Mordecai "Three Finger" Brown. Umpire Bill Klem was offered a bribe before the game (see also **Gambling and Fixed Games**). Mathewson's arm was throbbing, but he managed to get through the game. Joe Tinker hit the decisive blow, a triple over the head of Cy Seymour, after Mathewson had asked Seymour to play deeper.

Merkle was remembered for causing his team to lose the pennant, but many forget that the team lost five other games after his mistake, including the October 8 replay to determine the pennant winner. He lost 15 pounds brooding about the loss through the end of the season and endured an off-season of ridicule in the press and in vaudeville:

"Inexcusable stupidity." — *Sporting Life*.

"Minor league brains lost the Giants' game today after they had it fairly and cleanly won by a score of 2 to 1. In the ninth round, Merkle did a bone-head running stunt...." — *Chicago Tribune* sportswriter Charles Dryden.

"I call my name Merkle, because it has a bone head." — A vaudeville line.

Merkle stayed with the Giants until 1916 when, ironically, he was traded to the Cubs. In another bit of irony, he drove in the go-ahead run in the 9th inning for the Giants in the 1912 World Series game in which teammate Fred Snodgrass was immortalized for an **Error** in the bottom of the inning that purportedly cost the Giants the Series.

Merkle finished his 16-year career in 1926 with a .273 batting average. Merkle was bitter about the incident for the rest of his life, refusing interviews in his later years to avoid discussing it. After he retired he did not appear publicly again until 1950 when he showed up for a Giants Oldtimers Game.

When Merkle died in 1956 the New York papers highlighted the mistake in their headlines and text. A sample from the *New York Times*: "Fred Merkle, former Major League Baseball player who was best remembered for a 'boner' that cost the New York Giants the pennant in 1908, died today."

Heinie Zimmerman.

"Fate has set apart a 'goat' in every world's series. Zimmerman became the burden bearer in the 1917 title clash, but undeservedly so. Critics, after a second sober thought, could devise no strategy which would have relieved Heinie of the responsibility which had been thrust upon him by others." — G.W. Axelson in "*Commy*" (1919), referring to Giants third baseman Heinie Zimmerman's futile attempt to catch White Sox runner Eddie Collins dashing home with the winning run in Game 6 of the 1917 Series. It was not Zimmerman's fault, as catcher Bill Rariden abandoned home plate during a rundown and Zimmerman had no one to throw to.

George "Highpockets" Kelly. On June 14, 1924, Kelly became the first player in the 20th century to hit three home runs in a game twice in his career. The third home run in the second attempt was controversial. It was a game winner, and the crowd ran on the field to embrace him. As was sometimes the case, Kelly abandoned his trot around the bases at second and headed for the Polo Grounds clubhouse despite a warning from umpire Ernie Quigley. After an inquiry, National League president John Heydler allowed the home run, but admonished Kelly and indicated that such acts would be closely scrutinized in the future and the rules clarified to require all bases to be touched.

Dodger Daffiness.

"The Headless Horseman of Ebbets Field." — Pitcher Dazzy Vance's description of Babe Herman, after Herman's errant base running led to three Dodger runners on third base, resulting in a famous double play. This was one of the incidents in the 1920s that led to the inept Dodgers being dubbed "The Daffiness Boys."

On August 15, 1926, Herman was batting with the bases loaded against pitcher George Mogridge of the Braves. Hermann slammed a ball off the right field wall and Hank DeBerry scored. Dazzy Vance, running from second, was caught between third and home in a rundown and retreated to third base. Chuck Fewster, running from first base, slowed up between second and third because of Vance's predicament. Herman, running all out, passed Fewster and ran into third base. Herman was out for passing Fewster; Fewster was out for ending up on third with Vance because Vance was entitled to the bag.

The regular Dodger coach for many years was Otto Miller, and he has often been wrongly accused of orchestrating the mess at third base. However, he had been replaced earlier in the game by Mickey O'Neill at Miller's request.

Enos Slaughter. Red Sox shortstop Johnny Pesky is considered the goat of the 1946 World Series. During Game 7 he purportedly held the ball as Enos Slaughter of the Cardinals ran from first base to score the go-ahead run on a single by Harry Walker. Slaughter supposedly ran through a stop sign by the third base coach. Walker's hit has widely been reported as a single, but he officially was credited with a double.

Slaughter had been hit in the arm by a pitch in Game 5 and it was hemorrhaging badly, though he was unaware that he had broken his elbow. He was told by the doctors that he was through for the Series. Some sources contend that he was warned that it might have to be amputated if it got any worse from the internal bleeding.

Slaughter may well have been thrown out at the plate (or not even tried to score) had there not been a key injury an inning earlier. The Red Sox tied the score in the 7th inning, but center fielder Dom DiMaggio, one of the league's premier fielders, tore a calf muscle running the bases during the inning (some sources report that he sprained an ankle). He was replaced in center field by Leon Culberson, who had a much weaker arm. Slaughter presumably had this in mind when he took off from first base.

Shortstop Johnny Pesky took the relay throw from Culberson, but purportedly hesitated as he turned toward the plate with the ball. His throw was wide and up the line and far too late to get Slaughter. Though many newspapers reported that Pesky hesitated before throwing, film clips of the incident (which Pesky has seen "hundreds of times") clearly show that he took the throw, turned and threw all in one motion.

Another incident also may have inspired Slaughter. In the 4th inning of Game 1 of the Series, coach Mike Gonzalez held Slaughter at third on a possible inside-the-park home run. Slaughter was stranded and Boston went on to win 3–2. Slaughter apparently was not about to let it happen again, but Gonzalez swore that he was waving him home in Game 7: "Hell no, Gonzalez insisted later.

With the bottom of the batting order up next, he was down the line waving his arms like a windmill, urging Slaughter to keep going: 'I say, "Go on, go on!" and he go.'" — Gonzalez as quoted by John B. Holway in his essay, "The Myth of Pesky's Throw," in *The Ol' Ball Game* (1990). Holway's account is a thorough analysis of the various newspaper reports made of each aspect of the play, including the coaching, throwing and base running. Red Smith's account is perhaps the most eloquently incorrect: "[Pesky] stood morosely studying Ford Frick's signature on the ball.... At length, he turned dreamily, gave a small start of astonishment ... and threw in sudden panic."

The event was re-created 25 years later with many of the original players at a 1971 Cardinals Oldtimers Game.

Henry Aaron. Aaron was involved in a base running mistake at the end of Harvey Haddix's lost **Perfect Game** attempt when he thought teammate Joe Adcock's home run had not cleared the fence.

Lou Brock. Brock was the top **Stolen Base** leader of his era, but his base running error may have cost the Cardinals the 1968 World Series. He made a crucial mistake in Game 5 that may have turned the tide to the Tigers, who trailed 3–1 in the Series. In the 5th inning the Cardinals were leading 3–2. Brock tried to score from second on a single to left, but he failed to slide. As he tried to score standing up, Brock's foot hit Detroit catcher Bill Freehan's foot as Freehan tagged him and Brock was called out. The Tigers later scored three runs for a 5–3 victory and won the last two games for the Series title.

Mike Schmidt. Schmidt once scored from first base on a wild pitch. The ball hit the backstop and caromed toward the dugout. As the ball rolled along the dugout toward third base, the catcher chased it and left home plate unoccupied, allowing Schmidt to score.

Chris Chambliss. In the 1976 American League Championship Game, Yankees first baseman Chris Chambliss hit a game- and series-ending home run, but never touched most of the bases. Donald Honig described what happened in his book, *Baseball America:* "Chambliss never completed his circle of the bases. By the time he reached first base, he was mobbed, by the time he fought his way to second, the bag was already gone, and reportedly he reached out and touched it, whereupon he gave up and broke for the safety of the dugout."

Lonnie Smith. In Game 7 of the 1991 World Series the Braves lost to the Twins 1–0 in 10 innings. Bad base running by Braves outfielder Lonnie Smith in the 8th inning prevented his club from taking the lead. He led off with a single and was given the steal sign. He decided to wait and do a delayed steal because he was not sure he could pull off a straight steal. Batter Terry Pendleton thought Smith would be running and swung away, driving a ball to the left-center field gap. The ball went between the outfielders and caromed off the wall to the ground. Twins second baseman Chuck Knoblauch decoyed Smith by faking a play on a ground ball, but contrary to newspaper reports and the broadcasters' analysis during the play, Smith did not buy the fake. He knew the ball had been hit to the outfield in the direction of Kirby Puckett, but he did not know where. He had to slow up to see if the ball would drop and could only make third base.

Smith was severely criticized for his base running and received hate mail after the Series. What is often overlooked is that the Braves had men on second and third with no outs and could not score. Ron Gant hit a hard grounder to the drawn-in first baseman for the first out. After an intentional walk to David Justice, the extremely slow Sid Bream grounded into a double play.

Orioles Daffiness. On April 17, 1993, the Orioles had the bases loaded when Mike Devereaux hit a line drive that was trapped by Angel center fielder Chad Curtis. The three runners were Jeff Tackett on third base, Brady Anderson on second and Chito Martinez on first. All managed to end up on third as Tackett thought the ball had been caught and stayed put. Angels catcher John Horton tagged all three, ending the inning with a double play. The play prompted Angels third baseman Rene Gonzales to comment: "It wouldn't have been the stupidest play until Chito arrived at third. I think he thought there was a fight, so he ran across the field to get in it."

Somersaults. Carl Sawyer of the 1915–1916 Senators, who once rigged a bat to explode when it hit a ball, was called out on the bases for an acrobatic somersault over the third baseman. The umpire's reason: he was out of the base path.

Nickname. Steve Lyons earned the nickname Psycho in part because of his base running. As recounted in Jay Johnstone's, *Some of My Best Friends Are Crazy*, with Rick Talley (1990), Lyons' most memorable base running occurred in a 1985 game for the Red Sox.

With the Red Sox down 1–0 to the Rangers in the 10th inning, Lyons singled and moved to second on a wild pick-off throw. Marty Barrett then hit a soft liner to right field. Lyons ran hard all the way to third before deciding to return to second, thinking the ball might be caught. Barrett was by then barreling into second and they slid in at the same time. Lyons got up and ran back to third and right fielder George Wright threw the ball between the third baseman's legs, through the pitcher backing up, and into the dugout. Both runners scored and the Red Sox won 2–1.

Too Excited. In 1961 Gary Geiger of the home team Red Sox hit an 11th-inning triple that drove in the tying run against the Angels. Thinking he had instead won the game, Geiger ran straight across the third base bag into the dugout, where he was tagged out. Carl Yastrzemski then hit what would have been a game-winning sacrifice fly. The game ended at 1:15 a.m. in a curfew-mandated tie.

Home Run Trot. When Mark McGwire hit his 62nd home run in 1998 to break the season record held by Roger Maris, McGwire was so caught up in the moment that he missed first base as he rounded the bag. He had to return to touch it, led back by first base coach Dave McKay.

Rundowns.

"You stay in it for as long as you can until something happens. Then you look for someone to run into." — Mark Belanger on how to beat a rundown.

"Career highlights? I had two. I got an intentional walk from Sandy Koufax and I got out of a rundown against the Mets." — Bob Uecker.

"In all baseball, there's hardly a moment more exciting than when the runner leaps from Third, hustling into the irretrievable danger. Many a swift young man has been trapped there between those archons, the squat Catcher in his devil-mask, and the swifter Third Baseman like lithe graceful Death running him down!" — Robert Kelly in "A Pastoral Dialogue in the Game of the Quadrature" (1966).

The umpires goofed in the 6th inning of a game between the Royals and Yankees on May 9, 1997. Jeff King of the Royals was caught in a rundown between third and home, but umpire Dale Ford called him out before he was tagged. Ford thought that King had passed the preceding baserunner, Jose Offerman, but Offerman had already been forced at third base. Royals manager Bob Boone successfully argued that King should be able to return to third base and the other Royals runner (the original batter on the play) was allowed to stay at second base. The next batter, Chili Davis, lined a two-run single to tie the score and the Royals won 7–5 in 12

innings. The Yankees appealed to the league office, but president Gene Budig dismissed the appeal, arguing that King might have escaped the rundown and should have been allowed to return to third.

Broadcaster Vin Scully recalled on the air a game in which all nine Houston Astros players on the field touched the ball during a rundown play involving the Dodgers.

On September 16, 2004, the Brewers defense had a wild rundown that involved every base, and included two assists by right-fielder Brady Clark. Scoring on the play: 5-2-9-4-9-1-6, described as the "Powerball" rundown by coach Rich Donnelly.

Missed Bases. After **Fred Merkle's "Boner"** for the 1908 Giants, the second most memorable failure to touch a base may have been on an apparent triple hit by immortal Mets first baseman Marv Throneberry on June 17, 1962, against the Cubs at the Polo Grounds. Cubs first baseman Ernie Banks noticed that Throneberry missed first base, and he was called out on an appeal. Mets center fielder Richie Ashburn acknowledged that the entire team could see that Throneberry had not come close to first base; all except manager Casey Stengel. He dashed out onto the field, but was intercepted by second base umpire Dusty Boggess, who told Stengel that Throneberry had also missed second base. Stengel's immortal reply: "Well, I know he touched third, because he's standing on it."

Note that Throneberry's initials were M.E.T. (middle name Eugene).

Running Inside the Base Paths. The three-foot baseline designation on the first base foul line was created in 1882 to require runners to stay within that line when running to first base. Rule 6.05(k) covers batter-runner interference in the last half of the distance from home base to first base. Although it is agreed that a batter-runner who is running outside the 45-foot long three-foot wide box is called out for interference when struck by a thrown ball, the batter-runner does not have to be hit by a thrown ball to be charged with interference.

On May 29, 1882, umpire James L. Hickey called out Cleveland outfielder John Richmond for running inside the three-foot line while jogging to first on a base on balls.

One of the more controversial base running incidents in World Series history occurred in Game 4 of the 1969 Series between the Mets and Orioles. In the bottom of the 10th inning Mets catcher J.C. Martin bunted to Orioles pitcher Pete Richert, whose throw to first struck Martin on the wrist and ricocheted into short right field. That allowed pinch runner Rod Gaspar to score the winning run from second. Orioles manager Earl Weaver formally protested (he had already been ejected) because the television replay confirmed that Martin was not running in the three-foot strip. Umpire Shag Crawford's decision was upheld because it was an on-field judgment call within the umpire's discretion. The Mets won the game and took a 3–1 Series lead.

Another such call occurred during the 1988 World Series between the Dodgers and A's. Oakland's Dave Parker was batting in the 4th inning with Jose Canseco on first base. Parker hit a roller to Dodger pitcher Tim Leary, who tossed wildly past first baseman Franklin Stubbs. Parker was called out for batter interference even though he was never struck by the ball. Parker's illegal position while running the last half distance between home and first may have confused Leary when he made the throw.

Virgin Territory. Pitcher Jerry Koosman was 0-for-44 as a batter at the start of his career. He then doubled for his first Major League hit, but was called out for missing first base.

Bold Running. On September 3, 1983, White Sox infielder

Jerry Dybzinski batted with one out and runners on first and second. On an 0–2 pitch, Dybzinski bunted at the ball, which hit him. The first base umpire called Dybzinski out (apparently for the third strike bunt attempt) as the batter jogged to first base on the apparent hit-by-pitch. While they argued the call, both runners advanced one base. After play resumed, both runners were allowed to stay at their new bases. This was an incorrect call, as Rule 6.08(b) provides that "when a batter is touched by a pitched ball which does not entitle him to first base, the ball is dead and no runner may advance." The umpire's later admitted they blew the call, but it was not protested.

Running Bases in Reverse Order.

"He did everything — except steal first base. And I think he did that in the dead of night." — Rube Bressler on Ty Cobb.

On September 4, 1908, the Tigers and Indians were tied in the 9th inning. Germany Schaefer of the Tigers was on first base and Davy Jones was on third. Schaefer signaled Jones for a double steal and ran to second. The Indians catcher did not throw and Jones held at third. On the next pitch, Schaefer, known to be a comedian at times, ran back to first. He went to second on the next pitch and catcher Nig Clarke threw the ball away and Jones scored the winning run from third. Some sources report that Schaefer tried the stunt as late as 1911, but was unsuccessful.

Apparently Harry Davis was successful with the ploy in 1902 for the A's.

It was also done on May 7, 1906, by Mickey Doolan, who was trying to force a throw so that the runner on third, Sherry Magee, could score. He ran back twice, but drew no throw. The batter eventually walked, loading the bases, and frustrated pitcher Ed Pfeffer hit the next batter, forcing in the run.

A batter now is not allowed to run the bases in reverse order.

Johnny Vrain was a 19-year-old pitcher with the Cubs in 1902. He appeared in 12 games as a pitcher who threw left-handed and batted right-handed. In his first few games he never once put the ball into play as a hitter. His manager then forced him to bat left-handed, his natural side. He then grounded to Honus Wagner at shortstop, and purportedly ran to *third base*. He finished his abbreviated career with an .097 batting average.

Baseball

"This is a simple game. You throw the ball. You hit the ball. You catch the ball." — The manager in *Bull Durham*.

"There is no game now in vogue of which is more simple than that of base ball, and hence its attraction for the masses.... And yet to excel in the game as a noted expert requires not only the possession of the physical attributes of endurance, agility, strength, good throwing and running and power, together with plenty of courage, luck and nerve; but also the mental powers of sound judgment, quick perception, thorough control of temper and the presence of mind to act promptly in critical emergencies." — Henry Chadwick in 1876.

"I see great things in baseball. It's our game — the American game. It will take our people out-of-doors, fill them with oxygen, give them a larger physical stoicism. Tend to relieve us from being a nervous dyspeptic set. Anything that will repair such losses may be regarded as a blessing to the race." — Walt Whitman in 1888.

"Whoever wants to know the heart and mind of America had better learn baseball, the rules and realities of the game — and do it by watching first some high school or small-town teams." — Jacques Barzun, in his book, *God's Country and Mine: A Declaration of Love Spiced with a Few Harsh Words* (1954). Eliot Asinof,

author of *Eight Men Out*, once asked Barzun what he meant by the quote, and Barzum said he didn't know exactly what he had meant. Paul Dickson believes that Barzun's sentence is "the most re-quoted line on the game in the era since World War II." Criticism of *Bartlett's Quotations'* failure to go beyond the shopworn Barzun quote: "The boys of summer have had their innings. Now it's the season for carping. Your chief complaint this fall may be that the World Series is over, or that your team wasn't in it. Not mine. From my bleacher seat, possibly out in left field, I see leaves turning, some to be read and savored, others to be raked and burned, and too few of the best pressed into books. What rankles me most is that America's oldest and best known compendium of notable remarks persists in printing just one sentence from Jacques Barzun." — John E. Adams in "Keywords: Baseball, Bartlett's, & Barzun" (Adams' favorite author).

"A boy's game, with no more possibilities in it than a boy could master, a game bounded by walls which kept out novelty or danger, change or adventure." — F. Scott Fitzgerald.

"Baseball is like a language in several ways. We draw meaning from its events and records. If you say one guy is a .300 hitter, it means something. If you say another guy can't hit his weight, that means something too. Statistics, as Bill James has shown to the world, mean different things in different places and times." — Jim Allen, reporter for the *Daily Yomiuri* in Japan, who maintains a webpage on Japanese baseball.

"The crowded ground floor of the House of Baseball housed a bewildering assortment of amateurs and quasi amateurs, including collegians, town team players, industrial players, semipros, soldiers and sailors, and softballers. In the basement reside Indians and prisoners. An annex lodged women players. In an outbuilding almost hidden from view were squeezed black players, segregated by the occupants of the big house except when it was advantageous for them to have dealings with the outcasts. The upper floor of the House of Baseball came to serve professional teams and leagues in a form eventually known as Organized Baseball." — Harold Seymour in *Baseball: The People's Game* (1990).

"I have seen 344 home runs, four triple plays and two no-hit games. Baseball has been one of the greatest pleasures of my life. I have seen 906 speaking plays, 1,050 movies, and I have attended 4,510 church services and read 2,000 books; but I think I have gotten the most good out of my 1,134 ball games." — Frederick S. Tyler.

"Baseball, it is said, is only a game. True. And the Grand Canyon is only a hole in Arizona." — George F. Will, in *Men at Work: The Craft of Baseball* (1990).

"Baseball is one of the symbols of those things constant in American Life. Not even the toxic intrusion of artificial grass and megabuck contracts can spoil the naïveté and optimism that is baseball. Millions of Americans look to it for a nonviolent escape from the weariness that exists in the world beyond the centerfield wall. Baseball is constant and no matter how bad things get there is always next year. As Emily Dickinson put it, 'a little madness in the spring is wholesome even for a king.'" — *New York Times* editorial on June 5, 1984.

"THE GAME IS PERFECT. IT'S THE PEOPLE WHO SCREW IT UP." — Sign at Yankee Stadium just before the 1994 player strike.

"Baseball is the only thing beside the paper clip that hasn't changed." — Bill Veeck.

"The charm of baseball is that, dull as it may be on the field, it is endlessly fascinating as a rehash." — Jim Murray.

"The great thing about baseball is that there's a crisis every game." — General manager Gabe Paul.

"No game in the world is as tidy and dramatically neat as baseball, with cause and effect, crime and punishment, motive and result, so cleanly defined." — Paul Gallico.

"The American civilization will be remembered for three things 2,000 years from now: the Constitution, jazz music and baseball." — Gerald Early, director of the African and Afro-American Studies Department at Washington University in St. Louis.

"Baseball, almost alone among our sports, traffics unashamedly and gloriously in nostalgia, for only baseball understands time and treats it with respect. The history of other sports seems to begin anew with each generation, but baseball, that wondrous myth of twentieth century America, gets passed on like an inheritance." — Stanley Cohen.

"The game is played with a round bat and a round ball, the players run around the bases, and what goes around comes around." — Blue Jays rookie Frank Wills when called up in 1989.

"All winter long, I can't wait for baseball. It gets you back to doing the stuff you love and makes you wish the youthfulness of your life could stay with you forever." — Pitcher Tommy John in 1988.

"Baseball is a game where a curve is an optical illusion, a screwball can be a pitch or a person, stealing is legal, and you can spit anywhere you like except in the umpire's eye or on the ball." — Jim Murray.

See also *Balls*, *Historians*, *National Pastime* and *Origins of Baseball*.

"Base Ball" v. "Baseball."

"One spring morning in 1875, when baseball still was written as two words and newspapers were clucking over scandals in the Grant administration and releasing lurid details from Reverend Henry Ward Beecher's adultery trial..." — Darryl Brock in *The National Pastime* (1994).

The phrases "base ball" or "Base Ball" were the original spellings used in print until the 1920s. The earliest written reference to "base ball" was in a letter in the *National Advocate* newspaper in New York City on April 25, 1823. There is no evidence to show why the change was made, but gradually through that decade the spelling "baseball" (with no space) came to dominate. Some of the official baseball guides held out for the original spelling into the 1940s, when virtually all publications had switched to "baseball."

Effect on Other Sports.

"It is my thesis that baseball is a pioneer sports form which came to be widely imitated. In time other American team sports like football, hockey, and basketball imitated baseball's structural pattern in order to compete as commercialized spectacles." — David Quentin Voigt in *American Baseball* (1966).

Books. See *Books* — Best General Books.

Baseball Annies See *Sex*

Baseball Assistance Team (1986–)

"B.A.T. recognizes that the lives of our heroes continue after their active careers end. For some, particularly those who played before the days of escalating salaries and generous pension plans, events and circumstances can become difficult and trying when the cheering ends." — MLB.com.

Known as B.A.T., the organization raises money for indigent and needy retired ballplayers and others associated with the game. Joe Garagiola was instrumental in forming the organization and helped lead it for many years. By the 1990s BAT was raising more than $500,000 annually.

The group annually holds a dinner to honor its own, and presents the Bart Giamatti Award to the member of the "baseball family" who best exemplifies the humanitarian spirit and compassion of Giamatti. Roger Clemens was the 2004 honoree.

Baseball Camps See *Fantasy Camps* (for adults) and *Instructional Camps* (for kids)

Baseball Cards

"It wasn't that long ago that the buying of baseball cards reflected, believe it or not, a love of baseball. Those were innocent times. Now, collecting baseball cards reflects a love of something green, all right, but it has nothing to do with Astroturf." — Michael K. Evans in *GQ* magazine.

"They were beautiful and reassuring to behold, brand new and glistening crisply in their packages ... stuck behind glassed partitions and stacked on counters. An indication that the world was still in order, a promise of pleasant days and easeful nights." — Brendan

An oversized Topps 1964 baseball card featuring Sandy Koufax.

C. Boyd and Fred C. Harris in *The Great American Baseball Card Flipping, Trading and Bubble-Gum Book* (1973).

"But one evening my father came home from New York with the ultimate birthday present — a box of one hundred baseball cards. I unwrapped them with high expectations, only to find that twenty-eight of them were Horace Fords. Ford had departed from the majors in 1933 after a long and undistinguished career as an infielder in the National League, and the gum company apparently was trying urgently to reduce its inventory." — Frank Graham, Jr., in *Farewell to Heroes* (1981).

19th Century. The earliest commercially produced baseball cards in quantity were made in the 1880s as part of cigarette packages. Machine-made cigarettes were a new phenomenon at the time and for many years considered effeminate (see also *Tobacco*). Manufacturers tried to boost sales to men by including pictures of famous ballplayers on stiff cardboard.

The most prominent cards were the Old Judge cigarette cards produced by Goodwin & Company in New York, produced from 1887 through 1890. The series included 500 different players from various Major and minor leagues. The posed shots featured players swinging at balls on a string. Other companies marketed cards in the 1890s, but nothing as comprehensive as the Old Judge series.

1900–1945. Cards again were popular around 1910, when the American Tobacco Company issued its "White Bordered Set" of 400 players. This is the set that included today's **Most Valuable Card**, featuring Honus Wagner. Candy companies and sports magazines also produced cards as promotional items. The Zeenut Candy Company once had the longest continuous series of baseball cards (1911–1939). Cracker Jack began a short-lived series of cards prior to 1920.

Early 20th century card production tapered off until after World War I ended in 1918. A few series were issued in the 1920s, but cards were not especially popular until the 1930s. The primary card manufacturer was the Gouday Gum Company, which first produced a 240-card set in 1933. Gouday's last production year was 1941, and baseball cards all but disappeared during World War II because of the serious shortage of paper and rubber.

1945– . The modern era of cards was ushered in by the Bowman Gum Company in 1948 and Topps Gum Company in 1950. In 1948 the Leaf Company of Chicago issued a set of colorized picture cards with bubble gum and Red Man Tobacco issued a set from 1952 until 1955. Bowman's first issue contained 48 cards in black and white along with a slab of gum in each penny pack. Full color cards were first issued in 1950. Bowman's popularity peaked in 1951 and Topps' first big year was 1952.

Topps was founded in 1938 by four brothers, Abram, Ira, Joe and Phil Shorin. The last of them, Abram, died at age 91 in 1990. Joe's son Arthur ran the company into the 2000s. Abram is credited by some with the idea of packaging **Gum** with baseball cards and is credited incorrectly with adding **Statistics** to the backs of cards. The card size was standardized in 1957 at 2½ by 3½ inch cardboard rectangle, an invention credited to Topps employee Sy Berger. Berger is also credited with dumping thousands of unsold 1952 Mickey Mantle cards in the Atlantic Ocean.

As Topps began to dominate the market in the early 1950s, players had to choose a card company with whom to sign and could not appear on the others' cards. As more shifted to Topps, that company bought out Bowman in 1955 and Topps was virtually alone until the card explosion of the 1980s.

Cards were not terribly popular by 1970, and one serious collector stated that in 1972 there were only about ten card dealers in the New York area who would meet informally on Friday nights.

In the mid–1970s Topps sold 250 million cards annually, but lost its card monopoly after a court action that ended in 1981. As a result, card revenues exploded and there was a corresponding increase in licensing revenues to the Major League Players Association. Revenues increased from $2 million annually in 1981 to $70 million in 1992.

By 1988 card companies were selling five billion cards annually. The craze caused a number of companies to enter the field and older companies to resurrect their baseball card series with even more elaborate sets. Fleer had put out cards for four years until 1963, but reappeared in 1981 riding the general boom in collecting. Donruss began marketing cards again in 1981. The new companies included the extremely successful **Upper Deck**, which began in 1988, Sportflics in 1986 and Score (later called Pinnacle) in 1988.

It was reported by the card manufacturers association that the leading companies combined for $928 million in sales in 1991 and $922 million in 1992. In 1994 the major card producers were Topps, Fleer, Leaf/Donruss, Pacific Trading Cards, Pinnacle, Ted Williams Card Co. and Upper Deck. In 1995 there were over 50 different sets of baseball cards, though production levels were down over prior years by as much as 75% because of the player strike. In 1995 Topps had its lowest production in 30 years.

By 1996 Pinnacle was considered the top card company after it purchased the right to market cards under the Donruss name. Donruss had been owned by a Finnish conglomerate that also marketed hockey cards. Donruss took a downturn when both hockey and baseball suffered labor problems.

One source reported that sports card sales dropped from $1.1 billion in wholesale sales in 1991 to $350 million to $400 million by the 2000s. It has been estimated that in the 2000s there were between 5 million and 6 million sports card collectors in the United States.

Upper Deck. This card company started from scratch in 1988 and by 1992 it had sales of $250 million. Upper Deck introduced a number of innovations, including a hologram on each card to prevent counterfeiting. The company produced fewer cards, making them potentially more valuable, and the cards were wrapped in foil to help protect them.

When Upper Deck was struggling to get started, its attorney loaned the company $100,000 to buy an order of paper that it desperately needed to keep afloat. In gratitude, the company gave him 3% of the company in stock. He never sought repayment of the loan, but when the 3% was worth $33 million, he asked for the shares and had to sue to try to enforce his interest. Because he had not followed California's rigid rules regarding attorney-client relationships, as the court pointed out, "his apparent home run became simply a long out."

In 1992 Reggie Jackson signed with Upper Deck for $500,000 and was appointed to the board of directors. This was in addition to the seven-figure deal he signed with Upper Deck Authenticated, which was formed to market expensive replica memorabilia.

Statistics. Mecca cards were distributed by a tobacco company until 1918 and they were one of the earliest sets to include statistics on the back. Contrary to apparently popular belief, Topps was not the first manufacturer to include statistics. Card companies pay statistics services such as the *Elias Sports Bureau* a flat rate per card for the statistics.

Most Valuable Card. The baseball card craze of the 1980s led to a number of strange "finds" of valuable cards (and fakes) in odd places. In Maine in April 1990, a 12-year-old boy found a rusty tobacco can wedged in the foundation of a burned-down barn. Inside was a damaged card that, according to two experts, was a genuine Honus Wagner card. Because the card was in poor shape, it was probably worth between $15,000 and $40,000.

A number of reprints and fakes turned up to capitalize on the enormous run-up in prices during the 1980s. Experts claim that there were probably only 40 genuine Honus Wagner cards issued with Sweet Caporal cigarettes and probably 20,000 reproductions (some sources report 150 originals). Wagner's card was on the market for only a few months in 1910. The cards were printed and distributed for only a short time before Wagner, supposedly a "staunch opponent of tobacco," forced the company to stop distribution of his card. At least one source reported that Wagner was not a staunch opponent of tobacco, in part because one baseball card bearing his likeness shows him dipping into a pouch of chewing tobacco. Wagner may have objected to the use of his likeness on the previous card because he was not paid for it.

In the late 1980s a genuine Wagner card in top condition was thought to be worth over $100,000. A reflection of the soaring prices of all cards came in 1991 when Los Angeles Kings hockey club owner Bruce McNall (later to declare bankruptcy and be convicted of bank fraud) and star player Wayne Gretzky paid $451,000 for a single Honus Wagner card. The previous owner had paid $110,000 four years earlier. In March 1995 Gretzky bought out McNall's interest in the card for $225,000. In 1996 Wal-Mart held a contest to give away one of the Wagner cards. A female postal worker in Florida won the contest and expected to auction it for approximately $500,000. In July 2000 collector Brian Seigel from Tustin, California, bought a Wagner card on eBay for $1.265 million. Seigel has since said that he turned down offers of over $2 million for the card.

In the 1930s, most cards were selling for 50 cents, but the Wagner card brought brought $50. One uncut printer's sheet of five cards, including the Wagner card, still exists. It was reportedly found folded in the pocket of a uniform Wagner left in his attic of a former home.

In 1984 *Memorabilia* collector Barry Halper presented to the Hall of Fame one of the Wagner cards, officially called the 1909 T206 Honus Wagner tobacco card. The second most valuable card is a 1932 U.S. Caramel card featuring Fred Lindstrom, listed in the early 1990s at $24,000.

In the October 1993 issue of *Sports Card* magazine, perhaps at the peak of the market, the top cards were rated according to value. The T-206 Honus Wagner Card from the 1909 series was valued at $300,000 in 1993, down from the $451,000 paid by McNall and Gretzky. In 1994 a T-206 of lesser quality sold for $63,000.

In second and third place were two other cards from the 1909 series, both valued at $30,000. No. 4 was a 1933 Nap Lajoie card, also valued at 30,000. Mickey Mantle's 1952 Topps rookie card was in the top five at $30,000 and was the newest card in the ranking. Among more recent cards, Mantle is the biggest seller. In 1991 a mint set of 1952 Topps cards, including a Mantle rookie card, sold for $145,000.

The 1980s saw prices skyrocket, as the price of the Mantle and other key cards went up more than tenfold during the decade. The incredible rise in prices has ended and the best bets for appreciation are pre–1956 cards and pre–1987 cards of rookies who have Hall of Fame potential.

Cards generally are issued in a series, usually one series each month during the season, with the cards numbered from one to the last card of the last series. The last series each year, containing the so-called "high number" cards, is usually the one with the shortest life span because it is issued in August or September. It traditionally is the most valuable because the fewest number of cards are printed and purchased.

Industry Collapse. By the mid–1990s the card industry had collapsed from saturation. In 1995–1996 there were 23 sports card lines distributed by Topps, 22 by Fleer, 22 by Pinnacle, 15 by Upper Deck, seven by Donruss, seven by Pacific, four by Collectors Edge, three by Classic and two by Play-off. Topps' stock, traded on the NASDAQ, topped out at $20.25 in 1992 and then fell to a low of $4.25 in 1995 and back over $5.00 in 1996. By 1996 a number of card companies had combined. Pinnacle bought the largest race car line of cards. Marvel bought Fleer in 1992 and then Skybox, the dominant basketball card producer. A Finnish conglomerate that owned Leaf and its Donruss unit sold Donruss to Pinnacle.

Feud. In 1991 a dispute between a 12-year-old card collector and a dealer made national news. The boy bought a Nolan Ryan 1969 "Rookie Stars" card for $12.00 from an uninformed clerk at the dealer's store, who did not realize that the card was actually priced at $1,200. When the boy refused to return the card on the advice of his father, the dealer sued and the case went to trial. Before the trial was completed, the parties agreed to auction the card for charity.

Extra Card. The 1933 Nap Lajoie No. 106 card in the Gouday set has a unique history. That year the 240-card set of active players did not contain a number 106. The following year, in response to collectors' demands, the company put out its last set of the year with an extra card: a No. 106 that clearly followed the 1934 design, rather than 1933, and bore Lajoie's picture.

Price Guide. The *Beckett's Price Guide* is a monthly publication that has emerged as the definitive guide to baseball card prices.

Relative Value. A 1967 set of cards featured historical figures, including William Shakespeare and Sandy Koufax. By 2003, the Shakespeare card was worth $70, the Koufax card $450.

Retired Number.

"I believe everyone should carry some type of religious artifact on his or her person at all times." — Bob Costas, who carries Mickey Mantle's baseball card in his wallet.

After Mantle's death, Topps announced that it would no longer print a card in its annual series bearing number 7. In 1996 Mantle's estate won $4.9 million against Upper Deck for breach of a 1994 contract after the card company sold Mantle memorabilia following his death.

Clientele. Baseball card shows began in the 1970s and flourished through the mid–1990s. Boys ages 7 to 12 account for between 75% and 90% of card purchases.

Rookie Cards. These are generally the most valuable of all cards. Cards for old New York stars also tend to command higher prices. Even though Mickey Mantle's rookie year was 1951, Topps' first Mantle card was issued in 1952 and that card is considered his rookie card.

Topps 1952/Rarest Card. Andy Pafko was a journeyman outfielder most famous for watching Bobby Thomson's 1951 "shot heard 'round the world" go over his head in left field as it headed for the bleachers. Nevertheless, Pafko's 1952 Topps baseball card is the rarest of the famous set because it was No. 1 in the series. That card is now in short supply in good condition, as years of rubber band damage — it was on top of all the other cards in the set that youngsters collected — has left precious few available. The finest known Pafko card sold in 1998 for $83,870.

Mark McGwire. Miami resident Stanley Jackson died in 1997, but his wife, Wendy, a successful real estate broker, carried on his passion for McGwire's cards. By 1998 she had 3,000 McGwire cards, the most valuable of which was the 1984 card featuring him with the U.S. Olympic team. His 1985 Topps rookie card was worth more than $1,400.

Player Collector. Catcher Gary Carter was an avid collector, who by 1994 had every Topps card from 1959 through 1993 except for 1962.

Identity Problem. In 1969 Topps photographed the Angels batboy, thinking he was third baseman Aurelio Rodriguez. The card was issued with the batboy's picture.

Premium "Memorabilia" Cards.

"It goes against everything we would do, to grind up something rather than preserve it."—John Ralph, a spokesman for the Hall of Fame.

"This is our way to spread the wealth."—Mary Mancera, an Upper Deck spokeswoman.

Upper Deck decided to carve up a bat that Babe Ruth used in games into small pieces for mounting on trading cards, which were inserted into hundreds of thousands of 1999 card packs. The company was criticized for cutting up a piece of history, but Ruth never did anything noteworthy with the bat, and it cost them $23,000 for it, so, as one commentator noted, "this lets even poorer people own a small piece of history." Quite magnanimous of Upper Deck. In 2004 the company went to the extreme of releasing a set of five NBA cards that cost $500.

Promotion. In May 2004 the Ottawa Lynx of the Class AAA International League held a promotion on eBay to allow a fan to have his own baseball card as part of the team's 2004 set.

Stock Exchange. In 1990 baseball fan and stockbroker Ric Apter began the Apter Card Average (ACA) system to chart the prices of key baseball cards. The system was similar to the Dow Jones Industrial Average of 30 key national companies. Apter chose "blue chip" cards and sets from various years to get the best possible feel for the market. It was recalculated every month and Apter published a monthly guide, the *Card Collector Commentary*, but it had disappeared by the early 2000s.

Topps Baseball Card Auction. In 1990 Brooklyn-based Topps auctioned off its voluminous archives. The most popular items were 3" × 5" paintings of Willie Mays, Bob Feller, Roy Campanella, Whitey Ford, Jackie Robinson and Mickey Mantle. They were used to design the Topps 1952 and 1953 cards. The Robinson painting sold for over $78,000 and Mantle's sold for $121,000.

Japanese Cards. Japanese baseball cards became popular in the late 1980s, though the two most valuable cards are probably worth only in the $400–$500 range. Japanese cards were introduced in the 1930s and late 1940s on a limited basis, but have always been used primarily as promotional items for other products, as was originally done with U.S. cards.

Unlike American cards, which feature all active Major Leaguers, only stars are featured on Japanese cards. Cards recently have been featured with products such as potato chips, gum, candy and as part of a dice game.

Fee. For many years the fee to a player was $5 upon signing with Topps and another $250 when the card was issued. The latter fee is now $500. Players get most of their revenue through licensing agreements that the Players Association has with the various card companies. They also receive free copies of their cards.

Gum. Gum was a long-time staple of the baseball card packet, first appearing in 1933 when the Gouday Gum Company popularized the practice. One of the brothers who owned the Topps Company, Abram Shorin, is credited by some erroneously as the first to put gum in packets of baseball cards. When gum sales slumped after World War II, Topps created the Bazooka Joe eye-patched mascot, perhaps named after Arthur's father. In 1951 the company started putting baseball cards with Topps taffy. In 1952 Topps put cards with its bubble gum, which still features Bazooka Joe.

Based on an early 1960s court ruling, only Topps was allowed to issue cards with gum in the packets. The last of four early Fleer series, issued in 1963, contained cookies instead of gum because of the court decision. In 1991 Topps announced that it would no longer include sticks of gum in its card packages. The company said that the gum sometimes stained the cards, decreasing their value to collectors.

Players' Likenesses. The players voluntarily share baseball card licensing money equally with trainers and coaches. If two or more players appear in a baseball card picture in uniform (or on candy or other products), the Players Association receives 10% of the gross revenue, which it voluntarily shares with trainers and coaches to supplement their incomes. In 1980 there was very little of this revenue, in part because Topps still had a monopoly on baseball cards. In 1984 the revenue was up to $25 million and in 1993 it was almost $100 million, virtually all of it from baseball cards.

Parody. An Oklahoma card company produced Cardtoons, featuring parody cards with names such as Andre Awesome, Steve Bravery, Kirby Plunkit, Steve Saxophone, Robin Adventura, Dennis Excellency of the Pathetics, Rob Quibble, Lee Smite, Carlton Fist, Darryl Razzberry, Don Battingly, Tommy Lasagna, Greg Maddogs and Treasury Bonds. The images of the real players were used to sell the cards. The Players Association did not license the Cardtoons series, so the individual players had the right to prevent their distribution. The Players Association's rights were not infringed because the players did not appear in uniform.

Another card company, Pro Set, planned on distributing a set of cards parodying Topps, called Flopps. However, after the Major League Players Association threatened never to award a legitimate set of cards to Pro Set, the company backed away from its plans.

Collaboration. In 1995 the six Major League-licensed card companies collaborated to produce an 18-card set called the National Packtime. Donruss, Fleer, Pacific, Pinnacle, Topps and Upper Deck collaborated with the Players Association and Major League Baseball Properties. Each company contributed three cards. It was a follow-up to the highly successful five-card Roberto Clemente set that was introduced at the 1995 All-Star Game. Five of the six companies (not Pacific) participated in the Clemente Series.

Books. Mark Stewart, *The Ultimate Insider's Guide to Baseball Cards* (1993), which exposes certain facets of the industry that card companies and dealers would rather not surface.

John Alvis, Where Are You? This author once owned approximately 8,000 baseball cards, including 50% of the late 1950s and 1962–1969 complete. At age 13 in 1970 this author sold them to John Alvis for $20 to raise money for his stamp collection. If Alvis held on to the author's cards and his own, he is easily a millionaire today.

The Baseball Encyclopedia (1969–)

"It takes a lot of reading to know all this stuff. I wasted two years of my education reading *The Baseball Encyclopedia*."—SABR member Scott Flatow in 1986.

"And finally, for those who can't even get a sock or an unusual belt buckle in the Hall, there is still a form of immortality to be had even by you, because baseball also has its own Good Book, in which your deeds are inscribed forever, or at least as long as you and print and baseball are around to care. Whether your name is Aaron or Zwilling, whether you have been to bat in the majors 10,000 times or just once, there it all is in the Baseball Encyclopedia to be discovered and committed to memory by insomniacs yet unborn. (In fact, if you change your last name to Zyzmanski, you might even find your name mentioned in essays like this.)" — Wilfrid Sheed in *The Face of Baseball* (1990).

See also **Statistics.**

Published by Macmillan beginning 1969, "Big Mac" contained the most comprehensive compilation of individual players' Major League statistics. It later included players' individual lifetime and season records, separated by pitchers and position players; managers; annual team performances; home/road performances; League Championship Series and World Series; All-Star Games; trades; rule changes; no-hitters; Hall of Famers; all Major Leagues; National Association players; Negro League players; and All-American Girls Professional Baseball League players (AAGPBL).

Joseph L. Reichler was the editor through the first seven editions. Rick Wolff took over in 1987. New editions generally came out every three years. The book was subtitled *The Complete and Official Record of Major League Baseball.* Fairchild Publications put up a large amount of money to finance the project at its inception, which turned out initially to be a big loser. *The Baseball Encyclopedia* lost Major League Baseball's official endorsement in 1995 in favor of **Total Baseball,** and Macmillan discontinued publication after the ninth edition in 1993 (much to the author's dismay, who favored it over its excellent rival because of the simplicity of its organization and focus). It returned in a large softcover format in 2004, with updated statistics and new categories.

The 1969 and 1974 editions of *The Baseball Encyclopedia* contained full listings only for those players who had at least 25 at-bats in the Major Leagues. The 1976 edition was the first to contain entries for every player, no matter how few at-bats. Entries on the Negro Leagues and AAGPBL appeared in subsequent editions.

Baseball Guides (1860–)

"The National game of base-ball now stands pre-eminent as the American field-sport of the age." — First line of the original *DeWitt's Base Ball Guide* of 1876.

"In presenting this work to our readers, we claim for it the merit of being the first publication of its kind yet issued." — Preamble to *Beadle's Dime Base-Ball Player.*

See also **Books, Magazines, Newspapers, The Reach Guide, The Spalding Guide** and **The Sporting News.**

In 1860 sportswriter Henry Chadwick published, through Beadle and Adams, *Beadle's Dime Base-Ball Player,* the first baseball guide. It was the preeminent guide until 1866 and lasted until 1881. The 1860 edition published the newly adopted New York Rules and contained descriptions and rules for **Rounders** and **Townball.**

In 1867 the *Ballplayer's Book of Reference* was introduced, selling 65,000 copies that year. They were the only baseball publications until the mid–1870s, when Albert Spalding began publishing his *Spalding Guide.* The *Spalding Guide* was the official annual publication of the National League until it ceased publication in 1941. *Spalding's Official Base Ball Record* was first published in 1908.

The **Reach Guide** was first published in 1876.

DeWitt's Base Ball Guide was an early publication that lasted from 1876 until 1885.

Sol White's Official Baseball Guide was published in 1907 and reprinted in 1984.

Wright & Ditson's Guide was published in 1884, 1886 and 1910–1912.

The *Nap Lajoie Baseball Guide* was published between 1906 and 1908.

The Sporting News Baseball Guide covers all statistics from the previous year.

The Sporting News Baseball Register covers lifetime records for active players.

The American League publishes the *Red Book* and the National League publishes the *Green Book,* both of which contain annual statistical summaries.

The minor league National Association publishes a number of annual guides: *Minor League Digest, Major League Year & Notebook,* the *Blue Book,* a complete directory of Organized Baseball, and the *Orange Book,* an annual chronicle of the minor leagues. The *Blue Book* has been published since 1909 and is the primary guide clubs teams use for basic information during the season.

The *Baseball Bulletin* began publication in 1975.

The Baseball League

This was a proposed new Major League announced in 1989 during a period of player unrest. Real estate entrepreneur Donald Trump was to be involved with a team in New Jersey, but the plans never materialized.

Baseball Schools See **Fantasy Camps, Instructional Camps,** and **Umpires — Schools**

Baseball Writers Association of America ("BBWAA") (1908–)

"At noon a Kiwanis bunch in Braintree had a place setting with my name on it, and a chapter of the Baseball Writers of America wanted me to yammer with them at one of their overpriced meetings in a downtown sports bar. I told them I never went near those places, and they told me to come anyway. In my emeritus and celebrated state, my dance card was clogged." — From the mystery *Fear in Fenway,* by Crabbe Evers (1993).

See also **Sportswriters.**

Origins. The BBWAA had its origins in the short-lived **Base Ball Reporters Association** of 1887–1890.

Formation.

"The Association ... assure[d] the writers of a proper seat from which they could do their daily stint, without interference. It's pretty difficult to turn out deathless prose with a typewriter perched precariously on your knee, and your posterior balanced on an upturned beer case borrowed from a sympathetic concessionaire; it's doubly difficult when you face the added obstacle of free loading spectators, yelling in your ear, stomping on your feet, and waving madly to friends, while you try to write." — Former sportswriter Ford Frick in *Games, Asterisks and People* (1973). Frick related in his autobiography that the BBWAA supposedly was created after actor Louis Mann took sportswriter Hugh Fullerton's seat in the press box during the 1908 World Series in Chicago. Mann refused to move and Fullerton sat in his lap during an entire game. The indignant writers supposedly met that evening and formed the new association.

Discussions among writers to form a new association increased in 1906, but the Baseball Writers Association of America was not officially formed until 1908. St. Louis writer Sid Mercer and 32-year veteran Cincinnati writer Jack Ryder were instrumental in forming the BBWAA. The organization was created on October 14, 1908, at the Hotel Ponchartrain in Detroit. *Detroit Free Press* sports editor Joseph Stansfield Jackson was a key figure in the initial organizing effort and was president for 10 years.

There were 21 original members and the annual membership fee was $1. The emblem of the BBWAA was a green baseball diamond with the initials of the organization, together with a bat and pen criss-crossed in gold.

When the association was formed it had three goals: 1) to encourage a "square deal in baseball"; 2) to promote uniform scoring and simplified rules; and 3) to create better facilities for reporters and regulation of box scores during the postseason.

In 1910 National League president Harry Pulliam supported an effort by the Giants and Yankees to give some measure of acknowledgement of the BBWAA. The teams allowed only BBWAA reporters to use the press box during an intra-city game between the clubs.

Secretaries/Membership. The secretary is the key position in the BBWAA. There were only six in the first 75 years of the organization: William G. Weart and Joseph M. McCready, both of Philadelphia; Henry P. Edwards of Cleveland and Chicago; Ken Smith of New York; Hy Hurwitz of Boston; and Jack Lang of New York.

Membership in the BBWAA is signified by a card re-issued annually to each member. The number on the card signifies seniority, with No. 1 designating the most senior current member of the association.

Awards. All 10-year members of the BBWAA vote for induction into the *Hall of Fame*, though originally all members voted. The BBWAA is credited with resurrecting the leagues' Most Valuable Player Awards in 1931 after both the National and American Leagues abandoned them in the 1920s. The BBWAA started a Rookie of the Year Award in 1947. Two writers in each city vote for the awards, though early on three did so. The secretary of the BBWAA has the honor of first contacting the players named MVP and Cy Young Award winners, as well as Hall of Fame electees.

Black Members. The first black member of the BBWAA was Sam Lacy in 1948, a long-time writer who spearheaded efforts to integrate baseball in the 1940s. Wendell Smith, Jackie Robinson's roommate during the 1947 season, also was admitted in 1948 (see also *Integration* and *Sportswriters*).

Jack Lang. Lang may be the best-known of the organization's leaders. He was the secretary-treasurer of the group from 1966 through 1988, when he became executive secretary. In 1946 he began his career as a New York sportswriter and in 1986 received the J.G. Taylor Spink Award.

College. The National Collegiate Baseball Writers Association was established to improve media coverage of college baseball.

Baselines See *Base Running*—Running Inside the Base Paths and *Foul Lines*

Bases

"To the base is attached a hidden bell, with mechanism to sound the same upon sudden and forcible pressure of its top. An improved base for the game of baseball, constructed with a case, or box, elastic supporting-columns, cap-plate, and a bell or other enunciating device, arranged to be operated substantially in the manner and for the purpose set forth."—1875 patent application for a new base.

See also *Base Running*.

Early Versions. Prior to the 1850s bases often were holes in the ground or poles stuck in the ground. The 1846 Knickerbockers used canvas bases. Home plate was a flat circular iron disc painted or enameled white.

In 1863 players were required to touch the bags. Previously, it was acceptable for a player to come "close" to the bag. This new rule probably increased the frequency of sliding, and most sources credit the first *Slide* as occurring around 1865.

The home plate at Cincinnati's 19th century Bank Street Grounds was made of stone.

When the National League began play in 1876, 15-inch canvas bags were required to cover the bases and they were to be "filled with some soft material." Some sources report that this rule was not enacted until 1877.

Around 1900 sawdust sacks were often used for bases, but these would slide away and tear apart. Straps were used to hold down bases as late as the 1960s.

Modern Major League bases are held down by a subsurface 10" × 10" concrete block weighing 25 pounds. An anchor stake eight inches long comes up out of the block to one inch below the ground. Another anchor, fastened to the base, fits over the top of the embedded anchor. Modern bags are 15-inch squares, three inches thick, and are made of bonded polyester padding with a vinyl cover. Six to eight sets are needed each season for training camp and the home stadium. The cost of three bases is approximately $250.

Position of Bases/Home Plate. Prior to 1887 all three bags were centered within a 90-degree square, with the first and third bases half in fair territory and half in foul territory. In 1877 home plate was moved from just outside the diamond to just inside the diamond, its present location. In 1887 first and third were moved inside the foul lines, but second base remains outside the 90-foot square at its corner.

Home Plate Dimensions/Composition. In 1860 *Beadle's Dime Base-Ball Player* printed rules by Henry Chadwick in which it was provided that home plate should be no less than nine inches in diameter. Home "bases" were to be about 14 inches by 17 inches, but "as long as it covers one square foot of ground … the requirements of the rules will be fulfilled." Chadwick also edited the *DeWitt's Guide*, which provided that the bases were to be 18 inches square.

In 1868 the rules first noted that home plate was to cover essentially the same size as the other bases (12 square inches). In 1872 the plate was no longer to be of iron, but made of "white marble or stone, so fixed in the ground as to be even with the surface." For one season in 1876 home plate could be made of wood. In 1885 home plate could no longer be made of marble. It had to be made of either white rubber or white stone. The American Association allowed only white rubber to prevent slipping.

Before 1900, home plate was a circle, evolved into a square, and then became five-sided. The five-sided configuration was believed to make it easier for umpires to call balls and strikes. In a 1900 letter to *The Sporting News*, pitcher Crazy Schmidt claimed that he suggested that the Major Leagues adopt the five-sided home plate.

A modern home plate weighs about 20 pounds, so no anchoring is needed. It is one piece of molded vinyl four inches thick, with beveled edges. A plate is five-sided and is 17 inches wide, not including a one-inch strip of black around the border. It is 23 inches from front to rear. It is 12 inches on the sides and 8½ inches on the diagonal to the point facing the pitcher. Seven plates are required per ball park, at a cost of $60 each: four for the two bullpens, two for pre-game warm-ups (though generally they are not replaced during batting practice), and one for the field during a game.

Stunt. In 1990 Reds manager Lou Piniella gained a measure of notoriety by tossing a base in a fit of anger over a bad call. Two days later the *Cincinnati Enquirer* newspaper held a base-throwing contest. A television news anchorwoman wearing high heels and 75 others threw a base farther than Piniella.

Protest. In 2001 Pirates manager Lloyd McClendon picked up third base and carried it into the dugout to protest the umpire's call.

Inventions. It is estimated that there are 1.7 million amateur and professional sliding injuries each year, resulting in medical costs of $2 billion. As a result, in many amateur leagues, there is now a breakaway base patented to allow for the base to slide off its pedestal when struck with a severe blow.

Perhaps the best simple invention is the safety base, enabling young runners to tag an orange first base that is outside the foul line, but physically attached to the base that the first baseman steps on — avoiding collisions.

Another invention was a paper towel dispenser on home plate. When the towel got dirty, the umpire could simply pull another sheet across the plate. There is no evidence that this gimmick was used in a professional game.

Novel Approach. Ronald Reagan was fond of telling the story of the wife who explains to her baseball-crazed husband how to put a diaper on their newborn; bring the diaper's "third base" over to "first base" and tuck "second base" and "home plate" into the waist. "And if it starts to rain, start the whole thing over again."

Bases Loaded

"Luck and unconsciousness helps." — Pat Tabler, explaining why a lifetime .280s hitter was a star with the bases loaded. By 1990 he had 40 hits in 80 at-bats with the bases loaded.

"A man once told me to walk with the Lord. I'd rather walk with the bases loaded." — Ken Singleton, after forcing in a run with a walk in the 1983 World Series.

"The real test comes when you are pitching with men on bases. Do not worry. Try to appear jolly and unconcerned. I have smiled often with the bases full with two strikes and three balls on the batter. This seems to unnerve ..." — Andrew "Rube" Foster in an article in *History of Colored Baseball*, by Sol White (1907).

See also **Grand Slams**.

Slow Death. On June 23, 2002, the San Diego Padres beat the Marlins 18–2, with a club-record 10 hits in a nine-run 5th inning. The final 11 Padres in the inning all batted with the bases loaded as the Padres scored eight runs, one base at a time.

Basic Agreement See Collective Bargaining Agreements and Unions

Basketball

"No. The ball is too big and there's no chance of a rainout." — Pitcher Eric Hillman, who is 6'10", asked if he ever played basketball.

"Not unless [former Indiana Hoosiers coach] Bobby Knight was a baseball coach." — Former A's pitcher Brian Kingman, asked if he could have imagined a worse situation than playing for Billy Martin.

"Baseball is the only game left for people. To play basketball, you have to be 7 feet 6 inches. To play football, you have to be the same width." — Bill Veeck in 1975.

Comparison to Baseball.

"The NBA picked our pocket. While we were sleeping, talking about tradition and being America's pastime, [NBA commissioner] David Stern forged marketing relationships that were brilliant." — Entrepreneurial minor league owner Mike Veeck.

In 2002 Los Angeles Lakers coach Phil Jackson stated that it was easy to lose focus in baseball because it is such a boring game. Replied *Dallas Morning News* columnist Blackie Sherrod: "Rather like a December NBA game, Coach?"

Danny Ainge.

"No matter how long he played, he could never have hit a fastball to the left of the first base coach." — Jim Palmer on the right-handed Ainge.

The Boston Celtics star played three years of professional baseball, some of it in the Major Leagues with the Blue Jays, who drafted him in the 15th round, from 1979 through 1981. He batted .220 for Toronto before giving up baseball to play full-time with the Celtics, who had drafted him out of college. The Blue Jays filed a lawsuit in which a jury eventually ruled that their baseball contract could prevent Ainge from playing professional basketball. Ainge solved the problem by quitting baseball.

Frankie Baumholtz. The Reds outfielder finished fifth in the 1947 National League Rookie of the Year voting. He played baseball after two seasons of professional basketball in the National Basketball League and Basketball Association of America.

Bruce Benedict. The former Braves catcher became an NCAA basketball referee.

Larry Bird Retirement. When the Boston Celtics star announced his retirement in mid-1992, various baseball players honored him in their own ways. For example, Angels shortstop Gary DiSarcina changed his uniform number to Bird's number 33. DiSarcina's high school basketball teammate, Braves pitcher Tom Glavine, wrote the number 33 on his cap for a game.

Lou Boudreau. The Indians shortstop was All-Big 10 in basketball and played in the National Basketball League in 1938 and 1939. He played for the Hammond Ciesar All-Americans, a team that featured at guard former All-American and future UCLA basketball coach John Wooden.

Brooklyn Dodgers. The club had an off-season basketball team for one year during the 1950s. It played its games at the Paramount Theater in Brooklyn.

Scott Burrell. Burrell played for Connecticut and won an NBA championship with the Chicago Bulls in 1998. He is the only person drafted in the first round in both basketball and baseball.

Gene Conley.

"It was about equal. Neither one of them was a picnic." — Conley on pitching to Mickey Mantle and posting up against Wilt Chamberlain.

"It'll take him six weeks to get out of shape." — Celtics teammate Bill Russell when Conley left the NBA to play Major League Baseball.

"I like all sports. When it's basketball season, I like basketball and when it's baseball season I like baseball." — Conley, who played for two teams that won at least one world championship. He pitched for the 1957 Milwaukee Braves and played basketball for the NBA champion Boston Celtics in 1959, 1960 and 1961. His Major League career lasted from 1952 through 1963, during which he compiled a 91–96 record. In late 1952 he signed with the Celtics after the minor league baseball season and earned $4,500 playing basketball during the 1952–1953 season.

In 1953 he was Minor League Player of the Year with Toledo and the Braves offered him $1,000 not to play for the Celtics. He took it and did not play basketball again until late 1958. After the 1958 baseball season, in which he played poorly, he again signed with the Celtics and helped them win an NBA championship. He returned to the Braves for spring training in 1959 only to find out that he had been traded to the Phillies. After a decent two years with the Phillies, he returned to the Red Sox for the 1961–1963 seasons.

Chuck Connors. The long-time actor played both sports professionally (see also *Television Shows*).

Dave DeBusschere. The New York Knicks basketball star received $75,000 when he signed with the White Sox in 1962 and according to one source "promptly pitched a shutout." However, that season he made 12 appearances with no starts and no record. It was the next year, 1963, in which he had his shutout and a 3–4 record in what was to be his last Major League season. He was made player-coach of the Detroit Pistons at age 24 in 1964 before moving on to the Knicks and becoming a five-time all-star.

Dick Groat. The Pirates shortstop from 1955 through 1967 was a basketball All-American at Duke University and averaged 12 points per game for the NBA Fort Wayne Pistons in 1952–1953.

Tony Gwynn. The Padres outfielder was drafted by the NBA San Diego Clippers in the 10th round after attending San Diego State. He was drafted by the club only after it selected 80-year-old UCLA trainer Ducky Drake and UCLA football All-American and future NFL All-Pro Kenny Easley. These kinds of lower-round basketball draft farces ended when the NBA eliminated all but the first two rounds of its draft.

Steve Hamilton. The left-hander pitched primarily for the Yankees in the 1960s and developed his own version of the *Eephus Pitch*, known as the Folly Floater. At 6'6" he played for the Minneapolis Lakers in the 1950s.

Harlem Globetrotters. On the day in 1951 that Ned Garver won his 20th game for the lowly St. Louis Browns (52–102 that season), the Globetrotters were a pre-game attraction in a game against the Browns players (except Garver, who was disappointed that he couldn't play against them because he needed to rest for the baseball game).

Cardinals pitcher Bob Gibson played for the Harlem Globetrotters in the late 1950s. The Cardinals later paid him $1,000 *not* to play for the Globetrotters because the club feared that its star pitcher might be injured. He took the money and never again played basketball.

Donn Clendenon of the Pirates turned down a contract offer by the Globetrotters.

Bucky Harris. The Senators second baseman played professional basketball during the off-season early in his career in the 1920s.

Mark Hendrickson. On June 21, 2003, the former NBA player became the first Blue Jay pitcher to hit a home run, in an interleague game against the Expos. The 6'9" pitcher played baseball and basketball at Washington State, and later played professionally between 1996 and 2000 for four NBA teams and once scored 19 points in a game. He made his Major League debut in August 2002 for the Blue Jays, becoming the tenth NBA player to play in the Major Leagues.

Frank Howard. The 6'7" slugger was drafted by the NBA Philadelphia Warriors in the third round after having been an All-Big Ten Conference forward at Ohio State. Instead, he signed for $108,000 with the Dodgers and never played pro basketball.

LeBron James. In mid-2003 the basketball phenom, who had yet to play a pro game, took batting practice with the Reds. He missed the first nine pitches from pitching coach Tom Hume. Responded Tom Fitzgerald of the *San Francisco Chronicle*: "Maybe he really is the next [Michael] Jordan."

Kevin Johnson. The Phoenix Suns guard appeared in two games at shortstop in the California League for Modesto in 1986. He was 0-for-2.

Michael Jordan.

"Could Bump Head While Skying For Fly Ball in Seattle."

"Could Bite Tongue Off in Outfield Collision with Dan Pasqua."

"Tough to look spectacular running out routine grounders."

"Former Pete Rose associates might come out of the woodwork."

"Tough for Greatest Athlete of all time to bat behind Ron Karkovice in batting order." — Sportswriter Mike Ricigliano on the problems Chicago Bulls star Michael Jordan might experience as he prepared to go to spring training with the White Sox in 1994. Jordan was 3-for-20 for the White Sox in 13 spring training games before being moved to the minor league club.

Jordan played the entire season with the Class AA Birmingham Barons. He made his professional debut with an 0-for-3 performance on April 8, 1994. He got his first hits, a pair of bloop singles, two days later. Jordan finished the year with a .202 average for the Barons with 114 strikeouts in 436 at-bats. He had three home runs and 51 RBIs while stealing 30 bases in 48 attempts. He committed 11 errors in the outfield.

Jordan showed his dedication to baseball by playing in the Arizona Winter League for the Scottsdale Scorpions. He batted .252 with no home runs. His club's games accounted for 87% of the league's attendance. In apparent frustration over the baseball strike, Jordan returned to the Bulls in March 1995 in time for the NBA play-offs. See also Jim Patton, *Rookie: Michael Jordan's Year in Baseball* (1995).

Jerry Krause. In 2004 the Yankees hired the long-time Chicago Bulls general manager to evaluate baseball talent. Before his 18 seasons with the Bulls (including the Michael Jordan years), Krause had been a Major League scout for 16 years, including time with the Indians, A's, Mariners and White Sox.

Tommy Lasorda. The future Dodger manager and former minor league pitcher was an NBA rookie referee in 1963. After working two exhibition games he was bounced for allegedly having too foul a mouth. A few months later, Dodger general manager Al Campanis hired Lasorda to scout in Southern California full-time.

Kenny Lofton. The Gold Glove outfielder was the starting point guard on the University of Arizona basketball team that made it to the NCAA Final Four in 1989. He didn't play on the school's baseball team until his junior year.

Graig Nettles. The third baseman attended San Diego State University on a basketball scholarship.

Ernie Nevers. The *Football* great is the only Major League player to also play professional football and basketball. He played five games for the Chicago Bruins of the American Basketball League of the late 1920s (coached by football great George Halas). In 1927 Nevers served up one of Babe Ruth's 60 home runs.

Del Rice. The catcher played primarily for the 1950s Cardinals and Braves. He was 6'5" (erroneously 6'7" in some sources) and played professional basketball.

Robin Roberts. The Phillies pitcher was a 6'1" forward who received a basketball scholarship to Michigan State.

Jackie Robinson. At least one source, John Isaacs, who played for the all-black New York Rens in the 1930s, told the *New York Times* that Robinson was the first player to dunk a basketball, even though he was only 5'11". Robinson apparently could leap, as he was the 1940 NCAA long jump champion at 24' 10½".

Vin Scully. The long-time Dodger broadcaster played varsity basketball for Fordham University.

Bill Sharman. Sharman was an NBA player, Los Angeles Lakers coach and front office executive for more than 30 years. Before that he was on the Dodgers bench as a player on September 27,

1951, during a heated pennant race. He had been called up from Class AA Fort Worth after hitting .286. He was ejected from the game (along with catcher Roy Campanella and pitcher Preacher Roe) by umpire Frank Dascoli for bench jockeying and never played in a Major League game.

Dolly Stark. The 1930s National League umpire coached the Dartmouth College basketball team for 12 years.

Tim Stoddard. The future Orioles pitcher was a 6'7" forward on the 1974 NCAA champion North Carolina State basketball team. He and Kenny Lofton are the only two Major Leaguers to play in an NCAA basketball Final Four and a World Series.

Honus Wagner. Wagner sponsored the "Honus Wagners" basketball team in the early 20th century.

John Wooden. In addition to playing alongside **Lou Boudreau,** the former UCLA basketball coach was in Anaheim to throw out the first pitch of Game 2 of the 2002 World Series between the Angels and Giants.

Assists. Tim Wiles, Director of Research at the Hall of Fame, has been called by former football player and now journalist Billy Sample, "The John Stockton of baseball research." Stockton is the NBA's all-time assist leader. Another Wiles acolyte, Chicagoan Brian A. Bernardoni, a Wrigley Field tour guide, calls Wiles "a fucking Godsend."

Bat Racks

"To wake up the bats." — Pitcher Roger McDowell's explanation for why he threw firecrackers into the bat racks.

Well into the 20th century, bats commonly were left in front of the players' bench or near home plate. It was not until the 1920s that bat racks were routinely installed. In 1954 bat racks were required to be vertical instead of horizontal, but that rule was later abandoned.

Bat Speed

"Typically, the batter's center-of-mass moves forward a little less than 18 inches in the one-fifth second required to swing the bat. The considerable energy of about 0.6 horsepower-seconds transferred to the bat in one fifth of a second ... is generated largely by the large muscles of the thighs and torso." — Robert K. Adair in *The Physics of Baseball* (1990).

Major League batters swing the bat at approximately 70 miles per hour. It is estimated that for every mile an hour faster on the swing, five feet are added to the distance of a hit. Recent sluggers favor lighter bats to increase bat speed, but the smaller barrel slightly increases the likelihood of missing the ball and striking out.

In an interleague game in Seattle on June 24, 1997, Mariner's pitcher Randy Johnson was clocked at 97 mph; radar caught the pitch leaving Mark McGwire's bat at 105 mph on its way to a 538-foot home run.

Batboys

"The glamour job for a youthful fan was that of batboy, so remote that it seemed unattainable. However, one Sunday in 1924 I was standing near the press gate at Ebbets Field hoping to get in on an extra pass when the Brooklyn clubhouse man, Babe Hamburger, happened along and asked if I wanted to mind the bats for the Cincinnati team ..." — Harold Seymour in *Baseball: The Peo-*

ple's Game (1990), describing his start as a Dodger batboy for three summers.

"I'll take any way to get into the Hall of Fame. If they want a batboy, I'll go in as a batboy." — Phil Rizzuto in 1981; he finally was elected in 1995.

See also **Mascots** and **Women in Baseball**—Batgirls.

Giants manager John McGraw once had a hunchbacked batboy named Eddie Morrow. One source claimed that Morrow was the inspiration for Bill Veeck's use of **Midget** Eddie Gaedel for one at-bat in 1951 for the Browns.

Pitcher Rube Marquard, holder of the longest winning streak in Major League history, was a batboy for the Indians early in the 20th century.

Actor George Raft had been a batboy for the Yankees. Raft was later a buddy of Dodger manager Leo Durocher. Durocher was at one point told to stop associating with Raft (who often played gangster parts) and his alleged racketeering friends. This conduct in part led to Durocher's **Suspension** for the entire 1947 season by commissioner Happy Chandler.

Batboy Robert Scanlon lucked out in 1944 when he worked home games for the Cardinals and Browns. Both teams made it to the World Series and both voted Scanlon a World Series share of $500.

Actor William Bendix, who played Babe Ruth in a 1948 movie, purportedly was a batboy for the Yankees. He also is said to have been the batboy who bought mass quantities of hot dogs and soda from which Ruth supposedly developed the "bellyache heard 'round the world." Bendix allegedly was fired after this incident. Though it is improbable that Bendix was a Yankee batboy, it is even more improbable that he was the specific batboy who caused the severe gastrointestinal problems suffered by Ruth early in the 1925 season (which actually was syphilis, but the sportswriters covered it up).

John Hallahan began as a batboy with the Pirates in 1947, became the club's equipment man in 1957 and remained with the club into the 1990s.

When the Dodgers played their first game in Dodger Stadium, their bat boy was James Hahn, future Los Angeles City Attorney and son of one of the men responsible for bringing the Dodgers to Los Angeles, long-time supervisor Kenneth Hahn.

Long-time Braves executive Donald Davidson, a dwarf, was a batboy for the Braves and Red Sox in 1939 (see also **Midgets**).

Dodger bat racks closely guarded by svelte former hockey player-turned broadcaster Stu Nahan.

Mets general manager Joe McDonald was a batboy for the Dodgers in the 1950s.

Manager Sparky Anderson was a batboy for the USC Trojans in the 1940s.

In the early 1970s future rap star M.C. Hammer (later simply Hammer) was a batboy and general "gofer" for A's owner Charlie Finley. Hammer was at the time known as Stanley Burrell. Finley used Hammer to spy on his players and to provide telephonic play-by-play to Finley at his home in Illinois. Hammer threw out the first pitch at the 1990 All-Star Game in Oakland, his hometown.

Salary. In 1955 the Giants paid their batboys $3.75 for day games, $4.50 for night games and $6.00 for doubleheaders. That same year the Yankees paid their batboys only $2.50 per game, but collectively they received $1,200 in World Series money. Florida Marlins manager Rene Lachemann earned $5 per game as a Dodger batboy in the late 1950s in Los Angeles. His older brother was a prospect and the club wanted to help ensure that he would sign with them. By the 1990s the standard batboy salary was $40 per game.

Labor Violation. In 1993, 14-year-old batboy Tommy McCoy of the Class A Savannah Cardinals was fired after the U.S. Department of Labor advised the team that it was violating child labor laws that limited work hours for children under 16. Labor Secretary Robert Reich, batboy-ready at 4'10", intervened and suspended the rule for batboys and batgirls, calling the original decision "off base."

World Series Wackiness/Age Change. The 2002 World Series was the scene of one of the more bizarre incidents in baseball history. The Giants had stocked their dugout with batboys; children of various players, including Barry Bonds' son. Among them was three-year-old Darren Baker, son of manager Dusty Baker.

During Game 5, Darren wanted to be the first batboy out of the dugout to retrieve the bat of his favorite player, Kenny Lofton. To beat out the other batboy vying for the bat, Darren ran from the dugout before the play was completed and before the runners on second and third had scored. On a long double by Lofton, J.T. Snow came in from third as David Bell rounded third and headed for home. Snow arrived at the plate at full speed just as Darren Baker was there to pick up the bat. As the catcher and umpire looked on in horror at the potential collision, Snow slowed only slightly to scoop up Darren by his jacket collar and hoisted him into his arms, avoiding a potential collision by Bell and Angels catcher Benji Molina.

Dusty Baker's mother and wife scolded the manager about the incident and wanted to keep Darren out of the dugout for the final games. Baker let Darren stay in the dugout, but monitored him closely. As a result of this near-disaster, Major League Baseball instituted a rule after the season that batboys had to be at least 14 years old.

Books. Mets batboy Dominic Ardovino, *The Bat Boy* (1967); Neil D. Isaacs, *Innocence and Wonder: Baseball Through the Eyes of Batboys*, (1994); batboy Paul Wick with Bob Wolf, *Batboy of the Braves* (1957).

Bats

"The underprivileged people of the Americas play some strange game with a bat which looks like an overgrown rolling pin."—Fred Trueman.

"[Bats can be] wide-grain, tight-grain, slim and thick-handled, heavy or small-barreled, solid tan, yellow, black, two-toned, banded, big- and small-knobbed, end-cupped or non-cupped."—Richard Saul Wurman in *Baseball Access* (1988).

Aluminum.

"Mr. Speaker, I rise to condemn the desecration of a great American symbol. No, I am not referring to flag burning; I am referring to the baseball bat.

Several experts tell us that the wooden baseball bat is doomed to extinction, that Major League Baseball players will soon be standing at home plate with aluminum bats in their hands. Baseball fans have been forced to endure countless indignities by those who just cannot leave well enough alone.

Designated hitters, plastic grass, uniforms that look like pajamas, chicken clowns dancing on the baselines, and of course the most heinous sacrilege — lights in Wrigley Field.

Are we willing to hear the crack of a bat replaced by the dinky ping? Are we ready to see the Louisville Slugger replaced by the aluminum ping dinger? Is nothing sacred?

Please, do not tell me that wooden bats are too expensive when players who cannot hit their weight are being paid more money than the President of the United States.

Please, do not sell me on the notion that these metal clubs will make better hitters.

What is next? Teflon baseballs? Radar-enhanced gloves? I ask you.

I do not want to hear about saving trees. Any tree in America would gladly give its life for the glory of a day at home plate.

I do not know if it will take a constitutional amendment to keep the baseball traditions alive, but if we forsake the great Americana of broken-bat singles and pine tar, we will have certainly lost our way as a nation."—A July 26, 1989 speech by Congressman Dick Durbin of Illinois on the floor of the House of Representatives.

In 1990 an aluminum bat controversy erupted after an article in *Sports Illustrated* mentioned the dwindling wood supply for bats. Though aluminum bats add up to 30 feet to the flight of the ball, aluminum bat manufacturers claim that they can "tune" an aluminum bat to equal the distance given to the ball by a wood bat.

Studies have revealed that it is not so much the aluminum per se that makes the ball go farther. Instead, balls will go farther because there is a much larger "sweet spot" on an aluminum bat. In addition, balls hit off the handle will go farther because the bat will not shatter.

Wood bats at the Major League level are not profitable to bat makers, so it may be inevitable that aluminum bats will be the norm in the Major Leagues in the next 20 years. Aluminum bats can cost as much as $200 each, but last significantly longer. An aluminum bat will yield about 500 hits before it starts to suffer from metal fatigue. Aluminum bats have been used in college games since 1972 and were officially approved throughout college baseball in 1974.

Hillerich & Bradsby sold 6.9 million wood bats in 1971 and less than 200,000 aluminum bats. In 1991 the total for wood was 1.25 million, with aluminum up to approximately 800,000. In 1995 the company for the first time sold more aluminum bats (almost 1.5 million) than wood (1 million) (see also **Manufacturers**).

On April 1, 1990, ESPN aired an April Fool's story in which Jose Canseco, Mark McGwire, Dave Stewart and Glenn Davis commented on how their game would be affected that season because wood bats were soon to be replaced by more durable aluminum bats.

A member of the 1930s House of David team used a bat made out of aluminum. He worked for an aluminum manufacturing plant.

Bat Day. See *Promotions*.

Bottle Bat. Heinie Groh of the Reds, Giants and Pirates (1912–1927) was famous for using a 19th century style longer-barreled bat for greater control. He punched at the ball, resulting in a .292 lifetime average, but only 26 home runs.

Broken Bats.

"I struck out with two men on base. I was so angry, so frustrated, I turned and without even thinking about it, snapped my bat over my thigh. The bat split right in half. Afterward, reporters asked me if it was the first time I'd ever broken a bat over my thigh. 'I broke an aluminum bat over my knee in college,' I said. I was just kidding." — Bo Jackson.

Handles have become thinner in recent years to make them easier to swing for home runs. This is why bats are broken much more frequently. About 500 bats per team are broken each season.

Fastball pitcher Chris Short once broke nine Dodger bats in a game.

In a 1952 minor league game, Bud Hardin of Houston in the Texas League hit a ground ball toward third base, splitting his bat. The broken part flew toward third base, striking the ball before it got to the fielder and knocking it into the stands. The batter was ruled out for striking the ball twice.

Rip Collins of the Cardinals saved broken bats and built a fence out of them at his home.

Yankee infielder Tony Kubek has three distinct memories of broken-bat home runs by Mickey Mantle.

In 1947 Stan Musial fouled off a pitch from Schoolboy Rowe and his bat broke in two. The top part flew into the infield and struck Rowe on the arm.

In a 1993 game late in a pennant race between the Giants and Dodgers, third baseman Matt Williams of the Giants tried to field a ground ball to end a Dodger threat. The barrel end of the broken bat flew at Williams at the same time as the ball and he was unable to make the play.

Mike Piazza and Roger Clemens were at the center of a broken bat controversy during the 2000 World Series (see ***Beanballs—Mike Piazza***).

Care of Bats.

"Bats, like ballplayers, didn't like cold weather." — Shoeless Joe Jackson on why he took his bats home to the South each winter.

Bats should be oiled with linseed or tung oil over the winter, or Vaseline can be applied. Bats should be kept dry and some recommend rubbing the bat with a bone to keep it smooth and hard. More recently, however, in *The Physics of Baseball* (1990), Robert K. Adair explained why the hardening of a bat actually had a negative effect on the distance of the flight of the ball.

Pete Rose applied alcohol to his bats.

Honus Wagner boiled his bats in creosote.

Frankie Frisch hung his bats in a barn during the off-season to cure them like meat.

Eddie Collins buried his bats in cow dung piles to "keep them alive."

While playing in Candlestick Park for the Giants, Bobby Murcer stored his bats in the clubhouse sauna to keep them out of the cold.

Ty Cobb rubbed his bats with tobacco juice to keep out moisture.

According to Billy Martin, Joe DiMaggio rubbed his bats with olive oil.

Honus Wagner selecting his bat.

Future Royals manager and minor league batting champion Jim Frey soaked his bats in motor oil.

Color. Bats are traditionally left in their natural color, but some bats have been stained black or lacquered to achieve a darker shade. The color of the bat is determined by the number of layers of lacquer that are applied. Color also is affected by a colored wood filler that is applied to the wood's pores.

Goose Goslin attempted to use a striped bat on Opening Day in 1932, but the umpires tossed it out.

Harry "The Hat" Walker used two-tone bats that had a white handle and brown barrel.

A's owner Charlie Finley briefly introduced gold and green bats during spring training to match his team's colors.

Hillerich & Bradsby made a black bat for Pat Kelly of the White Sox in 1975. It was the first time a black bat had been used since the 1930s.

In 1981 Pete Rose used a red bat made by Mizuno and Dave Winfield used a blue bat made by Adirondack, but both used them only during batting practice.

Colored bats must be approved by the Major League Rules Committee, which has approved black and brown. Some hitters have advocated dark bats at night to make it more difficult for fielders to follow the ball off the bat.

Construction. After 10 to 18 months of air-drying, billets of wood are cut to even lengths of 37 to 40 inches, sorted and weighed. Then they are shaped by lathes and measured with calipers to achieve exact specifications. They are sanded and flame-treated to harden the surface and bring out the grain. The flame-treating sometimes depends on the specifications of a particular hitter.

Corked Bats.

"I'm going to get myself a corked bat and blast one out of here. What's the suspension for Oldtimers Games, 10 years?" — Retired Reds outfielder Vada Pinson.

"Obsession with home runs has led to a plague of corked bats and steroids. There isn't a physicist worth his weight in newtons [neutrons?] who thinks that a corked bat adds so much as a foot to the distance of a home run." — Allen Barra.

Corked bats are a phenomenon introduced as early as the 1860s, when a Connecticut team cut out the core of basswood bats and inserted cork.

A corked bat increases bat speed by reducing the weight of the bat by approximately 1½ ounces. The cork itself has no effect, but one less ounce can add one more mile per hour of bat speed, which can add five feet onto the distance of a hit. Part of the reason is the cork doesn't add anything is because the energy transfer is ineffective given that the bat is in contact with the ball for only a thousandth of a second.

Bats can be sawed off at the end, filled with cork, and the end glued back on. Players have also drilled holes and filled them with cork. Apparently unaware of the bat speed principle, some old-time players put iron in their bats. Ted Kluszewski of the 1950s Reds embedded nails in his bat barrel. In a game on July 22, 1925, umpire Charley Moran examined a bat brought to the plate by Phillie George Harper, and discovered nails embedded in the wood. Harper was not allowed to use the bat and struck out on three pitches.

A manager can ask to have one bat from the opposing team checked during a game. As soon as the inspection occurs, players could use a corked bat without fear of punishment unless the bat breaks.

Albert Belle. In July 1994 the Indians outfielder was found to have a corked bat under unusual circumstances. Umpires confiscated the bat during a game and immediately locked it in a cabinet in their dressing room. Some time during the game someone climbed into the room through the ceiling and took the bat. Miraculously, the bat reappeared in Belle's locker, with Paul Sorrento's name burned into it. The problem, as noted by shortstop Omar Vizquel in his autobiography, was that all of Belle's bats were corked. Belle was suspended for seven days after losing his appeal, though the suspension was reduced from 10 games. Red Sox reliever Steve Farr claimed that while he was with the Indians the club had a private woodworking shop to manufacture corked bats.

During Game 2 of the 1995 division play-off between the Indians and Red Sox, Belle again was accused of corking his bat. As the bat was removed from the game, Belle flexed his biceps and kissed them, implying that he did not need cork. No evidence of corking was detected.

Norm Cash. The Tigers outfielder hit an American League–leading .361 in 1961, using a later-revealed cork-centered bat that gave him by far his highest single-season average. When Cash was suspected of using the bat, opposing batters would yell, "check his bat," prompting Cash to turn around and return to the dugout for another bat. After he retired, Cash demonstrated for *Sports Illustrated* how he drilled an eight-inch hole in the barrel and then filled it with glue, cork and sawdust.

Lenny Dykstra.
"I corked my bats in the minor leagues ... did it perfect, too. But I never corked in the big leagues.... What would happen if they suspended you? Damn, that would be weak to miss the World Series because of corking." — Dykstra.

Dan Ford. In the early 1980s the Angels outfielder was suspended for using a corked bat; it was during the same season that he started two brawls and also posed nude for *Playgirl* magazine.

Wilton Guerrero. On June 1, 1997, the rookie led off for the Dodgers against the Cardinals and grounded out. His bat shattered, and instead of running to first base, Guerrero ran to pick up the pieces of the bat. Suspicious home plate umpire Steve Rippley show the bat to crew chief Bruce Froemming, who ejected Guerrero after finding cork. Guerrero was fined $1,000 and suspended for eight games.

Billy Hatcher. On September 1, 1987, the Astros outfielder was ejected from a game against the Cubs after his bat split, revealing a cork center. Hatcher claimed that he did not know the bat was corked and that he had borrowed it from relief pitcher Dave Smith. Smith claimed that he used it only in batting practice. Hatcher received a 10-day suspension.

Howard Johnson.
"I thought he was coming back to be a coach, either that or to cork our bats." — Mets pitcher John Franco on teammate Howard Johnson, who un-retired after a year as a minor league coach during the 1996 season. Johnson came back in spring training but failed to make the club.

Cardinals manager Whitey Herzog once revealed that the club had an X-ray machine at Busch Stadium and one night the club checked out the Mets' bats. He said that they found four corked bats, including one used by Johnson (who was caught in 1987). Johnson went from 10 home runs to 36, which made the Cardinals suspicious. Umpire Paul Runge confiscated a Johnson bat early in a game, but gave it back later; it was never seen again.

Graig Nettles. On September 7, 1974, the Yankee third baseman was ejected from a game when rubber was found in his bat when it broke after a single. Tigers catcher Bill Freehan raced around home plate picking up the evidence — six vulcanized rubber superballs. Ironically, Nettles once reported on a minor league player who put mercury in his bat. The centrifugal force of the mercury whipped toward the end of the bat and made it heavier. Nettles' comment about the superballs: "I didn't know there was anything wrong with the bat. That was the first time I used it. Some Yankees fan in Chicago gave it to me and said it would bring me good luck. There's no brand name on it or anything. Maybe the guy made it himself. It had been in the bat rack, and I picked it up by mistake, because it looked like the bat I had been using the last few days."

Nettles had homered earlier in the game, and it was allowed to stand to preserve the 1–0 victory.

Amos Otis. After he retired, the Royals outfielder revealed that he used a corked bat for most of his career that, according to Otis, had "had enough cork and superballs in there to blow away anything." He had a friend stuff the bat with cork and superballs. Otis claimed that he was caught only once, in 1971 when the bat shattered. Umpire Nestor Chylak kicked the bat out of the way because of a close play at home. Chylak reprimanded Otis but no formal action was taken. Teammate Hal McRae also was accused of using corked bats, but the one time one of his bats was confiscated and cut into, officials found nothing.

Tony Phillips. In June 1995, the Angels outfielder was accused of having a corked bat. X-rays showed no signs of tampering or illegal substances.

Pete Rose. Tommy Gioiosa, Rose's gofer for several years, later swore that Rose showed him a corked bat he was using near the end of his chase for Ty Cobb's record for most hits. When Gioiosa asked Rose what would happen if the bat broke, Rose responded: "There'd be fucking cork all over the place."

As reported in a *Vanity Fair* article, Rose allegedly told Gioiosa that he would lay off pitches that might cause the bat to break, and that he scuffed the bat on the concrete floor to avoid detection.

Chris Sabo.
"I don't have a drill press in my house, and I don't have cork. I can barely change a light bulb. Look at my stats. I have three home runs and 16 RBIs, which is certainly no endorsement for the cork industry." — Sabo, then with the Reds, who was ejected on July 29, 1996, when his borrowed bat broke apart after a hit and cork flew

out. His original bat used during the at-bat cracked on a foul ball and he picked from among three that the batboy brought out to him. He claimed that it was not his bat that contained the cork. He was suspended for seven days.

Sammy Sosa.

"It's one of the farthest balls I've ever seen. If I didn't know Sammy, I'd think there was a cork in the bat." — Brewers manager Jim Lefebvre after Sosa hit his 61st home run of the season on September 19, 1999. It landed on a street outside of Wrigley Field, hit a car, and landed on the front lawn of a nearby home.

"Sosa said he keeps a corked bat to use during batting practice because 'I like to put on a show for the fans. I like to make people happy and show off.' I believe that. I believe gangsters keep shotguns in their trunks to shoot rabbits. I believe the Tooth Fairy is married to the Easter Bunny. I believe — I guarantee I believe — that Sosa is a liar." — Rick Telander of the *Chicago Sun-Times*.

"Cork popped out of Sammy Sosa's broken bat, which confused the Cubs. They'd never seen a cork pop." — Craig Kilborn.

"My mind was clouded by anabolic steroids." — No. 10 on David Letterman's list of reasons why Sammy Sosa corked his bat in 2003. No. 3: "If you hit home runs you get paid $20 million a year, dumb ass."

Sosa created a sensation in June 2003 when his bat broke and cork was found. Sosa was ejected in the 1st inning of the Cubs' 3–2 victory over the Devil Rays on June 3, 2003. His bat splintered as he hit a ground ball to second base. Catcher Toby Hall retrieved the pieces and showed them to plate umpire Tim McClelland. There was a half-dollar sized piece of cork in the bat, about half way down the barrel. His eight-game suspension later was reduced to seven, for no apparent reason. In his first game back from the suspension, Sosa hit a home run to a chorus of boos from Reds fans.

Sosa said later that the bat was for practice, and he used it to dazzle fans with home runs during batting practice. After the game, Major League officials collected every bat in Sosa's lockers, which totaled 75.

The Yankees were at Wrigley Field the following weekend with Roger Clemens going for win No. 300 when Sosa was in the middle of the controversy. Major League Baseball didn't dare suspend him for that series, and his appeal was pending during that weekend.

The day before the controversy erupted, the U.S. House of Representatives voted 372–0 to congratulate Sosa on hitting his 500th home run and praise him as a role model. There was a reconsideration, but the resolution was upheld and Sosa received his commendation.

The Hall of Fame X-rayed each of the five Sosa bats it had on display, and each passed the test.

Cost. Bats in the 19th century cost approximately 75 cents. Bats in the early 1960s cost $4. By the mid–1980s, the price had increased to $12. By the early 1990s Major League bats retailed for approximately $17. By the mid–1990s the Glomar company out of Southern California was making Major League bats that retailed for $39.95. Louisville Slugger sold its pro model for $24.99. Major League clubs each spend approximately $70,000 annually on about 200 dozen bats for their players each season.

Curved Bats. In the 19th century Emile Kinst invented a curved bat in the shape of a question mark to put spin on the batted ball and helped eliminate foul balls. A variation of this theme has been used in slo-pitch softball, in which an "ess" curve at the grip area helps generate additional torque during the swing and forces a more level swing.

Dimples. In 1994 an M.I.T. professor introduced small dimples to bats that improved bat speed by five percent. He estimated that they could add another 15 feet to Major League hits. He discovered the phenomenon while discussing aerodynamics of a cylinder using a bat. By adding dimples similar to golf balls, air would stay on the bat longer and reduce drag. However, Major League rules prohibit use of such a bat. They require the bat to be "a smooth, round stick.... No laminated or experimental bats shall be used in the professional game."

Fan Injuries. In 1958 Ted Williams threw his bat after taking a called third strike. The bat caught on the pine tar in his hand and flew into the stands. It struck a 60-year-old woman, Mrs. Gladys Heffernan. She turned out to be the housekeeper for general manager Joe Cronin.

Indians outfielder Cory Snyder once threw his bat in frustration after a bad at-bat. His hand stuck to the pine tar and the bat flew into the stands. It injured two fans, breaking the nose of one and the dental plate of another.

On July 5, 1994, Angels shortstop Gary DiSarcina seriously injured two boys attending their first Major League game when his bat flew out of his hands during an at-bat.

On June 25, 2003, a 15-year-old girl and a 4-year-old boy were hurt when Carl Everett of the Rangers lost control of his bat and it flew into the stands near the Rangers dugout. Both were bleeding but conscious; the girl, Elizabeth Spence, was taken to the hospital, but the boy, Sean Haynes, was treated at the stadium and left with his family. He later had six stitches put in. She suffered a skull fracture and blood clot, but was released a day after the incident.

Flat-sided. Flat-sided bats were legal and used from 1885 until the controversy over their use ended with their formal elimination in 1893. These bats were used most frequently for bunting because they allowed for greater accuracy.

Fungoes. Fungo bats are extra long and slim bats used by coaches to hit batting practice fly balls (see also *Fungoes*).

Grain. See **Wood**.

Illegal Substances. Players may not apply any substances to the bat within 18 inches from the end of the barrel. Players are subject to a minimum three-day suspension for violations. See also **Corked Bats** and *Pine Tar*.

Knob. The baberuth.com website contends that Babe Ruth was the first player to order a bat with a knob.

Label.

"I didn't come up here to read." — Henry Aaron when told his bat label was facing the wrong way while at bat.

Tradition has it that the flame-branded bat label should face away from the ball because the unmarked flat surface on the side opposite the label is less likely to break when struck.

Hillerich & Bradsby's Louisville Slugger trademark was registered in 1894. Use of the trademark and the actual branding of the bats gave rise to the practice of branding players' names on the wood. Before that, players carved their names or initials in their bats or used some other identifying mark on the barrel or knob of the bat. Before the 20th century, teams or manufacturers would use dyes with block letters to brand the bats. The "125" burned into the Louisville Slugger signifies the highest grade of wood used by the bat maker, which is used on all Major League bats.

Lamination.

"The advantages of a bat with a separate piece of wood in the end appealed only to one of Ken Williams' temperament. If the genius of home runs for the Browns had been presented with a bat painted bright blue, and he had managed to get a few homers with it, he probably would [have] just as vociferously stated bright blue bats had more hits in them than bats painted red." — *The Sporting*

News in 1923 after American League president Ban Johnson chastised 1920s slugger Ken Williams for using a bat with a piece of hickory laminated into the ash. Johnson also told Babe Ruth to stop using a laminated bat.

In 1939 laminated bats were banned, but in 1954 the rule was changed to allow laminated bats only if they were approved by the Major Leagues. So far, no laminated bats have been submitted for approval.

Length. See **Size.**

Luck/Skill. Paul Waner once had six straight hits in a game with six different bats; he grabbed a bat at random the first time up, got a hit, and then continued the pattern on each at-bat.

Manufacturers.

"Powerized" — Hillerich & Bradsby's trademarked slogan burned onto all of the company's bats.

"For it is true: a Louisville Slugger, for the American male, is a talisman — a piece of property that carries such symbolic weight and meaning that words of description do not do it justice. I have a friend who has two photographs mounted above his desk at work. One photo shows Elvis Presley kissing a woman. The other shows Ted Williams kissing his Louisville Slugger. No one ever asks my friend the meaning of those pictures; the meaning, of course, is quite clear without any explanation." — Bob Greene.

"If my endorsement of your Red Band Trademark Bats is worth anything I cheerfully give it. They are the best made." — Cap Anson's endorsement of A.J. Reach's "red-band trademark" bats.

In the 1880s Charles Burlingame, a Providence carpenter, turned out bats for teams in Providence, Boston and other professional teams.

Hillerich & Bradsby and Adirondack (the latter owned by Rawlings) are the two primary wood bat makers. Hillerich & Bradsby evolved from the work of John Andrew "Bud" Hillerich, the son of German immigrants who had a wood-turning business in Louisville, Kentucky. Prior to entering the bat-making business in the early 1880s, Hillerich's primary business was butter churning.

Baseball lore has it that the first custom bat was designed by 18-year-old Bud Hillerich in 1884 for Pete Browning. Browning was the original "Louisville Slugger," and the bat was named after his nickname. Browning supposedly went 3-for-3 the day after receiving the bat and word spread of the custom-made bat. Not really true, but a good story. The first mention of any connection between Browning and Hillerich is found in a September 1914 article in the *Louisville Herald*, titled "Every Knock is a Boost For the Louisville Slugger Bat." Research by Bob Bailey suggests that it was all made up, and continued to be embellished in future articles, such as in a March 1939 article by Sam Severance in *The Sporting Goods Dealer*, a trade publication. This version is repeated in the 1939 *Famous Slugger Yearbook*, produced by, not surprisingly, Hillerich & Bradsby. Bailey uncovered an interview with Arlie Latham by Clifford Bloodgood that was published in *Baseball Magazine* in November 1937, in which Latham claims that he received the first Hillerich bat. As occurred with other claims by 19th century players (e.g., Cap Anson), Latham may simply have burnished his image a bit and there was no one around to dispute him. Bailey concludes that Gus Weyhing is the most likely claimant to the first Hillerich bat, based on additional information contained in the Dudley article. Weyhing was a childhood friend of Bud Hillerich and went on to win 264 games in the Major Leagues.

In 1894, Hillerich and his father, J. Frederich Hillerich, registered the Louisville Slugger name. Frank Bradsby joined the firm in 1911 and in 1916 the company changed its name to Hillerich & Bradsby.

By the mid–1880s, Hillerich had more than 300 different models designed for Major League use. That number is about the same today, though the company has 20,000 different bat specifications in its files (as requested by players), accumulated over almost the entire history of Major League Baseball.

By the 1980s, Hillerich was making over three million wood bats per year and grossing nearly $100 million. Today bats are made by the company at Slugger Park in Indiana, near the Kentucky border, which opened in 1974. Hillerich cuts down approximately 20,000 trees each year to makes its bats for professional players. Another 200,000 trees are cut for bats for amateurs at all levels, though aluminum is used far more than wood at those levels. Hillerich & Bradsby usually ships 70,000–80,000 bats to Major League clubs prior to the start of the season. At their peak, manufacturers produced 7 million wood bats, but that figure is now reduced to 1.4 million.

About 65% of Class AAA and Major League players use Hillerich & Bradsby bats. About 90% of lower minor leaguers use the brand. Hillerich also controls about 25–30% of the **Aluminum Bat** market, second to Easton.

Of the 80 firms who have made wood bats, only a few remained into the 1990s. Canada-based Irwin Sports' Cooper Division sells about 100,000 wood bats each year. It claims to sell to about 30% of Major Leaguers.

Rawlings' Adirondack bat is used by about 25–30% of Major Leaguer players.

The most popular bat among Major Leaguers in 2003 was the Hillerich & Bradsby Louisville Slugger number M110. The number stands for Eddie "Bud" Malone, who was the 110th "M" player to have his own model, which was designed in 1939. It is 35 inches long and weighs 32 ounces. Through 2003, 13 Hall of Famers used the bat, including Mickey Mantle.

Worth supplies about 5% of Major Leaguers, including Frank Thomas.

Mizuno has a small niche in the market, with about 10 Major Leaguers endorsing its product.

During spring training some of the bat manufacturers tour the team sites with their "batmobiles" and can make a new bat to specification in 35 minutes.

During World War II proper wood was difficult to find and there was a shortage of bats. The Senators arranged for a few bats to be made by the Glenn Martin Company, an aircraft manufacturer in Baltimore. Martin was a Senators fan and he engineered a design for a bat shaped like an airplane wing. It was tapered at the hitting end, supposedly making it aerodynamically sound. The club used 10–12 dozen of the bats, but they broke easily and were not used again.

Memorabilia. See *Memorabilia — Bats.*

Names. Nineteenth-century star Pete Browning had over 200 bats. He was somewhat eccentric (and illiterate) and frequently named his bats, often giving them biblical names. He was eventually committed to an insane asylum and died at age 44 in 1905.

Shoeless Joe Jackson had 18 bats at one time. Each one had a name, including Big Jim, Caroliny and Old Ginril. In August 2001, Rob Mitchell of Pottstown, Pennsylvania, paid $577,610 for Jackson's famous "Black Betsy." It was believed to be the highest price ever paid for a bat.

When Babe Ruth hit 59 home runs in 1921, his bats were known collectively as Black Betsy. When he hit 60 in 1927, he used Big Bertha and Beautiful Bella.

Al Bumbry of the 1970s Orioles referred to his bat as "My Soul Pole."

Jay Johnstone of the Dodgers called his bat "My Business Partner."

Kirk Gibson's bat was "Thumper."

No Bat. In 1980 pitcher Bob Walk was a 23-year-old rookie pitcher who stepped up to the plate to bat in his second Major League game. Unfortunately, he forgot his bat. He believes it was the day he earned his nickname, Whirlybird.

Number Used By Players. Babe Ruth ordered 170 bats one season. Presumably many of them were given away. That same year, Lou Gehrig used only six bats and in 1930 Bill Terry used two bats the entire year while batting .401. A modern player orders an average of 70 bats each season. Though thinner handles on modern bats facilitate home run power, bats break more frequently.

Phil Rizzuto of the 1950s Yankees said that players received only six bats for free, and if they all broke, they would use another player's bats.

Tommy Agee of the Mets once used 22 different bats during a 22-game hitting streak in which he had only 23 hits in 22 days.

See also **Manufacturers.**

Pine Tar. See *Illegal Substances* and *Pine Tar.*

Size and Weight.

"When a bat feels just right, the balance is so perfect that it almost feels weightless. I've looked all my life for a bat that felt as good as the broom handles I used to play stickball with as a kid in the Bronx."—Ken Singleton.

The 1840s Knickerbocker club used a bat with uniform thickness (i.e., not tapered at the handle), but the length was unlimited. Bat circumference was restricted by the amateur National Association in 1858 and in 1876 the National League set the maximum length at 42 inches.

In 1880 the maximum allowable diameter was 2½ inches. In 1894 the maximum allowable diameter was increased to 2¾ inches. One source erroneously claimed that the standard bat width in 1895 was 2¼ inches.

Babe Ruth generally used a 35½ inch (or 36-inch) bat. Henry Aaron used a 35-inch bat. Al "Bucketfoot" Simmons used a 38-inch bat, the longest in history, and Wee Willie Keeler used a 30½-inch bat, the shortest.

According to some sources, Babe Ruth supposedly used a 52-ounce bat early in his career. Another more authoritative source reported that bat manufacturer Hillerich & Bradsby has a record of an order from Ruth for a 52-ounce bat, but apparently it was never used. Ruth favored a 42-ounce bat (some sources report 44 ounces) and never used one lighter than 38 ounces. Ruth used a 42-ounce bat in 1920 when he first hit over 50 home runs.

Ken Williams of the 1920s Browns reportedly used a 48-ounce bat on occasion.

Reds outfielder Edd Roush used a 48-ounce bat, the heaviest ever used regularly, which carried him to a .323 average in 1926.

Catcher Ernie Lombardi used a 46-ounce bat.

Ty Cobb purportedly used a 44-ounce bat, but was down to a 38-ounce bat by the time he retired.

Hack Miller, who hit .301 in 1923, regularly used a 47-ounce bat.

Although only 5'6", Hack Wilson used a 40-ounce bat that was extremely thin at the handle to accommodate his small fingers.

Reds second baseman Joe Morgan used the smallest bat on record, weighing only 30 ounces, but hit 268 home runs. 1950s Red Sox infielder Billy Goodman also used a 30-ounce bat.

Roger Maris and Mickey Mantle used 33-ounce bats. Ted Williams used bats weighing between 31 and 34 ounces.

Today's bats are much lighter than the large 36- to 43-ounce bats used primarily in the 1920s and 1930s. Average weights today are between 31 and 33 ounces and are 34 inches long. In the 1990s, the biggest bat was used by Kevin Mitchell, who used a 36-inch, 35-ounce bat.

Players today often hollow out the end of the bat to reduce weight and thereby increase bat speed without losing circumference. Hollow or cupped bats were first used in Japan. Jose Cardenal of the 1976 Cubs was the first National Leaguer to use these bats. Lou Brock was another early National League user of the bats.

Ted Williams had some interesting theories and practices regarding bat weight. Early in the season bats absorb moisture and therefore are heavier. Williams took his bats to the local post office to weigh them on its exact scales. Later on, he was able to persuade the Red Sox to install small scales in the clubhouse. Mr. Hillerich of Hillerich & Bradsby once laid out six bats on a bed, with one bat one-half ounce heavier than the rest. Williams picked out the offending bat two times in a row.

During Joe DiMaggio's 56-game hitting streak in 1941, there was a crisis when his favorite bat was stolen by a fan between games of a doubleheader when the streak was at 40. Tommy Henrich was using another DiMaggio bat, so the problem was solved. Nevertheless, DiMaggio wanted his original bat because he had sandpapered the handle to take off some weight. The thief and the bat were located a short time later because the culprit was bragging about the incident.

Superstition. See *Superstitions*—Bats.

Trademark. See **Label.**

Weight. See **Size and Weight.**

Wood.

"They can make 250 bats out of one good tree. How's that for a statistic, baseball fans?"— Noted baseball hater and "60 Minutes" television columnist Andy Rooney.

"Base Ball Bats of every variety of wood kept constantly on hand."—1870s advertisement.

Bats were originally made from strong hickory, but ash is lighter and springier and is today's wood of choice. Willow was so flexible that it was disallowed in the 1890s when it was ruled that bats must be made of hard wood. This came after John Montgomery Ward's teams used the willow bat exclusively for bunting.

In the 19th century, manufacturers advertised for used wagon tongues to obtain seasoned wood out of which they made bats. Cap Anson had over 500 pieces of wood that he seasoned in his cellar rafters. He used pieces of wood from logs, cart shafts and fence posts.

In the 1880s a bat "manufacturer" named Perring supposedly made bats out of the wooden scaffolding from a dismantled Ohio penitentiary. This was actually a single ballplayer, George Perring, who took wood from the penitentiary in 1880 and made a hickory bat which he passed on to his son, who played for the Indians and Kansas City in the Federal League. In 1910 a sportswriter wrote of the junior Perring: "George permits no one else to touch his bat, much less take it up to the plate. He carries it to and from the park in a special case. The timber from which the hang man's rope dangled in the long ago has been punishing the pitches during more than 30 years."

Modern bats are constructed of northern white ash timber that is 40–50 years old (or 60–80 years old, depending on the manufacturer's source). Most of the wood comes from the Adirondack and Catskill ranges of New York and northern Pennsylvania. Second-growth trees are used and ash is preferred because it grows slower and therefore is harder.

Depending on the size, a tree will normally supply enough wood for 60–250 bats. Wide-grain bats are generally considered better because they have less chance of splintering. Stan Musial always requested wide-grain bats and spring wood cuttings because he believed the wood was harder. Each grain line in a bat indicates a year of growth. George Brett's famous **Pine Tar** bat was a seven-grain bat. In contrast, Ted Williams looked for narrow grain bats, believing they were harder. One source reported that Williams was the only modern Major Leaguer ever allowed by Hillerich & Bradsby to hand-pick his own wood for his bats. Nineteenth-century star Hugh Duffy frequented the Hillerich shop and would drop blocks of wood on a concrete floor to find those with the proper "ring."

In the 1990s Sam Holman of Ottawa, Canada, began constructing his bats from "rock" maple, which has a density of 63 to 65, compared to the traditional ash's 60 density (wood density is measured in pounds per cubic foot). The maple barrel is smaller at 2¼ inches, versus 2½ for the ash bats. The smaller circumference allows the batter to generate greater torque by decreasing drag and increasing bat speed. Maple bats apparently are more durable and last longer than ash bats. The "Sam Bats," as they are known, were approved by Major League Baseball in 1998 and their use expanded significantly by 2000. Jose Canseco and Barry Bonds were adherents, among others, including Joe Carter, who raved about the bat: "When you first use them, it's a totally different feel from a normal bat. I mean, totally different. After you use them, you don't want to go back."

Batter's Box

"Get the keys to the batter's box."— Prank played on rookies that 17-year-old catcher Tim McCarver apparently fell for. When he asked for directions from minor leaguer Dick Rand, McCarver was told that they were "next to the glove stretcher"; as told in *The Minor Leagues*, by Mike Blake (1991).

"Dave Winfield thinks mighty well of himself, likes to spread himself out, take up all the space that his six-foot-six frame permits. Naturally, he's the only man who's in danger of obliterating both the front and back lines of the batter's box."— Thomas Boswell in *The Heart of the Order* (1984).

In 1886 the batter's box was increased from 6' × 4' to 7' × 4'. It is now 6' × 4'.

The 1901 Spalding Athletic catalog featured corner plates for each of the two batter's boxes. They were made out of rubber and were used as a "guide for the umpire to keep the batsmen within the box."

In 1906 umpire Hank O'Day suggested that the chalked batter's box lines be outlined instead with rubber lines so they could not be rubbed out by cheating batters. The batter may touch the lines, but may not go outside the lines.

Henry Aaron lost a home run on August 18, 1965, at Sportsman's Park in St. Louis when catcher Bob Uecker noticed that his foot was out of the batter's box. On the pitch from Curt Simmons, Aaron hit a home run ball on the ballpark's roof, but umpire Chris Pelekoudas called Aaron out.

In 1981 Mariners manager Maury Wills was suspended for two games for doctoring the batter's box by extending it a foot (to seven feet) in the direction of the pitcher. The head groundskeeper said he had acted under orders from Wills. A's manager Billy Martin noticed, because it allowed batters to step up closer to pitcher Rick Langford, who relied on a big curveball that the batters could hit before the ball's break took full effect.

Batting Averages

"The precise moment of maturity, when your son will be eager to view the ball game as a ball game, rather than a haphazard picnic, is easily stated. It is the moment he learns to do 'long division' accurately. That is the moment when his intellect has arrived at the comprehension of baseball; and all baseball percentages are arrived at by long division."—Fred Schwed, Jr., in *How to Watch a Baseball Game* (1957).

"Baseball is a harbor, a seclusion from failure that really matters, a playful utopia in which virtuosity can be savored to the third decimal place of a batting average."— Mark Kramer.

"Carew babies his batting average with the tender care of an orchid gardener."— Columnist Blackie Sherrod.

See also **Batting Champions**, **Four Hundred Hitters**, **Hits**, **Hitting**, **Hitting Streaks** and **Three Hundred Hitters**.

Early Record Keeping. "Batting average" was first called "percentage of hits per times at bat." Batting averages supposedly were first kept officially in 1865, but many players were unaware of exactly what they were batting. One source notes that in the National Association's first year in 1871, averages were kept formally only by Boston and Cleveland. Before that, teams maintained only records of runs.

Base on Balls. In 1887 batting averages were calculated to include base on balls as hits. This allowed 11 men to hit over .400. The rule was abandoned after the season.

Worst Team Leader. According to one source, the all-time worst team-leading batting average was .243 by Al Burch for the Dodgers in 1908. He also supposedly had only 39 RBIs. However, *The Baseball Encyclopedia* shows that the top batting average on that team was .247 (still terrible) by Tim Jordan, who had 60 RBIs. Harry Lumley had 39 RBIs, third-best on the team, while Burch had 18.

Bad Years.

"There were times last year when people looked at the scoreboard and thought my batting average was the temperature."— Buck Martinez.

"It's not easy to hit .215. You have to be going terrible and have bad luck, too."— Steve Kemp.

Low batting averages in 1906 (e.g., Chicago's "Hitless Wonders") prompted many to consider lengthening the pitching distance by 10 feet or more.

In 1968 Major League hitters combined for an overall .237 batting average, the worst ever. This led to changes in the **Pitching Mound** and **Strike Zone**. By comparison, Major Leaguers averaged .266 in 1946, the first full post–World War II year to feature a number of returning stars.

The 1973 World Series was the first to feature two teams, the A's and Mets, which did not have a single .300 hitter. The Mets were also the first club to win a pennant without a .300 hitter or a 20-game winner.

Mendoza Line. Mario Mendoza played sporadically in the 1970s and early 1980s, usually batting near .200. It became a running joke in the Major Leagues that a player batting below .200 was "under the Mendoza line," a phrase supposedly coined by George Brett. Other sources report that the phrase was created in 1979 by Bruce Bochte and Tom Paciorek of the Mariners. It was passed on by Brett to ESPN broadcaster Chris Berman, who has referred to it periodically during broadcasts. In nine Major League seasons Mendoza hit .215. He later managed in the minor leagues and ironically was hired as a batting instructor by the Angels in 1992.

Price Index. During the 1991 season, a Seattle bar used catcher

Dave Valle's batting average to price its drinks every Tuesday. For example, .152 translated to $1.52. Valle finished the season batting $1.94.

Effect of Umpires. A 1986 study revealed a 40% differential in batting averages depending on the strike zone of certain umpires.

Worst.

"If the meek shall inherit the earth, then the Dodger batters are in great shape." — Radio commentator Bret Lewis on the anemic 2003 Dodgers.

From 1955 until his retirement after the 1970 season, left-handed pitcher Hank Aguirre batted near .040 seven times, contributing to his .085 lifetime average.

Catcher Bill Bergen had the worst lifetime batting average, .170, of any player with at least 2,500 at-bats. He batted .139 in 1909, the lowest ever for a batting qualifier.

See also **Hitters**—*Pitchers as Hitters.*

Highest .300 Team Average. The 1930 Giants had a .319 average, the highest team average in the 20th century. The last club to average .300 or better was the 1950 Red Sox.

Batting Champions

"I've got to be first, all the time." — Ty Cobb, whose .367 is the highest lifetime batting average in Major League history.

Rules for Qualifying. Before 1920 it was the custom that a player had to appear in 60% of his team's scheduled games to qualify for the batting title. From 1921 through 1950 the leagues required that a player appear in at least 100 games to qualify for the title. Although Taffy Wright appeared in exactly 100 games in 1938, hitting .350, he had only 263 at-bats. Despite the 100-game rule, the American League awarded Jimmie Foxx the title with a .349 average in 149 games and 565 at-bats. A classic example of the effect of this liberal rule was catcher Bubbles Hargrave, who in 1926 had only 326 at-bats in 105 games. He won the batting title with a .353 average.

For the 1951 season the rule was modified to require that the champion must have at least 400 at-bats. The rule carried an exception that allowed a batter to be champion even if he had less than 400 at-bats; so long as he would have won the title even if additional at-bats were added to his statistics to get to 400. In 1955 the rule was modified to require that the 400 at-bats actually occur. Reds catcher Ernie Lombardi was the last man to win a batting championship with less than 400 at-bats, hitting .330 in 309 official at-bats in 105 games in 1942 for the Dodgers. The rule cost Ted Williams a batting title in 1954 (see also **Close Races**).

In 1967 the leagues changed the rule to require 3.1 *Plate Appearances* for each game played by the batter's team. Plate appearances include unofficial at-bats such as base on balls and hit by pitch. The leagues also adopted a similar version of the 1951 exception: a batter could win the title with less official plate appearances if additional appearances when added to his actual appearances still gave the batter the championship.

This rule is still in effect, though no player had won the title with less than the required plate appearances until 1996. That year Tony Gwynn hit a league-leading .353 despite not finishing the season due to a torn achilles tendon. He did not have the required number of plate appearances, but an 0–4 performance (which would have gotten him to the required number) still left him with enough of a margin over the second place finisher, Ellis Burks, who finished at .344.

Brothers. Dixie Walker won the 1944 title with a .357 average for the Dodgers. His brother Harry, playing for both the Cardinals and Phillies in 1947, won the title with a .363 average.

Batting champions Matty and Felipe Alou are the only brothers to finish 1–2 in a batting race. In 1966 Matty hit .342 for the Pirates and Felipe hit .327 for the Braves. Third brother Jesus hit .259 for the Giants.

Catchers.

"Did you ever try to figure out why a catcher's batting average isn't usually as high as that of most other players? The answer: his hands are swollen and always in pain. Try swinging a bat when your hands hurt." — Catcher Tim McCarver.

Ernie Lombardi is the only catcher to win two batting titles, in 1938 with the Reds and 1942 with the Dodgers. He certainly had no "leg" hits in the process: he stole only eight bases in his 1,853-game career.

Mike Piazza of the Dodgers made a run at the batting title in 1995, but Tony Gwynn and Piazza's sore wrist prevented him from taking the lead late in the season. Gwynn finished at .368 to Piazza's .346.

Win, Place and Show. The 1993 Blue Jays featured the top three hitters in the league: John Olerud hit .363 for the title; Paul Molitor hit .332 and Roberto Alomar hit .326, one point ahead of Kenny Lofton. In 2001 Larry Walker led the league for the Rockies at .350 and teammate Todd Helton finished second at .336.

The 1893 Phillies also had the top three hitters in the National League: Billy Hamilton at .380, Sam Thompson at .370 and Ed Delahanty at .368.

Consecutive/Controversy.

"Tie game stats are now counted, even retrospectively, and the Anson error has been corrected, so Hines is listed in *Total Baseball* as having the highest batting average for the two years, but is deprived of the batting championship–the result of a compromise with Major League Baseball in *Total Baseball's* successful effort to become recognized as the official Major League Baseball encyclopedia. Baseball stats and Baseball politics make intriguing bedfellows." — Former SABR Executive Director Frederick Ivor-Campbell on why two-time batting leader Paul Hines is not officially credited with two batting championships.

In 1878 and 1879 Paul Hines of the Providence Grays arguably won two batting titles (the first to win consecutively) and a Triple Crown. In 1878 Abner Dalrymple was credited at the time with the title because statistics from tie games were not counted that year. In 1879 Cap Anson was awarded the title because of a huge mistake by the league in computing Anson's number of hits. The tie game statistics are now counted and the Anson hit total has been corrected. Although Hines is listed as having the highest batting average for those seasons in *Total Baseball*, he is not credited with the two batting championships; this was the result of a compromise between Major League Baseball and the book publisher's successful effort to be recognized as the official encyclopedia of Major League Baseball.

Highest Average. In the modern era, Rogers Hornsby had the highest season average at .424 in 1924, with his best average that year against the Braves at .480. His worst average was against the Cubs at .387. He had 227 hits in only 536 at-bats.

In 1887 Tip O'Neil hit .435 when base on balls were added as hits. Hornsby would have hit .506 in 1924 under that system.

The first professional batting champion, Levi Meyerle of the 1871 National Association, hit .492 (.471 in some earlier sources).

Led Both Leagues. Ed Delahanty led the National League with the Phillies in 1899 with a .410 average. In 1902 he led the American League with a .376 average for the Senators.

Higher Career Average. Through 2004, the following players have won batting championships with averages lower than their career averages:

Player	Team	Year	Avg.	Career
Dan Brouthers	Dodgers	1892	.335	.342
Elmer Flick	Indians	1905	.306	.313
Ty Cobb	Tigers	1907	.350	.367
Ty Cobb	Tigers	1908	.324	.367
Edd Roush	Reds	1919	.321	.325
Ted Williams	Red Sox	1947	.343	.344
Ted Williams	Red Sox	1958	.328	.344
Rod Carew	Twins	1972	.318	.328
Tony Gwynn	Padres	1988	.313	.338

Lowest Leader. Elmer Flick of the Indians had a league-leading average of .306 in 1905. In 1968, "The Year of the Pitcher," Carl Yastrzemski of the Red Sox hit an all-time league-leading low of .301.

In 2003 Bill Mueller of the Red Sox won the title with a .326 average, the lowest in the American League since Rod Carew hit .318 in 1972.

Most Consecutive. Ty Cobb won nine straight batting titles from 1907 through 1915. He hit .371 in 1916, losing the title to Tris Speaker's .386. He came back to win the next three titles. These three were his last, despite later hitting, .389, .401 and .378. Except for a .240 average in 41 games his first season, he never hit lower than the .320 in his second season. He batted over .400 three times, with a high of .420 in 1911.

Most Titles (through 2004).

12 Ty Cobb
 8 Honus Wagner
    Tony Gwynn
 7 Rogers Hornsby
    Stan Musial
 6 Ted Williams
    Rod Carew

Negro Leagues. James "Cool Papa" Bell of the Homestead Grays reportedly forfeited the 1946 Negro League batting championship to Monte Irvin to enhance the younger Irvin's chances of making it to the Major Leagues. Bell was leading the Negro League batting race over Irvin, .402 to .398, with two games to play. Bell needed to play in both games to have enough games to qualify for the title. Irvin was considerably younger than Bell and had a chance to play in the Major Leagues with a good showing that season. In order for Irvin to put a batting title among his accomplishments to impress Major League owners, Bell intentionally sat out the second game of the doubleheader to forfeit the title to Irvin. According to Bell: "The fans were mad, but they didn't know what we were doing. We wanted to give Irvin a chance to go to the Majors. We would rather pass something on to a young guy to help the future of the black man. And I'm not the only older guy who kept his average down. We didn't have a future. We were too old."

Despite this testimony, the available statistics show that Irvin batted .401 and Bell batted .430 in 25 recorded games.

No Home Runs. In 1973 Rod Carew of the Twins won the batting title while hitting no home runs, the first time since Zack Wheat of the Dodgers in 1918.

No Longer in the League. In 1990 Willie McGee of the Cardinals was leading the National League in batting when he was traded to the A's. He had already qualified for the National League title and as a result Lenny Dykstra of the Phillies was competing against a player who no longer batted in his league. McGee prevailed in the batting race with a .335 average as Dykstra faded to fourth at .325. Eddie Murray finished at .330. McGee then signed himself back into the National League with the Giants for $13 million over four years.

Pitcher/Batting Title. Guy Hecker of the 1886 American Association Louisville club is the only pitcher to win a batting title. In 84 games he batted .341, defeating Pete Browning by .002. He also won 26 games for the club. For years there was a dispute over the batting champion that season because each newspaper kept its own statistics. Hecker is the only American Association player to hit three home runs in a game and holds the Major League record with seven runs scored in a game.

World War II Quality. Tony Cuccinello of the White Sox was runner-up for the 1945 American League batting title. Two weeks before the end of the season the 37-year-old was handed his release. One source reported that he won the title, but he actually lost out by one percentage point to Snuffy Stirnweiss of the Yankees.

Youngest. In 1955 Tigers outfielder Al Kaline became the youngest batting champion, with a .340 average at age 20.

Oldest. In 1957 Ted Williams became the oldest batting champion at age 39, hitting .388. He repeated as champion the following year with a .328 average. In 2002 Barry Bonds hit .370 to lead the National League at age 38.

Most Hits/No Title. Paul Molitor is the all-time hits leader (3,319) without winning a batting title.

Close Races Since 1901.

1903.

National League. Honus Wagner hit .355 to edge out teammate Fred Clarke at .351.

1905.

American League. Elmer Flick hit .306 to Willie Keeler's .302.

1906.

American League. George Stone's .358 edged out Nap Lajoie's .355.

1910.

American League.

"It is believed that factional troubles also existed, which were apparently augmented by rows growing out of Cobb's personal ambition and his desire to win an automobile offered as a batting prize."—The *Reach Guide* on the decline of the Tigers and Ty Cobb's effort to win a batting title and thus a **Chalmers Award** automobile.

Cobb officially finished at .3851 and Nap Lajoie of the A's at .3841. Much later research indicates that Lajoie should have won the championship. The race was marked by controversy, culminating with odd events in Lajoie's last game of the season. The official scorer in that game scored as hits a series of bunts by Lajoie to Browns third baseman John "Red" Corriden. The Browns players supposedly knew the bunts were coming but failed to make the plays because they wanted Lajoie to beat out the hated Cobb.

In his first at-bat of the game, Lajoie hit a triple that supposedly was "lost in the sun." He followed up with six straight bunt singles. After each hit by Lajoie, A's coach Harry Howell went to the press box to see how it was scored.

In his last at-bat, Lajoie hit a ground ball to shortstop Bobby Wallace, who bobbled it. The scorer ruled it an error, but a few minutes later a signed message arrived in the press box from Howell, stating that if the sportswriter who was scoring would change the play to a hit, he would receive a new suit. The scorekeeper would not change his decision, but the matter did not end there. The sportswriter, E. V. Parrish, is erroneously identified in one source as a woman (a sexist belief because clothing was involved?).

American League president Ban Johnson investigated the game and then blacklisted Browns manager Jack O'Connor. Corriden, a rookie, was sent back to the minor leagues. Another source reported that Johnson did not ban O'Connor, but that owner Robert Hedges fired him (this may have been done under pressure from Johnson). O'Connor sued for and received his 1911 salary, but never received another job in baseball.

Research in 1981 by *The Sporting News* disclosed that there had been a phantom 2-for-3 entry for Cobb in the official American League records and two unrecorded hitless at-bats that should have dropped his average from .385 to .382. Lajoie also had an extra at-bat to move him down to .383. Although the research clearly showed that Lajoie was the champion, the Baseball Records Committee rejected the findings, citing as controlling a prior investigation by Ban Johnson as definitive (though presumably that investigation related only to the last game).

One source suggested that Johnson simply gave Cobb two more hits in the official statistics to give him the title. However, this more likely occurred in 1922 when Johnson apparently altered the statistics to give Cobb the coveted .400 average (.401). The rival National League had its own .400 hitter that season when George Sisler hit .420 and Johnson did not want his league to be upstaged (see also *Four Hundred Hitters*).

1911.

American League. In his book, *My Life in Baseball: The True Record* (1961), Ty Cobb claimed that he won the batting championship by psyching out challenger Shoeless Joe Jackson in the last six-game series of the year. Cobb claimed that Jackson led by nine points going into the games and that giving the cold shoulder to Jackson during the season psyched him out. Cobb took the batting lead in May, however, and never fell behind again. The closest Jackson got was nine points in August and the teams had only a three-game series at the end of the season. Cobb batted .420 to Jackson's .408. The ploy perhaps occurred early in September 1913, when Cobb hit .390 to Jackson's .373.

National League. Honus Wagner of the Pirates finished at .334 and Doc Miller of the Braves at .333, though Wagner had 100 fewer at-bats. Chief Meyer of the Giants finished at .332.

1918.

National League. Zack Wheat won the title with a .335 average. Edd Roush finished at .333, but the elimination of two protested games (in which the individual statistics were not counted — the National League rule between 1910 and 1919), cost Roush the title. In one of the disallowed games he had two hits in three at-bats. In another protested game Wheat was 0-for-5. The change would have given Roush a .336 average to Wheat's .331.

1919.

National League. Edd Roush of the Reds hit .321 to Rogers Hornsby's .318 for the Cardinals.

1921.

American League. Ty Cobb apparently had won the title with a .391 average to teammate Harry Heilmann's .390. However, when the official statistics came out from the league office, Cobb was at .389 and Heilmann was at .394 for the title.

1923.

American League. Harry Heilmann batted .403 to beat out Babe Ruth and his .393 average. Ruth came close to winning the Triple Crown, as he was the home run and RBI leader that season.

1925.

American League. Harry Heilmann batted .393 and beat out Tris Speaker on the last day with a 6-for-9 doubleheader performance against the Browns. Speaker finished at .389, but did not play regularly due to injury and only pinch-hit the last few weeks.

1926.

American League. Tiger Heinie Manush, a lifetime .330 hit-

ter, battled teammates Harry Heilmann and Bob Fothergill, as well as Babe Ruth, for the title. On the last day of the season, Manush went 6-for-9 in a doubleheader to overtake Ruth and win with a .378 average. Ruth finished at .372. Ruth won the other two legs of the Triple Crown with 47 home runs and 145 RBIs and this was his best attempt at winning all three.

National League. Bubbles Hargrave of the Reds hit .353 to teammate Cuckoo Christensen's .350.

1927.

American League. Harry Heilmann went into the last day of the season in a battle with Al Simmons of the A's. The Tigers had a doubleheader in Detroit, while the A's had a single game. Simmons was up two percentage points going into the game and Heilmann was able to follow Simmons' progress because of the time differential.

Heilmann doubled in each of his first two at-bats and Simmons went 2-for-5 and finished at .392. Heilmann was out on a bunt attempt his third time up, but bunted successfully in his fourth at-bat. He had clinched the title and did not need to bat again. Nevertheless, in his next at-bat he hit a home run and in the second game he hit a single, double and home run in four at-bats to go 7-for-9 for the day. He finished with a .398 average to win the title, completing a string of three batting championships every other year for five years.

1928.

American League. Senators outfielder Goose Goslin led Heinie Manush of the Browns by 20 points most of the season but Manush gained on him near the end of the year. It came down to the last at-bat of the season when Goslin received a note from the press box that a hit or an out would determine the crown. If he did not bat, he would win the title. Manager Bucky Harris let Goslin make the decision and Goslin decided to remain on the bench. This led to a debate among his teammates as to whether it would be a "cheap" crown. After a long discussion he decided to bat.

His next idea was to try to get thrown out of the game after reaching a 0–2 count. Umpire Bill Guthrie let him rail for five minutes before announcing that Goslin could not say anything that would get him thrown out of the game. Goslin hit a lucky infield single to culminate a 7-for-15 performance over his last three games. He finished at .379 to Manush's .378.

1929.

American League. Lew Fonseca of the Indians hit .369 to beat out Al Simmons of the A's at .365.

1930.

American League. Al Simmons of the A's led the league with a .381 average. On the last day of the season he beat out Lou Gehrig, who finished at .379.

1931.

National League. Chick Hafey of the Cardinals finished at .3489, Bill Terry of the Giants finished at .3486 and Jim Bottomley of the Cardinals finished at .3482, the closest three-way race in history. It was the first time that the averages had to be calculated out to four digits to determine the winner.

1932.

American League. Tiger Dale Alexander finished at .367 to Red Sox star Jimmie Foxx's .364.

1935.

American League. Buddy Myer of the Senators won the American League title on the last day by going 4-for-5 to beat out Joe Vosmik of the Indians. Vosmik, who was leading the race going into the last day, sat out the first game of a doubleheader. He played the second game and lost by one percentage point. If he had sat out both games the two players would have tied. Myer beat out two bunts among his four hits to finish at .349 to Vosmik's .348.

1945.

American League. Snuffy Stirnweiss of the Yankees finished at .3085 and Tony Cuccinello of the White Sox at .3084. To cap off the disappointment, Cuccinello was released by the White Sox after the wartime season to end his Major League playing career, though he later became a coach.

1949.

American League. George Kell and Ted Williams went down to the last day after Kell came back from an injury and got hot at the end of the season. The Tigers and Kell were at home against the Indians and Bob Lemon. The Red Sox and Williams were at New York for the pennant-decider. Williams went 0-for-2. Kell singled and doubled in his first two at-bats and then struck out against reliever Bob Feller.

Kell knew that he would win the championship if he did not have to bat in the 9th inning, but he was due up fourth. Manager Red Rolfe told him he could come out, but he declined. The first batter grounded out. The second batter singled. Luckily for Kell, the third batter, Eddie Lake, perhaps intentionally grounded into a double play. Kell won .3429 to .3427, only the second time that four digits were needed to determine the American League winner and the first time a third baseman won the batting title. Not only did Williams lose the title, but the Red Sox lost the pennant to the Yankees.

1953.

American League. Mickey Vernon of the Senators finished at .337 and Al Rosen of the Indians finished at .336. Had Rosen overtaken Vernon on the last day of the season, he would have won the Triple Crown (he was the unanimous MVP winner as consolation).

Rosen had three hits that day and would have won the title if he had beaten out a slow grounder in the 9th inning. He lunged for the bag and missed by only a few inches, requiring him to take a short stutter step with his other foot to touch the bag. The slight delay allowed the throw to beat him.

Rosen could have won anyway had Vernon's teammates not conspired to arrange for him not to bat in the 9th inning of their last game. An out by Vernon in that at-bat would have given Rosen the title. In the 8th inning, Mickey Grasso doubled and then allowed himself to be picked off. In the 9th inning, Kite Thomas singled but was called out after trying to stretch it into an unstretchable double. Eddie Yost, a good contact hitter, popped out by swinging at a ball over his head. Pete Runnels struck out, which left Vernon in the on-deck circle with the title.

1954.

American League. Ted Williams batted .345 to Bobby Avila's .341. However, the rules required a player to have 400 at-bats and Williams fell 14 shy, giving the title to Avila.

National League. Willie Mays hit 36 home runs in his first 99 games, but his average was suffering. He hit only five more for the season, but raised his average to .345 and won the batting title on the last day of the season over teammate Don Mueller, who finished at .342.

1958.

American League. Ted Williams defeated teammate Pete Runnels on the last day of the season. They went into the last two games virtually tied at close to .322. In the first game, Runnels tripled, singled, homered and flied out. Williams was still slightly behind after walking, singling twice and hitting a home run. On the last day, Williams homered and singled to defeat Runnels .328 to .322.

1962.

National League. The race was so close that it took the three-

game play-off series between the Giants and Dodgers for Tommy Davis of the Dodgers to surpass Frank Robinson's .342 average. Davis finished at .346.

1968.

National League.

"You look like an old woman the way you're swinging the bat."—Tommy Helms to Reds teammate Pete Rose the day before Rose took extra batting practice and won the title on the last day of the season.

On the second-to-last day of the season Rose was slightly ahead of Matty Alou of the Pirates. Alou went 4-for-4, but Rose cracked his fifth hit of the day to go ahead by two percentage points. Rose finished the season 6-for-9 to beat out Alou .335 to .332.

1969.

National League.

"The batting championship, on the last day of the season, two years in a row. Players talking to me, fans talking to me, and what I got to do is hit. I got to block out all the talk and hit. When a young ballplayer comes 'round and asks me about pressure, I have a couple of pretty good stories to tell him, am I right?"—Rose in *Pete Rose: My Story*, by Rose and Roger Kahn (1989).

Rose and Roberto Clemente were tied going into the last game of the season. Clemente went 3-for-3 the last day, but Rose used a bunt single in his last at-bat to win the title, .348 to .345. Rose later said that fans in the right field bleachers were keeping him apprised of Clemente's progress via portable radios.

1970.

American League.

"The most disgraceful act in the history of the American League."—Mild response of a Boston newspaper after Alex Johnson clinched the batting title over Carl Yastrzemski.

The Angels outfielder won the title on the last day over Yastrzemski by going 2-for-3 and then leaving the game because Yastrzemski was already finished. Johnson hit .3289 to Yastrzemski's .3286 and Johnson was 10-for-14 to conclude the season. Angels manager Lefty Phillips claimed that he took out Johnson without consulting him when he determined that Johnson had clinched the title. It was only the third time in American League history that the averages had to be calculated to four digits to determine the winner. The enigmatic Johnson's response to the criticism: "I'm just paid to hit."

1976.

National League. Going into the last game, Bill Madlock was at .333 and Ken Griffey at .337. Madlock had been mugged the previous night and was still weak and hurting. Griffey decided to sit out the game and protect his average. Madlock banged out three hits in three at-bats and tied Griffey at .337. His fourth hit put him in the lead, .339 to .337. Madlock then left the game for a pinch hitter. The Reds and Griffey learned of Madlock's hits and Griffey came up to pinch hit. He struck out and finished three percentage points behind at .336.

1976.

American League.

"Brett could get good wood on an aspirin tablet."—Royals manager Jim Frey.

Royals teammates George Brett and Hal McRae went into the last game in a dead heat. In the 9th inning, Brett needed a hit to win the title. He hit what has been described as a routine fly ball to left field. However, Twins outfielder Steve Brye allowed the ball to fall in front of him and it bounced over his head for an inside-the-park home run. Later in the inning, McRae grounded out to shortstop, losing the title .3320 to .3333. McRae, who is black, was furious at the Twins and claimed racism because Brye had apparently made only a token attempt to catch the ball. The American League office briefly investigated and then dropped the matter. Brye later was quoted as saying that Brett was more deserving of the batting title as a position player than McRae, a designated hitter.

1982.

American League.

"I didn't want to win by sneaking in the back door, but I did sneak in the back door. My pride told me to play, but my common sense told me not to. I went with my common sense." — Royals outfielder Willie Wilson on sitting out the last game of the 1982 season to clinch the batting title. Wilson hit .3316, Robin Yount .3307 and Rod Carew .3305.

1984.

American League. Don Mattingly and Dave Winfield of the Yankees went into the last game with Winfield leading .340 to .339. Winfield went 1-for-4 to finish at .340 and Mattingly went 4-for-5 to finish at .343 for the title.

1989.

National League. Tony Gwynn of the Padres had three hits on the last day against the Giants to edge Will Clark, .336 to .333. Gwynn became the first player to win three straight National League titles since Stan Musial. Late in the season the Padres were playing the Giants and Gwynn hit a sinking line drive to center field that Brett Butler caught. Gwynn, standing next to Clark at first base, refused to leave the field as the Giants trotted in to the dugout after the third out. Gwynn stood alone at the bag and signaled "safe." The umpires then conferred, the catch was ruled a "trap," and Gwynn was awarded his single. At the time, Clark was one percentage point ahead of Gwynn.

1990.

American League. George Brett finished the season at .329 to Rickey Henderson's .325.

1991.

National League. Terry Pendleton of the Braves sat out the last game of the season after the Braves clinched the division the day before. His .319 average, 87 points better than 1990, was good enough to defeat Reds first baseman Hal Morris, who finished at .318. Morris had led over most of the last few weeks and was 3-for-4 on the last day, but could not catch Pendleton. Padre Tony Gwynn had a shot at the title but hurt a knee and missed the last few weeks. He finished at .317.

1998.

American League. Bernie Williams of the Yankees won the title on the last day of the season with a .339 average. Mo Vaughn was second at .337. Vaughn led by a point going into the last weekend after two hits on Friday, then singled on Saturday to drop to .335537 as he extended his hitting streak to 15 games. Williams went 1-for-3 to end the day at .336016. On Sunday, Vaughn had two hits in four at-bats, including a home run, but Williams had two hits in two at-bats before removing himself from the game with the batting title secured.

2002.

American League. On September 22, 2002, Mike Sweeney of the Royals and Manny Ramirez of the Red Sox were locked in a tight race for the batting title. Sweeney led by less than .001, with an average of .346578 to Ramirez's .346062. Ramirez chipped away at the lead and took over for good late in the final week. On Friday, Sweeney fell four points behind at .343 after going 1-for-4. He dropped to .340 after going 0-for-4 on Saturday and Ramirez moved up to .347 to lock up the title.

2003.

American League. Bill Mueller of the Red Sox beat out teammate Manny Ramirez, .326 (.32634) to .325 (.32513). Derek Jeter was a close third at .324.

National League. On the last day of the season, Albert Pujols of the Cardinals and Todd Helton of the Rockies were virtually tied. Pujols had an infield single to finish with three hits for the day, and the lead over Helton. Helton came up later in the day in the 8th inning for his last at-bat of the season. Padres manager Bruce Bochy had been thrown out of the game and he and his coaches were not aware that Helton needed a hit to win the title. Because the game situation dictated it, the Padres intentionally walked Helton, thus depriving him of an opportunity to win the title. After the game, Bochy said that had he and his coaches known the situation for Helton, they would have pitched to him. Pujols won the title in the closest race in National League history, .35871 to 35849.

Batting Circles

"'Take it easy …' and he noticed now the guy was shaking. Mike went back to the batter's circle and spat his contempt. He'd give half his pay to be in this guy's spot right now, but the Redhead didn't know whether to piss or go blind." — From "The Rookie," by Eliot Asinof (1954); though this "batting circle" is the on-deck circle and is different from the batting circle referenced in this section.

The **On-Deck Circle** is designated for the next batter. A separate batting circle near home plate just outside the foul lines is designated for the **Fungo** hitters during fielding and batting practice. This circle marks an area out of the line of the batting practice cage so that the fungo hitter, usually a coach, is protected.

Batting Coaches

"One is tempted to see in [Walt] Hriniak yet another incarnation of an Eastern master, but in doing so there is a danger of overlooking this special quality of showing up before anyone else at the crack of dawn and leaving after everyone else has gone home. His labor is as much a glory to traditional Yankee stick-to-itiveness as to whispers of the East. In either case, the labor is defined by his relationships. And out of these relationships, carried on through the medium of 'quality' hard work, there has emerged this sense that is Hriniak's own, of sharing with a hitter that most elusive and private mystery: hitting a baseball well." — David Falkner in *The Short Season* (1986).

Early Batting Coaches. In the 1950s Harry Walker and Wally Moses were two of the earliest formal batting instructors. Before the 1950s teams rarely had more than three coaches; two base coaches and one in the bullpen.

It has been reported that the first batting coach may have been Bill Dickey, who returned to the Yankees in the 1950s to help out. First baseman Moose Skowron was unimpressed: "He didn't do anything for us. All Dickey ever said was, 'Stay back and wait for the ball. Don't lunge.'"

Charlie Lau. Batting guru Lau was a lifetime .180 hitter when he radically altered his stance to win a job with the Orioles in 1962. He changed to a classic 19th century stance with feet wide apart and bat parallel to the ground. He improved from .194 in 1961 to .294 in 1962 and finished his career in 1967 with a .255 lifetime average.

Lau's book, *The Art of Hitting .300* (1980), replaced *The Science of Hitting*, by Ted Williams (1971), as the Bible of batting. Lau also wrote *The Winning Hitter*, with Alfred Glossbrenner (1974). His greatest notoriety came with the Royals, where he counseled Hal McRae, George Brett and Willie Wilson. Lau proved, through videotape, that a batter does not "roll his wrist" on the top hand as he strikes the ball. He died of colon cancer in March 1984 at age 50 while at the peak of his fame.

Walt Hriniak. Hriniak is probably the best-known successor to Lau as the guru of batting instructors. He achieved his greatest success with the Red Sox in the 1980s and the White Sox between 1989 and 1995. Like Lau, he never had much success in the Major Leagues, batting .253 in 47 Major League games. However, he believed that he made it to the Majors at all because of what he learned from one of his minor league managers, Charlie Lau.

Batting Gloves

"He's advertising his determination [at the plate] just as Thurman Munson's batting glove fidgets and neck twitches held menace."—Thomas Boswell in *The Heart of the Order* (1989).

The first batting glove was introduced to baseball in 1949 by golf pro Danny Lawyer, who gave one to Bobby Thomson. Batting gloves were used only for batting practice and spring training until 1964, when Ken "Hawk" Harrelson began using one regularly after a day of golf hurt his hands.

Batting Grips

"Cadillacs are down at the end of the bat."—Slugger Ralph Kiner on why he never choked up on the bat and always tried to hit home runs. Kiner claimed that the correct quote was "singles hitters drive Fords" and that he never said either one. Rather, Fritz Ostermueller said it about Kiner.

Split-Hand Grip. The split-hand grip, with the hands spread 2–3 inches apart, was the most popular during the 19th century. Ty Cobb supposedly was one of the last 20th century players to use this grip, which was popular among the placement and "punch" hitters who predominated during the dead ball era. Pitcher Smoky Joe Wood disputed that Cobb spread his hands, but recalled that Harry Heilmann of the Tigers did. Rube Bressler used the grip much of his career for a lifetime .301 average from 1914 through 1932.

Cobb was disgusted with the power surge of the 1920s and felt slighted that Babe Ruth was recognized as the greatest hitter of the era. To prove that he, too, could hit the long ball, Cobb intentionally swung for the fences on May 5, 1925. He hit three home runs that day and two the next.

Interlocking Hands. Catcher Ernie Lombardi interlocked his right-hand pinky and left-hand index finger so he could get a better grip near the end of the bat. He used the league's heaviest bat at the time.

Cross-Handed Grip. Henry Aaron began his professional baseball career in the Negro Leagues with the Indianapolis Clowns. At age 18, he had a cross-handed grip that supposedly was not corrected until he entered the Braves' minor league system. In his autobiography, Aaron reported it with a slight difference. While he was with the Clowns a Major League scout asked him why he used a cross-handed grip. He did not have a reason and changed immediately. He hit a two-run home run in the game that day.

Batting Helmets

"I can really get off on a good helmet throw. A connoisseur appreciates that, doesn't boo and watches the game as if it were Nureyev defying gravity."—Pitcher Bill Lee.

"Players have finally been persuaded to wear protective caps while batting. Say what you will about ball players, they are generally a rather boyish lot. It took a generation since Chapman's time to persuade them to do this simple thing. It hurt their manly pride. They were always willing to protect their meat hand with a glove and their shins with a guard and their digestions with patent medicines. But to protect themselves from sudden and undeserved death in their prime, that was asking too much. That would be womanish."—Fred Schwed, Jr., in *How to Watch a Baseball Game* (1957).

"I'm not stupid. I don't need to be no stinking tough dude hero. I'm 33. I want to see my kids grow up."—Brewers third baseman Kevin Seitzer on the special batting helmet with face guard he wore in 1995 to avoid another shot to the face (which would have been his third to the face and fourth beanball in a year).

Early Helmets. In January 1905 A.J. Reach patented a "pneumatic head protector" that sold for $5. After being beaned, catcher Roger Bresnahan tried it and liked it. Bresnahan had been hit so severely it was feared that he might die, but he recovered in one month. The first pitcher he faced upon returning was Andy Coakley, who had beaned him. The helmet resembled a football helmet cut in half. Bresnahan suggested that his team have one for both left and right-handed batters. It was never adopted and the idea of helmets languished until the 1940s.

Spalding Sporting Goods made some prototype helmets in 1939 at the request of the International League president. The president's argument for helmets was persuasive: "Don't you think our League by adopting head protection would be doing a great thing for players in the small leagues playing under lights and facing a lot of wild kid pitchers? It is certain that if we adopt a protective head covering that other leagues will follow our example."

Later in the season the equipment became official in the International League and a seven-ounce "safety helmet" was first worn by Newark's Buster Mills.

In 1940 Joe Medwick of the Dodgers was hit in the head by Cardinals pitcher Bob Bowman at Ebbets Field. While Medwick was hurt, the Dodgers brought up Pee Wee Reese to play shortstop. Reese was beaned almost immediately and was out for three weeks. Dodger general manager Larry MacPhail was furious (see also **Beanballs**) and ordered fiber inner cap linings for his players to wear while batting.

Some sources credit Jackie Hayes with the first batting helmet. The White Sox second baseman was blind in one eye. In 1940 he made a homemade helmet that also covered his ears.

The Giants used a form of plastic helmets in a game against the Pirates on June 6, 1941.

Effa Manley, the woman owner of the Newark Eagles of the Negro Leagues, is credited by some with developing the batting helmet. She patterned her design from construction site hard hats. Negro League player Willie Wells (who played from 1924 through 1954) is credited by some with using a batting helmet well before Manley or the Major Leagues introduced the protective device. In 1942 Wells, playing for Manley's Eagles, wore a workman's hard hat after being knocked unconscious by a Bill Burke fastball a week earlier.

Creighton Hale, long-time Little League president, is credited by some with inventing the modern batting helmet. However, Hale only invented the ear flap in the late 1950s.

Some sources report that in 1951 Phil Rizzuto of the Yankees was the first player to wear a full batting helmet in a Major League game.

In the early 1950s, the Pirates under general manager Branch Rickey were the first Major League team to introduce full temple plastic helmets. Batting helmets were first worn by the entire team in the field and at bat on September 15, 1952. They were originally called miner's caps. The players quickly stopped wearing the helmets in the field. Pirates manager Fred Haney also began wearing one of the new batting helmets in the dugout because he kept bumping his head on the dugout roof. Not coincidentally, Rickey was an officer of the American Baseball Cap Company, which manufactured plastic helmets.

Brooks Robinson is credited as the first Major League player to wear an ear flap for protection. He also cut back the bill of his helmet for greater visibility.

Rules. In 1957 the National League required all players to wear protective headgear (cap liners, rather than full helmets, were sufficient). Current players who objected were not required to comply. In 1958 the American League followed suit; Ted Williams initially said he would not comply, but later relented by wearing a liner inside his cap.

In 1962 the American League reportedly ruled that inner linings were not enough and that helmets had to be worn. However, there is no evidence of enforcement until the 1970s. The last player to wear only a hard liner in his regular cap was Red Sox catcher Bob Montgomery, who retired in 1979.

In 1971 Organized Baseball introduced Rule 116, which required players at all levels to wear helmets and Rookie League and Class A players to wear ear flaps. The ear flap rule was gradually extended through all levels of professional baseball to include the Major Leagues. At least one source erroneously reported that the mandatory helmet rule was instituted by the American League in 1957.

In 1981 the double ear flap helmets were required in the minor leagues. In 1987 batboys and ball girls in the minors were required to wear such helmets. By 1994 single ear flaps were mandatory in the Major Leagues.

Composition. Helmets in the 1950s were made of fiberglass, but this has been replaced by Cycolac, a modern plastic. Modern helmets have about a two-season lifespan and the more popular models are made by the American Baseball Cap Company. Helmets have polycarbonate alloy shells and two-ply foam pads to absorb impact and keep the helmet snug against the head.

Rawlings introduced the MPH helmet in the 1990s, which protects batters from pitches thrown up to 90 mph. The helmet contains an expanded polypropylene liner that absorbs shock.

Assist. In April 1992 Kirk Gibson's helmet went flying as he headed for second base on a ground ball by Pittsburgh's Jay Bell. The ball hit Gibson's helmet, bounced to Cubs second baseman Ryne Sandberg, who threw to third base and forced Gibson into a rundown. Third baseman Chico Walker threw to shortstop Luis Salazar, who tagged out Gibson. Andy Van Slyke scored it: "7½ to 4 to 5 to 6"

Use in the Field/By Catchers. Johnny Bench is credited as the first catcher to wear a batting helmet behind the plate to protect against errant bats.

Dick Allen is one of the earlier players to regularly wear his protective helmet while playing defense to protect against objects thrown by fans.

Abuse. Ron Swoboda once stomped on his batting helmet in the dugout in such a fit of anger that it could not be pried off his spikes in time for him to take the field for the next inning.

Batting Order

"The majority of American males put themselves to sleep by striking out the batting order of the New York Yankees." — James Thurber.

"They've dropped him to the gristle of the batting order." — Kevin Kerrane describing Mike Schmidt's drop in the order due to a slump, in "Season Openers," part of *Baseball Diamonds*, edited by Kerrane and Richard Grossinger (1980).

Discretion. Cap Anson would wait to see how his first batters did before committing himself to a line-up. If the first two batters did not get on, he might hold himself out for later in the batting order when runners were on base. In 1881 a new rule required a set batting order before the game started.

Pitchers. Babe Ruth is the only pitcher in World Series history to bat anywhere but ninth in the order (other than shifts due to pinch hitting). That occurred in 1918 when he batted sixth in Game 4.

In the opening game of 1952, Red Sox manager Lou Boudreau batted pitcher Mel Parnell seventh in the line-up. Parnell had hit .309 in 1951, but returned to a pitcher's usual level with an .095 average in 1952.

On July 9, 1998, against the Houston Astros, the Cardinals batted pitcher Todd Stottlemyre eighth, allowing shortstop Royce Clayton, who was returning from a rib-cage injury, to bat ninth. It marked the first time since Steve Carlton in 1979 that a pitcher batted anywhere besides last in the order.

Poor Hitters. Yankee manager Casey Stengel thought so little of second baseman Jerry Coleman's hitting ability that he sometimes batted Coleman ninth in the order.

Switch. In June 1939 Connie Mack was so fed up with his team's batting that he changed his batting order; he checked the average for his starting eight hitters and put their names on a napkin in the order of their averages. The top average player batted first in the order and so on down through the number eight position. He did it for a few games, which seemed to bring the club out of a tailspin (however briefly).

In May 1996 Cal Ripken, Jr., batted seventh for the first time since his streak began.

Batting Practice

"Batting practice is the time to stand around in the outfield and tell each other stories." — Jim Bouton in *Ball Four* (1970).

"My name is Ted Fucking Williams and I'm the greatest hitter in baseball." — Williams psyching himself up during batting practice.

"All baseball fans can be divided into two groups: those who come to batting practice and the others. Only those in the first category have much chance of amounting to anything." — Thomas Boswell in *How Life Imitates the World Series* (1982).

Early Batting Practice. Harry Wright of the Boston Red Stockings started batting practice in the 1880s, but it was not popular until the 1890s. Before that, players simply hit fungoes to each other.

Time for BP. In 1894 the Senators often conducted batting practice at 8:00 a.m. even though game time was not until 4:30 p.m. Dodger manager Charles Ebbets is credited with setting specific times for batting practice.

Organization. Batting practice is a highly regimented routine with as many as six balls active on the field at one time.

Cost of Equipment. A batting cage costs about $8,000, but lasts for years. The net on the ground in front of home plate to protect the grass costs $2,500. The five protective screens around the infield and on the mound cost $400–$600.

Break with Tradition. In a public relations move following the 1994–1995 player strike, the White Sox switched the order of batting practice to allow more fans to watch the home team. The home team traditionally goes first to allow the players more rest before the game starts.

Screens. One source reported that batting practice screens to protect pitchers might have prevented Walter Johnson's career-ending broken ankle while pitching spring training batting practice to Joe Judge in 1928. Nevertheless, Johnson was only 5–6 in 1927 and was not likely to have played much of a role in 1928. Grantland Rice reported in his autobiography, *The Tumult and the Shouting* (1954), that the injury occurred in 1927 and that in Johnson's first game back he pitched a shutout.

Batting Practice Pitcher. In 1977 at approximately age 71, Satchel Paige pitched batting practice for New Orleans of the American Association.

In 1937 the Yankees became the first club to carry a regular batting practice pitcher, Paul Schraber. One source reported that Schraber had been a Major League pitcher prior to joining the Yankees that year. He supposedly was activated in 1945 during World War II at age 42 and pitched against the Tigers. However, *The Baseball Encyclopedia* carries no entry for him.

Tommy Lasorda was still pitching batting practice for the Dodgers at age 65.

Cage. Pittsburgh's Forbes Field was so cavernous that the club stored the batting practice cage on the grass in dead center field.

Batting Stance

"He's standing confidentially at the plate." — Broadcaster Dizzy Dean.

"Boston's Nomar Garciaparra, the opposite of a fat man walking — he is, in fact, so energetically fidgety at the plate that he looks like a rawboned, long-legged Little Leaguer who has to go to the bathroom." — Roy Blount, Jr.

"For a ballplayer, the search for a batting stance is a kind of search for athletic identity. Is anything in sports so undeniably a signature as The Stance?" — Thomas Boswell in *The Heart of the Order* (1989).

"You know you're going bad when your wife takes you aside and tries to change your batting stance. And you take her advice." — Thomas Boswell in *How Life Imitates the World Series* (1982).

"The secret of hitting is the stance at the plate, an open stance for pull hitting and a closed one for pushing the ball — just like golf. If you're a left-handed batter, never try to pull on a left-handed pitcher." — Ty Cobb.

"Mel Ott, the little right fielder who, when about to swing at a pitch, lifted his right leg so high that he looked, as somebody said, like a dog peeing against a fire hydrant." — Frank Graham, Jr., in *Farewell to Heroes* (1981).

"I don't like the way he stands at the plate. He bends his front knee inward and moves his foot just before he takes a swing. That's exactly what I do just before I drive a golf ball and knowing what happens to the golf balls I drive, I don't believe this kid will ever hit half a Singer midget's weight in a bathing suit." — Former infielder Bill Cunningham on Ted Williams during spring training in 1938.

Mike "King" Kelly's stance required him to stand with his back square to the catcher to "look the pitcher straight in the eye." He held his bat down and waited until the last moment to raise it so as not to give away the direction he was hitting.

According to sportswriter Fred Lieb, Rogers Hornsby stood extremely far back from home plate. His was the most unusual batting stance of the era, as he combined the positioning with a low

crouch in the style later used by Pete Rose and Rickey Henderson.

Babe Ruth and Stan Musial stood with their feet close together.

Heinie Groh of bottle bat fame stood with both feet facing the pitcher.

Al Simmons was known as "Bucketfoot" for putting his foot "in the bucket" — stepping almost out of the box toward the foul line to start his swing.

Mel Ott and Sadaharu Oh each made an exaggerated lift of the front foot as they strode into the ball.

Joe DiMaggio stood with his feet spread wide, as did Kirk Gibson.

Joe Morgan cocked his back elbow twice just before receiving the pitch.

Rickey Henderson crouched as low as possible waiting for the pitch.

Batting Tees

"There is hope for the [1996] Detroit Tigers if the American League, as expected, brings in the proposed T-Ball rule." — Nick Canepa of the *San Diego Union Tribune*. The tee was co-invented by author Bert Dunne, who wrote *Play Ball!* in 1948 (which this author's father, Robert Light, helped publish).

Beanballs

"He did not waste a pitch, unless it was to throw a ball at a batter's head, and he did not consider that a waste." — Philip Roth in *The Great American Novel* (1973).

"I wish I had knew then that he was stealing my girl and I would of made Callahan pitch me against him. And when he come up to bat I would of beaned him." — Jack Keefe in Ring Lardner's *You Know Me Al* (1914).

"Look out!" — Braves pitcher Lew Burdette, known to be a head hunter, as he threw a slider on the outside corner.

"The pitch missed by a millimeter, to the profound regret of uncounted millions." — Writer John Lardner when a pitch by Hi Bithorn of the Cubs just missed the head of highly unpopular Leo Durocher.

See also **Brushback Pitches** and **Fights**.

Rules Against.

"'Look, Slots, I'll suspend his ass if he starts in with that beanball stuff. He'll be sittin' on the bench so long they'll be pickin' splinters out of him past Thanksgiving.'" — Michael Geller in *Major League Murder* (1988).

In 1917 the National Commission tried to legislate against the beanball by instituting a five-year ban on a convicted player. However, no such ban was ever implemented.

Umpires have the right to warn teams before games if adversarial conditions warrant it.

In 1978 umpires were given the right to remove both a pitcher and his manager if the umpires believed that the pitcher was intentionally throwing at batters.

In 1987 National League president Bart Giamatti issued a rule prohibiting "acts clearly intended to maim or injure another player." Major League umpires were granted the right to issue a warning to one team's pitcher and then *either* team's pitcher could be ejected.

Death. Indians shortstop Ray Chapman is the only man to die as a direct result of an on-field Major League injury, when he was beaned in 1920 by Carl Mays (see also **Deaths**).

A modified version of the batting tee for spring training practice.

There were at least four minor leaguers killed between 1910 and 1920 because of pitches to the head.

John Dodge played in the Major Leagues in 1912 and 1913, primarily at third base for the Reds. He was hit in the face by a pitch in a 1916 minor league game and died the next night.

Hughie Jennings. Star pitcher Amos Rusie, the first true New York baseball hero in the early 20th century, once beaned Baltimore shortstop Hughie Jennings. Jennings finished the last six innings of the game before lapsing into unconsciousness for four days. He managed to return to the line-up a few days later. The batter who followed Jennings in the line-up hit a ball that struck Rusie in the ear, causing permanent hearing damage (see also *Injuries and Illness—Head*).

Frank Chance. The Cubs first baseman was beaned many times, which caused severe headaches and hearing problems. The cumulative effect forced him to undergo brain surgery after he retired in 1914 and he died in 1924 at age 47.

Ken Williams. The Browns outfielder was considered one of the best players of the early 1920s when he teamed with George Sisler of the Browns. Williams was at the time second only to Babe Ruth in home run prowess. He began his Major League career at age 29 in 1919 after very brief appearances with the Reds in 1915 and 1916 and the Browns in 1918. From 1921 through 1924 he had home run years of 24, 39, 29 and 18 (broken ankle), hitting no less than .324 and driving in a high of 155 RBIs.

Williams might have continued his success but for a beaning on August 14, 1925. He had 25 home runs that season before the injury. He spent 10 days in the hospital and did not play again that sea-

son. Headaches and dizziness continued through the winter and by spring it was clear that he was no longer the same player. He managed to play another four years, still batting well, but his power was gone and he was no longer the feared long-ball hitter of the past (see also *Home Runs*).

Ossie Bluege. The Senators third baseman was beaned during Game 2 of the 1925 World Series. He was carried from the field on a stretcher and taken to the hospital. The x-rays were negative as reported by the doctors to owner Clark Griffith: "In fact, it may interest you to know that Mr. Bluege's skull is the thickest we've ever X-rayed at Hopkins, for which he can be grateful."

Chick Galloway. In 1928 the lifetime .268 hitter for the A's and Tigers had his skull fractured by a pitched ball and his 10-year career was over.

Mickey Cochrane. The Hall of Fame catcher was beaned on May 25, 1937, by Irving (Bump) Hadley. The injury ended his playing career and shortened his managerial career. He was often sick after the incident and was unable to manage effectively. He retired from managing the following season after only 98 games (though he recovered sufficiently to manage military teams during World War II).

Joe Medwick. During the 1940 season the Dodger outfielder was beaned by Bob Bowman of the Cardinals in Medwick's first at-bat after being traded from the Cardinals to the Dodgers. The two supposedly had argued in an elevator before the game.

Another version of the story had Dodger manager Charlie Dressen stealing signs from the third base coaching box. He whistled on the curve ball and Bowman picked up on this. The next time he heard the whistle he threw a fastball. Medwick stepped into the pitch and was nailed. Enos Slaughter of the Cardinals said later that the beanball was not intentional. Given that Dressen did not manage the club until the early 1950s, this version likely applies to Frank McCormick (see below).

Dodger general manager Larry MacPhail was furious and stormed on the field attempting to have Bowman arrested. He referred to the Cardinals as "Beanball, Inc.," in sarcastic reference to the Mafia's moniker, "Murder, Inc." MacPhail demanded that Bowman be banned for life and asked for an investigation. The prosecutor who had severely hurt Murder, Inc., with a number of convictions was brought in to interview a number of players in formal hearings, but no punitive action was taken. Years later when MacPhail was interviewed about the incident, he swore he never went on the field despite a number of eyewitness accounts to the contrary. During Medwick's absence, the Dodgers brought up shortstop Pee Wee Reese, who was promptly beaned and was out three weeks (see also **Batting Helmets**).

Frank McCormick. The Reds first baseman was the inadvertent victim of a beanball in the early 1950s. Dodger pitcher Kirby Higbe did not believe manager Charlie Dressen's accurate claim that the Reds were stealing the Dodgers' signs. Higbe told his catcher to signal for a curve, but to be ready for a fastball. Higbe threw a fastball at McCormick's head and the batter did not move, thinking the ball would curve.

Joe Adcock. The Braves first baseman hit four **Home Runs** against the Dodgers on July 31, 1954. The next day he was beaned by Dodger pitcher Clem Labine after he had been thrown at earlier in the game. Adcock was wearing a metal cap liner and was not hurt. After the game, Labine went to the clubhouse to apologize, claiming that he was not trying to hit him.

Ted Williams. He was hit in the head only once, in the minor leagues. He never wore a batting helmet during his career, but wore a cap liner late in his career.

Don Zimmer.

"In contrast, dimwit American sportscasters like to use *plate* as a verb, as in 'Canseco's single plated Will Clark.' Even third-grade English students can tell you: In baseball, *plate* should only be used as a noun. As in, 'Don Zimmer has a plate in his head.'" — Steve Rushin in *Sports Illustrated*.

Zimmer was a promising shortstop prospect for the Dodgers in the 1950s when he was beaned in the minor leagues. He suited up in Brooklyn and sat on the bench even though he could not speak for some time after the beaning. He later had a plate inserted in his head and never reached his potential. Maury Wills was the backup and was almost the subject of a **Trade** around the time Zimmer was hurt.

Jim Ray Hart. The Giants third baseman was a rookie when he was beaned by Curt Simmons in 1963 and missed the remainder of the season. He had already missed playing time after his shoulder blade was broken by a Bob Gibson fastball. He returned in 1964 to hit 31 home runs.

Tony Conigliaro. The Red Sox star was 19 when he hit .290 with 24 home runs and was voted 1964 Rookie of the Year in the American League. At age 20 in 1965, he hit 32 home runs to become the youngest player ever to lead the American League in that category. On August 18, 1967, with two outs and no one on he was hit in the face by Jack Hamilton's first pitch to him (some believe it was a spitball). Jose Tartabull pinch-ran and scored the first run of a 3–2 win.

The pitch caused bone fragments to lodge in Conigliaro's right eye, his face swelled up terribly, and he suffered blurred vision. He

was out for the year at a point when the club was only 3½ games out of first place in its pennant-winning season.

Conigliaro missed the 1968 season, but he made a miraculous comeback in 1969, hitting 20 home runs and driving in 83 runs. In 1970 he hit 36 home runs and drove in 116 runs. However, blurred vision returned and he retired during the 1971 season while with the Angels. He resurfaced briefly for 21 games with the Red Sox in 1975 at age 30, becoming along with Rico Petrocelli and Carl Yastrzemski the only players to play on both the 1967 and 1975 Red Sox pennant winners. Insiders later claimed that he had no sight in his left eye and spent hours practicing his hitting with his head tilted so that one eye could do the job.

In 1982 he was broadcasting for the Giants when he received an offer to do color commentary for the Red Sox. On the way to the airport with his brother Billy, he suffered a massive heart attack and substantial brain damage from which he never fully recovered. He was only 37 years old. As a result of these complications, he died at age 45 in 1990. See also Tony Conigliaro, *Seeing It Through* (1970); Bob Rubin, *Tony Conigliaro — Up from Despair* (1971).

Chico Fernandez. In 1968 this Orioles infielder was beaned and almost killed. He was in a coma for 11 days and it took over 18 months for him to learn to speak again. He had a steel plate placed in his head and never played again.

Paul Blair. The Orioles outfielder was beaned in 1970 by Ken Tatum of the Angels. Blair first tried hypnosis to get over his fear and then tried switch hitting. He abandoned the switch hitting attempt after going 11-for-57. However, *The Baseball Encyclopedia* has no record of him switch-hitting.

Dick Dietz. The Giants catcher had his head bandaged for the remainder of the 1971 season after being beaned. The team needed him behind the plate during its successful pennant run.

Ron Cey. During the 1981 World Series, the Dodger third baseman was beaned by Yankee reliever Goose Gossage with a 95-mph fastball. Cey went down as if he had been shot, but was able to return later in the Series.

Dickie Thon. The shortstop from Puerto Rico had a big year for the Astros in 1983. He hit .286 with 20 home runs, 79 RBIs and 34 stolen bases. On April 8, 1984, at the age of 25, he was beaned by Mike Torrez of the Mets. Thon had been called out on an outside fastball in his first at-bat and he was leaning in on a 2–1 pitch his next time up. An inside fastball caught him above the eye. He had poor depth perception and swelling behind the eye. His 20/20 vision went to 20/150 in that eye, but eventually returned to 20–40. Thon managed to make it back as a platoon player in 1985 and 1986, with a more open stance to allow his good eye to be used more.

In 1987 he left training camp in frustration and then went down to Class AAA. He retired in July 1987 after hitting .212 in just 32 games. The eye was better in 1988 and he was picked up by the Padres in a back-up roll. In 1989 he was even better and had a good year with the Phillies. This earned him a new $1.1 million contract and he continued in the Majors through the 1993 season, retiring in early 1994.

Mike Piazza and Roger Clemens. During a July 8, 2000, interleague game between the Mets and Yankees (and the second between the two that day, in different ballparks), pitcher Roger Clemens nailed catcher Mike Piazza with a fastball to the helmet. Piazza dropped to the ground, but was able to walk away without severe damage to his head (though suffering a concussion). After Clemens beaned Piazza, Clemens learned that Mets pitcher Shawn Estes was assigned to retaliate against him. Clemens apparently passed along a message to Estes telling him "not to worry about"; just do it and get it over with. Estes hit a home run and beat Clemens 8–0. He didn't hit Clemens, but threw a pitch behind him in the 3rd inning.

The drama returned during the 2000 World Series when Clemens again faced Piazza. Incredibly, Piazza fouled a ball off and his bat splintered, sending the barrel in Clemens' direction. Clemens stormed after the bat piece, almost trance-like, picked it up and flung it toward the foul line, almost hitting Piazza as he ran to first. Clemens was not disciplined for the incident and claimed that he had no idea he was flinging the piece of bat toward Piazza.

When Clemens joined the National League in 2004, he had such a good first half that he was named to start the All-Star Game. His catcher that night: Mike Piazza. Clemens gave up six runs, the most ever by the American League in the 1st inning.

Alan Wiggins/Pascual Perez. On August 12, 1984, Braves pitcher Pascual Perez beaned the Padres' first batter, Alan Wiggins, and kept throwing at him nearly the entire game. A fight broke out when Wiggins was hit by relief pitcher Craig Lefferts in the 8th inning. Both benches emptied and five fans ran onto the field and joined the fight. During a second fight in the 9th inning, Atlanta's Chris Chambliss and Jerry Royster tackled a fan who was trying to take a loose helmet near third base.

Jaret Wright. In June 1999 American League President Gene Budig met with Indians pitcher Jaret Wright, who had already beaned two batters that season and buzzed two others, and precipitated two brawls. Wright's excuse was that he was simply trying to move the batters off the plate.

Ted Lilly. In August 2001, Yankee pitcher Ted Lilly was suspended for six games for hitting the Angels' Scott Spiezio in the head. Yankees manager Joe Torre blasted discipline czar Frank Robinson for the harsh decision, because Lilly was not even thrown out of the game.

Pedro Martinez. Martinez and an alleged beanball were at the center of controversy during the 2003 ALCS against the Yankees (see *Fights*).

Early Black Major League Players.
"Black players, particularly those pioneering in a new league, faced greater danger than the average performers." — Jules Tygiel in *Baseball's Great Experiment* (1983).

The first year in which significant numbers of black players appeared in the minor leagues was 1949. One in four non-pitching black players reportedly was hospitalized because of a beanball incident. Phillies pitcher Ken Raffensberger said many years later that racist manager Ben Chapman ordered his pitchers to throw at Jackie Robinson whenever he had two strikes on him.

Incentive Plan. In 2000 a police officer in Pennsylvania lost his job after he was found guilty of paying a Little League pitcher $2 to bean the other team's 10-year-old batter.

Beards See *Facial Hair*

Jake Beckley (1867–1918)

Hall of Fame (VC) 1971
"Chickazoola!" — Beckley's rallying cry to rattle pitchers whenever he was on a hitting terror.

Beckley batted .308 as a first baseman over 20 Major League seasons beginning in 1888.

Born in Missouri, Jacob Peter Beckley was a mediocre left-handed second baseman when he played for Leavenworth of the Western League in 1886. After switching to first base and batting .401 in 1887, he arrived in the Major Leagues in 1888 with the Pirates, hitting .343 in 71 games. Over the next 19 years he established himself as one of the premier first basemen in the Major Leagues.

He played with the Pirates until midway through the 1896 season, except for a one-year stint with the 1890 Players League entry in Pittsburgh. He batted over .300 six times while in Pittsburgh and led the league twice in triples. After a short stay with the Giants he moved over to Cincinnati, where he remained for six full seasons and batted over .300 five times. He had a 25-game hitting streak in 1899.

Beckley played for the Cardinals from 1904 until his retirement in 1907, when he became a minor league player-manager for a short time. He played minor league ball until 1911, his 26th professional season, when he ended his career with a club in the Class D Central Association. He returned to Kansas City to manage a semipro team and finished out his connection with baseball by umpiring in the Federal League in 1913.

He had a .308 lifetime batting average with 2,931 hits and is fourth all-time with 243 triples. Until Eddie Murray passed him in 1994, Beckley held the record for most games played at first base with 2,377. During his 20-year career he made a record 23,721 putouts at first base.

Bed Checks

"The trouble with bed checks is you usually disturb your best players." — Long-time pitcher and coach Dick Siebert, who obviously was not including Mickey Mantle in this assessment.

"Chuck Tanner used to have a bed check just for me every night. No problem. My bed was always there." — Pitcher Jim Rooker.

See also *Curfews*.

Beer See *Alcoholic Beverages*

Bees See *Insects*

Belgium

Japanese shipping crews taught the game to locals in the 1920s.

James "Cool Papa" Bell (1903–1991)

Hall of Fame (NLC) 1974
"Papa's way was cerebral, improvisational; he was a master of the little things, the nuances that are the ambrosia of baseball for those who care to understand the game. Power is stark, power shocks, it is the stuff of immortality, but Papa's jewel-like skills were the object of shoptalk for 28 winters." — Sportswriter Mark Kram in *Sports Illustrated*.

"Because of baseball, I smelled the rose of life." — Bell.

"Funny, but I don't have any regrets about not playing in the majors. At that time the doors were not open only in baseball, but in other avenues that we couldn't enter. They say that I was born too soon. I say the doors were opened up too late." — Bell.

Bell was one of the finest outfielders in Negro League history between 1922 and 1946.

James "Cool Papa" Bell was a native of Starkville, Mississippi, and turned professional at age 19 when he signed with the St. Louis Stars. He hit .417 in 22 recorded games for the Stars and his career took off. As an outfielder he had blazing speed and was considered one of the ***Fastest Runners*** ever to play professional ball. By his own account he once stole 175 bases during a 200-game season.

He played 10 seasons for the Stars before moving on, playing primarily with the Pittsburgh Crawfords in the mid–1930s and in the Mexican Leagues from 1938 through 1941. He finished his career with the Washington Homestead Grays from 1943 through 1946.

He retired at age 44 shortly before Jackie Robinson played in the Major Leagues. He purportedly forfeited the 1946 Negro League batting championship to Monte Irvin to increase Irvin's chances of making it to the Major Leagues. In 1951 at age 48, Bell declined an invitation from Browns owner Bill Veeck to play for his team.

Bell finished his 20-year Negro League career with a .337 lifetime average, according to the somewhat sketchy statistics available in *The Baseball Encyclopedia*. He also batted over .350 against Major League pitching in exhibition games. He later worked as a night watchman for 21 years. He was the second Negro League star elected to the Hall of Fame and died in 1991 in St. Louis at age 87.

Book. Shaun McCormack, *Cool Papa Bell* (2002).

Johnny Bench (1947–)

Hall of Fame 1989

"To Johnny Bench, a Hall of Famer for sure."—During spring training in 1968 Ted Williams signed a baseball with this inscription.

"I want to win, but there's the grind. There's so much responsibility for a catcher.... My arm feels good. My legs will be all right. How long will I go on? How long can I go on? How long will I want to go on playing baseball? Is this what it's like to be thirty?"—Bench.

"I can throw out any man alive."—Bench.

Bench starred primarily at catcher for the Reds from 1967 through 1983.

Oklahoma native and part–Cherokee Indian Johnny Lee Bench arrived in the Major Leagues with the Reds in 1967. He had been the Reds' second draft choice in 1965 and tore up the Carolina League in 1966, hitting .294 in 98 games with 22 home runs and 68 RBIs.

In 1968 he became the first catcher to win Rookie of the Year honors, while batting .275 with 15 home runs. He exploded in 1970 with 45 home runs and 148 RBIs to win the MVP award and set a record for catchers in both categories.

He had another MVP season in 1972, hitting 40 home runs and driving in 125, both league highs. He had a scare after the season when a lesion was discovered on one of his lungs. After two hours of surgery it was found to be benign. However, the surgery cut into important pectoral muscles and apparently caused a loss in power. He never hit more than 33 home runs after that, though he led the league with 129 RBIs in 1974.

Bench is considered by some to be the best catcher of all time and certainly the premier catcher of the 1970s. The wear and tear of the position finally got to him and he switched to third base for the final two years of his 17-year career. He played catcher in the last game of his career in 1983.

Bench finished with 389 home runs and 1,376 RBIs. He also hit 10 postseason home runs as the Reds were the dominant National League club of the 1970s. He had a television show during his playing days and after retirement he moved into the broadcast booth locally and with CBS radio nationally.

Books. Johnny Bench and William Brashler, *Catch You Later* (1979); Johnny Bench, *From Behind the Plate* (1972), a photographic diary of the 1971–1972 seasons.

Bench Jockeys

"Bench jockeying in baseball is, like sculpture and lyric poetry, one of the fine arts."—Charles Einstein.

"In Casey Stengel's book, Billy Martin is a 'fresh kid who's always sassing everybody and getting away with it.' In everybody's book, Martin is a pest, a vicious jockey, and perhaps the damnedest rider of them all."—Sportswriter Ray Robinson.

"A bench jockey is a player who is riding the bench and tends to spur the tender epidermis of the umpire with taunts."—Charlene Gibson and Michael Rich in *A Wife's Guide to Baseball* (1970).

"He knew how to ride a guy."—Clyde King on Leo Durocher.

"There was no limit to what they'd say. They'd learn things about you. They would research you. If these guys did research in school the way they did research for jockeying, they'd all be college professors."—Joe Garagiola on the old days of bench jockeying.

Bench jockeying became somewhat of a lost art in the late 1960s. This was in part because there were more sophisticated former college players who did not adopt the crudest forms of bench jockeying. Another reason for the decline is that more trades decreased team loyalty and long-term relationships by players with clubs. As a result, players became less likely to berate former and prospective teammates.

Pitcher Lew Burdette once told Jackie Robinson that his use of the term "watermelon" directed at Robinson was in reference to Robinson's waistline: "I don't ride a man about his race. I'm hard in the dugout. But not on things like that."

Chief Bender (1884–1954)

Hall of Fame (VC) 1953

"If I had all the men I've ever handled and they were in their prime and there was one game I wanted to win above all others—Albert would be my man. He was my greatest 'money pitcher.'"—Connie Mack, who managed Bender for 12 seasons.

Bender was one of the premier pitchers of the early 20th century, winning 210 games over 16 seasons.

A's owner Connie Mack saw ***Native American*** Albert "Chief" Bender defeat the Cubs in a 1902 exhibition and quickly signed him to a contract for $1,800 annually. Bender pitched 12 solid seasons for the A's between 1903 and 1914 and appeared in five World Series, winning six games.

He moved over to Baltimore in the Federal League for the 1915 season, but his career was fading and he won only four games. After two more mediocre seasons in 1916 and 1917 for the Phillies, he pitched and managed in the minor leagues for a number of years. He made a cameo appearance in 1925 for the White Sox, pitching one inning and giving up two runs.

Over 16 seasons Bender won 210 games and won 20 or more

games in a season twice. He had 41 shutouts and 2,645 strikeouts. Bender also saved 34 games, including a league-high 13 in 1913. That was the same year in which he won 21 games in only 22 starts, appearing in a total of 48 games with six relief wins. Bender was also a fair hitter, batting .212 over his career with six home runs.

Bender was highly educated and well versed about jewelry and diamonds. He was also an expert trap shooter and billiards player.

Benefit Games

"Babe Breaks Leg in Sandlot Game." — Tongue-in-cheek nightmare headline envisioned when Ruth agreed to play in a sandlot game for a church team to raise money to pay off a new enclosed field. On September 4, 1923, as a favor to a Philadelphia priest, Ruth played first base for the Ascension Catholic club, a strong local semipro team. He finished the Yankee game that day and rushed by cab to the local ballpark for the twilight game. Yankee pitcher Sad Sam Jones helped Ruth arrive on time by no-hitting the A's in 1 hour and 23 minutes. The event is described in Edward "Dutch" Doyle's essay, "Sandlot Babe," in *The Ol' Ball Game*, edited by Mark Alvarez (1990).

See also *Charity*.

Destitute. Christopher Von der Ahe, the flamboyant owner of the St. Louis Browns in the 1880s and 1890s, went bankrupt in 1900. In 1908 as a result of a Major League benefit game held for him, he was presented with $4,294.

One source reported that in 1928 a benefit game was held for the destitute Eddie Plank, who ended his extraordinary pitching career in 1917. The only problem with the report is that Plank died in 1926 at age 51.

Stories circulated through reporter Al Stump that Ty Cobb sent Mickey Cochrane checks in the 1950s because Cochrane was destitute. Stump apparently never checked out the story, which seems to have emanated from Cobb. Cochrane's daughter repeatedly denied the story in later years.

Death. On June 30, 1910, the A's hosted a benefit game to help the widow and children of catcher Doc Powers, who had died of an intestinal problem two weeks after he was the starting catcher for the A's on the day that Shibe Park opened in 1909. The club raised almost $8,000 for the family.

On July 24, 1911, a group of American League stars played the Indians in a benefit game for the family of recently deceased pitcher Addie Joss.

When 19th century player and sportswriter Tim Murnane died in 1917 at age 64, his colleagues staged a fundraising game in which Babe Ruth shut out an all-star team managed by Connie Mack. The event raised $10,000.

World War I. In 1914 Organized Baseball held a Red Cross Day to raise money for that organization's World War I effort. Major League Baseball later created the Ball and Bat Fund to raise money for baseball equipment during the war.

Christy Mathewson Testimonial Game. Mathewson suffered from mustard gas inhalation in France during *World War I*. After he returned to the States in ill health, his money depleted quickly, although he had invested relatively well. It was decided that there should be a game in his honor with the proceeds donated to him, supposedly a first for any player (not true). The game was held at the Polo Grounds in late 1921 between the Giants and Braves. The first *Oldtimers Game* was played as part of the event, a promotion suggested by sportswriter Fred Lieb.

As a precaution the promoters purchased $25,000 worth of rain insurance. After the pregame festivities and the Oldtimers Game, the rain came and the insurance proceeds were paid out. Mathewson also received $45,000 from ticket sales and $5,000 from autographed baseballs that were auctioned off during the game.

Movie Stars. In the 1920s and 1930s movie stars such as Douglas Fairbanks, Sr., and Tom Mix played in baseball "all-star" games to provide proceeds for the Association of Professional Ball Players of America (APBPA).

Irish Relief. On May 12, 1921, the Giants turned over the receipts of the game to the Irish Relief Fund during Ireland's rebellion that resulted in independence from Great Britain in 1923.

The Depression. During the Depression there were many interleague exhibition games to raise money for the unemployed. After the 1931 World Series, such games raised $250,000.

Hospital. On June 14, 1937, four Major League teams played in West Virginia to raise money for a children's hospital.

World War II. At the 1940 All-Star Game, Major League Baseball raised $20,000 for the Finnish Relief Fund.

From 1942 through 1944 each Major League team staged at least one annual Army and Navy Relief Fund game. In May 1942 at Ebbets Field, the two teams raised $60,000 and the event included an exhibition in which 54-year-old Walter Johnson threw 17 pitches to 42-year-old Babe Ruth. Ruth hit two home runs.

On July 7, 1942, Major League Baseball and the military staged an all-star game between the American League All-Stars and an all-star service team. The game was played at Cleveland's Municipal Stadium and raised $62,000.

In a game on May 24, 1943, called the "greatest show ever" by Yankee shortstop Phil Rizzuto, $2,125,375 in war bonds were sold as the Senators played a group of military all-stars. The goal was to buy a cruiser for the Navy. A box seat sold for a $1,000 war bond, with lesser prices for lesser seats, down to 50 cents for general admission. Bing Crosby and Kate Smith sang, baseball clown Al Schacht entertained and Babe Ruth appeared in uniform.

On June 26, 1944, the three New York clubs (Dodgers, Giants, Yankees) played a round-robin format in a single game at the Polo Grounds that raised $6.5 million in war bond sales. Over 50,000 fans watched each team play six innings. The Yankees scored six runs, the Dodgers scored five, and the Giants were held scoreless.

Major League Baseball raised $363,000 for war relief from the 1942 World Series. The owners ultimately contributed a collective $2.9 million to the war effort.

Don Black. In 1948 Indians pitcher Don Black, who had a chronic drinking problem, suffered a cerebral hemorrhage while batting. He was still in critical condition when an exhibition game for his benefit was held on September 13 that year. He received $40,380 from the Indians thanks to owner Bill Veeck. Black came back from the injury enough to pitch in an exhibition game against the Pirates on September 22, 1949, but he never again pitched in a regular season game.

Roy Campanella. On May 7, 1959, the Dodgers held a benefit game in the Los Angeles Memorial Coliseum for their paralyzed catcher. Campanella had been hurt in a car accident in Harlem the winter before the Dodgers began play in Los Angeles. A record crowd of 93,103 showed up for the game and the Dodgers donated between $50,000 and $75,000 to Campanella. The Yankees gave their share of the gate receipts to charities.

MTV. In the late 1980s and 1990s MTV staged an annual Rock 'n' Jock charity softball game. Major Leaguers played alongside stars from the music industry.

Yogi Berra (1925–)

Hall of Fame 1972

"Right now, Berra does about everything wrong, but Casey warned me about that. The main thing is he has speed and agility behind the plate and a strong enough arm. He just needs to be taught to throw properly. I know he can hit. I'd say Berra has the makings of a good catcher, I won't say great, but certainly a good one." — Yankee catcher Bill Dickey, who was Berra's tutor in the late 1940s. Dickey remarked in 1980 that Berra later became "one of the truly all-time great catchers in baseball history."

Berra played 19 Major League seasons beginning in 1946 and was a three-time MVP.

Lawrence Peter Berra, the master of the malapropism (though this attribute has been embellished heavily over the years), grew up in an Italian neighborhood in St. Louis with Joe Garagiola. He had a tryout with the Cardinals in 1942 but rejected a $250 bonus. He later signed with the Yankees for $500 and played at Norfolk in 1943. After military service during World War II he played in 1946 at Newark before being called up for a few games with the Yankees. He homered in his first two Major League games.

Although he began as an outfielder, he was converted to catcher and through hard work and tutelage under Bill Dickey, he became the premier catcher in the American League. Only Roy Campanella rivaled him in the National League in the 1950s.

Berra was the regular Yankee catcher from 1949 until 1959, when he began to share the duties with Elston Howard and Johnny Blanchard. Berra batted over .300 four times and hit over 20 home runs 11 times. He knocked in more than 100 runs five times over his 19-year career and won MVP Awards in 1951, 1954 and 1955. After the 1963 season he retired to become Yankee manager. Though he led the club to the 1964 World Series, he was fired the day after the club lost the seven-game series to the Cardinals and the Yankees hired Cardinals manager Johnny Keane.

Berra then signed to coach with the Mets under Casey Stengel and appeared in four games. He finished his career with 358 home runs and 1,430 RBIs while batting .285. He appeared in 1,696 games at catcher. In his 18 years with the Yankees the club played in 14 World Series. Berra is first all-time in a number of categories and is second in runs (41) and RBIs (39).

Berra became the Mets manager in 1972, a year after Gil Hodges died suddenly. He led the club to a pennant in 1973 and remained with the club through two-thirds of the 1975 season. He coached for a number of years and then returned to manage the Yankees in 1984 (finishing third) and for 16 games in 1985. He continued to coach into the 1990s and appeared in several television commercials.

Books. Yogi Berra and Ed Fitzgerald, *Yogi* (1961); Yogi Berra with Tom Horton, *Yogi, It Ain't Over...* (1989); Yogi Berra and Dave Kaplan, *Ten Rings: My Championship Seasons* (2003); Yogi Berra and Dave Kaplan, *What Time Is It? You Mean Now?: Advice for Life from the Zennest Master of Them All* (2002); Phil Pepe, *The Wit and Wisdom of Yogi Berra* (1974).

Bibliographies See *Books*

Biographies See *Books*

Birds

"Robin Roberts, George Crowe, Chicken Hawks, Frank Bird, Sparrow McCaffrey, Craig Swan, Ducky Swan, Jiggs Parrott, Johnny Peacock, Andy Swan, Hawk Taylor, Birdie Tebbetts, Joe Finch, Bob Swift, Jay Partridge, Goose Goslin, Turkey Gross, Ed Hawk, Alan Storke, Thorny Hawkes, Ducky Hem, Sparrow Morton, Mike Parrott, Birdie Cree, Sam Crane, Red Bird, Doug Bird, Webbo Clark, Ivy Wingo, Conrad Cardinal, Cuckoo Christensen, Joey Jay, Hal Peck, White Wings Tebeau, Chick Cargo, Henry Cote, Jim Duckworth, Wingo Anderson"

"Back to the coop with the hoodoo hen in the wail of the southsiders. She is low browed and dotty, and doesn't know her lines. After Mr. Comiskey had imported her from the west side, at severe expense, the hoodoo hen laid goose eggs for the wrong party. So much for the perversity of the female species in general." — *Chicago Tribune* sportswriter Charles Dryden writing about Game 4 of the 1906 World Series in which Three Finger Brown of the Cubs pitched a 1–0 shutout against Dryden's White Sox.

"That's the first time I've ever seen a 'fowl' in fair territory." — Fran Healy broadcasting for the Yankees in Toronto, on a flock of ducks on the field.

"Let's put it this way — pigeons have been roosting on him for two years." — Broadcaster Vin Scully on aging and immobile third baseman Ron Cey, after Cey had moved on to the Cubs.

"The Goose should do more pitching and less quacking." — George Steinbrenner on pitcher Rich "Goose" Gossage after Gossage accused Steinbrenner of treating the Yankee players like children.

"[T]he Senators were in sixth and moving toward seventh, their customary habitat, with all the singleness of purpose of a homing pigeon." — Douglas Wallop in *The Year the Yankees Lost the Pennant* (1954), later made into the more famous theatre production *Damn Yankees.*

"The birds are in play. Just play it off the bird." — Yankee manager Buck Showalter after checking with the umpires during a game in Milwaukee in which hundreds of seagulls descended on the field.

"It was a cross between a dove and a pigeon. It was a digeon." — Pirates outfielder Andy Van Slyke after recording the last four outs of Game 5 of the 1991 National League Championship Series. He watched a bird graze in the outfield the entire time. Van Slyke said that it: "was one of the greatest games I've ever been privileged to be a part of, and all I could think of was that bird."

Rule. A ball which strikes a bird is considered still in play. If the ball is caught on the fly after striking a bird, the ball is live and the play is not scored as an out.

Carrier Pigeons. In 1883 Philadelphia zookeeper Jim Murray sent carrier pigeons from ballparks to telegraph offices to relay scores at the half inning of games.

Pigeon Problem. In the 1950s Fenway Park had a pigeon problem and the groundskeeper came up with a novel solution. He threw grain on the field to attract the birds and then Ted Williams, owner Tom Yawkey and others had a "pigeon shoot" to thin out the flock. Word got out that Williams participated and he was chastised by the press and the local humane society. Williams reportedly was known to use the Fenway Park scoreboard lights for target practice.

Part of the club's frustration may have come from an incident on May 17, 1947, when a seagull dropped a three-pound fish on the mound during a game. Ellis Kinder was pitching at the time.

Window Dressing. In 1884 Henry Lucas, owner of the Union Association St. Louis club, had dozens of caged canaries placed around the stands.

Pet. Early 20th century pitcher Rube Waddell supposedly owned a mockingbird until it became so disruptive that one of Waddell's teammates strangled it.

Stunt. A famous story has it that outfielder Casey Stengel once found an injured sparrow in the field at the start of a game. The incident occurred on June 6, 1918, when he visited his old club, the Dodgers, as a member of the Pirates. He put the bird under his cap for protection and finished the 1st inning in the outfield. When he came up to bat in the top of the 2nd inning he was booed by the hostile crowd, and as a gesture to the crowd he doffed his cap. Out flew the bird, and he was deemed to have "given the bird" to the fans (a common obscenity using the middle finger). Stengel later denied he had planned the incident, saying that he merely had forgotten that the bird was there. Some sources report that Stengel was still popular in Brooklyn and was saluting the fans' ovation.

Joe DiMaggio. With one exception, DiMaggio claimed that he was never caught overrunning a base. He once thought a bird sitting in the outfield was the ball and believed he had time to take a bigger lead rounding second on a double. He was caught off the base and tagged out.

"Struck Out." In 1945 at Fenway Park, A's outfielder Hal Peck made a throw to home plate that hit a pigeon and deflected to the second baseman, who tagged Skeeter Newsome sliding into second base. The pigeon lived. Another version of the story had Newsome hitting the bird with his hit, turning a single into a double.

In 1974 at Fenway Park, Willie Horton killed a pigeon with a foul ball.

Eric Davis struck a bird with a batted ball in a 1981 minor league game.

In April 1987 Dion James of the Braves hit a fly ball against the Mets which struck a dove. The hit was ruled a ground rule double on what otherwise would have been an easy fly ball out. Shortstop Rafael Santana fielded the bird and gave it to a ball girl, though reports conflict as to whether or not the bird was killed.

In a 2001 spring training game, pitcher Randy Johnson threw a fastball that hit a dove, which exploded in a burst of white feathers. The blow prompted this comment from radio show host Jim Rome: "The bird was crowding the plate and needed to be backed off."

Dave Winfield.

"They say he hit the gull on purpose. They wouldn't say that if they'd seen the throws he's been making all year. It's the first time he's hit the cut-off man."—Yankee manager Billy Martin on outfielder Dave Winfield after Winfield struck a seagull during warm-up tosses before the 5th inning during a game in Toronto on August 4, 1983. He doffed his cap in mock sorrow, and the crowd laughed. Later that night he was brought before the Ontario Provincial Police on a charge of cruelty to animals and forced to post a $500 bond, but the charges were dropped the next day. Winfield later commissioned paintings of seagulls that raised $65,000 for Easter Seals. Apparently he didn't kill the bird. Winfield was sorry: "I am truly sorry that a fowl of Canada is no longer with us."

Bird Hunting. In April 2003, minor league pitcher Jae-kuk Ryu, a 19-year-old South Korean pitcher for the Class A Daytona Beach Cubs, knocked an osprey named Ozzy from its perch during pregame practice. It appeared that he had done it intentionally, prompting an investigation by the Florida Fish and Wildlife Conservation Commission. The bird, protected as a "species of special concern," sustained a serious eye injury and died three days later. The pitcher was then demoted to the Lansing Lugnuts of the Midwest League, fined $500 and placed on six months' probation. In January 2004 a judge ruled that he could not pay his way out of doing community service for killing the osprey.

Decoy. When the ballpark in Texas opened for the 1994 season, the club placed plastic owls in the rafters to scare off dive-bombing pigeons.

Mound Visit. On July 17, 2002, a seagull visited a pitcher on the mound for the third consecutive game. Pitcher Rick Reed had to shoo away the gull, but managed to avoid the distraction and pick up the win. The visit was probably about as productive as most mound conferences.

Birth Defects

"Which big league ballplayers have had physical deformities? No Neck Williams, Three Finger Brown and Sixto Lezcano."—Sportswriter Mike Downey.

See also *Deaf Ballplayers.*

Joe Black. The Dodger pitcher had a condition with two of his pitching hand fingers that apparently existed since birth. Black was unable to lift his middle and index fingers and they simply "sat" on the ball when he threw. It did not affect his pitching, as he won 15 games and had 15 saves in his rookie season in 1952. The following spring he changed his grip in an attempt to add another pitch to his repertoire. He never found his rhythm again and was largely ineffective until his retirement in 1957.

Buddy Daley. The left-hander pitched in the American League for 10 years with a withered right arm that was injured at birth. He won 60 games, including one in the 1961 World Series.

Jim Abbott. Abbott is easily the most famous person to become a Major League player and have a significant birth defect. His right hand never fully formed. He gripped his glove with the remnants of his right hand and shifted the glove to his left hand after his pitching follow-through. He played on the 1988 U.S. Olympic team that won the gold medal and was on the mound for the last out. He went straight to the Angels without any minor league experience.

By 1993 Abbott was considered to have the best "stuff" of any left-hander in the American League, but his pitches were considered easy to follow because he could not conceal the ball in his glove (he later faded badly). He capped the 1993 season with a no-hitter for the Yankees against the Indians on September 4, 1993.

As a high school senior he batted cleanup and batted .427 with seven home runs. At Michigan, he batted three times and got two hits. His batting ability became an issue when interleague play required him to bat, but he recorded his first Major League in June 1999 in a game against the Cubs while playing for the Brewers.

The Angels released him in early 1997 when he refused to be sent down to the minor leagues. The club ate the remaining $5.6 million of his contract. He made a comeback with the White Sox in late 1998, posting a 5–0 record for the club. He was 2–8 for the Brewers in 1999 before retiring.

See also Bob Bernotas, *Nothing to Prove: The Jim Abbot Story* (1995).

Antonio Alfonseca. The 2000s reliever was nicknamed El Pulpo (octopus) because he was born with six fingers on each hand and six toes on each foot.

Chad Bentz. The Expos pitcher has a deformed right hand. A 7th round draft pick in 2001, he was 1–4 with 16 saves in Class AA during the 2003 season and started 2004 on the Expos roster. The lefthander gave up a hit in two-thirds of an inning in his debut on April 7, 2004, helping to preserve a 3–2 win over the Marlins.

Birthdays

"I occasionally get birthday cards from fans. But it's often the same message: They hope it's my last." — Umpire Al Forman.

"How old would you be if you didn't know how old you was?" — Satchel Paige, whose birthdate was always a source of mystery and controversy. Paige later said that his birthdate was never a mystery, but that it became a publicity stunt perpetuated by Browns owner Bill Veeck. Paige's birthday has been confirmed as July 7, 1906.

Early Major Leaguer. Dickey Pearce was born in 1836 in Brooklyn and he had one of the earliest birthdates of any National League player. He played in a few games over two seasons for St. Louis before retiring.

Birthday Cake/Song.

"Well, we was going to get you one, but we figured you'd drop it." — Mets manager Casey Stengel to stone-handed Marv Throneberry after the first baseman complained that he did not receive a birthday cake.

When Bill Veeck owned the American Association Milwaukee Millers, he once bought manager Charlie Grimm a birthday present. It was left-handed pitcher Jose Acosta, who jumped out of a giant birthday cake upon his arrival with the club.

On August 24, 1960, Vin Scully was broadcasting for the Dodgers at the Los Angeles Coliseum. He noticed that it was umpire Frank Secory's birthday. Scully said through the microphone to the assembled crowd, many of whom had transistor radios: "Today is Frank Secory's birthday. Let's have some fun. As soon as the inning is over I'll count to three and on three everybody yell, 'Happy birthday, Frank!'"

The crowd responded as requested and Secory was astounded.

False Information.

"He's 33. What, in dog years?" — Phillies catcher Darren Daulton on new teammate Fernando Valenzuela. It was always suspected that Valenzuela had misstated his birthdate when he arrived with the Dodgers in 1980. The Mexican player claimed to be 19 years old, but many suspected that he was at least five years older.

"I'm only 32 in the Dominican Republic." — Tim Raines, retired outfielder, on being a 42-year-old Major Leaguer with the Florida Marlins in 2002.

"Them ain't lies, them's scoops." — Dizzy Dean explaining why he began giving sportswriters different locales for his birthplace.

"We're excited he's gained those years of knowledge." — Angels spokesman Tim Mead in 2003, after learning that pitcher Ramon Ortiz had aged three years after the U.S. Consulate in the Dominican Republic announced that his birth certificate showed that he was 28, not 25 as reflected on his passport.

In compiling their 1951 *The Official Encyclopedia of Baseball*, the editors claimed they found that 95% of the ballplayers had lied about their birthdates. The practice was common among many of the Negro League stars who were late in joining the Major Leagues. For example, Luke Easter was announced to be 33 when he broke into the Major Leagues, though there was speculation that he was 40. *The Baseball Encyclopedia* now lists him at 35 when he broke in.

Latin ballplayers have been notorious for faking birth certificates and lying about their ages. One 29-year-old Dominican used a birth certificate held by his much younger *sister*.

In 2000, when Braves infielder Rafael Furcal made his debut, it was noted that he was the first player born in the 1980s to make it to the Major Leagues. It was later determined that he had cut two years from his birth certificate, and actually was born in 1978.

In late 1999 controversy erupted over Dodger third baseman Adrian Beltre, who had just completed a breakout season at what was thought to be age 21. His agent, Scott Boras, learned from his client that he was only 20, and then confronted the Dodgers with the information. Boras said he had proof the Dodgers knowingly signed Beltre at age 15, one year earlier than allowed. Boras also alleged that the club altered documents that reflected Beltre's true age by using correction fluid. He claimed that the Dodgers delayed responding to his inquiry for several months, and responded only after Boras had acquired a certified, unaltered birth certificate. The Dodgers had signed Beltre for $23,000 in 1994, and many believed that he could have received far more had he been exposed to more teams at an older age.

In other situations, players signed under age were granted free agency. Those cases generally involved minor league players in which much less was at stake, but Beltre potentially could have commanded several million dollars annually on the open market.

The Dodgers already were barred from signing international players until after January 1, 2000, because scout Pablo Peguero violated rules while signing Cuban players Juan Carlos Diaz and Josue Perez. Those players were granted free agency, and the Dodgers were fined $200,000. Peguero had also signed Beltre, and eventually the Dodgers were fined, but allowed to keep Beltre. See also **Dominican Republic** for the Dodgers' ban on scouting due to signing underage players.

Early Signings. Mary Francis Veeck, wife of Bill Veeck, conceived the "Brownie Baby Promotion" for the Browns. The club mailed special contracts to parents of St. Louis newborns, inviting their sons to a tryout when they turned 18.

Leap Year. Pepper Martin was born February 29, 1904. He started his Major League career in 1928 and ended it in 1944. All were leap years.

Long Lost Twin? 1994 is the only year in which each league chose a first baseman for its MVP Award. Frank Thomas of the White Sox and Jeff Bagwell of the Astros have something else in common — they were both born May 27, 1968.

Birthday Uniform. White Sox outfielder Carlos May is probably the only player to wear his birthdate on his back: May 17.

Surprise. The bodyguard for author Danielle Steele, Danny Molieri, was a childhood friend of Barry Bonds in San Mateo, California. In 2004 Steele arranged to have dinner with Bonds, but his limo driver was asked to stop at a Hollywood bowling alley to meet Steele, who was out with her daughter. When Bonds and his second wife, Liz, arrived, they discovered 310 people waiting to celebrate his birthday. Bonds response: "This is amazing. They say I don't have any friends. Look at all these people here."

Gift. Roger Clemens gave comedian Bob Hope the jersey from his 301st victory as a present for Hope's 100th birthday. During the off-season Clemens traveled to the Middle East to visit U.S. troops.

Home Runs. Al Simmons had the most birthday home runs, with five.

Namesake. Bob Costas (dubbed the "Cupid of Baseball" by writer Frank Deford) named his first born boy after Kirby Puckett. Given Puckett's recent negative publicity, Costas may be regretting his choice.

Birth.

"Baseball likes euphemism. And so the game is again [in 2002] enduring 'labor difficulties' (in the way that Mrs. Powell, when giving birth to Boog, endured 'labor difficulties')." — Steve Rushin.

According to a game summary in the *Chicago Tribune*, a baby was born in the stands during an October 1908 game between the Cubs and Pirates. This would have been during the heat of the pennant race that featured the famous Merkle Boner incident. The excitement may have induced labor.

In July 1982 Oriole pitcher Mike Flanagan's wife had the world's fourth test-tube baby through artificial insemination. Flanagan immediately went on a seven-game winning streak and lost only one game through the end of the season.

On August 2, 2003, Abraham Nunez, Jr., was born 2½ hours before his father took the field for the Pirates. In the 2nd inning, Nunez drove in the only run of the game against the Rockies.

On May 28, 2004, Pittsburgh's Rob Mackowiak celebrated the birth that day of his first child in grand style. He hit a 9th inning walk-off grand slam in the first game of a doubleheader and hit a game-tying two-run blast in the second game that helped the Pirates win in extra innings.

Planned Parenthood. The babycenter.com website offered a Sports Conflict Catcher to help prospective parents plan births to not interfere with major sporting events.

Black "Firsts"

"The gentleman was the first black major league player in the United States." — Engraving on the tombstone of Moses Fleetwood Walker (though perhaps now that is not true).

See also *Integration*.

First Professional. The first known black professional player was Bud Fowler, whose real name purportedly was John Jackson. He played for the 1872 Newcastle Club of Pennsylvania.

First in Major League Baseball. The first known black players in Major League Baseball were for decades thought to be Moses Fleetwood Walker, a catcher, and his brother, Welday Walker, an outfielder. They played for Toledo of the Major League American Association in 1884. They also played for the 1883 Toledo club when it was in the Northwestern League. They had attended Oberlin College, where they were on the school's first varsity baseball team (see also *Integration* for more detail on the Walkers).

In 2004, SABR researcher Peter Morris discovered evidence that the first black player in the Major Leagues was William Edward White, born in 1860, who played one game at first base for the Providence Grays of the National League on June 21, 1879. Morris concluded that White was the son of A.J. White, a Milner, Georgia, white philanthropist and bachelor who fathered a child with a mulatto woman named Hannah White. She lived as a slave, then as a servant in A.J. White's house. Morris believed that the best evidence of the relationship was A.J. White's will, which left land to "William Edward White [and his two sisters] … the children of my servant Hannah." William Edward White was attending Brown University when he played the game for Providence.

Black Versus White Team. The first recorded instance of an all-black team playing an all-white team occurred September 18, 1869, when a white club defeated the City Items of Philadelphia.

20th Century/First Officially Recognized Black Player. A number of Cuban and other Latin players of the 1920s and 1930s were almost as dark-complexioned as Jackie Robinson. Because they were not considered Negroes they were not barred from Organized Baseball.

Robinson was the first prominently recognized black player to play Organized Baseball in the modern era, during the push for *Integration* in other fields (particularly the military) which occurred in the 1940s. Robinson first appeared in a minor league game in 1946 (see *Integration* for other black players who played minor league ball in the 20th century before Robinson). He first appeared in a Major League game for the Dodgers in April 1947.

Jackie Robinson in his 1946 Montreal Royals uniform, as the first formally recognized black minor league player in the 20th century.

First American League Player.

"And in a society where most people cannot name the most recent, or perhaps even the current, vice-president of the United States, we relegate number two to an undeserved obscurity." — Joseph Thomas Moore in the preface to his book, *Pride and Prejudice* (1988), the story of Larry Doby.

On July 5, 1947, 11 weeks after Jackie Robinson played for the Dodgers, 22-year-old Larry Doby broke the American League color line when he pinch-hit for the Indians against the White Sox in Chicago.

Baseball Writers Association Member. In 1948 Baltimore writer Sam Lacy became the first black *Sportswriter* admitted to the Baseball Writers Association of America (BBWAA). Spink Award winner Wendell Smith also was admitted in 1948, but it is unclear who was admitted first.

Batting Champions. In 1949 Jackie Robinson won the National League batting title and in 1964 Tony Oliva, a Cuban playing for the Twins, became the first black player to win the American League title. The first African American to win was Frank Robinson in 1966.

Broadcaster. Former pitcher Jim "Mudcat" Grant reportedly was the first black color commentator (no pun intended), for Channel 8 in Cleveland. When Bill White became National League president, he was the only black regular broadcaster for a Major League team (Yankees).

Brothers. The first black brothers to play in the modern Major Leagues were Sammy Drake with the 1960 Cubs and Solly Drake with the 1956 Cubs.

Coach. The first black Major League coach was Buck O'Neil with the Cubs in the early 1960s. He had managed the Kansas City Monarchs in the early 1950s. At least one source claimed that the first black coach was Jim Gilliam of the Dodgers in 1965, though Gilliam may only have been the first to coach a base.

By 1983 only 13 of 123 Major League coaches were black. Even in early 1991, Jerry Manuel of the Expos was the only black third base coach in the Major Leagues. The Expos also had Tommy Harper, who is black, as their first base coach. By late 1991 there were only six black base coaches in the Major Leagues.

Cy Young Award. In 1956 Don Newcombe of the Dodgers became the first black Cy Young Award winner. It was the first year in which the award was presented because Cy Young had died the previous winter. Newcombe was also the first black pitcher to lead a league in strikeouts (164 in 1951) and wins (27 in 1956).

General Manager. The first black general manager was Atlanta's Bill Lucas in 1977.

Hall of Fame.

"It took baseball over fifty years to admit Negroes to our 'national' pastime—a fact of life that should make it always hang its head in shame.... They fell all over themselves because nobody wants to mess with Jackie. If they slammed the door of the Hall of Fame on *Him*, he'd kick it in. He'd make it if he had to come in a spike-high slide and some of baseball's most hallowed custodians would have spike wounds from ankle to ear."—Jim Murray.

See also *Hall of Fame.*

Jackie Robinson was elected to the Hall of Fame in 1962. Every voting writer had Robinson on his ballot.

In 1969 Roy Campanella became the second black player elected to the Hall of Fame. By that time, approximately 25% of the 600 Major League players were black.

Home Run Leader. Larry Doby led the American League in 1952 with 32 home runs and Willie Mays led the National League in 1955 with 51 home runs.

Manager/Minor Leagues. The first black minor league manager was Nate Moreland, who managed Calexico of the Class C Arizona-Mexican League in 1959. The second black manager in Organized Baseball was Gene Baker in 1961, who was one of the first two black players for the Cubs (along with Ernie Banks). Former pitcher Dan Bankhead is sometimes identified as the first black minor league manager, at Farnham, Quebec, in Canada's Provincial League. However, the Provincial League was not part of Organized Baseball. It is noteworthy that all three made their managerial debuts with clubs located outside the United States.

Manager/Major Leagues.

"And don't think drinking with the boss isn't important. I think that's the real reason there has never been a black manager in the big leagues. Most managerial jobs are given to old drinking buddies, cronies, friends of friends. Baseball owners and general managers don't have old black friends. *Or* young black friends. Not personal friends, anyway. And they're not about to *start* going out drinking with a black, or sit in planes with one, or trade girl friends with one, or lounge around a hotel suite discussing trades with one."—Jim Bouton in *I Managed Good, but Boy, Did They Play Bad,"* by Bouton with Neil Offen (1973).

"Someday I'd like to be able to look over at third base and see a black man managing the ball club.... I'd like to live to see a black manager."—Jackie Robinson at the 1972 World Series, nine days before he died.

"If I had one wish I was sure would be granted, it would be that Jackie Robinson could be here, seated alongside me today."—Frank Robinson on October 3, 1974, during a press conference announcing his hiring as manager of the Indians for the 1975 season. Commissioner Bowie Kuhn and American League president Lee MacPhail attended the event, the first time that a commissioner or league president had ever attended the announcement of the hiring of a manager.

Robinson wrote a description of his first year managing, *Frank: The First Year*, with Dave Anderson (1976); see also Russell J. Schneider, *Frank Robinson, Making of a Manager* (1976). The Indians finished fourth in '76, and he was fired in 1977 when the club was in sixth place.

Robinson took over the Giants for the 1981–1984 seasons and then returned to managing with the Orioles in early 1988. He stayed with the club for 37 games into the 1991 season. His best finish was in 1989, when the Orioles finished second. He later managed the Expos when Major League Baseball took over the club's ownership.

The second black manager hired in the National League was Don Baylor of the Rockies. He and Dusty Baker of the Giants took over their clubs for the 1993 season. Hal McRae and Davey Lopes are among the black managers of the late 1990s and 2000s.

See also *Managers—Black and Latin Managers.*

Attempts to Hire Black Managers Before Robinson.

"It's true there haven't been many lately."—Yankee manager Ralph Houk before there were *any* black Major League managers.

Bill Veeck was planning to buy the Senators for the 1968 season. Veeck offered the managing job to former Yankee catcher Elston Howard, but the sale fell through and the offer went with it. The Blue Jays talked to Howard about managing the new franchise in 1977, but nothing came of it.

Giants manager Herman Franks attempted unsuccessfully to put together a group to buy the club in the late 1960s and install Willie Mays as the Major League's first black manager.

When Henry Aaron broke Ruth's home run record in 1974 he thought that he would get the Braves managing job. When he did not, he forced his trade to the Brewers.

Buck O'Neil might have become the first black Major League manager, however briefly, for the Cubs and their *College of Coaches* in 1962. O'Neil was part of the coaching staff that had no manager. A few of the coaches rotated into the managerial role but Charlie Grimm was in the front office and ordered the other coaches to ensure that O'Neil was never allowed to be a base coach or ever substitute as a manager even for a moment.

Most Valuable Player.

"If I have to thank *you* to win, I don't want the fucking thing."—Jackie Robinson to a sportswriter after he was told by him that he needed to show gratitude if he expected to win the award. In 1949 Robinson became the first black Major League player to win an MVP Award. In 1963 catcher Elston Howard became the first black player to win the American League MVP Award. Beginning in 1949, 15 of the next 20 National League MVPs were black or Latin.

No-Hitter. On May 12, 1955, Sad Sam "Toothpick" Jones of the Cubs pitched the first no-hitter by a black Major League pitcher. It was a 4–0 shutout against the Pirates in front of 2,918 fans at Wrigley Field. He struck out the side in a bases loaded 9th inning.

Outfield. The first all-black starting outfield took the field during a 1951 play-off game between the Giants and Dodgers. Due to an injury, Hank Thompson was inserted into the Giants outfield along with regular black starters Monte Irvin and Willie Mays.

Photograph. One of the earliest photographs of black and white Major League players in a congratulatory hug was taken in 1948.

Indians pitcher Steve Gromek, who was white, and outfielder Larry Doby, who was black, were shown together after Doby hit the game-winning home run in Game 4 of the 1948 World Series. The hit made Gromek a winner of the 2–1 game.

Pitching Appearance. On August 8, 1947, against the Pirates, Dan Bankhead of the Dodgers made the first appearance by a black pitcher in a Major League game. He came in to relieve in the second inning, pitched 3⅓ innings and gave up 10 hits and six runs. He also homered in his first at-bat against Fritz Ostermueller. That year Bankhead appeared in four games and had one save. He was 9–5 over his 52-game career.

Pitcher Versus Batter. Batter Hank Thompson of the Giants and pitcher Don Newcombe of the Dodgers faced each other at Ebbets Field on July 8, 1949. It was the first time that a black batter and pitcher faced each other in the Major Leagues.

President. In September 2002 Ulice Payne, Jr., then 47, became the first Black team president, when he took over the Milwaukee Brewers from Bud Selig's daughter, Wendy.

Roommates/Interracial. Bobby Grich and Don Baylor of the Orioles were two of the earliest interracial roommates.

Second-Generation Players. Sam Hairston played catcher for a few games in 1951 for the White Sox. His son Jerry played in the Major Leagues from 1973 through 1989, primarily for the White Sox, although from 1978 to 1980 he spent time in Mexico and in other minor leagues. Jerry was signed by his dad while he was a scout for the White Sox. Another son, John, played three games at catcher for the Cubs. A third son, Sam, Jr., played catcher in the minor leagues in the White Sox organization. The Hairston sons are the first black Major League players to have had their father play in the Major Leagues.

Starting Line-Up. On July 17, 1954, the Dodgers fielded five black players among their nine starters against the Milwaukee Braves (who had black players Bill Bruton and Henry Aaron in the line-up): Jim Gilliam at second base, Jackie Robinson at third base, Sandy Amoros in left field, Roy Campanella at catcher and Don Newcombe on the mound. It was the first time that a majority of players on a starting nine were black. Some sources erroneously report the year as 1955.

The first all-black starting line-up was fielded by the Pirates on September 1, 1971: Al Oliver at first base, Rennie Stennett at second base, Jackie Hernandez at shortstop, Dave Cash at third base, Gene Clines, Roberto Clemente and Willie Stargell in the outfield, Manny Sanguillen catching and Dock Ellis pitching. The Pirates won the game 10–7.

Team Captain. Willie Mays was the first black team captain in Major League history. He became captain of the Giants in 1964, eight years after his manager, Alvin Dark, had been the Giants' last team captain.

In 1965 Maury Wills became the team captain of the Dodgers, the first for the club since Pee Wee Reese.

In 1969 Henry Aaron was selected as team captain of the Braves.

Telegrapher. In April 1961 in San Francisco, Spencer Allen became the first black telegraph operator to work from the press box during a Major League game.

Twenty Game Winner. The first black 20-game winner was Brooklyn's Don Newcombe in 1955. The first black pitcher to win 20 games in the minor leagues was Jim "Mudcat" Grant ("Mud" to his friends).

Umpire.
"Now you've got the decision in black and white."—Black home plate umpire Emmett Ashford to manager Leo Durocher, after Ashford conferred with the white first base umpire on a checked

swing. Ashford was the first black Major League umpire, working from 1966 through 1977 in the American League. One source reported that he was hired at age 51 so that he could obtain the five years of service necessary to qualify for the pension plan. He was noted for his flamboyant attitude and dapper dress, including flashy cufflinks on the field. He started his career in Organized Baseball in 1952 in the Class C Southwest International League.

Ashford's first Major League game was the season opener in Washington, D.C. Vice-President Hubert Humphrey was scheduled to throw out the first ball. Ashford arrived in a cab and there was a long delay while he and the driver convinced the Secret Service agent at the gate that he was one of the umpires.

Ashford stated that only two or three players and one or two managers really gave him a hard time throughout his career. He also had a hard time from some of the other umpires, who were not ready to accept him into the fraternity.

Art Williams was the first black National League umpire, working from 1973 through 1977.

By 1979 one professional umpire out of 60 was black.

World Series Pitching Winner. In 1952 Joe Black of the Dodgers became the first black pitcher to win a World Series game.

Yankee Hall of Famer. Reggie Jackson chose to be depicted in a Yankee cap and uniform for his Hall of Fame plaque, acknowledging that he was the first black Yankee in the Hall of Fame (among the 36 to that point who had played for the Yankees and had been inducted).

Black Sox Scandal (1919–1920)

"The idea staggered me. I remembered, of course, that the World Series had been fixed in 1919, but if I thought of it at all I would have thought of it as something that merely *happened*, the end of some inevitable chain. It never occurred to me that one man could start to play with the faith of fifty million people."— F. Scott Fitzgerald in *The Great Gatsby* (1925).

"To me baseball is as honorable as any other business. It is the most honest pastime in the world. It has to be or it could not last a season out. Crookedness and baseball do not mix. It has become immeasurably more popular as the years have gone by. It will be greater yet. This year, 1919, is the greatest season of them all."—White Sox owner Charles Comiskey quoted in his biography, "*Commy*" (1919), just before the start of the fateful 1919 season.

Synopsis. Eight members of the 1919 White Sox conspired with gamblers to throw the 1919 World Series. The conspiracy succeeded, as the underdog Reds won the nine-game Series 5–3. One year later the players were indicted, but were acquitted after a jury trial. Three months later in November 1920, Judge Landis was appointed as the first commissioner of baseball. His first act was to permanently bar the eight players from Organized Baseball.

The Eight Men Out. The White Sox players banned for life by Landis were pitcher Eddie Cicotte, outfielder Happy Felsch, outfielder Joe Jackson, first baseman Chick Gandil, infielder Swede Risberg, infielder Buck Weaver, pitcher Lefty Williams and third baseman Fred McMullin.

Why It Happened. Most analysts point to two forces: the greed of players who believed they were underpaid by penurious owner Charles Comiskey; and the greed of gamblers who were drawn to a "can't miss" proposition. Comiskey had one of the lowest payrolls in the Major Leagues and was the stingiest for benefits such as meal money.

Despite having some of the top players in the game, Comiskey refused to pay even close to top dollar. Eddie Cicotte led the Major

"Eight members of the Chicago American League baseball club have been indicted by the Chicago grand jury for conspiracy in connection with a plot to throw the World Series in 1919. Eddie Cicotte has confessed that he got $10,000. Other players he says were double-crossed by the gamblers. More indictments of National League players and gamblers are expected at any time" (original newspaper caption).

Front row (the indicted eight players capitalized): Eddie Collins (2B), Nemo Leibold (OF), EDDIE CICOTTE (P), Erskine Mayer (P), LEFTY WILLIAMS (P), Byrd Lynn (C). Middle row: Ray Schalk (C), Shano Collins (OF), Harvey McClellan (U), Dickie Kerr (P), HAPPY FELSCH (OF), CHICK GANDIL(1B), BUCK WEAVER (3B). Back row: Kid Gleason (MGR), John Sullivan (P), Roy Wilkinson (P), Grover Lowdermilk (P), SWEDE RISBERG (SS), FRED McMULLIN (3B), Bill James (P), Eddie Murphy (OF), JOE JACKSON (OF), Joe Jenkins (C).

Leagues in 1917 with 28 wins and again in 1919 with 29, but made only $5,500 in 1919. Joe Jackson was one of the top hitters in the game, but also was low paid. Honest Eddie Collins was the highest paid White Sox player at $15,000 and Gandil earned $6,000, the highest salary of anyone in his dishonest group (see **Salaries** for comparisons).

Origin of the "Black Sox" Name. During the 1918 season Comiskey refused to pay for cleaning the team's uniforms and the players began wearing the increasingly dirty uniforms for weeks at a time. After a while they began to refer derisively to themselves as the Black Sox.

Factions on the Team. There were two distinct cliques on the team. Eddie Collins had not spoken to Gandil for two years and Ray Schalk talked only to the pitchers and never to anyone off the field.

The Gamblers. Chick Gandil approached Joseph "Sport" Sullivan, who was a front for big-time gambler Arnold Rothstein. Rothstein, Sullivan and boxer Abe Attell agreed to pay off the White Sox and bet heavily on the Reds. In later years Attell was known at Toots Shor's for pinning a phallic-shaped cork to the pants of drunks at the bar. Bill "Sleepy" Burns was a former player who acted as the intermediary with the Black Sox. He failed to produce some of the promised money and the players almost decided to give up the fix during the Series. Reds shortstop Edd Roush said that gamblers who knew that the White Sox were trying to lose tried to bribe the Reds players $5,000 to try to lose.

The Money. The eight players divided $80,000, though first baseman and ringleader Chick Gandil took $35,000 of it.

The Signal. The tip-off that Cicotte and the others were going to make good on the fix was for Cicotte to hit the first batter of the

Series. On the second pitch of the game, Cicotte hit Morrie Rath in the back.

The Shoddy Play.

Game 1. Cicotte lost the first game 9–1 after posting a 29–7 record and a 1.82 ERA during the season. He made an error on a ground ball to help give the Reds a run.

Game 2. Pitcher Lefty Williams was unusually wild, walking three in the 4th inning to hand the Reds three runs. The Reds won the game 4–2 to take a 2–0 Series lead.

Game 3. Dickie Kerr was not in on the fix and pitched a 2–0 shutout.

Game 4. Cicotte made two errors in the 5th inning to give the Reds the only two runs scored in the game.

Game 5. Williams lost as the Reds posted a 5–0 shutout for a 4–1 Series lead. The best-of-nine Series was now down to the last chance for the White Sox to redeem themselves.

Game 6. Kerr won in 10 innings to give the White Sox their second victory.

Game 7. Cicotte won with a four-hitter to make the Series 4–3 Reds.

Game 8. Williams was approached before Game 8 and told in no uncertain terms that he was not to last the 1st inning or he and his wife would be in grave danger. He complied by giving up four hits and three runs to the Reds before being removed with one out in the 1st inning. The Reds won 10–5 to clinch the Series 5–3.

Suspicion During the Series. Comiskey and other influential baseball men were aware of rumors about a fix, but refused to follow up on them. Manager Kid Gleason approached Comiskey about his suspicions during the Series. Because of Comiskey's poor relationship with Ban Johnson, Comiskey bypassed Johnson with Gleason's information and spoke with National League president John Heydler.

No immediate action was taken and it was not until a year later that an Illinois grand jury investigated the incident. After the season Comiskey offered a $10,000 reward ($20,000 in some sources) to anyone with information about the claimed scandal.

The 1920 Season, Investigation, and the Story Breaks. No investigation was made of the allegations during that winter and the early part of the 1920 season. All but Gandil among the conspirators returned to the club that year. Gandil retired to California with his earnings.

Late in the season, American League president Ban Johnson began providing information to the Illinois grand jury, in part because he was trying to disgrace his former friend and now hated enemy, Comiskey (see also *American League Presidents*).

The story began to unfold after an investigation of a 1920 Cubs/Phillies game that allegedly was fixed. The next big break in the case was an article in a Philadelphia newspaper regarding Bill Maharg, a small-time gambler who said that the first two games of the 1919 Series were fixed. The next day Eddie Cicotte and Joe Jackson confessed and implicated others. Cicotte reportedly had been urged by a priest to tell Comiskey the story.

All eight were exposed publicly during the last week of the 1920 season and were indicted on September 28, 1920. The indictment included the eight Black Sox, gambler Joseph "Sport" Sullivan and Nat Evans. Joe Gedeon was also suspended for knowing about the scandal. Comiskey wrote checks for $1,500 to the honest players on his club; the difference between the winning and losing shares in the 1919 World Series. The eight were immediately suspended despite three games to play in the season and a tight pennant race with the Indians.

An additional indictment was handed down October 23, which included 13 people: the eight Black Sox, former featherweight boxing champion Abe Attell, Sullivan, "Rachel Brown" (Nat Evans' pseudoym), first baseman Hal Chase and former American League player Bill Burns. Chase and Burns were accused of acting as the go-betweens for the players and the gamblers.

Public Perception. The magnitude of the scandal in the public mind cannot be underestimated. It completely wiped off the front pages the major news of the communist takeover in Russia, the "Red Scare."

Trial Testimony/Confessions.
"The state must prove that it was the intent of the ballplayers and gamblers ... to defraud the public and others and not merely to throw ballgames."—Pro-defendant jury instruction of Judge Hugo Friend.

Philadelphia gambler Billy Marber was an important witness at the trial who described several meetings at Chicago's Hotel Sherman. Buck Weaver sat in on two meetings, but said he never took any money and played hard during the Series. Cicotte, Jackson and Williams signed confessions; Felsch confessed orally to a newsman. All later recanted the confessions.

Rothstein said that Burns and Attell approached him and that he turned down the proposition. He claimed that he bet $6,000 on the White Sox as proof that he rejected the scheme.

The written confessions were stolen late in 1920 and the Chicago district attorney was going to drop the charges for lack of evidence. However, at least one source contends that Ban Johnson began a tenacious investigation to pull together enough evidence to prosecute.

The Verdict.
"I guess that'll learn Ban Johnson he can't frame an honest bunch of ballplayers."—Chick Gandil at the moment the jury's "not guilty" verdict was read.

On August 2, 1921, the jury returned a verdict of not guilty after only three hours of deliberation. The players celebrated their victory in a West Side Italian restaurant. The jurors supposedly were by coincidence celebrating in an adjacent room; the doors were opened and both groups joined for a party; they had assumed that all would be forgiven. They were wrong.

Landis Acts.
"Regardless of the verdict of juries, no player that throws a ball game, no player that sits in a conference with ... crooked players and gamblers where the ways and means of throwing games are discussed, and does not promptly tell his club about it, will never play professional baseball. Just keep in mind that regardless of the verdict of juries, baseball is entirely competent to protect itself against the crooks both inside and outside the game."—Judge Landis, banning the eight Black Sox players after the jury acquitted them. Landis became commissioner in November and one of his first acts was to recognize that despite the jury's acquittal, the players were guilty in the eyes of baseball people and should be punished. He barred each of the eight players from any future contact with Organized Baseball at any level. The players were also prohibited from buying tickets to or attending any Major or minor league games.

The Eight and Their Fate.
"The gambler has done his worst again. He is the respecter of no game. He would as quickly buy the youth in the lot as the professional in the arena, if he could. He has tried both. He will try again. The honest ballplayer need have no fear of any gambler. There are thousands and thousands of honest ballplayers. There is another small group—they were ballplayers once—to be immured in the Chamber of Oblivion. There let them rest."—The *Spalding Guide* in 1921.

Eddie Cicotte. Cicotte pitched and intentionally lost Games 1 and 4, though he won Game 7 (of 8). He went on to become a farmer and game warden in Michigan.

Happy Felsch. Felsch was the number five hitter in the line-up and was not an enthusiastic participant in the fix, but his meager sacrifice bunts during the Series were his contribution. He opened a bar in Milwaukee.

Chick Gandil. Gandil was the primary instigator of the plot by contacting Boston gamblers three weeks before the Series. Gandil retired to California to become a plumber and then moved to Napa Valley in northern California.

Joe Jackson. Jackson claimed that he tried his best during the Series despite knowledge of the plot, as evidenced by his .375 average. He played semipro ball in Georgia for many years, opened a dry cleaning business and later owned a tavern.

In November 1999 the U.S. House of Representatives passed a resolution calling for Jackson to be honored, though it did not call for him to be inducted into the Hall of Fame. It was introduced by Rep. Jim DeMint, who represented Jackson's home town of Greenville, South Carolina. This followed a 1998 call by Ted Williams for Jackson to enter the Hall, in an essay posted on a SABR website. The two-page essay began with "I want Baseball to right an injustice," and ended with "Come on in, Joe, I'd say, your wait is over. Let's talk hitting." See also David L. Fleitz, *Shoeless: The Life and Times of Joe Jackson* (2001).

Fred McMullin. McMullin had minimal impact on the Series with one hit in two at-bats. He moved West and died in Los Angeles in 1952.

Swede Risberg. Risberg batted .088 at shortstop and contributed four errors. He later worked on a dairy farm in Minnesota, moved to California and then ran a tavern in Oregon.

Buck Weaver. Weaver backed out of the plot but was still banned because he did not reveal the conspiracy. Throughout the rest of his life Weaver repeatedly attempted to have his name cleared. Though he attended two conspiracy meetings, he did not participate in the fix and received no money. Each commissioner to whom he appealed denied his request.

Lefty Williams. Williams contributed by losing three World Series games. He ran a saloon after being barred and then moved to California to run a plant nursery.

Movie. *Eight Men Out* was filmed at Bush Stadium in Indianapolis and starred Charlie Sheen. In 1979 author Eliot Asinof wrote *Bleeding Between the Lines*, his account of how he tried and failed to make a movie out of his book, *Eight Men Out*. He was not involved in the movie that was finally made.

Books. Eliot Asinof, *Eight Men Out* (1963); William A. Cook, *The 1919 World Series: What Really Happened?* (2001); Victor Luhrs, *The Great Baseball Mystery* (1966); Donald Gropman, *Say It Ain't So Joe* (1979); Brendan Boyd, *Blue Ruin* (1991) (fiction); Irving M. Stein, *The Ginger Kid* (1992) (about Buck Weaver); James Farrell's, *My Baseball Diary* (1957) (Weaver's last interview); Leo Katcher, *The Big Bankroll: The Life and Times of Arnold Rothstein* (1958).

Blacklists

"In the East [in 1875], Chadwick exposed the pernicious influence of gamblers, the selling of games by players, the mismanagement of directors, and the generally hostile reaction of the public. In demanding reform, he called for a convention that would stop fraudulent play by punishing crooked officials and blacklisting corrupt players."— David Quentin Voigt in *American Baseball* (1966).

"Gaban's voice had not changed, though. It still was a penetrating brassy bellow and it had inspired the nickname which he now was called with affection by ten million fans. Gaban had put the nickname and the affection to work by talking himself into the managership of the Drakes, and it was no surprise to Messlin. Anyone, he reflected, who could talk himself off the commissioner's blacklist and out of jail was a cinch to talk himself into a job."— Stanley Frank in "The Name of the Game" (1949).

See also **Barred from Baseball** and **Gambling and Fixed Games.**

The first formal National League blacklist was started in 1881 by National League president William Hulbert. At least 34 players and one umpire were blacklisted. Players were often blacklisted for "dissipation" (excessive drinking or gambling) or "general insubordination." Teams could therefore release players for no reason and other clubs could not negotiate with them.

Blacklisting was useful during the 1884 Union Association war when the American Association and National League threatened their players with blacklisting if they signed with the new league.

An early example of blacklisting involved Charley Jones, who played for Arthur Soden's Boston Red Stockings in 1880. Jones claimed that Soden owed him money and he refused to play. He was fined $100, suspended, and then blacklisted and expelled from the National League. He sued to be reinstated and collect his salary, and one source reported that a jury found for the club. A more authoritative source reported that he won $378 on his 1880 salary, levying on the club's gate receipts at Cleveland in 1881. He operated a laundry and played outlaw ball in Ohio before signing with Cincinnati of the American Association for the 1883 season.

Blackout

On July 13, 1976, the Cubs were playing the Mets at Shea Stadium when a blackout swept over the northeastern United States at 9:28 p.m. More than 30,000 fans were left in darkness and the game was suspended at 10:40 p.m. On September 16, 1976, the game was completed with the Cubs winning 5–2.

In August 2003 there was a massive blackout across the northeastern United States, forcing cancellation of the Mets' game against the Giants at Shea Stadium.

Giants outfielder Tony Torcato was called up by the club in mid-August 2003 from its Class AAA club in Fresno. He arrived in New York City to join the team on August 14, the day of the blackout that shut down the entire northeast part of the country. He slept on the floor of the airport before driving to Hartford, then caught a plane to meet the club in Montreal. He went 0-for-3 in two games against the Expos and then was sent back down.

Blocking the Plate   See *Catchers*— **Blocking the Plate**

Bloomer Girls

Bloomer Girls was a generic name for women's professional baseball teams that toured the country beginning in the 1890s (see also **Women in Baseball**—Bloomer Girls).

Bomb Threat

"They keep me pretty much in the dark about everything. If it had blown up I wouldn't have known a thing about it."— Dennis "Oil Can" Boyd, on not being informed of a bomb threat against the Red Sox team plane.

On August 25, 1970, a bomb threat was phoned into Minnesota's Metropolitan Stadium, causing fans to run out onto the field.

Bonus Babies

"He is improving in the outfield. To be sure, he hasn't caught a ball yet, but he's getting closer to them."— Cleveland sportswriter Gordon Cobbledick on disappointing bonus baby Dave Nicholson.

"Ownership must eliminate the bonus. It is bad for the boy, say an eighteen-year-old youth, to come into possession of unheard-of sums of money, unearned to begin with, and probably ill-spent to end with…. Something for nothing may be an objective among many slothful, unthrifty segments of our people, who seem to believe that the world or the nation or the community owes them a living, but it has no place in baseball because it tends to damn the player, wreck the club, and bankrupt the owner."— Branch Rickey in *The American Diamond*, with Robert Riger (1965).

"I received a $3,000 signing bonus. That was much more than my dad could really afford."— Bob Uecker, deadpanning at his Hall of Fame induction speech in 2003, when he received the Ford C. Frick Award for broadcasting excellence.

See also **Drafts.**

Origins/Rule. With very few exceptions, signing bonuses were not substantial until shortly after World War II, when six players first received at least $50,000 to sign. The poorer clubs were at a disadvantage because the wealthier clubs could stockpile bonus players in the minor leagues. In response, in the late 1940s the Major Leagues implemented a bonus baby rule that was modified in the 1950s.

The rule in 1949 was that if a player signed for $6,000 or more he could play on a minor league farm team for only one season. In 1952 the rule was modified to require a bonus baby to remain on a Major League club for two seasons. In 1953, 14 players were signed to bonuses greater than $6,000; a total of $457,000 in bonuses. There were four such bonuses paid in 1954 ($170,000). If a player was sent down to the minor leagues during the two seasons, he could be signed by another club. This is how the Dodgers lost **Roberto Clemente** to the Pirates in the mid–1950s.

By 1954 bonus babies receiving more than $4,000 had to spend the first two years of their careers with the parent club.

The bonus rule was abolished at the 1957 winter meetings because of persistent cheating and lack of enforceability. A total of 21 bonus players were being carried on Major League rosters at the time, including 12 signed in 1957. The 21 players were allowed to be farmed out without restriction beginning in 1958.

Bonus spending increased dramatically after the rule was repealed. To curb the spending, the Major and minor leagues approved an unlimited draft, but it took five years to implement after introduction of the idea at the 1959 winter meetings.

Dick Wakefield.

"In 43 years, the American League produced only four players who, in themselves, were great gate magnets—Ty Cobb, Walter Johnson, Babe Ruth and Bob Feller. Ted Williams, when he enlisted in the Navy Air Corps, was on his way. Now there is another whose star rides towards the orbit of Cobb, Ruth, Johnson and Feller. He is the Rookie of the Year—Dick Wakefield."—J.G. Taylor Spink in October 1943.

Wakefield, a sophomore outfielder at the University of Michigan with only one year of college ball, was the first Major League bonus baby. He signed with the Tigers for $52,000 in 1941 and reportedly received a new Cadillac from the club. The car's horn played the Michigan fight song. In a later interview, Wakefield claimed that *he* bought the car and that it was not a Cadillac, but a Lincoln Zephyr.

In his rookie year of 1943, Wakefield hit .316 and led the American League with 200 hits and 38 doubles. In the 1943 All-Star Game, manager Joe McCarthy gave him the bunt sign. Wakefield doubled instead and later told McCarthy that he had not missed the sign: he just knew that he could hit that pitcher anytime he wanted. He hit .355 in the first half of 1944 before going off to war.

Wakefield supposedly predicted that he would be better than Ted Williams, but that comment may have evolved from a friendly bet that he and Williams made during the war. He bet Williams that he would receive the salary he was going to demand when he returned and would beat out Williams in certain offensive categories. These were separate bets, on which he broke even. He received the salary, but a series of injuries (including a broken wrist and arm) prevented him from producing on the field.

After the war he never came close to his earlier batting accomplishments, finally retiring after the 1952 season. He claimed that he was forced out of the Major Leagues for making salary demands and landed in Oakland of the Pacific Coast League.

Wakefield was later involved in developing the players' *Pension* system and twice ran unsuccessfully for Congress. His father, Howard, was a Major League catcher from 1905 through 1907, batting .249 in 112 games for the Indians and Senators before his arm went dead and he faded.

Frank House. In 1949 House was an Alabama high school catcher who signed for $67,500 and two cars. He lasted 10 years beginning in 1950, compiling a .248 average and 47 home runs.

Paul Pettit. The "Wizard of Whiff," of Narbonne High in Los Angeles, received $100,000 in 1950 to become the first player to receive a six-figure bonus immediately after being drafted. Pettit signed a contract through an agent while still in high school. Although the move appeared to be illegal, commissioner Happy Chandler did not void the contract.

Pettit hurt his elbow and shoulder in the minor leagues and was never effective. In 1951 he made it to the Major Leagues with the Pirates, pitching 2⅔ innings over two games. In 1953 he appeared in the Major Leagues for the last time, with a record of 1–2 in 10 games for the Pirates.

Johnny Antonelli. The pitcher received $65,000 from the Braves in 1948. His best season was 1954, when he won 21 games for the Giants.

Roberto Clemente. The Dodgers paid Clemente $10,000 in 1953, but there was no room for him in Brooklyn. The club attempted to hide him in Montreal, but Branch Rickey found out and drafted him for the Pirates.

Bobby Brown. The future doctor and American League president received a $50,000 signing bonus.

Herb Score. The fastball pitcher accepted $60,000 from the Indians even though he was offered $80,000 by other clubs.

Carl Yastrzemski. Yastrzemski's father insisted that his son receive a $100,000 signing bonus when he graduated as class president of his New York high school. The Phillies offered $95,000 and an immediate spot in the starting line-up, but the family rejected the offer and Yastrzemski went to Notre Dame on a half-basketball, half-baseball scholarship. He finally received $108,000 from the Red Sox in 1958 (reported as $100,000 in some sources).

Bob Bailey. The third baseman received a reported $175,000 when he signed in 1961 out of Long Beach, California. Bailey was Minor League Player of the Year in 1962. He played third base for the Pirates in four full seasons starting in 1963 and then moved around the Majors through 1978. He was not much of a fielder, prompting an opponent to comment: "They called him Beetle, after the comic strip character, because he fielded like a comic strip character."

Tony Cloninger. The pitcher received $100,000 to sign with the Braves. Because of his "bonus baby" status and apparent potential he was promoted to Class AA ball despite an 0–9 record in his first season in Class B (and was a teammate of future author Pat Jordan).

Bob Taylor. The pitcher reportedly received $150,000 in 1956 from the Braves, but he never pitched in the Major Leagues.

Ted Kazanski. The infielder signed for a reported $100,000 from the Phillies and appeared in the Major Leagues for the first time at age 19 in 1953. He was largely a bust, batting .217 in 417 games between 1953 and 1958.

Willie Crawford. The outfielder received $100,000 from the Dodgers in the early 1960s. He first played in the Major Leagues in 1964 and over 14 seasons batted .268.

Ray Culp. The pitcher received $100,000 from the Phillies in 1959 and went on to post a 122–101 record from 1963 through 1973, primarily for the Reds.

Rick Reichardt. The highly touted star received $200,000 ($175,000 in some sources) from the Angels in 1964, the last and highest paid of the bonus babies before the amateur draft was instituted in 1965. Joe Garagiola was impressed: "The first time I saw him I thought he fell off a Wheaties box."

Kidney problems limited Reichardt's effectiveness and he had to have a kidney removed while still an active player.

Rick Monday. The first player chosen in the first amateur draft in 1965 received $104,000 from the A's. See *Drafts* for all first draft choices over the years.

Sandy Koufax. Koufax was one of many players negatively affected by the bonus rule. He did little in his first six Major League seasons after he signed at age 19 as a freshman out of the University of Cincinnati and had to be kept on the Major League roster during his first season.

Eddie Mathews. The infielder reportedly signed for $5,999 in the early 1950s to avoid having to remain on a Major League roster, required if he had signed for $6,000.

Comparison. Lou Brock signed for $30,000 in the late 1950s and Glenn Beckert for $8,000 in 1961. Generally, however, black players of comparable skill to white players received considerably lower bonus.

Not-So-Bonus Babies.

"[Johnny] Beazley was offered $200 to sign a contract. He didn't think there was that much money in one place in all the world. He certainly had never thought he'd have it, so he took the $200, sent it back to Mom, and signed the contract quickly, before anybody could change his mind."—Sportswriter J. Roy Stockton on the future Cardinals pitcher in *The Gas House Gang and a couple of other guys* (1945).

"I was a bonus baby. I got two autographed baseballs and a scorecard from the 1935 All-Star Game."—Hall of Famer Bob Feller commenting on his meager signing bonus.

During World War II the Cardinals instituted a public relations gimmick by which the club "signed" newborn babies in the city to future contracts: "Terry Morton Beazley, four-week-old son of Lt. Johnny Beazley, former Cardinal pitching hero, today received a St. Louis contract calling for $400 monthly for the season of 1962.... 'He's gonna sign with the Cardinals now, but I guess he'll have to write with a safety pin.'"—*The Stars and Stripes* military newspaper.

Hal Newhouser came from a poor family and at age 17 he and his father signed for $500 with the Tigers. His father took the five $100 bills and handed one of them to Newhouser. A short time later scout Cy Slapnicka and Bob Feller of the Indians showed up and handed them a certified check for $15,000. Newhouser had to tell them that he had already signed.

Young Bonus Baby. Joe Moeller was a pitcher for the Dodgers in the 1960s, at one time the youngest player in the Major Leagues at age 19. At age six he was a California state archery champion (his parents were itinerant professional archers). At 10 he wanted to quit archery and play baseball. His father allowed him to quit only after he won the national age group championship in archery. At age 12 Moeller was six feet tall and already considered a pitching prospect. The Red Sox thought so much of him that they paid his father $5,000 for a right of first refusal on any bonus contract he was about to sign. He was still 12 years old. He eventually signed with the Dodgers for $70,000.

Latin Bonus Babies. Texas Rangers scout Omar Minaya signed Sammy Sosa for $3,500 in 1985 out of the Dominican. In 1988, the Dodgers signed pitcher Pedro Martinez for $8,000, but by the late 1990s agents were getting to the young players first and obtaining much larger monetary figures for their clients. In 1998 a Dominican player named Wily Mo Pena signed with the Mets for $15,000, but the contract was invalidated by the Commissioner's office after Pena's father saw an opportunity and pointed out that the required date was inserted by a family friend after the fact. When Pena signed a legitimate contract, it was with the Yankees for $3.7 million. Pena's family reportedly gave 1 million pesos (about $60,600) to the family friend who initially reported the

missing date. The scout who had signed Pena with the Mets, and who forgot to put in the date, lost his job. Pena made it up to the Reds in 2002, where he remained through 2004.

In 2000 Willy Aybar, a third baseman, signed with the Dodgers for $1.4 million. He had not made it to the Major Leagues by 2004.

Books. Brent Kelley, *Bonus Babies* (1995).

Bonus Clauses and Incentives

"Million Dollar Kid"—Nickname for Lew Moren when he pitched in the Major Leagues between 1903 and 1910 (though in the minors in 1905–1906). He earned the name because his father, a steamboat owner, reportedly paid him $100 every time he won a game. He made $4,800 on the deal based on his 48–57 Major League record.

Incentives. In 1914 Schuyler Parsons Britton (husband of Cardinals owner Helene Britton) offered a 20% flat salary increase for a third-place finish or better. It worked, as the club came in third.

Attendance. Bob Feller had an attendance clause in his post–World War II contracts. Reggie Jackson had an attendance clause with the Angels which paid him 50 cents for each paid admission over two million.

The White Sox had attendance bonuses for their players as early as the late 1930s.

In 1953 Warren Spahn chose a straight $25,000 salary instead of an offer of 10 cents for each paid admission over 800,000. It seemed a good decision at the time because the Boston Braves looked like a poor bet to reach that figure. He realized his mistake when the Braves left for Milwaukee over the winter and drew over 1.8 million in its new home. He would have received an extra $100,000.

Mark McGwire had an attendance clause in his 1998 contract that kicked in during his record-setting home run tear (see *Home Runs*)

Banned. Long-time Tigers owner Walter Briggs twice bought one of his players a suit after a strong performance. As a result, the American League instituted a rule prohibiting bonuses for single-game efforts. However, pitchers have frequently received bonuses or other incentives for pitching no-hitters. Carl Erskine of the Dodgers received an extra $500 for his no-hitter on May 12, 1955. Owners circumvented the rule by rewriting the player's contract to include what would otherwise be the bonus.

This became a major area of abuse for another reason during the mid–1950s. Clubs were paying large signing bonuses to amateur players, but trying to hide them in the contracts as "annual salary" to avoid having to keep the players on their Major League rosters.

Manager Alvin Dark and the Indians were fined $5,000 in the early 1970s for entering into illegal incentive contracts.

Reverse Incentive. In 1959 slugger Rocky Colavito supposedly had a contract clause that gave him a bonus if he did *not* hit 40 home runs in an effort to cut down on strikeouts.

Hit By Pitch. With the bases loaded in an extra inning tie, 1940s Dodger manager Leo Durocher told his batter, Howie Schultz, that he would give him $100 if he allowed himself to be hit by the pitch. Schultz was not quick enough to get in the way of the ball and he ended up slapping a ball up the middle to drive in two runs and win the game. Durocher gave him the bonus anyway.

Free-Swinging Encouraged. Cubs owner Phil Wrigley wanted 1940s hitter Lou Novikoff to be *less* discriminating in his choice of pitches: he offered him a bonus of $5 every time he struck out swinging. It seemed to work, as Novikoff batted .300 in 1942, his first (and only) season as a regular. He walked only 24 times and it did not cost the club much because he struck out only 28 times (no record of how many times swinging).

House Payment. At least one source reported that when Chief Bender won the deciding game in the 1911 World Series, A's owner Connie Mack presented him with a bonus check equal to the amount of the mortgage on his house, $3,500.

Just Short. Dennis "Oil Can" Boyd had a clause that allowed him to receive $100,000 if he made 32 starts for the Expos. He was scheduled to start number 32 on the last day of the season. The club started someone else and Boyd filed a grievance that ultimately was settled.

All-Star Game. Curt Schilling received $100,000 for making the 2004 All-Star team, and an additional $50,000 if he started the game. For 2004, 43 players earned $2.05 million in bonuses for making the team.

Books

"'Why does not somebody write 1 decent book about baseball, Krazy? There never been a good book yet.'

'There been dozens of good books,' said he.

'There has only been fairy tales,' I said."— Mark Harris's character in *The Southpaw* (1953).

"Indeed, it may be fairly said that among all of mankind's games and sports, only chess, with its advantage of over a thousand years of existence and its international exposure, surpasses the literary outpourings devoted to baseball!"— David Quentin Voigt in the Foreword to Myron J. Smith, Jr.'s, prodigious *Baseball: A Comprehensive Bibliography* (1986), which contains over 21,000 entries.

"Sparky's the only guy I know who's written more books than he's read."— Ernie Harwell on Sparky Anderson.

"I've only read two books in my life: *Baseball Sparkplug* and *Love Story*."— George Brett.

"There are superb books about golf, very good books about baseball, not many good books about football, and very few good books about basketball. There are no good books about beach balls."— Writer George Plimpton on the inverse correlation between the size of the ball and the quality of the writing.

"All literary men are Red Sox fans. To be a Yankee fan in literary society is to endanger your life."— John Cheever.

"You will find many exaggerations, inconsistencies, stretched truths, and, yes, downright lies in this book. Such is human memory. Facts stream into our memory banks, and when we try to make a withdrawal some years later, we often find ourselves short-changed. But something is gained from this loss of memory, for along with these transmogrified facts comes a deeper knowledge, a cured, metamorphosed truth, more accurate than fact, more revealing than the damn score."— John Tullus in *I'd Rather Be a Yankee* (1986).

"The literature of baseball is voluminous; some of it is extremely valuable but most of it is riddled with clichés and empty analysis."— Ralph Andreano in *No Joy in Mudville* (1965).

"I WOULD RATHER BE A POOR MAN IN A GARRET WITH PLENTY OF BOOKS THAN A KING WHO DID NOT LOVE READING"— Sign over the reading chair of master *Spy* and Major League catcher Moe Berg.

This section contains a sampling from different genres of baseball books and a subjective selection of some of the best baseball books ever written.

Early History Books. Some sources credit Harry C. Palmer with writing the first history of baseball in 1889, as part of a book entitled *Athletic Sports in America*. It has been called the best sports book of the 19th century.

A good source of basic information about the early amateur baseball club teams is Charles Peverelly's *The Book of American Pastimes* (1866).

Another early book is *Sphere and Ash: History of Base Ball*, by Jacob Morse (1888) (reprinted in 1984).

One of the earlier and most complete histories of the game is Albert Spalding's 1911 work, *Base Ball—America's National Game* (reprinted in 1991). Another early book is *Balldom: "The Britannica of Baseball,"* by George L. Moreland (1914).

Some consider the best early non-encyclopedic baseball book of miscellaneous information to be Harold "Speed" Johnson's, *Who's Who in Major League Base Ball* (1933). It includes biographies of 358 players, managers, executives, trainers, statisticians, umpires and radio announcers.

Early Fiction.

"The heroes of those potboilers were so clean-cut as to make even Horatio Alger characters seem dissolute in comparison."— Ron Fimrite on the saccharin writing of the early 20th century baseball fiction writers.

"Most baseball books before and shortly after the Second World War were specialized works, intended largely for lifelong teen-agers (a group in which I sometimes number myself) who could read game-by-game recapitulations of long-dead baseball seasons and never feel their interest flag, no matter that the writing was pure journalese of the least-inspired sort."— Robert Smith in *Baseball* (1970).

Once source cited an 1880 work as the first baseball fiction book, *The Fairport Nine*, by Noah Brooks. Another source cited *Changing Base*, by William Everet (1868). That same source also identified the next work as *Double Play*, also by Everett. Another early fiction book is *Our Baseball Club and How It Won the Championship of 1884*, by Brooks (1884).

Dime novels about baseball were especially popular during the 1890s. The Frank Merriwell stories began in 1896, written by Gilbert William Patten, who used the pen name Burt Standish. Patten gained his insight into the sport from having managed a semi-pro team in Maine.

The *Baseball Joe* series was written by Edward Stratemeyer under the name Lester Chadwick. It was one of 65 pseudonyms that Stratemeyer and his assistants used to pump out over 800 titles, including the *Rover Boys* and *Tom Swift* series. See also Albert Johannsen, *The House of Beadle and Adams and Its Dime and Nickel Novel: The Story of a Vanished Literature* (1950).

Zane Grey wrote baseball fiction early in the 20th century after playing semipro ball.

The first adult baseball novel was *You Know Me Al*, by **Ring Lardner** (1916). No writer ever used baseball as a source of serious literature until Lardner's effort. The series consisted of 15 books published over 16 years. Lardner also wrote "Alibi Ike," which was the nickname for the lead character, Frank X. Farrell (see **Alibis**).

See also Debra Dagavarian, *A Century of Children's Baseball Stories* (1990).

Modern Fiction. Jim Bouton (*Ball Four*) and Eliot Asinof (*Eight Men Out*) teamed up to write *Strike Zone* (1994), a fictional account of the last game of a pennant race in which the umpire may be crooked.

Mark Harris, later an Arizona State University professor, wrote three of the definitive baseball fiction works: *The Southpaw* (1953), *Ticket for a Seamstitch* (1956), and *Bang the Drum Slowly* (1956).

Bernard Malamud wrote the classic 1950s baseball book, *The Natural* (1952).

Often called the best baseball fiction book is Robert Coover's, *The Universal Baseball Association Inc. J. Henry Waugh Prop.* (1968). It is the story of a Strat-O-Matic-type **Tabletop Game** nut who has taken the game to psychological and emotional extremes.

William P. Kinsella, a Canadian English professor in Calgary, wrote *Shoeless Joe* (1982), the basis for the **Movie Field of Dreams**. Kinsella also wrote the mystical *The Iowa Baseball Confederacy* (1968). Kinsella, born in Canada but who taught extensively in Iowa, based his 1982 *Shoeless Joe* on a short story revolving around reclusive author J.D. Salinger (*Catcher in the Rye*) and Major Leaguer Moonlight Graham, who played an inning in the outfield for the Giants in 1905 and never came to bat.

See also Cordelia Candelaria, *Seeking the Perfect Game: Baseball in American Literature* (1989); Andy McCue, *Baseball by the Books: A History and Complete Bibliography of Baseball Fiction* (1990).

First Autobiography.

"It was said that the first book Mickey Mantle ever finished reading was his own autobiography." — Joseph McBride in *High and Inside* (1980).

One of the first ballplayer autobiographies was Cap Anson's *A Ballplayer's Career* (ghostwritten in 1900). At least one source credits the first autobiography to Mike "King" Kelly, who played primarily in the 1880s.

Early Instructional Books. The first instructional book was written by John F. Morrell in 1884, *Batting and Pitching, with Fine Illustrations of Attitudes*.

John McGraw wrote a 1913 instructional book, *How to Play Baseball*.

In 1910 Cubs second baseman Johnny Evers collaborated with sportswriter Hugh Fullerton to write *Touching Second*, containing many of Evers' views on baseball strategy.

One of the most prominent and frequently updated instructional books of the mid–20th century, *Baseball*, was by former Major Leaguer Ethan Allen, who coached baseball at Yale University.

Mystery. *Death on the Diamond*, written by Cortland Fitzsimmons in 1934, is considered the first baseball mystery.

In 1991 "Crabbe Evers" wrote *Murder in Wrigley Field*. The pseudonym, actually for two writers, William Brashler and Reinder Van Til, is for Johnny Evers of the Cubs and his nickname, "the Crab" (he was frequently grouchy). The authors wrote a series of baseball mysteries set in Major League ballparks, including *Fear in Fenway* (1993), *Murderer's Row* (1991), *Murder in Wrigley Field* (1993) and *Tigers Burning* (1994). The books feature a retired Chicago sportswriter named Duffy House and his niece, Petrinella Biggers. *The Plot to Kill Jackie Robinson* (1992), is a different genre than normal for long-time baseball writer Donald Honig.

Tom Seaver went out of his element to collaborate on a mystery with Herb Resnicow, *Beanball: Murder at the World Series* (1989).

Strike Three, You're Dead, by J.D. Rosen (1984), is considered by many as the best baseball mystery.

See also Troy Soos, *Murder at Ebbets Field* (1995).

Robert B. Parker's, *Double Play* (2004) focuses on Jackie Robinson's white bodyguard in 1947

Horror. Stephen King once remarked that he had never written a horror story about baseball. "I have," replied sportswriter Dan Shaughnessy, referring to his writing on the 1986 Bill Buckner/Red Sox World Series.

Philosophy. See Eric Bronson (ed.), William Irwin, *Baseball and Philosophy: Thinking Outside the Batter's Box* (2004).

By Active Player.

"Fuck You, Shakespeare!" — Pete Rose yelling to Jim Bouton on the mound after Bouton's book came out. Bouton wrote the then-controversial *Ball Four* in 1970, which he co-authored with *Look* magazine editor Leonard Schechter. The book was a bombshell when first published, but would be considered somewhat tame today. The

The author and his nine-year old identical twin daughters, Katherine (left) and Elena at the Hall of Fame's gift shop/book store in April 2000; *The Cultural Encyclopedia of Baseball* (1st ed.) is featured on the shelves. Elena holds a baseball she found in the street outside the Hall.

book prompted an audience with commissioner Bowie Kuhn: "I advised Mr. Bouton of my displeasure with these writings and have warned him against future writings of this character."

After the 1970 Yankees Oldtimers game, Bouton was barred from any Oldtimers celebrations at Yankee Stadium after his book came out. That changed in July 1998, when he was invited to Yankee Stadium after his son suggested it in an article he wrote in the *New York Times.* In 2003 Bouton came out with *Foul Ball: My Life and Hard Times Trying to Save an Old Ballpark,* in which he decries the use of public funds to build new ballparks.

Pitcher Jim "Professor" Brosnan wrote *The Long Season* while still an active player for the Reds in 1960. In 1964 he wrote *Pennant Race,* the story of the Reds' pennant-winning 1961 season.

"[John Montgomery Ward] was the first ball player to write a book, *Baseball: How to Become a Player,* though it still is suspected that Henry Chadwick's ghost had much to do with the job."—Fred Lieb in *The Baseball Story* (1950). Ward is said to have written the first book by an active player, *Base-Ball: How to Become a Player* (1888). Ward was an attorney and presumably literate enough to have written it himself.

Kiss-and-tell books by current or former players proliferated in the 1970s and 1980s, as did run-of-the-mill autobiographies by players. One of the 2000s books that caused a stir was by David Wells, *Perfect I'm Not: Boomer on Beer, Brawls, Backaches, and Baseball* (2003).

Humor by Players.

"The other is the recorded fact that Joe Garagiola, one of the best-known .257 hitters in the history of baseball, actually hit .316 for the St. Louis Cardinals that year in the World Series against the Boston Red Sox and made headlines without telling a single joke or writing a single best-selling book."—Ed Fitzgerald.

Former catcher Joe Garagiola (see also **Broadcasters**) wrote one of the earliest nonfiction humor books by a player about his baseball experiences. *Baseball Is a Funny Game* (1960) has been reprinted numerous times and dozens of this genre have followed over the next 36 years. Garagiola came back in 1988 with *It's Anybody's Ballgame.*

In 1993 Brewers pitcher Bob McClure wrote *Rotting: The Craze of the '90s,* about "doing nothing; looking like you're doing nothing, but not feeling guilty about it."

Best Books. In 2003 *Sports Illustrated* selected its "Top 100 sports books of all-time." Roger Kahn's *The Boys of Summer* (1971) was second, Jim Bouton's *Ball Four* (1970) was third, and Ring Lardner's *You Know Me Al* (1914), a collection of short stories, was fifth, as the only baseball books to make it into the top 10. A.J. Liebling's *The Sweet Science* (1956), a collection of boxing essays for *The New Yorker,* was number one.

Spitball is a literary baseball magazine that each year recognizes the best baseball book of the year with its "Casey" Award. The winners:

1983 *The Celebrant,* by Eric Rolfe Greenberg
1984 *Bums,* by Peter Golenbock
1985 *Good Enough to Dream,* by Roger Kahn
1986 *The Bill James Historical Abstract,* by Bill James
1987 *Diamonds Are Forever,* by Paul M. Sommers
1988 *Blackball Stars,* by John B. Holway
1989 *The Pitch That Killed,* by Mike Sowell
1990 *Baseball: The People's Game,* by Harold Seymour
1991 *To Every Thing a Season,* by Bruce Kuklick
1992 *The Glory of Their Times (2d ed.),* by Lawrence Ritter
1993 *Diamonds: The Evolution of the Ballpark,* by Michael Gershman

1994 *Lords of the Realm: "The Real History of Baseball,"* by John Helyar
1995 *Walter Johnson: Baseball's Big Train,* by Henry W. Thomas
1996 *Slide, Kelly, Slide,* by Marty Appel
1997 *Play for a Kingdom,* by Thomas Dyja
1998 *Judge and Jury: Kenesaw Mountain Landis,* by David Pietrusza
1999 *Slouching Toward Fargo,* by Neal Karlen
2000 *Cy Young,* by Reed Browning
2001 *The Final Season,* by Tom Stanton
2002 *Shut Out,* by Howard Bryant
2003 *Moneyball,* by Michael Lewis

Mike Shannon's *Diamond Classics* (1989) analyzes his choices for the best 100 baseball books ever written.

Charles C. Alexander wrote *Our Game* (1991), which Roger Kahn described as "a work that will surely be accepted as the best one-volume history of baseball in America." It also contains a good bibliography of other baseball works.

Baseball Lives, by Mike Bryan (1989), chronicles many of the "little people" of baseball (and a few heavyweights), who work behind the scenes to make it all work in and out of the ballpark.

In 2002 *Sports Illustrated* named Roger Kahn's *The Boys of Summer* the second-greatest sports book of all time, behind A.J. Liebling's boxing book, *The Sweet Science.*

Managers. See **Managers—Books.**

By Former Player.

"A nothing sports book with a recognizable name on the cover is guaranteed to sell 5000 copies. Harmless. And everybody makes a little money. Some stock to push while trying to move the top of the line."—Jim Bouton in "*I Managed Good, But Boy Did They Play Bad,*" with Neil Offen (1973).

"I guess I should have written two books of my life, one for the adults and another for the kids."—Babe Ruth shortly before his death.

One of the best is Pat Jordan's *A False Spring* (1973), the story of his minor league pitching experience. Jordan has written a number of books, including a non-baseball fiction work that contains some baseball references, *The Cheat* (1984).

Best Biographies. Generally considered to be two of the best biographies are Robert W. Creamer's *Babe, the Legend Comes to Life* (1974), and Charles C. Alexander's *Ty Cobb* (1984).

Biographical Compilations.

"Having a biography prepared has always seemed to me as either superfluous or in the nature of an epitaph. The omission of both sometimes would seem to be of an advantage to the living."—Charles Comiskey, quoted in his biography, "*Commy,*" by G.W. Axelson (1919).

See also Gene Karst and Martin J. Jones, Jr., *Who's Who in Professional Baseball* (1973); David L. Porter (ed.), *Biographical Dictionary of American Sports: Baseball* (1987); Mike Shatzkin (ed.), *The Ballplayers* (1990).

Ghostwriters. Players have frequently had their autobiographies written by those qualified to put words on a page. The collaborations have now been legitimized by including the writer as one of the authors ("Lenny Dykstra with..."). However, in the early days of autobiographies or instructional books, the player's name was the only one credited for the book. For example, Christy Mathewson's *Pitching in a Pinch* (1912) was ghostwritten by John Wheeler.

Sportswriter Fred Lieb ghostwrote the Babe Ruth autobiography officially written by Ruth with Bob Considine, *The Babe Ruth Story* (1948). Lieb claimed that he dictated the book before the 1947 World Series.

Review. The Society for Baseball Research publishes an annual review of baseball books in its "SABR Review of Books."

Umpires. See *Umpires—Books.*

Out of Their Element. W. R. Burnett wrote *The Roar of the Crowd* (1964), on his views of baseball. He earlier wrote *The Blackboard Jungle* (1954), which became a successful movie starring Glen Ford.

Political columnist George Will wrote *Men at Work* (1990), an exhaustive look at the nuances of baseball as seen primarily through the eyes of four men: A's manager Tony LaRussa, Dodger pitcher Orel Hershiser, Padres outfielder Tony Gwynn and Orioles shortstop Cal Ripken, Jr. Will, a baseball enthusiastic, was named commissioner in 1995 of the new Texas-Louisiana Professional Baseball League.

Best General Books. Lee Allen, *100 Years of Baseball* (1950); Roger Angell, *Season Ticket* (1988); Roger Angell, *Late Innings* (1982); Roger Angell, *The Summer Game* (1972); Thomas Boswell, *The Heart of the Order* (1989); Thomas Boswell, *How Life Imitates the World Series* (1982); Thomas Boswell, *Why Time Begins on Opening Day* (1984); James Charlton (ed.), *The Baseball Chronology* (1991); Tristram P. Coffin, *The Old Ball Game—Baseball in Folklore and Fiction* (1971); John E. Dreifort (ed.), *Baseball History from Outside the Lines: A Reader* (2001); Charles Einstein (ed.), *The Fireside Book of Baseball* (1956); Donald Honig, *The Illustrated History of America's Game* (1990); Bill James, *The Bill James Historical Baseball Abstract* (1988); Roger Kahn, *The Boys of Summer* (1972); Leonard Koppett, *A Thinking Man's Guide to Baseball* (1967); Leonard Koppett, *The New Thinking Man's Guide to Baseball* (1991); Fred Lieb, *The Baseball Story* (1950); Daniel Okrent, *Nine Innings* (1985); Daniel Okrent and Harris Lewine, *The Ultimate Baseball Book* (1979); Benjamin Rader, *Baseball: A History of America's Game* (1994); Lawrence Ritter, *The Glory of Their Times* (1966 and 1984); Lawrence Ritter and Donald Honig, *The Image of Their Greatness* (1979); Curt Smith, Ed., National Baseball Hall of Fame and Museum Staff, Ed., *What Baseball Means to Me* (2001); Robert Smith, *Baseball* (1947, 1970); Robert Smith, *Baseball in America* (1961); Dean A. Sullivan, (ed.), *Early Innings: A Documentary History of Baseball, 1825–1908* (1995); Dean A. Sullivan, (ed.), *Documentary History of Baseball, Middle Innings, 1900–1948* (1998); John Thorn, *The Armchair Book of Baseball* (1985); John Thorn and Pete Palmer, *The Hidden Game of Baseball* (1984); Brandon Toropov, *50 Biggest Baseball Myths* (1997); Jules Tygiel, *Past Time: Baseball as History* (2000); Douglas Wallop, *Baseball: An Informal History* (1970); Joel Zoss and John Bowman, *The Untold History of Baseball* (1989).

Bibliography. Myron J. Smith, Jr., *Baseball: A Comprehensive Bibliography* (1986) (covering almost all non-newspaper baseball items published from 1840 through 1984, and the author followed it up with supplements covering 1985 through 1997; a new edition, 1840 through 2004, is forthcoming in 2005); see also Anton Grobani, *Guide to Baseball Literature* (1975) (listing over 3,000 publications in 33 categories); Andy McCue, *Baseball by the Books* (1991) (a complete bibliography of baseball fiction); James Mote, *Everything Baseball* (1989) (covering one man's "best baseball novels"); Donald E. Walker and B. Lee Cooper, *Baseball and American Culture: A Thematic Bibliography of Over 4,500 Works* (1995).

Boos

"Booing can be therapeutic — sometimes to prod a child to sudden speedy growth at the age of 31."— Writer William Saroyan in *Sports Illustrated.*

"When I'm on the road, my greatest ambition is to get a standing boo."— Reliever Al "Mad Hungarian" Hrabosky.

"You know what they do when the game is rained out? They go to the airport and boo bad landings."— Bob Uecker on fans in Philadelphia.

"Philadelphia fans would boo funerals, an Easter egg hunt, a parade of armless war vets, and the Liberty Bell."— Pitcher Bo Belinsky.

"Fans don't boo nobodies."— Reggie Jackson.

"The highlight of my baseball career came in Philadelphia's Connie Mack Stadium when I saw a fan fall out of the upper deck. When he got up and walked away, the crowd booed."— Bob Uecker.

"No one booed an Astro player. No one got into a fight; a fight at the Astrodome would be as shocking as fisticuffs in the College of Cardinals."— Roger Angell.

"It was the shortest honeymoon in history not involving someone named Zsa Zsa [Gabor]."— Mike Downey in the *Chicago Tribune* on new Mets pitcher Tom Glavine being booed after only his second batter in front of the home crowd in 2003.

"When I came to bat, the Washington crowd gave me a standing 'boovation.'"— Senators infielder Tim Cullen after making three errors in one game (but who also played an entire season with only three errors).

Credo. General Douglas MacArthur reportedly once said that he was proud to protect American freedoms, "such as the freedom to boo umpires."

Earplugs. In 1992 Bobby Bonilla began play in New York for the Mets after signing a huge free agent contract. After batting .147 to start the season, he began wearing earplugs to drown out the boos. He raised his average to .347 before cooling off. Red Sox leftfielder Carl Yastrzemski did the same thing, though using cotton balls. After running to his position, he made a great show of removing the cotton from his ears.

Boston

"All of us who live and work in New England, including Johnny Pesky, firmly believe it far superior to all other places on the globe (as, for that matter, does the *Boston Globe*), and we are boastful about the advantages we enjoy, except for the damned weather."— George V. Higgins in *The Progress of the Seasons* (1989).

Boston has a long history of baseball. The first prominent clubs were the Olympics of 1854 and the Boston Elm Trees, formed in 1855. The Elm Trees featured a "junior" club known as the Hancocks. Many Boston businesses of that era closed down on Saturday afternoons to allow employees to play or attend baseball games.

Professional Teams.

National Association Red Stockings (1871–1875)

National League Red Stockings/Braves (1876–1952)

Union Association Reds (1884)

Players League Reds (1890)

American Association Reds (1891)

American League Red Sox (1901–)

Books. Will Anderson, *The Lost New England Nine: The Best of New England's Forgotten Ballplayers* (2004); Stephen Hardy, *How Boston Played: Sport, Recreation and Community 1865–1915* (1982).

Boston Braves/Red Stockings

National League 1876–1952

"It is doubtful if any single day of baseball in Boston ever will attract more paid admissions than were collected for the pre- and post-luncheon games with New York that Labor Day September 7, 1914 ... [Owner John] Gaffney announced a total of 74,163 paid admissions for the two games."—Tom Meany in *Baseball's Greatest Teams* (1949), on the stretch drive of the 1914 Miracle Braves, one of the few bright spots in the history of National League baseball in Boston.

Origins. Originally known as the Red Stockings, the Boston club was a charter member of the National League in 1876. The club had dominated the last four seasons of the National Association.

First Game. The Red Stockings played their first National League game on April 22, 1876. They defeated the Athletics 6–5 in the first *National League* game ever played.

Key Owners.

Arthur Soden/1876–1906.

"The Dean of the National League"

Soden was a roofing tycoon who bought three shares of the team's stock for $15 in 1876. Principal owner Nick Apollonio soon bowed out and Soden increased his holdings. The notoriously cheap Soden rose in prominence to become a pillar of the National League for 30 years along with Albert Spalding. He was the principal owner of the club until 1906 (along with, at times, 17 minority owners).

By 1903 Soden began refusing to spend the money sufficient to compete with the American League's new entry in Boston, the Red Sox. The team weakened as a result of losing many good players and finished last in Soden's final year of ownership. After the 1906 season Soden sold out to the Dovey brothers.

George B. Dovey and John Dovey/1906–1910.

"Personally he is most affable and companionable, a good talker and 'mixer' and a man who makes friends readily and having made them, holds them; in short, he is just such a man as is needed to regain a National League following in Boston."—Francis Richter on George Dovey in 1906.

George was the leader of the brothers and had been a trolley magnate in St. Louis after moving from Kentucky. His family owned coal interests in Kentucky before business went bad. The brothers supposedly had played semipro ball under pseudonyms while in school. When they bought the club, a small interest was purchased by Fred Tenney.

The Doveys were friends of Pittsburgh owner Barney Dreyfuss, who had been the owner of the Louisville franchise. They were ineffective owners and the club wallowed in the second division. George died suddenly in June 1909 and John took over the club for a year before selling out to William Hepburn Russell.

William Hepburn Russell/1910–1911. Russell was a Missouri native and an attorney, a "man of large affairs" and a boyhood friend of Mark Twain. He became the editor of the *Hanibal Morning Journal* and then moved his law practice to New York in 1895 and Boston in 1900. He had a number of business ventures that made him wealthy. His interest in baseball apparently stemmed from his play at second base and as a pitcher for Hanibal, described as the leading amateur club in Missouri in the late 19th century. He was active in New York politics and construction before buying the club in 1910 for approximately $100,000. In 1911 he bought out his co-purchasers and sold out for $175,000 later in the year.

James Gaffney/1911–1916.

"It will thus be seen that Mr. Gaffney is a big man in business. Personally, he is extremely popular, owing to his genial disposition, unaffected ways and his loyalty to his friends."—*Sporting Life* in August 1915.

Gaffney started out as a policeman but eventually made some of his fortune by securing the contract for the excavation of the Pennsylvania railroad and tunnel station in New York. He also built a number of New York docks. The Tammany Hall–connected Gaffney was close friends with Yankee owner Frank Farrell, who encouraged him to buy out the interest held by Russell. Gaffney, wealthy sportsman Robert Davis and James Carroll paid $175,000 for Russell's interest in August 1911. In the fall of 1912 Gaffney bought out Davis and Carroll. Gaffney is credited with helping to settle the Federal League war, but illness forced him to sell in early 1916; some sources report that he had made a large profit of $300,000 from the club's 1914 success and wanted to cash out.

Gaffney was the brother-in-law of Cubs owner Charles Murphy (himself a model of ineffectiveness—see *Chicago Cubs*). Gaffney hired attorney and former player John Montgomery Ward to run the club but soon fired him. Perhaps Gaffney's primary claim to fame was changing the club's name to Braves. Gaffney sold out to a group fronted by Percy Haughton in early 1916.

Percy Haughton/1916–1919.

"What is baseball's gain in the acquisition of Haughton is unquestionably football's loss, as Haughton is the leading light in football to-day and perhaps the greatest football coach of all time."—Sportswriter Fred Lieb.

Percy Haughton was Harvard's nationally recognized football coach at the time of the purchase from Gaffney. It was a surprise purchase, as Haughton was the front man for an investment banking firm that financed the purchase (Millet, Roe & Haggen). The group had financed the construction of Braves Field and included local politicians Louis A. Fothingham and David I. Walsh. Manager George Stallings also owned some of the stock.

George Washington Grant/1919–1922.

"It was never proven, but it was generally believed, that with the advent of Grant the Braves fell under the control of the Giants."—Harold Kaese in *The Boston Braves* (1948).

In 1919 the club was sold for approximately $400,000 to a New York group (apparently with ties to the Giants owners) headed by "the derby-wearing, cane-carrying" George Washington Grant. Grant had been a pioneer of the motion picture industry in England before selling out in 1917. He also had been a baseball fan in Cincinnati, a fight manager and was a close friend of former Cubs owner Charles Murphy. Grant ran the group until 1922, when Judge Emil Fuchs took a controlling interest in the club.

Judge Emil Fuchs/1922–1935.

"In the 13 years he was to be connected with the club, the Braves were to experience a succession of weird adventures that would have left even [Tarzan creator] Edgar Rice Burroughs cold and unbelieving. But Boston fans who went along on the wild ride were too dizzy at the finish to have any doubts about the reality of their experience."—Harold Kaese in *The Boston Braves* (1948).

Fuchs, who was an attorney but never a judge, dominated the new ownership group after he purchased the club from George Washington Grant. Christy Mathewson was briefly the president of the club in 1923 and was a part-owner. Fuchs allowed Babe Ruth to take an ownership interest when he played for the club briefly in 1935 and Fuchs managed the club for one season (see also *Managers*—Owners as Managers).

The two primary financial backers of Judge Fuchs were friends of future Braves owner Charles Adams. Fuchs turned over some of his stock to Adams as his financial situation deteriorated. At one point the league took over the Braves' lease on the ballpark and sublet the property to the club. Fuchs signed Ruth with the hope of turning around his finances, but when Ruth left the club Fuchs was forced to give up control in August 1935.

Charles F. Adams/1935–1941.

"When Charles F. Adams first began to dabble in the affairs of the Braves, he had no more intention of taking control of the club then he had of playing left field for it. Adams was first and foremost a business man, and one of the most successful in the country."— Al Hirshberg in *The Braves, the Pick and the Shovel* (1948).

In 1935 Charles Adams formed a syndicate to buy the club. Adams had established major league hockey in Boston and owned Suffolk Downs racetrack in Massachusetts. This made it difficult for Adams to remain in baseball because of Judge Landis's intense dislike of baseball mixing with horse racing. As a result, Adams was forced to sell out to another syndicate in 1941.

Louis Perini/1941–1953.

"The Three Steam Shovels"— Nickname of Perini and his two partners in the Braves, each of whom made a fortune in construction during World War II. In 1941 Louis R. Perini bought the team with partners Guido Rugo and Joseph Maney and a few lesser investors. Perini held a 50% interest and controlled the club's direction. Beginning in 1943 the Three Steam Shovels began buying out the other investors.

In 1951 and 1952 Perini bought out the other two primary owners and controlled virtually the entire block of stock. Perini owned the club through the move to Milwaukee in 1953 and until November 1962.

The Move to Milwaukee/1953. Attendance slipped badly from the pennant year of 1948 through 1952:

1948	1,455,431
1949	1,081,795
1950	844,391
1951	487,475
1952	281,278

In 1952 the team lost over $600,000, the largest one-season loss in Major League history up to that time. The club's attendance had dropped almost to the 1935 level of 232,754, less than 3,000 per game. Perini also owned the minor league Milwaukee franchise, which was a Boston farm team. Having bought out his partners, he was in a position to pursue a *Franchise Shift*.

Milwaukee had been lobbying for a Major League team and Perini received permission to move. The Braves announced the move during spring training on March 13, 1953, a date that became known as Black Friday to the [few] Boston faithful.

The Braves left on March 18, 1953, ending a 79-year relationship with the city of Boston. The move paid off for the club from the outset, as the Milwaukee Braves drew 1.8 million and finished second in their first season.

Nicknames. The team originally was known as the Red Stockings or Red Caps, which lasted through the 1882 season. From then until 1906 the team was known primarily as the Beaneaters. The Doves name was used while the Dovey brothers owned the club in 1906–1910. The club was known as the Rustlers in 1910 because of owner William Hepburn Russell. It was known at times as the Pilgrims in approximately 1909–1911.

When James Gaffney purchased the club he changed the name to Braves for the 1912 season. That name has survived two franchise shifts and remains today despite being criticized as insulting to *Native Americans*. From 1936 through 1940, as a gimmick when the team was a chronic loser, the club was called the Bees and Braves Field was known as the Beehive. The Braves name was restored for the 1941 season and that name remained through the team's departure to Milwaukee in 1953.

"Lasts." Eddie Mathews hit the last Boston Braves home run on September 27, 1952, when he hit three on the road in the club's last victory. Virgil Jester earned the last of his lifetime three victories in an 11–3 win over the Dodgers and pitcher Joe Black. The last home run hit in Boston was by Walker Cooper a few days earlier. The club played its last game on September 28, 1952, a 12-inning tie called for darkness at Ebbets Field.

Mathews is the only player to play for all three versions of the Braves (Boston, Milwaukee, Atlanta). Robin Roberts is the only pitcher to face all three clubs.

Key Seasons.

1877. The Red Stockings won the pennant under manager Harry Wright with a 42–18 record. Tommy Bond led the league with 40 wins and a 2.11 ERA. Jim "Deacon" White was the batting champion with a .387 average and a league-leading 49 RBIs.

1878. The Red Stockings repeated as champions with a 41–19 record. Tommy Bond again led the league with 40 wins.

1883. The club won the pennant by four games over the White Stockings. Second baseman Jack Burdock hit .330 with 88 RBIs and Jim Whitney won 37 games. There was no championship series with the American Association because the A's declined to play.

1891. Boston won the pennant by 3½ games over the White Stockings as John Clarkson and Kid Nichols each won at least 30 games. There was no championship series because the American Association was about to fold.

1892. The Red Stockings repeated as pennant winners with 102 wins. Hugh Duffy hit .301 and Kid Nichols and Jack Stivetts each won 35 games. The league tried a split-season format and first-half winner Boston defeated the Cleveland Spiders in a five-game sweep (with one tie).

1893. The Red Stockings won their third straight pennant after the National League eliminated the split-season format. No championship series was played. Kid Nichols won 33 games and Hugh Duffy batted .363.

1897. Boston was back on top by two games over the Orioles. Kid Nichols led the league with 30 wins, Hugh Duffy led with 11 home runs, and seven of the club's eight starters batted over .300. Billy Hamilton stole 70 bases.

1898. The Red Stockings repeated as league champions with a 102–47 record. Kid Nichols again led the league with 29 wins and Jimmy Collins led with 15 home runs. Billy Hamilton batted .369. The club finished second in 1899 and then was mediocre or far worse until 1914.

1914. After more than a decade of mediocrity in the second division, this was the year of the Miracle Braves. The club was in last place on July 4, but won 60 of its last 76 to win the pennant by 10½ games. Manager George Stallings then led the club to a sweep of the Philadelphia A's in the World Series. After two more decent seasons, the Braves were mostly buried in the second division through the mid–1940s.

1948.

"Spahn and Sain and Pray for Rain."— The shorthand version of the fans' lament for a two-man pitching rotation late in the season.

"No one could have guessed how spectacularly the month would unfold or that a thirteen-day string of games and a bit of simple newspaper doggerel would make two members of the Braves mound corps legends forever."— Richard "Dixie" Tourangeau.

The original poem by *Boston Post* sports editor Gerry Hern:
"First we'll use Spahn, then we'll use Sain,
Then an off day, followed by rain.

Back will come Spahn, followed by Sain,
And followed, we hope, by two days of rain."
See also *Poetry*.

The Braves broke into the first division when they finished fourth in 1946 under Billy Southworth, who had enormous success with the Cardinals over the previous five years. He took the Braves to third place in 1947 and then won the pennant in 1948. Pitchers Warren Spahn (15–12) and Johnny Sain (24–15) led the club. The Braves lost the World Series to the Indians in six games and never placed as high as third place again before moving to Milwaukee.

Key Players.

John Clarkson (HF) had four seasons between 1888 and 1891 in which he posted records of 33–20, 49–19, 25–18 and 33–19.

Kid Nichols (HF) spent the first 12 seasons of his career pitching for the Red Stockings. During that span he led the league in wins four times, winning 30 or more games seven times and pitching 44 shutouts.

Jimmy Collins (HF) played only five seasons at third base for the Braves, but hit over .300 three times and led the league with 15 home runs in 1898.

Warren Spahn (HF) pitched the first eight seasons of his 21-year career for the Braves before the club moved to Milwaukee. He won more than 20 games four times during his days in Boston.

Key Managers.

Harry Wright (HF) led the club from 1876 through 1881. He won pennants in 1877 and 1878 and finished second in 1879.

Frank Selee was Boston's manager from 1890 through 1901, though he had no Major League playing experience. During the 1890s he led the club to five first-place finishes and second- through fifth-place finishes one time each. In 1900 he finished fourth and after finishing 69–69 in 1901 he moved on to the Cubs.

George Stallings.

"Stallings knew baseball as Einstein knows Algebra."—Major League catcher and coach Tom Daly.

Stallings took over the club in 1913 with almost no Major League experience (six games in which he batted .100). He started the 1914 season with little confidence in his pitchers: "I have 16 pitchers, all of them rotten."

The club was nicknamed the Miracle Braves after going from last place on July 4 to the pennant and a sweep of the powerful A's in the World Series. Stallings' clubs faded after that season and he left after finishing seventh in 1920.

Rogers Hornsby (HF) took over the club part-way through the 1928 season and managed the team to a dismal 39–83 finish.

Judge Emil Fuchs, who owned the club for several years, managed the club to a last-place finish in 1929 (see also *Managers—Owners as Managers*).

Casey Stengel (HF) managed the club from 1938 through 1943, always finishing in the second division. His next stop was the Oakland Oaks in 1944, where his great success led him to the Yankees job starting in 1949.

Billy Southworth managed the club from 1946 through 1951. He had been successful with the Cardinals from 1941 through 1945, finishing first three times and second twice. He improved the Braves' standing from fourth the first year to a pennant in 1948, finishing 91–62. The club lost the Series 4–2 to the Indians. After mediocre seasons in 1949 and 1950, the club was 28–31 when he was fired in 1951.

Charlie Grimm was the club's last manager in Boston, finishing 7th with a 64–89 record in 1952. He continued as manager when the club moved to Milwaukee.

Ballparks. The 19th century Red Stockings played in the South End Grounds from their start in the National League until September 1887, when the old ballpark was torn down (it had been in use since at least 1871).

The Red Stockings used the new South End Grounds from 1888 through 1894. The ballpark seated 6,800. The park burned down on May 15, 1894. While a new facility was being constructed, the club occupied the Congress Street Grounds, which was home to the 1890 Players League entry and 1891 American Association club.

A new South End Grounds was ready by midseason 1891, and the Braves played there until August 11, 1914. The club borrowed larger Fenway Park for the rest of that pennant-winning season and in the World Series that year. The Braves also used Fenway for most of the 1915 season before moving into Braves Field on August 18, 1915. At the end of that season, the Braves reciprocated by loaning Braves Field to the Red Sox to give them a larger site for the World Series.

Braves Field.

"No one will ever hit a home run out of this ballpark."—Ty Cobb shortly after the ballpark opened.

Braves Field was built in 1915 and the Braves opened the field on August 18, 1915, with a 3–1 victory over the Cardinals. Over 42,000 attended the game, the largest crowd in Major League history to that date. Built over an old golf course, the ballpark had dimensions from left to right field of 402–440–402 (though 550 at its deepest point). It was built with 750 tons of steel and 8.2 million pounds of cement. The dimensions were changed at least 15 times over the years. The ballpark originally seated 40,000, but capacity increased to 46,000 in 1926 and then fluctuated over the years to 37,106 in 1948. It was a single-decked stadium and a streetcar looped inside the outer walls. The 2,000-seat right field bleachers were called the "Jury Box."

It took 10 years for a home run to be hit over the left field wall, by Frank "Pancho" Snyder of the Giants. Wind off the Charles River made hitting very difficult and at various times in 1928 the fences were moved in significantly to create dimensions of 353–330–417–402–364. The final dimensions were 337–355–370–355–319 (with a deepest point of 520 in center field at the flagpole).

It has often been reported that a few horses and mules were buried alive in a cave-in during construction and remained buried beneath the third base line throughout the life of the ballpark. The ballpark is now the site of the Boston University football stadium and the former ticket office became the Boston University Police Station.

Key Broadcasters. Fred Hoey was the club's broadcaster until 1938 (see also *Boston Red Sox—Broadcasters*), when former shortstop Frankie Frisch replaced him for the 1939 season. Jim Britt broadcast for the Braves and Red Sox from 1939 through 1951. In 1950 he broadcast exclusively for the Braves when the two Boston clubs decided to use separate announcers. After the Braves left town before the 1953 season, Britt did television for the Indians in 1954–1955. Long-time Red Sox announcer Curt Gowdy started his Major Leaguer broadcasting career with the Braves in 1951.

Books. Al Hirshberg, *The Braves, the Pick and the Shovel* (1948); Harold Kaese, *The Boston Braves* (1948).

Boston Red Sox

American League 1901–

"An almost inexorable baseball law: A Red Sox ship with a single leak will always find a way to sink…. No team is worshipped with such a perverse sense of fatality."—Thomas Boswell.

"Why did Johnson bat for Willoughby? Where were you when you heard Denny Galehouse was pitching against the Indians? How could Slaughter have scored from first? Why was Buckner still in the game?"—Rhetorical questions addressing the Red Sox Curse, which many contend began with the trade of Babe Ruth in 1919. Dan Shaughnessy's book on the subject is *The Curse of the Bambino* (1990). Add to that: "Why didn't Grady take out Pedro?" after Martinez labored in the 7th inning of Game 7 of the 2003 ALCS game won by the hated Yankees. Manager Grady Little left Martinez in to take a pounding in the 8th inning, when the Yankees went ahead for good.

To answer the other questions:

Red Sox reliever Jim Willoughby was lifted by manager Darrell Johnson for pinch hitter Cecil Cooper, who fouled out for the last out of the bottom of the 8th inning; otherwise Willoughby would have pitched the top of the 9th inning of Game 7 of the 1975 World Series, in which the Reds scored the winning run.

Aging veteran Galehouse was chosen to pitch the one-game *Play-Off* against the Indians for the 1948 pennant. He was bombed, including two home runs by Indians player-manager Lou Boudreau.

Enos Slaughter of the Cardinals scored from first on a single in the 8th inning of Game 7 of the 1946 World Series when shortstop Johnny Pesky purportedly was slow in relaying the ball home (see *Base Running*).

Mookie Wilson dribbled a ball between Buckner's ailing legs to score the winning run in Game 6 of the 1986 World Series and

Pitcher Babe Ruth of the Boston Red Sox in the late 1910s.

the Mets went on to win Game 7. Buckner usually was lifted late in games because his bad ankles gave him little mobility (see *Errors*).

In 2004 the Northeast League Brockton Rox scheduled a May 29, 2004, Grady Little Appreciation Night, which was to include 1,000 Little Bobblearm Dolls, on which the right arm moves to a summon a new pitcher in from the bullpen. Angry fans demanded cancellation of the promotion and club president Jim Lucas complied: "I thought that the wounds would have healed seven months later. I underestimated how raw this still is for people."

Origins. Ban Johnson initially hesitated to put an American League franchise in Boston because of the history of strong support for the National League in the city. The American League's franchise was financed initially by Charles Somers, whose money was used to finance at least three other teams.

First Game. The Red Sox started their first season on the road and did not play at home until May 8, 1901, a day that the rival National League club was playing just across the railroad tracks. The Red Sox were 2–7 when they arrived home to defeat the A's 12–4 in front of 11,500 fans as Cy Young got the win. The National League club drew only 2,000 for a game that day against the Dodgers.

Key Owners.

Henry Killilea/1902–1904.

"Criticized by the press for keeping his owner's share of the World Series take … and for other 'skinflint' business practices (like charging visiting baseball writers for their series seats), Killilea first replaced his unpopular business manager, then decided to sell the club to local ownership."—Peter C. Bjarkman in *Encyclopedia of Major League Baseball* (1993) (who uses the moniker "Doctor of Baseball" after his name).

Milwaukee attorney Henry Killilea bought the club in 1902 and reportedly sold it for a fast profit after winning the 1903 World Series. Other sources report that a ticket scandal at the World Series created bad publicity for the league and that Ban Johnson, who controlled the club from behind the scenes, forced him to sell the club in early 1904.

The Taylor Family/1904–1911. Henry Killilea sold the club to General Charles H. Taylor, owner and publisher of the *Boston Globe* newspaper, and his playboy son, John Irving Taylor. The younger Taylor ran the club. Though Boston repeated as American League champions in 1904, his strange trades and clubhouse tirades alienated the players and manager Jimmy Collins, who departed during the 1906 season. Taylor was criticized for his handling of the club, but he signed a number of players who were the foundation of the club's pennant years starting in 1912: Tris Speaker, Harry Hooper, Joe Wood, Duffy Lewis and Bill Carrigan.

Jim McAleer and Ban Johnson/1911–1913. Near the end of the club's first decade in 1911, Ban Johnson engineered the sale of 50% of the Taylors' interest to former outfielder Jim McAleer and Robert B. McRoy, American League secretary and Johnson's right-hand man. Taylor became a vice-president and relinquished control of the club. Former Boston player Jake Stahl was a part-owner and shortly thereafter became player-manager, though it was clear that this group was merely a front for Johnson. They paid $148,000, outbidding Ned Hanlon, who had offered $125,000. When Stahl became manager, other investors (all bankers) were brought in from Chicago, including Stahl's brother, Garland.

Joe Lannin/1913–1916.

"It was a moderate 55 degrees on the dark Boston streets as the great grandfathers of today's Red Sox fans made their way home.

None of them could have known that inside the walls of the building on 60 Congress Street, well heeled gentlemen sat around a mahogany conference table, smoking cigars and toasting a transaction that would prove to be the first snag in the unraveling with the Boston Red Sox."—Dan Shaughnessy on Lannin's sale to Harry Frazee in *The Curse of the Bambino* (1990).

Lannin, a Garden City, New Jersey, hotel man, bought the club in early 1913. After two mediocre seasons, the club won the 1915 and 1916 pennants behind the pitching of Babe Ruth, Ernie Shore and Dutch Leonard, but Lannin took his profits and sold out.

Harry Frazee/1916–1923.

"He made more sense drunk than most people do sober."—Songwriter Irving Ceaser expressing the minority view.

Frazee was a theater producer who bought the club from Joe Lannin in mid–December 1916. Frazee's big hit was *No, No, Nanette*, which was a huge money-maker on Broadway. Nevertheless, Frazee was often deeply in debt, depending on the fortunes of his most recent theater production.

The Red Sox initially fared well under his ownership, finishing second in 1917 and winning the World Series in 1918. After those successes, the team began to crumble. Frazee sold Ernie Shore, Dutch Leonard and Duffy Lewis to the Yankees for three players and $50,000. He sent Carl Mays to the Yankees for $40,000. On January 9, 1920, he sold Babe Ruth to the Yankees for $100,000 and a $350,000 loan secured by a lien on Fenway Park (in part to secure financing for *No, No, Nanette*). Frazee went on to sell another 10 players to the Yankees. Even general manager Ed Barrow, who owned a piece of the Red Sox in 1918, moved on to the Yankees to become general manager.

As a result of Frazee's efforts to obtain ready cash, the club slipped to sixth in 1919, fifth in 1920–1921, and last in 1922. Mercifully, he sold the club during the 1923 season, but a losing tradition remained for the next decade.

Bob Quinn/1923–1932. J.A. Robert "Bob" Quinn headed a Midwestern group that bought the club from Frazee for $1.5 million in 1923. Quinn had last been with the Browns as general manager. Aristocratically-named Palmer Winslow was a glassworks manufacturer who had the money to back Quinn. Another group of backers was from Columbus, Ohio, and it was rumored that Ban Johnson found these money men and engineered the deal to force out the despised and inept Frazee.

Despite competent management, the club finished last in 1923, seventh in 1924, and then finished in the cellar for six straight years. The club's owners still did not have enough money to bring it out of the doldrums, and Quinn was always scrambling to make ends meet. Winslow died in 1926 and no money was funneled to the club from his estate.

Whenever a competent player developed, he was sold to raise cash. For example, pitcher Red Ruffing was sold to the Yankees for $50,000 in 1930 ($17,500 in some sources; though that may have been his salary). In 1932 the club drew only 182,150 (averaging 2,236 per home game), and Quinn was $350,000 in debt and in need of a buyer. In 1933 Quinn had to borrow against his life insurance policy to make the spring payroll.

Quinn's son John later became general manager of the Braves for 23 years. In 1988 his grandson Robert became general manager of the NFL New York Giants.

Tom Yawkey/1933–1976 (HF).

"I don't intend to mess around with a loser."—Yawkey upon purchasing the Red Sox.

On February 25, 1933, future Hall of Fame inductee *Tom*

Yawkey bought the club from Quinn and his Columbus associates. Hall of Fame third baseman Eddie Collins also bought some of the stock and became vice president and general manager. Collins had attended the same prep school as Yawkey, and Yawkey bought the club primarily on Collins' advice.

Yawkey inherited $4 million from his mother and $3,408,650 from his foster father, who was his uncle and owner of the Tigers at one time. Yawkey had mixed with a number of Tiger players when his father owned the club. He went on to Yale and then was living in New York when he bought the club. He did not receive his fortune until age 30 under the terms of his father's will, but as soon as he did he bought the club four days later for $1 million. Yawkey previously was a prospective buyer of the Dodgers.

Yawkey planned to spend $250,000 in rebuilding the Red Sox, but the total exceeded $1 million (see also *Trades and Player Sales*). He instructed Collins to buy up players to quickly build a winning team. The buying frenzy climaxed in 1934 with the purchase of Joe Cronin from the Senators for $250,000 and shortstop Lyn Lary. He also picked up Jimmie Foxx and others from the fading A's.

All the effort landed the club in fourth place in 1935, the first time it had been in the first division in 16 years. This was as high as the Red Sox could get in the short term, as they dropped back to sixth place in 1936 and fifth in 1937. As a result, Yawkey abandoned the buying spree in favor of developing a farm system.

Yawkey was loved by his players, in part because he was extremely generous with them. Some contended that the players were not hungry enough because of the high salaries and therefore fell short of a pennant in every season during Yawkey's reign except 1946, 1967 and 1975.

Yawkey controlled the club until his death on July 9, 1976. He died during extended hold-outs by Fred Lynn, Rick Burleson and Carlton Fisk, though each continued to play in the wake of the free agent rulings the previous winter. He died of pneumonia (apparently related to his leukemia), but some attributed his death to the "heartache prompted by the audacity of the new free agents brought on by the seminal Messersmith/McNally reserve clause decision."

Jean Yawkey/1976–1992.

"What a terrific gal she was."—Ted Williams.

Tom Yawkey's death put the club into the Yawkey Trust, which was controlled by his widow, Jean Yawkey, executor Joseph LaCour, and California attorney James Curran. Yawkey provided in his will that it was to be run by the trust and then sold to someone else, but everyone underestimated the resolve of Jean Yawkey to retain control. His death led to attempts to buy the club by various groups, including one led by Dom and Joe DiMaggio.

Jean (née Hollander) Yawkey began feuding with team executives Haywood Sullivan and Buddy LeRoux, and she waged a bitter but successful battle for control of the club. She maintained that control through the 1980s until her death from a stroke at age 83 in February 1992. A former model, she and Yawkey were married, both for the second time, in 1944. They watched the game from separate rooftop boxes so she would not hear him swear.

In the late 1970s the team physician, Dr. Arthur Pappas, received about 5% of the club. His conflicts of interest over player injuries became a source of embarrassment in the 1990s. The most publicized event was second baseman Marty Barrett's lawsuit against him for failing to tell him that he had removed the anterior cruciate ligament in his knee during an operation, which shortened his career. Barrett received $1.7 million in a jury verdict against Pappas.

Haywood Sullivan and John Harrington/1992–1993. The club was controlled next by general manager Haywood Sullivan and John Harrington, the latter the co-executor of the estate of Jean Yawkey and the president of her corporation, JRY, which owned the Yawkey stock. Sullivan and Harrington battled each other for control after Yawkey's death, until Sullivan sold out in late 1993.

A former Red Sox back-up catcher and A's manager in 1965, Sullivan joined the Red Sox front office in 1977 and was named general manager. In 1978 Sullivan bought a general partner's share of the club with a $1 million interest-free loan from Jean Yawkey. He later owned a quarter and then a third of the team. In 1992 he was estimated to be worth $40 million based on the value of the club.

John Harrington/1993–2001.

"Red Sox CEO John Harrington is one of the most influential members of baseball's power elite. He heads up several ownership committees, and he was a major collaborator in management's ill-fated attempt to convince the Major League Baseball Players Association to accept a salary cap."—Peter Schmuck.

Harrington continued as president of JRY Corp., which controlled the franchise. He had become a close confidante of the Yawkeys and was the executor of Jean Yawkey's estate. In 2000 the Trust put the club up for sale because of the struggle to obtain public financing for a new ballpark. In December 2001 the partners voted to sell the team to the highest sealed bidder.

John Henry and Tom Werner/2001– .

"[John] Henry, 53 [in 2003], looks, talks and acts more like a college professor than a team owner. In real life, he's been called the world's foremost commodities trader."—Hal Bodley.

In December 2001, a group of investors led by Florida Marlins owner John Henry bought the franchise for a record $660 million—more than double the previous record price for a Major League Baseball team. The agreement included Fenway Park and 80% of the New England Sports Network. It also included assumption of $40 million in debt and doubled the record for the price paid for a ballclub. Henry sold the Marlins to Montreal Expos owner Jeffrey Loria to facilitate the Red Sox deal. He also had to give up his 1% interest in the Yankees.

Henry's group included television producer and former San Diego Padres owner Tom Werner, and former Padres and Baltimore Orioles president Larry Lucchino, skiing entrepreneur Les Otten and former Senate Majority Leader George Mitchell. The group also includes the New York Times Co., which owns the *Boston Globe* newspaper.

Henry, 52 at the time of the purchase, was a Boca Raton commodities trader and hedge fund manager. Lucchino had completed a stint as special adviser to commissioner Bud Selig to determine the feasibility of building a new ballpark in south Florida.

The Massachusetts Attorney General (AG) initially opposed the bid, which was the lowest offered by about $90 million, because the AG represented several charities designated in the Yawkey Trust to receive some of the proceeds. The Trust owned 53% of the club. The Trust and limited partners rejected a $790 million offer made by a group led by Wall Street lawyer Miles Prentice. The Red Sox said Prentice's offer was rejected in part because one of his key investors had not been approved by major league baseball.

Nicknames. The club was known originally as the "Somersets," named after 1901 owner Charles W. Somers. The team tried other names, most notably Pilgrims, Puritans and Plymouth Rocks.

When the National League Boston Braves discarded their traditional Red Stockings name, the Puritans switched to red socks, or Red Sox. This name was finally settled on in 1912 (attributed by one source to Boston president John Irving Taylor in 1907).

Key Seasons.

"The Boston Red Sox are not so much a baseball team as a religion that offers fewer pennants than hair shirts."—Sportswriter Tim Cohane.

"Buckner or Little
It doesn't really matter
Someone will fuck up.

Hey, wait till next year:
Every eighty-six years
Like Clockwork. Go Sox."—Haiku from redsoxhaiku.com.

1901. In the American League's inaugural season the Red Sox finished second, four games behind the White Sox. They were led by Cy Young's league-best 33 wins and Jimmy Collins at third base, who batted .332.

1903. Jimmy Collins managed and played the club to its first pennant. Cy Young led the league with 28 wins, but the Red Sox lost the inaugural World Series to the Pirates.

1904. The Red Sox repeated as American League champions, but the peevish Giants would not participate in the World Series. Cy Young led the club with 26 wins, one of three Boston pitchers to win over 20.

1912. Smoky Joe Wood won 34 games and Tris Speaker hit .383 as the club won 105 games and the pennant by 14 games over the Senators. In the famous Fred Snodgrass World Series (see *Errors*), the Red Sox won in eight games (one tie).

1915. After a second-place finish in 1914, the Red Sox beat out the Tigers by 3½ games to win the pennant. Babe Ruth won 18 games and Tris Speaker hit .322 to lead the club. Boston won the World Series over the Phillies in five games.

1916. The club repeated as American League champions, winning the pennant by two games over the White Sox. Babe Ruth won 23 games to lead the team. The Red Sox repeated as World Champions by defeating the Dodgers in the World Series.

1918. After finishing second in 1917, the Red Sox won an abbreviated season by 2½ games over the Indians. Carl Mays won 21 games and Babe Ruth won 13 games and led the league with 11 home runs. The Red Sox won the World Series over the Cubs; it was to be the club's last World Series victory in the 20th century. See also Ty Waterman and Mel Spring, *The Year the Red Sox Won the Series* (1999).

1920s. There were no "key seasons" in the 1920s, as the Red Sox finished last eight of nine years starting in 1922, though owner Harry Frazee's *No, No, Nanette* was number one at the box office.

1930s/Early 1940s. The Red Sox began developing talent through their farm system, bringing up players such as Ted Williams, Bobby Doerr, Johnny Pesky and Dom DiMaggio. Unfortunately, the Yankees were still world-beaters and the Red Sox were perennial bridesmaids. Boston finished second in 1938, 1939, 1941 and 1942, then did poorly during the rest of the war years.

1946.

"We beat Hitler and the Japs in '45, and in '46 Joe Cronin and the Sox won the pennant, with a machine's patience. Joe Cronin did for baseball what the war effort did for this country, I'd say."—Donald Challenger in "White River Spools" (1976).

The Red Sox finally broke through in 1946, winning 104 games to run away with the pennant. Though Boo Ferriss won 25 games and Ted Williams batted .342 for the season, the Red Sox lost the World Series in seven games to the Cardinals on Enos Slaughter's *Baserunning* heroics.

1948.

"Meditating, no doubt, on the predestination emphasized by their religion, some of the faithful have been seen to wander around bumping into doors and excusing themselves. A few have been known even to slip across the frontiers of sanity. They staged an exodus over the line after the Red Sox lost successive pennants in 1948 and '49, each by one game on the last day." — Sportswriter Tim Cohane.

The Red Sox lost a heartbreak one-game *Play-Off* to the Indians to finish second. Ted Williams led the league with a .369 average.

1949. The Red Sox repeated the anguish with a last-day loss to the Yankees on Jerry Coleman's three-run double. Ted Williams finished second in the league in hitting with a .349 average and led in virtually every other important offensive category.

1967.

"The Impossible Dream"

The Red Sox went from ninth place in 1966 to a pennant in 1967 behind Carl Yastrzemski's Triple Crown and Jim Lonborg's league-leading 22 wins. The club lost the Series in seven games to the Cardinals and Bob Gibson. See also Ken Coleman, *The Impossible Dream Remembered: The 1967 Red Sox* (1987); Herbert F. Crehan and James W. Ryan, *Lightning in a Bottle* (1992); Jeff Miller, *Down to the Wire* (1992); Bill Reynolds, *Lost Summer* (1992).

1972. The Red Sox lost the Eastern Division title to the Tigers by one-half game. The fractional finish was caused by an early season strike that forced the cancellation of a few games that were never made up.

1975.

"We're going to win this thing in spite of the manager." — Red Sox slogan during the pennant-winning 1975 season in which there was player unrest under manager Darrell Johnson. Despite the World Series Game 6 heroics of Bernie Carbo's 8th inning, three-run home run and Carlton Fisk's 12th-inning game-winning home run, the Red Sox lost in Game 7 on a 9th inning, two-out single by Cincinnati's Joe Morgan. The Reds won the game 4–3, overcoming a 3–0 deficit in the process. Rookies Fred Lynn and Jim Rice each drove in more than 100 runs and hit over 20 home runs. Bill Lee, Luis Tiant and Rick Wise each won at least 17 games.

1978. The Red Sox were 11 games in front of the Yankees in August, but fell behind and had to catch the Yankees on the last day of the season. In a one-game *Play-Off* the Yankees held off the Red Sox to win the Eastern Division title. Jim Rice led the league with 46 home runs and 139 RBIs. Dennis Eckersley won 20 games.

1986. The Red Sox suffered perhaps the most stunning defeat in their history when they were one strike away from a World Series championship against the Mets in Game 6. Three singles, a wild pitch and a costly *Error* by Bill Buckner, and the Mets were winners in extra innings. In Game 7 the Red Sox blew a 3–0 lead (shades of 1975!) for an 8–5 loss. See also Dan Shaughnessy, *One Strike Away* (1987).

Don Baylor hit 31 home runs and Jim Rice drove in 110. Buckner drove in 102 runs and hit 18 homers. Roger Clemens was almost unbeatable with a 24–4 record and 2.48 ERA.

1990. The Red Sox won the division by two games over the Blue Jays, but were swept by the A's in the ALCS. Roger Clemens won 21 games and Ellis Burks hit 21 home runs.

1995. The Red Sox ran away with the Eastern Division title, but were swept by the Indians in the division play-offs. Mo Vaughn hit 39 home runs with 126 RBIs and shortstop John Valentin hit 27 home runs with 102 RBIs. Knuckleballer Tim Wakefield made a comeback with a 16–8 record.

1999. The Red Sox finished the season in second place with a record of 94–68 and a wild card spot in the play-offs. They lost the first two games of the division series against the Indians, but stormed back (23–7 in Game 4) to win in five games. They met the Yankees in the ALCS, losing in five games. Nomar Garciaparra hit .357 with 27 home runs and 104 RBIs. Troy O'Leary had 28 home runs and 103 RBIs. Pedro Martinez was dominant with a 23–4 record and a 2.04 ERA. Relievers Derek Lowe and Tim Wakefield combined for 15 saves each.

2003.

"Boone Dents Red Sox." — Headline in the *Los Angeles Times* after Aaron Boone won Game 7 of the 2003 ALCS with a home run; the headline was a tribute to Bucky Dent's 1978 play-off home for the Yankees that knocked the Red Sox out of the postseason.

The Red Sox were the wild card team after finishing second to the Yankees with a 95–67 record. They came back from an 0–2 deficit to beat the A's in the division series, and then lost a heartbreaker to the Yankees in Game 7 of the ALCS. The club was led by Manny Ramirez and his 37 home runs (one of six players with at least 25). Ramirez, David Ortiz and Nomar Garciaparra each had over 100 RBIs. Derek Lowe led the club with 17 wins and a sore-shouldered Pedro Martinez had 14.

2004.

"The Idiots" — Self-described name for the postseason Red Sox, who staged their own certified miracle with a guy who looked like Jesus leading off (Johnny Damon of long hair and beard), a sloppy-fielding outfielder in dreadlocks (Manny Ramirez), and the only white guy in America with cornrows (pitcher Bronson Arroyo).

The Red Sox were again the wild card team after finishing three games behind the Yankees with a 98–64 record. Manny Ramirez led the club with 43 home runs and David Ortiz led with 139 RBIs (along with 41 home runs). Johnny Damon batted .304 and scored 123 runs. Curt Schilling was 21–6 after leaving the Diamondbacks and Pedro Martinez was 16–9. Keith Foulke had 32 saves.

The Red Sox swept the Angels in the division series and then faced elimination after losing the first three games of the ALCS to the Yankees. In Game 4 the Red Sox trailed by a run in the 9th inning with Yankee reliever Mariano Rivera on the mound. Pinch runner Dave Roberts stole second and the rest is history. The Bosox came back with extra-inning wins in Games 4 and 5, won Game 6 back in New York, and then blew out the Yankees 10–3 in Game 7. It was the first time in Major League history that a team came back to win a seven-game series after being down 3–0. The Red Sox continued to beat back the Curse with a four-game sweep of the Cardinals to win their first World Series since 1918. Horror writer and New England native Stephen King picked a good year to write a chronicle of the 2004 Red Sox season, *Faithful*, also by Stewart O'Nan.

Key Players.

Cy Young (HF) was induced to move from the Cardinals to the new American League for the 1901 season. He won 119 games over the next four years and 192 games over eight years for the Red Sox before being traded to the Indians.

Babe Ruth (HF) was the premier left-handed pitcher in baseball while with the Red Sox from 1914 through 1919. He won 89 games for the club, including seasons of 23 and 24 wins in 1916 and 1917. He also provided solid evidence of his home run prowess with 29 in 1919.

Tris Speaker (HF) played the first nine seasons of his career with the Red Sox, batting over .300 in each of his seven full seasons starting in 1907. He helped the club to two World Series appearances in 1912 and 1915.

Joe Cronin (HF) played the last 11 seasons of his 20-year career with the Red Sox, seven of them as the club's starting shortstop. He also managed the club throughout his playing days and continued on for two years after his retirement as a player. He batted over .300 six times for the Red Sox and was considered one of the premier shortstops of the 1930s.

Ted Williams (HF) was the all-time greatest Red Sox player, starring for the club from 1939 through 1960, with interruptions for both World War II and the Korean War as a fighter pilot. He batted .344, sixth all-time, and hit 521 home runs over 19 seasons.

Bobby Doerr (HF) played his entire 14-year career with the Red Sox, batting .288 and playing a stellar second base to anchor the infield along with Joe Cronin.

Carl Yastrzemski (HF) was the successor to Ted Williams in left field and held down the position for most of the next 23 seasons until his retirement in 1983. He batted .285 and hit 452 home runs to go with 1,844 RBIs, 11th all-time. He won the Triple Crown in 1967.

Fred Lynn won the MVP and Rookie of the Year Awards in 1975 when he and Jim Rice led the Red Sox to the World Series. He played with the club for seven years before moving on to the Angels. He batted over .300 five times and won the American League batting title in 1979 with a .333 average.

Jim Rice played his entire 16-year career with the Red Sox from 1974 through 1989. He batted over .300 in seven seasons and finished his career at .298 with 382 home runs. His best season was 1978 when he hit .315 and led the league in slugging average (.600), at-bats (677), hits (213), triples (15), home runs (46) and RBIs (139).

Wade Boggs played the first 11 years of his career with the Red Sox, batting .338 and leading the league in hitting five times.

Roger Clemens was the premier pitcher in the Major Leagues from 1986 through 1992 before arm trouble slowed him. He won 20 games three times, with a top season of 24–4 in 1986. He won no more than 11 games between 1993 and 1996, finishing with a total of 192 wins for the club after signing with the Blue Jays for the 1997.

Nomar Garciaparra began with the Red Sox in 1996 and through 2003 he had a lifetime .323 average, with consecutive batting titles in 1999 (.357) and 2000 (.372) before a wrist injury slowed him down and he was traded in 2004.

Key Managers.

Jimmy Collins (HF) was the first Red Sox manager. He was considered the premier third baseman of the era when he moved across town from the Braves to become the player-manager. He put together a team that contended for the next decade, though he was fired after finishing last in 1906. He led the team to a second-place finish in 1901 and third in 1902, and then two pennant-winning seasons in 1903 and 1904.

Bill "Rough" Carrigan managed the club from 1913 through 1916, including pennants in 1915 and 1916 with Babe Ruth pitching. He was 30 years old and seven years out of college at Holy Cross when he took over the Red Sox. He came back to manage the club for three years starting in 1927, but the club finished last each time during a decade of disastrous seasons.

Joe Cronin (HF).

"But Red Sox rooters have been second-guessing Cronin with vengeance of late, especially in his handling of pitchers. In support of their arguments they cite the cases of such moundsmen as Jim Bagby of the Indians, Buck Newsom of the Athletics, Fritz Ostermueller of the Pirates, Nelson Potter of the Browns and others unable to win under Cronin who became stars after leaving the Sox." — *The Stars and Stripes* military newspaper.

Cronin was the next manager who spent more than three years with the club, from 1935 through 1947. Owner Tom Yawkey purchased him from the Senators and he was the club's player-manager until he retired as a player in 1945. Along with Ted Williams, he led the Red Sox to a number of second-place finishes in the late 1930s and early 1940s. He managed the Red Sox to their first pennant since 1918 when the club won 104 games in 1946, only to lose to the Cardinals in the World Series. Cronin later was the club's general manager before moving on to become president of the American League.

Joe McCarthy (HF) managed the club from 1948 through mid–1950 after retiring from the Yankees for health reasons (he was a chronic alcoholic — see ***Alcoholism***). His 1948 Red Sox club lost in a play-off to the Indians and in 1949 the club lost to the Yankees on the last day of the season. He retired midway through the 1950 season while the club was in fourth place.

Dick Williams managed the Red Sox from 1967 through 1969, leading the club to the 1967 American League pennant after it had finished ninth in 1966. He was fired after the club finished third in 1969. He moved on to the Oakland A's in 1971, where he had tremendous success in the early 1970s. See also Dick Williams and Bill Plaschke, *No More Mr. Nice Guy* (1990).

Don Zimmer took over during the 1976 season when the club began to falter after its 1975 pennant-winning season under Darrell Johnson. Zimmer managed the Red Sox through 1980, but his infamous notoriety was for leading the club during the 1978 pennant race collapse and play-off loss to the Yankees.

John McNamara managed the Red Sox from 1985 through the 1988 All-Star break, when he was fired. He led the club to the 1986 American League pennant, but lost the World Series to the Mets in a heartbreaker. He was voted Manager of the Year that season, but the club could not win a division title under his leadership after 1986.

Joe Morgan led the club for three seasons, coming in first in first in 1990 and second in 1991 before being fired.

Kevin Kennedy won a division title in 1995 and then was fired after finishing third in 1996.

Jimy Williams led the club for five seasons beginning in 1997, and the club was the American League wild card winner in 1998 and 1999, but could not get past the Yankees. Williams was fired after the 2001 season.

Grady Little was hired for the 2002 season and the Red Sox finished second. They repeated in second in 2003, but were the wild card team. After the highly public ALCS seven-game fiasco against the Yankees, he was terminated.

Ballparks.

"Boston's Fenway Park is normally best on the worst days, in raw, misty spring and foggy fall. The streets around the Fens are crowded, narrow, and damp. Taxis blow their horns at the herds of Soxers in Lansdowne Street." — Thomas Boswell in *How Life Imitates the World Series* (1982).

The first American League playing field in Boston was at the Huntington Avenue Grounds, the predecessor to Fenway Park. It was the site of the first World Series game, played in 1903. The first lease on the park was signed by Connie Mack, acting as Ban Johnson's advance man when Johnson was establishing the American League in Boston. The park seated 9,000, though some sources erroneously put the figure at 16,000. The dimensions from left to right field were 350–530–280 when the club first used the park, but were altered in 1908. Tufts Medical College now stands on part of the site. The club moved to ***Fenway Park*** for the 1912 season and has been there ever since.

Key Broadcasters. The Red Sox originally broadcast over the New England–based Yankee Network. The network always broke for the news at 6:00 p.m., no matter what was happening in the game. Fred Hoey, a former sportswriter, started in Boston in 1933 and broadcast until 1939 for both Major League clubs in the city. Hoey died at age 64 in 1949 and is credited by some as instrumental in building up baseball broadcasting. Former shortstop Frankie Frisch briefly replaced him and bombed.

Jim Britt broadcast simultaneously for the Braves and Red Sox in the 1940s and 1950, and then broadcast exclusively with the Braves in 1951. Curt Gowdy began broadcasting for the Red Sox and Braves in 1951, ending his relationship with the Braves when they moved to Milwaukee. He stayed with the Red Sox through the 1965 season, when he left to broadcast NBC's Game of the Week. His partners through the 16 years with the Red Sox were Bob Delaney (1950–1953), Bob Murphy (1954–1959), Art Gleesen (1960–1964) and Mel Parnell (1965).

Boston native Ken Coleman took over in 1966, went to Cincinnati for four years in the late 1960s, then returned as the voice of the Red Sox through 1989. Ned Martin was a broadcast fixture with the Red Sox starting in 1961, on radio until 1978 and then television for a few more years into the 1980s. Joe Castiglione, who wrote, along with Douglas B. Lyons, *I Saw It On the Radio with the Boston Red Sox* (2004), started on radio for the club in 1983 and became the lead announcer through the 2004 season. Sean McDonough has been the club's primary television broadcaster since 1988.

Books.

"Are you kidding? People actually write books about one of the worst franchises in the history of sports?… The Red Sox and the word dream should never go together in a sentence. Unless of course it's used in the context of destroying people's dreams."— Anonymous on-line book review for Glenn Stout's *Impossible Dreams: A Red Sox Collection* (2003).

Ellery H. Clark, Jr., *Red Sox Forever* (1977); Peter Gammons, *Beyond the Sixth Game* (1985); Derek Gentile, *The Complete Boston Red Sox* (2003); Peter Golenbock, *Fenway* (1992); David Halberstam, *The Teammates* (2004); Al Hirshberg, *The Red Sox, the Bean & the Cod* (1947); Jack Lautier, *Fenway Voices* (1994); Fred Lieb, *The Boston Red Sox* (1947); Johnny Pesky with Phil Pepe, *Few are Chosen* (2004); Dan Riley (ed.), *The Red Sox Reader* (1987); Dan Shaughnessy, *The Curse of the Bambino* (1990); George Sullivan, *Picture History of the Boston Red Sox* (1979).

Movie. *Still, We Believe: The Boston Red Sox Movie*, was released in July 2004. It chronicled eight Red Sox fans from February 2003 through Game 7 of the 2003 ALCS loss against the Yankees. Fan Angry Bill summed it up: "I wouldn't know what to do if they won. Would you know what to do?"

Boston Red Stockings

National Association 1871–1875

"The announcement that the home Nine were again defeated by their red-hosed [Boston] adversaries will occasion no unusual surprise. There was a time when a thunderbolt from a serene sky would cause less astonishment in this city than the news of the Club's defeat…"—*Chicago Tribune* story quoted in *Baseball and Mr. Spalding*, by Arthur Bartlett (1951).

This was an early 1870s professional team formed when the core players of the original Cincinnati Red Stockings, including George Wright, quit and moved to Boston for the 1871 season. The Red

Stockings were original members of the National Association and won four straight pennants beginning in 1872 behind the underhand pitching of Albert Spalding. In 1875 the team was 71–8 and lost only one game at home. Boston had the top four hitters in the league and eight of the top 20, resulting in a pennant by 15 games. After the National Association collapsed, the Red Stockings moved into the National League (see *Boston Braves/Red Stockings*).

Boston Red Stockings   See *Boston Braves/Red Stockings*

Boston Reds

Union Association 1884

"In Boston, Spalding's old teammate and fellow sporting goods dealer, George Wright, was persuaded to organize a Union club. Because of Wright's standing and reputation, this gave the whole movement additional strength."—Arthur Bartlett in *Baseball and Mr. Spalding* (1951).

Also known as the Unions, the club finished the season in fifth place with a record of 58–51. The Reds were led by first baseman, manager and future sportswriter Tim Murnane. George Wright, of Cincinnati Red Stockings and Boston Red Stockings fame, was the club's president.

Boston Reds

Players League 1890

Charles A. Prince owned the Reds and the club won the pennant by 5½ games. They were led by catcher Mike "King" Kelly, first baseman Dan Brouthers and pitcher Old Hoss Radbourn, who won 27 games. After the Players League folded, the Reds moved over to the American Association for the 1891 season.

Boston Reds

American Association 1891

After the 1890 Players League folded, the Boston entry shifted to the American Association with a few of the same players (most notably Dan Brouthers). The 1891 club won the pennant with a 93–42 record behind Brouthers and Hugh Duffy. The club was barred from using the "Boston" name on its uniforms because of the rival National League team already in the city.

Boston Unions   See *Boston Reds*

Jim Bottomley (1900–1950)

Hall of Fame (VC) 1974

"With a touch of swagger, a constant smile and a cap perched at a rakish angle, Bottomley came by his nickname of 'Sunny Jim' honestly and, in his bachelor days, he was certain to attract thousands of extra customers to Ladies Days at Sportsman's Park."— Lowell Reidenbaugh in *Cooperstown* (1986).

Bottomley played first base primarily for the Cardinals and Reds from 1922 through 1937, batting .310.

James LeRoy "Sunny Jim" Bottomley was in the Cardinals farm system when he was promoted to the Major Leagues in 1922. He remained with the Cardinals at first base until after the 1932 season, when he was traded to the Reds. He batted over .300 eight times for the Cardinals and helped lead them to four pennants. His best season with the club was 1928, when he batted .325 and had a league-leading 20 triples as the league's MVP.

On September 16, 1924, Bottomley set a since-tied Major League record when he drove in 12 runs. He also went 6-for-6 that day and is one of only three Major Leaguers to do it twice in his career.

He played three seasons with the Reds and batted a high of .284 in 1934. He was traded to the Browns for the 1936 season and batted .298. He ended his career primarily as a pinch hitter in 65 games in 1937 and managed the club for part of the season. He finished with a lifetime .310 average and 1,422 RBIs in 1,991 games.

Bottomley managed in the minor leagues for a short time before retiring to his Missouri cattle ranch. He returned briefly to scout for the Cubs and manage in the minor leagues in 1957, but a heart condition forced him out after only two games at the helm. He died two years later.

Lou Boudreau (1917–)

Hall of Fame 1970

"There is nothing very unusual about a man who works desperately, refusing to spare himself in any way, in order to attain a specific goal. There is, however, a rare halo of good luck drawn around the head of the man who experiences the satisfaction of reaching that goal. I enjoyed that good luck and that satisfaction." — Boudreau in his autobiography, *Player-Manager*, with Ed Fitzgerald (1949), shortly after his Indians won the 1948 World Series.

Boudreau was a player-manager for most of his shortstop career for the Red Sox and Indians between 1938 and 1952.

Louis Boudreau graduated from the University of Illinois after being declared ineligible for college ball because he had signed an agreement with the Indians to play following graduation. He appeared in one Major League game in 1938 and played for the Buffalo Bisons for most of 1939.

He appeared in 53 games for the Indians in 1939 and became the club's starting shortstop at age 22 in 1940. He played 13 years in Cleveland, leading the league in hitting with a .327 average in 1944 and batting over .300 four times. He managed the club from 1942 (at age 24) through 1950 when he was fired and traded to the Red Sox. He was almost released when Bill Veeck bought the Indians in 1946, but a public outcry put a stop to the move.

Boudreau's best season was 1948 when he batted .355 and led the club to a tie with the Red Sox. In a one-game play-off he hit two home runs to put the Indians into the World Series. The club defeated the Braves in six games and Boudreau's season was capped off when he was named the American League MVP.

He finished his career in 1952 with a .295 lifetime average and a reputation as a strong fielder and manager. In his nine seasons as Cleveland's manager the club finished first once and third twice. Under his leadership again, the Red Sox finished no better than fourth between 1952 and 1954, and he had no success with the Athletics in 1955–1957.

He broadcast for the Cubs before one more unsuccessful effort at the helm for most of 1960. After posting a 54–83 record to end the season in seventh place he returned to a long and popular career as a broadcaster.

Books. Lou Boudreau with Ed Fitzgerald, *Player-Manager* (1949); Lou Boudreau with Russell Schneider, *Lou Boudreau: Covering All the Bases* (1994).

Bowling

"It's only the start. So many heads are going to roll it's going to look like a bowling alley around here." — Red Sox second baseman Jerry Remy after the firing of manager Don Zimmer after the 1980 season.

"… Lawrence Peter Berra, the squire of Montclair, New Jersey, home-run hitter par excellence, bowling alley proprietor, Yoo-Hoo Chocolate Drink vice-president, promising golfer (he's been promising to break 80 for years), and now author…" — Sportswriter Ed Fitzgerald.

"Never bowl with a guy who shows up with a ball called a Piranha." — Sportswriter Gordon Edes on pitcher John Burkett, who had rolled ten 300 games through 2003 and has participated in professional bowling events in the off-season.

"Charlie Bowles, Steve Bowling, Grant Bowler"

Denny McLain credited an off-season bowling regimen for the strength and stamina he needed to win 30 games for the Tigers in 1968. He made the wild claim that he bowled 60 lines each day.

Box Scores

"My idea of courage is the guy who has $500,000 tied up in the stock market and turns to the box scores first." — Entertainment writer Earl Wilson.

"If anyone got it, he did." — Official scorer Bozeman Bulger arbitrarily crediting Larry Doyle with a hit after the sportswriter's box score did not add up.

"The box score is the catechism of baseball, ready to surrender its truth to the knowing eye." — Stanley Cohen in *The Man in the Crowd* (1981).

"The baseball box score is the pithiest form of written communication in America today. It is abbreviated history. It is two or three hours (the box score even gives *that* item to the minute) of complex activity, virtually inscribed on the head of a pin, yet no knowing reader suffers from eyestrain." — Fred Schwed, Jr., in *How to Watch a Baseball Game* (1957).

Origins. Famed 19th century sportswriter **Henry Chadwick** is credited with inventing the box score, which first appeared in 1863 in the *New York Clipper* newspaper (though some sources erroneously put the date as 1859). Box scores were not unheard of, as a form of box score was already in use for cricket matches.

Format. Ernest Lanigan, originally of the *New York Press* (and succeeded there by sportswriter Fred Lieb), is credited with adding two categories to the box score: RBIs and "thrown out stealing," the latter listing the names of those caught stealing by the catchers.

In 1958 the Associated Press (AP) and United Press International (UPI) wire services changed their box scores, but *The Sporting News* continued the old format until 1961. The old format used five columns: at-bats, runs, hits, putouts, and assists. Under the new format, the defensive statistics were eliminated and RBIs were added, creating a four-column format still in use. Before 1925 the home team was often shown on the left of the box score or at the top of the line score.

In 1965 umpires were dropped from box scores, but were reinstated a few years later. In 1992 the *Los Angeles Times* and other newspapers began using a more comprehensive box score that included a player's average. It followed the format established by *USA Today*.

Minor League Box Scores. Because of the great interest in all baseball shortly after 1900, newspapers in Major League cities began carrying minor league box scores. It appears that the Major Leagues were stable enough at that point not to be threatened by the minor leagues and the Major League clubs no longer needed to exert pressure on the local media to refrain from printing other clubs' box scores.

Name Problems. Pete Jablonowski showed up in the box score as "Jblnsi." He changed his name to Appleton (which still would not fit) and won 14 games for the Senators in 1936.

No At-Bat. Pitcher Amos Rusie supposedly once refused to bat and the next day's box score carried a cryptic note to explain why there were only 26 outs recorded.

Books/Key Games. Joseph J. Dittmar, *Baseball's Benchmark Boxscores* (1990); box scores of 119 games with significant milestones in various statistical categories.

BASE BALL PLAY—The subjoined is the result of the return match between the New York Base Ball Club and the Brooklyn players, which came off on the ground of the Brooklyn Star Cricket Club yesterday. Messrs. Johnson, Wheaton and Van Nostrand were the umpires.

NEW YORK BALL CLUB.	Hands out.	Runs.	BROOKLYN CLUB.	Hands out.	Runs
Davis	2	4	Hunt	1	3
Murphy	0	6	Hines	2	2
Vail	2	4	Gilmore	3	2
Kline	1	4	Hardy	2	2
Miller	2	5	Sharp	2	2
Case	2	4	Meyers	0	3
Tucker	2	4	Whaley	2	2
Winslow	1	6	Forman	1	3
	12	37		12	19

Box score from the *New York Herald*, game of October 25, 1845.

UNION VS EXCELSIOR.—The match between these clubs which was played on the Excelsior grounds, South Brooklyn, on the 15th inst., resulted in favor of the Unions by a score of 20 to 9. The Excelsiors played as if entirely out of practice, and were sadly lacking in that fine display we were once accustomed to witness at their hands.

BATTING.

EXCELSIOR.	H.L.	RUNS	UNION.	H.L.	RUNS
Flanly, 2d b	0	5	Nicholson, 1st b	5	0
Smith, p	5	0	E Durell, l f	3	2
Masten, 3d b	2	1	Abrams, 2d b	4	2
Whiting, 1st b	3	1	Hannegan, p	3	3
McKenzie, l f	4	0	Birdsall, c	3	3
H Brainard, s s	2	2	Hyatt, 3d b	2	3
Cline, c	4	0	Gaynor, s s	4	2
Fairbanks, r f	3	0	Collins, c f	1	2
Leggett, c f	4	0	F Durell, r f	2	3
Total		9	Total		20

RUNS MADE IN EACH INNINGS.

	1st	2d	3d	4th	5th	6th	7th	8th	9th	
Excelsiors	2	0	2	1	1	1	1	0	1-	9
Union	4	1	2	1	3	1	3	2	3-	20

Umpire—Mr. Pearce, of the Atlantic club.
Scorers—Messrs. Holt and Travers.
Home runs—Hyatt, 1.
Struck out—Smith, 1.
Catches missed—Leggett, 1; Masten, 1; Smith, 1; Fairbanks, 1; Birdsall, 2; F. Durell, 1.
Put out at first base—Excelsiors, twice; Unions, 9 times.
Put out at home base—E. Durell, By Masten.
Fly catches made—Masten, 2; Fairbanks, 1; H. Brainard, 1; McKenzie, 1; Flanly, 2; Cline, 1; Abrams, 3; Birdsall, 4; E. Durell, 1; Hannegan, 1; Hyatt, 2; Nicholson, 2.
Put out on foul balls—Excelsiors, 16 times; Unions, 8 times.
Time of the game—three hours and thirty minutes.

Box score from the *New York Clipper*, game of August 22, 1863.

The Chicagos Vanquish the Mutuals.
[Special Despatch to The Boston Globe.]
NEW YORK, September 10.—The eighth game in the championship series was played on the Union grounds yesterday, and resulted in a victory for the Chicagos by the following score:

CHICAGOS.	R.	1B.	PO.	A.	E.	MUTUALS.	R.	1B.	PO.	A.	E.
Barnes, 2b	3	2	6	1	1	Start, 1b	1	1	4	1	1
Anson, 3b	4	3	3	3	1	Treacy, r. f.	2	3	0	0	1
McVey, c.	1	2	4	8	0	Hallinan, s. s.	1	2	2	1	1
Peters, s. s.	0	2	1	1	0	Craver, c.	0	2	9	3	2
White, l. f.	1	1	3	0	3	Hayes, l. f.	0	0	2	6	0
Spalding, p.	1	2	2	0	0	Booth, c. f.	0	1	2	1	2
Hines, c. f.	1	1	1	0	0	Matthews, p.	0	0	1	0	1
Gleason, 1b	1	2	5	0	0	Nichols, 3b	0	0	2	1	3
Addy, r. f.	1	2	2	0	1	West, 2b	0	0	1	3	0
Totals	13	18	27	6	6	Totals	4	11	27	10	12

Innings	1	2	3	4	5	6	7	8	9	
Chicagos	2	0	5	2	0	0	0	4	0—	13
Mutuals	0	0	0	1	0	2	1	0	0—	4

Umpire—Mr. Ducharme of the Oceola Club. First base by errors—Chicagos, 5; Mutuals, 2. Runs earned—Chicagos, 3; Mutuals, 4. Time of game—1 hour 35 minutes.

Box score from *The Sporting News*, game of September 10, 1876.

Box Seats

"I have discovered in 20 years of moving around a ballpark that the knowledge of the game is usually in inverse proportion to the price of the seats." — Entrepreneurial owner Bill Veeck, Jr.

"A man who pays for a box seat has a right to see the game without getting a pain in the neck." — Cubs owner Phil Wrigley on the new box seats that faced more toward the infield than the outfield.

See also *Tickets*.

In 1871 William H. Cammeyer, ballpark builder and owner of the New York Mutuals of the National Association, installed seats in front and above the dressing room, charged extra for them and called them box seats.

Boxing

"Today is Opening Day in baseball. Out in Yankee Stadium Billy Martin just threw out the first punch." — "Tonight Show" host Johnny Carson.

"I didn't raise my son to be a catcher." — Mrs. Marciano on why her son Rocky did not sign a contract with the Cubs.

"George 'Babe' Ruth and Old Jack Dempsey, both Sultans of Swat, One hits where the other people are, the other where they're not." — John Lardner.

See also *Fights*.

19th Century. On November 2, 1883, heavyweight champion John L. Sullivan pitched against the St. Louis Browns of the American Association in an exhibition. In front of a large crowd it was soon evident that he could neither pitch nor hit. In spite of that, he did receive 60% of the gate receipts.

Sullivan later managed an independent professional baseball team in New England, his qualifications to manage coming from growing up near the South End Grounds in Boston. He sometimes appeared on the field before games and let players throw balls at his chest.

Gentleman Jim Corbett, heavyweight champion of the 1890s, attempted to sign with Baltimore of the National League in 1894. He supposedly was offered $10,000 to play with the team on a road trip in July and August of that year. He had been a decent player with a San Francisco team, but the plan was abandoned after an uproar by the other owners. He did manage to play first base in cameo appearances for a number of minor league teams in the mid–1890s.

YANKS WIN AGAIN; RUTH MAKES 35TH

McNally and McInnis Pull Off Triple Play, but Red Sox Lose.

NEW YORK, July 25.—New York easily defeated Boston here today, 8 to 2. Mays held the Red Sox to four hits, two of which were of the scratch variety. Hoyt pitched well except in the fifth when the Yankees got to him for six hits, one of which was Babe Ruth's thirty-fifth home run of the season, the ball going into the lower right field stand.

The fielding feature was a triple play executed by McNally and McInnis in the third. Peckinpaugh was passed and moved to second when McNally fumbled Pipp's grounder. Pratt then lined to McNally, who touched second before Peckinpaugh could return to the bag and then whipped the ball to McInnis, retiring Pipp, who had started for second.

Boston	A	R	H	O	A		New York	A	R	H	O	A
Hooper,rf.	4	0	0	3	0		Peckinp'gh,s	2	2	1	1	5
Vitt,3	3	1	0	0	1		Pipp,1	3	2	1	16	0
Menosky,lf	3	0	0	2	0		Pratt,2	4	2	3	4	4
Schang,cf	4	0	1	1	0		Ruth,lf	3	2	3	0	
McInnis,1	4	0	0	9	1		Meusel,rf	3	0	2	0	0
Scott,s	4	0	2	2	3		Bodie,cf	4	0	0	1	0
McNally,2	3	1	0	4	1		Ward,3	4	0	1	1	5
Walters,c	3	0	1	3	2		Ruel,c	4	1	1	1	1
Hoyt,p	2	0	0	0	0		Mays,p	3	0	0	0	2
*Karr	1	0	0	0	0							
Fortune,p	0	0	0	0	0		Totals	30	8	11	27	17
Totals	31	2	4	24	8							

*Batted for Hoyt in eighth.

Boston ....0 0 0 0 1 1 0 0 0—2
New York ....2 0 0 5 0 1 0 *—8

Errors—Hooper, McNally, Bodie. Two-base hits—Ruth, Pratt. Three-base hit—Schang. Home run—Ruth. Stolen base—McNally. Sacrifices—Meusel, Ruth. Double plays—Scott to McInnis to Walters; Peckinpaugh to Pratt to Pipp. Triple play—McNally to McInnis. Left on bases—Boston 4, New York 3. Bases on balls—Off Hoyt 3, off Mays 2. Hits—Off Hoyt 11 in 7 innings; off Fortune none in 1 inning. Struck out—By Hoyt 2, by Mays 1. Umpires—Nallin and Connolly. Time—1.35.

Box score from *The Sporting News*, game of July 25, 1920.

In 1896 the Baltimore Orioles signed Corbett's brother, Joe, who won 24 games for the club in 1897. Joe also supposedly became his brother's sparring partner after he lost his effectiveness as a pitcher. Joe later coached at Santa Clara College in California, where future Major League star Hal Chase played for him.

In the 19th century boxers were popular as guest umpires at minor league games. Honorary umpires included John L. Sullivan, Jim Corbett, Jim Jeffries and Bob Fitzsimmons.

Black heavyweight boxing champion Jack Johnson, a former first baseman, masqueraded as a player with the Negro American Giants around 1910 to flee Mann Act prosecution for transporting an underage female across state lines (apparently she was his fiancée). He fled to Canada and later moved to Europe.

Umpires/Referees. Umpire Honest John Kelly was one of the King of the Umpires in the 1880s. After trying his hand at managing and horse racing, he refereed a few prominent boxing matches in the 1890s.

Settling Differences. Jim Coates was considered a racist member of the Yankees in the 1950s. He was openly hostile to the first black player on the club, catcher Elston Howard. After an exhibition game against Army at West Point, Mickey Mantle led the team into an adjacent gymnasium for some basketball. There was a boxing ring and, after much prodding, Howard agreed to box against Coates. Howard decked him. Coates was known around the league for throwing at black players. Vic Power got revenge with four home runs over his career against Coates, all on special days such as Memorial Day, Father's Day and Mother's Day.

Boxing Career. An early King of the Umpires was Billy McLean, an ex-prize fighter who worked in the National Association in the early 1870s. He umpired in the National League through 1884.

Umpire George Magerkurth fought 70 professional fights before becoming a National League umpire in 1929. One source noted that he "[f]ought several times afterward, but these altercations cost fines, suspensions, damage to ego." (Gene Karst and Martin J. Jones, Jr., *Who's Who in Professional Baseball* (1973)) (see also **Fights**).

Long-time catcher Rick Ferrell had a brief boxing career before going into baseball.

Don Hoak, Pirate third baseman on the 1960 World Championship team, was a professional boxer as a teenager. He was knocked out seven straight times before retiring.

Art "The Great" Shires TKO'd Al Spohrer in a boxing match at the Boston Garden in 1930. Shires played 82 games for the Braves two years later and was Spohrer's teammate. Shires later tried to arrange a bout with Cubs outfielder Hack Wilson, but Judge Landis intervened. Shires had shown signs of pugilistic prowess, having brawled twice during the 1929 season with manager Lena Blackburne. Shires also signed to fight one Dan Daly, who took a dive in the fight. Shires' boxing career ended quickly when Judge Landis told him to quit fighting or quit baseball. Shires' Major League career lasted from 1928 through 1932.

Sportswriter. Paul Gallico, a longtime baseball writer and sports editor at the *New York Daily News*, who wrote *The Poseidon Adventure*, was KO'd by a left hook from Jack Dempsey in 1923. He was the first writer to step into the ring with a professional fighter, which George Plimpton (of *Sidd Finch* fame) did almost 40 years later.

Big Brother. Future heavyweight boxing champion Mike Tyson lived and trained in the Catskill Mountains in the early 1980s, trying to avoid juvenile delinquency at trainer Cus D'Amato's headquarters. Tyson's *de facto* big brother at the camp was future Seattle Mariner Mickey Brantley.

Death. The brother of 1930s and 1940s first baseman Dolf Camilli died in the ring fighting heavyweight champion Max Baer.

Banned. In 1923 Ban Johnson banned boxing matches in Major League ballparks at a time of anti-gambling sentiment. The view faded by the 1930s and the ban was never seriously enforced.

First Pitch. Muhammad Ali threw out the first pitch of the 2004 All-Star Game in Houston.

Good Clean Fun. Dodger pitcher Hugh Casey, who delivered the swinging third strike dropped by Mickey Owen in the 1941 World Series (see also *Passed Balls*), was a heavy drinker. He once met up for a party with writer *Ernest Hemingway* during a Dodger spring training in Cuba. Hemingway proposed a boxing match while the two were drinking heavily. Hemingway got in a few shots of little consequence, while Casey toyed with him good-naturedly. When Hemingway finally connected, Casey responded by decking him with one shot—end of boxing match. Coincidentally, both committed suicide, Casey two years after he retired. Some sources report that the two were dove-hunting companions and regularly beat each other up at Hemingway's house.

Bad Choice. During the 1970 Puerto Rican winter league, pitcher Bill Lee slugged local catcher Eliseo Rodriguez when Rodriguez charged the mound after being hit by a pitch. Lee later learned that Rodriguez was a Golden Gloves boxing champion. His brothers found Lee on their next road trip and beat him up.

Hall of Fame. In 2002, the Summit County (Ohio) Boxing Club Hall of Fame named Pete Rose as a candidate for induction on the strength of Rose's 1973 on-field play-off game fight with Mets shortstop Bud Harrelson.

Equipment. In 1988 Angels manager Cookie Rojas placed a punching bag in the dugout runway to let his players blow off steam without breaking their hands on the water cooler.

Boys Baseball League

This league consists of separate leagues for 8–12-year olds (Junior League), 13- and 14-year-olds (*Pony League*), and 15- and 16-year-olds (*Colt League*). The league is headquartered in Washington, Pennsylvania, and is not affiliated with Little League baseball.

Roger Bresnahan (1879–1944)

Hall of Fame (VC) 1945

"The old Giant catcher from way back — the guy who caught Mathewson and Marquard and all the rest of them, the man who invented shin guards back in 1908 or so…. Mr. Bresnahan helped me a great deal. He more or less showed me the ropes and taught me how to catch…. Except for Bresnahan, nobody paid any attention to me…. They didn't want a rookie to come in and take one of their buddies' jobs. But they weren't *too* bad. They just more or less ignored me."—Bob O'Farrell quoted in *The Glory of Their Times*, by Lawrence Ritter (1966).

Bresnahan was one of the premier catchers around the turn of the century and is credited by some with introducing shin guards to the Major Leagues.

Though born in Toledo, Ohio, in 1879 (1880 in older sources), Roger Philip Bresnahan was known as the Duke of Tralee because of the mistaken belief by many that he was born in Ireland (only his parents were). He started his career as a pitcher (a six-hit shutout in his 1897 debut with Washington), but later was best known as one of the outstanding catchers of his era. Washington released him before the 1898 season when he asked for more money, and he went back to the minors.

He did not establish himself in the Major Leagues until he played 86 games primarily at catcher for Baltimore in the American League in 1901. He went with John McGraw when McGraw made a mid–1902 jump to the National League Giants. Bresnahan stayed with the Giants for six more full seasons and was the catcher when Christy Mathewson pitched three shutouts in the 1905 World Series.

Bresnahan moved on to the Cardinals as player-manager for the 1909 season and continued in that role until he was fired midway through 1912. Bresnahan sued for the balance of his long-term contract, finally obtaining a $20,000 settlement. He played three more years with the Cubs before retiring in 1915 after 17 years in the Major Leagues. He had a .280 lifetime average while playing in 1,430 games, 974 of them at catcher.

Bresnahan later owned and managed the Toledo Mud Hens and coached for the Giants and Tigers. He is best known for popularizing shin guards (see *Catcher's Equipment*) and was the first Major Leaguer known to wear a *Batting Helmet* (after a beaning), although only for a brief time. He died in Toledo in 1944.

George Brett (1953–)

Hall of Fame 1999

"I love George Brett, George is everything that's right about baseball, and not just because he's a good hitter. I want you to know that George Brett will never be a selfish player. My only worry about him is that he plays without fear, and that he might hurt himself—end his career. He doesn't fear the baseball, which frightens you. An injury could cost him. How much? You'll laugh, but if George doesn't hurt himself seriously, someday you'll see him in the Hall of Fame. I played with Hank Aaron and Eddie Mathews and some other great players. George will be in that class."—Hitting guru Charlie Lau.

Brett hit .305 in a 21-year career mostly at third base for the Kansas City Royals from 1973 to 1993.

Southern California native George Howard Brett was drafted by the Royals in the second round in 1971 and made his Major League debut in August 1973. In his first full season in 1974 he hit .282 with 21 doubles. In 1975 he began to establish himself as a star, hitting .308 and leading the American League in hits and triples. In 1976 Brett led the Royals to the first of three consecutive American League West titles (losing the pennant to the Yankees each time), pacing the league in hits, triples, total bases and winning his first batting crown with a .333 average.

In 1980 Brett carried a .400 hitting mark well into September, eventually finishing at .390 to lead the league. He also led the league in slugging at .664. To these numbers Brett added 24 home runs, 118 RBIs, a 30-game hitting streak and the league MVP Award. Brett hit .375 in a six-game World Series loss to the Philadelphia Phillies.

Brett and the Royals would finally get their World Series title in 1985. For the season Brett hit .335 with 30 home runs and 112 RBIs, and a league-leading .585 slugging percentage. Brett also won the only Gold Glove of his career. In the seven game Series win over the Cardinals, Brett hit .370.

Brett was an outstanding postseason performer. In 27 division series and ALCS games, he hit .340 with nine home runs and 19 RBIs. In 13 World Series games Brett batted .373.

In 1990 Brett won another batting title, hitting .329 with a league-leading 45 doubles. On September 30, 1992, Brett recorded his 3,000th hit. He hit over .300 11 times, led the American League three times in average, hits, slugging and triples. He finished his career with 317 home runs and 1,595 RBIs. Brett's 3,154 base hits are 14th all-time, his 665 career doubles 5th. He was elected to the Hall of Fame with 98.19% of the vote.

Books. George Brett, with Steve Cameron, *George Brett: From Here To Cooperstown* (2002); Mark Zeligman, *George Brett: A Royal Hero* (1999).

Bribes See *Gambling and Fixed Games*

Briggs Stadium See *Tiger Stadium*

Broadcasters

"On warm humid nights through transistors and earphones, they whisper to us — like lovers across a pillow. On hot sunny days, through stereo speakers in the back of the car, they shout at us like happy children on the way to summer camp. They are the local baseball announcers for the local teams on the local radio stations, as much a sound of summer as the singing of birds, the chirping of crickets, and the hissing of lawn sprinklers." — Joe Lapointe in the *New York Times*.

"What a racket. You golf, swim, or shoot pool during the day, go to the park and b.s. with the manager and players a little before the game, do the game, b.s. some more, and go home. It's tough, real tough." — Cardinals broadcaster Jack Buck.

"Ya see, I said 'fuck' to ruin his audio. Then when I started scratching my ass I was ruining his video. He ain't gonna ask me a question like that again." — Casey Stengel, after a reporter asked him if his team had choked in the World Series.

"Pretty much shut up." — Advice from Bob Costas and others before *Sports Illustrated* columnist Rick Reilly broadcast three innings in 2003 at a Rockies game during a Fox Sports telecast.

"Going, going, gone!!" — Harry Hartman, who broadcast primarily for the Reds in the 1930s. In 1929 he became the first broadcaster to use this familiar refrain to describe a home run ball. The phrase was later popularized by Yankee broadcaster Mel Allen.

"And that ball is out of here. No it's not. Yes, it is. No, it's not. What happened?" — Yankee broadcaster Phil Rizzuto.

"The first pitch to Tucker Ashford is grounded into left field. No, wait a minute. It's ball one, low and outside." — Padres broadcaster Jerry Coleman.

See also *Radio, Re-Creations, Television* and **Key Broadcasters** in team histories.

Early Broadcaster. The first well-known broadcaster was Graham McNamee, a professional singer who did color commentary for the 1923 World Series. He sat in a ground level chair to conduct the broadcasts from the Polo Grounds and Yankee Stadium. During his broadcast career he covered 10 separate sports and many foreign coronations until his death at age 53 in May 1942.

Selected Former Players.

"Men without intellect, without training, without my background at law, without the spontaneity of articulation that I possess." — Howard Cosell on ex-ballplayers as broadcasters.

"Last night I neglected to mention something that bears repeating." — Ron Fairly.

"Radio Announcing I Have Did" — Tongue-in-cheek title of a lecture on radio broadcasting that the semi-literate Dizzy Dean gave at Southern Methodist University. Dean began broadcasting in St. Louis in 1941. In 1944 Judge Landis, in one of his last acts before he died the following winter, removed Dean from the World Series broadcast as "unfit for a national broadcaster."

Dean spent one year with the Yankees in 1951 and then left to broadcast for the Browns. He broadcast the CBS "Game of the Week" from 1955 until 1959 with Buddy Blattner, a former minor league player (see also *Television*). Dean was often criticized for his abuse of the English language, reportedly prompting these retorts: "You learn 'em English and I'll learn 'em baseball." "A lot of people that ain't saying 'ain't', ain't eating."

Dean said that the latter remark was made by his friend Will Rogers in reference to the Depression. Whichever one said it, the remark apparently was made in 1935 when Dean was not yet a broadcaster.

"Goddamnit!" — Ron Santo's first words on the air as the Cubs' color man on radio. Play-by-play man Thom Brennaman had just said, "The Cubs are on the air!," when a gust of wind blew over a cup of coffee on Santo's scorecard and statistics.

Jack Graney.

"You could worship from afar, of course, taking the daily scripture in the paper, or listening to games on the radio, whose bullfrog voice, former Indian Jack Graney, took a few liberties in those untelevised days. A few? Very little was routine that happened before the eyes of the imaginative and histrionic Graney…" — Tennis commentator Bud Collins in *Cult Baseball Players*, by Danny Peary (ed.) (1990).

Graney was the first player to move into the radio broadcast booth, with the Indians in 1932. He was also the first ex-player to broadcast a World Series game, on October 2, 1935. In addition to his broadcasting notoriety, Graney was the first 20th century Major League player to appear at bat with a number on his uniform and the first to bat against Babe Ruth in the Major Leagues. He was also Ray Chapman's roommate when Chapman was killed by a pitched ball.

Harry Heilmann. The Hall of Fame outfielder was a Tiger broadcaster for a number of years over WXYZ, which covered all of Michigan except Detroit.

Frankie Frisch. The college-educated shortstop (who graduated from Vin Scully's alma mater, Fordham), broadcast poorly for the 1939 Braves and the 1947 Giants.

Waite Hoyt. The Hall of Fame pitcher broadcast 24 seasons for the Reds. He also did a vaudeville act with comedian Jimmy Durante and became famous for his stories during *Rain Delays*. Hoyt had a difficult time getting a job, as noted by his niece in a 1988 article, because the booth was not deemed an acceptable place for a former player — at least according to baseball executives and radio executives.

George Kell. After finishing his career at third base for the Orioles, Kell moved into the broadcast booth. He was succeeded on the field by Brooks Robinson, who later broadcast for the club.

Met Ott. The former slugger broadcast for the Tigers for a short time until his death in a car accident in November 1958.

Ralph Kiner.

"By a rather mysterious procedure, Kiner's slips of the tongue end up in sort of an unofficial clearing house, where they are tallied by dedicated students of broadcasting errata. In a highly competitive field, Kiner is in a class by himself, as superior to his rivals as he was at hitting home runs way back when." — Roy McHugh in *Executive Report*, a business magazine.

Kiner broadcast for many years with the Mets, resulting in a number of "Kinerisms": "Throneberry" for Strawberry; Gary "Cooper" for Gary Carter; Ryne "Duren" for Ryne Sandberg. He also identified Marie Osmond as Marie "Osburg" and Father's Day as Mother's Day (or vice versa).

Jimmy Piersall. During his broadcast days in the 1970s, Piersall

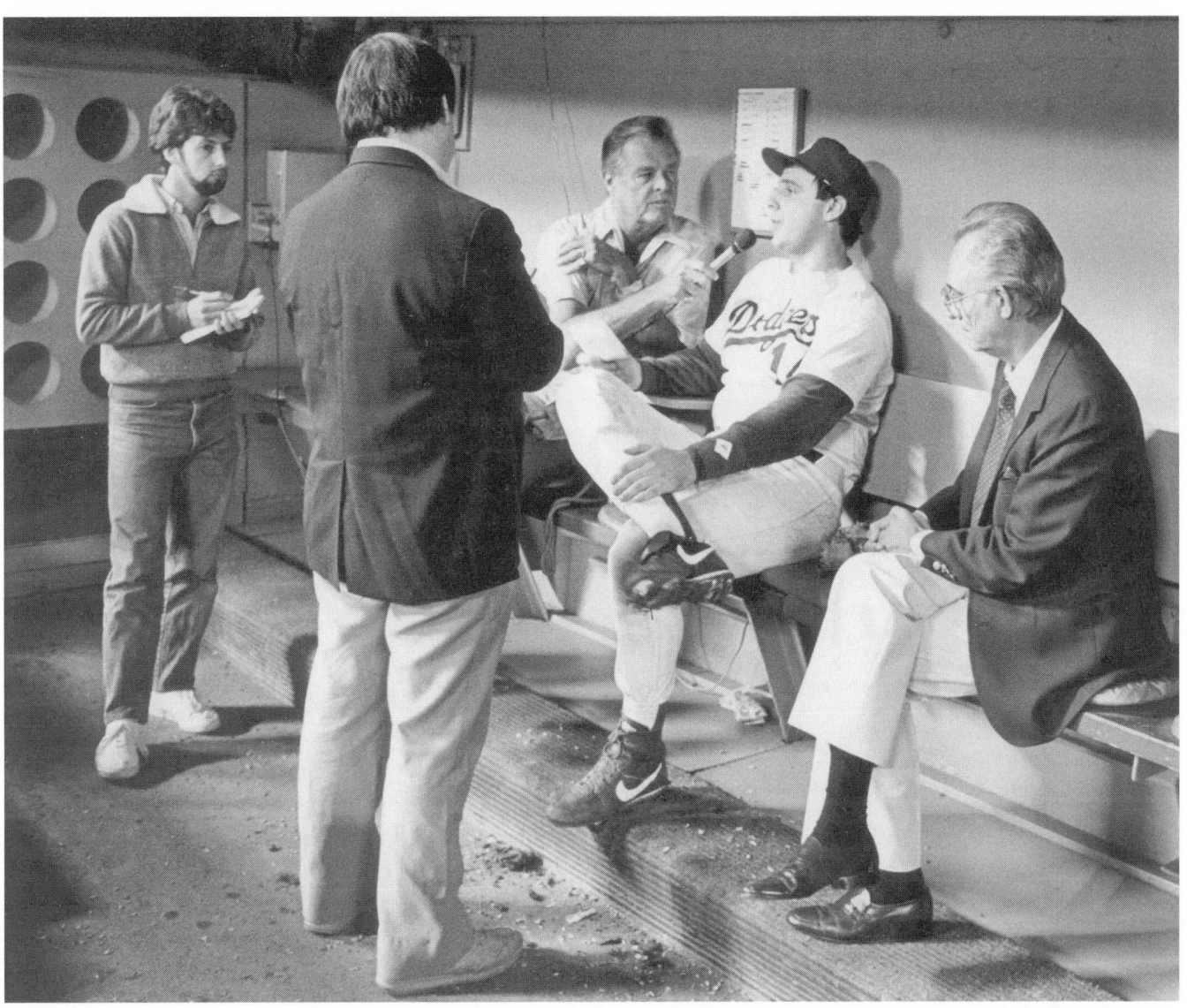

Former pitcher Don Drysdale interviews Dodger catcher Mike Scioscia.

called Mrs. Bill Veeck (his employer's wife) a colossal bore and once tried to choke a visiting sportswriter over the scoring of a past game.

Joe Garagiola. The mediocre catcher finished his career as a Major Leaguer in 1954 and began broadcasting for the Cardinals in 1955. In 1961 he signed with NBC to do the "Game of the Week." He was in continuous service with NBC on the show until his forced retirement in 1988. For a short time in 1965 Garagiola replaced Mel Allen as a Yankee broadcaster. In 1969 he was hired to host NBC's morning "Today" show, where he stayed until 1973. He returned to the "Today" show for a few years in the 1990s before retiring for good.

Tony Kubek. The Yankee shortstop went into the broadcast booth when he retired prematurely at age 28 after the 1965 season (see *Injuries and Illness* — Neck). He was given a job in 1966 as a color commentator on the NBC "Game of the Week." His six-week trial lasted 24 years and he also went on to broadcast for the Blue Jays.

Jerry Coleman. The Padres and CBS Radio Network broadcaster and former Yankee second baseman is famed for his malapropisms, which are chronicled throughout this book.

Ernie Johnson. Johnson was a Braves pitcher in the 1950s (40–23 lifetime record) who broadcast for the club beginning in 1962.

1980s. By the late 1980s a number of former players could be heard on the airways, establishing a trend into the 1990s: Ron Fairly, Joe Morgan, Tito Fuentes (in Spanish) and Duane Kuiper for the Giants; Joe Nuxhall and Johnny Bench for the Reds; Jerry Coleman and Rick Monday for the Padres; Jim Palmer, John Lowenstein and Brooks Robinson for the Orioles; Don Sutton for the Braves; Jerry Remy for the Red Sox; George Kell, Jim Northrup and Al Kaline for the Tigers; Phil Rizzuto and Jay Johnstone for the Yankees; Harmon Killebrew and Jim Kaat for the Twins; Larry Dierker for the Astros; Steve Busby for the Rangers; Claude Raymond (in French) and Ken Singleton for the Expos; Pete Vuckovich for the Brewers; Paul Splittorff for the Royals; Ralph Kiner, Fran Healy, Rusty Staub and Tim McCarver for the Mets; Steve Blass and Jim Rooker for the Pirates; Herb Score for the Indians; Al Hrabosky and Mike Shannon for the Cardinals; Tony Kubek and Buck Martinez for the Blue Jays; Joe Torre and Ken Brett for the Angels; Don Drysdale for the Dodgers; Ray Fosse for the A's; and Garry Maddox and Richie Ashburn for the Phillies.

1990– . See individual team sections for **Broadcasters** who played Major League Baseball.

Nerves. After his retirement following the 1966 season, NBC hired Sandy Koufax to conduct pregame television interviews for its "Game of the Week." He was so nervous and uncomfortable in his new role that he quit before his contract was up. He was to have received $1 million over 10 years. After he quit, he was replaced by Maury Wills, prompting this comment by writer Melvin Durslag: "Maury Wills knows as much about journalism as Edith Bunker [of "All in the Family"] knows about stealing second."

Joe DiMaggio had a similar problem with nerves. He had a one-year stint hosting a children's instructional television show. He also did a few interviews on Yankee telecasts, but his on-camera discomfort was evident.

Practice Makes Perfect. Don Drysdale began his broadcast career by "announcing" games in the bullpen between starts. He later broadcast for the White Sox before settling in with the Dodgers.

Longest Together. The Mets team of Lindsey Nelson, Ralph Kiner and Bob Murphy was the longest running threesome in Major League history. They broadcast for the Mets from 1962 into the early 1990s when Nelson retired.

First Paired Team. The first broadcasters to team up on the air simultaneously for an entire game were Red Barber and Al Helfer for the Dodgers in 1940. Prior to this pairing, broadcasters would split the air time and do innings separately.

Birthday Gift. Cardinals broadcaster Jack Buck gave his son Joe a surprise 18th birthday present. On April 25, 1987, in the 5th inning of a Mets-Cardinals game, Jack turned over the play-by-play to Joe and left the booth.

Awkward 500th. When Reds center fielder Ken Griffey, Jr., was pursuing home run No. 500 in 2004, he asked that longtime radio announcers Joe Nuxhall or Marty Brennaman be behind the microphone, rather than first-year man Steve Stewart. Stewart graciously stepped aside, but Brennaman in particular was uncomfortable with the request.

"Discovered." Dodger manager Tommy Lasorda claimed to have "discovered" broadcaster Al Michaels in Hawaii in 1971. Lasorda was the manager of the Class AAA Spokane club when they were playing the Hawaiian Islanders. Lasorda heard Michaels broadcasting several games in a row and reported on his quality to Dodger general manager Al Campanis. Lasorda's explanation for hearing so much of Michaels was that Lasorda had been thrown out of six games in a row and spent several hours in the clubhouse listening to the game broadcast.

Family.

"Take it easy, kid. Not everyone knows we're father and son."— Broadcaster Jack Buck to broadcaster son Joe, after Joe gave his father their customary hug and kiss on the cheek.

Harry Caray once broadcast from the bleachers while drinking beer. Son Skip (Harry II) Caray began broadcasting for the Braves in 1976, though he made his debut in an emergency fill-in role on May 30, 1965, when Mel Allen attended his mother's funeral. Grandson Chip Caray also broadcast Major League games, including stints in Texas and Seattle. For awhile, Harry broadcast with Thom Brennaman, son of long-time Reds broadcaster Marty Brenneman. By the mid–1990s Skip Caray and Jack Buck's son Joe were broadcasting for Fox television.

By 2000, Joe Buck had become Fox's lead broadcaster. In 2002 he became only the third broadcaster to be his network's number one for both football and baseball (following Curt Gowdy and Al Michaels). Joe began his career in 1989 as voice of the Class AAA

Louisville Cardinals. At 21, he was broadcasting with his father in St. Louis. In 1996 he became the second youngest, at 27, to broadcast a World Series game (Vin Scully was 25 in 1953). In 2004 Buck also became the primary broadcaster for Fox's NFL telecasts.

When Harry had a stroke in February 1987, WGN replaced him with a succession of celebrities: Bill Murray, George Wendt, Jim Belushi, George Will, Mike Royko, Pat Summerall, Dick Enberg, Brent Musberger, Bob Costas and Skip Caray.

New Blood. Sean McDonough took over in 1992 as the top television broadcaster for CBS. His father, Will, was a sports columnist at that time with the *Boston Globe* and also did some television work. Sean, who began his Major League broadcasting career with the Red Sox, replaced long-time broadcaster Jack Buck.

Pete Rose. In 1991 after he was released from prison for tax evasion, Rose filled in as a substitute sports anchor for WLWT-TV in Cincinnati. He also did a daily baseball commentary for a local radio station while completing his required community service, and he appeared on four nightly television newscasts during a ratings sweeps week. His first broadcast, described by critics as "average," received a 27 share, the highest for any Cincinnati newscast over the previous month (a share is the percentage of sets turned on that are tuned to a particular show).

Spanish. By the early 1990s seven Major League teams broadcast their games in Spanish. In the 1990s CBS television sold World Series broadcasts to 35 U.S. and 200 Latin American Spanish-language stations.

Hall of Famer Jaime Jarrin broadcast Dodger games in Spanish from 1958, when the club arrived in Los Angeles into the 2004 season. Fernando Valenzuela joined the Dodgers' Spanish-language broadcast team in mid–2003. Jarrin was Valenzuela's translator when the pitcher arrived with the club in 1980.

Eli "Buck" Canel broadcast the 1937 World Series in Spanish, beginning a streak of broadcasting 42 consecutive World Series. In 1985 he received the Ford Frick Award and admittance to the broadcast wing of the Hall of Fame. Despite his notoriety, he is not referenced in Curt Smith's otherwise definitive book on baseball broadcasters, *Voices of the Game* (1987).

Juan Vene broadcast the Spanish language version of "This Week in Baseball" for many years from its inception in 1977.

Manager. Larry Dierker left the Astros' broadcast booth to take over the club in 1997.

Multiple Languages. In 1993 the Dodgers became the first club to have their games regularly broadcast in four languages: English, Spanish, Korean and Chinese (and French when playing the Expos).

Fill-In. In the early 1950s in Battle Creek, Michigan, the Dodgers put broadcaster Vin Scully in a uniform to fill in during an exhibition game for Gil Hodges, whose wife had just had a baby. After somehow catching a line drive in the outfield during batting practice, the diminutive Scully decided that he had had enough.

Blind Color Man. Don Wardlaw, though blind, broadcast for the New Britain Red Sox. He did color commentary for the telecasts with his partner, Jim Lucas. In 1994 the Marlins invited the pair to work three innings of their June 23 game against the Cubs.

Big Talkers. Leonard Koppett has estimated that the average broadcaster utters 20,000 words during his share of a radio broadcast.

Mistakes.

"What'll it be tonight, Howard? Do you bullshit me or do I bullshit you?"— Pitcher Tracy Stallard to Howard Cosell when he thought the microphone was off before a radio interview.

Mel Allen received his first Yankee broadcast assignment as Arch

McDonald's assistant in 1939. He replaced an announcer who twice read an Ivory Soap commercial as "Ovary Soap."

"Game of the Week." See *Television — "Game of the Week."*

Trade. In 1948 Branch Rickey of the Dodgers traded minor league catcher Cliff Draper to the Atlanta Crackers in return for broadcaster Ernie Harwell.

P.A. Announcers. For many years some radio broadcasters did double-duty as the public address announcer in the ballpark.

Past Tense. Waite Hoyt was probably the only play-by-play broadcaster to speak in the past tense.

Fantasy Broadcasters. In the late 1980s the A's were the first club to allow fans to broadcast from a booth (complete with color commentary) for a fee. Fantasy broadcasting evolved into a lucrative business for creative entrepreneurs.

Umpire. When umpire Ron Luciano retired to be a writer and broadcaster, long-time nemesis Earl Weaver (see *Ejections*) took one last shot: "I hope he takes this job more seriously than he did his last one."

World Series.

"I tried to play it pretty cool. I was living at home with my mother and father and sister, and before the first game I sat down with them for breakfast as if it was just another day. Then I went upstairs and [lost] my entire breakfast." — Vin Scully on his first World Series broadcast, in 1953. He did 22 World Series for television, radio, or a combination of both.

Curt Gowdy broadcast 78 World Series games. Tim McCarver passed him during the 2003 World Series.

Hall of Fame Broadcasters. Since 1978 broadcasters have been honored with the *Ford C. Frick Award.*

The Greatest. In July 2000, the American Sportscasters Association named Dodgers legend *Vin Scully* as the No. 1 sportscaster of the 20th century. Howard Cosell was second, followed by *Mel Allen* and *Red Barber*.

Simulcast. It is believed that Vin Scully was the first broadcaster to air both television and radio at the same time.

Payment. Red Barber was paid $280 to broadcast the entire 1939 World Series, when the commissioner began choosing the broadcasters. By 1952 Barber was receiving only $200 per game. That was his 13th and last Series, as he finally refused to work for such low pay.

Books. Ted Patterson, *The Golden Voices of Baseball* (2002); Curt Smith, *Voices of the Game* (1987), the author's favorite baseball book (a made-for-television movie version of the book aired on ESPN in 1995); Curt Smith, *The Storytellers: Baseball Tales from the Broadcast Booth* (1995). In 2000 broadcaster Bob Costas wrote *Fair Ball: A Fan's Case for Baseball* (2001), in which he lamented the loss of competitive balance among the "haves" and "have nots" in baseball. See also Classicradio.com.

Lou Brock (1939–)

Hall of Fame 1985

"I'll tell you with my lead that I'm going to steal second base. You know I'm going to, but there's nothing you can do to stop it." — Brock.

"He just sits back very still, looking like a statue. Then all of a sudden he leaps, and you sit there, wondering how anyone can move from zero velocity to the speed of him like that." — Ernie Banks.

Brock is second on the all-time base stealing list and starred primarily for the Cardinals over a 19-year career beginning in 1961.

See also *Stolen Bases*.

Louis Clark Brock was a junior at Southern University in Louisiana when he signed for a $30,000 bonus from the Cubs. He hit the first pitch of his professional career for a home run and the Cubs brought him up for four games late in 1961.

Brock stayed with the Cubs until 52 games into the 1964 season, when he was traded to the Cardinals for Ernie Broglio in one of the worst trades in league history. He hit .348 in 103 games and helped the Cardinals into the World Series, where he hit .300.

In his first full season with the Cardinals he hit .288 and had 63 stolen bases. In 1966 he began a streak in which he won the league stolen base title in eight of nine years. He capped the string in 1974 when he stole a then-record 118 bases at age 35.

He finished his 19-year career in 1979 with 938 stolen bases, now second all-time. He also batted .293 with eight seasons over .300. He batted .391 in three World Series, second all-time, and is the World Series leader with 14 stolen bases.

Despite being elected to the Hall of Fame on his first try, he has been criticized for his high number of strikeouts (most by any player when he retired) and defensive shortcomings. He struck out over 100 times in nine seasons and regularly hit double figures in outfield errors.

Book. Lou Brock with Franz Schulze, *Stealing Is My Game* (1976).

Brooklyn

"Flatbush, of course, was then a charming, leafy suburban village languid as the motion of its ladies' parasols and billowing yards of skirt." — Harold Peterson in *The Man Who Invented Baseball* (1969).

"Brooklyn is the only city of two million people that doesn't have an airport, a newspaper, and a ballclub." — Sportswriter Tommy Holmes after the Dodgers left town and the *Brooklyn Eagle* newspaper shut down.

"Even when they lose, they got heart. That's why the people of Brooklyn love 'em so much. Now if only those crooked politicians running this borough had half the brains of those baseball players, we'd be in a lot better shape." — David Ritz in *The Man Who Brought the Dodgers Back to Brooklyn* (1981).

Amateur Clubs. Amateur Brooklyn teams of the 1850s included the Excelsiors, Putnams, Eckfords, Atlantics and Morrisania Unions.

Brooklyn baseball teams dominated New York during the early 1860s, at a time when Brooklyn was still a separate city. It was not until 1867 that a non–Brooklyn team won a championship. The Brooklyn Atlantics won a series of 1860s "whip pennants," except in 1862 and 1863, when the Brooklyn Eckfords prevailed. These championships were actually only championships for New York City and nearby cities, and consisted primarily of challenge matches.

Brooklyn teams of the 1860s played their games at sites such as Carroll Park, Bedford Park and the Capitoline Grounds. In 1868 curveball specialist Candy Cummings played for a team known as the Stars of Brooklyn, a group calling itself the "Championship Team of the U.S. and Canada." The team had disappeared by 1877.

Professional Teams.

National Association Brooklyn Atlantics (1872–1875)
National Association Brooklyn Eckfords (1872)
American Association Brooklyn Dodgers (1884–1889)
American Association Brooklyn Gladiators (1890)
Players League Brooklyn Wonders (1890)
National League Brooklyn Dodgers (1890–1957)
Federal League Brooklyn Tip-Tops (1914–1915)

In 2001 the borough again was home to professional baseball. The Brooklyn Cyclones, a Mets rookie league entry, began play in June 2001 in a new, 6,500-seat stadium in Coney Island. Named for the famed Cyclone rollercoaster, the club played in the New York-Penn League.

Book. James L. Terry, *Long Before the Dodgers: Baseball in Brooklyn, 1855–1884* (2002).

Brooklyn Atlantics

National Association 1872–1875

"Other teams in the league were hapless. Just five of them played at a .500 clip that 1875 season. The Brooklyn team was a joke with a 2 and 42 record..."—Harvey Frommer in *Primitive Baseball* (1988).

Prior to becoming a professional club, the Atlantics were members of the amateur National Association. They were 19–0 in 1864 and undefeated until early 1866. The Atlantics were the unofficial self-described 1865 national champion. They were also the first team to defeat the Cincinnati Red Stockings during their 1869–1870 undefeated streak.

Despite their success as an amateur club, the Atlantics were perennial doormats in the professional National Association in the 1870s, finishing at 9–28 in their inaugural season and 2–42 in 1875 before dropping out of the league late in the season.

Brooklyn Brown Dodgers See **United States League**

Brooklyn Dodgers

American Association 1884–1889

In late 1883 James Gordon Bennett was the owner of the *New York Herald* newspaper when he supposedly agreed to finance the Brooklyn Dodgers for the team's first American Association season in 1884. Not true. Though the idea supposedly originated with *Herald* night city editor George Taylor, then 30 years old, Taylor went to real estate agent Charles H. Byrne for backing.

Joining Byrne to finance the club were gambling establishment owners Joseph J. Doyle and Ferdinand H. Abel. Some sources report that Byrne had earlier owned a Brooklyn franchise in the Interstate League, which was loosely affiliated with the American Association, but sold it to buy into the new American Association team. The truth is that Byrne affiliated his new Brooklyn Dodgers with the Interstate League in 1883 while waiting to join the American Association the following year. Future National League owner Charles Ebbets was a young bookkeeper with the club beginning in 1883.

Taylor managed the club in 1884, but did poorly and was replaced. Doyle managed the club for a few games in 1885 and Byrne managed from mid–1885 through 1887. The club was known as the Trolley Dodgers from the beginning. The Dodgers received a number of players from the National Association Cleveland club for the 1885 season after Cleveland folded under pressure from the 1884 Union Association challenge.

Bill McGunnigle took over as manager in 1888 and guided the team to a championship in 1889. Dissatisfied with events in the **American Association**, Brooklyn moved into the National League for the 1890 season. The 1890 club was replaced by a new American Association entry in Brooklyn known as the Gladiators.

Brooklyn Dodgers

National League 1890–1957

"They brought me up to the Brooklyn Dodgers, which at that time was in Brooklyn."—Casey Stengel in 1962.

Origins. The Dodgers were an American Association entry beginning in 1884, but switched over to the National League for the 1890 season as the league's 26th entry.

Key Owners.

Charles H. Byrne, Joseph Doyle and Ferdinand Abel/1890–1898.

"The Napoleon of Baseball"—Byrne's nickname.

The Dodgers technically disbanded after the 1890 season and reorganized with new capital of over $200,000. The ownership was a combination of National League and Players League owners, with the National League people holding the controlling interest. National Leaguer Charles Byrne remained as president and Joseph Doyle and Ferdinand Abel held large interests. Each had been prominent members of the American Association version of the Dodgers which preceded this National League entry. Players League representatives Wendell Goodwin and George Chauncey led a group that held slightly less than 50% of the franchise.

Abel, Hanlon, Von Der Horst and Ebbets/1898–1902. The Players League owners eventually sold most of their interest in the club to Abel and Byrne. Doyle also sold out to Abel. Abel held a controlling interest in the team for a short period after Byrne's death in 1897. In the late 1890s Abel traded some of his stock so that he ended up owning 40% of both Brooklyn and Baltimore, while Ned Hanlon and Harry Von der Horst (Baltimore owners) took a combined 50% interest in both clubs. Bookkeeper Charles Ebbets held 10% in both and was elected Dodgers club president. This was typical of the Syndicate Ball era, when **Cross-Ownership** of clubs was common.

Von der Horst and Hanlon bought Byrne's stock and moved the best Baltimore players to Brooklyn. The goal was to strengthen the Dodgers because they were in the larger market. The Dodgers won the 1899 flag while Hanlon was president of Brooklyn and manager of Baltimore. The Orioles finished fourth under John McGraw.

Charles H. Ebbets/1902–1925.

"Ebbets was now thirty-two years old, curly-haired, mustached, hard-working, conscientious, ambitious, and ingratiating. No task was too hard for him, no day too long.... He ... attended to all the little drudgeries in the business office that the other employees were glad to shirk, and made friends for the club by his good humor and his patience."—Frank Graham in *The Brooklyn Dodgers* (1945).

Charles Ebbets was a bookkeeper when he first joined the team, reported as 1890 in some sources. However, he had been affiliated with the club as early as 1883 when it was a year away from joining the American Association. Some sources report that Ebbets also had been affiliated with Players League owner George Chauncey, who touted Ebbets to the National League Dodgers. As an inducement for Ebbets to come to the team, Chauncey sold him a small percentage of his ownership interest.

Before moving to the Dodgers, Ebbets supposedly had been the architect of an amusement park, a hotel and other buildings. More accurately, he had been a draftsmen on parts of these projects. He was also a publisher and later became active in politics as a state assemblyman and alderman (losing for city council by one vote and later losing for state senate). In his spare time he was a bowling fanatic.

In 1896 Ebbets became secretary of the club after Joseph Doyle died. When club president and chief stockholder Charles Byrne died in January 1898, the same month in which Brooklyn officially became a borough of New York City, Ebbets was elected president. However, he still did not hold a controlling interest in the club. His first act as president was to move the club back to play in South Brooklyn after it had been in Northeast New York City.

In 1902 Ferdinand Abel sold his interest to Ebbets at a point when most American and National League clubs were suffering financially because of their interleague feud. Von der Horst was ill and wanted out also. There was a power struggle between Ebbets and Hanlon, which Ebbets ultimately won after Hanlon tried to block Ebbets with a court action. Ebbets borrowed money from Henry W. Medicus to buy out Hanlon, although Hanlon continued as manager until he finished last in 1905. In the power struggle, Ebbets increased his own salary from $4,000 to $10,000 and reduced Hanlon's from $11,500 to $7,500. In 1909 there were 2,500 shares of stock owned by Ebbets or his son and another 749 shares owned by Medicus.

Charles Ebbets and the McKeever Brothers/1913–1925. In 1913, when he was building Ebbets Field, Ebbets ran short of cash to finish the ballpark. To raise money, he sold half his interest in the club for $500,000 to his friends, construction moguls and brothers Steve W. and Edward J. McKeever. The McKeevers had solidified their fortune when they secured the contract for delivery of quarried rock for the New York Central's railroad line to Buffalo.

As part of the sale to the McKeevers, Medicus was bought out and two corporations were created, one to own the team (Brooklyn National League Club) and one to own the ballpark and land under it (Ebbets/McKeever Exhibition Company). Ebbets became one of the dominant forces in the National League in the early 20th century, along with Barney Dreyfuss of the Pirates and Garry Herrmann of the Reds. Ebbets died of heart problems on April 18, 1925.

Wilbert Robinson and Steve McKeever/1925–1938. One week after Ebbets died, Ed McKeever died of pneumonia after supposedly catching cold at Ebbets' funeral. Ed had been the more outgoing of the McKeever brothers and it was then necessary for the more reticent Steve to take control. As a result of the deaths, Wilbert Robinson became club president. This began a period of acrimony between Robinson and Steve McKeever, in part over Robinson's continuing feud with the New York press over the team's habitually poor showing (the team finished sixth in five out of six seasons from 1924 through 1929).

By 1929 the board of directors was divided into two camps. One side was with McKeever (and his brother's heirs) and the other with Robinson. National League president John Heydler arranged for a fifth director to be appointed, neutral attorney Walter F. "Dutch" Carter.

Robinson resigned under pressure following a fourth-place finish in 1931 and after 18 years as Dodger manager. A ray of hope arrived in 1934 when prominent baseball man Bob Quinn signed on as general manager at age 63. Quinn had been part-owner of the Red Sox for nine years before selling out to Tom Yawkey. Quinn lasted only one season before leaving for the Braves.

Brooklyn Trust Company/1938–1943.
"Their nickname of 'Bums' was at this time very appropriate. It could have referred to any checks the organization cashed." — Dodger executive Fresco Thompson.

In 1937 the club was continuing to struggle and was in debt to the Brooklyn Trust Company. Board members included the now ancient Steve McKeever, Joe Gilleaudeau, James Mulvey, William A. Hughes and George Barnewall. Barnewall was a banker who represented the interest of the Trust, whose board for a time approved all waiver purchases of $6,000 or more.

National League president Ford Frick suggested the Reds' Larry MacPhail as the new Dodger general manager. MacPhail had been out of baseball in 1936 after having success with the Reds. The Dodgers were near bankruptcy in 1938 when MacPhail met with the National League powers. The National League and the Dodger board of directors agreed to appoint MacPhail as the executive vice president with virtually unlimited power. MacPhail was announced as the club's new leader on January 19, 1938.

The changing of the guard was made complete when Steve McKeever died on March 6, 1938. His 25% interest continued to be held by his daughter, Mrs. James (Dearie) Mulvey. The rest of the stock was held by the heirs of Edward McKeever and Charles Ebbets.

A new era had truly begun when Leo Durocher was hired as manager after the 1938 season. This began an era of prosperity for the Dodgers over the next 18 years that was matched only by the Yankees. In 1939 Branch Rickey, Jr. (whose father later would join the club as general manager), became director of the Dodger farm system.

Walter F. O'Malley and Branch Rickey/1943–1950.
"O'Malley has the kind of face that even Dale Carnegie would want to punch." — Bill Veeck, Jr.

Larry MacPhail had developed a strong, consistent contender when he decided to enter the army in 1943 (after a daring **World War I** adventure). Branch Rickey succeeded him as general manager. MacPhail and Rickey had attended law school at the University of Michigan.

In 1944 Rickey, Walter O'Malley (an attorney for the Brooklyn Trust Company) and insurance man Andrew J. Schmitz bought the 25% interest originally held by Ed McKeever and which had been controlled by the Brooklyn Trust Company. They paid $347,000. O'Malley had made a good deal of money selling a handbook for building subcontractors, the first of its kind. Schmitz was the front man for John Smith, who owned Pfizer Pharmaceutical (later to hold the patent for penicillin). This left 50% in the hands of the Ebbets heirs and the remaining 25% with James and Dearie Mulvey (Steve McKeever's daughter).

In 1945 Rickey, O'Malley and Smith bought the Ebbets 50% interest for $750,000, giving each of them a 25% interest in the club. O'Malley controlled Smith's vote and there was a 50% split whenever Rickey and Mulvey combined.

By the late 1940s a serious rift had developed between O'Malley and Rickey. Near the end of 1950 Rickey's contract as president expired and O'Malley was voted in as president on October 26, 1950. Rickey then wanted to sell his interest in the club. He wanted $1 million for his shares, for which he, like O'Malley, had paid $320,000 in 1943. O'Malley offered $320,000. The 1943 partnership agreement provided O'Malley with a right of first refusal and he invoked it when Rickey found a buyer for $1 million, real estate tycoon William Zeckendorf. O'Malley paid the $1 million to increase his interest to 66.2%, plus $50,000 to Zeckendorf as required under the partnership agreement. O'Malley felt cheated out of the $50,000 and had the cancelled check framed and put in his office. When Rickey left for the Pirates in 1951, Buzzie Bavasi became general manager and remained in that position through the Dodgers' move to Los Angeles.

Walter F. O'Malley/1950–1957.
"Baseball isn't a business; it's more like a disease." — O'Malley, who remained at the helm until his death in 1979, long after the club became the **Los Angeles Dodgers** for the 1958 season. When

the Dodgers moved, 25% of the stock was still owned by the Steve McKeever heirs (the Mulveys), but the O'Malley family controlled the club and the Smith 25% interest.

Departure for Los Angeles.

"This is the obit on the Brooklyn Dodgers. Preliminary diagnosis indicates that the cause of death was an acute case of greed, followed by severe political complications." — New York columnist Dick Young.

Much has been written about the Dodgers' move to Los Angeles. During the mid–1950s, Walter O'Malley supposedly made impossible demands on Brooklyn to immediately build a new ballpark. It is possible that O'Malley only made a show of trying to stay in Brooklyn when all along he intended to leave for the potentially lucrative Los Angeles market.

Other sources report that O'Malley made a legitimate effort to remain in Brooklyn. He supposedly even contemplated a domed stadium for Brooklyn, and had Ed Roebuck hit fungoes to see how high the roof needed to be. O'Malley talked to architects about the project and envisioned a park at Flatbush and Atlantic in Brooklyn.

O'Malley eventually was offered a site in Flushing Meadow (where Shea Stadium later was built), but O'Malley thought the rent would be too high. O'Malley obviously saw the potential of the West Coast, because Brooklyn was still profitable before the move. In fact, the franchise made more money in the 10 years prior to the move than any other National League club. Nevertheless, attendance had declined from a high of 78% of capacity to 45% by 1956.

The team played a few games in Jersey City, New Jersey, in 1956 and 1957, which was viewed as a sign that the team intended to move. In February 1957 California politicians visited O'Malley and offered to build a park for him. When Brooklyn realized that O'Malley was leaving, it formed a sports authority headed by prominent parks commissioner Robert Moses, whose mandate was to find another team for Brooklyn.

O'Malley sold Ebbets Field to real estate operator Marvin Kratter at the end of 1956 for $4 million, with an agreement to stay and play there until 1959 (with cancellation options which O'Malley exercised). O'Malley also sold the Dodgers' minor league Montreal ballpark for $1 million to raise additional cash for the move. He then prepared for the move by buying the Cubs' Los Angeles franchise in the Pacific Coast League and its Los Angeles ballpark, also known as Wrigley Field (and with the same design as Chicago's Wrigley Field). The Dodgers announced their *Franchise Shift* on October 8, 1957.

Nicknames.

"Dem Bums"

"The Daffiness Boys"

The team was known as the Brooklyn Trolley Dodgers from its earliest days in the American Association. "Dodgers" originated from the maze of trolley cars at the end of the Brooklyn Bridge and the Brooklyn inhabitants were called Trolley Dodgers. The name was later shortened to Dodgers. The club has had other names over the years, often depending upon its manager.

Author Bill McNeil points out that the earliest reference to Trolley Dodgers that he found was 1895 or 1896, and that the electric trolley cars did not appear until 1890; so it may be unlikely that the nickname was used in the 1880s. Perhaps there were horse drawn trolleys prior to 1890.

The club was known as the Bridegrooms for a short time around 1890. The name was given by writer Francis C. Richter of Philadelphia after four Brooklyn players were married before the 1888 (or 1890) season — Bobby Caruthers, Bill "Adonis" Terry, George "Germany" Smith and Ed Silch.

In 1899 Ned Hanlon managed the club to a pennant. The club was known as Hanlon's Superbas, after a vaudeville troupe of the same name (though some sources erroneously claim that Hanlon was in the act). The name was also used for a short time after Hanlon left in 1905. The Dodgers name was again used generally until 1914, when Wilbert Robinson became the Brooklyn manager after he was fired as Giants coach in 1913 by John McGraw of the Giants.

After Robinson arrived, the team was often known as the "Robins" until Robinson was forced to resign in 1931. The team was sometimes referred to as the "Flock" in honor of Robinson. In 1914 Brooklyn was also known as the Nationals, apparently to distinguish it from the rival Federal League entry known as the TipTops or BrookFeds.

"Lasts." The last Dodger game in Brooklyn was on September 29, 1957, when the club lost to the Phillies 2–1 as Seth Moreland defeated Roger Craig. The last Brooklyn Dodger home run was by Ransom Jackson on September 28, 1957. The last active Major Leaguer who played in Brooklyn was Bob Aspromonte. He appeared briefly with the team in 1956 (striking out in one at-bat). He was sent down to the minor leagues and then came back to the Majors for the 1960–1971 seasons, primarily with the Astros.

Key Seasons.

"Wait 'til next year!" — Perennial slogan of Dodger fans.

"THIS IS NEXT YEAR" — Headline in the *New York Daily News* after the Dodgers finally won their first World Series in 1955.

"If the Dodgers aren't careful, overconfidence might cost them 7th place." — Eddie Murphy on the pitiful 1930s Dodgers.

"Brooklyn, unquestionably." — New York sportswriter Sid Mercer when asked which team gave Dodger pitcher Nap Rucker the most trouble (referring to the poor teams for whom the excellent Rucker had to play).

1890. Brooklyn is the only franchise to win pennants in two leagues in consecutive seasons, moving from the American Association in 1889 to the National League in 1890. Led by Oyster Burns' league-leading 128 RBIs, the Dodgers won the pennant by six games over the White Stockings.

1916. The Dodgers were the weakest of the New York teams until they won the National League pennant in 1916 under Wilbert Robinson. Jeff Pfeffer won 25 games and Zack Wheat batted .312. The Dodgers lost the World Series in five games to the Red Sox and pitcher Babe Ruth.

1920. The Dodgers were led by Burleigh Grimes' 23 wins and won the pennant by seven games over the Giants. They lost to the Indians 5–2 in a nine-game Series.

1941. The Dodgers waited another 21 years to win a pennant, this time with Leo Durocher at the helm, but they again lost the World Series. The Yankees beat them in five games after Dodger catcher Mickey Owen let what would have been the last pitch of Game 4 get by him and the Yankees went on to win the game and the Series in five games (see also *Passed Balls*). Pete Reiser led the league with a .343 average and Dolf Camilli led with 34 home runs and 120 RBIs. Kirby Higbe and Whit Wyatt both led the league with 22 wins.

1942. The Dodgers became the second team to win at least 100 games (104) and not win a pennant (described erroneously as the first in many sources — see also *Wins*). The Cardinals had 106 wins.

1946–1955. If the Dodgers had won their last game of the season in 1946, 1950 and 1951, they would have won 9 of 11 pennants, including five in a row (see *Pennant Races* and *Play-Offs*). They won pennants in 1947, 1949, 1952, 1953, 1955 and 1956. They finally won their first and only Brooklyn World Series in 1955.

1946. The Dodgers finished tied with the Cardinals at 96–58 and then lost a three-game play-off series. Dixie Walker led the club with a .319 average and 116 RBIs.

1947. The club won the pennant by five games over the Cardinals. Ralph Branca had 21 wins and Dixie Walker batted .306 with 94 RBIs. The Dodgers lost the World Series in seven games to the Yankees when Joe Page shut them out over the last five innings of Game 7.

1949. The Dodgers won the pennant with 97 wins, one game ahead of the Cardinals. Jackie Robinson was the National League MVP with a league-leading .342 average. The Yankees beat the Dodgers in five games to win the World Series.

1950. The Dodgers lost the pennant on the last day of the season to the Phillies. Gil Hodges, Duke Snider and Roy Campanella each hit over 30 home runs to lead the club.

1951. The Dodgers lost a heartbreaking *Play-Off* series to the Giants in three games, as Bobby Thomson hit the "Shot Heard 'Round the World." Gil Hodges hit 40 home runs and Don Newcombe and Preacher Roe each won at least 20 games.

1952.
"If you were a Dodger fan, you really suffered in 1952 and 1953." — Sportswriter Ed Fitzgerald.

The Dodgers won the pennant by 4½ games over the Giants as Jackie Robinson and Duke Snider each hit over .300 and Gil Hodges drove in 102 runs. The Yankees continued their domination of the Dodgers with a seven-game victory in the World Series. The Yankees won Games 6 and 7 to capture the crown.

1953. Brooklyn ran away with the flag with 105 wins. Carl Furillo led the league with a .344 average and Roy Campanella was the MVP with a league-leading 142 RBIs. The Yankees once again beat the Dodgers in the World Series, this time with a six-game victory; again winning the last two games of the Series.

1955.
"Please don't interrupt, because you haven't heard this one before. Brooklyn Dodgers, champions of the baseball world. Honest." — *Washington Post* columnist Shirley Povich in the lead to his story on the Dodgers' victory.

"Far into the night rang shouts of revelry in Flatbush. Brooklyn at long last has won a World Series and now let someone suggest moving the Dodgers elsewhere!" — *New York Times* sportswriter John Drebinger.

The Dodgers won the pennant with 98 wins as Duke Snider led the league with 136 RBIs and hit 42 home runs. They finally won their first World Series as Sandy Amoros preserved a 2–0 shutout in Game 7 with a running catch to rob the Yankees of two runs. See also Stewart Wolpin, *Bums No More: The Championship Season of the 1955 Brooklyn Dodgers* (1995).

1956. The Brooklyn Dodgers made their last appearance in the World Series after winning the pennant by one game over the Braves. Duke Snider led the league with 43 home runs and Don Newcombe won a league-best 27 games. Among the Series highlights was Don Larsen's perfect Game 5, as the Yankees blew out the Dodgers 9–0 in Game 7. See also Michael Shapiro, *The Last Good Season* (2003).

1957. In their last season in Brooklyn, the Dodgers finished third with an 84–70 record.

Key Players.
"Once a Dodger, always a Dodger." — Long-time club slogan beginning in the 1920s; though player Oscar Roettger decided that the slogan should change after a series of trades during the dismal 1930s: "Once a Dodger, always seeking employment."

Zack Wheat (HF) was a fixture in the Dodger outfield from 1909 through 1926, covering 18 of his 19 seasons. He batted over .300 12 times, including a league-leading .335 in 1918 (with zero home runs). He batted .283 in two World Series for the Dodgers.

Dazzy Vance (HF) was one of the best pitchers in the Major Leagues in the 1920s, playing for the Dodgers from 1922 through 1932. He won 20 games three times, including a league-leading 28 in 1924. He returned to the club for his final season in 1935, finishing with a total of 190 wins for Brooklyn.

Babe Herman played only six seasons for the Dodgers, but established himself as one of the best batters in the National League when he hit .381 and .393 in 1929 and 1930.

Pee Wee Reese (HF) anchored the Dodger infield at shortstop for 15 of his 16 years with the club from 1940 through 1958 (losing three full seasons to the war). He hit .269 lifetime and helped lead the club to seven National League pennants. He batted .272 in the World Series.

Duke Snider (HF) joined the Dodgers in 1947 and was a star from 1949 until the club left for Los Angeles in 1958. He hit 40 or more home runs five straight seasons beginning in 1953, batted over .300 five times and drove in over 100 runs six times.

Jackie Robinson (HF) joined the Dodgers in 1947 at age 28 to become the first black Major League player in the 20th century. He hit .311 over 10 seasons with the Dodgers, leading the league in batting in 1949 with a .342 average to become the first black MVP.

Roy Campanella (HF) was a three-time National League MVP for the Dodgers over his 10-year career with the club. He batted .276 lifetime and along with Yogi Berra of the Yankees was considered the best catcher in baseball in the 1950s.

Don Newcombe was the top Dodger pitcher of the 1950s, arriving with the club in 1949 to win 17 games and departing during the 1958 season when he began to fade. He won 20 games or more three times, including a league-leading 27 in 1956.

Key Managers.
Ned Hanlon (HF) led the Dodgers for seven seasons beginning in 1899, when he won the pennant. His teams faded after his initial success and he eventually finished last in 1905 and was fired.

Wilbert Robinson (HF).
"Uncle Robbie, as everyone in baseball knows him, defies every law of leadership since Gideon led his band. The Brooklyn team is a debating society to all outward appearances. The rotund Robbie, who hasn't played for many years, sits on the bench in uniform with his boys. He argues with them, yells at them and shakes a finger under their noses, and they argue, yell and shake fingers back at him. The Robins are a soviet to the casual eye, but make no mistake! Robbie runs the team in his own peculiar way, but he runs it." — Sportswriter Cullen Cain in a 1926 article in the *Saturday Evening Post*.

Robinson managed the Dodgers from 1914 through 1931. A former catcher, he had been a coach with the Giants for three years under John McGraw before they had a falling out. Brooklyn originally wanted him only as a coach, the club's first choice being Hughie Jennings of the Tigers. After American League president Ban Johnson blocked Detroit from letting Jennings go, the Dodgers settled on Robinson.

Robinson took the club to its first modern pennant in 1916 and again in 1920, but had few successes in the 1920s. He ended his managerial career after the 1931 season with 1,375 Dodger wins.

Leo Durocher (HF)
"Durocher claims he was sacked forty times [by Larry MacPhail] in his five years as Dodger manager; but I was there, and I can verify only twenty-seven." — Harold Parrott in *The Lords of Baseball* (1976).

Durocher began his 24-year managerial career with a nine-year stint with the Dodgers in 1939. He came to the Dodgers as a short-stop in a trade from St. Louis in 1938 and quickly succeeded Burleigh Grimes to become the last Dodger player-manager. In 1941 he led the team to its first pennant in 21 years and compiled a lifetime 740 wins with the Dodgers. He was suspended for the entire 1947 season for allegedly having ties with gamblers (see *Suspensions*) but returned to the team in 1948. Durocher knew his days were numbered by Dodger general manager Branch Rickey's attitude toward him in 1948, and near the end of the season he was sent to the hated Giants and managed there for eight seasons.

Burt Shotten.

"Hold 'em close boys, I'll think of something." — Shotten, who took over for the suspended Leo Durocher during 1947 and guided the team to a pennant. This quote is also attributed to Shotten's successor, Charlie Dressen. Shotten then succeeded the reinstated Durocher midway through the 1948 season. He guided the team to another pennant in 1949 and a second-place finish in 1950. See also David Gough, *Burt Shotton, Dodgers Manager: A Baseball Biography* (1994), primarily focusing on the 1947 season.

Charlie Dressen.

"Squat, sad-eyed, his thin hair slicked back, Dressen seemed to cry out for sympathy. A boyish ego contended endlessly in him with a dark suspicion of inferiority, and no matter how well he was doing one always had the feeling that he was going to end up with egg on his face." — Frank Graham, Jr., in *Farewell to Heroes* (1981).

Dressen, who had been one of Leo Durocher's coaches, took over the team in 1951. The club finished second after Bobby Thomson's home run for the Giants in the play-offs. Dressen took the team to pennants in 1952 and 1953, but after demanding a three-year contract after the 1953 season, the Dodgers fired him and hired Walter Alston.

Walter Alston (HF).

"Walter Who?" — New York newspaper headline when the little-known Alston was hired.

Pee Wee Reese was approached first as Charlie Dressen's successor, but declined. Alston started his 33-year Hall of Fame managerial career with the Dodgers in July 1944 with their Trenton team. The Dodgers announced Alston as their choice to manage the Major League club on November 23, 1953, signing the first of 23 straight one-year contracts.

Alston, who spanned the Brooklyn and Los Angeles eras, led the Brooklyn Dodgers to second place in 1954 and their first World Championship in 1955. He also guided the team to Game 7 of the 1956 World Series. The team slipped to third in 1957 before moving to Los Angeles.

Key Ballparks. Brooklyn's earliest field was Washington Park. It was built by long-time Dodger owner and realtor Charles Byrne between Fourth and Fifth Avenues and Third and Fifth Streets in Brooklyn. It had been built to house Byrne's Brooklyn Dodgers minor league team that was the predecessor to the American Association team of 1884. The site was called Washington Park because George Washington's army had fought the Battle of Long Island in the area. It burned in 1889 and was rebuilt for use in 1890 by the National League Dodgers.

Many sources are confused about the various parks that the Dodgers played in, but they played seven seasons in Eastern Park starting in 1891. The Dodgers moved to a rebuilt Washington Park for the 1898 season and remained there through 1912.

Washington Park seated 12,000, with overhanging seats from nearby buildings also put to use. After *Ebbets Field* opened in 1913, Washington Park was leased by the Brooklyn Federal League team for the 1914 and 1915 seasons. Ebbets Field remained home to the Dodgers until the club's departure for Los Angeles after the 1957 season. In 1956 and 1957 the Dodgers played a few games at Jersey City's Roosevelt Stadium, a WPA landmark. This occurred only after the city lost its Class AAA minor league franchise.

Key Broadcasters.

"[Red] Barber, a dapper little man with a knack for turning hill-country sayings into personal trademarks ... was a perfectionist. Once in his booth, he was all business, and he expected those around him — the other announcers, the engineers, and the ball club's publicity department, to keep to his standards." — Frank Graham, Jr., a member of the Dodger publicity department, in *Farewell to Heroes* (1981).

Hall of Famer **Red Barber** began broadcasting for the Dodgers in 1939 and stayed until 1954, when he moved over to the Yankees after a dispute over World Series pay with the commissioner in which the Dodgers failed to back him. Prior to 1939 the Dodgers had been part of a five-year agreement with the Giants and Yankees prohibiting radio broadcasts in New York. After the 1938 season, new Dodger general manager Larry MacPhail refused to renew the agreement and hired Barber away from the Reds.

The Dodgers sent their broadcasters on the road for the first time in 1946. Nevertheless, Nat Albright did re-creations for the Dodgers from 1950 (the first year of the Dodger Network) through 1962 (from Brooklyn). The re-creations were aired over a network of 100 stations, including one in Washington, D.C. The Washington broadcast had a higher rating than the lowly Senators' live broadcasts. Three stations in Washington were airing the re-creations and the 75-mile broadcast encroachment limit was ignored.

In 1950, 22-year-old Fordham graduate **Vin Scully** joined the announcing team. He replaced future long-time Tiger broadcaster Ernie Harwell, who joined Russ Hodges with the Giants. The regular announcing team when Walter O'Malley bought a controlling interest in 1950 consisted of Red Barber, Vin Scully and Connie Desmond.

In 1956 Jerry Doggett was hired to replace the alcoholic Desmond. Doggett had broadcast for 18 years in the minor leagues before joining the Dodgers. Doggett and Scully were the Dodger announcers when the club moved to Los Angeles for the 1958 season.

Books. Stanley Cohen, *Dodgers! The First 100 Years* (1990); Richard Goldstein, *Superstars and Screwballs* (1991); Peter Golenbock, *Bums* (1984); Frank Graham, *The Brooklyn Dodgers* (1945); Roger Kahn, *The Boys of Summer* (1972); Rudy Marzano, *The Brooklyn Dodgers in the 1940s* (2004); Andrew Paul Mele, *A Brooklyn Dodgers Reader* (2004); Mark Rucker, *Brooklyn Dodgers* (2002).

Brooklyn Eckfords

National Association 1872

"Replacing the western entry were the Brooklyn Eckfords, which had refused to join earlier on the grounds that the entry fee was too high. As prodigal sons, all they could hope for was money, because the terms of their belated entry stated that their won-loss record would not count." — David Quentin Voigt in *American Baseball* (1966).

The Eckfords of Greenpoint later became the prominent Brooklyn amateur team of the 1860s. The team was owned by a Scottish shipbuilder, Henry Eckford, and was known as a workingman's team as opposed to some of the more elitist teams such as the Knickerbockers. The team won the 1862 and 1863 New York City championship, often referred to as the informal "national championship." The club joined the National Association for the 1872 season, finishing with a 3–26 record.

Brooklyn Excelsiors

"JYBBBC"—Jolly Young Bachelors' Base Ball Club, nickname of the Excelsiors.

The Excelsiors were an early amateur team that made the first road tour, playing first in Albany, Buffalo and Rochester with nine players on the team. The Excelsiors won all their games, and then went on to Philadelphia, Wilmington and Baltimore. They won 15 in a row in front of crowds sometimes as high as 3,000.

Nineteen-year-old Jim Creighton, the team's star pitcher, was probably the game's first famous player. He had excellent control and a "wrist-throw" pitch, which was rudiment of the curve ball. Creighton later died from an injury he suffered at age 21 while batting (see *Deaths*). J. B. Leggett was the club's driving force and manager.

Brooklyn Gladiators

American Association 1890

When the American Association Brooklyn Dodgers left for the National League after the 1889 season, a new Brooklyn club attempted to fill the void. The Gladiators finished last with a 26–73 record.

Brooklyn Tiptops

Federal League 1914–1915

Federal League president James Gilmore supposedly told Robert Ward of Ward Brothers Bakery in New York that he could obtain national recognition for his TipTop bread if he financed a team in Brooklyn. Ward wanted the club's name to be TipTops, but supposedly the New York writers vetoed the name and instead primarily used Brookfeds in their reporting.

In 1914 the Tiptops finished in fifth place with a 77–77 record. In 1915 the club finished seventh at 70–82, despite the league-leading .342 batting average of outfielder Benny Kauff.

Brooklyn Wonders

Players League 1890

The Wonders were owned by Wendell Goodwin, a streetcar executive who was controlled by wealthy real estate tycoon George Chauncey. Chauncey and Goodwin helped finance a reconstituted National League franchise in Brooklyn for 1891.

The Wonders finished second with a 76–56 record, 6½ games behind Boston. The club's key players were John Montgomery Ward, who batted .337 and led the league in various defensive categories at shortstop, and George Van Haltren, who won 15 games and batted .335 as a utility player.

Brotherhood of Professional Base Ball Players (1885–1890)

The Brotherhood of Professional Baseball Players was the first true *Union*. It was founded in 1885 and became stronger until the death of the Players League after the 1890 season, when the Brotherhood quickly expired.

Brothers

"If I had known what Paul was gonna do, I would have pitched one, too."—Dizzy Dean, who pitched a one-hitter in the first game of a doubleheader, only to see his brother pitch a no-hitter in the second game. Good quote, but it never happened.

Major Leaguers. There have been over 335 brother combinations among the approximately 15,000 players who have made it to the Major Leagues. Twenty-five Hall of Famers had a brother who appeared in the Major Leagues.

Brother's Brief Appearances. Tom Paciorek's older brother John was called up from Class A Modesto in late 1963. He played in one Major League game on the last day of the season for the Houston Colt 45's. He played right field and went 3-for-3 (in five plate appearances) and is the only one of the players who hit 1.000 in the Major Leagues to do so with as many as three at-bats. Spinal fusion to relieve a chronic back problem ended his shot at the Major Leagues, but he bounced around the minors until 1969. He later graduated from the University of Houston and became a teacher.

In 1971 Robin Yount's older brother Larry threw a few warm-up pitches on the mound in a regular season game for the Astros. He hurt his arm during the warm-up and never again appeared in a Major League game. He is listed in the Major League's official baseball records because he was officially announced into the game.

World Series Opponents. Ken and Clete Boyer played against each other in the 1964 World Series. Each hit a home run in Game 7, won by Ken's Cardinals over Clete's Yankees. Third brother Cloyd was a Major League pitcher briefly in the 1950s.

All-Star Game. Mort and Walker Cooper were the first brothers selected to play in the same All-Star Game, in 1942 and 1943. Other brothers who were selected together:

Dixie and Harry Walker (1943 and 1947)
Joe and Dom DiMaggio (1941, 1949 and 1950)
Felipe and Matty Alou (1968)
Carlos and Lee May (1969)
Jim and Gaylord Perry (1970)
Sandy and Roberto Alomar (1991)

Ballpark Christeners. Felipe, Matty and Jesus Alou each was the first batter in a new ballpark: Atlanta's Felipe at Busch Stadium in St. Louis on May 12, 1966; Houston's Jesus at San Diego on April 8, 1969; and Pittsburgh's Matty at Atlanta on April 12, 1966.

Four In A Game/Infielders. On September 27, 1998, the Reds featured four Major League brothers in the lineup, all in the infield, when they brought up Barry Larkin's brother, Stephen (1B), a career minor leaguer, to join Aaron (3B) and Bret Boone (2B). Stephen had one hit on the day for a lifetime .333 average. He had a productive season for Chattanooga that season, but in August he had to have his heart's pacemaker replaced. When the Reds called up Aaron Boone in June 1997, they made room on their roster by sending down his brother, Bret, who was hitting .205. Bret quickly made it back to the Majors, however.

Three in Uniform. Only four sets of three or more brothers (out of 12 sets in Major League history) have been in uniform at the same time:

George, Sam and Harry Wright (manager) for the National League Boston Red Stockings (1876)

Felipe, Matty and Jesus Alou for the Giants (1960s); On September 10, 1963, Jesus was called up and all three brothers batted in the same half inning, which had never been done before or since, against pitcher Carlton Wiley of the Mets.

Jose, Hector and Tommy Cruz all played for the Cardinals in 1973.

Jose (Angels), Benji (Angels) and Yadier Molina (Cardinals) all were in the Major Leagues in 2004.

Same Outfield. The Alou brothers simultaneously played one game as starters for the Giants on September 15, 1963, shortly after

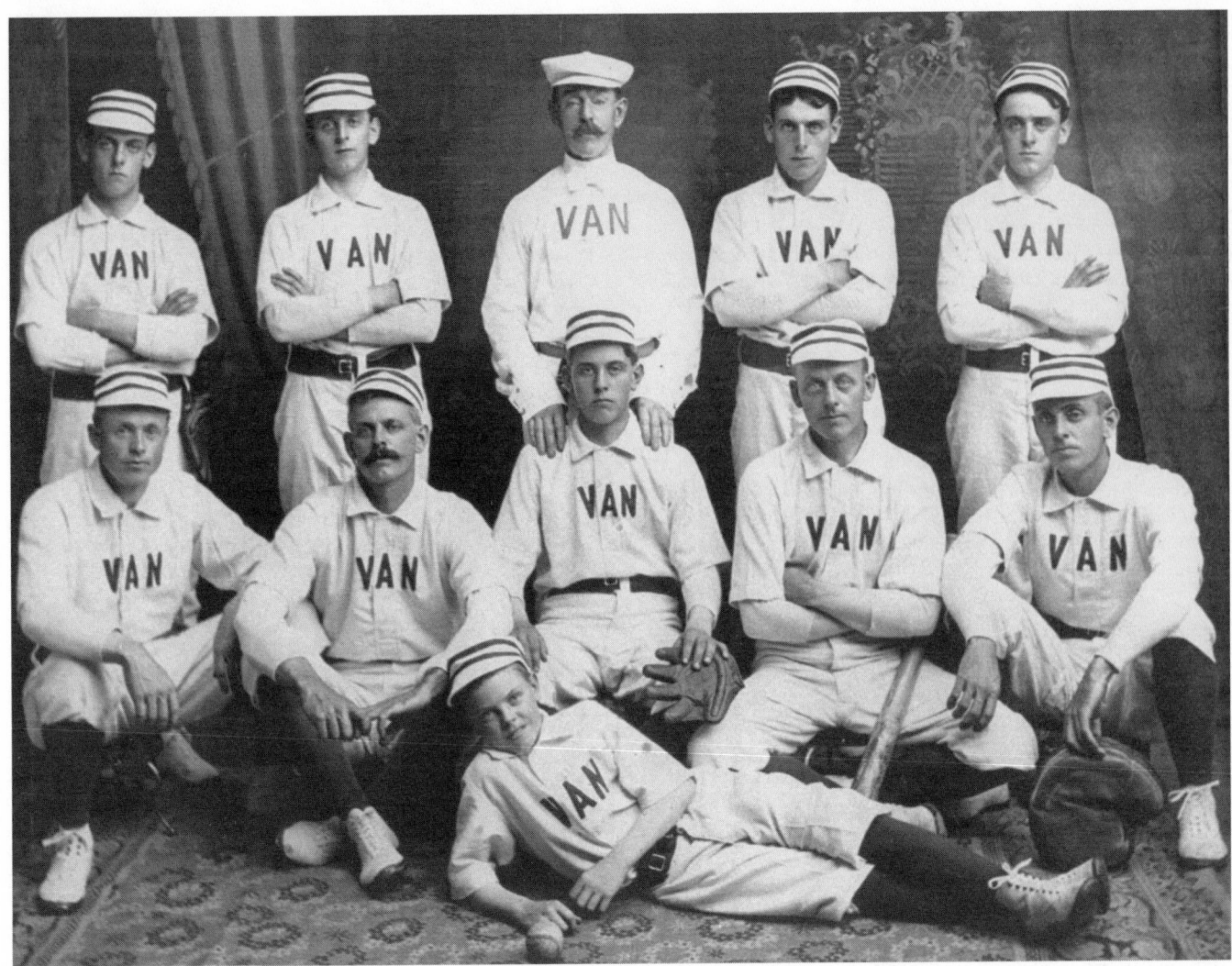

The Van Tassel Brothers Baseball Team of Pennsylvania. *First row, left to right:* Levi, George, Paul, Seymour, John, Avery. *Top row, left to right:* Grover, Jefferson, George W., Charles, William.

Jesus was brought up from the minor leagues. Matty went on to become the all-time leader in pinch hits (since surpassed). Felipe managed the Expos in the 1990s and Jesus became a hitting instructor.

Back-to-Back Home Runs. Cliff Melton is the only pitcher to give up back-to-back home runs to brothers, Lloyd and Paul Waner, on September 15, 1938. It was Lloyd's 27th and last home run of his career.

Battery. Joe and Luke Sewell and Mort and Walker Cooper are two brother batteries who played together.

Double Play Combination. Cal and Billy Ripken played shortstop and second base for the Orioles, at times for their father, manager Cal, Sr.

Hits.

"If [Mrs. Niekro] had a couple more kids I'd have had 5,000 hits." — Pete Rose, who had more than 100 hits off pitchers Phil and Joe Niekro.

"The Waners were a pair of slight, keen-eyed hitters who had learned how to hit by swinging broom handles at wickedly thrown corncobs on their father's farm in Harrah, Oklahoma." — Lawrence Ritter and Donald Honig in *The Image of Their Greatness* (1976).

Paul and Lloyd Waner combined for 5,611 hits. The three Alou

brothers had 5,094, the three DiMaggios had 4,853, and the five Delahanty brothers had 4,211.

Most Home Runs/Season. The record for most home runs in a season by brothers is 61, by Jason (41) and Jeremy (20) Giambi in 2002, topping the 59 by Joe (46) and Vince (13) DiMaggio in 1937. Dom once led the American League in stolen bases and was probably the best defensive player of the three DiMaggio brothers. He later wrote *Real Grass, Real Heroes*, with Bill Gilbert (1990).

Opposing Teams/Home Runs. On July 5, 1935, Tony Cuccinello of the Dodger and his brother Al of the Giants each hit home runs in the same game to mark the first time in Major League history that brothers on opposing teams connected for home runs. Brooklyn beat New York 14–4. Most recently Bret (Padres/Braves) and Aaron (Reds) Boone did it in 1999 and 2000, Felipe (Giants) and Cesar (Padres) Crespo did it in 2001, and Hector (Cubs) and Jose (Astros) Cruz did it in 1981.

Most Years Between Debuts. Jessie Fowler began in the Major Leagues in 1924 at age 25. Thirty years later his brother Art appeared at age 21.

No-Hitters.

"Hey, man, we signed the wrong brother." — Barry Bonds to

pitcher Mark Leiter, after his brother Al pitched a no-hitter for the Marlins in May 1996.

Bob and Ken Forsch are the only brothers to pitch no-hitters. Bob did it for the Cardinals against the Phillies on April 16, 1978, winning 5–0. Ken did it for the Astros against the Braves on April 7, 1979, winning 6–0.

Not Brothers. For many years through much of the 1980s, Chick and Jake Stahl were identified as brothers. Not true, despite being teammates briefly and each managing the Boston franchise in the American League. Also confused were Bill and Patsy Donovan. Chick committed *Suicide* while still a player in 1907and Jake later became an owner of the Boston franchise and died in 1922 of tuberculosis while still in his mid–40s.

Pitcher Versus Pitcher. On July 5, 1967, Phil Niekro of the Braves and Joe Niekro of the Cubs started against each other, the first of many times in their careers. Phil won 8–3. It was the first such game since May 3, 1927, when Jesse Barnes of the Dodgers was a 7–6 winner over brother Virgil of the Giants.

Pitchers Harry and Stan Coveleski had opportunities to face each other between 1916 and 1918, but Harry apparently did not want to pitch against his brother.

On September 29, 1986, rookies and brothers Greg Maddux of the Cubs and Mike Maddux of the Phillies were the starting pitchers. Mike won 8–3, but Greg went on to become the star, winning Cy Young awards in four straight seasons beginning in 1992.

On July 2, 1999, Jeff Zimmerman of the Rangers defeated his brother, Jordan, a left-handed pitcher for the Mariners.

On September 6, 2002, the Cardinals defeated the Cubs 11–2 as brothers Andy and Alan Benes opposed each other in the seventh matchup of brothers in Major League history. Andy got the win.

Amateur Draft. For the first time, in June 1997 brothers were drafted in the first round together. J.D. Drew was drafted by the Phillies as the second pick overall out of Florida State, ignoring his warning that he was going to demand a lot of money (see **Draft** for the problems that followed). His brother, Tim, was drafted No. 28 by the Indians. He played two seasons for the club, pitching nine innings and winning one game during his Major League career.

Brotherly Love? Houston pitcher Joe Niekro hit the only home run of his career off his brother Phil on May 29, 1976. The blow came in the 7th inning and won the game 4–3.

Several brothers have hit home runs off each other.

Substitute. In late 2003 Tom Glavine's younger brother, Mike, started at first base for the Mets, and a few games later pinch hit for Tom.

Managers. In 1995 Marcel Lachemann of the Angels and Rene Lachemann of the Marlins were the first brothers to manage at the same time in the Major Leagues since George and Harry Wright in the National League in 1879. George managed Boston and Harry managed Providence.

Rene Lachemann was fired as Marlins manager in mid–1996. A few weeks later Marcel "resigned" as manager of the Angels. Two days later interim Angels manager John McNamara was ejected from a game. He was replaced by bench manager Bill Lachemann, brother of Marcel and Rene.

Perez Brothers.

"He'll be a good pitcher if he stays sane." — Expos manager Felipe Alou on pitcher Carlos Perez.

Pascual Perez of the Braves, Yankees and others had two other brothers in the Major Leagues, Melido of the White Sox and Carlos of the Expos. They also had three other brothers who did not make it to the Major Leagues: Vladimir was in the Mets organization; Ruben Dario was in the Royals organization; Valerio played

in the Royals organization in the early 1980s and finished his career with a professional team in Taiwan known as Brother Elephants.

Recent Entries. Pitchers Livan and Orlando Hernandez came up to the Major Leagues from Cuba. Every-day players Wilton and Vladimir Guerrero came from the Dominican Republic. Jason and Jeremy Giambi of California have played in the Major Leagues since 1995 (Jason) and 1998 (Jeremy).

Same Team. In 2004, when the Braves brought up right-handed pitcher Tim Drew to play with his brother, J.D., it was the 12th time that siblings had played together for the Braves.

Twin Brothers. See *Twins.*

Lifetime Wins. Brothers Joe and Phil Niekro combined for 539 wins. They passed Jim and Gaylord Perry, who combined for 529 wins.

Christy Mathewson and his brother Henry won a combined 373 games, but Henry contributed no wins even though he pitched in a number of games. Christy's brother Henry died; other brother Nicholas, a pitcher at Lafayette College and thought to someday be the equal of Christy, committed suicide at the family farm.

One More Dean. Dizzy and Paul Dean had a brother named Elmer, nicknamed Goober because he was a peanut vendor at Sportsman's Park in St. Louis. Goober played briefly with Paul and Dizzy on a House of David team.

Wins/One Day. On July 20, 1969, Gaylord and Jim Perry between them won three games.

Most. There were five Delahanty brothers in the Major Leagues, though the most playing at one time was three. There were four O'Neil brothers, but only two played at one time.

Shutout. While with the Cubs, Rick and Paul Reuschel became the only brothers to combine on a shutout.

20-Game Winners. Jim and Gaylord Perry are the first brothers to each win 20 games in the same year, 1970.

Umpire. On July 14, 1972, umpire Bill Haller worked the plate while his brother Tom played catcher for the Tigers.

In August 2003, Marlins pitcher Mark Redman criticized umpire Jim Wolf and said there was a "perception problem," because Wolf's brother, Randy, pitched for the Phillies at a time when the Marlins and Phillies were locked in a battle for the wild card slot. The Marlins eventually prevailed and the umpire issue subsided. Wolf, a Class AAA umpire, had been filling in for vacationing Major League umpires. Redman complained after TV replays confirmed that Wolf had blown a call against the Marlins, who were playing the Dodgers at the time. In 2004 Wolf was hired as a full-time National League umpire. The commissioner's office ruled that Wolf could work his brother's games, but could not work home plate.

World Series. In 1920 Jimmy and Doc Johnson became the first brothers to face each other in a World Series, a year before the Meusel brothers did it.

Hall of Fame. Paul and Lloyd Waner and George and Harry Wright are the only brothers to be elected to the Hall of Fame.

Speechless. Bret Boone was in the television broadcast booth when his brother, Aaron, hit the game-ending home run against the Red Sox that sent the Yankees to the 2003 World Series. Bret was criticized for having nothing to say, but apparently he had hit the mute button because he was choked up over his brother's heroics. Others believed that he simply couldn't think of anything to say, after going innings without saying a word in the booth. For more than three minutes Bret said nothing, even though broadcaster Joe Buck looked expectantly at him at least twice.

Books. L. Robert Davids (ed.), *Insider's Baseball* (1983) (section on brothers by Larry Amman); David Nemec, *Great Baseball Feats, Facts & Firsts* (1987).

Dan Brouthers (1858–1932)

Hall of Fame 1945

"The ball touched Mother Earth sixty feet from the fence on the outside of the grounds. Then it galloped up an alley to Calvert Street and assaulted a Blue Line car. A policeman arrested it and returned it to the Union Park box office. Secretary Herman Vonderhorst had it safe in his possession last night. He will have it gilded and hung in the baseball headquarters, with an appropriate inscription."—Newspaper description of a long blast by Brouthers, quoted in *Baseball's Famous First Basemen*, by Ira L. Smith (1956).

Brouthers was a slugging star from 1879 through 1896, batting .342.

Dennis Joseph Brouthers began his professional baseball career in New York in 1876. At 6'2" and 207 pounds he was a large first baseman for the era. He made it to the Major Leagues in 1879 when he played for Troy. In 1881 he was traded to Buffalo and led the league in batting with .368 and .374 averages in 1882 and 1883. They were part of a 16-year streak in which he hit over .300. He moved to Detroit when Buffalo disbanded after the 1885 season.

Brouthers was part of the trade of the "Big Four" of Detroit to Boston when Detroit folded after the 1888 season. He led the National League in 1889 with a .373 average. He bounced to six clubs over the next seven years and finished his career in 1896 with Philadelphia. He came back to play cameo roles in two games for the Giants in 1904.

He finished his career with a .342 average, having led the league in batting five times and in slugging average seven times, including six years in a row in the 1880s. After leaving the National League he played in the minor leagues for a few years. At age 48 in 1904, while managing and playing for Poughkeepsie in the Hudson River League, he was 6-for-6 in one game and led the league with a .373 average.

After his playing career ended, he was a minor league club owner before becoming a scout for the Giants. He later became a ticket taker in charge of the press gate at the Polo Grounds. He died in August 1932 while still working the ballpark gate.

Mordecai "Three Finger" Brown (1876–1948)

Hall of Fame 1949

"But you haven't space enough to tell of all the grand deeds of Brownie on and off the field. Plenty of nerve, ability and willingness to work at all times under any conditions, the crowds never bothered him. There never was a finer character—charitable and friendly to his foes and ever willing to help a youngster breaking in."—Johnny Evers quoted in *Kings of the Diamond*, by Lee Allen and Tom Meany (1966).

Brown won 239 games over 14 seasons beginning in 1903.

Mordecai Peter Centennial Brown was born in Nyesville, Indiana, and became one of the premier pitchers of the early 20th century. He had mangled two fingers in childhood accidents (see also *Amputees*), but the injuries helped him get movement on his pitches. He was known primarily for his curveball and his fielding ability.

The Cardinals purchased his contract for the 1903 season and he won nine games. He was traded to the Cubs after the season and spent the next nine years in Chicago, winning 20 games or more in six straight seasons (1906–1911). In 1908 Brown won one of the most famous games ever played, the season-ending replay of the Cubs/Giants Merkle Boner game. Another measure of his ability is that he defeated the great Christy Mathewson (considered by many to be the best of that era) nine straight times between July 12, 1905, and September 8, 1908.

His career tapered off after his years with the Cubs. Beginning in 1913 he spent three years struggling with the Reds and two Federal League clubs. He returned briefly to the Cubs in 1916 and won the last two of his 239 Major League victories. After his Major League career ended he played in the minor leagues for a few seasons before retiring.

Brown won five World Series games and pitched three shutouts among his nine appearances in four Series. His regular-season career ERA of 2.06 is the third highest all-time. He pitched seven one-hitters, but a no-hitter eluded him.

Brush Resolution   See *Umpires—Attacks*

Brushback Pitches

"Driving the Batsman away from the plate is an essential part of baseball."—Jouett Meekin, 1890s Giants pitcher.

"When I broke in you knew damned well that pitchers were throwing at you. The first month I was in the league, I spent three weeks on my back at the plate."—Casey Stengel, who said that one of his biggest mistakes in baseball was when he managed the Boston Braves; he sent Warren Spahn back to the minors because Spahn wouldn't throw at Dodger shortstop Pee Wee Reese during an exhibition game.

"Know how I'd pitch to you? I'd throw the old tie ball. You can't hit on your back."—Satchel Paige to Ernie Banks.

"It's always the same. Combs walks. Koenig singles. Ruth hits one out of the park. Gehrig doubles. Lazzeri triples. Then Dugan goes in the dirt on his can."—Yankee infielder Joe Dugan.

"In the olden days, the umpire didn't have to take any courses in mind reading. The pitcher *told* you he was going to throw at you."—Leo Durocher in *Nice Guys Finish Last* (1975).

"If one of our guys went down, I just doubled it. No confusion there. It didn't require a Rhodes Scholar."—Don Drysdale, who is credited by Jim Brosnan for making the brushback pitch 90% of his repertoire, rather than the standard 10%.

"Don Drysdale said something I've always enjoyed. He said, 'The most important pitch of the game is the second knockdown pitch.' Then the hitter knows the first one wasn't an accident. That's the way it is when I bust a guy twice."—Roger Clemens.

"The pitcher has to find out if the hitter is timid. And if the hitter is timid, he has to remind the hitter he's timid."—Don Drysdale in the *New York* Times in 1979.

"You all done? You comfortable? Well, send for the groundskeeper and get a shovel because that's where they're gonna bury you."—Dizzy Dean to a batter who dug in at the plate.

"I'd brush back my own grandmother if she crowded the plate on me."—Pitcher Early Wynn denies ever saying this.

"Is that called dustin' Hoffman?"—Angels broadcaster Joe Torre after A's pitcher Curt Young threw a brushback pitch at Glenn Hoffman.

"George Porgie, he might buy the whole league, but he doesn't have enough money to buy fear to put in my heart."—Red Sox pitcher Pedro Martinez, after Yankees owner George Steinbrenner accused Martinez of throwing at Derek Jeter and Alfonso Soriano.

See also *Beanballs* and *Fights*.

Hughie Jennings. Jennings learned not to step away from close pitches by standing against a wall and having teammate John McGraw pitch inside to him.

Sal Maglie. Sal "The Barber" Maglie was known for his brushback proclivities in the 1940s and 1950s.

Jim Lonborg. The Red Sox pitcher was known as a friendly pitcher who was easy to hit because he rarely challenged the hitters inside. He changed his demeanor for the pennant-winning 1967 season and hit 19 batters. He notched each hit batter on the back of his glove in black ink.

Wild Game. In 1984, after a brushback-filled game between the Braves and Padres, two managers and five players were suspended, and two coaches and another nine players were fined. Things became so wild that five players who had already been ejected from the game returned to the field and took part in later fights. Managers Joe Torre (Braves) and Dick Williams (Padres) were suspended for three and 10 days; the five players were suspended for two or three days.

Japan. The brushback pitch was unheard of in Japan until 1966.

Buffalo Bisons

National League 1879–1885

The Bisons finished third in their first National League season behind the pitching of Pud Galvin, who won 37 games. The club was strong again from 1881 through 1884 with player-manager Jim O'Rourke, Deacon White and Galvin leading the club. However, the club could never get beyond third place in any of those seasons. In 1885 Buffalo finished 38–74 with essentially the same players and the club dropped out of the league after the season.

All the players were sold before the end of the 1885 season for $7,000 to Detroit pharmaceutical man Frederick Kimball Stearns of the National League. The key to the deal was four players: Deacon White, Dan Brouthers, Jack Rowe and Hardie Richardson (Galvin had faded by this time to 13 wins). The sale before the end of the season violated the National Agreement. New National League president Nick Young ordered the four returned to Buffalo, but they refused and were allowed to leave in early 1886 when Detroit persuaded them to sign.

Buffalo Bisons

Players League 1890

The Bisons finished last with a 42–96 record as pitcher George Haddock led the league with 26 losses. No regular on the club batted over .300.

Buffalo BufFeds/Blues

Federal League 1914–1915

"Share in the profits of the game you patronize. That's the aim of the Federal Baseball League in giving everyone in the Buffalo and vicinity a chance to become financially interested in the new major league project. The major league is no longer an experiment. It is an assured fact and promises one of the greatest financial successes in the history of baseball."—Advertisement to invest in the club reprinted in Marc Okonnen's *The Federal League of 1914–1915* (1989).

One of the great pitchers of the early 20th century, Cubs star Mordecai Peter Centennial Brown, better known as "Three Finger" Brown because of a childhood accident that cost him parts of three fingers: the index finger and parts of the middle finger and pinkie (see *Amputees*).

Buffalo finished fourth in 1914 with an 80–71 record behind the play of first baseman Hal Chase, who batted .347. Chase had a league-leading 17 home runs in 1915, but the club finished sixth with a 74–78 record under four managers. The club was known as the BufFeds in 1914 and Blues in 1915.

Morgan G. Bulkeley (1837–1922)

Hall of Fame 1937

Bulkeley was the first *National League President*.

Bullpens

"I've come to the conclusion that the two most important things in life are good friends and a good bullpen."—Long-time pitcher and manager Bob Lemon.

Derivation. The term "Bullpen" arose when fans were allowed into games for 10 cents if they arrived after the 1st inning in the early years in the National League; latecomers were penned in "like bulls" behind ropes in foul territory beyond first and third base. Relief pitchers warmed up along the sidelines near these areas.

First. Though the term was not used until about 1915 to describe where pitchers warmed up, the first formal bullpen area was at the Polo Grounds in 1905.

Bullpen Obstructions. On July 1, 1958, Giants rookie outfielder Leon Wagner was fooled by the Cubs bullpen bench in Wrigley Field (which is on the field adjacent to the outfield foul lines). Tony Taylor hit a ball into the Cubs bullpen. The opposing players sitting on the bench peered under the bench to decoy Wagner. The ball was 45 feet away in a rain gutter and by the time Wagner found the ball, Taylor had an inside-the-park home run.

Location. Reds general manager Bob Howsam made sure that Riverfront Stadium, built in the late 1960s, had a bullpen that was within sight of the fans. He believed that it was a source of interest and should not be hidden away.

Bullpen Transportation.

"I could never play in New York. The first time I ever came into a game there, I got in the bullpen car and they told me to lock the doors."—Mike Flanagan on the tough New York fans.

Various modes of transportation have been used to move relief pitchers from the bullpen to the pitching mound. Other than walking, players have been brought in by mule, scooter, golf cart and automobile.

Indians general manager Hank Greenberg was the first to use transportation to drive relievers in from the bullpen. In the 1950s his club used, among other cars, a Nash Rambler, which he tried to give to pitcher Bob Lemon. Lemon rejected "that piece of junk."

In the 1970s and 1980s Cleveland relievers, embarrassed, sometimes jogged next to the transportation donated by a sponsor. Seattle Mariners owner George Argyros created a tugboat-shaped cart that pitchers were too embarrassed to ride in.

The Yankees stopped using transportation when rats chewed through the engine cables and fans threw trash at the carts. But the main reason, according to Hall of Fame historian Russell Wolinsky, was that "the players hated them."

The origins of golf cart use can be traced to the Los Angeles Angels and their Palm Springs spring training site. In 1963 the local booster club gave the Angels a golf cart for shuttling relief pitchers from the bullpen to the mound. The Angels liked the idea and used the cart all season, starting a trend throughout the Major Leagues.

A's owner Charlie Finley used a mule to take a new pitcher into the game. Pitcher Catfish Hunter derisively recalled riding in from the bullpen with the mule and having it stop at the railing to eat popcorn from fans during a tight 2–1 game.

During the 1950s the White Sox used a station wagon to bring in relief pitchers from the bullpen. It was also used for visiting pitchers, but the Yankees refused to use it and walked in, prompting one Yankee pitcher to remark that the Yankees "only ride in Cadillacs." The next time the Yankees visited Comiskey Park, White Sox general manager Frank Lane rented a black Cadillac hearse to carry the Yankee relievers into the game.

During home games in the 1970s, the White Sox bullpen catcher restored a 1929 Ford. After wins he drove the "Big White Machine" around the field.

Boston's Fenway Park used a scooter to bring in pitchers in the late 1950s and early 1960s, though the pitchers looked uncomfortable perched behind the driver.

Vegetables. Baltimore's Memorial Stadium, replaced for the 1992 season, had a tomato patch growing behind the right field line. It was tended at times by manager Earl Weaver.

Jim Bunning (1931–)

Hall of Fame (VC) 1996

"For weeks after the season ended, all I could think of was how we blew the thing. Sandy Grady, the fine columnist of the *Philadelphia Bulletin*, asked me if I felt like pulling a Floyd Patterson, wearing a fake beard and dark glasses and pulling all the shades down in the house. No, I didn't. But it was almost as bad."—Bunning on the 1964 collapse of the Phillies after leading the league by 10 games with 12 days left in the season; in *The Story of Jim Bunning*, by Bunning as told to Ralph Bernstein (1965).

Bunning won 224 games primarily for the Tigers and Phillies between 1955 and 1971.

James Paul David Bunning began his pro career in 1950 with Richmond in the Ohio-Indiana League. He made it up to the Tigers for 15 games in 1955, but spent most of 1956 with Charleston in the American Association. He finished the 1956 season with a 5–1 record for the Tigers and blossomed in 1957 with an American League–leading 20–8 record.

Bunning spent another six seasons with the Tigers, though he never again reached 20 wins. He pitched a no-hitter against the Red Sox in 1958. He was traded to the Phillies in 1964, for whom he pitched a perfect game against the Mets on Father's Day that season before the last-week fade by the club to lose the pennant.

The sidearm fastball pitcher won 19 games three times for the Phillies before moving on to the Pirates in 1968. After a poor 4–14 season he spent 1969 with the Pirates and Dodgers, winning a total of 13 games. He finished his career with two more seasons for the Phillies, winning 15 games through 1971.

He finished his 17-year career with a 224–184 record and a 3.27 ERA. He pitched 40 shutouts and led the league in strikeouts three times; second only to Walter Johnson in career strikeouts when he retired. He was the first pitcher since Cy Young to win at least 100 games in each league. During the off-season the native Kentuckian was a stockbroker. After he retired he became a Kentucky state legislator and later lost a bid for governor. In 1986 he was elected to the House of Representatives, where he served for several years.

Bunts

"The hitters who get under my skin are the pests who bunt and drag, or poke at the ball. They're hard to fool."—Lefty Grove.

"Boys, bunting is like jacking off. Once you learn how you never forget."—Pilots manager Joe Schultz.

"I was surprised by the bunt [sign]. I don't know how to bunt."—Reds outfielder Wily Mo Pena after failing twice to get down a bunt and then tripling.

"Sure, I screwed up that sacrifice bunt, but look at it this way. I'm a better bunter than a billion Chinese. Those poor suckers can't bunt at all."—John Lowenstein.

Bats. John Montgomery Ward's teams used a soft willow bat to bunt, but it was quickly outlawed (see also **Bats—Wood**).

Fan Dislike. Many early fans disliked the bunt and booed its use. In 1892 prominent "baseballists" Ned Hanlon and Cap Anson agreed that there should be consideration given to banning use of the bunt because the "baby play" required no skill. A compromise may have been reached when flat-sided bats were banned in 1893. These bats were the easiest to use when trying to bunt.

First Bunters. Dickey Pearce is credited by some with the first bunt in the 1860s.

John McGraw is credited with regularly using the bunt while leading off for the Baltimore Orioles of the 1890s. Wilbert Robinson, catcher for the team and later the Dodger manager, said that McGraw's ability to dump the ball was "astounding."

Fair/Foul Bunt. The fair-foul bunt supposedly was perfected by the Brooklyn Atlantics in the 1860s. The hit was a bunt that began in fair territory and then rolled foul, usually far out of play. This was considered a legal hit until after the National League's first season in 1876. The new rule required the ball to be in fair territory when it passed first or third base or be in fair territory if it stopped short of either base.

Dickey Pearce, who had the key hit that stopped the 1869–1870 Cincinnati Red Stockings' streak, was a prominent practitioner of the fair/foul hit. According to one source, the rule was changed because Ross Barnes of the White Stockings had become so adept at hitting fair/foul balls. After the rule change, his batting average dropped from a league-leading .429 in 1876 (.404 in early sources) to .272 in 1877. His average dropped, however, because he played only 22 games while suffering from a progressively worse malaria-like condition known as ague. It caused debilitating sweats and chills, and Barnes apparently never fully recovered.

Another man who early on was adept at the fair/foul bunt was Tommy Barlow, whose first season of professional ball was for the National Association Atlantics in 1872. His career ended quickly in 1874 after he became addicted to the morphine he was given after suffering a severe on-field injury.

John McGraw claimed that the fair-foul ball rule was changed because he was able to bunt safely 24 straight times using this method. A bit of a fabrication considering that McGraw was only four years old when the National League rule was changed.

Rules/Third Strike. In 1894 the rules were changed to require a third strike call on a bunt attempt that went foul.

Sacrifice Bunt.

"To order the sacrifice bunt as a matter of routine whenever the situation arises is about as productive for the manager as attempting to marry his sister." — Earnshaw Cook in *Percentage Baseball* (1964).

The sacrifice bunt was introduced into the rules in 1889, but the batter was still charged with an at-bat. In 1894 it was ruled that a bunt that advances a base runner would be considered a sacrifice hit and the batter would not be charged with an at-bat. The rule was not uniformly adopted by all scorers until 1897.

Drag Bunt/Pitcher Retaliation. During spring training in 1963 Mickey Mantle put down a drag bunt on Don Drysdale. Drysdale was late in reaching the bag and Mantle was safe, but Drysdale caught up with Mantle after passing the bag and stepped hard on Mantle's foot. Drysdale told Mantle never to drag bunt on him again, and Mantle agreed. Drysdale told Mantle that he would not forget what Mantle did. At the World Series that year, Drysdale walked up to Mantle during batting practice and asked him, "Where do you want it," meaning a hit by pitch in retaliation for the bunt. Mantle believes that Drysdale must have softened because he did not nail him during the Series.

Defensive Strategy. Fielder Jones, a turn-of-the-century star outfielder primarily with the White Sox, is credited with creating the infield motion shift to defend against bunts (corners in toward the plate, shortstop to second, second baseman covering first).

Never Bunted.

"I don't know — nor have I any intention of ever finding out"— Yankee manager Joe McCarthy, asked if Joe DiMaggio could bunt.

Harmon Killebrew never bunted in 8,147 at-bats. Frank Robinson laid down his first bunt in 12 years only after crashing into the railing at Fenway Park in the previous half inning. He was unable to breathe due to damaged ribs and could barely swing.

Frequency. According to George Will, in 1988 only 3% of all batted balls put into play were bunts.

Field. Connie Mack Stadium had a third base line known as Ashburn's Ridge, which helped bunters such as the Phillies' Richie Ashburn keep bunted balls from rolling foul.

Tiger Stadium had an area between third base and home plate known as "Cobb's Lake," which was watered down to slow Ty Cobb's bunts so the opposing club's third baseman could not reach them in time.

Argument. On October 7, 1998, in the ALCS between the Indians and Yankees, the game was tied in the 12th inning with the Indians at bat. On a close bunt play at first, Yankees second baseman Chuck Knoblauch argued the call rather than throwing home as the lead runner scored. The Indians went on to win 4–1.

Burials and Cemeteries

"Let's put the *fun* back in *funeral*." — License plate frame observed by this author.

"All relations and immediate friends are well informed that I desire to be buried in my baseball suit, and wrapped in the original flag of the old Knickerbockers of 1845, now festooned over my bureau…" — Instructions of James Whyte Davis.

"You should always go to other people's funerals, otherwise, they won't come to yours." — Yogi Berra.

"The Phillies beat the Cubs today in a doubleheader. That puts another keg in the Cubs' coffin." — Jerry Coleman.

"Paul Waner retired as a big leaguer last May 13 [1945]. At present he is in the concrete burial vault business…" — The *Stars and Stripes* military newspaper in September 1945.

"Billy Martin has just been hired by Forest Lawn to kick dirt." — "Tonight Show" host Johnny Carson.

"Anybody lookin' for me, tell 'em I'm being embalmed." — Casey Stengel to a group of sportswriters after an early morning breakfast and on his way for a nap.

"You can have money piled to the ceiling, but the size of your funeral is still going to depend on the weather." — Pirates manager Chuck Tanner.

Braves pitcher Tony Cloninger lays down a bunt as Mets catcher Choo Choo Coleman crouches behind the plate. Cloninger is the only pitcher to hit two grand slams in one game.

"Dodger Stadium was his address, but every ballpark was his home." — Tommy Lasorda's proposed epitaph after he as denied the right to be buried under the pitching mound at Dodger Stadium. At Vero Beach one year, Dodger owner Walter O'Malley presented Lasorda with a 50-pound granite (or marble) tombstone bearing his name and a heart with a drop of Dodger blue blood. Lasorda always has said that he wanted the Dodger schedule on his tombstone so fans will know if the Dodgers are in town.

William Hulbert. The National League founder is buried in Graceland Cemetery in Chicago. His tombstone is a baseball 20 inches in diameter carved from red granite.

Christopher Von der Ahe. The 19th century St. Louis Browns owner commissioned a statue of himself and placed it in front of his ballpark. The statue later was moved to a cemetery as the headstone on his grave.

Baltimore Orioles. The nucleus of the 1890s Baltimore Orioles are all buried in New Cathedral Cemetery in Baltimore: John McGraw, Wilbert Robinson, Ned Hanlon, Bobby Mathews and Joe Kelley.

Addie Joss. When the early 20th century Cleveland pitching star died of meningitis while the club was on the road, his teammates petitioned to attend his funeral. The club initially refused and the players threatened to strike. Ultimately the game was cancelled and the players returned briefly to Cleveland for the funeral.

Ban Johnson. His grave in Seymour, Indiana, is marked with a simple headstone: "Byron Bancroft Johnson. Founder of the American League"

Lou Gehrig. His original will is located in the files of the Hall of Fame (it was buried in a file located by this author during a research trek to the Hall).

Henry Chadwick. Nineteenth-century sportswriter Henry Chadwick's burial plot is in the same cemetery in Brooklyn as that of one of the first professionals, Jim Creighton. Creighton's burial site, an early pilgrimage mecca, is now roped off to ward off tourists.

When Chadwick died, the Major Leagues purchased his headstone in a gesture of respect for the penniless sportswriter who had done so much to promote the sport. Four stones were laid out to simulate a baseball diamond. The names of all the National League teams at the time were engraved on the headstone.

Rube Waddell. When Waddell died of tuberculosis on April 1, 1914 (only four years after he retired), his grave was marked by a simple wooden stake in a San Antonio cemetery. When the president of the Texas League heard about the gravesite, he obtained $500 from Connie Mack, John McGraw and others to purchase an appropriate tombstone to mark the grave.

Charlie Grimm. The Cubs player, coach, manager and broadcaster secretly arranged to have his ashes spread over Wrigley Field after he died in 1983.

Johnny Orlando. The Red Sox equipment manager was a favorite of Ted Williams. Though many sources report that he retired shortly after Williams retired, he was actually fired for his chronically heavy drinking the spring before Williams' last season in 1960. When he died in 1974, a bartender friend of his secretly scattered his ashes on the infield and left field grass of Fenway Park.

Waite Hoyt. The Yankee pitcher had a father-in-law who was a mortician. Hoyt once supposedly did him a favor by picking up a corpse near Yankee Stadium before a game. He left the body in the trunk of his car during the game, pitched a shutout, and then delivered the corpse.

Charles Ebbets. When the Dodger owner died in 1925,

National League president John Heydler postponed the Tuesday schedule in honor of Ebbets' funeral.

Ty Cobb. When Cobb died in 1961, there were 400 in attendance at his funeral (many of whom were Little Leaguers), but only three Major League Baseball people: Mickey Cochrane, Ray Schalk and Hall of Fame Director Sid Keener.

Richie Hebner. Hebner was a gravedigger in the off-season for his dad, who was the foreman of a Boston cemetery.

Tom Gorman. The long-time umpire, who died in 1986, was buried as requested in his umpire suit with the indicator in his hand set at a 3–2 count. His autobiography is *Three and Two* (1979).

Dusty Boggess. The umpire carried a ball that was signed by every umpire he ever worked with over a career covering 21 years in the minor leagues and 18 years in the National League (1944–1962). The signed ball was buried with him as specified in his will.

Project Remember. This was a national effort to document the gravesites of notable Americans, including a number of baseball players. The Foundation was located in Lunenburg, Massachusetts, and the project was undertaken during the early 1980s.

Babe Ruth.

"May the divine spirit that animated Babe Ruth to win the crucial game of life inspire the youth of America!" — Cardinal Spellman quoted on Ruth's headstone.

Ruth is buried at the Gate of Heaven cemetery in Hawthorne, New York. When Ruth died in 1948, his body lay in state inside the home plate entrance to Yankee Stadium for a huge public viewing. Joe DiMaggio was the only active player who served as a pallbearer at Ruth's funeral.

When Ruth visited Hawaii in 1939 he laid a wreath at the grave of New York Knickerbocker Alexander Cartwright. Ruth's original will is in the collection of **Memorabilia** king Barry Halper.

Promotion. In 2003 the Class A Hagerstown (Maryland) Suns promised a free funeral to the fan who presented the most creative plans for his or her own service. A funeral home sponsored the $4,000 funeral as a means of promoting people's awareness of the need to plan for the afterlife. Finalists were asked to read their essays at a game.

Bad Hands. The pilot of a small plane carrying the remains of an avid Mariners' fan attempted to drop the ashes above Safeco Field, but the canister bounced off the stadium roof and landed on the street. Fear of an attack brought police and firemen rushing to the stadium.

Bereavement Program. In 2004 the Association of Professional Ballplayers of America (APBPA), in conjunction with the Major League Baseball Players Alumni Association (MLBPA) and the Baseball Assistance Team (BAT), announced the development of a bereavement program for Major League and Minor League baseball. A network of baseball representatives throughout the world was being created to attend funeral and memorial services of current or former baseball people.

Book. Peter J. Nash, *Baseball Legends of Brooklyn's Green-Wood Cemetery* (2004).

Jesse Burkett (1868–1953)

Hall of Fame 1946

"Jesse Burkett didn't get tagged 'Crab' in his later years on the ball field because he was the picture of joy and gaiety. Bleacherites reportedly hung the nickname on him because of his retorts to the critical comments they shouted at him. Mainly, the bleacher jockeys rode him on account of his advancing years. Born not very long after gunfire of the Civil War died down, he was still cavorting as a major leaguer when he was close to forty." — Ira L. Smith in *Baseball's Famous Outfielders* (1954).

Burkett played outfield for 16 years in the Major Leagues beginning in 1890, batting .339.

Jesse Cail Burkett was raised in West Virginia and reported to Scranton of the Central League as a left-handed pitcher in 1888. After a weak Major League pitching debut with the Giants (while batting .309), he returned to the minor leagues and moved to the outfield. He joined the National League Cleveland Spiders for part of the 1891 season and remained a fixture in the Spiders outfield for the next seven years. He batted no less than .348 for the club beginning 1893, with league highs of .409 and .410 in 1895 and 1896.

Burkett was one of the players who was switched to St. Louis when the Robison brothers purchased the club. Until recently he was credited with a third .400 season in 1899 for the Cardinals, but that figure has been revised downward from .402 to .396. He spent two more seasons with the Cardinals and batted a league-high .382 in 1901. He moved over to the Browns in 1902 and began to fade. In 1905 he played his last season in the Major Leagues, batting .257 for the Red Sox.

He finished with a lifetime .339 average and 2,853 hits. He led the league three times in batting average and hits. At only 5'8" and 155 pounds, he was a surly player whose nickname "The Crab" reflected his abusive treatment of fans, umpires and opposing players.

After he left the Major Leagues he was player-manager and part-owner of Worcester in the New England League from 1906 through 1913. He won a batting championship in 1906 with a .344 average. He coached at Holy Cross from 1917 through 1920 and then returned to the National League as a scout and coach for the Giants.

Buses

"I'd like to stay in baseball long enough to buy a bus — then set fire to it." — Senators reliever Joe Grzenda after 11 years of grueling minor league road trips.

"Free bus fumes while you work out." — One of David Letterman's "Top Ten Good Things About Playing Baseball in New York," presented by outfielder Bernie Williams.

See also *Transportation*.

See *Deaths* for the story of Lucky Lohrke's brush with death in a bus accident.

Prank. During the 1982 pennant race, Giants pitcher Greg Minton decided to loosen things up by stealing the team bus and driving it to the ballpark in Houston — with a stop to buy some boots. He was fined $120.

Bus Accident. In the early morning of May 21, 1992, one of the Angels' team buses turned over on the expressway on its way from New York to Baltimore while on the New Jersey turnpike. Manager Buck Rogers sustained the worst injuries, suffering a broken rib and wrist and a severely damaged knee.

Miscommunication, Rickey Style. Tradition over the last several years is that veterans get two seats each on buses taking players to the ballpark. In the mid–1990s, when Rickey Henderson was with the Padres, he got on the bus and saw that there were no two seats available. General Manager Kevin Tower told Henderson: "Tell one of the young players to move because you've got tenure." Henderson, who often spoke in the third person, said, "No, Rickey got 15 year."

Lost and Found. Thanks to an honest bus cleaner, Reds reliever Danny Graves recovered his wallet. In May 2004 the man found Graves' wallet after the players had been dropped off at the airport in San Diego. He mailed it to Graves' home, but not before converting the $1,400 in the wallet to travelers' checks, so they wouldn't be stolen in the mail. He told Graves in a cover letter, "I borrowed $26 to overnight it to you." He asked only that Graves sign an autograph for his father. Graves promised a lot more than that.

The Business of Baseball

"The baseball mania has run its course. It has no future as a professional endeavor." — The 1879 *Cincinnati Gazette*.

"Baseball is a game, yes. It is also a business. But what it most truly is is disguised combat. For all its gentility, its almost leisurely pace, baseball is violence under wraps." — Willie Mays, according to one source [Hard to believe that the relatively unsophisticated Mays spoke these words].

"As baseball is no longer a sport, but a business, and a rather low business at that, it must be treated like the stove business and the express business whenever it obstructs the sidewalks or interferes with the clear right of way of pedestrians." — The 1891 *New York Times*.

"Baseball is too much of a sport to be a business and too much of a business to be a sport." — Phil Wrigley.

"The umpires always say 'Play ball.' They don't say 'Work ball.'" — Willie Stargell.

"Is baseball a business? If it isn't, General Motors is a sport." — Jim Murray.

See also *Profits, Income and Expenses*.

Books. Ralph Andreano, *No Joy in Mudville* (1965); Scott Barzilla, *The State of Baseball Management: Decision-Making in the Best and Worst Teams, 1993–2003* (2004); Robert F. Burk, *Never Just a Game: Players, Owners and American Baseball to 1920* (1984); Robert F. Burk, *Never Just a Game: Players, Owners and American Baseball Since 1921* (2001); John Helyar, *Lords of the Realm: How the Business of Baseball Has Taken Over America's Game* (1994); Kenneth Jennings, *Balls and Strikes: The Money Game in Professional Baseball* (1990); Gerald Scully, *The Business of Major League Baseball* (1989); Andrew S. Zimbalist, *Baseball and Billions* (1992); Andrew S. Zimbalist, *May the Best Team Win: Baseball Economics and Public Policy* (2003).

"**C** is for Cobb,
Who grew spikes and not corn,
And made all the basemen
Wish they weren't born."
— Ogden Nash on Ty Cobb.

California

"The people of California … a level-headed, practical folk, who know a good thing when they see it." — Campaign statement by Albert Spalding when he unsuccessfully ran for the U.S. Senate after moving to San Diego in the early 20th century.

The first organized baseball team in California was the Eagles, formed in 1859. The team was named after the New York Eagles, many of whose players had migrated West. In 1861 the San Francisco Knickerbockers were formed by a few migrating New York Knickerbocker players. Local newspapers welcomed the men from the "direct center of the Baseball Universe." Other pre–Civil War teams were the Em Quads and Rovers. In 1866 the convention of the state's baseball organization was attended by 100 clubs.

California has had the following Major League clubs (none of which has ever left the state):

Los Angeles Dodgers (1958–)
San Francisco Giants (1958–)
Los Angeles/California/Anaheim Angels (1961–)
Oakland Athletics (1968–)
San Diego Padres (1969–).

"Called Shot" (1932)

"No way. [Pitcher Charlie] Root would have put the next pitch in his ear if Ruth had tried that on him."—Cubs first baseman Charlie Grimm on whether Babe Ruth actually pointed to center field before his famous home run during the 1932 World Series.

In the 5th inning of Game 3 of the 1932 World Series at Wrigley Field in Chicago, Babe Ruth is supposed to have "called his shot," a home run to center field off pitcher Charlie Root. Most historians dispute this claim. Amid heavy bench jockeying between the clubs, someone from the Cubs dugout rolled a lemon in Ruth's path, infuriating him. Ruth supposedly pointed to the center field bleachers after letting two strikes go by. He then belted a home run to center field on a low-and-outside change-up curveball.

Root and others said that Ruth was simply pointing at Root. Catcher Gabby Hartnett said that Ruth only pointed to the Cubs dugout and said that "it only took one to hit." Year-end baseball summary digests contained no reference to the "Called Shot."

According to sportswriter Fred Lieb, Lou Gehrig supported the notion of Ruth's called shot, but Gehrig was the one who actually called his shot. When Ruth headed for the dugout after his blast, he told Gehrig, "Why don't you do the same thing?" Gehrig's response: "I will." He did. Ruth also hit a three-run shot off Root in the 1st inning.

There is so much confusion surrounding the event that no one is even sure of the pitch count. It has been reported as 2–2 (historian Robert Creamer and writer Paul Gallico, with differing accounts of how it was reached), 0–2 (Ruth and Root), and 3–2 (one umpire and the *New York Times*).

Ruth both confirmed and denied the story. In one of his last commentaries on the subject, in the May 23, 1944, edition of *The Sporting News*, he said that he pointed to the outfield, but not to any particular spot.

Cubs public address announcer Pat Peiper, who traditionally sat on a stool on the field said, "Don't let anybody tell you differently. Babe definitely pointed." Bill Dickey of the Yankees said that Ruth came back to the bench and reported that he was pointing only at Root, angry that Root tried to quick pitch him.

In 1986 the tongue-in-cheek Court of Historic Review and Appeals heard testimony from both sides. The court's ruling: "It is not important if the incidents referred to in ... legends really did in fact happen. What is important is that a large segment of the people believe that they did occur, and it is for us as individuals to place whatever credence or value on these stories as we might desire....

"It is the Court's opinion that the legend of Babe Ruth pointing to the center-field fence in the 1932 World Series shall remain intact for future generations of baseball fans and sportswriters to argue about.

"The petition before this Court to rule against the Babe Ruth legend is therefore denied."

Other Called Shots.

Prankster Germany Schaefer of the 1905–1909 Tigers supposedly once announced as he approached the plate that he intended to hit a home run: "Ladies and gentlemen, permit me to introduce myself, Herman Schaefer, the premier batsman of the world. No pitcher can throw the ball hard enough to throw it past me. I will now hit a home run to demonstrate my marvelous skill."

White Sox pitcher Doc White was enraged and did exactly what Schaefer guessed he would; he threw a fastball down the middle of the plate. Schaefer of course hit a home run, but the thrills were not over. He slid into each base as he circled them on his home run. It was the only home run he hit that season (apparently 1907).

Camera Day See *Photography*

Roy Campanella (1921–1993)

Hall of Fame 1969

"To be good, you've gotta have a lot of little boy in you. When you see Willie Mays and Ted Williams jumping and hopping around the bases after hitting a home run, and the kissing and hugging that goes on at home plate, you realize they have to be little boys."—The full text of Campanella's signature line.

Campanella starred as the Brooklyn Dodgers catcher from 1948 through 1957 before a car accident left him a quadriplegic.

Roy (NMI) Campanella was the child of a black mother and Italian father who grew up in Philadelphia. He played American Legion ball and then signed with the Baltimore Elite Giants of the Negro National League at age 15. By 1938 at age 17 he was playing full-time with the team, having played only on weekends while still in school. In 1939 he became the first-string catcher for the club.

Campanella played in the Mexican League in 1942 and 1943 and then returned to the Elite Giants through 1945. He signed with the Dodgers after the season and played in Organized Baseball for the first time in 1946 with Nashua, a New Hampshire Class B Eastern League team affiliated with the Dodgers.

He moved up to the Class AAA Montreal Royals in 1947. He was more than ready for the Major Leagues in early 1948, but Branch Rickey wanted him to integrate the American Association first. He made it to Brooklyn at age 26 in mid–1948, batting .258 in 83 games. Over his nine full Major League seasons he hit over .300 three times, hit more than 30 home runs four times and drove in over 100 runs three times. His best season was 1953 when he hit .312 with 41 home runs and 142 RBIs. He was named National League MVP in 1951, 1953 and 1955.

He was preparing to move with the club to Los Angeles for the 1958 season, but his career (and almost his life) ended when his car skidded on an icy street in Harlem over the winter. He was paralyzed from the neck down and endured years of therapy. He became a goodwill ambassador for the Dodgers and lived far longer than the typical quadriplegic.

Books. Roy Campanella, *It's Good to Be Alive* (1959); Gene Schoor, *Roy Campanella* (1959); Milton Shapiro, *The Roy Campanella Story* (1958).

Canada

"Bunting is a very Canadian thing to do: obedient, modest, self-effacing.... As a baseball tactic, it practically screams out, 'Excuse me.'"—Alison Gordon in *Sports Illustrated*.

"I talked to Canada yesterday."—Giants second baseman Jeff Kent during the 2002 World Series, declining a pregame interview with a Canadian sports network.

Early Canadian Baseball.

"Baseball having been so well established in Canada at that time [1872], it would seem that Canada ought to have had a professional league long ago. Perhaps the decisive defeats were discouraging."—Jacob Morse in *Sphere and Ash* (1888), noting that the Boston club had toured Canada and defeated local clubs 68–0, 52–4, 64–1 and 63–3.

One source reported that the first recorded baseball game in Canada was an 1838 game in Beachville, Ontario. This came to light 50 years later in a letter from a doctor to *Sporting Life* magazine in 1888. Sounds suspiciously like the Cooperstown/Doubleday letter that allegedly explained the *Origins of Baseball*.

Canada has had minor league baseball since the earliest days of Organized Baseball. The first formal minor league was the 1877 *International League*, which had clubs in Canada.

Attempted Restriction. In 1894 a U.S. Immigration Inspector asked the Treasury Department if baseball is a "recognized profession" in order to determine if Buffalo has violated the alien contract labor law by signing two Canadians. Before he received a reply, Buffalo decided to play only Americans.

George Sleeman.

"Arguably, the father of Canadian baseball."—Canadian baseball historian Bill Humber.

Sleeman was inducted into the Canadian Baseball Hall of Fame after pioneering teams and leagues in the 1860s and 1870s. He was also the owner of a large brewery. He managed the Guelph (Ontario) Maple Leafs, one of Canada's first teams to employ professional players in the 1870s. He founded Canada's first baseball league, the 1876 Canadian Association of Base Ball Players. He was also Guelph's mayor three times before passing away in 1926.

First Canadian Major Leaguers. The first Canadian Major Leaguers appeared in 1879.

First Round Draft Pick. In June 1997 Stetson University shortstop Kevin Nicholson, the MVP of the Cape Code League in 1996, was drafted No. 27 by the Padres. A native of Surrey, British Columbia, he was the first Canadian ever drafted in the first round.

Amateurs. The Canadian Amateur Baseball Association was founded in 1893.

Hall of Fame. The Canadian Baseball Hall of Fame and Museum was located in Toronto until 1995, when it was moved to St. Mary's, Ontario. In 1987 two boys broke into the Hall and stole two balls, which they threw into Lake Ontario when they were about to be caught. The balls had been signed by Babe Ruth and the entire 1925 Cleveland Indians.

The 2004 inductees were Andre Dawson (Expos star, but not a Canadian) and long-time umpire Jim McKean, a Canadian. On the ballot for 2005 were Pete Rose and Ted Giannoulas, the "famous chicken" mascot.

Players.

"Who lumbers like a goalie and talks like a waiter and looks like a slacker and pitches like the devil?"—Bill Plaschke of the *Los Angeles Times* on Dodger reliever Eric Gagne. When Gagne was recruited by Oklahoma's Seminole State (junior) College, he didn't speak a word of English. In 2003 he received his second consecutive Tip O'Neill Award as the best Canadian player in the Major Leagues.

Of the over 160 Canadian players who have made it to the Major Leagues, the most prominent are Hall of Famer Ferguson Jenkins, Jeff Heath, George Selkirk, Jack Graney, Claude Raymond, Terry Puhl, John Hiller, Dick Fowler, Reggie Cleveland and Larry Walker.

More recent players have included Corey Koskie, Rheal Cormier, Jason Dickson, Michael Johnson, Paul Quantrill, Paul Spoljaric, Jeff Zimmerman, Matt Stairs and David Wainhouse.

Dennis Boucher of Quebec was drafted by the Blue Jays, but made his first appearance in the Major Leagues with the Expos on September 6, 1993. It was the first time that a native Canadian res-

ident had appeared on a Major League team since Claude Raymond with the Expos in 1971. Soon after Boucher arrived, Joe Siddall of Ontario, Canada, made the club as Boucher's catcher and the two combined to become the first all–Canadian battery in Major League history.

Opposing Pitchers. On September 7, 1999, Canadians Eric Gagne (of Quebec) of the Dodgers and Ryan Dempster (British Columbia) of the Marlins were the starters, but neither got a decision in the Marlins' 2–1 win.

On July 1, 2000, Canada's 133rd birthday, Florida's Ryan Dempster (Edmonton, Alberta) and Montreal's Mike Johnson (Sechelt, British Columbia) faced each other as the starters that day.

First Major League Home Run in Canada. Mack Jones of the Expos hit 22 home runs for the club in its inaugural season in 1969. On April 14 that year he became the first Major League player to hit a home run in Canada.

First Regular Season Game/Expos v. Blue Jays. Interleague play in 1997 allowed the two Canadian teams to play each other in the regular season. On June 30, 1997, the Expos beat the Blue Jays 2–1 at the Toronto Skydome. Pedro Martinez allowed three hits, including a solo shot by Carlos Delgado, and struck out 10. The Expos won the next game of the three-game series, beating Roger Clemens. The Blue Jays salvaged the third game with a 7–6 win.

Most by Canadian. Larry Walker set a record in 1995 with the most home runs (36) by a native Canadian. He broke the record of 27 set by Jeff Heath of the 1947 Browns.

Language Barrier.

"I just look stupid, shrug my shoulders and laugh a lot. They figure it out; then they start speaking English."—Expos first baseman Randy Milligan on encountering Quebec's French-speaking natives.

New League. In 2003 former Major League pitcher Ferguson Jenkins threw out the first pitch of the Canadian Baseball League and had a three-year contract to serve as the league's first commissioner. The league started with a 72-game season.

Prank. In mid–2003 commissioner Bud Selig was duped into a 12-minute phone call with a Canadian comedian named Marc-Antoine Audette, who posed as Canadian Prime Minister Jean Chretien. The purpose of the call was to inquire about the fate of the Expos. Selig said that saving them was "mission impossible" and that the actions of the former owners was "appalling." The conversation was played on Montreal radio.

Grudge. In 1995 Dodger broadcaster Rick Monday was detained at Canadian customs. When asked by the customs agent if he knew why he was being detained, Monday responded correctly that it was because of his 1981 9th inning home run that clinched the NLCS for the Dodgers over the Expos.

Books. John Bell (ed.), *The Grand Slam Book of Canadian Baseball Writing* (1994); William Humber, *Diamonds of the North: A Concise History of Baseball in Canada* (1995); William Humber and John St. James (eds.), *All I Thought About Was Baseball: Writings on a Canadian Pastime* (1996); Jim Shearson, *Canada's Baseball Legends* (1994); Don Turner, *Heroes, Bums and Ordinary Men: Profiles in Canadian Baseball* (1988).

Cancelled Games See *Postponed Games*

Candlestick Park (1960–1999)

"Don't blame the architect. After all, it's his first ballpark."—Herb Caen in the *San Francisco Chronicle*.

"How Not to Build a Ballpark" — Title of an August 1961 *Harper's* magazine article.

"It don't bother Willie Mays." — Mets manager Casey Stengel when asked in 1963 why his Mets were having so much trouble fielding in Candlestick Park.

"Sitting in the dugout is like sitting in the bottom of a toilet. All that tissue blows in, and no one flushes it." — Whitey Herzog.

"You know it's summertime at Candlestick when the fog rolls in, the wind kicks up, and you see the center fielder slicing open a caribou to survive the 9th inning." — Bob Sarlette.

Candlestick Park was built at a cost of $15 million by contractor Charles Harney, who also sold the land to the county. It was the only stadium up to that time that was built completely of reinforced concrete.

First Win. Sad Sam Jones pitched the Giants to a 3–1 win on April 12, 1960, the club's first game in Candlestick Park.

Dimensions. Candlestick's dimensions from left to right field originally were 330–397–420–397–330. The dimensions created too many left field fly ball outs because of the prevailing wind. The center field backdrop made it difficult for batters to see pitched balls. These impediments resulted in only 80 home runs by both the home team and the visitors in 1960, a National League ballpark low that year. The following season the club moved the left field fence in 10 feet and installed a 40-foot green backdrop. The Giants responded with 174 home runs, led by Orlando Cepeda with 46 and Willie Mays with 40.

Capacity. The original capacity was 43,000, but in 1971 Candlestick's seating was increased to 58,000 to accommodate the NFL's 49ers, who moved from Kezar Stadium. It was increased again to its final capacity of 62,000.

Weather Problems.

"Never mind the coffee, get a priest." — Broadcaster Joe Garagiola commenting on the cold weather and its effect on the Giants' outdoor radio booth.

The wind at Candlestick was notorious. Willie McCovey once hit a pop fly to the vicinity of the second baseman that got caught in the jet stream and went for a grand slam. Game time was moved from 1:30 p.m. to 1 p.m. in an attempt to avoid some of the wind that arrived by 2 p.m.

The "King of Torts," San Francisco attorney Melvin Belli, once filed a lawsuit seeking recovery of his 1961 season ticket money based on alleged misrepresentations as to the "comforts" of the new ballpark. One of his witnesses at trial was an Abercrombie and Fitch salesman who testified on outfitting arctic groups with cold weather gear.

When Candlestick Park was enclosed in 1971 to accommodate the 49ers, the architect's series of baffles behind the upper deck's seats were designed to diminish the effect of the wind. They did not work.

The original stadium clock had a second hand that often could not move past the one-half hour mark because of the force of the wind. When it hit that point it would shoot backward.

Limerick. In 1999 website SFGate held a contest for the best limerick memorializing recently abandoned Candlestick Park. The winning entry referenced the *Croiz de Candlestick*, which was handed out to fans who stayed through extra innings and freezing weather:

"The boy's look he mistook for awe,
He was frozen, his face would not thaw.
'We'll wait for Mike Ivie,'
My dad said beside me,
'Then you can sleep in the heat with your "Croix.'"'
— Nels Johnson, titled "Bottom of the 12th, 1978."

Surface. Candlestick had natural turf until 1971, when *Artificial Turf* was installed to accommodate the football 49ers. The infield remained dirt until the following season, when the dirt was covered over with artificial turf except at the bases. Natural turf was restored for the 1979 season (erroneously 1980 in some sources).

Original Name. The ballpark is named for the tall trees and jagged rocks in a nearby area known as Candlestick Point (the site of the parking lot). It was also known as "The Stick."

1995 Name Change.

"Believe us, locals are not pleased with the new name [3Com Park]. One native said it was like selling the Golden Gate Bridge to a hamburger chain and renaming it 'McDonald's Golden Arches Bridge.'" — Dan Shaughnessy in the *Boston Globe*.

"Mayor Frank Jordan of San Francisco blithely declared 'the city can take great pride' in the name 3Com Park. Right. And Telegraph Hill can be renamed after a garbage-bag company." — George Vecsey in the *New York Times*.

In mid-1995 the city of San Francisco, the 49ers and 3Com Corporation announced that the new name of the park would be 3Com Park. The corporation was located in nearby Santa Clara and was a leading computer data networking company with annual sales of $1.3 billion. The city had been seeking a corporate sponsor to offset the $35 million in improvements needed before Super Bowl XXXIII. However, it was reported that 3Com paid only $500,000 for the honor.

Last Game. The last game was played September 30, 1999, as Juan Marichal threw out the first pitch and three members of The Grateful Dead sang the National Anthem. Dusty Baker and four previous managers — Bill Rigney, Herman Franks, Charlie Fox and Roger Craig — delivered the line-up card. After an 8–4 Dodger win, the Giants introduced over 60 players from the San Francisco era (each going to his position in the field), capped with Willie Mays emerging from behind the centerfield wall. He threw one last pitch on the mound to his godson, Barry Bonds, a helicopter rented from the Highway Patrol carried away home plate, and the crowd watched on the scoreboard as it was installed at the new ballpark.

The Giants recorded their last out at Candlestick Park at 4:35 p.m., the same minute as their last out at the Polo Grounds.

New Ballpark. See *San Francisco Giants — Ballparks*.

Candy

"If I played in New York, they'd name a candy bar after me." — Reggie Jackson before he began playing in New York. Jackson's Reggie Bar was marketed in response to the three home runs that he hit for the Yankees during Game 6 of the 1977 World Series against the Dodgers. At the first home game of 1978, on April 13, the Yankees passed out 72,000 of the bars as a promotional item. When Jackson immediately homered off pitcher Wilbur Wood, fans stood and cheered for a full five minutes, showering the field with the candy and covering much of the grass in the outfield. Bob Lemon said that there were "people starving all over the world and there are 30 billion calories lying on the field." It was such a big moment that the *New York Times* did a feature on the story 20 years later.

"When you unwrap one, it tells you how good it is." — Catfish Hunter on the Reggie Bar.

"It's the only candy bar that tastes like a hot dog." — Columnist Dave Anderson on the Reggie Bar, a 25-cent concoction of chocolate, peanuts and corn syrup wrapped in a square, with a picture of Jackson in mid-swing.

"For years I heard 'eat another pizza,' or 'eat another burger.'"

Now I yell back, 'eat another candy bar.'" — Rotund Tiger first baseman Cecil Fielder on his new candy bar.

"Brooks [Robinson] never asked anyone to name a candy bar after him. In Baltimore, people named their children after him." — Gordon Beard.

"I don't make these things up, I just sign the papers." — Chipper Jones on the new "Chocolate Chipper" named after him, although he said he didn't like chocolate. It was a blended milk chocolate with crisped rice (sounds like a Nestlé's Crunch bar in disguise). Chipper's response upon sampling the delicacy: "Wow. I expected it to be good, but it exceeded my expectations."

"Charlie See, Frank Hershey, Sugar Cain, Taffy Wright, Les Sweetland, Candy Maldonado, Candy LaChance, Buttercup Dickerson, Ralph Glaze"

See also *Endorsements* and *Gum*.

Cap Anson. Anson may have been the first ballplayer to have had a candy named after him.

Ty Cobb. Cobb had a short-lived endorsement contract with the Benjamin Candy Company.

Babe Ruth. "Babe Ruth Home Run Candy" was marketed in the 1920s. However, the owner of the competing Baby Ruth candy bar — named after President Cleveland's infant daughter, Ruth, the first child born in the White House — appealed to the federal trademark office on an infringement claim. The office held that there was infringement and Babe Ruth's Home Run Candy was out of business. In 1995 the makers of Baby Ruth bars for the first time used Babe Ruth's likeness as a tie-in to their product.

Mantle and Maris. Sales of M & M candies skyrocketed during the 1961 season because Roger Maris and Mickey Mantle, known as the M & M boys, were on a home run tear. Nevertheless, no endorsement deal was cut between the company and the two players.

Ken Griffey, Jr. The Seattle area was inundated with the Ken Griffey, Jr., candy bar during his rookie season in 1989.

Kirby Puckett. In 1994 Puckett endorsed his own "Kirby Puckett Bar — A Bundle of Energy."

Albert Belle. In 1995 Malley's Chocolates introduced a chocolate crunch candy bar named after the Indians slugger. Belle failed to show at the news conference announcing the new candy. He said he had not slept well.

Ejection. On May 12, 1995, Expos manager Felipe Alou was ejected from the game on his birthday. Montreal fans, in the tradition of their hockey team, the Canadiens, had begun tossing "Oh Henry!" candy bars on the field whenever popular slugger Henry Rodriguez got a big hit. Alou was ejected after arguing with Harry Wendelstedt over the umpire's decision to stop play after an excessive amount of candy was thrown on the field.

Fading Pastime.

"Now the only food at Yankee Stadium with a surprise inside are the hot dogs." — Alex Kaseberg in May 2004, after the Yankees switched from Cracker Jack to Crunch 'n Munch as its caramel popcorn. The move was made in part because Cracker Jack switched from boxes to bags, prompting this comment from Tom FitzGerald of the *San Francisco Chronicle*: "That's baseball for you. Penalize somebody for thinking outside the box."

After fans complained (another "public outcry"?), three weeks later the snack returned, in part because, as one vendor said, "Crunch 'n Munch doesn't have a prize."

By 1997 only 23 stadiums offered Cracker Jack.

Caps

"I'm just happy to be here. I'll take whatever they give me. If they took off my hat and shit in it, I'd put it right back on my head and say thanks." — Jerry Stephenson of the Pilots.

"How do I know? I'm not in shape yet." — Yogi Berra when asked his cap size by former pitcher Lefty Gomez during spring training. Gomez supposedly was a measurer for a sporting goods company.

"If he'd just tip his cap once, he could be elected mayor of Boston in five minutes." — Eddie Collins on Ted Williams, whose feud with the Boston media caused him never to tip his cap to the fans after the first few years of his career.

"That was silly, because generally the Boston fan was so great." — Ted Williams, then in his 80s, on his failure to doff his cap in appreciation of the fans.

"They had all season to see me play." — Injured Blue Jays second baseman Roberto Alomar, refusing to come out of the dugout and tip his cap to the fans during the last game of the season.

19th Century. The advent of the glove ended the practice of catching balls in caps to avoid further punishment to raw hands. According to some sources, Albert Spalding's proficiency with his cap led to formal abolition of the practice. Caps in the 19th century were flannel or "merino" (soft wool or soft wool and cotton) and sold for 60 cents.

Albert Spalding created a different colored cap for each position, resembling, according to the *Chicago Tribune*, "a Dutch bed of Tulips." The colors were designed to enable fans to determine the player's position, but the color-coding was quickly abandoned.

Caps in the 1870s National Association were tams or beanie-style hats. Some clubs wore small derbies. The Chicago White Stockings featured the cake box or pillbox hat.

In 1976 many Major League clubs wore the pillbox style caps to commemorate the league's 100th anniversary. Every club except the Pirates returned to the regular style the following season. The Pirates wore the style from 1976 through 1985.

20th Century. The turn of the century brought a new style of cap, which was similar to modern caps except the bills were somewhat shorter. About this time clubs began to put their cities' initials on their caps. The bills were longer by the 1930s.

Poor Judgment. In *The Bill James Historical Baseball Abstract* (1988), James related a story told to him by Milt Litvin: A's first baseman Gene Hasson once ran after an errant throw by a third baseman, but stopped to pick up his cap while the ball was still in play. According to Litvin, Hasson was sent down to the minors the next day because of his breach of on-field etiquette.

Psychologist. The 1972 Reds changed the underside of their cap bills from green to gray after a club official read a study of the effects of these colors and light on humans. The study was prepared by Dr. John Nash and was entitled "Health and Light." The gray supposedly had a positive emotional effect on the players.

Two-Toned. The Red Sox switched to two-toned caps in the 1970s. Pitcher Bill Lee registered his disdain by attaching a propeller to his first time he took the field wearing the new cap.

Extra Large. Catcher Bruce Bochy was known for the size of his head — a huge size 8. He always had to bring his helmet with him when he was traded because equipment managers had difficulty finding a helmet large enough to fit him. After once hitting a game-winning home run his teammates set out a red carpet to his locker and put ice and a six-pack of beer *inside* his helmet.

Tribute. On June 28, 1997, Yankees pitcher David Wells started the game wearing Babe Ruth's autographed cap from the 1934 season. Manager Joe Torre forced him to change caps after the 1st inning, because it did not conform to team uniform rules. Without the cap, Wells blew a 3–0 lead and the Indians won 12–8.

Captains See *Team Captains*

Harry Caray (1923–1998)

Hall of Fame (Frick Award) 1989

"Booze, broads and bullshit. If you got all that, what else do you need?"—Caray.

"I'm reduced to drinking O'Doul's. Can you imagine Harry Caray unable to drink a martini! Without a cold Budweiser? It's not me."—Caray in 1994 after being forced to cut out alcohol due to an irregular heartbeat.

"I'd rather be miserable and alive than happy and dead."—Caray on why he followed his doctor's orders to quit drinking.

"One is tempted to call Harry Caray a throwback, but a throwback to *what*? He's unique. He charges through his professional and personal lives with the throttle wide open. He's a ham. He's colorful, controversial, complicated, compulsive, impulsive, flamboyant, opinionated and outspoken."—Bob Rubin in *Inside Sports*.

"Stein Renburg"—Caray's butchering of Ryne Sandberg's name.

"Hello again, everybody. It's a bee-yooo-tiful day for baseball."—Caray.

Caray was a Major League broadcaster from 1945 through the late 1990s.

Orphaned at 10, Harry Carabina started his Major League broadcast career in 1945 in St. Louis for the Cardinals. He was the voice of the Cardinals through their purchase in 1953 by August Busch and the Budweiser Brewery and lasted 25 years with the club. He teamed with Joe Garagiola for the catcher's first broadcast job.

In November 1968 Caray was struck by a car and seriously injured, but recovered in time to broadcast the 1969 season for the Cardinals. He was fired at the end of the season. He spent a year with the A's in 1970 before being fired and moving on to the White Sox for 11 years through 1981. He hooked up with the Cubs in 1982, where he remained until his death.

Caray suffered a stroke in 1986 but recovered to continue his career. He collapsed in June 1994 from heat exhaustion, but recovered to broadcast a few games before the August strike. He was believed to be in his mid–70s at the time. He continued to broadcast a partial schedule in the mid–1990s, and continued to sing his trademark "Take Me Out to the Ball Game." In 1989 Caray received the Ford C. Frick Award and two years later he broadcast a game with his son Skip of the Braves and grandson Chip, also a Major League broadcaster (see also *Broadcasters*).

Book. Harry Caray and Bob Verdi, *Holy Cow!* (1989).

Career Year

"Baseball is like this. Have one good year and you can fool them for five more, because for five more years they expect you to have another good year."—Frankie Frisch.

A clinical study by Professor Harvey C. Lehman of Ohio University was titled, "The Most Proficient Years at Sports and Games." He concluded that baseball pitchers peak at age 27 and the peak lasts 4.39 years. Non-pitchers peak at 28 and it lasts 4.04 years. All athletes were determined to peak between the ages of 27 and 29.

Rod Carew (1945–)

Hall of Fame 1991

"Watching Rod Carew bat is like watching Bulova make a watch, DeBeers cut a diamond…. Rod Carew doesn't make hits, he composes them."—Jim Murray.

"There is a special sensation in getting good wood on the ball and driving a double down the left field line as the crowd in the ballpark rises to its feet and cheers. But I also remember how much fun I had as a skinny barefoot kid hitting a tennis ball with a broomstick on a quiet, dusty street in Panama."—Carew.

Carew was an infielder for the Twins and Angels from 1967 through 1985.

Rodney Carew was born in Panama on a train and moved to New York at age 17. He signed with the Twins out of high school in 1964 and began his professional career with the Melbourne and Orlando clubs in Florida. He made it to the Twins as a second baseman in 1967, hitting .292 in 137 games and was named Rookie of the Year. He remained at second base for the Twins until 1975, when he switched over to first base after winning his fourth straight batting title. The move was made in part because of a serious knee injury he suffered in 1970.

After two more batting titles in 1977 and 1978 he was traded to the Angels after announcing that he would become a free agent. He hit .305 or better for the Angels in each of the next five seasons before dropping below .300 for the first time since 1968. His career ended when he was cut by the club in the spring of 1986.

Carew batted .328 with 3,053 hits over 19 seasons for the Twins and Angels. He led the American League in batting six times, including a .388 average in 1977 when he was the league's MVP. He hit .300 or better 15 straight times and stole 353 bases, including seven steals of home in 1969.

Carew later became a batting instructor for the Angels and endured a highly public battle for his daughter Michelle's life. She was stricken with leukemia in 1995 and died in April 1996. In 2004 Carew joined the Twins front office in public relations.

Book. Rod Carew and Ira Berkow, *Carew* (1979).

Max Carey (1890–1976)

Hall of Fame (VC) 1961

"I know if I can get the proper start, the greatest catcher who ever lived cannot prevent me from stealing second. All my attention is centered rather on the pitcher. He is the man I have to outwit and if I can do so, the catcher doesn't count in my calculations."—Carey.

Carey was the premier National League center fielder primarily for the Pirates from 1910 through 1929.

Carey was born Maximilian Carnarius and supposedly used Carey in his early professional days to protect his college eligibility. Other sources report that he gave up divinity school for baseball when he ran out of money, but apparently he graduated in 1909 from Concordia College.

Carey played for the Pirates from 1910 through most of 1926, hitting over .300 seven times. He was considered the finest National League base stealer of the early 20th century. He led the league in stolen bases 10 times, finishing his 20-year career with 738 steals. He was also the best center fielder of his era and his lifetime 339 assists are a National League record.

He was traded to the Dodgers in late 1926 after an internal dispute among the Pirate players. He faded after that, finishing his playing career in 1929. He was a lifetime .285 hitter who excelled at getting on base, and also had 159 triples.

Carey managed the Dodgers in 1932 and 1933, finishing third and sixth, before scouting and managing in the minor leagues until 1956.

Caribbean Series

"The group also decided to cap off their own seasons with a tournament among the champions of each country's winter league. To make the competition even stiffer, the countries agreed that each team could bring along five reinforcements from the rosters of the defeated teams in their league. Since the North American Major Leagues considered their own championship to be the World Series, the founders of this new tourney had to qualify it by calling it the *Caribbean* World Series."— Michael M. Oleksak and Mary Adams Oleksak in *Beisbol* (1991).

See also **Latin Ballplayers**.

Origins. This Latin American World Series was first staged in 1949 among Cuba, Puerto Rico, Panama and Venezuela. Cuba was a regular participant until Castro took control in the early 1960s. It is now held as a winter event among various Latin American countries.

Pan-American Series. In 1958 Nicaragua, Colombia and Mexico staged the first and only Pan-American Series, in Nicaragua. These countries were unable to participate in the Caribbean Series, held among Cuba, Panama, Venezuela and Puerto Rico. Marv Throneberry starred for the Nicaraguans, but Mexico won the round-robin series.

Steve Carlton (1944–)

Hall of Fame 1994

"When Steve and I die, we are going to be buried in the same cemetery, 60'6" apart."— Batterymate Tim McCarver.

Carlton was a left-handed Major League pitcher from 1965 through 1988 who recorded 329 career wins.

Steven Norman Carlton signed with the Cardinals for $5,000 and began his professional career in 1964 with Rock Hill, South Carolina. Between stints in Winnipeg and Tulsa he made it to the Cardinals for 15 games in 1965 and nine in 1966. He stuck for good in 1967, winning 14 games. He won 20 games for the first time in 1971, but was traded to the Phillies for the 1972 season after the second of two acrimonious salary disputes.

In 1972 the Phillies were pitiful, but Carlton, known as "Lefty," was amazing. He won 27 games, had an ERA of 1.97, and struck out 310 batters while completing 30 games. He was a unanimous MVP and Cy Young Award winner, becoming the first winner on a last-place team.

Carlton slumped to 13–20 in 1973, but rebounded with four seasons of 20 or more wins over the next 12 years for the Phillies. He led them to the 1980 World Championship with 24 regular-season victories, winning a League Championship game and two World Series games en route.

In 1986 the Phillies sent him to the Giants after 16 appearances. He then bounced to various Major League clubs after that as his career was winding down. His last full season was 1987, when he was 6–14 for the Indians and Twins. He attempted one more season in 1988, but was cut after four appearances in which he posted a 16.76 ERA.

Carlton finished his 24-year career with a 329–244 record, ninth in career wins, and 4,136 strikeouts, second all-time. In 1969 he struck out a National League–record 19 Mets in a losing effort.

After his retirement the reclusive Carlton still would not talk to reporters, but opened up around the time of his induction into the Hall of Fame. He made a number of curious statements that indicated a strong tendency toward **Racism**.

Gary Carter (1954–)

Hall of Fame 2003

"The best in the business"—1983 *Sports Illustrated* cover.

"I also think that what Johnny [Bench] saw in me was the hustle of Pete Rose and similar desire and love of the game that he had, and that with that combination, he was saying this kid might be as good if not better than me and might make it to the Hall of Fame."— Carter's induction speech.

Carter played 19 seasons from 1974 to 1992, primarily as a catcher for the Expos and Mets.

Gary Edmund Carter ("The Kid"), a Southern California native, was drafted in the 3rd round by Montreal in 1972 and received a $35,000 bonus. He had been a shortstop and pitcher in high school, and an All-American football player who was rumored to be going to UCLA to play quarterback. The rumor was spread by Expos scout Bob Zuk.

By 1974 Carter had reached Class AAA Memphis of the International League. He was one of the top players in the league that year, batting .268 with 23 home runs and 83 RBIs.

Carter's first full season in Montreal was 1975. He batted .270 with 17 home runs and 68 RBIs, splitting time between catcher and right field. He would not land permanently at catcher until 1977, hitting .284 with 31 home runs. It would be the first of 11 straight years of steady production from Carter, which established him as the premier National League catcher of the era. In 1980 he hit 29 home runs with 101 RBIs while leading the league's catchers in fielding and winning his first Gold Glove.

In 1982 he hit .293 with 29 home runs and won his third consecutive Gold Glove. In 1983 he had a career high 37 doubles and led National League catchers in fielding. The following year, his last in Montreal, Carter led the league with 106 RBIs and hit a career high .294.

Carter moved via free agency to the Mets in 1985, and in 1986 the club won 108 games and the pennant. In the World Series against Boston, Carter batted .276 with nine RBIs and two home runs. His most crucial contribution was a Game 6 two-out single that touched off the Mets' famous rally that culminated with the infamous Wilson/Buckner ground ball and an improbable Mets win.

Carter spent five seasons with the Mets, followed by single seasons in Los Angeles, San Francisco and Montreal, closing out his career in 1992. He retired as the all time leader among catchers with 11,785 career putouts. He holds the National League mark for games played at the position with 2,056. He led National League catchers in putouts eight times and batted .262 with 324 home runs. He played in 11 All-Star Games and was the MVP twice.

Book. Ray Buck, *Gary Carter: The Kid* (1984).

Cartoons See *Comic Strips and Cartoons*

Alexander Joy Cartwright, Jr. (1820–1892)

Hall of Fame 1938

"*The Man Who Invented Baseball*"— Title of Harold Peterson's biography of Cartwright subtitled, *No, It Wasn't Abner Doubleday...* (1973).

Cartwright was a member of the 1840s New York Knicker-bockers and has been described as the "Johnny Appleseed" of 19th century baseball.

Cartwright's contribution to baseball in the mid–19th century was largely forgotten until 1938 when his journals were reviewed more closely. For the next 40 years he was considered a true *Father of Baseball* because of his contribution to the 1840s Knickerbocker club and the codification of the rules. Revisionist historians have downplayed Cartwright's contribution with the Knickerbockers (see also *Origins of Baseball*). He was certainly involved, but recent historians have merely included him among a few others in developing more standardized rules and memorializing games in scorebooks. Nevertheless, his efforts are symbolic of the work of those connected with the club.

Born in 1820, "Alick" Cartwright was the descendant of British sea captains. He was big for his time, 6'2" (or 6'3") and 210 pounds, and played baseball with the Knickerbocker club in the mid–1840s. Focus seemed to fall on Cartwright because supposedly he was a surveyor and therefore seemingly more qualified to come up with the geometric lines of the playing field. In fact, he was a bank clerk and then book dealer.

Cartwright worked for the Union Bank of New York in 1845. Coincidentally, his boss was E.A. Ebbets, the father of future Brooklyn Dodgers owner Charles Ebbets. It is possible that E.A.'s brother, another Charles, played with the Knickerbockers in 1846. When the bank burned down at the end of 1845, Cartwright became a book dealer.

Just as the game was exploding in the New York area, on March 1, 1849, Cartwright left the city for good to head for the California gold rush. Traveling first by train and then covered wagon beyond St. Louis, Cartwright and his traveling companions demonstrated the game to Indians along the way. His diary notation of April 23, 1849, in Independence, Missouri, is illustrative of the 156-day trip: "During the past week we have passed the time in fixing wagon covers ... etc., varied by hunting and fishing and playing baseball. It is comical to see the mountain men and Indians playing the new game. I have the ball with me that we used back home."

Some sources report erroneously that his ultimate destination was China. He supposedly set off for China from California and arrived in Hawaii in 1850. After recovering from a violent bout of seasickness he decided to remain in Hawaii and never returned to the mainland. What may have happened is that Cartwright bought a mining enterprise in California, but soon contracted dysentery and was advised by his brother to join him in Hawaii to recover. Other accounts report that the settlers suffered dysentery on the trail, and lost most of their wagons and mules, were starving, and came under Indian attack. His brother, Alfred DeForest, wrote: "Alick arrived here on 10th August. They had what they had upon their backs, a cup and a spoon apiece left, his journal, the original rules of the Knickerbocker Base Ball Club, his rifle and ammunition, and that was all."

When Cartwright arrived, he saw no future in the mining operations and had heard of the Sandwich Islands (Hawaii). His brother apparently already was there and prospering. Another version has it that a friend of his brother enticed him to come to Hawaii, so he loaded a ship with retail goods and set sail.

Cartwright's plan was to depart Hawaii for China when he was well and then book passage back to New York. Another version had him returning around South America. He arrived in Honolulu on August 28, 1849, and decided to stay. He and his brother pooled their money, chartered a ship, and sent fruit and vegetables to San Francisco. He later became a representative for whaling ships.

Alexander Joy Cartwright, Jr., wearing his Honolulu fire chief's helmet and posing with his hailer. The photograph is in the Hawaii state archives.

He established the Masonic Lodge in Honolulu, the Chamber of Commerce and the Honolulu Library, among other institutions in the islands. He supposedly laid out the first diamond in the islands in 1852, at least according to Anne Cartwright, widow of Cartwright's great-grandson, William E. Cartwright (1913–1989).

Though he is credited with spreading baseball to Hawaii, the sport was played there before Cartwright arrived. In a famous photograph taken around 1870, Cartwright is shown in his uniform as the fire chief of Honolulu. Employing his banking background, he managed the finances of Hawaii's royal family. He died July 13, 1892, and is buried at Nuuanu in Honolulu. Babe Ruth laid a wreath at the site during a visit in the 1930s following a barnstorming trip to Japan.

Cartwright's diaries came to light when his grandson wrote to the commissioner's office in the mid–1930s attempting to clarify the origins of baseball. He had read about the plan to open a Hall of Fame in Cooperstown based on the activities of Abner Doubleday.

In 1996 the non-profit Alexander Joy Cartwright, Jr. Baseball Foundation, Inc., was founded and memorabilia collector Barry Halper was the organization's first president. It was established to preserve baseball's history, artifacts and related materials. Its goal was to establish a permanent museum somewhere near Hoboken, New Jersey, where the Knickerbockers and Cartwright played their early games.

"Casey at the Bat" (1888)

"Love has its sonnets galore; war has its epics in heroic verse; tragedy its sombre story in measured lines and baseball has its 'Casey at the Bat.'"—Albert Spalding.

Origins. This 19th century poem was written by Ernest Lawrence Thayer (1863–1940), an 1885 *magna cum laude* Harvard graduate and native of Worcester, Massachusetts. Thayer had been the editor of the school's *Harvard Lampoon* and some sources credit him erroneously with constructing the first catcher's mask (that was Harvard's *Fred* Thayer).

When George Hearst decided to run for senator from California in 1885, he bought the *San Francisco Examiner* to promote his political ambitions. He later gave the paper to his son, William Randolph Hearst, who had just graduated from Harvard College. While in college the younger Hearst had been editor of the *Harvard Lampoon*. When he went to California to edit the *Examiner*, he took along with him three members of the *Lampoon* staff; Eugene Lent, F. H. Briggs, and Ernest L. Thayer. Each had nicknames—Thayer's was "Phin." He wrote a humorous column on a regular basis for the *Examiner* and signed his columns with his nickname.

Thayer was not a career newspaperman, however. He traveled to Europe after graduation to avoid going into his father's wool milling business, but to no avail after his brief stint with the *Examiner*. He retired from the wool business in 1912 and spent his years in Santa Barbara, California, until his death in 1940. He always thought of the poem as "nonsense" and told one publisher, "All I ask is never to be reminded of it again."

The poem first appeared in print in the *San Francisco Daily Examiner*'s Sunday morning edition of June 3, 1888, under Thayer's byline, "Phin." It was subtitled "A Ballad of the Republic, Sung in the Year 1888."

Inspiration. A number of men have claimed to be the inspiration for Casey: John Cahill played primarily in the Pacific Coast League, but had a few years in the 1880s in the Major Leagues. He played for Stockton in the PCL, which he claimed was the original "Mudville." Support for his claim came from the fact that the players named in the poem actually played in the PCL in the 1880s.

The most widely promoted claim came from Dan Casey, who pitched primarily for Philadelphia in the National League in the 1880s. His claim surfaced in 1938 when a radio broadcaster let him tell his story. He supported his story by noting that the area around the Philadelphia ballpark was known as "Mudville." His facts were off, however, and his claim was discounted by those who checked into his statements. Nevertheless, he was awarded a lifetime pass to all Major League games.

Other sources report that the inspiration for "Casey" was a Worcester, Massachusetts, bully from Thayer's youth. The Mudville name reportedly came from a train station stop outside San Francisco, near where Thayer was working when he wrote the poem. Thayer himself later acknowledged that the name was inspired by a high school acquaintance who was not a ballplayer.

Some sources reported that Mike "King" Kelly was the inspira-

tion for the poem, though this probably arose when bastardized versions of the poem were published in the *Sporting Times* in 1888 using Kelly's name.

Author Controversy. Months went by during which several people laid claim to the poem. Finally, Thayer came forward, commenting that the "the poem's persistent vogue is unaccountable" and that the authorship claims "certainly filled me with disgust."

Because Thayer made little effort to identify himself with the poem, there was an ongoing debate for a number of years as to its author. At least eight of the 13 stanzas were claimed to be written by one George D'Vys in 1886, but research around 1900 by a Columbia University professor concluded that his claim was groundless.

Public Performances. The poem was first recited publicly by DeWolf Hopper at Wallack's Theatre in New York in May 1889 between acts of a play in which he was appearing. Some sources report erroneously that it was on May 13, 1888, or August 14, 1888. Hopper recited it after receiving a newspaper clipping given to him by novelist Archibald Gunter. An actor in the stage play *Prince Methusalem*, Hopper first performed it at one of his shows attended by members of the New York Giants and Chicago White Stockings. It became a classic and transformed Hopper's career because he became obligated to recite it at every theatre performance he gave.

He recited the poem at least 10,000 times and always did it in exactly 5 minutes 40 seconds. Hopper was later married to Hollywood gossip columnist Hedda Hopper. The poem was part of the inaugural program at Radio City Music Hall on December 27, 1932.

There have been at least 75 imitations of the original poem through opera, theatre, books and other poems. In many sequels Casey hits a home run off the same pitcher.

Book. Eugene C. Murdock, *Mighty Casey—All-American* (1984), a detailed chronology of Casey-related poems and historical minutiae; Jim Moore and Natalie Vermilyea, *Ernest Thayer's "Casey at the Bat": Background and Characters of Baseball's Most Famous Poem* (1994); Barry Moser, *Casey at the Bat Centennial Edition* (1994).

Movie Cartoon. The Disney full-length cartoon feature *Make Mine Music*, contained a nine-minute segment of "Casey at the Bat." Disney released a sequel in 1954 called "Casey Bats Again."

Nickname. The Class A Stockton Ports of the California League are owned by "Joy in Mudville Inc."

The Poem. The poem has appeared in many different forms, including an updated version that Thayer prepared himself around 1909. The following is exactly how it appeared in its newspaper debut (including the original punctuation):

Casey at the Bat

A Ballad of the Republic, Sung in the Year 1888

The outlook wasn't brilliant for the Mudville nine that day,
The score stood four to two with but one inning more to play;
And then when Cooney died at first and Barrows did the same,
A sickly silence fell upon the patrons of the game.
A straggling few got up to go in deep despair. The rest
Clung to that hope which springs eternal in the human breast;
They thought if only Casey could but get a whack at that—
We'd put up even money now with Casey at the bat.
But Flynn preceded Casey, as did also Jimmy Blake,
And the former was a lulu and the latter was a cake;
So upon that stricken multitude grim melancholy sat,

For there seemed but little chance of Casey's getting to the bat.
But Flynn let drive a single, to the wonderment of all,
And Blake, the much despised, tore the cover off the ball;
And when the dust had lifted, and the men saw what had occurred,
There was Jimmy safe at second and Flynn a-hugging third.
Then from 5,000 throats and more there rose a lusty yell,
It rumbled through the valley, it rattled in the dell;
It knocked upon the mountain and recoiled upon the flat,
For Casey, mighty Casey, was advancing to the bat.
There was ease in Casey's manner as he stepped into his place,
There was pride in Casey's bearing and a smile on Casey's face;
And when responding to the cheers, he lightly doffed his hat,
No stranger in the crowd could doubt 'twas Casey at the bat.
Ten thousand eyes were on him as he rubbed his hands with dirt,
Five thousand tongues applauded when he wiped them on his shirt;
Then while the writhing pitcher ground the ball into his hip,
Defiance gleamed in Casey's eye, a sneer curled Casey's lip.
And now the leather-covered sphere came hurtling through the air;
And Casey stood a-watching it in haughty grandeur there;
Close by the sturdy batsman the ball unheeded sped —
"That ain't my style," said Casey. "Strike one," the umpire said.
From the benches, black with people, there went up a muffled roar,
Like the beating of the storm-waves on a stern and distant shore;
"Kill him! Kill the umpire!" shouted some one on the stand,
And it's likely they'd have killed him had not Casey raised his hand.
With a smile of Christian charity great Casey's visage shone,
He stilled the rising tumult; he bade the game go on;
He signaled to the pitcher, and once more the spheroid flew,
But Casey still ignored it, and the umpire said, "Strike two."
"Fraud!" cried the maddened thousands, and echo answered fraud,
But one scornful look from Casey and the audience was awed;
They saw his face grow stern and cold, they saw his muscles strain,
And they knew that Casey wouldn't let that ball go by again.
The sneer is gone from Casey's lip, his teeth are clenched in hate,
He pounds with cruel violence his bat upon the plate;
And now the pitcher holds the ball, and now he lets it go,
And now the air is shattered by the force of Casey's blow.
Oh, somewhere in this favored land the sun is shining bright,
The band is playing somewhere, and somewhere hearts are light;
And somewhere men are laughing, and somewhere children shout,
But there is no joy in Mudville — mighty Casey has struck out.
—"Phin"

8th Inning. One source noted that because there was "but one inning to play," it suggests that the Mudville club was batting in the bottom of the 8th inning instead of the 9th.

Sequels. The following is a representative sample of the many sequels to the original that began to appear as early as 1895. It was later determined that this version was written by Grantland Rice using a pseudonym. This is supported by the fact that Rice included it in an anthology of his work in 1910, *Baseball Ballads*. A slightly modified version appeared in later anthologies. This is how the version appeared in *Baseball Ballads*:

Casey's Revenge
By James Wilson

There were saddened hearts in Mudville for a week or even more,
There were muttered oaths and curses — every fan in town was sore;
"Just think," said one, "how soft it looked with Casey at the bat,
And then to think he'd go and spring a bush league trick like that!"
All his past fame was forgotten — he was now a hopeless "shine,"

They called him "Strike-out Casey" from the mayor down the line;
And as he came to bat each day his bosom heaved a sigh,
While a look of hopeless fury shone in Casey's eye.
He pondered in the days gone by that he had been their king,
That when he strolled up to the plate they made the welkin ring;
But now his nerve had vanished for when he heard them hoot,
He "fanned" or "popped out" daily, like some minor league recruit.
He soon began to sulk and loaf — his batting eye went lame,
No home runs on the score card now were chalked against his name;
The fans without exception gave the manager no peace,
For one and all kept clamoring for Casey's quick release.
The lane is long, some one has said, that never turns again,
And Fate, though fickle, often gives another chance to men;
And Casey smiled — his rugged face no longer wore a frown —
The pitcher who had started all the trouble came to town.
All Mudville had assembled — ten thousand fans had come,
To see the twirler who had put big Casey on the bum;
And when he stepped into the box the multitude went wild,
He doffed his cap in proud disdain — but Casey only smiled.
"Play ball!" the umpire's voice rang out — and then the game began,
But in that throng of thousands there was not a single fan
Who thought that Mudville had a chance, and with the setting sun,
Their hopes sank low — the rival team was leading "four to one."
The last half of the ninth came round, with no change in the score,
But when the first man up hit safe, the crowd began to roar;
The din increased — the echo of ten thousand shouts was heard,
When the pitcher hit the second and gave "four balls" to the third.
Three men on base — nobody out — three runs to tie the game!
A triple meant the highest niche in Mudville's hall of fame;
But here the rally ended and the gloom was deep as night,
When the fourth one "fouled to catcher" and the fifth "flew out to right."
A dismal, groaning chorus came, a scowl was on each face,
When Casey walked up, bat in hand, and slowly took his place;
His bloodshot eyes in fury gleamed, his teeth were clenched in hate,
He gave his cap a vicious hook and pounded on the plate.
The pitcher smiled and cut one loose — across the plate it sped,
Another hiss, another groan, "Strike one!" the umpire said;
Zip! Like a shot the second curve broke just below the knee,
"Strike two!" the umpire roared aloud, but Casey made no plea.
No roasting for the umpire now — his was an easy lot,
But here the pitcher whirled again — was that a rifle shot?
A whack, a crack, and out through the space the leather pellet flew,
A blot against the distant sky, a speck against the blue.
Above the fence in center field in rapid whirling flight,
The sphere sailed on — the blot grew dim and then was lost to sight;
Ten thousand hats were thrown in air, ten thousand threw a fit,
But no one ever found the ball that mighty Casey hit.
O, somewhere in this favored land dark clouds may hide the sun,
And somewhere bands no longer play and children have no fun!
And somewhere over blighted lives there hangs a heavy pall,
But Mudville hearts are happy now, for Casey hit the ball.

Catchers

"A good catcher is the quarterback, the carburetor, the lead dog, the pulse taker, the traffic cop and sometimes a lot of unprintable things, but no team gets very far without one." — Yankee manager Miller Huggins.

"The infield is like a steel net held in the hands of the catcher. He is the psychologist and historian for the staff—or else his signals will give the opposition hits. The value of his headpiece is shown by the ironmongery worn to protect it."—Jacques Barzun in "From God's Country and Mine" (1954).

"There must be some reason why we're the only ones facing the wrong way."—Catcher Jeff Torborg.

"There are two requisites to being a catcher. You've got to be big and you've got to be dumb, and I qualify on both counts." —1960s Twins catcher Earl Battey, 6'1" and 220 pounds [though any ballplayer who uses "requisite" in a sentence must be smarter than he may be given credit].

"Pudge Rodriguez is my favorite catcher. He's built more like me than the others."—Yogi Berra in 2003.

See also *Catcher's Equipment*.

All-Time Greats.

"I got one that can throw, but can't catch, and one that can catch but can't throw; and one who can hit but can't do either."—Casey Stengel while managing the Mets; who for a time did have an aging Yogi Berra, who could still do all three relatively well.

"Two hundred million Americans, and there ain't two good catchers among 'em."—Casey Stengel.

Buck Ewing was considered the greatest catcher of the 19th century. He was captain of the New York Giants, batted a lifetime .303 and was elected to the Hall of Fame in 1939. Though his statistics are not incredible, contemporary observers always chose him as the greatest catcher of the era, if not the greatest player. Cap Anson might be the other choice for greatest everyday player of the era.

Johnny Kling of the Cubs was probably the best of the early 20th century.

Yankee manager Joe McCarthy said that Gabby Hartnett of the 1930s was "the perfect catcher."

Bill Dickey and Mickey Cochrane were considered by most as the greatest of the 1920s and 1930s.

Yogi Berra of the Yankees and Roy Campanella of the Dodgers were the preeminent catchers of the 1950s. Between them they won six MVP Awards.

Cubs iron man Randy Hundley was the class of the 1960s, prompting this comment from pitcher Ferguson Jenkins: "Having Hundley catch for you was like sitting down to a steak dinner with a steak knife. Without Hundley all you had was a fork."

Yogi Berra blocks the plate as Dodger catcher Al Walker heads home during a 1956 spring training game. Umpire Tom Gorman is in position to call the play.

Bill Freehan was the best American League catcher of the 1960s, playing for the Tigers from 1961 through 1976.

Johnny Bench was the star of the 1970s and possibly the greatest of all time. He won 10 straight Gold Glove Awards. The Orioles had scouted him and were exchanging scouting information with the Reds that year. The Reds used that information to draft him in the second round even though he had played only eight high school games.

Gary Carter was the best of the late 1970s and early 1980s.

Ivan Rodriguez was acknowledged as the best defensive catcher of the 1990s and early 2000s. He was also perhaps the best-hitting catcher in the American League for the Rangers (Mike Piazza in the National League), though his greatest heroics occurred in 2003 when he signed with the Marlins and was the NLCS MVP before leading the club to a victory in the World Series. He didn't re-sign with the Marlins, after few clubs expressed interest in him, and he considered playing in Japan in 2004. He ended up signing a $30 million, three-year deal with the last-place Tigers, who began 2004 remarkably well.

Backing Up Throws. Ray Schalk of the 1912–1928 White Sox is credited as the first catcher to back up infield throws to first base.

Balk By Catcher. See *Balks — Catcher's Balk*.

Barehanded Catch.

"But that Ernie Lombardi was something special. He wasn't just a hitter, he was a great catcher, too. Enormous hands; he could wrap his fingers completely around a baseball so that you couldn't see it. Twice I saw him do something I never saw another catcher do, or even try to do. Once it was with Vander Meer pitching, the other time I think it was Derringer. They threw balls outside that were going to be wild pitches. Lombardi couldn't get his glove across in time, so he just stuck out that big hand and plucked the ball right out of the air as easily as you'd pluck an apple off of a tree." — Billy Werber quoted in *Baseball Between the Lines*, by Donald Honig (1976).

Batting Leader.

"Most people don't understand catchers. For example, Jerry Grote is a catcher who hits. Johnny Bench is a hitter who catches. There is a big difference." — Catcher Joe Torre.

Johnny Bench was the first catcher to lead the Major Leagues in home runs and RBIs in the same season. He did it in 1970 with 45 home runs and 148 RBIs. He did it again in 1972 with 40 home runs and 125 RBIs. Mike Piazza has come closest to repeating the feat, with 40 home runs and 124 RBIs in 1997 to finish fourth in both categories.

Blocking the Plate. The rules specifically require that the catcher must have the ball in order to block the plate (Rule 7.06 B). Until 1940 or so the rule was enforced. However, today's catchers routinely block the plate without the ball, hoping that it gets there in time for a tag. Mike "King" Kelly is reported by some as the first catcher to throw his mask in the way of a runner.

Catcher's Box. In 1955 the catcher's box was reduced to 43 inches wide. The catchers complained because it restricted their movement. As a result, the rule was modified to allow catchers more flexibility in moving to catch inside and outside pitches. It was within the umpire's judgment to determine if the catcher was intentionally moving outside the new box. See also *Balks – Catcher's Balk*.

Errors. See *Errors*.

Most Games/Career. After being voted 1972 American League Rookie of the Year, Carlton Fisk went on to break the Major League record for most games played by a catcher. On June 22, 1993, catching for the White Sox, Fisk played in his 2,226th game as a catcher, breaking the record held by Bob Boone. Fisk played 22 seasons to reach the milestone, but was released shortly after breaking the record. He played in a total of 2,499 games.

After Fisk was dumped he swallowed his pride at the end of the season and returned to Comiskey Park to congratulate his teammates before they began the American League Championship Series. A security guard refused to allow him into the clubhouse, saying it was against Major League rules. Fisk stormed out and vowed never to return.

Most Games/Season. Frankie Hayes holds the American League record for most games caught in a season, playing in 155 games for the A's in 1944. Randy Hundley holds the Major League record, catching in 160 games (147 of them complete) in 1968 (and 152 in 1967). After 151 games caught in 1969, he dropped to a total of 82 games over the next two seasons.

Consecutive Games. During World War II, Ray Mueller caught 233 straight games for the Reds to set a Major League record.

Home Runs.

"I was thinking of making a comeback until I pulled a muscle — vacuuming." — Johnny Bench, on how he felt about Carlton Fisk breaking his record for career home runs by a catcher.

"Congratulations on breaking my record last night. I always thought the record would stand until it was broken." — Yogi Berra in a telegram to Johnny Bench after Bench broke Berra's record of 313 home runs by a catcher. Bench's record was broken by Carlton Fisk with 351. Fisk is also the only catcher in history to hit 100 home runs and steal 100 bases. He hit over 50 home runs after age 40. Mike Piazza had nine consecutive seasons with 30 or more home runs and on May 5, 2004 he broke Fisk's record before playing more frequently at first base.

Injuries/Early Mortality.

"Shaking hands with an old catcher is like shaking hands with a bag of peanuts." — Baseball adage attributed to many.

"A catcher and his body are like the outlaw and his horse. He's got to ride that nag till it drops." — Johnny Bench, whose body forced him to third base for the last few years of his career. Bench is a prime example of the wear and tear on catchers. He suffered a broken right ankle, six broken bones in his left foot, five broken bones in his right foot, a broken finger, cartilage tears in his left shoulder, a ruined elbow, ruined knees and back. He also underwent lung surgery in 1972. Though the surgery was unrelated to baseball, surgeons were forced to cut through his pectoral muscles and his power was reduced.

Catchers often did not catch every day in the 19th century, in part because they were more vulnerable to injury due to the lack of protective equipment.

Nineteenth-century catcher Silver Flint once was in a train wreck. When a physician saw his mangled fingers after the accident, he started to splint them until Flint supposedly told him that they got that way from catching for the Chicago White Stockings.

Innings Caught/Day. A's catcher Ossee Schreckengost caught all 28 innings of a doubleheader on July 4, 1905. In the second game, Rube Waddell and Cy Young each went the distance in a 20-inning marathon, won by Waddell and the A's 4–2.

Intimidation. Catcher Ossee Schreckengost soaked his mitt with water before catching Rube Waddell. The loud crack into the mitt supposedly intimidated hitters.

Left-Handed. See *Left-Handed — Catchers*.

MVP. Catchers who have won a league MVP Award (through 2004):

1934 Mickey Cochrane (Detroit Tigers)
1935 Gabby Hartnett (Chicago Cubs)

1938 Ernie Lombardi (Cincinnati Reds)
1951 Roy Campanella (Brooklyn Dodgers)
1951 Yogi Berra (New York Yankees)
1953 Roy Campanella (Brooklyn Dodgers)
1954 Yogi Berra (New York Yankees)
1955 Roy Campanella (Brooklyn Dodgers)
1955 Yogi Berra (New York Yankees)
1963 Elston Howard (New York Yankees)
1970 Johnny Bench (Cincinnati Reds)
1972 Johnny Bench (Cincinnati Reds)
1976 Thurman Munson (New York Yankees)
1999 Ivan Rodriguez (Texas Rangers)

No-Hitters/Perfect Games Caught. See *No-Hitters*.

Playing Close to Home Plate.

"Player after player went down before his unfaltering nerve, and although struck four times during the game — once squarely on the mouth by the ball and once on the chest and twice with the bat — he could not be driven away from his position." — Newspaper account of 1860s catcher Nat Hicks of the New York Mutuals when he began playing close behind the batter. Before that, catchers played farther back to catch the ball on one bounce, which could be recorded as an out on a foul tip.

F.R. Boerum is credited as the first catcher to move up behind the plate following an experimental ruling in 1859. Previously, catchers would stand approximately 15 feet behind the batter and catch the ball on one bounce. Jim "Deacon" White is credited as the first professional to play directly behind the plate in 1875. The practice was still rare until well into the early years of Major League Baseball in the 1880s. It did not become standard until the turn of the century unless men were on base (to throw out potential base stealers).

Two factors encouraged catchers to move up. Protective equipment made it safer and a rule change eliminated the catcher's ability to make a putout on a one-bounce foul tip. Catchers moved close behind the plate permanently in 1901 when the first two foul balls were ruled as strikes.

Yogi Berra played farther behind the hitter than the other prominent Yankee catcher of the 1950s and 1960s, Elston Howard. Because Howard could catch the ball before it dropped out of the strike zone, he was credited by the Yankee pitchers with getting more low strike calls.

Rookie of the Year.

1968 Johnny Bench (Cincinnati Reds)
1970 Thurman Munson (New York Yankees)
1971 Earl Williams (Atlanta Braves)
1972 Carlton Fisk (Boston Red Sox)
1987 Benito Santiago (San Diego Padres)
1990 Sandy Alomar, Jr. (Cleveland Indians)
1993 Mike Piazza (Los Angeles Dodgers)

Squat or Snap Throws.

"My catcher showed up and he must have been Old Man Moses. He was so old he didn't have to crouch." — Satchel Paige.

Buck Ewing is credited as the first catcher to throw from a crouch to second base (although one source referred to him as Buck "Williams"). This came to be known as the "snap" throw.

Catcher Jimmy Archer played in the National League from 1904 through 1918. Before he made it to the Major Leagues, his arm had been burned by hot tar in an industrial accident. In healing the muscles, they became shortened, giving him additional strength and leading to his trademark squat throw on stolen bases.

Benito Santiago of the Padres and Marlins is the modern catcher who most often employed the squat throw, although an analysis of his statistics reveals that he is not particularly effective against base runners attempting to steal.

Stolen Bases by Catcher. See *Stolen Bases* — Catcher.

Throwing Out Base Stealers.

"Every time [Johnny] Bench throws, everybody in baseball drools." — Long-time Orioles general manager Harry Dalton.

On August 23, 1909, Bill Bergen threw out six Cardinals (erroneously seven in older sources) and was considered one of the best defensive catchers of the era (though he couldn't hit, evidenced by his .139 average that season — lowest ever for a batting title qualifier).

In 1914 in one inning, Les Nunamaker of the Yankees threw out three Indians runners attempting to steal.

Branch Rickey's Major League catching career of 119 games beginning in 1905 was far from stellar. While playing for the Yankees on June 28, 1907, he allowed 13 stolen bases to the Senators.

Lou Brock said that Mets catcher Jerry Grote was the toughest for him to steal on, though most runners focus on the pitcher (see also *Stolen Bases*).

Mike Piazza, despite his hitting prowess, was considered only an average catcher. In June 2002, he broke a string of 51 consecutive runners who successfully stole on him; not counting one runner who was thrown out on a 1–3–6 play (started by a throw to first by Piazza on a pick-off). He has been as low as a 13% success rate in throwing out runners.

Good Career Move. According to one source, Roy Campanella became a catcher by accident. In ninth grade he was encouraged by a teacher to go out for the baseball team. He was sent to the gym for tryouts and the coach had placed circles on the floor designating certain positions. No one was standing in the catcher's circle, so Campanella took the spot.

Catcher's Equipment

"The Tools of Ignorance" — Catcher Muddy Ruel, circa 1920s, who was a practicing lawyer in the off-season. Ruel stepped in his catcher's mask in the bottom of the 12th inning of Game 7 of the 1924 World Series trying to catch a foul ball. He dropped the ball and the batter then doubled, starting a rally that ended with a ***Bad Hop*** single over third baseman Fred Lindstrom that drove in the winning run. Walter Johnson got the victory with four innings of relief.

"We used no mattress on our hands,
No cage upon our face;
We stood right up and caught the ball
With courage and with grace." — George Ellard, one of the organizers of the 1869 Cincinnati Red Stockings.

See *Umpires* — Equipment.

Batting Helmet. Johnny Bench is credited as the first catcher to wear a batting helmet to protect his head from foul balls and errant bat swings.

Catcher's Mask.

"There is a good deal of beastly humbug in contrivances to protect men from things that don't happen. There is about as much sense in putting a lightning rod on a catcher as a mask." — A 19th century sportswriter quoted in Harvey Frommer's *Primitive Baseball* (1988).

Invention. The first catcher's mask was developed in 1877 by Fred Winthrop Thayer, captain of the Harvard baseball team and later a prominent Boston attorney. He conceived the idea from a fencing mask. After commissioning a tinsmith to construct the mask, Thayer presented it to Harvard catcher James Tyng, who first wore it in a game. Thayer later obtained a patent on the design. Some sources identify him erroneously as the author of "Casey at the Bat," which was written by *Ernest* Thayer, also a Harvard man. In 1886 Thayer successfully sued Spalding Sporting Goods for infringement of his patented mask. In 1995 *Sports Illustrated* reported that the first to use Thayer's mask was Harry Thatcher, and that the mask is now in Barry Halper's **Memorabilia** collection.

Major League catcher Deacon White read about "The Man in the Iron Mask" (Tyng) and decided to try it. He did not like the fit because it was too clumsy. Instead, White had an iron worker make him a steel wire mask which he padded. He added an elastic band to hold it in place on his head.

White is also credited as the first catcher to see the value of a "target" for his pitchers. He used that target to help his brother Will win 43 games in 75 starting appearances in 1879. The large number of starts might have been tough on Will's arm, as he was 18–42 the next season.

Rule Change. The use of the catcher's mask was encouraged by the abolition of a rule that enabled catchers to make a putout on one bounce of a foul-tipped ball. The mask allowed catchers to move closer to the plate to catch foul tips on the fly.

Danger. Early catcher's masks were not particularly helpful at times because of the weak metal used in their construction: balls sometimes drove the metal into the catcher's face. Roger Bresnahan is credited erroneously by some as the first to add leather padding to the wire-framed catcher's mask in 1908, shortly after he wore shin guards for the first time.

Odd Invention. In 1904 James Bennett invented a cage to be worn by the catcher. The pitcher threw at the cage, which collapsed inward at impact. The ball would hit the padded chest of the catcher and drop through a hole into the catcher's hand. There is no evidence that anybody ever used it in a game.

Throat Guard. In 1977 Dodger catcher Steve Yeager began using the metal throat guard, or "turkey waddle," which attaches to the face mask. Other catchers began putting a hard metal wire down below the mask to cover the same area.

Tooth Protector. Before the catcher's mask, George Wright of Cincinnati Red Stockings fame had some success marketing a rubber mouth protector. He received a patent on the device, which was also worn by fielders, including Wright himself at shortstop. The device lost popularity as catcher's masks became more prevalent,

which generally coincided with the use of at least some types of fielding gloves. This made it less likely for a ball to get by a fielder and hit him in the mouth. When memorabilia from the 1869 Cincinnati Red Stockings was auctioned off in 1916, among the items was a rubber mouthpiece used by catcher Doug Allison.

Catcher's Mitt. See *Gloves—Catchers Mitts*.

Shin Guards.

"Roger Bresnahan makes an entrance, accompanied by a dresser who does him and undoes him in his natty mattress and knee pads."—*New York Times* article of September 24, 1908.

"Well, I'm a little weak on ground balls."— Young infielder to Casey Stengel at an early Mets tryout, on why he was wearing shin guards but not playing catcher.

Roger Bresnahan is credited by many with wearing the first shin guards in 1907 or 1908. The guards rode high up on the thighs and Bresnahan was criticized by some for providing a reminder of cricket guards. The version he wore was an updated design of a leather and fiber-filled model used by Hughie Ahearn of Baltimore around the same time. Pirates manager Fred Clarke complained about the new equipment and threatened to have his infielders wear them.

Another source credits early 20th century Negro League player Bill Monroe as the first catcher to wear shin guards, while still another credits Matty Fitzgerald of Albany, New York. Bud Fowler, one of the early black players and the first to play on a white team, is credited by some with inventing shin guards because of all the white players that kept sliding into him. He began taping pieces of wood to his legs to protect himself.

Red Dooin wore shin guards and an inside chest protector two years earlier than Bresnahan and admitted it only after Bresnahan did it openly. Dooin substituted paper mâché for rattan to make the guards lighter.

Negro League shortstop Pop Lloyd wore metal shin guards to avoid the spikes of sliding base runners.

Modern shin guards are made of plastic with thick extensions to shield feet and ankles from foul tips and wild pitches.

Chest Protector.

"But Berra was nervous. The Dodgers stole everything from him except his chest protector."— Sportswriter Arthur Daley about Yogi Berra's mediocre defensive performance against the Dodgers in the 1947 World Series.

"Made of the best rubber, inflated with air, light and pliable and do not interfere with the movements of the wearer under any conditions."— Advertisement for chest protectors in the 1901 Spalding catalog.

The first chest protector was sheepskin worn inside the catcher's jersey. Jack Clements is said to have used a chest protector as a left-handed catcher for the Philadelphia Keystones in the one-year Union Association in 1884. Charlie Bennett of the 1885 Detroit Wolverines secretly used a padded vest. When he was found out he created a sensation by having pitchers throw fastballs at his chest. Chest protectors in the 1890s were made of canvas with cotton batting inside.

The first outside chest protector was created in 1903 when Giants groundskeeper Henry Fabian made a homemade version with cotton stuffing. It was used by catcher Tom Moran on a Dallas minor league club. As it evolved, Fabian's basic design became air-filled.

Cubs catcher Clyde McCullough was so tough that he sometimes played without a chest protector during a 15-year career spanning the 1940s and early 1950s.

Chest protectors have become smaller over the years, as catchers have reduced the bulky protectors to allow for more mobility.

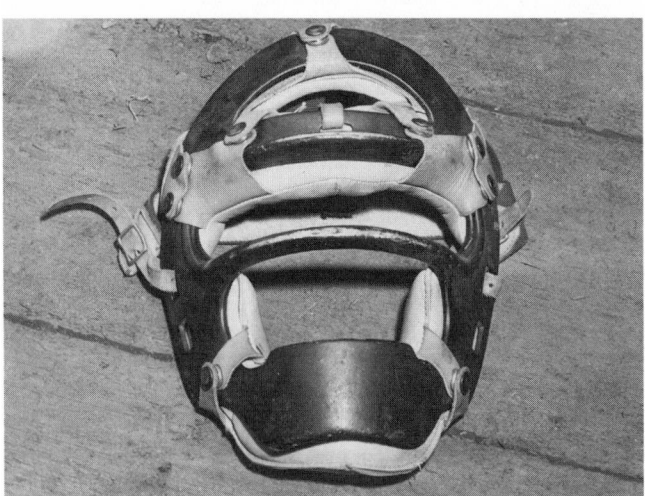

Catcher's mask of the vintage worn by Yogi Berra, circa 1957.

Weight. Modern catcher's equipment weighs between 8½ and 10 pounds. Like other position players in the early days (which continued well into the 20th century for outfielders), catchers often left some of their equipment on the field.

Catcher's Interference See *Interference*

Celebration

"They poured out of the stands like deranged lemmings, like the mob attacking the Bastille, like barbarians scaling the walls of ancient Rome, like maddened initiates in some Dionysian rite, driven, however, by pure joy, by ecstasies beyond hope of control. Their destructiveness was spontaneous, unreasoned, free of malice."—Leonard Koppett describing Mets fans at the moment their club won the Eastern Division title in 1969, in *The New York Mets—The Whole Story* (1970). The Mets clinched on a 6–0 shutout by Gary Gentry during the club's last home game of the season.

"Then, in a rush, came … the sprint for life (Met fans are not the most excited pennant locusts I have ever seen, but they are the quickest off the mark and the most thorough)…"—Roger Angell in *The Summer Game* (1972), describing the same celebration.

"What the hell are cops doing on the field? I've never seen cops on the field before. They ought to be back at the university where they belong."—Manager Ralph Houk, also describing the same time event, near the height of the Vietnam War protests on college campuses around the country.

The Mets clinched the 1969 Eastern Division crown on September 24. The fans held a three-hour impromptu celebration in Shea Stadium, stealing everything that was or was not nailed down. The flag, home plate, scoreboard parts and approximately 1,500 square feet of sod were carted away. Fans painted graffiti on the outfield fence and the usual four-hour clean-up job was expanded to four days.

See also *Alcoholism*.

No Raid. In 1959 after the White Sox locked up the pennant, Chicago mayor Richard Daley set off air raid sirens, scaring many people who thought the Russians were invading.

Sammy Sosa. At the conclusion of the homer-happy 1998 season, New York City honored Sosa in Washington Heights, home of tens of thousands of Dominican immigrants. A ceremony on October 17, 1998, capped three days of celebration for Sosa, who received an award from John Cardinal O'Connor for his relief efforts for victims of Hurricane Georges in the Dominican Republic. He also received a ticker-tape parade in the Canyon of Heroes in lower Manhattan.

Celestial Bodies

"Blue Moon Odom, Charlie Starr, Moonlight Graham, Joe Cusp, Bill DeMars, Wally Moon, Memo Luna, Skyrocket Smith, Pat Rockett"

Cemeteries See *Burials and Cemeteries*

Center Fielders

"On a baseball diamond, the most commanding and far-reaching assignment. It is an unwritten decree that when the centerfielder calls for the ball, all others cease pursuit. 'He takes whatever he can get' … no other player has so imperative a mandate. He is a player whose boundaries are defined solely by his speed and his daring."—Donald Honig in *Mays, Mantle, Snider* (1987).

"Willie Mays was a center fielder, as much a man defined by his territory as George Washington or Peter the Great. But he was also Frank Lloyd Wright, creator of spaces. He played center field but what he did speaks to all fielders everywhere from the first hunter to Billy Hunter."—David Falkner in *Nine Sides of the Diamond* (1990).

"It is the sport that a foreigner is least likely to take to. You have to grow up playing it, you have to accept the lore of the bubble gum card, and believe that if the answer to the Mays-Mantle-Snider question is found, then the universe will be a simpler and more ordered place."—David Halberstam.

The top five center fielders at their peak according to Bill James:
1. Mickey Mantle
2. Willie Mays
3. Joe DiMaggio
4. Ty Cobb
5. Tris Speaker

Most historians would put Speaker ahead of Cobb for defensive purposes and Mays or DiMaggio ahead of Mantle defensively.

Until Willie Mays arrived in the early 1950s, the best center fielder in National League history was considered to be Hall of Famer Max Carey. Carey starred in the years before and after 1920 and led the league 10 times in stolen bases.

Mickey Mantle at his peak was considered by many as the top center fielder of the 1950s, an era which included Duke Snider and Willie Mays.

Bill James makes the case for Richie Ashburn of the Phillies as the best defensive center fielder of all time. Much of the credit may go to the ballpark, as Connie Mack Stadium was huge and gave Ashburn room to roam. The Phillies were lousy, which produced many base runners for Ashburn to throw out. It should be noted, however, that Ashburn was considered to have a relatively weak arm.

Albert Spalding chose Bill Lange of the 1890s White Stockings as the greatest center fielder of the 19th century (see *Marriage* for Lange's fate).

Devon White was considered by many as the best defensive center fielder of the 1980s. Ken Griffey, Jr., was probably the best center fielder of the 1990s.

Orlando Cepeda (1937–)

Hall of Fame (VC) 1999

"When Major League baseball first came to the Bay Area in 1958, the city of San Francisco was far more cohesive than it is now. The City by the Bay had its proper share of common heroes and common passions: columnist Herb Caen; symphony conductor Pierre Monteux; a football team called the 49ers; and an exciting rookie first baseman and slugger supreme, 20-year-old Orlando Cepeda, baseball's inimitable 'Baby Bull.'"—Herb Fagen.

Cepeda played most of his 17 seasons in the late 1950s and 1960s with the Giants, Cardinals and Braves as a power-hitting first baseman.

The son of Puerto Rican Winter League star Pedro Cepeda, Orlando was a teenage Puerto Rican amateur when he signed with the Giants. Cepeda mastered the Giant farm system quickly. In 1955, at Kokomo (Indiana) of the Midwest League he hit .393 with 21 home runs. By 1957 Cepeda was at Class AAA Minneapolis of the American Association, hitting .309 with 25 home runs.

Cepeda debuted as an original San Francisco Giant in 1958,

batting .312 with 25 home runs and 96 RBIs, and his 38 doubles led the league. He was unanimously selected National League Rookie of the Year. He may have been even better as a sophomore, hitting .317 with 27 home runs and 105 RBIs. After slipping slightly in 1960, Cepeda returned with an impressive 1961, posting career high marks of 46 home runs and 142 RBIs.

Cepeda lost most of the 1965 season to a knee injury and then was traded to the Cardinals early in the 1966 season. In 1967 the Cardinals won 101 games and the pennant, and Cepeda was the unanimous selection as league MVP. He hit .325 with 25 home runs, a league-leading 111 RBIs, and 37 doubles. Cepeda again had a quiet World Series, hitting only .103. In 1968 the Cardinals repeated as league champions and Cepeda contributed a pair of three-run home runs over the seven game series won by the Tigers.

In 1969 Cepeda was traded to the Atlanta Braves for Joe Torre and the Braves won their division. In 1970 the Braves returned to mediocrity, but Cepeda excelled. He hit over .300 for the ninth time in his career, with 34 home runs and 111 RBIs.

Over the last four years of his career Cepeda appeared with four clubs, with a notable stop in Boston. In 1973 he hit .289 with 20 home runs for the Red Sox as one of the American League's original designated hitters. He retired in 1974.

For his career Cepeda hit 379 home runs with 1,365 RBIs. His 2,351 hits include 417 doubles. He scored 1,131 runs and had a lifetime .297 batting average.

Cepeda fell on hard times when he was convicted of cocaine possession and trafficking in the 1980s. After serving prison time in Puerto Rico, he returned to the U.S. and bounced around in various jobs. He eventually landed with the Giants as a goodwill ambassador and was a perennial runner-up for Hall of Fame consideration until elected.

Book. Orlando Cepeda and Bob Markus, *High and Inside* (1983).

Henry Chadwick (1824–1908)

Hall of Fame 1938

"In young manhood he became an authority on the playing of

the game, and was personally instrumental in the working out of many improvements in the game itself. Aside from his acknowledged gifts as a writer of pure and forceful English, Mr. Chadwick possessed a peculiar penchant for statistics. To this attribute of Mr. Chadwick more than to any other source is attributable the perfectly accurate records covering the entire professional field and for which the game is to-day indebted."—Albert Spalding in *America's National Game* (1911).

Chadwick was the most prominent baseball writer of the 19th century.

Called the ***Father of Baseball*** by many, Chadwick was born in England and moved to the United States as a young teenager in 1837. He primarily played rounders in his youth, but played some version of baseball in his 20s.

He was a reporter for the *New York Times* in 1856, then went to the *New York Clipper*, the *Herald-Tribune* and the *Brooklyn Eagle*. At the latter he spent 45 years. One source reported that he played for the Washington Nationals, though that may have been a cameo appearance (if it occurred).

His initial journalistic interest in cricket (still a prominent sport) shifted to baseball and he soon became a key figure in the development of baseball in the New York area. He crusaded to rid the sport of gambling and was the official scorer for many key games, some involving the Cincinnati Red Stockings of 1869–1870 (including the club's first loss in 1870).

Chadwick was chairman of the Rules Committee of the National Association in 1871 and later was an official member of the National League Rules Committee. For most of the last 27 years of his life he edited the *Spalding Guide*.

Chadwick headed an effort to form the ***Baseball Writers Association*** in 1887, but a writers' association did not become permanent until the year Chadwick died, 1908. Chadwick is the only sportswriter (or broadcaster) voted directly into the Hall of Fame as opposed to being voted into a special wing of the Hall based on a contribution in a particular category.

Chadwick is credited by some with inventing the scorebook scoring system and the ***Box Score***. He bridged the evolutionary development of baseball, watched the old Knickerbockers prior to 1850 and witnessed the first World Series in 1903.

Chadwick fell on hard times in the early 20th century and the National League Rules Committee voted him a $600 annual pension. In 1908 he had a cold, but insisted on attending the Dodger home opener on a cold, damp day. He contracted pneumonia and died a few days later.

Chalmers Award (1911–1914)

"All the [1914] Braves rode home, for they all had purchased cars out of their series shares, all but Johnny Evers, who had won a Chalmers car as the National League's most valuable player for 1914. Stallings knew the make of every car owned by his players and in that 1915 season, he prefaced his derogatory remarks to his men by inserting the name of the automobile. Thus Rabbit Maranville became a 'Jack-rabbit bonehead,' others were 'Packard dunces,' 'Stanley Steamer clowns' and 'White simpletons.'"—Tom Meany in *Baseball's Greatest Teams* (1949).

From 1911 through 1914 the Chalmers Automobile Company presented a car (a Chalmers) to each league's MVP. The prize was known as the Chalmers Touring Car Award. Chalmers presented a car to each league's batting champion in 1910, but the award was

Henry Chadwick, one of the 19th century Fathers of Baseball.

modified for 1911 so that an MVP was chosen based on overall performance and not just batting average. This probably occurred because of the controversy that arose over Nap Lajoie's last game of the 1910 season and his efforts to overtake Ty Cobb for the batting title (see also **Batting Champions**).

In 1911 one sportswriter from each Major League city was chosen to be a voter, for a total of 11. A writer could vote once for each league in his city. The Chalmers Award prohibited repeat winners of the automobile, a tradition continued by the American League in 1922 when it started its own MVP Award. The National League did not follow suit in 1924 and the American League quickly abandoned the no-repeat rule (see also **Most Valuable Player**). The Chalmers Award was discontinued after the 1914 season and the outbreak of World War I in Europe.

Championship Series

"The World Championship Series"—Name given to interleague championship games in 1885 by Alfred Spink, publisher of *The Sporting News.*

See also **World Series**.

Prior to the first official World Series in 1903 between the National and American Leagues, championship games were played between members of various leagues or independent teams. At times in the press the winners were referred to as "World's Champions." Some sources contend that the term World Series was first formally used in 1903 when the modern World Series began. However, the *Dickson Baseball Dictionary* notes that the first-known usage in print of the term "World Series" was in 1887.

1859/Massachusetts. The 1859 "championship" of Massachusetts lasted 1½ days and took 101 innings to score the required 100 runs. The losers scored only 71.

Amateur Championships/1860s. A championship team in the amateur years up to 1870 usually had to be defeated twice to be dethroned as the informal national champion (see also **Amateur Teams**).

1860–1861. In 1860 the **Brooklyn Atlantics** played a three-game series against the Brooklyn Excelsiors for the championship. In Game 3 the Excelsiors were leading 8–6 when Atlantic fans started a riot. The game was cancelled and apparently called a draw, so the Atlantics were considered the champions that year because they did not formally lose the series.

1862–1863. The **Brooklyn Eckfords** were champions in both seasons. The club was undefeated in 1863, the only club other than the 1869 Cincinnati Red Stockings to accomplish the feat over an entire season (though playing less games than Cincinnati).

1864–1866. The Brooklyn Atlantics were back on top for all three seasons.

1867. The Unions of Morrisania (Brooklyn) were the top team, though the Washington Nationals were the best outside of New York and may have been the best of that season.

1868. The Washington Nationals were probably the top club in the nation.

1869–1870. The **Cincinnati Red Stockings** went undefeated in 1869 and then won almost every game in 1870. They lost to the powerful Brooklyn Atlantics in 1870 but most sources report that the Red Stockings were still the top club in 1870.

1871–1881. From 1871 through 1881 the National Association and then the National League had no direct professional competition, so some contend that their pennant winners may rightfully be considered the best clubs each year. However, many newspapers ranked the best clubs in the country each season regardless of league affiliation, and a few independent clubs were included among the league clubs that usually were ranked at or near the top.

Results of 19th Century Championship Series (1882–1897)

1882. The first attempt at a formal Major League championship series was in 1882 between the new American Association's Cincinnati Red Stockings and the Chicago White Stockings of the National League.

These games were not a formal championship series because other exhibitions were already scheduled and the Association had a rule prohibiting games with National League clubs. Cincinnati supposedly tried to circumvent the rule by releasing all of its players on October 1 and then re-signing a "new team" the next day.

Cincinnati won the first game 4–0 and then lost 2–0. After those two games the Association president, Denny McKnight, supposedly threatened to expel the Reds for playing with the "enemy" and the team was fined $100. Another source indicated that McKnight did not cancel any games and that the series was only scheduled for two games because of a number of exhibition games that the clubs were playing against other teams. Still another source reported that Cincinnati was ready to defy the Association, but White Stockings leader Cap Anson pulled his club out "for the good of both teams."

1883. The National League Boston Red Stockings challenged the American Association's Philadelphia A's, but the A's had played poorly in seven of eight exhibition games earlier in October. As a result, the A's declined to play the series against the Red Stockings.

1884. The first full championship series was played between Providence of the National League and New York of the American Association. Providence prevailed with a three-game sweep of the five-game series. Old Hoss Radbourn pitched on three straight days and won 6–0, 3–1 and 12–2 (or 11–2). Tim Keefe pitched the first two games for New York and umpired the third game. He called a halt to the third game allegedly due to darkness when the rout was on.

1885. The National League Chicago White Stockings played Charles Comiskey's St. Louis Browns of the American Association. A pot of $1,000 was to go to the winning team. As part of a barnstorming tour, the games were played in Cincinnati, St. Louis, Pittsburgh and Chicago. There was violence in the stands, slanted news coverage and umpire disputes. The series was stopped after six games when the players were not being paid and the play had deteriorated: 100 errors amid 97 hits.

The Browns won the series 3–2 after a tie in the first game and a forfeit to the Browns in the second game, which Chicago did not recognize. Some sources ignore the forfeit and call the series a 3–3 tie.

1886. This was the first season in which there was a scheduled seven-game series that was actually played to conclusion. In a repeat of 1885, the St. Louis Browns played the National League White Stockings over seven days.

Three games were played in Chicago, three in St. Louis, and a never-played seventh game was scheduled for a neutral site. The compact schedule was required because the Browns had scheduled a nine-game series with their cross-town rivals, the St. Louis Maroons of the National League. The Browns played part of the series with the Maroons before beginning the series with Chicago. The Browns were swept four straight by the Maroons, which did not bode well for their series against Chicago.

The Browns and White Stockings split the first four games and the Browns won the fifth game to set the stage for the deciding and dramatic sixth game. With 10,000 fans at Sportsman's Park, the Browns scored the winning run in the bottom of the 10th inning.

Curt Welch was hit by a pitch to lead off the inning for the Browns. Cap Anson protested that he was too close to the plate and made no effort to move out of the way. Welch was then ordered to bat again and he singled. He made his way to third and stole home to win the game. White Stockings catcher Mike "King" Kelly anticipated the steal by calling for a pitchout, but he bobbled it. Another source reported that it was a wild pitch and Welch could have jogged home with no slide necessary. The steal of home later was referred to as "The $15,000 Slide" because of the winner-take-all format. Browns owner Christopher Von der Ahe supposedly gave all the money to his players, but another source reported that he received $13,000, gave $850 to each of his players, and pocketed the rest.

It was the American Association's only undisputed championship and marked the first time that all games were played in the home parks of the two clubs.

1887. The National League Detroit Wolverines played the St. Louis Browns in a 15-game series in 10 different cities. There were low gate receipts due to low attendance (only 51,455 over the 15 games), as the fans simply wore out. Detroit won 10 of the 15, but had already clinched the series after 11 games, winning eight of them. Arlie Latham stole 12 bases for the Browns and there was a triple play in one game.

1888. After selling five regulars, the St. Louis Browns still won the American Association pennant for the fourth straight season. They were opposed by the New York Giants of the National League in the championship series. The Giants clinched the series in eight games, winning six of the eight before giving away the last two. St. Louis blamed the umpires and tried to make a scapegoat of shortstop Bill White, whose error cost the team one game. John Montgomery Ward was the catalyst for the Giants.

The extravagances of the series supposedly cost St. Louis owner Christopher Von der Ahe $50,000. This was the first year in which the championship *Dauvray Cup* was offered as an incentive to the winning club (the cup was named for Helen Dauvray, actress wife of John Montgomery Ward).

1889. The National League New York Giants defeated the American Association Brooklyn Dodgers in nine games (6–3) after Brooklyn won three of the first four games. In the pivotal sixth game, a Giants runner on second scored the winning run on an infield hit with two out. See Jean-Pierre Caillaut, *A Tale of Four Cities: Nineteenth-Century Baseball's Most Exciting Season, 1889, in Contemporary Accounts* (2003)

1890. Louisville of the American Association faced Brooklyn, which had moved to the National League after winning the American Association championship the year before. Louisville supposedly quit the series when it was tied 3–3, with one tie. The Louisville players purportedly were "tuckered out," but the real reason may have been dwindling gate receipts. More than 5,000 fans attended the first game, but that total steadily dropped to only 300 by the last game. In addition, the series was not particularly popular because so many star players had played that year in the Players League. A usually accurate source reported that a deciding 8th game was started but called off due to bad weather.

1891. There was no series because the failing American Association was not in a position to do much of anything except fold after the season.

National League Results: 1892–1897. After the 1891 season, the American Association dissolved and all that was left at the Major League level was the 12-team National League. Various postseason intraleague series continued sporadically in one form or another over the next few years.

1892. The National League's 12 teams played a split season. The winners of each half met for the league championship. Boston defeated Cleveland 5–0 (with one tie) in this one-year experiment.

1893. The National League eliminated the split-season format and no series was played.

1894–1897. Additional championship series in the 1890s were between the first- and second-place finishers in the National League. These teams played a seven-game series for the *Temple Cup*, presented by the Pittsburgh club's owner, but there was not much fan interest and the series was played only from 1894 through 1897.

1894. The second-place New York Giants swept the first-place Baltimore Orioles in four games.

1895. The second-place Cleveland Spiders defeated first-place Baltimore in five games.

1896. First-place Baltimore defeated second-place Cleveland in five games.

1897. Second-place Baltimore defeated Boston in five games after the Red Stockings won the regular season championship in a tight pennant race.

Major League Results: 1898–1902. The National League abandoned all postseason play after 1897 and did not play the American League in the World Series until after the Major Leagues ended their war in 1902.

1898–1899. There was no postseason play among National League clubs.

1900. Though the Western League had changed its name to American League, it was not yet recognized as a Major League and there was no postseason competition between the National and American Leagues.

1901–1902. The American League was recognized as a Major League, but feuding with the National League prevented any postseason play.

1903 and Beyond. With the exception of 1904 and 1994, the *World Series* has been played every year since 1903.

Books. Larry G. Bowman, *Before the World Series: Pride, Profits, and Baseball's First Championships* (2004); Jerry Lansche, *The Forgotten Championships: Postseason Baseball, 1882–1891* (1989); Jerry Lansche, *Glory Fades Away* (1991), covering all pre–1900 championship games; John Phillips, *The Fall Classics of the 1890s: The Temple Cup of 1894–1897 and the Championship Series of 1892* (1989); John C. Tattersall, *The Early World Series, 1884–1890* (1976).

Frank Chance (1877–1924)

Hall of Fame 1946

"You're ballplayers and not society dancers at a pink tea."—Chance to a group of his players, one of whom he fined $10 for shaking hands with a rival player.

Chance starred primarily as a first baseman over a 17-year career that began in 1898.

Born in Fresno, California, to a relatively wealthy family, Frank Leroy Chance studied medicine before turning full-time to baseball. Discovered by Chicago star Bill Lange, who recommended him to Cap Anson, Chance reported to the National League White Stockings as a catcher in 1898.

When Chance was often injured playing catcher and Johnny Kling arrived to play the position, Chance shifted to first base in 1902 under new Cubs manager Frank Selee. Chance was appointed captain of the team in 1904 and player-manager in 1905, becoming known as "The Peerless Leader." In his first full season as player-manager in 1906, the Cubs won a Major League record 116 games.

Chance hit .296 over his 17-year career, with four seasons over .300. He rarely played a full season because of injuries, including a number of beanings that affected his hearing. Chance was the anchor of the famous *Tinker to Evers to Chance* infield and managed the club through 1912, with four pennants and two World Championships (1907 and 1908). He has the highest managerial winning percentage in National League history at .652, with a record of 768–389.

He moved to the American League and the Yankees in 1913 and 1914, but ill health forced him to retire to California. He managed the Los Angeles Angels in the Pacific Coast League in 1916 and 1917 and then returned to the Major Leagues in 1923 to manage the Red Sox to a last-place finish. He was scheduled to manage the White Sox in 1924, but his health deteriorated and he died in September of that year. His .593 Major League winning percentage is sixth all-time.

Chances

"Napoleon Lajoie made five errors in one game [on April 22, 1915], but how many 40-year-old men could get near five chances?" — Philadelphia sportswriter James C. Isaminger in *Sporting Life* in May 1915.

"An opportunity to make a fielding play that results in an out or assist."—Technical definition of the term.

The all-time leader in chances accepted is 19th century National League first baseman Jake Beckley, with 25,024. The National League record since 1900 is 21,914 by Pirates and Cubs first baseman Charlie Grimm. The American League record is 21,198 by Senators first baseman Mickey Vernon.

Shortstop Ron Hansen of the White Sox tied an American League record on August 29, 1965, when he handled 18 chances in the first game of a doubleheader. He also had 10 chances in the second game.

The Major League record for outfielders is held by Tony Armas, who handled 12 chances for the A's in an 8–1 win over the Blue Jays on June 12, 1982. Harry "Silk Stocking" Schafer had established the record of 11 chances in 1877, which had been matched four times; the last by Bake McBride in 1978.

A.B. "Happy" Chandler (1907–1991)

Chandler was appointed *Commissioner* of baseball in April 1945 and stayed in the position until forced out in 1950.

Change-Up See *Pitches*

Ray Chapman (1891–1920)

"You can have it, it wouldn't do me any good."—Chapman to an umpire purportedly after declining to use up his last strike during a fruitless at-bat against Walter Johnson.

Chapman is the only Major League player killed as a direct result of action on the playing field. He was struck by a Carl Mays pitch on August 16, 1920, and died the next day (see *Deaths*).

Charity

"There is no charity in baseball. I want to win the pennant every year."—Yankee owner Jacob Ruppert.

See also *Benefit Games, Disaster Relief, Pension System — Charity Cases, World War I* and *World War II.*

King Kelly. After 19th century star Mike "King" Kelly died, Major League owners raised $1,400 for his widow.

Grover Cleveland Alexander. Cardinals owner Sam Breadon funneled money through the National League so that aging and alcoholic Grover Cleveland Alexander would think that he was receiving an official pension check from the league.

Early Pension. Out of the proceeds of the first All-Star Game in 1933, the leagues donated $45,000 to the Oldtimers Baseball Fund.

Titanic. In 1912 the Reds raised $9,000 for victims of the *Titanic* disaster.

Jimmy Fund. This is the name of the long-time fundraising efforts of the Red Sox and Ted Williams, in tribute to a young Boston fan named, curiously, Einar.

Fundraising. "Passing the hat" among fans was not uncommon in the 1940s. In 1949 on Joe DiMaggio Day, the fans collected $7,197 for DiMaggio to give to charity.

Balls. Dave Winfield auctioned off the balls from hits 2,968 to 2,995 for the benefit of the David M. Winfield Foundation. He reserved for himself and the Hall of Fame the last five balls in his quest for 3,000.

Performance Incentives. In the 1990s a number of players joined the Caring Team of Athletes, who generated contributions for each hit they made, up to $60,000 a week. In 1993 the Caring Team raised more than $1.8 million to help children who could not afford health care.

AIDS. In early August 1994 the Giants wore red ribbons on their uniforms and donated $1 for each ticket sold to benefit an AIDS care organization in the Bay Area.

Lou Gehrig's Disease. The Orioles sold 260 special temporary on-field seats for Cal Ripken's record-breaking game on September 6, 1995. Each seat sold for $5,000 and it was the first time that special field seating was approved by the league for a regular season game. The seats raised $1.3 million for ALS research (Lou Gehrig's Disease) and the Orioles contributed another $700,000 to the effort.

Players Union. In 1996 the Players Association announced the creation of the Players Trust for Children, the first charitable foundation established and run by professional athletes. Each Major League player contributed a minimum of 2% of his annual licensing royalty.

McGwire Home Run Ball.
"I want to raise awareness. What better way to publicize the cause than to tie it to the home run derby? I hope when sportscasters talk about the money, they'll also talk about the cause."—Anonymous fan. On September 5, 1998, the *New York Times* reported the fan's offer of $1 million for Mark McGwire's 62nd home run ball, which was yet to be hit. The anonymous fan wanted to buy a $650,000 annuity that would pay the fan $50,000 annually for 20 years. His plan was to resell the ball, and any profits above $650,000 would go to the Lawyer's Committee for Human Rights, a New York-based organization that represents victims' families and promotes human rights around the world. The money would go to help in the continuing search for justice in the 1980 murders of three American nuns and a lay worker in El Salvador. If there was no profit, the fan would donate $75,000. It does not appear that this pledge was ever fulfilled, as the fan apparently was unable to purchase the ball.

9/11/2001. After the tragedy of September 11, 2001, Red Sox catcher and union representative Scott Hatteberg abandoned plans for a team donation to victims after some of his teammates refused to give up a day's pay.

Shea Stadium served as a relief center after the terrorist attacks. Most of the gate areas were filled with food, supplies and temporary shelters for the massive rescue effort. On September 21, the Mets made an emotional return against the Atlanta Braves in front of 41,275 fans, including Mayor Rudolph Giuliani.

Major League Baseball and the Players Association donated $10 million and created the MLB–MLBPA Disaster Relief Fund to aid victims of the terrorist attacks.

Jeopardy!. Mike Piazza appeared on a celebrity version of the television show "Jeopardy!" in early 1997 and won $15,000 for a Los Angeles children's hospital.

Alomar/Hirschbeck. Roberto Alomar forever linked himself to umpire John Hirschbeck when he spat on Hirschbeck after the umpire called him out on strikes in late September 1996 (See *Umpires—Attacks*). The event spilled into 1997 when Alomar was suspended at the beginning of the season and Hirschbeck went out of his way to avoid Alomar; even going to so far as to position himself on the shortstop side of second base to avoid Alomar as much as possible.

Alomar had exacerbated the situation when he said that Hirschbeck was under stress because of the death of Hirschbeck's son, eight-year-old John Drew, three years earlier in 1993. His son died of a rare brain disease known as adrenoleukodystrophy (ALD). Only about 1,000 people contract it each year, and it is hereditary. Unfortunately, Hirschbeck's other son, Michael, had the disease, and therein lies the link that brought Alomar and Hirschbeck together.

When Alomar apologized for the spitting incident, he made a $50,000 donation to Hirschbeck's foundation that he uses to raise money to fight the disease. Two years later Hirschbeck made the first overture to try to repair the relationship, using Cleveland's umpire room manager, Jack Efta. As a result, in 1999 Alomar and his brother, Sandy, donated signed Indians jerseys for a charity auction Hirschbeck runs each year, and then in 2000 had all the Indians players wear jerseys that were signed by each and then auctioned off. Hirschbeck's son Michael has been an Indians batboy, but he too is likely to die of the disease. He was 13 in 2000, with the mental capacity of a first grader.

Hirschbeck now says: "If that's the worst thing Robbie ever does in his life, he'll lead a real good life," Hirschbeck said. "People make mistakes. You forgive, you forget and you move on."

Lisa Pollack of the *Baltimore Sun* won a Pulitzer Prize for an article about Hirschbeck and his family.

Don Zimmer. During the 2003 American League championship series, Zimmer was fined $5,000 for charging Pedro Martinez. Fans started a website to collect money to pay the fine, which Zimmer and his grandson arranged to be donated to charity.

Nun. In May 2004 a nun won $10,000 in a contest sponsored during a game by the Cincinnati Reds. Sister Susanna Helms won the money after her name was drawn and Barry Larkin and Sean Casey hit back-to-back home runs in the 5th inning of a game against the Marlins. Helms said she would donate the money to her religious order, the Sisters of St. Francis in Oldenburg, Indiana.

Oscar Charleston (1896–1954)

Hall of Fame (VC) 1976

"He was brute strength looking. We used to say he was strong enough to go bear huntin' with a switch, didn't need a gun."— Satchel Paige.

Charleston was a Negro League star center fielder for 26 seasons beginning in 1915.

Oscar Charleston was raised in Indianapolis and joined the military before playing with the Indianapolis ABCs in 1915. He also played with the Lincoln Stars before moving on to the Chicago American Giants. Considered by some as the best center fielder of all time in any league, Charleston moved to various teams in the 1920s. A showboat, he often played directly behind second base, but old-timers swore that a ball never went over his head.

In 1925 he batted .445 to lead the Eastern Colored League. After the league collapsed he moved to the Philadelphia Hilldale Club, the Homestead Grays in 1930, and the Pittsburgh Crawfords in 1932.

Charleston was player-manager for the Crawfords in 1935 and led them to the Negro National League championship. He switched to first base as he got older, but he kept on hitting. Over his 26 seasons he hit a recorded .350, but that average reflects only a small percentage of the games he played.

Charleston continued to manage in the 1940s and then scouted for the Brooklyn Dodgers for what was thought to be a new team of black stars for the short-lived Brooklyn Brown Dodgers of the almost-mythical *United States League*. He then worked for the railroad in Pennsylvania before returning to professional baseball. In 1954 he managed the Indianapolis Clowns to a championship and then suffered a stroke that killed him in October of that year.

Chatter

"The art of enlightened conversation."— Catcher Biz Mackey, who taught Roy Campanella the fine art of breaking the batter's concentration.

"Gabby Hartnett, Orator Shaffer, Spoke Emery, Lew Say, Mike Witt, Orel Hershiser, Oral Hildebrand, Tris Speaker, Bob Speake"

Yogi Berra was considered one of the great chattering catchers, but he said that he simply liked to talk.

Jack Chesbro (1874–1931)

Hall of Fame 1946

"Aside from Ed Walsh, Chesbro was the best-known of the spitters *and* the wettest. Many errors were made behind him because he sprayed the ball so liberally. His form was flawless and he threw almost straight overhanded."— Lee Allen and Tom Meany in *Kings of the Diamond* (1965).

Chesbro was one of the leading pitchers of the early American League, with a modern season record 41 wins in 1904.

John Dwight Chesbro has the distinction of being the only Hall of Famer to have played professionally in Cooperstown. He pitched in 1896 for the Cooperstown Athletics, a semipro team. After pitching in the New York League and with Richmond in 1899, Chesbro signed with the National League Pirates late that season. He won a league-leading 28 games for the Pirates in 1902 before jumping to the rival American League.

Chesbro won 21 games for the Highlanders (Yankees) in 1903 and peaked in 1904 when he won a 20th century record 41 games in 51 starts. Three of those wins were in relief, a league high. Chesbro was known as one of the great spitball pitchers of the era, but allegedly it was a spitball that sailed over his catcher's head in 1904 that cost his club the pennant (see also *Wild Pitches*).

Chesbro's career lasted only 11 years, but his 199 wins, 41 in one season, and relatively brief stardom in New York, solidified his work in the minds of historians. He finished his career in 1909, appearing in nine games for the Highlanders and one game for the

Red Sox. He went back to his hometown of North Adams, Massachusetts, where he operated a lumberyard and sawmill. He coached at Amherst College in 1911 and pitched occasionally in semipro games.

Chest Protectors See *Catcher's Equipment*

"Chew"

"When it was discovered at the turn of the century that tuberculosis was transmitted through expectoration, chewing and spitting became socially unacceptable and in some places illegal, but the baseball park, always a universe of its own, continued to be a haven for tobacco users."—Joel Zoss and John Bowman in *Diamonds in the Rough* (1989).

"I don't like tobacco because it causes diseases. Dirt is free and nobody bums it off you."—Minor league pitcher Todd Welborn, who wedged dirt in his cheek.

See also *Gum* and *Tobacco*.

Bologna. Pitcher Harry Coveleski put bologna in his back pocket and chewed it during games. Observing that it was an obsession with Coveleski, Giants manager John McGraw ordered his players to repeatedly ask Coveleski for a bite of his bologna. It upset Coveleski and he had a hard time pitching. He supposedly never beat the Giants again after destroying them in the final days of the 1908 season. After word got around the league about the bologna fetish, other clubs harassed him and it drove him back to the minor leagues for four seasons. His brother said "what a lot of bull that story is," because the real story was that Harry hurt his arm and it took a few years for him to recover.

Bathroom Tissue. Tobacco made 1960s pitcher Joe Horlen sick, so he chewed bathroom tissue.

Fingernails. Pitcher Greg Swindell bit off a fingernail and kept it inside his cheek during games that he pitched. He did not like gum and was afraid he would swallow tobacco.

Chicago

"I'd rather be a lamppost in Chicago than a millionaire in any other city."—William Hulbert recruiting Albert Spalding to the White Stockings from the Boston Red Stockings.

"If I were traded to another team, especially a Chicago team, I wouldn't go, I'd just quit.... The only two things that should never happen again is the rearming of Germany and a pennant in Chicago."—"Stu the stockbroker" quoted in Richard Grossinger's *The Temple of Baseball* (1985).

"Beyond the walls, beyond the bleachers, lay the big-shouldered city of Carl Sandburg and Theodore Dreiser. There the vista was unmistakably Chicago: slaughter house tough streets, lined with modest one-family houses and neighborhood bars that served a shot-and-a-beer more often than cognac on the stem."—Stanley Cohen in *A Magic Summer—The '69 Mets* (1988).

Chicago has always been an extraordinarily strong baseball town; Chicago and Boston are the only cities to have Major League representation continuously since 1876. Chicago is the only club to have a National League representative continuously since that season.

Amateur Teams. The first organized team in Chicago was the Chicago Unions of 1856, which adopted the style of baseball known as the New York Game. There also was a prominent amateur Chicago team of the 1860s known as the Cubs.

Professional Teams.

National Association Chicago White Stockings (1871, 1874–1875)

National League Chicago White Stockings/Cubs (1876–)
Union Association Chicago Browns/Unions (1884)
Players League Chicago Pirates (1890)
American League Chicago White Sox (1901–)
Federal League Chicago Whales (1914–1915)

Chicago Black Sox See *Black Sox Scandal*

Chicago Browns/Unions

Union Association 1884
"The Chicago Unions are a busted community ... a complete cleanout."—Albert Spalding in a September 1884 letter to Abraham Mills after the rival club failed.

This club had a 34–39 record before transferring to Pittsburgh in August 1884 because of the strong competition from the National League Chicago White Stockings. The club played its games in the original South Side Park.

Chicago Chi-Feds See *Chicago Whales*

Chicago Cubs/White Stockings

National League 1876–
"*Bunker Hill, Indiana*—Elva A. Kling Reyburn, an avid Chicago Cubs Baseball fan who has waited since 1908 for her favorite team to win the World Series, has died at age 108."—1990 obituary.

"Top 10 Lies Told at Wrigley Field:
  1. The Strike wasn't about money.
  2. August is our month.
  3. Dunston just needs a few years to develop.
  4. The Tribune Company really cares about the fans.
  5. Harry's not drunk.
  6. We don't need Maddux.
  7. There will never be lights in Wrigley Field.
  8. Wait 'til next year.
  9. Parking is no problem.
  10. Bleacher bums drink in moderation."—Seen on a tee shirt at the ballpark.

Origins. The Chicago White Stockings were members of the National Association when owner William Hulbert spearheaded formation of the National League and included his club among the first members of the new league.

In June 1875 Hulbert induced star pitcher Albert Spalding to move from the Boston Red Stockings to his National Association Chicago White Stockings. Spalding came and brought three other players with him; Jim "Deacon" White, Cal McVey and Ross Barnes. They were known collectively as "The Big Four." After the inaugural season Hulbert also signed the "Philadelphia Phenom," Cap Anson.

Key Owners.
William Hulbert (HF)/1876–1882.
"A strong, forceful and self-reliant ... man of tremendous energy—and courage."—Albert Spalding.

Hulbert controlled the club until his premature death in 1882. During his reign the club won the first National League pennant in 1876 and then won three straight beginning in 1880. Hulbert's legacy is the founding and stabilizing of the *National League* in its infancy. He was *National League President* from 1877 until his death.

Albert Spalding (HF)/1882–1891.

"Intelligent and gentlemanly ... both on and off the baseball field conducts himself in a manner well calculated to remove the public's bad impression as to professional ball tossers, created by swearing, gambling, specimens who form the black sheep of the flock." — Henry Chadwick.

Spalding became a minority owner of the club while still a player and began devoting significant time to his sporting goods business (see also *Spalding Sporting Goods*). When William Hulbert died in 1882, Spalding took over majority ownership of the club with minority owner John L. Walsh, a prominent Chicago banker. In 1891 Spalding retired from active control of the team to devote himself full-time to his sporting goods business. However, many sources give the erroneous impression that he sold his interest in 1891. Spalding was involved in virtually all of the significant events of 19th century Major League Baseball while holding his interest in the White Stockings into the early 20th century.

James A. Hart/1891–1905.

"[O]f course everyone knows Al Spalding, the owner of the Chicago Club. Al's mouthpiece is Jim Hart, the nominal president of the club. Al pulls the string and Jim spiels." — *The Sporting News* commentary in 1891.

When Spalding stepped down he selected Hart, who had managed in the minor leagues, to run the club. Hart had been Chicago's business manager on the team's world tour of 1888. Hart was still nominally in charge in 1901 and eventually took over full ownership of the team until he sold out in 1905. Prior to Hart becoming the majority owner, the club was controlled by Spalding, with ownership interests held by Chicago Board of Trade member Charles T. Trego and banker John Walsh.

Cap Anson's Claim.

"I found myself something in the position of a politician who had announced his candidate, had the wires all set, convention packed, election assured, but my candidate would not run." — Albert Spalding after Anson refused a tribute dinner after he was forced to leave the White Stockings, quoted in *A.G. Spalding and the Rise of Baseball*, by Peter Levine (1985).

Cap Anson played 22 years with the club from 1876 through 1897 and managed it from 1879 through 1897, winning five pennants. Anson claimed that Spalding promised him a controlling interest in the club when Spalding stepped down, but Spalding allegedly reneged on the promise. A disgruntled Anson retired at the end of the 1897 season at the age of 46, although there is some sentiment that he could have continued playing because he was in such good shape.

Some contend that it is more accurate to say that president and minority owner James Hart got rid of him, probably because Anson was seen as a threat, and also because of a running feud between Hart and Anson. Among other problems and slights, Anson had refused to chip in for an expensive gift for Hart after Hart had coordinated the club's 1888 world tour. Spalding never confirmed or denied Anson's claims. Other sources reported that Spalding fired Anson when he refused to step down as manager.

Charles Murphy/1905–1914.

"It was while he was hospitalized that owner Murphy came through with a statement denouncing the Cubs as strayers from the straight and narrow path of training. Among other things, he said that the Cubs of 1913 would have to get along without their rum ration." — Warren Brown in *The Chicago Cubs* (1946).

Murphy was a New York Giants press agent and newspaperman in Cincinnati who later became the highly unpopular Cubs owner. He was finally forced out during the Federal League war. He took over majority ownership in early 1905 by paying James Hart $105,000. First baseman and manager Frank Chance also had an ownership interest in the club. Chance supposedly earned his 10% interest as a result of a base stealing feat that he performed to win a game. He was offered the 10% for $10,000, which Murphy loaned him.

Charles P. Taft, wealthy half-brother of U.S. President William Howard Taft, put up the money for Murphy. Taft and Murphy initially were interested in the Phillies, because Mrs. Taft owned the land underneath the Philadelphia ballpark.

The abrasive Murphy was considered an embarrassment to the league from the outset, but managed to hang onto the club until 1914. The Cubs won four pennants and two World Series during his ownership, but after finishing third in 1912 he arranged to sell off his championship players. They included Joe Tinker, Three Finger Brown and Johnny Evers. He also sold off players during the Federal League challenge two years later. The other National League owners reacted negatively to Murphy's erratic action, which culminated in a successful effort to drive him out of the league.

National League president John Tener arranged for Charles Taft to buy Murphy's 53 shares for $503,500. When Murphy was forced out, his assistant, William Hale Thompson, became president of the club and Taft was simply a caretaker owner until a new buyer could be found. Following Murphy's ouster, *Sporting Life* celebrated:

"Brought to the leash and smashed in the jaw,
Evers to Tener to Taft.
Hounded and hustled outside of the law,
Evers to Tener to Taft.
Torn from the Cubs and glitter of gold,
Stripped of the guerdons [rewards] and glory untold
Kicked in the stomach and cut from the fold,
Evers to Tener to Taft."

Actually, Murphy contended he made a tidy profit and went willingly: "It was not hard for me to take a half-million dollars for my franchise. No force was required. Despite that fact I read every once in a while that I was forced out of baseball — knocked down the back steps, as it were, and kicked into the yards behind. That is simply camouflage. It is true that the Chief Executive of the National League at that time was not 'crazy' about me and that he called a meeting to have me quartered and boiled in oil, or shot at sunrise, I don't know which.... Before the meeting I sold out to Mr. Charles P. Taft and without force.... One or two baseball politicians shouted with glee over my retirement, but I think events have since shown that the laughing was all on my side, because I got out at the psychological moment."

Charles Weegham/1916–1918.

"I have devoted my time, my energy and my money to help bring this project to the point where it stands today. What success I have attained in a business way I owe to the loyal patronage of the general Chicago public, and in this effort to further clean sport and to bring to a large section of the city an opportunity to enjoy the national pastime I am doing more than my natural loyalty to this community demands." — Weegham.

Weegham, owner of the Federal League Chicago Whales, was granted the right to buy the Cubs with other investors as part of the settlement among the three Major Leagues. The best players from the Whales moved to the Cubs. One of the minority investors was William Wrigley, who would soon own a controlling interest in the club.

Weegham was worth about $50 million in 2000 dollars. Nevertheless, Weegham apparently began to have financial problems and started borrowing from Wrigley, using Cubs stock as collateral. In 1918 Weegham was ousted as club president and Wrigley took control.

The Wrigley Family/1918–1981.

"He's the only owner I ever knew who would vote against his own best interests if he thought it was good for baseball." — Bill Veeck, Jr., on long-time Cubs owner Phil Wrigley.

"It is hard to understand how a father and son can be as completely different as William and Phil Wrigley. The father, who practically invented chewing gum, was the last of the super salesmen, a man who made his name synonymous with his product. He was a well-upholstered, jovial man who liked people and knew what made them tick. The son is one of those men who is difficult to describe in a quick few words…. If he has any particular feeling for baseball, any real liking for it, he has disguised it magnificently." — Bill Veeck, Jr., in *Veeck—As in Wreck*, with Ed Linn (1962).

"The most valuable and least imitated magnate in major-league baseball is a dour, puffy-eyed individual … [who] has developed a perfect misunderstanding of himself: 'I have decided,' he once said glumly, 'that I am not a very impressive person.'" — William B. Furlong on Phil Wrigley in 1972.

Chewing gum magnate William Wrigley bought into the club in 1916 and took control in late 1918. Wrigley's father had manufactured soap and baking soda and Wrigley became a traveling soap salesman while still a young teenager. He gave away banana chewing gum (known as chicle at the time) as a premium and. When the product became popular, and Wrigley realized that it was less expensive to ship it, he changed his production lines to gum in 1891, when he was 30 years old. He reportedly had amassed a fortune of $30 million at his death. In 1919 he bought Catalina Island off the California coast for $3 million, owning all but one acre in the middle of the island.

When Wrigley bought the Cubs he also immediately hired Bill Veeck, Sr., as the general manager of the club. Wrigley's son Phil bought stock in the club in 1926 and was appointed to the board of directors in 1929. Though primarily interested in yachting, in 1932 Phil inherited his father's shares and in 1934 he took over as president. He ran the club for most of the next 43 years. Film comedian Joe E. Brown was a part-owner of the team beginning in the 1940s. His son later was an executive with the Pirates.

Phil Wrigley died at age 82 on April 12, 1977, leaving the team to his son, William Wrigley, Jr. Late in the 1981 season the Wrigley family sold the club to the Tribune Company, owner of the *Chicago Tribune* newspaper.

The Tribune Company/1981–.

"An editorial in the Chicago Tribune, miffed because it was constantly reporting on the one-sided losses of the local team, reflected the mood of the time." — Apparently little has changed in the Cubs' fortunes; this was written in 1869, quoted in *Primitive Baseball*, by Harvey Frommer (1988).

The Tribune Company purchased the club late in the 1981 season. The newspaper's biggest break with tradition was the commencement of **Night Baseball** at Wrigley Field in 1988.

Nicknames.

"At the turn of the century, bustling, civic-minded Chicagoans insisted the team should have a name indicative of 'bear-like strength and a playful disposition.' Whereupon some fast thinker, whose name has been lost to posterity, came up with Cubs." — Frank C. True.

The original name of the club was White Stockings, which existed before the formation of the National Association in 1871 and the National League in 1876.

In 1890 the club was referred to as the Colts because of the depletion of the club due to defections to the Players League and the signing of many young players from the minor leagues to fill the team's roster.

One source reported another origin of the Colts name. Manager Cap Anson appeared in an 1896 theatre production called *A Runaway Colt* (referred to as a silent film in one source). Other 19th century names reportedly included the Zephyrs, Panamas, Recruits, Rough Riders, Cowboys, Broncos and Rainmakers.

When the disgruntled Anson left the team in 1897 to manage the Giants, the club was nicknamed the Orphans because it had been abandoned by its long-time field leader. One recent source erroneously reported that Anson's death was the reason for his departure from the club.

The names Orphans and White Stockings reportedly lasted until 1899, when a Chicago newspaperman held a contest to name the team: Cubs was the winner. Another source attributed the Cubs name to sportswriters Fred Hayner and George Rice, who referred to the young players on the team as Cubs. Yet another source reported that in 1901 a local writer first referred to the inexperienced team as the Cubs after the club had signed a number of young pitchers when players were jumping clubs during the National League war with the new American League.

Key Seasons.

"Wrigley Field fans go in for resigned sarcasm; it befits a franchise whose top-level incompetence has been a marvel of consistency since World War II." — Thomas Boswell in *Why Time Begins on Opening Day* (1984).

"Every player should be accorded the privilege of at least one season with the Chicago Cubs. That's baseball as it should be played — in God's own sunshine. And that's really living." — Alvin Dark.

"TO: CHICAGO CUBS FANS

"The Cub management wants you to know we appreciate the wonderful support you are giving to the ball club. We want you fans and Charlie Grimm to have a team that can be up at the top — the kind of team that both of you deserve.

"We also know that this year's rebuilding job has been a flop. But we're not content — and have never been — to just go along with an eye on attendance only — we want a winner, just as you do, and we will do everything possible to get one.

"If one system does not work, we will try another. Your loyal support when we are down is a real incentive for us to try even harder to do everything in our power to give us all a winner.

"Thanks — THE CHICAGO CUBS" — Open letter in all major Chicago newspapers after the 1948 season.

"Anybody can have a bad century." — Numerous pundits on the Cubs' 20th century woes.

"What does a mama bear on the pill have in common with the World Series? No cubs." — Harry Caray.

Through 2004 the post–1900 Cubs have won a wild card title (1998) three division titles (1984, 1989 and 2003), 16 pennants (none since 1945) and two World Series (1907 and 1908).

1876. Pitcher Albert Spalding led the White Stockings to the league's first pennant by six games with a 52–14 record. Spalding also led the league with 47 wins and second baseman Ross Barnes led the league with a .429 batting average, .590 slugging average, 138 hits, 21 doubles, 14 triples, 126 runs scored and 20 base on balls.

1880. The club won the pennant by 15 games with a 67–17

record. Larry Corcoran won 43 games and George Gore led the league with a .360 average.

1881. The White Stockings repeated as champions by nine games over the second-place Providence Grays. Cap Anson led the league with a .399 average.

1882. Player-manager Cap Anson led the club to its third straight pennant. The first **Championship Series**, between Chicago and the American Association champion Cincinnati Red Stockings, resulted in a tie when the series was called after two games.

1885. Anson again led the club to a pennant, this time by two games over the New York Giants. John Clarkson led the league with 53 wins and Anson was the league leader with 114 RBIs. In the **Championship Series** the St. Louis Brown Stockings beat Chicago 3–2 in a disputed series. The White Stockings considered a sixth game to be a win, though most contemporary sources reported it as a forfeit.

1886. Chicago won the pennant by three games, with Mike "King" Kelly leading the league with a .388 average. The Brown Stockings again defeated Chicago in the **Championship Series**, a six-game win culminating in the famous "$15,000 Slide." This was to be Cap Anson's last pennant as manager of the White Stockings.

1906. The Cubs won a Major League–record 116 games. Three Finger Brown won 26 games and led the league with a 1.04 ERA. In the World Series the Cubs lost in six games to the White Sox.

1907. The club won 107 games under manager Frank Chance to repeat as National League champions. The Cubs won their first World Series with a sweep of the Tigers. Orval Overall led the club with 23 wins and Jack Pfeister led the league with a 1.15 ERA while compiling a record of 15–9.

1908.

"The last time the Cubs were the champions of the national pastime, Babe Ruth was a baby. He wasn't *the* Bambino — he was *a* Bambino. Well, almost. A growing lad, let's say." — Columnist Mike Downey.

Chicago won its third straight pennant behind the 29 wins of Three Finger Brown. This was the famous Merkle Boner season (see **Base Running**) when the Cubs beat out the Giants by one game. The Cubs again faced the Tigers and won the Series, this time in five games. It was to be their last Series victory of the 20th century.

1910. After finishing second with 104 wins in 1909, the Cubs returned as pennant winners with another 104 wins. Though Three Finger Brown won 25 games and the Cubs won the pennant by 13 games, they lost the World Series to the A's in five games.

1918. The Cubs captured the pennant on pitcher Hippo Vaughn's league-leading 22 wins and 1.74 ERA, but lost the World Series in six games to the Red Sox and pitcher Babe Ruth.

1929.

"Hornsby's virile bat had helped put the Cubs in the world series, and all was well with the Wrigley vanity." — Joe Williams in the *Saturday Evening Post*.

The Cubs won the pennant by 10½ games under manager Joe McCarthy. They were led by Hack Wilson's 159 RBIs and Rogers Hornsby's .380 batting average. Chicago lost the Series to the A's in five games.

1932. The club won the pennant with a 90–64 record, but was swept by the Yankees, managed by former Cubs manager Joe McCarthy, in the World Series. Kiki Cuyler batted .291 with 77 RBIs, catcher Gabby Hartnett was solid behind the plate, and Riggs Stephenson batted .324. Lon Warneke was 22–6 to lead the club.

1935. The Cubs won the pennant by four games over the Cardinals, but again lost in the Series, this time to the Tigers in six games. Lon Warneke and Bill Lee each won 20 games and Billy

Herman batted .341. See Doug Feldmann, *September Streak: The 1935 Chicago Cubs Chase the Pennant* (2003).

1938. After Gabby Hartnett's **Homer in the Gloamin'**, the club went to the World Series only to be swept by the Yankees. Bill Lee led the league with 22 wins and a 2.66 ERA, but no batter had more than 13 home runs or 69 RBIs.

1945.

"The 1945 pennant was less a trend than a wartime freak." — William B. Furlong.

The club won the pennant by three games over the Cardinals. They lost the Series to the Tigers in seven games after the Cubs gambled by throwing pitcher Hank Borowy in Game 7 on only one day's rest. He was bombed for five runs in the 1st inning and could not get anyone out. Phil Cavarretta won the batting title with a .355 average, Andy Pafko drove in 110 runs and Hank Wyse won 22 games.

1969.

"New York didn't need that 1969 pennant … all Cub fans wanted was that one measly pennant. It would have kept us happy until the twenty-first century. But New York took that from us and I can never forgive that." — Mike Royko.

The 1960s Cubs were strong, but their fate was epitomized by the collapse at the end of the 1969 season. The Mets overcame the Cubs' 8½-game lead in September and the Cubs finished second. See also Rick Talley, *The Cubs of '69* (1989).

1984. The club won the Eastern Division title but lost the NLCS to the Padres in five games. The Cubs won the first two games of the series, but the key blow was Padre Steve Garvey's home run in the bottom of the 9th inning of a tied Game 4 to force a deciding Game 5. In the final game the Cubs led 3–0 after five innings, but Leon Durham's error in the 7th inning opened the door to four runs and a 6–3 Padre win. Rick Sutcliffe was 16–1 and Ron Cey, Jody Davis and Leon Durham each drove in more than 90 runs.

1989. The club won the Eastern Division title by six games over the Mets but lost the NLCS to the Giants in five games. Greg Maddux won 19 games and Ryne Sandberg hit 30 home runs.

1998. The club won a one-game **Play-Off** with the Giants to get into the postseason, only to be swept by the Braves in three games. Sammy Sosa had 66 home runs and 158 RBIs, Kevin Tapani won 19 games, and Rod Beck saved 51.

2003.

"Cork, Dork, No Fork" — Robert Ostrove on the highlights of the Cubs season: Sammy Sosa's corked bat incident; Steve Bartman's attempted catch of the infamous foul ball (see **Interference — Fans**); and Dusty Baker's failure to take out a tired and laboring Kerry Wood ("stick a fork in him, he's done") in Game 7 of the NLCS.

The Cubs were 88–74 to win the Central Division. They beat the Braves in five games in the division playoff, the Cubs' first postseason series victory since 1908. Then they lost in seven games to the Marlins after leading in Game 7. The Cubs were led by Sammy Sosa with 40 home runs and 103 RBIs (in 137 games), Mark Prior with a record of 18–6, and Joe Borowski with 33 saves. See *Chicago Tribune, Out of the Blue* (2004).

Key Players.

Albert Spalding (HF) was the club's first star, winning a league-leading 47 games in 1876 to help lead the club to the first National League pennant.

Cap Anson (HF) is the all-time Cubs leader in hits (2,995 — reduced from 3,041 and 3,000 in earlier editions of *The Baseball Encyclopedia*), doubles (528 — down from 532), runs scored (1,719 — no change), and RBIs (1,715 — down from 1,879 in some sources).

He played 22 seasons for the White Stockings/Cubs between 1876 and 1897.

John Clarkson (HF) was the club's star pitcher in the 1880s. He won 326 games in only 12 years, including high seasons of 53, 49 and 38.

Mordecai "Three Finger" Brown (HF) was a National League pitching star while with the Cubs from 1904 through 1912, winning more than 20 games six times. He had an ERA under 2.00 six times for the Cubs and won five World Series games.

Joe Tinker, Johnny Evers and Frank Chance (HF). See *Tinker to Evers to Chance*, who played together for the club from 1902 through 1912.

Gabby Hartnett (HF) played catcher for the Cubs from 1922 through 1940, hitting 236 home runs and batting .297.

Hack Wilson (HF) had his best years in the Major Leagues while with the Cubs from 1926 through 1931. He had home run years of 21, 30, 31, 39 and 56, and batted .313 or better five times.

Ernie Banks (HF).

"Without him, the Cubs would finish in Albuquerque." — Manager Jimmy Dykes.

Banks was the charismatic star of the Cubs from 1953 through his retirement after the 1971 season. Over those 19 years he batted .274 and hit 512 home runs. He won back-to-back MVP awards in 1958 and 1959, but the club was never able to make it to the World Series.

Billy Williams (HF) played for the Cubs from 1959 through 1974, hitting close to 400 of his 426 home runs with the club and batting almost .300.

Ron Santo.

"Five runs ahead and he'd knock in all the runs I could ask for. One run behind and he was going to kill me." — Manager Leo Durocher on Ron Santo.

Santo played 14 of his 15 Major League seasons with the Cubs (finishing his career with the White Sox). He hit 337 home runs and had 1,290 RBIs for the club while anchoring the infield at third base and suffering from diabetes throughout his career.

Ferguson Jenkins (HF) was traded to the Cubs in 1966, and in 1967 he began a streak of six straight seasons with 20 or more wins for the club.

Ryne Sandberg was considered the premier second baseman of the 1980s after being traded from the Phillies at the start of his career in 1981. He had a high of 40 home runs in 1990 and was the 1984 MVP. He retired abruptly early in the 1994 season, citing burnout and a desire to be with his family. He returned to the club for the 1996 season and finished two more years before retiring for good. He hit 282 home runs and had 1,061 RBIs for the Cubs.

Sammy Sosa was one of the most prolific home run hitters of the late 1990s and 2000s, with at least 63 home runs three times and 40 or more seven times between 1996 and 2003. He had 506 home runs for the Cubs through the 2003 season and in 2004 he became the Cubs' all-time leader when he surpassed Ernie Banks at 512.

Key Managers.

"For the moment he was the most famous baseball manager in the nation, the man guiding the Chicago Cubs toward their first pennant in half a century; everyone wanted to talk baseball, none gave a damn about his dreams....

"'Gentlemen, for the past several weeks I have been having prophetic dreams. It is my considered opinion that if the Chicago Cubs win the National League pennant, the world is going to end.'" — W.P. Kinsella in "The Last Pennant Before Armageddon," in *The Thrill of the Grass* (1977).

Cap Anson (HF) and his teams were often called the "Heroic Legion of Baseball" and were physically large teams in comparison to most others. He was player-manager of the club from 1879 through 1897 when he retired as a player and resigned under pressure. Over those 19 years he led the club to five early pennants (1880–1882, 1885–1886) and then generally finished in the first division until 1891. During the balance of the 1890s the club was mediocre or worse.

Frank Chance (HF) managed the club from 1905 through 1912, leading the Cubs to four pennants and two World Championships. Chance was fired after the 1912 season when the club faced the Chicago White Sox in the annual City Series. When the White Sox scored six runs in the 1st inning, erratic owner Charles Murphy reportedly fired Chance, who moved over to the Yankees for the 1913 season. The firing may have been caused by Chance's third-place finish that season after a string of first- and second-place finishes over the previous six years.

Joe McCarthy (HF) was hired by the Cubs in 1926 after they finished last for the first time in their history. He had never managed or played in the Major Leagues. He led the Cubs for five seasons, capped by a pennant in 1929. The club was in second place in 1930 when he was fired with four games remaining. Cubs owner William Wrigley had lost confidence in him, in part because the Cubs lost the 1929 World Series to the Yankees. Ironically, McCarthy went on to achieve his greatest success with the Yankees and beat the Cubs in the 1932 World Series.

Charlie Grimm played for the Cubs from 1925 through 1936 and also managed the club to pennants in 1932, 1935 and 1945, but never won a World Series. He returned for a brief managing stint in 1960, but was fired after 17 games and a 6–11 record. He returned to the Cubs' broadcast booth for the remainder of the season, but managed again in 1961 as an original member of the club's ill-fated *College of Coaches*. See also Charlie Grimm, *Jolly Cholly's Story* (1968).

Leo Durocher led the club from 1966 through mid-1972, finishing second twice. He was the manager during the Cubs' famous 1969 flameout when the Amazin' Mets beat them out for the division title and won the World Series.

Don Zimmer was nicknamed the "Gerbil" by pitcher Bill Lee because of his big puffy cheeks. He managed the Cubs from 1988 through 1991, leading the club to a division title in 1989.

Jim Riggleman managed the club for five seasons beginning in 1995, with a best finish of second in 1998.

Don Baylor took over in 2000 and was fired on July 5, 2002. In three seasons the club could do no better than third in 2001.

Dusty Baker left the Giants after going to the World Series in 2002, and promptly led the 2003 Cubs to the brink of their first World Series appearance since 1945.

Ballparks. In 1876 and 1877 the team played in a rickety wooden park on the West Side between 23rd and 24th on Dearborn, known as the 23rd Street Grounds (built following the Great Chicago *Fire*).

From 1878 through 1884 the club played in two parks known as Lakefront Park, though most sources identify them as a single park. The club moved to the better-known version for the 1883 season. Its dimensions were unbelievably small; from left to right field they were 186–280–300–252–196. All "home runs" hit over the short right field fence prior to 1884 were ruled doubles, but the ground rule double was eliminated in 1884 and the team's high home run statistics are distorted for that year. Ned Williamson set a dubious seasonal home run record with 27, and the club hit 131 home runs in 56 home games. The team hit a more realistic 10 on the road.

The White Stockings opened the 1884 season on the road because the Illinois Central Railroad offered $800,000 to the city of Chicago for the ballpark site as a depot. The club was allowed to finish its 1884 schedule when the club promised to build a site later known as the West Side Grounds. The park was located at Congress, Loomis, Harrison and Throop on the Near West Side (sometimes identified as the Congress Street Grounds). The club also played at South Side Park from 1891 through 1893, though in 1891 the White Stockings split time between West Side Park and South Side Park.

The club played at the West Side Grounds from 1894 through 1915. It had a capacity of 16,000 and had dimensions from left to right field of 340–560–316.

Wrigley Field was built in 1914 as a Federal League ballpark for the Chicago Whales. It was known originally as Weeghman Park after the club's owner, Charles Weeghman. When the Federal League disbanded, Weeghman bought the Cubs and combined the teams. The Cubs played their games at Weeghman Park beginning in 1916 and the name was changed to Cubs Park. It remained Cubs Park until the mid–1920s, when the name was changed permanently to Wrigley Field after owner Phil Wrigley.

Key Broadcasters.

"Overnight, Chicago became the baseball radio center of the nation. Hal Totten, Bob Elson, and Pat Flanagan were names to conjure with in fan circles — pioneers in a new and startling industry that would, in less than a decade, draw hundreds of millions of listeners to the parlor sets of a nation, and revolutionize the entire American sports industry." — Ford Frick in *Games, Asterisks and People* (1973).

"We don't care who wins, as long as it's the Cubs!" — Motto of long-time Cubs broadcaster Bert Wilson, who was heard over WIND from 1944 through 1955.

"If you're from the Midwest, given the words 'Hey-Hey,' who comes to mind in an instant? Unless you have spent the last thirty-plus years under an Arctic snow drift, the answer is elementary — Jack Brickhouse." — Cubs game program in the early 1980s.

The club's first radio broadcast was on October 1, 1924, for a Cubs/White Sox City Series exhibition game. Sen Kaney broadcast over WGN radio. The first regular season broadcast was on April 14, 1925, with Quin Ryan broadcasting from the grandstand roof. By the mid–1920s, five stations were broadcasting baseball in Chicago; the Cubs on three stations and the White Sox on two. Phil Wrigley wanted as many stations as possible broadcasting his club's games, believing that the exposure would generate greater attendance at games.

Hall of Famer Jack Brickhouse was Bob Elson's assistant with the Cubs in 1940, helping him to re-create Cubs and White Sox games until 1942. Elson went into the Navy, so in 1943 Brickhouse took over. Brickhouse aired 5,060 games over the next 42 years, retiring after the 1981 season. He also handled the White Sox announcing from 1948–67 and was the radio voice for the Chicago Bears from 1953 through 1976. He even broadcast Bulls games in the 1960s, signing the deal for WGN over cocktails with the team's owner.

Wrigley built the first glass-partitioned broadcast booth and the Cubs debuted on television on April 20, 1946, with Whispering Joe Wilson over WBKB-TV. That season the Cubs became the first club to televise all their home games. WGN-TV, the current flagship station, debuted on April 5, 1948, with Brickhouse at the microphone.

Jack Quinlan was the voice of the Cubs from 1956 until his death in a car accident at age 38 in March 1965. From 1958 through 1964 he teamed with Lou Boudreau, who was in the Cubs broadcast booth for almost 30 years.

Charlie Grimm broadcast for the Cubs during most of the late 1930s and 1940s. In between he managed the club three times and was part of the College of Coaches in the early 1960s.

Brickhouse was succeeded in 1982 by Harry Caray, who moved over from the White Sox. When Caray suffered a stroke and missed the early part of 1987, a number of celebrities filled in for him until his return, including actor/comedian Bill Murray and national columnist and writer George Will. President Reagan once broadcast a few innings with him. Caray was still going strong in 1997, his 53rd season, though he had cut back to three television innings and only selected road trips. He died in February 1998.

Ron Santo began broadcasting in 1990 and was still at it in 2003 for WGN despite severe health problems caused by diabetes. Joe Carter and Bob Brenley were among the former players to broadcast for the club in the 2000s. The club's primary broadcasters in the late 1990s and 2000s were Chip Caray and Pat Hughes.

Books. Warren Brown, *The Chicago Cubs* (1946); Bruce Chadwick, *Chicago Cubs: Memories and Memorabilia of the Wrigley Wonders* (1994); Derek Gentile, *The Complete Chicago Cubs: The Total Encyclopedia of the Team* (2002); Barry Gifford, *The Neighborhood of Baseball* (1981); Eddie Gold and Art Ahrens, *The Golden Era Cubs* (1985), covering the Cubs players from 1876 through 1940; Eddie Gold and Art Ahrens, *The New Era Cubs* (1985), covering 1941 through 1984; Eddie Gold and Art Ahrens, *The Renewal Era Cubs* (1991), covering players from 1985 through 1989; Peter Golenbock, *Wrigleyville* (1999); Fredrick C. Klein and Mark Anderson, *For the Love of the Cubs* (2004); Jim Langford, *The Game Is Never Over* (1980); Carrie Muskat (ed.), *Banks to Sandberg to Grace: Five Decades of Love and Frustration with the Chicago Cubs* (2001); Doug Myers, *Essential Cubs* (1999).

Chicago Pirates

Players League 1890

Charles Comiskey managed the club to a 75–62 record and a fourth-place finish. The Pirates featured Fred Pfeffer, Hugh Duffy and Jimmy Ryan, who batted .340. John Addison owned the Pirates and after the 1890 season he sold out to Albert Spalding of the rival White Stockings. As part of the sale, Addison took a $15,000 interest in the newly restructured New York Giants. The Pirates played their games at South Side Park, almost at the exact location on which Comiskey Park was built.

Chicago Whales/ChiFeds

Federal League 1914–1915

Chicago cafeteria magnate Charles Weeghman owned the Whales. During its first season the club was known as the ChiFeds. A contest was then held to name the club and Whales was chosen. The winner was D.J. Eichoff of 1451 Hood Avenue, Chicago. He said that the name Whales appealed to him because the best commercial whales were found in the north; the team played on the north side of Chicago; to whale means "to lash, thrash or drub"; and a whale is anything extraordinary in size.

The club finished second in 1914 with Joe Tinker as manager, only 1½ games out of first. In 1915 the club finished first by one percentage point with an 86–66 record (.566) to an 87–67 record (.565) for St. Louis. After the two-year Federal League folded, Weeghman was allowed to buy the National League Cubs and the best players from the Whales were included on the Cubs roster for the following season. The Whales played their games at a ballpark built for them, Weegham Park. It was later renamed **Wrigley Field**.

Chicago White Sox

American League 1901–

"If there is any justice in this world, to be a White Sox fan frees a man from any other form of penance."—Bill Veeck, Jr.

"Being a White Sox fan meant measuring victory in terms of defeat. A 6–5 defeat was a good day. A big rally was Wally Moses doubling down the right field line."—Jean Shepherd.

Origins. The White Sox were founded in 1900 by Charles Comiskey, who moved his St. Paul club in the Western League to Chicago as part of the new American League's bid to compete with the National League.

First Game. The White Sox were involved in the first game played in the American League, against Cleveland on April 24, 1901. The White Sox won 8–2 in front of 9,000 fans as all other games that day were rained out. Roy Patterson pitched a six-hitter in a game umpired by Tom Connolly.

The first game played by the club before the American League was recognized as a Major League was in 1900. The White Sox lost 5–4 to Milwaukee on April 21, 1900, but went on to win the pennant.

Key Owners.
Charles A. Comiskey/1901–1931.

"It has always been the contention of Comiskey that the only useful owner in baseball has been the one who has been through the mill as a player and manager, and the sentiment has not been in disparagement of that host of sportsmen-capitalists who have had a hand in upbuilding the game."—G.W. Axelson in "*Commy*" (1919).

Charles Comiskey owned the club from its American League debut as a Major League club in 1901 until he died in October 1931. The Hall of Famer was one of the most powerful owners in the history of the *American League* and went from a close relationship with *American League President* Ban Johnson to openly hostile.

J. Louis Comiskey/1931–1939.

"His pioneer heritage was left to J. Louis Comiskey, the only surviving [male] member of his immediate family, who had honeymooned with the former Grace Reidy on that 1914 trip around the world and had been quietly groomed to take his father's place."—John Carmichael in *The American League*, edited by Ed Fitzgerald (1959).

Charles Comiskey's son Lou was a vice-president under his father, weighed 360 pounds and was an invalid from the time he contracted scarlet fever in 1912. Nevertheless, he ran the club after his father's death until his own death in 1939. Lou is credited with starting the White Sox farm system.

Grace Comiskey and Children/1939–1959.

"To state it bluntly, Mrs. Comiskey, for reasons sufficient unto herself, had thought it better to leave the club under the control of her daughter rather than her son."—Bill Veeck, Jr.

"Chuck had grown up firmly convinced that the divine order of the universe called for the earth to spin on its axis, the sun to rise in the east and Charles Comiskey II to preside over the fortunes of the White Sox."—Veeck on the contentious and litigious grandson of club founder Charles Comiskey.

When Lou Comiskey died, the family's interest was put into a trust controlled by the First National Bank on behalf of his widow, Grace Comiskey, and her children. The estate was valued at $2,325,000. Before the 1940 season the bank petitioned the court for authority to sell the club and ballpark. Mrs. Comiskey immediately took steps to block the sale by renouncing the will in favor of her "dower" rights in the estate as provided by law. A year later the bank formally withdrew as trustee and transferred the estate to Mrs. Comiskey.

Grace Comiskey controlled the club until her death in December 1956. She arranged for her daughter Dorothy to take control of the club with a 54% interest. Son Charles A. "Chuck" Comiskey II received the other 46%. Dorothy eventually tired of the family wrangling with Chuck and decided to sell out. Though she preferred to sell to her brother (at least according to buyer Bill Veeck), Chuck's legal maneuvering and lowball offer for his sister's interest eventually forced her to sell to Veeck.

Although Dorothy married White Sox pitcher Johnny Rigney (later an executive with the club), one source erroneously reported that she married Major League player and manager *Bill* Rigney.

It has been reported that during the 1940s the Comiskeys turned down $2.5 million for the franchise and that Bill Veeck tried to buy the club before he bought the Indians in the 1940s.

Bill Veeck, Jr./1959–1961.

"It does seem only fair that I should return to baseball, if only to enjoy some slight taste, one might say, of my own cake — or, at least, to find out whether I can find some new way of blowing it."—Veeck shortly after he sold the club in 1961, in his autobiography *Veeck—As in Wreck*, with Ed Linn (1962).

Veeck and former slugger Hank Greenberg and their financial backers bought the club in March 1959 for $2.7 million and helped guide the White Sox to their first pennant since 1919. The deal was financed by the Allyn family, who had been backers of Veeck with the Indians and Browns. Chuck Comiskey continued to hold his 46% interest in the club and his refusal to sell cost the Veeck group (and Comiskey) more than $1 million in extra taxes. Charlie Finley initially was to be one of the members of the syndicate that purchased the club, but he tried to cut his own deal with the Wrigley family in the event that Veeck's deal fell through. In retaliation, Veeck dropped him from the group.

Veeck was forced to sell out in 1961 due to illness. He and Greenberg sold their interest to the primary investors with Veeck, the Allyn brothers.

Arthur Allyn, Jr., and John Allyn/1961–1975.

"One of the few indisputable characteristics of the human animal is that he's happier while playing than compelled to forage for food and security. There will always be a minority of self-centered buzzer-pushing unimaginative gransegniors who, despite their ulcers and prematurely gray hair, will dispute that philosophy, but Arthur C. Allyn, president of the Chicago White Sox, isn't among them."—Columnist Frank True.

Arthur Allyn was a butterfly collector, amateur pilot, pianist and former chemist. In 1973 he opened the Allyn Museum of Entomology to house his collection of 850,000 butterflies. His father founded his family's investment firm and was a partner with Bill Veeck when Veeck owned the Indians and Browns in the late 1940s and early 1950s. Arthur took over the family's investment business when his father died in 1959 and financed Bill Veeck's purchase of the club.

Arthur and his brother John bought a controlling interest in the club from Veeck in 1961 through the family company, Artnell. Chuck Comiskey refused to sell his 46% interest to the Allyns and gave an option to the group that eventually bought the Milwaukee Braves. The Milwaukee group later bought Chuck's interest on the erroneous promise from an anonymous source that they would be able to buy out the Allyns. The Milwaukee group instead bought the Braves and sold their minority interest in the White Sox to the Allyns in June 1962.

In the mid–1960s Arthur Allyn tried to sell the club to interests in Milwaukee who wanted to replace the departed Braves. When Arthur was unsuccessful in the sale, he bowed out in 1969 and sold his interest to his brother. The Allyn/Veeck association was resurrected when Veeck bought the White Sox from the Allyns in the 1970s and they retained a minority interest.

Bill Veeck, Jr./1975–1981.

"Chicago White Sox Trading Post"— Sign in the hotel lobby the morning after Veeck closed the deal to buy the team in December 1975. He made six deals involving 22 players in 48 hours. It has also been reported that the sign said "Open for Business by Appointment Only."

Veeck's investment group again included Hank Greenberg and the Allyn brothers, who maintained a minority interest in the club. Veeck paid about $10 million and tried to revive the moribund franchise, but limited resources, a rundown ballpark and a poor team made matters worse. When he bought the club the White Sox had finished last that season, as did every one of their farm clubs.

Financial problems forced Veeck to put the club up for sale in late 1980. The intended buyer was Edward DeBartolo, who instead bought the San Francisco 49ers in the NFL. DeBartolo was estimated to be worth $600 million, but the Major League owners would not approve the sale because DeBartolo also owned racetracks and did not live in Illinois (Ohio resident).

Eddie Einhorn and Jerry Reinsdorf/1981–.

"Reinsdorf runs the owners, enough of them anyway, the way O'Malley once did. He is that kind of boss, even as he hides behind Selig. Reinsdorf is the one who took out Fay Vincent. He is the real author of this strike. The cleanup hitter for Murderers Row. In the process of murdering a baseball season."— Columnist Mike Lupica.

In January 1981 Eddie Einhorn and Jerry Reinsdorf formed a limited partnership to buy the club. Reinsdorf and Einhorn met while both were in law school at Northwestern. Reinsdorf had sports franchise experience, owning the Chicago Bulls into the mid–1990s. He made his money in real estate development and sold his company to American Express for $50 million. Einhorn's background was as a television executive and syndicator of sporting events through a company that he later sold for $5 million. The pair continued their ownership of the club into the 2000s and became one of the driving forces in Major League Baseball.

Nicknames.

"What is the singular of Sox? In the days when ballplayers were often fairly happy where they were, there were frequent stories about this fact, usually with headlines like 'It's great to be a Yankee!' Could Mike Proly, then, write an article entitled 'It's great to be a White Sock'?"— Art Hill in *I Don't Care if I Never Come Back* (1980).

Charles Comiskey originally chose the White Stockings name as an insult to the cross-town National League rival Cubs, who had been known as the White Stockings but changed their name early in 1900.

In 1902 the name was shortened to Sox, supposedly because it fit better into newspaper headlines. Another source credits newspaperman Cy Sanborn with reviving the old White Stockings name, and he may have been the one to simply shorten the name to Sox.

In 1906 the White Sox were known as the Hitless Wonders for their league-low team batting average while winning the pennant.

The 1918 club was known as the Black Sox for their dirty uniforms and the 1919 club was given the same name for its involvement in the Black Sox gambling scandal.

The late 1950s White Sox were known as the Go-Go Sox because of their team speed.

Key Seasons.

"I'll believe a World Series when I see one. When the 1959 season was over and we baby Soxers were told by our parents to stop crying because, 'there'll be another World Series.' Well, mommy, daddy, you Big Fat Liars!"— Mike Downey in the *Chicago Tribune.*

The White Sox won the American League pennant in 1901, 1906, 1917, 1919 and 1959. They won the World Series in 1906 and 1917 (no World Series was played in 1901). The club won division titles in 1983 and 1993, but each time lost the League Championship Series. They were leading the American League Central Division in 1994 when the season was cancelled due to the player strike.

On August 31, 1920, the club was in first place, but finished second. They were never in first place again that late in the season until 1959, though the club was in first place for 44 days in 1951. The White Sox did not finish as high as second from 1921 through 1957.

1901. The club was led by the pitching of future Senators owner Clark Griffith and won the pennant by four games over Boston. Because of the feud between the leagues, no World Series was played until 1903.

1906.

"Putting any construction one pleases on the race as a whole, it was patent to any observer that the Sox had bluffed their way through."— G.W. Axelson in "*Commy*" (1919).

The club was known as the "Hitless Wonders" because it had by far the lowest batting average in the league at .228. Thirteen players batted over .300 that season in the American League, though none was from the White Sox. Nevertheless, the club won 19 straight in August, including eight shutouts, to vault into the lead and then defeat the Cubs in the World Series.

1908. Though the White Sox did not win the pennant, the season was one of the wildest of all time as the club finished third by 1½ games. See also G.H. Fleming, *The Unforgettable Season* (1981).

1917. This club had virtually the same players as the Black Sox of 1919. They won 100 games, captured the pennant by nine games and beat the Giants in the World Series 4–2. Eddie Cicotte led the league with 28 wins and Happy Felsch had 102 RBIs and a .308 average.

1919. The White Sox won the pennant and then took a dive in the World Series in what became known as the ***Black Sox Scandal.*** The Reds won the nine-game series 5–3. Eddie Cicotte led the league with 29 wins and Joe Jackson hit .351.

1959. The Go-Go Sox, who had been strong throughout the 1950s, finally overcame the powerful Yankees and Indians to capture the pennant. The club lost to the Dodgers in the World Series in six games. Early Wynn led the league with 22 wins, Turk Lown led with 15 saves and Luis Aparicio led with 56 stolen bases.

1983. The White Sox ran away with the Western Division crown behind LaMarr Hoyt's league-leading 24 wins and Richard Dotson's 22 wins. Ron Kittle hit 35 home runs with 100 RBIs. The White Sox lost the ALCS to the Orioles in four games.

1993. The White Sox won the Western Division by eight games over the Rangers and then fell in the ALCS to the eventual World Series champions, the Blue Jays. Frank Thomas hit .317 with 48 home runs and 128 RBIs. Jack McDowell won 22 games to lead the league.

1994. The club was leading the new American League Central

Division by one game when the season was cancelled in August because of the player strike.

2000. After four straight second-place finishes (albeit three with losing records), the White Sox won the Central Division with a 95–67 record but were swept by the Mariners in the division series. Frank Thomas had 43 home runs and 143 RBIs, Mike Sirotka (!) led the club with 15 wins and Keith Foulke had 34 saves.

Key Players.

Ed Walsh (HF) had a lifetime 1.81 ERA for the White Sox and pitched 57 shutouts from 1904 through 1917. Over his 13 years with the club he won 195 games, including 40 in 1908.

Joe Jackson is the club's all-time career batting leader with a .339 average. He was banned from Organized Baseball after the Black Sox Scandal of 1919.

Eddie Collins (HF), a stellar second baseman, had a .331 lifetime average for the White Sox and 2,007 of his hits from 1915 through 1926 in Chicago. He played 12 of his 25 Major League seasons for the club, batting over .300 in 10 of those years.

Ted Lyons (HF) is the club's all-time leader in pitching wins, with 260 over a 21-year Major League career spent entirely with the White Sox from 1923 through 1946.

Luke Appling (HF) was voted by Chicago writers in 1969 as the greatest living White Sox player. He is the club's all-time hit leader with 2,749 over 20 seasons, and also the club leader in runs, games, hits, doubles, total bases, RBIs, base on balls and at-bats. He is third in triples with 102.

Nellie Fox (HF) played second base for the White Sox in the 1950s and early 1960s and is second in many of the team's statistical categories behind Luke Appling.

Luis Aparicio (HF).

"He made plays that opponents at first viewed with amazement, and then gloomily came to accept as his normal performance."— Sportswriter Ed Prell.

Aparicio played 10 of his 18 Major League seasons with the White Sox in 1956–1962 and 1968–1970. In each of his first seven seasons, all with the Sox, he led the American League in stolen bases.

Hoyt Wilhelm (HF) is the club's all-time relief pitcher with 41 wins and was the leader with 98 saves. He was passed in 1990 by Bobby Thigpen, who set a Major League record with 57 saves that season.

Carlton Fisk (HF), though long recognized as a Red Sox catcher, was the all-time White Sox home run leader before being surpassed by Frank Thomas. Fisk played for the club from 1981 through 1993, when he retired after setting the record for most games played by a catcher.

Frank Thomas, known as The Big Hurt after being the 7th pick in the 1989 draft, won consecutive MVP Awards in 1993 and 1994. He hit 418 home runs for the White Sox between 1990 and 2003 while batting .310.

Key Managers.

Clark Griffith (HF), later to own the Senators, took over as manager in 1901 and immediately won a pennant. He lasted only one more year before moving over to the Highlanders/Yankees.

Pants Rowland, later president of the Pacific Coast League, took over the White Sox managerial duties in 1915 and oversaw a resurgence of the club through a number of key player purchases. The club finished third in 1915, second in 1916 and first in 1917. After a drop to sixth in 1918, Rowland was released.

William "Kid" Gleason managed the club during the ill-fated 1919 Black Sox season and led the 1920 club to a second-place finish. After the scandal surfaced, the club was decimated and he endured three more seasons of mediocre second-division ball. He was replaced after the 1923 season.

Jimmy Dykes.

"Most Dykes stories bubble over with the irrepressible good humor and witticisms of that effervescent character."— Sportswriter Arthur Daley.

Dykes managed the club from early 1934 until 40 games into the 1946 season. Known as the "Round Man," he smoked between 20 and 40 cigars a day. His best seasons were third-place finishes in 1936, 1937 and 1941. See also Jimmy Dykes and Charles O. Dexter, *You Can't Steal First Base* (1967).

Paul Richards took over the club in 1951, leading it to a fourth-place finish and then three straight third-place finishes behind the powerful Indians and Yankees. He moved to the Orioles for the 1955 season to become both manager and general manager.

Al Lopez (HF) began his managerial career with the Indians in 1951. After five second-place finishes and a pennant in 1954, he moved on to the White Sox for the 1957 season. He led the club to second-place finishes in 1957 and 1958 before winning the pennant in 1959. He continued to manage the club through 1969 (with two years off in 1967 and 1968), with his best years in 1963, 1964 and 1965, when the club finished second.

Tony LaRussa.

"The toughest thing for me as a younger manager is the fact that a lot of these guys saw me play. So it's hard for me to instruct them in anything, because they know how bad I was."— LaRussa as manager of the White Sox in 1981 after a Major League career in which he batted .199. He managed the club for eight years from 1979 through 1986, winning a division title in 1983.

Jerry Manuel managed the club to four second-place finishes and a division title between 1997 and 2003 before being replaced.

Key Ballparks.

"[It's] not exactly sterile, but it has roughly the charm of a clean utensil drawer."— Rick Telander on New Comiskey Park, which changed its name in 2002 to U.S. Cellular Field for a fee of $68 million over 20 years.

When the club was part of the new American League in 1900, it played its games in a small wooden ballpark at 39th and Wentworth. The facility had been the home of the Chicago Wanderers Cricket Club. Charles Comiskey obtained loans to renovate the ballpark and its capacity was increased from 7,500 to 15,000 (though some sources reported that the capacity never exceeded 7,500).

The club stayed in this facility until **Comiskey Park** opened four blocks away on July 1, 1910. The team began play in New Comiskey Park at the start of the 1991 season (see **Comiskey Park**). That park changed its named to U.S. Cellular Field for the 2003 season, after the company agreed to pay the club $68 million over 20 years for 23 years of naming rights.

Key Broadcasters.

"He made it sound as if broadcasting White Sox games was going to be more like joining the French Foreign Legion than playing the Palace."— Harry Caray in *Holy Cow!* (1989), describing the sales pitch to him by White Sox management in 1970; the club had just lost 106 games in 1970, the worst showing in its history.

Bob Elson first broadcast White Sox and Cubs games in 1928 and remained as the primary Chicago broadcaster for 40 years. He broadcast 12 World Series and nine All-Star Games. When he went into the military during World War II, President Roosevelt intervened to obtain him leave to broadcast the 1943 World Series. Following the war he broadcast exclusively for the White Sox through late 1970. He then followed Harry Caray to Oakland, and Caray returned to the White Sox. Jack Brickhouse broadcast for the club from 1940 through 1945 and then left briefly for New York. He returned and was the television broadcaster for both the Cubs and White Sox in the 1950s and mid–1960s before broadcasting exclusively for the Cubs in the late 1960s.

Harry Caray broadcast for the club from 1970 through the 1981 season before moving over to the Cubs. Jimmy Piersall was his broadcast partner for a good portion of his tenure with the Sox. See also Jack Brickhouse with Jack Rosenberg and Ned Colleti, *Thanks for Listening* (1986), referred to by one reviewer as "so badly written it's hard to believe three people worked on it."

Former player Ken Harrelson started in the booth for the club in 1991 and was still with the club through the 2004 season. John Rooney has been the primary radio broadcaster beginning in 1989, and former player Tom Paciorek broadcast for almost the entire 1990s.

Books. Warren Brown, *The Chicago White Sox* (1952); Richard Lindberg, *The Chicago White Sox Story: Who's on Third* (1983); Richard Lindberg, *Stealing First in a Two-Team Town: The White Sox from Comiskey to Reinsdorf* (1994); Richard Whittingham, *White Sox: The Illustrated Story* (1997).

Chicago White Stockings

National Association 1871, 1874–1875

This club was the predecessor to the team of the same name that was a founding member of the National League in 1876. William Hulbert was a stockholder in the club, but did not become president until early 1875 and then was the catalyst for creation of the National League the following season.

The club finished second in 1871 (19–9) and then missed the 1872 and 1873 seasons because of the Great Chicago *Fire* of October 1871, which destroyed their ballpark. The club returned in 1874 and 1875 to finish fifth and sixth before moving on to the National League. The White Stockings played their games at the Union Base-Ball Grounds in 1871 and at the 23rd Street Grounds in 1874 and 1875.

Chicago White Stockings See *Chicago Cubs/White Stockings*

Chicken See *Food*

Nester Chylak (1922–1982)

Hall of Fame (VC) 1999

"I umpired for 25 years and can honestly say I never called on wrong in my heart. The way I see it, an umpire must be perfect on the first day of the season and then get better every day." — Chylak.

Chylak was an American League umpire from 1954 until 1978.

Nestor Chylak was born in Peckville, Pennsylvania, in 1922. He served in World War II and was wounded in Europe in 1945. Temporarily blinded by his injuries, Chylak was awarded the Purple Heart. He began his umpiring career in 1947 working in the Class D PONY (Pennsylvania-Ontario-New York) League. He reached the Class AAA International League in 1952 and made the Major Leagues in 1954. He would officiate in the American League from 1954 until 1978 and would work five World Series, four American League Championship Series and three All-Star Games.

Chylak was the home plate umpire when Bill Mazeroski's home run ended the 1960 World Series. More infamously he also umpired the Cleveland Indians 10 cent "Beer Night" in 1978 which ended when Chylak forfeited the game to the Texas Rangers after hundreds of passionate Indian fans stormed the field. He was considered best post-war umpire during his tenure on the field.

Following his retirement from active umpiring Chylak served as the American League's assistant supervisor of umpires. Chylak suffered a heart attack in 1982 and passed away in Dunmore, Pennsylvania, at age 59.

Cigarette Cards See *Baseball Cards*

Cigarettes See *Tobacco*

Cincinnati

"Cincy is a dry town — as dry as the Atlantic Ocean." — Damon Runyon on the eve of the 1919 World Series in Cincinnati.

"When the world ends, I want to be in Cincinnati because it's always 20 years behind the times." — Supposedly said by Mark Twain.

"As Johnny Bench says, Cincinnati is a city of jocks. Sport is a central part of the local culture, and baseball is at the city's sporting heart.... Cincinnati not only gives baseball primacy, as Mayor Ruehlmann and Dave Parker both observe, but it uses baseball in some special ways. The city and the game keep inventing one another." — Robert Harris "Hub" Walker in *Cincinnati and the Big Red Machine* (1988).

"It's a good thing I stayed in Cincinnati for four years — It took me that long to learn how to spell it." — Rocky Bridges.

In 1915 it was reported that Matthew Yorston was the father of baseball in Cincinnati. He reportedly organized Cincinnati's first ballclub in 1859, which was made up of hospital interns. He also supposedly constructed the first bat in Cincinnati.

Most sources report that the game of Town Ball arrived in 1860 and the first organized baseball club in Cincinnati was the Live Oak Club formed immediately after the Civil War. Cincinnati was always considered a strong baseball town and local teams played to "immense" crowds in 1867. That same year the Ohio Baseball Federation was formed and became affiliated with the 1860s amateur National Association. The most famous early professional team was the all-professional *Cincinnati Red Stockings* of 1869–1870.

Major League Teams. Cincinnati has had the following Major League teams:

National League Cincinnati Red Stockings (1876–1877)
National League Cincinnati Reds (1878–1880)
National League Cincinnati Reds (1890–)
American Association Cincinnati Red Stockings (1882–1889)
American Association Cincinnati Kellys (1891)
Union Association Cincinnati Outlaw Reds (1884)

Book. Lonnie Wheeler and John Baskin, *The Cincinnati Game* (1988).

Cincinnati Kellys

American Association 1891

"But the King [Mike Kelly] was on his royal last legs when he came to Cincinnati again and formed the Killers. This weird team was absolutely without discipline.... On one occasion Kelly, stimulated by one of the post-game bacchanals, stripped down to his underwear and swam across the Ohio River to the Kentucky shore." — Lee Allen in *The National League*, edited by Ed Fitzgerald (1959).

The Kellys were formed after the Association's Cincinnati Red Stockings moved to the National League after the 1889 season. When the National League was at war with the American Association again during the winter of 1890–1891 (over the division of players from the Players League), the American Association allowed former Cincinnati owner Al Johnson back in as an owner.

The National League immediately tried to buy out Johnson to eliminate the threat to John Brush's National League Cincinnati club. A court action ensued that blocked the payment, and it was not resolved until 1901 when Johnson died and the money was divided. After the National League attempted to buy out Johnson, he was forced out by the American Association and it formed another team with Mike "King" Kelly as manager. St. Louis Browns owner Christopher Von der Ahe held a 75% interest in the club. Kelly's Killers played their games in Pendleton, a Cincinnati suburb.

By August of 1891 Von der Ahe was losing money and negotiating with National League Reds owner John Brush to sell out for $12,000 and move the team to Milwaukee. His plan was to combine with the Western League entry for a new American Association team in Milwaukee. The Kellys left town in August, before the end of the season, finishing in seventh place with a 43–57 record.

Cincinnati Outlaw Reds

Union Association 1884

"In Cincinnati the union entry managed to snag the lease from under the association team, thus forcing the Reds to relocate in an abandoned brickyard. This provoked heated rivalry between the two, and at times hired thugs menaced players of both nines." — David Quentin Voigt in *American Baseball* (1966).

The Outlaws finished second with a 69–36 record, 21 games out of first place with players primarily from the National League's Cleveland franchise. Key players were catcher Mike "King" Kelly and pitcher George Bradley, who was 25–15. The Outlaws played their games at the Bank Street Grounds, which had been trashed before the season by the former tenants, the American Association Red Stockings.

Cincinnati Red Stockings (1869–1870)

"We are a band of baseball players
from Cincinnati City.
We come to toss the Ball around
And to sing to you our ditty.
And if you listen to our song
We are about to sing,
We'll tell you all about baseball
and make the welkin ring.
Hurrah, Hurrah,
for the noble game, hurrah.
Red Stockings all will toss the ball
and shout our loud hurrah." — 1860 Red Stockings song sung to the tune of "Bonnie Blue Flag." The players lined up hand-in-hand at home plate before all games and sang to the crowd.

First Recognized All-Professional Team. This version of the Cincinnati Red Stockings was organized in 1867 and then reformed for the 1868 season by a 26-year-old attorney and entrepreneur, Aaron Burr Champion. The team was sometimes referred to as the Porkopolitans in reference to Cincinnati's unofficial nickname, Porkopolis, for its pig slaughterhouses and meat processing plants.

The 1868 team had four paid players. In 1869 all the players were paid and the club is recognized by most historians (and Major League Baseball) as the first all-professional baseball team. The club was managed by Harry Wright, sometimes acknowledged as a *Father of Baseball*. Wright hired eastern players and found them outside jobs, including his brother George from the Washington Nationals. The team may not have been the first all-professional team, but it was certainly the first all-salaried team to tour the country with players having binding season-long contracts.

Team Members. The team members and their ages, occupations, positions and salaries:

Andy Leonard	23	Hatter	LF	$	800
Doug Allison	22	Marble Cutter	C		800
Asa Brainard	25	Insurance	P		1,100
Charles Sweasy	21	Hatter	2B		800
Cal McVey	20	Piano Maker	RF		800
Charles Gould	21	Bookkeeper	1B		800
(The only Cincinnati native)					
Harry Wright	35	Jeweler	CF*		1,200
George Wright	22	Engraver	SS		1,400
(from Morrisania Unions of New York)					
Fred Waterman	23	Insurance	3B		1,100
Richard Hurley	20	Unknown	Sub		600

(from Cincinnati Buckeyes)
*and relief pitcher

Undefeated Streak. The team was undefeated in 1869 and for part of the 1870 season, with only one tie to mar its record. There have been various totals given over the years for the number of games won by the Red Stockings in 1869: 57, 58, 60, 61 and 65. The team went approximately 130 games over two seasons without a loss.

The 1869 Season. Asa Brainard made the first pitch of the season on April 17, 1869, beating a Cincinnati amateur team 24–15. The Red Stockings beat various local teams and then went on the road to play in Cleveland, Troy, Rochester, Buffalo, Albany, Syracuse, Boston and New Haven. The club had a 17–0 record before moving on to New York.

The team's toughest game during the streak was a 4–2 victory against the New York Mutuals on June 15, 1869, at the Union Grounds in front of 10,000 fans in Ridgewood, New York. The team then played in Philadelphia, Baltimore, Washington, Wheeling (W.Va.), Rockford (Ill.), St. Louis and Milwaukee. The last game of the season was on November 5, 1869, when they again beat the Mutuals 17–8.

The team barnstormed approximately 12,000 miles and played in front of 200,000 fans. Receipts for the season were $29,726.26. Salaries and expenses were $29,724.87, leaving a net profit from the tour of $1.39. The only injuries suffered by the players during the season were an assortment of broken fingers. When the players returned to Cincinnati they were presented with a 27-foot wooden baseball bat from the Cincinnati Lumber Company.

The Tie Game. The only blemish on Cincinnati's 1869 undefeated streak was a 17–17 tie against the Haymakers of Troy, New York. The game was called after five innings due to an argument and Troy walked off the field. It was later reportedly determined that the team quit so that Troy owner John Morrissey and other New York gamblers could avoid paying off bets if their team lost.

First Loss. The team's first loss was against the Brooklyn Atlantics on June 14, 1870. Cincinnati lost 8–7 in 11 innings in front of 9,000 (or 20,000) fans, who each paid 50 cents to watch the game at the Capitoline Grounds in Brooklyn. The game was tied 5–5 at the end of nine innings. The game's official scorer, sportswriter Henry Chadwick, decided that the game was to be played to completion.

In the top of the 11th inning the Red Stockings scored two runs to lead 7–5. The Atlantics rebounded with three in the bottom of the inning for the victory. Some accounts report that Red Stockings outfielder Joe Start tried to field a key hit during the inning while a fan was jumping on his back. The ball fell for a triple and the Atlantics won the game.

The 1870 Season and Dissolution. The team lost six games in 1870. The first loss to the Atlantics caused interest in the team to decline and "penny pinching" began to erode the team when A.P. Bonte took over as the club's president. Bonte later announced that there would be no team in 1871 because of "enormous salary demands" by the players. One director of the Red Stockings later admitted that the threat to disband the team over salary disputes was a bluff that did not work.

Because of financial problems the bulk of the team's key players moved to the Boston Red Stockings. They included George and Harry Wright, Cal McVey and Charlie Gould. Every player from the 1869 team signed with clubs in the new National Association in 1871. One writer noted that the legacy of the Red Stockings was to stimulate local interest in having a "representative" club for an entire city.

Ballpark. The club played its home games at the Lincoln Park Grounds, opened for the 1869 season.

Books. Harry Ellard, *Baseball in Cincinnati* (1907) (Ellard's ancestor, George S. Ellard, was instrumental in helping form the Red Stockings); John Erardi and Greg Rhodes, *The First Boys of Summer* (1994).

Cincinnati Red Stockings

National League 1876–1880

"Si Keck's Stink Factory"—Nickname for club owner Keck's waste-burning facility at the edge of the city. The name might have been applied to the Red Stockings, who finished last in four of their five seasons.

The Red Stockings were a charter member of the National League in 1876. The team was so bad that it finished last with a record of 9–56. It played its games in the Chester Park area in a ballpark with a capacity of 3,000, but which was rarely even half full.

The owner of the team was Josiah "Si" L. Keck, a meatpacker who had suffered stormy times in Cincinnati. In 1868 he started the Cincinnati Fertilizing Factory with a contract to remove animal and vegetable waste from the city.

Keck lost money during the 1876 season and the situation did not improve in 1877. On June 16, 1877, he announced his resignation as owner, disbanded the team, and released the players. It was unclear whether the team would still be part of the league, but eight local businessmen stepped up with money to keep the team afloat. To make matters worse, Keck's field was inaccessible because of heavy rains that had washed out a number of games.

When Keck made his announcement, White Stockings owner and National League leader William Hulbert immediately signed two players from the Cincinnati roster. Outfielder Charley Jones played two games for Chicago and then went back to Cincinnati when the new owners stepped in. The other player, Jimmy Hallinan, remained in Chicago.

It was not until December 1877 that the league decided whether the Cincinnati games for 1877 counted. The league initially determined that the games with Cincinnati were null and void although no reason was given for the decision. *The Baseball Encyclopedia* records all of the club's games that season, as it finished with a full-season record of 15–42, good for a distant last place.

The club was back in 1878 — by then known as the Reds — and it rebounded with a second-place finish before finishing fifth in 1879. During the 1880 season the club was struggling in last place. The Reds attempted to raise money by selling beer during games and leasing the park to other clubs for Sunday baseball. There was vocal opposition to both practices from the "puritanical" Worcester club. Cincinnati club president W.H. Kennett was adamant regarding the sale of beer and said the team would quit the league if there was to be no drinking. As a result of the rift, the Reds were replaced in the National League by Detroit after the 1880 season.

One source noted that this was only the "announced" reason for dropping the Reds. The "real" reason was that Kennett opposed the newly instituted reserve clause. National League president Hulbert wanted the reserve clause and is said to have enlisted the New England clubs, including Worcester, to push the beer issue as a smokescreen. Cincinnati fans were angry at the loss of their club and one local reporter, upset over the puritanical objection to beer sales, noted: "that while the league is in the missionary field ... they should turn their attention to Chicago and prohibit the admission to the Lake Front Grounds of the great number of prostitutes who patronize the game up there."

The Red Stockings played their games at the Chester Avenue Grounds from 1876 through 1879 and then moved to the Bank Street Grounds for the 1880 season.

Cincinnati Red Stockings

American Association 1882–1889

When the Cincinnati Red Stockings were kicked out of the National League following the 1880 season, Cincinnati *Sportswriter* O.P. Caylor combined with the Spink family in St. Louis to help form the American Association. The National League Cincinnati club was bankrupt and the receiver, a Colonel Harris, worked hard to persuade local businessmen to back a new club. Clothing man Aaron Stern bought the principal interest in the club and a strong Cincinnati team won the Association's first pennant in 1882.

In February 1886 John Hauck, the wealthiest brewer in Cincinnati, bought into the team and by then Caylor was managing the club. He took them to a second-place finish in 1885 before fading to fourth in 1886. The Reds finished second under a new manager in 1887 and then faded over the next two seasons. Pitcher Tony Mullane was the club's best pitcher in the mid–1880s. Outfielder Charley Jones and second baseman Bid McPhee also were key players.

By 1889 owner Aaron Stern was fed up with the Association's leadership and tried to force a change at the 1889 winter meetings. A deadlock in the voting for a new president was broken only after the Reds and the Brooklyn Dodgers resigned from the Association and moved over to the National League.

In 1882 and 1883 the Reds played their games at the Bank Street Grounds. The players ransacked the ballpark just before the 1884 season when the new Union Association club was about to occupy it. In 1884 the Reds built a park at Findlay and Western Avenues, where Crosley Field eventually stood. The club was briefly known as the Pioneers in 1886.

Cincinnati Reds

National League 1890–

"There is, however, a legendary team of the 1970s. It lives of all places in Cincinnati, Ohio, a conservative, Middle Western community of German ancestry. It is an industrial community located on the Ohio River where Ohio, Indiana, and Kentucky seem to become one. It is, in the ever-expanding big league scene, the third smallest of major league cities. It is also the best baseball city anywhere."—Bob Hertzel in *The Big Red Machine* (1976).

Origins. During the 1890 Players League, a group of Players League backers bought this National League club from long-time owner Aaron Stern, who had owned the club in the American Association from 1882 until it moved to the National League after the 1889 season. After the dust settled from the events of 1890, former Indianapolis owner John Brush was awarded the National League franchise in Cincinnati. Matters were so confused during 1891 that some investors owned a piece of both the National League and American Association clubs in Cincinnati.

First Game.

"A few over 6,000 assembled in the Cincinnati Park this afternoon to witness the opening game of the National League between the local club and the Chicagoes. It was not a model for ballplaying as it was quite cold. The Chicagoes outplayed the Cincinnatis in the field and won the game by fortunate bunching of their hits and their opponent's errors."—Game day report.

The Reds played their first game on April 19, 1890, in front of 6,000 fans. The Chicago White Stockings beat them 5–4.

Key Owners.

Aaron Stern/1890. Stern had been the owner of the American Association version of this club through the 1880s and was instrumental in moving the club to the National League for the 1890 season. He was forced out during the season, a casualty of the Players League war.

John Brush/1891–1902. Brush owned the club from its second season in the National League until 1902, when he sold the team for $125,000 to Garry Herrmann, who became president. Brush parlayed that sale into a purchase of the more lucrative New York Giants, eliminating the hated Andrew Freedman as an owner (see *American League* for details of the interrelationship of these sales and the ultimate effort by the American League to bring a team to New York). Brush was considered one of the most influential owners of the 1890s.

August "Garry" Herrmann/1902–1927.

"He was the personification of Cincinnati Culture. To remember him is to remember the outdoor beer gardens and vaudeville, the surging waiters, the foaming steins of beer, the Liederkrantz sandwiches, the belching, guffawing laughter of long-forgotten nights."—Ethan Allen quoted in *Cincinnati and the Big Red Machine*, by Robert Harris "Hub" Walker (1988).

Herrmann was president of the Reds from 1902 through 1927 and shared ownership with his political crony, mayor George B.

Sliding drills at the Reds spring training in 1939. Eddie Joost (8) applies the tag as manager Bill McKechnie (glasses) looks on.

"Boss" Cox. Herrmann also headed the Cincinnati Waterworks and served as Grand Exalted Ruler of All the Elks in America. Herrmann's nickname of Garry came from his early years as a printer, when he was nicknamed Garibaldi — later shortened to Garry.

Herrmann was chairman of the National Commission from 1903 until 1920, when Judge Landis was appointed commissioner and the Commission was abolished. Other owners during Herrmann's tenure were Max and Julius Fleischmann. Their father Charles founded the Fleischmann Yeast Company (of margarine fame) and Julius later became the youngest mayor in the history of Cincinnati. The Fleischmann brothers had a plant in New York and therefore had contact with Yankee owner Frank Farrell, who encouraged them to buy into the Reds.

Herrmann's personal papers chronicling the years 1902–1925 are contained in over 70 boxes at the Hall of Fame. Herrmann retired in 1927, in part due to blindness and other health problems. After he relinquished control of the club, the business affairs of the

Though not a Major Leaguer for the Reds, comedian Jonathan Winters always sported his favorite team's uniform when he played in celebrity games in the 1970s. As provided by Winters' son, Jay, to the author, Winters had written on the back of the photograph: "In pain? you bet your sweet_____! I singled off Del Crandall (coach of Angels during benefit game at Anaheim — hard ball). Slid home but suffered a hematoma (blood clot) below right knee cap — has taken almost two months for it to go away. July 30, 1977, age 51 (last hard ball game I play in) Nothin' worse than an 'old jock.' P.S. Also a grim look because the Reds didn't win the pennant!"

club passed to C. J. McDiarmod, who sold the club in 1930. Ty Cobb unsuccessfully offered $275,000 for the club in 1928.

Sidney Weil/1930–1933.

"If I had bought the Cincinnati club in 1930 at $300,000, would have lost my shirt. Team drew under 500,000 ten years.... Horseshit town today." — Entry in Ty Cobb's 1946 diary, now part of Barry Halper's *Memorabilia* collection.

Weil owned a Ford automobile dealership and a number of Cincinnati garages when he bought the club. He lost his fortune in the stock market crash and lost the Reds to bankruptcy in 1933. He later became a millionaire again after learning to sell life insurance.

Powell Crosley, Jr./1934–1961.

"Apparently there was no one in Cincinnati interested in becoming an angel for the ballclub. After a considerable selling job [by Larry MacPhail] sold me the idea of becoming interested.... I do have sufficient civic pride and my makeup did not want to see Cincinnati, the birthplace of major league baseball, become a minor league town." — Powell Crosley, Jr., in a 1939 interview.

After Weil filed for bankruptcy, a bank repossessed the team and hired Larry MacPhail to become general manager. MacPhail immediately appealed to local broadcaster Powell Crosley to invest in the failing club for $450,000.

Crosley's company manufactured appliances, radios and automobile bodies. He also owned the Crosley Broadcasting Company, which included the leading Cincinnati radio station, WLW. He started the station in 1922 with 500 watts, and it grew to an astonishing 500,000 watts. It was so powerful that it could be heard in Australia and people in Cincinnati sometimes complained that they picked up the signal in the fillings of their teeth. After World War II the power was reduced to 50,000 watts, the highest now allowable.

Gabe Paul was the driving force behind the Reds for many years, working for the team from 1937 until 1960. He left to help pursue a new franchise in Houston. He started as publicity director and moved through the team's front office as traveling secretary, assistant to the president, vice president and general manager. Future National League president Warren Giles was president of the Reds in 1946.

Crosley died during spring training in 1961, but his brother continued to control the family's foundation that owned the club. They sold out in 1963 to a group headed by Bill DeWitt, who had taken over as general manager in early 1961.

Bill DeWitt/1963–1967. DeWitt held the club until late 1966, when he offered to sell out under pressure. He was unhappy with the leasing situation at Crosley Field because of the NFL's insistence that a new stadium would be required in Cincinnati before the NFL would commit to a football franchise for the city. DeWitt agreed to sell out, but only to local interests. That occurred in early 1967, when he received $7 million for the club.

Francis Dale, et al./1967–1973. The publisher of the *Cincinnati Enquirer* newspaper, Francis Dale, became president of the Reds and a 15% shareholder. He headed a group of 12 buyers (11 from Cincinnati) who raised $7 million to buy the club. The owners were incorporated as "617, Inc.," which was the street address of the *Cincinnati Enquirer*.

Bob Howsam took over as general manager in 1967 after having been with the Cardinals for three years. He had also been president of Denver in the American Association by age 30. He attended the University of Colorado, where Branch Rickey had taught and recommended him to the Cardinals. In 1973 Howsam succeeded Francis Dale as club president, though Dale remained an investor. However, the *Enquirer* had divested itself of its interest by this time and Louis Nippert increased his holdings to a majority interest.

Louis Nippert/1973–1981. By 1973 Louis Nippert, one of the original members of the syndicate that bought the club in 1967, had increased his ownership interest to 51%. By 1980 he had obtained 90% of the club. The remaining 10% was owned by his brother James, Andrew Hoppel, David Gamble and Barry Buse. All were members of the original syndicate that purchased the club in 1967.

The Williams Brothers, et al./1981–1985. A new partnership was created in 1981, to be headed by the Williams brothers, James and William. They were Cincinnati financiers who had been minority shareholders with the Francis Dale syndicate in the late 1960s. Louis Nippert remained as a limited partner. Other limited partners were Lloyd Miller, Marge Schott, Morley Baldwin and Carl Kroch. Kroch owned a chain of Chicago bookstores.

Marge Schott/1985–1999.

"She does the dumbest things." — Former commissioner Fay Vincent.

"I just wish she'd get out. We all wish she'd get out. She's a despicable person." — One of Schott's partners.

"Red Menace." — *Sports Illustrated*'s May 20, 1996, cover of Schott.

Schott bought into the team as a limited partner in 1981, became the managing general partner in 1985 and later owned more than 40% of the club. When she bought the club to avoid its departure from the city, she called it a "Christmas present" for the city.

She also ran two car dealerships and more than 10 other businesses and held a sizable stake in General Motors stock. She was from a strict German family and was raised in a convent. Her father had made a fortune in plywood and veneer. When her husband died in 1968 she successfully fought to keep the dealerships and increased sales dramatically in the first two years. Schott called everyone "honey" because she couldn't remember names.

Other investors during the Schott era included financier Carl Lindner, Frisch's Restaurants, Carl Kroch, Multimedia, Inc., Louis Nippert, William Reich, Jr. and TF Corporation.

In 1991 several limited partners sued Schott for the $17.69 million they claimed she failed to disperse to them. The case later settled. In the early 1990s she was suspended for a year for making racist remarks. In 1994 and 1995 Schott threatened to move the club to Louisville or another site if the city did not capitulate to her demands. In 1997 Schott sold her Chevrolet-Geo dealership after General Motors accused her of faking sales to meet quotas.

She was the center of controversy again in 1996 for ***Racism*** issues and was again suspended. John Allen was named the interim managing executive in June 1996 and Schott was barred from day-to-day operations through the 1998 season. Minority owners Barry Nussbaum and Jerry Ruyan, owners of Frisch's Restaurants, wanted to sell 6.6% of the club in spring 1997 for $10 million.

In April 1999 Schott finally gave in to pressure from Major League Baseball and sold out to Carl Lindner and the other partners for $67 million. She did so two years before their partnership agreement was to end. At the time, she was again under investigation by General Motors for irregularities in the running of her car dealership.

A chain smoker who was hospitalized for severe breathing problems, Schott died in 2004 at age 75. See also Mike Bass, *Unleashed* (1994).

Carl Lindner/1999–

"only in america. gee, am I lucky." — On business cards handed out by Lindner.

One of the wealthiest men in America, Lindner owns 40% of Chiquita Bananas and is the largest shareholder of insurance company American Financial Group, worth about $14 billion. A devout Baptist, he does not swear, drink or smoke, and is a former owner of the *Cincinnati Enquirer*. He was instrumental in fighting the exhibition of Robert Mapplethorpe's controversial sexually explicit art in the city in 1990.

Born in Ohio, Lindner dropped out of high school and started out working in his father's ice cream shop. He built it into a chain of 200 United Dairy Farmers stores, run by his brother. Lindner used the profits to buy into financial institutions (his long-time lawyer was Lincoln Savings' scandalized leader Charles Keating). He then moved into insurance, often using junk bond king Michael Milkin to finance his deals.

Nicknames.

"We were known as the Reds before the Communists. Let them change their name." — Sportswriter Tom Swope in the early 1950s. During the Communist scare led by Senator Joe McCarthy in the early 1950s, the Reds were persuaded to change their nickname to "Redlegs" from 1953 through 1958.

"Nobody's gone after Reds with this much vigor since Joe McCarthy." — Jeff Blair of the *Montreal Gazette*, on the Expos' Shane Andrews, who hit .471 (16-for-34) with six homers and 21 RBIs against Cincinnati in August 1996.

The team has always been known as the Red Stockings, Reds or Redlegs. The 1970s powerhouse was known as The Big Red Machine (see also ***Dynasties***).

Key Seasons. The Reds did not win a pennant from 1890 until 1919, when they won the first of nine. They have won the World Series five times (1919, 1940, 1975, 1976 and 1990). They won division titles in 1973, 1979 and 1995.

1919. The club won the pennant by nine games and then upset the heavily favored White (Black) Sox in the tainted World Series. Edd Roush led the league with a .322 average and Slim Sallee won 21 games.

1939. The club won 97 games and the pennant over the Cardinals by 4½ games, led by pitcher Bucky Walters' league-leading 27 victories and Frank McCormick's league-leading 128 RBIs. The Reds were swept in the World Series by the Yankees.

1940. The Reds repeated as pennant winners and won 100 games for the first time in their history. They went on to defeat the Tigers in a seven-game World Series. Bucky Walters again led the league with 22 wins and Frank McCormick hit .309 with 127 RBIs.

1961. The Reds won a close pennant race over the Dodgers by four games but lost the World Series in five games to the powerful Yankees. Joey Jay led the league with 21 wins and Frank Robinson hit 37 home runs and had 124 RBIs.

1970. Rookie manager Sparky Anderson led the Reds to a pennant with 102 wins and a victory over the Pirates in the NLCS. They lost to the Orioles in the World Series as Brooks Robinson almost single-handedly beat them. Johnny Bench had a league-leading 45 home runs and 148 RBIs.

1972. After an off-season in 1971 the club won the Western Division by 10½ games and beat the Pirates for the pennant. They lost the World Series in seven games to the A's. Johnny Bench again led the league with 40 home runs and 125 RBIs. Clay Carroll led the league with 37 saves.

1973. The Reds were division winners but lost to the Mets for the pennant. Pete Rose led the league with a .338 average and both Tony Perez and Johnny Bench had over 100 RBIs.

1975. After winning 98 games in 1974 but finishing second to the Dodgers, the Reds won the 1975 pennant and a dramatic seven-game Series over the Red Sox to capture their first World Championship since 1940. Joe Morgan was the league MVP with a .327 average, 17 home runs, 94 RBIs, 132 walks, 122 runs scored and 58 stolen bases. Tom Adelman, *The Long Ball: The Summer of '75—Spaceman, Catfish, Charlie Hustle, and the Greatest World Series Ever Played* (2004).

1976. The Reds repeated as National League champions with a 102-win season. They beat the Phillies for the pennant and went on to sweep the Yankees in the World Series for their second consecutive championship. Joe Morgan won another MVP award and George Foster led the league with 121 RBIs. Rawley Eastwick was the league leader with 26 saves.

1979. After two strong second-place finishes in 1977 and 1978, the Reds bounced back to win the Western Division in 1979 by 1½ games over the Astros before losing to the Pirates in the NLCS. George Foster had 30 home runs and 98 RBIs.

1990. This club was the first since the 1984 Tigers to go wire-to-wire for a division title. They beat the Pirates in six games, with four of them decided by one run. Led by Eric Davis and his 24 home runs, the Reds went on to sweep the World Series against the A's.

1995. The Reds won the Central Division title behind the 18 wins of Pete Schourek and 28 home runs by Reggie Sanders. National League MVP Barry Larkin anchored the club at shortstop while batting .319 and stealing 51 bases. The Reds swept the Dodgers in the division play-offs and then were swept by the Braves in the NLCS.

1999. The Reds finished the season in second place in the National League Central with a 96–66, then lost a one-game play-off with the Mets for the wild card spot (thereby finishing with a 96–67 season record). Greg Vaughn had 45 home runs and 118 RBIs. Pete Harnisch was 16–10 and relievers Danny Graves (27) and Scott Williamson (19) combined for 46 saves.

Key Players.

Edd Roush (HF) starred for the Reds from 1917, when he hit .341, until 1926. He never hit below .323 during his 11 years with the club.

Eppa Rixey (HF) was the winningest left-hander in National League history until Warren Spahn came along. Rixey won 179 games in 13 seasons with the club, including a league-high 25 in 1922.

Bucky Walters was a star pitcher for the Reds from the late 1930s through the mid–1940s. He won 27 games in 1939 and 22 in 1940, both years leading the club to the pennant. Between 1939 and 1944, he won 121 games before fading.

Ted Kluszewski played 11 seasons for the Reds from 1947 through 1957. During that span he hit 251 home runs, including a league-high 49 in 1954 and 47 in 1955. He also batted over .300 seven times for the club and drove in more than 100 runs five times.

Frank Robinson (HF) played 10 solid seasons for the Reds before being traded to the Orioles after the 1965 season (exploding in 1966 to win the Triple Crown). He batted over .300 five times for the Reds and hit 29 or more home runs nine times. He also led the league in slugging average three times while with the Reds.

Johnny Bench (HF) was perhaps the greatest catcher of all time. He won two MVP awards and starred for the Reds from 1967 through 1983. He batted .267 lifetime and hit 389 home runs, twice hitting 40 or more in a season.

Joe Morgan (HF) played only eight seasons for the Reds during the 1970s (after nine in Houston), but he made the most of them. He won consecutive MVP Awards in 1975 and 1976, batting

.327 and .320, with slugging averages of .508 and .576. He was the sparkplug of the club and helped anchor the infield at second base. Though only 5'7" and 150 pounds, he hit 22 or more home runs four times for the club.

Pete Rose played the first 16 and last three seasons of his 24-year career with the Reds (1963–1978, 1984–1986). He led the league in batting three times and had over 200 hits for the club nine times. He also led the league in runs scored four times.

Eric Davis played eight seasons for the Reds from 1984 through 1991 and hit 24 or more home runs five times. Though injury-prone, he led the club to a World Championship in 1990. He returned to the club in 1996 after a series of injuries and drug problems.

Barry Larkin. In 18 seasons through 2003, Larkin had 2,240 hits and a career-high 35 home runs in 1996 while anchoring the Reds' infield at shortstop.

Key Managers.

Pat Moran took over the club in 1919 and immediately led it to its first pennant, defeating the Black Sox in the World Series. He managed the club four more years, finishing second in 1922 and 1923.

Bill McKechnie (HF) managed for 25 Major League seasons, including nine years with the Reds at the end of his career. He led the club from 1938 until near the end of the 1946 season. He won two pennants and one World Series (1940), and finished in the first division in five other seasons.

Fred Hutchinson.

"For five innings, it's the pitcher's game. After that, it's mine."—Hutchinson.

Hutchinson led the Reds from mid–1959 through most of the 1964 season, when he was diagnosed with cancer and died in November of that year. He led the Reds to a pennant in 1961 and the club finished second in 1964.

Sparky Anderson (HF).

"I refuse to call a 56-year-old man with white hair Sparky."—Umpire Al Clark.

George Anderson led the Big Red Machine of the 1970s to the club's greatest success. He took over in 1970 and immediately led the Reds to a pennant. He managed the club through the 1978 season and won two World Series along with four pennants and five division crowns. See also Sparky Anderson with Si Burick, *The Main Spark* (1978); Sparky Anderson with Dan Ewald, *Sparky!* (1990).

Pete Rose was manager or player-manager of the club for most of the 1980s. He led the club to three consecutive second-place finishes from 1985 through 1987. The end of his tenure was marked by a suspension due to a run-in with umpire Dave Pallone and surfacing *Gambling* allegations. The club finished second in 1988. Rose was barred from baseball in mid–1989 when the club was in fourth place.

Lou Piniella led the club to a championship in his first season in 1990, faded to fifth in 1991 and returned to second place in 1992. He then departed after conflicts with erratic owner Marge Schott.

Ballparks.

Early Ballparks and *Crosley Field*.

"Cincinnati, 1958, entering a major-league ballpark for the first time."—National Public Radio "Morning Edition" host Bob Edwards, asked in *Vanity Fair*, "When and where were you happiest?"

The Reds first played in League Park in an area known as Chester Park. The ballpark was rebuilt in 1894 and the club played in that facility until 1901. It was rebuilt for the 1902 season to become the Palace of the Fans. It was improved in 1911 and remained essentially the same facility until 1970. It was first known primarily as Redland Field and later *Crosley Field* after 1930s owner Powell Crosley.

Riverfront Stadium/Cinergy Field. The first proposal for a new riverfront ballpark in the historic downtown business district was made in 1948 as part of a 15-Volume "Plan of 1948" Redevelopment Plan for the city. The plan was developed by the nationally known father of urban planning, attorney Alfred Bettman.

The key decisions to build the new stadium were made in 1966–1967. Owner Bill DeWitt did not favor the eventual site because of potential flooding. The immediately adjacent river had overflowed by over 80 feet in 1937, so the stadium eventually was designed with the field 80 feet above the river.

Pro football wanted to be in Cincinnati, but DeWitt would not give football the 40-year lease that was required by the National Football League. The NFL said that if there were no stadium by 1970, Cincinnati would not be awarded a franchise. Because of the stand-off, DeWitt agreed to sell out and the new owners agreed to the lease.

Riverfront Stadium was built at a cost of $48 million. Capacity originally was 51,050 and later fluctuated slightly above that amount. The dimensions from left to right field were 330–375–404–375–330.

Local contests were held to name the ballpark. In order of popularity: Astronaut Neil Armstrong; Senator Taft; President Eisenhower; Governor Rhodes; former owner Powell Crosley; Fred Hutchinson (who had managed in the 1960s and died of cancer shortly after resigning). Also popular were Regal Stadium, People's Stadium, Buckeye Bowl, Ohio Stadium, Red Bengal Stadium and Queen City Stadium.

Five weeks before it opened, the facility still had no name. Mayor Eugene Ruehlmann, who had spearheaded the stadium's development, wrote a letter on May 30, 1970, in which he identified the facility as "The Cincinnati Riverfront Stadium," in reference to the same designation given to the site in the 1948 Redevelopment Plan. The name stuck.

The Reds played their first game in Riverfront on June 30, 1970, against the Braves in front of 51,051 fans (one more than capacity!). The Braves jumped off to a 3–0 lead in part on a home run by Henry Aaron. The Braves won 8–2 but the Reds won the National League pennant with a club-record season attendance of 1,803,568.

On July 14, 1970, the All-Star Game was held in this stadium, only two weeks after it opened. In the first regular season game the scoreboard and sound system were only temporary; the plumbing was unfinished and the team had to install temporary elevators to accommodate fans.

The ballpark was renamed Cinergy Field for the 1997 season and closed after the 2002 season. On September 22, 2002, the Reds played their final game at Cinergy Field, a 4–3 loss to the Phillies. The facility was demolished in December 2002 to become the western concourse of the new facility and included the Reds' new Hall of Fame.

Great American Ball Park.

"Maybe we could rename it "Pretty Good American Ballpark." — Paul Daugherty of the *Cincinnati Enquirer*.

This new facility opened in 2003 after Great American Insurance paid for the naming rights in 2000, paying $75 million over 30 years. In 1996 voters approved a tax increase to build two new facilities, one for the Reds and one for the Bengals of the NFL. The budget for both was $544 million, but the Bengals' stadium alone exceeded that amount. Voters again approved another ballpark for

the Reds in 1998 and construction began in 2000 along the banks of the Ohio River.

The Reds lost the first game there, 10–1 to the Pirates, on March 31, 2003. Capacity is 42,036 (or 42,059) and the dimensions from left to right are 328–404–325.

Key Broadcasters.

"And this one belongs to the Reds." — Hall of Fame broadcaster Marty Brennaman's signature sign-off after all Reds wins.

"The biggest fear I have is that I'll wake up and sound like Pee Wee Herman and my career will be over." — Brenneman on his 1990 throat surgery.

"Rounding third and heading for home" — Signature sign-off of broadcaster Joe Nuxhall.

"I talked to several of the players ... and I was about to leave when I was spotted by Joe Nuxhall, once a pitcher but now a fat radio announcer." — Sportswriter Glenn Dickey.

Harry Hartman broadcast in the 1920s as both the public address announcer and occasional radio commentator. The first regular Reds broadcasts began in 1929 with Bob Burdette.

Red Barber first broadcast in Cincinnati in 1934, primarily doing re-creations, though he broadcast 20 games directly from Crosley Field. Owner Powell Crosley used his Burger Beer Baseball Network to broadcast Reds games to southern Ohio, Indiana, Kentucky, West Virginia and Northern Tennessee. One source erroneously reported that former pitcher Waite Hoyt and Barber broadcast together during the 1930s before Barber followed general manager Larry MacPhail to Brooklyn in 1939. Hoyt was still pitching until 1938 and did not begin broadcasting with the Reds until 1942, where he remained until 1965 (maybe he made a few guest appearances between starts?).

Hoyt was criticized by Reds president Warren Giles for not being more positive on the air about the team, in contrast to Cubs broadcaster Bert Wilson. Hoyt's rather pointed response, as recounted in Curt Smith's *Voices of the Game*: "Why the shit *shouldn't* Bert Wilson cheer? They won the pennant last year, didn't they? They've got a great park to play in and they've got some stars, they win some games. But us ... your top hitter's a lousy .267 or whatever the hell it is. Your top pitcher's won eight games. What is there to *cheer* about? Christ, if I cheered like Bert Wilson with the bums we've got, people would think I was blind or the village idiot ... or maybe both."

Former Reds pitcher Joe Nuxhall and Marty Brennaman later had long tenures as Reds broadcasters and ABC's Al Michaels broadcast for the Reds early in his career. Brennaman, a 2000 Frick Award winner, began with the club in 1974 and was still going strong through 2004. Nuxhall started a couple of years later and signed a deal that took him through the 2004 season, making it 28 straight seasons with Brennaman. George Grande has been the television voice since 1993. Former pitcher Chris Welsh began his ninth season broadcasting with the club in 2004.

Books. Lee Allen, *The Cincinnati Reds* (1948); Bruce Chadwick, *Cincinnati Reds: Memories and Memorabilia of the Big Red Machine* (1994); Harry Ellard, *Base Ball in Cincinnati* (1987 reprint of a 1907 edition); Earl Lawson, Cincinnati *Reds: My 34 Years with the Reds* (1985); Greg Rhodes and John Snyder, *Redleg Journal: Year by Year and Day by Day With the Cincinnati Reds Since 1866* (2000); Chris W. Sehnert, *Cincinnati Reds (America's Game)* (1997); Robert Harris "Hub" Walker, *Cincinnati and the Big Red Machine* (1988); Lonnie Wheeler, *The Cincinnati Game* (1988).

Civil War (1861–1865)

"It had a been a great war for baseball."—Arthur Bartlett in *Baseball and Mr. Spalding* (1951), referring to the war as a catalyst for spreading baseball to the masses.

"If U.S. Grant had been leading a team of baseball players, they'd have second guessed him all the way to the doorknob of the Appomattox Courthouse."—Bill Veeck.

"War is an organized bore."—Justice Oliver Wendell Holmes, suggesting that players had plenty of down-time to play ball during the war.

"So baseball is the old army game. Previous to the Civil War, it was played almost entirely in New York and Boston and their vicinities. Those players introduced it to the [prison] camps. The South's army learned it from captured Union soldiers. At the close of the war, soldiers of both armies carried the game to every city, town, and hamlet. In this manner, baseball was nationalized."— 19th century star Jim "Deacon" White, as told to Gene Kessler in *The Birth of a Nation's Pastime* (1933). This quote is not entirely accurate, as Southerners had already learned the game and it was played in many Southern towns before the Civil War. For example, New Orleans was a hotbed of prewar baseball. Nevertheless, the Civil War was important to the popularity of baseball because it helped spread the game to new enthusiasts. Prior to the war, it was played most frequently by a relatively small and sometimes elite group.

The number of amateur teams plummeted at the outset of the Civil War as club members and potential players became soldiers. New York alone went from 92 to 28 teams in the first two years of the war, which began on April 12, 1861, at Fort Sumter in Charles Harbor, South Carolina.

During the war, truces were arranged at the front lines to play baseball games (though not between Northern and Southern teams). On Christmas Day 1862 at Hilton Head, South Carolina, a game was arranged involving the 165th New York Volunteers Infantry (Duryea's Zouaves), played in front of 40,000 soldiers. The game purportedly was the talk of the military for months afterward. Future National League presidents Nick Young and A.G. Mills brought baseball equipment with them while serving in the Civil War and supposedly played often during breaks in the fighting.

There are claims that the first baseball played in Texas was in 1863 by Union prisoners at Camp Ford.

No Yankees Allowed. Gee and Harvey "Hub" Walker were graduates of the University of Mississippi. Their Confederate mother supposedly would not let them wear a "Yankees" uniform because of the Civil War connotation, so both signed with the Tigers and debuted with the club in 1931.

Book. George B. Kirsch, *Baseball In Blue and Gray* (2004).

Fred Clarke (1872–1960)

Hall of Fame (VC) 1945

"He was one of the fastest base runners of all time. He used his elbows in running as much as his legs and tried to jar the ball loose whenever the infielders held it, a style that led to numerous altercations."—Lee Allen.

Clarke starred as an outfielder and manager for Louisville and Pittsburgh beginning in 1894.

Born in Iowa, Clarke began his professional career in Nebraska in 1892. He made it to the Major Leagues as an outfielder in 1894 with Louisville of the National League, going a record 5-for-5 in

his first game. At age 25 in 1895 he was named manager of the club, a position he held through Louisville's move to Pittsburgh through the 1915 season.

Clarke was a player-manager who succeeded at both for the Pirates. He batted .312 as an outfielder over his 21-year career, including 11 seasons over .300. He hit 220 triples, seventh all-time. His last game was in 1915 on Fred Clarke Day, when he played four innings and had a single.

As a manager, he won 1,602 games over 19 years, including three straight pennants starting in 1901 and a pennant in 1909. The club lost the first World Series in 1903 but won the 1909 Series in seven games over the Tigers.

After the 1915 season Clarke retired to his Kansas ranch, known as Little Pirate Ranch. He occasionally surfaced in baseball circles, but his primary concern was the fortune in wheat he made at the ranch. He died of pneumonia in 1960, just short of his 88th birthday.

John Clarkson (1861–1909)

Hall of Fame (VC) 1963

"Many regard him as the greatest, but not many know of his peculiar temperament and the amount of encouragement needed to keep him going. Scold him, find fault with him, and he could not pitch at all. Praise him and he was unbeatable. In knowing exactly what kind of a ball a batter could not hit and in his ability to serve up just that kind of a ball, I don't think I have ever seen the equal of Clarkson."—Cap Anson on learning of Clarkson's death.

Clarkson was a National League pitching star in the 1880s and 1890s who won 326 Major League games.

John Gibson Clarkson and two of his younger brothers became Major League pitchers, although John was the star of the group. He won 326 games in only 12 years, with highs of 53 in 1885 and 49 in 1889. He was discovered by Cap Anson and the White Stockings in 1884 while pitching at Grand Rapids, though he had pitched in 1882 in the National League for Worcester. He was obtained in exchange for fading pitcher Larry Corcoran. He led the White Stockings to pennants in 1885 and 1886 while winning 88 games.

He was traded to the Boston Red Stockings in 1888 and went on to win 165 games over the next five seasons. He finished his career with Cleveland, to whom he was traded during the 1892 season. He has the distinction of playing for both pennant winners that season, as Boston and Cleveland each won one of the split-season races. He won a total of 24 games for Cleveland in 1893 and 1894 before a sore arm forced him to retire. He opened a cigar store in Michigan and died at age 47 in 1909.

Roberto Clemente (1934–1972)

Hall of Fame 1973

"I would like to be remembered as a ballplayer who gave all he had to give."—Clemente.

"I would be lost without baseball. I don't think I could stand being away from it as long as I was alive."—Clemente.

Clemente hit .317 in 18 seasons for the Pirates beginning in 1955 and was the greatest sports star in Puerto Rican history.

Roberto Walker Clemente ("Bob" on some of his Topps baseball cards) signed with the Dodgers in 1954 and played that season for their Class AAA club in Montreal. Because he had received a bonus of over $4,000 and had not played with the Major League club in 1954, he was available to be drafted by another club. The

Pirates grabbed him and at 20 years old in 1955 he was Pittsburgh's starting right fielder.

Clemente hit over .300 in 1956, the first of 13 .300 seasons in 18 years. He led the league in hitting in 1961, 1964, 1965 and 1967 and led the Pirates to the World Series in 1960 and 1971. He was named National League MVP in 1966 when he hit .357 with a league-leading 209 hits.

Clemente batted a lifetime .317 with 440 doubles, 166 triples and 240 home runs. He batted .362 in two World Series. He was known for his defensive prowess in right field and was considered to have the best arm in the Major Leagues during his career (see also **Defensive Gems**).

He reached exactly 3,000 hits on the last day of the 1972 season. On New Year's Eve 1972, he was killed on a mercy flight to Nicaraguan earthquake victims (see also **Deaths**). He was elected to the Hall of Fame by special vote in early 1973.

Books. Bruce Markusen, *Roberto Clemente: The Great One* (2004); Jim O'Brien, *Remembering Roberto* (1994); Kal Wagenheim, *Clemente* (1973).

Cleveland

"Cleveland was the kind of city that Neil Simon thought about when he was stuck for one-liners." — David Falkner in *The Short Season* (1986).

"The A's leave after this game for Cleveland. It was only by a 13–12 vote that they decided to go." — A's announcer Lon Simmons.

Cleveland had daily baseball in its public square as early as 1857. Local authorities tried to find an ordinance prohibiting the game, but were unsuccessful. Cleveland has had the following professional clubs:

National Association Forest Citys (1871–1872)
National League Cleveland Blues (1879–1884)
National League Cleveland Spiders (1889–1899)
American Association Cleveland Blues (1887–1888)
Players League Cleveland Infants (1890)
American League Cleveland Blues/Naps/Indians (1901–)

Cleveland Blues

American Association 1887–1888

The club finished last in 1887 with a 39–92 record. The Blues improved to 50–82 in 1888, but were dropped from the league after the season.

Cleveland Blues

National League 1879–1884

"The Clevelands played their last game of the season in this city yesterday, and that they come no more is not a matter of serious regret. It may have been the weather, but all the men in the field seemed in the ugliest possible mood." — *Buffalo Express* article of August 31, 1881.

The Blues were added to the National League in 1879 and lasted through the 1884 season. The club was mediocre or worse until 1883, when it finished 55–42 and only 7½ games out of first place. Nevertheless, the club was in financial trouble in 1883 and pressure from the Union Association in 1884 hurt it badly.

The Union Association raided its star players, including shortstop Jack Glasscock and pitcher Jim McCormick, forcing the Blues to pick up players from the recently disbanded Grand Rapids club.

Blues president C.H. Bulkley needed the National League's help and was given an indirect subsidy of 50% of road receipts instead of the usual 30%.

Cleveland staggered to a seventh-place finish in 1884 and sold all of its players to Brooklyn of the American Association for "delivery" in 1885. The sale and delivery of the players during the 1884 season was a technical violation of the National Agreement, as players could not be sold before October.

Cleveland Forest Citys

National Association 1871–1872

In 1871 this mediocre club finished eighth in a nine-team league with a record of 10–19. The following year the club had a 6–15 record prior to disbanding before the end of the season. The Forest Citys played their games at the 3,000-seat National Association Grounds.

Cleveland Indians

American League 1901–

"One thing about the Cleveland Indians: They may, in the words of a once-popular song, have been a headache, but they never were a bore." — Gordon Cobbledick in *The American League*, edited by Ed Fitzgerald (1959).

Origins. The Indians were created in 1900 when the Western Association changed its name to American League. The club was a charter member in 1901 when the league achieved Major League status.

Key Owners.

"The reader is introduced to businessmen behind the scenes who were the true culprits of Cleveland's decline. They include a dubious fraternity of hacks, drunks and womanizers who gutted the farm system, forcing questionable personnel moves that dispatched talented players to other teams while sending local fans fleeing in droves." — *Baseball Weekly* book review of Jack Torry's *Endless Summers: The Fall and Rise of the Cleveland Indians* (1995).

Charles Somers and Jack Kilfoyl/1901–1916.

"But they did have one big advantage and that was Somers's bank account. Charley was a handsome young man who was willing to take almost any kind of a gamble, in business or in sports." — *The Sporting News.*

The original American League franchise owners were Charles Somers and Jack Kilfoyl. Somers was in the coal business with his father and Kilfoyl owned a men's clothing business in Cleveland. When they assumed control of the Cleveland franchise in the new American League in early 1900, there was no team, no players and no ballpark. They worked out an arrangement to lease old League Park from Frank and Stanley Robison, who still owned the ballpark and also the National League franchise in St. Louis (and had owned the Cleveland Spiders).

Kilfoyl remained with the club until 1908 when ill health, brought on in part "by the stress he suffered from each agonizing defeat," forced him to sell his interest. Future American League president Ernest Sargent Barnard became associated with the club in 1904 as traveling secretary and, after Kilfoyl retired, Barnard became vice-president and general manager. By 1916 Somers was almost $2 million in debt and was forced to relinquish control of the club to the American League.

Jim Dunn and Family/1916–1927.

"The old flu came pretty near to taking the sun out of Sunny Jim Dunn, president and principal owner of the Cleveland Indi-

Members of the 1910 Cleveland Indians.

ans, this spring…. He's of the sort that the game needs — eager to win, if he can fairly, but the same old smile if his team loses; the even temperament that has brought him the nickname of 'Sunny Jim.' In fact, he feels insulted if anyone calls him 'Mr. Dunn'; He is 'Jim' to everybody, which indicates pretty well the sort of stuff that he's made of." — *The Sporting News* in 1922.

Sunny Jim Dunn was a railroad contractor based in Chicago who agreed to take over the failing club from Somers, though not without financial assistance from other American League owners. Ernest Barnard remained with the club as general manager through this period. Charles Comiskey loaned Dunn $100,000, as did American League president Ban Johnson. The total purchase price was $500,000 and the balance of the proceeds came from other investors known by Dunn.

Dunn saw the club's quality increase in the late 1910s, with two second-place finishes and a World Series victory in 1920. Dunn died in 1922 and the club passed to his widow, though Barnard remained as club president until becoming American League president in 1927.

Alva Bradley/1927–1946.

"When Alva Bradley, president of the Cleveland Indians,

scratched baseball men the wrong way by saying he didn't think the game would last the [wartime 1944] season out ... some unkind soul asked what kind of baseball Bradley thought he'd been giving Cleveland fans the past few years. The Indians have done less with good material than any other club in the circuit, because of front office and managerial blunders."—The *Stars and Stripes* military newspaper.

On November 27, 1927, the club was sold for about $1 million to a group headed by Cleveland banker John Sherwin. Alva Bradley was named president of the club and he chose former umpire Billy Evans as general manager. The Indians spent lavishly on new players and jumped from seventh to third in two years. However, the 1929 stock market crash forced the owners to stop spending on the club. Despite a number of first division finishes, the Indians never seriously challenged for the pennant during the remainder of Bradley's tenure. On June 21, 1946, Bradley sold the club for $1.6 million to Bill Veeck, Jr., who had recently recovered from his World War II wounds.

Bill Veeck, Jr./1946–1949.

"Then, as the army and navy veterans came back in 1946, Cleveland baseball reached its most significant turning point. Bill Veeck, a war-damaged ex-marine, hit the town with the explosive force of a hydrogen bomb."—Gordon Cobbledick in *The American League*, edited by Ed Fitzgerald (1959).

Veeck took over the club after Alva Bradley's associates forced a sale in June 1946. Under Veeck's stewardship the Indians reversed their fortunes and two seasons later won a pennant and set a new season attendance record. After the club fell flat in 1949 Veeck sold out later that year.

Ellis Ryan/1949–1953. Ellis Ryan was an insurance executive who headed the group that purchased the club from Veeck in November 1949 for $2.2 million. Bob Hope retained his small interest in the club and Hank Greenberg bought into the club. Greenberg was elevated to general manager and manager Al Lopez guided the club to a series of strong finishes in the early 1950s.

Ryan sold his interest in 1953 after a dispute among the major stockholders. He advocated that all games except Sunday games be played at night and he was on the selection committee that chose Ford Frick to succeed Happy Chandler as commissioner. Ryan was forced out of the presidency when six members of an opposition faction came onto the board.

Myron Wilson/1953–1963. When Ellis Ryan was forced out, Myron Wilson became club president in 1953 and headed the syndicate that owned the club until early 1963.

Gabe Paul/1963–1966. In 1963 long-time baseball man Gabe Paul put together a group that bought the club. Paul was the largest shareholder with a 21% interest.

Vern Stouffer/1966–1972. Stouffer, of frozen food and restaurant fame, bought a controlling interest in the club in 1966 for over $8.3 million. Gabe Paul remained as club president until the end of Stouffer's ownership in 1972.

Stouffer's family opened a restaurant in 1924 and his father had a butter manufacturing business that evolved into a frozen food empire and a series of lunch counters. When Stouffer bought the club, he had just sold his company to Litton Industries in a stock transaction. Stouffer took Litton stock, which plummeted throughout his ownership and forced him to sell when he was short on cash.

Nick Mileti/1972–1975. Mileti and four other Cleveland businessmen bought a controlling interest in 1972. Mileti was a 40-year-old attorney who owned the Cleveland Cavaliers of the NBA and the Cleveland Barons of the American Hockey League. Mileti reportedly withdrew from the group in April 1975, replaced by the

IBC Corporation and Ted Bonda. However, Mileti sold only a portion and remained as a minority owner.

Ted Bonda/1975–1977. IBC Corporation was headed by Bonda, who had been club president for the previous three years. He was one of the founding members of APCOA, the largest parking lot company in the country. Bonda remained in control of the club through late 1977.

Steve O'Neill/1977–1986. O'Neill bought 57% of the Indians and brought Gabe Paul back to the club. Paul had been with the club from 1963 through 1971 and remained with the club from 1977 through 1985. The O'Neill group owned the Indians through late 1986, when the Jacobs brothers bought the club.

Richard and David Jacobs/1986–1999. When they purchased the club in December 1986, Richard and David Jacobs owned 43 shopping malls, six hotels and six office buildings. They continued to own the club into the 1990s, but Richard died in 1992. In 1994 David Jacobs paid over $13 million to have the club's new ballpark named after his family. In 1994 he was reported to be worth $275 million.

On June 4th, 1998, the Indians went public and quickly raised $60 million by selling out all four million shares of common stock at $15 each in about one hour. After the offering sold out, the stock was trading in the $14.75 to $15.25 range. The club is still the only publicly traded team in Major League Baseball. In May 1999 owner Richard Jacobs announced that he was putting the club up for sale.

Larry Dolan/1999– .

"George Steinbrenner and his Yankees play in a dilapidated, old, concrete-falling, 1920s stadium.... The Indians play in a brand-new ... luxury-suite-filled stadium.... Dolan has been cheating Americans out of their cable money for thousands of years.... So next time you want to throw stones, make sure you don't live in a glass house."—Peter Brown in *The Sporting News*.

"I will be the CEO. I will control 100 percent of the voting rights. The balance of ownership will be held by Dolan family trusts. My brother Charles will not be involved in the ownership of the team or in these family trusts in any way. Cablevision is not involved in the ownership either."—Dolan.

In November 1999, Cleveland attorney Larry Dolan, 68 at the time, agreed to buy the Indians from Richard Jacobs for $320 million ($323 million in some sources), a record at the time. The sale was approved in January 2000. Dolan was part of a cable television empire and had wanted to buy the Reds. His brother, Charles Dolan, was chairman of Cablevision Systems Corp., the nation's sixth-largest cable television provider who was at the time the 312th richest person on the *Forbes* 400. The brothers had attempted to buy the Reds (and had a purchase agreement with Marge Schott executed), Yankees, Washington Redskins and Cleveland Browns. Most of Larry's wealth was as a result of stock ownership in the cable company founded by Charles.

The cable company's operations were primarily in the New York, Cleveland and Boston metropolitan areas. Based in New York, the company had a 50% ownership interest in Fox Sports Net, a national sports programming network that fed most of the country's sports networks. Larry Dolan brought Cablevision to the Cleveland area in the early 1980s. Until that time, he had spent most of his time as an attorney in the courtroom representing developers, insurance companies and white-collar crime defendants.

Nicknames.

"Instead of Naps, they ought to be 'Napkins,' the way they fold up."—A Cleveland sportswriter commenting on the club's inability to win a pennant under manager Nap Lajoie.

Various sources report slightly different versions of how the various Cleveland nicknames were created. Some report that the team was known as the Blues from 1901–1904 in honor of the club's uniform colors. Others report that the club was known as the Blues only for their first Major League season in 1901, but that the players chose Broncos for 1902. The name did not stick, in part because newspapermen could not find a convenient way to shorten it for headlines. From 1905 through 1914 the club was known as the Naps for Nap Lajoie, who managed the club from 1905 through 1909 and was its star player until traded to the A's after the 1914 season. Other sources report that Naps was chosen in a newspaper poll in 1903, an unlikely occurrence given that Lajoie had been with the club for less than a year and was not yet manager.

In early 1915 a newspaper contest reportedly was held to pick a new name. The name "Indians" supposedly was chosen to honor former Cleveland player Louis Sockalexis, the first *Native American* thought to have played Major League Baseball. Baseball historians, using research by Ithaca College professor Ellen Staurowsky, now believe that no such naming contest was held and that the club simply took the name to promote a "warrior" image. In addition, Jim Toy was probably the first *Native American* player in the Major Leagues.

Key Seasons.

"In Cleveland, pennant fever usually ends up being just a 48-hour virus."—Frank Robinson.

"I always liked working Indian games because they were usually out of the pennant race by the end of April and there was never much pressure on the umpires."—Former umpire Ron Luciano.

The Indians won pennants in 1920, 1948, 1954, 1995 and 1997, and have been runners-up 12 times. They won the World Series in 1920 and 1948. Between 1959 and 1993 the club did not finish within 10 games of first place.

1908. The club came close to a pennant for the first time, but lost out to the Tigers on the last day of the season despite a perfect game by Addie Joss the day before.

1920. Mediocrity prevailed through the 1910s until 1917, the season after Tris Speaker arrived. The club finished third that year, second in 1918 and second again in 1919 under new manager Speaker. The tumultuous 1920 season featured the *Death* of Indians shortstop Ray Chapman in August and revelations about the Black Sox of 1919. Though the Indians fell out of first place shortly after the Chapman beanball incident, the club rallied behind new shortstop Joe Sewell and won the pennant by two games over the White Sox and defeated the Dodgers 5–2 in a nine-game World Series for their first championship. Jim Bagby led the league with 31 wins and Tris Speaker, Elmer Smith and Larry Gardner each drove in more than 100 runs.

1940. The Indians finished second by one game to the Tigers. Bob Feller led the league with 27 wins and a 2.61 ERA.

1948. Player-manager Lou Boudreau led the club to a tie for the American League championship and his two home runs helped beat the Red Sox in a one-game play-off for the pennant. The Indians went on to defeat the Braves in six games to capture their first World Series in 28 years.

1954. The Indians won a then league-record 111 games, but the Giants swept them in the World Series. The Indians were led by Bobby Avila's league-leading .341 average and Larry Doby's league-leading 32 home runs and 126 RBIs. Pitchers Early Wynn and Bob Lemon each won a league-leading 23 games. See also Bruce Dudley, *The 1954 Cleveland Indians Revisited* (1995).

1994.

"For the first time since 1954, it's the—yes!—first-place Indians. Talk about a real-life 'Field of Dreams.' It don't get any better

than this."—Walter Shapiro in *Time* magazine, fantasizing about late-season 1994 baseball without a strike.

The club was in first place at the All-Star break for the first time since 1959. When the strike-shortened season ended, the Indians were still leading their division.

1995. The Indians won the Central Division by 30 games and then beat the Red Sox in the division play-offs. They beat the Mariners in six games for the American League pennant, but lost the World Series in six games to the Braves. Albert Belle hit 50 home runs in only 144 games.

1996. The Indians won the American League Central Division by 14½ games over the White Sox before losing to the Orioles in the first round of the postseason. Albert Belle hit 48 home runs and had 148 RBIs, and Jim Thome hit 38 home runs. Jose Mesa had 39 saves.

1997. The Indians ran away with the American League Central and then beat the Yankees in five games in the division playoff. They beat the Orioles in six games for the American League pennant, but lost the World Series to the Marlins in a thrilling extra-inning Game 7 after leading in the 9th inning. Jim Thome, Matt Williams and David Justice each had over 100 RBIs and Thome had 40 home runs. Charles Nagy won 15 games and Jose Mesa and Mike Jackson combined for 31 saves.

1999. The Indians won the Central Division with a 97–65 record. They won the first two games of their five-game division series against the Red Sox, but Boston came back to sweep three straight for the series win, including 23 runs in Game 4. Manny Ramirez hit 44 home runs and drove in 165. Jim Thome and Roberto Alomar each drove in 108 runs or more, and Dave Burba, Charles Nagy and Bartolo Colon each recorded at least 15 wins. Mike Jackson had 39 saves.

2000. The club missed the wild card spot by one game, finishing with a 90–72 record behind the A's and Mariners.

Key Players.

"The first thing they do in Cleveland if you have talent is trade you for three guys who don't."—Pitcher Jim Kern.

Nap Lajoie (HF) starred for the Indians from his arrival in mid–1902 until his departure after the 1914 season. The second baseman led the league in hitting with .355 and .381 averages in 1903 and 1904 and hit over .300 11 times.

Addie Joss (HF) was one of the premier pitchers in baseball from 1902 through 1909. He won 20 or more games in four straight seasons and had the second-lowest career ERA at 1.88. He faded in 1910 and early in 1911 he contracted meningitis and died a few weeks later.

Joe Jackson played for the Indians from 1910 (appearing in 20 games) to mid–1915, batting .331 or better each season. He hit .408 in 1911, the highest rookie average of all time. In 1915 he was sold during the season to the White Sox when owner Charles Somers was strapped for cash.

Tris Speaker (HF) played for the Indians from 1916 through 1926 and was player-manager beginning in 1919. He hit over .300 ten times for the club, including years of .386, .388, .380 and .389. He also led the league in doubles seven times while with the Indians and was the premier center fielder in the Major Leagues.

Joe Sewell (HF) arrived from the University of Alabama shortly after the death of shortstop Ray Chapman in 1920. Sewell finished the season with a .329 average, fielded well, and remained as Cleveland's shortstop (and later the club's third baseman) through the 1930 season. He hit over .300 nine times, including a .353 average in 1923. He struck out only 99 times in 11 seasons for the Indians.

Wes Ferrell won 21 or more games four straight seasons with the Indians from 1929 through 1932.

Mel Harder pitched for 20 years in the Major Leagues, all with the Indians. He won 223 games from 1928 through 1947 and had two seasons of 20 or more wins.

Lou Boudreau (HF) played 13 seasons for the Indians, leading them to a World Series victory in 1948 after two home runs in a one-game play-off against the Red Sox to capture the pennant. He was player-manager of the club from 1942 until his departure to Boston in 1950. He was the team's shortstop and catalyst, batting over .300 four times, including a league-leading .327 in 1944.

Bob Feller (HF) won 266 games over an 18-year career with the Indians that was interrupted for three seasons during World War II. Feller led the league with 24, 27 and 25 wins from 1939 through 1941 before going into the military. He returned for a few games in 1945, and in 1946 and 1947 led the league with 26 and 20 wins. He led the league in strikeouts seven times and pitched 46 shutouts.

Bob Lemon (HF) won 207 games for the Indians in only 13 Major League seasons. He started late because of a position change and military duty during World War II, reaching the club at age 25 in 1946. He won 20 or more games seven times and pitched 10 shutouts in 1948 when the Indians won the World Series.

Rocky Colavito had two terms with the Indians totaling eight seasons. He was the club's most popular player from 1956 through 1959. He hit 41 home runs in 1958 and led the league with 42 in 1959 before being traded to the Tigers in 1960. He returned to Cleveland in 1965 and hit 26 home runs and led the league with 108 RBIs. After 30 home runs in 1966 he was traded during the 1967 season. In 1976 Colavito was voted Cleveland's "Most Memorable Player." See also Gordon Cobbledick, *Don't Knock the Rock* (1966).

Sam McDowell pitched 11 years for the Indians from 1961 through 1971. He won 122 games, including 20 in 1970, but he is best remembered for his blazing fastball that led him to five strikeout titles (see also *Alcoholism*).

Albert Belle was one of a cadre of young talent that improved the Indians during the 1990s. He blossomed in 1991 with 28 home runs and went on to hit 50 during the strike-shortened 1995 season. After eight seasons ending in 1996 he left for the White Sox.

Jim Thome played 12 seasons with the Indians after being drafted in the 13th round by the club in 1989. He hit 334 home runs for the club and had 927 RBIs before leaving in 2003 for the Phillies.

Key Managers.

"A three-time loser is a baseball manager on his way to Cleveland in an Edsel." — Indians manager Bobby Bragan.

Nap Lajoie (HF) took over the club as player-manager in late 1904. After disappointing finishes from 1905 through 1907, the club went down to the last day of the 1908 season before losing the pennant to the White Sox. Lajoie lasted through August 1909 when he resigned after being criticized constantly for his short temper and poor handling of his pitching staff.

Tris Speaker (HF) took over as player-manager in 1919 and guided the club to a second-place finish, only 3½ games behind the White Sox (soon to become the Black Sox). He stayed with the club as player-manager through the 1926 season, when claims about his *Gambling* forced the club to release him. During his tenure the club won the 1920 World Series and finished second in 1926.

Roger Peckinpaugh managed the club from 1928 until June 1933, finishing as high as third in 1929. He also managed the club in 1941, finishing fourth.

Lou Boudreau (HF).

"... Bill Veeck let it be known that he thought Boudreau was a

$150,000 shortstop but a ten-cent manager and that he would like nothing better than to get rid of him. The fans loved Louie in Cleveland as if he were one of the family, and they did everything but ride Veeck out of town on a rail." — Sportswriter Ed Fitzgerald.

Boudreau was the first Indians manager since Roger Peckinpaugh to last more than three seasons. He was player-manager of the club from 1942 until 1950, when he was traded to the Red Sox. During that span the club won the 1948 World Series, but otherwise never finished higher than third.

Al Lopez (HF) managed the club from 1951 through 1956. But for the Yankees he might have been considered one of the best managers of all time. His clubs finished second five times and won the pennant in 1954 before being swept by the Giants in the World Series.

Frank Robinson (HF).

"I had no trouble communicating. The players just didn't like what I had to say." — Robinson, who became the first black manager in the Major Leagues in 1975. He led the Indians to two fourth-place finishes before being fired 57 games into the 1977 season when the club was in last place.

Mike Hargrove took over the club midway through the 1991 season, when the Indians finished seventh. After mediocre (fourth) and bad (sixth) seasons in 1992 and 1993, the club was in first place in 1994 when the season was cancelled. Hargrove then led the Indians to the World Series in 1995 and 1997, with three other first place finishes (1996, 1998 and 1999) before leaving for the Orioles after the 1999 season.

Charlie Manuel led the club to second and first place finishes in 2000 and 2001 before being replaced midway through the 2002 season.

Ballparks.

League Park. The ballpark was built in 1891 by the club's new owner, Frank DeHaas Robison. In 1910 the structure was rebuilt as baseball's fourth concrete and steel stadium. It was known as Dunn Field until owner James Dunn died in 1927. The park crisscrossed two rail lines at Lexington Avenue and East 66th Street.

Its dimensions from left to right field were 374–415–420–400–290, with a 40-foot screen in right. Its original capacity was only 9,000, but was expanded to 21,000 in 1910 and 22,500 in 1939. The small park was abandoned by the Indians in 1946. Most of it was torn down in 1950 and the site is now a public park.

Starting in 1932 the Indians were in the unique position of having two ballparks available to play in because cavernous Municipal Stadium was completed that year.

In the early years of both ballparks, only holiday and Sunday games were scheduled for larger Municipal Stadium. League Park could handle the smaller weekday crowds.

Municipal Stadium.

"Cleveland's Municipal Stadium ... is a monument to architectural homeliness. Vastness is its only virtue. When it is empty, there is no greater emptiness." — Jane Leavy in *Squeeze Play* (1990).

The first game in Municipal Stadium was played on July 31, 1932, after it had been built in a swift 370 days for $2.8 million (the first ballpark built with public funds). The Indians lost to the A's 1–0 in front of 80,284 (76,979 in other sources) as Lefty Grove defeated Mel Harder. The ballpark was known as Lakefront Stadium when it opened and also Cleveland Public Municipal Stadium before the name was shortened to Municipal Stadium.

During the second half of 1932 and all of 1933 the Indians played exclusively in Municipal Stadium. In 1934 the club returned to League Park except on Sundays and holidays and split time in both ballparks through 1946. In 1947 the Indians moved into Municipal Stadium full-time.

The original capacity of Municipal Stadium was 78,000. Though it held about 75,000 beginning in the 1950s, 84,587 squeezed into the park on September 12, 1954, for a game against the Yankees. The dimensions from left to right field originally were 322–435–470– 395–385. They were shortened somewhat in subsequent seasons, though increased in 1991 on the theory that the Indians had few power hitters and their hitters would benefit by larger gaps in the power alleys for extra base hits.

No home runs were ever been hit to dead center field. The longest home run hit in the ballpark was a 477-foot blast into the right field upper deck by first baseman Luke Easter on June 23, 1950.

The Indians played their last game in the ballpark at the end of 1993, though it continued to be used by the NFL Cleveland Browns until they left town after the 1995 football season (and was then used by the new version of the Browns that was created by the NFL). In 1997, the city sold bricks from the ballpark for $10,000 in a gift box with a certificate of authenticity. See also Dan Cook and Jim Toman, *Cleveland Municipal Stadium* (1981).

Jacobs Field.

"I think there's a nice symmetry to the relationship between the town and the fans because the team has driven people to drink for 40 years now, and the liquor tax was used to build the new stadium."— Sportswriter Bud Shaw of the *Cleveland Plain Dealer*.

The new ballpark, originally to be known as the Gateway Sports Complex, hosted its first game on April 4, 1994, as the Indians beat the Mariners 4–3 in 11 innings in front of 41,459 fans. It was built at a cost of $169 million, though the total project, which included an adjacent indoor arena, cost $362 million. It was paid for from both public and private funds and had 125 luxury suites. Club owner David Jacobs paid $13.8 million to have the stadium named after his family, though he has no ownership interest in the facility. The dimensions from left to right field are 325–368–400–375–325 and capacity is 42,000.

The team keeps all money from parking, signage, and concessions, as well as all the money from 2,400 premium club seats and luxury suites. The Indians pay no rent for the first 1.85 million annual admissions, then 75 cents per ticket for the next 400,000 admissions, $1 per ticket for the next 250,000; and $1.25 per person over 2.5 million. Even though they sold out every home game for several years beginning June 12, 1995, the Indians paid less than $1.5 million per year in rent.

Key Broadcasters.

"Bob Neal is a disgrace to the broadcasting industry … there aren't ten percent of the fans in Cleveland who enjoy listening to him. Right now, we have a bush-league announcer, and point out that I emphasize the word now. I sure hope that Neal enjoys his job next year, wherever it is, because I think most of the people — not just the players — are fed up with him. There's such a thing as adding by subtraction in broadcasting, too."— Indians pitcher Sam McDowell during his feud with the 1960s Indians broadcaster.

The first Indians broadcasts began in 1925 with Tom Manning behind the microphone. He had started with the club as a stadium announcer with a megaphone in the early 1920s. The first regular radio broadcasts in Cleveland began in 1928.

The voice of the Indians from 1948 through 1967 was Jimmy Dudley. Dudley's broadcast network extended from Maine to Mississippi. Former Major Leaguer Jack Graney was Dudley's partner from 1948 through 1954. Dudley moved on to become the voice of the Seattle Pilots for its one season in 1969. Bob Neal broadcast for

the club in the 1950s before leaving in 1961. He returned in 1965 for seven seasons.

Former pitcher Herb Score did television for the Indians from 1963 through 1968. In 1969 he switched to radio and Mel Allen broadcast televised games for the club in 1968. Score was still with the club in the mid–1990s. The club at times featured former Major Leaguers Rocky Colavito, Jim "Mudcat" Grant, Bob Feller, Mike Hegan and Rick Manning.

Tom Hamilton began his 15th season with the club in 2004 and John Sanders began his 14th season.

Books. The Cleveland Press, *The Cleveland Indians (1920–1982)* (1983); Franklin Lewis, *The Cleveland Indians* (1949); Tim Long and Don Fox, *Indians Memories: Heroes, Heartaches and Highlights from the Last 50 Years of Cleveland Indians* (1997); Terry Pluto, *The Curse of Rocky Colavito: A Loving Look at a Thirty-Year Slump of the Cleveland Indians* (1994); John Thorn, Pete Palmer, Michael Gershman, David Pietrusza and Paul Hoynes (eds.), *Total Indians* (1996); Jack Torry, *Endless Summers: The Fall and Rise of the Cleveland Indians* (1996).

Cleveland Infants

Players League 1890
The club finished seventh with a 55–75 record in its one season of play in Brotherhood Park.

Cleveland Spiders

National League 1889–1899
"The only person who had the misfortune to watch all our games."— Inscription on the locket presented to the club's traveling secretary by the Spider players after their last game.

Key Owners/Seasons. Some sources reported that a new National League franchise in Cleveland was created to counter the 1890 Players League challenge. However, the National League Spiders existed in 1889, finishing sixth under manager Tom Loftus. The club won the first half of the 1892 split season, followed by up-and-down years in the 12-team National League until 1898.

By 1898 the owners were brothers and tractor magnates Frank DeHaas Robison and Matthew Stanley Robison. They bought the St. Louis Browns in 1899, forcing out Browns owner Christopher Von der Ahe. The Robisons were unhappy that the Spiders had not drawn fans even though they had a .544 winning percentage in 1898. Their response was to swap the best players of their St. Louis and Cleveland clubs, with Jesse Burkett and Cy Young going to the National League St. Louis Browns. Before the swap, the brothers had tried to sell the Spiders to Detroit interests, but the National League vetoed the sale to a smaller city.

The 1899 club was so bad that the Spiders began playing home games on the road and at neutral sites. In 1898 and 1899 the Spiders averaged only $25 in gate receipts at the club's few home games. The National League folded the Spiders after the 1899 season, in which the club had a .130 winning percentage and a 20–134 record. The club had an 8–30 start, mixed results in the middle of the season, and then won only four of its last 74 games. The team lost 11 or more games six times and only once won two games in a row. The team lost 102 of 113 road games and played only on the road after June.

Last Game. In the club's last game, Eddie Kolb, reportedly a cigar stand clerk at the Queen City Hotel, pitched and lost, 19–3. It was the only game he ever pitched in the Major Leagues.

Nicknames. The players wore white and dark blue uniforms and a club executive assessing their shapes supposedly said: "They look skinny and spindly, just like spiders. Might as well call them Spiders and be done with it."

Other sources point out that the uniforms had thin stripes and were black and red, leading to the nickname. Because of the club's incompetence, the players were on a permanent road trip in the second half of the season; earning nicknames such as "Exiles," "Barnstormers," "Wanderers," and "Forsakens."

Ballpark. The club played its games at League Park, which seated approximately 9,000 fans.

Book. J. Thomas Hetrick, *Misfits!* (1991), covers the 1899 club.

Clichés

"Learn your clichés. Study them. Know them. They're your friend."—Crash Davis in the movie *Bull Durham.*

"Baseball, however, has an adage for every occasion, and so another one had to be trundled out…"—Lawrence Ritter and Donald Honig in *The Image of Their Greatness* (1979).

"Big-league baseball is customarily played by brilliant outfielders, veteran hurlers, powerful sluggers, knuckle-ball artists, towering first basemen, key moundsmen, fleet base runners, ace southpaws, scrappy little shortstops, sensational war vets, ex-college stars, relief artists, rifle-armed twirlers, dependable mainstays, doughty right-handers, streamlined backstops, power-hitting batsmen, redoubtable infielders, erstwhile Dodgers, veteran sparkplugs, sterling moundsmen, aging twirlers, and rookie sensations."—Sportswriter Frank Sullivan in a column titled "The Cliché Expert Testifies on Baseball," first appearing in *The New Yorker* in 1949.

"There is one final tradition which deserves mention. It is said, as a cliché, that the team scoring the most runs wins the most games and that fans pay to see home-runs, not walks and singles."—Ralph Andreano in *No Joy in Mudville* (1965), who cited statistical evidence for the 1947–1960 seasons to demonstrate that there was no correlation between home runs or runs scored and total attendance.

"When we left the park, the Christian guard was still there. 'Did the Lord explain His purpose to you?' he asked us. 'Oh, yeah,' I told him. 'He said to take two an' hit to left, play for the tie at home an' the win on the road, don't run until you bunt the ball, an' never put the winning run on base.' 'Oh,' he said. 'The Lord told you all that?' 'At least we *thought* it was the Lord. Turned out just to be a sportswriter.'"—From *Sometimes You See It Coming*, a novel by Kevin Baker (1993).

"It seems that what today's sports figures are saying is that if they try very hard and play better than their opponents, then it is possible to win a game by beating the other team, but only if, at the end of the game, they have more points by at least one."—Steve Martin in *The New Yorker*, distilling the cliché-ridden comments of a player.

A cliché sampling:

Take two and hit to right.

Anything can happen in a short series.

He came to play.

Don't get behind in the count.

Don't throw a strike on an 0–2 pitch.

Keep the batter off balance.

Fundamentals win ballgames.

Play for a tie at home and play to win on the road.

Play .500 against the top clubs and do better against the second division teams.

His contribution doesn't show up in the box score.

I'm just trying to help the ballclub.

It's a game of inches.

We're taking one game at a time.

The pressure's on them [even though they may be in first place].

We're not playing fundamental baseball.

We're not watching the scoreboard.

It's a line drive in the box score.

Clocks

"Baseball has no clock. Yes, you were waiting for that. The comeback, from three or more scores behind, is far more common in baseball than football."—Thomas Boswell in "99 Reasons Why Baseball Is Better Than Football," in *The Heart of the Order* (1989).

"Baseball games end in their own terms, they do not end because a clock runs out: one thus sees that anything can happen up until the time that last out is made…. Time has neither power nor meaning in this game…. It is the ball that controls the game."—Gilbert Sorrentino in "Baseball" (1977).

"Only nine innings may be lawfully overgone [in sports]—baseball having no clock and, indeed moving counterclockwise, so anxious is it to establish its own rhythms and patterns independent of clock time."—A. Bartlett Giamatti in *Take Time for Paradise* (1989).

"You can't sit on a lead and run a few plays into the line and just kill the clock. You've got to throw the ball over the goddamn plate and give the other man his chance. That's why baseball is the greatest game of them all. "—Orioles manager Earl Weaver.

It has been reported that a clock first appeared in a Major League ballpark on July 4, 1915, in Fenway Park, at the suggestion of one George E. Hamilton.

A clock on top of the main scoreboard in left field of Cincinnati's Great American Ball Park is a replica of the Longines analog clock that was at Crosley Field.

Clothing See *Dress Code and Clothing*

Clowns/Clown Princes of Baseball

"Baseball is a circus, and as is the case with many a circus, the clowns and the side shows frequently are more interesting than the big stuff in the main tent."—Sportswriter Bill McGeehan.

Al Schacht.

"I came into this world very homely and haven't changed a bit since."—The first line of Schacht's autobiography, *My Own Particular Screwball*, with Ed Keyes (1955).

"That was Al's greatest talent when he was a pitcher—getting the ball over the plate. The batters usually got it over the fence."—The *Stars and Stripes* military newspaper.

Schacht, born in 1892, was the first man dubbed the "Clown Prince of Baseball" for his diamond antics before and during games. He had a brief Major League pitching career before turning to comedy. He signed with the Senators as a result of repeated letters to Senators owner Clark Griffith from someone signed "A Fan" talking up the right-handed pitcher. Years later Griffith learned that "A Fan" was A. Schacht. From 1919 through 1921 Schacht won 14 Major League games with the Senators before settling down as the clown prince.

Schacht managed the Senators as a temporary fill-in in 1934, though it was apparently done as a gimmick and he is not credited in *The Baseball Encyclopedia*. He also appeared on the "Information, Please" radio show. In 1944 Schacht was scheduled to legitimately broadcast Yankees and Giants home games, but quit during spring training, noting that he is "a pantomimist and out of character before a microphone." He died in 1984.

See also Al Schacht, *Clowning Through Baseball* (1941); Al Schacht with Murray Goodman, *G.I. Had Fun* (1945), describing his days with the USO during World War II.

Max Patkin.

"?"—Patkin's uniform number.

Patkin, born in 1920, succeeded Schacht as the Clown Prince of Baseball. After pitching briefly at the Class A level in the 1940s, he began a 40-year career as a baseball clown.

His first performance was in 1944 when the 6'3", 185-pounder threw a gopher ball to Joe DiMaggio in a charity game between two military teams. At the time a minor league pitcher, Patkin followed DiMaggio around the bases imitating his home run trot. He was then escorted back to the mound by DiMaggio's teammates.

Patkin was known for his ability to twist his body into odd positions. He made a cameo appearance in 1987's *Bull Durham*, starring Kevin Costner. In addition to what was shown in the movie, the director filmed scenes in which Patkin dies during a routine and his ashes are sprinkled on the mound. The scenes never left the editing studio.

At age 71 in 1991 Patkin was inducted into the Clown Hall of Fame in Wisconsin and presented with its Laughter Achievement Award. He died in 1999. See also Max Patkin with Stan Hochman, *The Clown Prince of Baseball* (1994).

Nick Altrock.

"Altrock often mimicked umpire's movements; walked foul line as though it were tightrope; threw and caught baseballs in impossible positions; used baseballs like bowling balls; engaged in shadow boxing; plus dozens of other crowd-pleasing antics."—Gene Karst and Martin J. Jones, Jr., in *Who's Who in Professional Baseball* (1973), on the otherwise ill-tempered Altrock.

"What would you get if you mixed the clowning of Max Patkin, the crafty southpaw pitching of Jimmy Key, and the organizational loyalty of Jimmie Reese with the endurance of ageless Minnie Minoso? The result of this unlikely baseball recipe might be something like Nick Altrock, a man who pitched, coached, clowned, and yes, drank his way through the major leagues for almost sixty years."—Jim Blenko.

Altrock had a successful Major League career as a pitcher in the early 20th century, but earned a reputation as a baseball clown from the Senators' third base coaching box. He first teamed with former ballplayer Germany Schaefer to mix coaching with antics. After Schaefer left the Senators, Altrock teamed with Al Schacht, but the two stopped speaking even though their new act flourished. They reenacted the famous "long count" boxing match between Jack Dempsey and Gene Tunney, as well as a tennis match between stars of the day Helen Wills and Suzanne Lenglen. From 1921 until the early 1930s, they appeared at every World Series and they became regulars in vaudeville and even toured Europe.

There was great speculation about why they never spoke, but Schacht said, years after Altrock's death, that it was because of a nasty remark that Altrock had made about Schacht's Jewish heritage. Whatever the reason, Schacht left the Senators in 1935 to join Joe Cronin and the Red Sox.

Altrock continued to appear as a pinch hitter for the Senators in late-season games, even coming in at age 57 and getting a triple (probably a gift from the opposing team).

Altrock retired in 1953 and died in 1965. To measure his celebrity in his era, researcher Jim Blenko notes that at the 1931 World Series,

there were three important celebrities lined up before a game giving autographs: Babe Ruth, John McGraw and Altrock.

Emmett Kelly.

"I got enough make-believe clowns around, so I don't need no real ones."—Umpire Jocko Conlan tossing the famous clown off the field during a game at Ebbets Field. Kelly was not so much the Brooklyn Dodgers mascot in 1957, but rather the symbol of the club as drawn by New York cartoonist Willard Mullin. Mullin had asked Kelly many years earlier if he could use his likeness to illustrate the Dodgers. Kelly said that Mullin "thought my sad clown [Weary Willie] character typified the Dodgers."

When the Dodgers were known early in 1957 to be ending their relationship with Brooklyn after that season, the club hired him to entertain the fans during that melancholy year. He would sit on home plate and spread out his picnic lunch while the managers exchanged line-up cards with the umpires and the display various antics during the game. He would go on the road to the Dodger minor league locations when the Major League club was on the road.

Clubhouses and Clubhouse Men

"Visitors' Clubhouse—No Visitors Allowed"—Sign over the visitors' clubhouse at Tiger Stadium.

"They wouldn't have made good pig pens."—Description in the 1892 *Cleveland Plain Dealer* of the typical visitors' locker room.

"They never talk about baseball or politics. It's usually about their kids, or clothes, or cars. They all like sporty good-looking cars. They do crossword puzzles, look at TV or listen to the radio. But mostly they all play a card game called 'Crazy Eight.'"—Astute observation of a baseball clubhouse by early 1960s Dodger batboy Jim Reynolds; a bit sanitized perhaps, as he left out any discussion of women.

Former Site. The Philadelphia Athletics clubhouse of 1865 had been the site of the 1833 Olympic Town Ball club headquarters.

Dressing Quarters. Visiting players originally dressed in their hotel rooms and were taken by carriage or trolley to the ballpark. In 1906 Charles Ebbets successfully pushed the National League to require all parks to have dressing rooms with lockers and hot water for visiting players.

During the 1923 World Series between the Giants and Yankees, Giants manager John McGraw had his team dress in the Polo Grounds locker room and take taxis to Yankee Stadium—despite the fact that Yankee Stadium was new and had excellent visitors' locker room facilities.

Clubhouse Man. Pete Sheehy spent over 50 years as clubhouse man for the Yankees. He started in 1926 moving a few trunks for clubhouse man Fred Logan in return for a free pass to the game. He returned the next day and Michael Joseph Sheehy became known as "Silent Pete." That was shortened to Pete and forever after he was known as Pete Sheehy.

Clubs

The term "club" was used to describe early teams because of the genteel or "club-like" atmosphere of teams such as the Knickerbockers and their more sophisticated players.

Coaches

"The best qualification a coach can have is being the manager's drinking buddy."—Jim Bouton.

"In the old days, the coaches were mostly fat guys who had outlived their usefulness in other capacities.... They were little or no help, and their duties consisted of hitting and infield practice, and counting the practice baseballs to see if any had been stolen or lost. As a rule they had a hard time seeing around their bellies."—"The Old Timer" in W.R. Burnett's, *The Roar of the Crowd* (1964).

"It's a boring job. But people who become coaches are not easily bored. You ever see a baby play with a rattle for two hours."—Jim Bouton in *Ball Four* (1970).

"The First Base Coach's Workout: Demonstrates major league training techniques, such as the one-handed scratch, the crossed-ankle lean, the backpocket wrist rest and the perpetually exploring finger. Pigeons are optional. (Deluxe version includes guest slouching by place kickers and relief pitchers)."—Proposed Christmas DVD by *Rocky Mountain News* columnist Bernie Lincicome.

"Coaching third with a pitcher on base is like being a member of a bomb disposal squad. The thing could blow up in your face at any moment."—Rocky Bridges.

Rules. Base coaches were officially recognized in the rules in 1887 (see also ***Coaching Boxes***).

First Formal Coach. In the 1880s Arlie Latham of the St. Louis Browns coached his teammates. In 1907 (1909 in some sources) he was hired by John McGraw purportedly as the first coach with a formal contract.

Major League Coaches. *Total Baseball* contains a list of Major League coaches during the 20th century.

Batting Coaches. See ***Batting Coaches***.

The Depression. During the ***Depression*** of the 1930s, teams tried to cut out their coaches to economize. This effort was unsuccessful at the Major League level, but the International League required its members to eliminate coaches by May 5, 1933. It is unclear whether all teams complied.

Hand Signals. The first coach to use hand signals reportedly was Harry Wright, a 19th century star with the Cincinnati Red Stockings and Boston Red Stockings. See also **Signs**.

Longest Tenure.

"For 25 years Steinbrenner called me 'Zimmer' and I called him 'Boss.' From now on, as far as I'm concerned, he's just Steinbrenner."—After the 2003 World Series, Yankee bench coach Don Zimmer announced he was quitting after several sparring matches with owner George Steinbrenner. Zimmer, with over 50 years in the game, had sealed his fate when he engaged in a shoving match with Red Sox pitcher Pedro Martinez during the ALCS, and was fined $5,000 by the American League office. Zimmer then signed as a special consultant to the Devil Rays and manager Lou Piniella, prompting this comment from Zimmer: "I don't worry about Steinbrenner anymore. I've got new bosses that treat me like a human being."

The Cleveland Indians change in their clubhouse after a 1952 spring training game in Daytona Beach.

Nick Altrock coached 46 seasons for the Senators from 1912 through 1957, though for the last few years he was largely inactive. Frank Crosetti coached for three clubs (primarily the Yankees) for 26 years, 1946 through 1971.

In April 1997, long-time Red Sox coach Johnny Pesky was banished by the team from the dugout at age 77, but was told that he could continue to hit ground balls during fielding practice. He would then have to change out of his uniform and sit in the press box for games. Pesky was disappointed: "It hurts me quite a bit, to be honest with you. I don't have much time left and I was hoping they would let me stay in the dugout. I think some of the players like having me around there."

Pesky was still at it in 2004, hitting ground balls during infield practice. He had been a player, manager, broadcaster, coach and instructor for the club in eight decades beginning in 1939.

Oldest. Jimmie Reese roomed with Babe Ruth in the 1920s and coached for the Angels in the 1990s. He was worshiped by many players, including Nolan Ryan. He died at age 92 on July 13, 1994. The Angels wore their batting uniforms for a few games with a special patch on the left sleeve. They were waiting for approval from Major League Baseball to wear a patch above their hearts on game uniforms to honor Reese, but the player strike intervened and the plan was never implemented.

Most in an Inning. In 1968 the Senators had four first base coaches in a single inning. Coach Nellie Fox was ejected in the 9th inning. Replacement coach Bernie Allen was called to pinch-hit. Cap Peterson took over, but was announced as a pinch hitter and was replaced by Camilo Pascual. Despite the musical chairs, the Senators won the game.

Number Allowed. Clubs are allowed to have six coaches in the dugout at any one time.

Pitching Coaches. *Pitching Coaches* were used with some frequency in the 1910–1920 era and thereafter became mainstays of the coaching ranks.

Celebrity Coaches. Babe Ruth appeared as a celebrity coach for the Dodgers at Johnny Vander Meer's second no-hitter (the first night game at Ebbets Field). There was such a commotion near the first base box that Dodger general manager Larry MacPhail decided to hire Ruth as the first base coach. He did not last long because he kept missing the signs.

Mickey Mantle was a base coach for the Yankees during the middle three innings for two weeks during August 1970 and then abruptly quit.

Joe DiMaggio coached for the A's for a short time in the late 1960s. DiMaggio made the mistake of asking owner Charlie Finley for a desk to sit at so he could answer his huge volume of mail. Finley refused, citing the expense.

Miscommunication. In the bottom of the 9th inning of Game 6 of the 1975 World Series, the Reds and Red Sox were tied 6–6. The Red Sox had the bases loaded and nobody out. Denny Doyle was the runner on third base when Fred Lynn hit a fly ball to left fielder George Foster 170 feet from home plate. Third base coach Don Zimmer yelled, "No, no!" Doyle thought he said "Go, Go" and tagged up. Foster threw him out at the plate and the clubs remained tied into extra innings before Carlton's Fisk's dramatic home run in the 12th inning.

See *Base Running* – **Enos Slaughter** for the coach's role in Slaughter's dash from first base in Game 7 of the 1946 World Series.

Barred. In the 1980s coaches were barred from the press box after the Orioles accused the White Sox of stealing their pitching signs. Electronic communication also was banned.

No Control. In June 1999 Mets manager Bobby Valentine read in the paper that one of his coaches, Bob Apodaca, had been fired. When he arrived at the park, he discovered that Mets general manager Steve Phillips has fired two other of Valentine's coaches and replaced all three with new men without Valentine's approval or input.

Coaching Boxes

"Frank [Frisch] was coaching at third base and by mid-game he had the fans completely hypnotized by his antics. In the seventh inning a Pittsburgh player was called on strikes. Frank let out a yell of anguish that could be heard in Hoboken, clutched his chest, and toppled over to the ground like a man suffering from a fatal heart attack. Tremors raced up and down his legs, his torso shook, and then he stiffened out, his eyes fixed on the sky and his arms extended at right angles to his body." — Ford Frick in *Games, Asterisks and People* (1973). The postscript as reported by Frick; umpire Bill Klem raced out from behind the plate and said: "I've had it! If you're not dead when I get there, you're out of the game!"

The Early Years. Cap Anson is credited as the first manager to coach from the baselines, but the blowhard probably spread the rumor himself. In the 1880s rowdy teams in the American Association, particularly St. Louis (with Charles Comiskey, Bill Gleason and Arlie Latham), constantly abused other teams by having their coaches run up and down the baseline shouting insults. This led to the establishment of coaching boxes in 1887.

Eating. Germany Schaefer once coached such a poor team that he started eating popcorn in the coaching box. He was promptly thrown out of the game.

Dimensions. The coaching boxes are 10 feet by 20 feet.

Chalk Lines. Umpire Al Barlick once delayed a game at Shea Stadium to have the coaching boxes re-chalked to make sure that the coaches did not stray from their designated areas.

Good Tackle. In 1977 baserunner Bobby Murcer tried to score on a single despite a "stop sign" from third base coach Peanuts Lowrey. In order to enforce his signal, Lowrey simply stepped out and tackled Murcer. Murcer was called out because Lowry touched him.

Honored. On April 5, 1999, the Orioles honored Cal Ripken, Sr., by painting his uniform number in the third base coach's box. He had died three weeks earlier from lung cancer.

Ty Cobb (1886–1961)

Hall of Fame 1936

"He played under the law of the survival of the fittest." — Sportswriter Fred Lieb.

"Aside from [40 Major League records], he had everything to hide: unquestionably a womanizer, a wife beater and a venomous racist, he was possibly a murderer and a fixer of ball games." — Richard Schickel in his *Time* review of the movie *Cobb* (see also **Murder**).

"Ty Cobb was a fascinating man. He could graciously dine with bankers and presidents, yet he was vulgar, violent and despised by every player in the league, including his own teammates." — Cobb biographer Al Stump.

"Having to live alone, I spent all my time thinking baseball — of plays I could make ... of tricks I could try. Baseball was one hundred per cent of my life." — Cobb as told to Grantland Rice.

Playing primarily for the Tigers from 1905 through 1928, Cobb holds the highest batting average in Major League history at .367.

Tyrus Raymond Cobb was born and raised in Georgia and carried a chip on his shoulder not only during his playing career, but throughout his life. His professional career began inauspiciously when he was released after batting .237 for Augusta in the South Atlantic League. After another minor league attempt he attracted scouts and signed with the Tigers, but batted only .240 in 41 games for Detroit in 1905.

In 1906 Cobb started in the outfield for the Tigers and had the first of 23 straight seasons in which he hit over .300. In 1907 he led the league in hitting for the first of nine straight seasons. In 1909 he won the as-yet-unnamed Triple Crown with a .377 average, nine home runs and 107 RBIs. He also led the league with 76 stolen bases. From 1907 through 1909 the Tigers won the American League pennant, but could not win a World Series as Cobb batted a collective .262.

In 1911 and 1912 Cobb had consecutive seasons over .400. He hit .401 in 1922 but was not the league leader. He was player-manager of the Tigers from 1921 through 1926 but never finished higher than second. He was traded to the A's for two years after he was implicated in a **Gambling** scandal along with Tris Speaker.

He ended his 24-year career in 1928 with the A's, finishing with a lifetime .367 average, best all-time. He had 4,191 hits and 297 triples, both second all-time (see **Four Thousand Hits**). His 892 **Stolen Bases** are third all-time and his 2,245 runs scored are second all-time. He also finished with 1,937 RBIs (adjusted down from 1,961), fifth all-time.

Cobb made a fortune in Coca-Cola and General Motors stock (among others) and never worked in baseball after he retired. His Coke stock was estimated to be worth $12 million when he died. He spent most of the rest of his life on the fringes of baseball with few friends but many admirers for his competitive fire and baseball skills.

Books. Charles C. Alexander, *Ty Cobb* (1984); Richard Bak, *Ty Cobb: His Tumultuous Life and Times* (1994); Ty Cobb (ghostwritten by John N. Wheeler and reprinted by McFarland), *Busting 'Em and Other Big League Stories* (1914); Ty Cobb with Al Stump, *Ty Cobb: My Life in Baseball* (1961); John D. McCallum, *Ty Cobb* (1975); Al Stump, *Cobb: The Life & Times of the Meanest Man Who Ever Played Baseball* (1994).

Mickey Cochrane (1903–1962)

Hall of Fame 1947

"[Cochrane] literally lifted himself by his bootstraps from obscurity to the peak of his profession … the personification of the ideal diamond athlete … the picture of sublime courage, of energy, pep. Eyes flashing, his fist quivering as a flaunting pennon [banner on a lance] of battle, Cochrane in the thick of things personifies faith, fight, confidence, courage, and give-'em-hell and victory!"— Bill Dooley in *The Sporting News*.

One of the best catchers of all time, Cochrane played for the A's and Tigers from 1925 through 1937.

Born in Massachusetts, Gordon Stanley Cochrane attended Boston University and starred as the quarterback and punter on the football team. He played semipro baseball in upstate New York until moving down to the Dover minor league club in 1924. In the process, he moved from the outfield to catcher. He played for Portland in the Pacific Coast League before signing with the Philadelphia A's for the 1925 season.

One of the best catchers of all time, "Black Mike" hit .330 his first season and had another eight seasons in which he bettered .300. He played nine years with the A's, leading the club to pennants in three consecutive seasons beginning in 1929. He won the MVP Award in 1928 for his leadership and catching, though he hit only .293 and committed a career-high 25 errors.

In 1933 he batted .322 and made only seven errors in 124 games behind the plate. Nevertheless, he was traded to the Tigers because the cash-poor A's were suffering during the Depression. He became player-manager and continued his strong hitting in 1934, leading the Tigers to the American League pennant. In 1935 he batted .319 as the club won the World Series over the Cubs.

He slipped in 1936 after injuries slowed him. After only 27 games in 1937, he suffered a severe **Beanball** injury and his career was over. The injury seriously hampered him and his Major League managerial career ended midway through the next season. He finished his playing career with a .320 average over 13 seasons.

He recovered sufficiently to manage a military team during World War II, winning 33 straight with Major Leaguers Johnny Mize, Gene Woodling and Schoolboy Rowe. He later held positions with the A's, Yankees and Tigers. His children have discredited claims by Ty Cobb that Cobb supplied Cochrane with cash over the years because he was destitute.

Book. Charlie Bevis, *Mickey Cochrane: The Life of a Baseball Hall of Fame Catcher* (2004); Gordon S. "Mickey" Cochrane, *Baseball, the Fan's Game* (1939).

Collective Bargaining Agreements (1967)

"The Infield Fly Rule is obviously not a core principle of baseball…. Without the Infield Fly Rule, baseball does not degenerate into bladderball the way the collective bargaining process degenerates into economic warfare when good faith is absent."—*Penn Law Review* (1975).

"Workers have a long history of organizing and acting together to achieve better working conditions and better pay. The relationship between professional baseball players and team owners is similar to that of other American workers and business owners."— Baseball Hall of Fame exhibit. After hearing part of the exhibit text, long-time Players Association labor leader Marvin Miller pronounced "pretty fair, pretty accurate." After hearing the exhibit's description of the reserve clause, which before free agency left players at the mercy of their employers, the retired labor leader said: "that's pretty good. That's not bad. At least it says what it was."

See also **Arbitration, Free Agents, Strikes and Lockouts** and **Unions**.

1967–1970. The first collective bargaining agreement was negotiated by Marvin Miller, the new head of the Players Association.

1970–1973. There were no dramatic changes in the basic agreement, although arbitration was expanded to include player salaries in certain circumstances. Negotiations dragged on four two years, in part because of the highly anticipated **Arbitration** decisions of December 1995.

1976–1979. A new basic agreement was signed during the 1976 All-Star break, after the owners staged a lock-out during spring training to force the players to sign a more restrictive agreement. The new agreement followed the December 1975 free agency ruling that changed baseball permanently.

1980–1983. A new agreement was signed in July 1981 after a two-month strike by the players. It retroactively covered 1980 through 1983. It provided for free agent compensation based on a two-year statistical ranking of players by position. There was compensation for Type A players (ranked in the top 20% at their position) and compensation for Type B players (ranked between 20% and 30% at their position). Teams losing such players received a supplemental draft pick between the first and second rounds of the amateur draft.

1983–1986. The agreement made a few changes to the arbitration provisions but contained no dramatic changes from prior contracts.

1986–1989. The agreement abolished professional player compensation through draft choices.

1990–1993. The collective bargaining agreement was scheduled to expire in December 1993, but the owners voted 15–13 in December 1992 to reopen talks early, as they were allowed to do under the agreement. Talks began in January 1993, but no progress was made. Part of the owners' motivation for reopening the negotiations was to prevent a repeat of the $500 million they spent on signing players over the winter of 1992–1993.

In August 1993 the owners met in Wisconsin to attempt to hammer out a consensus on their side. Some owners predicted a revenue-sharing resolution shortly. With 21 votes needed to approve a new economic system, a coalition of 10 high-revenue clubs, including the Dodgers and Yankees, consistently amended formulas proposed by the small-market clubs. Ironically, the owners met in Kohler, Wisconsin, the site of the longest labor strike in American history. For 8½ years beginning in 1954 the United Auto Workers were out on strike against Kohler Manufacturing.

1994–1995. The owners pledged that they would not lock out the players during spring training in 1994. The players went out on strike in August 1994 and the impasse continued into 1996 even though the players returned to the field in May 1995. Under federal law the parties were required to operate under the old agreement, until a trial of the players' claim that the owners conducted unfair labor practices in their negotiating during the strike (see also ***Strikes and Lockouts***).

1996–2001. The newest contract was the result of protracted negotiations and the infamous player strike of 1995–1996. There was to be a payroll tax of about 35% on payrolls in the $50 million range, with the threshold increasing in subsequent years.

The new agreement included a tax in 1997–1999, with no tax in 2000, and a union option, which was exercised, to extend the plan to 2001 in return for a payment from the players and a reduction in playoff money. The tax threshold was halfway between the fifth-highest and sixth-highest payrolls if that is higher. This meant that the tax would apply to no more than five teams.

There was also a tax across the board of 2.5% retroactively in 1996, and in 1997 as well. The tax was used to fund the shortfall caused by the phase-in of revenue sharing; $10 million was used for this purpose in 1997, and the remaining $2 million was distributed among the five American League teams with the lowest net local revenues.

The owners approved the agreement on November 26, 1996, by a 26–4 vote. Many owners were angry at White Sox owner Jerry Reinsdorf, who had led the movement for tighter salary control which caused the deal to be rejected. He then signed Albert Belle for $10 million a year. This gave the appearance that he had opposed the deal for his own interests, because he would have had to pay a tax on Belle's salary, and would have lost Alex Fernandez to free agency. The union approved the new deal on December 5, 1996 and the final agreement was signed on March 14, 1997.

The new collective bargaining agreement provided that players with less than two years of service, along with the 83% of players with the least amount of service among third-year players, had no negotiating rights and had to accept the Major League minimum, if offered. They could not bargain with any other club. Players above the minimum service time could go to arbitration, but the club could release the player rather than agree to arbitration. If released, the club could not bargain with him until after May 1 of the following year, and the team that released him could not receive any compensation from another club who signed the player.

Players with less than six years of service were required to accept arbitration. More senior players could become free agents. Clubs still had to compensate a player's former club under the complicated Type A, B or C **Free Agent** rating rules.

2002– . Avoiding a threatened strike, the 2002 agreement increased revenue sharing and the so-called competitive-balance tax on the high payroll clubs. The agreement called for a 17.5% tax on all payroll above $117 million in 2003. If that percentage had been applied in 2002, only the Yankees, Rangers and Dodgers would have been affected (see ***Salaries***). The Yankees would have paid $10.2 million, the Rangers $2.3 million, and the Dodgers $525,000. The tax threshold increased in each of the four years of the agreement, and repeat offenders were to be penalized.

In 2003 the Yankees were so far above the cap that they paid more than $60 million in luxury taxes and revenue sharing (see ***Profits, Losses and Revenue*** for a discussion of revenue sharing).

The Yankees paid a $22.5 million luxury tax on its $195.5 million payroll in 2004. The Red Sox were assessed $2 million. The money is used for player benefits, an industry growth fund and player development in less organized countries, such as the Dominican Republic.

Website. Cbaforfans.com contains simple explanations for each bargaining agreement.

College Baseball

"The only reason I played college baseball was to get out of spring football."— Tom Paciorek, long-time Major Leaguer and former linebacker for the University of Houston.

"If a man comes from a university, he's dumb, and the higher the university the greater the degree of dumbness in [Rogers] Hornsby's estimation."— J. Roy Stockton of the *St. Louis Post-Dispatch*.

"Rip Radcliffe, Hub Perdue, Yale Murphy, Ad Yale, Dean Stone"

First College Game. Amherst and Williams met in the first collegiate game on July 1, 1859, at Pittsfield, Massachusetts. Amherst won 73–32 (although one source had the score at 66–32) in a game lasting 26 innings. The game was played under the Massachusetts Game rules, using 13 players on each side. Each team provided a ball. Victorious Amherst kept them and still has them on display. Amherst's pitcher, "Hyde," may have been baseball's first ringer. Part of the festivities was a chess match between the clubs, which Amherst also won. Amherst catcher James Clafin captained the chess team. The two-sport confrontation led to the following headline in the *Amherst Express*:

"Williams and Amherst
Baseball and Chess!
Muscle and Mind!"

The 19th Century. Yale, Harvard and Princeton dominated the intercollegiate game once those schools formally started playing baseball in the 1860s. Between 1868 and 1879, Harvard won nine titles, Yale two and Princeton one. In 1869 Harvard defeated various professional teams, including the Philadelphia Athletics and the Philadelphia Keystones. In 1870 Harvard lost to the Cincinnati Red Stockings 46–15 and 20–17.

Michigan and Chicago dominated western play from the 1880s through the early 20th century. See also *Walter Camp's Book of College Sports* (1893) for coverage of college baseball and its rules, including recollections of early Harvard/Yale games.

Despite the strength of the Ivy League teams, an editorial in the Yale newspaper cast a negative eye on baseball: "We are not an admirer of the National game. As to amount of amusement to be obtained by this means, it is just about what might be extracted from a certain number of sand bags and basewood clubs; and common balls by educated enlightened men under other circumstances. On the question of bodily damage we would suggest that the immense increase of accident insurance companies is probably due to no other cause; and if the mania does not presently cease the country will be without able-bodied men."

College teams played competitively against National Association teams in the early 1870s and baseball was the primary sport among colleges in that decade. The best college teams of the 1880s were still on a par with the best minor league clubs and close to Major League caliber.

As late as 1895 certain colleges did not require their players to enroll before playing for the baseball team. This and other aspects of the game caused Harvard president Charles W. Eliot to speak out against the sport: "I think baseball is a wretched game; but as an object of ambition for youth to go to college for, really it is a little weak. There are only nine men who can play the game, and there are 950 men in college; and out of those nine there are only two desirable positions, I understand— pitcher and catcher— so there is little chance for the youth to gratify his ambition. I call it one of the worst games, although I know it is called the American national game."

The American College Baseball Association was formed in 1880, but there was a rift in 1887 and it was not until the 1920s that organized college baseball leagues were formed. The first was the Eastern Intercollegiate (Ivy) League.

Early and Mid–20th Century. Baseball was popular on Southern campuses, but the college game was sluggish during the first half of the 20th century because of the increasing popularity of college football. There was an early 20th century move by some schools to eliminate baseball from college campuses because it was a professional sport.

In 1945 the American Association of College Baseball Coaches was formed, giving a boost to the game. In 1946 this organization sponsored the first College All-Star Game, which evolved into the *College World Series* in 1947.

In 1950 only 20% of the players who signed a pro contract before they finished college stayed in the professional ranks more than one year. The majority of those who failed did not return to college.

Major Leaguers as College Coaches. Joe Judge, an outstanding first baseman primarily for the Senators in the 1920s and 1930s, was the coach at Georgetown almost continuously from 1937 through 1958.

Smoky Joe Wood was the coach at Yale for 20 years from the 1920s through the 1940s.

New York Giants star Jack Chesbro coached the Harvard pitchers in the early 20th century.

College Players to the Major Leagues.

"If I can't talk you out of it or preach you out of it, I'll beat you out of it."—Pitcher Norm Charlton on his triple major in college of speech, religion and physical education.

In the early days, almost no professional players attended college and by the early 20th century it was still a novelty. John Montgomery Ward was one of the exceptions, having played at Penn State before turning professional in 1877.

By the 1890s more college players began to join the professional ranks. When the Western League made its bid to become a second Major League as the renamed American League in 1900–1901, the move was looked on favorably, in part because the league had a number of former college players who were viewed as having a cleaner image.

In 1906 Eddie Grant graduated from Harvard and after a nine-year Major League career became the most prominent former player killed during *World War I.*

The 1910 A's signed five players straight out of college who went directly to the Major Leagues: Eddie Collins, Jack Barry, Chief Bender, Jack Coombs and Eddie Plank.

Collins had been captain of the Columbia squad in his junior year, but played professionally during his senior year under the name Eddie Sullivan and apparently did not play for Columbia that season.

Hal Chase played for Santa Clara College in California, but there is no record of him ever taking a class, and researcher Martin D. Kohout points out that there is some doubt that he graduated from high school.

When pitcher Christy Mathewson became famous in New York

Three 1895 college men from Holy Cross in Massachusetts: left to right, outfielder Louis Sockalexis, later with the Cleveland Spiders (1897–1899); catcher/first baseman Michael Riley "Doc" Powers, later primarily with the Philadelphia Athletics (9 of 11 seasons); and second baseman Walter J. "Doc" Curley, later briefly with the 1899 Chicago Cubs (10 games). Holy Cross has seen 77 of its alumni play Major League Baseball.

in the early 1900s, his college background at Bucknell made baseball more acceptable to the New York gentry.

Shortstop Frankie Frisch, nicknamed the "Fordham Flash" after being a three-sport college star, played for the Giants and Cardinals in the 1920s and 1930s.

Harry Hooper was another college graduate, playing for the Red Sox from 1909 through 1925. Hall of Fame catcher Mickey Cochrane was a five-sport star at Boston University: baseball, track, basketball, boxing and football.

Lou Gehrig played professionally as "Lewis" to protect his eligibility at Columbia, where he also played football. He worked out with the Giants at the Polo Grounds but received little attention. He signed with the Yankees before he graduated, but the deal was kept secret until after graduation.

By 1927 one third of all starters in Major League Baseball had played at least some college ball. Other sources point out that college players were a primary source of talent only until 1920, but their Major League numbers dropped off dramatically in the 1920s. This has been attributed to the explosion of the minor leagues in that decade due to the prosperity that followed World War I. As a result, the enormous spread of clubs into rural areas produced a huge increase by the 1930s in the number of less-educated players making it to the Major Leagues. The *Depression* also had an effect, as fewer men could afford to attend college.

By the 1960s there were still only 20–25 former college players among the 600 Major Leaguers, but that figure increased steadily into the 1990s. This is reflected in the ratio of high school versus college players in the amateur *Draft* each year. For example, the number of first round players in 1975 included 16 high schoolers and eight college players. By 1985 the numbers were reversed, with nine from high school and 17 from college (although that trend shifted back in the 2000s).

After 1960 players, especially pitchers, still rarely went straight to the Major Leagues from college. In 2001 Paul Prior pitched for the Cubs immediately after leaving USC. He was the first pitcher to go to the Majors straight out of college since Eddie Bane in 1973. Less than a month after he pitched in the College World Series for Arizona State, Bane was pitching for the Twins. He lasted only two seasons, but not because he felt he was rushed to the Majors. He lost his curveball and was never the same, a fact he did not attribute to his quick arrival in the Major Leagues.

In 2004 it was calculated that, with Mark Prior just receiving his degree in business administration, there were only 17 Major League players with college degrees.

Fraternity. Lou Gehrig's mother was a cook in a fraternity house. His own fraternity later established an *Award* in his honor.

Eligibility. Native American Louis Sockalexis attended Notre Dame and Holy Cross. One source reported that Cleveland Spiders manager Patsy Tebeau supposedly arranged to have Sockalexis get drunk so that he would be kicked out of school and be able to play professional baseball. Most good college players in the 19th century played for pay during the summers at resorts that had seasonal town teams.

In 1915 five University of Michigan players were discovered to be professional athletes and virtually the entire squad had been paid to play ball during the summer.

George Sisler signed with a minor league club and then decided to enroll at the University of Michigan and play for Branch Rickey. He never played professionally while in school, but his contract was assigned to different clubs during his college career. The Pirates ultimately held his contract, but upon appeal from Sisler, the National Commission voided the contract.

Early signings were made with many schools' knowledge. Frank Navin of the Tigers signed Eppa Rixey out of the University of Virginia in 1912, assuring coach Hugh Lanigan that: "His signing with our club will not be made public until he is ready to report to our team."

Future Indians shortstop Lou Boudreau was barred from University of Illinois intercollegiate sports after he entered into a contract in which he agreed to sign with Cleveland at a later date.

Low Pay. Ken MacKenzie was a Yale graduate and the only pitcher on the 1962 Mets with a winning record at 5–4. When he pointed out to manager Casey Stengel that he was the lowest paid member of his graduating class, Stengel responded that MacKenzie also had the highest ERA at 4.95.

Perseverance. Guy Cartwright was a 30-year-old rookie with the White Sox in 1943. He probably would never have made it but for the shortage of qualified Major League players during World War II. During nine years in the minor leagues he earned a Master's Degree from the University of Missouri.

Successful College Programs.
USC.
"Bill Lee. Another USC man. When they come out of USC, they go directly to the moon."—Giants broadcaster Lon Simmons on the rather eccentric and outspoken pitcher, referring in part to Lee's nickname, "Spaceman." USC has produced a number of Major League players, including Mark McGwire, Dave Kingman, Ron Fairly, Randy Johnson, Tom Seaver and Mark Prior. Long-time coach Rod Dedeaux had success right from the start; five players

from his 1947 team (his first) made the Major Leagues, and the batboy made the Hall of Fame—Sparky Anderson. Dedeaux, who turned 90 in 2004, had a plain philosophy: "My tastes are simple. All I demand is perfection."

He won 11 national championships during his 45 years as head coach at USC beginning in 1942, including five consecutive from 1970 through 1974. He was named "Coach of the Century" by *Baseball America* and *Collegiate Baseball*. He had a lifetime record of 1,332–571–11 (.699) and sent 200 players to professional baseball. Dedeaux was offered a chance to coach with Casey Stengel and the Yankees in the 1950s and with Walter Alston and the Dodgers in the early 1970s, both situations with an eye to eventually taking over the clubs. He turned both down. Dedeaux was also unhappy that NCAA sanctions, directed primarily at the football team, cost him the chance at perhaps six additional national championships.

Arizona State.
"The Notre Dame of College Baseball"—Roger Angell in *The Summer Game* (1972). The ASU program may be the most successful, producing Rick Monday, Reggie Jackson, Sal Bando, Craig Swan, Ken Landreaux, Floyd Bannister, Alan Bannister, Bob Horner, Gary Gentry, Lenny Randle and Paul Lo Duca. See also Jim Brock with Joe Gilmartin, *The Devil's Coach* (1977), an autobiography of the ASU coach.

Texas. Texas has historically been a strong college program, and in 1983 Roger Clemens led the club to the College World Series championship.

St. Mary's. This small private college in northern California turned out 55 Major League players from the 19th century through 1998, including Hall of Famer Harry Hooper, Joe Oeschger, Gus Triandos, Von Hayes, Tom Candiotti and James Mouton.

LSU. The Louisiana school won five College World Series between 1991 and the early 2000s.

National Championships. The top schools:

12 USC
 5 Arizona State
   Louisiana State
   Texas
 4 Cal State Fullerton
   Miami

Big Game. Future Mets star Ron Darling of Yale pitched an 11 inning no-hitter against future Twins star Frank Viola and St. Johns University in an NCAA play-off game in the 1970s. Darling lost the game in the 12th inning. An account of the game is contained in *Late Innings*, by Roger Angell (1982). Angell had at his side during the game former Yale coach and Major League star Smoky Joe Wood, who was 91 at the time. The next time that Darling and Viola faced each other was on April 27, 1994. Viola and the Red Sox beat Darling and the A's 1–0.

Top Coaches. The winningest coach in college baseball history is Cliff Gustafson of the University of Texas, whose alumni include Greg Swindell and Roger Clemens. When he won his 1,333rd game he passed USC's Rod Dedeaux for first on the all-time list. The top five through 2003 (active coaches in bold):

Record	Yrs.	Coach	School
1,423–373	29	Cliff Gustafson	Texas
1,380–666	34	**Augie Garrido**	Cal St. Fullerton/Texas
1,357–422	25	**Gene Stephenson**	Wichita St.
1,338–305	43	**Chuck Hartman**	Virginia Tech
1,332–571	45	Rod Dedeaux	USC

Most Runs Scored. See *Runs*.

Designated Hitter. It was ironic that Jeff Conine made it into the 1994 All-Star Game as a first baseman/left fielder. In three years at UCLA he was a pitcher and never batted.

Scouting College Players. Connie Mack has been credited as the first manager to use colleges as a proving ground and source for players. In contrast, George Stovall was fired by the St. Louis Browns in 1914 (and went to the Federal League) in part for his absolute refusal to give tryouts to college players. Stoval was replaced by Branch Rickey, who had been in the club's front office in 1913. Stoval's playing days are best remembered for smashing a chair over the head of his manager, Nap Lajoie, in a hotel lobby fight.

Brainy. M.I.T. graduate Jason Szuminski, reported as the first ever Major Leaguer from that school, induced Barry Bonds to fly out as the third batter faced by the pitcher in his Major League career. Actually, Major League/M.I.T. alumni include 1970s reliever Skip Lockwood and Art Merewether, who played one game for the Pirates in 1922. He and Lockwood both attended M.I.T. after their playing days. M.I.T. grad Alan Dopfel was drafted in the third round by the Angels in 1972 and struck out Reggie Jackson in a spring training game, but never made it past Class AAA.

Dick Howser Trophy. This award is presented to the nation's outstanding college player and is named for the former Royals manager who died of a brain tumor in 1987.

Rules Differences. College baseball has a few rules that differ from Major League Baseball:
1. No roll blocks while sliding;
2. No tobacco products of any kind;
3. Double ear flaps on helmets required;
4. Relaxed balk rule; the pitcher need not step toward the base before throwing;
5. Aluminum bats are used.

Tuition.
"Mr. Mack paid for my entire education without ever asking for an accounting or my signature on a contract."—Wayne Ambler, Duke University graduate, on refusing a $5,000 bonus to sign with a National League club in favor of Mack's A's.

In 1962 Organized Baseball inaugurated a college tuition plan that enabled a player to attend college with an eight-semester financial contribution from baseball. In the 1960s it was $1,000 per semester.

College Degree. In 2003, when Sammy Sosa got caught using a corked bat, a reporter tracked down Albert Belle (a previous cork offender) in Arizona for a comment. Belle was incensed that the reporter would find him only for that purpose: "Isn't it interesting that you and your editor care enough to find my house and ask me about this, but no one cares that I've been taking classes at [Arizona State] and I'm about to get my undergraduate accounting degree? What does that say?"

Power Elite. In 1994 the top NCAA Division I programs created a new partnership to ensure a power elite that would include 50–75 colleges.

Greatest Team. Many believe that the greatest college team of all time was the 1976 Arizona State Wildcats. Among the 12 players from that team who played in the Majors were pitcher Floyd Bannister and outfielder Ken Landreaux.

Grammar Problem. An old joke is that an outfielder yelling "I have it!" was a sandlotter trying to sound like a collegian. "I got it" was a college player trying to sound like a sandlot player.

Book. Cappy Gagnon, *Notre Dame Baseball Greats* (2004) (including over 70 Major Leaguers).

College of Coaches (1961–1965)

"He probably wanted two tables of bridge."—Sarcastic comment about Phil Wrigley's eight coaches rotating as manager of the Cubs in the early 1960s.

On December 21, 1960, Cubs owner Phil Wrigley announced that he was abolishing the manager's position and would have a rotating group of eight coaches. The original members were Rip Collins, Charlie Grimm, Elvin Tappe, Goldie Holt, Vedie Himsl, Harry Craft, Bobby Adams and Rube Walker. *The Baseball Encyclopedia* credits only three with managing the club in 1961 when the Cubs finished seventh: Tappe (42–54), Himsl (10–21) and Craft (7–9).

Later members of the college were Bob Kennedy, Buck O'Neil (the first black coach in the Major Leagues), Lou Klein, Charlie Metro, Al Dark, Freddie Martin, Mel Wright and Mel Harder. *The Baseball Encyclopedia* credits only three for 1962: Tappe (4–16), Klein (12–18) and Metro (43–69).

In the winter of 1962 Bob Kennedy became "Head Coach," but the college officially continued for three more seasons. The college ended on October 25, 1965, when Leo Durocher was hired as Cubs manager, but not before some verbal sparring: "We have found from long experience that it doesn't make any difference what title a team leader has as long as he has the ability to take charge."— Cubs team official on the hiring of Durocher, to which Durocher responded: "I just gave myself a title. I'm not the head coach here. I'm the manager."

College World Series (1947–)

"That was real baseball. We weren't playing for the money. We got Mickey Mouse watches that ran backwards."—Pitcher Bill Lee on the College World Series.

In the inaugural College World Series, played in 1947, Yale was led by future **President** George "Spikes" Bush at first base. Yale lost to the University of California, but Bush's team also reached the 1948 final, where they lost again, this time to USC. In losing Game 1 in 1948 by a score of 3–1, with Bush on deck, Yale's Jerry Breen hit into a bases-loaded triple play in the bottom of the 9th inning.

The World Series was played in Kalamazoo in 1947 and 1948 and then moved permanently to Omaha, Nebraska.

The NCAA tournament was expanded to 48 teams in 1987. In 1994 the field was expanded to include six more conference champions.

Eddie Collins (1887–1951)

Hall of Fame 1939
"Eddie Collins was the greatest second baseman I ever saw and one of the best ballplayers. He could hit, he could run, throw, field, and he had it upstairs too. Smartest baseball man I ever met. Eddie could stand at third coaching and I don't care who was pitching, in two innings he'd have their signs; he'd know what that pitcher was going to throw and call them."—American League outfielder Doc Cramer.

Collins starred at second base for the A's and White Sox from 1906 through the late 1920s.

Edward Trowbridge Collins was a star infielder at Columbia University when supposedly he was discovered by Andy Coakley, then a pitcher with the A's who was on his honeymoon during the 1906 season. Collins signed almost immediately with the A's at age 19 and played six games for the club that year under the name Eddie Sullivan to protect his eligibility.

Having lost his eligibility at Columbia after being found out, Collins played 14 games for the A's in 1907, but increased that total to 102 in 1908, batting .273. After that he blossomed, hitting over .300 in 18 of the next 20 seasons while starring at second base.

Collins was the leader of Connie Mack's "$100,000 Infield" and led the club to pennants in all but one season from 1909 through 1914. After the 1914 season Mack disbanded the club in the face of competition from the Federal League. Collins was traded to the White Sox, for whom he starred over the next 12 years. He missed part of the 1918 season when he joined the Marine Corp, but was back in time to be one of the honest players on the 1919 Black Sox. He was player-manager of the club in 1925 and 1926, finishing fifth both seasons. He moved back to the A's in 1927, but his career was almost over. He played parts of the 1927 and 1928 seasons, but made only cameo appearances in 1929 and 1930.

He had 743 stolen bases and 3,311 hits over his 25-year career. When his playing days ended, he was promised a chance to manage the A's, but the offer did not materialize as Connie Mack stayed at the helm for what seemed like forever. Collins moved into the front office of the Red Sox in 1933, where he worked until his death in 1951 at age 64.

Jimmy Collins (1870–1943)

Hall of Fame 1945

"With a swoop like that of a chicken hawk, Collins would gather up the bunt and throw it accurately to whomever should receive it. The beauty about him was that he could throw from any angle, any position on the ground or in the air."—John B. Foster in the 1902 *Spalding Guide.*

Collins starred at third base at the turn of the century primarily for the National and American League clubs in Boston.

New York native James Joseph Collins began his Major League career with the National League Boston Red Stockings in 1895, but was quickly loaned to the Louisville Colonels for the balance of the season. Moving to third base with the Colonels, he established himself over the next 14 years as the greatest third baseman of the era.

Collins returned to the Red Stockings through 1900 and then moved over to the new American League club in Boston in 1901. He managed the club for the first six years of its existence, compiling a .548 winning percentage. He was player-manager of the first World Series winners in 1903. The club won the pennant in 1904, but the Giants refused to play in the World Series against the rival American League.

Collins starred in Boston until 1907, when he was fired as manager and traded midseason to the A's. He played two more mediocre seasons and then retired. Collins finished with a .294 lifetime average, hitting over .300 five times. He led the National League in home runs with 15 in 1898.

After Collins retired from the A's, he played in the minor leagues in his native Buffalo until 1911. He was heavily involved in real estate in that city, but was wiped out by the 1930s Depression and went to work for the local park service. He died of pneumonia in 1943, two years before his election to the Hall of Fame.

Collusion

"To the best of my knowledge and information, there is no conspiracy, there are no rules, there are no bulletins, there are no regulations that exist that control the behavior of the clubs."— Barry Rona, the owners' chief labor lawyer, referring to 1985–1986.

1986. In 1986 Major League owners were accused of conspiring among themselves ("collusion") to forego negotiating with free agents. Three separate arbitration rulings found them guilty and total damages of $280 million were assessed against them in the first phase of the damage payments. The money was to be divided among those players who had been free agents from 1986 through 1991.

A total of 843 players filed 3,000 claims totaling $1,321,948,295 by the deadline of May 20, 1991. Clubs put the $280 million into a bank account for the players as of January 2, 1991, and the union was given the task of dispersing the money. The big winners were Jack Clark, Andre Dawson and Lance Parrish, each of whom was awarded $1 million or more in damages from the pool of money. The $280 million was inadequate to cover all claims and the union was taken to arbitration by some players dissatisfied with the distribution.

After a second round of collusion damage payments in early 1995, Mike Hargrove received $476,000 of the $9.9 million available. The biggest winners were Dave Kingman with $829,850 for 1987 and Rod Carew with $782,036 for 1986. Ten players were awarded money for 1986 and 11 for 1987.

Some players renegotiated their contracts due to collusion, most notably Rickey Henderson, who had signed an artificially low contract. After the scandal, owners agreed through collective bargaining to treble damages for future collusion.

2003. The issue resurfaced in late 2003 when high-priced free agents claimed that clubs conspired to keep prices down over the slow-signing winter of 2002–2003. The union requested and received team documents that suggested to the union that the clubs were reporting offers through a "central command" in New York and using the 60–40 debt ratio rule as a form of salary cap. The rule prohibits clubs from having debt larger than 40% of its assets.

Colombia

Colombian brothers Ibraham and Gonzalo Zuniga Angel are responsible for bringing baseball to Colombia in the 19th century. Some sources credit the Cubans with introducing the game in 1903. Colombia had a professional league into the 1970s, but it disbanded when foreign players became fearful of playing winter ball there.

The first Colombian to play in the Major Leagues was Luis "Jud" Castro, who played for the 1902 Athletics. Colombia was the second Latin American country represented in the Major Leagues, following only Cuba. In the mid–1990s Edgar Renteria of the Mariners became the fourth Colombian to play in the Major Leagues.

Jolbert Cabrera of the Dodgers wears No. 6 because he's the sixth Major League player from Colombia.

Colorado Rockies

National League 1993–

"I really don't understand why baseball traditionalists are so opposed to the concept of interleague play. There has been de facto interleague play—between the major and minor leagues—since big league teams began playing in Colorado in 1993."—Fan Andy Schwich in a letter to the *Los Angeles Times* after the Dodgers and Rockies combined to score 84 runs in a four-game series; capped by a 16–15 comeback win by the Rockies in the last game.

"Cows"—*Denver Post* columnist Woody Paige's proposed nickname of the expected-to-be lousy Colorado Rockies; so that fans could say "things will be different when the Cows come home," after a losing streak on the road.

Origins. Denver was to have received a franchise in the early 1960s when the American League expanded, but Gene Autry's Angels took the spot originally thought to have been reserved for Denver. The *Continental League* plans included a team in Denver, but when the league was scrapped before its formation, Denver lost out.

The Rockies were one of the two National League *Expansion* franchises that started play in 1993 (see also *Expansion Draft*).

First Game. In their first game, played April 5, 1993, the Rockies played the Mets in Shea Stadium. The Rockies' first draft pick, Dave Nied, lost 3–0 as the recently deposed Fay Vincent threw out the first ball. The Rockies set an Opening Day attendance record when they drew 80,277 on April 9, 1993, in Mile High Stadium. They defeated the Expos 11–4 for their first victory.

Key Owner.

Jerry McMorris/1993–. The leader of the original ownership contingent was Jerry McMorris, who was estimated to be worth $130 million at the time the club was formed. He owned approximately 30% of the club and was the managing general partner. Son of a trucker, he began his own three-truck operation as a 19-year-old and built it into a trucking company with 1992 revenues of $500 million. Another of the principal owners, John Antonucci, owns a chain of drugstores and markets in the Midwest. The Coors Brewing company is also a minority owner of the club.

John McHale, Jr., son of long-time Montreal general manager John McHale, Sr., was named the club's first Director of Baseball Operations (the 1990s name for general manager).

In July 2004 News Corp.'s Fox cable networks announced the purchase of a minority interest in the Rockies, whose games the network had broadcast since 1997. The stake was reported to be worth $20 million.

Nickname. The minor league club that preceded the Rockies was the Denver Bears. An NHL hockey franchise in Denver was known as the Rockies for the mountain range that is adjacent to the city.

Key Seasons.

1995. The Rockies were the wild-card team behind the 30+ home run performances of Larry Walker, Andres Galarraga, Vinny Castilla and Dante Bichette. The Braves beat the Rockies in the division play-offs.

Key Ballplayers.

Dante Bichette.

"Bichette Happens"— Headline in *Sport* magazine.

Bichette hit 21 and 19 home runs for the club in its first two seasons and then exploded for 40 home runs and 128 RBIs in 1995.

Larry Walker went from 19 home runs in 1994 in Montreal to 36 home runs and 101 RBIs in 1995, his first season in Colorado. Eight years later, through 2003, he had reached highs of 49 home runs and 130 RBIs (both in 1997), along with 208 hits in a season and a .366 batting average (also in 1997). He had four seasons with over 100 RBIs in Colorado and had hit 252 home runs there through 2003.

Todd Helton emerged has perhaps the best hitter of his generation, compiling a .337 lifetime average over seven seasons beginning in 1997. He had at least 109 RBIs and 30 home runs in five straight years through 2003, with a peak year of 2000; he batted .372 with 216 hits, 42 home runs and 147 RBIs.

Key Managers.

Don Baylor was the club's first manager and led them to the play-offs in 1995, only their third season, and he was named Manager of the Year. His clubs were 83–79 in 1996 and 1997 and he had the best expansion club record in history at the time with a

record of 363–384. His relationship with the front office deteriorated in 1998 and the club's 77–85 fourth-place finish got him fired.

Ballparks.

Mile High Stadium.

The Rockies' first ballpark was Mile High Stadium, built for baseball in 1948 and originally known as Bears Stadium. It was the home of the Class A Denver Bears of the Western League (later to move up to Class AAA). The ballpark initially had a seating capacity of 19,000 but was expanded over the years, primarily to accommodate the NFL's Denver Broncos. The dimensions from right to left field were 335–375–423–400–370 and capacity was 76,037 in 1994. The huge ballpark enabled the club to set a number of Major League *Attendance* records.

The Rockies cut a sweetheart deal with the city of Denver, which owned Mile High Stadium. The club paid no rent the first two years and kept 40% of all concessions, worth at least $10 million.

Coors Field.

"Pops, I gotta say, this Coors Field ain't bad. It's got all the cool old-time stuff, like a hand-operated scoreboard in rightfield, and all the cool new stuff, like one of those microbrew pubs just beyond rightfield. Only thing was, we were freezing because all we had on were our leather jackets, and everybody else looked like they were ready to hit the slopes."— Rick Reilly in *Sports Illustrated* on the club's second ballpark.

"The Boom Box"— Nickname given the new home run-friendly ballpark by Norm Clarke of the *Rocky Mountain News*. Both ballparks yielded large numbers of home runs because of Denver's high *Altitude*.

"I don't put a lot of credibility into what they do in Colorado. [Hitting in] Coors Field is like hitting in the lobby of a Doubletree."— Reggie Jackson.

"There is no fat lady at Coors Field."— Vin Scully.

By the 1970s Denver's minor league ballpark was known as Coors Field (for the Colorado-based brewery). The new Major League ballpark that opened for the 1995 season was known by the same name. The new ballpark was built for $141.5 million and opened in April 1995. It originally was to seat 43,800, but after the club's first season shattered Major League attendance records, seating capacity design was expanded to 50,249.

Dimensions from right to left field are 347–390–415–375–350. Coors Brewery paid $15 million to name the new ballpark. The site was a former Union Pacific rail yard and dinosaur bones were found in the area that were estimated to be 70 million years old. Every one of the 1.4 million bricks on the facade is stamped with the Coors Field name.

Key Broadcasters. The club's first number one broadcaster was Wayne Hagin, who had spent 11 years broadcasting for the A's, Giants and White Sox. Also in the booth was Jeff Kingery, who had 11 seasons as the voice of the Denver Nuggets and broadcast for the Denver Bears minor league club. The Rockies broadcast network covered 12 states in its first season. Hagin lasted through the 2002 season before moving over to the Cardinals, but Kingery remained through 2004. The Rockies later added former player George Frazier (1998–) and long-time Indians broadcaster Jack Corrigan (2003).

Books. Lew Cady, *They've Got Rockies in Their Heads!* (1994); Fulcrum (publisher), *Colorado Rockies: The Inaugural Season* (1994); Bob Italia and Paul Joseph, *Colorado Rockies (America's Game)* (1997); Bob Kravitz, *Mile High Madness: A Year With the Colorado Rockies* (1993); Wayne Stewart, *The History of the Colorado Rockies* (2002).

Colorado Silver Bullets See *Women in Baseball*

Colors

"Dick Green, Pink Hawley, Dallas Green, Pinky Hargrove, Jimmy Lavender, Red Blum, Carmen Hill, George Carmen, Dick Gray, Ike Brown, Gates Brown, Gil Blanco, Whitey Witt, Whitey Ford, Frank White, Fuzz White, Whitey Oak, Don Black, Lu Blue, Blackie Schwamb, Bud Black, Vida Blue, Bill Black, Bill White"
See *Uniforms—Color.*

Colt League

This youth league was founded in 1953 in Martin's Ferry, Ohio, for boys 15 and 16 years old. In 1959 it merged with *Pony League Baseball* and other leagues to form "Boys' Baseball," headquartered in Washington, Pennsylvania. These leagues are not affiliated with *Little League Baseball.*

Columbian League (1912)

"WARNING TO PLAYERS! Ballplayers Under Contract or Reservation to Clubs in Organized Ball Should Not Permit Themselves to be Blinded or Cajoled by the Specious Promises of Promoters of Shadowy Outlaw Leagues."—*Sporting Life* headline in January 1912.

In 1912 the backers of this league attempted to form a rival major league. Their leader was John Powers, who had been the organizer of the Class D Wisconsin State League in 1904. The Columbian League was to be located in various Midwestern cities, but it never opened the season. When St. Louis brewer Otto Steifel backed out, the league collapsed. Steifel became an owner in the 1914–1915 Federal League.

Columbus Buckeyes

American Association 1883–1884, 1889–1891

"Columbus was a major-league town in 1883, 1884, 1889, 1890, and 1891, when the American Association was major league. Since then it has been a bastion of minor-league Triple A ball. But the latter-day Columbus Redbirds are no more. In baseball, as in most other matters, Ohio State University is the only thing left in Columbus."—Harold Peterson in *The Man Who Invented Baseball* (1969).

1883–1884. Led by manager Hustling Horace Phillips, the Buckeyes were terrible in 1883 with a 32–65 record. Frank Mountain led the league with 33 losses. In 1884 the club rebounded with a 69–39 record and a second-place finish, but the financial pressure from the Union Association forced the club out of the league.

1889–1991. The owner of the 1889–1891 club was Allan W. Thurman, who tried to engineer peace between the leagues after the 1890 Players League almost wiped out the American Association. After a poor 1889 season, the club finished second in 1890 behind Hank Gastright's 30 wins. The club faded to sixth in 1891 and was eliminated when the American Association folded and only its four strongest clubs merged into the National League.

Earle Combs (1899–1976)

Hall of Fame (VC) 1970

"As I went after [the dropped ball], I was tempted to keep right on going, climb the fence, and not stop running until I got back to Pebworth."—Combs, fearing manager Joe McCarthy, in *I'd Rather Be a Yankee* by John Tullus (1986).

Combs starred in center field for the Yankees from 1924 through 1935, batting .325 lifetime.

Earle Bryan Combs received his teaching certificate in Tennessee while he was the player-manager of a local semipro club. After a successful minor league stint in Louisville starting in 1922 (batting .344, .380 and .368), the Yankees reportedly offered $50,000 to Louisville for his contract. He played a few games for the Yankees in 1924 and then became the starting center fielder in 1925. He batted .342 and was the club's lead-off hitter well into the 1930s.

Combs batted over .300 nine times and led the league in triples three times. His 231 hits in 1927 were a team record until the 1980s and he had a lifetime average of .325 over 12 seasons. His good speed allowed him to hit 154 triples and he hit .350 in four World Series.

In July 1934 he crashed into the wall at Sportsman's Park in St. Louis and smashed his head. He was forced to retire after a brief comeback in 1935. He coached for the Yankees until 1944, then moved to the Browns in 1947, the Red Sox in 1948–1952 and the Phillies in 1954. After he retired from baseball he spent most of his years farming.

Comebacks and Comeback Player of the Year

"This winter I'm working out every day, throwing at a wall. I'm 11 and 0 against the wall."—Jim Bouton on his comeback attempt at age 38.

"You know what that [award] tells you? It tells you were terrible the year before."—Rick Sutcliffe when asked in early 1992 about his chances for the award after starting the season 9–4. He finished at 16–15 after going 6–5 and 0–2 the previous two seasons.

"Expansion's coming up [in 1998], pitching is thin and I'm left-handed."—Former pitcher Tom Browning, who was considering a comeback after retiring early in 1997 when he was unable to make the Royals' pitching staff.

"I don't know how to say this, but for a guy who's going to be in the Hall of Fame, your mechanics are awful."—Miami University assistant pitching coach Lazaro Collazo, who assisted pitcher Jim Palmer in his comeback attempt. At age 45 in 1991 Palmer attempted a spring training comeback with the Orioles. No Hall of Fame inductee had ever attempted a serious comeback. Palmer shredded a hamstring in his first outing and aborted his plans.

Season Comebacks/Player. In 1960 both Ted Williams and Stan Musial won the award. Williams hit .316 with 29 home runs in his final year, after hitting .254 with 10 home runs in 1959. The basis for Musial's award is not as clear. He hit .275 with 17 home runs in 1960 after hitting .255 with 14 home runs the year before.

Dick Ellsworth became the first player to win the award in each league. He won the first time at age 23 in 1963 when he won 22 games for the Cubs after going 9–20 the year before. In 1967 he won 16 games for the Red Sox after going 6–7 the year before.

In spring 1997 Dennis Martinez successfully attempted a comeback with the Mariners at age 41, after retiring a year earlier with the Indians. He was only three wins shy of Juan Marichal's record number of lifetime wins for *Latin* pitchers, which he later broke by two wins, finishing with 245.

In 1998 Blue Jays pitcher Dave Stieb tried a comeback at age 40, after six years out of baseball. He joined the club during spring training as a guest instructor. He made it back to the mound when he gave up three hits in an inning of scoreless relief in June 1998 in his first appearance of the season. In August he got the win in a

14–7 victory over the Twins. It was his first win since 1993. He gave up four earned runs in five innings. He finished the year at 1–2 and then retired for good.

In April 2001, Cubs reliever Jeff Fassero recorded saves on two consecutive nights, his first since June 30, 1993.

On April 2, 2002, Cincinnati's Jose Rijo made his first start in almost seven years. He allowed one earned run in five innings and earned his first victory since July 13, 1995. He saw his first Major League action after several inactive years, when he appeared in relief in August 2001.

On September 2, 2002, Pirates starter Salomon Torres, age 30, pitched 8⅓ innings in a 3–0 win over the Pirates. It was his first appearance in the Major Leagues since July 20, 1997. He also collected his first hit since 1994. Torres had been Montreal's pitching coach in the Dominican Summer League before signing with the Pirates in January 2002.

Chris Hammond pitched remarkably well in 2002 after being out of baseball for two seasons. He posted an ERA below 1.00 while pitching 70+ innings for the Yankees, only the third pitcher since 1900 to do so. After the season, the Yankees offered him and two other pitchers, Mike Stanton and Mark Guthrie, identical $4.8 million contracts and gave them 15 minutes to decide whether to accept. Hammond was the only one of the three to sign.

Jose Lima returned to the Major Leagues in 2003 after scouts for the Royals spotted him pitching for the Newark Bears of the independent Atlantic League. He won six straight before injuring his groin.

Mariners right-hander Gil Meche in 2003 became the first pitcher to win 15 games after a two year absence from the Major Leagues since Whitey Ford in 1953.

In April 2003, David Cone pitched for the first time since 2001, and was the winning pitcher in a 4–0 victory for the Mets over the Expos. Throwing mostly breaking balls, he struck out five and walked three in five innings, giving up two hits on 84 pitches.

Reliever Rod Beck (who attended the author's high school) had reconstructive elbow surgery that put him out of action for part of 2001 and all of 2002. He returned to the minor leagues for two months in early 2003, living in a 36-foot Winnebago next door to the Sec Taylor ballpark in Des Moines, Iowa, while pitching for the Class AAA Iowa Cubs. After games, he would invite fans back for a beer. He was signed by the Padres and converted all 20 saves he had through the end of the 2003 season. He signed with the club for 2004, but went on a mysterious "personal leave" during spring training. He returned in May without explanation.

Mark McGwire. McGwire has to be considered a comeback story after hitting a total of only 18 home runs over the 1993–1994 seasons. He had surgery for various injuries and many thought his career was in severe decline, if not over. In 1995 he returned to form with 39 home runs, and then exploded over the next four seasons with home run totals of 52, 58, 70 and 65, before injuries slowed him again.

Come-from-Behind Games. See *Divisional Play and Play-Offs, League Championship Series, Play-Offs, Runs* and *World Series.*

In 1995 the Indians had 43 come-from-behind games, 26 in their last at-bat. The 1995 Braves had 25 last at-bat victories.

College. In 1973 the USC Trojans were down 7–0 in the 9th inning of the semifinals of the College World Series. Minnesota's Dave Winfield was pitching a one-hitter, but the Trojans rallied to win the game and then won the championship the next day with a 9th inning rally after being down 3–2 against Arizona State.

Comic Strips and Cartoons

"If that's so silly, how come every time I put one down, somebody else picks it up?"—Yogi Berra, sensitive about his love of comic books.

"Buck Rogers, Charley Brown, Moon Mullen"

Cartoons.

"Honestly, at one time I though Babe Ruth was a cartoon character. I really did, I mean I wasn't born until 1961 and I grew up in Indiana."—Don Mattingly.

One of the earliest baseball cartoons was published in 1877 in Buffalo by Christopher Smith, who featured local teams. The early 20th century saw the emergence of the sports cartoonist, as exemplified by "TAD," the byline for Theodore A. Dorgan, who popularized the term *Hot Dog.*

Willard Mullin's sports cartoons appeared in the *New York World-Telegram* six days a week for over 30 years. In 1971 he was named the sports cartoonist of the century by the Cartoonists' Association.

Comic Strips.

"I think it's a mistake to be unfaithful to your readers, always to be letting them down."—"Peanuts" creator Charles Schultz on the strip he began in 1952. At the start of the 1993 baseball season, on March 30, Schultz finally allowed Charlie Brown to hit his first home run after 43 years of futility. He hit it in the 9th inning and won the game.

Ray Gotto's "Ozark Ike" has been the only national comic strip with baseball as the primary theme. The strip first appeared in late 1945 and lasted until 1959. Gotto left the strip in the mid–1950s and started a similar strip called "Cotton Woods."

Cartoonist. Red Sox pitcher Bob Cremins, who faced Babe Ruth in his first Major League appearance on the mound, died at age 98 in early 2004. He had been a cartoonist for many years for the *Philadelphia Evening Bulletin.*

Too Much Television. Reliever Mitch Williams had a tattoo of movie cartoon character Speedy Gonzalez on his right calf. His dad had a Tasmanian Devil and Yosemite Sam tattoo. His brother had Gumby and Pokey.

Cartoon History. In 1989 Eddie Germano published a cartoon history of the Red Sox from 1964 through 1988 entitled *Red Sox Drawing Board: 25 Years of Cartoons.*

Books. Robert Mankoff and Michael Crawford (eds.), *The New Yorker Book of Baseball Cartoons* (2003); James Mote, *Everything Baseball* (1989), covering every comic strip and cartoon ever written primarily for baseball; S. Gross and James Charlton (eds.), *Baseball: A Treasury of Hilarious Cartoons* (1991).

Charles Comiskey (1859–1931)

Hall of Fame 1939

"In the Centennial year of 1876 there appeared on Chicago's diamonds a tall and lanky youth known to local fame as a pitcher. He brought into the game a sinewy right arm, a pair of speedy legs and a strong individuality. An eventful career of forty-three years has well-nigh robbed him of all but the last."—G. W. Axelson in *"Commy"* (1919).

Comiskey was a 19th century first baseman and the long-time owner of the Chicago White Sox.

The son of a prominent Chicago politician, Comiskey was known as "Commy," the "Noblest Roman in the League," or the "Old Roman" as the founder and long-time owner of the *Chicago White Sox.* He ran the club from its American League debut in 1901 until his death in 1931. He has been described as the second most powerful man in the American League, behind only Ban Johnson.

Prior to owning the White Sox, Comiskey played baseball primarily in the American Association for the St. Louis Brown Stockings. From 1882 through 1889 he was a solid, though not spectacular, first baseman for the club. He later played for Chicago in the Players League and Cincinnati in the National League. He batted .264 over 13 seasons and is credited by some with innovations in defensive play, such as playing away from the bag and putting on infield shifts. He also helped lead the Brown Stockings to four league titles between 1885 and 1888.

In the 1890s Comiskey became close friends with future American League president Ban Johnson. Comiskey purchased the Sioux City franchise of the Western Association, which he moved to St. Paul before settling in Chicago in 1900. There the club became known as the White Sox. His clubs won American League titles in 1901, 1906, 1917 and 1919. His legendary penny-pinching contributed to the fixed games by the 1919 Black Sox. His friendship with Johnson eventually turned to a mutual loathing and the two died within a few months of each other.

His son, J. Louis "Lou" Comiskey, died in 1939 after overseeing the team following his father's death. (Lou's daughter was a movie actress known professionally as June Travis. She played opposite James Cagney in the movie *Ceiling Zero*, in which this author's father had a supporting role. She and the author's father spent a number of afternoons eating box lunches while flying over the Burbank, California, movie lot. The plane was used in the movie and was piloted for them by the movie's technical director.)

Book. G.W. Axelson, *"Commy"* (1919).

Comiskey Park (1910–1990)

"The Baseball Palace of the World"—Name bestowed on Comiskey Park at its opening on July 1, 1910.

Construction and Dedication. As early as 1903 Charles Comiskey began formulating plans to move his club to a modern facility. In January 1909 he purchased the needed land from Roxanna Bowen. It was located in the Canal Trustees Subdivision east of 35th and Wentworth, four blocks from the club's existing ballpark (although many sources report that it was on the same site). It had been owned by Major Long John Wentworth during the Civil War and supposedly was the city dump in that era. Other sources note that it was a truck farm and junkyard at the time of Comiskey's purchase. Shortstop Luke Appling once supposedly tripped over a protruding copper kettle in the infield. Appling said he pulled a blue and white coffee pot out of the shortstop area and once cut his leg on a bottle sticking out of the ground near home plate.

Comiskey spent $100,000 to buy the land and more than $500,000 to build the park during 1909 and early 1910. It was the third steel and concrete ballpark constructed in the United States.

The architect who designed the park, Zachary Taylor Davis, also designed Wrigley Field in Chicago and Wrigley Field in Los Angeles. Pitcher Ed Walsh consulted in the design of Comiskey Park and suggested that the fences be far back, resulting in a notorious pitcher's park. Ironically, Walsh lost the opener to the Browns 2–0.

The new park was dedicated on July 1, 1910, in front of 30,000 fans. The club barely made the construction deadline because there had been a labor strike as a result of a carpenter's death during construction.

Comiskey Park was unique in its time, dwarfing all other ballparks previously constructed. It had an upper deck from third base to first base and two detached grandstands.

Additions/Remodeling. In the 1920s the wooden bleachers were replaced by steel and concrete. Double-decking in the bleachers was added in 1927 at a cost of $100,000.

As part of a 1941 remodeling, the seats were changed and much of the green brick was painted white. The center field wall was torn down to make room for a picnic area. A new scoreboard was installed in 1950.

During a 1982 construction of luxury boxes, engineers discovered serious structural problems with the ballpark, making it imperative that a new stadium be built. It was reported that the upper deck would have collapsed within two years. This led to the construction of **New Comiskey Park**.

Capacity. Upon completion in 1910 there were 6,400 box seats, 12,600 grandstand seats and 16,000 pavilion/bleacher seats, for a total of approximately 35,000. Shortly before 1920, Comiskey expanded the park to 41,000, and the ballpark was the site of a crowd of 43,825 in 1925 for the City Series between the Cubs and White Sox.

By 1927 the ballpark seated 52,000 but was reduced to 46,550 in 1941 when curved seats replaced the straight-backed seats. The all-time attendance was 55,555 on May 20, 1973, but seating was scaled back in the late 1970s to 44,492.

Name. The invitations to the first game referred to the park as White Sox Park, but it was known as Comiskey Park as early as 1913.

Dimensions. The original dimensions from left to right field were 363–382–420–382–362. In 1934 home plate was moved 14 feet closer to the fences to accommodate slugger Al Simmons. The plate was moved back for 1937.

The fences were moved closer early in 1949 (chicken wire was installed at the warning track) and then moved back three days later after the Senators hit seven home runs while the White Sox barely benefited from the change. However, those three days of shorter distances allowed Chicago's Floyd Baker to hit his only Major League home run in 2,280 at-bats over 13 years.

Center field remained at 400 feet into the 1980s, and by 1980 the foul lines were 363 feet. In 1983 the infield was again moved closer to the outfield wall to increase home run production.

Home Runs. The first home run in the park was hit by Lee Tannehill, a shortstop on the 1910 team. It was a grand slam that rolled down the foul line through the fence. Only seven home runs were hit the first year. Jimmie Foxx and Babe Ruth are two of the few players to hit a ball completely out of the park.

Grass. In 1969 artificial turf ("Sox Sod") was installed for the first time in an American League ballpark. When Bill Veeck took over again in late 1975, he ordered removal of the synthetic surface. It was the only ballpark ever to have artificial turf in the outfield and grass in the infield.

Scoreboard. Comiskey Park had a "Chesterfield! It's a hit!" sign that lit up on every White Sox hit. When Veeck took over he decided that a new scoreboard was necessary and in 1959 he built the first exploding *Scoreboard*. It stood for 21 years until replaced by a DiamondVision board in 1982.

Tenants. The Chicago American Giants of the Negro American League played in Comiskey Park from 1941 through 1950, and the ballpark was host to the Negro All-Star Game each year from 1933 through 1950.

The Cubs used the park for the 1918 World Series and the Chicago Cardinals (later the Bears) of the National Football League were tenants in 1922, 1925, 1929–1930, and 1939–1958.

Other Events. The ballpark has hosted other big events, including the 1937 heavyweight fight in which Joe Louis won the crown from Jim Braddock and the 1957 title fight in which Sonny Liston defeated Floyd Patterson. The Beatles, Frank Sinatra and Michael Jackson also appeared there.

New Comiskey Park.

"The White Sox, according to owner Arthur Allyn, will be playing in a new stadium by 1972, regardless of whether plans for a new sports complex at Dearborn Station are ever carried to completion."—1967 newspaper account; only 23 years later ground was broken for the new ballpark.

Whether or not the White Sox stayed in Chicago hinged on whether the city and state approved financing for a new ballpark. Beginning in 1986 concrete efforts were undertaken to assure that the club stayed in Chicago. The agreement to build a new ballpark was ceremoniously signed at home plate in Comiskey Park on January 19, 1987, but it took another two years to finalize the financing for the deal.

New Comiskey Park was built directly across the parking lot from the original Comiskey Park. Amid constant speculation that the White Sox would leave the city, ground was broken on May 7, 1990. Its opening in 1991 ended use of the Major League's oldest existing ballpark. Built at a cost of $150 (or $135) million, the new facility was the first baseball-only stadium built since Kansas City's Royals Stadium opened in 1972.

The Baseball gods apparently were not happy about the new ballpark. In the first game played there on April 18, 1991, with a capacity crowd of 44,702 on hand, the White Sox lost 16–0 to the Tigers and Frank Tanana. The club lost again in 12 innings and then won 5–4 with two runs in the 9th inning in a Sunday game.

The new facility has 85 suites on two levels. The highest seat in the upper deck of New Comiskey Park is almost twice as high as the same seat in the original Comiskey Park. The dimensions from left to right field are 347–383–400–383–347.

Books. Frank Budreck, *Goodbye Old Friend* (1991); Douglas Bukowski, *Baseball Palace of the World* (1991) (chronicle of the ballpark's last season).

Commissioners

"Charlie Finley wouldn't think God would make a good commissioner."—Warren Giles.

"It's not in the best interests of baseball."—The commissioner's fallback position when logic and law do not prevail.

"The Commissioner may take such steps as he may deem necessary and proper in the interest and morale of the players and the honor of the game."—Article 1, section 4 of the Major League Agreement of 1921, the formal language of the previous quote.

"We can't have a commissioner who makes too many mistakes. We have a big investment in this business. Baseball is big business."—Anonymous Major League owner.

The Commissioners.

Kenesaw Mountain Landis	1920–1944
Leslie O'Connor (interim)	1944–1945
Albert B. "Happy" Chandler	1945–1951
Ford C. Frick	1951–1965
William D. Eckert	1965–1969
Bowie Kuhn	1969–1984
Peter Ueberroth	1984–1989
A. Bartlett Giamatti	1989
Fay Vincent	1989–1992
Bud Selig (interim 1992–1998)	1992–

Attempts to Appoint a Commissioner.

Diminutive, no-nonsense and iron-willed Kenesaw Mountain Landis, the first commissioner of Major League Baseball, in front of an American Airlines plane.

"Baseball Peace Declared; Landis Named Dictator"—*New York Times* headline announcing the appointment of Landis.

National League president Abraham Mills anticipated the need for a commissioner in writing to Albert Spalding in 1886, recommending that a single man be appointed to oversee baseball.

It has often been assumed that the 1919 Black Sox Scandal was the primary impetus for the appointment of Judge Landis as commissioner. Even though the selection was made shortly after the scandal surfaced in the press, the owners had been pushing hard for a commissioner to replace the unworkable three-man National Commission and to curb the power of autocratic American League president Ban Johnson.

Illinois federal judge Kenesaw Mountain Landis was considered along with New York senator and former New York City mayor James J. "Jimmy" Walker. Also considered were generals John J. Pershing and Leonard Wood of World War I fame. National League president John Heydler actively sought to have Landis appointed commissioner. Heydler had finally concluded that the National Commission would not work after the fiasco surrounding the sharing of gate receipts at the 1918 World Series (see *World Series—Player Shares*).

Certain American League owners, including Harry Frazee of the Red Sox, backed former U.S. President William Howard Taft. Taft's brother Charles had been the owner of the Chicago Cubs.

Another alternative considered was to change the configuration of the National Commission by adding a player representative (Sam Crawford was mentioned) and a minor league representative.

Events Immediately Preceding Appointment. On October 2, 1920, Albert D. Lasker, a Chicago advertising man and part-owner of the Cubs, presented a plan to create a new three-man board to govern baseball. The National League quickly approved the plan, but Ban Johnson did not like losing his power.

At a meeting on October 18, 1920, the National League clubs and three American League clubs (Yankees, Red Sox and White Sox) were in agreement. They formed a committee to implement the new plan and gave the dissident five American League clubs an ultimatum. The five were to meet with the larger group by November 1 or the three would move to the National League and form a 12-team league with one new team to be placed in Detroit. On November 8, after the five clubs ignored the demand, the "New National League" was quietly formed. National League president John Heydler was elected to head the league, with Judge Landis at the top of the list to head the three-man committee that would oversee the league. It appears that this may have been posturing to force the five other clubs to conform.

At the annual meeting of the minor leagues, there was significant behind-the-scenes negotiating to break the impasse. The minor leagues voted to exclude the two Major League presidents from the proceedings, a move described as the "final humiliation" to Ban Johnson.

The five teams caved in and Landis was elected at a meeting in Chicago on November 12, 1920. Young attorney Leslie O'Connor was named his assistant. Landis officially took over on January 12, 1921, though he had been in control for a few weeks. The owners abandoned a plan to bring in the other two members as originally envisioned under the Lasker proposal. See also Bill Veeck, Jr., *The Hustler's Handbook* (1965), containing a chapter entitled "Harry's Diary," covering the selection of Landis and a mysterious diary describing the events.

Kenesaw Mountain Landis (1866–1944)
Served 1920–1944
Hall of Fame 1939

"The Ballplayer's Friend"—Landis' nickname for himself.

"Don't go to those owners if you get into trouble, come to me. I'm your friend. They're no good."—Landis.

"A wild-eyed nut."—Ban Johnson.

"An erratic and irresponsible despot."—J.G. Taylor Spink in 1923; though the Ban Johnson–supporting Spink later wrote a flattering biography of Landis.

"He got his job when somebody said, 'get that old boy who sits behind first base all the time. He's out there every day anyhow.' So they offered him a season's pass and he jumped at it."—Will Rogers.

"That middle name tells you all there is to know about how tough he was…"—Fay Vincent.

Kenesaw Mountain Landis was the first commissioner of baseball, ruling from his appointment on November 12, 1920, to his death on November 25, 1944.

Landis was born November 20, 1866, in Millville, Ohio. His father, Dr. Abraham Landis, was a surgeon in the Union Army and was wounded at Kennesaw (different spelling) Mountain, Tennessee. Kenesaw Landis stood only 5'7" and weighed 125 pounds but was a ruthless, narrow-minded autocrat who commanded and demanded the spotlight at all times. These traits later earned him the names "Boss," "Czar," and "Second Most Powerful Man in America."

He became a prominent federal court judge in Chicago and presided over a number of antitrust cases in the early part of the 20th century. Most notably, in 1907 he imposed a $29 million fine against Standard Oil Company for antitrust violations. The judgment later was overturned.

Landis was a baseball fan who often attended White Sox games. His first formal contact with the game was when he presided over the Federal League's 1915 lawsuit against Organized Baseball. The case was filed in January that year and his apparent strategy was to delay the case until late in the year. By then the Federal League was weakened sufficiently, a settlement was reached and the lawsuit was dropped. Landis made comments at the time that undoubtedly helped lead to his subsequent appointment as commissioner: "Both sides may understand that any blow at the thing called baseball would be regarded by this court as a blow to a national institution."

He was considered a good choice for other reasons. He was virulently pro–American in the jingoistic World War I era that immediately preceded his appointment. He was said to have routinely inquired into the war record of attorneys who appeared before him and he convicted the "Wobblies," the communist International Workers of the World, for obstructing the war effort. Baseball was also in the midst of appealing an antitrust violation fine of $240,000, arising from a lawsuit filed by one of the defunct Federal League clubs, the Baltimore Terrapins. It was overturned in a 1922 U.S. Supreme Court decision (see also *Antitrust*).

Landis was appointed commissioner in November 1920, just after the September verdict in the Black Sox Scandal; though this was not the sole or possibly even primary motivation for choosing a commissioner. Baseball owners had been feuding for some time with their respective league presidents and the three-man National Commission was no longer effective. Amid the fervor to clean up baseball and resolve the constant infighting between the Major Leagues and among the owners, Landis was given power to rule on "all matters detrimental to baseball."

Landis received a seven-year contract at $50,000 annually when he was appointed at age 54, a significant increase over his $7,500 salary as a federal judge; though he kept that job for a time. His salary later was raised to $65,000, but he voluntarily reduced it to $40,000 during the Depression. In 1940 he received another contract extension through January 1946, but died on November 20, 1944. He oversaw the immense popularity of the game in the 1920s, the tough times during the Depression-era 1930s and the talent-thin World War II years.

Landis was ill during the 1944 World Series and did not attend the event. He became seriously ill in St. Luke's Hospital in early November after suffering a heart attack and died of coronary thrombosis at age 78. At his request there was no funeral. Leslie O'Connor was named interim commissioner and the Major League Advisory Council ran baseball until Happy Chandler was appointed in April 1945.

At the age of 34, O'Connor became Landis' secretary in 1921.

He left his position in the commissioner's office in late 1945 after Happy Chandler took over earlier in the year. He went on to become president of the White Sox. The newspapers graciously and erroneously reported that O'Connor was often mentioned as a successor to Landis, but that O'Connor dismissed the suggestion in "deference to Landis' memory."

In 1947 J.G. Taylor Spink of *The Sporting News* wrote a biography of the first commissioner: *Judge Landis and Twenty-Five Years of Baseball* (reprinted in 1974).

Albert B. "Happy" Chandler (1907–1991)
Served 1945–1951
Hall of Fame (VC) 1982

"The Ballplayers' Commissioner"—Nickname adopted by Chandler.

"Keep Happy's big fat foot out of Happy's Big Fat Mouth."—Red Smith's 1945 advice to former catcher and then-attorney Muddy Ruel. Ruel had just been hired as chief aide to Chandler, who was already in trouble with the owners.

"The astonishing contrast between straight-laced, stern Judge Landis and his ebullient, sophomoric successor, Senator Chandler, has been as productive of goose pimples to baseball as a midnight sprint through a graveyard."—Sportswriter Dan Parker in the *Saturday Evening Post* in 1945.

"Commissioner Happy Chandler, who is the current target for every cute crack and barb the writers can invent, drew a round of boos from the fans when he tossed out the first ball in Wrigley Field [during the 1945 World Series]..."—The *Stars and Stripes* military newspaper.

When Judge Landis died in November 1944, his aide, Leslie O'Connor, was chosen as interim commissioner, and he worked in the position until Happy Chandler was elected on April 24, 1945. Before he accepted, Chandler made a show of rejecting the appointment because World War II was still on. However, 16 days after the war ended in Europe, he relented.

Larry MacPhail supposedly had been a candidate, but another source noted that Chandler was strongly promoted by MacPhail and Giants owner Horace Stoneham. Long-time Yankee general manager Ed Barrow was offered the job, but he declined because of poor health. Ford Frick was considered, but only Chandler and Postmaster General Robert Hannegan were on the owners' ballot. Hannegan received four votes, so on the second ballot it was unanimous for Chandler. Hannegan later bought into the Cardinals.

Chandler, who had graduated from the University of Kentucky Law School, began his term at age 46 after resigning as the junior senator from Kentucky. He had also been in the Kentucky state legislature and served as lieutenant governor and governor.

Chandler's salary was increased from $10,000 annually as a senator to $50,000 as commissioner. It was later increased to $65,000. He began his connection with professional baseball at an early age when he played briefly for the Class D Lexington Reos.

Chandler was in trouble with the owners as early as September 1945, though some historians considered him a mouthpiece for the wealthier club owners. For example, he allowed the Yankees to waive Hank Borowy, a good pitcher, to go to the Cubs for the 1945 pennant race under dubious circumstances. On the other hand, he was instrumental in breaking the color line in baseball (see also *Integration*), contrary to the near-unanimous opposition of the owners. He also broke the *Mexican League* challenge by the Pascual brothers. Others claim that he did a poor job of handling the Mexican League issue and subjected baseball to further congressional scrutiny in the early 1950s on antitrust issues such as the

reserve clause. He also allowed the players to establish a *Pension System*, another blow to the owners' power.

In 1950 he received a bare majority vote of confidence from the owners, but not the needed two thirds. As a result, a committee of owners was formed to find a new commissioner. Chandler immediately announced that he was a candidate, but soon became disenchanted with the situation and resigned under pressure on July 15, 1951, before his term was scheduled to end. Red Smith summed up the situation: "Happy left office for reasons of health; that is, the owners got sick of him."

The owners voted almost immediately to elevate Ford Frick from the National League presidency. Chandler came close to being George Wallace's running mate in the 1968 presidential election. His autobiography is *Heroes, Plain Folks and Skunks* (1989).

Ford Frick (1895–1978)
Served 1951–1965
Hall of Fame (VC) 1970

"Ford Frick isn't the worst commissioner in baseball history, but he's in the photo. He could get up in the last few strides with Happy Chandler, but I don't think anybody can catch Happy Chandler at the wire."—Jim Murray.

See also *National League Presidents*.

Frick was prominently mentioned as the successor to Judge Landis in 1944 while he was National League president, but lost out to Chandler. When Chandler fell out of favor, Frick was appointed commissioner on September 20, 1951. One source claimed that General Douglas MacArthur was the owners' first choice. Just before he became commissioner, Frick, a former newspaperman, almost took a job with the Maytag family running a newspaper in Colorado. He asked future Dodger general manager Buzzie Bavasi to go with him, but Bavasi declined. According to Bavasi, Frick then declined himself and took the commissioner's job. Frick remained in the position until November 16, 1965.

Frick was known as a low key guy, a good administrator and persuasive with the owners. He helped guide the Major Leagues through the trauma and upheaval of franchise shifts of the 1950s and expansion in the early 1960s. Considered "likeable" and "well-read," he was elected to the Hall of Fame in 1970 and died in 1978. His autobiography is *Games, Asterisks and People* (1973).

General William Dole "Spike" Eckert (1909–1971)
Served 1965–1968

"Jeez. They went and got the unknown soldier."—Sportswriter Larry Fox on an unknown retired Air Force general as the choice for commissioner.

"Baseball today acknowledged a grave error of three years' duration by accepting the 'resignation' of its Commissioner, William D. Eckert."—*Baltimore Sun* article in December 1968.

Eckert was a 56-year-old retired Air Force general who was elected to a seven-year term at $65,000 per year commencing November 17, 1965. Baseball owners interviewed 156 candidates for the position, but the list was cut to 15 four months before the decision. Eckert was not even on the original list and was a huge surprise choice. He had not attended a Major League game in 10 years.

He was a major failure and the situation deteriorated so badly that the owners directed him to appoint American League stalwart Lee MacPhail as a key administrator to help out. The Major Leagues ended the relationship by buying out his contract and electing little-known National League attorney Bowie Kuhn. Eckert technically resigned under pressure in December 1968.

The best that could be said was that he tried hard but simply was not up to the job. Part of the problem was that he was perceived as not being strong enough to stand up to Major League Players Association executive director Marvin Miller, who took control of the union in 1966.

Bowie Kuhn (1926–)
Served 1969–1984
"When [Dodger owner Walter] O'Malley sends out for coffee, Bowie Kuhn asks 'one lump or two?'"—Reference to the close relationship between O'Malley and Kuhn.

"I believe in the Rip Van Winkle Theory: that a man from 1910 must be able to wake up after being asleep for seventy years, walk into a ballpark and understand baseball perfectly."—Kuhn.

"An empty car pulled up and Bowie Kuhn got out."—Red Smith, who disliked Kuhn intensely.

"Mr. Kuhn, a tall, Princeton-educated Wall Street lawyer who has been a devout fan and student of the game, set to work instantly, advising all parties to cool it and forcing a sensible compromise … His subsequent operations have shown more sure-handedness, intelligence, and courage than have been customarily visible in the Commissioner's office in recent decades…"—Roger Angell in *The Summer Game* (1972), who noted later in his book that Kuhn was "another victim of the legendary sophomore jinx."

Bowie Kent Kuhn was elected as the fifth commissioner on February 4, 1969. He was a 42-year-old lawyer at a prominent law firm in New York City. He had represented the National League in legal matters and had been active in baseball law since 1950. At the time of his appointment he was legal counsel to the Major League owners' Player Relations Committee.

He was hired for one year as pro-tem chief executive at a salary of $100,000. Kuhn was a compromise choice after baseball failed in December 1968 to agree on the two most prominent available choices within baseball circles, CBS executive and Yankee president Mike Burke and San Francisco Giants president Chub Feeney.

It was generally assumed that Kuhn was an interim choice until baseball found a more prominent figure. He emerged as a stronger leader than expected, however, and finished with the second-longest tenure of any commissioner.

Kuhn persuaded both leagues to move their headquarters to New York City, the first time this had occurred. He presided over the dark years of Major League Baseball in the late 1960s and early 1970s when football emerged as king. He also enjoyed the renaissance years of the late 1970s before the 1981 player strike tarnished his image.

He suffered through the Curt Flood case (See *Reserve Clause*) and the rise of free agency. Kuhn gave in to the demands of television, which made the owners far richer, but he was criticized for abandoning tradition. In 1971 Kuhn sanctioned the first night game in World Series history (see also *Underwear*).

His approximately $200,000 annual contract was not renewed at a meeting of the owners on November 1, 1982. It would have been his third seven-year term. Baseball was in limbo for two years while Kuhn fought to stay, though other sources indicate that he was simply asked to stay through the 1983 season while a successor was found. The search lasted through almost the entire 1984 season. He resigned only after Peter Ueberroth was selected and had finished his Olympic Games commitment.

Kuhn was *The Sporting News* Man of the Year in 1983, apparently as a gesture of thanks knowing that he would be unable to save his job. He officially resigned September 30, 1984, the day before Ueberroth took over.

By the mid–1980s, Kuhn was involved in buying and selling minor league franchises. He was with the law firm of Wilkie, Farr & Gallagher and then founded a new firm in 1988 with a trial lawyer named Harvey Myerson, but the firm collapsed in bankruptcy two years later and Myerson later was convicted of bilking clients. Kuhn moved to Florida where the laws were more favorable to people in bankruptcy. He then became a partner in a franchise brokering business. In the mid–1990s, he became a consultant to the Caribbean Professional Baseball Confederation, the governing body for the Latin American winter leagues. Kuhn's autobiography is *Hardball* (1987).

Peter Ueberroth (1939–)
Served 1984–1989
"A lot of substance and not much style."—Ueberroth's assessment of his tenure as commissioner.

"It is unfortunate that he did not seem to have the deep attachment to the game itself that would have motivated him to stay on. It is probable that he never envisioned his role in baseball as more than a temporary one."—Lee MacPhail in his autobiography, *My Nine Innings* (1989).

Ueberroth was independently wealthy, having made his fortune in the airline and travel business after graduating from San Jose State University in California. By the late 1970s his company was annually grossing $300 million as the country's second-largest travel agency.

He was chosen as head of the Los Angeles Olympic Organizing Committee (LAOOC) to oversee the 1984 Olympic Games. One source reported that on October 1, 1984, near the end of his tenure in that position, it was announced that he would take over as the new commissioner of baseball. However, it was known that he was the choice a few months earlier but he could not end his relationship with the Olympics until October.

Ueberroth encouraged more dialogue among owners, such as exchange of salary information. That effort led to almost no free agent bidding and subsequent successful *Collusion* claims by the players. Ueberroth's official policy was to stay away from labor matters, but he worked behind the scenes during the 1984–1985 labor negotiations and was instrumental in limiting a player strike to one day.

Ueberroth was responsible for increased marketing, big television contracts and did a fair job of dealing with the *Drug* problems facing Organized Baseball. He resigned before the 1989 season when he saw the commissioner's power diminishing and he wanted to consider a political career, but he never entered politics (other than an aborted attempt to win the California governorship when Arnold Schwarzenegger won the election in late 2003). In 1995 he and an investment group lost out to the Disney Company in an effort to buy a controlling interest in the California Angels.

In the mid–1990s he made an unsuccessful bid to buy Eastern Airlines and was involved in attracting corporate investment to Los Angeles after the 1992 riots, but resigned as chairman of Rebuild L.A. in May 1993.

A. Bartlett Giamatti (1938–1989)
Served 1989
"It has long been my conviction that we can learn far more about the conditions, and values, of a society by contemplating how it chooses to play, to use its free time, to take its leisure, than by examining how it goes about its work."—The preface to Giamatti's *Take Time for Paradise* (1989).

Giamatti became commissioner in April 1989 after serving as *National League President* since December 1986. He opposed interleague play; dealt effectively with the players union early in the season; and banned Pete Rose in August 1989 for *Gambling*. He died one week later of a heart attack at only 51, prompting the following negative quote: "Like a Pope who died after just a few weeks in office, Giamatti has almost taken on the aura of sainthood; a philosophic scholar who descended on baseball from some higher level — or at least a higher level than most of the newspaper and magazine writers who quoted his pretentious, overripe prose with awe, without bothering to figure out the content of his precious emissions." — Players Association leader Marvin Miller in his autobiography, *A Whole Different Ball Game* (1991).

See also James Reston, Jr., *Collision at Home* (1991), about Giamatti's feud with Pete Rose; Anthony Valerio, *Bart: A Life of A. Bartlett Giamatti* (1991).

Fay Vincent (1938–)
Served 1989–1992

"The game will survive long past you or I [sic]." — Vincent after the earthquake during the 1989 World Series.

Deputy commissioner Vincent took over when Bart Giamatti died of a heart attack in August 1989. Vincent was formally elected on September 13, 1989. In 1978 Vincent was a $47,000-per-year Securities and Exchange Commission lawyer who was tapped to head Columbia Pictures. He lasted 10 years before moving to Coca Cola, which had bought Columbia. At one point he tried to land a job at Columbia for his friend, Bart Giamatti.

As commissioner, Vincent faced problems with the purchase of the Seattle Mariners by Japanese interests, lock-outs and a huge escalation of player salaries. The owners quickly became disenchanted with Vincent, whose term was not scheduled to end until 1994. He angered many owners when he unilaterally attempted to impose a realignment of the National League divisions in 1992. He was also seen as a weak negotiator in the face of serious player relations issues.

During the summer of 1992 Vincent sent a letter to the owners saying he would never quit. However, after 18 owners voted "no confidence" against him, he stepped down a few days later. Teams that supported him in the vote were reported to be the Orioles, Red Sox, Marlins, Astros, Expos, Mets, A's and Rangers. The Royals may have been the ninth team that supported him. The Reds abstained when owner Marge Schott left early.

Nelson Doubleday, co-owner of the Mets, voted to retain Vincent. As a show of support for Vincent and a snub of the other owners, Doubleday invited Vincent to throw out the first ball at Shea Stadium on Opening Day 1993.

In 1994 Vincent dropped his plans for a book when excerpts from his manuscript were leaked to the press. His descriptions included the following: National League president Bill White was a "good man" but "incompetent"; George Steinbrenner was "the most hated man in baseball"; White Sox owner Jerry Reinsdorf was "dangerous" and more to blame for the "poor state of baseball than anyone else"; Peter O'Malley was a "nitwit and bigot."

Vincent moved to England, where he spent 1993 in a country house writing a book. He was appointed to the Time Warner board of directors, but turned down Fred Wilpon's offer to be the Mets president. He then settled in as an investment banker with Shearson Lehman's Peter Solomon.

See Fay Vincent, *The Last Commissioner: A Baseball Valentine* (2004).

Bud Selig (1934–)
Served 1992– ("Interim" 1992–1998)

"Baseball will hire Billy Crystal as next commissioner, on the premise that if you're going to laugh at the guy in charge, there might as well be a legitimate reason." — Columnist Art Spander.

"I won't say the temporary leadership-by-committee structure is inefficient, but if baseball were a movie, the committee would be played by the Three Stooges." — Columnist Scott Ostler.

"When does the name 'interim' disappear from in front of Bud Selig's name. Presidents have had shorter terms." — Bob Costas during the 1995 World Series.

"Commissioner Landis banned the eight "Black Sox" players from baseball for life after a jury *acquitted* them of throwing the 1919 World Series. By contrast, Mr. Selig can't even get Barry Bonds to urinate in a cup." — *The Wall Street Journal* in 2004, critical of efforts by Congress to impose regulations on baseball in light of the steroid scandal that rocked baseball that year.

"But if Selig won't force the owners to address problems of their own creation, the least he can do is to stop whining and shut up. The *most* he can do is to resign in favor of a knowledgeable outsider, *and* insist that this outsider be given the necessary authority to solve anything the owners themselves describe as a problem. Don't hold your breath. Mortality tables suggest that the 67-year-old Selig is likely to live another 15 years, so look for a new Commissioner around 2016." — Doug Pappas, chair of SABR's Business of Baseball committee.

Brewers owner Bud Selig was immediately chosen as Vincent's interim successor in September 1992. In the wake of Vincent's departure, respected deputy commissioner Steve Greenberg resigned in early 1993, leaving a complete vacuum in the commissioner's office.

After Vincent was forced out, various others were mentioned as possible successors: former American League president Lee MacPhail; Player Relations Committee president Richard Ravitch; former Expos executive John McHale; Democratic National Committee chairman Ron Brown; White House Chief of Staff James A. Baker III; NBA commissioner David Stern; Blue Jays president Paul Beeston; CBS Sports president Neal Pilson; A's general manager Sandy Alderson; and Twins general manager Andy MacPhail.

By mid–1993 the owners had whittled the list down from 187 to 20. At the January 1994 owners' meeting, it was widely expected that a new commissioner would be chosen from a short list of two: Arnold Weber, the outgoing president of Northwestern University, and Harvey Schiller, executive president of the U.S. Olympic Committee. The surprise result was that no commissioner was chosen and Bud Selig remained as the Major League's titular commissioner.

Another late candidate was Senate majority leader George J. Mitchell of Maine, who announced his retirement from politics in early 1994. This Red Sox fan was also considered for a position on the U.S. Supreme Court. He ultimately withdrew from consideration for both positions and Bud Selig remained as interim commissioner. In 1994 Selig received a $1 million bonus for his efforts.

In mid–1996 rumors circulated that Selig was contemplating a move to full-time commissioner and turning over the control of the Brewers to his daughter, Wendy Selig-Prieb. He finally made that step on July 9, 1998, signing a five-year contract. He had been earning $2.5 million as chairman of the Executive Council, and it was believed that his salary was bumped to $3 million when he officially agreed to be the full-time commissioner.

In January 2000 Major League owners voted to give the commissioner power "without limitation" to ensure "there is an appropriate level of long-term competitive balance among the clubs." He could override baseball's rules and could have imposed a salary cap for 2001 if it was deemed necessary to strike an agreement with the players.

During August 2004 Selig was confirmed for another three year term. He signed another contract through 2006, at a reported $4 million per season.

Rules for Choosing. The Major League Agreement requires that the reelection of a commissioner must be considered at a joint owners meeting not more than 15 months nor less than six months before the end of his term; although this could be waived. A three-fourths majority is required for election.

Address. The Commissioner's Office is in the same building that simultaneously housed the American League and National League offices, 350 Park Avenue, New York, N.Y.

Book. Larry Moffi, *The Conscience of the Game* (2004).

Complete Games

"Now you get the manager outraging traditionalists like myself when he signs a pitcher and says, 'I hope you can give me five good innings.' If you pitched only five good innings in the old days you were a bum."—Columnist Shirley Povich.

"I came from the mind-set that it was your game, you were the starter and you had every intention of finishing it…. You weren't remotely interested in turning it over to somebody. That's just the way it was. You thought nothing of it."—Nolan Ryan.

"Maybe now he'll get a complete game."—Pirates third base coach Rich Donnelly after pitcher Bob Walk retired to the broadcast booth. Walk had only 16 complete games in over 240 starts over 13 seasons.

Historical Analysis.

"It was not for nothing that Sam Lewis, the pitcher, was known through the unfeeling medium of the sports pages as Six-Inning Sam. Six innings was his ball game, lately. It was as far as he went."—Charles Einstein in "Reflex Curve," first appearing in *Collier's* (1952).

Complete games by pitchers were the norm in the 19th century. For example, in 1876 of 260 games played and 520 starts made, there were 473 complete games, or 91%. By the 1890s complete games were pitched 80% of the time. Selected figures in the 20th century show the dramatic drop in Major League complete games:

1930 44%
1950 40%
1970 22%
1972 27% (American League only)
1988 15% (16% in the American League)
1989 12%
1993 11%

The last large block of complete games was pitched by the A's of the early 1980s under manager Billy Martin. The 1980 club pitched a modern record 94 complete games, 93 of them by the five regular starting pitchers. The National League record since 1961 (162-game schedule) for team complete games was set in 1968 by the Giants with 77. Rick Langford, who had lost 19 games in 1977, won 19 games in 1980 with 28 complete games (22 consecutive). He had 18 complete games the next year. He and a number of the A's pitchers suffered permanent arm problems because of alleged overuse by Martin, though Langford never blamed Martin for his problems.

As further evidence of the inability of recent pitchers to throw complete games, in 1991 there were 94 shutouts in the American League in which more than one pitcher was needed.

No pitcher since 1920 has thrown more than 40 complete games. In 1995 there were only 12 games out of 4,586 in which both pitchers went the distance. In 1920 Major League pitchers threw 1395 complete games (16 teams). In 2002, with 30 teams, there were only 224 complete games. Arizona led with 14 (8 by Randy Johnson, who tied Bartolo Colon of the Indians for the lead).

In 1974 there were 1,089 complete games in the Major Leagues. In 2003 there were 209.

Most. Cy Young completed 749 of the 815 games that he started (750 in older sources).

The 1899 Cubs set a National League record with 147 complete games. In 1904 the Red Sox set the Major League record with 148 complete games out of 157 played. The 1904 Cardinals set the modern National League record with 146 out of 155 complete games that season.

Among post-war players, Warren Spahn, the winningest left-hander of all-time with 363, completed 382 of his 665 starts.

Consecutive. Jack Taylor of the Cubs and Cardinals completed all but two of his 173 start between 1902 and 1906. One source reported that he completed every start in those years, but *The Baseball Encyclopedia* shows one game not completed in 1904 (39 of 40 completed) and 1906 (32 of 33 completed). He was 151–139 over 10 seasons beginning in 1898, but apparently was susceptible to bribery (see *Gambling and Fixed Games*). He completed 39 straight games from April 14 through October 6, 1904. Overall he completed 278 of the 286 games he started.

Worst Team Effort. The 1991 Yankees pitching staff set a then–Major League record with only three complete games. In 1995 the Rockies pitchers topped that record when they threw one complete game.

In April 1999 the Brewers ended a National League record 113-game streak in which none of their pitchers went the distance.

In 1999 the Angels set a record of 140 straight games from the start of the season without a pitcher completing one. The Mets reached 139 that season.

The 2001 Cubs were the first club in Major League history to prevent every opposing starting pitcher from throwing a complete game against them.

On May 21, 2002, the Devil Rays' Joe Kennedy pitched a four-hit shutout, ending the club's record 194-game streak without a complete game by one of its pitchers.

In July 2002 the Reds ended a 151-game streak of no complete games.

The 2003 Astros had one complete game.

Double Duty. Buck Ewing, considered the premier catcher of the 19th century, once filled in when his team was short of pitchers and pitched two complete games as his team won the pennant by one game in 1899. He only appeared as a pitcher in three games all season.

Strong Start. Mickey Welch went all the way in his first 105 starts beginning in 1880.

Two in Same Day/No Strikeouts. Emil Levsen of the Indians once pitched two complete game victories in the same day against the Yankees while striking out none.

World Series. In the inaugural World Series of 1903, Charles "Deacon" Phillippe of the Pirates pitched five complete games against the Red Sox. He won Game 1, won Game 3 on one day's rest, won Game 4 on three days' rest, lost Game 7 on two days' rest and lost Game 8 of the best-of-nine series on two days' rest.

By the end of the 2003 regular season, Marlins starter Josh Beckett had pitched in 88 professional games since being drafted in 1999, and had completed none of them. In the NLCS he shut out the Cubs and then in the deciding Game 6 of the World Series against the Yankees, he pitched another complete-game shutout.

Longest. The Dodgers and Braves played a 26-inning 1–1 tie on May 1, 1920. The game was called because of darkness after only 3 hours and 50 minutes (see also *Longest Games*—Most Innings).

Leon Cadore of the Dodgers and Joe Oeschger of the Braves both pitched the entire game for their clubs.

Harley "Doc" Parker pitched for the Cubs and Reds from 1893 through 1901. In 1901 he lost a 26-hit, 21-run complete game.

The longest complete game victory was a 20-inning 2–1 game pitched by Ed Reulbach of the Chicago Cubs. Reulbach also holds the record for most wins against one team in a season when he beat the Dodgers nine times in 1908.

In the American League, on August 9, 1921, Dixie Davis pitched a 19-inning complete game for the Browns against the Senators. He pitched a no-hitter over the last nine innings. In the 16th inning, one of the Browns hit an inside-the-park home run but was out for failing to touch first base. Nevertheless, the Browns finally won 8–6.

Babe Ruth of the Red Sox had the longest complete game in a World Series, pitching 14 innings for a 2–1 win in Game 2 of the 1916 Series against the Dodgers. The only run against him was a 1st inning inside-the-park home run by catcher Chief Meyers.

Statistical Anomaly. On September 26, 1942, in the bottom of the 8th inning, the Giants were at home and leading the Braves 5–2. Youngsters who had brought scrap metal to the game for the war effort, and had been admitted free, swarmed onto the field. Unable to clear the field, the umpires forfeited the game to the Braves.

Though Braves pitcher Warren Spahn was credited with a complete game (individual statistics count in forfeits), he did not get credit for a win or a loss. Because he had no other decisions that season, he shows a record of 0–0 and one complete game (which normally requires a decision).

Good to His Bullpen. On days he pitched, Yankee ace Whitey Ford was so confident that he would do well that he supposedly set up a table for the bullpen pitchers with a tablecloth, a bottle of wine and hero sandwiches. It makes a nice story, but while Ford was dominant he had a proportionately low number of complete games for the era in which he pitched (1950–1967). Although he led the league with 18 complete games in 1955, he generally finished between seven and 13 games, on the low side for a starting pitcher in those years.

Foreign Ritual. Connie Mack led a group of Major Leaguers on a tour of the Far East in 1934 that included the Philippines. He described a routine that the Philippine pitcher was required to follow: when a new pitcher entered the game, he was required to stand on the sideline and pitch to his catcher to show that he was in good condition to finish the game. It was considered a dishonor if a relief pitcher had to be brought in.

Incomplete Game. According to research by SABR member Al Kermisch, on April 13, 1894, Cap Anson's Chicago Colts played seven innings to their opponents' nine. The Colts led Minneapolis of the Western League in an exhibition game 6–1 and Minneapolis had to catch a train, so Anson skipped his club's last at-bats and let Minneapolis play their full nine innings. The score didn't change and apparently Minneapolis made its train.

Concessions and Concessionaires

"If you cut that big slob in half, most of the concessions at Yankee Stadium would come pouring out." — Pitcher Waite Hoyt on teammate Babe Ruth.

"The most amazing thing I've ever seen was Jay Johnstone, in uniform, in line at a concession stand in Dodger Stadium after the game had already started." — Fred Claire.

"Could a hawker of peanuts and pennants as easily sell ice cream from a truck or refrigerator at Sears? Sure, and more profitably,

too. But peanuts and pennants get him into the ballpark…. If life is, as Freud said, love and work, they have made baseball their life." — John Thorn in *The Game for All America* (1988).

"Outrageous, really outrageous. I'm not sure I wouldn't want to eat before I come." — Braves owner Ted Turner on the high food prices at new Turner Field.

"They can bring it in their tummies." — Braves owner Ted Turner after his club announced in early 1997 that fans could not bring their own food into his new Turner Field.

Earliest Prominent Concessionaire. The King of the Concessionaires, though not the first, was Englishman Harry Stevens, an 1880s scorecard hawker who expanded his services into a modern empire of sports concessions. During a strike at a Columbus, Ohio, steel plant where Stevens was working, he began selling books door-to-door in 1886 (apparently a logical extension of his Shakespearean scholar background). He went to his first baseball game around that time and supposedly did not understand it. The next day he called the Columbus baseball executives and obtained the exclusive right to sell a card listing the names of the players with empty spaces to write highlights. He sold advertising space on the cards to cover the $700 fee he paid the owners.

By the 1890s he had contracts with many parks and was the foremost purveyor of scorecards and concessions. Known as "Hustling Harry" and "The Scorecard Man," he began selling peanuts at ballparks in 1894. The Polo Grounds was his primary concession, where he sold peanuts, scorecards, beer, cigars and soft drinks. The name for his **Hot Dogs** was coined by New York cartoonist Theodore Dorgan.

Stevens teamed with future Yankee general manager Ed Barrow to obtain the Pirates concession in 1890 and many others into the 20th century. Stevens tried early on to persuade owners to put numbers on players' backs, but the players resisted.

By 1910 the Stevens letterhead stated that he sold concessions from the "Hudson to the Rio Grande." Though he died in 1934, the Stevens empire was perpetuated by his grandsons, and by the 1980s the family-run company annually grossed over $100 million.

1990s-2000s Concessionaires. The Stevens company had a number of competitors by the 1990s and only had contracts with the Astrodome, Fenway Park and Shea Stadium by early 1995. In 1995 Stevens was bought out by its chief competitor, Aramark (formerly ARA Services). As a result, the following is a breakdown of concessionaires and the ballparks with which they had contracts by the mid–1990s: Aramark: Atlanta, Baltimore, Boston, Colorado, Houston, Los Angeles, Montreal, New York (Shea) and Pittsburgh.

SportService: St. Louis, Chicago (Comiskey), Cleveland, Milwaukee, Cincinnati, Detroit and Texas.

Volume Services: Kansas City, Minnesota, New York (Yankee Stadium), Oakland and San Francisco.

Ogden: California, Chicago (Wrigley), Philadelphia and Seattle.

Fine Host: Miami.

McDonald's: Toronto.

Service America: San Diego.

The "Vendor Queen" of the 1990s was Rhonda Zechella, who criss-crossed the country training ballpark vendors. She began in 1969 as a concession worker at Crosley Field, where she spent 31 seasons.

By 2001, the Major League ballpark concessions business was dominated by three contractors. Aramark Corp. was the leader, with 13 contracts, followed by the SportService division of Delaware North Companies, and Volume Services America, each with seven. Boston Concessions Group had the contract at Miami's Pro Player

Top: The Peanut Man at Dodger Stadium, Roger Owens. Owens was so well known that he made an appearance on the "Tonight Show" with Johnny Carson and threw out the first "pitch" (a bag of peanuts) for one of the Dodger Opening Days. *Bottom:* Trash detail at Dodger Stadium.

Stadium, while ProDine, a former division of Restaura, Inc., had the contract at Bank One Ballpark in Phoenix (ProDine was not part of Aramark's 1998 acquisition of Restaura). The only self-operated concessions are in Detroit's Comerica Park, where Tigers owner Mike Ilitch uses his experience as founder and owner of the Little Caesar's pizza chain.

Partnerships with restaurants began to proliferate in the late 1990s. Vendors at Qualcomm Stadium in San Diego began selling Krispy Kreme donuts. The first Outback Steakhouse in a baseball park opened in 2001 at PNC Park in Pittsburgh. At 400 seats, it was the largest unit in the chain, and was open year-round. Famed chef Wolfgang Puck began working at Dodger Stadium in Los Angeles.

Financiers. SportsService owner Emprise has made several loans to floundering franchises over the years in return for lucrative concession contracts. Bill Veeck and Connie Mack both borrowed money from Emprise around 1950 when they were struggling. Emprise more recently loaned money to the owners of the Pilots, White Sox, Brewers, Expos and Tigers.

Concession Stands. Charles Weeghman of the Chicago Whales of the 1914–1915 Federal League was the first to build permanent concession stands. He built stalls behind the seats to sell refreshments so that vendors would not block the fans' view of the field. In the 19th century, Chicago's Albert Spalding would not allow vendors in the stands. Washington's 19th century Olympic Park had a full restaurant.

Beer. The first Major League team to sell **Beer** in its ballpark was Cincinnati in 1880.

General Concessions. Concessions in the 1910s included pie, tobacco, tripe, onions, chocolate, peanuts, hot dogs, soft drinks and gum. By the late 1910s, bars and hard liquor were eliminated and beer was sold more discreetly in ballparks.

Consumption. In 1950 it was estimated that average consumption per year per ballpark was 700,000 sodas, 600,000 hot dogs, 500,000 ice cream bars, and 400,000 bags of peanuts.

At the 1971 World Series in Pittsburgh, 700 employees served 70,000 soft drinks, 60,000 hot dogs, 20,000 bags of popcorn and peanuts, 130 kegs of beer and 2,000 cases of beer.

It was estimated that on Opening Day in 1999 the following amount of food was consumed at seven Major League stadiums:

—15 miles worth of hot dogs (110,000) if laid end to end

— 272,000 cups of beer, enough to fill a 25,000 gallon swimming pool

— 29,000 servings of nachos, equal to the weight of about 18 baseball players

— 26,000 soft pretzels, enough to feed 369 busloads of fans

—10,000 orders of fries, enough to fill 1,250 baseball hats

— 25,000 bags of popcorn, enough to fill two professional baseball dugouts

— 94,000 cups of soda, which if placed side-by-side would completely cover a baseball infield two times

No Glass. In the mid–1930s owners were urged to replace bottles because they were "dangerous missiles." The process was slow, but by the late 1960s bottles were eliminated, primarily as a result of action by the Major League Umpires Association. Soda bottles were last sold at Busch Stadium on April 28, 1953, when a riot forced an end to the sale of bottled products in the ballpark.

Drinking Fountains. In 1915 the House of Representatives passed a bill requiring all ballparks in the District of Columbia to provide free drinking water to fans: "Rooters here are up in arms over the new regulation, as they fear that it may drive the 'pop' bottle men out of business. As one ardent fan remarked; 'what's the

use of trying to 'bean' an umpire with a paper cup?'"—January 23, 1915, newspaper commentary.

When Dodger owner Walter O'Malley designed Dodger Stadium without drinking fountains, the city building inspectors required him to install them.

Peanut Vendors.

"I'm the only pitcher in the Majors making less than $1 million a year."—Peanut vendor extraordinaire Roger Owens, who worked Dodger Stadium through 1996. Owens became famous for his bag-throwing expertise, but in 1976 his antics were halted when an ice cream sandwich vendor hit a woman in the head with an errant throw. After a fan protest and boycott, bag throwing was reinstated.

On Opening Day in 1977 at Dodger Stadium, Owens threw out the first ball from the second deck. He appeared on the "Tonight Show" with Johnny Carson and once sold 1,500 bags of peanuts during a single game. He often receives $2,000 in prepaid season orders from wealthy "season-peanut holders." In 1995 Owens threw out the first pitch of the season — a perfect strike of a bag of peanuts thrown behind the back from the mound to the plate. In 2003 Owens began his 45th season as a Dodger vendor. A sales representative for a trucking company by day, he told this author that coming into a potential customer's facility and throwing out peanuts to the staff was a far more effective sales tool than a fancy lunch with the owner.

The top vendors in the country were invited to Pittsburgh for the 1994 All-Star Game and also for the 2004 Game.

Seniority. There is a hierarchy among ballpark vendors, with the longest tenured vendors selling beer, hot dogs and soft drinks. Some ballparks do not have beer or hot dog vendors in the stands, so the top vendors only sell peanuts. The next level of vendors sell pretzels and popcorn. Rookies get Cracker Jack. One empirical study (by the author) found that the veteran vendors primarily sold peanuts — easier on the shoulder and legs, no spilling, no melting. Dodger vendor Roger Owens said in 2003 that it would take 18–20 years for a new vendor to reach the pinnacle of his "sport," selling peanuts.

A typical stadium employs approximately 75 vendors who sell in the aisles, with another few hundred selling from refreshment stands. Aisle vendors typically are strictly on commission and earn between $80 and $100 per night. Concession stand employees are paid about $6-$7 per hour.

Conditioning

"The only thing running and exercising can do for you is make you healthy."—Rotund Tiger pitcher Mickey Lolich, who won three games in the 1968 World Series. After Lolich retired he bought a donut shop.

"All the fat guys watch me and say to their Mrs., 'see, there's a fat guy doing ok. Bring me another beer.'"—Lolich.

"The easiest day I have is the day I pitch."—Roger Clemens on his intense workout regimen on the days between starts. He referred to his off-day training as his "Navy SEALs workouts."

"I've been doing my 2½ miles every day and I've gained two pounds. My stomach is getting smaller but my butt's getting bigger."—Mickey Rivers in response to the Texas Rangers' training methods of 1981.

"To suppose that a man can play ball properly who guzzles beer daily, or indulges in spiritous liquors, or who sets up nightly gambling or does worse by still more enervating habits at brothels is nonsense."—19th century sportswriter Henry Chadwick.

"The increase of strength from playing base ball is providing many of our weak young men with strong chests and tall, robust, muscular figures."—Article in an August 1866 issue of Philadelphia's *City Item*.

"I believe in training by rising gently up and down from the bench."—Satchel Paige.

"John Kruk looks like a guy who went to a fantasy camp and decided to stay."—Broadcaster Don Sutton on the mashed potato-shaped Kruk.

"Lady, I'm not an athlete, I'm a baseball player."—Kruk, after a fan complained that he smoked; he used the phrase as the title of his 1994 autobiography.

"Do not pitch when you have an off day; when you do not feel able to do yourself justice, don't try to pitch hard. Let your average be considered less than your arm; but, to be in good form, a pitcher must practise about an hour morning and afternoon, holidays included. If the thermometer is below 60, vigorous pitching is risky, and the danger increases as the temperature falls. Never use liniments. They are not good. Rubbing too is bad. Hot water is good, as is also mild galvanism [electric stimulation]."—19th century sports medicine found in *Sphere and Ash*, by Jacob Morse (1888).

"I'll leave the working and conditioning to [others] forever. They can write a book and do videos. They can make money on that, on how to last 20 years in the big leagues by conditioning. I'll write the one, 'How Not to Work out.'"—Yankee pitcher David Wells, whose bad back forced him out of Game 5 of the 2003 World Series, which the Marlins won 6–4.

"The likes of Kirby Puckett among outfielders and Rick Reuschel among pitchers are probably as eccentrically designed as ever, and all bets are off with catchers, who still reserve the right to look like fireplugs. But in general, today's ballplayers are manifestly athlete-athletes, with well-tended physiques and wholesome faces, who could easily pass for track stars or squash players and not just for the first team at McGonnigle's Saloon, as their forebears [sic] usually did."—Wilfrid Sheed in *The Face of Baseball* (1990).

"I was eating too well and getting too much rest. I take my old lady dancing every night now. Doin' the bump keeps your legs in shape."—Mickey Rivers' response to a 1975 interview question of why he started playing better.

19th Century. See also ***Medical Treatment***. During the off-season in the 19th century, players often corresponded with management to reassure them that they were performing a diligent off-season training regimen.

Weight Training.

"When I played, you came to spring training with a ten-pound winter beer belly on, and you ran about thirty wind sprints and you sweated with a sweat jacket and you got yourself in condition. Now the players do Nautilus all winter, they play racquetball, they swim, they exercise and they come to spring training looking like Tarzan."—Pirates manager Jim Leyland.

"I never lifted weights, never touched them. To me, those were like kryptonite to Superman. I was scared of them. The first person I saw who lifted was Kenny Singleton. He looked like a million bucks, but when he did that over the winter, I don't think he swung a bat or threw a ball. That sent a red flag up for me."—Eddie Murray.

"You see guys hitting the weight room so much, you'd think they were football players. That's a big trend, and it works. Hitters are now strong enough to totally dominate baseball."—Frank Thomas, who is 6'5" and 257 pounds with 4% body fat.

"The heaviest thing I ever lifted was a glass of wine."—1960s pitcher Bob Gibson on the weightlifting trend in the 1990s.

Sportswriter Henry Chadwick advocated weightlifting for ballplayers as far back as 1886, but it was not in vogue until the 1980s. Weightlifting (and, apparently, steroids) became popular among home run-conscious players and the muscle-bound look appeared not to hamper their play. Through the 1960s it was felt that loose muscles were better for baseball and therefore weight training was discouraged.

Pitcher's Regimen/Running.

"You don't run the damn ball over the plate."—Pitching coach Johnny Sain.

"Heck, if running is so important, Jesse Owens would be a 20-game winner."—Phillies pitching coach Art Fowler.

"It doesn't 'loosen you up.' It very quickly tightens you up. It doesn't make you strong. After a certain point, it's more likely to weaken the heel, knee and back. I don't advocate running for ballplayers. For eight years I've tried to get it out of baseball."—Conditioning coach Gus Hoefling of the 1980s Phillies.

In 1906 Danny Green of the White Sox was given half the club to manage during spring training. He had his players go roller skating instead of jogging. The management was not impressed with the regimen and he was dismissed soon after.

Bob Feller used to toss eight-pound metal balls to strengthen his forearm and hand.

Nolan Ryan was known as a fanatic about conditioning. After throwing his seventh no-hitter in 1991 he stuck to his post-game routine: he rode the exercise bike for 45 minutes as friends and family waited to celebrate. Houston reporter Mickey Herskowitz started a story that Ryan developed his arm strength from throwing newspapers on his paper route. However, Ryan said later that he threw the papers left-handed.

In the 1990s the Braves pitchers, unlike most pitchers, threw twice between starts, including once the day before their next start. In 1995 Dodger pitcher Hideo Nomo followed this regimen and it underscored what the Braves had been doing for some time under pitching coach Leo Mazzone.

Testing. From 1963 through 1972 Phillies owner Bob Carpenter underwrote a "Research Program for Baseball." It was a series of tests designed to measure eyesight and bat speed conceived by professors at the University of Delaware and researchers at DuPont. It was generally ignored by baseball people.

Pouting. Vida Blue later admitted that after Charlie Finley refused to give him a raise after his stellar rookie season ("he treated me like a colored boy"), he didn't work out as hard as he could have.

Boxed Out. In March 1999 Alex Rodriguez was injured while jumping over boxes in an agility drill and was sidelined for six weeks.

Confidence

"Confidence is a mental thing."—Twins pitcher Scott Erickson. See also ***Pyschology***.

In the mid–1930s shortstop Joe Cronin temporarily lost confidence in his fielding ability and began going down on one knee to field ground balls. Sportswriters began calling the maneuver the "$250,000 squat," referring to the price paid to the Senators for him by Red Sox owner Tom Yawkey.

John "Jocko" Conlan (1899–1989)

Hall of Fame (VC) 1974

"Conlan was a mediocre White Sox outfielder in 1935 when umpire Red Ormsby collapsed from the summer heat. Conlan was nominated to replace Ormsby. The following season he had a new career to which he brought a polka-dot bow tie, a willingness to jaw with the most cantankerous of players, and a keen ability to judge the plays of the game." — *The Baseball Hall of Fame Anniversary Book*, edited by Gerald Astor (1988).

Conlan was a one-time Major Leaguer who umpired in the National League for 25 years starting in 1941.

Conlan played in the minor leagues for most of the 1920s and early 1930s before making it to the Major Leagues in 1934 with the White Sox. He lasted two seasons as an outfielder with the club, batting .263. When umpire Red Ormsby suffered from heatstroke during a 1935 game, Conlan came off the Chicago bench to fill in. He umpired impartially, even calling out teammate Luke Appling on an attempted triple. He soon abandoned his mediocre playing career (he was already 35) and became a full-time minor league umpire the following season.

Beginning in 1941 Conlan spent 25 years umpiring in the National League and had many well-publicized run-ins with various managers, including a shin-kicking episode with Leo Durocher. Conlan was allowed to use his trademark outside chest protector for five years after the National League switched to inside protectors.

Tom Connolly (1870–1961)

Hall of Fame (VC) 1953

"Tommy was a slight, quiet, little man in an era when most umpires were big, brawny, and boisterous. He was British born, with all of the reticence and reserve of an English gentleman. He was an extremely religious man, too, in an age of violent argument and colorful profanity.... But he had a ready wit and a quiet sense of humor that usually quelled the most serious detractors." — Ford Frick in *Games, Asterisks, and People* (1973).

Connolly was primarily an American League umpire from 1898 through 1931.

The English native never saw a baseball game until he was 15 and had emigrated to America. By 1894 he had established himself as a fine minor league umpire and was spotted by National League umpire Tim Hurst. He began in the New England League that season and moved on to the National League in 1898. After two years he moved on to the American League and umpired the first game in the new league. He also umpired the first World Series and in seven other Series. He umpired alone during the regular season until 1907.

Connolly had a temper and was known to toss players quickly. That reputation caused most players never to cause a problem. The last player Connolly threw out of a game was Babe Ruth in 1922. He umpired through the 1931 season and then became Chief Umpire until 1954. He continued to sit on the Rules Committee for most of the last years of his life.

Roger Connor (1857–1931)

Hall of Fame (VC) 1976

"Who wants to see big Roger Connor — who ... can hit the ball a mile ... make a puny little feminine bunt." — Sam Crane of the *New York Evening Journal*.

Connor was a National League first baseman and power hitter from 1880 through 1897.

One of the largest players of the 19th century at 6'3" and 220 pounds, Connor was considered by many as the best first baseman of the 1880s. He began with the Troy Haymakers in 1880 and was a star by the time the club shifted to New York in 1883.

Connor starred for the Giants through the 1889 season, when he jumped to the Players League that he helped form. He returned to the Giants in 1891, left for the Phillies in 1892, and then returned to the Giants for most of the next two years. He finished his career in St. Louis in 1897. He batted over .300 11 times, including a league-leading .371 in 1885.

Over 18 seasons he batted .317 and is fifth all-time with 233 triples. His 136 home runs were the career record until Babe Ruth came along. When his Major League career ended, he bought franchises in the minor leagues and continued playing until age 46 in 1903.

Consecutive Games Played

"I don't know what made me stay in there, and I doubt if Gehrig knows why he does it, either. I played when I should have been on the bench. So I punished myself and probably handicapped my team." — Everett Scott about his 1,307-consecutive game streak.

The List.

2,632	Cal Ripken
2,130	Lou Gehrig
1,307	Everett Scott
1,207	Steve Garvey
1,117	Billy Williams
1,103	Joe Sewell
895	Stan Musial
829	Eddie Yost
822	Gus Suhr
798	Nellie Fox
756	Miguel Tejada (through 2004)
745	Pete Rose
740	Dale Murphy
730	Richie Ashburn
717	Ernie Banks

Charlie Gehringer is the only player to have two streaks of 500 games or more (501 and 511).

Steve Brodie. Brodie had a streak of 574 games in the early 1890s for St. Louis and Baltimore in the National League.

George Pinckney. The American Association Brooklyn shortstop had a streak of 577 games from September 20, 1885, through May 7, 1890, when he was spiked and did not play for eight days. Some sources report that Pinckney's streak was unknown until the 1920s. However, Pinckney's record was known at least by 1919, when it was reported in a supplement to George Moreland's 1914 encyclopedia, *Balldom*.

Buck Freeman. The outfielder played in 535 straight games for the Red Sox at the start of the 20th century.

Candy LaChance. The first baseman played in 540 consecutive games at the turn of the century, starting with 138 for the Red Sox in 1902.

Fred Luderus. The Phillies first baseman had a consecutive game streak of 533. On September 24, 1919, he broke what was reported in some publications at the time to be the then-current record of 525. It is unclear whose record purportedly was 525, because none of the prior record holders was at that number and George Pinckney's record of 577 was not referenced in the press at the time (perhaps Buck Freeman's 535).

Aaron Ward. The second baseman played in 565 straight games for the Yankees in the early 1920s.

Everett Scott. Scott was a 5'8", 138-pound shortstop for 13 Major League seasons primarily for the Red Sox and Yankees. He had a .249 lifetime average and was Yankee captain from 1922 through 1925. He was also one of the nation's top bowlers. He started his then–American League record 1,307-game streak with the Red Sox on June 16, 1916, and eventually passed the 577-game mark of Brooklyn shortstop George Pinckney.

Scott was honored on May 2, 1923, before playing in his 1,000th consecutive game against the Senators. Unnoticed that day was Walter Johnson's 100th career shutout for the Senators.

Scott's streak ended May 6, 1925, when Yankee manager Miller Huggins replaced him with Pee Wee Wanninger. This was only one month before Lou Gehrig's streak began. Scott had been playing poorly, as were most of the Yankees while Babe Ruth was out with his famous stomachache (actually a venereal disease). Scott was released later that season.

Joe Sewell. Sewell began a streak of 1,103 consecutive games for the Indians on September 13, 1922. One source claimed that Sewell's streak ended in 1932 due to a bad flu virus. However, Sewell only appeared in 109 games in 1930 and the streak ended on April 30 of that year.

Lou Gehrig.

"I took the two most expensive aspirin in history." — Wally Pipp, who sat out a game with a headache in favor of Lou Gehrig.

The streak began on June 1, 1925, when Gehrig pinch-hit for Pee Wee Wanninger, who coincidentally had replaced Everett Scott on May 6 to end Scott's streak. On June 2, regular first baseman Wally Pipp was hit in the head by a ball thrown by the batting practice pitcher and he was unable to start. Gehrig not only replaced him in the line-up that day, he took over permanently. The year before, Pipp had hit .295 and led the league in triples.

There has been some confusion among historians about the actual first day of the streak because of Gehrig's pinch-hitting duty on June 1 and his start on June 2.

One source noted that by an odd coincidence the day before, manager Miller Huggins benched Everett Scott, ending his streak at 1,307. As discussed above, this occurred a month earlier.

Another source claimed that when Gehrig reached 1,308 games on August 17, 1933, breaking Scott's record, his teammate that day was Joe Sewell, "whose record Scott broke a few years earlier." Though Gehrig and Sewell were teammates in 1933, Scott could not have broken Sewell's record because Sewell's streak of 1,103 games ended in 1930, four years after Scott retired.

When Gehrig broke the record, there was very little media attention for the game against the Browns in St. Louis. No one in New York heard the game on radio. The game was stopped in the 1st inning and Gehrig was presented with a silver statuette from American League president Will Harridge. Scott, whose record was broken, was in Fort Wayne, Indiana, and did not attend.

Gehrig began having trouble with his coordination during a dismal start to the 1939 season. He then made the fateful decision: "I decided on it Sunday night. I knew after Sunday's game that I ought to get out of there. I got up four times with men on base. Once there were two on. A hit any of those times would have won us the ball game. But I left all five men on…. McCarthy's been swell about it. He'd let me go until the cows came home, he's that considerate of my feelings. Well, maybe a rest will do me good."

The Tigers public address announcer was succinct at the game of May 2, 1939: "Ladies and gentleman, Lou Gehrig has taken himself out of the line-up for the first time in 2,130 games."

According to Tommy Henrich, Gehrig sat sobbing on the bench during the announcement and pitcher Lefty Gomez broke the tension by telling Gehrig: "What the heck, now you know how we feel when we get knocked out of the box."

Gehrig's last game was April 30, 1939, and ended his streak at 2,130 games. He was only 35 years old, but was batting .143 over eight games and never played again. He had played in a total of 2,164 games. Gehrig also ended 885 consecutive games at first base. See *Lou Gehrig* for the specifics of the disease that ended his career and ultimately his life.

Wally Pipp, whom Gehrig replaced in the line-up in 1925, was on hand as a spectator on May 2 when Gehrig finally sat out (no game on May 1). He was the only Yankee to be present at the beginning and end of Gehrig's streak. Pipp was a salesman in his home-town of Grand Rapids, Michigan, when he drove down to Briggs Stadium in Detroit for the game. He was one of 11,379 fans that day who witnessed Gehrig's replacement, Babe Dahlgren, get two hits and two RBIs in the Yankees' 22–2 defeat of the Tigers.

Partial Appearances. Gehrig had cheap games in the streak, such as when he was announced as the shortstop and lead-off hitter to allow him to take one at-bat and then come out of the game for Frank Crosetti. The specifics of the 76 games he did not finish: he was taken out eight times for a pinch hitter, four times for a pinch-runner, and was replaced at first base in 64 other games. He failed to start only two games.

Gehrig's only serious injury that would have put him out of action was a broken hand he suffered during a tour of Japan in 1931. The streak was in jeopardy in the summer of 1934 after an exhibition game against a Yankee farm club in Norfolk. After hitting a home run, Gehrig was beaned. He was unconscious for five minutes before being helped off the field. In his next start, in Washington, he hit three triples before the game was washed out due to rain.

Many felt that the streak should not have been perpetuated. Among them was Babe Ruth: "This iron man stuff is just baloney. The guy ought to learn to sit on the bench and rest."

Gus Suhr. The first baseman played in 822 straight games for the Pirates in the mid–1930s.

Stan Musial. Musial had a streak of 895 consecutive games, mixing games in the outfield and at first base.

Eddie Yost. The third baseman played in 829 consecutive games for the Senators in the early 1950s.

Nellie Fox. The White Sox infielder holds the record for second basemen, with 798 consecutive games from August 7, 1956, through September 3, 1960.

Billy Williams.

"When you're in a streak, you can't do things other guys on the team do. You can't go out and enjoy yourself at night because you know you have to get your rest for the next day, all the games having taken a toll on you physically and mentally. You literally start to watch every step, afraid you're going to twist an ankle or something. I've heard Cal say that the streak has taken on a life of its own, and that's true. I think the Gehrig record and Joe DiMaggio's streak are the toughest in baseball to break." — Williams.

The Hall of Famer played left field for the Cubs in the 1960s, beginning his 1,117-game streak on September 22, 1963, and ending it on September 2, 1970. He and manager Leo Durocher attempted to end the then–National League record streak a day earlier because he was tired, but Durocher used him as a pinch hitter in a game he was supposed to sit out. Durocher then told Williams to stay home the next day so that Durocher could not use him in the game.

Steve Garvey.

"I started to dream about getting caught in rush-hour traffic and the streak ending because I didn't get to the stadium until the final out. I started to dream about going for a drink between games of a doubleheader and the manager refusing to play me because I returned late for the second game. Those of us playing in streaks are a small fraternity — we know what it takes. It takes a physical, mental and spiritual commitment — spiritual in the sense that you have to be one with the sport." — Garvey.

Garvey's National League record 1,207-game streak began with the Dodgers in 1974 and ended with the Padres in 1983, when he broke his thumb sliding into home plate. He also played every game in 1984 and 1985 and 155 games in 1986. Had he not broken his thumb he would have added at least 500 more games to the streak, for a total of more than 1,700.

Cal Ripken, Jr.

"I think the good feeling that is starting to generate about the streak comes from our love of baseball. It's not necessarily about me. It's about statistics and history and the game we all love." — Ripken in 1995.

"What if we collide on a short fly ball? What if I knock him out of the lineup? I'll need more Secret Service men than Reagan, Bush and Clinton combined." — Orioles center fielder Andy Van Slyke near the end of Ripken's quest to break Lou Gehrig's record.

"Cal Ripken is to baseball what Ernest Hemingway and John Steinbeck are to the literary world. Deion Sanders is to baseball what John Grisham is to the literary world. This is the difference between grace and integrity, and greed and egoism." — Jon Meyer.

Ripken's first Major League game was August 10, 1981, when he was a pinch runner for Ken Singleton in the 12th inning and scored on John Lowenstein's single. The streak started in the second game of a doubleheader on May 29, 1982. Ripken played the first game of a doubleheader the night before but sat out the nightcap in favor of Floyd Rayford. In May 1992 Ripken played in his 1,620th straight game exactly 10 years from the day that the streak began.

Ripken reached 2,000 games on August 1, 1994, 11 days before the strike started. He went 0-for-4 in the game but was batting .312 at the time.

Through the 1994 strike-shortened season, Ripken had played in 2,009 consecutive games and was scheduled to break Gehrig's record in early September 1995. Luckily the strike ended and replacement players were not used during the regular season, so Ripken's streak was not affected.

The starting shortstops on the day that Ripken's streak began (doubleheaders for some clubs):

California	Tim Foli
Chicago	Bill Almon
Cleveland	Jerry Dybzinski
Detroit	Alan Trammell
Detroit	Mark DeJohn
Kansas City	Onix Concepcion
Milwaukee	Robin Yount
Minnesota	Len Faedo
New York	Roy Smalley, Jr.
Oakland	Tony Phillips
Oakland	Fred Stanley
Seattle	Todd Cruz
Texas	Mark Wagner
Toronto	Alfredo Griffin
Atlanta	Rafael Ramirez
Chicago	Larry Bowa
Cincinnati	Dave Concepcion
Houston	Craig Reynolds
Los Angeles	Mark Belanger
Montreal	Chris Speier
New York	Tom Veryzer
Philadelphia	Ivan DeJesus
Pittsburgh	Jimmy Smith
St. Louis	Ozzie Smith
San Diego	Garry Templeton
San Francisco	Johnnie LeMaster

Ripken played 8,243 consecutive *Innings* beginning on May 30, 1982, in what is believed to be the longest streak of its kind. On September 14, 1987, the Blue Jays hit a Major League–record 10 home runs in an 18–3 victory over the Orioles and Ripken was replaced at shortstop by Ron Washington in the 8th inning. From 1982 through 1992 Ripken played in all but 128 of a possible 15,787 innings. The closest he came to ending the streak was in June 1993 when he hurt his knee during an on-field fight. At the 1996 All-Star Game, reliever Roberto Hernandez accidentally broke Ripken's nose during the team picture, but Ripken didn't miss the game.

Ripken tied Gehrig's record on September 5, 1995, and broke it the next night against the Angels. When Ripken broke the record, the Orioles donated $1 million to ALS research.

Three of the highlights of the record-breaking game: Ripken's home run in the 4th inning (and at-bat in the 5th inning with the bases loaded — he hit a soft liner that was caught by the second baseman for the third out), his lap around the field during the 22-minute 5th-inning break, and his post-game speech that included tribute to Eddie Murray for showing him the ropes. Michael Stim, who caught the home run, sold it in December 1995 to a Maryland businessman for $41,736.

Ripken was hit by a pitch 45 times during his career up to the game in which he broke the record, but it knocked him out of the line-up only once. In May 1982, less than four weeks before the streak began, he was beaned by Mike Moore and missed one game. Ripken started every game during his streak. During the streak there were 340 other Major League shortstops and 3,700 players on the disabled list. Ripken finished the 1995 season at 2,153 straight games played. He reached 2,500 on April 25, 1998. At the time, his streak was longer than the next 22 active streaks combined.

The top streaks when Ripken set the new record:

233	Frank Thomas
225	Travis Fryman
215	Chad Curtis
206	Barry Bonds

Of all players who were active between 1982 and 1995, the five players with the fewest games missed other than Ripken:

116	Eddie Murray
166	Tim Wallach
170	Brett Butler
211	Wade Boggs
239	Harold Baines

The Streak Ends.

"I'll probably hear from God or Cal when it's time, and I'll probably hear it sooner from God." — Orioles manager Davey Johnson in March 1997, on when Ripken should end his streak.

Ripken continued the streak into the 1997 season, even after he moved over to third base. Mike Bordick replaced him at shortstop and Bordick validated the move when he set a shortstop record for errorless games. On September 20, 1998, the streak finally ended at 2,632 when Ripken chose to sit out a game. Over the 15-plus years of the streak, the Baltimore Orioles used 289 other players, had 32 different coaches, and eight different managers. At the time the streak ended, Ripken had played in 502 more consecutive games than Gehrig and over twice as many as the player in third place, Everett Scott. Ripken was replaced in the line-up by Ryan Minor, who went 1-for-4 that night. The longest streak at the time was by Craig Biggio, whose streak ended in 1998 at 494 games.

Ripken was 38 when the streak ended and he was batting .273 with 14 home runs and 61 RBIs, giving the Orioles the worst third base run production in the American League. The late change in the Orioles lineup was not visible until minutes before the start of the game. When the name of Ryan Minor was inserted in Ripken's place at third base on the scoreboard, only a few fans at Camden Yards reacted, pointing at the change. After Chuck Knoblauch of the Yankees, the game's first batter, grounded out to shortstop, the entire Yankees team emerged from the visiting dugout and tipped their caps to Ripken, who was across the field. Ripken burst from the Orioles' dugout, playfully waving for the fans to sit, but they would not stop cheering and the Yankees would not stop clapping. Ripken returned to the Orioles' dugout and the standing ovation continued. Derek Jeter, on deck, stood out of the batter's box, and the Orioles' pitcher, Doug Johns, waited, having no intention of interfering. The cheers lasted for about three minutes, until Ripken gave Johns the sign to throw his next pitch, and the game went on. After the game at a post-game news conference, missing his first game since 1982, Ripken wanted back in the lineup: "I don't feel a sense of relief. I don't feel much different. Now that I know what it feels like, I don't want to sit and watch a game anymore."

For the first time in his career, Ripken went on the disabled list due to back irritation on April 19, 1999. Though he played just 86 games that season (a second trip to the disabled list cost him 28 games in August), and subsequent back surgery sidelined him for the final 13 games of the year, he had batted well for the season.

Since the streak began in 1982, only two players before 2003 had streaks in excess of 500 games: Dale Murphy with 740 and Joe Carter with 507. In 2004 Miguel Tejada reached 756. In 1999 Albert Belle had the longest active streak at 392, but he was benched by Orioles manager Ray Miller for failing to run out a ground ball.

Rule.

"A consecutive-game playing streak shall be extended if the player plays one half-inning on defense, or if he completes a time at-bat by reaching base or being put out. A pinch-running appearance only shall not extend the streak. If a player is ejected from a game by an umpire before he can comply with the requirements of this rule, his streak shall continue."—Rule 10.24(C). In short, pinch-running will not extend and an early ejection will not end a streak.

Japanese Leagues. Sachio Kinugasa of the Hiroshima Toyo Carp of Japan's Central League played in his 2,131st consecutive game on June 13, 1987, to break Lou Gehrig's then-professional record. The streak began in 1970, as Kinugasa primarily played catcher and once played with a broken shoulder. In 1987 he also hit his 500th home run. Kinugasa played third base later in his career and pinch-hit or played only a few innings in approximately 100 games. His streak ended at 2,215 games on October 22, 1987. Ripken broke his record against the Royals on June 14, 1996, with Kinugasa in attendance.

When Kazuo Matsui jumped to the Mets from the Japanese Leagues for the 2004 season, he had extended his consecutive games played streak in Japan to 1,143 games.

Mexican Leagues. The record in the Mexican Leagues was 1,165 games, set by Rolando Camarero between 1968 and 1976. In 1996 his record was broken by Gerardo Sanchez.

Consecutive Wins See **Wins and Winning Streaks**

Contact Lenses See **Glasses**

Continental League (1920)

"It is not likely that the major league club owners will view the proposed organization with any great alarm."—The *New York Times*.

This league was the brainchild of Boston-based Andy Lawson, who had been one of the organizers of the short-lived **United States League** of 1912. The league was chartered in December 1920 and was to be a league represented by states. Lawson spent the next few months organizing teams, but the league never got off the ground. One of the distinguishing features of the league was that it was considering the use of black players. The league postponed its scheduled April 1921 commencement and then disappeared.

Continental League (1960)

"The Continental League was Branch Rickey's final moment in the baseball sun."—Charles C. Alexander in *Our Game* (1991).

This league was conceived by New York attorney Bill Shea in the late 1950s. He recruited future Mets owner Joan Payson to help finance this proposed third major league. It appears that Shea may have been trying only to leverage an attempt to obtain a new National League franchise to replace the Dodgers and Giants in the New York area.

The new league was announced on July 27, 1960, with franchises to be located in New York, Houston, Toronto, Denver, Minneapolis and three cities to be named. Branch Rickey was to be the president of the league. Financial backing came from Jack Kent Cooke in Toronto, who was to become the long-time owner of the NBA Lakers and NFL Redskins, and Lamar Hunt in Dallas, who would become the owner of the AFL Kansas City Chiefs (who started in Dallas). The league scheduled 154 games and was set to meet formally on August 18 with commissioner Ford Frick and a six-man Major League committee to achieve cooperation among the leagues. Frick had allegedly admitted in private to Rickey that he was in favor of a third Major League, but could not do so publicly.

Frick had already met with Shea on the subject and learned that each new owner was to contribute $50,000 as a franchise fee and each was prepared to spend $2.5 million on a new club.

The formal meeting never took place and the idea died on August 2, 1960, when Major League Baseball announced that it would be expanding by two teams in each league. This effectively put a stop to the Continental League's plans because key prospective owners were to be awarded new franchises in the American or National League. At a secret meeting it was decided that the Major Leagues would absorb proposed clubs in four Continental League cities. They were to be New York, Houston, Minneapolis and Denver. Despite promises that Continental League owners would be included, they were largely ignored and Rickey was outraged: "Their action was not only unfair to the Continental League ... but it was unfair to the American public in defeating any proper concept of major league expansion into a number of great cities throughout our country.... It is difficult to understand how reputable gentlemen will explain this breach of good faith."

The American League expanded first in late 1960. Denver lost out to Los Angeles, which took on the Angels and Gene Autry. Calvin Griffith's Senators moved to Minnesota and a group unrelated to the Continental League bought the new Washington franchise.

The National League was more cooperative with the Continental League proponents. Shea's group bought the Mets franchise and Continental League participant Judge Roy Hofheinz took the Houston club.

Contraction

"Such a draft would stir far greater interest than the 1997 expansion draft, bringing the Hot Stove League to a full boil. There's only one problem: If contraction occurs, it almost certainly would mean that Major League Baseball is setting its house on fire. And once again, the owners would be holding the matches."— Ken Rosenthal in *The Sporting News*.

"On November 4, [2001] fans thrilled to the ninth-inning, seventh-game conclusion of the most exciting World Series in years. Two days later, Major League Baseball's owners, led by Commissioner-for-Life Bud Selig, destroyed all the goodwill the Series had produced by declaring that two of MLB's thirty teams would be eliminated during the off-season."— Doug Pappas, chair of SABR's Business of Baseball committee.

In 2000 Major Leagues owners quietly listed eight potential targets for contraction: Arizona, Florida, Kansas City, Minnesota, Montreal, Oakland, San Diego and Tampa Bay. In 2001 they expanded the list to include the Angels, when Disney was eager to unload the club. The thought was that the Angels would be eliminated and the A's would move to Anaheim.

Immediately following the conclusion of the 2001 World Series, Commissioner Bud Selig announced his intention to seek contraction of the Major Leagues by eliminating two of the financially weakest teams. Cutting from 30 to 28 teams would eliminate 50 player jobs and the league would have saved $40 million of the $160 million it was sending in subsidies to low-level clubs such as the Expos.

The two most frequently mentioned were the Twins and Devil Rays, with the Expos being moved to another city. Selig proposed to vacate the nation's 14th-largest television market (Minneapolis-St. Paul), 16th-largest (Miami), and Montreal, which averaged only 7,648 in 2001, fewer than those of 10 minor league clubs. It was estimated that the elimination of these franchises would require buyouts to their owners totaling $150 million to $200 million each.

Vladimir Guerrero of the Expos was the most coveted player that would be placed in the proposed dispersal draft. It was thought that the draft would depress the free agent market because of the glut of talent that would be picked up by teams without having to pay premiums through free agency. The owners took the position that contraction was not something on which they had to bargain with the players union, and of course that resulted in a grievance being filed by the union.

In January 2002, Representative John Conyers, Jr., of Michigan said publicly that Bud Selig should resign because he appeared to violate Major League rules in a 1995 loan from a company controlled by the owner of the Twins. Conyers, The House Judiciary Committee's ranking Democrat at the time, said the loan created an "irreparable conflict of interest" for Selig in his plan to fold two franchises (which at the time included the Twins). Selig rejected the idea: "The suggestions made in your letter are wholly unacceptable."

A similar sentiment against Selig was expressed by Marvin Miller, the former head of the Players Association. Selig wasn't happy, and commented: "St. Louis is closer to Minneapolis than Milwaukee is [not true]. Are the Red Sox going to benefit if Montreal is contracted? No. I don't think the Brewers will gain either. Its so outrageous and not worthy of comment."

The Florida attorney general vowed to fight any attempt to move the Devil Rays and the team was locked into a long-term lease. In November 2001, a Minnesota judge issued an injunction prohibiting any action involving the Twins for the 2002 season.

As a result of the new *Collective Bargaining Agreement* signed in September 2002, contraction was taken off the table through the end of that agreement. Ironically, the Twins made it to the postseason, losing to the Angels in the ALCS. Montreal managed a strong showing, leading its division early in the season under manager Frank Robinson and finishing in second place with an 83–79 record. Major League owners nevertheless collectively bought the club and ran it until a suitable buyer could be found.

In June 2003 Major League Baseball won an important court decision that prevented the media from gaining access to internal memos and financial documents that were generated during the attempt to eliminate the Twins. The Minnesota Supreme Court refused to issue an order allowing access to the information, which was part of the Metropolitan Sports Facilities Commission's successful lawsuit to prevent elimination of the Twins. After signing the new collective bargaining agreement, the Expos could not be contracted prior to 2007 and plans were made to move the club to another city.

Contracts

"In your haste to accept terms you forgot to sign contract."— Telegram response by the Indians to the return of an unsigned contract by Hank Greenberg.

"In your haste to give me a raise you put in the wrong figure."— Greenberg's response to the response.

"Ocala, Florida February 14, 1891
To the Directors of the Ocala Base Ball Association
Gentlemen: We the undersigned base ball players, and members of the Ocala Giants, agree to play with the Ocala Club, until further notified, for board, shaving and washing expenses; also a cigar once a week.
[Signed] John J. McGraw
C.F. Thorp
J. Conner
Ed. Mars
Frank Stanton"

Contracts originally were only for the duration of the baseball season rather than annualized over a full year. This was formalized in the 1883 National Agreement, which set the contract period from April 1 to October 30. By the 1890s teams began to allow payment over the entire year, rather than over seven months. By 1910 as teams attempted to exert more control over their players, contracts were routinely extended to a full year. However, many players still received their money only during the season and many were broke by the start of the next spring training. Advances during the winter were common.

The sale of the Browns to Phil Ball after the Federal League disbanded was complicated because the buyer and seller had to reconcile thousands of dollars of advances made to players by owner Robert Hedges.

Lawsuits. One of the first reported instances in which professional baseball went to court was to settle a dispute in 1888 involving the American Association and National League. The American Association Cincinnati club sought to enjoin the National League Boston club from using a player who had jumped to the Cincinnati club (see also *American Association*).

The National League Phillies and American League A's feuded over players during the 1901–1902 battle between the leagues. Nap

Lajoie, Bill Bernhard and Chick Fraser all played with the Phillies before jumping to the A's. The Phillies filed a lawsuit seeking to prohibit the three from playing for the A's. The Pennsylvania Supreme Court ruled that the players had to return to the Phillies. Fraser complied, but American League president Ban Johnson arranged for Lajoie and Bernhard to be traded to Cleveland to avoid the jurisdiction of the Pennsylvania court. When Cleveland played in Philadelphia, the two players were given paid vacations out of the state.

Appeal. When Judge Landis became commissioner in 1920, the basic contract was amended to provide that any ballplayer could appeal to the commissioner a club's decision on any matter relating to his contract.

Uniform Player Contract. The first standard player contract was recognized in 1887. The first basic agreement resulting from collective bargaining was signed in 1967. In 1946, as a result of efforts by the players to form a *Union*, the owners agreed to a number of changes in the basic agreement: 1) owners were required to mail new contracts to players no later than February 1 of each year; 2) there would be a cap of 25% on the amount that a player's contract could be reduced from year-to-year; 3) player contracts were guaranteed through the end of the year even if they were reassigned to another Major League club or to a minor league club.

The mailing date was important to Carlton Fisk in 1981. The Red Sox mailed his contract late, so he was allowed to become a free agent and sign with the White Sox. On Opening Day that year he hit a three-run home run in the 9th inning at Fenway Park to defeat his former club.

Multi-Year Contracts/Early 20th Century. It has often been reported that early contracts were almost always for a single year rather than multi-year. However, there were a number of exceptions. Multi-year contracts were often the product of a competitive market caused by the presence of a new league. In 1889 when the Players League was forming for one season in 1890, its clubs signed players to three-year deals to prevent them from jumping back to the more established leagues. The same phenomenon occurred during the Federal League challenge of 1914–1915. In 1914 Eddie Collins received a multi-year contract when Connie Mack sold him to the White Sox. Many other prominent players such as Babe Ruth received multi-year contracts.

Sandy Koufax and Don Drysdale tried to become the first Dodgers with multi-year contracts by staging a *Hold-Out* in 1966. Although they received large increases, the contracts were for one year each.

Free Agency/Multi-Year Contracts. The first large multi-year contract during the early free-agency era was signed by John Mayberry with the Royals. He signed for $1 million over five years shortly after the free agent explosion in the mid–1970s. The Royals made a conscious decision not to sign free agents and instead tied up their best players with long-term deals.

By 1980, 42% of all contracts were long-term, led by Bruce Sutter's, which called for him to receive $43 million over 30 years. In 1993 Bret Saberhagen signed a contract extension with the Mets that deferred $250,000 annually from 2004 through 2028.

A request for a multi-year contract by Dodger manager Burt Shotten cost him his job in the early 1950s. His successor, Walter Alston, signed 23 consecutive one-year contracts with the club.

1990s Trends. In 1993 the Expos, perhaps starting a new trend in baseball, put their entire team on one-year contracts with nothing guaranteed for 1994.

The Indians' 1990s strategy was to sign most of their young players to multi-year contracts before they proved themselves. By doing this the club could ensure having a cohesive group of players for a number of years with the hope that enough of them would develop into stars to carry the team to success. The strategy might have paid off in 1994 when the Indians were leading their division, but the player strike ended the season. It clearly paid off in 1995 when the club made it to the postseason, and then in 1997 the Indians were within an out of a World Series win over the Marlins.

Bonuses and Incentives. See *Bonus Clauses and Incentives*.

No Team. Rupert Mills signed to play first base for Harry Sinclair's Newark club in the 1916 Federal League. The league failed before the season started and the team folded. Mills would not accept a $600 settlement on his $3,000 contract, so he continued working out for the nonexistent team until July when he accepted a larger settlement offer.

Blank Check. In the early 1990s an arbitrator ruled that baseball owners had committed *Collusion* in 1987 to keep player salaries down. Andre Dawson was perhaps the best player available that year, but he could not find a place to play as the owners shut down the market for free agents by refusing to bid on them. Dawson finally agreed to play for the Cubs after he told the club to fill in a blank check with an amount of their choosing. He signed for $500,000, extremely low for that year, and went on to have an MVP season, the first time that a player from a last-place club won the award. He signed the next year for over $1.5 million.

Publicity. The earliest player contracts required the player to cooperate in at least some publicity on behalf of the club.

Negotiations.

"I'm the greatest pitcher that ever lived. The greatest game that was ever pitched in baseball wasn't good enough to beat me, so I've got to be the greatest." — Lew Burdette's pitch to management for a raise after the 1959 season. Burdette won the game in which opposing pitcher Harvey Haddix threw a *Perfect Game* for 12 innings, only to lose in the 13th inning. No indication whether Burdette received the $10,000 raise he was seeking.

In 1950 Indians owner Bill Veeck left 25 blank contracts on his desk and told each of his players to fill in an amount. He had only one argument, because third baseman Ken Kelner had cut his own pay by $5,000.

Control Pitchers

"Some people throw to spots, some people throw to zones. Renie throws to continents." — Reliever Dan Quisenberry on fellow Royals pitcher Renie Martin's inability to hit the strike zone.

"Alex could throw a ball into a tin cup. I have never seen such control." — Grantland Rice on Grover Cleveland Alexander.

"His control is so good, I would be willing to put on the gear and catch any pitch he throws with my eyes closed, because I know he's going to hit some part of the glove with every pitch." — Orioles manager Johnny Oates on starter-turned-ace-reliever Dennis Eckersley.

See also *Base on Balls*.

Pinpoint Control.

"He can throw all day within a two-inch space, in, out, up or down. I've never seen anyone as good as that." — Henry Aaron on Juan Marichal.

"There are a lot of shots in golf I can't hit, but I try to hit them anyway. The frustration is not there, because I'm still learning. But I really know how to do this. I'm not just hoping to get it where I want it.... Let the other guys do it half-assed." — Greg Maddux, when asked why he got so angry at himself for two bad pitches thrown in a hundred during practice, in an article by Thomas Boswell in *Playboy*.

"My brothers and I must have thrown a zillion pitches to each other growing up. Every two years the smokehouse door would splinter to pieces from the pounding it took. Hour after hour day after day, pitch after pitch. It's funny folks always wondered where I got such great control. The answer is written all over those smokehouse doors." — Jim "Catfish" Hunter.

Bob Feller was not noted for his control. In a pregame exhibition in 1936 as a rookie, he and other pitchers on both teams attempted to throw five balls through a square the size of an 8½" by 11" picture frame. In front of 65,000 fans, he watched as George Uhle led the other pitchers by throwing two of five through the small square. Feller then got up last and threw all five balls through the square.

Loss of Control.
Steve Blass.
"Baseball men said they could recall no other case in which the ability left a player that quickly. It made no sense to them; it made no sense to the Pirates either, and, against their better judgment, they kept giving him fresh chances. But it was like playing the man off the street; he could go through the motions convincingly enough from having played as a kid and from having watched enough games, but there was no way he could get real hitters out. And in the end they stop asking questions and say simply: — He lost it. They're sorry." — Richard Grossinger on Steve Blass in *The Unfinished Business of Doctor Hermes* (1973).

Blass pitched effectively for the Pirates until the spring of 1973, when he totally lost his ability to get the ball over the plate. He experimented with psychotherapy, meditation and other psychological methods but was never able to return to form. He had posted a 19–8 record in 1972, but then struggled to a 3–9 record in 1973 after a disastrous spring. He never returned to the Major Leagues after one game in 1974, when he walked seven batters and gave up five hits in five innings.

In January 1973 Blass delivered the eulogy at the funeral of Pirate teammate Roberto Clemente. Some people (but not Blass) claimed that Clemente's death affected Blass's ability to pitch the following spring.

When he was an announcer for the Pirates, Blass injured two fans after he tried to drop a foul ball from the booth to a young fan waiting for it in the second deck. Blass missed, and the ball hit a man on the head and bounced to the lower deck, where it struck a child on the head.

Mitch "The Wild Thing" Williams. Williams lost his control and was released by the Angels on June 19, 1995, and then tried a comeback with the Royals during spring training in 1997. It lasted through May 13, when the Royals released him with an 0–1 record and 10.80 ERA. See also *Base on Balls.*

Mark Wohlers. Wohlers was the ace of the Braves' reliever corps in the mid–1990s. In early 1998 he suffered a torn muscle in his side and never regained his form. He was sent down to Class AAA Richmond, but it didn't help. In his remaining time with the Braves he gave up 15 walks and 13 runs in only 4⅓ innings. The club gave up on him in April 1999 and traded him to the Reds. In a minor league rehab stint in May that year he walked five of the seven batters he faced and threw four wild pitches.

Cooperstown

"The game of baseball was invented and first played in Cooperstown in 1839. Few statements of historical fact can be supported by the decision of a commission of experts especially appointed to examine the evidence and render a verdict, but in fixing the origin of baseball it is exactly this solemn form of procedure that has placed the matter beyond doubt." — Ralph Birdsall's 1918 (and 1948 edition), *The Story of Cooperstown*, a history of the town. This is the lead paragraph of his chapter on "The Birth of Baseball."

Cooperstown is home to the baseball *Hall of Fame* and Baseball Museum (as well as a llama farm just down the road). One Abner Graves claimed in the early 20th century that *Abner Doubleday* spontaneously invented baseball in Cooperstown. Graves made his claim in connection with an "investigation" into the *Origins of Baseball* conducted by Albert Spalding and his so-called Mills Commission. Graves identified the "[Elihu] Phinney Lot" in Cooperstown as the site of the first game. Organized Baseball ded-

Idyllic Cooperstown frames Doubleday Field as high schoolers from the region pay a small fee to play a game on the "hallowed grounds."

icated the site as Doubleday Field on September 20, 1939, in connection with the opening of the Hall.

If not for the erroneous claim that Cooperstown was the site of the first baseball game, the town would still be most famous for James Fenimore Cooper and his book, *Last of the Mohicans* (1826). The book was used in an analogy by famous elocutionist Mickey Rivers in describing a teammate who had just played his first game: "He was lost out there. He was the Lost Mohegan."

In 1939 writer Eliot Asinof played in an all-stars versus local amateurs game under portable lights at a Cooperstown baseball field.

In 1995 the town rejected a minor league baseball franchise on the ground that Cooperstown is "really not a baseball town, per se."

Corked Bats See Bats—Corked Bats

Stan Coveleski (1889–1984)

Hall of Fame (VC) 1969

"It's tomorrow that counts. So you worry all the time. It never ends. Lord, baseball is a worrying thing."—Coveleski.

Coveleski pitched in the American League primarily for the Indians from 1916 through 1924, winning more than 20 games four seasons in a row.

Stanley "Kowaleski" began his pro career in 1908 in the Atlantic League and had a brief Major League appearance in 1912 with the Phillies, pitching a shutout in his debut. He went back to the minor leagues on the West Coast and returned to the Major Leagues with the Indians in 1916. He won 19 games in 1917 with a 1.81 ERA and then reeled off four straight seasons with more than 20 wins. He peaked in the 1920 World Series when he beat the Dodgers in three complete games with pitch counts of 72, 78 and 82.

In 1925 he was traded to the Senators, for whom he won 20 games and led the league with a 2.84 ERA. He lost two games in the World Series and had only one more decent full season in 1926 (14–11) before fading. He retired after posting a 5–1 record in 12 games in 1928 for the Yankees.

In 14 seasons Coveleski compiled a 215–142 record and a .602 winning percentage. His brother Harry played nine years in the Major Leagues. Stan was one of 17 pitchers who were allowed to continue using the spitball after it was banned in 1920. After his retirement he operated a service station in South Bend, Indiana.

Cracker Jack See Candy and Oldtimers Games

Sam Crawford (1880–1968)

Hall of Fame (VC) 1957

"Boy, here I am still talking. Hard to believe. I hope I haven't said anything I shouldn't. There are a lot of the old-timers still left, you know, and they're liable to say, 'That fathead, who the hell does he think he is, anyway, popping off like that!'"—Part of Crawford's closing words in his conversation with Lawrence S. Ritter in *The Glory of Their Times* (1966).

Crawford was an outfielder for the Reds and Tigers from 1899 through 1917, batting .309.

A native of Wahoo, Nebraska, Samuel Earl ("Wahoo Sam") Crawford broke in with Cincinnati in 1899, knocking out five hits in a doubleheader against two different Major League clubs on the same day. The Reds had a regular game against the Louisville Colonels and also scheduled another game against the vagabond Cleveland Spiders, who were horrible that season and had stopped playing home games. Crawford played for the Reds through the 1902 season, when he jumped to the Tigers during the war between the leagues.

In 1906 Crawford began 12 seasons alongside Ty Cobb in the Tigers outfield. Though he despised Cobb, the two worked the basepaths perfectly, often executing complicated double steals.

Crawford led the National League with 16 home runs in 1901 and later led the American League with seven home runs in 1908. He hit over .300 eight times for the Tigers, including .378 in 1911. Crawford retired after batting .173 in 1917, finishing only 36 hits shy of 3,000. He played four more years in the Pacific Coast League with Los Angeles, batting .318 in 175 games in 1921 (one prominent recent source reported that he umpired in the league during those four years).

Crawford's primary claim to fame was his all-time record 312 triples, though he also stole 366 bases and drove in more than 100 runs six times. He had a lifetime .309 average to go with his 1,525 RBIs. After his playing days ended, he stayed in the Los Angeles area and died in Hollywood in 1968.

Cricket

"Baseball is better than cricket because it is sooner ended."—George Bernard Shaw.

"Cricket is a splendid game for Britons. It is a genteel game, a conventional game—and our cousins across the Atlantic are nothing if not conventional. They play cricket because it accords with the tradition of their country to do so; because it is easy and does not overtax their energy or their thought."—Albert Spalding bashing Britons in his 1911 memoir, *Base Ball—America's National Game*.

"To have some idea what it's like, stand in the outside lane of a motorway, get your mate to drive his car at you at 95 mph and wait until he's 12 yards away, before you decide which way to jump."—Geoffrey Boycott in 1989, on how a cricket batsman feels when facing a fast bowler.

"England and America should scrap cricket and Baseball and come up with a new game that they both can play. Like Baseball, for example."—Robert Benchley.

"Though I like the various forms of football in the world, I don't think they begin to compare with these two great Anglo-Saxon ball games for sophisticated elegance and symbolism. Baseball and cricket are beautiful and highly stylized medieval war substitutes, chess made flesh, a mixture of proud chivalry and base—in both senses—greed. With football we are back to the monotonous clashing armor of the brontosaurus."—Cricketeer John Fowl.

"Of course, ignorant disdain has for much more than a century been the attitude of most Americans toward cricket and most Englishmen toward baseball."—Patrick Carroll.

"I'm helplessly and permanently a Red Sox fan. It was like first love.... You never forget. It's special. It's the first time I saw a ballpark. I'd thought nothing would ever replace cricket. Wow! Fenway Park at 7 o'clock in the evening. Oh, just magic beyond magic: never got over that."—Art Historian Simon Schama in *History in Brilliant Brushstrokes* (1999).

Cricket is recognized as one of the predecessors of baseball and was popular in the Northeastern United States through the Civil War. Cricket remained a strong attraction into the 1880s to the wealthier inhabitants of certain major cities, including Boston, Philadelphia, Chicago and New York. At times it was more popular than baseball; in 1859, 24,000 fans jammed Elysian Park in

New Jersey to watch an England–United States cricket match. Baseball matters were first included among the more prominent cricket news in early newspaper accounts.

Cricket was popular among Americans of British descent, but the heavy wave of Irish immigrants in the mid–19th century (caused in part by the Irish potato famine) created a backlash against the British. The resulting influx of Irish players to baseball helped strengthen and promote it as the *National Pastime* after the Civil War ended in 1865.

Four reasons why Cricket declined in popularity in the United States:

1. It required more skill than baseball.
2. It was a game controlled by Englishmen.
3. It had less action than baseball.
4. The game could not be modified and was already too structured to meet the needs of the lower classes who needed an unstructured game such as baseball (which was still being refined).

Common Terminology. Cricket uses the terms batter, umpire, runs and innings.

Pro League. American Pro Cricket debuted in July 2004 on Staten Island, New York, as 1,000 fans watched the Florida Thunder beat the New York Storm. Funding was deemed sufficient to last three years. Radical changes to the rules shortened games to under three hours.

Book. George B. Kirsch, *The Creation of American Team Sports: Baseball and Cricket* (1989).

Joe Cronin (1906–1984)

Hall of Fame 1956

"Nobody in the world was nicer and easier to play for than Joe Cronin. He was a big, good-looking Irishman, and everybody liked Joe Cronin. God, he was a hitter's manager if there ever was one…. He was always optimistic and enthusiastic and always trying to stir up good conversation with the youngsters about baseball, and especially hitting. We'd sit around for hours in the clubhouse, in the hotels, on the trains talking pitchers and the psychology of the game. He was a real heads-up guy, and he kept us thinking."—Ted Williams quoted in *Voices from Cooperstown*, by Anthony J. Connor (1982).

Cronin was primarily an American League shortstop for 20 years beginning in 1926, and was a long-time player-manager and later American League president.

Cronin was born the year that his father lost everything in the 1906 San Francisco earthquake. He was not particularly impressive in his minor league days in the early 1920s after turning down a college scholarship. He debuted in the National League with the Pirates in 1926 and after a second mediocre season in and out of the Major Leagues he was traded to the Senators.

He blossomed with the Senators when he hit .346 in 1930 in 154 games at shortstop. It was the first of 11 seasons in which he hit over .300. He was the starting shortstop for the Senators through 1934 and became player-manager in 1933. Red Sox owner Tom Yawkey purchased him in 1935 and he was the player-manager of the Red Sox from 1935 through his retirement as a player in 1945. He managed two more years in Boston before moving to the club's front office. He remained with the Red Sox until he became the fourth *American League President*, serving from 1959 through 1973.

Over 20 seasons Cronin batted .301 and drove in over 100 runs eight times. During his 15-year managerial career he won two pennants, one each for the Senators and Red Sox, and finished second four times.

Crosley Field (1912–1970)

"Palace of the Fans"—1920s name for the ballpark.

Origins. Crosley Field was home to the Reds from its dedication on May 18, 1912, through the 1970 season. It was built out of the remnants of League Park, which burned in 1911 and then was renovated for $225,000. In 1920 the owners undertook further renovation to the park, which was located at Finley and Western Avenues.

Dimensions. Left field was 387 feet deep, with a towering scoreboard above the fence that was in play. In 1938 left field was shortened to 328 feet. Right field was 366 feet or 342 feet, depending on the year and whether the bullpen area (the "Goat Run") was in or out of play. This terraced area often was replaced with bleachers for special games such as Opening Day.

Home Runs. Until 1921 no player hit a ball out of the park in fair territory. On June 2, 1921, Reds outfielder Pat Duncan hit one over the left field wall. Later in 1921 during an exhibition, Babe Ruth became the first player to hit balls over the center field and right field fences.

Capacity. Seating capacity initially was 25,000, but was expanded a few times beginning in 1927 to 29,000 and fluctuated around that mark after that.

Name. Before the park and the club were purchased by Powell Crosley in the 1930s, the facility was known as Redland Field. After Crosley took over, the name was changed.

Demolition. In 1972 the abandoned ballpark was demolished and the area was developed into an industrial park.

Replica. A replica of the park was built in Blue Ash, Ohio, by Marvin Thompson. He obtained some wood from the original park from a Kentucky fan who had done the same thing, but the Kentucky park mysteriously disappeared.

Books. Greg Rhodes and John Erardi, *Cincinnati's Crosley Field: An Illustrated History of a Classic Ballpark* (1995); Mark Rohrk, *Crosley Field* (1986).

Cross-Ownership

"One Grand Confederacy"—Sportswriter Francis Richter's 1880s *Millennium Plan*, which envisioned ownership of all clubs by a single entity—the ultimate form of cross-ownership.

Syndicate Ball. Cross-ownership of Major League clubs, known as Syndicate Ball, was rampant in the early years of professional baseball and through the 1920s. Syndicate Ball was especially popular in the late 1880s and early 1890s as teams struggled for operating capital in the face of competition from rival leagues and declining attendance.

The Players League folded in 1890 and the American Association collapsed before the 1892 season, forcing the weakest clubs in the 12-team National League to survive only with cash infusions from other owners. The strong teams would buy into the weaker clubs and siphon off the better players. This created a mini-farm system that kept the poor clubs perpetually at the bottom of the standings.

New York Giants. In 1883 when Giants owner John Day was in financial trouble, he persuaded Albert Spalding of Chicago and John Brush of Cincinnati to invest in the club. Boston Red Stockings (later Braves) owner Arthur Soden also purchased an interest in the club that year. Even after Soden left baseball in 1906 and later died, his heirs held their Giants stock until 1928.

Brooklyn Dodgers and Baltimore Orioles. The Dodgers and Orioles of the late 1890s together were another classic example of

19th century Syndicate Ball. Their owners each held the same percentage interest in both clubs and for a short time transferred players somewhat randomly.

Garry Herrmann. Herrmann, principal owner of the Cincinnati Reds in the early 20th century, owned stock in the Phillies and Cardinals. He also made loans to help owners Frank Robison (Cardinals) and Charles Ebbets (Dodgers).

Ned Hanlon. After he was fired as Dodger manager in 1905, Hanlon managed the Reds while still holding a 10% interest in the Dodgers. He was also a principal owner of the minor league club in Baltimore.

Barney Dreyfuss. The Pirates owner held stock in the Phillies for a year and also gave the team three players to help out the club.

Boston Braves. When the Braves were sold in 1919 to a New York group headed by George W. Grant (a friend of Giants manager John McGraw), it was rumored that Charles Stoneham of the Giants loaned Grant $100,000 to make the purchase.

Charles Somers. The Cleveland owner financed at least four of the early American League clubs, including the Indians and Red Sox. The entire American League cooperated in running the Senators until financially independent owners were found. American League president Ban Johnson owned stock in the Red Sox and he and White Sox owner Charlie Comiskey owned a portion of the Indians for a number of years.

Banned. Cross-ownership was officially banned by the Major Leagues in 1927, though team owners had long been afraid of the *Antitrust* implications of cross-ownership, particularly in the early part of the 20th century when trust-busting was a national obsession. The American League had officially banned cross-ownership in 1910, but unofficially allowed it in "emergency" situations. Loans still could be made, however, and that practice continued into the 2000s.

Crotch

"I'm not sure what it means, but whenever the ball is not in play, somebody grabs his crotch." — Bobbie Bouton, former wife of pitcher Jim Bouton.

"Hitters get to scratch themselves only once per at-bat." — Columnist Tom Weir on how to speed up baseball.

"When I began playing the game baseball was as gentlemanly as a kick in the crotch." — Ty Cobb in *My Life in Baseball* (1961).

"Every time a player grabs himself you hear this sound [slide whistle]." — One of David Letterman's "Top Ten Ways Major League Baseball Teams Can Win Back The Fans."

"Like it or not, the crotch is essential in sports. No football play begins without passing the ball through the crotch. No at bat begins without the pitcher staring intently at his catcher's crotch. Roseanne Barr couldn't have finished her sentimental rendition of the national anthem without the crotch." — Rick Reilly.

See also *Protective Cup*.

Cuba

"I had heard that Cubans are a deeply religious people. In two days here I have learned that baseball is their religion." — Sportswriter Sam Lacy in 1947.

"From the start, baseball has been strangely tangled up with politics. Cubans embraced it as a statement of rebellion because it was a modern and sophisticated export from democratic America, rather than an imposition of imperial Spanish culture on the island. It was also played by people of all races, not just the white elite,

which added to its political allure, and Cubans fleeing Spanish oppression took it with them to Venezuela, Puerto Rico, and the Dominican Republic." — Susan Orlean in *The New Yorker*.

See also *Latin Baseball and Major League Players/Managers*.

Origins. Baseball was introduced to Cuba in the 1860s by Cuban students returning from the U.S. (specifically 1866 in some sources). Other sources report that the country was first exposed to baseball in 1876 by a group of American barnstormers. It quickly became popular, to the dismay of the ruling Spaniards, who moved to ban the sport in 1895 (and sent violators to prison) because supposedly it was used to raise money to support insurrection against the Spanish government.

Popularity. Baseball is the dominant sport in Cuba, followed distantly by volleyball, basketball and soccer.

American Presence.

"El Mono Amarillo" — "Yellow Monkey," the Cubans' nickname for John McGraw during his playing days there in the 1891.

"Lee MacPhail, Public Enemy Number 1 of Cuban Baseball." — Havana headlines in 1960 when Orioles general manager Lee MacPhail announced the cancellation of an exhibition game in Havana between the Orioles and Reds. The communist takeover by Fidel Castro made scheduling in Cuba problematic for U.S. clubs. Neither club wanted to play the game, but MacPhail agreed to take the heat because the Reds had a working agreement with the Havana club.

The island nation began a league during the winter of 1878–1879, about the same time that manager Frank Bancroft toured the Caribbean with his team. John McGraw is credited with helping foster baseball in Cuba after first visiting the island in 1889 and visiting regularly thereafter.

The Giants visited Cuba during spring training in 1911 and in subsequent years, leading to McGraw's financial interest in a racetrack and hotel near Havana. He and Giants owner Charles Stoneham were forced to sell their interest in the property when Judge Landis became commissioner and objected to the gambling venture. Havana was a popular spring training site in the 1920s, due primarily to the town's lack of Prohibition-era restrictions on alcohol.

Amateur Organization. The National League of Amateur Baseball of Cuba was formed in 1914 and baseball flourished. Today, by age 13, outstanding players are admitted to a Sports Initiation School, a Soviet-style athletic program that Castro created in 1961. The best players are sent at age 16 to an Advanced School for Athletic Perfection. The Cuban equivalent of Little League is *Categoria Pequeña.*

Professional Leagues.

"When you get hungry enough, you find yourself speaking Spanish pretty well." — Josh Gibson on playing in Cuba.

Newspaper editor Carlos Ayala founded the first professional Cuban league in the 19th century. Cuba had 10 professional leagues by 1950 and the Havana Sugar Kings were members of the Class AAA International League. Many Negro League players went to Cuba for the winter league. Cuba's relationship with Organized Baseball ended when Fidel Castro's communist regime took over in 1960. Since then the island has had two independent professional leagues and strong international teams.

Pitcher Fidel Castro.

"I'd love to meet Fidel Castro. Heck, he's been on the cover of *Time* as much as I've been on *Sports Illustrated.*" — Pete Rose.

Castro supposedly claimed to have been offered $5,000 to play for the Giants after being a star pitcher in college in Cuba. Though he claimed to have played professionally in winter ball, he supposedly pitched only to one batter (Major Leaguer Don Hoak) before being thrown out of his only game. The Hoak story has been told often, but is untrue. Hoak apparently conspired in June 1964 with writer Myron Cope and the editors of *Sport* magazine to create the fictional tale.

Several sources unwittingly elaborated on the hoax, including Kevin Kerrane in *Dollar Sign on the Muscle*, the Oleksaks in *Beisbol: Latin Americans and the Grand Old Game* and a *Harper's* article in 1989 by David Truby that said Horace Stoneham and his New York Giants were pursuing Castro, who was "a star pitcher for the University of Havana baseball team." The article also quotes from never-before- and never-since-reported scouting reports about Castro's prowess.

There are a number of inconsistencies in the story, including the year in which it purportedly occurred. Hoak only played in Cuba during the 1953–1954 winter season and Castro was in jail the entire time. When Castro's communist regime took over in the late 1950s he quickly cut off the supply of baseball talent to Organized Baseball. Castro sometimes pitched in exhibition games for a club known as the Bearded Ones. The first Cuban national series was in 1962, after Castro outlined professional sports in the country in 1961, by virtue of National Decree 83A.

Former presidential candidate Eugene McCarthy advocated in 1984 having Castro serve as Baseball's commissioner because the sport needed "an experienced dictator."

One of Cuba's few international stages for its talented players was the Olympic Games when the sport was added in 1984. By 1993 there were indications that Castro was beginning to soften his stance on Cubans playing Major League Baseball.

A supermarket tabloid once reported that Castro attended the 1993 World Series in Philadelphia. Castro supposedly "sat in expensive field level seats, drank beer and rooted for John Kruk and the Phillies."

In 1998 Castro expressed the desire for a ball signed by Joe DiMaggio, which he had "always dreamed of owning." DiMaggio initially balked, but later relented and sent Castro the signed ball. As noted by a DiMaggio friend, as reported by the Associated Press: "He doesn't approve of Castro's politics, but he figured, if it helps relations between Cuba and the U.S., then OK."

Euphemism. The term "Cuban player" as used in the 19th and early 20th century often meant that the player or team was black. For example, the Cuban Giants were a black team from the United States and had no connection with Cuba. There are numerous documented attempts to pass off black players as "Cuban" to circumvent the racial prohibitions imposed by Organized Baseball until the 1940s.

Greatest Player. Hall of Famer Martin DiHigo was a Negro League pitching and outfield star and possibly the greatest all-around player of all time, white or black.

Early Major League Players.

"Clark Griffith's Good Neighbor Policy"—The Senators owner was famous for his Cuban pipeline of players in the 1930s and 1940s. Senators scout Joseph Cambria signed over 400 Cuban players over the years.

Vincent Nava. Nava was a Spanish caucasian considered by some to be the first Cuban player in the Major Leagues, though he was born in San Francisco and died in Baltimore. He played five 19th century seasons for Providence in the National League and Baltimore in the American Association.

Armando Marsans and Rafael Almeida. When these Cubans were recruited to play for the Reds around 1911, someone from the club purportedly made a special trip to Cuba to verify that both were "pure Caucasians." Marsans was a versatile fielder who batted .269 over eight seasons spread over the American, National and Federal Leagues between 1911 and 1918. Almeida batted .270 over parts of three seasons for the Reds beginning in 1911.

Mike Gonzalez. In 1912 Gonzalez began a 17-year career as a catcher and managed the Cardinals briefly in 1938 and 1940.

Dolf Luque. "The Pride of Havana" pitched for 20 years in the National League. His best season was 1923 when he won 27 games for the Reds and pitched six shutouts.

Last Major Leaguers Until the 1990s. Bert (Dagoberto) Campaneris, Tito (Rigoberto) Fuentes and Luis Tiant were the last Cubans to play in the Major Leagues until the 1990s.

Top Recent Major League Players.

"My family fled Cuba because my parents wanted a better life for us, They wanted to give us a better chance. When I was growing up, I just wanted to be a big league baseball player. That's all that I ever thought about. I'd tell my friends and everybody that I knew that that's what I was going to be. Knowing that the percentage of players making it was so small, everybody said, 'You're crazy; you need to do something else.' But, you know, I thought, 'Well there are people up there playing, so why not me?' I saw my dad come to a country where he didn't speak the language, didn't have a penny to his name. He came here with 3 little kids and a wife and had no place to live, and I saw that as a young kid. I saw him as a hero, as somebody who worked really hard and didn't accept any handouts or gifts from anyone. And just by watching him, I learned to work for the things that I wanted to achieve. He made time every day after work. He worked in construction most of his life, and he'd come home about 4:00, 4:30 and eat something, change his clothes, then we'd go to the ballpark. Every day. He pushed me as hard as he could and kept me focused."—Rafael Palmeiro.

Luis Tiant.

"A barrel-chested man who looked fatter than he really was, he would emerge from the shower with a cigar in his mouth, look at his naked body in the mirror and declare 'good-lookeen sonofabeech' in his exaggerated Spanish accent."— Mark Armour.

"Tiant's first season with the Tigers was equivalent to 'The Perils of Pauline.'"—Tiant and Joe Fitzgerald in *El Tiante* (1976). Tiant won 229 games over a 19-year career almost exclusively in the American League. He had four seasons of 20 or more wins and won two World Series games for the Red Sox in 1975.

In 1975 Senator George McGovern made an unofficial visit to Cuba to see Fidel Castro. He carried a letter from Senator Edward Brooke of Massachusetts asking that Tiant's parents be allowed to visit Tiant in Boston. Castro approved the request and three months later they were in Boston together.

Zoilo Versalles. The Twins shortstop was the American League MVP in 1965 when he led the club to the pennant. See also James Terzian, *The Kid from Cuba* (1967).

Mike Cuellar. Cuellar pitched primarily for the Orioles from 1964 through 1977, compiling a 185–130 record and a 3.14 ERA. He won 20 games, in 1969, 1970 and 1971 and was the Cy Young Award winner in 1969. His primary pitch was a palmball.

Jose Cardenal. He hit .278 in a career lasting from 1963 through 1980.

Jose and Ozzie Canseco. The twin brothers emigrated from Cuba with their family when they were young boys.

Defectors.

"Maybe one day they will come back to Cuba and bring their money with them."—Fidel Castro on the recent defectors.

"Defective?"—Headline in *Sports Illustrated* about the underachieving Cuban defectors who were signed to big contracts to pitch in the Major Leagues.

Rene Arocha. Arocha was with the Cuban national team in Miami International Airport when he bolted for the exit and sought asylum on July 10, 1991. He won his Major League debut for the Cardinals on April 9, 1993, an 8–2 victory over the Reds. Arocha was 18–17 in four seasons primarily for the Cardinals.

Rey Ordonez. Ordonez defected in 1993 and by 1996 was a dazzling defensive shortstop for the Mets. He was a steady but injury-prone player for the club through 2002 and then moved over to Tampa Bay.

Ariel Prieto. The Cuban exile was drafted by the A's in the first round of the June 1995 amateur draft and he began pitching immediately for the club. Tendinitis limited his effectiveness that season. Prieto was 14–21 when he left the Major Leagues after the 1997 season.

Osvaldo Fernandez and Livan Hernandez. In mid–1995 pitchers and Osvaldo Fernandez and Livan Hernandez defected to the United States from Cuba. Fernandez was the star Cuban pitcher during the 1992 Olympics and was 22–0 in international competition. Early in 1996 both signed multi-million dollar deals with Major League clubs. Fernandez won his debut for the Giants in April 1996 but struggled over four seasons. Hernandez had far more success after a slow start, winning 57 games for the Giants and Expos in four seasons beginning in 2000.

Orlando Hernandez. "El Duque" signed with the Yankees and debuted with the club in 1998.

Rolando Arrojo. Arrojo received a $7 million signing bonus from the Devil Rays in early 1998. After winning 14 games in his debut season, he struggled and did not pitch in the Major Leagues after 2002.

Tony Fossas was a middle reliever for several clubs over 12 seasons beginning in 1988.

Andy Morales. In March 2001, the Yankees signed the third baseman and defector to a four-year contract. He bombed with his minor league club and was waived a few months later. The club tried to back out of the deal because he had lied about his age by three years. As a result of the disastrous results with Morales and particularly with several Cuban pitchers who never panned out, U.S. clubs began to shy away from big deals for Cuban players.

Jose Contreras signed with the Yankees for the 2003 season and was 7–2 in nine starts and 18 total appearances. He was reunited with his family in June 2004 after his wife and two daughters crossed the Caribbean to Florida in a small boat.

Major League Managers. Carlos Tosca managed the Blue Jays in 2002 through mid–2004 before being fired. He had no prior Major League or minor league experience as a player.

Japan. In the 1990s Castro allowed some of the best Cuban players to take sabbaticals in Japan, and a few stars played there for two seasons.

Free Pass. On October 23, 1998, the Yankees held a parade for their World Series sweep of the Padres. The parade was up the Canyon of Heroes on lower Broadway to celebrate their World Series sweep over the Padres. It was especially significant for pitcher Orlando Hernandez, who had his mother, children, and ex-wife present because they were granted permission by the Cuban government to visit the United States and attend the Yankees homecoming parade on a 30-day visa.

Cultural Exchange. On May 3, 1999, the Cuban national team played the Orioles at Camden Yards, as part of a cultural exchange that had begun in March, when the Orioles played the national team in Havana. The Cubans won 12–6 in Baltimore, and lost

pitching coach Rigoberto Herrera, who defected and requested asylum. On March 28, 1999, for the first time in 40 years, Americans played a professional game in Cuba as the Orioles beat the Cuban team 3–2 in 11 innings.

In late January 2004 the USC Trojans baseball team traveled to Cuba for a three-game series.

Protest. On April 25, 2000, several Cuban Major Leaguers and coaches sat out their games to protest the handling of the situation involving Cuban refugee Elian Gonzalez in Florida. Gonzalez was the young boy who was taken from his relatives' home in Florida by U.S. immigration officials and reunited with his father in Cuba.

World War II. See *World War II— Cuban Players.*

Book. Jorge S. Figuerido, *Beisbol Cubano* (2004 Spanish); S. L. Price and Victor Baldizon (Photographer), *Pitching Around Fidel: A Journey into the Heart of Cuban Sports* (2002).

Candy Cummings (1848–1924)

Hall of Fame 1939

"This thing of examining scores of games in which the Cincinnati Reds play, and seeing from 18 to 25 hits each day being piled up against Cummings' record, is getting sickening. His presence on the team is demoralizing. Unless the evil is remedied, the club on its return will not attract 100 people to the games. No change could be for the worse."—1877 Cincinnati newspaper editorial as Cummings' National League career was ending.

Cummings played primarily in the 1871–1875 National Association and is credited with inventing the curveball.

Credited by early sources for bringing the *Curveball* to professional baseball, diminutive (5'9", 120 lbs.) William Arthur Cummings played for the Stars of Brooklyn team in the 1860s and then moved on to clubs in the National Association. His best season was 1875 when he won 35 games for Hartford for a total of 124 wins over four seasons.

Cummings pitched briefly in the National League for Hartford in 1876. He was still reasonably good with a 16–8 record and a 1.67 ERA with five shutouts. By 1877 his underhand pitching style was obsolete because pitchers were allowed to throw at higher angles. He was 5–14 for Cincinnati and never pitched again in the Major Leagues.

When Cummings retired he became president of the International League, the first formal minor league. Given the debate over the evolution of the curveball, the only thing historians can be sure Cummings invented was a railroad coupling device for which he was paid significant royalties. He was elected to the Hall of Fame solely on the strength of his claim to the curveball.

Curaçao

"It means a lot for a little island"— Braves outfielder and Curaçao native Andruw Jones, after his small island nation's (population 192,000) Little League team won the 2004 Little League World Series against a team from Thousand Oaks, California. Curaçao, off the coast of Venezuela, had sent a team to Williamsport in each of the previous four seasons before winning. Pitcher Carlos Pineda was the largest player in the tournament at 5'11" and 169 pounds. Jones collected on a bet with California native and teammate Robert Fick.

Curfews

"I'm rooming with a suitcase."— Yankee Ping Bodie alluding to his night owl roommate Babe Ruth. Bodie may have used the term "valise" in the original quote.

"The only thing he fears is sleep." — Manager Jimmy Dykes on pitcher Don Larsen after Larsen's pre-dawn spring training car accident.

"He slept from 'Last Call' to 'Play Ball!'." — *Sports Illustrated* on Andy Van Slyke's minor league escapades.

"What is harmful to a ball player is not liquor by itself, nor sex (licit or illicit) by itself, but the prolonged pursuit of either or both. It's the night spent pub-crawling, or woman-hunting, at the expense of some decent amount of rest, that really does the damage. That's why many managers have a curfew, formal or informal. The idea is not to force grown men to be teetotalers or to act like celibates; it is to get them to bed at a decent hour, whatever they did before." — Leonard Koppett in *A Thinking Man's Guide to Baseball* (1967).

"A guy who's basically a good, hard-nosed player, having a good year, if I catch him out at four a.m. with a broad, I'll tend to look the other way." — Jerry Coleman on why he got along so well with his players during his brief stint as a manager.

See also **Bed Checks**.

Babe Ruth. Future Yankee general manager Ed Barrow was the Red Sox manager in 1918 when Babe Ruth was still with the team. Ruth was such a problem with curfews that Barrow had to fine and suspend him. It had no effect on Ruth, but it only demoralized Ruth's teammates to have him out of the line-up. As a result, Barrow arranged for Ruth to report to him each morning the time he had gone to bed the night before — regardless of whether or not it violated curfew.

Clock Trick. Boots Poffenberger was notorious for breaking curfew. In 1939 while with the Dodgers under manager Leo Durocher, Poffenberger supposedly used the international clocks at the Bellevue Stratford Hotel to win a curfew argument with Durocher.

Autographs. Charlie Dressen, Dodger manager in the late 1940s and early 1950s, secretly directed a hotel clerk to have his ballplayers autograph a baseball as they came in for the night. It was his way of determining which players were in by curfew. Manager Jimmy Dykes is known to have made the same arrangement with an elevator operator.

Guilty Conscience. In 1968 Mets manager Gil Hodges recognized four of his players out after curfew. The next day he announced a $50 fine and told the team that he expected the four unnamed offenders to leave their checks in his desk and they would not be identified publicly. If the four checks were not there, he was going to double the fine and name names. He received seven checks.

Double Standard. Reds manager Sparky Anderson had a curfew for his younger players, but not for his stars.

Game Rules. The National League had no limit on how late a game may be played. In the American League, for many years no inning could begin after 1 a.m. Now, there are no set rules, and curfews would be governed by any local ordinances in effect. Rule 9.04 (Time Limits) provides that the umpires are instructed to inform the teams beforehand "if a time limit has been set." In Rule 4.12 (Suspension of games) there is a reference to terminating games because of "a curfew imposed by law."

Curses See *Superstitions*

Curtain Calls

"Though we thumped, wept, chanted 'We want Ted' for minutes after he hid in the dugout, he did not come back. Our noise for some seconds passed beyond excitement into a kind of immense open anguish, a wailing, a cry to be saved. But immortality is nontransferable. The papers said that the other players, and even the umpires on the field, begged him to come out and acknowledge us in some way, but he refused. Gods do not answer letters." — John Updike in "Hub Fans Bid Kid Adieu" (1960).

The first curtain calls by players (stepping out of the dugout for a bow) are said to be after either Dale Long's home run in his eighth consecutive game in 1956 or after Roger Maris' 60th and 61st home runs in 1961.

Curveballs

"Oh the joys and miseries it has caused." — Long-time coach-emeritus Hub Kittle.

"Don't tell me about the world. Not today. It's springtime and they're knocking baseball around fields where the grass is damp and green in the morning and the kids are trying to hit the curve ball." — Pete Hamill.

"Tommy Lasorda's curveball has as much hang time as a Ray Guy punt." — Rocky Bridges.

Discovery.

"How it originated has not been satisfactorily explained, there being conflicting claims in the amateur and professional ranks as to the credit of the discovery." — Jacob Morse in *Sphere and Ash* (1888), which devotes considerable space and expert discourse on the mechanics of the pitch.

"I said not a word, and saw many a batter at that game throw down his stick in disgust. Every time I was successful I could scarcely keep from dancing for pure joy. The secret was mine." — Hall of Famer Candy Cummings on an 1867 game in which he supposedly introduced the curveball to batters. He is credited by many with discovering the curveball in 1863 at age 14. Cummings claimed that he noticed how clam shells curved in flight as he tossed them on the beach.

This information was first gleaned from Cummings in an interview with him in *The Sporting News* on December 29, 1921, less than three years before he died. It was also reported in a story by Harold C. Burr that appeared in *The Sporting News* on November 19, 1942, based on research by Guy Smith of Danville, Illinois. Henry Chadwick, Harry Wright and Albert Spalding all said at least once that Cummings was the first. However, in 1898 Chadwick claimed that he saw a Rochester pitcher throw a curveball in the 1850s. Cummings probably was not the first to throw a curveball, but he could have thrown one of the first that many batters saw.

Other claimants to the first curveball were Fred McSweeney of the New York Mutuals in 1866 and Bobby Mathews in 1867 (who is credited by some with throwing the first **Spitball**). It has been reported that all of the top pitchers of the 1860s threw curveballs, which means that Cummings was among many to do so; and means that whoever spoke up to take credit for a "first" tended to receive credit regardless of the facts (something Cap Anson worked to perfection in the early 20th century).

Alphonse "Phoney" Martin also claimed to be the inventor of the curveball, but at age 87 in 1932 he dropped his claim in favor of Mathews. Other early users were Fred Goldsmith of New Haven and Edmund Davis and Joseph Mann of Princeton College in the 1860s.

In 1948 Frank W. Blair claimed that Ivy League players first used the curveball in 1874. In an article in the *Amherst Graduates Quarterly*, he claimed that Charles Hammond Avery used the curveball for Yale against Harvard in 1874, supposedly becoming the first to use the curveball in a "game of record."

Physics.

"Where: d equals displacement from a straight line; cl equals circulation of air generated by friction when the ball is spinning; P equals the density of the air (normal at .002378); V equals the speed of the ball; t equals the time for delivery; g equals the acceleration of gravity (32.2 feet per second to the second power); C equals the circumference of the ball (9 inches); and W equals the ball's weight (.3125 pounds); while the number 7,230 relates other values of pounds, inches, feet, seconds, etc., to arrive at an answer in feet." — The formula for the curveball, printed in a 1953 edition of *American Mercury* magazine in an article by Joseph F. Drury, Jr., entitled, "The Hell it Don't Curve." The mathematical formula: d = Cl P V2 t2 g C2 over 7230 W × feet.

The batter sees a greater break than actually occurs because the ball is coming toward him — an optical illusion that only the laws of physics could help explain.

Attempts to Prove Its Existence.

"I am not positive whether a ball curves or not, but if this pitch does not curve, it would be well to notify a lot of baseball players who were forced to quit the game they love because of this pitch and may now be reached at numerous gas stations, river docks, and mental institutions." — 1950s Phillies manager Eddie Sawyer.

Sportswriter Henry Chadwick covered what was claimed at the time to be the first of many demonstrations attempting to prove the existence of the curveball. On August 16, 1870, he attended a demonstration at Capitoline Park in Brooklyn by Fred Goldsmith of Connecticut. Goldsmith threw the ball around two poles set in the ground 20 feet apart over the 45-foot pitching distance then in use.

One source reported that Candy Cummings threw the first curveball in 1867 for the Brooklyn Excelsiors against Harvard and that the Harvard Physics Department showed up to dispute the existence of the pitch.

In the September 15, 1941, issue of *Life* magazine, there was an article with photographs purportedly confirming that the curveball is an optical illusion. Photographer Gjou Mili took high speed photos of right-handed Phillies pitcher Cy Blanton and Hall of Fame left-handed screwballer Carl Hubbell. The pictures supposedly demonstrated that the ball did not curve.

In July 1952 Ernest Lowery, a fervent Canadian opponent of the curveball, claimed that the curveball was a hoax and suggested bringing lawsuits against all writers who supported its existence.

In 1953 *Life* magazine tried again with photographer Mili. He photographed pitcher Ken Raffensberger's curves by painting the ball half black. The pitches were thrown at 43 mph, the speed of a very slow curveball. The photographs were accompanied by calculations provided by aeronautical engineer Joseph Bickwell of M.I.T. Once again an optical illusion was claimed.

In November 1982 *Science* magazine proved the curveball's existence. Pitchers Ray Miller and Scott McGregor threw for the Tulane Department of Engineering to help prove that the ball curved.

Best Curveball.

"He had terrific speed. He was a big, loose, lanky fellow who was almost as fast as Johnson. And his curve was even better than his speed. The Rube had the fastest and deepest curve I've ever seen." — Connie Mack on Rube Waddell.

Many claim that the modern pitcher with the best curveball was Bert Blyleven, who won 287 games over a 22-year career and is ninth all-time with 60 shutouts.

Curveball Hitters.

"I'll be home soon, ma. The pitchers are starting to curve me." — Rookie's spring training lament.

Only a few hitters have professed to hitting curveballs better than they hit fastballs; including Rogers Hornsby, Moose Skowron, Roy Sievers, Ducky Medwick and Al Simmons.

Practice. Pitcher Bob Muncrief of the 1940s Browns worked on his curveball on the road by pitching into a pillow in his hotel room (must have been a *long* room).

How To Throw. The first two fingers are placed against a seam and the pitcher snaps the wrist when throwing it. Scientists supposedly have determined that the optimum speed for throwing it is 68 mph, though most batters would probably rather face a 68 mph curve with a big break than Sandy Koufax's 90 mph curveball with a little less break.

Poetry. Jay Hook, a mediocre 1960s Mets pitcher, was an engineer who wrote an article on how curveballs curve. In response, a group of New York sportswriters penned a poem to the lyric of "I Could Write a Book," from the Broadway musical *Pal Joey*:

"If they asked me I could write a book,
About the way a baseball's spin makes it hook;
I know all the theories, the complex math,
That explains a curving ball's path.
I compute compression of the air,
Counting gravity as one-half times Gee Tee squared.
But with all I know of trajectory,
They keep hitting homers off me."

Book. Martin Quigley, *The Crooked Pitch* (1988).

Cut-Off Plays

"[Disco Dan] Ford needed to be back in Anaheim, where baseball illiterati play with a beach ball during the late innings of tied games. There, like Ford, they don't even know what a cutoff man *is*. And they don't care. They cheer one-handed catches, enjoy a smile after an error and think two runners trapped on one base is cute." — Thomas Boswell in *Why Time Begins on Opening Day* (1984).

The 1890s Dodgers are credited with developing the cut-off play, whereby an infielder cuts off throws from the outfield.

Until the 1850s many shortstops played like an extra outfielder and acted as a universal cut-off man.

In *Mitts* (1985), author William Curran claimed that the cut-off play was not used until 1922.

Kiki Cuyler (1899–1950)

Hall of Fame (VC) 1968

"Memory sketched a picture of a dark, vivid face with a big nose, of square shoulders that gave the effect of stockiness to a middle-sized figure that moved in a blur of speed across National League outfields and around the bases." — Red Smith.

Cuyler played 18 years in the National League from 1921 through 1938, batting .321 as an outfielder primarily for the Pirates and Cubs.

Hazen Shirley Cuyler attended West Point during World War I and was a football star before withdrawing from school. He began minor league play in Michigan and appeared in one game in both 1921 and 1922 for the Pirates. He finally stuck with the club in 1924, hitting .354 in 117 games. He had a .357 average and 26 triples in 1925 and helped the Pirates into the World Series.

After another season over .300 he was traded to the Cubs, for whom he led the league in stolen bases three straight seasons. He was still going strong in 1935 when he was traded to the Reds midseason. He batted .326 in 144 games in 1936 and dropped to .271

in 1937. He finished his 18-year career with the Dodgers in 1938. Cuyler had a .321 lifetime average with 157 triples and batted .281 in three World Series for the Pirates and Cubs.

Cuyler became a successful minor league manager and coached for the Cubs and Red Sox in the 1940s. He died suddenly in 1950 while ice fishing at age 50.

Cy Young Award (1956–)

"When Ford Frick was commissioner, he was disturbed by the back-of-my-hand-to-you-treatment [of pitchers] from the baseball writers in the annual polls for MVP. So Ford suggested a companion award for the outstanding pitcher."—*New York Times* columnist Arthur Daley.

"I didn't cheat when I won the twenty-five games in 1961. I don't want anybody to get any ideas and take my Cy Young Award away. And I didn't cheat in 1963 when I won twenty-four games. Well, maybe just a little."—Whitey Ford in his autobiography, *Slick*, with Phil Pepe (1987).

The Cy Young Award for pitching excellence was established in 1956 after commissioner Ford Frick pushed for its creation. Pitchers rarely earned the MVP Award and Frick wanted to see pitchers recognized separately. Young died in 1955 and the award was established in his name the following year.

Only one award for the entire Major Leagues was given until 1967, when one winner for each league was chosen. Because Frick had favored only one award, the two-award system was implemented two years after he retired.

Unanimous Choice. During the 1956–1966 single-award period, Sandy Koufax was the only unanimous winner, a feat he achieved each of the three times that he won the award: 1963, 1965 and 1966.

Tie. In 1969 Mike Cuellar and Denny McLain tied under a system that allowed only one vote per sportswriter. After that season, sportswriters were allowed to make first, second and third choices, which made ties almost impossible.

Consecutive. Greg Maddux of the Braves won a record fourth consecutive Cy Young Award in 1995.

Pedro Martinez won his second consecutive award in 2002, giving him three in four years.

In 2002 Randy Johnson won his fourth straight Cy Young Award (and fifth overall), a unanimous pick over teammate Curt Schilling. Johnson earned $4 million for winning the award; a $1 million bonus and a $3 million increase in his $12 million salary for 2003. It was his fifth award overall, two short of Roger Clemens' record of seven (Clemens won his last in 2004). Johnson matched Maddux with four straight starting in 1999 and he and Schilling became the first pitchers to finish one-two in the voting in consecutive years.

Both Leagues. Gaylord Perry won the Award in 1972 for Cleveland in the American League, and then again for the Padres in the National League in 1978. Randy Johnson duplicated the feat when he won the award for the Mariners in 1995 and then four straight for the National League Diamondbacks between 1999 and 2002. Roger Clemens left the Yankees after the 2003 season, skipped retirement, and won the National League Cy Young Award for the Astros in 2004.

Cycle

"In batting practice, I don't think I hit one ball hard. It was frustrating, that bat was no good."—Rockies outfielder Dante Bichette,

Steve Carlton's 1980 National League Cy Young Award.

who hit for the cycle after flinging into the stands the bat he was using for batting practice.

Protocol. "Hitting for the cycle" means that a player hits a home run, triple, double and single all in one game. Fewer players have hit for the cycle (since 1901, 212 times through July 2001—106 in the National League) than have pitched no-hitters.

Both Leagues. Bob Watson is the only player to hit for the cycle in both leagues, with the Astros and Red Sox. He did it on June 24, 1977 for the Houston Astros and on September 15, 1979 for the Boston Red Sox.

Most. Bob Meusel and Babe Herman hold the record for hitting for the cycle three times each.

In Order. Several players have done it in order (single, double, triple and then home run), including Bob Fothergill, the first, in 1926, and Tigers second baseman Charlie Gehringer, against the Indians on May 27, 1939.

The last was White Sox shortstop Jose Valentin, who did it on April 27, 2000, as the White Sox beat the Orioles 13–4. He hit a single, double and triple in the 1st, 2nd and 3rd innings, and then homered in the 7th.

Oldest. Dave Winfield became the oldest player to hit for the cycle when he did it for the Angels in 1991 at age 39.

World Series. No player has hit for the cycle in the World Series, but three have come close. On October 6, 1968, Lou Brock of the Cardinals hit a double, triple and home run against the Tigers. On October 12, 1979, Kiko Garcia of the Orioles collected two singles, one double and one triple against the Pirates. On October 17, 1990, Billy Hatcher of the Reds had a single, two doubles and one triple against the Oakland A's.

Stars. Lou Gehrig did it twice, but Babe Ruth came up empty. Ty Cobb, Henry Aaron and Willie Mays never did it, but the immortal Chris Speier did it twice.

Teammates. George Brett and Frank White of the Royals are believed to be the only teammates to each do it twice for the same team.

Pitcher. No pitcher has ever hit for the cycle in a game, and only 11 pitchers have done it over a season. The last was Catfish Hunter in 1971 for the A's. In the National League, Don Newcombe of the Dodgers did it in 1955.

Fewest Triples. John Olerud of the Mariners hit for the cycle twice in his career despite hitting only 12 triples in his first 13 seasons. The next fewest triples with two cycles was by Wally Westlake, who had 33.

Longest Drought. Travis Fryman of the Detroit Tigers hit for the cycle on July 28, 1993, the first time in 43 years that a Tiger had done it. When he broke the dry spell, it left the Philadelphia Phillies with the longest drought. Johnny Callison of the Phillies did it on June 27, 1963.

Inning. On May 20, 1998, the Class AAA Indianapolis Indians hit for the "homer cycle" in the same inning, the 5th, against Pawtucket. Pete Rose, Jr., hit a solo home run to start the inning, Jason Williams then hit a three-run shot, Glenn Murray hit a grand slam, and Guillermo Garcia hit a two-run homer to finish the inning's scoring. The Indians won 11–4.

Putting on the Brakes. On August 17, 2001, Jeff Frye of the Blue Jays hit for the cycle in an 11–3 victory over Texas. His last hit, in the 9th inning, was a line drive to deep right-center that would have easily gone for a double. Instead, with Toronto up by several runs, Frye stopped at first base for the cycle.

Reward. The traditional post-game reward for hitting for the cycle is to find a bicycle at the player's locker.

"**D** is for Dean.
The grammatical Diz,
When they asked, Who's the tops?
Said correctly, I is."
—Ogden Nash on Dizzy Dean.

Ray Dandridge (1913–1994)

Hall of Fame (VC) 1987
"That was the greatest ball player ever put on a uniform! There's nothing he couldn't do. Oh, that was the most beautiful player I've ever seen! I'll say that the rest of my life. Ray Dandridge was a hell of a ball player — excuse the expression."—Negro League pitching star Dave Barnhill.

Dandridge was a Negro and Mexican League star at third base in the 1930s and 1940s before a brief minor league career in Organized Baseball.

Raymond Emmett Dandridge, Sr., is considered the premier third baseman in Negro League history, with a better arm than Brooks Robinson of the Orioles and his equal in fielding ability (and a much better hitter). He was born in Richmond, Virginia, about two blocks from famed singer Bill "Bojangles" Robinson. Dandridge spent most of his teenage years in Buffalo.

The bowlegged infielder starred in the Negro Leagues from 1933 through 1944 and then left for the Mexican League for nine seasons. He batted .343 in the Mexican League and then returned to the States with the New York Cubans. Earlier statistics credit him with a .355 Negro National League average, but the most recently confirmed (though spotty) statistics credit him with a .322 average. He batted .545 in 10 Negro League All-Star Games.

Dandridge had a chance to play in the Major Leagues after Jackie Robinson signed with the Dodgers, but apparently he refused to leave the Mexican League without a bonus from Indians owner Bill Veeck. He played in the minor leagues in 1950 in Minneapolis, winning the MVP award his first season. He helped Willie Mays when Mays played briefly in Minneapolis before Mays moved on to the Giants. Dandridge batted .318 in five seasons in the white minor leagues late in his career.

Dandridge thought he had been forgotten by baseball, but in 1987 he received the call that he had been inducted into the Hall of Fame. In an informal vote of Negro League stars who gathered in 1982, Dandridge and Judy Johnson were voted the all-time best players.

Book. James A. Riley, *Dandy, Day and the Devil* (1987).

Darkness

"The game, scheduled as a double-header for Saturday only, was suspended at dusk on July 5, with the score still tied after eighty-five innings of play. A truly superhuman effort was extended by both teams. The starting pitchers, Three Finger Brown for the Cubs and Arsenic O'Reilly for the Confederacy, were still flinging the ball when darkness forced suspension of the contest."—W. P. Kinsella in *The Iowa Baseball Confederacy* (1986), the story of a game between members of the amateur (and mythical) Iowa Baseball Confederacy and the Cubs that lasted more than 2,000 innings.

See also **Longest Games, Postponed Games** and **Tie Games.**

During Game 1 of the 1922 World Series, Judge Landis inexplicably ended a 3–3 tie because of darkness, even though it was only 4:40 p.m. and not dark. A near riot ensued and Landis decided that the proceeds from the game, $120,554, would be given to charity in order to placate the fans and dispel the complaint that the commissioner was trying to extend the Series to increase gate receipts. The money was given to a World War I disabled veterans fund.

Nineteenth century pitcher John Clarkson supposedly once threw a lemon to the plate as dusk set in. When umpire Jack Kerin called it a strike, catcher Wilbert Robinson showed the lemon to him as proof that it was too dark to play. The game was called immediately. This is a good anecdote, but according to *The Baseball Encyclopedia*, the two never played together on a Major League team (perhaps in an exhibition game or in the minor leagues?).

Dauvray Cup (1887–1889)

"Whenever he [Monte Ward] made a brilliant play, her plump little palms would patter with ecstacy, and she became so enthusiastic at a time when New York was still in the race for the pennant that she offered a $500 silver trophy for the winning club."—Commentary on Helen Dauvray's donation of a championship cup in her name.

In 1887 the Dauvrey Cup was first presented to the winner of the **Championship Series** between the National League and American Association. It was named for Helen Dauvray, New York actress and wife of shortstop John Montgomery Ward. She had grown up in California and Nevada, pursued a successful child stage career in San Francisco and New York, and then as an adult in Europe before settling in New York in 1885 to further her career there. In 1886, when the Giants were experiencing success, it became fashionable for the New York stage actors to appear at the Polo Grounds.

The cup was awarded only through the 1889 season, when the Giants won it for a second time. It had been decided that the team that first won three championship series would get to keep the cup permanently. It never happened and the cup has been lost.

It was widely publicized that this was Dauvray's second marriage after a divorce. She and Ward married in 1887 but lived together for only one year. They were legally divorced in 1893, though some authoritative sources report the divorce year as 1890 and even 1903; rather, they signed a separation agreement in 1890 and Dauvray moved to Europe. Ward went to England to reconcile after the failure of the Players League, and she agreed to return. They separated again and then divorced. She remarried (her third; she was married briefly before Ward) a Naval officer and lived in Washington, D.C. until her death in 1923.

George Davis (1870–1940)

Hall of Fame (VC) 1998

"Never mind, Matty, it was worth it. This game ought to teach you not to pitch your head off when you don't need to."—Davis' sage advice to rookie Christy Mathewson, quoted in Mathewson's *Pitching In a Pinch* (1912), after the pitcher went too hard early in the game and gave up four in the 9th inning to lose. Mathewson added, "It did. I have never forgotten that lesson." With today's reliever corps, he wouldn't have to learn it in the first place.

Davis was a switch hitter whose 20-year career, spent mostly at shortstop, spanned from the 1890's in the National League to dead-ball era play in the fledgling American League.

Overshadowed perhaps by contemporaries like Nap Lajoie and Honus Wagner, George Stacey Davis nevertheless was one of the finest players of a generation of baseball supermen. He began his Major League career as a 19-year-old outfielder with the Cleveland Spiders of the National League. In 1890 he hit .264 with 73 RBIs in his rookie season for the second division Spiders.

In 1891 Davis raised his batting average to .289 with 35 doubles, second in the league and finished fourth in both hits and total bases. He also made his only three pitching appearances in the Major Leagues, compiling an 0–1 record while surrendering eight hits and eight runs in four innings pitched. His performance slipped overall in 1892 and he was traded to the Giants for Buck Ewing.

At third base for the Giants in 1893, he hit .355 with 119 RBI and 27 triples (seventh best season total ever). He also put together a 33-game hitting streak, the Giants club record. Although the Giants were a second division club the remainder of his career with them, Davis was superb. From 1893 to 1901 he hit over .300 in nine consecutive seasons, including three years in which he hit over .350. Davis also had three 100+ RBI seasons, leading the league with 136 in 1897. He moved full time to shortstop in 1897 and led the league in fielding in 1899 and 1900.

Davis also dabbled in managing with somewhat less success. He managed the Giants in parts of both 1895 and 1900. He took the helm full-time in 1901, guiding the club to a 7th place finish. For his career Davis' managerial record was 107–139 for a .435 winning percentage.

Davis jumped to the American League and the Chicago White Sox in 1902, hitting .299 and leading the league's shortstops in fielding. He attempted to return to the Giants in 1903 and in the ensuing squabble sat out nearly the entire season. Davis returned to the White Sox in 1904 to begin a six year stretch with the club. He continued to excel at shortstop, leading the league in fielding in 1905. Although Davis' offense declined in these years, he was still productive in a defensive era, topping 100 runs scored four straight years from 1904–1907. In 1906 the White Sox won the pennant with Davis hitting .277 with 80 RBIs. In the all-Chicago World Series Davis only appeared in three games because of injury, but managed three doubles among his four hits, and six RBIs in his only career appearance in the postseason.

Davis retired after the 1909 season. He finished his career with a .295 batting average, 2,665 hits, 1,439 RBIs and 1,545 runs scored. He passed away in Philadelphia in 1940.

Leon Day (1916–1995)

Hall of Fame (VC) 1995

"People don't know what a great pitcher Leon Day was. He was as good or better than Bob Gibson. He was a better fielder, a better hitter, could run like a deer. And just as good a pitcher. When he pitched against Satchel, Satchel didn't have an edge. You thought Don Newcombe could pitch. You should have seen Day! One of the most complete athletes I've ever seen."— Monte Irvin quoted in *Blackball Stars*, by John B. Holway (1988).

Day was a Negro League star primarily as a pitcher and outfielder between 1934 and 1950 before playing briefly in Organized Baseball.

Leon Day grew up in Baltimore and his first semipro club was the Silver Spoons. He began his Negro League career as a pitcher in 1934 with Baltimore of the Negro National League. In 1935 at age 19 he moved to the Brooklyn Eagles for a season before the club and Day settled in Newark. Day remained there through 1946, with a two-year interruption while he served in the military and one year playing for Vera Cruz in Mexico in 1940.

Throughout most of his career he played winter ball in the Caribbean, usually pitching and filling in for injured fielders. He was known as one of the most complete ballplayers of all time, though he was only 5'7" and 140 pounds. He hit well over .300 in most seasons in addition to having a strong no-wind-up pitching repertoire. In 1942 he struck out 18 for the Negro League record and pitched a no-hitter in his first game back from the war in 1946. He played in Mexico in 1947 and 1948 after hurting his arm and then returned to Baltimore for the 1949 season.

Day played in the International League for Toronto in 1951 and had an ERA of 1.58. He posted a 13–9 record in the Red Sox chain in 1952 and then began to barnstorm, though he played one more season with Edmonton. His arm had been gone for some time and he retired to his hometown of Baltimore. He died in March 1995, only one week after learning that he had been voted into the Hall of Fame.

"Days"

"Some teams have Bat Day and Cap Day. 'Round the Ides of September, the Orioles had Divine Intervention Week."—Thomas Boswell in *Why Time Begins on Opening Day* (1984), on the 1982 Orioles and their September comeback against the Yankees.

"I didn't get a lot of awards as a player. But they did have a Bob Uecker Day Off for me once in Philly."—Bob Uecker.

See also *Field Days* and *Promotions*.

Tiger pitcher Joe Sparma interrupted Mickey Mantle Day in 1965 when he shook Mantle's hand as he came up to bat. Sparma then induced him to pop out.

In 2004 Major League Baseball decided to designate every April 15 as Jackie Robinson Day. In 2004 balls with the number 42 on them were used and Jackie Robinson scholars threw out the first pitch.

Dead Ball Eras See *Ball*—Dead Ball Eras

Deaf Ballplayers

"Curiously enough, a rare exception to this rule [aloofness by ballplayers] is Luther [Dummy] Taylor, of the New York Nationals, who is deaf and dumb. Wherever Taylor goes he will always be visited by scores of the silent fraternity among whom he is regarded as a prodigy. Taylor has a genial, humorous spirit that covets companionship…. Taylor's friends are different from the general run of baseball enthusiasts. The deaf mutes have not only a genuine admiration, but sympathy for, and adherence to, their champion, while, so far as I have observed, every other kind of a 'fan' is fickle."—Allen Sangree in a 1905 article in the *Saturday Evening Post*.

Dummy Taylor. Though almost totally deaf, Taylor won 21 games for the 1904 Giants and 112 games in nine years. Giants manager John McGraw supposedly instituted coaching signs at third base to aid Taylor. McGraw also reportedly required his players to learn American Sign Language to communicate with Taylor and they began using it to talk to each other on the field.

Dummy Hoy. Hoy was probably the best-known deaf (and mute) ballplayer. He was only 5'4" and 148 pounds, which was probably more of a handicap than his deafness. Because of these factors he did not get his shot in the Major Leagues until 1888 when he was 26. In 14 Major League seasons he had over 2,000 hits and a lifetime average of .288.

Hoy is credited with inspiring umpires to use hand signals. Lack of electronic scoreboards and public address systems more likely contributed to their use for the benefit of the fans. Hoy purportedly was once thrown out of a game for insulting umpire Hank O'Day in sign language. It is unclear how O'Day knew what was being said, unless Hoy used some sort of "universal" sign language.

At age 99 Hoy threw out the first ball for Game 3 of the 1961 World Series in Cincinnati. One source credited him with being over 100 years old when he died, but he missed by five months when he passed away in December 1961.

Dick Sipek. When he was five years old in 1928, Sipek fell down a flight of stairs and suffered head injuries that left him almost totally deaf. He attended an Illinois school for the deaf, where one of the housefathers was deaf former Major Leaguer Dummy Taylor.

Sipek hit .336 in 1943 and .319 in 1944 for the Southern Association Memphis club (teaming with one-armed Pete Gray in 1943). He played 82 games in 1945 for the Reds, primarily pinch-hitting his way to a .244 average.

Pete Browning. Nicknamed the ***Louisville Slugger***, Browning was virtually deaf as a result of mastoiditis. He was also an illiterate alcoholic.

Frank Chance. The first baseman suffered so many beanballs that he was deaf in one ear.

Curtis Pride. In 1993 Pride made his debut in the Major Leagues for the Expos. He doubled in his first Major League at-bat during the late-season pennant race. Pride was 95% deaf but attended regular schools through high school and college at William & Mary. He also played point guard for the school's basketball team and had been a world-ranked soccer player as a teenager.

He signed with the Mets in 1986 and spent a number of years in the minor leagues before the Expos picked him up. He bounced up and down with various Major League clubs through 2004. His best season was 1996, when he hit 10 home runs for the Tigers.

Scout. Roy Largent was a scout for the White Sox from 1924 through 1939. He traveled with his wife, who would interpret for him because he was totally deaf.

Dizzy Dean (1911–1974)

Hall of Fame 1953

"I want to thank the Lord for givin' me a good right arm, a strong back and a weak mind."—Part of Dean's Hall of Fame induction speech.

"I'm a man of some intelligence. I've had some education, passed the bar, practiced law. I've been a teacher, and I deal with men of substance, statesmen, business leaders, the clergy. Then why, *why* do I spend my time arguing with Dizzy Dean."—Branch Rickey.

Dean starred for the Cardinals from 1932 through 1937, but a broken toe and resulting sore arm slowed his career and he moved into broadcasting in the 1940s.

Despite numerous stories to the contrary by him, Jay Hannah Dean was born in Lucas, Arkansas, in 1911. He signed in 1930 with the Cardinals and spent the season in the Western League, where he was 17–8 with St. Joseph. He moved up to Houston in the Texas League late in the season, where he was 8–2. He pitched and won a game for the Cardinals on the last day of the season. Though he was probably ready for the Major Leagues in 1931, he stayed in Houston, winning 26 games with a 1.57 ERA.

He was an immediate success in 1932 for the Cardinals, posting an 18–15 record and leading the league in strikeouts and shutouts. He increased his total to 20 wins in 1933 before exploding for 30 wins in 1934 and 28 wins in 1935. He was the strikeout leader in each of those seasons. He was the star of the National League at that point, winning another 24 games in 1936.

At the 1937 All-Star Game he was hit on the toe by a line drive from Earl Averill. He changed his pitching motion to accommodate the bad toe and it caused bursitis in his shoulder.

Traded to the Cubs at the start of the 1938 season, he won seven games in 13 appearances (10 starts), but his arm was gone. He made only 30 more appearances until he retired in 1941 at age 30.

He immediately moved into the broadcast booth, but took the mound once for the Browns in 1947, shutting out the White Sox for four innings in the last game of the season. He became a hugely popular ***Broadcaster*** in the 1950s, moving to national prominence with the "Game of the Week" (see also ***Television***).

Dean was 150–83 in 230 starts and 317 total appearances, with 26 shutouts and 30 saves. He was also a decent hitter, with a .225 lifetime average and eight home runs. Despite having only five stellar seasons over his 12-year career, Dean was easily elected to the Hall of Fame in 1953.

Books. Robert Gregory, *Diz* (1992); Curt Smith, *America's Dizzy Dean* (1978); Vince Staten, *Ol' Diz* (1988).

Deaths

"Andre Dawson has a bruised knee and is listed as day-to-day [pause]. Aren't we all?"—Vin Scully.

"He can be lethal death."—Jerry Coleman.

"He's dead at the present time."—Casey Stengel on the status of a colleague.

"Most people my age are dead—you could look it up."—Stengel.

"How did the Mets do today?"—Supposedly Moe Berg's last words, spoken to the nurse attending to him.

"Baseball is a game dominated by vital ghosts; it's a fraternity, like no other we have of the active and the no longer so, the living and the dead."—Richard Gilman.

"The season during which Clarence Van Puyster pitched for the Giants is destined to live long in the memory of followers of baseball. Probably never in the history of the game has there been such persistent and widespread mortality among the more distant relatives of office-boys and junior clerks. Statisticians have estimated that if all the grandmothers alone who perished between the months of April and October that year could have been placed end to end they would have reached considerably further than Minneapolis."— "The Pitcher and the Plutocrat," by P.G. Wodehouse (1924) (also known as "The Goalkeeper and the Plutocrat").

"If anybody talks about a dead guy during a broadcast, I'll sack 'em. I'm sick of dead guys. Whenever I turn on baseball, all I hear about is dead guys. If I hear a name, I'm going to ask: 'Is he dead?' And if he is, you're fired."— David Hill, president of Fox Sports Television, in 1996.

"He had a drinking problem, got into barroom brawls, and three decades after leaving baseball was sent to a state prison in California for growing marijuana."— Touching 2001 obituary in the *New York Times* for two-time American League batting champion Ferris Fain.

"Boy, I hope I never see my name up there."— Yogi Berra, on a list of deceased Yankee greats that appeared on the scoreboard at an Oldtimers' Day.

See also ***Burial and Cemeteries, Injuries and Illness, Murder, Umpires—*Deaths** and various wars.

Premature Notice. On January 24, 1999, NBC ran a "crawl" across the bottom of television screens announcing the death of Joe DiMaggio. DiMaggio didn't die until March that year and reportedly saw the crawl on television.

On Field Incidents.

"With nearly a quarter of a million balls being pitched during a big league season alone, helmets or no, the miracle remains that there are not more killings, especially with night baseball in such vogue."— Grantland Rice in 1954.

"Whitper passed third and eased up a bit. As he neared home, he turned his head and yelled some epithet at the uncomfortable Higgins. He faced front and clutched at his side. His stride broke, he began to wobble. There was an expression of horrified amazement on his face as he staggered, stumbled and fell sideways, face forward about eight feet short of the plate. He lay still, a crumpled mass."— From *Death on the Diamond*, by Cortland Fitzsimmons (1934), regarded as the first baseball mystery.

Ray Chapman. The Indians shortstop is the only Major League player killed as a direct result of an on-field incident. He was hit in the head on a gloomy and rainy Monday, August 16, 1920, on a pitch by submarine and sidearm pitcher Carl Mays of the Yankees (who won 26 games that season). Chapman died the next day.

Chapman was known to crowd the plate and the drag bunt was one of his favorite plays, leaning far over the plate to do it. Mays saw Chapman shift his back foot into a bunting position, so Mays threw high and tight to make it more difficult to bunt. The fastball hit Chapman and bounced all the way back to Mays on the pitching mound. Mays thought the ball had hit Chapman's bat and he threw it to first base. Other accounts report that the ball was fielded by third baseman Aaron Ward or catcher Muddy Ruel. Ruel thought the ball would have been a strike, which is possible considering how much Chapman crowded the plate. Harry Lunte came in to run for Chapman. The Indians won the game 4–3 after leading 3–0 when Chapman was beaned.

After he was hit, Chapman got up briefly and walked around before collapsing, bleeding from both ears. According to Grantland Rice and others, Chapman supposedly regained consciousness in the clubhouse long enough to say, "Tell Mays not to worry." His skull was crushed and he died at 5 a.m. the next morning. A wreath was placed on his grave, which included a blanket of 20,000 flowers purchased for 10 cents each by fans. Two days after the funeral Mays pitched and won, despite public opinion that he should wait and despite an attempt by Cleveland fans to force a boycott of the game.

One source reported that Mays was very cavalier about the death; he said he was not nervous about pitching again and that the incident had merely given him a "headache." Another reported that he was quoted as having "deep regret." Chapman's teammates did not believe that Mays was trying to hit him. Mays was not well-liked, however, and had a reputation as a headhunter. One catcher claimed that Mays had a sign for the beanball. The Chapman ball was Mays' 55th hit-by-pitch in six Major League seasons.

After the Indians won the 1920 World Series, the Cleveland players voted Chapman's widow a $1,000 share. The 29-year-old Chapman had spoken before the 1920 season about retiring after the season to concentrate on business with his new father-in-law, the president of a gas company.

Fred Lieb's *Baseball as I Have Known It* (1977) contains a detailed account of this incident; see also Mike Sowell, *The Pitch That Killed* (1989).

Jim Creighton. This early pitcher is considered by many to be the first professional player. He died after suffering an internal injury while batting for the Brooklyn Excelsiors in 1862. Depending on the source, he either ruptured his spleen, suffered an "internal injury occasioned by strain while batting," or ruptured his bladder. Some sources report that he thought he had snapped his belt. Others report that he was circling the bases on a home run when he sustained the injury and fainted on home plate. He died at his home four days later. On his tombstone are engraved crossed bats, scorebook, base and cap, with a baseball engraved on the headstone.

Semipro Game. It has often been reported that in a 20th-century semipro game a runner rounding third base died of heart failure. The runner behind him did not realize he had died and picked him up and crossed the plate.

Chief Bender's Brother. Pitcher Chief Bender's brother died on the mound while pitching in the minor leagues on September 25, 1911.

Disaster Plan. See ***Airline Travel—*Disaster Plan.**

Accidents During the Season.

Thurman Munson.

"Ah, hell, Lou, there's no need to worry."— Munson to teammate Lou Piniella shortly before he was killed in a plane crash on August 2, 1979.

"I could see myself racing across the tarmac of that airport near Canton, Ohio, tearing open the door of the plane and dragging Thurman Munson's body to safety, gripping him under the arms like a two-hundred-and-twenty-five-pound sack of flour and backing away from the flaming wreckage. Later, when I was interviewed by television and newspaper reporters, I would speak modestly of my accomplishment, displaying my bandaged hands. I would be known as The Man Who Rescued Thurman Munson."— W.P. Kinsella in "The Night Manny Mota Tied the Record" (1984).

Munson was killed while practicing take-offs and landings in his private plane at a short runway in Canton, Ohio. He was the first Yankee team captain since Lou Gehrig and the only Yankee ever to win both the Rookie of the Year Award and the MVP Award. When Munson died, a song was published in his honor called "Playing Catch with the Babe." Consideration was given to voting him into the Hall of Fame immediately in the same manner as Roberto Clemente, but the Hall's nominating committee rejected the idea and Munson has never been elected. See also Bill Libby, *Thurman*

Munson, Pressure Player (1978); Thurman Munson and Martin Appell, *Thurman Munson* (1978).

Ed Delahanty. On July 2, 1903, the Washington star was returning with the club by train from Detroit through upstate New York. Stories vary as to what happened next. What is known is that he was drinking heavily and disrupting the club car. The train stopped on a bridge as it neared Niagara Falls. He had an argument with a guard and either was put off the train or voluntarily got off.

One source reported that Delahanty had been drinking heavily "to forget a bad winter at a New Orleans racetrack." Another source reported that he had been suspended by manager Tom Loftus. Still another reported that Delahanty wrote his wife saying that he was coming home to Buffalo from Detroit and asked her to meet the train, the Michigan Central Express. Just before crossing the falls at the International Bridge at Fort Erie, Ontario, he left the train. He apparently tried to run up the track and reboard the train, but the drawbridge was open and he fell in and was carried to Niagara Falls. His left arm was mangled, and one newspaper article presumed that he was caught in the propeller of the "Maid of the Mist" tourist boat. In another reporter's embellished story, his body supposedly was found a week later by honeymooners.

Delahanty jumped to so many clubs during his career that he was known as "The Human Grasshopper." Though he was playing for the Senators at the time of his death, he had purportedly accepted a $4,500 advance to play for the New York Giants.

In his book, *July 2, 1903* (1992), Mike Sowell attempted to piece together the events surrounding Delahanty's death. Sowell may be fixated by morbid events, as that book followed *The Pitch That Killed* (1989), a chronicle of Ray Chapman's death. See also Jerrold I. Casway, *Ed Delahanty in the Emerald Age of Baseball* (2004).

Lucky Lohrke. See *Luck* for the story of Lohrke and his not-so-fortunate minor league teammates.

Duluth. On July 24, 1948, four players and the manager of the Duluth, Minnesota, team of the Northern League were killed when their bus collided with a truck near St. Paul. The truck driver also was killed.

Tom Gastall. The Orioles catcher was killed in a plane crash on September 20, 1956. The plane he was piloting crashed into Chesapeake Bay.

Steve Olin and Tim Crews. On Monday, March 23, 1993, during spring training in Florida, Indians pitcher Tim Crews was showing off his new lakefront home near the club's spring training site in Winter Haven. On the club's one off-day that spring, he went fishing on Little Lake Nellie with teammates Steve Olin and Bob Ojeda. On the way back in Crews' bass fishing boat in the dark at about 7:35 p.m., they rammed a dock while traveling at about 35 mph. Olin was killed instantly and Crews died a few hours later of massive head injuries. Ojeda suffered severe head lacerations but made a full recovery, at least physically (his depression was understandable). It was later discovered that Crews was legally drunk, having taken at least a case of beer and screwdriver drink makings on the boat.

The Indians had moved their spring training operation from Arizona to Florida for that season. However, its planned operation at Homestead, Florida, had to be moved to Winter Haven because Hurricane Andrew wiped out the facility.

The club wore a patch in honor of both Olin (No. 31) and Crews (No. 52). The Dodgers wore a patch in honor of Crews, who had been a popular player with the club through the 1992 season. The wives of Olin and Crews were presented with their uniforms at the club's first game that season, a 9–1 loss to the Yankees in front of the second largest opening day crowd in American League his-

tory. With wife Patti Olin's approval, team members wore pieces of Olin's clothing.

Ojeda returned to the mound for the Indians on August 7, 1993, pitching two innings in Baltimore and giving up two runs on four hits. He made his first start on August 16, giving up three runs in the 1st inning to the Blue Jays, but holding them scoreless for the balance of the five innings he pitched. His comment: "It was hard coming through that [bullpen] gate and onto the field. But I did it. Hopefully it will get easier. I'm glad that part's over. That was for the guys, my dead buds."

Mike Sharperson. In 1996 the former Dodger utilityman was playing for the Las Vegas minor league affiliate of the Padres. On May 26, 1996, he was en route from Las Vegas to join the Padres in Montreal when he was killed in a single-car crash. He missed a turn-off and tried to swerve onto a freeway ramp. His car turned over and he was ejected from the sunroof (no seatbelt).

Ken Robinson. On February 28, 1999, the minor league and former Major League pitcher was killed in a car accident in Arizona. His teammate, John Rosengren, was charged with second-degree murder in the alcohol-related death.

Brian Cole. In March 2001 the Mets' top prospect, age 22, was killed when he was hit head-on by another car and his car flipped over while driving home to Mississippi from spring training. He had been voted the New York organization's player of the year in 2000.

Gerik Baxter. The San Diego minor league pitcher died on July 29, 2001, at age 21. A tire blew on his pickup truck, causing the vehicle to swerve into another car and roll several times.

Mike Darr. On February 15, 2002, the Padres outfielder was killed in an early morning accident when his car rolled over in Phoenix near the club's spring training site. Teammate Ben Howard was in the car and survived. He was sitting in the back seat and was wearing a seatbelt. Darr was legally drunk at the time of the crash, just hours before the start of spring training.

Darr's father, also Mike, had one start for the Blue Jays on September 6, 1977, but lasted only 1⅓ innings (giving up a grand slam to Carlton Fisk), in his only Major League appearance.

In-Season Deaths Due to Illness.

Hal Carlson. See *Injuries and Illness*—**Stomach** for Carlson's in-season death.

Darryl Kile.

"I think that one of the coolest things my dad and I had was, we were friends. He was always showing me different things and I'd ask him questions, and if he didn't know the answer we'd go work it out together, we'd go look it up. That meant a lot to me. So hopefully as my children grow up, I'll be able to help them learn things more than tell them what to do."—Darryl Kile on June 11, 2002, 11 days before he died.

On June 22, 2002, the Cardinals pitcher was found dead in his hotel room prior to the Saturday game against the Cubs. His room was locked from the inside and it was believed that he died in his sleep from a heart irregularity. The game was postponed.

Phoenix radio disc jockey Beau Duran made an on-air prank call to Kile's widow in her hotel room during a postseason game between the Cardinals and Diamondbacks. He told her she "looked hot" and asked if she had a date for the game that night. Duran was fired and the station said, a few days later, that the prank "was not intended to be hurtful or malicious in any way."

Steve Bechler. The Orioles pitcher died at age 23 the day after collapsing during spring training in Fort Lauderdale on February 16, 2003. His body temperature rose to 108 degrees and a bottle of xenadrine RFA-1 was found in his locker. Toxicology tests confirmed "significant amounts" of the over-the-counter muscle-building supplement containing ephedra led to his heatstroke. The ephedra acted as a diuretic, causing fluid loss that contributed to the high temperature. The Major Leagues quickly banned the substance.

In July 2003, Bechler's widow, Kiley, sued the manufacturer for $600 million. Nutraquest, Inc., formerly known as Cytodyne Technologies, Inc., the manufacturer, asked a court for permission to sue the Orioles, claiming the team was responsible for Bechler's death.

Randy Burden. The Angels minor leaguer died on December 6, 2002, at age 23, suffering heart failure while sleeping.

John Leroy. The minor league pitcher died June 25, 2001, at age 26, of an aneurysm.

Doug Million. The Colorado minor league pitcher died September 24, 1997, at age 21. He suffered a severe asthma attack in Arizona during the fall Instructional League.

Randy Donisthorpe. The Cincinnati minor league pitcher died March 20, 1997, at age 23, after suffering a seizure while sleeping.

Off-Season Deaths of Active Players.

"George [Brett] is getting to be such a monster that I'd hate to die in a car wreck with the guy. You'd be listed as: Others Killed."—Clint Hurdle in 1981.

Thomas J. O'Brien. In late 1900 some of the Dodgers and Giants players left for Cuba to play a series of exhibition games. Thomas J. O'Brien, who had played for the Pirates that year, but had been with the Giants the year before, was asked to participate. He was told that if he drank a large amount of sea water on the voyage he would be seasick for a brief period and then would be fine. He overindulged, along with Kid Gleason, and became extremely ill. Gleason recovered, but O'Brien's internal organs were affected and he was unable to play. He returned to the States and went to Arizona to regain his health, but became worse and died on February 4, 1901, two weeks before his 29th birthday.

Marvin Goodwin. The Reds pitcher was killed when the plane he was piloting crashed on October 18, 1925. He was one of the spitball pitchers allowed to continue using the pitch after it was banned in 1920.

Tony Boeckel. In 1923 the Boston Braves third baseman finished his seventh season with a .298 average. He was killed the following February 15 after a collision with a truck.

Walt Lerian. The starting catcher for the 1929 Phillies died on October 22, 1929, when hit by a car that veered onto the sidewalk.

Alvin Montgomery. On April 26, 1942, the Braves catcher was killed in a car accident in West Virginia. He was on his way from spring training to open the season in the minor leagues after playing 42 games for the Braves in 1941.

Ken Hubbs. The Cubs second baseman was killed in a plane crash on February 15, 1964. Hubbs was Rookie of the Year in 1962 and went a then-record 78 games at second base (1962–1963) without an error. The Cubs inaugurated the Ken Hubbs Memorial Award following his death.

Charlie Peete. The Cardinals rookie outfielder was in Venezuela playing winter baseball when he was killed on November 27, 1956.

Roberto Clemente.

"Every time I get on an airplane, I think of Roberto Clemente. At takeoff, feminists may seek the vanished spirit of Amelia Earhart, soul singers may reach for the final crescendo of the Big Bopper. For a ball fan, the great Pittsburgh Pirate right fielder serves as the friendly skies' emblematic fatality."—John Krich in *El Beisbol* (1989).

The most prominent off-season death of an active player was that of Hall of Famer Roberto Clemente, who died in a plane crash

on New Year's Eve 1972. He was aboard a DC-7 four-engine prop jet taking off from his native Puerto Rico carrying relief supplies for earthquake victims in Nicaragua. The overloaded plane had trouble on take-off and tried to return to the airport, but the engines failed and the plane crashed into the ocean. One source erroneously reported that the plane crashed into a fence when the brakes failed. Fellow Puerto Rican Vic Power claimed that the pilot was drunk and that the plane's engine would not start on the first three tries.

Witnesses say they saw fire on the left side of the plane as it took off. When it tried to return to the airport, it dropped into the ocean over a mile offshore. What was not known until later was that the co-pilot and owner, Arthur Rivera, had his license suspended for 180 days earlier in the year and had once slammed the same plane into a concrete wall while taxiing. The flight engineer was an unqualified mechanic and the cargo was over the weight limit by two tons.

Clemente had been in Nicaragua two weeks earlier with the Puerto Rican National Team. At least one source reported that he made the fatal trip to see a girlfriend.

Chico Ruiz. The Reds and Angels infielder was killed in a car accident on February 9, 1972. In the mid–1970s the Braves had a rookie second baseman also named Chico Ruiz. During a televised game, Howard Cosell began talking about how the Braves had a knack of resurrecting old ballplayers, referring mistakenly to the Ruiz who had been killed.

Bob Moose. The Pirates pitcher was killed in a car accident on October 9, 1976.

Danny Frisella. On New Year's Day 1977, the Brewers pitcher was killed in a dune buggy accident.

Mike Miley. The Angels shortstop was killed in a car accident on January 6, 1977.

Scout. Recently retired Dodger scout John Corriden sat down in his living room to watch his minor league protege, Larry Sherry, pitch during the 1959 play-off between the Dodgers and Braves. Sherry won 3–2 in relief, while Corriden died of a heart attack on his couch during the game.

Ted Williams.

"Ted Williams got the living part right. He was a war hero, an ace fisherman, the greatest hitter who ever lived. Then he went and died. Big mistake."—Mark Bradley of the *Atlanta Journal-Constitution* on the fiasco surrounding Williams' cryogenic preservation following his death.

"Sooner AND Later"—Letter signed by Dr. Jerry Lemler, known as "Dr. Feelgood" around Alcor Life Extension Foundation in Scottsdale, Arizona, the company that cut off Ted Williams' head (however clumsily) and froze it cryogenically.

"But wouldn't it be neat to sell Dad's DNA? There are lots of people who would pay big bucks to have little Ted Williams running around."—John Henry Williams, the son of Ted.

"If you can call living without a body 'life.' Even if you (your head) had to sit all day and watch TV, you couldn't even work the remote to mute the commercials, let alone change the channel. What kind of life is that?"—Doug Lyons.

Williams was billed $120,000 (and had paid only $25,000) for the "head-only suspension," known at Alcor, the company that performed the dubious task, as "neuros." This stands for neuroseparation, the procedure of cutting off the head, which was perhaps not done properly. His head was shaved, drilled with holes, accidentally cracked as many as 10 times and moved twice to different receptacles. Apparently there was some dispute about whether there was to be a neuroseparation. Just before the surgery, a call was placed to John Henry, who apparently okayed the separation procedure.

As of the time of a 2003 *Sports Illustrated* investigative report, there were 630 living Alcor members who paid monthly dues to be future patients.

The only evidence that Williams wanted to be cryogenically preserved was a scrap of paper stained with motor oil dated November 2, 2000. It contained the signatures of his son, John Henry, John's younger half-sister Claudia, and Ted. All three supposedly pledged to be subject to the cryogenic procedure. Nevertheless, Claudia and John Henry never signed a "consent to be suspended" form after this document was signed. John Henry allegedly found the document in the trunk of his car. There is a fair amount of evidence to show that the document may be a sham perpetrated by John Henry.

By mid–2003 investigators were trying to determine if a felony had occurred based on claims that Williams had not actually signed the release that allowed his body to be frozen. The complaint was lodged by the husband of Williams' eldest daughter, and only after the *Sports Illustrated* article revealed details of the state of Williams' (headless) body.

John Henry received a measure of sympathy late in the 2003 season when he was discovered to have a form of leukemia (with remission rates of 70–80%). At age 34, he had been a right-handed hitting first baseman for the independent Baton Rouge River Bats, hitting .153 (11 for 72). He also played briefly for the Schaumsburg (Illinois) Flyers of the Northern League, going 0–7 with five strikeouts. He died in March 2004 at age 35 despite a bone marrow transplant from Claudia. His body was flown to Arizona to be with his father in the family "plot."

Williams' daughter and son-in-law, Bobby-Jo and Mark Ferrell, dropped their lawsuit when the money ran out, having spent over $100,000 to try to end the fight with Alcor. Mike Piazza had offered to help them, but abandoned the effort when told that his involvement could embroil him in legal action. Bobby-Jo said that Williams' will called for him to be cremated and his ashes spread over his favorite fishing area off the Florida coast.

The fight continued into mid–2004, when Williams' nephews obtained a court order requiring the company to produce a document, if it existed, showing Williams' intent to gift his body. The order was pursuant to the Uniform Anatomical Gift Act.

Book. Bill Lee, *Baseball Necrology: The Post-Baseball Lives and Deaths of More than 7,600 Major League Players and Others* (2003).

Debuts See *At-Bats, First Game of Career* and *Home Runs*—First At-Bat

Defamation

"He operated on my pocketbook, too."—Walter O'Malley commenting on a bill from the surgeon who unsuccessfully operated on Roy Campanella's hand before the 1954 season. O'Malley settled the resulting defamation suit.

Ban Johnson and John Montgomery Ward. Ward, a prominent player of the 19th century, later became a well-known New York attorney and was considered for the National League presidency in 1909. American League president Ban Johnson announced that he was unalterably opposed to Ward being his counterpart on the three-man National Commission because Ward was a "trickster" and a "menace." Ward sued for libel and won $1,000, although much of the case was thrown out.

According to some, the hatred between Ward and Johnson apparently stemmed from Ward's representation of George Davis, a player who was at the center of a fight between the National and American Leagues. Ward had drafted a contract for Davis when he jumped from the Giants to the White Sox for the 1902 season. He then represented Davis in court when the National League forced him back to the Giants. Davis did not play for the White Sox in 1903 due to an injunction and then played only four games for the Giants that season. He returned to the White Sox in 1904 for the last six years of his 20-year career. Given that Ward was fighting to keep Davis in the American League, it is illogical that Johnson disliked Ward for this reason.

Phil Ball and His Players. In 1917 the Browns owner publicly berated his players for poor play and threatened to fine them $100 for every $1,000 he lost on the team. Two of his infielders, shortstop Doc Lavan (a medical doctor) and second baseman Del Pratt, filed suits against Ball. No evidence as to the outcome, but Ball traded them both during the winter.

Sam Breadon and Branch Rickey. When Rickey left the Cardinals for the Dodgers, Cardinals owner Sam Breadon accused him of being disloyal and breaking his contract. Rickey sued for defamation and the case was settled.

Billy Martin and Dale Ford. Umpire Dale Ford filed suit in 1983 against Billy Martin after Martin had called him a "stone liar" in an interview. It later settled.

Lou Piniella and Gary Darling. In 1991 Reds manager Lou Piniella accused umpire Gary Darling of being biased against the Reds. The umpires union filed a $5 million defamation lawsuit against Piniella and the Reds, which later settled.

John Montefusco. Montefusco sued ESPN after the network compared him to O.J. Simpson following his conviction of simple assault against his former wife in 2000. The court threw out the case, declaring that ESPN's conduct did not amount to defamation.

Defensive Gems

"A great catch is like watching girls go by. The last one you see is always the prettiest."—Hall of Fame pitcher Bob Gibson.

"There's hardly a greater staple of the Hot Stove League than retelling stories of great catches in the outfield…. Bring three or four vintage baseball fans together on a winter's evening, the refrigerator filled with beer and nothing better on television than basketball, hockey or demolition derby, and chances are they will begin to regale one another with tales of acrobatic catches they have seen."—William Curran in *Mitts* (1985).

See also *Fielding and Fielding Average*.

Greatest Catch. A poll of Major League players in the 1980s voted the best catch ever as one that was repeated during the opening credits of the television program "This Week in Baseball." The catch was made by Masafuri Yamamori, left fielder for the Hankyu Braves in the Japanese Leagues. Yamamori climbed atop the left field fence to grab a sure home run.

Ground Ball. On April 20, 1978 Ozzie Smith made what is considered by some to be the greatest defensive play in Major League history. On a hard ground ball hit up the middle, Smith dove and stretched out his glove hand toward second base as the ball took a bad hop back toward third. It looked to be a clean single. Suddenly, while prone in the air, Ozzie reached up with his bare hand and caught the ball. He hit the ground, popped up, and made a perfect throw to get the runner out at first.

Babe Ruth. Ruth reportedly entertained fans late in a meaningless game by chasing a puppy around in the outfield while on all-fours. He tossed his glove at the dog at the same time that the opposing batter hit a fly ball to him. He caught it barehanded (the ball, not the dog).

Willie Mays.

"Harvey Kuenn gave it an honest pursuit, but the only man who could have caught it, hit it." — Sportswriter Bob Stevens on a triple by Willie Mays to win the 1959 All-Star Game.

"I won't believe that play until I see him do it again." — Dodger manager Charlie Dressen on another terrific catch by Mays. When Mays made an amazing catch as a rookie, manager Leo Durocher told his players to give him the silent treatment; but Pirates general manager Branch Rickey sent Mays a note: "That was the finest catch I have ever seen … and the finest I ever expect to see."

"I have always thought that this play defined what defense in baseball is all about. There was nothing defensive in it. It was not only a game winner, it was game, match, and series." — David Falkner in *Nine Sides of the Diamond* (1990), on Mays' catch of Vic Wertz's drive in Game 1 of the 1954 World Series.

"Well, I got my man." — Giants pitcher Don Liddle upon returning to the bench after coming in to face one batter, Vic Wertz of the Indians, in Game 1 of the 1954 World Series. Wertz blasted a drive on which Mays made his most famous catch, possibly the most-recalled defensive play in Major League history.

Mays caught Wertz's 460-foot smash running with his back to home plate and then whirled and threw back to the infield to hold the runner. The catch was important because the game was tied 2–2 in the 9th inning. The Giants won 5–2 in the 10th inning on a three-run homer by Dusty Rhodes.

In the top of the 10th inning Mays made another outstanding play to prevent Wertz from hitting a possible inside-the-park home run, holding him to a double and allowing the Giants to go on to win the game. Wertz was hot that game, with two singles, a double and a triple.

For a description of the entire game, see Arnold Hano, *A Day in the Bleachers* (1955), who once wrote about the throw: "But the throw! What an astonishing throw, to make all other throws ever before it, even those four Mays himself had made during fielding practice, appear the flings of teen-age girls. This was the throw of a giant, the throw of a howitzer made human, arriving at second base…."

Mays later said that he had many catches better than the one off Wertz. In 1952 he made a catch running into the outfield wall at Ebbets Field, knocking himself unconscious. The umpire had to run out to check his glove for the out call. Another time he went back on a ball at Forbes Field, turned, but could not get his glove on the ball — so he barehanded it; many years later he had the following exchange with Giants outfielder Kevin Mitchell, who also barehanded a catch: "I didn't teach you that. Catch the ball with your glove."

Perhaps another catch that surpassed the Wertz catch was in 1970 at Candlestick Park in a game against the Reds. Mays and right fielder Bobby Bonds both went after a long drive to right center field by Bobby Tolan. Neither made the call, and the ball appeared headed over the wire fence; both leaped and collided in midair, but Mays made the catch while being knocked unconscious.

Al Gionfriddo.

"Swung on. And belted. It's a long one deep to left field. Back goes Gionfriddo. Back … Back … Back. It may be out of here. No! Gionfriddo makes a one-handed catch against the bullpen fence. Ohhh, *doctor*!" — Red Barber's call of Gionfriddo's somewhat overrated catch in Game 6 of the 1947 World Series. Gionfriddo was playing center field for the Dodgers, who held an 8–5 lead in the bottom of the 6th inning when Joe DiMaggio stepped to the plate

with two on and two out and drove the ball to the 415-foot sign. Gionfriddo's catch preserved the lead and the Dodgers won the game. The Dodgers still lost Game 7 (5–2) and the Series.

Sandy Amoros.

"I dunno. I just run like hell." — Response by Amoros on his sensational catch of a drive by Yankee catcher Yogi Berra to help win the 1955 World Series for the Dodgers. Amoros made his Series-saving catch in the 6th inning of Game 7. He preserved a 2–0 lead with a running catch near the left field foul pole with two Yankees on base. His relay to Pee Wee Reese helped double up Gil McDougald at first base. Hank Bauer then grounded out to end the inning.

After Amoros retired in 1961 he returned to Cuba, where Fidel Castro asked him to manage a team in Cuba's pro league. After Amoros refused, Castro stripped him of his assets, including a ranch, and Amoros left in 1967. He died in Miami in 1992 after undergoing a leg amputation in 1987 and other complications resulting from diabetes.

Roberto Clemente. In 1960 Clemente made a catch that many say was superior to the catch by Willie Mays in the 1954 World Series. With the Pirates leading the Giants 1–0 in the 7th inning, Clemente took off after a drive by, ironically, Mays. He slammed into the right field concrete wall at Forbes Field and fell to the ground. As he rose, blood gushing from his chin, he held up his glove to signal that he had the ball.

Known for his rifle arm in right field, Clemente once made a throw from the right center field fence in Forbes Field to home plate. The catcher never had to move his glove to haul in the 416-foot throw and nail the runner.

Clemente did have a problem on a throw on at least one occasion. He once attempted a throw from Wrigley Field's outfield ivy that did not make it very far: the ball turned out to be an empty white soft drink cup.

Ron Swoboda. Swoboda made two stellar catches for the Mets in the 1969 World Series against the Orioles. They both came in the 9th inning of Game 4 with the Mets leading 1–0. With runners on first and third, he made a diving catch of a fly ball in right center field hit by Brooks Robinson. The runner scored, but the rally was cut short when Swoboda made a good running catch on a line drive to end the inning and preserve the tie. The Mets won the game in the 10th inning. Swoboda drove in the deciding run in the final game of the Series.

Brooks Robinson.

"Brooks is not a fast man, but his arms and legs move very quickly." — Broadcaster Curt Gowdy.

The Orioles third baseman almost single-handedly dismantled the Reds in the 1970 World Series and was voted into the Hall of Fame almost exclusively on the strength of his defensive skills. What is forgotten is that on the first chance that Robinson had in the Series, he made an error on a ball hit by Lee Maye.

Dwight Evans. Red Sox right fielder Dwight Evans made what may have been, "given its significance, one of the two greatest catches ever made," according to opposing manager Sparky Anderson. It occurred in the top of the 11th inning of Game 6 of the 1975 Series between the Red Sox and Reds. Evans ran back and stabbed at Reds second baseman Joe Morgan's line drive that was heading for at least the base of the Fenway Park right field wall. The catch robbed Morgan of at least a double and possibly a home run, and turned it into a double play. After the catch, he relayed the throw from the wall to first baseman Carl Yastrzemski, who fired to first base, then being covered by Rick Burleson. He had raced over from shortstop to double up the runner.

Bo Jackson.

"The Throw"

On June 5, 1989, the Royals were playing the Mariners in the Kingdome. The clubs were tied 3–3 in the bottom of the 10th inning with the Mariners batting. Runner Harold Reynolds took off for second base on a hit and run when Scott Bradley lined a ball into the left field corner. Left fielder Jackson caught the ball off the 310-foot wall while standing flat-footed with one foot on the artificial turf and one foot on the warning track. Reynolds was already rounding third base when Jackson caught the ball. Without taking a stride, Jackson threw a line drive strike on the fly to catcher Bob Boone, who tagged out Reynolds. The out preserved the tie, and the Royals went on to win 5–3 in 13 innings.

Devon White. In the 1992 World Series for the Blue Jays, White made a tremendous catch at the center field wall and began what should have been a *Triple Play* (but for a bad call by the umpire on what would have been the third out).

Derek Jeter.

"In my mind everything happened in slow motion. When I watched it later I just looked at it really as what I was supposed to do. We'd practiced that play in spring training."—Jeter in *Playboy*.

Perhaps the most famous non-World Series postseason defensive play of recent years was Jeter's backhanded flip to his catcher during the 2001 division series against the A's that changed the course of the series. The A's had won both games in New York and the Yankees were trying to preserve a 1–0 lead in Game 3 in Oakland, created by catcher Jorge Posada's 5th inning homer. In the 7th inning with two outs, Jeremy Giambi singled for the A's. Terrence Long then drilled a pitch to the right field corner that Yankees outfielder Shane Spencer fielded and threw back toward first base — but threw high. Jeter ran across the field from shortstop toward the first base line to cut off the throw in case it went over second baseman Alfonso Soriano, the first cut-off man, and the second cut-off man, first baseman Tino Martinez. It did, and Jeter caught it in full stride as he crossed the foul line and made a backhanded flip to catcher Jorge Posada, who applied the tag on a shocked Giambi, who failed to slide. Asked by *Playboy* what the play was called, as no one had ever seen it before, Jeter said it was called, simply, "The Play."

Jeter made another spectacular play ("greatest catch I've even seen"—Alex Rodriguez) on July 1, 2004, when he dove head first into the stands to catch a foul pop-up by Trot Nixon with two runners on base in the 12th inning of a game against the Red Sox. He left the game for the hospital with a face full of blood, but was back in the line-up the next night. Alex Rodriguez moved over to shortstop for the first time that season.

Good Day At The Plate. On June 10, 1997, A's center fielder Damon Mashore threw out three runners at home plate. Nevertheless, despite five double plays, the A's lost to the Tigers 6–4.

Fence Busters. For many years 1890s star outfielder Bill Lange was credited with crashing through an outfield fence making a catch. Later research determined that the fence was left intact.

Vancouver outfielder Rodney McCray had the defensive gem of 1991. Playing in the Pacific Coast League he ran straight through a wooden fence while making an unbelievable catch. The play was caught on film for posterity.

Out At First. On June 7, 2000, rookie pitcher Clayton Andrews of the Blue Jays blooped what appeared to be his first Major League hit to right field, but Brian Jordan threw him out at first. It was one of three times that season that Jordan threw runners out at first base.

Possible Faked Catches. See *World Series—Controversial Calls*

for Josh DeVore's alleged catch in Game 3 of the 1912 World Series and Sam Rice's alleged catch in Game 3 of the 1925 World Series.

Catcher. The best defensive play by a catcher ever witnessed by the author was in a girls softball game in 2003. With no outs and runners on first and third, the batter bunted a ball just up the first base line. The catcher leaped out and grabbed the ball as the runner on third momentarily hesitated. As the runner broke from third, the catcher threw out the runner at first and then rushed back to home plate to take the return throw by the first baseman. The ball came in high and away toward the first base side, so the catcher had to leap to successfully backhand the throw. In one motion she threw her body back toward the plate, diving as she stretched for a lay-out tag of the runner sliding in. Meanwhile, the runner on first was heading for third, so the catcher jumped to her feet and threw a strike to the bag, and the third baseman tagged out the runner. Triple play. The catcher was the author's 12-year-old all-star catcher, Katherine Fraser Light [her identical twin sister, Elena Rose, had been a good pitcher (making for quite a battery), before pursuing a ballet career].

Ed Delahanty (1867–1903)

Hall of Fame 1945

"Men who met him had to admit he was a handsome fellow, although there was an air about him that indicated he was a roughneck at heart and no man to tamper with. He had that wide-eyed, half-smiling, ready-for-anything look that is characteristic of a certain type of Irishman. He had a towering impatience too, and a taste for liquor and excitement. He created plenty of excitement for opponents and spectators when he laid his tremendous bat against a pitch."—Robert Smith in *Baseball* (1970).

"Del was a whole-souled fellow, socially inclined, and even when under the fatherly management and watchful core of the veteran Harry Wright he never grasped the idea that the game afforded a field for improvement and betterment of habits and character that could have firmly established him in life as a prosperous and successful man."—Sam Crane of the *New York Evening Journal*.

Delahanty was one of the premier hitters in the National League in the late 19th century before his mysterious death in 1903.

Born in Cleveland, Edward James Delahanty joined the Ohio State League in 1887 and moved to the Major Leagues as an outfielder in 1888 for the Phillies. Except for one year with Cleveland in the 1890 Players League he played 13 straight seasons in Philadelphia. He was primarily an outfielder, but he played over 500 games among each of the infield positions. In those years he batted .400 or better three times and had seven seasons over .300. He also led the league in slugging average four times and drove in more than 100 runs seven times.

Delahanty played the last two years of his career (1902–1903) with the Senators in the American League, batting .376 and .333. He holds the fifth-highest batting average in Major League history at .346 over 16 seasons. He finished with 2,597 hits and had 455 stolen bases and 520 doubles. Notwithstanding his enormous batting talents, he is remembered primarily for the strange circumstances of his *Death* over Niagara Falls while still an active player. He was one of five Delahanty brothers to play in the Major Leagues.

Book. Mike Sowell, *July 2, 1903* (1992).

Dentists

"Batting against Don Drysdale is the same as making a date with the dentist."—Pirate shortstop Dick Groat.

See also *Teeth*.

Aborted Career. The most famous would-be dentist in baseball history was Casey Stengel. After his 1910 minor league season, Stengel's friend Billy Brummage planned to study dentistry at Western Dental College in Kansas City and Stengel tagged along.

Stengel was eligible to enter the college despite the absence of a high school diploma. He spent the fall and winter of 1910–1911 in school and returned again after the 1911 season. According to biographer Robert Creamer, "if Casey had not made it as a ballplayer he almost certainly would have been a dentist." It has been reported that Stengel's dental school had a baseball team until the dean made them stop playing because it was hurting their fingers.

Dentists. Doc Bushong played 12 years as a catcher in the 19th century while also pursuing a dental career.

Doc (Guy Harris) White was a dentist who pitched for 13 years at the beginning of the 20th century, winning 190 games.

Ed Lafitte left the Tigers after the 1911 season to finish dental school. He later signed with the Brooklyn Tip-Tops of the Federal League and pitched the Federal League's first no-hitter, defeating Kansas City 6–2 on September 19, 1914.

James T. "Doc" Prothro was a dental school alumnus who managed the Phillies from 1939 through 1941, after playing third base in the Major Leagues in the 1920s.

Dick Hoblitzell became a dentist after an 11-year Major League career from 1908 through 1918. One source referred to him as "Doc" Hoblitzel (with one "l" at the end of his name), but *The Baseball Encyclopedia* makes no reference to the nickname.

Purported Dentist. In Harold Seymour's *Baseball: The Early Years* (1960), he reported that 19th century player "Dick" Allen was a dentist and even went on to teach at the University of Buffalo Dental School. There is no record of a "Dick" or Richard Allen as a 19th century Major Leaguer, so "Dick" must be a nickname for another Allen of that era.

The Depression (1930s)

"Great is Baseball the National Tonic, the reviver of hope, the restorer of confidence." — An editorial in *The Sporting News* during the Depression in 1931.

The Great Depression of the 1930s had a negative impact on Organized Baseball. Many teams slashed salaries, but there were few complaints from players simply because they had jobs, unlike a third of the general population. In 1933 *Attendance* in Organized Baseball reached its lowest level since the World War I–related year of 1919 when schedules were shortened before the season in anticipation of another poor year. In 1934 there was an improvement in Major League attendance, but it was not until 1936 that baseball had its first big year since the prosperous 1920s.

The Depression devastated the minor leagues, which received only a temporary reprieve due to the introduction of night baseball in the mid–1930s. Bad economic times also caused many teams to eliminate coaches. The coach-firing plan failed to interest Major League clubs, but the International League tried to require clubs to eliminate coaches by May 5, 1933. The plan was quickly abandoned.

Major League teams that suffered the most were the Braves, Phillies, Browns and Senators. Not coincidentally, all but one of the teams was located in a two-team city; areas where the Depression made it difficult to support two clubs simultaneously. Despite general assumptions to the contrary, during the 1930s clubs suffered heavy losses only in 1932, 1933 and 1934. For the rest of the decade most clubs were at least marginally profitable.

It has been suggested that three major changes occurred as a result of the Depression: 1) the popularity of radio skyrocketed; 2) night baseball was instituted; and 3) baseball saw the emergence of modern business techniques such as advertising and marketing.

Rosters. To lower team expenses, roster sizes were cut from 25 to 23 players.

Salary Cuts. There was almost a national obsession with a pay cut for Babe Ruth during the Depression. He received cuts from $80,000 in 1930 to $75,000 in 1931 and to $62,000 in 1932. There was also pressure on Judge Landis to take a cut. Within a week he voluntarily cut his annual salary 40% to $40,000. In another symbolic gesture, National League president John Heydler volunteered to take a pay cut.

Spring Training. In 1933 groups of tired and hungry young men appeared uninvited at Florida's Major League spring training sites trying to catch on with a professional team.

Book. William B. Mead, *Baseball in the Depression, 1930–1939* (1990).

Designated Hitter (1973–)

"Let's not even start on the Designated Hitter. It's baseball's abortion issue. We won't go there." — Dan Holmes in TheBaseballPage.com.

"The designated hitter rule is like letting someone else take Wilt Chamberlain's free throws." — National League pitcher and decent-hitting Rick Wise in 1974 [note to the young reader: Wilt, as great as he was on the basketball court (and in the bedroom), was a terrible free throw shooter, just as pitchers generally are terrible hitters].

"While it would be preferable if both leagues followed identical playing rules, the situation in the National League with respect to offensive/defensive balance is dissimilar to ours because most of their parks have artificial turf— an innovation which has changed the game as much as the designated hitter rule." — American League president Lee MacPhail trying to justify use of the designated hitter.

"Baseball is a game of teams which emphasizes individuals in competition. Use of the designated hitter takes something away from the game. Baseball has always been the hardest game to play because any player must be a whole athlete— able to do everything." — National League president Chub Feeney in opposition to the designated hitter.

"Designated Hitter, in a pennant race and making about $7 million a year." — Washington Redskins center John Gesek, asked what position he would like to play in any sport.

"Almost everything wrong in American society stems from the DH rule … it is a symbol of the permissiveness that has eroded our values." — Political writer David Broder in 1997 in the *Seattle Times*.

"It seems like Satan has thrown the DH into our game." — Andy Van Slyke.

"Vote for Mudville and we promise: To restore the laundry room of the White House. A chicken or tofurkey in every pot. Draft beer for every veteran. A tacks [sic] increase. And, most controversial, the elimination of the Designated Hitter. Let no one call us soft on the issues!... You'll wish we ran this country someday. We know it." — Publishers of *Mudville* magazine.

See also *Interleague Play* and *Rover*.

Early Proposals.

"The suggestion, often made, that the pitcher be denied a chance to bat, and a substitute player sent up to hit every time, has been brought to life again, and will come up for consideration when the American and National League Committees on rules get together. This time Connie Mack is credited with having made the suggestion. He argues that a pitcher is usually such a poor hitter that his time at the bat is a farce, and the game would be helped by eliminating him in favor of a better hitter. Against the change there are many strong points to be made. It is a cardinal principle of baseball that every member of the team should both field and bat. The better remedy would be to teach [pitchers] how to hit the ball."—*Sporting Life* commentary on February 3, 1906.

The designated hitter was first proposed in the 1890s. An early argument in favor of a DH was that a pitcher batting late in a game made him an easy out because of fatigue from pitching. If he actually got a hit, he would be exhausted running the bases.

In 1928 National League president John Heydler proposed use of a DH and a 10-man team. After unanimous National League approval, the plan was rejected by the American League and Judge Landis. Nevertheless, Heydler almost had the National League owners convinced to use it during spring training in 1929.

Major League Implementation. A semipro baseball tournament has been held for many years in Bridgeton, New Jersey. The tournament is unusual because the clubs are regulated by a clock. For example, batters must get in the box in a certain amount of time and pitchers must throw within time restrictions. In 1969 Monte Irvin appeared at the tournament when he was working in the commissioner's office. He later stated that it was the first time that he had seen the designated hitter used in regular play. He used that as a springboard for advocating use of the DH in the Major Leagues.

On January 11, 1973, with a boost from maverick but innovative A's owner Charlie Finley, the American League voted 8–4 to institute the rule for three years. Originally known as the Designated Pinch Hitter (DPH), it was rejected by the National League on a split vote. The DH rule became official in the American League in 1976 and the National League still refuses to use it.

Rule. The designated hitter may only be used to substitute for the pitcher at the start of a game. If a DH switches to a fielding position, then there will be no more DH for the game.

First Spring Training DH. The DH was used by the American League in a few exhibition games in 1969, but the National League refused to participate. The first Major League DH in an exhibition game after the rule was approved in 1973 was Larry Hisle of the Twins, who hit two home runs against the Pirates. Ironically, he never DH'd during that season.

In an exhibition game against the Padres, A's pitcher Steve McCatty came to the plate holding a 15-inch toy bat on the instructions of manager Billy Martin, who was upset that his club was not allowed to use a DH in spring training games at National League parks. Home plate umpire Jim Quick refused to let McCatty use the bat, and McCatty took three called strikes.

The First Official Major League DH.
"And all because I pulled my hamstring in spring training 20 years ago." — Ron Blomberg of the Yankees reminiscing on why he became the first DH. Otherwise, it would have been Felipe Alou or Johnny Callison.

Ron Blomberg was the first DH on Opening Day, April 6, 1973. He batted at 1:53 p.m. for the Yankees against the Red Sox in Fenway Park. Blomberg batted sixth in the Yankee order and was assured of a 1st inning at-bat and immortality when the Yankees scored three times in the top of the 1st. He walked against pitcher Luis Tiant, but drove in a run because the bases were loaded. He was 1-for-3 in a 15–5 loss.

Because he was Jewish, Blomberg sometimes referred to himself as the "Designated Hebrew." He DH'd in 55 games in 1973 and played first base in 41 games.

Even though Blomberg was the first to bat, Orlando Cepeda of the Red Sox is arguably the first DH because he was the first one actually designated on a line-up card: the home team Red Sox turned in their line-up card first.

First-Year DHs. The top DHs in 1973:

	Avg.	HR	RBI
Tommy Davis (Balt)	.306	7	89
Orlando Cepeda (Bos)	.289	20	86
Tony Oliva (Minn)	.291	16	92
Frank Robinson (Cal)	.266	30	97
Deron Johnson (Oak)	.246	19	81
Jim Ray Hart (NY)	.254	13	52

Full-Time DH. The first player to DH in all 162 games was Rusty Staub of the Tigers in 1978.

World Series DH. The World Series first saw the DH in 1976, when the leagues agreed to use it every other year. Dan Driessen of the Reds became the first official DH when he batted against the Yankees. However, a runner was picked off before he received a pitch, so some contend that Lou Piniella was actually the first DH later in the game for the Yankees. In 1986 the leagues shifted to a format that allowed the DH to be used in any World Series game played in an American League park.

Other Firsts and Lasts. Tony Oliva was the first DH to hit a home run. He did it for the Twins on the same day as Blomberg's first start as a DH.

Until the 1980s the last American League pitcher to get a hit during a regular season game was Ferguson Jenkins of the Rangers, against Minnesota on October 2, 1974. It was the last game of the season and manager Billy Martin inserted Jenkins as a hitter. Jenkins broke up a no-hitter with the hit and was the only pitcher to bat that year. In addition to his .500 batting average (1-for-2), Jenkins had a 25–12 pitching record that season.

Prior to Jenkins during the DH era, American League pitchers who had hits were Ed Figueroa and Catfish Hunter in 1973 and Tom Murphy in 1974.

Pitcher Tim Lollar of the Red Sox had a hit as a pinch hitter against the Royals on August 12, 1986. Ken Brett, generally a good-hitting pitcher, also had a hit in 1986.

On August 2, 1991, Rangers pitcher Mike Jeffcoat was inserted into the game as the DH. He had a single and, according to at least one source, the first RBI by a pitcher in the DH era in a 15–1 win over the Brewers. However, Rick Rhoden had a sacrifice fly for an RBI in 1988 when he started a game as the DH for the Yankees. The last RBI by a pitcher before the DH era was by Bert Blyleven, who had an RBI-double on October 4, 1972.

Brewers pitcher Matt Maysey had a hit in 1993. In 1998 the Brewers returned to the National League for the first time in 98 years. On April 15, 1998, the Brewers beat the Expos 7–4. Scott Karl became the first Milwaukee pitcher to score a run since 1989.

The last pre–DH American League pitcher to hit a home run was Orioles pitcher Roric Harrison, who hit it on October 3, 1972, against the Indians.

The last American League pitcher to hit a grand slam was Indians pitcher Steve Dunning. He hit it on May 11, 1971, against Diego Segui of the A's.

See *Interleague Play* for pitchers who hit again.

Home Runs. In May 2004 Edgar Martinez broke Harold Baines' DH home run record, when he hit his 236th as a DH (he had 301 overall).

National League. The first National League designated hitter was Glenallen Hill, who appeared in an ***Interleague Game*** for the Giants against the Rangers on June 12, 1997.

On June 30, 1997, Bobby Witt of the Rangers hit the first American League home run by a pitcher since Roric Harrison in 1972. He did it in an interleague game against the Dodgers, which he won 3–2.

On June 13, 1997, Tigers pitcher Omar Olivares hit the first triple by an American League pitcher in 24 years, in an interleague game against the Expos. Olivares lost the game 4–3 despite going 2-for-3.

Rule Change. Pitcher Steve Stone of the Orioles was used as a designated hitter 12 times for the Orioles in 1980 but never batted. His efforts were the result of a September 8 incident in which the Orioles knocked Tigers starter Milt Wilcox out of the game before he faced DH Lee May. Orioles manager Earl Weaver was upset because May had to face a reliever against whom historically he was not effective. Weaver left May in so as not to waste a pinch hitter. From that point to the end of the season, Weaver filled out his line-up card with a pitcher as the DH and then batted for him when he came up the first time. Weaver penciled in Stone one night even though Stone had gone ahead to Toronto because of a Jewish holiday. The next night Weaver started reliever Tippy Martinez even though Martinez was in Colorado at a funeral. After the season the Rules Committee responded by instituting a requirement that the DH make at least one plate appearance.

Weaver wrote in his book, *Weaver on Strategy*, "When my team was on the road, I would list someone else as our leadoff hitter and shortstop. Often it was Royle Stillman, a young outfielder we brought up from Rochester." He would bat Stillman for weak-hitting shortstop Mark Belanger. Stillman batted 4-for-9 during this period.

Effect on Hitting. The American League has had a higher overall batting average than the National League in every season since the DH rule was instituted. The American League has also generally outscored the National League by half a run per game. Nevertheless, there has been only a marginal increase in hitting and scoring due to the DH. In its first season of use, American League averages were up from .239 to .259, but so were National League averages: .248 to .254.

Initially, the change caused more complete games, but had a negligible effect on home run production. The American League hit 1,552 home runs in 1973, only two more than the National League total of 1,550.

Over the first eight years of DH use, American League batting averages were 21 points higher than the previous eight years (.262 vs. .241) and ERAs were 48 points higher (3.37 vs. 3.85). However, batting averages in the National League also rose, from .251 to .257, and ERAs rose 15 points from 3.51 to 3.66.

In the DH's first 17 seasons, the American League averaged 8.5 runs per game to the National League's eight runs.

Disenchantment. By 1996 when interleague play was approved, the American League voted 7–7 in a straw poll to eliminate the DH. Elimination was viewed as a cost-cutting measure because one less high-priced star would remain on a club.

Minor Leagues. The only minor leagues that do not currently use a DH are at the Class AAA level, and then only when two National League affiliates play each other.

The Class AAA International League first instituted the DH rule for the 1969 season. The league abandoned the rule after the season and resurrected it in the 1970s.

Passing Time. DHs have used various methods of passing time between at-bats. Blomberg ate. Kurt Bevacqua hung upside down

from a gyro machine. Mike Easler swung a bat against a boxing heavy bag. Greg Luzinski would tie and untie his shoes. George Brett brought out his wedge and chipped golf balls into a box on the clubhouse shelf. John Lowenstein claimed that he kept his wrists strong by flushing the toilet between at-bats.

Out of Practice.

"They told me to hit. Nobody said anything about running."— Blue Jays pitcher Jimmy Key after hitting an apparent single to the outfield in a rare plate appearance during spring training. He was thrown out at first base.

"You can get yourself hurt out there."— Pitcher David Wells, getting in some batting practice after moving over to the Padres for the 2004 season. Former Yankee Andy Pettitte began with the Astros that season, and promptly pulled an elbow tendon on a check swing, landing him on the disabled list.

In July 1996 Mariners designated hitter Edgar Martinez played his first inning of the season in the field. While playing third base he collided with catcher John Marzano and suffered bruised ribs that put him out of action. Marzano suffered a cut over his eye that required 30 stitches. Martinez was on pace to break Earl Webb's record for most doubles in a season.

Japan. Only Japan's Pacific League has a designated hitter. The Central League follows the National League's tradition of having pitchers bat.

Book. G. Richard McKelvey, *All Bat, No Glove* (2004).

Detectives

"The Yankees should have been easy to stalk because, belonging to a high-class ball club, they drank martinis and left a trail of olives."— Sportswriter John Lardner on the hiring of detectives by Yankee manager Bucky Harris.

"I ain't gonna save this ballclub no more money by doubling up."— Giants outfielder Casey Stengel in the early 1920s, after splitting up with Irish Meusel during their nightly barhopping escapades so that the club would need two detectives to keep track of them.

Albert Spalding once assigned detectives to follow star catcher Mike "King" Kelly. The report concluded that Kelly had been in a bar at 3 a.m. drinking lemonade. Kelly protested the accusation: "It was straight whiskey. I never drank a lemonade at that hour in my life."

Christopher Von der Ahe. In 1894 the eccentric St. Louis Browns owner purportedly presented his players with suits that matched his own. During spring training he told detectives that they could find his players out on the town without permission by identifying their suits. They found three players, who were fined $25 each. The fines were later rescinded.

Yankees. In 1922 the Yankees hired a detective to track their players by posing as a sportswriter covering the club. At parties during the Prohibition era he took photographs that supposedly were autographed by the players in attendance. The photographs were passed on to Judge Landis, who visited the Yankee clubhouse to lecture the players on their behavior.

Waite Hoyt was traded by the Yankees early in the 1930 season supposedly as a result of his night life exploits uncovered by a detective traveling incognito with the team.

According to Yankee shortstop Tony Kubek, general manager George Weiss had a number of Yankee players trailed during losing periods in the 1950s. If the club started winning the detectives disappeared.

Phillies. In 1954 Phillies shortstop Granny Hamner's complaints over being shadowed by a detective received widespread media coverage.

Dodgers. Dodger general manager Branch Rickey often employed detectives to follow his players, particularly when they were playing exhibition games in freewheeling Cuba.

Charlie Finley. When Finley announced his plan to buy into the Kansas City A's, American League owners hired a detective to investigate him. The detective's conclusion: "Don't let him in."

Detroit

"Some people laugh at us. They poke all kinds of fun at Detroit. We're right up there with Buffalo and Cleveland on the joke list. Maybe we've even taken over the top spot. Ever see a travel poster inviting you to visit Detroit on vacation?"—Joe Falls in *The Detroit Tigers* (1989).

Detroit's earliest organized team was the Franklin Club of 1857. This is also thought to be the earliest Midwestern baseball club. The city had a National League entry, the Wolverines, from 1881 through 1888. It also had an entry in the International League and then was part of Ban Johnson's Western League before that league was renamed the American League. Detroit was a charter member of the American League in 1901 and later had entries in the Negro Leagues.

Detroit Tigers

American League 1901–

"High or low in the standings, the Detroit Tigers have always been a fighting baseball club, snarling and scrapping to the finish."—Dust jacket commentary to Fred Lieb's *The Detroit Tigers* (1946).

"One of the major characteristics of guyhood is that we guys don't spend a lot of time pondering our deep innermost feelings. There is a serious question in my mind about whether guys actually *have* deep innermost feelings, unless you count, for example, loyalty to the Detroit Tigers or fear of bridal showers."—Dave Barry in *Dave Barry's Complete Guide to Guys* (1995).

Origins. In 1889 Western League president Ban Johnson accepted the National League's Detroit club, which became one of the original American League franchises in 1901. The club almost shifted to New York in 1902 when Johnson was negotiating for peace with the National League. The agreement provided that Johnson could put a team in New York to compete with the National League Giants, but not against the Pirates in Pittsburgh. Johnson had wanted to shift the small-market Detroit franchise, but ultimately left it in place.

First Game. Detroit's first American League game was played on April 25, 1901. A total of 10,023 fans jammed the 6,000-seat park. Detroit was down 13–4 to Milwaukee in the 9th inning, but won 14–13 in one of the greatest 9th inning comebacks in Major League history (see also ***Runs*—Comebacks**).

Key Owners.

Frank Navin/1902–1935.

"Frank Navin, first of the influential owners of the Tigers, kept an accounting of the day's receipts in his vest pocket. It was that simple an operation. He was the owner, general manager, business manager, farm director, and publicity man and, if things got busy, he'd be down in the booth selling tickets on the side."—Joe Falls in *Baseball Greatest Teams: Detroit Tigers* (1975).

Insurance man Sam Angus purchased the club in 1902 and appointed his employee, Navin, as the club's bookkeeper. Angus was Ban Johnson's personal choice after numerous disputes with the previous owners. Angus consistently lost money, so Navin was charged with finding a buyer. He almost had a deal consummated with lumber Baron William Clyman Yawkey (then the richest man in Michigan), but Yawkey died suddenly during the deal. Yawkey left $10 million to his 28-year-old son, William Hoover Yawkey. William, who died at age 43 (supposedly "in Ty Cobb's arms" in Georgia), left his then–$40 million fortune to Thomas Austin Yawkey, his foster son (later the long-time owner of the Boston Red Sox).

Navin persuaded William Hoover Yawkey to finish the deal started by his father to buy the Tigers for $50,000. At the same time, Navin bought a $5,000 interest in the club. Future Yankee general manager Ed Barrow was the team's general manager, and he was given $2,500 in stock in the club.

Known as "Old Poker Face," Navin controlled the operations of the club and gradually increased his holdings. After the 1909 World Series provided Navin with $51,273.67, he was able to buy out Yawkey completely and control the club outright.

Navin was considered by some as the most influential man in baseball during his tenure. He was sought out by other owners and team presidents, and Judge Landis is said to have called 20 times a day on occasion. Like other owners of the era who relied on the club as their sole source of income (including Comiskey, Mack and Griffith), Navin was known for being extremely tight-fisted.

Walter O. Briggs, Sr., and Family/1935–1956.

"Oh so very prejudiced. He's the major league combination of Simon Legree and Adolf Hitler."—Black sportswriter Wendell Smith on the extremely prejudiced Briggs, quoted in *Baseball's Great Experiment*, by Jules Tygiel (1983). The Tigers signed no black players until after Briggs' death in 1952.

The second dominant figure in Detroit history, Walter O. Briggs, Sr., owned an auto body manufacturing plant. Briggs, called a "true fan" since 1900, paid $250,000 for a 25% interest in the club in 1920. When another investor, tire manufacturer John Kelsey, died during the 1920s, Briggs bought Kelsey's 25% interest. Though Briggs then held an equal share of the club with Frank Navin, he never interfered with the club's operation.

Navin died at age 64 in a horseback riding accident (or had a heart attack while riding) only a month after the Tigers won their first World Series in 1935. By prior agreement Briggs paid $1 million for the interest in the club held by Navin's heirs.

Briggs owned the club through the rest of the Depression, when season attendance dipped to a low of 320,000, through World War II and the postwar baseball boom. Though Briggs was an anachronism on issues of integration and night baseball, he spent lavishly on players and Briggs Stadium.

He died in January 1952 and a strange sequence of events followed. Briggs' son, Walter O. (Spike) Briggs, Jr., became president, but his father's estate trustees were told by the probate court that the club was not a prudent investment for the minor heirs of the estate and it was ordered sold. In 1955 and 1956 Briggs was unsuccessful in selling the club. In late 1956 the trustees announced a competitive sealed bid sale of the team. Before the announcement, Spike Briggs supposedly tried to buy it from his sisters, who refused his lowball offer of $3.5 million.

John Fetzer/1956–1983.

"John Fetzer had built a broadcasting empire and bought a major league team. He had helped put baseball on national TV, opening a vault that made owners and players rich. His ballclub had won a world championship. He had kept the Tigers in Detroit. As he grew older, he became fascinated with eastern religions and less interested in worldly affairs." — Michael Betzold and Casey Ethan in *Queen of Diamonds: The Tiger Stadium Story* (1991).

Fetzer, a local radio mogul, did not want to buy the club, but one of his executives, Fred Knorr, did. Upon Knorr's urging, Fetzer put together a syndicate to make a bid. There were three bidders who joined together, consisting of Fetzer, Knorr and Kenyon Brown. Bill Veeck tried to buy the club, but many felt that his personal style doomed his chances of a successful bid. Fetzer bid $5.5 million, which overbid Veeck, and then Veeck tried to raise his bid to $6 million, but it was too late when the bids were unsealed on July 3, 1956. Football and basketball owner Jack Kent Cooke tried to buy the club during this time frame, but lost out to Fetzer and his group.

The "Three Wise Men" (Fetzer, Knorr and Kenyon) now owned the team. Fetzer was president and Spike Briggs was initially retained as general manager. On May 1, 1957, John McHale became the general manager after a dispute between Fetzer and Briggs on whom to hire as manager.

In 1959 Kenyon Brown wanted out so Fetzer bought his interest. Knorr later died in a bathtub accident and Fetzer purchased the stock from his estate on November 14, 1961. Fetzer became the sole owner of the team and held the club until 1983, when he sold out at age 82.

Tom Monaghan/1983–1992.

"The only fun I had [as a child living in an orphanage] was listening to the Tigers on the radio. That's why I can't believe I own the team." — Monaghan quoted in *Queen of Diamonds: The Tiger Stadium Story*, by Michael Betzold and Casey Ethan (1991).

Domino's Pizza king Tom Monaghan paid Fetzer $53 million for the club on October 10, 1983. Monaghan was 46 years old. He was blessed with a World Series victory the following season. Despite the general success of the team, Monaghan's pizza empire began to suffer so he tried to sell the club beginning in 1991. One of the potential buyers was Ford Motor Company heir Edsel Ford II.

Mike Ilitch/1992– .

"I resent being tabbed as greedy. I could handle dumb." — Ilitch.

"GROIN" — Acronym for an Internet website established by Stephen T. Tremp, standing for "Get Rid Of Ilitch Now."

Monaghan sold to Mike Ilitch, owner of the National Hockey League Detroit Red Wings and the Little Caesar's pizza chain. Ilitch had tried to buy the club in 1983 when Monaghan won out. Ilitch was once signed by the Tigers at the urging of Hall of Famer Charlie Gehringer for salary and bonuses totaling $5,000. Ilitch met his wife while playing for the minor league Detroit Smokers. They opened their first pizza parlor in 1959 and by the 1990s had over 4,000 stores. In 1994 Ilitch was worth $900 million, but his pizza chain suffered significant losses over the next decade.

Nicknames. The club originally was called the Detroits or simply Detroit, although some sources claim that Wolverines was used from the outset (Michigan is the Wolverine State). During its Western League days, a local writer dubbed the club the Creams after it purchased a number of players from California teams ("Cream of California Baseball").

As for the Tigers name, one version has it that in 1896, after manager George Stallings switched the uniform socks to orange stripes from solid color, Detroit newspaper editor Philip J. Reid dubbed them the Tigers. The name caught on and was adopted by the team. This version is disputed because the *Detroit Free Press* used the Tigers name in a headline on April 16, 1895, and *Sporting Life* also used the Tigers name in May 1895.

Another source pointed out that the club's uniforms included striped socks. The stripes and the colors reminded people of the Princeton University Tigers. During Ty Cobb's tenure as manager of the club, it was sometimes referred to by the press as the "Tygers."

Key Seasons.

"The Tigers … have a peculiar history of winning championships with shortstops who could barely carry a bat to the plate." — Art Hill in *I Don't Care If I Never Come Back* (1980); citing Dick Bartell's .233 average in 1940, Skeeter Webb's .199 in 1945 and Ray Oyler's 29 hits and .135 average in 1968.

1907. The club won the pennant under manager Hughie Jennings, finishing 1½ games ahead of the A's. Ty Cobb led the league with a .350 average and 116 RBIs. In the World Series they were swept by the Cubs after an opening-game tie.

1908. The Tigers won their second pennant by only one-half game over the Indians. This led to a rule change requiring all games to be played that affected the outcome of the pennant race. Ty Cobb was again the batting champion with a .324 average and Ed Summers won 24 games. In a virtual repeat of the 1907 Series, the Tigers lost to the Cubs in five games.

1909. The Tigers again prevailed in the American League, this time by three games over the A's. Ty Cobb won the Triple Crown, and George Mullin won 29 games to lead the league. In a much closer Series than the prior two, the Tigers lost to the Pirates in seven games.

1915. The Tigers became the first American League team to win 100 games and not win a pennant, finishing one game out to the Red Sox. Ty Cobb led the league with a .369 average and Bobby Veach and Sam Crawford were co–RBI leaders with 112 each.

1934. The club won the pennant, only to lose the World Series to Dizzy Dean and the Cardinals in seven games. The Tigers had four players with 100 or more RBIs and two 20-game winners, Tommy Bridges and Schoolboy Rowe.

1935. The Tigers defeated the Cubs in the World Series with basically the same players as on the 1934 club (though one source reported erroneously that Al Simmons of the A's had joined the club — but he did not arrive until 1936). Hank Greenberg led the league with 36 home runs and 170 RBIs. The Tigers finished second in both 1936 and 1937.

1940. The Tigers won the pennant but lost to the Reds in the World Series. Hank Greenberg led the league with 41 home runs and 150 RBIs and Bobo Newsom won 21 games. Al Benton led the league with 17 saves.

1945. In the last war year, the Tigers won the pennant by one game over the Senators and then defeated the Cubs in the World Series. Hal Newhouser led the league with 25 wins, but the club had no player with more than 18 home runs or 93 RBIs.

1952. The Tigers finished last for the first time in their history.

1968. The Tigers won the pennant on the strength of Denny McLain's 31 wins and then were down 3–1 in games to the Cardinals in the World Series. Behind the pitching of Mickey Lolich the Tigers won the dramatic Game 7 for the championship. Willie Horton hit 36 home runs.

1972. The club won the American League East by one-half game over the Red Sox after an early season player strike created an unequal schedule for some clubs. The Tigers lost the pennant to the A's after losing the final game of the ALCS 2–1. Mickey Lolich won 22 games but the club had no batter with more than 61 RBIs.

1984. After winning 92 games in 1983, the Tigers started the 1984 season with a 35–4 run and never looked back. They beat the Royals in the ALCS and beat the Padres in the World Series, as Kirk Gibson hit two home runs in the fifth and final game. See also

Sparky Anderson, *Bless You Boys* (1984); George Cantor, *Wire-To-Wire: Inside the 1984 Detroit Tigers Championship Season* (2004); Roger Craig and Vern Plagenhoef, *Inside Pitch* (1984).

2003. The Tigers generated some interested in 2003 when they had a good chance to pass the 1962 Mets (40–120) as the worst team of the modern era. With a last-week surge the club managed to finish at 43–119. Pitcher Mike Maroth became the first 20-game loser (9–21) since Brian Kingman was 8–20 for the A's in 1980.

Key Players.

Ty Cobb (HF) came up to the Tigers in 1905 and played 22 years before moving on to the A's in 1927 for two seasons. He finished his career with a .367 average, first all-time, and 4,191 hits, now second all-time behind Pete Rose. He is third all-time in steals with 892.

Charlie Gehringer (HF) played 19 seasons for the Tigers and batted .320 while establishing himself as the premier second baseman of the 1930s. He batted over .300 in 13 seasons and led the league with a .371 average in 1937. He appeared in three World Series for the Tigers, batting .321.

Hank Greenberg (HF) played 12 seasons for the Tigers, interrupted by injury and World War II. He had four seasons with 40 or more home runs and in 1938 he hit .315 with 58 home runs and 146 RBIs. He appeared in four World Series for the Tigers.

Mickey Cochrane (HF) played two stellar seasons for the Tigers as their player-manager. He batted over .300 and led the club to World Series appearances each year.

Hal Newhouser (HF) was elected belatedly to the Hall of Fame after dominating the mid–1940s with season win totals of 29, 25, 26 and 21. In his 15 seasons with the club he won exactly 200 games.

Al Kaline (HF) played his entire 22-year career with the Tigers, batting .297 and hitting 399 home runs. He had eight seasons over .300 and led the club to a 1968 World Series victory.

Bill Freehan was an All-Star catcher who played 15 seasons for the Tigers beginning in 1961, batting .262 with 200 home runs.

Denny McLain played eight seasons for the Tigers, with three good and two great seasons. He had seasons of 16, 20 and 17 wins before exploding for 31 victories in 1968 to lead the Tigers to the World Series. He followed up with 24 wins and nine shutouts in 1969 to lead the league in both categories.

Jack Morris pitched 14 seasons for the Tigers, winning 198 games from 1977 through 1990. He won more games in the 1980s than any other Major League pitcher, with highs of 20 in 1983 and 21 in 1986. He also had 24 shutouts for the club.

Alan Trammell played shortstop for the club from 1977 through the 1996 season. He hit .285 with 185 home runs and 236 stolen bases.

Lou Whitaker played second base for the Tigers from 1977 through 1995, hitting 243 home runs and driving in 1,040 runs.

Key Managers.

"Through the years, Detroit has had some of the most colorful characters on the manager's seat. They have been aggressive, hard-driving martinets or free-and-easy chaps who led with tact and diplomacy, but they all have been colorful figures."—Fred Lieb in *The Detroit Tigers* (1946).

Hughie Jennings (HF) managed the team from 1907 through 1920. Jennings won pennants his first three years and then never won again. He was an alcoholic during his last years as manager and was replaced by Ty Cobb on December 18, 1920. Allegedly Cobb did not want the job, but took it after learning that it was to be taken by Pants Rowland, whom Cobb disliked.

Ty Cobb (HF).

"Kid Gleason should have succeeded Hughie Jennings as man-

ager of the Tigers. Instead, it was forced upon me. After which I suffered torture."—Cobb in *My Life in Baseball*, with Al Stump (1961).

Cobb managed the club from 1921 until he was forced out of the position by Judge Landis after an alleged *Gambling* scandal surfaced in 1926. Cobb won no pennants during his tenure, finished second once and third twice.

Mickey Cochrane (HF) managed the team from 1934 until midway through the 1938 season. He came over to the Tigers in a trade with the A's and as player-manager led the club to the 1934 World Series, losing to the Cardinals in seven games. The club repeated as American League champions in 1935, this time defeating the Cubs in the World Series. Cochrane was still player-manager when he was beaned on May 25, 1937. He was often dizzy and sick after that and could not manage effectively. He was replaced on August 6, 1938.

Steve O'Neill.

"The greatest thrill in the life of Stephen Francis O'Neill, proud and happy manager of the conquering Detroit Tigers, came yesterday at the age of 54."—The *Stars and Stripes* military newspaper after the Tigers won Game 7 of the 1945 World Series. O'Neill managed the Tigers from 1943 through 1948, winning one pennant and finishing second three times.

Miscellaneous Unhealthy Managers. After a series of undistinguished managers (though Del Baker and Steve O'Neill won pennants), Red Rolfe managed the team from 1949 until 1952, but suffered from colitis and was forced to retire.

In 1961 Casey Stengel was set to take over the team, but a health examination resulted in a negative recommendation by the doctor. The Tigers signed Bob Scheffing instead. Scheffing quit in mid-1963 and Charlie Dressen took over. Dressen had a heart attack during spring training in 1965 and coach Bob Swift ran the club until Dressen returned three months later. He managed briefly until May 15, 1966, when he retired. He died on August 10 of that year. Swift managed again during the summer of 1966 but he had cancer and died on October 17, 1966. Coach Frank Skaff took over from Swift before the end of the season and was replaced by Mayo Smith to start 1967.

Mayo Smith.

"Open up a ballplayer's head and you know what you'd find? A lot of little broads and a jazz band."—Smith, who had immediate success with the Tigers. He led them to a second-place finish in 1967 and won the World Series in 1968. After subsequent second- and fourth-place finishes he was fired.

Billy Martin replaced Mayo Smith for the 1971 season and won the Eastern Division title in 1972. He was fired September 2, 1973, after saying that he ordered his pitchers to throw spitters. The pitchers said that they had done it on their own, ostensibly getting Martin off the hook, and Martin left the city as a martyr.

Sparky Anderson (HF).

"Sparky came here two years ago promising to build a team in his own image, and now the club is looking for small white-haired infielders with .212 batting averages."—Tigers broadcaster Al Ackerman in 1981.

Anderson followed his tremendous success with the Reds with 17 seasons as the Tigers manager from 1979 through 1995. He led the club to first-place finishes in 1984 and 1987 and produced four second-place finishes. See also Sparky Anderson and Dan Ewald, *Sparky!* (1990).

Ballparks.

Tiger Stadium. The Tigers played in the same ballpark (with modifications and name changes) from their arrival in the American League in 1901 through the end of the century. Bennett Park was home to 19th century Major League clubs in Detroit. The ballpark was renamed Navin Field in 1912, renamed Briggs Stadium in 1938, and finally renamed *Tiger Stadium* in 1960. In 1901 on Sundays the club played in Burns Park, which was also known as West End Park.

Comerica Park.

"To paraphrase Joni Mitchell, Detroit paved paradise and put up an amusement park."—Doug Pappas.

"Tigers owner Mike Ilitch is a father of seven kids with short attention spans. So he wanted a ballpark where you can spend a few hours doing things other than just watching baseball."—W. Blake Gray.

In 2000 the Tigers moved to Comerica Park, which featured two enormous tiger statues at the entrance. The first game at the new facility was played on April 11, 2000, as the Tigers beat the Mariners 5–2.

In 1992 voters rejected the spending of public money, but in late 1995 plans were announced to spend $235 million for a new downtown ballpark and in 1996 a new vote was held that favored public monies to help pay the cost. It won with 80% of the vote, as supporters outspent the opposition by 60 to 1 and portrayed the opponents as suburbanites who had allowed Detroit to become a symbol of urban decay. After it passed, the club agreed to pay 60% of the cost and to cover any overruns, and construction began in 1997. The stadium ended up costing $361 million ($395 million in some sources), and additional taxes were raised to increase public spending on the project to $250 million.

Comerica Park has a brick exterior, 42,000 seats, a small foul territory, and outfield dimensions from left to right of 345–420–335.

Comerica's 102 luxury suites rent for between $90,000 and $125,000 a year, providing the club with another $10 million in annual revenue. The Ilitch family controls concessions, merchandise and parking rights at the stadium, and owns many of the nearby garages. The city owns Comerica but receives no rent from the Tigers and needs the club's consent to use the park for any purpose. There is a 50-foot ferris wheel with baseball-shaped cars. A carousel sits behind first base and a water fountain adorns center field next to the "world's largest scoreboard."

Key Broadcasters. Former player Harry Heilmann broadcast primarily during the 1940s to all of Michigan except Detroit. Metropolitan Detroit was reserved for Ty Tyson. After being one of the premier broadcasters in the 1930s, Tyson retired from radio in 1942 and was on the first Tiger television broadcasts in 1948. In 1949 Van Patrick joined the Tigers with Heilmann, but Heilmann died in 1951. Patrick was the voice of the team from 1952 through 1959, working with former players Dizzy Trout, Mel Ott (until he was killed in November 1958), and then George Kell.

Patrick was succeeded by *Ernie Harwell* in 1960. Harwell's broadcast partners were George Kell (1960–1963), Bob Scheffing (1964), Gene Osborne (1965–1966), Ray Lane (1967–1972) and Paul Carey (1973–1991). Harwell was 73 when he was fired after the 1991 season. Under new club management he was rehired for the 1993 season. Harwell broadcast his last game on Sunday September 29, 2002, at age 84 and after 42 seasons with the Tigers—and 55 years of calling Major League games.

Al Kaline began broadcasting for the club in 1976 and was still with the Tigers until he finished the 2001 season. Kell broadcast through the 1996 season. Jim Northrup had eight seasons with the club behind the microphone until he departed after the 1994 season. Kirk Gibson broadcast from 1998 through 2002,

Lance Parrish was on the air in 2002 only, and Jack Morris started in 2003.

Frank Beckmann has been the voice of the Tigers since 1995, and former Major League catcher Jim Price worked his way up from cable to radio play-by-play in 1998.

Books. William M. Anderson, *The Detroit Tigers* (pictorial history) (1991); Richard Bak, *Cobb Would Have Caught It* (1994); Joe Falls, *The Detroit Tigers* (1975); Patrick J. Harrigan and Patrick Harrigan, *The Detroit Tigers: Club and Community, 1945–1995* (1997); Jim Hawkins, Dan Ewald and George Van Dusen, *Detroit Tigers Encyclopedia* (2003); Art Hill, *I Don't Care If I Never Come Back* (1980); Bob Italia, *The Detroit Tigers* (1997); Fred Lieb, *The Detroit Tigers* (1946); David Lee Poremba, *Baseball in Detroit* (1998).

Detroit Wolverines

National League 1881–1888

"In Detroit, they are not concerned with what happened in the years B.C. (Before Cobb). I very much doubt whether 100 people in the city can name the individual members of the 'Big Four' who won the pennant and post-season series in 1887."—Sportswriter H.G. Salsinger in *The American League*, edited by Ed Fitzgerald (1959).

In 1881 the Detroit club joined the National League as a replacement for the banished Cincinnati Red Stockings. The club was owned by W.G. Thompson, mayor of the city and first president of the Wolverines. The team's office was at the mayor's business address.

In 1885 Frederick Kimball Stearns bought the club and spent heavily to improve it. Stearns was the heir to a pharmaceutical company and is credited with suggesting the use of two umpires for the 1887 championship series. His partner was Charles W. Smith, a shoe manufacturer.

After Stearns paid $4,000 for "The Big Four"—Dan Brouthers, Deacon White, Hardie Richardson and Jack Rowe—Detroit won the 1887 pennant and challenged the American Association's winner, the St. Louis Browns, to a 15-game cross-country series. Detroit won the championship series in 11 games. In addition to the players purchased by Stearns, the team had Charlie Bennett (see also *Amputees*), considered the second-best catcher of his era behind Buck Ewing.

Stearns planned to reap profits on the road because the team did not draw well at home, but other owners changed the gate receipt rules and Detroit slipped due to financial problems. After a fifth-place finish in 1888, Stearns and Smith sold their "pack of tramps" for $45,000 and quit the league. The team folded and the city had no Major League Baseball until the American League was recognized as a Major League for the 1901 season.

The first Detroit Wolverines games were played in the 1880s at Helen and Lafayette in the east end of the city. In 1881 Recreation Park was built near Brush and Brady streets and the Wolverines played there throughout the 1880s.

Bill Dickey (1907–1993)

Hall of Fame 1954

"So they pitched to Dickey. When I saw that—and this is the absolute gospel truth—I turned around and picked up my glove, because I knew the game was going to be over right now. And it was. Dickey singled into center field. One way or another, he was going to get that run in. No doubt about it. He was one of your best money players."— Yankee outfielder Tommy Henrich on teammate Dickey's winning hit in the bottom of the 9th inning of Game 1 of the 1939 World Series; quoted in *Baseball Between the Lines*, by Donald Honig (1976).

Dickey starred at catcher for the Yankees over 17 seasons beginning in 1928.

William Malcolm Dickey was a native of Louisiana who played professionally in Mississippi and Arkansas before moving up to the Major Leagues. He played a few games for the Yankees in 1928 and exploded in 1929 with a .324 average in 130 games. He hit over .300 in nine of the next 10 years and had a career high 29 home runs in 1937.

Dickey played in eight World Series for the Yankees, hitting five home runs and batting .255. He finished his 17-year career in 1946 with a .313 average and 202 home runs, with 11 All-Star appearances starting with the inaugural event in 1933.

Dickey was considered the premier catcher of the 1930s and early 1940s, setting a then–Major League record with 13 straight seasons in which he caught 100 or more games. He might have extended his career statistics if he had not entered the military during the 1943 season at age 36. He was batting .351 when he left and missed the next two seasons. When he returned in 1946 he hit .261 in 54 games and then retired.

Dickey took over as manager of the club early in the 1946 season, finishing third. He later became a Yankee coach from 1949 through 1957. Dickey is credited with developing catcher Yogi Berra before leaving baseball to become an investment banker in Little Rock, Arkansas.

Dieting See *Food*

Martin DiHigo (1905–1971)

Hall of Fame (NLC) 1977

"Virtually everyone who saw Martin DiHigo agrees that he was the greatest all-round ball player who ever lived, black or white.... Only two men in baseball history, Babe Ruth and Bullet Joe Rogan, could rival him as a double threat man with the bat and on the pitching mound."— John B. Holway in *Blackball Stars* (1988).

DiHigo starred in the Negro, Mexican and various Caribbean Leagues from the early 1920s through the mid–1940s.

Martin DiHigo was born in Cuba and began professionally with the Havana Reds at age 17 at shortstop and moved up to the Cuban Stars the following year. In the mid–1920s he improved his hitting and became one of the premier hitters in the game. By the late 1920s he had begun to pitch for the Stars and various Negro League clubs. In 1933 he moved to the Venezuelan League for three seasons.

He played two more years in the United States and then left for the Mexican Leagues and other Caribbean leagues for the rest of his career (with a brief return to the States in 1945). From 1937 through 1942 he starred as both a hitter and a pitcher. He hit over .300 and led the league in strikeouts as a pitcher at least four times. He ended his career in 1946 at age 41, hitting .316 and compiling an 11–4 pitching mark in the Mexican League and finishing in Cuba with a 1–3 record. His spotty 12-year Negro League statistics show him to have hit .319.

DiHigo was by far the most popular player in Cuba and moved into the broadcast booth there in the 1950s. His popularity waned when he supported Fidel Castro's fledgling revolution. After baseball fan Castro came to power, DiHigo again surfaced as a national hero until his death in 1971. He was inducted into the Hall of Fame in 1977, though Satchel Paige insisted that DiHigo should have

been the first Negro League star to go in. He is also a member of the Cuban and Mexican baseball Halls of Fame.

As a result of his versatility, in an early 1980s poll of black stars, DiHigo was named by one group as the best all-time outfielder and third baseman. Another group named him to the all-time Negro League All-star team at second base.

Joe DiMaggio (1914–1999)

Hall of Fame 1955

"He was a guy who knew he was the greatest baseball player in America and he was proud of it. He knew what the press and the fans and the kids expected of him, and he was always trying to live up to that image."— Lefty Grove.

"There was an aura about him. He walked like no one else walked. He did things so easily. He was immaculate in everything he did. Kings of State wanted to meet him and be with him. He carried himself so well. He could fit in any place in the world."— Phil Rizzuto.

"A gawky, awkward kid, all arms and legs like a colt, and inclined to be surly."— Local newspaper report on DiMaggio during his first spring training with the San Francisco Seals, quoted in DiMaggio's ghostwritten autobiography, *Lucky to Be a Yankee* (1951).

"Where Have You Gone, Joe DiMaggio."— Lyric from Paul Simon's song, "Mrs. Robinson," from the movie *The Graduate*.

"I told myself not to worry: someday there would be another DiMaggio."— The last line of Red Smith's last column.

"He'll live in baseball's Hall of Fame.
He got there blow by blow.
Our kids will tell their kids,
Joltin' Joe DiMaggio's his name."— Lyric from a 1941 song by Allan Courtney and Ben Horner, introduced by Les Brown and his orchestra.

"But I must think, he thought. Because it is all I have left. That and baseball. I wonder how the great DiMaggio would have liked the way I hit him [the shark] in the brain."— Santiago, the old fisherman, losing consciousness, in Ernest Hemingway's *The Old Man and the Sea* (1952).

DiMaggio was the epitome of the Yankee dynasty while in center field from 1936 through 1951.

A native of San Francisco and son of Italian immigrants, Joseph Paul (Guiseppi Paolo) DiMaggio was the middle of three brothers to make it to the Major Leagues. Younger brother Dom batted .298 in 11 years with the Red Sox. Older brother Vince batted .249 in 10 years in the National League, leading the league in strikeouts six times.

DiMaggio starred almost from the outset in the Pacific Coast League. He began as a 17-year-old shortstop and at 18 he had a 61-game hitting streak for the San Francisco Seals. Though a damaged knee (see *Injuries and Illness*) made him somewhat less desirable, the Yankees gave him a clean bill of health and signed him for $25,000. He remained in San Francisco in 1935 and hit .398 before joining the Yankees for the 1936 season. He hit .323 and then exploded with a .346 average in 1937 and a league-leading 46 home runs and 151 runs scored. He also had 167 RBIs.

He led the league in batting in 1939 (.381) and 1940 (.352) and then had a 56-game hitting streak in 1941. He missed all of the 1943–1945 seasons due to World War II, but returned for six more years. Though hampered by injuries after the war, he led the league with 39 home runs and 155 RBIs in 1948. His last strong season was 1950, when he hit .301 with 32 home runs and 122 RBIs. He retired after hitting .263 in 1951.

The "Yankee Clipper" played only 13 seasons with the Yankees. Injuries plagued him throughout his career, but he hit .325 and placed sixth all-time in slugging average at .579. He also hit 361 home runs and drove in 1,537 runs. He batted .271 in 10 World Series and hit eight postseason home runs. When he retired, only Ruth (714), Foxx (536), Ott (511) and Gehrig (493) had hit more home runs.

DiMaggio's high-profile life continued after retirement when he had a short **Marriage** to Marilyn Monroe. He returned briefly to baseball in 1967 as an executive vice president and **Coach** with the A's under Charlie Finley. He was one of the best-known and best-loved sports figures in history. His "Mr. Coffee" commercials of the 1970s and 1980s continued his fame and then the sports memorabilia craze of the mid–1980s and 1990s kept him in the spotlight. In 1969 he was voted the game's greatest living player, but that title ended when he died in 1999.

Books. Richard Ben Cramer, *Joe DiMaggio: The Hero's Life* (2000); Joe DiMaggio, *The DiMaggio Albums* (1989); Joe DiMaggio, *Lucky to Be a Yankee* (1946 and 1951); Joseph Durso, *Joe DiMaggio: The Last American Knight* (1995); Morris Engelberg and Marv Schneider (foreword by Henry Kissinger), *DiMaggio: Setting the Record Straight* (2003) (Engelberg was DiMaggio's agent and confidante at the end of his life); Dick Johnson and Glenn Stout, *DiMaggio: An Illustrated Life* (1995); Jack Moore, *Joe DiMaggio: A Bio-Bibliography* (1986); Michael Seidel, *Streak: Joe DiMaggio and the Summer of '41* (1988); Al Silverman, *Joe DiMaggio, The Golden Year 1941* (1969).

Dirt See *Infield and Dirt*

Disabled List

"The Yankees are pretty strong, but they are weak on the disabled list. That's why they picked up Butch Hobson, so they can put him on the disabled list."—Giants broadcaster Hank Greenwald in 1982.

"Managers really encouraged players to talk it up on the bench. That was important. You had to keep those guys from falling asleep, because I've seen guys fall right off that bench and onto the disabled list."—Bob Feller.

"Derek Jeter is off the disabled list and Chuck Knoblauch is not throwing the ball away. All is right with the world."—Actress Sarah Jessica Parker.

"I felt fine a week ago, so I was getting pretty anxious. There's only so much rehab you can do, only so much batting practice you can take, and my wife is already pregnant. I needed to get back out there and play again."—Brewers infielder Pat Listach, finding his options limited as he waited to come off the disabled list.

See also *Injuries and Illness.*

Current Rules. There currently are 15-day and 60-day disabled lists. There is no limit on the number of players who may be placed on either list. A player may not be put on the 60-day list until his club has 40 players on its reserve list. A player put on the 60-day list after August 1 will be ineligible for postseason play. Players on the 15-day list count against the reserve limit of 40, but not against the active limit of 25. Players on the 60-day list do not count against either total. For many years there was a 21-day disabled list, but it has been abandoned.

To be placed on the disabled list, the player must be certified as unable to play, with a specific diagnosis made by the team physician. A signed form is then sent to the Office of the Commissioner.

Players on the disabled list are allowed to sit on the bench, but may not "jockey opposing players or umpires."

Frequency. From the 1989 season through the 1999 season, 3,282 players were on the disabled list for a total of 195,671 disabled list days. The average number of disabled list days per team was 640.6 per season. The number and length of disabled list days increased dramatically in that decade. In 1989 teams averaged 10.2 disabled list reports per season, for a total of 571.9 days per team. By 1999 the averages were 12.2 reports per season for a total of 787.1 days per team.

Injury Rehab Assignment. An injury rehabilitation assignment to the minor leagues for a player coming off the disabled list can last no more than 20 days.

Unfair Treatment. During the 1973 World Series, A's owner Charlie Finley embarrassed second baseman Mike Andrews after he made two errors in the 12th inning of Game 2. The errors gave the Mets four runs and led to their 10–7 victory. Finley forced Andrews onto the disabled list as a subterfuge for what amounted to an improper suspension, but commissioner Bowie Kuhn reinstated him immediately. Andrews made only one more appearance in the Series, pinch-hitting late in Game 4.

Multiple Appearances. After he signed for $105 million with the Dodgers in 1998, pitcher Kevin Brown went on the disabled list six times through 2002. He signed with the Yankees and went on their disabled list in June 2003 with a strained lower back.

Disaster Relief See *Benefit Games, Charity* and *Earthquakes*

Diseases See *Injuries and Illness*

Divisional Play and Play-Offs

"Baseball, to be sure, is like the nation that created it: too resilient to be counted out no matter how dire the forecasts. If the game can survive cartoonish owners (George Steinbrenner, Marge Schott), self-indulgent players (the entire New York Mets roster), 19th century labor relations and a defrocked commissioner [Fay Vincent]…, perhaps this latest wild-card wackiness will prove to be little more than an unfortunate rain delay. But don't wait till next year; this may be our last and best September."—Walter Shapiro in a 1993 *Time* magazine article on the 1994 realignment into three divisions in each league.

"'All right, already,' concedes the browbeaten wild card fan. 'You may have a point. Maybe the wild card hasn't been all it was cracked up to be, at least as far as competition is concerned. Maybe it was all shuck and jive, just a sales pitch, when they said it would give more teams a chance to reach the playoffs. But that first argument in its favor still holds, right? Baseball still gets all that extra money from the expanded playoffs. That's got to be good for the health of the game, right? We can trust the owners to take advantage of their increased revenues and do what's best for the game, can't we?'"—Stephen Taylor.

"I made my arguments and history will prove me right."—Texas Rangers general partner George W. Bush in 1993, voting against the wild card format. Wrong again.

See also *Expansion, Interleague Play, League Championship Series* and *Scheduling*.

19th Century. In the 1890s when the National League was bloated with 12 teams, the league made plans for two six-team divisions. The idea was quickly abandoned and instead the league tried a split-season format for one year in 1892. The first half winner played the second half winner in a championship series.

1969 Divisional Placements. When the Major Leagues expanded by four teams for the 1969 season, the unwieldy 12-team leagues were divided into two divisions each. Because of problems with *Scheduling* and feuding among owners to retain lucrative playing dates with popular road teams, strange pairings were made. For example, eastern teams Cincinnati and Atlanta were put in the Western Division of the National League.

The realignment was important to the owners because teams played more games against clubs in their own division. Mets chairman M. Donald Grant did not want to lose lucrative playing dates with the popular Dodgers and Giants. However, neither of those teams could be in the Eastern Division because of their West Coast locale. The league granted Grant's request that the Cardinals, also a lucrative draw, be put in the Eastern Division instead of the Reds. Cincinnati at that time was a doormat, although that status changed dramatically in the 1970s when the Big Red Machine emerged.

The Cardinals refused to be placed in the Western Division because they would lose profitable games with natural rival Chicago. A compromise was reached when both St. Louis and Chicago were put in the East, replacing eastern cities Cincinnati and Atlanta.

The new National League franchises were the Montreal Expos in the Eastern Division and San Diego Padres in the Western Division.

The new American League franchises were the Kansas City Royals and Seattle Pilots, both of which were placed in the Western Division. The 1969 alignment:

National League

Western Division	*Eastern Division*
Atlanta Braves	Chicago Cubs
Cincinnati Reds	Montreal Expos
Houston Astros	New York Mets
Los Angeles Dodgers	Philadelphia Phillies
San Diego Padres	Pittsburgh Pirates
San Francisco Giants	St. Louis Cardinals

American League

Western Division	*Eastern Division*
California Angels	Baltimore Orioles
Chicago White Sox	Boston Red Sox
Kansas City Royals	Cleveland Indians
Minnesota Twins	Detroit Tigers
Oakland Athletics	New York Yankees
Seattle Pilots	Washington Senators

1969/New Postseason Format. With the start of divisional play in 1969, a *League Championship Series* play-off system was created to determine the pennant winners. The format was a best-of-five series until 1985, when it was expanded to a seven-game format.

1970–1972 Shifts. The Seattle Pilots moved to Milwaukee for the 1970 season, forcing the new Brewers to play in the Western Division until 1972. When the Washington Senators moved to Texas to become the Rangers for the 1972 season, the Rangers shifted to the Western Division and the Brewers moved to the Eastern Division.

1977 Expansion. When the Toronto Blue Jays and Seattle Mariners joined the American League in 1977, the Blue Jays entered the Eastern Division and the Mariners entered the Western Division.

1992 Realignment Attempted. The National League expanded

into Colorado and Florida for the 1993 season. The Rockies went into the Western Division and the Marlins moved into the Eastern Division. In July 1992 in connection with the expansion plans, Commissioner Fay Vincent attempted to impose a realignment of the National League's divisions. Citing the commissioner's inherent right to "act in the best interests of baseball," Vincent usurped the power of National League president Bill White and the club owners by ordering that Cincinnati and Atlanta shift to the Eastern Division and Chicago and St. Louis shift to the Western Division.

Vincent made the move because the vast majority of National League clubs were in favor of the shift for economic reasons: the move of eastern cities Cincinnati and Atlanta would cut down travel costs and wear and tear on players.

Four clubs initially opposed the move: the Cubs and Cardinals, who had been in the Eastern Division since 1969; the Mets, primarily because they were showing support for the Cubs' position; and the Dodgers, apparently because they opposed the commissioner's intervention in what the club viewed as within the league's jurisdiction. The changes eventually received a 10–2 favorable vote by the National League clubs, more than the required 75% needed. However, any team subject to a change of division was required to vote in favor of the move; the relocating Cubs (along with the Mets) voted against it.

Although the switch was a natural move from a geographic standpoint, the Cubs were the most vocal about the negative aspects of the changes. The club cited the problem it would have in scheduling televised games from the West Coast that would start at 9:30 p.m. in Chicago. In response the West Coast clubs considered moving their game time up from 7:30 to 7:00 to help alleviate the problem.

Scheduling was also an issue, as most clubs favored an alignment that gave them 13 games against each club in their own division and 12 outside the division. A few clubs, including the Braves, favored a schedule that would allow 20 games against clubs within the division and only six against the other division's clubs. The 13–12 schedule had already been adopted by the American League.

The Cubs sought an injunction in federal district court in Chicago and successfully blocked the move. Vincent appealed to the Seventh Circuit Court of Appeal, which was to be heard September 30, 1992. Former commissioners Bowie Kuhn and Peter Ueberroth submitted affidavits in support of Vincent's effort. The plan and the Cubs' lawsuit were dropped before the hearing when Vincent stepped down from his position in August 1992 (see also *Commissioners*).

1994 Realignment. In 1993 the Major League clubs introduced a plan for three divisions in each league. There would be either four or five clubs in a division beginning in 1994. The plan was for the three division winners in each league and the best second-place club to meet in postseason play. The winners would then play for the pennant before moving on to the World Series. The Rangers and Tigers voted against the proposal, which was not defined completely at the time. The alignment:

National League

Western Division	*Central Division*	*Eastern Division*
Colorado Rockies	Chicago Cubs	Atlanta Braves
Houston Astros	Cincinnati Reds	Florida Marlins
Los Angeles Dodgers	Houston Astros	Montreal Expos
San Diego Padres	Pittsburgh Pirates	New York Mets
	St. Louis Cardinals	Philadelphia Phillies

Placement of the Indians and Pirates was the most problematic because both logically belonged in the Eastern Division of their respective leagues. They finally approved a move to the Central Division. The Indians' decision allowed the Tigers to stay in the Eastern Division. The Pirates' move allowed the Braves to move to the Eastern Division. The new alignment passed in September 1993 by a 27–1 vote, with Texas casting the only negative vote.

1998 Expansion and Realignment. Expansion to 30 teams in 1993 evened out the six divisions with five teams each. That changed in 1998 with two new **Expansion** teams in Tampa Bay and Phoenix. The 15 teams to a league would have forced interleague play on a regular basis; otherwise one team in each league would always be idle. There was no decision through early 1996 regarding the new divisional alignment or the placement of the two new clubs. Limited interleague play was scheduled for 1997 in anticipation of 1998. In 1998, when the Diamonbacks (National League) and Devil Rays (American League) entered the Major Leagues, the Milwaukee Brewers moved to the National League Central division, becoming the first team since 1898 to switch leagues. This created an even number of teams in each league (16 and 14), eliminating the need for an unbalanced schedule. Nevertheless, there was still discontent over the current system: "While there's a great deal of dissatisfaction (at least here) with the game's current division structure, I'm confident that few will be taken in by the current realignment proposals being floated by baseball's combed-over Bozo, Bud Selig. It's clear we need to get Budzilla (my nickname for the Man Who Trampled the World Series) another hobby; all his mindless, inept tinkering is doing little other than conjuring images of slapstick comedy. But Bud and his banana peel have long since ceased to be funny."— Don Malcom at BigBadBaseball.com.

Getting Old. In 2003 the American League East clubs finished in the same order for the sixth consecutive season.

Division Play-Offs.

"The format is harder to understand than the essay question on a Russian literature final exam. The American League's official media guide, the *Red Book*, even got it wrong. When an Indian official telephoned both the American and National League offices to find out which league champion has the home field advantage in the World Series, he received two different answers."— Tom Verducci in *Sports Illustrated* late in the 1995 season.

Best Division Play-Off.

"These games were totally incredible, they went right down to the last second. You can't ask for anything more. My hat goes off to the Yankees. It's a shame someone had to lose."— Jay Buhner after a wild five-game series between the Yankees and Mariners in 1995.

All future division play-offs will be hard-pressed to top the Mariners/Yankees series in 1995. The Yankees took a 2–0 series lead when Jim Leyritz hit a home run in the 13th inning after both clubs had scored in the 12th. The Mariners returned home to take three straight games and the series. In Game 5 the Mariners were down 4–2 when they scored two runs in the 8th inning to tie. In the top of the 11th the Yankees scored a run to go ahead, but the Mariners scored two in the bottom of the inning to win the Series

on a single by Edgar Martinez that scored Ken Griffey, Jr., from first.

Down at Home. The 2001 Yankees were the first club to lose the first two games at home and come back to win the five-game series, against the A's. Derek Jeter broke Pete Rose's postseason record for hits, with 87. The 2003 Red Sox did the same thing to the A's, who couldn't seem to make it out of the first round.

Dixie Series

This is the championship series between the Class AA Southern Association and Texas League.

Larry Doby (1923–2003)

Hall of Fame (VC) 1998

"There is something on the bottle that says you should forgive and forget. Well, you might forgive, but boy, it is tough to forget."— Doby on the abuse he endured as the first black American League player in 1947.

Doby was the first black player in the American League and lasted 13 years in the Major Leagues as an outfielder primarily with the Cleveland Indians and Chicago White Sox (see **Black "Firsts"** and **Integration**).

Born in South Carolina, Lawrence Eugene Doby was the son of a semipro baseball player who died when Doby was eight. After that, Doby moved with his family to New Jersey. In 1942, at age 18 he joined the Newark Eagles, for a time playing under the name of Larry Walker to protect his amateur status. Following a two-year stint in the Navy during World War II, he returned to Newark in 1946, helping a strong Eagles team win the Negro National League and the Negro World Series over the Kansas City Monarchs. In 1947 Doby was hitting .414 with Newark when he was signed by Cleveland owner Bill Veeck and played his first American League game on July 5, 1947, in Comiskey Park (see **Integration**).

Primarily a second baseman with Newark, Doby moved permanently to the outfield with Cleveland. He established himself quickly in his new league. In 1948, his first full season, Doby scored 84 runs and hit .301 with 23 doubles. The Indians won the pennant and his solo home run in Game 4 of the World Series (a 2–1 Indians victory) helped the club beat the Boston Braves in six games. In 1950 Doby hit .326 with 25 home runs, 102 RBIs and 110 runs scored. In 1952 he led the league in runs, home runs and slugging and began a three year run in which he had over 100 RBIs each season.

In 1954 the Indians won 111 games and the pennant with Doby leading the league in home runs and RBIs (second in MVP balloting), but he hit only .125 in the World Series sweep by the Giants. Doby was traded to the Chicago White Sox for the 1956 season and hit 24 home runs with 102 RBIs. He began to tail off after that, finishing in 1959 with short stints in Detroit and Chicago. He also played briefly for the Chunichi Dragons of the Japanese leagues in 1962.

After retiring Doby coached with several teams and became the second black manager in Major League history when he led the Chicago White Sox for 87 games in 1978. He later had front office jobs with the Indians, Expos and White Sox before working in community relations with the commissioner's office in New York.

For his 13-year Major League career Doby hit .283 with 253 home runs. He drove in 100 or more runs five times and scored 100 or more runs three times. Doby appeared in the Negro League East-West All-Star game in 1946 and was named to seven consecutive Major League All-Star teams between 1949 and 1955. He is also one of just four men to appear in both the Negro League and Major League World Series. Doby died in New Jersey in June 2003.

Doctors

"Dr. B.C. Miller, who takes the greatest delight in being present to repair fractured knee-pans and disjointed fingers, and bind up the general wounds of the victims of a too hot ball or other unlucky accidents, immediately attended to Glenn."—The *Chicago Tribune* in 1874, referring to a doctor attending to a player who cut his hand stealing second base. He cut it on the iron plate which held the bag.

"It's one of those nights you wished you had listened to your parents and went to medical school."—Cubs first baseman Mark Grace after his club lost 18–1 to the Braves.

Players.
"The Physician of Pitching Emergency"—Writer Damon Runyon on relief pitcher and physician James Otis "Doc" Crandall, also known as "The Doctor of Sick Ballgames." Crandall won 102 Major League games, including 21 in 1915 for the St. Louis team in the Federal League.

Arlie Pond was a licensed physician while playing Major League Baseball in the late 1890s. He left for the Philippines during the 1898 Spanish-American War and remained there permanently.

On August 4, 1905, the Highlanders battery consisted of two doctors: pitcher Jim Newton and catcher Mike Powers.

First baseman Frank Chance, son of well-to-do parents in Fresno, California, studied medicine before abandoning it for a 17-year baseball career.

George Stallings, manager of the 1914 Miracle Braves, was a Virginia Military Institute graduate who was studying medicine when he was called to play professional baseball.

Browns pitcher Bob Poser was signed to a contract by Rogers Hornsby when Poser was on a break from medical school. He had a five-game pitching career in the Major Leagues in the 1930s.

Joe Sewell graduated from the University of Alabama in 1920 and intended to become a doctor like his father. That summer he played professionally in New Orleans and planned to begin medical school in September. He was called up by the Indians when shortstop Ray Chapman was killed after being struck by a Carl Mays pitch. Sewell left for the Indians after only 45 days of professional baseball and never went to medical school.

Bobby Brown was a Yankee infielder in the late 1940s and early 1950s. After only eight seasons he retired at age 29 before the 1955 season. He entered medical school and became a successful cardiologist in Ft. Worth, Texas. He later was a part-owner of the Rangers and became *American League President*.

George "Doc" Medich pitched for the Yankees in the 1970s while holding his medical degree. In his first Major League start in September 1972, Medich drew a walk in the top of the 1st inning when the Yankees batted around. In the bottom of the 1st he could not get anybody out and was lifted for a reliever. He started medical school at Pittsburgh the next day. He returned in 1973 to begin a moderately successful career over 11 seasons with a 124–105 record.

Blue Jays manager and former outfielder Felipe Alou spent one year in medical school in the Dominican Republic in 1956 before embarking on a professional baseball career in the United States.

Team Physician. The 1890 Brooklyn Dodgers were one of the early clubs to have a team physician.

Association. The Association of Professional Baseball Physicians is located in Minneapolis. Modern Major League team doctors are members of the Major League Physicians Association.

"Pre-Med." Ron Taylor was the team physician for the Blue Jays in the 1980s. Prior to that he played for the World Champion 1964 Cardinals and 1969 Mets. In 1964, after the Cardinals' World Series locker room champagne celebration, the entire team except Taylor went to Stan Musial's home for a victory party. A security guard at the stadium purportedly found Taylor passed out under a pile of clothes in the locker room.

Bobby Doerr (1918–)

Hall of Fame (VC) 1986
"Doerr, and not Ted Williams, is the No. 1 player on the team. He rates the Most Valuable Player in the American League."—Babe Ruth on the 1946 American League MVP Award (won by Williams).

"I used to think, at a time when I knew less about these things than I know now, that Bobby Doerr was one of the unrecognized greats of history."—Bill James in *The Bill James Historical Baseball Abstract* (1988), who concluded that Joe Gordon was a better second baseman. James contended that Doerr was consistently among the best at his position, though not in the top 10 all-time list that he had compiled.

Doerr was the second base anchor of the Red Sox from 1938 through 1951.

Robert Pershing (born April 1918 during World War I—to honor General Pershing, presumably) Doerr grew up in Los Angeles and began his professional career with Hollywood of the Pacific Coast League in 1934. He hit .342 with San Diego in 1936 (playing with Ted Williams) and moved up to the Red Sox for 55 games in 1937.

He was Boston's regular second baseman for the next 13 seasons, except 1945 when he was in the military. He finished his career in 1951 with a .288 lifetime average. He hit 223 home runs and was considered one of the premier infielders of the era. He led the American League in slugging average in 1944 at .528 and was the league's MVP.

Doerr led the league in double plays five times and held various double play and errorless game marks during his career. He once went 414 chances without an error, an American League record at the time.

Doerr scouted for the Red Sox from 1958 through 1966 and then coached for the club for several years. He also coached for the Blue Jays in the early 1980s before retiring and spending the rest of his life in Oregon.

Dominican Republic

"Nowadays the [Dominican] baseball 'training complex' is as recognizable a mark of foreign domination as the sugar mill…. The clubs justify these combination soup kitchens, boot camps, and holding cells in terms of the welfare of the athlete…. Basic instruction in English supplements advanced seminars in coaches' sleeve-wiping coupled with a crash course in the gringo way of life. These kids from poor families have to learn not only how to handle umpires but a knife and fork."—John Krich in *El Beisbol* (1989).

"When will we have a World Series of Baseball, to show what a real world tournament might be like in a game we do care about [as opposed to soccer]. The Japanese, the Cubans, even the Canadians, for goodness' sake. And the Dominicans! Imagine a team with A.Rod, Sosa, Pedro Martinez, and Vladimir Guerrero, and Felipe Alou to manage—it would be the Brazil of Baseball."—Adam Gopnik in *The New Yorker*.

Early Play. At least one source reported that the Dominican Republic had teams competing for the Silver Ball Trophy as early as 1871. The teams were sponsored by sugar cane and other companies that built diamonds for their clubs. By the 1970s this legacy had enabled the country to become the largest base for Major League talent other than the United States. The country supplanted Cuba, whose doors were closed when Fidel Castro took power in the late 1950s.

One source reported that baseball was introduced to the Dominican Republic far later than the 1870s. It contended that, unlike other Latin American countries where baseball was introduced by students returning from the U.S., baseball was introduced to the country by refugees fleeing the Cuban revolution of the 1890s. Still another source reported that baseball was introduced in 1891 by a group of Cuban sportsmen led by brothers Ignacio and Ubaldo Aloma.

There was professional baseball in the Dominican until the late 1920s, but the professional game died out between 1929 and 1935. In 1936 a number of U.S. Negro League stars came to the island and the professional game was reestablished for two years. Between 1937 and 1950 there was no professional baseball in the Dominican. In 1951 the modern leagues were established and Dominican baseball became affiliated with Organized Baseball in 1955. By 1995 the most prominent Dominican league had the following teams:

Leones del Escojido (Santo Domingo)
Tigres del Licey (Santo Domingo)
Aguilas del Cibao (Santiago)
Azucareros del Este (La Romana)
Estrellas Orientales (San Pedro de Macoris)

Teams are limited to six foreign players. By the late 1980s the Dodgers owned two Dominican franchises and operated a baseball academy on the island.

Shortstops/San Pedro de Marcoris. This baseball hotbed of the Dominican Republic is legendary for turning out Major League shortstops, including Tony Fernandez, Rafael Santana, Alfredo Griffin, Rufino Linares, Jose Offerman and Rafael Ramirez.

Major League Players. When the 2000 season opened, 71 of 750 players on Major League rosters—nearly 10 percent—were from the Dominican Republic. In 1998, 860 foreign-born players were signed to professional contracts by Major League clubs. Of that number, 473, or 55%, were from the Dominican Republic.

Key Major League Players.

"[Raul] Mondesi … who'd grown up playing ball with the standard equipment of a poor Dominican kid: a milk carton for a glove, a sock stuffed with paper for a ball and a guava tree limb hewn into a bat."—Johnette Howard in *Sports Illustrated* on the then-new defensive star of the Dodgers.

Ossie Virgil. Virgil was the first Dominican player to arrive in the Major Leagues, in the 1950s. The utilityman batted .231 in 324 games over nine seasons.

Juan Marichal. Known as the Dominican Dandy, Marichal compiled 243 wins over 16 years and was elected to the Hall of Fame in 1983.

Rico Carty. Carty was a career .299 hitter who batted over .300 eight times, but was often felled by injury or illness. He lost the 1968 season due to tuberculosis and the 1971 season to a broken leg.

Jesus, Matty and Felipe Alou. Each of the three brothers had a solid Major League career. Matty was a lifetime .307 hitter over 15 seasons. Jesus hit .280 over 15 seasons and Felipe, the oldest, hit .286 over 17 seasons and went on to manage the Expos.

Joaquin Andujar. Billing himself as "One Tough Dominican," Andujar pitched 13 seasons in the Major Leagues, winning at least 20 games in 1984 and 1985. He lost his temper during Game 7 of the 1985 World Series, and was thrown out of the game during an 11–0 loss to the Royals. He was never again an effective pitcher.

Pedro Guerrero. Guerrero starred for the Dodgers and Cardinals at first base primarily in the 1980s.

Tony Pena. The stand-out catcher played for the Cardinals, Pirates and Red Sox primarily in the 1980s and early 1990s and went on to manage the Royals in the 2000s.

George Bell. Bell starred for nine years with the Blue Jays before moving on to a series of clubs. His career year was 1987, when he hit 47 home runs and drove in 134 RBIs. See also George Bell and Bob Elliot, *Hardball* (1990).

Julio Franco. The second baseman for the Indians, Rangers and White Sox in the 1980s and 1990s played in Japan in 1995. He returned to the Major Leagues in 1996 for the Indians, then missed another three years, but returned in 2001 with the Braves, where he appeared in over 100 games in both 2002 and 2003. He was still playing for the Braves in 2004 at age 44.

Sammy Sosa. Sosa emerged as the one of the premier home run hitters of all time after being traded from the Rangers to the Cubs. Sosa became the second Dominican, after Felipe Alou, to have 2,000 hits and 200 home runs.

Ramon and Pedro Martinez. Martinez pitched for the Dodgers in the 1990s and became the then-highest paid pitcher in Dodger history at $4 million annually. Pedro replaced Ramon as the premier Martinez pitcher, winning the Cy Young Award in 1999 and 2000.

Alex Rodriguez. Although Rodriguez was born in New York City and grew up in Miami, his parents were Dominican immigrants.

Miguel Tejada. The A's shortstop blossomed in the late 1990s, hitting 156 home runs in his first seven seasons before leaving for the Orioles in 2004. He was the 2002 American League MVP.

Managers.

Felipe Alou. Alou was the first Dominican manager in the Major Leagues, when the Expos hired him at age 57 in 1992. He was still going strong with the Giants in 2003, leading them to a division title.

Tony Pena. Pena took over as manager of the Royals in 2002 and was named Manager of the Year in 2003 when he led the mediocre team to a winning record.

Violation. In December 1999, the Dodgers were fined $50,000 and banned from scouting any Dominican players for one year. This was the penalty for signing third baseman Adrian Beltre when he was only 15 years old (below the mandatory age minimum of 16). Beltre was not allowed to become a free agent because, according to the commissioner, he participated in the scheme and because his claim for free agency was made too late.

Books. Alan M. Klein, *Sugarball* (1991), a sociological examination of the seamy underside of Dominican baseball; Rob Ruck, *The Tropic of Baseball* (1993), covering the history of baseball in the Dominican Republic.

Donut

"Elston Howard's On-Deck Bat Weight"—Official name of the Donut.

"Elston Howard, forever seeking ways to help himself and fellow hitters against the 'Amalgamated Association of Puzzling Pitchers,' has received a favorable response from a batting device he introduced."—Neal Russo.

The batting warm-up accessory is used to add weight when taking practice swings with a bat; it was invented by Yankee catcher Elston Howard, who obtained a patent on it. The Cardinals were the first team to buy his device in 1968. Howard supposedly had been passed over by the club as a player in the 1950s because he was black.

Double Plays

"He always said if you feel like you're going to hit into a double play, strike out." — Don Baylor on Orioles manager Earl Weaver.

"A double play takes 3.8 seconds. Even as dumb as I am, I can concentrate that long." — Umpire Ron Luciano; it actually takes about 4.3 seconds to turn the average double play, about the same time it takes most right-handed batters to go to first base.

"The poet or storyteller who feels that he is competing with a superb double play in the World Series is a lost man. One would not want as a reader a man who did not appreciate the finesse of a double play." — John Cheever.

"I'm workin' every day for a double play combination. Why, do you know a double play is two-twenty-sevenths of the ball game?" — Casey Stengel while with the double-play combination-less Mets.

"Give me the Hoover!" — Pirates broadcaster Bob Prince asking for a double play to suck the bases clean.

Barry Bonds displays the modern batting "donut" contraption. "Robo-bat" fits its owner. Note the custom "Barry" and "Bonds" elbow body armor.

See also *Infield Fly Rule.*

1860s Stars. Dickey Pearce is credited by many with the first recorded double play (a trapped pop up) and the first **Bunt**. Another source credits George Wright with the honor in 1870 while with Cincinnati in a game against the Brooklyn Atlantics.

Error. In 1898 it was ruled that an infielder would not be charged with a throwing error attempting to complete a double play unless the throw was so wild that it gave the base runner an additional base.

3-6-3 DP. One source credits first baseman Fred Tenney in 1897 with initiating the first double play from first to second and back to first (3-6-3 in the scorebook). It seems a bit unlikely that it took that long to occur. Another source reported that Tenney first originated the play while with Brown University in the early 1890s.

Statistics. The National League began compiling official double play statistics in 1933. The American League began the practice in 1940.

Tinker to Evers to Chance. According to research conducted by Chicago sportswriter Warren Brown, only 54 double plays were turned by the trio between 1906 and 1909. Another source reported it as 56 4-6-3 or 6-4-3 double plays (see also *Tinker to Evers to Chance*).

Longest Played Together.

"We've been together longer than lots of husbands and wives." — Lou Whitaker.

The longest-running second base/shortstop combination was Lou Whitaker and Alan Trammell of the Tigers. They played a few games together in 1977 and then played side-by-side through 1993. Though they began to tail off and play less frequently, they remained teammates until Whitaker retired after the 1995 season.

Whitaker was the American League Rookie of the Year in 1978 and won three Gold Gloves. Whitaker and Hall of Famer Joe Morgan are the only second basemen to play in 2,000 games, collect 2,000 hits and hit 200 home runs. Trammell was the 1984 World Series MVP and arguably should have been the league MVP in 1987 with a .343 average, 28 home runs and 105 RBIs.

The Dodger pair of shortstop Bill Russell and second baseman Davey Lopes played together for 11 years from 1972 through 1981, after which Lopes was traded to the Cubs.

Hardest to Double Up. In 4,553 Major League at-bats, Don Buford of the Orioles hit into only 33 double plays.

In 1934 Augie Galan became the first every day player to go an entire season without hitting into a double play. Ironically, he hit into one triple play in his 646 at-bats that season.

In 1968, Dick McAuliffe went an entire season without grounding into a double play and played in every game.

Astros second baseman Craig Biggio went 658 at-bats without hitting into a double play, including all of 1997, a streak that ended on Opening Day 1998 in his second at-bat of the season.

Consecutive At-Bats/No DP. The Major League record for most at-bats without grounding into a double play is held by Tony Womack of the Pirates. He broke Pete Reiser's record of 887, which Reiser set between July 20, 1941 and June 24, 1946 (gone for most of the war, however). Womack broke the record on July 27, 1998, and finished the streak with 918 consecutive at-bats over 212 games.

Hit into Most. Henry Aaron grounded into a then–Major League record 328 double plays. Cal Ripken broke the record with 350, after breaking the American League record of 323, held by Carl Yastrzemski.

In 2002 Brad Ausmus recorded his 1,000th career hit, but also tied the National League record with his 30th time grounding into

Ron Bush of the independent minor league Sioux Falls Canaries completes a double play.

a double play that season. The record he tied was set by catcher Ernie Lombardi in 1938.

The record for career double plays grounded into in the World Series is seven, by Joe DiMaggio.

Bad Day. Mike Kreevich of the 1940s Browns once hit into four double plays in one game, reportedly the first player to accomplish this dubious feat. However, Tiger outfielder Goose Goslin hit into four straight double plays in a game against the Indians in 1934.

On July 21, 1975, Joe Torre of the Mets grounded into four double plays. Felix Millan had four singles, but was wiped out each time by Torre.

On April 9, 1998, Orioles catcher Chris Hoiles was involved in four double plays in a single game.

Most by Batting Champion. Catcher Ernie Lombardi of the Reds grounded into 30 double plays while batting a league-leading .342 in 1938.

Red Sox third baseman Wade Boggs grounded into 23 double plays while batting .366 to lead the American League in 1988.

Outfielders. See also *Assists.* The most double plays in a game participated in by an outfielder is three, held by a number of players.

Red Sox outfielder Tris Speaker had six unassisted double plays, though most record books only credit him with four.

Good Defensive Day. On May 4, 1979, the Astros set a Major League record by turning seven double plays against the Giants.

On June 16, 1994, the Cardinals tied the record with seven double plays. The last club to tie the record had been the Braves in 1982.

On August 21, 2004, the Giants and Mets combined for 10 double plays, a Major League record, as the Mets won 11–9 in 12 innings.

Controversy. On the last day of the 1943 season, the Reds infield had a chance to break their double play record set in 1928 and tied in 1931. The Dodger runners were ordered to steal by manager Leo Durocher to prevent double plays. Durocher claimed that the Reds were equally at fault because pitcher Johnny Vander Meer intentionally walked a number of Dodger batters to set up double plays. The National League investigated the six double plays by the two clubs, but no action was taken.

Most Hit into/Teams. On July 18, 1990, the Red Sox and Twins combined on 10 double plays, setting a Major League record. The previous record of nine was set by the Angels and Red Sox in 1966. The Red Sox also set an American League record against the Twins by grounding into six double plays. The next day the Red Sox became the first team to hit into two triple plays in one game.

Phantom Double Plays.

"I cheated. I was the biggest cheat you ever want to see. I touched the bag but was across it before I got the ball. That way I got the ball away quicker. I was headed toward the shortstop or third baseman when I got it. Another result was that no baserunner ever took me out of a DP. Not once. I was far off the base when they came roaring in." — A's second baseman Pete Suder, who helped the club set a Major League record with 217 double plays in 1949.

Until 1978 umpires routinely allowed the "phantom" double play, in which the fielder does not actually touch second base before throwing to first base. Umpires were lenient because it afforded the shortstop and second baseman greater protection from base runners and their spikes, so long as the fielders were at least in the immediate vicinity of the bag before the runner. Beginning in 1978, umpires officially were to enforce the rule more stringently, but it appears that their prior leniency still exists.

Abner Doubleday (1819–1893)

"You ask for some information as to how I passed my youth. I was brought up in a book store and early imbibed a taste for reading. I was fond of poetry and art and much interested in mathematical studies. In my outdoor sports I was addicted to topographical work — even as a boy I amused myself by making maps of the country around my father's residence which was in Auburn." — This makes it reasonably clear that Doubleday had nothing to do with baseball in his youth despite claims to the contrary.

"Abner Doubleday died in 1893 without ever learning that he was the inventor of baseball." — Art Hill in *I Don't Care If I Never Come Back* (1980).

Doubleday was dubbed the **Father of Baseball** after a trumped-up 1907 committee known as the Mills Commission was formed by Albert Spalding to determine the **Origins of Baseball**. Doubleday was said to have invented the game spontaneously as a boy one day in 1839 in **Cooperstown**. However, Doubleday was a West Point cadet by 1838.

He is properly credited with the order to fire the first shot at Fort Sumter, the site of the start of the Civil War. Though he was relieved of his command nine days later, he returned to help lead the Union Army as a major general at Gettysburg.

Doubleday was a prolific writer after he retired from the Army in 1873, including 67 diaries, but never once mentioned baseball. His obituary in the *New York Times* on January 28, 1893, also made no mention of the game.

Doubleheaders

"Let's Play Two!" — Ernie Banks.

"Doubleheader tomorrow, barring nuclear holocaust." — Politically attuned Ron Taylor of the 1969 Mets.

"The only thing worse than a Mets game is a Mets doubleheader." — Casey Stengel.

See also **Tripleheaders**.

First Recorded Doubleheader. The first doubleheader may have been played on June 19, 1846, between the Knickerbockers and the Murray Hill players. This date has historically been cited as the date of the first formal baseball game, but there is clear evidence of games played by the Knickerbockers in 1845. Nevertheless, on June 19 the clubs played the first game of the day, with the Knickerbockers winning 23–1. The clubs then scrambled their players and played a second game, score unknown.

First National League Doubleheader. On September 9, 1876, Candy Cummings pitched the first Major League doubleheader, winning 14–4 and 8–4 for Hartford over Cincinnati. This was not a true doubleheader, however, because one game was scheduled in the morning and one in the afternoon, with separate crowds for each. The first true doubleheader (though not scheduled — it was due to rain) was on September 25, 1882, as Worcester and Providence split a pair.

Scheduled Doubleheaders. The first scheduled Major League doubleheaders are believed to have originated in the 1880s in Cleveland and were known as "bargain bills" by at least 1884. In her book, *The Real McGraw* (1953), Mrs. John McGraw credits the first Major League doubleheader to Baltimore in the American Association, played on October 4, 1884. Other sources, including sportswriter Fred Lieb, claim that the first doubleheader was on October 9, 1886, when Philadelphia played at Detroit in the National League.

Scheduled doubleheaders were rare until the 1930s. In the 1920s John McGraw said that scheduled doubleheaders were a good idea in the minor leagues and correctly predicted that the Major Leagues eventually would adopt the practice on a regular basis.

In the 1930s Cardinals general manager Sam Breadon began staggering his rotation so that Dizzy Dean could start on Sundays. This ensured a sell-out crowd for the usually lucrative Sunday games. Breadon is credited with introducing the modern scheduled doubleheader over the objection of other Major League clubs. He first instituted the scheduled doubleheader, primarily on Sundays, with his Houston farm team and attendance tripled.

The number of scheduled doubleheaders increased into the 1950s and then gradually decreased to almost zero. In 1992 there was only one scheduled doubleheader, between the Indians and Red Sox on April 12. The night before, the teams played a 19-inning game won by Boston 7–5. In the opener of the doubleheader, Matt Young pitched a no-hitter and lost.

In 1996 the Twins scheduled a doubleheader for the first time ever in the Metrodome. It was the only one scheduled that year.

The Phillies played a doubleheader on August 2, 2003, their first scheduled doubleheader since August 10, 1985. The Rockies played their first-ever scheduled doubleheader in May 2004.

See also **Scheduling — Days Off Comparison**.

Consecutive. The Braves played nine consecutive doubleheaders between September 4 and September 15, 1928. During that span they lost five consecutive doubleheaders, the first team to do so.

Opening Day. The Cubs played a doubleheader against the Dodgers on Opening Day 1935. The clubs may have agreed on this unusual step in order to boost attendance during the Depression.

Famous. Possibly the most famous doubleheader in baseball history was on July 2, 1933, at the Polo Grounds between the Giants and Cardinals. In the first game Carl Hubbell pitched 18 scoreless innings in a 1–0 defeat of Tex Carleton. In the second game Cardinals pitcher Dizzy Dean lost 9–0. Over the years some sources have confused the pitching match-ups by incorrectly reporting that Dean and Hubbell pitched against each other in the 1–0 game.

Both Ends Pitched/20th Century. In 1903 Iron Man Joe McGinnity pitched three doubleheaders in one month and won each of them. The strain of many innings apparently had no effect, as he pitched in the minor leagues until he was 54.

Big Ed Walsh, "The Man of Steel," frequently pitched both ends of a doubleheader in the early 20th century.

In 1916 Grover Cleveland Alexander won his 30th and 31st games in a doubleheader, winning 7–3 and 4–0 against the Reds. He completed the second game in 1 hour and 7 minutes.

Some sources erroneously reported that the last player to pitch a complete game in both ends of a doubleheader was Emil Levsen of the Indians. He defeated the Red Sox 6–1 and 5–1 on August 28, 1926. Subsequent pitchers accomplished the feat, however. For example, on June 19, 1927, 35-year-old Jack Scott, pitching for the Phillies, beat the Reds in Cincinnati 3–1 and 3–0. Dodger pitcher Don Newcombe pitched both ends of a doubleheader in the mid–1950s, winning 2–1 and losing 2–1.

Recent Winners of Doubleheaders. On May 26, 2002, Corry Bailey of the Royals won both ends of a doubleheader. He was the first pitcher to do so since David Wells in 1989. He pitched the top of the 9th in the first game trailing the Rangers, 5–4; but a 3-run rally gave him the victory. In the second game, Bailey got two outs to end the top of the 6th after the Rangers tied the game 7–7. The Royals rallied to take a 9–7 lead in the bottom half and went on to win 9–8.

Longest Doubleheader. See **Longest Games**.

Lead-off Home Runs/Both Games. See **Lead-Off Hitters**.

Seven Innings. The Montreal Royals were for many years a Dodger farm team in the International League. Typical of minor league doubleheaders was that the second game went only seven innings. In 1969 at the first home game played by the Major League Montreal Expos, the public address announcer made sure that the crowd understood the new rules: "When Montreal has a doubleheader, the second game will go the full nine innings, not seven."

Fewest Hits/Doubleheader. On April 12, 1992, Matt Young of the Red Sox pitched an eight-inning no-hitter at Cleveland, but lost 2–1. Young was not credited with an official *No-Hitter* under the new rule interpretation. In the second game the Indians managed only two hits off Roger Clemens to set a Major League record for fewest hits in a doubleheader by one team.

Two Ballpark Doubleheader. The Mets and Yankees played a day-night doubleheader in their respective ballparks on July 8, 2000. The opener was played at Shea Stadium, and the Yankees won both games 4–2. Dwight Gooden won his first game since returning to the Yankees. It was also the day on which Roger Clemens hit Mike Piazza in the head with a pitch (see *Beanballs*).

Three-Team Doubleheader. On September 25, 2000, the Indians played the second three team doubleheader since 1900, at Jacobs Field in Cleveland. The Indians beat the White Sox 9–2 in the opener, then lost the second game to the Twins in a makeup. The last three-team doubleheader was in 1951.

Good Season. The 1945 pennant-winning Cubs swept a record 20 doubleheaders.

Unusual. On August 4, 1997, the Mets played an unusual doubleheader with one of their minor league teams at Shea Stadium. The Mets beat the Cardinals 4–2 in a rain-interrupted game. In an earlier nine-inning game, the Pittsfield Mets beat the New Jersey Cardinals in a New York-Penn League game.

Doubles

"I don't know if this is what you're asking. But I feel closest to God, like after I'm rounding second base after I hit a double."—Eight-year-old Jewish boy, quoted in "The Children's God" in *Psychology Today.*

"He slides into second with a stand up double."—Jerry Coleman.

Most/Teams. On July 12, 1931, the Cardinals and Cubs hit 23 doubles, 13 by the Cardinals. Fans were crowded in the outfield, creating a number of ground rule doubles. It broke the record of 18 set by Chicago and Buffalo on July 3, 1883. Chicago set the team record with 14 on that date.

On August 11, 2003, the Royals and Yankees set a new American League record with 19 doubles in a 12–9 Kansas City win. The Royals had 11 of them.

On July 13, 1996, the Indians and Twins combined to tie the then-American League record of 18 doubles in a game. The Indians tied the American League record of 12 doubles in a game. The record was set by the Red Sox against the Tigers on July 29, 1990.

Most/Career. Tris Speaker had 792 doubles to set the all-time record. Pete Rose is second with 746. Stan Musial (725) and Ty Cobb (724) are the only other players with more than 700 career doubles. Speaker had 40 or more doubles ten times in his Hall of Fame career. He is followed by Stan Musial with nine seasons, and Harry Heilmann and Wade Boggs with eight apiece.

Most/Season. In 1931 Earl Webb of the Red Sox hit 67 doubles. Though Fenway Park's Green Monster was not yet in place, a large fence contributed to the high number. The closest anyone

has come to that record since 1950 is Hal McRae with 54 in 1977 and John Olerud with 54 in 1993.

Game. On June 16, 1997, Sandy Alomar of the Indians tied a Major League record with four doubles in four at-bats. On August 29, 1999, Albert Belle became the 40th player to do it. He did it again on September 23 that season.

Consecutive. On July 27, 2003, Marcus Giles of the Braves had four consecutive doubles, the first player to do so since Billy Williams in 1969.

Home Runs. Only three players have led the Major Leagues in both home runs and doubles: Albert Belle for the Indians in 1995, Willie Stargell for the Pirates in 1973 and Tommy Holmes for the Braves in 1945.

50/50. In 1995 Indians outfielder Albert Belle became the first player to hit 50 home runs and 50 doubles in the same season. Amazingly, he did it in a 144-game season due to the player strike.

Tris Speaker in 1912 and Craig Biggio in 1998 are the only two players to reach 50 doubles and 50 steals in the same season.

Team Record/Season. The 1930 Cardinals hit a Major League record 373 doubles.

Elite Group. On August 28, 1998, Paul Molitor of the Twins, in a 7–6 win over the Blue Jays, drove in four runs, hit his 500th career double in the 1st inning and joined Ty Cobb and Honus Wagner as the only players in history with 3,000 hits, 500 doubles and 500 stolen bases.

Draft

"These deals damage the system that rewards players for what they do as Major Leaguers. We're rewarding players who haven't played an inning as a professional. When you give $1.5 million to an 18-year-old, how eager is that player going to be to listen to a pitching coach.... He can say, 'Here's how I hold it, and look what I got—$1.5 million.' Players in the minors have been motivated to tap into the unbelievable rainbow when they get to the Majors. Now they're tapped in already."—Astros general manager Bill Wood after 1991 first draft pick Brien Taylor signed with the Yankees for $1.5 million.

"After the Series, the league above the Major Leagues will draft Orel Hershiser as number one."—outfielder Mike Marshall, after Hershiser shut out Oakland on three hits and had three hits himself in Game 2 of the 1988 World Series.

See also *Expansion Draft.*

Two types of drafts have been created over the years. The first is the minor league draft by which Major League clubs may pick players from other clubs' minor league rosters after each season, subject to certain restrictions. A form of this draft has existed since the 19th century and is now known as the Rule V draft. The second draft is the amateur draft of high school and college players, instituted in June 1965.

19th Century Minor League Draft. Player drafts were proposed as early as the 1880s. They were created primarily to protect minor league teams from being raided by the wealthier Major League clubs.

As part of the Compromise of 1892 involving all of Organized Baseball and its revised National Agreement, the National League instituted a minor league player draft. This allowed the best minor leaguers to be purchased by Major League clubs for a set minimum price.

That initial agreement provided that participating minor leagues could retain reserved players, but at the end of the season the Major League teams could draft other players at fixed prices. High minor league clubs could have their players drafted for $1,000 and lower minor league clubs for $500. This plan was created by *Sporting Life* editor Francis Richter, who also spearheaded the implementation of a program that allowed each minor league team to protect ("reserve") 14 players from being drafted by Major League clubs.

20th Century/Rule V Draft. By the early 20th century, most minor league clubs had signed the draft agreement and their players could be purchased for up to $5,000. A notable exception was the International League, led by Jack Dunn and his Baltimore Orioles. Under his influence the league refused to participate in the draft until 1924, when the Major Leagues modified the agreement to allow minor league clubs to hold a player for a few years before he was draftable.

The minor league draft has remained intact into the 1990s, with some modifications. In the modern Rule V draft, a club may select a player off another club's minor league roster if that player has played professionally for three or four years (depending on his age) and is not on the Major League club's 40-man protected list. The selecting club must pay the original club $50,000 and place the player on its active Major League roster. He cannot be sent down to the minor leagues that same season unless he is offered back to his original team for $25,000.

There is also a minor league phase of the Rule V draft. Class AAA teams can draft players for $12,000 and Class AA teams can draft for $4,000 per player. Players selected in the minor league portion of the draft do not have to be offered back to their original clubs. Under Rule V, a minor league player with six years of continuous minor league service may become a free agent.

20th Century/High School and College Free Agents. By the 1950s Major League clubs were competing fiercely to pay large signing bonuses to untried high school and college players (see also *Bonus Babies*). This gave an advantage to the wealthier clubs. Major League Baseball finally abandoned that system in the mid–1960s by creating an amateur free agent player draft that has been fine-tuned over the years.

First Amateur Draft/June 1965. The first amateur free agent player draft, known as the Rule 4 draft, was inaugurated after the 1964 season. The draft, held on June 8–9, 1965 (erroneously reported as January in some sources), included all high school seniors and college players. A total of 813 (or 814) prospects were drafted (identified erroneously as 600 in some sources). The Astros drafted the most players, 22. Clubs could draft as long as they desired regardless of whether other clubs stopped choosing players. Of the total drafted, 426 signed before the next draft. Of the 70 players selected by the Orioles, only three made it to the Major Leagues, a typical result. The first player to reach the Majors was Joe Coleman of the Senators, the third pick overall.

Draft Procedure. At first there were to be three drafts each year, but that was quickly reduced to June and January drafts. The first phase of each draft, held in June around graduation, involves players who are truly free agents. The second special phase was held in January for previously drafted players who did not sign with their clubs. This January Free Agent Amateur Draft was added in 1966. There were 95 prospects selected in the inaugural phase of this draft.

Each season the worst team in the National League alternates with the worst team in the American League for the first pick in the draft. The National League drafts first in even-numbered years. In the first round, clubs draft in reverse order of finish in the previous season's standings. After the first round, the clubs draft by lot on a rotating basis. Any player drafted at any level had to be retained for at least 90 days. A club is required to offer any drafted player a contract within 15 days, and negotiation could continue until 15 days before the next draft.

Originally if a player was not signed within 15 days of the next draft, he was put back into the next draft and the process continued until 1) he signed 2) he enrolled in a four-year college; or 3) he was no longer drafted. If the player went to a four-year college, he could not be drafted until he turned 21 or his class had graduated. The latter rule has been relaxed because of antitrust threats, which received media attention because of other sports (i.e., basketball and football) draft of prominent college underclassmen.

In 1976 college players who had completed their junior year of eligibility could be drafted regardless of their birthdate. A drafted player that does not sign and attends a junior college will still be controlled by the club that drafted him and he can sign only with that club after his initial junior college season. Today, players may be drafted as seniors in high school, while attending junior college, after their junior years at four year colleges, or if they turn 21 within 45 days of the draft.

In 1986 the last January draft was conducted. In 1987, instead of conducting a January draft of junior college players and unsigned players whose eligibility had expired, teams which failed to sign a first round selection were given a supplemental first round selection the following year, in the Rule 4 June draft.

On May 18, 1998, arbitrator Dana Eischen, in a seven-page decision, invalidated changes teams made to the Major League Rules in September 1997 that were designed to close draft loopholes. The charge was brought by J.D. Drew, the former Florida State outfielder, who tried to find a loophole in the amateur draft rules. He did not win free agency, however. Eischen said the player's status "is a matter for initial determination by the commissioner/executive council." Philadelphia lost rights to Drew after not being able to get a deal completed by the May 25, 1998 midnight deadline (15 days before the next draft).

Under the original draft procedure, each Major League club received one player in the draft, Class AAA clubs received two choices, Class AA clubs four choices, and Class A clubs unlimited picks, resulting in a record 101 rounds in 1990. However, because the Major League clubs controlled their minor league affiliates, in effect each Major League club had unlimited choices. Baseball eventually ended the facade of restricting the number of choices by level and created a 50-round draft in 1992. That restriction was lifted a few years later and then reinstated for the 1999 draft after 1,432 players were chosen during a then-record 74 rounds in 1998. A total of 855 were signed and all but one of the first-round picks signed. In June 1994 Major League clubs drafted 1,703 players. In 1999 there were 1,474 picks over 50 rounds, which was about average for the five years through 2004.

Warm-Weather States. California and Florida traditionally have dominated the drafts. For example, in the June 1989 draft those two states were home to 36% of the players drafted in the first five rounds. Through 1998, 11,308 California players and 4,412 Florida players had been drafted. Texans were third at 3,025. The fourth-place state was Illinois at 1,582 players (college players are credited to the state where they went to college).

High School Versus College Players. There was a tremendous shift in the focus of the draft as college baseball programs expanded and improved. The shift is reflected in the number of first round draft picks who were in high school in 1965 versus 1992, but then the trend drifted back toward high school picks in the late 1990s:

Year	High School	College
1965	15	5
1975	16	8
1985	19	7
1992	7	21
1998	14	16
2001	18	12 (including 9 of the top 11 from high school)

The seminal year was 1980, when 34 of the first 50 players selected were from college programs, more than double the previous highest total. An anomaly occurred in 1989, when 597 high school players were drafted, the most since 1970's total of 646. By 1995 the overall totals were 769 high school players and 886 college players drafted. In 2003 there were 1,480 picks, more than half of which were college players.

High school pitchers are the favorites of scouts, but are the least likely to make it to the Major Leagues: half as likely as college pitchers, and 75% less likely to make it as college position players.

Jim Callis prepared a statistical analysis of all players drafted and signed in the first 10 rounds between 1990 and 1997, and concluded that college players actually reach the Major Leagues more frequently, but by only two percentage points; and those who become Major League regulars arrive almost equally from college and high school.

Same High School. In June 1997 two players were drafted in the first round from the same high school. Shortstop Michael Cuddyer was the 9th pick, by the Twins. Pitcher John Curtice was the 17th pick, by the Red Sox. Cuddyer played briefly for the Twins in 2001, but Curtice never made it to the Majors.

Most First Round. The Orioles had four first round picks in 1999, the most ever. Only one, outfielder Larry Bigbie, has played more than one game in the Major Leagues (171).

All Signed. In 2003, for the first time, every player drafted in the first two rounds came to terms with his team.

Decrease in Bonuses. The commissioner's office made a strong effort to encourage clubs to reduce bonuses in 2003, and that is exactly what happened. In addition, the commissioner's office had to approve any bonus of more than $150,000 that was offered to a player drafted after the sixth round.

Free Fall. Matt Harrington went from No. 7 in the draft to No. 711. He turned down $4 million from the Rockies in 2000 as a high school senior and the fourth pick in the draft, and $1.25 million from the Padres when they took him in the second round in 2001. He was drafted in the 13th round by the Devil Rays in 2002, but he didn't sign. In 2003 as a 21-year-old, he was drafted 711th by the Reds in the 24th round and earned $1,000 per month with the Fort Worth Cats after receiving a nominal bonus. He had been one of the most coveted high school pitchers in 2000, but injuries and then poor minor league outings derailed his career.

Chances of Success. A first round draft pick has a 1 in 4 chance of making it to the Major Leagues. A second round pick has a 1 in 10 chance; a fifth round pick has a 1 in 20 chance.

Between 1965 and 1995, 774 first round picks reached the Major Leagues, and 8% of players in the first 10 rounds became regular players.

Canadian Players. Canadians were included in the draft for the first time in 1991. The highest Canadian draft pick in the first three years was by the Expos, who made the 55th pick right-handed pitcher Martin Mainville of L'Academie du Baseball Canada in Montreal (who never made it to the Major Leagues). Many scouts believed that he should not have been picked that high, but the Expos had been criticized in the past for passing up Canadian-born free agents. See also *Canada*.

Latin American Countries. The draft has no effect on Latin American players because only U.S. residents (including the Virgin Islands and Puerto Rico) and Canadians are subject to the draft. To cut down on the price of signing Latin American ballplayers, in 2000 commissioner Bud Selig proposed to make Latin American players subject to the draft, in part to prevent large-market teams from signing the high-priced talent. In response, Victor Garcia Sued, a former senator in the Dominican government, wanted to organize opposition from the Latin American countries. Sued had a vested interested, as he ran an independent baseball academy in the Dominican. Garcia said that the Dominicans would be at a disadvantage because most Latin players come from poor backgrounds and suffer from substandard nutrition. He said that boys in the United States and the Far East are two to three years ahead of Dominican players in physical development. Also, and obviously, Garcia said that an international draft would eliminate competition among teams for Latin players and keep salaries and signing bonuses down.

Foreign Players in U.S. Schools. The so-called Juan Nieves rule was created in the mid–1980s to permit drafting of foreign players who were currently attending school in the United States. Nieves was from Puerto Rico but was playing ball for an American university.

Trades. By the 1980s, once a player was drafted, his team was prohibited from trading him for one year; this became known as the Pete Incaviglia Rule. He was drafted by the Expos as the 8th pick of the June 1985 draft, but was traded that November to the Texas Rangers.

Drafted By Same Club. A player may not be drafted by the same club in two consecutive drafts without the player's written permission.

American Legion Draft. In the first two years of the amateur draft, a special supplemental draft was held to cover American Legion players. The draft was phased out after only 11 selections were made in 1965 and eight in 1966.

Last Round Major Leaguers. Selected Major Leaguers who were last-round draft choices (with the round listed):

Doug Griffin	Angels	1965	21
Dick Billings	Senators	1965	25
Steve Hovley	Angels	1966	35
John Wockenfuss	Senators	1967	42
Andy McGaffigan	Reds	1974	36
David Palmer	Expos	1976	21
Howard Johnson	Yankees	1978	23
Rick Aguilera	Cardinals	1980	37
Jeff Robinson	Padres	1980	40
Jeff Hamilton	Dodgers	1982	29
Mike Piazza	Dodgers	1988	62

High school senior Tony Gwynn went undrafted through all 72 rounds of the 1978 free agent draft. He went on to win eight batting titles.

The lowest round draft pick to make it to the Major Leagues was, at the time, Yankee pinch-hitter Scott Seabol, drafted in the 88th round in 1996. He first appeared in the Major Leagues in April 2001. Eleven days later, Travis Phelps of the Devil Rays appeared in the Major Leagues after being drafted in the 89th round in 1996.

Results of the First Draft. Rick Monday was the first pick of the first draft held in June 1965. He signed with the A's for $104,000.

The Red Sox drafted the fewest players, 20, while the Astros picked the most with 72. On the first day of the draft, players were drafted at the rate of about one per minute.

Drafting players often is an inexact science, confirmed by a review of the results of the first round of the first draft (drafting club in parentheses):

1. Rick Monday (A's): 19-year-old Arizona State sophomore who hit .371 in college. Monday spent 19 years in the Major Leagues beginning in 1966, hitting .264 with 241 home runs. Monday was among 10 future Major Leaguers chosen by the A's, creating the nucleus for their pennant runs in the early 1970s.

2. Les Rohr (Mets): 19-year-old left-handed college pitcher from Montana who was 2–3 for the Mets from 1967 through 1969.

3. Joe (Joel at the time) Coleman, Jr. (Senators): 17-year-old high school pitcher who played 15 years in the Majors, compiling a 142–135 record primarily for the Senators and Tigers from 1965 through 1979. He was the first draftee to reach the Major Leagues.

4. Alex Barret (Astros): 18-year-old high school shortstop who never made the Major Leagues.

5. Billy Conigliaro (Red Sox): 17-year-old high school player (brother of Tony Conigliaro) who lasted five years in the Major Leagues from 1969 through 1973, hitting .256 with 40 home runs.

6. Richard James (Cubs): 17-year-old high school pitcher who was 0–1 in 1967, his only year with the Cubs.

7. Ray Fosse (Indians): 18-year-old catcher who played 12 years in the Major Leagues, hitting .256 with 61 home runs from 1967 through 1979.

8. John Wyatt (Dodgers): High school pitcher who never made it to the Major Leagues.

9. Ed Leon (Twins): The Twins failed to sign Leon, an 18-year-old shortstop who eventually played in the Major Leagues for eight years, hitting .236 for the White Sox, Yankees and Indians from 1968 through 1975.

10. Douglas Dickerson (Pirates): 17-year-old high school outfielder who never made it to the Major Leagues.

11. Jim Spencer (Angels): 17-year-old high school player who played 15 years in the Major Leagues from 1968 through 1982, hitting .250 with 146 home runs.

12. William Grant (Braves): First baseman who never made it to the Major Leagues.

13. William (Gene) LaMont (Tigers): 18-year-old catcher who played five years with the Tigers from 1970 through 1975, hitting .233 with four home runs.

14. Alan Gallagher (Giants): 19-year-old third baseman who played four years in the Majors Leagues from 1970 through 1973, hitting .263 with 11 home runs.

15. Scott MacDonald (Orioles): 18-year-old pitcher who never made it to the Major Leagues.

16. Bernardo (Bernie) Carbo (Reds): 17-year-old third baseman who played 11 years in the Major Leagues from 1969 through 1980. His crowning moment was a three-run home run in the 8th inning of Game 6 of the 1975 World Series for the Red Sox against the Reds.

17. Kenneth Plesha (White Sox): 19-year-old catcher who never made it to the Major Leagues.

18. John Michael Adamson (Phillies): The Phillies failed to sign this 18-year-old pitcher, who never made it to the Major Leagues.

19. William Burbach (Yankees): 17-year-old pitcher who never made it to the Major Leagues.

20. Joe DiFabio (Cardinals): 21-year-old pitcher who never made it to the Major Leagues.

Number One Picks and Other Notables.

1965. Rick Monday was drafted by the A's out of Arizona State University (see above). He signed for $104,000.

1966. High school catcher Steve Chilcott was drafted by the Mets, but shoulder problems kept him out of the Major Leagues after six years in the minors. Chilcott signed for $75,000 and is the only pre–1990s number one pick never to play in the Major Leagues. The A's made Reggie Jackson of Arizona State the second pick overall.

1967. High school first baseman Ron Blomberg, later to be the first *Designated Hitter*, signed for $75,000 with the Yankees. The Red Sox made Carlton Fisk the fourth pick of the January draft (previously drafted but unsigned). Other first round notables were Ken Brett (4th by the Red Sox), Richie Hebner (15th by the Pirates) and Carlos May (18th by the White Sox).

1968. Tim Foli was drafted at shortstop by the Mets. Foli accepted a football scholarship to play for John McKay at USC, but abandoned that plan when the Mets signed him for $75,000. He made it to the Major Leagues three years later and played 14 seasons. Thurman Munson was selected 4th by the Yankees out of Kent State and Greg Luzinski was selected 11th by the Phillies.

1969. California high schooler Jeff Burroughs was drafted as an outfielder by the Senators at age 19 and signed for $88,000. He blossomed into a star with the Rangers and was American League MVP in 1974, hitting 41 home runs and driving in 114 runs. He was traded to the Braves in 1977 and finished his career in 1985 with 240 home runs and a .261 average. Reds pitcher Don Gullett was selected 14th and was the first player from this draft to make it to the Major Leagues. J.R. Richard was chosen 2nd overall by the Astros.

1970. Georgia high school player Mike Ivie was drafted by the Padres as a catcher and signed for $80,000, though he played catcher in only nine games over an 11-year career. He hated the position so much that late in his career he had a contract clause that prohibited the club from using him at catcher. Many future stars went in the January draft, including Chris Chambliss, Doug DeCinces, Rick Burleson and Bill Madlock. The Brewers made catcher Darrell Porter the 4th selection in the June draft.

1971. Illinois high schooler Danny Goodwin was the first pick in the draft, by the White Sox, but decided to stay in school as a pre-med student. He was drafted number one again in 1975, when he signed with the Angels (see below). The Angels drafted Frank Tanana 13th and the Red Sox made Jim Rice the 15th pick.

1972. The Padres made third baseman Dave Roberts the first pick in the draft. Roberts signed for $60,000 and left the University of Oregon campus to play immediately in the Major Leagues in 1972, batting .244 in 100 games. He lasted 10 years and compiled a lifetime .239 average. The Indians made shortstop Rick Manning the second pick and Scott McGregor was the 14th pick, by the Yankees.

1973. High school player David Clyde signed with the Rangers for $125,000. He went straight from high school (one of three players drafted who went straight to the Majors) to the Rangers, for whom he started 39 games in two years, winning only seven. He suffered arm trouble almost the entire time and ended his five-year career with an 18–33 record.

Clyde retired to run a lumberyard for 22 years, and in 2005 a movie about his life, *Walk On*, was scheduled for release and was to co-star Jessica Simpson as his former wife. Clyde said he preferred a "young Harrison Ford" to portray him. By 2004 Clyde was giving private baseball lessons near his home in Houston.

Dave Winfield, drafted 4th, went immediately to the Padres

outfield from the University of Minnesota. The Twins also brought Arizona State pitcher Eddie Bane straight to the Major Leagues, as the 11th overall pick. Shortstop Robin Yount was the third overall pick, by the Brewers.

1974. Brown University infielder Bill Almon was the first pick by the Padres, who paid him $90,000 to sign ($100,000 in some sources). Almon played 15 years and compiled a .254 average. Twelve of the first 13 picks played in the Major Leagues, including Lonnie Smith (3rd, by the Phillies), Dale Murphy (5th, as a catcher, by the Braves) and Garry Templeton (13th, by the Cardinals). Lance Parrish was the 16th pick, by the Tigers, and the Dodgers selected Rick Sutcliffe as the 21st pick.

1975. Southern University catcher Danny Goodwin signed for $125,000 with the Angels (after he had been drafted number one in 1971 but decided to go to college). Arm injuries limited his playing and he hit .236 with 13 home runs in a 252-game career as a DH and first baseman. The Indians selected catcher Rick Cerone as the 7th pick and Dale Berra was selected 20th by the Pirates.

1976. Pitcher Floyd Bannister of Arizona State was the first pick of the draft, by the Astros. He signed for $100,000 and pitched into the 1990s. The first 10 selections in that draft made it to the Majors, including Ken Landreaux (6th, by the Angels) and Steve Trout (8th, by the White Sox). Leon Durham was selected 15th by the Cardinals and Mike Scioscia was selected 19th by the Dodgers.

1977. Outfielder Harold Baines was drafted by the White Sox and general manager Paul Richards predicted that he would make the Hall of Fame. Baines, who signed for $40,000, was first scouted by White Sox owner Bill Veeck, who watched him as a Little Leaguer in Maryland in 1971 and monitored his progress as a teenager. In 1975 Baines showed up illegally at a tryout camp at age 15. He made it to the Major Leagues in 1980 and played 22 seasons through 2001, ranking 23rd in RBIs, ahead of such luminaries as George Brett and Mike Schmidt.

The Expos drafted pitcher Bill Gullickson as the 2nd pick. He was from Illinois, and many assumed that Veeck would take him for the White Sox. Paul Molitor was the 3rd pick, by the Brewers, out of the University of Minnesota. Catcher Terry Kennedy was drafted 6th by the Cardinals and pitcher Bob Welch was selected 20th by the Dodgers.

1978. The Braves chose third baseman Bob Horner out of Arizona State University. He signed for $175,000. The powerful but often-injured Horner lasted 10 years in the Major Leagues, hitting 218 home runs. Lloyd Moseby was the second pick overall, by the Blue Jays. Hubie Brooks of Arizona State was selected third by the Mets. Pitcher Mike Morgan, selected 4th by the A's, was one of four players to go directly to the Major Leagues. The others were Horner, A's pitcher Tim Conroy, drafted 20th, and Brian Milner, drafted in the second round by the Blue Jays. Kirk Gibson of Michigan State was drafted 12th by the Tigers.

1979. The Mariners chose Pennsylvania high school outfielder Al Chambers, who signed for $60,000. He played 57 games for the Mariners from 1983 through 1985, compiling a .208 average. Pitcher Tim Leary was drafted second by the Mets out of UCLA. The Expos selected Tim Wallach as the 10th pick overall. Don Mattingly was not drafted by the Yankees until the 19th round.

1980. The Mets chose Los Angeles high school outfielder Darryl Strawberry, who signed for $210,000. He made it to the Major Leagues in 1983 (Rookie of the Year) and went on to star for the Mets before fading in the 1990s with the Dodgers. Pitcher Ken Dayley was selected 3rd by the Braves.

1981. Pitcher Mike Moore of Oral Roberts University signed with the Mariners for $100,000 and started 27 games in 1982. He

pitched adequately for various clubs into the mid–1990s. Joe Carter of Wichita State was the second pick in the draft, by the Cubs. High school shortstop Dick Schofield was selected 3rd by the Angels. Ron Darling of Yale was the 9th pick, by the Rangers.

1982. The Cubs made Shawon Dunston the first pick after he hit .790 in his senior year in high school in Brooklyn. He signed for $100,000 and made it to the Major Leagues in 1985 but back problems slowed his career. Dwight Gooden was selected 5th by the Mets and Todd Worrell was the 21st pick by the Cardinals. The Yankees selected Bo Jackson in the second round.

1983. The Twins chose pitcher Tim Belcher, but he did not sign and stayed in junior college. He made it to the Major Leagues with the Dodgers in 1987. High school shortstop Kurt Stillwell was the second pick overall, by the Reds. Roger Clemens was selected 19th by the Red Sox out of the University of Texas. High schooler Ricky Jordan was selected 22nd by the Phillies and pitcher Dan Plesac was selected 26th by the Brewers out of North Carolina State.

In 1981 Roger Clemens was drafted in the 12th round by the Mets out of San Jacinto Junior College in Texas. The Mets rejected his demand for a $25,000 bonus and he chose to go to the University of Texas instead. The Red Sox drafted him 19th overall in 1983, one spot ahead of the Mets, who wanted him. Five days later he won his final college game to give Texas the College World Series title over Alabama.

1984. The Mets chose Pennsylvania high school outfielder Shawn Abner, who signed for $150,000 and made it to the Major Leagues with San Diego in 1987. His older brother, Ben, was selected in the 5th round by the Mets. Of the 25 first round selections, 17 made it to the Major Leagues by 1988. Sixteen of the 17 had been on the 30-man Olympic Games roster and a record 18 first-rounders were from college programs. The Reds finally selected a college player in the first round, Seton Hall's Pat Pacillo (5th overall). Shortstop Cory Snyder of BYU was selected 4th by the Indians. Mark McGwire of USC was selected 10th by the A's.

1985. University of North Carolina catcher B.J. Surhoff was selected by the Brewers and signed for $150,000. He made it to the Major Leagues in 1987. Will Clark of Mississippi State went 2nd, by the Giants, University of Michigan shortstop Barry Larkin was selected 4th by the Reds, Barry Bonds of Arizona State was selected 6th by the Pirates, and Rafael Palmeiro was selected 22nd out of Mississippi State by the Cubs.

1986. Third baseman Jeff King was selected by the Pirates and signed for $160,000. He made it to the Major Leagues in 1989. Pitcher Greg Swindell of the University of Texas was the second overall pick, by the Indians. University of Nevada-Las Vegas shortstop Matt Williams was 3rd, by the Giants, and Georgia Tech pitcher Kevin Brown was 4th, by the Rangers. Florida high school shortstop Gary Sheffield was selected 6th by the Brewers.

1987. The Mariners selected Cincinnati high school outfielder Ken Griffey, Jr., and signed him for $169,000 ($160,000 in some sources). He made it to the Major Leagues in 1989. Stanford pitcher Jack McDowell was selected 5th by the White Sox. California junior college pitcher Kevin Appier was selected 9th by the Royals. Catcher Craig Biggio of Seton Hall was selected 22nd by the Astros.

1988. The Padres selected University of Evansville pitcher Andy Benes as the first pick and signed him for $235,000. He made it to the Major Leagues in 1989 and won six games that season. He pitched through the 2002 season, with a record of 155–139. Oklahoma State third baseman Robin Ventura was selected 10th by the White Sox and first baseman Tino Martinez was selected 14th by the Mariners out of the University of Tampa.

1989. LSU pitcher Ben McDonald was drafted by the Orioles and signed for $350,000 as part of a $1.1 million, three-year deal. He made it to the Major Leagues that same season, winning one game in six appearances. He struggled over a nine-year career, but had win totals of 14, 13, 13 and 12 during his most productive seasons. Frank Thomas was selected 7th by the White Sox out of Auburn.

1990. Switch-hitting Florida high school shortstop Chipper Jones was chosen by the Braves and signed for $275,000. In 1992 he was simultaneously chosen Class AA and Class A Player of the Year by *Baseball America*. He first played for the Braves at the end of 1993. California high school outfielder Tony Clark was selected 2nd by the Tigers and California high school catcher Mike Lieberthal was selected 3rd. Stanford pitcher Mike Mussina was selected 20th by the Orioles.

High school pitching phenomenon Todd Van Poppel made it clear that he would go to college rather than turn professional. Nevertheless, the A's took a chance and made him their first-round draft choice (14th overall). They persuaded him to accept a three-year deal worth $1.2 million, including a $500,000 signing bonus. He debuted with mixed results at age 19 with the A's on September 11, 1991. Van Poppel suffered shoulder weakness in 1992 and did not pitch for much of the season, but pitched regularly (though erratically) starting in 1993.

1991.

"In high school nobody ever got on base, so I've got some adjusting to do."— Brien Taylor, after his minor league debut in which he threw a 90-mph fastball, struck out five in five innings and left with a 4–3 lead.

In a cutthroat and heated battle for his services, North Carolina high school pitcher Brien Taylor signed with the Yankees for $1.55 million. He signed the night he was supposed to start college. He received another $250,000 for a baseball card contract.

The Yankees put tremendous pressure on him and his mother to force him to sign a much smaller contract. The family held firm and finally received more than they were seeking, which was the $1.2 million paid to Ben McDonald in 1990. The heavy-handed negotiations were featured on a segment of the CBS news show "60 Minutes."

Taylor pitched in the minor leagues from 1991 through 1993. Over the following winter (December 18) he was in a fight in a trailer park in North Carolina (Florida in some sources) and hurt his shoulder sufficient enough to require surgery and put him out for the 1994 season. He had previously refused a Florida Instructional League assignment to work on holding runners and fielding. He never pitched in the Major Leagues, the only No. 1 pick between 1990 and 1998 who didn't make it.

California high school outfielder Dmitri Young was selected 4th by the Cardinals. New York high school outfielder Manny Ramirez was the 13th pick, by the Indians, and California high school outfielder Shawn Green was selected 16th by the Blue Jays.

1992. Cal State Fullerton third baseman Phil Nevin, 21, was chosen No. 1 by the Astros. In his final year of college he hit .398 with 21 home runs and 81 RBIs. He quickly signed with the Astros, in part because he wanted to concentrate on his preparation for the Olympic Games. He began the 1993 season in Class AAA and made it to the Major Leagues in 1995. The contract terms were not disclosed, but it was known that Nevin received at least a $700,000 signing bonus. In 1990 the Dodgers had drafted him in the third round and he turned down a $100,000 bonus. The highest-drafted high school player, shortstop Derek Jeter (drafted 6th) from Michigan, received $700,000 from the Yankees.

1993. Alex Rodriguez was a 17-year-old high school shortstop from Miami who was drafted by the Mariners. He was seeking more than $2 million, but signed for $1,259,000 in August 1993 on the eve of starting college classes ($1 million in some sources). Rodriguez made his Major League debut on July 8, 1994, after suffering a severe knee injury in spring training that year.

Second pick Darren Dreifort, a pitcher from Wichita State, signed with the Dodgers for $1.3 million and started the 1994 season with the club without any prior minor league experience. He lasted only a few weeks before he was sent down for more seasoning. He later signed a $55 million, five-year deal with the Dodgers, but was plagued by shoulder and knee injuries.

Arizona high school outfielder Torii Hunter was drafted 20th by the Twins.

1994. Florida State pitcher Paul Wilson was selected first by the Mets and received a $1.55 million contract. Wilson was a 6'5" Florida State junior with a 95 mph fastball. He pitched reasonably well in Class A in late 1994, but failed to win a game. He moved up to Class AA in 1995 and then the Mets late in the season. Wilson had surgery in November 1996 and was 5–12 as a rookie in 1996. He had several more surgeries, including Tommy John ligament surgery in 1999, and never regained his form. Wilson was still at in 2003, having been traded by the Mets in 2000 to the Devil Rays. He signed with the Reds before the 2003 season, but continued to struggle. Wilson finally had a small measure of success in early 2004 when he began the season with six straight wins.

The Florida Marlins paid high school star Josh Booty, the 5th pick, $1.6 million, the largest signing bonus ever. Texas high schooler Ben Grieve was the 2nd pick, by the A's. Nomar Garciaparra was drafted 12th by the Red Sox out of Georgia Tech.

1995. The Angels selected Darin Erstad, a junior outfielder at Nebraska. He had been drafted by the Mets in the 13th round of the 1992 draft. Erstad was recruited to punt for Nebraska's football team but ended up playing baseball. He hit .410 with 19 home runs and 76 RBIs in 58 games during his junior year. He was still with the Angels in 2004.

The second pick in the draft, Pennsylvania high school catcher Ben Davis, received a $1.3 million signing bonus from the Padres and made it to the Majors for good in 1999. Texas high school pitcher Kerry Wood was drafted 4th by the Cubs. The Rockies selected Todd Helton 8th, from the University of Tennessee.

1996. The Pirates drafted Clemson pitcher Kris Benson, a member of the 1996 U.S. Olympic team. His college teammate, Billy Koch, was drafted 4th by the Blue Jays. When Benson won his first start, he was only the second No. 1 draft pick, with David Clyde in 1973, to do so.

The second pick was Travis Lee by the Twins out of San Diego State.

Matt White was drafted by the Giants but did not sign (his agent was Scott Boras, who represented J.D. Drew the following year). He became a free agent and received $10.2 million bonus from the Diamondbacks, the largest ever. In 2003 he relieved in six games for Boston and Seattle, losing one, in his only Major League appearances.

The A's drafted third baseman Eric Chavez, a San Diego high school player.

1997. The Tigers selected Matt Anderson, a relief pitcher from Rice University. Anderson was named the top pitching prospect by *Baseball America*. He made it to the Majors in 1998 after only a few weeks of Class A ball and posted a 5–1 record and 3.27 ERA in 42 appearances for the Tigers. He slipped in 1999 after suffering control problems, but remained with the club into the 2000s.

Second pick J.D. Drew rejected the Phillies' offer of $2.6 million plus $100,000 a season through 2001. He was forced back into the draft after an arbitrator's ruling and signed with the Cardinals the following year. In May 1998 arbitrator Dana E. Eischen ruled that Drew was subject to the draft and was not a free agent. Drew and his agent, Scott Boras, had argued that because Drew played in the independent Northern League the prior season, he was a true free agent. The Phillies would not meet Drew's demand for $11 million. The Tigers had skipped signing him because of the anticipated cost. Drew was the first college player to hit 30 home runs and steal 30 bases in a season.

Troy Glaus was selected 3rd by the Angels out of UCLA. Lance Berkman was drafted 16th by the Astros out of Rice. Shortstop Adam Kennedy was selected 20th by the Cardinals out of Cal State Northridge.

1998. University of Miami (Fl.) first baseman Pat Burrell was selected first by the Phillies and signed for over $3 million. His .888 slugging percentage was second in NCAA history. Michigan State pitcher Mark Mulder was selected second by the A's and received $3.2 million. High school player Corey Patterson was taken third by the Cubs and signed for a record $3.9 million.

J.D. Drew was selected fifth by the Cardinals after he failed to sign with the Phillies the year before. The Cardinals signed him to an $8.5 million contract.

High school third baseman Sean Burroughs, son of Major Leaguer Jeff Burroughs, was selected 9th by the Padres.

1999. North Carolina high school outfielder Josh Hamilton received a $3.96 million bonus from Tampa Bay. He was the first high school number one pick since 1993. As of 2004, he still had not made it to the Major Leagues, and his *Psychological Problems* made a successful career unlikely.

The No. 2 pick was high schooler Josh Beckett, who signed for $3.625 million. He pitched a two-hit shutout for the Marlins in the 2003 World Series against the Yankees and also won the deciding Game 6.

Catcher Eric Munson was chosen third by the Tigers and signed for $3.65 million (he was drafted in the second round by the Braves in 1996).

A total of 34 players (all but one first-rounder) sign for $1 million or more, and 76 players in the first 10 rounds received $500,000 or more. The Pirates signed their 39th round pick, Patrick O'Brien, for $500,000.

2000. California high school first baseman Adrian Gonzalez was drafted by the Marlins and signed for $3 million. They traded him to the Rangers in mid–2003 in return for reliever Urgueth Urbina. Gonzalez had made it to Class AA by that time. The Cubs chose Miami high school shortstop Luis Montanez as the third pick. The Twins made the second pick Cal State Fullerton pitcher Adam Johnson.

The White Sox selected as the 12th pick Stanford football player Joe Borchard, who signed for $5.3 million, the highest bonus in the draft.

2001. Hometown favorite Joe Mauer was drafted as a catcher by the Twins. He was the first catcher drafted at No. 1 since B.J. Surhoff in 1985. At 6'4" and 220 pounds, Mauer was *USA Today's* offensive player of the year in football and received a scholarship to play football at Florida State. He was named *Baseball America's* 2003 minor league player of the year.

The second pick in the draft, USC pitcher Mark Prior, made a much faster impact in the Major Leagues with the Cubs. Prior had previously turned down $1.7 million from the Yankees when he graduated from high school.

2002. The Pirates paid $4 million to Ball State pitcher Bryan Bullington. The next seven picks were high schoolers, including No. 2 pick Melvin Upton, a shortstop selected by Tampa Bay. The No. 6 pick was Prince Fielder, selected by the Brewers and the son of former Major Leaguer Cecil Fielder.

2003.

"We should be able to win that World Series title before 2010." — Delmon Young. Young, the 6'3", 205-pound brother of Tigers outfielder Dmitri Young (No. 4 pick in 1991 by the Cardinals), signed out of Camarillo High School in California (the same school as 2000 draftee Joe Borchard) by the Devil Rays for $5.8 million over five years. He received a $3.7 million signing bonus. The first player to make it to the Major Leagues was Ryan Wagner, a pitcher drafted 14th overall by the Reds out of the University of Houston. The No. 2 pick was Ricky Weeks, a Southern University second baseman drafted by the Brewers.

2004. San Diego high school shortstop Matt Bush signed with the Padres for $3.15 million and was to start in rookie ball for the club. The 18-year-old was suspended by the club two weeks after the draft when he was arrested at an Arizona nightclub for investigation of trespass, disorderly conduct and assault. Apparently he bit one of the bouncers who escorted him off the premises. After glowing statements about him on draft day, Padres general manager Kevin Towers was asked if the arrest had changed his opinion: "It certainly hasn't helped."

Worst Choices. The 1968 Expos (at the time a new franchise) and the 1981 Braves are the only clubs to have drafted no players who made it to the Major Leagues.

Expansion Club Participation. All expansion clubs in 1968 participated in the June phase of the amateur draft, but not the earlier January phase. Some sources reported erroneously that 1977 was the first year in which expansion clubs participated in the draft. Still other sources reported that in expansion years prior to the 1990s, new expansion clubs were not allowed to participate in that year's regular draft of high school and college players. The confusion may lie in the fact that the 1969 expansion clubs did not participate in the first three rounds of the June 1968 draft. The 1977 clubs did not participate in the 1976 draft, but were allowed to make selections as the last two teams of the first round in the 1977 draft.

Drafting Pattern. The Twins under the penurious Calvin Griffith historically drafted college seniors because they had the least amount of bargaining leverage and could be signed for the lowest amounts.

Low Round Drafting. Clubs are not required to keep drafting until all rounds are completed. For example, in 2003 there were 50 rounds, but the A's were the first club to stop drafting, after the 31st round.

Court Challenges. In 1979 high school pitcher Bill Bordley threatened an antitrust lawsuit over the legality of the draft because he was not allowed to sign with a West Coast team after being drafted by the Reds. The commissioner's office publicly defended the draft while it quietly negotiated a deal to send Bordley from the Reds to the Giants.

Tampering. In June 1980, the Yankees selected high school star Billy Cannon, Jr., son of former Heisman Trophy winner Billy Cannon. The father had written to 25 teams explaining that his son planned to attend college and therefore they should not draft him. Cannon would otherwise have been a first round selection. The Yankees selected him in the third round, but Commissioner Bowie Kuhn voided the selection after it was determined that the club had colluded with the Cannons. Cannon then decided to attend Texas

A&M on a football scholarship and later was drafted by the Dallas Cowboys.

Father/Son Picks. Rangers general manager Tom Grieve was taken by the Senators in the first round of the 1966 draft. His son Ben was drafted second in the 1994 draft and received $1.2 million from the A's.

In 1977 catcher Terry Kennedy, son of then–Cubs general manager Bob Kennedy, was drafted by the Cardinals as the sixth pick overall.

Strike Season/1994. The Expos had the best record in the Major Leagues during the strike-shortened 1994 season. Even though they received no reward for the strong finish, they were required to draft last based on the regular practice of drafting in reverse order of finish.

Book. W. C. Madden, *Baseball's First-Year Player Draft, Team by Team through 1999* (2001); Allan Simpson (ed.), *The Baseball Draft: The First 25 Years* (1990).

Dragging the Infield   See *Groundskeepers*—Dragging the Infield

Dress Code and Clothing

"The wardrobe acquired by Phil Rizzuto, Is as tasty as melon and prosciutto."—Line from an Ogden Nash poem, "The Diamond Dude."

"There goes my wardrobe."—Jason Thompson after Tigers manager Sparky Anderson banned denim jeans on road trips.

"Zito dresses like a '70s porn star."—Mychael Urban on A's pitcher Barry Zito.

"You're a Major League player. You get paid like a Major League player. At least resemble one when you get to the ballpark."—Devil Rays manager Lou Piniella in 2003, who decreed that his players wear dress pants to home games.

"He's [Carl Yastrzemski] a dull, boring potato farmer from Long Island who just happened to be a great ballplayer. But he was the worst dresser in Organized Baseball. He made Inspector Clouseau look like a candidate for Mr. Blackwell's list of best-dressed men. He had the same London Fog raincoat during his entire career. We'd throw it in trashcans all around the league, and somehow it mysteriously made its way back."—Pitcher Bill Lee.

"The man's idea of a three-piece suit is a shirt, ironed jeans and a pair of cowboy boots."—Bob Nightengale on Dodger manager Bill Russell.

"Jess Buckles, John Cuff, Levi Meyerle, Tex Jeanes, Socks Seybold, Boots Poffenberger, Boots Day, Royce Lint, Cotton Tierney, Rags Faircloth, Bunny Fabrique, Hal Leathers, Button Briggs, Orval Overall, Jim Bluejacket, Jim Coates, Slicker Parks, Dickey Pearce, Ty Cline, George Derby, Cap Anson, Wally Hood"

See also *Uniforms.*

Sartorial Splendor.

"Standing six-foot-three in what was left of his stockings, he was wearing a suit of Arizona store clothes that would have been a fair fit for Singer's youngest Midget and looked like he had pressed it with a tractor that had been parked on a river bottom…. But when you seen his shirt, you wondered if he hadn't rode in the cab and loaned it to the fireman for a washcloth."—Ring Lardner in "Hurry Kane" (1929).

Long-time Red Sox scout "Broadway" Charlie Wagner was once described by *Esquire* magazine as one of the best-dressed men in America.

Neck Ties.

"[Bill Veeck] wears his sport shirt collar open all the time just to show that he did not come by any 'bad habits' in the Marines when he was, of course, forced to wear a necktie."—The *Stars and Stripes* military newspaper.

"I still think neckties are designed to get in your soup."—Ted Williams, who supposedly was sent down to the minor leagues for refusing to wear a tie in the hotel where the team was staying. This bit of folklore is never mentioned in his autobiography, though he is legendary for hating ties.

Prank. In June 1996 Korean pitcher Chan Ho Park of the Dodgers was the subject of a rookie prank to which he did not respond well. After he had won a game with his bat, his teammates shredded his suit and shirt and replaced them in his locker with a hideous disco outfit. As was customary, Park was expected to wear the outfit through the airport. Park apparently did not understand or appreciate the humor; as soon as he saw the torn clothing he began screaming obscenities and refused to wear the new clothes. He did not cool down until the next day when he responded more calmly to the media about the prank.

Drug Use and Abuse

"Well I'm not, so that's 49% right there."—Rickey Henderson, responding to claims that 50% of Major League players were using steroids."

"Freud would have taken to baseball the way he took to cocaine. Mid-European intellectuals have an *organ* for baseball."—Andrei Codrescu in *The Temple of Baseball*, edited by Richard Grossinger (1985).

"Dock Ellis had the greatest sporting achievement of the 20th century, as far as I'm concerned. He pitched a no-hitter on acid."—Dan Reed, lead singer of a popular band in Cincinnati in the 1990s known as Dock Ellis. Ellis admitted that he was sometimes high on drugs on the mound during the 1960s and 1970s.

"I hope the guys I play against do it. I don't give a shit. It is just going to make my job easier."—Pete Rose in *Playboy*.

"If the [hockey] Canadians are the Habs, our pitching staff is the Rehabs."—Expos publicist Richard Griffin on the number of Expo pitchers coming out of drug and alcohol rehabilitation programs.

"Players can't do drugs unless they bring enough to go around."—One of David Letterman's "Top ten ways Major League Baseball teams can win back the fans."

"Mike Marshall is going back to Los Angeles to get cocaine for his injured foot."—Broadcaster Harry Caray in 1984; he was quickly corrected by broadcast partner Steve Stone: "Novocain."

Late 19th and Early 20th Century.

"Pure elixir of malt and hops beats all the drugs and all the drops."—1880s refrain in support of beer over drugs.

As early as 1886 newspapers accused Washington players of using opium. Before World War I the use of cocaine, heroin and marijuana was not uncommon because each was legal.

Amphetamines.

"Amphetamines improved my performance about 5%. Unfortunately, in my case, that wasn't enough."—Pilots pitcher Jim Bouton.

"True grit: trying to make it through a hangover without a greenie."—Pilots catcher Jim Pagliaroni on using amphetamines.

At least since World War II, "uppers" have probably been the drug of choice among Major League ballplayers. Willie Mays was known for his "red juice" amphetamines and Pete Rose was said to have been the primary distributor among the Reds.

Writer George Vecsey told of one of the best pitchers of the 1960s, "a model of conservative propriety," who, because of amphetamines, was at least once "babbling a blue streak in the clubhouse" just before going out to pitch.

Marijuana.

"Boys, if you get caught with Mary Jane, you better be hitting four-fucking-eighty at the All-Star break." — An anonymous coach on marijuana.

While still an active Major League pitcher, Bill Lee admitted sprinkling marijuana on buckwheat cakes, prompting a $250 fine by commissioner Bowie Kuhn. The money was donated to a charity of Lee's choice, an Alaskan mission, prompting Lee to comment about Kuhn: "If I had sent it to a charity of his choice, I'm sure it would have been [President] Nixon."

As part of a 2003 investigation into sexual abuse by a long-time Boston Red Sox clubhouse attendant, a police report indicated that a 13-year-old attendant would be given $250 by former reliever Dennis Eckersley to buy marijuana, and to "keep the change." Eckersley's response: "I don't recall anything that happened over 20 years ago. That's what I'm sticking to."

Team Use.

Washington Senators. It was known that pitchers on the 1970 Senators were using anabolic steroids with the club's blessing in an effort to create greater strength.

Kansas City Royals. In 1983 the Royals suffered through a drug scandal. Willie Wilson, Willie Mays Aikens, Jerry Martin and Vida Blue were implicated in cocaine purchases based on federal investigators' wiretaps. Martin served three months at the Fort Worth Correctional Institute. All but Blue were reinstated (with other teams) on May 15, 1984, and Blue came back in 1985 after serving a short prison term. He pitched for the Giants and then went to Oakland for the 1987 season. However, he failed his spring training urine test and retired rather than face further scandal.

After his drug conviction, Aikens starred in the Mexican League in an attempt to get his career on track, but never returned to the Major Leagues. He was convicted in 1994 of drug trafficking (70 grams of cocaine) and went to prison for 20 years without possibility of parole.

1985 Pittsburgh Drug Trial.

"A demon in me." — Keith Hernandez on cocaine.

Pittsburgh was the site of a 1985 drug trial in which it was revealed that at least 19 Major League players had used drugs. Among those implicated were Willie Stargell, Dave Parker, Bill Madlock, Dale Berra, John Milner and Keith Hernandez. A number of players were granted prosecutorial immunity for testifying against the suppliers, which included a Philadelphia caterer.

Commissioner Peter Ueberroth gave most of the players the option of being suspended or doing 50–200 hours of community service and donating 5–10% of their 1986 salaries to drug treatment centers. Most of the penalties were not enforced, apparently through negligence of the commissioner's office.

Parker had signed a huge multi-year contract in 1979, with much of the salary deferred to 1987. When it came due, the Pirates refused to pay based on the morals clause in the contract, citing Parker's alleged association with a drug dealer who frequented the Pirate clubhouse. Parker sued and then settled for $1.8 million of the $5.3 million he claimed the club owed him.

2003–2004 BALCO Scandal.

"A galaxy of stars is insisting that Victor Conte, founder of the Bay Area health-supplement firm BALCO, did *not* supply them with steroids. Rather, he was simply the scientist best qualified to provide world-class nutritional analysis, based on his previous job as bassist for the soul band Tower of Power." — Steve Rushin.

"Y'all act like it's a big deal to gain weight when you get old. I got it down to an exact science." — Basketball commentator Charles Barkley ("The Round Mound of Rebound") on Barry Bonds' weight gain.

Late in the 2003 season Victor Conte became the poster boy for beefed-up Major Leaguers and other athletes. He was a sports nutritionist who counted Barry Bonds among his clients. His lab was the source of a new performance-enhancing steroid called tetrahydrogestrinone (THG), which was extremely hard to detect by drug testing labs. The scandal touched on Olympians, the NFL and Major Leaguer players that included Bonds and Yankee outfielders Jason Giambi and Gary Sheffield.

Conte's lab, the Bay Area Laboratory Cooperative (BALCO), was under investigation by the FBI, which raided the facility in September 2003. The investigations began after the U.S. Anti-Doping Agency (USADA) received an anonymous call from someone claiming to be a "high-profile coach" who had evidence of an undetectable steroid, THG.

Apparently Conte's notoriety expanded greatly among athletes after NFL linebacker Bill Romanowski began touting his supplements in the mid–1990s. Conte had been a bass player for the 1970s band Tower of Power.

Bonds' childhood friend and trainer, Greg Anderson, was a target of the investigation, and both men were subpoenaed to testify regarding distribution of the drug by BALCO. In December 2003 several players from different sports were called to testify before a San Francisco grand jury. They included Jason and Jeremy Giambi, Gary Sheffield, as well as boxer Shane Mosley and Oakland Raiders players Bill Romanowski and Barret Robbins.

During spring training 2004, steroids dominated the news. Bonds took exception to public comments about his alleged steroid use. Pitcher Turk Wendell said it was "obvious he did it" and it was "clear just seeing his body" that Bonds had used steroids. Bonds was discovered to be on a list of players who allegedly received steroids from the BALCO men, who were indicted early in 2004. The list included Gary Sheffield and Jason Giambi.

In January 2004, President Bush made war on steroids in baseball a priority in his State of the Union address. Giambi showed up at spring training considerably less buff, but contended that he had lost only four pounds. In March 2004 Sheffield denied using steroids and said he would take a drug test. In early 2004 Donald Fehr and Bud Selig were jointly called to testify before Congress, as both were interested in heading off any legislative intervention into baseball's drug issues.

On February 10, 2004, the grand jury subpoenaed baseball's drug testing results. Three days later, the BALCO officials, founder Victor Conte, Vice President James Valente, personal trainer Greg Anderson, and world-class track coach Remi Korchemny pleaded not guilty to distributing steroids to sports stars. On February 17, 2004, Anderson admitted distributing the drugs to several unidentified baseball players. On February 27, 2004, it was disclosed that Bonds' name appeared on a seized document listing steroids and dosages. Bonds' lawyer denied the accusation.

The product that the ballplayers were alleged to have taken was known as "The Clear," because it could not be detected by conventional testing procedures. World record holder in the 100 meters, Tim Montgomery (Marion Jones' boyfriend), reportedly was told by Conte that Barry Bonds was using The Clear. In June 2004 Conte agreed to plead guilty in exchange for a plea bargain. In July 2004 BALCO was fined $772,000 by the California Department of Health Services, the largest fine ever levied against a California lab.

Ephedra. See *Deaths* – Steve Bechler.

Derrick Turnbow. In January 2004 Turnbow became the first Major League player publicly identified to have used a banned steroid. He was at the U.S. national team's Olympic qualifying camp when he tested positive on October 7, 2003, for metabolites of a steroid, either nandrolone or 19-norandrostenedione (the test didn't distinguish between the two types of "andro"). Turnbow was stunned, saying he had taken an over-the-counter dietary supplement containing "19-nor." Although banned from international competition, Turnbow could receive virtually no punishment under the Major League's policies. Andro was banned by the International Olympic Committee, but not Major league baseball in 1998 when Mark McGwire was known to use it. It was later banned in the minor leagues but remained unregulated in the Major Leagues until 2004.

Testing.

"The other day they asked me about mandatory drug testing. I said I believed in drug testing a long time ago. All through the '60s I tested everything." — Pitcher Bill Lee.

"What baseball needs is promotional Steroid Days at ballparks. Fans would get to vote on which visiting ballplayer will take a drug test following the game. A failed test means an automatic forfeit. that would give baseball back to the fans in more ways than one." — Fan Jeff Stillman, writing to *Sports Illustrated*, with the perfect solution.

"Baseball is free of drugs." — Peter Ueberroth, apparently based on nothing. In the 1980s during Ueberroth's tenure as commissioner, baseball attempted to impose mandatory testing of all players, but the players union fought the effort and prevailed. Only players who had a history of drug problems could be randomly tested until new rules were instituted as part of the 2002 collective bargaining agreement. Nevertheless, performance-enhancing drug use was believed to be rampant. By the 2000s, several pitchers were believed to use steroids to enhance muscle mass and build strength. One relief pitcher was known by other players as "Mr. Anabolic."

In August 2002 Major League Baseball unveiled a new drug testing program that had almost no teeth in it. The steroid testing was ridiculed by the drug testing experts. One player representative said that the owners approached the union and said "come up with something to make this [image problem] go away."

Baseball would only test for Schedule III steroids, which are illegal without a prescription. Muscle enhancers and human growth hormones used for dwarfism were not to be tested. Nor would they test for androstenedione, which the body converts to testosterone, and which both the International Olympic Committee and the NFL ban. Baseball also was not going to perform off-season testing, unlike the NFL. The plan was for half the players to be tested during spring training and the other half to be tested during the season. Players could easily dope up in the off-season and be clean by the start of the season. The agreement required that if 5% of the players tested positive then all players would be subject to random testing over the ensuing two years.

Of baseball's 1,200 Major League players, 700 were tested in the spring, 500 were tested during the season, and 240 were randomly tested twice, with the testing going into September 2003. After the season, the results indicated that over 5% of the players had tested positive, and Major League Baseball instituted the prearranged plan for testing. In 2004 all players were to be tested, with penalties for a positive test ranging from a 30-day suspension to a one-year suspension without pay or fines of $10,000 to $100,000. Testing was

to continue until positive results dropped below 2.5% in two consecutive years.

It was widely believed that the drop in home runs in 2003 was directly attributable to the new testing.

Of the 1,438 anonymous survey samples, 5%-7% were positive. There were 1,198 players who submitted samples, some more than one. In comparison, Olympic athletes usually hit less than .5% positive. Most experts believed that the Baseball results were very low, in part because there was no off-season testing, no testing for androstenedione (the stuff Mark McGwire admitted using), no testing for human growth hormone, no testing for THG (what four Oakland Raiders tested positive for in November 2003).

Dick Pound, chairman of the World Anti-Doping Agency characterized baseball's testing program as "quite an insult." Players could only be tested from March 2 through the end of the season, leaving them four months to get the benefit of the illegal drugs and time to get the chemicals out of their systems.

Under the program, first time offenders were referred to a medical professional and treatment program. There was no suspension or fine. A second offense earns a 15 day suspension and up to a $10,000 fine. Suspensions increase to 35 days and fines to $25,000 for a third positive test, 50 days and $50,000 for a fourth and one year and up to $100,000 for a fifth. The suspensions would be without pay. There was skepticism over the enforcement process: "They want people to think they're getting their house in order, but it's disingenuous because it has so many loopholes. It's unacceptable." — Dr. Gary Wadler, professor at NYU's medical school.

Major League owners delayed testing many players during the 2004 season because they feared that players would resume steroid use after being tested.

Other Sports' Testing Programs. The NBA tests rookies up to four times a year, and veterans are subject to one random test during training camp. Penalties range from game suspensions to lifetime bans.

The NFL bans steroids and players are randomly tested. A positive test can result in game suspensions.

The NHL has no mandatory testing policy, unless the player is already in the league's substance abuse aftercare program.

The NCAA randomly tests athletes at NCAA championship events and football bowl games. Athletes testing positive are ruled ineligible by their schools for at least 365 days and lose a year of eligibility.

Testing in Minor Leagues/Latin America. The commissioner's office began testing minor leagues in the United States in 2001, and then expanded its program in 2004 to Latin America. The expansion came after the *Washington Post* ran an article reporting that many Dominican prospects had injected themselves with veterinary drugs, including steroids. Minor leaguers can undergo up to three random tests a year.

Special Delivery. In October 1998 Tigers reliever Matt Anderson signed for delivery of a package that contained a small amount of marijuana. He admitted signing for it, but said that it was for his roommate, future Braves first baseman Robert Fick.

Individual Players.

"Hats off to drug abusers everywhere." — Jerry Coleman [what??].

Francisco Barrios. A relief pitcher with the White Sox in the late 1970s and early 1980s, Barrios was heavily into drugs during the 1981 season and died of an overdose in April 1982. He appeared in only 11 games over the 1980 and 1981 seasons.

Ken Caminiti.

"That was a real eye-opener for me. Walking down the corridors in prison and having people walk up and say 'Hey, Caminiti, sign my crack pipe."—Caminiti pleaded guilty in 2003 to possession of crack cocaine, for which he served time in prison. The plea arose out of his arrest in November 2001, right after he retired following his final season with the Rangers and Braves.

In May 2002 in an article in *Sports Illustrated*, Caminiti said that about 50% of current Major League players used some form of steroids, and that he used performance-enhancing drugs during his MVP year. He failed four mandatory drug tests after going on probation for possession of cocaine in 2002, and died of an apparent overdose in fall 2004.

During the October 2004 postseason, Caminiti died from what was initially described by his agent as a heart attack. It was later reported that caminiti was last seen in New York City in the presence of two known drug dealers and his death was ruled a drug overdose.

Jose Canseco.

"The Canseco Shake"—Derogatory reference to the possibility that beefy slugger Jose Canseco had used steroids.

"You know, I've never said I have and I've never said I haven't."—Canseco in 2003, on whether he used steroids.

A number of late 1980s and early 1990s several players were accused of using steroids to build muscle mass. Canseco was the most prominent among them, in part because of his striking and significantly bulkier build than his twin brother. However, brother Ozzie gained over 20 pounds between the 1989 and 1990 seasons, weighing in at 225 pounds. Jose was 230 pounds, so the possibility of his using steroids diminished unless Ozzie also began using them. During the 1988 play-offs Red Sox fans chanted "Steroids! Steroids!" at Canseco, who responded by flexing his right biceps.

In June 2003, Canseco was serving a two-year house arrest following a 30-day jail sentence for violating terms of his probation following a 2001 fight in a Miami Beach nightclub. That month he was arrested after testing positive for steroids—a condition of his house arrest was that he submit to random drug testing. In November 2003, Canseco added to the medical annals with the following analysis: "Steroids, if used the right way with human growth hormones, can have a profound affect on your life. We're supposed to be built to live 120–130 years, and the combination of steroids and human growth hormones, taken properly, can add 30 years to your life."

In November 2003 Ozzie was sentenced to four months in jail for possessing an anabolic steroid and driving with a suspended license. Jose, who promised a tell-all book in late 2004, coyly said in spring 2004 (after a failed tryout with the Dodgers) that he could now pass a drug test: "No one knows if in the past I could have passed, because no one ever tested me."

Leon Durham. As a result of admitted cocaine use, Durham was suspended in 1988 by the Cubs and again in late 1989 by the Cardinals after 29 games. He never returned to the Major Leagues, but was still playing in the minor leagues in the mid–1990s. He was on the first club to defeat the all-women Colorado Silver Bullets in 1994.

Dwight Gooden.

"Yesterday in Texas, Dwight Gooden made his debut as a Yankee, pitching against the Texas Rangers. Even though it was a road game, Gooden received a standing ovation from the beer vendors."—David Letterman in early 1996.

In the late 1980s the Mets pitcher revealed a cocaine addiction and entered a rehabilitation program. It appeared that he had made a successful recovery, but in May 1994 he tested positive and was suspended for 60 days. He failed another series of tests during the 1994 strike and was suspended for the 1995 season. He signed with the Yankees for 1996 and capped his comeback with a no-hitter on

May 14. He pitched through the 2000 season, going 6–5 for three clubs that year before retiring. See also Bob Klapisch, *High and Tight* (1996) (covering Gooden and Darryl Strawberry).

Steve Howe.

"They get two bases, and I get a urine test."—Often-suspended pitcher Steve Howe, after tossing an appeal throw over the head of third baseman Charlie Hayes and into the stands, allowing a runner at third to score and a runner at first to advance to third.

Howe was first caught using cocaine in 1983 and was suspended for the entire 1984 season after his third offense. He attempted comebacks in 1985, 1987 and 1989, finally making it back to the Majors in 1991 after 3½ years away. He returned in May of that year with the Yankees and posted a 3–1 record with three saves and a 1.68 ERA. He was required to undergo weekly drug tests, all of which he passed that season.

He signed a contract for 1992 worth a minimum of $600,000, but which contained incentives that could push the amount to $2.2 million. During the 1991–1992 off-season, however, he was arrested in Montana on a cocaine-related charge. After the bust, he stayed with the Yankees through spring training and opened the season with the club. He plea-bargained his way out of a trial, pleading guilty to cocaine possession, and was allowed to continue pitching for a few weeks. After a hearing by commissioner Fay Vincent and a subsequent appeal, Howe was suspended from Major League baseball for the seventh time on June 8, 1992.

If Howe had stayed on the Yankee roster for six more days he would have received a $200,000 bonus. Had he made six more appearances, he would have received an additional $300,000. Howe then appealed the decision to arbitrator George Nicolau, who ruled in late 1992 that Howe had to be reinstated; but that if he was caught again, he would be banned for life (again). The decision prompted severe criticism from Vincent: "It makes baseball look silly and I think there'll be a lot of adverse reaction. I don't think there was any doubt about my having just cause. I think the arbitrator substituted his judgment for mine, and the arbitrator was wrong…. I think it's a bad development for baseball. Why is eight [suspensions] different from seven?"

Howe remained with the Yankees into the 1996 season, appearing in 25 games that year before his career ended.

LaMarr Hoyt. The pitcher revealed his drug problem in 1986 and was suspended for the 1987 season, never returning to baseball. He also received a 45-day prison sentence for possession of drugs. He was arrested again after drugs were found in his home, and then arrested one more time after being caught carrying amphetamines across the Mexican border into California. For the last offense he served time in a federal prison in Georgia. He had a 98–68 record in eight seasons and was the 1983 Cy Young Award winner

Rex Hudler. Hudler, an Angels broadcaster at the time, was arrested at a Kansas City airport in September 2003 after inspectors found marijuana and drug paraphernalia in his luggage. He was reinstated to his position with the team after a brief suspension.

Doug Johns. Apparently to celebrate the painting of Cal Ripken, Sr.'s, number in the Orioles third base coaching box earlier in the day, on April 5, 1998, the Orioles pitcher was arrested for drunk driving and marijuana possession. He was arrested again in October 1999 for driving while under the influence of marijuana.

Ron LeFlore. The outfielder later admitted coming to the ballpark under the influence of drugs.

Mark McGwire. In August 1998 during his 70-homer season, McGwire admitted to using over-the-counter, easily available enhancements: creatine, an amino-acid powder that builds muscle; and androstenedione, a nutritional supplement that raises the level of testosterone to build lean muscle mass and promote recovery from injury. On Sunday, August 23, 1998, the Cardinals released a statement defending McGwire, saying, "It has neither proven anabolic steroid effects nor significant side effects…. Taken approximately one hour before, it may make one's workout more efficient. Due to current research that lacks any documentary evidence of any adverse side effects, the Cardinals medical staff cannot object to Mark's choice to use this legal over-the-counter supplement." Androstenedione was at the time banned by the National Football League and the International Olympic Committee.

Eddie Milner. Milner was a solid center fielder for the Reds in the early 1980s. During the spring of 1987 he checked into a drug rehabilitation program and managed to return for over 100 games that season. He ended his career only a few games into the 1988 season at age 32.

Paul Molitor. Molitor admitted using cocaine briefly in the late 1970s.

Otis Nixon. In the heat of the 1991 pennant race, the Braves left fielder and lead-off catalyst was suspended for 60 days after testing positive for cocaine. He was a prior offender who was required to undergo random drug testing. The suspension took him out of not only the pennant race, but the play-offs and World Series. At the time, Nixon was batting .297 with 72 stolen bases and 81 runs scored and would have been a lock for Comeback Player of the Year. The Braves were also talking about a new three-year contract worth $5.5 million. Nevertheless, he returned for the 1992 season and helped the Braves into the World Series.

Pascual Perez. In early 1992 the Yankee pitcher was suspended from baseball for one year as a result of again testing positive for cocaine. He forfeited a salary of $1.9 million and never returned to the Major Leagues. He had first tested positive in 1989 and to be reinstated he was required to undergo periodic testing.

Tony Phillips. On August 19, 1997, the Angels utilityman was arrested for allegedly purchasing a small quantity of crack cocaine at an Anaheim motel. He later pleaded guilty to a misdemeanor and was ordered into a drug diversion program.

Darrell Porter. The Royals catcher wrote *Snap Me Perfect*, with William Deerfield (1984), about his life with drugs and later religious conversion.

Tim Raines. Raines once admitted sliding head first to avoid breaking a vial of cocaine in his pocket.

Pete Rose. Pete Rose's "gofer," Tommy Gioiosa, told a *Vanity Fair* magazine interviewer in 2001 that in the mid–1980s Rose expressed interest in investing in cocaine trafficking. Gioiosa was running a Gold's Gym in Cincinnati owned by two men later convicted of drug trafficking. Gioiosa allegedly went to Rose's house and received a large quantity of cash that he drove to Florida to invest in the drug. Paul Janszen, another gofer used by Rose and who apparently replaced Gioiosa, has stated that Rose expressed interest in cocaine trafficking in early 1987.

Eric Show. The Padre pitcher retired in 1991 after a bizarre series of injuries. The last was during spring training with the A's, when he explained that the multiple cuts on his hands were from climbing a barbed wire fence fleeing an attacker. He was cut and dropped out of the public eye. He died of a cocaine and heroin overdose on Opening Day 1994, almost at the same time that the Padres were honoring him that day as the club's all-time winningest pitcher with 100 victories. At the time of his death, he had prematurely ended his third stay in a rehabilitation center in two years.

Chick Stahl.

"Boys, I couldn't help it. It drove me to it."—Stahl from his deathbed, allegedly in reference to drug addiction.

Stahl was an outfielder for the Boston Red Stockings of the National League and Boston Red Sox of the American League around the turn of the century. He died in mid-career in 1906 under "mysterious" conditions at age 33. His wife died 18 months later. Based on the circumstances of their deaths and commentary surrounding them, it is probable that they were drug addicts.

One source reported that Stahl was blackmailed by a "baseball Sadie" claiming to be carrying his child. He purportedly committed suicide by drinking four ounces of carbolic acid.

Darryl Strawberry.

"The Yankees are the first team in history to have two players forbidden by law from associating with one another."—Comedian Bob Lacey on drug abusers Steve Howe and Darryl Strawberry, who were joined by drug abuser Dwight Gooden in 1996.

"I never had a problem hitting. I had a problem living."—Strawberry.

Strawberry missed the last spring training game of 1994 with the Dodgers and then admitted that he had a drug problem. Rumors had been circulating for at least three years that he dabbled with cocaine, though the nature of the drug problem was never formally disclosed. Strawberry checked into a California drug rehabilitation center. After his discharge the Dodgers bought out his contract and cut him. Strawberry was paid $642,857 by the Dodgers while in drug rehabilitation and settled the balance of his salary claim for another $4,857,143.

Robert Shapiro, one of the lawyers who represented O.J. Simpson, filed a lawsuit against Strawberry in August 1998, claiming that Strawberry failed to pay about $100,000 in fees for his work in settling the action with the Dodgers. Strawberry's reaction: "It's a wrong suit. He's just trying to claim something back that he didn't do. Major League Baseball did it; the Players Association did it."

Strawberry recovered sufficiently from his addiction in time to join the Giants shortly before the 1994 All-Star Game, but was out of baseball again at the start of the 1995 season when he was suspended for 60 days for testing positive for cocaine. He was reinstated on June 23 and signed with the Yankees, but was released at the end of the season.

In May 1996 Strawberry signed with Mike Veeck's Class AA St. Paul Saints as he tried to play his way back to the Major Leagues; he then signed with the Yankees. He never made it back, and later served several stints in a halfway house.

On April 14, 1999, Strawberry apparently had too much time on his hands while working out during an extended spring training following colon cancer surgery the previous October. He was arrested for soliciting a prostitute and possession of cocaine. In May 1999 he pleaded no contest and was sentenced to 18 months probation. In June 1999 he was suspended for 120 days for violating baseball's drug policy and aftercare program (later reduced a week; for good behavior?).

In January 2000 he was found to have cocaine in his system and because it was his third offense he was suspended from baseball for one year. In September 2000 he was sentenced to two years' house arrest after admitting he violated probation by driving under the influence of medication and leaving the scene of an accident. On October 25, 2000, he was arrested and jailed after leaving a treatment center following a weekend drug binge.

On April 2, 2001, he was arrested at a Tampa hospital for violation of a probation warrant. He had been missing for four days after leaving his drug treatment center. On April 29, 2002, he was sentenced to 18 months in prison for violating the terms of his probation six times.

In late 2003, Strawberry signed on as a batting and "player

development" instructor with the Yankees for 2004. He had just been released from Florida's Gainsborough Correctional Institute after serving 11 months of the 18-month sentence stemming from a parole violation after a conviction for cocaine possession and soliciting prostitution. Strawberry said he felt qualified to help young players avoid the hazards of high living and drug use. He resigned abruptly a few weeks later.

David Wells. Wells wasn't accused of using drugs, but in February 2003, he claimed in his book, *Perfect I'm Not! Boomer on Beer, Brawls, Backaches and Baseball*, that between 20% and 40% of all Major League players "are juiced." In addition: "Down in the minors, where virtually every flat-broke, baloney-sandwich-eating double-A prospect is chasing after the same, elusive, multimillion-dollar payday, the use of anabolic homer-helpers is flat-out booming. At just about 12 bucks per shot, those steroid vials must be seen as a really solid investment."

He also claimed that players ate caffeine pills, drank Red Bull and Ripped Fuel, and even took Ritalin.

Alan Wiggins. Wiggins was a star for the Padres at second base starting in 1982, but drug abuse wiped out his career after a series of rehabilitation efforts failed. He was released by the Orioles after the 1987 season. He later contracted AIDS (apparently from dirty needles) and died at age 32 in 1991.

Maury Wills.

"Letting him manage in the Major Leagues is like sending Bo Derek through cellblock A without a bodyguard." — Statistician Bill James on Wills, who had some problems with cocaine and alcohol. One story has it that Wills was ready to pull the pitcher during a bad outing, and started out of the dugout. His coaches had to remind him that it was the *other* team's pitcher on the mound. Wills managed to get things back under control and by the 2000s was working with the Dodgers.

Books. Edward F. Dolan, Jr., *Drugs in Sports* (1986); Tom Donohoe and Neil Johnson, *Foul Play: Drug Abuse in Sports* (1988); Richard E. Lapchick (ed.), *Fractured Focus: Sport as a Reflection of Society* (1986); Ray Tricker and David L. Cook (eds.), *Athletes at Risk: Drugs and Sports* (1990).

Don Drysdale (1936–1993)

Hall of Fame 1984

"I hate all hitters. I start a game mad and I stay that way until it's over. I guess I'm a perfectionist. When I throw a curve that hangs, and it goes for a hit, I want to chew up my glove." — Drysdale.

Drysdale pitched for the Dodgers from 1956 through 1969, winning 209 games.

Donald Scott Drysdale was born and raised in a Los Angeles suburb before moving on to the Dodgers' minor league system. He arrived with the Dodgers in 1956 and was 17–9 in 1957, the club's last season in Brooklyn. His greatest season was 1962, when he was 25–9 and led the league with 232 strikeouts.

He is perhaps best known for his menacing demeanor on the mound and his propensity for brushing back batters. His crowning moment was in 1968, when he pitched 58⅔ straight **Scoreless Innings**, a record he held until Dodger pitcher Orel Hershiser broke it in 1988.

Drysdale's career ended with a torn rotator cuff in 1969. He finished with a record of 209–166, 2,486 strikeouts and 49 shutouts. He was also a decent-hitting pitcher, with 29 home runs in his career and a .186 average.

After his pitching career ended, Drysdale moved to the broadcast booth with the Rangers and White Sox. He arrived back with the Dodgers as a broadcaster beginning in the late 1980s. He died during the 1993 season when he suffered a heart attack in his hotel room in Montreal a few hours before he was to broadcast the Dodger game that night. His widow was former UCLA basketball star Anne Meyers.

Book. Don Drysdale with Bob Verdi, *Once a Bum, Always a Bum* (1990).

Hugh Duffy (1866–1954)

Hall of Fame 1945

"The length of time required for those events indicate something of the extent of Duffy's career. For Hugh signed his first player contract for Salem of the New England League in 1887 and he was still on the payroll of the Red Sox when he died at eighty-seven in 1954, spending his last days as a scout. His record of sixty-eight years in the professional game has been exceeded only by Connie Mack." — Lee Allen and Tom Meany in *Kings of the Diamond* (1965).

Duffy starred primarily as an outfielder for the 1890s Boston Red Stockings.

Hugh Duffy began his professional career in 1886 with Hartford in the New England League and moved to Cap Anson's Chicago White Stockings in 1888. He bounced to various clubs until 1892, when he became a star outfielder for the Boston Red Stockings. He peaked with a Major League record batting average of .438 in 1894, the first season after the pitching distance was increased to 60'6". He followed with six more seasons hitting .300 or better.

Duffy became player-manager for Milwaukee in the American League in 1901. After a two-year playing hiatus, he was back with the National League Phillies in 1904 through 1906 as player-manager to finish out his career. He is one of a handful of players to appear in four Major Leagues (National League, American Association, Players League and American League). Duffy finished with a .324 average in 17 seasons from 1888 through 1906.

After he retired, Duffy managed the White Sox (1910–1911) and Red Sox (1921–1922) to mediocre results or worse. He later became a Red Sox coach and directed tryouts camps in New England. He and Red Stockings teammate Tommy McCarthy were known as the "Heavenly Twins" and the mediocre McCarthy rode Duffy's coattails into the Hall of Fame in 1945.

Dugouts

"The dugout is the worst place to watch a ballgame. From such a side angle, the diamond is cross-sectioned and ceases to hold shape or gleam. A fine strata of mica chipping is all one sees. As through a periscope, the horizon flattens…. Viewed at ground level, the game is a progression of groaning knee-bends, prompted by the bats' metronomic aerobic class." — John Krich in *El Beisbol* (1989).

"If everybody on this team commenced breaking up the furniture every time we did bad, there'd be no place to sit." — Casey Stengel after Ron Swoboda of the Mets tore up the dugout.

Rule. According to the official rules, only players in uniform, the manager, coaches and trainers are allowed in the dugout during games.

Sunken Dugouts. The enclosed and sunken dugout was popularized when the first steel and concrete stadiums were built in the early 20th century. The Dodgers paid to install sunken dugouts when they moved into the Los Angeles Coliseum for the 1958–1961 seasons.

No Dugout. The first modern non-dugout (field level) dugout was built in Candlestick Park in San Francisco.

Length. When Roy Hofheinz built the Astrodome in the mid–1960s, he insisted that the dugouts be an extravagant 120 feet long. He did so not to accommodate the players, but to allow more fans to receive tickets "behind the dugout."

Home Team Side. There is no requirement that home teams have their dugouts on a particular side of the field. It is sometimes based on the whim of the owner, in part depending upon where the owner's executive suite is and whether the dugout can be seen from that vantage point.

Most visiting dugouts are on the first base side because they face the sun. The New York Yankees originally had their home dugout on the third base side, but later switched it to the first base side.

The tradition of the home team dugout on the first base side ended in the early 1970s. By 2000 at least 12 home teams occupied the third base dugout.

Weather Controls. Many home dugouts have air conditioning or heat, but visiting dugouts usually do not contain such amenities.

Dugout Disaster. The Angels spent a fortune on slugger Mo Vaughn, who joined the team for the 1999 season. In the opening game of the year, the first baseman fell into the Indians' dugout chasing a pop fly and injured his ankle. Although he only missed 15 days, the injury lingered all season and eventually he had surgery to repair ligament damage. He still managed over 30 home runs and over 100 RBIs, so the Angels poor results couldn't be blamed entirely on him (though many tried, in part because of his poor attitude).

Rule Change. On July 4, 1966, catcher Jerry Grote of the Mets went into the Phillies dugout to make a catch. Phillies manager Gene Mauch hit Grote's arms and Grote dropped the ball. There was no interference called because the then-existing rule did not prohibit an interference call when a defensive player ventured into the dugout to make a catch. After the season the rule was changed to allow a defensive player to go into the dugout to make a catch without interference.

Dumbest Players

"Stengel is the world's greatest ballplayer—from the neck down."—Dodger owner Charles Ebbets after fining Stengel $50 for sliding into second base with a man already there.

"You talk something like Dizzy Dean. Only you couldn't be Dean. You sound much too intelligent."—Blindfolded "What's My Line?" panelist Dorothy Kilgallen to Dean, who was the mystery guest that night.

"[Catcher] Choo-Choo Coleman would give you the sign and then look down to see what it was."—Mets pitcher Roger Craig.

"I'll just accept that I'm stupid."—Yankee pitcher Dwight Gooden after Jose Canseco blasted a Gooden curveball for a home run. Gooden was aware that Canseco was a notoriously good off-speed hitter.

"He can run, hit, throw and field. Thy only thing Willie Davis has never been able to do is think."—Buzzie Bavasi.

"A ballplayer could go to college and be a sportswriter. But what writer could be a ballplayer? And tell me this: What college did the twelve apostles go to?"—A's manager Billy Martin defending a claim that ballplayers were dumb.

"As usual—nothing."—Jim Hickman on what he was thinking while rounding the bases after a game-winning home run.

"No brain, no headache."—Adage that a dumb ballplayer doesn't outthink himself.

"There's something to be said for the 'dumb jock,' because his intelligence doesn't get in the way."—Barry Zito.

"One of these fine days some bold person may find gumption enough to write a voluminous book titled, 'The Contents of a Peanut Shell, or the Brain of a Ballplayer.'"—A December 1915 article in the *Pittsburgh Gazette* criticizing successful pitcher Al Mamaux for agreeing to play football and basketball in the off-season. The criticism may have been justified; after a 21–15 record in 1916, Mamaux slipped to 2–12 in only 18 appearances over the following two seasons.

"Baseball is the favorite American sport because it's so slow. Any idiot can follow it. And just about any idiot can play it."—Gene Vidal, father of Gore Vidal, quoted in Gore's *Matters of Fact and Fiction* (1979); with a reply by writer Art Hill in *I Don't Care If I Never Come Back* (1980): "Gore Vidal doesn't like baseball because there is almost nothing he does like. If he liked more things he would be a less interesting writer but, on occasion, a more reliable source. As for his father, I suspect that Gene Vidal, like many great athletes (e.g., Jim Thorpe), couldn't hit a curveball. You may have noticed how often people who can do certain things well find that the things they can't do are, after all, not worth doing."

Davey Johnson. The Orioles infielder had a clause in his contract that paid him a bonus if he recorded a certain number of doubles. Teammate Jim Palmer related a story in which Johnson smashed a ball that should have been an easy triple, but Johnson stopped at second. Palmer asked Johnson why he didn't go for the triple. "Because I have a doubles clause." Palmer's response: "Don't you think they'd give you credit for a double on a triple?" Johnson's response: "I've got a doubles clause." Palmer said after that they starting calling Johnson "Dum-Dum." Nevertheless, Johnson had a successful Major League managing career.

Leo Durocher (1905–1991)

Hall of Fame (VC) 1993

"Synonymous with controversy, noise, argument, shouting, rhubarbs, litigation, Durocher has been supreme egotist, brash loudmouth, natural ham, narcissistic monologist, hunch player, strategist. Has been strutting clothes horse, manicured, pedicured, perfumed, ruthless, sarcastic, bitter, amiable, affable, flirtatious, charming, dapper."—Gene Karst and Martin J. Jones, Jr., in *Who's Who in Professional Baseball* (1973).

"I didn't like Leo. He didn't treat all the players the same. He played favorites. He wasn't trustworthy; too often he didn't tell you the truth, and he would do everything he could to protect himself, no matter what it did to you."—Billy Herman quoted in *Bums*, by Peter Golenbock (1984).

"Leo Durocher must be livid someplace today. He has achieved his lifelong dream. He's in the baseball Hall of Fame. He got in Sunday. Trouble is, it's too late. Durocher wanted to get in while he could smell the roses, hear the applause, maybe get a license plate saluting his achievement. The last time I saw Durocher, a year or two before he died, he was bitter that he hadn't been inducted."—Jim Murray in 1993.

A 17-year Major League shortstop beginning in 1925, Durocher made his mark primarily as a long-time manager.

Known as "The Lip" and sometimes "The Most Hated Man in Baseball" (per sportswriter Arthur Mann), Leo Ernest Durocher was known for his combative attitude on the field and gregarious nature off it in a playing and managing career that lasted from 1925 through 1973.

The son of a French-Canadian railroad engineer and born in

Massachusetts, Durocher began his professional career at Hartford in 1925 and batted once for the Yankees that season. He played in the minors in 1926 and 1927 before returning to the Yankees in 1928. He batted .270 in 102 games while splitting time at second base and shortstop. After a decent season in 1928 he moved over to the Reds for three years as the club's starting shortstop.

He achieved his greatest fame as a player when he moved to the Cardinals in 1933 and anchored the Gas House Gang until 1937. He was traded to the Dodgers in 1938, and in 1939 he became player-manager. His playing tapered off through 1945 and he ended 17 years on the field with a .247 average.

After a third-place finish under Durocher in 1939, the 1940 Dodgers finished second and in 1941 Durocher led them to the World Series. He continued to manage the club through 1946, with best finishes of second in 1942 (104 wins) and 1946 (96 wins). He was *Suspended* for the entire 1947 season for associating with gamblers and crime figures. After returning for 73 games in 1948, he was hired mid-season to manage the rival Giants.

Durocher led the Giants to the World Series in 1951 and won his only championship with a sweep of the Indians in 1954. He ended his relationship with the Giants in 1955 and went into the broadcast booth at NBC for a few years. He returned to coaching in 1961 with the Dodgers and then managed the Cubs for seven years beginning in 1966. He brought the club back to respectability with two second-place finishes in 1969 and 1970. He took over the Astros in late 1972, and in 1973 he led the club to a fourth-place finish in his last season as a manager. Some believe that he was becoming senile during that season (he was 68), failing to recognize a number of his players for weeks at a time.

Durocher finished his 24-year managerial career with 2,008 victories, now 8th all-time. In the 20 seasons in which he managed a full season, his clubs finished in the second division only five times.

In his later years, Durocher was the most prominent baseball man not in the Hall of Fame, primarily because of his maverick attitude and negative behavior over the years. When he died in 1991 in Palm Springs, he was still bitter toward the baseball establishment and had instructed his friends not to accept a posthumous entry into the Hall—which finally came in 1993 and was accepted.

For perhaps the best inside look at Durocher's true persona, and highlights of some of the reasons why he never made it into the Hall during his lifetime, see William Barry Furlong's "How Durocher Blew the Pennant," which is reprinted from a 1970 *Look* magazine article in *"I Managed Good, But Boy Did They Play Bad,"* by Jim Bouton with Neil Offen (1973).

Books. Leo Durocher with Ed Linn, *Nice Guys Finish Last* (1975); Gerald Eskenazi, *The Lip* (1993).

Dynasties

"Rooting for the Yankees is like rooting for U.S. Steel."—Red Smith on the 1950s Yankees (also attributed to Joe E. Brown). In 1969 during baseball's centennial celebration the 1927 New York Yankees were voted the greatest club of all time.

"Rooting for the Yankees once was like rooting for U.S. Steel. Now it's like rooting for Ringling Bros. and Barnum & Bailey."—Sportswriter Frank Dolson on the 1970s feuding Yankees.

"Perhaps the truest axiom in baseball is that the toughest thing to do is repeat. The tendency to relax without even knowing it, the feeling being, 'We did it last year, so we can do it again.'"—Dodger manager Walter Alston.

St. Louis Browns/1885–1888. The Browns won four straight American Association pennants and were contenders in most other seasons in the 1880s.

Baltimore Orioles and Boston Red Stockings/1890s. According to historian Harold Seymour, Baltimore's mythic place in baseball history is attributable to the six players from that National League club who eventually became managers and continued to extol to the press the virtues of the team well into the 1920s and 1930s. The real dynasty of that era arguably was the Boston Red Stockings, who won National League pennants in 1891, 1892, 1893, 1897 and 1898. The Orioles won in 1894, 1895 and 1896.

New York Giants/1903–1925. Manager John McGraw led the Giants for 32 years from 1902 through mid–1932. From 1903 through 1925 the club finished first or second in all but four seasons. The Giants won the pennant nine times and the World Series three times in that span.

Chicago Cubs/1906–1910. The Cubs won the pennant in four of five seasons between 1906 and 1910. In the year they did not win the pennant, they won 104 games to finish second.

Philadelphia A's/1927–1932. This was the last club that was put together exclusively from players purchased from minor league clubs (no farm system). Sandwiched between the long Yankee dynasty, the club finished first or second from 1927 through 1932, with three straight first place finishes starting in 1929 and World Series victories in 1929 and 1930.

New York Yankees/1921–1964.

"Yesterday the Senators beat the Yankees at their own game—baseball."—1950s game story in the *New York Times*.

"A mystique of history and heritage surrounds the New York Yankees. It's like the old days revived. We're loved and hated, but always in larger doses than any other team. We're the only team in any sport whose name and uniform and insignia are synonymous with their entire sport all over the world ... the Yankees mean baseball to more people than all the other teams combined."—Paul Blair, quoted in the *Washington Post* in June 1978.

Between 1921 and 1964, covering 45 seasons, the Yankees became the preeminent dynasty in the history of Major League Baseball, if not all of professional sports. They won 29 American League pennants and 20 World Series titles. They won four straight World Series titles under Joe McCarthy (1936–1939) and five straight under Casey Stengel (1949–1953). Over the 45 seasons, the club finished second or third seven times each, and finished fourth or seventh one time each.

As early as 1923, the success of the Yankees was attributed by one Midwestern writer to the "potency of the New York checkbook." Fifteen of the first 32 American League MVPs were Yankees. The Yankees of the 1950s and early 1960s sewed the seeds of ultimate decline when general manager George Weiss stopped paying large signing bonuses and the team could not keep key bonus players on its star-laden roster. The free agent draft also hurt the team because it could no longer monopolize free agent signings with a big checkbook. To signal the end of the era, the team finished first in 1964 and sixth in 1965, the first year in which a player draft was held (though that draft would not have had any impact on the 1965 Major League club). The team continued a steep decline until George Steinbrenner purchased the club in the early 1970s and began spending heavily in the new free agent market in the 1970s.

Among the great Yankee eras, 1936–1942 stands out. The club won six pennants and five World Series, and eight players from the team played during this entire period: Red Ruffing, Lefty Gomez, Johnny Murphy, Bill Dickey, Red Rolfe, Frank Crosetti, Joe DiMaggio and George Selkirk.

St. Louis Cardinals/1930–1949. Branch Rickey's *Farm System* helped the Cardinals become the preeminent National League team of the 1930s and 1940s. The most prominent of these Cardinal teams was the Gas House Gang of the 1930s, led by Dizzy Dean, Leo Durocher and Pepper Martin. The Cardinals won pennants in 1930, 1931, 1934, 1942, 1943, 1944 and 1946. They finished second in 1935, 1939, 1941, 1945, 1947, 1948 and 1949.

Brooklyn Dodgers/1941–1956.

"The Boys of Summer"—Roger Kahn.

The Dodgers were perennial National League contenders in this era, winning pennants in 1941, 1947, 1949, 1952, 1953, 1955 and 1956. Had the club won its last game of the season in 1946 (a *Play-Off*), 1950 and 1951 (a *Play-Off*), it would have won five straight National League championships (1949–1953) and nine in 11 years. Despite all the pennants, the club won only one World Series, a seven-game victory over the Yankees in 1955.

Oakland A's/1971–1976.

"The Angry A's"

Charlie Finley's players feuded with Finley and among themselves almost constantly. Nevertheless, the club won three straight World Series crowns in 1972, 1973 and 1974. The A's also won the American League's Western Division in 1971 and 1975 and finished second in 1976 before fading for the rest of the decade.

Baltimore Orioles/1969–1979.

"The Orioles don't do it with money or attendance or publicity or a beautiful stadium. They rank in the middle of baseball in all of those areas. The most basic reason for their superiority, say the O's, is always the same: Fundamentals are the Orioles' edge."—Thomas Boswell in *How Life Imitates the World Series* (1982). Boswell also noted that the Orioles won more games than any other Major League club between 1960 and 1981, almost 50 more than the second-place Reds. The Orioles do not usually receive credit as a baseball dynasty, but their record between 1969 and 1979 speaks for itself. The club won division titles in 1969, 1970, 1971, 1973, 1974 and 1979, pennants in 1969, 1970, 1971 and 1979, and the World Series in 1970. They finished second in 1975, 1976 and 1977.

Cincinnati Reds/1970–1978.

"Cincinnati's Big Red Machine is about the third best team in fundamentals that I've seen—behind the Taiwan Little Leaguers and the USC NCAA champions in 1968. The Reds act like a drill team; they should be managed by 'Dragnet's' Jack Webb."—Pitcher Bill Lee on the Reds' 1970s dynasty. The clubs were led by a powerful line-up of superstars, including Johnny Bench, Joe Morgan, Tony Perez and Pete Rose. The team's batting prowess made up for generally average pitching.

"You give us the pitching some of these clubs have and no one could touch us. But God has a way of not arranging that, because it isn't as much fun."—Reds manager Sparky Anderson.

The Reds used the same line-up to win consecutive World Series in 1975 and 1976: Tony Perez at first base, two-time (consecutive) MVP Joe Morgan at second base, Dave Concepcion at shortstop, Pete Rose at third base, Johnny Bench at catcher, and outfielders George Foster, Ken Griffey, Sr., and Cesar Geronimo. The club also won the National League title in 1970 and 1972, the Western Division title in 1973, and finished second in 1974, 1977 and 1978.

The 1976 Reds were the only modern team to lead the league in runs, stolen bases and home runs. They had five regulars who each eventually had at least 2,000 hits.

Atlanta Braves. The Braves won every division crown between 1991 and 2003 (with 1994 washed out due to the strike—they were in second place at the time). The run included three National League pennants and one World Series victory (1995). Unfortu-nately, between 1997 and 2003, the club lost every division series except one.

New York Yankees. Between 1993 and 2004 the Yankees finished first in their division nine times (including six straight) and finished second three times. They won four World Series titles (1996, 1998–2000) and had two other World Series appearances.

"**E** is for Evers,
His jaw in advance;
Never afraid
To Tinker with Chance."
—Ogden Nash on Johnny Evers.

Early Retirement See *Last Seasons*

Earned Run Averages (ERAs)

"I expected it. Let's face it, would you want me on your pitching staff."—Tigers pitcher Kurt Knudsen after being sent down in 1994 with an ERA of 13.50.

Definition. Earned run average is the number of runs scored per nine innings without benefit of an error. For example, if a pitcher allowed four earned runs in 18 innings (regardless of how many games it took to pitch those innings), his ERA would be 2.00.

Early Rules. Prior to 1912 there were seasons when earned runs were not officially tabulated. During some of this early period, base on balls, hit batsmen and wild pitches often were considered errors in computing earned run average.

In 1897 it was ruled that an earned run could be credited only on a hit. In 1917 it was ruled that earned runs would include runs scored as a result of stolen bases. Earned runs now are also tallied when forced home on a walk with the bases loaded.

Official Use. Earned run averages were not officially kept until 1912 (1917 in some sources), although researchers for *The Baseball Encyclopedia* went back and calculated ERAs for earlier years. National League historian Lee Allen claimed that National League president John Heydler "revived" the ERA in 1911, an indication that the ERA had been used previously. Another source indicated that the National League formally adopted the ERA in 1884, suggesting that it was abandoned at some point later. Still another source reported that in 1913 the Western League became the first league to formally adopt the ERA.

Changed Statistics. Later research determined that Walter Johnson's ERA in 1913 was not 1.09, but rather 1.14. This allowed Bob Gibson and his 1.12 ERA in 1968 to move into third ahead of Johnson on the all-time single season ERA list behind Dutch Leonard's 1.01 in 1914 and Three Finger Brown's 1.04 in 1906. The change in Johnson's ERA occurred because he pitched in a meaningless late season game in which he allowed two batters to score as a joke. Originally, the game was ignored in calculating season statistics.

Trends. After World War II, teams hit more home runs, which normally increases strikeouts and lowers batting averages, but batting averages continued to rise. This had a negative effect on ERAs. Indicative is Early Wynn's 1950 American League–leading earned run average of 3.20, the highest ever for a league leader.

By 1968 the trend had shifted, as the *average* ERA in both leagues was under 3.00. ERAs then began a slow rise through the late 1980s as pitching deteriorated, but were still considerably lower than 40 years earlier. By 1989 the average Major League ERA was 3.70, while the average Major League ERA in 1950 was 4.36.

Qualifying for ERA Title. In order to qualify for the ERA title prior to 1950, a pitcher was required to throw 10 complete games and pitch 100 innings, though the complete game rule usually was ignored. In recognition of the role of relief pitchers, the rule was changed to require a pitcher to throw as many innings as his team had games.

In 1952 Hoyt Wilhelm became the first reliever to win the title, with 159 innings in 154 games. He was 15–3 without starting any games and had 11 saves with his 2.43 ERA during his rookie season.

No Qualifiers. The 1957 A's are the only team in history without a season ERA qualifier. Of the team's 20 pitchers that year, none had over the required 154 innings. The highest was 145 innings by former Browns ace Ned Garver, who was 6–13.

League Leader. Lefty Grove led the American League in ERA nine times, the most in Major League history.

In 2000 Pedro Martinez had an ERA of 1.74. His nearest challenger was Roger Clemens of the Yankees at 3.70.

Consecutive Seasons. In 1995 Greg Maddux recorded his second straight sub–1.80 season ERA, the first time it had been done since Walter Johnson in 1918 and 1919. Maddux was 19–2 with a 1.63 ERA. He had a 1.56 ERA in strike-shortened 1994.

Lowest Lifetime. Ed Walsh had a 1.82 lifetime ERA on his way to 195 wins. Addie Joss, who pitched from 1902 through 1910, is second with a 1.88 ERA.

Worst ERA. The worst ERA for a pitcher with more than 75 career innings is 6.36 by Pretzels Pezzullo of the 1935–1936 Philadelphia Phillies.

Joe Cleary had an ERA of 189.00 for the 1945 Senators. He pitched one third of an inning, walking three and allowing five hits. It was the same game in which one-legged Bert Shepard pitched his one game for the club (see also *Amputees*).

Andy Sommerville started one game for the Dodgers in 1894. He gave up one hit and walked five in one third of an inning and registered an ERA of 162.00.

Roy Halladay won the Cy Young Award in 2003. He had been sent all the way to the Class A Florida State League in 2001, following his 10.64 ERA in 2000, the worst in Major League history for an ERA qualifier.

In 1996 the Tigers set an American League record with a 6.38 ERA en route to 109 losses.

ERA Title and Losing Record. Six pitchers have won the league ERA title with a losing record: Ted Breitenstein had a 19–20 record and a 3.18 ERA for the 1893 St. Louis Browns.

Rube Waddell had an 8–13 record and a 2.37 ERA for the 1900 Pirates. He also led in strikeouts and relief losses.

Dolf Luque had a 16–18 record and a 2.63 ERA for the 1925 Reds. He also led the league with four shutouts.

Dave Koslo had an 11–14 record and a 2.50 ERA for the 1949 Giants.

Stu Miller had a 6–9 record and a 2.47 ERA for the 1958 Giants.

Joe Magrane had a 5–9 record and a 2.18 ERA for the 1988 Cardinal.

Earthquakes

"I was standing in right field. At first I thought it was another of my migraines, but it was just an earthquake." — Jose Canseco on the 1989 earthquake that rocked the World Series at Candlestick Park in San Francisco. During Game 3 of the Series, ABC's Al Michaels was broadcasting the pregame show from Candlestick Park when a 7.1 earthquake struck the San Francisco area. The

game was postponed and the Series was resumed a week later when the A's finished their four-game sweep of the Giants. Twelve ordinary citizens simultaneously threw out first balls before Game 3. Each had performed emergency services during the quake. In early May 1996 the Giants experienced another earthquake during a game, this time a 3.2 quake that was barely strong enough to be felt by some. See Ron Fimrite, et al., *Three Weeks in October: Three Weeks in the Life of the Bay Area, the 1989 World Series, and the Loma Prieta Earthquake* (1990).

San Francisco/1906. The National League sent $1,000 to San Francisco for earthquake relief in 1906. The Dodgers raised $12,000 for earthquake relief the same year.

Long Beach/1933. Bill Terry and the Giants were playing an exhibition in Los Angeles during the disastrous 1933 Long Beach earthquake.

Los Angeles/1994. During the severe January 1994 earthquake in Los Angeles, the Anaheim Stadium scoreboard fell into the bleachers, causing almost $4 million in damage.

Japan/1995. On July 24, 1995, a group of Japanese All-Stars played a group of American players who were on Japanese teams. The game, the first of its kind, was played to benefit victims of the Kobe earthquake, which killed more than 6,000. The "Foreign Dreams," as the Americans were dubbed, won 5–3.

Seattle/1996. On May 2, 1996, the Mariners game was suspended when a 5.4 earthquake struck during the 6th inning. A Seattle minor league game was once cancelled because of "seismic shocks."

San Francisco/2002. On May 13, 2002, the Giants beat the Braves 7–6 in 11 innings after an earthquake jolted Pac Bell Park during the 9th inning. The game was not stopped by the quake.

"Quakes." Because the San Andreas earthquake fault runs through Rancho Cucamonga, California, the city's California League team is known as the Earthquakes. Its mascot is a character named Tremor whose uniform number is 4.8.

Ebbets Field (1913–1957)

"Ebbets Field itself had something to do with the love affair. It was a tiny, comfortable park seating only 32,000, not one of the massive ball yards, such as the Polo Grounds or Yankee Stadium. Ebbets Field was personal and familiar, and the fans responded to that. It was a suitable place for falling in love with the game." — Peter Golenbock in *Bums* (1984).

"The rotunda that Fred Wilpon remembers so fondly was a small crowded area that looked more like the peanut concession at an amusement park than the entrance to a ball park. The grandstands were usually dirty and smelled of a stale beer. The aisles were narrow, the seats jammed together. The playing field was cramped. The dugouts were inadequate. The home team club house was so small that the players were crowded against each other amid a jumble of equipment trunks. The visiting team clubhouse was worse." — Robert W. Creamer of the *New York Times* on the deterioration of Ebbets Field by the mid–1950s.

Origins. Ebbets Field was home to the Brooklyn Dodgers from 1913 through the club's departure for the West Coast after the 1957 season.

Brooklyn's Washington Park, located at two different sites over the years (see also ***Brooklyn Dodgers — Ballparks***), was considered too small and poorly located for the club by the early 20th century. As a result, owner Charles Ebbets began buying up approximately 40 different ownership interests covering a 40-acre site bordered by Bedford Avenue, Sullivan Street, Franklin Avenue and

Montgomery Street in an accessible shantytown area on the fringes of Brooklyn known as Pigtown.

Ebbets secured the final piece of land in December 1911, paying a total of $200,000 for all the necessary parcels. He broke ground on March 4, 1912, but underestimated the cost of the park by $500,000. In order to finance its completion, he agreed to sell half of his interest in the team to two contractors, brothers Steve and Ed McKeever.

Dimensions. The park had jagged dimensions. The left field foul pole was 343 feet from home plate. Center field was 393 feet deep and jagged across to the right field line: going in to 384 and then out to 409 in right center field, moving in to 376, and then 297 down the right field line. The original dimensions were modified in the 1930s to 351 in left center field and 388 in center field. By the 1950s the dimensions from left to right field generally were 348–351–384– 352–297.

First Game.

"Even the grand opening of Ebbets Field in 1913 was symptomatic of the entire operation. It was discovered that they had forgotten to build a press box. This discovery was slightly delayed because the valet assigned to unlocking the gates had forgotten to bring the keys. But the big moment eventually arrived, the grand march to the flagpole for the big ceremony. Trumpets blared. No flag-raising, though. They had forgotten the flag." — Sportswriter Tim Cohane.

The first game in the ballpark was an April 5, 1913, exhibition on a rainy day against the Yankees. Charles Ebbets' daughter Genevieve threw out the first ball and Nap Rucker beat the Yankees 3–2.

The first official game was Opening Day on April 13, 1913. There was only a frozen dirt skin in the outfield and there was no grass until midsummer. The announced 25,000 SRO capacity crowd (with 18,000 seats) watched as Otto Knabe doubled for the only hit in Johnny Seaton's 1–0 shutout for the Phillies over Rucker. Other sources report that the crowd was 12,000.

Capacity/Seating. The original capacity was 18,000, though some sources have reported 22,000 and 25,000 (which did not occur until the 1920s). The high was 35,000 in 1937 and then

dropped to between 31,000 and 34,000 in the 1950s. There were no left field bleacher seats until a few years after the park opened (there were never any right field seats). In 1930 the team decided to rip out the wooden bleachers and put in concrete stands. They were partially ready by mid–1931 and completed by 1932. It was thought that the new construction would add more seating, but the engineers miscalculated and the capacity did not change.

Flags. Ebbets Field flew flags from left field to right field showing the league standings each day.

First Home Run. The first home run in Ebbets Field was an inside-the-park shot by Giants outfielder Casey Stengel that skidded in the hard dirt to the outfield wall.

Name. The name of the park came supposedly from a discussion at the groundbreaking ceremony when reporter Len Wooster of the *New York Times* asked Ebbets what he intended to name the park. Ebbets responded with Washington Park, after the earlier parks' names. Wooster said that Washington Park had no meaning to that part of Brooklyn and suggested that it be named Ebbets Field. Another source reported that the name was determined by an informal vote of local sportswriters.

Lasts. The last game in Ebbets Field was played between the Dodgers and Pirates on September 24, 1957, with 6,673 fans in attendance. Danny McDevitt defeated the Pirates 2–0 as Bennie Daniels lost his first Major League start. The last out was made by Dee Fondy of the Pirates. Duke Snider hit the last two home runs in Ebbets Field on September 22, 1957.

Demolition.

"I have been trying to find a single memory so vivid and so real that one can understand, with the shock of recognition, what the place called Ebbets Field once meant. It was my ballpark and before that it was my father's ballpark…. It was the Elysium of boyhood. The wrecker's ball, crashing against Furillo's wall, destroying mortar, laying waste a monument. Steam shovels assaulting soil that had felt the spikes of Reese and Robinson. We thought, we had always thought, that Ebbets Field would stand for centuries." — Roger Kahn.

"It was a terrible psychic blow … Ebbets Field was replaced by a housing project. How could a father tell his son where Duke Snider used to hit one? Point out Apartment 5Q?" — Joe Flaherty.

On February 23, 1960, fans held a ceremony at home plate just prior to the start of demolition. In attendance were public address announcer Tex Rickard, and players Ralph Branca, Carl Erskine and Roy Campanella. The park became the site of the Jackie Robinson Housing Project.

Spelling. Some authoritative modern sources incorrectly spell Ebbets with an extra "t": "Ebbetts."

Eccentrics

"He showed them it was a game and they locked him up." — Yippie (and later suicide victim) Abbie Hoffman, on Jimmy Piersall (see also *Psychological Problems*).

"In baseball, you're supposed to sit on your ass, spit tobacco and nod at stupid things." — Noted offbeat pitcher Bill Lee.

"He may well be the only person named for John Milton who has never heard of John Milton." — Roger Kahn on John Milton ("Mickey") Rivers.

"Roger McDowell was the incarnation of a living, breathing horror film when he pitched for the Mets." — Angus G. Garber III in *The Baseball Companion* (1989).

"Ten million years from now, when the sun burns out and

The Ebbets Field scoreboard. Note Abe Stark's "HIT SIGN WIN SUIT" ad underneath the scoreboard.

the Earth is just a frozen iceball hurtling through space, nobody's going to care whether or not I got this guy out." — Noted screwball Tug McGraw.

"I threw about 90% fastballs and sliders, 50% fastballs and 50% sliders…. I'm starting to sound like Mickey Rivers." — John Butcher.

"That ball has a hit in it, so I want it to get back in the ball bag and goof around with the other balls in there. Maybe it'll learn some sense and come out as a pop out next time." — Mark Fidrych. See *Pitching Mound* for the Tiger pitcher's atypical behavior.

"What makes him unusual is that he thinks he's normal and everyone else is nuts." — Manager Danny Ozark on Jay Johnstone.

Jim "Deacon" White. The 19th century catcher firmly believed that the earth was flat and when he was with Detroit he tried to convince his teammates of this. Shortstop Jack Rowe reportedly became a believer after White explained that a ball hit in the air could not be caught if the earth was revolving.

Germany Schaefer. The early 20th century infielder purportedly convinced teammate Davy Jones that the earth was flat by pointing out that the bath water was flat.

Rube Waddell. The Hall of Fame pitcher was perhaps the greatest eccentric in baseball history. In 1902, after pitching in six straight games against the Tigers, he supposedly came into a game in the last inning, called in all three of his outfielders and then struck out the side. Some sources report that this happened only during spring training.

He once jumped the team for 10 days to go fishing and supposedly ran after a fire truck over the center field wall during a game (variations on this story do not place him on the mound). He was also found posing as a clothes mannequin in a department store.

He once cartwheeled to the clubhouse after 14- and nine-inning doubleheader victories. The cartwheel trick was also attributed to a complete game, 20-inning 4–2 victory against Cy Young on July 4, 1905. Waddell also pitched in the first game of the doubleheader that day.

Ossee Schreckengost, Waddell's catcher and roommate, purportedly arranged for it to be written in Waddell's contract that he could not eat animal crackers in bed.

Carlos Perez. The Expos pitcher is the youngest brother of pitchers Pascual and Melido Perez. He was considered somewhat eccentric for throwing his hands wildly in the air when he struck out a batter, for patting the mound, and high-hurdling the foul line each inning for good luck.

Dennis Eckersley (1954–)

Hall of Fame 2003

"He was Mr. Automatic. He got it done really quick." — Rickey Henderson.

"It was magic. We expected to win and I expected to save games. That's how it was." — Eckersley.

"Just for the heck of it, I watched the whole game on *ESPN Classics* the other night. I couldn't get over how young I looked." — Eckersley on Game 1 of the 1988 World Series, in which he gave up Kirk Gibson's game-winning home run.

Eckersley was a right-handed pitcher who both started and relieved during a 24-season career.

Born in Oakland, Dennis Lee Eckersley was drafted in the third round of the 1972 draft by Cleveland. "Eck" spent two seasons in Class A ball with Reno of the California League before being promoted to Class AA in 1974. Playing with San Antonio of the Texas

League, Eckersley posted a 14–3 mark with a 3.40 ERA, leading to a spot with the Indians in 1975. After beginning the season in the bullpen, he was awarded his first start on May 25. He made the most of it, crafting a three-hit, 6–0 complete game shutout of Oakland. He finished the season with a 13–7 won-lost record and a 2.60 ERA, third best in the American League. In May of 1977 he no-hit California 1–0. Eckersley would win 40 games for Cleveland over three years before being traded to Boston in 1978.

In 1978 he had his only 20-win season, finishing 20–8 with a 2.99 ERA. He followed with another fine season in 1979, fashioning an identical 2.99 ERA, a 17–10 record and 17 complete games. Eckersley would pitch for six seasons in Boston, compiling an 84–70 record before being traded to the Chicago Cubs during the 1984 season. His stay with the Cubs was brief and he was traded to Oakland for the 1987 season. Acquired to be a spot starter and long reliever, Eckersley inherited the closer role for the A's after the incumbent, Jay Howell, was lost with an injury. Eckersley earned 16 saves that season and a bullpen star was born.

In 1988 he led the league in saves with 45. He was the MVP of the A's ALCS sweep of Boston, earning four saves while not allowing a run in six innings pitched. In the World Series that year Eckersley's accomplishments would be ultimately overshadowed by Kirk Gibson's game-winning Game 1 home run off Eckersley and the Dodgers' subsequent upset win. In 1989 he saved 33 games with a 1.56 ERA, walking just three batters in 57 innings. He again excelled in the ALCS, earning three saves. In the World Series Eckersley recorded the last out in the A's four-game sweep of San Francisco. In 1990 he recorded 48 saves while allowing just four walks and nine runs in 73 innings In 1991 he finished second in the league with 43 saves. In 1992 Eckersley capped his brilliant five-year run with a 7–1 record, a 1.91 ERA and a league-leading 51 saves, earning both the Cy Young and MVP Awards.

Eckersley finished his career with brief stints in St Louis and Boston, retiring after the 1998 season. Upon retiring he had a 197–171 record with 100 complete games and 390 saves. A superb control pitcher, Eckersley allowed just 738 walks in 3,285 innings pitched.

General William D. "Spike" Eckert (1909–1971)

Eckert was a retired Air Force Lt. General when he was chosen as *Commissioner* of baseball in 1965.

Eephus Pitch

"It's a nothin' pitch, and eephus ain't nothin." —1940s Pirates benchwarmer Maurice Van Robays, credited with naming the pitch.

"I don't name them — I just throw them." — Pittsburgh Pirate pitcher Rip Sewell, who originated and perfected this 20-foot high-arc pitch. Sewell first threw the pitch in an exhibition game in 1941 against the Tigers. He used it against bonus baby Dick Wakefield, who struck out.

Catcher Al Lopez later recalled the origin of the pitch. He caught regularly for Sewell in the bullpen when he was warming up, and the last pitch was always a blooper ball that he invariably lobbed in for a strike.

The pitch made its regular season debut in 1941 in a 1–0 game against the Cubs. In the 9th inning with two outs, the Cubs had the bases loaded and Sewell had a full count on Dom ("Dim Dom") Dallessandro. Sewell threw the pitch for a called strike three. Dallessandro's response: "You SOB, if this was a rifle, I'd shoot you right between the eyes."

After its debut, the pitch was first referred to as the "blooper." It was also known as the "rainbow ball," "whoopsy-do," "sky-scraper" and "parachute pitch." Some baseball people thought the pitch should be outlawed as a balk, but National League umpires approved the pitch. Sewell blew off much of his foot in a hunting accident following the 1941 season, but he came back and had a number of solid seasons through the war years.

In the 1946 All-Star Game, Ted Williams took revenge against Sewell and the eephus pitch with a long home run to right field. Sewell came into the game with the American League ahead 8–0. With two men on he threw the first blooper outside. Williams hit the second pitch for a long foul. The third pitch, a fastball, was outside for a 1–2 count. On the fourth pitch, Williams took three steps forward and hit the eephus pitch out of the park. It was the only home run ever hit off the pitch. Williams later said that Yankee catcher and All-Star teammate Bill Dickey told him to run up on the ball to generate enough power to combat the slowness and arc of the pitch.

The next batter, Charlie "King Kong" Keller, swung extremely hard at an eephus pitch and hit a five-foot pop-up. The catcher was laughing so hard that he almost dropped the ball.

"Spitter." Whitey Kurowski made a regular habit of spitting at the pitch when it came in.

Potato Man. In 1944 Luke "Hot Potato" Hamlin returned to the Major Leagues and introduced his version of the Eephus pitch, the "soft potato."

Folly Floater. The "Folly Floater" was essentially the eephus pitch reincarnated. It was thrown by Steve Hamilton primarily for the Yankees from 1961 until 1972.

Tony Horton once popped out on Hamilton's Floater, dropped his bat and literally crawled back to the dugout. Everyone thought Horton was clowning around, but a short time later he left baseball and was hospitalized for emotional problems. Manager Alvin Dark described it as "the most sorrowful incident I was ever involved in in my baseball career."

LaLob. Relief pitcher Dave LaRoche developed "LaLob," a legal version of the eephus pitch that he used occasionally in the 1970s and 1980s. It was once clocked at 28 mph when LaRoche was pitching for the Yankees.

In 1981 slugger Gorman Thomas struck out on the pitch, threw his batting helmet in the air and then shattered it with his bat. On June 30, 1982, LaRoche gave him another chance. This time he threw Thomas seven straight LaLobs. After taking the first one for a ball, Thomas fouled off five straight and then singled to left field. Upon reaching first base he stuck his tongue out at LaRoche.

On August 6, 1982, Lamar Johnson had somewhat less success. LaRoche had two strikes on him with two outs in the 9th inning. He then threw the LaLob; Johnson swung, missed and collapsed on home plate. Umpire Ken Kaiser counted him out like a fallen boxer and then helped him up to a standing ovation from the fans.

"Leephus Pitch." On August 24, 1975, Bill "Spaceman" Lee of the pennant-winning Red Sox shut out the White Sox in the rain using his version of the eephus, dubbed the "Leephus." He used it in Game 7 of the 1975 World Series and Reds first baseman Tony Perez hit it for a home run.

Mark McGwire. On June 28, 1998, in the middle of his torrid home run pace, Mark McGwire was slowed down by Twins pitcher Bob Tewksbury and his version of the pitch. On 44-mph lobs, McGwire grounded out in the lst inning and popped out in the 4th. Tewksbury also used the pitch to retire Ray Lankford in the 6th inning.

Ejections

"Young man, if that bat comes down, you're out of the game."—Umpire Bill Klem to batter Al Lopez, who had flung his bat 20 feet in the air in protest.

"Damn, I'm going so bad that I don't even get thrown out of the game right. Aren't they supposed to give you a chance to stand around and argue?"—Oscar Gamble of the Yankees.

"No, everyone just seemed to be gathered around me."—Manager Alvin Dark when asked if he intentionally touched an umpire during a 1961 argument which resulted in his ejection.

"When I first went into the American League, Johnny Rice told me that the toughest call an umpire has to make is not the half-swing; the toughest call is throwing a guy out of the game after you blew the hell out of the play."—umpire Bill Kinnamon.

"Throwing people out of a game is like learning to ride a bicycle—once you get the hang of it, it can be a lot of fun."—Umpire Ron Luciano.

See also *Fights*, *Fines*, *Protests* and *Suspensions*.

Early Rules. By the 1890s umpires had the power to throw players out of a game. The Fleischmann Resolution of 1902 and the Brush Amendment of 1904 made it mandatory to fine players $10 if they were ejected from a game. If the league president suspended the player after that, another $10 fine was levied. Players were also fined an additional $10 for each day of the suspension. The owners undermined this effort at discipline by paying the fines for the players.

Silence. Whitey Lockman was tossed out by umpire Frank Dascoli, supposedly prompting this exchange: "But I didn't say anything."

"No, but I knew what you were going to say and it's the same thing."

Sleeping. Edd Roush purportedly was ejected from a game for sleeping on his glove in center field during an argument in the infield.

Babe Ruth. In 1922 Ruth tried to go into the stands after a heckler, but umpire Tom Connolly blocked his path and ejected him. The last time in his career that Ruth was ejected was in 1931, four years before he retired.

Distractions. The Phillies were playing the Giants on August 11, 1950. Giants second baseman Eddie Stanky was waving his arms whenever Andy Seminick of the Phillies batted. Phillies manager Eddie Sawyer protested and Giants manager Leo Durocher told Stanky to stop until league president Ford Frick ruled on the conduct. The next day Stanky froze at second base when Seminick batted early in the game. Later in the game, Giants catcher Hank Gowdy was knocked unconscious in a collision at the plate. Durocher was upset about the incident and let Stanky wave his arms at Seminick when he batted. Stanky was ejected and a huge brawl ensued.

Raincoat. On September 29, 1949, Connie Ryan wore a raincoat in the on-deck circle to protest the decision not to call a game due to rain. He was tossed out by umpire George Barr. Frankie Frisch and many others have pulled the same protest stunt, sometimes using an umbrella.

All Is Forgiven. On April 25, 1928, umpire Charley Moran ejected Rabbit Maranville from a game but allowed him to return in the 14th inning because the Cardinals were running out of players.

Dizzy Dean of the Cardinals was ejected on August 10, 1936, but was allowed to continue pitching after Cubs manager Charlie Grimm asked for an exception so as not to disappoint the large Ladies Day crowd.

Video Helper. On June 6, 1986, Padres manager Steve Boros was ejected before the first pitch of the game when he tried to give umpire Charlie Williams a videotape of a disputed play in the previous night's 4–2 loss to the Braves.

Airline Reservations. Jim Bouton claimed that an unidentified umpire threw out a player knowing that the player needed to make an early flight.

Bill Sharman. See *Basketball*.

Family Honor. In 1961 Rocky Colavito was ejected for going into the stands to protect his father, who was being harassed by fans.

Elite Group. Only four men have been ejected from a Major league game in six different decades: Casey Stengel, Leo Durocher, Frank Robinson and Don Zimmer.

Most Ejections/Manager.

"Durocher has been banished to the showers more times than B.O."—Charles Dexter in *Collier's* magazine.

The all-time leaders in managerial ejections are John McGraw with 131, Leo Durocher with 121, and Bobby Cox with 108 through 2003.

Orioles manager Earl Weaver holds the American League record with at least 91 ejections (98 in earlier sources). He had 61 in his first 9½ years as a manager and was suspended four times.

It took 14 years for Joe McCarthy to be ejected from a Major League game. It finally happened in August 1945.

Suffer. In the mid–1980s Cubs manager Lee Elia was desperate to shake up his losing team, so he asked umpire Frank Pulli to kick him out of the next game. Pulli said "no problem." During the game there was a close play at the plate, and Elia ran out to argue. Pulli wouldn't run him, however: "If I've got to watch this for five more innings, you're going to watch it with me."

Luciano/Weaver Feud. Minor league umpire and future author Ron Luciano ejected future Orioles manager Earl Weaver in four straight games when the two first met in the International League. This began a near-legendary feud that lasted through most of Weaver's career as a Major League manager. Luciano ejected him eight times in Major League games and the American League finally reassigned Luciano from all Orioles games. Luciano committed suicide in January 1995 and Weaver was elected to the Hall of Fame in 1996.

Touching Umpire. On October 1, 1964, Dave Wickersham was 19–12 for the Tigers and in his last start against the Yankees was trying for his first 20-win season. In the 7th inning on a close play at first, Wickersham touched umpire Bill Valentine trying to get his attention. First baseman Norm Cash was yelling in Valentine's ear, so Wickersham tapped him on the shoulder to get his attention to call time out. Valentine whirled around and tossed Wickersham for touching him. This resulted in an automatic ejection from a game that the Tigers eventually won 4–2, but Wickersham did not get credit for the win. He never again won more than 12 games in a season.

In later years, Valentine, who spent almost 30 years as the general manager of the Angels' Class AA affiliate in Arkansas, regretted being "too impulsive" on the ejection. In a 2003 letter to the former umpire, Wickersham, by then 68, acknowledged that Valentine made the right decision and forgave him for costing him a chance at win No. 20.

Manager/Doubleheader. On June 9, 1946, Met Ott of the Giants became the first manager to be ejected from both ends of a doubleheader.

Double Ejection. On August 23, 1952, the Giants' Bob Elliott complained and kicked dirt arguing over a called strike two.

Umpire Augie Donatelli ejected him from the game. Bobby Hoffman finished the at-bat by being called out on strikes and also was ejected by Donatelli for arguing the call.

Mark McGwire. On August 29, 1998, in St. Louis, a crowd erupted in fury when McGwire was thrown out of the game in the 1st inning for arguing over strike calls by the umpire, Sam Holbrook. The crowd of 47,627 came mainly to see and to cheer on McGwire in his pursuit of the home run record he set that year. The crowd reacted with boos and threw baseballs, golf balls, bottles and other objects onto the field.

To Be Continued. On July 17, 2001, Expos coach Ozzie Guillen was thrown out before the first pitch was thrown after continuing an argument from the previous night with umpire Greg Gibson.

Disguise. On June 9, 1999, Mets manager Bobby Valentine was ejected from the game in the 12th inning of a 3–2 loss to the Red Sox. He quickly returned to the bench wearing dark glasses and a moustache penciled in with eye black. He was suspended for two games and fined $5,000 for the prank.

Longest Wait. It took Nolan Ryan 26 years to get thrown out of a game. In his last season in 1993 he was tossed by umpire Richie Garcia after he was accused of intentionally throwing at Willie Wilson. After Wilson and Ryan had exchanged curses, Wilson tripled and they continued their exchange. The next time up, Ryan hit Wilson with a pitch and was ejected.

On July 18, 2001, the Mets beat the Marlins 4–3 in 11 innings. Marlins manager Tony Perez was ejected for arguing a call. It was his first ejection in 31 seasons and more than 3,800 games as a player and manager.

Postseason Play.

"I'd seen enough."—Cardinals manager Whitey Herzog after getting thrown out of Game 7 of the 1985 World Series; his club lost 11–0 to the Royals. Cardinals pitcher Joaquin Andujar lost his composure on the mound and earned an ejection during the game.

Heinie Manush of the Senators made history in 1933 when he became the first player ejected from a World Series game. He earned the hook after protesting a call by snapping the elastic on the bow tie of umpire Charley Moran. Judge Landis ruled that in the future only he could eject a player during the World Series, but it was too late for Manush. The commissioner-only rule never was implemented, although Ducky Medwick was taken out of a game in 1934 by Judge Landis after Tiger fans rained fruit and vegetables down on him during Game 7 of the Series (see also *Fans—Fan Attacks on Players*).

Roger Clemens was tossed out in the 2nd inning of Game 4 of the 1990 League Championship Series between the Red Sox and A's. There was much debate over Clemens' inability to control his temper in crucial situations. It was already a lost cause, however, as the A's won the game and swept the Series.

Japanese Leagues. American Rob Ducey of the Nippon Ham Fighters fought with Kevin Reimer of the Fukuoka Daiei Hawks on September 16, 1995. Ducey was ejected from that game and the game the next day. It was the first time that a player in the Japanese leagues was ejected in consecutive games. He received a 300,000 yen fine (about $3,000) and a two-game suspension.

Milton Bradley. In a crucial game in the last week of the 2004 season, the Dodger right fielder, always edgy and temperamental and having been ejected three times already that season, dropped a fly ball trying to make a basket catch in the 8th inning to give the Rockies two runs and a 4–0 lead. Fans booed and someone threw an empty plastic water bottle about 20 feet from him. He grabbed the bottle and ran toward the low right field seats screaming and cussing at the fans (the wrong fans, it turned out), some of whom were cussing back at him. He had already had a temper tantrum earlier in the game when he broke his bat over his knee after a strikeout and then threw his helmet wildly in the dugout after another strikeout.

Bradley had to be restrained by teammates in the outfield and then was ejected from the game. As he left the field he tore off his uniform and then raised his hands to urge the fans to boo more. He missed the wild 9th inning when the Dodgers rallied for five runs and won 5–4.

Little Misunderstanding. In mid–2004 Roger Clemens attended his 10-year-old son's tournament baseball game in Colorado. His son, Kacy, appeared to be safe at second on a stolen base attempt, but was called out against a team from Bakersfield, California. When the umpire came over to the dugout to discuss the call, he felt a sunflower seed hit his pants leg. He pointed at Clemens sitting in a lawn chair close behind the fence, and said, "He's out of here."

Clemens quickly received an apology from the tournament's president for being "unjustly" ejected from the game: "Mr. Clemens was a non-aggressor and a victim of mistaken identity and confusion by an upset umpire."

Elias Sports Bureau (1913–)

"I don't care what or who, a record is a record. A triumph. Something to be cherished."—Seymour Siwoff of the Elias Sports Bureau.

This sports statistics service was founded in 1913 by Al Munro Elias (1872–1939). His nephew Lester Goodman continued the Bureau after Elias died. The Bureau originally sold scorecards and statistics primarily to fans and saloons.

Many newspapers refused to accept the Bureau's statistics until 1916, but by 1919 Elias was the official statistician of the National League and International League. The Bureau later published the *Red* and *Green Books*, which contain the official statistics of each Major League (see also **Statistics**).

Seymour Siwoff became the head of the organization in the late 1950s. He was planning to join the FBI before reviving the Elias Bureau in the early 1960s. In addition to baseball, Elias began supplying statistics to the NFL in 1961 and basketball later in the decade. In the 1960s and 1970s, Elias earned $1.25 for each version of a Topps baseball card that contained its statistics, but earned nothing for copies.

In 1970 Elias assigned some of its statisticians to the ABC broadcast booth during "Monday Night Baseball." It was a breakthrough in the use of statistics and many more teams began using the service. In 1975 Elias was entirely computerized, as were its competitors. By then its primary income was from selling statistics for various purposes other than baseball cards. Initially, however, Elias could not persuade enough clubs to buy its more comprehensive computer-generated materials. About one in five purchased the statistics, but it was not enough to recoup the $300,000 Siwoff had invested. By the early 1980s, however, Elias had good penetration of the marketplace with its materials.

The first mass public display of the organization's wares was in 1985, with the publication of the first *Elias Baseball Analyst*. Sales eventually tailed off and the publication ceased after 1994.

Elizabeth Resolutes

National Association 1873
"Pathetic" and "Wretched"—The *New York Times*.

This dismal club located in Waverly, New Jersey, had a record of 2–21 before dropping out of the Association.

Emblems   See *Logos*

Encyclopedias

"He can walk to school."—Babe Herman of the 1930s Cubs, when Chuck Klein suggested that he buy his son an encyclopedia after Herman complained that the kid was asking too many questions.

"There are many people who say that the era of print encyclopedias has passed. Let us hope that Lucifer is saving those people a nice warm spot. I want a bumper sticker: You can have my *Baseball Encyclopedia* when you tear it from my cold, dead hands. Sure, you can stumble across Cliff Dapper in cyberspace, but what are the odds? If you don't have a print encyclopedia, what are your real chances of discovering that Milo Candini could actually hit? Major league players don't deserve the wispy, ephemeral immortality of buzzing electrons; they deserve the cold, marble permanence of black ink on white pages. You owe it to every baseball player you hated as a child to buy this book and confirm that Tommy Boggs was every bit as bad as you thought he was."—Historian and statistician Bill James (amen!).

The Official Encyclopedia of Baseball.
"This book is dedicated to those men whose devotion to the decimal point and rabid research for records in the past hundred years accumulated the baseball statistics which have come to be recognized as the lifeblood of the game."—Dedication to *The Official Encyclopedia of Baseball*, edited by Hy Turkin and S.C. Thompson (1951). This edition was the first encyclopedia of baseball statistics officially sanctioned by Major League Baseball. The Executive Council authorized the work in February 1949. The first edition was the Jubilee Edition in celebration of 50 years of the American League and 75 years of the National League. Revised hardcover and softcover editions (as well as pocket editions by Gillette) were published into the 1970s.

The Baseball Encyclopedia. In the mid–1960s, a group of baseball historians decided to publish a new volume that received official sanction from Major League Baseball. Macmillan's **The Baseball Encyclopedia** was first published in 1969 as part of the game's celebration of 100 years of professional baseball.

Total Baseball. A later book that is comprehensive in its own right is **Total Baseball**, by John Thorn and Peter Palmer (1990). For its 1995 and subsequent editions the book received official status from Major League Baseball and *The Baseball Encyclopedia* lost its official status.

Other Encyclopedias. Statistician Ernest J. Lanigan, *The Baseball Cyclopedia* (1922–1933); George Moreland, *Balldom* (1914), with updates in 1926–1927 (Horton Publishing reprinted the 1914 edition in 1989); David S. Neft, *Sports Encyclopedia: Baseball* (1991); Murray Olderman, *Nelson's 20th Century Encyclopedia of Baseball* (1963); Joseph Reichler (ed.), *Ronald Encyclopedia of Baseball* (1962).

Endorsements

"What do you eat every morning, Lou?"—
"A heaping bowlful of Wheaties!"—Lou Gehrig's response on the radio show, "Ripley's Believe It or Not." Unfortunately, Gehrig

was paid to say "Post Toasties." Later, however, he was the first player featured on a Wheaties box (in 1934), but on the back. Pole vault champion Bob Richards was the first to appear on the front of the box, in 1958.

"I drink Coca Cola myself, and advise all the team to drink it. I think it is good for them."—Connie Mack in a 1912 advertisement.

"Goldsmith Company
Dear Sir:

Please send me a black [Fred] Snodgrass model glove. I used that model last season and led the American League in fielding with an average of .967. Also had wonderful luck with it in the World Series.

My success with your gloves include—a run of 24 straight games with 148 chances and no errors (World Record), a .960 fielding average for 3 years; and a .960 average in 10 World Series games. These are exceptionally high averages for a short-stop.

If you care to use these facts and my name in your advertising you can do so by sending me *two gloves each year "gratis."* Many firms have made me better offers, but yours is the only glove that I can use with success.

If you can't or don't care to use this send me the glove C.O.D. at once and oblige."

Yours respectfully, Everett Scott
Short-stop Boston American World Champs."—1916 letter by Red Sox shortstop Everett Scott.

"Carl Yastrzemski has finally landed where all the great ones eventually land: 'Home Shopping Network.'"—Sportswriter Dan Shaughnessy.

"The Babe's greatest legacy may well be the universal application of athletic fame to huckstering, a principle reflected constantly in the media of today."—Michael Roberts in *Fans!* (1976).

"We soothe babies' backsides, not baseballs."—The makers of Vaseline, rejecting an endorsement offer by spitball artist Gaylord Perry.

"A promise made, a promise kept."—1980 Owens Corning ware advertising slogan featuring footage of Babe Ruth hitting his "*Called Shot*" home run.

"The Mantle in the Gray Flannel Suit"—Sportswriter Shirley Povich's description of Mickey Mantle and his quest for endorsement money. Povich estimated that in 1956 Mantle took in about $59,000 in endorsement money, almost double his $30,000 salary from the Yankees. Including his World Series share, Mantle earned about $100,000 that year.

"I ain't got to please nobody. All those white sponsors aren't going to use me for endorsements anyway."—Barry Bonds.

"Steve Hertz, Fred Lear, Dick Kenworthy, Dick Hoover, Joe Hoover, Bill Singer, Walter Tappen, Dennis Kinney, Ken Sears, Ed Roebuck, Hooks Warner, Morrie Schick, Zeke Wrigley, Evar Swanson, Jim Ritz, Clarence Kraft, Steve Libby, Wally Gerber, Soup Campbell, Bill Kellogg, Curt Schilling, Joe Borden"

See also ***Advertising, Candy, Cigarette Cards*** and ***Underwear.***

Earliest. The earliest endorsements were by players featured on 19th-century cigarette cards. Players were soon featured in connection with paint, gum and general tobacco products.

Coke. Ty Cobb claimed in an ad that he kept a "Coca Cola case in the dugout to prevent fatigue." He became a multi-millionaire in part because of his Coca Cola stock ownership.

Remedies and Tobacco. In 1887 Charles Comiskey endorsed Menell's Penetrating Oil, cigars and chewing tobacco.

Cereal? 2000s Indians outfielder Coco Crisp definitely merited an endorsement deal.

Wagons. Hack Wilson, a small (5'6") but mighty slugger, endorsed children's wagons.

Bathtub Mat. Zeke Barnes was fined $100 by Giants manager John McGraw after he hurt his ankle and wrist in a bathtub accident while drinking. On the upside, Barnes received a $200 fee to endorse a bathtub mat manufacturer.

Disparity. When Harry Hooper received $50 to push a patent medicine in 1920, Babe Ruth was receiving $10,000 to hawk Home Run cigarettes.

Just Missed. Joe DiMaggio was talking with Heinz 57 Steak Sauce makers for an endorsement deal should his hitting streak end at 57. Heinz apparently was unwilling to change to "Heinz 56" and the deal fell through. DiMaggio endorsed "Mr. Coffee" in the 1970s and his television commercials for the product were revived in 1990.

Yoo-Hoo. Yogi Berra endorsed Yoo-Hoo soft drinks and owned stock in the drink's maker. He once persuaded the entire Yankee team to wear tee shirts bearing the Yoo-Hoo logo. Berra did his own television spots for the soft drink.

M & M's. After Mickey Mantle and Roger Maris had outstanding home run numbers in 1961, they endorsed men's and boys' clothes for $45,000 each year for three years. Curiously, although sales for M & M's candy skyrocketed while the "M & M Boys" were hitting all their home runs, they never negotiated an endorsement deal with the candy maker. The two did star in a movie made in 1962, *Safe at Home.*

Death Threats. Jackie Robinson received 10 death threats in seven years and for a while turned down all appearances for commercial endorsements.

Pepsi. During his wild 1968 season, Denny McLain had an endorsement contract with, and a dog named, Pepsi.

Magnavox. When Henry Aaron broke Babe Ruth's home run record in 1974 he received only one significant national endorsement, for Magnavox television sets. He received a $1 million, five-year deal.

Cereal.

"Meanwhile, it's Albert Belle who just put his name on a new breakfast cereal, which is called 'Albert Belle's Slugger Cereal,' but should be released in Baltimore under the name 'Albert's Not-So-Cheeri-Os.'"—Peter Schmuck on the sourpuss Belle.

In the 1990s Ken Griffey, Jr., made the cover of a Kellogg's Frosted Flakes box, the first time in 40 years that Tony the Tiger shared the cover with someone else. In the 1990s Kellogg's marketed a Roberto Clemente memorial cereal box in Puerto Rico and Miami.

Endorsement Value After Death. Many states allow the heirs of a famous person to continue protecting that person's likeness and receive licensing royalties. For example, California allows the heirs to control the likeness for 50 years after death. The rules in other states differ widely. Oklahoma allows protection for 100 years and Tennessee for 10 years.

Babe Ruth's family received $400,000 from such licensing in 1989 and almost $1 million in 1990. It took awhile for his heirs to cash in on this bonanza, as the total 1984 income from licensing his likeness was a mere $100.

Drop in Endorsements/1990s. National endorsements dropped significantly as baseball declined in popularity in the 1990s. In the late 1970s and early 1980s, George Brett, Reggie Jackson, Steve Garvey and other players had national contracts. By the early 1990s only aging Nolan Ryan and Brett had national endorsement contracts, and both were for pain remedies.

England

"Attention GIs from Brooklyn! You will be astounded to learn that the fame of Dem Bums has failed to span the Atlantic. A London newspaper, scouting for information yesterday, telephoned the sports desk of The Stars and Stripes to inquire if the Brooklyn Dodgers were a 'fencing team or a baseball team.'" — The *Stars and Stripes* military newspaper in 1944.

See also *Cricket, International Tours, Rounders* and *Royalty*.

The National Base Ball League of Great Britain was formed in the late 19th century, though Albert Spalding unsuccessfully attempted to organize an English baseball league in the 1890s.

In 1938 the United States Olympic Baseball team played a series of games in England. The tour was in preparation for the 1940 Olympic baseball tournament scheduled for Japan. The Americans lost four of five games.

Compliment. When John McGraw went to England in 1924 he met writer George Bernard Shaw, who declared that he had "at last discovered the real and authentic Most Remarkable Man in America."

Player. A native of Bedford, England, Lance Painter attended Wisconsin before being drafted by the Padres in 1990 and spending 10 seasons (through 2003) as a middle reliever.

Book. Alistair Cooke, *Fun and Games with Alistair Cooke: On Sports and Other Amusements* (1995).

Entertainers

See also *Clown Princes of Baseball, Musicians, Organs, Singers, Songs* and *Television Shows*.

Ballplayers of the 19th century often appeared at theaters to be introduced to the audience and many performed vaudeville routines.

Pitcher Rube Marquard once appeared as a female impersonator.

Equipment See *Balls, Bats, Catcher's Equipment, Gloves, Shoes, Umpires* — Equipment and *Uniforms*

Errors

"Errors are part of the game, but Abner Doubleday was a jerk for inventing them." — Rangers second baseman Billy Ripken.

"It's too perfect. Errors are part of the excitement. It wasn't like this when I was playing." — 19th century curveball artist Candy Cummings watching a 1921 game at Fenway Park.

"To err is human. To forgive is a Mets fan." — 1960s banner at Shea Stadium.

"If ever an error had "F" [sic] written on it, that grounder did." — Jerry Coleman.

"Over the course of a season, a miscue will cost you more games than a good play." — Jerry Coleman.

"Things could be worse. Suppose your errors were counted and published every day, like those of a baseball player." — Unknown.

Early Rules and Statistics. Prior to 1889 a number of plays were scored as errors: base on balls, wild pitches, passed balls, balks, and hit batters. In the 1910s an attempt was made in some box scores to categorize the different kinds of errors. They included references to "First Base on Errors," "Fumbles," "Muffed Flies," "Muffed Foul Fly," "Muffed Thrown Ball" and "Wild Throw."

Errors were not credited to earlier 19th-century infielders unless there was a bad throw on a runner and the runner was able to advance an extra base.

Modern Rule. An error may be charged to a fielder even if the fielder does not touch the ball.

Fred Snodgrass.

"Boston fans are mentioning his name only in whispers, and deepest gloom prevails [in New York] wherever baseball is discussed." — Hugh Fullerton in a late 1912 edition of the *New York Times*.

Giants outfielder Fred Snodgrass dropped a fly ball during the last game of the 1912 World Series. The error supposedly led directly to the loss of the Series to the Red Sox (it did not). The fly ball, however, was never forgotten.

In the top of the 10th inning of the deciding Game 8 (there had been a tie), the Giants scored a run to go ahead 2–1. It was driven in by Fred Merkle, the most famous player credited wrongly with losing a pennant (see also *Base Running*).

In the bottom of the 10th inning, the first batter flied to center field within 10 feet of Snodgrass. There was a mix-up among the outfielders and Snodgrass dropped the ball for a two-base error. Despite the error, the Giants should have been able to get out of the inning unscathed and claim the championship.

Snodgrass played shallow on the next batter, Harry Hooper, figuring a bunt was in order. Hooper hit a hard line drive on which Snodgrass made his "best catch ever" and almost doubled off the runner at second base. With one out and men on first and second after a walk, Tris Speaker hit a pop foul off first base. It should have been caught for the second out. First baseman Merkle, pitcher Christy Mathewson and catcher Chief Meyers all froze and the ball dropped untouched. Speaker then singled in the tying run and the other runner advanced to third while Speaker took second on the throw home. After an intentional walk loaded the bases, a long sacrifice fly by Larry Gardner ended the game and the Series.

Snodgrass was forever-after credited with losing the Series for the Giants. Giants manager John McGraw never publicly blamed him and helped him obtain a $1,000 raise the next year. McGraw publicly blamed the loss on a dropped fly ball in the 7th inning by Art Fletcher that led to a run. The error plagued Snodgrass even after his death: "Fred Snodgrass; 86, Dead; Ballplayer muffed 1912 fly." — *New York Times* obituary of April 6, 1974.

Bill Buckner.

"I'm off the hook! I'm off the hook!" — Repeatedly yelled by broadcaster and former Red Sox pitcher Mike Torrez in the Red Sox locker room immediately after Buckner's error in Game 6 of the 1986 World Series. Torrez had never been forgiven by Red Sox fans after he gave up Bucky Dent's dramatic three-run home run in the 1978 *Play-Off* game between the Yankees and Red Sox.

Buckner became the goat of the 1986 World Series between the Mets and Red Sox. In Game 6 the Red Sox led the Series 3–2 and the game 5–3 going into the bottom of the 10th inning (Roger Clemens had earlier been the pitcher of record after leaving with a 3–2 lead). After two quick outs, the Red Sox needed one more strike on Mets catcher Gary Carter to clinch the club's first World Series since 1918.

Carter singled to keep the Mets' hopes alive. Kevin Mitchell, who had been taking off his uniform in the clubhouse, quickly dressed and lined an 0–1 pitch for a single to center and Carter stopped at second. Ray Knight blooped an 0–2 pitch for a single to center and Carter scored to make it 5–4, with Mitchell taking third. Mookie Wilson stepped to the plate as reliever Bob Stanley replaced Calvin Schiraldi. Stanley threw a wild pitch on a 2–2 count and Mitchell scored to tie the game. On a 3–2 count Wilson hit a weak ground ball to the gimpy Buckner, who was playing well behind the first base bag. Buckner's commentary: "It bounced and bounced and just then it didn't bounce. It just skipped. I can't remember the last time I missed a ground ball. I'll remember that one."

The ball went through Buckner's legs and the winning run scored. Red Sox manager John McNamara later was criticized for not bringing in a defensive replacement for the sore-ankled Buckner (see *Injuries and Illness* – **Ankle** for the extent of his problems), who was barely mobile in the field. The Mets won Game 7 and the Series after the Red Sox took a 3–0 lead into the bottom of the 6th inning.

Immediately after the play the first base umpire supposedly gave the ball to Mets public relations director Milton Richman, who gave it to Buckner. In 1992 actor Charlie Sheen paid $93,500 for the ball. Sheen paid more than 10 times the presale estimate. Buckner later said that he still had the ball and that Sheen bought a fake.

In 1993 the pressure of Buckner's negative celebrity finally forced him to move to Idaho from Andover, Massachusetts. However, he returned to baseball in 1995 as a hitting coach.

Career Errors. From 1889 through 1904 shortstop Herman Long made over 1,000 errors. It would have taken 1970s star shortstop Larry Bowa 85 years to make that many errors. Three errors per game by a team was common in the 1890s. Third baseman Bill Shindle made 122 errors in 1890 for Philadelphia of the Players League. In the pre-glove days, one in every six chances was turned into an error. Today one in 50 chances is booted.

Bill Keister, a turn-of-the-century shortstop, holds the record for the lowest 20th century season fielding average. He had an .851 average for Baltimore in 1901, with a 20th century record 97 errors in 115 games.

The most National League errors in a 20th century season was 81 by shortstop Rudy Hulswitt for the 1903 Phillies. In 1913 shortstop Buck Weaver of the White Sox became the last player to commit 70 errors in a season.

Most/Game. On May 21, 1904, outfielder Bill O'Neill of the Red Sox filled in at shortstop for the injured Freddy Parent. O'Neill made six errors to set a 20th-century single-game record.

Most/Game/Team.

"The Boston Red Sox field the ball as if it contains mad cow samples." — Mike Lupica on the club's pathetic early 1996 fielding. The 1901 Tigers and 1903 White Sox each made 12 errors in a game to set the 20th century record.

In May 1995 the Dodgers and Cardinals combined for 12 errors in an 8–4 Dodger victory. It was the most errors in a game since June 11, 1959, when the Pirates made seven and the Giants made five in a 12–9 Pittsburgh win.

Four in an Inning. Cubs shortstop Lenny Merullo committed four errors in the same inning on consecutive plays on September 13, 1942. Merullo's son Leonard, Jr., was born on that day and both father and son were thereafter nicknamed Boots. On the plus side, Merullo also participated in three triple plays during his career.

Mike Grady, utilityman for the 1899 Giants (also reported as 1895 Phillies — he played for both), committed four errors on the same play. Playing third one day, he booted a ground ball and then threw it wildly over the first baseman's head. Grady dropped the return throw as the runner came into third base. He picked up the ball and threw home trying to nail the runner — except that he threw the ball into the stands.

On September 14, 1986, Giants catcher Bob Brenley played third base against the Braves. In the 4th inning he made four errors as the Braves took a 4–0 lead. He began his redemption in the 5th inning when he hit a solo homer. In the 7th inning he hit a two-run single to tie the game at six. In the bottom of the 9th he hit another home run to give the Giants a 7–6 victory.

Four in a Game. On April 22, 1972, Rich McKinney of the Yankees made four errors on ground balls to third base, all of which figured in Boston's scoring of nine runs to beat New York 11–7.

Pokey Reese started at shortstop on Opening Day 1998 for the Reds in place of the injured Barry Larkin. Reese made four errors on his first three chances as the Reds lost 10–2 to the Padres.

Three in an Inning.

"If the Dodgers don't want him, I'll take him." — Hank Bauer on Willie Davis.

Dodger centerfielder Willie Davis committed three errors during the 5th inning of Game 2 of the 1966 World Series against the Orioles. He lost two fly balls in the sun and made a wild throw past third (caught by first baseman Wes Parker, the answer to a trivia question about who was backing up third base). The inning was part of the inauspicious conclusion to the career of injured pitcher Sandy Koufax, who pitched six innings in a 6–0 loss to rookie Jim Palmer.

On May 18, 1950, third baseman Tommy Glaviano of the Cardinals committed three consecutive errors in the 9th inning to give the Dodgers four runs and a 9–8 victory. The Cardinals had held an 8–0 lead, but gave up four runs in the 8th and one in the 9th before Glaviano's "heroics" led to four additional runs. He had four errors for the game.

In 1937 at Wrigley Field, Reds second baseman Alex Kampouris was honored before a game by the Chicago Hellenic Society, which gave him a car. Kampouris responded with three errors in one inning.

Hard-Headed.

"I thought I had it. I was twisting around like this. It grazed my glove, hit me on the head, and bounced over. I'll be on ESPN for about a month." — Jose Canseco.

"He wore a glove for only one reason. It was a league custom. The glove would last him a minimum of six years, because he rarely made contact with a ball." — Dodger executive Fresco Thompson on outfielder Babe Herman. Herman always insisted that he had never been hit in the head with a fly ball. He once told reporters that if he ever did get hit in the head, he would walk off the field and quit on the spot. When asked by sportswriter Tom Meany if the promise included getting hit on the shoulder, Herman responded: "Oh, no, the shoulder don't count."

Creative Excuse.

"Third baseman Joe Foy and shortstop Rico Petrocelli ... were both subject to fatal spells of introspection when approaching ground balls." — Roger Angell in *The Summer Game* (1972) on the Red Sox infielders of the mid–1960s.

"I did my job. The ball didn't do its job." — Indians outfielder Coco Crisp after dropping a routine fly ball in 2004.

Early 20th century outfielder Josh DeVore once dropped a fly ball and supposedly claimed that he was "momentarily blinded by the sun" from the reflection off his newly manicured fingernails.

Dodger third baseman Billy Cox also was blinded by the sun — on a ground ball (see also *Sun*).

Symmetry. During the 1950 season, utility infielder Pete Castiglione of the Pirates committed one error at first base, two errors at second base, three errors at third base and four errors at shortstop.

Pennant Lost. In 1945 the Senators went down to the last day of the season one-half game behind the Tigers. In the first game of their doubleheader, the Senators lost to the A's in extra innings after leading 3–0 in the 8th inning. The A's scored three unearned runs in the 8th to tie the game on a strange error call by umpire Eddie Rommel.

Senators outfielder Buddy Lewis caught a fly ball for the out and in one motion underhanded the ball back to the infield. His hand and the ball hit his baggy pant leg and the ball rolled to the ground. The crowd roared, the umpire turned around, assumed that Lewis had dropped the ball and called an error. The A's went on to score three runs and win in extra innings, clinching the pennant for the Tigers. The winning run scored as a result of a fly ball lost in the sun because outfielder Bingo Binks was not wearing dark *Glasses*.

Consecutive Errorless Games/Team. The 1975 Reds had 15 consecutive errorless games, the Major League record. The American League record is 14, set by the 1991 Angels.

Uniform Problem. In 1945 A's infielder Irv Hall hit a line drive to Senators pitcher Dutch Leonard. Leonard got his glove on the ball and then lost it down the inside of his pants.

In 1948 A's shortstop Eddie Joost fielded a ground ball from Billy Goodman of the Red Sox. The ball went up his sleeve and into his shirt. Runner Ted Williams was laughing so hard on third base that he could not run home.

Brain Lock. On April 24, 1994, in the 3rd inning of an eventual 7–1 Dodger win over the Expos, Dodger shortstop Jose Offerman was on first base with one out and Mike Piazza at bat. Expos first baseman Larry Walker caught Piazza's pop fly foul ball as he ran away from the infield down the line. Thinking the inning was over, Walker flipped the ball to a young fan. He turned to walked toward the dugout and saw Offerman running to third base. Walker ran back to the fan, six-year-old Sebastian Napier, retrieved the ball and threw it back to the infield. Offerman ended up on third. Tim Wallach then hit the first of his two home runs that night.

On August 12, 2000, the Mets beat the Giants 3–2, despite a mental error by outfielder Benny Agbayani. He caught a fly ball for the second out of the 4th inning, and then handed the ball to a seven-year-old boy in the stands. Agbayani thought it was the third out, and two Giants runners score.

World Series. Senators manager Roger Peckinpaugh played shortstop for the club in the 1925 World Series. Although he was the league MVP that season, he had eight of his team's nine errors in the Series, six of which led directly to runs. The Senators lost to the Pirates in seven games, though they led 6–4 after six innings in the last game and Peckinpaugh had homered early in the game.

In his last Major League appearance, in Game 2 of the 1973 World Series, center fielder Willie Mays dropped a fly ball in the 9th inning against the A's to allow in the tying run. He had been brought in as a defensive replacement that inning. What is often forgotten is that Mays later in the game had the game-winning hit off premier reliever Rollie Fingers.

Wrong Way Turner. Padres outfielder Jerry Turner once wheeled to make a throw to nail a runner at the plate. He threw so hard that the force of his body turned him around and he nailed the outfield wall with the ball.

Bad Timing. The Cubs were leading the Brewers 7–5 in the bottom of the 9th on the Wednesday before the last weekend of the 1998 season, September 23. A win would put them a half game up on the Mets for the wild card spot. With the bases loaded and Rod Beck on the mound, Cubs outfielder Brant Brown dropped a routine fly ball, three runs scored, and the Brewers won the game even after the Cubs had built a 7–0 lead on two home runs by Sammy Sosa.

The Cubs were forced into a one-game *Play-Off* for the wild card spot, and managed to hold on to beat the Giants 5–3. The Cubs traded Brown after the season, but he landed back with them briefly in 2000.

Making the Most of It. On April 22, 1998, White Sox second baseman Ray Durham tied a Major League record by reaching base three times on errors. He also had three hits and scored four runs. He also advanced to third on a throwing error on his stolen base, and then after tripling he scored on an error on the play.

Catchers. Until 1997, Buddy Rosar of the 1946 A's was one of only five catchers to play an entire season without making an error. He played in 117 games that year. The others were Yogi Berra (85 games for the 1958 Yankees), Lou Berberet (77 games for the 1957 Senators), Pete Daley (77 games for the 1957 Red Sox) and Rick Cerone (83 games for the 1988 Red Sox). Between July 1957 and May 1959 Berra handled 950 consecutive chances without an error.

Marlins catcher Charles Johnson caught 123 games in 1997 without an error, but had one passed ball. He set a record with 160 straight games without an error when he broke Rick Cerone's record of 159. His streak ended at 172 when he made an error in the 1st inning of the first game of 1998. He made up for the mistake with a three-run home run in the bottom of the 1st and the Marlins won 6–1.

Thurman Munson made only one error behind the plate during 117 games in 1971, and on that play he was knocked unconscious in a home plate collision.

Wally Schang made an American League-record 218 errors in 1,439 games between 1913 and 1931. Ivy Wingo holds the modern Major League and National League record with 234 errors in 1,231 games between 1911 and 1929.

Pitchers.

"I wanted to dig a hole behind the mound and crawl in and hope that no one would see me." — Astros pitcher Wade Miller in April 2003, after his throw to an uncovered third base allowed three runs to score by the Reds.

Pitcher Al Downing once went 244 games without making an error. Pitcher Ed Walsh committed an American League-record 55 errors in 430 games between 1904 and 1916. Hippo Vaughn holds the modern Major League and National League record with 64 errors in 390 games between 1913 and 1921.

First Basemen.

"He was, I believe, the worst-fielding first baseman I ever saw. He played the position so badly that he *looked* dumb.... [Though he went to college], when Bonura went after a ground ball to his right, it was hard to believe he was an educated man." — Art Hill in *I Don't Care If I Never Come Back* (1980).

Zeke Bonura was a stone-handed first baseman for the White Sox in the 1930s. In one game with the bases loaded and two outs, Bonura allowed four runs to score on one play as he dropped a ground ball, dropped it again, dropped it *again*, kicked it, and then threw the ball in the dugout trying to get the batter coming in to home plate.

A 1963 movie entitled *Dr. Strangelove* was the basis for the nickname "Dr. Strangeglove" given to Pirate first baseman Dick Stuart. Stuart led the league in errors at first base seven of nine years, but also led the league in putouts and assists one year and holds the record (with others) of three assists in one inning. Stuart once received a standing ovation for successfully picking up a hot dog wrapper in Fenway Park. Stuart's response: "Errors are a part of my image."

Steve Garvey played 193 straight games without an error and in 1984 for the Padres became the first player to go an entire season at first base without making an error.

On April 18, 1991, Orioles first baseman Glenn Davis had four errors against the Brewers. Three of the errors were awarded immediately, but the fourth was not awarded until the next day after a scoring change.

Hal Chase made a Major League and American League record 285 errors in 1,117 games between 1905 and 1914. Fred Tenney holds the modern National League record with 252 errors in 1,807 games between 1900 and 1911.

Don Mattingly finished his career with a .996 fielding percentage, tied only by Steve Garvey and Wes Parker for first basemen with at least 1,000 games played.

Second Basemen. In 1990 Ryne Sandberg of the Cubs broke the Major League record with 123 consecutive errorless games by a second baseman. The streak, which began in 1989, ended when Sandberg barehanded a shot that had skipped off first baseman Mark Grace's glove. Sandberg's off-balance throw went between Grace and pitcher Mike Harkey, who was attempting to cover first base. Sandberg once went four years without making a throwing error.

Blue Jays second baseman Roberto Alomar set a new American League record with his 90th consecutive errorless game on June 17, 1995. He broke the record of 89 set by Jerry Adair for the Orioles in 1964 and 1965.

In 1990 Jose Oquendo of the Cardinals set a National League record with three errors in a game at second base. The American League record is five, held by three players.

Eddie Collins made an American League record 435 errors in 2,650 games between 1908 and 1928. Larry Doyle holds the modern Major League and National League record with 443 errors in 1,730 games between 1907 and 1920.

Shortstops. When Cal Ripken, Jr., set the Major League record with only three errors by a shortstop during the 1990 season, he broke Eddie Brinkman's record of seven in 156 games in 1972 for the Tigers. Ripken holds the record for the most consecutive chances in a single season without an error, 431 set in 1990.

Larry Bowa holds the National League record for fewest errors by a shortstop playing in 150 or more games in a season. He had only nine errors in 152 games for the 1972 Phillies (and only six over 146 games for the 1979 Phillies).

Rey Ordonez once held the record among shortstops for flawless play in the most consecutive games. From June 14 through October 4, 1999, he played in 100 consecutive errorless games for the Mets, handling 411 chances without a miscue. In his second game of the 2000 season, played in the Tokyo Dome, he made an error on the artificial turf and the streak ended at 101.

The American League record was for a time held by Cal Ripken, who played in 95 straight games for the Orioles without an error from April 14 through July 27 in 1990, a stretch during which he handled 429 chances. Both records were broken by Mike Bordick in 2002, when he played in 110 consecutive errorless games and handled a record 543 chances. The streak ended on April 1, 2003, the first game of the season, on his second chance of the game.

Donie Bush made an American League and modern Major League record 689 errors in 1,886 games at shortstop between 1908 and 1921, mostly for the Tigers. Honus Wagner committed a modern National League record 676 errors in 1,887 games between 1901 and 1917.

Third Basemen.

"You've gone from a human vacuum cleaner to a litterbug." — Orioles pitcher Dave McNally to teammate Brooks Robinson after Robinson had a bad day at third base.

In April 2002, Jeff Cirillo tied the Major League mark for third baseman by playing in his 99th straight errorless game. His streak was broken the next day.

Don Money committed five errors for the Brewers in 157 games in 1974 for the American League season record. Ken Reitz of the Cardinals holds the National League record, with five in 150 games in 1980.

Jimmy Austin made a modern Major League and American League record 359 errors in 1,433 games between 1909 and 1929. Pie Traynor made a National League record 324 errors in 1,864 games between 1921 and 1937.

Outfielders.

"I partied the night before — I was out until 5 a.m. — and then I had a day game. It was a real sunny day, and Gary Allenson hit the ball into left-center field. I flipped my glasses down. They went into my eyes and I lost sight of the ball." — White Sox outfielder Ron LeFlore, on how he was hit in the head by a routine fly ball in a 1982 game in Boston.

"I find it more and more difficult to stop myself from yelling 'Mayday!' every time a ball heads Roger Cedeno's way." — Mike Royko in 2003 on the Mets center fielder.

Darren Lewis of the Giants holds the Major League record for all players with 392 straight errorless games. The streak began in the first game of his career in 1991 and ended on June 30, 1994. He charged a ball hit by Montreal's Cliff Floyd and let it skip under his glove. His last error was on May 10, 1991, for Class AAA Phoenix. He handled 938 Major League chances without a mistake. Nevertheless, he did not win a Gold Glove Award.

Lewis broke the record of 266 straight games set by infielder/outfielder Don Demeter between 1962 and 1965. Lewis also set a record for most errorless games from the start of a career, breaking outfielder Doug Dascenzo's record of 242 games beginning in 1988.

On August 23, 2003, centerfielder Kenny Lofton of the Cubs ended an errorless streak of 265 games dating back to September 2, 2001, while with Cleveland.

In 1942 Danny Litwhiler became the first outfielder (and regular at any position) to go through an entire season (151 games) without making an error. Rocky Colavito handled 274 chances without an error over 162 games in 1965. Curt Flood handled 568 chances between 1965 and 1967 without making an error.

Hall of Famer Lou Brock led the National League in outfield errors seven times.

Nineteenth-century star Pete Browning batted .343, tenth all-time, but his .791 lifetime fielding percentage is the lowest ever for an outfielder.

Ty Cobb made an American League record 271 errors in 2,934 games in the outfield between 1905 and 1928. Max Carey made a National League record 235 errors in 2,422 games between 1910 and 1929.

Team/Fewest. The 1999 Mets set a record for fewest errors in a season, with 68, breaking the record of 81 set by the 1998 Orioles.

ESPN See *Television*

Ethnicity

"The Mick, the Sheeney, the Wop, the Dutch and the Chink, the Cuban, the Indian, the Jap or the so-called Anglo-Saxon — his nationality is never a matter of moment if he can pitch, hit, or field." — 1920s editorial in *The Sporting News*, which "of course" did not include the "Ethiopian" in the Major League ethnic mix.

"Irish, German, Polish, Italian, Hispanic, Black." — Progression of ethnic groups into Major League Baseball.

"The Yankees are the real America. Where else can whites,

blacks, Asians and Hispanics play happily together except on a team worth $180 million? If I were an Inuit second baseman with a good on-base percentage, I'd get my résumé to the Bronx as soon as possible." — Joel Stein in *Time*.

"That, and $4.50, will get you a cup of beer." — Angels owner Arte Moreno, on being ranked by *Sports Illustrated* as the most influential minority in American sports. The Arizona native referred to himself as an American, and not a Latino.

"The International House of Pitchers" — Vin Scully on the 1996 Dodger pitching rotation after Ramon Martinez went out with an injury: Ismael Valdez of Mexico, Chan Ho Park of Korea, Hideo Nomo of Japan, Tom Candiotti of the U.S. and Pedro Astacio of the Dominican Republic.

"Your first name's white, your second is Hispanic, and your third belongs to a black. No wonder you don't know who you are." — Yankee outfielder Mickey Rivers to teammate Reginald Martinez (Reggie) Jackson; though one of the great ethnically confused names of all time belongs to late 1970s and 1980s pitcher Juan Tyrone Eichelberger, who was born in St. Louis.

See also **Black "Firsts*,*" Integration, Jewish Ballplayers, Latin Ballplayers, Native Americans, Negro Leagues, Racism** and entries for specific ethnic groups and countries.

British descendants dominated the early amateur and very early professional teams, though Irish Americans were prominent and later predominated in the late 19th century. Some of the early amateur clubs such as the Knickerbockers attempted to exclude the lower classes from the game. They were unsuccessful and many of the early **Amateur Teams** were dominated by the lower middle classes.

Approximately one third of all Major League players in the 1890s were of Irish descent, in part because baseball was considered an urban game and most Irish immigrants had settled in the more heavily populated northeastern cities. This led to a belief that Irish players were superior in ability.

As Irish players retired they moved into the management ranks, reflected in the 11 of 16 Major League managers in 1915 who were Irish. German players began to proliferate late in the 19th century as the game expanded into the Midwest.

In 1897 only three of 168 National League players were from south of Virginia. Seven were from the West and one third were from Pennsylvania and Massachusetts. Most were of German or Irish descent. By the early 1900s, 90% of the players were of Irish, German or English descent.

The first well-known player of Dutch origin was pitcher Rynie Wolters with the New York Mutuals in 1871. In 1872 Oscar Bielaski, of Polish descent, began to play for the Washington Nationals. The first Italian player of note was Ed Abbaticchio with Philadelphia in 1897. However, Italians did not begin to dominate the game until the 1930s and 1940s.

By 1941 Slavic Americans made up 9.3% of the Major League rosters and Italians 8%; in each case the percentage was twice that of the general population. Slavs included the following players (some of whom appeared earlier than the 1940s): Stan Musial, George Kroski, Stan and Harry Coveleski, Al Simmons (Syzmanski), Ted Wilks, Erv Palica, Pete Appleton (Jablonowski), Cass Michaels (Cassimere Kwietniewski), Chet Laabs, Dick Kokos, Mike Ryba, Hank Borowy, Ray Mack (Mlckovsky), Hank Majeski, Elmer Valo, Sig Jakucki and Andy Seminick.

A few Latin players made it to the Major Leagues prior to the 1940s, usually light-skinned Cubans or Puerto Ricans.

Black players began to populate Major League clubs in the late 1940s and 1950s, while large numbers of Latin players were on Major League rosters beginning in the 1960s and 1970s, primarily from Puerto Rico and the Dominican Republic.

Umpires. Going into the 2001 season, the Major Leagues listed 68 umpires (17 crews), including three umpires of Latin descent: Angel Hernandez, Lazaro Diaz and Alfonso Marquez. At that point, Hernandez had completed eight years of service in the Major Leagues; Diaz and Marquez, two years or less.

Etymology   See *Terminology*

Billy Evans (1884–1956)

Hall of Fame (VC) 1973

"Versatile: umpire, sports writer, baseball front office man, football executive — capable in all." — Gene Karst and Martin J. Jones, Jr., in *Who's Who in Professional Baseball* (1973).

Evans was a long-time American League umpire beginning in 1906 who later became a Major League front office executive.

After embarking on a college education to become an attorney, William G. Evans dropped out in 1903 to help support his family. He became a reporter in Ohio and umpired a game in the Ohio-Pennsylvania League when the regular umpire failed to show up. After umpiring and sportswriting for two more years he made umpiring his full-time profession and a year later in 1906 was hired by the American League.

He became the premier umpire in the league and was on the American League staff through 1927. He umpired in six World Series during his career and added decorum to an otherwise boisterous field of play. Nevertheless, he was not above going under the stands once to fight Ty Cobb after Cobb questioned his calls. Evans lost.

Evans continued his writing habit with a syndicated column in over 100 newspapers that he wrote from 1920 through 1927, "Billy Evans Says." After leaving the umpiring profession he moved into the Indians front office, where he served as the club's general manager until 1936. He held the same position with the Tigers from 1947 through 1951. In between, he was the Braves farm director (1936–1940), general manager of the Cleveland Rams in the National Football League (1941) and president of the Southern Association (1942–1946).

Johnny Evers (1883–1947)

Hall of Fame 1946

"He would go to bed each night with a rule book, a copy of *The Sporting News*, and a couple of bars of candy, studying the game from every conceivable angle to try to gain some advantage on the field." — Lee Allen and Tom Meany in *Kings of the Diamond* (1965).

"I have played baseball when literally thousands of people were yelling at me.... I could yell as loud as any of them but not as loud as all of them put together. They had the floor, so I went about my business." — Evers.

Evers was the second base component of the famous trio and the grouch of the group.

An Irishman from Troy, New York, John Joseph Evers weighed all of 115 pounds when he began his professional career. Known as "The Crab" for his rotten disposition, Evers began his Major League career with the Cubs in 1902. In 1903 he became the club's regular second baseman and became part of the famous double play combination known as **Tinker to Evers to Chance**.

Evers generally batted around .270 for the club, though he hit

.341 in 1912. After 12 seasons with the Cubs he was released after managing the club to a third-place finish in 1913. He signed with the Braves for three full seasons before being traded early in the 1917 season to the Phillies. He finished his career that year, though he made two cameo appearances during the 1920s. He had a .270 average over his 18 seasons.

He began a long career as a coach, manager and scout, including brief stints managing the Cubs (1921) and White Sox (1924). He later owned the Albany club in the Eastern League and ran a sporting goods store in that city. John J. Evers and Hugh S. Fullerton, *Touching Second* (1910; 2004 reprint).

Buck Ewing (1859–1906)

Hall of Fame 1939

"Ewing was as near to being free from any weakness as a ballplayer as Ty Cobb is today. As a thrower to bases, he was in a class by himself. He was not an unusually fast runner, but he was the best stealer of bases on the Giant team, outside of John Montgomery Ward. As a batter and run-getter, he had few superiors." — Sportswriter and former Major Leaguer Sam Crane, writing for the *New York Journal*. Connie Mack believed that Ewing was the best catcher ever.

"We have always been inclined to consider Catcher-Manager William ("Buck") Ewing in his prime from 1884–1890 as the greatest player of the game from the standpoint of supreme excellence in all departments — batting, catching, fielding, base running, throwing and base ball brains — a player without a weakness of any kind, physical, mental or temperamental." — Francis Richter in the 1919 *Reach Guide*.

Ewing was one of the supreme players of the 19th century, starring primarily at catcher while batting .303.

William Ewing grew up in Cincinnati in the 1870s, earning his nickname from his boyhood friends. He began his Major League career in 1880 with Troy of the National League, playing in 14 games and batting .178. He was among the Troy players who moved to the New York Giants in 1883. He played the next seven years with the Giants, batting over .300 in all but one of those seasons. He played for New York of the Players League in 1890 before returning to the Giants for two seasons. He was traded to Cleveland in 1893 and hit a career-high .344.

After the 1890 season Ewing played only a few games at catcher, though even before that he never played more than 97 games in a season. He returned to his native Cincinnati for the 1895 season, again batting over .300. He played 69 games at first base in 1896 and then appeared in one game in 1897 to close out his career.

Ewing finished with a .303 lifetime average and 336 stolen bases, though stolen bases were not recorded for the first few years of his career. He managed the Reds from 1895 through 1900 before returning to his hometown. He died six years later of diabetes.

Executives

"The winner, and possibly all-time heavyweight champion of executive bungling is, of course, George Steinbrenner ... an architect with the wrecking ball.... Above all else stands Steinbrenner's greatest talent — nay, genius: his uncanny knack of never being responsible for anything that goes wrong." — Sportswriter Scott Ostler.

"George Weiss was tighter than a Speedo two sizes two small." — Sportswriter Steve Rushin.

"With so many guinea pigs at his disposal, [Pirates general manager Syd] Thrift turned into the closest thing to a mad scientist that baseball has yet spawned, bringing to his campus a steady procession of physicists, time-lapse photographers, ballistics engineers, meteorologists, optometrists, audiologists, physiologists and psychologists to try to prove (often with peculiar-looking machines) his belief that the human animal can be trained to see a ball better, throw it harder, get off to a faster start and feel more emotionally fit than had previously been supposed." — William Zinsser in *Spring Training* (1989).

"An assortment of half-wits, nincompoops, and Neanderthals like Don Drysdale and Don Zimmer [who] are not only allowed to pontificate on whatever strikes them, but are actually solicited and employed to do this." — Bill James on Baseball's "organization men."

See **Racism** for a discussion of blacks and other minorities in the front office (and lack thereof).

Hall of Fame.

"Front office brilliance in baseball is rarer than a triple play." — Roger Angell in *Late Innings* (1982).

The following baseball executives or owners have been voted into the Hall of Fame for meritorious service (with year of induction):

Edward Grant Barrow, general manager of the Yankees (1953)

Morgan Bulkeley, owner of the Hartford club and first president of the National League (1937)

William G. Evans, former umpire and front office executive primarily with the Tigers (1973)

Andrew "Rube" Foster, driving force behind the Negro Leagues (1981)

William Hulbert, owner of the Chicago White Stockings and founder of the National League (1995)

Leland Stanford "Larry" MacPhail, maverick general manager of the Reds, Dodgers and Yankees in the 1930s and 1940s (1978)

Branch Rickey, former player, manager and general manager of the Browns, Cardinals, Dodgers and Pirates (1967)

Albert Spalding, owner of the Chicago White Stockings (1939)

Bill Veeck, innovative and maverick owner of the Indians, Browns and White Sox (1991)

George M. Weiss, general manager of the Yankees and Mets from the mid–1940s through the mid–1960s (1971)

Tom Yawkey, long-time owner of the Boston Red Sox (1980)

Award. Among the annual awards is the Major League Baseball Executive of the Year Award, presented by *The Sporting News*.

"**Award.**" In 1997 website TheBaseballPage.com established the Harry Frazee Award for front office incompetence. Frazee was the Boston Red Sox owner credited with dismantling the 1910s powerhouse, including the trade of Babe Ruth to the Yankees after the 1919 season. Woody Woodward of the Mariners was the first recipient for failing to find a bullpen to support Ken Griffey, Jr., Alex Rodriguez and Randy Johnson. Runner-up was Marge Schott: "Marge has been suspended since 1996, which predates our Frazee award, but she has committed so many crimes against the game that she merits a mention here."

Terminology.

"Both men worked under the same title: General Manager. There was nothing unusual about that. There had been many general managers before them, usually glorified flunkies without business experience, content to busy themselves at unimaginative details, without either pride or program. Barrow and Rickey were different." — Ford Frick in *Games, Asterisks and People* (1973).

The term "general manager" was first applied to former umpire Billy Evans, who became general manager of the Indians in 1927.

In the 19th century the same person was usually referred to as the business manager or simply manager, and the field manager was often called the team captain.

Expansion Exodus. After the Marlins were formed in 1992 but had not started play, there was a mass exodus of 10 Expos front office personnel to the Marlins over several months. National League president Bill White finally stepped in and stopped the flow until after the season ended.

College Courses. In the past few years there has been a proliferation of college curricula for sports management. It is estimated that close to 20% of the off-field jobs in sports (especially baseball) are held by people with sports-related business degrees.

Traveling Secretary.

"I never lost a trunk or a newspaper man." — Mark Roth, Yankee traveling secretary from 1903 through 1942. He died in early 1944.

Interesting Explanation. Orioles general manager Frank Wren signed a three year $1.35 million contract in October 1998, but was dumped after the 1999 season following a series of problems with his performance, including an odd confrontation involving Cal Ripken missing a team flight in mid-September.

Ripken was stuck in traffic and called ahead to say that he would be there in 10 minutes. There was no problem in holding the plane the extra few minutes, but Wren demanded that the plane take off. In a statement issued by the team at the time of his termination, Wren's problems were addressed: "In the opinion of management, there was no need for such an arbitrary and inflexible decision. In the meeting, Wren defiantly dismissed our concerns, characterized them as 'silly' and insisted he would invoke the same takeoff order no matter what the extenuating circumstances. The Orioles management cannot and will not abide having a GM operate in such an unreasonable, authoritarian manner and treat anyone this way, especially someone such as Cal who has done so much for the Orioles and for baseball."

Turnover.

"Why would you want to stay manager and be second-guessed by me when you can come up into the front-office and be one of the second-guessers?" — George Steinbrenner to Gene Michael after firing him as manager. Steinbrenner had 15 general managers between 1973 and 1995.

Popularity.

"It does bother me. I'm going to be a household word — like 'toilet.'" — Twins general manager Andy McPhail, on not signing popular pitcher Jack Morris with the Twins.

In 2003 A's general manager Billy Beane achieved some notoriety with the release of a new book, *Moneyball*, by Michael Lewis, but many in the business chastised him for his candor about other GMs and certain players. Beane had been a former first round draft pick who struggled to a .213 career average over six seasons in the Major Leagues in the mid–1980s.

After the season, there were rumors flying that Beane was going to take over the Los Angeles Dodgers (after the purchase by Frank McCourt). Dodger general manager Dan Evans confronted Beane in a phone call, prompting this comment from a miffed Beane: "Unfortunately, rumor and speculation have a tendency to create insecurities. I'm not sure I was the best therapist."

Soon after, the Dodgers hired Beane's number one assistant, 31-year-old Harvard graduate Paul DePodesta.

In April 2001, Dodgers general manager Kevin Malone resigned under pressure. Although already unpopular in the front office, the final event was a verbal altercation he had with a fan during a game.

Minority Combination. In 2000 Ken Williams, then 36, became the third black general manager when he took over the White Sox. He had played Major League Baseball after playing wide receiver at Stanford. He and manager Jerry Manuel became the first all-minority general manager/manager combination in Major League history.

Latin. In the 2000s, the first Latino general manager was Omar Minaya, who took over the Montreal Expos. He had been an assistant general manager with the Mets and before that a Rangers scout best known for signing Sammy Sosa.

Youngest.

"The best advice I got was given by [former Dodgers and Angels executive] Buzzie Bavasi. He said to remember that every time you're about to make a deal, the guy on the other end of the phone is just as smart as you are, probably smarter." — Red Sox general manager Theo Epstein, in late 2002 when the Red Sox owners hired the 28 year old to be the general manager of their club.

The second-youngest 20th century general manager was 29-year-old Randy Smith, who succeeded Joe McIlvaine with the Padres in 1993. Smith is the son of respected baseball executive Tal Smith. Jim Bowden was hired at age 32 by Marge Schott of the Reds. He was fired in mid–2003.

When Bob Watson resigned as Mets general manager in 1998, he was replaced by 30-year-old Brian Cashman.

Paul DePodesta, the assistant general manager for the A's under Billy Beane, was hired by the Dodgers in to be the club's general manager in early 2004 at the age of 31.

Website. Thedeadballera.com contains a list of general managers and other executives during the deadball era.

Books. Scott Barzilla, *The State of Baseball Management* (2004); Bing Devine and Tom Wheatley, *The Memoirs of Bing Devine: Stealing Lou Brock and Other Winning Moves by a Master GM* (2004); Robert S. Fuchs and Wayne Soini, *The MacPhails: Baseball's First Family of the Front Office* (2004); Michael Lewis, *Moneyball* (2003).

Exhibition Games

"What kind of dumb fucking question is that? This is the fucking exhibition season, and you're wasting my time with a crappy question like that." — Senators manager Ted Williams to sportswriter Russ White.

"Never knock in the tying run in the ninth inning of an exhibition game. Far better to lose than go extra innings in spring training." — One of Rick Reilly's Unwritten Rules of Sport.

"Is your team white or colored? Kindly let me hear from you by return mail." —1906 letter to Rutherford Hayes Jones, owner of the Negro League Washington Giants, from a promoter organizing a series of games.

See also *Barnstorming*, *International Tours* and *Spring Training*.

One of the first highly publicized exhibition games was between the Brooklyn Excelsiors and the Harvards of Cambridge in the 1850s.

After the National League formally organized, exhibitions were played frequently during the season because teams played only three league games each week. By 1882, however, only the American Association allowed exhibition games to be interspersed with scheduled league games.

In 1903 Joe McGinnity pitched two games per week for the Giants and his contract allowed him to pitch on Sundays for a New Jersey team.

In the 1910s the American League schedule sometimes finished a week or so ahead of the National League, so the American Leaguers often organized an all-star squad to play the pennant-winner while waiting for the World Series to start.

The 1914 standard player contract barred exhibition games, though the prohibition was generally ignored until Judge Landis became commissioner and the rule was modified. Exhibitions normally were allowed for 10 days after the conclusion of the season, though that number was expanded to 30 following the 1947 season.

The 1927 New York Yankees were so relaxed that they played exhibitions on open dates during the season. This was not uncommon in those years as a way to pick up extra cash. They covered such towns as Dayton, St. Paul, Buffalo and Indianapolis, as well as Sing Sing Prison.

Lou Gehrig made more money on an exhibition tour after the 1927 season than he earned in salary from the Yankees during the regular season.

Rogers Hornsby was fired as the Cardinals manager immediately after the 1926 season even though he guided the team to the World Championship that year. It was generally thought that his termination was because of the high salary he was demanding and his rotten attitude. One source reported that it was due to Hornsby's blunt and negative response to owner Sam Breadon upon hearing that Breadon wanted the team to play an exhibition game after the World Series.

The first 20th century exhibitions between same-city Major League clubs occurred in St. Louis and Philadelphia immediately after World War I. The clubs in Boston, New York and Chicago reportedly took longer to agree on playing such games because of lingering animosity between the teams. However, the Chicago clubs played intracity games prior to 1910.

Modern clubs play few exhibition games other than during spring training. Some Major League teams will play a game against their primary Class AAA affiliate some time during the regular season. Two clubs also play an exhibition game at Doubleday Field during the Hall of Fame induction week.

Expansion

"The next great American invention may be a mass production method for big league teams to fill the demand at $8.98 in the five-and-dime store. Meanwhile, there are only sixteen franchises, and these are hard to get and even harder to move." — Joe King in *The San Francisco Giants* (1958).

See also *Expansion Drafts*, *Franchise Shifts* and entries for each expansion team.

1950s discussions. When the American League voted to allow the Browns to move to Baltimore for the 1953 season, it was done with the American League owners' agreement that the league was paving the way for American League expansion to San Francisco and Los Angeles.

In January 1955 National League president Warren Giles said that the league was abandoning the idea of expanding to 10 teams, primarily because: it would dilute the talent of the other eight clubs; there were already too many second division teams; and there were not enough players of Major League caliber.

1961–1962 Expansion. After the Dodgers and Giants left for the West Coast in the late 1950s, the mayor of New York City asked attorney Bill Shea to lead a committee formed to bring National League baseball back to New York. The committee included former Postmaster General James A. Farley, Bernard Gimbel of department store fame (whose daughter was married to for-

mer Tigers star Hank Greenberg), and Clint Blume, a real estate executive.

Shea was a Brooklyn native and attorney for the Brooklyn Trust Company, the entity that held the promissory notes on the Brooklyn Dodgers in the 1930s and 1940s before fellow Trust Company attorney Walter O'Malley took over the club. Shea first tried to interest the Pirates and Reds in moving to New York, but those overtures were rejected. He then worked quietly with Branch Rickey to develop the **Continental League**, a proposed rival third major league. Once their plan was made public late in the 1960 season, the National League preempted it in October 1960 by announcing an expansion plan for 1962 that would add clubs in New York and Houston, to be owned by Continental League owners.

The American League was upset that the National League had acted unilaterally. The American League believed that it was important to grab big-market Los Angeles as a franchise city (ultimately placing the Angels there) because New York had been granted a new National League city to compete with the Yankees. A unanimous vote of the National League owners was required to place a team in the other league's city (and vice versa), which is what occurred when the Mets were placed in New York.

There was concern among some owners in 1960 that the leagues would expand into small markets which already had clubs. This problem was blocking smooth sailing for the large-city and single-city expansion proposals. At one of the key meetings, it was proposed that no second Major League club could be established in a city with a population of less than 4 million people. This cleared the way for Los Angeles and New York, while protecting the smaller market cities.

At its 1960 winter meetings one week after the National League announced its 1962 expansion plan, the American League announced that it would expand immediately for the 1961 season into Los Angeles and Washington, D.C. Washington may not have been the first choice for expansion, but the Senators were moving to Minnesota and the city of Washington was threatening a lawsuit against Major League Baseball over the loss of the team. The American League approved a new Washington franchise headed by General Elwood Quesada, head of the Federal Aviation Administration.

The American League approved the Washington franchise on November 17 and the Los Angeles franchise on December 6. It was only one week before the expansion draft.

1969 Expansion. On October 18, 1967, the American League's approval of a franchise shift from Kansas City to Oakland was made with the understanding that there would be new franchises in Kansas City and Seattle by at least 1971. As a result, the Kansas City Royals and Seattle Pilots were created for the 1969 season.

On May 27, 1968, the National League formally approved franchises in San Diego and Montreal. Cities which lost out on bids were Buffalo, Dallas, Ft. Worth and Milwaukee. Montreal and San Diego were chosen only after at least 16 ballots. The increase to 12 teams required each league to divide into two divisions (see also *Divisional Play*).

1977 Expansion.

"In 1977, the AL voted to expand to fourteen teams so each owner could grab a couple of million dollars as his slice of the expansion fees paid by Toronto and Seattle. These 'fees' are the bribes baseball requires to get into its monopolistic social club." — Thomas Boswell in *Why Time Begins on Opening Day* (1984).

In 1977 the American League expanded by two teams to 14. The Toronto Blue Jays were added to the Eastern Division and the

Seattle Mariners to the West. The National League did not expand and the American League expansion created unwieldy seven-team divisions which made *Scheduling* awkward. One team always had to finish the season with a string of games against teams outside its division. The new clubs each paid $7 million for the privilege of joining the league, though Seattle's entry fee was discounted by $1 million because of the pending lawsuit by the city to force the league to place a franchise in its city to replace the Pilots.

1993 Expansion. In 1991 the National League voted to expand to 14 clubs for the 1993 season. There was controversy over whether the American League would share in the enormous entry fee put up by each club: $95 million, a figure apparently tied to the claimed value of a typical Major League franchise.

The National League finally agreed to allow each American League club to receive $3 million, for a total of $42 million out of the $190 million put up by the two expansion clubs. In return, the American League agreed to contribute players to the *Expansion Draft* to stock the new teams. Start-up costs for the new clubs, in addition to the $95 million entry fee, were estimated to be $35 million each.

Denver and Miami were finally chosen from among finalists that included Washington, Buffalo, Orlando, and Tampa/St. Petersburg. One writer pointed out that the 1988–1990 minor league Miami Miracle had 49 rainouts, whereas the average number of rainouts for a Major League club was two per season. This seemed to make Miami a poor choice. Denver was the only Major League city located in the mountain time zone and was more than 600 miles from any other Major League club.

Orlando, which lost out to Miami, was to be called the Sun-Rays and had the backing of the Amway Company founders. Long-time catcher Bob Boone was set to manage the team.

Washington was deemed too small a market and too close to Baltimore, and its track record with clubs was a negative. Tampa/St. Petersburg had a domed stadium but it lost out to the stronger Miami bid.

Buffalo, though a terrific minor league baseball town for many years, did not have the population base to support a Major League club. Nor was it within driving distance of other towns and cities that could help support the club.

David Whitford wrote *Playing Hardball* (1993), a look at the behind-the-scenes fight for the 1993 National League franchises; see also Bob Andelman, *Stadium for Rent: Tampa Bay's Quest for Major League Baseball* (1993).

1998 Expansion. In 1994 Major League Baseball began to solicit proposals for expansion franchises. In early 1995 Phoenix and Tampa/St. Petersburg were awarded franchises. Areas which lost out were Orlando, Northern Virginia, Mexico City, Monterrey (Mexico) and Vancouver.

The Arizona Diamondbacks and Tampa Devil Rays were each required to pay $130 million to enter the Major Leagues. However, the actual price was $155 million because each received $5 million less each year for five years from Major League Baseball's central fund (composed primarily of television and licensing revenues).

Expansion Teams/First Year Finishes.

1961	Angels	70–91	8th
1961	Senators	61–100	10th
1962	Astros	64–96	8th
1962	Mets	40–120	10th
1969	Royals	69–93	4th

(Note: Divisional play started in 1969)

1969	Pilots	64–98	6th
1969	Expos	52–110	6th
1969	Padres	52–110	6th
1977	Mariners	64–98	6th
1977	Blue Jays	54–107	7th
1993	Marlins	64–98	6th
1993	Rockies	67–95	6th
1998	D'Backs	65–97	6th
1998	Devil Rays	63–99	6th

Expansion's Effect on Travel. The 1961 expansion of the American League, the first increase in teams in 60 years, added to a team's average annual travel by 16,400 miles, more than double the old amount. The number of time zones crossed or entered doubled to four for many clubs. For example, the Red Sox played 127 games in the eastern time zone (versus 134 in 1946), 27 in the central time zone (five more than 1946), and nine on the West Coast (none in 1946). By 1969, with the second wave of expansion adding slightly more miles, teams traveled an average of 35,000 miles each year.

Expansion's Effect on Hitting. The 1961 expansion created a hitter's paradise, with eight more games and 20 pitchers who otherwise would not have been in the Major Leagues. Roger Maris and Mickey Mantle combined for 115 home runs. Jim Gentile hit 46 home runs, one fourth of his career total. Norm Cash hit .361 with 41 home runs (although with a corked bat), 90 points above his career average.

Short Term Success. The only expansion team to have at least a .500 record after 10 games was the 1998 Tampa Bay Devil Rays, at 6–4.

Expansion Club Attendance.

1993	Rockies	4,483,350
1998	Diamondbacks	3,600,412
1993	Marlins	3,064,847
1998	Devil Rays	2,506,023
1977	Blue Jays	1,701,052
1977	Mariners	1,338,511
1969	Expos	1,212,608
1962	Colt 45's	924,456
1962	Mets	922,530
1969	Royals	902,414
1969	Pilots	677,944
1961	Angels	603,510
1961	Senators	597,287
1969	Padres	512,970

See also *Attendance.*

Expansion Drafts

"Why don't we just give [the other owners] the money and not take the players." — Royals owner Ewing Kauffman, after picking three players in the 1976 expansion draft and determining that there were no more quality players available.

The 1961 American League Draft. Late in 1960 the new American League teams each drafted 28 Major League players for $75,000 per player. Two minor league players were chosen by each club for $25,000 each, bringing the total cost for each team's players to $2.15 million.

Each existing club was required to submit 15 names from its 40-man roster. At least seven of the players were required to have been on the club's 25-man roster prior to the previous September 1. The expansion teams could pick up to four players from each team's roster. The new clubs were also required to choose 10 pitchers, two catchers, six infielders and four outfielders. Six picks were unrestricted as to position. Coin flips determined the first selection for each position, with the Angels winning three of four first picks.

The Senators made their first pick White Sox pitcher Dick Donovan and the Angels chose Yankee pitcher Eli Grba (also reported inaccurately as pitcher Fred Newman of the Red Sox).

The 1962 National League Draft.

"In the 1962 draft creating two new teams, the National League owners, ignoring the much fairer system inaugurated by the American League the previous year, protected their player investment so carefully that the squads were manned entirely by a miserable collection of culls and aging castoffs…"—Roger Angell in *The Summer Game* (1972).

"[The expansion clubs were never promised] pennant contending teams or even first-division outfits … [and I'm] sure the Colts and Mets didn't enter the league with the expectation that we'd furnish them—at any price—with a sure-fire pennant winner."—Cardinals general manager Bing Devine responding to charges the National League talent pool was absurdly weak.

The draft was held the day after the World Series on October 10, 1961. It was conducted at National League headquarters in Cincinnati and each expansion team drafted 22 players. The first 16 players cost $75,000 each and the next four cost $50,000 each. The last two each were selected from a "premium player" list and cost $125,000 each. Unlike the 1961 American League draft, the National League clubs were not required to pick a set number of players from each position.

Each existing club was required to put up 15 Major League players for bid, seven of whom had to be on the club's 25-man roster as of August 31, 1961. The draft procedure was revealed during the 1961 season and resulted in a number of key young Major League players being sent back to the minor leagues before August 31. This ploy put them among the minor leaguers who were protected from the draft. For example, the Giants sent down catcher Tom Haller, who later was their first-string catcher for a number of years. This same phenomenon occurred in 1992 in anticipation of the 1993 draft.

Houston won the coin flip and drafted first. The club chose shortstop Ed Bressoud of the Giants, although one source erroneously reported that it was Joey Amalfitano of the Giants.

The Mets chose catcher Hobie Landrith of the Giants. One source identified their first pick as Cardinals pitcher Bob Miller, but Miller was the club's first "premium" player pick for $125,000. The clubs each paid $1.8 million for their players.

Although Landrith was the first Mets pick, the first to sign a contract was infielder Ted Lepcio (although he was cut during spring training). He was described by his 1960 manager, Eddie Sawyer, as "the worst player I ever saw." The Mets' strategy was to sign some familiar New York names such as Roger Craig, Don Zimmer and Gil Hodges. By 1965 all but two of the originally-drafted Mets were gone; only Jim Hickman and Chris Cannazzaro remained.

The 1969 National League Draft. The draft was held on October 14, 1968, to stock the Padres and Expos. Each club made 30 picks. The Padres made their first choice Ollie Brown, an outfielder with the Giants. The Expos chose Pirates outfielder Manny Mota. The clubs paid $200,000 for each player chosen in the draft. The last original Padre was catcher Fred Kendall, who was traded to the Indians in 1976.

The 1969 American League Draft. The first draft choice of the Royals was Orioles pitcher Roger Nelson. The Pilots chose Angels first baseman Don Mincher. All players in the American League draft cost $175,000, $25,000 less than their National League counterparts. Each existing club was entitled to protect 15 players.

The 1977 American League Draft. The Blue Jays took infielder Bob Bailor of the Orioles as their number one pick. The Mariners chose Ruppert Jones from the Royals. Both clubs paid $175,000 for each player. Each club made 30 picks.

The 1993 National League Draft. The draft procedure to stock the 1993 teams was to be much more equitable than earlier drafts. Each existing team was entitled to freeze 15 players. After one player was selected from a team, that team was entitled to protect another three players. After a second player was taken from that team, another three players could be protected.

Another significant change was that the American League teams contributed players as a result of the $42 million that the National League agreed to give them from the expansion payments by the two new teams. Though the American League received 22% of the $190 million expansion money, the league was forced to contribute 55% of the players.

On November 17, 1992, the Rockies chose Braves pitcher David Nied as the first pick in the draft. Nied started the Rockies' first game but never pitched in more than 22 games a year over parts of four seasons because of injuries and personal problems. He compiled a lifetime 17–18 record with a 5.07 ERA for Colorado and Atlanta.

The Marlins picked Blue Jays infielder Nigel Wilson. Colorado's second pick was Yankee third baseman Charlie Hayes, who blossomed in the thin Denver air. The Marlins made their second pick Jose Martinez, a right-handed pitcher from the Mets. The clubs each picked 36 players. Seven of the Rockies' first 13 picks had played Major League Baseball, while only two of the first 13 Marlins had any experience at that level.

The 1998 National and American League Drafts.

"Bor-ring! Bor-ing!"—Chant by the small gallery of fans after the two expansion clubs selected Esteban Yan, Hanley Frias, Steve Cox and Chris Clemons.

The draft took place in November 1997, early enough to allow the new clubs to compete for the many free agents on the market. The Diamondbacks made their first pick Indians lefthander Brian Anderson. The club also signed third baseman Jay Bell to a $34 million contract.

The Devil Rays made their first pick Marlins rookie pitcher Tony Saunders. One of the key players in the draft was Bobby Abreu, who became the Phillies' everyday right fielder after he was acquired from Houston through Tampa Bay. The Astros left him unprotected, and the Devil Rays picked him and then traded him to Philadelphia for shortstop Kevin Stocker.

Of the 70 players selected, 39 were pitchers and 10 of the 70 were immediately traded. The only players over 30 were Colorado outfielder Quinton McCracken, Boston pitcher Jeff Suppan, White Sox catcher Jorge Fabregas and Anaheim knuckleballer Dennis Springer.

Expansion Man. Phil Roof has the distinction of playing on the first-year teams of the Oakland A's, Milwaukee Brewers and Toronto Blue Jays. Bobby Shantz (Astros, Senators) and Al Fitzmorris (Royals, Jays) are the only two players ever picked in two expansion drafts.

Best Last Choice. Cito Gaston, later to manage the Blue Jays to two World Championships, may have been the best last draft choice by an expansion club. The Padres took him as their 30th pick. He hit 70 home runs over his 11-year career and was named to the All-Star Game in 1970.

Postseason Success. The Marlins won the 1997 World Series, only four years after being created. They beat the 1969 Mets by three years. Both teams were eclipsed by the 2001 Diamondbacks, who did it in three years after beating the Yankees in Game 7. They also made the play-offs in their second season, the fastest ever to reach the postseason.

Expenses See *Profits, Losses and Expenses*

Extra Base Hits

"That's the fourth extra-base hit for the Padres—two doubles and a triple."—Broadcaster Jerry Coleman.

"Half of Jeff King's extra base hits last year were extra base hits."—Mets broadcaster Ralph Kiner.

"It was less a game than it was a relay race with bats."—John Holway in *The Sluggers* (1989), on the May 17, 1979, game between the Cubs and Phillies that yielded 50 hits, a Major League-record 24 of them for extra bases. The Phillies won 23–22 in 10 innings and Mike Schmidt hit four home runs.

On May 28, 1995, the Tigers and White Sox combined for 21 extra base hits for the American League record. The previous league record of 19 was set by the Twins and Blue Jays in 1979.

See also *Doubles*, *Triples* and *Home Runs*.

Consecutive. Elmer Smith of the Indians holds the record for most consecutive extra base hits, seven, set in 1921.

On May 21–22, 1996, Larry Walker of the Rockies set the National League record with six straight extra base hits.

Most/Player/Game. The most extra base hits in a game is five. Joe Adcock of the Braves had four home runs and a double on July 31, 1954. Lou Boudreau of the Indians had four doubles and a home run on July 14, 1946. On August 28, 1977, Dodger Steve Garvey had five extra base hits—three doubles and two home runs in five at-bats, including a grand slam. On May 23, 2002, Shawn Green had four homers and a double (and one single).

Most/Season. In 1995 Albert Belle became the eighth player to record 100 extra base hits in a season. Babe Ruth is the all-time leader with 119 in 1921, followed by Lou Gehrig with 117 in 1927. In 2001 Barry Bonds tied Chuck Klein's National League mark of 107, which Klein achieved in 1930. A total of 11 players have reached 100 extra base hits in a season.

Jim "Mudcat" Grant of the Indians after he pitched 14 innings for the win in a 1959 game.

Rookie. In 2001, Albert Pujols of the Cardinals hit his first Major League grand slam to give him 83 extra base hits in his rookie season, breaking the record of 82 set by Brooklyn's Johnny Frederick in 1929.

100/Back-To-Back. In 2001 Todd Helton had 100 extra base hits to become the first to reach that milestone in back-to-back seasons. Lou Gehrig and Chuck Klein are the only other players to do it twice in their careers.

Streak. On April 20, 1998, Alex Rodriguez of the Mariners had his eighth extra base hit in three games, tying the American League record set by Earl Sheehy in 1926.

Extra Innings

"It was nothing to nothing at the end of the tenth. And the prospects good it would last to the nth."—Poet Robert Frost writing for *Sports Illustrated* during the July 1956 All-Star game (though this rhyme was not about that game). The phrase was preceded by the following: "… one of my unfulfilled promises on earth was to my fellow in art, Alfred Kreymborg, of an epic poem someday about a ball batted so hard by Babe Ruth that it never came back, but got to going round and round the world like a satellite. I got up the idea long before any artificial moon was thought up by the scientists. I meant to begin something like this."

See also *Longest Games*.

National League First. The first extra inning game in National League history was played April 29, 1876, between the Boston Red Stockings and Hartford Dark Blues. Hartford's Tommy Bond defeated Boston 3–2 in 10 innings.

American League First. Boston played Philadelphia on April 30, 1901. Boston won 8–6 in 10 innings with two runs in the 9th inning and two in the 10th.

Best Extra Inning Comeback. On April 21, 1991, the Pirates were five runs down in extra innings to the Expos but scored six runs for the victory in the greatest comeback ever in extra innings.

Most Runs. The National League record for most runs in an extra inning is nine by the 1995 Padres and 1947 Reds.

Bad Year. The 2003 last-place Mets set a futility record with a total of two runs scored during all the extra innings they played that season.

Jinx. In 1997 Mets reliever Joe Crawford twice lost games after giving up runs in the 15th inning.

Home Runs. On May 31, 2002, in a 10–7 win over the Rangers, Carlos Beltran of the Royals hit a grand slam early in the game and then hit a solo shot in the 11th inning. It was the first of three consecutive home runs in the 11th inning (Mike Sweeney and Joe Randa helped out). It was only the second time that a team hit at least three consecutive home runs in extra innings. The Twins hit four straight in the 11th inning on May 2, 1964, by Tony Oliva, Bob Allison, Jimmie Hall and Harmon Killebrew.

Eyesight

"How can I read this? If it's yours, it must be in Braille."—Infielder Fresco Thompson after an umpire waved a rulebook in his face during an argument.

See also *Glasses*, *Injuries and Illness* – Eye, and *Superstitions*.

One Good Eye.

"Cal had one of every different color, just to impress the annies. He'd have blue eyes he'd wear for nights out, green eyes he'd wear for road trips. He'd stick with one particular color for a few days if we got hot, bein' superstitious like everybody else in baseball. An' he wore a patch over it for big games." — Kevin Baker on fictional one-eyed manager Cal Rigby in *Sometimes You See It Coming* (1993).

Tom Sunkel, who pitched in the 1930s and 1940s, had a cataract and was blind in one eye. He had a lifetime record of 9–15 over six seasons.

Bill Irwin of Cincinnati's 1886 American Association club was blind in one eye. He pitched two complete games and lost them both.

Harry "Hi" Jasper had been hit in one eye and blinded, but he played four years in the Major Leagues and compiled a 10–12 pitching record for three clubs beginning in 1914.

Paul O'Dea had only one good eye while playing Major League Baseball for two years during World War II. He peaked with a .318 average in 76 games for the Indians in 1944.

Blindness. Big Bill Lee was a pitcher primarily for the Cubs in the 1930s and 1940s. He compiled 169 wins despite failing eyesight. He had trouble seeing the catcher's signals, so he began using glasses in 1942 and won 13 games. After he retired he had surgery for detached retinas but eventually lost his sight.

Batting Eye. Rogers Hornsby would not go to the movies for fear of losing his batting eye. Nor would he look out train windows or read any more than necessary.

According to *The Sporting News*, in 1961 one Johnny Hughes suggested that the Reds spring training include target practice with BB guns to improve hand-eye coordination: "It wasn't long before Hughes had the players plinking pennies which were tossed in the air. There was no time for eye squinting. A player just put the gun to his shoulder, pulled the trigger and bingo — a direct hit."

Umpires.
"I've never questioned the integrity of an umpire. Their eyesight, yes." — Leo Durocher.

"I can see the sun okay, and that's 93 million miles away." — Umpire Bruce Froemming having his eyesight called into question.

"The first guy who lays a finger on this blind old man is fined fifty bucks!" — Expos manager Gene Mauch, when his players rushed at the umpire to dispute a call.

Eye Tests.
"If he can hit .350, we (Missouri driver's license bureau) figured he could see." — Harley Duncan on why they waived the eye test for George Brett.

In 1911 National League president Tom Lynch ordered all umpires to take eye tests. The worst result among the crew was still in the normal range.

Southern Association umpire Harry "Steamboat" Johnson carried a notarized declaration from an eye doctor attesting to his 20/20 vision.

Umpire Bob Emslie called balls and strikes in both the American Association and National League from 1890 through 1924. John McGraw once referred to him as "the blind robber" and Emslie took offense. As the story goes, Emslie went to a Giants practice and placed a dime on the pitching mound. He then went behind home plate, pulled out a pistol and shot out the dime. Emslie is the umpire who missed the famous Merkle Boner play at second base during the 1908 pennant race (see *Base Running*).

Long-time American League umpire Cal Hubbard was found to have 20/10 vision, better even than Ted Williams (who was legendary for his eyesight).

Eye Doctor. On May 22, 1961, Roger Maris was hitting .210 with four home runs and was sent to the eye doctor for a checkup. After the appointment he had to come out of the game that day due to a bad reaction to the eye drops used for the test. After that he went on a batting tear and finished with 61 home runs.

In 1999 Boston eye doctor Carmen Puliafito offered free surgery for Major League umpires during the postseason after umpires blew three calls against the Red Sox during the ALCS. Puliafito, who chaired the ophthalmology department at the Tufts University School of Medicine, suspected that some umpires are secretly nearsighted: "That's the only explanation I have for these three horrible calls."

Accountant. Senators third baseman Ossie Bluege played from 1922 through 1939. He was an accountant in the off-season and owner Clark Griffith ordered him to quit that job because it affected his eyesight. He refused, though apparently this did not annoy Griffith because he and his son, Calvin, repeatedly promoted Bluege in the organization after his playing days ended. Bluege became comptroller of the team from 1957 through 1971 after he had been a coach, manager and farm director.

Blinking. Max Butcher constantly blinked while on the mound and was known to have pitched only between blinks. He blinked his way to 95 wins over 10 years, with a high of 17 in 1941 for the Pirates.

Eye Chart. Fans at Comiskey Park often brought oversized eye charts to the park and held them up on bad calls by the umpires.

Eye Wash. Babe Ruth reportedly had a superstition that he had to wash out his eyes before each game. Someone supposedly switched his special eyewash bottle one day and the bat boy unknowingly brought Ruth a bottle of turpentine. After applying the turpentine, Ruth screamed and rinsed his eyes repeatedly — and then (as legend has it) went out and hit a home run and two doubles.

New System. In 1992 *Sports Illustrated* reported on an eye therapist who founded the Institute for Sports Vision. The Institute's program improved the vision of professional athletes, including a few Major Leaguers. The therapy forced players to focus more efficiently, find the seams on a ball and not follow the spot where the ball had just moved from. The system also taught players to keep their heads still, which makes it easier to focus.

"**F** is for Fordham
and Frankie and Frisch;
I wish he were back
With the Giants, I wish."
—Ogden Nash on Frankie Frisch.

Red Faber (1888–1976)

Hall of Fame (VC) 1964
"The winning hit in that closing contest was made off Urban Faber, who had been loaned to the Giants for the trip. No rookie had been put to a more severe test than was the youngster from Cascade, Iowa. Not only was it up to him to hold his own against Jim Scott and Joe Benz, veteran slabsmen, but in addition, he was pitching under the gaze of a monarch and a great crowd of diplomatic notables." — G.W. Axelson in *"Commy"* (1919), describing Faber's efforts during the 1913 international tour led by Charles Comiskey and John McGraw. Faber had not yet appeared in a Major League game when he made the trip and pitched in front of the King of England.

Faber was one of the all-time best *Spitball* pitchers, winning 254 games in a career spanning 20 years.

Born in Iowa of farmers from Luxembourg, Urban Charles Faber made his professional debut in 1909 for Dubuque. Though the Pirates were watching him, he signed with the White Sox and remained there his entire career. When he reported to Chicago in late September 1913, the club was about to leave for an international tour with the Giants. When Giants pitcher Christy Mathewson decided not to make the trip, Faber replaced him and defeated his future club in Hong Kong, Cairo, Brisbane and Melbourne, losing only in London.

The spitball pitcher won 24 games in 1915 and had three straight seasons over 20 wins starting in 1920. He had a number of decent but not stellar seasons for the White Sox after 1922 until his retirement in 1933. He finished with a 3.15 ERA and 30 shutouts and won three games for the White Sox in the 1917 World Series.

Faber was plagued by arm injuries during his career and turned primarily to relieving the last three years, appearing in 78 games with seven starts and saving 11. After he retired following the 1933 season, he coached for the White Sox and then worked as a surveyor for Chicago's Cook County well into his 80s.

Facial Hair

"Gorman Thomas looks like he could grate cheese with his beard stubble."— Scott Ostler.

"Some of these guys wear beards to make them look intimidating, but they don't look so tough when they have to deliver the ball. Their abilities and attitudes don't back up their beards."— Don Drysdale.

"He could be a caveman at times, crude and rude and always unshaven, but all he cared about was winning."— Tim Kurkjian on Kirk Gibson.

"From time immemorial beards have been in the public domain, and in that respect all men have rights in common."— Judge John M. Woolsey in an opinion in which he ruled that the **House of David** did not have the exclusive right to have its players wear beards. In its infringement action, the House prevailed in forcing a competitor to stop using the House of David name for its bootleg barnstorming team, but the outlaw club could wear beards.

"How can I intimidate batters if I look like a goddamn golf pro."— Pitcher Al Hrabosky, owner of a wild moustache and sideburns, when ordered to shave in the 1970s. After Hrabosky failed to be named to the 1974 All-Star team, Cardinals fans brought banners to the ballpark in his support on: "We Hlove Hraboski Hbanner Hday"

"Fuzz White, Curly Onis, Johnny Schaive, Nub Kleinke, Razor Ledbetter, Dave Beard, Ted Beard"

19th Century. Moustaches were popular among players in the 19th century, but they disappeared early in the 20th century. Nineteenth century star Cap Anson, in response to criticism about his advanced age late in his career, once donned a white beard for a game.

Wally Schang. Schang is reported to have been the last Major Leaguer to wear a moustache in an official game (in 1914) until Reggie Jackson did it in 1972. Schang shaved his off under mild duress. One source reported that in the early 1960s Bobby Lowe wore the first moustache by a Cubs player since 1903; suggesting that Jackson was not the first recent player to sport facial hair.

Frenchy Bordagaray. A moustache (and goatee in some sources) appeared briefly in 1936 (1935 in some sources) on Stanley "Frenchy" Bordagaray when he showed up at the Dodgers' spring training camp. Manager Casey Stengel was not happy and forced him to shave it off. Bordagaray then conveniently blamed a hitting slump on the shave.

A's.

"The 'Mustache Gang' was a breath of fresh air or it was evil, depending on your perspective. The 1972 World Series pitting the A's against the Reds was like Microsoft playing the Luddites. Today long sideburns, goatees, ear rings, tattoos, and bleached hair have the AL and NL looking more like the WWF."— Dan Holmes at TheBaseballPage.com.

The "Moustache Gang" was the Oakland A's of the early 1970s, led by maverick owner Charlie Finley. Finley paid $300 to each player on the 1972 team who grew a moustache. When Finley staged a moustache promotion day, 7,000 fans who sported moustaches were let in free. The game was Vida Blue's first start after his hold-out for more pay, and he shaved off his moustache before the game in protest of Finley's handling of his salary negotiation.

Steve Yeager. The Dodgers had a policy against facial hair, but allowed 1970s catcher Steve Yeager to wear a beard because his catcher's mask irritated his face. Some black players have been given special permission by clubs to wear beards to avoid a skin condition caused by shaving that almost exclusively affects African-Americans.

Reds. As late as 1996 the Reds banned facial hair because of the policies instituted by general manager Dick Howsam in the early 1970s. He had three rules: black shoes, high socks and clean shaves. These rules have often been attributed to Sparky Anderson, but Anderson credits Howsam. The Reds finally dropped the policy for the 1999 season after newly acquired Greg Vaughn persuaded Marge Schott to change the policy.

Half-and-Half. Pitcher Bill Caudill once came out of the dugout in a lopsided game with half his beard shaved off.

Fu Manchu Cult. During 1992 a number of players began sporting fu manchu moustaches and goatees: most prominent were Mark McGwire, Jack McDowell and Roger Clemens. They were preceded by 1970s star pitcher Luis Tiant.

Fire Sale. In 2003 Tim Hudson's goatee hairs sold at an auction for $2,405, which included dirt from the pitcher's cleats.

Bad Look. Perhaps the worst-looking chin hair in 2003 was the wad on Cubs pitcher Matt Clement. The big round puff looked like a brown sno-cone glued to his chin. Really ugly.

Yankees. In 2004 pitcher Esteban Loaiza was traded by the White Sox to the Yankees mid-season, forcing him to shave off his moustache to comply with the club's "no facial hair" policy.

Drug Test. After Red Sox infielder Johnny Damon had his beard shaved off for charity in 2004, his remaining thick mop of hair prompted this from Jim Armstrong of the *Denver Post*: "Steroids? They need to test Damon for Rogaine."

Fair Territory

"Leon Wagner hits a fly ball deep to right.... Will it be fair? Will it be foul?... It is!"— Broadcaster Herb Score.

Pursuant to Rule 4.03 all defensive players except the catcher must be in fair territory when the ball is pitched. This rule was created to prohibit a fielder from standing behind the catcher during an intentional walk to guard against passed balls and wild pitches.

Fan Appreciation Day See *Promotions*

Fan Interference See *Interference*

Fans

"One of the chief duties of the fans is to engage in arguments with the man behind him. This department of the game has been allowed to run down fearfully."— Humorist Robert Benchley.

"At a Dodger baseball game in Los Angeles, I asked Will Durant if he was ninety-four or ninety-five. 'Ninety-four,' he said. 'You don't think I'd be doing anything as foolish as this if I were ninety-five, do you?'"—Norman Cousins.

"When you are ten, you know more about your team than you ever will know again."—Dan Shaughnessy.

"What is both surprising and delightful is that spectators are allowed, and even expected, to join in the vocal part of the game.... There is no reason why the field should not try to put the batsman off his stroke at the critical moment by neatly timed disparagements of his wife's fidelity and his mother's respectability."—George Bernard Shaw.

"Baseball is not necessarily an obsessive-compulsive disorder, like washing your hands 100 times a day, but it's beginning to seem that way. We're reaching the point where you can be a truly dedicated, state-of-the-art fan or you can have a life. Take your pick."—Thomas Boswell in the *Washington Post*.

"I don't love baseball. I don't love most of today's players. I don't love the owners. I do love, however, the baseball that is in the heads of baseball fans. I love the dreams of glory of 10-year-olds, the reminiscences of 70-year-olds. The greatest baseball arena is in our heads, what we bring to the games, to the telecasts, to reading newspaper reports."—Stan Isaacs in *Newsday*.

"We would never be part of that golden company on the field, which each of us, certainly for one moment of his life, had wanted more than anything else in the world to join."—Roger Angell in *Game Time* (2003).

"I believe in exciting games, but the style of play should be limited to the intelligence of the people who pay to see the games."—American League president Ban Johnson expressing disdain in 1901 for the new "scientific" baseball style.

"It is also necessary at this season to establish firm emotional connections with a Major League ball club, to share in the agonies of their defeats and the ecstacies of their triumphs. Without these simple marriages, none of us could survive."—Writer E.B. White.

"I've been in love five times, once with a girl and four times with big league ball clubs. That sets no record for either course but it does raise a question. Constancy would seem to be as excellent a virtue in a man's relationship with his ball club as with his lady, and indeed there are cynics around who would claim it is more readily found there."—Sportswriter Ed Fitzgerald.

"Met fans—once the devoted vegetarians of baseball—have put aside wheat germ and carrot juice, completely forgotten the air of self-congratulation with which they once consumed them, and, having tasted protein, have suddenly taken to howling for blood just like fans in Chicago, Pittsburgh and St. Louis."—Paul O'Neil in *Life* magazine during the Mets' 1969 pennant run.

"The guy with the biggest stomach will be the first to take off his shirt at a baseball game."—Sportswriter Glenn Dickey.

"Time is of the essence. The crowd and the players
Are the same age always, but the man in the crowd
Is older every season. Come on, play ball!"—Last lines of a poem about the Polo Grounds by Rolfe Humphreys.

Fan Attacks on Players/Owners/Coaches.

"Major League Baseball is now issuing stiffer penalties to crazed fans who run onto the field. Under the new policy, the only shirtless fans allowed on the field are Jennifer Anniston, Buffy the Vampire Slayer, and whomever Derek Jeter is dating."—From CBS's "The Late Show."

"I got so I could feel a brick coming when I couldn't see it."—Turkey Mike Donlin of the 1906 Giants.

"In my day they just called you a bum."—Joe DiMaggio.

"Please stop throwing things. This is an important game! Now quit this!"—Twins announcer Bob Casey, after Minnesota fans showered former Twins player Chuck Knoblauch with objects in left field during a game against the Yankees in 2001.

"The man who has done the most for baseball in Boston this year."—Boston sportswriter Dave Egan on the cabdriver who ran over Braves manager Casey Stengel.

"Imagine the worst kind of New York Yankee fan, on his way out of his cave to watch his team play a postseason game at Yankee Stadium, conducting a last-minute check of necessities. *Game ticket, lucky cap, Mattingly T-shirt, subway token and Titleist for beaning other team's second baseman. All set.* He is armed and dangerous."—Tom Verducci in *Sports Illustrated*, after Yankee fans pelted Mariners players during the 1995 play-offs. Players were showered with a softball, a shot glass, a Walkman, a golf ball, plastic bottles, batteries, beer and coins.

"I know why they threw at me. What I can't figure out is why they brought it to the ball park in the first place."—Cardinals outfielder Ducky Medwick on the vegetables thrown at him by fans during Game 7 of the 1934 World Series after he slid hard into third baseman Marv Owen of the Tigers. When Medwick came out to left field after the inning, fans showered him with fruit and vegetables. The Cardinals were leading 9–0 when Judge Landis decided to force Medwick out of the game for his own safety. Medwick's lament many years later: "I don't want to be remembered as the guy who got thrown out of a World Series game. I don't want to be remembered as some kind of freak, like Wrong Way Corrigan or the guy who ran the wrong way in the Rose Bowl. I want to be remembered as Joe Medwick, the ballplayer."

Third baseman Marv Owen 25 years later: "It was my fault. I was on the bag, faking as if the throw coming was coming to me and Joe did what any runner would do."

Early 20th century fans in Brooklyn were known to fashion spears from umbrella tips and the Giants carried rocks in their carriages to throw back at Philadelphia fans.

In 1896 Patsy Tebeau of the visiting Cleveland Spiders rode the umpire throughout a game and the umpire later called the game for darkness. The crowd mobbed the umpire and attacked Tebeau and his team. Tebeau and the umpire spent the night in jail. Tebeau was fined $200 by the league, but the team's owner, Stanley Robison, obtained an injunction prohibiting collection of the fine and prohibiting the league from boycotting games in which Tebeau played based on his failure to pay.

In 1906 after John McGraw's Giants brawled with the Phillies, hostile Philadelphia fans threw debris at the Giants' departing carriages. Catcher Roger Bresnahan stood up and lost his balance, falling into the crowd. He ran into a corner store, barricaded himself in a small room and waited for the police to arrive.

During a key 1922 stretch drive game between the Yankees and Browns, Yankee center fielder Whitey Witt was struck by a bottle in the 9th inning. Blood streamed down Witt's face as he was taken from the field. Though he was thought to be seriously injured, he returned the next day and had a key hit in a 3–2 Yankee victory.

In 1960 a fan came out of the stands at Yankee Stadium and punched Mickey Mantle in the jaw.

In Detroit during the 1961 season a fan ripped a chair out of the concrete and threw it at Roger Maris. The same thing happened during a 1924 brawl between the Tigers and Yankees in Detroit. The Yankees were leading 10–6 in the 9th inning when Tiger pitcher Bert Cole hit Bob Meusel in the back with a pitch. During the ensuing 30-minute brawl, fans ripped out seats and threw them at the players. The umpires forfeited the game to the Yankees and Meusel and Cole were suspended for 10 days.

Twice within three weeks in 1961, both in Sunday doubleheaders against the Yankees in Yankee Stadium, Jimmy Piersall was the object of a potential fan attack. On the first occasion, a large fan ran toward Piersall in center field. He wanted to shake his hand. "You touch me and I'll kick you in the rear," Piersall said, reasoning the man could have a knife. The fan squared off against Piersall, then decided against a fight and ran. In the second incident, two fans, 17 and 18, charged him, calling him a nut and throwing punches after Piersall had yelled at the fans in center field in defense of Vic Power, who was being booed. Piersall landed punches against both of the perpetrators as teammate Johnny Temple and then the police intervened. Piersall refused to press charges after the melee: "I've had 117 fights and that's the first time I've ever won."

When Texas Rangers owner Bob Short appeared at a game in Baltimore shortly after he moved the club from Washington, a woman broke into a special box behind the visitors' box and poured a beer over Short's head — though initially she claimed to have slipped: "I'll tell you something, I didn't slip. I purposely poured a cup of beer over that bum Short's head. And I'd do it again."

On August 26, 1986, a "fan" threw a Bowie hunting knife with a five-inch blade at California Angels rookie Wally Joyner after his team's 2–0 defeat of the Yankees in Yankee Stadium. Joyner was grazed on the left arm by the butt end of the weapon, but was unhurt.

On Opening Day 1986 in Toronto, 35 Blue Jays fans were arrested and 126 ejected when a large group in the bleachers repeatedly ran on the field and disrupted the game.

"If he throws another home run, I'm going to run out there and give him what for." — Brother of Cubs fan John Murray quoting him about reliever Randy Myers during a game on September 28, 1995. Myers then gave up the offending home run during a crucial late season game between the Cubs and Astros, giving the Astros a 9–7 lead. Murray ran on the field and attacked Myers on the mound. The 6'1", 230-pound Myers was adept at martial arts and got in a few punches before other players pulled Myers off. Murray was a bond trader at the Chicago Board of Trade and his wife first learned of his actions on the evening news. Cubs shortstop Shawon Dunston was not ready for serious injury: "I knew Randy was going to do one of those martial-arts moves. I was afraid Randy was going to snap his neck. I would have gotten sick, thrown up on the spot."

Murray's response: "I was watching the game with some friends and I told them if Myers gives up another homer to a guy I'm going to run out on the field and yell at him. In retrospect, it was a bad move on my part."

During a game on September 24, 1999, Berley W. Visgar, a 23-year-old from South Beloit, Illinois, jumped out of the stands in Milwaukee and tackled Astros right fielder Bill Spiers in the bottom of the 6th inning. Spiers suffered a welt under his left eye, a bloody nose and whiplash before Houston starter Mike Hampton grabbed the fan and beat on him before his teammates came from the bench and bullpen. The Astros won 9–4. In April 2000, Visgar was sentenced to 90 days in jail and fined $1,000.

On September 19, 2002, a drunken and shirtless father and son combination jumped out of the stands at Comiskey Park and attacked Royals first base coach Tom Gamboa. William Ligue, Jr., age 34, led his 15-year-old son in the attack during a meaningless game, and later pleaded guilty after he blamed the incident on drugs and alcohol. Father and son tackled Gamboa from behind, causing his head to snap back and smack into the ground. He went into shock as they turned him over and the father punched him. Gamboa kicked once at the father before Kansas City players swarmed them. There was also a knife lying on the grass, although it wasn't used in the attack. When Gamboa saw the knife, he flashed back to tennis player Monica Seles and the attack she suffered in Germany in 1993, when a crazed fan stabbed her in the back in an effort to see fellow German Steffi Graf secure the world number one ranking. Ligue was sentenced to 30 months' probation in August 2003 after pleading guilty to two counts of aggravated battery. He also was required to perform community service and remain in a substance abuse program. Gamboa was not happy: "To me, probation is nothing." The son received six months in a boot camp. Gamboa suffered permanent hearing damage.

"I'm no threat to society. I just had a rough time in my life." — Ligue, after he was recognized at the U.S. Open golf tournament outside of Chicago in June 2003. He was wearing a legitimate vendor's badge after being hired to clean up hospitality tents. In December 2003 Ligue tested positive for marijuana use and prosecutors sought to revoke his probation.

Gamboa was terminated by the Royals after the 2003 season. Many within the organization apparently resented it when he was surrounded by media and fans for autographs and comment throughout the 2003 season. Gamboa said that manager Tony Pena told him it was the players who should be talking to the media, but Gamboa felt it would be rude if didn't talk to the media. To avoid some of the notoriety, he was moved from the coaching box to bullpen coach.

In mid–2003 a fan at Oakland's Network

Yankee fans, 1947.

Associates Coliseum threw a cell phone at Rangers outfielder Carl Everett and hit him in the back of the head.

Eric Dybas, 24, ran on the field in Chicago during a game on April 15, 2003, between the Royals and White Sox. He tried to tackle umpire Laz Diaz, but was subdued by Royals players before he could hurt Diaz. In December 2003 he was sentenced to six months in jail. (see also *Umpires—Attacks* for fan attacks on umpires).

Attacks on Fans. In 1909 in Atlanta a fan was prosecuted for hitting another fan who kept putting his feet on his seat. The fan was acquitted after the attack was ruled justifiable.

On June 23, 1910, Art Devlin of the Giants belted a fan sitting in the Ebbets Field box seats. He was suspended for five days but was not criminally prosecuted.

On May 15, 1912, Ty Cobb went into the stands and attacked a particularly vehement heckler. Cobb apparently ignored the fact that the fan had lost his hands in a printing accident. Cobb was suspended for 10 days.

In 1922 Babe Ruth was suspended by Judge Landis for the first few weeks of the season because of a barnstorming tour the previous winter. Five days after returning to the line-up he went after a heckler in the stands. He received another suspension and was stripped of his position as Yankee captain.

On May 10, 1991, Indians outfielder Albert Belle, a recovering alcoholic, was harassed in his home park by a fan who yelled, "Hey Joey, keg party at my house after the game. C'mon over." Belle then hurled a ball into the fan's chest from a distance of 20 feet. Belle was suspended for seven days by the American League. Soon after the attack fans began wearing tee shirts with a bulls-eye on the front and "Albert Belle Fan Club" on the back. In September 1993 Belle was at it again: he attacked a fan with a ping pong paddle.

In 1995 Angels designated hitter Chili Davis poked a man who he thought had been heckling him in Milwaukee. He poked the wrong man. Davis was fined $5,000 by the American League and security was increased after Davis received anonymous telephone threats.

In 1995 a 15-year-old fan accused Twins second baseman Chuck Knoblauch of pushing him against a wall and grabbing him by the neck. The fan had insulted Knoblauch after he refused to sign an autograph.

On May 15, 1996, Tony Phillips of the White Sox went into the stands to attack a heckler who had been yelling racial epithets. He was ordered to appear in court after punching 23-year-old Chris Hovorka, who denied making any racial comments and claimed to have had only two beers.

On May 16, 2000, Dodger backup catcher Chad Kreuter was sitting in the bullpen at Wrigley Field, which is an open area on a bench next to the fans down the line. A fan hit him in the head and stole his cap. Kreuter and several teammates went into the stands and there was a brawl. Sixteen Los Angeles players and three coaches were given suspensions. The Dodgers won 6–5. The commissioner's office ordered suspensions and fines against the Dodgers totaling 45 games and $71,000. Fan Ronald Camacho, who was arrested at the time for disorderly conduct, was awarded $775,000 in civil penalties assessed against the Cubs and Dodgers.

On September 13, 2004, A's fans spent the night screaming at Rangers pitchers in their bullpen. In the top of the 9th inning, the Texas players got into a fight with the fans, and reliever Frank Francisco (Rookie of the Month in August) threw a chair into the stands. The folding chair injured a male fan in the head and broke the nose of a female fan. The melee caused a 19-minute delay and the area was cleared of spectators. The A's won 7–6 in the bottom of the 10th inning. Francisco was arrested after the game and posted a $15,000 bond to be available in the bullpen for the next game. He was later suspended for the remainder of the season.

The woman who was injured, 41-year-old Jennifer Bueno, intended to sue, prompting this comment from Joe Gutierrez to *Los Angeles Times* columnist Larry Stewart: "I guess that means Francisco is going to be paying through the nose."

Fan Deaths. On August 8, 1903, in Philadelphia, a fight erupted outside the ballpark and fans inside went to the rail of the stands to watch. The steel underpinning collapsed, killing 12 and injuring 300. One source reported that there were so many lawsuits that owners A. J. Reach and John Rogers were "delighted" to sell the club to Philadelphia socialite James Potter (though it is likely that the pending lawsuits were factored into the sale price).

During the 1908 Cubs/Giants make-up game to end the season following the Merkle Boner game, a fan fell off the elevated railroad tracks while viewing the game. He died instantly, but according to *The Sporting News* "his vacant place was quickly filled."

After the Angels beat the Giants in Game 7 of the 2002 World Series, a fan was stabbed to death during a postgame tailgate party at Edison Field.

In September 2003 a fan was shot to death in the Dodger Stadium parking lot after a game. There did not appear to be any connection between the game and the shooting.

See also *Fires*.

Gifts from Fans. White Sox manager Jimmy Dykes was considered a terror with umpires during the 1930s and 1940s. He once stalled a bullpen move so that Boston's 6 p.m. curfew would prevent further play. He was fined $250 by the league, but on his next visit to Fenway Park the fans presented him with a $250 watch as a token of their admiration. (see also *Umpires—Fan Appreciation*).

Notable Characters. Frank H. Wood was a well-known 19th century New York Giants fan famous for saying in a loud voice, "Well, Well, Well." He was mentioned in one of *Zane Grey*'s baseball stories, *The Red Headed Outfield* (1915).

Perhaps the first well-known fan was Arthur Dixwell of Boston, who was prominent during the 1880s. He was independently wealthy and gave rewards to players. He also awarded New England and Boston minor leaguers the Dixwell Trophy for outstanding performance. He was known as "Hi!Hi! Dixwell."

Mary Ott (no relation to Mel) was known as the Horse Lady of St. Louis. She drove opponents crazy in Sportsman's Park for 25 years by sitting behind the visitors' dugout and screeching at the players. She was a large woman who attended games while her husband supposedly was at home cooking.

In the 1920s Al the Milkman sat in the bleachers in Cincinnati and gave floral pieces to Reds home run hitters.

Abie the Iceman parked his ice wagon outside Ebbets Field in the 1920s and yelled "Ya Bums Ya" as the Dodger players entered the ballpark. Manager Wilbert Robinson finally offered him a pass to games to stop the razzing but Abie declined it so he could continue his heckling.

"Howling Hilda" Chester was known as The First Lady of Flatbush as the star fan of Ebbets Field from the 1930s until the early 1950s. She was given a cowbell by the Dodger players in the late 1930s so that she would stop bringing her frying pan to games. She did no more yelling after suffering a heart attack, but still attended games. One source reported that she turned her attention to the Mets when they arrived in 1962, but in actuality she had died a few years earlier. Chester's daughter Bea was an infielder on the South Bend Blue Sox of the All-American Girls Professional Baseball League in the late 1940s.

On September 24, 1940, with Leo Durocher managing the Dodgers, pitcher Whit Wyatt was leading the Giants 5–0. Late in the game Chester thought that Wyatt was losing his stuff, so she wrote a note to Durocher telling him to take him out. She gave the note to Dodger outfielder Pete Reiser at the railing by the dugout. He put it in his pocket and ran to his outfield position. After the inning Reiser stopped by the box seats and talked briefly about something else with Dodger general manager Larry MacPhail. Reiser then walked into the dugout and handed the note to Durocher.

Durocher pulled Wyatt from the game but afterward was furious, thinking that MacPhail had sent the note and interfered with Durocher's managerial responsibilities. When Durocher found out who really sent the note, he was in shock: "I've heard of front office interference, but how about me listening to that crazy dame with the cowbell."

The Dodgers had Shorty Laurice and his Dodger Sym-Phoney Band (see also **Musicians**), as well as Eddie Bettan with his tin whistle and explorer helmet.

Jack (or Jake) Pierce was another Ebbets Field character of the 1930s and 1940s. The wealthy restaurant owner would always buy 10 seats and bring two large boxes of balloons, a hydrogen tank and a bottle of scotch. Whenever Cookie Lavagetto did something good, Pierce would wave a gray banner and burst balloons.

Leather-lunged Pete Adelis, an A's fan, once was barred from Ebbets Field. He was only six feet tall, but supposedly weighed 620 pounds. The Yankees once hired him to heckle the Indians during a crucial series in the 1940s.

Cincinnati's Harry Thobe was a retired bricklayer who danced a jig continuously at all games during the World War II era. He wore a white suit with red stripes and had one red and one white shoe. He carried a red and white parasol and had 12 gold teeth. He always danced on top of the dugout.

Patsy O'Toole was an especially loud Tigers fan. During one World Series game, President Roosevelt's aides arranged for O'Toole to be moved to a less prominent seat in the stands.

A Pirates fan known as "The Coal Man" could bark like a seal for a full nine innings.

The 1970s Orioles had Wild Bill Hagy, a taxi driver who spelled out each letter of "ORIOLES" by twisting his body on the roof of the club's dugout.

Groups of Fans.

"From the time a team leaves the [New York] Sheraton on Seventh Avenue until it pulls up safely at the [Yankee] Stadium entrance, ballplayers sound like a bunch of maiden aunts who are certain that they're about to be hijacked to Yemen."—Thomas Boswell in *Why Time Begins on Opening Day* (1984), on players' fears of playing in New York.

"Detroit fans don't know anything about baseball. They couldn't tell the difference between baseball players and Japanese aviators."—Tigers manager Mayo Smith.

Boston Red Sox.

"If Mrs. Custer had been an eyewitness to the massacre, she would not have been more traumatized than I was by the unhappy event forever linked to Buckner. And after it I had a deep sense of foreboding that I was witnessing the unfolding of a Greek tragedy and that there was no way they would win the seventh game. Being a died-in-the-wool Red Sox fan should be a disease category in the Diagnostic and Statistical Manual of the American Psychiatric Association. How one can get one's hopes up when they advance to the postseason is clearly a psychotic break with reality. The condition is, alas, incurable."—Manitoba University professor Barney

Sneiderman in an email to the author in 1999, well before the 2003 fiasco against the Yankees in the postseason.

"Boston fans [have a] world view born of bitterness and a deep-seated pessimism. The residents of Red Sox Nation (roughly, New England, north of New Haven) have seen more than enough to be wary of anything presenting itself as new and better..."—Ben McGrath in *The New Yorker*.

Boston's Royal (or Loyal) Rooters of the early 20th century were led by saloon keeper "Nuf Ced (or Sedd)" McGreevey. McGreevey owned a saloon nearby called the Third Base Saloon because, as he explained, "you always need to touch third before heading home." They led parades as early as the 1903 World Series. Boston mayor John "Honey Fitz" Fitzgerald (John F. Kennedy's grandfather) led similar parades in 1914 and 1916. The Royal Rooters turned a popular song of the day from this:

"Tessie, you make me feel so sadly
Why don't you turn around
Tessie, you know I love you madly
Babe, my heart weighs a pound."
To this:
"Honus, why do you hit so badly
Take a back seat and sit down
Honus, at bat you look so sadly
Hey, why don't you get out of town."

Early in the 20th century there were fan groups organized as the White Sox Rooters, Cleveland Bards and Pittsburgh Stove League.

Chicago Cubs Fans.

"The fuckers don't even work! That's why they're out at the fucking game! Tell 'em to go out and get a fucking job and find out what it's like to earn a fucking living! Eighty-five percent of the fucking world works, the other 15 come here!"—Cubs manager Lee Elia after Cubs fans were a bit rough on him.

"Let's all just admit it. It's better this way. It's better that the Cubs and Red Sox don't win the World Series. If they ever won, then the Wrigley faithful and Red Sox Nation would be just another group of fans."—Patrick Mallon in a 2003 letter to the *Los Angeles Times*.

"So now everybody is making a big deal about the Cubs, their fans who have been loyally supporting them through decade after decade of losing—as if we should APPLAUD them because they wasted generations of perfectly good fan energy rooting for a team that traditionally had as much chance of winning the World Series as the von Trapp family singers, with Julie Andrews pitching."—Dave Barry.

The Cubs have their Bleacher Bums, celebrated in a long-running stage play of the same name (see also **Theater**). The Bums, reported in most sources as formed in 1969 during the Mets/Cubs pennant race, originally were a group of construction workers who manned the bleachers. Actually, the Bums were formed by 10 fans in 1966, but only came to prominence during the 1969 pennant race. Cubs reliever Dick Selma was their cheerleader. Members of the Bums once threw white mice at outfielder Lou Brock and a battery at pitcher Jim "Mudcat" Grant. Cubs owner Phil Wrigley once paid $10,000 to send the Bleacher Bums on a road trip with the club.

Cleveland Fans.

"When you wake up in the morning and you read in the *New York Times* about Cleveland fans talking about a sports player's dead mother, that's not how we want to be known."—Cleveland Mayor Michael R. White in an October 15, 1998, letter to David Wells, George Steinbrenner and Mayor Rudy Giuliani, apologizing for comments Indians fans made about Wells' mother, who had died in 1997.

Japanese Fan Support. Japanese fans who support the Hanshin Tigers have a tradition when the club wins a league title. As happened in 2003, thousands of fans jumped off the Ebisubashi Bridge into the "murky" Dotonbori River.

Devoted Attendance. Edwin A. Lowenthal of Evansville, Indiana, saw his first Major League game in 1916 and all but five Reds games between 1934 and 1966. He never missed a game between 1947 and 1966.

Jimmie McCullough of Atlantic City began a streak in 1926 of 50 years attendance at all World Series games.

Lou Schulte missed seven Reds home games in 24 years.

During the 1940s, Braves fan Arthur Felch camped out in a cardboard crate outside the bleachers of each year's World Series site so that he would be the first one in.

At 90 years old, Pat Olsen continued a streak of 283 straight World Series games through Game 7 of the 1991 Series.

John Franzen, Jr., attended 2,137 Brewers games from the club's arrival in 1970 through the 1994 season. He had his streak of 1,090 games broken at the start of the 1987 season when he suffered a heart attack in the spring. He missed the club's 13–0 start and attended only 10 games in 1987.

Earliest Fans. Some of the earliest fans were the invited guests of the Knickerbocker Club, who witnessed a "genteel affair" complete with tents and hors d'orveures.

Terminology. Fans, or "fanatics," originally were called "Kranks" and after games were allowed on the field to carry the hero of the day around on their shoulders.

Fan "Appreciation." In late 1995 Deion Sanders debuted with the Giants after a trade from the Reds. Near the end of the game a fan ran out to Sanders in center field and imitated Sanders' touchdown celebration dance, drawing a laugh and a high five from Sanders.

Fan Injuries. See *Bats*—Fan Injuries and *Foul Balls*.

On July 2, 2003, 32 people were sent to the hospital after an escalator at Coors Field accelerated and caused dozens of fans to fall on each other after a game. Nine remained at the hospital for serious injuries.

In April 1999 a Florida jury awarded Linda Postlethwaite $2.7 million after her nose was broken by a wild pitch thrown by "Wild Thing" Mitch Williams in a game between the Phillies and Marlins on August 8, 1993.

Fan Interference. See *Interference*.

Fans as Managers.

"There are three things that the average man thinks he can do better than anybody else. Build a fire, run a hotel and manage a baseball team."— Rocky Bridges.

On August 24, 1951, six days after the famous Eddie Gaedel *Midget* stunt, Bill Veeck's Browns allowed 1,115 "Grandstand Managers" to make strategy decisions during the game. These fans, chosen from letters to a local newspaper, were given signs with a "Yes" or a "No." They sat behind the dugout while coaches held up signs asking the fans what to do, such as "Bunt?" or "Hit and Run?"

The Browns won the game against the A's, which took only 2 hours and 11 minutes to play despite the "fan interference." The fans' most important decision came in the 1st inning. After Browns pitcher Ned Garver allowed hits by five of the first six A's batters, the fans voted to allow him to stay in. He went all the way for the 5–3 victory, allowing only two more hits. Any dispute among the fans was decided by applause. To gauge the applause, the team hired a local municipal court judge to rule. One source reported that among those in the stands with cards was the owner of the visiting A's, Connie Mack.

At one point Garver refused to pitch with the infield in, so one of Veeck's assistants successfully implored the crowd to change its decision. A fireworks display at the end of the game spelled out a thank you to the fans: "Thank you G.S. [Grand Stand] Managers for a swell job. Zack [Taylor] manages tomorrow."

Fan on the Field.

"Please don't throw anything—or anybody—onto the playing field."— Twins announcer Bob Casey's standard pregame admonition.

On May 21, 1998, in a game between the Rangers and Mariners, while Rangers manager Johnny Oates was involved in an animated argument with third base umpire Brian O'Nora over a call on a stolen base in the top of the 9th, a fan holding onto his cap like former Orioles manager Earl Weaver (for whom Oates played) came out of the third base stands to join the discussion and was escorted away by security.

Flagpole Sitter. Indians fan Charlie Lupica sat on a flagpole on May 31, 1949, and vowed not to come down until the Indians were in first place. On September 25, 1949, when the team was mathematically eliminated from the race, owner Bill Veeck had the flagpole platform moved to Municipal Stadium and Lupica came down after 117 days. The Indians were in seventh place when he went up and were in fourth place when he came down, eventually finishing third.

Leaving Early.

"The stadium seems to be suffering from premature evacuation."— Giants broadcaster Ted Robinson on the mass exodus of fans from the ballpark while the Giants were beating up on the Phillies at Veterans Stadium.

"This is the president of the Eight-Inning Club. What can I say? We beat the traffic. That's the important thing."— A radio talk show caller after he left early and missed Francisco Cabrerra sending the Braves to the 1992 World Series with a bottom-of-the-9th-inning single to defeat the Pirates in the League Championship Series.

"Things were so bad in Chicago last summer that by the 5th inning we were selling hot dogs to go."— Ken Brett on the 1975 White Sox.

"It is interesting about people that leave early from ball games. It's almost as if they came out to the ballgame to see if they can beat the traffic home."— A's broadcaster Lon Simmons on Dodger fans who are notorious for leaving early, even during close games.

"The Dodgers drew their 100 millionth fan in Los Angeles on Tuesday and their 70 millionth to leave early."— Allan Malamud of the *Los Angeles Times*.

Yogi Berra left during the 9th inning of the 1951 Giants/Dodgers play-off game in which Bobby Thomson hit his famous game-ending home run off Ralph Branca. Leaving before all the heroics, Berra said that he heard the ending on his car radio.

Football coach and then-announcer Mike Ditka carried this concept to the extreme during a Monday Night Football telecast in 2001. During the middle of the second half, he told his fellow radio announcers that he was leaving because he wanted to beat the traffic. He then got up and left the booth. And they thought baseball was boring.

Seating. In the early years of the Los Angeles Angels franchise in the 1960s, the club roped off a section of seats exclusively for fans who were originally from the city whose team was playing the Angels that day.

Streakers. Streaking was in vogue in the early 1970s. The practice consisted of getting naked and running through crowds of clothed people for the shock value (it happened at the Oscar

Awards show in the early 1970s). The practice surfaced again on July 17, 1991. Two Braves fans streaked down the first base line at Atlanta's Fulton County Stadium and slid into home plate (*sans* sliding pads).

On August 17, 2002, in a game between the Padres and Expos, a streaker, wearing shorts, ran across the field and slid into second base at infielder Gene Kingsale's feet. Kingsale had capped a four-run 8th inning with a two-run double.

Women Fans.

"It may not be amiss to offer a suggestion unrelated at first glance to the central concern of this book: the fact that so many women view televised baseball games suggests the tedium and emptiness of their own lives. Perhaps they seek wish fulfillment from viewing virile males, and if this is so it may have important policy implications for baseball..."—Ralph Andreano in *No Joy in Mudville* (1965).

By the late 1980s, 43% of baseball television viewers were women, while 35% of fans attending games were women. The highest percentage of women fans attend minor league games.

In 2000 Major League Baseball finished a study on women fans. The study showed that baseball was the favorite professional sport among women, in part because attendance at a game provides the quality time and atmosphere they want for their families. The study was part of The Commissioner's Initiative on Women and Baseball, an effort to help clubs build stronger relationships with female audiences. The Initiative was established in 1999 as a pilot program in six Major League cities.

African American Fans.

"In seats all around us there seemed to be a new category of fan—black people who came out to root just for Dwight [Gooden], not the Mets. They danced in the aisles and gave high and low fives for his strike-outs, then left for the concession stands during the Met at-bats. It was as though he were Michael Jackson or some sparkling young break-dancer from New York."—Richard Grossinger in *The Temple of Baseball* (1985).

From 1969 through 1984 African Americans comprised less than 5% of baseball fans. In a 1985 survey the percentage was up to 5%, though that ethnic group made up 11.7% of the general population. In a 1986 study, African Americans comprised 6.8% of baseball fans, 7.5% of football fans, and 17% of basketball fans.

In 1982 even though African Americans comprised 25.2% of New York City's population, only 6% of Mets fans were black.

In 1987 the White Sox had no black season ticket holders, even though the club played its games in a predominately black section of the city. Don Newcombe of the Dodgers' front office staff noted that in 1987 less than 50 of the approximately 26,000 season ticket holders were black.

Fan Association. The National Baseball Fan Association is the representative for fans in the Commissioner's Office.

In 1995 the National Unhappy Fedup Fan Association (NUFFA) was formed.

Protest. At the Mets home opener in April 1995 following the end of the player strike, three fans ran onto the field wearing tee shirts with "GREED" hand-lettered on the front and threw $150 worth of $1 bills at the players. They stood at second base briefly with clenched fists in the air as fans cheered. Later in the game another fan ran onto the field to rip out third base and try to climb back into the stands with it.

In May 1999, to protest the discrepancies between the rich teams and the poor ones, more than 2,500 Royals fans staged a walkout during their team's game with the Yankees. They littered the warning track in left field with fake dollar bills and then left in the top

of the 4th inning, taping to their seats paper skull and crossbones that read "Small markets are dying."

The Wave.

"I'm waiting for the day we see the 'wave' at the Metropolitan Opera."—Broadcaster Al Michaels on the phenomenon of fans standing up in unison in serpentine fashion around a ballpark and waving their arms.

The wave apparently was introduced at University of Michigan football games in 1983 and first appeared in a Major League ballpark in Detroit during the Tigers' championship season in 1984. Precision versions of the wave were performed by capacity crowds at Dodger Stadium during the final game of the 1984 Olympics.

The Sporting News carried an account of a game between the National League New York Giants and the American Association's Brooklyn Bridegrooms in the championship series of 1889. It included a description of what may have been the first Wave: "As the seventh opened somebody cried, 'Stretch for Luck!' And instantly the vast throng on the grand stand rose gradually and then settled down, just as long grass bends to the breath of the zephyr."

Beach Balls.

"Patrons engaged in the handling of inflatable objects or in any way interfering with the enjoyment of the game by others will be subject to immediate ejection from the ball park."—Sign at Fenway Park.

Dodger Stadium was the site of the first beach balls, which are now ubiquitous throughout Dodger games. The tradition has been expanded to other stadiums, and has sometimes included inflatable, anatomically correct, dolls.

Best Fan Story. Andy Strasberg was the Public Relations Director of the Padres for many years. When he was a boy he became a fan of Yankee outfielder Roger Maris. Maris befriended Strasberg and delivered on promises to give him balls and broken bats when Strasberg attended games at Yankee Stadium. As Strasberg moved into his teens, the relationship continued.

When Strasberg moved to college in Chicago, he and five friends traveled to St. Louis to attend the first game Maris played in the National League on Opening Day. Strasberg introduced his friends to Maris, who (to the surprise of Strasberg's doubting friends) acknowledged that Strasberg was his "greatest fan." Maris hit his first National League home run during the game into the right field bleachers full of fans. Strasberg caught the ball, a miracle verified by Maris.

The two continued to correspond until Maris's death from cancer in 1985. Strasberg spoke at his funeral and organized an annual memorial golf tournament. Maris' family acknowledged how important Strasberg had been to Maris and one of Maris' children named his son after Strasberg, who became the boy's godparent. The story was featured in *Sports Illustrated* and in Mike Bryan's *Baseball Lives* (1989).

Fantasy Camps

"There have long been summer baseball camps for young boys, sponsored by some star who may put in a brief appearance and pass on a few pointers, but the latest variation on this is baseball camps for grown men, where for a few thousand dollars aging frustrated jocks can get into the uniform of their favorite team, mix with some of the former players, and play ball."—Joel Zoss and John Bowman in *Diamonds in the Rough* (1989).

Fantasy camps sprang up in the 1980s, allowing the common man to rub elbows with former Major League ballplayers. Many sources reported erroneously that the Cubs held the first fantasy camp in 1983. The error is that former Cubs catcher Randy Hundley started the first camp on his own in 1983 and it was never affiliated with the Cubs or any other Major League club. He charged $2,295 for the first camp, for which 65 people signed up. A wonderful description of Hundley's camp was written by Roy Blount, Jr., called "We Had a Ball," in *The Armchair Book of Baseball*, edited by John Thorn (1985). Camps in the 1990s and 2000s cost between $3,000 and $6,000 per week.

See *Baseball Camps* for instructional camps geared to children and young adults.

Fantasy League Baseball

"You smell like a goat. You're unshaven. You work endless hours in dimly lit caves. You speak a language understood only by others of your kind. You fear women and put prices on men's heads. And legions of enemies long to destroy you."—Rick Reilly on fantasy league owners.

"An official scorer will be fired in a fantasy league scandal."—Bill Plaschke in an early 1997 prediction.

"It's hard to accept that so many fans have traded sunshine and the roar of the crowd for the anemic glow of a [computer] monitor and the whir of a hard drive."—Dick McSweeney in a letter to *Baseball Weekly*.

"And I, for one, would rather have Herve Villachaize recite census data into my ear than listen to some lawyer pontificate about why Gary Varsho was a real bargain at $15."—Steve Wulf in *Sports Illustrated*; Villachaize was the dwarf on the television series, "Fantasy Island" ["de plane, boss; de plane!"].

These "newspaper" leagues are based on the day-to-day performances of players in the Major Leagues. Prior to fantasy league baseball, most fans played Strat-o-Matic or other **Tabletop Games** involving chance and historical statistics. Fantasy leagues provide fans an opportunity to "manage" their own team of active Major League players and win or lose based on the players' current daily performance.

"Owners" draft Major League talent onto their teams and follow key statistics such as stolen bases, batting averages, home runs, RBIs, wins, losses, ERAs and saves. The total of these categories for a "team" dictates the final standings of the teams in each fantasy league. Elaborate statistics services have become a cottage industry to service the large number of leagues.

The most prominent of these leagues is Rotisserie League Baseball, created in 1980. It was founded by *Life* magazine editor Daniel Okrent and others at a now-defunct Manhattan restaurant, La Rotisserie Francaise. It claims to be the granddaddy of all newspaper leagues, but this author's Beer Drinkin' Association of Major League Baseball (BDA) was formed in 1979 and the author has been the commissioner since its inception. Founding members include league godfather Michael Parmley, David Bordeaux, former Padres minority owner Michael W. Monk (the BDA stopped playing for money during his ownership), and Bruce Smart. Subsequent owners include Bob Johnsen, Tom "Felix" Housel, Bill Creim, John Erickson and former motorcycle racer Keith Smart.

When 12-year-old Emerlee Erickson asked her father, John (a BDA member), to take her to a model horse show, his incredulous response was: "Model horse show! Are you kidding?!"

Emerlee's response was succinct: "Fantasy League Baseball?! Are you kidding?!"

Touché.

The estimated number of fantasy league players ranged from 500,000 to one million in 1991. By 1993 some estimates were as high as four million. By 2002, it was estimated that 15% of Americans over 18 had been in one or more fantasy sports leagues. By 2004 there were 15 million fantasy league players and it was a billion dollar industry.

Celebrity Owners. Several celebrities are fantasy league devotees, including singer Meat Loaf, Olympic softball pitcher Jennie Finch, Major League pitcher Curt Schilling, retired NFL football player Dan Marino and actor Michael J. Fox.

Scoring System. The United Sports Fans of America came up with a tongue-in-cheek suggested fantasy league scoring system for various transgressions by players, causing a reduction in player points for each of the following (point reduction noted):

1 Suspension from play (points returned upon successful appeal)
3 Declaration of bankruptcy
4 Refusal to play in All-Star Game
5 DUI arrest/conviction
6 Barroom brawl arrest
7 Domestic disturbance arrest
8 Physical abuse of media/fans
9 Loss of civil suit or making cover of *GQ*
10 Rape conviction
15 Banned from MLB for one year
20 Other felony conviction
50 Murder conviction or throwing pitch that kills a batter
100 Doing cartwheels while running the bases after home run

Farm System

"Chain Store Baseball"—Common 1930s nickname for the system.

"Perhaps the story originally got around from some of the ball players in the Cardinal chain who complained about slave wages, but according to Lt. John Silliard one of the Nazi propaganda lines fed German children was the idea that slavery existed in the United States. Silliard, a military intelligence officer, said the Nazis illustrated the point by calling attention to the fact that American baseball clubs sold players."—The *Stars and Stripes* military newspaper in August 1945.

"Just when the change from the general-store concept to big-business principles first made itself felt in baseball is speculative. Easier to mark, historically, is the spot where the illusion of managerial omniscience first began to show its slip. This was a tiny cell (now a shrine, no doubt) in Branch Rickey's brain where the farm system was spawned. There can be no doubt that Rickey, a leader in so many things, including the art of advanced circumlocution, was the first to demonstrate the wisdom and practicality of going to the source for material and bringing it along by degrees and in quantity."—Sportswriter Joe Williams.

See also *Minor Leagues*.

Early "Farm" Teams. The original farm team may have been formed by the 1867 Brooklyn Excelsiors. The team recruited 20–30 ballplayers ages 15–20 and gave them uniforms. These players were trained to replace the first nine Excelsiors and were called the Excelsior Juniors. Young players on these junior teams were usually referred to as muffins.

John Brush owned the Cincinnati Red Stockings in the 1890s and used Indianapolis of the Western League as a farm team to feed players to his Major League club. This practice was not widely copied at the time.

Cleveland Indians. In Ed Fitzgerald's *American League* (1959), sportswriter Gordon Cobbledick noted that the Indians had a modest farm system as early as 1912, though the club's lack of success probably caused most people to ignore the idea. Two early players that came through the system were Major League pitchers Stan Coveleski and Jim Bagby.

Branch Rickey and the St. Louis Cardinals.

"Out of quantity comes quality." — Rickey.

Rickey and the Cardinals are credited with implementing the first modern farm system by placing young Cardinal players on minor league teams to control and train them. After a brief stint as a catcher, Rickey began his Major League managing/general managing career when he was hired to manage the Browns from late 1913 through 1915. In 1917 he joined the Cardinals as president and became manager in 1919 under owner Sam Breadon.

The Cardinals soon sold Sportsman's Park for $350,000 and rented it back from the Browns. The proceeds were used to finance the original farm system. Rickey's theory was that the Cardinals were too cash poor to buy players, so the club started developing players through the minor leagues. Before their farm system was created, almost every time the Cardinals made an offer to a minor league team for a quality player, the Giants or another powerful team would outbid them.

The Cardinals had only one scout at the start of Rickey's tenure, Charley Barrett. Rickey quickly developed a network of college coaches who fed him information. Rickey is credited with inventing the "working agreement," whereby he would exchange players from his Major League club to help stock a minor league club in return for first choice at the end of the season for the minor league club's most talented players.

Rickey's first farm team was Houston in the Texas League in late 1919, in which the Cardinals held an 18% interest. Rickey's second farm team was the Ft. Smith, Arkansas, team in the new Western Association. The Cardinals owned a 100% interest in that club. In 1921 the Cardinals purchased a 50% interest in Syracuse of the International League.

Jim Bottomley was the first Major League starter developed in the Cardinals farm system, coming up in 1922. Bob Feller's father purportedly turned down a contract for his son with the Cardinals because he felt there were too many players in the Cardinals farm system.

At one point the Cardinals had a working agreement with or owned every team in the Nebraska State League and the Arkansas-Missouri League. By 1940 the club owned 32 teams and had eight working agreements. One source reported that at one time the team had 50 minor league clubs under contract in one form or another, covering 800 players. By 1941 and the start of World War II, however, the Cardinals were down to approximately 30 farm teams, owning half of them outright. Judge Landis later ruled that a team could have only one team affiliation in a league.

Rickey's strategy appears to have been well conceived, as his Major League club won pennants in 1926, 1928, 1930, 1931 and 1934. In 1942 Cardinal farm teams won one or both halves of every significant minor league, and the Major League club won 106 games and the pennant. That season 22 of the 25 players on the club's roster were developed in its farm system.

The number of minor league teams diminished due to the war, and the Cardinals only had 23 club affiliations in 1942. This was still 13 more than any other Major League club. Even though World War II decimated the Major and minor leagues, the strength of the Cardinals farm system helped the club to win pennants in 1943 and 1944.

Judge Landis' Dislike of the Farm System.

"It is intolerable and un–American when a group of ballplayers can be boxed into a minor league and advance only at the whim of their employer." — Landis.

Judge Landis referred to the farm system as a prison "chain gang" in reference to the Southern connection of the Cardinals. Landis believed that minor league teams should be owned and run at the local level. He tried to find and create loopholes in the system, but he never totally succeeded and the farm system flourished. See *Free Agents* for instances in which Landis penalized Major League clubs for their improper stockpiling of minor leaguers. One source claimed that the Cubs delayed implementing a farm system in deference to opposition to the system by Landis. Cy Slapnicka of the Indians was a contract manipulator disciplined frequently by Landis: "Slap spent so much time on Judge Landis' carpet as to be practically indistinguishable from the nap."

Farm Systems by Other Clubs.

"It's the stupidest idea in baseball. What Rickey is trying to do can't be done." — Giants manager John McGraw on Branch Rickey's experiment. Though McGraw departed in 1932, the Giants waited until 1937 to implement a farm system, the last Major League club to do so.

Yankees general manager Ed Barrow initially saw no value to having a farm system because of the expense involved. The first Yankee farm club was the Newark Bears around 1930. The Yankees were said to have "perfected" the farm system by the late 1930s with about 15 clubs. In 1937 the Cardinals had 33 farm teams and the Phillies had two.

Red Sox owner Tom Yawkey financed Boston's first farm system in the mid–1930s. The system finally paid off after World War II when the Red Sox had strong teams, though only one American League pennant. Tigers general manager Jack Zeller was a zealous critic of the farm system during the 1940s. One of his speeches advocating the abolition of the system brought this response from minor league leader Judge William Bramham, who saw Major League support for the minor leagues as essential: "[Zeller's remarks] can be charitably attributed only to a loquacious imbecility."

Curbing the Yankees. In 1939 Senators owner Clark Griffith attempted to curb the strength of the cash-rich Yankees by proposing that a Major League team could own only one team in the minor leagues at each level above Class D. The American League rejected this proposal, but the league adopted for one year in 1940 a rule that the league's pennant winner could not execute any interleague *Trades*. This backfired when the Yankees did not win the pennant that season after four straight pennants.

Modern Farm Systems. Since the early 1960s there have been far less elaborate farm systems because of the elimination of all minor leagues below Class A except rookie leagues (see also *Minor Leagues*).

Fastballs

"Every hitter likes fastballs; just like everybody likes ice cream. But you don't like it when someone's stuffing it into you by the gallon." — Reggie Jackson on Nolan Ryan's fastball.

"I don't mind catching your fastball at all. Naturally, I'd want to have a glove on in case you might be having an especially good day." — Gene Green, to pitcher Jim Brosnan.

"It's no fun throwing fastballs to guys who can't hit them. The real challenge is getting them out on stuff they can hit." — Sam McDowell.

"Lady Godiva Fastball." — Tug McGraw's description of his fastball, because it had nothing on it. McGraw was not original, as this phrase was used as early as 1907 to describe the fastball of Tigers pitcher Eddie Siever.

"The Peggy Lee Fastball."—McGraw's other nickname for his weak fastball, based on Lee's famous song, "Is That All There Is?" He also had the "John Jameson fastball," which was straight, "like Irish Whiskey should be." He also had his "Cutty Sark fastball," which sailed.

"I'm throwing as hard as I ever did. The ball's just not getting there as fast."—Yankee pitcher Lefty Gomez after suffering arm problems.

"He's got a fastball you could catch in your teeth. Three pitch speeds: slow, slower and reverse."—Jim Murray on junkball pitcher Stu Miller.

See also *Fastest Pitchers*, *Pitching Speeds* and *Speed Guns*.

Only Pitch. Amos Rusie and Walter Johnson are possibly the only pitchers to win for prolonged periods without using any pitch except a fastball.

Speed. The average fastball travels 85 mph.

Four-Seam Fastball. This is the most basic pitch. The index and middle fingers are placed across the horseshoe of the ball with the fingertips just across the top seam. It rotates bottom to top, giving the appearance of four spinning seams to the batter. It has less movement than other pitches, but at high speed it will tail in or away to the batter.

Two-Seam Fastball. The first two fingers are placed over the seams at their narrowest point. The arm motion is the same as the four-seam fastball, but the ball moves in the direction of the pitcher's throwing arm and sometimes down.

Cut Fastball. A cut fastball is similar to a slider, whereby the pitcher breaks his wrist slightly to make the ball drop.

Fastest Games

"What do you want me to do? Let them sons of bitches stand up there and think on my time?"—Grover Cleveland Alexander on why he pitched so quickly.

See also *Length of Games* and *Slowest Games.*

The fastest known nine-inning Major League game was on September 28, 1919, when the Giants defeated the Phillies in the first game of an end-of-season doubleheader, winning 6–1 in 51 minutes. Jesse Barnes was on the mound for the Giants and won his 25th game as Lee Meadows lost his 20th.

On September 26, 1926, the Browns beat the Yankees 6–2 in 55 minutes in the second game of a doubleheader.

On August 30, 1918, the Giants beat the Dodgers 1–0 in 57 minutes.

On September 21, 1919, the White Sox beat the Red Sox 3–2 in 58 minutes.

One source erroneously reported that on August 8, 1920, Howard Ehmke of the Tigers pitched the "fastest game in Major League history," 1 hour and 13 minutes, a 1–0 victory over the Yankees.

Another source erroneously reported that the fastest nine-inning game in American League history was played on May 21, 1943, when the White Sox defeated the Senators 1–0 in 1 hour and 29 minutes.

On April 6, 1997, Greg Maddux led the Braves to a 4–0 victory over the Cubs in 1 hour, 47 minutes. It was the fastest game since October 4, 1992, when the Dodgers and Astros played a game in 1 hour, 44 minutes.

On July 24, 2002, the Tigers shut out the Royals 3–0 in 1 hour and 41 minutes, the fastest nine–inning game in the Major Leagues since 1984.

World Series. The fastest game in World Series history was the deciding Game 5 of the 1908 Series. The Cubs finished off the Tigers in Detroit behind the three-hit pitching of Orval Overall. They did it in 1 hour and 25 minutes in front of a record-low World Series crowd of 6,210.

The likely last under-two-hour World Series game was Game 4 of the 1966 Series, when Dave McNally beat the Dodgers and Don Drysdale 1–0 in 1:45 to sweep the Series. Think of all the revenue-producing commercials that never aired.

Minor Leagues.

"There was nothing phony about the game. With no previous agreement the two teams went to work to finish things off as fast as they could and they did not realize they were setting a world's record, so I am told. A double play and a triple play speeded things up. Each side made five hits and only one error was committed."—Game summary of one of the shortest minor league games on record, played September 19, 1910, the last day of the season between Atlanta and Mobile in Atlanta. The game took 32 minutes and Mobile won 2–1.

On August 30, 1916, Asheville, North Carolina, pitcher Doc Lowe lost 2–1 to Winston-Salem. It was the closing day of the Class D North Carolina League season. The Asheville club wanted to catch the late afternoon train home and asked to start early. Apparently "we really made a farce of it." Each batter swung at the first pitch lobbed over the plate. Novelist Thomas Wolfe was a 15-year-old spectator at the game.

Fastest Pitchers

"You can't hit what you can't see."—Either Ping Bodie about Walter Johnson or Joe Tinker about Rube Marquard.

"Mister, no man alive can throw a baseball harder than Joe Wood."—Walter Johnson, whom many considered the fastest ever, believed that Smoky Joe Wood was the fastest pitcher of his era. Wood was 34–5 in 1912 at age 22, then flamed out at age 23 and spent the rest of his career as a moderately successful outfielder (see also *Injuries and Illness*—Thumb).

"I threw so hard I thought my arm would fly right off my body."—Smoky Joe Wood.

"He was the fastest pitcher who ever lived."—Ford Frick on Lefty Grove.

"But his real fast one was faster than that first one he threw, and before the week was over we looked at speed that made it seem like Johnson had never pitched nothing but toy balloons."—Ring Lardner in "Hurry Kane" (1929).

"Either he throws the fastest ball I've ever seen, or I'm going blind."—Richie Ashburn on Sandy Koufax.

"He can throw the ball through a car wash and not get it wet."—Johnny Bench on teammate Don Gullett's fastball.

"You can talk about the speed of Walter Johnson or Amos Rusie, but I doubt that either had any more speed than Bender when he was at his best. He was not physically as strong as some others, but he had long, tapering fingers and a peculiar whip to his arm that certainly drove that baseball through the air."—Eddie Collins.

See also *Fastballs*, *Pitching Speeds* and *Speed Guns*.

Pre–1980 Alleged Fastest Clockings.

Bob Feller	107.9 mph	1946
Bob Feller	104.0 mph	1941
Nolan Ryan	100.8 mph	1974
J.R. Richard	100.0 mph	1978
Walter Johnson	99.7 mph	1914
Jim Maloney	99.5 mph	1965

Walter Johnson.

"There is no question but that [Walter] Johnson was the speediest pitcher of all time. Mechanical tests mean nothing. Johnson might have been asked to come out to Harvard or Yale or M.I.T. for a test he probably did not think it did not mean future quoting of record, he might not have had his baseball shoes even, he might be slated to pitch that day or the next or night, or might have pitched the day before, etc.... Grove was fast, Feller of Cleveland, but never let anyone tell you from now on that *any* pitcher was as fast as Johnson. Yes, and by quite a margin."— Ty Cobb in a letter dated April 18, 1944, to fan Edwin E. Jones of Stockton, California.

"Walter Johnson's fastball looked about the size of a watermelon seed and it hissed at you as it passed."— Cobb.

"He knows where he's throwing because if he didn't there would be dead bodies strewn all over Idaho."— Scouting report on Walter Johnson.

In 1914 Johnson was clocked against a motorcycle at 97 mph (or 99.7, depending on the source).

Bob Feller.

"If anybody threw that ball any harder than Rapid Robert, then the human eye couldn't follow it."— Satchel Paige.

Feller was clocked at least at 98 mph using various contraptions, including a speeding motorcycle and a ballistics tester at Aberdeen Proving Grounds. Feller claims that in 1941 he was clocked at 104 mph at Lincoln Park in Chicago. Two cameras measured the speed against a motorcycle in a stunt set up by American League film coordinator and former player Lew Fonseca. Feller also claimed that he was clocked at 107.9 mph in a demonstration in 1946 at Griffith Stadium.

Perhaps a fair comparison comes from Charlie Gehringer, who batted against both Lefty Grove and Feller, and he claimed that Grove was much faster.

Nolan Ryan.

"Others will throw harder, but no one will throw harder for longer."— Rangers pitching coach Tom House on Nolan Ryan.

Using two different **Speed Guns**, Ryan was clocked at 100 mph at Anaheim Stadium while pitching for the Angels on August 20, 1974.

Steve Dalkowski.

"To understand how Dalkowski, a chunky little man with thick glasses and a perpetually dazed expression, became a 'legend in his own time'..."— Pat Jordan in *The Suitors of Spring* (1974).

The fastest pitcher ever may have been 1950s phenom and flame-out Steve Dalkowski. Dalkowski signed with the Orioles in 1957 at age 21. After nine years of erratic pitching he was released in 1966, never having made it to the Major Leagues. Despite his failure, he has been described as the fastest pitcher ever.

Ted Williams once stood in a spring training batting cage and took one pitch from Dalkowski. Williams swore he never saw the ball and claimed that Dalkowski probably was the fastest pitcher who ever lived. Others who claimed he was the fastest ever were Paul Richards, Harry Brecheen and Earl Weaver. They all thought he was faster than Bob Feller and Walter Johnson, though none of them probably saw Johnson pitch.

In 1958 the Orioles sent Dalkowski to the Aberdeen Proving Grounds, a military installation where Feller was once clocked at 98.6 mph. Dalkowski was clocked at only 93.5, but a few mitigating factors existed:

1) Dalkowski had pitched in a game the day before, so he could be expected to throw 5–10 mph slower than usual;

2) there was no mound to pitch from, which Feller had enjoyed, and this would drop his velocity by 5–8 mph;

3) he had to pitch for 40 minutes before the machine could measure his speed, and he was exhausted by the time there was a reading. Other sources reported that the measuring device was a tube and that he took a long time to finally throw one into the tube.

It was estimated that Dalkowski's fastball at times reached 105 mph. Dalkowski was not physically imposing, standing only 5'8" and wearing thick glasses. He had legendary wildness, which kept him out of the Major Leagues. In 995 minor league innings, he walked 1,354 batters and struck out 1,396. He walked 21 in one minor league game and struck out 21 in another. In high school he pitched a no-hitter while walking 18 and striking out 18.

He threw 283 pitches in a complete game against Aberdeen and once threw 120 pitches in only two innings. He played in nine leagues in nine years.

In 1963 for Elmira he finally started throwing strikes. During spring training in 1964, Dalkowski was with the Major League club. After fielding a sacrifice bunt by pitcher Jim Bouton in spring training, Dalkowski's arm went dead and he never recovered. He drifted to various jobs and landed in Bakersfield, California, where he was arrested many times for fighting.

He once threw a ball at least 450 feet on a bet. He was supposed to throw the ball from the outfield wall to home plate, but he threw it well above the plate into the press box. He once threw a pitch so hard that the catcher missed the ball and it shattered an umpire's mask. Dalkowski was the basis for wild fastball pitcher Nuke LaLoosh in the movie *Bull Durham*.

Jim Maloney. Some sources report that Reds pitcher Jim Maloney posted speeds of 99.5 mph in 1965, the year he went 20–9 and pitched two of his three no-hitters.

1990s–2000s.

"You should see the scouts. They're like kids with new toys when they see that 100 light up on their guns. Three digits! Nobody else in the league can do that."— Braves scout and speed gun handler Jim Guadagno on Braves reliever Mark Wohlers, who hit 103 mph on the gun in spring 1995 and was considered the fastest pitcher in the Major Leagues, but later lost his ability to get it over the plate. A number of players reached 100 mph by the mid–1990s and beyond.

Reds pitcher Rob Dibble supposedly registered 100 mph on a speed gun in Candlestick Park in 1992. Other sources report that he was clocked at 95 mph "or more" before he blew out his arm in late 1993.

Robb Nen of the Giants threw a pitch 101 mph at Pro Players Park in October 1997.

Mariners pitcher Randy Johnson has been clocked at speeds in excess of 97 mph, including one reading at 102 mph in 2002 and another in 2000 at 101.

Mets reliever Armando Benitez reached 102 mph in 2002 at Shea Stadium.

Indians reliever Jose Mesa was considered the fastest American League pitcher of the mid–1990s with a fastball often clocked at over 100 mph.

A.J. Burnett, a starter for the Marlins, regularly threw at or above 100 mph in the 2000s.

Negro Leagues.

"Smokey Joe [Williams] could throw harder than all of them."— Satchel Paige quoted in *Blackball Stars*, by John B. Holway (1988).

Many historians routinely choose Satchel Paige as the fastest of the Negro League pitchers. However, those more knowledgeable cite Smokey Joe Williams of the Homestead Grays as the fastest.

100 MPH. According to Bill James, in 2003 Billy Wagner threw

159 pitches clocked at 100 mph or more. During the same season, there were only 40 such pitches thrown by all other Major Leaguers.

Fastest Runners

"Having speed—and knowing what to do with it—are two different things. There are many who are swift of foot, but too slow of mind to use that speed effectively."—H.A. Dorfman and Karl Kuehl in *The Mental Game of Baseball* (1989).

"The only constant in baseball is speed."—Maury Wills.

"I don't know why, but I can run faster in tight pants."—Phil Linz.

"I'm not bad. I'm no Joe Morgan, but I'm pretty good for a white guy."—Pete Rose, on his speed.

"Bob Swift, Fleet Walker, Dasher Troy, Darcy Fast, Ed Quick, Horace Speed, Bob Rush, Rod Scurry, Skeeter Webb, Jim Quick, Zip Collins"

See also **Pinch Runners** and **Stolen Bases**; because the fastest runners are not necessarily the best base stealers—and vice versa, as the following will attest: "Speed is a great asset; but it's greater when it's combined with quickness—and there's a big difference."—Ty Cobb quoted by Grantland Rice.

Lip Pike was considered the fastest player in the National League in the 1870s. On August 27, 1873, he beat a horse in a race over 100 yards, with the horse having a 25-yard head start.

Future evangelist Billy Sunday (see **Religion**) supposedly was the first to circle the bases in under 13 seconds during the 1880s, but this is unlikely in light of modern clockings in which players have never broken 13 seconds.

Hans Lobert, who played 14 years in the Major Leagues beginning in 1903, stole 316 bases and once ran the bases in 13.8 seconds. Lobert once ran a match race around the bases with a horse. In 1913 at Oxnard, California, with John McGraw as Lobert's manager and Bill Klem umpiring, the horse raced around the outside of the bases, with Lobert on the inside "track." The horse won the race, but Lobert always claimed that the horse had crowded him between second and third base. Klem claimed that the horse won by a nose. The event is described by Lobert in *Glory of Their Times*, by Lawrence Ritter (1966).

Evar Swanson was considered the Major League's fastest runner during the first half of the 20th century. In 1931 he circled the bases in 13.3 seconds. An outfielder, Swanson played five years starting in 1929, with a high of 33 stolen bases in his rookie season.

Stolen base king Max Carey reportedly tied Swanson's record of 13.3 during a pregame Field Day in Cincinnati in the 1930s.

One source reported that Maurice Archdeacon, who had a 127-game Major League career, once circled the bases in 13.4 seconds during an exhibition that preceded a 1921 minor league game.

Though not famous for his speed, Rogers Hornsby sometimes offered $500 to anyone in the league who could beat him in a footrace. Apparently no one ever took him up on the offer.

George Case was considered the fastest runner of the 1940s. He ran five match races before games in 1946, losing only to track star and Olympic champion Jesse Owens. Case ran the bases in 13.5 seconds in 1943 while with Washington, but claims that Evar Swanson's earlier 13.3 (or 13.2, as Case recalls), was an invalid time because there was only one watch on Swanson. General Eisenhower attended one of the 1946 races primarily because Case was running. Case received $1,000 for one of the exhibitions.

In 1965 the Mets hired Jesse Owens to teach running and fast starts. During one of his training sessions he suffered a pinched nerve and had to have surgery.

Modern runners are not regularly clocked in circling the bases (only home to first). Running exhibitions are not held anymore because players do not need the extra cash and management would not want to risk injury (as when Reds shortstop Barry Larkin hurt his elbow in a throwing exhibition during an All-Star Game). Presumably the modern stolen base leaders are among the fastest runners, though Lou Brock was, by his own admission, not particularly fast.

By the 2000s, the fastest runners were considered to be Luis Castillo of the Marlins and Ichiro Suzuki of the Mariners.

Cool Papa Bell.

"If Cool Papa had known about colleges or if colleges had known about Cool Papa, Jesse Owens would have looked like he was walking."—Satchel Paige on Bell's blazing speed. The Negro League star supposedly once circled the bases in 13.1 seconds and claimed to have done it on a dry field in 12.0 seconds (one source even reported it as 11 seconds, which would mean 120 yards in a circle faster than a world class sprint could do it on a straight track). Bell was considered one of the fastest, if not the fastest, player in the Negro Leagues. Two apocryphal stories are about his speed. One was told by Paige, who said that Bell could turn off the light switch and be in bed before the lights went out (there was a short in the wiring). Another had Bell hitting a ground ball up the middle that hit him in the back as he slid into second base.

Fat and Weight

"David Wells is fat. Not phat. Fat. He is not a work in progress, not a lug trying to shed some pounds, not a Weight Watchers washout…. Wells is a fat guy who is content being fat."—Jeff Pearlman.

"Watching Fernando Valenzuela force himself into a Los Angeles Dodgers uniform is something like seeing Kate Smith ["it ain't over until the fat lady sings"] struggling to fit into a pair of Brooke Shields' designer jeans."—Sportswriter H.G. Reza.

"Fernando Valenzuela apparently wants to be paid by the pound."—Sportswriter Furman Bisher.

"I was getting old, I had problems with my back, my neck, my knees. I thought I had a few more years left, so I was gonna get after it. I took one day off after the 1999 season and started lifting weights. I bounced on the trampoline with a medicine ball, rode the stationary bike every day for 40 minutes, busting my tail. I got my weight down … and then I blew my arm out. It goes right back to the statement I made a few years ago. I ain't never seen a guy on the disabled list with pulled fat."—Rod Beck.

"Foxx is, in his own estimation, 12 pounds overweight at 212, and now he has double chins along with his double X's."—The *Stars and Stripes* on Jimmie Foxx's 1944 comeback.

"I only eat two meals a day, I just like snacks."—Tiger slugger Willie Horton, who invariably reported to spring training seriously overweight.

"Look at Gossage. He's six feet four and most of it is fat. He pitches maybe an inning a week. And for that, they pay him a million dollars a year. And you know what? He's worth it."—Yankee teammate Rudy May.

"Question: What does Sid [Fernandez] think the Eat to Win diet is? Answer: The more he eats, the more he wins."—Bob Klapisch and John Harper in *The Worst Team Money Could Buy* (1993); Fernandez ballooned to 260 pounds before shedding 45 pounds and regaining some of his form (pitching, not physique).

"Chubby Dean, Jerry Lumpe, Bill Pounds, Fatty Briody, Fats Dantonio, Jack Berly, Jumbo Shoeneck, Jumbo Brown, Stumpy Eddington, Stubby Overmire, Tubby Spencer"

See also *Height* and *Umpires* — Weight Problem.

Carlton Molesworth, a pitcher for the Washington Nationals in the 1890s, was 5'6" and weighed 200 pounds.

The inappropriately named Larry McLean was one of the heaviest player of the early 20th century with 228 pounds on his 6'5" frame. He managed to get into a crouch as a catcher for 761 Major League games.

Bob Fothergill's nickname was "Fats," in reference to his 5'10", 230-pound frame. Two apocryphal stories about him: Leo Durocher once complained that there were two men in the batter's box when Fothergill was batting. Fothergill supposedly bit an umpire after complaining about a third strike call while he was fasting to lose weight. Fothergill had a lifetime pinch-hitting average of over .300 from 1922 through 1933, the highest for any player with 200 or more pinch hit at-bats.

Jumbo Brown was a 6'4", 265 (or 295)-pound pitcher in the early 1930s with a lifetime record of 33–31 for five clubs. Yankee manager Joe McCarthy only started him against the pitiful A's in Philadelphia because: "It's the only way I know to fill Shibe Park."

Tigers pitcher Mickey Lolich was not known for his svelte figure, but capped his career with three wins in the 1968 World Series. After he retired, he bought a donut shop.

In the 1960s, 6'6" Frank Howard weighed in at as much as 315 pounds, even though he was supposed to stay under 260 pounds or risk being fined.

Charles Kerfeld was a 6'6" relief pitcher for the Astros who ate his way out of the National League in the 1980s. His weight, over 260 pounds, coupled with later arm problems, forced him down to the minor leagues.

Dwight Eisenhower once asked Dizzy Dean on the golf course how such a great athlete could let himself become so overweight (close to 300 pounds). Dean's response: "Mr. President. I was on a diet for 25 years. Now that I'm makin' some money, I'm makin' sure that I eat enough to make up for the lean years."

C.C. Sabathia of the Indians pitched in the 2000s at 6'7" and 290 pounds.

In college at Rice, Lance Berkman was known as "Lumpy Lance" and "Lumpy Kruk," in honor of poorly sculpted John Kruk. Nevertheless, Berkman hit 41 home runs, drove in 138 runners, and hit .438 during his career there.

Cutting Remarks.

"A fat tub of goo." — Television host David Letterman describing pitcher Terry Forster. Forster is generously listed in *The Baseball Encyclopedia* as 6'3" and 200 pounds, but by the end of his career he weighed well over 200 pounds. Forster's retort: "A waist is a terrible thing to mind."

The full text of Letterman's comments: "The fattest man in all of professional sports. I mean the guy is a balloon. He must weight 300 pounds. The guys doing the ballgame, not once do they mention that this guy is enormous. They pretend the guy couldn't be in better shape. He's a load. Not once, when they see this mammoth figure, this silo, get up in the bullpen…. I just want them to say, 'Terry Forster's warming up. He's a lefthander, an ERA of 3.5. What a fat tub of goo.'"

Weight Loss During Season.

"It looks like the same thing George Scott wore around his waist when he was trying to lose weight." — Pitcher Bill Lee on the retractable roof at Montreal's Olympic Stadium.

Red Sox catcher Carlton Fisk once lost almost 40 pounds over the course of a season because of the demands of his position.

During one of his typically underachieving seasons, Braves third baseman Bob Horner received a bonus of $7,692.31 each time he weighed in at no more than 215 pounds on every Friday that the club played a home game. There is no record of how many times he collected.

Faux Pas. In the late 1990s this author attended a Dodger Stadium game with his fantasy league compatriot, Michael Monk, a former Padres owner. Monk still had access to the owner's field box seats in visiting ballparks, so we sat in the second row behind Padres owner John Moores' wife. She was friendly and engaging, and when aging and rotund Tony Gwynn walked by us on the field, this author asked jokingly if she could do something about Gwynn's enormous weight gain. She politely "shushed" the author, whispering that Gwynn's wife was sitting in the seat next to her (with Don Newcombe's wife). Oops.

Trend Toward Heavier Players. The Reds studied their players between 1981 and 1989 and determined that the average weight had increased from 189 to 205 pounds, while body fat declined from 15 to 10 percent.

Playing Weight. In 1882 in Buffalo, teams known as the "Phats" and "Leans" played a series of games. The Phats were composed of players weighing at least 200 pounds and the Leans a maximum of 140 pounds.

Though accurate height and weight figures from the first quarter of the 20th century are sketchy, most players stood between 5–8 and 5–11 and weighed between 150 and 180 pounds.

Father of Baseball

"Although [Alexander] Cartwright was the 'father of baseball,' he did not stay around long enough to see the growth of his child." — Harvey Frommer in *Primitive Baseball* (1988).

"In his time, Henry Chadwick was known as the Father of Baseball, and the title fits him as well as anyone. Originator of the box score and block-style standings, codifier of rules and statistics, grand proselytizer for the nascent sport, Chadwick was indispensable to the early growth of the game." — Tom Nawrocki in *The National Pastime*.

See also *Origins of Baseball*.

A number of individuals have at one time been dubbed "The Father of Baseball":

Abner Doubleday was often erroneously credited in the early 20th century as the Father of Baseball because he supposedly invented the game in 1839 in *Cooperstown*.

Alexander Cartwright might be the most qualified to hold the title as a symbol of the efforts of members of the 1840s New York Knickerbockers to codify the rules of the game and begin organized play. However, revisionist historians might choose a lesser-known candidate from that club. Dr. D. I. Adams served for 15 years on the Knickerbocker rules committee and in 1895 *The Sporting News* called him the Father of Baseball.

The Alexander Cartwright claim as the Father of Baseball may be attributable to 19th century sports historian Charles A. Peverelly, who wrote a general sports history in 1866. *The Book of American Pastimes* chronicled virtually every state's baseball association and the more prominent teams of the era, and he attributed the rise of the sport to Cartwright.

Henry Chadwick, often referred to in early 20th century baseball writing as "Father Chadwick," received distinction because of his extensive involvement in developing the rules of the game, promoting baseball through sportswriting, editing baseball guides and creating the box score.

Harry Wright of the 1869 professional Cincinnati Red Stockings and the 1870s Boston Red Stockings has been called the father of *professional* baseball. The choice is based on his leadership in innovative training methods, ballpark administration, equipment evolution, an international trip to Britain, and his participation in forming the National Association in 1871.

Fathers and Sons

"The only thing my father and I have in common is that our similarities are different." — Dale Berra, Pittsburgh Pirate shortstop and son of noted linguist Yogi Berra.

"Baseball's unique possession is the fan's memory of the times his daddy took him to see the great players of his youth. The excitement of those hours, the step they represented in his growth and the part those afternoons — even one afternoon — played in his relationship with his father are bound up in his feelings toward the game. When he takes his own son to the game, as his father once took him, there is a spanning of the generations that is warm and rich and — if I may use the word — lovely." — Bill Veeck, Jr., in *The Hustler's Handbook* (1965).

"I'm glad Mel, Sr., can't still pitch." — White Sox manager Jeff Torborg about 1960s Yankee pitcher Mel Stottlemyre, after Torborg watched Stottlemyre's sons Mel, Jr., of the Royals and Todd of the Blue Jays defeat the White Sox in the same week.

"[H]e was not an orphan (if he was, he was the only orphan whose father watched him pitch for the Red Sox)." — Lee Allen and Tom Meany in *Kings of the Diamond* (1965), on claims that Babe Ruth was an orphan.

"It must be her. My dad doesn't do anything but sit on the couch and watch TV." — Pitcher Sidney Ponson on getting his athletic genes from his mother.

"Freddy Parent, Mark Parent, Stan Papi, Pop Lytle, Pop Rising, Dad Hale, Dad Clark, Dad Meek, John Papa, Pop Boy Smith, Kid Baldwin, Kid Nichols, Kid Camp, Harry Child"

All-Star Game. Bret Boone of Cincinnati was a 1998 All-Star replacement for the injured Sammy Sosa, which raised the number to six for father-son All-Stars. His father, Bob Boone, played in the 1976–1979 All-Star Games. The other five All-Star sons and their four fathers:

Moises and Felipe Alou
Barry and Bobby Bonds
Ken Griffey, Jr. and Sr.

Alomars, two sons, Roberto and Sandy, Jr., and father Sandy Sr.

In the Majors. Over 100 father/son combinations have played in the Major Leagues.

Playing Together.

Griffeys.

"No. I don't give Kenny too many tips. He never listens to anything I say." — Ken Griffey, Sr.

The Griffeys are the first father/son combination to play in the Major Leagues at the same time. Junior played for the Seattle Mariners and Senior originally played for the Reds. He returned to the Reds near the end of his career and the club released him during the 1990 season to enable him to clear waivers into the American League. He signed with the Mariners so that he could play with Junior.

On August 31, 1990, father and son started in the outfield together in a 5–2 defeat of the Royals. They hit back-to-back home runs on September 14, 1990.

Raines.

In 2001, Tim Raines joined the Orioles near the end of his career after overcoming Lupus, joining his son, Tim, Jr., on the ros-

ter. On October 4, 2001, Junior played centerfield and Senior played left field in the Orioles 5–4 loss.

McRaes.

During spring training in 1986 there was talk among the Royals of having son Brian McRae stay with the parent club so that father Hal McRae could play with him. Although Brian was sent down to the minors before they played together in a regular-season game (he later acknowledged that he was not ready for the Majors), the two played together in one spring training game.

Executive Decisions. In the early 1930s Bill Veeck, Sr., hired temperamental Rogers Hornsby to manage the Cubs. In the early 1950s, Bill Veeck, Jr., hired him to manage the Browns. When Junior signed Hornsby, his mother wrote him to ask: "What makes you think you're smarter than your daddy was?"

On the day Hornsby was fired, mom purportedly wrote again: "What did I tell you?"

Grandfather/Father/Son.

Boones.

"Bowden has taken the pressure off me. Now he can give Bret his allowance." — 1997 Royals manager Bob Boone on the Reds signing his son, Bret, to a new $11.45 million contract over four years. Jim Bowden was the Reds' general manager.

Ray Boone played infield primarily in the 1950s for various American League clubs. Son Bob Boone was a long-time catcher for the Phillies, Angels and Royals. Grandson Bret, a former USC player, started at second base for the Mariners late in the 1992 season to complete the cycle.

Bells.

Gus, Buddy and David Bell became the second three-generation baseball players when David came up to the Indians in 1995. On July 20, 2000, another grandson, Mike, joined Buddy and Gus as the first three-generation family to play for the same team, the Reds.

Home Runs. Thornton Lee of the White Sox gave up a home run to Ted Williams on September 17, 1939. His son, Don Lee of the Senators, gave up a home run to Williams on September 2, 1960.

The record for most home runs by a father and son in the Major Leagues was held by Yogi and Dale Berra, who totaled 407. Bobby and Barry Bonds broke that record in 1989, and Barry continues to add to his dad's total of 332.

Most Hits.

"They will surpass the father-son tandem of Buddy Bell and Yogi Berra [sic]." — Ralph Kiner on the Bonds family.

Gus and Buddy Bell amassed 4,090 hits in their careers, the leaders until the 2000s. The Ken Griffeys (Jr. and Sr.) had 4,223 hits through the 2003 season. Barry and Bobby Bonds had 4,481 hits through the 2003 season.

Hitting Records. Pitcher Dave LaRoche's son, Adam, made his mark when he tied the Major League record with four doubles in a game for the Braves, on May 15, 2004. The record had last been tied by Braves second baseman Marcus Giles, who broke his collarbone during LaRoche's big day.

Pitchers. Father Dizzy (170) and son Steve (88) Trout combined for 258 career wins.

On August 15th, 1998, it was father versus son, as Todd Stottlemyre came to Yankee Stadium to pitch for his team, the Texas Rangers. His father, Mel, was the pitching coach for the New York Yankees. The person who was in the middle was Todd's mother, Jean, who had to choose between cheering for her husband or her son. Mel said, "She'll be rooting for Todd. No mother alive could watch her son and not root for him. It'll be very difficult for her."

Mel was circumspect: "It's going to be very difficult for me, too. I'm going to make myself enjoy the game and whatever happens, happens. I'm still going to enjoy it. I'll probably try to hold my emotions inside as much as I can and realize I've got a son pitching on the other side and I've got a job to do." Todd got the win, 16–5.

Managing Their Children. Earle Mack is one of only a handful of Major League players who played for their fathers. In Earle's first Major League game under Connie in 1910 for the A's, he hit a single and a triple. He played in only four more games (two each in 1911 and 1914) and had no more hits in 16 Major League at-bats before moving into the front office. It was generally assumed that the Mack brothers would take over management of the club when their father retired. However, one sportswriter claimed that "Connie Mack's sons became senile before Connie did."

Billy and Cal Ripken, Jr., played for their father, Cal, Sr., while dad managed the Orioles in 1987 and for a few games in 1988. Cal also played for dad in 1985.

Dale Berra played for his father, Yogi, while they were both with the Yankees in 1985.

In 1991 Hal McRae managed his son Brian while both were with the Royals. They were together into the 1994 season.

In May 1992 former outfielder Felipe Alou was appointed manager of the Expos. Later in the month his son Moises hit his first Major League home run for the club. They were together through 1996.

Aaron Boone played for his father, Bob, with the Reds in 2001–2003.

Player Against Manager Dad. On May 25, 1998, second baseman David Bell of the Indians played against his dad's Tigers, winning 7–4. The only other players to take the field against their fathers up to that time were Bump Wills and Moises Alou.

On May 19, 2004, Giants manager Felipe Alou brought in another reliever to face his son, Moises, playing for the Cubs. Moises hit a 3–2 pitch for a home run and a 4–3 Cubs victory in the bottom of the 10th inning.

Playing Against Each Other. On August 21, 2001, the Raines family created a "first" when Tim Raines, Jr., and Tim Raines faced each other in a doubleheader between Ottawa and Rochester in the International League. Each went 1-for-3 in the opener, while Junior outperformed Senior in the second game, going 1-for-4. In spring training they faced each other when Junior was a minor leaguer hoping to make the Major League roster.

Most in the Game. On June 18, 1997, the Giants and Mariners set a Major League record when they combined to have four sons of Major Leaguers in their lineups: Stan Javier, Ken Griffey, Jr., Barry Bonds, and Jose Cruz, Jr.

Negro Leagues. Reggie Jackson's father played for the Bacharach Giants in the Negro Leagues. The fathers of Major Leaguers Jerry Hairston and Lyman Bostock also played in the Negro Leagues.

Umpires. In a 1984 spring training game, infielder Jeff Kunkel of the Rangers presented the line-up card to his father, umpire Bill Kunkel. During the game, Jeff hit a double and tried to stretch it into a triple. His father was umpiring at third base and called him out on a questionable decision. Jeff lay face-down for some time, then finally rolled over, looked at his father and said: "*You* explain it to Mom."

Major League umpires Mike Di Muro (Lou), Jerry Crawford (Shag) and Brian Gorman (Tom) all are sons of Major League umpires. All three sons umpired together for the first time in April 2000. Umpire Harry Wendelstedt's son, Hunter, also umpired in the Major Leagues.

World Series. Catcher Billy Sullivan, Sr., played for the White Sox in the 1906 World Series. Billy Sullivan, Jr., played catcher for the Tigers in the 1940 World Series. They were the first father and son to appear in the Series.

Sportswriter. Hall of Fame (Spink Award) and *Los Angeles Times* sportswriter Ross Newhan's son, David, played in the Major Leagues in 1999, but injuries forced him out. After a long rehabilitation he finally made it back in 2004, hitting a home run in his first at-bat for the Orioles.

First in Major Leagues. Herman Doscher played third base for Troy in 1879. His son Jack pitched primarily for the Dodgers in the first few years of the 20th century.

Most Years in Between Careers. Charlie Ganzel played for St. Paul of the Union Association in 1884. In 1927, 43 years later, his son Babe Ganzel played for the Senators, 13 years after his father died.

Jack Lively pitched for the 1911 Tigers. His son Bud pitched in the Major Leagues 36 years later for the 1947 Reds.

Same Team/Same Decade. Earle Brucker, Sr., and Earle Brucker, Jr., played catcher for the A's at different times in the 1940s.

Most Sons in One Year. In 1990, 25 sons of former Major Leaguers appeared in the Major Leagues. Another eight sons were drafted in the June 1991 draft. One theory has it that recent ex–Major Leaguers have been more successful financially and have the leisure time to help their sons develop into quality ballplayers.

Cecil Fielder's Son. In 1997 Cecil Fielder's son, 12-year-old Prince, was a 5'9", 200-pound seventh grader who had hit balls over the fences of the Seattle Kingdome, Milwaukee County Stadium and Tiger Stadium — at least according to his dad. He hit several balls out of the park at the Yankees' spring training site in Tampa in front of about 50 fans.

Like Father, Like Son. On April 22, 2004, senior Mike Rickert pitched a perfect game for Bowler (Wisconsin) High School against Iola-Scandinavia High. Twenty-two years earlier, to the day, his dad, Raymond, also pitched a perfect game for Bowler while a senior, against the same school and for the same coach.

Recent Draft Picks. In 2003 Tony Gwynn's son, Anthony, was drafted 39th out of San Diego State (the senior Gwynn's alma mater and where he was the coach). Fernando Valenzuela, Jr., was drafted out of UNLV in the 10th round by the Padres. Gary Gaetti's son, Joe, was drafted in the 12th round by the Rockies out of North Carolina State.

Ballpark. Felipe Alou was the first Brave to bat at Atlanta-Fulton County Stadium, in 1966. His son, Moises, playing for Montreal at the time, was the last (regular season), in 1996.

Strikeout Families. In August 1993, Nolan Ryan struck out Eduardo Perez, son of Tony Perez. The Perez family joined seven other father-son combinations to strike out against Ryan.

Mickey Mantle.

"... Mantle began talking about his father. He described his strength in holding his family together during the Depression and his courage in the last year of his life, when he knew he was dying of Hodgkin's disease but did not tell Mickey, who was in his precarious rookie season with the Yankees. 'My father was the bravest man I ever knew,' he said."—Robert Creamer in *Sports Illustrated* shortly after Mantle died.

"It was the turning point in my life."— Mantle after his father arrived in Kansas City from Oklahoma when Mantle was in a slump at the start of his career with the Yankees. When Mantle complained that he did not think he could make it in the Major Leagues, his dad started packing for them to return to work in the lead and zinc mines of his home state. After a long talk the younger Mantle was convinced to stay with baseball.

No Sympathy. Mickey Mantle related a story of a bad day at the plate in the 1950s. He was in the locker room after the game with his head in his hands, feeling like he was going to cry. Timmy Berra, Yogi Berra's young son, came over and tapped him on the knee. Mantle assumed that Timmy would console him in a boyish manner, but Timmy looked at him and said, "you stink."

Honor Thy Father. In 1994 it was discovered that a fan had placed a photograph of his father in a baseball uniform under the display case of an exhibit at the Hall of Fame. It was found during a refurbishing of the area and an intensive search began to discover the name of the father and son. It was learned that the son was Pat O'Donnell, then a 47-year-old tavern owner. His father Big Joe had died in 1966. He had played catcher for Sinclair Oil, whose company team was featured in the photo. After the refurbishing and a flood of letters to O'Donnell and the Hall, the photograph was placed back underneath the case and a story about the incident was placed in the exhibit.

Ted/John Henry Williams. See *Deaths*—Ted Williams.

Pete Rose, Jr. Rose made his Major League debut on September 1, 1997, for the Reds at Riverfront Stadium, prompting 15,000 walk-up ticket sales. Rose struck out in his first at-bat, but later singled during a 1-for-3 performance. He played in a total of 11 games, batting .143 with no home runs or RBIs.

In July 2004 Rose signed with the Lincoln Saltdogs of the Northern League. Earlier that month he had taken over on an interim basis as the manager of the Florence Freedom of the Frontier League, replacing former Reds pitcher Tom Browning. In 2002 and 2003, Rose played for the Winnipeg Goldeyes.

Ironic Choice. A 2001 Father's Day feature on ESPN aired footage of famous athletes with their fathers or children. So far, so good. The music for the piece, however, was Marvin Gaye's rendition of "How Sweet It Is to Be Loved By You." Gaye, again addicted to cocaine, was murdered by his father (who he was named after) on April Fool's Day 1984.

Books. Dick Wimmer took a summer tour of Major League parks with his two teenage sons, interviewing Major Leaguers about their dads and how they affected their Major League careers. His book about the experience is *Baseball Fathers, Baseball Sons* (1988); see also Wayne Stewart, *Fathers, Sons and Baseball* (2002).

Federal League (1914–1915)

"The Flapjack Circuit"—Dubbed by writer Joe Vila because of the number of food business owners who financed the league.

Formation. By 1912 baseball was perceived as a money-making operation and many felt that a third Major League was possible. However, a number of factors worked against the Federal League's success: fear of possible war with tensions in Europe increasing by 1915; and the automobile, movies and other leisure activities competing for fans' time, interest and money.

The Federal League was created out of the remnants of the short-lived 1912 *United States League* and operated as a minor league in 1913. A few of the Federal League owners had been owners in the United States League. The first Federal League president was John T. Powers of Chicago, who had unsuccessfully tried to start the *Columbian League* in 1912.

Ballparks. Within three months in early 1913, six ballparks were built or renovated. In Baltimore, park construction began on February 1 and was completed at a cost of $82,000. It was built directly across the street from the International League Baltimore ballpark.

Brooklyn and Chicago built parks using the same plans, which means that a version of what later was known as *Wrigley Field* was built in Brooklyn on the old Washington Park site.

Financial Backing.

"I'll stand at the battery [Manhattan's waterfront] and I'll take on any of them [Major League owners] in pitching dollars into the sea; and we'll see who quits first."—Harry Sinclair, the wealthiest Federal League owner, with a net worth in excess of $50 million. He had so much money that during the Depression on May 2, 1936, he bet $500,000 on Kentucky Derby entry "Brevity." The horse lost by a nose.

When Brooklyn owner Robert Ward died in October 1918, he had lost $1 million in the Federal League venture.

Structure of the Organization. The Federal League was structured with a single corporation at the head. The corporation was given a $25,000 guarantee by each club and the league held each stadium lease. This was done to insure that the teams finished the season.

1913/Minor League Season. The Federal League was considered a minor league in 1913, with six teams completing a 120-game schedule. The first teams were in Chicago, Cleveland, Covington (later Cincinnati and then Kansas City 41 games into the season), Indianapolis, Pittsburgh and St. Louis. No major stars were signed for the 1913 season, though retired pitcher Cy Young managed the Cleveland club.

Transition to Major League Status.

"I believe that man Gilmore not only can convince a millionaire that the moon is made of green cheese, but can induce him to invest money in a cheese factory on the moon."—National League president John Tener on Federal League president James A. Gilmore.

At a secret meeting in Indianapolis on August 2, 1913, James Gilmore was elected president. He succeeded John Powers, who was perceived as too weak for the job. Gilmore was a wealthy Chicagoan who was president of a manufacturing company that produced ventilation machines. He has also been described as a coal and paper executive.

Gilmore immediately took a number of former Major League Baseball executives into his league office. They included Horace S. Fogel, the bitter former owner of the Philadelphia Phillies. Fogel announced his intent to run teams in New York and Philadelphia, but he never received the chance.

Roster Limits. Because they had no minor league affiliations, all Federal League clubs had to carry 30 players in order to control players being developed. At one point, however, the Federal League warehoused players in the northeastern Colonial League. That minor league was part of Organized Baseball and was allowing the arrangement in contravention of the National Agreement, which barred its member leagues from affiliating with leagues that were not part of Organized Baseball.

Major League Response. American League president Ban Johnson proposed to fight the Federal League by creating a new Major League consisting of the better American Association and International League teams. The Pacific Coast League, always agitating to be a third Major League, objected to Johnson's proposal on the ground that it violated the National Agreement of 1903. Whether or not the PCL's objection carried any weight, the plan never went forward.

The American and National Leagues also talked seriously of expanding to 10 teams each to combat the Federal League. Instead, they chose the less costly path of blacklisting all departed players. At a secret meeting in February 1915 between Gilmore and Ban

Johnson, Johnson rejected Gilmore's plan for recognition of the Federal League as a third Major League.

Players Signed. At first the Federal League only signed players who were not under contract with a team in Organized Baseball. As competition became nastier (in part because of a lawsuit filed against the Chicago Whales to invalidate one of its player contracts), the Federal League went after all players in Organized Baseball whether or not they had an existing contract. Because the National and American Leagues were afraid of how the courts would treat the reserve clause, the clause was not used by the established leagues as the basis for retrieving their ballplayers through court.

The only established stars signed early by Federal League teams for the 1914 season were pitchers Chief Bender and Eddie Plank. Both were key pitchers in the 1914 World Series and both had signed contracts with Federal League clubs before the Series was completed. By April 1, 1914, 59 former Major League players were on Federal League rosters (39 National Leaguers and 20 American Leaguers). Each club averaged seven former National or American League players. Among them were Joe Tinker, who was nearing the end of his career, Hal Chase and Three Finger Brown.

The Federal League eventually signed 221 players who had been in Organized Baseball, including 81 Major Leaguers and 140 minor leaguers. A total of 18 Major Leaguers and 25 minor leaguers jumped contracts to play in the Federal League. At least 63 Major League players and 115 minor leaguers disregarded the reserve clause to play in the Federal League. Eventually there were 264 Federal League players, of which 60% had previous Major League experience.

1914–1915 Federal League Clubs.
Baltimore Terrapins (1914–1915)
Brooklyn Feds/TipTops (1914–1915)
Buffalo BufFeds (1914) Blues (1915)
Chicago ChiFeds (1914) Whales (1915)
Indianapolis Hoosiers/Feds (1914)
Kansas City Packers (1914–1915)
Newark Peppers (1915)
Pittsburgh Rebels (1914–1915)
St. Louis Terriers (1914–1915)

1914/First Major League Season. The Federal League expanded to eight teams in 1914, dropping Cleveland and adding Brooklyn, Buffalo and Baltimore. Indianapolis was the winner of the 1914 Federal League pennant and the league's war with Organized Baseball was front-page news for the entire season.

First Game. The first Federal League game was played on April 13, 1914, as Buffalo visited Baltimore's Terrapin Park. Over 27,000 fans paid their way in while a total of approximately 30,000 watched the game. Baltimore defeated Buffalo 3–1 behind the pitching of Jack Quinn.

At the same time, directly across the street at Oriole Park, only 1,500 fans watched the National League Giants under John McGraw play an exhibition against Jack Dunn's International League Orioles. Dunn's Orioles suffered from the Federal League competition that season, which eventually forced him to sell some of his stars, including Babe Ruth, to the Red Sox.

1915 Pennant Winner. Because Indianapolis had been so strong in winning the 1914 pennant, the club was moved to Newark for the 1915 season to have a second New York area presence. However, the 1915 club drew poorly and was a flop. The Chicago Whales were the 1915 pennant winners with an 86–66 record under manager Joe Tinker, just ahead of St. Louis and its 87–67 record. The mayor of Chicago tried to arrange a round-robin World Series, but the established leagues would have nothing to do with it.

Effect on Major League Salaries. See *Salaries*.

Effect on Major League Profits. Only three National League and three American League clubs made a profit in 1914, as did only two Federal League clubs. The Federal League had to cut base ticket prices in many cities from 50 cents to 25 cents.

Clubs with Minor League Rivals. Kansas City, Indianapolis and Baltimore of the Federal League competed in their cities with local minor league clubs.

Antitrust Litigation. In January 1915 the Federal League filed an *Antitrust* suit against Major League Baseball. It was filed in federal court in Chicago and was presided over by future commissioner Kenesaw Mountain Landis. The trial took two weeks and Federal League stars Three Finger Brown and Joe Tinker testified.

Landis delayed ruling on the case for almost a year while the Federal League fell apart. The suit was eventually dropped and is different from (though often confused with) the *Antitrust* lawsuit later filed by the Baltimore Federal League club that did not share in the settlement proceeds distributed by the Major Leagues to certain Federal League clubs (see below).

Settlement with the Major Leagues. The Federal League struggled through the 1915 season, but the enormous wealth of Harry Sinclair and other owners would have allowed the league to last through 1916. When Sinclair decided to move his team from New Jersey to New York for the 1916 season and continue the battle, the National League showed a willingness to compromise. At a secret meeting between National League president John Tener, Pittsburgh owner Barney Dreyfuss, and James Gaffney, Gilmore and Sinclair of the Federal League, a compromise was worked out.

The settlement was not finalized until December 1916, supposedly because of Ban Johnson's refusal to make the agreed-upon settlement payments. Part of the plan called for Sinclair to take over a number of Federal League player contracts and sell them to the National and American Leagues.

A total of $600,000 was paid to key Federal League owners. The Wards received $400,000, Sinclair received $100,000 and $40,000 went to Edward Gwinner of the Pittsburgh Rebels. The Wards received $20,000 a year for 20 years and retained title to their Brooklyn ballpark. Sinclair received $10,000 per year for 10 years and the Pittsburgh owners received $10,000 per year over four years.

As a result of the settlement, Phil Ball was allowed to buy the American League club in St. Louis and the National League paid $50,000 to help him do it. Chicago Whales owner Charles Weegham was allowed to buy the Cubs, which enabled the National League to rid itself of the embarrassing Charles Murphy.

Kansas City and Buffalo were weak Federal League franchises and were left out of the settlement. The Baltimore owners were offered $50,000, but rejected it and challenged the Major Leagues in court on *Antitrust* grounds. Baltimore won at the lower court level but lost in the U.S. Supreme Court in 1922. Justice Oliver Wendell Holmes wrote the opinion, holding that baseball was exempt from the federal antitrust laws because it was "not trade or commerce in commonly accepted use of those words." This ruling helped preserve the reserve clause until late 1975.

Dispersal of Federal League Players. Except for the Chicago and St. Louis players (who were absorbed by the Cubs and Browns), the Federal League players were put into a pool to be bid for by National and American League clubs. Baltimore was not paid any settlement money and its players were left out of the pool because it appeared that Baltimore would move into the International League. Many Federal League stars were not picked up by the two established Major Leagues when the war ended. Among them were Steve Evans, Ted Easterly, Vin Campbell and Rebel Oakes.

Benny Kauff, the premier star of the Federal League, received $35,000 from the Giants, but later was barred from baseball because of a criminal charge which many believed was a pretext to blackball him because of his Federal League involvement (see also *Felons*).

Some sources contend that the shortage of players brought on by World War I helped integrate the Federal League players back into the Major Leagues. However, the Federal League dissolved after the 1915 season and World War I had no appreciable effect on Major League Baseball until mid–1918. A total of 137 former Federal League players signed with teams in Organized Baseball, including 36 with the National League and 21 with the American League.

Hall of Fame. Six players from the Federal League made it to the Hall of Fame: Chief Bender, Three Finger Brown, Eddie Plank, Bill McKechnie, Edd Roush and Joe Tinker.

Chicago Fixtures. Rollie Zeider and Dutch Zwilling are the only Major Leaguers to play for all three 20th century Chicago teams; the White Sox, Cubs and Whales.

Book. Marc Okonnen, *The Federal League, 1914–1915: Baseball's Third Major League* (1989).

Donald Fehr (1948–)

"Baseball has nothing to fear but Fehr itself." — The *Village Voice* on the eve of the 1994 baseball strike.

Donald Fehr has been the executive director of the players union since 1983.

Fehr became executive director of the Major League Baseball Players Association (MLBPA) in 1983 at the age of 35. When Fehr was between the ages of nine and 12 he read the entire *World Book Encyclopedia*. A graduate of Missouri Law School, he clerked for a federal judge before beginning practice with a Kansas City firm specializing in labor law. He handled Andy Messersmith's free-agency case and successfully represented the players union in the owners' appeal.

When the case concluded, an impressed Marvin Miller asked Fehr to join the MLBPA in 1977 as general counsel. When Miller retired in December 1982, former federal mediator Kenneth Moffett took over the union. The players replaced him with Fehr 11 months later. By 1993 Fehr's annual salary was $550,000. During the 1994 strike he became the focal point of the public's perception of the players' greed.

Bob Feller (1918–)

Hall of Fame 1962

"And like the man biting the dog, it's news when Rapid Robert loses a ball game." — The *Stars and Stripes* military newspaper.

"You talk about a ballplayer having magnetism, Bob Feller had it, with plenty to spare. He was continually hounded by the press, by well-wishers, by fans, by people wanting something from him.... But I'll say this, with it all, he kept a pretty level head. There weren't many ballplayers who had that kind of magnetism." — George Case.

Feller was the preeminent pitcher of the late 1930s and 1940s, winning 266 games over 17 war-interrupted seasons.

See also *Fastest Pitchers*.

Robert William Andrew Feller, "Rapid Robert," from Van Meter, Iowa, had his father guide his early baseball career. Dad signed his 17-year-old son to a contract with the Indians. Feller had 15 strikeouts in his first start at age 17, 17 in a game three weeks

later, 18 in a game at age 19, a no-hitter at 21 and 107 wins by the time he was 22 after the 1941 season.

His career was interrupted by **World War II** and he missed almost four full seasons. He returned spectacularly, winning 26 games to lead the league in his first full season back. He also had 10 shutouts that year on his way to 46 for his career. He won 20 games in 1947 to lead the league and won 22 games in 1951 to lead again. Feller began to fade after that and retired after posting an 0–4 record in 1956. He won 266 games over 17 full seasons, including three no-hitters.

Feller was a superb businessman who formed a business corporation while still a player. He earned large sums on postseason barnstorming tours and product endorsements. He became an insurance executive in Ohio and in 1969 was voted baseball's greatest living right-handed pitcher.

Books. Bob Feller, *Strikeout Story* (1947); Bob Feller and Bill Gilbert, *Now Pitching, Bob Feller* (1990); Gene Schoor, *Bob Feller* (1962); John Sickels, *Bob Feller: Ace of the Greatest Generation* (2003).

Felons (and Arrests, Misdemeanors and Miscellaneous Other Non-Felony Acts)

"I'm an escaped car thief. I broke out of prison to see the Cubs in the World Series." — Jim Belushi in *Taking Care of Business* (1990).

"You have to remember that most of Billy's boyhood friends are in San Quentin." — Broadcaster Jerry Coleman on Billy Martin's tough Oakland neighborhood.

"I'm convinced that every boy, in his heart, would rather steal second base than an automobile." — Justice Tom Clark.

"What they should do is give Candlestick Park back to the city and use it as a prison. Then, they could sentence the convicts to playing baseball … naked." — Giants coach Jim Lefebvre.

"Leo [Durocher] would play a convicted rapist if he could turn the double play." — Jim Bouton in *"I Managed Good, But Boy Did They Play Bad,"* with Neil Offen (1973).

"Knowing that if we ever got to the seventh game of the World Series, that with one phone call, we could get the opposing pitcher whacked." — One of David Letterman's "Top Ten Good Things About Playing Baseball in New York," presented by manager Buck Showalter.

"The prosecutors in the Kobe Bryant case are the '62 Mets of jurisprudence." — Michael Ventre on MSNBC after the Colorado prosecutors had another setback in the prosecution of the basketball star.

"Con Lucid, Jimmy Outlaw, Tom Crooks, Wally Hood, Don Hood"

See also *Alcoholism*, *Drug Abuse*, *Gambling and Fixed Games* and *Murder*.

Benny Kauff. Kauff was the "Ty Cobb of the Federal League," but in 1920 while with the Giants he was ruled ineligible for the Major Leagues by Judge Landis. The ban was not for gambling on baseball, but for being implicated in a stolen car ring.

Kauff was defended at trial by future Boston Braves owner Judge Emil Fuchs (never a judge, but an attorney). Kauff was acquitted, but Judge Landis disagreed with the verdict and refused to reinstate him. Kauff obtained an injunction allowing him to play, but then dropped the suit and never returned to baseball.

Edwin "Alabama" Pitts. At age 19 in 1930, Pitts was convicted of armed robbery for stealing $76 from a grocery store. He was sent to Sing Sing prison in upstate New York. After five years in prison he was eligible for parole and signed a $200-per-month contract with Albany, managed by former Cubs star Johnny Evers. The contract was voided by both the International League president and the National Association president because Pitts was a convicted felon. Despite an enormous national groundswell of public support for Pitts (he even appeared on the "Kate Smith Hour" on NBC Radio), the National Association executive committee rejected his attempt to play. The committee then asked that the issue be submitted to Judge Landis. After supporting the committee's view in a written report, at the end of the document he nevertheless reversed the decision by concluding that it would have a "destructive effect" on Pitts' rehabilitation.

Following his reinstatement, Pitts hit only .233 in 43 games for Albany and fielded poorly. After the season he played football in the NFL with the Philadelphia Eagles. He returned for a few more minor league games over the next five years but had little success. He died after being stabbed on June 6, 1941. His killer was pardoned after the governor concluded that Pitts had been drinking heavily and forced himself on the killer's girlfriend.

Ron LeFlore. Perhaps the most celebrated ex-convict to play Major League Baseball was LeFlore, whose life story was later made into a book, *Breakout*, by LeFlore with Jim Hawkins (1978). It was made into a television movie, "One in a Million," starring LeVar Burton of "Roots" fame.

At 17 LeFlore was convicted of robbing a liquor store. He received a 5-to-15 year sentence as a first offender. He was in Jackson State prison in southern Michigan when Major League scouts discovered him. LeFlore had been befriended by an inmate who had some coaching experience.

As LeFlore was nearing his parole date, the Tigers and manager Billy Martin met him and prison officials inside the prison. He was given a tryout during a furlough to Tiger Stadium on his 24th birthday, June 16, 1972. LeFlore had no high school experience in baseball or football, though he was also scouted in prison as a halfback by Dick "Night Train" Lane for Wilberforce College. A little more than a year later, after only a few months in the minor leagues, he was in the Major Leagues with the Tigers. LeFlore first claimed to be born in 1952, then 1950, and finally admitted to 1948.

LeFlore is the only Major Leaguer to lead both leagues in steals: the American League with 68 for the Tigers in 1978 and the National League with 97 for the Expos in 1980. He finished his nine-year career in 1982 with a .288 average and 455 stolen bases. He later ran successful baseball schools in Florida, tried his hand as an umpire, played in the ill-fated Senior Baseball League and managed a year in the independent Northeast League.

Denny McLain. Despite McLain's infamy over his later felony convictions, his first brush with the law involved *Gambling*.

Gates Brown.

"I took a little English, a little math, some science, a few hubcaps, and some wheelcovers." — The Tigers pinch hitter on his high school felony record in Ohio. Brown received a 1-to-5 year prison sentence for breaking and entering while still a teenager. He served 21 months and then signed a $7,000 bonus contract with the Tigers. He hit a pinch home run in his first Major League at-bat.

Mitch Williams. In November 1995, former pitcher Mitch "Wild Thing" Williams was cleared of rape charges filed against him by a Kentucky woman in February 1994.

Jose/Ozzie Canseco.

"This just in. The Hall of Fame has announced that if Jose Canseco is inducted, he'll go in wearing an orange jumpsuit and his jersey No. 168943." — Jim Armstrong of the *Denver Post*.

"If you're a real baseball purist like me, you know the season doesn't really begin until Jose Canseco gets arrested." — David Letterman on the fast-driving Canseco. In 2002, after he retired in May of that year, Canseco and his twin brother Ozzie pleaded guilty to charges they beat up two men in a nightclub fight on Halloween night, 2001. The plea bargain allowed the two former Major Leaguers to avoid jail time, as they agreed to probation and community service. They were also ordered to attend anger management classes. See also *Drugs and Drug Abuse.*

John D'Acquisto. In December 1995, the former Major Leaguer pitcher was arrested on charges of trying to pass off a forged $200 million certificate of deposit as collateral on a deal at Prudential Securities.

Jose Mesa. In April 1997 the Indians reliever went to trial on claims of rape, gross sexual imposition and theft. He was acquitted later in the month. A second trial for possession of a loaded gun was dropped after a judge ruled that the gun was illegally obtained in a search of Mesa's vehicle. Mesa received a standing ovation when he appeared in his first game of the season (the home opener) two days after the verdict.

Wil Cordero. In June 1997 the Red Sox outfielder was arrested and charged with assaulting his wife. He was alleged to have slapped her, hit her on the head with a phone, and threatening to kill her. In November 1997 he pleaded guilty and was sentenced to a 90-day jail sentence, suspended for two years.

Mark Whiten. The Yankees outfielder, who played for seven teams during one six-season stretch, was arrested for allegedly sexually assaulting a 31-year-old woman in July 1997, only four days after the birth of his second child.

Bobby Chouinard. In October 2000, the Rockies pitcher pleaded guilty to aggravated assault for abusing his wife and agreed to serve a year in jail. Chouinard served his time in Colorado during the off-season. Chouinard was under contract to the Diamondbacks when he was arrested in December 1999 at his Phoenix home after he hit his wife, Erica, and held a loaded gun to her head while she begged for her life, police said. The Diamondbacks had released him at his request in February 2000.

Richard Ankiel. In May 2000, the father of then-Cardinals rookie pitcher Rick Ankiel was arrested for allegedly throwing a loaded handgun from his car. The elder Ankiel later began serving an almost six-year sentence for participating in a cocaine and marijuana trafficking operation.

Kirby Puckett. A member of the World Sports Humanitarian Hall of Fame, in 2003 Puckett was found not guilty of false imprisonment, fifth-degree criminal sexual conduct and fifth-degree assault. A woman claimed that in September 2002 Puckett forced her into a men's room and groped her breast hard enough to cause a bruise. The jury didn't believe Puckett, but followed the law exactly, which required his intent to injure the woman. Puckett's community ambassador contract with the Twins was not renewed in October 2002, after he was in that position since his retirement in 1996. Puckett's stellar reputation was sullied further in 2002 when various publications reported on his numerous infidelities before his divorce that year. He was also fat, fat, fat, by 2002.

Toe Nash. Nash was a teenage phenom in the late 1990s who dropped out of high school at 15 and was discovered by an agent living near New Orleans. His physical attributes made up for his raw talent, and clubs drooled over the possibilities. He was signed by the Devil Rays, who then released him in September 2002 when he was released from jail after serving eight months for having sex with a 15-year-old girl. The Reds then picked him up, but terminated his contract in February 2003 for "legal reasons." That ended Nash's attempts to play professionally.

Terry Adams. In September 2003 the Phillies reliever was charged with misdemeanor assault charges for allegedly attacking his wife in a New York hotel room.

Ramon Castro. The backup catcher for the Marlins was charged with raping a woman in his hotel room in 2003.

Milton Bradley. Bradley was given a three-day jail sentence for bad behavior while being issued a speeding ticket on August 30, 2003. He refused to sign the ticket, rolled up his window and drove away.

Spousal Abuse in Reverse. On April 2, 2002, sometime actress Tawny Kitaen, age 40, was arrested for attacking husband Chuck Finley, who was pitching for the Indians at the time. Finley was scratched from his start (and scratched up) after Kitaen was charged with spousal abuse and battery.

Sting Operation. In 1991 federal marshals in Chicago arrested 17 felons who responded to a letter offering complimentary season tickets to the White Sox home opener. The sting, dubbed Operation Home Run, sent out 2,500 letters to "winners," promising free tickets, sportswear and door prizes. When asked why so few responded to a White Sox promotion, the attorney handling the operation said: "There are a lot of Cubs fans out there."

Television Exposure. On August 30, 2004, Reds fan Charles Baker, age 27, caught Adam Dunn's 40th home run ball in Cincinnati. He chatted on-air with television broadcaster Chris Welsh during the game. An off-duty policeman recognized Baker as wanted in Ohio for various criminal infractions, and called the Cincinnati police. Unfortunately, Baker was gone before police could catch up to him. In May 2003 a man wanted for parole violation was spotted on the "Kiss Cam" at Great American Ballpark, and he was quickly apprehended.

Petty Theft.

"Roy Weatherly, the Yankee outfielder, was deprived of gasoline rations for six months for allegedly falsifying a request for auto fuel. Roy isn't much worried as he's due to go in the Army soon."—The *Stars and Stripes* military newspaper in March 1944.

Blue Jays pitching prospect Pasqual Coco was released by the club in March 2003 after reportedly stealing money from teammate Diegomar Markwell's locker. Coco told reporters that there was a "good reason" he took the money.

Prison Break. In the 1930s at California's Folsom prison, an annual game between Major Leaguers and the prison team was stopped when it was discovered that two prisoners had escaped. With the professionals leading 24–5 at the end of the 7th inning, the game was cancelled and guards went after the two prisoners, who were found three hours later. The Major League players included Ernie Lombardi, Ernie Bonham, Gus Suhr, Joe Marty and Johnny Babich.

O.J. Simpson. On the night in October 1995 when Simpson was acquitted of double-murder charges in Los Angeles, the Dodgers played their first play-off game against the Reds at Dodger Stadium. Six fans in the upper deck took off their shirts to reveal "G-U-I-L-T-Y" spelled out on their chests in blue paint. Many in the crowd began chanting "guilty" along with the six exhibitionists.

Mark Fuhrman, one of the cops heavily involved in the Simpson murder case and trial, was in the dugout at the Yankees' workout at the Seattle Kingdome in early 1997. His brother was a long-time friend of pitcher David Wells. The relationship dispelled a rumor by Tom Keegan of the *New York Post* that Fuhrman was "brought to Seattle to throw out the first glove." [remember attorney Johnny Cochrane's mantra: "If the glove don't fit, you can't convict."]

Swift Justice. The basement of Philadelphia's ballpark contains a sitting magistrate to handle rowdy fans who get out of control. They are immediately charged and arraigned before the game is complete (this is usually done at football games, however).

Yankee Scam. In 2002 six persons were indicted for bilking the New York Mets ownership out of more than $2 million. A former executive with the club, Russell Richardson, used his insider position to work with others by creating dummy vendor invoices and other schemes.

Promotions. In 2004 the St. Paul Saints passed out mugs containing mug shots of various felons. One lucky fan received a one-off mug featuring mug shots of actor Robert Downey, Jr.

The independent River City Rascals cancelled plans in June 2004 to stage "Sports Criminals Night," by offering free admission to any fan wearing the jersey of a pro athlete convicted of a crime.

Award. Indians pitcher Carl Sadler and Royals pitcher Brian Anderson received the Steve Palermo Award for their heroism in apprehending a purse snatcher in 2003. The award is named after the former *Umpire*, who sustained serious injury while coming to the aid of an attack victim.

Oh, Martha. After Martha Stewart was convicted in 2004, the minor league Richmond Roosters offered free admission to any fan named Martha Stewart.

Random Shooter. On September 29, 2004, the Cleveland Indians team bus took a bullet near the airport in Kansas City after a game against the Royals. The apparently random shot struck the right calf of pitcher Kyle Denney. He was in the middle of a rookie hazing evening and thus wearing white cheerleader boots, which he credited with absorbing some of the bullet's impact.

Umpire Memorabilia Fraud. For umpire Al Clark's transgressions, see *Memorabilia—Umpire Fraud*.

Website. See cracksmoker.com.

Fences

"When franchises, such as Cleveland and Texas, constantly move their fences in or out … it's a giveaway that the club has, in its indecision, constructed a team that can't even play in its own park. Ever hear the Dodgers talk about a new wall for Chavez Ravine?"—Thomas Boswell in *Why Time Begins on Opening Day* (1984).

See also *Fields and Field Dimensions* and *Warning Tracks*.

Fan Enclosure. Many early fields had a four-foot fence to keep fans off the field. In 1884 Baltimore put a barbed wire fence around its field to contain fans.

Painting. In 1895 the Cincinnati Red Stockings painted their center field fence black because outfielder Bug Holliday could not see pitched balls due to the white advertisements on the wall. He batted .383 in 1894 despite the handicap.

Required Distances. After the 1884 season (1888 in one source), the National League ruled that any ball hit over a fence that was 210 feet or shorter would be ruled a ground rule double. This was done to legislate out the inequities of Chicago's ridiculously small park. It had right and left field distances of less than 200 feet, leading to 127 *Home Runs* by the home club White Stockings, an unheard-of total in that era.

In 1892 it was ruled that any ball hit over a fence that was less than 235 feet would be considered a ground rule double instead of a home run. After 1916 the National League required all new outfield fences to be at least 270 feet from home plate. Another source reported that in 1926 all new parks were required to have outfield distances of at least 250 feet.

In 1959 Rule 104a was created to require any professional field constructed after June 1, 1958, to have a minimum distance of 325 feet down the foul lines and a minimum of 400 feet to the center field fence. Nevertheless, Enron Field in Houston and PacBell Park in San Francisco, both constructed in 1999, had fences to both right and left field that were only 315 feet.

Fathoms. From 1977 to 1980 the Seattle Kingdome had its outfield wall distances marked in nautical fathoms (one fathom equals six feet).

Metric. Riverfront Stadium in Cincinnati was the first Major League ballpark to post on its outfield fences the distances using the metric system.

Fair Trade. In 1920 Lefty Grove was sold by his minor league club for $3,000 to Baltimore, which was enough to pay for a fence for the club's dilapidated ballpark. Baltimore later sold him for over $100,000 to the A's.

Movement of Outfield Fences and Rules. During the 1890s fences were often moved during the season to help certain hitters. In 1895 Charles Comiskey, owner of the St. Paul franchise in the Western League, moved in his right field fence to accommodate the seven left-handed hitters in his lineup. After being severely criticized by the league, he reverted to the prior configuration.

In the 1920s the Tigers moved temporary bleachers into place when weak hitting teams came to town and removed them when power teams arrived.

In 1928 the Braves traded for Rogers Hornsby. Braves owner Judge Emil Fuchs thought Hornsby would greatly increase the club's home run numbers, so he brought in the left field fence by installing a group of seats that became known as the jury box. Unfortunately for the Braves, only opposing batters were taking advantage of the new distance. The climax came in June when the Reds arrived. In each game of the three-game series, a Reds pitcher hit a home run into the jury box. Immediately after the third game, Fuchs had the seats removed.

When Charlie Finley took over the A's in 1960, he was required to sign a four-year lease with the city for use of its ballpark. Finley was unhappy with that arrangement and in protest he installed a "Pennant Porch," a low fence in right field modeled after the 296-foot right field fence in Yankee Stadium. He claimed that the Yankees had built a powerhouse due to the short porch. He moved the existing fence from 338 feet (or 353, based on a photograph that shows that number) to the Major League–minimum 325 feet and angled the fence down to 296 feet at the foul pole.

He painted the fence with the words "K-C Pennant Porch." The fence was up for two exhibition games before American League president Joe Cronin and commissioner Ford Frick ordered it removed. Finley then put up a "One Half Pennant Porch" at 325 feet and a bleacher roof that cut the distance to 296 feet. This was also disallowed. In response, Finley installed a 40-foot screen at the 296-foot mark. It too was disallowed and the fence was expanded to the minimum legal distance of 325 feet.

Current rules require fences to remain in the same place for a full season. This prohibits such abuses as Browns owner Bill Veeck's in the early 1950s. He had a retractable cyclone fence that he moved in and out on a daily basis depending on which team was in town. The American League later ruled that a club could move its fences only one time during the season. This was in response to the White Sox moving their fences whenever the Yankees came to town.

Padding. In the 1950s the Pirates became the first club to pad its outfield walls when general manager Branch Rickey ordered padding only for the concrete right and right center field walls. Padding became common in the 1970s, but a number of clubs still had not adopted the practice. The Reds decided to pad their outfield walls for the 1992 season after being criticized when Phillies outfielder Lenny Dykstra broke his collarbone, crashing into the wall.

Red Sox owner Tom Yawkey decided to pad Fenway Park's walls after rookie sensation Fred Lynn crashed into the wall in the 5th inning of Game 6 of the 1975 World Series. After Lynn lay motionless while Ken Griffey went to third with a triple, Yawkey told scouting director Haywood Sullivan that the walls had to be padded before the 1976 season.

1912 World Series. The Red Sox Royal Rooters stormed the field in protest over losing their seats for Game 7 of the 1912 World Series (there was one tie, so this was not the final game). Mounted police had to disperse them, but in the process the Rooters knocked down the low left-field bleacher fence. The game was delayed while the fence was repaired. In the meantime, the arm of Red Sox starter Smoky Joe Wood tightened up. He gave up six runs in the 1st inning and was knocked out of the box.

High Walls. The Green Monster at Fenway Park is 37 feet high. Connie Mack Stadium in Philadelphia had a right field wall that stood 50 feet high between 1934 and 1956. Washington's Griffith Stadium had a 30-foot high wall in right field, hardly necessary given the ballpark's large dimensions (372 in right center tapering to 320 at the foul pole).

Fence Buster. In college at Rice, Astros first baseman Lance Berkman was an outfielder. He once raced to the foul line and slid trying to make a catch. The ball got away from him and fell into a pile of trash in a swirling wind. Berkman's leg caught in the chain-link fence as he grabbed the ball and threw. The ball amazingly went right into a plastic bag swirling about 30 feet in front of Berkman, and the package died a few feet further away. As the runner rounded the bases for an inside-the-park home run, Berkman was stuck in the fence and could only watch helplessly.

Home Run or Out? If an outfielder catches a ball in the seats, the catch is recorded as an out if the fielder returns immediately to the field with the ball.

Minnesota. The Minnesota Metrodome's plastic fence is called the Hefty Bag because it is a soft sheet of canvas that has considerable give when it is hit by a ball or an outfielder.

Fenway Park (1912–)

"Fenway Park, Boston, is a lyric little bandbox of a ball park. Everything is painted green and seems in curiously sharp focus, like the inside of an old-fashioned peeping-type Easter egg." — Writer John Updike.

"A crazy-quilt violation of city planning principles, an irregular pile of architecture, a menace to marketing consultants, Fenway Park works. It works as a symbol of New England's pride, as a repository of evergreen hopes, as a tabernacle of lost innocence. It works as a place to watch baseball." — Martin F. Nolan in *A Ballpark, Not A Stadium* (1999).

"I came to love Fenway. It was a place that rejuvenated me after a road trip; the fans right on top of you, the nutty angles. And the Wall. That was my baby, the left-field wall, the Green Monster." — Carl Yastrzemski.

"As I grew up, I knew that as a building Fenway Park was on the level of Mount Olympus, the Pyramid at Giza, the nation's capitol, the czar's Winter Palace, and the Louvre — except, of course, that is better than all those inconsequential places." — Commissioner Bart Giamatti.

"I can't wait to see the new park when it's done. I want Boston to have the best. If any city needed a new park, it's Boston. I won't shed a tear."— Ted Williams.

Fenway Park has been home to the Boston Red Sox since it was built for the 1912 season. It was originally a single-decked red brick ballpark taking up a city block. Jersey Street (now Yawkey Way) is on the third base side and Van Ness Street is on the first base side. Ipswich is on the left field side and Landsdown is behind home plate.

The ballpark was built by John I. Taylor of the Taylor newspaper family. The name comes from

Through the looking glass, the mystical "Green Monster" at Fenway Park, dressed up for the 1999 All-Star Game.

the Fens, a marshy area of the city where the park was built. It was originally known as Fenway Park Grounds or Red Sox Park.

Dedication. John F. Kennedy's grandfather, Boston mayor John "Honey Fitz" Fitzgerald, threw out the first ball at the dedication on April 20, 1912. Fifty years later President Kennedy threw out the first ball in Washington to start the 1962 season.

Capacity. Fenway Park has had various capacities over the years, in part depending on the source of such information. Its initial capacity was approximately 35,000, and that total has fluctuated around that amount to its 1990s total of approximately 34,000. Modern sources have put the 1990s capacity at 34,171, 33,536 and 33,583. The sell-out attendance at the 1975 World Series was 35,205. The largest crowd (including SRO) was 49,000 to see the Yankees on September 22, 1935. The rooftop seats were added in 1988 and there are now 44 luxury boxes.

For the 2003 season, 280 seats were added in new bleachers above the Green Monster, at $50 per ticket. In 2004 the club added 200 seats above the retired numbers on the right field façade. Capacity remained about the same, as the club sold fewer SRO seats. Additional seats were added on the right-field roof for 2004, bringing capacity to 36,298. Plans were then announced to add another 2,000 seats for the 2005 season.

Dimensions. The early dimensions from left to right field were 324–379–488–405–313, with one spot near center field reaching 593 feet in 1931 (though there is controversy about the accuracy of this distance). The dimensions are jagged because of the numerous twists and turns in the outfield wall. Modern dimensions from left to right field are approximately 315–379–389–383–302.

The recent official distance in left field has been 315 feet, but research seems to support 304 in left field and 380 in center field (instead of 389).

The Green Monster.
"Do they leave it there during games?"— Pitcher Bill Lee disturbed at the sight of the close proximity of the Green Monster.

The Green Monster in left field is 37'2" high and was created in 1947 when all the advertisements were removed and the fence was painted green (the wall was already there). A 23-foot screen was added

over the 37-foot wall to keep balls off the street. The only advertisement that remained was one for the Jimmy Fund, a Boston institution created to raise money for cancer research and patient care.

The first home run over the left field fence was by first baseman Hugh Bradley of the 1912 Red Sox. It was his only home run that year. The first home run over the Green Monster was on April 15, 1947, by Eddie Pellagrini in the 3rd inning of the club's season opener off Early Wynn.

In 1997 Coca-Cola paid to install a 20-foot Coke bottle at the top of the light standard above the Green Monster. The 427-foot shot would earn the batter $1,000 to donate to the charity of his choice. Jerry Naehring was the first player to hit the bottle, with a grand slam, although at least one source reported that it was Wil Cordero (who did it later in the game).

In 2002–2003 the Red Sox spent $20 million to renovate the stadium, including adding seats above the Green Monster to increase capacity. The 23-foot screen above it was removed to make room for the seats.

Duffy's Cliff.
"Like something half goat and half steeplejack, Duffy scrambled up the Cliff to spear fly balls against the wall."— Sportswriter Tim Cohane.

Before there was the Green Monster in left field, there was an eight-foot embankment that started 25 feet from the left field fence and gradually sloped upward to the fence. It was known as "Duffy's Cliff" for long-time (1910–1917) Red Sox left fielder Duffy Lewis. In 1934 the slope was reduced considerably.

Bad Luck. There were two rainouts before the park debuted on April 20, 1912. Though the Red Sox won 7–6, it was an ominous start because it was the same time that news arrived of the sinking of the *Titanic* (which sank between April 14 and 15).

Tenant. The Braves played at Fenway Park from September 7 through September 29, 1914, later that season during the 1914 World Series, and during the first half of the 1915 season.

Book. John Boswell and David Fisher, *Fenway Park* (1992); Bill Nowlin and Cecilia Tan (eds.), *The Fenway Project* (2004); Dan Shaughnessy, Stan Grossfeld and Chris Coffin (eds.), (1999).

Rick Ferrell (1905–1995)

Hall of Fame (VC) 1984

"Brother or no brother, … he was a real classy receiver. You never saw him lunge for the ball; he never took a strike away from you. He'd get more strikes for a pitcher than anybody I ever saw, because he made catching look easy."—Ferrell's brother and Major League pitcher Wes Ferrell.

Ferrell was one of the top American League catchers during the 1930s.

Before reaching the Major Leagues in 1929, Richard Benjamin Ferrell attended Guilford College beginning in 1922 at age 17. He signed with the Tigers, who assigned him to the Virginia League. He began to be recognized as a top catching prospect when Judge Landis intervened. Landis ruled that the Tigers had improperly signed Ferrell and he was declared a free agent.

The Browns signed Ferrell and he first played for them in 1929. He became the club's first-string catcher in 1930 and batted over .300 in 1931 and 1932. He then moved to various other clubs in the American League during his 18-year career. The highlights were seasons with the Red Sox when he batted over .300 twice in the mid–1930s. He bounced back and forth between the Senators and Browns starting in 1937, with diminishing totals in each season until his retirement in 1947 after missing the 1946 season.

Ferrell finished his career with a .281 batting average and only 28 home runs (less than his brother, pitcher Wes Ferrell). Nevertheless, Rick established himself as a premier American League catcher during the 1930s and played 1,805 games at the position. After his retirement Ferrell coached for the Senators and then held various positions with the Tigers into his 80s.

Feuds

"There's nothing in the world I wouldn't do for Walter O'Malley. There's nothing he wouldn't do for me. That's the way it is. We go through life doing nothing for each other."—Gene Autry on Walter O'Malley, owner of the crosstown rival Dodgers and Autry's landlord when the Angels played in Dodger Stadium in the early 1960s.

This section covers feuds between individuals; see *Rivalries* for feuds between teams.

See *Tinker to Evers to Chance* for the long-standing feud between Joe Tinker and Johnny Evers.

See *Suspensions*—Leo Durocher for the feud among Durocher, Dodger general manager Branch Rickey and Yankee general manager Larry MacPhail.

Babe Ruth and Lou Gehrig. The teammates feuded for years, supposedly because Gehrig's mother criticized the way that Ruth's wife Claire dressed their daughter. The information got back to Claire and Ruth then told off "Ma" Gehrig.

Another incident that apparently added to the rift was recalled by Yankee catcher Bill Dickey, Gehrig's best friend on the team. Dickey said that Ruth turned on the charm to a beautiful woman who then dropped Gehrig. Dickey recalls that even though Gehrig appeared to reconcile with Ruth in later years, he never forgave him.

One source claimed that Ruth did not speak to Gehrig until he knew that Gehrig was dying, although this seems contrary to a number of instances in which the two appear to have spoken. Gehrig's wife Eleanor claimed that Gehrig never resented Ruth and that there was no feud.

Ty Cobb and Babe Ruth. Cobb supposedly feuded with Ruth, whom he surely resented for stealing the headlines during the 1920s.

Cobb often sneered at Ruth's style of power baseball. In one on-field incident involving the Yankees and Tigers, a brawl erupted near home plate. Cobb supposedly raced in from center field and headed straight for Ruth.

In another incident, Cobb was to room with Ruth on a hunting trip during the off-season. Cobb's response: "I've never bedded down with a nigger before and I'm not going to start now." This was in reference to Ruth's broad nose and other facial features that led a few people to conclude that he was black (see also *Racism*). Ruth and Cobb supposedly patched up their differences at a war bond rally during World War II and there are a number of photographs showing the two happily — though competitively — playing golf together.

Ty Cobb and Ted Williams.

"Those two writers, Ty Cobb and Ted Williams, recently have been waging a public vendetta. You may recall that Cobb said that the old timers were much better ball players. Ted countered by saying the moderns outranked the former stars and that he could name many men better than the players of Cobb's day. 'All except Cobb and Ruth,' wrote Williams. 'They stand alone.'"—Grantland Rice in *The Tumult and the Shouting* (1954).

Cobb and Williams supposedly had a falling out when they tried to decide who was the best second baseman of all time. Williams favored Rogers Hornsby, a Cobb rival of that era. Cobb disagreed and purportedly never spoke to him again.

John McGraw and Wilbert Robinson. The two were teammates, friends, and Giants manager and coach for many years before a purported falling out during the 1913 World Series. Robinson was coaching first base for the Giants while McGraw was coaching third and managing the club. Robinson ignored a sign by McGraw and sent a runner to second base. Robinson supposedly was fired over this incident and they became bitter enemies after Robinson was hired to manage the Dodgers beginning in 1914. Other sources report that McGraw once berated the entire Giants team and Robinson took offense.

At a ceremony in 1927 to mark McGraw's 25 years as manager, Robinson was persuaded to attend and supposedly patched things up with his old friend. McGraw had a 197–190 record against the Dodgers while they were managed by Robinson.

John McGraw and Ban Johnson. There was a feud between McGraw and American League president Johnson over McGraw's 1902 midseason departure for the National League Giants from the American League Orioles (see also *American League*). However, Mrs. John McGraw claimed in her 1953 book, *The Real McGraw*, that there was no such feud. She contended (unconvincingly) that it was an elaborate charade to allow McGraw to move to the National League in return for the American League placing a club in New York, the largest market available.

Charles Comiskey and Ban Johnson. See *American League Presidents*—Ban Johnson.

Connie Mack and Silk O'Loughlin. Mack and umpire O'Loughlin supposedly feuded for the rest of their lives after O'Loughlin made a crucial call against the A's during their 1907 *Pennant Race* with the Tigers. O'Loughlin nullified an apparent extra-inning ground-rule double by Harry Davis against the Tigers. O'Loughlin called Davis out after concluding that a policeman interfered with outfielder Sam Crawford's attempt to catch the ball. The next A's batter singled, which would have scored Davis and probably given the game to the A's. The A's lost the pennant race by 1½ games.

Roger Maris and Mickey Mantle. Maris and Mantle supposedly feuded during the hectic 1961 season, but it is clear that this was a fabrication created by a few sportswriters.

Charlie Finley and Bowie Kuhn.

"I have often called Bowie Kuhn a village idiot. I apologize to the village idiots of America. He is the nation's idiot."—Finley on Kuhn in 1981 after Finley sold the A's.

Finley feuded with almost everyone in Major League Baseball, but he held particular ill-will toward Kuhn. Among other things, Kuhn cancelled a number of *Trades and Player Sales* attempted by Finley and vetoed Finley's punishment of infielder Mike Epstein's two errors during the 1972 World Series. Finley had immediately put Epstein on the *Disabled List* for the duration of the series.

Johnny Bench and Pete Rose. Bench and Rose began feuding in the 1990s when Bench stated publicly that Rose was placing bets on baseball games when they were teammates.

Umpires/Players.

"He's so incompetent that he couldn't be crew chief on a sunken submarine."—A's manager Billy Martin on umpire Jerry Neudecker.

"You're still the second best umpire in the league."—Dick Groat, in his last game, to umpire Shag Crawford, after Groat was called out on a close play at second base. Groat noted that the other 19 umpires were tied for first.

See *Ejections* for the feud between Orioles manager Earl Weaver and umpire Ron Luciano.

See *Barred From Baseball* for George Steinbrenner's feud with Dave Winfield.

Field Days

In the 19th century and into the 1940s, clubs staged pregame Field Days in which players put on exhibitions of running and throwing for fans (see also *Fastest Runners* and *Longest Throws*).

Fielder's Choice

"It looked more like 'fielder's indifference.'"—Angels broadcaster Bob Starr on a botched comebacker by pitcher Randy Johnson.

A fielder's choice occurs with a man on base and a ground ball to an infielder. The infielder chooses to get the force play on the runner while the batter takes first base on what would otherwise be a putout of the batter.

Field Dimensions   See *Fields and Field Dimensions*

Fielding and Fielding Averages

"In our day you didn't see the plays you do today. I can't remember anybody catching one by jumping over the fence and it would stick in the big glove, 'cause it wouldn't. Maybe I dove for a ball once or twice, but you'd only hurt yourself probably and still wouldn't do more than knock it down. Now [the balls] stick and you can get up and throw them out if they're hit hard. Nobody seemed to think fielding was that important ... hitting made all the difference."—Charlie Gehringer of the 1924–1942 Tigers.

"Batting averages are terribly important to a player's reputation and salary, but fielding averages are scarcely regarded."—Fred Schwed, Jr., in *How to Watch a Baseball Game* (1957).

"What the hell were you doing last night? Jesus Christ! You looked like a monkey trying to fuck a football out there."—George Steinbrenner laying into one of his players after a bad game on the field.

"'It takes a lot of years of watching baseball to learn *not* to follow the ball every second. The true beauty of the game is the ebb and flow of the fielders, the kaleidoscopic arrangements and rearrangements of the players in response to a foul ball, an extra-base hit, or an attempted stolen base.'"—Gideon's father in W.P. Kinsella's *The Iowa Baseball Confederacy* (1986).

See also *Errors, Gloves, Gold Glove Award* and *Strategy— Williams Shift,* as well as entries by position.

Fielding Rules. If a fielder throws his shoe or cap at the ball, the batter receives two bases. If he throws his glove at it, the batter receives three bases (no explanation for the difference).

Fielding Average. Fielding average is calculated by totaling the number of assists and errors and dividing them into the number of putouts and assists. Fielding averages have increased dramatically since 1900 as the quality (and size) of gloves and playing surfaces have improved.

Qualifying as League Leader. In 1920 it was ruled that for a fielder to qualify as the league leader in fielding percentage, he had to play in at least 100 games. Prior to that there was no rule, but it was common practice that a player had to play in at least 60% of his team's scheduled games. The new rule was slightly different for catchers, who had to play in 90 games to qualify.

In 1957 the rule was modified to require a fielder to play in at least two-thirds of his team's scheduled games at the specific fielding position in order to qualify. It was also ruled that a catcher had to catch in at least half of his team's scheduled games to qualify.

To qualify for a league fielding title, pitchers must complete as many innings (162) as games scheduled for each club in their league that season. The exception is if another pitcher has a fielding average as high or higher, and has handled more chances in a lesser number of innings; if so, he shall be the fielding champion.

Early Rules. Prior to the Civil War, a batter was out if the ball was caught on one bounce. The rule spared fielders from the effects of catching hard balls with no gloves. Fouls were also outs if caught on one bounce. These rules were eliminated in 1864, though gloves were not yet in vogue.

Early fielders played near the foul line because the rules allowed any ball to be in play if it started fair and then went foul. The fielders had to be near the line to go for what would today be considered foul balls.

A few sources credit first baseman Charles Comiskey with having his infielders back up throws from the outfield. This may have contributed to his four straight pennants with the Browns in 1885–1888. Ned Hanlon's Baltimore Orioles of the 1890s have also been credited with first backing up throws and shifting as the batter hit the ball—part of the "inside baseball" played by the club. However, it is more likely that these strategies were developed fully before the Browns and Orioles rose to prominence and that these claims are simply part of the efforts by prominent 20th century baseball people to overstate their 19th century contributions to baseball.

One-Handed Catches.

"When you have hands as bad as mine, one hand is better than two."—1960s outfielder Ken Harrelson on why he caught balls one-handed. His nickname of "Hawk" was based on his prominent nose and not his outfield prowess.

In 1882 American Association Cincinnati Red Stockings first baseman Henry Luff one-handed a catch and was fined $5 for such poor fielding technique.

In the 1950s first baseman Vic Power was one of the first players to exclusively employ the one-handed catch on all plays. In part because he was black, he was criticized as a hot dog and even received mail about it when he one-handed a foul ball pop-up for the last out of a no-hitter.

Apocryphal Hidden Outfielder Trick. In 1912 in the Southern League, Casey Stengel was playing left field for Montgomery. In the 7th inning while standing in the outfield, he purportedly found an underground case in the outfield containing water pipes. He crawled inside and waited for the pitch. When one of the batters hit a ball to left field, Stengel crawled out of the box and made the catch.

Outfield Play. Late 19th century Phillies outfielder Sam Thompson is credited by at least one source with being the first to use a one-bounce throw into the infield. This seems unlikely given that infielders prior to the 1890s did not have gloves and outfielders probably bounced the throws to the infield to make them easier to catch.

Tris Speaker played a shallow center field, occasionally taking pick-off throws at second base from the pitcher. Speaker also had a number of unassisted double plays by catching fly balls in shallow center field and doubling a runner off second himself. He once performed this feat in the World Series. He was able to play so shallow in part because of the dead ball used during part of his career.

Outfield Communication. Joe DiMaggio positioned the Yankee outfielders by wiggling his glove a certain way.

During the 1962 inaugural season of the Mets, Venezuelan shortstop Elio Chacon had a habit of taking every fly ball he could reach. Center fielder Richie Ashburn decided to solve the problem by learning how to say "I got it" in Spanish. Bilingual teammate Joe Christopher informed him that it was "Yo la tengo." On the next fly ball in the area, Chacon ventured out to Ashburn's territory and Ashburn yelled, "Yo la tengo! Yo la tengo!" Chacon backed off just as left fielder Frank Thomas, a Pittsburgh native and English-only speaker, smashed into Ashburn and knocked the ball out of his glove.

Fielding Percentage/Shortstops. Lou Boudreau is the only player to lead the league in fielding percentage at shortstop nine years in a row. Boudreau was not known for his speed, however: "He is easily the slowest ballplayer since [notoriously slow catcher Ernie] Lombardi tried to stretch a double into a single."—Sportswriter Stanley Frank.

Ernie Banks is the only shortstop ever to lead the league in home runs and fielding percentage in the same season. Banks also won two consecutive MVP Awards while hitting over 40 home runs in five of six seasons over one stretch of his career at shortstop. In contrast, in 1973 seven of the Major League's 24 starting shortstops hit no home runs.

Cal Ripken set a record in 1990 with only three errors and a .996 fielding percentage.

Pitchers.

"He belonged to that venerable pitchers' union that called the dirt circling the mound the extent of their fielding range."—Fresco Thompson in *Every Diamond Doesn't Sparkle* (1964).

A pitcher's fielding played an important role in Game 7 of the 1960 World Series. In the 8th inning, in which the Pirates scored five runs to take the lead, slow-footed pitcher Jim Coates replaced excellent fielding pitcher Bobby Shantz of the Yankees. On a key play that would have prevented the big inning, Coates was late in covering first base on a slow roller and the runners were safe. The next batter, Hal Smith, hit a three-run homer to put the Pirates ahead. The Yankees tied the game in the top of the 9th inning, but the Pirates won in the bottom of the 9th on Bill Mazeroski's home run.

Importance. Branch Rickey considered fielding to be the least important quality of a Major League prospect. He believed that fielding could be taught and that running speed was paramount.

Books. William Curran, *Mitts: A Celebration of the Art of Fielding* (1985); David Falkner, *Nine Sides of the Diamond* (1990).

Fields and Field Dimensions

"The patterns of the game are of themselves interesting and pleasing to the eye. The rich chocolate-brown or pale tan of the infield is contrasted with the fine soothing green of the outfield. The base paths are neatly geometrical, and the white foul lines on either side of the home plate start their differing roads toward infinity. There is a place for everyone and every place is neatly marked off with white lines."—Paul Gallico in *Farewell to Sport* (1938).

"Down the left-field and right-field lines, it's 99 liters [sic], whatever that means."—Mets broadcaster Ralph Kiner during a French-dominated Montreal Expos game.

"90 feet between bases is the nearest thing to perfection that man has yet achieved."—Red Smith.

"The ball field itself is a mystic creation, the Stonehenge of America."—Roger Kahn in *A Season in the Sun* (1977).

"It is desirable that the line from home base through the pitchers plate to second base shall run east-north-east."—Official rule on the placement of the field to avoid the **Sun**.

See also **Ballparks**, **Bases**, **Fences**, **Infields and Dirt**, and **Pitching Distances**.

Engineers. During the 1890s clubs were required to have an engineer lay out the field to ensure accuracy.

Before one National League game in 1887, the umpire noticed that the diamond was laid out wrong. It turned out that workmen had mistaken grading stakes for the baseline markers.

New Dimension. In 1893 one Clifford Spencer suggested that with the mound further from the plate at 60'6", the field should be a pentagon with four bases and one home plate. This would create fewer fouls, more stealing and higher status for the second baseman.

Backstops. In 1931 the required distance between home plate and the backstop was reduced from 90 to 60 feet.

Square Feet. The average ballpark field contains 90,000 square feet between the foul lines.

Distance Between Bases. The distance between first and second, and second and third, at their closest point is actually 88'1½" because first and third base are placed inside the foul lines and second base is not inside the "diamond," but straddles it. The distance between home plate and second base is 127 feet.

The early rules proposed a distance of 42 paces between first and third base and between home plate and second base. This resulted in a distance of 30 paces (about three feet each) from home to first, first to second, etc.

Drainage. Infields are built with a slight crown in the middle to promote good drainage. This can lead to a pitchers mound being even higher than is allowed. Newer parks have better drainage, so a higher crown is not necessary (unlike older Dodger Stadium).

Fights

"[I]n all of these extra-curricular fights there runs a strain of striking similarity — namely, that while no end of blows may fill the air, few if any ever find their mark. Still and all, this profound ignorance of fisticuffs has never lessened the zeal and enthusiasm ball players put in their roundhouse swings and the results have been most startling."—*New York Times* sportswriter John Drebinger.

"Flailing fists. Bumping beer bellies. To the untrained eye, the typical bench-clearing, bullpen-emptying baseball brawl appears anything but organized. But beneath the standard elements — the pushing, the pulling, the inevitable dog-piling — lies a hidden order. It's an unwritten code of conduct as rigidly mannered as one of the dutiful, repressed English butlers in a Merchant-Ivory film." — Patrick Hruby.

"[Van Lingle] Mungo and I get along fine. I just tell him I won't stand for no nonsense — and then I duck." — Casey Stengel.

"I watched him turn red, purple, then blue. I could have held him 45 more seconds until he turned black. Maybe now he holds more value for life, because I spared him this time." — Astros coach and former wrestler Ed Ott describing a 1992 brawl in which he had a choke hold on Reds reliever Rob Dibble.

"No one got into a fight; a fight at the Astrodome would be as shocking as fisticuffs in the College of Cardinals." — Roger Angell in *The Summer Game* (1972).

"George Gore, Al Maul, Punch Knoll, John Strike, Rip Williams, Bruce Hitt, Swat McCabe, Stan Hack, John Slappery, Pinch Thomas, Enos Slaughter, Joe Bash, Buck Thrasher, Bump Wills, Rip Sewell, Roy Shook, Adrian Lynch, Boom Boom Beck, Cy Slapnicka, Sterling Slaughter"

See also **Beanballs**, **Boxers**, **Fans**, **Fines**, **Suspensions** and **Umpires**.

Fights were much more common on the field in the 19th and early 20th centuries. The late 1890s were marked by frequent fights and umpire abuse in the National League, which contributed to a downturn in the sport's popularity.

In 1933 National League president John Heydler wrote a memo to team owners requesting less fraternization among players from different teams and a more aggressive attitude on the field. It is unclear whether this led to more fighting on the field.

Fights increased in the 1990s as players took offense at every slight by the opposition, but primarily at **Brushback Pitches**.

Fighters.

"Nobody knew how well Dolph [Dolf Camilli] could fight because, quite frankly, nobody had ever wanted to find out." — Leo Durocher in *Nice Guys Finish Last* (1975).

"The greatest amateur brawler in the world." — Heavyweight boxing champion Jim Corbett on Frank Chance.

Arlie Latham. This 19th century third baseman was known as "The Freshest Man on Earth" because of so many brawls. He once had more than 20 fights scheduled for after the season, five against his own teammates. This behavior seems out of character for him because he had a tremendous sense of humor and was known for his comedy in the coaching boxes in later years. After returning from living in Europe at the start of World War II, he was given a job in the Giants press box entertaining reporters with his anecdotes. At age 89 in 1949 he still had the job.

Ad Brennan. The Phillies pitcher once decked Giants manager John McGraw during a fight beneath the stands.

Clark Griffith. The New York Highlanders manager once hit a photographer under the stands. The photographer arranged for a warrant to be served on Griffith and the matter was settled for $4.50 after the photographer demanded $5.

Buck Herzog and Ty Cobb. "I got beat, but I knocked the bum down and he'll never forget a little guy like me having him on the floor." — Herzog on his fight with Cobb in a Dallas Hotel. Herzog was 5'11" and 160 pounds; Cobb was 6'1" and 175 pounds. In 1917 during a spring training exhibition tour, Herzog of the Giants and Cobb staged a fight in Cobb's hotel room, refereed by Tiger trainer Harry Tuttle. Herzog decked Cobb with the first punch before Cobb pummeled him. According to Tuttle "they fought like a couple of washerwomen" over a spiking incident earlier in the day.

Leo Durocher and Babe Ruth. Durocher once pushed Ruth into a locker when both were with the Dodgers (Ruth as a coach) after Ruth had threatened to punch him. The two had played together briefly with the Yankees when Ruth dubbed Durocher "The All-American Out."

Casey Stengel. When Stengel was the Dodger manager, he bloodied the lip of Cardinals shortstop Leo Durocher during a fight under the stands.

Mickey Owen. The Cardinals catcher attacked Dodger player-manager Leo Durocher after a force-out at second base in Brooklyn in 1940. In 1941 Owen was traded to the Dodgers and played for Durocher.

Art Ditmar. In the late 1940s a brutal fight was instigated by the Yankee pitcher against the White Sox. American League color-line breaker Larry Doby was at bat and Ditmar was throwing head-high brushback pitches. In the huge brawl that followed, former football player Moose Skowron leveled Doby with a hard tackle.

Carl Furillo. The Dodger outfielder once suffered a broken finger in a fight after a confrontation with Giants manager Leo Durocher. Furillo had been hit by a pitch just before the fight started.

Jim Tobin. Only 36 hours before he relieved in Game 1 of the 1945 World Series, the Tigers pitcher was involved in a bar fight in Detroit. He was slugged on the head with a beer bottle, knocked down and kicked, but did not suffer any serious injuries. He declined to prosecute his assailants and pitched his only three innings of the Series, giving up four hits and two runs in the Tigers' 9–0 loss.

Frank Robinson and Eddie Mathews. In 1959 Robinson slid hard into the Braves third baseman and a memorable brawl ensued, one of the first between high-profile black and white players. Robinson was booed following the fight, but responded immediately with a grand slam. Robinson apologized the next time they were near each other and Mathews told him that there were no hard feelings.

Billy Martin.

"He's a feisty little son of a bitch. He's the kind of guy you'd like to kill if he's playing for the other team, but you'd like 10 of him on your side, the little bastard." — Indians general manager Frank Lane.

Martin was legendary for his drinking and brawling, which eventually got him traded by the Yankees. He began to create that image in 1952, when he brawled with Jimmy Piersall after Piersall insulted his nose and ears. Martin also had a fight with the much larger Clint Courtney of the Browns in June 1950, though another source pegs the date as Martin's rookie season in 1953. Courtney ("The meanest man I know" — Satchel Paige) was fined $250 and Martin $150.

To celebrate Martin's birthday on May 15, 1957, a few of the Yankees went to the Copacabana Club in New York City. Hank Bauer, Mickey Mantle, Whitey Ford, Yogi Berra and Johnny Kucks celebrated with Martin. Bauer was accused of hitting a patron, a brawl followed and this gave the Yankees the excuse they needed to trade Martin to Kansas City one month later.

First baseman Vic Power later said that the fight started when Martin called entertainer Sammy Davis, Jr., "Mau Mau," in reference to the black African terrorists active in Kenya in the 1950s. Power, who was black, had called other black players Mau Mau and the nickname spread among the few black players in the American

League. Martin's use of the term was not appreciated by a group of black patrons sitting next to him and a fight broke out. Another source reported that a group of bowlers began heckling Davis with racial insults.

Martin charged the mound in 1960 and broke the jaw of Cubs rookie pitcher Jim Brewer. Brewer sued and settled for $10,000. After Brewer filed suit for $1 million, Martin responded by saying: "How do they want it, cash or check?"

While he was manager of the Twins, Martin knocked out one of his own players, pitcher Dave Boswell (who, according to one source, also recovered $10,000 from Martin). Two years earlier, Martin had broken up a fight between Boswell and Bob Allison. Martin later lost a managerial job after a fight in a bar with a marshmallow salesman.

Martin was killed in a winter driving accident when both the pick-up truck's driver and passenger Martin were drinking when the vehicle skidded off the road.

Juan Marichal. On August 22, 1965, the Giants pitcher was batting against Dodger pitcher Sandy Koufax. Marichal concluded that Dodger catcher John Roseboro had thrown too close to him on the return throw to the mound. Marichal then hit Roseboro in the head with his bat, drawing blood. A brawl was avoided after quick action by the umpires and Willie Mays.

Earlier in the game, Marichal had brushed back Maury Wills and Ron Fairly. When Roseboro responded by asking Koufax to nail Marichal, Koufax allegedly refused and Roseboro did it on his own with the close throw.

Jeff Torborg came in to replace the injured Roseboro and Bob Schroeder replaced Marichal at the plate and struck out. Ron Herbel came in to replace Marichal on the mound and went 5⅓ innings for a 4–3 win.

The incident was preceded by bad blood a few days earlier over catcher's interference calls. Wills allegedly had tipped catcher Tom Haller's mitt with his bat, and Matty Alou retaliated by tipping the mask of Dodger catcher John Roseboro. Roseboro responded by almost beaning Alou on the return throw to the mound.

Marichal was suspended for eight games and fined $1,750, reportedly the largest player fine by the National League up to that point. Roseboro later sued Marichal for damages and the case settled before going to trial. Ironically, Marichal finished his career with two ineffective appearances for the Dodgers in 1975 and Roseboro helped campaign for Marichal's successful entry into the Hall of Fame. Roseboro's perspective is contained in his autobiography, *Glory Days with the Dodgers*, with Bill Libby (1978).

Tommy John. In 1967 the White Sox pitcher got into a fight with Tigers shortstop Dick McAuliffe that put John out for part of the season and may have cost Chicago the pennant.

Henry Aaron and Rico Carty. While with the Braves, Aaron and the arrogant Carty had a fight on one of the team's airline flights.

Lenny Randle. In 1977 the Texas Rangers second baseman beat up manager Frank Lucchesi, resulting in a $10,000 *Fine*, the largest player fine in history at that point.

Cliff Johnson. In a 1970s Yankee clubhouse fight, the volatile Johnson once broke the thumb of star relief pitcher Goose Gossage.

Don Sutton and Steve Garvey. Sutton and Garvey had a fight in the clubhouse in the late 1970s and then made amends on national television. The fight supposedly was precipitated by a column written by Thomas Boswell, though Boswell claimed that another paper had misrepresented his column.

Bill Russell. In the 1970s the mild-mannered Dodger shortstop was hit in the rear end by pitcher Tug McGraw after McGraw gave up a hit to Joe Ferguson. Russell charged the mound, only to be tackled by Pete Rose. The next day, Russell and McGraw posed together with boxing gloves.

Pascual Perez. On August 12, 1984, the Braves and Padres staged a brawl after a long day of attempted and hit batsmen. Braves pitcher Pascual Perez was the focal point and was finally hit by a pitch in the 8th inning. The brawl also included fans, who jumped the rail and pitched in. The appearance of fans on the field united the two teams against the fans' onslaught.

Glenn Davis. The Orioles first baseman suffered a broken jaw in a bar fight while on a minor league rehabilitation assignment in 1993.

Robin Ventura. One of the more memorable recent fights occurred in mid–1993 when the White Sox third baseman charged the mound against Nolan Ryan during Ryan's last season. The 26-year-old Ventura took a beating from the 46-year-old Ryan. Ryan got Ventura in a headlock and punched him six times in the head and throat before Ventura could grab his arm and other players rushed in.

Albert Belle. See *Fines*.

Tony Phillips.

"Phillips thinks a doubleheader is a nine-inning game followed by a grandstand fistfight." — Bill Plaschke of the *Los Angeles Times*.

The American League outfielder had a reputation for fighting. On May 15, 1996, while with the Tigers, he came out of a game in the 6th inning and changed into street clothes. He immediately went into the stands to beat up a fan who had been heckling him nonstop. Phillips was fined $5,000 for his efforts.

Antonio Alfonseca. In March 2002 the Florida Marlins reliever got into an argument while working out with conditioning coach Dale Torborg. Although Alfonseca is 6'5" and 258 pounds, Torborg is 6'6" and 270 pounds, and wrestles professionally as "The Demon." After Alfonseca cursed at Torborg and Torborg went after him, he locked himself in the trainer's office. He was traded a week later.

George Steinbrenner.

"I clocked them. There are two guys in this town looking for their teeth." — Yankee owner George Steinbrenner after a fight in an elevator in Los Angeles during the 1981 World Series between the Dodgers and Yankees.

"He probably did punch out those two Dodger fans, as long as they were nine and 10." — Reggie Jackson.

"I understand exactly how you must have felt in that elevator. I only hope you don't have a good-behavior clause in your contract. By the way, the marshmallow man I hit was saying bad things about New York and the Yankees…" — Billy Martin, by then manager of the A's, in a telegram to Steinbrenner.

Out of Uniform. During a 1984 Atlanta Braves/San Diego Padres fight, injured Brave Bob Horner — who was watching the game from the press box — raced down to the clubhouse, put on his uniform and ended up in the middle of the dispute on the field.

Sudakis/Dempsey (Rick, not Jack). On September 30, 1974, the Yankees had just arrived at Milwaukee's Pfeister Hotel after a flight delay. There were two games left in the season and the Yankees were only one game behind the Orioles. Because of the delay, many of the Yankee players had been drinking at a local Cleveland bar, where third baseman Bill Sudakis had been getting on catcher Rick Dempsey all night. According to outfielder Bobby Murcer, this was nothing new. "Everybody used to get on everybody all the time."

Dempsey finally tired of the abuse from Sudakis, so he smacked him in the lobby while they were getting their room keys. They broke furniture and knocked pictures off the walls while players, including Murcer, tried to break it up. Murcer ended up on the bottom of the pile and someone stepped on his finger and broke it. The finger kept him out of the lineup the next day, and the Yankees lost to the Brewers 3–2 in 10 innings while the Orioles won and clinched the division championship.

The Pfeister Hotel Again. On May 25, 1998, Pirates relief pitcher Jeff Tabaka suffered a fractured jaw after being punched during a hotel lobby fight, apparently in a dispute over a card game. The scene took place at the Pfeister Hotel in Milwaukee between Tabaka and reliever Marc Wilkins.

Mariners and Orioles. In August 1993 the Mariners and Orioles staged a 20-minute brawl that left several players bloodied and resulted in eight ejections, including Mariners manager Lou Piniella.

Yankees and Orioles.

"I took a couple of knocks. It was like a hockey game."—Darryl Strawberry

"I haven't seen anything like it in 25 years."—George Steinbrenner.

"I had a feeling he'd throw at him. I didn't think he'd throw at his head like he did."—Drew Coble, home plate umpire.

"It was the most gutless thing I've seen in my life."—Yankee general manager Brian Cashman.

In Yankee Stadium on May 19, 1998, the Orioles and Yankees got into a bench-clearing brawl. In the 8th inning, Yankee outfielder Bernie Williams hit a three-run homer with two outs to give the Yankees a 7–5 lead. Orioles reliever Armando Benitez then drilled Yankee first baseman Tino Martinez in the upper back. Martinez fell over in pain, and umpire Drew Coble threw out Benitez immediately. Benitez, however, stepped toward home plate, where Martinez stood back up, with both of them glaring at each other. Players on both teams started to walk on the field, including the 6'6" Darryl Strawberry pointing at Benitez. The Yankee relievers stormed the mound from the bullpen, led by Graeme Lloyd, who ran straight for Benitez and started to throw punches. Benitez retreated to the mouth of Baltimore's bullpen, but the Yankee players followed him, including third baseman Scott Brosius.

Meanwhile, Yankee reliever Mike Stanton wrestled with Orioles catcher Chris Hoiles near the stands. Other players tried to hold Martinez back from attacking Benitez. Manager Joe Torre said, "It was like fires were breaking out all over." Yankee reliever Jeff Nelson broke away from Baltimore's Norm Charlton and began swinging at Benitez. Strawberry hit Benitez with an overhand swing to Benitez's face. At that point, Orioles pitcher Alan Mills jumped on top of Strawberry and with Martinez still struggling to reach Benitez, the fight moved to the Orioles dugout. The whole event lasted for about 10 minutes, in front of a crowd of 31,311. The umpires ejected Benitez, Lloyd (who Coble said bumped him), Strawberry, Nelson and Mills. The Yankees won the game, 9–5.

Benitez received an eight-game suspension. Mills got two games for punching Strawberry, who got three games for leading the charge out of the Yankee dugout. Lloyd received three games for running out of the Yankee bullpen to join the melee along with Jeff Nelson, who was suspended for two games. Benitez was fined $2,000, Strawberry and Lloyd $1,000 each. Nelson and Mills paid $500 each.

Darryl Strawberry. On September 14, 1998, the Yankee outfielder was suspended for three games for a fight he had three days earlier with members of the Toronto Blue Jays. He was also fined $1,000. Infielder Homer Bush and coach Don Zimmer were each fined $300 by Gene Budig, president of the American League. Bill Risley, a Toronto reliever, was suspended two games and fined $1,000.

David Wells. After a September 2002 fight, New York bartender Rocco Graziosa was sentenced to 45 days in jail after punching Yankee pitcher David Wells in a Manhattan diner. Wells claimed at the trial that Graziosa had made fun of Wells' weight after the pitcher ordered an egg-white omelet, saying "Why don't you order a fucking cheeseburger?" Wells then approached Graziosa, who is 5'7" and weighed 150 pounds (Wells was 6'4" and 235 pounds at the time), and knocked out Wells' two front teeth with one punch. When Wells was asked during his call to 911 what his emergency was, he responded by saying, with profanity tossed in, "My emergency is I just got offended."

Postseason/Yankees-Red Sox. One of the more bizarre fights occurred during Game 3 of the 2003 ALCS between the Yankees and Red Sox. In the 4th inning at Fenway Park, Red Sox pitcher Pedro Martinez, with men on base, threw high and right behind batter Karim Garcia. The ball appeared to graze Garcia's back or possibly hit his bat, which never left his shoulder. It was called a ball as Garcia walked out to challenge Martinez. The benches started to empty and then calm was restored. Martinez later gestured to Garcia that he would have hit him in the head if he had meant to hit him. Garcia retaliated by sliding hard and late into second baseman Todd Walker. Martinez also made a threatening gesture to Yankee catcher Jorge Posada, suggesting that he would hit him in the head. Martinez's rather lame response for the pitch after the game: "I was just trying to make sure I got a fastball up and in…. I just held on to the ball too long."

In the bottom of the inning, Yankee pitcher Roger Clemens appeared to barely retaliate when he threw high, but nowhere near tight, to mercurial Red Sox batter Manny Ramirez. Ramirez, assuming it was headed for his head, ducked. He came up cussing at Clemens and walked toward the mound. The benches emptied as umpires tried to keep the teams apart. In the middle of the typical milling around pseudo-fight, 72-year-old Yankee coach Don Zimmer charged out and tried to attack Pedro Martinez. Martinez saw him coming and pushed him away. Zimmer stumbled and hit the ground, making it appear that Martinez hit him. Zimmer looked bewildered (not an unusual pose even on his best day). The Yankee trainer applied a band-aid between Zimmer's eyes and play resumed. Clemens then struck out Ramirez on the next pitch and went on to win 4–3.

Later in the game a Fenway Park groundskeeper, Paul Williams, a middle school teacher from New Hampshire, supposedly went into the Yankee bullpen in right field and caused trouble. He was waving a rally towel and inciting the crowd to root against the Yankees. He was jumped on by various Yankee players, including pitcher Jeff Nelson and right fielder Karim Garcia, who hurdled the low fence to get into the action. Garcia cut his hand but was available to play in Game 5. The groundskeeper was led away by police and taken to the hospital with spike marks on his body from the "attack." It appears that Williams had been stationed in the Yankee bullpen, but the players took exception to his open rooting for the Red Sox, including the waving of a towel. Garcia and Nelson later sued Williams (and vice versa).

The incident inevitably led to a comment by David Letterman: "Happy birthday to the world's oldest man [who] yesterday, ladies and gentlemen, turned 114 years old [true]. Today, he was tossed to the ground by Pedro Martinez."

Zimmer was fined $5,000 by Bob Watson, baseball's vice president in charge of discipline. Martinez was fined $50,000, Ramirez $25,000 and Garcia $10,000. Zimmer's press conference the next day was brief: "I'm embarrassed at what happened. I'm embarrassed for the Yankees, the Red Sox, the fans, the umpires and my family. That's all I have to say."

Then he choked up and Joe Torre gave him a pat on the back.

Many Red Sox players were fed up with the antics of their teammates, and even manager Grady Little said that his players were "fed up" with discussing actions of players who "refused to speak for themselves."

Yankees/Red Sox Regular Season. On July 24, 2004, the Yankees and Red Sox had another brawl that resulted in suspensions for Alex Rodriguez (Yankees) and Jason Varitek (Red Sox). Six other players were either fined or suspended by Bob Watson. Varitek and Rodriguez went at it relatively fiercely, bloodying Varitek, and the normally rational Rodriguez was clearly observed uttering "Fuck You, motherfucker!" at Varitek.

Minor Leaguers. On May 22, 1995, Winston-Salem Warthogs pitcher Glenn Cullop had his jaw broken during a one-half hour brawl against the Durham Bulls on "Strike Out Domestic Violence Night." Durham reliever Earl Nelson was suspended for six games after kicking Cullop in the head and groin. Cullop gave up Michael Jordan's last minor league home run.

Fights Started by Umpires.

"Which one of you wants to take me on? How about you?" — Umpire Al Barlick to the Milwaukee Braves and specifically Eddie Mathews, while they were all standing naked in the Braves shower. Barlick was fed up with the taunts by the Braves and challenged them to a brawl after running naked out of the umpires' shower room. Cooler heads prevailed and calm was restored.

Umpire Tim Hurst worked in the National League from 1891 through 1897 and later in the American League. He sometimes hit players with his mask and reportedly once chased New York Highlanders manager Clark Griffith into the dugout and knocked him out. In 1909 he spit in the eye of star second baseman Eddie Collins, almost starting a riot. Appropriately, Hurst later worked as a boxing referee.

Umpire George Magerkurth had a fight with 1940s Giants shortstop Billy Jurges after an argument over a fair or foul home run call. Magerkurth, long known for his short temper, was umpiring first base when another umpire made the call down the left field line. Magerkurth admitted to spitting in Jurges' face and National League president Ford Frick suspended both player and umpire for 10 days and fined them each $250.

Magerkurth was scheduled to umpire the 1941 World Series but was pulled at the last moment when the Dodgers were the National League entry. He had been having a running feud with Dodger manager Leo Durocher.

Sportswriter/Player. Senators first baseman Joe Kuhel once took a swing at sportswriter Shirley Povich of the *Washington Post*. Kuhel mistakenly thought that Povich had credited him with an error. Owner Clark Griffith fined him $100. A few days later Kuhel received a fan letter with a $50 bill and the following: "I'd send you the other half if you hadn't missed."

Karate Kid. In June 1999 Dodgers pitcher Chan Ho Park kicked Angels pitcher Tim Belcher during an on-field fight and was fined $3,000 and suspended for seven games.

I'm Just the Poor Catcher. In July 2001, Pawtucket's Izzy Alcantara became the star of ESPN when he wasn't happy with an inside pitch. He turned and drop-kicked Wilkes Barre/Scranton catcher Jeremy Salazer and then charged the mound. His kung fu movie impression earned him a seven-game suspension and a dis-

invitation to the International League all-star game. As a reward, the Red Sox called him up to the Major Leagues on September 1 that season.

Little League. In 2004 a Massachusetts mother was charged with assault and battery for beating and kicking an 11-year-old boy who rooted against her son's Little League team.

Road Warrior. In 2003 Hall of Fame pitcher Bob Gibson was sued over a case of "road rage," in which he allegedly hit another driver. The incident prompted this from Tom FitzGerald in the *San Francisco Chronicle*: "Gibson's lawyers are expected to argue that the former pitcher was merely painting the blacktop, trying to establish the inside half of the plate."

Sidd Finch

"The publishers have made the mistake of calling this book a novel. It is not, of course, as anyone who turns the pages will realize. A chronicle might be a more apt description — since it details the career in the National League of the Buddhist scholar, Sidd Finch."

On April 1, 1985, not coincidentally April Fool's Day, *Sports Illustrated* ran a cover story on an alleged wonder pitcher named Sidd Finch. He could throw a fastball 165 mph using an unorthodox cricket-style delivery. His curveball traveled at 140 mph. Finch also studied in Tibet, was a Buddhist monk and played the tuba.

Many readers believed the story, as reflected in the next issue's letters to the editors. Some fans were indignant that they had been duped by a supposedly "upstanding" magazine. The story was released later as a more comprehensive book by George Plimpton, *The Curious Case of Sidd Finch* (1987).

Fines

"The fine was a little more than I expectorated." — Frenchy Bordagaray after being fined $500 and suspended for spitting in an umpire's eye (though this phrase probably was written by a creative sportswriter).

"Play him, fine him, and play him again." — Gene Mauch, Phillies manager, on how to handle the phenomenal, but temperamental, Richie (later Dick) Allen.

"Connie Mack cracked down on the deportment of his Philadelphia A's today, instituting a rigid set of training rules. Henceforth, there'll be no drinking, nickel and dime poker only, and prompt attendance at meals. Stiff fines await transgressors, Mack warned." — The *Stars and Stripes* military newspaper.

See also *Fights* and *Suspensions*.

First Fine. The first recorded fine was during a New York Knickerbocker game on October 6, 1845. Archibald T. Bourie, a Wall Street broker, was fined six cents for swearing.

Rules. In 1878 or 1879 (depending on the source), umpires were empowered by the National League to levy fines against players and managers. Umpires could levy fines of up to $20 and could eject rowdy fans from the ballpark. This power was not revoked until 1950 when umpires were required to submit reports to the league presidents, who decided on the amount of fines.

Appeal. Any fine by a club of $500 or less cannot be grieved to the union by a player.

Dirty Pants. During the 1880s the National League began cracking down on discipline problems, but some owners went too far. St. Louis Browns owner Christopher Von der Ahe purportedly suspended Yank Robinson and fined him $25 for having dirty pants. The players revolted and manager Charles Comiskey intervened and quelled the insurrection.

Fan Generosity. Fans of 1880s second baseman Fred Pfeffer once raised $500 to pay his fine. That would have been at least 10% of his salary and is probably overstated.

Andrew Freeman and Amos Rusie. See *Hold-Outs*.

John McGraw. In 1917 the Giants manager had a run-in with National League president John Tener after McGraw blasted him in the newspapers. McGraw was called to the league office and signed a retraction in which he repudiated all his remarks. The sportswriters were upset with McGraw before he told them that he signed the retraction under duress. This forced another round with Tener, who fined him another $1,000.

Babe Ruth. In the 1920s Ruth was fined $5,000 for insubordination and suspended by Yankee manager Miller Huggins. Ruth was required to pay the fine to end his suspension. At least one source reported that after Huggins died in 1929 owner Jacob Ruppert returned the money to Ruth.

Bill Dickey. When the Yankee catcher punched Carl Reynolds on the jaw on July 4, 1932, he was fined $1,000, believed by some to be the largest fine up to that time. However, John McGraw reportedly was fined $1,000 for knocking down umpire Bill Byron well before the Dickey/Reynolds incident. Reynolds was out six weeks and Dickey received a 30-day suspension.

Uniforms. Dizzy Dean and brother Paul staged a brief walk-out in 1934 when manager Frankie Frisch fined them for missing a train. The Deans protested the fine by tearing up their uniforms. Reporters and photographers missed it, so they asked the pair to do it again for the cameras. They obliged by tearing up their road uniforms. Judge Landis responded by telling them to "grow up." Their fines included $36 for the cost of the uniforms.

Ted Williams. After rounding the bases upon hitting his 400th home run, Williams dramatically spit toward the Fenway Park press box to show his disdain for the writers. He was officially fined $5,000 by the team, though he later claimed that he never paid the fine. Red Smith had his own view of the situation: "It was a $4,998 mistake when Ted Williams chose puritanical and antiseptic New England for his celebrated exhibition of spitting for height and distance. In easygoing New York's sanitary subway the price is only $2…. The price the Boston general manager set upon a minute quantity of genuine Williams saliva, making it the most expensive spittle in Massachusetts, suggests that the stuff is rarer than rubies."

When Williams was in his prime, the Yankees purportedly had a standing automatic fine of their pitchers if Williams beat them in the 7th, 8th and 9th innings.

Lenny Randle. In 1977 the Rangers infielder was levied the largest player fine to that date, $10,000, for punching out manager Frank Lucchesi in front of a crowd during spring training. Randle was irritated that he had not made it as a starter that spring. He was suspended and immediately traded to the Mets, where he had his best year, batting .304 with 33 stolen bases. Lucchesi suffered a black eye, fractured cheekbone and other injuries. He later sued Randle and the case was settled.

Payment. By at least the early part of the 20th century, fines were to be paid to the National Commission or the commissioner's office within five days. Although fines were to be paid with a player's personal check, teams usually reimbursed their players.

Commissioner's Office/Rule. When the commissioner's office was created, fines initially could not exceed $5,000. By the 1980s the maximum allowable fine against an individual owner was $25,000. Fines of $250,000 could be levied against a club.

With the abolition of the two league presidents, in February 2000 the commissioner's office designated Frank Robinson as the new arbiter of on-field discipline. In February 2002 Robinson was appointed to manage the Expos, and Bob Watson replaced him.

Self-Imposed. In May 1997 Reds manager Ray Knight announced that he was fining himself $250 for not knowing how many outs there were when he gave the bunt sign in a 3–2 win over the Dodgers. Knight was fired in July when the Reds were 25–25.

Golf Balls. Giants manager Alvin Dark often made his players pay their club fines with golf balls.

Incentive. Don Newcombe said that Dodger manager Charlie Dressen fined his pitchers $50 if they let Willie Mays hit the first pitch of an at-bat.

Umpires. After the 1934 World Series, premier but arrogant umpire Bill Klem lectured Tiger outfielder Goose Goslin about his behavior during the Series. Judge Landis took exception to Klem's conduct and fined him $50 for "abusive language to a ballplayer." One source reported erroneously that Klem never again received a World Series assignment from Landis.

Indians manager Frank Robinson hated umpire Ron Luciano and fined his players $200 if they talked to him during a game. Robinson's animosity probably stemmed from his days with the Orioles when Luciano and manager Earl Weaver regularly feuded (see also *Ejections*).

On September 20, 1999, umpire John Shulock went out toward the mound to confront pitcher Wilson Alvarez, after the pitcher had hit him with a pitch. American League president Gene Budig suspended Shulock for three games and fined him for his "overly aggressive behavior, display of temper, inappropriate remarks and physical contact."

George Steinbrenner. The Yankees owner incurred a number of fines after taking over in 1973 as the managing partner of the club. In 1983 he was fined $5,000 for a shouting match in which he traded insults with White Sox owners Eddie Einhorn and Jerry Reinsdorf, who were each fined $2,500.

Steinbrenner was fined $50,000 one spring training when he insulted National League umpires. He was also suspended for a week by American League president Lee MacPhail for blasting an American League umpire after Dave Winfield was ejected from a game. It was his feud with Winfield that led to Steinbrenner being *Barred From Baseball* and a huge fine by the commissioner.

In October 1998 Steinbrenner was fined $25,000 for "inappropriate comments" about the umpiring during Game 2 of the ALCS. Steinbrenner told reporters that home plate umpire Ted Hendry was known to be among the worst umpires in the league and that it was "too bad this great game had to be decided by a call like that." Hendry did not call interference on a play at first base in the 12th inning of Game 2. The Indians scored the lead run and went on to win 4–1.

Steinbrenner also levied a few fines of his own. Sparky Lyle and Ed Figueroa were once fined for sleeping through a Steinbrenner speech.

Ted Turner. The Braves owner was fined $25,000 in August 1983 when he prematurely told Braves outfielder Brett Butler that he would be the "player to be named later" in an uncompleted trade with the Indians. Bowie Kuhn nevertheless allowed Butler to finish the season with the Braves.

George Argyros. In the 1980s the Mariners owner was planning to sell the club and buy the Padres. He was fined $10,000 for tampering when he phoned Padres manager Larry Bowa to offer congratulations after his club beat the Dodgers in a regular season game. He had been warned not to have any contact with the Padres during the ultimately unsuccessful negotiations.

Largest/Albert Belle. In spring 1996 Albert Belle was fined

$50,000 for his profanity-filled tirade against NBC-TV reporter Hannah Storm during the World Series. It was the largest player fine in history. By accepting the fine, Belle avoided a suspension.

In early May 1996 Belle was accused of hitting *Sports Illustrated* photographer Tony Tomsic. Reportedly there was a question whether Belle had acted intentionally, but most reports made it clear that Belle threw two balls at the photographer with the intent of having him leave the field during warm-ups. One ball broke the skin on Tomsic's hand. He had complied with Belle's request that he stop photographing the players while they were stretching near the dugout. When they moved to the outfield to warm-up, Tomsic moved to the edge of the tarp for more photographs. Belle was quickly ordered to get counseling for his aggressive behavior. In response, he hit two home runs that night.

On May 31, 1996, Belle smashed into Brewers second baseman Fernando Vina with a forearm shot to the neck, triggering a brawl that resulted in a three-day suspension for Belle.

Rollie Fingers (1946–)

Hall of Fame 1992

"A fellow has to have faith in God above and Rollie Fingers in the bullpen." — A's manager Alvin Dark.

"Rollie Fingers is married to a sportswriter. She writes a column for a suburban newspaper. One year she gave him a two-foot high statue of W.C. Fields for his birthday. His heroes are not baseball players. His hero is the late comedian, and the walls of his home are covered by life-sized posters of this funny man. Fingers is funny himself.... With a rubber arm, a sharp slider, and good control, the slender, towering hurler is a superb specialist." — Bill Libby in *Charlie O & the Angry A's* (1975).

The second true reliever elected to the Hall of Fame, Fingers saved 341 games over a 17-year career that began in 1968.

Before becoming the premier reliever of the early 1970s, Roland Glen Fingers was raised in California by a father who had played in the Cardinals organization. After starring in American Legion ball and junior college, Fingers signed with the A's in 1965 and made it to the Major Leagues in 1968 for one game.

"Matchbox" sculpture using bats on display at the Great American Ballpark in Cincinnati.

Fingers was a starter from 1969 through most of 1971, though he saved 17 games in 1971. He blossomed in 1972 with 11 relief wins and 21 saves to lead the A's to the World Series. Fingers then established himself as the premier reliever of the 1970s, saving 20 or more games six times in an era when the "closer" first became an essential component of a Major League club.

Fingers stayed with the A's for 10 years until signing with the Padres for four seasons beginning in 1977. In 1981 he was traded to the Brewers and helped them into the postseason with a league-leading 28 saves and 1.04 ERA on his way to receiving the MVP and Cy Young Awards.

Fingers missed the 1983 season due to injury and then came back with the Brewers to post 23 saves in 1984 and 17 in 1985 before retiring. He finished his 17-year career with 341 saves and a 114–118 record to go with a 2.90 ERA. He is the purported answer to a trivia question, "Who is the only Hall of Fame pitcher with a losing record?": except that the question is a misnomer — Satchel Paige had a 28–31 record in the Major Leagues.

Fire

"Let L.A. burn. I don't live there anymore." — Disgruntled Dodger outfielder Darryl Strawberry when informed of devastating November 1993 fires in his hometown.

"You think Ron Davis isn't trying to get traded? He's done everything but light himself on fire at Minnesota." — Broadcaster Al Michaels in 1982. Davis apparently needed a little more lighter fluid: he was not traded until 1986.

"Things have been bad enough. That's like pouring more fire on the gasoline." — A Sparky Anderson malapropism when asked if he was concerned that the 2003 Tigers could break the Mets' 1962 record for futility.

"Britt Burns, Wildfire Schulte, Sparky Lyle, Flame Delhi, Al Stokes, Smoky Burgess, Tully Sparks"

19th Century Ballparks. Fire was a constant problem for the old wooden structures that predated the steel and concrete ballparks built shortly after 1900. Ballparks in the early years only lasted about five years because fire and rapid decay were major problems.

Fire damaged the St. Louis park six times in 10 years during the 19th century. In 1894 fires erupted in Baltimore, Philadelphia, Boston and Chicago. At one point three parks burned within a few weeks and people feared that there was a baseball arsonist on the loose.

Great Chicago Fire. The Great Chicago Fire of 1871 may have cost the Chicago White Stockings the National Association championship that season. The White Stockings lost their park, uniforms and equipment and the club had no money to replace them. Nevertheless, the team completed the season and only lost the pennant on the last day of the season to the Athletics, losing 6–1 in a game played in Brooklyn. After that season, Chicago did not field a National Association team until 1874.

St. Louis. On April 16, 1898, the St. Louis grandstand collapsed due to fire and over 100 fans were injured. With the help of the players, temporary circus seats were erected and St. Louis defeated Chicago 14–1.

Cincinnati. When Cincinnati's new park opened in 1902 it was billed as "The Palace of the Fans" and "fireproof."

Fenway Park. The left field foul line bleachers at Fenway Park burned down on May 8, 1926. The ballpark was renovated over the winter of 1933–1934, but a fire on January 5, 1934, burned most of the new wooden grandstands. They were replaced in time for the season opener in April.

Braves Mascot. In 1970 Braves mascot Chief Noc-A-Homa accidently set fire to his tepee while attempting to send up smoke signals. Fans helped put out the fire by emptying their beer cups on the Chief.

Luxury Box. On July 20, 1993, a fire broke out on the club level of Atlanta-Fulton County Stadium about 90 minutes before a Braves game against the Cardinals. The club was just about to introduce new first baseman Fred McGriff to the press when a food-warming unit tipped over in a luxury box near the press box. The fire burned for more than an hour, torching a radio booth and five luxury boxes.

Firecrackers

"It's not like we were in the car plotting, like, to blow up a plane or anything." — Eric Davis after being in a car with Vince Coleman when Coleman tossed the equivalent of a third of a stick of dynamite (M-100) into a crowd of fans outside Dodger Stadium. The incident occurred on July 24, 1993 and an 11-year-old boy and a 2 _ year-old girl were injured. Coleman plea-bargained a felony charge down to a misdemeanor possession of an explosive device.

The Mets then released Coleman despite a press conference in which Coleman, surrounded by his family, pathetically attempted to apologize for the incident. The response of Mets owner Fred Wilpon: "Vince Coleman was a total mistake by this organization."

Bret Saberhagen. On July 7, 1993, Bret Saberhagen threw a lighted firecracker near reporters after the game. Three weeks later he used a water gun to spray writers with bleach. He was suspended by the club for the first five days of the 1994 season.

Fan Injury. In July 1994 four fans were sent to the hospital and 29 were injured at Royals Stadium when a noisemaker exploded in the right field stands.

On July 8, 2003, in Oakland, a fan threw a cherry bomb in the left-field stands, injuring an eight-year-old boy enough to send him to the hospital. The 21-year-old fan, Travares Moore, was identified and arrested.

Fireman of the Year

"Larry Bearnarth and Tom Sturdivant, the [1964 Mets] relievers, have been uneven to date; the latter two might as well sleep with their rubber boots on, for they will be summoned to a lot of dangerous fires this summer." — Roger Angell in *The Summer Game* (1972).

See also *Relief Pitchers* and *Saves*.

In 1960 the first winners of this relief pitcher award were Lindy McDaniel of the Cardinals with 26 saves and Mike Fornieles of the Red Sox with a 10–5 record and 14 saves. However, the save was not yet an official statistic.

First At-Bat
See *At-Bats, First Game of Career* and *Home Runs — First At-Bat*

First Base

"I Can't Get to First Base with You" — Song written and recorded in 1935 by Eleanor Gehrig (Eleanor Twitchell) and Fred Fisher.

"There are some people who know absolutely nothing about baseball. They not only cannot get to first base; they do not know where first base is.*

*It is to the right." — Fred Schwed, Jr., in *How to Watch a Baseball Game* (1957).

In 1894 the rules first provided that a runner could run past first base without being tagged out. However, the practice had been in effect for a number of years (see also *Baserunning*).

First Basemen

"The first baseman is a big stiff, and since the beginning of time, big stiffs have played first base. He can't run, he can't field, he can't even bend over ... that's because their real position is batter.... There is a formula for first basemen — the more homers they hit, the fewer balls they have to catch." — Pete Franklin in *You Could Argue but You'd Be Wrong* (1988).

See also *Errors*.

Fielding.

"One of the most tenacious of these [myths].... This story has been repeated so many times that it has long since become baseball gospel." — Harold Seymour on Charles Comiskey's purported first base innovations, in *Baseball: The Early Years* (1960). Comiskey has often been credited as the first to play off the bag, in the 1880s. However, the practice was common by the 1860s and others credit Joe Start of the National Association New York Mutuals with beginning this fielding strategy. Comiskey is also credited with moving the first baseman back and away from the bag and having his pitchers cover first base on certain plays.

Best Defensive First Basemen.

"Others will feel that I should pick Lou Gehrig over Chase. Or George Sisler over both of them. But I pick [Hal] Chase.... He was so much better than anybody I ever saw on first base that — to me — it was no contest, and I still feel that way." — Babe Ruth. Chase was considered a wizard around first base, but his propensity for throwing games made him unreliable (see also *Gambling and Fixed Games*). See also Donald Dewey and Nicholas Acocella, *The Black Prince of Baseball* (2004); Martin Donell Kohout, *Hal Chase: The Defiant Life and Turbulent Times of Baseball's Biggest Crook* (2004).

Jack Dunn, Jr., manager of the International League's Baltimore Orioles, once observed about Mickey Vernon: "Mickey was so smooth around the bag that he could have played first base wearing a tuxedo!"

George Sisler starred at first base for the Browns from 1915 through 1927 before being traded.

Keith Hernandez may have been the top defensive first baseman of his era, winning 11 Gold Glove Awards in the 1970s and 1980s.

Best Overall. Lou Gehrig and Jimmie Foxx are considered the two greatest first basemen of all time, primarily because of their outstanding batting skills. Hank Greenberg is a close third for the same reason

Most Games. In 1994 Eddie Murray played in his 2,369th game at first base, the most in Major League history. He finished his career in 1997 with 2,413. Nineteenth century first baseman Jake Beckley previously held the record.

Books. Donald Honig, *The Greatest First Basemen of All Time* (1988); Ira L. Smith, *Baseball's Famous First Basemen* (1956).

First Game of Career

"This is his first Major League debut." — Cubs broadcaster Steve Stone when Giants reliever Bill VanLandingham made a relief appearance in 1994.

"There is a certain amount of fascination to the big-league debut of any athlete. Sometimes they are incredible successes. Sometimes they are frenetic failures. Sometimes they are tinted with comedy, tragedy, pathos…." — Sportswriter Arthur Daley.

See also **Home Runs—First At-Bat.**

A sampling of Major League debuts:

Henry Aaron. Aaron was 0-for-5 (0-for-4 in his autobiography) on Opening Day, April 13, 1954, against Bud Podbielan and the Reds. The immortal Jim Greengrass of the Reds hit four doubles in the game.

Fred Clarke and Cecil Travis. On June 30, 1894, Clarke of the Louisville Colonels of the National League was 5-for-5 in his first game (a Major League record), on his way to a career total of 2,703 hits. The only other Major League player to debut so successfully was Cecil Travis of the Senators on May 16, 1933. Travis had five hits in 12 innings.

Ty Cobb. The Tiger rookie doubled off Jack Chesbro in a 5–3 victory on August 30, 1905.

Dizzy Dean. Dean pitched a three-hitter against the Pirates on the last day of the 1930 season but was called up too late (after August 31) to pitch in the World Series that year. He then spent the entire 1931 season in the minor leagues after a spring training fight with catcher Gabby Street.

Joe DiMaggio. DiMaggio's first hit was a single to left field off Jack Knott of the Browns. He had two singles and a triple in a 14–5 victory in 1936.

Bob Feller. The teenage pitching star debuted against Major League talent in an exhibition game against the Cardinals. He struck out eight in three innings and Leo Durocher was his first strikeout victim. In his first official Major League game in 1936 Feller pitched two innings of a 16–3 victory over the A's. He allowed one run, three hits and struck out two.

Jason Jennings. On August 24, 2001, the Rockies pitcher beat the Mets 10–0 in his Major League debut. He pitched a five-hit shutout, and had three hits, including a home run. He was the first pitcher since 1900 to pitch a shutout and hit a home run in his first Major League game.

Walter Johnson. On August 2, 1907, the new Senators pitcher faced the Tigers, giving up six hits in six innings. Though he left the game trailing 2–1, his debut was described as "impressive." It became commonplace for fans to brag that they had attended Johnson's Major League debut. At a game in the 1930s the Senators invited all fans who had been in attendance to sit in a special section with commemorative badges. Only 2,841 fans attended the 1907 debut, but over 8,000 showed up to receive the commemorative badges.

Addie Joss. Joss pitched a one-hitter in his Major League debut in 1902.

Juan Marichal. On July 19, 1960, the Giants pitcher threw a one-hit 2–0 shutout against the Phillies at Candlestick Park. He gave up only an 8th inning single to catcher Clay Dalrymple, while walking one and striking out 12. Four days later, Marichal pitched a four-hitter against the pennant-bound Pirates.

Christy Mathewson.

"The untried semi-professional possessed great speed and plenty of confidence in himself but could not control his curves." — Newspaper account of Mathewson's Major League pitching debut on July 17, 1900. He came in to relieve in the 5th inning for the Giants.

Willie Mays.

"I can't do it, Mr. Leo. You better bench me." — Mays, who played his first Major League game on May 25, 1950, going 0-for-5 in an 8–5 Giants win. He did not get a hit for 12 at-bats until homering off Warren Spahn. He then went 0-for-13 for a 1-for-25 start in the Major Leagues. It was during this streak that he told manager Leo Durocher he could not succeed. Spahn later commented that had he not given up the home run, National League pitchers may never have been terrorized by Mays for the next 20 years.

Stan Musial. Musial had a single and triple in his first game, played April 14, 1942.

Willie McCovey. McCovey had two triples and two singles in his first game for the Giants on July 30, 1959, hitting them against future Hall of Fame pitcher Robin Roberts. McCovey went on to bat .354 and was voted Rookie of the Year.

Satchel Paige. The Negro League star debuted in the Major Leagues on his birthday, July 7, 1948, pitching two scoreless innings for the Indians at age 42.

Casey Stengel.

"I broke in with four hits and the writers promptly decided they had seen the new Ty Cobb. It took me only a few days to correct that impression." — Stengel about his debut on July 27, 1912.

George Van Haltren. On June 27, 1887, Van Haltren debuted as a pitcher for the Chicago White Stockings. He struck out the first batter and then walked a National League record 16 batters in a 17–11 loss. Nevertheless, he went on to a stellar Major League career and is a borderline candidate for the Hall of Fame.

Ted Williams. Williams had a double in four at-bats in his debut on April 20, 1939, against the Yankees.

Cy Young. Pitching for Cleveland on August 6, 1890, Young defeated the White Stockings 8–1 while giving up three hits.

Pitchers. On April 2, 2003 the Tigers became the first team in history to debut four pitchers in the same game: Jeremy Bonderman, Wilfredo Ledezma, Chris Spurling and Matt Roney.

Washout. On September 19, 2002, Twins rookie outfielder Mike Ryan had two hits, scored two runs, and drove home two runs, all in the 1st inning of his Major League debut. Unfortunately, the game was rained out after two innings and all records were washed away.

Consecutive Hits/Start of Career. Ted Cox of the 1977 Red Sox holds the record of six consecutive hits in his first six official at-bats (over two games), the most in a row at the start of a career. He broke the record set by Cecil Travis, who had five in an extra inning game for the Senators in 1933. He also tied the Major League record for most hits in his first game, four. Willie McCovey and Casey Stengel are among the players who share the record.

Fish

"Lefty Herring, Catfish Hunter, Dizzy Trout, Marlin Stuart, Catfish Metkovich, Bobby Sturgeon, Newt Fish, Roger Salmon, Newt Randall, Doc Bass, Chico Salmon, George Barnicle, Art Herring, Preacher Roe, Bill Whaling, Dick Bass, Oyster Burns, Thornton Kipper, Dick Conger, Snapper Kennedy, Ernie Koy, George Gill, Jim Gill, Fin Wilson, Jay Hook"

See **Florida Marlins** and **Food.**

Carlton Fisk (1947–)

Hall of Fame 2000

"You don't play baseball. You are involved in it. You work at it." — Fisk.

"It's not often a player or a person of any profession has a moment in the universe that is just yours … and that was mine." — Fisk on his 1975 World Series Game 6 home run.

Fisk caught a record 2,226 Major League games over 24 seasons with the Red Sox and White Sox.

A child of New England, born in 1947 in Vermont, Carlton Ernest "Pudge" Fisk was Boston's No. 1 pick in the 1967 draft after briefly attending the University of New Hampshire. His minor league career was a smooth, unspectacular march through the Red Sox system. He made brief appearances with the big club in 1969 and 1971, and his first full year in 1972 was sensational. A right-handed batter, Fisk hit .293 with 22 home runs. He tied for the league lead in triples with nine and won the Gold Glove. He was voted Rookie of the Year unanimously.

The rest of his years in Boston were marked by a steady excellence that would become the hallmark of his career. His best overall season with the Red Sox was perhaps 1977 when he hit .315 with 106 runs, 102 RBIs and 26 home runs. Certainly his famed, extra-inning home run at Fenway Park to win Game 6 of the 1975 World Series against the Reds was the most memorable single moment of his career.

In 1981 Fisk moved via free agency to Chicago, where his methodical success continued. He established career marks for home runs and RBIs with 37 and 107 in 1985. Fisk reached numerous catching milestones with the White Sox. In 1988 he broke the American league record for games caught with 1,807. In successive years, 1989 and 1990, he broke the American League and then-Major League marks for career home runs by a catcher.

Fisk continued to catch full time and produce offensively well into his 40's. In 1990 at the age of 43 he managed to catch 116 games while hitting .285 with 18 home runs. On June 22, 1993, Fisk caught his 2,226th career game to set the Major League mark. He was released six days later and his bitter relationship with White Sox ownership simmered for years.

Fisk finished his career as the finest catcher of his generation, with 1,276 runs scored and 2,356 hits. He had a career .269 batting average, 376 home runs and 1,330 RBIs. Defensively he recorded 11,369 putouts, second all-time, and a .988 fielding average. Despite playing more career games in Chicago, Fisk entered the Hall of Fame in 2000 wearing a Red Sox cap.

Fitness See Conditioning

Five Decade Players See Four and Five Decade Players and Longest Careers

Five Hundred Wins See Three Hundred Wins

Fixed Games See Gambling and Fixed Games

Flags

"For several years now I've found myself trembling whenever the National Anthem is played at sporting events, not out of patriotic sentiment but of fear that some flag-crazed lunatic sitting in back of me will be overcome by his emotions and seize the opportunity to bludgeon me from behind with his souvenir Louisville Slugger."— George Kimball in "Opening Day at Fenway" (1973).

Upside Down. In 1928 the Giants hosted the Braves in their home opener. As Mayor Jimmy Walker and 35,000 fans watched, the American flag was raised — upside down.

As part of the pregame ceremonies for Game 2 of the 1992 World Series in Atlanta, the local Marine Corp detachment marched on the field carrying the American and Canadian flags. They failed to notice that they carried the maple leaf on the Cana-

dian flag upside down. The uproar ended when the Marines asked for and received permission to carry the flag properly at the first game in Toronto. The Canadian Mounties carried the American flag (properly). Deputy commissioner Steve Greenberg received a two-page fax showing the Canadian flag and the word "Top" printed across the top.

Rick Monday.
"If you're going to burn the flag, don't do it in front of me. I've been to too many veterans' hospitals and seen too many broken bodies of guys who tried to protect it."— Monday.

On April 25, 1976, in the bottom of the 4th inning at Dodger Stadium, Rick Monday was in center field for the Cubs against the Dodgers when a man and his 11-year-old son ran onto the field and tried to light an American flag on fire. The man reportedly was trying to draw attention to his wife's supposed "imprisonment" in a mental hospital.

Monday raced over and grabbed the flag before the fire protest began, prompting a standing ovation from the 25,167 fans. At the end of the inning the crowd stood and sang "God Bless America." Monday was saluted throughout the country and received congratulatory telegrams from President Ford and former President Nixon. The man and his son were fined $80 each and sentenced to two years' probation. The flag now hangs in Monday's den. Cubs left fielder Jose Cardenal had ignored the flag bearers and later was not terribly amused by the attention Monday received: "Now we have three great patriots ... Lincoln, Washington and Monday."

In Play. Minute Maid Park in Houston has a flagpole in play on a hill in dead center field.

Patriot. In 2004 pitcher Keith Foulke wore a Red Sox cap that bore a U.S. flag. His father was in the Air Force and he wore it most of the season to show support for the troops in Iraq. After a letter of rebuke from the commissioner, he took it off. This was consistent with the collective bargaining agreement, which prevents players from making individual changes to hats, jerseys and anything else they wear. On July 4, 2004, all Major League players wore flags on their hats.

Elmer Flick (1876-1971)

Hall of Fame (VC) 1963
"Flick reported with a bat that he had turned out for himself on a lathe and kept in a canvas bag, and he began to wield it so efficiently that Francis Richter, a Philadelphia scribe, wrote: 'Flick is going to make the other outfielders hustle to hold their positions. He is the fastest and most promising youngster the Phillies have ever had.'"— Lee Allen and Tom Meany in Kings of the Diamond (1965).

Flick hit .313 in 13 Major League seasons for the Phillies, A's and Indians beginning in 1898.

An Ohio native, Elmer Harrison Flick began his professional career in late 1896 when he hit .438 in 31 games for Youngstown. By 1898 he was in the Major Leagues with the Phillies as an outfielder, batting .302 in 134 games. He peaked at .367 in 1900 and hit .336 in 1901. He jumped to the Athletics of the new American League in 1902, but the Phillies obtained an injunction against him and he could no longer play in Pennsylvania. He moved over to the Indians, where he remained for the duration of his 13-year career.

Flick had the distinction of having the lowest league-leading batting average in American League history when he hit .306 in 1905 — until Carl Yastrzemski led the league with a .301 average in 1968.

Known as one of the best all-around players in the game, Flick

Giants manager Bill Terry and New York City mayor Fiorello LaGuardia raise the flag to kick off the 1938 season at the Polo Grounds.

led the league in RBIs with 110 in 1900, stolen bases in 1904 and 1906, triples from 1905 through 1907, runs in 1906 and batting average and slugging average in 1905. The Indians once turned down a trade for Ty Cobb in exchange for Flick. Flick's career faded after he developed a stomach ailment, and his last three partial seasons were unproductive as his weight dropped from 165 to the 130s.

He finished his Major League career in 1910 with a .313 average and 334 stolen bases. He played two more seasons for Toledo of the American Association. After his retirement he was a part-time scout for the Indians.

Curt Flood Case See *Reserve Clause*

Floods

"Day Twelve. The rain continues. The ball diamond being on high ground is all that enables the game to carry on.

"Behind the Cubs' bench, under the empty bleacher, Little Walter has built a small fire inside a tiny circle of stones, and over a makeshift grill he dries out baseballs. There are only about a dozen available, and after each one comes in contact with the mud of the infield or the water of the outfield, it is tossed to the midget, who sees it smoked and toasted until he considers it suitable to pass

back to Bill Klem."—W.P. Kinsella in his mystical *The Iowa Baseball Confederacy* (1986).

"SURELY HOODOOED. Pirates Have Had Nothing but Hard Luck. Rains Have Prevented Most of Their Games on the Road and Their Park Is Underwater."—1901 dispatch in *The Sporting News*.

See also *Weather*.

Johnstown Flood. In 1889 the American Association's Louisville club was 27–111. On a midseason road trip during which they lost 21 games, they were mistakenly reported lost in the famous Pennsylvania flood.

Pittsburgh's Problems. In the 19th century the Pirates experienced flooding of their ballpark (a problem even into the 1960s). In 1901 a strong wind ripped off the roof.

On July 4, 1902, at Exposition Park, a special ground rule was used because of flooding in the outfield. Any ball hit into "Lake Dreyfuss" (after owner Barney Dreyfuss) was ruled a ground rule single (double in one source). By the second game of the doubleheader that day, the water was only 20 feet behind second base. Nevertheless, the clubs finished both games and the Pirates swept.

Cincinnati. In 1937 Crosley Field was flooded with 20 feet of water and Gene Schott and Lee Grissom rowed out to the outfield, a stunt captured in a famous photograph.

Astrodome. The Astros cancelled a few games at the Astrodome due to heavy rains that caused flooding in the vicinity of the stadium.

Florida Marlins

National League 1993–

"The 1993 Florida Marlins are going to smell worse fresh than other fish do after a week."—Columnist Dave George in anticipation of a weak expansion team in Florida.

Origins. The Marlins were one of the two National League **Expansion** clubs for the 1993 season. In 1991 Miami was selected as the club's home despite intense bidding for a Florida-based club by Orlando and St. Petersburg.

First Game.

"The ghost of knuckleballs past."—Marlins outfielder Jeff Conine during the 2003 postseason, asked to compare the Marlins' brief history (begun with a knuckleball) with the fabled ghosts of Yankee Stadium.

The Marlins debuted on April 5, 1993, in front of 46,115 fans (or 42,234) at Joe Robbie Stadium in Miami. A U.S. mail carrier delivered the first ball from the Hall of Fame to Joe DiMaggio, who made the ceremonial first pitch. Charlie Hough threw a knuckleball for a strike on the first pitch and earned the first win for the club, a 6–3 victory over Hough's former team, the Dodgers. *Sports Illustrated* noted that Florida began its existence with a 1–0 record and the Dodgers slipped to 7,506–6,849.

Key Owners.

H. Wayne Huizenga/1993–1999. Huizenga was 51 when he was awarded the franchise on June 10, 1991. He purchased a 50% interest in Joe Robbie Stadium in 1990 and owned 15% of the Miami Dolphins and the new NHL Panthers. He had lived in South Florida since 1953, starting a one-truck waste collection route in 1962 in Fort Lauderdale. By 1971 he had merged with a relative in Chicago to form Waste Management, Inc., the largest waste hauler in the country. He resigned from the company in 1984 to pursue other interests. In 1987 he bought Blockbuster Video with 19 stores. By 1992 the company had grown to over 3,000 stores.

Huizenga created the college football Blockbuster Bowl and was reported to be worth $600 million in 1994. He owned the NFL Miami Dolphins at the time he purchased the Marlins.

Huizenga bought the Marlins franchise for the entry fee of $95 million. Controversy arose in mid–1991 when it was revealed that Pirates president Carl Barger was on the Miami club's board during the franchise bidding process and that Barger intended to become the Marlins' president after the 1991 season. He was named president of the Marlins in July 1991, but died suddenly at baseball's December 1992 winter meetings. Former Expos general manager Dave Dombrowski was named the club's first general manager in September 1991.

After Huizenga sold the club he still received an estimated 62.5% of the Marlins' parking revenue, 30% of profits from concessions, and $2 million a year from the state as a piece of the $60 million in tax incentives he initially was given to place the Marlins in Florida. His sale to John Henry was approved in January 1999.

John W. Henry (1999–2002).

"Perhaps the world's foremost commodities trader."—*Money* magazine.

Born in Illinois in 1949, Henry grew up in Arkansas on farms owned by his father. When Henry was 25, his father died and the son was charged with running the family's crop operations. From there he became a commodities trader focusing on corn, soybeans and wheat. He sold most of his farm holdings in 1980, based on his "trend analysis" style of investing that made him one of the leading commodities investment advisors. By 1992 he was managing an almost $700 million investment fund portfolio, and it was over $1 billion by 1994. In 1996 he was estimated to be worth at least $40 million.

Henry got his start in baseball in the late 1980s, when he became principal owner of the Tucson Toros, a Class AAA team, and the West Palm Beach Tropics of the short-lived **Senior Professional Baseball Association**. He attended several mostly California colleges, including UCLA, but never graduated.

In the 1990s he moved his base of operation from the Northeast to South Florida, and that led to his purchase of the Marlins from Huizenga. He wanted to purchase the Red Sox, and that goal came to fruition in 2002 through a complicated three-way deal with Jeffrey Loria.

Jeffrey Loria (2002–)

"Marlins owner Jeffrey Loria is Churchill, custodian of an empire that is, even in the first hours of the victory celebration, already dead."—Steve Rushin comparing post-war Britain to the 2003 Marlins' World Series victory and subsequent dismantling (*à la* 1997).

John Henry sold the club for $158.5 million to Loria, who had been credited with $120 million from Major League owners to buy him out of the **Montreal Expos** so that he could purchase the Marlins. Henry used his money to help buy the Red Sox. Loria, based in New York, had been dealing in 20th century art for almost 40 years.

Nickname. Huizenga picked the Marlins name for his favorite form of recreation, sportfishing, and because "the fish is a fierce fighter and adversary that tests your mettle." The name also had historic basis, as Miami had the minor league Marlins from 1956 through 1970 and from 1982 through 1988.

Key Seasons. In their first 11 seasons the Marlins finished above .500 twice. Both times they won the World Series.

1993. The Marlins were decent for a first-year club with a record of 64–98 and finished ahead of the Mets by five games. Orestes Destrade hit 20 home runs and Jeff Conine batted .292.

1997. The Marlins reached the World Series faster than any other expansion team to that time. The Marlins were the National League wild card team with a 92–70 record, finishing nine games behind the Braves. They swept the Giants in the division series and then beat the Braves in six games for the National League pennant. In the World Series, they beat the Indians in seven games, winning in extra innings. Edgar Renteria drove in Craig Counsell in the bottom of the 11th inning for the victory. Moises Alou had 23 home runs and 115 RBIs. Alex Fernandez won 17 games and Kevin Brown won 16, while closer Robb Nen had 35 saves.

1998. After the 1997 season the club dropped its payroll by $20 million and finished last with a 54–108 record. It was the first time in Major League history that a team won the World Series and then finished last the following season.

2003.

"It's a great story. Maybe the story of the century." [maybe not!]—Marlins manager Jack McKeon after the club won the 2003 World Series.

"I'm a huge Marlins fan. I've been following this plucky team ever since they beat the San Francisco Giants, which was what, nearly a week ago. I live and die by this team! When they win I drink champagne and dance a lot. This is also what I do when they lose, because there is no point in wasting champagne. But I dance in a more subdued manner."—Dave Barry in October 2003.

Led by 72-year-old manager Jack McKeon, the Marlins were the wild card team with a record of 91–71. They surprised the Giants in the division series and then beat the Cubs in seven games before taking out the Yankees in six games. The club was led by catcher Ivan Rodriguez who hit .297 and appeared in 139 games. Pitcher Dontrelle Willis was named Rookie of the Year while compiling a record of 14–6, and Josh Beckett had two postseason shutouts. See Dan Schlossberg with Kevin Baxter, *Miracle Over Miami: How the 2003 Marlins Shocked the World* (2004).

Key Player.

Jeff Conine emerged as a hitting star for the Marlins, batting .302 and driving in 105 runs. He missed only 11 games in the club's first three seasons.

Preston Wilson hit over 100 home runs for the club in four seasons before leaving for the Rockies in 2003.

Luis Castillo hit .292 for the club and played a stellar second base beginning in 1996 and into the 2004 season.

Derek Lee played six seasons for the Marlins and hit 129 home runs while batting over .270 four times.

Key Managers.

"I was hoping we'd be opening at Joe Robbie Stadium against Elmer Milktoast and the Gigiville nine. But unfortunately, it's Bobby Cox and the world champion Atlanta Braves in Atlanta."— Florida Marlins manager John Boles on his managerial debut in 1996. He was fired near the end of the season, but returned to manage the club in 1999 and lasted through 48 games of the 2001 season.

Rene Lachemann was the club's first manager, lasting into the 1996 season with marginal success. He was fired in early July 1996 with a record of 39–47. His clubs never finished higher than third as he compiled a record of 221–285 over 3 1/2 seasons.

Jim Leyland had one stellar and one horrific season for the club. The Marlins won the World Series under Leyland in 1997, but after the team was decimated in the off-season, the club finished 54–108 and Leyland was fired.

Jack McKeon took over the struggling club in May 2003 and led them to the best record in the National League over the balance of the season and to a World Series victory over the Yankees. He was rewarded for his efforts by being named Manager of the Year.

Ballpark.

"There are roughly 1,000 projects more deserving of tax dollars than a new tank for Billy the Marlin.... One of the problems with professional sports franchises is their inherent sense of self-importance. It's as if South Florida, minus the Marlins, suddenly would shrink in size and relevance to Yeehaw Junction."— Jeff Miller of the *Miami Herald*.

The Marlins play their games at Pro Player Stadium, originally known as Joe Robbie Stadium. "Pro Player" is the apparel brand of Fruit of the Loom. During a 1992 exhibition game it was discovered that the facility had no bullpens. The dimensions from left to right field are 330–385–404–385–345 and seating capacity is 47,662.

In 1999 the club announced plans to build a retractable roof stadium in downtown Miami, but by 2004 still nothing had come of it. In December 2003 Miami leaders approved asking the county to approve a half-penny sales tax to raise $225 million for a new stadium; and nothing may come of it: "I will eat my hat if they can build a downtown, retractable dome stadium for $325 million."— Baseball economist Andrew Zimbalist, on Miami leaders' plan to build a ballpark for that price.

Key Broadcasters. Jay Randolph called 18 seasons with the Car-

dinals and had been associated with NBC sports since 1968 when he was tapped to become the club's first number one broadcaster; but the relationship never materialized and he stayed with the seniors golf tour.

Before regular season Major League Baseball came to Florida for the 1993 season, Floridians had access to at least 18 Major League teams through radio and television network broadcasts.

The radio play-by-play was first handled by long-time Major League broadcaster Joel Angel. He stayed from 1993 through 2000, and then was fired in favor of Dave Van Horne. Van Horne had broadcast 22 years for the Expos before moving South. Felo Ramirez broadcast in Spanish for the club from its inception in 1993 through 2004. Former player Tommy Hutton began broadcasting on television for the club in 1997, coming over from the Blue Jays.

Books.

"If the Marlins win the World Series, the unlikeliest of outcomes for a team major league owners considered killing two years ago, someone ought to write a book about it."— Bill Shaikin before the 2003 Series.

Gordon Edes and Robert Mayer, *Marlins Mania: The Rookie Season of the Florida Marlins* (1993); Bob Italia, *Florida Marlins* (1997); Dan LeBatard, *Marlins! Top of the First* (1993); Kevin M. McCarthy, *Baseball in Florida* (1996); John Nichols, *The Florida Marlins* (2003).

Fly Ball

"All the Padres need is a fly ball in the air."— Jerry Coleman.

"Only Joe DiMaggio, says Jimmy Cannon of the *New York Post*, 'had more natural grace and superior instinct [than Willie Mays] to anticipate a ball's flight by a system of calculation that can't be defined and never taught.'"— Sportswriter Irv Goodman.

"If a woman has to choose between catching a fly ball and saving an infant's life, she will choose to save the infant's life without even considering if there are men on base."— Dave Barry.

"The revolutionary plan called for a batter to stand still at the plate, instead of running to first base, when he hit a fly ball to the outfield. He would stay at the plate until the ball was caught. Then he would tag up and sprint toward first, exactly like a baserunner heads for home when he is trying to score on a sacrifice fly.

"The outfielder would throw to first base as soon as he caught the ball. It would then be up to the player who had hit the ball to beat the throw to first. If the first baseman caught the ball before he crossed the bag, he would be called out, just as if he had been thrown out on a ground ball hit to an infielder."— Suggested rule change by a fan in a letter to Johnny Mize, reported in *Baseball's First Basemen*, by Ira. L. Smith (1956).

In 1864 it was ruled that balls caught on one bounce would no longer be recorded as outs. This rule was originally proposed in 1857 but was rejected by the prominent but fading New York Knickerbockers because of safety concerns (no gloves) and the continued reliance on some aspects of cricket. During the 1850s and 1860s, individual games had their own fly ball rule depending on prior agreement of the teams.

Deal. Gil Hodges, a converted catcher who played first base for the Dodgers, was unsteady trying to catch pop flies. He supposedly cut a deal with second baseman Jackie Robinson that Hodges would pay Robinson $5 every time Robinson caught a popup in Hodges' territory. They had an argument during the 1952 World Series when Robinson insisted on $10 for a World Series catch. After general manager Buzzie Bavasi intervened, Hodges told him they had settled the dispute at $7.50.

No Action. In 2003 Diamondbacks sinkerball pitcher Brandon Webb retired 78 consecutive batters on groundouts, strikeouts or infield putouts.

Flying See *Airline Travel*

Foliage

"Ken Ash, Howard Maple, Forrest Crawford, Harvey Branch, Pete LePine, Estel Crabtree, Alan Ashby, Orval Grove, Limb Mc-Henry, Wilbur Wood"

"Guy Bush, Bush Bates, Ron Reed, Jeff Holly, Bob Sprout, Ducky Hemp, Ed Holly, Cactus Keck, Jack Reed, Charlie Root, Algie McBride"

"George Daisy, Ben Flowers, Jim Lillie, Daisy Davis, Clint Blume, Garland Buckeye, Fred Stem, Jake Flowers, Pete Rose"

"Lee Moss, Ray Moss, Ivy Olson, Mike Ivie, Ivy Wingo"

Food

"There should be more on sunflower seeds in your book. They're the regular food of baseball and softball." — Seven-year-old Katherine Fraser Light.

"Jeter is a six-tool player. I've never eaten with him so I can't tell you if he has good table manners, but I would imagine he has those too." — Rangers manager Johnny Oates in 1999.

"I prefer fast food." — Rocky Bridges, on why he won't eat snails.

"I've started taking food orally again." — Red Sox president Larry Lucchino a few days after the Red Sox lost their 2003 postseason series to the Yankees.

See also *Candy, Endorsements* and *Hot Dogs.*

Beef.

"Buy a steak for a player on another club after the game, but don't even speak to him on the field. Get out there and beat them to death." — Leo Durocher.

"Watch this!" — Former 1930s outfielder Jake Powell just before he choked to death trying to eat an entire steak in one bite three years after he retired.

According to Albert Spalding, Jim "Orator" O'Rourke once ordered six plates of roast beef at a luncheon and then had five base hits that afternoon against the White Stockings.

Designated hitter Ron Blomberg claims to have eaten 28 hamburgers in one sitting.

Bread. In the 1960s Carl Yastrzemski endorsed Big Yaz Special Fitness White Bread.

Cake. A piece of Joe DiMaggio's wedding cake, from his marriage in 1939 to actress Dorothy Arnold, sold at a 2002 auction for $1,742. The cake was petrified.

Cereal. See *Endorsements.*

Chicken.

"To get a better piece of chicken, you'd have to be a rooster." — Slogan proposed by Mickey Mantle for his unsuccessful fried chicken restaurant chain. It was not used.

"You can't make chicken salad out of chickenshit." — Senators manager Joe Kuhel lamenting the sorry state of the Senators, when he was fired in 1949 after finishing last.

In 2004 the Giants passed out rubber chickens to fans, at $10 a pop (money donated to charity), which they waved whenever an opposing pitcher intentionally walked Barry Bonds. Francine Bradley was interviewed on the issue. She said it was wrong to consider chickens cowards and, "as a poultry scientist, it disturbs me greatly." Her comment prompted this from newscaster Bret Lewis:

"She's a poultry scientist. Imagine how disturbed her parents must be."

In 1867 Charlie Pabor ate only chicken while in training with the Brooklyn Atlantics.

Red Sox third baseman Wade Boggs carried chicken-eating to an extreme. He ate it before virtually every game and published chicken recipes.

Roy Campanella once played for Class B Nashau in New Hampshire. A local businessman offered 100 chickens to any home run hitter; Campanella hit 13. When chicken owner Jack Fallgren went out of business, Campanella bought out his remaining stock of 3,000 birds and went into the chicken business.

Cheese.

"The few thousand chilly Cheeseheads remaining from the crowd of 10,059 erupted into a bubbling fondue as they stood and cheered." — Kelly Whiteside in *Sports Illustrated* reporting on Brewers fans.

On December 3, 1987, a disgruntled fan drove his car into Pittsburgh's Three Rivers Stadium and tipped over a 70-gallon vat of cheese dip.

Donuts. In 2003 Krispy Kreme donuts staged a season-long promotion in which they gave away a dozen donuts to fans who attended games in which the Kansas City Royals recorded at least 12 hits. It seemed a good idea after the Royals had lost 100 games in 2002. The surprising 2003 club did it 27 times, costing Krispy Kreme 6.8 million donuts. Should have made it a baker's dozen.

Kosher Food.

"I thought it was a shanda that the city with the most Jews and the most baseball teams in America didn't provide a kosher option for observant families. Now kosher families can root and nosh at the same time." — New York City public advocate Mark Green in May 1998, on the new Kosher Food Stand at Shea Stadium. Another such stand opened at Yankee Stadium. The stands were to be closed on the Jewish Sabbath. David Senter, a graduate of Kol Yakkov Torah Center in New York, used his rabbinical degree to open these food courts, the first for-profit Orthodox Kosher concession stands in the Major Leagues.

In Baltimore, with the 21st largest Jewish population in the country, there was a certified kosher hot dog stand behind home plate run by Orthodox Jewish teenagers earning money to travel to Israel, but by 1998 the stand was a money-loser. At the end of the 5th inning the group held a prayer service that often attracted over 30 Orthodox fans. Also in 1998 a kosher restaurant at Joe Robbie Stadium in Miami (6th largest group) closed due to poor patronage.

Sweets.

"Cookie Cuckerillo, Pie Traynor, Brownie Foreman, Cookie Rojas, Honey Barnes, Rick Honeycutt, Mark Lemongello"

Parsimonious Reds owner Marge Schott presented many of her staff members with boxes of chocolate for Christmas in 1995. Inside each sealed box was a trading card company's promotion of a free trip to the *1991* Grammy Awards.

Relief pitcher Bob Locker claimed that he derived all his power from consuming honey.

In 1987 Astros reliever Charles Kerfeld asked for and received a contract clause giving him 37 boxes of Jello; which he used for miscellaneous clubhouse pranks.

Dieting.

"Nine teams in this league have managers, but Boston has a dietician." — Anonymous Angels player after Red Sox manager Dick Williams benched George Scott in 1967 for being overweight. It was later noted that the dietician led his club to a pennant.

"Science in 1941 consisted of laying off booze and fats."—Joe DiMaggio recalling the diet regimen of ballplayers.

"You mix two jiggers of Scotch to one jigger of Metrecal. So far I've lost five pounds and my driver's license."—Rocky Bridges describing his favorite diet drink.

"I never fill my stomach. My mother was a great cook, but my father told me, 'she's only filling your stomach so another woman never gets to. She's just trying to hold on to you.' Ever since I *can* eat more, but I never do."—91-year-old former Negro Leaguer Buck O'Neil on one of the secrets to a long life.

When George Steinbrenner arrived back with the Yankees in 1993 after a suspension, the first thing he did was place a copy of a new book in front of each player's locker during spring training. The book was *Home Plate Strategy: A Guide to Good Eating for Baseball Players.*

Egg. Joe Charboneau of the Indians once swallowed a raw egg in its shell, but it got stuck in his throat. A hard slap on the back broke the egg and he never performed the stunt again.

Soup.

"Soup Campbell, Noodles Hahn, Frank 'Noodles' Zupo"

Spice Rack.

"Laurin Pepper, George Curry, Pepper Martin, Salty Parker, Bob Spice, Herb Score, Bob Pepper, Tom Curry, Ray Pepper, Henry Sage, Herb Brett, Pat Carroway"

Favorite Foods. In a 1955 survey of the 36-man Giants roster during spring training, steak was the favorite of 20 of the players. Fried chicken was the choice of four; calves' liver, lamb chops, chicken, roast beef and roast pork all received one vote. Nevertheless, according to *The Sporting News*: "[N]one of these was Dusty's [Rhodes] choice. His? Macaroni and cheese."

Exotica. By 1997 fans could sample a wide variety of foods in Major League ballparks: edamame (soy beans), calamari and ahi tuna (San Francisco); California Roll sushi (Anaheim); Chili with chocolate and cinnamon (Cincinnati); biscotti, pierogies and eggrolls (Cleveland); carrot juice and herbal tea (Oakland); wild duck salad (New York—Shea Stadium); seafood martinis, crab cakes and Polynesian hot dogs (Baltimore); arepas (South American cornmeal crepes with cheese), rice and beans, and media noche ("midnight" sandwich made with a sweet bread, roasted pork leg, ham, swiss cheese, mustard, mayo and pickles), plantains, flan and Cuban ham croquettes (Miami); tuscan bruschetta and Willie's chili, named after Willie Stargell (Pittsburgh); Beaver Tails (fried dough shaped like a beaver's tail and dipped in cinnamon sugar or chocolate and hazelnuts.) (Montreal and Toronto); bison meat hot dogs (Atlanta). Atlanta also has a "Taste of the Majors" concession featuring a regional cuisine of the visiting team, such as Philly cheesesteaks when the Philadelphia Phillies are in town.

Fish.

"I've got a new invention. It's a revolving bowl for tired goldfish."—Yankee pitcher Lefty Gomez.

"No thanks, I don't drink."—Phillies outfielder Jeff Stone when offered a shrimp cocktail before dinner.

Before each start, pitcher Ben McDonald ate a can of mustard sardines.

Lou Gehrig's mother supposedly supplied the Yankees with pickled eel to keep them hitting.

Al Lopez once ate kippered herring and eggs for breakfast 17 days in a row because he was in a hitting streak.

In the 1980s Dodger Stadium began serving sushi at some of its food concessions. Sales increased dramatically with the success of Hideo Nomo in 1995 and vendors began roaming the stands with prepackaged sushi. The Florida Marlins also served sushi during games.

Fruit.

"Luke Appling, Peaches O'Neill, Frank Pears, Homer Peel, Bob Lemon, Gordon Pitts, Charlie Berry"

Meal Money. See *Meal Money*.

Pizza. In 1990 the Expos were flying from San Francisco to Montreal when they learned that they would have to refuel in Cleveland. The club's media relations director called ahead from the plane's phone and ordered eight large pizzas, which were delivered to the team's plane at 1:30 a.m.

Postgame Spread.

"I remember when I was in Atlanta and [manager] Eddie Mathews tipped over the spread. As soon as he left the room, we washed off the hot dogs and dipped them in mustard. So what good does that do?"—Braves outfielder Dusty Baker on why it did no good for the manager to tip over the postgame food table.

"Now, anybody who has ever seen baseball players attack a [postgame] spread is reminded anew how recently we've been promoted from the animal kingdom…. As with any postgame meal, it was probably enough that no one got hurt…"—Richard Hoffer in *Sports Illustrated*.

"It also might spare the Seattle Mariners a hefty clubhouse catering bill. Fans kept hearing how hungry scabs were to play, but this is ridiculous. The replacement Mariners scarfed down chips, ice cream and cheese at such an alarming rate in the Arizona Faux League that Seattle manager Lou Piniella, upon noticing the bulging waistlines, ordered lunchtime rations of half a sandwich and a bowl of soup."—Tim Kurkjian in *Sports Illustrated*.

Restaurants.

"Had Comiskey not taken to baseball he could have made a living as a cook. His skill in peeling potatoes, boning a bass and skinning an onion, is second to none. He takes the greatest pleasure in superintending cooking operations and, while others have their tussles with the muskie and bass, he labors over the stewpan and coffee pot in some clearing in the brush."—G.W. Axelson in "*Commy*" (1919).

"I've seen him order everything on the menu except, 'Thank you for dining with us.'"—Jerry Royster on teammate Dale Murphy.

"When we win, I'm so happy I eat a lot. When we lose, I'm so depressed I eat a lot. When we're rained out, I'm so disappointed I eat a lot."—Tommy Lasorda, who owned an Italian restaurant in Los Angeles that once was cited for health violations.

"People were not coming in anymore."—Reason given by a spokesman for Don Mattingly after he closed his restaurant, "Mattingly's 23," in Evansville, Indiana.

"To lure him out of the pantry, the Tigers would have to guarantee him a million dollars over the next five years. If they won't, *zut alors!* it's off to *la cuisine*, where his gentle touch with a *creme caramel* (with control, in the patois of the trade) is properly appreciated."—Art Hill in *I Don't Care If I Never Come Back* (1980), on New York restaurant owner and noted gourmet chef and former Expos slugger Rusty Staub.

After his release from prison for tax evasion, Pete Rose opened the Pete Rose Ballpark Cafe in Boca Raton, Florida. Consistent with Rose's merchandising mentality, he had a sign on the entrance: "No merchandise may be brought in from the outside to be autographed."

A number of other players have opened restaurants, including Mickey Mantle in New York.

In 1995 players were warned to stay away from Ruben Sierra's New York restaurant because it was frequented by unsavory characters.

Babe Ruth was a legendary eater. He had a special barbecue spot in St. Louis where he ordered hundreds of ribs and took them on the train. He would lock them in a bathroom and sell them to teammates along with free beer.

Rockies slugger Dante Bichette owned a restaurant in Denver.

Salad. In 1926 the Salt Lake City Bees relocated to become the Hollywood Stars of the Pacific Coast League. The club was also known as the Sheiks when Rudolph Valentino was at his peak. One of the club's owners over the years was the owner of the Brown Derby restaurant in Hollywood, Bob Cobb, for whom the Cobb Salad is named. Nevertheless, in the 1990s, a restaurant known as Danny J's in Burbank, California, had on its menu a "Ty Cobb Salad," calling it the original Brown Derby recipe.

The author's father, a screen and stage actor in the 1930s, was friends with Bob Cobb and the two would shag flies together before Hollywood Stars games. Cobb was married to actress Gail Patrick.

Vegetarian.

"Polyunsaturated Pam [Huizenga, vegetarian daughter of Marlins owner Wayne] also passed out a free bumper sticker to each customer, reading, 'Don't Have a Cow, Eat Vegetarian.' At a ballgame? Yuck. I'd rather eat Yogi Berra's socks."—Sportswriter Mike Downey.

After being ordered to go on a diet of vegetables and soy by manager Tatusro Hirooka, the Seibu Lions climbed from last place the year before to win the 1983 Pacific League Championship. They beat the Nippon Ham Fighters in a series sportswriters dubbed the "Vegetable-Meat War."

"Gene Leek, Harry Colliflower, Hap Collard, Pea Ridge Day, Joe Bean, Yam Yaryan, Spud Davis, Spud Chandler, Belue Bean, Ty Cobb, Beany Jacobson, Pickles Dillhoefer, George Gerken, Larry Gerkin, Peanuts Lowrey, Bill Almon"

"Joe Staples, Johnny Oates, Del Rice, Zack Wheat, Pretzels Pezzullo, Bun Troy, Gene Rye, Bob Seeds"

Soul Food. In his autobiography, *Cleon* (1970), Cleon Jones of the 1969 Mets included his recipe for a soul food dinner.

Food Injury. Brewers' fan Jason Freitag attended the 2001 Opening Day at Miller Park as a guest of the team. During a game in 2000 he had been hit on the head by a 10-pound box of frozen bratwurst dropped from an overhead ramp.

Meat.

"Ham Wade, Fletcher Franks, Eddie Bacon, Ham Peterson, Bob Veale, Herb Hash, Jim Spencer, Harry Salisbury, Stew Boland, Coot Veal, Turkey Tyson, Sweetbreads Bailey, Wally Berger, Gordon Maltzberger, Chili Davis"

Football

"Haven't they suffered enough."—Football analyst and former coach Beano Cook after commissioner Bowie Kuhn announced that the 1979–1980 Iran hostages would receive lifetime passes to Major League Baseball games.

"If God wanted football played in the spring, he would not have invented Baseball."—Former football player Sam Rutigliano, on the United States Football League.

"Football may be the 'disco beat' of modern sports, but Baseball is Chopin or the mystique of Mozart. Every baseball game is new with the pristine beauty of the notes of Beethoven's Ninth."—Phillip Gerstle.

"What do you want, son, a career or a limp?"—Fresco Thompson to a high school player deciding whether to play football or baseball.

"Baseball players are smarter than football players. How often do you see a baseball team penalized for too many men on the field?"—Jim Bouton.

"Football combines the two worst features of American life: violence and committee meetings."—Columnist George Will.

"It ain't like football—you can't make up no trick plays."—Yankee manager Yogi Berra when asked what he was going to do after losing Game 1 of the 1964 World Series.

"No other sporting event can compare with a good Series. The Super Bowl is a three-hour interruption in a week of drink and Rotarian parties."—Roger Kahn.

"Baseball is my favorite sport. I was too chicken to play football."—Cubs pitcher Burt Hooton.

"For football has returned, as it does every August, to knock the books from baseball's arms, steal its lunch money and leave the sport suspended in obscurity—hanging, by its Hanes, from a hook in a locker…. On the surface the two sports have much in common—armored men with Popeye arms playing games that end 17–10. But one's thriving and one's dying. One's cool and one's not. It's the difference between John Wayne and John Wayne Bobbitt."—Steve Rushin.

Team Nicknames. In the early days of the NFL and other professional football leagues, using baseball nicknames was a common practice. The Chicago Bears were named by owner George Halas (a former Yankee) to capitalize on the Cubs name. Only the New York Giants remain as a tie to baseball, though the Phoenix Cardinals carry on the St. Louis connection to baseball.

Boston Fans. Before the 2004 Super Bowl, the Carolina Panthers' lack of marquee players presented a problem for the New England Patriots. *Boston Globe* columnist Dan Shaughnessy wrote that an appropriate target would be Panthers tackle Brenston Buckner: "New England fans have serious issues with players named Buckner."

Broadcaster. Long-time baseball broadcaster Jack Buck was the broadcaster on the first American Football League (AFL) broadcast.

Amateur Baseball Draft. Long-time Oakland Raiders quarterback Ken Stabler was drafted by the Yankees in the 10th round of the 1966 amateur draft. Future Oilers quarterback Dan Pastorini was selected by the Mets in the 32nd round that year. In 1971 five future NFL quarterbacks were drafted, included Archie Manning, Steve Bartkowski and Joe Theismann. In 1979 several future NFL players were drafted, including Dan Marino and John Elway (Kansas City), Jack Thompson (Seattle), Curt Warner (Philadelphia), Kevin House (St. Louis) and Jay Schroeder (Toronto). Michigan quarterback Rick Leach was drafted by the Tigers in the first round and went on to a Major League career. Elway did not sign and was drafted again in 1981 by the Yankees, signing a contract that allowed him to play baseball and football. After a few games with Oneonta in 1982, Elway abandoned baseball to pursue his hall of fame football career.

Two-Sport Players. A number of Major League Baseball players, managers and umpires have had connections with professional and college football. A sampling:

Red Badgro. Badgro hit .257 for the Browns in 1929–1930. He played end at USC and performed for all three professional football teams in New York during that era. He was elected to the pro football Hall of Fame in 1981, the oldest inductee up to that time.

Albert Belle. The future Indians outfielder was offered a scholarship to play quarterback for Notre Dame under coach Gerry Faust.

Charlie Berry. Berry played NFL football for the Pottsville Maroons in 1925–1926 before moving full-time to baseball. He was a catcher primarily for the Red Sox from 1925 through 1938 and umpired in the American League for 21 years starting in 1942. He led the NFL in scoring in 1925 and was the head linesman in the 1958 NFL overtime championship game that put professional football into the mainstream of television and the public's awareness. He had been a first-team All-American at end.

Hugo Bezdek. Bezdek coached the Rose Bowl–winning Oregon Ducks in 1917 and managed the Pirates that year, finishing as the last of three managers for the club with a 30–59 record (the team finished eighth). He also managed the club in 1918 and 1919 and coached the Cleveland Rams in 1937. Bezdek never played either sport in college or professionally.

Tom Brookshier. The Philadelphia Eagles player and longtime CBS broadcaster was 7–1 in 1959 for Class C Roswell of the Longhorn League. After spending two years in the Air Force after that season, he decided to concentrate on football and returned to the Eagles, for whom he had played in 1953.

Tom Brown. Formerly of the University of Maryland, Brown played for the Senators in 1966, hitting .147 in 61 games. He also started at safety for the Green Bay Packers from 1964 through 1968. He played in the first two Super Bowls for the Packers in 1966 and 1967, as well as the 1969 Super Bowl for the Redskins. He was the only man to play Major League Baseball and appear in a Super Bowl until **Deion Sanders** in 1995 (49ers) and 1996 (Cowboys).

Garland Buckeye. Buckeye played guard for the Chicago Cardinals in the early 1920s and then pitched in the American League from 1925 through 1928. He and football great Ernie Nevers each gave up one of Babe Ruth's 60 home runs in 1927.

Gary Carter. At seven years old, the future Major League catcher won a national Punt, Pass and Kick competition and later turned down a football scholarship to UCLA.

Galen Cisco. Cisco was a Mets pitcher in the 1960s who co-captained the 1957 Ohio State football national champions.

Charlie Connerly. Branch Rickey once offered quarterback Charlie Connerly $3,000 to sign, after which Connerly signed for $60,000 with another team.

D.J. Dozier. Dozier played outfield briefly for the Mets in 1992 and was a running back for the Minnesota Vikings and Detroit Lions from 1987 through 1991. He was traded to the Padres organization, but never made it back to the Major Leagues. In 1994 Dozier ended his baseball career and decided to join the ministry. He hit .191 in 25 games with the Mets in 1992 and in 393 minor league games hit .272 with 39 home runs.

Charlie Dressen. The future Dodger manager played quarterback for George Halas' Decatur Staleys (forerunner of the Bears) and the Racine Legion of the early NFL.

John Elway. The quarterback of the Denver Broncos played one year of pro baseball at Oneonta in upstate New York. At the 1998 All-Star Game, Elway swung a baseball bat in competition for the first time since he was a minor leaguer in the Yankees' farm system in the early 1980's. Elway, then 38, was a participant in the All-Star hitting challenge that featured four teams made up of a major league rookie, a retired All-Star and a celebrity. Teams earned points based on the distance of each hit, while bonus points were awarded for every home run. Elway's team finished last despite a respectable performance by the Super Bowl-winning quarterback.

Chuck Essegian. Essegian played for Stanford in the 1952 Rose Bowl and had two pinch-hit home runs for the Dodgers in the 1959 World Series.

Steve Filipowicz. Filipowicz played three seasons in the National League in the 1940s, batting .223 in 57 games. He also played quarterback for the NFL New York Giants.

Walter French. French played professional football for the Pottsville Maroons in 1925. He also had a lifetime .303 average for the A's, playing in 1923 and from 1925 through 1929.

Frankie Frisch. The leader of the Cardinals Gas House Gang was selected to Walter Camp's second All-America football team while playing at Fordham in 1917.

Lou Gehrig. Gehrig's scholarship to Columbia University was in football.

Warren Giles. The future National League president was also a football referee.

Bobby Grich. The future American League star was a freshman at UCLA in the late 1960s, where he was being groomed to succeed star quarterback Gary Beban. Grich left after his sophomore season to pursue professional baseball.

Frank Grube. Grube played primarily for the White Sox as a catcher from 1931 through 1936, replacing holdout Moe Berg, who was traded to the Indians for the waiver price. Grube had played in the NFL before moving on to baseball.

Bruno Haas. The A's pitcher walked an American League record 16 Yankees in nine innings on June 23, 1915. He played no more Major League Baseball and in 1921 joined the new National Football League.

Hinkey Haines. Haines played outfield for the Yankees in 1923, batting .160 in 28 games. He also saw action in two World Series games that year. He later was a running back in the NFL, including the Giants' first championship team in 1927.

George Halas. "Papa Bear" was a founder of the National Football League and long-time owner of the Chicago Bears. He briefly played right field at the end of the 1919 season for the Yankees, with two hits in 22 at-bats. A trivia question has circulated in which Halas is identified as Babe Ruth's immediate predecessor at that position for the Yankees. In fact, Sammy Vick played right field for most of the 1919 season before Ruth arrived from Boston for the 1920 season.

Halas expected to contribute to the Yankees in 1920 but broke his leg before the season and went home to be athletic director at the Staley Starch Company in Decatur, Illinois. The football team he put together eventually moved into the NFL. Future Dodger manager Charlie Dressen was the team's quarterback.

Carroll Hardy. Hardy, who is a footnote in baseball history as the only *Pinch Hitter* for Ted Williams, played wide receiver and defensive back for the San Francisco 49ers in 1955. Although he had a strong season, Indians' general manager Hank Greenberg made him pick, and he liked baseball more because it was not so physically demanding.

After his baseball career ended in 1968 (a brief stint to qualify for his pension), he returned to football and became a scout for the Denver Broncos until 1987, when he became the team's Director of Player Personnel. He later scouted for the Chiefs. Hardy is also the only Major Leaguer to play in the same backfield with three football Hall of Famers at the University of Colorado. In his last college game he rushed for 238 yards and three touchdowns in an upset of Kansas State.

Brian Harper. Harper played pro football for the Atlanta Falcons in the 1990s while also playing Major League Baseball for the Cardinals. He finally opted for full-time play with the Cardinals when he rejected a July 1992 offer from the Falcons.

Todd Helton. Helton was a quarterback at Tennessee just before Peyton Manning arrived.

Drew Henson. In 2003 the former University of Michigan quarterback was called up by the Yankees, with whom he signed a six-year, $17 million contract. The third baseman played poorly both in the Majors and minors, but swore he would not return to football, even though he was projected as the top pick in 2001. The Houston Texans drafted him in the sixth round of the 2003 draft, just in case he changed his mind. He did. In February 2004 Henson gave up on baseball and agreed to give up the $12 million remaining on his $17 million six-year deal with the Yankees that he signed in 2001. He signed with the Texans and played in 2004. In two seasons with the Yankees he batted .111 in nine at-bats with no home runs.

Cal Hubbard. The long-time American League umpire (1936–1951) is the only man to be enshrined in both the baseball and football Halls of Fame. At 6'3" and 250 pounds, he was captain of the Green Bay Packers in 1933 and played nine years for the club as a lineman from 1927 through 1933 and in 1935 and 1936.

Don Hutson. The all-time NFL receiver played two seasons in the Reds organization before focusing exclusively on football.

Bo Jackson. Jackson played professional football for the Oakland Raiders and outfield primarily for the Kansas City Royals. He first played baseball for the minor league Memphis Chicks after leaving college and had not yet played professional football. He hit .277 and struck out 81 times in 184 at-bats. After the season he picked football and signed with the team that took a chance and drafted him, the Raiders. He then decided to play both sports.

He usually joined the Los Angeles Raiders in mid–football season after a week's rest following the baseball season. In 1991 he became the first player to participate in the all-star game for each sport. His football career was cut short after a hip injury suffered in a play-off game against the Denver Broncos.

It was thought that his sports career was over because of the hip problem, but he made a brief comeback at the end of the 1991 season with the White Sox. The hip pain returned in the spring of 1992 and Jackson underwent hip replacement surgery in April 1992. He returned miraculously and dramatically to the White Sox on Opening Day in 1993, though without much of the power that made him so special at the plate (see *Injuries and Illness* — Hip). He retired after the 1994 season.

Vic Janowicz. Until Bo Jackson, Janowicz was the only man to win the Heisman Trophy and play Major League Baseball. In 1950 he was a star halfback for Ohio State. He then played 83 games at catcher and third base for the Pirates in 1953 and 1954, hitting .214 with two home runs. In 1954 and 1955 he played football for the Washington Redskins, leading the team in rushing and scoring. His career was cut short by a serious auto accident in 1956.

Jackie Jensen. Jensen played in the 1949 Rose Bowl for California and in the 1950 World Series for the Yankees. He is the only baseball MVP that was also a college football All-American. He could easily have played pro football, but the pay and prestige were vastly different at that time and he chose baseball. See George L. Martin, *The Golden Boy: A Biography of Jackie Jensen* (2004).

Brian Jordan. Jordan was with the Cardinals when he was sent to Class AAA Louisville early in the 1993 season after signing a three-year $2.2 million deal in 1992 to give up football. He had been an all-pro safety for the Atlanta Falcons through 1991. Jordan again officially ended his football career in October 1995 when he agreed to a three-year, baseball-only contract reportedly worth $10.5 million.

Jim Levey. Levey played four years for the Browns beginning in 1930. He made 147 errors during three of those seasons as the starting shortstop. After leaving the club in 1933 he played three seasons at halfback for the NFL Pittsburgh Steelers.

Ron Luciano. The outspoken umpire played in the 1959 Pro-College All-Star Football Game and played briefly with the AFL Buffalo Bills before becoming an umpire.

Jim McKean. McKean was an umpire in the American League from 1974 through 1987. Prior to that he played in the Canadian Football League and was elected to the league's Hall of Fame.

Pepper Martin. Branch Rickey formed the Brooklyn Dodgers football team in 1948 and hired 44-year-old Pepper Martin of St. Louis Gas House Gang fame as a baseball scout and placekicker. Martin had never kicked before, but supposedly he was making 30–40 yard field goals in the preseason. However, he tore a leg muscle and never kicked in a league game. Former Dodger pitcher Freddie Fitzsimmons was the general manager of the club.

Christy Mathewson. The pitching star very briefly played professional football in the pre–NFL days before World War I. His career consisted of one game at fullback for the Pittsburgh Stars in November 1902. The club was owned by Ben Shibe and managed by Connie Mack.

Charley Moran. Moran played a few games at catcher for the Cardinals in 1903 and 1908 and umpired in the National League from 1917 through 1939. He also was a successful college football coach primarily in the 1920s. In 1921 his tiny Centre College Praying Colonels (see also *Religion*) handed Harvard its first defeat in three years. In 1927 he coached the Frankford Yellow Jackets in the NFL.

Earle "Greasy" Neale. The outfielder led the Reds in batting in the 1919 World Series and averaged .259 in seven Major League seasons between 1916 and 1922. He also coached tiny Washington and Jefferson College to a 0–0 tie with mighty California in the 1922 Rose Bowl. Neale later coached the Philadelphia Eagles to NFL championships in 1948 and 1949.

Ernie Nevers. Nevers is a football Hall of Famer who gave up two of Babe Ruth's 60 homers in 1927, number eight on May 11 and number 41 on August 27.

Ace Parker. Parker is in the pro football Hall of Fame and hit a home run in his first Major League at-bat. Parker played two seasons for the A's beginning in 1937 and hit a total of three home runs.

Edwin "Alabama" Pitts. Pitts appealed to Judge Landis to play minor league baseball after his parole from prison (see also *Felons*). After a nationally publicized effort to allow him to play, he had an undistinguished season in the minor leagues before playing briefly in the NFL with the Philadelphia Eagles in the 1930s.

Pid Purdy. Purdy played 181 games in the outfield for the White Sox and Reds in the 1920s. He also was a running back for the Green Bay Packers.

Jackie Robinson. In the spring of 1941 the former UCLA halfback played pro football in Hawaii for the Honolulu Bears. He finished the season and sailed for the mainland on December 5, 1941, two days before Pearl Harbor was bombed by the Japanese.

Ryne Sandberg. The long-time Cubs second baseman was a *Parade* high school All-America football player in Spokane.

Deion Sanders.

"Atlanta's most celebrated cross-dresser" — Atlanta sportswriter Len Pascarelli.

"In some ways Sanders, a.k.a. Neon Deion (which he hates) and Prime Time (which he embraces), seems from yet another time. He has Satchel Paige's wit and flair for self-promotion, Cab Calloway's sense of outrageous style and Jim Thorpe's mind-boggling athletic ability." — Steve Wulf in *Time* magazine before the 1995 Super Bowl.

Sanders played sparingly and poorly for the New York Yankees over two seasons in 1989 and 1990 while starting as a defensive back for the Atlanta Falcons. He returned a punt for a touchdown the first time he touched a football in a professional game and he hit a home run for the Yankees in his first Major League game.

Sanders was traded to the Braves during the 1991 season, but during the pennant race he left the team to concentrate on football. He returned to the Braves for part-time duty during the final two weeks of the season.

In 1992 Sanders apparently made a firmer commitment to baseball when he decided to stay with the Braves for the entire season despite a contract clause that allowed him to leave the club for the Atlanta Falcons any time after July 31. Nevertheless, he signed with the Falcons late in the baseball season and began commuting by helicopter between Braves games and the Falcons' training and in-season practice camps.

On Saturday, October 10, 1992, Sanders sat on the bench while the Braves lost to the Pirates in Pittsburgh during the National League Championship Series. That night he took a flight to Miami so that he could play in Sunday's football game against the Dolphins. He finished the game and flew back to Pittsburgh, again sitting on the bench as the Braves lost that night.

At the end of 1992 Sanders signed a three-year, $11 million contract with the Braves. It required him to finish the baseball season before playing football.

Early in the 1993 season he failed to return to the Braves after attending his father's funeral. He left because he was unhappy with his playing time but was reinstated with the club a few weeks later. In 1994 he was traded to the Reds and played football for the San Francisco 49ers. He became the second player to play Major League Baseball and appear in the Super Bowl when he played cornerback for the 49ers in the 1995 Super Bowl.

He played for the Reds for part of 1995 and signed with the Dallas Cowboys in late summer for $17 million. He appeared in the 1996 Super Bowl for the Cowboys, but did not play baseball in 1996. After his first round of batting practice in 1997 with the Reds, Sanders said: "That's more hits than I had the entire football season."

He played with the Cowboys in 1996–1997 and did not play baseball in 1996. He had a terrific return with the Reds in 1997 and was leading the league with 56 stolen bases when he left the 4th-place club on September 5 to join the Cowboys. It was his last appearance in Major League Baseball. In nine seasons Sanders hit .263 and stole 186 bases (with 48 football interceptions).

Rick Sofield. Sofield played for the Twins in 1980 and 1981, but he ended his career with a .207 average and switched to football. He became the starting quarterback for the University of South Carolina in 1983.

Amos Alonzo Stagg. The legendary football coach pitched for Yale and once had 20 strikeouts in a nine-inning game. He spent seven years pitching for the school, four as an undergraduate and three as a divinity student.

Bobby Valentine. Valentine was the first three-time high school All-State football player from Connecticut.

Rube Waddell. The eccentric pitcher played professional football in 1902 on a team run by Connie Mack. He was a lineman of reasonable ability, but missed out on a game against Christy Mathewson at fullback over Thanksgiving weekend in 1902.

Waddell had been playing football so that Mack could keep an eye on him, but the night before the big game Waddell was out gambling on an important billiards match. When he returned late, Mack confronted him and when Waddell reached for a handkerchief in his pocket, a revolver popped out and discharged when it hit the floor. The bullet came close to Mack's head and Mack suspended him from the next football game.

Chris Weinke. Weinke played minor league baseball for several years before going back to college at Florida State. As a 28-year-

old senior quarterback, he became the oldest player ever to win the Heisman Trophy.

Home Run/Touchdown/Same Season. Six players have hit a home run in the Major Leagues and scored a touchdown in the NFL in the same season:

Deion Sanders—1994 Braves and 49ers; 1995 Giants and Reds and Cowboys

Bo Jackson—1987 Royals and Raiders

Steve Filipowicz—1945 Giants and Giants

Ace Parker—1937 A's and Dodgers

Red Badgro—1930 Browns and Giants

Pid Purdy—1927 Reds and Packers

Writer. Writer Bob Broeg of St. Louis was a member of the baseball Hall of Fame Board of Directors and was for many years the only man ever eligible to vote for the baseball, professional football and college football Halls of Fame.

Training Technique.

"I don't know, but we lead the league in third-down conversions."—Rangers pitcher Charlie Hough when asked about the effectiveness of a unique training regimen instituted by pitching coach Tom House in the mid–1980s. He had the pitchers throw footballs as a warm-up drill to help their mechanics. The idea was finally abandoned in 1992 amid speculation that House was on his way out (he was).

Books. Thomas Boswell, *The Heart of the Order* (1989), containing "99 Reasons Why Baseball is Better Than Football." Also not to be missed is comedian George Carlin's monologue comparison of baseball and football.

Forbes Field (1909–1970)

"At a forty-five-degree angle across the street and up Forbes Avenue a bit from the Cathedral stood Forbes Field. Surrounded by several blue-collar bars and fast-food restaurants, which filled with fans on game days, Forbes Field was the major drawing card for the area.... A fan attending a ball game at Forbes Field was treated to the beauty of an entire neighborhood geared toward baseball.... [The] Oakland [section] revolved around Forbes Field. Nothing in the city could match the atmosphere created by the field's ivy-coated outfield walls, the smell of the ball park's hot dogs and the chatter of Pirate fans in the street."—Willie Stargell in his autobiography, *Willie Stargell*, with Tom Bird (1984).

Pittsburgh's Forbes Field was completed in 1909 for $1 million. The club purportedly received thousands of suggestions for naming the facility. Owner Barney Dreyfuss finally decided on one of the founders of Pittsburgh, frontier general John Forbes, an Englishman who fought in the French and Indian War.

The ballpark originally featured triple-decked stands, electric lights (though not to light the field), elevators, telephones and maids in the ladies restrooms. For $100 a patron could have his name engraved on a brass plate on his box seat.

First Game. The first game was played on June 30, 1909. Johnny Evers had the first hit in the ballpark as the Pirates lost 3–2 to the Cubs.

Dimensions. The dimensions from left to right field originally were 360–406–422–408–376. In 1947 the Pirates obtained Hank Greenberg and paired him with Ralph Kiner, the top slugger in the Major Leagues immediately after World War II. The club created a double bullpen to shorten the distance in left field. The new bullpen was 30–50 feet deep and 200 feet long. It was first called Greenberg Gardens and later referred to as Kiner's Korner. The bullpen reduced the dimensions in left field from 365 to 335 down the line and from 406 to 355 in the left field power alley.

Capacity. The seating capacity originally was 23,000 and increased to 41,000 in 1925.

Tenants. The Negro League Homestead Grays played in Forbes Field from 1939 through 1948.

Home Run. Babe Ruth was the first player to hit a ball over the roof. The home run was one of three he hit on the same afternoon a few days before he retired in mid–1935 — the last three of his career.

No-Hitter. A notorious hitter's park, Forbes Field never hosted a no-hitter over 62 seasons and 4,700 games.

Triples. Because it was so large and known as a hitters park, it yielded more triples than any other ballpark. Coincidentally, its replacement, Three Rivers Stadium, is also conducive to triples.

Last Game. The last game was played on June 28, 1970, as the Pirates swept a doubleheader from the Cubs. Jim Nelson got the last win in front of 40,918 fans.

Demolition. The University of Pittsburgh graduate schools occupy the site of Forbes Field, but the actual brick wall over which Bill Mazeroski hit his 1960 World Series home run still stands, with a plaque to commemorate the moment. Home plate is preserved under glass on the campus in nearby Forbes Quadrangle.

Book. William Benswanger, *Forbes Field: 60th Birthday* (1969).

Whitey Ford (1926–)

Hall of Fame 1974

"Arm, heart, head."— Ford's three ingredients for successful pitching.

Ford won 236 games for the Yankees over 16 seasons beginning in 1950.

A native New Yorker dubbed "The Chairman of the Board" by Elston Howard and "Slick" by Casey Stengel, blonde-haired Edward Charles Ford was the premier Yankee pitcher during the club's glory years in the 1950s and early 1960s.

Ford began his professional career with a $7,000 signing bonus from the Yankees and in 1947 was 13–4 for Butler in the Mid-Atlantic League. After 12 games for Kansas City in the American Association in 1950 he was 9–3 and was brought up to the Yankees. Though he was bombed in his first appearance, he won his first nine games before losing in relief, finishing with a 9–1 record and a 2.81 ERA.

Ford missed the 1951 and 1952 seasons due to a military commitment, but returned with 18 wins in 1953. In 1955 he led the league with 18 wins and in 1956 he led the league with a .760 winning percentage and a 2.47 ERA.

During the mid– and late 1950s manager Casey Stengel limited Ford's starts to as few as 24, saving him for big games and giving him four days rest on most occasions. His two best seasons were 1961 and 1963, when he was 25–4 and 24–7 after new manager Ralph Houk let him start as many games as possible; he led the league in that category both seasons. However, he had far fewer complete games than most successful pitchers of the era.

Ford faded after injuring his arm and undergoing surgery in 1966. He retired abruptly following seven starts in 1967 after posting a 4–9 record over his final two partial seasons. He finished with a 236–106 record and the third-highest winning percentage of all time at .690.

Ford starred in the 11 World Series he played in for the Yankees. He had a World Series career record of 10–8, highest all-time in both categories. He also pitched the most innings in the World

Series and is second all-time with three shutouts. In the 1960, 1961 and 1962 World Series he pitched 33 straight shutout innings, breaking Babe Ruth's World Series record. In 1974 he was inducted into the Hall of Fame in his second season of eligibility. He went in with his long-time roommate Mickey Mantle.

Books. Whitey Ford and Phil Pepe, *Slick* (1987); Milton Shapiro, *The Whitey Ford Story* (1962).

Foreign Baseball

"After the season a rich friend of mine wants to take me on a trip around the world, but I told him I'd rather go someplace else."
— Babe Herman.

See also *Asia*, *International Baseball*, *Olympic Games* and specific countries: *Aruba*, *Australia*, *Belgium*, *Canada*, *Colombia*, *Cuba*, *Curacao*, *Dominican Republic*, *England*, *France*, *Ireland*, *Italy*, *Jamaica*, *Japan*, *Korea*, *Mexico*, *Netherlands*, *Nicaragua*, *Panama*, *Puerto Rico*, *Russia*, *Taiwan*, *Venezuela* and *Virgin Islands*.

Foreign-Born Major League Players

"For starting pitchers, we have two Dominicans, one Italian, one Mexican and one Japanese…. In the bullpen we have a Venezuelan, a Mexican, a guy from the United States and a guy from St. Louis."— Dodger manager Tommy Lasorda. In August 1999 the Dodgers started four pitchers in a series against the Giants who were from four countries covering three continents: Eric Gagne from Canada (before his relieving fame); Jeff Williams of Australia; Ismael Valdez from Mexico; and Chan Ho Park from Korea.

"We've got a problem here. Luis Tiant wants to use the bathroom, and it says no foreign objects in the toilets."— Graig Nettles.

See also *Ethnicity*, *Latin Ballplayers* and entries for specific countries.

Home Runs. Jose Canseco was the first foreign-born player (Cuba) to reach 400 home runs. Sammy Sosa (Dominican Republic) was the first foreign-born player to reach 500 home runs.

Major League Organizations. In 1996 the Dodgers led all Major League organizations with 45.2% of their Major and minor league players from foreign countries. They included the only players from Guatemala and Ecuador. The Expos were second at 42.7%. The Reds (12.7%), Cubs (12.4%) and Mariners (11.9%) had the lowest percentages.

Work Permits. In June 2004 Major League teams were informed that some of their draft picks could not play in their minor league systems that summer because the U.S. government told Major League officials that no new work visas were being issued to foreign-born players for several months.

Recent Percentages. Approximately 17% of the Major League players of the 1990s were not born in the United States. In 1995 a record 15 players on the World Series rosters were foreign-born.

In 2003, 26.1% of Major Leaguers were foreign-born, up from 25.3% in 2002. The Orioles had the most foreign-born players on its roster, with 12. The Dodgers and Expos had 11 each. In the minor leagues, among 5,781 players, 49.6% were born outside the U.S., led by the Dominican Republic with 1,536 and Venezuela with 738.

In 2003, of the 849 players on Opening Day Major League rosters or disabled lists, 222 were born outside the United States, among 15 foreign countries, Puerto Rico and the Virgin Islands. The totals:

74 Dominican Republic
38 Puerto Rico
38 Venezuela
18 Mexico
11 Cuba
11 Japan
10 Canada
7 Panama
3 Australia
3 Colombia
2 Aruba
2 Netherlands Antilles
2 Nicaragua
2 South Korea
1 Virgin Islands

Historical Survey: The following is a summary of foreign-born players who have played Major League Baseball from 1876 through the early 1990s:

145	Canada	10	Virgin Islands	3	Korea
120	Cuba	5	Italy	2	Jamaica
120	Puerto Rico	5	Scotland	2	Poland
90	Dominican Republic	5	Colombia	2	Norway
		4	Bahamas	2	Wales
50	Mexico	4	Czechoslovakia	2	Sweden
45	Venezuela	4	France	1	Greece
30	Ireland	4	Russia	1	Okinawa
25	Panama	4	Nicaragua	1	Denmark
20	England	3	Canal Zone	1	Canary Islands
20	Germany	3	Japan		

Foreign Substances See *Illegal Substances*

Foreign Tours See *International Tours*

Forfeits

"I foolishly put my name on the roster one night at the last minute to avoid a forfeit and before the season was over I played four games, a fat middle-aged man standing in the outfield, being eaten by mosquitoes and wishing he could lose 20 years for an hour and a half." — Richard Hugo in "The Anxious Fields of Play" (1977).

Grounds for Forfeit. A game *may* be forfeited by an umpire if:

a) a team fails to start play within five minutes of an umpire saying "play ball";

b) a team uses tactics to delay or shorten a game;

c) a team fails to resume play within one minute of the end of the suspension of play;

d) a team refuses to continue play;

e) a teams fails to comply immediately after an umpire warns of a rule violation;

f) a team fails to remove a player from the game after being ordered to do so;

g) a team fails to appear within 20 minutes for the start of the second game of a doubleheader.

A game *shall* be forfeited if:

a) the field is not playable after suspension of play and the groundskeeper fails to comply with umpire orders;

b) a team cannot field nine players.

Score/Statistics. If there is a forfeit, the winning team is credited with a 9-0 win. In contrast, football uses the minimum score possible, 2-0.

The modern rule (1940s) is that individual statistics will count if it is an "official game," meaning five innings have been completed before a forfeit is declared. The rule: "If a game is forfeited before it becomes a regulation game, include no records. Report only the fact of the forfeit." — Rule 10.03(e)(2).

Forfeited Games.

"Lasorda instigated the whole damn thing by running out there, waving his fat little arms." — Umpire crew chief Bob Davidson on the forfeit against the Dodgers on August 10, 1995. The Dodgers forfeited a 2-1 game to the Cardinals with one out in the 9th inning when fans threw souvenir baseballs on the field to protest called third strikes. Davidson also ejected Dodger right fielder Raul Mondesi in a 1995 postseason game against the Reds. It was the first forfeit in 16 years.

The earliest professional forfeited game may have been an 1871 National Association game between Rockport and Philadelphia. Rockport won two games over Philadelphia but used an ineligible player, W. Scott Hastings. Philadelphia was awarded the wins and was then able to capture the 1871 pennant. Its record of 22-7 was two games better than Chicago's 20-9.

Tom Murphy, an old Baltimore groundskeeper in the 19th century, supposedly planted balls in the outfield for his team. In a St. Louis/Baltimore game the umpires purportedly forfeited the game in favor of the Browns when both a planted ball and the real ball were simultaneously thrown back into the infield.

On October 14, 1899, Jimmy Sheckard of the Baltimore Orioles protested a call and was ejected from the game. After he refused to leave the field, umpire John Hunt forfeited the game. To appease the large Saturday crowd, Hunt ordered the second game of the series, which was not scheduled until the next day, to begin immediately. Baltimore lost the second game, though not by forfeit.

On June 28, 1902, umpire Tom Connolly was behind the plate when Baltimore runner Cy Seymour rounded third for home but was forced all the way back to second base during a rundown. He failed to touch third base on the return trip and was called out by Connolly. Orioles manager John McGraw asked the base umpire to rule on the play, but Connolly would not allow it and ordered McGraw off the field. McGraw refused, so Connolly forfeited the game and Ban Johnson quickly suspended McGraw. This hastened McGraw's move to the National League Giants.

In 1902 the American League Baltimore Orioles had lost so many players to the Highlanders/Yankees that the club was unable to field a team and forfeited a game in July against the Browns.

On August 6, 1906, umpire James Johnstone angered the Giants with his calls. The next day he was refused entry to the ballpark. Giants manager John McGraw picked pinch hitter Sammy Strang to umpire in his place, but the Cubs refused to play with him as a substitute. The second umpire, Bob Emslie, refused to start the game without Johnstone and forfeited the game to the Cubs. National League president Harry Pulliam upheld the forfeit and Johnstone returned to the field for the third game of the series.

In early 1907 the Giants were trailing the Phillies at the Polo Grounds in a game that was played following a snowstorm the night before. In the 8th inning fans began throwing snowballs on the field and umpire Bill Klem forfeited the game to the Phillies.

On Opening Day in 1912 at the Polo Grounds, Rube Marquard of the Giants was leading 18-3 in the 6th inning when fans became rowdy. One source reported that the game was forfeited to the opposing team. However, this was the date of the first of Marquard's record 19 straight wins so there could not have been a forfeit: it was actually called because of darkness and Marquard received credit for the win.

In 1924 bad-tempered Bob Meusel of the Yankees charged the mound with a bat after Tiger pitcher King Cole threw a brushback pitch. A huge fight followed and the game was forfeited to the Tigers.

In 1937 the Cardinals forfeited a late-running game after the umpires ruled that they were stalling. This wiped out the individual statistics, which would not be the case under today's rules if five innings were completed. Joe Medwick had homered, and the loss of that home run cost him sole possession of the league crown. He and Mel Ott both finished with 31, though Medwick is credited with winning the Triple Crown that season because he also led the league in batting average (.374) and RBIs (154).

In 1939 the Yankees were tied 5–5 with the Red Sox in Boston. In the top of the 8th inning the Yankees scored two runs and were hurrying to finish the game because it was only 20 minutes to curfew. Red Sox fans became unruly and threw debris at the players. The umpires forfeited the game to the Yankees and the league fined the Red Sox $1,000.

On August 15, 1941, the Senators were leading the Red Sox 6–3 in the 8th inning at home when it started to rain hard. The ground crew was intentionally slow in rolling out the tarp so that the game might be called with the Senators ahead. The umpires ruled that the action was deliberate and forfeited the game to the Red Sox.

On September 26, 1942, in the bottom of the 8th inning the Giants were at home and leading the Braves 5–2. Youngsters, who had brought scrap metal to the game for the war effort and had been admitted free, swarmed onto the field. Unable to clear the field, the umpires forfeited the game to the Braves. The forfeit resulted in a statistical anomaly. Though Braves pitcher Warren Spahn was credited with a complete game (individual statistics count in forfeits), he did not get credit for a win or a loss. Because he had no other decisions that season, he shows a record of 0–0 and one complete game (which normally requires a decision).

On August 21, 1949, the Phillies were home to the Giants. In the 9th inning with the Giants leading 4–2, Phillies outfielder Richie Ashburn was ruled to have trapped a ball. The fans would not stop littering the field, so the umpires forfeited the game to the Giants.

In 1954 the Cardinals forfeited a game to the Phillies after a brawl involving Eddie Stanky made it impossible for the umpires to control the game.

On September 30, 1971, the Senators played their last home game before moving to Texas. The Senators were leading 7–5 in the top of the 9th inning when fans ran onto the field and tore it up. The umpires forfeited the game to the Yankees. See also **Washington Senators** — "Lasts for the Second Franchise."

On June 4, 1974, the Indians and Rangers were in a 5–5 tie in the bottom of the 9th inning in Cleveland. When fans ran onto the field and began fighting with players, the umpires were unable to restore order and declared a forfeit to the Rangers.

National League umpire Al Barlick once forfeited a game to the visitors in Philadelphia when he was hit by a tomato and umpire Lee Ballanfant was hit by a bottle.

The White Sox forfeited a game on July 12, 1979, after a "Disco Demolition Night" **Promotion** that backfired.

In 1981 umpire Dale Ford threatened a forfeit against the White Sox after he accused broadcaster and occasional eccentric Jimmy Piersall of inciting the crowd.

Owner Popularity. An example of New York Giants owner Andrew Freedman's unpopularity at the turn of the century occurred in 1898. Ducky Holmes had been with the Giants in 1897 but played with Baltimore of the National League in 1898. During that season he had a rude exchange with a fan at the Polo Grounds in which Holmes made a snide remark about Freedman. Freedman heard about the remark and told the local police to eject Holmes from the ballpark. Umpire Tom Lynch refused to allow it; Freedman would not leave the field in protest, so Lynch forfeited the game to Baltimore.

Baltimore supposedly had already received its check for the game's gate receipts. After the forfeit, Freedman "reimbursed the fans" and demanded that Baltimore give back the check. Baltimore refused, so Freedman stopped payment. Baltimore then demanded that the Giants pay a $1,000 fine under the rules. Freedman deposited the money with National League president Nick Young and sailed for Europe. The league called a board meeting and upheld the forfeit and the fine but suspended Holmes for the season. The press condemned Young for Holmes' suspension and after pressure from other owners he responded by reversing his decision.

1995 Spring Training. The 1995 Orioles refused to field a replacement team during the strike. If the season had started without the club on the field, Cal Ripken's consecutive game streak would have ended.

Forkball See *Pitches*

Ft. Wayne Kekiongas

National Association 1871

"We take pleasure in announcing to you that our Professional Club is now in condition to meet all first class clubs, and herewith invite your club to visit us, guaranteeing that all will prove most satisfactory." — Club announcement in April 1871.

"Their economic arrangements varied widely, reflecting differences in the class composition of the club backers. At the top of the scale was the stock company of the White Sox; at the bottom were the clerks and salesmen who ran the Ft. Wayne club and offered their players, in lieu of a salary, a share of the gate receipts." — Ted Vincent in *Mudville's Revenge* (1981).

The club was 5–9 for the short time that it lasted in the National Association's first season. The Kekiongas had the distinction of playing the Association's first game on May 4, 1871, defeating Cleveland 2–0 in front of 200 fans at Hamilton Field in Ft. Wayne.

Forty-Year-Old Players See *Longest Careers* and *Oldest Players*

Rube Foster (1879–1930)

Hall of Fame (NLC) 1981

"Rube was a phenomenal pitcher, a magnificent manager, a powerful organizer, and even a greater humanitarian. He had the face of a teddy bear, the heart of Rocky Balboa, the legendary strength of John Henry, the soul of Malcolm X, the vision of Dr. Martin Luther King, the oratorical skills of James Earl Jones and the genius of Ray Charles. Rube Foster was the most perfect blend of baseball expertise ever assembled." — Dick Clark and Larry Lester (eds.) in *The Negro Leagues Book* (1994).

"White baseball has never seen anyone quite like Rube Foster. He was Christy Mathewson, John McGraw, Connie Mack, Al Spalding and Kenesaw Mountain Landis — great pitcher, manager, owner, league organizer, czar — all rolled into one." — John B. Holway in *Blackball Stars* (1988).

Foster was the father of the Negro Leagues and a strong pitcher before becoming an owner and promoter.

Andrew "Rube" Foster was the driving force behind the Negro Leagues of the 1920s, but he first had a stellar pitching career that began in the late 19th century in college and semipro ball, with the traveling Waco Yellow Jackets. He signed a pro contract at the turn of the century and then pitched for the Cuban X-Giants and Philadelphia Giants. He led his club to a victory over a white club that included pitcher Rube Waddell, and Foster thereby supposedly earned his nickname. Foster is credited by some with providing Christy Mathewson the pitching tips that sent him on his way to stardom.

Foster returned to the Chicago Leland Giants in 1907 and helped them to 48 straight wins. He learned baseball promotions and marketing from the master, Frank Leland, who owned the club. By 1910 Foster was the player-manager and the club was the dominant Negro club of the Midwest and in the integrated Chicago city leagues. In 1911 Foster and a white businessman, John Schorling, bought the old White Sox ballpark (Comiskey Park having opened) and it became home to the Chicago American Giants. Foster continued to star for the club through the decade.

In 1920 he was instrumental in creating the Negro National League in Kansas City. The Midwest-based league was dominated by Foster, though he helped maintain balance among the clubs and loaned money to many of the clubs. The league struggled and prospered at the same time, but Foster left the game in 1926 when he suffered from mental illness and was institutionalized. He died four years later. His half-brother, Bill Foster, a prominent Negro League player, is also in the Hall of Fame.

Book. Charles E. Whitehead, *A Man and His Diamonds* (1980).

Bill Foster (1904–1978)

Hall of Fame (VC) 1996

"If I could paint you white, I could get $150,000 for you." — Charlie Gehringer in 1929 after Foster shut out a group of American League all-stars.

"Willie Foster's greatness was that he had this terrific speed and a great, fast-breaking curveball and a drop ball, and he was really a master of the change-of-pace. He could throw you a real fast one and then use the same motion and bring it up a little slower, and then a little slower yet. And then he'd use the same motion again, and Z-zzz. He was really a great pitcher." — Negro League star Dave Malarcher.

Foster was a star pitcher in the Negro Leagues between 1923 and 1937.

Willie Hendrick "Big Bill" Foster was a left-handed Negro League pitcher who won at least 150 games over 15 seasons between 1923 and 1937. His half-brother Rube Foster was a pioneer Negro League owner and was elected to the Hall of Fame in 1981.

The Texas native played primarily for his brother's club, the Chicago American Giants, in the 1920s and 1930s. His best season was 1926, when he won 26 straight games and led his club to the Negro Leagues championship. In 1927 he was at least 21–3 for the Giants. He pitched in three Negro League World Series, winning four games for the Giants in 1926 and 1927 and one game for the Kansas City Monarchs in 1937. Foster won six of seven recorded games against white Major League players and won 11 of 21 pitching duels with Satchel Paige.

His last year in professional baseball was spent with a white semipro team in Elgin, Illinois, and with a black team called the Washington Browns in Yakima, Washington. After he retired he became a baseball coach and dean of men at his alma mater, Alcorn College. He coached from 1960 until shortly before his death in 1978.

Foul Ball

"There's a shot up the alley. Oh, it's just foul." — Jerry Coleman.

"McCovey swings and misses, and it's fouled back." — Jerry Coleman.

"C'mon Wallace, Morley Safer makes that catch!" — A Yankee fan yelling at CBS "60 Minutes" host Mike Wallace, after Wallace failed to catch a foul ball in his vicinity.

Foul Ball as an Out. In the 1880s each league at different times inaugurated a short-lived rule allowing a foul ball to be recorded as an out if it was caught on no more than one bounce: National League (1883); Union Association (1884); American Association (1885).

Advancing on Caught Foul Ball. When the National League started play in 1876, it adopted most of the National Association's foul ball rules. However, one new rule provided that a runner could return safely to a base without risk of being put out after a foul ball fell untouched. Another allowed a runner on a foul-fly catch to move up a base the same as on a fair-fly catch.

Fair or Foul. In the mid–1880s John Gaffney reportedly became the first umpire to call balls foul at the point they left the park, rather than where they landed or were last seen. This practice was not formally adopted by the Major Leagues until 1930 and was refined when **Foul Poles** were adopted. In the late 19th century ground balls were first ruled foul if they were foul as they passed first or third base.

Rule 48 required batted balls leaving the ballpark to be judged fair or foul not by where they left the ballpark, but rather where they landed or were last seen by the umpire. The rule was implemented after the 1930 season, except for a two-month period early in the 1920 season when the modern rule was briefly in effect. At least one source reported that Babe Ruth lost at least 50 home runs because of the rule and that he could have had another five or six during the 1927 season in which he officially hit 60.

On August 22, 1971, Don Buford hit the ball over the first base bag and umpire John Stevens ruled it foul, then signaled fair. The ball boy down the right field line picked up ball and then put it down in time for Rich Reese to pick it up and throw out runner Dave McNally at home.

Fair-Foul Bunt. See *Bunts.*

Foul Tip. In 1895 a strike was assessed on a foul *tip*, but not on a foul ball. The difference between a tip and a foul ball was within the umpire's discretion. Connie Mack claimed that he clicked his fingers into his glove to simulate the double-hit sound made when a foul tip is caught by the catcher.

Foul Ball Strike. See *Strikes and Strikeouts — Foul Balls.*

Foul Balls/Allowed to Keep.

"A child, male, wants to sit in the upper tier where he will have a chance to try to catch a foul fly. Fortunately his chances for this opportunity are astronomically against him." — Fred Schwed, Jr., in *How to Watch a Baseball Game* (1957).

"New rule: catch a foul ball, win the salary of the guy who hit it." — One of David Letterman's "Top Ten Ways Major League Baseball Teams Can Win Back the Fans."

In 1916 Federal League Chicago Whales owner Charles Weeghman allowed fans to keep balls hit into the stands. It was a few years before this practice was adopted by all Major League clubs.

In 1921 fan Reuben Berman refused to return a foul ball hit into the stands. He went to court and won, changing the rule forever.

Braves owner Judge Emil Fuchs was known to have gone into the stands to retrieve and reuse foul balls.

During World War II balls were returned from the stands because of a shortage of the materials, primarily rubber, needed to make them (see also *Balls — Balata Balls*). It was viewed as unpatriotic for a fan to keep a foul ball as a souvenir during the war. Fans were told that balls hit into the stands should be returned because they would be shipped to servicemen overseas.

In Japan only about half the 12 professional clubs allow their fans to keep foul balls hit into the stands.

In Cuba when a foul ball is hit into the stands, it is returned to a man in white gloves who holds it until needed again.

Injuries.

"Fright, fear, caution, joy, humor and hope — those are the contrasting emotions of a box seat crowd as a foul ball heads toward it."— Caption to a 1950 *Baseball Digest* photo.

By 1920 fans hit by foul balls were held to be subject to the law of "assumption of the risk." This doctrine means that a fan attending a baseball game is assumed to be aware of the risk of foul balls coming into the stands and must be properly attentive throughout the game. The courts also ruled that it was sufficient for clubs to put a screen behind home plate (but nowhere else) to guard against that species of foul ball.

In 1937 a fan trying to retrieve a ball from the backstop screen was beaten by ushers. He sued and recovered $7,500.

On August 17, 1957, Phillies outfielder Richie Ashburn lined a foul ball into the stands which struck grandmother Alice Roth. After the game was stopped for a few minutes while she was attended to for a broken nose, Ashburn lined another ball into the stands and hit her again while she was being carried away on a stretcher. At least one source reported that she was the wife of a sportswriter.

In 1990 Cubs fan Delbert Yates, Jr., surprisingly won a foul ball lawsuit when a Chicago judge awarded him $67,500 for being hit in the eye in 1983 by a foul ball off the bat of Cubs first baseman Leon Durham. Yates was 10 years old at the time of the injury.

On August 25, 1995, six-year-old Cameron Wilson survived a skull fracture on a foul ball hit by Rockies outfielder Eric Young.

In April 2000, a boy who was struck in the head with a baseball before a Florida Marlins game in 1997 was awarded $1.05 million by a state court jury. Andrew Klein suffered permanent brain damage after the injury during batting practice. He had taken part in a pregame "Bullpen Buddies" program with 100 other children at Pro Player Stadium. A line drive hit by Ray Lankford came into the stands and struck the boy in the left temple.

See also *Injuries and Illness — Head* for injuries to players.

Fouling Off Pitches. Nineteenth century star Billy Hamilton once supposedly fouled off 29 straight pitches. He also fouled off 27 straight against Cy Young, although these reports may relate to the same at-bat and the numbers may have been confused over the years.

Roy Thomas was a National League outfielder from 1899 through 1911 who is credited by some with perfecting the art of intentionally fouling off balls. Some sources report that he once hit 22 straight foul balls. His prowess purportedly led to the change in the rules whereby the first two foul balls were called strikes, prompting writer Bill James to comment: "Thomas' impressive walk totals dropped only slightly after that, which may show that if you have the ability to foul off twenty-two pitched balls, calling two of them strikes isn't going to make much difference."

Luke Appling of the White Sox is said to have fouled off 17 straight pitches in one at-bat before hitting a triple. Another story has him batting against Red Ruffing of the Yankees. Appling hit four foul balls, took a ball, then fouled off six more pitches before taking another ball. He then fouled off 14 more pitches before receiving a base on balls. Appling supposedly was told by his club to stop fouling off balls because it was costing too much to replace them. Still another source reported that he fouled off 33 straight pitches because he was annoyed that the club would not give him a few extra balls to give to friends.

Cardinals infielder Rabbit Maranville supposedly once fouled off 14 straight pitches and fidgeted long enough in the batters box to let the Braves' curfew take effect. It wiped out the previous half-inning in which their opponent scored the go-ahead run; the game ended in a tie.

Some sources report that Richie Ashburn of the Phillies once fouled off 16 pitches during an at-bat.

On September 29, 1992, lead-off batter Pat Listach of the Brewers forced A's pitcher Ron Darling to throw 17 pitches, most hit for foul balls, before drawing a walk.

Royals infielder Bip Roberts had a 14-minute 1st inning at-bat against Tigers pitcher Felipe Lira on May 18, 1997. The at-bat featured 18 pitches and nine pick-off attempts of runner Tom Goodwin; who also tried to steal second base six times during the at-bat (foul balls sent him back).

On May 12, 2004, light-hitting Dodger infielder Joey Cora fouled off 14 straight pitches during an 18-pitch at-bat against Cubs pitcher Matt Clement in the 7th inning, improbably culminating in a two-run homer that gave the Dodgers the win. For his trouble, Cora was hit on the arm in his first at-bat of the next game, in part because the Cubs took offense to him tossing his bat after the home run. Cora said he was just excited and did not mean to show up the Cubs after he hit the hanging slider on a 2–2 pitch. Clement had thrown 86 pitches before the at-bat, but was removed immediately after the home run, his pitch count having run to 104.

Glove Throwing. It has always been legal in the National League to throw a glove at a foul ball. It was not legal in the American League until 1954.

Mother's Day Gift. On Mother's Day 1939 at Comiskey Park, Bob Feller's mother came to see him pitch. She was struck in the face by a foul ball hit off Feller by third baseman Marv Owen that broke her glasses. After Feller supposedly came over to check on her, he went back and finished the game. In Feller's autobiography, he claims that he only looked over at her box to see her being taken away and he resisted the urge to go over to see how she was. He pitched a complete game win but gave up three runs in the inning in which she was hurt.

Blown Foul. Mariners third baseman Lenny Randle got on his hands and knees to blow a bunted ball foul during a game against Kansas City on May 27, 1981.

Bad Luck. Late 1930s and early 1940s first baseman Buddy Hassett swore that the following anecdote was true. An unidentified Braves hitter was playing against the Phillies late in the 1939 season and was obsessed with reaching 100 RBIs. A check of Braves players in statistical sources was inconclusive as to who it might have been, as no one came close to reaching that figure.

With men on second and third, this player popped out for the first out. He walked very slowly and dejectedly back to the dugout with his head down. The pitcher quickly threw to the next batter, Paul Waner, but it was a wild pitch in the direction of the dejected hitter. As it crossed his path and thinking it was a dead ball, he picked it up and flipped it to the catcher. The catcher tagged the runner coming home for the second out. The pitcher threw another wild pitch and the second runner scored. The next pitch was fouled into the Braves dugout, knocking the dejected batter cold. It could only have happened (if it did) on a team (the Braves) managed by Casey Stengel.

Dugout Interference. See *Interference*.

Foul Territory. Fenway Park has the smallest foul territory area of any Major League ballpark.

Fan Lawsuit. Hank O'Day was the umpire who made the famous Merkle Boner call during the 1908 pennant race between the Cubs and Giants (see *Base Running*). He was also involved in a critical call late that season against the Pirates, on an apparent grand slam by Ed Abbaticchio, that would have allowed the Pirates to end the season in a three-way tie with the Cubs and Giants.

As dusk set in, Abbaticchio hit a ball that was near the foul line that O'Day ruled foul. "Proof" that the ball was fair came a few months later when a female fan sued the Pirates, claiming that she was seriously injured by Abbaticchio's drive. She had sworn statements from witnesses and a ticket stub for her seat — in fair territory. The court threw out her case, in part because she was in fair territory when she was hit by the ball and had assumed the risk of injury by attending the game. One writer supposedly dug up the court records and determined that the ball was hit to right field, not left field as often reported, and that the woman was not in her seat, but in an overflow area that ringed the outfield.

Safe Territory. In 2004 a New Jersey trial court ruled that fans have an expectation of safety while in the concession area, and a man who was hit in the face by a foul ball while standing in line at a vendor's cart was allowed to proceed with his lawsuit.

Good Thinking. On August 7, 1999, J.T. Snow of the Giants hit a towering pop up in the 9th inning that eluded three Braves infielders and landed on the pitcher's mound after second baseman Bret Boone called off the other fielders and then couldn't reach the ball. After the ball hit, it ricocheted toward the third base line. Shortstop Ozzie Guillen yelled for everyone not to touch the ball as it harmlessly crossed into foul territory, where Guillen picked it up. Snow then flied out as the Braves won 15–4.

Phantom Foul. On October 11, 1997, the Orioles played the Indians in Game 3 of the ALCS. Mike Mussina of the Orioles struck out 15 in seven innings, but the Indians won in the bottom of the 12th inning on a botched played by Orioles catcher Lenny Webster. Webster was sure that a pitch was tipped by batter Omar Vizquel (who was trying to bunt), so he didn't chase after it when it got by him. Marques Griffin stole home on the play to win the game 2–1. Mussina struck out another 10 four days later, but the Orioles lost 1–0 and the Indians wrapped up the series.

Foul Language

"Obscene and indecent language between players and to the umpires reached such a pitch that … some of the magnates could not stand the raw work of the players, and protested continually against it. But the larger number of the magnates condoned and excused every act of rowdyism, no matter how flagrant." — Sportswriter Francis Richter on the National League owners of the 1890s.

"Trading profanities with Tommy Lasorda is like engaging in a dart duel with a porcupine." — Columnist Scott Ostler.

"He remembered how he'd really got his adjectival shoulders into a swing and had knocked the indelicacy ball against the Anglo-Saxon hotel out there." — Red Smith "paraphrasing" Babe Ruth's profane description of a home run.

"In fact, the Washington club had later on what we playfully called 'the cussin' battery': [Walter] Johnson's worst was 'goodness gracious sakes alive!' and catcher Muddy Ruel's, 'dog-gum it!'" —

Al Schacht in his autobiography, *My Own Particular Screwball* (1955).

"Repeat 100 times — Four-letter words like 'Dude' are fine. Others make me sound like some kid outside the 7-Eleven." — 2004 New Year's resolution for the foul-mouthed Josh Beckett, as proposed by Alan Schwartz.

Early Profanity. The New York Knickerbockers' 1846 scorebook reflects that players were fined six cents for using profanity.

Board of Discipline.

"The stenographer was a little lady straight out of 'Little House on the Prairie.' She couldn't believe what she heard after that. The poor old woman's hands were shaking. I'm thinking, I hope Little House on the Prairie makes it." — Roger Clemens recalling a 1990 hearing with Commission Fay Vincent after Clemens was ejected during the American League Championship Series (see *Ejections*). All parties were being polite during the hearing, until Vincent reminded them that they were all grown men and didn't have to edit their on-field language.

Reds owner John Brush, whose salary classification plan in part led to the formation of the Players League in 1890, introduced his "Purification Plan" in 1898. This was an attempt to eliminate foul language by players, which peaked in the 1890s in part because it was encouraged by most National League owners. A Board of Discipline was created, which consisted of three baseball management men: L.C. Krauthoff, Louis Kramer and Fred Stearns. This group only dealt with players and did not address problems with umpires, fans or club officials. In addition, the body did not rule on fighting, only on profanity and obscenity. The board was largely ineffective and soon disappeared.

Court Rulings. Courts have ruled that suspensions were unjustified for use of foul language because "players are entitled to use words stronger than those ordinarily used by the average citizen."

Prank. In 1989 a Billy Ripken baseball card was released showing him holding a bat. The knob of the bat contained a profanity and the card was reissued with the profanity blacked out.

Tommy Lasorda. Lasorda is legendary for his profanity and has been taped a number of times blowing up at players and sportswriters. Perhaps his most famous tirade was one in which he was asked, by a sportswriter after a Dodger loss, about Dave Kingman's performance that day against the Dodgers. Kingman had hit three home runs and driven in eight runs. "What do I think of Kingman's performance" started the tirade, which included the gamut of expletives.

Lasorda was caught on tape swearing repeatedly at Dodger pitcher Doug Rau on the mound after Rau had given up three hits in Game 4 of the 1977 World Series. Lasorda had forgotten that he was wearing a microphone. Dodger second baseman Davey Lopes had to come on the mound and calm down Lasorda.

Lasorda used even more expletives in a tirade against the Padres, and particularly utilityman Kurt Bevacqua, that included the following excerpt (profanity excluded): "When I was pitching, Bevacqua was the kind of player that I'd send a limousine for because Bevacqua couldn't hit water if he fell out of a boat."

This is a variation on a Casey Stengel quote about one of his players: "That boy couldn't hit the ground if he fell out of an airplane."

Good Judgment. Rick Bosetti of the Blue Jays once was fined for turning down a young fan's request for an autograph by using an obscenity. Two months later during the off-season he was hired as the team's goodwill ambassador.

Bad Day at Work. In September 2003 White Sox reliever Jose Paniagua was released one day after he made an obscene gesture at plate umpire Mark Carlson as he left the field during a game against the Twins. It was his first appearance in the Major Leagues in almost a year, and he gave up four four runs in a third of an inning. Paniagua apparently was upset at some of the umpire's home plate calls. After he was gone, the nameplate on his locker was replaced with "Lost and Found."

Insulting Animals. In spring training 1999, Yankee pitcher Hideki Irabu failed to cover first base. An upset George Steinbrenner called him a "fat pussy toad," but later apologized.

Flipping the "Bird"/Obscene Gestures.

Jack McDowell.

"The Yankee Flipper"—Nickname given the Yankee pitcher in 1995 after he flipped off fans while being booed during a poor outing. He raised his arm high in the air and gave the fans the "finger." The club fined him $5,000 and the league ordered him to buy a large number of tickets and distribute them to charities.

Byung-Hyun Kim. During the 2003 division play-off series between the Red Sox and A's, the Boston reliever blew a save early in the series in Oakland. When he was introduced to Boston fans for Game 3 as the players lined up on the foul lines, the fans booed him. He raised his right arm and touched the bill of his cap. When he brought his arm down, he raised it again without changing the smile on his face, and then put up his middle finger. He later apologized for the gesture in a statement likely written by the club's public relations department (given that Kim's English wasn't quite this sophisticated): "I apologize to the fans of the Red Sox, the people of New England and baseball fans throughout the world. It was an instant, reflexive reaction that I regret."

Kim had been obtained by the Red Sox from Arizona on May 29. He had 16 saves in 19 chances for the Red Sox during the regular season, but he had previously suffered from problems during another postseason, the 2001 World Series, when he gave up game-tying home runs by the Yankees when they played the Diamondbacks at Yankee Stadium.

Albert Belle. Belle left the Indians after the 1996 season and signed with the White Sox. In his first game back in Cleveland, on June 3, 1997, the loud, bell-ringing crowd was hostile toward him, but he responded with a three-run homer and two doubles to lead the White Sox to a 9–5 victory. After the game, Belle made an obscene gesture to the crowd, which cost him a $5,000 fine from the league, payable in game tickets to underprivileged children.

Joe Schultz. See *Seattle Pilots*—Managers for the legendary profanity-laced pep talks by Schultz.

Foul Lines

"Tell me. Are you responsible for putting down these nice straight lines?"—Female WCCO Minnesota television interviewer to the Twins groundskeeper, quoted in Roger Angell's *The Summer Game* (1972).

"Where is the foul line? It does not exist. It is the fair line. I have been meaning to write to the Rules Committee. There are many things I must correct."—Former catcher and Virgin Islander Valmy Thomas.

"And in all match games, a line connecting the home and first base and the home and third base, shall be marked by the use of chalk, or other suitable material, so as to be distinctly seen by the umpire." — Rules published in the 1861 *Beadle's Dime Base-Ball Player*.

Prior to 1869 foul lines were often dug with a furrow. Notwithstanding the 1861 reference in the *Beadle's Guide*, historian Lee Allen credited William Wing, a Cincinnati Redstockings groundskeeper, with first using a chalky lime substance in 1869.

National League president Harry Pulliam urged unsuccessfully that three-inch canvas or rubber strips be used to mark the foul lines. For 81 years the White Sox used flattened fire hoses painted white as the foul lines in Comiskey Park outfield.

The Tigers use white exterior latex paint on all foul lines and use chalk only in the batter's box. The club goes through 80 gallons of paint a year at a cost of $3,000.

Foul Poles

"Why don't they call it a fair pole?"—Headline in *Baseball Weekly*.

"I'm sort of a permanent fixture, like home plate and the foul pole."—Giants manager John McGraw.

"Foul Pole Polka."—Thomas Boswell's description of Carlton Fisk's 1975 World Series Game 6 dance to keep the ball fair and win the game for the Red Sox.

See also *Foul Balls*.

Origins. On July 15, 1939, Harry Craft hit a home run into the left field upper deck at the Polo Grounds. The Giants believed the ball was foul and an argument ensued. As a result, a 2'- to 3'-wide net was installed running the length of each Polo Grounds foul pole to help identify fair and foul balls. All modern ballparks are now equipped with foul pole nets. All poles must be at least 10 feet high.

Wrong Placement. When Dodger Stadium opened in 1962, the foul poles were completely in foul territory, rather than on the foul lines as they were supposed to be. During the off-season the Dodgers moved home plate to put the poles in fair territory.

When the Giants opened Candlestick Park, it was discovered that the foul poles were well inside fair territory.

The foul poles in San Diego's Jack Murphy Stadium were two feet behind the fence and one foot in front of the wall. This makes it possible to hit a curving fly ball that is fair when it goes over the wall but curves outside the foul pole for a foul ball.

Advertising. In 1996 the White Sox sold advertising rights to their foul poles.

Close Call.

"It's funny, but sometimes I have nightmares that when I hit that ball that it's going to curve foul. Every time I see it on TV it hits the pole and I can relax."—Carlton Fisk on his Game 6 home run of the 1975 World Series.

During Game 1 of the Yankees/Red Sox ALCS game on October 8, 2003, Todd Walker of the Red Sox hit a ball that was headed for the right field foul pole. The right field umpire ruled the ball foul, but the home plate umpire overruled him (in concurrence with three other umpires), saying the ball hit the foul pole. A fan, identified only as "Josh," appeared to get his hand on the ball, and he said that the ball hit his hand first, in foul territory, and then caromed into the pole. Replays seemed to suggest that the ball hit the foul pole.

Four and Five Decade Players   See *Longest Careers*

Four Hundred (.400) Hitters

"To hit .400 you need a great start and you can't have a slump. The year I did it, I was around .410, .412 all season, and I was really hitting the ball on the nose. Hitting is a business. With two strikes, you really protect that plate."—Bill Terry, the last player to bat over .400 in the National League. He hit .401 in 1930 for the Giants at age 33.

See also *Batting Average*, *Batting Champions*, *Hits*, *Hitters* and *Three Hundred Hitters*.

Ted Williams.

"If I'm going to be a .400 hitter, I want to have more than my toenails on the line."—Purported response of Ted Williams when manager Joe Cronin asked if he wanted to come out of the game after he had locked up a .400 batting average for the 1941 season. He hit .406 for the Red Sox in 1941, the last player to break the magic mark.

In his autobiography he claimed that an injury helped him do it. He only had to pinch-hit the first two weeks of the season because of a sore ankle. He never hit well during the cold April weeks and that year he had only a few at-bats during that period, reducing the negative impact on his average. He also credits his success that year to extra batting practice all season with pitcher Joe Dobson.

Williams needed to go 5-for-12 over the final three games to maintain his .401 average. In the first game he went 1-for-4 and his average dropped to .3995535 going into the final day's doubleheader. There would be no intentional walks in those games, as A's manager Connie Mack had instructed his players to pitch to him. The night before the doubleheader Williams walked 10 miles while eating ice cream. He then went 6-for-8 in Shibe Park to finish at .406 or, more accurately, .4057017. He hit .397 in September.

During the season Williams had the following batting averages against each club:

.471   Yankees
.444   Athletics
.426   Browns
.400   White Sox
.387   Indians
.381   Senators
.338   Tigers

Writer Ed Linn pointed out in *Hitter*, his 1993 biography of Williams, that Williams did not get the benefit of the sacrifice rule that Bill Terry enjoyed in 1930. Under the old rules a batter was not charged with an at-bat if any runner advanced a base. Under that system Williams would have batted .412.

The Last .400 Hitter, by John B. Holway (1991), is a day-by-day account of Williams' season-long quest for .400.

Williams would have had a second .400 season, in 1957, if he had delivered five more hits. He also had a remarkable 119 walks that season, 33 of them intentional.

.400 Three Times. Jesse Burkett, Ty Cobb and Rogers Hornsby are the only three-time .400 hitters.

20th Century .400 Hitters.

.424	1924	Rogers Hornsby
422	1901	Nap Lajoie
.420	1922	George Sisler
.420	1911	Ty Cobb
.410	1912	Ty Cobb
.408	1911	Joe Jackson
.407	1920	George Sisler
.406	1941	Ted Williams
.403	1925	Rogers Hornsby
.401	1922	Rogers Hornsby
.401	1922	Ty Cobb
.401	1930	Bill Terry

Just Missed.

"I hope somebody hits .400 soon. Then people can start pestering *that* guy with questions about the last guy to hit .400."—Ted Williams in 1980.

"I don't know if he can do it, but I tell you what: He's taking me to places that I haven't been in a long time, just watching him. His work ethic, the joy of playing the game.... I got to watch George [Brett] chase .400, too, and Todd has the same passion and respect for the game I saw in George."—Rockies hitting coach Clint Hurdle on Todd Helton, who was batting .394 going into September 2000, and last was at .400 that season on August 22. He finished the season at .372.

In 1927 Harry Heilmann and Al Simmons were locked in a race for the batting title, which overshadowed the fact that on the last day of the season Heilmann went 6-for-8 against the Indians and missed hitting .400 by one hit. He finished at .398, defeating Simmons, who finished at .392 (see also *Batting Champions*).

In 1929 Lefty O'Doul needed one more hit or three less at-bats to have reached .400.

In 1939 Joe DiMaggio had an excellent chance to hit .400. He was at .412 with about two weeks left in the season. He came down with an infection in his eye, which doctors injected with Novocain. The eye was tearing and painful, but manager Joe McCarthy didn't take him out of the lineup. With the bad eye, DiMaggio's average fell about 32 points in two weeks and he finished at .381.

In 1977 Rod Carew came within eight hits of .400 while accumulating 616 at-bats. He also had 15 intentional walks.

George Brett flirted with .400 for most of 1980, finishing at .390 after a 37-game hitting streak. During the season he suffered a bruised heel tendon and a torn ligament, causing him to miss 45 games. Since Ted Williams in 1941, Brett was at .400 the latest into the season: September 19, 1980.

In 1994 Tony Gwynn batted .394 during the strike-shortened season. He fell three hits shy of .400, but was well short of the required 502 plate appearances (assuming a full season of 162 games played). Factoring in the at-bats needed to qualify for the batting title in the short season, he would have needed another 27 hits to be credited with a legitimate .400 season.

Most .400 Hitters. In 1887 a rule change added walks to hits, allowing 20 hitters to bat .400 or better.

Rookie. Joe Jackson is the only rookie who qualified for the batting title to bat over .400. He hit .408 in 1911.

Controversy. In August 1922 sportswriter Fred Lieb was scoring a game at Yankee Stadium involving Ty Cobb. John Kieran was the official scorer at the ballpark, but Lieb scored for the Associated Press wire service. It had rained during the game and many writers had left the press box for cover in the grandstand.

Cobb grounded to Everett Scott at shortstop, who fumbled it a bit; the field was wet and the ball was hard to pick up. Lieb scored it a hit. Kieran, sitting elsewhere, scored it an error and, as was customary after the game, sent his scoring summary to the American League office.

At the end of the season the Associated Press had Cobb finishing at .401 based on Lieb's "hit" scoring. The American League office had him at .399 based on Kieran's official "error" call. Irwin Howe was the American League's official statistician. Howe resolved the controversy by relying on the more experienced Lieb's judgment and calling it a hit. The Baseball Writers Association voted in favor of Kieran's interpretation because he was the official scorer, and Lieb strongly supported this decision. Nevertheless, American League president Ban Johnson wanted a .400 hitter in his league because the few recent .400 hitters had been in the National League and Rogers Hornsby of the Cardinals hit .401 that season. Johnson supported the .401 result, which became official.

Pitchers. In 1925 Walter Johnson hit .433, with 42 hits in 97 at-bats.

In 1923 Jack Bentley of the Giants hit .427, with 38 hits in 89 at-bats.

Orel Hershiser of the Dodgers was over .400 for much of the 1993 season, finishing at .356.

Four Hundred Wins See *Three Hundred Wins*

Four Thousand Hits

"When the symbolic, the statistical and the historic intersect in sports, the larger world pauses in its rounds to pay attention and pass its judgment. Now in our national on-deck circle: Pete Rose."— Thomas Boswell in *The Heart of the Order* (1989), three hits before Rose broke Cobb's record.

Ty Cobb. Cobb reached 4,000 hits at age 40 on July 18, 1927 (erroneously the 17th and 19th in some sources), while playing for the A's. His double off the glove of former Tiger teammate Harry Heilmann was barely noticed in the press. The hit came off pitcher Sam Gibson in a 5–3 Tiger win. Even the Detroit papers paid no attention except for a reference in the game notes. He finished his career with 4,191 hits.

Pete Rose.

"It was also during this period [1985] that Rose became obsessed with breaking Ty Cobb's record for most hits…. But it was also clear to virtually everyone in baseball that as a hitter he was living on vapors, unable to hit with any of his former authority."— Buzz Bissinger in a September 2001 *Vanity Fair* story.

"When I get the record, all it will make me is the player with the most hits. I'm also the player with the most at-bats and the most outs. I never said I was a greater player than Cobb."— Rose.

Playing for the Expos, Rose reached 4,000 hits on April 13, 1984, the day before his 43rd birthday. It was a double in the 4th inning off Jerry Koosman of the Phillies. The hit came exactly 21 years after his first hit, a triple off Pittsburgh's Bob Friend (after an 0-for-11 career start). Rose hit number 2,000 on June 19, 1973.

Playing for the Reds, Rose tied Cobb's all-time record of 4,191 on September 8, 1985, with a single off Cubs pitcher Reggie Patterson at Wrigley Field. Rose hit number 4,192 on September 11, 1985. It was a 1st inning single to left field off Eric Show of the Padres. He did it on the same date as Cobb's last game. A circle was painted on the Three Rivers Stadium field to mark where the ball struck the ground. Rose set the new record in official at-bat number 13,768, while Cobb needed only 11,429 official at-bats to reach 4,191 hits. Rose finished with 4,256 hits. In a deal cut with the Reds, Rose received a percentage of all souvenirs relating to his pursuit of the record. See also Pete Rose and Hal Bodley, *Countdown to Cobb* (1985).

In November 1998 one of Rose's associates sold the record-breaking bat for $21,096.

Closest to 4,000. Henry Aaron reached 3,771 hits, third all-time.

Nellie Fox (1947–1975)

Hall of Fame (VC) 1997

"I just loved him as a second baseman. I rate him close to [Bobby] Doerr and [Joe] Gordon."— Ted Williams.

Playing primarily for the White Sox, Fox was the American League's premier second baseman in the 1950's and early 1960's.

Jacob Nelson Fox began his pro career in 1945 at 17 with Lancaster (Pennsylvania) of the Inter-State League. He spent 1946 in military service. Fox returned to Lancaster in 1947 and later that

year made his Major League debut briefly with the Philadelphia A's of the American League. In 1948 he moved to Lincoln, Nebraska, of the Western League and again appeared briefly (three games) with the A's.

Fox finally made the A's roster in 1949, hitting .255 in 88 games. After the 1949 season the White Sox acquired him, but his inauspicious 1950 debut with the club would prove to be an aberration. In 1951 Fox hit .313, finishing second in the league with 189 hits. In 1952 Fox led the league in hits with 192. For his career Fox would lead the league in hits four times, hitting over .300 six times. He led American League second baseman in fielding six times and putouts 10 consecutive years, a Major League record.

Fox began a spectacular 1959 season with five hits on Opening Day, the last American League player to do so. Fox hit .306 with a career high 34 doubles, won the American league MVP Award and led the White Sox to the pennant. In the World Series he hit .375 in a six-game loss to the Dodgers. After that his statistics began to decline and he was traded to Houston for the 1964 season. In 1965 he ceded second base to Joe Morgan, appearing in just 21 games before retiring.

Fox finished his career with a .288 batting average and 2,663 hits. A fine contact hitter, Fox's 216 strikeouts in 9,232 at bats is the third best ratio all time. He holds the American League record for career double plays with 1,568 and the Major League record for consecutive games at second base with 798. He was a 12-time All-Star and won three Gold Gloves. He was a Major League coach after his playing career, but died of cancer at age 47 in 1975.

Jimmie Foxx (1907–1967)

Hall of Fame 1951

"We were watching that ball for two innings."— A bullpen catcher on a long Foxx drive.

"I give him my best pitch and run to back up third."— Lefty Gomez on his pitching strategy for Foxx.

The first baseman hit 534 home runs primarily for the A's and Red Sox from 1925 through 1945.

Known as "The Beast" and "Double X," James Emory Foxx began his professional career at age 16 in 1924 in the Eastern Shore League under manager Frank "Home Run" Baker. Foxx played catcher, third base and outfield, positions he played at various times in the Major Leagues. He signed with the A's in 1925 and played briefly with the club after spending most of the year with Providence of the International League.

He played a few games with the A's in 1926 and 1927, finally sticking with the club in 1928 with 13 home runs in 118 games. He became the club's starting first baseman in 1929 and immediately established himself as one of the premier power hitters in the game with 33 home runs. This began a string of 12 seasons in which he never hit less than 30 home runs.

Foxx peaked in 1932 with 58 home runs and 169 RBIs to go with a .749 slugging average. The following season he won the Triple Crown with a .356 average, 48 home runs and 163 RBIs. He hit .344 with four home runs in three World Series for the A's from 1929 through 1931.

Foxx hit 36 home runs in 1935 the cash-poor A's sold him to the Red Sox, where he continued to star. He peaked with the Red Sox in 1938 with a .349 average and 50 home runs to go with 175 RBIs. He did not win the Triple Crown only because Hank Greenberg hit 58 home runs.

Foxx began to fade in 1941 with 19 home runs, though he still hit .300 and drove in 105 runs. He was traded to the Cubs in 1942 and finished his career in 1945 for the Phillies, for whom he hit seven home runs and pitched in nine games. Over his 20-year career he established the fourth-highest slugging average of all time among retired players at .609. He hit 534 home runs, good for twelfth, and drove in 1,922 runs, seventh all-time.

He managed and coached in the minor leagues, but his heavy drinking made it difficult for him to save money through a series of business failures. He broadcast briefly for the Red Sox in 1946, but bad business decisions left him broke by the late 1950s. He died in 1967 when he choked on a piece of meat during dinner.

Book. Bob Gorman, *Double X: Jimmie Foxx Baseball's Forgotten Slugger* (1990).

France

"Tuez l'arbitre."—"Kill the Ump."

"About the most knowledgeable non–American fan I ever saw a ball game with was a Frenchman who came to this country when he was thirty years old. They do many things in France but they don't play either cricket or baseball. He brought a completely blank mind to the game. He was fascinated; he studied hard; in record time he won his Phi Beta Kappa key in the American madness."— Fred Schwed, Jr., in *How to Watch a Baseball Game* (1957).

"The Mets, like France in the nineteen-twenties, have a missing generation between the too old and the too young."—Roger Angell in *The Summer Game* (1972), comparing the thin roster of the expansion Mets to the war-decimated able-bodied male population of France after World War I.

The Fédération Française de Baseball, de Softball et de Criket (Fede), was founded in 1924. The first club was the Ranelagh club, also founded in the 1920s. Baseball was popular during and after each of the World Wars, when occupying Americans introduced the game. The sport experienced a renaissance in France in the 1980s, expanding from 30 clubs and 2,500 registered players to 270 clubs and 12,000 players in 1992. The French baseball publication is called *Strike*.

French Baseball Terms.
Frappeur—Batter
Plaque—Home Plate
Le Batting Glove—Batting Glov
Gant—Glove

No-Hitter. In 1981 Charlie Lea of the Expos became the first French-born player to throw a no-hitter. He beat the Giants 4–0.

Language Barrier. When Gary Carter began his acceptance speech at the 2003 Hall of Fame induction ceremony, he started out speaking French, a language he learned from Berlitz tapes when he first joined the Expos in French-speaking Montreal.

Franchise Shifts

"Baseball is trying to operate as it did in 1900—and it can't be done. Population and business have gone West. Baseball must follow."—Ford Frick in October 1954.

"If a community fails to support a team, the solution was easy— move to a greener pasture. Franchise shifting was as much a part of normal procedure as expansion has become today. When a problem arose, a rule was passed to solve it. No questions asked. If a given rule failed to work it was replaced by a new one, with little fear of questioned legality or public condemnation."—Frick in *Games, Asterisks and People* (1973).

See also individual team entries.

Pre–World War II. Prior to 1900 only Chicago and Boston had continuous representation in the National League.

In 1905–1906 there was talk of shifting the Dodgers to Baltimore, but the move never materialized.

The Detroit Tigers were not well-supported by the city in their first 15 years starting in 1901, and some thought was given to moving the franchise to another city. However, the town was revitalized by the automobile boom over the next few years and by 1924 attendance had reached 1 million annually.

In 1916 serious consideration was given to moving the Washington Senators to Toronto. After a year of discussions, the move was abandoned.

In 1933 Cardinals owner Sam Breadon consulted with Judge Landis on the rules governing his desire to move his club to Detroit. According to Ford Frick, Landis ruled that it was a league matter and Breadon ultimately was unable to strike a deal with Tigers owner Frank Navin, whose approval was required.

Post–World War II. After World War II Americans had large amounts of leisure time compared to past years, allowing for more free time to attend baseball games. Many Major League clubs were losing money, however, in part because a number of ballparks were inconveniently located in decaying areas and had poor *Parking*. Public transportation was fast becoming only a secondary means of transporting fans to ballparks and adequate parking was needed. The older ballparks were built in residential neighborhoods that could not be leveled to accommodate more parking.

Other factors contributing to declining postwar attendance were population shifts from the northeast and the fact that only a few teams were dominating the Major Leagues: the New York teams (Dodgers, Giants, Yankees), Cardinals and Red Sox.

In 1951 Congress investigated baseball on *Antitrust* issues and recommended that it be expanded to cities that were ready for it. Not surprisingly, the most vocal supporter was a congressman from Los Angeles. By the 1970s the league rules required approval for a move by 10 of 14 National League owners and eight of 14 American League owners. No National or American League franchise shifts occurred between 1903 and 1953. There were 10 shifts between 1954 and 1972 and various attempts to move:

1. **Boston Braves to Milwaukee/1953.**

"… the time is not far distant when the Boston club of the National League will be shifted to some other city.…"—*The Sporting News* in 1919, 33 years before the club actually moved to Milwaukee.

The Braves shifted to Milwaukee for the 1953 season and Milwaukee's minor league franchise shifted to Toledo, Ohio. Braves owner Lou Perini was desperately attempting to leave Boston, but Milwaukee did not enter into his plans, at least initially. More prominently in his thoughts were Denver, Montreal, Toronto, Houston and Dallas.

Milwaukee had just completed a 35,000-seat stadium for its Class AAA club, which made it attractive to Perini. However, on March 7, 1953, Perini stopped his annual efforts to move when commissioner Ford Frick announced that he would not allow a move so late during spring training. Only six days later Frick backed down, stating that the National League did not need his approval of the move.

After it appeared that the deal was dead, Milwaukee County officials discovered that they could terminate their lease with the minor league Brewers on 30 days' notice, which they promptly did. Wisconsin politicians threatened to renew the recently completed congressional antitrust investigation of baseball if Perini failed to move forward with the shift to Milwaukee.

Perini announced on March 13 that the club was moving immediately, which required and received a unanimous vote of the National League owners.

2. St. Louis Browns to Baltimore/1954. In 1941 the Browns came close to moving to Los Angeles. A December 8, 1941, meeting to make a final decision on the move was cancelled due to the Pearl Harbor bombing. In addition, the Los Angeles Coliseum Commission had decided a few months earlier that it only wanted football in its stadium. There were no serious efforts to move clubs until after the war.

In 1950 it was clear that the Browns would be moving and it was only a question of where. William Zeckendorf of New York negotiated to buy the club and move it to Houston after he tried unsuccessfully tried to buy Branch Rickey's interest in the Dodgers. Despite Zeckendorf's efforts, Browns owner Bill Veeck eventually sold to Baltimore interests.

Before the Browns finally moved, many thought that the club would move to Toronto or Montreal rather than Baltimore, although Baltimore had been mentioned. When the vote was taken, it was done with the intent that the American League would later expand to 10 teams and absorb the Pacific Coast League cities of San Francisco and Los Angeles.

Many have claimed that the American League forced Veeck to sell the club because of animosity toward him by other owners. The Yankee owners approved the franchise shift only after Veeck was out and the other owners quickly fell in line. Other sources report that Senators owner Clark Griffith did not want the competition of a franchise in Baltimore, so he suggested to Veeck that he move to Los Angeles. At first Veeck rejected the idea but soon changed his mind. Hank Greenberg and Veeck then tried to put a team in Los Angeles, but that effort was rebuffed by the other American League owners.

Because of the general animosity toward Veeck by the other owners, at least one source reported that Greenberg might have succeeded on his own. Either way, the Browns' stockholders had other ideas. They wanted out of ownership and wanted the club out of the city. Veeck's partners forced a sale to Jerry Hoffberger, a Baltimore brewery owner, and the club moved to Baltimore for the 1954 season.

3. Philadelphia A's to Kansas City/1955.
"A third franchise shift in three years took place before the 1955 season.... If St. Louis had never been big enough to support two major-league clubs, then Philadelphia, still the nation's fourth-largest city, had always seemed to be. Yet besides being unable to play Sunday home dates until 1934, the Philadelphia teams had frequently offered wretched baseball, all too often in the same season." — Charles C. Alexander in *Our Game* (1991).

In 1954 Arnold Johnson bought the Philadelphia A's from Connie Mack's heirs and shifted the club to Kansas City for the 1955 season. It was the third Major League franchise shift in 20 months. The Senators and Indians voted against the shift, though one account reported erroneously that a unanimous vote was required (which was true only for the National League).

4–5. Brooklyn Dodgers to Los Angeles and New York Giants to San Francisco/1958.
"I never asked them to build me a ballpark. I said we'd build it on taxable land with our money at Atlantic and Flatbush. Robert Moses blocked this site and wanted his own in a poor location." — Dodger owner Walter O'Malley responding to claims that he made unreasonable demands on New York before moving to Los Angeles.

"My roots are in Brooklyn, so why should I move?" — Walter O'Malley before the announcement.

"I feel bad for the kids. I've seen lots of them at the Polo Grounds. But I haven't seen many of their fathers lately." — Giants owner Horace Stoneham after announcing that his club was moving to San Francisco.

In the mid–1950s the Dodgers and Giants publicly considered shifting their clubs to other cities. Walter O'Malley of the Dodgers and Horace Stoneham of the Giants cited small parks and inadequate parking as primary reasons for the moves. The Giants were drawing poorly. In 1956 they drew 629,267; only nine years earlier they had drawn 1,599,784. Attendance had dropped 50% over the previous three years alone.

By at least February 1957 the Giants were planning to leave for Minneapolis, where they had a farm team that allowed them to control the territorial rights to the area. Stoneham wanted to move to Minnesota because he liked the state and the fans knew many of his players because of their interest in the farm team. Walter O'Malley purportedly had to talk him out of going to Minnesota and persuade him to go to California so they could continue their rivalry.

On August 19, 1957, the New York Giants board of directors formally voted 8–1 to move to San Francisco. M. Donald Grant was the only dissenter and later he was instrumental in bringing the Mets to New York. The Dodgers had already been given clearance by the National League to move and on October 8, 1957, the league finally voted approval for the Giants to move.

O'Malley had to pay the Pacific Coast League (PCL) $900,000 to move into its most productive market. PCL president Leslie O'Connor opposed the move because he still held out hope that the PCL could become a third Major League. He was almost right, as each PCL city except Portland eventually obtained a Major League franchise (Oakland, San Francisco, Los Angeles, San Diego and Seattle).

O'Malley persuaded Cubs owner Phil Wrigley to sell Wrigley Field in Los Angeles and the minor league Los Angeles Angels in exchange for the Dodgers' Fort Worth ballpark and ballclub. Had Wrigley held onto the PCL franchise, O'Malley might not have moved.

By 1961 only Willie Mays among the Giants was left from the New York days. In contrast, the Dodgers still had 12 of their Brooklyn players. San Francisco fans did not warm up to the holdover New York players and adopted Orlando Cepeda and Willie McCovey rather than Mays.

The Giants initially did well to move, increasing attendance from 653,000 in 1957 in New York to 1,272,000 in 1958 in San Francisco. The Dodgers drew 1,845,556 in 1958 in Los Angeles, better than their all-time Brooklyn best of 1,807,000 in 1947.

The first Major League game on the West Coast was Opening Day, April 15, 1958, in Seals Stadium in San Francisco. Gino Cimoli of the Dodgers was the first batter. The Giants routed Don Drysdale behind an 8–0 shutout by Ruben Gomez. Orlando Cepeda had the first Major League home run on the West Coast. See also Neil J. Sullivan, *The Dodgers Move West* (1987).

6. Washington Senators to Minnesota/1961.
"You only have 15,000 blacks here ... you've got good hard-working white people here ... blacks don't go to ball games." — Minnesota Twins owner Calvin Griffith in a speech to a group of Minneapolis businessmen, on why he moved his franchise from predominantly black Washington, D.C., to predominantly white Minneapolis–St. Paul for the 1961 season. As part of the expansion of the American League in 1961, the Senators moved their franchise to Minnesota and a new Senators franchise was placed in Washington.

7. Milwaukee Braves to Atlanta/1966. Milwaukee's attendance began to fade in the early 1960s, in part due to bad teams and the arrival of the Twins in Minnesota. Their presence siphoned off many of Milwaukee's fans. From an average of 2.1 million from 1954 through 1957, the Braves drew less than 800,000 in 1962 and 1963.

In October 1964 the club announced that it would be moving to Atlanta for the 1965 season, but a local judge ruled that the team had to play one more season in Milwaukee. The case made its way to the state's Supreme Court, which ruled in a 4–3 decision that although baseball was a monopoly, the state had no power to regulate its conduct. Nevertheless, the Braves spent the 1965 season as a lame duck club in Milwaukee.

8. Kansas City A's to Oakland/1968.

"The luckiest city since Hiroshima."— Missouri Senator Stuart Symington on the city of Oakland after the late 1967 departure from Kansas City of the A's and contentious owner Charlie Finley.

Finley began looking for a new home immediately after taking over a majority interest in the A's in 1961. He considered moving to Seattle, Atlanta, Louisville or Oakland. A marketing report presented to him said that Seattle was the best choice, but he preferred Oakland.

The American League was serious about keeping Finley in Kansas City until the last possible moment because Symington threatened him with expulsion from the league if he did not honor his ballpark lease with the city; Finley had been forced to sign a new lease in 1961 as a condition of his purchasing a majority interest in the club.

9. Seattle Pilots To Milwaukee/1970.

"No doubt the AL's speed, in the first instance, was based on a desire to beat the NL to Seattle, considered a plum. But a plum, when squeezed too hard, turns sour. And that sour taste is in everyone's mouth. Nevertheless, we say in sincerity, 'good luck to Milwaukee.'"— Seattle newspaper article shortly after the Pilots left town.

After the one-year Pilots completed their dismal 1969 season, they failed to fulfill various conditions imposed by the league for upgrading the stadium. As a result, the club was sold and moved to Milwaukee, which had been without baseball since the Braves left for Atlanta after the 1965 season.

10. Washington Senators to Texas/1971.

"It would be unthinkable to have a 'National Pastime' that wasn't represented in the nation's capital. Think it over, boys."— Columnist Bob Addie in 1957.

"In terms of am-I-a-prisoner-in–Washington, I would rather make it work in Washington and break even than make a million dollars annually in Arlington, Texas, because for whatever it's worth, it stirs more genes. The fact that you make a million dollars in Arlington, Texas, who the hell knows about it except your banker, and the hell with him anyway…"— Owner Bob Short in May 1971, before the move.

"The fink has moved the club to Texas."— Washington newscaster in a live broadcast after the news was released.

In September 1971 the American League voted 10–2 to allow the Senators to shift to Texas. Only the Orioles and White Sox opposed the move. A Washington group offered $9.4 million to owner Bob Short in order to keep the club in Washington, but Short rejected it because it was the same amount he had paid for the team and he had already lost $3 million. Short probably would have moved the club sooner, but the stadium lease did not run out until after the 1971 season.

11. Montreal Expos to Washington D.C./2005. Late in the 2004 season it was announced that the Expos would be moving to Washington D.C. in 2005. There was objection from the Expos'

former minority owners, who had filed a lawsuit that included an attempt to block any move of the team, and from Peter Angelos, owner of the Baltimore Orioles, who felt that competition from Washington would cost him $30 million in revenue each season.

Miscellaneous Franchise Non-Shifts.

Cleveland Indians to ? In 1957 the Indians owners talked of shifting their franchise, which became a semi-constant topic of conversation until the club resolved to build a new ballpark in the early 1990s. Moves prominently discussed were to Seattle or New Orleans.

San Diego Padres to Washington/1973. Original Padres owner C. Arnholdt Smith's bank went under in the early 1970s. Smith was offered $12.5 million for the franchise by grocery store magnate Joe Danzansky, who planned to move the club to Washington, D.C., and hire Minnie Minoso to be the manager. The deal was accepted by Smith and would have been approved by the league except that the club was unable to get out of its stadium lease in San Diego.

San Francisco Giants to ?/1974. In late 1974 A's owner Charlie Finley offered Giants owner Horace Stoneham $3 million to move to another city, but Stoneham rejected the deal. At the time the Giants had attendance of 500,000, lowest in the Major Leagues. The A's also could not draw fans in 1974, with only 800,000 in their ballpark despite winning their fourth straight division title.

San Francisco Giants to Toronto/1976. In 1976 the Giants almost shifted to Toronto (before the Blue Jays were created), but the conditional deal was cancelled when Bob Lurie bought the team and kept it in the Bay Area.

San Francisco Giants to San Jose or St. Petersburg/1992.

"First they froze your extremities. Now they want to break your heart."— A 1992 ad for a *San Francisco Examiner* contest asking readers to explain in 25 words or less the best reason why the Giants should not leave for St. Petersburg, Florida.

In early 1992 the Giants announced that the club would be moving to nearby San Jose for the 1994 season. The move was contingent upon the passage of a referendum in San Jose earmarking bond money for a new ballpark. Three previous bond votes in San Francisco had failed.

In 1987 the Giants fell only 11,440 votes short, but in 1989 looked to be in a good position to prevail on the November ballot given the Giants' success that year in winning the National League pennant. A major *Earthquake* hit the Bay Area during the 1989 World Series and the local population's focus was on rebuilding the city rather than building a new stadium for the Giants. This time the Giants lost the referendum by only 2,054 votes.

The 1992 vote in San Jose was 55%–45% against the stadium, ending chances of the move to San Jose. Then a group of investors from St. Petersburg announced that they were purchasing the club from owner Bob Lurie. The deal looked to be a sure thing based on Lurie's statement: "No other offer could or would be considered."

On August 6, 1992, Lurie announced a sale for $115 million to a St. Petersburg group headed by George Shinn, owner of the NBA Charlotte Hornets. The Shinn group prompted a malapropism by broadcaster Ralph Kiner: "In the hunt to buy the San Francisco Giants was George Shinn, owner of the Charlotte Harlots."

Though Shinn was based in South Carolina, his group consisted primarily of Florida investors that included Vince Piazza. Piazza was a friend of Dodger manager Tommy Lasorda and the father of Mike Piazza, who made it to the Major Leagues with the Dodgers in 1992. That connection led to rumors that Lasorda would be the club's first manager.

A group of San Francisco–based investors led by supermarket

magnate Peter Magowan countered Shinn by announcing that they would attempt to put together a deal that would keep the club in San Francisco. The Shinn group quickly dropped out of the bidding, though not without filing a lawsuit that was later settled. The club remained in San Francisco under local ownership led by Magowan.

St. Petersburg Left at the Altar.

"St. Petersburg is 0–6 in teams courted since 1984."—Ray Ratto in the *San Francisco Examiner*.

The Seattle Mariners were never profitable and it was strongly rumored in 1991 and 1992 that the club would move to St. Petersburg and its Suncoast Dome. However, local Japanese interests were allowed to purchase a majority interest in the club and the Mariners remained in Seattle. The White Sox averted a move to St. Petersburg when they built New Comiskey Park.

St. Pete had also been teased by the Twins (1984), A's (1985) and Rangers (1988) before the debacle with the Giants in late 1992. As a result of the last effort, the city filed a $3.5 billion suit against Major League Baseball and the Giants. *Sports Illustrated* made perhaps the best observation about the empty Suncoast Dome in downtown St. Pete: "[It] reminded us of the segment in the movie *Mondo Cane* in which aborigines in New Guinea, enchanted by the big airplanes that fly overhead, clear a landing strip in the belief that it will lure the craft to their village."

Tampa Bay and St. Petersburg finally scored with the Devil Rays for the 1998 season.

Oakland A's.

"Why is there a baseball team in Oakland, California? The obvious answer is that no one has yet made Charlie Finley an offer he cannot refuse, free of restrictive conditions."—Art Hill in *I Don't Care If I Never Come Back* (1980).

The A's have often considered leaving their small market. The club's ballpark lease ran through 2000, but a clause allowed them to cancel the lease if they accumulated losses of $3.5 million within two consecutive seasons. In the late 1970s, when Charlie Finley owned the team, he almost sold it to oil millionaire Marvin Davis, who wanted to move the club to Denver. Finley actually made a deal, but the county, which owned the stadium, would not let him out of his lease.

Houston Astros to Northern Virginia/1995. By late 1995 Houston Astros owner Drayton McLane was making serious efforts to negotiate a sale of his club to interests in Northern Virginia. The deal called for his club to play two seasons in RFK Stadium in Washington before a suitable facility was available in Virginia. The National League indicated that it would try to block the move, while McLane said he would need $200 million to renovate the Astrodome and double his season ticket sales in order to stay in Houston. The club settled in when its new ballpark was ready for the 2000 season.

Montreal Expos to Anywhere/2000s. The Expos were the bane of the Major Leagues in the late 1990s and 2000s. They drew so poorly at home on a regular basis that visiting clubs had no chance of making any money on the trips. Major League Baseball intervened by buying the club while trying to find it a new home. In 2003 the Expos played 22 home games in **Puerto Rico** and drew relatively well (given the demographics and size of the ballpark). Washington, D.C., was a prime candidate, but not until it built a new ballpark (that city's RFK Stadium is considered a poor baseball facility). By mid 2003, Northern Virginia was competing with Washington D.C. and Portland, Oregon. In August 2003, the Oregon legislature approved a $150 million partial financing deal for a new stadium, a positive step forward for Portland's efforts to secure the Expos, but that option appeared dead by spring 2004.

In 2004 Las Vegas was making a pitch for the Expos, but there was no decent ballpark to house the franchise while a real facility was built. By mid–2004 it appeared that Washington D.C. was to be the choice (it was), though over the vociferous objection of nearby Orioles owner Peter Angelos. See **Washington Nationals**.

Fraternization

"Players of opposing teams shall not fraternize at any time while in uniform."—Rule 3.09. The rule has been referred to as the "Stargell Rule," because of Willie Stargell's friendliness with both teammates and opposing players.

During Game 2 of the 2000 World Series played between the Yankees and Mets, television cameras caught opponents John Franco and David Cone talking to each other over the Yankee Stadium bullpen fence during the 7th inning. Sandy Alderson, the executive vice president of baseball operations, said he would look into it since there were concerns about the rule prohibiting fraternization.

Freak Accidents

"There was no way to cover up the McDowell incident since he bled all over the salad."—Sportswriter Frank Luksa of the *Dallas Morning News* on Oddibe McDowell disabling himself after slicing his finger with a butter knife at a team luncheon. The comment came after the Rangers withheld for five days the news that Jose Canseco had injured his arm after a one-inning pitching stint (see also **Hitters Who Pitched**).

"There'll be no more pole-vaulting for members of the Cleveland Indians, Manager Lou Boudreau warned the players today. The ban went into effect after Vern Kennedy, veteran pitcher, fancied himself as a second Cornelius Warmerdam and successfully vaulted nine feet on the Purdue athletic field, where the Indians are training. He landed on his head."—The *Stars and Stripes* military newspaper.

"Some persons go through life accident-prone; [Tug] McGraw goes through life disaster-prone."—Sportswriter Joe Durso on the Mets reliever.

"Anything I do is dangerous. Getting out of bed is dangerous to me. I need to wear hockey pads all day."—Marlins pitcher Kevin Brown, who missed a start after bruising his ankle when he slipped on a dock during a fishing trip.

"I tripped over my dog. That's my story and I'm sticking to it."—Infielder Howard Johnson during spring training 1997, on why he showed up with a black eye.

See also **Injuries and Illness**.

Playing With Fire. Indians outfielder Earl Averill had an off-year in 1935 after burning his hands while testing fireworks.

Watch Where You Walk. Frenchy Bordagaray tore ligaments in his knee falling off the dugout bench.

Frank Crosetti tore knee ligaments crawling into the upper birth on a train.

Ruben Sierra sprained his ankle on an escalator. He missed three games, ending his consecutive games streak at 325.

Glenallen Hill suffered cuts to his feet, hands and elbows when he fell into a glass coffee table while sleepwalking in 1990. He spent 15 days on the disabled list.

In August 1993 Rich Gossage tripped over a ball bag and broke his wrist, almost ending his career

In August 1993 Ken Griffey, Jr., fell down a flight of stairs while moving furniture and sprained his back.

In 1995 Jerry Browne of the Marlins required nine stitches in his elbow after slipping in the bathtub at the team's hotel and cutting it on the soap dish.

In January 1997 Red Sox pitcher Tim Wakefield was hit by a car while out jogging, but escaped serious injury.

Liquid Non-Refreshment. In 1940 Lon Frey was the starting second baseman for the Reds. He was knocked out of the World Series that season after a water cooler lid fell on his foot and broke it.

Pitcher Joe Hoerner was celebrating along with the rest of the Cardinals after Game 7 of the 1964 World Series when an exploding champagne bottle cut tendons in his middle finger.

Pitcher Larry Anderson pulled a muscle in his chest when he slipped carrying two glasses of wine into a hot tub.

Off His Rocker. In the 1940s pitcher Freddie Fitzsimmons rolled over his fingers in a rocking chair accident during spring training.

Mets catcher Mackey Sasser accidentally set a chair down on Dwight Gooden's left foot, injuring his middle toe and causing him to miss a start. Gooden also missed a start when teammate Vince Coleman struck him with a golf club (nine-iron) in the locker room while practicing his swing. The Mets announced that Gooden had been "bumped."

Laughter Isn't the Best Medicine. Dom DiMaggio and Sam Mele were roommates on the road. One night DiMaggio's bed collapsed and Mele laughed so hard that he aggravated a sacroiliac condition and was forced out of the next game.

A Close Shave. Pitcher Evans Killeen was cut from the 1962 expansion Mets after missing a scheduled spring training start. He had failed to explain adequately how he managed to cut his thumb while shaving. His Major League career consisted of four no-decision appearances for the A's in 1959.

No Heavy Lifting. Second baseman Bobby Grich slipped a disc lifting an air conditioner.

Yardwork. Pitcher Pat Zachry suffered a severed toe while using his lawn mower. Pitcher Curt Simmons did the same thing in 1953, causing him to miss a month.

Bob Ojeda once severed a finger with hedge clippers (and narrowly avoided severing his head in a boating accident that killed Tim Crews and Steve Olin — see *Deaths*).

Bite-Sized. Clarence "Climax" Blethen was a 30-year-old rookie with the Red Sox in 1923. He pitched with his false teeth in his hip pocket. On September 21 that season, he had forgotten to put them back in his mouth while running the bases. He bit himself in the butt sliding into second base.

Car Problems. John Smiley had his pitching hand slammed in a taxi door.

Dick Allen severed tendons in his left wrist when he put his hand through a headlight pushing a stalled antique car in the rain. He was confronted by police and had difficulty convincing them that he was not stealing his own car.

Pitcher Bill Lee was on a training run on the streets of Montreal when he almost stepped on a cat. Lee leapt into the street out of the way and was hit by a taxi cab. The injuries put him on the disabled list.

The classic post-free agency injury: in 1992 Padres outfielder Tony Gwynn fractured the tip of his finger when he caught it in the door of his Porsche as he was rushing to go to the bank.

In May 1999 pitcher Esteban Loaiza slammed his hand in a car door and was out for several weeks.

Catcher Brent Mayne was put on the disabled list after wrenching his back and suffering severe muscle spasms in a parking lot — after turning to look for approaching cars.

Dress More Conservatively. Wade Boggs hurt his back pulling off his cowboy boots.

Nothing to Sneeze At.

"A double sneeze has put Cub slugger Sammy Sosa on the DL. According to witnesses, Sosa became vulnerable after falling behind in the pollen count." — Randy Hill. In May 2004 Sammy Sosa went on the disabled list for a month with a strained ligament in his lower back after injuring it during two "violent" sneezes.

Reliever Goose Gossage threw his back out sneezing.

In 1993 Angels reliever Joe Grahe suffered a pinched nerve after sniffing to clear his sinuses. His teammates began teasing him by calling him "Neckersley" in reference to ace reliever Dennis Eckersley.

In 1995 Marlins pitcher Marc Valdez aggravated a rib injury sneezing in a cab.

Stay Out of the Kitchen.

"I guess that means I can't get a job at Denny's." — Reds catcher Joe Oliver in July 1993 after he tripped unloading his dishwasher and stuck himself with a knife, requiring 12 stitches.

Brewers shortstop Jose Valentin cut his hand on a pineapple and missed a few games.

In September 2000 Cardinals catcher Mike Matheny cut his finger with a kitchen knife and missed the postseason.

In May 2004 pitcher David Wells of the Padres went on the disabled list after severing a tendon in his wrist. He fell over a bar stool in his kitchen and landed on a bottle of wine he knocked over during the fall — as well as a glass he was carrying — both of which shattered.

Don't Go Deep. Henry Cotto punctured an eardrum in 1985 when he was bumped by Ken Griffey, Sr., as he cleaned out his ear with a cotton swap.

Rob Dibble suffered a perforated ear drum in 1993 when he dove into a swimming pool during spring training.

Bad Directions. Terry Harper dislocated his shoulder waving in a runner at home plate.

Ironworker.

"What can I say. I'm domesticated." — Roger Clemens explaining a burn mark on the back of his pitching hand caused by an iron.

John Smoltz scalded his chest while he was ironing a shirt — one that he was wearing at the time.

Cleaners. While knocking dirt from his spikes with a bat, Lefty Gomez missed and hit his ankle, and had to be carried off the field.

Try a Handshake. In the early 1990s Dodger coach Joe Amalfitano broke his thumb giving a high five.

Not Man's Best Friend. During the 1993 season, pitcher Roger Clemens stopped on the freeway on the way to the ballpark to help an injured dog. The dog bit him on the thumb, causing him to miss a start.

Flicking Unbelievable. Greg Harris of the Rangers injured his pitching elbow in 1987 while flicking sunflower seeds into the stands.

Stick To Baseball. In 1989 Pirates pitcher Brian Fisher was leaning on a putter at a miniature golf course. The putter snapped and lacerated his arm.

Attempted Suicide. In 1991 pitcher Eric Show had to go on the 15-day disabled list when his finger became infected after he stabbed it with a toothpick.

Dial 411 Instead. Brewers pitcher Steve Sparks dislocated his shoulder during spring training while trying to tear a telephone book in half with his bare hands. He missed the entire 1997 season. The Angels signed him to a minor league contract for 1998. He went 0–10 before being promoted to the Majors, where he went 9–4 that season.

Cure Worse Than Ailment. Rickey Henderson missed a few games in 1993 when he suffered a case of "frozen foot" from frostbite caused by an ice pack.

Mariners outfielder Brian Turang once made a diving catch in the outfield in Detroit on a cold afternoon. He had taken a plastic hand warmer out to the field before the inning to keep warm, and he had put it in his back pocket. When he dove, the hot chunks broke open the bottle and burned his butt.

Try Walking. Jacob Brumfield missed a few games in 1993 when he suffered a gash on his shin after falling while riding a beach bike.

In March 2002 Giants second baseman Jeff Kent lied about the cause of his broken left wrist. Kent said he had slipped while washing his truck. Not so. He was seen falling off his motorcycle while performing a wheelie. He was lost for a large chunk of the season, though the Giants were able to get to the World Series. He was on bad terms with the club after that and signed with the Astros in December 2002.

Wash Well. Bret Barberie of the Marlins missed a game on May 5, 1994, because he was blinded by hot peppers. He failed to wash his hands thoroughly after eating the peppers and got juice on his contact lenses.

Humming is Safer. In 2001 Padres pitcher Adam Eaton missed a start after slicing open his stomach with a pocketknife while trying to open a new DVD.

Luggage Problems. In 1992 Expos pitcher Dennis Martinez strained a side muscle while throwing his suitcase onto an equipment truck. This prompted the club's publicity director, Richard Griffin, to announced that Martinez would miss a start due to "Samsanitis."

In 1996 Twins pitcher Rick Aguilera strained his shoulder while helping his wife with her bags during spring training.

Blue Jays pitcher Huck Flener flew to spring training in 1997, expecting to be the fifth starter for the Blue Jays. During the flight, an overhead compartment opened and a suitcase fell on his shoulder, causing a chipped collarbone. He ended up starting one game for the club and appeared in a total of eight that season.

In 2003 Mariners pitcher Kazuhiro Sasaki went on the disabled list after injuring his ribs when he fell on his suitcase.

TV Can Be Dangerous. In May 2000 Marlins pitcher Ricky Bones missed his start after injuring his lower back watching television while relaxing in a clubhouse recliner.

Hunting. In the winter of 1999 pitcher Carlton Loewer broke his leg while hunting (he fell out of a tree) and did not pitch again until June 2001.

Too Much Exercise. In March 1999 Moises Alou underwent surgery to repair torn knee ligaments suffered in the Dominican Republic. He was trying to adjust the speed of his treadmill when he fell.

Facial. In 2002 Orioles outfielder Marty Cordova sat out a day game to protect his face, which he had burned when he fell asleep in a tanning booth.

Perhaps Not So Freak. Jesse Orosco, who hadn't batted in nine years, was once put on the disabled list for pulling a muscle — during batting practice.

Snake-Bit. In 2002 Yankee pitcher Randy Keisler couldn't pick up a ball for a month after being bitten on the pinkie by a rattlesnake in Tampa.

Hooked. Orioles pitcher Jason Johnson received 11 stitches in his left buttock after a fishing hook lodged in his rear end while he was casting. He was put on the 15-day disabled list.

Free Agents

"Dodgers Can Feel Flush Even Without John." — Headline in *The Sporting News* after the Dodgers lost Tommy John to free agency.

"Not really. They lean toward cash." — White Sox owner Bill Veeck when asked if free agents were more likely to go to big cities.

"My four boys picked up my option and said, 'You're staying here.'" — Roger Clemens on rumors in November 2003 that he was not going to stay retired and would sign with one of the Texas teams. He declared for free agency rather than officially retire after the 2003 season. He signed with the Astros and reeled off seven straight wins to start the season.

"He said he was embarrassed by Atlanta's $4.2 million offer. We didn't want to add to the embarrassment." — Texas Rangers general manager Tom Grieve, explaining why his club wouldn't be signing free agent Bob Horner.

See also **Arbitration**, **Collusion**, **Drafts**, **Reserve Clause** and **Salaries**.

Lawsuit Against the Commissioner. Browns owner Phil Ball filed a lawsuit against Judge Landis in 1931. Ball unsuccessfully sought a restraining order when Landis granted free agency to a number of his players based on minor league **Farm System** contract violations.

Early Rulings. In 1940 Judge Landis ruled that certain players in the Tigers' farm system were **Free Agents** because the Tigers improperly hid key players in their farm system (including Johnny Sain). The team was also fined $47,250. Landis had allowed the same conduct by former Tigers boss Frank Navin, but Navin had been an advisor to Landis over the years. The Cubs and Browns attempted to sign some of these players early and were each fined $500.

The primary beneficiaries of the action were Roy Cullenbine, who sold himself to the Dodgers for $25,000, and Benny McCoy, who was purchased by Connie Mack for $45,000. One newspaper account estimated that over $500,000 in talent was released, which included pitcher Dizzy Trout, the Texas League MVP and future Major Leaguer.

As a result of the action taken against the Tigers, the club sold off all its minor league clubs. At the time, Tigers general manager Jack Zeller suggested to Judge Landis that all minor league players be put in a pool and distributed, but Landis rejected the idea. Ironically, the Tigers won the pennant that year.

Similar actions occurred in 1938 involving the Cardinals and Branch Rickey, in which 80 (or 91) players were declared free agents. Landis did not rule that the Cardinals were guilty of underhanded practices. Rather, Landis ruled that the entire system was out of control and the Cardinals suffered the most because they were the primary practitioners.

In the early 1930s Johnny Vander Meer and Tommy Henrich were declared free agents by Judge Landis as a result of abuses by their respective clubs.

Bob Feller signed with the Indians as a 17-year-old high school junior even though there was a rule against a Major League club signing an amateur player other than a high school graduate or a college-age player. The Western League challenged Cleveland's signing because Feller was in great demand. Judge Landis ruled that the Indians were within their rights, primarily because Feller wanted to join the club and because Landis wanted to prevent a stampede to Feller's door by minor league clubs.

Free Agent Draft. See **Drafts**.

Tom Seaver. Seaver was declared a free agent after he illegally signed for $50,000 (or $40,000) with the Braves in the 1960s. He signed after his college, USC, had already started its season by playing two nonscheduled exhibition games against a military team. The rule is that once the season starts, a player cannot sign during the remainder of the school year. The Dodgers blew the whistle on the Braves in an attempt to get Seaver. Some sources reported that the violation was because Seaver's class had not yet graduated.

The Phillies, Mets and Indians were allowed to vie for his services. The winning Mets drew Seaver's name out of a hat and were required to match the bonus offered by the Braves.

First Modern Free Agent. In 1974 Catfish Hunter was able to void his contract because A's owner Charlie Finley neglected to fulfill one of the contract provisions. Finley failed to pay one half of a $100,000 insurance premium called for under Hunter's contract.

After an arbitration panel ruled that Hunter was a free agent, Finley filed a lawsuit seeking a restraining order prohibiting other clubs from bidding on Hunter. The injunction was denied in December 1974 and Hunter signed with the Yankees on December 31 for $3.7 million, the highest salary paid to that point. The contract was broken down as a $1 million bonus; $200,000 for each of five years; a 10-year retirement plan at $50,000 per year; a $1 million life insurance policy; $25,000 for each of his children and $200,000 for attorney fees.

Negotiations/Rules Modification.

"I think what we've created here is a concrete glider." — A's president Roy Eisenhardt on the complicated 1981 free agency rules.

After the late 1975 arbitration decision by Peter Seitz that granted free agency to players, the owners fought the decision in court. After the lower court and the appellate court ruled that the reserve clause could be enforced for only one year, the owners attempted to have the players bargain away that right. Marvin Miller was the executive director of the players union at the time. He asked 974 Cy Young Award winner Mike Marshall to threaten publicly to sue the association if it bargained away free agency. This supposedly gave Miller some of the leverage he needed with the owners to keep free agency rights intact.

After the Seitz decision, the rules under the Basic Agreement were suspended until a new Basic Agreement could be signed. This resulted in a number of players who would become free agents after the 1976 season if they did not sign before the 1976 season. The new Basic Agreement, signed during the 1976 All-Star break, provided that any player with six years of Major League experience could become a free agent and put himself on the market. After five years a player could ask to be traded and could veto a trade to any of six clubs. If he was not traded, he became a free agent.

Under the agreement signed in mid–1976, a free agent could be selected by a maximum of 12 teams (13 in 1977 after expansion) drafting in reverse order of their finish in the standings. In addition, a player traded during a long-term contract could opt for free agency at the end of the season in which he was traded. Clubs were entitled to sign a maximum of two free agents. The draft was scrapped after a few seasons when it became unworkable.

Under a new agreement negotiated in the late 1970s, a player could decline a trade if he had played five years with one team and a total of 10 years in the league. The most recent rules require that a club may not trade a newly signed free agent until June 15.

In 1981 the season started under threat of a strike, which began on June 12 and ended July 31. As part of the settlement it was decided that clubs losing "premium" free agents would have their choice of players who were put in a pool by all clubs. Clubs losing players would be compensated from a dispersal fund contributed to by all owners. A two-year average of seven key statistics was created: plate appearances, batting average, on-base percentage, home runs, RBIs, fielding percentage and total chances. Only two players ever led in all seven categories over a two-year period: Don Mattingly in 1986–1987 and Cal Ripken in 1990–1991.

The rankings divide free agents into three groups based on the quality of their prior season's performance. The top 30% in each group receives an A ranking, the next 20% a B ranking and the group between 50 and 60% a C ranking. Depending on the ranking, the club then receives a certain position in the next minor league draft.

Andres Galarraga in 1993 is an example of a low-level Class C free agent. Based on his 1992 statistics, the Colorado Rockies were not required to give up a draft choice as compensation to the team that lost him. Galarraga then hovered around .400 for most of the year.

Clubs are now compensated by receiving a bonus choice in the free agent draft. After each of the first two rounds, the clubs which lost players have a special mini-draft round. For example, In 2001 the A's lost their three top players to free agency. First baseman Jason Giambi, outfielder Johnny Damon and reliever Jason Isringhausen signed with other clubs for a combined $33 million, only $5 million less than the entire A's payroll. The A's received three first round picks from those clubs who signed the players and three picks at the end of the first round.

The Elias Sports Bureau, the official Major League statisticians, came out with annual rankings of players based on a 100-point scale that it developed. In 2002 Manny Ramirez became only the fifth player to achieve a perfect score. The statistics, covering two years of performance, are used to decided whether a player is a Type A, B or C free agent.

Minor League Free Agents. Under Rule V (see *Drafts*), six-year minor leaguers are entitled to become free agents (originally seven years).

Mickey Lolich. The former Tigers pitching star played for the Mets in 1975 and 1976. He sat out the entire 1977 season to get out of his contract (just after true free agency was established) and then played two more seasons for the Padres.

The First Truly Free Agents.

"I didn't ask for the money, they offered it to me. No one was ever paid more than he was worth." — Wayne Garland.

The first crop of free agents were created in 1976 following the historic arbitration decision of Peter Seitz involving Andy Messersmith and Dave McNally (see also *Reserve Clause*). The pot of gold thought to be available to each free agent did not quite pan out in some cases, but a few players in the first group did extraordinarily well. The first 24 free agents averaged new salaries of $200,696, including Royle Stillman of the White Sox, who received only $25,000. The top 14 free agents received a total of $22 million.

Bobby Grich. The Orioles second baseman received a five-year contract worth $1.5 million after he had earned $68,000 the year before. However, before the 1977 season he hurt his back lifting an air conditioning unit and had two discs removed. In 1981 he cashed in again when he received a four-year/$4 million contract from the Angels.

Grich was a Long Beach, California, native and his father was a longshoreman, so he naturally wanted to play for his hometown Angels. He bypassed his agent and called Angels owner Gene Autry. He told Autry that the Yankees were offering more money, he knew that Autry had already opened his saddlebags for other free agents, but that he wanted to play for the Angels. The two cut a deal over the phone.

Bill Campbell. The Twins pitcher was the first new free agent to sign a contract, on November 4, 1976, 10 hours after the first free agent draft at the Plaza Hotel in New York. He signed a five-year deal with the Red Sox worth $1,050,000 (also reported as $1 million over four years). The year before, he had earned $22,000 when Twins owner Calvin Griffith said "take it or leave it" after Campbell asked for $30,000.

Campbell almost immediately suffered a sore shoulder, but hung on until 1986 with Montreal. By 1989 he was broke from poor investments in tax shelters and attempted an unsuccessful comeback with the Senior Professional Baseball Association.

Steve Stone. The Cubs pitcher played for the Cubs in 1974–1975, earning $60,000 annually prior to free agency. During 1976 he had arm problems, going 3–6 with a 4.08 ERA. Five teams drafted him and the White Sox and Rangers negotiated with him. He asked for $75,000, but was informed by the Rangers that the club wanted to pay $1 million for a pitcher, for publicity reasons, and he wasn't worth it.

Stone received $60,000 from the White Sox, the fourth-lowest amount among the 24 free agents who signed. He came back to win 15 games in 1977. He was the first player to become a free agent for a second time when he signed for $200,000 with the Orioles in 1978. He won the American League Cy Young Award in 1980 when he won 25 games for the Orioles. When he received the trophy in the mail, it was National League winner Steve Carlton's trophy. Stone was out of baseball with a bad arm after the 1981 season and became a restaurant owner and broadcaster for the Cubs.

Doyle Alexander. Alexander received the $1 million over several years that Steve Stone could not get from the Rangers.

Wayne Garland. Garland signed a 10-year deal with the Indians worth $2 million. In the previous season, 1976, he was 20–7 with a 2.68 ERA for the Orioles at age 26. He was 13–19 in 1977, suffered a rotator cuff tear in 1978, and never again won more than six games in a season. By 1990 all of the money was gone and he blew his arm out again while attempting a comeback in the Senior Professional Baseball League.

Reggie Jackson. The slugger was by far the most successful of the original free agents, receiving $3 million from the Yankees for five years after one season for the Orioles in 1976. His career exploded in part from the media attention in New York and he was a first round Hall of Famer in 1993.

"New Look" Free Agents. When arbitrators determined that the owners had practiced **Collusion** against the players, 15 "new-look" free agents were designated who were given until January 29, 1991, to entertain bids even though they were already under contract at the time.

Missed Payment. A player may declare himself a free agent 10 days after a club misses a salary payment.

1992–1993. In 1993, 153 players filed for free agency. Of that group, 91 signed with other Major League clubs, 24 agreed to Class AAA contracts, and three went to Japan. There were 250 player movements during the 1992–1993 off-season. These numbers are typical of the 1990s.

Effect on Player Movement. Long-time sports columnist and writer Leonard Koppett studied the number of player movements from 1961 through the early 1990s. He found that the number of players moving from one club to another did not increase significantly after 1977, the first full year of free agency. He concluded that only the manner in which they moved had changed, from trades to free agency (see also **Player Trades and Sales— Free Agency**).

Combating Free Agency. Former players union chief Marvin Miller once said that the smartest thing the owners could do would be to make every player a free agent each winter. This would create a glut of players and hold down salaries. It seemed to have worked beginning in 1993, as a number of mid-level players were shut out from decent contracts.

Filing Period. Players may declare themselves free agents the day after the World Series is completed. They have until 15 days after the World Series to make the filing. Teams must offer salary arbitration to their declared free agents no later than the first week in December each season. Players must accept or reject arbitration by early January. If no offer is made, the club may not negotiate with the player until early in the following season.

Japan. In Japan a player may declare free agency after completing 10 years in their major leagues.

Florida. Before their World Series-winning season in 1997, the Marlins spent $167 million on free agents. Then they jettisoned most of them immediately after the Series.

Book. Roger I. Abrams, *Money Pitch: Baseball Free Agency and Salary Arbitration* (2000).

Ford Frick (1895–1978)

Frick was **National League President** from 1935 until 1951 and **Commissioner** from 1951 until 1965.

Frick Award (1978–)

"I've wondered many times what the reaction of Ponselle, et al., must have been when they learned of my utter ineptness…. I'm sure they all heaved a sigh of relief when I finally left broadcasting to go with the National League."— Frick in *Games, Asterisks and People* (1973).

The Ford C. Frick Award is named for the former sportswriter, radio broadcaster, National League president and **Commissioner,** and is presented to outstanding baseball broadcasters "for major contributions to the game of baseball." The first recipients were Mel Allen and Red Barber in 1978, the year of Frick's death. The winners are inducted into the broadcast wing of the Hall of Fame.

The award is voted on by a seven-person committee appointed by the Hall of Fame Board of Directors. The 1994 committee consisted of Lee MacPhail, Bowie Kuhn, Jack Buck, Ernie Harwell, Jack Brickhouse, Mel Allen and Joe Garagiola. The award has been presented annually by Hall of Famer and Mets broadcaster Ralph Kiner. The inductees and their primary clubs:

1978   Mel Allen (Yankees), Red Barber (Dodgers, Yankees)
1979   Bob Elson (Cubs, White Sox)
1980   Russ Hodges (Giants)
1981   Ernie Harwell (Tigers)
1982   Vin Scully (Dodgers)
1983   Jack Brickhouse (Cubs, White Sox)
1984   Curt Gowdy (Red Sox, NBC)
1985   Eli "Buck" Canel (Yankees in Spanish)
1986   Bob Prince (Pirates)
1987   Jack Buck (Cardinals)
1988   Lindsey Nelson (Mets)
1989   Harry Caray (Cardinals, White Sox, Cubs)
1990   Byrum Saam (Phillies, A's)
1991   Joe Garagiola (Cardinals, NBC)
1992   Milo Hamilton (Cubs, Astros, Braves, Pirates)
1993   Chuck Thompson (Orioles)
1994   Bob Murphy (Mets)
1995   Bob Wolff (Senators)

1996   Herb Carneal (Twins)
1997   Jimmy Dudley (Indians)
1998   Jaime Jarrin (Dodgers in Spanish; Latin America)
1999   Arch McDonald (Senators)
2000   Marty Brennaman (Reds)
2001   Rafael "Felo" Ramirez (Marlins in Spanish
            and Latin America)
2002   Harry Kalas (Phillies)
2003   Bob Uecker (Brewers)
2004   Lon Simmons (Giants, A's)

Frankie Frisch (1898–1973)

Hall of Fame 1947

"The explosive Frisch is saved from being a victim of spontaneous combustion only by an enormous sense of humor.... On second thought he may be completely sane but a trifle uninhibited." — Sportswriter Arthur Daley.

Frisch was one of the all-time infielders and World Series competitors as a player, player-manager and manager from 1919 through 1951.

"Fordham Flash" Frank Francis Frisch of the Bronx moved straight from Fordham University to the Giants without playing in the minor leagues. Frisch played 54 games for the club in 1919 and in 1920 became the club's starting third baseman. He starred in 1921 when he hit .341 and led the league with 49 stolen bases while leading the Giants into the World Series. He gradually shifted over to second base for the remainder of his career.

Frisch remained with the Giants through 1926, hitting .314 or better every season and scoring over 100 runs four times. When the Giants slipped in 1925 and 1926, Frisch was traded to the Cardinals. Frisch continued to star, batting .300 or better through 1934. He led the league in stolen bases in 1927 and 1931 and led the Cardinals to the World Series in 1928, 1930 and 1931. In 1933 he became the club's player-manager and in 1934 led the Gas House Gang to another World Series.

Frisch finished his playing career in 1937, ending 19 years with a .316 average and 2,880 hits. He also stole 419 bases and hit 138 triples. His .970 fielding percentage was one of the best of the era. After his playing career ended he managed for most of 1938 with the Cardinals and took over the Pirates from 1940 through 1946. His best year with the club was 1944, when the Pirates finished second. He managed the Cubs for most of three seasons starting in 1949, finishing no better than seventh. He was a broadcaster for a short time, primarily with the Braves in 1939 and Giants in 1947.

Book. J. Roy Stockton, *Frank Frisch: The Fordham Flash* (1962).

Front Office Personnel See **Executives**

Funerals See **Burials and Cemeteries**

Fungoes

"All coaches religiously carry fungo bats in the spring to ward off suggestions that they are not working." — Jim Brosnan in *The Long Season* (1960).

"I just pretend I'm back in my playing days with the bases loaded and two out." — Rangers coach Steve Smith on hitting pop fly fungoes to his catchers in practice sessions.

"The fungo bat was as much a part of his uniform as his cap — the badge of his craft. No ode has been written to that elongated piece of wood, and even the *American Heritage Dictionary* doesn't know how it got its name, but where would spring training be without it?" — William Zinsser in *Spring Training* (1989); *The Dickson Baseball Dictionary* has six versions of the origin of the name.

"Edgerton left Reese's fungo in the whirlpool overnight. When we got to the clubhouse next morning, the thing had warped and flared out in all directions like some kind of weird flower. Jimmy just sat by the whirlpool and cried." — Orioles pitching coach Ray Miller, after elder statesman and fungo hitter extraordinaire Jimmie Reese ran overweight pitcher Bill Edgerton ragged with a specially made fungo bat.

Special extra-long thin-handled bats are used to hit fly balls during fielding practice. Fungoes were hit as early as the 1840s with the Knickerbocker club. Formal **Batting Practice** was not taken until much later. Outfielder Patsy Flaherty of the early 20th century was considered the best fungo hitter of his era.

In 1929 Babe Ruth set an unofficial record with a 447-foot fungo drive during a pregame contest at Yankee Stadium.

In the 1980s the mechanical Ponza Hammer was introduced to hit fungoes automatically.

"**G** is for Gehrig.
The Pride of the Stadium;
His record pure gold,
His courage, pure radium."
—Ogden Nash on Lou Gehrig.

Eddie Gaedel See **Midgets**

Pud Galvin (1856–1902)

Hall of Fame (VC) 1965

"A devoted family man, Galvin fathered nine children, two of whom still survive. When he retired from the field, he opened the largest cafe in Pittsburgh, a busy spa that employed nine bartenders. But 'Gentle Jeems' was not cut out for business. As a commentary on human nature, it can be observed that while Galvin was going broke, each of his bartenders opened a place of his own." — Lee Allen and Tom Meany in *Kings of the Diamond* (1966).

Galvin won 361 games from 1879 through 1892.

James Francis Galvin was a semipro and minor league pitching star in St. Louis in the 1870s. He began in the National League in 1879 with Buffalo, immediately winning 37 games with six shutouts. He won 46 games in both 1883 and 1884 for Buffalo, with 12 shutouts in 1884 (and 57 in his career). His last strong season was 1889, when he won 23 games for Pittsburgh. He won no more than 14 games over the following three seasons and retired after 12 games with St. Louis in 1892.

Galvin pitched the second-most innings in Major League history (behind only Cy Young) and is sixth all-time in wins with 361. He was known as an excellent control pitcher who relied chiefly on his fastball.

After he retired, Galvin opened a large restaurant in Pittsburgh but slowly went broke. He died of a stomach ailment at age 47 in 1902. Galvin had been a friend of President Grover Cleveland when Cleveland was the sheriff and mayor of Buffalo and Galvin starred for the local club.

Gambling and Fixed Games

"Any player or person connected with the club who shall promise or agree to lose, or attempt to lose, or fail to give his best efforts towards the winning of any baseball game … shall be declared permanently ineligible." — Rule 21 of the Major League rules.

"I shoulda stood in bed." — Boxing manager Joe Jacobs who got out of a sickbed to attend the 1935 World Series opener, on which he lost a considerable sum of money. Jacobs is also credited with the famous line, "We Wuz Robbed," when his fighter, Max Schmeling, lost to Jack Sharkey on June 21, 1932.

"Baseball is like a poker game, nobody wants to quit when he's losing: nobody wants you to quit when you're ahead." — Jackie Robinson.

"Bob Chance, Howard Luckey, Lee Gamble, Trick McSorley, Huck Betts, Ace Stewart, Spades Wood, Coot Deal, Ace Parker, Card Camper, Bob Spade"

See also **Black Sox Scandal**.

Earliest Gambling. One of the earliest reported instances of gambling on baseball was in 1860, when the Unions of Medway played the Upton Excelsiors for $1,000.

Earliest Fixes. The earliest known fixed game occurred on September 28, 1865, between the New York Mutuals and Brooklyn Eckfords. The Eckfords won 28–11, scoring 11 runs in an inning marred by a number of obvious errors. It was later revealed that three players conspired to throw the game. Thomas H. Devyr, E. Duffy and William Wansley of the Mutuals were accused of conspiring with two known gamblers and were expelled. All three played again as both teams needed players and had no desire to publicize the scandal.

One of the earliest public claims of scandal was during the 1867 tour by the Washington Nationals. After losing to the Forest Citys club 29–23, the Nationals moved into Chicago to play the Excelsiors. The local press assumed that the Excelsiors would defeat the Nationals based on the game against Forest Citys. Betting on Chicago was heavy, but the Nationals wiped them out with a 49–4 win amid claims that the Forest Citys loss had been deliberate to stimulate bets against the Nationals.

Cincinnati Red Stockings. The Cincinnati Red Stockings of 1869–1870 had a single tie with the Troy Haymakers to mar their record before finally losing. The tie was directly related to gambling. In the 6th inning, the Troy players walked off the field in protest of an umpire's call while the game was tied. It appears that the protest was orchestrated to enable Troy owner John Morrissey and other gamblers to avoid paying off $60,000 in bets on the game. It was thought that a tie was all the Troy team might achieve that day and the tie was enough to avoid a possible financial loss.

1870s–1890s.

"NO GAME PLAYED BETWEEN THESE TWO TEAMS IS TO BE TRUSTED." — Sign across the street from a 19th century ballpark.

Gambling was extremely popular in the ballparks of the pre–National League 1870s and after the National League and its rivals were formed beginning in 1876. In the 1870s the National Association prohibited players and umpires from wagering on games in which they were participants. Players would be permanently expelled if caught betting on their own games. The Philadelphia Pearls expelled John Radcliff for betting $350 against his own team.

Boston's park in the 1890s had a gamblers' area directly behind third base. *Runaway Colt*, a popular 1895 play about baseball, portrayed gambling inside Chicago's park.

Serious betting among owners was commonplace. In 1892 John

Montgomery Ward won 20 shares of New York stock from Edward Talcott, a club director, after Ward won a bet on where the Giants would finish in the standings. Cap Anson routinely bet on his own team.

According to sportswriter Henry Chadwick, betting pools were common, and owners and players often bet on their own teams to lose.

Early National League.

"William [Hulbert] ran with a fast crowd. He piled up some gambling debts. After reforming himself, he set out to reform the game. He thought a shot of virtue was better for the game than a shot of whiskey." — Susan Green Linder, whose grandmother was a niece of National League founder William Hulbert.

The National League's first charter provided that there was to be no gambling. William Hulbert led the founding of the National League in part to avoid the rampant gambling in the National Association. Nevertheless, the National League Troy Haymakers were said to be under the total control of gamblers.

In 1876 National League president Morgan Bulkeley, a Hartford banker, wanted the Philadelphia Athletics and New York Mutuals expelled from the league for allegedly throwing a game, but nothing came of it. Both were eventually expelled for failing to complete their schedules, which may have been a pretext for the gambling allegations.

The Louisville Colonels Scandal. In 1877 National League president William Hulbert expelled four Louisville Colonel players for life for throwing games: Jim Devlin, Bill Craver, George Hall and Al Nichols. The action led to the dissolution of their club after the season. Ironically, two of the four players became policemen.

In August 1877 Louisville was 27–13 and in first place. Bill Hague suffered from a boil in his armpit and needed to be replaced. George Hall, the team's number one hitter, recommended Al Nichols, formerly with the New York Mutuals and by then with an independent Pittsburgh club. When Nichols joined the club, strange things began to happen. The Colonels started losing amid warning telegrams from an anonymous source that the team would lose. Even when Nichols did not play, however, the team still lost. With 15 games to play, Louisville needed to win half of them, while Boston needed 13 of 15 to win the pennant. Louisville continued its tailspin by losing its last seven and Boston won the pennant.

Near the end of the season George Hall went to the owner and reported the fix. Al Nichols allegedly first proposed the scam, but others always believed that Hall was the main culprit. All of the four except shortstop Bill Craver allowed their telegrams to be inspected to show guilt or innocence, after which the owner immediately expelled them from the team. The word "SASH" in a telegram was code for "Fixed." Devlin allegedly was paid $100 for his complicity.

In December 1877 at the league's annual meeting, Louisville's expulsion of its players was confirmed by the league and the players were barred for life. Devlin and Craver repeatedly petitioned the league for reinstatement but were never allowed back.

According to legend, a few years later a disheveled and threadbare Devlin appeared in president Hulbert's office and dropped to his knees: "Please, Mr. Hulbert, have mercy on me and let me play again. Do it not for me — I am not worthy of your consideration — but do it for my wife and child."

Hulbert purportedly shook with emotion and tears welled up in his eyes. Taking out a $50 bill and giving it to Devlin, Hulbert supposedly said: "That's what I think of you personally, Devlin. But damn you, you are dishonest and you sold out a game. I can't trust you. Now go on your way, and never let me see your face again, for your act against the integrity of baseball never will be condoned as long as I live."

Devlin again tried unsuccessfully to return to baseball in any capacity. He wrote a touching letter to Harry Wright of the Red Stockings on Feb. 24, 1878 [spelling and punctuation left intact]: "as I am Deprived from Playing this year I thought I woed write you to see if you Coed do anything for me in the way of looking after your ground or anything in the way of work I Dont Know what I am to do I have tried hard to get work of any Kind But I canot get it do you Know of anyway that you think I Coed get to Play again I can asure you Harry that I was not Treated right and if Ever I Can see you to tell you the Case you will say I am not to Blame I amliving from hand to mouth all winter I have not got a Stich of Clothing or has my wife and child You Dont Know how I am Situated for I Know if you did you woed do Something for me I am honest Harry you need not Be afraid the Louisville People made me what I am to day a Begger I trust you will not Say anything to anyone about the Contents of this to any one if you Can do me this favor By letting me take Care of the ground or anything of that Kind I Beg of you to do it and god will reward you if I dont or let me Know if you have any Ide [Idea] of how I coed get Back I am Dumb Harry I dont Know how to go about it So I Trust you will answear this and do all you Can for me So I will Close by Sending you & Geo and all the Boys my verry Best wishes hoping to hear from you Soon I am yours Trouly

James A Devlin"

After all the efforts at reinstatement, the National League slammed the door for good by a resolution of December 8, 1880: "RESOLVED, That notice is hereby served on the persons named, and on their friends, defenders and apologists, that the Board of Directors of the National League will *never* remit the penalties inflicted on such persons, nor will they hereafter entertain any appeal from them or in their behalf."

Umpire.

"Some of ours is so crooked that they can lay in a berth only when the train's making a curve." — Ring Lardner on umpires.

"Fans and players boo and abuse umpires, but there isn't one umpire in the history of baseball who has ever been proved guilty of being dishonest. I'm very proud to have been an umpire." — Former player and umpire George Pipgras, who was wrong by at least one umpire.

One umpire has been banned from Major League Baseball for dishonesty. Richard (Dick) Higham was born in England and was the son of a famous English cricketer. He grew up in New York City, where he played for the New York Mutuals, a team known to have had a few suspicious games and players. As early as 1876 while still a player, the Chicago White Stockings benched him for "dubious play." He nevertheless was hired as a professional umpire in 1881.

In 1882 Higham was umpiring games for Detroit of the National League. He umpired 26 of Detroit's first 29 games and the club repeatedly received bad calls from him.

A Detroit fan purportedly found a letter in the street, signed "Dick," alerting a known gambler, James Todd, how to follow a code to bet games. After this was discovered, a league meeting was held and Higham was called to defend himself. Handwriting experts compared the incriminating letter to other Higham writing samples and they were found to be identical. After being expelled, Higham drifted to Chicago and became a bookie.

1891 Giants. In 1891 there were rumors that the Giants had thrown a few games to the Boston Red Stockings to ensure that the Chicago White Stockings and Cap Anson did not capture the pen-

nant. The Giants played a few late-season games without their stars, though a league investigation panel accepted the explanation that the players were injured or otherwise indisposed. No action was taken.

"Incentives." In 1893 Baltimore players were accused of offering Red Ehret of Pittsburgh a bribe of $500 to lose a key game at the end of the season. Baltimore captain Wilbert Robinson acknowledged semipublicly that Ehret received $100 to *win* the game and apparently such inducements were not uncommon in early years.

Early 20th Century. Gamblers were all around parks and hotels in the early part of the century, especially in Pittsburgh and Boston. Gamblers were not barred from ballparks, which allowed "Gamblers' Roosts" to flourish, most notably at Braves Field in Boston. There was also no formal rule at that time prohibiting a player from betting on his own team.

1903 World Series. Catcher Lou Criger was offered a bribe in connection with the 1903 Series. Criger rejected the attempt and caught all eight games of the Series, won by his Red Sox.

Jack Taylor. Taylor was a pitcher primarily for the Cubs and Cardinals early in the 20th century. Known for his ability to *Complete Games*, he is said to have thrown two games in a postseason City Series in 1903 between his Cubs and the White Sox. He may have thrown a 1904 game for the Cardinals after bystanders heard him remark about the 1903 series: "Why should I have pitched hard? [Cubs owner] James Hart paid me a hundred for winning, and I got $500 for losing." Taylor's conduct was investigated by the National Commission and he was exonerated. What may be more accurate is that his drinking and carousing tipped off gamblers that he was not in top shape for these games.

Garry Herrmann. In 1906 Reds owner Garry Herrmann bet $6,000 that Pittsburgh would not win the pennant. In support of the bet, he sold Cy Seymour to the Giants to help them win. It did not matter much, as both the Giants and Pirates finished at least 20 games behind the Cubs, who won 116 games.

1908 Giants. As part of the 1908 Merkle Boner game (see *Base Running*), it has been reported that umpire Bill Klem was offered a bribe in connection with the final game played between the Cubs and Giants when they were tied for the season at 98–55. Klem was twice told that "the Giants gotta win." News of the bribe came to light during the World Series that year and National League president Harry Pulliam called for an investigation.

It was later revealed that Giants team physician Dr. Joseph M. Creamer was responsible for the bribe attempt. Just before Klem took the field Creamer supposedly waved $2,500 in front of him that reportedly came from three Giants players. Creamer of course denied the story. He had an excellent reputation and was widely known in New York sports circles. He was the official physician at many boxing matches and bicycle races in the city. Pulliam nevertheless believed Klem; the doctor was barred from baseball and reportedly never heard from again in baseball circles.

1912 World Series. There were rumors that the 1912 World Series was fixed in favor of the New York Giants, but the Red Sox won the Series anyway.

Rube Waddell. Some sources reported that there was speculation that eccentric pitcher Rube Waddell was part of a scheme to cause his Philadelphia A's to lose the 1905 World Series when he purportedly hurt his shoulder near the end of the season while wrestling over a straw hat. The theory seems meritless in light of the fact that Waddell hurt his shoulder so far in advance of postseason play. The injury occurred on September 1 (August in some sources), the day when bowler hats were usually discarded to signal the end of summer. When Waddell refused to get rid of his, he had a fight with Andy Coakley which resulted in the injury (some sources referred to the hat as Coakley's).

Horace Fogel. The former sportswriter headed a syndicate that purchased the Philadelphia Phillies in 1909. Fogel was expelled from the league in late 1912 for alleging publicly that Roger Bresnahan of the Cardinals and other former Giants stars had rigged the season to allow John McGraw's Giants to win the pennant.

Fogel compounded his problems by also telling the New York writers that the season had been rigged in favor of the Giants by National League president Thomas Lynch and the umpires. He repeated this charge in a telegram to Reds owner Garry Herrmann. Fogel wrote the same allegations in a newspaper article after being encouraged to do so by his friend, generally despised Chicago Cubs owner Charles Murphy.

Fogel implicated Murphy as a participant in these allegations, but the league let Fogel be the sacrificial lamb. Fogel was found guilty in court on five of seven slander-related counts and barred from baseball. He went back to the newspaper business and died in 1928.

Effect of the Federal League/World War I. Historian Bill James attributes the upswing in fixed games from 1916 through 1918 to a sudden rise in salaries brought on by the Federal League in 1914–1915 (providing more disposable income to players), and the equally swift decline in salaries brought on by World War I and a declining economy starting in 1916 (creating a measure of desperation among players). White Sox owner Charles Comiskey was the most miserly of the owners, which was a key factor contributing to the Black Sox Scandal. Gamblers again became particularly focused on baseball during World War I because horse racing tracks were closed down.

1914 A's. One source claimed that Connie Mack may have suspected that his 1914 team threw the World Series to the Miracle Braves. He disbanded the team after the Series, though the primary reason was probably due to the financial impact of the Federal League challenge. One source advanced the argument that Mack broke up the team because six of the players were caught by the Internal Revenue Service for failing to report their World Series shares.

1916 Giants. In 1916 Giants manager John McGraw accused some of his players of aiding the Dodgers in late season games against the Phillies. The Dodgers had three key ex–Giants on its club, Fred Merkle, Rube Marquard and Chief Meyers, suggesting that their former teammates on the Giants wanted to see them win the pennant (which the Dodgers did). Following a brief postseason investigation, the matter was dropped.

Hal Chase and Lee Magee.

"That he can play first as it never was and perhaps never will be played is a well-known truth. That he will is a different matter."— 1913 column about Chase in *The Sporting News*.

First baseman Hal Chase was accused of throwing games as early as 1909, but no formal action was taken until 1918. In 1913 Yankee manager Frank Chance complained privately to a few sportswriters that Chase was throwing games. Sportswriter Heywood Broun printed the story. The Yankee owners were upset and traded Chase to the White Sox.

Chase was suspended for "indifferent play" by the Reds on August 9, 1918. He was accused of throwing games, bribery and betting, despite hitting .301 and being considered the best first baseman in baseball at the time.

A hearing before the National Commission was held on January 30, 1919. Teammate Jimmy Ring accused Chase of telling him to lose a game. After Ring unintentionally lost, the next day he was given $50 by Chase, who threw the money in his lap and walked away. Christy Mathewson was also a key witness to this incident, but he was away in the military in France during the hearing and testified by affidavit.

On February 5, 1919, Chase was acquitted for insufficient evidence amid a finding that he had merely been "careless." As soon as he was acquitted, the Giants announced that he had signed with them.

Late in the 1919 season Chase disappeared from the Giants. At the same time, former Reds second baseman Lee Magee (Leopold Hoernscheneyer), was playing for the Cubs with a two-year contract left over from his Cincinnati days. The Cubs released him and he sued for his 1920 salary. At the trial Magee described how Chase asked him to bet with him on a game between the Reds and Braves, which the Reds won. Chase told Magee that he had bet the Reds to lose, which was not Magee's understanding, and Magee stopped payment on his check to Chase.

Gambler Jim Costello, who took the bet, told a different story on the stand. He implicated Magee and Chase for unsuccessfully trying to fix the game. In a 2–2 tie in extra innings, Magee intentionally grounded weakly to the shortstop. The ball took a bad hop and broke the fielder's nose. Magee was on first when Edd Roush hit a home run for a 4–2 Reds victory. There was nothing Magee could do about the Reds' win and he and Chase lost their bet. As a result of the ensuing trial, both Magee and Chase were banned for life.

Prior to this incident, there had been no publicly aired betting scandals since 1877. Chase was also indicted by the court in the Black Sox Scandal, but California refused to extradite him. Rube Benton claimed that Chase won $40,000 betting on the 1919 World Series and Chase was prominently mentioned as one of the organizers of that escapade.

In 1920 Chase was banned from the Pacific Coast League for trying to bribe an umpire. He died in 1947 of beri beri in Colusa, California, after years of playing outlaw ball in the Southwest.

To illustrate Chase's character, Smoky Joe Wood later recounted a poker game in which Wood was having a streak of bad luck. Chase graciously told Wood not to cut the cards on the next deal, resulting in a winning four-of-a-kind hand for Wood. After Chase repeated the charitable act in the next hand, Wood always cut the cards when Chase shuffled.

Carl Mays and Joe Bush.

"Any ballplayers that played for me on either the Cardinals or Yankees could come to me if he were in need and I would give him a helping hand. I make only two exceptions, Carl Mays and Joe Bush. If they were in the gutter, I'd kick them."— Yankee manager Miller Huggins quoted by Fred Lieb in *Baseball as I Have Known It* (1966). Huggins apparently was referring to World Series games that the two pitchers may have thrown in 1921 (Mays) and 1922 (Bush). Mays was 1–2 in the 1921 Series and Bush was 0–2 in the 1922 Series.

Mays became depressed and pitched poorly after beaning and killing Ray Chapman in 1920, but rebounded in 1921 to win 27 games and help lead the Yankees to their first pennant. In 1922 Mays pitched adequately to a 13–14 record, but got no run support, and then lost Game 4 of the World Series. Manager Miller Huggins put him on waivers to punish him, and then in 1923 rarely used him; a "public shaming" that so disgusted shortstop Everett Scott and first baseman Wally Pipp that they walked off the field in a game in which the rusty Mays was getting pounded and Huggins wouldn't take him out. Huggins waived him again after the season and Cincinnati claimed him, but Huggins took one more shot when he wrote to Reds president Garry Herrmann and told him that Mays was difficult to handle and that Herrmann should cut his salary in half. He recovered to win 20 for the Reds but slipped after that.

The gambling story was reinforced many years later when writer Fred Lieb wrote about a man who approached Lieb after Game 4 and told him that Mays had thrown the game. Lieb took the man to Judge Landis's hotel suite and had the man repeat the story. Landis hired a detective to investigate Mays, but could find nothing suspicious. Mays was cleared, but Lieb's 1940s publication of the story further stained Mays' reputation (which wasn't so great given the Ray Chapman *Beanball* incident and Mays' 1919 suspension after leaving the Red Sox (see *Carl Mays Incident*).

Judge Landis. Landis was legendary for his near-fanatical opposition to mixing gambling and baseball. For example, he forced Giants owner Horace Stoneham and manager John McGraw to sell their interests in a Havana, Cuba, racetrack and casino to prevent any possible taint. Landis and Ban Johnson openly feuded with Red Sox owner Harry Frazee because Frazee allowed gambling in his ballpark. Landis was the key disciplinary figure in the *Black Sox Scandal*, but as reflected below that incident was only one of many in the era.

Joe Gedeon and Gene Paulette. The pair were expelled by Landis after the 1920 season for alleged gambling. Gedeon was accused of being peripherally involved in the Black Sox Scandal. Paulette was accused of accepting gifts from gamblers during the 1919 season, one of whom was involved in the Black Sox Scandal.

Paul Carter. The National League pitcher was released after allegedly attempting to fix Cubs games in 1920. Though not formally barred from baseball, he was secretly blacklisted and never again allowed to pitch in the Major Leagues.

Claude Hendrix. In August 1921 the Cubs pitcher was released after having allegedly bet $5,000 against his own club when he was scheduled to pitch against the Phillies. When club president Bill Veeck, Sr., received a phone tip about the plan, Hendrix was replaced at the last moment by Cubs ace Grover Cleveland Alexander. The Phillies still won 3–0. Hendrix was never officially barred from baseball, but he never again appeared in a Major League game. Hendrix had already been suspected of wrongdoing, having been summoned to testify before the grand jury investigating the Black Sox Scandal.

Phil Douglas. The heavy-drinking Giants pitcher once told an opposing team's player that he might throw a game. He was immediately barred from baseball by Judge Landis (see also *Alcoholism*).

Rube Benton. Benton was barred by the National League before the 1922 season, stemming from claims that he knew about the 1919 Black Sox fix and failed to report a bribe by Hal Chase and Heinie Zimmerman. However, his story was a key to blowing open the Black Sox Scandal. As a result, he was reinstated by Judge Landis and played for the Reds beginning in 1923.

Jimmy O'Connell and Cozy Dolan. O'Connell was an outfielder purchased by the Giants in 1923 from the Pacific Coast League San Francisco Seals for $75,000. He hit .250 that year for the Giants and was hitting .317 in 1924. Before a late-season game on September 27, 1924, he approached Phillies shortstop Heinie Sand, whose club was in a pennant race with the Dodgers. O'Connell said, "How do you feel about the game?" Sand replied, "We don't feel. We're going to beat you." O'Connell allegedly said, "I'll give you $500 if you don't bear down too hard." Sand: "Nothing doing." Sand then told manager Art Fletcher about the incident, who told National League president John Heydler, who called Judge Landis, who came to town to visit O'Connell.

O'Connell told Landis that he thought the entire Giants team knew of the "bribe" and that he made his comment to Sand because coach Cozy Dolan asked him to. O'Connell said that his teammates picked him as the spokesman to solicit the bribe because he knew Sand from the minor leagues. When interviewed, Dolan could not remember anything about the incident. O'Connell also implicated Ross Youngs, George Kelly and Frankie Frisch; all denied any involvement. The latter three were absolved by Landis, but Dolan and O'Connell were barred for life. Frisch, Kelly and Youngs were key players and future Hall of Famers, which may have contributed to the decision not to punish them.

American League president Ban Johnson was upset that he had not been part of the investigation. He wanted the second-place Dodgers (1½ games back) substituted in the World Series for the more powerful Giants, or alternatively to cancel the World Series. Barney Dreyfuss, owner of third-place Pittsburgh, also suggested more investigation and urged cancellation. Landis refused, saying that it was: "… a pretty good time for gentlemen who are not clothed with responsibility to keep their shirts on."

O'Connell left baseball and moved to California. Dolan said he would sue Landis, Dreyfuss and others. He even hired the attorney who defended gambler Arnold Rothstein in the Black Sox Scandal, New Yorker William J. Fallon. Dolan eventually lost interest in the case and it never went to trial.

Sammy Bohne and Pat Duncan. In 1923 a Chicago newspaper implied that Bohne and Duncan of the Reds were associated with gamblers. They were cleared by a federal judge and won a libel suit against the paper.

Ty Cobb and Tris Speaker. In 1926 pitcher Dutch Leonard wrote a letter accusing Ty Cobb and Tris Speaker of betting on a game seven years earlier — on September 25, 1919, between Cobb's Tigers and Speaker's Indians. Leonard refused to appear publicly to accuse them and it was widely believed that Leonard's motive in blowing the whistle on Cobb was because player-manager Cobb released Leonard from the Tigers in 1925.

The accusations also included Smoky Joe Wood, who did not appear in the 1919 game in question, but who was alleged to have placed the bets for Cobb and Speaker. Wood was the coach at Yale when the story broke. The basis for Leonard's claim were letters written in 1919 by the trio which appeared to implicate each of them. The Leonard accusation and the two letters:

Leonard's Accusation:

"We talked about getting money down on the game, that is, how to get up the dough and how much we would put up, and Cobb said he would send Fred West [a Detroit club employee who ran errands for the players] down to us.

I [Leonard] was to put up $1,500 and as I remember it Cobb $2,000 and Wood and Speaker $1,000 each. I had pitched the previous day and was through for the season and so I gave my check for $1,500 to Wood at the ball park and went to the hotel, packed my things, and left that night for Independence [Missouri].

Several days later, I received the Wood letter at Independence with a check for $1,630. He wrote that West was only able to get up part of the money and that my share of the winnings was only $130."

The Wood Letter:

"Cleveland, O., Friday

Enclosed please find certified check for sixteen hundred and thirty dollars ($1,630).

Dear Friend 'Dutch':

The only bet West could get up was $60 against $20 (10 to 7). Cobb did not get up a cent. He told us that and I believed him.

Could have put some at 5 to 2 on Detroit, but did not, as that would make us put up $1,000 to win $400.

We won the $420. I gave West $30, leaving $390, or $130 for each of us. Would not have cashed your check at all, but West thought he could get it up to 10–7, and I was going to put it all up at those odds. We would have won $1,750 for the $2,500 if we could have placed it.

If we ever get another chance like this we will know enough to try to get down early.

Let me hear from you, 'Dutch.'

With all good wishes to yourself and Mrs. Leonard, I am, always [signed] JOE WOOD"

The Cobb Letter:

"August, Ga., Oct. 23, '19

Dear Dutch:

Well, old boy, guess you are out in old California by this time and enjoying life.

I arrived home and found Mrs. Cobb only fair, but the baby girl was fine, and at this time Mrs. Cobb is very well, but I have been very busy getting acquainted with my family and have not tried to do any correspondence, hence my delay.

Wood and myself are considerably disappointed in our business proposition, as we had $2,000 to put into it and the other side quoted us $1,400, and when we finally secured that much money it was about two o'clock and they refused to deal with us, as they had men in Chicago to take the matter up with and they had no time, so we completely fell down and of course we felt badly over it.

Everything was open to Wood and he can tell you about it when we get together. It was quite a responsibility and I don't care for it again, I can assure you.

With kindest regards to Mrs. Leonard, I remain, sincerely, [signed] TY COBB"

There are at least two versions of how American League president Ban Johnson handled the matter after receiving the letters. One version is that Johnson tried to keep the matter quiet by letting Cobb and Speaker retire without scandal, though Johnson gave the letters to Judge Landis.

Another source reported that Johnson quietly barred the players and then hid the existence of the letters from Landis. Landis learned about the matter only after the letters were passed from Tigers outfielder Harry Heilmann (to whom Leonard had written) to Tigers owner Frank Navin (who did not like Johnson), and then to Landis (Navin's confidante). After the allegations were publicized, Leonard was unofficially barred from participating in any baseball activities such as oldtimers games. One source reported that Landis paid Leonard $15,000 to $25,000 for the two letters, which he used to invest in farmland in California.

Landis was not convinced that there was a problem. He made the story public in December 1926 and reinstated the players on January 27, 1927. Cobb and Wood admitted to writing the letters, but Speaker—who was not mentioned in them—denied everything. Some sources contend that Landis refused to bar the players because Leonard refused to appear for a hearing in front of Landis. Other sources contend that Speaker in particular simply was not guilty.

The two players' respective clubs did not want them back, so Cobb went to the A's and Speaker left the Indians for the Senators. Each played two more seasons, but neither was ever offered a managing job after being let go by their teams; even though both were player-managers in 1926 when the story broke.

Johnson was furious at Landis, accusing him of seeking public-ity. Landis supposedly acted consistent with public sentiment at the time, which meant not making a huge issue of the gambling incident during the wild 1920s. Club owners supported Landis, except Phil Ball of the Browns, who was more closely aligned with Johnson than most. The decision by Landis to reinstate the players was another blow to Johnson's power in the American League and he was forced to retire the same year.

Bill James. Another name that surfaced during the 1926 Cobb/Speaker incident was Bill James. James had been an American League pitcher from 1911 through 1919 who had retired long before Dutch Leonard's letters were made public. James was named in two gambling incidents, including having knowledge of the Cobb/Speaker affair.

The other involved a 1917 game in which James, a Tiger pitcher at the time, admitted collecting $850 from future Black Sox player Swede Risberg and paying it to various Tiger players. James claimed that it was for bearing down harder to help beat the Red Sox in an earlier series, rather than to throw a game.

Other versions of the incident differ. In December 1926 Risberg publicly revealed a story regarding the Tigers from September 1917. The Tigers purportedly threw a four-game series (two double-headers) to the White Sox. The White Sox were battling for the pennant and after they clinched they purportedly reciprocated by dropping two games to give the Tigers third place (except that the Tigers finished fourth, 9½ games behind the third-place Indians). Joe Jackson, Chick Gandil and Happy Felsch purportedly over-shifted on certain batters to be out of position in the thrown games.

In January 1927 Judge Landis held public hearings on this claim. Gandil supported Risberg's allegations, and it was revealed that there were 20 stolen bases in four games. Each White Sox player contributed $45 toward the $1,000 that went to the Tigers and Bill James distributed the money to his teammates. During the hearing, Black Sox player Buck Weaver stood up and asked for reinstatement, presenting a petition in his favor signed by 10,000 fans.

Until 1927 it was not uncommon for clubs to reward other pitchers who beat their rivals. After the 1917 Bill James incident was publicized, Judge Landis barred such payments.

Pants Rowland. Rowland was implicated in the Bill James scandal. Rowland had been the White Sox manager in 1917 and Swede Risberg charged that Rowland had participated in fixing the four games between the Tigers and White Sox. After investigation by Judge Landis, Rowland was absolved.

Starting Pitchers. In 1920 Indians manager Tris Speaker feared that gamblers might again attempt to influence the World Series, so he did not name his starting pitchers until game time. In 1931 Judge Landis temporarily halted the practice of announcing starting pitchers in an attempt to curb gambling. The short-lived plan backfired primarily because it hurt attendance when fans did not know in advance who was to pitch.

Team Gambling.

"Rules are made to be broken, so there won't be any rules."—Pirates manager Billy Herman, whose 1940s club was dubbed the "casino on wheels" for its heavy gambling on train trips.

While Dodger manager in 1941–1942, Leo Durocher allowed bookies in the clubhouse and there were frequent dice games, poker and horse betting. Durocher was deeply involved with all three. When Dodger general manager Larry MacPhail left for the military in late 1942, Branch Rickey replaced him and cracked down on all forms of gambling. Durocher was never disciplined over these incidents, but in spring training 1947 while still the Dodger manager he was suspended for a full year due to his association with various shady characters (see also ***Suspensions***).

In his autobiography, former commissioner Ford Frick reported that his chief investigator for gambling and other illegal activities was a former FBI agent, Buck Greene. During Frick's 15-year tenure there were 839 arrests of bookmakers, gamblers, scalpers and pickpockets. Over 430 suspicious taverns, nightclubs and restaurants were investigated and certain establishments were declared off limits. When Cardinals owner Gussie Busch was informed that a restaurant across from his ballpark hosted an illegal gambling operation, he bought the property and leveled the building for parking.

One 1990s story has it that when an FBI representative was making his annual spring training rounds to lecture on the evils of gambling, the players on one club made him wait while they finished filling out their NCAA basketball tournament pool.

William B. Cox. One of the last acts by Judge Landis before he died was to force Phillies owner Bill Cox to sell his interest for betting on games. Cox bought the team in 1943 and hired Bucky Harris as manager. He abruptly fired Harris in late July of that year and Freddie Fitzsimmons replaced him. The players were upset and took the field only after a personal appeal by Harris.

Harris told sportswriters that Cox was betting on the Phillies. Word of this got to Landis, who met with Cox. Cox first said the bets were made by associates of his in the lumber business. He then admitted making close to 20 bets on the Phillies, but only in the range of $25–$100. Landis nevertheless forced Cox to sell his stock in the club and barred him from further contact with Organized Baseball. Cox's interest was purchased by Robert R.M. Carpenter, Sr., the CEO of DuPont.

1944 Browns. In September 1944 a bogus story appeared in a magazine claiming that those who controlled Major League Baseball wanted the Browns to lose the American League pennant race because the club's ballpark would be too small for the World Series. The magazine later retracted the story.

On the last day of the 1944 season, the Browns and Tigers each had a chance to win the pennant. The Tigers were to play the Senators in Detroit and Senators knuckleballer Dutch Leonard (not the same Dutch Leonard who accused Cobb and Speaker 18 years earlier) was offered $20,000 to throw the game. He immediately reported the bribe to his manager and then went out and won 4–1 over Tigers pitcher Dizzy Trout, who pitched on one day's rest.

Evangeline League. The only known betting scandal to hit Organized Baseball since the 1919 Black Sox occurred in 1946. Five players in the Louisiana-based Evangeline League were barred for life for conspiring to fix play-off games that year between Houma and Alexandria. Of the five players, only pitcher Bill Thomas was reinstated. He had won 35 games that year and was 5–0 during the supposedly rigged games. In 1950 he won 23 minor league games at age 45.

Unjustly Accused. At the 1955 All-Star Game, first baseman Vic Power was sick and was told by American League manager Al Lopez to stay in the clubhouse for the entire game because he would not be required to play. In the 6th inning, however, Lopez (who had a reputation for not liking certain black players) sent word that he wanted Power to pinch-hit immediately. Power was not dressed and could not bat. It was reported in the next day's papers that "Vic Power didn't want to play in the All-Star Game because he had a bet." Power was exonerated after he was forced to go to New York to explain the situation to commissioner Ford Frick.

Modern Umpires. Late in the 1960 season umpires Ed Runge and Bill McKinley were picked up by two women in a bar. A short time later they were threatened with blackmail by two ex-convicts who had photographs of the married umpires with the women.

The felons threatened the umpires with publication of the negatives if they did not pay $5,000 or fix games. The umpires immediately met with the American League office and Maryland police and the plot was stopped.

In 1972 in a Baltimore suburb bookie raid, the police found the telephone numbers of 11 American League umpires. Commissioner Bowie Kuhn and the state attorney met on the matter but nothing came of the incident.

Denny McLain. On February 23, 1970, *Sports Illustrated* broke a story regarding a bookie operation involving Denny McLain. After an investigation by Bowie Kuhn, McLain received a three-month suspension from April until July. On October 9 of that year during the World Series, Kuhn took the unusual step of announcing that McLain had been traded to the Senators. Such announcements usually were made by club officials, so it was suspected that Kuhn was involved in the trade as a form of punishment of McLain.

In 1984 McLain was convicted of cocaine-trafficking offenses and was sent to prison, but the verdict was thrown out two years later and the government chose not to re-try him. In 1993 he and a partner bought Peet Packing and within a month stole $3 million from the company's pension fund and funneled it to the Cayman Islands. By 1995 the company was bankrupt. At the end of his prison term, McLain served a six-month term in a work-release program working at a 7-Eleven. He also remarried his wife, Sharyn, 40 years after their first marriage.

McLain's first comprehensive autobiography (with Dave Diles) was *Nobody's Perfect* (1975). After his release from prison in the mid–1980s he wrote *Strikeout*, with Mike Nahrstedt (1988).

Dizzy Dean. In 1970 Dizzy Dean was indicted in a gambling ring. At the time his co-conspirators were arrested in Las Vegas, police found $172,000 in cash and $450,000 in checks.

Clete Boyer.

"I'd go double or nothing with Bowie Kuhn, but I don't think he'd go for that." — Boyer on his $1,000 fine for gambling.

Boyer had played 30 games for the Atlanta Braves in 1971 when Bowie Kuhn called him regarding his creation of football betting pools in the clubhouse. Such pools were rampant around the Major Leagues, but Kuhn decided to make an example of Boyer and bar him from Major League Baseball. Boyer was forced to go to Japan to play and never returned to the Major Leagues after a 16-year career.

Pete Rose.

"Bud Selig is considering letting Pete Rose back into baseball, but reaction around the game is mixed. Current players favor it. Ted Williams was reportedly cool on the idea." — Comedian Alan Ray, after reports of Williams' cryogenics fiasco made headlines.

"You owe it to yourself to be the best you can possibly be — in baseball and in life." — Rose, who apparently tried to be the best gambler he could possibly be.

"Shoeless Joe, meet Clueless Schmoe." — Columnist Scott Ostler's player introductions in the gambling wing of baseball's hereafter.

"To millions of fans, Pete Rose was baseball, representing everything that was good and pure about the game. But despite all the hits he collected, despite the thousands of high-fives and fanny-pats he exchanged with teammates, despite the records that fell to him and the presidents who called, Rose remained very much an outsider within the game itself." — Michael Y. Sokolove in *Hustle: The Myth, Life, and Lies of Pete Rose* (1990).

Rose once said that he was "the best ambassador baseball has. My name is synonymous with the game." Added Bernie Lincicome of the *Rocky Mountain News*: "In the way that Lizzie Borden's name is connected with hand tools, maybe."

Except for the Black Sox Scandal, Rose's gambling escapades are probably the most celebrated — and certainly most scrutinized — in baseball history. Rose was long known to be a heavy bettor on all sporting events, though he repeatedly denied betting on baseball. The evidence derived from the 1988–1989 investigation overseen by commissioner Bart Giamatti suggested that Rose did indeed bet on baseball. He was linked to a number of known gamblers in Philadelphia and Cincinnati. Baseball interviewed over 100 people to confirm the allegations, and Rose was given an opportunity to have a hearing. Not only did his people fail to interview the group, Rose turned down the hearing offer.

John Dowd was a Justice Department lawyer who prosecuted mobsters and defended congressmen when Giamatti asked him to head the probe into Rose's gambling. In May 1989 Dowd issued his 225-page report stating that Rose placed more than 400 bets on Major League games from 1985 to 1987. Of those, 52 were on teams Rose managed. Dowd's guideline was that he needed three sources to confirm each allegation. Eight to 10 people testified that Rose bet on Reds games and bookies supplied betting slips, confirmed by FBI analysis of Rose's thumbprints on them. Phone records traced calls from Rose's office in Riverfront Stadium to his middleman, to his bookie, and back.

Dowd also felt he had some evidence that Rose had bet against the Reds, but couldn't quite prove it, and Major League Baseball mildly censured Dowd for the allegation. Dowd, speaking to a SABR group in 2004, said that he had evidence that Rose bet against the Reds in a game in San Diego, but because he had only two sources of proof, he omitted it from his report.

Dowd also referenced in his speech the fact that Major League Baseball had investigated Rose in the late 1970s for betting on baseball. Dowd said that Major League Baseball couldn't find the report and Dowd said that it was probably at "the bottom of the East River."

In a deposition Rose gave in connection with the investigation, he admitted to gambling on football and basketball, and to using his long-time gofer, Tommy Gioiosa, as the middleman. Gioiosa testified, however, that in 1985 Rose was betting $2,000 a game on baseball, and making the bets from his clubhouse office phone using a bookie named Ron Peters. Gioiosa also testified that Rose bet on the Reds, and was present when Rose called another Major League manager to get the scoop on that night's starting pitcher. Gioiosa said that Rose was making tens of thousands of dollars in bets each week and later evidence showed that Rose was at times betting $50,000 per week. Gioiosa, who used massive amounts of steroids in the mid–1980s, later was convicted of tax evasion and involvement with a cocaine trafficking ring, and then spent two years in prison. At his trial he admitted to receiving 10% of Rose's losses from their bookie, Ron Peters. Gioiosa later married and became a distributor for Herbalife.

Rose apparently arranged for Gioiosa to receive a baseball scholarship to the University of Cincinnati, where he wore Rose's No. 14. They spent eight years together until parting in 1987. Gioiosa told *Vanity Fair* during over 100 hours of interviews that Rose invested in cocaine trafficking and used a corked bat. They had met at a Florida hotel where Rose stayed during spring training and where Gioiosa's family stayed for two springs during a high school baseball excursion.

The IRS investigated Rose because of his failure to pay taxes on his voluminous memorabilia and autograph sales. He ultimately pleaded guilty to income tax evasion and was sentenced to a $50,000 fine, six months in jail, and 1,000 hours of community service. He also had to pay $366,043 in back taxes and penalties to the IRS. At the same time, Giamatti barred Rose from baseball, though Rose could request reinstatement at a later date. Rose was barred on August 24, 1989, and true to memorabilia-hawking form, he appeared on the Home Shopping Network that night. Perhaps in part because of the stress of the Rose incident, Giamatti suffered a fatal heart attack only a week after he disciplined Rose.

After Rose served his prison term, he relocated to Florida and remarried. In the 1990s Rose continued to sell memorabilia, was a paid spokesman for Maaco Enterprises, a paint-and-body-shop chain, and he licensed his name to two restaurants in South Florida. He remained married to his second wife and they have two children, one of whom is an actress.

He has not been reinstated to baseball and has not been eligible for induction into the *Hall of Fame*. He has waged a publicity campaign to gain favor with Major League Baseball in his attempt to gain reinstatement and thus eligibility for the Hall.

In 1993 on Cincinnati's all-sports radio station, WSAI, pro football cast-off and addicted gambler Art Schlichter's talk show was followed by Rose's show. Locals called the show the "Daily Double."

Rose's good-behavior voucher while serving time for tax evasion sold for $770 at a December 1993 auction. The winning bidder, Andy Gross, commented on his purchase: "I know it's a little twisted. But this little conversation piece will have cult value. I could display it next to the Gerald Ford letter pardoning Richard Nixon, which I own, in my new Hall of Guilt."

Rose was allowed to attend the on-field World Series ceremony in 1999 honoring the All-Century Team, to which he was chosen. As he walked off the field after the loudest ovation, he sharply rebuked on-air interviewer Jim Gray, who asked him to admit that he had bet on baseball: "I'm not going to admit to something that didn't happen."

Several of the Rose gambling investigation documents were donated to the Hall of Fame in 2003 by John Dowd, the attorney who headed the probe. They were not going to be available to the public for several years, as the Hall needed to catalog them.

In September 1997 Rose applied for reinstatement, but Commissioner Bud Selig saw no reason to lift the ban. They met again secretly on November 25, 2002, and Rose appeared hopeful that positive (for him) action would be taken. Rose admitted at the time to betting on baseball four or five times a week, "but I never bet against my own team, and I never made any bets from the clubhouse" (the latter contrary to other reports). When asked why he bet, Rose responded, "because I didn't think I'd get caught."

At age 62 in 2004, Rose came out with a new book, *My Prison Without Bars*. In it, he finally admitted his baseball use with an, uh, heartfelt apology: "I'm sure that I'm supposed to act all sorry or sad or guilty now that I've accepted that I've done something wrong. But you see, I'm just not built that way…. Let's move on."

To which former commissioner Fay Vincent said in a *Time* magazine essay: "If it is not in Pete Rose to be sorry or sad or to feel guilty, then it should not be in Commissioner Selig to feel merciful. For most of us, the premise of forgiveness is contrition. So, as Rose put it himself, 'Let's move on.'"

In his book, Rose indicated that he called other Major League managers and innocently pumped them for information about their players. Tommy Lasorda denied the statement, calling it a "lie." Several influential Veterans Committee members, including Bob Feller, publicly opposed Rose's reinstatement. Their opposition had intensified over the years when Rose would set up an autograph booth down the street from the Hall of Fame ceremonies in Cooperstown and would brag about the crowds he was drawing.

In November 1999, Rose created a website that allowed fans to add their names to a petition to Major League Baseball asking that Rose be reinstated.

With baseball fan Billy Crystal hosting the 2004 Oscars, it was inevitable that Rose would be referenced after being in the news earlier in the year. In the opening musical number sung by Crystal, he said "watch his nose as it grows," referencing Rose. In another segment, there was a clip from the movie, *The Last Samurai*. The scene had Crystal's head superimposed over Tom Cruise's head, in which the samurai brings a sword blade to within an inch of Cruise's neck. Crystal looks at the camera and says, "all right, I bet on baseball!"

See also Pete Rose, *The Pete Rose Story* (1970); Pete Rose and Roger Kahn, *Pete Rose: My Story* (1989); Michael Y. Sokolove, *Hustle: The Myth, Life, and Lies of Pete Rose* (1990).

Lenny Dykstra. Dykstra was warned by National League president Bill White not to play any more high stakes poker after going $80,000 in the hole against a Mississippi gambler named Herbert Kelso. Dykstra reportedly lost $114,000 during an October 1992 gambling trip and another $47,000 one night in Atlantic City.

Dykstra's mistress between 1993 and 1997, Lindsay Jones, filed a lawsuit against him in June 2004, alleging that he had drug problems and was in rehab four times. She also saw him lose $70,000 in a London casino. He owned several car washes, which allegedly financed his escapades.

Don Zimmer. In the early 1990s the Cubs manager bet from $3,000 to $5,000 each week on basketball and football. He later had a meeting in the commissioner's office about his activities.

1994 Strike. Las Vegas oddsmakers had a preseason disclaimer for paying off on the 1994 season winners. Teams were required to play 160 games before the oddsmakers would pay off on bets. Otherwise, the money was refunded.

Japan. In 1969 six Japanese players were banned for life for fixing games in the Yakusa-inspired "Black Mist Scandals."

Friendly Wager. In 1927 Babe Ruth bet pitcher Wilcy Moore that Moore would not get three hits all season. Ruth bet $300 to Moore's $100. Moore got five hits and used the money to buy two mules for his farm: "Babe" and "Ruth."

Walter Matthau. According to his biographers, Robert Edelman and Audrey Kupferberg, actor Walter Matthau once lost $183,000 betting on spring training baseball when he was in Florida shooting a television series, "Tallahassee 7000." His losses included $38,000 on a single game.

Over/Under Snafu. Robin Ventura hit a 15th inning grand slam for the Mets in Game 5 of the 1999 NLCS against the Diamondbacks. The hit was later ruled a single after the on-field celebration prevented Ventura from advancing past third. The final score was reduced from 5-3 to 4-3. The "over-under" line in Las Vegas was 7½ runs, but the scoring change came too late for gamblers on the lower end of the betting line to collect; the "overs" had already been paid by the time of the ruling.

Recent Efforts to Curtail. In 1987 Major League Baseball instituted a program of assigning a police officer to every big league club 12 months of the year. The agents do not conduct investigations, but alert players, umpires and team officials of gamblers, drug dealers and con men who may be around. The officers meet each year with rookies to stress the importance of staying away from these people.

Loss of Pension Benefits. The original pension plan required that any player who was declared permanently ineligible under Rule 21 (no gambling) would lose all pension benefits. This provision was negotiated out of the plan in 1976.

Las Vegas Odds.
"I can tell you that the Cubs winning the World Series would be a really bad result for the sports books. Now, we're at the point where there's so much money bet on the Cubs that they have become a huge liability to the sports books."—Tony Sinisi, senior oddsmaker for Las Vegas Sports Consultants. Fans had bet down the Cubs from 50-1 and 30-1 at the beginning of the 2003 season, to 4-1 by the beginning of the postseason.

Taiwan. In 1997 members of a Taiwanese professional club, the Eagles, confessed to deliberately losing games to help gamblers win their bets. One of the gamblers was accused of paying $360,000 to three players from the Eagles. Players said they were threatened by the gangsters and five members of the Elephants club were briefly abducted.

March Mad. Following gambling allegations against Albert Belle in early 1997, Major League Baseball informed all clubs that "March Madness" NCAA basketball pools would be disallowed. In a deposition in February 1997, Belle admitted that he had lost $40,000 gambling with friends, but denied ever betting on baseball.

Casino Advertising.
"After all, gambling is legal everywhere. So as life changes and society changes, frankly, we also have made some of those changes." — Commissioner Bud Selig, rationalizing Major League teams' acceptance of advertising by gambling establishments.

"I'm very surprised to hear this. A few years back, baseball wouldn't let Mantle and Mays associate with casinos, but apparently the game itself is now associating with casinos." — John Dowd, the Washington lawyer who conducted the investigation that led to the 1989 ban of Pete Rose.

It was reported in 1998 that at least five Major League teams accepted advertising money either directly from casinos or through umbrella organizations. The Florida Marlins and the Minnesota Twins accepted direct advertising from casinos. The Las Vegas Convention and Visitors Authority was a sponsor for the Los Angeles Dodgers, Chicago White Sox and Arizona Diamondbacks. At the Diamondbacks' internet site, visitors could link with the Las Vegas convention authority's home page. There, its "gaming guide" includes a page on sports books. Commissioner Selig said he found no trouble with the setup even though the gaming guide appears side by side with the Diamondbacks' logo and home page index. Selig said: "I still think there's enough of a firewall so that it doesn't affect our game or our integrity or the integrity of the game played on the field.

Little League. In 2004 several offshore on-line gambling sites started taking bets on the Little League World Series.

Book. Daniel E. Ginsburg, *The Fix Is In: A History of Baseball Gambling and Game Fixing Scandals* (1995).

Game of the Week See *Television* —Network Broadcasts/"Game of the Week"

Game Starting Time

"Play ball!"—Umpire's call to start a game; though the rules require only that the umpire say "Play."

"The Cards lead the Dodgers 4-2 after one inning and that one hasn't even started." — Broadcaster Jerry Coleman.

"... like those special afternoons in summer when you go to Yankee Stadium at two o'clock in the afternoon for an eight o'clock game. It's so big, so empty and so silent that you can almost hear the sounds that aren't there." — Ray Miller.

Games generally started in the early days at 3:00 or 3:30, so that fans could get home by 6:00.

Until 1912 the New York Giants started games at 4:00 to accommodate the Wall Street crowd and the stock market's 3:00 closing. Pressure from sportswriters trying to meet deadlines moved the time up to 3:30.

Game time for night games was 8:30 in the 1940s, 8:00 in the 1960s, 7:35 through most of the 1980s, and often 7:05 by the late 1980s to save on the light bill. Night games during the World Series often begin at 8:30 on the East Coast to accommodate West Coast viewers who are just arriving home from work.

See *Longest Games* for the second game of doubleheaders that started after midnight.

Twilight.

"Hitting at 5:15 p.m., with the shadows that are being cast, is like trying to swat flies with a string of spaghetti."—Pete Rose in *Charlie Hustle* (1974).

Early Start.

"Ten-thirty? I'm not even done throwing up at that hour."—Seattle Pilots catcher Jim Pagliaroni on an early game time.

"There was a kind of justice in the fact that the Metropolitans won both games, particularly since the hosts had elected to start a double-header at the bizarre hour of 10:30 a.m. on a field the approximate consistency of cold porridge. But it was reassuring and proper that the Pittsburgh management still be piratical."—Harold Peterson in *The Man Who Invented Baseball* (1969).

In 1988 the Pirates hosted the Dodgers in a Sunday game starting at the experimental hour of 10:30 a.m. The experiment was not repeated.

Because of incredibly cold evening weather in April 1997, the White Sox moved one of the start times from 5:05 pm to 11:05 am.

Late Start. In June 2004 the Braves and Marlins started a game at 11 p.m. because of a rain delay. They finished in a relatively quick 2 hours and 24 minutes.

Game Time See *Fastest Games, Game Starting Time, Length of Games, Longest Games* and *Scheduling*—Day Games

Game Winning RBIs (1980–1988)

"They should take that stat and shove it."—Broadcaster Phil Rizzuto in 1980.

This statistical category was added in 1980 and abandoned after the 1988 season. Keith Hernandez is the all-time leader with 129. Jack Clark won or tied for the National League title the first three years of the statistic's existence.

Games Played

Pete Rose is the all-time Major League leader with 3,562 games played. Others over 3,000 are Carl Yastrzemski, Henry Aaron, Ty Cobb and Stan Musial. Musial was the first player in the National League to play in over 3,000 games. In October 2001 Cal Ripken became the seventh player to reach 3,000 games played.

Prior to 1912 in the National League, appearances by pinch hitters, pinch runners and other substitutes were not credited with a game played. The American League recognized these players with a game played in 1907.

Among pitchers, Dennis Eckersley broke Hoyt Wilhelm's record on September 26, 1998, appearing in his 1,071st game for the Red Sox. When the Red Sox refused arbitration after the season, Eckersley retired (see also *Pitchers*).

Gas House Gang

"We could finish first or in an asylum."—Manager Frankie Frisch.

This term was used to describe the 1930s Cardinals. There are various stories describing its origin. One has it that Dizzy Dean walked up to Leo Durocher and *New York Sun* writer Frank Graham, who was commenting on the club's strength. Durocher replied, "but they wouldn't let us play in the American League; they'd just say we were a lot of gas house players." The *Dickson Baseball Dictionary* attributes Durocher's remark to Graham.

Another version involves a 1935 doubleheader in Boston. The team could not get its uniforms cleaned in time after a game in New York the day before. Leo Durocher claimed that when the team arrived in New York the uniforms were filthy from playing on wet fields. In their game stories the next day writers Frank Graham and Bill Corum talked of the "dirty kids on the tracks" looking like a gas house gang. The phrase was then retroactively applied to the 1934 World Championship team.

Durocher later said that the first time he saw the phrase in print was in a Willard Mullin cartoon in the *New York World Telegram*. The last survivor of the Gang was Pat Crawford, whose primary claim to fame was as the league leader in pinch hits and pinch hit at-bats in 1934.

Gate Receipts

"Base Ball, it will be remembered by old settlers, is a game played by eighteen persons wearing shirts and drawers. They scatter around the field and try to catch a cannon-ball covered with rawhide. The game is to get people to pay two shillings to come inside the fence."—1879 article in a Milwaukee newspaper.

See also *Tickets.*

Earliest Sharing. In 1862 William Cammeyer owned the Union and Capitoline Grounds in Brooklyn (two separate ballparks). He enclosed the Capitoline Grounds and apparently charged the first admission. The first such game supposedly was played on May 11, 1862. In return for gate receipts he allowed the Union Club of Brooklyn to play rent-free. This arrangement lasted one season until the club realized the money-making potential of selling tickets on a regular basis. The next season the club refused to play unless Cammeyer shared the gate receipts.

Revenue Splits. Because of the inequality in attendance that 19th century teams experienced in part because of the size of their respective markets, teams began sharing gate receipts. Before professional baseball was in full swing in the 1870s, the visiting team often received 50% of the base seat price.

If a home team charged a premium for better seats, the visiting club did not receive any percentage of the premium. This system gave the home team an incentive to upgrade many of its seats to box seats or reserved sections. This basic system eventually was adopted by professional leagues, though the percentage gradually decreased through the 20th century.

In 1877 the National League clubs agreed to pay the visiting team 15 cents for each patron, based on a 50-cent admission. This 30% allocation applied to all admissions except players, police and ten other categories of what were known as "deadheads." This system was similar to that used by the professional National Association of 1871–1875.

The National League's percentage split existed through the 1870s and early 1880s. By 1886 some of the more prosperous eastern clubs (who generally had larger populations from which to draw fans) were not making expenses on some of their poorly attended road trips. The eastern clubs demanded a $100 visiting team guarantee per game and threatened the league with departure if this was not implemented. A temporary compromise was reached whereby visiting teams received $125 per game except on holidays, when the teams split gate receipts evenly.

This new plan was in part implemented because of action taken by Detroit Wolverines owner Frederick Kimball Stearns, who realized that his small-market team could not draw well at home. He assumed that he would make more money on the road by receiving a percentage of the home team's gate and rescheduled a number of his club's games on the road.

The flat rate eventually was abandoned and the visitor's percentage fluctuated upward during the 1890s and then gradually dropped through the 20th century. It was 40% in 1892, 25% in 1901 (American League), 21% by 1929 and 14% by 1950. By the 1980s visiting National League clubs received 38 cents on every ticket, which was increased in the 1990s to 44 cents. A visiting American League team received 20% of the base price of a ticket. By the 1990s the Major League split was 85%-15%.

Modern Gate Receipts as Percentage of Revenue. By 1950 gate receipts were 74% of total team revenue, with concessions, radio and television the other primary sources. By 1989 gate receipts were only 37% of total revenue primarily because of the increase in broadcast revenues and merchandise sales (see also *Profits, Income and Expenses*).

In 1975, averaging 20,000 a game was enough to meet the expenses of running a Major League team. In 1995, with an 800% increase in player salaries over the previous 20 years, that amount could not come close to breaking even.

Dollars Through Turnstiles. In 2001, Major League gate receipts totaled $1,383,458,000, with the Yankees leading at $98 million and the Red Sox second at $89 million. Next were the Mariners at $76.5 million. Tops in the National League were the Mets at $73 million and the Cardinals and Giants at $67 million. At the bottom of the income levels were the Expos at a dismal $6 million, followed by the Twins, Devil Rays, Royals and Marlins, who were all between $16–$19 million.

World Series Percentages. The owners of the two World Series clubs each receive 8.5% of the gate for Games 1 through 4 and 21.25% of the gate of Games 5, 6 and 7. The percentage changes because the players receive percentages for Games 1 through 4 and nothing for the last three games. This is to avoid any incentive by the players to improperly stretch out the Series beyond the mandatory four games.

Lou Gehrig (1903–1941)

Hall of Fame 1939

"It may have been a child's perversity, but I like to think now that I was in tune with changing times when I selected not the Babe but Gehrig as my hero. Handsome, shy, put together along such rugged lines that he was once screen-tested—wrapped in a leopard skin—in Hollywood for the role of Tarzan, a devastating hitter with men on base, Gehrig served perfectly as the idol of a small boy soon to reach adolescence."—Frank Graham, Jr., in *Farewell to Heroes* (1981).

"Lou Gehrig was to baseball what Gary Cooper was to the movies: a figure of unimpeachable integrity, massive and incorruptible, a hero…. Today both are seen as paradigms of manly virtue. Decent and God-fearing, yet strongly charismatic and powerful."—Kevin Nelson in *The Greatest Stories Ever Told About Baseball* (1986).

"Biscuit Pants."—Nickname for the large size of Gehrig's rear end.

Gehrig batted .340 over 17 seasons for the Yankees beginning in 1923 and played in 2,130 straight games.

Born at 309 East 94th Street in New York City, Henry Louis Gehrig had an unimpressive workout with the Giants in 1921 and then entered Columbia University, where he played football and baseball. He played professionally for a few games in 1921, which cost him his freshman eligibility. He was reinstated for football in 1922 and then pitched and played first base for Columbia in 1923. He signed for $1,500 with the Yankees and played a few games for the club in both 1923 and 1924. In 1925 he became a regular at first base and started his famous streak in place of Wally Pipp. Gehrig eventually became the Yankee captain, the last until catcher Thurman Munson in the 1970s.

From 1925 through 1938 Gehrig appeared in every Yankee game played, earning the name "The Iron Horse." He batted .300 or better 12 straight seasons and drove in over 140 runs eight times. He led the league in RBIs five times and in runs scored four times. He also led the league in home runs three times, with a high of 49 in both 1934 and 1936. He won the Triple Crown in 1934 with a .363 average and 165 RBIs to go with his 49 home runs.

He slumped to a .295 average, 29 home runs and 114 RBIs in 1938, his last full season. He played only eight games in 1939 when he was forced to retire at age 35 after being diagnosed with Amyotrophic Lateral Sclerosis (see **The Illness**). His *Consecutive Games Played* ended at 2,130 and he never played another game.

Gehrig's slugging average of .632 is third all-time, as is his RBI total of 1,990. He finished his career with 493 home runs and a .340 average. Had he played only four more full seasons illness-free, his totals project to over 620 home runs and 2,400 RBIs. He hit a Major-League record 23 grand slams and holds the American League record with 184 RBIs in 1931. In seven World Series, Gehrig hit 10 home runs and batted .361.

Overshadowed by Others. Gehrig was continually overshadowed by Babe Ruth. When Gehrig hit 47 home runs in 1927, Ruth set his record of 60. In the 1932 World Series, Gehrig hit .529 with three home runs, but what everyone remembers is Ruth's "Called Shot" off Cubs pitcher Charlie Root. In 1935 Ruth was gone and Gehrig had a bad year. When Gehrig exploded for 49 home runs, 152 RBIs and a .354 batting average, the press and fans were more focused on rookie sensation Joe DiMaggio.

On June 3, 1932, Gehrig hit four home runs in a game, but the story of the day was John McGraw's resignation as manager of the New York Giants after over 30 years. When he played in his 2,000th consecutive game in 1938, the headlines were about Johnny Vander Meer's second no-hitter. Even when he died on June 2, 1941, it was on the same day as game 19 of Joe DiMaggio's 56-game hitting streak.

The Illness. Gehrig hit poorly (for him) in 1938 and pursued a rigorous off-season training regimen in response. However, the disease, Amyotrophic Lateral Sclerosis (ALS), had already set in and he was even having trouble stepping off curbs. He gave some indication that he was healthy when he hit two home runs and two singles (described as three home runs in some sources; regardless, they were over a short right field porch) against a Yankee farm club in Norfolk during spring training. However, he became progressively worse only a few games into the 1939 season. To boost his morale, he was even being congratulated by his teammates for routine fielding plays. He played five innings of an exhibition game on a western road trip and then went to the Mayo Clinic.

Gehrig took himself out of the lineup on May 2 and never played again. Within a few weeks he was diagnosed by the Mayo Clinic as having "infantile paralysis." ALS is a progressive muscle disease that gradually wipes out all muscle function. The illness was described by writer Fred Lieb as "turning of the marrow of the spinal cord to chalk." In 1993 scientists isolated the gene that causes the disease.

Gehrig stayed in uniform after he came out of the lineup. He went on road trips and roomed with Bill Dickey despite an unfounded rumor that the disease was contagious. He also worked for New York mayor Fiorello LaGuardia, going into the office until his disease made it impossible. Two years after his retirement he was dead.

Seven weeks after Gehrig took himself out of the line-up he gave his famous speech to 61,808 fans attending a "Lou Gehrig Day" doubleheader against the Senators on July 4, 1939: "Fans, for the past two weeks you have been reading about a bad break I got. Yet today I consider myself the luckiest man on the face of the earth. I have been in ballparks for 17 years, and have never received anything but kindness and encouragement from you fans.

"Look at these grand men. Which of you wouldn't consider it the highlight of his career just to associate with them for even one day?

"Sure, I'm lucky. Who wouldn't consider it an honor to have known Jacob Ruppert; also the builder of baseball's greatest empire, Ed Barrow; to have spent six years with that wonderful little fellow, Miller Huggins; then to have spent the next nine years with that outstanding leader, that smart student of psychology—the best manager in baseball today, Joe McCarthy?

"Sure, I'm lucky. When the New York Giants, a team you would give your right arm to beat, and vice versa, send you a gift—that's something. When everybody down to the groundskeepers and those boys in white coats remember you with trophies—that's something.

"When you have a wonderful mother-in-law who takes sides with you in squabbles against her own daughter—that's something. When you have a father and mother who work all their lives so that you can have an education and build your body—it's a blessing. When you have a wife who has been a tower of strength, and shown more courage than you dreamed existed—that's the finest I know.

"So, I close in saying that I might have had a tough break. But I have an awful lot to live for."

One source erroneously reported the phrasing somewhat different: "I have a wonderful wife. I have a wonderful mother and father, and wonderful friends. I have been privileged to play many years with the famous Yankees, the greatest team of all time. What young man wouldn't give anything to mingle with such men for a day, as I have for these years? You've been reading about my bad break for the past two weeks now. But today I can say that I consider myself the luckiest man on the face of the earth."

In 1999 the uniform he wore during the speech sold at auction for $451,541 to a south Florida man who was not identified.

Books. Richard Bak, *Lou Gehrig: An American Classic* (1995); Paul Gallico, *Lou Gehrig—Pride of the Yankees* (1942) (on which the movie was based); Eleanor Gehrig and Joseph Durso, *My Luke and I* (1976); Frank Graham, *Lou Gehrig—A Quiet Hero* (1942); Richard G. Hubler, *Lou Gehrig* (1941); Ray Robinson, *The Iron Horse* (1990).

Lou Gehrig Memorial Award (1955–)

"… most typically represents the spirit of the Hall of Fame first baseman."—The criteria for presentation of the award by the New York Baseball Writers Association. It was first presented in 1955 to Alvin Dark. Other early winners were Pee Wee Reese in 1956 and Stan Musial in 1957. More recent winners have included Ozzie Smith, George Brett, Cal Ripken, Brett Butler, Mark McGwire, John Franco and Danny Graves.

Charlie Gehringer (1903–1993)

Hall of Fame 1949

"There were the stars who lacked color or, if they had it, always kept it within the bounds of the organization…. If there were ever a stereotype of this player, it was Charlie Gehringer, the perfect second baseman of the Detroit Tigers. Called the 'Silent Knight' by Harold A. Fitzgerald, Gehringer looked like a 'Hollywood Star' and was dubbed the quiet man of baseball."—Richard C. Crepeau in *Baseball: America's Diamond Mind—1919–1941* (1980).

Gehringer starred at second base for the Tigers for 19 years beginning in 1924 and batted .320 lifetime.

A native of Michigan, Charles Leonard Gehringer, "The Mechanical Man," spent a year at the University of Michigan before signing with the Tigers in 1924. He played in the Michigan-Ontario League in 1924 and with Toronto of the International League in 1925. In each season he played a few games for the Tigers.

In 1926 Gehringer became the club's regular second baseman, a position he held through 1941. He went on to hit over .300 13 times, starting in 1927. He led the league in batting in 1937 with a .371 average and was the American League MVP. He had over 200 hits in a season seven times and led the league in runs scored twice. He hit .320 in 20 World Series games covering 1934, 1935 and 1940.

In 1942 he played in 45 games primarily as a pinch hitter before entering the Navy. He never again played in the Major Leagues. Gehringer hit .320 with 184 home runs and 1,427 RBIs in 19 seasons for the Tigers. He was a stellar second baseman, leading the league in fielding percentage nine times. After the war he returned to Detroit to become an auto interior supply salesman. In 1951 he became general manager of the Tigers for two years before stepping down to a vice president position until 1959. He returned to the auto supply business until his retirement in the 1970s.

General Managers See *Executives*

Ghostwriters See *Books* and *Sportswriters*

A. Bartlett Giamatti (1938–1989)

Giamatti was *National League President* from 1986 until 1989, when he was appointed *Commissioner* of baseball.

Bob Gibson (1935–)

Hall of Fame 1981

"The only people I ever felt intimidated by in my whole life were Bob Gibson and my daddy."—Dusty Baker.

"That would be my answer too."—Gibson, at the All-Century Team ceremony, on comments by others that he would be the choice for a Game 7 starting role.

"Nothing that has ever been said about Bob Gibson and his talent has ever been overstated. Everybody embellishes, but with Gibson, there is no way to do so out of the realm of fact."—Gibson's batterymate Tim McCarver.

"I've played a couple hundred games of tic-tac-toe with my little daughter and she hasn't beaten me yet. I've always had to win. I've got to win."—Gibson.

Gibson won 251 games over 17 seasons for the Cardinals beginning in 1959.

One of the most intense competitors of all time, Pack Robert Gibson attended Nebraska's Creighton University before signing with the Cardinals as a pitcher for $4,000 in 1957. He also played a few months with the Harlem Globetrotters. He pitched for Omaha, Columbus and Rochester in the minor leagues with brief stints with the Cardinals in 1959 and 1960. He came up for good in 1961, winning 13 games in 27 starts. In 1962 he was 15–13 and led the league with five shutouts.

Gibson established himself in 1963 with 18 wins. In 1964 he won 19 games during the regular season and won two World Series games against the Yankees, including Game 7. In 1965 he won 20 games,

the first of five seasons in which he reached that mark; it would have been a streak of six consecutive seasons, but a line drive broke his leg in 1967 and he finished at 13–7. He returned that year to lead the Cardinals in the World Series, winning three games over the Red Sox.

In 1968 Gibson had his finest season, winning 22 games while posting a 1.12 ERA and pitching 13 shutouts. He also won two games in the World Series, but lost Game 7 to the Tigers. In 1972 the injury-prone Gibson had his last fine season, winning 19 games with four shutouts. He retired after the 1975 season and finished with a 251–174 record, 3,117 strikeouts (second all-time when he retired), 56 shutouts and nine consecutive Gold Glove Awards.

After retiring he became a sports commentator and owned radio station interests in Nebraska. He later became a pitching coach but sometimes was at odds with his managers because of his combative nature. He left the coaching ranks in the early 1980s, but returned to the Cardinals as a coach in 1995 after an 11-year hiatus.

Book. Bob Gibson with Lonnie Wheeler, *Stranger to the Game: The Autobiography of Bob Gibson* (1994).

Josh Gibson (1911–1947)

Hall of Fame (NLC) 1972

"Gibson, without a doubt, was the greatest hitter I ever saw, black or white. He would have broken Ruth's record. The fans saw the Babe from the left side; they would have seen Josh from the right side."—Negro League and New York Giants star Monte Irvin.

"I couldn't carry Josh's glove. Anything I could do, he could do better."—Catcher Roy Campanella.

"Gibson was, at a minimum, two Yogi Berras."—Bill Veeck, Jr.

"Josh wanted to be the one to break the color barrier. When the Dodgers signed Jackie Robinson he knew it was over for him. He wasn't going to make the big leagues, and he also knew that because of his health and his bad knees his career with the Grays was about over. He didn't know what to do with himself. They say a man can't die of a broken heart, and I guess that's true. But I'll tell you this, all of this sure lessened Josh's will to keep going, to keep fighting to stay alive."—Ted Page on Josh Gibson.

Gibson was a Negro League catching star between 1930 and 1946 and possibly its greatest player of all time.

Joshua Gibson was born in Georgia and began work as an apprentice electrician in Pittsburgh. At age 19 he joined the Homestead Grays and between 1930 and 1946 Gibson starred for the Grays and Pittsburgh Crawfords. He got his start while attending a Grays game and was asked to play when Grays catcher Buck Ewing had to leave the game with an injured thumb.

In 1932, supposedly his best season, he is said to have hit 75 home runs and batted .380 in 123 games. The latest statistics available for his 1932 season show Gibson to have hit seven home runs in 46 games while batting .286. Gibson played briefly in Mexico and Puerto Rico, winning the 1941 MVP award in Puerto Rico with a .480 (or .440) average.

Gibson suffered a brain tumor and died at age 36 while still an active player, though his skills had eroded from the effects of the tumor that had been discovered in 1942. Some insiders contend that Gibson suffered brain damage caused by untreated syphilis.

Satchel Paige rated only Charlie Gehringer as close to Gibson as a hitter and Roy Campanella said he was the best player he ever saw, black or white. Gibson is the only player to hit a fair ball out of Yankee Stadium.

Books. William Brashler, *Josh Gibson: A Life in the Negro*

One of the greatest sluggers of all time, black or white, Josh Gibson of the Homestead Grays gets ready to pound the ball.

Leagues (1978); John B. Holway, *Josh and Satch* (1991), covers Gibson and Satchel Paige in a season-by-season account.

Warren Crandall Giles (1896–1979)

Giles was **National League President** from 1952 through 1969.

Glasses

"I was pitching one day when my glasses clouded up on me. I took them off to polish them. When I looked up to the plate, I saw Jimmie Foxx. The sight of him terrified me so much that I haven't been able to wear glasses since…"—Lefty Gomez.

"I was tired of being a dork."—Pitcher Greg Maddux on why he got corrective eye surgery, Lasik, in 1999, and gave up his glasses.

"Baseball doesn't make passes at players who wear glasses."—Baseball axiom.

"I know it, but I can't guarantee I'll see it."—Ryne Duren after manager Gene Mauch asked the myopic pitcher if he knew the bunt sign. Duren wore thick bottle glasses and was one of the wildest and fastest pitchers of the mid–1950s and early 1960s. He routinely hit the backstop during his warm-up and once walked in a run after 12 straight balls. In 10 seasons he won 27 games and had 57 saves, with a league-high 20 saves in 1958 for the Yankees.

"The man John McGraw said that with two good eyes he'd be the best player ever."—Scout Tom Sheehan on National League outfielder and Hall of Famer Chick Hafey. In 1931 Hafey became the first batting champion to wear glasses. He was plagued by chronic sinus problems requiring five operations, all of which affected his eyesight. The infections caused frequent changes to his eyesight and Hafey adjusted by using three different pairs of glasses. He began wearing the glasses not because of the sinus problems, but after a doctor recommended that he do so after a beaning.

First Major Leaguer. The first Major League player to wear glasses in a game was pitcher William Henry "Will" White. He wore them in 1877 for the Boston Red Stockings of the National League. White finished with 229 wins over a 10-year National League and American Association career that included 394 complete games out of 401 starts. He was the only 19th century Major League player to wear glasses on the field. No other player wore glasses in the Major Leagues for another 38 years.

First in 20th Century. In 1915 Lee Meadows pitched for the Cardinals while wearing glasses, the first 20th century player to do so. He won 188 games over 15 Major League seasons.

Second in 20th Century. The second 20th century Major Leaguer to wear glasses was pitcher Carmen Hill, who, like Meadows, first pitched in the Major Leagues in 1915. Hill pitched primarily for the Pirates, compiling a 49–33 record over a sporadic Major League career that lasted until 1930.

First Non-Pitcher. In 1921 George "Specs" Toporcer became the first infielder and non-pitcher to wear glasses. He hit .279 over his eight-year career for the Cardinals.

Mel Harder. The nearsighted pitcher threw for the Indians while wearing glasses, compiling a 223–186 record from 1928 through 1947.

Mel Ott. Ott wore glasses for the first time in June 1940.

Paul Waner. In 1943, the 40-year-old played the outfield and hit .311 for the Dodgers while supposedly wearing glasses for the first time. Other sources reported that he wore the glasses only off the field in 1943 and 1944 and wore the glasses on the field for the single game he played in 1945 for the Yankees.

MVPs. In 1950 relief pitcher Jim Konstanty of the Phillies became the first MVP to wear glasses. Dick Allen was the first American Leaguer to win the MVP while wearing glasses and consecutive MVPs wore glasses in 1972 (Allen), 1973 (Reggie Jackson) and 1974 (Jeff Burroughs).

Dodger reliever Eric Gagne, 2003 MVP Award winner, wore huge goggles, making him look almost comical on the mound (until he unleashed a nasty slider).

First Catcher. In 1952 Clint Courtney of the Browns became the first catcher to wear glasses. Over his 11-year career he hit .268.

Total Through 1950. Through 1950 at least 50 players reportedly wore glasses during parts of their careers.

Contact Lenses.

"When the pitcher threw a fastball low and outside, it looked like a fastball high and inside."—Junior Ortiz, Cleveland Indians catcher, after going 0-for-3 on June 8, 1992, while playing with his left contact lens in his right eye and his right lens in his left eye.

In 1971 Darrell Evans of the Braves may have become the first Major League player to wear contact lenses. By 1973 one in seven players used glasses or contact lenses. By the late 1970s it was estimated that one in five wore glasses and that at least 50 players wore contact lenses. Wade Boggs, with a lifetime average over .330, was below .300 in mid–1992. On July 22 that season he began wearing glasses and went 1-for-3 in his first game. He later switched to contact lenses.

Sunglasses.

"Here comes Andruw Jones, strutting through the Braves clubhouse slick as an oil stain, smiling, flashing more dimples than a Titleist. His sunglasses are on, though he is indoors, which does not matter because it is overcast outside anyway. His cell phone is pressed hard against his ear. A former teammate once said Jones walks around the Braves clubhouse 'like he's Willie Mays or something,' but you have to wonder if Willie Mays ever walked this proudly, ever wore his sunglasses inside on a cloudy day."—Sean Deveney.

One source cited Paul Hines of the Providence Grays in the 19th century as the first to use any style of sunglasses. Another source claimed that Harry Hooper was the first to wear sunglasses for the Red Sox in right field at Fenway Park around 1912. Another source reported that George Burns wore sunglasses as early as 1911 for the New York Giants in the Polo Grounds. He also wore a long-billed cap to give him extra protection from the sun. Still another source reported that in 1914 Fred Clarke of the Pirates became the first player to use flip-style sunglasses. Ty Cobb wore protective dark glasses for a short time after having growths removed from his eyes. He was concerned that he might not see beanballs in time to get out of the way.

Sunglasses might not have helped pitcher Billy Loes, who once claimed that he lost a ground ball in the sun. See **Pennant Races** for the story of how Senators outfielder Bingo Binks dropped a key fly ball in the sun that in part cost his club the 1945 American League pennant.

In the 1990s wraparound sunglasses became popular among many players. These replaced the standard flip-ups used for many years. Until the 1990s there were four shades of green lenses available to ballplayers, whose specially fitted glasses (made of polycarbonate plastic) were stored in a container that held 28 separate pairs of glasses.

Lamp Black. Ken "Hawk" Harrelson is credited with first using lamp black under the eyes to deflect the sun.

Umpire. On April 18, 1956, American League umpire Ed Rommel became the first umpire to wear glasses. Umpires are tested periodically, but 20–20 vision is not required. Near the end of his career, Larry Goetz became the first National League umpire to wear glasses. In 1974 the Major League Umpires Association formally won the right through collective bargaining for its umpires to wear glasses on the field (but not dark glasses).

In 1994 a mild controversy erupted over whether umpires should be able to wear sunglasses. Both supervising umpires were against the idea: "No. We want them to look like umpires, not Hollywood producers." — Ed Vargo of the National League.

"If an umpire can't handle the glare of the sun, he should get a job in a bank." — Marty Springstead of the American League.

Global Baseball League (1969)

"This League is hereby created to bring baseball to the people of the world so they can enjoy international sportsmanship, mutual respect, and the friendly rivalry which will encourage understanding, good will, and brotherhood." — Founder Walter Dilbeck.

This was an ill-fated league founded in the late 1960s by Walter J. Dilbeck of Evansville, Indiana. He planned to place teams in Latin America, Japan and the U.S. The league initially made progress domestically with plans for clubs in Milwaukee, Omaha, Jersey City and Dallas. By July 1968 Dilbeck had abandoned the project and was trying to buy a minor league franchise for Louisville.

In October 1968 Dilbeck resurrected the league for 1969 when he announced that there would be four clubs in Japan — Tokyo, Nagoya, Osaka and Yokohama — as well as clubs in Louisville and Jersey City.

When the 1969 Global League preseason actually began, there were clubs representing Japan, the Dominican Republic, New York and Los Angeles. The bankroll for the project came primarily from Tom Redmond, who owned the Las Vegas Cowboys of the Continental Football League.

Japanese players had been signed and 125 players were training in Daytona Beach and in the Caribbean in the spring of 1969. Checks began to bounce and American players were stuck in Venezuela due to the financial problems. The Major Leaguers who were swept up in the new league and were burned included Johnny Mize (who managed one club), Enos Slaughter and Stu Miller. The Tokyo Dragons trained in Florida and won seven of 11 games in Caracas before the collapse in May 1969.

The Global League eventually was purchased by the Baptist Foundation, which apparently was part of a complicated scheme to defraud investors. Dilbeck later pleaded guilty to false tax filings.

Glove Oil

"My first glove … was once soaked in linseed oil, because in the first stages of my growing addiction I confused linseed with neat's-foot oil, the proper glove preservative.

"My rather academic parents thought linseed sounded foolish enough to be correct, so into the oil bath went the new glove. The linseeded glove quickly dried up, cracked like a stoned windshield, and literally flaked away." — Thomas Boswell in *How Life Imitates the World Series* (1982).

"It's a secular country, so we forget: baseball contains primeval images, and we return to the game because of them, not because we are athletes. We go back to the memory of ourselves…. The smell from within the pocket of an oiled glove is as dizzying as tomato leaves or lemon flowers…" — Richard Grossinger in "The Baseball Junkies" (1977).

"It is worth noting that even with the disappearance of flannel, all the essential elements of baseball — ball, bat, glove, rosin bag and player — are biodegradable. High-speed photos show the bat bending in its arc like a sapling. The glove is kept supple by application of neat's-foot oil, which is rendered from the feet and shinbones of cattle." — Roy Blount, Jr.

Glove oil is used to soften the new leather in baseball gloves. Neat's foot oil has been the base product in most glove oils during most of the 20th century. The oil is a pale yellow oil that comes from cattle hooves. "Neat" is an old English term for cattle and the oil is made by boiling hooves and shinbones. The oil has been used to waterproof and soften leather and as a lubricant for delicate machinery.

Rawlings has sold its Glovolium neat's foot oil product since 1915. The product averages annual sales of approximately 75,000 four-ounce bottles.

In recent years a company called Accupack has supplied bat manufacturer Hillerich & Bradsby with a glove oil that it marketed under the name "Louisville Slugger Glove Softener." Regent Sports also has a baseball glove conditioner that contains some neat's foot oil.

Gloves

"He wore a glove for one reason: it was a league custom. The glove would last him a minimum of six

First baseman Betty Whiting of the All-American Girls Professional Baseball League displays good form at first base while wearing dark glasses during a game.

years because it rarely made contact with the ball." — Fresco Thompson on Babe Herman.

"It had a marvelous snap to it when a ball hit the pocket, but the pleasure diminished considerably when the padding began migrating to the outer edge of the glove. The snap then correlated so directly with pain that I found I couldn't hear anybody field a hot one without emitting a small Pavlovian wince." — Paul Dickson in *The Dickson Baseball Dictionary* (1989) on the mitt he purchased at age 47 to accommodate his son's desire to play catch.

"Garvey is the only first baseman who washes his glove." — Comedian Don Rickles on the squeaky-clean image of Steve Garvey (but see also *Sex*).

"It is better to have gloved and lost than never to have gloved at all." — Jokester and juggler Bob Nickerson.

Early Gloves.

"The first glove I ever saw on the hand of a ball player in a game was worn by Charles C. Waite in Boston in 1875. He had come from New Haven and was playing at first base. The glove worn by him was of flesh color, with a large, round opening in the back. Now, I had for a good while felt the need of some sort of hand protection for myself. In those days clubs did not carry an extra carload of pitchers, as now. For several years I had pitched in every game … and had developed severe bruises on the inside of my left hand. For every ball pitched it had to be returned, every swift one coming my way from infielders, outfielders or hot from the bat must be caught or stopped, some idea may be gained of the punishment received." — Albert Spalding.

Gloves were unknown until the 1860s. Catchers reportedly were the first to begin using gloves because of the wear and tear on their hands (see **Catcher's Mitts**). One 19th century newspaper reported that the first catcher's glove was worn in 1860 by a Mr. Delaverage of the Troy Victory club. The player wore them on both hands. In 1869 Cincinnati catcher Doug Allison wore buckskin mittens to protect bruised hands. Frank Flint used a thin leather glove filled with raw beefsteak.

As noted by Albert Spalding above, Charles Waite used a flesh-colored glove in 1875 at first base for New Haven, and he took abuse from other players for using it. He wore gloves on both hands and cut the fingers out of the right glove to allow easier throwing. This type of hand glove cost $2.50 in the 19th century. In 1877 Spalding began wearing a black glove when he moved from pitcher to first base.

After suffering a number of broken fingers, shortstop Arthur Irwin developed the first infielder's glove while playing for Providence in 1883. He used a buckskin driving glove several sizes too large. The glove style was adopted by shortstop John Montgomery Ward and the glove became widely used. Irwin also invented a form of football scoreboard (and later committed suicide).

Pitchers were the last position players to regularly wear gloves. In 1893 Nig Cuppy of the Cleveland Spiders became the first Major League pitcher to wear a glove.

No Glove. The last non-pitcher who never used a glove was Jeremiah Denny, a third baseman for Louisville who retired in 1894. He made 609 errors in 13 seasons.

Early 20th Century. By the early 20th century bigger and better gloves, along with rule changes such as counting foul balls as strikes before the third strike, were contributing to lower scoring games. These changes helped force the move to the lively ball by 1910 to spur more run production.

Manufacturers.

"Send Twelve Bill Doak Gloves Six Short Finger Stop Six Long Finger." — Ty Cobb's telegrammed request to Rawlings for more gloves.

Catcher Gus Triandos, who used the infamous "trash can lid" mitt to snag Hoyt Wilhelm's knuckleballs.

The Spalding glove was the most widely used glove in the 19th century. Draper & Maynard (D & M) also manufactured an early glove that was a standard for years. Rawlings introduced the "Sure Catch" in 1912, but the glove was still missing a key ingredient that was introduced a short time later.

Bill Doak was a spitball pitcher with the Cardinals from 1913 through 1924. Near the end of World War I, as a result of his questions to Rawlings, the company created a glove with a pocket and webbed thumb and finger, known thereafter as the "Doak Model." Rawlings introduced the revolutionary new glove in 1919 and the company paid Doak royalties until 1954 when the glove was phased out.

Harry "Bud" Latina, later known as "Doc," started at Rawlings in 1922 and stayed for 40 years. He obtained at least 30 glove patents while working with Rawlings. Among them were the Deep Well Pocket (1940), Trapper (1940), U Crotch (1941), Snugger Wrist Adjustment (1942), Palm Crotch Extension (1946), Laced Pocket Z (1946), Playmaker three-finger glove (1947), Web Controller (1949), Web (1950), Trap-Eze (1959), Edge-U-Cated Heel (1959) and Dual Step-Down Palm (1961). Latina died at age 84 in 1980. His son Rollie took over the glove operation in 1961 and stayed until 1984.

In 1956 Rawlings conducted a survey and learned that 83% of Major Leaguers used its gloves. By the late 1980s Rawlings was turning out about 100 gloves per day. In 1990 Rawlings and Nokona were the only two companies making gloves in the United States. The Rawlings plant was located in Ava, Missouri, producing 51 different glove styles and reportedly supplying 55% of all Major Leaguers. Other sources reported that by 1993 there were almost no Major League players using American-made gloves. Of the 3.7 million softball and baseball gloves sold in the U.S. in 1993, about 98 percent were made overseas, most of them in the Far East. Other manufacturers for the American market were Wilson, Louisville Slugger, Spalding, SSK, Mizuno, Cooper and Regent.

In Nocona, Texas, the Storey family has been making gloves since 1932. Nokona initially marketed its gloves in the 1940s and 1950s through the Fort Worth Cats of the Texas League. That Dodger farm team had a number of future Major Leaguers who used the glove, including future manager Dick Williams and shortstop Chico Carrasquel. Legend has it that Nolan Ryan's first glove was a 1953 Nokona model bought at a hardware store in Alvin, Texas.

In the 1930s Moe Berg was traveling in Japan when he advised Japanese manufacturer Mizuno on glove design and construction. Mizuno once developed a glove with a radio transmitter so that the pitcher and catcher could give signs without using their hands.

Cost. Nineteenth century gloves cost between $1.50 and $2.50. In the 1940s glove prices ranged from 50 cents to $12.00 for standard gloves. In the 1950s a good glove cost $15 and a decent off-the-rack glove cost $4.50. Today Major League–quality gloves costs around $150–$200. One of the most expensive gloves is a catcher's mitt put out by Rawlings, priced in the mid-$250s.

Construction. Modern gloves are made from 20 pieces of leather tied together with approximately 154 stitches. Each cow yields two hides, one from each side. Each hide yields up to four gloves. The best hides are saved for baseball gloves, and these usually come from summer hides (late May to early November), that are not as tough as weathered winter hides. The "heart" of the hide is best, at the top back of the cow, and is used for the pocket and fingers.

Gloves are sewn inside out and a sticky wax is spread inside and on the outside layer of the pocket before turning it right side out. Webbing is laced into the glove, padding is put in the heel and the heel is then sewn up. The glove is pounded and then inspected. It takes approximately six weeks for the glove to be created from the time the cow is slaughtered. Some newer gloves have nylon backs for better air circulation to keep the hand cooler.

Endorsement. Star players might receive $50,000 to $100,000 to use a particular glove, but most players receive far less or nothing except free gloves.

When Michael Jordan began playing professional baseball, Wilson came out with the Michael Jordan autograph glove.

Padding. There was little or no padding in non-catchers' gloves until 1908. Even then, infielders often cut the palms out of gloves to get a better feel for the ball. For extra padding, players sometimes improvised with raw meat or feathers. In the 1950s infielder Willie Miranda used a tongue depressor and socks as padding. Henry Fabian of New Orleans in the 19th century used two gloves and put a thin sheet of lead between them.

Origins. In 1872 catcher Deacon White used a buckskin glove and put padding in it. He claimed to be the first to use a catcher's mitt, but catchers Nat Hicks and Doug Allison claim that they were the first to do it in 1869 and 1870. William "Gunner" McGunnigle, who later pitched for Buffalo and Worcester, is credited by some with first using a catcher's mitt in 1875.

In the 1880s the puff pillow mitt appeared, which was the basic catcher's mitt used well into the 20th century. Either Joe Gunson of the Western League Kansas City Blues or Harry Decker of the National League Washington Statesmen invented it, but Buck Ewing popularized it. Decker's version was known as the "Decker Safety Catching Mitt." Gunson had suffered a series of split fingers and a swollen hand. He took a thin glove that others were using and stitched together the fingers. He added wool padding and placed it around the fingers and sewed it all together with buck-skin. He then stiffened it with paint can wire. This construction was the basis for the patent obtained in 1891 by Decker for Reach Sporting Goods.

Joe Gunson later wrote a letter in which he reported that there were two games scheduled on Decoration Day 1888 (Memorial Day). The other catcher was injured and Gunson had a crippled finger on his left hand, so he did the following to protect himself: "I stitched together the fingers of my left-hand glove, thus practically a 'mitt'; then I caught both games. It worked so well that I got to work, took an old paint-pot wire handle, the old flannel belts from our castoff jackets, rolled the cloth around the ends of the finger, and padded the thumb. Then I put sheepskins with the wool on it in the palm and covered it with buckskin, thus completing the mitt, and the suffering and punishment we endured at the then 50 foot distance was all over."

In 1891 catchers were officially allowed to wear padded mitts. Players often used additional padding in their mitts, sometimes called "falsies."

Finger Outside. Yogi Berra is credited with first putting the index finger outside his mitt. He did so because of a sore digit.

New Design Technique. In the 1950s journeyman catcher Gus Niarhos cut an opening in the pocket of his catcher's mitt to create a hinged joint. This allowed him to close the mitt around the ball with one hand. Under the puff pillow design in use for decades, the catcher had to cover the mitt and ball with his throwing hand to keep it in his mitt.

Elston Howard of the Yankees and Randy Hundley of the Cubs were the first prominent catchers to wear hinged gloves, although many sources also credit Yogi Berra with using the style. The hinged design led to a dramatic change in catching. A catcher no longer had to use both hands to catch a pitched ball, allowing him to protect his throwing hand. He could place it behind his back during a pitch to shield it from pitches and foul balls. The practice is now standard when there are no runners on base.

Defense. Sam Trott of the 1890s Washington Senators would throw away his unwieldy catcher's mitt to take throws from the outfield. In 1969 catcher Clay Dalrymple kept a fielder's glove in his pocket while using a catcher's mitt behind the plate. He would use the fielder's glove on fielding plays at home. The league office upheld the umpire's ruling disallowing the extra glove on the field.

Glove Size.

"They're playing infield with barn doors." — Remark made after 1880s infielder Lave Cross wore a larger catcher's mitt while playing third base. This type of abuse in part led to size restrictions on gloves in 1895. The rule required gloves to be 10 ounces or lighter and have no more than a 14-inch circumference at the palm. The current requirements for glove size are set forth in Rule 1.13. The rules by position:

Fielders/Pitchers:

"Has anyone ever seen Luis Polonia's glove over the years? From 1988–1991 the little flychaser used a glove that measured almost 17 inches. It looked more like a jai-lai cesta than a fielder's glove and far exceeded the 12-inch limit from the tip to heel. It took awhile, but to give credit where credit is due, the American League subsequently outlawed Polonia's illegal piece of leather." — Rich Marazzi.

Gloves may be no longer than 12 inches from heel to tip and no more than 7¾ inches wide. The webbing cannot be more than 4½ inches wide at the top. Gloves are usually about 9¼ inches from the heel to the tip. The rule limiting length was not regularly enforced until 1990.

Outfield gloves are usually the largest, although some pitchers like a large glove because it hides their choice of pitches. Infielders prefer smaller gloves to get the ball out faster. Outfielder Luis Polonia of the Yankees and Angels had probably the largest glove in recent years. Joe Morgan of the 1970s Reds probably had the smallest of the era. The rules for pitchers' gloves are the same as fielders' gloves, except that there are restrictions on color (no white or gray).

Pitcher Joe Orrell wore an oversized glove briefly while with the Tigers that was 14½ inches by 12¼ inches. He brought it to the Reds' training camp in 1939 to hide pitches, but it was disallowed.

First Basemen: Gloves may be no more than 12 inches long or eight inches across the palm. The web cannot be more than five inches high or four inches wide.

Hank Greenberg's first baseman's glove was once disallowed because it was too big: it had a four inch webbing at the top and was more than eight inches across at the palm. In the 1930s a rule was passed as a direct result of Greenberg's glove. It limited the length to 12 inches and the width to eight inches across at the palm.

Catchers:

"A giant trash can lid."— Description of the mitt worn by catcher Gus Triandos to catch Hoyt Wilhelm's elusive knuckleball.

A catcher's mitt may be no more than 38 inches in circumference or 15½ inches from top to bottom. The webbing can be no more than seven inches across the top or six inches to the base of the thumb. The size of a catcher's mitt was restricted after Triandos employed a huge mitt to catch Wilhelm's knuckleball. The Triandos mitt was 45 inches in circumference and 15½ inches from top to bottom. It was first used on May 27, 1960.

Rule. If a fielder makes a putout while using an illegal glove, and the manager of the other team objects, the out stands and the player must remove his glove from the game.

Babe Ruth. Ruth wore a white glove while with the Red Sox and was a left-handed catcher wearing a right-handed catcher's mitt while at St. Mary's School as a teenager.

Strap. In 1991 a company known as World of Truth Enterprises (WOTE Inc.) began the manufacture and distribution of a glove featuring a wrist strap to hold it in place on the hand.

Breaking In.

"Her skin is as tender as DiMaggio's glove."— Line from the song "Bloody Mary," from the 1949 musical, *South Pacific.*

Many ways of breaking in a new glove have been used over the years. Neat's Foot **Glove Oil** traditionally has been used to oil gloves. Another popular method is to soak the glove in water and pound it with a bat. Robin Yount threw his gloves into a training room whirlpool. Mike Gallego ran hot water over his glove and then put it in the dryer on the fluff cycle. Other players have used shaving cream, petroleum jelly, shoe polish, baby oil, olive oil, mink oil, saddle soap, tobacco juice, bubble gum juice, skin lotion and coffee (Eddie Brinkman's substance of choice).

Some teams have had designated "breaker-inners." Willie Stargell did it for the Pirates and Tim Ireland did it for the Padres. The accepted theory is that gloves should be broken in "horizontally" for wide target and vertically for longer reach.

Repair.

"They should have called a welder."— Broadcaster Richie Ashburn after poor-fielding Dave Kingman called for an equipment man to repair his glove.

Many glove manufacturers have roving "glove doctors" who make the rounds during spring training to repair and distribute gloves to Major Leaguer players.

Pitcher and glove repairman Bob Patterson of the late 1980s Pirates was known as The Glove Doctor, the True Value Man, and Emmett, after the fix-it man on "The Andy Griffith Show."

Color. In 2003 Ruben Sierra of the Yankees commissioned Mizuno to make him a green-white-and-blue glove. Given his rare number of appearances in the field, it probably didn't get much use.

Orange Strip. Dodger general manager Al Campanis obtained a patent on the fluorescent orange strip that is sometimes painted on the perimeter of a catcher's mitt for practice. This was the Rawlings "Campanis Target Mitt," Patent No. 3,898,696.

Illegal Patch. When Roger Clemens went to the mound in late May 2003 to try to win his 300th game against the Red Sox, he wore a special glove bearing a commemorative patch. Red Sox manager Grady Little complained to plate umpire Bill Miller, who went to the mound with crew chief Joe West and forced Clemens to replace the glove.

Sharing. In July 1995 Mark Grace of the Cubs used Expo first baseman David Segui's glove. Grace's equipment had not arrived from the All-Star Game and the Cubs did not have another left-handed mitt (see also **Kangaroo Court**).

Under the Table. Pete Rose's gofer, Tommy Gioiosa, said that Rose had him fly to San Francisco to meet a representative of Mizuno for an endorsement deal, and Gioiosa returned with a bag containing $50,000 in "stew," Rose's term for cash.

Nicknames. Some players have named their gloves. George Scott of the Red Sox won eight Gold Gloves with "Black Beauty." Gold Glove third baseman Aurelio Rodriguez wore the "Black Hand." Mel Hall had "Lucille" and Ted Simmons "The Big Trapper."

Assessing Blame.

"It's your fault, *your* damn fault!"— Pitcher Wes Ferrell leaving the mound and yelling at his glove in disgust after a pitching failure. He then ripped the glove in half and tossed it on the ground.

Twins shortstop Zoilo Versalles supposedly threw away his glove whenever he made an error (often reaching 30 errors in a season in the 1960s). As a result, his sponsoring company stopped supplying him with free gloves.

Interview.

"I'm beginning to see Brooks [Robinson] in my sleep. If I dropped a paper plate, he'd pick it up on one hop and throw me out at first."— Sparky Anderson.

During the 1970 World Series in which third baseman Brooks Robinson almost single-handedly beat the Reds defensively, a reporter took the unusual step of interviewing Robinson's glove.

Ball Stuck in Glove. On September 3, 1986, pitcher Terry Mulholland of the Giants fielded a hard ground ball hit by Mets first baseman Keith Hernandez. The ball stuck in Mulholland's Wilson A2000 glove, so he threw the entire package to first baseman Bob Brenley, who made the putout. Umpire Ed Montague called out Hernandez and Brenley dug out the ball and threw it around the infield as is customary after an out. Brenley's only regret: "I should have thrown the glove around [the infield]."

Quirks. Chicago Cubs outfielder Billy Williams threw his glove into the crowd after the last game of each season. Orioles utility infielder Rene Gonzales carried his glove wherever he went. He always carried it on airline flights in a Wonder Bread bag.

Innovation. Easton Sporting Goods came out with an oil-injected catcher's mitt, which gives the glove a soft feel and added ball-gripping ability. Easton and Wilson came out with miniature pumps for their gloves to give a surer fit on the hand.

Leaving Gloves on the Field. Leaving gloves on the field was outlawed after the 1953 season in Rule 3.14 (originally 3.16), although *The Sporting News* campaigned against the practice as early as the 1920s. There is no evidence that gloves on the field interfered with any important games over the years. Nevertheless, in a 1984 *Sports Illustrated* article, former Yankees manager Ralph

Houk described several instances in which gloves left on the field interfered with play.

Historically, the shortstop and second baseman threw their gloves onto the grass just behind the infield dirt. The third and first basemen dropped theirs into foul territory near their bags. The outfielders dumped there gloves wherever convenient on the grass. The pitcher and catcher placed their gloves on the top step of the dugout.

Players also played practical jokes on the glove owners, stuffing them with rocks, dirt, mice, frogs, lizards and snakes. Eddie Stanky, tabbed as one of the worst offenders, once hid Bill Rigney's glove under second base.

Pranks were played as a result of this long-time practice. A dead rat was put into Yankee Phil Rizzuto's glove, as he was deathly afraid of rodents. Johnny Pesky, a Hearts card player, found the deadly queen of spades in his glove.

Complimentary Gloves. Ballplayers in the high minors often receive two free gloves per season; generally four if they are in the Major Leagues. Premier shortstop Ozzie Smith received a new glove every six weeks (a 1959 TrapEze six-fingered model) so that it remained hard and stiff.

Throwing at Ball. Throwing a glove at a fair ball has always been illegal and results in an automatic triple. On July 27, 1947, Red Sox first baseman Jake Jones was credited with a triple after pitcher Fred Sanford threw his glove at the ball (see also *Foul Balls*).

Memorabilia Sales. See *Memorabilia—Gloves*.

Book. William Curran, *Mitts* (1985); Noah Liberman, *Glove Affairs: The Romance, History and Tradition of the Baseball Glove* (2003).

Gold Glove Award (1957–)

"You won't make any errors. You don't get to a ball until it stops rolling."—Joe Lovitto after slow-footed Jeff Burroughs announced his goal of winning a Gold Glove.

"The winner of the Idiotic Clause Award goes to [Milwaukee] Brewer DH Brian Harper, who gets $50,000 for [winning] a Gold Glove. For Brewer General Manager Sal Bando, giving in to that clause must have been like agreeing to not eat seal blubber for Lent."—Peter Gammons of the *Boston Globe*.

Origins. Rawlings Sporting Goods and *The Sporting News* inaugurated the Gold Glove Award in 1957. An award was presented to the best defensive player in the Major Leagues at each position. After the first season a Gold Glove was presented to players at each position in each league.

The Award. The award is a gold-finished leather glove or mitt consistent with the winner's position, mounted on a walnut stand and centered between a pair of gold, leather baseballs. It is approximately 17 inches high and 17 inches wide. Repeat winners receive a gold crest on their trophy.

Voting. When the award was first created the voters included the media, players and managers. It was modified later to include only coaches and managers. Winners are now selected based on a ballot distributed to every Major League manager and coach, who can vote for only one player at each position (three outfielders). They cannot vote for anyone on their own team and can vote only within their own league.

Gloves. Winners who use Rawlings gloves receive gloves the following year with the "Rawlings" name stamped in gold rather than the traditional red.

Hall of Fame.

"The only way I'm going to get a Gold Glove is with a can of spray paint."—Reggie Jackson.

In 1991 Rawlings established its Gold Glove Hall of Fame for Lifetime Achievement for Fielding Excellence. The first inductees were Brooks Robinson and Jim Kaat. The 1992 inductees were outfielders Willie Mays and Roberto Clemente. In 1993 the inductees were Johnny Bench, Reggie Jackson (!) and Curt Flood. Infielder Phil Rizzuto was the 1994 winner.

Rawlings acknowledged that Jackson's award was not for his fielding prowess, but rather for his long service to the company. More gloves were sold with his name on them than any other Major League player; though Ken Griffey, Jr., later surpassed him. Rawlings also is careful to call the award the "*Rawlings* Gold Glove Award" and has trademarked the name.

Switching Positions. Ryne Sandberg is the only man to win a Gold Glove Award the year after switching positions, from third base to second base.

Outfield Positions. Outfielders may be chosen from any of the three positions, which does a disservice to the specialties of each field. Many have advocated choosing an outfielder from each position. Willie Mays and and Roberto Clemente each won 12 straight Awards. Al Kaline and Ken Griffey each won 10 straight.

Catchers. Reds catcher Johnny Bench won 10 straight awards from 1968 through 1977. Rangers catcher Ivan Rodriguez also won 10 straight, between 1992 and 2001.

Domination. The Gold Glove Awards tend to be dominated by a few players. Once a player is established as the best at his position, he wins the award until his career starts to decline. For example, pitcher Jim Kaat won 14 straight awards (among his 16), Bob Gibson won nine straight, and pitcher Bobby Shantz won the first award and seven more after that for four different teams. Orioles third baseman Brooks Robinson won 16 straight awards from 1960 through 1975. First baseman Keith Hernandez won 11 consecutive awards from 1978 through 1988. Second baseman Robbie Alomar won 10 straight through 2001. Shortstop Ozzie Smith won 13 straight from 1980 through 1992. Pitcher Greg Maddux won 13 straight before the streak ended in 2003.

In 1968 the entire Reds infield won Gold Gloves, and the 1970s Reds won 25 Gold Gloves, including 10 straight by catcher Johnny Bench. From 1974 through 1977 Reds middle infielders Joe Morgan and Dave Concepcion won all Gold Glove Awards for their positions, as did outfielder Cesar Geronimo and Bench.

Golf

"Players who stand flat footed and swing with their arms are golfers, not hitters."—Rogers Hornsby.

"It took me seventeen years to get 3,000 hits in baseball. I did it in one afternoon on the golf course."—Henry Aaron.

"Show me a man who cheats at golf, and I'll show you a winner."—Casey Stengel, according to USC baseball coach Rod Dedeaux, who worked out with Stengel's Toledo Mudhens in the 1930s.

"I told them not to call me between tee times. I have one stipulation. I will not work for a living."—Johnny Bench in early 1997, acknowledging that his hiring as a "special consultant" to the Reds was more of a public relations move by the club.

"You can bring a picnic lunch to the tournament golf course, watch the best in the world and not spend a small fortune on food and drink. Try that at one of the taxpayer funded baseball or football stadiums. If you bring a soft drink into a ballpark, they'll give you two options — get rid of it or leave." — One of many reasons why golf is considered (by some) better than baseball or football.

"He was a high ball hitter." — Casey Stengel on golf legend Sam Snead, who once took batting practice with the Yankees. Standing on home plate, Snead hit a golf ball over the center field wall in Yankee Stadium. At Wrigley Field on April 17, 1951, using a two-iron, Snead hit a golf ball over the scoreboard in center field, becoming the only person ever to hit a ball of any kind over the scoreboard. No batted ball has ever hit the center field scoreboard, but two baseballs narrowly missed it. One was hit by Bill Nicholson of the Cubs for a homer onto Sheffield Avenue (right-center) in 1948, and the other was hit by Roberto Clemente of the Pirates onto Waveland Avenue (left-center) in 1959.

"And how about golf, where the prima-donna golf champion, getting ready to putt or drive, can't stand to have a pin drop or a bird fly over. The fan yells, 'Hit it out, will you, ya bum! You're way behind,' Women faint all over the course. The golfer has to be treated for shock. And the fan is sent to the psychiatric ward." — "The Old Timer" in W.R. Burnett's *The Roar of the Crowd* (1964).

"When I hit a ball, I want someone else to go chase it." — Rogers Hornsby on his preference for baseball over golf.

"Baseball players ought to try playing golf for a living. No guarantees, all expenses paid — by yourself. I'd like to hear them complain then." — Pro golfer Al Geiberger.

"There is nothing to hurt you in golf unless lightning strikes or somebody throws a club. And, gee, there's that golf ball, sitting right there for you to hit, and a flat-faced club to hit it with." — Ted Williams in *The Science of Hitting* (1968).

"Al Oliver is a great player but not as great as he thinks he is. In golf terms, he talks a seventy-two and shoots a seventy-six." — Oliver's teammate Richie Hebner.

"Yeah, but you don't have to go into the stands and play your foul balls." — Arnold Palmer to Ted Williams, on the relative difficulty of their two professions.

"Tick Teed and Harvey Shanks."

Ken Harrelson.

"In baseball you hit a home run over the right field fence, the left field fence, the center field fence. Nobody cares. In golf, everything has got to be right over second base." — Red Sox outfielder Ken "Hawk" Harrelson, who unsuccessfully attempted a professional golf career while still playing baseball. In 1969 the Red Sox found him expendable when Tony Conigliaro returned from his *Beanball* incident. Harrelson's feelings were hurt when he was traded to the Indians and he refused to report. Commissioner Bowie Kuhn intervened and Harrelson relented and finished out the season. After 17 games with the Indians in 1970, Harrelson retired to concentrate on golf. After aborting his professional golf career, he returned for 52 games with the Indians in 1971 and then retired at age 29. See also Ken Harrelson with Al Hirshberg, *Hawk* (1969).

Road Trips.

"That's what's the trouble with baseball. That's why pitchers can't work more than once a week. That's why we have to have special shift hitters for batters who can't hit left-handers. That's why the game is softening up." — Ed Barrow, Yankees general manager, in 1926, after two teams arrived at a spring training game with 40 sets of golf clubs.

Golf became a popular pastime among players in the 1920s and many teams had to crack down and prohibit players from bringing their golf clubs on road trips.

George Wright. One of the prominent names of 19th century baseball, George Wright abandoned baseball in 1904 to concentrate

on golf. He was "too high class" for baseball and laid out the first golf course in Boston, one of the first in the United States.

Jigger Statz. Statz played in two L.A. Open golf tournaments in the 1920s and 1930s. He played Major League Baseball from 1919 through 1928.

Sammy Byrd. Byrd, known affectionately as Babe Ruth's Caddy because he was a late-inning defensive replacement for Ruth, won two PGA tour events in 1945 after playing in professional golf events as early as 1923.

Lou Gehrig. Grantland Rice reported that Lou Gehrig would not play golf because he believed it would compromise his baseball swing. One time he witnessed Gehrig hit a long iron — his only shot of the day — smoothly over 200 yards.

Ralph Terry. Pitcher Ralph Terry joined the Seniors Golf Tour in the 1980s and had a fair amount of success.

George Brett. Brett founded the Pro Athletes Golf League, whose tournaments were televised by ESPN beginning in 1994. With six tournaments a year, the league featured former and current players from all major sports. Fred Lynn was among those who played in the league, as did the very accomplished Mike Schmidt.

Ryne Sandberg. After Sandberg's stunning early retirement announcement in June 1994, his first public appearance was as the caddie for golfer Mark Calcavecchia at the Western Open. Sandberg was a six-handicap golfer at the time and had always wanted to caddie on the pro tour.

Master Stroke. In the mid–1990s the Pirates' Class A team in Augusta, Georgia (site of the Masters) had as its nickname "The Green Jackets."

Phenom. In 1939, 12-year-old baseball fanatic and future professional golfer Bob Rosburg beat Ty Cobb in the club championship at The Olympic Club in San Francisco. The humiliated Cobb stormed out of the clubhouse and vowed never to return. Before playing golf professionally, Rosburg played baseball at Stanford and pitched in a semipro league after graduating in 1948. He became one of the few touring pros to use a baseball grip on his golf clubs. When Rosburg was 11, Cobb and Babe Ruth invited him to play the last two holes of a round with them. Ruth played to a six handicap, better than Cobb.

Phil Mickelson.

"He'll probably be effective because those guys haven't seen a 68-mph fastball since Little League." — Pro golfer Paul Azinger.

In August 2003 Michelson threw batting practice to the Toledo Mud Hens in an effort to sign a contract with the Tigers' Class AAA affiliate. Mickelson, who golfs left-handed and pitches right-handed, said "I know I don't have the talent the players here do, but this is a lifetime dream." The club didn't offer him anything after his 70 pitch workout, though no one hit a home run off him. He threw to 18 batters and did not use a protective screen. His fastball topped out at 68 mph, forcing him to use an array of off-speed pitches. The Mudhens wanted to sign him to a one-game deal to pitch in a cameo role, but the Tigers front office vetoed the idea. The workout must have cleared Mickelson's mind, as he won his first Major at The Masters in April 2004.

Olympic Games. The International Olympic Committee voted in 2002 to drop baseball from the Olympics and replace it with golf. The reason given was that the competition does not draw the best players, since Major League Baseball does not release their players to play.

Nice shot. On April 20, 2002, USC first baseman Bill Peavey homered for the second time in a game against the Washington State Cougars. The ball cleared the fence and landed on the university's adjacent nine-hole golf course. The equipment manager went to retrieve the ball and found it in the center hole of the practice green.

Native Americans. On August 13, 2002, the Twins staged Native American Heritage Day. Professional golfer Notah Begay, a Navajo, chipped the opening (baseball) pitch.

Dangerous Weapon. In 2003, Montreal Expos pitcher Livan Hernandez had charges reduced to a misdemeanor and community service after swinging golf clubs at a 65-year-old man.

Long Driver. In 2003 Mark McGwire participated in the ADT Skills Challenge in Florida and drove a golf ball 319 yards to outdistance pros Paul Azinger, Nick Faldo, Colin Montgomerie and Greg Norman.

First Pitch. In August 2004, Ryder Cup captain and golfer Hal Sutton chipped the opening pitch using a pitching wedge to hit a baseball from the mound to the catcher.

Lefty Gomez (1908–1989)

Hall of Fame (VC) 1972

"The image in [Yankee general manager Ed] Barrow's mind was that Gomez, the strikeout artist, was a husky young fellow with plenty of power. It was a shock and surprise for Barrow when he first set eyes on his 50 grand investment. Instead of the broad-shouldered, narrow-hipped westerner, he met a tall, skinny kid with big hands and shoe box feet. The boy had no more meat on him than a fence post. Barrow doubted that he could lift a baseball, much less heave one to the catcher." — Jimmy Powers in *Baseball Personalities* (1949).

Gomez won 189 games for the Yankees between 1930 and 1942, winning over 20 games four times.

Before starring with the Yankees in the 1930s, Vernon Louis Gomez was raised in California and pitched for Salt Lake City in 1928 and San Francisco in 1929. The Yankees bought him for $35,000 and he pitched part of the 1929 season in New York. In 1931, his first full Major League season, he won 21 games for the Yankees. He won 24 in 1932 and then peaked with a 26–5 record, a 2.33 ERA and six shutouts in 1934. His blazing fastball carried him to one more season of more than 20 wins in 1937 before he began to fade.

The Yankees sold Gomez to the Braves after the 1942 season, but he was released by the club without pitching and he signed with the Senators for one more appearance. He pitched briefly in 1946 and 1947 when he managed Binghamton of the Eastern League. He eventually worked for Wilson Sporting Goods as a goodwill ambassador.

The colorful and humorous pitcher led the league in strikeouts three times and his 189 lifetime wins put him near the top of Yankee pitchers all-time. He won six World Series games and never lost in seven starts.

Goose Goslin (1900–1971)

Hall of Fame (VC) 1968

"Heck, let's face it, I was just a big old country boy having the time of his life. It was all a lark to me, just a joy ride. Never feared a thing, never got nervous, just a big country kid from south Jersey, too dumb to know better. In those days I'd go out and fight a bull without a sword and never know the difference. Why, I never even realized it was supposed to be big doings. It was just a game, that's all it was. They didn't have to pay me. I'd have paid them to let me play. Listen, the truth is it was *more* than fun. It was heaven." — Goslin.

Goslin played in the outfield for 18 seasons beginning in 1921, batting .316 primarily for the Senators.

A 1920s star outfielder for the Senators, Leon Allen Goslin began his professional career of good hitting and poor fielding in the Sally League in 1920 and dominated that league in 1921. He came up to the Senators at age 20 in late 1921 for 14 games. He became a regular in the outfield in 1922, batting over .300 for the first of seven consecutive seasons. He led the league with a .379 average in 1928 and regularly had around 200 hits.

Goslin's best season for the Senators was 1924, when he led the league with 129 RBIs and hit .344. He also batted .344 in the 1924 World Series and returned to hit .308 in the Series the following season.

In 1930 the Senators traded him to the Browns, for whom he hit .326 that partial season and played solidly through 1932. He went back to the Senators for the 1933 season before moving to the Tigers from 1934 through 1937. He returned to the Senators for 38 games in 1938, finishing 18 seasons with a .316 average and 2,735 hits. After completing his Major League career, he played in the minor leagues through 1940 and managed from 1939 through 1941. He retired to run a boating concession in New Jersey.

Gossip

"[I read the gossip columns] even before the sports section. To make sure I'm not in them." — Derek Jeter.

Curt Gowdy (1919–)

Hall of Fame (Frick Award) 1984

"A typical week in Curt Gowdy's life is like a chapter in Jules Verne's *Around the World in 80 Days*." — Writer Jerry Lister alluding to Gowdy's vagabond life that included baseball games and miscellaneous locales on his show "The American Sportsman."

"As a kid I never wanted to be Joe Namath or Jerry West or even Jim Murray. All I wanted to be was Curt Gowdy, sports announcer and god." — Rick Reilly.

Gowdy was the primary broadcaster for the Red Sox and later NBC's "Game of the Week" between 1951 and 1975.

Curt Gowdy received his break when he was discovered broadcasting baseball games for the Oklahoma City Indians of the Texas League. He began his Major League broadcasting career as Mel Allen's assistant with the Yankees in 1949–1950. He had a year left on his Yankee contract when owner Dan Topping released him to work as the number one broadcaster for the Red Sox in 1951. He remained in Boston until moving to NBC in March 1966. From 1966 through 1975, Gowdy broadcast NBC's "Game of the Week." He also called every World Series and All-Star Game in that stretch and virtually every regular season network game. He broadcast 12 World Series and 15 All-Star Games. His total of 78 World Series games wasn't passed until Tim McCarver broadcast No. 79 during the 2003 World Series.

Gowdy also broadcast on all three major networks at the time for the AFL, NFL, Rose Bowls, Super Bowls, Olympics and NCAA basketball Final Fours.

Gowdy was three times voted Sportscaster of the Year and in 1970 became the first sportscaster to receive the George Peabody Award for excellence in broadcasting. In 1984 he received the Ford Frick Award from the Hall of Fame for excellence in broadcasting.

Book. Curt Gowdy, *Seasons to Remember: The Way It was in American Sports (1945–1960)* (1993).

Grand Slams

"As I remember it, the bases were loaded." — Garry Maddox's expansive comment to reporters after hitting a grand slam.

"I've reached the epitome of grand slamness." — Mariners pitcher Mike Schooler, who tied the Major League record in 1992 for most grand slams given up in a season, with four.

"Hitting your first grand slam is a thrill. I'll always remember this. (Reminded that he had hit a grand slam two years earlier) You're right, I guess I forgot about that one." — Steve Balboni, after hitting a grand slam.

Major League First. The first grand slam in the National League was by first baseman Roger Connor while playing for Troy in Albany. Connor was considered one of the first great power hitters in the league.

Pinch Hit. The first pinch hit grand slam was on September 24, 1916, by Marty Kavanaugh as the Indians defeated the Red Sox 5–3. The ball rolled down the third base line and through an opening in the left field fence. It was his only home run of the year.

Pinch Hit/Walk Off/Same Game. On May 28, 2004, in a game between the Cubs and Pirates, in the 7th inning Michael Barrett of the Cubs hit a pinch-hit grand slam. In the bottom of the 9th, Rob Mackowiak hit a walk-off grand slam to give the Pirates a 9–5 win. That was the first game of a doubleheader. In the nightcap, Mackowiak hit a two-run homer in the bottom of the 9th to send the game into extra innings, and the Pirates won in the 10th. Nice day, especially given that Mackowiak's wife gave birth to a son that same morning, their first child. The first game's excitement was the first time that there was a pinch hit and a walk-off grand slam in the same game.

World Series.

"Fate tried to conceal this lucky boy by naming him Smith, but with that tremendous slap Elmer shoved his commonplace identity up alongside the famous Smiths of history, which include Captain John, the Smith Brothers and the Village Smithy." — Sportswriter Harry Cross.

Elmer Smith hit the first World Series grand slam in 1920 for the Indians and holds the record for most consecutive extra base hits in the regular season (seven), set in 1921.

All-Star Game. In 1983 Fred Lynn hit the only All-Star Game grand slam, off Giants pitcher Atlee Hammaker.

First At-Bat. Pitcher Bill Duggleby is the only Major League player to hit a grand slam in his first at-bat. He did it for the Phillies on April 21, 1898, in the 2nd inning of a game against the New York Giants.

Bobby Bonds of the Giants is the only 20th century player to hit a grand slam as his first Major League hit. Bonds did it on June 25, 1968, in his third at-bat in the 6th inning of a 9–0 Giants victory over the Dodgers in San Francisco.

First Hit. On May 1, 1999, Red Sox rookie Creighton Gubanich hit a grand slam as his first Major League hit, only the fourth player do do so. It was the only home run of his 18-game Major League career.

Two in One Inning/Same Player. On April 23, 1999, Fernando Tatis of the Cardinals became the only player in Major League history to hit two grand slams in one inning. He did it against Chan Ho Park of the Dodgers at Dodger Stadium during an 11-run 3rd inning en route to a 12–5 victory. Tatis had a record eight RBIs during the inning. Park was only the second pitcher ever to give up two grand slams in an inning. The other was Bill Phillips of the Pirates in 1890.

On July 24, 2003, Bobby Abreu of the Phillies had a chance to tie Tatis, when he came up in the 6th inning of a game against the Cubs at Wrigley Field. After hitting a grand slam earlier in the inning, he hit a sacrifice fly to medium center field with the bases loaded.

Two in One Inning/Teammates. On July 18, 1962, in Minnesota, Bob Allison and Harmon Killebrew became the first players to each hit a grand slam in the same inning, for the Twins against the Indians. Their blasts were part of a team-record 11-run 1st inning.

On July 31, 1969, Jimmy Wynn and Dennis Menke hit grand slams for the Astros in the 9th inning against the Mets.

On April 12, 1980, Cecil Cooper and Don Money each hit a grand slam in the 2nd inning of an 18–1 Brewers victory over the Red Sox.

On August 24, 2003, Ramon Hernandez and Miguel Tejada of the A's hit grand slams in a 17–2 rout of the Blue Jays.

Two in One Game/Same Player. Tony Lazzeri of the Yankees was the first player to hit two grand slams in one game, against the Philadelphia A's on May 24, 1936. He also had a triple and drove in 11 runs, an American League record. In Game 2 of the 1936 World Series, Lazerri hit the second grand slam in World Series history.

Jim Gentile of the Orioles hit grand slams in both the 1st and 2nd innings of a game against the Twins on May 9, 1961.

Jim Tabor of the Red Sox accomplished the feat on July 4, 1939.

Rudy York did it for the Red Sox on July 27, 1946, in a 13–6 win over the Browns.

Tigers outfielder Jim Northrup did it in the 5th and 6th innings of a game on June 24, 1968.

Frank Robinson of the Orioles did it in the 5th and 6th innings of a game on June 26, 1970.

Robin Ventura of the White Sox hit two grand slams in a 14–3 win over the Rangers on September 4, 1995.

On August 14, 1998, Orioles catcher Chris Hoiles became the ninth Major Leaguer and first catcher to hit two grand slams in a game, leading the Baltimore Orioles to a 15–3 rout of the Cleveland Indians at Jacobs Field. They were the 7th and 8th grand slams of his career.

Pitcher/Two In a Game. Braves pitcher Tony Cloninger hit two grand slams against the Giants on July 3, 1966, in the 1st and 4th innings off Bob Priddy and Ray Sadecki. Atlanta won 17–3 as Cloninger also had an RBI single to set an RBI record for pitchers, with nine.

On May 24, 2000, Shawn Estes of the Giants hit a grand slam in an 18–0 win against the Expos and then narrowly missed another one.

Three in One Game/Team. There is only one known instance of a team hitting three grand slams in one game. In 1991 the Class AAA Calgary Cannons did it in a 22–7 victory over Tacoma.

All Runs Accounted For. On May 2, 1995, Mo Vaughn and John Valentin of the Red Sox hit grand slams in consecutive innings to defeat the Yankees 8–0. While it was the first time in Major League history that two grand slams accounted for all the scoring in a game, it was the 41st time that two grand slams were hit in a game.

Pinch Hit Grand Slams. Ron Northey hit the last of his three pinch hit grand slams for the Cubs on September 18, 1950.

Willie McCovey and Jim Northrup each hit three pinch hit grand slams during their careers.

On August 4, 1998, Darryl Strawberry hit his second pinch-hit grand slam of the season, tying Mike Ivie and Davey Johnson, who both did it in 1978. In 2004 Ben Broussard hit two pinch grand slams, as well as a third one as a starter.

Two in One Game/Pinch Hitters. On May 26, 1929, Les Bell of the Braves and Pat Crawford of the Giants hit pinch hit grand slams in the same game. It was the only time in Major League history that pinch hitters from different teams hit grand slams in the same game. The Giants won 15–8 after a nine-run 6th inning broke a 2–2 tie.

Pinch Hit/Both Leagues. Roy Sievers of the White Sox (June 21, 1961) and Phillies (May 26, 1963), and Jimmie Foxx of the Philadelphia A's (September 21, 1931) and Phillies (May 18, 1945), have hit pinch hit grand slams in both leagues.

Thanks for the Help. Chuck Estrada was the starting and winning pitcher in all games in which Orioles teammate Jim Gentile hit his five grand slams. Gentile hit two of them against the Twins on May 9, 1961.

Long Run. On July 20, 1965, Yankee pitcher Mel Stottlemyre hit an inside-the-park grand slam in Yankee Stadium off Bill Momboquette of the Red Sox.

Most/Career. Lou Gehrig hit a Major League record 23 grand slams in his career, the last coming off A's pitcher Lee Ross on August 28, 1938. Gehrig hit two off one pitcher, left-hander Lloyd Brown. Gehrig hit his first against Brown in 1931 when Brown was with the Washington Senators and the second in 1934 when he pitched for the Cleveland Indians.

Eddie Murray had 19, and Willie McCovey and Robin Ventura are the National League leaders with 18. When Ventura hit his 18th in September 2004, the active leaders were Manny Ramirez (17), Ken Griffey, Jr. (14) and Mike Piazza (14). Jimmie Foxx and Ted Williams each had 17.

When Shoeless Joe Jackson was barred from baseball in 1920, he was the all-time leader with five grand slams, all inside the park. One source reported that Babe Ruth hit only two grand slams, but he actually had 16.

Most/Season. Don Mattingly set the Major League season record in 1987 with six grand slams in a season. Before that year, Mattingly had never hit one. Mattingly had been only 13 for 52 with the bases loaded, with only one extra base hit. Jim Gentile in 1961 and Ernie Banks in 1955 both had five in a season.

Most/Month. The record for most grand slams in a month by a single player is three, a record last tied by Mike Blowers of the Mariners in August 1995 and accomplished by four American Leaguer players. In May 1987 Eric Davis became the first National League player to hit three grand slams in a month. Mike Piazza tied the record by hitting three during April 1998.

Most by Team/Season. Until 1997 the 1987 Yankees and 1938 Tigers held the Major League record with 10 grand slams in a season. The 1997 Braves hit 12 to set a new record. Before the Braves, the 1928 Cubs hit nine grand slams, a National League record tied by the Padres in 1995.

Both Leagues/Same Season. In 1996 Greg Vaughn hit grand slams for the Brewers in the American League and Padres in the National League. The only other player to do this was Will Clark for Baltimore and St. Louis in 2000.

Most in a Major League/Season. There were 48 grand slams during the 1961 American League and 1970 National League seasons.

Most in a Major League Day. A Major League record was set on August 9, 1999, when there were five slams hit in one day around the Majors.

Consecutive Games/Team. The 1978 Brewers and 1993 Tigers hold the record with grand slams in three consecutive games.

Consecutive Games/Player. On May 5, 1996, Eric Davis of the Reds became the 18th player in Major League history to hit grand slams in two consecutive games.

Mike Piazza did it in April 1998, and then later in the month hit a third to tie the record for most grand slams in a single month. He also hit three grand slams in 2000. The last one to do it was David Eckstein of the Angels on April 27–28, 2002.

Doubleheader/Player. On May 20, 1999, Robin Ventura hit a grand slam in each game of a doubleheader for the Mets, a first in the Major Leagues.

Same Inning/Two Teams. On May 18, 1950, at the Polo Grounds, Rube Walker hit a grand slam in the 6th inning for the Cubs. In the bottom of the inning, Monte Irvin hit a grand slam for the Giants, the first time in history that each team hit grand slams in the same inning.

Walk-Off Grand Slam. On May 17, 2002, after the Twins scored three times in the top of the 14th, Jason Giambi of the Yankees hit a one-out grand slam for a 13–12 New York victory. It was the 21st time that a player hit a grand slam to win the game when his club was down by three runs. Babe Ruth had done it for the Yankees in 1925.

Expansion Club Record. The 1961 Angels hold the expansion team record with six grand slams in a season.

Bad Base Running. On July 4, 1976, Tim McCarver hit a grand slam, but was called out for passing Garry Maddox on the basepaths. McCarver was credited with a three-run single.

Pitcher/World Series. Baltimore's Dave McNally is the only pitcher to hit a grand slam in the World Series. It came in the 6th inning of Game 3 of the 1970 Series between the Orioles and Reds. Coincidentally, McNally hit his grand slam off Tony Cloninger, who once hit two in one game.

Postseason Pinch Hit. The first postseason pinch hit grand slam was by Marc Lewis of the Reds. He did it on October 2, 1995, against the Dodgers in Game 3 of the division series and helped the Reds sweep the Dodgers.

Last by American League Pitcher. The last grand slam by an American League pitcher was by Steve Dunning of the Indians on May 11, 1971. He hit it off A's pitcher Diego Segui in the 2nd inning.

Most Homers/No Grand Slam. Braves third baseman Bob Horner held the record of 209 home runs without a grand slam, later broken by Sammy Sosa in 1998 with 247. Home run No. 248 was a grand slam. Amazingly, Sosa hit another grand slam the next night. Sosa went 4,428 at-bats before hitting the first slam.

Oldest To Hit. On June 3, 2004, 45-year-old Julio Franco of the Braves became the oldest player to hit a grand slam, surpassing Carlton Fisk in 1991, who was 43 at the time.

Most/Least Given Up.

"[Jim] Palmer is the greatest 'situation' pitcher I've ever seen. He makes them beat him on a single and one run at a time. Most of the homers he gives up are solos because he only works to their power when the bases are empty." — Oriole pitching coach Ray Miller.

Bob Feller gave up eight grand slams in his career, the record until Nolan Ryan surpassed him with 10. Jim Palmer never gave up one in the Major Leagues, but gave up one in a minor league game in 1967 to one Johnny Bench of Buffalo.

In 1996 the Giants pitchers gave up a National League record 10 grand slams. The Mariners gave up 10 in 1992 and the 1996 Tigers gave up a record 11 grand slams.

Reward. Rod Kanehl received 50,000 trading stamps when he hit the Mets' first grand slam on July 6, 1962.

Not In the Books. On October 17, 1999, the Mets were down 3–1 in games when they played the Braves in Game 5 of the NLCS. Robin Ventura hit a grand slam in the bottom of the 15th inning for the win, but his teammates mobbed him before he could reach second base. He was later credited with a single and the Mets won 4–3 instead of 7–3. Las Vegas had a problem, however, as it paid off all winners of the "over/under" betting line who chose the "overs"; because the original 7–3 score put the game over the middle line. The "unders" bettors never got paid, because of the way Las Vegas works—whatever the score is at the end of the game controls. If scorekeepers go back and make a change, as was done here, it is too late for the bettors.

Lucky Winner. On July 11, 1999, fan Gylene Hoyle won $1 million when Jay Bell hit a grand slam for the Diamondbacks in a game against the A's. She correctly picked the player and the inning in which he would get the prize-winning hit.

Grass

"They act like a team. If one or two get sick, the others take over. Some are hardier than others; some are greener. That's why we have nine. Come to think of it, that's one grass for every position on the field."— Royals groundskeeper George Toma on the new grass installed for the 1995 season. The Royals put in real grass for the first time in 22 seasons. Nine different varieties were used: five bluegrass—Princeton 104, Eclipse, Nassau, Glade and Suffolk; and four rye—Derby, Gator, Regal and Top Hat.

"Now more than ever, we need a change of pace in baseball. Ballparks should be happy places. They should always smell like freshly cut grass."—Bill Veeck in 1981.

"Lee Meadows, Jim Greengrass, Fred Snodgrass, Dale Green, Bill Parks, Hector Valle, Dave Valle, Luis Arroyo, Jim Field, Charlie Lea, Hub Knolls, Herman Hill, Fred Glade, Still Bill Hill, Hilly Layne, Punch Knoll, Grover Land"

See also **Artificial Turf** and **Groundskeepers**.

Dye Job. In 1937 the Reds became the first team to dye their grass after it became sunburned. The dye was approved by the golf-related United States Greens Association.

Front Lawn. When Fenway Park was resodded after the 1967 pennant-winning season, some of the old bluegrass in left field was put in Carl Yastrzemski's yard.

Primary Types of Grass and Cost. Reseeding a field costs approximately $50,000 and is always done in the fall. Bermuda grass is used on the West Coast and is kept at a height of one-half inch. It is not usable in cold climates because it cannot survive the winter, so bluegrass is used in the East and Midwest and is kept at 1½ to 2 inches high. These are the primary grasses, but groundskeepers often add other grasses to prevent disease and promote growth.

Underneath some Major League ballpark grass is a custom-designed system called Prescription Athletic Turf (PAT). The system provides maximum drainage by using only sand as the subsoil, which helps decrease the number of rain-outs. The negative side effect is that the grass is more delicate because the sand does not hold nutrients or water needed by the grass.

Mower. Infield grass is usually cut to between 1½ to 2 inches, and outfield grass typically is two inches.

New grass and dirt at soon-to-open Petco Park in San Diego, early 2004.

Greatest Athletes See also Greatest Players

In 1950 the Associated Press named its greatest athletes of the half-century. Decathlete and mediocre Major League Baseball player Jim Thorpe was first, followed by Babe Ruth, Jack Dempsey, Ty Cobb, Bobby Jones, Joe Louis, Red Grange, Bronco Nagurski, Jackie Robinson, and Bob Mathias. Babe Didrikson Zaharias was voted greatest female athlete and the Dempsey-Firpo heavyweight fight of 1923 was voted the greatest single event.

Greatest Feats

"The Yankee Clipper never was the luckiest of ballplayers but he is frank to admit that Dame Fortune accompanied him to the plate all during his hit harvest. Then she abruptly gave him the cold shoulder to end it."— Sportswriter Arthur Daley on Joe DiMaggio's 56-game hitting streak.

See also *Most Memorable Moments.*

In 1956 *The Sporting News* conducted a poll to determine the top 15 feats in baseball history; it has been updated with the author's literary license to include post–1956 feats:

1. Joe DiMaggio's 56-game hitting streak
2. Lou Gehrig's 2,130 consecutive game streak (now Cal Ripken's streak of 2,632 games).
3. Nolan Ryan's seven no-hitters and 5,000+ strikeouts
4. Babe Ruth's 60 home runs (then Roger Maris' 61 home runs, then Mark McGwire's 70, and then Barry Bonds' 73) and 714 career home runs (now Henry Aaron's 755)
5. Ty Cobb's 12 American League batting championships in 13 years
6. Rickey Henderson's 130 stolen bases (and Maury Wills' 104 in 1962)
7. Orel Hershiser's 58 straight scoreless innings
8. Cy Young's 511 wins; Walter Johnson's 412 wins and 110 shutouts
9. Johnny Vander Meer's two consecutive no-hitters
10. Rube Marquard's 19 straight wins in 1912
11. The 14 pennants in 16 years (1949–1964) won by the Yankees
12. Grover Cleveland Alexander's 16 shutouts for the 1916 Phillies
13. Ty Cobb's lifetime .367 lifetime average
14. Jack Chesbro's 40 wins in 1904 for the Highlanders
15. Rogers Hornsby's .424 batting average in 1924
16. Don Larsen's 1956 World Series perfect game

Greatest Games

"Don't people understand? Somebody wins the Series every year. There's only one game like that in a lifetime. I'd call it the greatest game in the history of American sports because baseball is the best and oldest game, and that's sure as hell the best baseball game I ever saw."— George Steinbrenner on the 1978 play-off game between the Red Sox and Yankees.

The National League celebrated its centennial in 1976 by voting Game 6 of the 1975 World Series as the most exciting game ever (even though Carlton Fisk's home run for the Red Sox won the game over the Reds — his home run ball sold in 1999 for $113,273. How soon they forget; what about Game 7 of the 1960 World Series, won by the Pirates?).

Greatest Players

"At my age, I'm just glad to be named the greatest living anything."— Joe DiMaggio after being named baseball's greatest living player during the sport's centennial celebration in 1969. Babe Ruth was named baseball's all-time greatest player.

"He was the best baseball player who ever lived. He was better than Ty Cobb, better than Joe DiMaggio, better than Ted Williams, better than Willie Mays, better than Henry Aaron, better than Bobby [sic] Bonds. He was by far the most flamboyant. There's never been anyone else like him."— Robert W. Creamer on Babe Ruth in *Smithsonian* magazine.

"If a man with a voice loud enough to make himself heard all over the United States should stand on top of Pike's Peak and ask, 'Who is the greatest ball player?' 27,806,009 persons would shout 'Wagner!' There are great baseball players, but only one Wagner.... He looked like a prosperous, contented German worker. One would have thought to watch the massive shoulders and the powerful bowed legs that probably he had been a brewery wagon driver or an iceman.... For a dozen years every player and every pitcher has searched for Wagner's weakness and found none. He has played every position in baseball, is as great in the outfield, perhaps greater than in the infield. He is the best batter, possibly excepting Cobb, in the land, he is the greatest baserunner...."— Hugh S. Fullerton in *The American* magazine.

"The redoubtable Tyrus Raymond Cobb, sharp of mind and spike, is dead. It would take a long parade of superlatives to re-enact his career, for his were talents of unmatched variety.... Of Ty Cobb let it be said simply that he was the world's greatest ballplayer."— Part of Cobb's obituary in the *New York Herald Tribune* on July 18, 1961; it was reprinted as the last page in Cobb's autobiography, *My Life In Baseball* (1961).

"Can you believe it? And [deceased] Ted Williams didn't get a single vote! Two of these same voters, in the last U.S. presidential election, wrote in Grover Cleveland Alexander."— Columnist Scott Ostler commenting on the Major League players who voted Babe Ruth as the greatest *living* baseball player in a 2003 *Sports Illustrated* poll.

"One of the silliest — and least resistible — baseball pastimes is picking the 'best' something. It's silly because sensible comparisons can't be made if different eras or different leagues are involved. But it's irresistible because all who follow the game love to wallow in contemplation of the qualities and feats of the greatest players, to discuss and compare the greatest accomplishments, to share dreams of approaches to perfection."— Leonard Koppett in *A Thinking Man's Guide to Baseball* (1967).

See also *Hitters*—Greatest, *The Perfect Player* and *Pitchers*—**The Perfect Pitcher.**

Major League Centennial. Major League Baseball celebrated its 100th year in 1969, using the 1869 all-professional Cincinnati Reds as the centennial reference point. To celebrate, fans were asked to select an all-time all-star team. Fan ballots were tallied and submitted to the Baseball Writers Association for final selection. The winning players were announced at a formal dinner in Washington, D.C., in connection with the All-Star Game that year. The results:

Greatest Living Players/Manager.

First Base. George Sisler and Stan Musial tied over Bill Terry.

Second Base. Charlie Gehringer over Jackie Robinson and Frankie Frisch.

Third Base. Pie Traynor over Jackie Robinson and Brooks Robinson.

Shortstop. Joe Cronin over Lou Boudreau, Luke Appling and Ernie Banks.

Outfield. Ted Williams, Joe DiMaggio and Willie Mays over Mickey Mantle, Stan Musial and Henry Aaron.

Catcher. Bill Dickey over Roy Campanella, Yogi Berra and Gabby Hartnett.

Right-Handed Pitcher. Bob Feller over Bob Gibson and Dizzy Dean.

Left-Handed Pitcher. Lefty Grove over Sandy Koufax, Warren Spahn and Carl Hubbell.

Manager.

"Thank you for voting me what I thought I was."— Casey Sten-

Perhaps the most famous Hall of Fame photograph. Ten of the greatest players of all time enshrined at the original induction ceremony in 1939. Seated, left to right, Eddie Collins, Babe Ruth (in need of new socks), Connie Mack and Cy Young; standing, left to right, Honus Wagner (needing tie-tying lessons), Grover Cleveland Alexander, Tris Speaker, Napoleon Lajoie, George Sisler and Walter Johnson.

gel, voted the greatest living manager over Walter Alston, Joe Mc-Carthy and Leo Durocher.

All-Time Greatest Team.

First Base. Lou Gehrig over George Sisler.

Second Base. Rogers Hornsby over Charlie Gehringer and Eddie Collins.

Third Base. Pie Traynor over Brooks Robinson and Jackie Robinson.

Shortstop. Honus Wagner over Joe Cronin and Ernie Banks.

Outfielders. Babe Ruth, Ty Cobb and Joe DiMaggio over Ted Williams, Tris Speaker and Willie Mays.

Catcher. Mickey Cochrane over Bill Dickey and Roy Campanella.

Right-Handed Pitcher. Walter Johnson over Christy Mathewson and Cy Young.

Left-Handed Pitcher. Lefty Grove over Sandy Koufax and Carl Hubbell.

Manager. John McGraw over Casey Stengel and Joe McCarthy.

The Sporting News noted that the only surprise was Joe DiMaggio beating out Tris Speaker in the outfield.

All-Century Team. On October 24, 1999, before Game 2 of the World Series, Major League Baseball unveiled its All-Century Team, with on-field appearances by the 18 living members at Turner Field in Atlanta. The best moment was when Willie Mays and Ken Griffey, Jr., helped 81-year-old Ted Williams to a seat, which was steadied by Henry Aaron. Aaron threw out the ceremonial first pitch, and then Mays also delivered a pitch without a catcher behind the plate.

A 25-man roster was selected by fans, and five more were added by a special panel of baseball executives, writers and historians (the five are noted with an asterisk). Babe Ruth received the most votes, 1,207,992, followed by Lou Gehrig with 1,158,044. Among the active players, Cal Ripken received the most votes (669,033). Pete Rose got 629,742. The active players were Ken Griffey, Jr., Cal Ripken, Roger Clemens and Mark McGwire (Barry Bonds was not on the list).

Pitcher: Nolan Ryan, Sandy Koufax, Roger Clemens, Bob Gibson, Walter Johnson, Lefty Grove, Warren Spahn (added at the insistence of Sandy Koufax) and Christy Mathewson.

Outfielder: Babe Ruth, Ty Cobb, Henry Aaron, Willie Mays, Ted Williams, Stan Musial, Ken Griffey, Jr., Joe DiMaggio, Mickey Mantle and Pete Rose. Rose received special permission to appear and received a raucous standing ovation. There was also a minor flap when reporter Jim Gray asked Rose at that moment if he would admit betting on baseball. Rose took offense and said it would have been more appropriate to ask the question in another setting. (Note that Rose was not present at the All-Star Game, when the 100 players on the ballot had been introduced.);

Catcher: Johnny Bench and Yogi Berra;

First Base: Lou Gehrig and Mark McGwire;

Second Base: Jackie Robinson and Rogers Hornsby;

Shortstop: Cal Ripken, Jr., Ernie Banks and Honus Wagner;

Third Base: Mike Schmidt and Brooks Robinson

A poll by *The Sporting News* placed Babe Ruth as the player of the century, with Willie Mays second.

Society for American Baseball Research.

"On the whole, the SABR list is similar to witnessing a pitcher hurl a no-hitter in which he walks four batters and his shortstop commits an error. Entertaining? Oh yeah, for sure. But, it's far from a perfecto."— Steve Lombardi.

In June 1999 SABR released its top 100 players of the century list, as voted on by 865 of its members. The top ten were, in order, Babe Ruth, Lou Gehrig, Ted Williams, Henry Aaron, Stan Musial, Joe DiMaggio, Ty Cobb, Willie Mays, Rogers Hornsby and Honus Wagner. The first two pitchers were Christy Mathewson at No. 12 and Warren Spahn at No. 15. No active player made the top 25.

Greatest Players/By Decade.

1890–1910. In a 1919 editorial, *Reach Guide* editor Francis Richter contended that Buck Ewing, Ty Cobb and Honus Wagner were the three greatest players ever. Ewing dominated the 1890s and Wagner and Cobb dominated the early part of the 20th century.

Sam Crawford and others contended that Honus Wagner was better than Cobb, particularly because of his fielding ability, which far overshadowed Cobb's work in center field.

1910s. Walter Johnson must be the top player of this decade. He won 30 games twice and won 264 games during this prime period of his career. He also pitched 74 shutouts during the 10-year stretch.

1920s. Babe Ruth clearly qualifies as the player of this decade, in which he *averaged* almost 47 home runs per year.

1930s. Jimmie Foxx probably qualifies as the best player of this decade, as they were the prime years of his career. He consistently hit around .340 (with two exceptions) and averaged over 41 home runs per year. Lou Gehrig in the first half of the decade and Joe DiMaggio in the second half of the decade also qualify.

1940s. Though the war years cut into their play, Joe DiMaggio and Ted Williams must qualify as the best players of the decade. Stan Musial would be a close third.

1946–1955. It has been reported that Bob Feller made the suggestion to *The Sporting News* to identify a Player of the Decade. The magazine selected Stan Musial the best player of the decade from 1946 through 1955.

1950s. Ted Williams was selected by *The Sporting News* as the best player of the 1950s. Mickey Mantle and Willie Mays are also contenders for this decade.

1960s. *The Sporting News* selected Willie Mays as the best player of the 1960s. However, many of his prime years were in the 1950s. Sandy Koufax should also be a strong contender despite retiring after the 1966 season. Roberto Clemente and Henry Aaron also are in the running.

1970s. Pete Rose was selected by *The Sporting News* as the best player of the 1970s, though teammate Johnny Bench might be a better overall choice.

1980s. *The Sporting News* selected Mike Schmidt as its Player of the Decade even though he retired mid-decade. Cal Ripken, Rickey Henderson and Roger Clemens are other strong candidates.

1990s. Possible candidates: Barry Bonds, Frank Thomas, Ken Griffey, Jr., Roger Clemens and Greg Maddux. Bonds had his greatest season in 2001, however. *The Sporting News* chose Bonds, while a panel of sportswriters chose Griffey.

2000s. Alex Rodriguez would likely be the choice through 2004; perhaps Albert Pujols will emerge for the entire decade based on his fast career start.

Miscellaneous Selections. Stan Musial ranked Willie Mays and Joe DiMaggio as the best he ever saw. Leo Durocher, obviously biased because he managed Mays, called Mays the best all-around player he ever saw.

Babe Ruth selected Negro League shortstop John Henry "Pop" Lloyd.

Historian Bill James rates Babe Ruth and Honus Wagner as the top two players of all time, both for their careers and at their peaks.

Smoky Joe Wood voted for Ty Cobb.

Connie Mack said that Rogers Hornsby was the best all-around player of all time.

Umpire Bill Klem chose Honus Wagner as the best player of all time.

In 1980 Miller Brewing Company sponsored a poll of sportswriters and sportscasters and determined that Babe Ruth was the all-time greatest athlete from any sport.

Good Prognostication. Before the 2001 season, *Total Baseball* ranked Barry Bonds as the 5th greatest player of all time, behind Ruth, Mays, Lajoie and Cobb. Although many were surprised, Bonds validated the selection with his incredible 2001 season. Not only did he break the single-season home run record, his .862 slugging percentage broke Ruth's seemingly unreachable single-season record of .846. He broke Rogers Hornsby's National League slugging percentage record by more than 100 points. He also broke Ruth's walk record of 172 and tied Chuck Klein's record for most extra base hits in a season. His .515 on-base percentage was the best in baseball since Ted Williams in 1957.

Books. Nick Acocella and Donald Dewey, *The All-Stars All Star Baseball Book* (1985), in which great players choose their all-time baseball teams and the reasons why; Charles F. Faber, *Baseball Ratings: The All-Time Best Players at Each Position* (1984); Bill James, *The Bill James Historical Baseball Abstract* (1988); Mark Maguire and Michael Sean Gormley, *100 Greatest Baseball Players of the 20th Century Ranked* (2000); Lawrence Ritter and Donald Honig, *The 100 Greatest Baseball Players of All Time* (1981); G. Scott Thomas, *Leveling the Field: The Revolutionary Formula That Ranks Baseball's Greatest Players and Their Achievements Throughout History* (2002); Warren Wilbert and Monte Irvin, *The Best of Baseball: The 20th Century's Greatest Players Ranked by Position* (2001).

Greatest Teams See ***Dynasties***

Hank Greenberg (1911–1986)

Hall of Fame 1956

"The Irish didn't like it when they heard of Greenberg's fame

For they thought a good first baseman should possess an Irish name;

And the Murphys and Mulrooneys said they never dreamed they'd see

A Jewish boy from Bronxville out where Casey used to be."— First lines of a poem by Edgar A. Guest.

Greenberg was one of the premier home run and RBI men of the 1930s and 1940s, primarily for the Tigers.

Henry Greenberg, the greatest hitting *Jewish Player* of all-time, was rejected by John McGraw and the Giants before the Yankees offered him $7,500. He turned that down and signed with the Tigers for $9,000 after one semester of college. He played in the Eastern League and Piedmont League in 1930 before playing one game for the Tigers that season. He remained in the minor leagues in 1931 and 1932.

Greenberg became the regular Tigers first baseman in 1933, hitting .301 in 117 games. He led the league with 36 home runs and 170 RBIs in 1935 and won the MVP Award. However, he suffered a broken wrist in the World Series and missed most of the 1936 season when he broke the wrist again after a collision only 12 games into the season.

Although it was feared that his career might be over, he hit 40 home runs in 1937 and led the league with 183 RBIs. He peaked with 58 home runs in 1938. He led the league again in 1940 with 41 home runs and won another MVP Award when he moved to the outfield for the Tigers. That season he batted .357 in his third World Series for the club.

Greenberg entered the military early in 1941 and played only 19 games that season. He missed the next three seasons and played only 75 games in 1945. In 1946 he returned to form, leading the league with 44 home runs and 127 RBIs.

The Tigers refused to increase his salary for 1947 and instead waived him out of the league. He signed with the Pirates for the first $100,000 *Salary*. He hit 25 home runs while playing in 125 games and then retired. He finished with 331 home runs in 13 seasons and his .605 slugging average is sixth all-time.

He became the farm system director for the Indians and then their general manager in 1950. He remained with the Indians through most of the 1950s and then became general manager of the White Sox in 1959. He left baseball in 1963 and became wealthy as an investment banker. His son Steve was a minor league ballplayer, sports attorney and deputy commissioner of baseball in the late 1980s.

Book. Hank Greenberg and Ira Berkow, *Hank Greenberg: The Story of My Life* (1989).

Zane Grey (1875–1939)

"Here's a story crowded with hard, fast baseball—and a dash of romance!"—Dust jacket description of Grey's baseball novel for boys, *The Young Pitcher* (1939 reprint of a 1911 edition).

"Zane Grey possesses no merit whatsoever either in style or in substance."—Literary critic Burton Rascoe.

"The substance of any two Zane Grey books could be written upon the back of a postage stamp."—Heywood Broun.

The author of 85 western novels played professional baseball and wrote a few baseball stories early in his writing career. He also spent time as a traveling tooth extractor. His western novels sold over 100 million copies worldwide and have been made into over 100 movies (though the *Encyclopedia Britannica* once reported only 54 novels selling 15 million copies).

The Red Headed Outfield was published in 1915 and reissued in 1920 as *The Red Headed Outfield and Other Stories*. The story was patterned after an all-redhead outfield that Grey played with in 1897 on the Buffalo Bisons. He also wrote *The Shortstop* (1909) and *The Young Pitcher* (1911).

Grey grew up in Zanesville with a real name of Pearl Zane Gray, with an "a" in his last name. He played professional baseball in the mid–1890s in the Interstate and Atlantic Leagues. In 1896 he helped a Pennsylvania club defeat the New York Giants with his outfield play. He also pitched during his career.

His brothers played professional baseball, but none made it to the Major Leagues. However, one SABR researcher claimed that Grey's brother Reddie played one game for the Pirates in 1903, but that his name was confused by the scorer with another Grey.

Clark Griffith (1869–1955)

Hall of Fame 1946

"Griffith, a small man himself, advised that size did not matter, and emphasized good control and a 'nervy heart' among the attributes a pitcher should have. He was one who practiced what he preached. He was not able to overpower the batters, so he relied on craft and artistry to fool them, and won for himself the nickname 'the Old Fox'."—Harold Seymour in *Baseball: The Early Years* (1960).

Griffith won 240 games before turning to managing and becoming the owner of the Senators.

"The Old Fox" was the long-time owner of the *Washington Senators*, taking over as manager and part-owner in 1912. He became president of the club in 1920 and remained so until his death at age 85 on October 27, 1955. Many forget, however, that Griffith also had a 21-year Major League pitching career in which he was 240–144. Although his career technically spanned 1891 through 1914, he never appeared in more than one game after 1907. He won 20 or more games seven times, including six years in a row from 1894 through 1899.

Griffith is credited with helping American League president Ban Johnson recruit players for the new league in 1901. He helped raid National League teams and was rewarded with the managerial position with the White Sox after leaving the Chicago Cubs of the National League. He is also credited by some with pioneering the use of relief pitchers.

When the American League needed a New York club, Griffith complied with Johnson's request and took over the New York Highlanders as manager. He was fired midway through the 1908 season, but soon became the manager of the National League Reds. After the 1911 season, again at Johnson's request, he returned permanently to the American League and the Senators.

He was the last surviving active member of the American League's original management structure. Because baseball was his sole source of income, his club was chronically in financial trouble and his teams were almost always at the bottom of the standings.

Griffith Stadium   See *Washington Senators*

Burleigh Grimes (1893–1985)

Hall of Fame (VC) 1964

"Ol' Stubblebeard"—Grimes' nickname, referring to his practice of not shaving for a few days before starts. Other sources report that he did not shave only on game days, because the slippery elm he chewed for his spitballs irritated his face.

Grimes won 270 games primarily for the Dodgers beginning in 1916.

Burleigh Arland Grimes was born in Wisconsin lumberjack country and made it to the Major Leagues in 1916 as a pitcher for the Pirates. After a terrible 3–16 season in 1917, he was traded to the Dodgers for Casey Stengel. His most productive years were in Brooklyn, where the long-time spitballer won over 20 games four times in nine seasons. He stayed with the club through 1926 and then moved on to the Giants. He won 19 games and then was traded to the Pirates, where he had his best season. He won 25 games in

1928 and led the league in games, games started, complete games, innings, wins and shutouts. He played another six seasons for various clubs through 1934 and won a total of 270 games in his career. He was the last legal spitballer to pitch in the Major Leagues.

Grimes took five no-hitters into the 9th inning, only to give up a hit each time. After his playing days ended, he managed the Dodgers for two seasons in 1937 and 1938 and then managed in the minor leagues for 10 years. He later scouted for the Orioles and died of cancer at age 92.

Ground Balls

"Quit trying to strike everybody out. Strikeouts are boring and besides that, they're fascist. Throw some ground balls. They're more democratic." — Catcher Crash Davis to pitcher Nuke LaLoosh in *Bull Durham.*

"There's a two-hopper to Eddie Leon, who catches it on the first bounce." — Broadcaster and former pitcher Herb Score.

See also *Bad Hops.*

Mickey Mantle sometimes did not run out ground balls that were sure outs, either to save his aching legs or because his superstar status allowed him to get away with it. He and first baseman Vic Power never got along and Power sometimes would pretend to miss the bag with his foot to force Mantle to run out the grounder. At the last moment, Power would then step on the bag.

Ground Rule Doubles

Rule. If a ball is touched by a fan or bounces over the outfield wall it is ruled a ground rule double. This became the rule in 1930 in the American League and in 1931 in the National League.

Large Crowd. In 1897 in a game between Boston and Baltimore, many in an overflow crowd of 25,000 stood almost immediately behind the infield, so the umpires ruled that any ball hit into the crowd was a ground rule double.

Blimps. Several years ago dirigibles (blimps) covered Major League games. The umpires ruled that any fly ball that hit a dirigible would be ruled a ground rule double. There is no record of the rule ever having to be invoked.

Pennant Loss. The lack of a ground rule double rule at Shibe Park in Philadelphia helped cost the Braves the 1949 pennant. On the last day of the season the Dodgers were playing the Phillies at Shibe, which had a ledge between the right field screen and the fence. Phillies pitcher Robin Roberts was leading the Dodgers 1–0 when Dodger shortstop Pee Wee Reese hit a ball that somehow stayed up on the ledge. As was customary at the time, the ball was ruled a home run even though it had not cleared the screen. The ground rules later were modified so that the ball would have been called a ground rule double. The Dodgers won the game and clinched the pennant.

Speaker Problems. See *Indoor Ballparks.*

Groundskeepers

"To a groundskeeper, the park is alive. The grass is his baby to be nursed, to be kept alive and beautiful. The soil is a soft cushion with feeling. The foul lines are the border to a beautiful centerpiece. The mound is a calculated summit suited to the great heights that can be reached there." — Joe Garagiola in *Baseball Is a Funny Game* (1960).

"[We are] a doctor, when the grass gets sick ... a pharmacist, preparing chemicals ... a dietician, prescribing the right food, adding minerals ... we're weathermen — we've got to know when to water, when not to water." — Royals groundskeeper George Toma, the dean of all groundskeepers, who also oversaw the grass for 38 straight Super Bowls.

"I made it as uncomfortable as the rules permit." — George Toma on the mound packing that he did to make life difficult for opposing pitcher Catfish Hunter, who liked a soft mound. Toma is considered the dean of Major League groundskeepers and he is well known outside of baseball circles. He and his crew were instrumental in rehabilitating the rain-damaged fields in San Francisco and Los Angeles for the 1992–1993 NFL play-offs and Super Bowl.

"He's finally earning his money." — Reds pitcher Mark Portugal in July 1996 after general manager Jim Bowden joined the grounds crew to sweep around second base.

Tampering. In the 1890s Baltimore groundskeeper Tom Murphy tapered the third base infield foul line to make bunts roll foul. He also loosened the dirt in front of the pitching rubber to make it harder on opposing pitchers Amos Rusie and Cy Young.

Economizing. Bill Stocksick, Sportsman's Park groundskeeper of the 1930s, saved money during the Depression by using goats to keep the grass trimmed.

Watering. The Tigers had an area in front of home plate known as Cobb's Lake, which the groundskeeper flooded to keep Ty Cobb's bunts in fair territory.

The Indians groundskeeper watered down the third base line to make life easier for third baseman Al Rosen, who suffered nine broken noses trying to field ground balls from 1947 through 1956.

Los Angeles Dodgers owner Walter O'Malley could not understand why his groundskeeper kept using a hose to water the outfield even though it was constructed with a $600,000 sprinkler system. O'Malley finally concluded that the groundskeeper had come with him from Brooklyn and he had used a hose there.

Ejection. At a Class A South Atlantic League game in May 2003, Bill Butler became what is believed to be the first groundskeeper to be thrown out of a game. It was raining steadily and both managers were ready to stop play. Butler tried to convince the umpires (a bit forcefully, apparently) that it was time to cover the field and give up. He was told to stay away, but when he returned with a copy of the weather radar report in hand, he was tossed. The umpires then told the rest of the ground crew to cover the field and they suspended the game.

Most Valuable Groundskeeper. Giants groundskeeper Matty Schwab played an integral role before the start of the 1962 National League play-off series between the Dodgers and Giants. Before the first game in Candlestick Park, Giants manager Alvin Dark (later dubbed the "Swamp Fox" because of this incident) asked Schwab to water down the area at first base. This was to slow down premier base stealer Maury Wills, who had set a new Major League record that year with 104 steals. Dark also had the groundskeepers water down the basepath between first and second base.

Veteran umpire Jocko Conlan saw what was happening and ordered Schwab and his crew to come back on the field and repair where the heavy watering had occurred. What Conlan did not realize was that the groundskeepers had also heavily watered the left side of the infield to slow down ground balls for the mediocre Giants infielders playing third base and shortstop. Another source reported that the umpire was Tom Gorman and that Gorman held up the start of the game for 1½ hours while the bases dried out. The Giants won the play-off and groundskeeper Schwab earned a full World Series share for his season-long efforts.

The Dodgers tried a similar tactic in 1978 against the Phillies in the National League Championship Series, but the umpires made them take out the excess dirt used to slow balls.

Dragging the Infield.

"You know you're having a bad day when the 5th inning rolls around, and they drag the warning track." — Orioles pitcher Mike Flanagan.

"And there the whole play lay recorded in the fresh infield dirt: the first baseman's footprints coming straight to the bag and Campaneris describing three hundred sixty degrees and ending in still-unsettled dust. Like the ripples from the day's first dive into a swimming pool — except that these prints persisted, less and less distinctly in the company of others, until the whole palimpsest was dragged smooth by the grounds crew after the top of the fourth." — Roy Blount, Jr.

5th Inning. Sometime between 1949 and 1952, Reds manager Luke Sewell asked groundskeeper Matty Schwab to drag the infield in the middle of the 5th inning. General manager Gabe Paul liked the idea because the extra time it took helped concession sales. The practice was gradually adopted by all teams.

Rule Change. On April 24, 1968, the Mets and Astros played in a 24-inning game won by the Astros on a bad hop on the dirt infield. Mets general manager Johnny Murphy successfully pushed for a new rule after the season requiring the infield to be dragged after every five innings, not just after the first five innings.

Fall from Grace. Joe Borden was the winner of the first National League game in 1876. By the end of the season his arm had gone dead and he became the team's groundskeeper.

Housing. Cubs groundskeeper Bobby Dorr lived in a six-room apartment at Wrigley Field in the 1930s. The site remains, but no groundskeeper lives there. Groundskeeper Matty Schwab worked at the Polo Grounds for the Giants and lived in a house built for him under the left field grandstand. When the club moved to San Francisco, he moved with it, but did not live at the new ballpark.

Insurance. When the Yankees traveled to Japan for the start of the 2004 season, the club took its own groundskeepers.

Dynasty. In 1936 in Cleveland Emil Bossard started a groundskeeping family dynasty that continued into the 1990s. Gene Bossard, who supervised Comiskey Park from 1940 to 1983, was succeeded by his son Roger, who maintained the family tradition as described in a 1998 Chicago Sun-Times obituary for Gene, who had died at age 80: "The Comiskey Park infield once was known as 'Bossard's Swamp' because he kept it watered for sinkerball pitchers Dick Donovan, Tommy John and Joel Horlen. He also soaked the area around first base when opposing base stealers came to town, and he kept the baselines raised so that Nellie Fox's bunts stayed fair."

Lefty Grove (1900–1975)

Hall of Fame 1947

"I never saw anything funny on a baseball field." — Grove, always serious and temperamental, in response to a reporter's question about the funniest thing he ever saw in baseball.

"If they said, 'Come on, here's a steak dinner,' and I had a chance to go out and play a game of ball, I'd go out and play the game and let the steak sit there. I would." — Grove.

Grove won exactly 300 games for the A's and Red Sox over 17 seasons beginning in 1925.

Robert Grove may have been the greatest left-handed pitcher of all time. He probably would have won many more than 300 Major League games, except that he pitched for five years with Baltimore in the minor leagues (1920–1924) before being sold for $100,600

to the A's at age 25. His 300–141 Major League record resulted in the fourth-highest winning percentage of all time, .680.

Using a blazing fastball, Grove won 20 or more games seven straight times and eight overall. He led the league in strikeouts in his first seven seasons, ERA eight times and shutouts three times. His greatest season was 1931 when he was 31–4 and had 16 straight **Wins.** Two of the losses were in relief and one was a late-season tune-up for the World Series. He won four games for the A's in the 1930 and 1931 World Series.

He was traded to the Red Sox after the 1933 season when Connie Mack was dismantling the A's to save money during the Depression. A bad arm ruined his first season with the Red Sox, but he came back to win 20 games in 1935 and 14 or more through the 1939 season. After he retired he opened a bowling alley in his hometown of Lonaconing, Maryland.

Book. Jim Kaplan, *Lefty Grove: American Original* (2000).

Gum

"Rocky Bridges chews tobacco because the chewing-gum industry wants no part of him." — Don Rickles.

"Harmon [Killebrew] told me never to chew gum at the plate. He said it makes your eyeballs bounce up and down." — Indians coach Charlie Manuel in 1988.

"I could barely close my lips. My cheeks were puffed out like a chipmunk's. I had to do it in four minutes, and I gagged a little bit." — Indians relief ace Steve Olin, after engaging in a 1992 bubble-gum chewing contest with fellow reliever Kevin Wickander. Olin chewed 50 pieces after Wickander chewed 42 and kept bragging about it. The next day Wickander chewed 55 and the two then chewed their way to a 71–71 tie.

See also *Baseball Cards — Gum.*

Baseball Card. Padres utility infielder Kurt Bevacqua won the Topps bubble gum blowing contest in 1975 (erroneously 1972 in some sources) and was pictured in a special 1976 baseball card showing Joe Garagiola measuring the winning bubble.

"Chew." "Big League Chew" is a pack of bubblegum that looks like a pack of chewing tobacco. The idea was conceived by 1960s Yankees pitcher Jim Bouton and a friend, who sold it to a corporation supposedly to prevent Bouton's ex-wife from receiving any of the profits.

Contest. During the 1976 World Series between the Reds and Yankees, there was a bubble gum blowing contest before Game 3 that featured two catchers, Johnny Oates of the Phillies and Gary Carter of the Expos. The televised mini-event called for each player to chew five or six sticks of gum and blow the biggest bubble. Joe Torre was the official scorer. Oates won with a bubble measuring 21 inches in diameter.

Cap. A number of players put their gum on the button of their caps while they batted, including Hal Chase, Eddie Collins, Frank Crosetti and Phil Rizzuto. One source reported that Collins had the strange habit of putting the gum in his mouth after he reached two strikes. His teammates once put pepper on the gum while it was on his cap. After two strikes he began chewing furiously on the pepper gum, lost his concentration and struck out.

Eyebrows. Early players sometimes put chewing gum on their eyebrows to ensure good luck at the plate.

Memorabilia. In 2002 Luis Gonzalez's chewed gum sold for $10,000 at an auction. A Bazooka Joe comic about Gonzalez's gum sold for $1,225 (the comics come inside the bubblegum).

Guns

"You're not gonna miss any plays today, big boy!"—Manager Jim Frey to umpire Ken Kaiser after a bad call the day before, as Frey held a starter's pistol to Kaiser's chest protector and pulled the trigger. The 6'5", 270-pound Kaiser first thought he had been shot; regaining his composure, he decked Frey.

"He's got a gun concealed about his person. They can't tell me he throws them balls with his arm."—Ring Lardner on Walter Johnson.

"The Angels had more guns in their clubhouse than the Jesse James gang."—Marvin Miller on the early 1970s Angels. Chico Ruiz of the Angels was accused in 1970 of pulling a gun on teammate Alex Johnson before being released by the club. At the same time, Angels outfielder Tony Conigliaro had a shotgun in his locker and reliever Eddie Fisher had several guns in his locker. Owner Gene Autry had been a singing cowboy and was known to bring guns into the locker room and pass them out as gifts to his players.

"Gene Schott, Tom Gunning, Cliff Darringer, John Carbine, Paul Derringer, Buckshot May, Manny Salvo, Cannonball Crane, Joe Cannon, Mace Brown, Cannonball Titcomb"

Celebration. In 1893 Louisville outfielder Farmer Weaver purportedly celebrated the Fourth of July by pulling out a pistol and putting five bullets in a fly ball before catching what was left of it.

Umpires. Many early umpires carried guns for protection. In 1909 a Chicago judge ruled that an umpire had no right to draw a gun even if faced with a mob.

Hoax. During an argument with an umpire, Jimmy Piersall once pulled out a squirt gun and shot him in the face.

Protection. In the late 1950s Frank Robinson began carrying a gun to protect himself from death threats. He purportedly was once arrested for brandishing it at a short order cook who refused to serve him.

Wake Up Call. When he was a minor league manager, Jack McKeon once used a starter's pistol with blanks to "shoot" a runner at third base who kept running through his stop signs.

Foul Ball Zeal. In 2001 an off-duty policeman dropped his gun on the field at Pittsburgh's PNC Park while reaching for a foul ball.

Denny McLain. Denny McLain was suspended by commissioner Bowie Kuhn near the end of the 1970 season for carrying a gun.

"H is for Hornsby;
When pitching to Rog,
The pitcher would pitch,
Then the pitcher would dodge."
—Ogden Nash on Rogers Hornsby.

Chick Hafey (1903–1973)

Hall of Fame (VC) 1971

"If Hafey had had good eyesight and good health he might have been the finest right-handed hitter baseball has ever known."—Branch Rickey, who is credited with discovering Hafey.

Hafey was a National League outfielder during the 1920s and 1930s, batting .317 lifetime.

A California native, Charles James Hafey began his Major League career late in 1924 with the Cardinals after being converted from a pitcher to an outfielder during the 1924 minor league season. Hafey increased his totals for the Major League club in 1925 and 1926 after starting each season in Syracuse. He stayed with the Cardinals for good in 1927, batting .329 and leading the league in slugging average. That started a string of six more years when he never batted lower than .336. He was the 1931 batting champion, beating out Bill Terry in the closest race in history.

Hafey might have extended his 13-year career except for serious sinus trouble that affected his eyes. He began wearing glasses as a result, one of the few players to do so in that era. It did not seem to affect his hitting. He suffered a beaning in 1926 and had three different sets of glasses to wear because his eyesight would change constantly. The Cardinals traded him after he held out for more money in 1932.

Hafey finished his career with the Reds from 1932 through 1937, as injuries slowed him down and his productivity slipped. After hitting .269 in 89 games in 1937 he retired to his California ranch.

He was considered the second-best hitter in the National League during his career, behind only Rogers Hornsby. He had a .317 lifetime batting average and a .526 slugging average.

Jesse Haines (1893–1978)

Hall of Fame (VC) 1970

"Jesse had strong right arm, burning fast ball. But this wasn't enough to make him fine pitcher until he learned two things — how to control his temper, how to throw knuckle ball."—Gene Karst and Martin J. Jones, Jr., in *Who's Who in Professional Baseball* (1973).

Haines won 210 games for the Cardinals over an 18-year career that lasted through the 1920s and most of the 1930s.

A native of Ohio, Jesse Joseph "Pop" Haines was pitching at age 26 for Kansas City of the American Association when he signed with the Cardinals in 1920. He had appeared in one game for the Reds in 1918 but did not remain for 1919. With the Cardinals over 18 seasons, he won more games for the club than anyone except Bob Gibson.

Haines had a fastball and later developed a knuckleball, which he used to extend his career. His best year was 1927, when he was 24–10 and pitched six shutouts. He won 20 games three times and won three games over four World Series. He was the winning pitcher in the 1926 World Series in which Grover Cleveland Alexander replaced him and struck out Tony Lazzeri with the bases loaded to preserve the Game 7 win for the Cardinals. Haines also had a .444 lifetime World Series batting average.

Haines pitched in the Major Leagues through his 44th birthday, coming in as a spot starter and reliever through the 1937 season. He finished with a record of 210–158, including 209 complete games and 24 shutouts. After retiring, he coached briefly for the Dodgers. Though he was able to attend his induction into the Hall of Fame in 1970, he was in ill health until his death eight years later at age 85.

Hair

"I have received many requests for autographs, bats, balls and equipment, but you are the first person to ask me for some of my hair. Therefore I feel I am obliged to comply with such a request at least once."—Babe Ruth, whose hair and the letter are now in the memorabilia collection of Barry Halper.

"It was a big thrill, all right. But I think the biggest was the night Yogi Berra phoned my room and asked me to go up and give him a haircut."—Reliever Tug McGraw, who worked his way through college as a barber, after beating Sandy Koufax at Shea Stadium.

"I think this stuff works. Every time I use it, I get a headache. I think that means that hair is trying to break through." — Yankee catcher Benny Bengough in 1927 on his new hair restoration product.

"The guy's got a fault? Dandruff, maybe." — Giants manager Leo Durocher on Frank Malzone, who had a fast career start and a slow finish.

"Brother Branch Rickey has been around a little too long to get panicky in a situation that sees the villagers clamoring for his scalp, slightly sprinkled with dandruff." — Sportswriter Joe Williams.

"Howard Cosell is the only guy who changed his name and put on a toupee to tell it like it was." — Sportswriter Jimmy Cannon.

"Anyone who has plastic hair is bound to have problems." — Jay Johnstone on the squeaky-clean image of Steve Garvey.

"He is said to have enough greasy kid stuff in his ultra-long curly hair to give [racer car driver] A.J. Foyt a lube job and an oil change." — Thomas Boswell in *Inside Sports*.

"The boorishness starts at the top, with manager Sparky Anderson.... He remains one of the troglodytes of the sport. Anderson is a short-hair freak. He requires that his players have short hair and be clean-shaven.... He actually believes that men with short hair are morally superior to those with long." — Sportswriter Glenn Dickey during the 1972 World Series between the clean-shaven and short-haired Reds and the long-haired and mustachioed A's. Dickey once described owner Charlie Finley as proud of the fact that his club was "The Hairiest Team in Baseball."

"Jerry Hairston, Earle Combs, Jeff Combe, Turner Barber"

Oscar Gamble played for the Yankees primarily in the 1970s. He was generally regarded as having the highest "Afro" haircut in Major League Baseball. He was ordered to cut off some of his hair because his batting helmet kept popping off.

Flaky Steve Hovley of the Pilots started the 1969 season with a crewcut. He refused to cut his hair during the season because he "didn't want to discriminate against any one hair."

At the height of his brief fame in 1976, Tigers pitcher Mark Fidrych went to the barber to shorten his curly blond hair. Young girls scrambled into the shop to pick up the cuttings from the floor.

In August 1991 Don Mattingly and the Yankees feuded over the length of Mattingly's hair. After he was forced to get a haircut, a New York radio station auctioned the hair for charity. New York policeman Tom Tumminia paid $3,000 for it and received a certificate of authenticity autographed by Mattingly, coach Carl Taylor, who did the cutting, and manager Stump Merrill.

Wahoo Sam Crawford was a barber with his father before playing professional baseball full-time.

Pitcher Larry Locke of the 1960s was known as a flake — and was a hairstylist.

Bill Veeck hired a barber to cut hair in the stands during White Sox games.

In the 1970s the Reds once sponsored Hairdressers Night and the Braves held a Farrah Fawcett look-alike contest.

In the 1990s barber Charlie Ciotta cut a deal with the Buffalo Bisons that allowed him to set up a barber chair in the stands at Pilot Field and trim hair for $2.50 a head during games.

Dodger infielder Delino DeShields and his father opened a hair salon in 1994 while DeShields was still an active player.

Hair Dryers/Hairpieces.

"Today they have more trouble packing hair dryers than baseball equipment." — Bob Feller.

"... champagne all over the nice red rug on the clubhouse floor, and also — hoo, hoo! ho, ho! — all over the Reds' other rug, which

Oscar Gamble sporting the largest afro in Major League history. He was actually ordered to trim it because his batting helmet kept popping off.

is Lee May's hairpiece." — Roger Angell in *The Summer Game* (1972), describing the 1970 NLCS celebration.

"Pepitone is the No. 1 member of baseball's mod set. He dresses in the newest fashions and wears hairpieces, including one partial wig which he refers to as 'my gamer.' He wears his gamer only on certain days, however, 'It depends on how I feel,' he explained." — Jerome Holtzman in *The Sporting News*.

"The Houston Astrodome is the biggest hairdryer in the world." — Joe Pepitone, who is credited with introducing the blow dryer to a Major League clubhouse in the 1960s; an interesting concept considering that he wore a hairpiece. Pepitone actually had two hairpieces, a large one which he wore when he went out and a smaller one to wear under his baseball cap (his "game piece"). Jim Bouton reported in *Ball Four* (1970) that he and Fritz Peterson once went into the Yankee clubhouse during a game and filled Pepitone's hair dryer with talcum powder. When he turned it on, Pepitone "looked like an Italian George Washington wearing a powdered wig."

Because he was prematurely bald and wore a hairpiece, early 20th century umpire Bob Emslie was given the nickname "Wig" (see **Pressure**).

Bad Hair Days.

"On the mound is Randy Jones, the left-hander with the Karl Marx hairdo." — Broadcaster Jerry Coleman, who presumably meant Harpo Marx.

"A pitcher with a damaged arm has about as much future as a bald Farrah Fawcett." — Umpire Ron Luciano in *Remembrances of Swings Past* (1988).

"You know what will make me look younger? More wins. That's what will make me look younger. And more important, feel younger." — Lou Piniella, after telling his pitiful 2003 Devil Rays players that he would let them dye his hair any (legitimate) color they wanted if they would win three games in a row. They finally delivered in July, and Piniella was turned into a blonde the next day. Stylist Wilber Bonilla, who had styled some of the Devil Rays players' hair, got up at 6:30 a.m. to make the 75-mile drive to Tropicana Field to make the 9 a.m. appointment.

Chili Davis was sometimes known as "Chili Bowl" in honor of chronically bad haircuts early in his career.

Red Sox outfielders Tris Speaker and Duffy Lewis supposedly feuded as a result of a bad haircut. On a trip west during the hot summer of 1915, the Red Sox players decided to shave their heads to keep cool. The dapper Lewis, known as a snappy dresser, had the misfortune of his hair not growing back after the haircut. Speaker began teasing him and repeatedly pulled his cap off in front of fans. Lewis took offense and eventually the two stopped speaking except to call for fly balls in the outfield.

Bald Is Beautiful.

"I won't have that problem." — Balding Giants slugger Matt Williams during his home run tear in 1994, commenting on the loss of hair by Roger Maris from the pressure of his 1961 record home run pace.

On May 14, 1972, 583 A's fans took advantage of free admission and baseball caps for bald men.

In 1989 broadcaster Tom Paciorek vowed to shave his head if the White Sox ever won eight games in a row. The White Sox delivered and Paciorek received a buzz cut and then put on a wig.

In 1994 the Mariners staged "Jay Buhner Haircut Night." More than 400 people lined up in front of 10 barber chairs to get a buzz cut just like the Mariners right fielder. Two women shaved their heads. Buhner's response to the evening: "It was crazy. Hair was flying everywhere. I should have collected some in case I need a weave someday."

By 1996 the Buhner Buzz Cut III saw 3,321 fans, including 28 women, have their heads shaved. It was estimated that over the years over 12,400 fans, including dozens of women, participated in Buhner Buzz cut nights. By 2001, during the seventh annual event on May 31, 6,246 fans, including 112 women, were admitted, bringing the seven-year total of baldies to 22,302.

In 1996 Rogaine was a sponsor of the Braves telecasts. Whenever the "Rogaine Leader Board" was flashed on the screen, the camera immediately panned to the baldest fan or player in view.

On June 10, 1998, the Giants staged Brian Johnson Buzz Cut night, and gave four box seats to any fan who was willing to have his head shaved like the San Francisco catcher.

Pressure. Bob Emslie umpired in the National League for more than 30 years. The pressure eventually got to him, as every hair follicle on his body died. Crew chief Bill Klem offered to continue umpiring with Emslie and allow Emslie to umpire only on the basepaths to reduce the stress. Reportedly this arrangement succeeded for several years.

Comb. Members of the minor league Newark Bears missed teammate Rickey Henderson when the Dodgers signed him for the Major League minimum $300,000. One night he couldn't find a comb for his new haircut, so he sauntered over to the postgame spread and used a fork.

Memorabilia. In 2003 some of Babe Ruth's hair sold for $102.51.

Some of Mickey Mantle's hair sold for $6,900, which was sold by his former lover — and agent.

Bad Timing. Mets infielder Rey Sanchez was in hot water with his teammates in May 2003 when he retired to the clubhouse during a lopsided loss and received a haircut from teammate Armando Benitez.

Hall of Fame (1939–)

"To the pioneers who were the moving spirits of the game in its infancy and to the players who have been elected to the Hall of Fame … we pay just tribute. But I should like to dedicate this museum to all America." — Judge Landis at the dedication of the National Baseball Museum and Hall of Fame on June 12, 1939.

"The personalities enshrined in the Baseball Hall of Fame represent a whole gamut of fictional characters and idiosyncrasies. Reading about them, and recalling their varied accomplishments and triumphs is like losing one-self in the great adventure classics of literature. Heroics, tragedies, derring-do, comic relief…" — Ken Smith in *Baseball's Hall of Fame* (1947).

"I read where Roger Clemens said it was a goal of his. To me, that's like planning for the 9th inning when you're in the 1st. I don't know many players who have set out to make the Hall of Fame, and I've played with both Frank [Robinson] and Brooks Robinson. I remember talking to Brooks about it one time, and it was like it hadn't even occurred to him. If Brooks Robinson didn't have the right to think about it, who did?" — Pitcher Jim Palmer.

Origins. *Cooperstown* became a baseball icon after the 1907 Mills Commission (see *Origins of Baseball*) erroneously determined that baseball was created in 1839 as the brainstorm of Cooperstown native *Abner Doubleday*. At the urging of Cooperstown locals, National League president John Tener and Giants president Harry Hempstead drove up to Cooperstown in 1916 to consider it as a site for a baseball museum.

In 1919 the Cooperstown Chamber of Commerce sent a delegation to National League president John Heydler to ask support for a plan to erect a baseball shrine. Heydler was from upstate New York, so he supported the idea of Cooperstown as the home of a museum. He was largely responsible for selling the idea to other important Major League figures.

American League president Ban Johnson was cool to the idea, in part because it was viewed as a National League proposal. Judge Landis liked the idea. After he threw his support to the plan in the early 1920s, Johnson grudgingly went along with it. In 1920 the people of Cooperstown established the first memorial to Doubleday.

Stephen Carlton Clark (1882–1960), a wealthy Cooperstown businessman and heir to the Singer Sewing Machine fortune (whose patriarch purportedly stole the patent from Elias Howe, uncle of the founder of the *Howe News Bureau*), collected the baseball memorabilia which formed the core of the original materials in the Hall. The display included an old baseball which purportedly was found in an old trunk. The ball supposedly was used by Abner Doubleday in the first baseball game in 1839. It is still on display at the Hall.

Clark later assigned Alexander Cleland to scour the country for authentic baseball artifacts to add to the collection. He obtained material from a number of prominent baseball people, including Connie Mack, Mrs. Christy Mathewson, Mrs. John McGraw, Clark Griffith, the Spink family and William Wrigley.

The exhibition drew large crowds and provided Clark and others the impetus to create a full museum. In the mid–1930s a town committee approached National League president Ford Frick for

The first Hall of Fame induction ceremony in 1939. Crowds were thick even then, but no Pete Rose signing autographs down the street.

help in establishing a National Museum at the site. Frick suggested a "Hall of Fame" and Clark and other locals initially contributed $40,000 for the building. The Otsego Historical Society paid $90,000 to build it in 1939.

Clark was president of the Museum from 1939 until his death in 1960. The wing which today houses the players' plaques was dedicated in 1949. By the early 1960s the Hall had doubled in size. The National Baseball Library was added in the late 1960s.

Doubleday Field. Dr. E. L. Pitcher [great name!] is credited by some with the idea of Cooperstown as a baseball mecca. He leased a plot of land for a public park and it was later renamed Doubleday Field when the local townspeople bought the plot in 1923. The first curator of the museum confirmed to sportswriter Fred Lieb that they did not know where the first baseball game was played, but that the site chosen "seemed appropriate." On September 6, 1920, National League president John Heydler umpired a charity game to raise $450 toward purchase of the site.

The field is approximately two blocks from what was to be the site of the Hall of Fame buildings. In 1933 the diamond was developed into what has been described incorrectly as a "Major League–quality" field, seating approximately 9,000 in the permanent stands, although

Cooperstown had only 3,000 inhabitants. The field now seats 9,791 and its dimensions from left to right field are 296–390–312.

Hall of Fame Game. The Hall of Fame game was born on June 13, 1940, to raise money to maintain the field and museum. Games between a National and American League team are played on the day after the Baseball Hall of Fame induction ceremony, a Monday in late July or early August. At its inception it had almost the prestige of the seven-year-old All-Star Game.

The games of 1944, 1962, 1990 and 1993 were rained out. The 1945 game was cancelled due to wartime restrictions. The 1981 game was cancelled because of the player strike and the 1989 game was cancelled due to mechanical problems with one of the team's planes. The 2003 game was rescheduled for the weekend following the induction ceremony weekend because of a conflict with the Major League schedule.

First Inductees/1936–1939. Voting for entry into the Hall of Fame began in 1936 and continued annually in 1937, 1938 and 1939 until the first induction ceremony in June 1939. For the 1936 vote, announced in January that year, Henry Edwards, secretary of the American League Service Bureau, polled the 226 members of the Baseball Writers Association of America using a ballot developed by a special six-person selection committee. A player was elected if he received at least two-thirds of the votes of the writers (today 75% is required).

Five players were elected in 1936. Ty Cobb received 222 of 226 votes, the highest percentage by any player until Tom Seaver in 1992. Babe Ruth and Honus Wagner received 215 votes, Christy Mathewson 205 and Walter Johnson 189.

Of the original 51 players who received votes, five made it in immediately. Another 38 of these candidates made it later through regular voting. The eight who never made were Hal Chase (11 votes), Johnny Kling (8), Lou Criger (7), Joe Jackson (2), Bill Bradley (1), Nap Rucker (1), Jake Daubert (1) and Kid Elberfeld (1). Of those who did not make it the first year, Nap Lajoie received the highest percentage of votes, 64.6% (146 votes).

There were supposed to be ten nominees selected in the first vote in 1936, five pre–1900 and five post–1900 players. The two groups were to be evaluated and selected by separate committees. However, the members of the committee to select the pre–1900 players argued among themselves and could not achieve a 75% committee vote for any player in order to submit him to a two-thirds vote by the writers. In addition, Cy Young had his votes split as to whether he was a pre– or post–1900 inductee. This may explain why he was not elected until 1937.

In 1937 three more players were elected: Nap Lajoie, Tris Speaker and Cy Young. In 1938 Grover Cleveland Alexander was elected and in 1939 the writers chose Eddie Collins, Willie Keeler, George Sisler and Lou Gehrig (the latter by special vote due to his illness).

Committee on Old-Timers. The predecessor to the Veterans' Committee, the Committee on Old-Timers, elected another 13 men to the Hall of Fame prior to the first induction ceremony in 1939: first National League president Morgan Bulkeley, Ban Johnson, Connie Mack, John McGraw and George Wright in 1937; Alexander Cartwright and Henry Chadwick in 1938; and Cap Anson, Albert Spalding, Charlie Comiskey, Candy Cummings, Buck Ewing and Charles Radbourn in 1939.

First Induction Ceremony and Exhibitions. Judge Landis made the dedication speech to officially open the Hall on June 12, 1939. Over 10,000 fans attended the first ceremony and the three games played that day at Cooperstown. The first game was a demonstration of the original *Town Ball* game, followed by a two-inning game of Knickerbocker ball. Each of the 41 existing minor leagues sent one player to comprise two teams that played a game using the original Cartwright Rules (see *Origins of Baseball*). The Doubledays defeated the Cartwrights 9–6. That exhibition was followed by a nine-inning game played by the stars of the day.

Among the initial inductees, Babe Ruth was the youngest and Connie Mack was the oldest living at 76. Wee Willie Keeler and Christy Mathewson had died.

On July 9, 1939, as part of the inaugural festivities to honor the National Association (the governing minor league body), all 41 minor leagues sent a star player to participate in a minor league all-star game in Cooperstown.

Attendance at Ceremony. Several inductees did not attend their ceremony, several apparently due to ill health, including Walter Alston in 1983. There was no ceremony in wartime 1942 and 1943, and so Roger Hornsby did not attend his induction in 1942. Eppa Rixey was the first inductee to die between his election and the ceremony, when he suffered a fatal heart attack in February 1963.

First Year of Eligibility/Elected. Between 1940 and 2004, 37

members of the Hall (players only) were elected in their first year of eligibility (in chronological order):

Bob Feller	1962	Joe Morgan	1990
Jackie Robinson	1962	Jim Palmer	1990
Ted Williams	1966	Rod Carew	1991
Stan Musial	1969	Tom Seaver	1992
Sandy Koufax	1971	Reggie Jackson	1993
Warren Spahn	1973	Steve Carlton	1994
Mickey Mantle	1974	Mike Schmidt	1995
Ernie Banks	1977	George Brett	1999
Willie Mays	1979	Nolan Ryan	1999
Al Kaline	1980	Robin Yount	1999
Bob Gibson	1981	Carlton Fisk	2000
Frank Robinson	1982	Kirby Puckett	2001
Henry Aaron	1982	Dave Winfield	2001
Brooks Robinson	1983	Ozzie Smith	2002
Lou Brock	1985	Gary Carter	2003
Willie McCovey	1986	Eddie Murray	2004
Willie Stargell	1988	Dennis Eckersley	2004
Carl Yastrzemski	1989	Paul Molitor	2004
Johnny Bench	1989		

Eligibility/Voting. Since 1936 the voting for candidates has been conducted by members of the *Baseball Writers Association of America* ("BBWAA"). This was decided by a Centennial Committee consisting of National League president Ford Frick, American League president Will Harridge, Judge Landis, former National League president John Heydler, and minor league executives Judge William Bramham and George Trautman. There was no voting in 1940, 1941, 1943 or 1944.

Balloting has changed over the years. By 1945 the BBWAA could vote only for players; a Veterans Committee voted for older players and others who contributed to baseball. By 1947 only 10-year members of the BBWAA could vote.

To be eligible a player must have been an active Major Leaguer for 10 years. Players are also eligible if they played 10 years in the Negro Leagues, or a combination of 10 years in both the Negro Leagues and Major Leagues. The 10-year rule was waived for pitcher Addie Joss, who died of meningitis while still active.

A player must also have been retired for five years, though there is confusion about when this rule was implemented. Some sources report that it was created in 1947, but Bill Guilfoile of the Hall of Fame reported that prior to 1953 there was no waiting period beyond one year. Any player who had retired prior to 1953 was not required to wait the five years. Players originally did not have to be retired to be eligible for the Hall, as evidenced by Mickey Cochrane's name on the original ballot. Joe DiMaggio received a single write-in vote in 1945 while he was still an active player (though in the military). DiMaggio retired in 1951 and received votes in 1954. He fell 14 votes short (175 of the required 189), but was elected in 1955.

The waiting period was waived for Roberto Clemente (Lou Gehrig was elected early, though before the rule was implemented). To avoid election of undeserving candidates because of the emotional impact of their premature deaths, the Hall eventually created a special system for the death of an active player or a player within the five-year waiting period. The player becomes eligible in the next election following six months after the date of death or six months after the five years, whichever occurs first. After Cardinals pitcher Darryl Kile died of an apparent heart attack during the 2002 season, he was added to the Hall of Fame ballot for 2003, but he received nowhere near the required number of votes.

A player must receive 75% of the votes cast. According to Ford

Frick, credit for the 75% rule goes to sportswriter Alan Gould of the Associated Press. Voting is based on the player's record, integrity, playing ability, sportsmanship, character, and contributions to his team.

The screening process is conducted by a panel of six baseball writers, among whom at least two must nominate a player. To stay eligible, candidates must be newly nominated or have received at least 5% of the prior year's vote (originally 10%). He may remain on the ballot for 15 years. Write-in candidates now are not permitted (or at least won't be considered), though write-ins still occur. Writers vote for 10. About 500 ballots are now mailed to the eligible writers and about 450 are returned.

Special Election. Lou Gehrig was elected to the Hall while he was still alive and within five years of his retirement, but the formal five-year rule did not exist until the late 1940s or early 1950s.

Judge Landis was elected by a special vote only two weeks before his death in 1944.

Shortly after suffering a broken hip midseason in 1966, Casey Stengel was elected by a special ballot circulated secretly a month before his induction as the 104th entrant. The Baseball Writers Association petitioned the Hall of Fame for a waiver of the normal rules, as it did for Gehrig.

Roberto Clemente was elected in 1973, only one year after his premature death in a plane crash. He received 393 of the 424 votes cast in the special election.

There was talk of taking early action for catcher Thurman Munson when he was killed in a plane crash during the 1979 season. However, the writers and the Hall agreed that early entrance would no longer be allowed, and it is doubtful that Munson will ever be elected.

Highest Percentage of Votes.

"If Jesus Christ were to show up with his old baseball glove, some guys wouldn't vote for him. He dropped the cross three times, didn't he."— Sportswriter Dick Young after Willie Mays failed to be elected unanimously. No player has ever been elected unanimously.

In 1992 Tom Seaver received 98.8% of the vote, topping Ty Cobb's previous all-time high of 98.2%. Every one of the top vote getters was omitted entirely from at least four ballots:

Year	Player	Votes	%	Omitted
1992	Tom Seaver	425/430	98.84	5
1999	Nolan Ryan	491/497	98.79	6
1936	Ty Cobb	222/226	98.23	4
1999	George Brett	488/497	98.19	9
1982	Henry Aaron	406/415	97.83	9
1995	Mike Schmidt	444/460	96.52	16
1989	Johnny Bench	431/447	96.42	16
1994	Steve Carlton	436/455	95.80	19
1936	Honus Wagner	215/226	95.13	11
1936	Babe Ruth	215/226	95.13	11
1979	Willie Mays	409/432	94.68	23

Mickey Mantle received only 88% of the votes cast. Bill Terry batted a lifetime .341 and once hit over .400. Nevertheless, he received only 77% of the vote 18 years after he retired. Some blamed the delay on his poor personality. The man who cut it the closest was Al Simmons, who received 75.38% of the vote in 1953 (199/264).

Veterans Committee. Although a Committee on Old-Timers existed during the initial selection process leading up to the 1939 opening of the Hall of Fame, the formal Hall of Fame Committee on Veterans was not created until 1945. Originally, to be inducted upon nomination of this committee, an inductee had to be retired

as a player for 25 years or otherwise have made a significant contribution to baseball (writer, broadcaster, owner, executive or umpire).

The committee, now changed completely, consisted of 18 members, six of whom had to be Hall of Fame players, six individuals who were members of the BBWAA or were broadcasters, and six individuals who were or had been connected with baseball (but not from the other two categories). Each committee member was appointed by the Hall of Fame board for a term of six years.

By the mid–1990s the Veterans Committee could choose up to four people — two from the regular veterans pool or a nonplayer, one from before 1920, and one from the Negro Leagues.

A screening committee consisting of three members of the Veterans Committee created a ballot of up to 15 candidates in each category. A player or nonplayer had to receive at least 75% of the committee votes cast, but only one winner from each category was allowed (if there were two players with at least 75% of the votes, only the top vote getter can be elected that year).

By 2001 the rules called for 60 BBWAA members, two from each Major League city and four from any city with two teams, to identify 25 players and 15 persons for the composite ballot (executives, managers and umpires). In addition, the Hall of Fame appointed a committee of six Hall of Fame members to identify five additional candidates for the Players Ballot. The final Players Ballot contains 25–30 names, depending on duplication between the two groups. Voting members receive ballot materials, including supporting documentation and statistics, in January of each year. Results are announced in February after being counted by an accounting firm in the presence of a Hall of Fame representative. Big Four accountants Ernst & Young was selected for the 2001 vote.

In 1978 the Veterans Committee was expanded to include jurisdiction over the Negro Leagues and the **Negro League Committee** was disbanded. The Veterans Committee expanded to 18 members, with three seats reserved for black members. Between 1979 and 1994 only two black veterans were elected by the committee, in contrast to 17 whites. Only four votes are needed to defeat a nominee from this committee. Of the total pre–Jackie Robinson players inducted into the Hall as of the early 1990s, there were 11 black players and 140 white players.

When a player has been passed over for the last time by the writers in the regular voting, he must wait three years before being considered by the Veterans Committee. Managers, umpires and executives who have been retired for five years are eligible. If they have reached age 65, then the waiting period is only six months. All players had to have 10 years in the Major Leagues and other person had to be affiliated with baseball for at least 10 years. In 2000 the Hall of Fame commissioned a study of African-American baseball from 1860 to 1960, and recommendations by that committee may affect voting on Negro League players.

In 1993 the Hall of Fame changed its eligibility rules for Veterans Committee consideration. Post–1945 veterans would still be eligible for consideration by the regular writers even after 25 years following their retirement if they 1) received at least 60% of the regular writers' votes in any one year; 2) or at least 100 votes by the regular writers in any year prior to February 1991. This positively affected Bill Mazeroski, Roger Maris, Maury Wills and Richie Ashburn, allowing each of them to remain eligible for consideration and not forcing them into Veterans Committee consideration. Ashburn and Mazeroski later were elected by the Veterans Committee. Under the new rule a player had to be retired for 23 years before being considered by the Veterans Committee: five years from retirement, 15 years of eligibility on the regular ballot, plus the three-year waiting period after becoming ineligible for the regular balloting.

With significant changes in 2001, the Hall of Fame eliminated a rule that any player who did not receive 5% of the vote in the Players Ballot in any year could never be considered by the Veterans Committee. Now, anyone who otherwise qualifies with 10 years of service is eternally eligible. This reinstated hope for 1,700 players who received less than 5% of the vote in a year. The special ballots for Negro League and 19th century players were eliminated after the 2001 voting.

In 2001 the committee was revamped to eliminate the 15-member committee and replace it with the living members of the Hall of Fame (61 people in 2001), the living recipients of the Spink Award for writers (13 in 2001) and Frick Award for broadcasters (also 13 in 2001), and then-current members of the Veterans Committee whose terms had not expired (3 in 2001). This increased the voters to 90 from the original 15.

In early 2002 an overview committee of 10 historians and veteran baseball writers selected 200 former players to make the first cut out of 1,400 listed for further voting by the Veterans Committee. The overview committee also selected 60 managers, umpires and executives.

The next step was for a screening committee appointed by the writers association to cut the eligible players to 25 and the others to 15. Another five players could be added by a six-member screening committee consisting of Hall of Famers. The final ballots were to be announced in fall 2002 and in early 2003 final voting would require a 75% vote to elect a candidate.

In 2003 the Veterans Committee consisted of 84 voters—82 Hall of Famers (including 58 players, 13 broadcasters and 11 writers), and two members of the former committee whose terms had not yet expired. Beginning in 2003, the Veterans Committee was to hold its election of players every other year. Voting for managers, executives and umpires would be every four years.

Most Inductees in One Year. In 1946, 11 people were elected to the Hall of Fame, all of them old-timers through the Veterans Committee. No players were regularly elected by the baseball writers. In 1945 the Veterans Committee selected 10 inductees.

Fewest Inductees. After the initial flurry of inductees in 1939, there were no regular elections until 1942, when Rogers Hornsby made it. Another five years passed before four more players were elected. No players were elected in 1950 and then from 1957 through 1961 no players were elected. No regular selections were made in 1963, 1965, 1971 and 1996.

Most Future Hall of Famers. The 1928 Athletics had seven Hall of Famers, including Eddie Collins, Tris Speaker, Ty Cobb, Mickey Cochrane, Jimmie Foxx, Al Simmons and Lefty Grove. The Yankees that season topped them with nine, including Leo Durocher, who made it in as a manager. The group: Leo Durocher, manager Miller Huggins, Babe Ruth, Lou Gehrig, Bill Dickey, Earle Combs, Tony Lazzeri, Herb Pennock and Waite Hoyt.

First Black Players. In 1962 Jackie Robinson became the first black player inducted into the Hall of Fame. Roy Campanella was the second in 1969.

Negro League Committee. Ted Williams was extremely vocal in urging the election of Negro League players to the Hall. At his August 1966 induction ceremony he was characteristically blunt, but also more eloquent than expected in both his personal thanks and his views on recognition of Negro League players: "I guess every player thinks about going into the Hall of Fame. Now that the moment has come for me, I find it difficult to say what is really in my heart, but I know that it is the greatest thrill of my life. I received 280-odd votes from the writers. I know I didn't have 280 close friends among the writers. I know that they voted for me because they felt in their minds, and some in their hearts, that I rated it, and I want to say to them thank you. Thank you from the bottom of my heart....

"Baseball gives every American boy a chance to excel, not just to be as good as someone else but to be better than someone else. This is the nature of man and the name of the game, and I've been a very lucky guy to have worn a baseball uniform, to have struck out or to have hit a tape-measure home run. And I hope that someday the names of Satchel Paige and Josh Gibson in some way can be added as a symbol of the great Negro players who are not here only because they were not given a chance...."

The Negro League Committee was formed in 1970, but there was a debate over the physical location of plaques for such players in the Hall. Commissioner Bowie Kuhn advocated a "special niche" at the Hall for Negro League players. After controversy erupted over the different treatment, it was agreed that full induction and placement among the white greats was appropriate. Satchel Paige was the first to be inducted in 1971 before the "niche" idea was abandoned, and he echoed the sentiments of many that this was tokenism: "The only change is that baseball has turned Paige from a second class citizen to a second class immortal."

Eight more Negro League inductees were selected after Paige until the committee was disbanded in 1978. Committee members and sportswriters revealed later that the committee had been given a quota of nine Negro League players. When the quota was filled the committee was disbanded.

When the Negro League Committee dissolved, the **Veterans Committee** was expanded to have jurisdiction over Negro League selections, but the makeup of the expanded committee has effectively excluded a number of deserving Negro League inductees. See also James A. Riley, *Too Dark for the Hall* (1991).

Jackie Robinson batting during the 1951 Hall of Fame Game at Doubleday Field.

Losing Record. Relief pitcher Rollie Fingers has often been described as the only pitcher in the Hall with a losing record (114–118). He had 341 saves over his 17-year career, first all-time when he retired. What is often forgotten is that Negro League star Satchel Paige had a losing record of 28–31 during his Major League career.

Newsletter. The Hall has a newsletter which it sends to members of the Hall.

Historian. The position disappeared after Cliff Kachline was unceremoniously dumped in 1982, and the position's functions are now spread out among several different people.

Ring. Those elected to the Hall receive a large ring, with a "stone" that is a large metal baseball (see *Jewelry*).

Writer's Wing. The J.G. Taylor *Spink Award* is presented to sportswriters upon their induction into the Hall of Fame Writers Wing.

Broadcasters. Broadcasters who are selected for the Hall receive the *Ford Frick Award*.

Fielders. Brooks Robinson is the first fielding phenomenon to make it into the Hall based primarily on that aspect of his game.

Fan Infiltration. See *Fathers and Sons — Honor Thy Father* for the story of the photograph that was slipped into a Hall of Fame exhibit by the son of a former amateur player.

Financial Support. The Hall receives no financial support from Major League Baseball and must generate all of its income from the sale of merchandise, Hall of Fame tours and a recently started national tour of Hall of Fame memorabilia that was expected to generate $20 million.

By Position. The number of Hall of Fame members who played each position through 2004 (A player who switched positions is listed only once):

66 Pitcher	11 Third Base
14 Catcher	19 Left Field
19 First Base	20 Center Field
16 Second Base	22 Center Field
22 Shortstop	1 Designated Hitter (Paul Molitor)

Not in the Hall.

"The beauty of baseball is that the older you get, the better you were. Pretty soon you think that you are Hall of Fame material. By God, there are a lot of us who were decent players, but we weren't Hall of Fame." — Johnny Pesky quoted in *For the Love of the Game*, by Cynthia J. Wilber (1992).

Joe Jackson has the highest batting average, .355, of any player not in the Hall. He has been excluded because of his involvement in the Black Sox Scandal.

Riggs Stephenson is not in the Hall even though he hit .336, the second highest of any player not elected. Though he played 14 seasons, he appeared in over 136 games in only four seasons.

Jim "Deacon" White was a star catcher from the 19th century who hit .303 over 15 seasons.

Between 1995 and 2004, Jim Rice received 2,180 votes, the most for any player not elected to the Hall. Second was Bruce Sutter, who received 1,914 votes.

See also Brent Kelley, *The Case for Those Overlooked by the Baseball Hall of Fame* (1992), covering 39 men who arguably should be in the Hall; Wil A. Linkugel and Edward J. Pappas, *They Tasted Glory: Among the Missing at the Baseball Hall of Fame* (1998) (17 whose careers were cut short by injury, death or circumstance); Mike Shalin, Neil Shalin, *Out by a Step: The 100 Best Players Not in the Baseball Hall of Fame*, (2002).

Belated Entry.

"'Look, I got a confession to make,' he said. 'I was born in Chicago Canaryville on the South Side. Played Little League in Armour Park. And I know your uncle. Man, do I. I read him in the *Daily News*. He tried to get Nellie Fox into Cooperstown, God love him. Nellie ever gets in, you know there's a God." — Crabbe Evers in *Fear in Fenway* (1993). Fox was a White Sox second baseman in the 1950s and a 12-time All-Star who died of cancer in his 40s. In his last year of eligibility, 1985, he received 295 of 395 votes, missing by two votes. Because his percentage was 74.7%, he came the closest of any player to being elected without making it in. He was finally elected by the Veteran's committee in 1997.

Hal Newhouser won 20 games four times in the 1940s with 170 wins to lead all pitchers in that decade. Until 1992 when he was elected, he had been the only two-time MVP (1944–1945) not to be elected to the Hall. Dale Murphy may end up in this category after winning MVP Awards in 1982 and 1983.

Pitcher Ferguson Jenkins was kept out for many years, apparently because of his 1980 cocaine possession conviction. He finally made it in 1991 by one vote (75.3%).

Until his 1980 election, Chuck Klein was the only man to have 2,000 or more hits with a .320 average or better not to be selected for the Hall of Fame. Klein is also the only man to have at least 120 RBIs during each of his first five full seasons, from 1929 through 1933.

Jim Bunning, who was finally elected by the Veterans committee in 1996, once received 317 out of 427 votes, leaving him only four short of the required 75%. However, nine New York writers protested marginal candidates by sending in blank ballots. If they had abstained instead, Bunning would have been elected.

American Association. No 19th century player who played a majority of his career in the old American Association is in the Hall of Fame. This may have occurred because of the lingering National League bias against its 1880s rival. Statistics show that when some of the best National League and American Association players were together in 1890 in the Players League, the American Association players led the league in most statistical categories. It should be noted, however, that when the four presumably strongest American Association teams were absorbed into the National League for the 1892 season, those teams all finished at the bottom of the pack. This suggests that the American Association players were generally inferior.

Owners. Tom Yawkey and Bill Veeck are the only owners in the Hall of Fame who were selected strictly as owners. Clark Griffith was the long-time owner of the Senators, but he managed for over 20 years at the beginning of the American League (winning his only pennant in his first season, 1901, with the White Sox).

Pete Rose/Barred.

"When Pete Rose is eligible, Mr. [Jack] Lang will count the ballots and you [the writers] will decide whether he belongs in the Hall." — Commissioner Bart Giamatti.

"The question 'Does Pete Rose belong in the Baseball Hall of Fame?' is as persistent as crabgrass but less interesting. Simply *seeing* it, here on the page, now fills me with an existential ennui, the boredom-induced despair common to long-haul Greyhound passengers." — Steve Rushin in 2003.

"OK: Here's the list. Before Rose can be elected to the Hall of Fame:

1. He has to pay the IRS

2. He has to admit that he bet on baseball

3. He has to enter and complete a gambler's rehab program

4. He has to stop going to Cooperstown on induction day and signing Pete Rose stuff just down the block

5. He has to apologize to Dennis Eckersley and Paul Molitor (his book came out the week their election was announced)

6. He has to apologize to Roger Kahn for the lies he told in his last autobiography

7. He has to disgorge all the profits he made from that book and the new one

8. He has to get a new haircut

9. He has to follow the advice Lou Grant gave to Ted Baxter the night before Baxter's wedding on 'The Mary Tyler Moore Show.'

Grant: 'Ted, you know the way you are?'

Baxter: 'Yes, Lou.'

Grant: 'Don't be like that any more.'

10. He has to make Pete Jr. retire." — Doug Lyons, co-author of *Out of Left Field* (multiple editions).

After Bart Giamatti barred Pete Rose from baseball in 1989 for **Gambling** indiscretions, there was great debate as to whether Rose should be eligible for the Hall of Fame. Giamatti's successor, Fay Vincent, dodged the issue, but on February 4, 1991 a special Hall of Fame committee decided that persons on baseball's ineligible list would also be ineligible for the Hall. The Baseball Writers Association was furious because the issue had been taken out of its control. The 10-man committee included former American League president Lee MacPhail, Cooperstown official Edwin Stack, and two members of the Baseball Writers Association, Jack Lang and Phil Pepe.

Rose would have been eligible for the 1992 election. The results of that vote were announced June 8, 1992, and Rose received 41 write-in votes. Overshadowed somewhat was Tom Seaver becoming the 23rd player to be voted in during his first year of eligibility. When Reggie Jackson was the sole inductee in 1993, Rose received 14 write-in votes. He received 10 votes in 1994 when Steve Carlton was elected and 14 in 1995 when Mike Schmidt went in. He received 19 votes in 1996 when no player was selected in the regular voting. He received 18 votes in 2003 and 15 votes in 2004.

In 2004 Rose was inducted into the World Wrestling Entertainment's Hall of Fame (for a fee, of course). WWE chairman Vince McMahon said that Rose "has a deep, abiding respect for what we do."

Cap Controversy.

"I play 20 years, work my tail off, they're not going to tell me what hat I'm wearing. I promise you that. There might be a vacant seat there. I'll take my mother and we'll go to Palm Springs and I'll invite all y'all and we'll have our own celebration." — Roger Clemens in 2003, who said he would go in as a Yankee or he wouldn't attend the ceremony. This prompted a reply by sportswriter Ross Newhan: "Why would Roger Clemens want to retire when he still has a lot of little boy in him, as evidenced by his childish snit over which cap he wants to be wearing on his Hall of Fame plaque?"

Gary Carter expressed a preference for a Mets cap in light of the 1986 World Series win, but the Hall chose an Expos cap, to which Carter did not object. Catfish Hunter solved the problem when he was inducted in 1987. He couldn't decide between the A's and Yankees, so his plaque does not have a cap.

Youngest. It has been reported that when Sandy Koufax was elected to the Hall of Fame in his first year of eligibility at age 36, he became the youngest person ever admitted to the Hall. However, Lou Gehrig was a few months younger than Koufax when he was elected.

Votes While Active Player. Several players received votes while they were still active, the most recent of which was pitcher Jose Rijo, who received one vote in 2003.

Visitors.

"It was as though Milton Hershey had said, 'Doug, come back here, I'll show you how we really make chocolate.'" — *Out of Left Field* author Doug Lyons, after a basement tour of the Hall of Fame, accompanying his brother and co-author, film critic Jeffrey Lyons, and actor James Earl Jones.

During its early years the Hall received 25,000 visitors annually. By the 1980s the total had reached 250,000 annually. During the peak summer months, attendance averages 5,000 per day. In August 9, 1995, 11-year-old Brett Hornby of Glen Ridge, New Jersey, was identified as the 10 millionth visitor to the Hall.

Address. The Hall of Fame's mailing address is Post Office Box 590, Cooperstown, New York 13326. The phone number is 607/547-7200.

Books. Gerald Astor, *Baseball Hall of Fame 50th Anniversary Book* (1988); Rudy A.S. Gafur, *Cooperstown is My Mecca* (1995); David L. Fleitz, *Ghosts in the Gallery at Cooperstown: Sixteen Little-Known Members of the Hall of Fame* (2004); Bill James, *The Politics of Glory: How the Hall of Fame Really Works* (1994); Lowell Reidenbaugh, *Cooperstown—Where Legends Live Forever* (1986); John C. Skipper, *Biographical Dictionary of the Baseball Hall of Fame* 1999); Ken Smith, *Baseball's Hall of Fame* (first published in 1947 and updated periodically); James F. Vail, *The Road To Cooperstown: A Critical History of Baseball's Hall of Fame Selection Process* (2001); James A. Vlasich, *A Legend for the Legendary: The Origin of the Baseball Hall of Fame* (1990).

Inductees. There have been 256 inductees into the Hall of Fame through 2004:

1936	1941
Ty Cobb	None (no voting)
Walter Johnson	**1942**
Christy Mathewson	Rogers Hornsby
Babe Ruth	VETERANS COMMITTEE:
Honus Wagner	None
1937	**1943**
Napoleon Lajoie	None (no voting)
Tris Speaker	**1944**
Cy Young	None (no voting)
VETERANS COMMITTEE:	VETERANS COMMITTEE:
Morgan G. Bulkeley	Kenesaw Mountain Landis
Byron Bancroft Johnson	**1945**
Connie Mack	None
John McGraw	VETERANS COMMITTEE:
George Wright	(first time officially known as
1938	the Committee on Veterans)
Grover Cleveland Alexander	Dan Brouthers
VETERANS COMMITTEE:	Fred Clarke
Alexander Cartwright	Jimmy Collins
Henry Chadwick	Ed Delahanty
1939	Hugh Duffy
Eddie Collins	Hughie Jennings
Lou Gehrig	Mike Kelly
Willie Keeler	Jim O'Rourke
George Sisler	Wilbert Robinson
VETERANS COMMITTEE:	Roger Bresnahan
Cap Anson	**1946**
Charles Comiskey	None
Candy Cummings	VETERANS COMMITTEE:
Buck Ewing	Jesse Burkett
Charles Radbourn	Frank Chance
Albert G. Spalding	Jack Chesbro
1940	Johnny Evers
None (no voting)	Clark Griffith

Tommy McCarthy
Joe McGinnity
Eddie Plank
Joe Tinker
Rube Waddell
Ed Walsh
1947
Mickey Cochrane
Frankie Frisch
Lefty Grove
Carl Hubbell
VETERANS COMMITTEE:
None
1948
Herb Pennock
Pie Traynor
VETERANS COMMITTEE:
None
1949
Charlie Gehringer
VETERANS COMMITTEE:
Three Finger Brown
Kid Nichols
1950
None
1951
Mel Ott
Jimmie Foxx
VETERANS COMMITTEE:
None
1952
Harry Heilmann
Paul Waner
VETERANS COMMITTEE:
None
1953
Dizzy Dean
Al Simmons
VETERANS COMMITTEE:
Ed Barrow
Chief Bender
Tommy Connolly
Bill Klem
Bobby Wallace
Harry Wright
1954
Bill Dickey
Rabbit Maranville
Bill Terry
VETERANS COMMITTEE:
None (no voting)
1955
Joe DiMaggio
Gabby Hartnett
Ted Lyons
Dazzy Vance
VETERANS COMMITTEE:
Frank Baker
Ray Schalk
1956
Joe Cronin
Hank Greenberg

VETERANS COMMITTEE:
None (no voting)
1957
None
VETERANS COMMITTEE:
Sam Crawford
Joe McCarthy
1958
None
1959
None
VETERANS COMMITTEE
Zack Wheat
1960
None
1961
None
VETERANS COMMITTEE:
Billy Hamilton
Max Carey
1962
Bob Feller
Jackie Robinson
VETERANS COMMITTEE:
Bill McKechnie
Edd Roush
1963
None
VETERANS COMMITTEE:
John Clarkson
Elmer Flick
Sam Rice
Eppa Rixey
1964
Luke Appling
VETERANS COMMITTEE:
Red Faber
Burleigh Grimes
Miller Huggins
Tim Keefe
Heinie Manush
John Montgomery Ward
1965
None
VETERANS COMMITTEE:
Pud Galvin
1966
Ted Williams
VETERANS COMMITTEE:
Casey Stengel
1967
Red Ruffing
VETERANS COMMITTEE:
Branch Rickey
Lloyd Waner
1968
Joe Medwick
VETERANS COMMITTEE:
Kiki Cuyler
Goose Goslin
1969
Roy Campanella

Stan Musial
VETERANS COMMITTEE:
Stan Coveleski
Waite Hoyt
1970
Lou Boudreau
VETERANS COMMITTEE:
Earle Combs
Ford Frick
Jesse Haines
1971
None
VETERANS COMMITTEE:
Dave Bancroft
Jake Beckley
Chick Hafey
Harry Hooper
Joe Kelley
Rube Marquard
George Weiss
NEGRO LEAGUE COMMITTEE:
Satchel Paige
1972
Yogi Berra
Sandy Koufax
Early Wynn
VETERANS COMMITTEE:
Lefty Gomez
Will Harridge
Ross Youngs
NEGRO LEAGUE COMMITTEE:
Josh Gibson
Buck Leonard
1973
Warren Spahn
Robert Clemente
VETERANS COMMITTEE:
Billy Evans
George Kelly
Mickey Welch
NEGRO LEAGUE COMMITTEE:
Monte Irvin
1974
Whitey Ford
Mickey Mantle
VETERANS COMMITTEE:
Jim Bottomley
Jocko Conlan
Sam Thompson
NEGRO LEAGUE COMMITTEE:
James "Cool Papa" Bell
1975
Ralph Kiner
VETERANS COMMITTEE:
Earl Averill
Bucky Harris
Billy Herman
NEGRO LEAGUE COMMITTEE:
Judy Johnson
1976
Bob Lemon
Robin Roberts

VETERANS COMMITTEE:
Roger Connor
Cal Hubbard
Fred Lindstrom
NEGRO LEAGUE COMMITTEE:
Oscar Charleston
1977
Ernie Banks
VETERANS COMMITTEE:
Al Lopez
Amos Rusie
Joe Sewell
NEGRO LEAGUE COMMITTEE:
Martin DiHigo
John "Pop" Lloyd
1978
Eddie Mathews
VETERANS COMMITTEE:
Addie Joss
Larry MacPhail
1979
Willie Mays
VETERANS COMMITTEE:
Hack Wilson
Warren Giles
1980
Al Kaline
VETERANS COMMITTEE:
Chuck Klein
Duke Snider
Tom Yawkey
1981
Bob Gibson
VETERANS COMMITTEE:
Johnny Mize
Rube Foster
1982
Henry Aaron
Frank Robinson
VETERANS COMMITTEE:
Travis Jackson
Happy Chandler
1983
Juan Marichal
Brooks Robinson
VETERANS COMMITTEE:
George Kell
Walter Alston
1984
Luis Aparicio
Don Drysdale
Harmon Killebrew
VETERANS COMMITTEE:
Rick Ferrell
Pee Wee Reese
1985
Lou Brock
Hoyt Wilhelm
VETERANS COMMITTEE:
Ray Dandridge
Enos Slaughter
Arky Vaughan

1986	1996
Willie McCovey	None
VETERANS COMMITTEE:	VETERANS COMMITTEE:
Bobby Doerr	Jim Bunning
Ernie Lombardi	Bill Foster
1987	Ned Hanlon
Catfish Hunter	Earl Weaver
Billy Williams	**1997**
VETERANS COMMITTEE:	Phil Niekro
None	VETERANS COMMITTEE:
1988	Nellie Fox
Willie Stargell	Tommy Lasorda
VETERANS COMMITTEE:	Willie Wells
None	**1998**
1989	Don Sutton
Johnny Bench	Larry Doby
Carl Yastrzemski	VETERANS COMMITTEE:
VETERANS COMMITTEE:	Lee MacPhail
Red Schoendienst	Bullet Joe Rogan
Al Barlick	George Davis
1990	**1999**
Joe Morgan	George Brett
Jim Palmer	Robin Yount
VETERANS COMMITTEE:	Nolan Ryan
None	VETERANS COMMITTEE:
1991	Orlando Cepeda
Rod Carew	Nestor Chylak
Ferguson Jenkins	Frank Selee
Gaylord Perry	Smokey Joe Williams
VETERANS COMMITTEE:	**2000**
Tony Lazzeri	Carlton Fisk
Bill Veeck	VETERANS COMMITTEE:
1992	Tony Perez
Rollie Fingers	Sparky Anderson
Tom Seaver	Bid McPhee
VETERANS COMMITTEE:	Turkey Stearns
Hal Newhouser	**2001**
Bill McGowan	Dave Winfield
1993	Kirby Puckett
Reggie Jackson	VETERANS COMMITTEE:
VETERANS COMMITTEE:	Bill Mazeroski
None	Hilton Smith
1994	**2002**
Steve Carlton	Ozzie Smith
VETERANS COMMITTEE:	**2003**
Leo Durocher	Gary Carter
Phil Rizzuto	Eddie Murray
1995	**2004**
Mike Schmidt	Dennis Eckesley
VETERANS COMMITTEE:	Paul Molitor
Leon Day	
William Hulbert	
Vic Willis	

Halls of Fame and Museums Other Than at Cooperstown

"If they ever start an Instructional League Hall of Fame, I'll be a charter member." — High school phenom and Major League bust David Clyde.

See also *Canada, Japan* and *Negro Leagues.*

The Baseball Reliquary. Terry Cannon founded The Baseball Reliquary in Orange County, California, in 1996. In 1999 he established the Shrine of the Eternals. Unlike the National Baseball Hall of Fame, the Shrine honors "rebels, radicals, and reprobates — those characters the establishment couldn't digest." One of the first inductees was Curt Flood, the St. Louis Cardinals outfielder.

African American. The Afro-American Hall of Fame is located in Detroit and contains a section on black baseball stars of the modern era and the Negro Leagues.

Latin America. See *Latin America* for the 2003 opening of a new Hall of Fame in Puerto Rico.

Association. The Association of Sports Museums and Halls of Fame is located in Wilmington, Delaware.

St. Louis Browns. A Browns Hall of Fame was established by Bill Borst at Maryville College. Borst founded the Browns Fan Club on October 4, 1984, exactly 40 years after the Browns defeated the Cardinals in Game 1 of the 1944 World Series.

Yogi Berra.
"Usually you have to be dead to get something like this." — Berra, at the 1998 opening of the Yogi Berra Museum and Learning Center in Montclair, New Jersey.

Dizzy Dean. In 1977 in Jackson, Mississippi, the Dizzy Dean Hall of Fame opened, but averaged only 3–4 visitors per day. By 1990 the Dean Hall directors were contemplating closing the exhibit and donating the memorabilia to the Baseball Hall of Fame in Cooperstown. In 1994 the Dean Hall did close, but the memorabilia was donated to the Cardinals Hall of Fame that opened at Busch Stadium in 1995.

Burleigh Grimes. The Burleigh Grimes Museum is located in Wisconsin.

Roger Maris. The Roger Maris Museum is located in Fargo, North Dakota.

Cincinnati Reds. When the Reds opened their Hall of Fame in 2004 they included a baseball for every one of Pete Rose's hits. In keeping with the Major League ban against Rose, however, they did not enshrine Rose in their Hall of Fame.

Media. The National Sportscasters and Sportswriters Hall of Fame is located in Salisbury, North Carolina.

Negro Leagues. The new Negro League Hall of Fame is located at 1601 E. 18th Street in Kansas City.

Red Sox. In 1995 the Red Sox announced plans for a Red Sox Hall of Fame to be housed in a building adjacent to Fenway Park until a new ballpark is opened. The initial inductees were Babe Ruth, Tris Speaker, Cy Young, Jimmy Collins, Lefty Grove, Jimmie Foxx, Joe Cronin, Ted Williams, Harry Hooper, Rick Ferrell, Bobby Doerr, Carl Yastrzemski, Eddie Collins and Tom Yawkey.

Babe Ruth. The Babe Ruth Museum was founded in Baltimore in 1974 at 216 Emory St., Ruth's birthplace in an upstairs bedroom. It was later expanded into three adjoining row houses, which were renovated and combined in 1983. They are only a few blocks from Camden Yards.

Ted Williams. The Ted Williams Retrospective Museum and Library opened in early 1994 in Hernando, 75 miles north of Tampa. In 2003 Pete Rose was elected to the Williams Hitters Hall of Fame located at the museum. He was selected along with Dom DiMaggio, Wade Boggs, Tony Gwynn and Williams (who didn't want to be honored while he was still alive). The Hitters Hall of Fame began in 1995 and Shoeless Joe Jackson — like Rose on the career banned list — was inducted in 1998. Later inductees have included Dave Winfield, Jim Rice, Robin Yount and Paul Molitor.

Nolan Ryan. The Nolan Ryan Museum opened in April 1999 in Alvin, Texas.

Book. Doug Gelbert, *Sports Halls of Fame: A Directory of Over 100 Sports Museums in the United States* (1992).

Billy Hamilton (1866–1940)

Hall of Fame (VC) 1961

"The object of a baseball team is to score runs. It is obvious that a club that scores as many as possible and holds its opponents to as few as possible is likely to win. And what is true of a team is also true of an individual player. That is why the run-getting ability of William Robert Hamilton made him a champion: of all the men who have played major league baseball for any length of time, only Hamilton and Harry Stovey [and George Gore] ended up with more runs scored than they had games played." — Lee Allen and Tom Meany in *Kings of the Diamond* (1965).

Hamilton played 14 seasons beginning in 1888 and stole 915 bases during his career.

William Robert "Sliding Billy" Hamilton started his career with Kansas City in the American Association for two years beginning in 1888. In 1890 he moved over to the National League Phillies, leading the league in stolen bases four times and winning batting titles in 1891 (.340) and 1893 (.380). In 1896 he was traded to the Boston Red Stockings, where he stayed for the remainder of his career.

Hamilton stole 915 bases over 14 seasons ending in 1901, though at times during his career taking the extra base on a hit was counted as a stolen base. He stole over 100 bases three times and over 95 bases twice. He had a high of 117 in 1889 and won the stolen base crown seven times.

Hamilton is one of only three Major League players to score more runs than games played (1,692 to 1,593). He hit .325 or better 10 times on his way to a .344 lifetime average, putting him eighth all-time. He also holds the Major League record with 196 runs scored in a season.

Knee and leg injuries shortened his Major League career, but he was able to play for minor league clubs until age 44 in 1910. He managed in the minor leagues until 1916 and later scouted for the Red Sox.

Ned Hanlon (1857–1937)

Hall of Fame (VC) 1996

"A coldhearted scalawag by the name of Ned Hanlon was determined to do in 1902 what a ruthless, money-hungry scalawag by the name of Water O'Malley ended up doing fifty-five years later: Hanlon wanted to transfer the borough's beloved baseball team out of Brooklyn. And Hanlon might well have gotten his way, except for one steadfastly loyal Dodger employee who not only loved Brooklyn passionately but had a deep and unwavering faith that there was something very special about playing there." — The first lines of Peter Golenbock's *Bums* (1984), on Charles Ebbets, who feuded with Hanlon over control of the club.

Hanlon played primarily in the 1880s and managed the 1890s Baltimore Orioles and early 20th century Dodger clubs to five pennants.

Edward Hugh Hanlon began a mediocre playing career for Cleveland in 1880, but spent the prime years of his career with the National League Detroit Wolverines from 1881 through 1888. He batted over .300 only once, in 1885, while playing center field for the club. In 1889 he moved over to Pittsburgh as player-manager and then became the player-manager of the 1890 Players League club in that city. After one more season in Pittsburgh — by then the

National League Pirates — and 11 games with the Orioles as player-manager in 1892, the injured Hanlon retired to manage full-time.

Hanlon led the Orioles to three straight pennants and two second-place finishes between 1892 and 1898. His club is credited with refining many of the "inside baseball" techniques such as the hit-and-run. He moved over to the Dodgers as a part-owner (the two clubs had common ownership for a number of years) and immediately won two straight pennants in 1899 and 1900. The Dodgers finished second in 1902, but after three poor finishes he left for the Reds. In 1906 and 1907 his clubs finished sixth and he never managed again.

After his retirement Hanlon became a fixture in Baltimore. He was president of the Eastern League club in 1908–1909 and was affiliated with the city's Federal League entry in 1914. He had various business interests in the city until his death there in 1937.

Will Harridge (1883–1971)

Harridge served as the third **American League President** from 1931 through early 1959.

Bucky Harris (1896–1977)

Hall of Fame (VC) 1975

"So I'll choose Harris for my best manager. He was most fair, and I don't think I ever heard him second-guess a player, no matter how lousy they'd done. He seemed to enjoy managing, and he didn't take it out on the players when things were going bad." — Hall of Famer Charlie Gehringer.

Harris played 12 Major League seasons and managed a number of clubs to over 2,100 wins between 1924 and 1956.

Following a stint in the Pennsylvania coal mines, Stanley Raymond Harris began his professional career in the Eastern Pennsylvania League in 1915 and continued in the game as a player, manager and scout until the 1960s.

After playing for Buffalo in the International League, Harris made it to the Major Leagues with the Senators in 1919 for eight games. In 1920 he became the club's regular second baseman, batting .300. He stayed with the Senators through the 1928 season and then played in 11 games with the Tigers in 1929 and 1931 while managing the club. Harris batted .274 over 12 seasons and played in the 1924 and 1925 World Series.

Harris made his primary mark as a manager, taking over the Senators in 1924 at age 27 (the "Boy Manager"), shortly after owner Clark Griffith tried to trade him to the White Sox. He led the club to pennants in both 1924 and 1925, winning the World Series in 1924 and losing in 1925. He lasted with the Senators until 1928, moved over to the Tigers from 1929 until 1933, went to the Red Sox for a season in 1934 and then returned to the Senators from 1935 through 1942. In 1943 the Phillies dumped him after 92 games at the helm — though only after he had a falling out with soon-to-be-barred owner William Cox (see also *Gambling*). He never finished higher than third (1927) between 1926 and 1943.

In 1947 Harris returned to manage in the Major Leagues, this time with the powerful Yankees. He guided the club to a World Series victory over the Dodgers but was fired after a third-place finish in 1948 despite 94 wins. He returned to manage the Senators from 1950 through 1954, never finishing higher than fifth. After two more seasons as manager of the Tigers in 1955 and 1956, he became a scout for the Senators. He is third on the all-time managerial list with 2,157 wins in 4,408 games, a .493 percentage.

Book. Bucky Harris, *Playing the Game: From Mine Boy to Manager* (1925).

Hartford Dark Blues

National Association 1874–1875

"Following the collapse of the Middletown Mansfields in 1872, G. B. Hubbell, a gentleman from Hartford who had been an officer in the old association in 1870, had declared that there would never again be a professional team in Connecticut. Two years later, he was proving his statement premature."—William J. Ryczek in *Blackguards and Red Stockings* (1992) on the opening of the season in Ft. Wayne on May 4, 1871.

The club was poor in 1874, finishing with a 17–37 record under manager Lip Pike. The following season the Blues prepared for entry into the National League by finishing in third place with a 54–28 record under manager Bob "Death to Flying Things" Ferguson.

Hartford Dark Blues

National League 1876–1877

"The Hartfords ought to have it, but they are an unruly set of fellows. They want more of the qualities which carry us on to glory every year. I mean brains…"—Albert Spalding quoted in *Baseball and Mr. Spalding*, by Arthur Bartlett (1951).

Hartford was a charter member of the National League, finishing the 1876 season in third place with a 47–21 record. Some sources reported that the team was so bad that in 1877 it played all its home games in Brooklyn to draw fans. The club was a contender and it is more likely that its owners, who had plans to move to New York, were simply looking to draw more fans from a much larger market by playing in Brooklyn.

The club finished third with a 31–27 record but folded after the season. Inaugural National League president Morgan Bulkeley was the team president in name only because he was deeply involved in Connecticut politics and the Aetna Insurance Company.

Gabby Hartnett (1900–1972)

Hall of Fame 1955

"The Perfect Catcher"—Yankee manager Joe McCarthy.

Hartnett was considered the premier catcher in the National League for the Cubs during the 1920s and 1930s.

Charles Leo Hartnett, "Old Tomato Face," was born in Rhode Island and worked in Worcester, Massachusetts, until he signed professionally with Worcester in the Eastern League. The Cubs bought him in 1922 for $2,500 and he appeared in 31 games for the club that year. He remained with the Cubs for another 18 years until 1941, when he moved over to the Giants for one season before retiring.

Hartnett was considered by many as the best National League catcher of all time (with apologies to Roy Campanella) until Johnny Bench arrived in the late 1960s. He hit over .300 six times for a lifetime average of .297. His best season was 1930, when he hit .339 with career highs of 37 home runs and 122 RBIs. He was the National League MVP in 1935 when he hit .344.

He broke his arm as a child and it did not heal properly. He exercised it constantly as a boy and later had arm problems that prevented him from catching more than one game during the 1929 season (though he pinch hit in 24 games).

Hartnett's greatest fame came with his ***Homer in the Gloamin'***

in 1938 when he knocked the Pirates out of the pennant race and the Cubs went on to the World Series.

Hartnett was player-manager for the Cubs from 1938 through 1940, leading them to the pennant in 1938 and the middle of the pack in 1939 and 1940. He was fired and moved to the Giants as a player-coach. He later managed in the minor leagues and in 1965 became a coach and then front office man for the A's.

Book. Jim Murphy, *The Gabby Hartnett Story: From a Milltown to Cooperstown* (1983).

Ernie Harwell (1918–)

Hall of Fame (Frick Award) 1981

"I've had a gratifying career as your Tiger announcer, and now I say goodbye. I'll never be able to repay all the warmth and affection you fans have shown me…. I agree with Satchel Paige and William Shakespeare. Old Satch said, 'Don't look back, something may be gaining on you.' And Mr. Shakespeare once wrote, 'To have done is to hang quite out of fashion'…. Thank you very much and God bless all of you."—Harwell's final words on what was thought to be his last broadcast for the Tigers to close the 1991 season.

Harwell was a Major League broadcaster primarily for the Orioles and Tigers from 1948 through 2002.

Harwell began his Major League broadcasting career with the Dodgers in 1948. He broadcast his first game on August 4, 1948, when he filled in for Red Barber on a Dodger broadcast against the Cubs. He had been traded from the Atlanta Crackers (where he had been broadcasting) to the Dodgers for minor league catcher Cliff Draper. He finally met Draper in September 2002 when the Tigers honored both men before one of Harwell's final broadcasts. Harwell moved to the Giants in 1950 and to the Orioles in 1954. In 1960 he began 32 consecutive seasons broadcasting for the Tigers.

Harwell broadcast two World Series (1963 and 1968) and 10 American League championships (1976–1983 and 1985–1986) for CBS radio. In 1984 he broadcast for the home town Tigers, who won the World Series. He also broadcast two All-Star Games (1958 and the second 1961 game).

During his broadcasts, Harwell used something he learned as a student debater. During the off-season, he would find anecdotes about the players and little-known baseball events, write them on index cards, and then grab a handful of them before each game and share them with the listeners.

In late 1990 the Tigers management asked him to announce his retirement after the 1991 season, but he refused. After a great uproar in the media, Harwell finished the 1991 season with the club and then retired. The Tigers at least had the decency to stage a "day" for him. Incredibly, none of the key Tiger executives showed up. Harwell's last broadcast that season was in Baltimore, which was saying goodbye to its old ballpark. Harwell had ushered in the Orioles as a Major League club in 1954 as its primary broadcaster.

Harwell broadcast a few games for the Angels and other clubs during the 1992 season before returning to the Tigers, who were under new management for the 1993 season. He broadcast until the end of the 2002 season, when he retired at age 84. He finished with 42 seasons for the Tigers, and a total of 55 years broadcasting Major League games. To honor Harwell, the club changed the press box name to "The Ernie Harwell Media Center" for the 2003 season. Harwell said his most memorable moment as a broadcaster was Game 7 of the 1968 World Series, when Jim Northrup's triple over Curt Flood's head gave the Tigers the victory over the Cardinals. Harwell unretired for one game on June 1, 2003, when he appeared as a guest television analyst for the Tigers when they played the Yankees in Detroit.

Harwell's "Ode to Baseball" is classic verse; first printed in *The Sporting News* in 1955, it is now in the Hall of Fame. He also has published music and written extensively.

Books. Ernie Harwell, *The Babe Signed My Shoe* (1994); Ernie Harwell, *Tuned to Baseball* (1985); Ernie Harwell, et al., *Stories From My Life In Baseball* (2001); Ernie Harwell, *Life After Baseball* (2004); Tom Keegan and Al Kaline, *Ernie Harwell: My 60 Years in Baseball* (2002).

Hawaii

"It is in Hawaii, however, that Base Ball has become most quickly acclimatized, and if the Kanakas persist in their pursuit of the game, we may soon expect to see a team of Hawaiian players traveling through the United States.... That Base Ball is popular in Hawaii is evident from the amount of newspaper space devoted to the accounts of games in Honolulu and elsewhere."—Circa 1900 article in the *New York Sun* quoted in Albert Spalding's *Base Ball—America's National Game* (1911).

See **Alexander Cartwright**, for his connection to Hawaii.

See **Home Teams** for the 1997 games between the Cardinals and Padres in Hawaii.

Minor League Team. Hawaii was home to the Class AAA Islanders until they departed for Colorado Springs in 1987.

Native. Pitcher Sid Fernandez wore No. 50 on his uniform to honor his home state. Mets outfielder Benny Agbayani was from Hawaii.

Winter League. The Hawaii Winter League lasted from 1993 through 1997 as an alternative to the Arizona Winter League and the Latin American winter leagues. Although the league was reasonably successfully and popular, the league suffered from a dispute with Major League Baseball over the payment of salaries. The league wanted the Major League clubs to pay more than 10% of the player salaries. It was the only league in the U.S. in which the league had to pay salaries and expenses. If the Major Leagues had paid $10,000 to $20,000 per team, it might have survived. Instead, local founder Duane Kurisu, a successful real estate entrepreneur, shut down the league.

The league featured the Hilo Stars, Kauai Emeralds, Honolulu Sharks and Maui Stingrays. The clubs were stocked with Major League prospects out of Class A and AA, as well as players from Taiwan, Japan and Korea. The Maui Stingrays once had on their roster Colorado Silver Bullets alumni Julie Croteau and Lee Anne Ketcham. Among the Major Leaguers who played in the league were Brad Fullmer, Gabe Kapler, David Kennedy, Preston Wilson and Chad Fonville.

Babe Ruth. In October 1933 Babe Ruth arrived in Honolulu to play two exhibition games, play golf and sign autographs before moving on to Japan. The Japanese leg, organized by impresario Herb Hunter, fell through. Ruth was guaranteed $10,000 for the two games, but Hunter claimed that the gate receipts were only $4,000 and so he lost money on the venture. Ruth agreed to go to Hilo for a third game to help make up the difference, with a promise by Hunter to split the gate receipts. Ruth planted a banyan tree that still sits on Hilo Bay.

Major League Games. In April 1997 the Padres and Cardinals played an official doubleheader in Hawaii on a Saturday and then finished the three-game series on Sunday. The games were played at Honolulu's Aloha Stadium. The Cardinals had to make an 11 hour all-night flight after a loss to the Marlins. The Padres arrived from Pittsburgh. The Cardinals swept the doubleheader (1–0 and 2–1), but the Padres came back to win 8–2 on Sunday.

Heaviest Players See *Fat and Weight*

Height

"Baseball is not a sport of the gods, it's a sport of mortals, and ballplayers are even more human than other athletes. They tend to be of average size and weight, unlike the *Star Wars* cantina of humanoids who participate in football and basketball."—Lev Grossman in *Time*.

See also **Tallest Players** and **Smallest Players**.

Casey Stengel once told his players to line up "alphabetically by height."

The 1927 "Murderers' Row" Yankees averaged only 5'11" and 176 pounds. Babe Ruth was 6'2", but would be taller than only 48% of players on Major League rosters at the start of the 2003 season.

The 1975 championship Reds ("The Big Red Machine") averaged 6'1" and 188 pounds.

The 2001 Yankees, winner of the three straight titles, averaged 6'2" and 204 pounds. In 2001, 20 pitchers on the Cardinals 40-man roster averaged 6'4", while the average American male was 5'11". At the start of 2001, only 15 of the 280 pitchers on American League rosters were under 6'0". Of course, 5'11", 170-pound Pedro Martinez won three Cy Young Awards, proving that size might not matter.

Heilbroner Baseball Bureau (1905–)

This baseball statistics bureau was formed in 1905 in Ft. Wayne, Indiana. It was founded by ex–Cardinals manager Louis Heilbroner, one of the few Jewish managers in Major League history, who had a 23–25 record for the club in 1900 after future Giants manager and current Cardinals third baseman John McGraw turned down the job. Heilbroner was the 4'9" business manager of the Cardinals when he was tapped for the position, but he held no real power over the plays; they generally answered only to McGraw.

The Bureau served all of professional baseball, maintaining personnel cards and transaction records for every organized league. Starting in 1909 the Bureau issued a *Baseball Blue Book* (first called the *Baseball Yearbook*), the most complete annual directory of the game. A form of the *Blue Book* has continued into the modern era, though the Bureau was absorbed by other statistical organizations.

Harry Heilmann (1894–1951)

Hall of Fame 1952

"I'm just not hitting right. This has lasted for weeks, and I'll just have to size myself and see exactly what it is that I'm doing wrong."—Heilmann, a lifetime .342 hitter, at a time when he was batting a mere .328.

Heilmann won four batting titles while playing outfield over a 17-year career for the Tigers beginning in 1914.

A native of San Francisco, Heilmann was a bookkeeper when he began playing for Portland in the Northwest League in 1913 and moved on to the Tigers in 1914. He was sent to San Francisco for the 1915 season and then stuck with the Tigers in 1916, batting .282. His career was interrupted briefly with a stint on a crude form of submarine during World War I.

He blossomed as an outfielder in 1919 with a .320 average and in four of the next eight years he hit over .390 for the Tigers.

Arthritic wrists made hitting difficult and forced him to miss the 1931 season. He came back in 1932 for 15 games with the Reds as a player-coach, but his career was over.

Despite being a heavy drinker, he hit .342 over his 17-year career and is considered by many to be among the top right-handed hitters of all time. He earned four batting titles every other year from 1921 through 1927 and had 2,660 career hits.

He hit 183 home runs with 542 doubles and 151 triples while playing half his games in Tiger Stadium, a good hitter's park. After he retired and was financially decimated in the stock market crash of 1929, he broadcast Tiger games for 17 years until he died of lung cancer in 1951.

Ernest Hemingway (1899–1961)

"What paper are you with, Ernie?"—Yogi Berra when introduced to the writer.

"He was the only guy who could make fishing sound interesting to me. Fishing, with me, has always been an excuse to drink in the daytime."—Sportswriter Jimmy Cannon.

Hemingway apparently wrote one piece on baseball; a 1918 article in the *Kansas City Star* when he reported on the hold-out staged that spring by Cubs pitcher Grover Cleveland Alexander. Hemingway once attended a boxing match in New York with Joe DiMaggio. No one recognized Hemingway so he began identifying himself as DiMaggio's doctor. See **Boxing—Good Clean Fun** for Hemingway's pugilist activities with Dodger pitcher Hugh Casey.

Billy Herman (1909–1992)

Hall of Fame (VC) 1975

"But I fiercely wanted to play ball, and I begged my way in. Signed for nothing. Would have paid to get that contract with the Louisville Colonels back in 1928 when they signed. I still wasn't any good…. I'd have been sent home because Class D is the end of the line. I'd have dropped out of baseball. Instead, I stuck with second base for the next 20 years [after switching from shortstop]."—Herman quoted in *Voices from Cooperstown*, by Anthony J. Connor (1982).

Herman was considered one of the premier second baseman of the 1930s while playing for the Cubs.

An Indiana farm boy, William Jennings Bryan Herman began his minor league career in 1928 with Louisville after playing second-string in high school. He played in the minor leagues until mid–1931 when the Cubs brought him up to replace Rogers Hornsby at second base. From then on he established himself as the best National League second baseman of the 1930s and early 1940s.

He starred for the Cubs from 1932, when he batted .314 and played in every game, through 1940, when he batted .292 in 135 games. His best season was 1935, when he hit .341 and led the league with 227 hits and 57 doubles.

Herman was traded to the Dodgers in early 1941, where he stayed through a stellar 1943 season (.330 in 153 games) before entering the military during World War II. He lost the entire 1944 and 1945 seasons before returning for most of the 1946 season with the Dodgers and Braves. After managing the Pirates for most of 1947 and playing in 15 games, he retired with a .304 lifetime average and 2,345 hits. He batted .242 in four World Series and played in 10 All-Star Games.

After his retirement from the Major Leagues, he played a few games in the minor leagues before coaching for various teams in the 1950s and early 1960s. He managed three mediocre Red Sox teams in the mid–1960s before the club's success in 1967, but by then Dick Williams was at the helm.

Heroes

"The small boy does not know that the best third baseman in baseball is human: that he fights with his wife, worries about bills and occasionally swears at the bat boy. All the small boy knows is that the third baseman is a hero, and a hero always does the right thing. It would be sinful to disillusion him, to tell him that Babe Ruth was a glutton, that Enos Slaughter has had five wives."—Robert Creamer in *Sports Illustrated*.

"I play for the poor man. I try to give a thrill to the lunch bucket fan. I know their plight. I worked in a factory in high school. The poor folk who lay out the hard bread to see a game. That's where my heart lies. The rich don't need heroes."—Former Angels player Leon "Daddy Wags" Wagner, who died in 2004 homeless (living in an outdoor closet) and penniless in Los Angeles.

John A. Heydler (1869–1956)

Heydler was interim **National League President** in 1909 and then held the position from 1918 through 1934.

Hickok Belt Award (1950–1976)

Ray and Alan Hickok created the award in 1949 as a tribute to their father, S. Rae Hickok. Their company manufactured high-end wallets, belts and other men's accessories.

The award was officially known as the S. Rae Hickok Professional Athlete of the Year Award and the alligator-skin belt was initially worth between $10,000 and $15,000 with a four-carat diamond and 26 gem chips requiring 250 man-hours to produce at the plant. Over 300 newspaper sports editors and sportswriters voted for a monthly award and then discarded those results to vote for an annual winner.

Until 1973 the winner was awarded the three-pound belt, reportedly worth $30,000 that year. The Tandy Corporation had purchased the company in 1971, and the format changed after 1973. For the next four years an automobile was presented instead. Hickok also awarded the Link Award, symbolizing a winner who is a link from the past. Hank Greenberg was the 1974 winner. When the company was sold, a clause guaranteed perpetuity of the award. However, it was discontinued after the 1976 presentation. See also Murray Goodman, *The Hickok Winners* (1976). The baseball winners:

Phil Rizzuto (1950)
Allie Reynolds (1951)
Willie Mays (1954)
Mickey Mantle (1956)
Bob Turley (1958)
Roger Maris (1961)
Maury Wills (1962)
Sandy Koufax (1963)
Sandy Koufax (1965) (erroneously Willie Mays in one source)
Frank Robinson (1966)
Carl Yastrzemski (1967)
Reggie Jackson (1968)
Tom Seaver (1969)
Brooks Robinson (1970)
Steve Carlton (1972)
Pete Rose (1975)

Hidden Ball Trick

"Even in the 19th century they were calling it ancient and moss-covered." — SABR historian Bill Deane on the origins of the ploy. Deane estimated that it has succeeded 141 times in the Major Leagues, most recently on June 26, 1999 by the Giants against the Dodgers.

How It Works. The infielder conceals the ball in his glove and fools the runner into believing that the pitcher has the ball in his glove. As the pitcher fakes his set position without the ball, the runner takes his lead, and the infielder tags him out.

Origins. One source first placed this ploy at around 1910. Others, including former Major Leaguer Arlie Latham, traced it to the earliest days of the Major Leagues. One source cited the first use by the 1870s National League Worcester club against Albany. Bill Deane cites May 25, 1876, when National League star Cap Anson was caught off base by Hartford Dark Blues shortstop Tom (Scoops) Carey, who threw to third baseman Bob Ferguson for the out. The play was banned briefly early in the 20th century because it often took too long to develop.

Lou Boudreau. Boudreau was once interviewed about the trick and said that there was no excuse for falling for it. The next day, Opening Day, he was the victim of White Sox third baseman Tony Cuccinello.

Frank Crosetti. The Yankee shortstop, who learned the play from Joe Cronin, once caught Cronin on the play.

Ernie Lombardi. The catcher once was caught off second base by the trick. He told second baseman Tony Cuccinello that he would punch him in the nose if he tagged him with the ball; he then walked off the field and was called out for leaving the basepath rather than be tagged out.

Jimmie Foxx. When the slugger returned briefly to the Major Leagues as a pitcher during World War II, he was immediately picked off second base using the hidden ball trick.

They Should Have Known Better. On May 6, 1978, Yankee second baseman Willie Randolph pulled the trick on Bump Wills of the Rangers in the 1st inning. In 1980 Randolph had it pulled on him and, as noted by Bill Deane, he and Orlando Cepeda are the only two players to do it and have it done to them.

Matt Williams. The Indians third baseman successfully pulled off the hidden ball trick for the third time on September 19, 1997. He used the same ruse each time, asking the runner to step off the bag so he could brush off the dirt. This time he got Royals rookie Jed Hansen.

High Fives

"High fives. And eights. And elevens. If you were ever lucky enough to be part of a winning team, at any level of play, you remember exactly how ecstatic these guys feel." — John Thorn in *The Game for All America* (1988).

"I'm glad I don't play anymore. I could never learn all those handshakes." — Phil Rizzuto.

"You don't see the Orioles screaming or yelling or giving high fives. They just beat you and say, 'See you tomorrow.' They're not out to show you up." — Sparky Anderson.

According to at least one source, the practice of slapping palms in the air was a phenomenon begun among black players in the late 1960s. Others attribute it to Glenn Burke, who played in the mid–1970s for the Dodgers and A's and who later disclosed his *Homosexuality* and died of AIDS in 1995. He purportedly first used the high five in 1977 to celebrate at home plate with Dusty Baker, who had hit his 30th home run.

Will Penny of the independent league Sioux Falls Canaries high fives a young player.

The *Dickson Baseball Dictionary* attributes high fives to the 1979 University of Louisville basketball players and reports that high fives first appeared in baseball in 1980.

High School Players

"I never played on the high school baseball team. Too much gee-whiz bullshit and girls jumping up in their skirts with no panties on just to drive you wacky." — Pitcher Bo Belinsky.

"He shouldn't have gone to high school. It took three years off his pension." — Walt Weiss on teenage star Ken Griffey, Jr.

"Schoolboy Rowe, Bid Teachout, Dave Chalk, Paul School, Dean Stone, Jim Proctor"

See also *Youngest Players*.

Straight from High School. Shortstop Roger Peckinpaugh joined the 1910 Indians line-up straight from Cleveland's East High School. Also in that category are pitchers David Clyde of the 1973 Rangers and Mike Morgan of the 1978 A's. See also *Drafts*.

Tampering. In 1947 George Zoeterman signed with the White Sox while still in high school. This prompted more stringent regulations regarding the signing of high school undergraduates. The White Sox supposedly were "thrown out" of the league for two weeks in the autumn of 1947 for failing to pay a fine over this incident.

Teammates. George Brett was not the best player on his high school championship team. Future Orioles pitcher Scott McGregor was the team MVP when El Segundo High (southwest of Los Angeles) won the 1971 regional championship.

Hall of Famers Eddie Murray and Ozzie Smith were teammates at Locke High in South Los Angeles.

Greatest Player. The greatest high school pitcher of all time was probably Jon Peters, who won a national-record 53 straight high

The Los Angeles High School baseball team, circa 1904. Future New York Giants outfielder Fred Snodgrass is top center. Note the "mascot" by the bats and gloves.

school games in the late 1980s and was on the cover of *Sports Illustrated*. After entering college he suffered various injuries and underwent arm surgery more than once. He pitched his last game on February 27, 1991, for Blinn College in Texas.

In 2002, in the 12th round, the Twins selected Marshalltown's Jeff Clement, the high school home run champion with a record 71 that year. He broke the mark of 70 set by Drew Henson in 1998.

Greatest Team. In *Darryl Strawberry and the Boys of Crenshaw* (2004), author Michael Sokolove said that scouts touted the 1979 Los Angeles Crenshaw High School team as the best ever, as it included Chris Brown and Strawberry. Nevertheless, the team lost the City championship to Granada Hills High School, led by future NFL quarterback John Elway.

Prodigy. Nolan Ryan's high school coach once recalled an anecdote from Ryan's 8th grade season. Players were lined up at the goalposts on a football field and threw softballs as far as they could. Most of the players threw the ball to the 30 or 40 yard line, approximately 50 yards. Ryan threw the ball between the goalposts on the opposite end of the field. He threw the ball at least 50 yards farther than any other boy on the field.

Long Journey. Gary Carter went to high school in Los Ange-

les with Tommy Lasorda's daughter, when Lasorda was a Class AAA manager for the Dodgers. Carter finally played for the Dodgers and Lasorda in 1991, as a back-up catcher to Mike Scioscia.

Highest Scoring Games See *Runs*

Hillerich & Bradsby See *Bats*—Manufacturers

Hippodroming

"With two pretenders to the 1892 [split-season] league championship, confused fans deluged local papers with queries as to the true champion. Although a play-off was the logical answer, Boston found itself accused of 'hippodroming,' of dragging its feet during the second half. It was such charges that prompted worried magnates to scrap the double championship, and to seriously consider junking the play-off by awarding the flag to Boston on the basis of its better overall record."—David Quentin Voigt in *American Baseball* (1966).

Most sources report that this was an 1860s term used to describe the practice of fixing games. Teams sometimes took turns losing to give the appearance of competitiveness, but suspicions about this practice hurt gate receipts. The term also has been used to describe promotional stunts to bring fans to baseball games.

Historians

"To the serious historian, tracking trends is the passion that spurs his working life.... Mischievous delights aside, baseball historians regularly shoulder the burden of enlightening the clueless and undoing the damage wrought by shallow research probing. Baseball historians are most likely to be plagued by soothsaying sportswriters spinning phony predictions."—Quintessential modern historian David Q. Voigt.

See also **Books**—Best General Books.

Early Historians. One of the earliest baseball historians was Charles Peverelly, who wrote an 1860s chronicle of American baseball. Jacob Morse, who wrote *Sphere and Ash* (1888), was another early chronicler of baseball. He attended Harvard College and graduated from Boston University Law School. He launched *Baseball Magazine* and was a correspondent for *Sporting Life*. He also managed the Boston Unions to a 46–28 record at the end of 1884.

A few baseball men, such as Albert Spalding, wrote anecdotal baseball histories or autobiographies at various times around the turn of the century. In the early 20th century George Moreland and others wrote encyclopedic compilations but were not necessarily considered historians.

True baseball historians before 1950 probably came only from the ranks of the sportswriters who covered the game, such as Fred Lieb and Frank Graham. Also included on the short list should be writer Robert Smith and New York librarian Robert William Henderson, both of whom wrote definitive baseball accounts in the 1940s.

Henderson was the author of *Ball, Bat and Bishop*, an authoritative 1947 volume that accurately recounted the history of baseball and clearly dispelled some of the mythology surrounding the origins of the game. Henderson was the supervisor of the main reading room at the New York Public Library on 42nd Street. He was also the librarian of the Racquet and Tennis Club of New York and his baseball volume was the result of 35 years of research.

Modern Historians.

Harold Seymour.

"Will grip every American who has invested part of his youth and dreams in the sport, and it will inform everyone else who is interested in an American phenomenon as native as apple pie."— The *New York Times* on baseball historian Harold Seymour's seminal *Baseball: The Early Years* (1960).

Seymour was probably the first true modern baseball historian, having devoted a doctoral thesis to the subject in the 1950s while at Cornell. Nevertheless, his efforts to create a college course in baseball history at Columbia University fell on deaf ears in those years. He also wrote three exhaustively detailed accounts of baseball, chronicling the years prior to World War II. A portion of the dissertation was edited for public consumption and published in 1960 as *Baseball—The Early Years* (described as "a valuable, serious, scholarly, though at times pretentious, study," by Ralph Andreano in *No Joy in Mudville* (1965). Seymour followed that with *Baseball—The Golden Years* in 1971 and *The People's Game* in 1990. Seymour died in September 1992 at age 82.

In 2004 Seymour's widow, Dorothy Jane Mills, published an autobiography that detailed her baseball writing partnership with her husband between 1949 and 1990. She is now recognized as the first female baseball historian, and had far more to do with the research and writing than ever revealed or imagined. See her book, *Woman's Work: Writing Baseball History with Harold Seymour*.

Lee Allen. In the late 1950s and early 1960s, the National League publicist and former **Sportswriter** became well known after he wrote various baseball histories.

Lawrence Ritter. The author of *Glory of Their Times* (1966), who died in 2004, traveled around the country in the 1960s, logging 75,000 miles to capture on reel-to-reel tape interviews with old-time ballplayers for his book. The tapes are now in the Hall of Fame.

Joseph Reichler. The Associated Press editor and reporter rose to prominence in the 1960s as the first editor of MacMillan's **The Baseball Encyclopedia** (1969).

David Quentin Voigt. After Harold Seymour, the college professor is probably the most preeminent of the more scholarly baseball historians who were prominent beginning in the 1960s. He wrote a three-volume series beginning in 1966 about the history of baseball, *American Baseball*. By the early 1990s Voigt was teaching a course at Albright College entitled "Baseball in American Culture." Voigt wrote the brief history contained in *The Baseball Encyclopedia*.

Bill James. James emerged in the 1980s with his *Historical Abstracts* and led the statistical avalanche of that decade. Much of the baseball analysis of the 1970s and later came through James' cohorts in the **Society for American Baseball Research** (SABR). Other prominent historians of the 1980s and beyond are John Thorn, Charles Alexander and John Holway.

Tom Shea. This researcher has been described by Dick Thompson as "baseball's greatest biographical researcher," having compiled player information since about 1926. He also probably should have received co-authorship credit on Hy Turkin's and S.C. Thompson's *Official Encyclopedia of Baseball*, first published in 1951.

Cliff Kachline. A staffer for *The Sporting News* beginning in 1943, Kachline wrote for the periodical for almost 25 years. In May 1967 he left to become public relations director of the newly formed United Soccer Association, but its successor folded and in 1969 he became the Hall of Fame's historian, a position he held until late 1982, when apparently he was forced out due to internal politics. He is credited with determining that Rube Waddell's strikeout total was 349, instead of the accepted 343, when Bob Feller was thought to have broken the record with 348 in 1946. He also was a central character in getting Major League Baseball to officially revise Hack Wilson's season-record RBI total from 190 to 191 (see **Statistics**).

Kachline spearheaded the effort to marshall the old paper records of the Major League clubs, and some had treasure troves of material dating back to the turn of the century. In 1983 he accepted the position of Executive Director of SABR, which he occupied for three years before retiring.

Jerome Holtzman. In 1999 long-time Chicago sportswriter Jerome Holtzman was named Major League Baseball's official historian.

Research Organization. The North American Society of Sports History (NASSH) is more academically oriented than SABR, looking more at the sociological impact of sports on society as a whole. Founded in 1972, it is headquartered at Penn State University. It publishes *The Journal of Sports History*.

As It Should Be. The 1998 Houghton Mifflin textbook on American History contained 33 lines on the Depression and Franklin Roosevelt's presidency. It devoted two pages to Cal Ripken, Jr.

Hit and Run

"Man may penetrate the outer reaches of the universe, he may solve the very secret of eternity itself, but for me, the ultimate human experience is to witness the flawless execution of the hit and run." — Branch Rickey.

Comparison to Run and Hit. The "run and hit" is different from the "hit and run" because, in a run and hit, when the runner takes off, the batter is not required to swing at the pitch to protect the runner. In a hit and run the batter is required to swing at virtually any pitch in order to protect the runner.

Origins. Various sources credit at least three teams with originating the hit and run. Earlier historians credit the 1890 Baltimore Orioles of Wee Willie Keeler, John McGraw and Hughie Jennings. The Orioles purportedly once succeeded on 13 straight hit and run plays. Revisionist historians point out that the players on the Orioles were prominent 20th century managers fond of promoting themselves as the originators of most of the key strategies of the late 19th century.

Some of these sources have cited Frank Selee, manager of the National League Boston Beaneaters from 1890 to 1901, as the first manager to use the hit and run play. Bill James disputes historian Harold Seymour's contention that Cap Anson executed the hit and run in the 1880s with the Chicago White Stockings. James claims that Wee Willie Keeler of the Orioles in the 1890s learned it from John Montgomery Ward, who saw it first executed by Boston's Tommy McCarthy.

Historian Lee Allen identified the first as 1880s catcher Mike "King" Kelly of the Chicago White Stockings. Louisville manager John J. McCloskey said that Cap Anson told him that the Chicago White Stockings used the play in 1883 and that Kelly had invented it.

Early Strategy. Originally the hit and run was faked first to see if the shortstop or the second baseman moved to cover the bag. On the next pitch the team executed the hit and run in the direction of the infielder who vacated his position to cover second base.

Hit and Run Bunt. Negro Leaguer patriarch Rube Foster is credited with developing the hit and run bunt.

Hit by Pitch

"Apologies by pitchers for hitting batsmen, Morgan 4, Neale 3." — 1877 *Utica Herald* game summary appendix.

"None of them." — Don Baylor's response when asked which of his all-time record 267 hit-by-pitches hurt the most. When Baylor was hit for the 190th time on August 29, 1985, he broke Minnie Minoso's Major League record of 189 (which is still the American League record).

"He gets good flesh on the ball." — Expos press guide on infielder Ron Hunt, who was hit by a pitch 243 times in his career.

"There's not a guy living who ever saw me rub." — Al Rosen.

"But I think I looked a little bit better than John Kruk." — Padres pitcher David Wells in June 2004 after being plunked on the forearm by a Randy Johnson fastball. He was alluding to Kruk's hilariously premature bailout on a Johnson pitch during an All-Star Game. Wells thought he might bat left-handed next time to avoid the pain.

"Andujar Cedeno to lead it off. He swings. And he is hit by a pitch. And it is hit over the wall and out of here for a home run." — Ralph Kiner.

"If somebody wants to hit me [with a pitch], he's doing me a favor." — Braves shortstop Jeff Blauser on hitting only .226.

"They ought to stop it before somebody gets hurt." — Detroit Tigers catcher Bill Freehan in September 1968, who had been hit 20 times that season.

See also *Beanballs*.

Origin. The rule allowing a batter to take first base after being hit by a pitch was created in 1884 by the American Association. It came about supposedly because John Schappert, pitching for St. Louis in 1882, threw at so many batters.

The National League adopted the rule in 1887, possibly after an important postseason encounter with the American Association the year before. The rule was in place for the 1886 championship series between the American Association St. Louis Browns and National League Chicago White Stockings. In a crucial last game situation, Browns outfielder Curt Welch let himself be hit in the shoulder by the White Stockings pitcher. White Stockings catcher Mike "King" Kelly protested the intentional act and Welch was forced to bat again. After getting a base hit, Welch came around to score to win the *Championship Series*.

No Attempt to Avoid. If the batter makes no attempt to get out of the way of the pitch, the umpire need not make a hit-by-pitch call. This became the rule in 1956 because Minnie Minoso crowded the plate so closely and was hit so often. This rule of interpretation was critical during Don Drysdale's consecutive *Scoreless Innings* streak of 1968.

Statistical Category. In 1889 the hit-by-pitch statistic was added to a pitcher's overall statistical record (along with strikeouts). At the same time the prior rule was eliminated that called for a hit-by-pitch to be recorded as an error by the pitcher. In 1909 National League president John Heydler added the hit by pitch to the official batting statistics.

19th Century Leaders. Hughie Jennings was hit by a pitch 51 times in 1896 (or 49 in some sources). Tommy Tucker was the 19th century career leader, reportedly absorbing 270 shots.

Most/Season/Batter.

"Some people give their bodies to science; I gave mine to baseball." — Mets infielder Ron Hunt.

Hunt was hit 50 times in 1971, including four times by Nolan Ryan. Only the Pirates failed to nail him at least once. The season's runner-up was teammate Rusty Staub, with nine. Don Baylor and early 20th century shortstop Kid Elberfeld hold the American League record of 36. Baylor tied the record in 1986 while with the Red Sox.

Most/Season/Rookie. Plate-crowder Frank Robinson was hit by a pitch 20 times in 1956, a rookie record.

Most/Season/Club. In 1971 the Expos set a record for most times hit by a pitch, with 76. They broke the 1956 mark of 75 set by the White Sox.

The 2002 Devil Rays pitchers hit a record 94 batters.

Most/Game/Batter. Bill Freehan and Tito Fuentes are two of the players who have been hit a Major League-record three times in one game. On May 30, 1904, Frank Chance of the Cubs had a particularly bruising day: he was hit by a pitch five times during a doubleheader. The last two players to be hit three times in a game are Damion Easley of the Red Sox on July 16, 2002, and Melvin Mora of the Orioles two days later.

Clean Living. The only players not to be hit by a pitch in their first 2,000 at-bats are John Kruk, Mickey Mantle, U.L. Washington and Herm Winningham.

In 1991 Braves pitcher Tom Glavine was in a situation calling for retaliation against the next Phillies batter. It happened to be his former teammate, Dale Murphy, one of the most well-liked players of the era and a devout Mormon with eight children. Glavine could not bring himself to nail Murphy, so he lobbed four half-speed pitches in his general direction. After Murphy easily dodged the last one and took first base on a base on balls, Glavine was ejected from the game.

Angels center fielder Garret Anderson went over six years without being hit by a pitch, from August 25, 1998, through early August 2004. In 10 years with the Angels, he was hit five times, none for 890 games and 3,807 plate appearances until Todd Williams of the Orioles plunked him.

Most/Career/Pitcher. Walter Johnson is said to have disliked coming inside to hitters for fear of hurting them with his blazing fastball. The facts do not bear this out. Johnson hit 206 batters in 5,924 innings, far more than the second- and third-place finishers in the 20th century, Nolan Ryan with 158 and Don Drysdale with 154. Ryan was ejected for it only once and three batters charged the mound against him in retaliation, the last of whom was Robin Ventura (see also *Fights*).

Chick Fraser hit 215 batters in 3,356 innings between 1896 and 1909 to become the all-time leader among 19th and 20th century pitchers.

Most/Season/Pitcher. Joe McGinnity hit 41 batters in 45 games in 1900 while pitching for the Dodgers to become the all-time National League season leader. Chick Fraser of the A's is the American League leader with 31 hit batters in 1901.

Most/Game/Pitcher. On June 2, 1996, Darryl Kile of the Astros became the 15th player to hit four batters in a game.

Dodger knuckleballer Tom Candiotti had control problems in a 5–1 loss to the Astros on September 13, 1997. He hit three Houston batters in the 1st inning, and another in the 2nd, to tie the Major League record.

On May 22, 1999, knuckleballer Steve Sparks couldn't control his pitch and hit a batter to load the bases, then hit the next two batters. He also hit Jose Canseco earlier in the game to tie the Major League record, and walked six. Nevertheless, the Angels won 8–6.

Three Straight/Pitcher. On August 3, 1998, Astros pitcher C.J. Nitkowski hit three straight Marlins batters in the 8th inning. Since 1900, only Dock Ellis in 1974 and Wilbur Wood in 1977 have hit three straight batters.

Most/Inning/Team. On April 30, 2003, the Red Sox scored three runs in the bottom of the 9th inning against the Royals and won in extra innings. It was the 17th time since 1900 that a team had hit three batters in one inning; and only the second time it had occurred in the 9th inning.

Most/Inning/Batter. On May 23, 1999, Brady Anderson of the Orioles was hit by a pitch twice in the same inning as the club batted around in a 15–6 win over the Rangers. He tied a record set by Willard Schmidt in 1959 and tied by Frank Thomas in 1961.

Black Sox Scandal. The signal for whether the fix was in for the 1919 World Series was a hit batsman. White Sox pitcher Eddie Cicotte was to hit the first batter of the Series to signal that he was going along with the gamblers. On the second pitch of Game 1, he hit Reds second baseman Morrie Rath between the shoulder blades.

Jackie Robinson. During his rookie season, Robinson was hit by a pitch nine times.

Stunt. On April 27, 1957, pitcher Moe Drabowsky had himself pushed to first base in a wheelchair after he was hit by a pitch thrown by rookie Dick Drott.

To the Minors. Warren Spahn pitched only two games for the Braves in his rookie year for manager Casey Stengel. Stengel ordered Spahn to hit Dodger shortstop Pee Wee Reese, but Spahn could not seem to do it no matter how many times he threw at him. A dis-gusted Stengel sent the future 363-game winner down to the minors "to learn more control." Stengel later admitted that it was the biggest mistake of his managing career.

Bad Start. Phillies reliever Andy Carter made his Major League debut on May 3, 1994. He was ejected after hitting two of the three Padre batters he faced.

Pinching. Manager John McGraw supposedly once pinched one of his batters to raise a welt that would support a claim that he was hit by a pitch.

Retaliation. On July 17, 2002, Minnesota's Torii Hunter, unhappy after he was hit by a pitch, picked up the ball and threw it at Indians pitcher Danys Baez in the 5th inning of an 8–5 Twins win. Hunter's throw hit Baez in the leg, but he stayed in the game. Afterward, Baez came into the Twins clubhouse and apologized.

Bad Day All Around. On April 19, 2000, the Astros beat the Dodgers 10–3 as Dodger starter Orel Hershiser tied a modern Major League record by hitting four batters in only 1⅓ innings. Astros outfielder Richard Hidalgo was hit by two of Hershiser's pitches, and was also nailed by reliever Matt Herges, to tie another Major League record. The five hit-by-pitches also tied another 20th century mark by both pitchers and batters, done by Atlanta and Cincinnati on July 2, 1969.

That number increased to six on April 22, 2001, when Pedro Astacio of Colorado hit four Diamondbacks and Arizona pitchers hit him twice.

Strategy. In 1930 Sparky Adams of the Cardinals was in the process of stealing home against Dodger pitcher Dazzy Vance. Seeing that he had no chance to get Adams, Vance quickly hit batter Chick Hafey with the pitch. The dead ball forced Adams back to third.

Honorable. Lefty Grove was a fierce competitor who reportedly threw brushback pitches to his teammates during batting practice and often tried to brush back Babe Ruth. Nevertheless, he never threw at the head and never threw at Lou Gehrig, reasoning that it was "best not to wake him up."

No Show-Offs. Yankee pitcher Jim Coates was warming up when next batter and noted 1950s eccentric Jimmy Piersall was showing off by swinging four practice bats near the batter's box. Coates, a known hothead, intentionally hit him with a practice pitch.

Digging In. Dodger utilityman Derrell Thomas once took extra-long to dig in at the plate against Bob Gibson. When he was finished, Gibson yelled down that he'd "better dig it deeper." Thomas stepped out of the box and began filling back in the hole he had dug. He still was knocked down on the next pitch.

Good Recovery. Late in the 1969 pennant race between the Cubs and Mets, New York's Tommy Agee was knocked down by the first pitch of a key game between those clubs. He grounded out, but the next time up he homered to help the Mets to a victory.

In Game 1 of the 1988 World Series, Jose Canseco was hit on the wrist by Tim Belcher in his first at-bat. In his next at-bat he hit a grand slam. The A's lost the game when Kirk Gibson hit his dramatic 9th inning home run.

Vendetta. Notorious gambler and game fixer Frank Chance, then with the Cubs, was hit by a pitch from Jack Harper of the Reds in late 1905. Chance was mad and vowed to run Harper out of baseball. Chance got his revenge a year later when the Reds owed the Cubs a player from a recent trade. Cubs player-manager Chance insisted that he receive Harper to complete the trade. Harper was earning $4,500 at the time. Chance offered him $1,500 on a take-it-or-leave-it basis. Harper left it after one appearance for the Cubs and never pitched in the Major Leagues again, losing out on a World Series share that year.

New Rule. In February 2001, Major League Baseball announced that umpires had been instructed to eject pitchers who threw at hitters, without giving them a warning first.

"Hitless Wonders"

"We were 'hitless wonders' but even 'hitless wonders' can hit hill billy tryout pitchers."—Outfielder Bill Bailey in "Voo and Doo," by Hoke Norris (1968).

"To those who have not seen the Sox in the wonderful winning streak, it is a wonder how they score so many runs on so few hits. Let them see the Sox take every advantage of misplays and let them dash daringly around the bases and invite wild throws. Let them follow the quick accurate work of the fielders and their keen teammates. These wonderful fans will solve for themselves the methods which are winning game after game."—Hugh Fullerton in the August 21, 1906 edition of the *Chicago Tribune.*

This was the name given to the 1906 Chicago White Sox, who captured the pennant with a record 116 wins despite an anemic .230 league-low team batting average. The Hitless Wonders nevertheless beat their crosstown rival Cubs in the World Series.

Hits

"There is an old saying that money can't buy happiness. If it could, I would buy myself four hits every game."—Pete Rose.

This section covers certain hitting records. Pitching records relating to hits are found under *Low-Hit Games, No-Hitters, Perfect Games* and *Pitchers.* See also *Three Thousand Hits, Four Thousand Hits* and *Hitting.*

Consecutive/Player. Pinky Higgins had 12 straight hits for the Red Sox in June 1938 and Walt Dropo of the Tigers had 12 straight in July 1952. Tris Speaker of the Indians had 11 straight hits in 1920. In August 2002 Yankees outfielder Bernie Williams had 11 straight hits to fall one short of the record.

Nine players have tied the National League record of 10 straight hits. Among them are Chick Hafey of the Cardinals in 1929 and Bip Roberts of the Reds in 1992. In late July 2003, Marcus Giles of the Braves had nine straight hits, one short of the record held by 10 players and last accomplished by Roberts.

Jimmy Dykes once had five straight hits on five straight pitches in a 1925 game.

Don Larsen holds the record for consecutive hits by a pitcher, with seven.

Equal Time. Stan Musial had 1,815 hits on the road and 1,815 hits at home, for a total of 3,630 in his career (the National League record when he retired). His last two hits were to the left and right of Pete Rose at second base. Rose later passed Musial to claim the all-time National League hit record. In another bit of consistency, Musial scored 1,949 runs and drove in 1,951 runs.

In 1948 Musial missed by one home run leading the league in all important offensive categories: home runs, triples, doubles, hits, slugging average, batting average, runs batted in and runs scored.

Only 20 players have accumulated 15 doubles, triples, home runs and stolen bases in one season. Bob Meusel and Babe Ruth did this as teammates in 1921 while driving in more than 300 runs between them. The last was Andy Van Slyke in 1988 for the Pirates.

19th Century Leader. Cap Anson was the premier hitter of the 19th century, compiling 2,995 hits over 22 Major league seasons. He usually played slightly over 100 games per season. His career hit total has been reduced periodically over the past 25 years since the 1969 inaugural edition of *The Baseball Encyclopedia.* Errors in various editions were not rectified until the 1990 edition, resulting in a downward fluctuation in his hit total to 2,998. *Total Baseball's* now official figures place him even lower at 2,995.

Minor League Record. The Pacific Coast League routinely scheduled over 180 games in a season. This enabled some incredible records to be set. Paul Strand of Salt Lake City holds the minor league record for most hits in a season, with 325 in 1923. He played in 194 games, with 825 at-bats and a .394 average.

Most in an Inning. Gene Stephens is one of only two players in modern history to record three hits in a single inning. He did it for the Red Sox against the Tigers on June 18, 1953. He had two singles and a double during a 17-run 7th inning that led to a 23–3 Red Sox victory. On June 27, 2003, Johnny Damon of the Red Sox had three hits in the 1st inning of a game in which the Red Sox scored 10 *Runs* before the Marlins recorded a single out. Damon had a single, double and triple in the 14-run 1st.

On April 23, 1955, catcher Sherm Lollar became one of three Major Leaguers to collect two hits in one inning twice in the same game. He hit two home runs as the White Sox beat the A's 29–6.

Giants outfielder Ross Youngs was the first player to have two hits in a World Series inning. In the 7th inning of Game 3 of the 1921 Series, he had a double and triple during an eight-run inning against the Yankees.

On April 18, 1950, Billy Martin debuted in the Major Leagues when he pinch-hit a double in the 8th inning against the Red Sox in Boston. Later in the inning he singled to become the only player to record two hits in an inning in his first game.

Most in an Inning Possible Without a Run. It is possible to have six hits in an inning without scoring a run: single; single; runner out stealing; runner picked off; three more singles to load the bases; ground ball hits a runner for the third out and batter is credited with a single: No runs, six hits, no errors, three left.

Most in a Game. On July 10, 1932, Indians shortstop Johnny Burnett had nine hits in 11 at-bats in an 18-inning game against the A's. It was his only season as a regular.

Wilbert Robinson of the National League's Baltimore Orioles had seven hits (and 11 RBIs) in a nine-inning game on June 10, 1892, against the St. Louis Browns. The newspapers paid no attention at the time. Nor did *Sporting Life* mention it in the lead of its story. The final score was 25–4 and the game took only 1 hour and 50 minutes to play. Robinson had all his hits in the first six innings; three singles, a double and then three more singles. The feat came to light 20 years later after Robinson spoke about it to sportswriter Heywood Broun, who publicized it.

Rennie Stennett tied Robinson's National League record on September 16, 1975, as the Pirates defeated the Cubs 22–0. In the most lopsided *Shutout* in history, Stennett also had two hits in one inning twice.

Tigers shortstop Cesar Gutierrez, who wore number 7, was the first American Leaguer to go 7-for-7. He did it in 12 innings in the second game of a doubleheader against the Indians on June 21, 1970. He had six singles and a double in a 9–8 Tigers win. It was his only season as a regular, during which he batted .243.

Selected Six-Hit Games.

"Royster has gone six-for-seven against Shirley this year ... and there's a single that makes him five-for-eight."—Jerry Coleman.

Jack Fournier was with the Dodgers on June 19, 1923, when Wilbert Robinson was managing and coaching third base for the club. Fournier was 6-for-6 when he was on deck against the Phillies in the 9th inning. With two out and a man on first, Robinson flashed the steal sign and the runner was thrown out for the last out. Fournier lost his chance to tie Robinson's record of seven hits in a game. The Dodgers had a big lead so the steal made no sense and Fournier never forgave Robinson. The story has also been reported that Robinson simply inserted a pinch hitter for Fournier to avoid a seventh at-bat.

Ty Cobb had three home runs, a double and two singles against the Browns on May 5, 1925.

Doc Cramer of the A's is the only American League player to twice have six hits in a game. He did it on June 20, 1932, and on July 13, 1935.

Roger Connor was 6-for-6 on June 1, 1895, playing for the St. Louis Browns against the Giants.

Sam Thompson of the Phillies hit for the cycle while going 6-for-7 in a game on August 17, 1894.

Two batters went 6-for-6 in the same game in 1897. Wee Willie Keeler had five singles and a triple for the Orioles and Jack Doyle had four singles and two doubles for the Orioles.

On September 16, 1924, Jim Bottomley set a since-tied Major League record when he drove in 12 runs during a 6-for-6 performance.

On May 9, 1937, Ernie Lombardi of the Reds went 6-for-6 in a 21–10 rout of the Phillies.

On July 6, 1949, Walker Cooper of the Reds went 6-for-7, including three home runs and 10 RBIs in a 23–4 victory over the Reds.

On June 20, 1951, Bobby Avila of the Indians hit three home runs, two doubles and a single in a 14–8 win over the Red Sox.

On August 30, 1987, Kirby Puckett of the Twins was 6-for-6 with two homers, two doubles and four RBIs in a 10–6 victory over the Brewers.

On July 2, 1993, Sammy Sosa became the first Cubs player to go 6-for-6 in a game in the 20th century.

Tony Gwynn went 6-for-7 on August 4, 1993, giving him four games with five or more hits in one season. That tied the Major League record held by Willie Keeler (1897), Ty Cobb (1922) and Stan Musial (1948).

On June 12, 1995, Rondell White of the Expos went 6-for-7 and hit for the cycle in a 13-inning game against the Giants.

On June 14, 1995, Mike Benjamin of the Giants went 6-for-7 in 13 innings as part of a record three-day spree (see below).

In late September 1995 Lance Johnson of the White Sox had six hits against the Twins, including three triples.

Gerald Williams became the second Yankee (after Myril Hoag) to record six hits in a game, in 15 innings on May 1, 1996.

On August 30, 1999, Edgardo Alfonzo of the Mets went 6-for-6 against the Astros in a 17–1 win, with a double, three home runs, five RBIs and six runs scored (the last tying the Major League mark). He was only the sixth player to hit three home runs while going 6-for-6.

On June 21, 2003, Nomar Garciaparra had six hits, all singles, for the Red Sox, becoming the fourth Boston player to achieve that milestone.

On May 1, 2004 Frank Catalanotto had six hits for the Blue Jays, including five singles and a double. The last player with six was Shawn Green on May 23, 2002, for the Dodgers, when he hit four home runs.

On August 31, 3004, the Indians pounded the Yankees 22–0, the worst defeat in their history. Cleveland shortstop Omar Vizquel had six hits.

Five or More in a Game. Ty Cobb is the all-time leader with 14 games with five or more hits. Pete Rose had 10 and Tony Gwynn

had nine. Five players had five-hit games four times in a season: Ichiro Suzuki, Tony Gwynn, Stan Musial, Ty Cobb and Willie Keeler.

Most in Two Games. Walt Dropo of the Tigers had 10 singles, a double and a triple in two games over July 14–15, 1952.

Mike Benjamin had 10 hits in two games on June 13–14, 1995.

Most in Three Games. Utilityman Mike Benjamin of the Giants had 14 hits over three games between June 11 and June 14, 1995. He finished off the streak with a 6-for-7 performance on June 14. Overall he was 14-for-18 during the streak. He had only one hit on June 15, but it broke up a perfect game.

Red Sox shortstop Joe Cronin holds the American League record of 13 hits in three games in 1933. He had 15 hits in four games during the streak, a record tied by Buddy Lewis of the Senators in 1937 and Walt Dropo of the Red Sox in 1952.

In May 1994 Tim Salmon of the Angels went 13-for-15 over three games to tie Cronin's record. Salmon was 4-for-5, 4-for-5 and 5-for-5.

Most in Four Games. The modern Major League record for hits in four games is 16, by Milt Stock of the Dodgers in 1925.

Most in a Month. Mariners outfielder Ichiro Suzuki had 56 hits in August 2004, the highest total since Jeff Heath had 58 for Cleveland in August 1938. Cleveland's Roy Weatherly also had 56, in July 1936.

Most in a Season. George Sisler of the Browns held the record with 257 in 1920, until Ichiro Suzuki of the Mariners passed him in Game 160 of the 2004 season. The highest totals before 2004 were Ichiro's 242 hits in 2001, and the 240 hits by Wade Boggs of the Red Sox in 1985 and Darin Erstad of the Angels in 2000. Ichiro finished the 2004 season with 262 hits.

Fast Career Start/200 Hits. In 2004 Ichiro Suzuki of the Mariners became the first player to record 200 hits in each of his first four seasons and had the most ever over that period at the start of a career, with 914. Paul Waner is second with 840 and Joe Medwick is third at 827.

Multiple Hit Games. George Brett had six consecutive three-hit games. Rip Repulski once had 10 straight games with two or more hits.

Most in a Doubleheader. Joe Kelley once went 9-for-9 in a doubleheader around the turn of the century.

Most at Start of Career. Ted Cox had six hits in the first six at-bats of his career for the Red Sox in 1977. Though he hit .362 in 13 games that year, he was traded to the Indians and bounced around the American League until 1981, compiling a .245 lifetime average.

Five-for-Five. In 1986 at age 45, Pete Rose of the Reds had his tenth five-hit game to set a National League record. He broke the record of nine held by Max Carey.

Tony Gwynn has had seven five-hit games, half of Ty Cobb's Major League–record 14.

Consecutive in an Inning. On September 4, 1992, the Blue Jays tied the American League record by recording 10 straight hits in the 2nd inning of a 16–5 victory over the Twins. The American League record was first set in 1901 by the Red Sox and tied by the 1983 Tigers. The Major League record of 12 was set in 1920 by the Cardinals.

On June 12, 1922, the Cardinals had 10 straight hits in the 6th inning of a game in which they defeated the Phillies 14–8.

Most in an Inning/Team. On August 3, 1989, the Reds scored 14 runs in the 1st inning and set a Major League record with 16 hits in the inning. They beat the Astros 18–2.

Most in a Game/Team. The all-time record is 36 hits by

Philadelphia against Louisville on August 17, 1894. The modern record is 33 by the Indians on July 10, 1932. In this 18-inning game in which Johnny Burnett had nine hits, the Indians won 18–17. The A's contributed 25 hits to help set the Major League record for two teams of 58.

On August 28, 1992, the Brewers had 31 hits in a 22–2 win over the Blue Jays. They broke the American League record of 30 in a nine-inning game by the Yankees against the Red Sox on September 2, 1923.

On June 9, 1901, the Giants set a 20th century National League record with a 31-hit game against the Reds in a 25–13 Giants victory. Al Selbach of the Giants was 6-for-7.

Multiple/By Team. On April 11, 1998, the Reds and Rockies had a total of eight players with at least three hits, tying a Major League record set in the 19th century. The Reds had six of them.

Most Runs/Fewest Hits. On April 22, 1959, the White Sox scored 11 runs against the A's in one inning on a single hit. The White Sox combined a single by Johnny Callison with three errors, a hit batter, and nine walks.

Consecutive Innings. On September 25, 2001, Craig Wilson of the Pirates had hits in each of the first three innings of a game against the Cubs in a 13–1 Pittsburgh victory. The night before, Wilson had three hits in each of the last three innings of the game. The six hits in six consecutive innings, all off different pitchers, was a Major League record.

1,000 Hits in Each League. The only players to reach 1,000 hits in each league are Dave Winfield and Frank Robinson.

No Hits/Season. The record for the highest number of at-bats in a season without a hit is held by the following (all pitchers):

Player	Team	Year	At-Bats
Bob Buhl	Braves/Cubs	1962	70
Bill Wight	White Sox	1950	61
Ron Herbel	Giants	1964	47
Karl Drews	Browns	1949	46
Dann Howitt	A's/Mariners	1992	43

(maybe he should have bought a vowel to go with all the consonants).

Pitchers as Hitters.

"I was the worst hitter ever. I never even broke a bat until last year. That was backing out of the garage." — Lefty Gomez.

"I know Koufax's weakness. He can't hit." — Whitey Ford.

"Imagine your worst nightmare; that's how bad I was. The only thing I can say for myself is that I stayed around long enough to get the record. I don't want anyone to break it, either. For all the abuse I put up with, I should have something to show for it." — Ron Herbel, whose one extra base hit was a double that he unsuccessfully tried to stretch into a triple. Herbel was the worst-hitting pitcher of all time (minimum 100 at-bats). He was 6-for-206 for a lifetime average of .029. Herbel had a pitching record of 42–37 from 1963 through 1971.

"I wish I were still active in baseball. The designated hitter rule was made for me." — Pitcher Dean Chance, who batted .066 lifetime.

"Parents, if there are any young children in the room, please beware. This is not going to be pretty." — Braves broadcaster Skip Caray on an at-bat by weak-hitting pitcher Rick Camp.

Bob Buhl struck out 45% of the time in compiling an .089 lifetime batting average.

Fred Gladding appeared as a pitcher in 450 games from 1961 through 1973. He had one hit in 63 at-bats. It came on July 30, 1969, off Ron Taylor of the Mets during an 11-run inning.

In 1969 pitcher Bill Stoneman of the Expos went 4-for-73 with 55 strikeouts.

Terry Forster, far from the most svelte player (see **Fat and Weight**) hit .526 the year before the designated hitter rule went into effect in the American League. He hit .397 lifetime (31-for-78).

George Uhle, a 200-game winner, has the highest batting average for a pitcher appearing in over 500 games. He hit .288 in 17 years and led the league with 11 pinch hits in 1924.

Johnny Sain hit .346 in 1947 and in 11 years struck out only 20 times while compiling a .245 average.

Hank Aguirre, one of the worst hitters of all time, decided to bat left-handed after batting right-handed for most of his career (he was a natural left-hander and pitched left-handed). After batting .053 as a right-hander for eight years, in 1963 he switched sides and batted .106 over the next eight seasons. The turnaround raised his lifetime average to .085.

Joey Hamilton of the Padres did not get a hit in his first 57 Major League at-bats. He surpassed the record from the start of a career set by Don Carman, who was 0-for-48.

World Series Comparison. Jack Sheehan is the only player to have as many hits (two) in the World Series as in his regular season career — two years with the Dodgers in 1920–1921 that included 17 at-bats.

Hits/Three Teammates. Jim Gantner, Robin Yount and Paul Molitor amassed 6,381 hits between 1978 and 1992. They broke the record of 5,748 set by the trio of the Waner brothers and Pie Traynor.

Young Hit Leaders. Johnny Pesky led the league in hits his first three years in the American League. In 1942 he had 205 hits, in 1946 he had 208, and in 1947 he had 207 (he missed three years due to World War II). He was voted *The Sporting News* Rookie of the Year in 1942.

Beginning in 1964 Tony Oliva of the Twins led the American League in hits his first three full years in the league. He had a total of only seven hits in limited appearances in 1962 and 1963.

One source reported that Joe Medwick had 1,064 hits in his first five seasons to become the all-time leader. However, that source failed to note that Medwick had 37 hits in 26 games in his first *partial* season and that the 1,064 total only covers Medwick's first five *full* seasons. Even if only full seasons are counted, however, Chuck Klein — and not Medwick — leads in this category with 1,118 in his first five full seasons (with hit totals of 219, 250, 200, 226 and 223). Klein had 986 hits in his first five full *or* partial seasons to become the all-time leader, just ahead of Wade Boggs with 978.

Kirby Puckett had 1,062 hits in his first six seasons, which the same source reported was the best effort after Medwick's. However, Klein had 1,209 hits in the first six years of his career to become the all-time leader, ahead of Boggs at 1,178 and Medwick at 1,101.

Wade Boggs played in only 104 games his first season in 1982. Beginning in 1983 he had seven straight seasons with 200 or more hits, the best effort in the 20th century. He dropped to 187 hits in 1990. Willie Keeler had eight straight 200-hit seasons in the 19th century.

Wee Willie Keeler had 2,065 hits in the first 10 years of his career, the most all-time. Kirby Puckett is second with 2,040.

Oldest and Youngest to Get a Hit.
See **Oldest Active Players** and **Youngest Players**.

Hitters Who Pitched

"Joe Klink! I can pitch better than Joe Klink." — Jose Canseco on his former teammate. Klink had a strong 1991 season, with a league-leading 10 relief wins.

"It was well-prepared from spring training. We allowed him to pitch in Oklahoma City, he did well. I knew in my heart and my mind I did it with good intention, not with malice or because I was reckless. I don't pay attention to the negativism." — Rangers manager Kevin Kennedy on his decision to allow Canseco to pitch in a regular-season game. Canseco suffered season-ending ligament damage in his elbow during his one-inning stint on May 29, 1993. He mopped up in a 15–1 loss to the Red Sox. He gave up three runs on two hits and three walks. After throwing 33 pitches during the 8th inning, he finished with an ERA of 27.00.

Canseco tuned up for the start with an April appearance against the Class AAA Oklahoma City 89ers. His fastball was clocked at 86 mph and his knuckleball was described as "good." After his regular season debut on the mound, he missed a few games with a sore arm and then it was announced that he had torn ligaments in his throwing elbow and would miss the remainder of the season. He underwent surgery and successfully returned in 1994.

This section covers hitters who made cameo appearances as pitchers. See **Players Who Switched Positions** for players who made permanent changes in their position, such as Babe Ruth, or pitched infrequently but not as a cameo, such as "Wonderful" Willie Smith.

Derek Bell. On the same date that Pirates catcher Brent Mayne was credited with a win, August 22, 2000, outfielder Derek Bell of the Mets mopped up in a 16–1 loss to the Padres. Bell kept his sunglasses on while tossing up easy pitches to 10 batters. He gave up three hits, three walks and five runs (four earned) in one inning.

Mike Benjamin. On June 21, 1997, the Red Sox were losing to the Tigers 15–2 in the 9th inning when they handed the ball to infielder Mike Benjamin. He retired the side, the first Red Sox pitcher to do so in the game.

Larry Biittner. Biittner pitched his only game in the Major Leagues on July 4, 1977, against the Montreal Expos, who beat the Cubs, 19–3. Biittner faced 10 batters over 1⅓ innings. He gave up six runs and five hits, including three homers, while walking one and striking out three. He finished with a career ERA of 54.00.

Bobby Bonilla. On April 17, 2001, Cardinals third baseman Bobby Bonilla gives up the last two runs in a 17–4 loss to the Diamondbacks.

John Cangelosi.
"It brought new meaning to the phrase short reliever." — The 5'8" Cangelosi after he mopped up in June 1995 for the Astros against the Cubs. He pitched a scoreless 9th inning. He also pitched two scoreless innings in 1988 for the Pirates against the Dodgers, prompting him to say: "Two thousand days between appearances, and the first pitch I threw was a strike — that was pretty good."

He pitched one last time for the Marlins on July 21, 1997, against the Padres in a 10–2 loss. He walked one and retired Wally Joyner on a fly ball to end the game.

Rick Cerone. The catcher pitched twice in 1987 for the Yankees, giving up no runs in two innings.

Rocky Colavito. The slugger pitched for the Indians against the Tigers on August 13, 1958. He did not give up a hit in three innings. He also pitched 2⅔ innings for the Yankees on August 25, 1968, and was credited with the win. He had the last pitching decision by a non-pitcher until Jose Oquendo lost a game in 1988 while with the Cardinals (see below). In 2000, Brent Mayne, a catcher, also won a game.

Steve Finley. On August 30, 2001, the Diamondbacks outfielder pitched one inning. He walked one and hit Jeff Kent, but got out of the inning with a double play.

Jimmie Foxx. Foxx pitched in one game in 1939, striking out one in one inning. Six years later during a war-induced player

shortage he pitched in nine games at age 37, compiling a 1–0 record and 1.59 ERA in 22⅔ innings.

Gary Gaetti. The third baseman gave up a home run in a short stint for the Cubs on July 3, 1999. The Cubs lost to the Phillies 21–8.

Ed Giovanola. On August 25, 1999, the Padres lost 15–1 and turned to their infielder to pitch. He last pitched in Little League, but managed ⅓ of an inning of scoreless relief.

Jeff Hamilton. When the Dodgers played 7 hours 14 minutes against the Astros on June 3, 1989, the third baseman was pressed into service. Eddie Murray moved over from first base to play third, and pitcher Fernando Valenzuela played first base. Hamilton had not pitched since his senior year in high school. One of his pitches was clocked at 91 mph. He attributed his speed to having a rested arm since he was pitching on "seven years' rest."

Elrod Hendricks. On June 26, 1978, the 37-year-old Orioles reserve catcher was called on with two outs in the 5th inning after the Blue Jays had scored 24 runs in their small home park, Exhibition Stadium. Hendricks pitched 2⅓ shutout innings, allowing a hit and a walk, with no strikeouts while throwing nothing but fastballs. Final score, 24–10.

George "Highpockets" Kelly. The first baseman played primarily for the Giants in the 1920s. In 1917 he won the only game he ever pitched, beating the Phillies in five innings of relief.

Pepper Martin. The Cardinals shortstop once came in to pitch for manager Frankie Frisch. Martin had always wanted to throw his knuckleball in a game, and with a number of sore-armed pitchers on the staff, Frisch gave him the chance. According to Frisch, Martin retired the side and got the first out of the next inning. He then called over Frisch, who related the rest of the story: "Martin says, 'Get another pitcher. I can't raise my arm.' After, that I have no more trouble with Pepper wanting to pitch." — Quoted in Martin Quigley's *The Crooked Pitch* (1984). The story is not quite consistent with the record books. Martin appeared on the mound one time each in 1934 and 1936, pitching in four innings while compiling no record and a 2.25 ERA. In the first outing he gave up a hit and a run. In the second he gave up a hit and two walks, but did not allow a run.

Brent Mayne. On August 22, 2000, the catcher came in for the Rockies after the club had used nine pitchers through 11 innings. As the tenth pitcher, Mayne helped set a National League record for most used in a game. He allowed a walk but no hits in a scoreless 12th and got Chipper Jones to ground out to end the inning. The Rockies scored in the bottom of the inning for a 7–6 win. It made Mayne the first position player to win a game since Rocky Colavito on August 25, 1968. Mayne was the first catcher to do so since Buck Ewing in 1889.

Stan Musial. The former minor league pitcher pitched to one Major League batter, Frankie Baumholtz of the Cubs, on the last day of the 1952 season. Musial and Baumholtz were the top two hitters in the batting race at the time, but Musial had already clinched (contrary to the inference in many sources that they were still battling for the title). In the 1st inning Baumholtz switched sides and batted right-handed against Musial. Baumholtz grounded the first pitch from Musial to the third baseman, who bobbled it for an error. Musial went 1-for-3 and finished at .336, and Baumholtz went 1-for-4 to finish at .325. (see also **Players Who Switched Positions**, for Musial's minor league transition from pitcher to outfielder).

Jose Oquendo. The Cardinals utility infielder pitched against the Braves in a game that began on July 4, 1987. The 19-inning affair was rain-delayed and ended near 4 a.m. He gave up three runs in the 19th inning for the loss, becoming the first nonpitcher since Rocky Colavito to get the decision (see also **Longest Games**).

Oquendo pitched once in 1988 for the Cardinals, giving up four hits and six walks in four innings. In 1991 he pitched for the last time, giving up two hits and two walks in one inning.

Keith Osik. The catcher pitched for the Pirates on May 20, 2000, in the 9th inning against the Cardinals with his club down 14–3. He had given up four runs in one inning in 1999, and this time gave up five runs on five hits, hit two batters, gave up a home run and had a wild pitch.

Kevin Seitzer. On May 2, 1993, the A's third baseman made one pitch and was credited with a strikeout against a batter he never faced. A's pitcher Kelly Downs and Indians batter Carlos Martinez were ejected for fighting, and Seitzer was brought in to pitch to replacement batter Glenallen Hill. With a 2–2 count left over from Martinez, Seitzer threw strike three past Hill. The rules credited Seitzer (and Martinez) with the strikeout.

Mark Whiten. On July 31, 1998, the Indians outfielder was brought in to pitch in what ultimately was a 10–2 loss to the A's. Down by nine runs, Whiten gave up a run on a double and two walks, but struck out three batters. He is the first player in Major League history, with at least one inning pitched, to get every out by strikeout.

Ted Williams. In one game in 1940 Williams pitched two innings and gave up three hits against the Tigers. He struck out Rudy York with a sidearm curveball with two men on. York later claimed that Williams quick-pitched him.

Todd Zeile. Zeile pitched an inning for the Mets on July 26, 2004. He gave up five earned runs for a 45.00 ERA.

Hitting

"It's the hardest thing to do in sports." — Ted Williams on hitting a baseball. His book, *The Science of Hitting*, with John Underwood (1971), is one of the definitive books on the subject.

"Keep your eyes clear and hit 'em where they ain't." — Wee Willie Keeler's successful strategy.

"He was the finest natural hitter in the history of the game. He never figured anything out or studied anything with the scientific approach I used. He just swung." — Ty Cobb on Shoeless Joe Jackson, whose hitting style admittedly was copied by Babe Ruth.

"With tears in my eyes." — Frank Sullivan, asked how he pitched to Mickey Mantle.

"I got a charge out of seeing Ted Williams hit. Once in a while they let me try and field some of them, which sort of dimmed my enthusiasm." — Rocky Bridges.

"I used to be a mad hitter. And then I learned the longer you wait out the ball, the better you see it. And the better you see it the harder you hit it. And the harder you hit it, the higher your average is going to be. And the higher your average is, the more money you're going to make." — George Brett.

"When you take a pitch and line it somewhere, it's like you've thought of something and put it with beautiful clarity." — Reggie Jackson.

"Suppose a pitcher has three good pitches: a fastball, a curve and a slider. What I do, after a lot of consideration and analyzing and studying, is to eliminate two of those pitches, since it's impossible against a good pitcher to keep all three possibilities on my mind at the plate…. When it comes, I'm ready. Now, I can have guessed wrong, and if I've set my mind for a fastball it's hard to do much with a curve short of nibbling it out over the infield. But the chances are that I'll eventually get what I'm looking for." — Henry Aaron quoted in *Sports Illustrated*.

"I don't guess, I know." — Stan Musial claimed never to guess what pitch was coming. He memorized the speed of delivery of each pitcher and each pitch. He picked up the speed in the first 30 feet and then knew how it would cross the plate. He later said that he knew the speed of each pitcher's fastball and then could adjust if he saw anything slower coming to the plate.

"There probably never has been what you would call the 'complete' hitter. Babe Ruth struck out more than he should have. Cobb didn't have the power, he didn't have great style. Harry Heilmann wasn't serious enough. I suppose Rogers Hornsby came the closest to being complete." — Ted Williams in *The Science of Hitting* (1971). Williams also recalled how, as a 20-year-old in spring training, he worked with Hornsby every day after practice.

"They can talk about Babe Ruth and Ty Cobb and Rogers Hornsby and Lou Gehrig and Joe DiMaggio and Stan Musial and all the rest, but I'm sure not one of them could hold cards and spades to [Ted] Williams in his sheer knowledge of hitting. He studied hitting the way a broker studies the stock market, and could spot at a glance mistakes that others couldn't see in a week." — Carl Yastrzemski.

"The pitcher has to throw a strike sooner or later, so why not hit the pitch you want to hit and not the one he wants you to hit?" — Johnny Mize.

"Whether that says he's better than Mays or Aaron or some of the best hitters of my generation I'm not sure. I've just never seen a hitter shown this much respect. I never saw Gibson or Drysdale or any of the other great pitchers have the respect for a hitter that pitchers and managers now do with [Barry] Bonds." — Dodger pitcher Don Newcombe, a 1950s star.

"Robin Yount in the first, Robin Yount in the fourth and Robin Yount in the seventh." — Pitcher Roger Clemens, asked to name the game's three most dangerous hitters.

"Good hitters don't just go up and swing. They always have a plan. Call it an educated deduction. You visualize. You're like a good negotiator. You know what you have, you know what he has, then you try to work it out." — Dave Winfield.

"He seemed to have an obligation to hit." — Lou Brock on Pete Rose.

"I'd rather hit than have sex." — Reggie Jackson, to which Roberto Alomar responded in 1996: "Better than sex? Maybe for him. He's a power hitter. I think Reggie is lying a little bit."

"Love is a Manny Splendored Thing" — Banner at Fenway honoring Manny Ramirez during Game 3 of the 2003 ALCS.

"I wish I was like Mark Johnson. He's like Ted Williams, Rod Carew, Ty Cobb and Tony Gwynn. Right now he's the best hitter I've ever seen in my life." — Pirates catcher Jason Kendall in early 1997 on teammate Mark Johnson. Johnson's career stats: .232 average and eight home runs in seven seasons. He hit .215 with four home runs in 78 games in 1997. [Note to GM's: don't hire Kendall as a scout].

See also **Batting Grips** and **Batting Stances**.

Split Second. The bat is on the ball for only .004 seconds and the batter has .4 seconds to decide what to do from the moment the ball leaves the pitcher's hand (see also **Pitching Speeds**).

Book. Rob Rains and Rawlings, *Rawlings Presents Big Stix: The Greatest Hitters in the History of the Major Leagues* (2004).

Hitting Streaks

"38 going for 56 sounds like Dolly Parton going through puberty." — "Tonight Show" host Johnny Carson during Pete Rose's 1978 hitting streak of 44 games.

Denny Lyons. Lyons, who played for the American Association Philadelphia A's, had a 52-game hitting streak in 1887. Under the rules in effect that season, walks counted as hits. Twice his streak was extended by games in which he only had base on balls.

Bill Dahlen. Dahlen had a 42-game hitting streak from June 20 to August 6, 1894. After going hitless on August 7, he hit in another 28 games, for a total of 70 out of 71 games. That season was the first in which the pitching distance was 60'6", resulting in a surge in batting averages.

Willie Keeler. In 1897 Keeler had a 44-game hitting streak and 243 hits (199 singles) in 128 games. The streak lasted from Opening Day on April 22 through June 18, 1897. The streak was actually 45 games, as Keeler had a hit on the last day of the 1896 season. An argument can be made that Keeler's record should be recognized as 49 because he also hit in each of the four games of the postseason Temple Cup the previous season.

Keeler's streak was virtually unknown until the publicity surrounding DiMaggio's streak in 1941 caused historians to review the record books. For example, the 1914 baseball encyclopedia *Balldom*, by George Moreland, reported that early 20th century outfielder Otis Clymer held the hitting streak record at 25 games.

Ty Cobb. Cobb hit in 40 straight games in 1911 to set the American League record.

George Sisler. In 1922 Sisler had hit in 39 straight games for the Browns and had a chance to tie Ty Cobb at 40. On September 11, 1922, Sisler was hitless going into the 9th inning against the Tigers and player-manager Cobb. Cobb could have walked Sisler to prevent him from beating the Tigers during a pennant race and from tying Cobb's record. Cobb did not want to be accused of preventing Sisler from attempting to tie his record and a walk would have forced the tying run into scoring position. Instead, Cobb realigned his outfield to cover the likely spot that Sisler would hit the ball. Sisler still managed a triple between Cobb in center field and the right fielder to drive in the tying run. Sisler went on to break Cobb's record three days later, ending the streak at 41.

Joe DiMaggio.

"Presented to Joe DiMaggio by his fellow players on the New York Yankees to express their admiration for his consecutive-game hitting record, 1941" — Inscription on a cigar humidor presented to DiMaggio by his teammates on August 29, 1941. The top featured a likeness of DiMaggio in midswing, with the numbers 56 (games) and 91 (hits).

DiMaggio became aware of the streak when writers told him about past records: the Yankee record of 29, held by Roger Peckinpaugh and Earle Combs; the American League record of 41 by George Sisler; and the Major League record of 44 by Willie Keeler.

DiMaggio's streak of 56 games began on May 15 and ended July 17, 1941. He had his last hits in the streak in game 56 on July 16 against the Indians in front of 67,468 fans at Cleveland's Municipal Stadium. In game 57 Indians third baseman Ken Keltner made two great defensive plays and pitchers Al Smith and Jim Bagby, Jr. controlled DiMaggio the rest of the game. Bagby's father, Jim, pitched for the Indians 20 years earlier.

In the 1st inning of game 57, DiMaggio hit a hard ground ball to third base that Keltner backhanded deep behind the bag for the out. He made a long throw from behind the bag, but DiMaggio was slow to get out of the box because of the wet field caused by heavy rains. He walked in his second at-bat. In his third at-bat in the 7th inning, he hit another ground ball down the line which Keltner grabbed on one hop and threw him out by a step.

In the 8th inning DiMaggio faced knuckleballer Bagby and grounded to shortstop Lou Boudreau for a double play. The ball took a bad hop, but Boudreau was able to stay with it. The Indians almost tied it in the 9th inning when the Yankees were leading 4–1. A two-run triple made it 4–3, but with nobody out the Indians stranded the runner at third. Had the game been tied, DiMaggio would have batted in the 10th inning.

He had 56 singles during his 56-game streak and scored 56 runs. During the streak the Yankees hit a home run in a since-broken Major League record 25 straight games, ending their streak in the 44th game of DiMaggio's streak.

DiMaggio extended the streak seven times in his last at-bat. He was 91-for-223 with 55 RBIs during the streak. After failing to get a hit in game 57, he hit in 16 straight games. On June 2, 1941, the day of game 19 of the streak, Lou Gehrig died.

A "Star Trek" chronology entitled *The History of the Future* (1993), predicted that DiMaggio's record would be broken in the year 2026 by a shortstop for the London Kings.

See also Michael Seidel, *Streak: Joe DiMaggio and The Summer of 1941* (1988); Al Silverman, *Joe DiMaggio — The Golden Year 1941* (1969).

Tommy Holmes. The Braves outfielder had a 37-game hitting streak between June 6 and July 8, 1945. Cubs pitcher Hank Wyse ended the streak on a day when Holmes did not come close to a hit.

Pete Rose.

"If Rose's streak was still intact, with that single to left, the fans would be throwing babies out of the upper deck." — Jerry Coleman on a hit in what would have been Rose's 57th straight game to break DiMaggio's record.

Rose's National League record 44-game streak started with two hits on June 14, 1978, and ended August 1, 1978. In game 45 Braves pitcher Gene Garber struck out Rose in the 9th inning after Rose had grounded into a double play in the 7th.

Paul Molitor. The Brewers infielder had a 39-game streak in 1987.

Luis Castillo. The Marlins second baseman had a 35-game hitting streak in May and June 2002.

Minor Leagues. In 1887 Daniel Stearns of the Topeka Golden Giants had a 69-game hitting streak, but walks counted as hits that year.

In 1919 Joe Wilhoit hit in 67 straight games for Wichita of the Western League. He played four years (five *games* in one source) in the Major Leagues, batting .257 in 283 games.

Joe DiMaggio had a 61-game hitting streak in 1933 for the San Francisco Seals of the Pacific Coast League. The streak ended in late July when he was shut down by Ed Walsh, Jr., son of the more famous Big Ed Walsh, a turn-of-the-century star for the Giants. DiMaggio had 104 hits in 257 at-bats during the streak and went 0–5 to end it.

Rookie. Nomar Garciaparra set the American League rookie record in 1997 when he had a 30-game streak in which he batted .383 during late July and most of August. He broke the record of 26 held by Guy Curtwright in 1943, a 30-year-old rookie who only played one season in the Major Leagues. In the process, Garciaparra broke the Red Sox rookie record of 20, set by Fred Lynn.

Padres catcher Benito Santiago set a National League rookie record in 1987 with a 34-game hitting streak.

Don Mattingly had a chance to set a new Yankee rookie hitting streak record of 25 games in 1983 but was stopped on July 24. He did not have a hit in the game when it presumably ended — but it was not over. It was the famous *Pine Tar* game involving George Brett. Mattingly was given a reprieve and one more at-bat in the bottom of the 9th inning a month later, but made a quick out against pitcher Dan Quisenberry and ended his streak at 24.

Stars' Streaks.

Babe Ruth	26
Henry Aaron	25
Ted Williams	23
Willie Mays	21
Lou Gehrig	19

Hoax

"It is extremely probable that when the Detroit baseball club again faces the Chicagoans, it will meet with such a terror in the pitcher's box as has never been known in baseball circles." — The *Chicago Mail* in 1887, describing the mysterious (and mythical) Teang Wong Foo, a "Coolie" from the village of Uwsachu in the Chicne province of Kiangton rumored to be headed for the White Sox. An "eyewitness" account in the newspaper described him in a demonstration pitching four straight curveballs that stuck on the end of a nail. Commented researcher David McDonald: "As yet, there is no listing for Teang Wong Foo in *The Baseball Encyclopedia*. Maybe he's having some kind of visa problem."

See also **Sidd Finch.**

The "Great Imposter of Sports," Barry Bremen, struck on Opening Night at Royals Stadium in 1980. He dressed up as an umpire and stood at home plate for the National Anthem. The real umpires noticed him after security failed to catch him going on the field. He quietly left the field after the anthem ended. He wore number 31, the same number he wore in a Yankee uniform when he showed up on the field at the All-Star Game in Los Angeles in 1979. He did the same thing in Seattle earlier that season, wearing number 13 in Yankee pinstripes.

Hockey

"Hockey is my kind of sport. You can get your feelings out on the ice. Baseball is you and the pitcher. Strike out and you gotta go back to the dugout and wait until the next time up.... I can't stand those feelings inside me. That's the trouble with ball. There's no outlet in the game." — Former infielder Richie Hebner, who was an All-American hockey player in Massachusetts and was offered a contract by the Boston Bruins.

"I wasn't scared. I just told them to give me all that hockey equipment." — Roger Clemens, who wore Mo Vaughn's forearm pad and Kevin Mitchell's shinguard to get his first Major League hit, after a series of shifts put the designated hitter in left field, forcing the Boston pitcher to bat.

"Introducing a revolutionary concept in professional sports: actual games." — Advertising slogan for the Chicago Wolves of the International Hockey League during the 1994 NHL hockey lockout and the Major League Baseball strike.

"It's our one chance to be hockey players." — Curt Schilling after a bench-clearing brawl.

"I'm not saying sports fans in Canada don't know much about baseball. However, upon hearing that favorite son Eric Gagne just set the record with 84 straight saves, the Montreal Canadiens immediately offered him a contract as a goalie." — Jim Greene.

Horace Stoneham. The long-time Giants owner was a prep school hockey star.

Ferguson Jenkins. The Canadian pitcher turned down offers from a number of professional hockey teams.

Tom Glavine. The Braves pitcher was a fourth-round draft pick of the Los Angeles Kings.

Orel Hershiser. The Dodger pitcher was an excellent high school hockey player.

Wayne Gretzky. In July 1980 the Blue Jays offered hockey great Wayne Gretzky a professional contract. They had seen him play in a semipro league in southern Ontario, where he purportedly batted .500 for the Brantford Red Sox of the Inter-County Major League.

Kirk McCaskill. The Angels and White Sox pitcher was an All-American hockey player at the University of Vermont and was runner-up for the Hobey Baker Award as the college hockey player of the year. He played professionally for the Sherbrooke Jets of the American Hockey League in 1983–1984.

Stanley Cup. In 1994 the New York Rangers won their first Stanley Cup since the 1940s. During the following off-season, the Cup is customarily carried to eateries and sporting venues throughout the winning city by the players. The Yankees issued a press credential that summer for Mr. Stanley Cup.

Bill Stewart. Stewart was a National League umpire for 22 years, and was also the first American referee to work in the National Hockey League in the baseball off-season. In 1938 he stopped being a referee and coached the Chicago Blackhawks to the Stanley Cup title, but the next year he was back on the ice as a referee. Stewart was the umpire in a famous **Pick-Off Throw** call during the 1948 World Series.

Octopi. In May 2002, the Tigers staged an octopus–throwing contest in honor of the Stanley Cup Western Conference Championship Series, which was being held that week at Detroit's Joe Louis Arena. Throwing boiled octopi on the ice is a hockey tradition in Detroit. Each participant threw an octopus at a target and the winner received a limo ride to the nearby Arena and tickets to the second game of the Conference Championship. Tiger pitchers Jeff Weaver and Matt Anderson competed along with fifty fans, but neither pitcher hit his target.

Tribute. In June 2000 the Expos announced that they would wear hockey immortal Maurice Richard's number 9 on their uniforms to honor the Montreal Canadians star who just died. It was believed to be the first time a Major League team had honored an athlete from another sport in this way.

Little Leaguer. Chris Drury was the NHL Rookie of the Year in 1998–1999. In 1989 he pitched and won the final game of the Little League World Series for Trumbull (Connecticut) against Taiwan.

Russ Hodges (1910–1971)

Hall of Fame (Frick Award) 1980

"The Giants Win the Pennant!" — Hodges' screaming broadcast call, repeated five times, of Bobby Thomson's 1951 **Play-Off** home run to give the Giants the pennant over the Dodgers.

"I'm guessing that you're probably not going to get a lot of 'Russ Hodges' replies." — Email from "The Commissioner" in response to a request on BaseballFever.com for comments on favorite broadcasters.

Hodges was the primary New York Giants broadcaster from 1949 until the club moved to San Francisco in 1958. He continued to broadcast for the Giants until his retirement due to illness in 1970. Prior to working with the Giants, he broadcast with Arch McDonald in Washington and assisted Mel Allen with the Yankees from 1946 through 1948.

Hodges is famous for his call of Thomson's off Dodger pitcher Ralph Branca. According to Hodges, the tape of his call was not recorded by the station. A Dodger fan, believing the Dodgers would win, taped the game off the radio to listen to later. Over the following winter the fan sent the tape to Hodges and Hodges sent him $10.

Book. Russ Hodges with Al Hirshberg, *My Giants* (1963).

Hold-Outs

"Bobo Newsom always held out just for exercise. He hated spring training." — Columnist Furman Bisher.

"You would have thought I had kidnapped Lindbergh's baby." — Joe DiMaggio on the hate mail and fan abuse he received after his aborted 1937 spring hold-out for $45,000 after hitting .346 with 46 home runs and 167 RBIs. He was told by general manager Ed Barrow that Lou Gehrig was only paid $41,000. Yankee catcher Bill Dickey said later, however, that Gehrig was making $33,000 at the time. Barrow offered $25,000 and DiMaggio finally signed for that amount in April 1938.

"Somehow, in these days of breadlines and jobless heads of families, one cannot sympathize too deeply with the well-fed bankroll-padded baseball holdout." — Columnist George Trevor during the Depression.

"Marv Throneberry got the Good Guy Award [which he received for cooperating with the press] mixed up with the Most Valuable Player Award." — Mets general manager George Weiss during Throneberry's 1963 spring hold-out.

"There's no reason to squabble…. I've done it all. It's not my fault that it hasn't been done in the Major Leagues." — Phillies catcher Bill Nahorodny during a hold-out, using his minor league statistics to support his case.

Terminology. The term "hold-out" was first used by the *New York Press* newspaper in 1888, though several players prior to that date were hold-outs.

George Gore. The outfielder played for the 1879 Chicago White Stockings and is credited by some as the first Major League hold-out. He wanted a contract worth $2,500, was offered $1,200 and finally settled for $1,900.

Tony "The Count" Mullane. The popular 19th century pitcher rebelled against pay cuts imposed by the National League after the American Association folded before the 1892 season. Most players were taking 40% cuts as a result of the failure of the American Association and the resulting lack of competition for the National League owners. Mullane refused to take a cut from $4,200 to $3,500 and held out the second half of the year. Mullane then signed the next year for $2,100.

Hugh Duffy. Duffy played for the 1890s Boston Red Stockings of the National League. He received a $12.50 per month raise after holding out, but the team retaliated by appointing him captain and putting him in charge of all bats and balls. If any were lost, he had to reimburse the team.

George Davis. The belated Hall of Famer played in the National League in the 1890s and early 20th century. In 1902 he jumped to the White Sox of the new American League and then moved back to the National League Giants. As part of the 1903 compromise that brought peace between the National and American Leagues, Davis was awarded to the White Sox. He sat out most of the 1903 season in protest and then played four games with the Giants at the end of the year. This precipitated a lawsuit between the American League and the Giants. Nineteenth century player and union leader John Montgomery Ward, who had become an attorney, represented Davis in court. They lost and Davis was forced to return to the White Sox.

Amos Rusie.

"The Giants without Rusie would be like Hamlet without the Melancholy Dane." — O.P. Caylor writing in the *New York Herald* about the frequent hold-out.

"It was a matter of policy with him to hold out almost every year. He despised spring training for one thing, and liked to miss that annual drill. But he always placed a high valuation on his services and, confronted with a contract that was not to his liking, he could be as stubborn as granite." — Lee Allen and Tom Meany on Rusie in *Kings of the Diamond* (1965).

The Giants pitcher held out in 1896 because penurious Giants owner Andrew Freedman would not meet his salary demands. Rusie was fined $200 and then demanded the $200 back, plus another $5,000 in attorney fees for the expense of his federal court lawsuit against Freedman. Before the case was decided, the other owners reportedly chipped in the price of his legal fees and he signed for $3,000 with the Giants. This was the same amount he received the previous season in which he played. Freedman later suspended him for breaking club rules.

Rusie also held out early in 1899 and then did not play in 1900 because of a marital dispute. He pitched in only three games in 1901 and retired. He won 243 games in only nine seasons (though playing in one game in a tenth) and was elected to the Hall of Fame by the Veterans Committee in 1977.

Thomas Lovett. The Dodger pitcher held out the entire 1892 season, sacrificing $3,000, and then signed in 1893 for a pay cut. A number of players took pay cuts for the 1892 season because the American Association had folded, leaving the National League with no Major League competition.

George "Rube" Ellis. Ellis held out in 1908, purportedly refusing to sign until he received $2.50 for a new glove from the Cardinals. This was before he had ever played in the Major Leagues. He signed and then played four years with the club.

Walter Johnson and Clyde Milan. These Senators teammates held out before the 1911 season. Johnson had won 25 games for the seventh-place Senators. He demanded an increase from $4,500 to $9,000, "as much as Ty Cobb." Milan wanted $4,000, a $1,000 raise after a decent season in which he hit .279 with 44 stolen bases. Milan signed for the $4,000, but Johnson refused to sign a three-year contract for $6,500 per year. Johnson went home to Coffeyville, but after a 30-hour hold-out he signed a three-year deal worth $7,000 annually.

Johnny Kling. The Cubs catcher was the premier catcher of the first 10 years of the 20th century. He held out for the entire 1909 season when the Cubs refused to raise his salary sufficiently after it won its third straight National League championship in 1908. When he returned for the 1910 season, the club again won the pennant after coming in second in 1909.

One source reported that after the 1908 season Kling won the world pocket billiards championship and decided to stick with pool in 1909. When he lost the title, only then did he return to the Cubs in 1910. In fact, Kling played for an outlaw baseball club in Kansas City in 1909 and made more money than he could have earned with the Cubs.

Frank "Home Run" Baker. In 1915 Baker held out the entire season in protest over A's owner Connie Mack's reduction of salaries due to competition from the Federal League. Baker instead played outlaw ball outside Organized Baseball for a club in Upland, Pennsylvania. Mack sold him for $35,000 to the Yankees for the 1916 season and he finished his career in New York.

Dickie Kerr. Kerr pitched honestly as a rookie for the 1919 Black Sox in the World Series. Despite his loyalty and strong pitching for the White Sox in 1921, Charles Comiskey as usual presented him with a lowball contract. Kerr finally rebelled and held out dur-

Rick Dempsey of the Orioles slides in as Carlton Fisk makes a late tag.

ing 1922. He played semipro ball and Judge Landis deemed him ineligible for Major League ball. He finally returned for 12 games in 1925, but with an 0–1 record he never again appeared in the Major Leagues.

Heinie Groh. In 1921 after holding out, the bottle bat hitter of the Reds signed in June on the promise of a trade. He was quickly traded to the Giants, but Judge Landis voided the deal. Groh was traded to the Giants after the season.

Babe Ruth and Lou Gehrig. The Yankee sluggers held out before the 1930 season, when Gehrig was making $39,000 and Ruth $70,000. Ruth eventually received $80,000, his highest salary.

Bill Terry.

"Terry, back in his playing days, had the highly deserved reputation of being able to handle money matters as well as he batted and fielded baseballs. Each spring, as regularly as the trees turned green, he was a 'holdout,' demanding an increase in salary. And, just as regularly, he won in his salary disputes."—Ira L. Smith in *Baseball's Famous First Basemen* (1956). Terry held out almost every year while with the Giants in the 1920s, making it somewhat ironic that owner Charles Stoneham chose him to succeed John McGraw as manager in 1932.

Edd Roush. In 1930 the Giants outfielder held out the entire year, returning for only one more season in 1931. He had hurt his stomach muscles in 1928 and had a poor 1929 season. The Giants cut his salary to $15,000 for 1930 and added a clause that it would be cut further if the stomach injury returned. He refused to sign the contract and sat out the season. He returned for one more season with the Reds, with whom he had starred during the prime of his career.

Ernie Lombardi. The Reds catcher held out each year from 1936 through 1938.

Don Drysdale and Sandy Koufax. The Dodger pitchers staged

a highly publicized joint hold-out in the spring of 1966. They finally agreed to contracts of $125,000 (Koufax) and $110,000 (Drysdale).

Joe Azcue. Azcue played for the Angels in 1970 and then sat out the entire 1971 season. He returned for three games with the club in 1972 before being traded to the Brewers. He played 11 more games for the Brewers before retiring.

Vida Blue. The A's pitcher received $14,750 during his first full season in 1971 when he won the Cy Young and MVP Awards after compiling a 24–8 record. He held out in 1972 and sought a $115,000 salary. He eventually signed for $63,500, but his record in 1972 was only 6–10. It has been claimed that this was the first year in which he started using drugs.

Home Games See *Home Teams* and *Scheduling*

Home Games Out of Town See *Home Teams*

Home Plate See *Bases*

Home Plate Collisions

"Home-plate umpire Ken Burkhart, apparently forgetting all about the base-runner, stepped forward ... and Jim Palmer, approaching from the mound, had an incomparable view of the ensuing carnage.... Burkhart, now horribly resembling a dog on a highway, was struck simultaneously from two directions. He landed on the seat of his pants, facing the outfield, but bravely raised his fist in the air for the 'out' sign."—Roger Angell in *The Summer Game* (1972), describing a home plate collision during the 1970 World Series (see also *Tag*, because catcher Elrod Hendricks had the ball in his throwing hand when he tagged the runner with his empty glove).

"It's unfair that catching, a job with so much toil and peril of pain from pitch to pitch, also requires its practitioner from time to time to stand still while someone runs into him." — John Lowe.

"The guy was built like Apollo Creed and could run like Carl Lewis." — Mike Scioscia on the man who hit him the hardest at the plate, Chili Davis. Davis hurt his shoulder in the collision and Scioscia, who was staggered, made no attempt to pick up his mask and helmet: "All I could think about was rolling the ball back to the mound. I ended up rolling it to the third base coaching box. I was woozy for a week, and they told me I hit real well that week. Maybe I should have been hit more often."

Ernie Lombardi. The Reds catcher was knocked senseless in Game 4 (the final game) of the 1939 World Series. With Yankee runners on first and third in the top of the 10th inning, Joe DiMaggio singled to right. Ival Goodman bobbled the ball and then threw home to Lombardi with Charlie "King Kong" Keller bearing down on him. Keller hit Lombardi in the groin and knocked him down and out. Lombardi lay dazed on the ground with the ball a few feet away as DiMaggio circled the bases. The play made the score 7–4 and the Yankees closed out the game and the Series in the bottom of the inning. Lombardi was considered the goat of the Series and never lived down the image. His misfortune was described by sportswriters as "the Lombardi coma," "the sleeping beauty act," and "the dying swan."

Ray Fosse. The Indians catcher was behind the plate for the American League during the 1970 All-Star Game. In the bottom of the 12th inning Pete Rose of the Reds bowled him over to score the winning run for the National League. Fosse suffered a separated shoulder and was never again the same player.

Buck Martinez. The Blue Jays catcher never recovered from a collision in July 1985. After tagging out the lead runner at the plate and suffering a broken leg and dislocated ankle in the collision, he threw wide to third while lying on the ground. The runner on third broke for home and Martinez took the return throw and tagged him out before collapsing. He missed the rest of the season and then returned briefly in 1986 before retiring after 17 years in the Major Leagues.

Harry Bemis. Indians catcher Harry Bemis once smashed a ball into Ty Cobb's head after Cobb had knocked him down in a home plate collision and the ball came lose.

Albert Belle. On May 18, 1997, Belle scored for the White Sox in a game against the A's. As he crossed the plate, he threw an elbow at the face of A's catcher George Williams. In his next at-bat, Belle was hit on the leg by A's pitcher Aaron Small.

Division Decider. In the deciding game of the 2003 division series between the Giants and eventual champion Marlins, J.T. Snow of the Giants came barreling home with the tying run in the 9th inning with two outs. The throw from left field beat him by yards as he slammed into catcher Ivan Rodriguez, who held the ball for the final out.

Home Run Trots

"I wanted to go into my home-run trot, but then I realized I didn't have one." — White Sox catcher Jim Essian on his first Major League home run.

"There is room for only one clown on this team." — Mets manager Casey Stengel after releasing Jimmy Piersall shortly after he circled the bases running backwards on his 100th home run on June 23, 1963. The pitch to Piersall, a hanging curve, came from future Phillies and Cubs manager and general manager Dallas Green, who also threw Pete Rose's only grand slam. Piersall had wanted to run the bases in reverse order, but the umpires vetoed the attempt. It was Piersall's only home run in 40 games for the Mets. The National League immediately enacted a new rule requiring runners to face the bases.

Babe Ruth. When Ruth hit his 56th home run in 1927, it was a dramatic two-run game-winning blast. He decided to carry the bat with him around the bases. A young fan leaped out of the stands and ran after Ruth around the bases, grabbing onto the bat. Ruth would not give up the bat and the boy would not let go, so Ruth carried bat and boy across home plate.

Jeffrey Leonard. Known as "penitentiary face" for his perpetual scowl, Leonard incurred the wrath of opposing teams by circling the bases in a ridiculously slow fashion. He did so with his "flap down," meaning his left arm was straight down at his side.

Mel Hall. Yankee outfielder Mel Hall took 33 seconds to circle the bases after hitting a home run in a 12–0 win over the Twins on May 23, 1990. The next time up, the pitcher threw close to his head, prompting words between Hall and Twins catcher Brian Harper. After the game, Hall, who once said that he thought he could beat heavyweight boxing champion Mike Tyson, said that Harper's chances were not too good: "He's better off going out and getting hit by a car."

Premature Trot. The 1990 National League Championship Series graphically illustrated the risk of the modern phenomenon of prematurely breaking into a home run trot. The Reds beat the Pirates in six games, but in Game 4 Pittsburgh's Bobby Bonilla was at the plate as the potential tying run in the bottom of the 8th inning with the Pirates down 2–1 in games. Bonilla hit a shot to left center field that looked like a home run and then died at the last moment and smashed off the wall back toward the infield.

Center fielder Billy Hatcher leaped and missed the shot and the replay analysis and press reports touted the outstanding back-up by left fielder Eric Davis. He took the ball off the wall, wheeled and threw a strike to third baseman Chris Sabo, who tagged out Bonilla. Barry Bonds then singled, which would have driven in Bonilla.

What the commentators ignored was that Bonilla lost the triple within 20 feet of leaving home plate. Bonilla started to trot toward first as he admired his apparent home run. Considering that he was thrown out by a matter of inches, the time lost at the start of his trek around the bases was the deciding factor.

Trot Injuries. Zack Wheat is credited with the "longest" home run ever hit when he rounded first base and collapsed with a cramp. He was on the ground for five minutes. He got up and completed his trip around the bases.

Jack Clark tore a calf muscle during a home run trot in a spring training game in the 1980s.

On the night that Cal Ripken set his consecutive games played record, Mets second baseman Jeff Kent sat out a game after suffering a pulled quadriceps muscle the night before while in his home run trot.

Henry Aaron. Aaron always looked down during his home run trot and never saw the ball clear the fence. This was supposedly because he had lost his first home run in the minor leagues when he missed first base admiring his work and was called out on an appeal.

Home Runs

"McGookins knocked the first ball pitched into the right-field stands, and started on an exotic, thrill-laden, round-the bases tour.

"First base! The thrill of landing at a distant goal! The feel of canvas under one's feet, the sheen of green grass stretching limitless into the outfield! And then, good-by to first base, with new lands, new faces, new adventures lying ahead.

"Second base! The land of the keystone sack! The soil that Cobb, Speaker, the great Ruth himself, have trod before you. The centerfield bleachers on the distant horizon. Strange noises from thousands on thousands of foreign throats. And so — perhaps with a sigh of regret — it is farewell to second base with its glamorous memories.

"Third base! Ah, to round third base, celebrated in song and story as the Land of the Long Heave to First! The famed Hot Corner! The distant land that many never reach in a lifetime. And now, 'tis homeward bound we are.

"Home at last! Broadened, educated, with golden memories that will live forever. The greetings of friends, the fond handclasps. Congratulations ringing in your ears. Danny, the bat boy, to meet you, joyously, heartily: 'That's socking 'em, kid!' Ah, yes, it's good to be home again! Ah, travel, life's precious boon!

"Rourke grounded out to short, ending the inning."—"The Home Run" ("As the Travel Agent Would Describe It"), by Parke Cummings, as it appeared in the *Saturday Evening Post* in 1939.

"Jacks are home runs. So are dongs, bombs and big flies. Baseball people express their fondness for a thing by thinking up lots of different ways to say it."— Michael Lewis in *Moneyball* (2003).

"No one can stop a home run. No one can understand what it really is, unless you have felt it in your own hands and body.... As the ball makes its high, long arc beyond the playing field, the diamond and the stands suddenly belong to one man. In that brief, brief time, you are free of all demands and complications."— Sadaharu Oh.

"Reggie Smith of the Dodgers and Gary Matthews of the homers hit Braves in that game."— Jerry Coleman.

See also *Grand Slams*, *Home Run Trots*, *Inside-the-Park Home Runs* and *Pinch Hitters*.

Home Run Log. The Baseball Hall of Fame contains home run logs for Major League players. Each log covers the day and circumstance of every home run hit by the logged player. Many of the logs were prepared by SABR researchers as part of an ongoing project known as the Tattersall-McConnell Home Run Log. The project has logged every home run in Major League history.

Early Home Run Leaders.

"Kenneth Williams, this new home run feature of the American League, is a funny sort of guy. He actually plays ball as if he liked the game. Yessir, never golfs, or signs up with the movies or anything — like that — he talks baseball night and day. He's so different from Babe Ruth that it's almost a crime."— *The Sporting News* on Browns slugger Ken Williams. He was the other notable home run hitter of the 1920s. His biggest year was 1922 when he hit 39 home runs and drove in 155 runs for the Browns. His career slowed after he suffered a debilitating *Beanball*, but prior to that he hit 135 home runs in his five most productive seasons beginning in 1921.

Buck Freeman. Freeman hit 25 home runs in 1899 for the Washington Nationals and finished his career with 82 home runs. It was the highest legitimate season total before Ruth's 29 in 1919.

Ned Williamson. Williamson holds an illegitimate 19th century season record of 27 home runs for the Chicago White Stockings during the 1884 National League season. His total was a fluke. He had hit only three home runs in 1882 and two in 1883, but in 1884 the team played its home games at Lakefront Park, which had a left field fence of 180 feet and a right field fence of 196 feet (215

in some sources). In previous seasons balls hit over those fences had been declared ground rule doubles. In 1884 balls hit over the right field fence were ruled home runs. Williams hit 25 of his 27 home runs at his home park (see also *Fences*).

Williamson tore up his knee sliding on a field near the Eiffel Tower during the 1888 international tour sponsored by Albert Spalding, but Spalding refused to pay for Williamson's medical bills, and he limped into the next season. He died weighing 300 pounds (up from 170) in 1894, only ten years after his home run record was set. Williamson was voted by twelve 19th century greats as the best of the era, in a poll taken in the year of his death.

In 1882 the entire National League hit only 126 home runs and in 1883 hit 124. In 1884 the White Stockings had four players with 21 to 27 home runs each, for a total of 142, three times the next best team. The following year the club had 54 home runs when balls hit over the short fence were again ruled ground rule doubles.

Roger Connor. At 6'3" and 220 pounds, Connor was considered the first great power hitter of the 19th century. He had 136 home runs and 227 triples over a career lasting from 1880 through 1897. He reportedly once was given a $500 gold watch for hitting a ball out of the Polo Grounds.

Dan Brouthers. Brouthers was another player considered the Babe Ruth of his day at 6'2" and 207 pounds. In 1886 he hit a shot out of Washington's Capitol Park that was the "tape measure" home run of its time (in part confirmed by writer Zane Grey's reference to it in one of his few early 20th century baseball novels). Brouthers was the first National League player to win back-to-back batting titles and he hit 106 home runs over 19 Major League seasons from 1879 through 1896 (with a two-game cameo appearance in 1904).

Frank "Home Run" Baker. Baker led the American League in home runs from 1911 through 1914, with totals of 11, 10, 12 and 9 (9, 10, 12 and 8 in older sources). He hit two home runs in the 1911 World Series to earn his nickname.

Socks Seybold. Seybold set the American League season home run record of 16 in 1902 while with the A's. He had 51 home runs over his nine-year career.

Gavvy Cravath. The Phillies outfielder (who usually receives an extra "v" in his first name), born Clifford Carlton Cravath, set the post–1900 Major League record with 24 home runs in 1915. He was the league leader in six of seven seasons between 1913 and 1919 and was the home run champion of the 1910s. His 1915 total was more than 10% of the National League total. He learned to hit to the opposite field to take advantage of Baker Bowl's 272-foot right field fence (though it had a 60-foot wall and screen).

Ruth in the Minor Leagues. Babe Ruth hit one home run in the minor leagues, for Providence in the International League. It was a three-run smash on September 5, 1914. He also pitched a one-hitter that day in a 9–0 victory over Toronto.

Ruth's 29 in 1919.

"Perhaps, and most likely, Ruth will not be so successful in 1920. The pitchers will eye him with more than ordinary caution and they will twist their fingers into knots to get more curve and still more curve on the ball. They will give one another private little tips."— The 1920 *Spalding Guide* after Ruth hit 29 home runs in 1919. Its suggested strategy was unsuccessful, as Ruth had an astonishing 54 in 1920. There was not much indication early in 1919 that Ruth would explode to 29 home runs that season. He had only seven by the end of June, but hit 14 after mid–August to finish with a flourish and a new record.

Ruth captured the nation's attention in 1920 when he began to hit home runs at prodigious rates and distances for the Yankees.

This coincided with the permanency of the lively ball and the official elimination of trick pitches such as the spitball.

Ruth may have hit far more than 29 home runs in 1919, but for four factors. First, spitballs and other "substance abuse" pitches were not limited until 1920. Second, Ruth played in only 130 of the shortened 140-game 1919 season. Third, in 1919 Ruth played in difficult Fenway Park. He moved into the Polo Grounds, with its short foul line dimensions, with the Yankees for the 1920 season. Fourth, it was the year before the livelier ball was introduced permanently (although there is evidence to suggest that the ball was already in use).

All-time Leader. One modern source reported that Ruth became the all-time home run leader on June 10, 1921, when he hit number 120. However, Roger Connor hit 136 home runs in the 19th century, so it was actually a few weeks later that Ruth broke the record.

Rules. In some 19th century ballparks home runs were only counted if they were hit between the fielders "in grounds," rather than over the fielders' heads.

Home Run Percentage. The ratio of home runs per game steadily increased into the 1950s, with a slight dip in the 1940s during the lower-quality baseball of the war years. Home run production dropped off through the 1970s, rose again in the 1980s, dipped steadily in the 1990s and then exploded in the 2000s:

1870s–1920	.33 per game
1920s	.80
1930s	1.12
1940s	1.05
1950s	1.69
1960s	1.64
1970s	1.47
1980s	1.60
1990–1995	1.55
2001	1.44
2002	2.09

Home Run Percentage/Player. Barry Bonds set the record for best home run percentage in a season when he hit one every 6.52 at-bats during his 73-home run season in 2001. That broke Mark McGwire's 1998 record of 7.27. Bonds' 15.34 homers per 100 at-bats broke McGwire's 1998 record of 13.75.

Major League Record/Season. The 1901 season saw a combined 455 home runs. The first time the leagues saw 1,000 home runs was 1922, with 1,055. In 1950 the Major Leagues broke 2,000. They reached 3,001 in 1962, an expansion year (the previous expansion year, 1961, saw 2,730, a new record).

In 1987 there was an aberrational increase to 4,458, far more than had ever been hit, and more than 1,000 higher than would be hit until 1993. In 1996 the record increased in 1996 to 4,962. The 5,000 milestone was reached in 1998 with 5,064 and two new expansion teams. The all-time peak was 2000, when 30 teams combined to hit 5,693. The National League had a record 3,005 that season. The American League record is 2,742, set in 1996.

The First National League Season. In the National League's first season in 1876 there were 39 home runs. League leader George Hall had five.

Low Output/Team/Season. The third-place 1908 White Sox hit only three home runs. The Browns and A's each hit 21 to lead the league. The modern National League record low is nine, by Pittsburgh in 1917 in cavernous Forbes Field.

High Output/Team/Season. The 1997 Mariners hit 264 home runs for the American League record, breaking the 1996 record of 257 set by the Orioles. The 2000 Astros hit 249 for the National League record. The 1996 Rockies had tied the National League record of 221, set by the 1956 Reds and 1947 Giants.

500 Home Runs. See Bob Allen and Bill Gilbert, *The 500 Home Run Club* (2002).

"This is no mere record about to be marked up in perishable chalk. It is the middle of an epoch."—The *New York Evening World* describing Babe Ruth's 500th home run in 1929.

"Last night's homer was Willie Stargell's 399th career home run, leaving him one shy of 500 [sic]."—Jerry Coleman.

"I checked [the Dodgers website]to see how the 'Guess What Day Fred McGriff hits his 500th home run' contest was going, and found no more mention of it. I presume if you replied 'not in my lifetime,' you won—although it might be hard to collect."—T.J. Simers in the *Los Angeles Times*, after McGriff was an injured bust with the 2003 Dodgers. He returned to the Majors with Tampa Bay in May 2004, but had a slow start and didn't make it to 500.

See below for more information on the 600- and 700-home run clubs.

The 20 members of the 500-Home Run Club (through 2004, in date order), along with their first, 500th and last home runs:

1. Babe Ruth.

"From 1926 through 1931, as he aged from 32 to 37, he put on the best sustained streak of power hitting that baseball has ever seen or—I'd bet the farm on this—will ever see again."—Robert W. Creamer in the late 1990s.

"I'd kinda like to have that one."—Babe Ruth to a policeman, crossing the plate after hitting his 500th home run.

"The next batter made a hit that will live in the memory of all who saw it. That clouter was George Ruth, the southpaw from St. Mary's school. The ball carried so far to right field that he walked around the bases."—Account of Ruth's home run in the Orioles' first intrasquad game on March 7, 1914, a week after he had left St. Mary's Academy.

Ruth hit his 500th home run against Willis Hudlin of the Indians on August 11, 1929, at Cleveland. It was Ruth's 30th home run of the year. He was 34 years old.

Ruth hit his first home run off Jack Warhop of the Yankees on May 6, 1915, at the Polo Grounds in New York.

"Boys, that last one felt good."—Ruth, sitting on the bench of the rival Pirates after hitting the last of his three home runs of his career, on his way to the visitor's clubhouse. He hit his 714th home run (one of three that day) off Guy Bush of the Pirates on May 25, 1935, at Pittsburgh (see below).

2. Jimmie Foxx. Foxx hit his 500th home run on September 24, 1940, off George Caster of the A's. Foxx was 32 years old, the youngest player ever to reach 500. The inning almost featured five consecutive home runs (see below).

Foxx hit his first off Urban Shocker of the Yankees on May 31, 1927, at Philadelphia.

He hit No. 534, his last, on September 9, 1945, off Johnny Lanning of the Pirates at Pittsburgh.

3. Mel Ott. Ott was managing the Giants when he hit his 500th home run against the Braves on August 1, 1945, at the Polo Grounds. The hit came in the third inning off Johnny Hutchings in a 9–2 Giants victory. Ott was 36 years old.

His first home run was on July 18, 1927, against Hal Carlson of the Cubs in the Polo Grounds.

His last, number 511, was on April 16, 1946, against Oscar Juddy of the Phillies at the Polo Grounds. Ott hit more home runs in a single ballpark, 323 in the Polo Grounds, than any other player.

4. Ted Williams. Williams hit his 500th home run on June 17,

1960, in a 3–1 win at Cleveland against Wynn Hawkins. He was 41 years old.

His first home run was on April 23, 1939, at Fenway Park against A's pitcher Bud Thomas.

In the **Last At-Bat** of his career on September 28, 1960, against Jack Fisher of the Orioles, he hit a dramatic home run at Fenway Park, number 521.

5. Willie Mays. Mays hit number 500 in the Astrodome off Houston's Don Nottebart on September 13, 1965. He was 34 years old.

He hit number 1 against Warren Spahn on May 28, 1951, over the left field roof at the Polo Grounds. It was his first hit in the Major Leagues and prompted the following comment from manager Leo Durocher: "I never saw a fucking ball get out of a fucking ball park so fucking fast in my fucking life."

Spahn's reaction: "Gentlemen, for the first 60 feet, that was a hell of a pitch."

He hit his last home run, number 660, on August 17, 1973, in Shea Stadium for the Mets against Reds pitcher Don Gullett.

6. Mickey Mantle.

"There is no sound in baseball akin to the sound of Mantle hitting a home run, the crunchy sound of an axe biting into a tree, yet magnified a hundred times in the vast, cavernous, echo-making hollows of a ball field." — Arnold Hano in *Baseball Stars of 1958*.

Mantle hit his 500th home run on May 14, 1967, against Orioles pitcher Stu Miller at Yankee Stadium. He was 35 years old.

He hit his first off Randy Gumpert of the White Sox at Comiskey Park on May 1, 1951.

Mantle hit number 536 off Red Sox pitcher Jim Lonborg on September 20, 1968, at Yankee Stadium. It is well known that during Denny McLain's 31st victory of the 1968 season, he grooved a pitch to Mantle for the next-to-last home run of his career. It allowed Mantle to pass Jimmie Foxx on the all-time list. McLain alerted Mantle that he was going to groove him, but Mantle did not believe it. He looked at the first two pitches — cream-puff fastballs down the middle — before connecting on the third pitch.

7. Eddie Mathews. At age 35 Mathews was playing for the Astros when he hit his 500th home run off Giants pitcher Juan Marichal on July 14, 1967, at Candlestick Park in San Francisco.

His first home run was on April 19, 1952, off Ken Heintzelman of the Phillies in Philadelphia.

His last home run, number 512, was on May 27, 1968, at Anaheim Stadium against Sammy Ellis.

8. Henry Aaron.

Aaron hit his 500th home run at age 34 on July 14, 1968, against Mike McCormick of the Giants in Atlanta.

He hit his first home run on April 23, 1954, against Vic Raschi of the Cardinals in a 7–5 victory by Milwaukee.

He hit number 755 on July 20, 1976, at Milwaukee off Angels pitcher Dick Drago (see below).

9. Ernie Banks. Banks hit his 500th home run on May 12, 1970 (1969 in two incorrect sources), against Braves pitcher Pat Jarvis in Chicago. He was 39 years old.

He hit number 1 on September 20, 1953, in St. Louis off Gerry Staley of the Cardinals.

His last home run, number 512, was against Jim McGlothlin of the Reds in Wrigley Field on August 24, 1971.

10. Harmon Killebrew. Killebrew hit his 500th home run on August 10 (erroneously 11 in some sources), 1971, against Mike Cuellar of the Orioles in Minnesota. He was 35 years old. The umpire behind the plate was Bill Kunkel, who had surrendered

three home runs to Killebrew when Kunkel was an American League pitcher.

He hit his first home run on June 24, 1955, in Washington against Tigers starter Billy Hoeft.

He hit number 573 while playing for the Royals on September 18, 1975, at Minnesota off Ed Bane of the Twins.

11. Frank Robinson. Robinson hit his 500th home run on September 13 (erroneously September 14 in some sources), 1971, against Tiger pitcher Fred Scherman in Baltimore. He was 36 years old and it was his last season with the Orioles.

His first home run was on April 28, 1956, off Cubs pitcher Paul Minner in Cincinnati.

His last home run, number 586 while he was a player-manager, was for the Indians in Anaheim Stadium off Sid Monge of the Angels on July 6, 1976.

12. Willie McCovey. McCovey hit number 500 for the Giants against Braves pitcher Jamie Easterly in Atlanta on June 30, 1978. He was 40 years old.

He hit number 1 against Ron Kline of the Pirates in San Francisco on August 2, 1959.

His last home run, number 521 (tying him with Ted Williams), was off Montreal's Scott Sanderson on May 3, 1980, in Montreal.

13. Reggie Jackson. Jackson hit number 500 on September 17, 1984, off Royals pitcher Bud Black at home for the Angels.

He hit his first home run while with the A's on September 17, 1967, against Jim Weaver of the Angels in Anaheim Stadium.

He hit his last home run, number 563, on August 17, 1987, against Mike Witt of the Angels in Anaheim.

14. Mike Schmidt. Schmidt hit number 500 for the Phillies off Don Robinson in Pittsburgh on April 18, 1987, with two outs in the 9th inning to rally the Phillies to an 8–6 win over the Pirates.

He hit his first home run on September 16, 1972, off Balor Moore of Montreal.

He hit his last home run, number 548, on May 2, 1989, off Houston's Jim DeShaies. Schmidt retired a few days later.

15. Eddie Murray. Murray hit number 500 on September 6, 1996, for the Orioles against Tigers pitcher Felipe Lira. The 7th inning blast was on the one-year anniversary of teammate Cal Ripken breaking Lou Gehrig's consecutive game streak. Psychic Friends Network owner Michael Laskey, a former sports handicapper, reportedly paid $500,000 for the ball in the largest memorabilia purchase of all time (until two weeks later when a collector paid over $700,000 for a Honus Wagner baseball card). Actually, Laskey paid $280,000, and the money was put into an annuity that would pay out $500,000 over several years.

Murray hit his first home run while with the Orioles on April 18, 1977, off Tom Buskey of the Indians.

Murray hit his last home run on May 30, 1997, for the Angels off Bob Tewksbury of the Twins.

16. Mark McGwire. McGwire hit No. 500 on August 5, 1999, off Andy Ashby of the Padres. He was the fastest to reach 500, doing it in 5,487 at-bats. When McGwire reached 400 home runs on May 8, 1998, he did it in 4,726 at-bats, fewer than anyone in history.

He hit his first home run on August 25, 1986, off Walt Terrell of the Tigers.

He hit his last home run, No. 583, on October 4, 2001, off Rocky Coppinger of the Brewers. It was the same day that Barry Bonds tied McGwire's season-record 70 home runs.

17. Barry Bonds.

"After he hit his 500th home run, I called to congratulate him. Most people would say, 'Thank you very much.' He told me, 'If you had brought me up earlier, I'd have hit it sooner.'"—Former Pirates general manager Syd Thrift.

Bonds hit No. 500 on April 17, 2001, off Dodger reliever Terry Adams. He did it in 7,502 at-bats. He also hit home runs in five straight games to get to 500.

He hit his first home run, a solo shot, on June 4, 1986, off Craig McMurtry of the Braves in the 5th inning. He had his first RBI in the 4th inning of the game.

18. Sammy Sosa.

"I know what it means to get close to 500. I gave up almost 500."—Pitcher Bert Blyleven, empathizing with the pressure Sosa was under as he approached the magic mark.

Sosa hit No. 500 on April 4, 2003, off Scott Sullivan in Cincinnati's new Great American Ballpark in a 10–9 loss to the Reds. Fan Zach Kirk, 22, scraped his knees and knuckles in coming up with the ball, and later rejected a $20,000 offer for the ball. Sosa was only the fifth player to reach 500 before his 35th birthday (he was 34). The others were Ruth, Aaron, Mays and Foxx.

Sosa hit his first home run on June 21, 1989, while with the Rangers, off Roger Clemens.

19. Rafael Palmeiro. Palmeiro hit No. 500 on May 11, 2003, off Dave Elder of the Indians. It was the first time that a team had players with 300, 400 and 500 home runs playing at the same time. Juan Gonzalez had 417 and Alex Rodriguez had 309.

He hit his first home on September 9, 1986, off Kevin Gross of the Phillies while playing for the Cubs.

20. Ken Griffey, Jr.

"It's about time!"—Teammate Barry Larkin.

Griffey's 500th home run was delayed because of injuries, but he finally delivered on Father's Day, June 20, 2004, off Cardinals pitcher Matt Morris at Busch Stadium in St. Louis. He was 34 years old at the time, the sixth youngest to reach the milestone, and gave a hug to his dad sitting in the stands after the blow. Griffey said it was a nice present, as he usually gives his dad "Old Spice and underwear." Mark Crummley, 19, caught the ball and returned it to Griffey, who gave Crummley the jersey he was wearing and a bag full of memorabilia. Stan Musial, who shares Griffey's birthday and was born in Griffey's home town of Donora, Pennsylvania, was in the stands.

600 Home Runs.

"Why me? Why did it have to be me?"—Padres pitcher Mike Corkins on giving up Willie Mays' 600th home run.

Babe Ruth. Ruth hit his 600th home run on August 21, 1931, against George Blaeholder of the Browns in St. Louis. Ruth paid $10 and provided a new ball to the fan who caught the ball. When Ruth hit No. 600, second on the all-time list was Rogers Hornsby with 293. Ruth was ejected from the game for arguing a home run hit over him that bounced off the top of the wall and bounced back over his head.

Willie Mays. Mays hit his 600th home run on Monday, September 22, 1969, in the 7th inning off Mike Corkins ("Corcoran" in one source). He was pinch-hitting for rookie George Foster in a 4–2 victory over the Padres. See also *Promotions—Promotions That Backfired* for a false story about the home run by former Padres general manager Buzzie Bavasi. In the game, Bobby Bonds set a new record for most strikeouts in a season (later broken) with 176.

Henry Aaron. Aaron hit number 600 off Gaylord Perry on April 28 (erroneously 27 in some sources), 1971, in a 6–5 loss to the Giants. The Giants won on a 10th inning single by Willie Mays. Aaron passed Mays, who was still active, with his 644th home run on June 11, 1972.

Barry Bonds. Bonds hit No. 600 on August 7, 2002, off Kip Wells in a 4–3 loss to the Pirates.

Bonds hit No. 660 to tie Willie Mays on April 13, 2004. He hit No. 661 later in the game. Both balls dropped into McCovey Cove, and both were recovered by "the dude in the kayak wearing an Arnold Schwarzenegger mask," Larry Ellison, a 53-year-old computer executive. He easily scooped up the first blast, but there was a frenzied scramble for the second, as one kayaker missed the ball with his net and Ellison rowed over to grab it, missed, and then dove in after it. He and his son, Jeremy, decided to give Bonds No. 660, but kept the other ball for sale. Ellison kayaked at about 15 games a season and had tickets to the game, but decided to give Bonds another shot for No. 660. Up to that point there had been 38 splashdowns into McCovey Cove, 29 by Bonds. Bonds hit the tying drive off Matt Kinney, a 442-foot blast in the 5th inning. Willie Mays came onto the field and embraced Bonds.

Ruth's 700th Home Run.

"Ruth's Record of 700 Home Runs Likely to Stand for All Times in Major Leagues"—Headline in the *New York Times*.

"The only number I care about is Babe Ruth's because as a left-handed hitter, I wiped him out. And in the baseball world, Babe Ruth's everything, right?"—Barry Bonds in 2003.

"When I pass Babe Ruth's 714 home runs in last weekend of the season, resist urge to thump chest, point to the heavens and yell, 'Take that, you big, fat, white guy.'"—Proposed New Year's resolution for Bonds in 2004, by Alan Schwartz.

Ruth hit his 700th home run off Tigers pitcher Tommy Bridges on July 13, 1934, in a 4–2 victory over Detroit.

Ruth's Last American League Home Run. Ruth's last American League home run before moving over to the Braves for the 1935 season was number 708, hit on September 29, 1934, off Syd Cohen of the Senators.

Ruth's Last Home Run/714.

"I never saw a ball hit so hard before or since. He was fat and old, but he still had that great swing. Even when he missed you could hear the bat go *swish*. I can't remember anything about the first home run he hit off me that day.... But I can't forget that last one. It's probably still going."—Pitcher Guy Bush on the ball he served up.

Guy Bush gave up Ruth's 714th (and 713th) home run on May 25, 1935, while Ruth was playing for the Boston Braves. It was the day after the first night game in Major League history. Ruth hit three home runs that day against the Pirates and retired less than two weeks later.

Ruth's last home run, off a fastball, was hit over the Forbes Field roof, the first time anyone had done it. The ball sailed over the heads of a group of boys on a street corner and bounced into a construction site, where it was retrieved by Henry "Wiggy" Diorio. He took it around to the Schenly Hotel and got Ruth's autograph on the ball. Ruth's former Yankee teammate, Waite Hoyt, was the winning pitcher for the Pirates that day as the Braves lost 11–7.

Ruth would have quit at that point, but the team had a western road trip scheduled. Ruth had committed to making "farewell" appearances in the cities on the trip, which meant a much bigger gate if he played.

When Ruth retired he had far more than twice as many home runs as his nearest competitor. Only two players had over 300 at the time; Rogers Hornsby with 301 and Lou Gehrig with 314. Jimmie Foxx needed most of the rest of the 1935 season to reach 300. See *Foul Balls—Fair or Foul* for a discussion of the 50 home runs that Ruth lost because of an early foul ball rule.

Aaron's 700th Home Run.

"Why should I read about a man playing a game I couldn't get into at the time." — Aaron when asked whether in his youth he was aware of the exploits of Babe Ruth.

"I don't care how many home runs Mr. Aaron hits. I just want to be left alone." — Claire (Mrs. Babe) Ruth, after constant questioning during Aaron's pursuit of her husband's record.

Aaron was 34 years old on July 21 (erroneously 23 in some sources), 1973, when he hit his 700th home run on a 1–1 fastball in the 6th inning off Ken Brett in Philadelphia. The Phillies won the game 8–4. The home run was caught by Robert Winborne, who received 700 silver dollars in return for the ball.

Bonds' 700th Home Run.

"Friends describe the usually surly slugger as now merely grouchy." — Greg Cote of the *Miami Herald* on Bonds, after the slugger passed Willie Mays.

"Even No. 500 and No. 600 had a bit more oomph to them, it seems. The first one because nobody had any idea he'd go this much further, the second because everybody was shocked he'd gone so far so fast…. And, truth be told, a milestone just doesn't rank up with a record. This certainly isn't the traveling circus that the Road to 73 was in 2001, or anything like the Big Mac-Sammy Show of '98. And it won't change the American landscape the way 715 did. It's mostly just a cool number: 700." — John Schlegel at MLB.com.

Bonds hit home run No. 700 on Friday, September 17, 2004, off Jake Peavey of the Padres in the 3rd inning of a 4–1 Giants victory. The ball went into the left field stands 392 feet away and was caught on the fly by a fan. It was Bonds' 42nd homer of the season. At the time, Bonds had 79 home runs against the Padres, by far the most he had against any club.

Of course, the home run resulted in another lawsuit, as 40-year-old Timothy Murphy sued 26-year-old Steve Williams after Williams allegedly yanked the ball away from under Murphy's leg. Williams' lawyers naturally estimated the ball's worth at $500,000 and Murphy's lawsuit contended that he had "possession, dominion and control over the ball by sitting on it and securing it with his right leg" before Williams "systematically reached under [his] body, striking him and hitting him as they did so." A judge immediately ruled that Williams was the owner and could sell the ball.

Aaron's 714th Home Run.

"It wasn't a bad pitch, but it wasn't good enough against Hank Aaron." — Jack Billingham.

In 1973 at age 39 Aaron hit .301 with 40 home runs and 96 RBIs in only 392 at-bats. He finished the season with 713 home runs, one short of Ruth. He received death threats in "fan" mail during the off-season (see also **Racism**): "There is six months until the '74 season begins. Until then, one can break a leg, his back, develop sickle cell anemia or drop dead. Babe Ruth's 714 record will never be tied or broken."

Aaron hit number 714 on Opening Day in Cincinnati, April 4, 1974. He hit it off Reds pitcher Jack Billingham in his first at-bat of the season in front of Cincinnati's largest opening day crowd in its history, 52,154. The Braves were going to hold Aaron out of early road games so that he would hit the tying and record-breaking home runs in Atlanta, but commissioner Bowie Kuhn vetoed the plan.

Aaron's 715th Home Run.

"Here's the pitch by Downing … Swinging…. There's a drive into left center field. That ball is gonna beeee … OUTA HERE! IT'S 715! There's a new home run champion of all time and it's Henry Aaron!" — Braves broadcaster Milo Hamilton.

"This means that Americans will be treated, *ad nauseam*, to one of the worst calls in the history of radio play-by-play. Milo Hamilton is the guilty party and he screamed for the entire time that it took Aaron to circle the bases. All he needed to say was, 'There it is … number 715,' and shut up [which is what Vin Scully did while calling the game for the Dodgers]." — Sportswriter John Steigerwald of the *Pittsburgh Post-Gazette* on the 20th anniversary of Aaron's record home run.

On April 8, 1974, the Braves held their first home game of the season versus the Dodgers in front of 53,775 fans, the largest crowd in Atlanta history. Aaron walked his first time up in the 2nd inning.

In the 4th inning with Darrell Evans on base, Dusty Baker on deck, the Dodgers leading 3–1, Al Downing pitching and Joe Ferguson catching, Aaron drove a slider into the Braves bullpen at 9:07 p.m. Atlanta pitcher Tom House caught the ball and ran it in to Aaron. Aaron's mother Alfredia Aaron ran on the field and jumped into his arms — not out of happiness — out of fear for her son's life, at least according to Aaron.

Both Downing and Aaron were wearing number 44. Downing was in uniform for the Yankees on the day that Roger Maris hit his 61st home run of the 1961 season.

Each ball thrown to Aaron had been stamped to avoid fakery. In 1973 the balls were stamped with an invisible diamond with a number inside. In 1974 there were two sets of numbers and a marked pattern that lit up under a fluorescent lamp.

The ball Aaron hit for 715 was marked with a pair of 12's and two 2's. The number 12 was arbitrarily picked by Braves equipment manager Bill Acree.

Each of the Braves pitchers was stationed along the outfield fence, with the veterans getting the choice spots near the left field foul pole. House was the last pitcher before center field and did not think he had a chance. Sammy Davis, Jr., and an anonymous Venezuelan offered $25,000 for the ball. Aaron still keeps the ball in a bank vault.

The two young fans who ran onto the field and followed Aaron around the basepaths were Cliff Courtney and Britt Gaston. They were arrested for the stunt, but Aaron helped in having the charges dropped. Both later became successful businessmen. See also George Plimpton, *One for the Record* (1974).

Aaron's Last National League Home Run.
Aaron's last National League home run was number 733, given up by Reds pitcher Rawley Eastwick on October 2, 1974. Aaron returned to Milwaukee (American League Brewers) for the 1975 season.

Aaron's Last Home Run/755.

"I would like people not to think in terms of the 755 home runs I hit but think in terms of what I've accomplished off the field and some of the things I stood for." — Henry Aaron.

"I'm mad at Hank for deciding to play one more season. I threw him his last home run and thought I'd be remembered forever. Now I'll have to throw him another." — Pitcher Bill Lee.

"While he had a total of 40 home runs in his first two big-league seasons, it is unlikely that Aaron will break any records in this department." — Furman Bisher, in the *Saturday Evening Post*.

Dick Drago of the Angels gave up Aaron's last home run, number 755, on July 20, 1976. Including postseason play and All-Star Games, Aaron hit 763 Major League home runs.

Milwaukee Brewers groundskeeper Richard Arndt caught number 755. He decided to keep the ball after Milwaukee management asked him to give it to Aaron. He was fired the next day and his final paycheck had a $5 deduction for the cost of the ball. He later asked Aaron to sign the ball, but Aaron refused. For many years Aaron told reporters that he had the ball in a safety deposit box. Arndt tried to get *Sports Illustrated* to set the record straight, but the magazine stuck by its story that Aaron had the ball. Arndt's claim was validated later by Aaron, who mentioned it in his 1991 autobiography, *I Had a Hammer*, with Lonnie Wheeler.

Most to Ruth. Rube Walberg of the Giants, A's and Red Sox gave up 17 home runs to Babe Ruth over a pitching career that lasted from 1923 through 1937.

Most to Aaron. Don Drysdale gave up 17 home runs to Henry Aaron, the most by any pitcher. Second was Claude Osteen with 13. Drysdale and Osteen had been teammates in the 1960s, and when Osteen was about to face Aaron later in his career, Drysdale would call him and say: "Now, Claude, don't let down. That record is within *reach*."

Most to Mays. Warren Spahn gave up 17 home runs to Willie Mays, including Mays' first and 200th. Spahn gave up 433 home runs in his career.

Most to Bonds. As of Bonds' 700th home run, four pitchers had given up eight of them: Greg Maddux, John Smoltz, Curt Schilling and Terry Mulholland.

Most to Single Player. Brooklyn Dodger center fielder Duke Snider holds the record for most home runs in a career off one pitcher with 19 against Phillies Hall of Famer Robin Roberts. Others (career total in parentheses):

Henry Aaron (755) 17 off Don Drysdale
Babe Ruth (714) 17 off Rube Walberg
Barry Bonds (at 700 in late 2004) 8 off John Smoltz, Greg Maddux, Terry Mulholland and Curt Schilling
Willie Mays (660) 18 off Warren Spahn
Frank Robinson (586) 10 off Larry Jackson
Mark McGwire (583) 7 off Frank Tanana
Harmon Killebrew (573) 9 off Earl Wilson
Reggie Jackson (563) 8 off Wilbur Wood
Mike Schmidt (548) 11 off Bob Forsch

Ruth's 60 Home Runs in 1927.

"If I'd a known it was going to be a famous record, I'd a stuck it in his ear."—Pitcher Tom Zachary, who gave up number 60.

"If you really want to know the truth, I'd rather have thrown at his big, fat head."—Zachary.

On the second-to-last day of the season, September 30, 1927, Senators pitcher Tom Zachary gave up the 60th home run hit by Babe Ruth that year. The ball was caught in the right field bleachers barely in fair territory by 40-year-old Joe Forner, who lived at 1937 1st Avenue in Manhattan. As Ruth hit it, Zachary yelled "foul ball," but it landed about 10 feet fair. Mark Koenig had tripled and was on third base. It was Ruth's 17 home run of the month and it came in his last at-bat of the season.

The crowd threw "Homer 60" hats into the air as Ruth's ball cleared the fence. The game was Walter Johnson's last in the Major Leagues; he pinch-hit for Zachary in the 9th inning to receive one last ovation from the crowd.

Zachary was the only pitcher to give up at least two of Ruth's home runs that year for two separate teams. In addition to number 60 with the Senators, he gave up number 22 on June 16 while with the Browns.

That season 33 different pitchers gave up home runs to Ruth, including two by football star Ernie Nevers. Nineteen were hit against left-handers and 28 were at Yankee Stadium. Before Ruth got hot in September, most writers felt that Ruth's record of 59 home runs in 1921 was safe and instead they concentrated more on Lou Gehrig's unsuccessful assault on 200 RBIs.

In 1930 Ruth was on a pace to break 60. He had 32 home runs when he was 20 games ahead of the pace, but he tore off a nail at midseason and ended up hitting only 49.

Maris' 60th Home Run in 1961. Roger Maris hit his 60th home run of 1961 off Jack Fisher of the Red Sox on September 26, in the 158th game of the year. It came with two outs in the 3rd inning at Yankee Stadium. The ball bounced back onto the field to Orioles outfielder Earl Robinson. Babe Ruth's widow Claire attended the game, as well as the game in which Maris hit number 61. She claimed that Maris' 60th was "too late" to tie her husband because it was after Game 154.

Maris' 61st Home Run in 1961.

"Here's the wind-up ... fastball hit deep to RIGHT, THIS COULD BE IT! WAY BACK THERE! HOLY COW, HE DID IT! *61* HOME RUNS!"—Yankee broadcaster Phil Rizzuto.

"If I never hit another home run, this is the one they can never take away from me."—Roger Maris.

"As a ballplayer, I would be delighted to do it again. As an individual, I doubt if I could possibly go through it again."—Maris, on the pressure.

"They've been pitching me low and wide and tight.
I've been tense and nervous, drawn and pallid,
But my prayers are full of joy tonight,
Thank you, God, for Tracy Stallard."—Yankee public address announcer Bob Sheppard's ode to the pitcher who served up number 61 to Maris.

"I don't want to be him. Everybody knows *who* he is. Nobody knows *where* he is."—Pitcher Ray Sadecki, referring to Tracy Stallard, on the difficulty of being a high-profile goat.

"Hey, Maris, the only thing you have in common with Ruth is a belly."—Anonymous fan in 1961.

"Why can't they understand? I don't want to be Babe Ruth. He was a great ballplayer. I'm not trying to replace him. The record is there, and damn right I want to break it, but that isn't replacing Babe Ruth."—Maris.

After hitting number 60 in game 158, Maris was shut out in games 159 through 161. In the last game of the season the Red Sox faced the Yankees on October 1, 1961, in front of 23,154 fans. Some contended that the game was anticlimactic because the 61st home run came after the 154-game period thought to be allowed by commissioner Ford Frick to break any existing records (see also *Asterisks*) because 1961 was an expansion year and the schedule had been increased by eight games.

The entire Yankee pitching staff was sitting in the bullpen hoping to catch the ball. In the 4th inning (erroneously the 3rd in one source), Red Sox pitcher Tracy Stallard threw one ball outside and one in the dirt to a chorus of boos. On a 2–0 pitch Stallard gave up the home run, which landed in the right field bleachers about 40 feet to the left of Ruth's 60th home run (to the *right* in most sources). It was about 360 feet from the plate and 15 rows deep. It was the only run of the game and Maris's 30th home run in Yankee Stadium that season.

After Maris circled the bases he tried to enter the dugout but his teammates kept pushing him back out onto the field. After the fourth *Curtain Call* (one of the earliest on record in baseball), Maris finally was allowed back.

Nineteen-year-old Sal Durante caught the ball, although the ball first landed in another fan's coat held above his head to catch the ball. Durante simply grabbed the ball off the coat. Contrary to this account, *Sports Illustrated* reported in 1994 that Durante made a one-handed grab from his seat (No. 4 in box 163D in section 33).

Durante received $5,000 and two trips to the West Coast in return for the ball. The money was offered by Sam Gordon, owner of Sam's Ranch Wagon Restaurant in California. See also Maury

Allen, *Roger Maris—A Man for All Seasons* (1986); Harvey Rosenfeld, *A Title to Fame* (1991).

McGwire's 60th, 61st, 62nd and 70th Home Runs in 1998.

"I am in awe of myself right now."—McGwire near the end of his 70-home run 1998 season.

McGwire started the 1998 season in style, hitting a grand slam against the Dodgers in his first game. He also homered in his first four games to tie a record set by Willie Mays for start-of-the-season home run games. Ironically, McGwire's streak ended in hitter-friendly Colorado.

McGwire hit his 60th home run on September 5, 1998. He did it in the Cardinals' 142nd game, which included a tie that doesn't appear in the records. Ruth hit number 60 in the 154th game of the year, and Maris in game 159. The ball was returned to him by the fan who caught it, 22-year-old Deni Allen. Allen only wanted to take batting practice and receive a few season tickets for his family. McGwire called the gesture "outstanding." The Cardinals also threw in some bats, balls and hats.

"It will mean more to him and baseball than it will to me."—Mike Davidson, on returning McGwire's 61st home run ball, hit on September 7, 1998. Davidson was a 28-year-old catering manager who had lived in St. Louis all his life. He decided to give the ball to McGwire, passing up a chance to cash in for $100,000 or more from collectors. Davidson got the ticket for Bush Stadium's section 281, Row 1, seat 1, from his brother-in-law, who had to work. McGwire hit the home run off Cubs pitcher Mike Morgan in the 1st inning of a 1–0 victory in front of 50,530 home fans. McGwire did it in 144 games and 7.4 at-bats per home run; it took Maris 163 games (the Yankees had a tie game) and 9.7 at-bats per home run.

The next night, September 8, McGwire hit his 62nd home run against Steve Trachsel in the 4th inning in a game the Cardinals won 4–0. It was only 341 feet, just making it over the wall near the left-field foul poll. After all the predictions about the game ball, who would get it, and what they'd do with it (and the IRS reports about possible taxation), the ball landed in a vacant area, where it was run down by Tim Forneris, who was part of the Busch Stadium grounds crew. At a post-game ceremony, he presented McGwire with the ball saying, "Mr. McGwire, I think I have something that belongs to you." Earlier, there was some confusion when an unidentified man handed a ball to McGwire shortly after the home run. But McGwire knew that it wasn't the ball, because it said "Official League" on it, and not "National League," so McGwire gave it back.

Immediately after McGwire hit No. 62, Cubs right fielder Sammy Sosa ran in from right field to hug McGwire. They bashed their arms together, and McGwire gave Sosa a fake punch to the stomach. Sosa responded with his trademark: kissing his fingers, tapping his heart, holding up his fingers in a V in honor of late announcer Harry Caray.

After McGwire's 63rd home run, on September 15, 1998, a fan finally decided he wanted to cash in on a home run ball. John Grass, a 46-year-old from St. Louis said, "The ball is worth something to someone, and I'd like to have something for it myself." Grass was a groundskeeper for a St. Louis County school district. For the time being, he was going to put it in his safety deposit box. Grass said, "He makes millions of dollars. I don't think there is anything wrong with something coming to me." McGwire, however, previously said he would not pay for any baseballs returned by fans, but would trade items such as bats and tickets. Grass was the first person who would not give up the ball since McGwire's 55th home run.

On September 27, 1998, in the Cardinals' last game of the season, at home in front of 43,688 fans, McGwire hit home runs number 69 and 70 against the Expos. It was announced as the Cardinals' 14th consecutive sellout crowd of 46,110. The attendance bonus in his contract—$1 for each ticket sold over 2.8 million—provided McGwire an extra payday of $395,021 above his $9.5 million salary. Number 69 came off Mike Thurman in the 3rd inning. Kerry Woodson, a 22-year-old body-shop worker from Maryland Heights, Missouri, wound up with the ball:

"I reached up, closed my eyes, and it landed in my glove. It's a dream come true. I hope he doesn't hit any more today."

He didn't get his wish, as McGwire connected on his last swing of the season off Carl Pavano with two outs and two runners on base in the 7th inning of a 6–3 Cardinals' win. The ball landed in a party box and was grabbed by Phil Ozersky, 26, of Olivette, Missouri, attending the game with a group of Washington University research lab scientists. He said he didn't know what he'd do with the ball, which had a standing $1 million offer from collectors. A dollmaker wanted to buy the ball, and shred it out up into one million threads, and then insert it into Mark McGwire dolls with a piece of the ball in each one. Ozersky had a different idea: "I'd like to see it end up in the Hall of Fame. It'd make me very happy to see my parents live very comfortable for the rest of their lives, too. My parents aren't inanimate objects and the ball is. That's all going to go into my thinking."

McGwire's 70th home run ball was bought by Todd McFarlane, creator of the *Spawn* comic book series and an empire of adult-oriented action figures that specialize in realistic depictions of their subjects. McFarlane paid $2.7 million ($3.2 million according to *Vanity Fair*), far more than it was thought to be worth. He also bought Bonds' record-breaking No. 73, but paid a more rational (comparatively) $450,000 in June 2003.

After the game the club presented McGwire with a red Corvette and he drove it around the field, his son in the passenger seat. McGwire led the home run race all season except when Sammy Sosa twice passed him briefly—and then for a total of only 103 minutes. McGwire's five home runs on the last weekend, for 70, set a standard that most people thought would last for many years.

Sosa's 66th Home Run in 1998.

Sosa reached 66 home runs in a season before any other player, beating Mark McGwire by less than two hours.

Bonds' 70th, 71st, 72nd and 73rd Home Runs in 2001.

"I think it will stand for a while. I know how grueling it is to do what I've done this year. Will it be broken someday? It could be. Will I be alive? Possibly."—Mark McGwire after his 70-homer season in 1998. He was alive and well in 2001.

"Then there was Barry Bonds's home run record, though his case lacked the excitement of Mark McGwire's three years earlier. It may be that home run records, even at 73, have become commonplace, that they require amiable accomplices, or that Bonds, who has more attitude than Ichiro ever will, can't command a nation's attention, or affection."—Richard Hoffer in *Sports Illustrated*.

Barry Bonds had one of the greatest all-around years in Major League history in 2001, a season that propelled him to an unprecedented fourth MVP award. He hit 73 home runs to break Mark McGwire's single season record of 70. He led the Major Leagues with 122 homers over two seasons (8 more than Sammy Sosa), breaking Babe Ruth's record 114 by a left-hander. Of the 73, 47 either gave the Giants the lead (24), tied the game (7), extended a one-run lead (10), or brought the club within one run of the lead (6). He had 137 RBIs and a Major League-record slugging percentage of .863.

Bonds went into the second-to-last series of the season against the Astros with 69 home runs, where he stayed until the last game of the series. The Astros walked him eight times in three games before he hit No. 70 off rookie Wilfredo Rodriguez. The next night, a Friday, against the Dodgers, he hit Nos. 71 and 72. The first was off Chan Ho Park to break the record.

He didn't start Saturday's game, but hit a pinch single on the only good pitch he saw. On Sunday, September 30, 2001, the final day of the season, he hit No. 73 against soft-throwing knuckleballer Dennis Springer. It was a solo shot in the 1st inning that helped give the Giants a 2–1 victory. He also singled in the third, popped out in the sixth and flied out in the eighth.

Bonds had said, gratuitously or otherwise, that his 73 home runs in 2001 should not be recognized as a record because of the 84 that Josh Gibson is credited with by some during one of his stellar Negro League seasons. Bonds hit 49 the following season and had never hit more than 49 prior to 2001. Through 2004 he still had not reached 50 again.

The 73rd generated a protracted legal battle over ownership of the ball. Alex Popov, a 38-year-old fan, caught the ball, but in the skirmish immediately following, 37-year-old Patrick Hayashi came up with the ball. Popov sued, claiming to be the rightful owner. The ball was ordered placed in a bank's safe deposit box pending a court decision. In December 2002, San Francisco Superior Court judge Kevin McCarthy ruled that the players would share ownership and sell it jointly. The judge had reviewed a tape of the incident and concluded that the ball first struck the webbing of Popov's softball glove, but after that a mob descended and the judge concluded that it was unclear what happened next ("we do not know when or how Mr. Popov lost the ball"). The judge rejected Hayashi's claim that Popov bit the leg of another spectator during the melee.

Sources in the memorabilia field valued the ball at between $1 million and $1.5 million, but ultimately, despite its notoriety, it sold for only $515,000 ($450,000 in some sources). Popov's lawyer immediately filed an injunction preventing Popov's share from being distributed to him; the lawyer claimed that Popov owed him $473,530.32 in legal fees. Hayashi's lawyers agreed to less than their agreed-upon contingency fee of 20% of Hayashi's share of the proceeds from the sale. Popov sawed another baseball in half and sent out Christmas card photos of himself with the ball, with the inscription, "Halfy Holidays."

In 2003 a steroid controversy erupted that tainted the records set by both Bonds and Mark McGwire (see *Drugs*).

1927/1961 Ruth/Maris/Mantle Comparison. After 82 games Ruth had 27 home runs, Maris had 31 and Mantle had 29. By the end of July, Mantle had 36 and Maris had 35. On August 4, after four home runs and eight RBIs in a doubleheader, Maris was 25 games ahead of Ruth's pace. In early September, Mantle hurt his right forearm and could barely swing the bat. Nevertheless, in his first game after being hurt, he hit two home runs.

When Maris hit number 53 (and Mantle number 50 in the same game), he was eight games ahead of Ruth's pace. When Maris hit number 55, he was seven games ahead of Ruth. On September 10 Maris had 56 home runs with nine games left to 154 total games. Mantle still had 53.

The next day Mantle went in to have a flu shot from a doctor recommended by Yankee broadcaster Mel Allen. Later to become known as "The Shot" because it so debilitated Mantle, the injection hit bone and Mantle's side became infected. He had a 104-degree temperature, and a large abscess on his hip had to be lanced. From then on Mantle was not a factor in the home run race.

Many claimed that Maris and Mantle had an easy time of it

because of the dilution of pitching due to expansion in 1961. This is partially true. On the other hand, Ruth hit seven home runs off rookie pitchers and six off two Boston pitchers who were a combined 51–103 lifetime, Tony Welzer and Slim Harriss.

It should also be noted that Maris was far ahead of Ruth early in 1960, with 27 home runs in his first 70 games. He was then involved in a collision with Baltimore's Billy Gardner and suffered severe bruises. As a result, he finished with only 39 home runs.

Season/Career Assaults on Ruth Before Maris. Jimmie Foxx hit 58 home runs for the A's in 1932. He might have broken the record had he not injured his wrist falling off a stepladder in late August or early September. He also supposedly hit five would-be home runs into the screen at Sportsman's Park in St. Louis. More recent research has concluded that only one of those screen shots would have been a home run without the screen. In 1927 there was no screen for Ruth, though it has been determined that he would have lost only one home run.

Foxx also hit three would-be home run balls into a screen in Cleveland and again there was no screen in place for Ruth in 1927. Foxx also lost two home runs when partial games were washed out by rain.

In 1938 Tigers first baseman Hank Greenberg came close to Ruth's record when he finished the season by hitting 12 home runs in his last 24 games for a total of 58. The right-handed Greenberg had the handicap of aiming at a 340-foot left field fence in Detroit, while the left-handed Ruth had the advantage of a 296-foot right field fence.

Number 57 should have been a single, but Greenberg turned it into an inside-the-park home run. He said later that he should have been called out at the plate.

Greenberg had 58 home runs with five games left to play. The first two were against the Browns in Detroit. In the first game Greenberg walked four times and in the second game he had one single in four at-bats.

The last three games originally were scheduled in tiny League Park in Cleveland, a hitter's paradise. Unfortunately for Greenberg the Indians heavily promoted the game and moved it to Municipal Stadium because it held far more fans; it also had cavernous dimensions from left to right field of 375–415–460. One source erroneously identified the site of the games as League Park, but the club often played important games and Sunday games at Municipal Stadium.

Greenberg was hitless in the first game on Friday. Saturday's game was called off to create a Sunday doubleheader that would attract a larger crowd in the new park. In the first game on Sunday, Bob Feller struck out 18 to set a new Major League record and Greenberg helped him out by striking out twice. In the second game he doubled twice. One of the doubles would have been a home run under the ballpark's later configuration (inner fences were installed) and in any other park in the league. The game had to be called due to darkness in the 6th inning by umpire George Moriarty; Greenberg agreed with the decision.

It was reported in one source that as Greenberg approached the record, the word was out not to let a Jew break Babe Ruth's record of 60. In a documentary about him, Greenberg said, "I wasn't bitter at all."

Eddie Mathews was given a shot at beating Ruth's career record because he had 190 home runs at age 25, the youngest ever to reach that mark. Injuries slowed him down and he finished with 512.

In the 1960s Harmon Killebrew seemed to have the best shot at breaking Ruth's career record. At age 31 after the 1967 season, he had 380 home runs, more than Ruth at the same age. Injuries soon slowed him, though he finished fifth all-time with 573.

Ruth Outhitting Entire Teams. In 1920 and 1927, Babe Ruth hit more home runs (54 and 60) than every other American League *team's* total. In 1920 only the last-place Phillies, playing in tiny Baker Bowl, had more home runs than Ruth among National League teams. The 1920 National League leader was Cy Williams with 15.

In 1920 there were 369 home runs hit in the American League and 261 in the National League, making Ruth's 54 home runs 8.6% of the Major League total of 630. Ruth's 60 home runs in 1927 were 13% of the total hit that year in the American League (439) and 6.5% of the Major League total (922).

Ruth averaged an incredible 46 home runs per season over a 14-year period. He also had the advantage of hitting at home in the hitter-friendly Polo Grounds until equally friendly Yankee Stadium opened in 1923.

Ruth Exhibition. On February 27, 1927, Ruth spent an hour hitting off a series of pitchers, hitting 125 balls into the stands.

Domination of Ruth. Hubert "Hub" Pruett was a lifetime 29–48 pitcher with the St. Louis Browns. In Ruth's first 11 at-bats against Pruett, he struck out eight times, walked twice and grounded back to the mound. Ruth struck out 13 times against Pruett in 1922, presumably on his best pitch, the screwball. In 33 plate appearances over 14 games, Ruth struck out 14 times in 25 official at-bats. For his career against Pruett, he hit .208 with two home runs and seven hits. Older sources erroneously reported that Ruth struck out against him 19 times in 31 career plate appearances.

Ruth/Mantle Eras. Al Benton is the only pitcher to face both Babe Ruth and Mickey Mantle. He did it in 1934 against Ruth while with the A's and in 1952 against Mantle while with the Red Sox. Bobo Newsom is often credited with accomplishing the same feat, but he only pitched against Ruth in 1934 while with the Browns. In 41 games with the Senators and A's in 1952 and 1953, Newsom pitched against the Yankees in one inning of relief, but Mantle was injured and did not play.

National League Leader. In 1930 Cubs slugger Hack Wilson hit 56 home runs, the National League record until Mark McGwire (and Sammy Sosa) in 1998, and then Barry Bonds in 2001. Wilson should have been credited with 57 that year. In a game at Crosley Field in Cincinnati, Wilson hit a ball near the Reds bullpen that the Reds relief pitchers saw bounce off the seats and back onto the field. The umpire assumed that the ball hit the screen and had not made it out of the park and ruled it a double.

50 Home Runs/Season. Through 2004, 36 players have hit 50 or more home runs in a season, 19 of them since 1990. Those with 54 or more:

73	2001 Barry Bonds (Giants)
70	1998 Mark McGwire (Cardinals)
66	1998 Sammy Sosa (Cubs)
65	1999 Mark McGwire (Cardinals)
64	2001 Sammy Sosa (Cardinals)
63	1999 Sammy Sosa (Cubs)
61	1961 Roger Maris (Yankees)
60	1927 Babe Ruth (Yankees)
59	1921 Babe Ruth (Yankees)
58	1932 Jimmie Foxx (A's)
	1938 Hank Greenberg (Tigers)
	1997 Mark McGwire (Cardinals)
57	2001 Luis Gonzalez (Diamondbacks)
	2002 Alex Rodriguez (Rangers)
56	1930 Hack Wilson (Cubs)
	1997 Ken Griffey, Jr. (Mariners)
	1998 Ken Griffey, Jr. (Mariners)

54	1920 Babe Ruth (Yankees)
	1928 Babe Ruth (Yankees)
	1949 Ralph Kiner (Pirates)
	1961 Mickey Mantle (Yankees)

30/Season/Consecutive. Jimmie Foxx led all players with 12 consecutive 30 home run seasons between 1929 and 1940, until Barry Bonds tied the record in 2003 and then broke it in 2004 with 13. Lou Gehrig (1929–1937), Eddie Mathews (1953–1961) and Mike Schmidt (1979–1987) each had nine straight. Mickey Mantle (1955–1962) and Babe Ruth (1926–1933) had eight straight.

Only two players through 2004 have nine seasons with 35 home runs and 100 RBIs, Jimmie Foxx and Rafael Palmeiro.

40/Season/Consecutive. Only Babe Ruth and Rafael Palmeiro hit at least 40 home runs in seven consecutive seasons.

Minor League Season Record.

Joe Bauman. Bauman was a 32-year-old first baseman in 1954 for the Roswell (New Mexico) Rockets of the Class C Longhorn League when he hit 72 home runs. Roswell was located at an altitude of 3,500 feet, is the unofficial UFO capital of the world, and is the birthplace of actress Demi Moore.

Bauman had 64 home runs going into the last few games of the season. On August 31, with six games remaining, he hit four home runs and then hit another two nights later to tie the minor league record of 69 with four games to play. He did not hit a home run in the next two days and then played a doubleheader on the last day of the season. He moved to the lead-off spot that day to get extra at-bats. In the 1st inning of the first game he hit a 2–2 pitch over the right field wall for number 70 and a new record. He then jogged along the stadium wall to collect dollars the fans had pushed through the fence — still a minor league custom in those days.

In the second game, with the pressure off, Bauman hit two more home runs for a total of 72 over 138 games. He had 224 RBIs, 199 hits, a .398 batting average, 150 walks and a .916 slugging average.

After the season he received no Major League offers and only one from a Class AAA team, the San Francisco Seals. Admittedly not a hitter of Major League or even Class AAA caliber, Bauman declined the offer and followed through with his preseason decision to retire.

Joe Hauser. In 1930 Hauser hit 63 home runs for Baltimore of the International League. In 1933 he hit a then-minor league record 69 for the Minneapolis Millers of the American Association. Hauser hit 79 home runs in 629 Major League games.

Bob Crues. Hauser's then-season record of 69 was tied by Bob Crues of the Amarillo Gold Sox in 1948.

Most/College Game. On May 9, 1999, Florida State junior second baseman Marshall McDougall hit six consecutive home runs while going 7-for-7 with a record 16 RBIs. The home runs broke the record of five in 1985, set by Henry Rochelle of Campbell. The Seminoles beat Maryland 26–2.

Most Home Runs/Not in Hall of Fame. The retired players with the most home runs who have not been elected to the Hall of Fame:

462	Jose Canseco
442	Dave Kingman
382	Frank Howard
377	Norm Cash

Road Games. In 2001, Barry Bonds broke Mark McGwire's (1998) and Babe Ruth's (1927) record of 32 road game home runs, hitting 36 in foreign parks.

Four in One Game. Fifteen Major League players have hit four home runs in one game:

1. Bobby Lowe. On May 30, 1894, Decoration Day (now

Memorial Day), Lowe played second base and led off for Boston at the Congress Street Grounds in Boston during the second game of a doubleheader. He hit four home runs off Elton "Icebox" Chamberlain of the visiting Reds. Lowe hit his home runs consecutively among six at-bats, all over the 250-foot left field wall. The Grounds were the club's temporary home while their regular ballpark was being repaired. After Lowe's fourth shot, the game was stopped and he received $160 in silver from the fans.

Lowe had no hits in the team's 13–10 win in the first game of the day's doubleheader. He and his wife had shared a large seafood lunch before the second game, which might have contributed to his second-game barrage.

2. Ed Delahanty. On July 13, 1896, Delahanty of the Philadelphia Phillies hit four home runs in Chicago off William "Adonis" Terry. All were inside-the-park. He also singled and after the game he received four boxes of chewing gum as a reward.

3. Lou Gehrig. On June 3, 1932, Gehrig hit four home runs for the Yankees against the A's in Shibe Park. Gehrig almost had five home runs, but Al Simmons hauled a ball in that was headed over the fence. The feat was largely ignored in the next day's newspapers because this was the same day that John McGraw resigned after 31 years as manager of the New York Giants. The *New York Daily News* did carry a large picture of Gehrig, but with a headline blaring "Terry Succeeds McGraw."

Prior to a mid–1930s spring training game, Bobby Lowe approached Gehrig for an autograph after Gehrig joined him and Ed Delahanty as one of only three men to hit four home runs in a game. When asked what Gehrig said to him, Lowe responded: "Nothing, I didn't tell him who I was."

4. Chuck Klein. On July 10, 1936, Klein of the Phillies hit four home runs in a 10-inning game. The Phillies beat the Pirates 9–6.

5. Pat Seerey. On July 18, 1948, Seerey hit four home runs for the White Sox against the A's, the last in the 11th inning for a 12–11 win. He hit only eight more in his career, all in 1948. He had 86 over his seven-year career, which ended when he was only 26 in early 1949. His penchant for strikeouts (102 in 363 at-bats in 1948) were his downfall.

6. Gil Hodges. On August 31, 1950, the Dodger first baseman became the first 20th century National League player to hit four home runs in a nine-inning game. In a 19–3 win over the Braves, Hodges had nine RBIs in six at-bats and tied the National League record with 17 total bases (he also had a single and ground out).

7. Joe Adcock. On July 31, 1954, Adcock hit four home runs for the Braves in a 13–7 victory over the Dodgers at Ebbets Field. Adcock had 18 *Total Bases* (he added a double), which broke the existing record for total bases. The two teams combined for 10 home runs in the game. Adcock suffered a *Beanball* by a Dodger pitcher the next day.

8. Rocky Colavito. On June 10, 1959, Colavito hit four home runs for the Indians in an 11–8 victory over the Orioles at Baltimore. He was the third player to do it in successive at-bats (with Lowe and Gehrig), and did it in a park that had relinquished the fewest home runs of any ballpark in the Major Leagues since Baltimore came back into the American League in 1954.

9. Willie Mays. On April 30, 1961, Mays hit four home runs for the Giants in a 14–4 victory over the Braves in Milwaukee. Mays also hit a line drive to deep center field that was caught by Henry Aaron and Mays was on deck in the 9th inning when the last out was made. The Giants hit eight home runs in the game and 13 over two days.

Before the game Mays had been in a slump. He also was sick from eating barbecued ribs ordered the night before by roommate Willie McCovey. Mays told a local writer that he would get four hits that day to break out of the slump. He never swung and missed during the game and did not hit a foul ball. It has been reported that Mays knew what pitches were coming because Giants coach Wes Westrum was stealing the signs and waving a towel to tip off Mays.

Pitcher Billy Loes was on one of the two teams in the games in which Mays, Colavito, Hodges and Adcock each hit their four home runs.

10. Mike Schmidt. On April 17, 1976, the Phillies third baseman hit four home runs. Philadelphia trailed the Cubs 12–1 and 13–2 on a windy day in Wrigley Field that ended 23–22 Phillies. The Phillies tied the National League record for comebacks, tying the game in the 9th inning and then winning it in the 10th on Schmidt's fourth home run. It was the second time a player accomplished the feat in extra innings.

11. Bob Horner. On July 6, 1986, Horner of the Atlanta Braves, touted as the successor to Ruth and Aaron, hit four home runs against the Expos in Atlanta. It was only the second time a player hit four during a losing cause (Ed Delahanty was the first). Slowed by injuries, Horner never fulfilled his potential after coming directly to the Major Leagues from Arizona State University. In 1987 Horner played in Japan and then returned to the Cardinals for 60 games in 1988 before retiring.

12. Mark Whiten.
"Every time I hit it, I was like, amazed."

On September 7, 1993, the Cardinals outfielder hit four home runs against the Reds in Cincinnati and drove in 12 runs to tie the Major League record. He was 4-for-5 in the game, played in front of 22,206 fans and with an eight-mph wind. All four home run balls were returned to Whiten.

The game was the second of a doubleheader. In the opener Whiten misplayed a line drive by Reggie Sanders of the Reds to allow Cincinnati to win 14–13. He atoned by hitting a grand slam in the 1st inning of the second game and then homered three more times.

13. Mike Cameron. On May 2, 2002, the Mariners outfielder hit four home runs in a game against the White Sox, but not before he and teammate Bret Boone made history. Cameron and Boone each hit two home runs in the same inning, connecting back-to-back twice during Seattle's 10-run 1st inning. Cameron also had solo shots in the 3rd and 5th innings as the Mariners won 15–4. White Sox pitchers Jon Rauch and Jim Parque served up the four contributions to the 1st inning history.

14. Shawn Green. On May 23, 2002, in Milwaukee's Miller Park, the Dodger outfielder became the second player that season to hit four in a game. The Dodgers beat the Brewers 16–3 as Green went 6-for-6, scored six runs, had seven RBIs, and set a Major League record with 19 *Total Bases*. He was the first player to have six hits while hitting four home runs. Before the game, Green had gone 0-for-15 and had been benched on May 18. Later in the season he had four in a row over two games.

15. Carlos Delgado.
"I wish I could do it more often."

On September 25, 2003, Delgado hit his 300th home run (the 98th player to do so) among four he hit that day. He took cold medicine and a nap before the game, which obviously perked him up. The last came in the 8th inning off Devil Rays pitcher Lance Carter and tied the score at 8. Delgado was only the sixth player to do it in consecutive at-bats. He had six RBIs for the night.

Josh Gibson. Negro League Star Josh Gibson hit four home runs in one game at cavernous Griffith Stadium in Washington.

This is the same park in which the entire Washington Senators team once hit only one home run all year and it was an *Inside-the-Park Home Run.*

Sadaharu Oh. Oh hit four in a game in Japan on May 3, 1964.

Four in a Row Over Multiple Games.

"You may not believe this, but I was trying to knock him down with the pitch. That shows you the kind of control I had that night."— Pitcher Paul Foytack, on a pitch to Indians infielder Larry Brown, who hit the fourth of four straight home runs off Foytack over multiple games in 1963.

"I feel terrible, but every time I take a swing at the ball it goes out of the park."— Ted Williams on his four consecutive pinch-hit home runs, as quoted in John Updike's "Hub Fans Bid Kid Adieu" (1960). Williams had home runs in four consecutive official at-bats in 1957. Returning from a lung ailment, he hit a pinch-hit home run against the A's. The next day he pinch-hit and walked. In the next game he hit the only home run of his career against Whitey Ford, pinch-hitting in the 9th inning to break up Ford's shutout. In the third game he started and hit his 15th grand slam to go with three walks. In game four he homered in his first at-bat. The streak was part of 16 straight plate appearances in which he got on base, an all-time record (see *Reaching Base*).

On May 3, 1959, Tigers outfielder Charlie Maxwell hit four consecutive home runs in a doubleheader sweep of the Yankees at Briggs Stadium.

In his book, *Sixty-One* (1987), Tony Kubek recalled that Yankee catcher Johnny Blanchard hit two consecutive pinch-hit home runs in 1961. Both were in the 9th inning of games against the Red Sox. The first was a grand slam to win the game and the second was a solo shot that tied the game. In Blanchard's first at-bat of the next game that he started after the pinch hits (with no intervening appearances), he homered. In his next at-bat he homered again for his fourth home run in four straight at-bats.

Willie Kirkland of the Indians hit four home runs in four official at-bats over two games. On July 9, 1961, he hit three in a row off pitcher Cal McLish, all on two-strike pitches. He walked and sacrificed in his next two at-bats in the game. In his next game, after the All-Star break, he homered in his first official at-bat against the Twins for four in a row.

Mickey Mantle hit two home runs in his final two at-bats on July 4, 1964, and his first two at-bats on July 5.

On June 24, 1970, Yankee outfielder Bobby Murcer hit three consecutive home runs against the Indians after homering in his last at-bat of a doubleheader the day before.

On May 8–9, 1973, Johnny Bench hit four home runs in four straight official at-bats.

Beginning on June 23, 1973, pitcher Ken Brett hit a home run in each of four consecutive games in which he pitched, though they were not in consecutive at-bats.

During the 1977 World Series Reggie Jackson hit a home run in his last at-bat of Game 5. In the famous Game 6, Jackson walked on four pitches in his first at-bat. He then hit three straight home runs on three consecutive pitches to clinch the Series for the Yankees. His heroics prompted the following comment by Bill Lee: "I think there are going to be a lot of Reggies born in this town."

In 1990 Bo Jackson of the Royals hit a two-run home run in the 1st inning, a two-run home run in the 3rd inning and a three-run home run in the 5th inning. In the bottom of the 5th inning he dove for a fly ball by Yankee outfielder Deion Sanders. The ball skipped under his glove for an inside-the-park home run and Jackson came out of the game with a shoulder separation that put him

on the disabled list. When he came off the disabled list, he hit a home run in his first at-bat.

Over three games on June 8–10, 1995, Jeff Manto of the Orioles became the 24th player to hit home runs in four consecutive official at-bats.

On September 16, 1998, Manny Ramirez of the Indians hit his 41st and 42nd homers, tying the Major League record with homers in four straight at-bats (and five in two games). He homered three times on September 15, and then again in his first at-bat the next day. After grounding out his second time up, he homered again for his fifth in two days.

On May 20, 2001, Barry Bonds hit four consecutive home runs over two games. He hit seven home runs in four games during the streak, and then hit another in the fifth game for a Major League record.

On June 14–15, 2002, Dodger outfielder Shawn Green hit four home runs over two games a few weeks after he hit four in one game.

Troy Glaus of the Angels hit four straight over September 15–16, 2002, and Andruw Jones did it for the Braves on September 7 and 10 that season.

A Chance at Four in One Game. On May 22, 1930, Babe Ruth hit three home runs against the A's. In his fourth at-bat that day, the left-handed Ruth purportedly batted right-handed and struck out. The fifth time up, he supposedly batted right-handed for the first two strikes and then switched to the left side, still striking out.

Willie Stargell came close on May 22, 1963, when he hit the left field railing for a double on what would have been his fourth home run of the day.

Perfect Day. On August 27, 1951, back-up catcher Del Wilber of the Phillies hit three home runs on three swings in three at-bats. The next day regular catcher Andy Seminick pretended to be sick so that Wilber could start the game and get a chance to hit a fourth consecutive home run. Wilber hit a ball to deep left field but it was caught.

Wilber is the only undefeated manager in Major League history. In 1973 he had been the Class AAA manager for the Rangers when he managed one game near the end of the Major League season between Whitey Herzog's firing and Billy Martin's hiring. Wilber's daughter, Cynthia J. Wilber, interviewed over 40 Major League players for her book, *For the Love of the Game* (1992).

Five in a Doubleheader. On May 2, 1954, Stan Musial hit five home runs against the Giants in a doubleheader at Sportsman's Park (then called Busch Stadium). The last two by Musial were off Hall of Fame knuckleballer Hoyt Wilhelm. The Cardinals won the first game 10–6 but lost the second 9–7.

Musial almost had a sixth home run that day, but Willie Mays hauled in a drive 410 feet from home plate just in front of the bleachers.

Eight-year-old Nate Colbert attended the game. Eighteen years later, on August 1, 1972, in Atlanta, Colbert duplicated the feat for the Padres. Colbert started the day with severe back pains but used a new bat during a brief batting practice. He put 10 of 10 balls over the fence, three just foul.

Colbert drove in 13 runs and had 22 total bases that day, both records for a doubleheader. He also hit all five home runs off different pitchers. Four of the five homers came on the first pitch. The other came on the second pitch. He missed a sixth home run (and four in one game) when he hit a ball just foul and then walked.

Five on Consecutive Days. At last 20 players have hit five home runs on consecutive days. Mark McGwire and Ralph Kiner are the only players to do it twice. Shawn Green did it in May 2002 after hitting four on the first day of the streak. He tied another record with 25 *Total Bases* in those two games.

Only Home Runs. In August 2001 Mark McGwire had a streak of 11 straight hits (going 11-for-72) in which each hit was a home run. In 1995 Albert Belle had eight straight hits that were all home runs.

Minor League Record/Game. On June 15, 1902, Nig Clarke hit eight home runs in eight at-bats for Corsicana against Texarkana of the Texas League. He had 16 RBIs in the 51–3 rout, in which Corsicana scored 27 runs in one inning. Texarkana was so bad that it was dropped from the league in midseason. In his Major League career, Clarke hit six home runs in nine years and 1,536 at-bats.

A Mr. DeWitt was the only pitcher for Texarkana that day, pitching a 53-hitter. His father, C.B. DeWitt, owned the club and insisted that manager Cy Mulkey use his son, prompting one local to comment: "On that day for that kid, giving up a double is a moral victory."

On May 6, 1938, Bob Seeds of the Newark Bears homered in four consecutive innings against Buffalo in the International League. He ended the day 6-for-6 and then homered in his first three official at-bats in the next day's game. That gave him nine consecutive hits and seven home runs in eight at-bats. He struck out to end the streak. Seeds later spent nine years in the Major Leagues, homering only 28 times in 1,937 at-bats.

Lowest Batting Average. In 1946 Hank Greenberg became the first player to hit 40 home runs with less than a .300 average (.277). That dubious feat has been accomplished many times since. For example, Harmon Killebrew, Reggie Jackson and Gorman Thomas twice hit 40 or more home runs and batted less than .250.

Most Multiple Home Run Games. Babe Ruth had 72 multiple home run games, not including four such games in the World Series. The leaders after Ruth through 2004:

68 Barry Bonds
67 Mark McGwire
66 Sammy Sosa
63 Willie Mays
62 Henry Aaron
55 Jimmie Foxx
54 Frank Robinson
50 Ken Griffey, Jr.

When Hank Greenberg hit 58 home runs in 1938 for the Tigers, he broke Babe Ruth's single-season record by hitting at least two home runs in one game 11 times. Sammy Sosa tied the record with 11 in 1998 (Mark McGwire had 10 that season).

Four players have had multi-homer games three straight times: Lee May (1969 Reds), Frank Thomas (1962 Mets), Gus Zernial (1951 Athletics) and Jeff DaVanon (2003 Angels).

Two in One Game/First. On June 17, 1876, George Hall of the Phillies became the first Major Leaguer to hit two home runs in one game. He hit five home runs for the year to lead the league.

Three in One Game/First. In 1884 Ned Williamson hit three home runs in one game in his home park in Chicago. It should be remembered that the home runs were tainted by a 196-foot right field fence. The ballpark had a one-season (1884) rule that balls hit over that fence would be scored as home runs instead of ground rule doubles, as had been the rule in the past.

Three in a Game/Different Leagues. Claudell Washington, Johnny Mize and Babe Ruth are the only players to hit three home runs in a game in different leagues. Washington did it for the White Sox in 1979 and the Mets in 1980. Mize did it for the Cardinals in 1938 and 1940, the Giants in 1947 and the Yankees in 1950. Ruth did it for the Yankees in 1930 and with the Braves (his last three) in 1935.

Three in a Game/Career. Johnny Mize is the only man to hit three home runs in a game six times, and he did it for three different clubs.

Joe Carter and Lou Gehrig hold the American League record with four three-home run games.

Babe Ruth had two three-homer games, but no four-homer games.

Three in a Game/Multiple in a Season. In 2001 Sammy Sosa became the first player to hit three homes in a game three times in the same season. Through 2004 there have been 12 players who have done it twice in the same season.

Most Consecutive Years. Ty Cobb and Rickey Henderson each hit a home run in 24 straight Major League seasons.

Three Consecutive Innings. On June 25, 1995, Andres Galarraga of the Expos hit home runs in three consecutive innings starting in the 6th. He lost his chance at a fourth when Larry Walker struck out with the bases loaded to end the game. The other players to accomplish this are Larry Parrish of the Expos in 1978, George Kelly of the Giants in 1923 and Carl Reynolds of the White Sox in 1930.

Most Against One Team/Season. Lou Gehrig hit 14 home runs against the Indians in 1936.

Teammates.

"You see, throughout history, great sluggers have come in partnership. Look it up. Take the greatest sluggers in history — Babe Ruth and Henry Aaron. Ruth was part of that middle-of-the-lineup crash attack — Ruth and Lou Gehrig. Aaron came with Eddie Mathews attached." — Jim Murray.

Henry Aaron and Eddie Mathews had 894 home runs between them, breaking Ruth's and Gehrig's record of 793. Mark McGwire and Jose Canseco averaged over 69 home runs together for the five full seasons they were together between 1987 and 1991.

Fathers and Sons. See *Fathers and Sons*.

First At-Bat.

See also **First Pitch of Career**.

George "White Wings" Tebeau and Mike Griffin were the first Major Leaguers to hit home runs in their first at-bats. They did so on the same day, April 16, 1887, the start of the American Association season for both players. Griffin hit his for Baltimore against Philadelphia. Tebeau did it for Cincinnati against Cleveland.

Earl Averill was the first American League player to hit a home run in his first Major League at-bat. He did it for the Indians on Opening Day, April 16, 1929.

One source claimed that Giants third baseman Art Devlin's first home run, supposedly in his first at-bat, was a grand slam. After that he averaged only one home run per year (10 in 10 years between 1904 and 1913). Devlin's first hit was a grand slam, but it was not in his first at-bat.

Ernie Koy of the Dodgers and Emmett Mueller of the Phillies are the only players to hit home runs in their first Major League at-bats in the same game. They did so in the 1st inning of an Opening Day game on April 19, 1938, at Baker Bowl. The Dodgers won 12–5.

Dan Bankhead, the first black pitcher in the Major Leagues, hit a home run in his first Major League at-bat for the 1947 Brooklyn Dodgers. He never hit another.

On April 25, 1952, knuckleball pitcher Hoyt Wilhelm homered in his first Major League at-bat and never homered again. He tripled in his second at-bat and never repeated that performance during a career in which he hit .088. Wilhelm's home run was off Dick Hoover, who only gave up one home run in his two-year career.

Gary Gaetti was the 41st player to do so, on September 20, 1981. In the same game, Tim Laudner and Kent Hrbek hit home runs in their first Major League game, but neither did it in his first at-bat.

Jose Offerman, rookie shortstop for the Dodgers in 1990, hit a home run in his first Major League at-bat after hitting no home runs in 454 minor league at-bats earlier in the year. He then went another 659 plate appearances before homering again.

Will Clark hit a home run in his first Major League at-bat and also in his first professional at-bat, for Class A Fresno.

It has been reported that Minnie Minoso's home run in his first at-bat came in the same game in which Mickey Mantle hit his first home run. However, Minoso's home run was not in his first at-bat.

In 1963 Gates Brown became the first player in the American League to hit a **Pinch Hit** home run in his first at-bat. Eddie Morgan was the first National Leaguer to do it. Chuck Tanner was the first National Leaguer to do it on the first *pitch*, in 1955 (but is sometimes erroneously credited as the first National League pinch hitter to hit a first at-bat home run).

The Full List of First At-Bat Home Runs (through 2004).
American Association
George Tebeau, Cincinnati, 1887
Mike Griffin, Baltimore, 1887
National League
Joe Harrington, Boston, 1885
Bill Duggleby, Philadelphia, 1898
Johnny Bates, Boston, 1906
Walter Mueller, Pittsburgh, 1922
Clise Dudley, Brooklyn, 1929
Gordon Slade, Brooklyn, 1930
Eddie Morgan, St. Louis, 1936
Ernie Koy, Brooklyn, 1938
Heinie Mueller, Philadelphia, 1938
Clyde Vollmer, Cincinnati, 1942
Paul Gillespie, Chicago, 1942
Buddy Kerr, New York, 1943
Whitey Lockman, New York, 1945
Dan Bankhead, Brooklyn, 1947
Les Layton, New York, 1948
Ed Sanicki, Philadelphia, 1949
Ted Tappe, Cincinnati, 1950
Hoyt Wilhelm, New York, 1952
Wally Moon, St. Louis, 1954
Chuck Tanner, Milwaukee, 1955
Bill White, New York, 1956
Frank Ernaga, Chicago, 1957
Don Leppert, Pittsburgh, 1961
Cuno Barragan, Chicago, 1961
Benny Ayala, New York, 1974
John Montefusco, San Francisco, 1974
Jose Sosa, Houston, 1975
Johnnie LeMaster, San Francisco, 1975
Tim Wallach, Montreal, 1980
Carmelo Martinez, Chicago, 1983
Mike Fitzgerald, New York, 1983
Will Clark, San Francisco, 1986
Ricky Jordan, Philadelphia, 1988
Jose Offerman, Los Angeles, 1990
Dave Eiland, San Diego, 1992
Jim Bullinger, Chicago, 1992
Jay Gainer, Colorado, 1993
Mitch Lyden, Florida, 1993
Garey Ingram, Los Angeles, 1994

Jermaine Dye, Atlanta, 1996
Dustin Hermanson, Montreal, 1997 (it was only his third at bat for the reliever in four seasons of professional baseball)
Brad Fullmer, Montreal, 1997
Marlon Anderson, Philadelphia 1998 (14th pinch hitter)
Guillermo Mota, Montreal, 1999
Alex Cabrera, Arizona, 2000
Keith McDonald, St. Louis, 2000 (and second at-bat)
Chris Richard, St. Louis, 2000 (second Cardinal in two weeks)
Gene Stechschulte, St. Louis, 2001 (15th pitcher; and first pitch of career)
Dave Matranga, Houston, 2003
Kaz Matsui, Mets, 2004
American League
Luke Stuart, St. Louis, 1921
Earl Averill, Cleveland, 1929
Ace Parker, Philadelphia, 1937
Gene Hasson, Philadelphia, 1937
Bill LeFebvre, Boston, 1938
Hack Miller, Detroit, 1944
Eddie Pellagrini, Boston, 1946
George Vico, Detroit, 1948
Bob Nieman, St. Louis, 1951 (and second at-bat)
Bob Tillman, Boston, 1962
John Kennedy, Washington, 1962
Buster Narum, Baltimore, 1963
Gates Brown, Detroit, 1963
Bert Campaneris, Kansas City, 1964
Bill Roman, Detroit, 1964
Brant Alyea, Washington, 1965
John Miller, New York, 1966
Rick Renick, Minnesota, 1968
Joe Keough, Oakland, 1968
Gene Lamont, Detroit, 1970
Don Rose, California, 1972
Reggie Sanders, Detroit, 1974
Dave McKay, Minnesota, 1975
Al Woods, Toronto, 1977
David Machemer, California, 1978
Gary Gaetti, Minnesota, 1981
Andre David, Minnesota, 1984
Terry Steinbach, Oakland, 1986
Jay Bell, Cleveland, 1986
Junior Felix, Toronto, 1989
Rusty Greer, Texas, 1994
Jon Nunnally, Kansas City, 1995
Carlos Lee, Chicago, 1999
Esteban Yan, Tampa Bay, 2000
Marcus Thames, New York, 2002 (off Randy Johnson)
Miguel Olivo, Chicago, 2002
Eric Munson, Tigers, 2002

Gary Gaetti is the all-time home run leader among players who hit one in their first Major League at-bat, with 360. He passed Earl Averill, who had 238. Tim Wallach and Will Clark passed Averill in the 1990s. At least 10 players on the above list never hit another.

First Pitch of Career.
"I told the guys at Triple A that I was going to swing at the first pitch and try to hit one out. But I was joking. No one does that. Afterward, I was thinking, My God, what did I do? It was like I did something I shouldn't have done." — Rockies first baseman Jay Gainer, who hit the first pitch of his Major League career for a home run in 1993.

The only player to hit a grand slam on the first pitch to him in the Major Leagues was Bill Duggleby, who did it on April 21, 1898, for the Philadelphia Phillies.

Dodger pitcher Clise Dudley hit the first pitch thrown to him for a home run. He did it on April 27, 1929, on a pitch thrown by Claude Willoughby of the Phillies.

On April 14, 1936, Eddie Morgan of the Cardinals hit the first pitch for a home run. He played in 39 Major League games and this was his only home run.

On June 10, 1938, Red Sox pitcher Bill LeFebvre hit the only home run of his career on the first pitch thrown to him. It was his only at-bat of the season.

On May 31, 1942, Clyde Vollmer of the Reds hit the first pitch for a home run.

On April 20, 1948, George Vico of the Tigers hit the first pitch thrown to him for a home run.

On April 12, 1955, Chuck Tanner of the Braves hit the first pitch thrown to him for a home run. He was the first pinch hitter to hit a home run on the first pitch of his career. Some sources erroneously report that he was the second (or third) player to hit a home run on the first pitch of his career, possibly confusing this with his pinch hit record.

On July 23, 1964, Bert Campaneris of the A's hit a home run on the first pitch thrown to him in the Major Leagues, by Jim Kaat of the Twins. He hit another one later in the game.

On September 12, 1965, pinch hitter Brant Alyea of the Senators hit the first pitch of his Major League career for a home run.

On May 24, 1972, Don Rose of the Angels hit the first pitch of his career for a home run. It occurred during his second season in the Major Leagues. It was the year before the designated hitter rule went into effect, so Rose was the last American League pitcher to homer in his first at-bat until interleague play (see Esteban Yan below).

Gary Gaetti of the Twins hit the first pitch he faced for a home run on September 20, 1981.

Jay Bell of the Indians hit the first pitch of his Major League career for a home run. He did it off noted gopher ball specialist Bert Blyleven on September 29, 1986. He swung at the first pitch on the advice of Mike Hargrove. Blyleven, who had been traded for Bell a year earlier, struck Bell out the next two times he faced him in the game.

On May 4, 1989, Junior Felix hit of the Blue Jays hit the first pitch of his career for a home run.

Cubs relief pitcher Jim Bullinger hit the first pitch thrown to him for a home run off Rheal Cormier of the Cardinals on June 8, 1992. Bullinger had been a minor league shortstop before becoming a pitcher. He became only the tenth pitcher to hit a home run in his first at-bat.

On May 14, 1993, first baseman Jay Gainer of the Rockies hit the first pitch he saw for a home run. It wasn't enough, as the Reds beat the Rockies 13–5.

On June 4, 2000, Devil Rays pitcher Esteban Yan hit the first pitch he saw for a home run. It was the first first at-bat home run by an American League pitcher since Don Rose in 1972. Yan would not have batted but for the fact that this was an interleague game with the Mets in the National League ballpark. Yan did it in the 2nd inning of his 15–5 win over the Mets. On the next pitch, teammate Felix Ortiz hit the first home run of his career.

On July 17, 2000, Cardinals outfielder Chris Richard became the second Cardinal in two weeks to homer in his first at-bat, but Richard did it on the first pitch he saw in an 8–3 victory over the Twins in interleague play.

On April 17, 2001, Cardinals pitcher Gene Stechschulte hit a 6th inning home run on the first pitch he saw in his career, during a 17–4 loss to the Diamondbacks.

On June 10, 2002, outfielder Marcus Thames of the Yankees, in the first of his seven games for the club that season, homered on the first pitch he saw, off Randy Johnson.

On April 6, 2004, Mets shortstop Kaz Matsui, recently signed from the Japanese leagues, homered on the first pitch of his Major League career off Atlanta's Russ Ortiz.

Lou Brock hit the first pitch of his pro career for a home run, for St. Cloud of the Northern League.

Pitchers/First Batter Faced. The Baseball Almanac.com contains a list of 25 American League pitchers and 33 National League pitchers (through 2003) who surrendered a home run to their first Major League batter. The list includes Bob Gibson, Ken Holtzman, Kenny Rogers and Bert Blyleven.

First Two At-Bats. Bob Nieman of the Browns was the first player to hit home runs in his first two Major League at-bats, both given up by Mickey McDermott of the Red Sox on September 14, 1951.

Cardinals catcher Keith McDonald duplicated the feat in July 2000, in separate games. On July 4, 2000, just after the Cardinals bought his contract from their minor league affiliate, McDonald homered in a pinch hit appearance off Andy Larkin of the Reds. Two days later, on July 6, 2000, McDonald started the game and homered off Reds starter Osvaldo Hernandez. He walked his third time up.

Bert Campaneris of the A's is reported by some to have hit a home run in each of his first two Major League at-bats on July 23, 1964. The first was on the first pitch of his Major League career, but the second home run occurred in his fourth at-bat that day, in the 7th inning.

On October 9, 1889, Charlie Pierce of Columbus in the American Association hit two home runs in his first Major League game, but not in his first two at-bats as has sometimes been reported.

First and Last At-Bat. Paul Gillespie of the 1942–1945 Cubs hit a home run in his first and last regular season career at-bats.

John Miller hit home runs in the first and last at-bats of his career, and none in between. He hit the first in 1966 for the Yankees and the last for the Dodgers in 1969. In 61 career at-bats he hit .164.

Fast Career Starts. Kevin Maas of the Yankees hit 10 home runs in his first 77 at-bats in 1990, the fastest man to 10 in history. The previous record was held by George Scott of the Red Sox, who did it in 79 at-bats in 1966. Maas hit 21 in 254 at-bats. He hit 23 in 500 at-bats the following season. He was released by the Yankees before the 1994 season, finishing with 62 home runs.

In 1981 and 1982 Dave Hostetler of the Expos and then Rangers hit a record 12 home runs in his first 100 at-bats, but hit only 25 more in his career.

Sam Horn of the Red Sox hit 13 home runs in his first 123 at-bats in 1987, but faded after that and finished with 62 over seven seasons.

Bob Speake of the Cubs hit 10 home runs in his first 100 at-bats in 1955, but had only 21 more in his four-year career.

30 or More/First Four Seasons. Albert Pujols is the first player to hit 30 or more home runs in each of his first four seasons.

Mark McGwire was the first player to hit 30 or more home runs in each of his first four *full* seasons in the Major Leagues (1987–1990). McGwire had 81 in his first two full seasons. In 1991 he tailed off with only 22, but returned with a vengeance in 1992 before straining a rib cage muscle, which had curtailed his swing.

He still managed to finish with 42 for the year and began to peak again with 52 in 1996.

Frequency. From 1921 through 1940, hitting 40 or more homers in a season was accomplished 32 times by 12 different players. From 1941 through 1960, it was accomplished 44 times by 17 different sluggers. From 1961 through 1980, the number rose to 54 times that a player hit 40 homers in a season, reached by 30 different players. During the last 20 years (1981–2000), the number of 40-homer hitters jumped to 98, accomplished by 49 different players.

Most by Age 24.

168 Alex Rodriguez
153 Eddie Mathews
153 Mel Ott
130 Frank Robinson
124 Ken Griffey, Jr.
118 Ted Williams
118 Juan Gonzalez

Babe Ruth had 20 home runs by age 24 and Henry Aaron had 110. Albert Pujols had 114.

Most Home Runs by Age 30.

380 Alex Rodriguez
379 Jimmie Foxx
374 Mickey Mantle
370 Eddie Mathews
342 Henry Aaron
324 Frank Robinson
306 Mel Ott
297 Harmon Killebrew
287 Johnny Bench
284 Babe Ruth
280 Darryl Strawberry
279 Willie Mays

Youngest to 100. In July 1967 Tony Conigliaro became the youngest American League player to hit 100 home runs when he reached that mark at age 22 years, 197 days. Met Ott holds the Major League record at 22 years, 132 days. Eddie Mathews is third at 22 years, 292 days and Alex Rodriguez is fourth at 23 years, 16 days.

Only four players had 100 home runs through their third season: Joe DiMaggio, Ralph Kiner, Eddie Mathews and Albert Pujols.

Fastest to 200. Ralph Kiner reached 200 home runs in 2,537 at-bats, faster than any other player.

Youngest to 300. In 1998 Ken Griffey, Jr., became the second youngest player (at the time) to reach 300 home runs on April 13, 1998. He was 28 years, 143 days, and Jimmie Foxx was 27 years, 328 days when he hit No. 300. On April 2, 2003, Alex Rodriguez hit his 300th, to become the youngest ever to reach that milestone, at age 27 years, 249 days.

Youngest to 400. At age 30 years, 141 days, Ken Griffey, Jr., became the youngest player to reach 400 home runs, when he did it on April 10, 2000, during the Rockies' home opener. He did it on his father's 50th birthday. It was the fourth home run he had hit on his father's birthday, including No. 1 of his career. He beat out Jimmie Foxx, who was 30 years, 248 days. Alex Rodriguez will break this record in 2005.

Youngest to 500. Jimmie Foxx was the youngest player (age 32) to reach 500 home runs.

Rookies. Lou Gehrig was the first rookie to hit 20 home runs in a season. In 1987 Mark McGwire broke Wally Berger's rookie record for home runs by hitting 49 (see also **Rookies**).

Latest in a Game. Jack Reed of the Yankees hit a home run off Tigers pitcher Phil Regan in the 22nd inning of a game on June 24, 1962. It gave the Yankees a 9–7 victory and it was the only home run of Reed's career.

Lead-off/Career and Season. See *Lead-Off Hitters*.

Back-to-Back Twice/Same Game.

"We're so bad right now that for us back-to-back home runs means one today and another one tomorrow." — Earl Weaver.

On August 6, 1992, Gary Sheffield and Fred McGriff of the Padres twice hit back-to-back home runs in a 7–5 victory over the Astros. It has been done 17 times in a game, but no two Major League players until Sheffield and McGriff had done it in consecutive innings (1st and 2nd). Back-to-back home runs twice in a game never occurred between 1972 and 1991, but has happened several times since.

In 1993 Barry Bonds and Matt Williams of the Giants and Fred McGriff and Dave Justice of the Braves did it.

In April 1994, Julio Franco and Robin Ventura of the White Sox hit back-to-back home runs twice in a 7–6 loss to the Tigers. It also happened five days earlier, when Mo Vaughn and Tim Naehring of the Red Sox did it.

Lou Gehrig and Babe Ruth had 16 back-to-back home runs, but never did it twice in the same game.

Same Inning/Three Players/Twice In Game. On April 21, 2000, the Angels beat the Devil Rays 9–6 as Mo Vaughn, Tim Salmon and Troy Glaus did something never done before. All three hit home runs in the same inning, twice in the same game. Vaughn and Salmon did it back-to-back in the 4th inning, then did it again in the 9th inning. Glaus also homered in those two innings. Other teams have had three players hit two home runs in the same game, but never all three in the same inning each time.

Two In Same Inning/Two Players. Thirty-nine players had hit two home runs in an inning until Bret Boone and Mike Cameron each did it in the *same* inning on May 2, 2002 (and Cameron hit four in the game). It had never been done before by two players.

Two in One Inning/One Player. A sampling: On June 10, 1880, Charley Jones of the Boston Red Stockings became the first player to hit two home runs in an inning.

Andy Seminick was a catcher with the Phillies on June 2, 1949, when he hit two home runs in an inning in a 12–3 victory at Shibe Park. One of the two was among four consecutive home runs by the Phillies.

Von Hayes is the only player to hit two home runs in the 1st inning, on June 11, 1985, for the Phillies against the Mets.

On April 8, 1993, Carlos Baerga of the Indians became the first Major Leaguer to hit home runs from both sides of the plate in the same inning.

On August 29, 2002, Mark Bellhorn became the first National League player to hit home runs from both sides of the plate in the same inning, in the Cubs' 10-run 4th inning of a 13–10 win over the Brewers. (see also *Switch Hitters*).

Joe Carter of the Blue Jays hit two home runs in an inning on the last day of the 1993 season. He is the last American League player to do so.

Jeff Bagwell did it in 1994 for the Astros and in August 1995 Jeff King of the Pirates became the 16th National Leaguer to do it.

Willie McCovey, Andre Dawson and Jeff King are the only players to hit two home runs in an inning in two separate games.

On August 20, 2003, Reggie Sanders of the Pirates hit two homers in the same inning against the Cardinals in a 10-run outburst that was part of a 14–0 victory. The second homer was a grand slam, and the inning took so long that Sanders thought it was during a different inning.

Juan Rivera hit a grand slam and a two-run homer in the 2nd inning of a game for the Expos on June 19, 2004. His club almost blew an 11–1 lead, but held on for a 15–14 win over the White Sox.

Three in One Inning. No Major League player has ever hit three home runs in one inning. It is believed to have occurred only once in professional baseball, on August 6, 1930, by Gene Rye (Eugene Rudolph Mercantelli) of Waco in the Texas League. In 1931 in a brief appearance with the Red Sox he hit .179 with no home runs.

According to the National High School Sports Record Book, only one high school player has hit three home runs in an inning. On May 5, 1999, Bill Clayton of Chatham Glenwood High in Illinois hit three in the 2nd inning of the Redskins' 27–2 victory over Taylorville. Oh, and Clayton also pitched a no-hitter that day.

Consecutive/Start of a Game. On April 13, 1987, the first three Padres batters homered: Marvell Wynn, Tony Gwynn and John Kruk, all off Giants pitcher Roger Mason. The Giants still won the game 13–6.

On May 28, 2003, the Braves hit three home runs to start the game, en route to a 15–3 rout of the Reds. Rafael Furcal, Mark DeRosa, and Gary Sheffield homered off Jeff Austin. Before the inning was over, Javy Lopez knocked Austin out of the box. After the game, Austin was demoted to the minors. His response: "My goodness, this team is definitely better without me on it. I'm surprised I've stayed here this long."

Oldest Player. Pitcher Jack Quinn was 45 years and 357 days old on June 27, 1930, when he hit a home run for the A's against Chad Kimsey of the Browns.

Most/Fewest in a Park/Career. Mel Ott retired as the National League's all-time home run leader with 511, but he never hit one in nine years of trying at Shibe Park in Philadelphia (when the Phillies occupied the park). Ott had the most home runs in a single park, hitting 323 in the Polo Grounds over a 22-year career played exclusively for the Giants.

All Ballparks. Ellis Burks homered in a then-record Major-League record 41 ballparks, but in September 2002 Fred McGriff broke the record with his 42nd, and then hit one in new Petco Park in San Diego for No. 43.

Johnny Mize hit a home run in every Major League ballpark that existed during his career, as did Harry Heilmann and Jeff Heath.

Frank Robinson hit a home run in a then-record 32 different ballparks, the last two being Arlington Stadium in Texas in 1971 and Pittsburgh's Three River Stadium during the 1971 World Series. Rusty Staub also hit home runs in 32 ballparks.

Reggie Jackson holds the record for home runs in the most American League parks, with 19.

Henry Aaron hit balls out of 31 parks and holds the National League record with 22 different ballparks. Dave Winfield hit balls out of 30 ballparks.

In 1971 Willie Stargell hit balls out of a record 13 parks in one season as a result of a midseason shift by Pittsburgh from Forbes Field to Riverfront Stadium. One source reported that the record included the All-Star Game and World Series sites; this is illogical, or the record would have been 15 sites because of the two American League venues that season for those events. Stargell did not hit a home run at either event, though he participated in both.

In 1919 Babe Ruth became the first player to hit a home run in every park in his league in a single season, on his way to a record 29 for the season.

Warren Spahn is the only pitcher to hit a home run in every ballpark he pitched in during his career.

Most in a Ballpark/Season. In 1938 Hank Greenberg of the Tigers hit 39 home runs in Detroit's Briggs Stadium.

Most Against One Pitcher. Duke Snider holds the record for most home runs against a single pitcher, with 19 against Robin Roberts. Snider hit 407 home runs in his career. Henry Aaron had 17 against Don Drysdale, Babe Ruth had 17 against Rube Walberg, and Willie Mays had 18 against Warren Spahn. Barry Bonds had eight against four different players: Greg Maddux, Curt Schilling, Terry Mulholland and John Smoltz.

Ballpark Milestones.

"You can play for the three-run homer there a lot. Like every inning." — Former Rockies catcher Joe Girardi, on playing at Coors Field.

Atlanta's Fulton County Stadium is the only ballpark in which players have reached home run milestones of 100 (Bob Horner and Dale Murphy), 200 (Bob Horner), 300 (Murphy), 400 (Eddie Murray), 500 (Willie McCovey), 600 (Henry Aaron) and 700 (Aaron).

In 1993 Tiger Stadium became the first ballpark in which 10,000 home runs have been hit.

Consecutive Games/Team. The 2002 Texas Rangers hit in 26 straight in August and early September 2002.

Until 1998, only two teams had hit home runs in 25 straight games. The 1994 Tigers and the 1941 Yankees (during Joe DiMaggio's 51-game hitting streak). The Tigers hit 46 home runs during their streak and the Yankees hit 40.

In May 1998 the Yankees hit in 25 straight, and in April and May 1998 the Braves did it to break the National League record.

Consecutive Games/Team/Given Up. The 2004 Mariners gave up home runs in 26 consecutive games to tie the Major League record.

Team/Season. The 1998 Orioles set the Major League record with 257 home runs in a season by a team. The Astros set the National League record in 2000 with 249.

Consecutive Games. Dale Long hit at least one home run in each of eight straight games from May 21 through May 28, 1956. Don Newcombe stopped him in the ninth game. Long received a $2,500 raise to $16,500 during the streak. He broke the record of six held by Ken Williams, Don Hurst and Lou Gehrig when he hit a knuckleball off Art Flowers for a home run in the seventh game. Hurst, a first baseman for the 1929 Phillies, had one hit in each of six straight games, all home runs, from August 10 through August 19.

Long's record was tied by Don Mattingly from July 8 through July 18, 1987 (10 home runs in 8 games). On the night the streak ended (July 20), Mattingly tied the Major League record of 22 putouts by a first baseman in a nine-inning game.

Ken Griffey, Jr., had an eight-game home run streak from July 20 through July 28, 1993. Griffey's bid for nine straight ended when he singled and doubled before grounding out and popping out to second base. For what would have been the ninth game in Griffey's streak, the Mariners sold 30,220 game day tickets, the most in club history.

In April 2004 Barry Bonds hit a home run in seven straight games in which he had an official at-bat. In one game mid-streak, he was walked intentionally in a pinch hit appearance, so that game didn't count in the streak. He homered in six consecutive games twice during the 2001 season, when he hit a record 73.

Babe Ruth's best was five straight games in which he homered. In 2002 Jim Thome of the Indians had his streak stopped at seven games.

The rookie record for consecutive home run games is five:

1936 Rudy York (Tigers)
1962 George Alusik (A's)
1983 Ron Kittle (White Sox)
1995 Marty Cordova (Twins)

Bunches.

"It's hard to win when you can't keep the ball in the ballpark. I don't think they could hit more home runs if you told them what was coming. I don't think they could hit any more if it was batting practice." — Giants manager Dusty Baker, on his club giving up 24 home runs in one seven-game stretch.

Ralph Kiner hit eight home runs in four games over three days, September 10–12, 1947.

On June 21, 1930, Babe Ruth hit three home runs in a game and two in the first game of a doubleheader the next day. He hit another in the second game of the doubleheader for six in three games. Lou Gehrig hit three home runs in the first game of the doubleheader.

The Red Sox once hit 33 home runs over 10 straight games.

The Red Sox hit five home runs in a game against the Yankees on June 19, 1977, giving them a Major League record 16 in three games. In the three-game series the Yankees hit no home runs.

In August 1947 Hank Greenberg and the Pirates hit a National League record 16 home runs in five games, breaking the New York Giants' 1924 record of 15. In another streak over nine games (mostly pinch hitting), Greenberg hit nothing but home runs whenever he put the ball in play.

During Roger Maris' 1961 record-breaking season, he had only three home runs by May 16. Over the next 17 games he had 12 home runs and 25 RBIs. By the beginning of July, he had 30 home runs.

In 1968 Frank Howard hit 10 home runs in only 20 at-bats over six games. In May 2001 Barry Bonds tied Howard's record (twice in 1968) when he hit eight home runs in five games.

In a four-game series in late June 1996 in Colorado, the Rockies and Dodgers combined for 25 home runs. The clubs had 10 in the last game of the series.

The 1996 Orioles hit two or more home runs in nine consecutive games, tying the Major League record set by the 1962 Indians and 1987 Orioles.

In May 2001 Barry Bonds hit nine home runs in six games. It was the second time that season that he had hit home runs in six straight games.

Most in the Majors/Day. On July 3, 2002, a total of 62 home runs were hit in the Major Leagues, breaking the mark of 57 set on April 7, 2000. Nine players had multiple-home run games, breaking the previous record of eight.

Most in Three Games. On May 25, 2002, Shawn Green hit his seventh home run in three games (four in the first game of the streak).

On September 16, 1998, Manny Ramirez hit his 41st and 42nd homers, tying the Major League record with homers in four straight at-bats and five in two games. On the 17th, Ramirez tied a record by hitting his sixth home run in three games. Ramirez was the seventh player to accomplish the feat. He was the first to do it since Mike Schmidt of Philadelphia did it in 1976. He was the first American League player to do it since Gus Zernial of the Philadelphia Athletics in 1951. The other American League player with six homers in three games was Tony Lazzeri of the Yankees in 1936. The other National League players were Ralph Kiner of Pittsburgh, who did it twice in 1947; Frank Thomas of the Mets in 1962; and Lee May of Cincinnati in 1969.

Most in a Month.

"I knew June was Pedro [Guerrero]'s favorite month, so I told him that in the U.S., June had sixty days. I'd see him in July and say, 'Well, Pedro, it's June 52 and I see you're still hot.'" — Los Angeles Dodgers manager Tommy Lasorda, after Pedro Guerrero hit 15 home runs in June and batted .460 in July.

Until 1998, Rudy York of the Tigers held the Major League record with 18 home runs in August 1937, when he was a rookie. Sammy Sosa took over as the leader when he hit 20 in June 1998, including 15 in 16 games. That number also broke the National League record of 17, hit by Willie Mays in August 1965. The monthly league leaders:

April:

13	Ken Griffey, Jr., Mariners, 1997
	Luis Gonzalez, Diamondback, 2001
11	Graig Nettles, Yankees, 1974
	Brady Anderson, Orioles, 1996
11	Willie Stargell, Pirates, 1971
	Mike Schmidt, Phillies, 1976
	Barry Bonds, Giants, 1996
	Gary Sheffield, Marlins, 1996
	Larry Walker, Rockies, 1997

May:

| 16 | Mickey Mantle, Yankees, 1956 |
| 15 | Cy Williams, Phillies, 1923 |

June:

20	Sammy Sosa, Cubs, 1998
15	Babe Ruth, Yankees, 1930
	Bob Johnson, A's, 1934
	Roger Maris, Yankees, 1961
15	Pedro Guerrero, Dodgers, 1985

July:

16	Albert Belle, White Sox, 1998
15	Joe DiMaggio, Yankees, 1937
	Hank Greenberg, Tigers, 1938
	Juan Gonzalez, Rangers, 1996
15	Joe Adcock, Braves, 1956

August:

18	Rudy York, Tigers, 1937
17	Willie Mays, Giants, 1965
	Sammy Sosa, Cubs, 2001

September:

17	Babe Ruth, Yankees, 1927
	Albert Belle, Indians, 1995
16	Ralph Kiner, Pirates, 1949

First Two Months. In 1994 Ken Griffey, Jr., set the then Major League record for most home runs in the first two months of the season with 22 through May 30. Mickey Mantle had held the record with 20 in 1961. Griffey extended the record to 23 in 1997. In 1998 Mark McGwire broke the record with 25 before June 1. In 2001 Barry Bonds increased that record to 27 in 2001.

In 1994 Matt Williams of the Giants tied the National League record for most home runs in the first two months of the season, with 19. The record was set in 1987 by Eric Davis of the Reds before the 1998 onslaught by Mark McGwire and Sammy Sosa.

First Three Months. In 1994 Ken Griffey, Jr., set a then-Major League record for most home runs by June 30, with 32. It broke Babe Ruth's record of 30 set in 1928 and 1930. In 1994 Matt Williams set the National League record when he hit 29 home runs by June 30. Mark McGwire shattered all these records when he blasted 36 by June 30, 1998. Barry Bonds extended that record to 38 through June 30, 2001.

First Four Months. The record for most home runs through July is 41, established by Babe Ruth in 1928 and tied by Jimmie Foxx in 1932. Barry Bonds extended the record to 44 in 2001.

40/Three Players/Same Team. The 1973 Braves featured Henry Aaron with 40 home runs, second baseman Davey Johnson with 43 and third baseman Darrell Evans with 41. Johnson batted in front of the two greatest home run hitters of all time: Aaron and Sadaharu Oh (trick question, as Johnson played in the Japanese Leagues with Oh after his Major League career ended).

The 1996 Rockies also had three players with 40 home runs: Andres Galarraga with 47 and Vinny Castilla and Ellis Burks with 40 each.

30/Four Players/Same Team.

"Now we're the 30, 30, 30, 30 and 1 club."—Larry Walker after he and three teammates hit 30 home runs each in 1995 and shortstop Walt Weiss finally cracked his first home run of the season in late September. The four with 30: Andres Galarraga (31), Larry Walker (36), Vinny Castilla (32) and Dante Bichette (40). The Rockies repeated in 1996, but this time Ellis Burks replaced Larry Walker as the fourth member of the group. Walker would have been the fifth player to hit 30 on the club, except he suffered a midseason injury that put him out of action for several weeks. The totals: Gallaraga (47), Castilla (40), Bichette (31) and Burks (40).

The 1977 Dodgers had four players with 30 or more home runs: Steve Garvey (33), Ron Cey (30), Reggie Smith (32) and Dusty Baker (30).

Most Over 30. In 1987 there were 28 Major League players who hit 30 or more home runs. In 1996 there were 43. In 2002 there were 28 again.

Most Home Runs/Fewest Strikeouts. Tommy Holmes of the Braves hit 28 home runs in 1945 to lead the National League. He also led the league with the fewest strikeouts, nine, and had a then–National League record 37-game hitting streak.

Fewest Home Runs/Player.

"What's one home run. If you hit one, they're just going to want you to hit two."—Mick Kelleher of the Tigers, who had not hit one, on why it was a mistake to try. He never hit one in 1,081 at-bats over 11 years.

"I knew it was gone as soon as I hit it. Man, I've always wanted to say that."—Light-hitting Rangers shortstop Jeff Huson after hitting his second home run in four days in 1994.

"The Hostage."—Orioles second baseman Rich Dauer's nickname because, in the words of teammate Mike Flanagan: "Richie's been kept inside the fences longer than the hostages were held in Iran."

Dauer hit 43 home runs in 10 seasons, with a high of nine in 1979.

Bill Holbert played catcher and outfielder from 1876 through 1888. He had no home runs in 2,335 at-bats while batting .208.

A lifetime .251 hitter, third baseman Floyd Baker hit only one home run in 2,280 at-bats over 13 years from 1943 through 1955 (see also *Comiskey Park*—Home Runs for why he was able to hit the one).

In 1915 Babe Ruth led the Red Sox with four home runs while still pitching full-time. The next best total on the team was two.

Rabbit Maranville holds the single-season Major League record of 672 plate appearances in 1922 without hitting a home run.

Duane Kuiper hit a home run in at-bat number 1,381, on August 29, 1977. He did not hit another in his next 1,997 at-bats. He contended (presumably facetiously) that he intentionally did not hit another one over the balance of his career.

Light-hitting infielder Johnnie LeMaster hit only 22 home runs in a 12-year career covering 1,039 games and 3,191 official at-bats, but the 6'2", 165-pounder hit one in his first at-bat in the Major Leagues.

U.L. Washington and John Lucadello are the only players to hit only two home runs all season, in the same game, from both sides of the plate. Washington did it for the Royals on September 21, 1979, and Lucadello did it for the Browns on September 16, 1940. See also *Switch Hitters*.

Charlie Maxwell hit only three home runs in 1951 for the Red Sox and they were the first three hits of his career. All were pinch hits and all were off future Hall of Famers: Satchel Paige, Bob Feller and Bob Lemon.

Braves pitcher/outfielder Johnny Cooney did not hit a home run for 15 years and then hit two in two days. He did not hit another for the last five years of his career.

Tommy Thevenow hit a home run in the 1926 World Series for the Cardinals after hitting only two all season. He never hit another in 12 more seasons.

In 1982 Pete Rose did not win the batting title. Instead, he became the only first baseman on a pennant-winning team since the dead ball era to hit no home runs.

Al Newman retired in 1992 without hitting a home run in his last 1,971 at-bats, including 1,893 straight in the American League. In eight seasons he hit one home run.

Red Sox infielder Rey Sanchez went 1,094 at-bats between home runs.

On September 26, 1997, Rafael Belliard of the Braves hits his first home run in a decade, off Brian Bohanon of the Mets. Belliard's last one was on May 5, 1987, off Eric Show of the Padres.

Team Power Shortage. On September 7, 1945, Joe Kuhel of the Senators hit the only home run of the season by the Senators in cavernous Griffith Stadium. It was an inside-the-park shot. The team hit only 27 all season, with Harlond Clift leading with eight. Opposing teams hit only six out of the ballpark.

Minimum Results. In a 1991 game the A's hit six home runs against the Twins and scored only those six runs. The previous record for minimum RBIs was a five home run/five RBI day by the 1971 A's against the Senators.

Most/Without Two In a Game. Lou Piniella at one time held the record for most home runs without a multi-homer game, with 103. Braves outfielder Marquis Grissom broke the record and went on to reach 109 before hitting two in a game in September 1998.

Shared Home Run Title. Johnny Mize and Ralph Kiner shared the home run title twice. In 1947 they each hit 51 and in 1948 they each hit 40.

Joe Medwick of the Cardinals had 31 home runs in 1937, tying Mel Ott for the league title. Early in the season Medwick lost a home run because the curfew rules forced cancellation of a game before five innings were completed. The other team stalled to get to the curfew in a game they were losing 3–0. Umpire Bill Klem declared a 9–0 forfeit in favor of the Cardinals because of the obvious stalling tactics. However, the individual statistics did not count because five innings were not played.

Lou Gehrig could have had sole possession of the 1931 American League home run title. On April 26, he homered at Griffith Stadium, but runner Lyn Lary returned to second base thinking the ball was caught (some sources have him returning to the dugout). Gehrig passed him and nullified the home run as the Yankees lost 9–7. Gehrig ended the season tied at 46 home runs with Babe Ruth.

All-Time Switch Hitters. Mickey Mantle is the all-time switch-hitting home run leader with 536, followed by Eddie Murray (see also *Switch Hitters*).

Coincidence. Pitcher Jack Fisher gave up both Roger Maris' 60th home run and the last home run by Ted Williams (see *Last At-Bat*).

35 or More/Both Leagues. Only Dick Allen, Dick Stuart, Frank Robinson and Mark McGwire hit 35 or more home runs in a season in each league.

30 or More/Most Teams. In 2002 Fred McGriff became the first Major League player to hit 30 home runs in a season for five different teams. He did it in 2002 with the Cubs, joining Atlanta, Tampa Bay, Toronto (three times) and San Diego (twice).

Most Teams.

"A dubious honor." — Todd Zeile in April 2003 when he hit a home run for his tenth club, the Yankees. He also homered for the Expos in San Juan, Puerto Rico, on September 6, 2003, becoming the first player ever to homer for 11 different teams.

Youngest Champion. Tony Conigliaro became the Major League's youngest home run champion when he hit 32 home runs in 1965 at age 20.

Longest Home Runs.

"Anything that goes that far in the air ought to have a stewardess on it." — Pitcher Paul Splittorff on a George Brett home run (variations on this quote have been made by others).

"When the ball was last seen crossing the roof of the stand in deep right field at 315 feet, we wonder whether new baseballs conversing together in the original package ever remark: 'Join Ruth and see the world.'" — From a 1923 *New York World* column by Heywood Broun.

"When Neil Armstrong first set foot on the moon, he and all the space scientists were puzzled by an unidentifiable white object. That was a home run ball hit off me in 1937 by Jimmie Foxx." — Lefty Gomez.

"The ball went further than I ever went on vacation as a kid." — Gene Geiselmann, Cardinals trainer, on a home run hit by Juan Gonzalez.

"I am The Can, and I am going to come right at you with my best shit, and if you can hit it, I want to see how far Bo Jackson can hit The Oil Can." — Dennis "Oil Can" Boyd, Boston Red Sox pitcher, to Bo Jackson before Jackson hit his first pitch over the 71-foot high scoreboard in straightaway center field at Fenway Park. The ball reportedly landed 515 feet from home plate.

"It doesn't matter whether the ball went a mile or whether it scraped the back of the wall." — Ralph Kiner on the unimportance of distance on a home run.

"It's getting completely out of hand. A home run is nothing nowadays if you don't have to measure it. Pretty soon, anything under 400 feet will only count as a sacrifice fly." — Jim Murray.

"There have been a plethora of guys to hit it up there, but that was the plethorest." — The Marlins' publicist after Reds outfielder Kevin Mitchell pounded a ball into the upper deck of Joe Robbie Stadium.

"The best place to catch a baseball hit by [Mark] McGwire is definitely not within the confines of the playing field, or sometimes even the ballpark. Other players dial '1' for long distance. McGwire has to ask for an international operator." — Thomas Boswell in the *Washington Post*.

Note that many of these home run feats carry with them dubious claims of distance, and more authoritative sources have in later years corrected, or at least rationally disputed, these claims. Minnesota's Metropolitan Stadium was the first ballpark to estimate home run distances in the early 1960s. Major League Baseball began using IBM in the late 1980s to develop a program to compute home run distances based on seating charts.

Dan Brouthers was considered the Babe Ruth of his day. His 1886 shot out of Washington's Capitol Park was the tape measure shot of its era. Its notoriety is reflected in a reference to it in one of Zane Grey's baseball novels from the early 20th century. Brouthers was the first player to win back-to-back batting titles and continued playing in the high minors until age 48.

Babe Ruth hit a home run measuring 587 feet at a 1919 exhibition game in Tampa. Long-time sportswriter Fred Lieb recalls a 600-foot home run that Ruth hit in a New York/Boston game in 1919 in Tampa, which is probably the same shot.

On June 8, 1926, in Detroit's Navin Field (later Tiger Stadium), Ruth hit a 3–0 pitch from Lil Stoner out of the park that landed on Plum Street, an estimated 626 feet (606 on some sources). The field had not yet been double-decked and there was only a 12-foot wall. Future commissioner Ford Frick was a New York writer at the game that day. He noted that the ball rolled two blocks (he could see it from the press box), and calculated that it had gone 800–850 feet when it stopped rolling. More scientific sources, such as SABR researcher William J. Jenkinson in *The Home Run Encyclopedia*, puts the drive at more like 500 feet, and notes that there is no proof of a 600-foot blast.

One writer was more impressed with Ruth's second home run that day. It gave the Yankees an 11–9 win and hit the screen so hard that it "bounced back almost to second baseman Gehringer."

The Wells Motor Company car dealership on Grand Avenue in St. Louis, across the street from Sportsman's Park, put up a huge sign celebrating a home run during Game 4 of the 1926 World Series. One of Babe Ruth's three home runs had cracked the glass storefront.

In 1926 Tiger outfielder Harry Heilmann hit what was estimated (wildly!) at the time to be a 660-foot shot out of Navin Field.

Jimmie Foxx hit one over the left field bleachers in Comiskey Park in 1936. It landed in a playground over 100 feet from the fence for an estimated total of 620 feet.

Catcher Ernie Lombardi is said to have hit a ball over the center field fence and into a truck that carried the ball 30 miles.

In June 1946 Ted Williams hit a home run measuring 502 feet in Fenway Park. It supposedly landed on the straw hat of fan Joseph A. Boucher.

On April 17, 1953, Mickey Mantle hit one out of Griffith Stadium in Washington, D.C., off pitcher Chuck Stobbs that cleared the left field wall and landed in a yard behind a three-story tenement building. Yankee publicist Red Patterson said he personally measured the shot at 565 feet, the longest actually measured in a Major League game. The ball caromed off a football scoreboard before it landed in the back yard of the tenement. The bat and ball were put on display, later stolen and then returned. William J. Jenkinson estimates this drive at 510 feet and notes that the 565 mark was from where the ball was picked up by a boy, presumably after rolling some distance.

Originally, Patterson measured it at 563, but somehow two extra feet were added. The distance is a myth. Patterson much later told SABR researcher Jenkinson, "hey, I was supposed to make Mantle look good." Jenkinson said: "There is no authenticity to the story. Absolutely zero. Patterson didn't admit that he padded the distance, but he was clearly defensive about it."

Mantle later admitted that Patterson told him that there was no basis for the claim. What is true is that Mantle did hit a ball over the 55-foot fence, the first ever to do so.

On June 5, 1955, Mantle hit a ball off Chicago's Billy Pierce at Comiskey that was estimated to have traveled 550 feet.

Joe Adcock hit a ball over the center field bleachers in the Polo Grounds in 1953. Adcock was the first player to hit one in that area, a shot that was at least 487 feet. In 1963 Lou Brock became the second player to hit one there, and the next night Henry Aaron repeated the feat with a grand slam.

On September 10, 1960, Mantle hit a long home run off Tigers pitcher Paul Foytack. The ball cleared the right field roof at Briggs Stadium and landed in a lumberyard across the street from the park. The length of the drive was measured trigonomically in 1985 at 643 feet, but appears to have bounced several times to the point at which it was measured.

On May 22, 1963, Mantle hit the Yankee Stadium facade in right field with a home run off Bill Fischer of the A's. What made the shot remarkable was that the ball hit 118 feet up, into the upper grandstand facade, and was hit into a wind. It is estimated that the ball would have traveled 620 feet had it not hit the facade. Mantle hit the right field upper deck facade five times in his career.

On May 6,1964, Dave Nicholson of the White Sox reportedly hit a 573-foot home run at Comiskey Park. "White Sox mathematicians," of course never identified, apparently assumed that the ball had cleared the roof, which it did not. It hit the back of the roof and bounced beyond the stadium.

On May 8, 1966, Frank Robinson reportedly hit a 541-foot drive over the left-field wall of Baltimore's Memorial Stadium. It was the only ball ever hit completely out of the park.

On June 3, 1967, Harmon Killebrew hit a ball 522 feet at Metropolitan Stadium, the longest ball ever hit out of that ballpark.

Frank Howard hit a ball over the roof at Yankee Stadium on September 29, 1970, that was estimated to have traveled over 580 feet. But the umpire called it foul by four inches.

Reggie Jackson hit one out of Tiger Stadium during the 1971 All-Star Game. It went over the right field roof and hit a light standard or it would have traveled at least 600 feet. Jackson had been added to the team by Earl Weaver after Tony Oliva was injured. Ted Williams said it was the hardest hit ball he had ever seen. Jackson pinch hit for pitcher Vida Blue, who commented tongue-in-cheek on the wisdom of the substitution: "To be honest, I don't think I could have hit it that far."

On April 14, 1976, Dave Kingman hit an estimated 573-foot (or 550) home run against the side of a building on Waveland Avenue adjacent to Wrigley Field in Chicago. In struck the third house beyond Waveland Avenue, which is 530 feet from home plate. In 1979 while with the Cubs in Wrigley Field, Kingman allegedly sent one approximately 620 feet but was aided by 30–35 mph winds. These reports may have been about the same home run in 1976, as that home run has sometimes been reported as reaching 620 and 630 feet.

On August 3, 1977, George Foster reportedly hit a ball that "flight engineers" measured at 720 feet if it had not hit the stands.

On May 20, 1978, Willie Stargell hit a 535-foot blast in Montreal's Olympic Stadium, the longest home run in that ballpark.

On May 22, 1990, Jose Canseco hit a grand slam in Toronto's SkyDome that hit the fifth deck, nearly 600 feet away. One source reported that Canseco's longest drive was into the fifth level at Toronto's SkyDome during the 1989 American League playoffs, which was estimated at 484 feet.

In 1994 Frank Thomas hit a ball 519 feet at Pittsburgh's Three Rivers Stadium during the home run hitting contest at the 1994 All-Star Game. The club placed a star where the ball landed, which was 80 feet farther than any ball ever hit in the ballpark during a game.

On May 16, 1998, Mark McGwire hit a 548-foot home run (or 545 feet) against Marlins pitcher Livan Hernandez, the longest home run in Busch Stadium history. McGwire said it was the longest home run he ever hit. Four days earlier he had hit one 527 feet at Busch Stadium.

Negro League star John Beckwith hit a home run in Griffith Stadium that supposedly cleared the 460-foot marker and hit 40 feet above the left field bleachers.

The Sporting News reported in 1934 that Negro League star Josh Gibson hit a ball in Yankee Stadium that was estimated to be 580 feet and would have been 700 feet had the ball not hit two feet below the top of the roof. *The Sporting News* later reported another Gibson shot of at least 575 feet in Yankee Stadium.

On May 31, 1997, Andres Galarraga of the Rockies hit a 529-foot home run at Pro Player Stadium in Florida, but then was ejected from the game four innings later in the Rockies' 8–4 win.

In August 2004 Adam Dunn of the Reds hit a home run into the Ohio River that was estimated at 535 feet.

Measuring Device.

"It should be noted that those regular references over the years to 500- and 600-foot home runs were born out of scientific ignorance, misinformation, or even deliberate exaggeration. The most common cause for overstatement has been the basic misconception about the flight of a batted ball once it has reached its apex. Seeing great drives land atop distant upper-deck roof, sportswriters observing the occurrence from a press box would resort to their limited skills in mathematics without any regard for the laws of physics."—William J. Jenkinson in *The Home Run Encyclopedia*.

In 1982 IBM installed a device in several ballparks that measured the distance of home runs. Between 1982 and 1998, there was one home run measured by the system at over 500 feet. Cecil Fielder of the Tigers is credited with hitting a ball 502 feet in the air over the left-field bleachers at Milwaukee's County Stadium on September 14, 1991.

In the 1990s long distance telephone carrier MCI replaced IBM and co-sponsored with Major League Baseball a "longest home run" measuring system. They were determined by a grid system that took into consideration where the ball landed or would have landed had it not hit something other than the ground.

Bottom of the Last Inning ("Walk Off") Home Runs.

"The greatest thrill in the world is to end the game with a home run and watch everybody else walk off the field while you're running the bases on air."—Al Rosen.

"I'm telling you, it is illegal. You can't score runs after a game is over!"—Umpire Hank O'Day in 1920, still arguing at the rules committee meeting after the vote to allow home runs to count even after the winning run had already crossed the plate; as reported by the person who suggested the rule change, sportswriter Fred Lieb, in his book *Baseball as I Have Known It* (1977).

Until 1920 a ball that was hit out of the park in the bottom of the last inning was scored only as the hit sufficient to bring home the winning run. A total of 37 players lost home runs under the prior rule, including Babe Ruth on July 8, 1918. Fred Lieb was on the rules committee in early 1920 when he suggested a rule change that would give a batter credit for a home run in a bottom-of-the-last-inning situation.

In 1931 the rule was extended to hits other than home runs to allow the official scorer to credit the batter who drove in the winning run with a single, double or triple, depending on the number of bases the scorer believed would have been made by the batter.

The Japanese have for many years recorded game-ending home runs as an official statistic. The name: Sayonara Home Runs.

See also *World Series*—**Series Wins on Final Pitch.**

Walk-Off Home Run/Debut. In July 2003, Miguel Cabrera of the Marlins became only the third player since 1900 to hit a walk-off home run in his Major League debut. Indians rookie catcher

Josh Bard did also did it, on August 23, 2002, against the Mariners in the bottom of the 9th for a 4–2 win.

Fair/Foul. Into the 1920s, to be considered a fair ball, a ball had to stay in fair territory until it hit the ground. Today a ball need only pass the foul pole in fair territory to be considered a fair ball, even if it later curves foul (see also **Foul Balls**).

Two Teams/One Season/Led League. Braggo Roth was the first player to lead the league in home runs while splitting the season between two teams. He hit seven in 1915 for the Indians and White Sox.

In 1951 Gus Zernial became the second player to accomplish this by hitting 33 for the White Sox and A's. He also became the first player to lead the league in RBIs (129) while playing for two teams.

Pitchers (as Home Run Hitters).

"There will be a man on the moon before he hits a home run in the big leagues." — Giants manager Alvin Dark on weak-hitting pitcher Gaylord Perry in 1962 (also attributed to Perry himself). On July 20, 1969, 17 minutes after Apollo 11 landed on the moon, Perry hit his first Major League home run in a 7–3 win over the Dodgers.

See **Pitchers — Home Runs Allowed** for home runs given up by pitchers.

Pitcher Gary Peters hit back-to-back pinch home runs for the Red Sox in 1971.

Pitcher Jim Tobin hit three consecutive home runs in a game on May 13, 1942, for the Braves against the Cubs.

In 1955 Babe Birrer of the Tigers pitched four innings of relief and hit two three-run home runs. He never hit another home run.

In 1955 Dodger pitcher Clem Labine had three hits, all home runs.

Don Drysdale is the only pitcher to hit two home runs on Opening Day.

On September 4, 1955, Brooklyn pitcher Don Newcombe connected for his seventh homer of the season for a National League record for home runs by a pitcher. Mike Hampton of the Rockies hit seven in 2001 and Don Drysdale of the Dodgers hit seven in two separate seasons. Wes Ferrell hit nine home runs in 1931 for the Major League and American League record.

The all-time home run leaders among pitchers are Wes Ferrell with 36, Red Ruffing with 36 and Warren Spahn and Earl Wilson with 35. During a career that lasted mostly during the dead ball era, Walter Johnson hit 24 home runs.

Pitcher Reciprocity. Pitchers have homered off each other in a game only 10 times in the 20th century. The last to do so were Marvin Freeman of the Rockies and Kevin Foster of the Cubs in June 1995.

Pitcher Home Run/Only Run of Game. On August 28, 2002, Odalis Perez of the Dodgers hit a solo home run off Arizona's Rick Helling, for the only run of the game. He was the first pitcher (and 12th ever) since Bob Welch in 1983 to hit a solo home run for the only run of the game.

Last Home Run Before the Designated Hitter. See **Designated Hitters**.

Pinch Hit Home Runs. See **Pinch Hitters**.

Two-Out Home Runs. On July 18, 1998, the Red Sox set the American League record for two-out homers, with four in their 9–4 win over the Tigers. The Major League record is five, by the New York Giants against the Reds in 1939 (see below).

20 Home Runs/Team/Most Players. The 2003 Braves had six players with 20 or more home runs. The only other time this occurred was with the 1965 Braves, the year before they relocated from Milwaukee to Atlanta.

Consecutive/Three Players/First. The first game in the 20th century in which three players hit consecutive home runs occurred on June 30, 1902, by Cleveland's Nap Lajoie, Piano Legs Hickman and Bill Bradley.

Consecutive Home Runs/Team/Game.

"Denny, did it ever occur to you to throw anything but a fastball?" — Jim Northrup of the Tigers to pitcher Denny McLain, after the first two batters had homered on two fastballs and McLain then struck out the next three batters on fastballs. McLain's response: Why? When was the last time you saw anyone hit three home runs in a row?"

Three teams have hit four consecutive home runs in an inning. On June 8, 1961, Milwaukee's Eddie Mathews, Henry Aaron, Joe Adcock and Frank Thomas hit consecutive home runs in the 7th inning against the Reds.

On July 31, 1963, Cleveland's 8–9–1–2 men in the batting order hit consecutive home runs against the Angels: Woody Held, Paul Foytack, Tito Francona and Larry Brown.

On May 2, 1964, in the 11th inning at Kansas City, the Twins had four straight home runs by Harmon Killebrew, Tony Oliva, Bob Allison and Jimmie Hall.

Jimmie Foxx hit his 500th home run on September 24, 1940, in Boston during an inning that almost featured five consecutive home runs. Ted Williams and Joe Cronin hit home runs immediately before and after Foxx, for three in a row. They were followed by a triple by Bobby Doerr and many thought he could have scored for a fourth consecutive home run. Jim Tabor then homered. The Red Sox had six home runs, three triples, five doubles and nine singles in the 16–8 victory over the A's.

Most by Team/Inning. The Giants hit five home runs in the 4th inning of a 17–3 win over the Reds on June 6, 1939. On their way to eight runs that inning, Harry Danning, Al Demaree, Burgess Whitehead, Manny Salvo and Joe Moore all hit home runs with two outs.

On August 23, 1961, the Giants hit five home runs in the 9th inning, while scoring 12 runs en route to a 14–0 win over the Reds.

The Phillies hit five home runs in one inning on June 2, 1949. This included one by pitcher Schoolboy Rowe and two by Andy Seminick. A double by Granny Hamner missed being a home run by about a foot and a triple by Willie Jones was inches from the top of the fence. Jones also homered in the inning. The Phillies had 26 total bases in the inning and scored 10 runs en route to a 12–3 victory.

Most by Team/Game. On September 14, 1987, the Blue Jays hit 10 home runs against the Orioles in an 18–3 win. It was the same game in which Cal Ripken's consecutive innings streak ended at 8,243. The most by a single team in a game before that was eight, by the Twins against the Senators in a 14–2 win on August 29, 1963.

Most By Team/Two Games. The 2003 Angels hit 13 home runs in two straight games at Hi Bithorn Stadium in Puerto Rico, tying a record set by the 1939 Yankees.

Most by Team/Season. The 1996 Orioles hit 257 home runs to break the 1961 Yankees Major League season record. This contributed to a new Major League record of 4,962 home runs. The Orioles also set an American League record by having nine players hit 20 or more home runs.

Most/Two Teams in a Game. On May 28, 1995, the Tigers and White Sox combined for a Major League record 12 home runs at Tiger Stadium and an American League record 21 extra base hits. The 12 home runs broke the record of 11, which had been accomplished four times in each league. On July 2, 2002, the same two teams again combined for 12 home runs, as the White Sox won 17–9.

On May 17, 1979, the Phillies and Cubs combined for 11 home runs in a 23–22 Philadelphia victory on a windy day at Wrigley Field. Dave Kingman hit three of the 11.

On May 22, 1977, the Red Sox and Brewers combined for 11 home runs in a 14–10 Red Sox victory at Fenway Park. The Red Sox hit six of the 11.

On June 23, 1950, the Tigers and Yankees combined to hit 11 home runs. The Tigers hit five in their 10–9 victory.

On April 25, 1997, the Brewers and Indians hit 11 home runs as the Indians won 11–4.

In 1989 a devastating ***Earthquake*** in the San Francisco Bay area caused a 10-day postponement of Game 3 of the World Series because the games were being played in San Francisco and Oakland. When play resumed on October 27, the A's hit a World Series record-tying five home runs and the clubs combined for a series record seven home runs in one game. The A's won the game and went on to sweep the Giants with two more home runs in the final game.

Most by Two Teams/Doubleheader. On May 30, 1956, the Braves and Cubs combined for 15 home runs in a doubleheader. The Braves hit nine of them.

The Yankees and A's combined for 13 home runs in a doubleheader on June 23, 1939.

Solo Home Runs. On May 28, 1995, the Tigers and White Sox combined for 10 solo home runs, a Major League record. It broke the mark of seven set by the Blue Jays and Red Sox on July 4, 1977.

Catchers.

"That's Hendricks' 19th home run, one more and he hits double figures."—Jerry Coleman on Orioles catcher Elrod Hendricks.

The 1961 Yankees had three catchers with at least 20 home runs: Johnny Blanchard, Elston Howard and Yogi Berra.

Roy Campanella and Mickey Tettleton were the only catchers to have back-to-back 30-home run seasons until Mike Piazza did it three times in a row and later five times in a row after an off year due to injury. Surprisingly, Johnny Bench never did it, but he was the first catcher to lead the Major Leagues in home runs and RBIs in the same season.

In 1996 Todd Hundley of the Mets set a new record for catchers with 41 home runs.

Bad Day. On July 28, 2004, Twins rookie Justin Morneau had two home runs taken away from him after umpires reversed their calls in a game the Twins finally won over the White Sox. In the 2nd inning Morneau hit a fly ball that umpire Ed Montague ruled a home run. After argument by the White Sox, the umpires ruled (and replays confirmed) that the ball hit the top of the fence and bounced back on the field. In the 5th Morneau hit a home run down the right field line that the umpires first ruled fair, then foul.

Coincidence. On September 27, 1923, Lou Gehrig hit his first homer in the majors off Bill Piercy of the Red Sox. On the same date 15 years later, he hit his 493rd and last off Dutch Leonard of the Senators.

Who Was That Man? When Satchel Paige and his Negro all-star team played Bob Feller and his all-stars, Paige gave up a home run to Ralph Kiner. After the shot, Paige turned to teammate Buck O'Neil and asked who had hit the long shot off him. After O'Neil told him it was Kiner and that he had led the league in home runs that season, Paige said: "Oh yeah? Be sure to tell me when he comes up again."

Statistician. In 2004 this author was seeking an esoteric piece of home run data and the Hall of Fame's Gabriel Schechter had exhausted all his resources; he suggested the author email SABR's David Vincent, "the expert on HR records and breakdowns."

Within five minutes of sending the email, the author had the answer and the same information for 20 other top home run hitters.

Books. William Curran, *Big Sticks* (1990); Arthur Daley, *Kings of the Home Run* (1962); John Holway, *The Sluggers* (1989); Bob McConnell and David W. Vincent (eds.), *SABR Presents the Home Run Encyclopedia* (1996); Dan Valenti, *The Top Home Runs in Baseball History* (1989).

Home Teams

"Throughout the evolution of major American professional team sports, only baseball has escaped the curse of the distorting, infuriating, far-too-important home field advantage. That is, until the 1987 Minnesota Twins arrived."—Thomas Boswell in *The Heart of the Order* (1989). Most Major League clubs were about 4% better at home; the Twins were 15.8% better between 1982 and 1986 and were 35% better in 1987.

"Actually, the best thing about playing at home is that you are not on the road."—Cardinals catcher Darrell Porter.

"Sometimes."—Yogi Berra after being asked if he comes to all the Yankee home games.

See ***Road Games*** for clubs that were forced to play exclusively on the road due to problems with their ballparks.

See also ***Weather—Hurricane*** for games forced to be moved.

Coin Toss. In the earliest National League games, a coin toss determined the home team. In 1886 the home team captain was first allowed to decide which team batted first. This rule remained in effect until 1950, when it was made mandatory for the visiting team to bat first.

Home Team Bats First. On April 22, 1903, the New York Highlanders played the Senators in Washington. To open the first game of their first season, the Senators elected to bat first.

Bell. For a number of years a boxing ring bell was used to tell the home team to trot on the field to start the game.

Early Neutral Sites. In the late 19th and early 20th centuries, teams sometimes played in neutral cities to avoid the Sunday Blue Laws or to boost attendance late in the season. For example, in 1902–1905 Cleveland played homes games in Canton, Columbus, Dayton and Fort Wayne. Detroit played in Columbus, Toledo and Grand Rapids, while the Yankees played in Newark and the Braves played in Providence, Rhode Island.

Philip J. Lowry's *Green Cathedrals* (1992) identifies every ballpark in which a Major League game was played, allowing the reader to determine where neutral-site games were played throughout the history of Major League Baseball.

Chicago White Stockings. Fearing competition from the 1876 Chicago World's Fair, the White Stockings booked home games out of town. The team miscalculated the beneficial effect of the fair, and other teams in the league unsuccessfully tried to book their own home games in Chicago to capitalize on the enormous crowds in the city during that time.

Washington Nationals. In the 1880s the Washington Nationals received such a large visitor's share when they played Philadelphia that the team rescheduled all of its remaining home games with Philadelphia in Philadelphia. The league disallowed this move and fined Washington's owners $1,000.

Brooklyn Dodgers. The Dodgers played seven home games in 1956 in Roosevelt Stadium in Jersey City, New Jersey, and eight games there in 1957. The club was 11–4 in these games, the first Major League games played in Jersey City since the New York Giants played two games there to open the 1889 season.

One source reported that the Boston Braves sometimes played

in Jersey City, but there does not appear to be any evidence of this.

Chicago White Sox. The White Sox played 20 home games in Milwaukee County Stadium in 1968 and 1969. This was after the Braves left town for Atlanta in 1966 and before the Brewers arrived in 1970. The White Sox had a record of 8–12 in those games.

Montreal Expos. The Expos played 22 home games in **Puerto Rico** in both 2003 and 2004. In 2004 all the games were played before the All-Star break (presumably before it got so bloody hot and humid that it was like playing in St. Louis in the summertime).

Oakland A's. In 1996 the A's played their first six home games in Las Vegas because a $100 million renovation to their ballpark had not been completed. Cashman Field in Las Vegas seated only 8,000.

San Diego Padres. On August 16–18, 1996, the Padres and Mets played a three-game series in Monterrey, **Mexico**, that was considered a Padres home series.

Foreign Home Openers. See **Opening Day** for home openers played at international sites.

Hawaii. See **Hawaii** for a recent Major League series locale.

"Homer in the Gloamin'" See **Pennant Races**—1938
National League

Homestead Grays

Independent and Negro Leagues 1910–1950
"In 1931 Jud [Wilson] jumped to the Grays, which just might have been the greatest black team ever assembled."—John B. Holway in *Blackball Stars* (1988).

This club based in Pittsburgh was formed by a group of black steelworkers originally known as the Murdock Grays. The owner and leader of the club for most of its existence was Cum Posey. The Grays joined the American Negro League in 1929 for one season and the East-West League briefly in 1932. After a brief stint in the Negro National League in 1933, the club remained in the league from 1935 through 1949. The Grays won nine consecutive pennants from 1937 through 1945 and the Negro League World Series in 1943 and 1944.

Key early players were Smokey Joe Williams (possibly the best black left-handed pitcher of all time), Oscar Owens and Lefty Williams. Later stars were Josh Gibson, Oscar Charleston and Buck Leonard.

The Grays played most of their home games at Forbes Field in Pittsburgh and were named for an industrial area outside of the city. They also played home games as the Washington (D.C.) Homestead Grays at Griffith Stadium.

Book. Brad Snyder, *Beyond the Shadow of the Senators* (2002).

Homosexuals

"Consider the possibilities: in the middle of a pennant race, a team's star shortstop falls in love with his second baseman."—Dust jacket to Peter Lefcourt's *The Dreyfus Affair* (1992).

"In the world of pro sports, nothing has changed. Calling someone a 'homosexual' is still sports' worst insult. Come out of the closet? Ha! Put a double bolt on the door."—Bob Ryan of ESPN in 2004.

"[Fred Talbot is so tough that] fortunately we were able to convince him he was wrong. I wouldn't want to fight him. As far as he's concerned the Marquis of Queensberry is some fag hairdresser."—Jim Bouton in *Ball Four* (1970).

"Kid, I've been with this club a lot of years. We've had just two kinds of seasons: good ones and great ones. And I can remember them all, like they were yesterday. But I want you to know that nothing, *ever*, has meant more to me than beating those wimpy, limp-wristed, degenerate homos!"—From *Out at the Old Ball Game*, by Bernie Bookbinder (1995), about the fictional first all-gay Major League Baseball team composed of players who had been "outed."

"We're all sad to see Glenn Beckert leave. Before he goes, though, I hope he stops by so we can kiss him good-bye. He's that kind of guy."—Jerry Coleman.

"The fag's really blowing in center field."—Jerry Coleman on a blustery day in Candlestick Park.

"What's his name? Nomo? Homo?"—Always sensitive Reds owner Marge Schott on Dodger pitcher Hideo Nomo.

"Jeter's Gay"—Libelous T-shirt sold at the 2003 American League Championship Series between the Yankees and Red Sox.

Glenn Burke.
"Prejudice just won out."—Burke on his inability to stick in the Major Leagues during the 1970s. He admitted being gay after his career ended in 1979, but it was known in baseball circles before that. He died of AIDS in May 1995. In 1982 his companion wrote an article for *Inside Sports* entitled "The Double Life of a Gay Dodger." See also Glenn Burke with Erik Sherman, *Out at Home—The Glenn Burke Story* (1995).

Billy Bean.
"Overnight they would have found some way to kick me out, because some dad doesn't want his little kid watching some gay baseball player and saying, 'I want to grow up to be just like him.'"—Bean (not to be confused with Oakland A's general manager Billy Beane), a former Padres outfielder at times between 1987 to 1995, on why he couldn't admit publicly that he was gay until he retired. He spoke publicly for the first time in an August 30, 1999, article in the *New York Times*. He then became somewhat of an icon on behalf of gay athletes, although he was criticized by some in the gay community for being so pessimistic about the prospects of the typical player and fan accepting a gay Major Leaguer. Bean played in 272 games and batted .228 with five home runs (all in 1993) over his career.

Survey Response. In 1975 the gay magazine *The Advocate* sent out a survey and questionnaire to all Major League teams requesting interviews with "players living gay lifestyles." No record of how many responded, though the publicity director for the Twins responded by denouncing the "colossal gall in attempting to extend your perversion to an area of total manhood."

Dave Pallone. Umpire Dave Pallone admitted being gay after he was fired for erratic conduct (though the two were not necessarily related). His autobiography is *Behind the Mask* (1990).

Marge Schott. In 1994 Reds owner Marge Schott was quoted as saying that she was glad her players did not wear earrings because "only fruits wear earrings." She later issued a statement saying that she was not "prejudiced against any group, regardless of lifestyle preference."

In response to Schott, Dodger pitcher Roger McDowell bought earrings for the entire club and they wore them in the clubhouse in Cincinnati. Manager Tommy Lasorda would not let the players wear them on the field.

Lawsuit. In 2002 a group of rookie players for the Giants farm team in the Dominican Republic sued the Giants, claiming that their former chief Latin American scout sexually harassed the players and fired them if they refused his advances. The activity supposedly began in 1995.

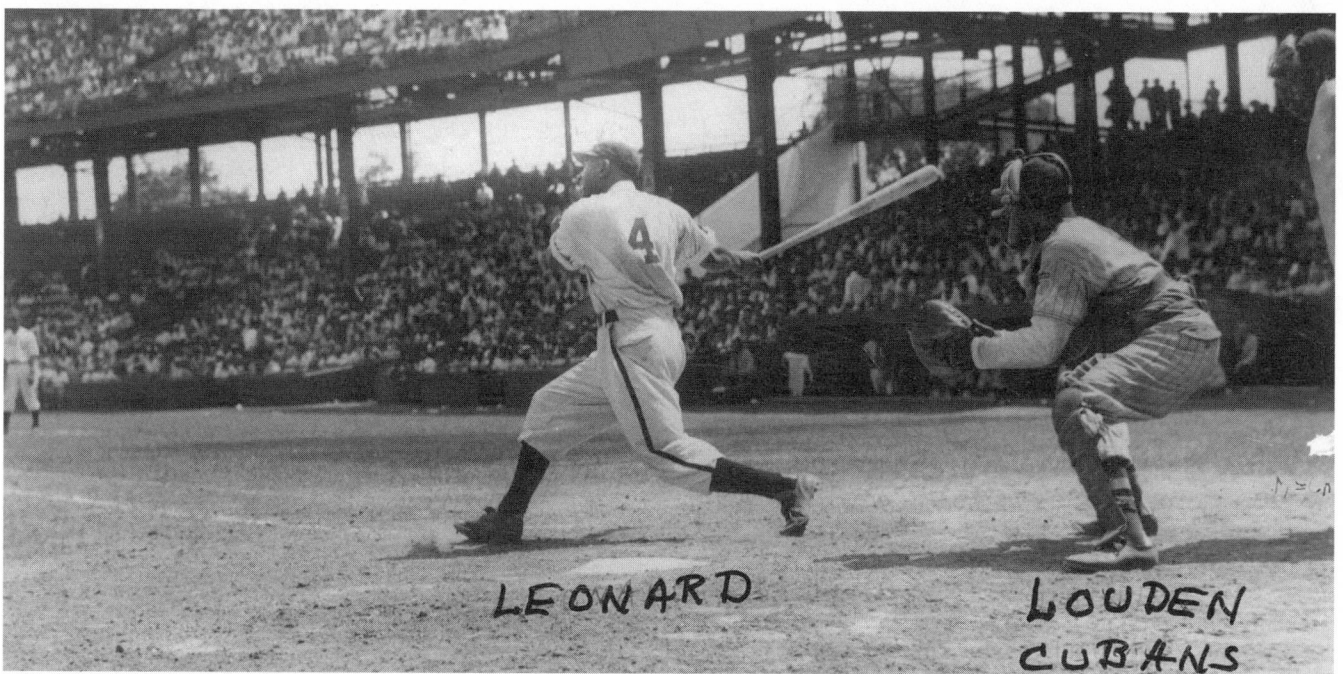

LEONARD   LOUDEN
CUBANS

Homestead Grays first baseman Buck Leonard crushes a ball to right field at Washington's Griffith Stadium in a 1944 game against the New York Cubans.

In late 2003 a New York state court threw out a lawsuit by a homosexual clubhouse worker who sued the Yankees and pitchers Mariano Rivera, Jeff Nelson and Bob Wickman in 1998. The worker, Paul Priore, claimed that he was harassed because he was gay and was HIV-positive.

Todd Jones. The Rockies pitcher told the *Denver Post* in April 2003: "I wouldn't want a gay guy being around me. It's got nothing to do with being scared. That's the problem: All these people say he's got all these rights. Yeah, he's got rights or whatever, but he shouldn't walk around proud. It's like he's rubbing it in our face. 'See me, hear me roar.' We're not trying to be close-minded, but then again, why be confrontational when you don't really have to be?"

The club responded that the remarks were "unfortunate" and Jones later apologized.

Mike Piazza. Piazza spent much of the 2002 season denying that he was a homosexual after rumors to that effect surface in the media. In a subsequent interview in *Playboy*, Piazza, who was dating Playmate Alicia Rickter at the time, said he always confesses to a priest after having sex.

Roger Angell. Angell wrote a hilarious article in the July 1, 2002, edition of *The New Yorker* around the time that Mike Piazza was forced to defend his sexuality. The article purported to be about a teammate of Babe Ruth who recounted with great nostalgia his romantic relationship with the Bambino. The Babe was devastated when he didn't get the part in "No, No, Nanette" (financed by the money Red Sox owner Harry Frazee obtained in the Ruth trade to the Yankees), and here's the reason: "Steroids. These were readily available in the early nineteen-twenties, in the form of breakfast food…. Babe went into a bit of a slump in the spring of '22 and, looking for a lift, downed a hundred and twenty-seven bowls of Weatnutz in one sitting. Typical Ruthean excess. By nightfall, his weight was up fourteen pounds and he'd turned contralto. The svelte Babe had gone forever, except at the ankles."

Julian Tavares. In April 28, 2001, the Cubs pitcher apologized to fans after making derogatory "faggot" remarks toward San Francisco fans. He was fined by the club, and over 2,000 gay Cubs fans appeared at a Cubs game on June 23, 2001, as part of a Gay Pride celebration.

Doug Funnel. Funnel is a gay baseball fan from Cleveland who has written over 5,000 letters to baseball players, front office executives and owners, trying to raise consciousness and a positive attitude about gays. He has received several positive written responses over the years, and occasionally some negative ones. For his Christmas card one year he had an actor dress up in a Kansas City Royals uniform and give him a kiss for the camera.

Brendan Lemon. In June 2001, the *Out* magazine editor wrote: "For the past year and a half, I have been having an affair with a pro baseball player from a major-league East Coast franchise, not his team's biggest star but a very recognizable media figure all the same. During this time, none of my friends has been privy to this liaison, a concealment that has been awkward at times but nothing in comparison to the maneuverings that my ballplayer has had to make. I am surprised that I have put up with this discretion requirement for so long. There is more than a little irony in the editor of the nation's largest-circulation gay magazine skulking around with someone so deep in the closet."

Billy Bean's response to the article was negative. He told Johnette Howard of *Newsday*: "I think it's easy to say those things when you're the editor of a gay and lesbian magazine. But if I were that ballplayer, I'd have cold sweats right now."

Sandy Koufax. Koufax cut ties with the Dodgers after a December 19, 2002, two-line gossip item in the *New York Post*, which was owned by the club's owner, Rupert Murdoch's News Corp.: "[The] Hall of Fame hero [had] cooperated with a best-selling biography only because the author promised to keep it secret that he is gay. The author kept her word, but big mouths at the publishing house can't keep from flapping."

Although Koufax was not specifically named, it came near the time of Jane Leavy's best-selling *Sandy Koufax: A Lefty's Legacy*, published in September 2002. Leavy's response called the report: "thoroughly erroneous on all counts. [The item] was blatantly unfair, scandalous and contemptible. It was thoroughly without basis insofar as it had to do with Sandy or any relationship I had with him professionally."

Koufax returned to Dodgertown during spring training in 2004 after Frank McCourt bought the club from Murdoch.

Movie Magic. In 2004 Indians pitcher Kaz Tadano confessed to a role in a gay porn video while he was in college. He appeared under the name Joel Foreskinner. Tadano said he was not a homosexual, but that he just needed the money. Bill Scheft in *Sports Illustrated* reported that it was not clear whether Tadano was "the setup man or the closer."

The Governor.

"It sure seems like a lot can happen when a governor admits he's gay."—Katherine Fraser Light.

In August 2004 New Jersey governor James E. McGreevey resigned after admitting his homosexuality and having propositioned a male worker on his staff. He made the announcement with his wife at his side. A few days later, minor league Atlantic City Surf announcer Greg Maiuro dedicated a between-innings rendition of the song "YMCA" to McGreevey during a game on August 17. The hit song by the Village People has long been associated with the gay community. The team fired Maiuro and then the governor asked that Maiuro be reinstated, indicating that an apology from Maiuro was sufficient. The night after Maiuro's antics, scoreboard operator Marco Cerino posted a message on the scoreboard, "Sponsored by Gov. Jim McGreevey," as the same song was played. Cerino resigned.

Harry Hooper (1887–1974)

Hall of Fame (VC) 1971

"A lucky combination of circumstances. One of the outfielders was hurt, and another had to go in and play first base because the first baseman was sick. They *had* to play me because they didn't have anybody else. Well, if I'd been ballyhooed as a wonder or something, I'd probably have been a little shaky. But the way it was, nobody expected anything of me, and I went out there determined to show them."—Hooper on his first Major League appearance, in which he drove in a run in his first at-bat; quoted in *The Glory of Their Times*, by Lawrence S. Ritter (1966).

Hooper was an outfield star for the Red Sox and White Sox from 1909 through 1925.

Harry Bartholomew Hooper graduated from St. Mary's College in California in 1907 with a degree in civil engineering and had no intention of playing baseball. He began playing in the California League in Sacramento only because he was promised a surveying job. Hooper signed with the Red Sox only two years later and never surveyed again.

He became a member of the "Million Dollar Outfield" with Tris Speaker and Duffy Lewis, playing right field for the Red Sox from 1909 through 1920. He hit .311 in 1911 and .312 in 1920, but never had more than 58 RBIs for the club. His value was in his all-around play and leadership. He helped lead the Red Sox to four world championships, batting .293, and hit two home runs in the 1915 Series.

Hooper moved on to the White Sox for the 1921 season, playing regularly until he retired after the 1925 season when owner Charles Comiskey reduced his salary. He batted .281 lifetime and had 2,466 hits over his 17-year career. He is credited with suggesting that Babe Ruth play regularly in the outfield.

After he quit he returned to California to capitalize on the real estate market and played 78 games with a Pacific Coast League club before retiring for good. He later coached at Princeton for two years and became a postmaster in California for over 25 years.

Book. Paul J. Zingg, *Harry Hooper: An American Baseball Life* (1993).

Rogers Hornsby (1896–1963)

Hall of Fame 1942

"If there had been a Pulitzer Prize for batting, Rogers Hornsby would have won several."—Howard Green, the youngest league president in Organized Baseball history.

"If consistency is a jewel, then Mr. Hornsby is a whole rope of pearls."—Sportswriter Joe Williams.

"He was frank to the point of cruelty and subtle as a belch."—Historian Lee Allen.

"But I'll tell you one guy nobody liked and that was our manager, Rogers Hornsby. Now there was a real p-r-i-c-k.... With Hornsby, except for his *Racing Forms*, there were no newspapers, no movies, no beer, nothing. Women and horses, that was his downfall."—1930s Browns pitcher Les Tietje.

"I've always played hard. If that's rough and tough, I can't help it. I don't believe there's any such thing as a good loser. I wouldn't sit down and play a game of cards with you right now without wanting to win. If I hadn't felt that way I wouldn't have got very far in baseball."—Hornsby.

Hornsby recorded the second-highest Major League batting average of all time with a .358 average over a 23-year career beginning in 1915.

The greatest right-handed hitter of all time, Rogers Hornsby ("The Rajah") began his professional career in 1914 in the Texas-Oklahoma League. He moved up to the Cardinals to play shortstop in 1915. By 1920 he was playing full-time at second base, where he remained with the Cardinals through the 1926 season. After single seasons as player-manager with the Giants and Cardinals in 1927 and 1928, the hard-nosed and often disagreeable Hornsby moved on to the Cubs from 1929 through 1932. After a brief stint with the Cardinals in 1933 he finished out the last five years of his 23-year career with the Browns as player-manager.

He won seven batting titles, including six in a row, with a modern high of .424 in 1924. He also batted over .400 in 1922 and 1925 to help him to a .358 lifetime average, second all-time behind Ty Cobb. Though only 5'11" and 175 pounds, he hit 301 home runs, including 42 in 1922 and 39 in 1925. He won the Triple Crown in both those seasons, with RBI totals of 152 and 143. He is seventh all-time with a .577 slugging average and finished with 2,930 hits in 2,259 games, while playing only 15 full seasons.

Hornsby managed a number of clubs between 1925 and 1953, though he won only one pennant, in 1926 with the Cardinals. In 15 seasons of managing, he finished third once and regularly finished in the second division. His difficult personality prompted this comment from Billy Herman, quoted in *Voices from Cooperstown*, by Anthony J. Connor (1982): "He was a real hard-nosed guy. He ran the clubhouse like a Gestapo camp. You couldn't smoke, drink a soft drink, eat a sandwich. Couldn't read a paper. When you walked in the clubhouse, you put your uniform on and got ready to play. That was *it*! No more kidding around, no joking, no laughing. He was dedicated to the game and made sure you were too. A very serious person. Tough guy to play for … a very odd person."

Hornsby also managed in the minor leagues and later coached in the Major Leagues, including a stint with the Mets in 1962.

Books. Charles C. Alexander, *Rogers Hornsby* (1995); Rogers Hornsby, *My Kind of Baseball* (1953); Rogers Hornsby and Bill Surface, *My War with Baseball* (1962).

Horse Racing

"Barney thinks he might as well try to lead an elephant to water with a cotton string as try to keep that gang of pony lovers in line when backed up against a race track."—1901 sports report about the Pirates and owner Barney Dreyfuss during spring training at Hot Springs, Arkansas. Dreyfuss often let his players give him money to bet at the track. If he lost, he supposedly returned their stake to them. If he won, they received all the profits.

"Yesterday I asked a player how he did at the track. He said, 'My horse won.' I said, 'How much did he pay?' The player said, 'No, coach. I didn't *bet* on the horse, I *own* it.'"—Mickey Vernon in 1985.

"You can't expect Mr. Ed to keep up with Secretariat."—Andy Van Slyke, on why the Pirates didn't catch the Mets one season.

"You can prepare a donkey to run in the Preakness, but he probably won't run very well."—Padres pitching coaching Greg Booker in 2003, considered the scapegoat for the failure of the Padres rotation to produce despite their Class AA credentials and collective short stints in the Majors in 2003.

"That's perfectly all right. Larry's in the business office. I'll crack down on anyone connected with the playing field who bets on horses."—Happy Chandler's weak response to reports that Yankees general manager Larry MacPhail had been playing the ponies. MacPhail engineered Chandler's surprise election as commissioner.

"They call me Seabiscuit now."—Brewers catcher Eddie Perez in 2003, after he scored from second on a wild pitch in a 4–3 win over the Mets [the movie of the same name came out that season, or otherwise there is a reasonable chance that Perez would never have known who Seabiscuit was].

"So's the stock market."—Rogers Hornsby, when told by Judge Landis to stop playing the horses because it was a form of gambling. St. Louis Browns owner Bill DeWitt arranged to have manager Hornsby's phone tapped to get information on his betting. Hornsby allegedly went so far as to have betting information delivered to him on the bench during games.

Hornsby once booked a $5 horse bet for umpire Cal Hubbard. Judge Landis found out about the bet and held Hubbard out of the 1937 World Series as punishment. Shortstop Jimmy Cooney recalled that Hornsby would read the racing form while Cardinals general manager Branch Rickey gave his pregame speeches.

Hornsby claimed that in 1943 he tried to pay off a $4,000 loan to the Browns owners that he had used to buy stock in the club. The club's owner, Don Barnes, and the general manager, Bill DeWitt, traced the check to a bookmaker after Hornsby acknowledged that he had won it betting the horses. According to Hornsby, they refused the money and fired him over the incident. The next year he managed Vera Cruz in the Mexican League.

Bill Dahlen. The turn-of-the-century shortstop was known to have himself deliberately ejected from games so that he could go to the racetrack.

Frank Navin. The long-time Tigers owner always took at least as many $1,000 bills to the racetrack as there were races on the card. He was known to bet as much as $25,000 on a single race. It is ironic that he was a confidante of and advisor to Judge Landis, who purportedly hated anything related to horse racing.

John "The Count" Montefusco. After he retired, the 1970s pitcher became a relatively successful harness racer.

John Galbreath. The Pirates owner once named a thoroughbred after Roberto Clemente. In 1972 the horse won the Epsom Derby, the most prestigious race in England.

Dick Allen. In 1969 Allen was suspended briefly for missing a game at Shea Stadium because he had a horse running at Monmouth Park in New Jersey. He later became a horse trainer and breeder.

Mitch "Wild Thing" Williams. The horse ranch owned by the erratic reliever and 1993 World Series goat was fittingly known as "3 & 2 Ranch."

Horse Races. See *Fastest Runners* for descriptions of races around the bases between players and horses.

Actor John Forsythe of "Dynasty" fame was the public address announcer for the Dodgers briefly during the 1940s. He once announced catcher Mickey Owen's race around the bases against a horse.

Triple Crown. Joe Medwick and War Admiral are the only Triple Crown winners in the same season, 1937.

Hot Dogs

"Nick Bierbrodt"—The perfect baseball food combination.

"There isn't enough mustard in the world to cover Reggie Jackson."—A's pitcher Darold Knowles.

"Yes, I am a hotdog. Look up all the baseball players who were ever called hotdogs. Every last one of those guys could play. You're not called a hotdog unless you *can* play. Unless you have style. Ever hear of a hotdog who couldn't play?"—Rickey Henderson in his book, *Off Base* (1992).

"A hot dog at the ball park is better than steak at the Ritz."—Humphrey Bogart.

"I regret that I can't sit in the stands and watch me."—Pitcher and playboy Bo Belinsky.

"A corked bat is a hollowed-out bat filled with cork, Styrofoam and ground up rubber balls. It's the same stuff they put in the hot dogs in Chicago."—David Letterman.

"Barry Bonds may land an endorsement deal with Amour Hot Dogs, according to the *Chicago Sun Times*. Whenever he pauses at the plate to admire his home run, it could be an Armour Hot Dog Moment."—Tom Fitzgerald.

Origins. Hot dogs originated in 1852 in Germany. Most sources credit Brooklyn vendor Charles Feltman with selling the first American hot dog on July 27, 1867.

Writer H.L. Mencken claims to have eaten "hot dogs" in his home town of Baltimore in 1896, long before an Irishman is said to have sold them at the Polo Grounds in New York. At least one source credits Christopher Von der Ahe, owner of the St. Louis Browns in the 1880s and 1890s, with introducing the hot dog at his ballpark.

Still others credit vendors at the 1893 Chicago World's Fair. *Concessionaire* Harry Stevens claimed to have introduced the hot dog at the Polo Grounds in the 1890s.

What is confirmed is that the first published use of the phrase "hot dog" was on August 12, 1906, in an article about Coney Island in the *New York Sun*. The phrase first appeared in a "Dorgan" cartoon on December 12, 1906. See also *Comic Strips and Cartoons*.

Confidence. Kyle Graham was a reliever for the Tigers in 1929. He had just bought a hot dog when he was told to go in and relieve against sluggers Mickey Cochrane, Al Simmons and Jimmie Foxx. His response to his bullpen teammates (as either a realist or a dreamer): "Leave this hot dog alone. I'll be right back."

Presidential Appetite. Lyndon Johnson once ate four hot dogs at an Opening Day game.

Big Eaters. Major League clubs use an average of 13,500 gallons of mustard and 9,800 gallons of relish during the season.

Alice Cooper. The rock star owned a restaurant, Alice Cooper'stown, in Phoenix, that featured a two-foot hot dog called the Big Unit (in honor of, uh, Randy Johnson). In an interview with *Sports Illustrated*, Cooper expressed dismay at not being inducted into the Rock and Roll Hall of Fame (still not in through 2004): "I'm think I'm being blackballed. But it's great to be the Pete Rose of rock and roll. I bet on my own bands."

No Sliding. Gates Brown was eating a hot dog at the end of the Tigers dugout during a game one day, when manager Mayo Smith told him to pinch hit. Not wanting to abandon his snack, Brown stuffed it inside his shirt and grabbed a bat: "Of all the times I didn't care if I got a hit, would you believe I hit one up the gap and had to go head first into second. When I got up, I had mustard and ketchup all over the front of my jersey."

Smith fined Brown $100.

Loss of Dignity. In 2003, when Rickey Henderson was playing for the minor league Newark Bears, he took part in a promotional race against people dressed up as oversized ketchup and mustard bottles.

Assault.

"They could have billed the race as the hot dog versus the condiments."—Steve Simmons of the *Toronto Sun*.

"It was the most spectacular baseball hot-dog incident since the A's Jason McDonald was knocked unconscious in 1998 when he collided with Rickey Henderson."—Janice Hough.

"The bratwurst, having lost three races in a row, has been sent down for more seasoning."—Columnist Scott Ostler.

On July 8, 2003, Pirates first baseman Randall Simon watched from the dugout a well-known Milwaukee Brewers promotion in which sausage and bratwurst mascots race around the field. As they passed him, Simon stuck out a bat and hit the bratwurst costume in the backside, worn by 18-year-old Mandy Block, a team employee. Block fell, but was uninjured. She was among four employees dressed as a bratwurst, a hot dog, and Italian and Polish sausages. Another employee dressed up like a sausage also fell, 21-year-old Veronica Piech. At their request, Simon presented them with signed bats.

The local sheriff's department cited Simon for disorderly conduct and fined him $432. Block took it in stride: "It wasn't that big of a blow. I think just because I'm so small and it's such a big costume that I tumbled, and the reason I couldn't get up right away is because I couldn't get up. I wasn't like I hurt so bad I couldn't get up. Luckily someone helped me up."

Commissioner Bud Selig was less forgiving: "Obviously, the type of behavior exhibited by Mr. Simon is anathema to the family entertainment that we are trying to provide in our ballparks and is wholly unacceptable."

Simon was suspended for three games and fined $2,000. Simon was traded a short time later to the Cubs. When the club visited Pittsburgh, 330 fans in a section behind first base received an Italian sausage courtesy of Simon.

The event was big enough to foster a David Letterman "Top 10" list of "Excuses of the Baseball Player Who Beat Up the Sausage." The list included "Looking to land a big endorsement deal with Jimmy Dean," "It was a Brewers-Pirates game. Somebody had to liven things up," and ""it's not whether you win or lose, it's how you blindside the opposing team's costumed racing mascot."

And finally, to beat a dead sausage out of its casing, weighing in from the National Hot Dog and Sausage Council, Josee Meehan said, "I think it probably raised awareness that there are all types of sausages out there."

Race. In June 1999 Pirate shortstop Pat Meares was recovering from hand surgery when he participated in a sausage race at Milwaukee County Stadium. Dressed as a 10-foot bratwurst, he beat a giant hot dog and Polish sausage. Two days earlier he had been caught on videotape sunbathing in the upper deck at Philadelphia's Veteran's Stadium during the first six innings of the game.

Inedible, but looking good, this hot dog sculpture made out of bats is on display at the Great American Ballpark in Cincinnati.

Hotel Rooms

"But the fullest, most expansive, most public talk is the talk in the lobby, baseball's second-favorite venue. The lobby is the park of talk; it is the enclosed place where the game is truly told, because told again and again. Each time it is played and replayed in the telling, the fable is refined, the nuances burnished the color of old silver."—A. Bartlett Giamatti in *Take Time for Paradise* (1989).

"Setting up the press headquarters before the American League playoffs in 1971, [A's owner Charlie] Finley decided on the Mark Hopkins in San Francisco, since the list of great hotels in Oakland has yet to get a first name on it."—Glenn Dickey in *The Jock Empire* (1974); Finley neglected to determine that the Mark Hopkins was the National League headquarters. Finley blamed the mistake on his public relations man, who soon quit.

"We are not sending him on the road because there are too many factors in the environment that we cannot control when you put him in a hotel on the road."—Columbus Clippers general manager Ken Schnacke on why Darryl Strawberry only played home games for the Yankee farm club.

"John Hilton, Ham Hyatt, Bill Marriott" See also **Roommates**.

Babe Ruth. Lefty Gomez once told a story involving Ruth when they were on an international barnstorming tour that included the Philippines. Ruth and his family were kept waiting in the lobby of the Manila Hotel for over an hour while the royal suite was prepared for them. According to Gomez, General Douglas MacArthur was asked to vacate the suite for the Ruths.

The Curse. Suite 818 of the Myles Standish Hall dormitory at Boston University was a hotel room where Babe Ruth usually slept when the Yankees played in Boston. It was occupied by five female students during the 2003 ALCS between the two clubs. One of the women, Lisa Kelly, was a confirmed Red Sox fan: "I'm praying that if I'm here and root hard enough and bring enough good Sox karma to the room that maybe this will be the year."

Henry Aaron. Late in his career Aaron always booked two rooms at a hotel. He booked one in his name, which was left empty, and one in the name of Bill Suber, which was a variation on the name of Aaron's second wife, Billye Suber. Another source (Aaron's autobiography) reported that in 1973 he registered as Victor Koplin. Koplin was the last name of one of Atlanta's office staff.

Directory. The baseball *Blue Book* provides an annual list of key hotels in Major League cities. Until recently many clubs listed their road hotels in their media guides.

House of David

"The Bearded Beauties"—Nickname for the House of David teams because of their trademark long beards.

The Israelite House of David was a communal colony established in 1903 at Benton Harbor, Michigan. The founder, King Benjamin Purnell, promised eternal life and an "overthrow" of the earth in 1999. In 1922 he was charged with taking "indecent liberties" with more than 100 underage girls among the sect. He disappeared, but four years later a female member of the group led police to a secret room at the colony where Purnell had been hiding. He died a short time later. At its peak there were over 1,000 members of the community. By the 1980s there were fewer than 100 members of the sect and no more than 15 remained by the 1990s.

By the 1920s the House of David became best known for its barnstorming baseball clubs. There were factional differences in the House, resulting in separate House of David teams that are often referred to interchangeably (but never part of Judaism).

The original House of David ballpark was completed in 1910. It was built primarily for Floyd Fitzsimmons' semipro "Speed Boys" (Fitzsimmons was Jack Dempsey's fight promoter) and the House of David used the ballpark when the Speed Boys were on the road.

The "Davidites" became a popular attraction and began traveling to play against Negro League clubs and others throughout the United States, Canada and northern Mexico. They often played close to 180 games each year. Because of better competition, the House of David was forced to pay outsiders to play on its clubs. Many of the Israelites received professional offers, including Dutch Faust, Dave Harrison and John Tucker.

Among the outside recruits, the most famous was Grover Cleveland Alexander, who played for the Israelites for three seasons and managed one of the clubs in 1933 and 1934. Satchel Paige also played a few games with the Israelites and once went on a two-month barnstorming tour featuring his Kansas City Monarchs against Alexander's House of David team. The Dean brothers, including third brother Goober, played briefly for the Israelites, as did Major Leaguers Sig Jakucki, Larry Jansen, Frank McCormick and Ossie Orwal. Female star Babe Didrikson Zaharias played two seasons for one of the teams. The teams often had tal-

ented players; one team beat the Cardinals in Sportsman's Park in 1931.

Various outlaw "House of David" impersonators grew beards or wore fake beards, causing the legitimate Israelites to bring suit, usually unsuccessfully (see also *Facial Hair*). When members entered in the military during World War II, they received special permission to retain their long hair and beards.

The House of David played several games in Cooperstown and was part of the centennial celebration held in July 1939. Its teams were phased out during World War II, but one barnstorming group revived in 1948 and continued to barnstorm until 1955. The last of the Israelite sports teams was the basketball squad that often played the Harlem Globetrotters. It disbanded in 1956, but one source credited the House of David basketball club with inspiring the Globetrotters' famous warm-up circle.

Houston Astros

National League 1962–

"Invented, along with the Mets, in the league expansion of 1962, they have consistently displayed a shabby competence that has kept them above New York in the standings every year, and has probably cost them the rich affection and attention generated by the Mets' anti-heroes."—Roger Angell in *The Summer Game* (1972).

"The Astros, by the way, haven't won a pennant during their 42 years of existence, were the first to inflict the scourge of AstroTurf upon the major leagues and initially named their new ballpark after Enron. As far as curses and cosmic comeuppances go, the Astros didn't need any additional kindling."—Mike Penner in the *Los Angeles Times*.

Origins. In the mid–1950s former Cardinals shortstop Marty Marion headed a group that paid $100,000 for the minor league club in Houston. They did so in the hope of eventually landing a Major League franchise in the city. They later sold out, however, to the group that eventually paid for the new National League franchise created for the 1962 season (see also *Expansion* and *Expansion Draft*).

The George Kirksey Story, by Campbell Titchener (1989), chronicles the sportswriter who worked the hardest to bring Major League Baseball to Houston.

First Game. On April 9, 1962, the Colt 45's beat the Cubs 11–2 as Bobby Shantz won in front of 25,271 fans. Ernie Banks hit his 299th home run.

Key Owners.

Judge Roy Hofheinz/1962–1970.

"He made P.T. Barnum look like 14 miles of bad road."—Hofheinz contemporary Willard Walbridge.

"Our fans are more like the ones they have out in California. We don't have any of those rowdies or semi-delinquents who follow the Mets."—Hofheinz in 1966.

"We combined baseball with a cocktail party."—Fred Hofheinz, son of owner Roy, on the Astros of the mid–1960s in the Astrodome.

Hofheinz was the original chairman of the board and president of the Houston Colt 45's. He passed the Texas bar at 19, was elected to the state legislature at 22 and became a judge at 24. At one time he was Lyndon Johnson's campaign manager, the mayor of Houston and the owner of the Ringling Bros. and Barnum & Bailey Circus. He served four terms as a county judge and two as Houston's mayor. Paul Richards was the club's first general manager, from 1961 through 1965, when Hofheinz fired him. Hofheinz feuded with his partner, oil magnate R. E. "Bob" Smith, causing Hofheinz to buy out Smith and take an 86% interest in the club.

In May 1970 Hofheinz suffered a stroke, which compounded his problems. The club was $30 million in debt because Hofheinz not only built the Astrodome, but a number of hotels and an entertainment complex in the nearby area. The debt load was horrendous and by the end of 1970 Hofheinz was bankrupt. He died in 1982 at age 70.

Creditors in Control/1970–1979. Miscellaneous creditors controlled the club during much of the 1970s, including the General Electric Credit Corporation and Ford Motor Credit Corporation. GE and Ford were the sole owners by the mid–1970s and Ford took over sole ownership in 1978.

John McMullen/1979–1992. In July 1979 McMullen and David LeFevre, a New York attorney, were the primary purchasers (among 25) of the Astros from Ford Motor Credit for about $19 million. The sale included the adjacent convention center and the lease on the Astrodome. McMullen had been a partner in the Yankees and was a New York resident. He made his fortune as a marine architect designing ships.

McMullen had a falling out with his partners in May 1980 when he fired general manager Tal Smith and hired Al Rosen. There was a shake-up in the ownership structure involving 17 minority owners, but McMullen remained in control. During the 1992 season, McMullen, who also owned the New Jersey Devils of the National Hockey League, completed the sale of the club to Texas businessman Drayton McLane, Jr.

Drayton McLane, Jr./1992– .

"He'd rather see the money go to charity than a second Mercedes for a bunch of ballplayers."—Astros vice-president Bob McClaren on owner Drayton McLane's frustration with the club's financial situation.

McLane, a graduate of Baylor University, took a small family grocery distributorship started by his grandfather in the 1890s and built it into a huge grocery chain. He sold out for $300 million to Wal-Mart owner Sam Walton in 1990. He is now a vice-chairman of Wal-Mart and in 1994 he was reported to be worth $400 million. By the end of 1995 he had lost $65 million since buying the club for $116 million from McMullen.

In 1995 McLane was in serious negotiations with Northern Virginia businessman Bill Collins. The asking price reportedly was over $150 million, but the negotiations stalled late in the year and McLane continued as the owner through 2004.

Nicknames.

"The Lastros"—Nickname given the team in 1992 when the club was stripped of all its quality players in an effort by management to cut costs and make the club more attractive to prospective buyers.

The club originally was known as the Colt 45's, but the name changed when they moved into the Astrodome in 1965. The name was changed because the Colt 45 gun manufacturing company would not allow its name to be used on novelties and other marketing items. Astros was derived from Astronauts because of Houston's connection with the NASA space program. The club was referred to as the 'Tros by sportswriters briefly after the name change. The club today is often referred to as the 'Stros.

Key Seasons.

1962. The Astros finished ahead of the Cubs and Mets with a 64–96 record in their inaugural season. The top hitter was outfielder Roman Mejias, who had 24 home runs and 76 RBIs.

1972. The Astros had their best finish through that season when they came in second to the Reds with an 84–69 record and scored the most runs in the league.

1979. Behind the pitching of J.R. Richard (18 wins) and Joe Niekro (league-leading 21 wins) the Astros finished second with an 89–73 record.

1980. The Astros led the division by three games with three to play against the Dodgers. The Dodgers won three straight to force a one-game *Play-Off*, which the Astros won to win the division. They lost to the Phillies in the deciding fifth game of the NLCS. Joe Niekro won 20 games and Jose Cruz batted .302 with 91 RBIs.

1981. The club won the second half of the strike-shortened split season, but lost to the Dodgers in the mini-playoffs to determine the division winner. Don Sutton and Nolan Ryan each won 11 games.

1984. The club finished tied for second with a record of 80–82.

1986. The Astros won the National League West with a 96–66 record behind the pitching of Mike Scott with 18 wins and a 2.22 ERA. They beat out the Reds by 10 games but lost to the Mets in a wild NLCS in which the Mets clinched the pennant in Game 6 with a 16-inning win.

1997. The Astros won the National League Central with an 84–78 record, but were swept by the Braves in the division series. Jeff Bagwell had 43 home runs and 135 RBIs. Craig Biggio batted .309 with 22 home runs and 81 RBIs. Darryl Kile was 19-7 and Billy Wagner had 23 saves.

1998. The Astros had perhaps their best season when they won the division with a 102–60 record, but once again lost in the division series, this time in four games to the Padres. Jeff Bagwell had 34 home runs and 111 RBIs, and Moises Alou had his best season with 38 home runs and 124 RBIs. Shane Reynolds led the team with 19 wins and Jose Lima won 16. Closer Billy Wagner saved 30 games while nursing a sore arm.

1999. The club won the division for the third straight season with a 97–65 record, but as usual lost in the division series, in four games to the Braves. Jeff Bagwell was stellar with 42 home runs and 126 RBIs, and Carl Everett had 25 home runs and 108 RBIs. Craig Biggio scored 123 runs and had 73 RBIs. Jose Lima had his best year with a 21–10 record, and Mike Hampton was an unbelievable 22–4 with a 2.90 ERA. Billy Wagner had 39 saves.

2001. After slipping to fourth place in 2000, the Astros returned to first with a 93–69 record, but in keeping with tradition they were swept in the division series by the Braves to continue their record of never having made it out of the first round of the play-offs. Jeff Bagwell continued his steady play with 39 home runs and 130 RBIs, and was joined this time by Lance Berkman with 34 home runs and 126 RBIs. Moises Alou had 27 home runs and 108 RBIs. Wade Miller led the staff with a 16–8 record, and both Roy Oswalt and Shane Reynolds won 14 games. Billy Wagner had another 39 saves.

2004. The Astros had a stellar second half and won the wild card spot by one game over the Giants. Jeff Kent, Craig Biggio, Jeff Bagwell and Lance Berkman each had between 24 and 30 home runs, and Kent (107) and Berkman (106) led the club in RBIs. Roger Clemens "un-retired" to win 18 games with a 2.98 ERA and Roy Oswalt won 20 games. Brad Lidge and Octavio Dotel combined for 44 saves. Against Atlanta in the division play-off, the Astros beat the Braves in the division series with a Game 5 cliff-hanger to win a postseason series for the first time in their history. They moved on to face the Cardinals in the NLCS, and were up 3–2 after five games, but the Cardinals came back to beat Roger Clemens in Game 7 and send the Astros home.

Key Players.

"The Astros are a curiosity, for they are a team without a star, present or past, unless one counts such mini-celebrities as Jimmy Wynn or Larry Dierker."—Roger Angell in *The Summer Game* (1972).

Joe Morgan (HF) played nine years for the Astros beginning in 1963. He became one of the premier second baseman in the league before being traded to the Reds for the 1972 season.

Larry Dierker was one of two good early Astros pitchers. He pitched in 13 seasons for the club beginning in 1964 and won 20 games in 1969.

Don Wilson was the other top Astros pitcher of the 1960s, winning 104 games over nine years beginning in 1966. He had two 16-win seasons, but committed *Suicide* in January 1975 at the age of 29 while still an active player.

Jimmy Wynn, nicknamed the Toy Cannon for his small but powerful build (5'10", 160 lbs.), hit 223 home runs for the Astros in 11 seasons beginning in 1963.

Doug Rader played third base for the Astros for nine seasons beginning in 1967. He hit over 20 home runs three times and anchored what was otherwise a mediocre infield. The sometimes irreverent and wild Rader was known as the Rooster for his red hair.

J.R. Richard was the most overpowering pitcher of the late 1970s. The 6'8" hurler won 20 games in 1976 to establish himself as one of the premier pitchers in the Major Leagues. He won 18 games in each of the next three seasons and led the league with over 300 strikeouts in 1978 and 1979. In mid–1980 he suffered a stroke and never returned to baseball, except for a brief attempt at the Senior Professional Baseball Association.

Jose Cruz was the most popular long-term player in the history of the Astros franchise. He played 13 seasons for the club beginning in 1975 and hit .300 or better six times.

Mike Scott was one of the best pitchers in the Major Leagues in the 1980s, pitching for the Astros for nine years from 1983 through 1991. He led the league with a 2.22 ERA in 1986 when he won 18 games and led the Astros to the National League West crown. The split-finger fastball pitcher won 20 games in 1989 to lead the league, but then faded with a sore arm.

Cesar Cedeno played 12 seasons for the Astros beginning in 1970. He was touted as a potential superstar but never quite made that level. He did lead the league in doubles twice, batted over .300 four times and stole 50 or more bases six times.

Craig Biggio began with the Astros in 1988 and was still going strong for the club in 2004. Through 2003 he had 2,461 hits, 210 home runs and 389 stolen bases. He had logged playing time at catcher (his original position), the outfield and at second base.

Jeff Bagwell began his Major League career with the Astros in 1991 and continued with the club into the 2004 season. He hit 419 home runs in 13 seasons through 2003 and drove in 1,421 runs.

Billy Wagner. In nine seasons beginning in 1995 Wagner saved 225 games before leaving for the Phillies after the 2003 season.

Key Managers.

Harry Walker led the club from early in the 1968 season to midway through the 1972 season. His best finishes were two fourth-place showings.

Bill Virdon managed the club beginning late in the 1975 season. He finished third in 1976 and 1977 and rose to second place in 1979 behind the pitching of J.R. Richard. The club won the National League West crown in 1980 in a play-off with the Dodgers, but lost to the Phillies in five games for the pennant. Houston won the second half of the 1981 strike-shortened split season, but lost to the Dodgers in the play-offs. Virdon was fired midway through the 1982 season.

Hal Lanier managed three seasons for the Astros beginning in 1986. He won a division crown in his first season, but the club dropped to third and then fifth before he was fired after the 1988 season.

Larry Dierker. Dierker came out of the broadcast booth in 1997 and led the club to four division titles in five years after the club had finished second three times under Terry Collins. Nevertheless, Dierker couldn't get past the first round in the playoffs and resigned after the 2001 season. See Larry Dierker, *This Ain't Brain Surgery: How to Win the Pennant Without Losing Your Mind* (2003).

Ballparks.

Colts Stadium. Colts Stadium preceded the Astrodome as the club's home from 1962 through 1964. The stadium was built quickly on South Main Street and had notoriously bad lighting. Its dimensions from left to right field were 360–420–360 and capacity was 32,000. It was later the site of the Astrodome's north parking lot. Two no-hitters were pitched in the park and it had a serious problem with *Insects*.

Astrodome. In 1965 the Astros moved into the *Astrodome*, the first indoor Major League ballpark.

Enron Field/Minute Maid Park. The new ballpark was originally to be called The Ballpark at Union Station, but a corporate sponsor was found before the facility opened.

Enron Field opened on April 7, 2000, with presidential candidate George W. Bush in attendance. The infamous Kenneth Lay of Enron threw out the first pitch in front of 41,583 fans as the Phillies beat the Astros 4–1. It had a $65 million retractable roof and featured a steam train that ran on tracks behind the left field wall. The outfield walls have 80 bends and the dimensions are generally from left to right 315–435–325. There is a 30-foot grass incline in center field (the league's deepest) and a flag pole that is in play. The Astros were allowed to violate the Major Leagues' minimum-distance rule by erecting a left-field fence only 315' from the plate, but with a 21-foot fence in left and seven- to nine-foot walls elsewhere. The ballpark seats 42,000 and has 59 luxury boxes. Construction costs came in under budget at $310 million, $248 million of which came from public funds.

After Enron fell from grace with its very public bankruptcy in 2001, the club temporarily named the park Astros Field until a new corporate sponsor could be found. The Astros paid Enron's bankruptcy trustee $1.2 million to get the name back. In mid–2002 Sunkist stepped forward and paid to have the stadium renamed Minute Maid Ballpark.

Key Broadcasters. Gene Elston was the first Voice of the Astros and remained with the club through 1986. He then went on to broadcast the CBS radio "Game of the Week" for 10 years. He had started with the Cubs in 1954 (through 1957) and also worked Mutual Broadcasting games. Joining Elston from 1962 through 1975 was Loel Passe. Long-time Phillies broadcaster Harry Kalas got his Major League start with the Astros between 1965 and 1970. After spending over 25 years with the Pirates, Bob Prince broadcast one year for the club in 1976.

Milo Hamilton joined the club in 1985 and remained through the 2004 season. Former pitcher Larry Dierker began in the broadcast booth in 1979 and remained there until 1996, when he took over as manager for five seasons. Bill Brown and Bill Worrell have been the television team since the mid–1980s, and former players Alan Ashby and Jim Deshaies have been with the broadcast team since the late 1990s. Former player Alex Trevino handles Spanish language broadcasts.

Books. Michael E. Goodman, *The History of the Houston Astros* (2002); Robert Reed and Rusty Staub, *A Six-Gun Salute: An Illustrated History of the Houston Colt .45s 1962–1964* (1999); Chris Sehnert, *Houston Astros* (1997).

Howe News Bureau (1910–)

This statistics service was founded by Irwin Howe in 1910 (or 1911) and later was operated by his son Fred. Howe tracked statistics as a hobby and decided to sell them to newspapers. His uncle, Elias Howe, invented the sewing machine but had the patent stolen from him by the founder of the Singer Sewing Machine company, Isaac M. Singer (see also **Hall of Fame—Origins**, for the connection between Singer's relative and the Hall).

Howe died in 1934, but his son Fred took over. By 1940 the bureau had 40 minor league subscribers and was the official statistician for the American League. By the 1990s Howe was known as Howe Sports Data International and was the statistician for all 17 minor leagues affiliated with the National Association, the independent Northern League, and all of the winter baseball leagues.

Waite Hoyt (1899–1984)

Hall of Fame (VC) 1969

"He was the best of the former athletes who went to the microphone, highly intelligent, industrious and a great story teller."— Hall of Fame broadcaster Red Barber on the Yankee pitcher and Reds broadcaster.

Hoyt pitched primarily for the Yankees in the 1920s and later became the most prominent former player to broadcast games.

Before starring for the Yankees in the 1920s, Hoyt first pitched professionally at age 16 in 1916. In early 1918 he tried out unsuccessfully with the Giants, whom he would beat in the 1921 World Series, but later in the year pitched one game for the club. He then played minor league ball until signing with the Red Sox in 1919. He was traded to the Yankees in December 1920 and won 19 games in 1921. His best seasons were 1927 and 1928, when he won 22 and 23 games for the club. He pitched in eight games for the Yankees in 1930 before being traded to the Tigers early in the season. He bounced around to various teams after the trade, with a best season of 15–6 in 1934 for the Pirates.

Hoyt won 237 games over 21 seasons, including 39 relief wins and 52 saves. He had an ERA of 3.59 and pitched 224 complete games. Hoyt pitched in 12 World Series games for the Yankees (11) and A's (1), winning six (all with the Yankees), with a World Series ERA of 1.83.

After retiring from the mound, Hoyt moved into the radio booth in 1939 for the Dodgers, broadcasting before and after the game. He moved to Cincinnati in 1941 and broadcast play-by-play for 25 years until his retirement in 1965. He was considered by many as the best former ballplayer of his era to broadcast Major League games (see also **Broadcasters** and **Rain Delays**).

Book. William A. Cook, *Waite Hoyt: A biography of the Yankees' Schoolboy Wonder* (2002).

Cal Hubbard (1900–1977)

Hall of Fame (VC) 1976

"There's no sense in both of us umpiring this game. The unfortunate part of the situation from your standpoint is that I'm being paid to stand behind the plate and umpire. You're not. You're only being paid to catch. One of us is obviously unnecessary and has to go. It breaks my heart to say so, but the guy who's gonna go is you."— Hubbard to Yogi Berra, prompting Berra to promise to keep his mouth shut.

"Boys, I'm one of those umpires that misses 'em every once in a while so if it's close, you'd better hit it."— Hubbard.

"Being an umpire wasn't such a tough job. You really have to understand only two things and that's maintaining discipline and knowing the rule book."— Hubbard.

Hubbard was an American League umpire from 1936 through 1951.

Future umpire Robert "Cal" Hubbard began his sports career playing as a nationally-recognized 6'2" tackle on the football teams at tiny Centenary and Geneva colleges. He went on to play professional football with the Giants and Packers from 1927 through 1933 and reportedly was the highest paid player in the game. After coaching football at Texas A&M, he began a full-time minor league umpiring career. He had been umpiring professionally during the football off-season.

After four years in the International League, he moved up to the American League in 1936. Over the next 15 years he umpired in four World Series and three All-Star Games. An eye injury forced him to retire in 1951, but he remained as off-field chief umpire for another 15 years. He was said to have 20–10 vision, better than even Ted Williams. Hubbard is the only man elected to the baseball, pro **Football** and college football Halls of Fame.

Book. Mary Bell Hubbard, *Strike 3—and You're Out!* (1976).

Carl Hubbell (1903–1988)

Hall of Fame 1947

"My own great pitcher, a southpaw, tall and elegant. Hub pitching: the loose motion; two slow, formal bows from the waist, glove and hands held almost in front of his face as he pivots, the long right leg (in long, peculiar pants) striding; and the ball, angling oddly, shooting past the batter. Hubbell walks gravely back to the bench, his pitching arm, as always, turned the wrong way round, with the palm out. Screwballer."— Roger Angell in *The Summer Game* (1972).

The screwball artist was considered one of the premier pitchers of all time when he won 20 or more games in five straight seasons during the 1930s.

Carl Owen Hubbell, an Oklahoma native, began his professional career in 1923. He later received a tryout with the Detroit farm system and signed for the 1926 season. The Tigers organization would not let him throw his **Screwball** because of the wear and tear on his arm. He made little progress in their farm system and never made a Major League appearance for the club.

Hubbell joined the Giants in 1928, winning 10 games in 20 appearances. Over the next four years he won between 14 and 18 games. In 1933 he exploded with five straight seasons of 21 or more victories and earned his nickname, "The Meal Ticket." His best season was 1933, when he won 23 games with a 1.66 ERA and 10 shutouts.

Hubbell's crowning moment was during the 1934 All-Star Game at the Polo Grounds when he struck out, in succession, Babe Ruth, Lou Gehrig, Jimmie Foxx, Al Simmons and Joe Cronin. Hubbell also pitched a no-hitter and once went 18 innings in a 1–0 victory without walking a batter.

The screwball eventually took its toll and after his fifth 20-game season Hubbell never won more than 13 games over the next six years. He ended his 16-year Major League career in 1943, winning 253 games exclusively for the Giants. He pitched 36 shutouts on his way to a lifetime ERA of 2.97. He also won four games in three World Series. After he retired, Hubbell eventually became director of the New York Giants farm system.

Miller Huggins (1879–1929)

Hall of Fame (VC) 1964

"Huggins was almost like a schoolmaster in the dugout. There was no goofing off. You watched the game, and you kept track not only of the score and the number of outs, but of the count on the batter. At any moment, Hug might ask you what the situation was." — Yankee pitcher Waite Hoyt.

After a 13-year playing career, Huggins led the Yankees to six pennants and three World Championships in the 1920s.

Miller James Huggins began his professional playing career in Ohio in 1899 under the name of Procter to protect his eligibility at the University of Cincinnati. After three years in St. Paul he joined the Cincinnati Reds in 1904, where he remained until 1909. The 5'6" infielder led the league in base on balls twice in those years and played a strong second base. He was traded to the Cardinals for the 1910–1916 seasons, finishing his 13-year career with a .265 average and nine home runs.

The "Mitey Mite" Huggins had become player-manager of the Cardinals in 1913, beginning the managing career that would lead him to the Hall of Fame. He guided the club to a third-place finish in 1914, its highest since joining the National League. He was hired away by the Yankees following the 1917 season, apparently after American League president Ban Johnson asked J.G. Taylor Spink of *The Sporting News* to approach him about the job.

Huggins began slowly with the Yankees, leading them to a fourth-place and two third-place finishes beginning in 1918. He then won three straight pennants in 1921–1923 and won the World Series on the third try. After finishing second and seventh in 1924 and 1925, the Yankees won pennants from 1926 through 1928 and won the Series the last two years. Huggins died late in the 1929 season while the club was in second place, from a skin condition known as erysipelas, caused by streptococci, which today is almost never fatal. Many claimed that the pressure of managing the Yankees and Babe Ruth, with whom he constantly feuded, was too much for the diminutive manager.

William Ambrose Hulbert (1832–1882)

Hulbert was the second **National League President** and the driving force in the formation of the **National League**.

Humor

Selected Books. Bill Adler, *Baseball Wit* (1986); Glenn Liebman, *Baseball Shorts: 1000 of the Game's Funniest One-Liners* (1994); Stan Lomax and Dave Stanley (eds.), *A Treasury of Baseball Humor* (1950); Tex Millard, *Cuttin' the Corners* (1966); Dan Morgan, *The Complete Baseball Jokebook* (1953); Kevin Nelson, *Baseball's Greatest Insults* (1984); F.S. Pearson, *Butchered Baseball* (1952); Michael J. Pellowski, *Baseball's Funniest People* (1997); Dick Schaap and Mort Gerberg (eds.), *Joy in Mudville: The Big Book of Baseball Humor* (1992); Fred Schwed, Jr., *How to Watch a Baseball Game* (1957); Ira L. Smith and H. Allen Smith, *Three Men on Third* (1951); Ira L. Smith and H. Allen Smith, *Low and Inside* (1949); Mike Whiteford, *How to Talk Baseball* (1983); Robert R. Whiting, *The Fat Mascot: 22 Wildly Funny Baseball Stories and More* (1987).

Jim "Catfish" Hunter (1946–1999)

Hall of Fame 1987

"We just gotta forget all this crap and go out there and play ball." — Hunter during the 1977 turmoil on the New York Yankees among Thurman Munson, Reggie Jackson and Billy Martin.

"A little girl who wears a Yankee cap and T-shirt lettered 'Catfood Hunter' has shown him her mimic routine and he likes it…" — Jerry Klinkowitz in *Short Season and Other Stories* (1988)

Hunter won 20 or more games five times on his way to 224 wins primarily in the 1970s.

James August Hunter grew up in North Carolina, where he threw five no-hitters (including one perfect game) as a high school pitcher before signing with the Kansas City A's for $75,000 in 1964. He made it to the Major Leagues without playing minor league ball. A hunting accident caused him to miss what would have been his first minor league season.

He was 8–8 as a rookie for the A's in 1965 and won between 9 and 13 games over the next four seasons. He pitched a perfect game against the Twins on May 8, 1968. In 1970 Hunter won 18 games and established himself as one of the premier pitchers in the game. He then rocketed to stardom by winning 21 or more games from 1971 through 1975. He peaked at 25 wins in 1974 and was declared a *Free Agent* when A's owner Charlie Finley failed to pay a portion of Hunter's insurance policy as had been agreed. Hunter became the highest paid player in history up to that time when he signed with the Yankees for what was worth $3.5 million spread over more than 15 years.

After winning 23 games for the Yankees in 1975 he dropped to 17 wins in 1976 and then arm trouble and diabetes ended his career at age 33 only three years later. He finished with 224 career wins, 42 shutouts and the 1974 Cy Young Award. He was a complete player, finishing three seasons without making an error and batting .226 lifetime (.350 in 1971). He also won five World Series games in 12 appearances, playing in three Series each with both the A's and Yankees.

Hunter was known for his control, good fastball and average curveball, regularly having a very good strikeout/walks ratio. After his retirement he worked for the Yankees part of the year and primarily worked his farm in North Carolina. He was diagnosed with Lou Gehrig's Disease in 1998 and died the following year.

Books. Catfish Hunter and Armen Keteyan, *Catfish — My Life in Baseball* (1988); Bill Libby, *Catfish — Million Dollar Pitcher* (1976).

Hurricane See **Weather**

"**I** is for Me,
Not a hard-sitting man,
But an outstanding all-time
Incurable fan."
—Ogden Nash.

Ice Baseball

"General Rules for the Game on Skates." — Section of the 1867 *DeWitt's Base Ball Guide*.

This form of baseball was played primarily in the 1860s and 1870s with its own rules to accommodate the ice, weather and skates. The first reported ice game on skates took place in 1861, when the Atlantic and Charter Oak clubs of Brooklyn faced off. At least 8,000 spectators witnessed the Atlantics' 20–9 victory. Powdered charcoal circles were used for bases. The ball was soft so it would not sting in the cold air and a runner was allowed to skate beyond the base/circle up to five feet.

In January 1885 the Brooklyn Atlantics played the New York Gothams on skates on a pond which had formed over a ballpark field.

Ice Skating See also *Hockey*

Lee Mazzilli. Though apparently not much of a hockey player, outfielder Lee Mazzilli won eight national speedskating championships.

Jackie Robinson. Dodger publicist Irving Rudd and his wife once went to the Catskill Mountains for a winter vacation with Jackie and Rachel Robinson. Robinson insisted that they ice skate, and then challenged Rudd to a race. Rudd had skated many times, but this was a first for Robinson, who flopped on his back on his initial attempt. By the end of the session, Robinson had beaten Rudd in a few races, despite falling several times.

Idols

"That's pretty good, considering Dave's previous idol was himself."—Willie Stargell on former teammate Dave Parker's statement that Stargell was his idol.

"I suppose I had forgotten how much I had idolized them. We go nuts over baseball stars when we are little boys; by the time we are teenagers our allegiance has switched to other folks—rock stars and the like—and we forget how much the baseball players meant to us. When I say 'we' and 'us,' I'm referring to my own generation; I really don't know if little boys today feel quite the same about the millionaire ballplayers with agents and financial advisers as we did about the men whose faces appeared on our Topps baseball cards."—Bob Greene.

Illegal Pitches/Substances

"Someday I expect to see a pitcher walk out to the mound with a utility belt on—file, chisel, screwdriver, glue…. He'll throw a ball to the plate with bolts attached to it."—Orioles pitching coach Ray Miller.

"I ain't never throwed an illegal pitch…. Just once in a while I used to toss one that ain't never been seen by this generation!"—Satchel Paige.

See also *Pine Tar* and *Spitballs*.

Early Debate.

"… all pitchers and infielders sewed emery paper on their gloves and you were a sissy if you didn't keep a man sized chew of tobacco in your mouth … when a new ball was put into the play the pitcher let the catcher's toss roll out to the second baseman or shortstop. Emery paper and tobacco juice had done a good job on the ball before it was tossed back to the pitcher who then worked on the seams.

"Nor was it unusual for a pitcher to scrape the cover with his spikes to give it grooves and cause it to wobble through the air. We often played five or six innings with one ball. And after two or three innings you thought you were hitting a rotten tomato."—Early 20th century second baseman Nap Lajoie on the tricks of the trade.

There was debate in the press at least by 1910 over whether to ban pitches using foreign substances. After the 1919 season Major League Baseball decided to curtail the use of such pitches, though an outright ban was not instituted until after the 1920 season and the death of Ray Chapman. He was struck in the head by a pitch, though his death was not the primary catalyst for the change. One direct result of Chapman's death, however, was that umpires made more of an effort to keep a clean ball in play to make it more visible to batters.

First Rule. Rule 8.02 was enacted on February 10, 1920, and outlawed the spitball and other "substance" pitches. A few recognized spitball pitchers were allowed to continue throwing the pitch for the duration of their careers. The rule prohibits a pitcher from having on his person or in his possession any slippery substance or anything with which to scuff or gouge the surface of the ball. The rule requires that: "The pitcher shall not: (1) apply a foreign substance of any kind to the ball or his glove; (2) expectorate either on the ball or his glove; (3) deface the ball in any manner; (4) deliver what is called the 'shine' ball, 'spit' ball, 'mud' ball, or 'emery' ball. The pitcher, of course, is allowed to rub the ball between his bare hands."

The commission to abolish trick pitches included National League president John Heydler, Cubs general manager Bill Veeck, Sr., National League umpire Hank O'Day, A's owner Connie Mack, Browns executive Bob Quinn, Senators owner Clark Griffith and Fred Lieb of the Baseball Writers Association.

Subsequent Rule. On May 16, 2003, Expos pitcher Zach Day was ejected for having glue on his finger. He claimed that it was there to protect against a newly developed blister. Under Rule 8.02(b), a pitcher is automatically ejected if he is found with any foreign substance on his fingers, and so Day had to go.

Slippery Elm.

"A mucilaginous demulcent made from the fragrant inner bark of the North American elm and used by American Indians as a scurvy preventive."—Dictionary definition of the stuff.

Prior to 1920 slippery elm was routinely chewed by spitball pitchers to help them keep up a good level of saliva. There is no evidence that scurvy increased among pitchers after the ban.

The Pitches.

"No, it's a hard slider."—Allison Perry, age five, asked if her father Gaylord threw a greaseball.

"Envious rivals insisted that the White Sox rode to the front on Cicotte's mysterious 'shine ball,' a delivery which blinded some of the greatest sluggers in the league. The 'jump ball' of Dave Danforth also served to clutter up President Johnson's desk with horsehide exhibits. Protests, strategy boards and chemical analysis, all failed and the riddle remains unsolved."—G.W. Axelson in "*Commy*" (1919).

Shine Ball. The shine ball describes pitches thrown with licorice, alum, tobacco juice or slippery elm saliva. The pitches were popular because of the visual distractions that pitchers could use to deceive batters into thinking they were applying a foreign substance to the ball. More modern substances are metamucil, hair tonic, vasoline and vaginal creams.

Mudball. Mudball is a generic term for pitches that curve because of the application of substances such as mud, beeswax, or fine cinders. The pitch became less popular because it was difficult to conceal these darker substances, though 1950s Yankee star Whitey Ford allegedly was an adherent of the mudball. Ford later admitted to building little mud pies around the mound to load up on the ball: "I used enough mud to build a dam." He also used a "gunk" ball, which combined baby oil, turpentine, and resin, which is what Yogi Berra once mistakenly used as his roll-on deodorant.

Emery ball. The emery ball required the surface of the ball to be roughened, usually with sandpaper, belt buckle, tack or steel phonograph needles. Russell Ford of the 1909–1913 Yankees among others, glued an emery board to the heel of his glove.

Talcum Powder Ball. Hod Eller, Eddie Cicotte and Chief Bender kept a bag of talcum in their pockets.

Soap. Ryne Duren of the Angels spread white soap flakes on his uniform and then applied them to balls.

Pine Tar. See *Pine Tar*—Use By Pitchers.

Enforcement.

1920. The penalty for violating the new ban on illegal substances was a 10-day suspension, a penalty still in effect. Shortly after the rule was enacted, umpire Bill Klem toured every spring training camp to explain the rule.

1962. Baseball ruled that a pitcher could not go to his mouth with his bare hand while on the mound. Exceptions now are allowed in cold weather, when pitchers may blow on their hands while on the mound.

1967. Baseball ruled that pitchers could blow on their hands while on the mound if both sides and the umpires agreed beforehand.

1968. The umpire became the "sole judge" for detection and enforcement and did not need approval from the league office. Reliever Phil "The Vulture" Regan of the Cubs was strongly suspected of throwing with foreign substances. He was searched many times during the 1968–1969 seasons and some of his pitches were called balls strictly based on their irregular flight, including one actually hit for a fly out.

On May 7, 1970, Regan came in to pitch against the Reds at Wrigley Field. Umpire Chris Pelekoudas searched everything on Regan and the pitcher objected to the "thoroughness" of the search. National League president Warren Giles found him innocent and less vigorous searches were used after that incident.

1974. Umpires were given even greater control over illegal substances. They could enforce penalties up to ejection and it was made easier for them to discipline pitchers. Previously, umpires were required to catch the pitcher applying the substance. The new rule allowed the umpire to impose punishment if he believed that a ball acted erratically based on the application of any foreign substance (regardless of whether he found the substance).

1980. The enforcement procedures were changed again. Umpires were now to ensure that each inning starts with an unscuffed ball. If the umpire sees a scuffed ball, he can search the pitcher or warn him, or both, and keep the ball. A second such ball can result in an ejection and an automatic 10-day suspension.

Pitchers Caught.

"That's not fair. Pascual [Perez] *is* a foreign substance." — Expos publicist Richard Griffin, after Dodger manager Tommy Lasorda asked the umpires to search the Dominican right-hander for foreign substances.

"If you can cheat, I wouldn't wait one pitch longer." — Pitching coach George Bamberger to a struggling Ross Grimsley in 1975.

Joe Niekro.

"I like to give pedicures to ballboys." — One of Niekro's Top 10 Reasons Why He Had An Emery Board In His Pocket, on David Letterman's show.

"The guy was so blatant. It was like a guy walking down the street carrying a bottle of booze during Prohibition." — Umpire Steve Palermo, who was at second base during a game in which Joe Niekro was caught with sandpaper in his pocket. As umpires approached, he reached into his pocket quickly and flipped out the sandpaper. Cameras caught it flying onto the ground as Niekro

concealed the motion by throwing his hands in the air in mock exasperation at being "frisked" once again.

Ted Lyons. The White Sox pitcher threw pitches so erratically from 1923 through 1946 that he was accused of doctoring balls with Mexican jumping beans. A few of the allegedly offending balls were sent to the American League office and cut in half. Nothing improper was found.

Don Sutton.

"Not true at all. Vaseline is manufactured right here in the United States." — Sutton, about the rumors that he used a foreign substance on the ball.

"You're getting warm. But it's not there." — Note left for umpires in Sutton's glove.

The Dodger pitcher often was accused of throwing scuffed balls. In one game, umpire Doug Harvey collected three allegedly scuffed balls and ejected Sutton. The National League withdrew a proposed suspension when Sutton threatened to take the league to court to obtain a restraining order prohibiting the suspension.

Rick Honeycutt. Near the end of the 1980 season, Mariners pitcher Rick Honeycutt was caught with an orange band-aid on his finger with a thumb tack sticking out. When umpires arrived on the mound they saw blood on his forehead, the result of Honeycutt absentmindedly scratching his head with the thumbtack finger. Honeycutt was given a 10-day suspension, which was not imposed until the first 10 days of the 1981 season; by that time he was with the Rangers. Ironically, he was caught by umpire Bill Kunkel, a former Major League pitcher who frequently was accused of using a spitball.

Kevin Gross. The Cubs pitcher was suspended for 10 days after getting caught for using sandpaper during a game on August 10, 1987. Three years later he called the commissioner's office and asked for his confiscated glove back.

Tim Leary. In June 1992 the Yankee pitcher appeared to put a piece of sandpaper in his mouth when confronted by the umpires. The umpires missed it, but it was picked up by the television cameras. Nevertheless, he was acquitted of any wrongdoing by the American League office.

Brian Moehler. On May 1, 1999, the Tigers pitcher was ejected from a game against the Devil Rays after umpire Larry Barnett found sandpaper taped to Moehler's thumb on his pitching hand. Moehler said it was dirt. He was suspended for 10 games.

Byung-Hyun Kim. On June 9, 1999, the Diamondbacks pitcher, recently called up by Arizona, was ejected from a game after a bandage containing heat balm flew out of his shirt sleeve. He claimed that he used the heat balm in Korea and forgot to take it out of his shirt before entering the game.

Cooking/Freezing Balls.

"You had to wipe the mildew off the balls before the game. First you'd take them out of the boxes, which were all rotted away anyway, wipe the mildew off and put them in new boxes. Then you gave them to the umpires and they never suspected a thing." — Jerry McNertney on manager Eddie Stanky and the White Sox of the mid–1960s. Stanky froze the balls to deaden them in support of his good pitching/poor hitting team.

Connie Mack's A's and the 1920s Pirates froze balls. The Pirates kept an icebox in their offices to freeze the balls overnight. Phillies manager Art Fletcher admitted in 1925 that the club had frozen the balls used in a two-hitter by pitcher Johnny Cooney. The 1890s Orioles may have cooked their balls in an oven to make them livelier.

Tricks of the Trade.

"I reckon I tried everything on the old apple but salt and pepper and chocolate sauce topping." — Gaylord Perry, who would try to psyche out opposing players by shaking hands with grease on his palm and fingers. Perry always claimed that he had Reggie Jackson so psyched out that he never needed to throw the spitter.

Eddie Cicotte. The Black Sox pitcher put transparent paraffin on his fingers to smooth out the ball. He also threw an emery ball.

Leo Durocher. The shortstop filed his belt buckle and scored the ball with it when it was thrown around the infield.

Don Drysdale. Dodger coach Preston Gomez later said that Drysdale used surgical jelly during his 1968 *Scoreless Innings* streak. He allegedly hid the stuff in a different spot each inning, including his hat, glove and body. Umpire Augie Donatelli once was so frustrated with Don Drysdale that he yanked off Drysdale's cap and grabbed his hair. After claiming that he had found grease, Donatelli ordered Drysdale to wash his hair between innings, but he was not ejected.

Whitey Ford. Ford had a rasp installed on his wedding ring so that he could use it to scuff the ball.

Marketing. In 1994 Gaylord Perry began marketing a jar of petroleum jelly for $39. The jars bore Perry's autograph and were numbered 1 through 3,534, his lifetime strikeout total.

Survey. In an informal survey conducted one year by pitcher and *Ball Four* writer Jim Bouton, 87% of all pitchers reported cheating in some fashion.

Movie.

"He reached up and grabbed the bottle. A larger one started to topple off the crowded shelf and he juggled the two bottles with his slippery wet hands. Vernon watched in agonized horror, involuntarily reaching out. But it was too late. The little bottle slipped from Dolan's hand and fell into the basin with a crash. Vernon stood there, dumb and helpless, watching the World Series running down the drain." — From *It Happens Every Spring*, by Valentine Davies (1949), made into a movie starring Ray Milland; he creates a substance that avoids wood and was a pitcher's dream.

Books. Dan Gutman, *It Ain't Cheatin' If You Don't Get Caught* (1990); Martin Quigley, *The Crooked Pitch* (1988).

Illegal Substances See *Drugs and Drug Abuse* and *Illegal Pitches/Substances*

Illness See *Injuries and Illness*

Incentive Clauses See *Bonuses and Incentive Clauses*

Income and Expenses See *Profits, Losses and Expenses*

Indianapolis

"No city is as reviled by our readers as the friendly Midwestern burg of Indianapolis." — *Forbes*.com on the lack of nightlife for singles (presumably including most ballplayers).

This city had Major League clubs in the National League (1878 and 1887–1889), American Association (1884) and Federal League (1914).

Indianapolis Hoosiers

American Association 1884

The Hoosiers were one of the doormats of the Association, finishing near the bottom of the pack with a 29–78 record.

Indianapolis Hoosiers

National League 1878, 1887–1889

"Milwaukee and Indianapolis folded, the owner of the latter team losing so much money that he was forced to flee the state to escape his creditors. A good portion of his debt had been incurred before the start of the season on his trip to Canada, from which he returned with most of the talent on the Guelph (Ontario) Maple Leafs of the IA." — Ted Vincent in *Mudville's Revenge* (1981).

1878. As a result of National League franchise failures in Hartford and St. Louis, the league placed a team in Indianapolis. Indianapolis had been an independent club and the National League ruled that it would accept independents who were the best of the group after beating other independents. The club finished the season with a 24–36 record behind the pitching of The Only Nolan. After that single season, the team folded.

1887–1889. Future Reds and Giants owner John T. Brush owned this club, which finished last in 1887 with a 37–89 record. The club finished seventh the following two seasons before dropping out of the league.

Indianapolis Hoosiers

Federal League 1914

"HooFeds" — The team's nickname.

The Hoosiers won the 1914 Federal League pennant with a record of 88–65. The club featured Benny Kauff in the outfield with a .370 average. The club also featured former National Leaguers Edd Roush and Bill McKechnie. Though the club did well in the standings, it did poorly at the gate. After the season, the Federal League shifted the franchise to New Jersey for new owner and oil tycoon Harry Sinclair, the wealthiest baseball man in any Major League. Kauff was shipped to the Brooklyn Tip-Tops.

Indians See *Native Americans*

Indoor Ballparks

"I got started too early in baseball. In air conditioning I could have lasted 20 years longer." — Stan Musial.

See also *Artificial Turf, Astrodome* and *Ballparks*.

Indoor Ballparks/Opening Dates.

Houston Astrodome (April 12, 1965)

Seattle Kingdome (April 6, 1977)

Stade Olympique (Olympic Stadium), Montreal (April 15, 1977 for baseball; 1976 for the Olympic Games)

Minnesota Metrodome (April 6, 1982)

Toronto Skydome (June 5, 1989) (retractable)

Bank One Ballpark, Phoenix (March 31, 1998) (retractable)

Tropicana Field, Tampa Bay (March 31, 1998) (all-dirt basepaths, first time in 20 years in the Major Leagues)

Seattle Kingdome (April 6, 1977)

Minute Maid Ballpark, Houston (April 7, 2000) (retractable three-section roof)

First World Series Game. The first World Series game played indoors was on October 17, 1987, when the Twins hosted the Cardinals in the Metrodome.

Speaker/Catwalk Problems.

"I hit one that far once. I did. And I still bogeyed the hole." — Ron Fairly on a Mike Schmidt home run off the Astrodome speakers in 1973.

Seattle. In 1979 Mariners slugger Willie Horton hit what looked to be his 300th home run in the Seattle Kingdome. The ball struck a low speaker in the outfield and dropped in for a hit. Horton hit number 300 the next night and the speakers were soon raised.

Ruppert Jones and Rickey Nelson both hit balls that lodged in the facility's speakers.

Philadelphia. On June 10, 1974, Mike Schmidt of the Phillies hit a drive off a speaker located in fair territory. It was ruled in play and the hit was only a long single. The speaker was 117 feet off the ground and 329 feet from home plate. Neither runner on base scored.

Montreal. On May 5, 1992, outfielder Larry Walker of the Expos hit a ball in Olympic Stadium that struck a speaker. The ballpark's ground rules required that it be called a home run. In 1995 Matt Williams became the only player to hit a ball off the Expos roof. It dropped down and was caught for an out.

On May 26, 1996, the Dodgers were up 4–1 in the bottom of the 9th inning of a game against the Expos in Montreal, having scored four runs in the top of the inning. With two on and no out, Expos batter Henry Rodriguez popped a foul ball that was easily catchable by the third baseman. However, the ball hit a speaker suspended from the roof and the ball was called dead. Rodriguez then singled to load the bases. The Expos scored twice but the Dodgers held on to win 4–3.

Minnesota. Balls hit by Dave Kingman and Alvaro Espinoza lodged in the facility's infrastructure. Kingman's got stuck in a drainage valve and Espinoza's lodged in an overhead speaker.

On May 29, 1992, Rob Deer hit two balls off the Metrodome roof (200 feet up) in back-to-back at-bats.

Tampa Bay. On June 28, 2002, Kevin Millar of the Marlins hit a high fly ball that landed in one of the catwalks that hangs from the stadium's dome. It never came down and was ruled a double. In 1999, Jose Canseco hit a home run that lodged in the same section.

Roof Problems.

Minnesota.

"The worst wedding of two white things since Lisa Marie [Presley] married Michael [Jackson]."— Steve Rushin on the Twins' white-ceiling Metrodome when a high pop fly heads its way.

On May 4, 1984, Dave Kingman hit a pop-up that went through a hole in the fabric of the Minnesota Metrodome's soft roof. The next night the Twins arranged for a ball to be dropped from the same spot in the roof. Mickey Hatcher was to catch the ball and step on first for the "out" call by the umpire and Kingman was to rush out to protest. Unfortunately, Hatcher lost track of the ball, it hit him on the thigh and he required medical attention.

On April 26, 1986, the Twins led the Angels 6–1 in the 9th inning at the Metrodome. High winds then blew a hole in the roof, which caused a 10-minute delay. When play resumed, the Angels scored six runs and won 7–6.

Montreal. Montreal's retractable roof could not be moved if winds exceeded 25 mph. On occasion the club suffered through rain delays because it was not able to move the roof in time. On August 29, 1986, the $117 million roof caught fire, postponing the game.

On May 19, 1998, the Expos played their first game without their roof, which had been removed on May 10 because of several tears and instability. Plans were made to install a new permanent roof after the season. It was the first outdoor game played at the stadium since 1991. In January 1999 a fiberglass panel fell from the roof and injured five people during the setup for an auto show at the facility.

Toronto. On June 7, 1989, the Blue Jays closed the Skydome's retractable roof during a game for the first time. The game started under the sky, but with dark clouds and thunder in the distance the roof was closed—a process that took 34 minutes (see also *Rainouts*).

On June 22, 1995, roof tiles from the Skydome fell during a game, injuring 30 fans. The most seriously injured was a teenaged woman who had cuts on her head. Inspectors pronounced the ceiling tiles safe after the 30-pound panels were reinforced.

On July 9, 1995, a worker installing lights for a computer trade show died after falling 25 feet from a scaffold in the Skydome. The worker was the fourth to die at the Skydome since it opened in June 1989. In November 1989 a worker was killed and another seriously injured in a fall while both were working on the roof. A month later two men washing windows died after falling more than 30 feet when a cherry-picker tipped over. In August 1991 a fan died after plunging more than 90 feet after leaving a Blue Jays game. It was believed that he had been jumping between ramps.

Seattle. On July 19, 1994, four 15-pound acoustic tiles dropped 180 feet from the Kingdome ceiling into choice seats behind home plate. The incident occurred several hours before the game that night and forced a postponement. A few days later two workmen were killed when their crane broke while removing defective tiles. The facility was closed through the strike date of August 12.

The Mariners tried to play their remaining pre-strike games at Tacoma's Cheney Stadium, but the players' union and the American League vetoed the move. The club played its games on the road in the interim. There was speculation that a $6 million renovation of the exterior of the roof in the spring had loosened the tiles. The ceiling spans seven acres and contains 80,000 wood fiber tiles, each one about three feet by four feet and held in place by metal frames.

Recent Costs/Roof. Retractable roof stadium costs:

$400 million — 2001 Milwaukee
$250 million — 2000 Houston
$525 million — 1999 Seattle
$319 million — 1998 Phoenix

Air Conditioning.

"This is a tough park for a hitter when the air conditioning is blowing in."— Bob Boone on the Astrodome.

Minnesota Metrodome maintenance superintendent Dick Ericson admitted to adjusting the ventilation system during the late innings of close games in an attempt to get baseballs to carry farther. He worked for the Twins from 1982 until he retired in 1995. The Twins won World Series titles in 1987 and 1991.

Shea Stadium. Shea Stadium was originally proposed to have a dome, but engineers determined that the foundations would not support the additional weight of the dome.

First Indoor Baseball Game. The first indoor ballgame was played in 1888 on Christmas Day in Philadelphia. The Downtowners defeated the Uptowners 6–1 in the State Fairgrounds Building.

In 1891 the Giants scheduled regular season games indoors at Madison Square Garden, but the games were never played there.

Early Indoor Baseball.

"[The Diamond] is more like a sheet of plate glass than a field of greensward. The bases have the unpardonable tendency to slide themselves when the runner throws himself upon them with some force…. [Spectators] "set up a howl of satisfaction at the result."— The *Utica Daily Press*, as reported by researcher Scott Fiesthumel, on the indoor baseball played in the late 19th and early 20th centuries.

Between 1897 and 1902 the Utica Indoor Baseball league flourished, based on early rules created by Chicagoan George Hancock, who invented the precursor to modern *Softball*. The playing surface had to be at least 40 feet by 60 feet and the balls were softball and larger: about 17 to 18 inches in circumference (present day softballs are 12 inches). Bats were undersized but the basic rules were otherwise the same as for regular baseball. The balls in Chicago most likely led to the game of Pillow Ball, which is still played in parts of Chicago using a larger, softball ball, pitched underhanded, and players do not wear gloves.

Japan. The Tokyo Dome, built in 1988, was Japan's first indoor ballpark.

Infield Covers See *Tarpaulins*

Infield Fly Rule

"Herndon seems to be bothered by insects at the plate. I don't know what species it is. Maybe it's an infield fly." — Broadcaster Hank Greenwald.

"I'll write about the Infield Fly Rule." — Red Smith when the *New York Times* killed his story advocating a boycott of the 1980 Moscow Olympics after the Soviet Union invaded Afghanistan.

Rule. The Infield Fly Rule was created in 1895 (1893 or 1894 in some sources). The rule applies when a team has fewer than two outs and runners on first and second or the bases are loaded. If the batter hits a pop-up in or near the infield which the umpire in his discretion believes can be caught easily, the batter is automatically out. This prevents a fielder from intentionally dropping the ball and making a double play.

The rule was initially applied when there was only one out, but for the 1901 season it was expanded to include none out. The rule first applied only to infielders, but was later expanded to include all fielders who may be near the infield to make a catch.

Non-Call. On September 1, 2000, the Orioles turned the season's fifth triple play on a disputed non-call of an infield pop-up at Jacobs Field. On a pop to short with no outs and runners on first and second, Orioles shortstop Melvin Mora let Sandy Alomar's ball drop, apparently intentionally, and started the triple play. The infield fly rule was not called. Indians manager Charlie Manuel was thrown out of the game for arguing, but Cleveland came back to win 5–2.

Infielders

"We have a Stonehenge defense. There have never been four such immobile infielders in the Boston infield." — Bob Ryan on the 1994 Red Sox.

"Rocky [Bridges] was a shortstop and second baseman by trade, a third baseman out of desperation and a left fielder for a third of an inning." — Jim Bouton in "*I Managed Good, But Boy Did They Play Bad*," by Bouton with Neil Offen (1990).

"I can play anywhere in the infield as long as the darned ball doesn't come to me." — Outfielder Kirby Puckett after playing second, third and shortstop in an extra-inning game.

See also entries by position and *Double Plays*.

Longest Together. The longest-playing infield was the Dodgers' of 1973–1981: Steve Garvey (1B), Davey Lopes (2B), Bill Russell (SS) and Ron Cey (3B). The Dodger quartet first played together as a unit on June 13, 1973, in a 16–3 loss to the Phillies. Their last game together was during the 1981 World Series against the Yankees. Lopes was traded after the season.

The Chicago White Stockings of 1883–1889 had an infield of Cap Anson (1B), Fred Pfeffer (2B), Tom Burns (SS) and Ned Williamson (3B).

Best Hitting. The greatest hitting infield arguably was the 1934 Tigers. Sportswriter Charles P. Ward dubbed the Tigers infield "the Battalion of Death." The four were Hank Greenberg at first base, Charlie Gehringer at second, Billy Rogell at shortstop and Marv Owen at third base. They played together from 1933 through 1937 and combined for a record 462 RBIs in 1934. In 1984 Owen designed and ordered commemorative Louisville Slugger bats for each member and had the RBI records for them all inscribed on the bats. The breakdown of the 1934 group and other top-hitting infields:

1B	139	Hank Greenberg
2B	127	Charlie Gehringer
SS	100	Billy Rogell
3B	96	Marv Owen

The 1948 Indians infield had 432 RBIs:

1B	83	Eddie Robinson
2B	124	Joe Gordon
SS	106	Lou Boudreau
3B	119	Ken Keltner

The 1936 Yankees had 409 RBIs:

1B	152	Lou Gehrig
2B	109	Tony Lazzeri
SS	78	Frank Crosetti
3B	70	Red Rolfe

The 1986 Tigers infielders all hit 20 or more home runs:

1B	29	Darrell Evans
2B	20	Lou Whitaker
SS	21	Alan Trammell
3B	20	Darnell Coles

Catcher Lance Parrish (22) and outfielder Kirk Gibson (28) also hit more than 20 home runs each.

Infields and Dirt

"You're standing on two tons of dirt. Why don't you rub some of it on the ball?" — Mets manager Casey Stengel to pitcher Roger Craig after Craig was having trouble holding onto the ball.

"This column is a tribute to baseball's unbroken connection to earth. Baseball remains the only American sport that has not dispensed altogether, in any arena, with American soil … and even the most thoroughly carpeted parks have patches of high-grade dirt at home plate and the mound, for pitchers and catchers and hitters to root in, and at the bases for runners to slide in." — Roy Blount, Jr.

"Everybody likes it different. Some like it soft. Some like it firm. Some like it wet. Some like it dry. So it's, you know, you try and satisfy everybody." — Pete Flynn, head groundskeeper at Shea Stadium.

See also *Artificial Turf, Bases* and *Fields and Field Dimensions*.

Dirt. The Partac Peat Company supplies dirt to at least nine Major League clubs and can match any color the team desires. The company uses separate mixes for the batter's box, the coaching boxes, the pitching mound and the infield. Dirt is pulverized, ground up and shredded, and then sand is added so that it will drain well.

Drainage. Infields are slightly raised in the center (sloping up to the pitcher's mound) to promote good drainage. For example, Wrigley Field's infield slopes four inches from the edge of the pitcher's mound to the edge of the infield dirt. The outfielder slopes 10 inches to each foul pole.

Yankee Stadium. Before Yankee Stadium was renovated in the mid–1970s, located under second base was a 15-foot deep vault containing electrical equipment for events such as boxing and concerts.

Injuries and Illness

"My goals are to hit .300, score 100 runs, and stay injury-prone."—Mickey Rivers.

"Once upon a time, you spit on a cut and rubbed a bruise. Now, if you don't feel perfect, a battery of trainers, doctors and masseurs try to decide whether you need diathermy, deep heat, whirlpool, ice, massage, ultrasound, acupuncture, cortisone, hypnotism or an L.A. shrink."—Thomas Boswell in *The Heart of the Order* (1989).

"The Human Virus"—*Sports Illustrated* writer Rick Telander on perennial malcontent Albert Belle.

"No sanitary measure that can be adopted … is so calculated to induce that healthy condition of the system which acts as a barrier to the progress of this disease as base ball exercises every afternoon."—Recommended cure for an 1886 cholera outbreak.

"Rick Folkers is throwing up in the bullpen."—Jerry Coleman.

"Ed Head, Dave Brain, No Neck Williams, Roy Face, Harry Cheek, Tom Lipp, Lip Pike, Don Gullett, Camp Skinner, Jimmy Bloodworth, Mike Overy, Bill Hart, Wes Livergood, Ribs Raney, Limb McHenry, Ed Armbrister, One Arm Daily, Mike Palm, Bill Hands, Rich Hand, Three Finger Brown, Pinky Higgins, Rollie Fingers, Butts Wagner, Heinie Meine, Jim Bottomley, Johnny Dickshot, Jack Glasscock, Doug McWeeny, Bones Ely, Buck Marrow, Ralph Shinners, Footsie Blair, Barry Foote, Sixto Lezcano, Arch Reilly, Arch McCarthy, Eddie Sicking, Dave Ricketts, Gary Serum, Cotton Nash, Charlie Chart"

See also ***All-Star Game*—Injuries, *Amputees*, *Beanballs*, *Birth Defects*, *Conditioning*, *Deaf Ballplayers*, *Deaths*, *Disabled List*, *Eyesight*, *Freak Accidents*, *Medical Treatment*** and ***World War II*—Injuries**.

The Baseball Encyclopedia. The 1969 inaugural edition of *The Baseball Encyclopedia* contained information on significant player injuries and illnesses (as well as suspensions and military duty). This helped to explain gaps in players' career statistics. These listings were discontinued for the second edition in 1974 and never reappeared.

Lost Salary. Injuries often were more catastrophic for early players, not only because of the lack of medical knowledge, but because early teams and leagues required players to play in order to get paid. Some clubs, including the Cleveland club of the 1890s, paid injured players. John McGraw was paid $1,200 after he went out with typhoid fever. However, the standard player contract of the era provided that the risk fell on the player: "All risk of accident or injury, in play or otherwise, and of illness from whatever cause, [is assumed by the player, and he] had no claim to wages."

Jackie Robinson showing off his fielding skills before Game 2 of the 1949 World Series at Yankee Stadium. Note the chalk "baselines" from first base heading toward second.

Clubs also required players to be examined at the player's expense, and it was within the club's discretion to determine if a player was hurt or not. In 1912 the National Commission declared that an injury would not cause a player to forfeit his salary.

Baseball versus Cricket. In an 1881 article in the *New York Times*, the writer editorialized against baseball and in favor of cricket because of the alleged number of baseball injuries. The writer claimed the following unsubstantiated average figures over the previous 10 years:

37,518 injuries, 5% of which were fatal

25,611 finger injuries

11,016 eye injuries

More Frequent Injuries.

"The answer is, there aren't more injuries. It just seems that way because today, through radio, television, and a different reporting attitude, the fan hears all about every injury, sometimes *ad nauseam*. In the old days, not only were injuries to familiar players less documented, but no one was aware of how many careers ended prematurely, before the player in question became familiar. Today, many players are kept going, and some thoroughly repaired, who simply would have had to quit under the conditions of two generations ago."—Leonard Koppett in *A Thinking Man's Guide to Baseball* (1967).

A number of hypotheses have been advanced to explain the increase in injuries and days on the disabled list over the past few years:

1. More injuries are detected because of the more sophisticated equipment available;

2. Clubs are more willing to put players on the disabled list sooner than later because of the enormous investment they have in them;

3. The "wimp factor" among athletes, particularly with the enormous guaranteed salaries that are a disincentive to playing hurt;

4. Players have taken on too much off-season conditioning (and, perhaps, performance-enhancing drugs), particularly weight training that puts on too much bulk and strains tendons, ligaments and joints;

5. Players warm up an hour and a half before game time and then negate the effectiveness of the warm-up by returning to an air-conditioned clubhouse and cooling down;

6. Artificial turf — though at least one doctor prefers artificial turf because there are no sprinklers, wet grass or torn-up turf;

7. Aluminum bats have caused pitchers to throw more breaking balls; college pitchers are not as successful throwing strictly fastballs to players who use aluminum. The resulting increase in breaking balls puts more strain on the arm;

8. Teams for a while were not using the 25th man that they are entitled to have on their rosters. This subtle difference puts somewhat more strain on the remaining players;

9. The heavy travel schedule.

In 1992 almost $100 million was paid to players on the disabled list. In a 2001 study by Stan Conte in *The American Journal of Sports Medicine*, it was determined that baseball accounts for more than 50,000 injuries per year, with rates per 100 participants ranging from two in Little League to 58 in Major League Baseball. Between 1990 and 2000, Major League pitchers constituted an average of 48.4% of the disabled list reports and 56.9% of the total disabled list days. Both the number of pitchers and the number of disabled list days lost by pitchers increased over the 11 years. This pattern was seen among both starting and relief pitchers. The number of disabled list reports from other positions was appreciably smaller than the number for pitchers (average of 5.1 for third basemen to 19.7 for outfielders). The study had hypothesized that injuries would decrease due to better training and conditioning, diagnostic methods and better surgical strategies, but the opposite was true.

Pitchers.

"Pitchers have torn muscles, broken bones, been operated on, had ligaments grafted; they have altered everything about their delivery and rhythm that made them a pitcher in the first place. They have come back from rotary cuff surgery, from not being able to lift their arms for a year and a half, and they have won ballgames. Occasionally, like Jim Palmer and Luis Tiant, they have pitched the best baseball of their lives after the actual physical equipment seemingly is taken away."— Richard Grossinger in *The Unfinished Business of Doctor Hermes* (1976).

"I was taught that ice was for Scotch, not your arm."— Reliever Rod Beck on why he doesn't ice down his reconstructed elbow.

An authoritative study by Tricia A. Murray suggests that muscle fatigue over the course of a game creates poor mechanics, resulting in damage to the shoulder and elbow. Tom Seaver, in his book, *The Art of Pitching*, said essentially the same thing, in that proper mechanics is the secret to "pitching mastery and longevity." Murray determined that shoulder and elbow symptoms prevent 50% of all professional pitchers from throwing at some time in their career. See also Will Carroll, *Saving the Pitcher* (2004).

Aches and Pains. In August 1996 Kevin Mitchell told Reds management that he was unable to play because he was suffering from "aches and pains." The strain on his body was exacerbated by the 50 pounds of excess weight that he was carrying at the time.

Achilles Tendon.

Tony Gwynn. Gwynn hit a league-leading .353 in 1996 despite a torn achilles tendon.

Allergy.

John McGraw. Because of severe allergies aggravated by sinusitis (caused by a throw that hit him in the face), the Giants manager often managed by phone from the clubhouse.

Amnesia.

Jim Kern. The noted prankster and reliever (who was known as Craziness, Inc., along with Tug McGraw) was once on the mound watching a foul ball hit into the stands when his catcher threw him a new ball. Kern was not looking and the ball hit him in the head. He fell backward off the mound with a concussion and claimed that he suffered temporary amnesia.

Amputees. See *Amputees*.

Amyotrophic Lateral Sclerosis. See **Lou Gehrig's Disease.**

Aneurysm.

John Olerud. When the Blue Jays first baseman was a junior at Washington State in the early 1990s, he underwent a life-threatening operation to repair an aneurysm at the base of his brain. Seven weeks later he was back playing.

David Cone. On May 16, 1996, the Yankee pitcher had surgery to repair an aneurysm in his shoulder. He was fully recovered by mid–1997, when he struck out 16 Tigers in a 5–2 win.

Ankle.

"You couldn't play on my Amazin' Mets without having held some kind of record, like one fella held the world's international all-time record for a pitcher getting hit on the ankles."— Casey Stengel.

Jeff Heath. On September 29, 1948, the outfielder for the pennant-winning Boston Braves was playing in a meaningless game when he slid into home and broke his ankle. He was out of the World Series against his former team, the Indians, and his missing power and average (.319) hurt the Braves. As he was lying on the ground writhing in pain, all he could say was, "Why did I slide?"

Bill Buckner. The long-time outfielder/infielder had the worst ankles in the Major Leagues. In January 1977 he underwent a bone spur operation. It resulted in a staph infection that was the beginning of his serious ankle problems. Cubs broadcaster Lou Boudreau (whose own ankle problems kept him out of World War II) said Buckner "looks like he's walking on eggs and can't take another step"— and Buckner still had another 10 years to play. He had to ice his ankles six to seven times a day and was in terrible pain all the time. He finally retired following the 1990 season, ending 22 years in the Major Leagues (see also *Errors*).

Robin Ventura. On March 21, 1997, during an exhibition game, the White Sox third baseman dislocated his ankle and fractured his lower right leg while trying to slide home. He was leading with his right leg while trying to protect a bruise on his left calf, but his spikes caught on the plate. He was out until mid-season.

Jason Kendall. On July 4, 1999, the Pirates catcher tried to break up a perfect game by laying down a bunt against Steve Woodard of the Brewers. Kendall hit first base awkwardly and severely dislocated his ankle, putting him out for the season.

Carl Crawford. In 2004 the Devil Rays leftfielder sprained his ankle trying to avoid a collision with the 10-year-old son of general manager Chuck LaMar while shagging flies during batting practice.

Appendicitis.

"They're hitting me all over the field and I can't get them out."— Pitcher Tiny Bonham as he lay dying after a 1949 appendectomy.

"With Bernie Williams uncertain for the [2004] season opener because of an appendectomy, the Yankees are trying to make a deal with God for DiMaggio."— Columnist Bud Geracie.

Joe Leonard. The utilityman played five seasons primarily for the Senators. In April 1920, after playing only one game that season, he was sent home ill. He died of a ruptured appendix on May 1.

Jake Daubert. In October 1924 the Reds first baseman underwent appendix and gallstone surgery. He died of complications a week later at age 40 after hitting .281 in 102 games that year. He had a lifetime .303 average.

Juan Guzman. The Blue Jays pitcher had an appendectomy late in the 1996, but nevertheless won the ERA title with a 2.93 mark after his season ended September 7.

Arm.

"My arm still bothered me every time I pitched. I just decided Mother Nature was going to take care of her own, so I did nothing. I figured that God only put a certain number of pitches in my arm and when I used them up, it was over. But I always hoped I didn't use that last one up with the bases loaded." — Milt Pappas.

"Don's the guts of the Angels, our triple threat. He can hit, run and lob." — Merv Rettenmund on chronically sore- and weak-armed Don Baylor.

"I knew it would ruin my arm, but one year of 25–7 is worth five of 15–15." — Steve Stone.

Goose Goslin. The outfielder once hurt his arm shotputting baseballs between batting cage at-bats.

Satchel Paige. In 1938 Paige suffered a broken arm while throwing a curve ball in Mexico City. Kansas City doctors told him he was through, but it healed properly and he resumed his career after a year's hiatus as a coach with the Monarchs.

Ken Burkhart. The minor league pitcher and future umpire suffered an arm injury during World War II. As a result, he switched to a shotput-type delivery that helped him to a 19–8 record for the Cardinals in 1945, his rookie year. He was largely ineffective after that, winning only nine more games over four seasons.

Jim Kaat. An arm injury to the Twins pitcher may have cost the club the 1967 American League pennant. He tore a forearm muscle in a September 30 game against the Red Sox. He left in the 3rd inning and eventual pennant-winner Boston went on to win 6–4. Kaat had won six games in September before the injury and the Twins lost the pennant by one game.

Rob Dibble. The 1980s Reds pitcher had seven screws and a metal plate inserted in his arm. To avoid problems with metal detectors in airports, he carried a photograph of the results of the operation to present to security guards.

Tom Browning. On May 9, 1994, the Reds pitcher broke his left arm while making a pitch in the 6th inning of a game against the Padres and had to be carried from the field. Reporters in the press box could hear the snap.

Eric Ludwick. On May 2, 1998, the Marlins pitcher tried to block a ball smashed off the bat of Padre Wally Joyner. It broke Ludwick's arm and he was out for three months.

Tony Saunders. On a pitch he threw on May 26, 1999, the Devil Rays pitcher broke the humerus bone in his left arm, the same bone that Dave Dravecky broke several years earlier (see *Amputees*). Saunders missed the rest of the season.

Rey Ordonez. On May 29, 2000, the Mets shortstop broke his arm and was out for the season when he applied a tag at second base and his arm collided with the helmet of runner F.P. Santangelo.

See **Elbow** for Sandy Koufax's legendary arm problems.

Attention-Deficit Disorder (ADD).

"If they did, I don't remember it." — Red Sox outfielder Manny Ramirez when asked if his former team, the Indians, had tested him for ADD.

Back.

"If you don't have a bad back by the time you're 60, then you haven't done anything in your life." — Red Sox manager Joe Morgan.

Charlie Keller. The player known as "King Kong" Keller had a chronic back problem that limited him to pinch-hitting duties late in his career for the Yankees and Tigers. With the exception of 1946, he never appeared in more than 83 games from 1945 through 1952. His son was a star minor leaguer before the same congenital back problem ended his career.

Ralph Kiner. The slugger's career ended prematurely at age 33 in 1955 because of a chronically bad back. He had led the league in home runs seven straight seasons beginning in his rookie season of 1946.

Juan Marichal. In 1970 the Giants pitcher suffered a severe reaction to penicillin that led to chronic arthritis and then a back injury when he tried to return too soon. He still managed to win 18 games for the Giants in 1971.

Joe Charboneau. The Indians outfielder was a rookie sensation in 1980. In 1981 he suffered a disc problem and was out for a long period of time. He returned briefly in 1982, but was soon out of baseball and became a bartender, softball player and successful local television broadcaster.

Cory Snyder. The Indians outfielder began his career with 81 home runs over his first three seasons beginning in 1986. He hurt his back in 1989 and his statistics plummeted.

Dave Winfield. The 6′6″ outfielder missed the entire 1989 season with back surgery. He returned to help lead the 1992 Blue Jays to a World Series victory and reached 3,000 hits in 1993.

Shawon Dunston. The Cubs shortstop had his career derailed in the early 1990s with a herniated disc in his lower back that required surgery. He missed all but 25 games over two seasons before returning to the club, but he was never as effective. Nevertheless, he continued to play through the 2002 season.

Randy Johnson. Johnson suffered a herniated disk in May 1996 and had surgery the following September. It came in the middle of a 16-game winning streak that began in 1995 and ended in 1997.

Beanballs. See *Beanballs*.

Blackballing.

Carl Furillo. The rifle-armed Dodger outfielder, a lifetime .299 hitter, claimed that he was dropped by the club in 1960 after he was hurt. Contending that he had been blackballed for complaining, he sued the team and recovered a $21,000 settlement.

Blood Clot.

Myril Hoag. On July 28, 1936, during his rookie season, while playing right field, Joe DiMaggio collided with center fielder Myril Hoag. Both collapsed and Hoag developed a blood clot on his brain. Pressure was relieved and he played another eight seasons (though he missed the rest of the 1936 season). As a result of the injury, DiMaggio moved to center field for the first time.

Roberto Hernandez. The White Sox pitcher made his Major League debut in late 1991, pitching seven innings of one-hit ball in a 5–1 win over the Royals. The game was only three months after an 8½-hour operation to remove two blood clots from his right forearm. He was told that he might have his arm amputated during the surgery, but it was saved by a transplant of a vein from his right leg into his forearm.

David Cone. In May 1996 the pitcher was diagnosed with a blood clot in his shoulder and underwent surgery that took him out of action for several weeks.

Blood Poisoning.

Nap Lajoie. In 1905 the Indians second baseman was spiked and was out two months with blood poisoning from the dye in his stockings (see also *Uniforms* — **Socks and Stirrups**).

Bone Chips.

Jeff Nelson. In late 2002 there was a bid of $23,000 on eBay for bone chips removed from the elbow of the Mariners pitcher; he had put them up for auction for charity. eBay prohibits selling body parts, so the listing was removed once it was discovered by eBay representatives.

Brain Tumor.

Austin McHenry. The outfielder played five seasons for the Cardinals from 1918 through 1922. Near the end of the 1922 season he began having difficulty following the flight of the ball. His doctors discovered a brain tumor and after an unsuccessful operation he died on November 27, 1922.

Josh Gibson. Considered the all-time greatest Negro League slugger, the Hall of Fame catcher died of a brain tumor while still a star at age 36 in 1947. On the morning of his death, Gibson correctly predicted to his mother that he would die that night. He had previously refused surgery on the tumor because he knew that it would end his career and probably leave him helpless. Some sources report that the tumor was a result of untreated syphilis.

Dick Brown. The Orioles catcher had his career cut short in 1965 when he was diagnosed with a brain tumor. He died in 1970.

Bunion.

"Mr. [Mike 'King'] Kelly's bunion was minced by a prominent jeweler, who paid $2.50 for it and sold the pieces at 50 cents apiece to sentimental young Boston women to wear on their bangles. Mr. Harris assures us that no Boston girl is considered au fait unless she flaunts a sample of Mr. Kelly's bunion on her bracelet." — Sportswriter Pete Dunne in 1887.

Cancer.

Jim Umbricht. The Astros pitcher died of cancer at age 33 on April 8, 1964.

Dave Dravecky. The pitcher's cancer led to amputation of his pitching arm (see *Amputees*).

Eli Marrero. On April 13, 1998, the Cardinals rookie tripled in his return to the lineup after undergoing surgery to remove a malignant tumor in his neck a month earlier.

Andres Galarraga. The slugger missed the entire 1999 season due to cancer surgery, but homered in his first game in 2000 for the Braves in a 2–0 victory over the Rockies. He had a recurrence in 2004 while still an active player at age 42, but again returned to the lineup with the Angels in September. He had 398 home runs and was trying to increase his total to 400, but they were in a tight pennant race and he barely batted.

See also entries for specific types of cancer.

Car Accident.

Art Houttemann. The Tiger pitcher's car was hit by a truck during spring training in 1951. He was given the last rites but recovered and returned in 1952 to pitch six more seasons. A few years later his wife was hurt and his child killed in a car accident.

Cast.

Bob Didier. The Braves catcher was wearing a protective cast on his wrist when the cast was hit by a foul ball and flew off toward the shortstop. Astros third base coach Salty Parker thought it was the ball and sent runner Norm Miller in from third. Miller was out at the plate.

Catcher's Injuries.

See *Catchers* — **Injuries/Early Mortality**.

Cheekbone. A number of players have played a portion of the season with a broken cheekbone or **Jaw**. Many wore football-type helmets with facemasks to protect the healing area while still playing.

Alfredo Griffin. In 1991 the Dodger shortstop wore a plastic face cover for much of the season to protect a broken cheek. He bore a strong resemblance to the Phantom of the Opera in clear plastic.

Cerebral Hemorrhage.

Kent Mercker. On May 11, 2000, the Angels pitcher was complaining of headaches and dizziness. The next day he was hospitalized with a hemorrhage in his brain. Doctors were quickly able to stop the bleeding and he was completely coherent. He returned to the mound later in the season.

Charley Horse. Research by Peter Morris that built on prior work by Gerald Cohen and found in Paul Dickson's *Baseball Dictionary* suggests that the term originated in Chicago in the 1880s, but the exact etymology is unclear. Etymologist Peter Tamony wrote: "When George Gore hit what should have been an inside-the-park homer and strained a thigh muscle rounding second, so that he had to limp into third, Billy [Sunday] cried, 'Here comes the Charley horse.'"

Collarbone.

"They got smoked, they really did. It was one of the worst things I've ever seen on the baseball field." — Pirates manager Jim Leyland on Dave Clark and Jacob Brumfield. On July 25, 1995, the Pirates outfielders had a violent collision in the outfield chasing down a drive to right-center field. Brumfield made a spectacular catch before slamming into the artificial turf. The game against the Braves was stopped for 23 minutes as an ambulance came out to treat both players. Clark lost a tooth and suffered a broken collarbone. Brumfield injured his hamstring.

Ted Williams. On March 9, 1954, surgeons spent more than one hour wiring his fractured collarbone. There was serious doubt that he would return, but he played 115 games that season, hitting 29 home runs and batting .348.

Larry Walker. In June 1996 the Rockies outfielder broke his collarbone when he crashed into the outfield fence at Coors Field. He was out for over two months.

Colon Cancer.

"Colon has solid outing." — 2004 Associated Press headline on pitcher Bartolo Colon.

Eric Davis. Davis was put on the Orioles' disabled list in mid–1997 and underwent surgery for colon cancer in June 1997. He had a cancerous growth removed from his intestine and then returned to action on September 15 that season (almost homering in his emotional first at-bat). In an odd coincidence, Davis's buddy on the Dodgers, Darryl Strawberry (they were rumored to have done several drugs together), had a cancerous growth removed from his colon in October 1998.

Darryl Strawberry. On October 3, 1998, the 36-year-old Yankees outfielder underwent what doctors said was a successful and uncomplicated three-hour operation to remove a walnut-sized tumor in his colon. The surgical team at Columbia Presbyterian Medical Center in Manhattan, headed by Dr. George J. Todd, said it removed a cancerous tumor that measured 2.4 inches in length and that nearly blocked Strawberry's intestine. There was no visible evidence that the cancer had spread, but he later had a kidney removed.

Concussion. See **Head**.

Corn.

Heinz Becker. In 1945 the Cubs infielder was suffering from severe corns on his feet. He played the last few innings of a late season game in his socks.

Deafness. See *Deaf Ballplayers*.

Diabetes.

"I look upon baseball as a kind of little extra burden that I have.

Some people have to live with diabetes, I have to live with a lousy baseball team." — Ted Turner.

Ron Santo. The Cubs third baseman was a diabetic while playing in the 1960s and 1970s. Santo, who broadcast for the Cubs, later had both legs amputated below the knee, and then faced surgery in 2003 for tumors in his bladder late in the season and was unable to attend the play-offs.

Catfish Hunter. The Hall of Fame pitcher was a diabetic while starring for the A's and Yankees primarily in the 1970s. He later died of **Lou Gehrig's Disease**.

Grover Cleveland Alexander. Alexander was a diabetic and an **Epileptic**, both surely aggravated by his legendary drinking habits.

Diphtheria.

Christy Mathewson. The Giants pitching star contracted diphtheria during spring training in 1906, causing his win total to drop to 22 after he returned in May.

Disc. See **Back** and **Neck**.

Elbow.

Sandy Koufax.

"Yeah, he's in pain except between the 1st and 9th innings." — Reds manager Dave Bristol.

"When I'm 40 years old I'd still like to be able to comb my hair." — Koufax on why he retired prematurely after the 1966 season at age 32 when his pitching elbow continuously swelled up due to arthritis. In 1962 Koufax missed half the season due to a circulatory problem in his pitching arm, known as Reynaud's Phenomenon, which caused him to lose feeling in his fingers. Koufax put strain on his arm in part because of a sidearm curve that he developed. He had to abandon the pitch because of the problems it caused. Jane Leavy's book, *Koufax* (2002), provides great detail on the excruciating pain Koufax suffered and the truly unbelievable effort it took to pitch despite these ailments.

Tommy John.

"When they operated, I told them to put in a Koufax fastball. They did — but it was a Mrs. Koufax fastball." — John after his radical surgery to replace a tendon in his pitching arm. John had surgery on July 17, 1974, after winning 13 games that season. He ruptured an elbow ligament and the surgeons transplanted a tendon from his right forearm into his left elbow. The operation later became known as "Tommy John surgery," and many players had their careers extended after successfully undergoing the procedure.

John sat out the entire 1975 season but threw out the ceremonial first ball at the All-Star Game that season. John returned to win 10 games in 1976 and won 20 games in 1977. He pitched long enough to be the Opening Day starter for the Yankees in 1989, winning 4–2 in what was to be his 26th and last Major League season.

Babe Ruth. He missed the last three games of the 1921 World Series with an abscessed elbow. The Giants won the Series 5–3 after the Yankees won the first two games by scores of 3–0.

Waite Hoyt. The Yankee pitcher lied to manager Miller Huggins about how he once hurt his elbow. He was actually throwing curveballs with lightweight baseballs at paper targets at a carnival but told Huggins something else to pacify the manager.

Enos Slaughter. The Cardinals outfielder is famous for his dash from first base in the 8th inning of Game 7 of the 1946 World Series against the Red Sox. On a pop fly single over second base by Harry Walker, Slaughter raced all the way home. He had a severely damaged elbow from being hit by a pitch earlier in the Series. It was bleeding internally and some sources reported that he was in danger of losing the arm if the bleeding intensified from further play (see also *Base Running*).

Joe DiMaggio. After the 1947 season he had surgery to remove bone chips in his elbow that were touching a nerve. He was barely able to throw during the 1947 season and his teammates covered for him by taking some balls and coming out to meet him on throws.

Ted Williams. He broke his elbow during the 1950 All-Star Game chasing down a fly ball against the outfield wall. He stayed in the game without knowing that it was broken, even singling in the winning run. It swelled up on the train home and he was put on the disabled list. He had shattered a key bone in the elbow and the standard surgery for that particular injury at the time was to fuse the bones. This would have ended his career. The doctors were able to avoid fusion and pieced the elbow back together.

Williams also suffered an elbow injury before the 1946 World Series. Some sources erroneously report that he was hurt in Game 1 of the Series. However, before the Series, the Cardinals were still in a play-off with the Dodgers for the National League pennant. The Red Sox scheduled a practice game to keep in shape before the Series started. The Red Sox played a group of American League all-stars on a cold day and Williams was hit on the elbow by a pitch. It swelled up tremendously and he was barely able to swing the bat. He had a miserable Series, batting .200.

Bruce Sutter. His career as a relief pitcher almost ended when he blew out his arm in 1972 during the second game of his minor league career. He paid to have the ulnar nerve rerouted in his elbow and could never straighten it after the operation. The Cubs called him in to release him, but changed their mind after Sutter revealed that he had paid for the operation himself.

Butch Hobson. Hobson played the 1978 season for the Red Sox with bone chips in his elbow, making 43 errors at third base. His manager, Don Zimmer, was aware of the problem: "Between pitches he adjusted the chips. Sometimes he didn't get them back in time, and he couldn't throw. He was tough."

Barry Larkin. At the 1989 All-Star break, the Reds shortstop was batting .340 when he was selected to start the All-Star Game. During an outfield-to-home relay contest before the game, he tore a ligament in his elbow and was out until September.

Nolan Ryan. Ryan's career ended in Seattle on September 22, 1993, after six batters and no outs in the 1st inning when a tendon snapped in his right elbow. He left with a 5–0 deficit after a grand slam by Dann Howitt, the tenth allowed by Ryan.

R.A. Dickey/Draft Pick. In 1996 the Rangers drafted University of Tennessee pitcher R.A. Dickey as the 18th player selected in the June draft. The club initially offered $810,000, but Dickey was forced to sign for $75,000 after a strange twist occurred. The Rangers' team doctor noticed Dickey's pitching elbow was at a strange angle on the cover of *Baseball America* magazine. X-rays revealed that Dickey had *no* ulnar collateral ligament in his elbow, the main support for the joint. He eventually would need "Tommy John" ligament replacement surgery, but he had been successful up to that point and could pitch without a full ligament in place. He made it up to the Rangers briefly in 2001, and then had a longer stint with the club in 2003.

Kerry Wood. Wood was the National League Rookie of the Year in 1998 after posting a 13–6 record and striking out 20 batters in a game. On March 16, 1999, during spring training, he suffered a torn ligament in his elbow and did not pitch again until 2000.

Jim Mecir. The Tampa Bay pitcher was shagging fly balls during batting practice when he collided with teammate Rick White, also a pitcher. Mecir suffered a broken elbow and was out for the 1999 season.

Jon Lieber. After winning 20 games in 2001, the Cubs starter underwent Tommy John ligament surgery in August 2002 and was sidelined through the 2003 season. He returned in mid–2004 with the Yankees.

Rick Ankiel. After a fast start in the Major Leagues in 2000 for the Cardinals, Ankiel couldn't control his wildness and washed out in 2001. He underwent Tommy John ligament replacement surgery to reconstruct his arm in 2003. He finally made it back to the Major Leagues on September 19, 2004, after a three-year wait following surgery and banishment to the minor leagues. In 22 innings before his call-up, he struck out 23 and walked two. In his first appearance he pitched two hitless innings and struck out four.

Darren Dreifort. The Dodger pitcher received a seven-year $55 million contract despite previously missing the 1995 season due to a torn medial collateral ligament (MCL) in his right elbow. In 1997 he had elbow tendonitis and missed 32 games. In 1998 he had soreness in his elbow and tightness in his shoulder, causing him to miss most of September. In 2001 he tore his MCL again and didn't pitch after June that year and for all of 2002. He also had right knee surgery during the layoff. In 2003 he was in the rotation but then tore the MCL in his right knee and missed the rest of the season. What a mess.

See *Hitters Who Pitched* for Jose Canseco's elbow injury while pitching.

Epilepsy.

Grover Cleveland Alexander.

"Alex's big problem was that he took epileptic fits on the bench, and that continued all the years we played together. Maybe two or three times a season he'd have an epileptic seizure on the bench. He'd froth at the mouth and shiver all over and thrash around and sort of lose consciousness. We'd hold him down and open his mouth and grab his tongue to keep him from choking himself. It was awful." — Hans Lobert on Alexander, who was an epileptic for the last 10 years of his career. He began having seizures after he served in France during World War I. Heavy shelling caused partial deafness and apparently brought on the seizures. He was also a heavy drinker, which probably did not help. During Game 7 of the 1926 World Series, he made a crucial *Strikeout* pitch in the 7th inning to fellow epileptic Tony Lazzeri with the bases loaded and two outs.

Tony Lazzeri. In 197 games for Salt Lake City in 1925, the epileptic second baseman hit 60 home runs with 222 RBIs and 202 runs scored. His roommate on the Yankees, shortstop Mark Koenig, later recalled that Lazzeri only had the seizures in the mornings and eventually died after a fall down stairs during a seizure.

Sherry Magee. The early 20th century Phillies outfielder was an epileptic. He once had a seizure which purportedly compelled him to hit umpire Bill Finneran in the mouth. Magee received a 30-day suspension.

Hal Lanier. When the Giants infielder was beaned in 1965 he began suffering from epilepsy. Though he was on the 1964 Topps All-Star Rookie team, after the beaning he never again hit above .233.

Buddy Bell. The third baseman played for 15 years with epilepsy. He did not disclose his condition until after he retired.

Eye.

"I remember I was batting more than .400 [in 1939], then I got this terrible allergy in my left eye, my batting eye, and I could hardly see out of it. [Yankee manager] Joe McCarthy didn't believe in cheese champions, so he made me play every day. I went into a terrible slump. McCarthy had to know the agony I was going through, but I'll never understand why he didn't give me a couple of days off. I guess it was the rule of the day — you played with anything short of a broken leg." — Joe DiMaggio quoted in *I'd Rather Be a Yankee*, by John Tullus (1986).

Willis Hudlin. In 1927 the Indians pitcher was hit between the eyes by a line drive but was out of action only two weeks and still managed to win 18 games.

Howie Judgson. The White Sox pitcher played his final season in 1954 knowing he might be going blind from a retina infection.

Herb Score. In 1957 the Indians pitcher was hit in the eye by a line drive off the bat of Yankee infielder Gil McDougald. Score's follow-through sometimes made it impossible for him to pick up line drives. Bob Lemon came in to relieve for 8⅓ innings for a 2–1 win over the Yankees.

Score was only 23 and considered a sure superstar after strong rookie (16–10) and sophomore (20–9) seasons. He set a rookie record with 245 strikeouts. A few weeks before the injury the Red Sox reportedly offered the Indians $1 million in cash for him.

Score's eye was never good again, but contrary to many reports he blamed his subsequent troubles on a sore arm rather than on the eye. He tore a shoulder tendon the following spring and threw for some time with a sore arm. He was only 17–26 after the eye injury, pitching through the 1962 season and retiring at age 29. Some have contended that McDougald, who inexplicably was hounded by fans, probably retired earlier than expected because he was so shaken by the incident. Other sources contend that McDougald ended his 10-year career with the Yankees rather than join the 1961 expansion Senators.

Art Fowler. The Angels pitcher was hit in the head during batting practice in 1962 and permanently lost the sight in his left eye.

Mookie Wilson. The Mets outfielder was participating in a spring training rundown drill one year when he was smashed in the eye with the ball while wearing sunglasses. The glass shards flew into his eye, but he sustained no permanent damage.

J.T. Snow and Chuck Finley. Angels outfielder J.T. Snow broke his eye socket on March 11, 1997, after being struck in the face by Mariners pitcher Randy Johnson. A few days later, Angels pitcher Chuck Finley was standing next to the batting cage when teammate Mike James was taking a practice swing. The bat flew out of the reliever's hand, striking Finley in the face and breaking his eye socket. Nineteen stitches were required to close the cut.

Sean Casey. On April 3, 1998, four days after being traded by Cleveland, the Reds first baseman broke his eye socket when he was struck by a ball thrown by teammate Damian Jackson during batting practice. He had surgery a few days later and was lost for several weeks.

Eyelashes.

Jose Cardenal. In 1974 the outfielder took himself out of a spring training game in Arizona, complaining that his eyelashes were stuck together. He recovered the next day after application of an eyewash solution overnight.

Face.

"It probably kept me off the cover of *GQ* magazine, and I had a headache for a while, but I could play." — Reds reliever Norm Charlton after being hit in the face by a Steve Finley line drive on May 27, 1995; he suffered a broken sinus cavity, a black eye and a cut that required stitches.

"At least [boxer] Frank Bruno got $6.3 million to get his face mashed. I didn't get squat." — Twins shortstop Denny Hocking during spring training in 1996 after he was hit in the face by a Jose Canseco line drive.

George McBride. He was considered by some as the premier defensive shortstop in the American League in the 1910s. While managing the Senators for one season in 1921, he was hit in the face by a batting practice ball and was paralyzed on one side of his face. He suffered a nervous breakdown and quit at the end of the season, though he later returned to coach for Ty Cobb in Detroit and lived to age 92.

Charley Moran. On October 8, 1938, during Game 3 of the World Series, umpire Charley Moran was hit in the face on a double play throw by Yankee second baseman Joe Gordon. Though bleeding profusely from the nose and mouth, he continued in the game.

Brad Holman. On August 8, 1993, the Mariners pitcher was hit in the face by a line drive, breaking his sinus cavity.

Ivan Rodriguez. The Rangers catcher had eight consecutive hits in July 1993 when he was hit in the face by the bat of Royals outfielder Hubie Brooks. He was out for several weeks and failed to get a hit in his first at-bat when he returned.

Lyle Mouton. On May 11, 1997, the White Sox outfielder broke a bone in his face when he collided with teammate Dave Martinez while trying to make a catch. Martinez suffered a slight concussion.

Bryce Florie. On September 8, 2000, the Red Sox pitcher was hit in the face on a live drive by Ryan Thompson. Although he had blood streaming down his face, Florie never lost consciousness and walked off the field. He suffered a fractured cheekbone and a fracture of the orbital socket, the bone that surrounds the eye, and retinal damage. He required surgery and returned to pitch in seven games in 2001, but his eight-year Major League career was over.

Fainting.

Willie Mays. During the heat of the 1962 pennant race, the Giants center fielder passed out for 20 minutes. He was out three days and then returned on September 16 to hit his 44th home run of the season.

Faked Injury.

Dan Brouthers. The 19th century star once faked an injury to his head in the second game of a doubleheader so he could take an early shower. Manager Tommy Byrne found out and purportedly persuaded the umpire to force him back into the game as punishment.

Maury Wills. During a 1965 game, the Dodger shortstop was asked to stall to give Dodger reliever Bob Miller more time to warm up. He did such an effective job of faking an eye injury that Miller came over with a towel to help him out.

Finger.

"Shaking hands with [battered old catcher] Steve O'Neill is just like grabbing into a bag of peanuts." — Charlie Grimm.

"Nice going, stupid!" — Telegram from Harmon Killebrew and Bobby Allison of the Twins to Al Kaline of the Tigers, after Kaline broke his finger throwing a bat into the bat rack during the 1969 American League pennant race.

Babe Ruth. The Red Sox pitcher had his 29-inning World Series scoreless innings streak snapped after he hurt his finger in a fight with a teammate on a train.

Claude Passeau. The pitcher used the smallest glove worn by any player in the Major Leagues because the third and little finger of his hand were bent down and useless. It did not seem to affect his fielding, as he went four years between 1942 and 1945 without making an error.

Roger Metzger. In 1980 the Giants infielder returned to the club for spring training after losing parts of four fingers in a hunting accident the previous winter. After hitting .074 in 28 games, he was released.

Paul Molitor. In 1990 Molitor broke his knuckle when he caught his left index finger in the opposing first baseman's glove while tying to run out a ground ball.

See also **Thumb.**

Fingernail.

"Am I the only person who finds it ironic that the day that Cal Ripken tied the iron man record by playing in 2,130 consecutive games, Hideo Nomo had to leave his game after five innings because of a broken fingernail?" — Ross Goldberg.

Claude Passeau. The Cubs pitcher lost the fingernail on his middle finger of his throwing hand when struck by a line drive off the bat of Tiger third baseman Jimmy Outlaw during Game 6 of the 1945 World Series. He stayed in the game but came out one inning later.

Ben McDonald. In 1991 the Orioles pitcher was scratched from his starting assignment because he "cut his fingernails too short and couldn't grip the ball."

Flu.

Warren Spahn. When the Braves pitcher had a bad case of flu before Game 7 of the 1957 World Series, he was scratched in favor of Lew Burdette. Burdette pitched a 5–0 shutout to clinch the Series over the Yankees.

Foot.

Mickey Mantle. In 1963 the Yankee outfielder was out for two months with a broken foot. He returned in dramatic fashion on August 4 with a pinch home run in the 9th inning to give the Yankees an 11–10 victory over the Orioles.

Matt Williams. In May 1995 the Giants third baseman was leading the league in each of the three Triple Crown categories when he fouled a pitch off his foot and broke it. He was out for several weeks.

Danny Tartabull. On February 20, 1997, the Phillies signed the free agent, but he broke his foot on Opening Day and sat out the season before retiring.

Foul Ball. See *Foul Balls — Injuries* for injuries to nonplayers from foul balls.

Freak Accidents. See *Freak Accidents*.

Gallstones.

Harvey McClellan. The White Sox infielder suffered through two gallstone operations in late 1924 that ended his career. He died the following year.

Glaucoma.

Kirby Puckett. In early 1996 the popular Twins outfielder started receiving treatment for symptoms of glaucoma. He was forced to retire midway through the season when surgery was unsuccessful, but continued to collect on his $6 million salary for the 1997 season.

Gout.

"Three steaks and you're gout." — Tom Fitzgerald in the *San Francisco Chronicle* after pitcher David Wells suffered from gout in early 1997. Wells weighed 248 pounds at the time and originally thought he was suffering from turf toe. The condition is caused by excess uric acid in the blood (sometimes from too much red meat or red wine).

Groin.

"Bad news for Red Sox fans. Roger Clemens is on the disabled list with a groin pull. If you ever watch baseball players, I'm sure you realize this is probably a self-inflicted injury." — Jay Leno.

"Clemens' Groin Remains Sensitive." — 1993 headline in the Worcester, Massachusetts, *Telegram and Gazette*.

"In twenty-five years, the two most exciting moments [in Cleveland] have been Tito Francona's TV commercials for Central National Bank and Valmy Thomas' groin injury." — Bennett Tramer of *Inside Sports*.

Hamstring.

"How can anyone who runs as slow as you pull a muscle?" — Pete Rose to teammate Tony Perez.

Harmon Killebrew.

"The team without Killebrew is like dressing up for a formal affair with a white tie and tails and then wearing muddy shoes."—Twins catcher Earl Battey.

Possibly the worst hamstring injury ever suffered was by the Twins first baseman in 1967. Playing first base, the thickly muscled slugger tore his hamstring, stretching for a low throw from shortstop Zoilo Versalles. He spent the off-season rehabilitating the leg and returned to be the American League's Most Valuable Player and Comeback Player of the Year.

Reggie Jackson. The slugger frequently suffered hamstring injuries, one of which kept him out of the 1972 World Series.

Hand.

"He was a careful tantrum thrower."—Ted Williams on Lefty Grove, noting that Grove always smashed lockers with his non-pitching hand.

Lou Gehrig. Late in his career the first baseman had his hands x-rayed. It revealed 17 different bone fractures (all apparently healed) which he never knew existed.

Roger Maris. The outfielder suffered a hand injury in 1963 that robbed him of his power. In June 1965 something popped in his hand and he was out for the year. After surgery he never had the strength that generated 130 home runs from 1960 through 1962.

Catchers. In 1970 Phillies catchers Tim McCarver and Mike Ryan each broke his hand in the same inning of the same game against the Giants. McCarver was hit in the back of the hand by a ball off the bat of Willie Mays. Ryan broke his hand while tagging out Willie McCovey at the plate.

Sammy Sosa. In August 1996 the Cubs outfielder had 40 home runs and 100 RBIs when he suffered a season-ending hand injury. He was on pace to hit 50 home runs for the first time in the National League since George Foster in 1977 and the first to hit 50 home runs and steal 20 bases since Willie Mays in 1956.

Kevin Millar. On the first pitch he saw in the Major Leagues, in 1998, the Marlins rookie swung and broke the hamate bone in his hand as he fouled off the pitch, forcing him on the disabled list.

Mike Lowell. The Marlins third baseman suffered a broken hand midway through the 2003 season after recovering from testicular cancer. He returned to the lineup very late in the season in a pinch-hitting role as he regained his stroke, but he delivered for the Marlins in Game 1 of the NLCS against the Cubs when he hit an 11th inning home run to dead center field to win the game.

Kevin Brown.

"Knife Going, Buddy" and "Punch Drunk"—Headlines in the *New York Post* in early September 2004, after Yankee pitcher Kevin Brown stupidly slammed his non-pitching hand into a locker in anger. He broke his hand and two pins had to be placed in it. He did not endear himself to his teammates, including Mike Mussina: "If you are going to get hurt playing the game, let's get hurt playing the game. But, to take yourself out for possibly the rest of the season, it's frustrating for the rest of the team."

Brown had previously inflicted vengeance on inanimate objects: a toilet in Florida, a wall display in San Diego, and a television in Chicago. Should have used his head (literally). He made it back for a game on September 26, 2004, but was bombed in the 1st inning while playing with a heavy pad in his glove to protect the hand.

Head.

"There's a fly to deep center field. Winfield is going back, back. He hits his head against the wall. It's rolling toward second base!"—Jerry Coleman.

"When the President of the United States comes to see old Bobo pitch, old Bobo ain't gonna let him down."—Bobo Newsom, who pitched a four-hit 1–0 shutout on Opening Day 1936 in front of Franklin Roosevelt. Newsom came through despite being struck in the head by his own third baseman, Ossie Bluege, on a throw across the diamond. Newsom was carried to the dugout after being struck but insisted on returning to the game.

Pete Reiser.

"Pete Reiser busted more fences than busted him—though the margin wasn't very big."—Sportswriter Charles Einstein.

"In Peck Memorial Hospital."—Reiser on where he thought he would finish the season.

"He was the best I ever had, with the possible exception of Mays. At that, he was even faster than Willie."—Manager Leo Durocher on Pete Reiser.

See also *Beanballs*.

Dodger outfielder Pete Reiser is probably the most famous player to suffer numerous head injuries, primarily because of collisions with outfield walls. Considered one of the finest pure hitters ever, he never reached his potential after a series of breaks, tears, concussions and beanings.

Reiser batted .343 during his rookie year in 1941. He was hitting .381 in July 1942 when he first crashed into a Major League outfield wall. He finished the season at .310 and he was on and off the field from then on with a series of injuries. Eleven times he was carried off the field; nine times he was knocked unconscious and woke up in the clubhouse or hospital. He broke or dislocated something seven times and was beaned twice.

He once had surgery for a blood clot on the brain and twice came out of the hospital against doctor's orders to make the game-winning hit (once hitting a pinch home run). In late 1946 he broke his leg sliding *back* into first base. In 1947 Reiser smashed into the center field wall at Ebbets Field. He suffered a skull fracture, two dislocated shoulders, went into a coma and was given the last rites.

Reiser was once counted out for the season by his doctor but quickly left the hospital and caught up with the Dodgers in Pittsburgh. He told manager Leo Durocher that he could not play, but in the 13th inning he came off the bench and hit what looked to be a sure triple—except that he collapsed rounding first base and was sent back to the hospital.

See Sidney Jacobson, *Pete Reiser: The Rough-and-Tumble Career of the Perfect Ballplayer* (2004).

Dizzy Dean.

"If I'd have known his head was there, I would have thrown the ball harder."—Tigers shortstop Billy Rogell after he nailed Dizzy Dean in the forehead with a throw at second base during the 1934 World Series. The Cardinals pitcher was hit in the head on a throw by Rogell as he slid into second base, prompting the famous "X-Ray Head; Find Nothing" headline. Coincidentally, in 1940 Rogell was released by the Cubs to make room for Dean on the roster.

The Cardinals pitcher once fell out of a car driven by one of his teammates. Though he landed on his head, he was not seriously injured.

Earle Combs. On July 24, 1934, the Yankee outfielder crashed into the center field wall of Sportsman's Park in St. Louis, suffering a fractured skull, knee and shoulder. As with all ballparks at the time, the field had no warning track or fence padding. Combs was near death for four days. He recovered, but after trying to make a comeback in 1935 at age 36, he retired to a coaching position in which he worked with Joe DiMaggio on his defensive play in center field.

Jim Wilson. Slugger Hank Greenberg hit Wilson in the head with a line drive. Wilson also had his leg broken by another line drive, though he later was able to pitch a no-hitter for the Braves.

Bill Dickey. When the Red Sox made their last out of the 1949 season to give the Yankees the pennant, the Yankee catcher jumped up so high in the dugout that he split open his head. The Yankees announced that it was the 74th disability on the team that year.

Jose Cardenal. In 1990, by then a coach, the former outfielder was hit in the head by a batted ball during a pregame drill. The injury resulted in a metal plate being placed in his head. In August 1993 he was hit on the head by a thrown ball during batting practice and was motionless on the ground for almost 10 minutes.

Jon Matlack. The Mets pitcher once had his skull fractured on a line drive by Marty Perez, but he was back pitching only 11 days later.

Matt Keough. During spring training on March 16, 1992, the pitcher was attempting a comeback with the Angels. He was struck in the head by a line drive foul ball while seated in the dugout and suffered a life-threatening blood clot in his brain. The pressure was relieved through surgery and he recovered, but his baseball career was over.

Carlos Perez. On June 25, 1995, the Expos pitcher was knocked unconscious by a foul ball while he sat in the dugout.

Kazuhisa Ishii. On September 8, 2002, the Dodger pitcher was hit in the forehead by a line drive off the bat of Astros outfielder Brian Hunter. Ishii suffered a concussion and underwent surgery to install a metal plate to help heal the fracture to his nasal area. He also suffered a forehead fracture, but no damage to his brain. He started the 2003 season showing no effects from the incident. He was 8–3 with a 2.94 ERA in 18 starts to begin the season, but finished only 9–7.

Jack Clark. During spring training 2003, the Dodger batting instructor wiped out on his motorcycle and suffered extensive injuries (not wearing a helmet). He finally returned mid-season, but his comments about management when the Dodgers couldn't hit caused him to lose his job.

Hee Seop Choi. On June 7, 2003, during a game in which Roger Clemens tried for win No. 300 for the first time, the Cubs first baseman, 6'5" and 240 pounds, was taken away by ambulance after a collision with pitcher Kerry Wood in the 4th inning. They both were heading for a pop fly. Wood's glove hit Choi in the face and he fell backward and hit his head on the third base path. Choi was unconscious for five minutes and stopped breathing for a brief period. It was 10 days before he began working out again.

Kevin Olsen. On June 27, 2003, during a 25–8 rout of the Marlins by the Red Sox, Florida pitcher Kevin Olsen was hit in the head by a line drive off the bat of Red Sox third baseman Todd Walker. The 7th inning line drive hit Olsen behind the ear and Olsen lay on the field for nine minutes, blinking his eyes and moving his legs, before being taken away on a stretcher. He was pronounced in good condition after a visit to the hospital. He was released from the hospital and immediately put on the disabled list.

Johnny Damon. In the 7th inning of Game 5 of the 2003 division series between the A's and Red Sox, the Boston center fielder collided brutally with his teammate, second baseman Damian Jackson. Jackson's forehead collided with the right side of Damon's head and created a gash next to Damon's right eye. Damon had to be taken off the field in an ambulance after being unconscious for almost two minutes. He managed to raise his right arm to acknowledge the hometown fans as he was loaded into the ambulance. Damon suffered a concussion, but he only missed one game.

Ernie Lombardi. See *Home Plate Collisions.*

Headache.

Hal Trosky, Sr. The Indians outfielder drove in over 100 RBIs six times in the 1930s, but his career was cut short when he began suffering from migraine headaches. He missed the entire 1942, 1943 and 1945 seasons because of the illness.

Ernie Camacho. The relief pitcher suffered headaches when pitching, apparently because he never blinked while on the mound.

Heart Problems.

"It's a good thing we won one or I'd be eating my heart out. As it is, I'm only eating out my right ventricle."—Ron Swoboda after striking out five times.

"The crowd seemed to be in the grip of angina, the cheers caught in their nervous throats."—Thomas Boswell in *How Life Imitates the World Series* (1982), describing the fans at the 1978 play-off between the Yankees and Red Sox.

"Speaking of technology, Joe, technology has kept [your brother] alive over the past five years…"—Fox television broadcaster Tim McCarver to Yankee manager Joe Torre in 2001, referring to the heart transplant received by Torre's brother.

"I don't have to sit here and rot, and the White Sox don't have to have a heart attack every time I come in the game."—Fallen reliever Billy Koch in 2004, after being traded to the Marlins to become a set-up man. He went from 44 saves for the A's in 2002 to a disaster in Chicago.

Urban Shocker. The 1927 Yankees pitcher was forced to retire early because of heart disease. He left the team in the spring of 1928 and died of complications from pneumonia in September of that year at age 38.

Babe Ruth. In 1929 Ruth complained of back and chest pains at age 34. While he was out of the line-up for a week, it was rumored that he had died of a heart attack. He had been suffering from an irregular heart beat brought on by emotional and physical exhaustion.

Roy Meeker. The 28-year-old A's pitcher was 5–12 for the 1924 A's and was at spring training for the Reds in 1929 when he suffered a fatal heart attack.

Duane Josephson. The hard-nosed catcher played primarily for the White Sox in the late 1960s. A heart problem forced his retirement in 1972.

John Hiller. The Tigers pitcher suffered a heart attack (some sources report it as a stroke) and missed the 1971 season. He made a comeback with the Tigers a year later and set a since-broken record of 38 saves.

Clyde Milan. The long-time Senators center fielder and coach was hitting fungoes for the club at age 65 during spring training in 1953 when he suffered a fatal heart attack.

Joe Hoerner. The pitcher apparently suffered from a weak heart. In response he switched to a sidearm delivery which supposedly was less strenuous. He pitched from 1963 through 1977 and recorded 77 saves.

Bunk Congalton. He played for the Red Sox from 1902 through 1907, batting .290. He died of a heart attack in 1937 at age 62 while watching Bob Feller pitch in a game at Cleveland.

Dave Leiper. On April 13, 1991, the minor league (and former Major League) pitcher had heart surgery to repair an irregular heartbeat caused by Wolfe-Parkinson-White Syndrome. He returned later in the season to a Class AAA team for rehabilitation but did not return to the Major Leagues.

Jason Schmidt. In spring training 1997, the Pirates pitcher was diagnosed with an irregular heartbeat after it was revealed that his heart stopped momentarily while he was resting. Luckily, it never stopped when he was exercising. Despite the problem, he was cleared to play.

Wally Bell. In May 1999 the Major League umpire returned to the diamond only 11 weeks after undergoing quintuple bypass surgery.

Kerry Wood. In October 1999 the Cubs pitcher revealed that he has a dime-sized hole in his heart, a condition known as atria septal defect. It can be treated, but it does not affect his pitching.

Darryl Kile. Kile died of a heart attack on June 22, 2002. See *Deaths.*

Jonny Gomes. On Christmas Eve 2002, the Devil Rays prospect, 22, discovered he had suffered a heart attack when he thought all he had was indigestion. The following spring, wearing a Major League uniform for the first time (playing in an exhibition game to rest the Major Leaguers), he hit a home run in his first at-bat. He broke down in tears after the game. He made it up to the Major League club for eight games in 2003.

Barry Bonds. When Bobby Bonds died in late August 2003, Barry Bonds was taken out of the line-up after rounding the bases following a home run. His heart rate had accelerated to 160 beats per minute. Bonds had sat out the six games following his father's death at age 57 on August 23. The elder Bonds had been ill with lung cancer and a brain tumor. His son had been on the bereavement list from August 14–18 that season.

Heel.

"Few business efforts receive the public attention accorded baseball. Every rhubarb is given nationwide consideration; the calcium deposit on the heel of a quasi-peon becomes the object of universal concern." — John Eckler, Esq., in the *University of Chicago Law Review* (1949).

Joe DiMaggio. The Yankee Clipper suffered from painful bone spurs in his heels which first required surgery in 1947. He had surgery on them again in late 1948, but the surgery was botched by the doctor and it was fixed by surgeons in a second surgery performed at Johns Hopkins University in the spring of 1949. DiMaggio also suffered painful and serious injuries to his knee, shoulder and elbow, all combining to force him to retire at the relatively young age of 36 after the 1951 season.

Rogers Hornsby. Hornsby suffered from bone spurs on his heels, which slowed him down significantly in his last eight years.

Barry Larkin. In May 1997 Larkin ruptured his heel running out a double and was lost for the season.

Hemorrhoids.

"My problems are, uh, behind me after the surgery." — George Brett after hemorrhoid surgery during the 1980 World Series.

Joe Cronin. Earl Johnson, a rookie with the Red Sox in 1940, later remembered the Red Sox player-manager stretched out on the trainer's table while the team doctor operated on him for hemorrhoids. After being bandaged up, Cronin supposedly went out and played both ends of a doubleheader.

Hepatitis.

"People don't know this but I helped the Cardinals win the pennant. I came down with hepatitis. The trainer injected me with it." — Bob Uecker.

Hip.

"Casey Stengel, New York"

"Man with the Broken Hip, New York City" — Fully-addressed envelopes received by Mets manager Casey Stengel when he broke his hip in 1965.

Britt Burns. The White Sox pitcher had a degenerative hip condition that forced him to retire at age 26 in 1986 after an 18–11 season in 1985.

Bo Jackson. The Royals outfielder had a degenerative hip condition that was aggravated primarily by professional *Football* with the Raiders. Many thought he would be forced to retire, but he staged a remarkable comeback in late 1991 with the White Sox as a designated hitter. Nevertheless, the pain continued and he had his hip replaced on April 4, 1992, supposedly ending his career.

A year later after intense rehabilitation, Jackson resumed his career in dramatic fashion on April 9, 1993, at New Comiskey Park. Jackson had batted 65 times during the spring without hitting a home run. In his first regular-season at-bat, pitcher Neal Heaton threw him a change-up for strike one and then threw another that Jackson ripped into the bleachers. Greg Ourednick, 16, caught the ball and returned it to Jackson. Ourednick was aware that Jackson had wanted to give the ball from his first official hit to his mother, who died three weeks after Jackson's hip surgery. Ourednick received another ball ("THANKS FOR THE BALL—BO JACKSON") and a signed bat. Jackson bronzed the ball and bolted it to his mother's tombstone.

Albert Belle. After signing a huge guaranteed contract extension and then playing sparingly in 1999, Belle had to go on the disabled list in early 2000 due to a chronic and degenerative right hip injury. In March 2001 the Orioles announced that Belle was "totally disabled and unable to perform as a Major League baseball player." He retired at age 35 and insurance covered 70% of the Orioles' salary obligation.

Hodgkin's Disease.

Scott Radinsky. The White Sox reliever was diagnosed with this form of cancer in early 1994. He made it back to earn a save on June 25, 1995, his first since August 14, 1993. He continued in the Major Leagues through 2001, but his last reasonably effective season was 1999, when he appeared in 43 games for the Cardinals.

Matt Turner. The Indians pitcher Turner contracted the disease in 1994. Just before the player strike hit in August 1994, the Indians released Turner so that they could continue to pay him — a gesture of good will on the club's part. He was making $139,000 that season.

Hypochondria.

"You never know with these psychosomatic injuries. You have to take your time with them." — Noted hypochondriac Jim Palmer.

"A few hours before, Mr. [Monte] Pearson, a better-than-fair performer in any hypochondriac league, had been bemoaning the desolate state of his health and crying out against the savage injustice of a capitalistic system which would permit a faithful hired hand to die in solitary misery." — Joe Williams on Monte Pearson, who pitched for 10 seasons during the 1930s, with a best of 19–7 for the Yankees in 1936. He also won one World Series game each year between 1936 and 1939 and his 1.01 Series ERA is seventh all-time.

"When Appling was around, the real blunder was to ask him, 'How do you feel?' It would sometimes take half an hour before he stopped telling you." — Maury Allen in *Big-Time Baseball* (1978) on White Sox shortstop Luke Appling, known as "Old Aches and Pains" for his constant complaints about his health. During his career Appling purportedly suffered from insomnia, gout, dizzy spells, torn leg tendons, fallen arches, seasickness, a sore throat, stiff neck, sore kneecap and astigmatism. When he dipped below .300 for the first time after nine straight seasons, he blamed it on having been completely healthy all season. Appling was healthy enough to hit a home run in the first Cracker Jack *Oldtimers Game* in 1982 at age 75, He died at age 83 in 1991.

"Sometimes when I wake up in the morning, I hurt so much I pray that I am still sleeping." — Roberto Clemente, legendary hypochondriac ("but if I was a hypochondriac I wouldn't be playing"). He had hurt his back in a 1954 auto accident, so he had at least one legitimate reason for the twists and turns he routinely made while at the plate or in the outfield. He also suffered from headaches, stomachaches, tonsillitis, insomnia, malaria, miscellaneous pulled muscles and bruised or chipped bones. A New York writer once upset Clemente when he wrote that Clemente was a hypochondriac and frequented witch doctors in Puerto Rico.

Jaw.

"The trouble with having a wired jaw is that you can never tell when you're sleepy—you can't yawn."—Rocky Bridges after his jaw was broken in 1958 by a Frank Lary fastball.

"I hope I never see a straw again."—Phillies outfielder Ricky Jordan, who broke his jaw on a beanball in early 1992 and had his mouth wired shut to allow it to heal. He faced a dangerous situation during his recovery when he craved real food instead of the milkshakes he had been forced to consume through a straw. He loaded up a blender with fried shrimp and fries and then drank the pureed concoction. It made him nauseous and he almost had to cut open the wiring, but he could not find the clippers. Water calmed his stomach and the potentially fatal crisis passed.

Carl Reynolds. Yankee catcher Bill Dickey punched the Senators outfielder on July 4, 1932. A few weeks into his recuperation Reynolds almost died when he was riding in a cab with his wife. His jaw was still wired shut when he became nauseous and began to vomit. He was beginning to choke to death when his wife, a nurse, pulled out manicure scissors and cut the wires holding his jaw closed.

George Kell. In 1948 Kell was playing third base with the bases loaded and Joe DiMaggio at the plate. DiMaggio lined a hard ground ball at him, which broke his jaw. Kell managed to pick up the ball and step on third base for the out before he collapsed. His jaw was wired shut and he was out for the season. Earlier in the season Kell's wrist was broken when hit by a pitch from Vic Raschi.

Bob Cerv. Cerv was out for a month with a broken jaw in 1958.

Glenn Davis. On June 7, 1993, the Orioles first baseman suffered a broken jaw during a bar fight. Later in the season he was struck just below the left ear and knocked unconscious by a foul ball.

Kirby Puckett. On September 28, 1995, Indians pitcher Dennis Martinez shattered his jaw with a pitch.

Willie Blair. He was hit in the face and broke his jaw by a ball hit by Indians infielder Julio Franco on May 4, 1997. Franco's shot was clocked at 107 mph. The blow was struck in the 6th inning, so Blair received credit for the 2–0 win.

Otis Nixon. On April 4, 1998, Nixon's jaw was broken when he slid into second base and was kicked by Royals shortstop Felix Martinez.

Kidney.

"Tom Griffin will be facing the heart of the order. Well, maybe not the heart, maybe just the kidneys."—Giants broadcaster Hank Greenwald.

"Explaining to your wife why *she* needs a penicillin shot for *your* kidney infection."—Mike Hegan on the toughest thing in baseball.

"I have kidney stones and I doubt I'll ever get rid of them. I have doubts that the national debt ever will be wiped out. But I have no doubts in my ability to win."—Ray Knight on becoming manager of the Reds.

"We're going to find out if chiles rellenos go with bagels and lox."—Albuquerque-born Dr. Julian Lopez of Las Vegas, after donating a kidney to his long-time friend, White Sox owner Eddie Einhorn. Einhorn recovered and was healthy at age 67 in 2004.

Ross Youngs. The Giants outfielder suffered from kidney problems that forced his retirement following the 1926 season after 10 years. He died of Bright's disease (kidney failure) in October 1927.

Oscar Melillo. The infielder played primarily for the Browns from 1926 through 1937, batting .260. His career was threatened with Bright's Disease, but he ate only spinach for as long as it took to cure him. Not surprisingly, his nickname was "Spinach."

Ewell Blackwell. The Reds pitcher had a kidney removed in January 1949 after he had already suffered an arm injury. He managed to return to the Reds to post 17- and 16-win seasons before retiring in 1955.

Norm Larker. Larker was a lifetime .275 hitter for six years in the late 1950s and early 1960s. He came within one hit of the 1960 batting title while playing with only one kidney.

Rick Reichardt. After receiving $200,000 as a bonus baby in 1964 and playing a few Major League games in 1964 and 1965, Reichardt batted .288 and hit 18 home runs in 89 games in 1966. After having a kidney removed late that season, he was never the same player, batting .261 with 116 home runs in 11 seasons.

Mike Shannon. The Cardinals infielder developed a kidney ailment that ended his career prematurely after nine years. He then moved into the Cardinals broadcast booth.

Eric Davis. During Game 4 of the 1990 World Series, the Reds outfielder lacerated a kidney when he crashed into the left field wall. He spent five days in the hospital and feuded with owner Marge Schott partly because Schott refused to pay for a private jet to bring him home from Oakland. The injury hampered his play in 1991, and he was traded to the Dodgers after the season.

Ozzie Guillen. In August 2004 the White Sox manager was hospitalized with kidney stones. He later said he wouldn't wish the experience on his worst enemy.

Knee.

"The Knee, subsequently operated on and now slowly on the mend, was the object of intense daily ministrations, rituals aspersions, invocations, and solemn preachments…"—Roger Angell in *The Summer Game* (1972) on pitcher Jim Lonborg's skiing accident after the 1967 season while with actress Jill St. John. He suffered a torn anterior cruciate ligament, from which he never fully recovered. He was never the same again, though he was not as bad as many sources imply. Although he won only 17 games over the next three years, he pitched for 12 more years after the accident, with a high of 18 wins for the Phillies in 1976.

Mickey Mantle. During Game 2 of the 1951 World Series, Willie Mays hit a fly ball into right center, which right fielder Mantle thought center fielder Joe DiMaggio would not get to because of painful ankle problems (DiMaggio retired after the Series). As Mantle raced for the ball, DiMaggio surprisingly camped under it and made the catch. At that moment Mantle's spike caught a sprinkler head and tore ligaments in his knee. He was only 19 years old and did not bother to rehabilitate it properly. It was the start of a series of problems with his legs.

In June 1963 Mantle suffered another serious knee injury and also a broken foot when he ran into the wall in Baltimore. He missed two-thirds of the season and limped through the next two seasons (see also **Leg, Osteomyelitis** and **Shoulder**).

Babe Ruth. In 1919 he suffered a knee injury that both the Red Sox and Yankees were aware of when he was sold to New York. The cartilage tear plagued him for the rest of his career and he finally had surgery on it in 1940, five years after he retired.

John McGraw. In 1924 the Giants manager suffered a knee injury that kept him away from the bench for seven weeks.

Joe DiMaggio. His Major League career almost ended before it began. In early 1934 while with the San Francisco Seals in the Pacific Coast League, he stepped out of a cab in San Francisco. His leg had fallen asleep and his knee buckled, tearing cartilage. A Los Angeles orthopedist checked him out and gave a positive report. As a result, the Yankees offered the Seals $25,000 and five players to obtain him. This was substantially lower than what had been expected, but a number of teams shied away from him after the injury. DiMaggio's debut with the Yankees was delayed a few weeks after he received a bad burn while using a diathermy machine on the knee (see also **Bone Spurs**).

Darren Daulton. The Phillies catcher tore the anterior cruciate ligament in each knee, one in 1986 and the other in 1995. The second one ended his catching and he tried to move to the outfield to extend his career. However, he failed to recover and retired during spring training in 1996.

Gary Carter. The Hall of Fame catcher endured nine knee operations, but still managed to average 148 games during an eight-year span of his 19-year career. He played in 2,056 games behind the plate, surpassed only by Carlton Fisk.

Kirk Gibson. Before Game 1 of the 1988 World Series, the Dodger outfielder and league MVP had a strained ligament in his right knee and a strained hamstring, and had taken a cortisone injection in his knee before the game and was unavailable. He told his wife to leave early in the 7th inning to beat the traffic, since he wouldn't be playing. In the bottom of the 9th inning, with the Dodgers down by a run, Gibson hit 10 pitches off a tee under the stands before telling a batboy to inform manager Tommy Lasorda that he was available. A stunned Lasorda brought him to the plate after a Mike Davis walk. With two outs, Gibson fouled off a couple of pitches and ran the count full. He then recalled a scouting report from Mel Didier saying that A's pitcher Dennis Eckersley liked to throw a "back door" slider on a full count. On the next pitch Gibson smacked a ball into the left field bleachers for a 5–4 victory, prompting national broadcaster Jack Buck to say, "I do not believe what I just saw!" Gibson pumped his arm low in a victory salute as he limped around the bases. It was his last appearance in the Series, which the Dodgers won in five games.

Benito Santiago. In January 1998 the catcher crashed his car into a tree in Florida and tore up his knee. He played in only 15 games for the Blue Jays in 1998 and his career came close to ending. He made a strong recovery and was still playing solidly, for the Giants by then, into the 2004 season.

Mark McGwire. McGwire announced his retirement in November 2001 as "unable to perform" because of his chronically bad knee. One knowledgeable source claimed that he had to get off performance-enhancing drugs so he could get married and "perform" his nuptial duties.

Mo Vaughn. Vaughn couldn't play in 2004 due to a bad knee, when he was owed $15 million by the Mets. Once he sat out 90 days that season, an insurance policy kicked in to pay 75% of the contract.

Aaron Boone. The hero for the Yankees with a 2003 ALCS homer to beat the Red Sox tore up his knee (ACL) in a pick-up basketball game early in 2004. Because his contract prohibited basketball, he forfeited his salary and then signed a $3.6 million deal with the Indians for 2004–05, but never played in 2004.

Kneecap.

Freddie Fitzsimmons. The Dodger pitcher was throwing a shutout against the Yankees for six innings in Game 3 of the 1941 World Series until a line drive in the 7th inning broke his kneecap and he came out of the game. The Yankees scored two runs in the 8th inning for a 2–1 victory.

Wilbur Wood. The White Sox pitcher suffered a broken kneecap on a line drive by Ron LeFlore in 1976 and he never pitched as well after that.

Jamie Moyer. The Mariners lefthander broke his kneecap during a postseason workout and missed the October 2000 league

championship series. Nevertheless, he was still pitching successfully at age 41 in 2004.

Knuckle. See **Finger**.

Leg.

"Never trust a baserunner who's limping. Comes a base hit and you'll think he just got back from Lourdes."—Joe Garagioloa.

"The body of a god. Only Mantle's legs are mortal."—Jerry Coleman.

"On two legs, Mickey Mantle would have been the greatest ballplayer who ever lived."—Second baseman Nellie Fox.

"He was the best one-legged player I ever saw play the game."—Casey Stengel on Mickey Mantle.

"If that guy were healthy, he'd hit 80 home runs."—Carl Yastrzemski on Mickey Mantle.

"Before every game he had to wrap his left leg from the ankle up with an Ace bandage wrapped as tight as a mummy. After every game, he would unwrap it, tears of pain on his face. Never said a word."—Former Major League player, broadcaster and later public address announcer Rex Barney on Mantle. See also **Knee** and **Osteomyelitis**.

Rabbit Maranville. The Braves shortstop was 42 years old during a 1934 spring training game against the Yankees. He slid into home, breaking both the tibia and fibula of his left leg. He returned for 23 games in 1935 but was finished at the Major League level. He batted .323 in 123 games in the minor leagues in 1936 at age 44.

Charley Gelbert. The Cardinal infielder's left leg was severely damaged in a hunting accident in 1932, two years after he had starred in the 1930 World Series for the Cardinals. Despite having most of the tendons in his left leg severed and about three inches of fibula that was totally unconnected, he made it back to the Major Leagues in 1935 after two years of hospital visits. He played five more years at shortstop.

Joe Green. The career minor leaguer superstitiously wore the same suit for the duration of a hitting streak that lasted for more than a month. His wife finally tired of the stench and took it to the laundry. He broke his leg the next day. Green had only a one-game Major League career for the A's in 1924, so this must have been in the minor leagues (contrary to the source that reported it).

Bob Gibson. The Cardinals pitcher broke his leg on July 15, 1967, after being struck by a line drive by Roberto Clemente. He was able to pitch to three more batters before coming out of the game. Gibson came back after only eight weeks, winning a total of 13 games, including the pennant-clincher against the Phillies. He capped the season with three wins in the World Series against the Red Sox.

Bobo Newsom. The often-traded pitcher broke both legs in a car accident. On the day the casts were removed he broke them again in another accident when he was kicked by a mule at a livestock show.

Bobby Thomson and Henry Aaron. Thomson was traded to the Braves in February 1954 and was expected to fill a hole in left field. During spring training he broke his leg sliding into second base. Henry Aaron was chosen among a number of candidates to take his place in the starting line-up. Otherwise, Aaron probably would have spent another year in the minor leagues.

On Labor Day weekend that season, Aaron broke his leg sliding into third base after going 5-for-5 that day. Ironically, he was replaced by Thomson in the line-up. Aaron nevertheless won the Rookie of the Year Award and avoided a military commitment because of the injury.

Bobby Valentine. The Angels outfielder severely broke his leg in 1973 when he collided with an outfield fence trying to catch up to a home run by Dick Green off pitcher Rudy May. The leg broke in two places and never healed properly. He played five more years in the Major Leagues, but his speed was gone and he was largely ineffective. Maybe that's why he was so grumpy while managing.

Buck Martinez. See *Home Plate Collisions*.

Moises Alou. In 1993 the Expos outfielder broke his leg and dislocated his ankle as he rounded first base. As he lay in the dirt his leg was dangling horribly in the wrong direction. It was so bad that the nearby umpires and players could not look at it. He returned successfully and was still playing well into the 2004 season.

Ron Gant. Early in 1994 the Braves outfielder broke his leg in a dirt bike accident. The Braves released him before the season rather than pay him $5.5 million for what little of the 1994 season he might have been able to play; as a result, the club was responsible for only $900,000.

Leg Cramps.

Bobby Tolan. The Reds outfielder suffered leg cramps during Game 7 of the 1972 World Series. He was unable to get to a 6th inning drive by Sal Bando, who drove in what turned out to be the winning run in a 3–2 A's victory.

Leukemia.

Harry Agganis. Agganis starred at quarterback for Boston University before playing first base for the Red Sox in the mid–1950s. Though a college football All-American, he signed with the Red Sox for $35,000 and was a future star. He was hitting .313 in May 1955 when he was forced to the sidelines with leukemia (also referenced as a heart ailment in some sources). He died at age 25 on June 27, 1955. His successor at quarterback for Boston University, Tommy Gastall, played catcher for the Orioles in 1955 and 1956 but was killed in a plane crash in September 1956.

Walt Bond. The outfielder had a high of 20 home runs and 85 RBIs for the Astros in 1964. He was diagnosed with leukemia during his career but it stayed in remission until he was with the Twins in 1967. After playing in only 10 games he was forced to retire and died in September of that year.

Lips.

"All he told me was, 'How do you burn your lip on the Astroturf?' That was worth a hug."—Twins manager Ron Gardenhire after center fielder Torii Hunter made a diving catch in the 9th inning to preserve a 3–2 win over the A's.

Liver.

"You're a sports journalist, aren't you?"—Dr. Goran Klintmalm of Baylor University during a press conference after giving Mickey Mantle a new liver; the questioner asked if the donor was still alive. As a result of the publicity surrounding Mantle's surgery, organ donor card sign-ups increased dramatically. More than one million cards featuring Mantle's photo and signature were distributed in September 1995 to encourage fans to sign up for the program.

Lou Gehrig's Disease.

Lou Gehrig. Certainly the most famous illness to strike a ballplayer while still active was Lou Gehrig's amyotrophic lateral sclerosis (ALS). He was diagnosed at the Mayo Clinic in Rochester, Minnesota. It was first announced that he had "chronic infantile paralysis" and that he would not get any worse (see also *Lou Gehrig*).

Catfish Hunter. In November 1998 the Hall of Fame pitcher announced that he had the disease, and he died less than a year later.

Lung Cancer.

Leonard "King" Cole. Cole, who was on the mound when Babe Ruth had his first Major League hit and scored his first run in 1914, died of lung cancer in January 1916 after an unremarkable

1915 season. He had starred in 1910 as one of the few rookies in history to have won 20 games and he pitched a shutout in his debut that season.

Lupus.

Tim Raines. In July 1999 Raines came out of a game complaining of dizziness and later was diagnosed with lupus. He sat out the rest of the year and 2000, but came back to play well in early 2001 before a shoulder injury curtailed his season. The 40-year-old Raines recovered sufficiently to play in the 2002 season and appear in a game with his son.

Malaria.

"I had malaria most o' the season. I wound up with .356."—Ring Lardner in "Alibi Ike" (1915).

"Baseball and malaria keep coming back."—Manager Gene Mauch after the 1981 strike.

Joe Cassidy. One of the first 20th century players to make it to the Major Leagues without any minor league experience, Cassidy died of malaria in the spring of 1906 when he was one of the top shortstops in baseball. He had played for the Senators in 1904–1905.

John McGraw. He once contracted malaria while playing for the 1890s Baltimore Orioles.

Doc McJames. The pitcher won 27 games for Baltimore in 1898 but contracted malaria late in the 1899 season. Though he returned to pitch in 13 games in 1901, he died that September.

Meningitis.

Addie Joss. The turn-of-the-century pitching star died of tubercular meningitis in April 1911 at age 28. Never particularly strong, Joss collapsed on the field during spring training and died a few days later. He had already won 160 Major League games (with four 20-game seasons), although he had won only 14 and five games his previous two seasons. He was plagued by arm injuries his final season in 1910 and might not have played much in 1911. He is second all-time with a lifetime ERA of 1.88. He was inducted into the Hall of Fame by the Veterans Committee in 1978 despite not having the requisite 10 years of Major League service.

Max Alvis. The Indians third baseman contracted meningitis and missed the last six weeks of the 1964 season. He recovered in time to make the 1965 All-Star team at third base.

Bruce Campbell. The Indians right fielder contracted meningitis in the mid–1930s, stayed in uniform but collapsed in May 1936. He was given a 50–50 chance to live but recovered and played through the 1942 season. He lived another 53 years until his death at age 85 in 1995.

Multiple Injuries.

Mike Marshall. The Dodger outfielder was almost legendary for the number of injuries he sustained over his career, starting with a beaning in early 1983. He followed with a foot operation in 1984, appendectomy in 1985, back strain in 1986, and a 1987 marked by wart removal, food poisoning, and wrist, back and ankle injuries. He once was held out of a game due to "general soreness."

Paul Molitor. The versatile Brewers star is another often-injured player of recent years. Despite outstanding numbers and a lifetime average over .300, the Hall of Famer suffered from pulled hamstrings, pulled ribcage muscles, a broken knuckle, torn ankle ligaments, and elbow injuries severe enough to warrant surgery in 1984.

Ken Griffey, Jr. After averaging 140 games for the Mariners during his first 12 seasons beginning in 1989 at age 19 (with only two seasons missing significant numbers of games), Griffey averaged only 95 games during his next four seasons with the Reds. The 2003 season epitomized his stay in Cincinnati. He dislocated his shoulder during the first weekend series, then tore tendons in his ankle after he returned in July. Both the ankle and the shoulder required surgery in August 2003.and put him out for the season. It was his sixth major surgery since joining the Reds in 2000. In November 2002 the Reds reached an agreement to trade Griffey for Phil Nevin (Phil Nevin?!), but Nevin voided the deal with his no-trade provision. A week after the Nevin deal went bad, the White Sox turned down a deal sending Griffey to Chicago in exchange for Magglio Ordonez.

Griffey pronounced himself ready for the 2004 season, but suffered a calf strain at the end of spring training and missed the first few games of the season. Nevertheless, he returned to make the cover of *Sports Illustrated* (always a risk) and hit his 500th home run to much fanfare. The SI Jinx kicked in shortly thereafter, when Griffey tore a hamstring on the Saturday before the All-Star break chasing down a ball hit to right center. The new injury put him out for the season after he tried to come back too soon.

Mumps.

Harlond Clift. The third baseman was traded by the Browns to the Senators in 1943, where he promptly got the mumps. He then fell off a horse and played only a few games for the Senators.

Neck.

"I tried to throw cheese [good fastballs], but it wasn't a sharp cheddar. It was more like a soft Brie." — Reliever Larry Anderson trying to come back while suffering with two bulging discs in his neck.

Ted Williams. He had the only poor year of his career in 1959 when he suffered a pinched nerve in his neck. Because he had 492 home runs, he wanted to play one more season to reach 500, even though owner Tom Yawkey wanted him to retire. He rebounded with 29 home runs in his final season.

Tony Kubek. After the 1961 World Series, the Yankee shortstop served in the U.S. Army Reserves during the Berlin Wall crisis. While playing touch football at Ft. Lewis, Kubek was hit while catching a pass. His neck hurt a little at the time, but after he returned to the Yankees he noticed that his left hand was often numb. Nevertheless, he hit a three-run home run in his first at-bat after returning from military duty.

Kubek's back continued to hurt and he visited the Mayo Clinic to determine the problem. The doctors discovered that he had broken a vertebrae in his neck and that it had not healed properly. He was told that he could be paralyzed if he had another collision, so he retired at age 29. He went to NBC sports for a tryout in 1966 and stayed through the 1989 season.

Earl Battey. In Game 3 of the 1965 World Series, the Twins catcher was chasing a foul ball when he ran into the dugout railing with his throat. He could barely move his neck for the rest of the Series, but he managed to throw out five runners, including Maury Wills twice.

Steve Yeager. In the late 1970s the Dodger catcher was in the on-deck circle waiting for shortstop Bill Russell to bat. When Russell fouled off a pitch, a piece of the bat flew off and lodged in Yeager's neck. He began to bleed profusely but quick action by the trainers may have saved his life.

Mike Jones. The Royals pitcher suffered a fractured neck in a 1981 auto accident. He managed to return to the Major Leagues with far less velocity on his fastball and lasted only parts of 1984 and 1985.

Nervous Breakdown. See *Psychological Problems*.

Nose.

"Oh, Nose! Angels break Yankees' streak, Posada's beak." — Headline in the *New York Post* in May 2004 when catcher Jorge Posada broke his nose during a collision at home plate.

"That noise in my earphones knocked my nose off and I had to pick it up and find it." — Jerry Coleman.

"Now you take Ernie Lombardi who's a big man and has a big nose and you take Martin who's a little man and has a bigger nose. How do you figger it?" — Casey Stengel.

"The last thing you want to do is go down in the history of All-Star game competition as the only injury sustained during the team picture." — Cal Ripken, whose nose was broken by Chicago White Sox reliever Roberto Hernandez, who momentarily lost his balance stepping down off a riser after the 1996 American League team picture was taken. Ripken, of course, did not miss any games.

Jake Gibbs. Mickey Mantle had a wicked knuckleball, but Casey Stengel never let him pitch in a game. Rookie catcher Gibbs decided not to put a mask on when Mantle told him he was going to unleash his best knuckleball during a pregame catch. Gibbs suffered a broken nose on the first pitch.

Al Rosen. The Indians third baseman broke his nose nine times trying to field ground balls.

Herschel Martin. During World War II Yankee outfielder Johnny Lindell spiked his teammate in the nose during an outfield collision.

Brendan Donnelly. The Angels reliever broke his nose in 20 places when hit by a fly ball during spring training in 2004. Due to excessive bleeding (no kidding!), he didn't return until late May that season.

Osteomyelitis.

"I know I could have set a lot of records that I didn't get a chance to because of my legs." — Mickey Mantle, whose bone disease kept him out of the Korean War and also hampered his play throughout his career. He suffered a bone bruise during a high school football practice that developed into the disease, which is an inflammation of the bone marrow. One source reported that Mantle missed World War II because of it, but he was 14 when the war ended (likely confused with the Korean War). Mantle also had a bad year in 1959, when he suffered injuries to his shoulder, finger and ankle, and contracted a severe case of Asian flu (see also **Knee**, **Leg** and **Shoulder**).

Paralysis.

Roy Campanella. The Dodger catcher was paralyzed in a car accident after the 1957 season, the club's last before moving to Los Angeles. He was leaving his liquor store in Harlem and at 35 mph skidded into a tree after hitting an icy patch. Ironically, his teammates hated to ride with him because he was such a slow driver.

Parasites. In 2004 Yankee pitcher Kevin Brown was diagnosed with intestinal parasites, joining teammate Jason Giambi with the ailment. Some attributed it to the club's opening game in Japan that season, as Brown began losing weight after the return. Giambi later was diagnosed with a benign **Tumor** for which he received treatment during the 2004 season. He finally returned to the line-up on September 14, 2004.

Pneumonia.

Joe DiMaggio. He suffered a case of pneumonia near the end of the 1949 season, but staged a dramatic comeback in two games against the Red Sox in a crucial Series.

Polio.

Vic Wertz. The Indians first baseman contracted non-paralytic polio in August 1955 but recovered to hit 60 home runs over the next two seasons.

Prostate Cancer.

Joe Torre. In March 1999 the Yankees manager was diagnosed with prostate cancer, but he made a full recovery. Don Zimmer ran the team in his absence. Torre returned on May 18, when the Yankees were in first place.

Psychological Problems. See *Psychological Problems*.

Ribs.

"My goal is to mess up every internal organ I have. I have been resting [the broken rib] so much that I have no idea how it will feel when I test it." — Orioles outfielder Brady Anderson in 1997 on his tender ribcage.

Pea Ridge Day. The 1920s pitcher had amazing strength. He impressed teammates with his ability to snap a belt wrapped around his chest by simply expanding his chest. His teammates had a special belt made by a harness maker, which Pea Ridge obligingly tried to break. He snapped three ribs in the attempt.

Ross River Fever.

"Let's just say a good case of Ross River leaves you feeling like a koala suffering from eucalyptus deprivation." — Sportswriter Bill Koenig. In early 1995 Brewers catcher and Aussie Dave Nilsson contracted this illness while at home during the off-season. The virus, which causes swelling in the joints, sore muscles and fatigue, is spread by mosquitoes. Only about 200 people contract it each year out of a population of three million.

Rotator Cuff. See **Shoulder**.

SARS. In response to an outbreak of this respiratory disease and resulting low attendance in early 2003, the Toronto Blue Jays offered tickets for one dollar to a game against the Rangers. They drew over 48,000 for the game.

Seizure.

Greg Walker. On July 30, 1988, the White Sox first baseman was taking infield practice before a game against the Angels. He suddenly suffered a seizure and swallowed his tongue. He was rescued by Chicago trainer Herman Schneider, who was able to pull Walker's tongue into place. A rare infection had invaded Walker's brain, but he was able to return the following season.

Larry Dierker. On June 13, 1999, the Astros manager suffered a grand mal seizure while sitting on the bench during the 8th inning of a game against the Padres. The game was suspended with the Astros leading 4–1. Dierker underwent surgery to removed tangled blood vessels in the brain. Dierker said later that he remembered nothing after the 2nd inning. Coach Matt Galante took over from Dierker until his return a month later. Most of the Astrodome fans greeted him with a sea of Hawaiian shirts and leis to honor his favorite non-uniform apparel.

Shin.

Carl Mays. In mid–1926 the submarine pitcher collapsed during his warm-up and his season was ended. In May he had been hit on the shin on a line drive by Kiki Cuyler and the leg somehow became infected. The Reds finished the year only two games behind the Cardindals, and Mays' presence might have made the difference. In 1927 Mays had a double hernia and didn't pitch much, and his career was essentially over.

Shoulder.

"Well, my bad shoulder feels good, but my good shoulder feels bad." — Roberto Clemente.

"The two leagues tried to sort things out on Monday by determining the sites and matchups for every possible tiebreaker combination, but American League President Gene Budig and National League President Len Coleman had to perform so many coin tosses — 20 — that they both could be candidates for rotator cuff surgery." — Peter Schmuck in the *Baltimore Sun*.

Johnny Vander Meer. The consecutive no-hitter pitcher was back in the minor leagues only two years after his brilliant 1938 performances. He had torn muscles in his shoulder warming up on a wet pitching mound and had a slow rehabilitation. After winning only eight Major League games in 1939 and 1940, he returned to form and led the National League in strikeouts from 1941 through 1943.

Whitey Ford. The Yankee pitcher had chronic problems with his shoulder, which is in part why he pitched so few complete games. He was criticized for not finishing more games, but had a .690 winning percentage and Yankee manager Casey Stengel sometimes skipped Ford's scheduled start against weaker teams to save him for big games. He had only three seasons with 15 or more complete games. Typical was 1961, when he had only 11 complete games while compiling a 24–7 record in 37 starts.

Mickey Mantle. During Game 3 of the 1957 World Series, Mantle was leading off second when Bob Buhl made a pick-off throw. As Mantle dived back to second base, Braves shortstop Red Schoendienst lunged for the wild throw and fell hard on Mantle's shoulder. Mantle said he was never the same again — no power from the left side — though he still continued to hit home runs from both sides of the plate.

Jerry May. On July 14, 1969, the Pirates catcher crashed into the Expos dugout chasing a foul ball. The ambulance taking him to the hospital was hit by another car and May suffered a serious shoulder injury. He lost his job to Manny Sanguillen and was a part-time performer for the rest of his career.

Ray Fosse. See *Home Plate Collisions*.

Ron LeFlore. In early 1979 the Tigers outfielder hurt his throwing shoulder while competing in weightlifting during a televised "Superstars" competition.

Kevin Elster. When the Mets shortstop had his right shoulder operated on, just before surgery he wrote "right" on his right shoulder and "wrong" on his left shoulder.

Bert Blyleven. The pitcher had major reconstructive surgery on his shoulder in early 1991 just before his 40th birthday. After almost two years of rehabilitation, he staged a near-miracle recovery in 1992, winning eight games for the Angels and increasing his lifetime total to 287 wins. He ended his career that season, finishing third (at the time) in strikeouts with 3,701 and ninth in shutouts with 60.

Kelly Gruber. In December 1992 the Blue Jays traded the third baseman to the Angels. In February 1993 Gruber underwent arthroscopic surgery to repair a rotator cuff injury to his non-throwing left shoulder. It was determined later that he was hurt during the 1992 World Series, but apparently the Blue Jays kept quiet about the injury. The Angels demanded that the Blue Jays pay Gruber's salary while he remained on the disabled list. The Blue Jays denied wrongdoing and refused to pay, but Gruber never returned to baseball.

Todd Worrell. The reliever signed with the Dodgers for $9.5 million over three years starting in 1993. The Dodgers insisted that he pass a physical before signing him but withdrew the demand after the Braves entered the bidding. Worrell had a bad shoulder and pitched very little for the club until 1995, when he saved 32 games.

David Justice. In May 1996 the Braves right fielder swung and missed a pitch by Denny Neagle and dislocated his shoulder. He had a similar injury in 1995, and it had never fully healed. He was out for the season. His replacement, Jermaine Dye, homered in his first Major League at-bat.

Davey Johnson. The Braves infielder was 30 years old in 1973 when he hit 43 home runs, 25 over his previous high of 18. He was able to reach the new high when he stopped trying to hit to the opposite field and a chronic shoulder injury stopped bothering him. He suffered a knee injury the following March and never came close to his 1973 power numbers.

Luis Gonzalez. In late September 2002, the Diamondbacks outfielder collided with teammate Tony Womack's knee and dislocated his shoulder. He was lost for the postseason.

Derek Jeter. On Opening Day, April 1, 2003, Jeter separated his left shoulder sliding head first into third base and colliding violently with Blue Jays catcher Ken Huckaby, who had come down to cover third.

Sinuses.

George Sisler.

"I felt sorry for the fans, for my teammates, for everyone except myself. I planned to get back into uniform for 1924. I just had to meet a ball with a good swing again, and then run. The doctors all said I'd never play again, but when you're desperate, when you're fighting for something that actually keeps you alive — well, the human will is all you need." — Sisler on his miserable time during the 1923, which the Browns first baseman missed while trying to recover after sinus surgery in late 1922. The surgery affected his eyesight, and for a time he saw double. He managed to return, however, and hit .320 for seven seasons after that, but he was not nearly as effective as he had been in the past, as those seasons dropped his lifetime average to .340.

Jimmie Foxx. The slugger suffered from serious sinus problems during the 1938 season, though he hit 58 home runs.

Skin Cancer. Several Major Leaguers and club personnel suffered from skin cancer in the 2000s, including Derek Lowe, Marlins manager Jeff Torborg and Tigers trainer Kevin Rand. Helping lead a crusade among ballplayers was Curt Schilling's wife, Shonda, who had six melanomas removed during the early 2000s. She organized free skin-cancer screenings for players and their families in Arizona, and other clubs then adopted the plan.

Skull Fractures. See **Head.**

Spinal Fusion.

Ron Kittle. The future White Sox slugger had a spinal fusion operation while in the Dodgers' minor league organization. After his release in 1977 he was working in construction when he received a tryout with the White Sox. He went on to become the 1983 American League Rookie of the Year and helped lead the White Sox to the division title.

Stomach.

"So it was with Ossee Schreckengost, his well-fed body of six decades cradled in a director's chair in a major-league clubhouse, when he suddenly took ill. He gagged, he choked, he clutched at his gut and at his throat. His eyes bugged in terror, then rolled in pain. His massive belly, the caldron of this sudden onslaught of dyspepsia — hell, of the Mother of all Gutaches — heaved and buckled and fairly roared with pain." — Near-opening lines of the murder mystery *Fear in Fenway*, by Crabbe Evers (1993).

"The stomachache heard around the world." — Description of the 1925 spring training gastrointestinal problem suffered by Babe Ruth. Sportswriters generously covered up the real reason for Ruth's problems, severe cases of syphilis and gonorrhea (see also *Sex*).

Doc Powers. The starting catcher for the A's on Opening Day at Shibe Park on April 12, 1909, was dead two weeks later from a gastrointestinal ailment that came on suddenly during the game.

Mickey Finn. The Phillies infielder died during the 1933 season after undergoing surgery for stomach pains.

Elmer Flick. The Indians outfielder saw his career fade after he developed a stomach ailment in late 1907. His last three partial seasons were unproductive as his weight dropped from 165 pounds to the 130s. He recovered sufficiently to live to age 94.

Ron Santo. The Cubs third baseman was once knocked out when hit in the stomach by a line drive off the bat of mammoth slugger Frank Howard.

Randy Moffitt. The pitcher suffered a stomach ailment that was so rare it was only the third case worldwide ever diagnosed. The fungus was burned out of his stomach and he was able to resume his career.

Hal Carlson. After 13 seasons and more than 100 wins, Carlson was pitching in May 1930 with the Cubs. After winning four of six games that season, he died after suffering a stomach hemorrhage in his hotel apartment. He called for a doctor and died 30 minutes later. Carlson had served in World War I and was gassed in combat, which appeared to cause his stomach ulcers. The next day's game was postponed.

Stroke.

"I had a brain spasm." — Cubs catcher Tim Blackwell when asked why he stopped between bases.

Dave Orr. The first baseman hit .373 in 1890 for Brooklyn of the Players League, the highest last-season average in history. He suffered a stroke in the off-season and never played again.

J.R. Richard. Early in the 1980 season the Astros pitcher experienced pain and numbness in his neck. Doctors initially did not believe his complaints. He then suffered a stroke after pitching batting practice in July 1980 while still suffering from an undiagnosed blood clot. He never again pitched in the Major Leagues.

At the time, Richard had a 10–4 record, a 1.89 ERA and 119 strikeouts as the most feared pitcher in the Major Leagues. He attempted a comeback after ballooning up to 300 pounds, but his skills were gone and his condition was further eroded by later-admitted drug use. In 1989 he tried to make it in the Senior Professional Baseball Association in Florida but was cut by the Orlando Juice after failing to drop his weight below 300 pounds.

Jeff Gray. On July 30, 1991, the Red Sox pitcher suffered a stroke. It occurred 11 years to the day after J.R. Richard suffered his stroke. Gray made moderate progress but never made it back as a player. After he retired, Gray thanked Red Sox manager Joe Morgan for advising him to obtain disability insurance prior to the 1991 season.

Syphilis.

Josh Gibson. Some sources report that his brain tumor was caused by an untreated case of syphilis.

Tendon.

"Whenever you get an inflamed tendon, you've got a problem. OK, here's the pitch to Gene Tendon [Tenace]." — Jerry Coleman.

Testicles.

Carlton Fisk. The catcher took a shot to the testicles while catching during spring training in 1974. Former teammate Reggie Smith, who had taken a few verbal shots from Fisk before Smith departed for the Cardinals, was in the other dugout when Fisk suffered the injury, shouting "I hope you die, you motherfucker!" He kept it up until one of the other Cardinals told him to be quiet. Fisk missed the first month of the season because of the injury.

Mike Gallego. The A's second baseman was diagnosed with testicular cancer in 1983 at age 22. He underwent radiation treatment for the highly treatable form of cancer. He recovered and played into the mid–1990s.

Tim Spehr. When Spehr arrived from Montreal to his new team and came in from his first practice, Red Sox pranksters greeted him with his protective cup cut in half. He had survived the removal of a cancerous testicle in 1985.

John Kruk. The Phillies first baseman was diagnosed with testicular cancer during the winter of 1993–1994. Surgery and chemotherapy apparently were successful, though he had a brief scare during the 1994 season when lumps were discovered at other places in his body. They were determined to be benign fatty masses; not surprising considering Kruk's lumpy out-of-shape physique.

Josias Manzanillo. In April 1997 the Mariners reliever almost lost a testicle after being struck there on a line drive by Manny Ramirez of the Indians. Manzanillo later had surgery to repair tears in both testicles as a result of the Ramirez shot.

Mike Lowell. In February 1999 the Marlins rookie third baseman underwent surgery for testicular cancer. He recovered in time for the 1999 season.

Thigh.

Paul Quantrill. In January 1999 the Blue Jays pitcher underwent surgery to repair a fractured thigh suffered in a snowmobiling accident. Doctors inserted a metal rod to stabilize the bone. He came back and pitched only a few games in 1999, finishing with a 3–2 record.

Throat Cancer.

Brett Butler. In May 1996 the Dodger center fielder was diagnosed with throat cancer. He went into the hospital to have his tonsils removed and doctors found a plum-sized malignant tumor. He had chewed tobacco for two to three years in the early 1980s, which might have led to his condition. Also contributing may have been the secondary smoke generated by his chain-smoking parents, both of whom died of lung cancer. The cancer had spread to at least one lymph node, which made his chances of survival more problematic.

Butler made a miraculous recovery and had an emotional return on September 6, 1996, scoring the winning run. A few days later he broke his hand when hit by a pitch trying to bunt and was out for the season. He had a scare in early 1997 with a swollen lymph node, but it turned out to be a virus.

Thumb.

"[Right-handed] setup man Paul Shuey has been told he needs surgery if he wants to have use of his right thumb, which he does…"—Jason Reid in the *Los Angeles Times*; how surprising that Shuey would actually want to use his thumb.

Leo Durocher.

"The [military] draft has so thoroughly mutilated the Brooklyn Dodgers' roster, it appears today that Manager Leo 'The Lip' Durocher will have to handle the short-stopping chores on his ageing under-pins, even if he requires the aid of a crutch or two."— The *Stars and Stripes* military newspaper. During wartime 1945, retired 38-year-old Dodger manager Leo Durocher inserted himself into the lineup at second base. Eighteen-year-old shortstop Gene Mauch made a bad feed on a double play ball and Durocher broke his thumb in two places. He quickly retired again after playing just two games.

Smoky Joe Wood. A broken thumb may have been the cause of the bad arm that suddenly ended the pitcher's fabulous but short-lived pitching career. After posting a 34–5 record in 1912, the following year he was pitching on a wet field in Detroit when he bent to field a bunt. He slipped and his thumb jammed into the ground. The fracture should have kept him out longer, but the team needed him in the rotation. The pain in his shoulder that plagued him began shortly after he returned to the mound prematurely. After that, he could pitch only once every two or three weeks, as he needed the extra time for his arm to recover sufficiently between starts. Even though he was able to pitch, his legendary fastball was gone and he moved to the outfield (see also ***Players Who Switched Position***).

Bobo Newsom. The Tigers pitcher broke his thumb during the 1940 season, but still won 21 games. He lost Game 7 of the World Series that season 2–1 to the Reds, giving up two runs in the 7th inning.

Carlos May. While on Marine reserve duty in August 1969, the White Sox outfielder lost part of his right thumb in a mortar accident. Though his season was cut short at 100 games, he was named Rookie of the Year by *The Sporting News*. He had to go through a series of skin grafts but returned to post a lifetime .274 average over 10 seasons ending in 1977.

Catfish Hunter. The A's pitcher took a 15–3 record into the 1973 All-Star Game. He tried to stop a Billy Williams line drive with his bare hand, breaking his thumb. He was out for 30 days and cost himself a chance to win 30 games. He finished with a record of 21–5.

Cecil Fielder. On July 15, 1997, the Yankees' 270-pound designated hitter/eater attempted to slide head first into home, trying to score from first base on a double. The resulting broken thumb put him out for two months.

Mike Piazza. The catcher suffered a thumb injury during the Mets' 1999 postseason. His replacement, Todd Pratt, hit an extra-inning home run in the division series Game 4 to send the Mets on to the NLCS. Piazza was back for Game 3 of the NLCS against the Braves, but cost them the 1–0 game when he threw a ball into center field on a double steal by runners on first and second.

Ivan Rodriguez. On July 24, 2000, the Rangers catcher broke his thumb on Mo Vaughn's bat attempting to throw a runner out. He missed the remainder of the season.

Jeff Kent. On March 1, 2002, the Giants second baseman broke his thumb while supposedly washing his truck. He was out more than a month, and rumors spread immediately that the accident had occurred while Kent was riding his motorcycle—an activity forbidden in the standard player's contract. There were two 911 calls about a motorcycle accident near the Giants spring training facility, but there was no police report and no accident. Kent sidestepped the issue: "I think what is sad is that this incident has become bigger than the game. There are so many good things that happen on this field with this team that are good for baseball. I'm not going to comment anymore on the issue."

His relationship with the club soured and he was traded to the Astros after the season.

Derek Jeter. The Yankee shortstop played the 2003 postseason with a ruptured ligament in his thumb.

Thyroid Cancer.

Jerry DiPoto. The Indians pitcher was diagnosed with thyroid cancer in 1994 after a strong rookie season. He rejoined the club in May 1994 after surgery and made a full recovery.

Danny Jackson. The pitcher had off-season surgery for thyroid cancer prior to the 1995 season. The Cardinals signed him for $10.8 million without fully researching the side effects of the surgery, such as fatigue. He started the season 0–9 and then took time off to rebuild his strength. He came back to pitch a shutout to end the skid.

Toe.

Dizzy Dean.

"Fractured, Hell! The damn thing's broke!"—Dizzy Dean after Earl Averill hit a line drive off his toe in the 1937 All-Star Game. Averill was thrown out at first, but Dean's toe was broken. The batter prior to Averill was Lou Gehrig. Dean shook off catcher Gabby Hartnett on a 3–2 pitch and threw Gehrig a fastball for a home run with two outs and Joe DiMaggio on first base.

Dean had been exhausted before the game and asked to sit it out, but Cardinals owner Sam Breadon urged him to play because of the publicity surrounding the game and the negative effect his absence would have on attendance. Breadon also pushed Dean to come back from his injury early because he was such a big draw. The toe had not completely healed and Dean altered his pitching motion to compensate, resulting in permanent shoulder damage that dramatically shortened his career.

Red Ruffing. Before he made it to the Major Leagues, the pitcher lost four toes in a mining accident. This forced him to change from a power hitter to a pitcher. This explains why he was such a strong-hitting pitcher during his career, batting .269 with 36 home runs.

Tooth.

Chris Brown.

"If that were Chris Brown, they'd be preparing him for open heart surgery."— Mike LaCoss after being hit hard in the chest by a ball, but managing to stay in the game. Brown, who played briefly at third base in the 1980s, was known as the "Tin Man" because he supposedly had no heart. He had a reputation for never playing with even the slightest injury: he once went on the disabled list with a "bruised tooth."

Brown resurfaced in 2004 when it was discovered that he was operating a $7 million crane in Houston and then drove a diesel truck in Iraq for Halliburton.

In 1926 *The Sporting News* reviewed the injury list and complained of "coddled" players who were out due to "upset stomach, sunburn and fear of an ulcerated tooth."

Tom Glavine.

"Since Glavine was a hockey player in high school, I'm surprised he had two front teeth to lose."— "StatsGuru" at Baseball-Musings.com. In August 2004 pitcher Tom Glavine was in a taxi that crashed on the way to the airport. He lost his two front teeth and was shaken up, causing him to miss a couple of starts.

Tourette's Syndrome.

Jim Eisenreich.

"Jim Eisenreich joins that hardy company of big leaguers who make playing merely 'hurt' seem sissy. These are men who defy impairments that would institutionalize less doughty mortals."— Jim Murray.

"Jim Eisenreich was a roommate of mine for about three days. I couldn't take it. He had that disease, and he would make me a nervous wreck. Seven o'clock, lights out, curtains closed, TV off, and he would just sit in bed and do his thing. I was young, none of us understood what was going on, and he scared me."— Len "The Vulture" Whitehouse, a pitcher with the Twins in 1983.

"Compared to what's wrong with most of us, Tourette's Syndrome is like having a common cold."— Phillies starter Curt Schilling, comparing the disorder suffered by teammate Jim Eisenrich to some of his other crazy teammates on the 1993 pennant-winning club. Eisenrich came up with the Twins in 1982 at age 23. He was hitting .303 early in the season, but his mysterious tic problem worsened as fans began abusing him. After only 34 games he was scratched from the lineup for the rest of the season. In 1983 and 1984 he played in a total of only 14 games. He was diagnosed as having agoraphobia, but he refused to take the prescribed medication because it made him sluggish.

After he retired following a brief and dismal 1984 season (.219 in 12 games), Eisenrich began taking medication on his own for what his doctors finally diagnosed as Tourette's Syndrome, a nervous disorder manifested by tics and uncontrollable speech pattern. He was able to bring the problem under control and after two years was picked up by the Royals, for whom he played 44 games in 1987. By 1989 he was a regular for the Royals and batted .301 in

1991. His career highlight was a home run in the 1993 World Series for the Phillies.

Tumor.

Jason Giambi. In mid–2004 the Yankee first baseman was diagnosed with a benign tumor after being out several weeks because of a parasite that weakened him. Giambi's response after finally being diagnosed: "I felt like a lab rat during those times. The not knowing, that was the worst part of it. You start to go, 'Why am I not getting better?'"

Typhoid.

John McGraw. The 1890s Orioles third baseman contracted typhoid while a player during the 19th century (also reported as **Malaria**).

Casey Stengel. In 1915 Casey Stengel reported to spring training 20 pounds lighter than his usual 175, and the weight loss was officially blamed on typhoid fever. Sportswriters apparently learned that it was actually caused by a venereal disease.

Trade. In July 1997 the Reds and Indians exchanged damaged goods. Of the five players involved in the trade, the three departing Reds pitchers had all had rotator cuff surgery, a fourth player was out for the year with a broken arm and the fifth had had knee surgery.

Umpires. See *Umpires—Injuries.*

Vertigo.

Nick Esasky. The first baseman had just established himself as a power hitter when he left the Red Sox to sign a big contract with the Braves for the 1990 season. Nine games into the season he had to quit because of a severe case of vertigo. He never returned to the Major Leagues.

Ken Dayley. In 1991 the pitcher signed a three-year contract with the Blue Jays worth $6.3 million, but pitched only five innings from 1991 through 1993 because of a severe case of vertigo.

Joe Carter. There was a brief scare in 1994 when the Blue Jays outfielder came down with a minor case of vertigo, but it disappeared quickly.

Wart.

Mike Mussina. In early 1998 the Orioles pitcher had to be placed on the disabled list because of a wart on his finger. He had just come off the disabled list when he was struck in the face by a line drive off the bat of Sandy Alomar. The resulting broken nose put him back on the disabled list.

Wrist.

Jim Rice. The Red Sox outfielder suffered a broken wrist when he was hit by a pitch in Detroit on September 21, 1975. The injury kept him out of the 1975 World Series between the Red Sox and Reds. Considering the closeness of the Series, his absence may have cost the Red Sox the championship.

Hank Greenberg. The Tigers first baseman broke his wrist during Game 2 of the 1935 World Series when he was hit by a pitch from Fabian Kowalik of the Cubs. The Tigers overcame the injury and defeated the Cubs in six games.

Early in the 1936 season, Greenberg hurt the wrist again in a baserunning collision and was labeled a "brittle" ballplayer. His season was a washout (he played in only 12 games), but he returned in 1937 to drive in 183 runs and hit 40 home runs. Despite missing almost four full seasons to World War II, almost one full season to injury, and retiring at only age 36, Greenberg still hit 331 home runs and is in the top 10 all-time in home run frequency.

Ken Griffey, Jr. In May 1995 the Mariners center fielder made a terrific catch against the center field wall but broke his left wrist as he braced his crash. He had to have surgery and was out for several months. He returned to lead the club to within two games of the World Series. Griffey broke another bone in his wrist in June 1996 after fouling a ball off it, but returned in early August.

Cliff Floyd. On May 15, 1995, the Expos first baseman suffered a badly damaged wrist when runner Todd Hundley of the Mets ran into him as he stretched across the bag for a throw. Floyd broke three small bones in his wrist and eight ligaments were mangled. It was also dislocated. Despite what many thought would be a career-ending injury, he returned on September 12 and made a diving catch in right field.

Nomar Garciaparra. In April 2001 the Red Sox shortstop suffered a split tendon in his wrist and was out for the season.

Book. Rick Swaine, *Beating the Breaks: Major League Ballplayers Who Overcame Disabilities* (2004).

Innings

"At dawn on Day Forty, in the bottom of the 2614th inning, O'Reilly approaches the umpire with the first line-up change in many days. Bill Klem casts a baleful glance toward the on-deck circle, where, ankle-deep in water, a huge Indian stands awkwardly, holding not a bat but a piece of root from the tree by the river..."—W.P. Kinsella in *The Iowa Baseball Confederacy* (1986).

Consecutive Played. Orioles shortstop Cal Ripken played 8,243 consecutive innings from May 30, 1982, to September 14, 1987, in what is believed to be the longest streak of its kind. The streak ended in an 18–3 loss to the Blue Jays, in which Ripken came out in the 8th inning. From 1982 through 1992, Ripken missed only 128 of 15,787 innings. Lou Gehrig played in every inning only during the 1931 season.

Innings Pitched. The official statistical category of innings pitched was added in the early 1900s. It had not been needed earlier because games pitched were usually complete games. The number of innings could be calculated fairly accurately by the number of games started.

Ed Walsh of the Giants holds the modern record of 464 innings pitched in 1908. See also *Pitchers*.

Hitless Innings/Pitcher. See *Pitchers*.

Insects

"Some of the bugs there are twin engine jobs."—Sandy Koufax on the large bugs at Colts Stadium, the original home of the Astros (then the Colt 45's).

"It tastes like a roach."—Pitcher Ron Reed when asked by the Braves trainer what kind of bug he had swallowed on the pitching mound.

"Hey, I got a kid to feed."—Twins designated hitter Matt Lecroy, after teammates paid him $550 to eat a black bettle that was crawling in the clubhouse.

"Spider Clark, Dave Beatle, Flea Clinton, Bug Holliday, Roxy Roach, Skel Roach, Bugs Raymond, Creepy Crespi, Terry Leach, Bugs Bennett, Freddy Leach, Buzz Boyle, Spider Jorgenson, Buzzy Wares"

Mosquitoes.

"Smart mosquitoes. They'd attack with a 3-and-2 count and runners in scoring position. They knew when you weren't paying attention to them."—Reds manager Davey Johnson in 1995 upon requiring blood pressure treatment after inhaling insect repellant fumes in the dugout.

Jimmy Piersall once called time during an at-bat, ran to the dugout and then returned to the plate. On the next pitch, he whipped out a can of mosquito spray and "fogged" the ball as it arrived at the plate. The ploy got a big laugh and Piersall continued his at-bat without incident.

Aphids. On August 3, 2001, the Blue Jays beat the Orioles 10–1, but a swarm of aphids in the 3rd inning impeded, but didn't delay, the game. Home plate umpire Tim Welke asked that the roof be closed and Toronto's Jeff Frye wore a dust mask in the dugout.

Gnats.

"From the way Denny's shaking his head, he's either got an injured shoulder or a gnat in his eye."—Jerry Coleman.

Ebbets Field. On September 15, 1946, during the second game of a doubleheader between the Cubs and Dodgers at Ebbets Field, a gnat swarm forced fans to wave their scorecards to fend off attacks. The umpires ruled that the scorecard waving was a hazard to players because they could not easily see the ball. As a result, the Dodgers were awarded a 2–0 win because the required five innings had been played.

Comiskey Park. On June 2, 1959, a swarm of gnats attacked Orioles pitcher Hoyt Wilhelm during a game at Chicago's Comiskey Park. The game was stopped as the batboys came running with bottles of bug spray. After the spray failed, the batboys unsuccessfully tried torches. A postgame fireworks display was brought in from center field and a smoke bomb was placed on the framework. The gnats finally departed and the Orioles won the game 3–2.

SkyDome. On August 27, 1990, the new Toronto Skydome experienced a 38-minute delay in the 6th inning when a swarm of gnats invaded the field. Officials opened the roof, the air conditioning was turned down and the gnats left the field.

New Name. In 1996 the Savannah, Georgia, Class A club renamed its club after a local nuisance, the Sand Gnats.

Bees.

"We haven't had so much excitement over bees since Barry Bonds and Bobby Bonilla left."—Pirates publicist Jim Trdinich after a swarm of bees forced the Pirates to call off batting practice in 1995.

"You need thick skin to play in New York."—Mariners first baseman John Olerud after teammate Bret Boone was stung by a bee in Yankee Stadium.

Bees invaded Riverfront Stadium in Cincinnati on April 17, 1976, causing a 35-minute delay after camping in the backstop screen. Invasions also occurred there on May 26, 1980, and May 10, 1987 (stinging pitcher Ted Power).

Inside Baseball

"In reality, this is the 'soft age' of baseball. Players are petted and pampered in a way unknown to the old-timers. While probably their equal mechanically, seldom do they devote much time to mastering the inside part of the game. Baseball was the life of a player 15 or 20 years ago."—*Los Angeles Times* sportswriter Harry A. Williams in 1920.

"Inside Baseball" was a phrase coined by the Baltimore Orioles for the "scientific" type of game the club played in the 1890s. Much of what the club did, however, was picked up from other clubs, most notably the Chicago White Stockings of the 1880s. The phrase apparently was overused early in the century: "... a much abused expression to denote clever team work much of which is the result of a vivid imagination."—John B. Foster in his 1908 glossary of baseball terms.

Inside-the-Park Home Runs

"Usually, someone has to go on the DL for me to get even a triple."—Robin Ventura in 2003 after hitting his first inside-the-park home run.

"The warped old legs, twisted and bent by many a year of baseball campaigning, just barely held out under Casey until he reached the plate, running his home run home. Then he collapsed."— Writer Damon Runyon on Casey Stengel's 1923 World Series home run. Stengel was playing for the Giants against the Yankees in newly opened Yankee Stadium. With two outs in the 9th inning of a 4–4 tie in Game 1, the 33-year-old Stengel lined a single over shortstop. The outfield was overshifted and the ball rolled on the hard ground 450 feet to the wall as Stengel tried to circle the bases. Rounding third base, he lost his shoe and staggered into a head first slide at home to score the winning run. It was the first World Series home run in Yankee Stadium history.

Four in a Game. On July 13, 1896, Ed Delahanty hit four *Home Runs* in a game, all inside the park. Delahanty, a strong right-handed batter with the Philadelphia Phillies, hit his homers against the Cubs at the West Side Grounds in Chicago. The Cubs played there from 1894 through 1915. The distance to left field was 340 feet and to right, 316 feet. However, it was the distance to straightaway center field — 560 feet — that probably helped Delahanty that day.

Career. Sam Crawford is the all-time leader with 51 inside-the-park home runs between 1909 and 1917.

Babe Ruth hit 10 inside-the-park home runs. Among players with at least 300 home runs, Rogers Hornsby is the leader with 30.

Catcher/Grand Slam. Only seven catchers have hit inside-the-park grand slams. The last was Dan Wilson of the Mariners, who did it on May 3, 1998.

Pitcher/Grand Slam. In 1964 Yankee pitcher Mel Stottlemyre became the first pitcher to hit an inside-the-park grand slam since 1910.

Season Total. Willie Wilson had six home runs for Kansas City in 1979; five were inside the park.

Two in a Game. On May 8, 1906, A's manager Connie Mack inserted pitcher Chief Bender as a substitute outfielder in the 6th inning. He responded by hitting two inside-the-park home runs.

In 1939 center fielder Terry Moore of the Cardinals hit two inside-the-park home runs in one game in Pittsburgh.

Dick Allen hit two inside-the-park home runs in a game against the Twins on July 31, 1972. It was the first time it had occurred since Hank Thompson did it in 1950.

On October 4, 1986, Twins shortstop Greg Gagne hit two inside-the-park home runs.

Only Home Run. Because of the enormous dimensions of Washington's Griffith Stadium, Joe Kuhel hit the only home run of any kind in 77 home games for the Senators in 1945, an inside-the-park drive. Despite the anemic output, the Senators only lost the pennant race on the last day of the season.

First Career Hit. On April 17, 1997, two days after debuting with Jackie Robinson's No. 42 (the last player to do so), Marc Sagmoen became the fourth player ever to hit an inside-the-park home run as his first hit. It was the only homer of his career, which lasted 21 games for the Rangers that season. Butch Henry of the Astros was the last to do it, on May 8, 1992. The others were Johnnie LeMaster in 1975 (among 22 total home runs over 12 seasons) and Brian Downing of the White Sox in 1973.

Back-to-Back. Back-to-back inside-the-park home runs were hit on June 23, 1946, at the Polo Grounds by the Cubs' Marv Rickert and Eddie Waitkus. The feat was duplicated on August 27, 1977, by Toby Harrah and Bump Wills of the Rangers.

Same Inning. Although not back-to-back, On May 26, 1997, Sammy Sosa and Tony Womack of the Cubs each hit an inside-the-park home run in a 2–1 win over the Pirates. Both came in the 6th inning. It was the first time this had occurred in the National League since Lou Brock and Hector Cruz did it for the Cardinals on June 18, 1976, against the Padres.

Instant Replay

"What other game includes errors as one of the line items? We know people are going to make errors. We publish errors: runs, hits and errors. We are human. We are fallible. We make errors. We are umpires, we make a mistake. It happens."— Commissioner Fay Vincent after stating that instant replay would not be a part of baseball.

"I don't believe it. Lou Brock could never make that play again — even on instant replay."— Bill Virdon.

First. The first television instant replay was used on station WPIX-TV in New York on July 17, 1959. Broadcaster Mel Allen asked that the tape of the break-up of Ralph Terry's no-hitter be replayed immediately, rather than during the postgame show.

Review. On June 3, 1997, the Padres played the Braves in Atlanta and were tied 2–2 in the 8th. When Keith Lockhart of the Braves hit a two-run 8th inning home run, the umpires immediately reviewed television tapes and ruled that Lockhart's ball was foul. Lockhart then grounded out to end the inning. The Padres scored three in the 9th for a 5–2 victory.

Controversy. The $1.5 million Atlanta scoreboard once replayed a controversial call which the umpire clearly missed. Bob Watson had scored on a passed ball on a close play at the plate. In protest, the umpires walked off the field. Braves executive Bill Lucas assured the umpires that no more close calls would be shown. This prompted the Major Leagues to ban replays of anything remotely resembling a close call.

Ejection. On May 9, 1984, umpire Joe West ejected two television cameramen from Shea Stadium after they allowed the Mets to review replays of a controversial call at the plate.

Poll. In a late 1980s poll, 75% of Major League players voted to keep umpires as the sole decision-makers on all calls and not use instant replay.

Instructional Camps

"I can teach you by mail to throw 32 different kinds of curves and to have absolute control over every one of them — out-curves, in-shoots, raise-balls and drops."— Sales pitch of the Ted A. Kennedy School of Scientific Baseball operating in St. Louis shortly after 1900.

First Camp. The first instructional camp was formed by Fred Pfeffer, second baseman for the Chicago White Stockings in the 1880s.

Bucky Dent. The Bucky Dent School in Florida features Little Fenway Park, a replica of the real thing (see *Errors— Bill Buckner*, for a story involving pitcher Mike Torrez and this field). Recently, in addition to Dent's baseball school, there have been schools bearing the names of Denny and Brian Doyle, Jim Rice, Mickey Owen, Jack Aker, Dusty Baker, Clint Hurdle, Steve Kemp, Geoff Zahn, Chet Lemon, Cal Ripken and Mickey Stanley.

Baseball Academy. From 1971 through 1974 Royals owner Ewing Kauffman underwrote a baseball academy that was mocked by most baseball people. Future Pirates general manager Syd Thrift was the first director of the Academy. Cost of construction was $1.5 million, with an additional $500,000 invested for the first year of operation.

In the first year 128 tryout camps were held for 7,682 candidates.

Three future Major Leaguers were in this first class: Bruce Miller, Ron Washington and Frank White. Also in the class was Hal Baird, who went on to coach at Auburn and tutor such stars as Bo Jackson, Frank Thomas, Tim Hudson and Gregg Olson.

White grew up in Kansas City and did not play baseball in high school because the sport was not offered. His coach on his amateur team encouraged him to try out, and his wife encouraged him to go. He got the day off from his sheet metal job. White was referred to in scouting circles as "The Six Million Dollar Man," in reference to how much Kauffman spent on the academy.

The academy was closed in May 1974. A total of 14 players made the Major Leagues, including U.L. Washington and Rodney Scott, out of the 40,000 prospects reviewed.

Instructional Leagues See *Winter League Baseball*

Integration

"Get That Nigger Off the Field."—Cap Anson in 1884 in Toledo; and the title of Art Rust, Jr.'s, book chronicling the history of racism and integration (or lack thereof) in Organized Baseball.

See also *Black "Firsts," Negro Leagues* and *Racism*.

19th Century Efforts to Ban Black Players.

"How far will this mania for engaging colored players go? At the present rate of progress, the International League may ere many moons change its name to 'Colored League.'"—1887 commentary in *Sporting Life*.

First Black Professional. The first well-known professional black player was Bud Fowler, who played for the 1872 Newcastle Club of Pennsylvania. That season marked the beginning of his 25-year career in and out of Organized Baseball. Ironically, Fowler was born in Cooperstown, New York. He was one of 55 black players known to have played in Organized Baseball before pervasive segregation formally blocked their play after 1887 (with a few short-lived exceptions).

First Known Major Leaguers.

"Colored people did not have a chance to play [during slavery], and so were late in developing proficiency. It was more than fifty years after the introduction of baseball before colored people in the United States had a chance to play it. Consequently, it was another fifty years before they arrived at the stage where they were important in the organized baseball picture."— Ford Frick's lame excuse for the delay in the appearance of black players in the Major Leagues.

Based on recent research, the first black Major League player was William Edward White (see *Black "Firsts"*).

Until 2003, the first known black players in Major League Baseball were catcher Moses Fleetwood "Fleet" Walker and his brother, outfielder Welday Walker. They played for the Toledo Mud Hens of the American Association in 1884 and for the same club when it was in the minor league Northwestern League the year before.

Fleet was born in 1857, the son of a physician. He played on the first varsity baseball team at Oberlin College in Ohio, the first U.S. school to officially adopt a policy of nondiscrimination. Fleet was 27 when he joined the Mud Hens in 1884 after studying law at Michigan. He hit .263 in 42 games for Toledo.

Welday was 24 when he joined the club after Fleet left late in the season, hitting .222 in five games. After their brief Major League stints, both played minor league ball.

There were many incidents of racism during the season and manager C.H. Morton received written death threats. Fleet com-mitted 37 errors, attributed by one source to pitcher Tony "The Count" Mullane "disliking Negroes" and therefore ignoring Walker's catching signals. Since signals were not yet in vogue, this is an unlikely reason; and the number of errors is not inordinate given the state of fielding and catcher's equipment in that era.

Fleet later owned an opera house and theater. He published the *Equator* newspaper, in which he and his brother urged black Americans to return to Africa. In 1908 Fleet wrote a booklet advocating emigration to Liberia and other countries to achieve equality and the brothers opened an office to help those who wanted to emigrate. Fleet died at age 67 in 1924 and Welday died at 77 in 1927. See also David W. Zang, *Fleet Walker's Divided Heart: The Life of Baseball's First Black Major Leaguer* (1995).

Other Early Black Professionals.

"… able to throw a ball at a flag-staff and make it curve into a water pail."—19th century writer on George Stovey.

Other early black ballplayers who played in Organized Baseball were pitcher George Stovey, infielders Frank Grant and James R. Jackson (at least one source reported that Jackson and Bud Fowler were the same person). Grant was considered by many as the best black player of the 19th century. He led the International League in hitting in 1887 with a .366 average. The best Major League second baseman of the era was black star Fred Dunlap. The best battery, often played up by the press because both were black, supposedly consisted of George Stovey and Moses Walker. Stovey set the International League record with 35 wins in 1887 and was considered the best black pitcher of the 19th century. There were approximately 20 black players on Major League teams in the 1880s.

Barred from Baseball.

"Philadelphia, Penn., Sept. 10 [1887]

To Chris Von der Ahe, Esq.

DEAR SIR: We, the undersigned, members of the St. Louis baseball club, do not agree to play against negroes tomorrow. We will cheerfully play against white people at any time, and think, by refusing to play, we are only doing what is right, taking everything into consideration and the shape the team is in at present.

[Signed] W. A. Latham, John Boyle, J.E. O'Neill, R. L. Caruthers, W. E. Gleason, W. H. Robinson [not Wilbert], Charles King, Curt Welch."

The records of the amateur National Association show that at the Association's convention in 1867 the group determined that any club with "persons of color" should not be admitted to the organization because it would cause a "division of feeling," and the "possibility of rupture being created on political grounds would be avoided."

On July 20, 1884, Chicago White Stockings captain and noted racist Cap Anson demanded that the Walker brothers not play for Toledo or the Chicago players would walk off the field. By 1888 Anson supposedly had initiated a purge of black players, which cost them 25 minor league jobs. Later historians have indicated that Anson's role has been overblown and that his views were shared by most players and management of that era. One source noted that Anson's racist attitudes may be explained by his supposedly having been "the first white child born among Indians in Iowa."

In 1887 the International League formally voted to exclude black players. Of the 10 teams represented at the meeting, the six with no black players voted for the bar and the four with black players voted against it. There was later an unwritten "gentleman's agreement" to ban black players from Organized Baseball, but many whites thought there was a formal law against integration. By restricting entry into the minor leagues, black players were effectively prohibited from pursuing the only logical route to the Major Leagues.

When the International League reorganized after the 1887 season, the color line was erased briefly. Fleet Walker signed with Buffalo and Dick Higgins signed with Syracuse. However, in an International League (then known as the International Association) exhibition game on September 27, 1888, Walker was not permitted to play against Anson's White Stockings. Walker played 89 games with Buffalo before being released.

It was not uncommon for white players to intentionally play poorly behind a black pitcher. Many whites also refused to sit for team portraits with black players.

"Passing." Players thought to be black were tossed out of their leagues in the 19th century. In the 1880s Lou Nava was forced out and in the 1890s George Treadway was forced out. The actions were taken based on suspicions arising from their appearance. John McGraw tried to sneak Charlie Grant onto the Baltimore Orioles of the 1890s, billing him as a "full-blooded Cherokee." Cincinnati Red Stockings manager Charles Comiskey supposedly recognized Grant from the black Chicago Columbus Eagles, and he was barred.

Last 19th Century Player. The last 19th century black player in Organized Baseball was Bert Jones, known as "The Yellow Kid." Jones was a left-handed pitcher in 1898 in the Kansas State League. Following Jones, with two brief exceptions (see below), there were no more known black players in Organized Baseball until 1946 unless they were passed off as "Indian" or "Cuban" (or they actually were Cuban). See also *Cuba* and *Native Americans*.

Early 20th Century Attempts to Break the Color Line.

"As it is, the field for the colored professional is limited to a very narrow scope in the baseball world. When he looks into the future he sees no place for him in the Chicago American or Nationals; nor the Athletics; or New York, even were he superior to Lajoie, or Wagner, Waddell or Mathewson, Kling or Schreck. Consequently he loses interest. He knows that; so far shall I go, and no farther, and as it is with the profession, so it is with his ability."— Sol White's *Official Base Ball Guide, History of Colored Ball* (*Spalding Guide* 1907).

Bill Thompson played an uneventful 1911 season in the Class D Twin State League of Vermont and New Hampshire. He played almost the entire season for the Bellows Falls team before being injured. Local papers made reference to his black heritage, so there was no question that he was not "passing" for something other than an African American.

On May 28, 1916, black pitcher Jimmy Claxton pitched for the Oakland Oaks of the Pacific Coast League. He was released on June 3, 1916, after seven days with the club, supposedly after it was learned that he was black. Based on his baseball card picture, it is hard to believe that anyone thought he was anything but black (he was extremely dark), but the team may have tried to hide his identity by claiming that he was "Cuban." Claxton played in 1932 for the Cuban Stars, on the same roster as Luis Tiant's father, Luis Sr. He died in 1970.

One source erroneously reported that the first black player on a 20th century minor league club was Alfred Wilson of the 1935 Granby Red Sox in the outlaw Quebec Provincial League in Canada.

1930s and Early 1940s.

"Beyond the fundamental requirement that a Major League player must have unique ability and good character and habits, I do not recall one instance where baseball has allowed either race, creed or color to enter into its selection of players."— Statement by National League president John Heydler in 1933.

"Each club is entirely free to employ Negro players to any and all extent it pleases. The matter is solely for each club's decision without restriction whatsoever."— Judge Landis in the 1930s.

"I've said everything to be said on the subject. The answer is no."— Judge Landis in the 1940s; he repeated this phrase at owners meetings whenever anyone raised the possibility of bringing a black player to the Major Leagues.

Informal Vote. At the 1933 annual baseball writers dinner in New York a vote was taken and all except Giants manager John McGraw were in favor of using black players in Organized Baseball.

Clark Griffith. In 1935 the Senators owner signed Roberto (Bobby) Estalella out of Cuba. He arguably was the first black player in the Major Leagues in the 20th century, as he was far from white even by Cuban standards of ethnicity.

In 1938 black sportswriter Sam Lacy (see also *Sportswriters*) approached Griffith regarding the use of black players on his club. Griffith used the likely demise of the Negro Leagues as his excuse for not employing black players. Another source reported that Griffith supposedly contacted Negro League stars Buck Leonard and Josh Gibson about playing with the club, but he decided not to disturb the status quo. Neither ever played in the Major Leagues, though Leonard was approached by Bill Veeck in the late 1940s. Leonard felt he was too old by that time and did not want to hurt the chances of those who might follow. At age 46 in 1953 Leonard played his only Organized Baseball, appearing in 10 games for Portsmouth of the Piedmont League and batting .333.

Bill Veeck. Veeck supposedly tried to break the color line when he owned Milwaukee of the American Association in the early 1940s. He tried to sign a black player, but Judge Landis threatened to throw him out of baseball. Veeck allegedly attempted to buy the Phillies prior to the 1944 season and had a deal all but finalized. He supposedly was turned down by the Major League owners when it was rumored that he intended to work with Harlem Globetrotters owner Abe Saperstein to stock the club with black players.

Veeck related this story during interviews in the 1960s and no one around in the 1940s ever corroborated it. No one ever attempted to verify Veeck's account until 1998, when baseball historians David M. Jordan, Larry R. Gerlach and John P. Rossi published a monograph in which they debunked virtually all aspects of Veeck's claim. In short, the trio showed convincingly that Veeck never had a deal to buy the Phillies, had no relationship with Saperstein, and no deal was quashed by Landis or National League president Ford Frick. Veeck said in his book that Frick had bragged "all over the baseball world … about how he had stopped me from contaminating the league." Yet, no other sources ever referenced this supposed statement by Frick. Veeck later gave inconsistent versions of the story to writers Donn Rogosin, Jules Tygiel and Shirley Povich.

Veeck supposedly had told people that he would not object to hiring Negro League players if he bought the Cleveland Indians. Again, however, it is unlikely that Major League owners would have approved the sale of the club to Veeck had they known of this intent. The monograph concludes with the following: "It is hardly surprising that historians have wanted Veeck's tale to be true. Bill Veeck is a more appealing crusader than the sanctimonious Branch Rickey, and his story has the added fillip of letting us believe that his plan was thwarted by the guardians of privilege and racism.... Nevertheless, we must face the fact that Bill Veeck falsified the historical record. This is unfortunate. His *actual* role in advancing the integration of major league baseball is admirable and can stand on its own merit."

Tryouts/*Daily Worker*. In the early 1940s Los Angeles of the Pacific Coast League invited black players for tryouts, but the invitations were cancelled without explanation. In 1942 *The Sporting News* continued to editorialize against the integration of baseball. That same year Dave Barnhill, a black pitcher weighing just 130 pounds but with a blazing fastball, received a telegram from Nat Low, sports editor of the communist *Daily Worker* newspaper. Low had arranged for a Major League tryout through William Benswanger, president of the Pirates. Benswanger backed out before the tryout was scheduled.

Lester Rodney was another writer for the *Daily Worker* who campaigned for the integration of baseball. As the Red Scare enveloped the nation in the 1950s, however, his contribution was obscured. It wasn't until 1997 when, as part of a 50th anniversary retrospective, his contributions were recognized. See Irwin Silber, *Press Box Red: The Story of Lester Rodney, the Communist Who Helped Break the Color Line in American Sports* (2003).

On September 1, 1942, the Indians issued a statement that they would try out three black players before the 1943 season. The three were third baseman Parnell Woods, pitcher Eugene Bremmer and outfielder Sam Jethroe. There is no record of the tryouts being held. Only Jethroe made it to the Major Leagues, though with the Braves and not the Indians.

The Dodgers held their 1945 spring training camp at Bear Mountain, New York. Two black players in their late 30s, pitcher Terris McDuffie and first baseman Dave "Showboat" Thomas, showed up and demanded tryouts with the team. They were accompanied by three newspapermen, two from black publications and communist newspaper editor Nat Low. Some sources described this as a publicity stunt forced on Rickey by one of the reporters, sports editor Joe Bostic of the black newspaper *People's Voice*.

Rickey watched the players but realized they were not good enough to make it. He purportedly told the entourage not to use force in their effort to achieve integration. For at least two years before this incident, Rickey had considered signing black players. He then announced the formation of a Negro League to be called the **United States League**, which was to include his Brooklyn Brown Dodgers. The club and league were to be used to develop black players for eventual transition into Organized Baseball. This gave him a reason to scout black players. At the same time, the Dodgers signed John Wright and Ray Partlow and assigned them to Three Rivers (a black team) before the end of 1945.

On April 16, 1945, after two of Boston's city council members threatened to revoke the Sunday Blue Law exemption for the Red Sox, the club relented and held a tryout for Jackie Robinson, Marvin Williams (who never played in the Major Leagues), and Sam Jethroe, but nothing came of it. Oddly, the team required the players to sign "tryout applications," something it had never done in the past. Manager Joe Cronin, in defense of the decision not to sign them, said that the club would have had to assign the players to Class AAA Louisville, which was not possible at that time because of the racial climate in that city.

Paul Robeson. At the urging of A's minority owner John Shibe and Cardinals owner Sam Breadon, in 1944 a delegation headed by black opera singer Paul Robeson visited Judge Landis and club owners at the winter meetings. Their appeal for integration was rejected.

St. Louis Segregation. In a small step toward integration, on May 4, 1944, both St. Louis clubs announced the elimination of their long-time policy of restricting black fans to the bleachers and pavilion at Sportsman's Park.

Integration Committees. In 1944 influential black sportswriter Sam Lacy was instrumental in having Organized Baseball appoint an integration committee that included him. Branch Rickey represented the National League and Larry MacPhail represented the American League. Also on the committee was Philadelphia magistrate Joseph H. Rainey. One source reported that the committee never met because MacPhail failed (refused?) to show up. According to Ford Frick, however, MacPhail participated on the committee and wrote in favor of integration, but his strong addition to this report was deleted at the last minute.

Other sources report the event somewhat differently. In 1945 New York mayor Fiorello H. LaGuardia formed a committee to survey "The Negro ... in Baseball." MacPhail submitted a paper on the subject in which he concluded that few blacks were capable of playing Major League Baseball. He reported that Negroes were deserving of a better deal and recommended that a few be allowed into Organized Baseball. By the time the report was issued, Rickey had signed Jackie Robinson to a contract with the Dodger farm club in Montreal.

Jackie Robinson Signs a Minor League Contract.

"To accept honors, public applause for signing a superlative ballplayer to a contract? I would be ashamed." — Branch Rickey.

"Do you really think a nigger's a human being?" — Montreal Royals manager Clay Hopper to Branch Rickey (according to Rickey), when Mississippi native Hopper begged Rickey not to make him the first manager of an integrated team. By the end of the season, Hopper reportedly had developed a deep respect for Robinson and thanked him for being on the team.

Robinson's signing came shortly after Rickey's famous meeting with him on August 28, 1945, in which Rickey counseled Robinson on the difficulties that lay ahead. Robinson signed for a $3,500 bonus and $600 per month to play for Montreal in 1946, the Dodgers' Class AAA club. Montreal general manager Hector Racine announced the signing on October 23, 1945. In contrast to Bill Veeck, who paid the Negro League Newark Eagles for Larry Doby's contract, Rickey refused to compensate the Negro League Kansas City Monarchs for Robinson's contract.

Rickey supposedly chose Robinson in part because he had learned discipline as an army officer. Robinson became an officer only after the intervention of heavyweight boxing champion Joe Louis (who often was criticized for being passive on integration issues) facilitated Robinson's entry into the Army's Officer Candidate School. Rickey undoubtedly was aware that Robinson had been discharged from the service in 1944 after he complained about segregated seating on military buses in Texas.

Organized Baseball's Integration in 1946.

"If a black boy can make it on Okinawa and Guadalcanal, hell, he can make it in baseball." — Statement by new commissioner Happy Chandler, supposedly made in March 1945 — though he did not take the job until April 1945, and it was probably imprudent for him to say that in March before he received the offer.

"It is ironical that America, supposedly the cradle of democracy, is forced to send the first two Negroes in baseball to Canada in order for them to be accepted." — Editorial of April 13, 1946, in the black newspaper, the *Chicago Defender*. Following Robinson, the second black player signed by Montreal was pitcher John Wright, but he was sent down a short time later. When Branch Rickey bought Robinson for the Royals in 1946, the team could not train in segregated Daytona and had to practice at nearby Kelly Field instead.

Robinson's first minor league game was on April 18, 1946, against the New Jersey Giants at Roosevelt Stadium in Jersey City. He had four hits, including a home run, four RBIs and two stolen bases. He also scored on a balk after distracting pitcher Phil Oates.

His first home game was on April 27. Robinson hit .349 for the season and Montreal won the International League pennant and Junior World Series against the American Association champions.

Shortly after Robinson began play for Montreal, Roy Campanella and Don Newcombe joined the New England League on a lower-level Dodger farm team.

Robinson to the Major Leagues.

"It wasn't my job to decide who could play baseball and who couldn't. It was my job to see that the game was played fairly and that everyone had an equal chance. I think I did that, and I think I can face my Maker with a clean conscience." — Commissioner Happy Chandler at age 88 reflecting on "Baseball's Great Experiment."

1) The right man off the field;

2) The right man on the field;

3) Positive reaction of black Americans;

4) Positive reaction of the press and public;

5) A place for him in the organization (Montreal, where race relations would be less of an issue);

6) Positive reaction of his teammates. — Branch Rickey's six-point criteria for making the Robinson "experiment" work, as reported by sportswriter Arthur Mann.

"After the game, Jackie Robinson came into our clubhouse and shook my hand. He said, 'You're a helluva ballplayer and you've got a great future.' I thought that was a classy gesture, one I wasn't then capable of making. I was a bad loser. What meant even more was what Jackie told the press, 'Mantle beat us. He was the difference between the two teams. They didn't miss DiMaggio.' I have to admit, I became a Jackie Robinson fan on the spot. And when I think of that World Series, his gesture is what comes to mind. Here was a player who had without doubt suffered more abuse and more taunts and more hatred than any player in the history of the game. And he had made a special effort to compliment and encourage a young white kid from Oklahoma." — Mickey Mantle.

According to Happy Chandler many years later, in late 1946 or early 1947 purportedly there was a secret "color line" vote by the Major League owners, who came out 15–1 against integration. The lone exception was Rickey and his Dodgers. The vote followed presentation of a secret report (the same as described above) written by National League president Ford Frick, American League president Will Harridge, Cubs owner Phil Wrigley, Cardinals owner Sam Breadon, Yankees general manager Larry MacPhail and Red Sox owner Tom Yawkey. The report allegedly recommended that black players be excluded. All copies of the January 1947 report were destroyed, although it has been speculated that Chandler secretly kept a copy.

Rickey purportedly walked out of the meeting claiming that "there will be riots in Brooklyn" due to the decision. The story of the vote first surfaced in 1970 when Chandler began circulating it, but there was never any corroboration. Some sources doubt Chandler's story that a vote occurred.

Despite the purported vote, Chandler allowed the Dodgers to move ahead with their plans for bringing Robinson to the Major Leagues. Others in the Dodger organization wanted Don Newcombe to be the first. Rickey vetoed their choice because Newcombe, playing for the Newark Eagles, was only 19, while Robinson was a more mature 28.

Many have assumed that Rickey broke the color line himself, but without Chandler's support it could not have happened. Chandler always contended that Rickey received too much of the credit, and that he, Chandler, deserved more. Long-time Dodger executive Buzzie Bavasi claimed in his autobiography that four people,

including Chandler, deserve the credit. Bavasi checked out Robinson's character; Rickey worked with the 11 New York newspapers to gauge their attitude toward the move; and scout Clyde Sukeforth followed Robinson everywhere in 1946 in Montreal to see if he was the right player physically. Bavasi claimed that the decision to bring up Robinson was kept secret from Chandler until the last moment.

Dodger manager Leo Durocher was suspended immediately before the 1947 season began for consorting with known gamblers (see also *Suspensions*). It has been reported that Robinson's first Major League manager was Burt Shotten, who replaced Durocher for the season. However, coach Clyde Sukeforth managed the club for the first two games of the season (winning both). Rickey had told his coaches that Shotten was coming in to manage and asked them to decide among themselves who would manage in the interim. For many years Sukeforth was credited with managing in only one game but later was correctly recognized for having managed the first two.

Dodger co-owner Walter O'Malley, who hated Rickey, told sportswriter Red Smith in 1950 that the idea to bring Robinson to the Dodgers was not Rickey's, but his.

Rickey later told Satchel Paige that if he had had his way, Paige would have been the first black player in the Major Leagues. Rickey did not elaborate and as Paige said, "Mr. Rickey, as the Bible says, sometimes spake in diverse tongues."

Having Robinson on the team was a financial windfall for the Dodgers from the outset. It increased black fan attendance at games and increased attendance overall because of the curiosity of having a black player on the team. The Dodgers sold out their southern barnstorming tour after spring training in 1947. Rickey was also in part trying to capitalize on the heavy northern migration of millions of blacks during and after World War II. Many black families had moved into large metropolitan areas that had Major League teams (primarily Chicago, St. Louis and New York).

Player Revolt.

"I don't care if the guy is yellow, black, or if he has stripes like a fuckin' zebra. I'm the manager of this team, and I say he plays." — Leo Durocher to his rebellious players.

During spring training in 1947, it was clear that Robinson would be playing with the Dodgers. Manager Leo Durocher quietly quelled a potential insurrection led by Dixie Walker and Eddie Stanky. On April 10, 1947, the club issued a press release: "Brooklyn announces the purchase of Jack Roosevelt Robinson from Montreal. He will report immediately." One source claimed that the announcement was made 'inconspicuously,' as it came during the media circus the day after Durocher was suspended for the season. After Robinson joined the Dodgers, five players supposedly asked to be traded: Dixie Walker, Bobby Bragan, Carl Furillo, Kirby Higbe and Pee Wee Reese. Ironically, Reese became Robinson's closest friend on the team; Furillo and Bragan relented and Bragan later admitted being "a better, more enlightened man" for having played with Robinson; Higbe was traded early in the season; and Walker was traded after sending the following letter to Rickey: "Recently the thought had occurred to me that a change of Ball clubs would benefit both the Brooklyn Baseball Club and myself. Therefore I would like to be traded as soon as a deal can be arranged. My association with you, the people of Brooklyn, the press and Radio has been very pleasant and one I can truthfully say I am sorry it has to end. For reasons I don't care to go into I feel my decision is the best for all concerned."

Walker was traded in December 1947. Many years later Walker would only say on the subject that "Jackie Robinson was a great ballplayer."

Robinson's First Major League Game.

"I know how to resolve this. Let's all put on No. 42 so they won't be able to tell the difference."— Gene Hermanski of the Dodgers in 1947, after the FBI met with the team to discuss death threats made against Jackie Robinson.

"It would be small compensation for the abuse the people of Brooklyn have taken from the incompetent and unfunny liars who describe them as Metropolitan hillbillys. There were 25,623 of them in the joint and they behaved with dignity and compassion."— Jimmy Cannon on Robinson's first game for the Dodgers on April 15, 1947, against the Braves at Ebbets Field. A full house of 26,623 saw the game, with reports that there were 14,000 black fans in the stands. Robinson played first base (Eddie Stanky played second base all season) and scratched out a bunt single in his first two games. One source reported incorrectly that he went hitless and was 0-for-20 in his first five games.

Robinson finished the season at .297, led the league in stolen bases and was voted Rookie of the Year. *When All Hell Broke Loose in Baseball* is broadcaster Red Barber's account of the 1947 season with the Dodgers.

Purported Strike/Cardinals.

"I do not care if half the league strikes. Those who do it will encounter quiet retribution. All will be suspended and I do not care if it wrecks the National League for five years. This is the United States of America and one citizen has as much right to play as another."— National League president Ford Frick, responding to threats of a strike by the Cardinals players over Robinson's appearance in the National League. However, Frick never said it quite that way and the Cardinals never threatened to strike.

Recent historians now claim that the strike threats never occurred, and the notion of a strike arose from a misunderstanding. Cardinals captain Terry Moore and team leader Marty Marion never mentioned a strike. It appears that owner Sam Breadon was unsure if manager Eddie Dyer had control of the club on matters other than integration, and this somehow evolved into an alleged threat to strike over Robinson's presence. Breadon supposedly said that anyone who struck would be suspended and National League president Ford Frick came out strongly in favor of Robinson.

New York Herald Tribune sports editor Stanley Woodward supposedly averted the strike by breaking the story. This is false, as his story appeared after the first Dodgers/Cardinals Series that supposedly precipitated the threat of a strike. It is also untrue that Stan Musial and Enos Slaughter had a fight over whether to strike against Robinson. The whole incident appeared to have stemmed from Sam Breadon's comments on his team's poor start — they lost 11 of their first 13 games.

Though a strike probably was never threatened, it is true that a beanball war with the Cardinals was quickly averted when the Dodgers threatened to throw at Musial in retaliation for beanballs directed at Robinson.

Honors to Robinson.

"I'm sixty-nine years old but never thought I'd live to see the day when I'd stand face-to-face with Ty Cobb in Technicolor."— Entertainer Bill "Bojangles" Robinson on the combativeness of Jackie Robinson, at a ceremony in Robinson's honor near the end of the 1947 season. The Rookie of the Year Award later was named after Robinson in his honor. On Opening Day 1987, to commemorate the 40th anniversary of Robinson's first game with the Dodgers, all ballparks staged a ceremony at second base, Robinson's primary Major League position. The anniversary also brought unintentionally racist comments by Dodger general manager Al Campanis that cost him his job (see *Racism*).

On April 1, 1997 commemorative baseballs were used in all Opening Day games to commemorative Robinson's breaking of the color barrier.

The April 15, 1997, game between the Dodgers and Mets at Shea Stadium was slated to honor the 50th anniversary of Robinson's appearance in a Major League line-up. Both teams objected to the planned 5th inning stoppage of play to honor Robinson after the game became official. The ceremony was to last 30 minutes, and needed to be held during the game because of security precautions involving President Clinton. He attended with Robinson's widow, Rachel.

The game was stopped after it became "official" in the 5th inning, and many of the 34,596 left after Clinton's remarks (the Mets had given away an additional 19,000 seats for the game). The Dodgers lost 5–0. Every team in the Major Leagues retired Robinson's No. 42 to commemorate the anniversary. The ceremonial first pitch was thrown out by Jesse Robinson Sims, a grandson of Robinson's who was born six years after Robinson died.

Frank Thomas of the White Sox was perhaps unfairly criticized at the time for being insensitive to the Robinson legacy, after being asked how Robinson affected the younger generation of players and whether he thinks about Robinson: "Not really. You know, I've got to be honest. I guess I'm more from the new age. I didn't know much about the history of that part of things."

Ken Griffey, Jr., wore No. 42 that night in his game for Seattle, instead of his usual No. 24. He also wore his black stockings almost at knee length to emulate the style of Robinson's day.

In 2004 Major League Baseball designated April 15 as permanent "Jackie Robinson Day" around the Major Leagues.

Larry Doby/American League Integration.

"Robinson has proved to be a real big leaguer. So I wanted to get the best of the available Negro boys while the grabbing was good. Why wait? Within ten years Negro players will be in regular service with big league teams."— Bill Veeck quoted in the Cleveland Plain Dealer on July 4, 1947.

Twenty-two-year-old Indians outfielder Larry Doby broke the American League color line on July 5, 1947. He pinch-hit against the White Sox in Chicago and struck out against journeyman Earl Harrist. Doby had played at Long Island University and in the Negro National League before moving on to Organized Baseball. He was playing for the Newark Eagles when Bill Veeck signed him, and Doby went on to a successful Major League career. He finally was elected to the Hall of Fame in 1998.

Hotel Accommodations. Former Dodger general manager Buzzie Bavasi surprisingly claimed in his autobiography that when the Dodgers began staying at desegregated hotels, the black players were unhappy because when they stayed at black hotels they were treated like kings and the accommodations were "beautiful."

Spring Training.

"Before their first season began, the Mets accomplished what the New York Yankees could not do in thirty years — they integrated St. Petersburg, Florida."— Leonard Schechter in *Once Upon a Time* (1970).

In 1961 Cardinals players Bob Gibson, George Crowe, Bill White (later National League president) and Curt Flood (who unsuccessfully tested the reserve clause in the early 1970s) led a successful effort to desegregate the Cardinals' spring training housing.

Military Team Integration. Integration of service baseball teams did not occur until 1948.

Historical Percentage of Black Players. In 1946 and 1947 a total of 16 black players were picked up by minor and Major League clubs. The most (five) played in Connecticut for the Class B Stamford Bombers of the Colonial League. By the end of 1949 six black players were in the National League. The minor leagues were absorbing more black players, but it was a truly miserable existence in many areas of the country. Nevertheless, the Negro Leagues were just about dead.

In 1950 there were eight black players and nine Latin players in the Major Leagues (2% each, 96% white). In 1957 there were 18 black players in the Major Leagues.

In 1967 there were 23 black players in the National League and 17 in the American League, a total of 40 out of 500 Major Leaguers. In 1990 the Major Leagues were 17% black and 11% Latin, with 159 black players and 107 Latin players. A 1973 study determined that teams with higher percentages of black players historically have had higher winning percentages.

By the 2000s the numbers had continued to drop, a fact lamented in many publications. The sparse numbers were attributed to the few numbers of organized baseball programs in black neighborhoods, the focus on football and basketball by black youth, and the lack of full college baseball scholarships.

In 2004, 24% of Major Leaguer players were Latin, down slightly from 2003. Only 83 African Americans were among the 827 Major Leaguers on rosters at the start of the 2004 season, down from 19% in the late 1980s and 27% in the 1970s. There were only four black pitchers in the Major Leagues, and Jerome Williams of the Giants was the only right-hander.

By Position. Since the 1960s the percentage of black players in the outfield has increased while the percentage of black pitchers and catchers has declined. In 1986, 70% of black players were outfielders. There were no black catchers and only 4% of black players were third basemen. Since 1983 an average of 80% of all black players have been in the outfield or at first base.

Star Players Only. In 1986 twice as many active black players as active white players had lifetime averages of .280 or above. More than 40% of active black pitchers had ERAs under 3.00, while only 11% of white pitchers did. These figures support the generally accepted notion in all of American professional sports that bench players will generally be white and that for a black player to make it to the highest level of his sport, he must be exceptional. Such criticism surfaced again in 1988 when the Mets were chastised for promoting supposedly average white players over supposedly average black players (see also *Racism*).

Front Office Jobs. See *Black "Firsts"* and *Racism*.

Team-by-Team Analysis.

"Many major league officials — Cincinnati's Bill DeWitt and Pittsburgh's Joe L. Brown, for instance — categorically state that the supremacy of the National League overall in the last decade is due to its quicker recognition of Negro talent." — Murray Olderman in *Nelson's 20th Century Encyclopedia of Baseball* (1963).

The National League pursued black and Latin ballplayers far sooner than the American League. Many contend that this contributed to the dominance of the National League during the 1960s, evidenced in part by that league's dominance of the All-Star Game in that era.

Integration/Chronological Order.
Brooklyn Dodgers, April 15, 1947
Cleveland Indians, July 5, 1947
St. Louis Browns, July 17, 1947
New York Giants, July 8, 1949
Boston Braves, April 18, 1950
Chicago White Sox, July 21 (or May 1), 1951
Philadelphia A's, September 13, 1953

Chicago Cubs, September 17, 1953
Pittsburgh Pirates, April 13, 1954
St. Louis Cardinals, April 13, 1954
Cincinnati Reds, April 17, 1954
Washington Senators, September 6, 1954
New York Yankees, April 14, 1955
Philadelphia Phillies, April 22, 1957
Detroit Tigers, June 6, 1958
Boston Red Sox, July 21, 1959

AMERICAN LEAGUE
Boston Red Sox.

"I have been connected with the Red Sox for 12 years and during that time we have never had a single request for a tryout by a colored applicant. It is beyond my understanding how anyone can insinuate or believe that all ballplayers, regardless of race, color or creed have not been treated in the American Way as having an equal opportunity to play for the Red Sox." — Red Sox general manager Eddie Collins in 1945.

"There would never be any niggers on my team." — Red Sox manager Pinky Higgins, who managed from 1955 through 1959, and again from mid–1960 through 1962.

Boston historically has been criticized by some as the most racist town in Major League Baseball (with St. Louis a close second). In 1951 the Red Sox signed their first black player into the organization. He was Piper Davis, a 34-year-old veteran of the Negro Leagues who never made it to the Major Leagues (he had also played for the Harlem Globetrotters). It was another eight years before a black player made it to the Major Leagues with the Red Sox.

The Red Sox were the last team to have a black player on their roster when infielder Pumpsie Green played for the club on July 21, 1959. The second black player for the club was pitcher Earl Wilson. In 1960 Willie Tasby became the club's first black regular. As late as 1989 Dennis "Oil Can" Boyd was the only black player on the roster.

An excellent telling of the team's racist past is by Howard Bryant, in *Shut Out: A Story of Race and Baseball in Boston* (2002).

Chicago White Sox. In 1951 the White Sox became the third American League team to integrate. Outfielder Minnie Minoso is sometimes credited as the first black player on the club, when he debuted on May 1. Others, perhaps more accurately, credit Sam Hairston as the first (father of Major Leaguer Jerry Hairston) because Minoso was a Latin player and not an African American. Hairston first played for the club on July 21, 1951.

Cleveland Indians. Outfielder Larry Doby was the first black player in the American League, making his debut shortly after Jackie Robinson on July 5, 1947 (see also **Integration After Jackie Robinson**).

In 1948 Satchel Paige became the second black player for the club. By 1953 the Indians and Dodgers each had the most black players, with five. There was speculation in 1953 that the Indians were not doing well because they had so many black players. Such talk ended with the club's 1954 pennant with virtually the same players on its roster.

Detroit Tigers. The Tigers were one of the last teams to integrate, followed only by the Red Sox. Not coincidentally, the club signed its first black player only after the death of long-time owner Walter Briggs, Sr., in the mid–1950s.

On June 6, 1958, infielder Ossie Virgil, then 25, became the first black player to see action for the club. He played third base for the Tigers after playing two years with the Giants. Some black players rejected Virgil's claim as the first because he was from the Dominican Republic, and they classified him as Latin. At the time, Detroit had only 19 black players under contract throughout the organization.

The second black player on the club was Larry Doby in 1959. The first Detroit regular was second baseman Jake Wood in 1961.

New York Yankees.

"When I finally get a nigger, I get the only one in the world who can't run." — Yankee manager Casey Stengel, who often used the "N" word, referring to catcher Elston Howard. The Yankees were slow to integrate. Howard was the first black player signed by the Yankees. He appeared in the line-up on April 14, 1955. Sportswriter Dan Daniel wrote in *The Sporting News* about Howard as the choice of the Yankees: "Howard … was chosen for that situation because of his quiet demeanor, his gentlemanly habits and instincts, and his lack of aggressive attitudes on race questions. He came to the Yankees determined to achieve the position he now occupies, not as a crusader."

See Arlene Howard, *Elston and Me: The Story of the First Black Yankee* (2004).

The second black player for the Yankees was Harry "Suitcase" Simpson in 1957. By 1964 they had only one black pitcher, Al Downing, and one black regular, Howard, who had become a starter in 1959. The club's lack of black players perhaps contributed to the decline of the Yankees in the 1960s.

Puerto Rican Vic Power probably would have been the first black player for the club, as he was playing first base for the Yankees' minor league Kansas City club in the early 1950s. The Yankee front office decided that Power was too flashy to be the first black Yankee and traded him late in 1953. Part of the criticism of Power was that he "liked white women," which some sources report was borne out by the fact that he married one; his wife was a light-skinned Puerto Rican. He batted .290 over his 12-year career and was a seven-time American League Gold Glove winner. He also hit better against the Yankees during his career than any other American League club.

Philadelphia Athletics. Pitcher Bob Trice played for the Athletics on September 13, 1953. In 1954 first baseman Vic Power became the club's first black starter.

St. Louis Browns. The Browns were the third team in the Major Leagues to integrate. Second baseman Hank Thompson, who came from the Negro Leagues and later played a number of years for the Giants, first played for the Browns on July 17, 1947.

Some sources reported that Willard Brown was the first to play for the club, but he did not join the Browns until the fall of 1947. He had been a star with the Negro League Kansas City Monarchs. After coming to the Browns at age 34, he hit only .179. Frustrated with the racial pressures and expressing exasperation at the poor quality of the team, he went back to the Monarchs after only 21 games. Before he departed, he hit the first American League home run by a black player.

Satchel Paige was the team's first black regular, pitching in 23 games in 1951.

Washington Senators. Outfielder Carlos Paula was the club's first black player and first black starter after debuting on September 6, 1954. The second was Joe Black in 1957, who had pitched for the Dodgers beginning in 1952.

NATIONAL LEAGUE

Boston Braves. Outfielder Sam Jethroe joined the club in 1950 and was the club's first regular. He played his first game on April 18 (erroneously 21 in some sources), 1950.

Brooklyn Dodgers. Jackie Robinson played his first Major League game on April 15, 1947 (see above).

Chicago Cubs. Shortstop Ernie Banks and second baseman Gene Baker were brought up at the end of 1953 and played in their first game simultaneously on September 17. Banks batted first, so he is often reported as the first black Cubs player to appear in a game. Both were regulars in 1954. Baker was one of the first black managers in the minor leagues.

Cincinnati Reds. Utilityman Nino Escalera was the first black player for the club, on April 17, 1954. The second was utilityman Chuck Harmon. Outfielder Frank Robinson became the first black regular in 1956.

New York Giants.

"No, we've got too many already." — Reply of Giants owner Horace Stoneham when manager Leo Durocher demanded that Willie Mays be brought up to the club.

The Giants were the second National League team to integrate when second baseman Hank Thompson played for the club on July 8, 1949. Outfielder Monte Irvin was the second black player on the club when he pinch-hit on July 27, 1949.

Willie Mays was brought up in 1951 to replace his minor league mentor, second baseman Artie Wilson. Wilson purportedly was sent down to maintain the early unspoken quota rule that no Major League team could have more than two black players on its roster.

Philadelphia Phillies. Third baseman John Kennedy was the first black player on the club, playing in five games in 1957 (his only Major League games) beginning on April 22. Utilityman Chuck Harmon was the second, also in 1957 (he also was the second for the Reds). Second baseman Tony Taylor and first baseman Pancho Herrera became regulars on the club in 1960. See Christopher Threston, *The Integration of Baseball in Philadelphia* (2002).

Pittsburgh Pirates. Second baseman Curt Roberts was the first black player, as well as the first regular, starting on April 13, 1954. Outfielder Sam Jethroe, who had been the first black player with the Browns in 1950, was the second black player for the Pirates.

St. Louis Cardinals. First baseman Tom Alston played for the club on April 13, 1954. The second black player on the club, pitcher Brooks Lawrence, also appeared in 1954 and posted a 15–6 record. Curt Flood was the first black nonpitching regular in 1958.

Books. Arthur Ashe, *Hard Road to Glory: A History of the Afro-American Athlete, 1919 to Present* (1988); Larry Moffi and Jonathan Kronstadt, *Crossing the Line: Black Major Leaguers, 1947–1959* (1994); Jackie Robinson and edited by Charles Dexter, *Baseball Has Done It* (1964); Art Rust, Jr., *Get That Nigger Off the Field* (1976); Jules Tygiel, *Baseball's Great Experiment* (1983).

Intentional Walks

"[Spitballer] Burleigh Grimes' idea of an intentional walk is four pitches at the batter's head." — Unknown.

"They're putting Bonds on base intentionally. They intentionally tried to keep me off because of what I could do once I was on." — Rickey Henderson, dismissing Bonds' **Base on Balls** record.

"Look at him. He knows he's going to hit me, and I know he's going to hit, so I'm going to walk him." — Harvey Haddix to his catcher, with Willie Mays at bat.

"I was such a dangerous hitter I even got intentional walks in batting practice." — Casey Stengel in 1967.

"That's an effective way to contain a hitter. Never throw him another strike the rest of his life." — Giants manager Felipe Alou on the number of intentional passes to Barry Bonds. At the time (late 2003) the batters who followed Bonds in 2003 had batted .167 with only 12 RBIs.

"Cook has vowed to avoid the tedious commute and will fax his next appearance from the bullpen."— Steve Abney after reliever Dennis Cook came in to throw two pitches to complete an intentional walk, and then was removed from Game 5 of the 1999 NLCS game between the Mets and Braves.

Rule. In 1925 Dodger pitcher Bill Hubbell threw to first base instead of the catcher while issuing an intentional walk. He did it again later in the season and National League president John Heydler threatened him with suspension if he did it again. The rule was changed the following year to require that the pitcher throw only to the catcher. The catcher is required to stay in the catcher's box to prevent him from moving up near the first base line to catch the pitch.

The statistic was not kept before 1955. In a 1956 American League exhibition game the teams experimented with eliminating intentional walks by allowing the batter to immediately go to first base without the necessity of throwing any pitches.

Most by Batter/Season/Game. Willie McCovey of the Giants received 45 intentional walks in 1969 and received 20 or more in a season five times. Barry Bonds was thought to have "shattered" the record in 2002 when he received 68 intentional walks. He also was walked intentionally three times in a nine-inning game, tying the record for a regulation game.

In 2004 when Bonds broke his own single season record of 68 (which he did before the All-Star break, with 71), he had 547 intentional walks to Rickey Henderson's 61. Bonds had 131 walks at the All-Star break that season and finished the year with an astounding 120 intentional walks among his new-record 232 base on balls. Second in 2004 was Jim Edmonds, with 26 intentional walks.

In 1993 Blue Jays first baseman John Olerud tied the American League record for intentional walks when he received 33. Ted Williams set the record in 1957.

Andre Dawson of the Cubs set a Major League record on May 22, 1990, when he was walked intentionally five times in a 16-inning, 2–1 Cubs victory over the Reds. Three of the walks came with first base occupied.

On June 5, 2001, Red Sox designated hitter Manny Ramirez was intentionally walked four times, tying the American League mark set by Roger Maris on May 22, 1962. Ramirez did it in 18 innings, Maris 12.

Most by Batter/Career. In April 1999 Barry Bonds broke Henry Aaron's National League record of 290 intentional walks, and in July 1999 Bonds broke Aaron's Major League record of 293 (Aaron had three while with the American League Brewers late in his career).

Strategy.

The strategy apparently began in 1896 when William "Kid" Gleason, captain of the New York Giants, had pitcher Jouett Meekin walk Chicago slugger Jimmy Ryan to get to George Decker, a weaker hitter. Decker struck out to end the game.

In 1915 Yankee manager Bill Donovan attracted media attention when he intentionally walked two batters with a man on third to set up a force play against the home team in the 9th inning of a tie game.

In 1957 Warren Spahn became the only pitcher ever to walk a batter intentionally in order to pitch to Stan Musial. This set up a double play, and Musial obliged.

During the 1961 home run barrage by Roger Maris, he never received an intentional walk. This might have been because the next batter in the lineup was named Mickey Mantle. Mantle had only nine intentional walks.

Harvey Haddix gave up home runs to Willie Mays in 1954 and 1959, both on low outside curveballs that Mays pulled out of the

park. Two weeks after the 1959 home run, Haddix decided to walk Mays intentionally with two outs and none on to avoid the same fate late in a tie game. He wanted to face rookie Willie McCovey, even though McCovey was in the middle of a 22-game hitting streak. Mays stole second base and McCovey singled him home to win the game.

In later years, Mays sometimes stayed at first base rather than attempt a double to enable McCovey to hit. Otherwise, McCovey was likely to receive an intentional walk with first base open.

In the 8th inning of Game 3 of the 1972 World Series, Reds batter Johnny Bench received a surprise from A's pitcher Rollie Fingers. The Reds were leading 1–0 with runners on first and third and one out. Bench, at the peak of his career, was an extremely dangerous hitter that the A's did not want to face. On a full count, manager Dick Williams and his infielders gathered for a mound conference and made it clear that they intended to intentionally walk Bench. Catcher Gene Tenace went back behind the plate and stood with his glove out, signaling for a ball-four intentional walk. Fingers threw a slider on the outside corner of the plate for a called strike three.

Chili Davis of the Angels suffered the same fate in July 1995 against the Indians. Indians catcher Tony Pena came out of his crouch and signaled for an intentional walk on a 3–2 pitch. Pitcher Dennis Martinez put a fastball over the plate for a called strike three.

Bases Loaded. Nap Lajoie of the A's is sometimes credited as the first batter to be walked intentionally with the bases loaded. It happened on May 23, 1901, against the White Sox. The Sox were ahead, 11–7, in the 9th. Fearing that Lajoie, who led the league with a .422 average, would hit a game-tying grand slam, Clark Griffith, then a pitcher-manager who was working in relief, walked Lajoie with no outs The next three batters grounded out and the Sox won, 11–10.

On July 23, 1944, Giants manager Mel Ott ordered his pitcher, Andy "Swede" Hansen, to intentionally walk Bill "Swish" Nicholson of the Cubs with the bases loaded. Nicholson had hit six home runs in four games within 48 hours. Hansen walked him and held on for a 12–10 win.

Mel Ott walked five times in the meaningless last game of the 1929 season, the last time perhaps intentionally with the bases loaded. He lost the home run title to Chuck Klein, 43 to 42, as Klein's manager, Burt Shotten, ordered his pitchers to walk Ott every time up. The last one came with two outs on a 3–2 pitch, and none of the writers mentioned it in the game stories. For this reason, Ott is generally not credited with an intentional walk with the bases loaded.

Barry Bonds is the only other batter walked intentionally with the bases loaded in the 20th century, on May 28, 1998. Arizona manager Buck Showalter, hanging on to an 8–6 lead, acknowledged Bonds as the career leader with 298 intentional walks when he came up with two outs in the 9th inning. Reliever Gregg Olson walked him to reduce the Diamondbacks' lead to 8–7. Brent Mayne hit a hard liner to right for the final out.

Erroneous Claims of Bases Loaded Intentional Walks.

Hub Pruett is said to have once intentionally walked Babe Ruth with the bases loaded, but the facts do not support this claim. On July 26, 1926, Joe Shanti of the Indians tried to walk Ruth with two outs and the bases loaded in the 6th inning of a game, but Ruth stepped across the plate and fouled off what would have been ball four. Umpire Brick Owens called him out for stepping out of the batter's box.

For many years, it was reported that Cardinals slugger Joe Medwick drew a bases-loaded walk during his 1937 Triple Crown season, but it has never been confirmed. Trying to check it out, Ev Parker, writing in *The National Pastime*, contacted Harry Danning, among others. Danning's response: "If you were a rival manager, would you walk Medwick to pitch to Johnny Mize?"

World Series. According to one source, Babe Ruth walked 12 straight times in the 1926 World Series. It makes a good story, but there were only 11 walks by the Yankees in the entire Series, and nothing close to 11 straight by anyone. In Game 7 with the Yankees behind 3–2 in the 9th inning, Ruth was intentionally walked. He tried to steal second and was tagged out for the last out of the Series (see also **Stolen Bases**).

Most by Pitcher/Season. Long-time Pirates reliever Kent Tekulve is the latest of three pitchers who have allowed 23 intentional walks in a season.

Gift. When Buddy Lewis returned to the Major Leagues from military service during World War II, the umpire called two balls on apparent strikes his first time up at the plate. The disgusted pitcher then intentionally walked Lewis. The umpire explained that it was the first time back for Lewis and he needed a break.

No Practicing Allowed. After serving a suspension for drug problems, Darryl Strawberry went to the minor leagues to hone his hitting stroke before joining the Yankees in 1995. In one game he was intentionally walked in each of his five at-bats.

Record-Breaking. On August 12, 2001, the Braves lost to the Diamondbacks 9–1, as Greg Maddux's National League record streak of innings without a walk ended at 72⅓. He intentionally walked Steve Finley in the 3rd inning to end the streak.

Interference

"Anyone interfering with a ball in play will be ejected from the park." — Public address announcement…

"I hope Stuart doesn't think that means him." — Pirates manager Danny Murtaugh referring to the routine public address announcement and first baseman Dick "Dr. Strangeglove" Stuart's poor fielding abilities.

Batted Ball Hitting Runner. In 1887 a batted ball was ruled dead if it struck a runner. Before that a runner was out if hit by a batted ball only in the umpire's discretion (apparently if a good faith effort had not been made to avoid being hit).

In 1888 a batter first received credit for a hit when a runner was struck by a batted ball and the runner was ruled out. In 1931 it was ruled that the out would be credited to the fielder nearest to the runner. Presumably, fielding statistics had become more important by this time and the ruling was necessary to account for all 27 outs in a game.

In April 1957 Don Hoak of the Reds exposed a loophole in the runner interference rules. In a game against the Braves, Hoak was on second base and Gus Bell was on first when Wally Post hit a double-play ground ball to the left side of the infield. Hoak, though he was a runner, fielded the ball with his bare hands and tossed the ball to surprised shortstop Johnny Logan. Houk was automatically out for interference, but not the batter, and Hoak thereby avoided an easy double play. After the Reds did this three times that season, the rule was changed effective immediately to also charge the batter with an out because of the obvious double play situation.

Fielder Interfering with Runner. The Giants and Red Sox went into extra innings during Game 2 of the 1912 World Series. In the bottom of the 10th inning Tris Speaker of the Red Sox tripled and attempted to score on the play. He was "hipped" by the third baseman, which broke his stride. He was called out at the plate,

which fueled a brawl after the umpire refused to call interference. The tie game was called in the 11th inning due to darkness.

In the bottom of the 10th inning of Game 3 of the 1975 World Series, umpire Larry Barnett called Reds pinch hitter Ed Armbrister safe on an interference call involving catcher Carlton Fisk. Replays show that the wrong call was made. Cesar Geronimo was on first base with none out when Armbrister attempted a sacrifice bunt. Fisk lunged for the ball but collided with Armbrister and threw erratically into center field trying to force out Geronimo. The Reds scored in the inning to win 6–5.

On July 8, 1966, Phillies third baseman Dick Allen ran into a runner while chasing a pop-up. Even though the runner was standing on the third base bag, the rule at the time required that the batter be called out for the runner's interference. The rule was changed after the season so that a runner touching the bag could not be called out for interference.

Umpire Interference. Normally an umpire is considered part of the playing field and cannot be held to interfere with play, even if struck by a ball. Nevertheless, in 1978 umpire Eric Gregg, weighing in at well over 300 pounds, called interference on himself when he bumped Cardinals catcher Ted Simmons attempting to throw out a Dodger base runner. The call nullified a double steal by the Dodgers.

Runner Interference. During the 2003 division series between the Cubs and Braves, Atlanta first baseman Robert Fick ran to first on an infield ground ball. As the throw came in to Cubs first baseman Eric Karros, Fick reacted by trying to hit the fielder's glove as it came near him. Fick knocked the glove loose, but also nailed Karros with his forearm as the glove and ball went flying. The commissioner's office fined him an undisclosed amount.

Obstruction. A Senators hitter once hit a ball into a center field fence box holding a flag. Outfielder Socks Seybold could not find the ball and the batter turned it into an inside-the-park home run.

A ball hit to the outfield by Jimmy McAleer purportedly lodged in a tomato can. Red Sox outfielder Hugh Duffy could not pry it loose so he threw the whole can in and the catcher tagged the runner. Though the runner appeared to be out, he was called safe.

Catcher's Interference. Catcher's interference is called when a catcher interferes with a batter's swing, usually by the bat striking the glove as the catcher attempts to catch the ball.

Catcher Connie Mack is credited with tipping the batter's bat, leading to the rule awarding first base to the batter on catcher's interference.

Catcher Dale Berra holds the Major League season record by interfering with batters seven times.

Andy Van Slyke reached base on catcher's interference 17 times in his career through 1995.

Pat Corrales is one of four catchers to have been called for catcher's interference twice in a game.

On August 12, 1995, the Dodgers beat the Pirates 11–10 in 11 innings when Pirates catcher Angelo Encarnacion lazily bent over and picked up the ball in the dirt with his mask. He was charged with catcher's interference, allowing Roberto Kelly to score from third to end the game.

Peanuts. During a game on June 9, 1962, Cubs fans in the right field bleachers threw peanuts at Dodger outfielder Frank Howard while he was trying to catch a fly ball. It was ruled a single after he dropped it.

Pistols. Gamblers would shoot off pistols at early Pacific Coast League games to disrupt outfielders on fly balls.

Physical Interference.

"Fans will not be permitted to jump on an outfielder's back while making a catch." — Early rule.

Running on Field. On September 18, 1993, at Yankee Stadium, a 15-year-old Yankee fan from a church group ran onto the field during what should have been the last out of the game between the Yankees and Red Sox. Boston reliever Greg Harris was pitching with two outs in the 9th inning with the Red Sox leading 3–1. Umpire Tim Welke noticed the fan running on the field as Harris induced Mike Stanley to hit a fly ball that would have ended the game. Welke signaled for a time out as Harris threw to the plate and the pitch was nullified. With a reprieve, the Yankees continued to bat and rallied for a 4–3 win.

Gloves.

Jeffrey Maier.

"Not since the O.J. Simpson trial has a black glove sparked such controversy."—Mike DiGiovanna of the *Los Angeles Times*.

In the first game of the 1996 American League Championship Series, 12-year-old Jeffrey Maier became a hero in New York. Sitting in the front row of the right field bleachers, he snagged a long fly ball with his black glove off the bat of Yankee Derek Jeter, turning a likely out into a home run. Maier had reached over the right field fence and took the ball away from a waiting Tony Tarasco. The home run tied the game and enabled the Yankees to win 5–4 in 11 innings.

Maier became an instant celebrity, appearing on the David Letterman show and receiving VIP treatment to Game 2 of the series. Ironically, Maier did not hang onto the ball, as his glove merely knocked the ball back into the stands and another fan grabbed it. The result should have been avoided under Rule 3.16: "When there is spectator interference with any thrown or batted ball, the ball shall be dead at the moment of interference and the umpire shall impose such penalties as in his opinion will nullify the act of interference. If spectator interference clearly prevents a fielder from catching a fly ball, the umpire shall declare the batter out."

Anonymous. On August 30, 1997, another fan interference situation involving the Yankees occurred that was similar to what happened in the ALCS in 1996. The Yankees lost to the Expos 7–2 after a fan reached over the right field wall and snagged a fly ball hit by Darrin Fletcher that was apparently heading for Yankee right fielder Paul O'Neill. The hit was ruled a home run. David Wells was on the mound for the Yankees, and after the game he berated owner George Steinbrenner for not having better security in the bleachers. Steinbrenner told him to stick to pitching, upon which Wells asked to be traded. Steinbrenner responded that no one wanted him. Wells then expressed the opinion that he wanted to deck The Boss.

Steve Bartman.

"Hey, it's Bill Buckner. You wanna hang out?"—No. 2 on David Letterman's list of 10 Top Messages Left on the Answering Machine of the Cubs Fan Who Tried to Catch the Foul Ball in Game 6. No. 1:

"Hi, Rush Limbaugh here. Gimme a buzz if you need something to take the edge off." [this was shortly after it was revealed that Limbaugh had entered rehab for painkiller addiction. His "source" was his maid.]

In one of the most infamous postseason incidents ever, 26-year-old Cubs fan Steve Bartman, a youth baseball coach, was forever branded when he tried to catch a foul pop fly at Wrigley Field during Game 6 of the 2003 NLCS game between the Cubs and Marlins. The Cubs led 3–0 in the 8th inning with pitcher Mark Prior in control and two innings away from their first World Series appearance since 1945.

With one out, Marlins center fielder Juan Pierre doubled. Luis Castillo looked to be the second out when he lifted a fly ball down the left field line near where Bartman was sitting in the front row wearing his Cubs sweatshirt and ballcap, headphones secured around his ears. Leftfielder Moises Alou had the ball in his sights as he reached into the stands, but Bartman tried to catch the ball barehanded and knocked it away at the last moment as it was headed for Alou's glove. Alou jumped back and hopped up and down screaming at Bartman as the entire stadium booed the poor fan. A shaken Prior then walked Castillo on a full-count wild pitch, advancing Pierre to third. Marlins catcher Ivan Rodriguez then singled home Pierre to make it 3–1.

Although many credit Bartman with costing the Cubs the game, the real crime was by Cubs shortstop Alex Gonzalez, who bobbled the next ball hit, an easy one-hopper that might have yielded a double play. Even one out (more likely on the slow grounder) would have given the Cubs a 3–1 lead with two outs and runners at the corners. The Cubs blew the lead and the game. A Chicago newspaper printed Bartman's name, home town, work location and phone number. The distraught Bartman issued an apology the day after the game: "I ask that Cub fans everywhere redirect the negative energy that has been vented toward my family, my friends and myself into the usual positive support for our beloved team on their way to being National League champs."

Bartman explained in his statement how the mishap occurred: "I had my eyes glued on the approaching ball the entire time and was so caught up in the moment that I did not even see Moises Alou, much less that he may have had a play on the ball. Had I thought for one second that the ball was playable or had I seen Alou approaching, I would have done whatever I could to get out of the way and give Alou a chance to make the catch."

Illinois governor Rod Blagojevich jokingly said that Bartman might need to get into the witness-protection program: "If he commits a crime, he won't get a pardon from this governor. You've got to be looking out for your team."

In a backhanded attempt at leniency toward Bartman from irate fans who made death threats toward him, the governor then said: "Nobody can justify any kind of threat to someone who does something stupid like reach for that ball."

Marlin fans were delighted, and one hotel owner offered Bartman a free three-month stay in Pompano Beach, Florida, with free airfare, dinner and drinks.

Former Cubs shortstop Don Kessinger defended Bartman's right to catch the ball (Bartman did not reach over the wall into the playing field): "I think he did what 40,000 people would have done."

ESPN was fooled by an imposter the following night. Someone claiming to be Bartman phoned ESPN and the network put him on the air live on its SportsCenter program at 6pm on the East coast. Shortly into the interview, the caller made reference to radio personality Howard Stern. At that point, anchor Dan Patrick said, "We've been had. That was not Steve Bartman."

Ten days after the game, commissioner Bud Selig called to offer some support.

The ball, picked up by another fan, a Chicago lawyer named "Jim," went up for auction on MastroNet on December 1, 2003, with a starting bid of $5,000. Wrote Dwight Perry in the *Seattle Times*: "The winning price, we assume, includes shipping and mishandling."

"Jim's" comment: "I don't look at it as profiting off [Bartman's] misfortune. I didn't cause his situation to occur.... He was just a random guy sitting in front of me."

Grant DePorter, a friend of Harry Caray and managing partner of Caray's restaurants, bought the ball for $106,600 at an auction. His plan was to destroy the ball on February 26, 2004, when the restaurant organized a worldwide toast to Caray. He solicited ideas from fans on how to destroy the ball. [author's idea: disassemble the ball and save the component parts for display; reassemble the ball if the Cubs ever win the World Series]. They blew up the ball at one of Caray's restaurants in March 2004. On hand to watch was Caray's widow, Dutchie.

Interleague Play (1997–)

"I can't tell if everyone appreciates the monumental thing that happened this week at a convention in a downtown Los Angeles hotel. I am not sure if baseball fans across America fully realize what happened at the owners' meetings, or what it means…. Baseball, finally, gloriously, will become a game of the future, not a game of the past."— Mike Downey in early 1996.

"Of course, for every great interleague series, there is a matchup that makes you wonder what Bud Selig was thinking when he championed this idea. The Marlins play host to the Orioles June 7–9 for a series in which fans can choose between fish or fowl and lose either way."— Peter Schmuck.

"The All-Cities-That-Begin-With-The-Letter-D Series"— Dave Krieger in the *Rocky Mountain News*, trying to generate some excitement over a 2003 Denver/Detroit interleague series.

Origins. In the early 20th century, suggestions were made to have regular-season interleague games, but nothing ever came of it. Discussions were renewed in the early 1990s, and the idea finally came to fruition later in the decade.

Beginning in 1997, National and American League clubs played each other around Memorial Day and Labor Day each season. The designated hitter is used in American League parks and not in National League parks, the same system used in the World Series. The proposal required the approval of the Players Association.

There were only a few interleague games in 1997. Western division clubs (four in the division) each played four games against four interleague clubs. Central and Eastern Division clubs (five in each division) played three games against five interleague clubs.

Interleague play became a fixture in 1998, and it was anticipated before the season that interleague play would be required every night because there were 15 clubs in each league with the addition of the Diamondbacks and Devil Rays. Without interleague play, one club in each league would always be idle because of the odd number of clubs in each league. The problem was solved when the Brewers left the American League and formed the 16-team National League.

First Game. The first regular-season interleague game was played June 12, 1997, between the Rangers and Giants at The Ballpark in Arlington, Texas. The Giants won 4–3 as Rod Beck got the first interleague save and Mark Gardner the first win. Darryl Hamilton had the first interleague hit and Stan Javier the first home run. Glenallen Hill was the first National League designated hitter.

Rainout. The first interleague rainout was in St. Louis on June 13 (a Friday), 1997, against the Indians.

Second Visit. When the Dodgers played an interleague game against the Red Sox at Fenway Park in 2004, it was their first appearance in the park. Broadcaster Vin Scully had been there once before, however, having broadcast his first network game there, for CBS in 1949. It was a football game between Boston University and Maryland, and he broadcast from the roof at a card table.

International Baseball

"Most of us will be here to see Major League Baseball on an international basis. Mexico, Venezuela, Cuba, Canada, Japan,

Puerto Rico and Panama are among the countries not only eager for it but ready for it. Further away, timewise, in baseball's global plans is Europe, with Holland and Italy the most advanced in interest, knowledge and facilities. Any new federal sport structures in those places, as well as many others, must include a baseball field."— Bowie Kuhn.

"If my teams loses a big one, and I strike out with the winning runs on base, are you aware that one billion Chinese don't care?"— Reggie Jackson to a reporter.

"Lucas Turk, Charlie Chech, France Pearce, Frenchy Bordagaray, Germany Schaefer, Les German, Charlie French, Charlie English, Greek George, Larry French, Egyptian Healy [Born in Cairo, Ill.], German Barranca, Turk Lown, Bill Roman, Swede Carlstrom, Dutch Distel, Roman Mejias, Frenchy Uhalt, Gus Brittain, Frank Brazill, Tim Ireland, Will Holland, Al Holland, Chile Gomez, Blas Monaco, Joe Malay, Hugh Poland, Ceylon Wright, Flame Delhi, Al Naples, Pat Capri, Paul Moskau, Rome Chambers, Sal Madrid, Zoilo Versalles"

See also *International Tours*, *Latin Baseball and Major League Players*, *Little League Basebal*, *World Cup*, and entries for specific countries: *Australia*, *Canada*, *Colombia*, *Cuba*, *Curaçao*, *Dominican Republic*, *England*, *France*, *Italy*, *Jamaica*, *Japan*, *Korea*, *Mexico*, *Netherlands*, *Nicaragua*, *Panama*, *Philippines*, *Puerto Rico*, *Russia*, *Taiwan*, *Venezuela* and *Virgin Islands*.

Tours by American players, wars and international spring training sites had long-lasting effects on international baseball. For example, American serviceman introduced baseball to the Philippines during the 1898 Spanish-American War. Many clubs held spring training in the Caribbean and various Latin American countries.

After World War I, many believed that baseball would take hold in France because so many servicemen played the game while stationed there. Despite the formation of amateur teams in the country, the game never completely caught on.

There were a number of barnstorming tours to Asia in the 1920s and 1930s, where baseball was already popular in Japan and to a lesser extent in Korea.

In 1946 a Madrid, Spain, club honored the Pittsburgh Pirates by notifying the Major League club that it had named its local club the Madrid Pirates. A scroll commemorating the name change was sent to the Pirates and owner Bill Benswanger was named honorary president of the club.

By 1950 the *American Baseball Congress* had affiliates in Argentina, Australia, Canada, Ecuador, Guatemala, India, Israel, Japan, Korea, Mexico, Netherlands Antilles, Nicaragua, Panama, Philippines, Taiwan and Venezuela. Also by 1950 baseball was a regular part of Central American and Caribbean sports tournaments.

Association. The International Baseball Association (IBA) is located in Indianapolis, Indiana, and governs international baseball events such as the Olympics, World Championships, the Pan American Games and various youth tournaments.

Youth Baseball. See also *Little League Baseball*.

The World Children's Baseball Fair was established in 1989 by Sadaharu Oh and Henry Aaron. Children ages 10 and 11 from around the world gather annually at a different international site for a week of baseball instruction.

Major League Baseball International. Major League Baseball launched an international expansion plan in 1994 designed to bring baseball to kids in other countries. The organization's Pitch, Hit and Run (PHR) program began in Australia and plans were made in 1996 to expand next to Germany, Great Britain, Japan, Korea and Taiwan.

Book. Joseph A. Reaves, *Taking In A Game: A History of Baseball in Asia* (2002).

International League (1877–1880, 1884–)

"But the International League is also broken dreams ... or broken ankles that end dreams."—Mike Blake in *The Minor Leagues* (1991).

Original Version. The International League was the first thoroughly organized minor league, formed in 1877 by James A. Williams of Columbus, Ohio. It was known initially as the International Organization of Professional Baseball Players and was not the same league as the modern version of the International League.

Seven clubs joined together at a convention in Pittsburgh on February 20, 1877. Candy Cummings of curveball fame was named the first president. The first teams were the Pittsburgh Alleghenys, Columbus Buckeyes, New Hampshire Manchesters, Rochester Hop Bitters, Lynn Live Oaks (Massachusetts), Guelph Maple Leafs (Ontario), and London Tecumsehs (Ontario).

The league had a loose 19-game schedule of games played only on weekends. As with most early clubs, the International League clubs scheduled games against non-league opponents, including members of the National League. However, the league was snubbed by most independent teams and had few teams against whom its clubs could play. In its second year, the league cooperated with certain other leagues and banned raiding of other clubs until after the season. This was sometimes referred to as the *League Alliance* and was a precursor of the *National Agreement* that maintained harmony among different leagues.

Tecumseh won the first International League pennant, and for 1878 the league expanded to 11 teams. In 1879 the league dropped the Canadian teams. The league could not maintain cohesion against the National League and changed its name to the National Association for its last two years before dying out at the end of the 1880 season.

Modern Version. In late 1883 the Eastern League was created and after numerous name changes became the International League of the modern era. The name change chronology:

1884	Eastern League
1885	New York State League
1886	International League
1888	International Association
1889	International League
1891	Eastern Association
1892	Eastern League
1912	International League
1918	New International League
1920	International League

In the 1930s the International League consisted of the Montreal Royals (the Dodger farm club where Jackie Robinson first played), Albany Senators, Buffalo Bisons, Toronto Maple Leafs, Syracuse Chiefs, Newark Bears, Rochester Red Wings, and Baltimore Orioles. In the 1940s a New York Giants farm club was added in Jersey City in place of Albany.

Former pitcher Tommy Lasorda is the Montreal Royals' all-time leader in career wins with 125.

Current Clubs. In the early 2000s the International League consisted of the following clubs: Rochester Red Wings, Pawtucket Red Sox, Ottawa Lynx, Scranton/Wilkes-Barre Barons, Syracuse Chiefs, Charlotte Knights, Richmond Braves, Columbus Clippers, Norfolk Tides and Toledo Mud Hens.

Book. Bill O'Neal, *The International League: A Baseball History 1884–1991* (1993).

International Tours

"Base Ball is a scientific game, more difficult than many ... can possibly imagine.... In the cricket field there is sometimes a wearisome monotony that is utterly unknown in Base Ball.... To see it played by experts will astonish those who only know it by written descriptions, for it is a fast game, full of change and excitement."—British newspaper column just prior to the arrival of an American baseball contingent in 1874. One source argued persuasively that this was written by American sportswriter Henry Chadwick and not a British journalist.

"Wherever there's summer there's baseball; Canada, the States, Mexico, Japan, all those little countries in Central America. I read once that they stop their wars for baseball games. They give the good left-handed guerrilla pitcher safe passage in from the hills. He pitches the game, goes back into hiding; the next day some of his team-mates try to hunt him down and kill him."—W.P. Kinsella in "Driving Toward the Moon" (1984).

First International Tour. In July 1874 the Boston Red Stockings and Philadelphia Athletics went on a tour of Ireland and England. Arranged in part by 23-year-old Albert Spalding, it was the first international tour by American baseball players. The entire National Association schedule was rearranged to accommodate the trip, which lasted from mid–July to mid–September.

The two teams played seven cricket matches with local clubs and 14 baseball games between themselves and against English teams. In their cricket matches, the American club was allowed to use 18 players against the usual 11 for the English club. Though more reliable sources report that the Americans lost all their cricket matches due to generally poor play, at least one modern source reported that the Americans won their matches despite "unorthodox play."

The British showed little interest in baseball and the tour was not considered a success. The two clubs lost $3,000 and claimed to be forced to impose pay cuts on their players.

Cuba. In 1879 Frank Bancroft led a group to Havana, but the trip was a failure. In 1886 the A's and Phillies again tried Cuba, and this time it was a financial success (see also *Cuba*).

First Around-the-World Tour.

"We found very little interest in athletic sports in Italy and France; in fact it was with the greatest difficulty that we could find a place to play a game of baseball in either of those countries, and not in a single place did we find an enclosed ground."—Albert Spalding on his 1888 international tour.

"... in a country where they use a stick for a plow, and hitch a donkey and a camel together to draw it and do many other things as they did twenty centuries ago it is hardly reasonable to expect that the modern game of base-ball will become one of its sports."—Spalding.

The first tour of American ballplayers to multiple countries began on October 20, 1888, when the Chicago White Stockings and a group of National League all-stars dubbed the "All-America Nine" embarked from Chicago. The teams stopped in a number of cities, including San Francisco, Honolulu, Auckland, Sydney, Melbourne, Ceylon, Cairo, Naples, Rome, Paris, London and Dublin. At least one source reported that the tour was first scheduled only for Australia, New Zealand and Honolulu, but after arriving in Australia, tour leader and sponsor Albert Spalding decided to go all the way around the world. Spalding was trying to export his sporting goods sales internationally

The 1888–1889 Albert Spalding–led international tour poses at the Coliseum in Rome (from the Barry Halper Archives).

The clubs played 50 games on the trip, which was profitable despite a cost of $50,000. The game was criticized in England in part because it relied too heavily on umpires' judgment calls. The tour culminated with a great banquet at Delmonico's restaurant in New York City attended by Mark Twain, New York police chief Teddy Roosevelt and New York senator Chauncey Depew. Twain spoke at the dinner and noted that the equator was created by the players "stealing bases on their bellies" and "leaving a nice deep trench along the way." Depew also spoke: "I believe that all men who have ever lived and achieved success in this world had lived in vain if they knew not baseball."

The definitive account of the 1888–1889 international tour is by Francis Richter contained in *Athletic Sports in America, England, and Australia, Also Including the Famous 'Around the World' Tour of American Baseball Teams*, edited by Harry C. Palmer (1889). This book has been called the best baseball book published in the 19th century.

Pre–World War I Tours.

"The twentieth century tourists were to exhibit before the little brown men of the Mikado's kingdom [Japanese], the almond-eyed celestials [Chinese] and before the reformed head hunters of Uncle Sam's island possessions [Filipinos]."—G.W. Axelson in *"Commy"* (1919), which contains a comprehensive account of many aspects of the 1913–1914 world tour by the White Sox and Giants, but especially the card-playing by the group: "He detailed it around the world and dwelt pathetically on the tragedy of the possessor of two pairs of threes, who swallowed a six-inch perfecto, ashes and all, when, after a long siege, he was given the privilege of gazing on four fives in the hands of John Sheridan."

In 1896 Orioles manager John McGraw led members of the team on a tour of Europe.

In 1908 the Reach All-American college team played in Japan and in 1909 the Wisconsin University team toured Japan. The first

barnstorming tour of American professionals to Japan and other Asian countries occurred in 1913, when John McGraw's Giants and Charles Comiskey's White Sox played in Tokyo, Yokohama, Kobe and Nagasaki. Some sources reported that the tour popularized baseball in Japan, but it was already a national phenomenon at the amateur level. The November 1913 departure from the States supposedly was arranged over drinks by Comiskey and McGraw, but actually had been in preparation for years. Over 139 days (142 in some sources) the White Sox won 24 games and lost 20 to their National League opponent.

The teams played 31 (or 44?) games in Shanghai, Hong Kong, Manila, Australia, Ceylon, Egypt, Italy (though the game was rained out), France and Britain. They returned from the European portion of the tour on the passenger ship *Lusitania*, whose 1917 sinking in part led to the United States entering World War I.

Post–World War I Tours. In 1921 American League president Ban Johnson led a successful tour to Mexico. A 1922 tour of Japan, China and the Philippines also was a success. It was the first multi-country tour after World War I and was organized by promoter and former Major League player Herb Hunter, who had business contacts in Japan, Korea and China.

In 1924 John McGraw and Charles Comiskey embarked on a world tour similar to their 1913 effort but returned home early after low attendance in England, Ireland and France. In 1926 Bucky Harris led a group to Europe that was not well received except in Ireland.

There were at least five appearances in *Japan* by American contingents during the 1920s and 1930s. After a 1934 tour of Japan led by Babe Ruth and Connie Mack, international tours were banned because of increased international tensions.

Post–World War II. After World War II it became traditional for American all-stars or individual teams to tour *Japan* after the season.

Internet

"I didn't know much about websites, and I still don't. You press something, or click something, and up it comes." — Peter O'Malley in 2003 on a new website dedicated to his father, Walter.

Early Sites. Skilton's Baseball Links was an early Internet site that by 1996 coordinated more than 1,000 separate baseball sites on the Web. In early 1996 the Dodgers became the 18th club to open an official website.

PornBall. Typing in "Angels.com" gets into an adult website.

On-Line Sales. Major League Baseball signed a deal with RealAudio Networks that was anticipated to bring them over $20-million in additional revenue by selling a season pass for Internet listeners.

Revenue Sharing. In January 2000 Major League owners voted to give all their Internet rights and revenue to the commissioner's office, to be doled out in equal shares.

Internet Auction. In 2003 a frustrated Yankees fan tried to auction off struggling pitcher Jeff Weaver on the Internet. The fan described the 6'5" Weaver as a pitcher "in fair-to-good condition, hardly used and showing minor wear." Bidding started at one cent and climbed to $300,000 after only 13 hours. The fan said he would accept a bag of batting practice balls in lieu of payment. Weaver justified the sale when he gave up the winning home run in Game 4 of the 2003 World Series, though he otherwise pitched well in the postseason.

Spam. Late in the 2003 season a disgruntled Phillies fan, Allan Eric Carlson, was arrested at his home in California after sending spam emails criticizing the Philadelphia front office. He was accused in a federal indictment of breaking into computers around the country and using the return addresses of reporters for the *Philadelphia Inquirer* and the *Philadelphia Daily News*.

All-Star Voting. In the 2000s Major League Baseball began allowing fans to vote for one member of each All-Star squad by way of the Internet. Hideki Matsui made the American League team in each of his first two seasons, both times through Internet voting (that included Japanese fans).

Best Sites. For the history of baseball and statistics: Retrosheet.org, Baseball-Reference.com, Baseballlibrary.com and BaseballAlmanac.com have been most useful to this author.

Inventions

"What if they did get a machine to replace us, you know what would happen to it? Why, the players would bust it to pieces every time it ruled against them. They'd clobber it with a bat." — Umpire Harry Wendelstedt in 1974.

"Mister Mack, who will be 86 years old next December, might almost ask for patent rights to the game of baseball if he had not signed away such claims by lending himself to the pretty fable that the sport was the handiwork of the late General Abner Doubleday." — Sportswriter Bob Considine.

Book. Dan Gutman, *Banana Bats and Ding-Dong Balls: A Century of Unique Baseball Inventions* (1993).

Iowa

"The road out." — Reliever Rod Beck on the best thing about Iowa, after he had a two-month pitching stint there in 2003, although he did have nice things to say about the people.

"Field of Dreams." — The Iowa cornfield turned into a baseball field in the movie of the same name.

Iowa had nine baseball teams by 1867, the year in which the Iowa State Baseball Association was formed. The Marshalltown club featured Cap Anson. Iowa never had a Major League club, but the Keokuk Westerns played briefly in the National Association in 1875.

Irish Players

"Jennings and McGann, Doyle and Callahan.
Hanlon, Scanlon, Kirk and Donlin,
Devlin, Keeler, Walsh and Conlin.
Joe McGinnity, Shea and Finnerty,
Farrell, Carroll, Darrell, and McAmes.
Connie Mack and John McGraw
All together shout hurrah!
They're all good American names."
—1911 Irish baseball song, "They're All Good American Names."

During the early days of professional baseball, the game was dominated by Irish players from the northeastern United States. Irish players comprised one-third of Major League rosters in the 1870s and 1880s, but that percentage decreased during the 1890s. German ballplayers became more prevalent as the game moved heavily into the Midwest, where the German and other northern European immigrant presence was heaviest (see also *Ethnicity*).

By the 1900s Irish dominance of the game had diminished further. Nevertheless, an older Irish element still was heavily involved in Major League Baseball, as 11 of 16 managers in 1915 were of Irish descent.

Monte Irvin (1919–)

Hall of Fame (NLC) 1973

"Irvin was a consummate gentleman of great poise as well as great talent, sort of the Sidney Poitier of baseball, and some people were quite upset that he was not chosen to be The One." — Historian Bill James on Irvin as the preferred choice over Jackie Robinson to integrate Major League Baseball.

Irwin was a Negro League star who played in the National League primarily in the 1950s.

Monford Merrill Irvin won 16 varsity letters at his New Jersey high school, with his best in the javelin and shot put. He played two years of baseball at Lincoln College while playing professionally under the name Jimmy Nelson.

Irvin played in the Negro Leagues beginning in 1939 with the Newark Eagles. He led the league in hitting in 1940 and 1941 before being drafted into the Army in 1942 for a three-year hitch. Though many considered him the best candidate to break the Major League color line, he later conceded that the layoff caused by his military commitment eroded his skills.

He joined the New York Giants in 1949 as an outfielder when he was past 30, and his first full season was 1950. He hit .299 that year and in 1951 he led the National League with 121 RBIs and had a .312 average. He led both clubs in the 1951 World Series with 11 hits and a .458 average. A broken ankle was the first of various injuries that slowed him down and shortened his career. He lasted eight years in the Major Leagues, compiling a .293 average before retiring in 1956.

Irvin scouted for the Mets in the 1960s and then worked for a number of years in the commissioner's office before retiring to Florida. After his election to the Hall of Fame by the Negro League Committee, he became a member of that committee and subsequently the Veterans Committee.

Italy

"Although he learned Italian first, Joe, now 24, speaks English without an accent and is otherwise adapted to United States mores. Instead of olive oil or smelly bear grease he keeps his hair slick with water. He never reeks of garlic and prefers chicken chow mein to spaghetti." — Comments about Joe DiMaggio appearing in the May 1939 issue of *Life* magazine.

"Well, Tony, how are the Wops going to vote this year?" — Babe Ruth to Tony Lazzeri in a live radio campaign ad for presidential candidate Al Smith. Ruth's interviewing career was cut short immediately by the Yankees. Considered the first superstar of Italian-American descent, belated Hall of Famer Lazzeri had a lifetime .292 average primarily with the Yankees.

"Mr. McCarthy, when someone again yells, 'throw it to the Dago!', will they please designate which Dago they mean?" — Yankee pitcher Lefty Gomez after a Yankee bench coach yelled during a play in which Gomez was faced with choosing between Italian shortstop Frank Crosetti or Italian second baseman Tony Lazzeri.

Major League Players. Ed Abbaticchio is recognized as the first prominent Major League player of Italian descent. He played from 1905 through 1908 and just missed clinching the 1908 pennant race for the eventual third-place Pirates when his grand slam attempt went just foul.

Italian players were slow to move into Major League Baseball, with only a few trickling into the Majors in the 1910s and 1920s. The pace increased in the 1930s, and by the 1940s Italians comprised 8% of Major League rosters (two times the national population percentage).

Early 20th century outfielder Ping Bodie's real name was Francesco Stephano Pezzolo.

Former player and later National League umpire Paul Sentele was an early 20th century player of Italian descent.

Hall of Fame. The National Italian-American Sports Hall of Fame is located in Arlington Heights, Illinois.

Italian Leagues. Club team matches began in Italy in 1919, and in 1931 an Italian amateur baseball association announced that it was sending 43 instructors to America to learn the game. Baseball became more popular after World War II and the Italian Baseball Federation was formed in 1950. That organization spearheaded the formation of the European Baseball Federation in 1953. Modern Italian professional teams are limited to two foreign players. Italy is considered the strongest European baseball country, closely followed only by the Netherlands.

Craig Minetto played in the Italian professional league in 1975. In 1978 he became the first player from that league to play in the Major Leagues. He played briefly for the A's from 1978 through 1981, compiling a 1–7 record before an arm injury ended his career.

Lenny Randle played in the Major Leagues before a brief stint in the Italian leagues. He returned to Major League Baseball at age 46 as a spring replacement player during the 1995 player strike.

Sign Language. Coaches in the Italian leagues must warn American players when they flash the sign for two outs not to raise the index finger and the pinkie. That is the *cornuto*, the horns, the worst insult one can give. It means, "Your wife is playing around," and can get a player kicked out of a game.

Book. Larry Freundlich and Tracy Brown (eds.), *Reaching for the Stars: A Celebration of Italian Americans In Major League Baseball* (2003).

"**J** is for Johnson
The Big Train in his prime
Was so fast he could throw
Three strikes at a time."
— Ogden Nash on Walter Johnson.

Reggie Jackson (1946–)

Hall of Fame 1993

"God, do I love to hit that little round sum-bitch out of the park and make 'em say 'Wow!'" — Jackson.

"I'm the straw that stirs the drink." — A partial quote by Jackson. The full quote was uttered in spring training 1977 and created bad blood with Yankee catcher Thurman Munson, who up to that point had tried to integrate the newly acquired Jackson into the team. More of what Jackson said: "I'm the straw that stirs the drink. It all comes down to me. Maybe I should say Munson and me, but he really doesn't enter into it. Munson thinks he can be the straw that stirs the drink but he can only stir it bad."

And then there was the fan's telegram to Jackson that alluded to the quote when teammate Dave Winfield was horrible during the 1981 World Series: "If you're the straw that stirs the drink, why don't you give Winfield a sip."

Jackson finished his 21-year American League career in 1987 with 563 home runs.

Reginald Martinez Jackson began and ended his career with the A's, also playing for the Orioles, Yankees and Angels. He is the only man to lead the league in home runs for three different teams. He hit 20 or more home runs in 16 seasons, leading the American League four times. His best season was 1969, when he burst onto the scene in his second full season with 47 home runs, 123 runs scored, and 118 RBIs.

Jackson hit 563 home runs from 1967 through 1987, sixth on the all-time list when he retired. He had 1,702 RBIs and a surprising 228 stolen bases despite frequent hamstring problems. He also had the most strikeouts in Major League history by a wide margin with 2,597.

Jackson's clubs won 11 division championships, five pennants and four World Series. He holds a number of postseason records, including a slugging average of .755. His greatest moment may have been Game 6 of the 1977 World Series against the Dodgers when he hit home runs on three consecutive pitches to clinch the Series for the Yankees. His "Mr. October" nickname was not appropriate for his postseason play for the Angels in 1982 and 1986; he was 7-for-40 with one home run.

After retiring, Jackson became a baseball ambassador primarily through his contract with Upper Deck baseball cards. He also worked for the Yankees in an advisory capacity. He received 396 of a possible 423 ballots (93.6%) to be elected to the Hall of Fame in his first year on the ballot, the 29th player to make it in his first year of eligibility. On the day that Jackson was inducted into the Hall of Fame, columnist Jim Murray wrote: "He had the most exciting at-bats in the history of baseball. He didn't swing at a pitch, he pounced on it like a leopard coming out of a tree. He finished his swing like a pretzel. His left leg was in a kneeling position on the ground, his right leg looked like a corkscrew. He went around like a window shade going up. You half expected to hear him flapping."

Books. Maury Allen, *Mr. October* (1981); Reggie Jackson and Mike Lupica, *Reggie* (1984).

Travis Jackson (1903–1987)

Hall of Fame (VC) 1982

"My greatest thrill. In 1921 I played for Little Rock in the Southern League and the first time I stepped on the field I was in awe. It held 4,500 people and I never saw a park that big. And there I was holding up my pants with a cotton rope."—Jackson quoted in the *National Hall of Fame Museum Yearbook*, edited by Bill Guilfoile (1989).

Jackson played 15 seasons at shortstop for the Giants beginning in 1922.

After attending Ouachita Baptist College in Arkansas, Jackson moved on to professional baseball in 1921 with Little Rock in the Southern Association. He was sold to the Giants in late 1922, playing in three games.

He played 96 games for the club in 1923 and became the regular shortstop in 1924. He remained in that role through early 1932, when a knee injury slowed him down for two seasons. He played a few games at third base in 1933, returned to his regular position in 1934, and then finished out his career at third base for his final two seasons.

Over his 15-year career he batted .291 with 135 home runs for the Giants. His best seasons were 1929 when he hit 21 home runs and 1930 when he hit .339. He hit over .300 six times and was considered one of the premier shortstops of the 1920s. He helped lead the Giants to four World Series, though he batted only .149 in postseason play. He coached for the Giants in 1939–1940 and 1947–1948 and managed a number of minor league clubs.

Jamaica

Chili Davis is one of two prominent Jamaican Major League ballplayer. He first played for the Giants in 1981 and had moderate success with the Giants, Twins and Angels through the mid–1990s.

Devon White hit 208 home runs in 17 seasons beginning in 1985 and played on three World Series winners.

Japan

"This country has got its national flag all wrong. Instead of a rising sun in the center, there should be a baseball."—British tourist quoted in Robert Whiting's *You Gotta Have Wa* (1989).

"Besuboru"—Baseball.

"Homu Ran"—Home run.

"Wa"—The sense of team spirit that subordinates all to the interest of the team, which historically has been the guiding principle of Japanese baseball.

Early American Influence. Baseball was first introduced in Tokyo in 1872 or 1873 by American teachers led by Horace Wilson. Students at Daigaku-Nanko (Kaisei Gakko) were the first Japanese baseball players. The game caught on fast because the Japanese perceived it as a form of martial arts.

Some sources report that the first team, the Shimbashi Athletic Club, was formed in 1878 by Hiroshi Hiraoka, a student who played the game in Boston. Other sources report that the first baseball club was organized in 1879 by a railroad engineer who had studied in the United States. Baseball may have been the first organized group game in Japan and became immensely popular first at the high school level. An early name for Japanese baseball was "Yakyu," or field ball. The first Japanese rule book was translated from an Englishman's work in 1865.

The emergence of baseball in the 19th century led to a strong intercollegiate baseball program before any professional programs began. Baseball became the country's most popular sport by the beginning of the 20th century and the Waseda University team made a tour of America in 1905, playing Stanford and USC, among others. Baseball at the college level strengthened during the first two decades of the 20th century, especially at Waseda and Keio Universities, two of the oldest private universities in Tokyo. They began playing each other in scheduled games in 1914.

In 1925 the Tokyo Six Universities League was founded and was a focal point for baseball until World War II. Two other college leagues were organized in 1931.

Japanese baseball was still an amateur sport through the 1920s, but the game received a boost from prominent barnstorming American Major Leaguers in the 1930s. Schools and universities are still farm teams for Japanese professional clubs in much the same way that American colleges are farm teams for professional football and basketball. A late summer month-long high school tournament, started in 1915, is still one of the biggest sporting event in Japan and the winning players become national heroes.

Fathers of Japanese Baseball. One of the early leaders of Japanese baseball was Suishu Tobita (1886–1965), who was known as the "God of Japanese Baseball" and the "Connie Mack of Japanese Baseball."

Some sources cite Dr. Isoo Abe as the father of Japanese baseball. He was educated in America and coached at Waseda University around 1900. In 1905 his team came to the United States to play baseball and returned to spread the game in Japan.

The Japan amateur baseball association was created in 1929. In 1990 all of the country's amateur organizations were united into the Baseball Federation of Japan.

The 1931 trip to Japan by American Major Leaguers was sponsored by the Japanese newspaper *Yomiuri Shimbun*. Sotaro Suzuki was the baseball representative from the newspaper and is considered by some as the father of Japanese professional baseball.

The greatest influence by an American on Japanese baseball probably was by Lefty O'Doul, who toured with the American all-stars in 1931. O'Doul taught in Japan sporadically and regularly returned to the country. He is credited with naming the Yomiuri (Tokyo) Giants professional baseball team.

Pre–World War II American Barnstorming.

"Beibu Rusu"—Babe Ruth, who barnstormed in Japan in 1934.

American college players toured Japan in 1908 and 1909, though some sources report that the first tour of college players was in 1910. The first barnstorming tour of American professionals was in 1908. They were the Reach All-Americans and included Major League reserves and Pacific Coast League players. The club won all of its 17 games against Japanese university and club teams.

The first tour exclusively of American Major Leaguers occurred in 1913, as John McGraw's Giants and Comiskey's White Sox were undefeated in games in Tokyo, Yokohama, Kobe and Nagasaki. The next American tour was in 1920 by the Herb Hunter All-Stars, who were undefeated in 20 games. The 1922 group of Hunter's All-Stars included Casey Stengel and suffered the first loss by an American squad (with a 15–1 record) (see also *International Tours*).

In 1924 and 1927 the Fresno Japanese American Baseball Team barnstormed the country, and groups of players that included Fresno-area players barnstormed in 1937, just before the ban on such trips.

A group of Negro League players from the Philadelphia Royal Giants toured the country in 1927, going undefeated in 23 games (one tie). They returned in 1932 and lost one of 24 games.

The 1922 American tour of Japan led by Herb Hunter. Note Hall of Famers Casey Stengel (front row, far left), Waite Hoyt (front row, center, with ball), and George "Highpockets" Kelly (tallest guy in the back row).

American Major Leaguers returned to go undefeated in a total of 33 games in 1931 and 1934. Sportswriter Fred Lieb organized and led the 1931 tour. Of the 17 games played in 1931, most were lopsided; the 3–2 and 2–0 games still resulted in a sweep by the Americans. Key American players were Lou Gehrig, Rabbit Maranville, Lefty O'Doul, Frankie Frisch, Lefty Grove and Mickey Cochrane. The most prominent members of the 1934 tour were Babe Ruth, Connie Mack, Lou Gehrig, Lefty Gomez, Jimmie Foxx and Charlie Gehringer. During that tour, catcher and *Spy* Moe Berg took a number of important photographs of Tokyo that were used by the U.S. during World War II bombing raids. Yokohama Park (now Yokohama Stadium) was the site of cricket matches early in its history, and at one time was named Lou Gehrig Field.

Although there was still no professional baseball in Japan at that time, the sport was already acknowledged as the "fall sport" in Japan. After the 1934 tour, barnstorming was banned because of increasing international tensions.

Japanese Professional Teams and World War II.

"Who won the World Series?"— Japanese prisoner of war in perfect English.

In 1932 National League president John Heydler expressed hope that there would be in the near future a Japan/U.S. World Series. The Yomiuri Giants were chartered under a different name as the first Japanese professional team on December 26, 1934; known then as the Dai Nippon Tokyo Yakyu Kurabu ("The Great Japan Tokyo Baseball Club"). The club changed its name while on a 1935 U.S. tour, in which they won 93 games against semipro and Pacific Coast League clubs. They returned in 1936 and played two spring training games in Tulsa. The Hanshin Tigers of Osaka were the second club, followed by the Chunichi Dragons of Nagoya and the Hankyu Braves. The first fully professional league began in 1936 as the Japan Professional Baseball League.

Japanese teams struggled during the war due to economic problems and resentment toward the American game. In the early 1940s the Japanese military government formally abolished baseball as an "American influence," but teams still played until midway through 1944. In 1942 *The Sporting News* supported the end of baseball in Japan, when it called for the United States to: "withdraw from Japan the gift of baseball which we made to that misguided and ill-begotten country."

Only six Japanese professional teams played in 1944, with a 35-game schedule cut short in August. Drab uniforms were used, Japanese lettering was substituted on uniforms and Americanized nicknames such as Senators, Tigers and Giants were changed to Japanese names. An April 1944 report in the *Stars and Stripes* newspaper: "The Japs apparently like American baseball even if they hate the American people. After a year of reports from Japan concerning bans and restrictions on baseball, the Domei News Agency today described the Japanese pro league's opening day game, with the Tokyo Giants defeating Sangyo, 2–0, in case anybody gives a hoot."

During World War II Japanese ballpark fields were used as vegetable gardens to help alleviate food shortages. There was no Japanese professional baseball in 1945.

Postwar American Tours.

"An hour after the game, you want to go out and play them again."— Rocky Bridges on playing the Japanese [shouldn't that be *Chinese*?].

The San Francisco Seals were undefeated in seven games in 1949 in the first postwar tour by American players. American Major League All-Stars returned in 1951 with Joe DiMaggio, losing one and tying two in 16 games.

DiMaggio and other Major League players traveled to Japan for an exhibition series in 1954. DiMaggio's wife, Marilyn Monroe, accompanied him before she went on to Korea for a GI show. By the 1980s American Major League teams or groups of All-Stars were making approximately biannual postseason tours of Japan.

Individual Major League teams toured Japan every few years after 1951, though by the mid–1980s the trips included Major League all-stars. After a dismal 1990 tour the Americans put together a more fiery contingent that had a 6–1–1 record in 1992. The Americans continued to have better success through the mid–1990s

In November 1996 the Major Leaguers were 4–2 with two ties in the eight-game series. Steve Finley was named MVP after going 8-for-20 with nine RBIs. Others players included Cal Ripken, Sammy Sosa, Barry Bonds, Mike Piazza, Hideo Nomo, Gary Sheffield and Alex Rodriguez. In 2002 a group led by Barry Bonds lost three straight games before winning.

See also *Ya Gotta Have Wa*, by Robert Whiting (1989), for a complete record of American tours through 1988.

See also **International Tours** for additional visits by American players.

Post-War Boom. Baseball in Japan rebounded after the war and by 1948 eight clubs were operating in the Japanese league. In 1950 the current structure was established when the Pacific League was formed to rival the Central League. Both leagues are governed by Nippon Professional Baseball (NPB), the Japanese equivalent of Major League Baseball and the commissioner's office. The leagues now play 140-game schedules among six clubs each, culminating in the Japan Series. The 1990s teams:

Central League	*Pacific League*
Yakult Swallows	Seibu Lions
Chunichi Dragons	Nippon Ham Fighters
Yomiuri (Tokyo) Giants	Orix Bluewave
Hanshin Tigers	Fukuoka Daiei Hawks
Yokohama Baystars	Chiba Lotte Marines
Hiroshima Toyo Carp	Kintetsu Buffaloes

Each team has a minor league affiliate in one of the two minor leagues, the Western League and the Central League. Clubs play in the World Series-equivalent Super Major Series, with the MVP of the losing team receiving the "Fighting Spirit Award."

2000s/Financial Problems. By 2004 several Japanese clubs were in financial trouble, in part caused by the drain of top talent to the American Major Leagues. Owners of the Osaka Kintetsu Buffaloes and the Orix Blue Wave began merger talks that season, creating a five-team league that would cause scheduling problems because the two Japanese Major Leagues did not have interleague play. The last time two Japanese teams merged was in 1957. The Japanese players union was weak, so it had little impact on the owners' efforts. Ultimately, no merger occurred.

Japanese owners support about 70 players on their Major and minor league clubs, but 4,000 high schools generate a huge amount of surplus talent. Japanese teams draw between 1.5 and 20 million viewers on television (Tokyo's Yomiuri Giants lead). The weaker Pacific League has lobbied for interleague play, but the Central League clubs have resisted. The Giants are "Japan's Team," having won 30 pennants since 1950. The Kintetsu club lost $36 million in 2003 and, as noted by *Los Angeles Times* sportswriter Bruce Wallace, many of the leagues' large corporate parents are in "an 0-for-the-decade slump" in corporate profits. The typical view is that because the teams are merely a small portion of the corporate picture, having one "division" of the company losing money is of no great moment. According to Japanese baseball historian Robert Whiting, many of the business people who run the teams are on loan from accounting departments and want to move on as soon as possible. See also **Strike.**

Amateur Baseball. The most popular form of amateur baseball in Japan is "nanshiki," played with a dimpled ball (though with raised seams) that is lighter than the average baseball and tends to pop out of the glove, as reported by Jim Allen, an American reporter based in Japan.

Best Pre-1990s Japanese League Players.

"No one can stop a home run. No one can understand what it really is, unless you have felt it in your own hands and body ... as the ball makes its high, long arc beyond the playing field, the diamond and the stands suddenly belong to one man. In that brief, brief time, you are free of all demands and complications."—Sadaharu Oh.

The Tokyo-born Oh is considered by many as the greatest Japanese League player of all time, belting 868 home runs in his career. His batting swing was similar to that of Mel Ott, who raised his front leg high off the ground before making contact. Oh retired at age 40 with a .301 average after helping the Yomiuri Giants win 14 league championships and 11 Japan Series titles.

Shigeru Chiba played for the Yomiuri Giants between 1938 and 1956. He is considered by many to be the greatest second baseman in Japanese baseball history, with the possible exception of American-born Johnny Sipin.

Yomiuri Giants third baseman Shigeo Nagashima has one of the highest lifetime batting averages in the history of Japanese baseball. The Giants were the only Japanese team never to sign an American player during the prime of its stars, Nagashima and Oh.

Iron Man Inao is considered one of the greatest Japanese pitchers of all time. He had a record of 276–137 and an ERA of 1.98 from 1956 through 1969 for the Nishitetsu Lions. He had what must be regarded as the greatest "Iron Man" performance in the history of baseball. At age 20 in 1958 he started or relieved in all of the Nishitetsu Lions' last nine games to propel them into the Japan Series against the Yomiuri Giants. Inao started five of the seven games against the Giants. The Giants took a 3–0 series lead, but Inao homered in the 10th inning of Game 4 to give the Lions a critical win. He then pitched three straight complete-game victories that included a 26-inning scoreless streak to clinch the series for the Lions.

Consecutive Games Played. See **Consecutive Games Played.**

American Gaijin.

"There's a new breed of Gaijin players—guys who are hungry and feel they still have a lot of career left. The guys who came over here years ago created a bad reputation for today's players. Those guys just came over for a final big payday, went through the motions, collected their million dollars and went home."—Former Major Leaguer Jack Howell.

"[Joe Pepitone] was playing in Japan. The last I heard he wasn't happy there, either. The Japanese people were very inconsiderate. They insisted upon speaking Japanese."—Leo Durocher in *Nice Guys Finish Last* (1975). A rift occurred in 1973 when Pepitone, a former Yankee, left his Japanese club without authority, and the Japanese leagues came close to banning American players after complaints that he was faking his injury (along with Don Money).

"If some major league team had offered me $1.5 million and told me I could play every day, I probably would have taken it.... But to walk away from that much money on the table in Japan, I don't think it would've been responsible for my family."—Former Marlins outfielder Kevin Millar, on his decision to play in Japan in 2003.

"I didn't learn nothing. I'll never take that long of a flight again."—Kevin Mitchell on what he learned in Japan. Mitchell signed the largest contract in Japanese baseball history at $4.5 mil-

The All Kanebo Team representing the city of Osaka at Korakuen Stadium in Tokyo, August 5, 1951.

lion (or $5.3 million) guaranteed for one season in 1995. His team thought he was malingering when he began to complain of a bad knee. In late March he left the club after being suspended earlier in the month but returned to finish the season.

Foreign baseball players who play in the Japanese professional leagues are known as Gaijin. Over 600 foreigners have played in the Japan Leagues (including players from Korea and Taiwan).

The first American to play in Japan was Wally Yonamine, who won three batting titles in the 1950s. His first season in Japanese baseball was 1951 when he played for the Yomiuri Giants. He was a Japanese-American from Hawaii who had played in a California minor league and with the NFL San Francisco 49ers.

The first Major Leaguer to play in Japan was Phil Paine, a former Braves pitcher. He played in the Japan Leagues in 1953 while in the Air Force. Larry Doby was an early Major Leaguer to play in Japan. Infielder Larry Raines played in Japan while on leave from the military and then played for the Indians in 1957 and 1958.

Pitcher Don Newcombe and outfielder Larry Doby were the first American Major League black stars to play in Japan. Both played for the Chunichi Dragons in 1962. Newcombe played first base and hit well.

In the mid–1960s Japanese teams began using ex–Major League ballplayers with some frequency. Nevertheless, the Japanese teams continued to honor the American reserve clause contained in player contracts.

Jim Marshall had a brief Major League career around 1960 before moving to Japan in 1963. He hit 78 home runs for the Chunichi Dragons over the next three years before returning to manage in the minor leagues.

After nine years in the Major Leagues ending in 1966, Willie Kirkland moved to the Japanese Leagues in 1968. He adjusted well by learning the language and marrying a Japanese woman.

George Altman played from 1968 through 1975 for the Hanshin team, batting .309 and hitting 205 home runs.

Slugger Frank Howard signed to play for a Japanese team in 1974. He hurt his back in his first game and never played again.

Dick Davis became a star in Japan with the Kintetsu Buffalos

after hitting .265 primarily with the Milwaukee Brewers from 1977 until 1982.

Career American minor-leaguer Randy Bass starred in the Japanese Leagues in the 1980s with the Hanshin Tigers, twice winning the Japanese Triple Crown. Despite his accomplishments and stature, he was released after going to San Francisco to be with his eight-year-old son, who had a brain tumor. The Hanshin Tigers CEO, Shingo Furuya, visited Bass in San Francisco in an attempt to convince him to return to the team. Unable to persuade Bass to come back, Furuya returned to Japan and committed suicide by jumping out a hotel window.

Orestes Destrade is a native Cuban whose family emigrated to the U.S. in 1968. He hit 154 home runs and had 366 RBIs in 3½ seasons in Japan to become the first foreigner to lead the Japanese Leagues in home runs three consecutive years. In 1993 he signed with the Florida Marlins for $3.5 million over two years.

Leron Lee batted .320 and hit 283 home runs in 11 years with the Lotte Orions.

John Sipin played 68 games for the San Diego Padres in 1969 but failed to stick with the club in 1970. After going back to the minor leagues he impressed Japanese scouts while playing for Hawaii in the Pacific Coast League. As a result, he went on to star for the Taiyo Whales in the 1970s.

Other Major Leaguers who played in Japan in the 1970s include Matty Alou, Tony Bernazard, Don Buford, Alvin Davis, Willie Davis, Mike Easler, Jim Lefebvre, Johnny Logan, Bill Madlock, Carlos May, Joey Meyer, Felix Millan, Ben Oglivie, Roger Repoz, Dick Stuart, Willie Upshaw, Roy White and Walt "No Neck" Williams.

Don Blasingame pitched, coached and managed in Japan (though he did not manage at the Japanese Major League level).

Davey Johnson signed in 1975 to play in Japan and had a good year there in 1976. He is the first American player to return to the U.S. Major Leagues after a career in Japan. The Yomiuri Giants were the last Japanese club to acquire an American when they signed Johnson.

Pete LaCock, son of "Hollywood Squares" game show host Peter Marshall, played in Japan in 1981.

Ken Macha played six years in the Major Leagues, primarily for the Expos in the 1970s. He moved to Japan from 1982 through 1985, hitting 82 home runs for the Chunichi Dragons over those four seasons.

Reggie Smith had difficulty hitting during his short stint in Japan due to injuries and cultural problems. He played for and highly respected manager Sadaharu Oh, and he helped lead the club to a pennant. Smith managed to have time to record an album while he was there. According to reliable sources, Americans are lucky that the album did not make it to the States.

Bert Campaneris played for the Seibu Lions after retiring in 1983.

Bob Horner played in 1987 for the Yakult Swallows. He was known as *Akaoni*, the Red Devil, a mythical red-skinned Buddhist ogre. After his one miserable season he moved on to the Cardinals, calling Japanese baseball "not real baseball." From his perspective, that might have been true, as he was called out throughout the season on pitches out of the strike zone.

Pitcher Bill Gullickson played for the Yomiuri Giants after signing a $2 million contract for one year.

Warren Cromartie played for the Expos from 1976 through 1983. He moved to Japan for the 1984 season, hitting 30 home runs in each of his first three seasons. He stayed through early in the 1991 season and then returned briefly to the Major Leagues with the Royals in 1992. See also his book, *Slugging It Out In Japan* (1991).

Cecil Fielder played for the Hanshin Tigers in 1989 and then returned to the Major Leagues with the Tigers and led the Major Leagues with 51 home runs in 1990 and 44 in 1991.

Anticipating a weak Major League market for mid-level players shortly after the 1992 season, Glenn Braggs and Mel Hall quickly signed with Japanese League clubs for $2 million each over two years.

Brook Jacoby played briefly for the Chunichi Dragons in 1993, suffered a knee injury and quit after hitting .183 in 18 games.

Jesse Barfield struggled with a bad wrist with the Yomiuri Giants in 1993.

Other Americans who played in Japan in 1993: Tom O'Malley, Bobby Rose, Rex Hudler, Jack Howell, Marty Brown, Alonzo Powell, Jim Paciorek, Lloyd Moseby, Matt Stairs, Mickey Brantley, Rick Schu, Ralph Bryant, Matt Winters, Kelvin Torve, R.J. Reynolds, Ty Gainey, Max Venable, George Wright, Darryl Motley and Jose Tolentino.

Rob Deer ended 10 years in the Major Leagues in 1993 and played for the Hanshin Tigers in 1994 for a reported $2.6 million.

When Dan Gladden played for the Yomiuri Giants in 1994, he commented that the Japanese media seemed to believe that if a player had ears of a certain size he could run faster.

Other 1994 Gaijin: Dion James, Mike Pagliarulo, Kevin Reimer, Hensley Meulens, Francisco Cabrera, Jerald Clark and Henry Cotto.

Julio Franco signed for $7 million for two seasons starting in 1995, but he was back in the Major Leagues in 1996. Shane Mack signed for $8.1 million for two years.

In 1995 Ken Griffey, Jr., was offered $12 million to play one season for an undisclosed Japanese team.

The 1996 American Gaijin included Bobby Rose, Shane Mack, Tom O'Malley, Darnell Coles, Glenn Braggs, Glenn Davis, Hensley Meulens, Rob Ducey, Troy Neel, Darrin Jackson, Chris Donnels, Randy Ready and Eric Hillman. Jackson signed with the Twins in 1997 and hit a grand slam in his first game.

In May 1997 the Rockies sold Darnell Coles to the Hanshin Tigers, who was to replace Mike Greenwell, recently arrived after being designated for assignment by the Red Sox after 10 seasons with the club. Greenwell suffered a broken leg shortly after starting play in Japan.

In 2003 the players included Steve Cox, Lou Pote and long-time Japanese league star Tuffy Rhodes. Mike Kinkaid signed for $809,000 in mid-2004 with the Hanshin Tigers, the Central League champions.

Gaijin Pitchers. American pitchers have been far less successful in Japan than their hitting counterparts. Matt Keough was the last American to win at least 10 games in the Japanese Leagues when he was 15-9 in 1989. The best American efforts were in 1964 when Joe Stanka won 26 games for the Nankai Hawks and Gene Bacque won 29 for the Hanshin Tigers.

Darrell May pitched in Japan for four years before coming up to Kansas City in 2002.

In a 1998 letter to this author from former UCLA pitching coach and ex-Major Leaguer Glenn Mickens, he reflected on his days as a pitcher in the Japanese Leagues between 1959 and 1963 for the pitiful Kintetsu Buffaloes. He said that Shigeru Chiba, perhaps the greatest second baseman in Japanese baseball history, was his manager in 1959. Mickens was pitching on a sweltering summer night and had a 2-1 lead going into the 8th inning against the Nankei Hawks. He sat next to Chiba in the bottom of the 7th, clearly exhausted: "I was sitting on the bench beside Chiba and he was wracking his brain to figure out how to stimulate me to beat the Hawks, as he knew I was out of gas. He said in broken English (he only knew a few), 'remember Pearl Harbor,' and I almost fell off the bench. Guess it worked, because I finished the game and we won 2-1."

Mickens said he was the first American to pitch in and win a Japanese all-star game.

Gaijin No-Hitters. In 1995 6'9" Terry Bross pitched the second no-hitter by an American in the Japanese Leagues. Bross, age 29, pitched a 4-0 no-hitter for the Yakult Swallows over the Yomiuri Giants in September. The first American to do it was Hanshin Tigers pitcher Gene Bacque in 1965.

Two-Time MVP. In 1993 Jack Howell became the first foreigner to win the MVP Award in consecutive seasons.

Trade. Clete Boyer was the first American player traded to a Japanese team in exchange for a player in the Japanese leagues. The trade occurred in 1971 after a minor **Gambling** incident while he was with the Braves. In return, his club received former Major Leaguer John Werhas from the Taiyo Whales. In 1972, after relationships with the two countries' leagues warmed after a trade controversy, the next such trade was Frank Johnson of the Giants to the Lotte Orions for pitcher Toru Hamaura, who never made it to the Major Leagues.

Home Run Title/Collusion Against American Players. Daryl Spencer had an outstanding career with the Hankyu Braves in 1964-1968 and 1971-1972. In 1965 long-time Japanese pitching star Masayaki Koyama walked Spencer four times on 16 straight pitches in a late season game to ensure that Katsuya Nomura would win the home run title over the American.

In 1971 American George Altman was in a tight batting race with Shinichi Eto. In a late-season game against Eto, the other team overshifted to allow Eto to go 4-for-4 and win the title. The manager of that team was Katsuya Nomura.

In 2001 former Major Leaguer Tuffy Rhodes of the Kintetsu Dragons tied Sadaharu Oh's record of 55 home runs. He was given nothing to hit in the last days of the season, and therefore had no chance to break Oh's record. Rhodes hit his 300th career home run in May 2004, the most by a foreigner, and the 28th player overall in Japanese professional baseball. He did it while playing for the Yomiuri Giants, to whom he was traded by the Kintetsu Buffaloes after eight season with the club.

In 2002 Venezuela's Alex Cabrera, who played 31 games in the U.S. Major Leagues in 2000 (after signing straight out of Venezuela with the Cubs in 1991), equaled Rhodes' season record. Cabrera had hit a pinch hit home run in his first Major League at-bat, for the Diamondbacks.

Batting Title. American Randy Bass holds the Japanese League season record with a .389 batting average. Ichiro Suzuki holds the record for most hits in a 140-game season, with 210 in 1994.

Apparently the Japanese were not as reverent of the batting title as they were the home run title, as Americans won the title in 1951 (Wally Yonamine), 1954 (Larry Raines), and 1962–1963 (Larry Raines).

There was some sentiment that after Oh passed Babe Ruth on the all-time home run list, it wouldn't be as disgraceful for an American to win an individual season's batting title.

No Gaijin Signings. The Yomiuri Giants were alone among Japanese teams in not signing American mainland players until the mid–1970s (signing Davey Johnson). The club's only American signees in the 1950s were of Hawaiian or Japanese descent.

All-Star Game. Unlike the American version, the Japanese play two all-star games on consecutive days. Players voted in by the fans must start at least one game. Only three foreigners are allowed on each all-star team, making it difficult for American stars on small-market teams to make the squad.

Cecil Fielder once led the Japanese leagues in home runs and RBIs at the all-star break but was not selected to the team.

In 1994 the all-star game was halted in the 5th inning for a "halftime show" of fireworks and music.

Gaijin Manager.

"No, it's not his job. My mouth is plenty big for both my feet."—Bobby Valentine in 2004, while managing in Japan for the second time, on his interpreter.

"Throw behind the runner."—Manager Bobby Valentine to his Japanese players; they never did, and he couldn't figure out why until his second tour as a manager in Japan. They thought he wanted them to throw at the baserunner's *behind.*

Don Blasingame was the first manager not of Japanese descent to lead a Japanese club when he was named manager of the Hanshin Tigers in December 1978. In 1957, Yoshio (Kaiser) Tanaka, an American citizen of Japanese descent, was named to manage the same club.

In 1994 Bobby Valentine he signed to manage the Chiba Lotte Marines of Japan's Pacific League. Valentine was fired after the season after it was revealed that two of his coaches sabotaged his signals and other managerial efforts. Ironically, the general manager who announced Valentine's departure had taken the job on the condition that he could hire an American manager. Prior to the announcement, 14,000 fans signed a petition asking the club to retain Valentine, who led the generally pitiful club to its best season since 1971 and attendance increased 16.9% over 1994.

In 1995 former Orioles infielder Lenn Sakata became a minor league manager in Japan.

Japanese Managers. Until 1970 no Japanese manager had ever been forced out during the season. Managers were simply sent away for rest and meditation before returning to the club.

Governing Document. The Japanese Professional Baseball Code is the governing document for the professional leagues in Japan.

Players Union. A Japanese players union was formed in 1985, but it has had a rocky and ineffective existence, despite the September 2004 player **Strike**.

Ballparks. Japanese ballparks are smaller than their American counterparts, with distances of 300 to 395 feet.

Japanese Hall of Fame. There are over 120 members of the Japanese Hall of Fame, which was established in 1959. There is one significant difference between the American and Japanese Halls. To be eligible in Japan, a player must be retired from all aspects of the professional game for five years. A former player who becomes a manager, such as Sadaharu Oh, is not eligible for the Hall. No Americans are in the Hall, though Hawaiian-born Tadashi Wakabayashi pitched his way into the shrine for various teams while earning the name Mr. Seven Colored Breaking Balls for his large selection of curveballs.

The Japanese Baseball Hall of Fame and Museum is located at 1–3–61 Koraku, Bunkyo-Ku, underneath the Tokyo Dome, home of the Yomiuri Giants.

Scheduling. The 12 teams in two leagues play 140-game schedules from early April through late September. There is no interleague play. Many games cancelled due to typhoons or rain are made up in October and the Japanese teams make up all postponed games regardless of their effect on the standings.

Ties. In the Pacific League games are called ties after 12 innings or four hours. In the Central League there is no time limit, but no more than 12 innings may be played. Ties count in the standings.

Scouting Presence. In May 1998 the Dodgers opened an Asian office, based in Tokyo.

Popularity. In the 1990s it was estimated that 10 million Japanese play baseball.

Pitching Award. Eiji Sawamura was a 17-year-old pitcher in 1934 when he struck out, in order, Babe Ruth, Jimmie Foxx, Charlie Gehringer and Lou Gehrig, en route to a 1–0 loss. He went on to record a 1.74 lifetime ERA in the Japanese Leagues. After he was killed during World War II in the battle for the Ryuku Islands, the Japanese version of the Cy Young Award was named after him. He was courted by the Pittsburgh Pirates after his spectacular strikeout exhibition, but he ignored them because of his virulent anti-American stance: "My problem is I hate America and I cannot make myself like Americans."

Greatest Game. The greatest game in Japanese baseball history, known as "The Emperor's Game," was played on June 26, 1959, between the Hanshin Tigers and the Yomiuri Giants at Tokyo's Korakuen Stadium. Emperor Hirohito and his wife were in attendance for the only time during his reign. Rookie Sadaharu Oh hit a home run to tie the game in the 7th inning and Shigeo Nagashima homered in the bottom of the 9th for the 5–4 victory. It was the first of 106 times that the two players homered in the same game, and they carried the Giants to nine pennants between 1965 and 1973.

Japan Series. The Japanese version of the World Series is traditionally played in late October.

Gambling Scandal. See *Gambling and Fixed Games*—Japan.

Free Agents/Reserve Clause. The reserve clause still exists in Japan. Masaichi Kaneda was a Korean pitcher who won at least 20 Japanese League games each season from 1951 through 1964. In 1963 he refused to pitch on less than three days' rest, creating a national uproar. In 1964 he became the first player to play out his option and switch teams.

The Japanese began a form of free agency after the 1993 season, resulting in the first multi-year contract ever offered to a native-born player. Hiromi Makihara was the beneficiary and he rewarded the club with a perfect game the following season.

Strike. In September 2004 the players voted to strike during weekend games to protest the proposed contraction of the league by two teams which had been struggling. The 752-member players association voted in August to carry out the strike, which occurred over the weekend of September 18–19, 2004. It was the talk of the nation and the two sides attempted further talks during the week of September 20 to avoid further upheaval in the schedule. Weekday games went on as scheduled. Fans overwhelmingly supported the players, but owners insisted that financial problems required a merger of weaker teams.

A second weekend strike was averted when the players gave in on a key demand and owners promised to find a way to add a team to make both leagues even at six each.

Japanese Ownership of American Teams. See *Seattle Mariners*.

Japanese Players in America.

Kenzo Nushida. In August 1932 it was reported that pitcher/infielder Kenzo Nushida was the first Japanese player to sign a contract in the Pacific Coast League with Sacramento. He was described as weighing slightly over 100 pounds and slightly under five feet tall.

Osaka Hawks. Most sources report that the first Japanese players to appear in an American professional league game were sent by the Osaka Hawks. The players were teenage former high school stars who competed in the Class A California League for Fresno in 1964.

Starting Pitchers. On May 5, 1972, for the first time, two Japanese-born pitchers were the starters in a U.S. professional game. Toru Homaura, pitching for Lodi in the Class A California League, defeated Masao Sato of Fresno. Lodi also had a Japanese starting catcher, Masaji Ishizuka.

Masanori Murakami. Murakami played for the San Francisco Giants in 1964 and 1965, winning five games in relief. Murakami bowed to Japanese pressure and returned to his homeland after 54 appearances. Legal problems over his transfer to the Giants caused a temporary suspension of relations between Japanese and U.S. Major Leagues. After 1965, he played the next 18 years in Japan but returned for one final attempt at the Major Leagues with the Giants in 1983. He was released during spring training.

Makoto Suzuki. In 1993 the Mariners signed 18-year-old Makoto ("Mac") Suzuki, who had a 92-mph fastball. He was trying to become the first Japanese player to reach the Major Leagues without starting his professional career in Japan. He played in the minor leagues beginning in 1994 and then pitched six Major League seasons through 2002. His best season was 2000, when he was 8–10 for Kansas City in 29 starts.

Hideo Nomo. The Dodger pitcher made his Major League debut against the Giants on May 2, 1995. The game was broadcast live on Japanese television and radio and was covered by 90 Japanese reporters and 29 Japanese news services. Nomo had been a winner of the Sawamura Award, the Japanese equivalent to the Cy Young Award. He set a Dodger rookie record with 16 strikeouts in June 1995 and pitched two straight shutouts during the month. This fostered a phenomenon known as Nomomania, similar to Fernandomania that occurred in 1981 when Fernando Valenzuela burst on the scene.

When Nomo was named National League Rookie of the Year for 1995 (the first by a Japanese player), it was the second time in his career that he received the award. In 1990 he was the Rookie of the Year in Japan's Pacific League for the Kintetsu Buffaloes. In Japan, playing professionally anywhere else disqualifies a player from winning the Rookie of the Year Award.

Katsuhiro Maeda. In 1996 the former Japanese minor leaguer pitched in Class AA for the Yankees. The orange-haired pitcher received a $1.5 million signing bonus, but never made it to the Major Leagues.

Shigatosi Hasagawa. Hasagawa first pitched in the Major Leagues for the Angels in 1997. He was the fourth Japanese player to play in the Major Leagues when he started against the Indians on April 5, 1997. He had played six seasons for the Orix Blue Wave of the Japanese Pacific League and had faced in Japan two Indians players who also played in his Major League debut, Kevin Mitchell and Julio Franco. Masanori Murakami was there for Hasagawa's debut to provide commentary for the Japanese broadcast of the game. Hasegawa later played for the Mariners.

Hideki Irabu. Irabu's rights were assigned to the Padres by his Japanese League club in January 1997, but San Diego was unable to sign him during that spring. He was then told that his old team, the Chiba Lotte Marines of Japan's Pacific League, would not take him back unless he apologized and signed a release saying that he would never try to play for an American Major League team. Irabu made it clear that he only wanted to negotiate with the Yankees, and in April 1997 the Yankees paid the Padres $3 million and traded two minor leaguers for the right to sign him. The Yankees sent the Padres injury-prone pitcher Ruben Rivera and pitcher Rafael Medina. The Padres gave up second baseman Homer Bush and outfielders Gordon Anderson and Vernon Maxwell.

The Yankees signed Irabu to a four-year deal worth $12.8 million. The deal included an $8.5 million signing bonus. Irabu made his Major League debut on July 10, 1997, striking out nine and winning 10–3 over the Tigers at Yankee Stadium. He was 13–9 and 11–7 for the Yankees in 1997 and 1998, but faded after that and finished up with 16 saves for the Rangers in 2002 before missing the last two months with blood clots in his lungs.

Kazuhiro Sasaki. In December 1999 the Mariners signed the Japanese Leagues' all-time save leader to a two-year contract. He responded with 37 saves to help the club into the play-offs and then saved 45 games the following season.

Masao Kida. On April 5, 1999, Kida came in to relieve for the Tigers in an 11–5 victory against the Rangers. He was the first Tokyo-born player to appear in the Major Leagues.

Ichiro Suzuki. Known simply as Ichiro, the outfielder became the most successful Japanese professional to play in the American Major Leagues when he signed with the Mariners in 2001 at age 27. He was the American League Rookie of the Year and MVP, and won a Gold Glove Award while leading off for the club. He had been a seven-time batting champion in Japan.

Kazuhisa Ishii. The highly-touted pitcher made his debut on April 6, 2002, pitching 5⅓ scoreless innings for the Dodgers in a 9–2 win.

Tsuyoshi Shinjo. In 2001 Shinjo debuted with the Mets, hitting 10 home runs with 56 RBIs in 123 games. He played in the Giants outfield in 2002 before returning to the Mets in 2003.

Satoru Komiyama. In December 2001 the Mets signed the star Japanese pitcher to a one-year contract. The 36-year-old Komiyama was a seven-time All-Star in Japan. He was 0–3 in 25 games for the Mets in 2002.

Hideki Matsui. Matsui was the biggest star in Japanese baseball in 2002, and Japanese fans went into mourning when the slugger signed a contract with the Yankees for 2003. He played well, coming in second for Rookie of the Year honors, and helped lead New York into the World Series. Matsui was a nine time all-star in Japan (332 home runs in 10 seasons) and was considered the most popular athlete in the country. At least 30 to 60 Japanese reporters showed up every day of the season, even in spring training, and the numbers increased to 100 during the World Series. When Matsui and Ichiro matched up early in the 2003 season, 50 million Japanese viewers tuned in live at 8 a.m. local time.

So Taguchi. Taguchi played for the Cardinals beginning in 2002.

Kazuo Matsui. After the 2003 season, Japanese shortstop Kazuo Matsui (no relation to Hideki) declared himself a free agent and said he would consider leaving for the U.S. Major Leagues. He hit a home run on the first pitch he saw for the Mets in April 2004. At age 24 in 2000, he was voted the greatest shortstop in Japanese league history.

Shingo Takatsu.

"Mr. Zero."

Takatsu lived up to his nickname when became the primary closer for the White Sox in mid–2004 after signing a one-year deal for $1 million.

High School Offer. In 2000 the Angels offered a $3 million signing bonus to Japanese high school pitcher Koji Uehara, but he turned it down and went on to star for the Yomiuri Giants.

Major League Face-Off. The first time that Japanese pitchers were on the mound at the same time in a Major League game was on June 18, 1997, when the Dodgers' Hideo Nomo was still in the game when the Angels' Shigetoshi Hasagawa came in to relieve in the 6th inning. The Dodgers won 7–5.

Salaries. In 1995 the average Japanese major leaguer received a salary of $553,529, an increase of 17.8% over 1994. The average did not include the salaries for foreigners. The average for foreigners, which consisted primarily of former U.S. Major League players, was estimated at $1.46 million.

The highest paid Japanese player was Hiromitsu Ochiai, who earned $4.4 million in 1995. Kevin Mitchell was the all-time highest paid American at between $4.5 and $5.3 million (depending on the source). By 2003 Tuffy Rhodes and Alex Cabrera were earning between $2 million and $3 million.

Gary Garland, perhaps the preeminent American source on Japanese baseball, reported at Baseballguru.com that minor leaguers in Japan make more than their American counterparts in the U.S. minor leagues. American minor leaguers who sign in Japan usually receive between $200,000 and $400,000 their first season. The Hiroshima club has a Carp Academy in the Dominican Republic, and those players earn between $35,000 and $50,000 in their first seasons in the Japanese major leagues. Alfonso Soriano of the Yankees and Rangers came up through that system.

Trades. Until the past few years, trades between Japanese teams were rare, as players stayed with teams for their entire careers as if they were Japanese factory workers (who, until recently, had jobs for life).

Spring Training. Training in the Japanese Leagues begins with "voluntary" workouts in mid–January at winter training camps. By February, teams conduct seven hour practices and evening strategy sessions. It is not uncommon for teams to have four-hour drills before regular season night games.

Since the 1980s a few Japanese teams have held at least part of their spring training camps in the United States. The Chiba Lotte Marines and Chunichi Dragons have held their spring training in Peoria, Arizona. The Yakult Swallows held their spring training in Yuma for a number of years.

Japanese clubs only scrimmage and practice at home before they play between 10 and 20 exhibition games on the road and at their regular season homes.

Player Agents. See *Agents.*

Umpires. Umpires in Japan are accorded far more respect than American umpires. Players bow to umpires before stepping into the batter's box and arguments are virtually unheard of. Leo Durocher horrified a large crowd in the late 1940s when he argued with an umpire. Later in the game he came out and bowed to apologize. The apology was accepted by both umpire and fans. The headline the next day in the Japanese papers: "Durocher Breaks Tradition."

In 1996 four American Major League umpires worked in Japanese spring training games in mid–March in Japan. Four Japanese umpires worked 16 Major League games earlier that spring.

Mike Di Muro, son of 20-year Major League umpire Lou Di Muro, was the only non-Japanese to umpire in Japan, in the mid–1990s. He left after a shoving incident with a Japanese league player, Taiwain's Yasuaki Taiho of the Chunichi Dragons.

American Opening Day. See *Opening Day* — **Japan,** for American Major League teams that opened their seasons in Japan.

The Seattle Mariners and Oakland A's were supposed to start the 2003 season in Japan in a late March three-game series, but security concerns related to the U.S. invasion of Iraq caused cancellation of the trip.

Books. Robert Obojski, *The Rise of Japanese Baseball Power* (1975); Sadaharu Oh with David Falkner, *Sadaharu Oh* (1983); Daniel E. Johnson, *Japanese Baseball: A Statistical Handbook* (1999); Fred N. Miike, *Baseball Mad Japan* (1955); Robert Whiting, *You Gotta Have Wa* (1983) (with a large bibliography); Robert Whiting, *The Chysanthemum and the Bat* (1977); Robert Whiting, *The Meaning of Ichiro: The New Wave From Japan and the Transformation of Our National Pastime* (2004). See also an excellent bibliography compiled by Paul Margiott at Jim Allen's Japanese Baseball Page (Allen writes a column for a Japanese newspaper).

Ferguson Jenkins (1943–)

Hall of Fame 1991

"He told me he was going to help me make a million dollars. He listed four things I had to do: 1) work hard; 2) concentrate, 3) make the batter hit my pitch; and 4) be ready to go out and pitch every fourth day." — Jenkins on former Cubs pitching coach Joe Becker.

Jenkins won 20 or more games seven times on his way to 284 career wins over 19 seasons beginning in 1965.

A native Canadian who starred in hockey and basketball as well as baseball, Ferguson Arthur "Fergie" Jenkins broke into the minor leagues with Miami in the Florida State League in 1962. In 1965 the Phillies called him up for seven appearances. He was traded to the Cubs early in the 1966 season and went on to star for Chicago after being converted from being primarily a relief pitcher. He won 20 games in 1967, the first of six straight seasons with 20 or more wins for the Cubs. A powerful strikeout pitcher, he led the league in 1969 and regularly amassed more than 200 strikeouts per season.

After slipping to 14 wins in 1973 the Cubs traded him to the Rangers. He pitched a one-hit shutout against the World Champion A's in his first American League start on his way to a 25–12 record. He moved on to the Red Sox in 1976 and back to the Rangers in 1978, when he won 18 games after three mediocre seasons. He returned to the Cubs in 1982 for his final two seasons, winning a total of 20 games in 63 starts.

Jenkins retired in 1983 with a 284–226 record, 3,192 strikeouts, 49 shutouts and a 3.34 ERA in 19 seasons. He won the Cy Young Award in 1971, when he led the National League with 24 victories for the Cubs. He regularly pitched 20 or more complete games, often because he was a decent hitter who was not lifted for a pinch hitter. For example, he hit six home runs and batted .243 in 1971.

His entry into the Hall of Fame was delayed a year or two because of a cocaine possession conviction a number of years earlier. In the early 1990s his girlfriend abducted his daughter from a prior marriage. She then killed the daughter and committed suicide, both by carbon monoxide poisoning while sitting in a car.

Jenkins was a pitching coach for a Rangers' minor league affiliate and then served in that capacity for Team Canada at the Pan Am Games in 1987. He also served as a roving instructor for the Reds and pitching coach of the Cubs between 1993 and 1996. He sold his Canadian cattle ranch in 1989 and moved to a new ranch in Oklahoma.

Book. Jenkins and George Vass, *Like Nobody Else: The Fergie Jenkins Story* (1973).

Hughie Jennings (1869–1928)

Hall of Fame 1945

"For many generations now ballplayers have come tumbling out of the Pennsylvania coal country as if they were bouncing down a chute, but the first of these to achieve real eminence in the game was Hughey Ambrose Jennings, an uneducated breaker boy from Moosic, between Pittston and Scranton, who bettered his condition in life through his ability to play baseball." — Lee Allen and Tom Meany in *Kings of the Diamond* (1965).

Jennings played infield primarily for the Baltimore Orioles in the 1890s on his way to a lifetime .312 average.

Hugh Ambrose Jennings began his minor league career in 1890 in Allentown, Pennsylvania, and then broke into the Major Leagues in 1891 with Louisville. Midway through the 1893 season he was traded and became the sparkplug of the powerful Baltimore Orioles of the 1890s. In five full seasons beginning in 1894 the shortstop batted at least .328, with a high of .401 in 1896 — a Major League record for shortstops. He also stole as many as 70 bases in a season to help lead the Orioles to the top of the National League.

Jennings moved over to the Dodgers in 1899 with the sharing of ownership between the two clubs. He also shifted primarily to first base to protect his sore arm. He played in at least 78 games through 1902 with the Dodgers and Phillies. He made a few appearances in 1903 back with the Dodgers, but his career was over except for cameo appearances while managing the Tigers from 1907 through 1920. Jennings hit .312 lifetime with 359 stolen bases. He was also hit by a large but number of pitches, approximately 287, including 51 (previously 49) in 1896.

A popular and colorful player, Jennings was equally popular and respected as a manager. Before managing the Tigers he was the player-manager of Baltimore in the Eastern League. With the Tigers he won pennants in his first three seasons at the helm beginning in 1907, though the club lost the World Series each time. He never again won a pennant, but his clubs finished second in 1911 and 1915. After the Tigers replaced him in 1921 with player-manager Ty Cobb, Jennings moved on to become a coach with the Giants and his old teammate John McGraw.

During the off-season in his playing days, Jennings earned a law degree and had a successful off-season practice in Pennsylvania. While coaching with the Giants, he contracted tuberculosis and was forced to retire in 1926. He died two years later at age 59.

Jewelry

"One chain, no rings — it's like being in the army." — Unhappy White Sox outfielder Ivan Calderon after being told that he could only wear one gold chain during games.

"I've got to spend it somehow, baby." — Pedro Guerrero on why he wore so many gold chains."

"Diamond-cutting is infinitely more complex and difficult [than playing baseball], not to say useful, but diamond-cutters can't even get the guy next to them on the bus to listen to them." — Jim Murray.

"Hope you enjoy my ring. The nightmare of 1986 is over! I'm off the hook. Your pal, Bill Buckner." — Buckner's note accompanying the sale of his World Series ring at a December 1993 auction. The note and ring brought $33,000.

"Silver King, Silver Flint, Sterling Slaughter, Mike Golden, Randy Sterling, Bill Cristall, Goldie Rapp, Jewel Ens"

World Series Rings. World Series commemorative rings were first awarded in 1912 (1922 in some sources). Before that, diamond stick pins were the norm for the victorious clubs. The tradition was not always followed, as rings were presented to players in 1922, 1926 and 1927, and then annually beginning in 1931.

The feud between 1940s Dodger co-owners Walter O'Malley and Branch Rickey spilled over to World Series rings. When Rickey ordered World Series rings for the Dodger players in 1949, O'Malley insisted that they turn in their 1947 rings before receiving new ones.

Theft. In 1994 Tim Raines had $95,000 worth of jewelry stolen from his Chicago apartment.

Search. During a minor league rehab assignment game in 2002, Red Sox outfielder Manny Ramirez held up the game for 15 minutes while he crawled around in the dirt looking for the $15,000 diamond stud he lost while sliding head first into third base. Should have bought a bigger earring.

Ouch. In 1995 David Justice made a new baseball fashion statement when it was revealed that he was wearing a nipple ring.

Distraction. On August 25, 2001, the Mariners beat the Indians 3–2 in 11 innings. In the 9th inning when Seattle's Arthur Rhodes came in to relieve, Indians batter Omar Vizquel complained that the sunlight was reflecting off the reliever's right earring. Rhodes started yelling at Vizquel and eventually was ejected by third base umpire Tim McClelland.

Paste. Pete Rose took the jewels from his Hickok Belt Award and replaced them with fakes. He used the jewels to make several pairs of earrings for girlfriends and others as gifts. He sold the belt for about $30,000 to a collector, who got revenge when the securities he paid Rose with turned out to be worthless.

Expensive Ring. On April 8, 2003, long-time Angels employee Phil Alger tried to auction off his World Series ring on eBay. The rings given to the players were worth about $15,000, and rings presented to employees were worth approximately $10,000. The club required each employee not to sell the rings. The $60,000-per-year employee resigned rather than be terminated for violating the agreement. He said that if he had sold it for $20,000, he would have rather used the money to put a down payment on a house.

Big Rings.

"He's talking all this smack about that ring. It better be good." — Marlins coach Ozzie Guillen after owner Jeffrey Loria promised the best championship rings ever after the club won the 2003 World Series. Loria apparently delivered. The rings included 228 white diamonds, 13 rubies and a single teal diamond in the eye of a marlin. The club made 85 rings and they weighed a quarter pound each, the largest ever, and twice as large as the Angels' rings the year before. The Marlins' rings were valued at $40,000 each.

The Celebrant. Eric Rolfe Greenberg's *The Celebrant* (1983) is a fiction-based-on-fact account of a championship ring-making jeweler's hero-worship of and relationship with New York Giants pitching star Christy Mathewson.

Jewish Players

"This is the story about a Manhattan Jewish boy, transplanted to the Bronx, who made good without getting into the ready-to-wear line."—Lead to a 1934 article in *The Sporting News* on new Jewish star Hank Greenberg.

"Though my disappointment was keen, my misfortune did not necessitate a change in plans for the future. Playing baseball was not what the Jewish boys of our lower-middle-class neighborhood were expected to do in later life for a living. Had I been cut from the high school itself, *then* there would have been hell to pay in my house, and much confusion and shame in me."— Philip Roth in *Portnoy's Complaint* (1969), on getting cut from the high school baseball team.

"Obviously, it's because they were honoring the Eighth Commandment."— Martin Abramowitz, chronicler of Jewish Major Leaguers, on why all 141 of them collectively had fewer stolen bases than Rickey Henderson.

"There is talk that I am Jewish—just because my father was Jewish, my mother is Jewish, I speak Yiddish and once studied to be a rabbi and a cantor. Well, that's how rumors get started."—Baseball clown Al Schacht in his autobiography, *My Own Particular Screwball* (1955).

"Because I'm David and I'm a star."— Dave Parker on why he wore a Star of David around his neck.

See also **Food—Kosher Food.**

Earliest. One baseball historian concluded from surname analysis that Jews played in the earliest known organized game involving the New York Knickerbockers in 1845 (Kline and Meyers).

Rainchecks for the four games hosted by the Twins during the 1965 World Series, which they lost in seven games to the Dodgers. The Dodgers were hoping for a rainout—a divine intervention to avoid Sandy Koufax missing Game One due to a Jewish holiday. He came back on two days rest to shut out the Twins 2–0 in Game 7.

19th Century Players. In addition to the famous Lipman Pike and his brother Boaz, other Jews were well-known 19th century players. Lip Pike's name appeared in a professional box score in 1858, supposedly only one week after his Bar Mitzvah at age 13. Other early Jewish players included 1880s outfielder Chief Jim Rosenman, versatile 1880s player Danny Stearns, 15-year third baseman Billy Nash and pitcher Harry Kane (aka Cohen).

Early 20th Century.

"In looking over the list of names comprising the American and National Leagues we fail to discover any of those well worn Semitic cognomens, such as Moses, Abraham, Ikey, Solomon, Aaron, etc., or the tribe of numerous 'Skys.' Something's wrong. Is the work too arduous?"—From a 1910 book of "humor" by Jack Regan and Will E. Stahl. These writers overlooked catcher Big Ed Reulbach among Jewish Major League players of the early 20th century.

Barney Pelty was known as the "Yiddish Curver," so presumably he was a Jewish Major Leaguer in the early part of the 20th century (92–117 record).

Erskine John Mayer was a right-handed pitcher in the 1910s who won 20 games in both 1914 and 1915 for the Phillies. His Jewish grandparents emigrated from Germany, where his great-grandfather had been a buyer for Otto Von Bismarck until he disappeared and was found buried under a stable.

Early Attempts to Find Jewish Players.

"There is not sufficient monetary inducement ... Jews are not inclined toward team sports.... In boxing, he is alone and the sport is more commercialized."—Widely held views espoused in *The Sporting News* on why Jews were not inclined to play baseball.

The New York teams of the first half of the 20th century, especially the Giants and manager John McGraw, tried to find talented Jewish ballplayers because of the large Jewish population in that city.

Moses Solomon. Solomon was the first highly touted Jewish player signed by a New York club, but he played only two games with the 1923 Giants. He was billed as "The Rabbi of Swat" in an effort to increase attendance to counter the big boost in attendance the Yankees were enjoying due to the opening of Yankee Stadium.

Solomon hit 49 home runs in 1923 for Class C Hutchinson, Kansas, the most in a season at any level except for Babe Ruth's totals. The Giants signed him late in the season and heavily publicized his presence on the team, but manager John McGraw held him out until the Giants had clinched the pennant. He was not a stellar fielder, having made 31 errors in 198 games in the minor leagues that year.

He finally appeared in the last home game of the season, playing in right field. He doubled in the winning run in the 10th inning, but otherwise was unsuccessful. He also played in the last road game of the season against the Dodgers, going 2-for-4. He returned home before the World Series because he was not on the Giants' World Series roster, and McGraw supposedly was miffed that his crowd-pleaser chose not to sit on the bench to cheer on his teammates. Solomon never made it back to the Major Leagues, finishing 3-for-8 in his career.

Johnny Kling. The Cubs catcher purportedly was the most well-known Jewish player in the era immediately before Babe Ruth began his home-run barrage in 1919. One of the better catchers of the first 13 years of the 20th century, his real name supposedly was Kline. Even though *The Baseball Encyclopedia* does not confirm the name change, one source reported that there is evidence that Kling used his real name when he played in the Texas League.

Kling later was a successful businessman in Kansas City and owned the Kansas City Blues of the American Association from 1934 to 1937. Perhaps thoughts of racism affected his pioneering decision to order the desegregation of the seating at the Blues' ballpark, Muehlebach Stadium. Nevertheless, research by David W. Anderson suggests that Kling was not Jewish. His wife later wrote the Hall of Fame to indicate he was baptized a Lutheran, though his daughters both married Jews, which perhaps created the confusion. Anderson also hypothesizes that because Kling was thought to be Jewish, it harmed his chances of entering the Hall of Fame during an era when he was still relatively well-known.

Andy Cohen. The best of the early 20th century Jewish players may have been Cohen, who came up as a second baseman with the Giants from the University of Alabama. He was touted as the first great Jewish ballplayer in New York, which would have been a major coup for any of the city's Major League clubs. He flamed out quickly (lasting only three seasons over four years in the late 1920s), though at first he was compared favorably to great second baseman Rogers Hornsby.

Moe Berg. The future *Spy* was a catcher in the 1920s and 1930s, known for his brilliant mind and eccentricities.

Wally Moses. Moses was thought to be Jewish, which made it easier to move up the baseball ladder on a New York team. However, his career supposedly was impeded when owners learned that he was not Jewish. Moses could not fit that role but still was a solid outfielder primarily for the A's and White Sox after he made it to the Major Leagues at age 24 in 1935.

Multiple Jewish Players. In 1941 the Giants had four Jewish players: Harry Danning, Morrie Arnovich, Hank Feldman and Sid Gordon. The 1946 Giants had Gordon, Arnovich, Feldman, Mike Schemer and Goody Rosen.

Ed Levy. When Larry MacPhail became general manager of the Yankees in the 1940s, he supposedly made Jewish Alabama-born Edward Clarence Whitner change his name to Ed Levy so Jewish fans in New York could more easily identify with him.

Jimmie Reese. Reese was one of Babe Ruth's roommates on the Yankees. He was still hitting fungoes for the Angels at age 90 in the early 1990s and was the honorary captain of the 1992 American League All-Star team. He was not known to be Jewish when he broke in with the Yankees in 1930, going 10-for-20 as a pinch hitter. According to Martin Abramowitz, who has created a set of baseball cards honoring Jewish Major Leaguers, Reese was batting one day against a Jewish battery who were speaking Yiddish to each other to call pitches. Late in the game the catcher commented to Reese on how well he was hitting against his pitcher that day. Reese responded, "well, my name is Hymie Solomon."

1960s-2000s. From the early 1960s through the 1990s, some of the more prominent Jewish players have been Steve Stone, Norm and Larry Sherry, Bo Belinsky, Mark Gilbert, Joel Horlen, Barry Latman, Steve Yeager, Ron Blomberg, Mike Epstein, Al Newman, Phil Weintraub, Dave Roberts and Scott Radinsky.

Kevin Youkilis, identified as the "Greek God of Walks" in the book *Moneyball,* is actually a Jew of Romanian descent. Jews comprised .08% of Major League players during the 20th century, despite comprising about 2% of the U.S. population at the time.

In the 2000s, some of the prominent Jewish players were Shawn Green, Gabe Kapler, Al Levine, Jason Marquis and Brad Ausmus. In November 1999, Green was traded to the Dodgers from the Blue Jays for disgruntled outfielder Raul Mondesi. Green acknowledged that he wanted to play in a cosmopolitan city with a large Jewish population, but apparently the California native forgot that Toronto fit that profile. In 1996 Green came to bat and exchanged greetings with catcher Jesse Lewis, also Jewish. They were joined by Jewish home plate umpire Al Clark.

Union Man. Players Association leader Marvin Miller is Jewish.

Hall of Fame Retrospective. In 2004 it was estimated that there were 141 Jewish Major Leaguers, and the Hall of Fame prepared a retrospective, "A Celebration of Jews in Baseball." The first kosher dinner in the Hall was planned for the August 2004 event. A set of baseball cards was issued at the time of the event. Harry Danning at age 92 was the oldest living Jewish Major Leaguer in 2004.

There have been six sets of Jewish brothers to make the Major Leagues, including Ike and Harry Danning, and the last pair, Norm and Larry Sherry.

Greatest.

"Henry Greenberg has already been scouted by the Giants, and he will never make a ballplayer."—John McGraw on Hank Greenberg after he shagged fly balls at the Polo Grounds in 1928 as a high school player.

"He's the greatest Jewish athlete since Samson."—Comedian George Jessel on Greenberg.

"Some Jew kid who'll never learn to pitch as long as he has a hole in his ass."—Carl Furillo identifying a young Sandy Koufax during an early tryout with the Dodgers.

Hank Greenberg and Sandy Koufax were probably the most famous and best Jewish ballplayers. Another top Jewish player was Ken Holtzman, who came to the Major Leagues in 1966 billed as "the next Sandy Koufax." He pitched two no-hitters and won 174 games in 15 years.

Ron Blomberg, though not a great ballplayer, was the first *Designated Hitter* and sometimes referred to himself as the Designated Jew.

Shawn Green is considered the best of the modern crop of Jewish ballplayers.

Holidays.

Sandy Koufax.

"God Knows." — Sandy Koufax commenting on why the 1965 World Series game scheduled on Yom Kippur was rained out. Koufax would not pitch on any Jewish holiday, which caused a problem during the 1965 World Series. Koufax was scheduled to pitch the first game of the Series against the Twins, but it fell on the holiday. Don Drysdale pitched instead and lost. Koufax came back to pitch Game 2 (losing) and Game 5 (winning) before pitching Game 7 on two days' rest (shutting out the Twins 2–0). Drysdale's comment to manager Walter Alston after losing Game 1: "Hey Skip, bet you wish I was Jewish today, too?"

Hank Greenberg.

"It was a constant thing. I think it was a spur for me to do better. Not only were you a bum; you were a Jewish bum." — Greenberg, who at first would not play baseball on any Jewish holidays. He then conferred with two rabbis and they determined that the Jewish religious tome, the Talmud, allowed him to play on Rosh Hashanah, the Jewish New Year. Yom Kippur, considered the holiest of Jewish holidays, was more important and Greenberg absolutely refused to play. When he sat out on the holiday in 1934, the *Detroit Free Press* printed Greenberg's picture above a caption in Hebrew: "Happy New Year Greetings."

A movie was made about Greenberg, *The Life and Times of Hank Greenberg*, a documentary film by Aviva Kempner. The film opens with actor Mandy Patinkin singing a Yiddish rendition of "Take Me Out to the Ballgame."

Shawn Green. In 2004 there was a bit of controversy surrounding Green's decision whether to play or sit out the Yom Kippur holiday on the second-to-last weekend of the season. The Dodgers had an important series scheduled with the Giants, and Green decided to play on Friday night and observe the holiday on Saturday. He hit a two-run homer to tie the game on Friday and the Dodgers won a close 3–2 victory. They lost 9–5 on Saturday.

Holiday Scheduling. There was an outcry among New York's huge Jewish population over the scheduling of two 1986 play-off games in New York during Yom Kippur. Once again there was divine intervention as it rained on the holier day of the two-day religious services and the game was cancelled.

Latin Jew. In 1994 Jose Bautista of the Cubs was the only known Jewish player on a Major League roster. Bautista was born in the Dominican Republic to a Catholic father and a Jewish mother from New York. Bautista's wife was a Conservative Jew whose family emigrated to Venezuela from Eastern Europe after World War II.

Wrong Religion. Indians third baseman Al Rosen made an "X" in the dirt before entering the batter's box. Sports columnist Ed Sullivan (yes, *the* Ed Sullivan) wrote that Rosen was making the sign of the cross because, though "of Jewish parentage, he is Catholic." Rosen publicly denied that he was Catholic, though not before receiving a Bible from a Philadelphia congregation.

Benny Kauff was a Federal League star thought for many years to be Jewish. He was barred from the New York Giants by Judge Landis after being accused of theft (see also *Felons*). Later research determined that Kauff was not Jewish.

Rod Carew never converted to Judaism, despite marrying a Jewish woman and raising his children in that faith.

Owners.

"Bar mitzvah age is when a Jewish boy learns he has a better chance of owning a professional sports team than of playing for one." — Sports agent Arn Tellem.

A sampling of Jewish baseball owners in history: Andrew Freedman owned the Giants at the turn of the century; Barney Dreyfuss and the Benswanger families owned the Pirates for many years; Judge Emil Fuchs owned the Braves in the 1920s–1930s; Sidney Weil purchased the Reds in the late 1930s; Jerry Hoffberger and his family owned the Orioles for many years; Commissioner Bud Selig owns the Milwaukee Brewers; Charles Bronfman of Seagram's owned the Expos for several years.

Nicknames. It was common for most Jewish players in the 1920s through the 1940s to be called "Moe," short for Moses.

Memorabilia. In 1995 B&J Collectibles of New Jersey offered yarmulkes signed by Sandy Koufax for $75 each.

Hall of Fame. The International Jewish Sports Hall of Fame is located in Tel Aviv, Israel, but has an office in Los Angeles.

Song. "Jake! Jake! The Yiddishe Ballplayer" was written in 1913.

Books. Peter S. Horvitz and Joachim Horvitz, *The Big Book of Jewish Baseball* (2001); Peter Levine, *Ellis Island to Ebbets Field: Sports and the American-Jewish Experience* (1992); Erwin Lynn, *The Jewish Baseball Hall of Fame: A Who's Who of Baseball Stars* (1987); Harold Ribalow, *The Jew in American Sports* (1963); Harold Ribalow, *Jewish Baseball Stars* (1984).

Jockstraps

"What would have happened had my team been the Browns or the Braves? ('I'm a Yankee fan, but you're an Athletic supporter,' I used to wisecrack to a young friend from Philadelphia.) I might have ended up besieged by insecurities, in the hands of a shrink." — Frank Graham, Jr., in *Farewell to Heroes* (1981).

"His sanitary socks and woolen stockings were slashed to shreds and all the other things were smeared black with shoe polish. He located his jock, with two red apples in it, swinging from a cord attached to the light globe, and both his shoes were nailed to the ceiling." — Bernard Malamud in *The Natural* (1952).

"Thanks for sharing that." — Broadcaster Joe Buck to seatmate Tim McCarver after the former catcher related the following story on the air during the 2003 World Series. After Don Larsen pitched his perfect game in the 1956 World Series, backup Yankees catcher Charlie Silvera asked Yogi Berra for a memento from the game. Berra gave him his used jockstrap.

See also *Underwear*.

Bike. In 1992 the Bike Athletic Company manufactured its 300,000th jockstrap. The Knoxville, Tennessee, firm claimed to have invented the athletic supporter in 1874.

Bare. Gas House Gang shortstop Pepper Martin did not wear a jockstrap or a protective cup.

Byron Bancroft "Ban" Johnson (1864–1931)

Johnson was the driving force in the formation of the *American League* and was the first *American League President*.

Judy Johnson (1900–1989)

Hall of Fame (NLC) 1975

"Johnson was one of the slickest fielding third basemen in the history of black baseball — or any other baseball." — John Holway in *Blackball Stars* (1988).

"If Judy Johnson was white, he could name his own price." — Connie Mack.

"We use to have a lot of fun — and there were some bad days too, but ... there was always sun shining someplace. So that's what we looked forward to, the big days, the best days." — Johnson.

"You have to take life in stride. Sometimes your heart may ache, but you can't let it get you down. There's always a better day coming." — Johnson.

Johnson was one of the premier third basemen of the Negro Leagues in the 1920s and 1930s.

William Julius "Judy" Johnson grew up in Wilmington, Delaware, and played on integrated community baseball and football teams. His high school team had no formal sports program, so he quit school. After World War I he began playing for the Chester Giants in Pennsylvania and then moved up to the Bacharach Giants and Philadelphia All-Stars. He got his nickname because of his resemblance to an older player, Judy Gals.

Johnson emerged as one of the top third basemen in the Negro Leagues by the mid–1920s, batting .392 in 1925, a mark he believed was his all-time high; though other sources report that he batted .401 with Hilldale in the Eastern Colored League. When that league folded in 1930 as a result of the Depression, Johnson moved on to the Homestead Grays as a player-coach. He later played for the Pittsburgh Crawfords and helped lead them to a Negro League World Series win in 1935. He eventually left baseball for a manufacturing job until 1951, when he returned as a Major League scout with the Philadelphia A's.

Johnson was known as an excellent teacher and scout; he is credited with discovering Josh Gibson in the Negro Leagues and helping to sign Dick Allen many years later. When he began working for Connie Mack and the A's, he tried unsuccessfully to persuade the club to sign future stars Minnie Minoso, Henry Aaron and Larry Doby. He moved over to the Phillies as a scout in the late 1950s and remained with the club until his retirement in 1973.

Book. Ellen Rendle, *Judy Johnson: Delaware's Invisible Hero* (1994).

Walter Johnson (1887–1946)

Hall of Fame 1936

"Everybody knew what was coming, but still couldn't hit him. Walter's right arm was different than yours or mine. It was special, like Caruso's lungs or Einstein's brain." — Chief Meyers, who caught for the Giants.

"You can't hit what you can't see." — Ping Bodie.

"The greatest pitcher of all-time." — Numerous.

"Forgetting the numbers, what pleased people most was that Johnson combined extraordinary baseball talent with a wholly admirable character. In a rowdy game, he was mild, modest, decent, friendly, and forbearing. Across the nation, beyond the confines of baseball, he personified values that Americans respected. He persisted into the lively ball era and the Jazz Age with his old-fashioned, almost Lincolnesque virtues intact." — A.D. Suehsdorf in *The Ballplayers* (1990).

"If Johnson had pitched night ball, Congress would have had to pass a law against him." — Nick Altrock.

"In his best years he had records as good as anybody for teams that weren't as good as anybody's." — Bill James.

Johnson won 416 games and pitched 110 shutouts over 21 seasons for the Senators beginning in 1907.

Known for his blazing fastball, Walter Perry Johnson, "The Big Train," was perhaps the greatest pitcher of all time. With the possible exception of Christy Mathewson, he was certainly the greatest pitcher of the first 30 years of the 20th century.

Johnson was born in Kansas but grew up in California. His first professional contract provided him with $75 per month to pitch and dig postholes for a telephone company in Idaho. He was discovered pitching there by Senators catcher Cliff Blankenship.

Johnson broke in with the Senators with a 5–9 record in 1907. In 1910 he won 25 games to begin a streak of 10 straight seasons with 20 or more wins. He peaked with 36 wins in 1913 with a 1.09 ERA and 11 shutouts. He led the league in strikeouts in eight straight seasons from 1912 through 1919 and led in shutouts seven times.

His career was ended by a broken ankle during spring training batting practice in 1927. He retired after 21 seasons for the usually mediocre Senators with 416 victories (second all-time) and 279 losses (fourth all-time). Early record books credit him with 3,501 strikeouts, but later sources put the figure at 3,509, ninth all-time. He is first all-time with 110 shutouts and pitched at least one shutout in every one of his Major League seasons.

After Johnson retired he managed in the minor leagues in 1928 and took over the Senators for four years starting in 1929, finishing second, third twice and fifth. He managed the Indians to two third-place finishes in 1934–1935 before retiring to his cattle ranch in Maryland. He died of a stroke caused by a brain tumor at age 59.

Books. Henry W. Thomas, *Walter Johnson: Baseball's Big Train* (1993); Roger Treat, *Walter Johnson* (1948).

Addie Joss (1880–1911)

Hall of Fame (VC) 1978

"With Addie Joss, baseball was a profession, as severe as that of any other, for it gave recreation to the masses, brought them out of the factories and the counting room into the open air and the sunlight and made them forget the petty annoyances of life. In taking his vocation seriously he was, in return, taken seriously by the people, who recognized in him a man of more than usual intelligence and one who would have adorned any profession in which he had elected to engage." — The *Toledo Blade* newspaper quoted in the *National Baseball Hall of Fame and Museum Yearbook*, edited by Bill Guilfoile (1989).

In a brief nine-year career beginning in 1902, Joss won 160 games and posted the second-lowest ERA of all time.

Adrian Joss pitched for the University of Wisconsin before playing professionally with Toledo of the Inter-State League in 1900. After a 25-win season for Toledo in 1901 (while it was in the Western Association), Joss moved to Cleveland for the 1902 season. He won 17 games and pitched five shutouts. Over the next eight seasons he won 20 or more games four straight times (1905–1908) and five times had an ERA below 2.00. He had a high of 27 wins in 1907 and his lowest ERA was 1.16 in 1908, with nine shutouts contributing to that total.

Joss threw a perfect game and a no-hitter for the Indians during his brief career. The perfect game came at the end of a close pennant race, when he beat 40-game winner Ed Walsh on October 2, 1908. In 1910 arm injuries caused him to fall to 5–5 and in the spring of 1911, to the shock of the baseball world, he died of tubular meningitis at age 31.

Joss finished with a 160–97 record and the second-lowest ERA of all time at 1.88. He completed 234 of his 260 starts and pitched 46 shutouts. His nine-year career disqualified him from the Hall of Fame for many years, but the Veterans Committee finally overlooked the 10-year career rule and elected him in 1978.

Jubilee Year

"We are reaching this year a right impressive milestone in the sport: the Diamond Jubilee of the National League and the Golden Anniversary of the American League and the National Association. Some sports have longer histories but none has made as great an impact on the people of any nation as baseball has made on Americans. The sport typifies the great American dream where a boy may rise from direct poverty to become a National Hero. No pull — no inside track is necessary." — Commissioner Happy Chandler in the preface to the Jubilee Edition of *The Official Encyclopedia of Baseball*, by Hy Turkin and S.C. Thompson (1951).

Baseball celebrated its so-called Jubilee Year in 1951. The milestones included 80 years of Major League Baseball (National Association in 1871), 75 years of the National League (1876), 50 years of the American League (1901) and 50 years of the minor league National Association of Professional Baseball Leagues (1901).

Judges

"Klem wore his chest protector beneath his coat and was as regal a figure as the Chief Justice of the Supreme Court." — Hall of Fame director Ken Smith.

"Joe Judge, Walt Justis, Joe Just, Barry Cort, Rudy Law, Law Daniels"

See also **Supreme Court**.

Gavvy Cravath. The outfielder later became a judge in Laguna, California. Some sources report that he was a judge while still playing. He was so easygoing that he eventually lost his judgeship.

Harry Taylor. The 19th century infielder later became a judge in New York's Erie County.

Judge Emil Fuchs. Fuchs owned the Braves in the 1930s. He was never a judge but earned his nickname as a result of practicing law for many years.

Lon Warneke. Warneke won 193 games in the 1930s and 1940s and later became a judge in Mt. Ida, Arkansas.

O.J. Simpson Trial. During the O.J. Simpson murder trial, prosecutor Christopher Darden asked defense witness Robert Heidstra what his favorite sports were:

"Soccer, what we call football in Europe," Heidstra replied.

"Anything else?"

"Oh yeah — ice hockey, basketball."

"American football?"

"Boring."

At which point Judge Lance Ito said, "Wait till you see baseball."

Jumping the Club

"I don't know why I did it." — Gene Conley, after leaving the Red Sox and trying to fly to Israel in 1962. A pitcher who also played **Basketball** for the Boston Celtics, Conley lost a game 13–3 and then jumped the club on July 26, 1962. The team bus was stuck in New York traffic when he decided to take off. He was gone four days and tried to book a flight to Israel, but he did not have a passport. Teammate Pumpsie Green left the bus with him and they lived it up together briefly before Green returned to the club after 48 hours.

Rube Waddell. The eccentric pitcher supposedly jumped the A's for 10 days, apparently to go fishing.

The Dean Brothers. In 1934 when Dizzy Dean won 31 games for the Cardinals, he and his brother Paul jumped the club. Paul made it back for his next start, but Dizzy missed almost two weeks.

Perhaps the greatest pitcher ever, the "Big Train," Walter Johnson.

He came back with stunning success, almost never losing to the end of the season.

Boots Poffenberger. Poffenberger, who won 16 games in the late 1930s, was a wild drinker and partier. He jumped the Boston/New York train in 1939 while with the Dodgers. To fool manager Leo Durocher, he left a dummy in his Pullman birth. He was sent back to the minors immediately and later joined the Marine Corps in 1943, ending his professional career. He never returned to the Major Leagues.

Junior World Series (1904–1962)

The minor league Junior World Series was played between the champions of the Class AAA International League and the American Association. A youth version of the series began in later years.

Book. Bob Bailey, *History of the Junior World Series* (2003).

"**K** is for Keeler,
As fresh as green paint,
The fustest and mostest
To hit where they ain't."
—Ogden Nash on Willie Keeler.

Al Kaline (1934–)

Hall of Fame 1980

"When I was a boy, life was a baseball game." — Kaline.

"When I was a kid I thought Al Kaline was responsible for the Alkaline battery." — Howard Cole.

Kaline starred for 22 seasons as an outfielder with the Tigers beginning in 1953.

Albert William Kaline, later to become "Mr. Tiger," signed with the Tigers for $30,000 (or $35,000) out of high school in Baltimore and never played minor league ball. He played in 30 games his first season in 1953 for the Tigers, batting .250 in 28 at-bats.

In 1954 at age 19 Kaline hit .276 over a full season and in 1955 he hit .340 to become the youngest Major League batting champion at age 20. The season included 27 home runs and 102 RBIs. He followed with six of the next eight seasons over .300, with a high of .327 in 1959.

In the mid–1960s he hit between 17 and 29 home runs until 1968, when he was injured and hit only 10. He still helped lead the club to the World Series, in which he batted .379 with two home runs as the Tigers beat the Cardinals in seven games.

Kaline hit 21 home runs in 1969 and then began to slow down, though he signed his first $100,000 contract for the 1972 season. He hit .313 in 106 games, but his power was down. He played two more seasons, including 147 games as a designated hitter in 1974, batting .262.

Kaline finished his 22-year career for the Tigers with a .297 average, 399 home runs and 3,007 hits. He would have done significantly better but for a series of injuries over the years, including a broken cheek bone, broken collar bone, broken finger, broken right arm, rib problems and a foot operation. He was also a solid right fielder, winning 10 Gold Gloves in 11 years between 1957 and 1967. After he retired he became a broadcaster for the Tigers.

Book. Hal Butler, *Al Kaline and the Detroit Tigers* (1973).

Kangaroo Court

"Among Oriole teammates, [Frank] Robinson was instigator, igniter, chief judge, prosecutor, and sole proprietor of a Marx Brothers instrument known as the Kangaroo Court. This burlesque of the Spanish Inquisition was designed to keep baseball and shared good times rolling together." — David Falkner in *The Short Season* (1986).

History. Kangaroo courts were said to have originated during the 1849 California gold rush as informal courts tried claim "jumpers" (those who stole mining claims).

Baseball Origins.

"A thing like that is all right for those college guys and such, but grown men don't need it." — Dodger manager Wilbert Robinson on why he disbanded his form of the kangaroo court. In the 1920s the Dodgers had their own version of the court when Robinson instituted the Bonehead Club to impose small fines for minor infractions. The first guilty party was Robinson himself, who wrote Ernie Lombardi as his catcher on the lineup card but sent in Al Lopez to catch.

It is unknown when the first baseball kangaroo courts convened, but they were perpetuated by veteran players to create a relaxed clubhouse atmosphere by assessing small fines for minor and usually humorous indiscretions by players. The proceeds usually went to a season-ending party or, more recently, to charity.

Stolen Gloves. In 1991 Giants center fielder Willie McGee's three gloves were stolen from the clubhouse at Shea Stadium in New York. The next day he used a glove owned by Mets center fielder Vince Coleman. McGee and Coleman had been teammates on the Cardinals for six years and they left the shared glove in center field after each half inning.

The clubs' respective kangaroo courts fined each player. McGee was fined $2 an inning. The Mets fined Coleman $5 for each catch made by McGee.

Kansas City

"Stay out of Kansas City…. You don't want to go there. The weather's too bad. Every spring it floods you out and every summer it bakes you out." — Indians groundskeeper Emil Bossard to groundskeeper guru George Toma quoted in *Baseball Lives*, by Mike Bryan (1989).

"Kansas City wasn't the fun spot in my day that it is now." — Casey Stengel in 1955.

With the exception of 1968, Kansas City has been represented by a professional baseball team since at least 1884. The first Major League club was the Cowboys of the 1884 Union Association. Kansas City had a National League team in 1886 and an American Association club in 1888 and 1889. One writer attributed the failure of the early Kansas City Major League teams to the primitive press in the city in those years, which was unable to properly market the teams and provide the necessary exposure to the public.

The city had an American League club in 1900, one year before the league received Major League status. The Federal League had a club in the city in 1914 and the Kansas City Blues were a longtime entry in the minor league American Association. The Kansas City Monarchs were a powerhouse of the Negro Leagues.

The Philadelphia A's arrived in 1955 and stayed through the 1967 season, when Charlie Finley moved the club to Oakland. The A's were the first Major League club moved west of St. Louis. The expansion Kansas City Royals began play in 1969.

Kansas City Athletics

American League 1955–1967

"Still unable to regain even a glimpse of the stature attained by the once-dominating team assembled by Connie Mack a full 30 years earlier…" — Capsule analysis of the 13 years that the Athletics were in Kansas City, in *The Encyclopedia of Baseball Managers*, by Thomas Aylesworth and Benton Minks (1990).

Origins. The Philadelphia Athletics franchise moved to Kansas City for the 1955 season after Arnold Johnson bought the club from Connie Mack and his family (see also *Franchise Shifts*).

First Games. On April 12, 1955, the A's beat the Tigers 6–2 in Detroit. On April 22, 1955, former President and Missouri native Harry Truman threw out one of two first balls at the inaugural A's home game. Also in attendance at Municipal Stadium was Connie Mack, who threw out the other first ball. A total of 32,147 fans attended the 6–2 victory over the Tigers. Alex Kellner was the winner and Bill Wilson homered for the first time by a Kansas City A's player.

Key Owners.
Arnold Johnson/1955–1960.

"Not in the slightest. I don't know a lot about baseball but enough so that this is one business I want no part of. I have headaches enough without inviting those which come with owning a Major League baseball team." — Johnson after selling his Kansas City stadium rights in the early 1950s and before he bought the club; quoted in *The Kansas City Athletics*, by Ernest Mehl (1956).

Johnson was a local industrialist, real estate owner and automat mogul. He reportedly paid $3.5 million for the club and held it until his unexpected death in 1960.

Charles O. Finley/1960–1967.

"I wanted to get into baseball in the worst way, which is the way I got in." — Finley on buying the pathetic A's.

Arnold Johnson died in 1960 and 42-year-old Charlie Finley bought a controlling 52% interest for $1.975 million at a probate sale on December 20, 1960. Finley had been trying to buy a Major League team for six years. He was approved by the sellers as an owner on the condition that he keep the team in Kansas City for at least five years. Finley kept the team there through 1967 and then left for Oakland (see *Oakland Athletics* for a more comprehensive biography of Finley).

Nickname. The Athletics continued the name brought from Philadelphia. It was one of the few things that Finley did not change.

Yankee Farm Club. The A's of the 1950s and early 1960s were virtually a farm club for the Yankees — which the Kansas City Colts of the American Association had been before the city achieved Major League status. Parke Carroll, an early general manager of the A's, was the manager of the Colts before the A's moved to town. The A's sold Roger Maris to the Yankees. Bob Cerv and Bill Renna were going downhill with the Yankees, so they were sold to Kansas City. Enos Slaughter was sent to Kansas City for 1½ years and then was "promoted" to the Yankees to help in a pennant race.

There were other connections with the Yankees. Yankee owner Del Webb, a contractor on major hotels and other construction projects, obtained the contract to expand Kansas City's Municipal Stadium to accommodate the new Major League club. The other Yankee co-owner, Dan Topping, was on the board of directors of Arnold Johnson's corporation. Johnson had owned the land under Yankee Stadium and Blues Stadium in Kansas City. As a condition of the sale, Johnson was required to sell his interest in the land under Yankee Stadium within 90 days of his purchase.

Key Seasons. The club compiled a dismal 829–1,222 record under 10 managers over its 13 seasons in Kansas City. There were no key seasons for the Kansas City A's; maybe 1966 when the club finished seventh and won 74 games, the most since 1952.

"Lasts." Dave Duncan hit the last Kansas City A's home run on October 1, 1967.

Key Ballplayers (Just Passing Through). A number of good players had short stints with the A's in the 1950s and early 1960s, including Vic Power (1955–1958), Roger Maris (1958), Billy Martin (1957), Ralph Terry (1957–1959), Virgil Trucks (1957–1958), Ned Garver (1957–1960), Diego Segui (1962–1965), Moe Drabowsky (1963–1965), Jose Tartabull (1962–1965) and Ken Harrelson (1963–1965).

Key Managers. No Kansas City manager distinguished himself, but mention should be made that the club was managed the longest by Lou Boudreau (2½ years beginning in 1955) and Alvin Dark (most of two years beginning in 1966).

Ballparks. The original Kansas City ballpark was Muehlenberg Field, built in 1923 and later renamed Ruppert Stadium after the Yankee owner. It was also known as Municipal Stadium and Blues Stadium, the latter for the minor league club of the same name. The ballpark seated 17,500 and was located at 22nd St. and Brooklyn Avenue. It was later double-decked and capacity was increased to 32,844 for the 1955 home opener and renamed Municipal Stadium. Its dimensions from left to right field initially were 353–421–353. Club owner Arnold Johnson bought the scoreboard from the then-defunct Boston Braves for $100,000 and installed it in the A's ballpark.

Key Broadcasters. In 1955 Merle Harmon succeeded long-time Philadelphia A's broadcaster Byrum Saam as the voice of the Athletics. Harmon was fired by Finley after the 1961 season. Monte Moore managed to last as the A's announcer for 16 seasons beginning in 1962 (see also *Oakland Athletics*).

Book. Ernest Mehl, *The Kansas City Athletics* (1956).

Kansas City Cowboys

Union Association 1884

Kansas City's first introduction to Major League Baseball was the Cowboys (or Unions) of the one-year Union Association. The team replaced Altoona six weeks into the 1884 season and finished with the worst record of the clubs that played most of the season. The Cowboys were 16–63, 61 games out of first place, and had a team batting average of .199.

Book. H.L. Dellinger, *The Kansas City Unions* (1977).

Kansas City Cowboys

National League 1886

The Cowboys were pitiful, finishing with a 30–91 record under manager Dave Rowe. Pitcher Stump Weidman led the league with 36 losses. Only Washington was worse with a 28–92 record.

Kansas City Cowboys

American Association 1888–1889

In 1888 the Cowboys finished last in the Association with a 43–89 record under three separate managers. Henry Porter led the league with 37 losses. In 1889 the club finished seventh with a 55–82 record before transferring to the minor league Western Association.

Kansas City Monarchs

Independent and Negro Leagues 1912–1960

"We were like the New York Yankees. We had that winning tradition, and we were *proud*. We had a strict dress code — coat and tie, no baseball jackets. We stayed in the best hotels in the world. They just *happened* to be owned by black people. We ate in the best restaurants in the world. They just *happened* to be run by blacks. And when we were in Kansas City, well, 18th and Vine was the center of the universe. We'd come to breakfast at Street's Hotel, and there might be Count Basie or Joe Louis or Billie Holliday or Lionel Hampton." — Negro League star Buck O'Neil quoted in *Sports Illustrated* in 1994.

The Monarchs originated from the *All-Nations Team* of 1912 organized by J.L. Wilkinson, who was white. The Monarchs were a charter member of the Negro National League in 1920 and remained in the league through 1930. During most of the 1930s the Monarchs barnstormed with quality players such as Satchel Paige and Buck O'Neil. Jackie Robinson played for the club in the early 1940s.

The Monarchs were a perennial powerhouse, rivaled only by the Homestead Grays for Negro League supremacy. The Monarchs peaked in the late 1930s and early 1940s when the Negro American League was formed and the club won four pennants in five years. Though most Negro League clubs disbanded by the early 1950s, the Monarchs remained on the barnstorming circuit until 1960.

Book. Janet Bruce, *The Kansas City Monarchs: Champions of Black Baseball* (1985).

Kansas City Packers

Federal League 1914–1915

"President Gilmore opted to appear in Kansas City, one of the more fragile franchises rescued from extinction through the generous efforts of local backers."—Marc Okonnen in *The Federal League of 1914–1915* (1989).

The Packers, also known as the KawFeds, finished sixth in 1914 with a 67–84 record under player-manager George Stovall. Duke Kenworthy led the league with 15 home runs. After the season the league tried to relocate the club to Newark for oil tycoon Harry Sinclair. When the Kansas City stockholders tried to block the franchise shift through the courts, the league backed down and instead moved the Indianapolis franchise.

The Packers were 81–72 in 1915, good for fourth place, but were financially strapped throughout the season. Other clubs had to make loans to the club and it did not share in the Federal League settlement with the established Major Leagues.

Kansas City Royals

American League 1969–

"At Kansas City the most prominent visible evidence of Alexander Cartwright's game, on the recreated trip, was a gaunt steel-and-concrete structure set close by the slums that were put to the torch in the season of rioting that attended the [Lyndon] Johnson Administration. This was Municipal Stadium. Looking at the whole milieu, one felt stirrings on an unexpected emotion: sympathy for Charles O. Finley, the much-disliked present Athletics owner, who moved the onetime Philadelphia team from Kansas City on to Oakland. But the new Royals' owner, Ewing Kauffman, did start with one big advantage: convenient new rubble-paved parking lots."—Harold Peterson in *The Man Who Invented Baseball* (1969).

Origins. Kansas City was granted an American League franchise as part of the 1968 **Expansion** for the 1969 season. Not coincidentally, Major League Baseball was still being threatened with losing its antitrust exemption through legislation authored by Missouri Senator Stuart Symington as a result of the loss of the Kansas City A's to Oakland.

First Game. The Royals beat the Twins 4–3 in their first game, played April 8, 1969, in front of 17,688 fans in Kansas City.

Key Owners.

Ewing Kauffman/1969–1993.

"No, I never had a desire to be a major-leaguer, and at fifty-four I don't think I want to get in condition to work out with the team like Gussie Busch. Anyway, I'd rather play golf."—Kauffman.

The Kansas City franchise was awarded to Ewing Kauffman, a Kansas City pharmaceutical magnate. In 1950 he founded Marion Laboratories with $5,000 and built it into a health care giant. In 1989 Kauffman received $675 million for his share of the company.

Kauffman was a pillar of the Kansas City community, though with little interest in baseball. When Charlie Finley moved the A's to Oakland after the 1967 season, local community leaders persuaded Kauffman to get involved with obtaining an expansion club. Kaufmann sold 19,000 shares of his company's stock to raise the cash necessary to buy the club.

Kauffman had no heirs. In the early 1980s when he became ill he entered into an agreement with Memphis real estate man Avron Fogelman. The deal gave Fogelman a stake in the club and he would have taken over majority ownership in 1991. Fogelman ran into financial difficulties, however, and fell out of the picture despite a loan from Kauffman. Fogelman had been a Memphis Little League teammate of former Cardinals catcher Tim McCarver.

Kauffman Foundation/David D. Glass et al./1993–2000. Kauffman died Aug 1, 1993, and the president and CEO of Wal-Mart, David D. Glass, was elected chairman and CEO of the club. A five-member board was selected before Kauffman's death to run the team while they looked for a permanent owner who would keep the club in Kansas City. The IRS later approved an ownership structure that allowed the franchise to be financed from Kauffman's estate, giving the club at least eight years to find a local buyer. The IRS designated the Royals as a city-held charity after a lengthy review.

In 1995 George Brett and an investment group offered $100 million to buy the club. The group reportedly included talk show host Rush Limbaugh, who had

Satchel Paige relaxing next to the dugout before a game for the Kansas City Monarchs.

once worked in the Royals' publicity department. The club lost $25 million in 1995 and another $10 million in 1996. It continued to be unprofitable until the 2000 sale to David Glass.

David D. Glass/2000– .

"But we're not kidding anybody here. There is no grand scheme of things in baseball, not in Kansas City. Nope, here it's baseball on a budget. You don't need a baseball cap and a scorebook to be a Royals fan, you need an accounting degree."—Joe Posananski of the *Kansas City Star.*

In April 2000 Major League owners approved a sale of the club to Glass for $96 million. Glass was the CEO of Wal-Mart and is listed on the *Forbes*' list of America's Most Powerful People. He has been on the Wal-Mart board of directors since 1977 and was 64 when he bought the club.

Nickname. The Royals name was chosen by a poll of fans.

Key Seasons.

1969. The Royals were 69–93 in their first season and finished fourth.

1971. Only two years after being created by expansion, the Royals finished a respectable second, though 16 games behind the A's.

1973. The club finished second again, this time six games behind the A's.

1975. Continuing the every-other-year tradition, the Royals finished second, seven games behind the A's.

1976. The Royals broke through with their first division title when they beat out the A's by three games. George Brett led the league with a .333 average and Dennis Leonard was the staff ace with 17 wins. The Royals lost a heartbreaking ALCS in five games when Yankee first baseman Chris Chambliss hit a home run in the bottom of the 9th inning to break a 6–6 tie.

1977. The Royals repeated as American League West champions with 102 wins, tops in the Major Leagues. They lost another heartbreaker to the Yankees in the ALCS after leading 3–1 going into the 8th inning of the fifth and deciding game. The Yankees scored one run in the 8th and three in the 9th to win 5–3. Dennis Leonard led the league with 20 wins and George Brett hit .312. Al Cowens had 112 RBIs and the club had four players with more than 20 home runs.

1978. The Royals won their division again, but lost to the Yankees in the ALCS for the third straight season. In Games 3 and 4 the Royals led, but the Yankees pulled out one-run victories in both games to clinch the pennant. Dennis Leonard won 21 games.

1980. After a second-place finish in 1979, the Royals blew away the division in 1980 and finally made it to the World Series with a sweep of the Yankees in the ALCS. They lost the World Series to the Phillies in six games, blowing the pivotal Game 5 when the Phillies scored two runs in the 9th inning for a 4–3 win. George Brett hit .390 and drove in 118 runs and Dan Quisenberry led the league with 33 saves.

1981. The Royals won the second half of the strike-shortened split season by one game over the A's. In the mini–play-off series to determine the division winner, the A's swept the Royals in three games. George Brett hit .314 and Willie Wilson hit .303.

1984. After finishing second in 1982 and 1983, the Royals won the American League West by three games over the Angels. The club was swept in three games by the Tigers in the ALCS. Dan Quisenberry led the league with 44 saves and Steve Balboni hit 28 home runs.

1985. The Royals won the division by one game over the Angels and then beat the Blue Jays in seven games to win the pennant. Dan Quisenberry led the league with 37 saves and George Brett batted

.335, hit 30 home runs and drove in 112 runs. Steve Balboni hit 36 home runs.

In the cross-state World Series with the Cardinals, the Royals received a huge break in the 9th inning of Game 6 when they scored two runs after a bad call at first base (see *World Series—Controversial Calls*). In Game 7 the Cardinals self-destructed in an 11–0 loss and the Royals became the sixth team to win the Series after trailing 3–1 in games.

1987. The Royals finished second, only two games behind the first-place Twins.

1989. The club finished second, seven games behind the A's, and then began a series of mediocre seasons into the 2000s.

Key Players.

George Brett (HF) is easily the greatest of all Royals players. He arrived in August 1973 and retired after the 1993 season with 317 home runs, 1,595 RBIs and a .305 batting average. He recorded his 3,000th hit late in the 1992 season and won batting titles in three different decades.

Frank White came up in June 1973 and played 18 years with the club through the 1990 season. He finished with a .255 average and was the club's regular second baseman for 14 years.

Freddie Patek, 5'5" and 148 pounds, was the club's starting shortstop for nine years and played in five League Championship Series between 1971 and 1979.

Hal McRae played the last 15 years of his career with the Royals from 1973 through 1987. He batted over .300 seven times and was the club's primary DH for 12 seasons.

Jeff Montgomery. Montgomery was traded by the Reds when Pete Rose said that Montgomery couldn't play for him. Montgomery blossomed in the 1990s and saved 304 games, all with the Royals, before hip problems forced him to retire. He had a career-high 45 saves in 1993.

Carlos Beltran. He was the club's only legitimate star when he was traded to the Astros in June 2004.

Key Managers.

Whitey Herzog.

"Be on time. Bust your butt. Play smart. And have some laughs along the way."—Herzog, who took over the club early in the 1975 season and led the Royals to second place. He then reeled off three first-place and one second-place finish through 1979. In each division-winning season the Royals lost a tough ALCS to the Yankees. Herzog moved over to the Cardinals in 1980.

Dick Howser.

"The reputation and the memories he left behind as his sliver of baseball history are, however, just right. What was within his power he handled as well as anyone could ask. He will be recalled, and for a long time, as a man who proved the difference between book and cover."—Thomas Boswell on Howser's premature death in 1987, in *The Heart of the Order* (1989).

Howser was the most successful of the Royals managers. After leading the Yankees to a first-place finish in 1980, he signed with the Royals, where his clubs finished first three times and second twice in six seasons. In 1985 the Royals won the World Series in seven games against the Cardinals. In mid–1986 Howser was diagnosed with a brain tumor and died in mid–1987. He was replaced by interim manager Mike Ferraro, who had overcome kidney cancer in 1983. The Dick Howser Award is now presented annually to the outstanding college baseball player in the nation.

Hal McRae led the club through a series of mediocre seasons starting in 1991. His clubs finished third each year from 1992 through 1994.

Tony Pena brought some hope and enthusiasm to the club with a third place finish in 2003, but the team faded badly in 2004. He was the fifth straight manager hired by the club without any previous managerial experience.

Ballpark.

"Like any Holiday Inn, the stadium appears forever new, and thus without history—the wrong overtones for a sport so devotedly attached to its ancestors and its family records."—Roger Angell in *Late Innings* (1982).

Kansas City Stadium opened in 1973 and was renamed Royals Stadium as the team nickname took hold. It was also known as the Harry S Truman Sports Complex, though more accurately it is part of the Truman Sports Complex, which includes Arrowhead Stadium, home of the Kansas City Chiefs. In 1993 the ballpark was renamed Ewing M. Kauffman Stadium after the death of the club's long-time owner.

The ballpark was budgeted to cost $43 million, but the final tab reached $70 million. It contained the Major League's first all-synthetic playing surface, but it was removed in favor of grass in 1995 (see also *Artificial Turf*). Capacity has always been around 40,600. Dimensions from left to right field are 330–375–405–375–330 after slight shifts in the outfield to make it deeper in 1980.

The stadium features an elaborate water show with the largest private fountain in the world that includes waterfalls, water, light and color shows.

Key Broadcasters. Buddy Blattner was the club's first number one broadcaster, remaining in that spot until 1975. Denny Matthews was chosen in 1969 from over 300 applicants for the number two broadcasting job. He took over the number one job in 1985 and remained in the job through 2004. Fred White was with the club from 1973 (excluding 1974) through 1998. Pitcher Paul Splittorff started broadcasting for the club in 1988 and remained with the club through 2004.

By 1984 the club had 115 stations in its radio broadcast network. The Kansas City market has only 1.4 million people, generating a television contract in the early 1990s of $4.2 million (compared to over $50 million for the Yankees).

Book. Sid Bordman, *Expansion to Excellence* (1981); Denny Matthews with Matt Fulks, *Tales from the Royals Dugout* (2004); Paul Joseph, *Kansas City Royals* (1997).

Tim Keefe (1857–1933)

Hall of Fame (VC) 1964

"The New York Club in traveling about the country, began to notice that as soon as they reached their hotel in any city they happened to be visiting, Keefe retired to his room, shut himself in and wasn't seen again excepting on the ball field. This conduct puzzled the club for a long time, until it was discovered that the big pitcher was studying short-hand, and studying it seriously too…. Under these circumstances, when the great pitcher of the New York Club concludes to abandon baseball, he will undoubtedly be able, with the influence he can command, to step at once into new employment of a lucrative character."—*Sporting Life* in 1988.

Keefe won 342 games over only 14 seasons beginning in 1880.

Timothy John Keefe's father was a native of Ireland and Keefe was born in Cambridge, Massachusetts on New Year's Day 1857. Though Keefe's father supposedly frowned on baseball, Keefe pitched his way through the ranks of semipro clubs in Massachusetts. He joined Troy of the National League in 1880 and beat Cincinnati 4–2 in his first Major League start.

Keefe primarily used a fastball and curveball, though he is credited by some as the first pitcher to use a change-up effectively.

When the Troy franchise was transferred to New York, Keefe played two years with the New York Metropolitans of the American Association before moving over to the National League Giants in 1885.

Keefe won 42 games in 1886 and more than 30 games in six straight seasons starting in 1883. In 1888 he won 19 straight games, though one of the games in the streak is suspect (see also **Wins— Consecutive by Pitcher**). He retired after the 1893 season with 342 wins, eighth all-time, and a .603 winning percentage (342–225). He pitched 557 complete games in 600 starts, third all-time. After his retirement he returned to Cambridge and became a prominent realtor. He died of heart trouble in 1933.

Willie Keeler (1872–1923)

Hall of Fame 1939

"Keep your eye clear and hit 'em where they ain't."—Keeler's batting philosophy.

"Wee Willie Keeler,
You have journeyed West;
Just an old Oriole
Flown to his rest.
Wee Willie Keeler
Smallest of them all;
But in height and manhood
You were mountains tall."

—Walter Trumbull of the *New York Herald* writing at Keeler's death.

Keeler was the sparkplug for the Baltimore Orioles and Brooklyn Dodgers of the 1890s, and later the Yankees/Highlanders of the early 20th century.

William Henry "Wee Willie" Keeler was a 5'4", 140-pound Brooklyn sandlot player who pitched and, though left-handed, played shortstop. He was playing for the New York Acmes semipro team when the Giants bought him for $800 late in the 1892 season and sold him to Brooklyn in early 1893. He moved to the Orioles in 1894 and was part of the core of players who made Baltimore one of the two top clubs of the 1890s.

Keeler had at least 200 hits eight years in a row, with a peak batting average of .424 in 1897 for the Orioles. He claimed he never struck out in 1898, and there are no official records to disprove him. He was an excellent hit-and-run man and was considered the fastest runner of his time. Keeler stole 495 bases in his career, with a high of 67 in 1896.

Keeler moved to Brooklyn in 1899 and continued his stellar batting for four seasons, with a high for the club of .379 in his first season (and a low of .333). In 1903 he began play for the American League New York Highlanders, where he continued to star. He batted .343 for the club in 1904 before beginning a slow slide toward retirement. He finished his career in 1910 with one season for the Giants, for whom he batted .300 in 19 games.

The outfielder had a lifetime .343 average, eighth all-time, and hit over .300 for 15 straight seasons over his 19-year career. He prospered in real estate after his career and reportedly turned down a chance to manage the Yankees.

George Kell (1922–)

Hall of Fame (VC) 1983

"George Kell is a thoroughbred."—Lou Boudreau.

"The Hall of Fame now can honor the Rick Ferrells and the George Kells. It can honor them by putting them in a class with the Yogi Berras and the Brooks Robinsons. But once they have sufficiently devalued the place, they'll lose the ability to do even that."—Bill James in *The Bill James Historical Baseball Abstract* (1988).

"Nothing can top being inducted into the Hall of Fame. I wanted to be selected so badly that when they notified me, my wife and I cried. I will never forget that weekend."—Kell quoted in *For the Love of the Game*, by Cynthia J. Wilber (1992).

"But when a guy is good, like Kell, you got to be able to take a lot of crap and not let it bother you. So a guy throws a rock [through his window]. So you get the window fixed. Listen, you hit three thirty, three forty like Kell, the pitchers are throwing crap and junk at you all the time and it's worse than any rocks because it's your living, it's what you *do*. You stand in there, that's all. When they come in with a good one you belt it."—Elmore Leonard in *The Big Bounce* (1969).

Kell started slowly but emerged as one of the premier third baseman of the late 1940s and early 1950s.

George Clyde Kell began his professional career in the Northeast Arkansas League in 1940. In 1943 his .396 average was the highest in Organized Baseball. Despite the impressive minor league statistics, Kell was slow to impress Major League executives. Bad knees and a series of injuries hampered him, but he overachieved his way into the Hall of Fame.

After one game for the A's in 1943, he became their starting third baseman in 1944 during the World War II player shortage. He played two full seasons for the A's and hit .268 and .272. In early 1946 the A's traded him to the Tigers.

Kell blossomed immediately with his new club, hitting .327 in 105 games. It was the first of seven straight seasons over .300 for the Tigers. He led the league with a .343 average in 1949, beating out Ted Williams for the crown on the last day of the season.

In 1950 Kell had a league-leading 218 hits and 56 doubles on his way to a .340 average. The Tigers traded him to the Red Sox midway through the 1952 season and he bounced to the White Sox and Orioles through 1957 before retiring at age 35.

Over 15 seasons he hit .306 and became one of the finest defensive third baseman of all time. After he retired he moved into the broadcast booth for CBS, conducting pregame interviews for "Game of the Week" telecasts. In 1959 he replaced Mel Ott in the broadcast booth for the Tigers. After quitting in 1963 he later returned to scout and broadcast for the Tigers.

Joe Kelley (1871–1943)

Hall of Fame (VC) 1971

"He unloosed his throwing arm and amazed the natives by the ease with which he threw in from the deepest field to the home plate. He scooted over all the outfield the same as a jackrabbit and he cared not if the sun shone in his eyes. When he had helped retire the foe and came himself to the plate, he swung mightily with the force of his giant strength, and they picked up the pieces a few miles further down the pike."—*Sporting Life* in 1911.

Kelley was one of the key players for the Baltimore Orioles in the 1890s.

Joseph James Kelley played in the New England League in 1891 before moving up briefly to the National League that season. He played another 66 Major League games in 1892 before establishing himself with the Orioles in their outfield. He batted over .300 in each of 11 seasons with three different clubs beginning in 1893, with a high of .393 in 1894 for the Orioles during their glory days.

When Ned Hanlon left for Brooklyn in 1902, Kelley went with him, but for only 60 games before jumping to the Reds. He stayed

with the Reds through 1906, batting a high of .316 in 1903. After a year as player-manager with Toronto in the Eastern League, he played one season for the Boston Braves in 1908, hitting .259 in 73 games.

Kelley stole 443 bases during his 17-year career, with a league-leading personal best of 87 in 1896. A strong outfielder, he hit 65 home runs in the dead ball era and is ninth all-time with 194 triples to go with his .317 average.

George Kelly (1895–1984)

Hall of Fame (VC) 1973

"In 1915 I was sold to the Giants for $1,500. There was one thought in my mind. McGraw wants ME. You cannot imagine the thrill I had as did every other player picked by McGraw. Hell, boy I felt I WAS a Giant—12 feet tall."—Kelly.

Kelly starred at first base for the Giants in the early 1920s.

George Lange "Highpockets" Kelly was 6'4" and 200 pounds, one of the larger players of the early 20th century. He began his professional career in 1914 in Victoria, British Columbia. He moved to the Giants in 1915 for 17 games. He played a few games in 1916 and 1917 for both the Giants and Pirates and then entered the military for the 1918 season.

In 1919 he played 32 games for the Giants and in 1920 became the club's regular first baseman. He remained in that role through 1924, batting over .300 three times and leading the league with 23 home runs in 1921. He had more than 100 RBIs four straight seasons beginning in 1922 and led the league twice in that category.

In 1925 he switched to second base to allow Bill Terry to remain in the line-up, but returned to first base the following season. He batted over .300 in 1925 and 1926 and then was traded to the Reds in 1927. He played decently, but his best years were behind him. He played briefly for the Cubs and Dodgers before finishing out his career with a few minor leagues games in 1932 and 1933.

Kelly finished with a lifetime .297 average over 16 Major League seasons and hit .248 in four straight World Series beginning in 1921. After his retirement he coached for the Reds and Braves until 1943. He also coached and managed in the minor leagues, including a stint with Oakland where he was credited with helping Billy Martin learn to throw to first base.

According to Bill James, despite somewhat marginal credentials — including only nine seasons as a regular — "for whatever reasons, the Veterans Committee of the Hall of Fame chose to subpoena him."

Mike "King" Kelly (1857–1894)

Hall of Fame (VC) 1945

"The inspiration of the immortal poem, 'Slide, Kelly, Slide,' was that most idolized ballplayer, Mike Kelly, one of the most fascinating figures ever to dig a cleated shoe into the diamond…. He was a slashing, dashing, devil-may-care athlete, good-natured, bighearted, sincere. He had perhaps the keenest brain that baseball ever knew."—Frank G. Menke in the *Encyclopedia of Sports* (1944).

"Slide, Kelly, Slide!
Your running's a disgrace!
Slide, Kelly, Slide!
Stay there, hold your base!
If some one doesn't steal you,
And your batting doesn't fail you,
They'll take you to Australia!
Slide, Kelly, Slide!"
—Popular song of the 1880s.

"He was a creator…. His strongest playing point was that he was always ready. He could take advantage of a misplay which others wouldn't see until afterward…. He played the umpire as intelligently as he did the opposing nine. He would make a friend of him, engage his confidence, and in various ways get the best of close decisions."— Teammate Fred Pfeffer.

The charismatic Kelly was the star catcher for the Chicago White Stockings in the 1880s.

A hard-drinking crowd favorite from Troy, New York, Michael Joseph Kelly was a star player for the 19th century Chicago White Stockings when Cap Anson managed the team. He played catcher and some right field and was considered one of the premier players of the era. At least one source credits him with developing the hit-and-run play.

After two National League seasons with Cincinnati beginning in 1878, Kelly moved over to the White Stockings and starred for the club through 1886. He batted a league leading .354 in 1884 and .388 in 1886. In 1887 Kelly was sold to the Boston Red Stockings for the then-outrageous sum of $10,000. He batted over .300 in two of his three seasons with Boston and then hit .326 for the Boston club in the 1890 Players League.

His Major League career ended in 1893 with a .308 average over 16 seasons. In 1894 he began managing in the Pennsylvania minor leagues. In November of that year he took a boat from New York to Boston for a vaudeville engagement at the Palace Theatre. He contracted pneumonia and died at a Boston hospital on November 8, 1894 at age 37.

Kelly is incorrectly reported by some to have inspired the "*Casey at the Bat*" poem that first appeared in 1888. Nevertheless, he often earned nearly $5,000 in the off-season by reciting the poem in vaudeville acts.

Keokuk Westerns

National Association 1875

"Declaring themselves champions of Iowa, they set their sights on the championship of the United States. Their ballpark and roster were more suited to a pursuit of the Iowa championship. Built on a corn field and known as Walte's Pasture, the field was bounded — rather encroached upon — by Pleasant Lake. The lake was not so pleasant for the outfielders who are reported to have tumbled in while in hot pursuit of a long fly ball."— William J. Ryczek in *Blackguards and Red Stockings* (1992).

This Iowa club had a 1–12 record before dropping out of the league early in the season.

Khoury Association of Baseball Leagues

"Good citizens can be built on baseball diamonds much better than in back alleys."— Motto of the Association, named for George Khoury.

Headquartered in St. Louis, this organization consists of over 65,000 baseball leagues organized by local civic, church and other community organizations.

Book. George Khoury, *Brothers, Bombshells and Baseball* (2003).

Kidnapping

"Perhaps the best commentary on Dean's value to the Cardinals was offered by John Henry Seadlund. Seadlund had been arrested by the FBI for the kidnapping of Charles S. Ross. When questioned by the agents of the Justice Department in 1938, he admit-

ted that he had toyed with the fantastic idea of kidnapping Dizzy Dean, but that he abandoned the plan because he doubted that [Branch] Rickey would pay $50,000 for Dean's release."— Jimmy Powers in *Baseball Personalities* (1949).

During the 1930 pennant race Flint Rhem was scheduled to pitch for the Cardinals against the Dodgers. He failed to show up for the game and later claimed that two men in a cab kidnapped him and took him to a house in New Jersey where they forced him to drink. Variations on this theme have been used by a number of players to explain away disappearances or drinking binges.

In August 2004 the mother of Tigers reliever Urgueth Urbina was kidnapped from her new home near Caracas, Venezuela. Urbina's father was murdered by robbers in 1994. It was believed that the four gunman, who posed as policeman, stole $520 and abducted a mechanic, were seeking a ransom from Urbina. Urbina and his family initially rejected ransom demands by the kidnappers and the situation was still unresolved by late 2004.

Harmon Killebrew (1936–)

Hall of Fame 1984

"If ever anyone wielded a blunt instrument at home plate, it was Harmon Killebrew. There was nothing subtle about the Idaho strongboy: it was always his intention to mash a pitched ball as hard and as far as he could."— Donald Honig in *The Power Hitters* (1989).

Killebrew was the most prolific home run hitter of the 1960s and finished with 573 over 22 seasons.

Idaho native Harmon Clayton Killebrew was one of the mid–1950s **Bonus Babies** required to stay on his Major League club, the Senators, for his first two seasons (1954–1955). He then spent most of the next three years in the Senators farm system.

His breakthrough year was 1959 when he hit 42 home runs to lead the American League. Over the next 11 seasons for the Senators and Twins he hit over 40 home runs seven times. His 393 home runs were the most in the 1960s. Many thought that he had an excellent shot at Babe Ruth's home run record when he had 380 by the end of 1967 at age 31 (more than Ruth at that age). Some sources contend that injuries, such as a dislocated elbow in 1965, a ruptured hamstring in 1968, and knee surgery in 1973, hampered his career. To some extent they did, but in 1969 he had his best season, with a career-high of 49 home runs and 140 RBIs to win the MVP Award.

The 13-time All-Star played a number of positions after beginning his career at second base. They included left field, third base and first base before he moved to designated hitter. He spent the 1975 season with the Royals before retiring to the broadcast booth with the Twins. Over his 22-year career he hit 573 home runs, now seventh all-time, and has the third-highest home run frequency in history. After his playing days, Killebrew worked in the Twins front office.

Books. Wayne J. Anderson, *Harmon Killebrew, Baseball Super Star* (1971); Hal Butler, *The Harmon Killebrew Story* (1966).

Ralph Kiner (1922–)

Hall of Fame 1975

"I guess I was always a power hitter … going all the way back to when I was eleven or twelve years old…; this was my style, what I was capable of doing, and what the game is all about anyway — putting solid wood on the ball, scoring runs, and winning games. I was always a fellow who hit tremendously high, long fly balls. I don't know why I sent them that way; it was just a natural part of my swing."—Kiner quoted in *Baseball Between the Lines*, by Donald Honig (1976).

Kiner led the National League in home runs in seven straight seasons starting in 1946.

Ralph McPherran Kiner began his minor league career at age 18 in the Eastern League in 1941, batting .279 for Albany. His rise to the Major Leagues was delayed when he enlisted in the Navy and lost the 1943–1945 seasons. He went to spring training with the Pirates in 1946 and was not slated to stay with the club. After 13 spring home runs he made the team and went on to lead the league with 23 home runs.

Kiner exploded for 51 home runs in 1947 after Hank Greenberg joined him in the lineup, continuing a streak of seven straight years in which he led the National League in home runs (though he tied three times). He peaked with 54 home runs in 1949, when he had a .310 average, .658 slugging average and 127 RBIs to establish himself as the greatest home run hitter of the early postwar era.

The perennially last-place Pirates traded him to the Cubs 41 games into the 1953 season and a chronically bad back began to affect his productivity. Though he hit 35 home runs in 1953 (his lowest total since his rookie season), his career was almost over. Two years later he retired at age 33 with 369 home runs and the second-highest home run percentage of all time behind only Babe Ruth.

After his 10-year career ended he served as general manager of the Pacific Coast League San Diego Padres. In 1961 he joined the White Sox as a broadcaster and moved to the Mets broadcast booth for their first season in 1962. He remained in that position through 2003, establishing a reputation for "Kinerisms" over the air (see also *Broadcasters*—Former Ballplayers).

Book. Ralph Kiner with Joe Gergen, *Kiner's Korner* (1987); Ralph Kiner and Danny Peary, *Baseball Forever* (2004).

Chuck Klein (1904–1958)

Hall of Fame (VC) 1980

"His final years bore no resemblance to the dominance that comprised the first third of his career, but this son of an Indianapolis steelworker had few regrets. Klein had started with a simple dream: to escape a lifestyle that offered little more than molten metal and blowtorches. In his quest he emblazoned the Klein name in NL record books and forged a bronze plaque for himself in the Hall of Fame."—Dave Masterson and Timm Boyle in *The MVPs* (1985).

The Phillies outfielder had the fastest start in Major League history beginning in 1928.

Indiana native Charles Herbert "Chuck" Klein began his professional career in 1927 and made it to the Phillies in 1928 at age 23. In tiny Baker Bowl he starred for the first six seasons of his Major League career, batting at least .337 every season and leading the league in home runs four times. He drove in at least 120 runs each season, with a high of 170 in 1930. Also in 1930 he had a record 44 assists in right field and twice had 26-game hitting streaks.

The Phillies traded him to the Cubs for the 1934 season and his production dropped dramatically in Wrigley Field. In his first season he hit only 20 home runs with a .301 batting average. He returned to the Phillies early in the 1936 season, but his production continued to drop. Except for a brief period in 1939 with the Pirates he played out his career with the Phillies, but he appeared in only a few games each season after 1940, hitting one home run.

Over 17 seasons Klein batted .320 and hit 300 home runs. He

won the Triple Crown in 1933 and hit four home runs in a game in 1936. After he retired he coached for the Phillies in 1945 and then ran a saloon, but heavy drinking caused serious medical problems, eventually resulting in a stroke that killed him at age 54.

Bill Klem (1874–1951)

Hall of Fame (VC) 1953
"King of the Umpires"
"The Old Arbitrator"
"Catfish"—Two appreciated and one despised nickname for the most famous Major League umpire. Catfish came from the fine spray he emitted when he called balls and strikes. Anyone calling him that name was automatically ejected.

"The foundation stone of our national pastime is its umpires. And the foundation stone on which that foundation stone rests is William J. Klem. He brought a dignity to the job that it never had before. He brought it respect and authority. He brought it a certain element of infallibility. 'I never missed one in my life,' he roared. And meant it."—Arthur Daley.

"I never thought eyesight was the most important thing in umpiring. The most important things are guts, honesty, common sense, a desire for fair play and an understanding of human nature."—Klem.

"But the greatest change in her is the way she sits there very quiet all afternoon, never once opening her yap, even when many of the customers around her are claiming that Umpire William Klem is Public Enemy No. 1 to 16 inclusive, because they think he calls a close one against the Giants."—Damon Runyon in "Baseball Hattie" (1954).

Klem was the most famous and well-respected umpire in Major League history.

William Klem (originally "Klimm") umpired regularly for 36 years in the Major Leagues from 1905 through 1940, and made a few appearances in 1941. Some prominent sources credit him with umpiring only through 1940, but near the end of the 1941 season he worked as an experimental fourth umpire on a crew. After probably blowing a call at second base he retired immediately after the game and assumed his full-time duties as chief umpire for the National League.

His first umpiring job in Organized Baseball was in the Connecticut League in 1902. In 1905 he was hired out of the American Association by National League president Harry Pulliam and began a string of 16 consecutive seasons behind the plate. He did not rotate with the other umpire during this period (two was the norm).

He worked 18 World Series and umpired a World Series game in each of the Major League cities that existed during his career. He presided over five no-hitters and the first All-Star Game in 1933.

Klem was credited with bringing integrity and dignity to 20th century umpiring. He was famous for "drawing a line in the dirt," over which arguing managers and players did not dare cross. Though John McGraw tested Klem's line drawing policy many times and had vicious arguments with him on the field, they apparently were good friends off the diamond. Klem is credited with using the inside chest protector, which enabled him to crouch and get a better look at the pitch.

After his retirement he lived in Florida in poor health until his death from a heart attack in 1951. Two years later he was elected to the Hall of Fame by the Veterans Committee. There was a short-lived Bill Klem Award presented in the 1950s to a deserving umpire. One of the recipients was Beans Reardon, who disliked Klem, and the award eventually was abandoned.

Knothole Gang

"I will not at any time skip school.

I will attend no game against the wishes of my parents.

I will practice clean speech, clean sport and clean habits.

I will try by attendance, deportment and effort at school or work to prove my worthiness to membership in the club." — Pledge of the early 20th century Knothole Gang formed by the Reds. Cards bearing the pledge were distributed to schoolchildren by their teachers.

Origins. Though credit for the Knothole Gang concept is generally given to 20th century creators, some sources credit Abner Powell, 1880s owner, manager, and one-time player with a prominent New Orleans club (Powell has been credited with the rain check and tarpaulin, among other innovations). He supposedly saw boys milling about outside the ballpark and let them in for free for two weeks.

St. Louis insurance man W.E. Bilheimer introduced the 20th century Knothole Gang with the Cardinals, apparently just before Branch Rickey joined the club in 1919. The team sold stock to the public to raise money and each $50 share provided one bleacher seat to a disadvantaged youth. These passes were channeled through local charitable organizations. Almost 65,000 kids were admitted free in 1920. The concept was not quickly adopted by other teams even though National League president John Tener encouraged it. Other sources credit St. Louis attorney J.C. Jones with starting the program.

Protest. When Dodger manager Leo Durocher was linked to gamblers and divorce in the mid–1940s, the Catholic Youth League pulled 50,000 kids out of the Dodgers' Knothole Gang. The Youth League deemed Durocher a "powerful force for undermining the moral and spiritual training of our young boys."

Modern Versions. Modern players often buy blocks of tickets to be distributed to disadvantaged youth and clubs still employ variations of the Knothole Gang.

Knuckleball

"There are two theories on hitting the knuckleball — unfortunately neither of them works." — Poor hitter but excellent batting coach Charlie Lau.

"God was never a catcher because, if He was, there would never have been a knuckleball pitcher." — Captain Jack Kirby, U.S. Navy Dental Corps.

"[A knuckleball is] a curve ball that doesn't give a damn." — Jimmy Cannon.

"I never seemed to feel as hostile toward the knuckleball when I listened to the French-speaking broadcasters in Montreal, who call it le papillon, the butterfly. You can't feel as bad about a passed ball knowing it was caused by le papillon. Striking out because you didn't hit le papillon makes you feel like you should get an award from some environmental group." — Joe Garagiola.

"Well, I always wanted to teach my kid to throw a knuckleball, to play seven card stud, and to fix the carburetor on an MG. I guess I'll just have to do that with a boy." — TV character Murphy Brown.

Origins. Future umpire Eddie Rommel is considered the father of the knuckleball (also known as the "dry spitter") because he was the first specialist to succeed in the Major Leagues. He developed a spitball before coming to the Major Leagues in 1920, but after it was outlawed he was sent back down to the minor leagues briefly after starting 12 games and making 33 appearances. There he met a Baltimore plumber who showed him how to throw the knuckleball. He was back up in 1921, with a 16–23 record for the A's.

In 1922 Rommell won 19 games as a starter and eight in relief for the A's, who won only 65 overall. He once gave up 29 hits in an extra-inning game. He had a high of 27 wins in 1922 for the A's and won 171 games over a 13-year career that included 51 shutouts.

Some sources credit Toad Ramsey as the first knuckleballer. Ramsey played for Louisville and St. Louis in the American Association from 1885 through 1890. He was a knuckleball pitcher out of necessity. When he was an apprentice bricklayer, a load was dropped on his hand, severing the tendon in his middle finger. As a result, he could not flex the finger or apply pressure, so he resorted to the knuckleball. He drank himself out of the league after winning 114 games in six years, including 24 in his last season. He died at age 42 in 1906.

No Knuckles Used. The knuckleball is thrown with the fingertips against the ball, rather than the whole hand, and the knuckles are not involved. The idea is to eliminate any rotation on the ball so that it "floats" erratically to the plate.

Knuckles Used. Jesse Haines is the only pitcher to have thrown the knuckleball with his knuckles. He managed to hang on in the Major Leagues until age 44. He was able to get more speed on the ball than most knuckleballers, resulting in 210 lifetime wins, second to Bob Gibson in Cardinals history. During Game 7 of the 1926 World Series, Haines developed a blister from throwing the knuckleball and he was replaced by Grover Cleveland Alexander. This set up the famous bases-loaded 7th inning confrontation in which Alexander struck out Tony Lazzeri of the Yankees. Indians pitcher Bob Lemon played Haines in the movie version of Alexander's life, *The Winning Team*, starring Ronald Reagan.

Team Effort. The 1945 Senators had four knuckleball pitchers who won a total of 60 games: Emil "Dutch" Leonard, Johnny Niggeling, Mickey Haefner and Roger Wolff. They each threw the pitch differently, with from one to four fingers on top of the ball. Hall of Fame umpire Cal Hubbard claimed that Wolff was the best knuckleball pitcher he ever saw. Leonard was second in lifetime wins for the Senators with 190, behind only Walter Johnson's 416.

Physics.

"I've been doing it practically forever, and I have no idea." — Phil Niekro on how the pitch works.

In its November 1975 edition, the *American Journal of Physics* analyzed the knuckleball and explained the principles which underlie its movement. The best scientific explanation for laymen is that rotation (or lack thereof) is the key, rather than speed. Martin Quigley's *The Crooked Pitch* (1984) contains a detailed explanation of the knuckleball and its properties.

Adaptability.

Larry Cheney. In 1915 the Cubs pitcher was struck by a line drive hit by Zack Wheat. The ball drove his thumb into his nose, breaking both. The next year, Cheney could not effectively grip the ball so he began using his nails to throw a knuckleball and learned the spitball from Ed Walsh. Despite the new pitches, he was never as successful after the injury. He had won over 20 games three straight years before the injury and then had only one good season among the last five he played.

Ted Lyons. Lyons was an instant success when he arrived in the Major Leagues in 1923 and pitched a no-hitter in 1926 for the White Sox. He developed a sore arm and learned the knuckleball from a picture of knuckleball pioneer Eddie Rommell holding the ball. Lyons went on to pitch another 20 years and ended up in the Hall of Fame.

Johnny Lindell. Lindell came up in 1942 with the Yankees while Joe McCarthy was still the manager. McCarthy did not like the knuckleball and made Lindell a left fielder, reasoning that: "When the ball breaks, the catcher misses it. If it doesn't break, the batter hits it out of sight."

Lindell hit .324 over eight seasons and played in three World Series for the Yankees. He then moved on to the Hollywood Stars in the Pacific Coast League. In 1952 he won 24 games with the knuckleball and at age 36 he was back in the Major Leagues for one season as a pitcher with the Pirates and Phillies, for whom he won six games in 1953.

1950s and 1960s.

"It's taken me 27 years and I still don't know why the ball does what it does. If a man asks me how to throw it down and in, I say he's talking to the wrong man." — Hoyt Wilhelm, who was the preeminent knuckleballer of the second half of the 20th century. The first Hall of Famer to be admitted on his relieving credentials, Wilhelm pitched from 1952 through 1972, retiring at age 49.

1970–1980s.

"Like some cult religion that barely survives, there has always been at least one but rarely more than five or six devotees throwing the knuckleball in the big leagues at the same time…. Not only can't pitchers control it, hitters can't hit it, catchers can't catch it, umpires can't call it, coaches can't coach it, and most pitchers can't learn it. The perfect pitch." — Ron Luciano in *Remembrances of Swings Past* (1988). Some baseball people contend that the knuckleball is dying out because teams are not willing to allow players the time in the minor leagues to develop the pitch. Clubs apparently have no patience with a pitcher trying to develop a knuckleball and are far more enamored of fastball pitchers.

Wilbur Wood. Wood was 19 when he made his Major League debut in 1961, "already looking like a roly-poly bear looking for a cave to sleep out the winter" (per Martin Quigley in *The Crooked Pitch* (1984)). He did not throw the knuckleball full time until he was in the Major Leagues. In his first 10 years he made only 21 starts, but in 1971 the White Sox allowed him to start more frequently. He started 224 games in the next five years, an average of almost 45 per year (20th century pitchers have rarely started more than 37 games in a season). Wood won 164 games, including 22 shutouts, over his 17-year career (see also ***Doubleheaders***).

Phil and Joe Niekro.

"Trying to hit [knuckleballer] Phil Niekro is like trying to eat jello with chopstick." — Yankee outfielder Bobby Murcer.

The Niekro brothers were the other top knuckleballers of the 1970s and 1980s. Phil won 318 games in the Major Leagues, though he had to pitch 24 seasons until age 48 to do it. Joe won 221 games over 22 seasons.

Charlie Hough. Hough began using the pitch when he hurt his arm in the minor leagues in the late 1960s and could not throw hard anymore. He was taught the pitch by scout Goldie Holt, and pitchers Hoyt Wilhelm and Jim Brewer helped him refine it. It allowed him to extend his Major League career from 1970 to age 46 in 1994, when a hip problem forced him to retire midseason.

1990s-2000s.

"That's a waste of electricity right there. He should have gone home and taken his wife out to dinner." — Pirates coach Rich Donnelly commenting on Dodger scout Mike Brito, whose job it was to hold up the radar gun throughout an August 26, 1992, knuckleball dual between Tom Candiotti and Tim Wakefield. It was the first time two knuckleballers were paired against each other since September 13, 1982, when brothers Joe and Phil Niekro faced off. Wakefield shut out the Dodgers 2–0.

Tom Candiotti. In 1991, other than an aging Charlie Hough, Tom Candiotti was the only pitcher using the knuckleball with any regularity. Candiotti bounced around among 13 teams in his first seven professional seasons. He finished having played for six Major League clubs over a 16-year career that lasted until he was age 41 in 1999.

Tim Wakefield. In 1992 Wakefield began his Major League career for the Pirates with a complete-game six-hitter in a 3–2 win over the Cardinals. He began his professional career as a first baseman but switched to pitching at age 23. He first learned the pitch while fooling around in the outfield in 1989 in Class A ball. Wakefield was something of a Major League sensation in 1992 with an 8–1 record in 13 starts and a 2.15 ERA.

Wakefield also pitched a complete-game victory against the Braves in the 1992 postseason. To help prepare against him, the Braves called in former pitchers Bruce Dal Canton and Phil Niekro to throw knuckleballs in batting practice. Niekro acknowledged that Wakefield had better control than he did, getting the ball in the strike zone about 70% of the time. Wakefield struggled after his rookie season and bounced back and forth to the minor leagues until 1995, when he returned to form with the Red Sox.

He was still going strong in 2003 for the Red Sox, capping the year with a stellar performance in Games 1 and 4 of the ALCS against the Yankees, resulting in the following headline in one newspaper: "Knuckle sandwich."

Jeff Reardon. Reardon became the all-time save leader in 1992, but by 1993 he was a has-been who began learning the knuckleball to resurrect his career. His problem was that he could not stop biting his nails, which prevented him from digging them into the seams of the ball to throw the pitch effectively. He made it back in 1993 for 58 appearances in a Reds uniform and then in 1994 he pitched in 11 games for the Yankees.

Steve Sparks. Not to be confused with pitcher Steve W. Sparks, who pitched three games for the Pirates in 2000, this Sparks is a knuckleballer who did well for the Tigers in the late 1990s and was still pitching in the early 2000s. He and Wakefield squared off on August 28, 1999, in what was believed to be the 27th confrontation by knuckleball pitchers. Wakefield's Red Sox beat the Angels 7–6.

Jared Fernandez. Fernandez debuted in September 2002 for the Reds and in August 2003 first pitched for the Marlins, throwing 56-mph knuckleballs, which contrasted nicely with closer Billy Wagner's 98-mph fastball.

Hard to Catch.

"The knuckler's like a dame. If you reach for it, you're licked. You've got to wait until it reaches for you." —1940s catcher Mike Sandlock.

"The way to stop a knuckleball is to wait until it stops rolling and then pick it up." —Catcher Bob Uecker.

Hoyt Wilhelm once dared any teammate to catch three of five knuckleballs bare-handed. None could, including Willie Mays.

On June 16, 1986, Charlie Hough watched a no-hitter go down the drain in the 9th inning. With one out, his Rangers led the Angels 1–0. The next batter hit a fly ball down the left field line. George Wright, who had come in for defensive purposes, overran the ball and it bounced off the heel of his glove for a three-base error. Rookie Wally Joyner then had the Angels' first hit when he singled in the runner to tie the game.

Catcher Orlando Mercado let a knuckleball get by and Joyner moved to second, forcing Hough to intentionally walk Reggie Jackson. Mercado let another ball get by and Joyner raced around third and headed for home. Mercado turned to throw to the plate, but Hough was standing on the mound shell-shocked from the turn of events and could not make the play. The Angels won 2–1 on one hit.

In May 1999, Tim Wakefield confounded catcher Jason Varitek when Varitek had five passed balls, one short of the Major League record. Varitek made up for it with three hits, including a home run in a 12–5 Red Sox win over the Indians.

In a game in 2002, Jared Fernandez's elusive pitch drove catcher Jason LaRue crazy, resulting in three consecutive passed balls and a wild pitch in the 1st inning.

Korea

See also *Korean War.*

American missionary P.L. Gillet is credited by some with introducing baseball to Korea in 1905. The Korean Baseball Association was formed prior to World War I and staged its first amateur championship in 1929. A new amateur baseball association was formed in 1946.

In the post–World War II years the most prominent Korean players went to Japan to play professionally, including Sadaharu Oh. Korean Isao Harimoto played in the Japan Leagues from 1959 through 1981 and in 1968 and 1969 the Dodgers and Giants considered buying him.

Since 1982 Korea has had a six-team professional league and is still one of the top amateur baseball nations in the world. Korea hosted the 1988 Olympics and finished fourth. In 1984 and 1992 Korea did not win a medal, but in 2000 at Sydney, Korea won a bronze medal.

Korean Players in the U.S.

Won Kuk Lee. This Korean pitcher signed with the Giants in 1964. He pitched ambidextrously during a brief spring training tryout with the club. After his release he pitched strictly right-handed and won more than 150 games in the Mexican Leagues.

Soon. A Korean player named Soon signed with the Brewers in 1979, but he did not get past Class AA.

Chel Sun "Sunny" Park. Another Korean-born player in the American minor league system was this right-handed pitcher, who played for the Stockton Ports in 1980–1981, going 7–9.

Chan Ho Park. Park made his debut with the Dodgers on April 9, 1994, but was in the minor leagues after two weeks (he returned in 1996). He signed with the Dodgers for a reported bonus of $1.2 million. When Park was introduced at Dodger Stadium for the first time, rookie public address announcer Mike Carlucci called him Ho Chan Park, but quickly corrected himself.

Sang-Hoon Lee. Lee pitched in nine games for the Red Sox in 2000, compiling a 3.17 ERA.

Byung-Hyun Kim. This reliever made his Major League debut for the Diamondbacks on May 29, 1999, striking out Mets catcher Mike Piazza to end the game and preserve an 8–7 victory. He had his ups and downs later, particularly during the 2001 World Series when he gave up two crucial 9th inning home runs to the Yankees in consecutive games. He was so erratic in 2004 that he was sent down to the minor leagues after returning from South Korea to have his sore back examined.

Jae Kuk-ryu. In June 2001 the Cubs signed this Korean high school pitcher to a contract. In 2003 while pitching in the minor leagues, he was cited for throwing balls at an osprey, a crime in Florida (see *Birds*).

Hee Seop Choi is the first Korean-born position player in the Major Leagues, and eight Korean reporters routinely follow him around in the 2000s.

Sun-Woo Kim. The pitcher attended Korea University and

then signed with the Red Sox and then the Expos, for whom he collectively appeared in almost 100 games between 2001 and 2004.

Home Run Record. In 1998, at Seoul, Korea's Chansil Stadium, 29–year–old American Tyrone Woods hit his 42nd homer to break the six–year–old Korean home run record. Woods, who played for the OB Bears, spent 11 years in the American minor leagues, the last with Pawtucket, before going to Korea. He was also named the Korean League MVP in 1998, which was the first year foreign players were allowed in the league.

In 2003 Korean Baseball Organization (KBO) Samsung Lions first baseman Seung-Yeop Lee, age 27 and known as the Lion King, became the all-time single-season home run leader in any Asian professional league. He hit 56 home runs to break Sadaharu Oh's Japanese League record in 1964, which was tied in 2001 by Tuffy Rhodes of the U.S. Lee had over 300 home runs by 2003, although the dimensions of his home park were a rather small 311 feet to the corners and 384 in center field. Lee's agent was Jihn Kim, part of superagent Arn Tellem's Los Angeles and San Francisco group.

The 6'1", 200-pound Lee hit .301 with 144 RBIs over the league's 135-game schedule. He also won his fifth straight KBO MVP Award. He had brief spring training appearances with the Cubs 2002 and Marlins 2003, but has not made it to the Major Leagues.

Scandal. In September 2004 four players on the LG Twins were dragged off the field by police during pregame warm-ups. They were among 50 professional baseball players accused of dodging the country's required military draft for all males over 20 who have no physical or mental disabilities. Apparently a "draft dodger broker" had been paid significant sums to teach several players how to fail the medical exam required for induction. Among the ploys was a medicine that caused the players to simulate a medical condition common among kidney patients.

Only a limited number of players are given exemptions from military service, and usually only for extraordinary results like an Olympic gold medal. American Major Leaguers Chan Ho Park and Byung-Hyun Kim have received the exemption.

North Korea. In the 1990s, North Korea renewed its interest in baseball, which had been played there prior to Japanese occupation of the country during World War II. The interest was spurred in part by China's interest in baseball fostered by the Barcelona Olympics in 1992. North Korean joined the International Baseball Association in 1990 and four Korean teams were formed. They now play an annual tournament under the auspices of the country's ruler, Kim Jong II.

Korean War (1950–1953)

"He was always coming back — back from Korea, back from a broken collarbone, a shattered elbow, a bruised heel, back from drastic bouts of flue and ptomaine poisoning."— John Updike on Ted Williams in "Hub Fans Bid Kid Adieu," first published in the *New Yorker* magazine (1960).

"Sorry Buzzie, I'm a Giants fan." — Response in the 1950s from Selective Service director Lewis B. Hershey to Dodgers General Manager Buzzie Bavasi. Bavasi had good-naturedly suggested that the Dodgers would contribute $5,000 a year to help Willie Mays support his family if the Army would retain him, rather than grant him a hardship deferment. Nevertheless, Mays lost two years to the military during the Korean War.

See also *Korea.*

Draftees. Only a few Major League players were drafted into the military during the Korean War, which lasted from June 1950 through July 1953. Phillies pitcher Curt Simmons was the first player drafted and missed the 1950 World Series. Among the most prominent players to be drafted was Willie Mays, who missed most of the 1952 and 1953 seasons. Others were Whitey Ford, Johnny Antonelli, Billy Martin and Dick Groat. A total of approximately 100 professional players who were in the military during the Korean War.

Ted Williams. Only the Marines called up World War II veterans for the Korean War, forcing Williams to lose most of the 1952 and 1953 seasons. Williams played in a highly publicized farewell game in 1952 before entering the military. Because he was 33 it was generally believed (including, apparently, by him) that this would be his last Major League game. He flew 39 combat missions over Korea and then returned to play through the 1960 season. He was future astronaut John Glenn's wingman on many of these missions.

Jerry Coleman. The Yankee second baseman flew 57 combat missions during the Korean War as a Marine Corp captain.

Jim Lemon. Lemon was an outfielder-first baseman primarily for the Senators and Twins. He began his career in 1950, but it was interrupted for the next two seasons by the war. Known as a power hitter, he came back to hit 27 home runs in 1956 and 38 in 1960, with 100 RBIs in both 1959 and 1960.

Bob Buhl. Buhl was a paratrooper in 1952 and began his delayed Major League career in 1953 as the number three starter in the Milwaukee Braves rotation behind mainstays Johnny Sain and Warren Spahn.

Deaths. Air Force Major Robert Neighbors played for the 1939 Browns, batting .182 in seven games. He is the only former Major League player known to have died in combat in Korea (missing in action). He survived military action in Europe, but was killed while piloting an aircraft during a mission over North Korea in August 1952.

Sandy Koufax (1935–)

Hall of Fame 1972

"I was always struck by his unique combination of immense power and absolute fragility. His dominance and his vulnerability, and his grace in never publicly acknowledging either, are what made his career so special and the memory of his prowess so sweet."— Sam Ludu in a letter to *Sports Illustrated*.

"Trying to hit him was like trying to drink coffee with a fork."— Willie Stargell.

"A foul ball was a moral victory."— Don Sutton on hitting against Koufax.

"Pitching is … the art of instilling fear."— Koufax.

"Don't you know that baseball stopped when Koufax retired."— Richard Sybert.

Possibly the best left-hander of all time, Koufax starred in the early 1960s for the Dodgers before a chronically bad elbow forced his premature retirement.

Leo Durocher saw the Brooklyn native pitch in a tryout with the Giants and passed on him because he was so wild. After a brief but stellar basketball and baseball career at the University of Cincinnati, Sanford Koufax (born Sanford Braun, but his stepfather adopted him and Koufax took his surname) debuted with the Dodgers in 1955. He was extremely wild early in his career and was only 36–40 after six seasons. He finally showed his talent in 1961, when he was 18–13.

From 1962 until his premature retirement after the 1966 season, Koufax led the league in ERA every year and won 25 or more games

three times. He was a unanimous Cy Young Award winner in 1963 (25–5), 1965 (26–8) and 1966 (27–9). He had a 165–87 record and a lifetime 2.76 ERA over his 12-year career. He had 40 shutouts and pitched no-hitters in four consecutive seasons, including a perfect game in 1965. He won four games in four World Series and is fifth all-time with a World Series ERA of 0.95.

Koufax suffered serious circulatory problems in his throwing arm throughout the 1960s and retired after the 1966 World Series at age 30. Considered by many as the greatest left-hander of all time, he was an NBC broadcaster briefly before retiring to his estate in New England. He kept his ties with the Dodgers and remained a periodic pitching coach for the club into the 1990s. He was elected to the Hall of Fame at age 36 and was only the sixth player elected in his first year of eligibility.

Books. Sandy Koufax with Ed Linn, *Koufax* (1966). Jane Leavy's celebrated book about Koufax, *Sandy Koufax: A Lefty's Legacy* (2002), was not influenced by Koufax. He declined to be interviewed, but agreed to verify biographical facts and then declined to read the manuscript: "It would be wrong for me to influence what you write."

"**L** is Lajoie
Whom Clevelanders love,
Napoleon himself,
With glue in his glove."
—Ogden Nash on Nap Lajoie.

Ladies Day

"They made the weirdest sound as they rushed at you screaming. It sounds like Ladies Day at Ebbets Field."— American soldier describing a 1944 Japanese banzai attack at Leyte Island.

"[With only men present] profanity, ill feeling, partisan prejudice and other characteristics of 'stag' gatherings are conspicuous features, while at the other the pride of gentlemen which curbs men's evil passions in the presence of ladies frowns upon all such exhibitions of partisan ill will, and order and decorum mark the presence of the civilizing influence of the fair sex."—1880s commentator on the value of Ladies Day.

Nineteenth Century. A number of teams and dates for the first Ladies Day have been cited, but the earliest known form of Ladies Day at a ballpark appears to have been in 1867. The New York Knickerbockers set aside the last Thursday each month for members to invite family and friends.

In the 1870s it was always Ladies Day at some ballparks, as women often were admitted free if accompanied by a man. It has been reported that there were Ladies Days in Cincinnati and Philadelphia in 1876. Providence is credited with staging a Ladies Day in 1882.

In 1883 the Philadelphia Athletics and Baltimore Orioles separately sponsored what some have reported as the first official Ladies Days in the Major Leagues. Women were only allowed in the bleachers. Another source reported that the first Ladies Day was held that year by the St. Louis Browns and owner Christopher Von der Ahe. Still another source credited Abner Powell in New Orleans in 1889, who is also credited by that source with starting **Rainchecks** and other innovations.

In 1884 Brooklyn of the American Association adopted the practice and provided special accommodations such as women-only restrooms. The Polo Grounds apparently was the site of a Ladies Day game between New York and Cleveland on June 16, 1883.

Some sources identify 1884 as the year. In Cincinnati in the late 1880s the team allowed women in free when "handsome and Irish" Tony Mullane pitched.

In 1897 the National League Washington Senators began the practice, and thousands of women showed up the first time to see popular George "Win" Mercer. Mercer was kicked out of the game for arguing with umpire Bill Carpenter. After a near-riot resulted, the Senators supposedly did not have another Ladies Day for many years. Given that the National League Senators/Nationals of the 1890s lasted only two more years, the lack of a Ladies Day must have continued into the 20th century with the American League club in Washington.

20th Century. Ladies Day was always on a weekday when women were admitted free with a male escort. In 1909 the National League abolished this practice while the American League clubs continued it. It caught on again in 1917 in St. Louis, Cincinnati and Chicago, and women were even admitted free without an escort.

Cardinals. From 1911 through 1916, Cardinals owner Helene Britton, the Major League's first woman owner and an early advocate of the Women's Suffrage Movement, tried to encourage female attendance by hiring a male singer and a band to entertain between innings. Some sources report that the Cardinals held a Ladies Day in 1912, despite the "official" 1909 ban.

Cubs. One source erroneously credited Phil Wrigley's Cubs with the first Ladies Day, in the 1920s. It may have been the first Ladies Day after the National League's 1909 ban was lifted. In 1930 the Cubs were in a pennant race and had to cut back on their Ladies Day promotion because 31,000 women showed up for a key June game and demanded to be admitted without charge. The club admitted 20,000 women and gave the rest priority for the next Ladies Day. The Cubs were then forced to distribute tickets at outlets around the city to avoid mob scenes at the ballpark.

Dodgers. One source reported that the first Ladies Day at Ebbets Field was in 1939 and was extremely successful. One day, however, two men dressed as women were discovered attempting to get into the park. They were trampled and later sued the club.

Yankees. In 1946 the Yankees promoted a Ladies Day by giving away 500 pairs of nylon stockings.

Night Game. The first Ladies "Night" reportedly was held in 1941 by the Giants.

Legal Implications. The practice died in the 1970s along with all other promotions giving women preferential treatment. Legal proceedings forced courts to ban these activities on grounds of discrimination against men.

Nap Lajoie (1874–1959)

Hall of Fame 1937

"When he got a hold of one, it usually hit the fence on the first bounce, traveling about five feet three inches above the ground most of the way and removing the ears of all infielders who didn't throw themselves flat on their stomachs the instant they saw him swing. They would have time to duck this ball, and after the battle there would be a meeting of earless infielders, threatening a general walkout if that big French gunman were allowed in the park again, even with a toothpick in his hand." — Ring Lardner writing in *The New Yorker* magazine.

Lajoie was a star second baseman for the Phillies and A's in the early 20th century.

Napoleon "Larry" Lajoie grew up in Rhode Island and was playing professionally at Fall River, Massachusetts, when the Phillies purchased him. He began his Major League career at first base in 1896, but in 1898 manager George Stallings moved him to second base due to an absence of quality players at the position.

Lajoie is considered one of the best of the early second basemen, proving his worth with the Phillies with averages of no less than .326 during his five years with the club. When the American League declared itself a Major League in 1901, Lajoie jumped across town to the A's for one year. He won the then-mythical Triple Crown that season with a .422 average, 14 home runs and 125 RBIs. He also led the league in hits, doubles, slugging average and runs scored.

Along with hitting .324 or better ten times for the Indians beginning in 1902, he managed the club for five years starting in 1905. His best year as manager was 1908, when the club just missed, losing the pennant by one-half game to the Tigers (rainouts were not made up).

Lajoie's 21-year Major League career ended in 1916 with two years back with the A's. He then managed in the minor leagues for two years. He finished his career with 3,244 hits and a .338 average, allowing him to become the sixth player elected to the Hall of Fame. Despite his individual success, he never played on or managed a pennant-winning team.

After he retired he left baseball and moved into business in Cleveland, though he spent increasing amounts of time in Florida and eventually moved there. He died of pneumonia in Daytona Beach in 1959.

Kenesaw Mountain Landis (1866–1944)

Landis was the first **Commissioner** of baseball, reigning from November 1920 until his death in November 1944.

Ring Lardner (1885–1933)

Hall of Fame (Spink Award) 1963

"Lardner is the Shakespeare of baseball, or the Boswell, if you like. A real classic American writer, one of the few, as American as hamburgers, hot dogs, and apple pie — and baseball." — "The Old Timer" in W.R. Burnett's *The Roar of the Crowd* (1964).

"During those years, when most men of promise achieve an adult education, if only in the school of war, Ring moved in the company of a few dozen illiterates playing a boy's game. A boy's game, with no more possibilities in it than a boy could master, a game bounded by walls which kept out novelty or danger, change or adventure…. However deeply Ring might cut into it, his cake had the diameter of Frank Chance's diamond." — F. Scott Fitzgerald speaking at Lardner's funeral in September 1933.

Ringgold Wilmer Lardner achieved baseball notoriety when he began a 1914 serial in the *Saturday Evening Post*. The first installment consisted of one letter from Jack Keefe to "Al," which began the "You Know Me Al" series. The letters were published as a novel in 1916. Lardner also wrote the famous "Alibi Ike" baseball story (see also *Alibis*). In later years Lardner claimed to hate his baseball work and sports in general. Lardner was the second recipient of the J.G. Taylor Spink Award (1963) for baseball writing.

Books. Matthew J. Bruccoli (ed.), *Ring Around the Bases: The Complete Baseball Stories of Ring Lardner* (1992); George W. Hilton (ed.), *The Annotated Baseball Stories of Ring W. Lardner 1914–1919* (1995).

Tommy Lasorda (1927–)

Hall of Fame (VC) 1997

"Lasorda was a master motivator. He didn't lie, exactly, he was just a kind of a novelist, and all his stories had happy endings."— Bill Plaschke.

"It couldn't have happened to a greater guy. Well, yes it could. It could have happened to me."— Lasorda on a Jerry Reuss no-hitter.

"He's got a lot of bluster, and a lot of the other things, but he's a baseball man. But if anyone ever said that baseball was his life, it would be Lasorda."— Dodger broadcaster Vin Scully.

Lasorda managed the Los Angeles Dodgers for 21 seasons, winning eight division titles, four National League pennants and two World Series.

As a player from a poor Italian neighborhood in Norristown, Pennsylvania, Thomas Charles Lasorda was a left-handed pitcher originally signed by the Phillies. He spent the bulk of his minor league playing career with Montreal of the International League, the Brooklyn Dodgers top farm club. Between 1950–1955 and 1958–1960 Lasorda won 98 games for Montreal (the all-time league record), helping them win five International League pennants.

Lasorda's Major League playing career was brief. He appeared in eight games for Brooklyn in 1954 and 1955, allowing 11 runs in 13 innings pitched, but was demoted to make room for Sandy Koufax. In 1956 he pitched for the Kansas City A's in the American League, walking 45 batters in 45 innings. Lasorda finished his Major League career with an 0–4 mark and a 6.48 ERA.

After his playing career was over, Lasorda worked as a scout and later a minor league manager in the Dodger organization. He became a major league coach in 1973 and succeeded Walter Alston as Dodger manager at the end of the 1976 season.

Lasorda won consecutive pennants in 1977 and 1978. Los Angeles lost both World Series to the New York Yankees in six games. After close second-place finishes in 1979 and 1980 (losing a one-game *Play-Off* to the Astros in 1980), his club won another pennant in strike-shortened 1981, this time besting the Yankees in six games to win his first World Series title. Lasorda won two more National League West crowns in 1983 and 1985, but the Dodgers were defeated in the playoffs by Philadelphia and St. Louis.

Lasorda won his second World Series in 1988, orchestrating upsets of the New York Mets and Oakland A's on the way to the title. Lasorda and the Dodgers won the West again in 1994 and 1995. A player strike cancelled the 1994 postseason and the Dodgers were swept by Cincinnati in 1995.

The long-time manager suffered a heart attack in mid–1996 and retired from managing that July to become a Dodger executive. He was named interim general manager in June 1998 when Fred Claire was fired.

Lasorda finished his managerial career with a 1,599–1,439 mark for a .526 winning percentage. Only one other manager, Gabby Street, won pennants in his first two seasons. Lasorda also managed nine Rookies of the Year, two Cy Young Award winners (Fernando Valenzuela and Orel Hershiser) and a National League MVP (Kirk Gibson). Lasorda was selected to manage the 2000 U.S. *Olympic* team and led them to a gold medal in Sydney.

Last At-Bat and Last Game of Career

"I want to hit a routine grounder to second and run all out to first base, then get thrown out by a half step. I want to leave an example to the young guys that that's how you play the game, all out."— George Brett in early 1992 when asked what he wanted to do in the last at-bat of his career. For his last game, at the end of the 1993 season, all of Brett's teammates wore their pant legs high and wrote Brett's No. 5 on their socks. In the 8th inning he hit a

ground ball up the middle past diving second baseman Jeff Treadway to drive in the tying run. He was removed for a pinch runner and never played again.

See also *Last Season*.

Selected last at-bats/last games:

Henry Aaron. Aaron singled in the 6th inning off Dave Roberts of the Tigers in the last game of the season on October 3, 1976.

Cap Anson. Anson was over 46 when he hit .302 in 114 games in 1897. He hit two home runs in his last game.

Johnny Bench. The Reds catcher switched to less-demanding third base for the last few years of his career. However, in the last game of his career in 1983 he played catcher for only the twelfth time in three years.

Gary Carter. Carter hit a game-winning double in the last of his 7,971 at-bats, in 1992.

Roger Clemens.

"That's been my makeup my entire career anyway. Fight and scratch even when I don't have my good stuff."— Clemens, after throwing 42 pitches in the 1st inning of his "last" start, on October 22, 2003, in the World Series against the Marlins. He was on track to lose the game when the Yankees rallied in the 9th inning to tie, but the Marlins won it in the 12th on a dramatic walk-off home run by shortstop Alex Gonzalez. Clemens threw 109 pitches in seven innings, giving up eight hits and three earned runs, striking out five and walking none.

When he faced his last batter in the 7th inning, the crowd knew it was his last appearance on the mound, as he was due to bat first in the 8th and the Yankees were losing. The Florida crowd gave him a standing ovation and flashbulbs popped through Luis Castillo's at-bat. Clemens finished him off with a 94-mph fastball for a called strike three. After the inning, fans continued to cheer, and Clemens emerged from the dugout and acknowledged fans in each direction of the stadium. The Marlins players stood at the top of their dugout and applauded, as did players on the field. See also *Retirement* for Clemens' 2004 return to the field with the Astros.

Larry French. On September 23, 1942, the Dodger pitcher threw a one-hitter against the Phillies. He faced the minimum number of batters thanks to a double play. He was 35 years old and went into the Navy soon after the game and never played professionally again.

Bob Gibson. Gibson gave up a grand slam to the last Major League batter he faced, Pete LaCock. Fifteen years later when Gibson faced LaCock in an oldtimers game, Gibson hit him in the back with a pitch.

Goose Goslin. Goslin had to be lifted for a pinch hitter after wrenching his back during his final at-bat in the Major Leagues in 1938. It was the only time he was ever replaced by a pinch hitter.

Tony Gwynn. On October 7, 2001, Gwynn pinch hit in the 9th inning and grounded out, then walked around the infield nailing shaking hands with the hometown crowd. Earlier in the game, Rickey Henderson had his 3,000th hit, a leadoff double, and then came out of the game, a 14–5 Rockies win.

Walter Johnson. Johnson appeared as a pinch hitter in the 9th inning of the last game of the 1927 season. He hit for pitcher Tom Zachary, who earlier in the game had given up Babe Ruth's 60th home run of the season.

Al Kaline. In the last game of his career in late 1974, Kaline batted once, lined out, and then took himself out of the game due to a bad shoulder.

Sandy Koufax. Koufax last pitched in Game 2 of the 1966 World Series against the Orioles. He gave up four runs in six innings primarily as a result of three errors in the 5th inning by center fielder Willie Davis.

Mark McGwire was 0-for-1 in a pinch-hitting appearance on the last day of the regular season in 2001. A bad knee had limited his appearances late that season.

Christy Mathewson and Three Finger Brown. Mathewson was the Reds manager in 1916 when he pitched his last game. One source erroneously reported that it was his only game of the season, but others reported that he appeared in upwards of 16 games, with 12 wins. *The Baseball Encyclopedia* credits him with 13 appearances and four wins for the season.

In his last game, Mathewson pitched against Three Finger Brown, who also was making his last Major League appearance. Mathewson won 10-8 as both pitchers staggered through nine innings. The Reds had 15 hits and the Cubs 19.

Willie Mays. Mays drove in one of four Mets runs in the 12th inning of Game 2 of the 1973 World Series against the A's. He had earlier made an error that allowed the A's to tie the game. The Mets won 10-7.

Stan Musial. Musial singled in the 6th inning off Jim Maloney in the last game of the year on September 29, 1963. He drove in Curt Flood for his last RBI.

John "Blue Moon" Odom. Odom combined with Francisco Barrios to throw a no-hitter in his final Major League outing in 1976.

Cal Ripken. On October 7, 2001, Ripken was on deck when Brady Anderson struck out to end the game. Ripken went 0-for-3 and had a putout and an assist at third base. Many fans had paid $500 premiums from scalpers for a game a week earlier, which would have been Ripken's regularly scheduled last game. The September 11 terrorist attacks pushed the season out an extra week to make up the cancelled games.

Babe Ruth. Ruth's last game was May 30, 1935, the first game of a doubleheader at Baker Bowl between his new club, the Braves, and the Phillies. He batted in the 1st inning against A's pitcher Jim Bivins, grounded out to first baseman Dolf Camilli and was replaced in left field by Hal Lee. One source reported that Ruth quit because of failing eyesight in one eye, although that is not mentioned in the most authoritative biographies.

Nolan Ryan. Ryan pitched in his last game on September 22, 1993. In the 1st inning he gave up five runs, including a grand slam by Dann Howitt. Ryan's arm had been getting progressively worse over the past two games, but he tried to fulfill his commitment to the fans. After the grand slam he went to a 3-1 count on Dave Magadan when he was taken out for the last time with ligament damage in his elbow. He had given up four base on balls and two hits. It was the third time in his career in which he was taken out of a game without retiring a batter (once each in 1971 and 1992).

Ted Williams.

"It's got a chance! It's got a chance! And it's gone!" — Broadcaster Curt Gowdy in a relatively restrained voice because he had thought an earlier fly ball out would be a home run and he had called it prematurely.

The most famous last at-bat occurred on September 26, 1960, in front of 10,454 fans. Williams homered off Orioles pitcher Jack Fisher in Fenway Park to spark an 8th inning rally and a 5-4 win, but nevertheless did not tip his cap or otherwise acknowledge the crowd. In his autobiography, Williams said that it was the closest he ever came to tipping his cap (at least after his first year when he stopped for good), but he could not change his habit at that point.

After the third out, he reluctantly went out to left field for the 9th inning, but was immediately replaced by Carroll Hardy so that he

could trot in to the cheers of the crowd. He did not make the final road trip to Yankee Stadium, though apparently he would have played against the Yankees but for the dramatic finale in Boston.

Williams had walked in the 1st inning of the game, hit a fly to deep center field in the 3rd, and in the 5th inning hit a tremendous blast to right center that was caught close to 400 feet from the plate.

The game was chronicled in John Updike's "Hub Fans Bid Kid Adieu," which first appeared in *The New Yorker* magazine. In the Crabbe Evers mystery novel, *Fear in Fenway* (1993), the first chapter is titled, "Hub Fans Bid Us Bonjour."

Cy Young and Grover Cleveland Alexander. In his last game in 1911, Young lost 1-0 to rookie Grover Cleveland Alexander. Young's last win was a 1-0 shutout against the Pirates on September 22, 1911. He retired the following spring.

In Alexander's last game, 19 years later in 1930, he was 43 years old. He had started three games for the Phillies that year and on May 28 he made his last appearance, a relief effort against the Braves. He gave up two runs in the 7th inning and pitched a scoreless 8th in a 5-1 Braves win.

Home Run. At least 35 players have homered in their last at-bat, including Jeff Tackett of the Orioles on August 2, 1994. The last to do it was Albert Belle in 2000.

Last Game of the Season

"I want this to be complete and so I must now before going on report an event that happened on the last day of the season. We were just playing out the string, all the standings were frozen because no win or loss would change them now and 'the pressure was off.' But the twin pitched like it was the seventh game of the world series, and he had a shut-out going through the sixth inning." — Outfielder Bill Bailey in "Voo and Doo," by Hoke Norris (1968).

Odd Results. Records set on the last day of the season were sometimes suspect because meaningless games often caused strange results and odd playing conditions.

Pitching Stunts. Babe Ruth pitched the last game of the 1933 season for the Yankees to draw a big crowd to the ballpark. At age 38 he pitched a complete game 6-5 win over the Red Sox. He walked three and struck out none.

In 1947 Dizzy Dean came out of a six-year retirement at age 36 to pitch in the season finale for the last-place Browns against the White Sox. He held them scoreless for four innings, with three strikeouts and one walk. After singling to left field and then sliding into second base, Dean's wife supposedly asked manager Muddy Ruel to remove him from the game for his own safety. He did.

Strikeouts. Bob Feller struck out 18 batters on the last day of the 1938 season.

David Cone struck out 19 batters for the Mets on the last day of the 1991 season.

Perfect Game. Rube Vickers of the A's pitched a five-inning perfect game against the Senators on the last day of the 1907 season. The game was the second of a doubleheader that day and was called because of darkness after Vickers won the first game with a 12-inning relief appearance.

Mike Witt pitched a 1-0 perfect game for the Angels against the Rangers on the last day of the 1984 season.

No-Hitter. Four A's pitchers, all used sparingly to rest them for the upcoming ALCS, combined to pitch a no-hitter against the Angels on September 28, 1975. They were Glenn Abbott, Vida Blue, Paul Lindblad and Rollie Fingers.

On September 28, 1951, Allie Reynolds pitched a no-hitter at

Yankee Stadium against the Red Sox. Yogi Berra dropped a foul ball by the last batter, Ted Williams. Berra then called for the same pitch, a high and tight fastball, and caught another foul ball hit by Williams.

Bill Stoneman pitched a 7–0 no-hitter for the Expos against the Mets on October 2, 1972.

Last Place Finishes

"Nice Guys Finish Last."—Leo Durocher's famous comment about Mel Ott's Giants; and the title of Durocher's autobiography. What Durocher actually said (sort of) to interviewer Frank Graham, Jr., on July 4, 1946: "There's Ott—he's a nice guy, and he's in last place. The Giants are nice guys. Finish last."

Long-time sportswriter Jack Lang set the record straight. He reported that Graham of the *New York Journal-American* and Lou Effrat of the *New York Times* were in the Dodger dugout at the Polo Grounds before the game, and they were talking about Eddie Stanky, whom Durocher described as a "scrappy, tough guy." To emphasize his point, Durocher pointed across the field to Mel Ott, manager of the Giants. "Take a look at number four over there," Durocher said of Ott. "A nicer guy never drew a breath, but where is he? In last place. Nice guys finish last." That quote was recorded by Graham, who had a photographic memory. In the *Times*, Effrat perhaps quoted Durocher more accurately as saying, "Nice guys finish eighth."

"Only in the American League West … does the luck of the draw run thin, bunching two expansion teams, the Seattle Pilots and the Kansas City Royals, with the White Sox and the Angels in a miserable heap of losers, and reminding us that this year's shallower cellars can be just as dank and gloomy as the old abolished dungeons of eighth place."—Roger Angell in *The Summer Game* (1972), noting that last place was still last place even after expansion prompted a move to divisional play in 1969.

See *Losing Teams and Pitchers.*

The A's finished in last place seven consecutive seasons between 1915 and 1921. The Tampa Bay Devil Rays finished last in every one of their seven seasons of existence between 1998 and 2004.

In 1952 the Tigers became the last of the original modern Major League clubs to finish in the cellar.

Last Place to First Place See *Losers to Winners*

Last Season

"I remember the last season I played. I went home after a ballgame one day, lay down on my bed, and tears came to my eyes. How can you explain that? It's like crying for your mother after she's gone. You cry because you love her. I cried, I guess, because I loved baseball and I knew I had to leave it."—Willie Mays.

"If I have to be a benchwarmer for the New York Mets I'll commit suicide."—Richie Ashburn of the expansion Mets on why he retired after a strong season in 1962. Ashburn is the last player to hit above .300 (.306) in his last year in the Major Leagues.

Batting Average. The highest last season average in the 20th century was .320 by Sam "Terrible Sammy" Dungan for the 1901 Senators. Bill Keister of the Phillies also hit .320 in his last season, 1903, but was dropped by the club after the season. The all-time last season leader was Dave Orr, who hit .373 for the 1890 Brooklyn Players League club. He suffered a stroke after the season and never played again.

RBIs. Smoky Joe Wood, who won 31 games in 1912 and then had to switch to the outfield due to a sore arm, drove in 92 runs in 1922, his last season in the Major Leagues.

Home Runs. Ted Williams hit 29 home runs in his last season, as did Mark McGwire.

Wins. Sandy Koufax won 27 games in 1966, his last season. It broke the 20th century National League record of Henry Schmidt, who won 21 games in 1903, his only Major League season. Schmidt pitched five shutouts but refused to sign his contract with the Dodgers, preferring to live on the West Coast and remain in the Pacific Coast League where he had been discovered.

The only American League pitchers to win at least 20 games in their final season were Black Sox pitchers Eddie Cicotte (21 wins) and Lefty Williams (22 wins).

Latin Baseball and Latin Major League Players/Managers

"Hector Torrez, how can you communicate with Enzo Hernandez when he speaks Spanish and you speak Mexican?"—Jerry Coleman.

"You're goin' to Cuba and the Dominican this summer. If there's any more of those creatures down there, I want 'em."—Pirates general manager Branch Rickey to scout Howie Haak after the Pirates had signed Roberto Clemente and he lit up the Pirates' spring training camp.

See also *Caribbean World Series* and entries for specific countries: *Aruba, Colombia, Cuba, Curaçao, Dominican Republic, Jamaica, Mexico, Nicaragua, Panama, Puerto Rico, Venezuela* and *Virgin Islands.*

Early Latin Players. Virtually all of the early Latin players were from *Cuba.* Cuban Esteban Bellan played for the Troy Haymakers in 1871. The Cubans are credited by some with introducing baseball to Venezuela in 1895, Colombia in 1903 and Panama in 1904.

The 1940s. It has been reported that from 1914 through 1947 there were approximately 50 Latin players in the Major Leagues. Latin players did not begin to proliferate until World War II, when they were less expensive and not generally subject to the United States military draft (see also *World War II*). In 1944 when there was no minimum Major League salary, Cuban players were signed for very little cost.

Discrimination.

"He was our Jackie Robinson. He was on a crusade to show the American public what a Hispanic man, a black Hispanic man, was capable of."—Rangers executive Luis Mayoral on his friend Roberto Clemente.

"I have always been convinced that Jackie Robinson was not the first black man in the modern Major Leagues. The Washington Senators in the mid–30s and 40s were loaded with Latin players of darker hue, who because they spoke Spanish got by with it."—Black sports editor and writer Art Rust, Jr.

Notwithstanding Rust's perspective, dark-skinned Latins often faced problems getting into the Major Leagues. Pitcher Jose Mendez was prohibited from playing in the Major Leagues even though he was good enough to be called "The Black Matty" in comparison with Christy Mathewson.

Giants manager Alvin Dark had a rule that his players could not speak Spanish while in uniform.

Reverse Discrimination. Catcher Jody Davis of the 1980s Cubs accused teammate and shortstop Ivan DeJesus of allowing fellow Latin players to slide safely into second base under his tags.

200-Game Winners. Three Latin pitchers have won 200 or more Major League games: Nicaraguan Dennis Martinez won 245, Dominican Juan Marichal won 243, and Cuban Luis Tiant won 229. Martinez passed Marichal in August 1998 and his last win was in September 1998.

MVP. The first Latin MVP was shortstop Zoilo Versalles, who led the 1965 Twins to the American League pennant.

Summer League. The only Latin country with a strong summer league is Mexico. All other Latin American countries have only strong winter leagues.

Confusion. Nicaraguan Dennis Martinez and Colorado native Tippy Martinez sat together in the Orioles' locker room to confuse sportswriters and broadcasters. They were not related and Tippy, a third-generation American, spoke no Spanish.

Managers. See *Managers — Black and Latin.*

Bowie Kuhn. In 1994 the former commissioner was appointed as a consultant to the Caribbean Professional Baseball Federation, which governs the Latin American winter leagues.

1990s. It has been estimated that by the 1990s more than 20% of all professional players in the United States came from Latin America. See also *Foreign-Born Players* and *Integration.*

Hall of Fame. The Latin American Baseball Hall of Fame Museum opened near San Juan, Puerto Rico, in 2003. Initial inductees included Venezuelan Luis Arroyo; Cubans Martin DiHigo, Tony Oliva and Orestes Minoso; Puerto Ricans Roberto Clemente and Orlando Cepeda; and Dominicans Juan Marichal, Rico Carty and Sammy Sosa.

Books. Peter C. Bjarkman, *Baseball with a Latin Beat: A History of the Latin American Game* (1994); John Krich, *El Beisbol* (1989); Michael M. Oleksak and Mary Adams Oleksak, *Beisbol* (1991); Nick C. Wilson, *Early Latino Ballplayers in the United States* (2004). Although not exclusively about Latin baseball, the most complete baseball history in Spanish is Bernardo Nunez B.'s, *Grandes Momentos del Beisbol de las Ligas Mayores en el Siglo XX, Ano tras Ano* (2004). Nunez organized many trips to the U.S. for the World Series and was Ambassador to the United Nations from his country, Panama.

Lawsuits

"The judges have taken the indicators away from the umpires." —1915 Opening Day newspaper commentary in the wake of a number of lawsuits arising from contract disputes during the Federal League war.

"Sometimes constables and other officers of the law come into the baseball field to discharge their duties, and that is where an umpire is really up against it. I am not sure what a court would say about which one had more authority, but I guess it goes with the side that can talk faster."—Minor league umpire Harry "Steamboat" Johnson in his autobiography, *Standing the Gaff* (1935).

See also *Arbitration, Carl Mays Incident, Contracts, Defamation, Fans*—Attacks on Players*, Foul Balls, Free Agents, Pine Tar, Reserve Clause, Strikes and Lockouts* and *Umpires.*

Puzzling. In May 1997 Dodger pitcher Hideo Nomo sued Tony Gwynn's wife, Alicia, for using, without permission, his name and likeness on a jigsaw puzzle she was marketing.

Cubs "Bleachers." In 2004 the Cubs settled a lawsuit with the owners of 10 rooftop locations adjacent to Wrigley Field. The settlement called for the club to receive 17% of the revenue generated by the bleacher businesses over the next 20 years.

They Call Me Coach. In February 2004 a Dominican court ruled that outfielder Raul Mondesi owed $640,000 to former Major Leaguer Mario Guerrero for helping improve his baseball skills. Mondesi was forced to play without pay in 2004 (the money from his $1.15 million contract was put into escrow) while the case was appealed. Guerrero claimed that he had an agreement in 1998 with Mondesi and a few other players to pay him 1% of their future earnings as payment for helping them improve their skills.

Mondesi went home to the Dominican Republic to sit out the season, prompting Tim Keown of ESPN to ask: "What knowledge could Mario Guerrero possibly know that would be worth $640,000?"

Mondesi was earning $1.15 million from the Pirates. He then signed with the Angels for $1.75 million and almost immediately tore up his hamstring and was lost for the season. The Angels released him a few weeks later after he repeatedly missed appointments to rehabilitate his leg.

The commissioner's office investigated the circumstances of Mondesi's departure from the last-place Pirates to determine if he left the club to avoid playing for them. He entertained offers from other clubs so soon after he left that suspicion arose. Nevertheless, the commissioner's office found "no manipulation of the system."

Books. Roger I. Abrams, *Legal Bases: Baseball and the Law* (1998); American Bar Association, *Entertainment and Sports Law Bibliography* (1986); Frederick J. Day, *Clubhouse Lawyer: The Sports Fan's Guide to Life and the Law* (2002); Spencer Weber Waller, Neil B. Cohen, and Paul Finkelman (eds.), *Baseball & the American Legal Mind* (1995).

Tony Lazzeri (1903–1946)

Hall of Fame (VC) 1991

"And you thought that of all of the ball players who have come up and stuck around for ten years or so Tony has changed less than almost any you could call to mind. Maybe this is because the mark of the busher never was on Lazzeri. He wasn't like some of these kids who come up out of the tank towns with their brakeman's hair cuts and their mail order clothes. Tony is a big-town guy. Born in San Francisco, which is a big town in all of its aspects."—Sportswriter Frank Graham.

"Tony Lazzeri is the key man of the Yankee infield—and a good one. No man in camp is hitting the ball harder than Tony—or holding up in the field with quite the same brilliance. A budding star last season, this year Lazzeri gives promise of full bloom to stardom."—Then-sportswriter and future commissioner Ford Frick reporting in the *New York Evening Journal* in March 1927.

Lazzeri starred at second base for the Yankees from the 1920s until the mid–1930s.

San Francisco native Anthony Michael Lazzeri, nicknamed "Poosh 'Em Up Tony," first played in the minor leagues at Salt Lake City in the Pacific Coast League, but with only moderate initial success. After later bouncing around the minors he became a star for Salt Lake in 1925, hitting .355 with 60 home runs and 222 RBIs in 197 games. He moved to the Yankees for the 1926 season as the starting second baseman, leading the league with 96 strikeouts while hitting .275.

For the next 11 years he was the starting second baseman for the Yankees, though he often played third base and sometimes shortstop. In seven of his seasons with New York he drove in more than 100 runs and five times hit .300 or better. His best season were 1930, when he hit .303 and drove in 121 runs, and 1932, when he hit .300, drove in 113 runs and hit 15 home runs.

He began to fade in the mid–1930s and after the 1937 season he was released by the Yankees and signed with the Cubs for 1938.

After playing a few games with the Dodgers and Giants in 1939 he ended his 14-year career with a .292 lifetime average and returned to San Francisco.

On May 24, 1936, Lazzeri had an American League–record 11 RBIs and became the first player to hit two **Grand Slams** in a game. Lazzeri hit .262 in 32 World Series games over seven seasons and had four postseason home runs. His epilepsy caused him lifelong problems and apparently caused his death at age 42 after a fall during a seizure.

Book. Paul Votano, *Tony Lazzeri* (2004).

Lead-Off Hitters

"Up here we'll call you the 'Waiter'. Whenever you get on base, you just wait there for Babe Ruth or Lou Gehrig or one of the other big fellows to send you the rest of the way around."—Yankee manager Miller Huggins to lead-off hitter and center fielder Earle Combs.

Catcher. Catcher Roger Bresnahan of shinguard fame often batted in the lead-off spot, an unusual role for a catcher. He must have had some speed, because he stole as many as 34 bases in a season.

MVP. Only three lead-off hitters have won the Most Valuable Player Award: outfielder Rickey Henderson of the 1990 A's; shortstop Zoilo Versalles of the 1965 Twins; and shortstop Phil Rizzuto of the 1950 Yankees. Henderson is the consensus best lead-off hitter of all time based on stolen bases (most ever) and power (81 lead-off home runs and 297 overall). He also had patience at the plate, evidenced by having led the league three times in base on balls and being second all-time in that category.

Best/Home Runs. When Rickey Henderson joined the Mariners in May 2000, he hit a lead-off home run in his first at-bat for the team. In May 2001, when he hit No. 79, the next two lead-off home run hitters were Brady Anderson with 44 and Bobby Bonds with 35.

In April 2003 Craig Biggio of the Astros broke the National League record for lead-off home runs when he hit No. 31. He was considered the best lead-off hitter in the National League in the 1990s. Biggio had 34 through the 2003 season.

Among Hall of Famers, Paul Molitor had 33 lead-off home runs, although it is inevitable that Rickey Henderson will be the new leader when he is elected (if he ever formally retires).

Kenny Lofton of the Indians was considered the top American League lead-off hitter of the late 1990s. Also in the 1990s, the profile of the average lead-off hitter changed dramatically. No longer the smallest guy on the team, the new lead-off hitter was epitomized by Brady Anderson, who hit 35 home runs in the lead-off role, tying a record, on his way to 50 home runs in 1996 (an aberration, as he never hit more than 24 in any other season).

Early in his career Red Sox shortstop Nomar Garciaparra was a lead-off hitter, setting a new Major League RBI record in 1997 with 98, breaking Harvey Kuenn's 1956 record of 85 for the Tigers. Darin Erstad of the Angels broke Garciaparra's record in 2000, with 100.

Lead-Off Home Runs/Season. Bobby Bonds holds the National League record with 11 home runs to lead off games, in 1973 for the Giants. Brady Anderson holds the Major League record with 12 in 1996 for the Orioles.

Back-to-Back/Leading off Game. Bobby Tolan and Pete Rose led off three games with back-to-back home runs. They are the only two players to do so more than once.

Doubleheader. On July 5, 1993, Rickey Henderson hit a lead-off home run in both ends of a doubleheader, the first time it had been done since Harry Hooper of the Red Sox against the Senators on May 30, 1913. Brady Anderson did it for the Orioles on August 21, 1999. Hooper hit only four homers all season.

League Alliance (1877–1883)

This was one of the two earliest minor leagues, formed in 1877. The league was a loose affiliation among former National League teams and various International League clubs. It disbanded in 1883 at the time of the signing of the **National Agreement**.

The league had no set schedule and included the New York Mutuals and the Philadelphia A's, formerly of the National League (both of whom had been kicked out of the league for failing to finish their schedules the year before). There were also League Alliance clubs in Indianapolis, Troy, Buffalo, Minneapolis, Milwaukee, Memphis, Providence, and St. Paul, among others, for a total of 13. The Alliance clubs were divided loosely into informal western and eastern groups.

League Championship Series

"The playoffs are the wedge between the season and the World Series. If you lose, it means you won't be going to the greatest sports event in this country. It's the quagmire before the promised land. It's the Red Sea that has to be crossed. If you don't cross in to the World Series, you're a loser. You're forgotten by Thanksgiving."—Tim McCarver in *Oh Baby, I Love It* (1987).

"Now three [TV attractions], with the addition of the inflationary autumn playoffs, the so-called Championship Series, which constitute television's first contribution to the game."—Roger Angell in *The Summer Game* (1972).

"Play-off baseball is all about who steps up and wins with the game on the line. There are always going to be a lot of shouldas, couldas and wouldas. God knows, we've gone through our share of those in the last four years."—Braves pitcher Tom Glavine in 1995.

Each Major League was divided into two divisions in 1969. As a result, a new League Championship Series (LCS) was established to determine the pennant winners. The original five-game series format was expanded to seven games in 1985. In mid–1993 the Major League owners voted 26–2 to add another round of **Division Play-Offs** to the postseason to go with the realignment into three divisions in each league.

After division play began in 1969, the second-best teams (at least that bad) in each league (based on won-lost record), have met in the World Series in 1969, 1970, 1971, 1976, 1978, 1979, 1982, 1986, 1997, 2000 (4th and 5th best in each league), 2001 and 2002 (4th and 3rd).

Best Game. Game 6 of the 1986 NLCS between the Mets and Astros may have been the greatest LCS game ever played. The Mets held a 3–2 series lead going into the game in Houston and wanted to close it out so they would not have to face the league's best pitcher in Game 7, Mike Scott.

Astros pitcher Bob Knepper held a 3–0 lead going into the 9th inning, but the Mets tied the game. In the 14th inning, the Mets pushed across a run, but Houston's Billy Hatcher tied the game with a lead-off home run in the bottom of the inning. In the 16th inning the Mets scored three times, but the Astros were not dead yet. In the bottom of the 16th, the Astros scored two runs and had the tying run at third base when reliever Jesse Orosco struck out Kevin Bass to end the game. See also Jerry Izenberg, *The Greatest Game Ever Played* (1987).

Comebacks.

1972 ALCS. On October 11, 1972, the Tigers played the A's in Game 4 of the five-game ALCS. The A's were leading 2–1 in games and could clinch with a win that day. The game went to the 10th inning, when the A's scored two runs in the top of the inning. The Tigers came back with three runs in the bottom of the inning to send the series to a fifth and final game. Despite the heroics, the Tigers lost 2–1 in Game 5.

1986 ALCS. Perhaps the best comeback came in the ALCS in 1986 between the Red Sox and Angels. In Game 4 of the seven-game series, the Angels scored three runs in the 9th inning and won it in the 11th to take a 3–1 series lead. In the 9th inning the next day, the Angels were one strike away from winning the first pennant in franchise history when Dave Henderson of the Red Sox hit a dramatic two-out, two-run homer that eventually led to a Boston victory that day. The Red Sox swept the last two games of the series in Boston to take the pennant. See also Mike Sowell, *One Pitch Away* (1995).

1988 NLCS. In Game 4 of the 1988 NLCS at Shea Stadium, the Mets had a chance to go ahead 3–1 in games when Doc Gooden was cruising against the Dodgers with a two-run lead going into the 9th inning. He had given up only three singles, none of them after the 4th inning. In the 9th inning he walked John Shelby. Dodger catcher Mike Scioscia, who had hit three home runs all season, hit a two-run homer to tie the game and Kirk Gibson hit an extra-inning home run to win the game and tie the series. The Dodgers went on to win it in seven games, preventing a World Series match-up of two 100-win teams (A's and Mets). Gibson hit another dramatic home run in Game 1 of the World Series off Dennis Eckersley.

2003 NLCS. The 2003 Marlins came back from a 3–1 deficit to beat the Cubs in seven games and go on to win the World Series (see **Best Series**).

Best Series. Creating a ratings bonanza for Fox Sports, the two 2003 LCS featured the Cubs/Marlins and Yankees/Red Sox in what lived up to the expected drama surrounding the perpetually futile Cubs and Red Sox. Both series went seven games, both had controversy, both featured bad late-inning managing by the Cubs and Red Sox (failure to bring in relievers soon enough), and both ended dramatically.

2003 ALCS.

"KA-BOONE!"— Headline in the *New York Post* when Aaron Boone ended the 2003 ALCS with an extra-inning home run to beat the Red Sox and send the Yankees to the World Series. Boone hit the first pitch of the 11th inning off knuckleballer Tim Wakefield in Game 7. This was after the Yankees had closed a three-run 8th inning deficit. With one out in the 8th, Derek Jeter hit a double to right and Bernie Williams hit a two-strike single to center, scoring Jeter to make the score 5–3.

Red Sox starter Pedro Martinez was clearly tired and ready to come out, but manager Grady Little left him in after a mound conference. Hideki Matsui hit an 0–2 pitch down the right field line for another double, moving Williams to third. Still, Martinez didn't come out. Jorge Posada hit a two-run double and the game was tied. The Boone blow prompted another headline in the *Philadelphia Daily News*: "Curse of the BOONE-BINO!"

2003 NLCS. The Marlins came back from a 3–1 series deficit to the Cubs to set up one of the most dramatic seventh games in LCS history. Game 6 featured the fan interference that helped push the Cubs to defeat (see ***Interference—Fans***).

W.P. Kinsella, who authored the book that was the basis for the movie *Field of Dreams*, once wrote a short story about the Cubs needing one win to clinch the National League pennant. The catch was that the world would end if the Cubs won. Not to worry, as the 2003 Cubs saved the world from extinction when poor decision-making by manager Dusty Baker led to a Marlins victory in Game 7 of the NLCS. Starter Kerry Wood labored in the 5th inning and gave up three runs (after a three-run homer against him in the 1st inning by Miguel Cabrera). Wood hit better than he pitched, belting a two-run homer in the 2nd inning to tie the game.

Book. G. Richard McKelvey, *Fisk's Homer, Willie's Catch and the Shot Heard Round the World: Classic Moments from Postseason Baseball, 1940–1996* (1998); Robert Obojski, *Great Moments of the Playoffs and World Series* (1988).

League Protective Players Association (1900–1903)

This attempt at a ***Union*** was in response to the National League's abusive treatment of players while it still had a monopoly on Major League play. It was also known as the Players Protective Association.

Leagues

"The country of baseball begins to take shape at the age of six.... Little League starts at six and stickball and cowpastureball at about the same age. At seven and eight and nine, the players begin to reside wholly in the country of baseball. For the people who will live there forever, the long summers take on form — time and space shaped by the sharp lozenge of the base paths. Then high school; maybe college, maybe rookie league, Class A, Double A, Triple A — the major leagues."— Donald Hall in *Dock Ellis in the Country of Baseball* (1976).

See also ***Major Leagues***, ***Minor Leagues*** and ***Negro Leagues***, entries for individual Major Leagues, attempts at Major Leagues and selected minor leagues, as well as various foreign leagues, amateur adult leagues, and youth leagues such as ***Little League Baseball*** and ***Pony League***.

The Patriot League is the mythical mid–20th century baseball league that was the subject of Philip Roth's *The Great American Novel* (1973).

Left Fielders

"On the very first play of the game, Yastrzemski made an incredible diving, sliding catch by the left field line off Horace Clarke's bat, rolled over and held the glove aloft. Now in the old days Jimmy Doyle from East Boston would've been yelling '*Atta boy, Carl Baby*' in his booming foghorn voice, a voice so loud that even in the middle of 35,000 fans Yaz would've heard him. But the ovation from the bleachers was only polite applause by comparison. '*That was a pretty nice catch,*' commented one of the kids behind me."— George Kimball in "Opening Day at Fenway" (1973).

"I felt alone out there, like I was on a desert island. I felt like Gilligan."— Mickey Rivers' response to playing left field for the first time.

Greatest.

"Being erect for the better part of a baseball game isn't that draining. And let's face it: We've seen Bonds play defense lately. Some solar-powered cars burn more energy."— Stephen Cannella on Barry Bonds, among the greatest for his hitting (see also, Ted Williams).

The greatest left fielders of all time are considered to be Ted Williams, Stan Musial, Carl Yastrzemski, Ralph Kiner, Willie Stargell, Rickey Henderson and Barry Bonds.

Pedigree. Between 1939 and 1980 the Red Sox had a virtually unbroken line of three left fielders: Ted Williams (1939–1960, except for years lost to military service), Carl Yastrzemski (1961–1974, with occasional years primarily at first base) and Fred Lynn (1975–1980).

Revolving Door. During his first eight seasons in Seattle, center fielder Ken Griffey, Jr., played alongside 46 different left fielders.

Phrase. The phrase, "he's out in left field," derives from Chicago's West Side Grounds of the 19th century. There was a mental institution next to the left field fence of the ballpark, which the Cubs occupied from 1893 through 1915.

Left-Handers

"Just because I'm left-handed and quotable doesn't mean I'm from another solar system."—Cardinals pitcher Joe Magrane.

"Left-handers have more enthusiasm for life. They sleep on the wrong side of the bed, and their head gets more stagnant on that side."—Casey Stengel.

"That felt good. I hadn't hit off a lefty in two months."—Mickey Rivers' post-game comment after hitting a double off Red Sox right-hander Bob Stanley.

"There ain't a left-hander in the world that could run a straight line. It's the gravitational pull on the axis of the earth that gets 'em."—Orioles pitching coach Ray Miller.

"Michael was left-handed and moved with that peculiar grace that left-handers always seemed to Federov to have in all sports. There had never been a left-hander before in Federov's family, nor in his wife's family that he knew of, and Federov sometimes wondered at this genetic variance and took it as a mark of distinction, a puzzling designation, though whether for good or ill he could not say."—Irwin Shaw in *Voices of a Summer Day* (1965).

"You are a lefthander, Henry. You always was. And the world needs all the lefthanders it can get, for it is a righthanded world. You are a southpaw in a starboarded atmosphere. Do you understand?"—From *The Southpaw*, by Mark Harris (1953).

"Man is naturally right-handed, and for that reason the right side of the body is always more fully developed and better able to stand a constant strain than the left side. What is more, a left-handed man may be regarded somewhat in the light of a freak, an unusual thing in nature. Also the swing of the left side is more likely to affect the heart than similar motions with the right side."—1892 newspaper article by a Dr. Burton, who concluded that left-handed pitchers have shorter careers than right-handed pitchers. It has been written that left-handed hitters in the earliest years of baseball were converted to right-handers, but the facts do not seem to support this. Nevertheless, left-handers were a scarce commodity in the 19th and early 20th centuries, reflecting the general bias against that persuasion.

Left-Handed Infielders. Hal Chase played 36 games at second base between 1905 and 1916.

Wee Willie Keeler played second base, third base and shortstop 71 times over his 19-year career.

Bill Hulen of the 1896 Phillies played 73 games at shortstop and two at second base in his only season with the club.

Baltimore Orioles third baseman and Hall of Famer Brooks Robinson was a natural left-hander except in the infield and at the plate.

Don Mattingly played four games at second base and third base despite being left-handed.

A teenaged Babe Ruth sports a left-handed catcher's mitt as he talks with his pitcher during a game.

Left-Handed Catchers.

Jack Clements caught over 1,000 Major League games between 1884 and 1900.

Pop Tate played 202 games at catcher, primarily for the 1880s Boston Red Stockings of the National League.

Fergy Malone caught a total of 21 games for the 1876 Philadelphia Athletics of the National League and the 1884 Philadelphia Keystones of the Union Association. He played no Major League Baseball in between.

Joe Wall caught seven games for the Giants and Dodgers in 1901–1902.

Tom Doran caught 46 games for the Red Sox and Tigers in 1904–1906.

First baseman Dale Long was a late-inning replacement at catcher for the Cubs on August 20, 1958. Regular catchers Sammy Taylor and Cal Neeman were already out of the game. Long came in with one out in the 9th inning and used his first baseman's glove behind the plate. He managed to pick off a runner at first base. He also caught during a game on September 21 of that year.

Long's catching was the residue of a failed experiment by him and Branch Rickey of the Pirates in the mid–1950s. Rickey purchased two left-handed catcher's mitts for Long to test whether left-handers might excel at the position. Rickey later supposedly said that left-handers could not throw a straight ball because of their "crooked arms."

Mike Squires was the last left-hander to catch in the American League. Normally a first baseman, he replaced Bruce Kimm for the White Sox late in games on May 4 and 7, 1980. He also played third base once in 1983 and 13 times in 1984.

On May 14, 1989, Benny Distefano of the Pirates caught left-handed in the 9th inning of a 5–2 loss to the Braves. He also caught two more times that season.

Babe Ruth began as a left-handed catcher using a right-handed mitt at St. Mary's School in Baltimore.

Percentage of Pitchers.

"Mike Caldwell, the Padres' right-handed southpaw, will pitch for San Diego tonight."—Jerry Coleman.

"Grimm Sends Prim to Trim Cards' Vim"—Headline in the *Stars and Stripes* military newspaper as Cubs manager Charlie Grimm sent left-handed pitcher Ray Prim to beat the Cardinals late in the Cubs' pennant-winning 1945 season.

Of the 52 National League pitchers in 1900, only 9, or 17%, were left-handers. In 1981, 21% of all National League pitchers were left-handed, compared to 36% in 1986.

See also **Relief Pitchers**—Left-Handed.

Starting Rotation. On April 9, 2004, the Royals made history when they started Jimmy Gobble to become the first team to start left-handed pitchers in its first four games of the season.

Most Wins Left-Handed. Warren Spahn won 363 games, the most all-time by a left-hander. He probably would have gone well over 400 wins had he not lost time to military service. He did not win his first game in the Major Leagues until age 25 in 1946 after appearing in a few games for the Braves in 1942.

Shortstops/Left-Handed Hitters. There have been only five Major League shortstops who have batted only left-handed for at least 1,000 games or 10 years: Arky Vaughan (1932–1948), Craig Reynolds (1975–1989), Joe Sewell (1920–1933) (although one source reported it as his catcher/brother Luke), Al Bridwell (1905–1915) and Arthur Irwin (1880–1894).

Injury. Pitcher Max Lanier (lifetime 108–82) was a left-hander only because he twice broke his right arm as a boy.

Batting Average. A 1946 statistical analysis revealed that left-handed batters had an 18-point advantage in batting average.

Oddity. Hal Chase was the only batting champion to bat right-handed and throw left-handed. He won the title with the Reds in 1916 with a .339 batting average.

Best Hitters. The best left-handed hitters have been Ty Cobb, George Sisler, Babe Ruth, Lou Gehrig, Charlie Gehringer, Ted Williams and Barry Bonds.

500 Home Runs. The left-handers who have hit 500 home runs (not including switch hitters Mickey Mantle and Eddie Murray): Babe Ruth, Mel Ott, Eddie Mathews, Ted Williams, Willie McCovey, Reggie Jackson, Barry Bonds, Rafael Palmeiro and Ken Griffey, Jr.

Left on Base

"It was Meet the Marlins Night."—Phillies first baseman John Kruk after the Marlins stranded 17 runners in a 1993 game.

"We set the table, but no one ate."—Rangers manager Johnny Oates after his team left 14 runners on base in an 8–3 loss to Oakland.

"We've been getting no hits when we got somebody on. Very aggravating. Well, I guess it's better to have somebody left on than not getting on at all."—Casey Stengel.

"In baseball, the journey begins at home, negotiates the twists and turns at first, and often founders far out at the edges of the ordered world at rocky second—the farthest point from home. Whoever remains out there is said to 'die' on base. Home is finally beyond reach in a hostile world full of quirks and tricks and hostile folk. There are no dragons in baseball, only shortstops, but they can emerge from nowhere to cut one down."—A. Bartlett Giamatti in *Take Time for Paradise* (1989).

Major League Record. On June 6, 1991, in a game that lasted 18 innings and 6 hours and 20 minutes, the Rangers lost 4–3 to the Royals. The Rangers set an American League record with 25 players left on base. The clubs tied the Major League record of 45 men left on base. The teams combined for 29 hits, 24 base on balls, three errors and one double play. Each club used seven pitchers.

National League Record. On September 8, 1905, the Pirates stranded a National League record 18 runners in an 8–3 loss to the Reds.

Postseason. The Braves left a record 19 men on base in an extra inning National League Championship Series game against the Mets on October 17, 1999. The Mets won 4–3 on a **Grand Slam**/single by Robin Ventura.

Shutout Loss. The record for most runners left on base in a shutout loss is 16, by the Cardinals against the Phillies in a 4–0 loss on May 24, 1994. On May 7, 1998, the Mariners tied the record by stranding 16 in a shutout by the Blue Jays.

The previous American League record was 15 by the A's against the Tigers in 1975. The previous National League record was 14, set by the Phillies against the Expos in 1971.

Batter. On August 10, 1901, batter Frank Isbell of the White Sox set a record by stranding 11 runners on base.

Legends

"Baseball's legends are, in some ways, the most enduring part of the game. Baseball has even more of them than the Civil War, and its fans prize them highly."—Civil War historian Bruce Catton.

Bob Lemon (1920–2000)

Hall of Fame 1976

"Today he's in the Hall of Fame, because he could throw a curve ball better than he could hit one."—Bob Feller.

The former outfielder won 20 or more games seven times for the Indians in the late 1940s and 1950s.

California native Robert Granville Lemon began his professional career in 1938 and played briefly as a third baseman for the Indians in 1941 and 1942. He lost three years to the war and returned to the Indians as a pitcher in 1946. He was 4–5 with a 2.49 ERA and had enough to be kept around for another season. He was 11–5 in 1947 and then began a string of three straight seasons with 20 or more wins.

After an off-season in 1951 Lemon again won more than 20 games in three straight seasons. He led the league in 1955 with 18 wins and once again won 20 games in 1956. During his nine prime seasons he pitched 30 shutouts. He faded in 1957 to 6–11 and ended his Major League career in 1958. He went to the Pacific Coast League briefly, winning two games for the Padres.

Lemon finished with a 207–128 Major League record and a .618 winning percentage. He pitched a no-hitter in 1948, the same season in which he had 10 shutouts. He won two games in the 1948 World Series but lost two in the 1954 Series. Lemon was one of the best-hitting pitchers of all time with a .232 average and 37 home runs. He was used frequently as a pinch hitter.

Lemon scouted for the Indians in 1959 and then coached for the Indians and Phillies before managing Hawaii in the Pacific Coast League in 1964. He coached in the Major and minor leagues until he was named to manage the Royals in mid–1970. He was fired after the 1972 season (with a best finish of second in 1971) and then managed the White Sox in 1977 and part of 1978. The White Sox won 90 games in 1977, good for third place, but Lemon was fired in 1978 when the club was 34–40. He took over the turmoil-ridden Yankees in mid–1978 and guided the then-third-place club to a World Series win over the Dodgers. He managed the Yankees for parts of the 1979, 1981 and 1982 seasons before returning to the coaching box. He had a .516 winning percentage as a Major League manager. He died in 2000 in Long Beach, California.

Length of Games

"By its nature, the watching of baseball appeals most strongly to imaginative people. The average major league games last approximately two hours and forty-five minutes. There is action for perhaps fifteen minutes of that time. The rest is either inaction or suspense, depending on imagination and point of view." — Roger Kahn in an article entitled "Intellectuals and Ballplayers" (1957).

"A critic once characterized baseball as six minutes of action crammed into two-and-one-half hours." — Columnist Ray Fitzgerald of the *Boston Globe*.

"There is, indeed, no agreement at all as to what baseball's greatest single virtue may be.... An ex-ballplayer said he liked the game chiefly because it had no clock to regulate its duration of play." — Sportswriter Charles Einstein in the preface to *The Fireside Book of Baseball* (1956).

"The home plate ump shall have a button. If a batter takes more than thirty seconds to adjust his uniform, tighten his batting glove, wiggle his toe, call for time and otherwise delay the game, the ump shall push the button. The button will open a trapdoor to a pit, full of reptiles, under the batter's box. This shall be known as the Rickey Henderson Hole, in honor of the potential Hall of Famer whose career was tragically cut short." — Thomas Boswell in *The Heart of the Order* (1989).

"The high strike will speed up the game? You want to speed up the game, here's how you speed up the game: No DH and no scratching below the waist." — Bob Hille.

"Any time I got those bang-bang plays at first base, I called them out. It made the game shorter." — Umpire Tom Gorman.

"[The pitcher] turns the ball around in his hand six times, wipes his forehead with his right hand, pulls a kink out of the seat of his pants, pulls out his handkerchief and wipes the sweat off his eyes, turns and asks what time it is, lays the ball between his feet, pats both his hands in the dust, wipes the dust off on his trousers, licks the ends of his fingers, pitches the ball over his left shoulder, absorbs a little more dust with his palms, tells the boys to look out, and pitches the ball. James Galvin is death to weak-nerved people." — The *Cincinnati Enquirer* in1879 on pitcher James "Pud" Galvin.

See also **Fastest Games** and **Longest Games**.

Average Length.

"Prohibit pitchers who reach base from asking for, receiving or being fitted for jackets. Not only does this ridiculous drama require delivery from the dugout, but the guy who brings it out, sensing his opportunity, always stays long enough to help the pitcher on with it rather than hand him the thing. He stops short of buttoning the thing and giving the pitcher a kiss on the cheek." — *Pittsburgh Post-Gazette* sportswriter Gene Collier's suggestion for speeding up the game.

19th Century. In Charles Peverelly's 1867 baseball book, he indicated that games were usually played in 2 hours and 30 minutes or less, more time than most sources report for that era. In 1892 Wilbert Robinson had seven hits in a 25–4 win that was played in 1 hour and 50 minutes.

1920s. Through the 1920s games were expected to take 1 hour and 30 minutes or 1 hour and 45 minutes. Anything more than 2 hours and 30 minutes was considered far too long. It has been reported that American League president Ban Johnson had a standing order early in the 20th century that for any game exceeding two hours, the umpire was required to submit an explanation. Note that early game times were rounded to the nearest five minutes in the box scores and daily records.

1930s. For a short time in the 1930s the American League

offered a cash prize to umpires with the lowest average completed game time. Bill Dinneen won, but the league office soon realized that the pitcher generally controlled the time of the game, not the umpire.

1940s–1970s. In 1943 the average game time was 1 hour and 58 minutes. In 1955 it was 2 hours and 31 minutes. Game 7 of the 1960 World Series, which the Pirates won 10–9 in 10 innings, took only 2 hours and 36 minutes. In 1977 American League games averaged 2 hours and 31 minutes and National League games 2 hours and 25 minutes. There was actually a drop in the length of games during the 1950s and early 1960s, which gave way to dramatic increases in the following decades.

1990s. In 1991 American League games lasted an average of 2 hours and 52 minutes, up 15 minutes over the prior 10 years. In 1992 a number of teams averaged over three hours, led by the ultra-slow Oakland A's. National League games averaged 2 hours and 46 minutes in 1991, up nine minutes from 1982 and 21 minutes from 1978. In 1992 American League games averaged 2 hours 53 minutes. National League games averaged 2 hours and 45 minutes. A number of factors may have contributed to the increase:

1) There are more commercials between innings, an average of 30 seconds longer;

2) There are more pitching changes in the era of fewer complete games;

3) Designated hitters mean more hitting, which means innings take longer;

4) Batters have become notorious for taking too much time between pitches;

5) Umpires are not enforcing the rule requiring a pitcher to deliver a pitch within 20 seconds when there is no one on base;

6) Umpires are not calling the high strike as required by the rules, which lengthens pitch counts;

7) The number of pick-off throws has increased.

1993 Goals.

"It's like cutting two pages from *War and Peace*." — Steven Rosenbloom of the *Chicago Sun-Times* on the one-minute reduction in the length of 1993 games.

"The games are so lengthy that CBS assigned the husband-and-wife team of Dick Stockton and Lesley Visser to the same series so that they could spend more quality time together." — Norman Chad in *Sports Illustrated* on the incredibly long 1993 postseason games. His other comment: "CBS's telecasts are starting to resemble telethons. The two-hour baseball game has gone the way of the doubleheader. (If teams still scheduled doubleheaders, they would have to include overnight accommodations as part of the ticket package.)"

In 1993 Major League Baseball set a goal of reducing game time by 20 minutes. Official guidelines called for batters to stay in the box, pitchers to work more quickly, catchers to cut the number of trips to the mound, managers to call for new pitchers as soon as they leave the dugout and pinch hitters to get ready in the on-deck circle.

The new rules were first implemented in the Arizona Fall League, but some believed that they would be less successful in the Major Leagues because there was no television in the Fall League and the generally younger players were more amenable to changing their habits to speed up games.

Early in the 1993 Major League season games were about 12 minutes faster. By midseason, the margin was five minutes. The season-ending statistics revealed that the Major Leagues shaved a whopping one minute off a nine-inning game — the American League from 2 hours and 53 minutes to 2 hours and 52 minutes;

the National League from 2 hours and 45 minutes to 2 hours and 44 minutes.

Sixteen teams played more quickly that year, led by the Indians with a nine-minute drop. The Tigers were the slowest at 3 hours and 4 minutes, including a nine-inning game that lasted 4 hours and 12 minutes against the Blue Jays, the **Longest Game** of nine innings in Major League history until 1996.

Matters worsened in 1994 and early 1995. In response, the Rules Committee adopted plans to speed up games by doing the following:

1. Raising the pitching mound to 12 or 13 inches from 10 inches;
2. Allowing pitchers to go to their mouths while on the mound;
3. Directing umpires to call the high strike.

2000s. Games in 2000 reached an all-time high of 2 hours and 58 minutes. The average dropped the next three seasons to a low of 2 hours and 46 minutes in 2003, the fastest average since 1989.

World Series/ First Three and Four Hour Games. The first three-hour World Series game was played in 1914. Game 3 was 12 innings and 3 hours and 6 minutes as Joe Bush of the A's went all the way but lost to the Braves 5–4.

The first three-hour nine-inning game was Game 3 of the 1947 World Series, when the Dodgers beat the Yankees 9–8 in 3 hours and 5 minutes.

The first four-hour nine-inning game was Game 2 of the 1973 Series, when the Yankees beat the A's 10–7 in 4 hours and 13 minutes. A record 116 batters came to the plate and this was the game that prompted A's owner Charles Finley to "fire" error-prone second baseman Mike Andrews (see **Disabled List—Unfair Treatment**).

Minor Leagues. In 1993 minor league games averaged 2 hours and 39 minutes, compared to 2 hours and 48 minutes in 1992. The longest games were in Class AAA (2:43) and the shortest games were in the Rookie Leagues (2:38) and Class A (2:37).

New College Rule. In 1994 college baseball attempted to speed things up by requiring batters to keep one foot in the batter's box between pitches. If the batter left the box he was assessed a strike.

Bad Influence. Catcher Carlton Fisk single-handedly added significant time to a game. The Elias Sports Bureau analyzed games in which he played in 1992 and determined that Fisk games averaged 3 hours and 1 minute. Games started by other White Sox catchers averaged 2 hours and 49 minutes. His mound conferences added at least 10 additional minutes to the game.

Actual Playing Time.

"Baseball provides far more time for disputation *during* the game than any sport. What other game could brag that it offers *discontinuous action?"*—Thomas Boswell in *How Life Imitates the World Series* (1982).

In 1994 a Seattle television station began a one-hour series featuring the day's Mariners game called "Mariners Fast Forward." The telecast featured the entire game, including each pitch, edited to 44 minutes and 50 seconds (not including commercials). The concept prompted this comment from *Sports Illustrated*: "'Fast Forward' is not perfect.... Still, if you've got only an hour, watching Ken Griffey Jr. bat five times beats the heck out of back-to-back episodes of 'Three's Company.'"

In 2002 Major League Baseball launched Condensed Games, which allowed fans to watch a shortened version of the previous day's games for a $4.95 seasonal fee. The games were reduced to eight minutes by showing the final pitch of each at-bat. The service attracted 130,000 subscribers, although Fox complained bitterly because it claimed the service was undermining television viewership. Its ratings were up slightly for the year, however.

Buck Leonard (1907–1997)

Hall of Fame (NLC) 1972

"Leonard hit pitchers like a tropical storm. With a strong turbulent stroke, he uprooted pitchers, knocked down fielders and destroyed teams from town to town. A powerful pull-hitter, Buck was a torrential terror at the plate."—Dick Clark and Larry Lester in *The Negro Leagues Book* (1994).

"You'd have to throw the ball 200 m.p.h. to get it by Buck. Ain't no doubt about it, Buck was a dude. Bad as you can get."—Negro Leaguer Connie Johnson.

Leonard was a star first baseman in the Negro Leagues primarily in the 1930s and 1940s.

North Carolina native Walter Fenner Leonard played in the Negro Leagues from 1933 through 1953 for the Baltimore Stars, Brooklyn Giants and most prominently for the Homestead Grays. He also played in Organized Baseball for 10 games in the Piedmont League for Portsmouth in 1953, batting .333.

A left-handed 5'10" first baseman for the Grays for 17 seasons, Leonard teamed with Josh Gibson to power the club to nine straight Negro National League championships from 1937 through 1945. He also helped the club to another championship at age 40 in 1948.

The available statistics show batting averages of over .400 two times and over .300 10 times. He played in the Mexican Leagues and retired with an unofficial batting average of .324. In seven recorded exhibition games against Major League pitchers he hit .421.

Bill Veeck tried to sign him at age 40 to play for the Indians, but Leonard considered himself too old and declined the offer. He later helped form a minor league club in the Class A Carolina League in the 1960s and served as a vice-president of the club.

Book. Buck Leonard and James A. Riley, *Buck Leonard: The Black Lou Gehrig* (1995).

Libraries

"You could look it up."—Caption on a portrait of Casey Stengel at the entrance to the research facilities at the National Baseball Library. The phrase originally came from Doc, manager Squawks Magrew's pal, in a 1941 James Thurber story in the *Saturday Evening Post*.

"Without libraries what have we? We have no past and no future."—Ray Bradbury.

"On this date in 1978 [February 25], it was announced that a junior high school in Lindsay, California, had been renamed after Steve Garvey.... If that isn't insane (or inane) enough for you, the school's library was named for Tom Lasorda, the Dodgers' manager, possibly in the belief that Tom has read a book."—Art Hill in *I Don't Care If I Never Come Back* (1980).

National Baseball Library. The largest collection of baseball books is housed in the National Baseball Library, located in the research facility next door to the baseball Hall of Fame in Cooperstown. The Library has over 19,000 baseball books and over five million newspaper articles and papers.

National Library of Sports. The National Library of Sports is located in the San Jose Public Library.

Library of Congress.

"Finally, my father, who worked at the Library of Congress, smuggled me into the off-limits-to-the-public stacks. There in a musty corridor of deck 29 with GV862 overhead, my father said those fateful words, 'Okay. Here is every book on baseball ever written. Don't go blind.'"—Thomas Boswell in *How Life Imitates the World Series* (1982). The Library of Congress contains the Branch Rickey papers on integration and the papers of sportswriter Arthur Mann on integration. The library also contains a number of other collections of baseball writings.

New York. The New York Public Library houses the Albert Spalding Collection of Historical Data and the original scrapbooks and diaries of Spalding, Henry Chadwick and Harry Wright. In 1921 Spalding's widow donated over 3,000 books and other materials to the library. The original pages from the New York Knickerbockers' "first game" scorebook were stolen from the library in approximately 1983.

Cleveland. The Cleveland Public Library has over 2,000 player biographies, the largest public collection in the country.

Chicago. The Chicago Public Library has many of the papers of Chicago White Stockings owner Albert G. Spalding and National League founder and White Stockings owner William Hulbert.

Detroit. The Detroit Public Library houses the Burton Historical and Ernie Harwell Collections, which cover the Detroit Tigers and broadcast history.

Japan. The Japanese Hall of Fame contains over 30,000 volumes, including a number of important early American baseball books.

Licensing   See *Logos/Licensing* and *Merchandising*

Lightning   See *Weather*

Lights   See *Night Games—Lights*

Fred Lindstrom (1905–1981)

Hall of Fame (VC) 1976

"We didn't need someone hitting us over the head to keep us in shape. In fact, we wouldn't take it—at least [Bill] Terry and I wouldn't. I don't think [Giants manager John] McGraw was able to adapt his methods of handling his men. On the field, yes, he adapted to the lively ball; but he wasn't able to cope with the more modern-style players. And after 1924 he never won another pennant."—Lindstrom quoted in *Voices from Cooperstown*, by Anthony J. Connor (1982).

Lindstrom played third base primarily for the New York Giants in the 1920s.

Frederick Charles Lindstrom made his Major League debut with the Giants in 1924 after a brief minor league career. At age 18 he played in 52 games for the Giants in the infield, batting .253. He played seven games in the World Series, becoming the youngest player ever to appear in the Series. He experienced a famous **Bad Hop** incident in the Series that led to the Senators scoring the winning run in Game 7 to clinch the championship.

In 1925 Lindstrom became the Giants' regular third baseman, hitting over .300 from 1926 through 1930. His best year was 1928 when he batted .358 and led the league with 231 hits. He moved to the outfield in 1931 after suffering back problems. He was miffed that he did not succeed John McGraw as manager in 1932 and asked to be traded. He was traded to the Pirates and batted .310 in 138 games.

He moved on to the Cubs in 1935 and appeared in four World Series games that season, batting .200 in the postseason. He played in 26 games for the Dodgers in 1936 and then retired at only 30 years old. He finished with a .311 lifetime average over 13 seasons, though he was a regular for only eight years.

Lindstrom managed in the minor leagues from 1940 through 1942 and then served as baseball coach at Northwestern University in the 1950s. He retired from the game to become a postmaster in Evanston, Illinois, and then moved to Florida in 1972.

Line-Up Cards/Line-Ups

"Willoughby and others."—Line-up card entry for the pitcher's spot by 1930 Phillies team captain Fresco Thompson when he took the card out to umpire Bill Klem. The designation for Jim Willoughby "and others" reflected the miserable state of pitching on the last-place club.

See also *Rosters*.

19th Century. In the 1880s, line-up cards were not required to be presented before the game. This allowed teams to change their **Batting Order** during the game. Eventually the home team was required to submit its line-up card first and now teams simultaneously exchange cards at home plate before a game.

Early Delivery. In the early part of the 20th century, managers often delivered their line-up cards to the sportswriters approximately 10 minutes before game time so that the afternoon papers could print them.

Burial. Chicago Cubs manager Charlie Grimm was coaching third base during an 8–0 loss. He was so disgusted with his team that he buried his line-up card in the coaching box dirt.

Error. On July 22, 1999, Indians manager Mike Hargrove presented an incorrect lineup card, which forced him to forfeit his designated hitter and bat pitcher Charles Nagy in the seventh spot in the order. Nagy failed to get a hit in two at-bats as the Indians lost 4–3 to the Blue Jays.

Multiple Lineups. In 2003 the Diamondbacks used 140 different lineups in their first 155 games.

Fan Advice. Casey Stengel once polled the fans on which line-up to use for one of his bad 1930s Brooklyn teams. Little did he know how bad it would get in the 1960s with the Mets.

Little League Baseball (1939–)

"Character, Courage, Loyalty."—The Little League motto.

"I think it's wonderful. It keeps the kids out of the house."—Yogi Berra on Little League Baseball.

"For the parents of Little Leaguers, a baseball game is simply a nervous breakdown divided into innings."—Columnist Earl Wilson.

Formation and Expansion. Little League Baseball began in 1939 in Williamsport, Pennsylvania, and soon moved into New Jersey. In the first game in the three-team league in Williamsport, on June 7, 1939, Lundy Lumber defeated Lycoming Dairy 23–8. The first Little League pitch was thrown by Lundy Lumber's Frank Sipe, who died in December 2002 at age 74.

Though there is some confusion as to its origins, Little League apparently was founded by Carl Stoltz, probably along with brothers George and Bert Bepples. Each coached one of the three original teams. In 1955 Stoltz became estranged from the National headquarters in a dispute over the exact origins of Little League. Stoltz died in 1992, having never reconciled with the organization.

International expansion began during the 1960s. By the 1980s there were 14,000 leagues around the world, covering 145,000 teams and 2.25 million kids in 30 countries (half of them in the U.S.). By 1990 the worldwide total had increased to 2.5 million, with leagues in 60 countries. It expanded to three million and 91 countries by 1995, a figure that held steady into the 2000s.

The author at age eight in 1965 (top right among players), the youngest and near-worst Little Leaguer on the 1–9 Pirates. In the 1950s, the same Van Nuys–Sherman Oaks Little League was home to television star Tom Selleck, who is now in the Little League Hall of Fame.

President. Creighton Hale served as Little League president for 16 years through the 1980s. He is credited by some with inventing the modern **Batting Helmet**, although he may have invented only the ear flap.

Girls.

"Girls are expected to play with dolls. We don't have that much experience playing baseball, but that doesn't mean we can't. I haven't played with dolls since I was seven years old."—Jenny Fulle, who unsuccessfully fought for the right to play Little League Baseball in the early 1970s.

"We have medical facts to back up our conclusion that it would be improper for girls to play Little League Baseball."—Little League official Creighton Hale.

In 1974 girls were allowed to compete in Little League for the first time, but only after court challenges brought the issue to a head. In 1972 the National Organization for Women (N.O.W.) filed a successful lawsuit against the Hoboken, New Jersey, Little League. In response, on December 26, 1974, the federal charter for Little League was changed to refer to "young people" instead of "boys." The subject of the suit, Maria Pepe, threw out the first pitch of the 2004 Little League World Series in Williamsport. For the first time that year, two teams had a girl on their World Series rosters.

The suit polarized many parents and teams, resulting in some leagues folding rather than admit girls. However, the flap soon subsided and girls began competing regularly.

Krissy Wendell was the first American girl to play on a Little League World Series team. She was the starting catcher for the 1994 Brooklyn team. She went on to help the U.S. Olympic hockey team win a silver medal at the 2002 Games in Salt Lake City. Another source reported that the first of 10 girls to play in the Little League World Series was Victoria Roche, who played for Belgium in 1984.

It is estimated that approximately 8,000 girls play Little League today. This averages out to 28 girls for every 10,000 players. Over 350,000 girls now play Little League softball, however.

Little League World Series. This event began in 1947. All-Star teams from various international zones compete for spots in the finals in Williamsport, Pennsylvania, held in late summer each year. The **Taiwan** Little League teams for a time dominated the Little League World Series, winning 14 times in their first 21 years starting in 1968. In 1997 Taiwan dropped out of the competition and refused to defend its 1996 title. The move came after a dispute related to possible rule violations.

Segregation. In 1955 a black all-star team was sidelined by a racial boycott in South Carolina that reached all the way to the National tournament in Williamsport, Pennsylvania. That season the city of Charleston had its first Little League for black kids: four teams sponsored by a local YMCA. The local Little League leaders refused to schedule the postseason tournament because the black players would be facing white players. The boycott spread to the state tournament, whose 61 teams withdrew rather than face the Cannon Street All-Stars.

The state group requested a segregated tournament, but the national officials refused. The state's teams broke off from Little League and formed the Little Boys League (later changed to Dixie Youth Baseball, which now covers 390 leagues in eight Southern states).

The Cannon Street All-Stars were invited to be spectators at the Little League World Series but were not allowed to compete because their state tournament had been canceled.

Older Boy Leagues. Little League eventually expanded to include leagues for older boys: Junior Division for 13 year olds; Senior Majors for 13–15 year olds; and Big Leagues for 16–18 year olds. These leagues are not affiliated with the Babe Ruth, Colt and Pony Leagues which are part of *Boys Baseball*.

1992 Scandal.

"Let's see, we've got dirty secrets, conflicting stories, a whole cast of unsavory characters and more overheated media coverage than all of Elizabeth Taylor's marriages put together. [Hollywood madam] Heidi Fleiss? Forget her. It's the Little League World Series I'm talking about." — Columnist Ron Rappaport.

In 1992 a Philippine Little League team from Zamboanga won the Little League World Series. The players were from the poor southernmost island of the country and were paid a total of $40,000 (one million pesos) for the victory, as promised by President Fidel Ramos. After a local journalist raised the issue, it was soon discovered that the players were too old and the victory was forfeited. A few of his countrymen sarcastically awarded the journalist the "Tokyo Rose Award for the Achievement of a Lifetime in the area of Treason" for exposing the illegal activity [Tokyo Rose broadcast propaganda from Japan to Allied soldiers during World War II].

The losing team from Long Beach, California, was instead awarded the victory. Most of the Filipino boys were 14–15 years old, rather than the maximum of 12 years old allowed by Little League rules. Some of the Philippine boys had to use Nair or tweezers to eliminate telltale pubic hairs.

This was not the first scandal involving Philippine teams. In 1984 Pony Baseball banned Philippine teams from international play for three years after the discovery of overage players. For the 1993 Series, Little League authorities disqualified the Dominican Republic and Taiwan for rules violations in connection with overage players.

2001 Scandal. Danny Almonte was the tall pitcher for the victorious Bronx team in the August 2001 Little League World Series. He pitched a perfect game in the opener, struck out 46, and allowed only three hits over the series games. Shortly after the series ended, it was discovered that his coach and his father had conspired to hide the fact that Almonte's real birth certificate in the Dominican Republic showed that he was two years older than claimed — 14 instead of the required maximum of 12. Almonte, his coach, and his father were all banned from Little League coaching and playing after the incident. Apopka, Florida, was declared the default winner.

Sports Illustrated investigative reporters found evidence of two birth registrations for Almonte. The second took two years off and the change was made only a few weeks before the boy entered the United States. Protests of racism against Dominicans prompted further investigations, which showed that Almonte and other players did not even attend school in the Bronx, did not play the requisite number of games with their Bronx team, that their coach had been banned from Caribbean Little League play in 1988 for using overage players, and that Danny's older brother was 14 when he played in 2000.

By 2004 Almonte was a New York high school pitching star.

Perfect Game. Before Danny Almonte's since-stricken-from-the-record-books perfect game, Angel Macias of Monterrey, Mexico, pitched one in the 1957 championship game against La Mesa Northern, in California. The only other pitcher who did not allow a batter to reach base was Fred Shapiro of Delaware Township, New Jersey, in 1956.

Back-to-Back Winners. The 1992 Long Beach club won again in 1993 when the team defeated Panama 3–2. Some sources reported that it was the first team to win back-to-back championships. However, back-to-back titles were won by the 1957–1958 Monterrey, Mexico, team and the 1984–1985 team from Seoul, South Korea. The leader of the 1993 Long Beach team was Sean Burroughs, son of former Major League slugger Jeff Burroughs. Sean made it to the Major Leagues in 2002 as a third baseman for the Padres.

1994 and 1995 Winners. The 1994 World Series winner was Maracaibo, Venezuela, which won the country's first title. They beat a club from Northridge, California, in a tight 4–3 game. Taiwan was back in 1995 for its 16th title with a 17–3 win over a team from Texas.

2003. In 2003 the Japanese team won behind 5'5", 181-pound pitcher Yuutaro Tanaka. The Japanese won three of the past five series through that season.

Hall of Fame. Nolan Ryan was elected to the Little League Hall of Fame, as was television star Tom Selleck. Selleck was elected for his heroics in the Van Nuys–Sherman Oaks, California, Little League (also this author's Little League, though he was the youngest and near-worst player on a 1–9 team and was personally responsible for injuries to the two best players on the team).

Major League/Little League Players. The first future Major Leaguer to play Little League Baseball was Joey Jay, who broke in as a pitcher with the Braves in 1953. His Little League attempted to bar him from playing at age 12 because he was so big (he grew to be 6'4" and 228 lbs.). While in the Major Leagues he wrote an article entitled "Don't Trap Your Son in Little League Madness."

The first Major Leaguer to play in a Major League World Series after appearing in a Little League World Series was Boog Powell. He played for the Baltimore Orioles in 1966 and a Lakeland, Florida, Little League team in 1954. Also on that team was Billy Connors, who had an 0–2 Major League pitching record in three seasons in the 1960s.

Others to play in both the Little League and Major League World Series are Jim Barbieri (Schenectady, N.Y., and the 1966 Dodgers), Rick Wise (Portland, Oregon, and the 1975 Red Sox), and Carney Lansford (Santa Clara, California, and the 1988–1990 Oakland A's). When Barbieri and Schenectady played, the shortstop on the losing Colton, California, club was future Cubs second baseman Ken Hubbs (who was killed in a plane crash after his second full season).

More recently, Lloyd McClendon, Charlie Hayes, Gary Sheffield, Derek Bell, Jason Varitek, Wilson Alvarez and Dan Wilson each played in the Little League World Series. Sheffield and Bell were teammates in Florida in 1980 and 1981 and Bell is the only Major League player to play in two Little League World Series. At least 20 Little League World Series players have made it to the Major Leagues (including those from Asian countries).

Ed Vosberg is the only Major Leaguer to play in a Little League World Series (1973), College World Series (1980) and Major League World Series (1997).

Disability. *Standing Tall*, by Paul Harisim (1993), chronicles the story of Tucker Church, a boy suffering from cerebral palsy who initially was prohibited from playing Little League Baseball in Houston.

Sex Offenders. After a *Sports Illustrated* article highlighted the subject, Little League Baseball mandated that all adult participants had to be checked against a state's data bank of sex offenders.

Softball. In 1974, as part of the aftermath of litigation, Little League inaugurated softball leagues for different age groups.

Books. Gary A. Fine, *With the Boys: Little League Baseball and Preadolescent Culture* (1987); Harvey Frommer, *Growing Up at Bat: 50 Years of Little League Baseball* (1989); Bill Geist, *Little League Confidential: One Coach's Completely Unauthorized Tale of Survival* (1999); John Janovy, Jr., *Fields of Friendly Strife* (1987); Jay Newkirk, *Hey Batter: The Little League Season* (1986); Rick Wolff, *Good Sports: The Concerned Parent's Guide to Little League and Other Competitive Youth Sports* (1993).

Little World Series   See *Minor Leagues*

John Henry "Pop" Lloyd (1884–1965)

Hall of Fame (NLC) 1977

"Where the money was. That's where I was." — Lloyd's answer to why he played for so many teams.

"Lloyd is the Jekyll and Hyde of baseball — a fierce competitor on the field, but a gentle, considerate man off the field." — Homestead Grays owner Cum Posey.

"They called him 'The Black Wagner,' and I was anxious to see him play. Well, one day I had an opportunity to go see him play, and after I saw him I felt honored that they would name such a great player after me." — Honus Wagner.

Lloyd starred as probably the best Negro League shortstop of all time beginning in 1905.

Considered by many as the greatest player of all time, Lloyd began his professional career in 1905 and played 27 seasons through 1932. Primarily a shortstop, Lloyd was considered the equal of Honus Wagner by no less than Connie Mack, and the greatest player ever by Babe Ruth.

Lloyd played for 13 teams in the United States and three teams in 13 years in Cuba during the winter. His most important early seasons were with Sol White's Philadelphia Giants (1907–1909) and Rube Foster's Leland Giants in 1910. After three seasons with the Lincoln Giants he played with the Chicago American Giants, one of the most powerful teams of all time. He regularly hit well over .300 and was perennially the premier shortstop in any league or independent circuit in which he played. He moved to second base and then first base as he slowed down near the end of his career.

Lloyd moved to a number of teams through the 1920s until 1926, when he returned to the New York Lincoln Giants for five full seasons while in his 40s. Age did not seem to slow him down, as he won a batting title at age 44 with a .564 average. He is said to have played until age 58.

In the games recorded in *The Baseball Encyclopedia* he batted .353 lifetime. After he retired he played semipro ball and was a janitor in Atlantic City, New Jersey.

Lockers

"Termites." — Pitcher Danny Jackson explaining how his locker was destroyed after he had a bad outing.

"I like being closer to the bats." — Don Mattingly on why he moved his locker.

See also ***Clubhouses and Clubhouse Men***.

Sealed. When Lou Gehrig died, his locker was permanently sealed and is now on display at the Hall of Fame.

Publicity Stunt. To honor Cal Ripken's retirement, the Rangers retired a locker, complete with shrine, in their visitors' clubhouse at The Ballpark in Arlington.

Lockouts   See *Strikes and Lockouts*

Logos/Licensing

"The down-to-earth artist of the Texas Rangers paints the team logo [in the grass] in satisfied solitude, knowing that in a matter of hours his art will be appreciated by an audience larger than most painters ever achieve 'in a lifetime.'" — John Thorn in *The Game for All America* (1988).

Earliest Use. The earliest use of team symbols in professional baseball is claimed to be the 1876 skull and crossbones of a Massachusetts team and the Maple Leafs of the club in Guelph, Ontario.

Advocacy. As early as 1934 *The Sporting News* called for adoption of a Major League logo for advertising purposes.

New Logo. In 1970 Organized Baseball promoted its new logo, called "BannerMark," to be used by amateurs and professionals from Little League to the Major Leagues. It consisted of a red, white and blue pennant with a white ball with red stitching in the center (a continuous single red line to denote the stitching). The logo from the 1969 commemorative ***Postage Stamp*** was adopted instead. Some sources contend that the silhouette is that of former Twins slugger Harmon Killebrew, but there is no evidence of this and the commissioner's office has informally denied this claim. Nevertheless, Killebrew later contended that coincidentally he was in the commissioner's office when they created the logo and used him as the model.

Prohibited Logo. The only logo not allowed on a Major League uniform is a baseball.

Longest Continuous Use. The longest-used Major League insignia is the Yankees' bat and top hat design, which dates to the mid–1940s. The logo was created by Lon Keller, a Pennsylvania artist. It first appeared during spring training in 1947 and was on the cover of the World Series program that season.

The Cardinals have the longest-used National League logo, its redbird in a circle used only since 1971. Team logos were not official in the American League until 1955 and in the National League until 1967.

Licensing.

"I think I've been misrepresented throughout my career as a bad guy, a bad person. [There's a perception that] 'Barry doesn't want to do anything.' This [move] gives the licensees the opportunity to get to know me and know who I am as a person and show the fans I am not a difficult person to deal with, I am not a difficult person to the fans. This is the ending part of my career. I want the public to see me for who I really am." — Barry Bonds in late 2003, allegedly trying to clean up his image with fans during the "twilight" of his career, but with the new steroid use allegations (see ***Drugs***), he was just as surly as ever. As part of his new marketing strategy, he opted out of the Major League licensing program, from which each union member received $30,000 in 2002. He would then cut his own deals with licensees.

One source reported that during commissioner Peter Ueberroth's tenure from 1984 through 1989, Major League teams began charging a minimum of $1,000 to anyone who sold equipment bearing Major League team's logo. However, the Major League

Promotions Corporation has been controlling such use since 1969 (see also **Merchandising** for licensing revenue).

In 1997 Yankee owner George Steinbrenner signed his own $95 million licensing deal with Adidas over 10 years. Major League Baseball argued that the agreement violated the Major League Agreement in which Major League Baseball as a whole negotiates licensing deals. Steinbrenner sued on antitrust grounds, but later dropped the suit and cancelled his contract. Dallas Cowboys owner Jerry Jones made a similar deal in the NFL, and that league didn't try to block it.

The Steinbrenner deal came four months after Major League owners rejected a league-wide 10-year deal with Nike and Reebok. Nike chairman Phil Knight said that "baseball has screwed up" by allowing the Yankees to cut its own deal and said that Nike would not rush in to sign individual teams. Steinbrenner refused to provide Major League Baseball with a copy of his Adidas contract.

Colorado Rockies. When the Rockies unveiled their inaugural caps with "CR" embroidered on them in black and silver, the Carbonic Reserve dry-ice company complained unsuccessfully that it was almost identical to their insignia. Despite not yet having played a game, the Rockies were ninth among all Major League teams in 1992 merchandise sales nationwide.

Restrictions. The proliferation of successfully merchandised minor league team logos led a number of clubs in the 1990s to switch colors and logos rather routinely. This forced the National Association to institute a rule forcing clubs to remain with the same logo for a minimum of three years.

Bad Karma. The ground crew for the Red Sox painted the 2003 World Series logo on the Fenway Park grass on the day that the Yankees beat the Sox in extra innings in the ALCS to knock them out of the World Series.

Ernie Lombardi (1908–1977)

Hall of Fame (VC) 1986

"The fact that he was slow robbed him of plenty of hits. A triple for an ordinary batter is a double for Lombardi. Once he hit a ball against the center field fence at the 399 foot mark and was thrown out sliding into second." — Jimmy Powers in *Baseball Personalities* (1949).

The slow-footed Lombardi was one of the best-hitting catchers of all time when he played in the National League in the 1930s and 1940s.

Oakland native Ernesto Natali Lombardi began his professional career with the Oakland Oaks of the Pacific Coast League in 1927. After a brief stint with Ogden he was back with Oakland for three years until 1930. He was sold to the Brooklyn Dodgers, for whom he hit .297 in 73 games in 1931 while catching 50 games.

Lombardi was traded to the Reds for the 1932 season, when he hit .303. He peaked with a league-leading .342 in 1938, the only time a catcher has led the league in batting. He hit over .300 seven times for the Reds before the club traded him to the Braves in 1942. He won another batting title with a .330 average and then moved to the Giants. He batted over .300 twice in the next five seasons before being released late in 1947. He went back to Oakland and Sacramento in the Pacific Coast League in 1948.

Lombardi was as slow as any runner in the history of Major League Baseball, stealing eight bases in 17 seasons. However, his catching was strong and he was an outstanding hitter with a .306 lifetime average and 190 home runs. He batted .235 in six World Series games in 1939 and 1940.

Longest Careers

"The second revolution occurred just the other day, and if one had to put a name on it, I'd say Steve Carlton, with Nolan Ryan seconding. The sight of these two aging flamethrowers outliving their spans, like creatures in mythology, snapped baseball's head around on the subject of conditioning…. So perhaps the Nautilus people deserve a footnote of their own in the Baseball Encyclopedia for their contribution to that unheard-of phenomenon, the 40-year-old superstar." — Wilfrid Sheed in *The Face of Baseball* (1990).

See also **Oldest Active Players**.

27 Seasons. When Nolan Ryan pitched in 1993 it was his 27th season in the Major Leagues. He won one game before going on the disabled list with torn cartilage in his knee. He suffered a hip problem midseason and returned for a few more games before ending his career with ligament damage to his elbow late in the season.

If the National Association were to count as a Major League, Cap Anson played 27 seasons from 1871 through 1897.

26 Seasons. Tommy John and his bionic elbow pitched for 26 seasons in the Major Leagues from 1963 through 1989. He finished his career with 288 wins in exactly 700 starts, sixth all-time. See Tommy and Sally John, *Our Life in Baseball* (1983); Tommy John and Dan Valenti, *My 26 Years in Baseball* (1991).

25 Seasons. Bobby Wallace primarily played shortstop for the Cardinals and Browns for 25 years between 1894 and 1918. However, he played in only 63 games over the final four seasons for the two clubs.

Eddie Collins played second base for 25 years between 1906 and 1930, although he appeared in only 12 games and had one hit over the last two seasons.

Pitcher Jim Kaat won 283 games over 25 seasons from 1959 through 1983.

Rickey Henderson signed with the Dodgers in mid–2003 after spending the first part of the season with the Newark Bears of the independent Atlantic League, where he was among the league leaders. It was his ninth team in 25 Major League seasons. He was paid the Major League minimum $300,000 and had two home runs and five stolen bases in 30 games. Henderson returned to the Bears at age 45 during the 2004 season, hit well, but no Major League team picked him up.

24 Seasons. Ty Cobb played 24 seasons between 1905 and 1928, all but two of them for the Tigers.

Steve Carlton pitched for 24 years in the Major Leagues, winning 329 games from 1965 through 1988.

Pete Rose played 24 seasons in the National League starting in 1963. He played his last games in 1986 while a player-manager for the Reds but did not formally retire until midseason 1987 after playing no games that year. He played in 3,562 games, first all-time.

In 1992 Carlton Fisk reached 23 years in the Major Leagues at age 44. Amazingly, he was still the regular catcher for the White Sox for part of the season. He retired after 24 seasons in mid–1993 after passing Bob Boone's record for most games behind the plate.

Left-handed reliever and Santa Barbara native Jesse Orosco started his Major League career in 1979 with the Mets, but was back in the minors for the entire 1980 season. He retired after the 2003 season at age 46, having appeared in the most games of any pitcher in history, 1,252, all but four in relief. He was 87–80 with 144 saves and a career ERA of 3.16 with nine teams over 24 seasons.

23 Seasons. Jack Quinn won 247 games in his career and saved 57 in an era (1909–1933) when saves were far less frequent.

Rabbit Maranville played shortstop and second base in the National League from 1912 through 1935. He hit .258 over 2,670 games.

Early Wynn was a starter to the end, starting 26 games and going 7–15 in his next-to-last year of a career that spanned 1939 through mid–1963. In his final year he started only five games, finishing 1–2 in a successful attempt to reach exactly 300 victories.

Henry Aaron played 23 seasons between 1954 and 1976, all but two of them for the Braves. He played in 3,298 games, third all-time.

Carl Yastrzemski played in 23 seasons for the Red Sox between 1961 and 1963. He played in 3,308 games, second all-time.

Four- and Five-Decade Players. Various players have played at least one game in each of four or, in one instance, five decades. Many of the four-decade players were still relatively active, though a number of them only made cameo appearances to reach the milestone.

Minnie Minoso. Minoso is the only Major League player to have appeared in at least one game in each of five decades. He played in nine games for the Indians in 1949 before playing throughout the 1950s and five seasons in the 1960s. He made cameo appearances in three games in 1976 for the White Sox. In 1980 he made two cameo appearances for the White Sox. He had one hit in 10 at-bats over these last five games. He tried to make it six decades in 1990, but commissioner Fay Vincent ruled that "it was not in the best interests of baseball." Minoso's response: "I'm not trying to insult the game, I have given my life to the game."

Minoso finally made it back for his sixth decade on June 30, 1993, but in the minor leagues. He appeared at age 70 as a DH for the St. Paul Saints. He grounded back to Thunder Bay pitcher Yoshi Seo in his only at-bat. Mike Veeck owned both the Miami Miracle, whose attempt to sign Minoso was blocked by the National Association, and the Saints. The Saints were in the independent Northern League, which was not under control of the minor league National Association or the commissioner's office.

On July 16, 2003, Minoso again appeared as the DH for the Saints, reportedly at age 77 (he was born in 1922, so he was 81 at the time). He drew a full count walk as he played in his seventh decade. See also Minnie Minoso with Herb Fagen, *Just Call Me Minnie: My Six Decades in Baseball* (1994).

19th Century Players. First baseman Dan Brouthers played in four decades from 1879 through 1896 and then again in 1904 in a cameo appearance.

Jim O'Rourke played from 1876 through 1893, with a cameo appearance in 1904.

Second baseman Kid Gleason played from 1888 until 1908 and then made an appearance in 1912.

Jack O'Connor played catcher from 1887 through 1907 and made one appearance in 1910.

Nick Altrock pitched from 1898 through 1909 and then made sporadic appearances through 1919. He made one final appearance in a game in 1924.

Early 20th Century Players. Shortstop Eddie Collins played from 1906 through 1930.

Jack Quinn pitched from 1909 through 1933.

1920s Through 1950s. Bobo Newsom pitched from 1929 through 1953 for 17 teams (including repeats).

1930s Through 1960s. Mickey Vernon played first base from 1939 through 1960.

Ted Williams played left field for the Red Sox from 1939 until 1960 (except for seasons lost to military service).

Early Wynn pitched from 1939 through 1963, when he finally won his 300th game.

1940s Through 1970s. No player's four-decade career included 1949 and 1970; Willie Mays came the closest with a career that lasted from 1951 through 1973.

1950s Through 1980s. Willie McCovey played from 1959 through 1980.

Jim Kaat pitched from 1959 through 1983.

1960s Through 1990s. Bill Buckner played from 1969 through 1990.

Nolan Ryan pitched from 1966 through 1993.

In 1990 Carlton Fisk became only the second modern catcher, along with Tim McCarver, to play in four decades. Fisk played in two games in 1969, was back in the minors in 1970, and then came up for good through the 1993 season. McCarver played from 1959 through 1980.

Pitcher Jerry Reuss came back on September 7, 1990, to pitch 1⅓ innings for the Pirates. He gave up two hits, one walk and no runs. He was the last player to reach the four-decade mark in the 1990s.

1970s Through 2000s. Jesse Orosco began his career in 1979 and was still pitching in 2003. In April 2002 Orosco, at the time a reliever for the Dodgers, scored just the third run of his career. He last scored while playing for the Mets on July 22, 1986.

Mike Morgan became the 25th player and ninth pitcher to play in four decades, 1978 through 2002.

Rickey Henderson began with the A's in 1979 and finished out with the Dodgers for a few games in 2003.

Tim Raines came back from lupus after missing the 2000 season and played in 2001 and 2002. He began his career in 1979 with the Expos.

Possible Four Decades. Elmer Valo was born in Czechoslovakia and officially began his Major League career in 1940 and ended it in 1961, playing primarily as an outfielder for the Philadelphia Athletics (through 1954). SABR member Jim Charlton followed up on a claim that Valo should be in the four-decade club when Charlton wrote to venerable sportswriter Red Smith in 1972.

Smith said that Valo pinch hit in the last game of 1939 for the A's, sent up to bat by manager Connie Mack on September 30, 1939. Mack had not yet formally signed Valo, and could have been fined by the league office. When the official scorer learned of the contract problem, he left Valo's name out of the official score. Valo walked, getting no official time at bat. The official scorer was of course Red Smith. In the 1980s, Charlton sent a letter to Valo trying to verify the story and some time later received a call from Valo, who didn't deny the story, but said "Listen, just forget about it." Charlton's review of the box score suggests that Valo could easily have pinch hit for pitcher Lynn Nelson, and there are two walks referenced in the box score. Nelson's official replacement, Chubby Dean, had two at-bats, while every other position player had four (suggesting that one of the at-bats was indeed Valo's).

No Four Decades. At least two sources have erroneously reported that Orlando Cepeda (1958–1974) and Ron Fairly (1958–1978) played in four decades. Another source reported that Tommy John pitched in four decades (1963–1989).

Career Length. A study of career length found that catchers have the longest Major League careers, followed by pitchers, outfielders and infielders.

Babe Ruth. When Ruth began the 1933 season (with two more years left in his career), he was one of only six Major League players still left from the 1914 season and the only star remaining.

Most Seasons with One Club. Players with the longest careers who have played with only one club:

Brooks Robinson (Orioles) 23 years
Carl Yastrzemski (Red Sox) 23
Al Kaline (Tigers) 22
Cap Anson (Cubs/White Stockings) 22
Stan Musial (Cardinals) 22
Mel Ott (Giants) 22
Ted Lyons (White Sox) 21
Walter Johnson (Senators) 21
George Brett (Royals) 21
Willie Stargell (Pirates) 21
Cal Ripken (Orioles) 21
Luke Appling (White Sox) 20
Robin Yount (Brewers) 20
Alan Trammell (Tigers) 20
Tony Gwynn (Padres) 20
Barry Larkin (Reds) 19, through 2004

Longest Games

"The game's not over 'til it's over."—Yogi Berra.

"The time occupied in playing the game under such rules is, we think, rather too much of a good thing."—1860 account of a game that covered six days, from 9:30 a.m. to 5:00 p.m. each day (with an hour for lunch), before reaching 100 "tallies."

"The clock doesn't matter in baseball. Time stands still or moves backward. Theoretically, one game could go on forever. Some seem to."—Columnist Herb Caen.

See also *Fastest Games*.

The longest Major League games are measured here both in number of innings and time elapsed. See *Length of Games* for a discussion of average game time and efforts to speed up play.

Most Innings/26.

"When darkness drew its mantle over the scene, both teams were still on their feet, interlocked in a death clutch and each praying for just one more inning in which to get in the knockout blow."—Ralph D. Blanpied quoted in *The Fireside Book of Baseball*, edited by Charles Einstein (1956).

"After the 26th inning, umpire (Barry) McCormick yawned twice and observed that it was nearly bedtime. He didn't seem particularly thrilled by what was going on. To him and his brother arbiter (Eugene) Hart, it was merely an infernally long day's work. McCormick held out his hand in the gloaming and thereupon called the game to the satisfaction of himself and Mr. Hart and to the chagrin of everybody else concerned."—Reporter for the *New York Times*, after the Dodgers and Braves played a 26-inning 1–1 tie on May 1, 1920, in front of 4,000 fans. The game was called because of darkness at 6:30 p.m. after only 3 hours and 50 minutes. Braves pitcher Joe Oeschger and Dodger pitcher Leon Cadore each pitched complete games. Cadore faced 95 batters, gave up 15 hits and allowed only a run in the 5th inning. Oeschger faced 85 batters and allowed a run in the 6th inning. The week before, the two pitchers had faced off and Cadore won 1–0 in 11 innings, as both pitched a complete game.

The only real chance at scoring during extra innings occurred in the 17th inning when the Dodgers had the bases loaded with one out. On a ground ball back to the pitcher, Cadore threw to catcher Hank Gowdy for the force out. Gowdy then threw wide to first and the runner on second tried to score. Gowdy took the throw back from first base and dove into the runner's spikes for the out.

The next day, May 2, the Dodgers played 13 innings against the Phillies, losing 4–3. On May 3 the Dodgers and Braves played 19 innings before the Braves won 2–1. The Dodgers had played 58 innings in three days and no relief pitchers were used in any of the three games. The Braves won a replay of the scoreless tie seven weeks later, but the Dodgers won the pennant by seven games.

The popular view was that the two pitchers had blown out their arms and would never be the same. Cadore said he couldn't raise his arm to comb his hair for three days. Oeschger shut out the Giants four days later. The next year Oeschger was 20–14, his only 20-win season. The following season, Cadore, always about a .500 pitcher, was 13–14, two wins less than his career high.

The longest previous National League game was a 21-inning affair between the Giants and Pirates on July 17, 1914. The Giants took 3 hours and 42 minutes to win that game 3–1.

25 Innings. On September 11, 1974, the Cardinals defeated the Mets 4–3 in a 25-inning game that lasted until 3:12 a.m. The total time for the game was 7 hours and 4 minutes. There were 50 players and 15 dozen balls used in the game and there were a then-record 202 plate appearances. Bake McBride scored from first base on a wild pick-off throw, giving the Cardinals the victory. A two-out, two-run homer by Ken Reitz of the Cardinals in the 9th inning sent the game into extra, extra innings.

On May 8–9, 1984, at Comiskey Park, the White Sox and Brewers played 25 innings in 8 hours and 6 minutes. The game was suspended at 1:05 a.m. after 17 innings on the first night. The White Sox scored two in the bottom of the 9th and three in the bottom of the 21st to keep the game tied. It ended with a Harold Baines home run when it was completed the next day before the regular game. Tom Seaver won both games for the White Sox.

24 Innings. On September 1, 1906, the Red Sox and A's played 24 innings before the A's won 4–1. Jack Coombs and Joe Harris both pitched complete games. Harris contracted typhoid a short time later and never pitched again.

The 1945 Tigers and A's went 24 innings without scoring before the game was called. Eight weeks later the game was replayed ("resumed" in some sources) and went another 16 innings before the A's finally won 3–2. Total number of innings: 40.

On April 15, 1968, the Mets defeated the Astros 1–0 in 24 innings, the longest shutout on record.

Longest in Time/Extra Innings.
Over Eight Hours.

"WHAT THE HELL IS GOING ON?"—Hastily scrawled sign draped on the outfield wall in the 18th inning of one of the longest games in time in Major League history.

On July 4, 1985, the Mets beat the Braves in Atlanta 16–13 in a 19-inning game that ended at 4:01 a.m. (3:55 in some sources) and lasted more than 8 hours and 30 minutes. The Braves then went ahead with the scheduled fireworks show and locals thought there was gunfire. The game featured a 1½ hour rain delay before the game started and two rain delays during the game.

The Braves tied the game at eight in the 9th inning. The Mets went ahead by two runs in the top of the 13th. Terry Harper of the Braves then hit a two-out, two-run homer to tie the game at 10. In the 17th inning Darryl Strawberry took a rest by getting thrown out of the game on a called third strike. Manager Davey Johnson was also thrown out on the call.

Braves pitcher Rick Camp hit the one home run of his career in the game. Camp, a career .074 hitter, hit his home run after 3:00 a.m. on an 0–2 pitch from Tom Gorman. He did it in the 18th inning to tie the score at 11 after the Mets had gone ahead in the top of the inning.

The Mets scored five in the 19th off Camp to take a 16–11 lead.

The Braves scored two runs in the bottom of the inning, and Camp came up as the tying run with two outs and two on. He struck out swinging off Ron Darling to end the game. The Mets had a team record 28 hits and the Braves had 18. Keith Hernandez hit for the cycle.

See **25 Innings** above for a game lasting 8 hours and 6 minutes.

Over 7 Hours. On June 24, 1962, the Tigers hosted the Yankees in a single Sunday game, which was rare in that era (doubleheaders usually were scheduled on Sundays). The game lasted 7 hours, from 1:30 to 8:30 in front of what started out as 35,638 fans. The Yankees won 9–7 in what up to then was the longest game in time on record. Six hundred pitches were thrown (316 by the Yankees) as Whitey Ford charted them all. The concession stands had to close at 8:15 that evening because women in Michigan were not allowed to work more than 10 hours on a Sunday. The Yankees used 21 of their 25 players and the Tigers 22 of 25. Yankee starter Bob Turley was knocked out in the 1st inning. The game was a 7–7 tie from the 6th inning on. It was broken up on a home run in the 22nd inning by pitcher Jack Reed, the only one of his career. Yogi Berra caught the entire game for the Yankees at age 37.

On June 3, 1989, the Dodgers and Astros played 22 innings in a Saturday night game that lasted 7 hours and 14 minutes. By the end of the game pitcher Fernando Valenzuela was at first base and first baseman Eddie Murray was at third. The Astros won 5–4 on a single by Rafael Ramirez off pitcher Jeff Hamilton, who normally played third base. The ball glanced off Valenzuela's glove for the Astros win.

Dodger broadcaster Vin Scully did the game by himself because both Don Drysdale and Ross Porter were unavailable. He had done 10 innings earlier in the day on an NBC Game of the Week national telecast. The Dodgers had another extra inning game the next day (13 innings), which they also lost, but the Dodgers had brought in local L.A. cable television announcer Eddie Ducette to help Scully.

Earlier Longest Games. The previous longest American League game in time was 4 hours and 58 minutes between the Orioles and Red Sox, a 17-inning game on June 23, 1954.

Night Games. On June 12, 1967, the Senators and White Sox played the longest night game in history to that point, 22 innings. It was also the longest night game in time to that point at 6 hours and 38 minutes. Catcher Paul Cassanova, who caught the entire game, singled in the winning run.

Longest Nine-Inning Game.

1. On October 5, 2001, Barry Bonds hit his 71st and 72nd home runs to set a new Major League record. He did it in the Giants' 11–10 loss to the Dodgers, which eliminated them from the playoffs. The game took 4 hours and 27 minutes, longest nine-inning game in Major League history.

2. On May 11, 2000, the Brewers beat the Cubs 14–8 in 4 hours and 22 minutes. The game featured 35 hits and 19 walks.

3. On April 30, 1996, the Yankees beat the Orioles 13–10 in 4 hours and 21 minutes.

4. On April 5, 1997, The White Sox and Tigers played a 4 hour and 20 minute game won by the Tigers 15–12. There were 23 mph winds throwing debris across the field and it rained several times during the game.

5. On June 30, 1996, in Colorado, the Rockies beat the Dodgers 16–15 in 4 hours and 20 minutes.

6. On October 2, 1962, the Dodgers beat the Giants 8–7 in 4 hours and 18 minutes.

7. On June 8, 1986, the Orioles beat the Yankees 18–9 in 4 hours and 16 minutes.

8. On September 15, 1993, the Blue Jays beat the Tigers 14–8 in 4 hours and 12 minutes.

9. On May 15, 1991, the Red Sox beat the White Sox 9–6 in 4 hours and 11 minutes.

Doubleheaders.

"I've just been watching the most incredible ball game. The Mets and Giants are in the 20th inning." — John Daly, after being introduced on the live television show, "What's My Line?," commenting on the game he had been watching on television.

The longest doubleheader on record was 32 innings on Sunday, May 31, 1964, between the Mets and Giants. Starting at 9:52 a.m., the Giants won the first game 5–3 in 2 hours and 29 minutes.

In the second game the Giants won again, 8–6 in 23 innings. The Giants scored two runs in the top of the 23rd inning and the game ended at 11:20 p.m. (11:25 in some sources). Game time was 7 hours and 23 minutes, the longest in history to that point and made the total elapsed time for the two games 9 hours and 52 minutes. Ed Sudol umpired home plate in both games.

Gaylord Perry pitched 10 innings in relief, which included a triple play. Perry later admitted that this was the first time he experimented with a spitball in a Major League game. Willie Mays played shortstop for part of one game. Attendance was 57,000 at the start of the day and 15,000 at the end.

Mets infielder Ed Kranepool played in a doubleheader the previous day for the Mets' farm club and ended up playing 50 innings in two days.

On May 24, 1995, the White Sox and Rangers took 7 hours and 39 minutes to play an 18-inning doubleheader. It eclipsed the old record for 18 innings by 49 minutes.

"Ponce, you want a shot and a beer? It's last call." — Padres catcher Kevin Higgins to home plate umpire Larry Poncino, after the first pitch of the second game of a doubleheader in Philadelphia that started at 1:28 a.m. The doubleheader lasted 12 hours and 5 minutes and included nearly six hours of rain delays. The first game started at 4:35 p.m. on July 2, 1993. The Padres won 5–2 at 1:03 a.m. after 8 hours and 28 minutes (5 hours and 54 minutes of rain delays).

The "morningcap" ended at 4:40 a.m., the latest finish of any game in Major League history. At least some of the 3 hour and 12 minute game was witnessed by about 5,000 fans (1,000 by the end of the game) of the original 54,617 in attendance.

On July 4, 1994, the Cubs and Rockies played a doubleheader that left 1,000 fans in their seats by the end of the day. The games lasted 10 hours and 10 minutes and included three rain delays and a 15-inning second game.

On July 20, 1998, the Tigers and Yankee played 17 innings in the first game of a doubleheader, with Detroit winning 4–3. The Yankees won the second game by the same score in nine innings, but the two games took almost nine hours to play.

Longest Championship Series Games. On October 15, 1986, the Mets and Astros played 16 innings in 4 hours and 42 minutes as the Mets outlasted the Astros 7–6.

On October 4, 1995, the Yankees and Mariners played 15 innings in 5 hours and 12 minutes as the Yankees beat the Mariners 7–5.

World Series/Nine Innings. On October 20, 1993, the Blue Jays rallied for a 15–14 win over the Phillies to take a 3–1 lead in the World Series. The nine-inning game took 4 hours and 14 minutes, the longest ever.

World Series/Extra Innings. Before 1993, the longest by innings was Game 2 of the 1916 Series, which went 14 innings. The game took only 2:32 to play, as Babe Ruth went the distance on the mound for the Red Sox, who won 2–1 (and the Series 4–1).

World Series/Time. In Game 1 of the 2000 World Series, the Yankees beat the Mets 4–3 in 12 innings. It took 4 hours and 51 minutes. The Mets led 3–2 going into the 9th inning, but Armando Benitez gave up the tying run on a sacrifice fly by Chuck Knoblauch.

Game 4 of the 1996 Series between the Yankees and Braves lasted 4 hours 17 minutes. The Yankees beat the Braves in 10 innings. Game 2 of the 1973 Series between the Mets and A's lasted 4 hours and 13 minutes, and was the game in which A's second baseman Mike Andrews committed two crucial extra-inning errors to give the Mets the win. Game 3 of the 1997 Series between the Indians and Marlins lasted 4 hours and 12 minutes.

Minor Leagues.

"We went the whole game without going to the bathroom."— Umpire crew chief Jack Lietz.

On April 18, 1981, the Pawtucket Red Sox (PawSox) and Rochester Red Wings of the International League began a game on Saturday night at Pawtucket's McCoy Stadium and continued to play into Easter Sunday morning until 4:09 (or 4:07) a.m., when the game was suspended. The game was delayed by a 32-minute power failure and then lasted for 8 hours and 7 minutes that night. After 32 innings and a 2–2 tie, the umpires called the game in the 28-degree predawn chill with only 17 fans left in the ballpark.

The game resumed on June 23 and lasted only one more inning before Pawtucket scored to win 3–2 on a bases-loaded bloop single by Dave Koza. The game lasted 8 hours and 25 minutes and produced 213 at-bats, 59 strikeouts and 156 balls used. A number of future Major League players appeared in the game: Cal Ripken, Wade Boggs, Rich Gedman, Marty Barrett, Bob Ojeda and Floyd Rayford.

The previous longest minor league game was 29 innings in the Florida State League in 1969.

Longest Professional Game/One Day. The longest single-day professional game without a rain delay was 8 hours and 16 minutes, played on June 26, 1988, between the Burlington (N.C.) Indians and the Bluefield Orioles of the Appalachian League. It was 3:37 a.m. when the game ended after 27 innings.

Longest Throws

See also *Defensive Gems*

Glen Gorbous. On August 1, 1957, Omaha outfielder Glen Gorbous threw a baseball 445'10". It may have been his most productive play that season, as he later appeared in only three games for the Phillies as a pinch hitter and never played in the field.

Don Grate. One source reported that a former Phillies outfielder named Don Grate threw a baseball 443'3½" on August 23, 1953. However, Mr. Grate does not appear in *The Baseball Encyclopedia*. *The Sporting News* reported that on September 7, 1952, Grate, of Chattanooga in the Southern Association, threw a ball 434 feet for the official minor league record.

Larry LeJeune. Grate's throw broke the record of 426'9" set by Sheldon "Larry" LeJeune in 1910. On October 12, 1910, in Cincinnati, soon-to-be Major Leaguer LeJeune threw a baseball "a record" 426'9" (also reported as ½ inch longer). It did not do him much good, as he appeared in only 24 games with the Dodgers and Pirates in 1911 and 1915. He had a .167 batting average and five errors in 61 chances (probably a lot of overthrows from the outfield).

Tony "The Count" Mullane. The ambidextrous 19th century pitcher was extremely strong and purportedly began throwing left-handed only after he hurt his right arm throwing a ball 416'7¾" in a contest. Most statistical sources show him as right-handed.

Women. In 1912 Amanda Clement set a women's record with a throw of 275 feet. Clement was the first woman to umpire professionally. Babe Didrikson once threw a ball 296 feet and reportedly threw a ball in a game 313 feet from the outfield wall to home plate.

One source reported that on August 18, 1957, Amelia Wershoven set the women's record by throwing a baseball 252'4½" (reported in the often unreliable *Sports Shorts*, by Mac Davis (1959)).

Injuries. When Arlie Latham won a throwing contest with Doc Bushong in the 1880s, he received $100 from manager Charlie Comiskey. Latham did not warm up, hurt his arm, and later became the butt of jokes for his feeble throws from third base.

Jimmy Piersall. Piersall had an excellent arm (considered the best of the era by some) but reportedly ruined it in a throwing contest with Willie Mays in 1954.

Lawsuit. According to SABR researcher Al Kermisch, former early 20th century Major Leaguer Mike Menosky was used as the court's expert in a case in which the defendant was accused of throwing a rock 250 feet through a railcar window. At age 57, Menosky, by then a probation officer, was asked to throw that far. He could do it with a baseball, but not a rock, so the judge concluded that the defendant couldn't do it either. Case dismissed.

Al Lopez (1908–)

Hall of Fame (VC) 1977

"In the course of time, Al Lopez, the manager of the Chicago White Sox, has been called, by various enlightened members of the working press, the Señor, the Stylish Señor, the Good Señor, the Happy Hidalgo, the Spanish Don, the Happy Castilian, the Cagey Castilian, the Calm Castilian, the Courtly Castilian, the Personable Skipper and Frolicsome Al…. For the most part, these sobriquets fairly delineate Lopez, and furthermore, inform those who might assume his name to be of Eskimo origin of his true lineage."—*Sports Illustrated* writer Gilbert Rogin on the 1950s manager of the Indians and White Sox, whose parents were Spanish.

"The manager is by himself. He can't mingle with his players. I enjoyed my players, but I couldn't socialize with them. So I spent a lot of time alone in my hotel room. Those four walls kind of close in on you."—Lopez.

"Living refutation of Durocher axiom, 'Nice guys finish last.'"—Gene Karst and Martin J. Jones, Jr., in *Who's Who in Professional Baseball* (1973).

The former catcher made his mark as a manager with the Indians and White Sox primarily in the 1950s and early 1960s.

Florida native Alfonso Ramon Lopez, of Spanish descent, began his 19-year Major League catching career with three appearances for the Dodgers in 1928. He came up for good in 1930 and played for the club through 1935 as the regular catcher. Perhaps his best season was 1933, when he had a career-high 10 stolen bases and batted .301 in 126 games. He also had a .991 fielding percentage behind the plate.

In 1936 Lopez moved over to the Braves, where he remained through part of 1940. His best season with the Braves was 1939, when he hit a career-best eight home runs and played in 131 games. He was traded to the Pirates, where he was the starting catcher through 1945. After part-time duty in 1946 he finished his career with 61 games for the Indians in 1947.

Lopez finished his playing career with a .261 lifetime average and 52 home runs in 1,950 games. He was then ready to begin a distinguished managing career. He led Indianapolis in 1948 and remained at the helm of that club until 1951, when he was hired to manage the Indians. He began a string of nine American League seasons in which his clubs finished either first or second, usually a few games behind the powerful Yankees.

Lopez led the Indians to a pennant in 1954 with 111 wins, but they were swept by the Giants in the World Series. In 1957 he took over the White Sox and led them to second-place finishes in 1957 and 1958 before winning the American League pennant in 1959 (losing the World Series to the Dodgers in six games). His White Sox clubs continued to be successful through the early 1960s, finishing second three more times between 1963 and 1965.

Lopez ended his managerial duties due to health problems in 1965, but returned for a few games in 1968 and 1969 as an interim manager for the White Sox. He finished 17 years of managing with a .584 winning percentage, fifth among the top 50 winningest managers of all time. As of 2004, he was No. 22 on the career win list, with 1,410.

Los Angeles

"Los Angeles is seven suburbs in search of a city." — Alfred Hitchcock, quoted by Bob Costas during the 1984 Olympics.

The city has had two Major League franchises, the Dodgers and Angels, as well as the Pacific Coast League Hollywood Stars and Los Angeles Angels.

Los Angeles Angels

See also *Anaheim Angels*.

The Los Angeles Angels were an original Pacific Coast League club beginning in 1903. Chicago Cubs owner William Wrigley purchased the club in the mid–1920s. The franchise remained in the city until it moved to Spokane after the 1957 season to make room for the Major League Dodgers. The Angels won 14 pennants over their minor league history.

In late 2004 the Angels ownership changed the name of the Anaheim Angels to "Los Angeles Angels of Anaheim," a move lamely attempting to placate the Anaheim city fathers who vehemently objected to the name change and who threatened litigation.

Los Angeles Dodgers

National League 1958–

"So the citizens of Los Angeles received in just two years the gift that had eluded Brooklyn for nearly three generations — a world championship. Others would soon follow, but first Angelenos would get a small taste of the torment that had cemented the relationship between the Dodgers and their followers over the years." — Stanley Cohen in *Dodgers! The First 100 Years* (1990).

Origins.

"The City of the Angels offered him [Walter O'Malley] more than the keys to the city. It gave him the keys to the Kingdom. New York balked at twelve acres. Los Angeles enthusiastically proffered 300 acres. This is the biggest haul since the Brink's robbery — except that it's legal." — Sportswriter Tim Cohane.

The Los Angeles Dodgers were the successors to the Brooklyn Dodgers, who moved to Los Angeles for the 1958 season (see also *Franchise Shifts*).

First Game. The Dodgers started the 1958 season in San Francisco, losing 8–0 on April 15 when pitcher Don Drysdale was shelled. In their first game in Los Angeles, the Dodgers defeated the Giants 6–5 at the Los Angeles Memorial Coliseum in front of 78,672 fans, a new Major League record. Giants rookie Jim Dav-

enport was called out for failing to touch third base after scoring on Willie Kirkland's triple in the 9th inning. The mistake preserved Carl Erskine's victory for the Dodgers (saved by Clem Labine).

Key Owners.

Walter and Peter O'Malley/1958– 1998.

"He was a portly, jowly, florid man, with a raspy voice, and he circulated with a kind of bonhomie that no one ever confused with charm. Socially, he had a tin ear." — Frank Graham, Jr., on the elder O'Malley in *Farewell to Heroes* (1981).

Ownership of the team remained primarily with the O'Malley family after the move from Brooklyn. The widow of John Smith of Pfizer Pharmaceutical remained on the board into the 1960s, but O'Malley bought her shares after her death. The heirs of Ed McKeever, the Mulveys, held their 33.8% interest into the 1970s but sold out in 1975 after the death of McKeever's daughter, Dearie Mulvey. At that point Walter O'Malley was the sole owner of the club. When he died in 1979, his shares were divided evenly between Peter O'Malley and his sister, Teresa O'Malley Seidler.

Walter O'Malley dominated the club and was a powerful Major League owner until the mid–1970s. His son Peter assumed the presidency shortly before his father's death in 1979. He remained a powerful force until the mid–1990s when his influence began to wane.

The Dodgers had remarkable continuity in the general manager position. Buzzie Bavasi was the general manager when the team arrived in Los Angeles until he left for the Padres in 1969. Al Campanis succeeded him until his ill-fated remarks about *Racism* in 1987. He was succeeded by Dodger publicist Fred Claire, who helped engineer the 1988 World Championship. Claire moved up the ranks from Director of Publicity starting in 1969, to Vice President of Public Relations in 1975, to General Manager 1987. See Fred Claire with Steve Spring, *My 30 Years in Dodger Blue* (2004).

The finances were not working for O'Malley and his family, and he needed to sell the club to provide cash for himself and relatives who had ownership stakes in the club. In March 1997 he announced his intent to sell the club and a deal was approved by Major League Baseball in March 1998. The 60-year-old O'Malley stayed on with the club for several months and then announced that he was leaving the organization after 48 years.

In January 2004, there were rumors that O'Malley would come back to run the Dodgers if a last-minute bid to buy the team by local real estate magnate Eli Broad had been successful. It wasn't, and he didn't.

Rupert Murdoch/Fox Sports Group/1998–2004.

"Press barons have always been feared, even hated, for the power they can wield over us. But until recently they have been the creatures of the neighborhood. Rupert Murdoch is the first press baron to be a monster of the entire world. That's globalization for you.... And monster is how many people do see Murdoch. He is subjected to far more criticism, if not abuse, than any other contemporary media mogul (except perhaps Bill Gates, and in both cases, mythomania plays a part). Throughout his life he has been attacked for his right-wing politics and for allegedly lowering the standards of everything he touches." — William Shawcross in *Time*.

Murdoch turned a small-town Australian newspaper into a worldwide communications conglomerate. He became an American citizen in the 1980s so he could buy American television stations, and eventually bought 20th Century Fox and Fox Television. He paid $311 million for the Dodgers, the largest paid for a sports franchise up to that point. It appeared that Murdoch bought the Dodgers as a vehicle for improving ratings on his Fox Network, in part by advertising the network's shows on the games. Murdoch's network also broadcast Major League Baseball regular and postseason games. In 1999 Robert Daly purchased a small interest in the club and became chairman and CEO.

The early front-runner for purchase of the club was Marvin Glaser, who owned the NFL Tampa Bay Buccaneers. He had trouble qualifying because of cross-ownership rules that prevented him from using his collateral in the NFL team to secure loans for purchase of the Dodgers. From the baseball side, Commissioner Bud Selig was vigorously enforcing a rule that prevented a club from having debt larger than 40% of its assets.

The Dodgers were reported to have lost $100 million in 2001 and 2002, making it difficult for Glaser to give up the lucrative Buccaneers (which appeared to be his only alternative). In mid–2003 Murdoch sold to Boston real estate magnate Frank McCourt, although it took into 2004 to obtain final approval of the sale. Despite never making the playoffs while owned by Murdoch, the club's winning percentage of .568 was better than that of the O'Malley family, at .550.

Frank H. McCourt, Jr., and Jamie McCourt/2004– .

"Ding, dong the Fox is dead…. This Frank McCourt, whoever he is, will soon discover that buying the Dodgers from Fox will be like buying lifeboats for Devil's Island."— Bill Plaschke of the *Los Angeles Times*.

"The Boston Parking Lot Attendant"— Derogatory name for McCourt by *Los Angeles Times* columnist T.J. Simers, referring to McCourt's ownership of parking lots in Boston.

"I can't believe this is my job."— Co-owner Jamie McCourt.

Frank McCourt was a 49-year-old Boston real estate developer when he and his attorney wife, Jamie McCourt, bought the club in mid–2003 for a highly-leveraged $430 million. In 2001 McCourt was outbid for the Red Sox and McCourt's grandfather was once a part-owner of the Boston Braves. McCourt also tried to buy the Angels in early 2003 before losing out to Arturo Moreno. McCourt was not listed in the *Forbes* 400 (minimum of $600 million) and there was speculation that he did not have enough assets to finance the purchase of the Dodgers. His paperwork submission was delayed until December 2003 and it took until January 2004 to obtain final approval from Major League Baseball. Part of the problem seemed to be the highly-leveraged nature of the transaction, which was being financed in part by the seller and by Aramark, a huge concessionaire for many Major League teams.

McCourt's bid was finally approved in late January 2004. At the last moment, however, Los Angeles real estate magnate Eli Broad made a cash offer as a backup in case the McCourt bid wasn't approved. McCourt's deal originally called for him to borrow $205 million from News Corp (Fox), but that was revised at the last minute to keep News Corp as a 20% minority owner to fall in line with the Major League equity rules.

The Dodgers reportedly were losing $40 million a year, and there was rampant speculation that McCourt would either try to build a football stadium in the Dodger Stadium parking lot or would move the ballpark to downtown Los Angeles (five minutes away) and turn the hillside ballpark's acreage (potentially worth hundreds of millions, if not more) into a residential development. There was also talk of renaming Dodger Stadium with the right corporate cash infusion.

Jamie McCourt was heavily involved in the day-to-day operations, with significant input into the hiring of general manager Paul DePodesta and overseeing the marketing operations.

Nickname. The Dodgers retained the name of the Brooklyn Dodgers.

Key Seasons.

1958. The Dodgers finished a dismal seventh in their first season in Los Angeles.

1959. The Dodgers defeated the Braves in a best-of-three National League ***Play-Off*** series after the clubs tied with records of 86–68. The Dodgers won the World Series in six games over the White Sox. Gil Hodges hit 25 home runs, Duke Snider batted .308 with 23 home runs and Don Drysdale won 17 games.

1962. The club finished the regular season tied with the Giants with 101–61 records and then lost to them in a three-game ***Play-Off*** to finish with a 102–63 record. Tommy Davis won the batting title with a .346 average and had a league-leading 153 RBIs. Don Drysdale led the league with 25 wins.

1963. The Dodgers won the pennant by six games over the Cardinals and then swept the hated Yankees in the World Series. Tommy Davis again won the batting title with a .326 average and Sandy Koufax led the league with 25 wins and a 1.88 ERA.

1965. The Dodgers won the pennant by two games over the Giants and then took seven games to defeat the Twins in the World Series behind the pitching of Don Drysdale and Sandy Koufax. Koufax led the league with 26 wins and a 2.04 ERA.

1966. The Dodgers repeated as National League champions, winning by 1½ games over the Giants. The club was swept by the Orioles in the World Series as Sandy Koufax pitched his last game. Koufax again led the league with 27 wins and a 1.73 ERA. Phil Regan led the league with 21 saves. This began a slide for the club that was not corrected until 1971.

1971. The Dodgers lost the National League West race to the Giants on the last night of the season, but the season was the beginning of a strong decade for the Dodgers.

1974. The Dodgers finished second in 1973 and then won the National League West in 1974 by four games over the Reds. They beat the Pirates in four games in the NLCS and then lost to the A's in the World Series in five games. Andy Messersmith led the league with 20 wins and Mike Marshall led with 21 saves. "Toy Cannon" Jimmy Wynn had 32 home runs and 108 RBIs.

1977. The Dodgers continued to be successful in 1975 and 1976 but each time finished second to the powerful Cincinnati Reds and the Big Red Machine, as the "Little Blue Wrecking Crew" just could not get the job done. Following Walter Alston's retirement in late 1976, the Dodgers won the 1977 division crown under Tommy Lasorda. The Dodgers beat the Phillies in four games for the pennant and then lost the World Series to the Yankees behind the three-home run barrage by Reggie Jackson in Game 6. Steve Garvey, Ron Cey, Reggie Smith and Dusty Baker each hit 30 or more home runs and Tommy John won 20 games.

1978. The Dodgers repeated as division champions by 2½ games over the Reds and again defeated the Phillies in four games to capture the pennant. The Yankees once again were waiting in the World Series and the Dodgers lost again in six games after taking a 2–0 Series lead. Burt Hooton led the club with 19 wins and Reggie Smith led with 29 home runs.

1980. The Dodgers swept a three-game series from the Astros on the last weekend of the season to finish in a tie. In a one-game ***Play-Off*** on the following Monday, pitcher Dave Goltz faded fast and the Astros beat the Dodgers.

1981. The Dodgers won the first half of the strike-shortened split season behind the pitching of rookie sensation Fernando Valenzuela. They finished a mediocre fourth in the second half, but had enough left to win the mini-series against the Astros in five games. They went on to beat the Expos in Game 5 of the NLCS on Rick Monday's 9th inning home run. In the World Series the Dodgers finally overcame the Yankees in six games. The Dodgers trailed 2–0 in games in both the Houston and New York series and were down 2–1 in games in the Montreal series.

1982. The Dodgers lost the division by one game when Joe

Morgan homered for the Giants to beat them on the last day of the season and propel the Braves into first place.

1983. The Dodgers won the National League West by three games over the Braves, but lost to the Phillies in the NLCS in four games. Pedro Guerrero led the club with 32 home runs and 103 RBIs.

1985. After a mediocre 1984 season, the Dodgers bounced back to win the Western Division championship by six games over the Reds. This time the Dodgers lost the pennant to the Cardinals in six games as Jack Clark hit a dramatic home run in the 9th inning to wipe out a Dodger lead that would have sent the series to a seventh game. Orel Hershiser was 19–3 and Pedro Guerrero led the club with 33 home runs.

1988. After back-to-back 73–89 records, the Dodgers' 1988 season was nothing short of miraculous. It started with a home run by Steve Sax on the first pitch of the season. The club capped the regular season with Orel Hershiser's *Scoreless Innings* streak and then defeated the Mets in a seven-game NLCS. Against the heavily favored Oakland A's in the World Series, the Dodgers won 4–1 after starting the series by winning Game 1 on a dramatic 9th inning, two-out home run by injured Kirk Gibson (National League MVP that year). Hershiser was 23–8 to lead the league and Gibson hit 25 home runs. See also Orel Hershiser with Jerry Jenkins, *Out of the Blue* (1989).

1991. The Dodgers and Braves fought for the pennant over the last two weeks, but the Dodgers were eliminated in the second-to-last game of the season, with the Giants once again knocking them out.

1994. The Dodgers surprised the league by leading the division when the season ended due to the player strike.

1995. The Dodgers won a tight pennant race over the Rockies, but were swept in the division play-offs by the Reds. Mike Piazza batted .346, Eric Karros had 32 home runs and 105 RBIs, and Hideo Nomo was the surprise of the season from Japan, winning 13 games and leading the league in strikeouts. Todd Worrell saved 32 games.

1996. Los Angeles blew a late season lead and finished as the wild card team behind the Padres. The Dodgers were then swept by the Braves in the first round of the postseason. Mike Piazza hit 36 home runs and Eric Karros hit 34. Todd Worrell saved 44 games.

2004. The Dodgers finally returned to the postseason after an eight-season wait, beating the Giants with a seven run 9th inning in the second-to-last game of the season to clinch the National League West. They finished the season with a record of 93–69, one game ahead of San Francisco. Adrian Beltre had a career year at third base with a .335 average, 200 hits, 48 home runs and 121 RBIs. Shawn Green had 28 home runs and 86 RBIs. The mediocre pitching staff had three starters with 13 wins (Jeff Weaver, Kaz Ishii and Jose Lima), but reliever Eric Gagne had 45 saves despite developing tendonitis late in the season. The powerful Cardinals blew out the Dodgers in the first two games of the five-game series, but Dodger pitcher Jose Lima managed to throw a 4–0 shutout in Game 3, the club's first postseason victory since they won the World Series in 1988. In Game 4, Albert Pujols hit a three-run homer to give the Cardinals a 4–1 lead and St. Louis went on to a 6–2 win to finish off the Dodgers.

Key Players.

Sandy Koufax (HF) qualifies as the all-time greatest Los Angeles Dodger. He finally blossomed in 1961, winning 18 games. He then had seasons of 14–7 (injured near the end of the season), 25–5, 19–5, 26–8 and 27–9 in 1966. He won three unanimous Cy Young Awards and then retired after the 1966 World Series because of circulatory problems and arthritis in his left elbow.

Don Drysdale (HF) starred in the 1960s for the Dodgers, cap-

ping his career with 58 consecutive *Scoreless Innings* in 1968. He was elected to the Hall of Fame in 1984 after winning 209 games over 14 years. His best season was 1962, when he was 25–9 and won the Cy Young Award.

Maury Wills exploded in his 1960 rookie season by leading the league in stolen bases and batting .295. He went on to lead the league in stolen bases for five straight seasons through 1965 and broke Ty Cobb's single-season stolen base record with 104 in 1962.

Steve Garvey was probably the Dodgers' best all-time hitter (with apologies to Tommy Davis, who led the league in hitting in 1962 and 1963). Garvey holds the National League record for most *Consecutive Games Played* and led the Dodgers to four World Series appearances. He batted over .300 seven times and had 200 or more hits for the Dodgers six times.

Fernando Valenzuela was the star Dodger pitcher of the early 1980s. He burst onto the scene in 1981 and fostered the "Fernandomania" craze by winning his first seven games that year (following two wins at the end of the 1980 season). His screwball failed him by the end of the decade and the Dodgers released him during spring training in 1991.

Orel Hershiser had a spectacular sophomore season in 1985 when he was 19–3. His career peaked in 1988 when he was 23–8 and broke Don Drysdale's *Scoreless Innings* streak with 59 shutout innings at the end of the season. He did ironman duty in the postseason that year as he led the Dodgers to an improbable World Series victory over the heavily favored A's. He had complete reconstructive shoulder surgery in 1990 but returned in 1991 to pitch adequately for the Dodgers through 1994.

Mike Piazza became the premier catcher in the National League in the mid–1990s, batting in the mid–.300s and generally hitting at least 30 home runs per season. Piazza was drafted 1,390th out of 1,433 players selected in the 1988 draft (62nd round). He was traded early in the 1998 season after a public feud with new owner Rupert Murdoch's management team over a new contract.

Eric Karros played for the Dodgers from 1991 until traded to the Cubs after the 2002 season. He hit 242 home runs and had 840 RBIs for the club in that span.

Eric Gagne. Gagne emerged in 2002 as the premier reliever in the Major Leagues after a mediocre to worse career as a starting pitcher. He saved a record 84 straight games between August 2002 and July 2004.

Managers.

Walter Alston (HF) was the only Los Angeles Dodger manager until he retired near the end of the 1976 season. While in Los Angeles he won five pennants (1959, 1963, 1965, 1966 and 1974) and three world championships (1959, 1963 and 1965). These added to his two pennants and one world championship for the *Brooklyn Dodgers*. In 1959, after a slow start following a seventh place finish the year before, Alston was on the verge of being fired and Pee Wee Reese was to take over the club. See also Walter Alston and Jack Tobin, *A Year at a Time* (1976); Walter Alston and Si Burick, *Alston and the Dodgers* (1966).

Tommy Lasorda (HF) took over as Dodger manager in late 1976 and remained at the helm until a heart attack ended his career in July 1996. Former general manager Buzzie Bavasi claimed that Lasorda was brought up to the Major Leagues in the late 1960s as a coach solely to reward him for being a long-term employee. Apparently, the Dodgers had no thought of making him manager, but he evidently was in the right place at the right time.

After serving as Alston's third base coach for four years, Lasorda immediately won the 1977 and 1978 National League pennants. He is only the second manager in National League history to reach the

World Series in his first two seasons. He compiled two World Championships (1981 and 1988), four National League pennants (including 1977 and 1978), and eight Western Division titles (including 1983, 1985, 1994 and 1995). He finished with a record of 1,599–1,439 and a .526 winning percentage over 20 seasons. See also Tommy Lasorda with David Fisher, *The Artful Dodger* (1985).

Following Lasorda, the Dodgers went through a series of short-term managers, starting with former shortstop Bill Russell.

Key Ballparks.

Los Angeles Coliseum.

"They had room at the Coliseum for 93,000 people and two left fielders."— Broadcaster Lindsey Nelson, referring to the short-porch left field created by the football-oriented Coliseum.

The Dodgers played their home games at the Los Angeles Memorial Coliseum from 1958 through 1961. The Coliseum had been expanded to 105,000 seats for the 1932 Olympics, but its baseball capacity was 93,600.

When the Dodgers arrived to play in the formerly football-only stadium, they paid for more lights, a sunken dugout, backstop and improved press box. The dimensions were odd because of the rectangular field. Left field was only 251 feet from home plate but had a 40-foot screen to prevent easy home runs. The dimensions expanded out from 320 in left center field to 410 in center field to 440 in right center field and then down to 300 in right field.

Although the left field shot was considered an easy home run, the Dodgers still hit fewer home runs than the year before in cozy Ebbets Field. Of the 193 home runs hit in the Coliseum the first season, 182 were over the short left field fence.

Dodger Stadium.

"The Taj Mahal, the Parthenon, and Westminster Abbey of baseball."— Jim Murray.

Chavez Ravine overlooks downtown Los Angeles and is the 300-acre site of Dodger Stadium, opened in 1962. The Dodgers looked at a site in Inglewood near where the Great Western Forum was built later for the Lakers, but it had a cemetery across the street and was owned by a private party.

In 1958 the Dodgers convinced the city of Los Angeles to condemn the downtown site and spend $3 million for access roads to the stadium. This required a referendum vote by the city to raise the money. The vote was extremely close and may have passed only because of a star-studded Sunday telethon held immediately before the Tuesday vote. Future politician Ronald Reagan participated in the telethon on behalf of the Dodgers. Ironically, the telethon was held on a station owned by future Angels owner Gene Autry.

One month later, a Los Angeles Superior Court judge ruled that the contract to sell the parcel through condemnation proceedings was illegal and blocked the deal. The ruling was later reversed and the sale proceeded. The condemnation of the site was upheld by the California Supreme Court because there was a "legitimate public purpose" in condemning the land to house a Major League Baseball team.

Chavez Ravine originally was primarily a landfill operation. It had a small store and a few homes in the largely Latino neighborhood. One of the homes, which was sold for $6,000, stood almost directly on top of what was later second base. The Dodgers paid the displaced homeowners, who almost uniformly opposed the development, a total of $150,000.

Although the city paid for access roads, the Dodgers paid to build the ballpark, which cost $22 million and was ready for the 1962 season. It was the first privately financed ballpark since Yankee Stadium was built in 1923.

The first game played in Dodger Stadium was on April 10, 1962,

as the Reds defeated the Dodgers 6–3. Mrs. Walter (Kay) O'Malley threw out the first ball. Dimensions from left to right field originally were 330–380–410–380–330, with a seating capacity of 56,000. In the 1970s center field was brought in 10 feet in what is known as a pitcher's park.

Willie Stargell is the only player to hit a ball completely out of the park. He did it on August 5, 1969 (500 feet off Alan Foster over the right field pavilion), and May 8, 1973 (470 feet).

Key Broadcasters. Hall of Famer *Vin Scully* and Jerry Doggett moved West with the Dodgers in 1958. In 1959, with both the Dodgers and Giants on the West Coast, future CBS Radio and Cardinals broadcaster Jack Buck broadcast 44 Dodger and Giant road games back to New York.

Ross Porter joined the broadcast team in the early 1980s, and he was fired after the 2004 season. When Doggett retired in 1987, Don Drysdale joined Scully and Porter until Drysdale's death at age 56 in July 1993, while on a road trip in Montreal, the city in which his pro baseball career began. He was replaced by former outfielder Rick Monday, who has an annoying habit of pronouncing the city as Los "Angle-less."

Hall of Famer Jaime Jarrin and Rene Cardenas broadcast Dodger games to a Spanish-speaking audience that reached upwards of 30 million internationally by the mid–1990s. Cardenas' grandfather had been the president of Nicaragua and Jarrin arrived from Ecuador in 1955. Jarrin broadcast continuously from 1958 when the Dodgers arrived through 2004. Cardenas interrupted his tour with the Dodgers with 13 years for the Astros and one with the Rangers. In 2003 former pitcher Fernando Valenzuela joined the Spanish language broadcast booth.

In the early 1990s the Dodgers broadcast selected games in Korean and Chinese. In 1995, with the arrival of pitcher Hideo Nomo, games were broadcast in Japanese and beamed back to Japan.

Books. Stanley Cohen, *Dodgers! The First 100 Years* (1990); Steve Delsohn, *True Blue: The Dramatic History of the Los Angeles Dodgers, Told by the Men Who Lived It* (2001); Frank Finch, *The Los Angeles Dodgers: The First Twenty Years* (1977); Cliff Gewecke, *Day by Day in Dodgers History* (1984); Tommy Holmes, Baseball's *Great Teams: The Dodgers* (1975); Mark Langill, *Images of Baseball, Los Angeles Dodgers* (2004); William F. McNeill, *The Dodgers Encyclopedia, 2nd Ed* (2000); Gene Schoor, *Pictorial History of the Dodgers* (1984); Myron J. Smith, *The Dodgers Bibliography* (1988); Glenn Stout, *The Dodgers: 120 Years of Dodgers Baseball* (2004); Paul Zimmerman, *The Los Angeles Dodgers* (1960).

Losers to Winners

"They are the first team to go from last to first since … us."—1991 Twins manager Tom Kelly on the resurgent 1991 Braves. The 1991 Twins and Braves became the first teams in modern Major League history to go from last to first in consecutive seasons. The Twins defeated the Braves in seven games in the World Series, winning 1–0 in 10 innings on a shutout by Jack Morris. Before 1991 the closest any two clubs came to duplicating the feat was when the Dodgers and Twins finished first in 1965. Each had finished sixth in 1964.

"the problem is that mets fans are by nature and training pessimists (unless they're eleven or under, but even then they learn quick). they have to be. even when we were weak, we blew the easy ones and split the hard ones, and so, now, if it's going good, you have an overwhelming feeling that everything is going to collapse in the next game."— joel oppenheimer in *the wrong season* (1973), in the author's lower case style.

The 1890 Louisville Eclipse club won the pennant with an 88–44 record after finishing 27–111 the year before. It was the first time that a club went from last to first in consecutive seasons.

The 1993 Phillies went from last in 1992 to the World Series the following season. The 1989 Orioles tied the 1967 Cubs for the most victories the year after losing 100 games. They won 87 games and spent 116 days in first place, including 98 straight days from May 26 to August 31. They did it with 40 players, 19 of whom had never played for them before that season and 22 of whom began 1989 with less than two years of Major League experience.

In 1999 the Diamondbacks finished 100–62, reversing their 1998 finish by 35 games (65–97), the largest single-season turnaround in modern history. They did it in their second year of existence.

In 2004 the Tampa Bay Devil Rays became the first club to go from 18 games under .500 to over .500 in the same season. They did it over about 35 games in May and June that season, but then faded badly over the second half.

The 2004 Tigers surpassed their 2003 win total just after the All-Star break, improving to 44–47 after going 43–119 in 2003. The club set a record for fewest games needed to surpass their prior year win total. The previous mark was 106 games by the 1962 Phillies (48–58 after going 47–107) and the 1989 Orioles (55–51 after 54–107).

Book. G. Richard McKelvey, *The Bounce: Baseball Teams' Great Falls and Comebacks* (2001).

Losing Streaks

"Losing streaks are funny. If you lose at the beginning, you got off to a bad start. If you lose in the middle of the season, you're in a slump. If you lose at the end, you're choking."—Gene Mauch.

"Things were so bad in Chicago last summer, that by the 5th inning the White Sox were selling hot dogs to go."—Ken Brett in 1977.

"Anybody can win a battle now and then, but it takes real genius to lose as consistently as the Macks have been losing lately."—Newspaper commentary during a 20-game losing streak by the A's in 1916.

"Every season has its peaks and valleys. What you have to try to do is eliminate the Grand Canyon."—Pirates outfielder Andy Van Slyke.

"Haven't they lost nine of their last eight?"—Braves owner Ted Turner.

"Now, a five-game losing streak is enough to make front-running mayor Rudy Giuliani sleep in his Mets jacket."—Peter Schmuck in 1999.

See also *Losing Teams.*

Longest Team Losing Streaks (Post–1900).

"Connie Mack is too grand a guy to list his team's deficiencies in this piece. However, Connie should lead the league in laughs, if nothing else, because Bobo Newsom wins the screwball title of the circuit hands down."—A 1944 preseason assessment of the A's following their horrendous 1943 season, which included a 20-game losing streak. The worst losing streaks, season record and finishing position:

American League

1988	Baltimore	21	(54–107/6th)
1906	Boston	20	(49–105/8th)
1916	Philadelphia	20	(36–117/8th)
1943	Philadelphia	20	(49–105/8th)
1975	Detroit	19	(57–102/6th)
1920	Philadelphia	18	(58–106/8th)
1948	Washington	18	(56–97/7th)
1959	Washington	18	(63–91/8th)
1926	Boston	17	(46–107/8th)

National League

1961	Philadelphia	23	(47–107/8th)
1969	Montreal	20	(52–110/6th)
1906	Boston	19	(49–102/8th)
1914	Cincinnati	19	(60–94/8th)
1962	New York	17	(40–120/10th)
1977	Atlanta	17	(61–101/6th)

On August 20, 1961, Phillies pitcher John Buzhart defeated the Braves 7–4 to end the longest losing streak in modern Major League history. The team's last win, also by Buzhart, was a 4–3 victory over the Giants on July 28. The Phillies started the streak 29 games out of first place and ended the streak with a record of 31–87.

19th Century Losers.

"Losing is the great American sin."—Writer John Tunis.

Cleveland Spiders.

"You can't win them all."—A's manager Connie Mack, after his club lost 117 games in 1916.

In 1899 the Cleveland Spiders, doormat of the National League, lost 24 straight games to set the all-time Major League futility record. The streak ended when rookie Jack Harper won his first start 5–4. The club finished with a record of 20–134, 84 games out of first place.

Pittsburgh Alleghenys. The 1890 National League Pittsburgh Alleghenys, decimated by Players League defections, lost 23 straight on their way to a 23–113 record, 66½ games out of first.

Louisville Colonels. One source reported that the 1889 American Association Louisville Colonels lost 26 straight on their way to a 27–111 record.

From Start of Season.

"This sets up the possibility of losing 162 games, which would probably be a record in the National League, at least."—Casey Stengel during the Mets' 0–9 streak at the start of the Mets franchise in 1962. After those nine games they were 9½ games out because the Pirates were 10–0. Ironically, the Mets defeated the Pirates for their first win. The club lost 120 games that season.

The 1988 Orioles lost a Major League–record 21 straight at the start of the season, costing Cal Ripken, Sr., his job after only six games of the streak. The streak broke the previous start-of-the-season losing streak of 13. The 1904 Senators and the 1920 Tigers lost their first 13.

The 1997 Cubs lost a National League record 14 games from the start of the season. On April 20, 1997, after losing the first game of a doubleheader for number 14, they beat the Mets for only their third win in 31 games dating back to September 1996. The Cubs were up 4–1 in the 9th when closer Mel Rojas left with a hamstring pull and Turk Wendell allowed two runners on with one out. Todd Hundley struck out, but Lance Johnson hit a two run double to make it 4–3. Manny Alexander, who was 4-for-7 in the doubleheader, then grounded out to end the game. The 14 straight losses broke the franchise record for losing streaks, 13, set in 1944 and tied in 1982 and 1985.

The Tigers, by losing their first nine in 2003, became the first club ever to lose their first nine games in consecutive seasons (they lost 11 straight in 2002). It took the 2003 Tigers three weeks to win their second game.

Consecutive Home Losses.

"Cubs bumper stickers removed here."—Sign in a Chicago gas station after the Cubs lost their first 12 home games of 1994. The National League record for consecutive losses at home is 15 by the

1911 Braves. In August 2002 the Mets were shut out by the Phillies for their 13th consecutive home defeat. The Mets became the first National League team to lose all their home games during a month. They finally won a home game on September 2, 2002, after losing 15 straight to tie the record.

In the American League, the 1913 Yankees lost 17 straight at home to start the season. In 1996 the Tigers lost their last 17 home games. They finally won on April 7, 1997, for their first home win since August 30, 1996.

Consecutive Road Losses. The Philadelphia A's lost 19 straight on the road in 1916, the American League record. The 1963 Mets lost 22 straight on the road in June and July that season for the Major League record. The 2004 Mariners lost 15 straight on the road, the most since the 1986 A's lost 15 straight.

Multiple Seasons/Consecutive Losses/Pitcher.

"It's not embarrassing. Someone has to win, someone has to lose. I'm just losing." — Mets pitcher Anthony Young on the day in 1993 on which he set the Major League record for consecutive losses by a pitcher.

Young lost his 23rd consecutive game on June 22, 1993, a 6–3 loss to the Expos. That tied the record set between June 13, 1910, and May 22, 1911, by Cliff Curtis of the Braves. Young broke the record in his next start a month later on July 24, 1993, when he walked home the winning run in the bottom of the 10th inning against the Dodgers in a 5–4 loss.

Young's streak ended with a 5–4 victory over the expansion Marlins in his next start on July 28, 1993. The Mets entered the 9th inning down by a run but rallied to give Young the win, his first since April 19, 1992. When his record reached 1–15 for 1993, he was sent down to Tidewater.

Young also broke the Mets' losing streak record by a pitcher, 19, set by Craig Anderson from 1962 through 1964. Young went 73 appearances without a victory. Montreal did the best against him during the streak, winning five games. When the streak ended, Young's career record stood at 4–32.

Most Appearances/No Wins. In April 2000 pitcher Vic Darensbourg finally got a win after 123 appearances and an 0–8 record since coming up with the Marlins in 1998. The 123 appearances without a win was a Major League record. He finished his career at 5–11.

Single Season Consecutive Losses/Pitcher.

"Charlie Finley gave me Catfish Hunter's old jersey. By the time I got it all the wins had been used up." — Matt Keough, who lost 14 straight in 1979 on his way to a 2–17 record. He tied the Major League record for losses at the start of a season.

The six longest single-season losing streaks by pitchers in modern Major League history:

Jack Nabors	A's	1916	19
Cliff Curtis	Braves	1910	18
Roger Craig	Mets	1963	18
Bob Groom	Senators	1909	16
Craig Anderson	Mets	1962	16
Mike Parrott	Mariners	1980	16

Jack Nabors. A's pitcher Johnny "Jack" Nabors lost a Major League–record 19 straight in 1916. According to at least one source he never again pitched in the Major Leagues, but he appeared in two games in 1917 with no record. His career record was 1–25.

Roger Craig.

"He pitched all that time with a team like that behind him? Well, he sure as hell deserves a lot more than a raise. He ought to bargain for a piece of the ballpark." — Teamsters union president Jimmy Hoffa, hearing that Craig pitched 233 innings for the Mets in 1963. Craig lost 18 straight in 1963, tying him for the longest personal losing streak over one season in National League history. He was 5–22 that year, a nice follow-up to the previous season when he was 10–24. Craig lost five 1–0 games in 1962 and became the first pitcher to have consecutive 20-loss seasons since Harry McIntire in 1905 and 1906 for the Brooklyn Dodgers. McIntire also lost 20 games in 1908.

Cliff Curtis. Curtis lost 18 straight games in 1910 as part of his then-record 23 games over two seasons.

Bob Groom. Groom lost 16 straight between June 19 and September 25, 1909. Groom was a Senators rookie who finished with a 7–26 record, one of the all-time worst American League records. His psyche remained intact, however, as he improved to 24–13 by 1912.

Craig Anderson. Anderson was 3–1 for the Mets early in 1962. He lost his next 16 that season and 19 straight over three seasons.

Russ Miller. Miller was 0–12 for the 1928 Phillies.

Pitching Losses/Start of Career. Guy Morton of the Indians lost the first 13 games of his career in 1914. He won his first game in September 1914, finishing the season with a 1–13 record and a 3.02 ERA. He recovered sufficiently to post a 16-win season in 1915 and won 98 games over 11 years.

Morton's record was broken in 1982 by Terry Felton of the Twins, who made 48 appearances that season and went 0–13. He had lost three games over three previous seasons for a total of 16 straight losses. He never again pitched in the Major Leagues.

Loss Avoidance. In 1997 and 1998, Mike DeJean of the Rockies set a Major League record for most appearances without a loss, 88, breaking the record set by Phil Paine. He went 7–0 during that stretch, but was 2–4 in 1999.

Losing Teams

"There is a special allure attached to rooting for a loser. It is a no-risk proposition that offers immunity from the despair of defeat while extending the promise of unexpected triumph. For the underdog, every victory has a spiritual message; it speaks of the conquest of forces larger than itself. Winners, and those who back them, carry with them always the relentless burden of their own success." — Stanley Cohen in *A Magic Summer — The '69 Mets* (1988).

"I managed a team that was so bad we considered a 2–0 count on the batter a rally." — Rich Donnelly, on managing in the minors.

"I'd hate to be associated with a team that goes down in history with the '64 Phillies and '67 Arabs." — Pitcher Bill Lee, delighted after being traded from the Red Sox.

"The more the California Angels play, the more they seem to be wearing those halos around their throats." — Tom Weir of *USA Today* on the Angels' slide in September 1995.

"There are a lot of changes coming in baseball. There will be an extra round of playoffs. There will be two new divisions, one in each league. And all the teams have agreed to pitch underhanded to the Mets." — David Letterman on the lousy 1993 Mets.

"The only way to prove you're a good sport is to lose." — Ernie Banks.

"One thing you learn as a Cub fan: when you bought your ticket, you could bank on seeing the bottom of the 9th inning." — Joe Garagiola.

"Waiting for the Dodgers and Angels to get into the pennant race is like leaving the porch light on for Amelia Earhart to return." — Radio personality Pat Buttram during the two clubs' dismal 1992 season.

"It seemed statistically unlikely that there could be, even in New

York, a forty- or fifty-thousand-man audience made up exclusively of born losers — leftover Landon voters, collectors of mongrel puppies, owners of stock in played out gold mines — who had been waiting years for a suitably hopeless cause." — Roger Angell writing about the 1962 Mets fans in *The Summer Game* (1972).

"1. There is everything to hope for and nothing to fear.

2. Defeats do not disturb one's sleep.

3. An occasional victory is a surprise and a delight.

4. There is no danger of any club passing you.

5. You are not asked 50 times a day, 'What is the score?' People take it for granted that you lost." — Cleveland writer Elmer E. Bates' philosophy on losing teams.

"They'll be two buses leaving the hotel for the park tomorrow. The 2 o'clock bus will be for those of you who need a little extra work. The empty bus will leave at 5 o'clock." — Giants manager Dave Bristol.

"There are lots of peaks and valleys in this game. We're in a valley — Death Valley." — Kirby Puckett on the 1995 Twins.

"Show me a good loser and I'll show you an idiot." — Charlie Gehringer.

"You know the old saying that you learn more from defeats than victories? We're going to become Einsteins." — Marlins manager John Boles in 2002. The club had a nice change in 2003 — the Marlins won the World Series, though not with Boles at the helm.

See also *Losing Streaks.*

Bad Franchise Start.

"I'd have to say no to that one." — Casey Stengel when asked on the last day of the 1962 season with the expansion Mets if the season had been fun.

The Mets were the losingest team of the 20th century, their 120 losses surpassing the 117 losses of the 1916 A's. At the start of the season, the Mets were in the unique position of being 9½ games out of first place after nine games (the Pirates had won 10 in a row). The Mets even lost ground after the regular season ended when the Giants and Dodgers squared off in a play-off that left the Mets another one-half game off the pace.

Best Losers. The 1915 Giants had a losing percentage of .454, the highest ever for a last-place team. The Giants finished only 14 games out of first place.

Consecutive Losing Seasons. The 1919–1933 Red Sox and the 1953–1967 Athletics share the American League record with 15 consecutive seasons with a sub–.500 record. The 1977–1990 Seattle Mariners came close with 14. The 1933–1948 Phillies hold the Major League record with 16 consecutive losing seasons.

Long-term Futility. Until the Browns won their first pennant in 1944, they were a combined 802½ games behind the Yankees over the previous 43 seasons in the American League.

Nolan Ryan lost more games than any other 20th century pitcher, 292, third all-time.

Shortstop Luke Appling of the White Sox holds the record for playing 20 consecutive noncontending seasons with the same team, 1930–1950 (he missed 1944 and most of 1945 due to a military commitment). The White Sox never finished higher than third in any of those years.

100 Game Losers. In 2002 the Brewers (56–106), Royals (62–100), Tigers (55–106) and Devil Rays (55–106) all lost at least 100 games, a first in Major League history. The last season with three 100-game losers was 1985 (Indians, Pirates and Giants).

2003 Detroit Tigers.

"We didn't have a farm system. We didn't have 100 years of background. And we didn't have any pitching. The only people we had were people the other teams didn't want. At least we had an excuse." — Former 1962 Mets player Rod Kanehl, comparing his losers to the 2003 Tigers.

"They don't deserve it. They're not bad enough to be the worst." — 1962 Mets member Ken Mackenzie, on whether the 2003 Tigers should be dubbed the worst team in modern Major League history. The club opened the season 0–12, making them the first club to start consecutive seasons with nine straight losses. They were also the first club to lose 60 games before July 1, with a record of 18–61 before that date. They lost 119 games to set the American League record. The Tigers hit bottom at 38–118, losing 10 in a row (and 16 of 17) to reach that nadir. They looked to be a lock to set the record for futility and overtake the 1962 Mets record of 40–120, but they won five of their last six (their best stretch of the season) to finish with a record of 43–119.

Time writer Joel Stein echoed the sentiment that the Tigers were taking themselves too seriously: "What the Tigers also don't understand is that no one is disgusted by losing…. Life is mostly losing. It's a series of imperfect essays full of jokes that don't quite work, of dreams that go unfulfilled, of passions that dwindle and ultimately, death. And if you don't figure out how to strive with the acceptance of guaranteed failure, how to find fulfillment in the eternal recurrence of imperfection, then you can have a brand-new stadium with a Ferris wheel, and no one is going to come. I'm rooting for the Tigers to win because they don't deserve to lose."

Bad Times In Chicago. In 2003 the Elias Sports Bureau calculated as 10,000 to 1 the odds of the Cubs and White Sox going a combined 180 years without winning a World Series.

Louisville Colonels

National League 1892–1899

"Yessah! Let the winds shriek through the night as they will; but then lightnings flash and the thunders roar; let the Heavens pour forth its floods, no man liveth now, nor will any man ever live who shall possess from Louisville the honor of having the last major-league game played on the home grounds!" — A.H. Tarvin in 1940. The last Major League game in Louisville was played September 2, 1899, as Louisville beat Washington 25–4.

American Association survivor Louisville had a series of mediocre to bad clubs through most of the 1890s. By 1896 the Colonels were the weakest team in the league and rivaled the Cleveland Spiders for mediocrity. In 1898 Harry Pulliam, later to become National League president, was running the club for other owners. He was forced to sell his interest to Barney Dreyfuss, who had been a penniless German immigrant who married into money and started in the liquor business. Dreyfuss bought the team for $25,000 and made himself president while he still owned the Pittsburgh club.

Louisville signed Honus Wagner for $2,100, purchasing him from a team run by Ed Barrow, future New York Yankees general manager during the Ruth years. Despite improved clubs by 1898, the National League eliminated Louisville after the 1899 season when the league cut back to eight teams. Dreyfuss shipped the best Louisville players to Pittsburgh, including Wagner and player-manager Fred Clarke. The club failed to recognize the potential of Rube Waddell and Nick Altrock and released them before the move.

Louisville played its games at the Eclipse Park, which was patterned after Sportsman's Park in St. Louis. In August 1899 the ballpark burned, but a temporary grandstand was built and stood for another 20 years.

Louisville Eclipse/Colonels

American Association 1882–1891

"He was as tight with a dollar as any of the more prominent robber barons of the era. But his miserly attitude was grounded in the reality that the Louisville franchise was severely short of cash."—Bob Bailey in *The National Pastime*.

Pete Browning starred for the club in 1882 and was one of the few top players the club ever had. The Eclipse name came from its ballpark of the same name, located at 28th and Elliott. The Eclipse name lasted only through 1883. In 1884 the club was officially known simply as the Louisville club before becoming the Colonels.

In 1889 the club struggled to one of the worst all-time records at 27–111 and suffered through a 26-game losing streak. The team was feared dead in the Johnstown Flood in Pennsylvania in May 1889. The club was known as the Cyclones in 1890 when they won the pennant with an 88–44 record. It was the first time that a club went from last to first in consecutive seasons. The name came from a cyclone that killed 75 Louisville residents in March of 1890. Louisville played miserably through the 1891 season and then was absorbed into the National League.

Louisville Grays

National League 1876–1877

"When this city entered the professional baseball business it was done with rather more judgment than is usual in a first adventure, and the nine was picked out with rather more good sense than is usual in like cases."—Lead paragraph in the *Chicago Tribune*'s report of the first game played by the National League White Stockings against the Colonels in Louisville on April 25, 1876.

The Grays were charter members of the National League in 1876. Walter Haldeman owned the club, which finished fifth. In 1877 the Grays lost a number of their final games under strange circumstances, including their last seven games to lose the pennant to the Boston Red Stockings. After a *Gambling* scandal surfaced over these losses, four players were barred for life by National League president William Hulbert: third baseman A.H. (Al) Nichols, outfielder George Hall, pitcher Jimmy Devlin and shortstop Bill Craver. As a result of the scandal, the club was expelled from the league at the 1877 winter meetings.

Louisville Slugger

Nineteenth century outfielder Pete Browning, a Louisville native, is mythologized as the original Louisville Slugger. Writers coined the phrase based on a bat allegedly made for him by John Hillerich (see also *Bats*—*Manufacturers*, for the likely true story).

Low-Hit Games   See *No-Hitters* and *One-Hitters*

Luck

"I'd rather be lucky than good."—Supposedly said by Yankee pitcher Lefty Gomez. Also attributed to Red Barrett, a 23-game winner with the Cardinals in 1945. The next year Barrett won only three games, but the Cardinals won the World Series.

"Luck is the residue of design. It's what's left after you have invested yourself fully in the job in front of you, with what intelligence you had, what information you can get, with what energy, what industry you can put into it—you give it all you've got and what comes out of it is luck. And if you haven't left very many loop-holes for negligence or mistakes—it's probably good luck."—Branch Rickey.

"I've seen guys pitch bad, and I've seen guys pitch in bad luck, but you've done an astonishing job of putting it all together."—Sparky Lyle on teammate Jim Kern, who was having a tough time on the mound.

"There is a lot of luck involved in baseball.... And what is luck? Luck is really just a lot of practice, a lot of work. I think it goes back to bouncing the ball off the steps a gillion times and my God, pretty soon you have to get pretty good."—Bobby Doerr.

"Luck's a hell of a thing. If you've got it, you can make bad moves and still come out good."—Rangers owner Bob Short on how he made his money.

"Luck? If the roof fell in and Diz was sitting in the middle of the room, everybody else would be buried and a gumdrop would drop in his mouth."—Leo Durocher about Dizzy Dean in *Nice Guys Finish Last* (1975).

See also *Superstitions*.

Lucky Lohrke. Lohrke was an infielder in the late 1940s and early 1950s with the Giants and Phillies who earned his nickname as a result of two incidents in the 1940s. On June 23, 1946, Lohrke was on the Spokane Indians team bus traveling to Bremerton, Washington. During a rest stop at a restaurant, he was told by phone that he had been sold to San Diego in the Pacific Coast League. He left his teammates and began hitchhiking back to Spokane. Soon after, the team bus veered down a 300-foot cliff in the Cascade Mountains, killing a number of the players and their manager. One of the injured players was Ben Geraghty, who later was Henry Aaron's favorite manager.

During World War II, Lohrke was on a military transport plane ready to leave for New Jersey from San Pedro, California. He was bumped off the flight by a higher ranking officer. The plane crashed and there were no survivors.

Lucky Pick-Up. Legend has it that Dick Kenworthy ("Duke" in one source), an infielder with the 1915 Kansas City Federal League team, saw a pebble of gold on the field, picked it up and used its sale proceeds to buy the ballpark.

Perhaps a more accurate version of this story involves a 1905 player for the Salt Lake City Rhyolites, first baseman William Griffiths. A ground ball came at Griffiths, but hit a small stone and caromed into the air. It flew into his glove and he beat the runner to first base. He picked up the stone and started to throw it off the field, when something caught his eye. He took a careful look at the stone and recognized free gold in it. He quietly slipped it into his pocket and went on with the game. He returned to the ballpark after the game and used a lantern to look for more rocks in the soil. He found enough to convince him that there was a fortune belowground. He and two friends quietly bought the ball park. The mine was called First Base.

Lottery. In early 1997 Reds pitcher Scott Service won $35,000 in Florida's lottery (5-for-5). Two weeks later he did it again, winning nearly $23,000. The luck prompted this comment from Peter Gammons: "If Pete Rose were still managing, Service would have guaranteed himself a job."

Luxury Tax   See *Collective Bargaining Agreements—2002–*

Thomas J. Lynch (1859–1924)

Lynch was a former "King of the Umpires" who was *National League President* from 1910 through 1912.

Ted Lyons (1900–1986)

Hall of Fame 1955

"He had a good knuckleball, and he was quick, and had an outstanding change-up. I used to hear stories about how physically strong he was.... The A's and the White Sox were on the same train going somewhere. Ted was walking through one of the cars and Jimmie ["The Beast"] Foxx was standing in the aisle. Jimmie was a playful guy and he wouldn't move out of the way. So Lyons just took hold of him, lifted him up and sat him in an upper berth and then walked on."—Mickey Vernon quoted in *Baseball Between the Lines*, by Donald Honig (1976).

Lyons pitched in 21 seasons for the White Sox beginning in 1923, winning 260 games.

Born in Louisiana, Theodore Amar Lyons was pitching for Baylor University in Texas when he was discovered by catcher Ray Schalk of the White Sox. Lyons went straight from college to Chicago, for whom he played his entire 21-year Major League career. He began in 1923 and won 21 games two years later. He won 22 games in both 1927 and 1930 and was generally effective through most of the 1930s.

An arm injury at age 31 cost him his fastball, so he developed a knuckleball and slow curve. By 1939 he was pitching only once a week on Sundays to rest his arm and take advantage of his popularity with large Sunday crowds. He ended his career in 1942 when he entered the military, though he returned at age 45 for five games in 1946. He won one game that season to bring his career record to 260–230.

Lyons pitched a no-hitter in 1926 and came within one out of another. After his retirement he managed the White Sox for three years before becoming a coach and scout. He retired from baseball in 1966 to help his sister manage a rice plantation in Louisiana.

"**M** is for Matty,
Who carried a charm
In the form of an extra
Brain in his arm."
—Ogden Nash on Christy Mathewson.

Joe McCarthy (1887–1978)

Hall of Fame (VC) 1957

"Joe McCarthy? I loved him. One of the greatest men I ever knew. I don't know where in the heck he learned all his psychology about ballplayers. He could handle almost anybody. And if he couldn't handle them he'd trade them.... He seemed always to know just how to talk to you. He knew when to jump on you, when to be your friend, when to give you a pat on the back, when to leave you alone. Best manager I ever knew or heard about. That's the way I felt about him, and I know quite a few other fellows who felt the same way."—Yankee outfielder Tommy Henrich quoted in *Baseball Between the Lines* by Donald Honig (1976).

"More than half of McCarthy's baseball life was spent in the brambles of mediocrity. He was the confirmed and perennial busher. He played the tank towns, rode the day coaches, had a gustatory acquaintance with all the greasy-spoon restaurants."—Joe Williams on McCarthy, whose broken kneecap as a teenager cost him his speed and a chance at the Major Leagues.

McCarthy managed the Cubs and Yankees to nine pennants and seven world championships beginning in 1929.

McCarthy was known primarily for his 16 years as manager of the Yankees, for whom he won eight pennants and seven World Series from 1931 through 1946. He had been a minor league second baseman for years, but never made it to the Major Leagues as a player. In a 1914 minor league game in Buffalo in which he appeared as a player, Babe Ruth made his professional debut.

McCarthy managed Louisville in the American Association from 1919 through 1925, winning the pennant his last season. In 1926 he debuted in the Major Leagues with the Cubs, which he managed through 1930 and won the 1929 pennant.

After his enormous success with the Yankees, he moved over to the Red Sox in 1948. His clubs finished second in 1948 and 1949 and McCarthy retired midway through the 1950 season. He was a severe *Alcoholic* who was finally fired by soft-hearted Red Sox owner Tom Yawkey, though it was reported that McCarthy resigned due to "ill health."

In 24 seasons his clubs won nine pennants and seven World Series. His teams finished in second place seven times. McCarthy's winning percentage of .615 is first all-time and his 2,125 career wins are fifth all-time. His World Series winning percentage of .698 is first all-time. Between 1929 and 1943 his clubs never finished below second, with one exception in 1940. None of his 24 Major League clubs finished in the second division.

Book. Alan H. Levy, *Joe McCarthy: Architect of the Yankee Dynasty* (2004).

Tommy McCarthy (1863–1922)

Hall of Fame (VC) 1946

"McCarthy looked something like an alderman, or a wrestling champion, a president of the Fat Man's Club, or that early movie star, John Bunny. But appearances can often be deceiving, for McCarthy [at 5'7" and 170 lbs.], from 1884 to 1896, was an agile, able right fielder, a good enough player on the championship Browns to be named field captain when he joined them."—Lee Allen and Tom Meany in *Kings of the Diamond* (1965).

McCarthy was a 19th century outfielder who had his greatest success with the St. Louis Browns of the American Association and the Boston Red Stockings of the National League.

Thomas Francis Michael McCarthy was a decent outfielder with marginal statistics who made it into the Hall of Fame on the coattails of his famous playing partner, Hugh Duffy. The pair, known as "The Heavenly Twins," played together for the powerful Boston Red Stockings from 1892 through 1895.

McCarthy first played in the Major Leagues for Boston of the Union Association in 1884, batting .215 in 53 games. He had a series of sub–.200 seasons before signing with the Browns of the American Association in 1888. His hitting improved to .350 in 1890 and .310 in 1891 before he moved over to the Red Stockings in 1892. His best year was 1894 when he hit .349 while legging out 13 home runs and 43 stolen bases.

He finished his career in 1896 for Brooklyn, compiling a .292 average over 13 seasons. He also stole 467 bases and scored 1,069 runs. McCarthy is best remembered for his contributions to baseball strategy. Various sources credit him with inventing or perfecting the hit-and-run and signals between runner and batter as well as the outfield trap play designed to freeze runners.

After retiring, McCarthy opened a saloon and pool hall with Duffy. He also scouted for the Reds from 1909 through 1912 and for the Braves in 1914 and 1917. He managed in the minor leagues in 1918 and later coached baseball at Holy Cross, Dartmouth and Boston College.

Willie McCovey (1938–)

Hall of Fame 1986

"Mr. Craig, where would you like us to defense McCovey: upper deck or lower deck?"—Mets manager Casey Stengel to pitcher Roger Craig before a series with the 1962 pennant-winning Giants.

McCovey hit 521 home runs primarily for the San Francisco Giants in the 1960s and 1970s.

The 6'4" Willie Lee McCovey, known as "Stretch" for his work at first base, began his professional baseball career in 1955 in the Georgia State League. He played for Phoenix of the Pacific Coast League in 1958 and early 1959 before breaking in with the Giants in mid–1959. He was named Rookie of the Year after batting .354 in only 52 games. He played decently for the Giants through 1962, but hit no more than 20 home runs each season and was sent down to the minor leagues briefly in 1960 after a deep slump.

McCovey exploded in 1963 with 44 home runs, and in 1965 he began a streak of six seasons in which he hit at least 31 home runs. He peaked in 1969 with 45 home runs, 126 RBIs and a .656 slugging average on his way to the MVP Award.

McCovey had occasional off-years due to injuries, but he was still going strong through 1977 with the Giants—though he had brief stints with San Diego beginning in 1974 and Oakland for 11 games in 1976. After mediocre seasons in 1978 and 1979, he finished his career with one home run for the Giants in 1980 to tie Eddie Mathews on the all-time list. He retired midseason and began work in the Giants' front office as a community relations specialist. By playing in 1980, he became one of only a few players to see action in four separate decades.

He finished his career with 521 home runs over 22 seasons. He drove in 1,555 runs and his home run percentage of 6.4% was 11th all-time when he retired, but now 22nd.

Joe McGinnity (1871–1929)

Hall of Fame (VC) 1946

"He established a personal fame that will live as long as baseball lives, and he was one of the most unassuming, amiable, and gentle mannered men who ever stood on a pitcher's plate and sailed the ball to that point where the batter most dreaded to swing at it, yet knew he must because it was good."—*The Sporting News*, eulogizing McGinnity.

"I saw a pitcher named McGinnity strike out twenty-two members of a girl's team at Van Buren, Arkansas, last year."—A friend of manager Honest John McCloskey, manager of Montgomery in the Southern League in 1893. McCloskey's reply, quoted in *Kings of the Diamond*, by Lee Allen and Tom Meany (1965): "Get him for me. If he can strike out twenty-two girls, perhaps he can strike out two men. And I don't have any pitchers who can."

McGinnity won 247 games over 10 seasons beginning in 1899 at age 28.

Joseph Jerome "Iron Man" McGinnity played a number of years in the minor leagues in the 1890s and also missed three seasons due to illness before reaching the Major Leagues with Baltimore in 1899 at age 28. He immediately led the league with 28 wins and then led the league again the following season with 29 wins for Brooklyn.

He moved on to Baltimore of the American League in 1901 and part of 1902 before jumping to the National League New York Giants and manager John McGraw. McGinnity led the league in 1903 and 1904 with 31 and 35 wins. He won 21 and 27 games in 1905 and 1906 before his Major League career tailed off.

McGinnity requested his release from the Giants after the 1908 season so that he could buy and manage the Newark minor league club. He continued to pitch until age 54 in 1925, finishing with a 6–6 record that season. He pitched another 14 years after completing his Major League career, winning 207 games. Including his minor league totals, McGinnity won 481 games. In 10 Major League seasons his record was 247–144 and he had an ERA of 2.64. After he retired as a player, he coached for the Dodgers in 1926 and scouted for the club until becoming an assistant coach at Williams College in 1929, the same year he died of cancer at age 58.

Bill McGowan (1896–1954)

Hall of Fame (VC) 1992

"McGowan … was more than a good umpire; he was a great one. He followed no rules of procedure, laughed uproariously when solemnity was indicated, kidded players when others would have been angry, was unexpectedly serious when levity seemed in order."—Ford Frick in *Games, Asterisks and People* (1973).

"'You're supposed to be the ace of umpires; but to me you're a pain in the ass, and if I ever ask you anything, it will be over my dead body.' But I have to say this: McGowan was the best umpire in the league."—American League umpire Joe Rue to (and about) McGowan, quoted in *The Men in Blue*, by Larry R. Gerlach (1980).

McGowan was an American League umpire for 30 seasons beginning in 1925.

William Aloysius McGowan debuted as a professional umpire at age 17 in the Tri-State League. He was elevated to umpire in the American League in 1925. He lasted through 1954, including 16½ seasons of 2,541 consecutive games. He umpired in four World Series and four All-Star Games, including the first in 1933. He was recognized as the best umpire in the league, and his nickname was "No. 1."

One of his claims to fame was calling Lou Gehrig out on an apparent home run for passing a runner on the basepaths. The lost home run cost Gehrig sole possession of the 1931 home run crown, as he finished tied with Babe Ruth at 46. Twice he was suspended by the American League office, once for throwing equipment at a player and using foul language, and once for failing to identify an ejected player to the press.

McGowan operated an umpiring school during the last 12 years of his life. Two days before he died in 1954, the American League voluntarily increased his pension amount from $3,000 annually to $6,000 for "brilliant service to the league."

John McGraw (1873–1934)

Hall of Fame 1937

"John McGraw off the field was a man in every old-fashioned sense of the word. He helped friends; he fought for his rightful due with words, fist or whatever came readily to hand; his charity knew neither restraint nor publicity."—Umpire Bill Klem, a long-time McGraw on-field nemesis.

"He is the incarnation of the American national sport…. There is no man in American baseball more coldly, cruelly commercial than John J. McGraw, manager and magnate, and no man more selflessly engrossed in the game's sake than Muggsy McGraw, baseball artist."—*The New Yorker* in 1925.

"[He] eats gunpowder every morning and washes it down with warm blood."—One of the umpires who had regular run-ins with the fiery manager.

"Life without baseball had very little meaning to him. It was his meat, drink, dream, his blood and breath, his very reason for existence." — McGraw's wife, Blanche.

"He looked like a person addicted with a permanent tumor of the buttock, which was not strange for a boy on the street or in school, but he was the only one who 'wore his tumor' at the church altar." — A neighbor of McGraw describing the hyperactive McGraw at age seven.

"The reason McGraw was a great manager — and he was the greatest — was because he knew how to handle men. Some players he rode, and others he didn't. He got the most out of each man. It wasn't so much knowing baseball. All of them know that. One manager knows about as much about the fundamentals of baseball as another. What makes the difference is knowing each player and how to handle him. And at that sort of thing nobody came close to McGraw." — Infielder Al Bridwell.

After starring for the 1890s Baltimore Orioles, McGraw managed the Giants for 31 years beginning in 1902.

Considered by many as the greatest manager of all time, the "Little Napoleon," John Joseph McGraw also had a distinguished playing career in the 19th century. He had a rough childhood that included an abusive father and the death from diphtheria of most of his family when he was 12.

McGraw began his professional baseball career in 1890 for Olean but was quickly released after supposedly making nine errors in one game. He improved at Cedar Rapids the following season and by the end of 1891 he had made it to the Baltimore Orioles of the American Association. The club was absorbed into the National League in 1892 and with McGraw at third base the club was one of the two dominant teams of the 1890s, along with the Boston Red Stockings.

McGraw played eight National League seasons for the Orioles, hitting well over .300 each year but one, including .391 in 1899 when he was player-manager for the club. He moved to the Cardinals in 1900, the American League Orioles as player-manager in 1901 and the Giants in 1902 after feuding with American League president Ban Johnson. As a player-manager for the Giants through 1906, he made only token appearances on the field. He finished his playing career with a .333 average over 16 seasons.

As manager of the Giants from 1902 through mid–1932, McGraw became one of the dominant figures in baseball. He won nine pennants in his first full 21 seasons with the Giants and 10 overall. His clubs also finished second 11 times. He ruled with an iron hand, which did not bring him great success in the mid– and late 1920s and early 1930s. Forty games into the 1932 season he retired in ill health, having not won a pennant since 1924. His clubs appeared in nine World Series though they won only three. McGraw is second all-time with 2,784 wins and 3rd all-time with a .587 winning percentage among the top 50 winningest managers.

Books. Charles C. Alexander, *John McGraw* (1988); Joseph Durso, *The Days of Mr. McGraw* (1969); Frank Graham, *McGraw of the Giants* (1944); Mrs. John J. (Blanche) McGraw and Arthur Mann, *The Real McGraw* (1953); John J. McGraw, *My Thirty Years in Baseball* (1923) (reprinted in 1995).

Connie Mack (1862–1956)

Hall of Fame 1937

"It's a pleasure for me to be here today. I'm retiring from baseball, and this is the way I'm retiring — as manager of the baseball club. I'm not quitting because I'm too old, but because I think the people want me to." — Part of Mack's retirement speech at age 88 on October 18, 1950.

Mack played Major League Baseball and then owned and managed the Philadelphia A's for 50 years starting in 1901.

Cornelius Alexander McGillicuddy, "The Tall Tactician," was born on December 22, 1862, and died at age 93 in 1956. He spent 72 years in professional baseball, 50 of them as owner and manager of the Philadelphia A's. He managed for 57 years from 1894 through 1950.

Mack began playing professionally with Meridien in the Connecticut League in 1884, played for Hartford in 1885 and then made it to the Major Leagues in 1886 with Washington in the National League. He spent 11 years on Major League clubs as a catcher, including a year with Buffalo of the 1890 Players League. He spent six years with the Pittsburgh Pirates beginning in 1891 and was player-manager from 1894 through 1896. He finished his playing career with a .245 average.

Mack managed Milwaukee of the Western League before taking over the Philadelphia A's as owner and manager in 1901 at the request of American League president Ban Johnson. Under his leadership the A's finished first nine times and last 16 times. He managed in 7,755 games, with a record of 3,731–3,948 (75 ties and one no decision) and a winning percentage of .486.

Mack was 6 feet and 150 pounds and knew he did not look good in a uniform while managing. He wore a suit instead, including high collar and either a straw or derby hat. He was never thrown out of a game in 50 years as A's manager. In 1929 Mack became the first sportsman to receive the $10,000 Bok Award from the *Ladies Home Journal* magazine for Greatest Service to Philadelphia.

By the late 1940s Mack had become somewhat senile. As he neared his retirement at age 88 in 1950, he was mistakenly calling on retired stars to pinch-hit. Third base coach Al Simmons was running the team on the field and Mack's sons Roy and Earle actually controlled the front office (see also **Fathers and Sons**). Third baseman George Kell said later that in the 1940s when the A's were losing by a lot early in a game, Mack would take his coat and leave the dugout to go up to the office for a nap and listen to the game on the radio.

Though Mack had an incredible managing career, he was technically enshrined in the Hall of Fame as a catcher in 1937. Columnist George Will pointed out that Mack was born the year after Fort Sumter was fired upon and died the year before Sputnik was launched.

Books. Connie Mack, *My 66 Years in the Big Leagues* (1950).

Bill McKechnie (1886–1965)

Hall of Fame (VC) 1962

"You can't even celebrate a victory. If you win today, you must start worrying about tomorrow. If you win a pennant, you start worrying about the World Series. As soon as that's over, you start worrying about the next season." — McKechnie quoted in *Baseball Wit and Wisdom*, by Frank Graham and Dick Hyman, Jr. (1962).

After a mediocre playing career, McKechnie managed in the National League for 25 Major League seasons beginning in 1922.

William Boyd "Deacon" McKechnie had an undistinguished playing career from 1907 through 1920, batting .251 as an infielder for various National League clubs, the Yankees for 44 games in 1913, and with two Federal League clubs in 1914 and 1915. His leadership capabilities and baseball knowledge were assets he used to develop a stellar Major League managing career.

He began 25 years at the helm in the Federal League with a fifth-place finish for Newark in 1915. In 1922, two years after his last day as a Major League player, he took over the Pirates and led them to four third-place finishes and a National League pennant in 1925. After losing to the Yankees in seven games, he managed the Pirates in 1926 before moving over to coach with the Cardinals in 1927.

McKechnie became the Cardinals manager in 1928 and immediately led the club to a pennant, but they were swept by the Yankees in the World Series. The series loss cost him his job and he managed Rochester in the International League before the Cardinals realized their mistake and reinstated him midway through the 1929 season.

McKechnie moved over to the Braves in 1930, but his talents could not bring that club out of mediocrity. He left the club after eight poor seasons to take over the Cincinnati Reds. With the Reds he won pennants in 1939 and 1940, winning a seven-game series in 1940 for the club's first championship.

He continued to manage the Reds through 1945 and resigned under pressure with only two games left in 1946 when the club was in 6th place. He finished with 1,896 wins over 25 years, 12th all-time. He moved to a coaching position with the Indians in the late 1940s.

Larry MacPhail (1890–1975)

Hall of Fame (VC) 1978
"There is a thin line between genius and insanity, and in Larry's case it was sometimes so thin you could see him drifting back and forth [or constantly wandering over the line]." — Leo Durocher, who managed for MacPhail's Dodger clubs in the late 1930s and early 1940s.

MacPhail was the maverick general manager of the Reds, Dodgers and Yankees in the 1930s and 1940s.

In the late 1920s Leland Stanford MacPhail, Sr., was a college football official and promoted golf tournaments in Ohio. Branch Rickey put him in charge of the Cardinals' Columbus club, where he quickly installed lights for night baseball. See **World War I** for a behind-enemy-lines kidnapping story involving MacPhail.

In the 1930s and 1940s, MacPhail was the maverick and mercurial redheaded general manager of the Reds (1934–1936), Dodgers (1938–1942) and Yankees (1946–1947). MacPhail is credited with introducing **Night Baseball** to the Major Leagues with the Reds in 1935 and for ending the ban on radio broadcasts in New York when he moved over to the Dodgers. During the Yankees' World Series victory celebration in 1947 he resigned in a drunken stupor and punched a writer. Yankee owners Dan Topping and Del Webb bought him out the next day.

MacPhail's son Lee became American League president and grandson Andy was the general manager of the Minnesota Twins in the 1980s and early 1990s until moving over to the Cubs.

Book. Don Warfield, *The Roaring Redhead* (1987).

Magazines

"This is the guy from Sports Thingy." — Marge Schott describing a reporter from *Sports Illustrated*.

See also **Baseball Guides** and specific entries for **The Reach Guide**, **Spalding Guide**, **The Sporting News** and **Sports Illustrated**.

Publications. *Porter's Spirit of the Times* was an early publication that was influential in popularizing baseball between 1852 and 1896.

Sporting Life was a rival to *The Sporting News* that was published between 1883 and 1917.

Weekly magazines of the 19th century included *The Ball Players' Chronicle* and *The Bat and Ball*.

Baseball Magazine published its second issue in 1908, claiming on its cover to be "For Red-Blooded Americans." It continued publication into the 1990s and was considered one of the best baseball magazines of the 20th century. It was edited from its inception for 27 years by F.C. Lane. Lane lived to be 99 and his monthly magazine focused on feature stories.

Baseball America is a twice-monthly publication that features information on the minor leagues.

In 1993 *The Diamond* magazine began publication as the official chronicle of Major League Baseball.

Circulation Levels. The following were approximate circulation levels in the 1990s:

Baseball America	50,000
Baseball Digest	275,000
Baseball Weekly	400,000
Inside Sports	500,000
Sport	932,000
Sports Illustrated	3,000,000
The Sporting News	725,000

Circulation generally declined during the 2000s due in part to the Internet.

Major League Baseball International　See *International Baseball*

Major League Baseball Players Alumni Association (MLBPAA)

The MLBPAA is a national association of former Major League players headquartered in Lakeland, Florida. It sponsors golf tournaments and other charity events involving former Major League players, including a spring training "Legends Game" featuring high-profile former Major Leaguers. The organization also maintains biographical information and assists players with drug and alcohol rehabilitation.

Major League Baseball Productions

This organization is the commercial branch of Major League Baseball. It produces films for sale, such as television's "*This Week in Baseball.*"

Major League Baseball Promotions Corporation
See *Merchandising*

Major League Executive Council (1946–)

This is now the governing body of Major League Baseball. For many years it was a seven-person committee consisting of the commissioner, the two league presidents and two club owners from each league. It was created in response to the **Union** efforts of Robert Murphy in 1946 to allow the Council to hear player grievances from elected player representatives.

Major League Players Association　See *Unions*

Major League Scouting Bureau　See *Scouting*

Major Leagues

"We have three big leagues now. There's the American, the National, and there's Ted Williams." — Red Sox pitcher Mickey Harris in 1946.

Designated Major Leagues. Numerous leagues have sprouted over the years since the first professional league was formed in 1871. Early sources often referred to the 1871–1875 National Association as a Major League, but various Major League records committees rejected it in part because of haphazard scheduling. Committees over the years have designated the following leagues as "Major" for statistical purposes:

National League (NL) (1876–)
Union Association (UA) (1884)
Players League (PL) (1890)
American Association (AA) (1882–1891)
American League (AL) (1901–)
Federal League (FL) (1914–1915)

Major League Cities.
Altoona (1884)
Anaheim (1965–)
Arlington (1972–)
Atlanta (1966–)
Baltimore (1882–1891, 1901–1902, 1954–)
Boston (1876–)
Brooklyn (1884–1957)
Buffalo (1879–1885, 1890, 1914–1915)
Chicago (1876–)
Cincinnati (1876–1880, 1882–)
Cleveland (1879–1884, 1887–1899, 1901–)
Columbus (1883–1884)
Denver (1993–)
Detroit (1881–1888, 1901–)
Hartford (1876–1877)
Houston (1962–)
Indianapolis (1878, 1884, 1887–1889, 1914)
Kansas City (1884, 1886, 1888–1889, 1914–1915, 1955–1967, 1969–)
Los Angeles (1958–)
Louisville (1876–1877, 1882–1899)
Miami (1993–)
Milwaukee (1878, 1884, 1891, 1901, 1953–1965, 1970–)
Minneapolis (1961–)
Montreal (1969–2004)
Newark (1915)
New York (1876, 1883–)
Philadelphia (1876, 1883–)
Phoenix (1998–)
Pittsburgh (1882–)
Providence (1878–1885)
Richmond (1884)
Rochester (1890)
San Diego (1969–)
San Francisco (1958–)
Seattle (1969, 1977–)
St. Louis (1876–1877, 1882–)
St. Paul (1884)
Syracuse (1879, 1890)
Tampa/St. Petersburg (1998–)
Toledo (1884, 1890)
Toronto (1977–)
Troy (1879–1882)
Washington (1884, 1886–1889, 1892–1899, 1901–1971, 2005–)

Wilmington (1884)
Worcester (1880–1882)

Number of Players.

"Less than one in twenty Class A players ever sets foot in a big league park, unless it's as a fan." — Jerry Klinkowitz in *Short Season and Other Stories* (1988).

"I was raised among major-league baseball players and all other things being equal I'd rather know a delicatessen owner, anytime." — Sportswriter Bill Slocum.

In 1985 it was calculated that from 1901 through 1985, 10,847 players had appeared in the Major Leagues. 6,038 were living, 4,737 were dead and 72 were missing. There were over 14,500 Major Leaguers by 1994 and 15,000 by 1999. There have been over 6,000 Major League pitchers.

It has been estimated that only about 8% of the players signed by 1990s scouts make it to the Major Leagues for even a single game. This is probably incorrect; 3% is more accurate.

Number of Major League teams. The number of Major League teams has fluctuated over the years, based on the number of leagues, expansion and contraction:

1876	8
1877–1878	6
1879–1881	8
1882	14
1883	16
1884	28
1885–1889	16
1890	24
1891	16
1892–1899	12
1900	8
1901–1913	16
1914–1915	24
1916–1960	16
1961	18
1962–1968	20
1969–1976	24
1977–1992	26
1993–1997	28
1998	30

Four Leagues Played In. Using the modern definition of Major Leagues, a player could not have played in four Major Leagues if he did not play before 1892. The best of a handful who played in four Major Leagues are the following (with league abbreviations):

1B	Joe Quinn	UA	NL	PL	AL
2B	Fred Dunlap	NL	UA	PL	AA
SS	Bill Hallman	NL	PL	AA	AL
3B	John Irwin	NL	UA	AA	PL
OF	Hugh Duffy	NL	PL	AA	AL
OF	Emmett Seery	UA	AL	PL	AA
OF	Dummy Hoy	NL	PL	AA	AL
C	Duke Farrell	NL	PL	AA	AL
P	Gus Weyhing	AA	PL	NL	AL

The last player to play in four Major Leagues was third baseman Lave Cross (1887–1907). Tom Loftus is the only person to manage in four Major Leagues: Milwaukee (UA), Cleveland (AA), Cleveland, Cincinnati, Chicago (NL), and Washington (AL).

Longest Between Major League Appearances.

Paul Schreiber. Schreiber pitched in 10 games for the 1922–1923 Dodgers, with no decisions and one save. He next appeared in the Major Leagues in September 1945 for the Yankees. He had been the Yankees' batting practice pitcher and was pressed into Major League service during World War II. He appeared in two games with no record.

Les "Buster" McCrabb. McCrabb pitched for the last-place A's for a few years until 1942. He did not appear in the Major Leagues again until 1950, pitching 1⅔ innings and giving up four earned runs.

Kevin Hickey. Hickey pitched for the White Sox in 1983, compiling a 1–2 record with five saves. His next Major League appearance was in 1989 for the Orioles. Hickey was later desperate for work after leaving baseball. He mentioned it during a radio interview in Chicago and the host quickly landed him a position as the doorman at Mike Ditka's restaurant.

American League/1900. There has been considerable debate over whether the American League should be classified as a Major League in 1900. League president Ban Johnson publicly acknowledged the league's status as a minor league that season, but many historians point out that he was simply playing politics to enable his league to place a club in Chicago. Historian Joe Wayman points out that 171 players (85%) of the 1900 American League players were in the Major Leagues before that season, and 112 (56%) remained in the Major Leagues after that season. SABR member David Shiner and others have concluded that the players were either not quite ready or over the hill, and thus the league does not deserve the elevated status.

Books. Peter Bjarkman, *Encyclopedia of Major League Baseball Histories* (1991); Donald Dewey and Nicholas Acocella, *Encyclopedia of Major League Baseball Teams* (1993); Donald D. Jones, *Former Major League Teams: An Encyclopedia* (1995); Michael LaBlanc (ed.), *Hot Dogs, Heroes and Hooligans: The Story of Baseball's Major League Teams* (1994); David Pietrusza, *Major Leagues: The Formation, Sometimes Absorption and Mostly Inevitable Demise of 18 professional Organizations, 1871 to Present* (1992); G. Edward White, *Creating the National Pastime: Baseball Transforms Itself, 1903–1953* (1996).

Manager of the Year

"Sharing a similarly curious fortune was a field general named Larry Shepard, who was fired a year ago as manager of the Pittsburgh Pirates after his team had won eighty-eight games; his successor, Danny Murtaugh, brought the Pirates home this year with eighty-*nine* victories and was instantly named Manager of the Year."—Roger Angell in *The Summer Game* (1972).

Awards. A separate Manager of the Year Award was presented annually by both the Associated Press and UPI until UPI folded. Now only AP presents the award. The Baseball Writers Association began presenting its Manager of the Year Award in 1983.

Lowest Finisher. Gene Mauch guided the 1962 Phillies to a seventh-place finish, the lowest ever for a manager who received the award.

Managers

"The secret of managing is to keep the five guys who hate you away from the guys who are undecided."—Casey Stengel.

"Out of 25 guys there should be 15 who would run through a wall for you, 2 or 3 who don't like you at all, 5 who are indifferent and maybe 3 undecided. My job is to keep the last two groups from going the wrong way."—Billy Martin.

"Playing for Yogi is like playing for your father; playing for Billy is like playing for your father-in-law."—Don Baylor, New York Yankees designated hitter, on Billy Martin and his predecessor, Yogi Berra.

"Managing is not running, hitting, or stealing. Managing is getting your players to put out one hundred percent year after year."—Sparky Anderson.

"He's going to sell Bobby Valentine. Most everyone in baseball does not like and does not respect Bobby Valentine. Closer to 100% than 50%."—Mets manager Dallas Green on his mid–1990s successor.

"Sometimes I think I'm in the greatest business in the world. Then I lose four straight and want to change places with a farmer."—Cubs, Yankees and Red Sox manager Joe McCarthy, who retired in 1949 after 24 years as a Major League manager with nine pennants and seven second-place finishes. He never had a club finish lower than fourth and won seven World Series titles.

"To all the managers who are constantly being second-guessed."—Dedication by Keith Hernandez in his book *Pure Baseball*, with Mike Bryan (1994).

Early Managers. In the early years of professional baseball the term "manager" generally was used to refer to what today is a general manager. "Team captain" usually referred to the bench manager. An 1876 National League rule barred managers from the players' bench. Bench managers were accepted by the 1880s and were more important by the 1890s. Frank Selee of Boston and Ned Hanlon of Baltimore were good examples of strong managers of the era. However, Brooklyn's Charles Ebbets was not alone in 1898 in refusing to pay for what he considered the excess baggage of a bench manager. He took over the club himself for most of the season.

Attempt to Hire. In 1907 Frank Navin of the Detroit Tigers attempted to hire Hughie Jennings as manager. However, American League president Ban Johnson did not want a member of the old Baltimore Orioles of the rival National League to manage in the American League. Navin told Johnson that if Jennings were prohibited from managing the club then Tigers owner Bill Yawkey would withdraw his enormous financial support. Johnson relented and Jennings went on to manage the team for 14 years. Navin's animosity toward Johnson is evidenced by the fact that Navin and Judge Landis, whom Johnson despised, were confidantes after Landis became commissioner.

Black and Latin Managers. In 1912 Cuban Mike Gonzalez began a 17-year career as a catcher and managed the Cardinals briefly in 1938 and 1940.

The first black manager in the Major Leagues was Frank Robinson, who was hired by the Cleveland Indians in 1975 (see also *Black "Firsts"*).

Larry Doby was the second black manager, taking over the White Sox in 1978, though he lasted only part of the season. His record was 37–50 and the club was in fifth place when he was fired.

Cuban-born Preston Gomez managed the Padres for four years beginning in 1969 and later managed the Astros and Cubs. He finished last every year except 1974 with the Astros, who finished fourth.

Maury Wills took over the Mariners in 1980 with 58 games to play and then lasted 25 games into the 1981 season. His erratic and combative behavior later was attributed to a drug problem which he acknowledged publicly.

Cuban-born Cookie Rojas managed the Angels for all but eight games in 1988, leading them to a fourth place finish.

Texas-born Clarence "Cito" Gaston was hired as the manager of the Blue Jays in mid–1989. In 1992 he led the Blue Jays to the first of two consecutive World Series victories. His clubs began to fade after that, and he was fired after the 1997 season.

Cardinals manager Red Schoendienst gives a clubhouse pep talk to the 1960s Cardinals.

Black and Latin managers were still a rarity in the early 1990s. In 1991 Hal McRae was the only black manager hired during the season and no other black or Latin managers were considered. Only Cito Gaston of the Blue Jays was a minority manager at the time.

During 1991 there were 10 Latin and 13 black minor league managers. Most of the Latin managers were at the rookie league level, where they were often only glorified interpreters for the young Latin players. Only one Latin managed at the Class AAA level. In early 1992 former outfielder Felipe Alou of the Dominican Republic was hired to manage the Expos. Alou has been one of the more successful of all managers of color. He was hired to manage the cash-poor Expos in 1992 and was named manager of the year in 1994. He lasted through part of 2001, and then in 2003 took the Giants to a division title.

Former slugger Tony Perez of Cuba was hired briefly in early 1993 to manage the Reds (see also **Shortest Tenure**).

In late 1992 Don Baylor was hired to be the first manager of the Rockies, and Dusty Baker was hired to manage the Giants. Baylor's club finished ahead of the Padres in 1993 and Baker's Giants finished only one game behind the Braves after leading the division for most of the season. Baylor lasted through the 1998 season, when the club finished fourth and he was fired. His best year was 1995, when the club finished second and he moved over to the Cubs for three seasons with mixed results. Baker managed the

Giants for 10 seasons, winning Manager of the Year honors three times and leading the Giants to the World Series in 2002. He left after that season and took over the Cubs, who he took to the 2003 NLCS before the club's heartbreaking loss to the Marlins.

It was often said that former Reds second baseman and two-time National League MVP Joe Morgan would be an excellent manager. However, Morgan became a successful broadcaster and has numerous business ventures to occupy his time. He has said that he is not interested because of his other pursuits and the grind of travel.

Cito Gaston has been perhaps the most successful of all Latin and black managers. He took the Blue Jays to the World Series in 1992 and 1993, and remained with the club through most of the 1997 season before being fired.

Tony Pena took over the Kansas City Royals in May 2002 and did a good job with the club in 2003.

On June 25, 2003, history was made when two Latin managers faced each other, Pena of the Royals and Luis Pujols of the Tigers.

Carlos Tosca of Cuba, with no professional playing experience, took over the Blue Jays in 2002 and lasted until midway into the 2004 season.

Bridesmaid. Al Lopez managed two pennant-winning clubs, the 1954 Indians and 1959 White Sox. These victories were sandwiched among 10 second-place finishes.

Celebrity Managers. Radio personality Larry King and broadcaster Bob Costas managed the all-star teams at the 1993 Class AA All-Star Game. Costas was the winner, allowing him to write one of King's columns in *USA Today*. King missed out on a chance to broadcast an inning of a Major League game.

Costas managed a 1992 spring training game for the A's in a 7–5 loss to the Mariners on his 40th birthday. After the loss, Costas noted that he had the same managerial record as Ted Turner (see **Owners as Managers.**).

Former *President* Dwight Eisenhower managed the Angels briefly during a spring training game in the early 1960s.

College Ranks to Major Leagues. Branch Rickey came off the campus of the University of Michigan to manage the Browns in 1913.

Bobby Winkles was the head coach at Arizona State before managing the Angels in 1973. The club finished fourth and in 1974 Winkles was fired after 75 games while the club was in last place. He took a Major League coaching position until he was hired to manage the A's during the 1977 season. He finished the year with a 37–71 record. He started 1978 by putting the A's in first place after 39 games, but resigned abruptly in May of that year.

Former Major League infielder Eddie Stanky left the head coaching job at Southern Alabama University to take over the Rangers in 1977. His managerial career lasted one day and he returned to Alabama (see also **Shortest Tenure**).

Fans as Managers. See *Fans*.

Firings.

"I wanted to make sure no one was in my uniform." — Don Zimmer on why he always arrived early at the ballpark.

"The two of them deserve each other. One's a born liar; the other's convicted." — Yankee manager Billy Martin on Reggie Jackson and George Steinbrenner. The comment led to Martin's firing for the second time.

"I TOLD YOU SO." — Telegram from 1890s Pittsburgh manager Connie Mack to his second-guessing owner. Mack was fired.

"Your letter came as a surprise, but we realize that ability should be rewarded. Therefore, I join with the fans of Worcester in expressing our appreciation for your outstanding services rendered and wish you luck in your new position; we congratulate Toledo on getting your valuable services." — Letter from club president Casey Stengel to manager Casey Stengel, releasing himself from his position at Worcester to move to Toledo. In the 1930s Stengel was the president, manager and a player for Worcester, a Boston Braves farm club.

"I can think of three managers who weren't fired. John McGraw of the Giants, who was sick and resigned; Miller Huggins of the Yankees, who died on the job; and Connie Mack of the Athletics, who owned the club." — Red Smith. Perhaps Tommy Lasorda should be included, when he resigned while ill in 1996.

"At least the day wasn't a total loss. George had somebody fired." — Yankee manager Dick Howser after the Yankees lost to the Red Sox and a hotel operator was fired after she refused to place a long distance call for Steinbrenner from the hotel bar.

At the end of the 1940 season the Indians players signed a petition calling for the firing of manager Ossie Vitt. The season started well, as Bob Feller pitched an Opening Day no-hitter, and the club finished second with an 89–65 record. Nevertheless, Vitt was an ineffective manager whom the players disliked and did not respect.

When Bill Veeck fired Rogers Hornsby as Browns manager in 1952, Veeck received a loving cup from the players in gratitude.

In July 1978 Yankee manager Billy Martin was on the verge of a nervous breakdown. The Yankees were doing poorly and he was feuding with his players, most notably Reggie Jackson. On July 24 Martin resigned abruptly under pressure from owner George Steinbrenner. Dick Howser was named interim manager for one game before Bob Lemon was hired.

The Yankees' Oldtimers Game was held on July 29, a few days after the managerial changes. There were chants and banners throughout the ballpark in support of Martin, but he was not seen. Near the end of the introductions, Yankee public address announcer Bob Sheppard made the following announcement: "Ladies and gentleman, your attention please. The Yankees announce today that Bob Lemon has agreed to a contract to continue as manager of the New York Yankees through the 1978 and 1979 seasons.... [Boos by crowd]....

"Your attention to the rest of this announcement. In 1980 Bob Lemon will become the general manager of the Yankees ... and the Yankees would like to announce that the manager for the 1980 season, and hopefully for many years after that, will be Number One ... [Billy Martin trotted onto the field to a huge ovation.]"

See also David Falkner, *The Last Yankee* (1992); Peter Golenbock, *Wild, High and Tight* (1994); Gene Schoor, *Number One: Billy Martin* (1980).

In September 1992 on Unemployment Night at San Diego's Jack Murphy Stadium, the Padres fired manager Greg Riddoch.

Greatest.

"McGraw, Mack and McCarthy were the best managers I ever saw." — Grantland Rice.

Edwin Pope's *Baseball's Greatest Managers* (1960), contains the greatest managers as chosen by a "jury" of 20 media experts. The almost unanimous selections were John McGraw, Connie Mack, Miller Huggins, Joe McCarthy and Casey Stengel. An updated list would probably include at least Sparky Anderson and Tony LaRussa.

At the 1969 centennial celebration of baseball, John McGraw of the Giants was named the all-time best in a poll of sportswriters.

Hall of Fame.

"Baseball is a simple game. If you have good players, and you keep them in the right frame of mind, the manager is a success. The players make the manager. It's never the other way." — Sparky Anderson.

The following 18 managers have been elected to the Hall of Fame:

Sparky Anderson (2000)
Walter Alston (1983)
Charles Comiskey (1939)
Leo Durocher (1994)
Clark Griffith (1946)
Bucky Harris (1975)
Miller Huggins (1964)
Tommy Lasorda (1997)
Al Lopez (1977)
Connie Mack (1937)
Joe McCarthy (1957)
John McGraw (1937)
Bill McKechnie (1962)
Wilbert Robinson (1945)
Casey Stengel (1966)
Earl Weaver (1996)
George Wright (1937)
Harry Wright (1953)

Japanese Managers. See *Japan*—Managers.

Latin Managers. See **Black and Latin Managers**.

Longevity.

"FIVE SKIPPERS FACING DATE WITH NOOSE" — September 1964 headline in *The Sporting News*.

Manager turnover has been far more frequent in recent years. In a study of managerial changes since 1946, the following results purportedly were illuminating:

1950s 58 fired or quit
1960s 90 fired or quit
1970s 95 fired or quit

The numbers may be deceiving for two reasons. First, there were more teams due to expansion beginning in the 1960s. Second, the expansion teams were mediocre to worse, causing high turnover among managers. Between 1946 and 1966, managers averaged 2.3 years on the job. The first time that four American League managers were replaced during the season was 1946. This began a trend toward more frequent firings. In 1991 a total of 13 managers were fired, the most in Major League history.

George Steinbrenner of the Yankees and Charlie Finley of the A's are the owners most notorious for making frequent managerial changes. Finley had 13 managers between 1961 and 1978. Steinbrenner had 21 managers between 1973 and 1995 (including repeats). Ironically, Billy Martin, who was hired and fired four times by Steinbrenner, turned down Finley's 1967 offer to manage. Martin managed the A's from 1980 through 1982 after Finley had sold the team.

When Buck Showalter managed his 472nd consecutive game in June 1995, he broke the record of 471 by Martin for the most consecutive by a Yankee manager under George Steinbrenner. Martin managed the club for a total of 941 games over five tours of duty under Steinbrenner. Joe Torre later shattered Showalter's record.

Between 1961 and 1995 the Yankees had 23 different managers; in that same span the Dodgers had two: Walter Alston and Tommy Lasorda. Between late 1976 when Lasorda took over the Dodgers and mid–1995, there were 200 managerial changes. Between 1954 and mid–1996, when Lasorda retired due to ill health, there were 404 managerial changes in the Major Leagues.

Longest Career (through 2004).

"Bob Hope can get only as many laughs out of his lines as his gagwriters put in them. It is the same with baseball managers. They stand or fall on the quality of their material. Naturally, some managers are quicker on the uptake than others and, as is true in any other field, the manager with superior attributes is going to be more successful than others less gifted. Even so, he isn't going to win pennants unless he has the players."— Sportswriter Joe Williams.

Manager	Years
Connie Mack	53
John McGraw	33
Bucky Harris	29
Tony LaRussa	27 (active)
Gene Mauch	26
Sparky Anderson	26
Casey Stengel	25
Bill McKechnie	25
Joe McCarthy	24
Leo Durocher	24
Walter Alston	23
Jimmy Dykes	21
Tommy Lasorda	21
Clark Griffith	20

Mack had two interruptions in service. In 1937 and 1939, Mack's son Earle managed the club for substantial periods of time.

Close Call Into Hall. Tommy Lasorda was forced to retire in mid–1996 after suffering a mild heart attack. He was elected to the Hall of Fame the following January, but almost didn't make it. Members of the Veteran's Committee thought he might try to come back and manage. Lasorda had said several times that he wanted to come back and manage (eventually he did, with the U.S. Olympic team — see **Olympic Games**). He told a newspaper reporter the weekend before the vote that he had managed his last game, perhaps in an attempt to convince the Veteran's Committee. Lasorda and the other veterans failed to reach the required 75% majority vote on the first vote, so the committee voted again on the six top vote getters. Lasorda received the required 12 votes, edging out former American League president Lee MacPhail and former Dodgers owner Walter O'Malley.

Longest with One Team.

50 years — Connie Mack, A's
30 years — John McGraw, Giants
23 years — Walter Alston, Dodgers
21 years — Tommy Lasorda, Dodgers (including a few games at the end of the 1976 season)

Major League Player. Since 1901 approximately 65 Major League managers have had no Major League playing experience.

Manager and Player Together. Don Drysdale of the Dodgers pitched under Walter Alston for 14 years, the longest period for any pitcher under one manager until the 1980s and 1990s. Drysdale's record is often reported as the most of any player until the 1980s, but Jimmy Dykes played 15 seasons for Connie Mack from 1918 through 1932.

Dodger catcher Mike Scioscia played in 1,441 games for Tommy Lasorda to set a record that was broken when infielders Alan Trammell and Lou Whitaker played 18 straight seasons for Sparky Anderson of the Tigers.

Manager Swap. The Tigers and Indians swapped managers in 1960 when Jimmy Dykes went to Cleveland and Joe Gordon went to Detroit.

Most Managers Played For. Nineteenth century star Deacon McGuire played for 23 managers in 26 years.

Most Teams Managed.

"I think they recycle more managers than cans."— Outfielder Billy North.

"The manager was fired twice, but was hired again on the grounds that he's a sound baseball man. A sound baseball man is anybody who has been fired twice."— Leonard Shechter in *The Jocks* (1970).

Bucky Harris ("The Boy Wonder") managed eight different clubs: the Red Sox, Yankees, Phillies, Tigers (twice) and Senators (three times). Harris managed from age 27 in 1924 (see also **Youngest Managers**) until 1956, missing only 1944–1946 and 1949. His managerial prowess was established at the outset of his career when he won pennants with the Senators in 1924 and 1925. His only other pennant, however, was in 1947 when he was with the Yankees. After 1928 his clubs finished in the first division only three other times (twice in fourth and once in third).

Most Wins (through 2004).

"So, you might think, if [Sparky] Anderson leaves his body to science and the Tigers prop him in the dugout and say, 'Ol' Spark sure has gotten quiet the last few years,' he might have a shot at Mack's record."— Thomas Boswell in *The Heart of the Order* (1989).

"As you have more years, you feel the performances a little deeper. After knowing what it feels like to win, the losing is tougher to accept. The bottom line in this league, you either get it done or you don't."— Tony LaRussa.

3,731	Connie Mack
2,784	John McGraw
2,194	Sparky Anderson
2,157	Bucky Harris

2,125	Joe McCarthy
2,112	Tony LaRussa (active)
2,040	Walter Alston
2,008	Leo Durocher
2,000	Bobby Cox (active)
1,905	Casey Stengel
1,902	Gene Mauch
1,896	Bill McKechnie

Most Wins/First 1,000 Games.

671	Frank Chance
636	Billy Southworth
617	Al Lopez
604	Earl Weaver
602	Sparky Anderson
597	John McGraw
593	Joe McCarthy
591	Davey Johnson
584	Bill Terry
583	Charlie Grimm

Most Wins/No Pennant/Career. Jimmy Dykes won 1,406 games in 21 years as manager of six teams but never won a pennant. Nor did Gene Mauch, despite winning 1,902 games over 26 years. He came close when the Angels won the 1982 Western Division title and then won the first two of five games with the Milwaukee Brewers in the ALCS. The Brewers then won three straight for the pennant.

Mauch came closest when the Angels won the 1986 division title and were one strike away from defeating the Red Sox in five games in the ALCS. Dave Henderson's 9th inning home run propelled the Red Sox to a seven-game victory for the pennant. Mauch also guided the 1964 Phillies to their late season collapse.

In all three debacles, Mauch, known as "The Little General" and "The Walking Computer," was accused of mismanaging his pitchers, in part by using them on only two days' rest late in the season or in the postseason.

Most World Series Winners. Joe McCarthy and Casey Stengel each managed the Yankees to seven World Series victories, the most by a manager in Major League history.

Not in the Hall of Fame. Billy Southworth is the only 20th century manager to win three or more pennants and not be elected to the Hall of Fame (excluding very recently retired or active managers). He led the Cardinals to pennants in 1942, 1943 and 1944, and the Boston Braves to a pennant in 1948. He also guided his clubs to World Series victories in 1942 and 1944. Winning pennants during the talent-thin war years and for an otherwise pitiful franchise (Boston) may have caused Southworth to be ignored despite winning 1,044 games over his 13-year managerial career while compiling the fifth-highest winning percentage of all time (.597).

Oldest Managers.

"I'm probably the oldest manager in the history of the game to win 800. I'll probably get a button from AARP."—Marlins manager Jack McKeon in 2003 at age 72, who led the Marlins to a victory over the Yankees in the World Series that year. He was the third-oldest manager in history (behind Connie Mack at 88 and Casey Stengel at 75), and the oldest to lead a team to the World Series (Stengel's last World Series appearance was at age 70 in 1960). McKeon led the Marlins to an NLCS victory over the Cubs after Chicago led 3–1 in games. The comeback was reminiscent of the 1984 NLCS when McKeon was general manager of the Padres. San Diego came back from a 2–0 game deficit to beat the Cubs in the five-game division series.

McKeon took over the Marlins on May 11, when the club was 16–22 under Jeff Torborg. The last manager to win a World Series after beginning the season in another capacity was Paul Owens, who led the 1980 Phillies to the championship. McKeon was rewarded with the Manager of the Year Award, which he also won in 1999 when he led the Reds.

Owners as Managers.

"Instead of identifying someone as manager, the Yankees should appoint him 'Vice President, Dugout Decisions.'"—*New York Times* columnist Dave Anderson on managing under meddlesome owner George Steinbrenner. Yankee manager Dallas Green was fired in 1989 in part for calling Steinbrenner "Manager George."

Other than legitimate managers such as Connie Mack and John McGraw and others who held an **Ownership Interest** in their teams, a few owners managed their clubs for a short time:

M.H. Davidson. In 1888 the Louisville Colonels were sold to Mordecai Davidson. The players threatened to *Strike* when pitcher Guy Hecker was named as manager. In response, Davidson put on a uniform to manage himself and announced that the players would be fined for errors. The team balked and wrote a letter stating their opposition. After forfeiting a game, the players relented. Davidson managed for the entire season and led the Colonels to a 26-game losing streak in 1889, an all-time record.

Charles Ebbets. Ebbets, who held a majority interest in the Dodgers in 1898, managed the club for most of the year primarily as a cost-saving measure. He started in ninth place and finished tenth, as his club won only 38 of 110 games under his leadership.

Christopher Von der Ahe. In 1892 the eccentric St. Louis Browns owner supposedly started a so-called "reign of terror" when he began managing the Browns after Charles Comiskey quit after the 1891 season. However, *The Baseball Encyclopedia* reports that Von der Ahe managed briefly only in subsequent years: winning one game in 1895, losing two games in 1896, and winning two of 12 games in 1897.

Horace Fogel. In 1902 Fogel managed the New York Giants for 44 games (42 in earlier sources), compiling an 18–23 record with three "no decisions" due to ties or darkness.

Judge Emil Fuchs. After the 1928 season the Braves owner traded player-manager Rogers Hornsby. Fuchs took over as field manager for the 1929 season, though he generally let Johnny Evers handle the club on the field. Fuchs guided the team to a 56–98 record and a last-place finish, and he took a few games off to try a case (he was never actually a judge, but was an attorney). He had a better winning percentage than Hornsby had in 122 games in 1928 when the team had a 39–83 record under him and finished seventh.

Ted Turner. Atlanta Braves owner Ted Turner managed the team for one game on May 11, 1977. Commissioner Bowie Kuhn supposedly stepped in and prohibited him from further managing on the ground that it was "not in the best interests of baseball."

The team was in a 16-game losing streak and Turner continued it with a 2–1 loss to the Pirates. Regular manager Dave Bristol was sent on a scouting trip and coach Vern Benson actually ran the team. Benson won the next game after Turner quit managing. Turner's response to the losing streak was philosophical: "This losing streak is bad for the fans, no doubt, but look at it this way. We're making a lot of people happy in other cities."

Ownership Interest. National League Rule 20(e) provides that a manager may not have a financial interest in a team without special permission from the league president. This rule may have been instituted because of the problems created when the Cardinals tried to unload Rogers Hornsby in the 1920s when he had a financial interest in the team. He held up his departure to another club by initially refusing to sell his stock in the Cardinals unless he received an exorbitant price.

Pennants First Three Years. Hughie Jennings (Tigers 1907–1909) and Ralph Houk (Yankees 1961–1963) are the only managers to win pennants in their first three seasons. Houk is also the only manager to win the World Series his first two years, 1961 and 1962. His club was swept by the Dodgers in 1963.

Pennants in Both Leagues. Only four managers have won pennants in both the National and American Leagues: Alvin Dark (1962 Giants and 1974–1975 A's), Joe McCarthy (1929 Cubs and 1932, 1936–1939, 1941–1943 Yankees), Sparky Anderson (1970, 1972, 1975, 1976 Reds and 1984 Tigers), Yogi Berra (1964 Yankees and 1973 Mets) and Dick Williams (1967 Red Sox, 1972–1973 A's and 1984 Padres).

The Perfect Manager.

"It's like you came to a controversy and a ball game breaks out." — Matt Keough, on a game between teams managed by Billy Martin and Earl Weaver.

Billy Martin/Leo Durocher	Competitiveness/fire
Walter Alston/Gil Hodges	Patience
Sparky Anderson	Leadership
Tommy Lasorda	Motivator
John McGraw and Tony LaRussa	Tactics

Player-Managers.

"I used to send myself up to the plate to pinch hit whenever the wind was blowing out from home plate."— Player-manager Joe Cronin.

Charles Ebbets of the Dodgers was a great believer in player-managers because they "lead by example." He also may have wanted to save a few dollars by not having to pay a bench manager.

As a cost-saving measure during the 1930s Depression, many teams hired player-managers to avoid paying two separate people. One source reported that on Opening Day 1934, seven of the eight National League managers also played. However, a review of the record does not bear this out. The only player-managers listed were Frankie Frisch (Cardinals), Bill Terry (Giants), Charlie Grimm (Cubs), Jimmie Wilson (Phillies) and Bob O'Farrell (Reds). Casey Stengel (Dodgers) and Bill McKechnie (Braves) were retired as players. Although George Gibson (Pirates) was retired, his successor that season, Pie Traynor, was a player-manager.

More accurately, there were eight player-managers in the Major Leagues at the start of the 1934 season, with two others added during the season. The American Leaguers were Mickey Cochrane (Tigers), Rogers Hornsby (Browns), Joe Cronin (Senators) and Jimmy Dykes (White Sox, hired midseason). All the player-managers except Bob O'Farrell started the 1935 season with the same clubs.

During and after World War II the player-manager became a rarity. In 1942 Mel Ott played in 152 games for the Giants. He was the last player-manager to play in as many games as his club had decisions (85–67). Lou Boudreau was the last player-manager to win a World Series, with the 1948 Cleveland Indians.

Between Lou Boudreau in 1952 with the Reds Sox and Frank Robinson in 1975–1976 with the Indians, the only player-managers were Phil Cavarretta with the Cubs in 1951–1953 and Solly Hemus when he played in 24 games in 1959 for the Cardinals. Robinson hit a home run the first time he appeared in a game as player-manager.

In 1977 Joe Torre was player-manager of the Mets and in 1979 Don Kessinger was player-manager of the White Sox. Torre finished the season for the Mets after Joe Frazier was fired, compiling a 49–68 record. Kessinger managed the White Sox to a 46–60 record before being replaced by Tony LaRussa.

Pete Rose was player-manager of the Reds from 1984 to midway

through the 1987 season, when he officially retired as a player. In 1984 he took over with 41 games remaining, compiling a 19–22 record. His club finished second the next three years. Though he was on the active roster for part of 1987, he never appeared in a game.

Since 1876 almost 150 managers have played in one or more of their team's games. Of that number, approximately 100 were true player-managers who made more than token appearances for their clubs. A complete list is contained in *Baseball from a Different Angle*, by Bob Broeg and William J. Miller, Jr. (1988). See also Fred Stein, *And the Skipper Bats Cleanup* (2002).

Player Revolt. Late in the 1971 season five Washington Senators players convened in the bathroom of the clubhouse at RFK Stadium in Washington. Led by Denny McLain and Bernie Allen, they inscribed their names on the wall as they solemnly swore to overthrow manager Ted Williams and his staff. The revolt culminated in a "Baptism" of new players on the club during a party at McLain's house in a spoof of a Ku Klux Klan meeting.

Resignation. Manager Dick Williams resigned during the victory celebration by the Oakland A's after winning the 1973 World Series. Williams then tried to sign with the Yankees, while Yankee manager Ralph Houk tried to sign with the Tigers, but Bowie Kuhn initially blocked the moves as "not in the best interests of baseball." Houk ended up with the Tigers and Williams went to the Angels.

Davey Johnson managed the Orioles to a 1997 division title and barely lost the ALCS to the Indians in six games. Hours before he was named American League Manager of the Year, Johnson resigned because Orioles owner Peter Angelos refused to give Johnson a vote of confidence after indicating earlier that Johnson would return for the 1998 season.

Rookie World Series Winners. The following managers have won the World Series in their first seasons at the helm:

Tris Speaker	1920 Indians
Bucky Harris	1924 Senators
Rogers Hornsby	1926 Cardinals
Bill Terry	1933 Giants
Frankie Frisch	1934 Cardinals
Eddie Dyer	1946 Cardinals
Ralph Houk	1961 Yankees
Bob Brenley	2001 Diamondbacks

Dallas Green of the 1980 Phillies and Tom Kelly of the 1987 Twins each won a World Series in his first full season as manager. Green managed for 30 games in 1979 and Kelly managed for 23 games in 1986.

Rotating Managers. The 1961–1965 Cubs had a series of rotating managers among their coaches, known as the *College of Coaches*.

Salaries. In 1928 Bucky Harris received $100,000 over three years to manage the Senators. Casey Stengel's $65,000 in 1951 with the Yankees was the highest for a manager up to that point. Stengel was later paid $100,000 to manage the Mets.

By the late 1980s, even the lowest paid managers were finally earning in excess of $100,000. At the highest end of the scale, Tommy Lasorda of the Dodgers earned $575,000 in 1991 and received a 43% raise for the 1992–1993 seasons.

In 1996 Ray Knight signed with the Reds for $250,000 per season in his first managing job. Davey Johnson signed for $750,000 per season.

Mike Scioscia signed a bargain-basement deal with the Angels for $3 million over four years starting in 2001. Lou Piniella left the Mariners after the 2002 season (making $2.5 million) and signed a multi-year deal with the Devil Rays for $13 million. Dusty Baker left the Giants after leading them to the World Series in 2002 and then signed with the Cubs for $14 million over four years.

Bobby Valentine earned $2.7 million in his last year with the Mets in 2003. In April 2004 Yankee manager Joe Torre signed a $19.2 million, three-year contract extension through 2007. He would remain as a consultant to the Yankees after managing at between $500,000 and $600,000 annually. He also received a $1 million bonus each time the Yankees won the World Series.

Broadcaster. In 2000 the Diamondbacks named broadcaster Bob Brenley as their manager and he won the World Series in his rookie year. Larry Dierker began managing the Astros after serving in the club's broadcast booth, and he led the club to four first-place finishes in five years beginning in 1997. Jerry Coleman left the booth to join the Padres for the 1980, but the club finished last and he returned to broadcasting.

Shortest Tenure.

"A manager is like a fellow swimming in the ocean with a cut on his arm. Sooner or later the sharks are going to get you."—Eddie Stanky on being named manager of the 1977 Rangers. Stanky beat the sharks to the punch; he managed one game for the Rangers and then returned to college baseball, saying he was homesick.

"I'm 49 and I want to live to be 50."—Eddie Sawyer, who lived to be 86. He managed the Phillies to an eighth-place finish in 1959. He managed the club on Opening Day 1960, a game they lost, and then retired with those words. He turned 50 on September 10 that year.

Early in the 1925 season new Cubs manager Rabbit Maranville ran through the club's Pullman cars at 2 a.m. yelling, "there will be no sleeping on this club under Maranville management." Maranville's sleepless tenure lasted 53 games with a 23–30 record.

The quickest in-season firings (and record at the time):

Cal Ripken, Sr.	6	(0–6)	1988	Orioles
Cy Young	6	(3–3)	1907	Red Sox
Preston Gomez	11	(4–7)	1972	Padres
Nick Leyva	13	(4–9)	1991	Phillies
Bob Lemon	14	(6–8)	1982	Yankees

Tony Perez of the Reds was fired after 44 games in 1993. Many believe that owner Marge Schott hired the popular Cuban to appear to soften her racist views that had forced her out of baseball for a year (see also *Racism*).

Snub. Manager Johnny Keane's Cardinals won the 1964 National League pennant and manager Yogi Berra's Yankees won the 1964 American League pennant. The Cardinals won the World Series. Both clubs had decided to get rid of their managers before the season ended when neither was expected to win a pennant. Both managers apparently were aware of their clubs' decisions. After the season, the Yankees moved forward with releasing Berra. The Cardinals changed their minds and fully expected Keane to renew his contract with the club. Keane held a press conference after the season at which he was expected to announce his signing of another contract with the Cardinals. Instead, he stunned everyone when he announced his signing with the Yankees.

Spring Training Firings. Two managers were fired during spring training after poor results the prior year. Alvin Dark was fired in 1978 by the Padres and Phil Cavarretta was fired by the Cubs in 1954 for having a "defeatist attitude." In 1977 Dark led the Padres to a fifth-place finish after taking over the club midway through the year and compiling a 48–65 record with a mediocre team. Cavaretta had managed the club for three years, finishing seventh twice (1951 and 1953) and fifth once (1952).

Stars as Managers.

Babe Ruth.

"How can he manage a ballclub when he can't manage himself."—Standard knock against Ruth's managerial abilities.

"There ain't anything to this masterminding business. All you've got to do is sit there and make out like you're trying to think."—Ruth in 1943, disgruntled at having never received a chance to manage in the Major Leagues.

Ruth desperately wanted to manage a team, but never had a real chance with the Yankees. However, he did have a chance to manage the Tigers in 1934. Tigers owner Frank Navin wanted Ruth (probably almost as much for his publicity value as for any alleged managerial skills), but Ruth demanded a share of the gate receipts and other concessions. Navin balked and hired player-manager Mickey Cochrane, who won pennants in 1934 and 1935. At least one source reported that when Ruth was approached by Navin to manage the Tigers, Ruth said that he could not meet because he was on his way to Hawaii. Ruth contacted the Browns to manage in the early 1940s but was turned down.

Ty Cobb. Cobb took over as Tigers manager in 1919 supposedly only after he heard that Pants Rowland, whom he despised, was taking the job. Cobb had one second-place and two third-place finishes in six seasons.

Walter Johnson. Johnson was a disaster as the manager of the Indians. The easy-going Johnson was described as "cordially hated" by his players though the club had a third-place finish in 1934 during his three-year tenure. He also managed the Senators from 1929 through 1931, finishing fifth, second and third.

Bill Terry. Terry succeeded John McGraw as manager of the Giants. In 10 seasons starting in 1932 he guided the club to three pennants and a World Series victory in 1933.

Ted Williams. Williams managed the Washington Senators/Texas Rangers for four years beginning in 1969. He had a winning record the first season (86–76). The .531 winning percentage was a significant increase over the club's .404 percentage the previous year. That was as high as he reached. The club finished no better than fifth in a six-team division over the next three years.

Frank Robinson. Robinson managed a number of clubs in the 1970s and 1980s with moderate success (see **Black "Firsts"**—**Managers**).

Pete Rose. Rose managed the Reds in the mid–1980s and finished second four times in six years.

Willie Mays. Mays contended in 1993 that he turned down an opportunity to manage the Mets in 1975.

Suspensions. See *Suspensions*.

Three Teams/Pennants. Dick Williams and Bill McKechnie are the only 20th century managers to win pennants for three different clubs. McKechnie won with the Pirates in 1925, the Cardinals in 1928 and the Reds in 1939 and 1940. Williams won with the Red Sox in 1967, the A's in 1971, 1972 and 1973, and the Padres in 1984.

Tongue Lashing? In September 2000 Yankee manager Joe Torre held a team meeting after a 16–3 loss to the Blue Jays. He blistered the team for poor play and thought that it might inspire them to play better. Sure. The Yankees lost their next seven games, 15–4, 2–1, 11–1, 11–3, 13–2, 9–1 and 7–3.

Umpire. Tim Hurst, an early "King of the Umpires" who often brawled with fans, managed the St. Louis Cardinals to a 39–111 record in 1898. He was later a boxing referee.

Uniforms. Managers usually wore uniforms even in the early days, primarily because field managers usually were also players. The tradition of wearing uniforms continued even after most managers were no longer player-managers. Connie Mack of the A's is the most famous manager to wear a suit and tie while managing. He was also the last to do so, which is unfortunate considering how bad some modern managers look in form-fitting double-knit uniforms (Tommy Lasorda's occasional diets notwithstanding). Burt Shotten also managed in street clothes; coincidentally his last year of managing was 1950, the same year in which Mack finally retired.

Jim Mutrie, who managed the New York Giants in the 19th century, often appeared in the dugout wearing gloves, spats and a silk top hat.

George Stallings of the 1914 Braves wore a suit instead of a uniform.

Youngest.

Roger Peckinpaugh. Peckinpaugh became the youngest manager of all time when he managed the Yankees for 20 games late in 1914 at age 23 years 7 months. He compiled a 10–10 record and moved the club from seventh to sixth. He did not manage again until age 37 with the Indians in 1928.

John Montgomery Ward. Ward was 24 in 1884 when he was the player-manager of the New York Giants.

Lou Boudreau. Boudreau was 24 years 9 months when he began the 1942 season as player-manager of the Indians. He succeeded another formerly young manager, Roger Peckinpaugh. Boudreau is the youngest to manage for an entire season.

Fred Clarke. Clarke was 24 when he began managing in 1897 for the National League Louisville club. He managed the club until it shifted to Pittsburgh in 1900. He continued as Pirates manager until 1915, when he left the club at age 43.

Fred Dunlap. Though reportedly illiterate, the second baseman managed the 1884 St. Louis Maroons at age 25.

John McGraw. McGraw took over the Baltimore Orioles in 1899 at age 26.

Bucky Harris. Harris managed Washington in 1924 at age 27, taking the club to a pennant that year and the next, earning the nickname "Boy Wonder." With one exception in 1947 with the Yankees, Harris never won another pennant over his 29-year career. Just before Clark Griffith surprised Harris with the news of his hiring, Griffith had asked him to switch to third base from second base in hopes of trading him to the White Sox for Eddie Collins. When the deal did not materialize, Griffith instead made Harris his manager.

Frank Chance. Chance managed the Cubs in 1905 at age 28. At 29 the next year, he managed the Cubs to 116 wins and a pennant. They repeated as pennant winners under Chance in three of the next four years.

Terry Francona. Francona was 37 when he took over the Phillies in 1997. He lasted four seasons and twice finished third.

Eric Wedge. Wedge was named manager of the Indians in October 2002 at age 35, and the club finished fourth in 2003 and third in 2004.

Books. Thomas Aylesworth and Benton Minks, *The Encyclopedia of Baseball Managers* (1990); Jim Bouton and Neil Offen, "*I Managed Good, But Boy Did They Play Bad*" (1973); Charles Cleveland, *Great Baseball Managers* (1950); Harvey Frommer, *Baseball's Greatest Managers* (1985); Leonard Koppett, *The Man in the Dugout* (1993); Hank Nuwer, *Strategies of the Great Baseball Managers* (1988); Ray Robinson, *Baseball's Most Colorful Managers* (1964); John C. Skipper, *A Biographical Dictionary of the Major League Baseball Managers* (2004).

Mickey Mantle (1931–1995)

Hall of Fame 1974

"To us, Mickey Mantle was the New York Yankees. You had to see Mickey day after day, year after year, and watch him play on days when his knees hurt so badly that he could barely walk to fully appreciate his greatness as a player."—Tony Kubek.

"Mantle was larger than life, symbolizing two eras—the golden years of an Eisenhower presidency and today's media-stained days when little distinguishes a celebrity's private life from his public persona."—Louis Berney in *Baseball Weekly*.

"All I had was natural ability."—Mickey Mantle.

"Mickey Mantle just was everything. At my Bar Mitzvah I had an Oklahoma accent."—Comedian Billy Crystal.

"And more than that, he was a presence in our lives—a fragile hero to whom we had an emotional attachment so strong and lasting that it defied logic. Mickey often said he didn't understand it, this enduring connection and affection—for men now in their 40s and 50s, otherwise perfectly sensible, who went dry in the mouth and stammered like schoolboys in the presence of Mickey Mantle."—Bob Costas in his eulogy delivered at Mantle's funeral.

"In the last year, Mickey Mantle, always so hard on himself, finally came to accept and appreciate the distinction between a role model and a hero. The first he was often not, the second he will always be."—Costas in his eulogy.

Mantle was the center field star of the Yankees in the 1950s and early 1960s before injuries and hard living took their toll.

Mickey Charles Mantle, "The Commerce Comet," grew up in Oklahoma and suffered osteomyelitis as a high school football player. In 1950 when Branch Rickey was the general manager of the Pirates, he supposedly offered the Yankees $500,000 and premier slugger Ralph Kiner for Mantle before he ever played in the Major Leagues.

Mantle broke in with the Yankees in 1951 and played right field beside Joe DiMaggio for one season. Mantle suffered the first of a number of debilitating injuries during the 1951 World Series. He tore ligaments in his knee when his spike caught on an outfield sprinkler. Injuries and general carousing shortened his career and reduced his abilities dramatically by 1964, only four years before he retired after 18 seasons at age 36.

Mantle had his best season in 1956 when he won the Triple Crown with a .353 average, 52 home runs and 130 RBIs. He also led in slugging average (.705) and runs scored (132). He hit 40 or more home runs four times and drove in over 100 runs four times. Mantle's best 10-year period included a .307 average, 323 home runs, 993 RBIs and 1,611 hits. He finished with a .298 lifetime average and 536 home runs. His home run percentage of 6.6 is seventh all-time among retired players (16th including active players as of 2004).

During retirement he traveled the banquet and memorabilia circuit for over 20 years before publicly acknowledging his alcoholism in the mid–1990s. Mantle summed up his retirement: "I'm really pretty good at my job, if I say so myself. Mainly it consists of playing golf and attending cocktail parties."

It finally caught up to him when he required a liver transplant in 1995. Shortly after the transplant it was discovered that his liver cancer had spread. He died a few weeks later.

Books. Tony Castro, *Mickey Mantle: America's Prodigal Son* (2002); Mark Gallagher, *Explosion! Mickey Mantle's Legendary Home Runs* (1987); Bill Liederman and Maury Allen, *Our Mickey* (2004); Howard Liss, *The Mickey Mantle Album* (1966); Mickey Mantle, *The Quality of Courage* (1964) (ghostwritten by Robert Creamer); Mickey Mantle with Lewis Early, *Mickey Mantle: The American Dream Comes to Life* (1993); Mickey Mantle and Herb Gluck, *The Mick* (1985); Mickey Mantle and Phil Pepe, *My Favorite Summer— 1956* (1991); Mickey Mantle with Mickey Herskowitz, *All My Octobers: My Memories of 12 World Series When the Yankees Ruled Baseball* (1994); *Sports Illustrated* (ed.), *Mantle Remembered* (1995).

Heinie Manush (1901–1971)

Hall of Fame (VC) 1964

"The Dodgers have not boasted a universally popular outfielder since Zack Wheat filled that role. Each of the others had his boosters and his berators. Heinie right now claims the place Wheat once held; and unless his ancient dogs grow too surly as the season progresses, Heinie will continue as the new baseball god of flatbush."— *The Sporting News.*

Manush was primarily an American League outfielder who batted .330 over 17 seasons beginning in 1923.

Henry Emmett Manush first played professionally in 1921 in western Canada and hit .374 in 1922 for Omaha. He broke in as an outfielder with the Tigers and Ty Cobb in 1923, seeing action in 109 games and hitting .334. Manush had a league-leading .378 average in 1926, but tapered off to .298 in 1927 and was traded to the Browns in 1928. He hit .378 (missing the batting title by .001) and led the league with 241 hits and 47 doubles.

Manush continued to hit over .300 for the Browns and then the Senators beginning midway through the 1930 season. He remained with the Senators through 1935, leading the league with 221 hits and 17 triples in 1933 and finishing third in the batting race in 1934. After a mediocre year in 1936 he was traded to the Dodgers and finished his career in 1938 and 1939 with the Pirates.

Manush had a lifetime .330 average and 2,524 hits in 2,009 games. He holds the distinction of being the first player ever thrown out of a World Series game, a feat he accomplished in 1933 in front of Franklin Roosevelt.

After his Major League career ended, he managed through the mid–1940s in the minor leagues and occasionally appeared as a player. He also scouted and coached at the Major League level through 1962.

Rabbit Maranville (1891–1954)

Hall of Fame 1954

"Carefree, frolicsome spirit who cavorted through 2,670 major league games … tried hand at managing Chicago Cubs and lasted less than two months. Drank more than his share of alcohol, relegated to minors. Reformed May 24, 1927…. Stories endless about clowning before his reformation. But infectious good humor lasted as long as he lived."— Gene Karst and Martin J. Jones, Jr., in *Who's Who in Professional Baseball* (1973).

Maranville mainly played shortstop and had over 2,600 hits in 23 seasons beginning in 1912.

Walter James Vincent Maranville was only 5'5", but played shortstop and second base in the Major Leagues for most of 23 seasons beginning in 1912. Serious alcoholism hampered his career, but he reformed in 1927 and his pranks and comedic flair were legendary both before and after he became sober.

He played in the New England League in 1911 and 1912 before joining the Braves late in the season. He remained with the club through 1920, though he missed most of 1918 while in the Navy serving in World War I. He was a consistent base stealer and extra-base man for the Braves, generally hitting slightly above or below .250. He batted .308 for the Braves in the 1914 World Series.

He was traded to the Pirates in 1921 and had his best season in 1922, batting .295 with 198 hits and 15 triples. From 1925 through 1927 he played partial seasons with three clubs because his alcoholism was taking its toll. He was sent to the minor leagues by the Cardinals in 1927 and stopped drinking in May of that season. He returned to the Cardinals in 1928 (again batting .308 in the World Series) and then returned to the Braves for five full seasons through 1933 and was one of the top shortstops or second basemen during that span. He broke his leg during spring training in 1934 at age 42 and sat out the season. He returned briefly in 1935, but the leg had not healed sufficiently.

Maranville finished his Major League career with 2,605 hits and a .258 average over 23 seasons to go with 177 triples and 291 stolen bases. He played a full season while player-manager at Elmira in 1936 and played a few more minor league games in 1947 while managing. He died a few weeks before being elected to the Hall of Fame in 1954.

Juan Marichal (1937–)

Hall of Fame 1983

"I could have had Juan Marichal when he was sixteen. Saw him at a tryout camp in the Dominican and just thought he was too little, not worth the risk of three hundred dollars."— Pirates scout Howie Haak quoted in Kevin Kerrane's *Dollar Sign on the Muscle* (1984).

Marichal was the first great pitcher from the Dominican Republic and the best San Francisco Giants pitcher of all time.

One of the first prominent players from the Dominican Republic, Juan Antonio Marichal Sanchez, the "Dominican Dandy," was 21 when he began play in the minor leagues in 1958 — though he was thought to be 19. Known for his high leg kick and variety of deliveries, his control was what made him one of the top pitchers of the 1960s.

Marichal made it to the Major Leagues with the Giants in 1960, pitching a one-hitter in his debut in July and a four-hitter in his next start. After decent seasons in 1960 and 1961 he won 18 games in 1962 and helped lead the Giants into the World Series, though a foot injury curtailed his effectiveness in September and in the Series.

He led the league with 25 wins in 1963 and won more than 20 games in five of the next six seasons. He led the league with 26 wins in 1968, and in 1965 and 1969 he led the league with 10 and eight shutouts. In 1970 Marichal suffered a serious reaction to penicillin and the resulting chronic arthritis diminished his skills. He still managed to win 18 games in 1971, but he suffered through two poor seasons before moving on to Boston in 1974. He was 5–1 for the Red Sox and then pitched in two games for the Dodgers in 1975 before retiring.

His stint with the Dodgers was ironic given his infamous altercation with Dodger catcher John Roseboro in August 1965. He hit Roseboro over the head with a bat and a wild brawl ensued (see also *Fights*). He received one of the largest fines in National League history and was suspended for a week.

Marichal was 243–142 with a 2.89 ERA over 16 seasons and pitched 52 shutouts. In 1983 he became the first Latin player inducted into the Hall of Fame through the regular election process (Roberto Clemente was inducted through a special election following his death). John Roseboro helped campaign for Marichal when he was ignored in the first two years of voting after he was eligible. Marichal was involved in a serious auto accident in the Dominican in April 1998, suffering serious leg, spine and head injuries.

Book. Juan Marichal with Charles Einstein, *A Pitcher's Story* (1967).

Rube Marquard (1886–1980)

Hall of Fame (VC) 1971

"I've never smoked or taken a drink in my life to this day. I always said you can't burn the candle at both ends. You want to be a ballplayer, be a ballplayer. If you want to go out and carouse and chase around, do that. But you can't do them both at once." — Marquard.

Marquard was a star pitcher primarily for the New York Giants early in the 20th century, winning 201 games over 18 seasons.

Richard William Marquard saw his first professional action with Canton of the Central League in 1907 at age 21 (Most sources erroneously report his birth year as 1889). He moved up to Indianapolis of the American Association in 1909 and won 28 games. The Giants signed him for $11,000 after he pitched a perfect game for Indianapolis, but he lost his only Major League appearance that season and was dubbed the "$11,000 Lemon."

After two poor seasons for the Giants he exploded in 1911 with a 24–7 record and a league-leading 237 strikeouts. Relying primarily on a forkball and change-up to go with pinpoint control, Marquard won 19 straight from Opening Day to July 3, 1912. Under modern rules he would have been credited with 20 straight **Wins**. He finished the season with a league-high 26 wins and won 23 the following season. He remained with the Giants until late 1915 when he moved over to the Dodgers under his old coach, Wilbert Robinson.

Marquard had peaked and never won 20 games again. He was 19–12 in 1917, but other than a 17–14 season for the Reds in 1921 he was largely mediocre. He finished his career with four seasons for the Braves, ending with a 2–8 record in 1925.

Over his 18-year career Marquard was 201–177 with a 3.08 ERA and 30 shutouts. He won two games in the 1912 World Series for the Giants but lost five other games in 11 World Series appearances. He pitched in the minor leagues through 1927 and then managed, coached and scouted for various clubs. He had a brief vaudeville career following his record winning streak, and after he retired he worked at racetracks in Florida and Maryland. The sophisticated Cleveland native received his nickname because he reminded sportswriters of A's eccentric Rube Waddell. Fortunately for Marquard, being left-handed was their only real similarity.

Book. Larry D. Mansch, *Rube Marquard: The Life and Times of a Baseball Hall of Famer* (1998).

Marriage

"No one is a pull hitter in his first year of marriage." — Baseball adage, though in Lou Gehrig's first year of marriage in 1934 he won the Triple Crown with a .360 average, 49 home runs and 165 RBIs.

"The club is a helluva lot of fun, like my wife, but there's no profit in either one." — Padres owner Ray Kroc.

"If you want to see a baseball game in the worst way, take your wife along." — Comedian Henny Youngman.

"If you were my husband, I'd give you poison." — A female fan to American League umpire Red Ormsby.

"Lady, if you were my wife, I'd take it." — Ormsby's response.

"When I asked, 'How would you like to be married to a major league manager?' my wife said, 'What, is Tommy Lasorda getting a divorce?'" — John Wathan, upon being named Kansas City Royals manager.

"A baseball park is the one place where a man's wife doesn't mind his getting excited over somebody else's curves." — Brendan Francis.

"I would argue that baseball would never have been considered the national pastime if the sport hadn't been so overcovered.... But I understood why this had happened. Sportswriters liked to get out of the house and on the road without their wives as much as ballplayers did." — Dan Jenkins in *You Gotta Play Hurt* (1991).

"Playing for Billy Martin is like being married to him. Right now, we're all sleeping on the couch." — Matt Keough.

"Billy Jurges of the Cubs was married yesterday morning to Miss Mary Huyette, of Reading, and he might do well to repeat the ceremony daily." — Philadelphia sports report in June 1933 after Jurges had a big day at bat and in the field.

"And the girl I'd been going out with since the seventh grade had decided that an assistant bank manager was a better bet as a marriage partner than a first baseman who couldn't hit a curve ball, except the odd one that hung." — John Craig in *All G.O.D.'s Children* (1975), described by H. Allen Smith as "the funniest (and the raunchiest) baseball book ever to come my way."

"Bob Groom, Algie McBride, Bucky Veil, Jake Virtue, Charlie Manlove, Grover Lovelace, Slim Love, Lynn Lovenguth, Frank Bliss, Dell Darling, Corky Valentine, Cupid Childs"

See *Dauvrey Cup* for the marriage between John Montgomery Ward and actress Helen Dauvrey.

Ballplayers' Wives.

"Let selfishness be no barrier to your happiness, but understand that each must often give up much, renounce himself, that both may enjoy delightful fruit. For you know that it is the sacrifice hit that adds to the number of runs and wins the game." — Marriage vows of Mr. and Mrs. John J. McGraw recounted in her book, *The Real McGraw*, with Arthur Mann (1953).

"The institution of baseball often treats the long-suffering pitcher as the institution of marriage treats the long-suffering wife. Both are subject to clods with no slightest sympathy for their most cherished graces, both seek to express themselves through nagging artifice, and both face the prospect of banishment to the shower room or the divorce courts without one word of comfort or approbation. The history of matrimony, as a result, is full of husbands who have been hit over the head with hot electric toasters at breakfast — or have had their liver blown out with their own shotguns — and the history of the national pastime is studded with pitchers who have slung their hard, round, white projectiles at batters rather than the plate. The sense of shock, surprise — and, above all, caution — which is visited upon surviving victims in each case is usually, to put it mildly, profound." — Paul O'Neil in *Life* magazine.

"How's the old lady? Oh, a pain in the ass. All women are pains in the ass. If you couldn't fuck 'em, they wouldn't be worth a thing in the world. Women have had too much to say for too long. This women's lib is a crock o' shit." — Noted women's libber Ted Williams quoted in Shelby Whitfield's *Kiss It Goodbye* (1973).

Wives have often had difficulty coping with their husbands as ballplayers. The definitive account of their plight is *Home Games* (1983), written by Bobbie [Jim] Bouton and Nancy [Mike] Marshall.

In the early 1970s Maryanne Simmons, wife of catcher Ted Simmons, began publishing a newsletter for baseball wives called *The Waiting Room*.

Jim Bouton's book *Ball Four* (1970) contains a detailed discussion of "Baseball Annies" (baseball groupies). After the book came out, the percentage of wives who began traveling with their husbands supposedly increased significantly.

Divorce.

"Psychologists tell us that man has a natural urge to produce results by striking objects with sticks. And it's equally natural, they say, to want to produce a change in our environment by tossing one object at another. Put these urges together and you have the kind of marriage that ends up in Reno ... or something completely different, and much more pleasant: baseball." — "A Housewife's Guide to Baseball" (1958).

"There was never any question about his [Enos Slaughter's] courage. He proved it by getting married four times." — Broadcaster Jack Brickhouse.

"'I've got nothing to show for 14 seasons but a tired right arm, three rich ex-wives, and a drinking problem,' one veteran pitcher told me, sitting naked in a clammy-floored locker room, staring into his Budweiser as if it were infinity." — W.P. Kinsella in "Barefoot and Pregnant in Des Moines" (1984).

"Saw lawyer re. divorce. She wants $5,000 per month. Will settle for less. And no $60,000 cash alimony. Extra problems keeping this out of the headlines." — January 3, 1946, entry in Ty Cobb's diary, now a part of Barry Halper's memorabilia collection.

"It was too bad I wasn't a second baseman; then I'd probably have seen a lot more of my husband." — Karolyn Rose, ex-wife of Pete, who had 746 doubles.

In the early 1970s so many Washington Senators got divorced that some of the ex-wives formed the Washington Area Ex-Players' Wives Club.

In a 1993 study by the National Center for Health Statistics, Denver psychologist Howard Markman determined that the divorce rate was 23% lower in cities with Major League Baseball teams. He also concluded that attending a baseball game was a positive force on a marriage because of the opportunities for "communication, fun and friendship."

In 1996 Braves slugger David Justice was divorcing actress Halle Berry. The divorce was announced during the same week in which Justice was stopped by police in an area frequented by prostitutes and drug dealers.

Bill Lange was an outfield star for the Cubs in the 1890s. He hit a team record .389 in 1895 and had six consecutive seasons over .300. In 1899 he retired at the peak of his career at age 28 to marry the daughter of a wealthy San Francisco real estate magnate who would not allow her to wed a baseball player. The relationship soon ended in divorce, but Lange never returned to Major League Baseball.

In 1934 Senators player-manager Joe Cronin was able to get married before the end of the season. He broke his wrist in early September and owner Calvin Griffith gave him the rest of the season off.

Entrepreneurial minor league owner Mike Veeck has staged Marriage Counseling Night, in which spouses air their grievances to the crowd, which votes using placards. If the couple can't resolve their differences, the club pays for the divorce.

All in the Family.

"You know it's time to quit when you've got a daughter old enough to marry a teammate." — Walker Cooper at age 42 and still a member of the Cardinals, when his daughter married teammate and second baseman Don Blasingame.

Infielder Jackie Hayes of the 1930s Senators married Thelma Griffith, the adopted daughter of Senators owner Clark Griffith. Hayes was later traded by the Senators but returned to the club as a coach, general manager and vice-president. He also moved with the club when it relocated to Minnesota in 1961.

Yankee pitcher Herb Pennock's daughter married Eddie Collins, Jr., son of the famous second baseman of the A's and White Sox. The resulting grandchildren had the unique claim of two grandfathers in the Hall of Fame.

Denny McLain's father-in-law was former Indians shortstop Lou Boudreau.

One source reported that infielder Bill Rigney, who later managed the Giants and Angels, married the daughter of White Sox owner Charles Comiskey. Wrong on two counts. It was former player John Rigney, who moved into the White Sox front office. He married Comiskey's granddaughter, who was the daughter of Lou Comiskey, who died in 1939.

See ***Trades and Player Sales*** for trades involving family members.

Quick on His Feet.

"Her name's Mrs. Coleman, and she likes me." — 1962 Mets utilityman Choo-Choo Coleman, when asked by broadcaster Ralph Kiner what his wife's name was, "and what's she like."

Good Thinking. During World War II the Pirates attended the afternoon wedding of teammate Vinnie Smith. The players arrived at the ballpark for a night game against the Reds drunk and in their tuxedos. They all marched to the Reds clubhouse and delivered cigars to Reds pitcher Ewell Blackwell to ensure that he did not hit them with a pitch during the game.

Romance.

"I came into [baseball] as a bachelor and kind of enjoy the life, doing my own thing." — Marlins pitcher Carl Pavano in 2004 after he broke off his months-long dating relationship with former child television star Alyssa Milano.

Road Trips/Reserve Clause Challenge. In the 1920s, some clubs (Giants, Reds and White Sox) allowed wives to go on road trips, but others (Pirates, Tigers and Browns) did not. In 1923 pitcher Urban Shocker challenged the St. Louis Browns and refused to go on the club's last eastern trip in protest. He was fined $1,000 and suspended. *The Sporting News* took management's side, but the *St. Louis Post-Dispatch* was a bit more realistic: "A tactical blunder appears to have been made, since the presence of a player's wife on a trip certainly should contribute to his good conduct, if he is the least inclined to waywardness."

Shocker appealed to Commissioner Landis's office, and a hearing was scheduled. Owners were worried that Landis might do something to appease Shocker, and Shocker had indicated that if he lost he would file a lawsuit challenging the Reserve Clause. This was fresh on everyone's minds after the 1922 Supreme Court decision on the subject.

In January 1924, a few days before the hearing, Shocker surprisingly withdrew his appeal. League president Ban Johnson had stepped in and signed Shocker to a new contract, but let the fine stand to appease owner Phil Ball (the contract was higher, to account for the fine). Johnson was in a running feud with Landis, and this move helped Johnson's waning stature. The crisis was averted and, as a result of Shocker's action, the owners agreed at the winter meetings to incorporate a clause that required players to abide by all present and future team rules.

The Babe. On the day Babe Ruth was married (at 6:30 a.m. to avoid a crowd) he hit a home run and stopped at second base to bow toward his new bride's box seat.

Trade. Agent and promoter Joe Tubiolo reported (to this author, during a Las Vegas poker game) that 1950s outfielder Jim Busby once was traded (among at least six trades) because his wife was so annoying to club officials.

Good Timing. Seventeen days after he gave up the fateful home run to Bobby Thomson in the 1951 Dodgers/Giants play-off game, pitcher Ralph Branca married Ann Mulvey. Her mother was Marie McKeever Mulvey, who owned 25% of the Dodgers.

Casey Stengel. Yankee photographer David Blumenthal positioned himself behind home plate for all games in the 1940s and 1950s. One day Joe DiMaggio brought down Marilyn Monroe before the game and asked Blumenthal to keep an eye on her. Edna Stengel, Casey's wife, quickly came down and began chatting with Monroe. Blumenthal told Mrs. Stengel that she would have to leave 10 minutes before the game. When she neglected to leave, Blumenthal repeatedly (but politely) asked her to leave. He finally had to be rude to her and she left. The next day Casey Stengel approached Blumenthal and asked if Blumenthal had been rude to his wife. Blumenthal acknowledged that he finally had been somewhat rude to get her to leave. Stengel replied, "well, next time don't let the damn woman into the area in the first place."

Bo Belinsky.
"I need her like Custer needed Indians."—Pitcher Bo Belinsky after breaking up with starlet Mamie Van Doren in the 1960s.

"If I did everything they said I did, I'd be in a jar at the Harvard Medical School."—Belinsky.

Belinsky was one of the more notable baseball playboys, marrying Van Doren, dating *Playboy* centerfold Jo Collins and a string of other well-known women. They included Ann-Margret, Tina Louise (of "Gilligan's Island"), Paulette Goddard, a DuPont heiress, and paper products heiress Jane Weyerhauser. He met Weyerhauser after saving her in the Hawaiian surf. Tony Conigliaro also dated Van Doren. To know Bo, read *Bo—Pitching and Wooing*, by Maury Allen (1973).

Leo Durocher. It seems impossible that wild Leo Durocher was married to actress Laraine Day during the late 1940s and early 1950s. Day was a strict Mormon who wrote a book about her life with Durocher and the Giants, *Day With the Giants* (1952).

Earlier in his career, Durocher married his first wife a few days before playing in the 1934 World Series and was publicly criticized for not staying focused on the game. Cardinals general manager Branch Rickey encouraged Durocher to marry the woman, a prosperous St. Louis dress designer. Her name was Grace L. Dozier, known nationally as Carol King. In her 1943 divorce papers she told a judge: "what all the National League umpires have known all along—that Leo is 'constantly of a nagging disposition and possessed of a very uneven temperament.'"

Joe DiMaggio.
"I don't know if it's good for baseball, but it beats the hell out of rooming with Phil Rizzuto."—Yogi Berra after being asked whether Joe DiMaggio's marriage to Marilyn Monroe was good for baseball. DiMaggio first saw his future wife with slugger Gus Zernial at a charity event and later inquired about her. Zernial had posed with her in a publicity shot. Zernial may have acted as intermediary for them through her agent, David March. March called Monroe and persuaded her to date DiMaggio. Their first meeting was a double-date with March and his date.

DiMaggio and Monroe had been married for 274 days when Monroe filed for divorce on October 5, 1954. She sought the divorce in part because she claimed that he never talked to her. Some sources report that he was preparing to ask her to remarry him at the time of her death in 1962. He arranged for a half-dozen long-stemmed red roses to be placed at her crypt on each Tuesday, Thursday and Saturday between 1962 and 1980. At the time of the divorce, pianist Oscar Levant made the following observation: "It proves that no man can be a success in two national pastimes."

Levant himself was no looker, as described by Anthony Lane in *The New Yorker*: "But Levant was a gargoyle, to be treasured as the ugliest runt ever to grace a movie screen."

Umpires/Strippers. Umpire Don Rudolph was married to stripper Patti Waggin. Umpire Dick Stello was married to stripper Chesty Morgan, reportedly the owner of a 73-inch bust.

Managing Technique. Detroit manager Bill Armour (1905–1906) purportedly asked his wife for her daily starting pitcher selections. She usually picked the pitcher with the cleanest uniform or the best looking. His club finished third in 1905 and sixth in 1906.

During the 1945 World Series, Tigers manager Steve O'Neill was criticized for using his son-in-law, shortstop Skeeter Webb, over shortstop Joe Hoover, who was acknowledged as the better hitter. Webb hit .185 in 27 at-bats and Hoover was 1-for-3. During the season Webb had hit .199 in 407 at-bats and Hoover had hit .257 in 222 at-bats.

Home Plate Wedding.
"We tried to get married in Riverfront, at home plate, but they said batting practice was more important."—Pete Rose on his second marriage, quoted in his autobiography, *Pete Rose: My Story*, with Roger Kahn (1989).

The first wedding known to have taken place at home plate was held on September 18, 1893, at the Western Avenue Grounds in Cincinnati. It was arranged by long-time promoter Frank Bancroft.

A few minutes after Game 2 of the 1995 American Association finals, Louisville Redbirds relief pitcher John Frascatore went back out to the mound and exchanged wedding vows with his bride, Kandria.

Walt Cruise, who played outfield for the Braves and Cardinals from 1916 through 1924, was married at home plate between games of a doubleheader. He did not play in the second game.

Don Zimmer was married at home plate at Elmira when he was an infielder in the Eastern League.

On July 9, 1998, Benny Agbayani was married at home plate to his fiancée, Neila, before the Class AAA All-Star Game. Agbayani is from Hawaii, so he and his bride wore flowered Hawaiian shirts. In his debut as a pinch-runner with the Mets the following day, he slipped trying to steal second in the 9th inning of an 8–8 tie and was tagged out. Another Mets runner was doubled off in the 10th and the Mets lost.

Married Couple. In 2003 Jake and Kendall Burnham became the first married couple to play professional baseball together. On May 14, 2003, 26-year-old Jake started at third base for the San Angelo (Texas) Colts of the independent Central League and Kendall, a 28-year-old infielder, struck out as a pinch hitter. She had been a star in the Women's Professional Softball League and had been an assistant softball coach for UNLV.

Married Couple? In March 2000 Padres outfielder Al Martin was arrested on charges that he exchanged punches with a woman who claimed to be his wife. Shawn Haggerty-Martin said the couple was married in Las Vegas two years earlier. Martin said the couple had the ceremony, but that he didn't think it was real. Haggerty-Martin contended that the outfielder was a bigamist.

Speeches. The White Sox defeated the Cubs to win the 1906 World Series. After the last game the players quickly left the field. The crowd demanded and received victory speeches from the White Sox wives, who had been sitting in a special box for the game.

Morals Clause? In 1996 Reds owner Marge Schott fired manager Davey Johnson, allegedly because she didn't approve of him living with his girlfriend before they were married. At first she named Ray Knight as "co-manager," before Knight formally replaced Johnson.

Wife Swap.
"It was March 5, 1973, and Yankee pitchers Fritz Peterson and Mike Kekich were explaining about their family trade at a press

conference. You remember that was the deal where Peterson traded his wife, their youngest child and their dog to Kekich, for his wife, their youngest child and their dog. They each kept their eldest child and their own house. The latest word was that Peterson's wife, child and dog refused to report and Kekich was demanding the return of his players." — Jim Bouton in *I Managed Good, But Boy Did They Play Bad*," by Bouton with Neil Offen (1973). The early 1970s wife swap between Yankee pitchers Mike Kekich and Fritz Peterson was half a success. Peterson stayed married to the former Mrs. Kekich, but the other two were married for only one year.

Indians center fielder Rick Manning moved in with Dennis Eckersley's wife Denise when they were separated. They later married, but Eckersley remained friends with them.

Bachelors. The Brooklyn Excelsiors of the 19th century were also known as the Jolly Young Bachelors.

Motivation. Lou Novikoff played primarily in the 1940s for the Cubs and had an interesting way of motivating himself at the plate. He arranged for his wife to sit down close to the field and yell derogatory comments about his playing ability.

Celebrity Wedding. Red Sox shortstop Nomar Garciaparra met soccer star Mia Hamm in 1998 at a charity soccer event at Harvard and they were engaged in November 2002, shortly after Hamm divorced her husband of six years. The two sports stars were married exactly a year later in a ceremony in Santa Barbara, California.

Honor Thy Father. Yankee catcher Thurman Munson's son, Michael, proposed to his girlfriend in front of his father's plaque in Monument Park in Yankee Stadium.

Mistaken Identity. Ace broadcaster Joe Buck executed a major faux pas at the end of the 2001 National League championship series while broadcasting for Fox. Interviewing the Diamondbacks' Tony Womack, they were joined on the field by a woman. Said Buck, "Who is this, Tony, your mom?" Responded Womack, "No, man, that's my wife."

Honeymoon. During the 1908 season, catcher Nig Clarke of Cleveland supposedly broke his finger on purpose so that he could go see his new wife and have an in-season honeymoon. He was out five weeks, which may or may not have affected his club's chances. The Indians finished one-half game out of first place.

Bedtime Precautions. New York Mets pitcher Tom Seaver required his wife to sleep on the left side of the bed in case she rolled over in the middle of the night. That way, she would roll on his left arm instead of his valuable right arm. Seaver almost had a nervous breakdown when he once woke up in the middle of the night and his pitching arm was "asleep." On the advice of semipro player Walt Payne, Seaver tried to do as many things as possible left-handed to save his right arm from strain.

Books by Baseball Wives.

"With the exception of guys who were devout Christians, virtually everybody had someone on the side. I would walk past the wives and think, They are either the dumbest or the most naïve people in the world. I mean, everybody knew it was going on." — Jeff Dubay of KFAN, a former Twins batboy.

Bobbie [Jim] Bouton and Nancy [Mike] Marshall, *Home Games* (1983); Charlene [Bob] Gibson and Michael Rich, *A Wife's Guide to Baseball* (1970); Danielle Gagnon [Mike] Torrez and Ken Lizotte, *High & Inside — Memoirs of a Baseball Wife* (1983); Cyndi [Steve] Garvey with Andy Meisler, *The Secret Life of Cyndi Garvey* (1989); Sharon [Mike] Hargrove, *Safe at Home: A Baseball Wife's Story* (1989).

Mascots

"Not at all. She thinks I'm a doctor in Wisconsin." — San Diego Chicken mascot extraordinaire Ted Giannoulas, when asked if his mother thought his occupation was foolish.

"They've got a broadcasters' wing and a players' wing. Maybe one day they'll have a chicken wing." — The San Diego Chicken on the Hall of Fame.

See also *Clowns.*

First Mascot. The New York Knickerbockers may have introduced the first mascot in 1846. At a party at the Fijux hotel, the son of the proprietor was adopted by the club and dubbed "Charles Knickerbocker Fijux," and his name was put on the roll of members.

Disabilities. It was not uncommon for many teams to have dwarfs, hunchbacks or retarded adults as mascots. Typical was the hunchback featured in *Zane Grey's The Shortstop* (1909).

Eddie Bennet. Born in 1903, Bennet was a hunchback fan who hung out at the Polo Grounds in 1917. At the start of one game, Chicago White Sox player Happy Felsch rubbed the hump for luck, not an uncommon superstition in those days. The White Sox defeated the Yankees that day. Felsch then took Bennet into the dugout for the next two games and the White Sox swept the series.

After that success Bennet was invited to be the club's bat boy and official mascot, and the White Sox went on to win the World Series that season. Bennet's luck became known to other clubs, and in 1920 they staged a minor bidding war for his services. The Dodgers got him and won the pennant. The Yankees signed him for the 1921 season and won three straight pennants (1921–1923) and then three more pennants after a two-year hiatus. Bennet was so popular as a mascot in those years that he supposedly made more money than many players.

Bennet remained with the Yankees until he was seriously hurt in an auto accident in 1933. When he died an alcoholic in 1935, the caretaker found photographs of four Yankee players on the wall of his small room on West 84th Street: Babe Ruth, Lou Gehrig, Herb Pennock and Waite Hoyt.

Li'l Rastus. At Detroit's Bennett Park in July 1908, Ty Cobb took on a young black boy as a good luck charm. It was not uncommon for players to rub a black child's head for good luck and Li'l Rastus served that purpose. Cobb took him on the road during the season and then abandoned him in late September, but the Cubs hired him when they played in the World Series that season against the Tigers. The Cubs won four of five games; as a result, Li'l Rastus was picked up by the Tigers for the entire 1909 pennant-winning season, but the Tigers still lost the World Series. When Cobb went home after the 1909 season he used Li'l Rastus as a domestic for a short time, but Rastus did not return for the 1910 season and his association with Major League Baseball apparently ended.

Charles "Victory" Faust. In 1911, 31-year-old Charles Victor "Victory" Faust attended a workout of John McGraw's Giants. Faust informed McGraw that a fortune teller had told him that if he pitched for the Giants, they would win the pennant. Tongue-in-cheek, McGraw arranged for the eccentric to pitch and hit during the team's practice. Faust was terrible, but he still went on the train with the team and warmed up every day.

Late in the season McGraw received permission from the other team for the nonroster Faust to play in a game. One source reported that he once batted when there were already three outs. A ground ball followed by a series of errors allowed him to circle the bases. He had no official at-bats, but the statistics supposedly showed that he scored a run and stole two bases. *The Baseball Encyclopedia*

Major League mascots Baxter (Diamondbacks) and Stomper (A's) at Atlanta Turner Field for a mascot gathering.

reports no plate appearances but shows two appearances as a pitcher, giving up two hits in two innings and compiling a 4.50 ERA with no record of wins or losses.

During the 1911, 1912 and 1913 seasons he hung around the team and it won the pennant each year. Near the end of the 1913 season his mental state deteriorated further and he did not stay with the team in 1914. In his absence, Boston's Miracle Braves won the pennant that season. After being institutionalized in the state of Washington, he died on June 18, 1915. Perhaps not coincidentally the Giants finished last that year.

Apropos Clarence Duval. Duval was the "Negro who has been with them round the world," traveling in 1889 on the international tour by the White Stockings and an "All America Base-Ball Team." He was later described on the tour by noted racist Cap Anson: "Outside of his dancing and his power of mimicry he was, however, a 'no account nigger,' and more than once did I wish that he had been left behind."

Schotzie.

"Marge just doesn't get it. Her only two concerns are her dog and money. We're hoping she buys the zoo and sells the team — then everyone will be happy." — Unidentified Reds player.

Schotzie the dog was the St. Bernard mascot of the Reds at the outset of Marge Schott's tenure as majority owner of the club. When Schotzie died in 1991, he was replaced by Schotzie 02, who was introduced to fans on June 2, 1992, at Schotzie 02 Appreciation Night. When shortstop Barry Larkin homered, the scoreboard dedicated it to the dog. The Schotzies were not popular with the players, as they often chased players during batting practice and always left a deposit on the field to be cleaned up by the ever-vigilant grounds crew. Schotzie 02 starred in the 1992 movie *Beethoven* and carried out the ball to start the last game of the 1992 season.

After numerous complaints by players, Schotzie 02 was banned from the pregame playing field. This decision by the Major League Baseball Executive Council prompted Marge Schott's attorney, Robert Bennett, to comment: "I'm really glad Major League Baseball is focusing on the major issues of the day. We're currently studying the case law, and we think there is a way Schotzie 02 can get on the field. We understand the San Diego chicken is really a man in a chicken suit. So, I think if we can get Schotzie in a chicken suit, he may be able to go on the field."

A letter sent to Major League Baseball addressed other issues affecting the dog's owner: "Moreover, to the best of my knowledge,

Schotzie 02 himself has never used racially or ethnically offensive language. If you are aware of any accusers, please bring them to my attention as soon as possible. I would, however, caution the Council to be wary of any claims made by cats. They are notorious prevaricators."

Schott saved a bag of the original Schotzie's hair and in 1995 she suggested that manager Davey Johnson rub the bag of hair on his players' chests for luck to end a bad start to the season. He politely refused but later relented when his players agreed. They immediately went out and scored nine runs in the last two innings to beat the Mets 13–11. They went on to win the division title.

In 1995 Schott took Schotzie 02 onto the field before a game to introduce the dog to the umpires. The dog crouched near home plate and urinated behind the batter's box a few seconds before the National Anthem. An umpire kicked dirt over the spot.

The San Diego Chicken.

"If you can't stand the heat, stay out of the chicken." — San Diego Chicken Ted Giannoulas during an uncomfortable heat wave. Giannoulas started his routine in 1974 for a San Diego radio station and survived a legal challenge by the Padres, who unsuccessfully claimed exclusive rights to the character. He originally put on the suit as part of a two-week promotion for the radio station. His job was to hand out candy and Easter eggs at the San Diego Zoo. His first baseball appearance was handing out free records at the Padres home opener a few days later. In the 1990s the Chicken made at least $7,000 per appearance (see also **Injury**).

Miscellaneous Characters.

"The man inside [Expos mascot] Youppi (a sort of dog or small bear) is actually a rather talented pantomime comedian. On the stage, or especially in a circus, he would probably be a smash. At a ball game, he's a pain in the ass." — Art Hill in *I Don't Care If I Never Come Back* (1980) on the character that was the Expos' mascot for many years beginning in 1979.

Monkey.

"Think of it: In the seventh inning of a tight game, you put a gyrating monkey on the big screen and 44,234 people scream and shout as if Mick Jagger has arrived. As a marketing tool, the whole thing is so dumb it's brilliant." — Dan Barreiro of the *Minneapolis Star-Tribune* on the Angels' 2002 Rally Monkey.

"Now most homes don't come equipped with air sickness bags, but Fox continued the nonsense by presenting us with "Rally Monkey Etiquette." — T.J. Simers in the *Los Angeles Times*.

In 1909 the New Orleans club had a real monkey for a mascot.

Bear. In 1916 the Cubs had Joa the Cubbie Bear, who briefly lived in a cage outside the stadium.

Beagle. The Mets' first mascot in 1962 was Homer the Beagle, who sat on a stage behind home plate that occupied four choice seats. The dog lived in the Waldorf Towers and was trained by Rudd Weatherwax, who trained the dogs that played Lassie on television. Homer held up a banner that said "Let's Go Mets" and this supposedly started the banner craze that is a staple of Mets games. However, the banner tradition is more properly attributable to the Banner Day held by the Mets early in their history. After Homer's affiliation with the club ended, he was brought back for the Mets' first Oldtimers Game in 1965.

Mule.

"I just wanted to see what happens when one mule confronts 300 asses." — A's owner Charlie Finley on bringing his mule mascot to a writers' luncheon during the World Series.

The 1979 Mets featured Mettle the Mule. It was a pet of Bebe De Roulet, given to her by her grandmother, Mets matriarch Joan Payson. De Roulet often rode the mule around the park sulky-style.

Elephant. In 1989 the elephant was restored as the A's team mascot and the club thought that it would be a good idea to use a pachyderm to throw out the first ball of the season. Akili the elephant froze in front of the crowd and instead of lobbing the ball to the plate as he had practiced, he kept dropping it on the ground. The A's promotion director then picked up the ball and threw it to home plate.

Animal Costumes. The 1970s and 1980s saw a proliferation of mascots created by individuals wearing oversized animal costumes. The San Diego Chicken and Phillie Phanatic are prime examples of the genre. Other mascots:

The Bird of the Orioles
Fred Bird of the Cardinals
Slider of the Indians
The Pirate Parrot
Orbit of the Astros
Homer the Brave
The Mariner Moose
Tony the Tiger (sponsored by Kellogg's)

In April 1997 the Red Sox introduced their new furry mascot, Wally the Green Monster.

Cat. *Rhubarb* was a 1950s movie based on an H. Allen Smith book of the same name in which a cat inherits a baseball team and leads it to a pennant as its mascot.

Totem Pole. For many years the Braves featured Big Victor, a large totem pole figure behind left field. His head tilted and eyes rolled when a Braves player hit a home run. He was replaced in 1967 by Chief Noc-A-Homa, who lasted until the early 1980s (See *Native Americans*—Mascots). He sat in a tepee behind the left field fence and emerged to celebrate Braves home runs (see also *Superstitions* for the Braves' ill-fated removal of the Chief's home).

Bernie Brewer. Until the late 1980s Bernie Brewer slid into a large beer stein in right center field after each Milwaukee home run.

Fish.

"Sorry, Miami, but this is one ugly fish. If you left it outside overnight, even the cats wouldn't go near it." — Rick Folstad of the *Naples* (Fla.) *Daily News* on the Florida Marlins' mascot.

Rejected Mascot. In 1984 the Giants polled their fans on whether to have a mascot. The fans voted overwhelmingly against the idea, but the club pressed ahead anyway. The San Francisco Crazy Crab would arrive in the middle of the 5th inning, but fans always booed the Crab and threw trash at it. The gimmick was discontinued after only a few games.

In late May 2004 the Dodgers announced plans to adopt a team mascot. "Dodger Dog" was proposed by some, but after a huge public outcry the team abandoned the effort a few days later.

Ejections. On May 21, 1993, the Blue Jays hosted the Twins. Minnesota outfielder Dave McCarty appeared to trap a fly ball against the wall, but it was ruled an out. When Blue Jays mascot B.J. Birdie gestured by flapping his wings and holding his nose, he was ejected from the ballpark by umpire Jim McKeon.

On August 8, 1996, Astros mascot Orbit was ejected from a game by umpire Gary Darling after making derogatory gestures following an unpopular call by Darling.

Best Behavior. In 2001 the *Philadelphia Daily News* reported that the Phillie Phanatic, about to appear with President Bush, was warned by a White House aide not to "pull any shit." The staff was nervous because another mascot had put the President's head in his mouth.

Injury. In late 1995 a 68-year-old man won a $128,000 judgment against the Phanatic, who was accused of knocking down the man at a 1991 church carnival.

During the 1995 postseason, the Mariners mascot — a roller-blading Moose — broke his ankle when he crashed into the outfield fence at the Kingdome while being towed by an all-terrain vehicle. Also during the 1995 postseason the Indians' mascot, a hairy, purple-colored blob known as "Slider," tore his anterior cruciate and medial collateral knee ligaments when he fell off the top of the right field fence.

In 1996 the San Diego Chicken lost a lawsuit to a basketball cheerleader. She won $375,000 after he injured her during good-natured roughhousing while performing a timeout routine.

Bad Timing. In early 2003, before the club's run through the World Series, in a cost-cutting move the Marlins fired their long-time mascot-wearer, John Routh, who earned $82,000 per year. One of his former assistants was hired at much less to don the outfit of Billy the Marlin.

Stolen. In 2004 the *Philadelphia Daily News* offered a $1,000 reward for the return of the head of the Phillie Phanatic, which was stolen at the team's charity auction. The Phanatic, Tom Burgoyne, had taken off the costume and gone on a break. The $3,000 head was described by him as having a "long snout, tongue, eyes, green fur and a little bit of body odor." The newspaper offered the reward with no questions asked: "Frankly, we wouldn't know what to ask anyway."

Book. Karen Ahearn and Art Ballant, *The Professional Mascot Handbook* (1982).

Massachusetts Game

"At about the same time that the New York Game was gaining acceptance all over the nation, in one area, at least — New England — the old style of play was being clung to tenaciously. There, particularly in the state of Massachusetts, the type of baseball most closely akin to town ball and rounders appeared to have its deepest roots. Indeed, the old game even seemed to flourish for a number of years and became known, in contrast to the New York Game, as the Massachusetts Game."— Irving A. Leitner in *Baseball: Diamond in the Rough* (1972).

The Massachusetts version of baseball was popular in New England into the 1860s. Only one photograph of Massachusetts Ball being played is known to exist. One of its key rules was that fielders were still allowed to throw at runners to record an out.

The game was played with a slightly smaller ball than that used in the more prevalent (and ultimately dominant) New York version of the game. There were 10–14 players to a side and wooden stakes were still used to mark bases. Bases usually were 60 feet apart and 100 runs were needed for victory.

At the first meeting of the Massachusetts Association of Base Ball Players, the organization dedicated itself to the Massachusetts game. Nevertheless, the Tri-Mountain team of Boston refused to adopt the Massachusetts game. Club President B.F. Guild had gone to study the New York game played by the Knickerbockers and other clubs and announced at the convention that his team would follow the New York rules. The Bowdoin Club of Boston also was influential in the switch to the New York Game.

Eddie Mathews (1931–2001)

Hall of Fame 1978

"I've only known three or four perfect swings in my time. This lad has one of them."— Ty Cobb.

Mathews played third base primarily for the Braves beginning in 1952, hitting 512 home runs over 17 seasons.

Edwin Lee Mathews, Jr., signed his first professional contract at his high school prom in 1949 while in a tuxedo. He spent the next two full years in the minor leagues before becoming the Braves' regular third baseman in 1952. He hit 25 home runs at age 20 and in 1953, the club's first year in Milwaukee, he hit 47 home runs to lead the league.

He played in Milwaukee through 1965, leading the league with 46 home runs in 1959 and hitting 40 or more in two other seasons. He drove in more than 100 runs five times while in Milwaukee. The club moved to Atlanta for 1966 and he began to fade. He played for Houston and Detroit in 1967 and finished his career with 31 games and three home runs for the Tigers in 1968.

The moody and contentious Mathews finished his 17-year career with 512 home runs and a .271 average. He appeared in three World Series and hit a 10th-inning home run in the 1957 Series to win Game 4. He was given a shot at Ruth's home run record until a back injury slowed and then ended his career somewhat prematurely.

He coached for the Braves from 1971 until he became the club's manager with 50 games left in the 1972 season. He remained as manager for 99 games into 1974 and then returned to coaching.

Book. Eddie Mathews and Bob Buege, *Eddie Mathews & the National Pastime* (1993).

Christy Mathewson (1880–1925)

Hall of Fame 1936

"The knightliest of all the game's paladins."— Grantland Rice.

"Mathewson pitched against Cincinnati yesterday. Another way of putting it is that Cincinnati lost a game of baseball. The first statement means the same as the second."— Damon Runyon.

"'They should erect over Matty's grave some hundred years or so from now the epitaph….' He done his damnedest — angels could do no more.'"— *World* reporter on the valiant effort of Mathewson after losing 3–1 on one day's rest in the 1913 World Series.

Mathewson was one of the top pitchers of all time, winning 373 games over 17 seasons primarily for the Giants beginning in 1901.

Christopher (NMI) Mathewson was born in Factoryville, just north of Scranton, Pennsylvania. He attended Bucknell University, where he starred in baseball, football and basketball. He also served in the glee club, two literary societies and was class president.

He began his professional baseball career with Taunton of the New England League in 1899. He moved on to Norfolk in the Virginia State League in 1900 for $90 per month. The Giants bought his contract in July for $1,500, but his poor showing sent him back to Norfolk for the remainder of the season.

The Reds drafted him for $100 and then traded him to the Giants for Amos Rusie. He won 20 games in 1901 for the Giants and manager Horace Fogel has been wrongly accused of trying to convert Mathewson into a first baseman (see also **Players Who Switched Positions**).

For 12 years beginning in 1903 Mathewson won at least 22 games each season and four times won 30 or more. He became famous throughout the country after pitching three shutouts in six days for the Giants in the 1905 World Series. His best season was 1908 when he was 37–11 with a 1.43 ERA and 12 shutouts.

His pitching arm began to weaken in 1915, and in 1916 he asked for his release so that he could manage Cincinnati. He pitched one last game for the Reds that season, a 10–8 victory over the Cubs and Three Finger Brown.

He won 373 games over his 17-year career, tied for third on the all-time list with Grover Cleveland Alexander. He had an ERA of

2.13, fifth all-time, and pitched 80 shutouts, third all-time. He was known for his control and once went 68 innings without giving up a *Base on Balls*.

Mathewson was probably the most charismatic and popular player of the first 20 years of the 20th century. His popularity was enhanced by his good looks and the fact that he played for the strong and large-market Giants.

Mathewson went into the military during World War I. During a training exercise in France he was gassed by his own army. Ty Cobb related a different story; he, Mathewson and others were instructed to put on masks in an air-tight chamber. Mathewson missed the signal and inhaled the poison gas, searing and permanently scarring his lungs. Other sources report that his lungs were scarred from repeated gas inhalation during training exercises and make no mention of Cobb.

Mathewson returned to serve as a coach for three years before poor health forced him into a sanitarium for the severe tuberculosis that he had developed. He briefly became a part owner of the Boston Braves, but the tuberculosis was terminal. He died at age 45 on the same day as Game 1 of the 1925 World Series. He was one of the five original inductees into the Hall of Fame.

Books. Eric Rolfe Greenberg, *The Celebrant* (1983) (fiction); Christy Mathewson, *Pitching in a Pinch* (1912, reprinted in 1994) (ghostwritten by Jack Wheeler); Christy Mathewson, *First Base Faulker* (1916) (also ghostwritten); Ronald A. Mayer, *Christy Mathewson* (1993); Ray Robinson, *Matty: An American Hero* (1993); Philip Seib, *The Player: Christy Mathewson, Baseball, and the American Century* (2004).

Carl Mays Incident (1919–1920)

"Those who are vitally interested in the case are confident that before another week has trickled its way across the calendar Justice Wagner will have decided whether or not the Mays injunction shall be made permanent…. Regardless of what Justice Wagner's ruling in the case is, baseball men are agreed that a bitter fight to oust Johnson from the presidency of the league will be launched during the winter, and will be fought to a finish…."— News account of September 15, 1919, in the *Pawtucket* (R.I.) *Evening Times*.

This 1919 incident was one in a series of disputes between American League president Ban Johnson and certain dissident American League owners (see also *American League*). It culminated in a reduction of Johnson's power and the appointment in 1920 of Judge Landis as commissioner of baseball.

By 1919 there were two factions in the league: Harry Frazee (Red Sox), Jacob Ruppert (Yankees) and Charlie Comiskey (White Sox) opposed Johnson almost routinely and were known as the "Insurrectionists." The other five owners generally supported Johnson and included Phil Ball (Browns), Connie Mack and Ben Shibe (A's), Jim Dunn (Indians) and Frank Navin (Tigers).

Mays left the Red Sox on July 13, 1919, after claiming that the team was not trying to win (according to one source he left "to go fishing"). Ban Johnson asked Red Sox owner Harry Frazee to suspend Mays and refrain from trading him as disciplinary action. Frazee ignored Johnson and sold Mays to the Yankees, who were in a pennant race. Johnson was furious and suspended Mays to void the deal. Johnson had a financial interest in the Cleveland club, which was also in the race with the Yankees. The Yankee owners pointed out that Johnson had conveniently approved the trade of outfielder Tris Speaker to the Indians in 1916 to bolster the club during a pennant race.

The Yankees went to court to block the Mays suspension. The

Christy Mathewson of the New York Giants, the most popular 20th century Major League player prior to Babe Ruth, a Bucknell graduate, and the toast of New York as the best pitcher in the National League.

judge ruled that Johnson had no right to interfere with a club's activities and enjoined his action. As a result, Mays first pitched for the Yankees on August 7, 1919, and finished the season with the club.

On February 10, 1920, the five-man American League board of directors (Johnson and Dunn dissenting) voted to leave Mays with the Yankees and upheld the Yankees' third-place finish. Detroit finished only one-half game behind the Yankees, so Tigers owner Frank Navin tried to claim that the Yankees' third-place share of World Series money was unfairly earned and should be forfeited to the Tigers because the Yankees had Mays.

Despite Mays' problems (including the beaning of Ray Chapman — see *Deaths*), he was one of the finest pitchers of the era. His statistics between 1915 and 1929 are better than every other pitcher except Walter Johnson and Grover Cleveland Alexander.

Willie Mays (1931–)

Hall of Fame 1979

"There have been only two true geniuses in the world: Willie Mays and Willie Shakespeare."— Actress and rabid Giants fan Tallulah Bankhead.

"[Mays] seems to inspect the pitcher as if he were a harmless but puzzling object recently deposited on the mound by the groundskeeper."— George Plimpton in *Sports Illustrated*.

"If he could cook, I'd marry him."— Leo Durocher, who managed Mays and said he was the best he ever saw.

"My longtime friend Bobby Bragan … always said that if you

gave a baseball test to a player and he simply answered Willie Mays to every question, he'd be certain to pass." — Maury Wills.

"I'm not sure what the hell charisma is, but I get the feeling it's Willie Mays." — Ted Kluszewski.

"Try that on an autograph-seeking kid who has been brushed off, a sportswriter who has been cursed, a manager who has tried to exercise authority, a black who has tried to get Mays to speak out against racial inequities.... Mays has an idolatrous press, but that has not made him cooperative. He talks only to the sycophants and those he thinks can help him. Questions from the others are met with obscenities or silence…" — Bay Area sportswriter Glenn Dickey in a 1970 column for which he received a good deal of hate mail.

Mays played 22 seasons beginning in 1951 and hit 660 home runs primarily for the Giants.

Willie Howard Mays began his professional career with the Birmingham Black Barons in the late 1940s. He was in 11th grade and Negro League star Piper Davis was the club's manager. Mays was the starting center fielder for the Barons in 1948 at age 17 and the club won the championship.

Mays made it to the Giants in 1951, hitting .274 in 121 games with 20 home runs. After finishing a military commitment during the Korean War, he played a full season in 1954 and led the league in batting (.345), slugging average (.667) and triples (13) to win the MVP Award. He hit a league-leading 51 home runs in 1955 and led the league in stolen bases for four straight seasons beginning in 1956.

From 1957 through 1963 Mays never hit below .300 and hit at least 29 home runs each season. He had two more huge seasons in 1964 and 1965, hitting 47 and 52 home runs and winning the MVP Award in 1965 at age 34. He continued to be relatively productive through 1970, when he hit 28 home runs. Nineteen games into the 1972 season he was traded to the Mets, for whom he finished his career in 1973.

Mays finished 22 seasons with 660 home runs, 3,283 hits and a .302 average. He was the first player to hit 300 home runs and steal 300 bases. He drove in 100 or more runs in eight straight seasons (1959–1966). He hit only .239 in four World Series and never hit a World Series home run in 71 at-bats.

In the 1970s Mays was barred from baseball by Bowie Kuhn for receiving a salary to represent an Atlantic City casino. Peter Ueberroth later rescinded the ban. When Peter Magowan led the group that bought the Giants in late 1992, Mays was hired "for life" as a coach with the club.

Books. Charles Einstein, *Willie Mays — Coast to Coast Giant* (1963); Charles Einstein, *Willie's Time* (1979); Willie Mays with Lou Sahadi, *Say Hey* (1988); Milton Shapiro, *The Willie Mays Story* (1960).

Bill Mazeroski (1936–)

Hall of Fame (VC) 2001

"I want to thank all the friends and family who made this long trip up here to listen to me speak and hear this crap." — Mazeroski just before cutting short his tearful induction speech.

"They can talk about all the great Pirates — and there have been a lot of them. But Maz represents the spirit of Pittsburgh and the Pirates as well or better than any of them. And what's really scary is that Maz set all those records not on a carpet but on the Forbes Field surface. A lot of visiting players wouldn't take infield at Forbes Field. Think about the numbers Maz would have put up if he'd have played on artificial turf and wouldn't have had all those bad

hops. They might have had to put him into the Hall of Fame five years before he retired." — Teammate Steve Blass.

Mazeroski starred at second base for the Pittsburgh Pirates during 17 seasons starting in 1956.

Born in West Virginia, William Stanley Mazeroski went straight from high school to Class A ball in 1954 at Williamsport. By 1956 he had vaulted to Class AAA Hollywood of the Pacific Coast League. Halfway through the 1956 season the Pirates decided they had waited long enough and the 19-year-old made his Major League debut in July. During his first full year in 1957 he hit .283. In 1958 he batted .275 with a career high 19 home runs.

Much celebrated for his superlative defense, in 1958 Mazeroski won the first of his eight Gold Gloves at second base. From 1956 until 1962 Mazeroski paired with Dick Groat at shortstop. Despite Groat leading National League shortstops in errors four times over this span, Mazeroski managed to lead the league in assists four times and double plays three times.

In 1960 the Pirates won the pennant and faced the Yankees in the World Series. It was Pittsburgh's first World Series since a sweep at the hands of a great Yankee team in 1927. In 1960 the Yankees outscored the Pirates by 29 runs in the seven game series. Nevertheless, the Pirates scraped out four wins with Mazeroski providing several key contributions. In both Games 1 and 5 he had 2 RBIs in close victories.

In Game 7 at Forbes Field Mazeroski stamped his career and baseball history with a singular moment. In a 9–9 tie game he led off the bottom of the 9th and lined a home run over the left field wall to win the Series title for Pittsburgh. Mazeroski would continue to excel over the next 10 years. In the 1960's he led league second baseman in fielding three times and in assists and double plays eight times each. In 1965 he received a new shortstop partner, Gene Alley. In 1966 they collaborated on Mazeroski's Major League record 161 double plays. Mazeroski also led the Pirates with 82 RBIs that year, a career high.

As a part-time player in 1971, he won his second World Series title, a seven game victory over the Orioles. He retired following the 1972 season and left heralded as one of the finest defenders to play the game, holding numerous defensive records for second baseman, including most years leading the National League in assists (nine) and in double plays (eight). His mark of career 1,706 double plays is the Major League record. Offensively, he produced 2,016 hits, 853 RBIs and a .260 batting average. Following his playing career he coached with both the Pirates and Mariners.

Meal Money

"There's something odd about going up to Michael Jordan and slipping him $16 a day." — Birmingham Barons manager Terry Francona on passing out meal money to the multimillionaire *Basketball* star.

"If Ed Sanmarda makes the major leagues he'll be the first starting shortstop who can feed an entire team for less than five dollars, another minor-league skill gone to waste in the bigs. By mid–June in his first year with Mason City he has fed his teammates, all twenty-two of them, on eight successive Sundays. Meal money is passed out Monday mornings and it never lasts a week." — Jerry Klinkowitz in *Short Season and Other Stories* (1988). He didn't make it.

"My biggest problem in the big leagues is that I can't figure out how to spend forty-three dollars in meal money." — Andy Van Slyke.

See also *Food*.

Payment. Until the 1920s it was common for players to be given meal money in cash. However, one story has it that irascible Browns owner Phil Ball wanted to know why his players were not in the hotel dining room eating when he arrived. He was told by the club's road secretary that the players took the $5 in meal money and ate for 75 cents at the local stand, pocketing the rest. Ball immediately ordered his players to eat in the hotel dining room and sign for their meals. This practice became the norm in the 1920s and remained so until food shortages and high prices in the 1930s brought a return to the earlier practice of passing out cash.

Black Sox Scandal. Supposedly a contributing factor in the Black Sox Scandal was the low meal money paid by the White Sox. Owner Charles Comiskey provided $3 per day, while other clubs paid at least $4.

Andy Carey. Andy Carey of the Yankees ate so much in the 1950s that the club supposedly stopped allowing players to sign for their meals in the hotel dining room.

Modern Meal Money. In 1972 Class A teams paid an average of $3.50 per day in meal money, while the Major Leagues paid $18 per day. The Class A meal allowance in the mid–1970s was $6.50 per day. It was increased to $8.50 in 1978. Class AAA meal money increased from $10 to $12 per day.

Major League meal money in the 1990s was $59 per day pursuant to the collective bargaining agreement ($52 during spring training). Based on about 134 days on the road, this comes to $7,902 per player. By 2004 meal money was $95 daily.

Medical Treatment

"I shall tell my doctors that baseball has more curative powers than all their medicine." — Former president Herbert Hoover at age 89, writing to National League president Warren Giles.

"My grandmother told me it was good for colds. It sure blows out those sinuses." — Outfielder Kevin Mitchell on why he *eats* Vicks VapoRub.

"It sends curative sensations vibrating about the muscles." — Satchel Paige on the deer oil that he supposedly obtained from the daughter of a Sioux Indian chief he met in North Dakota.

"The curbstone experts who couldn't see Detroit's infirm Tigers through the liniment fumes were swallowing a lot of wordage today…" — The *Stars and Stripes* military newspaper after the Tigers took a 3–2 advantage in the 1945 World Series against the Cubs.

See also **Conditioning** and **Injuries and Illness**.

Rehabilitation. Old Hoss Radbourn's routine for rehabilitating his pitching arm (which he often could not raise) was to put hot towels on the muscles; throw an iron ball underhanded; then throw a baseball 3–4 times the regular pitching distance to loosen it up (today's version of pregame "long toss").

Stove. Nineteenth century Cincinnati Reds owner John Brush believed in hot water for sprains and bruises and ordered a stove put in the Reds clubhouse.

Aspirin. National League pitcher Mort Cooper chewed aspirin on the mound in the 1940s to dull the pain in his arm.

Diathermy. Joe DiMaggio had to delay his Major League debut when he burned his foot in a diathermy machine during spring training.

Dale Alexander was a part-time player around 1930 when he used a diathermy machine on an injured knee. The new technology severely burned his leg and caused gangrene. He almost lost his leg and his career was over.

Hot Water Bottle. Yankee pitcher Whitey Ford had a circulation problem in his fingers, so on cold days he kept a small hot water bottle in his back pocket to keep his hand warm. Many thought he was wetting his fingers.

Pickle Brine. In 1968 Mets trainer Gus Mauch reportedly used pickle brine successfully to toughen Nolan Ryan's fingers against blisters that plagued him throughout much of his career. This bit of folklore is untrue, as the remedy never worked and Ryan had to spend two months on the disabled list that season because of blisters.

Lemon. Catcher Wilbert Robinson often went to bed with lemon wrapped around his bruised and swollen fingers. He broke all his fingers catching and his pinky was amputated to stop blood poisoning.

Potions. Guy Bush hurt his arm pitching for the Cubs in the 1930s. Trainer Andy Lotshaw thought the problem was psychosomatic, so he rubbed on a special potion that helped considerably. Lotshaw later admitted that the potion was Coca-Cola.

When pitcher Al Leiter found a cure for his blisters in Glutaraldehyde, he considered obtaining a patent and calling it "Leiter Fluid" (Nolan Ryan could have used this stuff).

Radiation Treatment. Unknown to the Yankee team doctor, various New York pitchers of the early 1950s took radiation treatment for sore shoulders. They included Johnny Sain, Ed Lopat, Allie Reynolds and Whitey Ford. The team doctor was upset about the treatments and later their use was outlawed even though there were no apparent side effects.

Rice. Pitcher Steve Carlton sometimes soaked his left arm in a vat of cooked rice. Roger Clemens had another use for a vat of rice, as he explained in a shoe commercial. He strengthened his arm by kneading the uncooked rice in the vat.

Joe "Ducky" Medwick (1911–1975)

Hall of Fame 1968

"I think there's a lot of personality in [getting into the Hall of Fame]. Look at Ducky Medwick. A great player and he went in on his last ballot, but he was antagonistic and difficult with the reporters and that hurt his chances of getting in. It shouldn't have anything to do with it, but the fact is, it does." — Ralph Kiner quoted in *Voices from Cooperstown*, by Anthony J. Connor (1982).

"This was the longest slump of my career. I had gone 0-for-20 before, but never 0-for-20 years." — Medwick at his Hall of Fame induction.

Medwick starred in the National League for 17 seasons beginning in 1932, batting .324 lifetime.

At age 18 in 1929, Joseph Michael Medwick hit .419 in his first professional season. After three more minor league seasons he made it to the Cardinals outfield for 26 games in late 1932. He hit .349 to begin a string of 11 straight seasons over .300.

Medwick was a starter in 1933 and 1934 and hit .379 in the 1934 World Series for St. Louis. He was removed by Judge Landis from Game 7 of the Series after Detroit fans pelted him with fruit and vegetables after he slid hard into the Tigers' third baseman (see also *Fans — Fan Attacks on Players*).

During six straight seasons in which he had more than 100 RBIs for the Cardinals, he hit .351 in 1936 and won the Triple Crown and MVP Award in 1937 with a .374 average, 31 home runs and 154 RBIs. He also led the league in slugging average, at-bats, hits, doubles and runs scored for one of the greatest seasons in the history of Major League Baseball.

Medwick again led the league in RBIs in 1938 but when his power numbers dropped in 1939 the Cardinals traded him to the Dodgers after 37 games in 1940. He hit .300 for the club, and in

1941 he helped lead them to a pennant with a .318 average. He was beaned that season and never returned to his previous form. He bounced around to various National League clubs in the 1940s before returning to the Cardinals in 1947 and 1948 to finish out his 17-year career.

Medwick had a lifetime .324 average with 2,471 hits and 1,383 RBIs. After leaving the Major Leagues he was a player-manager for various minor league clubs through 1952. He later became a hitting instructor for the Cardinals.

Memorabilia

"I had no idea it was worth $50,000. If I did, I'd be sleeping in it." — Mickey Mantle on one of his game jerseys; See *Mickey Mantle Memorabilia*, by Rick Hines, Mark Larson and Dave Platta (1994). Mantle's first home run ball sold for $41,250 in 1996. His 500th home run ball sold for $24,200 that year.

World War II. During World War II baseball memorabilia was sold at inflated prices as a popular means of auctioning off war bonds to support the war effort. At one bond rally Cardinal autographs went for $550, gloves for $1,000, a team picture for $9,500 and a portrait of Connie Mack for $16,000.

Top Collector. Barry Halper is considered the top collector in the country. It has not hurt that he has been a minority shareholder in the Yankees. Halper got his start in New Jersey collecting autographed balls. Lou Novikoff gave Halper an old road uniform worn by Barney McClosky to get Halper to stop pestering him. Word got around that the Newark teenager was collecting uniforms, and visiting players would make donations. Halper's wife was destined to marry him. Her father, uncle and aunt were George, Herman and Ruth.

Ball. See *Errors — Bill Buckner* for the story of actor Charlie Sheen's purchase of the ball that went through Buckner's legs to end Game 6 of the 1986 World Series.

Sammy Sosa's 500th home run ball sold for $44,823 in 2001. A college student caught the ball and decided to sell it to pay for college.

In July 2000 several items were sold at auction, including a baseball signed by the 1919 Black Sox and the umpires who worked the final game of the 1919 World Series, which sold for $93,666. A ball signed by the 1919 Reds sold for $11,208, and a ball autographed by Babe Ruth sold for $76,020.

Barry Bonds' 73rd Home Run Ball. See *Home Runs — Barry Bonds' 70th, 71st and 73rd).*

Bats. In 1994 Babe Ruth's bat from the 1921 season used to hit home run number 56 sold for $63,000. The previous record for a bat was $60,500, used by Ruth to hit his first home run of the 1924 season. The bat was sold along with an authenticating letter by Ruth.

Shoeless Joe Jackson's last Black Betty sold for $577,610 in the early 2000s.

Bat Fraud. In March 2002 Herbert John Derungs of San Francisco pleaded guilty to impersonating Derek Jeter and Nomar Garciaparra to obtain bats and then selling them on eBay. He sent emails to the Original Maple Bat Company which read: "I will place an order for 50–60 for the 2001 season, because my contract with Louisville Slugger is up, and I am trying to get a feel of what's out there before I decide what bats to use next year. The sooner the better. Thanks. Derek."

Bobblehead Doll. In 2003 the *San Francisco Chronicle* held a contest to determine the best use for a Tommy Lasorda bobblehead doll. Reader Steve Quinlan was the unofficial winner: "I put my Lasorda figurine in my refrigerator as a deterrent to late-night snacking."

Bone Chips. Pitcher Jeff Nelson's bone chips brought $23,600 at a 2003 auction.

Credit Card. Mickey Mantle's American Express card sold for $6,500 in the early 2000s.

Gehrig Fight. During World War II, Lou Gehrig's widow Eleanor auctioned off much of his memorabilia to raise money for war bonds. His parents objected and filed suit trying to block Eleanor's efforts. The case eventually settled, with Eleanor generally coming out ahead in the fight. Many of the court documents, including Gehrig's original will, are in the files of the Hall of Fame.

Gloves. Gloves traditionally have commanded much lower prices than uniforms. However, gloves belonging to Joe DiMaggio and Ty Cobb sold in the 1990s for $25,000. The gloves of current stars usually command prices of as little as $500.

Hat. Babe Ruth's straw hat sold at auction in 2003 for $6,065.36.

Umpire Fraud. In February 2004 former Major League umpire Al Clark pleaded guilty to fraud in connection with selling baseballs he falsely claimed had been used in memorable games, including the tying and record-breaking consecutive games played by Cal Ripken, Nolan Ryan's 300th victory, Dwight Gooden's 1986 no-hitter, and the 1978 Yankees/Red Sox play-off game. He was given four months in prison and ordered

Memorabilia from the Babe Ruth Museum in Baltimore.

to repay $40,000 he had received for the goods. His friend, memorabilia dealer Richard Graessle, Jr., pleaded guilty to tax evasion.

Clark became an umpire in 1977 and was terminated in 2001 after officials said he improperly used plane tickets in violation of his union's contract.

Uniforms. The uniform shirt that Tom Seaver wore during the 1969 World Series was auctioned for $55,000 in 1992.

Rachel Robinson consigned one of her husband Jackie's uniforms for sale at auction in 1993. It sold for $66,000.

Uniform Sacrilege.

"I don't mind including swatches from current players.... But only three Ruth uniforms! All in the name of the almighty dollar! What's next? Cut up a Revolutionary War uniform of George Washington for Donruss' 2004 Great Presidents series? Maybe pieces of an original Declaration of Independence?"—Memorabilia collector Jay O'Neill on the 2003 announcement that Donruss was going to cut up a game-worn Babe Ruth jersey from the 1925 Yankees and put the 1"x1" swatches in baseball card packets. One uniform would yield 2,100 pieces. Donruss purchased the uniform at auction for $264,210.

Joe DiMaggio. DiMaggio's memorabilia income increased from $4 million in 1992 to more than $7 million in 1993.

The Consummate Hustler. Pete Rose's gofer in the 1980s, Tommy Gioiosa, dutifully learned Rose's signature and Rose frequently critiqued him on the nuances of his signature; slapping him on the head playfully when Gioiosa did it wrong. Gioiosa also said he watched Rose put on several undershirts at one time on the night he was to break Ty Cobb's record for most hits. As Gioiosa remembered, Rose said, "I'll sell every one of these motherfuckers."

Pool Hall. Selling for $36,098 was a contract for the sale of a Chicago pool hall by Shoeless Joe Jackson to teammate Lefty Williams. The contract, dated October 6, 1921, was for $1.

The Big Show. The memorabilia industry's primary annual show is the National Sports Collectors Convention, which began in 1980.

FanFest. In 1995 at the FanFest extravaganza at the All-Star Game, jerseys and other items worn in the game were auctioned off. Dodger pitcher Hideo Nomo's jersey brought $11,000. Cal Ripken's brought $7,000, followed by Frank Thomas' and Greg Maddux's at $3,500.

Theft. In March 2002 Yankee outfielder Ruben Rivera stole Derek Jeter's glove out of his locker and sold it on the black market for $2,500. He also stole a bat from him. There were rumors that he took things from Roger Clemens, but Clemens denied it. The Yankees quickly released Rivera.

In May 1999 in Boston, Joseph Schnabel pleaded guilty to stealing wills signed by baseball Hall of Famers George Wright and 1920s umpire Tom Connolly, and selling them for more than $15,000. The discovery of the missing documents led authorities in other parts of the country to realize they had experienced similar thefts.

Toothpick. A Tom Seaver toothpick once sold for $440.

1990s Price Increases/Drops. The baseball memorabilia craze exploded in the 1980s with *Baseball Cards* leading the way, followed closely by *Autographs*. By 1992 the baseball card market had softened and other forms of memorabilia became more popular. Uniforms worn by players such as Gehrig, Mantle and DiMaggio have been offered at auction for prices starting at $300,000. A 1961 Roger Maris uniform sold for $132,000 in 1992. Babe Ruth's 60th home run ball sold for $100,000 and Lou Gehrig's bat sold for $27,500 in 1990. Prices slid after that, as authenticity became a problem.

Home Runs. Four seconds after Mark McGwire hit his 62nd home run in 1998, the QVC home shopping channel broke into its regular programming and offered commemorative 62nd Home Run Baseball merchandise. Before the day was over, customers had ordered over 100,000 items totaling more than $2.6 million.

After the 1998 season and the crush of home run record memorabilia, Posh International, Inc. (OTC Bulletin Board: POSE) announced its "Fielder's Choice" Collector Series Baseball Marbles, which one collectible industry veteran called "the hottest, freshest, most innovative sports collectible to be released in years." Sure.

Books. Bruce Chadwick and David Spindel began a series of books containing illustrations of collectibles from various teams; for example, *The Giants: Memories and Memorabilia from a Century of Baseball*; Douglas Congdon-Martin and John Kashmanian, *Baseball Treasures: Memorabilia from the National Pastime* (1993); Mark K. Larson, *Complete Guide to Baseball Memorabilia* (1994).

Mendoza Line See *Batting Averages*

Men's Senior Baseball League (1986–)

"Go ahead and play in the City League, and make everything serious. All it is, is Little League for big people."—Kevin Kerrane in "Season Openers" (1980).

The MSBL was formed in 1986 for players 30 and over. In 1995 it had 44,000 players in the U.S. and Canada alone. Former Major League pitcher Jim Barr won two games in the 1995 title series. Former Major Leaguers Jose Cardenal and Bob Oliver also played in the 1995 series. See Nelson W. Wolff, *Baseball for Real Men: Seven Spiritual Laws for Senior Players* (2000).

Merchandising

"Baseball has been a vehicle for merchandising since at least the 1870s, when scorecard publishers sold advertising to local restaurants, sporting goods emporiums, railway companies and brewers. Today baseball sells cars, clothing, cameras, computers—anything and everything."—John Thorn in *The Game for All America* (1988).

See also *Advertising* and *Logos/Licensing*.

Player Likenesses.

"[Ripken's] got endorsement deals ... and assorted memorabilia, including a bobble-head doll. (You can't establish a deathless baseball record without a bobble-head doll.)"—Richard Ben Cramer in *Sports Illustrated* as Cal Ripken chased Lou Gehrig's record in 1995.

Payment to Players. In 1966 union chief Marvin Miller convinced the players that they were being ripped off by Topps baseball cards. Topps paid each player $125 to use his likeness on baseball cards. Miller persuaded the players to hold out from signing their licensing contracts until Topps agreed to pay them a percentage of the gross revenue on the sale of the cards. This opened the floodgates in later years to huge revenue for the players for licensing of all types of baseball merchandise.

By 1993 royalties on likenesses were almost $100 million, resulting in payments of almost $100,000 per player per season. In 1993 the players began stockpiling their earnings into their strike fund, which reached over $175 million by the time they went on strike in August 1994.

Major League Baseball Promotions Corporation. This adjunct to the commissioner's office was created in the Bowie Kuhn era in the late 1960s to help promote baseball. One of its earliest promotions was a book celebrating 100 years of professional base-ball published in 1969. It is sometimes referred to as Major League Baseball "Properties."

Gross sales of Major League Baseball merchandise have risen from $200,000 in 1976, to $200 million in 1986, to $2 billion in 1991. By 1991 Major League Baseball had 400 licensees who man-ufactured 2,500 products. The corporation retains 11% of the pro-ceeds for operating and returns the remaining money to the clubs. The organization had projected sales of $2.8 billion in 1994, but the strike reduced that amount by $280 million to somewhat more than the $2.4 billion generated in 1993 ($3 million in some sources).

Strike Losses. The 1994–1995 strike cost Major League Base-ball over $700 million in unsold licensed merchandise.

Top Sellers/Teams. In 1994 the top Major League and minor league merchandise sellers (in order):

Major Leagues
Colorado Rockies
Atlanta Braves
Florida Marlins
Chicago White Sox
New York Yankees
Chicago Cubs
St. Louis Cardinals
Philadelphia Phillies
Cleveland Indians
Los Angeles Dodgers
Minor Leagues
Carolina Mudcats
Hickory Crawdads
Ottawa Lynx
Durham Bulls
Wilmington Blue Rocks
Toledo Mud Hens
Chattanooga Lookouts
Buffalo Bisons
Greensboro Hornets
Portland Beavers

In 1996 there was a shift, reflective of the success of certain clubs. The top-selling logos were, in order, the Indians, Braves, Dodgers, Yankees, White Sox, Rockies, Mariners, Orioles, Red Sox and Mar-lins. The minor league leaders were the Portland Sea Dogs, Nor-wich Navigators and Wisconsin Timber Rattlers.

Negro Leagues. Merchandising of Negro League items earned more than $3.4 million between July 1994 — when they first started — and the end of the year. This generated more than $143,000 in royalties for the Negro League Players Association, the Negro League Museum in Kansas City and the Jackie Robinson Foundation.

Merkle's Boner See Base Running

Mexico

"He wants Texas back." — Tom Lasorda, on Mexican pitcher Fernando Valenzuela's contract demands.

"The hottest tamale in the Mexican Baseball League today is that 48-year-old gay caballero, Rogers Hornsby…" — *The Sporting News* in the mid-1940s. Hornsby left Mexico a few days later and returned to the United States when he learned that he would be required to pay his own way on the road.

"Aw, how could he [Jorge Orta] lose the ball in the sun, he's from Mexico." — Broadcaster Harry Caray.

Origins. American railroad workers brought baseball to Mex-ico in the 1880s, though some sources claim that the game was first introduced when the White Sox toured the country in 1906.

Mexican Revolution. In 1914 Pancho Villa had troops ready to begin what later escalated into the Mexican Revolution. Accom-panying him was American newspaperman John Reed (featured in the movie *Reds*). Reed advised Villa that if he wanted headlines for his revolution in America, he should wait a few days until after the World Series. It makes a good story, but according to historians the dates do not jibe.

Professional Leagues. Professional baseball was first played in Mexico in 1925 and the first professional league was formed in the late 1930s. The first Mexican League lasted until 1953, and its teams signed a few Major League players after World War II. The Pas-cual brothers ran the league and signed a number of Negro League stars of the 1940s before going after Major League talent (see below).

Shortly after the league disbanded in the early 1950s, the north-ern clubs merged with the Arizona-Texas and Arizona-Mexico leagues at the Class AA level. The Mexican League reorganized in 1955 and has operated continuously since that date. It is now part of the National Association and recognized as a Class AAA league.

Other leagues were formed in Mexico over the years, but the only one with any impact was the Mexican Central League. In 1979 it merged with the Mexican League to form a 20-team league with four divisions. The combined league shrank to 14 teams after finan-cial problems in the early 1980s and then expanded to 16 teams by the 2000s. Only five foreigners may be on a roster.

There are now two Mexican professional leagues, one each in summer and winter. The summer league has a 132-game schedule and each team may have three foreign players. Willie Aikens is one of the more prominent Major Leaguers to play in the Mexican League. The winter league champion participates in the *Caribbean Series*.

1940s Raiding of American Teams.

"I'm perfectly happy here. My wife likes Mexico, and we moved into this super-modern apartment today and everything is dandy." — Catcher Mickey Owen, late of the St. Louis Cardinals and soon to regret his move to Mexico.

"There would be fierce resentment, I feel sure, if Man o' War were put to work pulling a vegetable wagon through his declining years, and the Society for the Prevention of Cruelty to Animals would take an immediate interest in the affair. But the baseball brethren will derive smug satisfaction from the fact that one of their immortals will play in the patched-roof circuit, and one of their idols will gather the dust of sleepy Mexican towns. He sinned against their narrow code, and as a sinner should he now get his comeuppance." — Sportswriter Dave Egan on horse racing lover Rogers Hornsby, recently defected to manage in the Mexican Leagues.

In his Hall of Fame induction speech, Phil Rizzuto gave his account of how he almost went to the Mexican League for $10,000 and a Cadillac. His wife Cora said that if he went, he would be going alone. He explained to the crowd: "It was a time when you couldn't get butter, you couldn't get stockings, you couldn't get a girdle. Not that she needed a girdle … she was pretty well built."

Jorge Pascual was a wealthy Mexican customs broker who had a financial interest in the Mexican League. In the mid-1940s Pas-cual and his four brothers used their $50 million empire to sup-port their raids of American Major Leaguers in an attempt to have the Mexican League compete directly with the Major Leagues. Pas-cual initially met Major Leaguer Danny Gardella in New York and induced him, Sal Maglie, Mickey Owen and others to jump south of the border.

When Indians shortstop Vern Stephens jumped to the rival league and played in two games there before heading home, commissioner Happy Chandler stepped in and ruled that all players who jumped to the Mexican League would be barred from Major League Baseball for five years if they did not come back to their teams by an arbitrarily imposed deadline. Nevertheless, a number of players accepted large salary increases and bonuses and left for Mexico. The first player of consequence to actually sign was Luis Olmo, a Dodger outfielder and hold-out who received $40,000 for three years.

The Pascual brothers also offered large salaries to a number of Major League stars: Ted Williams turned down $300,000 for three years and Stan Musial turned down $125,000 in each of five years and a $75,000 cash bonus (or, depending on the source, $65,000 up front and $130,000 for each of five years). Williams met with the Pascual brothers in Cuba during an exhibition tour and turned the money down while he was making $40,000 with the Red Sox.

Max Lanier was offered a $1,000 raise by the Cardinals (to $10,000) to induce him not to jump. Though he started the season with a 6–0 record with the Cardinals and was considered the best left-hander in the National League, he accepted the Mexican League's offer of $20,000 for each of five years, plus a $35,000 signing bonus. Terry Moore received $1,000 from owner Sam Breadon after he supposedly dissuaded Cardinal stars Stan Musial and Enos Slaughter from jumping to the Mexican League. Once word of the poor living and playing conditions in the Mexican League reached the Major Leaguers, the Mexican League raiders were no longer a threat.

Because of Happy Chandler's ruling that prohibited players from returning to the Major Leagues, Danny Gardella and others sued for reinstatement in 1949 on antitrust grounds. The owners agreed to lift the prohibition and paid off Gardella for $29,000 (Gardella later said it was $60,000) because they feared a challenge to the *Reserve Clause*. Gardella played only one more Major League game, with the Cardinals in 1950. Lou Klein was the first reinstated player to again play in the Major Leagues. Before that, many of the jumpers who left the Mexican League played in the outlaw Quebec Provincial League.

The Mexican League went bankrupt in the early 1950s and the remnants merged with the Class C Arizona-Texas League. The Mexican League raiding was important in indirectly helping to raise Major League salaries and accelerate approval of the *Pension* system.

The Major League players who jumped to the Mexican League (identifying those who returned to the Major Leagues):

New York Giants: Pitchers Adrian Zabala (a Cuban who returned briefly in 1949), Sal Maglie (returned), Harry Feldman and Art "Ace" Adams; infielders Roy Zimmerman, Nap Reyes (returned for one game in 1950), George Hausmann (returned for 16 games in 1949); outfielder Danny Gardella (returned for one game in 1950).

St. Louis Cardinals: Pitchers Max Lanier (returned) and Fred Martin (returned); infielder Lou Klein (returned).

Brooklyn Dodgers: Catcher Mickey Owen (returned) and outfielders Luis Olmo (a Puerto Rican who returned) and Canadian Roland Gladu.

Philadelphia A's: Outfielder Roberto Estalella (a Cuban who returned for eight games in 1949).

Washington Senators: Outfielder Roberto Ortiz (a Cuban who returned) and infielder Chile Gomez (a Mexican who had last played for the Senators in 1942).

Chicago White Sox: Pitcher Alex Carrasquel (a Venezuelan who returned for three games in 1949).

Detroit Tigers: Murray Franklin (who had last played for the Tigers in 1942).

Philadelphia Phillies: Cuban outfielder Rene Monteagudo.

Chicago Cubs: Catcher Sal "Chico" Hernandez (a Cuban who last played for the Cubs in 1943).

Greatest Player. Hector Espino hit 484 home runs over 25 years in the Mexican Leagues (1960–1984), a minor league record. He declined many offers to play in the United States though he did attempt to break into the Major Leagues when he played 32 games for Jacksonville in the International League in 1964. Although he hit .300, he quit because of racial discrimination and never again played on an American team.

Mexican Major League Players.

"A lot of Mexicans have bad foot speed. It's a genetic type thing. They have a different body type. Most all have good hands and good rhythm. That's why they dance so well. Rhythm is important in baseball, it means agility." — Orioles scout Fred Uhlman, Sr., in 1993, on why Mexican players rarely make it to the Major Leagues at any position except pitcher.

"There are two things that are rare in Mexicans: running speed and power. That's why the majority of Mexicans who reach the big leagues are pitchers." — Pirates scout Angel Figueroa.

"Mexicans, because of the Indian blood, can run to New York and not stop — just not fast." — Angel Figueroa.

The difficulty in signing most Mexican players is the highly structured Mexican Leagues. The leagues require Major League clubs to deal not only with a player and his agent, but also the club for whom he plays. Unlike Puerto Rican players, Mexican players are not subject to the American draft.

A total of 58 Mexican players had made it in the Major Leagues through the 1992 season, starting with Melo Almada with the Red Sox in 1933. In 1992 there were 48 Mexicans playing at any level of Organized Baseball, compared to 250 from Venezuela. Ten of the Mexican players were on Major League rosters. Of the 48, 16 were in the Dodgers organization and 13 with the Pirates.

Bobby Avila played second base primarily for the Indians from 1949 through 1959. He was the first Mexican to star in the Major Leagues, batting a lifetime .281. He was later president of the Mexican League and went into Mexican politics.

Winston Llenas was a star in the Mexican League before playing with the Angels for five years. He returned to the Mexican League in 1977 and played seven more seasons.

Fernando Valenzuela is easily the most famous Major League ballplayer to come out of Mexico. Fernandomania swept the country in 1981 when he recorded a number of shutouts and consecutive wins during the strike-shortened 1981 season. He won the Cy Young Award that year, although Tom Seaver might have been more deserving.

Valenzuela flamed out in the late 1980s and failed in a 1991 comeback attempt with the Angels, losing two games before being released. In 1993 he led Mazatlan to the Caribbean World Series. He then signed a minor league contract with the Orioles and capped the comeback with a two-hit shutout of the Indians in May 1994. Though sometimes erratic, he pitched decently for the Padres into the 1997 season.

Teddy Higuera pitched well for the Brewers, but injuries plagued his career. He was the first Mexican player to win 20 games in the Major Leagues, beating out Valenzuela for the honor by only a few days in 1986. After signing a $13 million four-year deal in 1990, he appeared in only eight games over the next three seasons due to shoulder problems.

Vinny Castilla hit 268 home runs in 13 seasons for four clubs (twice with the Braves), primarily the Rockies. His most productive seasons were with the Rockies between 1995 and 1999, when he hit between 32 and 46 home runs each season. He was still playing in 2004.

Esteban Loaiza. The Tijuana-born pitcher won 90 games in nine years for several clubs, with a peak of 21 wins in 2003 for the White Sox. He signed with the Dodgers for the 2004 season.

Erubiel Durazo struggled with the Diamondbacks for four seasons in Arizona beginning in 1999 before blossoming in Oakland with a full season and 21 home runs in 2003.

Others. Other Mexican players include Juan Castro, Francisco Cordova, Benji Gil and brother Geronimo, Armando Reynoso, Ricardo Rincon and Ismael Valdez.

Opening Day. See *Opening Day*—Opener In Mexico for the Padres/Rockies home opener in Mexico in 1999.

Umpire. Alfonso Marquez umpired behind the plate during Game 3 of the 2003 ALCS. He is a member of the Mexican Baseball Hall of Fame.

All-Stars. Through 2004 the seven Mexicans who have played in the Major League All-Star Game: Bobby Avila (1952, 1954, 1955), Jorge Orta (1975, 1980), Sid Monge (1979), Fernando Valenzuela (1981–1986), Aurelio Lopez (1983), Teddy Higuera (1986), Vinny Castilla (1995, 1998) and Esteban Loaiza (2002–2004).

Middletown Mansfields

National Association 1872
This Connecticut club had a 5–19 record in its only partial season and technically finished in ninth place.

Midgets

"I can't put you in a Giants uniform; you'd look like a Giant midget."—Then-scout and later Montreal Expos general manager Charlie Fox to Pete Rose (5'11") at a tryout for the Giants.

Eddie Gaedel.
"He'd have been great in a short series."—Browns owner Bill Veeck.

The midget stuntman and vaudeville actor appeared in a Major League game for the Browns on August 18, 1951 (though various sources erroneously put the date as the 13th or 19th). The event was witnessed by 18,369 fans (one source reported 20,299 fans) at Sportsman's Park in St. Louis against the Tigers. It was the largest home crowd for the Browns in four years. They were 36 games out of first place and the pressure was definitely off for the day's doubleheader.

Owner Bill Veeck had promised a "Festival of Surprises" that day, including jugglers, jitterbuggers and a band led by Satchel Paige and baseball clown Max Patkin. Veeck persuaded Falstaff brewery to promote the games, but the Falstaff people were disappointed that only the dancers and jugglers and a few other minor events were part of the between-game festivities as the "big surprise" promised by Veeck.

Between games Gaedel jumped out of a three-tiered papier-mâché birthday cake celebrating the American League's 50th anniversary. Everyone in the park thought this was the extent of Gaedel's participation, but they were proven wrong at the start of the second game.

The 3'7" Gaedel (3'8" in some sources) pinch-hit for right fielder Frank Saucier to lead off the bottom of the 1st inning. Saucier's career consisted of one hit in 14 Major League at-bats.

Gaedel wore elf shoes and came up to the plate swinging half a dozen 10-inch bats. He wore number "⅛" on the back of his uniform. He wore the uniform of batboy Bill DeWitt, Jr., whose father was a front office executive with the club.

Umpire Ed Hurley immediately questioned the status of the batter, but Browns manager Zack Taylor had Gaedel's contract in his pocket and a telegram to the American League office informing it of the "trade" for Gaedel. He had been signed for $100 per game and insured by Veeck for $1 million.

When Gaedel batted, Tigers catcher Bob Swift got on his knees and gave no sign to pitcher Bob Cain, who was not allowed to move up and pitch underhanded. Swift wanted to lie down but the umpire would not let him. Veeck estimated that Gaedel's strike zone when he was in a crouch was 1½ inches. Veeck threatened to shoot him if he tried to swing. Jim Delsing ran for Gaedel after he walked on four pitches. The Browns loaded the bases but could not score, eventually losing 6–2.

Veeck issued a tongue-in-cheek press release on Gaedel: 26 years old, lived in Chicago, "used to play shortstop when he was smaller, but went into semi-retirement several years ago when the big kids failed to pick him in a corner-lot game."

Gaedel was released the next day when American League president Will Harridge refused to approve the contract, saying that using midgets was "not in the best interests of baseball." After the game Gaedel was booked into television appearances on the Ed Sullivan and Bing Crosby shows, and promoted Buster Brown shoes.

The event mirrored a James Thurber story written 10 years earlier for the *Saturday Evening Post*, called "You Could Look It Up," featuring midget Pearl du Monville (see below). Another story has it that the inspiration for the stunt supposedly came from former Giants manager John McGraw. McGraw once had dinner with Veeck's father, who was president of the Cubs, and talked about a hunchback batboy named Eddie Morrow that he always wanted to send up to bat.

In 1959 Veeck again hired Gaedel, this time for the White Sox. On May 29 at Comiskey Park, Gaedel and three other little people dropped out of a helicopter dressed as Martians. They ceremoniously captured the diminutive White Sox double-play combination of Nellie Fox and Luis Aparicio (both 5'9"), made them honorary Martians and told the crowd that they had arrived to help the duo in their fight against the "giant earthlings."

Gaedel was back again in 1961 for the White Sox. Veeck hired him and seven other midgets as vendors because of fan complaints that they could not see around the regular vendors. The midgets worked the box seats on Opening Day and a few more games. A few weeks after the job ended, Gaedel was beaten up for $11 outside a bar and staggered home to his mother's house and went to bed. He was found dead the next morning at age 36 on June 18, 1961. The coroner determined that he died of a heart problem, though the beating may well have exacerbated the condition. According to his mother, a man claiming to be from the Hall of Fame swindled her out of Gaedel's bats and uniform.

Pitcher Bob Cain was the only baseball man known to have attended the funeral: "I owed him that much. Because in the many years I've been a goodwill man and speaker for the company, the midget was my best story—before and after he died."—Quoted in Bob Broeg's essay "Veeck and the Midget," in *The Ol' Ball Game* (1990).

Pearl du Monville. The 1941 James Thurber story appearing in the *Saturday Evening Post* was thought to be the inspiration for Veeck's stunt. The result was slightly different (though the manager did pull official papers from his pocket to validate the player's appearance); du Monville reaches ball three with the bases loaded and the game on the line with two out in the bottom of the 9th inning. Though told not to swing the bat, he swings and hits a dribbler: "'Fair ball!' yells the umpire, and the midget starts runnin' for first, still carryin' that little bat, and makin' maybe ninety foot an hour. Bethlehem breaks loose on that ball field and in them stands. They ain't never been nothin' like it since creation was begun."

The runners rounded the bases to score the tying and winning runs, but du Monville was still chugging to first base as the infielders fell over themselves trying to pick up the ball: "But Pearl is still maybe fifteen, twenty feet from the bag, toddlin' like a baby and yeepin' like a trapped rabbit, when the second baseman finely gets a hold of that ball and slams it over to first. The first baseman ketches it and stomps on the bag, the base umpire waves Pearl out, and there goes your old ball game, the craziest ball game ever played in the history of the organized world."

Poor Sport. Shortly after Veeck hired Rogers Hornsby as manager for the 1952 season, a group of midgets appeared on the field during spring training. Hornsby threw one of the little guys back over the railing and told them to leave.

Fielding Help. On August 26, 1946, in Fenway Park, the Indians were employing the "Williams Shift" against Ted Williams by overloading all but the left fielder to the right side of the field. Midget Marco Songini jumped out of the stands and briefly covered third base.

Donald Davidson.

"Sleeping sickness stunted my growth and deformed me when I was six. At age forty-six, I am only forty-eight inches tall, and the world obviously was not designed for four-foot adults."—Donald Davidson in his autobiography, *Caught Short*, with Jesse Outlar (1972).

The second-most famous little person in Major League history was Donald Davidson, a dwarf who had a long career with the Braves in front-office positions (starting as a bat boy), most notably as traveling secretary. His 30-year relationship with the club ended when he was fired on April 24, 1976.

In 1938 when Davidson was 13 and a batboy for the Red Sox, on the final day of the season manager Joe Cronin sent him up to the plate as a pinch hitter for Moe Berg. Umpire Bill Sommers told him to return to the dugout and refused to let him bat.

Midwest Baseball Association

"Northwestern Association of Base Ball Players"—Original name of the Midwest Baseball Association.

The first baseball association in the Midwest was established on December 6, 1865, as the Northwestern Association of Base Ball Players. It was formed in Chicago and had 16 clubs from Iowa, Missouri, Wisconsin, Illinois, Michigan, Indiana, Ohio and Minnesota. As the country's boundary's expanded, the name was changed to Midwest Baseball Association.

Military Baseball

"We owe a great deal to Base Ball.... It is one of the reasons why American soldiers are the best in the world—quick witted, swift to act, ready of judgment, capable of going into action without officers.... It is one of the reasons why as a nation we impress visitors as quick, alert, confident and trained for independent action."—The 1906 *Chicago American* newspaper.

"If you're so smart, how come you're still in the Army?"—Casey Stengel writing in response to a soldier's letter of criticism.

"Every member of our baseball team at West Point became a general: this proves the value of team sports."—General Omar Bradley.

"Admiral Schlei, Soldier Boy Murphy, Davy Force, Red Barron, Quincy Trouppe, War Sanders, Harry Spies, Lew Drill, Al Halt, Art Rebel, Yank Robinson, General Crowder, Colonel Snover, Phil Saylor, Ensign Cottrell, Jim Battle, General Stafford, Rebel Oakes, Wally Bunker, Ben Shields, Sumpter Clark"

Purchase. In the early 20th century a ballplayer could be purchased by a club right out of the military.

Douglas MacArthur. In the 1901 Army-Navy baseball game, the future general played left field. He went hitless but got on and stole a base.

Dwight Eisenhower. See *Presidents*.

Lefty Mills. Mills played briefly for the Browns in the late 1930s. He had been a mechanic on an aircraft carrier when he signed up for the ship's baseball team to get shore leave. He had never played baseball before that.

Military Leave. While a career naval officer, Willard Roland "Nemo" Gaines received a short-term leave to pitch for the Senators in 1921. He pitched four innings in four games, giving up no runs before returning to the service.

World War II. During the war, service teams flourished because of the abundance of Major League talent among their ranks. Many service games were played as *Benefit Games* and a number of games were organized between service players (including many former Major Leaguers) and then–Major Leaguers. The 1944 military world series was treated almost as the "real" World Series that year because of the number of quality ex–Major Leaguers on the squads.

The best military team during World War II may have been the 1942 Norfolk team that had a record of 92–8 and featured Bob Feller on the mound. The Great Lakes team, managed by Mickey Cochrane, was 63–14 in 1942, 52–10 in 1943 and 48–2 in 1945. The 1945 season included a 33-game winning streak and a 7–4 defeat of the Indians. Former Major League first baseman Zeke Bonura was in charge of all military baseball in North Africa.

Post-War Baseball. In 1953 quality military baseball was essentially extinct, replaced by fast-pitch softball. By then the Army had disallowed strengthening its teams with known military players for key games, a common practice in earlier years. Service championships in baseball disappeared by 1957.

Millennium Plan

"Condemning the financial inequality between wealthy and poor clubs, [Francis] Richter made an assortment of proposals. He wanted each league to grant only one player reservation per team, all the other players going into a pool, to be distributed annually by a lottery. The luck of the draw would equalize the strength of teams. The Millennium Plan was Richter's offer to those in the baseball fraternity who didn't like the way the reserve clause created dynasties by holding talent in one club year after year."—Ted Vincent in *Mudville's Revenge* (1981).

This was an 1888 and 1892 proposal presented by *Sporting Life* publisher Francis Richter, whereby minor league players would be subject to a *Draft* in an organized fashion and the then-existing 14 minor leagues would be better protected from raiding by the Major League clubs. A substantially different form of this proposal was incorporated into the National Agreement revisions of 1892.

American Marines play baseball on a South Seas Island during World War II. The original caption: "IT'S A HIT — PFC Robert Hogan, 20, of Waterloo, Ill.; catcher for one of the teams connects solidly for a base hit. Corp. Joseph Hargreves, 23, of 22 Branch Ave., Saylesville, R.I.; is the catcher. Sgt. Stanley R. Merrill, 25, of Redlands, Cal.; is umpiring."

Marvin Miller (1917–)

"The only way Marvin Miller will ever get into the Hall of Fame is through the janitor's entrance."— Anonymous Major League owner.

"The George Washington of the Union."— Gene Orza, associate general counsel for the players union.

"Marvin Miller, I suspect, is the most effective union organizer since John L. Lewis."— Studs Terkel.

Marvin Julian Miller was the powerful executive director of the Major League Players Association (see also **Unions**) from 1966 through December 1982. He had been a union negotiator and advisor to the president of the United Steelworkers. His baseball legacy is a vastly strengthened players union that saw the demise of the reserve clause and astronomical increases in player salaries.

Book. Marvin Miller, *A Whole Different Ball Game—The Sport and Business of Baseball* (1991).

Abraham G. Mills (1844–1929)

In December 1882 Mills was elected as the fourth **National League President** and served until 1884.

Mills Commission See *Origins of Baseball*

Milwaukee

"I opened my eyes to see if I was in heaven or if I was in Milwaukee."— Brewers infielder Kevin Seitzer after being hit in the face by a pitch from Yankee right-hander Melido Perez.

"The people of Milwaukee love the Brewers, and why not? The Brewers offered a diversion from the Great Depression and from several wars, and they gave Beer Town a chance to know some of baseball's most fascinating characters — some on the ascent to the majors, some on the decline, some going nowhere — but all heroes to the Wisconsin faithful."— Bob Buege in *The Milwaukee Braves, a Baseball Eulogy* (1988).

Milwaukee had a short-lived entry in the National League in 1878 known as the Cream Citys or Brewers. The city had an entry in the Western Association in the late 1880s and early 1890s. In early 1891 the soon-to-fold American Association moved its Cincinnati franchise to Milwaukee, and it combined with the existing Western League team for a one-year American Association entry known as the Brewers. Christopher Von der Ahe of the St. Louis Browns owned 75% of the club.

In 1900 Milwaukee had a one-season entry in the American League known as the Brewers before the league was designated a Major League. Milwaukee had no Major League entry until the National League Braves moved from Boston for the 1953 season. The Braves stayed in Milwaukee until they moved to Atlanta for the 1966 season. In 1970 the Seattle Pilots moved to Milwaukee to become the Brewers.

Milwaukee Braves

National League 1953–1965

"There was a big fuss in the newspapers in '57 over whether or not Casey Stengel had accused the Milwaukee fans of being 'bush.' Whether he said it or not doesn't matter. They are."— Sportswriter Ed Fitzgerald.

Origins. In 1953 the Boston Braves moved to Milwaukee (see **Franchise Shifts**) *and* its new $5 million stadium with 35,000 seats, ample parking (9,500 spaces) and enthusiastic fans. The move received the unanimous consent of all owners and it was announced during spring training on March 18, 1953. The short notice did not create many problems. It took only 13 home games for the Braves to exceed the club's entire 1952 attendance of 300,000. The 1953 season attendance was 1,826,397.

First Game. On April 13, 1953, the Braves defeated the Reds 2–0 in Cincinnati as Max Surkont got the win.

The Braves played their first home game on April 14, 1953, defeating the Cardinals 3–2 in front of 34,357 fans. The Braves got the win for starting pitcher Warren Spahn in the 10th inning on a home run by rookie Bill Bruton off Enos Slaughter's glove. Bruton was the first black player for the Braves in Milwaukee (Sam Jethroe had been the first when the club was in Boston). It was Bruton's only home run that year in 151 games.

Key Owners.

Lou Perini/1953–1962. Perini owned the **Boston Braves** and continued his ownership of the club until he sold out in 1962.

Bill Bartholomay/1962–1965. In 1962 two Chicago groups bought the club from Perini. The LaSalle Corporation was controlled by John McHale, Bill Bartholomay and four other businessmen, including John Reynolds. In 1963 Perini bought back 10% under an option. The LaSalle Corporation controlled the club through its move to Atlanta for the 1966 season.

Before Bartholomay and his group purchased the Braves, they had taken an option on and then purchased the 46% minority interest in the White Sox held by Chuck Comiskey (grandson of patriarch Charles). The group had understood that they would eventually be able to buy the remaining 54% held by the Allyn brothers, but that proved untrue. When Bartholomay's group was able to buy the Braves, they sold their minority interest in the White Sox to the Allyns in mid–1962.

Nickname. The club continued to use the Braves name that originated in Boston.

Key Seasons.

1953. The Braves enjoyed great success as soon as the club moved from Boston, finishing second in 1953. Eddie Mathews hit a league-leading 47 home runs and Warren Spahn won a league-leading 23 games.

1956. After finishing second in 1955, the Braves missed out on a pennant by one game to the Dodgers. Fred Haney took over as manager midseason, and Henry Aaron led the league with a .328 average.

1957.

"On the other hand, in Milwaukee in October 1957, the Braves, without Lucifer in cleanup, topped the dramatic appeal of the Senators in 'Damn Yankees.'" — Joe King in *The San Francisco Giants* (1958).

After consecutive second-place finishes in 1955 and 1956, the Braves won the National League pennant by eight games over the Cardinals and then beat the Yankees in seven games for the championship. Henry Aaron led the league with 44 home runs and 132 RBIs and Warren Spahn led the league with 21 wins.

1958. The Braves repeated as National League champions, winning by eight games over the Pirates. Warren Spahn again led the league with 22 wins. The Braves lost the World Series in seven games to the Yankees.

1959. The Braves lost the pennant to the Dodgers when they lost a three-game **Play-Off** after finishing the regular season in a tie. Eddie Mathews led the league with 46 home runs, Henry Aaron led with a .355 average, and Warren Spahn and Lew Burdette tied for the league lead with 21 wins each.

1960. The Braves finished second to the Pirates by seven games and then began a series of decent but not spectacular seasons before departing for Atlanta after the 1965 season.

The Move to Atlanta. Despite the continued success of the club, Milwaukee's attendance began to fade in the early 1960s, in part due to mediocre teams and because of the competition from the Twins in Minnesota. In October 1964 the Braves announced that they would be moving to Atlanta for the 1965 season, but a local judge ruled that the team had to play one more season in Milwaukee, which it did (see also **Franchise Shifts**).

"Lasts." The last home game of the lame duck season was played on September 22, 1965, in front of 12,577 fans. The last road game was on October 3, 1965, when the Braves lost to the Dodgers 3–0. Bob Miller defeated Bob Sadawski. Phil Niekro was the last active former Milwaukee Braves player.

Key Players.

Henry Aaron (HF) played in Milwaukee from the club's second season in 1954 until its departure for Atlanta after the 1965 season. During that span he hit over .300 10 times and averaged over 33 home runs per season.

Eddie Mathews (HF) was in his prime in Milwaukee, playing third base for 14 seasons from 1953 through the move to Atlanta. He hit over 40 home runs four times and led the league twice. He also had over 100 RBIs four times and scored more than 100 runs eight times.

Warren Spahn (HF) won 20 games or more eight times during his 12 seasons in Milwaukee, leading the league in that category six times. He also led the league in complete games seven straight seasons after he reached age 36.

Lew Burdette was the other key pitcher for the Braves, winning 173 games for the club in almost 11 seasons. He twice won 20 games and pitched 30 shutouts during that span. The pinnacle of his career came in 1957 when he won three games in the World Series to lead the Braves to the world championship over the Yankees.

Key Managers.

Charlie Grimm managed the club from 1953 until midway through the 1956 season. He guided the Braves to a 94–62 second-place finish in 1953 and second- and third-place finishes in 1954 and 1955. He was fired near the end of the 1956 season.

Fred Haney.

"Fred Haney didn't manage the club. He sat in one corner of the dugout, gulping down pills and saying to Crandall, 'What should we do, Del?'" — Pitcher Joey Jay of the 1959 Braves.

Haney followed up Charlie Grimm's success with a 68–40 record to finish the 1956 season at 92–62 in second place. In 1957 Haney won the pennant with a 95–59 record and the Braves won the World Series over the Yankees in seven game. He repeated in 1958 with a 92–62 record but lost the World Series in Game 7 as the Yankees took revenge. In 1959 Haney had the club in second place when he was fired. He went on to become general manager of the expansion Los Angeles Angels.

Ballpark. County Stadium was finished in early 1953 for $5 million, before the city had a Major League club. It originally seated 35,911 but was increased to 43,000 over the next few years. Its dimensions from left to right field generally were 320–402–315. It was the first Major League ballpark originally built with lights.

Key Broadcasters. Earl Gillespie was the Voice of the Braves from 1953 through 1963 after four years playing Class D ball and a short career in real estate with his father. He broadcast for the American Association Brewers in the early 1950s before the Braves arrived. He resigned after the 1963 season to be with his family and also because he sensed that the new owners were planning a move to Atlanta. It was Gillespie's "Holy Cow" that was adopted by Phil Rizzuto. He was also the first to use a fishing net to snag foul balls (later done by Harry Caray).

Gillespie was replaced by Merle Harmon, who endured two years of poor ratings and abuse due to the Braves' impending departure for Atlanta. Ernie Johnson, a former Braves pitcher, began broadcasting for the club in 1962 and moved with the team to Atlanta.

Books. Bob Allen, *The Fabulous Milwaukee Braves* (1960); Bob Buege, *The Milwaukee Braves: A Baseball Eulogy* (1988); Tom Meany, et al., *Milwaukee's Miracle Braves* (1954); John B. Parrott, *The Promise: A Baseball Odyssey* (2003).

Milwaukee Brewers

National League 1878
See *Milwaukee Cream Citys*.

Milwaukee Brewers

American Association 1891

The Milwaukee Brewers played in the Western Association during the second half of the 1880s, 1890 and part of 1891. In August 1891 the Brewers purportedly were in the middle of a game with the Sioux City club when they announced that they were forfeiting the game to move into the American Association to replace Cincinnati.

The Brewers' first game in the American Association was played on August 18 when the club defeated the powerful St. Louis Browns. The Brewers finished the season 21–15, though that record was blended into the former Cincinnati franchise's record of 64–72 for a fifth-place finish. The star of the club was Abner Dalrymple, who was ending his career where it had begun.

In 1892 the club was back in the Western League after the American Association folded. It remained there through the 1900 season, after which the league was renamed the American League (see below).

Book. Rex Hamann and Bob Koehler, *American Association Milwaukee Brewers* (2004).

Milwaukee Brewers

American League 1901

The Brewers were part of the newly named American League in 1900, finishing in second place under manager Connie Mack when the league was still considered a minor league circuit.

The club's 1901 season, the first in which the American League was considered a Major League, was a disaster. After finishing at 48–89, the city of Milwaukee was relegated to minor league status when the club was transferred to St. Louis to become the Browns. The team's best player was first baseman John Anderson, who hit .339.

The Brewers played their games at Athletic Park on 8th and Chambers Streets. That site was later used by the minor league Brewers from 1902 through 1952, when the ballpark was known as Borchert Field.

Milwaukee Brewers

American League 1970–1997
National League 1998–

"We didn't want to weaken the rest of the league." — Brewers manager Frank Lane in 1972 on why the club made no off-season trades.

Origins. When the Seattle Pilots folded after one ill-fated season in 1969, the franchise moved to Milwaukee to become the modern day Brewers (see *Franchise Shifts*).

First American League Game. On April 7, 1970, the club lost to the Angels 12–0.

First National League Game. On March 31, 1998, the Brewers played their first National League game and lost to the Braves 2–1.

Nickname. The club adopted the earlier Milwaukee team's nickname, based on the city's large number of breweries.

Key Owners.

Bud Selig/1970– . Long-time Brewers owner Bud Selig first tried to buy the White Sox in 1969 before taking the Seattle franchise in a purchase approved by a Seattle bankruptcy court. Selig had been on the board of directors of the Green Bay Packers. He continued to control the Brewers into the mid–1990s, eventually assuming the role of acting *Commissioner* after Fay Vincent was ousted.

Selig attended the University of Wisconsin and then returned to the family business selling Ford automobiles. He was distressed when the Braves moved out after the 1965 season and worked hard to bring the Brewers to the city. He became the largest shareholder in the Brewers by the time he was 29, at about 25% of the team. By 1998, due to his role as commissioner, his daughter, Wendy Selig-Prieb, was the new team president. The team switched leagues for the 1998 season.

In the early 2000s, Selig owned about 35% of the club, held in trust while he was commissioner. In 1995 Twins owner Carl Pohlad owned a financing firm that made a $3 million loan to Selig. The loan was made when the club was arranging long-term financing for its new ballpark, and was repaid within 90 days.

In 2002, completing the worst season in the franchise's 34-year history, the club replaced Selig–Prieb as president and Dean Taylor as general manager. Ulice Payne, Jr., took over as president and former player Doug Melvin replaced Taylor. By late 2003, the club reportedly was $110 million in debt. Selig owned 30% of the club in 2003.

Payne had his contract bought out in 2003 after he revealed that the board, chaired by Wendy, had ordered a reduction in salaries from $40 million to $30 million in 2004.

In October 2004 it was announced that Selig would be selling the team for $200 million to Los Angeles junk bond trader Mark L. Attanasio, a native of the Bronx. The fantasy baseball league player was 47 at the time and managed about $10 billion in high-yield bonds for his clients through his firm, TCW Group, Inc. (which itself controlled over $100 billion in such bonds). A large part of Attanasio's fortune is believed to have come from the money received in a sale of a majority interest in TCW by Societe Generale for $1.3 billion in 2001.

Key Seasons.

1970. The club was 65–97 in its first season, finishing fifth.

1978. The Brewers had their first good season, winning 93 games and finishing in third place.

1979. The club won 95 games and finished second, seven games behind the Orioles.

1981. The Brewers won the second half of the strike-shortened split-season but lost to the Yankees in a five-game play-off. Pete Vuckovich led the league with 14 wins. Gorman Thomas hit 21 home runs and Ben Oglivie drove in 72 runs.

1982. The Brewers won their first division crown with 95 wins, one game ahead of the Orioles. They were up by three games with four to play against the Orioles and lost three in a row before winning the last game of the season. The Brewers won the pennant over the Angels in five games after being down 2–0. In the World Series they lost in seven games to the Cardinals after being up 3–2.

Gorman Thomas led the league with 39 home runs and Cecil Cooper had 32 home runs and 121 RBIs. Robin Yount hit 29 home runs and drove in 114 runs while anchoring the infield at shortstop.

1992. It took another decade for the Brewers to reach second place again. They won 92 games to finish four games behind the Blue Jays.

1998. The Brewers rejoined the National League and finished fifth. Through 2004 the club had done no better than third place since 1992.

Key Players.

Robin Yount (HF) is the all-time Brewer, playing his entire 20-year career in Milwaukee from 1974 through 1993. He had a lifetime .285 average and hit 251 home runs to go along with 3,142 hits.

Paul Molitor (HF) played 15 seasons for the Brewers beginning in 1978 before moving on to the Blue Jays. He hit .303 and had 2,281 hits over an injury-prone career in Milwaukee.

Cecil Cooper played 11 seasons for the Brewers from 1977 through 1987. He hit over .300 six times and led the league in RBIs twice.

Jim Gantner played 17 seasons for the Brewers between 1976 and 1992. He batted .274 while playing second base.

Rob Deer and Jeremy Burnitz.

"Given that I've made about $8 zillion more in my career than I deserve and am about to play 81 games in Colorado, send parents a note thanking them for not having me nine years earlier, when I would have been Rob Deer."—Proposed 2004 New Year's resolution for Burnitz, by Alan Schwartz, alluding to his propensity to strike out and hit for low average. Burnitz played six seasons in Milwaukee, hitting over 30 home runs four times and driving in over 100 runs three times. Deer never made more than $900,000 with the Brewers through 1990, hitting 137 homers in five years, while Burnitz earned between $3.5 million and $5.5 million in each of his last three seasons with the Brewers ending in 2001.

Key Managers.

George Bamberger managed the Brewers in 1978, 1979 and some of 1980, again in 1985 and for most of 1986. His highest finish was second place in 1979.

Harvey Kuenn led the Brewers, known as Harvey's Wallbangers, to their only pennant in 1982, managing part of the season. He also managed one game in 1975 and for the entire 1983 season. The club finished fifth both times.

Phil Garner. Despite having poor personnel and no money to work with, Garner won more games than any other Brewers manager. He started with the club in 1992 and lasted through part of the 1999 season. The club finished second in Garner's first season with a 92–70 record, but then could do no better than third place twice, in 1996 and 1997.

Ballpark.

"They have the best bratwurst and the best tailgate parties in all of baseball here."—Philip J. Lowry in *Green Cathedrals* (1992).

Milwaukee County Stadium. The Brewers took over Milwaukee County Stadium, which had been used by the Milwaukee Braves. The ballpark originally had dimensions from left to right field of 320–404–320, but they were shortened slightly in subsequent years. It originally seated 35,911 in 1953, but was expanded over the years to 53,192 by 1981 (down from 54,187 at times in the 1970s and 1980). When the Brewers moved into the park in 1970, it seated 47,611.

In 1991 Cecil Fielder of the Tigers became the first player to hit a fair ball completely out of the ballpark. The shot was estimated to have traveled 520 feet. Another source reported that Jose Canseco is the only player to hit a ball over the roof. See also Gregg Hoffmann and Mario J. Ziino, *Down in the Valley: The History of Milwaukee County Stadium* (2000).

Miller Park.

A new stadium was proposed in the 1990s, with a cost estimated to be from $223.5 million to $600 million, depending on the source. In 1995 voters and the legislature barely approved financing for a $250 million stadium for the Brewers, $160 million of which would come from public financing. The bill barely made it out of committee, and the legislator who changed his vote (to make it 16–15) was the subject of the first successful recall effort in Wisconsin history. The Brewers then announced that they couldn't come up with their share of the money, in part because of Bud Selig's hard-line position during the labor dispute. The club was heavily collateralized already and couldn't obtain further loans. After four months of frantic effort, the American League loaned the club $10 million, local taxpayers put up $15 million, local businesses came up with another $14 million, and two local foundations contributed $21 million. The state also anted up another $72 million for infrastructure improvements. Miller Brewing paid $20 million for naming rights.

The designer proposed a roof that could open and close in 10 minutes. Groundbreaking occurred in late 1996 and was to be completed for the 1999 season, but later was revised to 2000. A crane accident on July 14, 1999, delayed the opening until 2001. A 50-story, 480-foot crane lifting a 400-ton section of the roof crashed to the ground in a 30-mph wind, killing three workers. In 2003 a Wisconsin court threw out a $94 million punitive damage award to the families of the three workers. The court left intact a $27 million compensatory damage award for the 1999 collapse. There were 74 skyboxes and seating was 10,000 less than the club's old park.

The first game was played on April 6, 2001, as President George W. Bush threw out the first pitch in front of 42,024 fans. The Brewers beat the Reds on an 8th-inning two-run homer by Richie Sexson. Reliever David Wells got the win.

Key Broadcasters.

"I've never worked for a team that had been over .500 in the Major Leagues."—Brewers radio broadcaster Jim Powell, who started with the club in 1996 and was still going in 2004.

In April 1970 Merle Harmon returned to Milwaukee after four seasons with the Twins. He had broadcast for the Milwaukee Braves before the team left for Atlanta. Harmon stayed with the Brewers until leaving for NBC in 1980 (leaving there in 1982).

Writer, television star and former catcher Bob Uecker, inducted into the broadcast wing of the Hall of Fame in 2003, has been a mainstay of the Brewers' broadcast booth since the club arrived from Seattle in 1970. Right after his induction in August 2003, he underwent double knee replacement surgery, a by-product of his years as a catcher. In the 1990s the Brewers had about 50 stations in their radio network.

Books. Chuck Carlson, *True Brew: A Quarter Century with the Milwaukee Brewers* (1993); Daniel Okrent, *Nine Innings* (1985); Don Olson, *Bambi's Bombers: The First Time Around* (1985); James R. Rothaus, *Milwaukee Brewers* (1989); Matt Silverman, *Brewers* (2000).

Milwaukee Cream Citys

National League 1878

The Milwaukee franchise filled a void (along with Indianapolis and Providence) when St. Louis, Hartford and Louisville all left or were expelled from the National League after the 1877 season.

The club's first game was on May 1, 1878, when the Cream Citys lost to the Reds 6–4. They did not win their first game until May 9, a 2–1, one-hitter at Indianapolis.

Milwaukee had financial problems, and on August 31 the players refused to take the field because they had not been paid. The club still managed to finish out the year, though in last place with a 15–45 record. The season was a disaster and over the following winter the National League stripped the city of its franchise.

Although known formally as the Cream Citys (dairy industry), the club is also referred to in some sources as the Brewers (beer makers) or Grays (uniforms). The club played its games in Athletic Park at 10th and Clyborn streets in downtown Milwaukee.

Milwaukee Unions/Cream Citys

Union Association 1884

Milwaukee started the 1884 season in the Northwest League as a minor league club, but the league collapsed in early September. Milwaukee and St. Paul were the only remaining solvent clubs. When Wilmington of the Union Association folded after losing 16 of 18 games late in the season it was replaced by Milwaukee for the last few games of the year.

In their first game the Unions shut out the Washington Nationals 3–0 and pitcher Ed Cushman pitched a no-hitter in their next game. The club played all of its games at the Wright Street Grounds and finished the season with an 8–4 record. When the Association folded after the season, the Unions joined the Western League and eventually were part of the American League in 1901.

Minnesota

"This region has long had America's friendliest and most unashamedly fickle fans. They enjoy, but do not trust, victory. They endure, but do not truly suffer from, defeat."— Thomas Boswell in *The Heart of the Order* (1989).

"Now, Minneapolis and St. Paul are wonderful hometowns, friendly and progressive, even urbane for their size, but to fans in *all* the less glamorous big league metropolises, it means a great deal when their players actually certify them by staying year-round. From F. Scott Fitzgerald to the Andrews Sisters, people from the Twin Cities have tended to become famous only after they've left the Twin Cities behind."— Frank Deford.

"You know, five years ago we had nothing here but the Lakers, and they were bush. Now we got the Vikings, we got the Twins, we got the pennant, and Hubert is Vice-President!"— Cabdriver to Roger Angell in *The Summer Game* (1972).

The earliest teams in Minnesota were formed by at least 1857 when the area was still a U.S. territory. Intercity play started in the state in 1865 and at a convention in 1867 the state's teams adopted the National Association rules.

The St. Paul Saints played in the one-season Union Association in 1884. The only other Major League team in Minnesota has been the Twins, who arrived from Washington for the 1961 season.

Books. Ross Bernstein, *Batter-Up: Celebrating a Century of Minnesota Baseball* (2004); Joel Rippel, *75 Memorable Moments in Minnesota Sports* (2004).

Minnesota Twins

American League 1961–

"You only have 15,000 blacks here … you've got good hardworking white people here … blacks don't go to ball games."— Twins owner Calvin Griffith when the Washington Senators moved to Minneapolis for the 1961 season.

Origins. In 1960 Washington Senators owner Calvin Griffith wanted to move his team to what was believed to be the more lucrative and hospitable environs of Minneapolis/St. Paul. He was allowed to move the club for the 1961 season after Washington, D.C., was awarded a new American League franchise (see also *Franchise Shifts*).

The new club in Minnesota initially was not much of an improvement over the old version, though Griffith rolled with the punches: "The fans like to see home runs, and we have assembled a pitching staff for their enjoyment."

Key Owners.

Calvin Griffith/1961–1984. Griffith maintained ownership and control of the club (with his sister, Thelma Haynes) until he sold out in September 1984 for $43 million. The parsimonious owner had trouble making ends meet in small-market Minneapolis in part because, unlike most other owners, he had no other source of income. On June 22, 1984, in a teary home plate ceremony before a Twins-White Sox game at the Metrodome, Griffith and his sister signed a letter of intent to sell their 52% interest in the club to Carl Pohlad. They had been involved in the team since 1922, when they were adopted by then-owner Clark Griffith.

In 1984 Tampa businessman Frank Morsani bought 42% of the club and planned to move the club to the Tampa Bay area. Commissioner Bowie Kuhn persuaded Morsani to sell out to Carl Pohlad "at cost" for "future considerations"—namely a shot at a new franchise. When the Denver and Miami franchises were awarded to others in 1992, Morsani was left out. He filed a lawsuit and it eventually settled.

Carl Pohlad/1984– .

"All my life I've suffered from an inferiority complex."

Pohlad was a Minneapolis banking tycoon who bought the club for a reported $43 million in September 1984 ($32 million in some sources). He was a decorated World War II hero who turned a small finance company into a group of 40 banks with more than $40 billion in assets. Pohlad also made money in soft drink bottling and corporate takeovers in the 1980s. He owned part of the Minnesota Vikings in the 1980s and early 1990s. In 1987 his personal fortune was estimated to be $550 million, and in 1994 he was reported to be worth $900 million.

In 2001 there was serious discussion regarding **Contraction** of Major League Baseball, with Minnesota a prime target. In November 2001, however, a judge issued an injunction that essentially forced the Twins to play the 2002 season (in which they made the playoffs). With the new labor agreement that year, contraction was pushed off into the distant future.

Nickname. The Twins name came from the fact that Minneapolis and St. Paul are separated only by the Mississippi River and are known as the Twin Cities.

Key Seasons.

1961. In their first season in Minnesota, the club finished seventh with a 70–90 record under three different managers. Pedro Ramos led the league with 20 wins and Harmon Killebrew hit 46 home runs.

1965. Despite the legacy of the lowly Senators, the Twins displayed remarkable power during the 1960s, with Harmon Killebrew and Rich Reese leading the way. The highlight of the decade was the 1965 American League pennant, though the Twins lost the World Series in seven games to the Dodgers and Sandy Koufax. Shortstop Zoilo Versalles was the league MVP, Jim "Mudcat" Grant led the league with 21 wins and Tony Oliva was the batting leader at .321.

1967. The Twins challenged for the pennant but lost out to the Red Sox on the last day of the season.

1969. The Twins won the division race by nine games over the

A's. They were swept in the ALCS by the Orioles. Harmon Killebrew led the league with 49 home runs and 140 RBIs.

1970. The Twins repeated as American League West champions but again lost to the Orioles for the pennant. Jim Perry led the league with 24 wins and Ron Perranoski led the league with 34 saves. Harmon Killebrew hit 41 home runs. The club faded in 1971 and was generally mediocre through the balance of the decade.

1987. The Twins continued their mediocrity at the start of the 1980s and had some truly pitiful clubs until finally emerging as a powerhouse in 1987. The club won the American League pennant and the World Series over the Cardinals in seven games. The pennant drive gave birth to the "Homer Hanky" handkerchief, distributed by a local newspaper. Frank Viola won 17 games and the Twins had four players with at least 28 home runs, led by Kent Hrbek's 34.

1991. After a last-place finish in 1990, the Twins won the American League pennant and defeated the Braves (also last in 1990) in the World Series. The thrilling seven-game series culminated in a 10-inning, 1–0 shutout by Twins pitcher Jack Morris. Scott Erickson led the league with 20 wins and Rick Aguilera had 42 saves.

2002. After almost being legislated into oblivion after the 2001 season (see *Contraction*), the Twins responded with a 94–67 record and a division title before losing to the Angels in the division series. Torii Hunter led the team with 29 home runs and 94 RBIs, Rick Reed was 15–7 and Eddie Guardado had 45 saves.

2003. The Twins repeated as division champions with a record of 90–72, but lost to the Yankees in four games in the first round of the play-offs. Torii Hunter again led the team with 26 home runs and 102 RBIs. Four pitchers had between 12 and 14 wins, and reliever Eddie Guardado recorded 41 saves.

2004. The Twins again won the division, this time by 9½ games over the White Sox with a 93–70 record. Corey Koskie, Jacque Jones and Torii Hunter each had between 23 and 25 home runs, and Hunter led the club with 81 RBIs. Johan Santana had a stellar season, finishing with a 20–6 record and 2.61 ERA. Carlos Silva was 14–8 and Joe Nathan had 44 saves.

The Twins split the first two games of the division series with the Yankees, and then New York came back to win Game 3 in Minnesota. The Twins led for most of Game 4, but the Yankees scored four in the 8th to tie and one in extra innings to win the series on a steal of third by Alex Rodriguez and then a wild pitch that brought him home with the go-ahead run.

Key Players.

Harmon Killebrew (HF) spent all but one of his 22 seasons with the Senators/Twins, hitting 559 of his 574 home runs for the club. He is seventh all-time in home runs. He was elected to the Hall of Fame in 1984, nine years after he retired.

Tony Oliva, a Cuban-born outfielder, spent his entire 15-year career with the Twins from 1962 through 1976. The lifetime .304 hitter led the league in batting three times. See also Tony Oliva with Bob Fowler, *Tony O!* (1973).

Jim Kaat was the club's premier pitcher through the 1960s. He broke in with the Senators in 1959 and emerged as a full-time starter in 1961. He peaked with the Twins in 1966 with 25 wins, contributing to his total of 283 over a 25-year career.

Rod Carew (HF), a Panamanian-born infielder, spent the first 12 of his 19-year career with the Twins. The lifetime .328 hitter led the league in hitting seven times, all while with the Twins.

Kirby Puckett (HF) was the club's preeminent player of the mid–1980s and 1990s. He came up in 1984 and emerged as a star in 1986 when he hit .328 with 223 hits and 31 home runs. His career was derailed in early 1996 when he was diagnosed with glau-

coma and then his life spiraled downward after allegations of sexual abuse and marital infidelity made headlines.

Kent Hrbek played 13 seasons for the Twins before retiring during the aborted 1994 season. He batted .282 with 293 lifetime home runs.

Brad Radke began with the club in 1995 and through 2003 had 116 wins for the club, including 20 in 1997.

Rick Aguilera was a reliever for the club for most of 10 seasons beginning in 1989, peaking with over 40 saves in both 1991 and 1992.

Torii Hunter is the club's most recent star, becoming a starter in 1999 and blossoming in 2001 with 27 home runs and 99 RBIs while patrolling center field.

Key Managers.

Sam Mele took over the club in mid–1961 and led it to a second-place finish in 1962. After two mediocre years the club won the 1965 pennant with a 102–60 record, losing to the Dodgers in the World Series. The club finished a close second in 1966, but when the Twins began poorly in 1967, Mele was fired.

Billy Martin.

"And Billy Martin, remember, who had done a good job at Minnesota, was fired because he wasn't a company man (which meant he wouldn't go drink with owner Calvin Griffith and listen to lineup suggestions)."—Jim Bouton in *"I Managed Good, But Boy Did They Play Bad,"* by Bouton with Neil Offen (1973).

Martin led the club to a first-place finish in 1969, but he could not get along with the front office and was fired after the Twins were swept by the Orioles in the 1969 ALCS.

Bill Rigney led the club for most of three seasons, winning the 1970 Western Division championship in his first year.

Tom Kelly emerged from nowhere to become one of the most respected managers in the Major Leagues. After a 49-game Major League career in 1975, he made it to the helm in late 1986. In his first complete season as manager in 1987, the Twins won the World Series. Though the club faded during the rest of the decade because of the strong A's, Kelly's club reappeared in the World Series in 1991, defeating the Braves in a seven-game series. He remained at the helm through 2001, when he retired after a second-place finish with a record of 1140–1244.

Ron Gardenhire took over the club in 2002 and promptly won three division crowns in his first three seasons, but couldn't get the club past the first round of the play-offs.

Ballparks.

Metropolitan Stadium. This ballpark was the first home to the Twins, from 1961 through 1981. It had dimensions from left to right field of 343–406–330 and a seating capacity of 45,919. The ballpark was demolished in early 1985 and replaced by a mall, convention center and amusement park. The location of home plate remained sacred, however, it became part of Camp Snoopy, a playground at the mall.

The Metrodome.

"If this is a ballpark, I'm a Chinese aviator."—Manager Billy Martin on the new Metrodome.

"I've come to hate the cartoonlike plastic appearance, narrow concourses, lack of rest rooms, excessive volume of the public address system, disappearing pop-ups, shoddy carpet, Hefty Bag outfield walls, dirty roof, malfunctioning scoreboard, blinding light structures and winds that push you out of the park after a game."—Twins fan Steve Mann, writing to *Sports Illustrated.*

"The House that Ruth Buzzi built."—Steve Rushin [Buzzi was a regular on television's "Laugh-In" in the late 1960s, playing a forlorn bag lady].

Metropolitan Stadium was replaced in 1982 by the Hubert H. Humphrey Metrodome, which originally seated 55,000 and has an air-supported fiberglass roof. In 1996 capacity was reduced to 48,126 because a giant white curtain was installed to cover the vast expanse of empty seats in right and right-center field. Its original dimensions from left to right field were 343–408–327. Balls traveled well, as evidenced by the 191 home runs hit in the park its first season. In its first 11 years, the park hosted only 10 1–0 games.

The fences eventually were raised in left field by 13 feet so that fewer home runs have been hit. One year the soft white roof collapsed, and in 1984 air conditioning was added to the park. The soft right field fence is known as the Hefty Bag.

In November 1997 the Minnesota state legislature, by a vote of 84–47, turned down the club's stadium financing proposal. In November 1999 the St. Paul voters rejected a referendum on a sales tax increase to cover one third of the $325 million needed for the stadium. The plan called for the Twins to pay one third and the legislature would provide the funding for the other one third. The team received a boost when Governor Jesse Ventura wrestled the legislature into approving a financing plan for a new $330 million stadium, but by late 2004 there were no concrete plans in place.

Key Broadcasters. Halsey Hall broadcast for the Twins from 1961 through 1972. Ray Scott, best known for his NFL broadcasts for the Packers and CBS, broadcast for the club from 1961 through 1966. He returned to call the club's televised games in 1973 and 1975.

In 1967 Merle Harmon began broadcasting for the Twins, which was as close as he could get to his first love, Milwaukee (which did not have a Major League club at the time after losing its franchise to Atlanta). Harmon stayed until April 1970 when he moved over to the Milwaukee Brewers for that team's inaugural season.

Herb Carneal worked with Ernie Harwell and the Orioles from 1957 through 1959 and then was the primary Voice of the Orioles until he joined the Twins in 1962. He remained as the Voice of the Twins through the mid–1990s and received the Ford C. Frick Award in 1996. The club also at times had former Major Leaguers Tommy John, Al Newman, Harmon Killebrew, Frank Quilici and Jim Kaat.

Bob Casey was at the microphone through the 2003 season at age 78, when he was inducted into the Twins Hall of Fame. Casey presented Kirby Puckett at Puckett's 2001 induction into the Hall of Fame.

Books. Dave Mona and Dave Jaryzna, *25 Seasons: The First Quarter Century of the Minnesota Twins* (1986); Bill Morlock and Rick Little, *Split Doubleheader: An Unauthorized History of the Minnesota Twins* (1979).

Minor League Drafts See *Drafts*

Minor Leagues (1877–)

"You know what the difference is between the Bigs and the minors?… Consistency. The whole thing is consistency. There are players in the minors who make spectacular plays and hit the ball just as hard as in the majors, but the guys in the Bigs are more consistent. They make the plays not just nine out of ten times but ninety-nine times out of a hundred."—Stan in "The Baseball Spur," by W.P. Kinsella (1985).

"I'm too lazy to work and too scared to steal."—Pitcher Tom Bolton, explaining why he kept playing despite seven years in the minors.

"The drama and melodrama of sport, the paradigm of entertainment, with its fun, naiveté, cold-hearted competition, big business and penny-ante operations, city slickers and country bumpkins, altruism and bigotry, success and failure, and the much-heralded thrill of victory and agony of defeat, are the flesh, the bone, and sinew of Minor League baseball."—Mike Blake in *The Minor Leagues* (1991).

See also *Drafts*, *Farm Systems*, *National Association of Professional Baseball Leagues* and selected minor leagues.

Overview. It has been estimated that there have been over 300 minor leagues, covering close to 3,500 franchises in at least 1,400 different cities. Somewhere in excess of 300,000 players have filtered through the minor leagues.

The National Association of Professional Baseball Leagues (now officially known as "Minor League Baseball") maintains a file card on every player who has played in Organized Baseball since 1911. It was estimated that there were 200,000 such cards by the mid–1970s. Earlier records maintained by the Association were destroyed by a fire at its headquarters in early 1911. It has been estimated that there were 75,000 players in Organized Baseball from 1876 through 1910. This does not include players on clubs in the 1871–1875 National Association and earlier well-known professional teams.

19th Century Leagues. The first organized minor league was the *International League*, which began play in 1877. It was joined that year by the *League Alliance*, which was a loose affiliation of 13 teams that disbanded that fall. The Alliance restarted with six teams the following season but did not last the entire year (though it restarted, and a form of the Alliance lasted into the early 1880s). There was also a small New England circuit in 1877, but it had no set schedule.

The original International League changed its name to the National Association for the 1879–1881 seasons, then died out. The Western League began in 1879 with four teams and the Eastern League followed in 1881.

In 1883 the newly created National Agreement that governed all of Organized Baseball gave more protection to the minor leagues by preventing raiding of their clubs by the Major Leagues. This helped foster additional and more prosperous minor leagues. In 1884 there were eight minor leagues, including the Eastern League, which evolved through various name changes into the International League of the modern era.

In 1885 the California League was formed and the Haverly Club of San Francisco was its first pennant winner. That year also saw formation of the Southern League, which evolved into the modern Southern Association. Also formed that year were the New England, Canadian and New York Leagues. The Texas League was formed in 1888. In 1895 the Atlantic League was formed with the help of future Yankee general manager Ed Barrow.

Minor League Structure. By the 1880s the minor leagues received protection from raiding by other leagues by having each club pay $250 to Organized Baseball as mandated by the National Agreement. In 1892 a compromise was reached whereby minor league teams could reserve some of their players and the Major Leagues—by then only the National League—could buy other players for a fixed price (see also *Drafts*).

Early Independence. Minor leagues originally were largely independent from the Major Leagues in the manner that the Mexican League is today. There was no particular urgency for players to be in the Major Leagues, as many minor league stars made as much or more as Major League players through the 1920s.

Turn of the Century/New Organization. In 1901 the National

Association of Professional Baseball Leagues (National Association) was formed and is still the governing body for the minor leagues. The minor leagues had a loosely organized national association prior to 1900, with future American League czar Ban Johnson as its president at one time.

The formation of the powerful National Association came in response to a rift that had been created by the National League's failure to recognize minor league rights in the face of the American League challenge at the turn of the century. The National League attempted to tie up as many quality players as possible to prevent the American League from becoming stronger.

The problems were substantially resolved in late 1902 after the peace between the Major Leagues. The minor leagues were back in the fold of Organized Baseball under a new National Agreement, with the National Association as their representative organization. The National Agreement, periodically renewed, has been the governing document between the Major and minor leagues since that date, with the exception of a period of disharmony in 1919 and 1920 before Judge Landis took over as commissioner.

One key problem was resolved by the 1902 agreement when Organized Baseball agreed to a purchase classification system that enabled minor league clubs to collect a minimum set price for a player. In addition, players could only be purchased between August 15 and October 15 each year. The original prices were $750 for Class A players (then the highest level), $500 for Class B, $300 for Class C and $200 for Class D. Minor league clubs could designate a set number of players that were eligible for the draft and teams in any of the higher classifications (or the Major Leagues) could draft their players. Minor league clubs were free to sell their protected players for whatever the market would bear. A form of this system had existed in the 19th century, but expiration of the 10-year agreement had created chaos in 1900–1902.

As a result of the harmony, the number of minor leagues in Organized Baseball grew from 15 in 1902 to 19 in 1903 (13 in less authoritative sources), and to 40 in 1913.

Classification System. The A, B, C and D minor league classification system was created in October 1901. Class AA was added in 1908 to designate the highest level and initially included only the Pacific Coast League and International League (then known as the Eastern International League).

In 1936 the minor leagues created the A-1 classification, which was between Class AA and Class A. It was applied to the Texas League and Southern Association.

In 1943 an E classification was created for the Twin Ports League in Minnesota and Wisconsin. It was abandoned at midseason.

In 1946 the Class AAA designation was first used for the Pacific Coast League and the International League. In 1952 the Pacific Coast League received an Open classification in recognition of its "almost" Major League status.

In 1958 the *Winter Instructional Leagues* were created. In 1963 the B, C and D classifications were abandoned and the Rookie Leagues created.

By the mid–1990s there was AAA, AA, A, Short-Season Class A, Rookie Advanced, and Rookie ball. Class AAA and AA are considered high minors, the rest are considered low minors. All teams play 140 games, except the short-season clubs, which play 76 games.

Independent Leagues. Some of the key minor leagues were not part of Organized Baseball when the National Association was formed at the beginning of the century. The newly revived American Association operated in 1902 independent of Organized Baseball due to a squabble with the Western Association, but folded late in the season due to floods and bad weather.

The Pacific Coast League was brought into the mainstream in February 1904 when Organized Baseball agreed to honor the PCL's player contracts. This occurred only after the PCL absorbed the weakened California League, which had been part of Organized Baseball. Some sources note simply (and erroneously) that the California League was the predecessor to the Pacific Coast League.

In 1905 the Tri-State League was formed in Pennsylvania. Its players were blacklisted by Organized Baseball until it signed the National Agreement in 1907. The California State League was another independent league formed in the early part of the century, but it was part of Organized Baseball by 1909.

1914–1919. In 1914 there were 42 minor leagues in Organized Baseball, up from 40 the previous year. This total dropped to 20 in 1918 as World War I decimated the minor leagues. Only the International League weathered the economic storm fully intact to finish the 1918 season though another eight leagues technically finished their schedules. The National Association finished the decade in turmoil because of the instability brought on by the war and friction with Major League clubs over player sales.

In 1913 because of fear over potential antitrust ramifications, the National Commission required all Major League teams to sell off their interests in minor league teams before January 1, 1914. There was much sidestepping of this rule, and it was increasingly abused as the National Commission lost power by the end of the decade. The rule was abandoned or completely ignored in the 1920s when Branch Rickey and the Cardinals began the first formalized and extensive *Farm System*.

Clubs in the National Association are now required to establish Major League affiliations or the Association will step in and make the matches.

The 1920s/Stability and Prosperity. In 1919 the minor leagues balked at the Major League player draft and player option requirements. In 1920 Judge Landis restored the protections for the minor leagues and their relationship with Major League Baseball was repaired.

In 1921 the National Association established a noncompulsory draft of players that was abandoned mid-decade. The draft was restored in 1931 due to economic problems brought on by the Depression. By 1925 there were 25 minor leagues, a figure that remained relatively constant through the balance of the decade.

Little World Series. The first Little World Series, played between the highest level minor league champions, was held in 1920. It featured the International League and American Association pennant winners. Prior to World War II the Pacific Coast League participated in the series for two years.

1930s and 1940s. The number of minor leagues dipped to 21 in 1930 and 16 in 1931 because of the economic problems of the Depression. In 1932 the minor leagues consisted of the following 17: American Association, International League, Pacific Coast League, Texas League, Western League, Central League, New York–Pennsylvania League, Piedmont League, Southeastern League, Three-I League, Cotton States League, Mid-Atlantic League, Western Association, Arizona-Texas League, Inter-State League, Mississippi Valley League and Nebraska State League.

By 1933 the total was only 14, although the minor leagues had instituted a major reform campaign in 1932 designed to save the system. Clubs were required to deposit money with their leagues to guarantee that they would last the season and to ensure payment to players should a club fold. The leagues also instituted a **Play-off System** that stimulated attendance.

As a result of the changes and the gradual turnaround in the

Sioux Falls Stadium, known as "The Birdcage," home of the Sioux Falls (North Dakota) Canaries.

economy, the number of leagues increased to 19 in 1934, 37 in 1938 and 41 in 1939. There was also an infusion of money into the minor leagues in the 1930s because the farm system concept had taken hold and most Major League teams adopted it by the end of the decade.

Play-Off System. In 1933 Montreal Royals general manager Frank Shaughnessy developed a postseason play-off plan that most minor leagues quickly adopted. Although there already were minor league "World Series" between leagues, Shaughnessy's plan called for the top four finishers in each league to have a postseason competition to determine the champion that would represent the league in further postseason play. Montreal's International League was the first to adopt it that season, followed by the Texas League the same year and the Pacific Coast League in 1936. Along with night baseball, the play-off plan, known as the Shaughnessy Play-offs, helped save the minor leagues. Attendance improved as more clubs were involved late in the season for the last play-off spots and postseason play.

1940s/Decline and Peak. World War II hurt the minor leagues because there were not enough players to fill out rosters. Over 4,000 Major and minor league players were in the military, and the minor leagues shrank to 10 leagues in 1943 and 1944 at the height of the war. They increased to 12 in 1945 and then exploded again to 42 leagues in 1946.

With the increase in the number of leagues after the war, the popularity of the minor leagues peaked in 1949 with attendance of a record 39,782,717, just before television and network radio became popular in the 1950s. The combination of those media brought Major League Baseball to areas of the country that had never experienced anything except minor league baseball. Rather than stimulate additional interest in the minor leagues, the beginning of this media saturation turned fans to Major League Baseball.

In 1949 there were 58 (or 59) minor leagues with 464 (or 448) teams and 9,000 players that had combined attendance of almost 42 million in the United States, Mexico, Cuba and Canada. In comparison, the Major Leagues drew 10 million fans among their 16 teams and 400 players.

By 1950 there were certain criteria that placed a club in a particular level of the minor league hierarchy:

	AAA	AA	A	B	C	D
Population	3m	1m	500k	250k	150k —	
Payment Req'd by MLB for player	$10k	$7.5k	$6k	$4k	$2.5	$2
Salary Limit	—	—	$5400	$4000	$3400	$2600
Roster Limit	25	19	17	—	—	—
Waiver Price	$5K	$2750	$1250	$ 500	$350	$100

1950s and 1960s. By 1952 there was a 40% decline in the number of minor leagues. From a high of 59 leagues in 1949, the total was 38 in 1953 and only 24 by 1958. Attendance also dropped dramatically, from a high of 41.8 million in 1949 to 25.3 million in 1952 and 13.2 million in 1958.

In 1956 Major League Baseball created a "Save the Minors Committee." It established a stabilization fund of $500,000, with each Major League club contributing. Another $1 million was added later. These efforts to save the minor leagues culminated in major changes instituted in 1962.

There were still seven levels of minor league play in the 1950s: Class AAA down through Class D and rookie leagues. Pursuant to an overhaul in late 1962, the minor leagues were reorganized into four levels of approximately 100 teams in 18 leagues: Class AAA (20 teams); Class AA (20 teams); Class A and rookie league (collectively 60 teams) for players in their first or second seasons. The B, C and D levels were eliminated.

The new rules required that each Major League club initially have ownership or affiliation with at least one club at each of the first three levels, with a total affiliation of five clubs. Expansion clubs for 1962 were required to affiliate with four clubs. Despite the consolidation and cash infusion, the minor leagues continued to struggle, and attendance was at a modern low of 9.9 million that season (in part because there were fewer leagues). By the early 1960s, over 90% of minor league clubs had a Major League affiliation.

In 1968 the number of leagues increased to a 1960s peak of 21 and attendance reached 10 million, the highest level since before the 1962 overhaul.

1970s. There were 18 leagues in 1973 (with two in Mexico), covering 136 teams and 2,500 players. Attendance was at 11.2 million, the highest since the late 1950s. By the mid–1970s the minor leagues included the following:

AAA: International League, Pacific Coast League, American Association and Mexican League

AA: Eastern League, Southern League and Texas League

A: California League, Carolina League, Florida State League, West Carolina League, Northwestern League, Midwest League, New York–Pennsylvania League and three Mexican Leagues

Rookie: Appalachian League, Gulf Coast League and Pioneer League

The standard operating contract of the 1970s between a Major League club and its minor league affiliates required the Major League team to provide from $2,500 to $8,000 of a player's annual salary. The Major League club paid for the trainer and manager for its minor league affiliates.

1980s–1990s Resurgence.

"A reasonable amount of virtue has combined with some economic realities and fortunate accidents to put minor-league baseball in a very special place." — Neil J. Sullivan in *Minors: The Struggle and the Triumph of Baseball's Poor Relation from 1876 to the Present* (1990).

In 1981 there were 17 leagues with 154 teams. By the late 1980s attendance was up 56% over the previous decade to more than 23 million. In 1988 the International League and the American Association combined to form the Triple A Alliance to stage interleague play and a postseason series.

As a reflection of the renewed popularity of minor league baseball, in 1987 the Class AA Midland Angels sold for $1 million. This price was consistent with the sale prices of other Class AA teams in the mid–1980s. Salinas of the Class A California League was purchased for one dollar in 1976 and sold for $1 million in 1987.

By the late 1980s the cost of a Class A club was $750,000 to $1 million; Class AA over $2 million; Class AAA close to $4 million and above.

In 1991 the celebrated Durham Bulls sold for $3 million, a dramatic increase over their 1980 sale price of $2,417. The Oklahoma City 89ers sold for $8 million in the 1990s and the Las Vegas franchise sold for $7 million in 1992. Some Class A franchises have sold for over $1 million, though 25% of the clubs still draw less than 1,000 per game.

There were 222 teams playing in 20 leagues in 1993. The minor league minimum salary in the 1990s was approximately $700 a month for a five month season. That figure stayed consistent through the decade, with 240 teams by 1998. Attendance also remained fairly constant after the Major League strike season of 1994–1995, with approximately 33 millions fans annually attending minor league games.

2000s. Attendance grew 40% between 1994 and 2003, and in 2003 minor league baseball had its second-highest total ever, 39,069,707, behind only 1949. In 2004 attendance was on track by July to break the all-time record, even though there were fewer games played. Class AAA clubs were selling for between $8 million and $20 million, Class AA for between $6 million and $15 million, and Class A for between $2 million and $8 million. Rookie League clubs sold for between $600,000 and $750,000. Profitability was still a difficult proposition, as one source estimated that 10% of the clubs earned 70% of the operating income. At Class AAA in 2001, the top nine clubs earned an average of $5.5 million, and the bottom nine earned an average of $1.72 million.

Modern Independent Leagues. By the 2000s there were over 60 teams in various independent leagues around the country. The leagues were often a risky investment, as seven of these leagues, unaffiliated with the Major Leagues, folded between 1995 and 2003. Others fared better. For example, the Frontier League, in the Midwest, had a franchise fee of $825,000 and an annual team operating budget of about $2.5 million. The salary cap was $60,000. The most prominent of the independents is the ***Northern League***, re-founded in 1993.

Celebrity Owners.

Roger Kahn. In 1985 the writer bought the Utica Blue Sox of the New York–Penn League and later wrote about the experience in *Good Enough to Dream* (1985).

Tim McCarver. The CBS broadcaster and former catcher became part-owner of the Memphis Chicks in 1992. The ballpark was renamed in his honor and the club retired his number.

Ken Brett. The former Major League pitcher, the youngest player to pitch in the World Series, was a part-owner of the Spokane Indians and the Spokane Chiefs minor league hockey club. He died of brain cancer in November 2003.

Bill Murray. The comedian has owned part of the Salt Lake City Trappers, the Charleston (S.C.) Rainbows, the Williamsport (Pa.) Bills and the Pompano Beach (Fla.) Miracle. He had two at-bats with the Grays Harbor (Wa.) Loggers.

In 2002 Murray and "Saturday Night Live" actor Jimmy Fallon were among the owners (with Mike Veeck) of the Brockton (Mass.) Rox, an independent minor league team.

Morganna. Morganna the Kissing Bandit (see also ***Sex***) has owned an interest in a northeastern minor league club.

Warren Buffet, the consummate financier, invested in minor league baseball teams in the 2000s.

20th Century Players Who Never Played in the Minor Leagues. In the 19th and early 20th century, the few Major League roster spots and the strong minor leagues made it highly unlikely that a player would begin his professional career in the Major Leagues. Those who did were usually discovered in semipro leagues, were a novelty (a young Mel Ott or Bob Feller), or came from good ***College Baseball*** programs (Frankie Frisch, the Fordham Flash). Eddie Plank of the A's came straight to the Major Leagues from Gettysburg College in 1901.

In the late 1940s and early 1950s, a few black players came straight from the Negro Leagues, which by then could be considered a minor league feeder to the Major Leagues.

By the 1980s a few more players were bypassing the minor leagues because they played in strong college programs. A sampling over the years:

Ethan Allen. Allen had a 13-year career in the Major Leagues and later was the Motion Picture Director of the National League and wrote a number of books on baseball technique.

Mel Ott. Ott was only 17 when he began playing for the Giants, though a number of sources report that he was 16; he turned 17 on March 2, 1926, and first played with the Giants later that year.

Bob Feller. In 1936 Feller was assigned to Fargo but refused to report. He was then assigned to Morehead and again refused to report. His contract was then sold to New Orleans, but once again he refused to report. The Indians gave up and brought him to the Major Leagues.

Al Kaline. Kaline came straight to the Major Leagues at age 18 and won a batting title at age 20, the youngest hitter ever to do so.

Ernie Banks. Banks played only in the Negro Leagues before coming to the Cubs in 1953.

Sandy Koufax. Koufax came straight to the Brooklyn Dodgers from Cincinnati University, where he had starred on the basketball team.

Dick Groat. The Pirates shortstop (1955–1967) never played in the minors, but played professional basketball before coming to the Pirates.

Catfish Hunter. The A's pitcher was assigned to Dayton but a hunting accident supposedly prevented him from reporting. He was in the Major Leagues with Oakland the next year. The real story is that Hunter's injury occurred before he signed with Oakland in June 1964 for $75,000. He played in the Florida Instructional League for a short time that winter before starting with the Major League club in spring training.

Mike Adamson. Adamson was the first post-draft player to skip the minors and go directly from college to the Majors. In 1967 he left USC and signed to pitch for the Orioles. In three seasons beginning in 1967 he was 0–4 in 11 appearances.

Dave Winfield. Winfield was unique in that he was drafted by teams in professional baseball, football and basketball after playing all three sports at the University of Minnesota. He was 8–1 as a pitcher in college and signed in 1973 for $75,000 with the Padres as an outfielder.

Other 1960s and 1970s Players. In 1969 pitcher Steve Dunning left Stanford and signed with the Indians. 1971 three players left school: pitcher Pete Broberg left Dartmouth for the Senators; outfielder Rob Ellis left Michigan State for the Brewers; and Burt Hooton left Texas for the Cubs. In 1972 third baseman Dave Roberts left Oregon to sign with the Padres. In 1973 pitcher Dick Ruthven left Fresno State to sign with the Phillies and pitcher Eddie Bane left Arizona State to sign with the Twins.

Late 1970s/1980s Players. Bob Horner (1978), Pete Incaviglia (1985), Jim Abbott (1988) and John Olerud (1989) all skipped the minor leagues after playing college ball. *Sports Illustrated* once reported that Olerud was only the 15th player to make his professional debut in the Majors, but rather he was the 15th since the 1965 amateur draft was initiated. Note that in August 1996, Abbott was 1–15 and the Angels sent him down to Vancouver to work on his throwing.

Darren Dreifort. The Dodger reliever went straight from Wichita State to the Major Leagues in 1994, but he was quickly sent down to the minor leagues.

The 15 Since 1965. Of the 15 players who went straight to the Majors since 1965, four were straight out of *High School* (pitcher David Clyde, 1973; pitcher Tim Conroy, 1978; catcher Brian Milner, 1978; pitcher Mike Morgan, 1978) and one was a Cuban defector (pitcher Ariel Prieto). The rest were all college players. The last college player to skip the minors was Xavier Nady in 2000, who played for Cal before signing with the Padres.

Few Minor League Games. Among a random sampling of current or future Hall of Famers, here are the number of minor leagues games they played:

64 Paul Molitor
130 Ken Griffey, Jr.
175 Tony Gwynn
177 Barry Bonds

Major League Players Who Finished Their Careers in the Minor Leagues.

"Be awful nice to people on your way up, because you're going to meet a lot of them on your way down again."—Yankee pitcher Herb Pennock.

Until the 1950s many Major League players finished out their professional careers with relatively long stints in the minor leagues. This was in part because the wage scale in the high minor leagues was not much below the Major League level. Even into the 1990s a few former Major Leaguers continued to chase the dream in the minor leagues. A few recent examples: Leon Durham, Dennis "Oil Can" Boyd, Steve Balboni (who made it up again at least once), and Jack Morris. Another option has been for players to go to Japan and earn Major League–level salaries. Other early examples:

Heinie Manush. The future Hall of Famer spent seven years in the minors after his Major League career ended in 1939.

Joe McGinnity. The "Iron Man" pitched in the minor leagues until age 54.

Lefty Grove. Grove had great success in the minors after he finished his Major League career, finishing his professional career with pitching records of 12–2, 25–10, 18–8, 27–10 and 27–6.

Dizzy Dean. Dean won eight games for Tulsa in the Texas League after finishing with the Cubs.

Best Minor League Clubs. Some sources cite the **Newark Bears** of the 1930s as the all-time best minor league club. It may be more accurate to state that the Bears had the most players who ultimately played (and often starred) in the Major Leagues.

Some contend that the 1956 Los Angeles Angels in the Pacific Coast League were the best. The club won 107 games, with a team batting average of .297 and six players with at least 20 home runs. Others cite the 1934 Angels, who were 137–50.

Best Minor League Players. In 1984 SABR members voted Buzz Arlett the best minor league player of all time. Between 1918 and 1922 he won 108 games in the Pacific Coast League and the hit .341 with 432 home runs as an outfielder through 1937 (shades of Babe Ruth). Arlett played one full season in the Major Leagues. In 1931 he hit .313 with 18 home runs in 121 games for the Phillies.

SABR voted Tony Freitas the best pitcher, with 342 wins, the most by a left-hander in minor league history. Freitas had a five-year Major League career, with a 25–32 record for the A's and Reds from 1932 through 1936.

Attendance. See *Attendance*—Minor Leagues/1945– .

Ballparks. See *Ballparks*—Minor League Ballparks.

Longest Return to Minors. In 1996 Chad Mottola hit three home runs for the Reds in 35 games after being drafted fifth overall in 1992. He then spent most of the next seven years in the minor leagues (a total of eight games for Toronto and Florida in 2001 and 2002), but on June 30, 2004, he hit another home run, this time for the Orioles, and had played in seven games through mid-September that season.

Territorial Rights. The minor leagues have a rule that no franchise may be established within 35 miles of an existing club's location.

Retired Minor League Uniform Numbers. See *Retired Numbers.*

Books and Website. Judith Blahnik and Phillip S. Schulz, *Mud Hens and Mavericks: The New Illustrated Guide to Minor League Baseball* (1995); Mike Blake, *The Minor Leagues* (1991); Bruce Chadwick, *Baseball's Hometown Teams: The Story of the Minor Leagues* (1994); Frank Dolson, *Beating the Bushes* (1982); Robert L. Finch, et al. (eds.), *The Story of Minor League Baseball* (1952); Steve Greenberg, *Minor League Road Trip: A Guide to America's 170 Minor League Teams* (1990); Arthur T. Johnson, *Minor League Baseball and Economic Development* (1994); Lloyd Johnson and Miles Wolff, *The Encyclopedia of Minor League Baseball* (1993); David Lamb, *Stolen Season: A Journey Through America and Baseball's Minor Leagues* (1991); Robert Obojski, *Bush League: Minor League Baseball* (1975); David Pietrusza, *Minor Miracles: The Legend and Lore of Minor League Baseball* (1995); Bob Ryan, *Wait Till I Make the Show* (1974); Neil J. Sullivan, *The Minors* (1990); Rick Wolff and Phil Pepe, *What's a Nice Harvard Boy Like You Doing in the Bushes* (1975). See MinorLeagueBaseball.com.

Johnny Mize (1913–1993)

Hall of Fame (VC) 1981

"I had a speech ready but somewhere along in 28 years it got lost." — Mize at his induction speech long after he retired.

"In the Navy for three years he worked hard during weeks just before his discharge to get rid of extra weight he had accumulated. On an island in the Pacific, he went into a tin hut at high noon each day. With all openings closed, the inside of that hut was just about the hottest spot in that part of the world. Mize had a mat on the floor and did a variety of strenuous exercises. He came out of that self-imposed conditioning program in fine physical condition to resume his baseball career." — Ira L. Smith in *Baseball's Famous First Basemen* (1956).

Mize was a home run-hitting first baseman primarily for the Cardinals and Giants in the 1930s and 1940s.

There was some doubt that John Robert Mize would play Major League Baseball when he underwent surgery for a bone spur high on the inside of his thigh in the spring of 1935. He had been in the Cardinals organization since 1930 and after the successful surgery he became a starter in 1936. Though considered a poor fielder, his big bat kept him in the lineup.

Known as "Big Cat," Mize had six straight seasons over .300 for the Cardinals and in 1939 he led the league with a .349 average and 28 home runs. The following season he had league-leading totals of 43 home runs and 137 RBIs.

The Giants traded for him in 1941, and he continued to hit .300 before entering the military and losing 1943 through 1945 to the war. He returned in 1946 with 22 home runs in 101 games. He hit 51 home runs for the Giants to lead the league in 1947 and led the league with 40 in 1948. The Yankees picked him up late in 1949 and he saw limited but productive action for the club through 1953. He hit three home runs for the Yankees in the 1952 World Series.

Mize is the only player to hit 50 or more home runs and strike out 50 or fewer times in the same season. He is also the only man to hit three home runs in a game six times. His slugging average of .562 is 21st all-time through 2004. He played 15 seasons with the Cardinals, Giants and Yankees, leading the league in home runs four times, batting once and RBIs three times. He drove in 100 or more RBIs from 1937 through 1941. Later in his career he led the American League in pinch hits three straight times.

Mize scouted for the Giants in the 1950s and coached for the A's in the early 1960s before retiring to his orange groves in Florida.

Paul Molitor (1956–)

Hall of Fame 2004

"The fans asked if I have any black-and-white tape of me when I first came into the league." — Molitor during his last season in 1998.

Molitor starred for three teams between 1978 and 1998, batting .306 while amassing 3,319 hits.

Paul Lee Molitor played baseball at the University of Minnesota and was drafted by the Brewers in the first round of the 1977 amateur draft. He played a single season in the minors, earning MVP honors of the Class A Midwest League.

Molitor arrived in the Major Leagues in 1978 as a second baseman and would also appear at shortstop, third base and in the outfield over the course of his career. Due to recurring injury problems, however, he would also spend significant time at designated hitter. He was *The Sporting News* Rookie of the Year in 1978.

Molitor played fifteen seasons in Milwaukee. Hitting primarily from the lead-off spot he batted over .300 eight times. As a Brewer he led the league in runs three times, batted over .300 in eight seasons and stole at least 40 bases four times. In 1987 he batted a career high .353 while hitting in 39 consecutive games, fourth longest streak in American League history. Molitor appeared in one World Series with the Brewers, in 1982 versus Philadelphia. In Game 1 he became the first player in Series history with five hits in one game. He hit .355 as the Brewers eventually fell in seven games to the Phillies.

Molitor moved to Toronto as a free agent in 1993 and had an outstanding year. He batted .332, scored 121 runs with 111 RBIs and led the league with 211 hits. In the World Series versus Philadelphia he was superb. Molitor went 12–24 with six extra base hits, including two home runs. He drove in eight runs and scored 10, the last run the Series winner in Game 6. He was an obvious choice for Series MVP.

Molitor played two more seasons in Toronto before returning to his birthplace, Minnesota, in 1996. His homecoming was sensational. Molitor batted .341 with 113 RBIs and led the league in hits with 225, the fourth 200-hit season of his career. On September 16 he tripled for his 3000th hit. He retired after the 1998 season.

Molitor finished his career with 1,782 runs scored, 1,307 RBIs, 234 home runs and 504 stolen bases. He hit over .300 twelve times and his 3,319 hits are 8th on the career list.

Following his retirement, Molitor worked as a Twins broadcaster in 1999, the Twins' bench coach in 2000 and 2001, the Twins' roving minor league baserunning and infield coordinator in 2003, and the Mariners' hitting coach for 2004.

Book. Paul Molitor, *Good Timing* (1994).

Montreal Expos

National League 1969–2004

"But in 1973 in Montreal it seemed possible to come to a game fresh and new, without the melancholy for the past. Parc Jarry was so small and local that it carried almost no memories of Yankee Stadium; the city was strange, the light was different, and the crowd could have been people from a tribe that didn't exist when I was a child." — Richard Grossinger, a Yankee fan as a youth in the 1950s, in "Public and Private Baseball: Notes on the 1984 Mets, with a

Retrospective of Mets History," in *The Temple of Baseball* (1984), which he edited.

"The place was always cold, and I got the feeling that the fans would have enjoyed baseball more if it had been played with a hockey puck." — Andre Dawson.

"The subject is baseball in French — or more properly, baseball in a French atmosphere. My first reaction was that it is revolting. But first reactions, conditioned to shock, are likely to be extreme. It is not revolting, especially when played by two good teams like the Expos and the Phillies. Irritating is what it is. Irritating as hell." — Art Hill in *I Don't Care If I Never Come Back* (1980).

Origins. Montreal was awarded a franchise in May 1968, based primarily on the success of the "Expo 67" World's Fair and on baseball's desire to place a Major League *Expansion* franchise in Canada. The driving force in obtaining the team for the French Canadian province was Montreal mayor Jean Drapeau.

First Game. The Expos' first Major League game on April 8, 1969, was an 11–10 victory over the Mets at Shea Stadium. The club's first home game was played April 14, 1969, the first Major League game ever played outside the United States. The Expos defeated the Cardinals 8–7 in front of 29,184 fans.

Key Owners.

Seagram's Distillery/1969–1991. Charles Bronfman of Seagram's Distillery Company, one of Canada's most prominent companies, held the position of owner and chairman from the club's inception until the Expos were sold in 1991. John McHale, former general manager of the Tigers and Braves, became the club's first president and CEO. Jim Fanning was the first general manager. Seagram's continued to hold a minority interest in the club through Jeffrey Loria's ownership.

Claude Brochu/1991–1998.

"Brochu was raked over the coals for allowing the once-proud club to become the laughing stock of professional sports. Until Jeffrey Loria, the carpetbagging art dealer from New York, came along and bought the team, Brochu was undoubtedly the most unpopular figure among Expos fans." — Ron Kaplan.

Brochu was the leader of the group that bought the Montreal Baseball Club on June 15, 1991, after already having led the club for several years. The investors were a combination of private investors and the city of Montreal. Brochu became president and general partner. He was a Seagram & Sons marketing executive when he was made club president in 1986, having been installed by the Bronfman family. Later, the Bronfmans directed him to sell the club. Brochu then decided to find the ownership himself and remain in control of the club.

Brochu owned about 7.5% of the team, among a total of 14 Expos owners who were primarily Quebec businessmen. He was estimated in 1996 to be worth $4 million, primarily based on his ownership interest in the club. He left the franchise in 1998 when Jeffrey Loria bought the club. See also, Claude Brochu, *My Turn At Bat* (2002).

Jeffrey Loria/1998–2002.

"No wonder everyone wants to leave Canada." — Loria complaining to a flight attendant in June 2000 after she asked him to turn off his cell phone.

Loria is a longtime New York fine art dealer whose father twice pitched to Lou Gehrig in high school, and Loria won a New York City High School championship as a second baseman. He majored in art history at Yale and worked with actor Vincent Price to mass market art.

Loria bought the Oklahoma City 89ers for $3.8 million in 1989, and then sold the Class AAA Rangers' affiliate for $8 mil-

lion in 1993. Loria had tried to buy the Orioles in 1993, but lost out to Peter Angelos. He ended up buying into the Expos for $75 million in 1998, a sale approved by Major League Baseball in early 1999.

The club drew poorly and ownership was losing money, and it was clear that the Expos were in turmoil by 2000, unable to sustain a viable franchise under Loria's stewardship. Major League Baseball finally intervened and threatened extinction through contraction, but negotiations with the Players Association in 2002 prevented contraction through the 2004 season.

When the Expos were looking for cash, Loria became managing partner with a $12 million investment for 24% of the club. His dispute with the other partners arose out of cash calls that he was entitled to seek from them, which they declined to do. This allowed Loria to fund them himself (for $18 million) and dilute the others' interest down to 6%. Loria was thus able to gain a 94% interest in the Expos for approximately $30 million. He then sold the team for four times that amount. The other owners, heavyweights in Canadian business such as the Bronfman family (Seagram's), said in their lawsuit that they didn't meet the cash calls because Loria "misrepresented important facts in an effort to destroy Major League Baseball in Montreal." Most commentators suggested that Loria had operated within his rights and that he would prevail in the litigation.

In February 2002, Major League owners finally formed a limited partnership, Baseball Expos LP, consisting of the 29 other owners, and paid Loria $120 million for the club. Loria applied that amount toward the $158.5 million purchase price of the *Florida Marlins* from John Henry, who then applied it to the purchase of the *Boston Red Sox*.

Major League Baseball/2002–2004.

The other Major League owners held equal ownership interests in the club while other cities tried to finalize their ballpark plans in order to attract the club. Portland, Northern Virginia and Washington D.C. initially were all in the running. Frank Robinson was hired to manage the club and Omar Minaya became the first Latino general manager in Major League Baseball.

In late 2002, Puerto Rican businessman Antonio Munoz guaranteed $6.6 million to Major League Baseball to stage 22 games in Puerto Rico in both 2003 and 2004. By mid–2004 it appeared that the club would be moved to either Northern Virginia or Washington, D.C., although other sites were considered (see *Franchise Shifts*).

In September 2004 the fight between Loria and the former minority owners continued. The minority group asked the court for an injunction prohibiting the movement of the team out of Montreal. At the same time, Major League Baseball announced that the club would move to Washington D.C. for the 2005 season.

French Canadian Player. The team's first French Canadian player was Claude Raymond, who was called "Frenchy" everywhere except Montreal. After he retired he broadcast for the club.

Nickname. Montreal hosted an international exposition in 1967 known as Expo '67. When the city was awarded a Major League franchise in 1969 it adopted the Expo name.

Key Seasons.

1969. The Expos started their existence with a last-place finish and a 52–110 record under manager Gene Mauch. Rusty Staub was one of the few bright spots, batting .302 with 29 home runs.

1979. Montreal had its first winning season, finishing second to the Pirates with a 95–65 record and only three games out of first. Bill Lee won 16 games and Gary Carter hit 22 home runs. Andre

Dawson had 25 home runs and 92 RBIs. See also Bob Snyder, *The Year the Expos Almost Won the Pennant* (1979).

1980. The Expos finished second again, this time only one game behind the Phillies. Steve Rogers won 16 games and Gary Carter hit 29 home runs with 101 RBIs to lead the club.

1981. The club won its first divisional championship by defeating the Phillies in a mini-series to resolve the strike-shortened split-season. The Expos then lost the NLCS to the Dodgers on Rick Monday's 9th inning solo home run in the final game. Andre Dawson hit .302 with 24 home runs and 64 RBIs.

1992. The Expos finished second to the Pirates with an 87–75 record. Larry Walker hit 23 home runs and drove in 93 runs.

1994. Montreal was in first place when the season ended with the player strike on August 12. Ken Hill was 16–5, Moises Alou hit 22 home runs and Larry Walker batted .322 with 44 doubles.

2002. Given up for dead with a likely franchise shift, Frank Robinson was installed by Major League Baseball as a caretaker manager and he led the club to a second-place finish. Vladimir Guerrero led the club with 39 home runs and 111 RBIs. Four pitchers, including Javier Vasquez and Bartolo Colon, combined for 45 wins.

2004. In what was declared their last season in Montreal, the Expos finished in last with a 67–95 record, 29 games out of first place.

Key Players.

Rusty Staub.

"Le Grande Orange"

The red-headed Staub was the club's first star, playing on Montreal's first three teams and batting over .300 twice and hitting 29, 30 and 19 home runs. See also John Robertson, *Rusty Staub of the Expos* (1971).

Steve Rogers was the premier long-time pitcher in Expos history. He won 158 games for the club over a 13-year career that began in 1973.

Andre Dawson was the club's first long-term hitting star. For 11 seasons beginning in 1976 he was the club's leader. He batted over .300 three times and hit 20 or more home runs seven times. After a contract dispute with the Expos after the 1986 season he signed with the Cubs and went on to become the National League MVP.

Tim "Rock" Raines arrived in 1979 and played for the Expos until leaving for the White Sox in 1991. He was one of the premier base stealers in the Major Leagues, winning four straight stolen base crowns. He batted over .300 five times while with the Expos and led the league in 1986 with a .334 average.

Gary Carter (HF) was, with the exception of a fading Johnny Bench, the preeminent catcher in the National League in the late 1970s. "The Kid" had become the premier catcher of the 1980s when he moved over to the Mets in 1985. Carter hit 20 or more home runs six times for the Expos and twice drove in more than 100 runs for the club.

Larry Walker. Signed by the Expos as an amateur free agent in 1984, the Canadian joined the club in 1989 and between 1990 and 1994 had five solid seasons for the club before departing for the Rockies. His best season for the club was 1992, when he hit .301 with 23 home runs and 93 RBIs.

Vladimir Guerrero. Between 1997 and 2003 (with nine games in 1996), Guerrero batted .323 and hit 234 home runs to become one of the stars of the game. He hit 34 or more home runs five times and twice stole 37 or more bases. After the 2003 season he signed with the Angels.

Key Managers.

Gene Mauch was the club's first manager, lasting from 1969 through 1975. The Expos improved under his leadership from last place the first two years to fourth in 1973 and 1974. After the club dropped to fifth in 1975, Mauch was fired.

Dick Williams was the manager from 1977 to near the end of the 1981 season. The Expos steadily improved over his tenure, but he was fired while the club was in second place in the second half of the strike-shortened season. Jim Fanning replaced him and led the club into first place.

Buck Rogers managed the club from 1985 through mid–1991, when he was fired after the club could not break its habit of finishing in the middle of the pack. He won 520 games as the club's manager.

Felipe Alou managed the club beginning in 1992 and lasted through the first third of the 2001 season. His clubs finished second three times, but after four straight seasons of fourth place finishes, he was dumped in May 2001 after 27 years with the organization.

The club was in first place when the 1994 season was aborted due to the player strike. He was offered the Dodger job in 1997 and turned it down, which he later called a "big mistake."

Frank Robinson came out of the commissioner's office to manage the club on behalf of the 29 other owners, who collectively owned the team in the 2000s. Miraculously, he led the team to a second-place finish in 2002 with an 83–79 record, and then finished fourth in 2003 and last in 2004.

Ballparks.

Jarry Park. The franchise was awarded based on a promise of a 55,000-seat stadium by 1971, but it took six years beyond that date to reach that goal. In the interim, Parc Jarry was the team's home until 1977. Jarry originally was a playground that seated only 3,000. It was expanded to 28,456 as a stopgap until a stadium was completed for the 1976 Olympics. Its dimensions from left to right field were 340–420–340.

Olympic Stadium.

"If, in some distant century, it becomes necessary to transport thousands of earth colonists to Alpha Centauri, I picture them making the trip in something that looks rather like the Stade Olympique."—Art Hill in *I Don't Care If I Never Come Back* (1980).

Montreal's Olympic Stadium (Le Stade Olympique) was built for the 1976 Olympics and was available for baseball in 1977. It has dimensions from left to right field of 325–375–404–375–325 and originally seated 58,838 for baseball. Capacity has increased slightly over the years to over 60,000.

After protracted efforts to complete the project, the ballpark received its fabled—and ill-fated—retractable roof in 1987. The entire project originally was to have cost $62.2 million, but the price tag eventually rose to $1.2 billion. With the addition of the repeatedly faulty roof, by 1991 taxpayers had shelled out over $2 billion for maintenance and interest payments.

See ***Puerto Rico*** for the Expos' part-time home field in that country, Hiram Bithorn Stadium, starting in 2003.

Key Broadcasters. The Expos are the only club to regularly broadcast in French, in recognition of the French-speaking population in the province of Quebec. Jacque Doucet has been the French radio voice of the Expos since 1972, and Rodger Brulotte has broadcast on French radio since 1984 (television since 1990). Former player Claude Raymond also broadcasts in French, doing so for the club since 1973.

Duke Snider broadcast for the Expos from 1973 to 1986. Dave Van Horne was the primary English language broadcaster for the Expos from 1969 through 2000, when he left for the Marlins. In

1996 he received a broadcasting award from the Canadian Baseball Hall of Fame.

Other Major Leaguers who broadcast for the club have included Tommy Hutton, Don Drysdale, Ken Singleton and Gary Carter, and coach Bobby Winkles.

Books. Floyd Connor, et al., *Day-by-Day in Montreal Expos History* (1984); Michael E. Goodman, *The History of the Montreal Expos* (2002); William Humber, *Cheering for the Home Team: The Story of Baseball in Canada* (1983).

Monuments

See also **Statues**.

In 1924 the U.S. House of Representatives passed a resolution authorizing creation of a $100,000 "Base Ball Monument" to be erected in East Potomac Park in Washington, D.C. It was to be built in conjunction with the Most Valuable Player Award and the winners' names were to be inscribed on the walls of the monument. It was to be a gift from the government to baseball. The resolution failed in the Senate and what might have become the Hall of Fame never again received support.

Yankee Stadium's collection of monuments and plaques honoring its greatest players is known as Monument Park.

See **Stunts** for attempts to catch balls dropped from the top of the Washington Monument.

Joe Morgan (1943–)

Hall of Fame 1990

"The smartest baseball man I ever met."—Pete Rose.

"Joe, it's funny how all those winning teams seem to follow you around."—Basketball player Bill Russell.

"I take my vote as a salute to the little guy, the one who doesn't hit five-hundred home runs. I was one of the guys that did all they could to win. I'm proud of my stats, but I don't think I ever got on for Joe Morgan. If I stole a base, it was to help us win a game, and I like to think that's what made me special."—Morgan.

"You guys got beat by a guy who looks like a Little Leaguer."—Phillies manager Gene Mauch after Morgan beat the Phillies with a hit in his Major League debut.

Morgan was a two-time MVP and second base star in the 1960s and 1970s for the Astros and Reds.

One of the premier second baseman of all time, the diminutive Joe Leonard Morgan (5'7" and maybe 160 pounds), began his professional career in 1963 with Modesto. After another year of minor league seasoning and brief stints with the Astros both years, he was named National League Rookie of the Year in 1965 after hitting .271, scoring 100 runs and leading the league with 97 base on balls.

He continued his stellar play at second base for the Astros through 1971, when he was sent to the Reds in a highly publicized trade. He immediately became a star with the powerful Big Red Machine, helping to lead the club to division titles five times. His best seasons were 1975 and 1976 when he won consecutive MVP awards while hitting .327 and .320. In eight seasons for the Reds he scored more than 100 runs six times, had more than 100 walks six times and stole more than 50 bases five times.

He moved to various clubs starting in 1980, helping lead the Astros to a division title in 1980 and the Phillies to a pennant in 1983. His postseason play was marginal as he batted .135 in 27 NLCS games and .235 in 23 World Series games. Nevertheless, his leadership skills and stellar fielding contributed greatly to the success of his clubs.

Morgan finished third (now fifth) all-time in base on balls, behind only Babe Ruth and Ted Williams. He is one of only 11 players through 2004 to win consecutive MVP Awards and was an All-Star nine times. He hit .271 lifetime with 1,133 RBIs, including a career high 111 in 1976. He also pounded out 268 home runs, with a career high of 27 in 1976.

After finishing his career with a season in Oakland in 1984, he went into the broadcast booth and became a respected commentator. His numerous business interests have led him to decline several offers to manage or move into the National League presidency. He was also considered for the commissioner's job before Bud Selig took over the position. According to former Dodger general manager Fred Claire, there was also a plan for Morgan to take over the Dodgers when Tommy Lasorda threatened to leave in the early 1990s, but it never materialized.

Book. Joe Morgan with David Falkner, *Joe Morgan: A Life in Baseball* (1993).

Most Influential Baseball Men

"On a higher level, A.G.'s contemporaries conferred on him the title, 'Mister Baseball.' The Philadelphia *LEDGER*'s obituary was headed, 'The Savior of Base Ball Is Dead.' The author of 'Baseball and Mr. Spalding' wrote this about his fellow author, 'Spalding was the top-ranked elder-statesman of baseball, who did more to build it into the nation's favorite sport than any other individual.' And *SPORTING LIFE* (the *SPORTS ILLUSTRATED* of the day) said, 'In the annals of baseball, he will always stand out as the game's chief constructive genius and its greatest missionary.'"—Samm Coombs and Bob West in the prologue to their 1991 reprint of Spalding's 1911 classic, *Base Ball—America's National Game*.

See also **Father of Baseball**.

The most influential baseball men by decade:

1870s. William Hulbert—Driving force behind the formation of the National League.

1880s–1890s. Albert Spalding—Former pitcher; owner of the Chicago White Stockings and founder of Spalding Sporting Goods.

1900s–1910s. Ban Johnson—Founder of the American League.

1920s. Babe Ruth—Revolutionized baseball with the power game.

1920s–1930s. Kenesaw Mountain Landis—First commissioner of baseball.

1930s–1940s. Branch Rickey—Created the farm system concept and helped modernize the role of the general manager.

1940s. Jackie Robinson—First black player in modern Organized Baseball.

1940s–1950s. Bill Veeck—Expanded baseball's promotional efforts.

1950s–1960s. Walter O'Malley—Driving force behind baseball's franchise shifts that helped result in the expansion of the 1960s.

1960–1970s. Marvin Miller—Leader of the Major League Players Association and the driving force behind the creation of free agency.

1980s–1990s. Players and Their Agents—Enormous increases in salaries changed the focus of baseball from the game on the field to contracts and money.

2000s. The Owners. The most recent collective bargaining agreement tended to favor the owners, and with Bud Selig—one of them—as commissioner, the owners seemed in greater control of the game.

Most Memorable Moments

"From Mickey Owen's passed ball to Bill Buckner's boot; Mazeroski's homer to Don Denkinger's blown call; the Babe's called shot to Fisk's foul pole polka; the Big Six's three shutouts to the pebble that finally gave the Big Train a Series win, baseball has consistently suspended disbelief in October."—Thomas Boswell in *The Heart of the Order* (1989).

"Well, a little while ago when we mentioned that this one, in typical fashion was going right to the wire, little did we know.... There's a swing and a high fly ball going deep to left! This may do it! Back to the wall goes Berra! It is ... over the fence—home run—the Pirates win!... Ladies and gentlemen, Mazeroski has hit a one-nothing pitch over the left field fence at Forbes Field to win the 1960 World Series for the Pittsburgh Pirates!"—Broadcaster Bob Prince.

"Some people still might not believe in us, but then, some people still think the world is flat."—Cleon Jones of the 1969 World Champion Mets.

See also *Greatest Feats*.

In 1975 Major League Baseball campaigned through the media to choose the most memorable moments in Major League history as part of the 1976 U.S. Bicentennial celebration. The results:

World Series/All-Star Games. Top five World Series moments:

1. Don Larsen's *Perfect Game*;
2. Bill Mazeroski's *World Series*–ending home run in 1960;
3. Babe Ruth's "*Called Shot*" in the 1932 World Series;
4. Carlton's Fisk's game-ending home run in Game 6 of the 1975 World Series;
5. The Mets' World Series victory over the Orioles in 1969.

The top two All-Star moments among the top World Series and All-Star Moments:

7. Carl Hubbell's 1934 *Strikeout* performance;
13. Pete Rose's 1970 *Home Plate Collision* with catcher Ray Fosse that scored the winning run.

National League.

1. Henry Aaron's 715th *Home Run* in 1974;
2. Bobby Thomson's 1951 *Play-Off* home run for the Giants to defeat the Dodgers;
3. Johnny Vander Meer's back-to-back *No-Hitters* in 1938;
4. Jackie Robinson's *Integration* of Major League Baseball in 1947;
5. Harvey Haddix's 12-inning *Perfect Game* in 1959 (since ruled not to be a perfect game).

American League.

1. Joe DiMaggio's 56-game *Hitting Streak* in 1941;
2. Roger Maris's 61st *Home Run* in 1961;
3. Lou Gehrig's 2,130 *Consecutive Game Streak*;
4. Ted Williams's six hits on the last day of the 1941 season to hit .400 (see also *Four Hundred Hitters*);
5. Ted Williams's final home run in the *Last At-Bat* of his career in 1960.

Most Memorable Moment for Each Team (as of 1976).
National League.

Atlanta Braves. Henry Aaron's 715th *Home Run* on April 8, 1974.

Chicago Cubs. Ernie Banks' 500th *Home Run* on May 12, 1970.

Cincinnati Reds. Johnny Vander Meer's consecutive *No-Hitters* in 1938.

Houston Astros. The first game in the Astrodome on April 9, 1965.

Los Angeles Dodgers. Sandy Koufax throwing a *Perfect Game* on September 9, 1965.

Montreal Expos. The Major League's first game outside the United States on April 14, 1969.

New York Mets. The club's World Series victory in 1969.

Philadelphia Phillies. Jim Bunning's *Perfect Game* on Father's Day, June 21, 1964.

Pittsburgh Pirates. Bill Mazeroski's 9th inning Game 7 home run to end the 1960 *World Series*.

San Diego Padres. Nate Colbert's five *Home Runs* and 13 RBIs in a doubleheader on August 1, 1972.

San Francisco Giants. The 1962 *Play-Off* victory over the Dodgers.

St. Louis Cardinals. Lou Brock's 105th stolen base of the 1974 season to break the record set by Maury Wills in 1962.

American League.

Baltimore Orioles. The club's 1970 World Series victory behind the amazing fielding of Brooks Robinson (see also *Defensive Gems*).

Boston Red Sox. The club's 1967 *Pennant Race* victory on the last day of the season.

California Angels. Nolan Ryan's fourth *No-Hitter* on June 1, 1975.

Chicago White Sox. The club's 1959 pennant, its first in 40 years.

Cleveland Indians. Frank Robinson's managerial debut on April 8, 1975, in which he also hit a home run (see also *Black "Firsts"*).

Detroit Tigers. Mickey Lolich's three World Series victories in 1968.

Kansas City Royals. Steve Busby's first no-hitter, on April 27, 1973.

Milwaukee Brewers. Major League Baseball returns to Milwaukee in 1970.

Minnesota Twins. Harmon Killebrew's 9th inning home run on July 11, 1965 against the Yankees to keep his club in first place.

New York Yankees. Don Larsen's World Series *Perfect Game* on October 8, 1956.

Oakland A's. Jim "Catfish" Hunter's *Perfect Game* against the Twins on May 8, 1968.

Texas Rangers. The successful Major League pitching debut of 18-year-old *High School Player* David Clyde on June 27, 1973.

Note that six clubs did not exist when the poll was taken and their most memorable moments come from a limited menu:

Arizona Diamondbacks. Game 7 of the 2001 World Series, bottom of the 9th inning comeback win.

Colorado Rockies. The 1995 pennant race.

Florida Marlins. Game 7 of the 1997 World Series, extra-inning win over the Indians.

Seattle Mariners. Ken Griffey's home runs in eight straight games in 1993; June 24, 1997, when Randy Johnson struck out 19; or perhaps Game 5 of the 1995 division play-off against the Yankees. Now it may be the 2001 season in which they won a record 116 games (but lost in the first round of the play-offs).

Toronto Blue Jays. Joe Carter's come-from-behind-bottom-of-the-9th-inning home run to beat the Phillies in Game 6 of the 1993 World Series to clinch the World Championship for the Blue Jays.

Most Memorable Moments Since 1976 (author's personal choice not in any particular order).

"The man who is the spearhead of the Dodger offense ... will not see any action."—The words of broadcaster Vin Scully that prompted Kirk Gibson to get ready to pinch-hit in the bottom of the 9th inning of Game 1 of the 1988 World Series. Gibson wrapped an ice bag on his knee in the clubhouse and got a batting tee. After a number of swings he sent batboy Mitch Poole out to tell manager Tommy Lasorda that he was available to pinch-hit if someone got on. After pinch hitter Mike Davis worked a walk against reliever Dennis Eckersley, Gibson came up and hit a 2–2 pitch for a two-run home run and a 6–5 victory.

1. Kirk Gibson's home run in Game 1 of the 1988 World Series;

2. Pete Rose's 44-game *Hitting Streak* in 1978;

3. Game 6 of the 1986 World Series;

4. Game 6 of the 1986 National League Championship Series (Mets over Astros in 16 innings);

5. Orel Hershiser's 59-inning *Scoreless Inning Streak* (especially given that Hershiser was on the author's fantasy league team at the time);

6. Cal Ripken's record-setting night in September 1995 to break Lou Gehrig's *Consecutive Games Played* streak;

7. Fernandomania in early 1981;

8. The 1981 player *Strike*;

9. Game 5 of the 1986 American League Championship Series (Angels one strike away from the pennant);

10. Nolan Ryan's fifth, sixth and seventh *No-Hitters*;

11. Jack Morris's 10-inning 1–0 win over the Braves in Game 7 of the 1991 World Series;

12. Joe Carter's 1993 World Series home run to defeat the Phillies;

13. The 1994 player *Strike* that ended the season prematurely;

14. Mark McGwire's 62nd home run in 1998;

15. Barry Bonds' 70th-73rd home runs in 2001;

16. Cubs/Red Sox joint flameout in the 2003 postseason (now the Bosox 2004 World Series win).

MasterCard Poll. In a poll sponsored by MasterCard in late 1989, nearly 500,000 ballots were cast for the most memorable moment: the winner was Henry Aaron's 715th home run. Five other events were runners-up: Ruth's called shot; Gehrig's farewell speech; Bobby Thomson's home run; Don Larsen's perfect game; and Kirk Gibson's home run.

Most Players Used See *Substitutions*

Most Seasons with One Club See *Longest Careers—* Most Seasons with One Club

Most Valuable Player Award

"Two basic trends stand out almost every year. MVP winners enjoy banner statistical campaigns, and, in more cases than not, are members of pennant- or division-winning ballclubs.... Home run hitters and big RBI men catch the attention of the voters, with the next significant qualification being a high batting average. Overall ability—hitting, running, throwing, and fielding—is important, but the greatest emphasis usually is placed on the player's might in wielding the bat."—Dave Masterson and Timm Boyle in *The MVPs* (1985).

"Shore is purty.... Shore am glad to get it. Got pretty nervous waiting for it, cause I've had to go to the bathroom since nine o'clock and didn't want to leave. Much obliged; now I can go."— Bill Dickey's entire speech in 1944 upon receiving a 1943 MVP Award (but not from the baseball writers) at a banquet in his honor that lasted until well after midnight.

"Most Valuable Player on the worst team ever? Just how did they mean that?"—Richie Ashburn on winning the team award with the Mets in 1962.

See also *Monuments*.

Chalmers Award. The *Chalmers Award* was presented by the Chalmers Automobile Company from 1910 through 1914. In 1910 it was given to the player in each league with the highest batting average. The rules were modified for 1911 and the award was presented to the "most valuable player" and not the batting champion.

League-Sponsored Awards. The National League began sponsoring an award in 1922, presenting $1,000 and a trophy to the winner. The American League inaugurated an MVP Award in 1924 when it presented $1,000 in gold to the winner.

The National League allowed repeat winners, which the American League prohibited initially. The American League also prohibited a player-manager from winning the award. The American League required that its sportswriters select one player from each team and then rank them in order. The National League allowed its writers to pick the best eight throughout the league and soon expanded the system to 10 names.

Both leagues' awards were discontinued at the end of the 1920s (National League in 1928 and American League in 1929). Historian Bill James reported that the National League owners got tired of giving money to the disliked Rogers Hornsby. Other sources blame it on the winners demanding too much money at contract time.

The Baseball Writers Step In. Most sources report that in 1931 the Baseball Writers Association started its own award to fill the void left by the leagues. However, there is evidence that a year earlier the writers voted the award to Hack Wilson.

***The Sporting News* and the Writers.** *The Sporting News* attempted to fill the void by presenting its own award from 1929 through 1945. It competed with the BBWAA until 1937 when they agreed that the writers would make the selection and the newspaper would provide the award. A one-city/one-writer system was abandoned in 1938 in favor of a 24-writer system (three covering each team) and the point system was modified to give greater weight to a first place vote (14–9–8–7 etc.).

The Sporting News and the writers cooperated until 1944 when the writers again split off and made their own selection. The writers called their award the Kenesaw Mountain Landis Memorial Plaque in honor of the ill and soon-to-die Landis. In 1946 *The Sporting News* agreed to end its official sponsorship, and the awards were combined into one presented by the writers. The same structure has remained into the 2000s.

Unfair Results.

Ted Williams. In 1947 Williams lost the award to Joe DiMaggio by one point, 202–201. Mel Webb, a Boston writer who constantly feuded with Williams, left Williams entirely off his ballot of 10 choices. A 10th place position was worth two points and that would have given Williams the award. Williams had 32 home runs, 114 RBIs and hit .343, while DiMaggio had 20 home runs, 97 RBIs and hit .315. DiMaggio helped his team win the pennant, however; always a relatively important factor. In fairness to DiMaggio, it should be noted that three voters failed to include DiMaggio on their ballots and three others had him no higher than eighth. In addition, the Yankee vote was split among three Yankees.

Williams probably should have won in 1942 when he won the Triple Crown with a .356 average, 36 home runs and 137 RBIs. Winner Joe Gordon of the Yankees had a .322 average, 18 home runs and 103 RBIs, along with a league-leading 28 errors, but the Yankees won the pennant by nine games over the Red Sox.

Rogers Hornsby. In 1924 Hornsby batted .424, but was passed over for the MVP Award in favor of pitcher Dazzy Vance with a 28–6 record. Sportswriter Jack Ryder left the disliked Hornsby entirely off his ballot of 10 nominees, effectively prohibiting Hornsby from winning under the format in effect at the time.

Pitchers. In 1968 Denny McLain in the American League and Bob Gibson in the National League were voted MVPs, the only season in which pitchers won in each league. The last pitcher to win an MVP Award was Dennis Eckersley in 1992.

Third Basemen. 1964 was the only year in which two third basemen were the MVP's: Ken Boyer of the Cardinals and Brooks Robinson of the Orioles.

Most Awards. Barry Bonds won his fourth MVP Award after his unprecedented 2001 season in which he hit 73 home runs. He went on to win three more awards in 2002, 2003 and 2004, for a total of seven through that season. At 39 in 2003, Bonds was the second-oldest winner, behind Willie Stargell, who was a few months older (but still 39) in 1979 when he was co-MVP with Keith Hernandez. In contrast with other sports, Wayne Gretzky won nine MVP Awards, Kareem Abdul-Jabbar won six, and Gordie Howe, Bill Russell and Michael Jordan each won five.

Biggest Gap. Willie Mays had the most number of seasons between wins, 11, when he won in 1954 and 1965. Cal Ripken, a two-time MVP, won the award eight years apart in 1983 and 1991.

One-Team Domination. The 1966 Orioles dominated the American League MVP voting: outfielder and Triple Crown winner Frank Robinson was first, third baseman Brooks Robinson was second, and first baseman Boog Powell was third.

Unanimous Choice. The first unanimous choice for Most Valuable Player in the National League was Orlando Cepeda in 1967. Unanimous choices in the American League have been Hank Greenberg (1935), Al Rosen (1953), Mickey Mantle (1956), Frank Robinson (1966) and Denny McLain (1968).

In 1967 Carl Yastrzemski won the Triple Crown and almost single-handedly carried the Red Sox to a miracle pennant in the last two weeks of the season. He would have been a unanimous choice for the MVP Award, except that one writer voted for Cesar Tovar of the Twins. Tovar hit .267 with six home runs and 47 RBIs. Perhaps not coincidentally the Twins were beaten out by the Red Sox on the last day of the season.

Multiple Winners/Same Team. The 1978 Reds are the only National League club to have four former MVP Award winners on the team at the same time: Johnny Bench (1970, 1972), Pete Rose (1973), Joe Morgan (1975–1976) and George Foster (1977). Despite all the stars, the Reds finished second to the Dodgers.

The 1982 Angels had four former MVPs: Reggie Jackson (1973), Fred Lynn (1975), Rod Carew (1977) and Don Baylor (1979). The Angels won their division but lost the ALCS to the Brewers in five games.

Winner in Both Leagues. Frank Robinson won the award in 1961 with the Reds and in 1966 with the Orioles.

Multiple Awards. Barry Bonds has won seven MVP Awards. Stan Musial, Mike Schmidt and Roy Campanella each won three.

Consecutive MVPs. Until Barry Bonds in 1992–1993 and 2002–2004, and Frank Thomas in 1993–1994, by coincidence exactly nine players, all at different positions, had won consecutive MVP Awards. It should be noted that before 1932 no repeat winners were allowed in the American League.

Yogi Berra (Yankees)	1954–1955	C
Hal Newhouser (Tigers)	1944–1945	P

The Kenesaw Mountain Landis National League MVP Award, presented in 1946 to Stan Musial of the Cardinals.

Jimmie Foxx (A's)	1932–1933	1B
Joe Morgan (Reds)	1975–1976	2B
Ernie Banks (Cubs)	1958–1959	SS
Mike Schmidt (Phillies)	1980–1981	3B
Mickey Mantle (Yankees)	1956–1957	OF
Roger Maris (Yankees)	1960–1961	OF
Dale Murphy (Braves)	1982–1983	OF

Ted Williams probably should have won in 1947 (see above), which would have given him two straight because of his 1946 win.

Rookie of the Year. In 1975 Fred Lynn of the Red Sox became the first rookie to win the Most Valuable Player Award. He also won the Rookie of the Year Award.

In 2001 Ichiro Suzuki of the Mariners duplicated the feat.

Different Position. Only three players have won the MVP Award at two different positions: Hank Greenberg (LF, 1B), Stan Musial (OF, 1B) and Robin Yount (SS, CF).

Tie. In 1979 Willie Stargell and Keith Hernandez tied for the MVP Award in the National League, the only tie in MVP history. Stargell led the Pirates to a World Series victory and Hernandez batted .344 and won a Gold Glove.

Most/Team. Through 2004 the Yankees lead with 20 MVPs. The Cardinals had 17, and are the only team with MVPs at each position, though Stan Musial won three MVP Awards at two different positions (1B and OF). The Dodgers are third with 12.

Fewest/Team. The Mets have never had an MVP, though seven players have won the award and at one time wore a Mets uniform.

Smart Negotiating. In 1997 it was reported that at least 33 players had incentive clauses providing for bonuses if they were named MVP in a division series. There is no MVP award for a division series.

Trophies. In 2003 Roy Campanella's wife sold his three MVP trophies at auction for $340,000.

Books. Milton Shapiro, *The Year They Won the Most Valuable Player Award* (1966); Dave Masterson and Timm Boyle, *The MVPs* (1985).

The Dodgers and Angels have for many years staged Hollywood celebrity baseball games during the season. The Angels hosted this game in the 1970s. Comedian Jonathan Winters (bottom row, near center) wears his trademark Reds uniform. Actor Jack Carter leans in two over from Winters' right. Hollywood impresario Johnny Grant is standing, second from left. Singer Pat Boone is standing (in uniform) third from right. The actor with his hand on Winters' left shoulder played for years on a Sunday slo-pitch softball team against this author; the guy fancied himself a shortstop (slow and bad hands, however), and always fielded his position with a cigar sticking out of his mouth. Fun to listen to, however.

Moustaches See *Facial Hair*

Movies

"I love baseball. You know it doesn't have to mean anything, it's just beautiful to watch." — Woody Allen in *Zelig* (1983).

"And who can say that the Mets didn't sense this, too — that they didn't know all along that this year [1969] at Shea life was imitating not just art but a United Artists production?" — Roger Angell in *The Summer Game* (1972).

"If you build it, he will come." — From 1989's *Field of Dreams*, starring Kevin Costner.

"There's no crying in baseball." — Tom Hanks in *A League of Their Own*. But see, *Crying: The Natural & Cultural History of Tears*, by Tom Lutz (1999), and the notable recent crying jags of Joe Torre, Don Zimmer, Jason Giambi and George Steinbrenner.

"I heard that actors start work at six o'clock in the morning. That sort of soured me on the whole thing." — Pitcher Bo Belinsky.

"Jeez. They're going to give me fifty thousand smackers just for *living*." — Dizzy Dean in 1951 after he optioned the film rights to his life.

"Duke Snider. I had sat in my bedroom as an eight year old, writing letters to him in care of the Dodgers in far-off Brooklyn, begging for an autographed picture. He was more glamorous to me than any movie star — because he wasn't acting; he was a real-life hero whose luster didn't fade when the film ended." — Bob Greene.

"*The Natural, Bull Durham, Field of Dreams* — they are to *The Babe Ruth Story* what *Citizen Kane* is to *Beach Blanket Bingo*." — Ron Fimrite.

"Jimmy Stewart, John Houseman, Eddie Murphy, Bill Murray" See *Batboys* for the story of actor William Bendix, who purportedly was a Yankee batboy and then played Ruth in *The Babe Ruth Story*.

Earliest Baseball Movies. In 1898 Thomas Edison released a movie that was a series of disoriented shots of baseball called *The Ball Game* (or *The Ballplayer*, depending on the source). An 1899 short without a plot was entitled *Casey*, but had no relation to the poem by Ernest Thayer. The earliest known baseball movie with a plot was a 1906 short by Edison called *How the Office Boy Saw the Ball Game*. His boss happened to be sitting next to him at the game. Another source reported that the earliest movie with a story line was a 1906 short entitled *Baseball on the Beach*.

In 1910 pitcher Christy Mathewson starred in a one-reel film.

Earliest Documentary. One source identified a 1908 filmed documentary of the World Series that year. Another noted that the 1911 World Series was the first to be filmed for commercial purposes. Others report that the National Commission sold the movie rights to the 1910 World Series for $500. The commission sold the 1911 rights for $3,500.

Instructional Film. In 1914 Harry E. Aitken, president of the Mutual Film Corporation, conceived the idea of movies of players for instructional purposes.

Color. The first color video of Major League players was shot in 1938. The Braves were the first club to make a highlight film in color.

1940s.

"My passion for baseball began with the Film *Pride of the Yankees*. I watched mystified but entranced as Gary Cooper, alias Lou Gehrig, tried to fulfill his promise to a crippled child to hit three home runs in the same game. The crouching man in the mask snarling exultantly every time Coop swung and missed was clearly the villain of the piece — more evil than Basil Rathbone as Sir Guy of Gisborne in *The Adventures of Robin Hood*." — Englishman Patrick Morley, a founder of the Bobby Thomson chapter of SABR in the United Kingdom (Thomson was Scottish).

The Pride of the Yankees (1942).

"When the movie Pride of the Yankees came out with Gary Cooper playing Lou Gehrig, I saw it maybe 15 times. When I first reported to the Dodger ball club in 1947, John Griffin, the club-house man asked me what number I'd like. Number 4 was available. That was Lou Gehrig's number. So I asked for number 4 and I wore it for my entire career."—Duke Snider.

The movie starred Gary Cooper as Lou Gehrig and featured Babe Ruth as himself. It was based on a script by writer Paul Gallico, and almost wasn't made. Studio head Samuel Goldwyn hated the script and thought the movie would bomb—until he saw a clip of Gehrig's famous speech.

The Babe Ruth Story (1948), starring William Bendix as the Babe. Bendix was often portrayed as a New York boy, but he never lived in New York and grew up in New Jersey.

Take Me Out to the Ballgame (1949), starring Gene Kelly and Frank Sinatra in a musical.

The Monte Stratton Story (1949), starring James Stewart as the pitcher who lost his leg in a hunting accident (see also **Amputees**).

The Kid from Cleveland (1949) wasn't very good, but had several Major Leaguers in it, including Hall of Famers Lou Boudreau, Tris Speaker, Satchel Paige, Bob Feller, Bob Lemon and Hank Greenberg. Bill Veeck has a voiceover monologue near the end.

1950s. *The Jackie Robinson Story* (1950), starring Jackie Robinson as himself.

The Pride of St. Louis (1952), starring Dan Dailey as Dizzy Dean.

The Winning Team (1952), starring Ronald Reagan as Grover Cleveland Alexander.

Big Leaguer (1953), starring Edward G. Robinson as ex–Major leaguer Hans Lobert running a Giants tryout camp. Carl Hubbell plays himself, and also appearing is former Dodgers general manager Al Campanis as the manager of one of the camp teams.

Fear Strikes Out (1957), starring Anthony Perkins as **Psychologically** troubled Jimmy Piersall.

Damn Yankees (1958), starring Ray Walston in the adaptation of the Broadway musical about a man who sells his soul to the devil to help the Senators beat the Yankees (see also **Theater**).

1960s. None of significance.

1970s. *Bang the Drum Slowly* (1973), a television version of the Mark Harris classic starring Robert DeNiro. Harris also wrote the screenplay.

The Bingo Long Traveling All-Stars and Motor Kings (1976) may have been the best baseball movie of the 1970s. It was a comedy/drama about a group of black professional ballplayers in 1939 who decide to start their own team. The cast included Richard Pryor, James Earl Jones and Billy Dee Williams.

The Bad News Bears (1976), starring Walter Matthau and Tatum O'Neal. It was about an irreverent and bumbling Little League team saved by Matthau's managerial skills and O'Neal's curveball.

It's Good to Be Alive (1974), starring Paul Winfield as Roy Campanella in the years after he became a quadriplegic (television movie).

One in a Million: The Ron LeFlore Story (1978), a television movie starring LeVar Burton and containing a cameo by Billy Martin (see also **Felons**).

1980s. *Don't Look Back* (1981), starring Louis Gossett, Jr., as Satchel Paige (television movie).

The Natural (1984), starring Robert Redford, Glenn Close and Kim Basinger in this film version of Bernard Malamud's classic. The ending in the movie is different from the ending in the book. Roy Hobbs hits a pennant-winning home run in the movie; in the book he strikes out.

A Winner Never Quits (1986), starring Keith Carradine as one-armed Pete Gray (television movie) (see also **Amputees**).

Eight Men Out (1988), starring Charlie Sheen in the well-made story of the **Black Sox Scandal**.

Bull Durham (1988) was an irreverent look at minor league baseball starring Kevin Costner as Crash Davis, an aging catcher sent to Durham to babysit a young pitcher, Nuke LaLoosh, played by Tim Robbins. Costner's character falls in love with a baseball groupie played by Susan Sarandon. Sarandon and Robbins began living together soon after the movie was made and had several children. Writer Ron Shelton said that the Nuke LaLoosh character was based on minor leaguer Steve Dalkowski, thought by many to be the **Fastest Pitcher** of all time.

In 2003 *Sports Illustrated* picked its top 50 movies of all time, across all sports. *Bull Durham* was listed at No. 1, but no other baseball movies made it into the top 10.

Field of Dreams (1989).

"The one constant through all the years, Ray, has been baseball. America has rolled by like an army of steamrollers. It's been erased like a blackboard, rebuilt, and erased again. But baseball has marked the time. This field, this game, is a part of our past, Ray. It reminds us of all that once was good, and that could be again. Oh people will come, Ray. People will most definitely come."—James Earl Jones as reclusive writer Terence Mann (patterned after J.D. Salinger), in *Field of Dreams*.

The movie starred Kevin Costner in the film version of William P. Kinsella's classic tale of a farmer who builds a ballpark for dead ballplayers, including Shoeless Joe Jackson, played by Ray Liotta. Burt Lancaster has an important roles in the picture as Moonlight Graham, a real-life Major Leaguer who appeared in one game, but did not bat.

Major League (1989) was a fictional account of the Cleveland Indians, but the ballpark shots were filmed primarily at Milwaukee's County Stadium. *Major League II* was a decent sequel and both included Charlie Sheen as a myopic pitcher.

1990s. *A League of Their Own* (1992) was the biggest baseball movie of the 1990s. It chronicled the women's professional league of the 1940s and early 1950s, the ***All-American Girls Professional Baseball League***. It starred Geena Davis, Tom Hanks and Madonna. Debra Winger dropped out, reportedly because she objected to Madonna's presence in the cast. The movie went $15 million over the $30 million budget, making it the most expensive baseball movie of all time to that point.

In *The Sandlot* (1993), unknown juveniles and James Earl Jones create a magical experience that made several 10 Top Baseball Movie lists.

Mr. Baseball (1991), starring Tom Selleck as a struggling Major League star traded to the Chunichi Dragons of Japan. Selleck once batted for the Tigers during a spring training game.

Two movies about Babe Ruth were released in the early 1990s. The first was a 1991 television version starring Mark Tinker, *Babe Ruth*, which contained a cameo by Pete Rose playing Ty Cobb. Commissioner Fay Vincent would not allow the barred-from-baseball Rose to appear on camera in a Major League uniform, so the scene was filmed in street clothes. A 1992 film about Ruth, *The Babe*, starring John Goodman, was released in movie theaters to relatively good reviews.

Angels in the Outfield (1994) was a remake of the 1951 original with William Bendix, in which angels help out a lousy ballclub.

Little Big League (1993) was about a young boy who inherits the Twins from his grandfather. Major Leaguers appearing in the movie included Ken Griffey, Jr., Randy Johnson, Rafael Palmeiro and Mickey Tettleton.

The Scout (1994), starring Albert Brooks, was described by *Time* magazine reviewer Richard Schickel as the "best baseball comedy ever." As a bush league baseball scout, Brooks is relegated to the deepest corner of Mexico where he discovers a fireballer named Steve Nebraska, who eventually receives a $55 million contract with the Yankees. Bret Saberhagen played himself in the movie, which was based on a story by Roger Angell.

Cobb (1994) starred Tommy Lee Jones as Cobb and included an appearance by Roger Clemens.

The Fan (1996) starred Robert DeNiro as a pathological baseball fan obsessed with an all-star San Francisco Giants outfielder played by Wesley Snipes.

Space Jam (1996) featured Michael Jordan plucked from the baseball diamond to help some hapless aliens win a basketball game in outer space.

Major League 3: Back to the Minors (1998) was a rehash of the terrific original.

In *For Love of the Game* (1999), Kevin Costner played Billy Chapel, a 40-year-old Major League pitcher in the twilight of his career. During the course of the final game of the season, he reflects on his life and his career while pitching what may be a perfect game. Vin Scully handled the play-by-play.

2000s. *61** (2001) was the Billy Crystal partly-financed story on HBO about Roger Maris's 1961 season.

The Rookie (2002) starred Dennis Quaid in the true story of high school chemistry teacher and baseball coach Jim Miller, who at age 35 in 1999 made it to the Major Leagues as a reliever within two months of getting a tryout with the Tampa Ray Devil Rays. See **Rookies**.

Mr. 3000, starring Bernie Mac.

In the Works. In 1996 Disney was planning a movie on the life of Roberto Clemente, and Spike Lee was working on a Jackie Robinson movie. There were plans to make a movie out of Bill Veeck's autobiography, *Veeck as in Wreck*. It was expected that Bill Murray would portray Veeck. By 2004 none of the movies had been made.

Movies by Decade.

"Can you even name ten movies with basketball or football as a major theme? After *Hoop Dreams* and *Brian's Song*, what have you got? *The Fish That Saved Pittsburgh* and *Necessary Roughness* is what."—Will Lingo in *Baseball America*.

One source reported that there were 72 baseball movies made between 1910 and 1992. However, other sources report that there were at least 80 in that period. In the same time frame other sports received even more attention:

Boxing—197
Horse Racing—138
Football—110
Auto Racing—85

The approximate reported baseball totals by decade through 2004:

1910–1919	8
1920–1929	9
1930–1939	7
1940–1949	7
1950–1959	13
1960–1969	1
1970–1979	7
1980–1989	14
1990–1999	22
2000–	7

Browns Futility. In a scene in 1944's *Going My Way*, Bing Crosby (who actually owned a small piece of the Pirates) is shown in the church basement wearing a Browns cap and jacket. Another character remarks that the Browns are "always in the cellar."

In the Blood. Pirates general manager Joe E. Brown's father was movie and vaudeville star Joe E. Brown, who had played professional baseball. The senior Brown played Ring Lardner's Alibi Ike and was in other baseball films, including *Save My Child*, a movie short about pitcher Rube Waddell and his fire engine-chasing antics.

Movie Magic. In 1942 Gary Cooper starred as Lou Gehrig in *Pride of the Yankees*. Gehrig batted left-handed and Cooper could not effectively duplicate the left-handed swing. To solve the problem the director had Cooper bat right-handed in close-ups, had the players wear reversed numbers and team names, and had Cooper run to *third* base after hitting the ball. The director then had his editor flip the negative to simulate left-handed hitting.

The only problem with this story is that another source reported that outfielder Babe Herman was chosen as Cooper's stand-in to do the batting scenes. Still other sources report that they simply flipped the negative only for scenes in which Cooper threw a ball.

Ballparks. In the 1960s suspense thriller *Experiment In Terror*, Glenn Ford plays a San Francisco cop trying to track down a killer. The final scene is at Candlestick Park, and scenes of various Dodgers and Giants are shown playing as the backdrop to the movie's tense finish; the climactic scene takes place on the mound.

Sharky's Machine (1976), a Burt Reynolds police drama set in Atlanta, had one scene with Reynolds and other cops sitting in Atlanta-Fulton County Stadium while two unidentified teams take batting practice. The stadium was featured in *The Slugger's Wife* (1987), based on a play by Neil Simon.

In *The Blues Brothers* (1980), Elwood P. Blues (played by John Belushi) gave his home address as 1060 Addison Street, Chicago, also known as Wrigley Field. A few other movies shot at Wrigley: *Ferris Bueller's Day Off*, *Rookie of the Year*, *The Babe*, *A League of Their Own*, *Kissing a Fool*, *About Last Night*, *V.I. Warshawsky* and *Running Scared*.

Arlington Stadium was the site of an interview scene in the movie *Bull Durham*.

Good Idea Gone Bad. In 1917 Tris Speaker and Marty McHale produced movies of Major League Baseball stars. They had $80,000 in 1918 theatre bookings lined up when World War I reached America and they were forced to pull the films. In an attempt to recoup some of their investment, they sold the material to the YMCA for European and shipboard viewing by military personnel.

Contract Clause. Actor William Frawley, who played Lucille Ball's neighbor, Fred Mertz, in the "I Love Lucy" television series, was a rabid baseball fan. When he signed with Paramount Pictures in 1933, he insisted that a clause be inserted into his contract that allowed him to attend the World Series each year. The same clause was in his "I Love Lucy" contract, except that he could only go if the Yankees were in the World Series (so he missed a lot of time in the 1950s).

Frawley was friends with baseball fan and tough-guy actor George Raft, who both were friends with Tigers star Mickey Cochrane.

Frawley wore a Cubs warm-up jacket in *Alibi Ike* (1935), a Yankees uniform in *Safe at Home* (1962), and played Baltimore manager Jack Dunn in *The Babe Ruth Story* (1948). He also appeared in *It Happened in Flatbush* (1942), *Kill the Umpire* (1950), and *Rhubarb* (1951, about an owner who dies and leaves $30 million and a baseball club to his cat; adapted from an H. Allen Smith book of the same name).

Bloodlines. Actor Paul Giamatti, who played a real radio station manager known as Pig Vomit in Howard Stern's movie, *Private Parts* (1997), and starred in *American Splendor* (2003) and *Sideways* (2004), is the son of former commissioner Bart Giamatti.

Movie Critic.

"He must have made that before he died."—Yogi Berra on a Steve McQueen movie. The frustrated movie critic was once hired to do one-minute movie reviews on television.

In 2003 Berra was asked who he would most like to catch. He replied, "Mike Mussina, because he throws a great curveball, and you don't see too many of those today." Yogi's wife, Carmen, was then asked whom she'd like to catch: "George Clooney."

Catchers. Prominent actors who have played catchers in movies: Buster Keaton (*College*), Robert DeNiro (*Bang the Drum Slowly*), James Earl Jones (*Bingo Long Traveling All-Stars and Motor Kings*), Kevin Costner (*Bull Durham*), Tom Berenger (*Major League*), and Geena Davis (*A League of Their Own*).

Home Movies. *When It Was a Game* (1992) was produced for cable TV and consists entirely of color home movies of players and games from 1934 through 1957.

Academy Award. Douglas Morrow received an Oscar in 1949 for Best Original Story for his work on *The [Monte] Stratton Story*.

Protest. The Hall of Fame had planned an April 2003 celebration of the fifteenth anniversary of *Bull Durham*, starring Tim Robbins and Susan Sarandon. In early April, however, Hall president Dale Petroskey sent a letter to the two stars calling off the gathering because of remarks the two had made in protest of the U.S. invasion of Iraq. Petroskey had been a White House Press Secretary under Ronald Reagan.

In response, Robbins sent a letter to Petroskey indicating that the Hall president "belong[ed] with the cowards and idealogues in a Hall of Infamy and Shame." Robbins ended the letter with "Long live democracy, free speech, and the '69 Mets—all improbable, glorious miracles that I have always believed in."

A Sampling of Players and Umpires in the Movies.

"I'm happy to sign a contract that doesn't have a reserve clause in it."—Vida Blue on signing a movie contract for a small role in *Shaft* (1971), soon after completing his acrimonious contract negotiations with A's owner Charlie Finley.

Rube Marquard. In 1912 Marquard won 19 straight games for the Giants. After the season he starred in a silent movie called *19 Straight*.

Ty Cobb. In the 1920s, Cobb starred in *Somewhere in Georgia*.

Mike Donlin. "Turkey" Mike Donlin was the first Major League player to have any long-term success in the movies. After he finished his baseball career in 1914, he spent almost 20 years in silent movies in Hollywood. Donlin was married to actress Mabel Hite. His first film, now lost, was the 1915 *Right Off the Bat*, in which he starred as himself in his only leading role.

Babe Ruth. Ruth appeared in the silent *The Babe Comes Home*, with Anna Q. Nilsson. It was made over the winter of 1928–1929 and Ruth insisted that his friend, sportswriter Marshall Hunt, be the film's technical advisor so that he could accompany Ruth to Hollywood. Ruth also appeared in *The Pride of the Yankees*, *Speedy* (1928), *Headin' Home* (1920), and *Home Run on the Keys* (short subject).

Joe DiMaggio. DiMaggio's first screen appearance came in 1937's *Manhattan Merry-Go-Round*.

Lou Gehrig starred in a 1938 B-Western, *Rawhide*.

Peanuts Lowrey. The National League outfielder appeared in

Pride of the Yankees in 1942 (his rookie season) and later *The Stratton Story*. He also was in silent films as a boy and had a speaking part in *The Winning Team* with Ronald Reagan.

Tommy Lasorda appeared in a Rodney Dangerfield comedy, *Ladybugs* (1992).

Ernie Orsatti. The Cardinals outfielder in the late 1920s and early 1930s, was a stunt double for actor Buster Keaton.

Bill Dickey. Dickey was the only active New York Yankee to play himself in *Pride of the Yankees*.

Chuck Connors. In addition to his prominent *Television* career, Connors appeared in a small role in *Three Stripes in the Sun* (1956), about an American solider stationed in post-war Japan.

Leo Durocher. Despite being married to actress Laraine Day, Durocher appeared in only one movie, a Red Skelton comedy called *Whistling in Brooklyn* (1943).

Bill Mazeroski. In *The Odd Couple* (1968), there is a scene in which sportswriter Oscar Madison watches from the press box as Bill Mazeroski of the Pirates hits into a triple play to end a game. Roberto Clemente was to have played the Mazeroski part, but he supposedly changed his mind after considering the effect on his native Puerto Ricans if he were shown failing so miserably.

Jim Bouton. The pitcher appeared in director Robert Altman's *The Long Goodbye* (1973).

Dodgers. Tom Lasorda, Tom Paciorek, Steve Yeager and Bill Buckner appeared in *The Godfather II* (1974).

Art Passarella. The long-time umpire went to Hollywood to become an actor. In *A Touch of Mink* (1962), with Cary Grant and Doris Day, he is shown umpiring a game in which Mickey Mantle, Roger Maris and Yogi Berra make cameo appearances. Mantle and Maris are thrown out of the game after Day, sitting on the bench, heckles Passarella.

Joe West. The Major League umpire appeared as an umpire in *The Naked Gun* (1992).

Books. Ronald Bergan, *Sports and the Movies* (1982); Gary E. Dickerson, *The Cinema of Baseball: Images of America, 1929–1989* (1991); Rob Edelman, *The Great Baseball Films: From Silent Days to the Present* (1994)—Edelman donated a trove of baseball movie materials to the Hall of Fame; Howard Good, *Diamonds in the Dark: America, Baseball, and the Movies* (1996); Hal Erickson, *Baseball in the Movies: A Comprehensive Reference, 1915–1991* (1992)—reviews all 81 feature-length films devoted to baseball over that time period; James Mote, *Everything Baseball* (1989) purportedly covers every movie ever made about baseball through the date of publication.

Mud

"Lena Blackburne Rubbing Mud"—Trade name of the special baseball mud.

"The procedure calls for an equal application of spit and mud. As we talked, [umpire] Bob Davidson spat on his hands five dozen times, scooped out a dab of Delaware River mud and rubbed the resulting mixture into the ball. Nothing in his manner suggested that it was a chore or an indignity; they were the motions of a man washing his car or of a cowboy saddling his horse."—William Zinsser in *Spring Training* (1989).

In 1930 Russell Aubrey "Lena" Blackburne, a former Browns player, briefly a manager, and at the time an A's coach, discovered a special mud by the Delaware River in South New Jersey, near the town of Palmyra. The mud dulled the gloss of the ball without significantly changing the color. The mud came specifically from Pennsauken Creek, a tributary of the Delaware. Blackburne's family still mines and markets the mud, which has the consistency of smooth silt. The mud is collected at ebb tide and is believed to contain a secret ingredient that gives it a creamy consistency. By 2000 a tub of the stuff cost $100; more specifically, a 32-ounce can cost $45.

When pitcher Bob Feller pitched an Opening Day no-hitter in 1940, he kept complaining to umpire Harry Geisel about the slickness of the balls. The complaints supposedly led to the Major Leagues formally adopting use of the Blackburne mud. Two years earlier in 1938, however, the American League was already requiring its umpires to undertake the 20-minute job of applying the mud to the game balls. The National League and minor league American Association and International League soon followed. The rules require umpires to rub down six dozen balls before each game, but they had quietly delegated that job to clubhouse attendants, a move which came under criticism in 2000. As a sign of the litigious times, the issue was put on the umpires' union bargaining table for future discussion.

Prior to discovery of the mud, new balls were rubbed up with dirt, which is now against the rules. Despite the use of dirt before the mud was used (and various illegal substances such as paraffin and talcum), a 1908 rule required that the ball not be soiled in any manner.

Before his death in 1968, Blackburne bequeathed the business to a childhood friend, John Haas. By 2000 it was owned by Burns Bintliff, whose first wife was the daughter of Haas. The mud came under criticism in 2000, apparently because it wasn't as effective as in past years. This was attributed by some to the drought that struck New Jersey that year. Because of that fact, a rumor began spreading that Bintliff had to procure his mud elsewhere, such as the Mississippi River.

Murder (and attempted murder)

"I'll never forget September 6, 1950. I got a letter threatening me, Hank Bauer, Yogi Berra and Johnny Mize. It said if I showed up in uniform against the Red Sox I'd be shot. I turned the letter over to the FBI and told my manager Casey Stengel about it. You know what Casey did? He gave me a different uniform and gave mine to Billy Martin. Can you imagine that! Guess Casey thought it'd be better if Billy got shot." — Phil Rizzuto.

"I'm sure that if Henry had been shot, he'd have called me." — Braves executive Donald Davidson after a 1973 rumor that Aaron had been shot. It was not an unreasonable concern given that Aaron received numerous death threats during his quest to overtake Babe Ruth's home run record (see also **Racism**).

Eddie Waitkus.

"It's extremely urgent that I see you as soon as possible." — Message left for Major Leaguer Eddie Waitkus by would-be murderer Ruth Ann Steinhagen.

"Why did that silly honey do that?" — Waitkus in an interview several months after the attempted murder.

On June 15, 1949, bachelor Waitkus of the Cubs received a message in his Edgewater Beach Hotel room in Chicago at 11:30 p.m.: a woman staying at the hotel wanted to see him. He went to her room, 1297-A, where she had checked in as Ruth Ann Burns. She was hiding in the closet when he arrived. He heard her say "come in" and he entered the room; she shot him near the heart with a .22 caliber rifle and called the house physician.

Waitkus was in critical condition for a few weeks but survived to play five more seasons. Club owner Bob Carpenter paid for his winter-long rehabilitation in Florida and sent along the team's trainer to assist. Waitkus's roommate, Russ Meyer, later said that Waitkus was never the same ballplayer after the attack.

The woman, a six-foot-tall typist, was schizophrenic 19-year-old Ruth Ann Steinhagen. She reportedly taught herself Lithuanian so that she could speak Waitkus's native language (or she at least listened to Lithuanian music). She had prior crushes on actor Alan Ladd and Major Leaguer Peanuts Lowrey. Her purported reason for the shooting was that Waitkus reminded her of her father. After the shooting she was committed to a mental institution: "Schizophrenia in an immature individual. She is committable to an institution for the mentally ill. At no time does she show concern, nor appear to realize the seriousness of her behavior. She discusses suicide freely and has thought of many methods that she would try. She should be under constant surveillance." — Steinhagen's diagnosis contained in a clinical report, as recounted in *The Fireside Book of Baseball*, edited by Charles Einstein (1956).

Steinhagen was released a few years later, though the Waitkus family tried hard to keep her confined. Waitkus feared a return engagement by her, but in fact never heard from her again. He was 53 when he died of cancer in 1972. Waitkus's son later said that his father became paranoid about going out, although he had been easygoing around strangers in the past. See John Theodore and Ira Berkow, *Baseball's Natural: The Story of Eddie Waitkus* (2002).

John Clarkson. The 19th century pitching star murdered his wife with a razor.

Ty Cobb.

"In 1912 — and you can write this down — I killed a man in Detroit. Left him there, not breathing, in his own rotten blood." — Cobb quoted by Al Stump in a 1961 article. According to Cobb, he had been jumped by three men and claimed that he tried to shoot them but his gun misfired. They cut him up and ran off, but Cobb chased down one and beat him to death with the pistol. Later research by Doug Roberts demonstrated that Cobb did not murder anyone. Contemporary newspaper reports contain accounts by Cobb that do not corroborate Cobb's statement. Nor does other information, including police and coroner's reports around that date. Roberts tracked down a man befriended by Cobb who put it best: "He might have been a son of a bitch, but he was not a killer."

Billy Jurges.

"An episode of unrequited love." — *The Sporting News*.

On July 6, 1932, Jurges was shot twice in Chicago's Carlos Hotel by a female admirer, showgirl Violet Popovich Valli. She shot Jurges in the hand and ribs. He recovered in three weeks and played 115 games that season, but hit only .253 and was replaced late in the year and in the World Series by former Yankee shortstop Mark Koenig.

Babe Ruth. Ruth was once chased through a railroad car by a woman wielding a knife. Ruth jumped off the train with her closely behind and then jumped back on as it left the station.

Big Ed Morris. During spring training in 1932, the Red Sox threw a party in honor of Morris, who had been with the team since 1928. During a late-night scuffle, he was knifed by a gas station operator (or, depending on the source, at a fish fry restaurant). He died three days later on March 3. General manager Bob Quinn purportedly had been set to sell Morris for $100,000. This seems unlikely given that Morris was 32 and had won only nine games over the previous two years.

Len Koenecke. In September 1935 Koenecke was released by Dodger manager Casey Stengel. Koenecke chartered a plane home but was killed on the flight after a supposedly drunken Koenecke made "improper advances" against the pilot and copilot. Koenecke was killed when the co-pilot struck him with a fire extinguisher during the fight.

Cesar Cedeno. On December 10, 1973, the 23-year-old Astros outfielder shot and killed Altagracia De La Cruz in a motel room in Santo Domingo, Dominican Republic. He was convicted of manslaughter and fined $100. He said the tragedy "will help me be a better person" and that he "would be ready for the start of spring training."

Gene Tenace. During the 1972 World Series the A's catcher was threatened by a man in the stands carrying a loaded gun after Tenace hit two home runs in the Series. Ten years later the man wrote to Tenace to apologize.

Lyman Bostock. The California Angels outfielder was murdered by an irate husband on September 23, 1978. Bostock was shot while he and a woman companion were sitting in a car at a stoplight in Gary, Indiana. Bostock had signed with the Angels at the start of the season and after getting only one hit over the entire month of April he offered to refund the club his salary for the month. Bostock's father played in the Negro Leagues.

Steve Palermo. In 1991 the American League umpire was in a Texas restaurant well past midnight after a game when two of the waitresses were accosted in the parking lot. Palermo and others ran out to help as all but one of the assailants fled in a car. As he helped subdue the remaining assailant, Palermo was shot by one of the fleeing robbers. Also shot was former pro football player Terence Mann. Palmero was partially paralyzed but managed to throw out the first pitch of the 1991 World Series. Permanently disabled but able to walk with great difficulty, he founded the Steve Palermo Foundation for Spinal Cord Injuries.

He broadcast for the Mariners in 1992, for The Baseball Network in 1994 and for the Yankees in 1995. In 1994 he became an assistant to the chairman of the Major League Executive Council. His first job was to study the length of games and make recommendations for shortening them. He later became a motivational speaker in addition to his baseball duties.

Roberto Alomar. In early July 1995 a woman was arrested in Toronto for carrying a gun and threatening to kill the Blue Jays second baseman. Tricia Miller had registered in the hotel at the ballpark complex where Alomar lived and was in the lobby carrying the gun. She had found out his room number and left a box of baseball cards, a chain with Alomar's No. 12 and a personal note outside his room. The 31-year-old unmarried Canadian factory worker apparently was upset over her inability to develop a relationship with Alomar, though she had never met him. She reportedly planned to kill Alomar and commit suicide. Alomar then hired his own security guard as a precaution.

Larry Walker. Walker found a dead body on his property in April 2004. The police reported that "Walker is not a suspect."

Replacement Player. During spring training 1995, replacement player David Shotkoski, a Braves pitcher, was shot to death during a robbery on March 24 in West Palm Beach, Florida.

Gary Sheffield. In October 1995 Sheffield was shot in the shoulder by an assailant who accosted him at a traffic light in Tampa. Sheffield was not seriously wounded during the attempted robbery.

Nick Bierbrodt. In June 2002 the Tampa Bay minor league pitcher was shot three times while sitting in a taxi as a fast food drive-in. He was in serious condition, but recovered and made it back to the Major Leagues in 2003.

Venezuela is a Dangerous Place.

Julio Machado. In early 1992 the Brewers pitcher was arrested in Venezuela for the admitted shooting death of a woman passen-

ger in a car that Machado believed was trying to force him off the road.

Gus Polidor. On April 28, 1995, in Venezuela, the former Major Leaguer had just returned from the United States in an attempt to make it as a replacement player. He was murdered by two men attempting to steal his car and take his one-year-old son.

Roger Blanco. The Braves minor league player was killed by robbers in Venezuela in November 1999. He had been traded for Mark Whiten in 1996.

Richard Hidalgo. In late 2002 the Astros outfielder was shot in the left forearm while waiting in his truck for a friend in Venezuela during an attempted carjacking. He recovered in time for the 2003 season.

Dernell Stenson.

"He's been drafted into the 'Supernatural League.' With as many people who love baseball, heaven's got to have a baseball team."— The Reverend Marshall Stenson describing his murdered nephew, Dernell Stenson.

Early on the morning of November 5, 2003, the 25-year-old Reds outfielder walked out of a bar in Arizona, where he had been playing in the Arizona Fall League. Teammates saw him around 11:30 p.m. sitting alone, and two hours later police found his body in a street six miles away. He had been shot in the head and run over, and indications were he had been dragged by a car. Four men were arrested for what was believed to have started out as a robbery attempt. Stenson had been a 1996 draft pick of the Red Sox and played 37 games for the Reds in 2003, batting .247 with three home runs and 13 RBIs, before heading to Arizona to play for the Scottsdale Scorpions.

Ivan Calderon. In December 2003 the former White Sox outfielder was killed after being shot in the back multiple times in a store in Loiza, Puerto Rico.

Targets. It has been calculated that in the first 75 years of the National League, 27 times as many of its former ballplayers were murdered as compared to American males generally.

Teammates. Kevin Mitchell was traded by the Mets in late 1986 reportedly because he threatened to kill teammate Darryl Strawberry.

Columbine. On April 20, 1999, the Rockies cancelled their game after 15 high school students were massacred at Columbine High School near Denver. The next day's game was cancelled and after that the Rockies wore a patch in memory of the tragedy.

Video. HBO's "Curb Your Enthusiasm" allowed an accused killer to substantiate his alibi. Juan Catalan was accused of killing a girl at the same time that he said he was at a Dodger game. His face appeared in some of the outtakes, which proved his claim. The episode showed Larry David taking a prostitute to the game so he could use the carpool lane on the freeway. David's response to Catalan's freedom: "I'm quitting the show to devote my life to freeing those unjustly incarcerated."

Murderer's Row

"Banned from appearing in most of the respectable ballparks of his day, Charles Babe Baudelaire was nevertheless a mainstay of the Oshkosh Opiumeaters notorious 'Merdeerer's Row.' Most Valuable Madman three times, he died after attempting to smoke one of the Minotaur's turds in the bullpen." — From "Nine Big League Poets," by Mikhail Horowitz, appearing in *Baseball Diamonds*, edited by Kevin Kerrane and Richard Grossinger (1980).

Many believe that the first Murderer's Row was the 1927 Yankee lineup of Lazzeri, Gehrig, Ruth, Combs and Meusel. A few sources note that the "original" Murderer's Row was the 1919 Yankees of Ping Bodie, Roger Peckinpaugh, Duffy Lewis and Home Run Baker. Other sources note that the phrase was used in baseball as early as 1858 when the term was borrowed from death row in The Tombs prison in New York.

The 1936 Yankees were even better than the 1927 club that became the most famous Murderer's Row. The 1936 team had 174 home runs versus 158 in 1927. The 1961 Yankees were even tougher, hitting 240 home runs over a 162-game schedule.

Eddie Murray (1956–)

Hall of Fame 2003

"A lot of things he made look easy, but he also understood that for other guys, thing were more of a struggle. But he supported guys, understood them, and made guys around him better. He has a great baseball mind and showed it as a teammate. When a guy like Cal Ripken … gives credit [during his speech after breaking the consecutive games record] to Eddie for helping him as a youngster … that puts into perspective the people he's touched in his career." — Mike Scioscia.

"Just Regular" — On a chain that Murray regularly wore, representing that he was just a regular member of the team, and not a pampered superstar.

"Few were as skilled in that mental game as Murray, who studied pitchers from the dugout, committed their patterns to memory, quickly deciphered what pitches an opponent couldn't throw for a strike on a given night and eliminated those from his thought process. The result: Murray guessed pitch and location better than most and was able to outsmart many a pitcher." — Sportswriter Mike DiGiovanna.

"Eddie Murray's bronze bust in Cooperstown will chatter only slightly less than the man himself. The first line of text on the monument should read: He spoke rarely and carried a mighty bat." — Sportswriter David Ginsburg.

"Did you ever notice it's always the same 10 or 15 athletes who get all the press in each sport? In basketball it's Jordan, Robinson, Rodman, O'Neal; in football it's Rice, Montana, Smith, Sanders; in baseball it's Bonds, Thomas, Strawberry. Well, I've had enough. Today I am making it my personal mission to get someone else's name in print. Not just someone different, but someone spectacular, incredible, driven, the greatest athlete in the history of professional sports. I'm talking about Eddie Murray, in case you hadn't guessed already from my description. Murray has been my hero since I was 7 years old and he was still sporting an Afro and corduroy bell-bottoms to Baltimore's Memorial Stadium." — Dominic Perella.

One of the finest switch hitters of all time, Murray hit 504 home runs in 21 seasons from 1977 to 1997.

Born in Los Angeles, Eddie Clarence Murray was drafted in the third round by the Baltimore Orioles in 1973. In 1977, appearing primarily as the Orioles' designated hitter, he had a fine rookie year, batting .283 with 27 home runs and 88 RBIs. Murray's first year would be indicative of seasons to come, as he would finish his career with a .287 batting average and post sixteen seasons with at least 20 home runs. After three remarkably similar seasons to start his career, Murray took his offensive production to a new level in 1980 with 32 home runs, 116 RBIs and a .300 batting average. Murray drove in 100 runs in four consecutive seasons beginning in 1982, with a career high 124 in 1985. During this period Murray also established his defensive prowess at first base, winning three Gold Gloves between 1982 and 1984. In 1983 Murray established

a career high with 33 home runs and Baltimore won the American League pennant. In Game 5 of the World Series against Philadelphia, Murray hit two home runs and the Orioles clinched the title.

In 1986 Murray's career would take an unfortunate twist. After suffering a hamstring injury he was accused of malingering by club owner Edward Bennett Williams. The situation rapidly deteriorated, Murray stopped speaking with the press, and eventually asked to be traded. The Orioles suffered through an abysmal 107 loss season in 1988 and Murray was traded to Los Angeles. He would spend three seasons with the Dodgers, hitting a career high .330 in 1990. In 1992 he signed as a free agent with the Mets, joining an infamously dysfunctional club of high priced veterans on the wrong sides of their careers, an association which did nothing for Murray's public persona. Despite the sixth 100 RBI season of his career in 1993, the Mets lost 103 games and Murray signed with Cleveland for the 1994 season. It was in Cleveland that the luster returned, with Murray credited as a steadying influence on talented young Indian clubs. In 1995 he batted .323, collected his 3000th hit and the Indians won the pennant.

In July 1996 Murray was traded back to the Orioles. On September 6 of that year he hit career home run number 500 at Camden Yards in Baltimore, becoming just the third player in history with 3,000 hits and 500 home runs.

Murray retired after the 1997 season with 3,255 hits and 1,917 RBIs. He then became a coach for the Orioles and then a batting instructor for the Indians.

Museums See *Hall of Fame* and *Halls of Fame and Museums Other Than at Cooperstown*

Stan Musial (1920–)

Hall of Fame 1969

"To Stanley Frank Musial, an emblem of esteem from his teammates. An outstanding artist in his profession; possessor of many baseball records; gentleman in every sense of word; adored and worshipped by countless thousands; perfect answer to a manager's prayer; to this, we, the Cardinals, attest with our signatures." — Plaque presented to Musial by his teammates to honor his 3,000th hit.

Musial had 3,630 hits and a .331 average over a 22-year career for the Cardinals that began in 1941.

Stanley Frank Musial was a Polish-American from Donora, Pennsylvania, who in 1972 became the only foreigner to receive the Polish government's highest sports award, the Merited Champions Medal. He avoided the local steel mills as a teenager by pitching in the minor leagues, but his true calling was as a hitter (see also *Players Who Switched Positions*).

Musial posted decent minor league pitching results after overcoming wildness, but he also played in the field when not pitching. A shoulder injury diving for a ball forced him to switch to hitting and in one season in 1941 he moved from Class D ball all the way to the Major Leagues, where he hit .426 in 12 games for the Cardinals.

Musial was one of the most consistent hitters in history, with 16 straight seasons at .310 or higher and the same number of career hits on the road as at home. His best season was 1948, when he hit .376 and led the league in virtually all offensive categories, missing the Triple Crown by one home run. He was a three-time MVP (1943, 1946, 1948), and in 1956 *The Sporting News* named him Player of the Decade (1946–1955). He finished his 22-year career with the Cardinals in 1963 with a lifetime .331 average, 475 home runs and a .559 slugging average, ninth all-time. He also had 1,951 RBIs, fifth all-time, and 1,949 runs, sixth all-time. He is fourth all-time with 3,630 hits and third all-time with 725 doubles.

After Musial retired, he moved into the Cardinals' front office and continued his restaurant and banking interests in St. Louis.

Books. James N. Giglio, *Stan Musial: From Stash to Stan the Man* (2001); Stan Musial with Bob Broeg, *Stan Musial—The Man's Own Story* (1964); Jerry Lansche, *Stan 'The Man' Musial: Born to Be a Ballplayer* (1994).

Musicians

"He doesn't have to march to the same drummer as long as he's in the same band." — Giants manager Dusty Baker on then three-time MVP Barry Bonds.

"It's like watching a man conduct an orchestra. All you see is him standing up there waving a baton. You don't see all those hours of rehearsal when he's working with the orchestra, trying to refine the music." — Eddie Sawyer on managing.

"Baseball is not precisely a team sport. It is more a series of concerts by the artists." — Jim Murray.

"Last year, more Americans went to symphonies than went to baseball games. This may be viewed as an alarming statistic, but I think that both baseball and the country will endure." — John F. Kennedy.

"Come over here and show me how to work this thing!" — Yogi Berra, calling a teammate about his new piano.

"The music world doesn't need it, any more than the sports world needs to see Elton John return a kickoff." — Sportswriter Mitch Albom on the new rap CD by Deion Sanders.

"… and I think it was on a two and one count that Rader hit a hard grass-cutter to Phillips who grabbed it, and in a motion like conductors make to the trumpets in the approach to the end of the fourth movement, Phillips laced it to first for the out." — Fielding Dawson in *Two Penny Lane* (1977).

"You don't tell Leonard Bernstein how to conduct the New York Philharmonic and we don't tell Mike Cuellar how to pitch. He's an artist." — Orioles scout Jim Russo on why, as part of the team's 1970 World Series preparation, he discussed the Reds hitters with all the Orioles pitchers except Cuellar.

"Roger Clemens going into the Hall of Fame as a New York Yankee is like George Harrison going into the Rock and Roll Hall of Fame as a traveling Wilbury." — Mike Bianchi in the *Orlando Sentinel* after Clemens announced he wouldn't wear a Red Sox cap on his Hall of Fame plaque.

"Jerry Cornett, Piano Legs Hickman, Buddy Bell, Keith Drumwright, Steve Sax, Gordie Windhorn"

See also *Entertainers*, *Opera*, *Organs*, *Singers*, *Songs* and *"Take Me Out to the Ballgame."*

Early Baseball Bands. Albert Spalding's 1880s Chicago ballpark featured an eight-piece band sitting in a pagoda. Cincinnati offered a three-piece regimental band and sometimes an orchestra during the 1880s.

Charles Ives.

"According to a biographer, Ives, concerned that his musical interests might make him appear effeminate, participated in amateur baseball well past adolescence in order to dispel any doubts about his masculinity." — Peter Levine in *A.G. Spalding and the Rise of Baseball* (1985).

Ives was one of the great innovators of American music near the turn of the century. His keyboard experiments included a musical

A collage of baseball sheet music.

version of a baseball game entitled, "1907 Giants v. Cubs and Willy [sic] Keeler at the Bat." Notations accompanying the sheet music indicated plays on the field that matched the music.

Dodger Sym-Phoney. A group of Brooklyn Dodger fans led by Shorty Laurice formed a band dubbed by broadcaster Red Barber as the Dodger Sym-Phoney. It was a mainstay of Ebbets Field from 1938 until the Dodgers departed after the 1957 season. They were located in Section 8, Row 1, Seats 1–6.

In July 1951 the American Federation of Musicians union questioned the amateur standing of the Sym-Phoney and threatened to picket the ballpark for using nonunion personnel. In response the Dodgers held "Musical Unappreciation Night" on which fans were admitted free if they brought a musical instrument to play. Included among the contributions were two full-sized pianos.

Accordion. Braves pitcher John Smoltz is an accomplished accordion player.

Harmonica.

Phil Linz. On August 23, 1964, the third-place Yankees, who had just lost four straight in Chicago, were in the team bus stuck in traffic. Infielder Phil Linz started playing "Mary Had a Little Lamb" on his harmonica. Manager Yogi Berra was irritated and yelled from the front of the bus for Linz to stop playing. The other Yankee players (supposedly Mickey Mantle in some sources) told Linz that Berra wanted him to play it louder, which he did. Berra went nuts, a fight followed, and Linz was fined $250. Linz netted some cash, however, as the Hohner harmonica company paid him $2,500 to endorse its product ($20,000 (!) in one source).

Jim Bouton later claimed that Mantle never said "play it louder." Linz simply continued playing until Berra charged to the back of the bus and Linz told off Berra and tossed him the harmonica. Linz good-naturedly reprised the song on the harmonica at Berra's 69th birthday party.

Stan Musial. Musial recorded a harmonica CD in the mid–1990s. He had been playing the harmonica at dinners for a number of years.

In March 1997 the Cardinals ended 50 years of spring training at Al Lang Field in St. Petersburg. Before the last game, Musial regaled the sellout crowd of 6,616 with two harmonica renditions of "Take Me Out To The Ballgame."

Union Problem. During the A's first season in Oakland in 1968, the club never played music in the ballpark because of a dispute between owner Charlie Finley and the local musicians union.

Music Night. In 1979 the Phillies sponsored a Music Night, on which fans were encouraged to bring musical instruments to the ballpark. Anyone without an instrument was given a kazoo, and the entire group played "Take Me Out to the Ballgame" during the 7th inning stretch. The club arranged to receive a certificate from the Guinness Book of Records for hosting the World's Largest Orchestra.

Musical Acts.

Gas House Gang. The Cardinals Gas House Gang was led by shortstop Pepper Martin and his Mississippi Mudcat Band. Martin played guitar, Bill McGee was on fiddle, and different players joined the group over time. At one point they had a vaudeville act paying $1,500 per week, but quit after four weeks on tour.

Eddie Basinski. The Dodger second baseman was known as "Fiddler" while with the club in 1944 because he was a violinist for his hometown Buffalo Philharmonic Orchestra in the off-season. He sometimes played his violin in the clubhouse.

Maury Wills. The Dodger shortstop played a banjo in his own nightclub act in the early 1960s.

Denny McLain. McLain put together a nightclub act after his 31-win season in 1968, featuring himself on the ***Organ.***

Ron Guidry. The Yankee pitcher once played drums with the Beach Boys in a postgame concert at Yankee Stadium.

Jack McDowell.

"Rock and roll musicians, they don't step on stage and get booed. Sixteen critics don't come backstage after a concert and say, 'You guys screwed up that C-to-the-A change there. Were you aware of that?'"—Pitcher and musician Jack McDowell.

The White Sox pitcher was the leader of an alternative rock band known as V.I.E.W. On one occasion he played a concert in the morning and was rocked in a game that night. During the 1991–1992 off-season, the band toured the country as the opening act for the Smithereens. The group's first album was Extendagenda and the drummer was pitcher Wayne Edwards, whose father played drums in the 1960s for the Hondells. In 1996 McDowell and his new band, Stick Figure, released a CD that was well received.

Scott Radinsky. The 1990s reliever played drums for a band in California known as Seared Straight. He later had an offseason punk rock band known as "Pulley" that played for crowds ranging from 150 to 1,600.

Joe West. The umpire cut several records with his "Texas Cookin' Band."

Bernie Williams. In 2003 former Beatle Paul McCartney signed Yankee centerfielder Bernie Williams to his music publishing company, MPL Communications. Williams, an accomplished guitarist, debuted with an album of original jazz songs and guest singers. McCartney's critique of Williams' work: "It's a home run." Original.

Cameo with the Boss.

"It was frightening. I had to down a couple of beers before I went out."—Mets pitcher and New Jersey native Al Leiter, who "played" the tambourine on stage at an October 3, 2003, show with Bruce Springsteen.

Infield Practice. During infield practice before one of the 1964 World Series games, prankster Bob Uecker of the Cardinals grabbed a tuba from a band member in the stands and began scooping up ground balls. It helped keep the team loose, but management apparently found little humor in it. After the Yankees presented the Cardinals with a bill for damage to the tuba, the club supposedly took the money out of Uecker's World Series check.

Babe Ruth's Piano. A suburban Boston pond allegedly was the site of a piano tossed in by Ruth in 1918, the last year the Red Sox won a World Series. In 2002 fans attempted to dredge the pond in hope of finding the lost piano and breaking the Red Sox Curse (see ***Superstitions***). The piano story had been part of local legend since Ruth rented a cottage near Willis Pond in 1917 and 1918. An infrared camera search of the pond revealed a large object about 15 feet deep, alleged to be the piano. Alas, divers never were able to recover a piano—player, upright or grand.

Japanese Band. A Japanese rock group named itself for Orestes Destrade, who starred in Japan before signing with the Marlins in 1993.

Class Act. The 1993 Phillies and their fans were known as a ragtag bunch as the club made it into the World Series. To spruce up their act during the NLCS, the Phillies hired the conductor of the Delaware Symphony Orchestra to lead them in a 7th inning stretch rendition of "Take Me Out to the Ballgame." As he directed the crowd from a special section in the stands, a fan reached out from above and stole his baton.

Violin Maker. Pitcher Marvin Freeman once made violin bows, but the finishing touches were left to a master, prompting Marvin's comment: "I was the middle reliever of bow making. He was the closer."

Image Upgrade. In 2004 Major League Baseball tried to improve its image with younger fans by sponsoring summer concerts. At the Ozzfest and Lollapalooza they pulled along the MLB Road Show, two 53-foot trailers filled with batting cages, radar guns, video games and memorabilia.

"**N** is for Newsom,
Bobo's favorite kin.
If you ask how he's here,
He talked himself in."
—Ogden Nash on Bobo Newsom.

Names

"I liked to have broken my jaw trying to pronounce that one, but I said his name just by holding my nose and sneezing."—Broadcaster Dizzy Dean explaining his pronunciation of Ed Hanyzewski.

"Members of the typographical union breathed a sigh of relief today when Cass Kwietniewski, White Sox rookie, changed his name to Kramer to fit the box scores."—1940s newspaper report.

"That's Blas Minor. I'm Blass Major."—Broadcaster and former Major League pitcher Steve Blass on the call-up of minor leaguer Blas Minor.

See also ***College Baseball*** (for players who changed their names to protect their eligibility) and ***Nicknames***.

The Classics.

"Drungo Hazewood, Togie Pittingo, Waddy MacPhee, Mysterious Walker, Scipio Spinks, Van Lingle Mungo, Putsy Caballero, Ping Bodie, Nig Cuppy, Phenomenal Smith, Bots Nekola, Claral Gillenwater, The Only Nolan, Brusie Ogradowski"

Alliteration.

"Pid Purdy, Coco Crisp, Snuffy Stirnweiss, Tuck Turner, Sibby Sisti, Twink Twining, Wash Williams, Jing Johnson, Lymie Linde, Stuffy Stewart, Slim Sallee"

All in the Family. A full nine-man squad of Major League players with the same surnames who played each position can be created from the following: Jones, Smith, Walsh, O'Neil, Wood, Collins, Williams, Murphy, Miller and White.

Bad Choice. When the Indians traded Stubby Clapp in 2004, Bud Geracie of the *San Jose Mercury News* said it was "for a player to be named better."

First.

"I owe it all to my parents." — David Aardsma, who in 2004 supplanted Henry Aaron as the first name in all baseball encyclopedias.

Namesake. Braves infielder Chipper Jones named his newborn son Shea because Jones had a .314 batting average and 17 home runs in the 66 games he had played at Shea Stadium in New York.

Memory Problem.

"It's a pleasure to be up here with Joe Torrez [sic]" — Somewhat clueless New York City mayor Michael Bloomberg in 2003 at the NYU commencement ceremony.

"If you ever worked with [Phil] Rizzuto you'd know my motivation. How would you like to work eighteen years with a guy who still doesn't know your first name?" — Former Mets broadcaster and National League president Bill White.

Casey Stengel often had trouble with names, calling the Mets the Knickerbockers and the Polo Grounds the Polar Grounds when he was introduced as the new manager of the Mets in 1962. He could not remember his starting right fielder when he went through his opening day line-up live for television announcer Lindsey Nelson. After making it through the other eight positions without a problem, Stengel got stuck: "He's a splendid man and he knows how to do it. He's been around and he swings the bat there in right field and he knows what to do. He's got a big family and he wants to provide for them, and he's a fine outstanding player, the fella in right field. You can be sure he'll be ready when the bell rings — and that's his name, *Bell*."

Good Breeding. Steve Dillon was a marginal pitcher who made the 1963 Mets primarily by the fact that his name was the same as the middle name of Mets manager Casey Stengel. Dillon appeared in three games in 1963 and 1964, compiling a 9.64 ERA with no record.

Strikeout pitcher Roger Clemens has named each of his four boys with a "K": Kody, Kory, Koby and Kacy. Clemens' home town is Katy, Texas. Pitcher Curt Schilling has a son named Gehrig, and Schilling and his wife have raised millions to support research into Lou Gehrig's Disease. When Schilling signed a huge contract extension in April 1997, Michael Ventre of MSNBC said about the son: "I'll bet he feels like the luckiest boy on the face of the earth."

Real Names/New Names.

Johnny Dickshot, a 1930s outfielder, had a real name of Dicksus.

According to Fred Lieb, early 20th century pitcher Rube Marquard's real name was Richard LeMarquis. *The Baseball Encyclopedia* makes no reference to this claim.

A's outfielder Al Simmons changed his name to fit into the box score: it was Szymanski.

Turn-of-the-century infielder Gene DeMontreville changed his name to Gene DeMont.

Lee Magee, barred from baseball for *Gambling* with Hal Chase, had a real name of Leopold Hoernscheneyer.

Sam Rice, who played for the 1915–1933 Senators, signed his name "Sam" Rice because he received the name Sam from a Washington sportswriter who did not know his first name. His real name was Edgar, which he preferred.

According to Lee Allen in *Kings of the Diamond* (1965), Nap Lajoie pronounced his name "Ladge-oh-way." In *Balldom* (1914), George Moreland reported that his name was pronounced "Lazhway." Both of these are contrary to some modern sources which report it as "Lazh-wa."

Eccentric pitcher Rube Waddell, whose real name was George Edward Waddell, once told a sportswriter that it was George Edward Harrison Reed Winchester Reuben Waddell.

Andy Coakley played as Jack McAllister in 1902.

Urban Shocker's original spelling was Shockcor, but he simplified it for reporters.

A's owner Charlie Finley offered Vida Blue $2,000 to change his name to True Blue.

Pitcher Eppa Rixey's middle name was Jephtha, but he adopted it only after a sportswriter invented it. According to one source, it was "inspired by the resonance it had when spoken between 'Eppa' and 'Rixey.'"

Sportswriter Charles Dryden of Chicago often bestowed fake middle names on players. Pitcher Ed Walsh was dubbed Edward Armstrong Walsh, though his middle name was Augustine.

In 2004 pitcher Ismael Valdez announced that his named be switched to "Valdez." He said that's how it is spelled on his birth certificate.

Extra Letters.

"What did they expect from a guy who can't spell his own name, to lead them to a pennant?" — Jim Armstrong after manager Jimy [sic] Williams was fired by the Astros in 2004.

Turn-of-the century Hall of Fame shortstop Bobby Wallace's real name was Rhoderick John Wallace. Most sources spell his first name without an "h." *The Baseball Encyclopedia* includes the "h" even though some sources report that the "h" is improper.

Some early sources reported that 19th century pitcher Charles Radbourn's name had an "e" on the end. However, in 1942 his sister made it clear at a Bloomington, Illinois, plaque unveiling for Radbourn that his family had abandoned the letter many generations earlier.

Eccentric. Super Joe Charboneau of the Indians, a bit of an eccentric, was a big talker, so he named his dog Diarrhea. He claimed that he named his daughter Dannon because he liked yogurt.

Coincidence. In his first at-bat of 1993, Scott Service of the Expos faced Scott Servais of the Astros.

Palindromes. Dave Otto is one of eight players in Major League history to have a palindromic last name (spelled the same way forward and backward). The others:

Robb and Dick Nen (father and son)

Truck Hannah

Mark Salas

Toby Harrah

Eddie Kazak

Johnny Reder

Vowels. Aurelio Rodriguez is one of the few Major League players to have every vowel in his first name.

Initials Only. U.L. Washington's first two names are "U" and "L." They do not stand for anything.

Jake Mooty's real name was J T Mooty (no periods, despite *The Baseball Encyclopedia*'s insistence on including them).

Superstition. In the introduction to *The Armchair Book of Baseball II* (1987), John Thorn reported that left-hander Bruce Hurst pitched a 1–0 shutout for the Red Sox in Game 1 of the 1986 World Series. Thorn then pointed out that the last time the Red Sox won a World Series was in 1918, when another left-hander pitched a 1–0 shutout for the Red Sox: "Whose shutout was it? Ruth's — an anagram of Hurst."

Best Name. In round 50 of the 1993 amateur draft, the Braves selected Tennessee State center fielder Wonderful Terrific Mons. He never made it to the Major Leagues, however.

Well, Well, Well. On September 2, 1999, pitcher David Wells of the Blue Jays faced pitcher Bob Wells of the Twins, who struck out Toronto's Vernon Wells.

Brown. On September 27, 1999, the Pirates' first three batters in the second game of a doubleheader were Adrian Brown, Emil Brown and Brant Brown.

Mirror Image. On May 11, 1999, Bobby M. Jones of Colorado beat Bobby J. Jones of the Mets, 10–3. The last time two pitchers with the same name started against each other was in the 19th century. George H. Bradley of Boston and George W. Bradley of St. Louis started against each other twice in 1876. On April 16, 1899, John B. Taylor of Cincinnati started against John W. Taylor of Chicago.

Snoozer. The 1999 Rangers had three players with last names starting with the letter "Z": Jeff Zimmerman, Todd Zeile and Greg Zaun. Only the 1916 Cubs duplicated this: Rollie Zeider, Heinie Zimmerman and Dutch Zwilling.

The Johnsons. On July 8, 1934, A's hitter Bob Johnson hit a pitch by Red Sox pitcher Hank Johnson to center field, where Roy Johnson caught it.

Reversal. Nomar Garciaparra is named in reverse for his father, Ramon.

Amnesia. Mets broadcaster Ralph Kiner referred to himself as "Ron Kiner" and "Ralph Korner" at least once each.

Longest.

"I told [general manager] Roland Hemond to go out and get me a big name pitcher. He said, 'Dave Wehrmeister's got 11 letters. Is that a big enough name for you?'" — White Sox owner Eddie Einhorn.

When Giants pitcher William VanLandingham beat Pirates pitcher Jason Christiansen on August 9, 1995, the 25 letters in their surnames was the most ever in a Major League game for the pitchers of record.

The longest surnames in baseball history contain 13 letters. There have been 13 such players, including VanLandingham and Ken Raffensberger, who pitched in the National League in the 1940s and 1950s. Kirk Dressendorfer pitched in the American League in the 1990s and 2000s. Todd Hollandsworth played for the Dodgers in the 1990s.

Edd J Roush.

"Then there is the matter of his name. His given name is not Edward or Edwin or Edmund, but Edd, and he has no idea where the extra 'd' came from any more than Jimmy Foxx knows where his grandfather picked up the extra 'x.' Nor does Roush's middle initial stand for anything. His two grandfathers were named Joseph and James respectively, and rather than offend either, his parents gave him the middle initial." — Lee Allen and Tom Meany in *Kings of the Diamond* (1965), who apparently spelled Jimmie Foxx's first name wrong.

The National See *The National Sports Daily*

National Agreement (1883–)

"During these years [1880s] of baseball prosperity, the National Agreement — the Blackstone of baseball law, as a contemporary writer called it — became more and more pervasive, as new minor leagues were organized and placed themselves under its rule." — Harold Seymour in *Baseball: The Early Years* (1960).

This often-amended agreement has helped guide all of *Organized Baseball* since its creation in 1883. It is one of five such governing documents.

1883 Creation. On February 17, 1883, the formal beginning of Organized Baseball occurred at a "harmony conference" in New York among the National League, American Association and Northwestern League, the latter a minor league operating in Michigan, Ohio and Illinois. Abraham G. Mills represented the National League, Denny McKnight the American Association and Elias Mather the Northwestern League. The representatives agreed on mutual recognition of reserved players and set up exclusive territories. The National League also formally recognized the American Association as a second Major League. The representatives extended the reserve clause to 11 players on each club and set a minimum salary of $1,000 for players in the National League and American Association.

1885 Amendments. In 1885 the "Saratoga Agreement" was negotiated to prevent open warfare for players between the National League and the American Association after the Union Association folded. The agreement added the origins of the *Waiver* rule, creating a 10-day period only after which one league could negotiate with another league's waived player. Postseason play between the National League and American Association resumed and blacklisting of club-jumping players was eliminated.

1890 Amendment. The National Agreement was rewritten after the Players League revolt of 1890. The new document was executed primarily between the American Association (soon to disband), the Western Association (later to be the American League), and the National League. Three board members were elected, one from each league, and they appointed a neutral chairman. They tried to bring Abraham Mills back into baseball to fill that post, but he declined. Mills had led the group that formulated the original National Agreement in 1883. The board ultimately selected Allan W. Thurman of the American Association as chair.

The reserve system was continued with some minor reforms. This was the last formal act to resolve the Players League war, but the fight between the American Association and National League continued and resulted in the extinction of the American Association after the 1891 season.

1900–1903 Fighting. The 10-year National Agreement expired at the end of 1900. It would not be renewed amicably unless the National League allowed the American League into the open cities of Baltimore and Washington, which the National League had abandoned in 1899.

In 1900 Ban Johnson and his newly named American League agreed to abide by the National Agreement, but would not honor the reserve clause contained in National League contracts. This resulted in bidding wars for players. During the season the National League refused to honor its contractual commitments to the minor leagues, so the minor leagues formed their own national association, the *National Association of Professional Baseball Leagues*. The disagreements were finally resolved with a new National Agreement in 1903, resulting in formation of the *National Commis-*

sion. The agreement also refined and formalized the minor league draft for the orderly disbursement of minor league players after each season.

1919. The National Agreement and Organized Baseball's unity were disrupted by the 1919 withdrawal of the minor leagues from the National Agreement because of a dispute with the Major Leagues over player purchases. At a 1919 meeting the National League owners voiced concern again for a neutral chair of the National Commission. Peace was restored after Judge Landis was appointed commissioner. Relative harmony existed for the balance of the 20th century until 1990.

1990. A new dispute involving the National Association arose between the Major and minor leagues because the Major Leagues were balking at continuing to underwrite major portions of the minor leagues' expenses. The issue came to a head when the parties refused to ratify a new version of the National Agreement. In December 1990 a seven-year deal was signed after the Major Leagues agreed to underwrite a smaller portion of the minor leagues' expenses.

1997. Minor and Major League Baseball reached agreement on a 10-year contract to guarantee a Major League player development contract for all 160 teams through the life of the contract.

National Amateur All-Star Baseball Tournament ("NAABT") (1993–)

This tournament for amateur players ages 16 to 18 was established in 1993. Various amateur associations participate in the event, whose first honorary commissioner was Steve Garvey. The original honorary team captains were Bill Madlock, Keith Hernandez, Willie Horton, Joe Charboneau and Joe Sambito. The first tournament was played in Battle Creek, Michigan.

National Amateur Baseball Federation (1914–)

This is the oldest amateur baseball organization in America, operating continuously since 1914. It coordinates "World Series" games for various U.S. amateur associations at different age levels.

National Anthem

"For Christ sakes, we're running a business here. Does Macy's play the 'Star Spangled Banner' before opening its doors every day?"— Sportswriter and later Hall of Fame director Ken Smith, criticizing the playing of the National Anthem before every game.

"I knew we were in for a long season when we lined up for the national anthem on openning day and one of my players said, 'Every time I hear that song I have a bad game.'"— Pirates manager Jim Leyland.

"As we stand here waiting/For the ball game to start...."— Comedian Albert Brooks on his version of the National Anthem.

"Instead of the National Anthem, sing 'In-a-Gadda-da-Vida' before every game."— One of David Letterman's "Top ten ways Major League Baseball teams can win back the fans."

"You might be a redneck if you think the last words to the 'Star Spangled Banner' are 'Play Ball.'"— Comedian Jeff Foxworthy.

Origin. "The Star Spangled Banner" was written by Francis Scott Key during the War of 1812 to the tune of an old British drinking song. He wrote the song in September 1814 while watching the seige of Baltimore and the shelling of Ft. McHenry by the British. "The Star Spangled Banner" was declared the National

Anthem by executive order of President Wilson in 1916. His order was confirmed by an act of Congress on March 3, 1931.

Earliest Baseball Connection. Although the National Baseball Library cannot document the first time the anthem was played at a baseball event, it is believed that the song was played on May 15, 1862, during the Civil War at the opening of the Capitoline Grounds in New York.

The tradition of playing "The Star Spangled Banner" before important events was not well established until after 1900. One of the earliest post–1900 playings was by the New York Highlanders (Yankees) on April 30, 1903. It usually was played only on special occasions with a band, since there was no recorded music. "Columbia, Gem of the Ocean," was actually more popular in ballparks for many years.

One source reported that the anthem was first played at a ballgame in 1916 at President Wilson's request. Another source reported that it was first played on Opening Day at Cleveland and New York in the American League in 1917.

World War I. The first well-documented playing of "The Star Spangled Banner" at a baseball game occurred at Wrigley Field during the 7th inning stretch of Game 1 of the 1918 World Series between the Cubs and Red Sox. The U.S. had just entered World War I and patriotic fervor was high.

As the band started to play, the players spontaneously faced the flag at attention and one saluted. The crowd began singing to great applause. During the 8th inning six biplanes flew in formation over the ballpark. The scene was repeated during the next two games, also in Chicago. When the series shifted to Boston, owner Harry Frazee had it played to start the game. This started a trend of playing it on Opening Day and for World Series games. It was also sometimes played at regular season games when a band was present.

Public Address Systems. The development of public address systems, the first of which was installed at Yankee Stadium in 1929, made it possible to play the anthem without a live band.

North v. South. There was sectional disagreement in the country over the choice of what had evolved into a civil war anthem as the country's national anthem. It would have been interesting to see how Major League teams handled the playing of the anthem in those early days had teams been located in Southern cities. Southern minor league teams refrained from playing the anthem due to the lingering animosity.

World War II. The patriotic fervor that accompanied World War II forced the playing of the anthem before all Major League games for the first time in 1942. That protocol continued after the conclusion of the war. Playing a national anthem before all regular season games first occurred in the Canadian cities of the International League because Canada entered the war in 1939.

In an exhibition game during the war, Jimmy Bloodworth was pitching during spring training. As a ground ball was hit back to him, the anthem came on the public address system. Bloodworth immediately stood at attention and the runner was safe at first.

Vietnam War. During the Vietnam War in 1972 the Royals announced that the anthem would only be played on Sundays and special occasions. Owner Ewing Kauffman made the decision after complaining that the anthem was not receiving the respect it deserved. After he received numerous calls and letters complaining about the decision, the anthem was restored to full-time play.

World Series Furor. The Tigers created an uproar during the 1968 World Series when they asked blind singer/guitarist Jose Feliciano to sing the national anthem before Game 5. He was invited at the suggestion of Tigers broadcaster Ernie Harwell. Feliciano sang the anthem in a folk-rock rhythm that offended and even outraged many.

In 1985 after the cross-state World Series between the Royals and Cardinals produced seven different versions of the anthem, a bill was introduced in the legislature requiring performers to "sing it straight." It never passed.

Player/Singer. A number of players have stepped up to sing the anthem before games. A small sampling: In 1977 Lamar Johnson of the White Sox sang the anthem and then had two home runs and a double, the only Chicago hits in a 2–1 victory.

After he retired, pitcher Nelson Briles sang the National Anthem at the 1973 World Series.

In August 1993 Dwight Smith sang the National Anthem at Wrigley Field before taking the field for the Cubs.

Cubs. Unlike all other Major League clubs, the Cubs played the anthem only on holidays and special occasions in the late 1950s and early 1960s.

White Sox. In 1966 the White Sox briefly played "God Bless America," but the fans responded with a city-wide ballot referendum in which 74% of the voters opted for "The Star Spangled Banner."

Orioles. Orioles fans chant "O" loudly in unison when the anthem reaches "O say does that star spangled banner…." The club stopped playing the anthem for a week during the 1954 season, attempting to play it only on holidays and special occasions. The city council responded by forcing it to be played at every game.

Roseanne Barr. The comedienne and television star created a furor in July 1990 when she performed the anthem at a San Diego Padres home game. The producer of her TV series and "The Cosby Show," Tom Werner, was at the time the primary owner of the club. Her performance was a screeching horror, and she concluded it with a grab of her crotch and a large spit wad in parody of the typical player.

Marathon.

"People ask me when I'm gonna spit and grab my crotch. The answer is, when hell freezes over." — Donna Greenwald, who in 1992 began a quest to sing the National Anthem in every Major League ballpark. She made it to number 13 in 1995 before the strike ended the season. She lived near Baltimore and regularly volunteered at the Babe Ruth Museum.

Late for Work. During the 1994 season Tommy Lasorda was still in the clubhouse and late for the National Anthem on a few occasions. Center fielder Brett Butler bought a life-size cut-out of Lasorda and brought it on the field during the anthem.

Fill-In. At the 2003 Hall of Fame Induction ceremony, Johnny Bench was a last-minute substitute to sing the Canadian national anthem. Bench did a credible job in place of Daniel Rodriguez, who was delayed by bad weather.

Youngest. On June 9, 1999, three-year-old Rex Spjute of Meridian, Idaho, performed the national anthem at Dodger Stadium to be become the youngest person ever to do so at a Major League game.

Japan. The Japanese national anthem is never played at regular season games.

National Association of Base Ball Players ("NABBP") (1858–1870)

"The National Association of Base Ball Players was formed (the *National* in the title was a trifle ambitious, since all the clubs were from New York) in 1858 and it insisted on amateurism and gen-

tlemanly behavior. It got neither." — Bill Bryson in *Made in America* (1994).

"The Knickerbocker Club, organized in 1845, was the pioneer organization, and for several years the only one in the field. Its first competitor was the Washington Club, which, however, only existed for a short period, many of its members taking part in the formation of the Gotham Club, in 1852. The Eagle Club was organized in 1854, but for several seasons the three clubs above mentioned were the only ones playing in the vicinity of New-York. They adopted a series of rules and regulations to govern the game, and these rules were adopted by all the clubs organized prior to 1857." — Preface to the NABBP constitution and by-laws.

1857–1858 Formation. The largely amateur NABBP was the central administrative body for baseball from 1858 through 1870. Amateur teams from the New York and Brooklyn area first met in 1857 to organize a formal baseball organization. The 16 teams set up a rules committee but did not formally establish the association, which explains why a number of sources cite 1857 as the year of formation.

In early 1858, 16 to 25 New York City and Brooklyn clubs (depending on the source) held another convention in New York City. This time they were successful in drafting a constitution and by-laws, officially forming the National Association of Base Ball Players. The group adopted a uniform set of rules patterned after the Knickerbocker Rules, but the new rules included a change to nine-inning games. Before that, the first team to score 21 "aces," or runs, was the winner.

Unlike modern leagues this was an organization of players rather than clubs. A two-thirds vote was needed to admit a club to the association. By the start of the 1858 season there were 26 clubs playing best-of-three series against each other. Through the rest of the decade generally 50 clubs existed in this Eastern-based organization, including members from Pennsylvania who joined in 1860.

Some clubs such as the Knickerbockers would not play socially inferior teams or professionals and attempted to keep the genteel club atmosphere prevalent in the 1840s. The balance of power was shifting, however, and the more society-based clubs were less powerful in the new association. None of the first year's officers were from the Knickerbockers, demonstrating the declining influence of the club.

The 1860s. By 1861 the association had approximately 200 club members, but the group languished during the Civil War. By 1867, two years after the war had ended, there were again over 200 member clubs. Great strides were made after the war. So many clubs joined that membership was limited to state organizations except in areas that had less than ten teams, the minimum to start a state organization. More than half the clubs were from the Midwest, so the eastern clubs (still primarily from New York) no longer controlled the association.

At the convention of 1868 there were delegates from 18 states and territories representing 400 clubs. Bowing to pressure from teams with at least some paid professionals on their rosters, the National Association repealed its prohibition against professional players participating in match games between National Association members.

By 1869 there were 1,000 active clubs, but there was a deepening rift between the purely amateur teams and those with professional players. The amateur association was unable to control gambling or enforce its rules, and many teams were openly defying decisions of the previously amateur-dominated body. In response, the association established two levels of players, "professionals" and "others."

In 1869 many games were marred by gambling scandals and the association was losing credibility. At an 1871 meeting the amateurs walked out, leaving the professional teams to develop a new organization. Thus was born the ***National Association of Professional Baseball Players***, the first formal league, commonly known as the 1871–1875 National Association.

Book. Warren Goldstein, *Playing for Keeps* (1989).

National Association of Professional Base Ball Players ("National Association") (1871–1875)

"The first professional league was hardly a financial success; very few teams turned a profit, and if any one group made out well it was the ball players, at least two dozen of them going on in later years to become directors or owners of ball clubs.... The Association helped the players and also helped to spread the professional game. Association clubs became drawing cards, and through 'exhibition' games with outside clubs helped bring fans to ball parks in many cities."— Ted Vincent in *Mudville's Revenge* (1981).

Origins. In response to the growing number of professionals in the game, a body separate from the amateur ***National Association of Base Ball Players*** was created in early 1871 to govern professional players. Again, however, the new body was an association of players rather than clubs with a centralized authority, which was a fundamental weakness not corrected until the National League was formed in 1876.

Formation. On March 17, 1871, representatives of 10 professional teams met at New York's Collier's Cafe on Broadway and 13th Street and formed the National Association of Professional Base Ball Players. The league started play that same summer, with an entry fee of $10 per player.

The first president was James N. Kerns, a U.S. Marshall and representative of the Philadelphia Athletics. Brooklyn player Robert V. "Death to Flying Things" Ferguson was the president for two of the first five years, although a few sources erroneously identify him as the first president.

Original Teams. The league started primarily in the Midwest and expanded eastward. The original teams were the Boston Red Stockings, Chicago White Stockings, Cleveland Forest Citys, Ft. Wayne Kekiongas, New York Mutuals (owned by Tammany Hall's Boss Tweed), Philadelphia Athletics, Rockford Forest Citys, Troy Haymakers and Washington Olympics. Some sources reported that the Ft. Wayne club was replaced midseason by the Brooklyn Eckfords, who attended the initial meeting but balked at the $10 fee because they thought the organization was precarious. However, *The Baseball Encyclopedia* reflects that the Eckfords did not play their first game in the league until 1872, their only season (the confusion may be because the Brooklyn Eckfords replaced another National *League* club in midseason 1876).

Later Teams. Added to the National Association after the first season were the Lord Baltimores (1872–1874), Baltimore Marylands (1873), Brooklyn Atlantics (1872–1875), Middletown (Conn.) Mansfields (1872), Elizabeth (Conn.) Resolutes (1873), Hartford Dark Blues (1874–1875), St. Louis Brown Stockings (1875), St. Louis Red Stockings (1875), Washington Nationals (1872 and 1875), New Haven Elm Citys (1875), Philadelphia Centennials (1875), Philadelphia Whites (1873–1875) and Keokuk (Iowa) Westerns (1875). See separate entries for each club.

Scheduling. Teams in 1871 played approximately 30 games in the league and another 50–60 games against nonleague opponents.

First Game. The first game played by National Association teams was between the Ft. Wayne Kekiongas and Cleveland Forest Citys on May 4, 1871. Bobby Mathews pitched the Kekiongas to a 2–0 victory, and the first recorded hit was by catcher Deacon Jim White off Mathews.

Problems. There were no centralized rules or centralized authority in the National Association. The Association was also marred by drinking, gambling and rowdiness. Attendance dwindled as Boston dominated and there clearly was no uniformity in scheduling; during one season Boston played 79 games (winning 71) and financially troubled Keokuk played 13 (winning 1) before dropping out. The association also suffered from constant "revolving," by which better players frequently switched teams.

In its last year in 1875 the league began with 13 teams but only seven finished the season. Many players often were too drunk to play. One source attributed the downfall of the association in part to the 1874 tour of England led by Albert Spalding of the Boston Red Stockings. The powerful Boston and Philadelphia clubs were absent from the National Association from mid–July to mid–September that year, which hurt gate receipts for a number of clubs. The association was sometimes known as the Players League, not to be confused with the Players League that operated for one season in 1890.

Pennant Winners. The Philadelphia Athletics won the first pennant with a 21–7 record that included two forfeit wins over Rockford, which had used an ineligible player. Chicago was hampered by the loss of its ballpark from the Great Chicago *Fire*. It still finished a close second at 19–9, so the Rockford forfeits to Philadelphia would have been important in today's pennant races. However, the clubs regularly played three-game series against each other, and some sources claim that it was the number of series wins that determined the champion (others report that it was percentage that counted). The Boston Red Stockings were favored, but finished third at 20–10 after suffering a number of injuries. Boston then went on to win the next four pennants by increasingly larger margins.

Attrition. After the 1871 season the Rockford club quit and star player Cap Anson moved to the Philadelphia Athletics. The Chicago club also left the league for two years because of the fire and the league had 11 teams in 1872. It had nine teams in 1873, eight in 1874 and nine in 1875 (with four additional clubs that were replacements during the season).

The Association Collapses. In 1875 Boston dominated the league with 71 wins and ended the season with 24 straight wins and a tie. Only two teams finished above .500, and Brooklyn came in at an abysmal 2–42.

The association was suffering from lack of funds, and it was also difficult for the western and eastern teams to travel to each other's locales. Most teams were not making enough money to sustain themselves, as reflected in the fact that 25 clubs played in the league in five years. Only three of the teams lasted the entire period: the Philadelphia Athletics, Boston Red Stockings and New York Mutuals.

After the 1875 season the National Association tried to reorganize itself after the National League was formed early in 1876, but the efforts were unsuccessful. Notwithstanding the weaknesses in the association, baseball as a spectator sport was about to emerge, spurred on by such factors as industrialism, urbanism and the railroads.

Major League Status. The National Association was considered a Major League by the 1951 *Encyclopedia of Baseball*, the first statistical reference officially sanctioned by Major League Baseball. The second sanctioned book, *The Baseball Encyclopedia*, published by MacMillan in 1969 and unrelated to the first work, declined to designate the National Association as a Major League. It did so in part because the Major League Records Committee determined that the association's scheduling was too haphazard.

Books. Harvey Frommer, *Primitive Baseball* (1988); Warren Goldstein, *Playing for Keeps* (1989); William J. Ryczek, *Blackguards and Redstockings* (1993).

National Association of Professional Baseball Leagues (1901–)

"This meeting, held in Chicago on September 5, marked the first time the Minor Leagues had joined together to accomplish anything and it set guidelines that were universally adopted."—Mike Blake in *The Minor Leagues* (1991), on the formation of this association of minor league clubs.

See also **Minor Leagues**.

Formation. This minor league association was formed after the National League abandoned its commitments to the minor leagues during the league's feud with the American League in 1900. The organization was formed in Chicago on September 5, 1901, and its first full year of operation was 1902. Charter members were the Class A Eastern and Western Leagues (Class AAA and AA did not yet exist), the Class B Southern Association, Western Association, New York State League, New England League and the Three I League (Indiana, Illinois and Iowa), and the Class C Pacific Northwest League and Connecticut League.

In 1903 the dispute between the minor and Major Leagues was resolved and the National Agreement again encompassed the minor leagues. Nevertheless, the new minor league organization remained intact. The association still governs minor league baseball and is the organization that negotiates on its behalf with the Major Leagues.

Key Officers. Western League president Thomas Jefferson Hickey supposedly was the first president. Other sources credit Patrick T. Powers, who also is credited with the organization's name. Powers was succeeded by Michael H. Sexton in 1909 and various others until 1933 when the position first took on significance in the organization. Before that, the executive secretary position held the power, and this was a post held for 32 years by John H. Farrell.

Judge William G. Bramham (who was never a judge but was nicknamed that by fellow law students), was known as the Czar of Minor League Baseball for the 14 years starting in 1933 in which he headed the National Association.

George Trautman was the general manager of the Detroit Tigers when he was elected president of the National Association in December 1946. He had pitched for Ohio State during college and was president of the American Association in 1933. He remained president until his death in 1963, which coincided with the near-death and reorganization of the minor leagues.

National Baseball Congress (1936–)

"National Semi-Pro Baseball Congress Kansas State Tournament"—Name of the first tournament organized by the Congress's founder.

This semipro organization was formed as the National Semipro Baseball Congress. It was founded as a result of a statewide amateur tournament in Kansas that had been successful since 1931. It was the brainchild of Raymond "Hap" Dumont, a Wichita sporting goods dealer and former newspaperman. After his first local tournament, he expanded to a nationwide tournament and invited

Satchel Paige's touring team to compete; guaranteeing Paige's group $1,000.

The first commissioner of the Congress was Honus Wagner, who was succeeded by George Sisler. J.G. Taylor Spink of *The Sporting News* became commissioner in the late 1940s. The Congress continues to sponsor semipro baseball on a national basis and holds its World Series in Wichita.

National Baseball Players Association (1922–1923)

This short-lived attempt at a **Union** was led by the attorney who represented some of the Black Sox players.

National Brotherhood of Professional Base Ball Players (1885–1891)

This **Union** was created in response to salary caps in the mid-1880s and remained strong through the 1890 Players League before fading.

National Commission (1903–1920)

"The Supreme Court of Baseball."

Formation. The National Commission was established in 1903 as a result of the truce between the National and American Leagues. The three-man commission replaced the old Board of Control and remained as the Major League's governing body until the commissioner's position was established in 1920. The National Commission ruled on fines and club disputes and was successful for a few years in bringing order and stability to the two Major Leagues.

Each league president and a third man acceptable to both comprised the commission, with the third acting as chairman. The only chairman that the commission ever had was Reds owner Garry Herrmann. He had been a friend of American League president Ban Johnson when Johnson was a Cincinnati sportswriter and therefore was acceptable to the American League. To the dismay of many in the National League, Herrmann often sided with Johnson on commission rulings.

Johnson was the American League representative throughout the commission's existence. A series of National League presidents were on the commission with Johnson and Herrmann.

Income Source. The National Commission's chief source of income was 10% of the gate receipts from the World Series. It also received income from fines levied on teams and players. Prior to the inception of the World Series tariff, the leagues each assessed their clubs 5% of gate receipts for the commission's operating expenses.

Minor Leagues. There was no minor league representation on the commission. The Major League owners believed that despite the lack of representation the minor leagues would support and receive protection from the National Commission in the face of competition from outlaw leagues. Both the minor leagues and the Major Leagues players periodically asked for and were denied representation on the commission.

Infighting Escalates and Dismantling of the Commission. Beginning in 1915 the owners were more contentious than in previous years. Many American League owners were particularly upset with their own president, Ban Johnson. This group of dissidents was led by Johnson's former friend, White Sox owner Charles

Comiskey, who had been angered over rulings against him made by Johnson. At the root of the final actions which led to the commission's dissolution were various disputes between clubs over player ownership.

Chairman Herrmann also was a source of irritation to the owners. For example, in 1916 Barney Dreyfuss of the Pirates had a dispute with Branch Rickey's Browns over the signing of future Major League star George Sisler. Sisler played college ball for Michigan, where Rickey had coached. The commission ruled against Dreyfuss; he was furious with Herrmann over the matter and tried to replace him.

During the 1914–1915 Federal League war, Major League owners considered abolishing the Commission, in part because of its ineffectiveness in dealing with the Federal League and the club-jumping American and National League players.

In June 1918 a dispute arose over ownership of pitcher Scott Perry (see also *Scott Perry Incident*). Connie Mack and the A's lost Perry to the Braves after the Commission ruled against Mack. He ignored the ruling and obtained an injunction prohibiting Perry from playing for the Braves. National League president John Tener refused to sit on the Commission unless Mack handed over the pitcher, which never happened (Perry pitched for the A's through 1921).

Tener and Johnson were already at odds over the handling of the Federal League competition. Tener also criticized Johnson when Johnson asked the government to give ballplayers draft exemptions during World War I. Tener eventually resigned and John Heydler was elected National League president in the winter of 1918–1919.

The commission's reputation was further damaged when it failed to quickly and quietly handle the 1918 World Series player strike (however brief it was) over World Series shares (see also *World Series*).

Possibly the most prominent dispute demonstrating the ineffectiveness of the commission was the *Carl Mays Incident*, which, like the Perry situation, was a fight over which team owned a player. In the Mays situation, however, the fight was among American League clubs and the National League was not involved.

The unity of Organized Baseball and the power of the commission were eroded further after the brief withdrawal of the minor leagues from the National Agreement in 1919. This was caused by the Major League's abuse of the draft system, whereby its clubs took players from minor league clubs.

All of these factors, including other matters closely related to Ban Johnson's abuse of power, led to the dismantling of the National Commission and creation of the Office of the Commissioner. It should be stressed that the National Commission was on its way out and a commissioner position on its way in well before the Black Sox Scandal broke in 1920. Many sources have erroneously characterized the scandal as the reason for creation of that office.

In 1920 the two league presidents staged their annual vote on Herrmann as the chair of the commission. This had been a formality in the past, but for the first time National League president John Heydler refused to vote for him. Johnson could not save Herrmann and Herrmann resigned June 8, 1920, though some sources report that Herrmann stayed in the position until Judge Landis became commissioner. More reliable sources report that a vacuum was created when Herrmann quit and there was no leadership from the breaking of the Black Sox Scandal in September 1920 through appointment of a commissioner in November 1920.

National Game See *National Pastime*

National League (1876–)

("National League of Professional Baseball Clubs")
"Gentleman, you have no occasion for uneasiness. I have locked the door simply to prevent any intrusions from without … and incidentally to make it impossible for any of you to leave until I have finished what I have to say. I promise not to take more than an hour." — William Hulbert to the assembled prospective National League owners just before launching into his pitch for the new professional league.

See also *National League Presidents*.

Formation. The National League was created as a result of the infighting among the 1871–1875 National Association owners. The most significant feature of the new National League was that it was a league of *clubs*, rather than players. By 1875 the National Association, organized by the players, was in shambles. It had 13 teams and almost one half did not finish the season. The Boston Red Stockings had a winning percentage of .899 and five teams had winning percentages below .200.

Chicago White Stockings owner William Hulbert was agitating for a new regime. The last incident that spurred formation of the National League was the National Association's actions involving Davy Force. Force switched teams repeatedly, an activity known as revolving, and the fight over ownership of this player created a lasting rift between Hulbert and the eastern clubs. The National Association's judiciary committee had ruled that Force should go to Hulbert's Chicago White Stockings. At a later National Association meeting in Philadelphia, a new president was chosen (Spering of Philadelphia). A new Judiciary Committee was formed and gave Force to Philadelphia. Hulbert was angry and moved forward with his plan to form the National League.

Hulbert was unpopular with the eastern club owners of the National Association in part because after the 1875 season he raided the Boston Red Stockings and brought star pitcher Albert Spalding and other players to his club. The eastern clubs apparently were considering expulsion of Hulbert and the White Stockings. Hulbert decided to preempt that action by forming his own league and forcing it on the eastern clubs.

In January 1876 in Louisville at the Galt House Hotel, Hulbert met secretly with Col. John A. Joyce of Cincinnati, Charles A. Fowle of St. Louis and Charles E. Chase of Louisville. All expressed interest in a new league and then Hulbert and Fowle wrote to eastern clubs to see who might be interested. G.W. Thompson, owner of the Philadelphia Athletics, William H. Cammeyer, noted builder of baseball parks and owner of the New York Mutuals, Morgan Bulkeley of the Hartford team, and Nathaniel T. "Nick" Apollonio of Boston all expressed interest.

Hulbert then called together representatives of eight choice cities with clubs in the earlier National Association: Chicago, St. Louis, Cincinnati, Louisville, New York, Philadelphia, Boston and Hartford. At a meeting at the Grand Hotel in New York on February 2, 1876, the league was formally established. Annual dues were set at $100 per club.

Teams were admitted to the league in the following order: Chicago White Stockings, Boston Red Stockings, New York Mutuals, Philadelphia Athletics, Hartford Blues, St. Louis Brown Stockings, Cincinnati Red Stockings and Louisville Grays.

The league issued a press release reporting that it had withdrawn from the National Association to show the lack of interest in the new league's activities. It took three days for the New York papers to report the event. In addition, once the National League started its season, the teams were not necessarily considered the elite. Typical was the 1877 *Louisville Commercial* newspaper, which printed standings of the best clubs in the country and had National League teams mixed in with independents.

Early baseball historians dated the National League's beginnings to 1871 because six of the eight 1876 National League clubs were identical to the clubs in the 1871–1875 National Association.

Cities and Their Teams/1876–1902. The National League was represented in 22 different cities with 31 separate teams over its first 27 years (championship seasons are in parentheses):

Baltimore	1892–1899 (1894–1896)
Boston	1876–1902 (1877–1878, 1883, 1891–1893, 1897–1898)
Brooklyn	1890–1902 (1890, 1899, 1900)
Buffalo	1879–1885
Chicago	1876–1902 (1876, 1880–1882, 1885–1886)
Cincinnati	1876–1880, 1890–1902
Cleveland	1874–1876, 1889–1899
Detroit	1881–1888 (1887)
Hartford	1876–1877
Indianapolis	1878, 1887–1889
Kansas City	1886
Louisville	1886–1877, 1892–1899
Milwaukee	1878
New York	1876, 1883–1902 (1888–1889)
Philadelphia	1876, 1883–1902
Pittsburgh	1887–1902 (1901–1902)
Providence	1878–85 (1879, 1884)
St. Louis	1876–1877, 1885–1886, 1892–1902
Syracuse	1879
Troy	1879–1882
Washington	1886–1889, 1892–1899
Worcester	1880–1882

National League Rules.

"First, to encourage, foster and elevate the game of baseball; second, to enact and enforce proper rules for the exhibition and conduct of the game; third, to make baseball playing respectable and honorable."— Preamble to the National League's new constitution.

The league's formal constitution was drawn by Campbell Orrick Bishop based on a draft by Hulbert. Bishop was an attorney and later a judge who had played with the St. Louis Unions of the 1860s. He had been a vice president of the National Association. Hulbert and Albert Spalding also issued what were later known as "Hulbert's Reforms":

1. The new organization was a league of clubs, not players;

2. $100 entry fee;

3. Only clubs in population areas of 75,000 or more allowed — although Troy and Syracuse were exceptions until they were ousted;

4. Clubs were required to be based a minimum of five (?) miles apart although this rule was not strictly enforced;

5. All player contracts were to be written — if a player was ineligible for one team, then ineligible for all;

6. Any player guilty of dishonesty would be barred by the league for life.

Among other reforms, clubs were required to complete their schedules (a major issue during the first season). The league set uniform admission prices and forced players to adhere to a standard player contract.

On disciplinary matters, only team captains (most of whom doubled as field managers) could dispute an umpire's decision. The

league was the first to supply police and to send results to a league secretary.

There would be no **Sunday Baseball**, though this rule was not strictly enforced before 1880. No alcohol would be sold, and no gambling would be tolerated on the grounds (not well enforced). There also was to be no player fraternization with the fans and unruly fans were subject to ejection by the umpire.

First President. Hulbert, who owned the Chicago White Stockings, chose Troy owner Morgan Bulkeley as the first league president. This choice supposedly occurred only after Hulbert declined the nomination, but a more logical explanation is that Hulbert orchestrated the selection of Bulkeley, whom he could control, to appease the eastern owners.

The First Game and Other Firsts. The first National League game was played on April 22, 1876, with Philadelphia hosting Boston. It was the only game played that day due to rainouts, so there were a number of confirmed firsts. Boston won 6–5, scoring two runs in the 9th inning in front of 3,000 fans. Game time was 2 hours and 45 minutes.

The first batter was Red Stockings shortstop George Wright, who grounded out to shortstop. Orator Jim O'Rourke of the Red Sox had the first hit, a two-out single in the 1st inning. Wes Fisler of the Athletics was the first player to get three hits in a game. Red Sox catcher Tim McGinley was the first to strike out and to score a run. Losing pitcher Alonzo "Lou" Knight of Boston made the first pitch. A's shortstop Davy Force had the first assist and Wes Fisler had the first putout. A's third baseman Edra Hutton had played in the first National Association game in 1871 while with Cleveland.

The winning pitcher was Joe Borden (apparently also known as Charles Joseph, according to some sources), who a year earlier had pitched the first professional no-hitter. Borden was 11–12 at midseason when he was dropped from the team. He then hired on as a groundskeeper and never pitched again in the National League.

Levi Meyerle of the A's had the first double and two days later hit the league's first triple. On May 2, ten days after the first game, Ross Barnes of the White Stockings hit the first home run off William Cherokee Fisher. Boston's Jack Manning had the first RBI, on a sacrifice fly, although this statistic was not recorded at that time.

First Game/20th Century. Jim O'Rourke was the only player to play in the first game in the National League and also play in the 20th century. He played in 1904 at age 52 for the Giants under John McGraw. He caught the first game of a doubleheader and had one hit. Joe McGinnity clinched the pennant for the Giants with a 7–5 win against the Reds.

Last Survivor. Tommy Bond was the last survivor of the National League's first season. He died in 1941 at age 85.

Rival League Attempt. In November 1876 the independent St. Louis Red Stockings called a convention for February 1877 for independent teams to meet and form a rival league. Future National League president Abraham Mills solicited help from Hulbert to reform certain aspects of the National League to prevent raiding by independent teams. This conciliatory gesture helped stave off the founding of a strong rival. Nevertheless, the convention went ahead and the teams formed the ***International League*** of Professional Base Ball Players, but the league was never a serious threat. The 23 International League teams occasionally played National League teams.

The Winter of 1876–1877. League president Morgan Bulkeley did not attend the league's December 7, 1876, winter meeting in Cleveland. Boston's Nick Apollonio, who had openly feuded with Hulbert over player sales (including Albert Spalding), was the eastern clubs' first choice for the presidency, but he said that he might not stay in baseball. As a result, Hulbert assumed the presidency and ran the league until his death in 1882.

Nicholas E. Young, a former player and umpire, and by then with the Washington club, was appointed league secretary. The league also ruled that two clubs from the same city would not be allowed in the league. Clubs were also prohibited from playing games in a city which was not in the league. This was done specifically to prevent teams from playing in large-market Philadelphia after the Athletics were expelled from the league for failing to play out the season (as were the New York Mutuals). This was a bold step given that these clubs were in the league's two largest cities. Clubs from these two cities were not readmitted for six years, and the league only had six teams for a time. Philadelphia had suffered financially due to competition from the Centennial Exposition and there were allegations of gambling against both clubs that may have been the real reason for their expulsion.

1877–1883/Tough Times of Infancy. In 1877 virtually every club lost money: St. Louis lost $8,000, Chicago $6,000, Hartford $2,500, Louisville $2,000, and Boston $1,500. Only Chicago made a profit.

Louisville quit after two seasons when four players were expelled for throwing games (see also *Gambling*). Hartford supposedly was so bad that it played its 1877 home games in Brooklyn and the club folded after the season. Its 1877 record of 31–27 seems to contradict this assertion.

St. Louis, with a record of 28–32, also folded after the 1877 season. Hartford, Brooklyn and St. Louis were replaced by teams in Indianapolis, Providence and Milwaukee. St. Louis and Milwaukee lasted only the 1878 season.

Only Boston and Chicago lasted through the mid–1880s. Things were so bad at times that Hulbert and one other owner were empowered to appoint another new club if one collapsed. When Abraham Mills took over as president in 1882, he intentionally did not list the names of the clubs on the letterhead because of the heavy turnover.

In 1879 Cleveland, Buffalo, Troy and Syracuse were added from 16 clubs trying to get into the league. This marked the last time that the National League had only six clubs. The National League recognized the quality of independent clubs and created a rule allowing admittance of one independent club each year if that club had beaten other key independents. Indianapolis was admitted on this basis.

Cincinnati was ousted in 1880 for selling beer. In 1882 Hulbert died of a heart ailment, though he left the league in good financial shape: most clubs made a profit in 1881. He was succeeded briefly by Arthur H. Soden, Boston club president for 30 years. Soden was an interim choice who was almost immediately replaced by Abraham Mills, who lasted two years.

1882/Troy and Worcester Out. In 1882 the rival American Association began play with clubs in National League cast-off cities Cincinnati, St. Louis and Louisville, as well as Pittsburgh, Philadelphia and Baltimore. The National League responded after the 1882 season by adding clubs in New York and Philadelphia. It dropped the unprofitable small-town clubs in Troy and Worcester, which were drawing less than 400 fans per game.

Both Worcester and Troy are technically still in the National League. According to the 1883 *Spalding Guide*, their resignations were accepted and the clubs were placed on the roll of honorary National League members. The two clubs were promised four exhibition games a year if they could field representative teams, but this never occurred.

1884–1890/Challenges from Rivals. Following the American Association's emergence in 1882, the Union Association appeared in 1884. By this time the National League had stabilized, teams were more profitable, and the league was able to handle the challenge of these new leagues. The most difficult challenge came from the Players League of 1890, and the National League barely survived, but then rallied to dominate.

1891/Fall of the American Association. In the fall of 1891 the American Association folded. The Louisville and Columbus franchises disbanded first and the National League supposedly persuaded American Association St. Louis Browns owner Christopher Von der Ahe to move to the National League. It is more likely that he orchestrated the move and brought three other strong clubs with him: Washington, Baltimore and a new Louisville team. The Association's Philadelphia owners were allowed to purchase the new National League club in Washington.

The realigned league technically was supposed to be the "National League and American Association of Professional Baseball Clubs," but the new name was never used and the American Association simply disappeared.

The 1890s and Monopoly.

"The 1899 season proved the last for the League in its twelve-club incarnation, and also brought the full ripening (or rotting) of syndicate baseball."—Charles Alexander in *Our Game* (1991).

When the Players League disbanded after the 1890 season and the American Association collapsed a year later, the National League's 12 clubs had no other Major League competition. Those clubs were Baltimore, Boston, Brooklyn, Chicago, Cincinnati, Cleveland, Louisville, New York, Philadelphia, Pittsburgh, St. Louis and Washington.

In 1892 the unwieldy 12-team league tried to create more fan interest by implementing a split-season format, with the winner of each half playing for the league title. The experience had been successful in the Eastern League but never took hold in the National League after the initial season. As part of the changes, the league increased its *Schedule* from 140 to 154 games.

With the 12-team monopoly, the owners could not agree on whether to cut back to eight teams or add four teams and create two eight-team divisions. The league remained paralyzed on the subject throughout the decade until shortly before the American League emerged in 1900–1901.

The Boston Red Stockings dominated the 1890s with a record of 706–400 and Baltimore was the other strong team of the decade. The St. Louis Browns were horrible, and after the 1898 season were bought by the Robison brothers, who also owned the abominable Cleveland Spiders.

The league was in trouble by the late 1890s because of waning interest and too many teams. In response to the financial crisis, the owners began combining their ownership interests (see also *Cross-Ownership*). They accused each other of cheating on the diminishing gate receipts, they slashed player salaries and the press became critical.

By 1899 the National League's troubles intensified and the owners were divided into two camps. One group was led by Giants owner Andrew Freedman and Reds owner John Brush. They headed the "[John] Brush Clique," also known as the "Big Eight." The second group was led by John I. Rogers of Philadelphia and was known as the "Little Four Rogers Faction."

To streamline the league, four clubs were designated for discard: Louisville, Cleveland, Baltimore and Washington. This left 80 players without clubs. The best Louisville players were moved to Pittsburgh by owner Barney Dreyfuss, who owned both clubs. The league considered selling the territorial rights to the abandoned cities to raise money and tax gate receipts to pay the buyout in the same manner that the league paid off the disbanded American Association teams in 1891.

To prevent the defunct teams from joining a possible new rival league (the American Association was trying to restart), the departing clubs technically remained part of the league for two years during the payoff period. The teams received payoffs totalling $111,500: $10,000 to Louisville; $25,000 to Cleveland; $30,000 to Baltimore; and $46,500 to Washington (some sources put the total at $150,000 for the group).

The eight remaining owners continued their infighting during 1900 and 1901 while the American League strengthened itself. In mid–1901 the National League's internal battle intensified and came to a head later that year.

Proposed Monopoly. During the summer of 1901 Giants owner Andrew Freedman controlled half the league's owners, including Arthur Soden of the Braves, John Brush of the Reds and the Robison brothers of the Cardinals. Freedman concocted a plan to turn the league into a trust with a single entity holding ownership that would control every aspect of the game. There would be a board of regents and stock ownership in the new entity. It was to be known as the National Baseball Trust, but the word "trust" carried a negative connotation in that trust-busting era. News of this plan leaked and the owners who opposed Freedman demanded a showdown. The opponents were Charles Hart of Chicago, Charles Ebbets of Brooklyn, Colonel John I. Rogers and Alfred J. Reach of Philadelphia, and Barney Dreyfuss of Pittsburgh.

Long-time baseball leader Albert Spalding, who still held a controlling interest in the White Stockings, had proposed his own plan for "Syndicate Ball" (complete cross-ownership) and met with Ban Johnson on the subject in an attempt to unite the National and American Leagues. Nothing came of it, however.

The Internal Battle for Control. On December 11, 1901, the National League power struggle came to a head at its winter meetings. National League president Nick Young was a puppet of Soden and Freedman. Barney Dreyfuss of the Pirates therefore nominated Albert Spalding as the league's new president. This resulted in a 4–4 voting deadlock, with the Freedman faction backing Young. After 25 ballots the groups were still deadlocked and they ended the voting for the night.

Late that same night Spalding persuaded Young to let him temporarily move the league's documents from Young's hotel room to another location in the hotel. This move apparently allowed Spalding to call another meeting, which became official when league secretary Fred Knowles momentarily (and unwittingly) walked into the room to create a quorum. Spalding was elected president by a 4–0 vote.

On January 24, 1902, Freedman and Brush countered the move by obtaining a court injunction to prevent Spalding from assuming the presidency. Spalding left the state before the court papers could be served. On March 29, 1902, Brush obtained a permanent injunction against Spalding. Spalding immediately resigned, and on April 3, 1902, the league's leaders created a three-man executive committee consisting of Arthur Soden, John Brush and Charles Hart, with Nick Young as secretary-treasurer. The owners failed to elect a president once again.

The three-man committee ran the league until Harry Pulliam was named president in 1903. He was a former club official with Louisville and Pittsburgh under Barney Dreyfuss. After all the intrigue, the universally despised Freedman gave up and was forced to sell his interest in the Giants. Now that the infighting among

National League owners was over, the league could turn its attention to resolving its battle with the American League.

National and American League Compromise of 1903. The National League was suffering from its internal problems and from competition with the American League for players and fans. The National League initiated complete merger discussions in late 1902, but the American League resisted.

When it became clear that the American League would not budge, a final agreement was reached in mid–January 1903. The agreement left the American League intact and allowed club movements into other cities. The American League was allowed to keep its club in New York and retain all of its former National League players. The American League agreed not to place a club in Pittsburgh and both leagues agreed to observe the reserve clause and honor the other league's contracts.

As part of the overall compromise, a new National Agreement was drawn to cover Organized Baseball at all levels, creating better cooperation among the Major and minor leagues (though not without a struggle; see also *Minor Leagues*).

19th Century in a Nutshell. In an August 1911 article in *Baseball* magazine, writer Allen Sangree divided the first 25 years of the National League into five eras: the War of the American Association; the War of the Union League; the Revolt of the Brotherhood; the Second War of the American Association; and the War of the American League. It might be appropriate to include an initial section for the birth and stabilization of the league in the late 1870s and a section entitled "Monopoly and Paralysis" to describe the 1890s after the American Association and before the American League.

20th Century Stability. The National League alignment remained stable until the 1950s, when the Boston Braves moved to Milwaukee, touching off a series of *Franchise Shifts* during that decade.

Expansion and Divisional Play. The 1962 and 1969 *Expansion* and *Divisional Play* altered the look of the National League, as did the addition of franchises in Colorado and Florida for the 1993 season and division realignment in 1994. In 1998 the Brewers joined the National League in order to allow for an even number of teams in each league (16 in the National, 14 in the American).

Books. Lee Allen, *The National League Story* (1961); Glenn Dickey, *The History of National League Baseball Since 1876* (1982); Ed Fitzgerald (ed.), *The National League* (1952); Harvey Frommer, *Primitive Baseball* (1988); Neil W. MacDonald, *The League That Lasted: 1876 and the Founding of the National League of Professional Base Ball Clubs* (2004); MacMillan (ed.), *A Baseball Century* (1976); Tom Melville, *Early Baseball and the Rise of the National League*; Charles Segar, *Official History of the National League* (1951). Tom Simon (ed.), *Deadball Stars of the National League* (2004).

National League Presidents (1876–1999)

"That to him alone is due the credit of having founded the National League, and to his able leadership, sound judgment, and impartial management is the success of the league chiefly due."— National League resolution upon the death of second president and driving force William Hulbert.

Morgan Bulkeley	1876
William Hulbert	1877–1882
Arthur Soden	1882 (interim)
Abraham Mills	1882–1884
Nicholas Young	1884–1902

[Note: no president for less than a year in 1902–1903 (reported erroneously as "abolished" in some sources)]

Harry Pulliam	1903–1909
John Heydler	1909 (interim)
Thomas J. Lynch	1910–1912
John Tener	1913–1918
John Heydler	1918–1934
Ford Frick	1934–1951
Warren Giles	1951–1969
Chub Feeney	1970–1986
A. Bartlett Giamatti	1986–1989
Bill White	1989–1994
Leonard S. Coleman, Jr.	1994–1999

Overview. There have been three National League presidents from politics (Mills, Tener and Bulkeley), five former club executives (Soden, Hulbert, Pulliam, Giles and Feeney), three with umpiring backgrounds (Young, Lynch and Heydler), two former Major League players (Tener again and White), one from academia (Giamatti), one businessman (Coleman), and one newspaperman (Frick).

Morgan Bulkeley (1837–1922)
Hall of Fame 1937
Served 1876

"In choosing officers, Hulbert named Morgan Bulkeley, a well-known Connecticut politician, as president. It was thought that such a name would go far towards endowing the league with respectability."— David Quentin Voigt in *American Baseball* (1966).

"Baseball has often been pictured as the typical American sport where the banker sits beside the bootblack to cheer, fan and eat peanuts. Bulkeley was probably the banker they had in mind."— Ken Smith in *The Baseball Hall of Fame* (1947).

Bulkeley practiced law in Brooklyn and served under General McLellan in the Civil War. He received a Masters of Arts degree from Yale. He founded and was president of the Hartford Club in 1876, the National League's first year.

Reports differ on how Bulkeley became the league's first president. One source reported that he was chosen by lot. Another reported that founder William Hulbert's name supposedly was drawn from a set of cards containing the team names. Hulbert was then entitled to choose the president. It is far more likely that Hulbert, a Midwesterner, simply selected his strong eastern supporter from the Hartford team to appease the other Eastern owners. Bulkeley was a figurehead who deferred to Hulbert and his term lasted only one year.

Bulkeley left baseball in 1877 to become president of Aetna Life Insurance Company, founded by his father. By 1913 that company was insuring eight of the Major League clubs. He also organized the U.S. Bank of Hartford in 1871. He was mayor of Hartford for eight years beginning in 1880 and later the governor of Connecticut and a U.S. Senator. Apparently demonstrating that his first love was not baseball, Bulkeley was president of the National Trotting Association for 30 years.

It appears that Bulkeley was elected to the Hall of Fame simply because his American League counterpart, founder Ban Johnson, was elected at the outset of Hall of Fame voting. At the time, no attention was paid to the fact that William Hulbert was the driving force behind the league.

William Hulbert (1832–1882)
Hall of Fame (VC) 1995
Served 1877–1882

"His great force of character, strong will, marked executive ability, unerring judgment of men and measures, and strict integrity and fairness, were of incalculable value to the league and he was rightly considered to be the brains and backbone of that organization."— *Chicago Tribune* editorial at Hulbert's death in 1882.

"It always has been the contention of the author that the role of this strong man of the Middle West in baseball has been grossly underplayed. No one in authority even has had the perspicacity to give him a plaque in the Cooperstown Hall of Fame."— Fred Lieb in *The Baseball Story* (1950); that error was finally rectified in 1995.

Hulbert was the original patriarch of the Chicago White Stockings and the driving force in the formation of the National League. After the league's first season in 1876, Hulbert became president and remained so until his death on April 10, 1882.

He was born in 1832 in Burlington Flats, Otsego County, New York, near Cooperstown, and attended Beloit College. He was a member of the Chicago Board of Trade stock exchange after growing up in that city in the early 1870s. He became involved in baseball when he bought into the Chicago White Stockings of the National Association. In 1875 he became chairman of the board of the club and moved quickly to establish the new professional league.

He was elected president of the National League for the 1877 season and was reelected for the 1882 season despite being terminally ill with heart problems in December 1881. He died at age 49 and should have been elected early on to the Hall of Fame for his work in organizing and running the league. However, the early nominating committee apparently did not realize that original National League president Morgan Bulkeley was merely a figurehead and that Hulbert ran the operation.

Abraham G. Mills (1844–1929)
Served 1882–1884

"The Bismarck of Baseball"— Mills' nickname, in reference to the German general of that era who was considered a respected and strong leader who held the public's trust.

Mills was a Civil War veteran who had been a baseball player and later served as president of the Washington Olympics club. An attorney, Mills took over as National League president in December 1882 after William Hulbert died (after a brief interim term by Boston's Arthur Soden). He then worked a compromise with the Northwestern League and the American Association that resulted in the National Agreement, which he was instrumental in drafting.

On November 19, 1884, at the league's ninth annual meeting, the National League's owners were ready to forgive the Union Association defectors after the 1884 season. They were prepared to allow the St. Louis Maroons of the Union Association to become a National League franchise. Mills opposed the move and resigned in protest because he did not want to see Maroons owner Henry Lucas (the driving force behind the Union Association) become a part of the National League.

Other sources report that Mills resigned in part because the job was too "onerous" and he had pressure from his other business interests, including his vice-presidency of the Otis Elevator Company. Still others report that Mills was voted out of office. Baseball continually but unsuccessfully tried to lure him back into the game over the next two decades.

Mills is best remembered for creating the National Agreement and for restoring order to the National League after numerous franchise moves disrupted the league. He also was given authority to discipline players, managers and umpires, and to appoint and remove umpires. He chaired the infamous tongue-in-cheek Mills Commission that investigated the ***Origins of Baseball***.

Nicholas "Nick" Young (1840–1916)
Served 1884–1902

"A naturally timid soul." — Charles C. Alexander in *Our Game* (1991).

As a result of the departure of Abraham Mills in 1884, "Uncle Nick" Young succeeded him as president. Young had been secretary of the league since its inception and the jobs of secretary and president were combined as a result of his election.

Young was born in Amsterdam, New York, and was an accomplished cricket player. He served in the New York army during the Civil War and played his first baseball game in the spring of 1863 when he was with the Twenty-Seventh New York Regiment. After the war he took a job with the Treasury Department in Washington.

In 1867 he helped organize the Washington Olympics Baseball club and played right field for four years. He managed the club in 1871 and helped organize the professional National Association, of which he was secretary. He managed the Olympics in 1872 and the Washington Nationals in 1873. Some sources report that he managed the Chicago White Stockings in 1874, but the records do not confirm this claim.

Young served as a National Association umpire in championship games held each of the five years of that league's existence. He was part of the group that formed the National League and was elected secretary on February 2, 1876. He served in that position until 1883.

Although Young was not a particularly forceful leader, the league prospered through the 1880s. He had help, as the influential Albert Spalding was still around to help stabilize the league. By the 1890s Spalding was in the sporting goods business full-time and was largely unavailable to help with problems brought on by monopoly and lack of competition from rival leagues. In part because of Young's ineffectiveness and in part because of the owners' contentiousness, the office of the president was largely benign under Young.

After leaving the presidency, Young served on the infamous Mills Commission that "determined" the *Origins of Baseball*.

Henry Clay "Harry" Pulliam (1869–1909)
Served 1903–1909

"He was an idealist and wished to place baseball on too high a plane for practical purposes." — Phillies owner James Potter.

Harry Pulliam became National League president at age 33 in 1903, coinciding with the end of the war between the National League and the new American League. He was born in Kentucky and received a law degree from the University of Virginia. He was one of many sportswriters who became sports executives; starting as a Louisville sportswriter he became secretary to the Louisville Colonels club and later secretary of the minor league American Association. He also spent two years in the Kentucky State Assembly.

Pulliam moved to Pittsburgh when owner Barney Dreyfus consolidated the Louisville and Pittsburgh clubs. He served the clubs as secretary-treasurer in 1900–1903 before becoming National League president.

Pulliam was effective early on and obtained unanimous support for reelection in 1904. By 1905 the vote was 7–1 as John Brush of the Giants was now his enemy and Pulliam became ill from the pressure. In 1906 the vote was 6–2 as Brush persuaded National Commission president and Reds owner Garry Herrmann to vote against him. By that year, Pulliam, a nervous and frail man, was becoming more arbitrary in his decisions.

There was an unsuccessful effort to oust him in 1907, and then two incidents in 1908 did him in. That year there was an investigation of a Cubs ticket scandal and Pulliam was under tremendous stress during the probe because of the importance of the matter (rather than any involvement by him in the scandal). Pulliam was also under pressure due to the famous Merkle Boner incident (see *Base Running*) that required a critical ruling on his part.

At a banquet in February 1909 a few months before his death, Pulliam summed up his position: "My days as a baseball man are numbered. The National League doesn't want me as president any more. It longs to go back to the days of dealing from the bottom of the deck, hiding the cards under the table, and to the days when the trade was the gum shoe. Because I am for dealing above board and playing in the open, my days are numbered. I can't afford to quit. But I will have to quit at the end of this year, for the club owners of the National League want to revert to the old methods."

Pulliam was known to be quite sick, and the speech finished to tumultuous applause. The next day he took a forced leave of absence after a second nervous breakdown and turned the presidency over to John Heydler. Miraculously, Pulliam quickly returned to his post, apparently healthier while living at the bachelors-only New York Athletic Club. Looks were deceiving, however, as he shot himself to death on July 28, 1909 (see also *Suicides*).

Thomas J. Lynch (1859–1924)
Served 1910–1912

"[Harry Pulliam's] death was followed by a period of bitter politicking over a successor, and the ensuing brief terms of men like former umpire Tom Lynch ... failed to provide strong leadership for the National League." — David Quentin Voigt in *American Baseball* (1966).

After Harry Pulliam committed suicide, John Heydler was a potential successor because he had filled in for Pulliam during Pulliam's illnesses. However, Heydler was seen as a weak choice even though he was the interim president in 1909 and 1910. Also considered was John Montgomery Ward, by then a wealthy and highly regarded New York attorney. However, he was intensely disliked by American League president Ban Johnson because Ward had represented players who had jumped from American League clubs in 1901 and 1902. If Ward had been elected, cooperation between the leagues would have been impossible.

Also in contention was Robert W. Brown, editor of the *Louisville Times* and a friend of Cincinnati Reds owner Garry Herrmann. As the voting began, Ward was supported by four teams: New York, Brooklyn, Chicago and St. Louis, all led by Giants owner John Brush. The other clubs backed Heydler. After four days of deadlocked votes, Brush offered up Thomas Lynch as a compromise choice, and it was accepted by the other clubs.

Lynch was a former National League umpire who was at the time managing a theatrical bureau in Connecticut and had been out of baseball since 1902. Brush supposedly advocated this former "King of the Umpires" on the theory that the National League president's primary duty was overseeing the umpires; but most sources fail to mention that Lynch was merely a compromise choice. Lynch was elected despite reservations by many of the league's owners. His secretary was Lenora Caylor, daughter of 1880s American Association leader and *Sportswriter* O.P. Caylor.

Almost from the outset Lynch was at odds with many of the owners. In August 1910 he fined Dodger owner Charles Ebbets $500 for improper conduct in connection with an option on a contract. The Robison brothers of St. Louis thought that Lynch's umpires were incompetent and Charles Murphy of the Cubs and Horace Fogel of the Phillies simply did not like him. In 1911 Reds owner Garry Herrmann again proposed newspaperman Robert

Brown for the presidency, but others wanted a national figure. Despite the dissatisfaction with Lynch, there still was not enough sentiment for league secretary Heydler. The controversy continued until early 1913, when a successor was chosen. After Lynch was forced out, he became bitter and reclusive until his death in 1924.

John K. Tener (1863–1946)
Served 1913–1918

"The Tener Regime, I should say, will go down in baseball history as a quasi-success. He tried to make his points in a dignified manner, and he tried to put sportsmanship and fair play ahead of everything else. He made his appeal to the best there was in a magnate, a manager, a player, an umpire — and I should say his stuff did not get over." — Ernest J. Lanigan of *The Sporting News* writing at Tener's death in 1946.

In late 1912 the National League dumped Thomas Lynch and elected Pennsylvania governor John Tener, who ran the league from Philadelphia starting in early 1913. Tener was supported most strongly by W.F. Baker, who became the Phillies' president and chief stockholder after Horace Fogel departed. Tener's salary was $25,000 per year for four years.

Tener was the first former Major League player to assume the presidency. He had played in the 1880s with Baltimore and Chicago of the National League and pitched for Pittsburgh's Players League club in 1890. He also participated in an international tour with the White Stockings in 1889. Sportswriter Fred Lieb claimed that Tener was 6'7", but *The Baseball Encyclopedia* lists him at 6'4", still very tall for a 19th century player.

When Tener took over, John Heydler continued to work under him as league secretary and did most of the work. Tener remained as Pennsylvania governor for the first two years of his presidency. After his four-year contract was up, Tener stayed for one more year, resigning August 6, 1918, because the owners failed to support him in a dispute with the American League over a player. This was the **Scott Perry Incident** in which the National League owners refused to hand over Perry to the American League, a decision with which Tener disagreed. The dispute over who would own this pitcher helped destroy the National Commission's effectiveness and contributed to the installation of Judge Landis as commissioner.

After the decision, Tener wanted to see the National League break with the American League. The owners did not support him and he resigned in a huff. Tener was also unhappy over the resolution of the Federal League dispute and feuded with Ban Johnson over draft deferment requests during World War I. Tener died in 1946 after years of regularly attending Pirates games.

John A. Heydler (1869–1956)
Served 1918–1934

"Congratulations to John Heydler and Casey. Long may you both live! [signed] Grover Cleveland." — Note to Heydler from the President of the United States after the youthful government clerk was summoned to the White House to deliver a document during a dinner party. The president asked Heydler if he could recite "Casey at the Bat" and Heydler obliged.

After John Tener's resignation, John Heydler finally received his chance at the presidency after serving as the league's secretary for more than a decade. He was elected at age 49 on October 10, 1918, at an initial salary of $12,000 a year for three years. He remained in the position for 16 years. His regime was marked by a general period of strength for baseball, though not necessarily because of his leadership.

Heydler originally was a linotype operator in Washington who kept baseball statistics as a hobby. When Harry Pulliam was named league president in 1903, Heydler was brought in to be Pulliam's secretary and statistician. He was interim president for a short time while Pulliam was ill and continued to serve under other presidents until he was elected in 1918.

After the 1934 World Series it was rumored that Heydler had detectives shadow the Gas House Gang of St. Louis as a precaution against gambling allegations. Heydler finally admitted the action and Cardinals owner Sam Breadon wrote Heydler a scathing and cruel letter (saying later that he immediately regretted mailing it). Heydler supposedly was hurt by the letter and resigned, retiring to California. After a tearful resignation speech, he was elected Chairman of the Board of the National League for life. Other sources charitably reported that Heydler resigned due to ill health — though he lived another 22 years.

Ford C. Frick (1895–1978)
Hall of Fame (VC) 1970
Served 1934–1951

"Maybe I'm a cockeyed optimist, but I have enough faith in management, in the players, and in the loyalty of the fans, to believe that proper answers will be found." — Frick on the labor-management strife of the early 1970s that preceded free agency; quoted in his autobiography, *Games, Asterisks and People* (1973).

Frick was born in Wawaka, Noble County, Indiana. He attended conservative DePauw College and went on to teach English at Colorado Springs, where he played semipro baseball.

He was working for the *Gazette and Telegraph News* in Colorado when a retired printer saw his work and sent it to newspaperman Arthur Brisbane of the Hearst organization. Brisbane offered Frick a job at the *New York American* newspaper. A year later Frick moved to the *Evening Journal*, usually covering the Yankees and ghostwriting in the Christy Walsh Syndicate for Babe Ruth. He also did a sports review on radio, which was considered one of the more accurate (i.e., not sensationalistic) radio reports of the day. The radio reporting made him well known in baseball and he was chosen to head the National League's publicity office as Service Bureau Chief in February 1934 at age 40.

In December 1934 Frick was elected president of the National League. Until 1941 Frick was faced with no real controversies as peace dominated the league. He then helped guide Major League Baseball through the war years and remained in the position until he was elected **Commissioner** of baseball in 1951.

Warren Giles (1896–1979)
Hall of Fame (VC) 1979
Served 1951–1969

"Most men connected with baseball are rabid fans. Warren is a triple-special. At World Series and at All-Star games, I think I get as much kick watching Warren as I do the performance on the field. When the game starts, he doffs his coat, rolls up his sleeves, and settles down to some plain and fancy rooting. He is the very epitome of everything that a loyal fan should be." — Ford Frick in his autobiography, *Games, Asterisks, and People* (1973).

"Quick to think. Slow to anger." — Giles' advice to his umpires.

Giles was the son of a painting contractor in Moline, Illinois. He attended Staunton Military Academy in Virginia and Washington and Lee University. He enlisted in the Army during World War I and was wounded while serving in France.

After the war he was active in the Three I League, where he was influential among the Moline team's fans, many of whom collectively owned the club. Giles was given the presidency of the club without pay in 1919, and one of his first moves was to arrange for Earle Mack (Connie Mack's son) to manage the team. Mack won pennants in 1921, 1922 and 1923. Giles then became an executive with St. Joseph in the Western League at a salary of $200 per month, though he quickly arranged to purchase the club with a local restaurant owner as his financial backer.

While a minor league manager, Giles once dealt fairly with the Cardinals after a clerical error would have allowed him to sell a player for a higher price to another Major League club. At the end of 1925, Branch Rickey of the Cardinals returned the favor and offered Giles the presidency of the Cardinals' Syracuse farm team in the International League. The club won four consecutive pennants under Giles. He later was president of the Rochester club in the International League and a member of the minor league National Association's Executive Committee.

In 1936 International League president Charles Knapp died and Giles was elected to replace him. When Larry MacPhail left the Reds in 1936, the Reds hired Giles as their general manager starting in 1937. He stayed for 15 years, winning pennants in 1939 and 1940 and becoming the club's president in 1948.

He was 56 when he was elected National League president on September 27, 1951, but almost became commissioner instead. When a successor to commissioner Happy Chandler was being chosen that year, the battle was between Giles and ultimate choice Ford Frick, who was then National League president. After a 17-ballot stalemate, Giles removed his name from the ballot and Frick was elected. When Frick was elevated to commissioner, Giles moved into the National League presidency.

Giles' Cincinnati headquarters had been only two blocks from Happy Chandler's commissioner's office, so Giles transferred the National League office into Chandler's old headquarters. When Giles was installed, he named *Sportswriter* and future baseball historian Lee Allen as the league's public relations director.

Giles led the league through a tremendous period of growth with franchise shifts in the 1950s and expansion in 1962 and 1969. He remained in office until 1969, when he was succeeded by former Giants executive Chub Feeney. Giles's son Bill later became president and a minority owner of the Phillies.

Charles S. "Chub" Feeney (1921–1994)
Served 1970–1986

"His saving grace was a sense of humor as constant as his cigar."
— Sportswriter Bob Broeg.

Feeney's grandfather was Charles Stoneham, the patriarch of the Giants in the 20th century. Feeney's full name was Charles Stoneham Feeney, and his mother was partners in the club with his uncle Horace Stoneham. Feeney attended Fordham Law School and passed the bar but never practiced law.

Feeney began his baseball career in 1946 with the Giants at age 25 after serving in the U.S. Navy during World War II. He moved west to San Francisco with the team in 1958. He eventually became the general manager of the club and moved on to the National League presidency in 1970. During his tenure baseball experienced the rise of free agency and a renaissance in popularity. He also was instrumental in refusing to adopt the designated hitter rule for the National League. At the time of his death he was a member of the board of directors of the Baseball Hall of Fame, and his daughter Katy was vice president of media relations for the National League.

A. Bartlett Giamatti (1938–1989)
Served 1986–1989

"There are a lot of people who know me who can't understand for the life of them why I would go to work on something as unserious as baseball. If they only knew."— Giamatti.

In December 1986 the long-time academician was appointed National League president, in part because of his handling of a difficult union situation while he was president of Yale University.

His appointment may have at least partially fulfilled the Red Sox fan's lifelong dream of becoming *American* League president.

Key actions during his tenure included the suspension of Pete Rose for 30 days for shoving umpire Dave Pallone. In April 1989 Giamatti was appointed ***Commissioner***.

Bill White (1934–)
Served 1989–1994

"Bill was selected as the best man for the job. Race did not enter into it."— National League selection committee chairman Peter O'Malley.

"A good man, but incompetent."— Former commissioner Fay Vincent.

William "Bill" White was appointed National League president in 1989, coming out of the Yankee broadcast booth. White was 55 when he took the job and became only the second player (after John Tener) to become National League president (and the first president to hit a home run in his first Major League at-bat in 1956).

More significantly, White became the first African-American to assume such a high position in American professional sports. New commissioner Bart Giamatti, whom White replaced, had been determined to find a qualified black candidate for the position.

Louis L. Hoynes was considered because he was the legal counsel to the National League. Simon Gourdine was a former NBA deputy commissioner and for a time was considered the leading candidate. Former Reds second baseman Joe Morgan was also considered, but he was too busy with business ventures and the broadcast booth.

White at times expressed that he felt more like a figurehead while in the position, in part because commissioner Fay Vincent on occasion intervened in National League affairs. For example, in 1990 umpire Joe West had a dispute with White, and umpire chief Richie Phillips successfully arranged for Vincent to intervene. As a result of this and other incidents White considered resigning midterm but held out until his contract ended on March 31, 1993. He stayed on for another year until a successor was found.

Former Los Angeles Lakers basketball star Tommy Hawkins was for a time considered to have the inside track to replace White. He was a media relations executive with the Dodgers during the time that Dodger president Peter O'Malley led the search committee.

Leonard S. Coleman, Jr. (1948–)
Served 1994–1999

"Going to baseball games."— Coleman on the best part of the job.

The search for a new National League president finally ended in March 1994, when Coleman, also black, was named. He had been the executive director of Major League Baseball's market development department. Coleman was 45 when he took over, having been an investment banker until he joined baseball in 1991. His four-year term called for an initial salary of $450,000 per year.

Coleman played baseball and football at Princeton before working as a missionary and later as New Jersey's commissioner of energy and community affairs. He is credited with helping to revitalize baseball among inner-city youth. Coleman was applauded for his firm leadership during the difficult 1995 season and some touted him for the commissioner's job.

The league presidents' jobs were merged into the commissioner's office after the 1999 season. Coleman concluded in September 1999 that his job was irrelevant and he resigned effective after the 1999 World Series. He then took a job as an administrator under commissioner Bud Selig.

National Pastime

"It is important to remember, in an imperfect and fretful world, that we have one institution which is practically above reproach and above criticism. Nobody worth mentioning wants to change its constitution or limit its powers. The government is not asked to inspect, regulate, suppress, guarantee, or own it.

"There is no movement afoot that we know of to uplift it, like the stage, or to abolish it, like marriage. No one complains that it is vulgar, like the newspapers, or that it assassinates genius, like the magazines. It rouses no class passions and, while it has magnates, they go unhung, with our approval.

"This one comparatively perfect flower of our sadly defective civilization is — of course — baseball, the only important institution, so far as we remember, which the United States regards with a practically universal approval." — 1909 *Saturday Evening Post* editorial.

"It is well to remember that a Martian observing his first baseball game would be quite correct in concluding that the last two words of the National Anthem are: PLAY BALL!" — Herbert H. Paper in the *Cincinnati Enquirer* on April 2, 1989.

"Love America and hate baseball? Hate America and love baseball? Neither is possible, except in the abstract." — John Krich.

"Baseball, like all sports, was always show business, but no one wanted to admit it. It preferred to take the position the sport was some kind of state religion. It reveled in the designation 'the National Pastime.'" — Jim Murray.

"Well it's our game; that's the chief fact in connection with it; it has the snap, go, fling of the American atmosphere; it belongs as much to our institutions, fits into them as significantly as our Constitution's laws; it is just as important in the sum total of our historic life." — Walt Whitman.

"Baseball, to me, is still the national pastime because it is a summer game. I feel that almost all Americans are summer people, that summer is what they think of when they think of their childhood. I think it stirs up an incredible emotion within people." — Pitcher Steve Busby.

"By now the sport is edging toward marginal, long past its national-pastime prime.... But any game that insists on a Hot Stove mentality in a Microwave Age is headed for trouble." — Richard Hoffer in *Sports Illustrated*.

"And one recalls the appropriate reference to the 'World Serious,' attributed to Ring Lardner, Sr.; Ernest L. Thayer's 'Casey at the Bat'; the ring 'Tinker to Evers to Chance'; and all the other happenings, habits, and superstitions about and around baseball that made it the 'National Pastime' or, depending upon the point of view, 'the great American tragedy.'" — Supreme Court Justice Harry Blackmun in the early lines of his opinion in the Curt Flood reserve clause lawsuit. The "tragedy" reference is to a quote by George Bernard Shaw writing in *The Sporting News* in 1943.

See also *Baseball*, *Origins of Baseball* and *Popularity*.

Baseball was widely referred to as the National Pastime as early as the 1890s but was extremely popular well before that date. Baseball was called "America's National Game" as early as the 1850s and clearly by 1866 from newspaper accounts in the *New York Herald*. Paul Dickson reported in the *Dickson Baseball Dictionary* (1989) that the term was used in 1857 in a letter reprinted in a popular sports publication of the era, *Porter's Spirit of the Times*.

By the 1850s baseball was spreading rapidly. One publication noted that Brooklyn, the "City of Churches," was fast becoming the "City of Base Ball Clubs," as "all available plots" within 10 miles were used as playing fields. Contrary to the fact of baseball's pop-

ularity, *Harper's Weekly* magazine took a different view as late as 1873: "Whether baseball is a better or worse game than cricket; we do not propose to inquire, but ... we see no evidence that baseball, or any other game, is so generally practised as to be fairly called a popular American Game."

There was no real competition for baseball as a participant sport for the masses, even though horse racing was the most popular sport of the second half of the 19th century. Baseball came to dominate: boxing was illegal, football was for the young and was marked by frequent injuries and brutality, and basketball had not yet been invented (1892). Baseball was well established before the 1890s bicycle craze, which quickly died with the coming of the horseless carriage.

Another factor which added to baseball's popularity was the fervor to develop a National Game that did not come directly from another country. This was fostered by intense nationalism during and immediately following the Civil War of 1861–1865. There was also formal promotion of health and physical fitness during the Civil War, evidenced by the formation of the United States Sanitary Commission.

The Civil War fostered strong anti–British feelings due to England's support of the South, so notwithstanding the clear relationship between cricket and baseball, many leading baseball people advanced the notion that baseball was American in origin. Abraham G. Mills, fourth National League president, said that "patriotism and research" had demonstrated that baseball was American in origin and that it was truly the American National Game.

Albert Spalding promoted the notion of a National Pastime to help sell his sporting goods. Possibly the original reference to a National "Pastime" was at a banquet at Delmonico's Restaurant in New York in 1889 honoring Major League players who were returning from an international touring group. The banquet was attended by Mark Twain and future long-time U.S. Senator from New York (1899–1911), Chauncey M. Depew. Depew's presence, but not his identity, is noted by almost all historians who have chronicled the event.

An example of the fervor over baseball as the National Pastime is captured in the following 19th century verse by an unknown author: "Here's a health to our Base Ball, and honor and fame, for 'tis many and hearty and free; Oh, may it flourish our National Game — Here's a health, good old Base Ball to thee."

Baseball's status as the National Pastime was invoked during **World War I** as a reason to continue play during wartime. The War Secretary was not much impressed and baseball suffered during this period.

Losing Popularity.

"Exactly when it ceased to be [the National Pastime] is not so precisely clear. But whereas once baseball was a reflection of the pace of the times, now it is out of sync, out of step, out of date. Baseball just doesn't appeal to high school kids anymore. Why? 'B-o-r-r-r-r-ing' is the reply." — Sportswriter Bill Lyon in the mid–1990s.

"The [1994] strike also made me aware that the notion of baseball as America's Game is a myth; it's a concept packaged and sold by owners, advertisers and players to gullible consumers like myself." — Stephen M. Haskioka in a letter to *Sports Illustrated*.

"To say that football has displaced baseball as the national pastime then, is laughably inadequate, like saying that TV has now edged quilting as a popular diversion." — Steve Rushin.

See also *Popularity* for baseball's popularity in comparison to other sports.

Name. The National League, American League and Major Leagues are the only American professional sports designations that do not contain the name of the sport in their title: contrast them with the National Basketball Association, National Football League, National Hockey League and Professional Golfer's Association.

Book. National Baseball Hall of Fame and Museum, *Baseball As America: Seeing Ourselves Through Our National Game* (2002).

National Senior Baseball

This organization was created to supervise amateur players age 19 through 22. It was formed to replace the *Pony League Baseball* level for this age group, known as Thoroughbred.

The National Sports Daily (1990–1991)

"It would have been a piece of cake if we were the *Wall Street Journal* and all our games were played in the daytime."—Frank Deford referring to the short-lived tabloid's distribution problems and inability to include late night box scores in the next day's edition.

This national sports daily newspaper commenced operation on January 31, 1990, primarily to satisfy the demand for increased baseball coverage that the *USA Today* newspaper had been tapping. The publication was founded by owner Emilio Azcarraga of Mexico, a broadcast mogul. The editor and publisher was sportswriter Frank Deford. The paper started out in four cities — Los Angeles, Chicago, Philadelphia and New York, and then expanded to a few others before folding.

The paper needed circulation of 500,000 to break even, but its high was 281,000 at a 50-cent price. When the price was raised to 75 cents in January 1991, circulation dropped to 200,000.

After 393 issues and $100 million in losses, the paper folded in June 1991. Part of the problem was distribution. *The National* had contracted with the *Wall Street Journal* to distribute its papers, but the *Journal's* trucks could not wait long enough for *The National* to get all of the late night box scores in for the next morning's edition, a must for the serious fan.

Native Americans

"In the box is 'Big Chief' Bender, pitching with a will;
Husky Meyers, nifty Redskin, waits to catch the pill. Firewater
   guards the first sack, second's Blue Nose's place;
short field's watched by Roaring Thunder, third by Ugly Face.
Flathead, Snakeskin and young Jim Thorpe, clever, fast and fit.
Caper in the outer pastures killing each long hit.
Cherokee, Piute, Apache, Injuns one and all,
Seminole, Choctaw and Moqui playing star baseball."— Ed
   Goewey in *Leslie's Illustrated Weekly* newspaper of March 18, 1915.

"[He] has given up the tomahawk and the scalping knife to don the mask and chest protector to judge the diamond plays. He is as good an umpire as his father was a fighter."—*Sporting Life* in August 1906 reporting that Sitting Bull, Jr., son of the famous chief, was a baseball umpire.

"Part Indian and part first baseman."— Sportswriter Tom Meany on clumsy Rudy York, who was part Native American and a mediocre first baseman.

"Birdie Cree, Squanto Wilson, Cherokee Fisher, Cesar Geronimo"

Nickname. Most Native Americans who played baseball suffered the indignity of the nickname "Chief." This occurred as late as the 1950s, when Allie Reynolds won 182 games for the Yankees and was known as "Superchief."

Early Play. One 1837 document referenced baseball played by Native Americans.

Earliest Known Major Leaguer. Although Louis Sockalexis is generally regarded as the first-known Native American to play in the Major Leagues, at least one source cites the first as James Madison "Jim" Toy, who played briefly in the American Association in 1887 and 1890.

Louis Sockalexis.

"During one dramatic game with the White Sox, he hit a grand slam in the ninth to put the Spiders ahead by a run. Then, in storybook fashion, Sockalexis made a game-saving catch. Afterward, teammates and fans carried him off the field and demanded that he lead them in a drinking fest to celebrate the victory. Sockalexis had never tasted alcohol before, but as the months went by, he fell under its spell."— Joanna Cohen in *Sports Illustrated*.

Sockalexis was a Penobscot Indian from Maine who played at Holy Cross College, reportedly after being expelled from Notre Dame due to heavy drinking. Some sources reported that he was the first full-blooded Indian in the Major Leagues, which is false (Jim Toy probably was). Sockalexis was not a full-blooded Penobscot because the last full-blooded Penobscot died in 1853.

Sockalexis began his career with much fanfare. He hit .331 during the first half of 1897 and was touted to become one of the best hitters ever, "but then he discovered whiskey." Despite his short career, he was considered by many to have the best arm of any player in the 1890s. He hit .338 in 1897 but played in only 21 games in 1898 and seven games in 1899. After two more years in the minor leagues he was finished. He became a woodcutter and street beggar in Maine and died at age 42 in 1913. When he was found, he had some of his old news clippings inside his shirt. In 1992 Luke Salisbury wrote *The Cleveland Indian*, a fictional history of his life. See also *Cleveland Indians*—Nickname for the story of the alleged relationship of Sockalexis to the club's long-time nickname. See Brian McDonald, *Indian Summer: The Forgotten Story of Louis Sockalexis...* (2004).

Chief Bender.

"You ignorant, ill-bred foreigners! If you don't like the way I'm doing things out there, why don't you just pack up and go back to your own countries."— Bender to jeering fans.

The Hall of Fame pitcher was one-half Chippewa Indian from Minnesota and attended the Carlisle School in Pennsylvania, made famous by Jim Thorpe. The highly educated Bender ignored the "Chief" nickname and signed his name "Charley Bender." After winning 210 Major League games, Bender coached in the Major Leagues (Giants, under John McGraw), managed in the minor leagues and coached at the United States Naval Academy.

Jim Thorpe. The Sac and Fox Indian supposedly was signed to a Major League contract by Giants manager John McGraw without any information about his baseball ability. Thorpe had just successfully completed the 1912 *Olympic Games* and had played some minor league baseball (which later cost him his Olympic medals). Thorpe signed for $7,500, the largest of the five offers he received.

He was a marginal Major League player who apparently had trouble with the curveball. He also had trouble with McGraw, who sent him down to the American Association. Thorpe began his Major League career in 1913 and lasted until 1919, batting a lifetime .252. He had a high of .327 in 62 games in his final season for the Giants and Braves.

Ed Pinnance. The Canadian pitched for the A's in two games in 1903. He supposedly arrived from his hometown carrying a suitcase made from an elk he had shot with a bow and arrow. He did not make much of an impression on the field, appearing in two Major League games and compiling no record.

Chief (George Howard) Johnson. The Winnebago Indian (born in Winnebago, Nebraska — reported as Kansas in one source) compiled a 41–43 pitching record with Cincinnati of the National League and Kansas City of the Federal League.

Chief (Elon Chester) Hogsett. The left-handed pitcher compiled a 63–87 record primarily for the Tigers during the 1930s.

Chief Meyers. Meyers, who signed his name John Tortes Meyers, was a California Mission Indian who later played on a Sioux City, Iowa, reservation team along with Jim Thorpe. Meyers was a catcher who played primarily for the Giants over his nine-year career in the National League from 1909 through 1917, batting .291.

Meyers had taken advantage of a scholarship which Dartmouth College reserved for Native Americans, but left school early to pursue his baseball career. He later revealed that he had been enrolled primarily to play baseball and that he had not graduated from high school. The 5'11" athlete was enrolled at Dartmouth as 5'6" red-headed scholar Ellis Williams.

Gene Locklear. The full-blooded Cherokee batted .274 over five seasons during the mid–1970s. He played in Japan for a year and then retired to be an artist.

Ernie (Chief) Koy. Koy was an outfielder primarily for the Dodgers before and during World War II. He batted .279 over five seasons.

Jack Aker. The Potowatomie compiled a 64–74 record in 495 career appearances. He was American League Fireman of the Year in 1966 while with the A's.

Cal McLish. His full name was Calvin Coolidge Julius Caesar Tuskamoha McLish; he was nicknamed Buster. He had seven brothers and sisters, and he was the only one his father was allowed to name.

Pepper Martin. The Cardinals outfielder and third baseman was a part–Native American born in Oklahoma and was known as "The Wild Hoss of the Osage."

Willie Stargell. The Pirates outfielder highlighted his Seminole heritage in his autobiography, *Willie Stargell*, with Tom Bird (1984).

Jim Willoughby. The 1970s Red Sox pitcher was a descendant of the Potawatomie Indians.

John Henry Johnson. The 1980s pitcher was a descendant of the Potawatomie Indians.

Johnny Bench. The 1970s catcher is part–Cherokee.

Others. Other players of Native American descent: Thurman Tucker, Early Wynn, Zack Wheat, Virgil Trucks, Joseph Tipton, Richard "Red" Smith, Nippy Jones, Howard Francis Fox, Clifford Fannin, Gene Bearden.

Passing Off as "Indian." It was the occasional practice in the late 19th and early 20th centuries to attempt to pass off black players as "Indian" or "Cuban" to avoid baseball's segregation rules. John McGraw orchestrated perhaps the most famous of these efforts.

McGraw discovered a ballplaying black bellhop in 1901 while at spring training in Hot Springs, Arkansas. Charles Grant was a light-skinned black second baseman. McGraw signed Grant and billed him as "Chief Tokohama, a full-blooded Cherokee Indian." The ruse worked during spring training for a short time until White Sox owner Charles Comiskey recognized Grant as having played for a Chicago-area team. He blew the whistle and McGraw's ploy ended before the season began.

Jim Thorpe, the most famous Native American athlete of all time, usually noted for his Olympic Games success and NFL football play. Nevertheless, he lasted six seasons as a Major League outfielder in the 1910s, primarily with the New York Giants.

General Custer. Reportedly there is evidence that General Custer's troops played baseball shortly before they were wiped out at the Little Big Horn in 1876.

Mascot Controversy.

"We were all rooting for the Reds and the Mariners." — Native American leader Vernon Bellecourt before the Braves and Indians won their respective League Championship Series against the Reds and Mariners.

There has been controversy over the use of Native American symbols as mascots. The issue came to a head during the success of the Atlanta Braves in the early 1990s. The club's mascot was Chief Noc-A-Homa and Braves fans began using the "Tomahawk Chop" as a rallying sign. The National Coalition of Racism in Sports and the Media was active in the fight to ban the Chop. Notwithstanding the controversy, the Braves did nothing to change the Chop, the chants or the mascot. The issue resurfaced when the Braves faced the Indians in the 1995 World Series.

In 1969 the Braves had an authentic Native American as Chief Noc-A-Homa III. He was Levi Walker, Jr., an Algonquin Indian.

Book. Joseph B. Oxendine, *American Indian Sports Heritage* (1988).

Negro Baseball Awards

"If you came here thinking you were going to see an old bitter black man, you're in the wrong place. I am old, I am black, but I'm not bitter because I played with, and against, some of the greatest athletes that ever walked the land. They just happened to be black." — Buck O'Neil on receiving the first Negro Baseball Lifetime Achievement Award, which was to bear his name in future years. The award was inaugurated in 1994 at a dinner held in New York City. Dave Winfield received the Josh Gibson Professional Achievement Award for his excellence on the field and commitment to causes outside the game. O'Neil was popular with many black stars of the Major Leagues as a mentor and inspiration: "He is a role model, a father, a mentor, a teacher, a sensei, a hero, a gentleman, a man. Who do you think I got my let's-play-two attitude from? From Buck O'Neil, that's who."—Ernie Banks, who played for O'Neil when he coached for the Cubs in the early 1960.

Negro Leagues

"Black baseball was a stone hard gig. It was three games a day, sometimes in three different towns miles apart. It was the heat and fumes and bounces from buses that moved your stomach up to your throat and it was greasy meals at fly-papered diners at three a.m. and uniforms that were seldom off your back."—Sportswriter Mark Kram in *Sports Illustrated*.

"Most of our baseball was run by gangsters. They were slick and slippery and sometimes dangerous. I didn't trust very many of them."—New York Black Yankees outfielder Clint Thomas quoted in *The Pittsburgh Crawfords*, by James Bankes (1991).

See individual entries for Negro League stars who have been elected to the Hall of Fame and entries for key Negro League teams.

Early Teams. One usually reliable source cited the earliest black team as the Pythians of Philadelphia, who defeated the City Items 27–17 on September 18, 1869. However, other sources noted that in 1867 black teams staged "Colored Championships" in Brooklyn, suggesting that black teams had been organized for at least a few years. Other top black teams of the era were the Philadelphia Excelsiors, Brooklyn Uniques and Brooklyn Monitors.

One of the first paid all-black teams was an 1885 group of black waiters recruited by waiter Frank Thompson at the Argyle Hotel in Babylon, Long Island. They spoke gibberish to fool whites into thinking they were Spanish and called themselves the Cuban Giants. In 1886 they defeated the Cincinnati Red Stockings of the American Association. In 1887 the club lost 6–4 to National League champion Detroit.

Early Leagues. The Southern League of Colored Base Ballists was formed in 1886 in Florida, but it never got off the ground.

In late 1886 writer Walter S. Brown of Pittsburgh announced the formation of the National Colored Base Ball League. It had a brief but widely publicized existence. Beginning in March 1887, the league featured the Cincinnati Browns, Pittsburgh Keystones, Capital Citys of Washington, Boston Resolutes, Falls City of Louisville, the Lord Baltimores, Philadelphia Pythians and New York Gorhams.

The players sometimes played in full dress suits to please the crowds. The league lasted for less than a month but was recognized by Organized Baseball as part of the National Agreement.

20th Century Leagues.

"Experts who have seen the Negro games in Chicago this year have been astonished at their wonderful progress and development, and now class some of the Negro teams with the best there is in the regular major leagues."—*The Sporting News* editor J.G. Taylor Spink.

There were five organized Negro Leagues in the 20th century:
Negro National League (1920–1930, 1933–1948)
Eastern Colored League (1923–1928)
Negro American League (1929, 1937–1950)
Negro Southern League (1932)
Negro East-West League (1932)

On February 13, 1920, the National Association of Colored Professional Base Ball Clubs (otherwise known as the Negro National League) was founded in Kansas City, Missouri. Former Chicago Lelands pitcher and future Hall of Famer Andrew "Rube" Foster, whom Honus Wagner called the "smartest pitcher ever," founded the league.

The original eight clubs in the midwest-based Negro National League were the American Giants (Chicago), Chicago Giants, Cuban Stars, Detroit Stars, St. Louis Stars, Indianapolis ABCs, Kansas City Monarchs and Dayton Marcos. Associate members were the Philadelphia Hilldales and the Atlantic City Bacharach Giants.

By the late 1920s, the Negro National League had declined to the point that the only viable franchises were in Detroit, Kansas City and St. Louis. The Eastern Colored League (ECL) was failing after more than five years, and it was replaced by the American Negro Baseball League (ANBL) in 1929. The independent Homestead Grays joined the few remaining ECL teams to establish the ANBL, but it folded in 1930. By 1931, near the bottom of the Depression, the Cuban Winter League failed and the Negro National League collapsed, ending the first era of organized Negro League baseball.

World Series Challenge. In 1906 the black Philadelphia X-Giants challenged the winner of the Major League World Series, but the white teams declined to play.

Latin Leagues. Most Negro Leaguers played winter ball in the Caribbean or Mexican leagues or barnstormed against Latin clubs.

Exhibitions/Black Versus White. Between 1887 and 1947 there were 432 recorded exhibition games played between black and white teams. Of those that were recorded, the black teams had a record of 266–166. As a result of the black teams' dominance in the 1930s, Judge Landis ruled that no more than three Major League players could be on an exhibition team roster against a black club and that the players could not wear their Major League uniforms. It does not appear that the rule was regularly enforced. Other sources report it more specifically: In the 1920s, pitcher Smokey Joe Williams and his team, the Lincoln Giants, supposedly shut out the National League champion Philadelphia Phillies 1 to 0 in an exhibition game in New York after the World Series. After that, no more exhibition games between whole Major League teams and black teams were permitted. This probably occurred in 1915, when Williams was at the height of his prowess, and the Phillies only won a pennant in 1915 and never in the 1920s.

Negro League All-Star Game. A Negro League All-Star game was first held in 1933, the same year as the first Major League All-Star Game. Both games were played at Chicago's Comiskey Park and the Negro League game became so popular that it regularly drew crowds of 50,000.

Attendance. Negro League games in Washington, D.C., in the 1930s routinely outdrew the Senators by 20,000 fans.

Negro World Series. The Kansas City Monarchs won the first Negro World Series, played in 1924. The last Negro World Series was played in 1948. The Washington Homestead Grays beat the Birmingham Black Barons.

Best Pitchers.

"There was no better teammate than Chet Brewer. He wanted to win so bad. He'll do anything to win. All the fellows respect him for that. There's no one like him. There were games he just refused to lose. He was so strong-willed. He had total concentration on the mound."—Second baseman Newt Allen on the pitcher who is reported to have won more than 600 games in the Negro Leagues between 1925 and 1948. The San Diego Padres staged a "Night" for him in 1989.

Satchel Paige (HF). Paige is acknowledged by many as the greatest Negro League pitcher of all time. He was placed on the *Pittsburgh Courier*'s all-time Negro League all-star team.

Dave Barnhill. Barnhill was a 130-pound sawed-off version of Paige and was said to be as fast as Paige.

Bill Foster (HF) is thought to be the best left-handed pitcher of the Negro Leagues.

Joe Williams (HF) was a stellar pitcher in the 1910s into the 1930s.

Hilton Smith (HF), though playing most of his career in Satchel Paige's shadow, the Hall of Famer starred for the Kansas City Monarchs with 20 wins or more in 12 seasons.

Bullet Joe Rogan (HF) pitched in the U.S. Army for several years before joining the Kansas City Monarchs in 1920.

Best Catchers.

Josh Gibson (HF). The Hall of Famer is another player considered by many to be the greatest player in the history of the Negro Leagues.

Biz Mackey. Mackey was viewed by many as the greatest defensive catcher of the Negro Leagues. He perfected the snap throw from the sitting position and taught the fine points to future Dodger catcher Roy Campanella.

Bruce Petway. Petway once threw out Ty Cobb three times in one game.

Best First Baseman.

Buck Leonard (HF). Leonard is the only Negro League first baseman enshrined in the Hall of Fame. He was dubbed the black Lou Gehrig while playing primarily for the Homestead Grays.

Best Second Basemen.

Martin DiHigo (HF). DiHigo is thought to be one of the best all-around players of all time at a number of positions, including pitcher, but on some lists he is the best second baseman.

Sammy Hughes. Hughes, considered one of the best of the Negro League second basemen, had a tryout scheduled with the Pirates in 1943 along with Roy Campanella, but the club reneged.

Newt Allen. Allen played for the Kansas City Monarchs from 1920 through 1948, batting .293 in 640 recorded games. Against Major League pitchers he batted .301 in 24 known games.

Bingo DeMoss. DeMoss was regarded as the top second baseman of the early 20th century.

Best Shortstops.

John Henry "Pop" Lloyd (HF) is acknowledged by some as the greatest baseball player of all time, white or black. The Hall of Famer was known as the Black Honus Wagner during his 26-year career. Wagner once commented that "it's a privilege to have been compared to him." Connie Mack once said: "Put Lloyd and Wagner in the same bag and whichever one you pulled out, you wouldn't go wrong."

In 29 known games against white Major Leaguers, Lloyd batted .321. Babe Ruth believed that the "greatest player anywhere" was Lloyd. Mrs. John McGraw had a collection of writings from her husband. They included a notation that he would have, if allowed, signed Negro Leaguers Pop Lloyd, Hall of Famer Willie Wells, Dick Redding and Spottswood Poles.

Best Third Basemen.

Ray Dandridge (HF). Dandridge batted a known .335 over his Negro and Mexican League career and was elected to the Hall of Fame in 1987.

Judy Johnson (HF). The Hall of Famer played 21 years at third base in the Negro Leagues, ending his career with the Pittsburgh Crawfords in 1938.

Best Outfielders.

Spottswood Poles. The Lincoln Giants featured Spottswood Poles, known as the "Black Ty Cobb." He was considered one of the best early 20th century Negro League players during most of his career from 1909 through 1923. He is said to have batted over .600 against white Major Leaguers.

Oscar Charleston (HF). The Hall of Famer was also known as the "Black Ty Cobb" and his modern counterpart is said to have been Willie Mays. His known batting average over 26 years was around .350, including an average over .400 in 1925.

Cool Papa Bell (HF). Hall of Famer James Thomas "Cool Papa" Bell played 25 years, with a known batting average of at least .330.

Hall of Fame. The following Negro League stars have made it into the Hall of Fame (through 2004), having been chosen initially by a special Negro League Committee (the first nine, one at each position) and then by the regular Veterans Committee (the last four) (See also *Hall of Fame*):

Satchel Paige, P (1971)
Josh Gibson, C (1972)
Buck Leonard, 1B (1972)
Monte Irvin, RF (1973)
Cool Papa Bell, LF (1974)
Judy Johnson, 3B (1975)
Oscar Charleston, CF (1976)
Martin DiHigo, 2B (1977)
John Henry "Pop" Lloyd, SS (1977)
Andrew "Rube" Foster, executive (1981)
Ray Dandridge, 3B (1987)
Leon Day, P (1995)
Bill Foster, P (1996)
Willie Wells, SS (1997)
Bullet Joe Rogan, P (1998)
Joe Williams, P (1999)
Turkey Stearnes, CF (2000)
Hilton Smith, P (2001)

Number of Players. About 3,200 men (and three women) played in the Negro Leagues, with less than 300 still alive by 1995. Although some sources report the figure as 285 (the number who received merchandise royalty checks in 1995), others say the figure was substantially lower, possibly 140 at most.

Tribute. On July 15, 2001, to celebrate Negro League Tribute Day, teams around the Major Leagues wore uniforms from the Negro League clubs. The Mets wore New York Cubans uniforms. Their opponents, the Blue Jays, wore the uniforms of the Chatham All-Stars. The Pirates wore the Homestead Grays uniforms and the Royals wore Kansas City Monarchs uniforms.

Negro League Hall of Fame and Baseball Reunion.

The first Negro Baseball Reunion was held in 1981 and brought together a number of Negro League players. The event coincided with an unsuccessful effort to establish a Negro League Hall of Fame in Ashland, Kentucky. In the early 1990s a Negro League Hall of Fame opened in Kansas City at 1601 E. 18th Street. The upgraded Negro League Museum opened in 1997 in Kansas City, moving from the temporary site on 18th Street in Washington D.C.

A new Negro League Legends Hall of Fame is scheduled to open in 2006 in Washington, D.C. It was to feature individual players more than the leagues.

Negro League Baseball Players Association, Inc. (NLBPA). This organization was formed in 1989 by music producer Richard Berg and New York attorney Ed Schander to promote and support Negro League ballplayers. Money is raised through card shows, exhibition games and corporate sponsorship. The first meeting was held in Baltimore in 1989 and the group initially had 80 members.

In 1993 Reggie Jackson's brother James was named president of the Negro League Baseball Players Association and the organization moved its headquarters to Carlsbad, California. James was ousted only a few months later.

Oldest. "Double Duty" Radcliffe, whose formal name was Theodore Roosevelt Radcliffe, turned 100 in 2003. He played primarily in the 1930s for an array of talented Negro League teams, including the St. Louis Stars (1930), the Homestead Grays (1931) and Pittsburgh Crawfords (1932).

Best 20th Century Teams. The Chicago Leland Giants and the New York Leland Giants were two excellent early 20th century teams organized by Frank C. Leland and led by Negro League founder Rube Foster. The Chicago American Giants had Smokey Joe Williams, who was 41–3 in 1914.

The key Negro League teams of the 1920s through the 1940s were the Birmingham Black Barons, Homestead Grays, Kansas City Monarchs, Pittsburgh Crawfords, Chattanooga Black Lookouts, Baltimore Elite Giants, Nashville Elite Giants, and New Orleans Black Pelicans.

The all-time best Negro League team may have been the 1936 Pittsburgh Crawfords of the Negro National League. The club featured future Hall of Famers Satchel Paige, Cool Papa Bell, Oscar Charleston, Josh Gibson and Judy Johnson.

The Newark Eagles operated in the Negro National League primarily in the 1930s and 1940s. The team was owned by Abe Manley, a "numbers" king, and his wife Effa, who apparently was white. She had a part in the development of the batting helmet. She passed for a light-skinned black, acting as a leader of the league and selling a number of players to the Major Leagues. The Eagles featured a few future Major League stars, including Don Newcombe, Larry Doby and Monte Irvin.

Owners. Rutherford Hayes Jones owned the Washington Giants in the early 20th century. In 2004 researchers discovered a suitcase owned by Jones that contained several artifacts from the Negro Leagues, including box scores, umpire salaries, receipts for team operation and numerous photos.

Kansas City Monarchs owner J. Leslie Wilkinson was the only acknowledged white owner in the early Negro Leagues. Effa Manley of the Newark Eagles apparently was white, though at times she passed for a light-skinned black woman during the 1930s and 1940s when she and her husband owned the Eagles. She was a leader in the desegregation of Harlem's department stores in the 1930s. See James Overmyer, *Queen of the Negro Leagues: Effa Manley and the Newark Eagles* (1998).

Some of the later eastern Negro clubs were owned by whites: Jim Keenan in New York; Nat Strong in Brooklyn; Charlie Spedden in Baltimore; and Tom Jackson in Atlantic City.

Celebrity Owners. In the 1930s, entertainers Cab Calloway and Louis Armstrong sponsored Negro teams. Armstrong's team was the "Secret Nine."

Future Major Leaguers. All of the early black Major Leaguers from the late 1940s and early 1950s initially played in the Negro Leagues. Frank Robinson, who broke into the Major Leagues in 1955, played for the Kansas City Monarchs. The Cubs purchased Ernie Banks from the Monarchs for $20,000 after he played one season in 1950, and he began his Major League career in 1953. Henry Aaron played for the Indianapolis Clowns in 1952 before signing with the Braves.

There were 72 Negro League players who made it to the Major Leagues in 1947 or later. The last was Ike Brown, who played for the Kansas City Monarchs in the early 1960s (long after the Negro Leagues were dead) and first played for the Tigers in June 1969. Eleven other Negro Leaguers played 20th century Major League Baseball before formal integration in 1947, but all were Latin players. The last active Major Leaguer to have played in the Negro Leagues was Henry Aaron, who retired in 1976.

Salaries. At the turn of the century, the average white player earned $2,000 per season, while the top black stars earned less than $500. It has been reported that Negro Leaguers earned approximately $230 per month in the 1920s. In the 1930s Monte Irvin earned about $150 a month with $1 a day for meal money. The average salary at the time reportedly was $170 per month. In 1937 Satchel Paige reportedly earned $350 per month.

Negro League players earned between $125 and $300 per month in the early 1940s, which was supplemented by winter ball salaries. In the mid–1940s Buck Leonard supposedly was the third-highest paid Negro League star at $10,000, behind only Josh Gibson and Satchel Paige.

Fathers and Sons. See *Fathers and Sons* for those Negro League players whose sons played in the Major Leagues.

Commemoration. In 1995 only the Seattle Mariners wore a patch to honor the 75th anniversary of the beginning of the Negro Leagues.

Books.

"Far from the least of the blacks' suffering arose from the maltreatment by Organized Baseball of black baseball players and leagues, recorded in accounts by Robert Peterson in his pioneer study, *Only the Ball Was White*, and in other praiseworthy books by John Holway, William Rogosin, Janet Bruce, and Rob Ruck."— Harold Seymour in *Baseball: The People's Game* (1990).

Bruce Chadwick, *When the Game Was Black and White: History of Baseball's Negro Leagues* (1992); Dick Clark and Larry Lester, *The Negro Leagues Book* (1994), with an extensive bibliography; Phil Dixon with Patrick J. Hannigan, *The Negro Leagues: A Photographic History* (1993) (photographs back to 1867); Wilmer Fields, *My Life in the Negro Leagues* (1992); John B. Holway, *Blackball Stars* (1988); John B. Holway, *Black Diamonds* (1989); John B. Holway, *Voices from the Great Black Baseball Leagues* (1975); Neil Lanctot, *Fair Dealing and Clean Playing: The Hilldale Club and the Development of Black Professional Baseball 1910–1932* (1994); Neil Lanctot, *Negro League Baseball: The Rise and Ruin of a Black Institution* (2004); Buck O'Neil with Steve Wulf, *I Was Right on Time* (1995); Robert Peterson, *Only the Ball Was White: A History of Legendary Black Players and All-Black Professional Teams* (1970); Robert D. Retort, *Pictorial Negro League Legends Album* (1992); Mark Ribowsky, *A Complete History of the Negro Leagues, 1884 to 1955* (1995); James A. Riley (ed.), *The Biographical Encyclopedia of the Negro Baseball Leagues* (1994); Donn Rogosin, *Invisible Men: Life in Baseball's Negro Leagues* (1983); Sol White, *History of Colored Baseball* (1907; reprinted in 1984 — White (1868–1948) was a 19-year-old black second baseman in 1887 when black players were barred from Organized Baseball); see also negroleaguebaseball.com.

Netherlands

"The only thing I know about it is that it's in New Jersey."— Dutch national team catcher Michael Crouhel after signing with the Phillies, on the location of Philadelphia. Crouhel never made it to the Major Leagues.

"Petey ... turned to face a muscled, black-haired guy at the tail end of his thirties. Half a head shorter than she, he had hard arms coming from a red golf shirt open to a hairy collarbone. If he wasn't Italian, then Rico Petrocelli was Dutch."— From *Fear in Fenway*, by Crabbe Evers (1993).

The Netherlands is one of two European countries (with Italy) to have decent amateur baseball teams. Baseball, known as *Honkbal*, was introduced in 1910 by physical education instructor J.C.G.

Grase after he returned from the United States. He was responsible for establishing the Dutch Baseball Federation in 1912. The Netherlands has won the most European Championships since the event started in 1954, but has not done well in international competition outside Europe.

Dutch baseball is organized at the club level. Three hundred clubs are active, with the highest level of play the 10-team *hoofdklasse*, or major league, which plays 45 games over a typical April–September season. Each club is allowed two American players.

Win Remmerswaal of the Netherlands played for the Red Sox, becoming the first Major League Baseball player to spend his entire amateur career in Europe. He won three games in two years for the Red Sox in 1979 and 1980.

In 1993 the Giants called up outfielder Rikkert Faneyte of the Netherlands. He hit .133 in seven games.

Netherlands-born Bert Blyleven returned to his homeland in 1993 to pitch in an international tournament. He had made an aborted attempt to return to the Major Leagues that spring, only 13 wins shy of 300.

In 2003 former Major League manager Davey Johnson led the Dutch national baseball team to its 18th European Championship with a win over Greece. Johnson agreed to manage the Dutch team after regular manager Robert Eenhoorn resigned following the death of his young son from cancer.

At the 2004 Olympic Games, the Dutch team won two games, including a win over Italy, but lost to Australia 22–2 and did not make it into the medal round.

New Haven Elm Citys

National Association 1875
"New Haven's continued existence was more of a tribute to their staying power than to ability…. The team began to gel as the season progressed, managing to add six more victories to the initial win to finish the campaign with a rousing 7–40 mark."—William J. Ryczek in *Blackguards and Red Stockings* (1992).

The club finished last in the league with a 7–40 record, 48 games out of first place.

New Orleans

"New Orleans is one of the two most ingrown, self-obsessed little cities in the United States. The other is San Francisco."—Screenwriter and director Nora Ephron.

"Arrive at New Orleans, a city of ships, steamers, flatboats, rafts, mud, fog, filth, stench, and a mixture of races and tongues."—President Rutherford B. Hayes.

This was one of many strong Southern baseball towns, with over 30 clubs as early as 1870. Baseball was fast becoming the popular pastime of the southern portion of the country. The South was also a strong baseball area before the **Civil War**, and it is more myth than fact that Confederate troops first learned the game from Union troops in prison camps.

New York

"There is no place like it, no place with an atom of its glory, pride, and exultancy. It lays its hand upon a man's bowels; he grows drunk with ecstasy; he grows young and full of glory, he feels that he can never die."—Thomas Wolfe.

"In a market like New York, there's a lot of pressure to win, and there's a lack of patience on the part of the fans to wait and see a player develop into a bona fide major leaguer. They'd rather have someone who has a name and can put people in their seats."—Steve Boros interviewed by Richard Grossinger in *The Temple of Baseball* (1985).

The earliest reference to baseball being played in the city was discovered in 2000, and pushed back the earliest known date to 1823. A number of amateur and professional teams have represented New York City, which was the primary cradle of modern baseball (see also **Amateur Teams** and **Brooklyn**):

Giants. The name eventually given to New York's second National League entry, which began play in the league in 1883 and left after the 1957 season.

The 1890 New York Players League entry was also known as the Giants.

Gothams. The name of an early amateur club team and the original name of the 1883 National League entry that eventually was named the Giants.

Highlanders. The original name of the American League entry that began play in 1903 and was later known as the Yankees.

Knickerbockers. An early amateur club team that first played in the 1840s and was dormant by the late 1860s and extinct by at least the 1880s.

Manhattans. An early amateur club composed of city policemen.

Mutuals. An early amateur club team composed primarily of firemen from the Mutual Hook & Ladder Co. No. 1.

A club of the same name was a member of the 1871–1875 National Association and later a charter member of the National League in 1876. The team lasted one year. New York returned to the National League in 1883 with entirely new ownership and a name, the Gothams, which was soon changed to Giants.

Metropolitans/Mets. An amateur club of the 1860s. There was also a future American Association club formed in September 1880 known as the Metropolitans. That club operated in the American Association from 1883 through 1887. Metropolitans is also the formal name of the modern National League New York Mets, who began play in 1962.

Phantoms. An early amateur club team composed primarily of bookkeepers.

Unions. One source identified a club known as the New York Unions as a member of the 1884 Union Association. No such club existed; nor was there any Union Association entry in the entire state of New York.

Yankees. Eventual name of the American League Highlanders.

All Clubs. Darryl Strawberry is the only player in Major League history to have played for all teams with New York ties: the Dodgers, Giants, Yankees and Mets.

Interleague Play. The first regular-season game between the Yankees and Mets was played on June 16, 1997, as the Mets won 6–0 at Yankee Stadium. The Yankees won the last two games of the series, which drew 168,719.

Book. Harvey Frommer, *Big Apple Baseball: An Illustrated History from the Boroughs to the Ballparks* (1995).

New York Game

This version of baseball began with the Knickerbockers and other local clubs in New York in the 1840s. It ultimately prevailed over other versions such as the **Massachusetts Game**. The essential differences were the configuration of the field and the ability to "soak" runners in the Massachusetts Game. Soaking consisted of throwing the ball at the runner while off base to make an out.

The New York Game field was virtually identical to modern playing configurations. Thirty yards separated the bases, and home plate was referred to as "Home Base." Fifteen yards separated home base and the pitcher's point. The bases were one-foot squares and the batter's box was referred to as the "Striker's Point."

Four New York clubs dominated the New York Game by 1854: the Knickerbockers, Gothams (originally the Washington club), Eagles and Empire Club. By the end of the 1850s, four Brooklyn clubs were also dominant: the Excelsiors, Putnams, Eckfords and Atlantics. Outside of New York City, the New York Game was strongest in Buffalo and Albany through the 1850s.

New York Giants

National League 1883–1957

"Giant fans were a different, more sophisticated, breed. Not for us were the emotional excesses or theatrics of the Dodger fan or the quiet calm of the Yankee adherents. Our elders had participated in McGraw's and Mathewson's victories before and after World War I and the Giants' championships of the 1920's. We, their lineal descendants, shared with quiet dignity in the Giants' hard-won titles in the 1930's and in the miseries of the team after those great years." — Fred Stein in *Under Coogan's Bluff* (1978).

"The Giants, the most intelligent, the quickest, strongest, and grittiest combination of baseball players that ever represented this city in any league, demonstrated beyond quibble paramount superiority over anything extant in diamond life today..." — Lloyd Lewis of the *New York Times* on the Giants' 1905 World Series victory.

Origins. The Giants were created in early 1883 and were known originally as the New York Gothams. They were the National League's 18th team, filling the spot vacated by Troy, New York, when Troy owner John Day brought his team to New York City.

Casey Stengel with the early 1920s New York Giants (and could be played by actor Ben Kingsley).

First Game. The Giants played their first game on May 2, 1883, in front of 15,000 fans. They defeated the Boston Red Stockings 7–5.

Key Owners.

John B. Day/1883–1894. The original New York Giants owner was John B. Day, active in local Democratic Tammany Hall politics. Day was a wholesale tobacco merchant who had pitched on a team he organized in Orange, New York. Day and his brother-in-law Joseph Gordon (later part owner of the Yankees) also concurrently owned the rival American Association New York Metropolitans.

An 1898 newspaper article in the *Brooklyn Times* reported that in the early 1880s the New York Metropolitans were playing an exhibition when Day, not associated with the club, asked if he could try his hand at pitching. After a miserable showing he was replaced after one or two innings. The article reported that after the game Day told Metropolitans manager Jimmy Clinton that he wanted to invest in a baseball venture. Jim Mutrie, "out of a job and disconsolate," was "hanging about the grounds on that day." Within a week Mutrie and Day had a partnership and a new club.

The American Association and National League fields were side-by-side in New York, with only a canvas fence separating them. The American Association manager was also under contract to the Giants (Mutrie), and he was accused of spying for the National League at early American Association meetings. Even though the American Association Metropolitans won the 1884 pennant, Day switched the two best players from that club to the Giants, Tim Keefe and Tom "Dude" Esterbrook. He also moved Mutrie over to manage the National League club.

Day struggled financially due to the proximity of a National League club in Brooklyn and rival clubs in the American Association. In 1890 Day was offered the presidency of the new Players League, but declined. The Players League further hurt Day's financial situation and he received loans from National League owners Arthur Soden of Boston, Albert Spalding of Chicago and John Brush of Cincinnati. This was the prime example of Syndicate Ball (see also **Cross-Ownership**), a major topic of discussion in that era. Soden made a $60,000 loan and his family received dividends on that investment well into the 20th century.

When the Players League folded after the 1890 season, its Brooklyn and New York franchises sold out to Day and his new partners. Day continued to own both the American Association and National League franchises through the Metropolitan Exhibition Company. The American Association franchise folded with the rest of the league after the 1891 season.

Day lost control of the Giants by 1894 due to financial problems but continued in the front office through the end of the decade. He even managed the club briefly in 1899 (29–35 in 66 games). He later became an inspector of players and umpires for the league. Although Day spent years building up baseball in New York, by 1923 he was almost broke, paralyzed and living in a one-room Manhattan apartment with his dying wife.

Andrew Freedman/1895–1903.

"Freedman is like a spoilt child when opposed. He will, metaphorically, throw himself on the floor and kick up his heels and refuse to play. He needs a spanking, and the press has spanked him hard, but like the parson's son, he refused to be good, and the other magnate boys have gone over to his yard to play, and taken with them all kinds of sweetmeats to conciliate their pouting playmate." — Early 20th century New York sportswriter.

"An astonishing faculty for making enemies." — *New York World* newspaper.

"George Steinbrenner on Quaaludes." — Baseball historian Bill James.

By 1894 the Giants were nearly broke and owner John Day had given away most of the stock in the club to raise cash. This enabled a number of influential people to own a piece of the club: Albert Spalding and his brother Walter; Arthur Soden, who owned the Boston Red Stockings; Cincinnati owner John Brush; Tammany Hall politico and Giants owner Andrew Freedman; and Edward Talcott, who had backed the Players League.

Freedman bought increasingly larger blocks of the club's stock, often purportedly as agent for James A. Bailey of the Barnum & Bailey Circus. Freedman took control of the club in early 1895 after sweeping into political power during the 1894 reform elections in the city, though he did not directly assume any of the elected or appointed positions.

Born in 1860 (died 1915) and a lifelong bachelor, Freedman attended City College of New York and made his fortune from real estate and transit contracts in "devious" means "no longer traceable" (*Dictionary of American Biography*). He is identified as an attorney in some sources. He later earned much of his income through his Tammany Hall connections that enabled him to receive a percentage of the insurance premiums paid by the city for its casualty insurance. He was instrumental in developing the city's infrastructure of subways and roads.

Freedman was the terror of the National League almost from the outset of his control of the Giants. As a result, rival minority owner John Brush attempted to seize control as early as 1896. Freedman also feuded with Brooklyn's owners, which in part led to a merger of the Brooklyn and Baltimore interests to bring the best players to Brooklyn. Freedman controlled the efforts to build the New York City subway lines in the 1890s and did his best to prevent them from stopping at any of the proposed ballpark sites that the Brooklyn club might have wanted.

By early 1902 Freedman had lost the support of the other owners and fans. Freedman lost his Tammany Hall influence after the November 1901 elections in New York City, when a reform slate reordered the power structure. He was fighting with umpires, insulting the other owners, banning newspapers critical of him and firing managers arbitrarily. Cap Anson had managed for him for three weeks in 1898, but quit in disgust with a 9–13 record.

After more internal club disputes and a league power struggle early in the 20th century (see also *National League*), Freedman sold out in early 1903. He was forced to sell control of the club to John Brush and to provide suitable land for building a ballpark for the American League franchise. One source reported that the only concession he received was that he could select the ownership of the American League team that was to be placed in New York. More accurately, he used his political influence to tie up all available ballpark sites until a compromise was reached.

John Brush and Heirs/1903–1919. John T. Brush, owner of the When Department Stores, exerted power over the club's direction due to his minority stock ownership in the 1890s. He persuaded John McGraw to manage the club midway through the 1902 season. However, McGraw's move was part of a larger plan that involved compromises between the National and American leagues and resulted in the placement of an American League club in New York. Brush also owned stock in the Cincinnati Reds and originally operated a club in Indianapolis.

In late 1902 or early 1903 the despised Andrew Freedman gave up and sold a majority interest to Brush for $200,000 ($125,000 in some sources, but this may have been Brush's share; along with minority owners the total may have been $200,000). Brush received a loan for some of the purchase price from the Fleischmanns of Cincinnati (of margarine fame).

Brush was a popular owner and theater people such as Douglas Fairbanks began attending games. Lillian Russell, the "sex pot of her day," also attended games. Brush, who retained stock in the Reds, owned the Giants until he died on November 12, 1912, of locomotor ataxia, which had confined him to a wheelchair.

Brush left the team to his wife and daughters. Harry Hempstead, who was one of Brush's clothing company officials and was married to one of his two daughters, took over official leadership of the club. Hempstead, co-executor of Brush's will, left the operations to club secretary John B. Foster. N. Ashley Lloyd of Norwood, Ohio, also owned a piece of the club.

Eddie Brannick was 12 years old when he was hired by Brush to help with the scoreboard. He spent 65 years as a Giants employee and ultimately became the club secretary.

Charles Stoneham/1919–1936. Harry Hempstead advised John Brush's daughters to sell in January 1919 for slightly over $1 million. This turned out to be a rock-bottom price because the economy was just about to explode in the early 1920s. One source reported that the sale apparently was made because of fears that wartime restrictions would force the team into debt. The deal was entered into shortly before the war ended on November 11, 1918, and closed early the next year.

On January 14, 1919, the club was formally sold to Wall Street stockbroker Charles A. Stoneham, along with Giants manager John McGraw and Judge Francis X. McQuade. Stoneham was unknown to baseball people, but was well known in Tammany Hall circles. Before the sale to Stoneham, McGraw had discussed the purchase of the club with former Federal League owner and oil magnate Harry Sinclair.

Stoneham purportedly paid $750,000 for his interest and contractor William Kenny purchased a block of shares, leaving Stoneham with control over slightly more than half the stock. Other sources report that Stoneham paid $1 million for 1,300 shares of the team's stock. John McGraw bought 70 shares for $50,000 and Francis McQuade also bought 70 shares for the same price and became the treasurer. Hempstead retained a small portion of the stock.

Stoneham ran the club through the prosperous 1920s, though McGraw's glory days had ended by the mid–1920s. Stoneham then suffered through the Depression before his death in 1936.

Horace Stoneham/1936–1957.

"Almost one-half of the Giant team was of German extraction, an overbalance that lends credence to the theory that Horace Stoneham admired more than anything else in his ballplayers the qualities of obedience, thoroughness, and discipline, however colorless they might be." — Thomas Kiernan in *The Miracle at Coogan's Bluff* (1975).

Charles Stoneham's son Horace took over the team when his father died in 1936. He continued his ownership through the club's departure to become the *San Francisco Giants* after the 1957 season (see also *Franchise Shifts*).

By the 1950s future Mets owner Joan Payson owned approximately 10% of the club's stock. When she took over the Mets, the National League allowed her to keep one share of the Giants in a symbolic gesture.

Nicknames. The classic story is that the team was named by manager Jim Mutrie in 1885 after he exclaimed after a great play that his players were, "My Big Fellows! My Giants!" One source reported that the name was derived from the fact that the club had a number of players over six feet tall. The term "Gotham Giants" was used early on by St. Louis newspaperman Joe Pritchard.

The Giants name was first used in print in 1885 as part of a verse entitled "The Pets of New York," written by Harry P. Keily and published in the August 26, 1885, issue of *Sporting Life*. Among the five stanzas was the phrase, "When out in the field the Giants never yield."

Key Seasons.

1884. Player-manager John Montgomery Ward led the Giants to a second-place finish, one game behind the Orioles. In the National League championship series of that era, the Giants beat the Orioles for the pennant.

1885. The club finished only two games behind Cap Anson's Chicago White Stockings.

1888. The Giants won their first pennant behind Tim Keefe's 19 straight wins, a record equaled by Giants pitcher Rube Marquard in 1912. Buck Ewing, John Montgomery Ward and Roger Connor also starred for the club. The Giants beat the American Association St. Louis Brown Stockings in the championship series.

1889. The Giants won the pennant on the last day as Tim Keefe defeated Cleveland 5–3. Boston, which was tied with the Giants, lost to Pittsburgh 6–1. The Giants defeated the American Association Brooklyn Dodgers in the championship series. Roger Connor led the league with 130 RBIs, and Mickey Welch and Tim Keefe each won at least 27 games.

1904. Manager John McGraw led the Giants to a 106–47 record, 13 games ahead of the second-place Cubs. As a result of lingering animosity between the National and American Leagues, the Giants refused to play in the World Series. Joe McGinnity led the league with 35 wins and a 1.61 ERA, and Christy Mathewson won 33 games.

1905. The Giants repeated as National League champions with a 105–48 record, nine games ahead of the Pirates. Led by Christy Mathewson's three shutouts in six days, the Giants beat the A's in five games in the World Series. Mathewson led the league with 31 wins and a 1.27 ERA and Sam Mertes drove in 108 runs.

1908. The famous "Merkle Boner" season (see *Base Running*) left the Giants with a 98–56 record, one game behind the Cubs. Christy Mathewson led the league with 37 wins and a 1.43 ERA, but he lost the final game of the season to give the Cubs the pennant.

1911. After a second-place finish in 1910, the Giants were back on top with a 99–54 record, 7½ games ahead of the Cubs. The Giants lost the World Series to the A's in six games. Christy Mathewson won 26 games and led the league with a 1.99 ERA and Rube Marquard won 24 games.

1912. The Giants repeated as National League champions with 103 wins as Christy Mathewson won 23 games and Rube Marquard won a league-leading 26 games. In the World Series the Red Sox beat the Giants in eight games (one tie), culminating in the famous Fred Snodgrass–dropped-fly-ball-game (see also *Errors*).

1913. The Giants won 101 games on their way to a third consecutive National League pennant. The club had three 20-game winners in Christy Mathewson, Rube Marquard and Jeff Tesreau. The Giants lost the World Series to the A's in five games.

1917. The Giants won the pennant by 10 games as Heinie Zimmerman led the league with 102 RBIs and Dave Robertson led with 12 home runs. The Giants lost the World Series in six games to the White Sox.

1921.

"I think we can win it — if my brain holds out." — Manager John McGraw during the heat of the 1921 pennant race.

After three straight second-place finishes, the Giants won the pennant by four games over the Pirates. George "Highpockets"

Kelly led the league with 23 home runs and batted .308. The Giants won the World Series in eight games (5–3) over the Yankees.

1922. The Giants repeated as National League champions and swept the Yankees in four games in the World Series. Irish Meusel and George Kelly each had over 100 RBIs and at least 16 home runs.

1923. The Giants won their third straight pennant by four games over the Reds. Irish Meusel led the club with 125 RBIs. In the World Series, the Yankees defeated the Giants in six games.

1924. The Giants won their fourth straight pennant by 1½ games over the Dodgers. George Kelly had a league-leading 136 RBIs. The Giants lost the World Series to the Senators in seven games when a *Bad Hop* ground ball went over third baseman Fred Lindstrom's head in the 12th inning of Game 7 to give Washington's Walter Johnson the victory.

1933. The Giants won the pennant in Bill Terry's first full season at the helm, finishing four games ahead of the Pirates. Carl Hubbell led the club with 23 wins, and they defeated the Senators in the World Series in five games. Hubbell won two of the Series games. The following year the Giants finished two games behind the pennant-winning Cardinals.

1936. The club won 92 games to win the pennant by five games over the Cubs. Mel Ott led the league with 33 home runs and Carl Hubbell led with 26 wins. The Giants lost to the Yankees in six games in the World Series.

1937. Carl Hubbell's 22 wins and Mel Ott's 31 home runs — both league highs — paced the club to its second straight National League pennant. In the World Series, the Yankees again beat the Giants, this time in five games.

1951.

"The Miracle at Coogan's Bluff"

The Giants staged a furious late-season rally to tie the Dodgers at the end of the regular season. In a three-game *Play-Off* series, Bobby Thomson hit a three-run homer in the bottom of the 9th inning of Game 3 to defeat the Dodgers 5–4. The exhausted Giants lost the World Series to the Yankees in six games.

1954. Willie Mays and his league-leading .345 average pushed the Giants to the pennant by five games over the Dodgers. Dusty Rhodes of the Giants hit two pinch home runs and had seven RBIs in the World Series to lead the club to a four-game sweep of the favored Indians.

1957. In their last season in New York, the Giants finished a dismal 69–85 under manager Bill Rigney.

Departure for San Francisco. Charles Stoneham always denied that he had any secret agreement with the Dodgers to move out West. He had planned to move to Minneapolis until Walter O'Malley suggested the West Coast. It would have been impractical for only one team to move West because of scheduling difficulties (see also *Franchise Shifts*).

"Lasts."

"They tore up the turf, they tore up the seats, they tore up home plate and if Giant owner Horace Stoneham had been around, they would have torn him up, too." — Sportswriter Milton Richman after the last game played by the Giants in New York.

The Giants played their last home game in New York on September 29, 1957. The Pirates beat them 9–1 as pitcher Johnny Antonelli took the loss. The last home run by a New York Giant was by Gail Harris on September 21, 1957. Bobby Thomson returned to the club near the end of the 1957 season and played the last game at third base "for old time's sake." Willie Mays was the last active Major Leaguer to play for the New York Giants. He retired in 1973.

Key Players.

Tim Keefe (HF) won 172 games for the Giants in only five seasons beginning in 1885. He peaked with 42 wins in 1886, with 62 complete games in 64 starts.

Mickey Welch (HF) won 239 games for the Giants between 1883 and 1891. He peaked with 44 wins in 1885 and won 22 or more games in seven straight seasons.

John Montgomery Ward (HF) starred for the club from 1883 through 1889 and then returned for two years in 1893. He hit .338 in 1887 and led the league with 111 stolen bases. He hit .328 in 1893 and finished his career with a .275 average.

George Van Haltren played the last 10 years of his career with the Giants beginning in 1894. He hit over .300 eight straight seasons and had 204 hits in 1898.

Christy Mathewson (HF) was, with the exception of Walter Johnson, the greatest pitcher of the early 20th century. In over 16 seasons with the Giants beginning in 1900, Mathewson won 20 or more games 13 times, including 12 straight starting in 1903. He also won 30 or more games four times, including a league-high 37 in 1908. His 2.13 ERA is fifth all-time and his 80 shutouts for the Giants are third all-time.

Rube Marquard (HF) exploded in 1911 with 24 wins for the Giants after three nondescript seasons. He led the league with 26 wins in 1912 (including 19 straight) and continued with 23 wins in 1913. He began to fade and was traded in 1915. He won two games for the Giants in the 1912 World Series.

Larry Doyle played second base for the Giants for 13 of his 14 Major League seasons. He hit over .300 five times for the Giants, including a league-leading .320 in 1915. He also helped lead the club to three consecutive World Series appearances starting in 1911.

Bill Terry (HF) played 14 seasons for the Giants beginning in 1923, finishing with a .341 lifetime average. He hit over .300 in 12 straight seasons, including a league-high .401 in 1930 when he had 254 hits. He led the club to three World Series, in which he batted .295. He had over 200 hits in a season six times and drove in over 100 runs in six seasons.

Mel Ott (HF) was the all-time National League home run leader when he retired in 1947 with 511 homers. In 22 seasons beginning in 1926, all with the Giants, Ott drove in 1,861 runs and hit .304. He led the club to three World Series appearances in the 1930s, hitting .295 with four home runs.

Carl Hubbell (HF) was the most dominant pitcher of the 1930s, the prime of his 16-year career. The screwball pitcher won more than 20 games five straight seasons beginning in 1933. His best year was 1933 when he won 23 games, had a 1.66 ERA and pitched 10 shutouts. He also won two games in the World Series that season. He finished with 253 lifetime wins and a 2.97 ERA.

Willie Mays (HF) played the first six of his 21 seasons with the Giants in New York. During that span he hit a league-leading .345 in 1954 and hit 51 home runs in 1955. He led the league in slugging average three times.

Key Managers.

Jim Mutrie.

"We are the people!"—Slogan of the early Giants manager.

Mutrie (of "My Giants" nickname fame) was the first prominent Giants manager, although it has been suggested that he was merely a figurehead and that star catcher Buck Ewing controlled the club on the field. Mutrie managed the Metropolitans of the American Association in 1883 and 1884 and then moved over to the National League Giants from 1885 through 1891. His .611 winning percentage is the second-best in Major League history. He won two National League championships with the Giants.

John McGraw (HF).

"It is probably impossible for a modern fan to appreciate the hold that the Giants had on the populace in the days when McGraw dominated baseball. For close to thirty years they were the darlings of New York."—Joseph Durso in *The Days of Mr. McGraw* (1969).

McGraw took over the Giants after they had floundered under 13 different managers after Mutrie left following the 1891 season, most of them hired by the despised Andrew Freedman. The trend ended when McGraw took over midway into the 1902 season. He began a 32-year Hall of Fame tenure for the Giants that lasted 40 games into the 1932 season. He managed in 4,456 games for the Giants, compiling a 2,606–1,801 record (with 51 ties or no decisions).

McGraw won 10 pennants, finished second 11 times and won three World Series out of the nine his clubs played in (no World Series in 1904). When he resigned due to ill health, he retained his stock in the club.

Bill Terry (HF) starred at first base for the Giants from 1923 through 1936, becoming player-manager in 1932 immediately after McGraw resigned. Following a poor first season, Terry led the club to a World Championship in 1933 and National League pennants in 1936 and 1937. The club began sinking in 1938, and Terry was fired after a fifth-place finish in 1941.

Mel Ott (HF) continued the club's tradition of hiring star player-managers when he was chosen to succeed Terry for the 1942 season. He led the club for seven years, never doing better than a third-place finish his first season. His last serious season as an active player was 1945, though he made a few appearances over the next two years. He was fired during the 1948 season while in fourth place and was replaced by Leo Durocher.

Leo Durocher (HF) became the Giants manager late in the 1948 season after managing the arch rival Dodgers. He had been suspended for the entire 1947 season (see also *Gambling*) while managing the Dodgers. He returned to the Dodgers in 1948, but the team was not doing well and not drawing fans. The Giants were also playing poorly and owner Horace Stoneham was looking for a manager to replace Mel Ott. On July 15, 1948, Stoneham and Dodger general manager Branch Rickey had a meeting at the Radio City offices of National League president Ford Frick. Stoneham told Rickey that Ott was resigning and he asked Rickey about the availability of Dodger coach Burt Shotten. Rickey said that Stoneham could not have Shotten but that Durocher was available. The deal was made and fans were stunned by the revelation that the hated Durocher would now be managing the Giants.

Durocher led the club to pennants in 1951 and 1954, with a World Series sweep of the Indians in 1954. In eight seasons he also finished second once and third twice.

Ballparks. The Giants occupied the *Polo Grounds* (or its predecessors of the same name) during their entire existence in New York.

Key Broadcasters.

"The Giants Win the Pennant!

The Giants Win the Pennant!"—Part of the famous cry of broadcaster Russ Hodges after Bobby Thomson's miracle home run to end the 1951 play-off against the Dodgers.

The Giants, Yankees and Dodgers all broadcast games for the first time in 1939. They had just concluded a five-year agreement with each other not to allow radio in the greater New York City area. In 1939 the Giants shared WABC with the Yankees but broadcast no road games.

The most famous Giants broadcaster was Hall of Famer *Russ Hodges*. He assisted Mel Allen with the Yankees from 1946 through 1948 and prior to that worked with Arch McDonald in Washington. He moved to the Giants in 1949 and began a nine-year run with the Giants before they moved to San Francisco for the 1958 season.

Hodges is best remembered for his call of the 1951 *Play-Off* home run by Bobby Thomson off Ralph Branca. The tape of Hodges was not recorded by the station. A Dodger fan had taped the game off the radio to listen to later (thinking the Dodgers would win). During the following winter the fan sent it to Hodges, and it was made into a record album.

Books. Frank Graham, *The New York Giants* (1952); Thomas Kiernan, *Miracle at Coogan's Bluff* (1975); Peter Williams, *When the Giants Were the Giants: Bill Terry and the Golden Age of New York Baseball* (1994).

New York Giants

Players League 1890

This club was owned by Colonel E. A. McAlpin, a New York real estate developer. The Giants finished the season in third place with a 74–57 record under manager Buck Ewing. Slugger Roger Connor was the star of the team with a .373 batting average and 124 RBIs.

New York Gothams

"Just as there were great composers before Beethoven, so indeed were there formidable baseball teams before the Cincinnati Red Stockings of 1869, but they were all amateur.... The old Knickerbocker Club was one of the very best, along with the New York Gothams."—Douglas Wallop in *Baseball—An Informal History* (1969).

This early amateur club was sometimes known as the Washington Club because it originated in Washington Heights on the northern end of Manhattan. It was also the name of the National League club that eventually was named the *New York Giants.*

New York Knickerbockers

"This silk-stocking aggregation, never able to play a brilliant game, was reluctant to accept challenges from shipwrights, boilermakers and other greasy mechanics."—Albert Spalding writing about the elitist Knickerbockers in *America's National Game* (1911).

This club team was formed in the early 1840s (see also *Origins of Baseball* and *Amateur Teams*). *Alexander Cartwright* was one of its early members. The Knickerbocker Base Ball Club was restricted to 40 males who initially paid annual dues of $2 ($5 in some sources). In addition to Elysian Field, early games were played at the Murray Hill and Parade Grounds located between 23rd and 34th Streets and 7th Avenue.

The Knickerbockers dominated the New York baseball scene for 10 years as the chief proponents of the *New York Game.* Social standing in the community was important to the club members and blackballing of potential new members was common. The team imposed a fine of 50 cents for disobeying the captain, 25 cents for disputing an umpire's decision and $1 if the captain neglected his duties.

The team was almost defunct by the 1860s (completely dead in some sources) because it failed to participate in the explosion of baseball across class lines and the professionalism of the game. It disbanded completely in the early 1880s.

New York Metropolitans

American Association 1883–1887

There was no Major League Baseball in New York in 1880 (the National League entry having been expelled), and so a nonleague team called the Metropolitans (or "Mets") was formed to play in 1881. It played 60 games against National League clubs, winning 18 (considered respectable for a nonleague club). The team then joined the *League Alliance*, a loose affiliation of teams friendly with the National League. This was done at the urging of National League president William Hulbert, who did not want to see the team join the fledgling American Association.

The team finally joined the American Association in 1883 for that league's second season. Joseph Gordon owned the club while his brother-in-law, John B. Day, owned the New York Giants, who had entered the National League. As a result, one entity controlled both clubs. The Metropolitans won the 1884 pennant, but lost $84,000 and in the spring of 1885 the team lost its two stars, Dude Esterbrook and Tim Keefe, to the National League Giants. The other American Association owners thought that the sale was a sham to give the Giants the better team in New York.

In retaliation for the sale, the Association immediately awarded the Metropolitans franchise to a Washington group, but Gordon and Day quickly sold the club to Erasmus Wiman of Staten Island for $25,000. Wiman was a millionaire promoter who owned the railroad ferry to Staten Island. In response, the American Association expelled the Metropolitans without Wiman's knowledge. Wiman then obtained an injunction and won his right to continue in the Association.

After three years of poor finishes and $30,000 in losses, Wiman sold the team to the American Association's Brooklyn franchise owners, who took the players and gave the franchise back to the Association. This effectively gave New York City to the National League Giants, as only Brooklyn remained in greater New York as part of the American Association.

New York Mets

National League 1962–

"Let's Go Mets!"—Mets cheer that began only a few weeks after the team started play in 1962 and which has stayed with the club into the 2000s. It was among the banners displayed in West Berlin during President Kennedy's visit in 1963.

Origins. At the 1961 World Series, Buzzie Bavasi of the Dodgers was approached by New York concessionaire Frank Stevens (heir to the Harry Stevens concession empire), and given a check for $1.8 million. This was to be the franchise fee for a new expansion club in New York. Stevens apparently did not want to own the club, but merely wanted the concession. It has not been uncommon for concessionaires to act as lenders in return for sweetened concession deals.

Despite the efforts of Stevens, the inside track on obtaining a new franchise in New York was always with New York attorney William Shea, who had been on the board of directors of the New York Giants. With M. Donald Grant, who represented the interests of future Mets owner Joan Payson, Shea pursued and won the new National League franchise. One source reported that the New York franchise was originally bought by Dwight F. "Pete" Davis (of the Davis Cup tennis family). Davis then supposedly brought in Payson as an investor and she designated Grant as her spokesman and soon gained full control (see also *Expansion* and *Expansion Draft*).

To help induce the National League to award his group the New York franchise, Shea made overtures about forming a rival **Continental League**. The established leagues took the threat seriously enough to absorb some of the proposed Continental League owners, which included Payson. Before that, however, Grant first tried to lure to New York the existing National League clubs in Pittsburgh, Cincinnati and Philadelphia.

First Game.

"Can't anybody here play this game?"—Manager Casey Stengel's frequent lament in the early years.

The club's first scheduled game against the Cardinals was rained out. In their debut on April 11, 1962, the Mets lost to the Cardinals in St. Louis 11–4 in front of 12,000 fans. Fittingly, the first play of the game was a ground ball to third baseman Charlie Neal that he fielded and threw into right field.

The Cardinals scored their first run on a balk by Roger Craig. This was characteristic of the Mets' first year, as the only team in the league not to have a winning record against the Mets were the Cubs, who were 9–9. An ominous sign was that the first home game played by the Mets was on Friday the 13th in front of 12,447 fans. Mrs. John McGraw was an honored guest at the game. The team won its first game on April 23, 1962, after starting the season with nine losses. Jay Hook was the winner.

Key Owners.

Joan Payson and Charles Shipman Payson/1962–1980.

"Let's Go Mets—Keep Mrs. Payson out of Debt."—Banner at the Polo Grounds in 1962.

The Mets were incorporated as the Metropolitan Baseball Club of New York, Inc. Payson's brother, Jock Whitney (referenced as her husband in many sources), was the owner of the *New York Herald Tribune* and had been ambassador to Great Britain.

The original purchasing group included Canadian sportswoman Dorothy J. Killiam, stockbroker G. Herbert Walker, M. Donald Grant and Payson. Payson originally owned 80% of the club, but the other investors (with the exception of Grant), all quickly sold out to Payson.

Branch Rickey, who helped orchestrate the Continental League challenge, originally was to run the team, but he wanted too much money and too much control. The Mets hired George Weiss instead, who had just been deposed as general manager of the Yankees. His Yankee buyout contract prohibited him from being general manager of another club, but the Yankees allowed him to move to the Mets.

Payson took great interest in the club until her death in September 1975. She left her interest to husband Charles Shipman Payson, who had little interest in baseball. Nevertheless, he held the club for five more years.

Doubleday Publishing, Nelson Doubleday, Jr., and Fred Wilpon/1980–2002.

"Owner Fred Wilpon in particular wanted to homogenize his ballclub, and began stressing family values long before the Republicans tried to make it an issue in the 1992 presidential campaign—with much the same success, as it turned out."—Bob Klapisch and John Harper in *The Worst Team Money Could Buy* (1993).

Charles Shipman Payson sold the club for a then-record $21.3 (or $21.1) million on January 24, 1980. Nelson Doubleday, Jr., of Doubleday Publishing purchased a 90% interest through his company. Real estate mogul Fred Wilpon purchased the balance (80%–20% in some sources). Wilpon, a graduate of the University of Michigan, also had a 10% interest in the New York Islanders hockey team and was a pitcher on the same Brooklyn high school team as Sandy Koufax. Doubleday is the great-great-grandnephew

Homer the Beagle, Mets mascot.

of alleged baseball inventor Abner Doubleday. Wilpon was the president and COO, while Doubleday served as chairman of the board.

Wilpon and Doubleday bought out the company's interest for $80.75 million in November 14, 1986, leaving each with a 50% interest in the club. This was after Doubleday sold the family publishing business in 1986 for $500 million, taking about $85 million for himself. The two continued to control the club into the 2000s, but friction had developed.

Fred Wilpon/2002– .

In August 2002 the two owners finally completed a deal to transfer full ownership to Wilpon, with a neutral arbitrator to establish the value of the club for purposes of establishing a sale price. They finally agreed upon $150 million that Wilpon had to pay to secure a 100% ownership interest in the club. Wilpon's company, Sterling Equities, technically owns the club, as well as the Brooklyn Cyclones, a Class A team that Wilpon placed near Coney Island to be a minor league affiliate of the Mets.

Nicknames. Payson originally wanted the name to be Meadowlarks. The finalists for nicknames were narrowed by newsmen and then the fans voted. Among the choices were Continentals, Skyliners, Mets, Jets, Meadowlarks, Burros, Skyscrapers, Rebels and Avengers. Mets finally won out after Payson called a news conference and gave her official blessing to the name ("I like Mets"). The name was made official on May 8, 1961, although reporters had used the name before that date.

In 2003 the Mets tried to register their name in Great Britain, but received resistance from the "Met Office," the British office of meteorology. The objection by the Met was rejected by the patent office with this explanation from spokesman Jeremy Philpott: "Have you ever gone out shopping intending to buy a Lotus car and come back with Lotus software?"

Key Seasons.

"The Amazin' Mets" — The nickname "Amazin's" first appeared in a newspaper headline.

1962.

"Everyone knew the Mets were going to stink, and they knew they were going to stink, and they stank with wild abandon." — Joel Stein in *Time*.

In their first season the club set a modern futility record by finishing 40–120. See Janet Paskin, *Tales From the 1962 New York Mets* (2004).

1963. One of the early Mets highlights was defeating the Yankees in the 1963 Mayor's Trophy Game. Other than Casey Stengel there was not much to talk about in the early years.

1966. The Mets climbed out of the cellar for the first time, finishing ninth.

1969.

"The only verifiable miracle since the parting of the Red Sea." — Comedian George Burns.

The turning point for the Mets may have been when Johnny Murphy was appointed general manager for the 1968 season after serving as a vice-president since 1964. Murphy had been an outstanding relief pitcher for the Yankees and Red Sox, and he became the architect of the team that won the "Miracle" World Championship in 1969.

Original general manager George Weiss retired after the 1966 season (coinciding with Stengel's departure), and Bing Devine from St. Louis lasted only the 1967 season as general manager.

The Mets came from 9½ games back of the Cubs to win the National League's first divisional crown and defeated the Braves in the NLCS. The Mets defeated a surprised powerhouse Baltimore club in five games. Tom Seaver won a league-leading 25 games and Tommy Agee led the club with 26 home runs. See also Stanley Cohen, *A Magic Summer: The 1969 Mets* (1988); Joseph Durso, *Amazing* (1970); Tom Seaver and Norman Lewis Smith, *The Perfect Game* (1974); Paul Zimmerman and Dick Schaap, *The Year the Mets Lost Last Place* (1969).

1973.

"Ya Gotta Believe!" — Reliever Tug McGraw's rallying cry.

The Mets made it to the World Series after compiling the worst regular season record of any pennant winner in history, 82–79. They beat the Reds for the National League pennant in a deciding fifth game, and then lost the Series to the Oakland A's in seven games (after being up 3–2 in games). Tom Seaver won 19 games and led the league with a 2.08 ERA and Tug McGraw saved 25 games. By 1977 the Mets virtually disappeared from the baseball map until the mid–1980s.

1986.

"The Siberia of Baseball" — Keith Hernandez on being traded to the Mets in 1983 before the club's turnaround in 1984.

After two strong finishes in 1984 and 1985, the Mets returned to postseason play in 1986 with a seven-game World Series victory over the Red Sox that was preceded by a thrilling six-game NLCS with the Astros. The Mets were one strike away from elimination in the World Series but broke New England hearts with a miracle comeback in Game 6 and a comeback from a 3–0 deficit in Game 7 (see also *Errors*). The Mets had six pitchers who won at least 10 games, and Darryl Strawberry led the club with 27 home runs. See also Gary Carter and John Hough, Jr., *Dream Season* (1987) and Jeff Pearlman, *The Bad Guys Won!* (2004).

1988. After a strong second-place finish in 1987, the Mets won the Eastern Division crown with 100 wins. However, they were eliminated by the underdog Dodgers in seven games in the NLCS.

David Cone won 20 games and Darryl Strawberry led the league with 39 home runs. The Mets fell back to second place in 1989 and then the club began a downward spiral in the early 1990s.

1999. The Mets finished second in the National League East with a 96–66 record, then won a one-game playoff with the Reds to determine the wild card winner (thereby finishing with a 97–66 season record). They beat the Diamondbacks in four games for the division series win. They fell behind 3–0 in games to the Braves in the NLCS, then won two to make it close, but lost Game 6 in extra innings. Mike Piazza hit .303, had 40 home runs and drove in 124 runs. Robin Ventura had 32 home runs and 120 RBIs. No pitcher had more than 13 wins (five had at least 10), and relievers Armando Benitez (22) and John Franco (19) combined for 41 saves.

2000. The club was the wild card team again, with a record of 98–68. The Mets beat the Giants in the division series in four games, and then won the pennant over the Cardinals in five games. In the subway World Series against the Yankees, the Mets lost in five games. Mike Piazza led the club with 38 home runs and 113 RBIs, while batting .324. Mike Hampton won 15 games and Al Leiter won 16, while Armando Benitez saved 41 games.

Key Players.

Ed Kranepool played his entire 18-year career with the Mets from 1962 through 1979. He hit .261 lifetime and batted .300 or better twice. Though he played first base and was 6'3" and 205 pounds, he hit only 118 home runs, with a high of 16 in 1966.

Cleon Jones played 12 seasons for the Mets beginning in 1963. He peaked in 1969 with a .340 average to help the Mets to the World Championship.

Tom Seaver (HF) played nine full seasons for the Mets at the start of his career in 1967. He quickly established himself as one of the premier pitchers in the Major Leagues. He led the league with 25 wins in 1969 and again in 1975 with 22. He also led the league in strikeouts five times and ERA three times. He played part of 1977 with the Mets and then returned for one season in 1983, when he was 9–14.

Jerry Grote was one of the premier catchers in the National League in the late 1960s and early 1970s. He played for over 11 seasons with the club, helping lead them to two World Series appearances in 1969 and 1973.

Bud Harrelson played shortstop for the Mets from 1965 through 1977.

Jerry Koosman pitched 12 seasons for the Mets beginning in 1967. He won 19 games in 1968 and 21 games in 1976.

Darryl Strawberry came up to the Mets in 1983 and established himself as the club's all-time home run leader with 252. He led the league with 39 home runs in 1988 and had over 100 RBIs three times before moving on to the Dodgers in 1991. He then began a downward spiral into *Drug Abuse* problems.

Dwight Gooden exploded with 24 wins, a 1.53 ERA and eight shutouts in 1985 before *Drug Abuse* and alcohol hurt his career. Even after suffering through a losing season in 1992, his career winning percentage was fourth all-time. He missed the 1995 season due to a drug suspension and signed with the Yankees for 1996.

Mike Piazza joined the club in 1999 and hit at least 33 home runs in each of the next four seasons before injuries slowed him in 2003. He batted .300 or better for the club three times while playing decently behind the plate. In 2004 he played more frequently at first base after becoming the all-time leader in home runs by a catcher.

Al Leiter won 85 games for the Mets between 1998 and 2003.

John Franco returned to his native New York (actually a Brooklyn native) in 1990 after five seasons with Cincinnati, and was still pitching for the club in 2003. He recorded almost 300 saves for the Mets over 13 seasons.

Key Managers.

Casey Stengel (HF).

"When Casey Stengel agreed to manage the Mets ... he leaned back into the deep swivel chair in the office of his bank ... and talked about how happy he was to be running the New York Knickerbockers. It was a half hour at least before he realized they were the Mets. And a week at least before he began calling them amazing."—Leonard Schechter in *Once Upon a Time* (1970).

George Weiss and Joan Payson wanted Stengel to manage the club after he departed from the Yankees. The club never finished out of the cellar in his four seasons from 1962 through mid–1965 (before a hip injury and advanced age ended his career).

Wes Westrum.

"Wesley Noreen Westrum was a squat, simple, humble man whose dedication to baseball could not be exceeded. His physical toughness was matched by an alert baseball mind that one became aware of only by knowing him well. He was instinctively self-effacing and anything but garrulous.... It is hard to describe what a sudden promotion to manager of a major league club means to a man like Westrum. It is the emotional equivalent of the pauper being made prince."—Leonard Koppett in *The New York Mets— The Whole Story* (1970).

Westrum joined the team after meeting with Casey Stengel during the 1963 All-Star game. Stengel thought Westrum had a good baseball mind and arranged for a trade with the Giants so that Westrum could become a Mets coach.

In 1964 there was much criticism of Stengel, led by Howard Cosell in a regular pregame radio show that aired during the season. Alvin Dark was considered a prime candidate to replace Stengel, but Dark's racist remarks about the Giants players took him out of the running.

Stengel's broken hip in 1965 led to Westrum taking over first as "interim" manager, which became permanent when it became clear that the 75-year-old Stengel would not be able to come back. Westrum lasted through most of the 1967 season, leading the Mets to their first finish out of the cellar in 1966.

Gil Hodges.

"He was a man of fundamental habits and beliefs — the type that might have been played by Gary Cooper in a John Ford western — and he imparted those fundamentals to his players in a matter-of-fact manner that left little to conjecture."—Stanley Cohen in *A Magic Summer—The '69 Mets* (1988).

When George Weiss retired, Donald Grant assumed a higher profile in the club's management. He hired Hodges for the 1968 season, which turned out to be an important step in the evolution of the 1969 championship team. Hodges had a heart attack in 1968 and in the spring of 1969 it was not clear whether he would be able to manage the team. He was able to return and guided the club through the miracle of 1969, third place finishes in 1970 and 1971, and then died during a round of golf on April 2, 1972.

See Marino Amoruso, *Gil Hodges: The Quiet Man* (1991), chronicling Hodges through the eyes of teammates and those he managed. Just before the 1969 season unfolded, Hodges wrote *The Game of Baseball* (1969), with Frank Slocum, a treatise on how to play and manage.

Davey Johnson.

"As the plane flew in here this morning, I knew I was back. I started looking for a Tums."—Johnson on starting to manage the Reds almost three years to the day after the Mets fired him.

Johnson took over the Mets in 1984 and guided the club to four

second-place finishes and two first-place finishes in six years before being fired in mid–1990. The Mets won the World Series over the Red Sox in 1986 and lost to the Dodgers in seven games in the 1988 Championship Series.

Bobby Valentine. Valentine and his brusque personality took over in mid–1996 and ran the club through 2002. The Mets had three consecutive second-place finishes behind the Braves, but were the wild card in 1999 and made it to the World Series as the wild card in 2001 before losing to the Yankees. After a fifth place finish in 2002, Valentine was let go in favor of Art Howe.

Ballparks.

Polo Grounds. Yankee Stadium was considered as a possible home for the Mets but was soon ruled out. The New York State Assembly vetoed a site in Flushing Meadow, in large part because the Yankees opposed it (led by then–Yankee general manager George Weiss). The day before the vote, Weiss joined the Mets and in a second vote the same site was approved for building what eventually became Shea Stadium. In the meantime, for $200,000 the *Polo Grounds* was renovated in 10 months to house the team for the 1962 and 1963 seasons while Shea Stadium was being built.

Shea Stadium.

"The Mets say they want to get out of Shea Stadium by the year 2000, and New Yorkers are outraged. They want them out now."— Jay Leno in 1995.

"William A. Shea Municipal Stadium"— Official name of Shea Stadium, after the central figure in the effort to bring a National League team back to New York after the departure of the Giants and Dodgers.

Ground was broken for the new ballpark on October 28, 1961. The facility was built in Flushing Meadow adjacent to the World's Fair site of 1939–1940 and 1964–1965, and was first known as Flushing Meadow Park. The ballpark was built at a total cost of $28.5 million ($20 million or $25.5 million in some sources), using municipal bonds. It was the first ballpark to have motorized tracks to convert the stadium grounds from a baseball diamond and outfield to a football field.

The Mets moved into Shea Stadium on April 17, 1964, just as the Polo Grounds were torn down. On the day of the game, some outfield grass was still to be put in and the fence was still being painted. Pittsburgh's Willie Stargell homered in a 4–3 Pirate victory in front of 50,312 fans.

At Shea Stadium's opening ceremonies, Bill Shea christened the Mets' new home with two symbolic bottles of water: one from the Gowanus Canal near Ebbets Field, former home of the Brooklyn Dodgers and one from the Harlem River near the Polo Grounds, where the New York Giants had played and later the Mets during the 1962 and 1963 seasons.

The park has a problem with airplanes flying out of nearby LaGuardia airport. It is considered a poor hitters' park because of the bad visibility and swirling winds.

The ballpark seated 55,300 when it first opened and capacity has fluctuated around that total since then. Early in its history there was a move to add another 15,000 seats and cover the ballpark, but a feasibility study determined that the pilings underneath the stadium were inadequate to support a dome. The dimensions from left to right field have remained at 341–358–410–358–341.

In April 1998 the Mets unveiled plans for a new ballpark patterned off old Ebbets Field, to contain a retractable roof and a retractable field suitable for multiple events.

Key Broadcasters. The expansion Mets wanted a three-man broadcast crew and 1,000 candidates applied. Although he did not apply for the job, Lindsey Nelson received an offer and broadcast for the team from 1962 until 1978, when he left for the Giants. Bob Murphy, who had worked with Curt Gowdy with the Red Sox and Orioles, campaigned actively for one of the positions and was selected as the second play-by-play man.

Former slugger Ralph Kiner had been general manager of the San Diego Padres in the Pacific Coast League and had one year of color commentary experience on the air with the White Sox. He became the color man on the broadcasts and this trio holds the record for longest continuous service with one team as a three-man crew—and the only broadcasters the club had for both radio and television through 1978. Kiner and Murphy continued to broadcast together until Kiner retired after the 1996 season.

Tim McCarver finished 16 seasons with the club in 1998. The Mets refused to offer him a contract for the 1999 season because he had been so critical of the club. He was replaced by Tom Seaver, who also signed on as a part-time coach.

Murphy, who received the Frick Award in 1994, signed off in late September 2003 after 42 years behind the microphone. The 78-year-old had been in ill health at times and decided to retire to Florida. The radio booth at Shea Stadium was renamed after him in 2002. His primary partner since the late 1980s was Gary Cohen. Murphy died of lung cancer in August 2004.

Other former players who have broadcast for the club include Art Shamsky, Fran Healy, Rusty Staub and Keith Hernandez. Seaver, Hernandez and Healy were all with the club in 2004.

Books. Maury Allen, *After the Miracle* (1989); Maury Allen, *Now Wait a Minute Casey* (1965); Peter Bjarkman, *New York Mets Encyclopedia, 2nd Ed.* (2003); Jimmy Breslin, *Can't Anybody Here Play This Game?* (1963); Peter Golenbock, *Amazin': The Miraculous History of New York's Most Beloved Baseball Team* (2003); Leonard Koppett, *The New York Mets—The Whole Story* (1970); Jack Lang and Peter Simon, *The New York Mets* (1987); Jerry Mitchell, *The Amazing Mets* (1970); Lindsey Nelson, *Backstage at the Mets* (1966); Jon Scher, *The New York Mets: A Photographic History*, photos by George Kalinsky (1995).

New York Mutuals

National Association 1871–1875

"There will be no more soft things and easy times for the hired men of the professional organizations, at least to the extent of loafing about doing nothing and being well paid for it when there is no match playing going on."—1872 pronouncement by club officials after the Mutuals suffered through a dismal 1871 season.

One of the original New York amateur teams of the 1850s, the Mutuals were originally composed of members of the Mutual Hook & Ladder Fire Company No. 1.

During the club's amateur days from 1860 through 1870, it was controlled by Boss Tweed of Tammany Hall fame. All players were on the city's payroll. Tweed later was convicted of stealing $6.5 million from the city and fled to Spain. He was tracked down and returned by Navy cruiser to New York, where he died in 1878.

The amateur version of this team joined the professional National Association in 1871 and was one of the original National League entries in 1876. William Cammeyer, builder of a number of ballparks, owned the National Association entry.

The club finished in the middle of the pack for the first three National Association seasons and then rose to second place in 1874. The club slipped back to seventh in 1875 before moving into the National League. The team sometimes was called the Green Stockings and Chocolate Sox.

New York Mutuals

National League 1876

"It is an old saying among the ball tossers that any kind of a nine with Mathews, Hicks and Start can win a game from the best club ever organized, and it is not difficult to name the reason. It is on account of Mathews' delivery."—April 9, 1876, newspaper article the day before Opening Day.

The club finished with a 21–35 record in sixth place under manager William Cammeyer. Bobby Mathews was the pitcher of record in all but one game, compiling a 21–34 record. The club was expelled from the league after the season for failing to complete the schedule, leaving New York without a National League franchise until 1883.

New York Yankees

American League 1903–

"In a tough age which called for tough men in baseball, the Yankees were the toughest. They were managed by a perfectionist, bossed by a president who hated second place, and owned by a man who could say, even with a seventeen-game lead in 1936, 'I can't stand this suspense. When are we going to clinch it?'"—David Quentin Voigt in *American Baseball: From the Commissioners to Continental Expansion* (1970).

"Hating the Yankees is as American as pizza pie, unwed mothers and cheating on your income tax."—Columnist Mike Royko.

"The Evil Empire"—Red Sox President Larry Lucchino.

"A baseball club is part of the chemistry of the city. A game isn't just an athletic contest. It's a picnic, a kind of town meeting."—Onetime Yankees president Mike Burke.

"A mystique of history and heritage surrounds the New York Yankees. It's like the old days revived. We're loved and hated, but always in larger doses than any other team. We're the only team in any sport whose name and uniform and insignia are synonymous with their entire sport all over the world ... the Yankees mean baseball to more people than all the other teams combined."—Outfielder Paul Blair.

Origins. The settlement by the American League and the National League during the war of 1901–1903 led to the formation of an *American League* club in New York.

First Game. The Yankees, known as the Highlanders for the first few years, played their inaugural game on April 22, 1903, a 3–1 road loss to the Senators. On April 30, 1903, the club hosted its first game, against the Senators. New York won 6–2 in front of 16,293 fans. Jack Chesbro was the winning pitcher and Willie Keeler had the first New York hit in the club's home park.

Key Owners.

Frank Farrell and Big Bill Devery/1903–1914. These kings of New York City graft and corruption were chosen by Ban Johnson to own the New York club because of their strong ties with the Tammany political machine. Farrell was a "pool room king," which was primarily a front for his bookmaking operations. One of his locations was at 6th Avenue and 30th Street. Police captain Big Bill Devery (also described as chief in some sources) worked out of the nearby 19th Precinct and was subject to numerous investigations for corruption and fraud. Most sources report that he was still a cop when he bought into the club. However, he was a real estate investor by the time he purchased the club. Farrell had contacts with the Fleischmanns (of margarine fame), who owned the Cincinnati Reds. The Fleischmanns had a plant in New York and, like Farrell, had a strong interest in horse racing.

Farrell and Devery paid $18,000 in 1903 to buy the former Baltimore franchise from the American League. They had been brought into the deal by reporter Joe Vila of the *New York Sun*, who was a friend of Ban Johnson from Johnson's reporting days. The first president of the club was local real estate developer Joseph Gordon (described as a coal merchant in some sources). Gordon lasted until 1907 as a figurehead, when Farrell and Devery formally took over his duties.

In 1914 the club had a bad year and Farrell and Devery were feuding and losing money. As a result, they sold out. They never spoke to each other after the sale and both died penniless; Devery in 1919 and Farrell in 1926.

Colonel Ruppert and Heirs (1915–1945) and Captain Huston/1915–1923.

"Unlike Ruppert, Cap Huston (who really was a military colonel) cared nothing for social standing and even less for how he looked. A big, gregarious, friendly man, Huston liked the company of ballplayers and sportswriters. He often wore the same suit for a week, and his pants were off the shelf and baggy. He also wore the same derby hat every day, and the players began to call him the Man in the Iron Hat. Not to his face, however."—John Tullus in *I'd Rather Be a Yankee* (1986).

"Master Builder in Baseball"

"Father of the Yankees"—Ruppert's nicknames.

"During the 1920s New York Yankee owner Jacob Ruppert once described his perfect afternoon at Yankee Stadium. 'It's when the Yankees score eight runs in the first inning,' Ruppert said, 'and then slowly pull away.'"—Peter Golenbock in *Dynasty: The New York Yankees 1949–1964* (1975).

Colonel Jacob Ruppert and Captain Tillinghast L'Hommedieu Huston had been friends with Giants manager John McGraw prior to buying the Yankees. They could have purchased the Cubs before opting for the Yankees.

Huston had been a civil engineer in Cuba for 10 years at the turn of the century, where he met McGraw during spring training. McGraw introduced Ruppert to Huston, and they attempted to buy the Giants using Ruppert's wealth from his prominent brewery. The pair finally entered baseball when they bought out Farrell and Devery for $460,000 in January 1915. Ruppert became president and Huston vice-president.

A rift between Ruppert and Huston began in 1918 while Huston was serving in the military in Europe during World War I. Huston wanted Wilbert Robinson named as manager and Ruppert wanted Miller Huggins based on the recommendation of Ban Johnson. The two owners waged a telegram war over this issue and the relationship never recovered.

The feud escalated after the Yankees lost the 1922 World Series in a sweep (including one tie), and Huston said that Huggins would never manage again. Ruppert disagreed because Huggins had already led the team to two pennants. Ruppert and Huston also had a number of other differences which led to their split. During the winter of 1922–1923, Ruppert bought out Huston's half of the team. The deal was consummated on May 23, 1923, when Ruppert reportedly paid $1.5 million for Huston's share. General manager Ed Barrow acted as a mediator.

After selling his interest in the Yankees, Huston had no further contact with baseball except for an attempt in the early 1930s to purchase the Dodgers for $1.7 million. He died on March 29, 1939, two months after the death of his former partner.

Ruppert presided over the Yankee dynasty through the 1920s and most of the 1930s. He became ill in early 1938 and attended only two games that season. He controlled the team until his death

in January 1939 when it was rumored that former Postmaster General James A. Farley was putting together a group to buy the club. World War II postponed any efforts to sell. After Ruppert's death, his estate continued to own the club until near the end of the war.

Del Webb and Dan Topping/1945–1964.

"I'm gonna buy the Yankees. I don't know what I'm going to pay for them, but I'm going to buy them."— Dan Topping shortly before buying the club.

"Only over my dead body will MacPhail buy the Yankees."— Ruppert-era general manager Ed Barrow. MacPhail indeed bought the Yankees with capital from Dan Topping and Del Webb. MacPhail also received a $300,000 no interest loan from Topping to purchase his share.

In January 25, 1945, former Reds and Dodger general manager Larry MacPhail used the money of Dan Topping and Del Webb to buy the Yankees from Jacob Ruppert's estate. MacPhail also bought a small interest in the club. Topping and Webb bought the club from Ruppert's nieces, who needed cash to pay estate taxes. They were Mrs. Joseph Holleran, Mrs. J. Basil Maguire and Miss Helen Weyant. The $2.8 million price included the team, the ballpark, and various minor league clubs, including Newark and Kansas City. The properties were estimated to be worth $7 million in 1939, but World War II had eroded much of that value.

Topping was a tin plating manufacturer and Webb was a building contractor based in Phoenix. Webb had built apartments and other developments, including a number of resorts in California, Arizona and Florida. Topping was married to Olympic ice skater Sonja Henie. General manager Ed Barrow was moved into a figurehead position when MacPhail took over. Barrow's subsequent illness probably prevented him from becoming commissioner when instead Happy Chandler was elected in 1945.

Amid the euphoria of the Yankees' 1947 World Series victory, MacPhail announced his resignation as general manager. Many claim that he did it as a grand gesture that would quickly be revoked, as were many of his managerial firings in fits of rage. However, as legend goes, Topping and Webb quickly accepted the resignation to be rid of the irritating MacPhail. Another account noted that MacPhail probably knew that he was very ill and that his doctors wanted to him to quit. Yet another source reported that MacPhail supposedly sold out in part over the furor regarding Leo Durocher of the Dodgers and his full-year *Suspension* for the 1947 season. MacPhail was unpopular with the Yankee players, who even threatened to strike early in the season. Writer Tim Cohane summed it up: "At a wet and wild world series victory party, he figuratively shook the pillars of the temple and smote his enemies with the jawbone of an ass. In the maelstrom, however, he did not neglect to sell his interest at a profit of $1 million."

Regardless of the reasons on both sides, the Yankees took MacPhail at his word and bought him out. They replaced him with George Weiss as general manager. Weiss had been with the club in various capacities since 1932. Topping and Webb owned the club through the 1950s and early 1960s. They sold out to CBS in 1964 for over $11 million, though Topping retained a small interest. Topping died on May 18, 1974, and Webb died two months later on July 4.

CBS/1964–1972.

"Baseball is like the United States of America. It's too big to be loused up by one man and one monumental mistake. It's even too great to be loused up by three recent monumental mistakes and a passel of small ones. The worst boner was the sale of the New York Yankees to the Columbia Broadcasting System and the clumsy manner in which it was consummated."—White Sox owner Arthur C. Allyn.

Members of the 1959 New York Yankees stand at attention for the National Anthem on Opening Day. Front row, left to right Tom Sturdivant, Enos Slaughter, Hank Bauer, manager Casey Stengel; second row, left to right, Whitey Ford, coach Jim Turner (who spent 51 years in professional baseball, 19 of them as the Yankees' pitching coach) Marv Throneberry, Elston Howard.

"The swan song of Yankee domination was the clandestine sale of the ballclub to CBS and the fumble-fingered attempt to get the sale approved without a proper meeting. This blatant disregard for league procedure jolted the owners out of their lethargy. Rather than accept the deal without question, they finally examined it in depth. To my knowledge, that was the first time anything the Yankees did was given such careful scrutiny."—Arthur C. Allyn.

"Here at NBC there is just one more reason to hate the Yankees."—NBC anchorman Chet Huntley.

CBS bought almost all the club in August 1964 for $11.2 million and held it through some horrible seasons through 1971. CBS initially bought 90% (80% in some sources) of the club and later bought out Dan Topping's remaining 10% interest. The sale of the Yankees was approved by the American League owners on an 8–2 vote, with Arthur Allyn of the White Sox and Charlie Finley of the A's against it. There were problems with conflicts of interest with other owners holding CBS stock, and there were network conflicts because CBS was required to vote on television bids. Mike Burke ran the club during the first down period in Yankee history since World War I.

George Steinbrenner, et al./1972– .

"I won't be active in the day-to-day operations of the club at all. I can't spread myself so thin. I've got enough headaches with my shipping company."—Steinbrenner in 1972.

"Nothing is more limited than being a limited partner of George's."—Steinbrenner limited partner John McMullen, who later bought the Astros.

"I'm gonna buy the Suez Canal. When one of his ships comes through there, I'm gonna blow it up."—Pitcher Dock Ellis on Steinbrenner.

"The Most Hated Man in Baseball"—Fay Vincent on Steinbrenner.

"Randy, it's not too late. Two words: George Steinbrenner."—Radio sportscaster Bret Lewis in response to Randy Johnson's claim that "I've done everything short of sell my soul to the devil to win."

"He really can be a miserable man."—Columnist Mike Lupica after Steinbrenner reneged on a handshake deal with Darryl Strawberry in 1995.

"He would come in and yell at us, or rip us in the newspaper. And if we played well after he ripped us, he thought that he actually spurred us on to the victory, which he didn't. But in his mind, he thought he did." — Graig Nettles.

"No kidding? George sold the Yankees?" — Former Yankee Bobby Murcer to a radio talk show host in mid–2003, after being told by the host that "the brutal dictator and his sons are no longer in power." [referring to Saddam Hussein. Murcer denied the comment.]

"Well, a lot of people won't be happy with that, but it's good news for me." — Steinbrenner, learning that nothing was wrong after he fainted in late December 2003.

"Winning is the most important thing in my life, after breathing. Breathing first, winning next." — Steinbrenner in 1998.

Yankee president Mike Burke was unsuccessful in putting together a syndicate to buy the club from CBS. Former Giants manager Herman Franks headed a group that tried to buy the club in 1972, but lost out to Steinbrenner and his group. Steinbrenner, 41 at the time of the purchase, was the major investor and met with Joe DiMaggio, whom he purportedly wanted to manage the club, but Steinbrenner never followed up with him.

Steinbrenner owned the Cleveland Pipers of the old American Basketball Association and had backed successful Broadway shows such as *Applause*. He was in the shipbuilding business and had been an assistant football coach at West Point. Steinbrenner's father graduated first in his class in naval architecture at MIT in 1927 and went into the family's shipping business. George was rejected by MIT, but graduated with a degree in English Literature from Williams College.

Steinbrenner bought a controlling interest with other partners in late 1972 for $10 million in a deal apparently facilitated by Gabe Paul, who was appointed president. Paul held a small interest in the club, selling out when he moved to the Indians. As part of the deal he sold a parking lot to the city of New York for $1.2 million, so the net sale price $8.8 million. Steinbrenner's personal cash contribution was $168,000.

After he bought the club, Steinbrenner was suspended for one year when he was convicted of illegal contributions to Richard Nixon's 1972 presidential campaign. See also Dick Schaap, *Steinbrenner!* (1982).

Steinbrenner continued his ownership interest into the 1990s. In August 1990 commissioner Fay Vincent forced Steinbrenner to resign as managing general partner because of Steinbrenner's involvement in an effort to discredit outfielder Dave Winfield. Steinbrenner continued to control the team with his 55% interest but could not remain in the day-to-day management of the club.

When Yankee fans learned of Steinbrenner's **Suspension** during a game, they responded with a standing ovation. The commissioner's office had conducted a four-month investigation of Steinbrenner's alleged violation of Major League rules. He had paid $40,000 to known gambler Howard Spira to have Spira investigate outfielder Dave Winfield. Steinbrenner and Winfield had been feuding for years, and Steinbrenner apparently was trying to uncover dirt on Winfield. During the season, Winfield was traded to the Angels for pitcher Mike Witt.

Steinbrenner's son-in-law, Joseph Molloy, initially took over as managing general partner but was replaced almost immediately by James Nederlander, a theater operator. Nederlander was out in 1992 after only 16 months. In mid–1992 Steinbrenner petitioned Vincent to be reinstated as managing general partner of the club. In August 1992 Vincent told him that he could resume his stewardship of the Yankees on May 1, 1993. Steinbrenner served two of the three years to which he was sentenced by Vincent.

In 1992 Steinbrenner was sued by the club's former chief oper-

ating officer, Leonard Kleinman. Vincent had told Steinbrenner that he would not consider reinstatement until the suits were dropped. Kleinman dismissed the action only after Steinbrenner paid him $1.05 million. In 1994 Steinbrenner was reported to be worth $225 million. In March 1995 minority owner Harvey L. Leighton placed an ad in the *Wall Street Journal* for sale of his 1% interest in the club for $2.95 million.

Steinbrenner continued to run the club into the mid–2004s, and began to be portrayed as an older (mid–70s), kinder, gentler George (as reflected in a sympathetic 2004 *Sports Illustrated* article). Steinbrenner's two sons, Hank and Hal, serve as general partners along with a son-in-law, Steve Swindal.

Nicknames. The Highlanders name supposedly was created when Joseph W. Gordon was appointed the first president of the team. At the time, there was a famous British regiment known as Gordon's Highlanders. In addition, the team played at the highest point in Manhattan, Washington Heights. Another version has them as the Highlanders because they played in Highlander Park (actually Hilltop Park). The new club was also known early on as the Invaders, Cliffmen, Burglars, Hill Dwellers and Porch Climbers.

There are several versions of how the name Yankees was adopted. The local Irish population objected to Highlanders because it was a Scottish nickname, so management supposedly decided on Yankees. Another has it that newspaper headliners objected to Highlanders as too long and that the name Yankees was coined by either Mark Roth of the *New York Globe* or Jim Price of the *New York Press*.

Apparently the Yankees name was in use long before 1912, the date usually given as the date of origination. *The Sporting News* carried an article from the *Boston Herald* of June 21, 1904, reporting on Patsy Dougherty being traded from Boston. "Dougherty as a Yankee" was the headline. A September 9, 1904, story in the same paper said "Yankees Take Two." In a 1906 column Grantland Rice referred to the club as Yankees, though Highlanders was still the predominant name.

One source reported that Jacob Ruppert supposedly was conned into buying one half of the Yankees in 1915 because he could change the team's name to Knickerbockers, which was the name of his beer. After the sale, he reportedly issued a statement that the name was changed, but New York writers refused to acknowledge it.

Key Seasons. The Yankees have never been overtaken after leading at any point in the season by at least 6½ games. The 1933 Yankees were ahead by six before falling to the Senators.

1903. The Yankees finished fourth in their first season and did not win a pennant through 1920. In the following 64 seasons, however, the team won 32 pennants and 22 World Series.

1921. In Babe Ruth's second season with the Yankees the club won the pennant by 4½ games over the Indians. Carl Mays led the league with 27 wins. Ruth had 59 home runs and 171 RBIs to go with his .378 average. The Yankees lost the World Series in eight games to the Giants.

1922. The Yankees repeated as American League champions, this time by only one game over the Browns. Ruth slipped to 35 home runs and 99 RBIs, and Bullet Joe Bush won 26 games. The club was swept in the World Series by the Giants.

1923.

"The Ruth is mighty and shall prevail." — The lead to Heywood Broun's story in the *New York World* on Game 3 of the 1923 World Series in which the Yankees beat the Giants 4–2. Babe Ruth hit two home runs.

After a third straight pennant and by then in their new ballpark, Yankee Stadium, the Yankees won their first World Series in six games over the Giants. Ruth led the league with 41 home runs and 131 RBIs.

1926. After slipping to second and seventh in 1925 and 1926, the Yankees and Ruth returned to form and won the pennant by three games over the Indians. They lost to the Cardinals in Game 7 of the World Series when Grover Cleveland Alexander struck out Tony Lazzeri in the 7th inning with the bases loaded and went on to save the game. Herb Pennock won 23 games and Babe Ruth led the league with 47 home runs and 145 RBIs.

1927. Babe Ruth hit 60 home runs as the Yankees won 110 games and swept the Pirates in the World Series. In 1969 as part of baseball's centennial, this club was voted the greatest team of all time.

1928. The Yankees won their third straight pennant with 101 wins as Lou Gehrig and Babe Ruth tied for the RBI crown with 142. The Yankees swept the Cardinals in the World Series.

1932. The Yankees won their last pennant with Babe Ruth, winning 107 games. The club swept the Cubs in the World Series for manager Joe McCarthy's first championship in New York. Lefty Gomez won 24 games and Ruth had 41 home runs and 137 RBIs. Lou Gehrig hit 34 home runs and drove in 151 runs.

1936. The Joe DiMaggio era began as Lou Gehrig led the league with 49 home runs and Red Ruffing won 20 games to give the Yankees 102 victories. The Yankees beat the Giants in six games to win the World Series.

1937. Both the Yankees and Giants repeated as pennant winners, and the Yankees again beat the Giants in the series, this time in five games. The Yankees repeated their 102 wins and this time Joe DiMaggio led with league with 46 home runs.

1938. Red Ruffing won 21 games to lead the Yankees to their third straight pennant. The Yankees swept the Cubs in the World Series. Joe DiMaggio hit a league-leading 46 home runs and drove in 167 runs. Lou Gehrig hit 37 home runs with 159 RBIs. Lefty Gomez led the league with 21 wins.

1939. The Yankees won 106 games and Joe DiMaggio led the league with a .381 batting average. The Yankees swept the Reds in the World Series for their fourth straight Series victory.

1941. After finishing third in 1940, the Yankees were back on top with 101 wins as Joe DiMaggio led the league with 125 RBIs, and reliever Johnny Murphy had 15 saves to lead the league. The Yankees and Dodgers squared off in the first of several memorable World Series clashes. The Yankees won in five games as they came back in Game 4 after the famous dropped third strike by Dodger catcher Mickey Owen (see also *Passed Balls*).

1942. The Yankees repeated with 103 wins but lost to the Cardinals in the World Series in five games. Ernie Bonham won 21 games and Joe DiMaggio had 21 home runs and 114 RBIs in his last season before leaving for the military.

1943. The Yankees won their seventh pennant in eight years by 13½ games over the Senators. They faced the Cardinals again, this time winning the Series in five games. It was the last pennant for manager Joe McCarthy. Spud Chandler led the league with 20 wins, Charlie Keller hit 31 home runs and Johnny Murphy led the league with 12 wins in relief.

1947. Under Bucky Harris the Yankees won the pennant by 12 games and beat the Dodgers in seven games in the World Series. Bill Bevens was two outs from a no-hitter for the Yankees in Game 4 when the Dodgers scored two runs to win 3–2. Spud Chandler led the league with 17 saves and Joe DiMaggio hit 20 home runs with 97 RBIs.

1949. In Casey Stengel's first season the club won the pennant by one game over the Red Sox. Joe Page's 27 saves led the league

and Joe DiMaggio hit .346 in an injury-shortened season. The Yankees beat the Dodgers in five games in the World Series.

1950. The Yankees beat out the Tigers by three games as Vic Raschi won 21 games and Joe DiMaggio hit 32 home runs with 122 RBIs in his last big season. The Yankees swept the Phillies in the World Series.

1951. The Yankees won their third straight pennant, beating out the Indians by five games. Vic Raschi won 21 games again and Eddie Lopat matched that total. Yogi Berra hit 27 home runs. In the World Series the Yankees beat the Giants in six games behind Lopat's two wins and 0.50 ERA.

1952. For the fourth straight season the Yankees won the pennant. They beat out the Indians again, this time by two games. Yogi Berra was the team leader with 30 home runs and 98 RBIs. Allie Reynolds won 20 games and led the league with a 2.06 ERA. The Yankees beat the Dodgers in the World Series, winning Game 7 by a score of 4–2.

1953. The Yankees won the pennant for the fifth consecutive season, edging out the Indians for the third straight time. Yogi Berra led the club with 27 home runs and 108 RBIs. In a rematch of 1952, the Yankees beat the Dodgers in six games.

1954. Though they won 103 games, the Yankees finished second to the Indians and their 111 wins.

1955. The Yankees were back on top, beating out the Indians by three games. Mickey Mantle led the league with 37 home runs and Whitey Ford led the league with 18 wins. In the World Series, the Dodgers won their first championship with a seven-game victory over the Yankees.

1956. The Yankees repeated as American League champions by nine games over the second-place Indians. Mickey Mantle won the Triple Crown and Yogi Berra had 30 home runs and 105 RBIs. Don Larsen's **Perfect Game** was the highlight of the World Series, as the Yankees beat the Dodgers in seven games.

1957. The Yankees won their eighth pennant in nine years, as Mickey Mantle had 34 home runs and Bob Grim led the league with 19 saves. The Braves surprised the Yankees with a seven-game World Series victory.

1958. Mickey Mantle's league-leading 42 home runs helped the Yankees to another pennant. Bob Turley contributed a league-leading 21 wins and Ryne Duren led the league with 20 saves. The Yankees avenged their 1957 Series loss with a seven-game victory over the Braves. The Yankees were the first team since 1925 to come back from a 3–1 game deficit to win the Series.

1960. After one off-year, the Yankees were back on top with 97 wins, as Roger Maris led the league with 112 RBIs and Mickey Mantle led with 40 home runs. The Yankees outscored the Pirates overall in the World Series, but the Pirates made their runs count and won Game 7 on Bill Mazeroski's 9th inning home run.

1961. Though the Tigers won 101 games, the Yankees ran away with the pennant with 109 wins. The highlights were the 61 home runs and 142 RBIs by Roger Maris, Mickey Mantle's 54 home runs, the league-leading 25 wins by Whitey Ford and league-leading 29 saves by Luis Arroyo. In the Series the Yankees blasted the Reds in five games. See also Tony Kubek and Terry Pluto, *Sixty-One* (1987).

1962. The Yankees won their third straight pennant, this time by five games over the Twins. Ralph Terry led the league with 23 wins and Roger Maris and Mickey Mantle each hit at least 30 home runs. The Yankees beat the Giants in seven games, as Willie McCovey lined out to second baseman Bobby Richardson with two on and two out in a 1–0 game to end the Series.

1963. The Yankees won 104 games to run away with the pennant again but were swept by the Dodgers in the World Series.

Whitey Ford led the league with 24 wins and four players hit at least 23 home runs.

1964.

"When I covered the Yankees in the '60s, they had players like Horace Clarke, Ross Moschitto, Jake Gibbs and Dooley Womack. It was like the first-team missed the bus."— Joe Garagiola, on the bad Yankee teams of the mid– and late 1960s.

The Yankees won their 14th pennant in 16 years by one game over the Indians. Jim Bouton won 18 games and Mickey Mantle hit 35 home runs and had 111 RBIs. The Yankee dynasty came to an end with a Game 7 loss to the Cardinals. By 1966 the club was in last place and was not a factor until the mid–1970s.

1976. After strong finishes in 1974 and 1975, the Yankees finally returned to the top under manager Billy Martin. Graig Nettles led the league with 33 home runs and Ed Figueroa won 19 games. The Yankees won the ALCS over the Royals on a Chris Chambliss home run in the bottom of the 9th inning of Game 5. After the exciting finish, the Yankees were swept in the World Series by the Reds.

1977. After adding Reggie Jackson to the line-up, the Yankees won 100 games to win the Eastern Division title. Jackson and Graig Nettles combined for 69 home runs. The Yankees again faced the Royals and again won in the last inning of Game 5. In the World Series, Jackson hit three consecutive home runs in Game 6 against the Dodgers to clinch the championship.

1978. The Yankees won their third straight division crown after trailing Boston for most of the season. Ron Guidry's 25 wins led the league, but part of the story was the turmoil surrounding ***Manager*** Billy Martin, who was replaced by Bob Lemon midway through the season.

The Yankees and Red Sox finished in a dead heat and the Yankees won a one-game ***Play-Off*** to move into the ALCS. They played the Royals for the third straight season and beat them in four games. They faced the Dodgers once more in the World Series and again the Yankees prevailed in six games. See also Sparky Lyle and Peter Golenbock, *The Bronx Zoo* (1979).

1980. The Yankees won 103 games to win the title by three games over the Orioles. Reggie Jackson led the league with 41 home runs. Kansas City finally made it into the World Series with a three-game sweep of the Yankees to win the American League pennant.

1981.

"If you want to get off this team you have to take a number."— Dave Revering on the 1981 Yankees.

The Yankees repeated as Eastern Division champions, winning the first half of the strike-shortened season and beating the Brewers in the mini-play-off for the division title. In the ALCS the Yankees swept the A's. The Dodgers finally beat the Yankees in the World Series, winning in six games. It was the last time the Yankees would make it into the postseason for 14 seasons.

1995. The Yankees were the wild card team on the strength of a number of strong but not outstanding individual efforts by their players. They lost the division series to the Mariners in the bottom of the 11th inning of Game 5 after leading in extra innings. Paul O'Neill hit 22 home runs and had 96 RBIs and Wade Boggs hit .324. John Wetteland saved 31 games.

1996. The Yankees held off the Orioles to win their first division title since 1981 and then knocked out the Rangers in the playoffs. The Yankees then beat the Orioles for the pennant with the help of a controversial interference call involving a young Yankee fan on a home run (See ***Interference***—Fan). The Yankees lost the first two games of the World Series to the powerful Braves but swept the next four (after being down 6–0 in Game 3). Bernie

Williams hit 29 home runs and Tino Martinez hit 25 and drove in 117 runs. Andy Pettitte won 21 games and John Wetteland saved 43.

1997. The Yankees came in second as the wild card to the Orioles by two games, with a 96–66 record, but lost to the Indians in the division series in five games. Tino Martinez had 44 home runs and 141 RBIs, and Bernie Williams and Paul O'Neill each had 100 or more RBIs. Andy Pettitte won 18 games and David Wells won 16, while Mariano Rivera had 43 saves

1998. The Yankees set a short-lived record with a 114–48 season, best ever in the Major Leagues (Seattle topped this three years later). The Yankees swept the Rangers in the division series and then beat the Indians in six games for the American League pennant. In the World Series, they swept the Padres to complete perhaps the best season ever by a Major League team. Four players had at least 23 home runs, and Tino Martinez led the club with 123 RBIs and Paul O'Neill had 116. David Cone was 20–7, David Wells 18–4 and Andy Pettitte 16–11. Mariano Rivera had 36 saves, a 3–0 record and a 1.91 ERA.

2000. The Yankees finished the regular season with a record of only 87–74, but won their division and then beat the A's 7–5 in the deciding Game 5. They went on to beat the Mariners in six games in the ALCS, and then beat the Mets in five games in the World Series. Bernie Williams led the club with 30 home runs and 121 RBIs, Andy Pettitte was 19–9 and Mariano Rivera saved 36 games.

2001. The Yankees again won the division, with a 95–65 record, and again beat the A's in five games in the division series, this time sweeping three games after losing the first two. In the ALCS, they again beat the Mariners, this time in five games. The World Series was one of the best ever, as the Yankees were down 2–0 in games and then came back twice to beat the Diamondbacks with 9th inning rallies off pitcher Byung-Hyun Kim. New York led going into the bottom of the 9th of Game 7, but the Diamondbacks rallied against reliever Mariano Rivera and scored two to win the Series. Tino Martinez led the club with 34 home runs and 113 RBIs, Derek Jeter hit .311 and Bernie Williams hit .307 with 94 RBIs. Roger Clemens was 20–3 and Mike Mussina won 17, and Mariano Rivera saved 50 games.

2002. Once again the club won the East, with a 103–58 record, but lost to the eventual champions, the Angels, in the division series in four games. Jason Giambi led the club with 41 home runs and 122 RBIs, second baseman Alfonso Soriano had 39 home runs and 102 RBIs, and Bernie Williams hit .333 with 102 RBIs. Mike Mussina won 18 games and David Wells won 19 games, as an injured Mariano Rivera saved 28.

2003.

"YANKEES SLEEP WITH THE FISH."— Headline in the *New York Post* after they lost to the Marlins in the 2003 World Series.

The Yankees won the East with a 101–61 record and beat the Twins in the division series in four games. They went seven games against the Red Sox to win the American League pennant, but lost the World Series in six games to the Florida Marlins. The Yankees were led by Jason Giambi with 41 home runs and Alfonso Soriano with 38. Hideki Matsui had 106 RBIs and Derek Jeter batted .324. Andy Pettitte was 21–8 in his last season with the club, and Roger Clemens (thought to be retiring) and Mike Mussina each won 17 games. Mariano Rivera saved 40 games.

2004. For the fifth straight season the Yankees won the East, this time with a 101–61 record, three games ahead of the Red Sox. Gary Sheffield and Alex Rodriguez each had 36 home runs, and Sheffield led the team with 121 RBIs. Hideki Matsui had 31 home runs and 108 RBIs, and Derek Jeter rebounded from a horrendous start to finish with a .292 average and 23 home runs. The starting pitching wasn't as strong as expected, as Javier Vasquez and Jon Lieber (a likely comeback player of the year) topped the club with 14 wins. Mike Mussina (12 wins) and Kevin Brown (10 wins) had off years, but Mariano Rivera had 53 saves. The Yankees beat the Twins in four games in the division series, and then took the first three games of the ALCS against the Red Sox. After winning Game 3 by a whopping 19–8, the Yankees looked ready to advance to another World Series. In Game 4, the Yankees led by a run in the 9th inning and were poised to sweep, but reliever Mariano Rivera blew the lead and the Red Sox won in extra innings on a home run by David Ortiz. The Red Sox then came back to win Games 5 (also in extra innings), 6 and 7, becoming the first team ever to win a seven-game series after losing the first three; and against the hated Yankees no less!

Key Players.

"It was a death struggle every day being a Yankee—you either won or you lost. There was no second place. Half of us were nuts by the end of a season."—Jerry Coleman.

Jack Chesbro (HF) won 41 games in 1904 for the Highlanders, a modern Major League record. He won 129 games for the club between 1903 and 1908.

Babe Ruth (HF) moved from the Red Sox to the Yankees for the 1920 season. He immediately had what many consider his greatest season when he hit .376 with 54 home runs and 137 RBIs. His .847 slugging average and home run percentage that season were the best ever until Barry Bonds in 2001. Ruth hit 659 of his 714 home runs for the Yankees. He led the league in home runs for the Yankees 10 times and slugging average 11 times.

Lou Gehrig (HF) played his entire 17-year career with the Yankees beginning in 1923. He hit 493 home runs and batted .361 in seven World Series. His .632 slugging average is third all-time. He had season RBI totals of 175, 174, 184 and 165, each time leading the league on his way to third all-time in the category.

Tony Lazzeri (HF) anchored the infield at second base from 1926 through 1937, driving in more than 100 runs seven times.

Bill Dickey (HF) batted over .300 in nine of his first 10 seasons in the American League beginning in 1928. Over his 17 years with the Yankees he batted .313 and was considered one of the premier catchers in the Major Leagues. He hit .255 in eight World Series.

Joe DiMaggio (HF) started his 13-year career with the Yankees in 1936. He hit .325 lifetime and is seventh all-time among retired players with a .579 slugging average. His career was interrupted for three prime years during World War II and he finished with 361 home runs. He hit .271 in 10 World Series.

Yogi Berra (HF) was the best American League catcher of the 1950s and led the Yankees to World Series appearances in 14 seasons. He hit .285 over his 18 years with the club beginning in 1946. He hit 358 home runs and is third all-time with 12 World Series home runs. He is first or second in many of the prominent World Series hitting categories.

Mickey Mantle (HF) arrived with the Yankees in 1951. Despite myriad injuries he lasted 18 seasons and hit 536 home runs. He finished with a .298 batting average and led the league in home runs four times. He won the Triple Crown in 1956 with a .353 average, 52 home runs and 130 RBIs. He appeared in 12 World Series and is first all-time with 18 World Series home runs.

Whitey Ford (HF).

"You kind of took it for granted around the Yankees that there was always going to be baseball in October."—Ford, who pitched 16 seasons for the Yankees starting in 1950. He won 236 games and pitched 45 shutouts. His .690 winning percentage is third all-time. Ford also won 10 games in the World Series, first all-time, and pitched three World Series shutouts.

Graig Nettles.

"It's a good thing Babe Ruth isn't here. If he was, George Steinbrenner would have him bat seventh and say he's overweight."—Nettles, during the turbulent late 1970s. He was the Yankee third baseman of the 1970s and early 1980s. He hit 20 or more home runs eight times for the club and appeared in four World Series. He led the league with 32 home runs in 1976.

Reggie Jackson (HF) played only five seasons for the Yankees, but he led the club to three World Series appearances in which he hit eight home runs. He led the league with 41 home runs in 1980.

Ron Guidry pitched for 14 seasons in New York, winning 25 games in 1978 and 22 in 1985. He finished with 170 wins and 26 shutouts for the club.

Don Mattingly.

"Everybody thinks I've changed, but I'm just a boy from the hills of Indiana. If you don't believe me, ask my butler, Reggie Jackson."—Mattingly, who was the only long-term Yankee star of the 1980s and early 1990s. He batted over .300 six times in the 1980s, including a league-leading .343 in 1984. He also led the league with 145 RBIs in 1985. Back problems cut down his power after 1989, but he was still the Yankee leader through 1995.

Derek Jeter. Drafted sixth overall in 1992 by the Yankees, Jeter was the American League Rookie of the Year in 1996 and continued to anchor the Yankees at shortstop through the 2004 season. He has batted .317 through 2003.

Bernie Williams began with the Yankees in 1991 and was still in center field for the club in 2004. Through 2003 he had five seasons with over 100 RBIs and batted over .300 in eight straight seasons.

Mariano Rivera, the premier reliever of his era, and the best ever in the postseason, saved 336 games between 1996 (his second season) and 2004, including highs of 53 in 2004, 50 in 2001 and 45 in 1999. In 21 postseason series between 1995 and 2003 he won seven games and saved 30.

Andy Pettitte pitched nine seasons for the Yankees between 1995 and 2003, before signing with the Astros in 2004 (and then was injured). His best seasons were 1996 and 2003, when he was 21–8. Overall, he had a record of 149–78 and a .656 winning percentage for the club.

Key Managers.

"The ideal Yankee manager isn't Joe McCarthy, it's Charlie McCarthy."—Peter Gammons alluding to the "Yes men" George Steinbrenner seemed to want running his club.

Clark Griffith (HF) was the first Yankee manager, leading the club for six seasons through 1908. His best finish was second place in 1904 and 1906. He later became the long-time owner of the Senators.

Miller Huggins (HF).

"There is a disposition to question Miller Huggins' ability, but I, for one, am convinced that the master of the Yankees is a smart and capable manager. No one but Huggins himself ever will know the problem he has had with his troupe of prima donnas."—Sportswriter Cullen Cain in a 1926 article in the *Saturday Evening Post.*

Huggins was managing the Cardinals when *The Sporting News* owner J.G. Taylor Spink urged him to meet with Jacob Ruppert about the Yankee job. Over the protest of co-owner Huston, Huggins was hired for the 1918 season and managed the club until his death in September 1929. He led the club to six pennants and three World Series victories.

Joe McCarthy (HF).

"Much to the chagrin of American League rivals, Joe McCarthy, boss-man of the New York Yankees, is a phenomenal seer when it comes to shuffling players from positions of their choosing to where Marse Joe thinks they should play." — The *Stars and Stripes* military newspaper in 1944.

"I want a man who can bring me a World's Championship." — Cubs owner William Wrigley, Jr., after firing McCarthy following the 1930 season. Ironically, McCarthy's Yankees swept the Cubs in the 1932 World Series. The alcoholic Hall of Fame manager led the Yankees through early 1946, winning eight pennants and seven World Championships.

Bucky Harris (HF) became the Yankee manager in 1947 and lasted two seasons before being replaced by Casey Stengel. One source reported that Stengel might never have become the Yankee manager except for a managerial move by Harris during the no-hitter attempt by Bill Bevens in the 1947 World Series. Harris ordered Bevens to walk Pete Reiser with Al Gionfriddo on second. Bevens had already walked a number of batters that day. Cookie Lavagetto then doubled. Harris was fired the next year when he finished third.

Casey Stengel (HF).

"Well, sirs and ladies, the Yankees have now been mathematically eliminated from the 1949 pennant race. They eliminated themselves when they engaged Perfesser Casey Stengel to mismanage them for the next two years, and you may be sure that the perfesser will oblige to the best of his unique ability." — Dave Egan of the *Boston Globe*.

Stengel was named Yankee manager on October 12, 1948, 25 years to the day after he hit the second of his two game-winning home runs in the 1923 World Series. Most beat writers in New York thought that he was too old and was merely a stopgap until a more qualified manager was found. He immediately led the club to five straight World Series victories and 10 World Series appearances in 12 years through 1960.

Stengel probably would have lost his job after the 1958 season if the Yankees had not defeated the Braves in the World Series in a rematch of the 1957 Series that the Yankees lost in 7 games. Owners Dan Topping and Del Webb were not happy with him, but it would have been a public relations nightmare to fire him after a World Series victory. They signed him to a two-year contract in January 1959, intending that it be his last contract. He might have been fired after the dismal 1959 season, but the owners did not want to eat the second year of the contract, worth $90,000. They used the 1960 Game 7 World Series loss to the Pirates to justify Stengel's "retirement" because he had turned 70. Stengel's response: "It's the last time I'll make the mistake of turning 70."

Yogi Berra (HF) was slated to be fired after his one season managing the club, but the Yankees finished first with a 99–63 record; though they lost to the Cardinals in seven games. Nevertheless, he was fired in favor of Cardinals manager Johnny Keane.

Ralph Houk managed from 1961 through 1963, winning pennants each season and claiming two World Series titles. Houk knew he would be gone after the 1963 season even before the Yankees were swept by the Dodgers in the World Series. Houk's close friend and pitching coach Johnny Sain was aware that long-time Yankee coach Frank Crosetti was quietly teaching Yogi Berra how to manage. Berra then took over for the 1964 season.

Billy Martin.

"To be manager of the Yankees under the malevolent dictator-

ship of George Steinbrenner is like being married to Zsa Zsa Gabor. The union is short and sweet." — Sportswriter Bob Rubin.

"If you approach Billy Martin right, he's Okay. I avoid him altogether." — Ron Guidry.

Martin managed the Yankees for most of the seasons between 1975 and 1979 (with some notable lapses in service — see *Managers*) and in 1983. He also managed the club for most of 1985 and a small portion of 1988. He won two pennants and one World Series for the Yankees.

Buck Showalter took over the Yankees in 1992 and remained at the helm through 1995 before leaving to manage the expansion Diamondbacks. The Yankees won the American League wild card spot in 1995. When he managed his 472nd consecutive game in June 1995, he broke the record of 471 by Billy Martin for the most consecutive by a Yankee manager under George Steinbrenner.

Joe Torre.

"Being a winner as a player is getting the most from your ability. Being a winner as a manager is not getting fired." — Torre.

"This really is fun, but you don't know it's fun until it's over." — Torre, after the 2003 ALCS nail-biter against the Red Sox.

For all his success, Torre holds the record of 15 seasons managing before winning his first pennant, which finally occurred in his first season with the Yankees. New York made it to the postseason every year that Torre managed the club beginning in 1996, through 2004. They won their division every year except 1997, when they were the wild card team. They won the World Series in four out of five years beginning in 1996, losing only in 1997 in the first round of the play-offs. The club won over 100 games three times under his stewardship, which continued through 2004.

Ballparks. The Yankees were the last early American League team to build a modern concrete and steel stadium in 1923. In 1903 the Yankee owners bought land and quickly built wooden Hilltop Park between 165th and 168th Streets. Hilltop had a capacity of 15,000 and is now the site of Columbia Presbyterian Hospital.

In 1913 Hilltop Park was run down, and relations with the Giants had improved. Yankee owner Frank Farrell signed a lease to play in the much larger Polo Grounds, home of the Giants. The Yankees remained tenants of the Giants until *Yankee Stadium* opened in 1923.

Key Broadcasters.

"I heard doctors revived a man who had been dead for 4–½ minutes. When they asked him what it was like being dead, he said it was like listening to Yankees announcer Phil Rizzuto during a rain delay." — David Letterman.

The first year in which the Yankees allowed broadcasts of their games was 1939. Before that, the club had an agreement with the Giants and Dodgers which prohibited broadcasts of New York games.

Arch McDonald moved from the Senators to the Yankees for one year in 1939, but a change in beer sponsorship ended the relationship and McDonald returned to Washington. McDonald's assistant during that year was *Mel Allen*, who took over the primary broadcasting duties. In 1943 Allen went into the Army, and there were no Yankee or Giants radio broadcasts because the teams could not find a sponsor. Gillette then came in to sponsor the games.

In 1946 Yankee general manager Larry MacPhail hired Allen when *Red Barber* refused to report after demanding $100,000 to broadcast Yankee games. In 1954 there were discussions about Barber, then with the Dodgers, and Mel Allen, switching teams; Barber would come to the Yankees and Allen would go to the Dodgers. Dodger owner Walter O'Malley disliked Barber, particularly because

Barber had been a close friend of former Dodger owner Branch Rickey, whom O'Malley despised. Yankee owner Dan Topping hated Allen. Over a drink in a bar, Topping and O'Malley agreed to swap announcers. Though the trade never materialized, Barber did move over to the Yankees that year.

Allen broadcast for the Yankees until he was fired in September 1964 and Barber lasted through the 1966 season. Phil Rizzuto was chosen to broadcast the 1964 World Series after broadcasting for the club since 1957. He continued in the Yankee broadcast booth until late in the 1995 season; remorseful at not attending Mickey Mantle's funeral, he abruptly resigned. He worked in the booth for a number of years with future National League president Bill White, a former Major League first baseman. White started in the Yankee broadcast booth in 1968.

Frank Messer began with the Yankees in 1968 and remained into the 1980s. In 1990 Tony Kubek broadcast for the club and remained through the mid–1990s. ESPN pioneer George Grande began with the Yankees in 1988 and remained through the 1990s. Tom Seaver broadcast in the early 1990s.

See David Halberstam, *Sports on New York Radio: A Play-By-Play History* (1999).

Books. Phil Bashe, *Dog Days: The New York Yankees' Fall from Grace and Eventual Redemption 1965–1976* (1994); Dom Forker, *The Men of Autumn* (1989); Dom Forker, *Sweet Seasons* (1990); Mark Gallagher, *The Yankee Encyclopedia* (1995); Mark and Neil Gallagher, *The Yankees* (1990); Derek Gentile, *The Complete New York Yankees: The Total Encyclopedia of the Team* (2001); Peter Golenbock, *Dynasty* (1975); Frank Graham, *The New York Yankees* (1943, 1958); David Hickey and Kerry Keene, *The Proudest Yankees of All: From the Bronx to Cooperstown* (2004); Donald Honig, *The New York Yankees* (1981); Richard A. Johnson, Dick Johnson, Glenn Stout, *Yankees Century: 100 Years of New York Yankees Baseball* (2002); Richard Lally, *Bombers: An Oral History of the New York Yankees* (2002); Ed Linn, *Steinbrenner's Yankees* (1982); Bill Madden and Moss Klein, *Damned Yankees* (1990); Jack Mann, *The Decline and Fall of the New York Yankees* (1967); Phil Pepe, *The Yankees* (1995); Lyle Spatz, *New York Yankee Openers* (1997); Lyle Spatz, *Yankees Coming, Yankees Going: New York Yankee Player Transactions, 1903 through 1999* (2000); Vic Ziegal, *Summer In the City: New York Baseball 1947–1957* (2003) (photos).

Newark Bears

"It would, in fact, have seemed to me an emotional thrill forsaken if, before the Newark Bears took on the hated enemy from across the marshes, the Jersey City Giants, we hadn't first to rise to our feet (my father, my brother, and I — along with our inimical countrymen, the city's Germans, Italians, Irish, Poles, and, out in the Africa of the bleachers, Newark's Negroes) to celebrate the America that had given to this unharmonious mob a game so grand and beautiful." — Philip Roth in *Portnoy's Complaint* (1969).

The 1937 Newark Bears won the International League's pennant by 25½ games and are considered by some as the greatest minor league team of all time. However, it may be more accurate to say that this was the best minor league club consisting of players who had future success in the Major Leagues. The Yankee farm team featured these future Major League position players:

George McQuinn	1B (starred with Browns)
Joe Gordon	2B (starred with Yankees)
Babe Dahlgren	3B (solid with the Yankees)
Jimmy Gleeson	SS (with Reds and Cubs as OF)
Bob Seeds	OF (with Indians, Red Sox, Yankees)
Charlie Keller	RF (starred with Yankees)
Willard Hershberger	C (Reds starter)
Buddy Rosar	C (Yankees, Indians, A's, Red Sox)

The team had no pitching stars, but each pitcher made the Major Leagues at least briefly.

Books. Ronald A. Mayer, *The 1937 Newark Bears* (1980).

Newark Peppers

Federal League 1915

The Peppers, also known as the NewFeds and Peps, replaced Indianapolis in the Federal League for the 1915 season. The owner was multimillionaire oilman Harry Sinclair, who later was implicated in the Teapot Dome political scandal. Newark finished fifth in the eight-team league with an 80–72 record. Bill McKechnie managed the club and played third base. The Peppers attempted to boost attendance by combining baseball with postgame bicycle races.

Hal Newhouser (1921–1998)

Hall of Fame (VC) 1992

"I cut him quite a bit because of the calibre of competition that he was facing, but his performance in 1946 and 1948 would put one through some fairly hefty contortions to show that he was not a worthy pitcher."— Bill James in *The Bill James Historical Baseball Abstract* (1988), commenting on the criticism of Newhouser because he had his greatest seasons during the talent-thin war years of 1944 and 1945.

Newhouser was the premier pitcher during World War II and had six strong seasons among his 17 years in the Major Leagues, almost exclusively for Detroit.

Harold Newhouser began his professional career with Alexandria in the Evangeline League and Beaumont in the Texas League. Near the end of the 1939 season he came up to the Tigers for one appearance. He remained with the Tigers for the next 14 seasons, including all of the war years. A congenital heart ailment kept him out of the service (and almost out of baseball), but he nevertheless became the dominant pitcher of the war years.

After four mediocre seasons, Newhouser erupted in 1944 with a 29–9 record and the MVP award. He won the award again in 1945 after posting 25 wins. Many have called the seasons flukes because of the poor competition created by the loss of players into the military. However, Newhouser posted 26 wins in 1946 and 21 in 1948 when the competition had returned.

He began to have shoulder trouble after the 1948 season and dropped to 18 wins in 1949 and 15 in 1950. He continued to fade and moved to the Indians for the 1954 season. He finished that year with seven wins and seven saves. In 1955 he appeared in only two games.

Newhouser finished his career with 207 wins, 33 shutouts and a 3.06 ERA. He is the only pitcher to win consecutive MVP Awards; although there was no Cy Young Award until 1956 and Sandy Koufax might have won consecutive awards had the Cy Young alternative not been available.

After his retirement Newhouser worked for a bank in Michigan and then scouted for the Orioles and Indians. He was on the bubble for the Hall of Fame for many years, receiving criticism for the short duration and wartime conditions of his peak seasons. The Veterans Committee finally elected him in 1992.

Book. David M. Jordan, *A Tiger in His Time* (1990).

Newspapers

"I know of no subject, save perhaps baseball, on which the average American newspaper discourses without unfailing sense and understanding." — Sports hater and writer/editor H.L. Mencken.

"I learned the English language more from the baseball columns than from the famous bard [Shakespeare]." — Francis Cardinal Spellman.

"There is a majesty about the printed word. There is life to it. I consider a newspaper my friend." — Moe Berg, who read many international newspapers each day and would refuse to read a newspaper if someone touched it before he finished it.

"In the relentlessly boring spitting contest between baseball labor and baseball management, the sole constructive purpose of daily journalism is to administer evenhanded beatings to all parties on a regular basis." — Thomas Boswell in *Cracking the Show* (1994).

"A ballplayer has two reputations, one with the other players and one with the fans. The first is based on ability. The second the newspapers gives him." — Johnny Evers.

"By the time the press of Boston has completed its daily treatment of Theodore S. Williams, there is no room in the papers for anything but two sticks of agate type about Truman and housing, and one column for the last Boston girl to be murdered on the beach." — John Lardner.

"And now his love for reading has gotten so out of hand, he'll even read a daily newspaper, starting with the sports section and reading his way forward, the way his dad does. He reads the sports section the way people read the wills of rich relatives, scouring the fine print, then rereading the parts he doesn't fully understand." — *Los Angeles Times* columnist Chris Erskine on his 12-year-old son's new-found love of reading.

See also **Magazines**, **The National Sports Daily** and **Sportswriters**.

Earliest Baseball Stories. Newspapers first carried baseball news in the 1850s. By the 1860s papers were printing inning-by-inning accounts of games and used a crude form of box score. They also began printing fan letters.

Many sources identify the first baseball article as written by Senator William Cauldwell, editor and owner of the *New York Sunday Mercury*. His April 1853 story referenced the upcoming game between the Knickerbockers and Gothams. The follow-up article was dated May 1, 1853, and reported a 12–12 tie after 12 innings. Another source identified the first baseball story as a July 10, 1853, article in the *Sunday Mercury*.

Still another source cites the first baseball newspaper coverage as an October 21, 1845, announcement in the *New York Herald* of a game between New York and Brooklyn clubs.

There was a reference to "Bass-Ball" in the July 13, 1825, edition of the *New York Gazette*. A challenge was issued to play games for $1.

The curtain was pulled back even further in the 2000s, when SABR research George A. Thompson, Jr., discovered an 1823 reference. On April 25, 1823 the *National Advocate* newspaper of New York carried a reference to "base base" and the fact that young men were in an "organized association." See also, **Origins of Baseball**.

New York Newspapers. In 1868 the *New York Times* sold its 12-page newspaper for one penny. Occasionally there appeared one half of a column titled "Sporting." It was also sometimes titled "Turf" or "Base Ball."

In 1911 New York City had seven English language morning papers and six afternoon papers. Newspapers in New York and other Major League cities of the early 20th century posted partial scores in their windows and published special baseball editions containing partial scores.

Morning/Afternoon Editions. The morning finals were always more detailed in their descriptions of games. The afternoon papers, printed almost immediately after games ended, often only had scores of the day's games and contained more detailed summaries of the previous day's games.

In the early days, reporters had afternoon deadlines immediately after games and therefore interviewed players prior to the game. The now-traditional postgame interview is a phenomenon that did not begin to proliferate until the 1920s.

Sports Departments. Joseph Pulitzer of the *New York World* is credited with organizing the first newspaper sports department. The paper started a full page of sports in the 1880s. In 1886 the *New York Times* contained 500 baseball columns over the summer months. The Hearst newspapers introduced a separate sports section in the late 19th century.

Standings. The team standings in the papers did not contain a "Games Behind Leader" column on a regular basis until 1938.

Newspaper Strike.

"Among the spectators was a pathetic little band of Detroit sportswriters, utterly orphaned by the five-month-old newspaper strike in their home town." — Roger Angell in *The Summer Game* (1972), writing during spring training in 1968.

During the 1978 American League East pennant race, the Yankees were under somewhat less pressure because of a New York newspaper strike during much of the second half of the season. Less media coverage meant less public scrutiny for the embattled players. The Yankees made a tremendous comeback in the standings and then beat the Red Sox in a play-off game before going on to win the World Series against the Dodgers in six games.

Newspaper Clippings. Gene Brown, *The Complete Book of Baseball* (1980), originally published as the *New York Times Book of Baseball History* (1975), contains 109 years of baseball as reported in the *Times*; Richard Cohen, et al., *The Scrapbook History of Baseball* (1975); Richard Whittingham, *The DiMaggio Albums* (1989). The two-volume DiMaggio set was beautiful on the outside but perhaps a little thin on the inside. It was a flop, originally retailing for $100 and dropping to $30 or less by the next year.

Dewey/Truman Redux. When the Yankees came back to the beat the Red Sox in Game 7 of the 2003 ALCS, the front and back pages of the October 17 *New York Post* featured full-page photos of Aaron Boone hitting the extra-inning home run that clinched it for the Yankees. Inside, however, a *Post* editorial lamented the Yankee loss: "The Curse of the Bambino boomeranged this year. The Fall Classic should be one helluva series — even without the Yanks.... Despite holding a 3–2 lead in games over the Boston Red Sox, the Yankees couldn't get the job done at home; their season ended last night in the seventh game of the American League Championship Series."

The paper had prepared two editorials, but when the game ended at 12:16 a.m. a copy editor ran the wrong one. The editorial ran in 200,000 of the paper's 650,000 copies. The newspaper committed a similar *faux pas* in spring 2004 when some of its editions erroneously announced the wrong running mate for presidential candidate John Kerry. The headlines blared "Kerry Chooses [Richard] Gephardt."

Nicaragua

"More than the national pastime, it is the national passion, played by Nicaraguans from six to sixty. Poets write about it; government leaders think about it; the newspapers are filled with columns about it; the games are carried over the radio and TV. Baseball, in fact, may be one of the few threads of unity left in the increasingly unraveling society of this country."—Joel Zoss and John Bowman in *Diamonds in the Rough* (1989).

According to some sources, baseball arrived in Nicaragua in the early 20th century, supposedly introduced by U.S. consul Carter Donaldson in 1905. Rather, one of the first prominent teams, the Boers, was established by Donaldson and remained in existence for many years. The U.S. Marines in the area popularized the sport over the next 20 years and baseball remains the country's most popular sport. The Boer club traveled to Costa Rica in 1924, for the country's first international contest.

Other sources more accurately report that in the 1880s, a local man became disenchanted with cricket, played by the occupying British. Albert Addlesberg convinced two of the cricket clubs to switch to baseball, and imported the necessary equipment from New Orleans. Two teams, the Southerns and the Roses, were established in 1887.

Nicaragua participated in several international tournaments and has hosted several, the first in 1948.

Professional League. Nicaragua had a professional league starting in the 1940s and it flourished in the late 1950s through the mid–1960s. It was officially abolished when the socialist government took over in the 1980s, but players are still paid. Marv Throneberry won the Nicaraguan League batting title in 1958 with a .344 average.

Major League Players. Pitcher Dennis Martinez is the first and most prominent Nicaraguan to play Major League Baseball. Martinez was so popular that in 1994 while still an active player he declined a request that he run for the country's presidency in the 1996 election. Other players who came up to the Major Leagues in the 1970s were Albert Williams, Tony Cheves and David Green (David Alejandro Green Casaya).

Marvin Bernard is one of two recent Nicaraguans to make it to the Major Leagues, playing in 1995 for the Giants and lasting through 2003. The other is Phillies pitcher Vincent Padilla.

Kid Nichols (1869–1953)

Hall of Fame (VC) 1949

"It was nothing for him to pitch over 400 innings a season, whereas even 300 is practically unheard of for present-day pitchers. Although he was not a big man, Nichols depended on sheer speed and good control."—Harold Seymour in *Baseball: The Early Years* (1960).

Nichols won 361 games in the National League between 1890 and 1906.

Charles Augustus Nichols grew up in Kansas City and was turned down at age 16 to play for the one-season (1886) National League club in that city. The next year he made the club, which by then was out of the National League. He was discovered by Frank Selee at Omaha in 1889 and Selee took Nichols with him when he moved on to manage the Boston Red Stockings in 1890.

Nichols won 329 games for the Red Stockings over 12 years from 1890 through 1901. Nichols won 30 or more games seven times for the club. He was hired to be player-manager for Kansas City in the Western League in 1902–1903. He was named player-manager of the Cardinals in 1904 and won 21 games for the club. He suffered from pleurisy in 1905 and was released as Cardinals manager. He completed his career with the Phillies, winning 10 games in late 1905 before finishing in 1906 with an 0–1 record in four appearances.

His 361 wins are sixth all-time and his 532 complete games are fourth all-time. He pitched 48 shutouts and had a winning percentage of .634. After retiring, he returned to Kansas City and opened a bowling alley.

Nicknames

"Finally there are the nicknames. All homogeneous groups love nicknames, and baseball people use them freely. Naturally, many of the nicknames remain within the confines of the profession and are not known to the average fan who becomes familiar only with those that the sportswriters and announcers use."—Tristram Coffin in *The Old Ball Game* (1971).

See also *Names*.

Groups of Players. The Chicago White Stockings infielders of the 1880s were known as "The Stone Wall" because of their superlative fielding skill.

Hugh Duffy and Tommy McCarthy of the 1890s Red Stockings were known as the "Heavenly Twins," and on the strength of that designation McCarthy rode Duffy's coattails into the Hall of Fame.

Stuffy McInnis, Eddie Collins, Jack Barry and Frank "Home Run" Baker were known as "The $100,000 Infield" because A's manager Connie Mack said that he would not take $100,000 for them. Despite the pronouncement by Mack, McInnis was traded to the Red Sox for three players in early 1918; Collins was traded to the White Sox in late 1914 for $50,000; Barry was traded to the Red Sox in mid–1915 for $8,000; and Baker was traded to the Yankees in early 1916 for $37,500.

A later A's infield consisting of Jimmie Foxx, Joe Boley, Max Bishop and Jimmy Dykes was known as "The Million Dollar Infield" (must have been inflation). They won three pennants and two World Series from 1929 through 1931. In late 1935 Foxx was traded to the Red Sox for two players and $150,000; Boley was traded to the Indians in mid–1932 for an undisclosed amount of cash; in late 1933 Bishop was traded to the Red Sox along with Lefty Grove for two players and $125,000; in late 1932 Dykes was traded to the White Sox with Al Simmons and Mule Haas for $100,000.

Harry Hooper became a member of the "Million Dollar Outfield" with Tris Speaker and Duffy Lewis for the Red Sox from 1909 through 1920.

Player Nicknames (a Sampling).

Grover Cleveland Alexander. Alexander got his nickname of "Old Pete" as a boy when he fell into a mud-alkali bog in Texas. Someone said, "Well, if it isn't old Alkali Pete, himself."

Frank "Home Run" Baker. Baker hit a high fastball for a home run thrown by Rube Marquard during Game 2 of the 1911 World Series. Marquard's teammate, Christy Mathewson, was unimpressed: "So what, he can't hit a low curve." In Game 3 Baker hit Mathewson's low curve for his second home run of the Series. Because of the infrequency of home runs in that period, and especially coming during a World Series, a legend was born in the name of Home Run Baker. He hit 96 home runs over 13 seasons.

Fido Baldwin. Residence in the manager's doghouse gave rise to the nickname of Fido. He won 154 games in seven years between 1887 and 1889, including a league-high 32 for Chicago of the 1890 Players League.

Lady Baldwin. Baldwin was a 19th century player who was given the nickname by teammates because he did not drink, smoke or cuss. Maybe his middle name of "Busted" kept him out of trouble.

Dave Bancroft. His nickname was "Beauty," from his habit of saying "beauty" whenever a pitcher threw one past him at the plate.

James "Cool Papa" Bell. Bell supposedly received his nickname pitching as a teenager against the black Babe Ruth, Oscar Charleston. After striking out Charleston he was described as Cool. Cool Bell did not seem appropriate to manager Bill Gatewood, who added the "Papa." Another version: Bell earned his nickname when he told his manager that he was not nervous during his debut because he had played in front of large crowds at home. This prompted a teammate to comment that he was "a cool one" and another to comment that he was "a cool papa."

Yogi Berra. As a kid, Berra and his friends saw a travelogue about India at a local movie theatre. His friend Jack Maguire, who later played shortstop for the Giants, thought that a Hindu yogi in the movie looked like Berra, and a nickname was born.

Ping Bodie. Bodie was given his name because of the sound of the ball off his bat.

Mickey Cochrane. Cochrane was baptized Gordon Stanley and "Mickey" was simply an Irish expression. He was known as "Black Mike," referring to his "black Irish" heritage.

Kiki Cuyler. Cuyler's real name was Hazen Shirley Cuyler. There are two versions of his nickname, which rhymes with "High High": Whenever he stuttered in pronouncing his last name, "Kiki" came out. He was called "Cuy" by his Nashville teammates. When a ball was hit to him in center field, the shortstop and second baseman would yell "Cuy" in succession to signify that it was Cuyler's ball. Fans picked up on the tandem cry and a sportswriter began calling him by that name.

Jay Hannah "Dizzy" Dean. Dean supposedly earned his nickname in 1930. Chicago White Sox coach Lena Blackburne (who discovered baseball *Mud*) was watching Dean pitch during spring training in Houston. Dean had struck out 18 batters and Blackburne yelled to the next batter: "You're letting that dizzy kid make a fool out of you. Are you going to take that from this dizzy kid?"

Joe DiMaggio. DiMaggio was named "Yankee Clipper" by broadcaster Arch McDonald, referring to the graceful ships.

Monk Dubiel. Dubiel had a uniform that was too tight and his teammates thought it looked like an organ grinder's monkey costume.

Dwight "Doc" Gooden. Gooden got his nickname in Little League when players would exhort "come on, Doctor, operate on 'em." Gooden later insisted that he always be referred to as Doc Gooden.

Jim "Mudcat" Grant. Grant was a rookie with the Indians in 1958. He did not come from Mississippi, the Mudcat State, but a teammate thought so and gave him the nickname. Grant was from Florida. For a while it was Mudman or Mudshoes, because he always had mud on his shoes. His friends call him "Mud," as Grant confirmed to this author at a delightful lunch in 2004.

Dolly Gray. Gray was named after a popular Spanish-American War ballad: "Goodbye, Dolly Gray."

Burleigh Grimes. The pitcher was known as Old Stubblebeard when he did not shave on game days because the slippery elm that he chewed caused his saliva to irritate his clean-shaven skin.

Harvey Haddix. Haddix was known as the "Kitten" because of his resemblance to Harry "The Cat" Brecheen and "because he was too small to be a cat" (5'9", 170 lbs.).

Gabby Hartnett. The catcher, Charles Leo Hartnett, was given his nickname because he was extremely shy as a rookie.

Jim "Catfish" Hunter. Hunter was never called Catfish until eccentric owner Charlie Finley decided that Hunter needed a nickname.

Walter Johnson.
"The Big Train comes to town today."— Grantland Rice's story on the arrival of Johnson to pitch in 1911. The fastball pitcher was also nicknamed "Barney" by roommate Clyde Milan, after mile-a-minute auto racer Barney Oldfield, who had won the Indianapolis 500. Johnson was for years also known as "The Big Swede," though his ancestry was Scot-German. His explanation, "the Swedes are nice people; I didn't want to offend them."

Willie "Puddin' Head" Jones. Jones was named for a song of the 1940s containing the lyric, "Wooden Head Puddin' Head Jones."

Peanuts Lowrey was given the nickname by his uncle, who noted his diminutive size at birth.

George Magerkurth. The umpire was sensitive to being called Meathead. Even a whisper of the word and a player or manager would be tossed. Umpire Beans Reardon had a habit of hiding behind doors and shouting "Meathead" at Magerkurth. Reardon's voice was unmistakable and the two rarely worked together because of their dislike for each other.

Pepper Martin. Martin was given the name "Pepper Pot," for his fiery style by Blake Harper, who operated the Fort Smith team in the Western Association in the late 1920s.

Christy Mathewson. There are a number of stories on how Mathewson received his nickname, "Big Six." Some claim he was named for a celebrated New York fire engine company. John McGraw claimed that it came from a prominent New York boxer and that Mathewson inherited it from him. Some claimed that it came from the Big Six Typographical Union in New York.

In 1923 Mathewson set the record straight in an article in *The Sporting News*. He said that Big Six was a contraction of "big six-footer," which was his height (actually 6'2").

Sudden Sam McDowell. The strikeout pitcher was so named because he pitched the ball to the plate "all of a sudden."

Joe "Iron Man" McGinnity. McGinnity supposedly got his nickname because of his ability to pitch both ends of a doubleheader on a few occasions. This is false. McGinnity was already known as "Iron Man" because in the off-season in his early years he worked in a foundry. The name was given to him in the minor leagues. Nevertheless, McGinnity did set a National League record for pitching 434 innings in 1903. He once won five games in six days during his rookie season with the Dodgers. In 1901 he pitched two doubleheaders and split both but went all the way in each. The nickname was used more generally after he won three complete-game doubleheaders during the heat of the 1904 pennant race, won by his Giants. At age 54 in 1925, McGinnity was still pitching in the Mississippi Valley League.

Willie Mays. When the shy outfielder arrived with the Giants, he said "Say Who?," "Say What?," and "Say Hey!" New York sportswriter Barney Kremenko started calling him "Say Hey" and broadcaster Russ Hodges promoted it on the air. *Say Hey* is the name of one of the Mays autobiographies.

Catfish Metkovich. Metkovich earned his nickname (supposedly from Casey Stengel) when he was getting a hook out of a catfish and stepped on the fish to hold it down. The fin cut through his crepe sole shoe and into his foot.

Felix Millan. The mid–1960s and 1970s infielder was named after television cartoon character Felix the Cat.

Johnny Mize. Mize was nicknamed "Big Cat" by Giants teammate Bill Rigney, who saw him on the pregame outfield grass sprawled out in the sun "looking just like a big cat."

Guillermo Mota. 2000s Dodger reliever Guillermo Mota was known as "The Big Filthy."

Stan "The Man" Musial. The nickname was popularized by Brooklyn fans who treated him well when he visited.

Bill "Swish" Nicholson. Nicholson was named because he repeatedly swung the bat both while warming up and waiting for the pitcher to deliver.

John "Blue Moon" Odom. Odom was nicknamed Moon as a kid for the shape of his face. His teammates added Blue because he was often downcast.

Spike Owen. His real name is Spike Lee Owen.

Satchel Paige. Paige received his nickname after he invented a contraption to carry four satchels at a time in the Mobile, Alabama, railroad station in which he worked as a kid.

Double Duty Radcliffe. Theodore Roosevelt "Double Duty" Radcliffe, former Negro League star who turned 100 in 2003, earned his nickname from writer Damon Runyon when Radcliffe came to New York with the Pittsburgh Crawfords for a double-header. He caught a shutout by Satchel Paige in the first game, then pitched one of his own in the second game.

Pee Wee Reese. Reese's nickname had nothing to do with his size (5'10"). It came from a prize marble he had as a boy.

Harold Patrick "Pete" Reiser. Reiser was known as Pete because of Two-Gun Pete of the movies.

Pete Rose. When Rose ran to first on a base on balls against the Yankees during spring training in his rookie year, Mickey Mantle asked who "Charlie Hustle" was.

George Herman Ruth. There are numerous accounts of how Babe Ruth received his nickname:

1. He was teased by the other boys at St. Mary's and cried, so they called him Babe.

2. The older boys would not let him play in their games because he was "just a Babe."

3. Baltimore Orioles owner Jack Dunn signed him when he was a minor, starting rumors that Dunn had adopted him. Around that time the writers began calling him Babe.

4. A Baltimore Orioles coach named Steinam gave him the nickname when he arrived, describing Ruth as club owner Jack Dunn's newest Babe.

5. An older player on the Orioles named him when he first came out to pitch.

6. Ruth was playing with the elevator in a hotel when got his head stuck in the door. He was bawled out by Dunn, who called him a babe in the woods.

Ruth was also known as Jidge, then a common derivative of George.

Bill "Moose" Skowron. Skowron did not get his nickname by being a big football player at Purdue, as many people believe. As a kid, he shaved his head (courtesy of his grandfather) and everyone called him "Mussolini" for his resemblance to the Italian dictator.

Tris Speaker. The Red Sox and Indians outfielder played the shallowest center field and nothing got by him, so he was known as the "Grey Eagle."

Marv Throneberry. Throneberry was named by his straight man, Mets outfielder Richie Ashburn. Ashburn even put up a "Marvelous" name plate over Throneberry's locker and the writers picked up on it.

Sloppy Thurston. Thurston was so named because he was such a classy dresser.

Pie Traynor. As a boy, he had to do the grocery shopping for his mother, carrying a long list from her. He always concluded the list by asking for a pie. The grocer's son, who played ball with Traynor, began calling him "Pie."

Dazzy Vance. Many thought that Vance earned his nickname by the way he threw a fastball. However, when he was a boy he knew a cowboy who had a favorite pistol. The cowboy referred to

it as a "Dazzy," instead of "daisy," as in "ain't it a daisy." Vance adopted it as his own and it stuck.

Harry "The Hat" Walker. Walker repeatedly took his cap off between pitches while batting.

John Montgomery Ward. Ward has been described in modern sources most frequently as Monte Ward when his full name has not been used. However, in a newspaper interview in the 19th century, the reporter noted that Ward was known as Johnny.

Walt "No Neck" Williams.

"Oh I suppose that Walt No Neck Williams did have *something* to connect his chest and chin, some sort of windpipe, but it was barely visible to the naked eye, let me tell you. I mean the man had absolutely no Adam's apple. He had more of an Adam's grape. Had he been the one who blabbed to Woodward and Bernstein, they would have immortalized him as 'Shallow Throat.' The poor guy could not even wear a necklace, because, you see, he was neckless." — Sportswriter Mike Downey.

Hack Wilson. Wilson was a colorful player who lasted 12 seasons with the Giants, Cubs, Dodgers and Phillies before alcoholism eroded his skills. He supposedly received his name from a newspaper contest in New York in 1924. The winning name was "Hackenschmidt," after the legendary wrestler. Another source reported that Hack is also another name for a brick, which is what the short and stocky Wilson was built like.

Cy Young. The name was derived from Cyclone, because the scouts thought he pitched so fast. Another version is that Young was from Iowa and it was common for farmers ("hayseeds") to be nicknamed Cyrus. Young himself said that he was trying to show his stuff to George Moreland, owner of Canton in the Tri-State League. He threw two balls so hard they tore boards off the grandstand. One of the men watching said that it looked like a cyclone had struck.

Hometowns. "Wahoo" Sam Crawford was from Wahoo, Nebraska.

"Hondo" Clint Hartung was from Hondo, Texas.

Bill Killefer (Grover Cleveland Alexander's catcher) and Tigers outfielder Charlie Maxwell were both nicknamed "Paw Paw" after their home town in Michigan (though Killefer was born in Bloomingdale and Maxwell was born in Lawton).

Wilmer "Vinegar Bend" Mizell came from a town of the same name in Alabama.

Nickname on Uniforms. Ken "Hawk" Harrelson had his nickname, which referred to his prominent nose, on his uniform. Ted Kluszewski had his nickname, "Klu," on the back of his uniform.

Name Recognition Problems. Babe Ruth called everyone "Kid," (or "Keed"), and Casey Stengel called everyone "Doctor," because they were both terrible at remembering names.

First Name. Ichiro Suzuki of the Mariners is known simply as "Ichiro," and that is what is on his uniform.

Longest Continuously Used Team Nickname. The Philadelphia Phillies have used their name continuously since they came into the National League in 1883. Philadelphia fans and sportswriters hated the name Bluejays, which was the winning suggestion in a name-this-team contest in 1944. The team owner relented and Phillies was again the official choice after the 1945 season, though it has been reported that the Blue Jays choice was simply a logo and not a formal name change (see *Philadelphia Phillies— Nicknames*).

Team Nicknames/Former Nicknames.

"Clearly legendary are the tales that concern the way in which major league franchises got their names, though such matters are of little concern to the players themselves." — Tristram Coffin in *The Old Ball Game* (1971).

"In case you're under the impression that in the distant past groups of stockholders spent hectic nights around a table concocting monikers for their athletes and held christening ceremonies at home plate, we have news for you."— Columnist Frank C. True.

"Say 'Dodgers' and people know you're talking about baseball. Say 'Braves' and they ask, 'What reservation?' Say 'Reds' and they think of communism. Say 'Padres' and they look around for a priest."— Dodger manager Tommy Lasorda.

"A professional sports team that doesn't end its nickname with an s doesn't end its season with a championship. The Boston Red Sox last won the World Series in 1918, and no NBA, NFL, NHL or major league baseball team without an s at the end of its nickname has won a world championship since."— Gerry Callahan in *Sports Illustrated*. True until 2004 (Red Sox) except for hockey (the Avalanche and Lightning have each won Stanley Cups).

See entries for individual teams.

When Johnny Evers came to the Major Leagues, he left a minor league club known as the Troy Cheer-Ups.

In addition to the traditional team names adopted over the years, many teams held other nicknames for short (and sometimes long) periods of their history. A few examples: The New York Giants ("Nationals") of the 1880s were known as the "$40,000 Nine" and "The Gilt-Edged Team."

The Brooklyn "Bums" name supposedly originated after the club lost the 1889 Championship Series.

The 1906 Chicago Cubs were known as the "Hitless Wonders" because they won the pennant despite having a league-low team batting average of only .228.

The St. Louis Cardinals were known as the *Gas House Gang* in the 1930s when they won pennants in 1930, 1931 and 1934. However, the name did not come into vogue until after 1931 and the 1930–1931 teams were retroactively known by that name.

During the late 1930s the Yankees were so powerful that pundits began calling the American League "Snow White and the Seven Dwarfs."

The National League champion 1950 Philadelphia Phillies were known as the Whiz Kids because of their youth.

The 1970s Cincinnati Reds were known as the Big Red Machine.

The 1970s Dodgers, who won three division titles over the Reds, were known as "The Little Blue Wrecking Crew."

Harvey's Wallbangers was the name given to the home run-hitting 1982 American League champion Milwaukee Brewers, after a popular drink and manager Harvey Kuenn.

Trademark Infringement. In 1989 the Los Angeles Dodgers filed suit against a Brooklyn sports bar known as The Brooklyn Dodgers Sports Bar & Restaurant. In 1993 the Dodgers lost the lawsuit when a federal court judge in New York ruled that the Dodgers abandoned the full name when they left Brooklyn.

Books. Frank Graham and Dick Hyman, *Baseball Wit & Wisdom* (1962); Mike Lessiter, *The Names of the Games: The Stories Behind the Nicknames of 102 Pro Football, Basketball, Baseball, and Hockey Teams* (1988); Louis Phillips and Burnham Holmes, *The Complete Book of Sports Nicknames* (1998); Tom Shea, *Baseball Nicknames 1870–1946* (1946); James K. Skipper, Jr., *Baseball Nicknames: A Dictionary of Origins and Meanings* (1992).

Phil Niekro (1939–)

Hall of Fame 1997
"He simply destroys your timing with that knuckleball. It comes flying in there dipping and hopping like crazy and you just can't hit it."— Ernie Banks.

"It giggles as it goes by."— Rick Monday on a Niekro knuckleball.

Niekro was a right-handed knuckleball pitcher from 1964 to 1987 who recorded 318 career wins.

Philip Henry Niekro began his professional career with Wellsville of the New York-Penn League in 1959, later moving on to McCook of the Nebraska State League. After serving in the military in 1963, Niekro made it to the Major League with the Milwaukee Braves in 1964. He appeared in 10 games with the Braves but spent most of the year with Denver of the Pacific Coast League. Niekro spent all of 1965 with the Braves as a reliever in 41 games.

In 1966 Niekro again split his year, appearing in 28 games for the newly relocated Atlanta Braves. Converted to a starter, Niekro went 11–9 in 1967 and led the National League with a 1.87 ERA. In 1969 the Braves were the top team in the National League West, with Niekro winning 23 games and posting a 2.59 ERA. In the NLCS the Braves were swept by the Mets with Niekro taking the loss in the first game. Unfortunately it would be 12 years before they would return to the postseason, with the team finishing above .500 just three times in that span.

Niekro's performance over the same period was exemplary. He twice led the league in wins, going 20–13 in 1974 and 21–20 in 1979. He also paced the National League in complete games and innings pitched four times, 1974 and 1977–1979. On August 5, 1973, Niekro pitched the first no-hitter in Braves history, 9–0 over the San Diego. The Braves won the division again in 1982, with Niekro winning 17 games, but were again swept in the NLCS, this time by St. Louis.

Niekro signed as a free agent with the Yankees for the 1984 season. He played two seasons in New York, posting 16 wins each year. His final start as a Yankee produced his 300th career win, 8–0 over Toronto, the oldest pitcher to ever throw a complete game shutout. Niekro finished his career with short stints in Cleveland and Toronto. He made one final appearance in a Braves uniform, pitching three innings on September 27, 1987, to close out his distinguished run.

Niekro finished his 24-year career with a 318–274 mark, 14th all-time in wins and 5th all-time in losses. Niekro's 5,404 innings pitched are 4th all-time and his 3,342 srikeouts place him 10th on the career list.

Book. Phil Niekro and Joe Niekro, *The Niekro Files* (1990).

Night Games

"Should the time ever come when by some system of illumination base ball could be played as well at night as in the day time the possibilities of the game's earnings could hardly be estimated.… But the chances are that the time will never come…"— O.P. Caylor in an 1893 *Sporting Life* column.

"Night ball has merit, but I don't think there will be a steady diet of it."— National League president Ford Frick in May 1935 when the first Major League night game was played.

"Night baseball is just a step above dog racing."—1934 editorial in *The Sporting News*.

"The night air is not like the day air; the man who goes to a baseball game after he has eaten a hearty meal is apt to have indigestion if he is nervous and excited; the disturbed and misanthropic fan will not sleep well after a night game. Who wants to go home in the dark when it is twice as pleasant to drive leisurely in the approaching twilight and sniff a good meal cooking on the range when the front door is opened and the aroma of a sputtering steak

spreads through the house?"—1930 editorial in *The Sporting News.*
"Watty Clark, Dennis Lamp, Eddie Watt, Alvin Dark"

See also *Scheduling*—Night Games.

Earliest Night Games.

"Not the least difficulty was found at the bat. With between 25 and 39 lights, there is no question but what electric light ball playing is an assured success."—*Sporting Life* on the first demonstration night game. The first baseball game played under lights was between two department store teams on September 2, 1880. The game was played at Oceanside Park on Nantasket Bay in Hull, Massachusetts, and was a demonstration put on by the Northern Electric Light Company.

Jordan Marsh & Co. and R.H. White & Co. played to a 16–16 tie in front of 300 fans. The game was called so that teams and fans could get back to the mainland on the last ferry boat for the evening. The incandescent light used in the game was invented the year before by Thomas Edison: as John Holway noted in *Blackball Stars* (1988), "Well, why else invent it?" Edison was by his own admission "always too busy a boy to indulge in baseball."

The next reported game was a seven-inning affair played June 2, 1883, in Fort Wayne, Indiana, between a Quincy, Illinois, professional team and the M.E. Church nine (some sources describe them as collegians). Quincy won 19–11 and the clubs and 2,000 fans endured two power failures.

The Giants scheduled night games at the Polo Grounds for the 1891 season, but the games were never played at night.

On July 2, 1893, a Los Angeles club in the California League (then not affiliated with Organized Baseball), played a night game against Stockton at Athletic Park in Los Angeles. Future evangelist Billy Sunday played center field in the game and had the game-winning hit. Twenty kerosene lamps were suspended from wires and a search light (!) was used to follow the flight of the ball. Los Angeles won 5–2 in front of 9,000 fans.

First Demonstration Game in a Major League Park.

"Night baseball has come to stay. It needs some further development, but proper lighting conditions will make the sport immensely popular."—Reds president Garry Herrmann after witnessing a demonstration of night baseball in 1909 and investing in its development.

"Night is the natural time for play, for amusement, for relaxation. I believe that man's greatest games, his outdoor manly sports, can and should be played at night."—Night game pioneer George Cahill.

In June 1909 at Redland Field (later Crosley Field), the Cincinnati Elks Lodge played Newport, Kentucky, in front of 3,000 fans. George Cahill of Massachusetts demonstrated his patented light tower for the Reds, who would play the first night game in Major League history in the same park 26 years later (a game also attended by Cahill). Cahill demonstrated his system in a game in front of 20,000 fans in Comiskey Park in 1910. Cahill and his brothers Thaddeus and Arthur owned a Holyoke, Massachusetts, floodlight manufacturing company.

First Negro League Games.

"We used to soak the ball in kerosene and light it on fire."—Double Duty Radcliffe, tongue-in-cheek, on playing night ball in the Negro Leagues.

"What talkies are to movies, lights will be to baseball."—J.L. Wilkinson, pioneer Negro League entrepreneur and owner of the Kansas City Monarchs. The Monarchs played their first night game on April 28, 1930. In the non-league game they defeated Phillips University in Enid, Oklahoma, by a score of 12–3.

On July 25, 1930, the Monarchs played the Pittsburgh Homestead Grays at Forbes Field in Pittsburgh in the first official Negro League game played under lights. Teenager and future legend Josh Gibson supposedly was pulled from the stands that night to play catcher because the regular catcher walked off the field in frustration over the portable lighting system. The manager who recruited Gibson was future Hall of Famer Judy Johnson. Portable lighting systems were often used by traveling Negro League teams.

First Minor League Games.

"Whether baseball fans like night games or not is a question the fans themselves have answered. They like night baseball because they turn out for the after-supper games in greater numbers every season, especially if they happen to have a winning club in that city."—Minor league umpire Harry "Steamboat" Johnson, writing in 1935.

An unofficial minor league game was played April 17, 1930, by the Independence Producers of the Western Association ("independent" team in some sources) against the House of David. Kansas City Monarchs owner J.L. Wilkinson witnessed the event and duplicated it 11 days later (see above). A month earlier the Major League White Sox and Giants had played an exhi-

Reds general manager Larry MacPhail manning the switch that will illuminate Crosley Field in Cincinnati for the first night game in Major League history. The photograph was taken by one of the designers of the lighting system, Earl D. Payne. In 1985 Payne's son, Robert, found an old family trunk containing a series of photographic negatives of the event, including this shot. Some sources later reported that the photograph was of Reds owner Powell Crosley, but through research and correspondence with Larry MacPhail's son, Lee, Robert Payne concluded that it is MacPhail (primarily by the tilt of the hat, the size of the ears, and because Crosley was about 6'5" and MacPhail was 5'8").

bition game under the lights in Houston.

On May 2, 1930, Lee E. Keyser's Des Moines club of the Western League installed lights at a cost of $19,000 for a game against Wichita that night. This was a heavily publicized event that was copied frequently by other minor league teams during the summer of 1930.

This was widely believed to be the first official minor league game under lights and many sources report it as such. Because Keyser had announced his plan beforehand, however, and the team's first game was on the road, the Independence Club of Washington, Kansas, in the Class C Western League, hastily installed a lighting system and played a minor league game on April 28, 1930 (April 30 in many sources). Independence Producers lost to Muskogee 13–3

Site of the first night game in Organized Baseball history, April 28, 1930, at Independence, Missouri.

in what is now considered the first official minor league night game. The crowd was so enthusiastic that another game was played the next night. The pitcher in the first game was Ron Vance and the catcher was Sherman Walker. The batter first batter was Muskogee (Oklahoma) Chiefs shortstop Hardy Buff, recently arrived from the University of Oklahoma.

At least one source reported on a minor league night game between home-team Lynn, Massachusetts, and Salem on June 24, 1922. Other sources report the game as being played in 1927.

By the end of the summer of 1930, 38 teams in 14 leagues had lights, including Los Angeles in the Pacific Coast League. By 1934, 15 of 16 minor leagues had at least one ballpark with lights. Night baseball gave the minor leagues some relief from the financial ruin brought on by the Depression, but the prosperity ended shortly after World War II because of television and the national dominance of the Major Leagues.

Major League Team Under Lights/Exhibition. On September 12, 1931, the Reds hosted the Dodgers in a day game at Crosley Field. Several hours later, the Reds and 1,000 fans hosted a team from Dayton, Ohio, using a portable lighting system used by the touring House of David team. Grover Cleveland Alexander, then 44, pitched three innings for Dayton and gave up five runs. The Reds were scheduled to play a doubleheader the next day and apparently were in no mood for the exhibition game, losing 14–7.

The Reds Get Permission. Major League club owners initially were hostile to night ball, with the exception of Cardinals owner Sam Breadon. When Larry MacPhail took over as general manager of the Reds in the early 1930s, he pushed for night baseball. The Reds were granted permission to play night games primarily because of the team's severe attendance problems during the Depression. MacPhail had been successful with the idea in 1932 with Columbus of the American Association. In 1935 the Reds were given permission to play seven night games, one against each team in the league, so long as the other team consented (all but the Giants did).

First Major League Game Under Lights.

"Manager Jimmie Wilson of the Phillies said the lights had nothing to do with the low hit total. 'Both pitchers just had all their

stuff working, that's all. You can see the ball coming up to the plate just as well under those lights as you can in daytime.'"—Associated Press story of the game.

"Staged under million watt after dark illumination, the closest approach to daylight ever attained on any outdoor field, the Reds inaugurated night baseball May 24, and wrote into the history of the game a chapter that may prove as epochal as that contributed by a Cincinnati club nearly seven decades ago in 1869 when the first professional team took the field under the banner of this city."—Edgar Brands, editor of *The Sporting News* who was in attendance at the first Major League night game.

"I think it was evident to everyone there that this was a night which would usher in a new era of baseball.... You could tell that night that baseball had come in like a tidal wave."—Red Barber in May 1985.

"No pun intended, but there was electricity in the air, on the field and in the dugout. The ballplayers did not get blasé, they got fired up, too."—Reds first baseman Billy Sullivan, Jr., in 1985, who played in his first National League game on May 24, 1935.

The first Major League night game was played between the Reds and Phillies at Cincinnati's Crosley Field on May 24, 1935. It was originally scheduled for the night before, but the game was postponed due to wet weather. The club enjoyed its third largest crowd of the season with 20,422 fans in attendance, about ten times the usual daytime crowd.

President Roosevelt pushed a gold Western Union telegraph key in the White House at 8:30 p.m. Eastern Standard Time and 1,090,000 watts from 632 lamps supposedly flooded the field. However, the key actually turned on only a light on a table on the field manned by Reds general manager Larry MacPhail. MacPhail then flipped a switch that lit the field. The Reds paid $72,000 (or $50,000) to General Electric for the lighting system, which was designed by engineers from the Cincinnati Gas & Electric Company, including Earl Payne and Wayne Conover.

National League president Ford Frick threw out the first pitch as the Reds defeated the Phillies 2–1 behind the pitching of Paul Derringer. The first batter was Lou Chiozza. Two long fly balls were dropped but scored as hits, and there were shadows in the corners of the outfield.

The Reds drew 130,337 fans to the seven games, an average of 18,619. One source erroneously put the average at 22,000, but the club only had three crowds over 20,000 all season. Attendance more than doubled in Cincinnati, from 206,000 in 1934 to more than 448,000 in 1935. The lights paid for themselves in the first three games. The system cost $50,000 to build; running the lights for one night cost about $250. The light bulbs were made by the Kenrad Light Company, which also made the tubes for Crosley's radio station. There were 616 (or 632) lights on eight light towers, more than twice the number of lights used at any other field at that time. The lights were designed to be at least twice as bright as any existing minor league ballpark.

First Home Night Game for Each Major League Club (the 16 that existed in the 1940s).

May 24, 1935	Cincinnati Reds
June 15, 1938	Brooklyn Dodgers
May 16, 1939	Philadelphia A's
June 1, 1939	Philadelphia Phillies
June 27, 1939	Cleveland Indians
August 14, 1939	Chicago White Sox
May 24, 1940	St. Louis Browns
May 24, 1940	New York Giants
June 4, 1940	St. Louis Cardinals
June 4, 1940	Pittsburgh Pirates
May 28, 1941	Washington Senators
May 11, 1946	Boston Braves
May 28, 1946	New York Yankees
June 13, 1947	Boston Red Sox
June 15, 1948	Detroit Tigers
August 9, 1988	Chicago Cubs

American League

Boston Red Sox. The Red Sox installed lights in 1947. The club's first night game was played on June 13, 1947, as the Red Sox defeated the White Sox 5–3. Owner Tom Yawkey was so delighted with the lighting system that he gave four permanent season tickets to the engineer who designed and installed the system. The engineer was entitled to choose seats anywhere in the ballpark. Unfortunately for his heirs, he chose a spot in the right field bleachers that provided the best view of his light towers.

Chicago White Sox. Charles Comiskey claimed that Comiskey Park, built in 1910, was designed with the idea that lights would someday be installed. His son, J. Louis Comiskey, was responsible for putting lights in the ballpark shortly before he died in 1939.

The first night game in Comiskey Park was played against the Browns on August 14, 1939, with 30,000 watching a 5–2 White Sox win behind the three-hit pitching of John Rigney.

Cleveland Indians. The Indians were the first American League club to install lights, but the second to host an American League night game (the A's beat them by a month). Cleveland's first night game at home was a 5–0 victory over the Tigers on June 27, 1939.

Detroit Tigers.

"It will be the beginning of the end of Major League Baseball." — Long-time Tigers owner Frank Navin, who died in the mid–1930s.

The Tigers were the last American League club to install lights. On June 15, 1948, 54,000 fans turned out to watch the Tigers defeat the A's 4–1. The field reportedly was illuminated by the equivalent of 6,000 full moons. The eight light towers had 1,458 lighting units providing 27,750,000 watts of power.

New York Yankees.

"I am more convinced than ever that there is absolutely no future in electric lighted play." — General manager Ed Barrow in the 1930s.

"It's a wart on the nose of the game." — Barrow in the early 1940s.

The Yankees hosted their first night game in Yankee Stadium only after World War II, on May 28, 1946. General Electric president Charles E. Wilson threw out the first ball in front of 49,917 fans as the Yankees lost to the Senators 2–1.

Philadelphia Athletics.

"The infield is better lighted than the average well-lighted office. It is several hundred times brighter than Times Square on New Year's Eve." — Engineers who directed the lighting installation at Shibe Park.

Connie Mack installed lights in Shibe Park in 1939 and the first night game was played on May 16, 1939. The A's defeated the Indians 8–3 in 10 innings in front of 15,109 fans. It was the first night game in American League history and the A's were the third Major League team to host a night game. The first batter was center fielder Roy Weatherly of the Indians. Eight steel towers supporting 780 floodlights, each with a capacity of 1,500 watts, made up the lighting system.

St. Louis Browns. The team's first night game was on May 24, 1940, as Bob Feller homered for the first time and pitched the Indians to a 3–2 win over the Browns. The crowd of 25,562 was the club's largest since 1928, though some sources report the crowd as 34,827. Judge Landis and American League president Will Harridge made speeches that night. The American League allowed the Browns to play 14 night games in 1940. Half the Browns' attendance of 240,000 was at the 14 night games.

Washington Senators.

"I don't believe night ball is destined to rival the daylight article, but I will say I was much surprised at the ease with which the game was played under tonight. Under improved lighting it will grow more popular." — Senators owner Clark Griffith in 1908 when he was the Reds manager during an exhibition in Cincinnati.

"There is no chance of night baseball ever becoming popular in the bigger cities because high-class baseball cannot be played under artificial lights." — Griffith in the 1930s.

"Baseball is made to be played in God's own sunshine." — Griffith.

In their first night game at home, the Senators lost to the Yankees 6–5 on May 28, 1941. Over 25,000 fans saw George Selkirk hit a pinch grand slam in the 8th inning for the Senators. Walter Johnson threw a strike across home plate that broke a beam of a light, switching on the new floodlights.

National League

Boston Braves. The Braves hosted their first night game on May 11, 1946, losing 5–1 to the Giants. The crowd of 35,945 was the club's largest in 13 seasons. The Braves wore new "sateen" uniforms "especially designed" for night play. National League president Ford Frick attended along with the governor of Massachusetts and the mayor of Boston.

Brooklyn Dodgers.

"You don't have to pay for sunshine." — Branch Rickey during the 1940s when he was the Dodger general manager and not a fan of night baseball. The Dodgers hosted their first night game before he arrived with the club.

The Dodgers were the second Major League club to host a night game, held June 15, 1938, against the Reds. The game featured Reds pitcher Johnny Vander Meer's second consecutive *No-Hitter*

(6–0) in front of 38,748 fans. The game was preceded by running races between players and track star Jesse Owens. Babe Ruth made a guest appearance and his popularity led to a brief stay with the Dodgers as a coach.

Chicago Cubs.

"I'll put in lights if we can disguise them as trees."—Cubs owner Phil Wrigley.

Wrigley had purchased the steel to erect light standards in Wrigley Field, but immediately after the outbreak of World War II he donated the materials to the war effort.

When the Tribune Company purchased the team in 1981, it announced that there was no plan to install lights. Nevertheless, economics and postseason play forced a change in policy. Night baseball finally came to Wrigley Field on August 9, 1988, when the Cubs defeated the Mets 6–4. The baseball gods may have had something to say about it because the game had been scheduled for the night before but was rained out after three innings. By agreement with the city, initially only 18 night games were scheduled each year, and they usually sold out quickly because of the novelty.

The first night baseball game of any kind in Wrigley Field was played in July 1943, when the All-American Girls Professional Baseball League held its All-Star Game under temporary lights in front of 7,000 fans.

Cincinnati Reds.

See **First Major League Game Under Lights**—May 24, 1935.

New York Giants.

"The throwing of the switches that set the eight light towers blazing put New York in the list of towns that play night baseball and marked a new era in the colorful history of the Polo Grounds. For those—and there may have been some in the crowd—who remember the old wooden stands and the horses and carriages in front of the old clubhouse where helmeted policemen stood guard, it must have been a strange sight. The light towers blazing and the field flooded with light on a misty night and the Giants and the Bees moving to their positions."—Sportswriter Frank Graham.

The Giants hosted their first night game on May 24, 1940, an 8–1 win over the Braves in front of 22,460 fans. This was the same night that the Browns held their first night game. The lighting system was excellent, diffusing 200 million candle power which, if concentrated on a single point, would provide reading light from eight miles away. *The Sporting News* considered the event an "outstanding artistic success," but "financially disappointing to its sponsors."

Philadelphia Phillies.

"Now, clubs don't spend more than $100,000 for lights to play to 8,000 fans at night, and it ought to sink in among owners that it is hazardous to start the night ball season before the middle of June. May, with its copyrighted fickle weather, is entirely out of the question."—*The Sporting News.*

The Phillies hosted their first night game in Shibe Park on June 1, 1939. They lost to the Pirates 5–2 as only 8,000 fans turned out in bad weather.

Pittsburgh Pirates. The Pirates defeated the Braves 14–2 on June 4, 1940. The crowd of 20,000 was disappointing, in part caused by the Ringling Bros. and Barnum & Bailey Circus, which had pitched tents just a few miles from "the nocturnal diamond scene." The Pirates were in last place at the time and were playing against a club that, according to *The Sporting News*, "wasn't exactly something you would want to write home about at that particular time." Judge Landis and Ford Frick were present.

St. Louis Cardinals. The Cardinals lost 10–1 to the Dodgers on June 4, 1940, the same night the Pirates hosted their first night

game. Ironically, *The Sporting News* devoted almost no regular coverage to the event, despite St. Louis being the publication's home city.

World War II Restrictions.

"Army officials decided that the glare would invite trouble at sea, perhaps guide some suicide flier bearing a grim message from Dizzy Adolf, and ordered the two ball parks blacked out."—*The Sporting News* on the blackouts at Ebbets Field and the Polo Grounds (Yankee Stadium did not have lights).

In early 1943 during World War II, Judge Landis barred night games in response to President Roosevelt's general request to save energy and prevent well-lit targets. Later in the season, however, the original seven games allowed the Reds were increased to 14, and before the season ended the Senators were allowed 21 games under the lights to accommodate fans working on day shifts for the government. A few months later, Landis approved unlimited night games for the Senators. They scheduled 43 home games at night to accommodate the heavy daytime workloads in the city. Among other American League clubs, the Browns scheduled 21 night games and a few other clubs that had lights scheduled 14. In July 1944 Landis approved unlimited night games for all Major League teams.

No night games were allowed on the West Coast during the war. In New York the Major League clubs scheduled "twights"—doubleheaders that were limited to one hour of artificial light at night.

Lights Out. In a game in Washington in the 1950s, the Tigers' powerful George Kell was at bat. Just as the pitcher was about to throw, the lights failed. When the lights came back on less than a minute later, every player on the field had hit the dirt—except the pitcher, who still had the ball.

First Home Run. Babe Herman hit the first night game home run for the Reds on July 10, 1935.

Sunday Rules. Prior to 1954 lights could not be turned on in Philadelphia to complete a Sunday game that began after 6 p.m.

Scheduling Under the Lights.

See *Scheduling*—Night Games.

First All-Star Night Game. The first All-Star Game officially played at night was in Philadelphia's Shibe Park on July 13, 1943, as the American League won 5–4. Game time was 8:45 p.m. Eastern Wartime. However, on July 6, 1942, the All-Star Game was played partially under lights in the Polo Grounds after a long rain delay. Darkness began to set in and the lights were turned on. The 1942 game ended shortly before 9:30, two minutes before the World War II blackout restrictions would have ended the game.

One source reported that the first officially scheduled All-Star night game was played at Anaheim Stadium on July 11, 1967. Another source reported that the 1944 game was the first night game.

World Series Games at Night. The first World Series game scheduled at night was Game 4 of the 1971 Series, played in Pittsburgh between the Pirates and Orioles on October 13, 1971. The Pirates won 4–3 in front of 51,378 fans and a television audience of 63 million who watched the game on 21 million television sets. At that time it was the largest television audience in history for a prime time sporting event.

Earlier World Series games were played under the lights only because day games ran long and the lights were turned on briefly. This occurred at least once during the 1949 World Series between the Dodgers and Yankees.

First Home Opener. In 1950 the Cardinals broke tradition by scheduling their home opener under lights. Despite protests from the scheduled opponent, the Pirates, the game went on at night and the Cardinals beat the Pirates 4–2 in front of 20,871 fans.

First Major League Ballpark Originally Built with Lights. In 1953 County Stadium in Milwaukee became the first current or future Major League ballpark built with lights, rather than having them added on later.

Attendance. On July 24, 1993, a crowd of 71,784 watched the Rockies host the Cardinals. It was the largest night game attendance in National League history.

Cost of Lights. It now costs about $2 million to outfit a Major League ballpark with new light bulbs. Teams pay light bills of about $50,000 per month for the halide light systems. Each light lasts about 3,000 hours.

Stunt. One source reported that Yankee general manager Ed Barrow opposed night baseball because of an incident in Wilmington when he was a manager many years earlier. In a night game, the opposing pitcher threw a firecracker instead of the ball. The batter hit it, it exploded, and singed the batter. The batter then chased the pitcher into center field. The batter supposedly was Honus Wagner.

In 1944 one newspaper reported on a plan to "put out the arc lights and paint the ball, bases, sidelines, equipment and such with phosphorescent paint."

Promotion. Bill Veeck's son, Mike, once staged a minor league ballpark seance to thank Thomas Edison for making night baseball possible. The medium failed to make contact with the inventor, claiming that someone named "Joe" kept interfering.

Book. David Pietrusza, *The Story of Night Baseball* (1995).

No-Hitters

"A no-hitter is an almost mystical feat, causing otherwise rational people to act very strangely indeed. In progress, it usually is not mentioned by anybody concerned lest the pitcher be jinxed, though some pitchers have been relaxed enough to mention it themselves. Ballplayers are reduced to whispers in the dugout and announcers are often forced to torturous circumlocutions to indicate to listeners that something important is happening without being able to tell them what." — Glenn Dickey in *The Great No-Hitters* (1976).

See also *Perfect Games*.

Back-to-Back by Different Pitchers. On September 17, 1968, at San Francisco, Gaylord Perry of the Giants no-hit the Cardinals and Bob Gibson 1–0. The next day Ray Washburn of the Cardinals reciprocated with a 2–0 no-hitter against the Giants.

Jim Maloney pitched a no-hitter on April 30, 1969, a 10–0 win for the Reds over the Astros. After the game the Reds made a number of disparaging remarks about the quality of the Houston ballplayers. Astros pitcher Don Wilson, irritated at the remarks, no-hit the Reds 4–0 the next day. Bobby Tolan is the only man to play in these two games as well as the consecutive no-hitters by Gaylord Perry and Ray Washburn.

On May 5, 1917, Ernie Koob of the Browns pitched a no-hitter against the White Sox. The next day in the second game of a doubleheader, Bob Groom of the Browns did it again against the White Sox. Groom also pitched the last two innings of the first game that day. Though not in consecutive games, the no-hitters were on consecutive days.

Bonuses. See *Bonuses* for pitchers who received bonuses for pitching no-hitters.

Brothers. Ken Forsch of the Astros pitched a 6–0 no-hitter against the Braves on April 7, 1979. Brother Bob of the Cardinals pitched a 5–0 no-hitter against the Phillies on April 16, 1978, and a 3–0 no-hitter against the Expos on September 26, 1983.

Wes Ferrell of the Indians pitched a no-hitter against the Browns on April 29, 1931. His brother Rick was the catcher for the Browns that day. On August 17, 1904, Jesse Tannehill of the Red Sox pitched a no-hitter against the White Sox. Tannehill's brother Lee played third base for the White Sox that day.

Catchers. Gus Triandos was the first catcher to catch no-hitters in both leagues (for Jim Bunning and Hoyt Wilhelm). Jeff Torborg duplicated the feat with Sandy Koufax and Nolan Ryan.

Hall of Famer Ray Schalk caught four no-hitters in 17 years: Joe Benz in 1914, Ed Cicotte in 1917, Charlie Robertson in 1922 (a perfect game) and Ted Lyons in 1926.

Catcher Jim Hegan caught three no-hitters: by Don Black in 1947, Bob Lemon in 1948 and Bob Feller in 1951.

Consecutive.

"After Vander Meer's no-hitter it's only fair to warn Adolph [sic] Hitler that if he does march into Czechoslovakia one of these fine hot days, he won't have the headlines in these parts if the Reds are playing — and particularly if Johnny Vander Meer is in the box." — *Cincinnati Enquirer* editorial.

Johnny Vander Meer pitched consecutive no-hitters for the Reds in 1938. The first game was against the Braves, a 3–0 shutout on June 11. Vander Meer was honored before the second game, attended by 700 of his friends and family.

Superstition about no-hitters meant that he would do poorly in the game following a no-hitter, but he defied the odds. His second no-hitter was the first **Night Game** at Ebbets Field against the Dodgers, a 6–0 victory on June 15, 1938. What is usually not noted is that this was the first time that a pitcher threw two no-hitters in the same season.

In the second game he threw three wild pitches to the first batter of the 9th inning, Buddy Hassett, who then grounded out. Vander Meer then walked the next three batters to load the bases. He got Ernie Koy on a fielder's choice for the second out. The last batter was Leo Durocher. Umpire Bill Stewart blew a game-ending third strike call and then Durocher flied out. As the game ended, Stewart ran out to Vander Meer and apologized for the bad call on the previous pitch. The toughest play in either game was a line drive in the second game by Buddy Hassett which Vander Meer knocked down and chased before throwing him out. Harry Craft caught the last out of the second no-hitter. Craft was Vander Meer's manager when he pitched a minor league no-hitter later in his career.

In the game before the two no-hitters, Vander Meer gave up two hits in the 1st inning to the Giants and then a bloop single in the 9th. Absent the 9th inning hit, he would have pitched over three games' worth of no-hit ball. Vander Meer's try for a third consecutive no-hitter ended in the 4th inning on June 19 against the Braves. Deb Garms got a hit, ending the streak at 21⅔ innings. Vander Meer ended the season at 15–10, finishing with nine straight wins.

Closest to Consecutive. Howard Ehmke almost had consecutive no-hitters in 1923 for the Red Sox. On September 7 he pitched a no-hitter against the A's when runner Slim Harriss missed first base and was called out on what would otherwise have been a double. In Ehmke's next start, Whitey Witt hit a dribbler to third baseman Howard Shanks of the Yankees, who let it bounce off his chest. Official scorer Fred Lieb scored it a hit (the only one of the game) and would not change his mind despite pressure from the other writers. In an effort to change the call, a few writers petitioned American League president Ban Johnson and presented a supporting affidavit by umpire Tommy Connolly. Johnson nevertheless upheld Lieb's call. Ehmke had his only 20-win season that year.

On September 13, 1925, Dazzy Vance pitched a no-hitter against the Phillies, winning 10–1. In his next start he gave up one hit with one out in the 9th inning.

On June 22, 1947, Ewell Blackwell of the Reds was two outs from his second consecutive no-hitter when Dodger infielders Eddie Stanky and Jackie Robinson singled. Stanky's ball went right back through the box and Blackwell probably should have stopped it.

There were connections between Blackwell and Vander Meer. As with Vander Meer, both games were in June in Cincinnati against the Braves and Dodgers, and Vander Meer was in the Reds dugout watching both games (he still pitched for the club).

The closest that Nolan Ryan came to consecutive no-hitters was after No. 2 in 1973. He held the Orioles hitless for seven innings before a bloop single by shortstop Mark Belanger. Ryan lost 3–1 in 11 innings.

After his fourth no-hitter, Ryan pitched five innings of hitless ball against the Brewers. Henry Aaron broke it up with a single with two outs in the 6th inning.

On September 24, 1988, Toronto's Dave Stieb had a no-hitter going with two outs in the 9th inning, and a 2–2 count. In his next start, on September 30, 1988, Stieb had a no-hitter going with two outs in the 9th inning, and a 2–2 count. He didn't come through with the no-hitter either time. He finally pitched a no-hitter on September 2, 1990, a 3–0 shutout of the Indians.

Consecutive No-Hit Innings. Cy Young had 23 innings of no-hit ball that included two innings in one game, six innings in the next, a perfect game in the third (May 5, 1904), and six innings in the fourth.

Johnny Vander Meer's consecutive hitless innings total was 21⅔ innings.

Double No-Hitters. Fred Toney of the Reds and Jim "Hippo" Vaughn of the Cubs each gave up no hits and two walks through the first nine innings of a scoreless game on May 2, 1917.

Olympic decathlon star Jim Thorpe was on "loan" from the Reds as a result of the friendly relationship between Giants manager John McGraw and Reds manager and former Giants pitcher Christy Mathewson. Thorpe had the winning hit in the 10th inning, a swinging bunt to drive in a runner from third after a dropped fly ball put him on base. Thorpe's hit was a high chopper to Vaughn that bounced off the plate and Vaughn had no time to throw out the speedy Thorpe. He threw home instead but could not get the runner. Vaughn later said that catcher Art Wilson stood paralyzed on Thorpe's hit. Vaughn grabbed the ball and threw to Wilson, but Wilson just stood there as the ball hit him in the chest protector and fell to the ground. The runner on third, Larry Kopf, stopped as Vaughn fielded the ball, but ran home when Wilson failed to make the play.

After the run scored, Toney retired the side in the bottom of the 10th inning for the win and the no-hitter. Umpire Al Orth had played with Vaughn on the Yankees in 1908. Toney also had a 17-inning no-hitter in the minor leagues on May 10, 1909, for Kentucky of the Bluegrass League.

On August 23, 1992, pitchers Andy Carter of the Class A Clearwater Phillies and Scott Bakkum of the Winter Haven Red Sox faced each other. Both pitched no-hitters in a 1–0 win by the Phillies. It was believed to be the first minor league double no-hitter in 40 years.

Kevin Brown of the Marlins pitched a 9–0 no-hitter against the Giants on June 10, 1997. Giants starter Bill Vanlandingham carried

a no-hitter into the 7th inning. Brown pitched a one-hitter a month later.

Earliest in the Year. Jack Morris of the Tigers pitched a no-hitter on April 7, 1984, and Ken Forsch of the Astros pitched a no-hitter on April 7, 1979. They were earlier in the year than the two **Opening Day No-Hitters** that have been pitched in the Major Leagues. Hideo Nomo topped everyone with a no-hitter for the Red Sox on April 4, 2001, a 3–0 shutout of the Orioles. He became only the fourth pitcher to throw one in each league.

Extra Inning No-Hitters.
See also **Nine Inning No-Hitters Lost in Extra Innings.**

There have been three complete game extra inning no-hitters in Major League history. There has been one no-hitter called due to darkness.

George "Hooks" Wiltse did it for the Giants against the Phillies on July 4, 1908, going 10 innings for a 1–0 victory.

Fred Toney of the Reds did it on May 2, 1917, in the famous **Double No-Hitter**, winning 1–0 in 10 innings.

On August 9, 1965, Jim Maloney of the Reds pitched a 10-inning no-hitter for a 1–0 victory. On June 14 that year Maloney pitched nine innings of no-hit ball, only to lose 1–0 in 10 innings against the Mets. He was given credit for a nine-inning no-hitter under the rules then in effect.

Two other games went into extra innings as no-hitters but were later disallowed by the Rules Committee: On October 4, 1884, Sam Kimber of Brooklyn in the American Association pitched a no-hitter for 11 innings that was called because of darkness in a scoreless tie against Toledo.

When Harvey Haddix pitched 12⅔ innings of perfect ball on May 26, 1959, no Major Leaguer had pitched a no-hitter for more than 11 innings or a perfect game for more than nine innings. Haddix's effort is no longer recognized as a no-hitter.

Fastest. In 1915 Rube Marquard pitched a no-hitter against the Dodgers in 1 hour and 16 minutes.

First Professional No-Hitter. The first professional no-hitter is credited to Joe Borden (also known as Joe Josephs) of Philadelphia on July 28, 1875, against National Association Chicago. Borden also won the first game ever played in the National League in 1876.

First in National League.
"The *Globe-Democrat* yesterday morning announced the fact that the St. Louis Base Ball Club intended accomplishing the greatest feat in the annals of the game, if sharp play could bring about the result prayed for, which was nothing less than the white-washing of the famous Hartford nine for the third consecutive time. They did it, and thereby covered themselves with glory and sent their admirers into ecstasies…. Bradley's pitching, and the magnificent backing given it by the fielders, won the day for St. Louis. For the first time in the annals of the League, nine innings were played without a single base hit being placed." — Game account in the *St. Louis Globe-Democrat* on the first no-hitter in National League history, a 2–0 shutout by George Bradley of St. Louis against Hartford on July 15, 1876. Bradley walked one and his team made three errors. Bradley was 45–19 that year and later became an umpire and then a traffic cop in Philadelphia.

Earlier sources credit Boston's Joe Borden with the first National League no-hitter, on May 23, 1876, in which he defeated the Red Stockings, but it is no longer recognized as a no-hitter. The official first no-hitter was by George Bradley of St. Louis, who did it on July 15 that season against Hartford.

First in American League. The first no-hitter in the American League was on September 20, 1902, when Jimmy Callahan of the

White Sox defeated the Tigers 3–0. On May 9, 1901, during the American League's inaugural Major League season, Earl Moore of the Indians pitched nine innings of no-hit ball against the White Sox. He gave up a hit in the 10th inning and lost 4–2. That effort is no longer recognized as a no-hitter even for nine innings.

First by Black Pitcher. See *Black "Firsts."*

First College No-Hitter. In his 1914 book *Balldom*, George Moreland reported that the first college no-hitter was pitched by Joseph McElroy Mann for Princeton against Yale on May 29, 1875.

First Start.

"That's all Bobo wants — a chance. I'm gonna make history." — Browns pitcher Bobo Holloman before pitching a no-hitter in his first Major League start on May 6, 1953. The 27-year-old Holloman also pitched the only complete game of his Major League career. When he defeated the A's 6–0, Holloman was so nervous in the 9th inning that he dropped two of the return throws from his catcher during his warm-up. Holloman had been slated to return to the minor league club when he was given a token start on a rainy night in front of 2,473 fans. He also had his only two hits in the Major Leagues. After posting a 3–7 record late in the season, he was farmed out and never returned to the Major Leagues.

Ted Breitenstein pitched a no-hitter in his first Major League start on October 4, 1891, an 8–0 win for St. Louis over Louisville in the American Association. Breitenstein is the only pitcher to throw no-hitters at both 50 feet and the modern 60'6" distance.

Charles Bumpus Jones pitched a 7–1 no-hitter on October 15, 1892, for the National League Cincinnati Red Stockings against the Pittsburgh Pirates in his first start (and first Major League appearance). It was the latest date in a season on which a no-hitter has been pitched.

On August 11, 1991, Wilson Olivares of the Baltimore Orioles pitched a no-hitter in his first Major League start. In his only previous Major League appearance two years earlier, he pitched to five batters in relief, giving up two hits and three walks before being taken out of the game.

On April 14, 1967, 21-year-old Bill Rohr of the Red Sox started his first Major League game on Opening Day in Yankee Stadium and lost a no-hitter in the bottom of the 9th inning. With two outs and a full count, Yankee catcher Elston Howard singled. The Red Sox had entered the 9th inning up 1–0 and finished with a 3–0 victory. Rohr soon left for military reserve duty and then hurt his arm. He later became a successful attorney.

Vida Blue of the A's came close, pitching a no-hitter in his third start on September 21, 1970, only 18 days after he was called up from the minor leagues. He defeated the Twins 6–0.

Bobby Shantz entered the game as a reliever in his first Major League appearance for the A's in 1949. He arrived in the 3rd inning and pitched nine innings of no-hit ball, getting the win when the A's scored in the 13th inning.

Frequency. From 1890 through 1984 there were 235,748 pitching decisions and 177 no-hitters of nine innings or longer. This translated to a no-hitter .075% of the time. Perfect games occurred once every 21,432 decisions, or .0046% of the time.

Home Run Pitcher. On April 27, 1944, Braves pitcher Jim Tobin became the first man to hit a home run and throw a no-hitter in the same game. He also hit three home runs in a game on May 13, 1942, to become the only National League pitcher to do so.

Rick Wise no-hit the Reds for the Phillies on June 23, 1971, a 4–0 victory in which he hit two home runs.

Improbable. On June 25, 1999, Cardinals starter Jose Jimenez became the 15th rookie to throw a no-hitter when he beat the Dia-

mondbacks in one of the most unlikely pitching performances in years. Jimenez had given up 55 runs and 73 hits in his past 57⅓ innings. He had one win in his previous 11 starts and was tied for the National League lead with 60 earned runs allowed. Adding to the improbability was that he was facing the National League's top-hitting team and its star pitcher, Randy Johnson. In the 1–0 Cardinals victory, Johnson had 14 strikeouts. The Cardinals scored on a broken-bat single with two outs in the 9th inning.

In his next game, Jimenez pitched a 1–0 two-hitter — once again against Randy Johnson, who struck out 12. Johnson lost his fourth straight in his next start, as the Diamondbacks failed to score for him again in a 2–0 loss. In August Jimenez joined Bobo Holloman as the only pitchers ever to be sent back to the minor leagues in the same season in which they pitched a no-hitter.

July 4th/Happy Birthday. Long-time Yankee reliever Dave Righetti pitched a no-hitter on owner George Steinbrenner's 53rd birthday on July 4, 1981. Righetti struck out the hard-to-get Wade Boggs to end the game, a 4–0 victory over the Red Sox.

Knuckleballs. On September 2, 1958, Hoyt Wilhelm became the only pitcher to throw almost nothing but knuckleballs during a no-hitter. Out of 99 pitches, he threw 87 knuckleballs and 12 balls that were either sinkers or curves.

Last Game of Season.

See *Last Game of the Season*.

Lopsided. The most lopsided no-hitter in Major League history was on September 6, 1905, when Frank Smith of the White Sox shut out the Tigers 15–0.

Losing No-Hitters.

"This is the greatest day of my life. It just doesn't feel like it yet." — Andy Hawkins.

On July 1, 1990, Yankee pitcher Andy Hawkins threw a complete game no-hitter against the White Sox in windy Comiskey Park, only to lose 4–0 on four unearned runs in the 8th inning. The wind and sun made playing conditions difficult. With two outs, White Sox left fielder Jim Leyritz (normally a catcher/infielder) dropped a fly ball for a two-base error. Hawkins then walked two batters and Leyritz dropped another ball for a three-base error. Right fielder Jesse Barfield then dropped a fly ball for the fourth run. A subsequent Major League scoring committee ruled that even though Hawkins pitched eight full innings, he would not be recognized as pitching a complete-game no-hitter because the Sox didn't come to bat in the 9th inning.

Matters did not improve in Hawkins' next four starts: first, he pitched 11 shutout innings, but lost 2–0 in 12 innings; on July 12 he was the losing pitcher in a rain-shortened 8–0 no-hitter thrown by Melido Perez; on July 17 he gave up three home runs in six innings to Bo Jackson in a 10–7 loss; on July 22 the Yankees scored 10 unearned runs late in a 10–6 victory over the Twins, but Hawkins pitched only 5⅔ innings and did not get the win.

On April 30, 1967, Steve Barber of the Orioles was leading the Tigers 1–0 and had a no-hitter going into the 9th inning. He had been wild up to that point, walking 10 and hitting two batters. He started the 9th inning by walking Norm Cash and Ray Oyler. A sacrifice bunt put runners on second and third. Willie Horton popped out for the second out. Barber had a 1–2 count on Mickey Stanley but wild-pitched in the tying run. The Orioles brought in Stu Miller to relieve. Stanley hit a smash to shortstop Luis Aparicio. Aparicio caught it, dropped it, then picked it up and flipped to Mark Belanger at second base, but Belanger dropped it. The runner scored the go-ahead run and then Al Kaline made the last out. The Orioles did not score in the bottom of the 9th, giving Barber and Miller a combined, but losing, no-hitter. Earlier in the year,

Barber won a game in which he pitched no-hit ball into the 9th inning before giving up a hit.

Ken Johnson of the Astros lost a 1–0 no-hitter to the Reds on April 23, 1964. Joe Nuxhall pitched a five-hitter for the Reds and Pete Rose scored the only run.

Most by a Pitcher.

Seven. Nolan Ryan threw seven no-hitters in his career. He pitched 12 *One-Hitters* and lost five no-hitters with hits in the 9th inning (all with one out; winning three, losing one, and getting a no-decision in the fifth). He also had 19 two-hitters and 31 three-hitters.

One of the one-hitters occurred in 1973 when second baseman Sandy Alomar let a pop fly drop untouched. Alomar's son, Roberto, struck out to end the seventh no-hitter.

During the second no-hitter, Norm Cash of the Tigers approached the plate in the 9th inning carrying a table leg. Umpire Ron Luciano made him get a bat and Ryan induced him to pop up to end the game.

Ryan pitched his first and last no-hitters 18 years apart, the seventh coming when he was 44. The last one might have been the most impressive, featuring 16 strikeouts (to tie his Rangers club record) and just two walks.

Four. Sandy Koufax pitched a no-hitter in 1962, 1963, 1964 and 1965, the last a perfect game. The dates: June 30, 1962 (5–0 over the Mets); May 11, 1963 (8–0 over the Giants); June 4, 1964 (3–0 over the Phillies); and September 9, 1965 (1–0 over the Cubs).

Three. Larry Corcoran, who was one of the early users of pitching signals, pitched three 19th-century no-hitters for the Chicago White Stockings. On August 19, 1880, he defeated the Boston Red Stockings 6–0. He did it again on September 20, 1882, defeating Worcester 5–0. The third no-hitter was on June 27, 1884, when he defeated Providence 6–0. He died of Bright's Disease (a kidney ailment) at age 32.

Cy Young pitched the first of his three no-hitters for the National League Cleveland Spiders on September 18, 1897, a 6–0 victory over the Reds. His May 5, 1904, effort for the Red Sox against the A's was a *Perfect Game*. In the third game, on June 30, 1908, he drove in four runs in an 8–0 Red Sox victory over the Yankees.

Bob Feller pitched the first of his three no-hitters on Opening Day, April 16, 1940, a 1–0 victory over the White Sox. The second was on April 30, 1946, a 1–0 shutout of the Yankees. The last was on July 1, 1951, as the Indians defeated the Tigers 2–1.

Satchel Paige. One source estimated that of the 8,000 games supposedly pitched by legendary Satchel Paige, 55 were no-hitters. Paige claimed that he pitched "only" 2,500 games, of which 100 were no-hitters.

Most Pitchers Used.

7. On June 11, 2003, six Astros pitchers combined on an 8–0 no-hitter against the Yankees in Yankee Stadium. Starter Roy Oswalt had to come out of the game with a strained groin, with none out in the 2nd inning. He was followed by Pete Munro, Kirk Saarloos, Brad Lidge, Octavio Dotel and Billy Wagner. The Yankees had gone 6,980 games without being no-hit, the longest streak in Major League history. The last time was in September 1958, when Hoyt Wilhelm beat them 1–0. It was the third no-hit game in interleague play, all of which occurred at Yankee Stadium.

The Yankees, in a class move, placed champagne at the lockers of each of the six pitchers. Luckily, Yankees owner George Steinbrenner chose to attended the New Jersey Nets play-off game that night.

5. In Oakland's 1975 season finale on September 28, manager Dick Williams wanted to use a number of pitchers as a tune-up for the ALCS. Vida Blue started and went five innings against the Angels at Oakland. Glenn Abbott came on in the 6th and Paul Lindblad in the 7th. Rollie Fingers pitched the 8th and 9th innings to complete the no-hitter. Reggie Jackson had two home runs in the 5–0 victory.

Most Played In. Bert Campaneris played in nine no-hitters. Rickey Henderson is second with seven (not including Nolan Ryan).

No-Hitters Lost in Extra Innings.

1901/Earl Moore. On May 9, 1901, the Indians rookie pitcher threw nine hitless innings against the White Sox before Sam Mertes singled in the 10th inning and the Indians lost 4–2. Because of rain, only 400 people attended.

1904/Robert Wicker. On June 11, 1904, the Cubs pitcher threw nine hitless before New York's Sam Mertes broke up another extra inning no-hitter with a single. Wicker won 1–0 in 12 innings, pitching a one-hitter.

1906/Harry McIntire. On August 1, 1906, the Dodger pitcher threw 10⅔ hitless innings before Pittsburgh's Claude Richey singled. McIntire lost 1–0 on four hits in 12 innings.

1909/Leon Ames. On April 15, 1909, the Giants pitcher threw 9⅓ hitless innings before Charles Alperman singled. Ames lost 3–0 on seven hits in 13 innings.

1910/Tom Hughes. On August 30, 1910, the Yankee pitcher threw 9⅓ hitless innings before Cleveland's Harry Niles singled. Hughes lost 5–0 on seven hits in 11 innings.

1914/James Scott. On May 14, 1914, the White Sox pitcher threw nine hitless innings before Washington's Chick Gandil singled. Scott lost 1–0 on two hits in 10 innings.

1917/Hippo Vaughn. On May 2, 1917, the Cubs pitcher threw 9⅓ hitless innings before Cincinnati's Larry Kopf singled. Vaughn lost 1–0 on two hits in 10 innings.

1934/Bobo Newsom. On September 18, 1934, the Browns pitcher threw 9⅔ hitless innings before Boston's Roy Johnson singled. Newsom lost 2–1 on one hit in 10 innings.

1956/Three Reds Pitchers. On May 26, 1956, a trio of Reds pitchers combined to pitch 9⅔ hitless innings: Johnny Klippstein (seven innings), Hershell Freeman (one inning) and Joe Black (2⅔ innings). Milwaukee's Jack Dittmar doubled with two outs in the 10th inning and Black lost 2–1 on three hits in 11 innings.

1959/Harvey Haddix. On May 26, 1959, the Pirates pitcher threw 12 perfect innings against the Braves before Joe Adcock doubled. Haddix lost 1–0 on one hit in 12⅔ innings.

1965/Jim Maloney. On June 14, 1965, the Reds pitcher threw 10 hitless innings before New York's Johnny Lewis homered. Maloney lost 1–0 on two hits in 11 innings.

1991/Mark Gardner. On July 26, 1991, the Expos pitcher threw nine hitless innings against the Dodgers before losing 1–0 in 10 innings.

1995/Pedro Martinez. On June 3, 1995, the Expos pitcher threw nine perfect innings before Bip Roberts doubled. Martinez was lifted and Mel Rojas saved a 10-inning 1–0 victory.

Oldest to Pitch No-Hitter. Nolan Ryan pitched a no-hitter at age 43 on June 11, 1990, a 5–0 victory over the A's. The previous oldest was Cy Young, who did it at age 41 on June 30, 1908, an 8–0 Red Sox win over the Yankees.

Recognition. Until the early 20th century, no-hitters were not always recognized as something special. Some commentators have suggested that the no-hitter was popularized when the *Reach Guide* began recognizing low-hit games in its season-ending summaries.

Two in One Season/One Pitcher. Johnny Vander Meer of the

Reds was the first pitcher to record two no-hitters in the same season, in 1938 (see **Consecutive No-Hitters**).

Allie Reynolds did it in 1951 for the Yankees on July 12 (1–0 over the Indians) and September 28 (8–0 over the Red Sox).

Virgil Trucks of the Tigers had two 1–0 no-hitters in 1952, on May 15 against the Senators and August 25 against the Yankees. The rest of the season was dismal, as he finished the year with a 5–19 record for the last-place Tigers.

Jim Maloney first did it on June 14, 1965, though he gave up a hit and lost the game in the 10th inning and that effort is no longer officially recognized. His second no-hitter of the season was on August 9, a 10-inning victory over the Cubs.

Nolan Ryan did it in 1973 while pitching for the Angels on May 15 and July 15. He shut out the Royals (3–0) and Tigers (6–0).

Most in a Season/Major Leagues. The 1990 season broke all records by producing nine no-hitters (one is now not recognized as a no-hitter). The previous record was seven in 1917. Each of the nine had something out of the ordinary attached to it other than the fact of the no-hitter:

1. The first was a combined 1–0 no-hitter by Mark Langston and Mike Witt of the Angels on April 11, just after the teams started play following a spring training lockout.

2. The second was by Randy Johnson of the Seattle Mariners on June 2, a 2–0 victory over the Tigers. Johnson is the ***Tallest Player*** in Major League history at 6'10".

3. The third was Nolan Ryan's sixth no-hitter, coming on June 11 in a 5–0 victory over eventual American League champion Oakland. His next start was in Seattle on June 16. The Mariners staged "Guaranteed No-Hitter Night" and the fans were to receive free tickets to another game if a no-hitter was pitched. Ryan did not come through, but Mariners pitcher Matt Young came close with a three-hitter.

4–5. The fourth and fifth occurred on the same night, June 29. A's pitcher Dave Stewart shut out the Blue Jays 5–0. Dodger pitcher Fernando Valenzuela defeated the Cardinals 6–0. On the last play of the game, former Dodger Pedro Guerrero grounded a ball through Valenzuela's legs that was fielded on second base by Alfredo Griffin, who threw out Guerrero at first.

6. The sixth was on July 1, a 4–0 loss by New York Yankee pitcher Andy Hawkins (See **Losing No-Hitters**).

7. The seventh was on July 12 by Chicago White Sox pitcher Melido Perez, who defeated the Yankees 8–0 in a 6-inning rain-shortened game (now not recognized as a no-hitter because it did not go nine innings).

8.. The eighth was a 6–0 shutout on August 15 by Phillies pitcher Terry Mulholland against the Giants. Mulholland came within a foot of a perfect game. In the 8th inning third baseman Charlie Hayes threw wide to first base, drawing the fielder off the bag for an error. It was the first no-hitter for a Phillies pitcher since 1906.

9. The ninth was by Dave Stieb of the Blue Jays on September 2, 1990, against the Indians. It was the first no-hitter in franchise history and it came after Stieb had twice blown no-hitters with two outs in the 9th inning.

No Confidence by Manager. Padres and Astros manager Preston Gomez lifted two pitchers in the eighth inning of no-hitters. On July 22, 1970, Clay Kirby of the Padres was losing 1–0 to the Mets when Gomez pinch-hit for him. The Mets eventually won 3–0.

In 1973 Don Wilson of the Astros had a no-hitter in the 8th inning against the Reds when Gomez sent in Tommy Helms to pinch-hit for him in a scoreless tie. Ironically, Clay Kirby was in the Reds dugout and when asked by teammate Don Gullett whether Gomez would pinch-hit for Wilson, Kirby said, "I guarantee he will."

None by Team. Through 2004 no pitcher on the Rockies, Devil Rays, Padres or Mets had ever pitched a no-hitter. Tom Seaver came close for the Mets on July 9, 1969, when he retired 25 consecutive Cubs batters until Jimmy Qualls singled with one out in the 9th inning. In May 2004 Tom Glavine came close for the Mets, taking a perfect game into the 7th inning and a no-hitter through two outs in the 8th before giving up a double.

In the early 1960s, the King Corn company offered a prize for the correct guess as to when the first Mets no-hitter would be pitched. The company is not in business any longer.

Only Win of the Season. On September 9, 1945, Dick Fowler of the A's no-hit the Browns 1–0 for his only victory of the season. He was 1–2 in seven appearances.

Opening Day. Bob Feller pitched a no-hitter against the White Sox on Opening Day, April 16, 1940. The no-hitter was saved on a diving stop by second baseman Ray Mack to end the game. White Sox shortstop Luke Appling always claimed that the no-hitter was tainted because with two out in the 9th inning he hit a line drive down the line that brought up chalk, but the umpire ruled it a foul ball.

Leon "Red" Ames of the Giants pitched nine innings of no-hit ball at the Polo Grounds on Opening Day, April 15, 1909. He lost the game in the 13th inning after giving up a hit in the 10th.

Rule Change. In August 1991 Commissioner Fay Vincent and a special rules committee redefined the no-hitter rules. The rules were modified to define a no-hitter as a game that went nine innings or more and was completed. The ruling deleted from the record books 38 rain-shortened no-hitters and 12 in which the pitcher went nine no-hit innings but gave up a hit in extra innings. This included Harvey Haddix's 12 perfect innings in 1959 against the Braves. In wiping out 50 no-hitters, the committee left 226 intact at the time of its ruling at the end of 1991.

Same Day. On April 22, 1898, Ted Breitenstein of Cincinnati no-hit Pittsburgh 11–0. On the same day, Jim Hughes of Baltimore no-hit Boston 8–0.

On June 29, 1990, Dave Stewart of the A's no-hit the Blue Jays and Fernando Valenzuela of the Dodgers no-hit the Cardinals.

See also **Double No-Hitters**.

Superstition. See ***Superstitions*** — **No-Hitters**.

Tainted. In July 1886 Toad Ramsey pitched a no-hitter for American Association Louisville against the Baltimore Orioles, striking out 16. However, a hit was later added to the line score for Baltimore center fielder Pat O'Connell, negating the no-hitter.

When commissioner Fay Vincent's special rules committee analyzed all no-hitters in 1991 to create new rules, the committee decided to retain the August 7, 1899, no-hitter allegedly pitched by Vic Willis for Boston, though there is considerable evidence that he gave up a hit. Willis defeated Washington 7–1.

On May 5 1917, Ernie Koob of the Browns gave up an infield single to the White Sox in the 1st inning for the only hit of the game. After the game, the sportswriters met with the official scorer and they all agreed to call it an error.

On June 12, 1959, Mike McCormick received credit for a five-inning no-hitter after a 6th inning hit was washed out by rain under the former rule allowing less-than-nine-inning no-hitters. McCormick defeated the Phillies 4–0.

One of the two no-hitters thrown by Virgil Trucks for the Tigers in 1952 had a minor controversy that some thought tainted it. On August 25, 1952, Trucks threw a no-hitter for the Tigers against the Yankees. One batted ball was scored originally as an error by John Drebinger of the *New York Times*. Dan Daniel of the *World Telegram* challenged that decision. Drebinger called Johnny Pesky, who committed the error, from a special phone in the press box to the dugout. Pesky agreed that it was an error.

Earlier in the year Trucks entered the 9th inning with a no-hitter in a scoreless game, but Vic Wertz hit a two-out home run to win it for the Indians. Trucks lost a no-hitter in the 10th inning while in the minor leagues.

Televised No-Hitter. On May 12, 1955, Carl Erskine pitched a no-hitter in the first coast-to-coast telecast of NBC's Saturday "Game of the Week."

World Series No-Hitter Attempt.

"Bevens, hitherto a pitcher of minor distinction, now stood at the brink of baseball immortality."—Lawrence Ritter and Donald Honig in *The Image of Their Greatness* (1976).

Yankee pitcher Bill Bevens went into the bottom of the 9th inning with a no-hitter in Game 4 of the 1947 World Series. The Yankees led the game 2–1. The Dodgers had scored without benefit of a hit on two walks, a sacrifice and a ground out. With one out in the 9th, Dodger outfielder Carl Furillo walked and Spider Jorgensen fouled out for the second out. Al Gionfriddo pinch-ran for Furillo. Pete Reiser was intentionally walked and Eddie Miskis ran for him. Cookie Lavagetto hit the second pitch from Bevens for a double off the wall to score Gionfriddo and Miskis to win the game 3–2 on one hit.

Bevens was released over the winter, never to pitch in the Major Leagues again. It also was Lavagetto's last game in the Major Leagues.

Youngest. Vida Blue was 21 years 3 months when he pitched a no-hitter in his fourth start on September 21, 1970. He walked Harmon Killebrew in the 4th inning for the only runner of the game.

Books. Rich Coberly, *The No-Hit Hall of Fame* (1985); Glenn Dickey, *The Great No-Hitters* (1976); Phil Pepe, *No-Hitter* (1968); Rich Westcott, *No-Hitter* (2000).

North American Baseball League

This was a 1984 effort to form a new international major league, but nothing came of it.

Northern League (1993–)

"Today, the Northern League is acknowledged to be *the* pre-eminent modern era independent league. Its success contributed to a growth in independent baseball that today includes seven leagues across the United States. With attendance increasing annually and continued interest from communities and ownership groups hoping for expansion, the future of the Northern League will surely prove to be as dynamic as its storied and proud history."—Northern League website.

This minor league has become the most prominent of the independent leagues after its birth in 1993. Previous Northern Leagues had been affiliated with minor league baseball, but the last version disappeared after the 1971 season. Miles Wolff is credited with resurrecting the concept of a league independent from Organized Baseball, and the six-team league began play in the Midwest in 1993. In 1998 the Northern League merged with the Northeast League to form a super-independent 16-team league with 14 franchises in 12 states and two in Canada.

Major Leaguers who spent time in the league include Rey Ordonez, J.D. Drew, Kevin Millar, Darryl Strawberry and Jeff Zimmerman. The league allows four veterans (five or more years) per team and requires at least five rookies.

Northwestern League

This was an early minor league founded in 1879 with teams in Dubuque, Omaha, Davenport and Rockport (Iowa, Illinois and Nebraska). The league was an indirect descendent of the American League (first evolving into the Western League), but was hurt by club-jumping players and no set schedule.

The league lasted one year, but was revived in 1883 and approached the National League for reciprocity rights regarding player movement. This opened the door to the *National Agreement* of 1883, which kept peace among the American Association, National League and the minor leagues. Their unity led to the downfall of the outlaw Union Association after one season in 1884.

Despite the Northwestern League's close relationship with the Major Leagues, league secretary Samuel G. Morton was accused of feeding his league's players to the upstart 1884 Union Association. Morton worked as a clerk for National League Chicago White Stockings owner Albert Spalding, who some claim may have secretly helped the Union Association. The basis for that claim is unclear.

Novels See *Books*

Number of Players See *Rosters*

Numbers on Uniforms See *Uniforms—Numbers*

"**O** is for Ott
Of the restless right foot.
When he leaned on the pellet,
The pellet stayed put."
—Ogden Nash on Mel Ott.

Oakland

"… there is no *there* there."—Gertrude Stein.

Baseball in Oakland mirrored the expansion of the game in San Francisco in the 1850s and 1860s. The most prominent of the area's clubs was the Oakland Oaks, a minor league team in the outlaw California League around 1900. It was a member of the Pacific Coast League when it organized in 1903.

The Oaks were controlled by J. Cal Ewing, who for many years also controlled the San Francisco Seals until Judge Landis forced him to sell the club because Ewing held a monopoly in the area. The Oaks played their games in nearby Emeryville and won one of their last pennants under Casey Stengel in 1948. The Oaks won their last pennant in 1950 and after the 1955 season moved to Vancouver, British Columbia.

Professional baseball did not return to Oakland until Charlie Finley moved the Kansas City A's to Oakland for the 1968 season.

Oakland Athletics

American League 1968–

"In a dozen years, Finley's A's had five general managers, 2 managers, 27 coaches, five scouting directors, seven farm directors, eight publicity directors, and 16 broadcasters, to say nothing of more ticket managers, secretaries, and switchboard operators than one can correctly count."—Bill Libby in *Charlie O & the Angry A's* (1975).

Origins. Major League Baseball returned to Oakland for the 1968 season when *Kansas City Athletics* owner Charlie Finley received permission to make the move (see also *Franchise Shifts*).

First Game. The A's played their first home game on April 17, 1968, with California governor Ronald Reagan throwing out the first ball. Reagan's comment to the crowd, two days after tax day: "One thing I'm sure of is that a lot of you paid your taxes [crowd boos]. Up to a few moments ago, I was happy to be here."

Key Owners.

Charles O. Finley/1968–1980.

"I like Charlie Finley. He's a refreshing guy, a fine business executive and a man with the courage of his own convictions. I admire his stand on many issues and I have stood shoulder to shoulder with him several times."—1960s White Sox owner Arthur Allyn expressing the minority view.

"Why was Charlie Finley disliked by just about every other owner during his tenure as owner of the A's? Well, it could have been because Finley was an outspoken, vulgar, penny-pinching bastard, capable of bringing embarrassment to the entire game with every flap of his gums. It could also have been because the other owners were (justifiably) jealous of Finley's ability to *have an original thought*."—Dan Holmes.

"When Charlie Finley had his heart operation, it took eight hours—seven just to find his heart."—A's pitcher Steve McCatty.

"A self-made man who worships his creator."—Jim Murray.

"Finley is an incredible man, bombastic, energetic, vulgar, inventive … the list of adjectives could go on and on. He careens through life like a bowling ball, and woe be it to anyone who gets in his way."—Glenn Dickey in *The History of American League Baseball* (1980).

See also *Kansas City Athletics*—Key Owners.

Finley owned 100% of the A's through the 1970s. He watched his championship clubs of the early 1970s fade into an abyss of poor teams and poor attendance near the end of the decade.

Finley alienated almost everyone in baseball, from his players and managers on up to commissioner Bowie Kuhn. He supposedly ended his semipro baseball career as a first baseman and manager in Indiana when he contracted tuberculosis in 1946. Finley made his initial fortune selling a group insurance policy to the American College of Surgeons and earning a commission of $441,563.

Finley is credited by many with suggesting or implementing a number of innovations (some good, most bad): playing World Series games at night; using multi-colored uniforms; the designated hitter; orange baseballs; the designated runner; and the three-ball walk and two-strike strikeout system to increase action. The pitch count innovation was tried in a spring game to speed it up, but there were too many walks and the games were actually longer

In the late 1970s Finley tried to sell the club to oil mogul Marvin Davis, who intended to move the club to his home in Denver. The deal fell through when the County Board of Supervisors, the A's landlord in Oakland/Alameda County Stadium, refused to release the team from the remaining 10 years on its lease. The county said it would allow the sale if the crosstown Giants would agree to play 41 games in the Oakland Coliseum. The Giants agreed, but the plan was vetoed by their landlord, the Alameda County Supervisors.

Finley died in 1996 at age 78. See Herbert Michelson, *Charlie O.—Charles Oscar Finley Versus the Baseball Establishment* (1975).

Walter A. Haas, Jr./1980–1995. Walter Haas and his family owned the Levi Strauss Co. and bought the club in August 1980 for $12.7 million. In 1994 Haas was reported to be worth $620 million (or $490 million) and was the great-great-grandnephew of Levi Strauss. The club's key move was to hire Sandy Alderson as the club's general manager in the mid–1980s. He led them to a series of successes late in the decade.

Wally Haas, son of the patriarch and the family member who ran the club, announced in May 1994 that the club was for sale. The asking price was $85 million, and they attempted to find a buyer who would keep the club in Oakland. The club was sold in September 1995, only a few weeks before Walter Haas died of prostate cancer at age 79.

Steve Schott and Ken Hofmann/1995– . Local businessmen Steve Schott and Ken Hofmann bought the club in mid–1995 for the $85 million asking price. Schott graduated from Santa Clara University and later built a 1,500 baseball stadium at the school. His construction company, Citation, has been one of the largest home builders in California.

By the 2000s the owners needed a new ballpark, and were complaining that the club was headed the way of the Expos. But the club kept winning despite having a revenue stream that was ranked 23rd out of 30 teams. The club was profitable by $1.5 million in 2003, but there were still rumors of the club moving to another state. Hofmann, 81 in 2004, was also rumored to be contemplating a sale of his interest, though the club's structure might not change dramatically because Schott was the managing general partner.

Nickname. The A's retained the nickname that originated with the Philadelphia Athletics when they joined the American League in 1901.

Key Seasons.

1971. After second-place finishes in 1969 and 1970, the A's won their first division crown. They won 101 games behind the combined 45 wins of Vida Blue and Catfish Hunter and Reggie Jackson's 32 home runs. They were swept by the Orioles in the ALCS.

1972.

"This fucking city can't do anything right."—Charlie Finley after a small turnout for a World Series victory celebration.

The A's won their second division title by 5½ games over the White Sox and were led by Catfish Hunter's 21 wins. The A's beat the Tigers in the ALCS, winning the deciding Game 5 when Vida Blue pitched four shutout innings to preserve a 2–1 win and earn the save. The A's beat the Reds in seven games in the World Series, winning 3–2 in Game 7 as Rollie Fingers earned the save.

1973. The A's again won the division with 94 wins, led by Reggie Jackson's league-leading 32 home runs and 117 RBIs. Ken Holtzman, Vida Blue and Catfish Hunter all won at least 20 games. The A's beat the Orioles in five games for the pennant and went on to defeat the Mets in a seven-game World Series. Immediately after the last game, A's manager Dick Williams resigned.

1974. The dynasty continued with a fourth straight division title behind Catfish Hunter's 25 wins. The A's again defeated the Orioles for the pennant and then beat the Dodgers in the World Series for their third straight crown. All but one of the five games was decided by one run as reliever Rollie Fingers had three saves and a win.

1975. The A's won their fifth consecutive division title behind Reggie Jackson's league-leading 36 home runs and Vida Blue's 22 wins. Oakland's pennant string was broken when the Red Sox swept them in the ALCS.

1981. After a second-place finish in 1980, the A's returned to win one half of the split-season format and then swept the Royals to win the Western Division. The Yankees swept the A's in the ALCS.

1988. Manager Tony LaRussa led the club to 104 wins behind Jose Canseco's league-leading 42 home runs and 124 RBIs, Dave Stewart's 21 wins and Dennis Eckersley's 45 saves. The A's swept the Red Sox in the ALCS but were surprised by the underdog Dodgers in the World Series. The Dodgers won in five games after a miracle 9th inning home run by Kirk Gibson off Dennis Eckersley to win Game 1.

1989. The A's won 99 games and the division title by seven games and beat the Blue Jays in five games for the pennant. The World Series was interrupted for a week by a major *Earthquake* in the Bay Area, but the A's nevertheless swept the Giants for the title. Dave Stewart won 21 games and Mark McGwire hit 33 home runs.

1990. The A's won 103 games and were led by Bob Welch's league-leading 27 wins and Dennis Eckersley's 48 saves. They swept the Red Sox in the ALCS and then were swept by the Reds in the World Series.

1992. Mark McGwire's 42 home runs and Dennis Eckersley's 51 saves led the club to another division title. The A's lost the ALCS in six games to the Blue Jays and then began a slide into mediocrity.

2000. After a second-place finish in 1999, the A's were division champions with a 91–70 record, but in what was to become a pattern, lost the division series to the Yankees in five games. Jason Giambi was the star of the club with 43 home runs and 137 RBIs while batting .333, and shortstop Miguel Tejada hit 30 home runs and drove in 115 runs. Tim Hudson led the club with a 20–6 record, and Jason Isringhausen had 33 saves.

2001. The A's were the American League wild card team with a 102–60 record, but again lost to the Yankees in five games in the division series despite winning the first two games. Jason Giambi again led the club, this time with 38 home runs and 120 RBIs. Eric Chavez and Miguel Tejada each had at least 31 home runs and 113 RBIs. Mark Mulder won 21 games, Tim Hudson won 18 and Barry Zito won 17. Jason Isringhausen saved 34 games.

2002. The A's won the division title with a 103–59 record, but lost the division series again in five games, this time to the Twins. Eric Chavez and Miguel Tejada (American League MVP) each hit 34 home runs, and Tejada had 131 RBIs. Barry Zito was 23–5 and Mark Mulder was 19–7, as new reliever Billy Koch recorded 44 saves.

2003. The A's again won the division title, with a 96–66 record, and for the fourth straight season lost the division series in five games, this time to the Red Sox, again despite winning the first two games. Miguel Tejada (27 home runs and 106 RBIs) and Eric Chavez (29/101) led the team, but Ramon Hernandez and Erubiel Durazo also each hit 21 home runs. Barry Zito, Tim Hudson and Mark Mulder each won 14 or more games, and Keith Foulke recorded 43 saves.

Key Players.

Vida Blue pitched for nine seasons in Oakland beginning in 1969. He exploded in his first full season in 1971 with 24 wins. He won 20 games in 1973 and 22 games in 1975. Drug problems later shortened his career. See also Bill Libby and Vida Blue, *Vida, His Own Story* (1972).

Reggie Jackson (HF) played nine seasons in Oakland, leading the league in home runs in 1973 and 1975 after peaking in 1969 with 47 home runs. He played in five championship series for the club and led the A's to three World Championships. Jackson had 268 home runs for the club, the most until Mark McGwire surpassed him.

Catfish Hunter (HF) pitched the first nine years of his career for the A's. He blossomed in 1971 with 21 wins, the first of four straight seasons of 20 or more wins for the club. He led the league with 25 wins and a 2.49 ERA in 1974 before departing for the Yankees. He won four World Series games for the A's.

Rollie Fingers (HF) played nine seasons for the A's, saving 136 regular season games and six World Series games.

Jose Canseco played seven seasons for the A's beginning in 1985. He hit more than 30 home runs five times, including a league-leading 42 in 1988 and 44 in 1991. He played part of 1992 for the A's before being traded to the Rangers. He hit seven postseason home runs for the A's.

Mark McGwire began with the A's in 1986 but exploded during his official rookie season in 1987 with a rookie record 49 home runs. He hit 42 home runs in 1992 and 52 in 1996 before being traded to the Cardinals in mid–1997.

Dave Stewart was traded to the A's in 1987 at a point when his mediocre career was thought to be nearing the close. However, he surprised with a league-leading 20 wins in 1987, the first of four straight seasons with 20 or more wins. He won eight postseason games for the A's between 1988 and 1992.

Dennis Eckersley (HF) was a starter for his entire career until he moved to the A's in 1987 when his career was fading. He saved 16 games that season and exploded with 45 saves in 1988. He followed that with seasons of 33, 48, 43 and 51 saves through 1992 before slowing substantially by mid-decade. He saved 11 postseason games for the A's.

Jason Giambi played seven years in Oakland before signing as a free agent with the Yankees in 2002. He hit 181 homers for the club over his six top seasons, with a best of 43 in 2000.

Miguel Tejada played seven seasons for the A's beginning in 1997, with three straight seasons of 30 or more home runs and four straight seasons over 100 RBIs. He was the 2002 American League MVP, when he batted .308 and had a slugging percentage of .508.

Key Managers.

Dick Williams managed the club from 1971 through 1973, winning three straight division titles and two World Series. He announced his resignation immediately after winning the 1973 Series.

Alvin Dark managed the club in 1974 and 1975, winning the division title both seasons. He led the club to its third straight World Series title in 1974, but his club was swept by the Red Sox in the 1975 ALCS. See also Alvin Dark and John Underwood, *When in Doubt, Fire the Manager* (1980).

Tony LaRussa managed the club starting in 1986, winning four division titles between 1988 through 1992. He led the club into the World Series three straight seasons beginning in 1988 and won the title in 1989. He left after the 1995 season following a series of mediocre finishes.

Art Howe managed the A's from 1996 through the 2002 season, but could never get past the first round of the postseason. His clubs finished first twice and was the wild card once (during his last four seasons), before he left for the Mets in 2003.

Ballpark.

"It's nice pitching in an airport." — Vida Blue on the spacious dimensions of the Oakland Coliseum.

The Oakland Coliseum (Oakland/Alameda County Stadium) was new for the A's first season in 1968. It originally had dimensions from left to right field of 330–378–410–378–330, which were reduced slightly in later years. Its original seating capacity was 50,000, increased and then reduced to 47,450 by the early 1990s. The park had no scoreboard for the first two months of the 1968 season before owner Charlie Finley's $1 million exploding scoreboard was installed in right field. An even more elaborate scoreboard, called the Finley Fun Board, was installed in left field for the 1969 season. Extensive renovations were undertaken after the 1995 season but they were not completed by opening day in 1996. As a result, the A's played their first six games in Las Vegas (see also **Home Teams**).

The stadium was called UMAX Coliseum for part of 1997 and 1998. The name reverted briefly back to Oakland-Alameda County Coliseum in 1998 until it was renamed Network Associates Coliseum that same year.

Key Broadcasters (or lack thereof).

"Charlie has this one little weakness: He doesn't treat people like human beings." — Broadcaster Bob Elson, one of seven broadcasters in the first six years in Oakland.

"Finley uses him as a pipeline to the players; he once had to establish a mandatory $1,000 fine for any player who hit Moore." — Bay area sportswriter Glenn Dickey in *The Jock Empire* (1974), on Monte Moore, the longest-lasting of the A's broadcasters in the late 1960s and mid–1970s.

Monte Moore had been the A's broadcaster since 1962 in Kansas City and stayed with the club through 1977. In the early 1970s there were years when the A's won the pennant and their games were broadcast over only a local college station. During that period Finley hired a young black teenager to telephone him in Chicago and "broadcast" the game to him over the open line. That teenager, Stanley Burrell, later became a rap music star in the late 1980s, M.C. Hammer. Curt Flood broadcast briefly for the A's in 1979.

In 1981 broadcaster Lon Simmons went from San Francisco to the A's when KSFO lost the Giants due to a conflict between the station and owner Bob Lurie. Long-time Oakland Raiders broadcaster Bill King joined the A's in 1981 and was still with them in the mid–1990s. Former catcher Ray Fosse began broadcasting for the club in 1985.

Books. Tom Clark, *Champagne and Baloney* (1976); Glenn Dickey, *Champions: The Story of the First Two Oakland A's Dynasties and the Building of a Third* (2002); Michael Lewis, *Moneyball* (2003); Bill Libby, *Charlie O. and the Angry A's* (1975); Bruce Markusen, *A Baseball Dynasty: Charlie Finley's Swingin' A's* (2002); John Shea and John Hickey, *Magic by the Bay* (1990).

Official Game

"I do not know how we got through it. I do not even know how yours truly got through it. I do not remember much. It was 3–0 after 4½, official now, and now we begun stalling, claiming it was raining, claiming the ball was wet and we were libel [sic] to be beaned, which Washington said would make no difference to fellows with heads as hard as us." — Mark Harris in *Bang the Drum Slowly* (1956).

See also **Pitchers—Starting Pitcher Win/No 5 Innings.**

A game becomes official after five innings, or 4½ innings if the home team is ahead. This rule has been in effect since at least 1857.

Official Scorer

"Right now there are two very nervous people in the park; the pitcher and the official scorer." — Broadcaster Lindsey Nelson when pitcher Jerry Reuss was a few outs away from a no-hitter in 1980.

"Baloney, it was a clean single up the middle." — Yogi Berra after complaining to the official scorer that one of his hits had not shown up in the box score and being told that it was a typographical error.

Early History. Scoring was somewhat haphazard in the early years and sometimes the identity of the official scorer was kept secret. With the lack of communication, information often was not disseminated until after the season and players were not aware until then how they had fared. Writers did their own scoring and different papers often showed different hit totals.

From 1882 through 1891, Albert Spalding kept secret the identity of the Chicago White Stockings official scorer. It turned out to be Elisa Green Williams, who usually sat between the wives of Cap Anson and Abner Dalrymple, who never suspected. Williams was the mother of team treasurer C.C. Williams.

In 1897 Washington owner George Wagner admitted to persuading the official league scorer to add 40 hits to Gene DeMontreville's season total to get him well over .300. This allowed Wagner to sell the ."300 hitter" to Baltimore at a higher price than otherwise might have been warranted. Wagner said that he was not the first owner to succeed with the official scorer in such a situation. According to *The Baseball Encyclopedia*, DeMontreville officially batted .341 in 1897 before being sold to Baltimore. The added hits seem to be overkill if all they were trying to achieve was a .300 batting average.

In 1911 sportswriter Fred Lieb received an extra $300 as official scorer for the season on all New York Yankee games and prepared a box score after each game. The Giants paid $250 for the same job.

World Series. Judge Landis decided that the president of the Baseball Writers Association of America would be chief scorer of all World Series games. The other two official scorers were to come from among writers who worked in the cities hosting the World Series.

Modern Selection Process. By 1966 regular season official scorers technically were selected by each league president. In reality, the Baseball Writers Association drew a list of eligible writers and divided up the games. There is one official scorer per game, usually a local sportswriter. In 1966 the scorers received $30 per game.

By 1993 scorers were paid $75 per game. Most are hired solely on the basis of recommendations of clubs' public relations directors. The American League does not test its scorers. The National League administers an open-book test. Neither league requires an eye exam and both leagues have a rule that scorers must watch at least 100 games in each of three successive seasons before serving as a scorer. Since the late 1970s, many newspapers have forbidden their writers to score games because of the possibility that the writer might become part of the story of a game.

Scoring Change. Any scoring change based on a judgment call must be made within 24 hours of the game.

See **Four Hundred Hitters** for an official scorer controversy surrounding Ty Cobb's pursuit of a .400 average in 1922.

The pitiful 1992 Mariners (64–98) found a scapegoat: they signed a petition to have their official scorer replaced.

Official Statistics   See *Statistics and Statisticians*

Old Age and Oldest Living Former Player

"Age is a question of mind over matter: If you don't mind, it doesn't matter." — Satchel Paige.

"First you forget names;
then you forget faces;
then you forget to zip up your fly;
and then you forget to unzip your fly."
— Branch Rickey on senility.

"Good black don't crack."—Negro Leaguer Buck O'Neil's explanation for turning 91 without a line on his face. Bill Buckner has described O'Neil as the "classiest man I ever met in all my years in baseball."

See also *Retirement*.

The only Major League player to reach 100 years old through 1989 was Ralph Miller, who pitched for Brooklyn and Baltimore in the National League in 1898–1899. He was born on March 15, 1873, and died on May 8, 1973. He was the last man to have played in the Major Leagues in the 19th century.

Paul Franklin "Bill" Otis lived to be 100. His one hit in the Major Leagues was off Walter Johnson in 1912. He died on December 15, 1990, nine days short of his 101st birthday.

In June 1991 former Yankee and Cardinal pitcher Red Hoff celebrated his 100th birthday, prompting him to comment: "I think I could still pitch nine innings. Cripes, I might give it a try, considering the salaries they're making now."

Hoff died on September 17, 1998, at age 107, the oldest ex–Major Leaguer ever. He struck out Ty Cobb as the first batter he faced in his first pitching stint in the Major Leagues.

Smoky Joe Wood was almost 96 years old before passing away in July 1985.

Former Reds outfielder Dummy Hoy, who was *Deaf*, was 99 when he threw out the first pitch of Game 3 of the 1961 World Series. He died in December that year.

In 1984 infielder Art Butler died after being the then-oldest living former player at age 97.

In January 1996 pitcher Milt Gaston turned 100, the eighth former Major Leaguer to reach that milestone. He died three months later.

A 1992 Nike shoe television ad featured the Kids and Kubs Baseball League for players 75 years old or older. George Bakewell was one of the players featured. He noted that "if Babe Ruth were alive today, he'd be two years younger than me." Bakewell was 100 years old at the time and attributed his longevity to the shoes and to oysters.

Oldest Active Players

"I don't mind paying a player, but I don't want to pay for his funeral."—Blue Jays general manager Pat Gillick after Rico Carty sought a three-year contract at age 39.

"Bruce Sutter has been around for a while and he's pretty old. He's thirty-five years old. That will give you some idea of how old he is."—Broadcaster Ron Fairly in 1988.

"These guys are so old they're eligible for meals on wheels."—Mickey Rivers commenting on the age of Texas Rangers teammates Bill Stein and Larry Bittner.

"Shows everyone that even though I'm 40, I am still … I'm sorry, I lost my train of thought."—One of David Letterman's Top 10 Great Things About Throwing a Perfect Game, after 40-year-old Randy Johnson did it in May 2004.

"When you first sign that contract as a kid, they tell you your whole future is ahead of you. But they forget to tell you that your future stops at 35."—Pitcher Hal Jeffcoat.

"Baseball is a peculiar profession, possibly the only one which capitalizes on a boyhood pleasure, unfits the athlete for any other career, keeps him young in mind and spirit, and then rejects him as too old, before he has yet attained the prime of life."—Gerald Beaumont.

"Oscar is so old that when he broke into the Majors he was still a Negro."—Yankee coach Stan Williams on Oscar Gamble, who

began his Major League career in 1969 and retired in 1985 at the not-so-old age of 35.

This section separates players who extended their careers well past age 40 from those players who returned for a cameo appearance years after they retired. The early practice of having former players appear in meaningless late-season games was the predecessor to full-scale *Oldtimers Games*.

See also *Longest Careers* and *Rookies—Oldest*.

Older Player Trend.

"Larry Lajoie was on second, but he was 41 years old, hit .246 and covered as much ground as the waterbucket. He quit after that year."—Pitcher Tom Sheehan quoted by Jack Orr in "The Worst Team of All," the 1916 A's.

In 1950 only three Major League players 35 years or older appeared in 100 or more games. In 1990 that figure was 25.

Oldest Non-Cameo Players.

"No. I only got old."—Negro Leaguer Cool Papa Bell, when asked if he tired of playing 29 seasons, 1922–1950, including winter ball. He retired at age 47.

"I want to see his autopsy."—A young pitcher about Nolan Ryan's arm. Ryan retired at age 46 after the 1993 season.

Cap Anson. Anson was 46½ when he hit .302 in 114 games in 1897. He hit two home runs in his last game.

Grover Cleveland Alexander. Alexander was the first pitcher over 40 to win 20 games in the National League. He pitched until age 43.

Jack Quinn. Quinn pitched regularly in the Major Leagues until age 49. He was the oldest player to pitch in the World Series when he appeared in 1930 at age 46.

Joe McGinnity. The early 20th century star was still pitching in the minor leagues at age 54.

George Brunet. Brunet spent 32 years (1953–1984) pitching professionally until age 49. In addition to 69 Major League wins, he posted 244 minor league victories. His 3,175 strikeouts are the minor league record.

Satchel Paige. Paige was 42 when he debuted in the Major Leagues with the Indians in 1948. He was 46 when he won a 12-inning, 1–0 game against Virgil Trucks of the Tigers on August 6, 1952. He made **Cameo Appearances** in the minor and Major Leagues a few years later. See also *Rookies—Oldest*.

Warren Spahn. Spahn was 23–7 for the Braves at age 42 in 1963, with 22 complete games to lead the league. He had a .767 winning percentage, 2.60 ERA and seven shutouts. He pitched until age 44 in 1965.

Don McMahon. McMahon pitched until he was 44 with the Giants in 1974.

Hoyt Wilhelm. Wilhelm was released by the Dodgers on July 21, 1972, only five days short of his 49th birthday. Wilhelm had an ERA under 2.00 for five seasons after age 40.

Tommy John. John pitched through his 46th birthday in 1989. He finished with 288 wins over 26 seasons—a season longevity record since broken by Nolan Ryan. See Tommy John with Dan Valenti, *T.J. My 26 Years in Baseball* (1991).

Phil and Joe Niekro. The brothers used their knuckleball talents to extend their careers well into their 40s. Phil retired after the 1987 season at age 48 with 318 lifetime wins. Joe turned 44 late in November 1988, after pitching in his 22nd and last season, and finished with a record of 221–204.

Nolan Ryan. Ryan arguably was the most successful pitcher over 40, throwing his 7th no-hitter at age 44 and reaching 5,000 strikeouts. He retired after the 1993 season, his 27th in the Major Leagues.

Charlie Hough.

"When I came out of high school, I didn't picture myself throwing a baseball for 28 years. It's been fun."—Hough on the day of his forced retirement. He ended his career in July 1994 after a degenerative hip condition finally became intolerable and he required hip replacement surgery. He became the second-oldest player to throw a shutout when he beat the Cardinals 7–0 in June 1994. It was his last victory. Hough finished with a 216–216 career record in 858 games, including 440 starts and 418 relief appearances.

Dave Winfield. Winfield played through the 1995 season, in which he turned 44 on October 3 (though he was not on the Indians' postseason roster after a dismal season. He is the oldest player to hit for the cycle; oldest to hit a postseason home run; and oldest to reach 100 RBIs in a season.

Jesse Orosco.

"He'll be placed in their way-over-40-man roster."

Steve Rushin on the Padres signing 46-year-old reliever Jesse Orosco for the 2003 season. He was traded to the Yankees in July and struck out the first batter he faced. He finally retired before the start of the 2004 season, though he had been offered a contract.

Relief Corp. The Cardinals started the 1997 season with 42-year-old Dennis Eckersley as their closer and 42-year-old Rick Honeycutt as his set-up man. It didn't last long, as Honeycutt only pitched in two games. Eckersley, however, had 36 saves.

40 v. 40. After divisional play began in 1969, it took until 1993 for two 40-year-olds to face each other on the mound. Forty-five-year-old Charlie Hough of the Marlins beat 40-year-old Frank Tanana of the Mets. Tanana attempted to steal the first base of his career but was thrown out.

Modern Position Players. Ted Williams was a starter through the 1960 season when he retired at age 42. He played only 19 seasons, however, missing almost five full years to the military. Dave Winfield played primarily as a designated hitter, appearing in the field only 63 times over his last four seasons. At age 39 he played 115 games in the outfield for the Angels.

In April 2004 Julio Franco, age 45, became the oldest non-pitcher to appear in a game since Carlton Fisk at age 45 in 1993. Other than 1995, 1998 and 2000 (when he generally was playing in the Japanese leagues), Franco played 2,144 Major League games between 1986 and 2003, and then returned to the Braves in 2004.

Pete Rose played 24 seasons until age 45. Though he did not formally retire until midway through the 1987 season, Rose did not play any games after 1986.

World Series Starting Pitcher. In 1995 Dennis Martinez of the Indians became the oldest World Series starter at age 40 since Grover Cleveland Alexander in 1928 for the Cardinals.

Cameo Appearances.

Minnie Minoso.

"Cheers caused me no see ball."—A teary-eyed Minoso, after striking out in his first at-bat in a cameo six-at-bat appearance at age 53 in a 1976 game for the Chicago White Sox. In eight at-bats in three games as the designated hitter that season he had one hit. One source erroneously reported that he had three hits on September 12, 1976, but he had one hit in three at-bats as the designated hitter against the Angels.

Minoso appeared in two games for the White Sox at age 57 in 1980, with no hits in two at-bats. See also *Four- and Five-Decade Players*, for his attempt to play in 1990.

Jim O'Rourke. In September 1904 at age 54, 11 years after he retired with a .310 lifetime average, Jim O'Rouke talked manager John McGraw into letting him catch for the Giants. He played

well, going 1-for-4 and scoring a run. O'Rourke continued to play catcher in minor league ball until age 57 and later was instrumental in forming the Connecticut League.

Sam Thompson. Thompson played eight games at age 46 for the 1906 Tigers after being out of Major League Baseball since 1898. He reportedly played some third base, but *The Baseball Encyclopedia* credits him only with playing in the outfield and handling 14 chances without an error. He batted .226 in 31 at-bats.

Deacon Jim McGuire. At age 48 McGuire played one game for the Tigers in 1912 after appearing in two games in 1908 and one game in 1910. In the 1912 game he played with a pick-up team of collegiate and semipro players who were fielded by the Tigers after the regular squad protested the *Suspension* of teammate Ty Cobb by sitting out the game. McGuire had one hit in the 24–2 loss to the A's.

Hughie Jennings. The Tigers manager supposedly pinch-hit at ages 43 and 49 for the Tigers. However, he only pinch-hit at age 43 in 1912 and he failed to get a hit. He played first base at age 49 in 1918, making two putouts, but did not bat.

Clark Griffith. In 1914, the 45-year-old Senators manager pitched one inning, an almost annual rite he pursued in 1909, 1910, 1912 and 1913. In his last appearance, he gave up a hit, no runs, and had a base hit for a 1.000 season batting average.

Jimmy Austin played one game at third base at age 50 in 1929 for the Browns. He played three innings, batted once and had two assists. He also played in one game for the Browns in 1923, 1925 and 1926, with one hit in three at-bats. In 1926 he doubled and stole home, though the latter may have been a gift from the opposing pitcher in a meaningless game.

Nick Altrock. On October 6, 1929, long-time Senators player, coach and clown Nick Altrock played right field and had a hit for the Senators at age 53.

Johnny Evers. Evers played one inning for the Braves in 1929 at age 47. He made an error and failed to get a hit in his only at-bat.

Gabby Street. Street caught three innings for the Cardinals at age 49 on September 20, 1931. He went hitless in one at-bat.

Charlie O'Leary. The 52-year-old ex-infielder played first base for the Browns on September 30, 1934, after finishing his 11-year Major League career at shortstop in 1913. He had one hit and scored a run in the game.

Jimmie Wilson. One of the best "elder statesman" stories arose from the *Suicide* of Willard Hershberger of the 1940 Reds. The Reds made it into the World Series, but without a regular catcher. Hershberger was dead and the other regular catcher, Ernie Lombardi, had sprained an ankle. Coach Jimmie Wilson, 40, was pressed into service after catching only two games in three seasons. He caught six of the seven series games for the victorious Reds and hit .353, though he was in terrible pain from all the squatting.

Lefty O'Doul. At age 59 in 1956, the former batting star batted for Vancouver of the Pacific Coast League.

Satchel Paige. When he was at least 59, Paige made a cameo appearance with the A's on September 25, 1965. He gave up a double to Carl Yastrzemski in three innings against the Red Sox and was leading 1–0 when he came out of the game. At age 61 in 1967, Paige pitched in an exhibition game for the Braves against their Class AAA affiliate, Richmond.

Hub Kittle. The long-time pitching coach began his career in 1936 with the Los Angeles Angels of the Pacific Coast League. In 1980, at age 63, he pitched a perfect inning for a Class AAA team.

Oldest Statistical Leaders

"But Williams, though sick and old ... emerged from his cave in the Hotel Somerset haggard but irresistible.... He ended the [1957] season with thirty-eight home runs and an average of .388, the highest in either league since his own .406, and, coming from a decrepit man of thirty-nine, an even more supernal figure." — John Updike in "Hub Fans Bid Kid Adieu" (1960). Ted Williams also led the league at age 40 in 1958 with a .328 average.

Jack Quinn was 47 when he led the Major Leagues with 15 saves in 1931. At 48 he led the National League with eight saves.

Warren Spahn led the league in complete games for seven straight seasons starting at age 36 in 1957.

Nolan Ryan led the league in strikeouts for four straight seasons starting at age 40 in 1987.

Oldtimers Games

"Oldtimers Weekends and airplane landings are alike. They're successful if you can walk away from them." — Casey Stengel.

"It's a mere moment in a man's life between the all-star game and the oldtimer's game." — Vin Scully.

Early Games. As part of a 1921 *Benefit Game* for an ill Christy Mathewson, sportswriter Fred Lieb suggested that the Giants host an oldtimers exhibition game of five innings between the 1905 National League pennant-winning Giants and other 1905 players. The club also rounded up players from the championship 1911, 1912 and 1913 teams.

Another early oldtimer's game was a reunion of the 1934 Cardinals staged by general manager Branch Rickey.

Babe Ruth. One source claimed that the first true Oldtimers Day was in 1947 to commemorate Babe Ruth's years with the Yankees. The proceeds were donated to Ruth's Foundation for Boys.

On August 28, 1943, to raise money for the war effort, Ruth faced Walter Johnson in a pregame show. After two pop flies, Ruth hit a home run to right field.

True Oldtimers Day. As reported by SABR member Tom Knight, one of the earliest Oldtimers Games was on September 22, 1940, when Brooklyn general manager Larry MacPhail organized two groups of veteran Dodgers to play a three-inning exhibition. Earlier "Days" did not feature retired players suiting up to actually play a game.

Joe DiMaggio. DiMaggio traditionally was introduced last at all Yankee Oldtimers games. However, the year after Mickey Mantle retired, Mantle was introduced last. The long ovation for Mantle supposedly insulted DiMaggio and thereafter the Yankees always introduced DiMaggio last.

Cracker Jack Oldtimers Games.

"The Ben-Gay Bowl." — The first game's nickname.

"I'm sure glad the season is over." — Luke Appling, age 75, after hitting a home run in the first Cracker Jack Old-Timers' Classic in Washington, D.C., on July 19, 1982. Cracker Jack candy began sponsoring a nationwide tour of oldtimers that season. The first game was at RFK Stadium in front of 29,000 fans as the American League won 7–2. Appling's "career" was resurrected when he led off the game by stroking a home run off Warren Spahn over a makeshift 260-foot fence in left field of the cavernous stadium. The proceeds went to one of the organizations that provides support to retired professional ballplayers. Henry Aaron, playing in right field, let a ball hit him in the chin. After Cracker Jack started the tradition, various companies have sponsored oldtimers games in conjunction with the All-Star Game, including Upper Deck baseball cards.

International Oldtimers. In 1995 a group of American Major League oldtimers played a group of Japanese oldtimers in Japan.

Olympic Games

"I suspect that if a professional baseball player discovered one day that he could make more money by going back home and laying bricks for a living, he'd go home and lay bricks." — Long-time International Olympic Committee president Avery Brundage, a staunch advocate of amateur play.

See also *Softball*.

1904/St. Louis. It has been reported that baseball was a demonstration sport at the 1904 Olympics in St. Louis. More accurately, anything remotely related to sports was billed as part of the World's Fair that year. The fair was not related whatsoever to the Olympics, and most authoritative sources make no reference to the exhibition that was played.

1912/Stockholm.

"Excusable on account of nervousness." — Reason provided for the number of errors by the Swedish team that lost to the Americans 13–3 in a demonstration game in front of less than 2,000 fans. The umpire was the venerable 19th century professional, George Wright.

Vesteras was Sweden's first *Basebol* club, formed in 1910. The club played six innings against the Americans, a few of whom were drawn from other sports at the Games. The Americans loaned a pitcher and catcher to the Swedes to help even things out.

Contrary to some reports, Jim Thorpe did not play in the demonstration game because it was at the same time as the second day of Thorpe's gold medal performance in the decathlon. Other sources report that the game was played on July 15, after the official competition was completed. The game was played on a field without a mound that had been used for equestrian events during the Olympics.

After the Olympics, Thorpe joined a group of American baseball players on an *International Tour* and returned home to play Major League Baseball.

1928/Amsterdam. Baseball was not included, but *Kaasten*, a Dutch version of cricket, was played.

1932/Los Angeles. Cleveland's Municipal Stadium was built with the hope that the city would be the site of the 1932 Olympics, which eventually were awarded to Los Angeles. A demonstration baseball game was planned for the Olympics, but it was shelved in favor of a football game. It has been reported that a group of Americans petitioned the U.S. Olympic Committee to make baseball a part of the 1932 Olympics, but that the request was too late.

1936/Berlin.

"There is reason to believe that Germany has been made immune to baseball." — Sportswriter Joe Williams of the *New York Times* after a crowd of over 100,000 witnessed a boring 2–0 game between two American amateur teams on August 12, 1936. Other sources report that the game was played on August 18, on the last day of the competition, and the final score was 6–5. The teams were dubbed the World Amateurs and the USA Olympics; the Amateurs won 6–5. White athletic tape was used to mark the field.

It has been reported that Hitler's girlfriend, Eva Braun, was fascinated with baseball. She met with the Americans and discussed strategy in well-spoken English.

1940/Tokyo. Baseball was to be a demonstration sport in baseball-strong Japan, but World War II forced cancellation of the Games. The nine competing teams were to be from China, the

Philippines, Hawaii, the U.S., England, Germany, Mexico, Cuba and Japan.

1952/Helsinki. *Pesapallo* was a Finnish version of baseball that was demonstrated at the Games. The American soccer coach was asked to put together a team of Americans to play a Finnish baseball club (described in some sources as the Finnish soccer champions) in a demonstration *Pesapallo* game. The Americans won 19–1. Lloyd Mosely pitched for the U.S. team in front of 4,000 spectators.

1956/Melbourne. More than 114,000 fans slowly filled the main track and field stadium for the regular day's events during an exhibition game won by American sailors 11–5 over an Australian team.

1964/Tokyo. USC baseball coach Rod Dedeaux led a 19-man squad to Japan for a demonstration game against a Japanese amateur all-star club. The Americans won 6–2 after completing a tour of the Far East. On the team were future Major Leaguers Chuck Dobson, Ken Suarez, Gary Sutherland and Mike Epstein.

The Japanese Olympic team was made up entirely of college players.

1984/Los Angeles. Baseball was a demonstration sport featuring eight teams from Nicaragua, Canada, Korea, Japan, Dominican Republic, Italy and the U.S. The finals were held at Dodger Stadium, where Japan won the gold medal, the Americans won the silver and Taiwan won the bronze. A number of Major Leaguers emerged from the American team: pitcher Mike Dunne, outfielders Oddibe McDowell, Shane Mack and Cory Snyder, shortstop Barry Larkin, third baseman B. J. Surhoff, and first basemen Will Clark and Mark McGwire.

The three players from the American team who never made it to the Major Leagues were Flavia Alfaro, Bob Caffrey and Sid Akins. All were drafted but never made it.

Sandy Koufax looking like he could still "bring it" at a 1980s Oldtime Day at Dodger Stadium

1988/Seoul. The powerful Cuban club boycotted the Games. The participating countries were the U.S., Puerto Rico, Korea, Japan, Canada and Australia. In the semifinals Ben McDonald beat Puerto Rico, and Japan defeated Korea to set up a rematch of the 1984 gold medal game. Jim Abbott won the final to give the U.S. the gold over the Japanese. The American players included future Major Leaguers Robin Ventura, Charles Nagy, Pat Combs, Ed Sprague, Dave Silvestri, Ty Griffin and Tino Martinez.

1992/Barcelona. After boycotting the 1984 and 1988 Olympics, Cuba won the gold medal. The Barcelona competition was the first Olympics in which baseball was an official sport. The tradition of an eight-team tournament continued and the U.S. finished fourth after losing to Japan. Taiwan won the silver and Japan won the bronze.

Olympian Ed Sprague (1988) hit a 9th inning home in Game 2 of the 1992 World Series to give the Toronto Blue Jays the victory — the first by a Canadian team in the World Series. His wife, American Kristin Babb-Sprague, won the gold medal in synchronized swimming in Barcelona that year. Ironically, she beat out a Canadian in a controversial situation in which the Canadian would have won the gold but for an admitted electronic scoring error by a judge.

1996/Atlanta. The eight participants in the tournament were Australia, Cuba, Italy, Japan, Korea, the Netherlands, Nicaragua and the U.S. The Cubans defeated Japan 13–9 for the gold medal. The U.S. defeated Nicaragua 10–3 for the bronze.

The U.S. women's softball team won the gold medal over China in the first year in which softball was an official event. There was talk of the Olympics dropping both baseball and softball from the Olympic schedule for the 2000 Games in Sydney (the events remained), which intensified in the 2000s.

2000/Sydney.

"Lasorda pumped so much sunshine into his players that they needed an SPF 60 sunblock." — Michael Farber.

Former Dodger manager Tommy Lasorda, 73 at the time, led the young American team to the gold medal, beating Cuba 4–0 behind future Brewers pitcher Ben Sheets. Catching was former World Series MVP Pat Borders, the old man of the team at 37. The Cubans had previously beaten the Americans 6–1 in round-robin play. Tim Raines was invited to play on the team and made it to the last cut before being let go in favor of younger players. He had been battling lupus and sat out the 2000 Major League season.

2004/Athens.

"Boston is the Athens of America, and America, the Athens of baseball, will not be playing baseball in Athens. The U.S. team didn't qualify for next summer's Olympics, though there's little shame in that. After all, we don't send our best players, and the Netherlands does." — Steve Rushin.

Frank Robinson led the squad that attempted to qualify for the 2004 Olympics, but they were defeated 2–1 by Mexico in a qualifying round despite winning their three previous games by a combined 20–0. The loss was seen as perhaps a death knell for baseball in the Olympics because of the lack of international support for the sport. The IOC had tabled the issue until 2005 in hopes that the U.S. would allow Major Leaguers to play in the Olympics, though there had been a 2002 vote to eliminate baseball from the Olympics and replace it with golf. There were also private comments by Olympic officials that Major League Baseball didn't want its players subjected to its strict drug testing.

The Cubans won the gold medal over Australia 6–2, and Japan beat Canada 11–2 for the bronze medal. The Japanese were expected to contend for the gold medal, as their team was stocked with high-level pros, but they were stunned 1–0 by Australia in the semi-finals.

The Rockies refused to allow their top pitching prospect, Jeff Francis, to pitch for his home country of Canada in the 2004 Olympics.

The Greeks, as hosts, were allowed to place a team in the base-ball competition. They did so by allowing any foreign player (i.e., Americans) to play if they could prove that at least a great-grand-parent was Greek. Eighteen of the 24 players on the 2004 Greek Olympic baseball team were Americans. Greek lessons were pro-vided every day for the Americans. Only two of the players were born in Greece. Baltimore Orioles owner Peter Angelos helped pay for some of the lineage research to establish eligibility. Sixteen of the 18 women on the Greek softball team were also Americans, as were more than a third of the Greek women's soccer team.

The Greek baseball team included former Yankee utilityman Clay Bellinger. Unfortunately, the baseball team's coach, Rob Derksen, collapsed and died of a heart attack in New York at age 44 three months before the Olympics. He had also been a coach with the Orioles and managed the Australian Olympic team in 1996 and the Guam team that attempted to make the Olympics in 2000. His son Nick continued to be a batboy for the club. The team was outscored 25–5 in its first four games and didn't win a game.

Goodwill Ambassador. In 1987 former Orioles pitcher Moe Drabowsky went to Poland to help form the first Olympic baseball team from that country.

Canada. Rheal Cormier pitched for the 1988 Canadian Olympic team and made it to the Major Leagues with the Cardinals in 1991.

Dominican Republic. Ramon Martinez was 17 when he pitched in relief for the Dominican Republic team in 1984.

Amateur Associations. The International Association of Ama-teur Baseball (AINBA) was formed immediately after the 1936 Olympics. The United States Baseball Federation is now responsi-ble for all amateur American baseball, including the Olympics, based on the Amateur Sports Act of 1978.

On-Base Percentage

"For one thing, batting average is less meaningful than on-base percentage, since on-base average is a far better indicator of a player's ability to foment or maintain a rally."—Thomas Boswell in *How Life Imitates the World Series* (1982).

See *Reaching Base* for consecutive times reaching base.

Rule. On-base percentage is calculated by totaling a player's at-bats, base on balls and hit by pitch, and dividing the num-ber of hits, base on balls and hit by pitches. Some commentators have argued that this is the most important statistic for evaluat-ing pitcher performance, because it includes hits, walks and hit batters.

Introduction. This statistic was introduced by statistician Allan Roth in the 1950s and did not become official until 1984. Ted Williams said that he first heard the term in the mid–1940s from gamblers who frequented Fenway Park and told him that he was an even money bet to get on base any time he came to the plate (he was at .483 for his career).

Lowest/.300 Season. In 1997 Cubs shortstop Shawon Dun-ston had an on-base percentage of .312, the lowest in the 20th cen-tury for a player who hit .300 in the same season (the Cubs traded him late in the season to the Pirates).

Season. The highest season on-base percentage before 2002 was .551 by Ted Williams in 1941. Barry Bonds shattered his record

with a .582 percentage in 2002 for the Giants. He also has the sixth highest percentage, with .529 in 2003. Bonds shattered the record again with a .609 on-base percentage in 2004.

John McGraw is next at .547 in 1899. Babe Ruth follows at .545 in 1923 and with a .530 mark in 1920. Williams has the ninth and 11th highest marks and Ruth has the 12th, 14th and 15th marks.

Joe Morgan of the Reds came the closest to .500 before Bonds when he reached .470 in 1975. Bonds' on-base percentage of .515 in 2001 was the best in the Majors since Ted Williams in 1957.

Lifetime. Ted Williams is the lifetime leader with a .483 on-base percentage, followed by Babe Ruth at .474 and John McGraw at .464. Sliding Billy Hamilton's .456 is estimated because there is no definitive number of hit by pitches calculated for him. Lou Gehrig is fourth at .447; Rogers Hornsby follows at .434, and Ty Cobb and Barry Bonds (through 2003) at .433.

Most Times Led League. Ted Williams led the league 12 times in on-base percentage, which was every year that he qualified for the title except his rookie season. Babe Ruth led the league 10 times and Ty Cobb six. Barry Bonds led the league eight times through 2004, and finished second another three times.

On-Deck Circle

"Al Deck is in the on-dark circle."—Braves broadcaster Earl Gillespie referring to Alvin Dark.

"And so the Cubs and the Red Sox are endlessly returned to whence they came, outside looking in, forever on the brink, await-ing a turn that never comes. It's not the circle of life, exactly, but something more poignant. It's the on-deck circle of life."—Steve Rushin in November 2003 on the futility of the Cubs and Red Sox.

"The place before the hitting place; what do you call it?"—Baseball sophisticate Angela Rains Light.

The team at bat must have a player in the on-deck circle at all times.

Orlando Cepeda was on deck when Willie McCovey of the Giants lined out to end the 1962 World Series. Some sources report that it was Willie Mays. Mays was on deck when Bobby Thomson hit his miraculous home run in the 1951 play-off game for the Giants against the Dodgers.

One-Club Players See *Longest Careers*—Most Seasons with One Club

One-Game Career

"Being struck out by Lon Warneke is about my only distinction as a player in the major leagues. I still say that one inning and one at bat isn't much of a test. But in those days, with hundreds and hundreds of players, that's what a lot of guys got. Some didn't even get that."—Walter Alston in his autobiography, *A Year at a Time*, with Jack Tobin (1976).

See *At-Bats* for one at-bat Major League careers, including that of long-time Dodger manager Walter Alston.

Worst. Eddie Kolb was a cigar store clerk and semipro pitcher in Cincinnati when he was asked to pitch the last game of the 1899 season for the pitiful Cleveland Spiders. He had a complete game 19–3 loss.

On July 27, 1918, Brooklyn pitcher Henry Heitman started and finished his Major League career. He pitched to four Cardinals, giv-ing up four consecutive hits before leaving the game. He never played professionally again.

Fred Bruckbauer pitched in one game for the Twins on April 25, 1961, during a 20–2 pasting by the A's. He gave up three hits and a walk, allowed three earned runs, and got no one out. He thus became the last player to retire with an ERA of infinity, and only the second player since World War II. Gordie Sundin was the other, for the 1956 Orioles.

Best. See *Brothers* for a description of the 3-for-3 one-game career of Tom Paciorek's brother.

On September 30, 1910, Ray Jansen of the Browns went 4-for-5, the all-time record for hits in a one-game career. He had three errors at third base, however, in the 9–1 loss to the White Sox.

White Sox catcher Chuck Lindstrom, son of Hall of Famer Fred Lindstrom, played one game in 1958. He tripled and walked for a 1.000 batting average and 3.000 slugging average, the highest ever.

A Piece of History. Hank Hulvey, starting for the A's on September 5, 1923, gave up Babe Ruth's 230th home run in his only Major League appearance.

Multi-Tasker. Katsy Keifer pitched in one game for the Indianapolis Hoosiers of the Federal League, on October 8, 1914, the last game of the season. He had an RBI, a hit and a win, to become the only player ever to perform the hat trick in his only game in the Major Leagues.

John Kull is the only player to have a perfect batting and pitching record (1–1 and 1–0), and a flawless fielding record (handled one chance), in his only Major League game. He relieved for the A's on October 2, 1909, the last game of the season.

One-Hitters

"He pitched a flawless game from a center of poise so striking that for that night he was the Natural, the archetypal pitcher: old baseball shining through even the media hyperbole."—Richard Grossinger in *The Temple of Baseball* (1985), describing a 1984 one-hitter by Dwight Gooden.

"It was Feller's ninth one-hitter. By now the newspapers were getting blasé and gave hardly any space to the feat."—John B. Holway in *The Ol' Ball Game* (1990), in an essay in which he chronicles each of Feller's 12 one-hitters and shows how close he came to pitching a total of 10 no-hitters (including the three he actually pitched). Only five of the 12 one-hitters were on clean hits. Feller's one-hitter record was tied by Nolan Ryan. Next on the all-time list with seven: Walter Johnson and Addie Joss.

"That was a maximization of a minimization of hits."—Royals catcher Mike Macfarlane after his club beat the A's 3–1 on only one hit.

There has been one game in Major League history in which there was only one hit. On September 9, 1965, Dodger pitcher Sandy Koufax defeated the Cubs in a 1–0 perfect game. Cubs pitcher Bob Hendley gave up one hit, a double to Lou Johnson in the 7th inning. The lone unearned run was scored in the 5th when Johnson walked, moved to second on a sacrifice and stole third. He came home on Cubs catcher Chris Krug's high throw to third on the stolen base.

In the American League the fewest number of hits in a game is two, one each given up by Bob Feller of the Indians and Bob Cain of the Browns in a 1–0 win by the Browns on April 23, 1952. The only run came on a triple in the first inning.

In 1915 Grover Cleveland Alexander pitched four one-hitters on his way to 31 wins and 12 shutouts (only his second-best season in both categories!).

Steve Carlton holds the National League record with six one-hitters.

There were 14 one-hitters in 1965, a record for one season.

Only nine clubs in Major League history have thrown consecutive one-hitters. The last was the Rangers on May 3–4, 1996. They were the third American League club to do it.

One-Run Games

"There ought to be a third column in the baseball standings: GAT, for games almost tied."—Jim Bouton in *Ball Four* (1970), alluding to the number of one-run games the Seattle Pilots lost in 1969.

"Most one-run games are lost, not won."—Gene Mauch.

One-Year Wonders

"Perhaps he blinked while Rogelio was up. Rogelio's cup of coffee in the bigs was a demitasse."—Tom Verducci in *Sports Illustrated*.

Jocko Flynn won 24 games for the 1886 White Stockings and led the league in winning percentage. He pitched in one game in 1887 and then was out of Major League Baseball.

Irv Waldron played one year in 1901 with Milwaukee and Washington, hitting .311, scoring 102 runs and leading the league in at-bats. Waldron disappeared after the season but *The Baseball Encyclopedia* notes that he lived until 1944. The only information available at the Hall of Fame is that his nickname was Torpedo Boat.

In 1903 Henry Schmidt won 21 games for the Dodgers, including an opening day defeat of Christy Mathewson and three straight shutouts. After the season he wrote Dodger owner Charles Ebbets, indicating that he did not like living in the East and would not report for the 1904 season. He never again appeared in the Major Leagues.

In July 1957 outfielder Bob Hazle was called up by the Braves after a six-game stint with the Reds in 1955. He finished the season with a .403 average in 41 games and a 2-for-13 performance in the World Series. He was hit by a pitch in spring training the following year and was quickly traded to the Tigers, where he played 63 games and batted .211. He never again appeared in the Major Leagues.

Long-time manager Sparky Anderson played 152 games for the 1959 Phillies, the most of any Major Leaguer whose career lasted only one year.

Mark Fidrych won 19 games as a rookie in 1976 with the Tigers. He had been a nonroster player in spring training that year and did not start a game until May 19. The following season he developed arm trouble and won only 10 more games over four years in the Major Leagues. See also Mark Fidrych and Tom Clark, *No Big Deal* (1977).

Joe Charboneau had one strong season for the Indians in 1980 before back problems cut his career short. He hit .289 with 23 home runs and was named Rookie of the Year before fading with only 70 appearances over the next two seasons. Charboneau later operated a baseball school for kids in Ohio and had a television series for which he won a local Emmy award. See also Joe Charboneau and Burt Graeff, *Super Joe—The Life and Legend of Joe Charboneau* (1981).

Books. Michael Fedo, *One Shining Season* (1991); Dennis Snelling, *A Glimpse of Fame* (1993).

Opening Day

"Commencement of the Season."—Notation on the scoresheet for the first game of the 1846 Knickerbocker season, played on Good Friday, April 10, 1846 (a game umpired by Alexander Cartwright).

"It isn't only baseball that has its Opening Days; lives and memories have them too."—George V. Higgins in *The Progress of the Seasons* (1989), on his first visit to Fenway Park as a seven-year-old.

"There is no sports event like Opening Day of baseball, the sense of beating back the forces of darkness and the National Football League."—George Vecsey in *A Year in the Sun* (1989).

See also ***Throwing Out the First Pitch***.

See also ***Home Games Out of Town***—Opening Day for games played outside a team's home city.

Opening Day Honors.

"However, at Cincinnati the first game is *always* played there. This is because the Citizens of this Ohio city do not consider Opening Day just as Opening Day. They consider it one small notch below Christmas."—Fred Schwed, Jr., in *How to Watch a Baseball Game* (1957).

With few exceptions, Cincinnati always had the honor of hosting the first National League game each season because of the status of the 1869 Cincinnati Red Stockings as the first all-professional team. That honor was missed by the club in 1877 due to three days of rain and also from 1881 until 1889 when the city did not have a National League club. In 1994 because of a scheduling change, the Cardinals hosted opening "night" on a Sunday prime time game to accommodate ESPN's new TV contract. The Reds always have a city-wide parade in connection with their first home game.

In 1995 the Marlins were scheduled to host the first game of the season on a Sunday night. The Marlins were to play the Mets for only one game on April 2 and the Mets were to return home for an April 4 game. The games were never played because of the strike which delayed the start of the season.

Baltimore now usually hosts the first game in the American League because the U.S. president often attends. The honor went to the Senators before they left town for Texas in the early 1970s.

Pitching Consistency. Walter Johnson made a record 14 Opening Day starts over 21 seasons and won nine times. His last opener was April 13, 1926, a 1–0, 15-inning win at age 38. He also threw a one-hit Opening Day shutout on April 14, 1910, one of his seven Opening Day shutouts.

Jack Morris tied Johnson's American League appearance record when he made his 14th Opening Day start in 1993.

Tom Seaver won seven of his 16 Opening Day starts over 20 seasons.

No-Hitters. See ***No-Hitters***—Opening Day.

Presidents.

"The attendance of Presidents at the Washington Lidlifters is now a tradition."—*The Sporting News*.

See ***Presidents***.

Most Runs. On April 19, 1900, the Phillies beat the Braves 19–17 in 10 innings, setting a Major League record for most runs scored by two clubs on Opening Day. This game also featured one of the great ***Comebacks***, as the Braves scored nine runs in the 9th inning to force extra innings.

On Opening Day 1925 the Indians defeated the Browns 21–14, capped by 12 runs in the 8th inning.

Longest. On March 31, 1998, the Mets and Phillies went 14 innings, tying the National League record for longest Opening Day game, a 1–0 Mets win.

Home Runs. Frank Robinson holds the record for hitting home runs on the most Opening Days (eight) for the Reds in 1959, 1961 and 1963; for the Orioles in 1966, 1969 and 1970; for the Angels in 1973, and for the Indians in 1975.

In 2001 Scott Rolen of the Phillies matched a record held by Willie Mays and Ken Griffey, Jr., by hitting an Opening Day home run in three consecutive seasons. Mays accomplished the feat in 1962, 1963 and 1964 for the San Francisco Giants, while Griffey hit Opening Day homers in 1997, 1998 and 1999 for the Mariners.

In the Giants opener in 2002 Barry Bonds hit two home runs. He tied a record held by Eddie Mathews when he hit two more in the second game of the season.

Winning Streak. Opening Day of 1912 was the start of Rube Marquard's record 19-game ***Winning Streak***.

Bad Starts. The Mets lost their first eight Opening Day games, including the 1969 "Miracle Mets" year.

Oldest Starting Pitcher. Nolan Ryan was the Opening Day starter for the Rangers in 1993, becoming the oldest pitcher in history at age 46 to start the season opener.

Oldest Winner.

"How many guys can crank it up at that age? Most are lucky they can get out of bed."—Yankee manager Dallas Green on Tommy John's successful 1989 Opening Day start for the Yankees against the Twins at age 45. Nolan Ryan was the second-oldest winner in the Rangers' home opener in 1990 at age 43.

Charlie Bennett. Bennett was the Detroit Wolverines catcher whose legs were amputated after an 1894 train accident (see also ***Amputees***). From 1896, when what would be built into Tiger Stadium opened as Bennett Park, until his death in 1927, Bennett threw out every Opening Day pitch.

Opener In Mexico. On April 4, 1999, the Padres and Rockies played their opening game in Monterrey, Mexico. It was the first Major League season opener played outside the United States or Canada. The Rockies won 8–2 in front of a sellout crowd of 27,104. Mexican star Vinny Castilla had four hits.

Opener In Japan.

"Opening day belongs within U.S. borders.... Certain traditions belong in cocoons and shouldn't be broken 15 time zones away, inside a noisy dome called the Big Egg, where drums beat and rocking fans chant for hours while eating a cup of noodles."—Jay Mariotti in the *Chicago Sun-Times*.

On March 29, 2000, the Cubs beat the Mets 5–3 in their home opener, played in the Tokyo Dome in Japan. Jon Lieber beat the Mets' new ace, Mike Hampton. It was the first Major League game played outside of North America. In the second game of the series, the Mets won 5–1 in 11 innings on Benny Agbayani's grand slam.

In late March 2004 the Yankees and Devil Rays kicked off the Major League season in Japan's Tokyo Dome after exhibition games against the Hanshin Tigers and Yomiuri Giants.

The Seattle Mariners and Oakland A's were supposed to start the 2003 season in Japan in a late March three-game series, but security concerns related to the U.S. invasion of Iraq caused cancellation of the trip.

Opener In Puerto Rico. On April 1, 2001, the Blue Jays beat the Rangers 8–1 to start the season in San Juan, Puerto Rico.

Opera

"Opera in English is about as sensible as baseball in Italian."—H.L. Mencken.

The Mighty Casey was a 1953 opera written by William Schuman. It was never recorded, but the Glimmerglass Opera in Coop-erstown revived it in the 1980s.

In 1888 John Philip Sousa wrote a comic baseball opera called *Angela*, or *The Umpire's Revenge*, about a college player from Yale and a New York girl.

Options and Option Year

A ballclub may assign a Major League player to the minor leagues three times. After the third time the player is out of "options" and if the Major League club brings him back and then wants to reassign him to the minor leagues, the player may declare himself a free agent rather than be sent down.

A player's "option year" is the year after his contract expires. The club may automatically renew his contract against his wishes for that option year at a set percentage increase in pay. After the option season, the player may become a free agent. The option year was at the heart of the **Reserve Clause** controversy of the mid–1970s that created free agency; clubs historically contended that the renewal of the contract each season created a perpetually new option year.

As part of the collective bargaining agreements and free agency rulings of the 1970s, a player could play out his option and move to another club if he had five years with that club and 10 years in the Major Leagues. A total of 24 players played out their options in 1976 and 89 did so in 1977. The practice became commonplace after that (see also **Free Agents** and **Salaries**).

Organized Baseball

"The ambition, power, and organizing ability of the profes-sional entrepreneurs made themselves felt, and before long the pro-fessional clubs, combined in a system called Organized Baseball, would dominate the game, fix its pattern, and point its direction throughout the United States and even abroad."—Harold Seymour in *Baseball: The Early Years* (1989).

The first semblance of what is now referred to as Organized Baseball occurred when the National League was created in 1876 and two minor leagues formed in 1877, the International League and the League Alliance.

Baseball was truly organized after the 1883 National Agreement was created among the National League, American Association, League Alliance and Northwestern League. This was the vision of National League president A.G. Mills in negotiating peace among the rival leagues. Organized Baseball is governed by five documents:

1. Major League Agreement
2. Major League Rules
3. Major-Minor League Agreement (also known as the Player Development Contract)
4. Major-Minor League Rules
5. National Association Rules (For minor leagues)

The commissioner of baseball has jurisdiction over all leagues in Organized Baseball. All contracts between clubs and their play-ers (as well as their staffs) require a clause binding them to disci-pline by the commissioner.

The Executive Council which governs Organized Baseball con-sists of the commissioner, the two Major League presidents, and two elected minor league representatives. If a player grievance is at issue, two players are added.

Organized baseball was initially confined to the northeast quad-rant of the country, expanding to the South in 1885, to the upper Midwest in 1886, to California in 1887, Texas in 1888 and the Pacific Northwest in 1890. In 1950 there were 10,000 professional players in 59 leagues that comprised Organized Baseball. This was the peak number in both cate-gories in the history of profes-sional baseball.

Organs/Organists

"Baseball players are the weirdest of all. I think it's that organ music."—Writer Peter Gent.

First Ballpark Organ. The Cubs are credited with installing the first organ in a Major League ballpark, in 1941. Roy Nelson first played the organ for the club on April 26, 1941. It was not played every day until 1967. When night games began, it was not played after 10 p.m. so as not to dis-pute the neighbors.

Ballpark Organists. At the end of the last game at Ebbets Field in Brooklyn in 1957, long-time organist Gladys Gooding played "Say It Isn't So." She had been playing at Dodger games with the club since May 8, 1942 (erroneously May 1941 in one source).

Opening Day 1965 at the Mets' home park, Shea Stadium, before a game against the Dodgers.

Long-time White Sox organist Nancy Faust recorded two albums, including "Crowd Pleasing Favorites."

Long-time Yankee organist Eddie Layton retired following the 2003 World Series after 37 years playing the pipes.

Big Moment. When Carlton Fisk hit his game-winning home run in the 13th inning of Game 6 of the 1975 World Series for the Red Sox, Fenway Park organist John Kiley played the opening notes of Handel's "Hallelujah Chorus."

Denny McLain. In 1968 McLain cut two albums featuring himself playing the organ. His comment at the time: "When all is said and done, some day in the future, I hope they will remember Denny McLain as a professional musician."

It was not likely in light of his 31-win season and subsequent scrapes with the law over drugs, gambling and theft. He resumed his organ playing in the late 1980s, sometimes playing in a Michigan bar where former heavyweight champion Leon Spinks worked as a bartender. During a 1993 *Sports Illustrated* interview he commented on the success of his albums in 1968, "Denny McLain at the Organ" and "Denny McLain in Las Vegas": "If you'd like to hear it, I can sell you a couple thousand copies."

Poor Sound. Atlanta's ballpark features an 80-year-old calliope organ that was installed in 1971. During the 1992 play-offs between the Pirates and Braves, Atlanta organist Carolyn King received complaints that she was playing the Braves' war chant, which accompanies the tomahawk chop, in the wrong key. Fans complained that it made the chant sound dreary.

Organist Ejection. Wilbur Snapp is the only organist ever ejected from a professional baseball game. He has played the Kawai at Phillies' spring training games for 18 years. For a decade, he also played at the Clearwater Phillies' minor-league games, 70 nights each summer. Although he can't read music, Snapp has a 2,000 song repertoire.

In 1985 he played "Three Blind Mice" after "the worst umpire's call I've ever seen in hundreds of baseball games." Ricky Jordan was on first base for the Clearwater Phillies when the next batter hit a sinking liner to right field. The outfielder made a shoestring catch and Jordan dove back into first base and grabbed the bag with both hands. Although clearly safe, the umpire called Jordan out. So Snapp played "Three Blind Mice" and the umpire walked up to the screen, pointed straight at him and ejected him. He was fined $100, but the fine later was rescinded.

Manager Ejection. On April 24, 2002, Tulsa Drillers manager Tim Ireland was ejected from a Texas League game for arguing about organ music at Rich Winder Field in Little Rock, Arkansas. Organist Rich Pharris began playing "I've Been Working on the Railroad" while Trent Durrington batted in the 6th inning. Durrington tried twice to call time to end the distraction, but umpire Jason Markley refused. Durrington, an Australian, was greeted the day before with "Tie Me Kangaroo Down, Boy." He asked Pharris to replace the song with "anything else." Ireland complained to the umpire, who threw him out of the game. Nevertheless, Markley ordered Pharris to play only between innings. As Ireland left the field, Pharris played "Happy Trails."

Origins of Baseball

"To ascertain who invented baseball would be equivalent to trying to locate the discoverer of fire." — Harold Seymour in a 1956 essay in the *New-York Historical Society Quarterly*, reprinted in *The Armchair Book of Baseball*, edited by John Thorn (1985).

"Ever since our caveman ancestry, men and boys liked to hit something that resembled a ball with a club." — First line of Fred Lieb's *The Baseball Story* (1950).

"In the beginning, there was no baseball. But ever since, there have been few beginnings as good as the start of a new baseball season. It is the most splendid time in sports." — B.J. Phillips in *Time*.

"No one really knows who originated the game of baseball. Perhaps it all started when a shaggy, irate fellow named Oog tossed a rock at his neighbor, Urg. And when Urg, instead of ducking, blasted the boulder with his club, then sprinted to the shelter of the nearest cave where his wife declared him 'safe.'" — "A Housewife's Guide to Baseball," a 1958 booklet distributed by the Dodgers' first radio affiliate in Los Angeles.

See also *Baseball* and *National Pastime*.

Earliest Connections to Baseball.

"We as a nation ca n recognize modern baseball's larger cosmic connections. In a way, the ancient Egyptians are still alive in us, and we are their cultural heirs through our baseball games." — Peter Piccione, professor of Egyptian history at the College of Charleston.

The earliest "origins" of baseball can be found in 5,000-year-old Egyptian paintings depicting "batting" priests in mock combat contests at crop planting time. These activities were in honor of the Egyptian God of Agriculture, Osiris. By 2000 B.C. Egyptian women were depicted with bats and balls. Crude variations of these bat-and-ball games were carried to Europe by the Moors. In Sparta, the word for "youth" and "ball player" were the same, and there are pictures of Roman men playing ball.

Historian Peter Piccione believes that the origins can be traced to an Egyptian game called *seker-hemat* (roughly translated as "batting the ball"), a game played by royalty during certain festivals. He cites as one of the top batters the pharaoh Thutmose III, who played around 1475 B.C.. Piccione created baseball-style cards depicting the Egyptians playing their bat and ball games, with the decoded inscription "Catching it for him by the servants of god." The pharaoh, known as "P-3" by Piccione, is mummified in an Egyptian museum, and was described: "As a muscular mummy, maybe 5'7". He was a Hall of Fame military man with 37 victories in 37 campaigns. Like Roberto Clemente, he was heroic. Like Brooks Robinson, he had a good disposition. Like Ty Cobb, he took no guff. And like Joe DiMaggio, he wears his wrappings nattily."

European Evolution. In Europe, Christian Easter ceremonies included ball games involving the kicking or hitting of a ball with a stick. A 10th century Norse game called *knatteleik* required Viking batters to swing at balls of leather or wood. In 12th century France a game known as *la soule* was an offshoot that resulted in lacrosse and soccer.

Creag was a medieval bat and ball game played by the son of King Edward I (1272–1307). *Club ball* is also referenced in medieval times, with drawings showing a bat and ball. *Hand-in-and-hand-out* was popular in Scotland and England. Tree stumps were used and holes dug, and the object was for the bowler (pitcher) to keep the batter away from the holes. Sticks were later added to mark the holes, an apparent precursor to cricket. Cricket is referenced as early as 1344.

In the 1790s a Belgian-French game known as *Katt* was imported to England by returning students. A tradition since the 1750s, *Katt* used a very hard ball somewhat larger than a golf ball. There was also the French game *tcheque*, which was imported into the United States by French Huguenots who settled in New York.

An 1822 French book entitled *Les Jeux des Jeunes Garçons* depicted a bat-and-ball game for children.

Pesapallo is the Finnish national game, which bears some resemblance to baseball.

European Rounders. The European variations of baseball crossed the channel to England by the 1600s, where stool ball was an early game. The pitcher tried to hit an upturned stool with a ball before a batter could hit the ball with a stick, similar to cricket. More stools, or "bases," were added which were put in a circle. This evolved into *Rounders* when a rule was added that the runner was out if struck by a ball. Rounders was the name of the game in the West of Britain. It was known as Feeder in London and base ball in the South of England. According to John Thorn in the preface to a reprint of Jacob Morse's *Sphere and Ash* (1888), Morse "unashamedly acknowledged" that baseball was derived from rounders.

Early References to Base Ball. The earliest written reference to "Base Ball" was in 1700 when an English clergyman of Maidstone complained that boys were "playing Base Ball on the Sabbath." Base Ball is also referred to in a 1744 London publication, *A Pretty Little Pocket-Book*, by John Newberry. It was reprinted in America in 1762, marking the first appearance of the words "Base Ball" in a North American writing. This book also contained the first-known picture of a baseball game.

In 1748 a Lady Hervey wrote a letter in which she describes family activities of Frederick, Prince of Wales. She refers to family members "diverting themselves in baseball, a play all who are or have been schoolboys are well acquainted with."

In *Northanger Abbey*, written in the 1790s, author Jane Austen described a game called "base-ball" developed from cricket and rounders, which at the time was primarily a girl's game in England. Base Ball faded as Victorian England discouraged such sport by women in the mid–19th century. Austen's reference: "… and it was not very wonderful that Catherine should prefer cricket, base-ball, riding on horseback, and running about the country, at the age of fourteen, to books."

In 2004 the city of Pittsfield, Massachusetts, along with baseball historian John Thorn, discovered a 1791 bylaw that was created to protect windows in Pittsfield's new meeting house by prohibiting the playing of baseball within 80 yards of the building. Thorn was conducting research on the origins of baseball when he discovered a reference to the law in an 1869 book on the town's history. He shared his find with local resident and former Major League pitcher Jim Bouton. A librarian found the document in a vault at the Berkshire Athenaeum library and its age was authenticated by researchers at a local conservation center. The find prompted this comment from Pittsfield mayor James Ruberto: "Pittsfield is baseball's Garden of Eden."

The game is described as "Base Ball" in William Clark's *The Boy's Own Book*, published in London in 1828 or 1829. There was an express reference to Base Ball, but the rules basically described what was also referred to as rounders. The book was reprinted in the U.S. the same year. Another book, *The Boy's & Girl's Book of Sports*, by Robin Carver, was published in the U.S. in 1834 or 1835. It copied the earlier book's rules, but called it Base or Goal Ball instead of Rounders. Carver acknowledged being indebted to the *The Boy's Own Book*. His description: "BASE, OR GOAL BALL This game is known under a variety of names. It is sometimes called 'round ball,' but I believe that 'base' or 'goal ball' are the names generally adopted in our country. The players divide into two equal parties, and chance decides which shall have the first innings. Four stones or stakes are placed from twelve to twenty yards asunder [in a diamond shape per diagram].

"One of the party who is out places himself at [pitching area]. He tosses the ball gently toward [home plate], on the right of which one of the in-party places himself, and strikes the ball, if possible, with his bat. If he miss three times, or if the ball, when struck, be caught by any of the players of the opposite side who are scattered about the field, he is out, another takes his place. If none of these accidents take place, on striking the ball he drops the bat and runs toward [*third*] base] … they play at the ball by turns, until they all get out. Then, of course, the out-players take their places."

The first printed reference of American origin was thought to be in the July 13, 1825 edition of the *Delhi (N.Y.) Gazette*, which had a notice listing the names of nine men challenging any group in Delaware County to a game of baseball at the home of Edward B. Chace for $1 per game.

Later research by SABR member George A. Thompson, Jr., a New York University librarian, revealed that the first written reference to "base ball" in the United States was found in a letter to the editor in the April 25, 1823, edition of *National Advocate*, a New York City newspaper: "I was last Saturday much pleased in witnessing a company of active young men playing the manly and athletic game of 'base ball' at the Retreat in Broadway (Jones'). I am informed they are an organized association, and that a very interesting game will be played on Saturday next at the above place, to commence at half past 3 o'clock, PM. Any person fond of witnessing this game may avail himself of seeing it played with consummate skill and wonderful dexterity. It is surprising, and to be regretted that the young men of our city do not engage more in this manual sport; it is innocent amusement, and healthy exercise, attended with but little expense and has no demoralizing tendency.—A Spectator."

The "Retreat" was on the west side of Broadway between what is now Washington Place and 8th Street.

Late 18th and Early 19th Century Versions. Early versions of what closely approximated baseball were called "One Old Cat," "Two Old Cat," and "Town Ball." At least one source suggested that the name was One "Hole" Cat, rather than One "Old" Cat. Variations of One Old Cat were still played in Brooklyn in the 1920s. The ball was thrown at the runners as a means of getting them out; this was called "plugging," "soaking" or "stinging." The game also was called "Bittle and Battle" by the Dutch in New Netherland (New York), as well as "stool ball," "feeder," "Goal Ball," and "Baste Ball." Some of these early games had the runners going clockwise (consistent with Carver's description above). The conservative Plymouth New Englanders saw enough evil in baseball to ban all versions of the game.

There is evidence that a form of baseball was played by George Washington's troops at Valley Forge in 1778, and Supreme Court Justice Oliver Wendell Holmes described playing "Base Ball" in 1829.

The New York Knickerbockers and Other Early Clubs. Prominent 1860s American sports historian Charles A. Peverelly credited the *New York Knickerbockers* of the 1840s with standardizing the rules and publishing them. Peverelly's well-known book helped perpetuate the belief that the Knickerbockers, led by *Alexander Cartwright*, were the first organized club and played the first organized game.

The Knickerbocker club members were probably playing as early as 1842 but did not formally organize until 1845. There is evidence of other organized clubs playing even earlier, as reflected in the fact that the New York Base Ball Club held its "second anniversary dinner" on November 11, 1845. The Brooklyn Club also played at Elysian Field in Hoboken in 1845, and there is evidence of even earlier clubs playing in Rochester in 1825 and in Philadelphia in the 1830s (see also *Amateur Teams*).

One source suggests that the game may have evolved more

quickly in Canada as there are reports of a game played there on June 4, 1838. There is also now evidence of organized games as early as 1823, per the above *Newspaper* article referencing such activity.

Supposed First Organized Game.

"Let them hit it, you've got your fielders behind you." — Purportedly said by Alexander Cartwright as reported in *The Crooked Pitch*, by Martin Quigley (1984).

The first organized game of baseball was for many years assumed to be on Sunday, June 19, 1846, between the Knickerbockers and the New York Nine club from Manhattan. Later research determined that earlier games were played by the Knickerbockers and other clubs, but this game has been chronicled in detail by many sources in part because there were scorebook entries for the game.

The players for that game ferried to the Elysian Field of Hoboken, New Jersey, an old Cricket ground. Alexander Cartwright, then 25 years old, supposedly was the umpire, and some sources indicate that he was injured and could not play. More recent historians report that there is nothing to suggest that Cartwright actually umpired this game. However, there is reference to Cartwright umpiring the club's first game of the 1846 season, played on April 10.

The typical historian's report of the June game has the captains picking the teams and setting positions, purportedly a relatively new innovation. Players were fined six cents for swearing. The New York Nine defeated the Knickerbockers 23–1 in a game lasting four innings. Many historians have expressed surprise at the outcome, believing that the more organized Knickerbockers should not have lost to a "pick-up" team. However, it is clear that other clubs existed by this time and there is nothing to suggest that the Knickerbockers' opponent that day was unorganized or merely a pick-up team. Another source reported that some of the best Knickerbocker players sat out the game, which was played primarily between old Murray Hill players who were former or future Knickerbocker stars. Elysian Field is now the site of a Heinz Foods facility.

In George Moreland's encyclopedic *Balldom* (1914), it was erroneously reported that "not another game was played until June 3, 1851, when a team calling themselves the Washington Club … issued a challenge that the Knickerbockers accepted."

Actual First Organized Game. It is impossible to know when the first organized game occurred. What is known is that the Knickerbocker club recorded many of its games in a scorebook, and historians have for years relied on a scorebook page from the game of June 19, 1846, in assuming that it was the first organized game.

The scorebook reflects, however, at least 12 games played in 1845, the earliest recorded on October 6 of that year (October 21 in some sources). The game was played with seven players to a side; there were 10 players to a side in the often-cited game of June 19, 1846.

Knickerbocker/Cartwright's Rules. What is clear is that the Knickerbocker club formally set down in writing a set of rules that became fairly standardized in New York by 1847. Contrary to popular belief, there is nothing to suggest that Alexander Cartwright was the driving force behind these rules. He was not among the club representatives who signed the first set of rules.

The rules were close to the basic modern rules. The club codified foul lines and established nearly 90 foot bases. It is incorrect to say, however, that 90 feet was the chosen distance. Rather, 42 paces was indicated between first and third base and between home plate and second base, which created approximately 90 feet between bases by pacing standards of that time.

A batter could try for first base on a dropped third strike. No innings limit was set, and the winner was the first team to reach 21 "Aces," or runs. The ball could not be thrown at the runner; rather, he had to be touched or the base had to be touched. The pitching distance was 45 feet with nine players to each side (though evidence suggests 10 to a side in some early games). Catching a ball on the fly or on one bounce constituted an out. More than half the original rules still exist. The formal rules, adopted September 23, 1845.

1st — Members must strictly observe the time agreed upon for exercise, and be punctual in their attendance.

2nd — When assembled for exercise, the President, or in his absence the Vice-President, shall appoint an Umpire, who shall keep the game in a book provided for that purpose, and note all violations of the By-Laws and Rules during the time of exercise.

3rd — The presiding officer shall designate two members as Captains, who shall retire and make the match to be played, observing at the same time that the players put opposite to each other should be as nearly equal as possible; the choice of sides to be then tossed for, and the first in hand to be decided in like manner.

4th — The bases shall be from "home" to second base, forty-two paces; from first to third base, forty-two paces, equidistant.

5th — No stump match shall be played on a regular day of exercise.

6th — If there should not be a sufficient number of members of the Club present at the time agreed upon to commence exercise, gentleman not members may be chosen in to make up the match, which shall not be broken up to take in members that may afterwards appear; but, in all cases, members shall have the preference, when present, at the making of a match.

7th — If members appear after the game is commenced they may be chosen in if mutually agreed upon.

8th — The game to consist of twenty-one counts, or aces; but at the conclusion an equal number of hands must be played.

9th — The ball must be pitched, and not thrown, for the bat.

10th — A ball knocked out the field, or outside the range of the first or third base, is foul.

11th — Three balls being struck at and missed and the last one caught is a hand out; if not caught is considered fair, and the striker bound to run.

12th — If a ball be struck, or tipped, and caught, either flying or on the first bound, it is a hand out.

13th — A player running the bases shall be out, if the ball is in the hands of an adversary on the base, or the runner is touched with it before he makes his base; it being understood, however, that in no instance is a ball to be thrown at him.

14th — A player running who shall prevent an adversary from getting the ball before making his base, is a hand out.

15th — Three hands out, all out.

16th — Players must take their strike in regular turn.

17th — All disputes and differences relative to the game, to be decided by the Umpire, from which there is no appeal.

18th — No ace or base can be made on a foul strike.

19th — A runner cannot be put out in making one base, when a balk is made by the pitcher.

20th — But one base allowed when a ball bounds out of the field when struck.

[Signed]
William R. Wheaton,
William H. Tucker
Committee on By-Laws.

Abner Doubleday, the "American Origin" Thesis, and the Mills Commission.

"The only thing Abner Doubleday started was the Civil War." —

Branch Rickey referring to Abner Doubleday having ordered the firing of the first shot at Fort Sumter by the Union army.

"This myth, possibly the greatest hoax since Piltdown Man…"—Art Hill in *I Don't Care If I Never Come Back* (1980). Piltdown Man was thought to be a "missing link" fossil between apes and man, but turned out to be an elaborate ruse.

Despite the clear link between baseball and rounders, many prominent Americans of the late 19th century promoted the game as purely American in origin. White Stockings owner Albert Spalding did so in part to promote his sporting goods company, though his 1878 *Spalding Guide* reported to the contrary: "Baseball 'unquestionably thus originated' from Rounders."

He expanded upon the nationalism fostered by the Civil War and the effort to create a purely American tradition with baseball: "Baseball must be free from the trammels of English traditions, customs, and conventionalities…. Baseball is the exponent of American courage, confidence, combativeness; American dash, discipline, determination; American energy, eagerness, enthusiasm."

In the early 20th century this fallacy was promoted by Spalding even more heavily when he formed the Mills Commission to research the origins of baseball. The commission supposedly was created out of what may have been a tongue-in-cheek argument a few years earlier between prominent sportswriter Henry Chadwick and Spalding over the origins of baseball.

Spalding added distinguished Americans to his committee to give it some credibility. Nevertheless, Spalding did most of the work and the other commission members were primarily window-dressing. Former National League president Abraham G. Mills chaired the committee. The other committee members:

1. Alfred J. Reach, a Philadelphia second baseman from the 1870s, who founded A.J. Reach & Co., a bat and ball manufacturer (owned by Spalding by then) and publisher of the *Reach Guide*;

2. George Wright, a star shortstop of the 1869 Cincinnati Red Stockings and considered a **Father of Baseball**; in 1907 he was head of Wright & Ditson Sporting Goods (also owned by Spalding);

3. Morgan G. Bulkeley, former National League president and former governor of Connecticut;

4. Nicholas E. Young, fourth president of the National League;

5. James E. Sullivan, president of the Amateur Athletic Union (of **Sullivan Award** fame); and

6. Arthur P. Gorman, former United States senator from Maryland, who owned baseball clubs in Baltimore at various times.

What has been described as a three-year study by the Mills Commission culminated in a December 30, 1907, written finding that baseball was first played at Cooperstown in 1839 by Abner Doubleday, a friend of Mills. Mills had great respect for Doubleday and had served in the same military unit with him. The eight-paragraph report was actually written as an afterthought by Spalding after the commission's purpose was largely forgotten by all involved.

Sullivan, a vociferous Irishman who hated the British, did some of the legwork with Spalding (what there was of it) in compiling the commission's report. There are only a few documents remaining from the effort, as the bulk of the records was burned in a 1911 fire at Spalding's publishing company, the American Sports Publications Company.

The report's conclusion was based almost entirely on a letter by one Abner Graves, a former mining engineer in Denver, who wrote to the commission during its well-publicized investigation. Graves reported that he went to grade school with Doubleday in Cooperstown and was present the day that Doubleday organized a base-

ball game with four bases. One authoritative source noted that Graves would have been five years old in 1839, putting him in his early 70s when he wrote the letter. However, most sources report that Graves was over 80 when he wrote the letter, putting him at about age 22 for the fateful game. Graves later shot his wife and died in an asylum, so his credibility is suspect.

Most damaging to Graves' claim is that Doubleday was 20 years old and at West Point when Graves claims he developed the game. However, there was an Abner Doubleday that could have been with Graves in 1839; there was a 10-year-old cousin of the same name.

The commission misquoted Graves' letter, incorrectly giving Doubleday credit for eliminating "soaking" as a means of getting a batter out. A portion of Graves' letter (the entirety of which is in Spalding's 1911 book, *Our National Game*): "The American game of baseball was invented by Abner Doubleday of Cooperstown, N.Y., either the spring prior to or following the 'Log Cabin and Hard Cider' campaign of General William H. Harrison for the presidency. The pupils of Otsego Academy and of Green's Select School were then playing the old game of Town Ball in the following manner: A 'tosser' stood close to the 'home goal' and tossing the ball straight upward about six feet for the batsmen to strike at on its fall, the latter using a four-inch flatboard bat. All others wanting to play were scattered about the field, far and near, to catch the ball when hit. The lucky catcher took his innings at bat. When a batsman struck the ball he ran for a goal fifty feet distant and returned. If the ball was not caught, or if he was not 'plunked' by a thrown ball, while running, he retained his innings…."

Doubleday then improved Town Ball, to limit the number of players, as many were hurt in collisions. From twenty to fifty boys took part in the game I have described. He also designed the game to be played by definite sides or teams. Doubleday called the game 'Base Ball' for there were four bases to it. Three were places where the runner could rest free from being put out, provided he kept his feet on the flat stone base…. There were eleven players on a side."

The commission apparently ignored another letter that suggested an alternative origin: "J.A. Mendum of 591 Dudley Street, Dorchester, Mass., who is now eighty-three years old, states that … in 1830, he, with other pupils of the grammar school in School Street, Portsmouth, N.H., played the genuine game of base ball regularly during the summer…. Mr. Stoddard says: 'Four Old Cat and Three Old Cat were as well known to Massachusetts boys as was Round Ball. My father played them between 1800 and 1820. The games then bore the same relationship to Rounders that 'scrub' now bears to baseball. If the boys assembled and found there were not enough on hand to make up a team of Round Ball, they would content themselves with Four Old Cat or Three Old Cat.'"

Doubleday wrote many letters and books, none of which mentioned baseball. Unfortunately, most of Doubleday's papers were destroyed in a fire. Abraham Mills had known Doubleday for years when Mills participated in a grand celebration of baseball at Delmonico's restaurant in New York in 1889. When the speakers were extolling the virtues of baseball as a purely American game, Mills could have mentioned Doubleday's alleged contribution. A final comment on the commission: "[The Mills Commission report was like] the infallibility of the Pope, which, as a Catholic savant once remarked to me, is 'a dogma we unfortunately have to believe.'"—Journalist Rollin L. Hartt.

To get over the problem of how the game was transported from Cooperstown in 1839 to the Knickerbocker Club and others in New York City, the commission concluded that a Mr. Wadsworth had delivered plans of the game to New York City players. One of the first encyclopedias of baseball statistics and history was George

Moreland's *Balldom: "The Britannica of Baseball"* (1914). He concocted a fictitious connection between Doubleday and, apparently, Alexander Cartwright: "The idea of the diamond was not that of Mr. Doubleday, but of a gentleman named Cartwright, who was one of the players. He brought a rough sketch of what he termed a baseball diamond and after much wrangling the boys decided to try it. After a thorough trial, the players continued playing on the diamond as planned."

In a letter to Mills, sportswriter Henry Chadwick commented on the commission's findings: "Your decision in the case of *Chadwick v. Spalding* ... is a masterly piece of special pleading which lets my dear old friend Albert [Spalding] escape a bad defeat.... The whole matter was a joke between Albert and myself."

In his autobiography, Ford Frick recounted a 1926 conversation with the elderly but alert Mills at the National League's 50th anniversary dinner celebration. Mills acknowledged the tenuousness of the Mills Commission's findings to sportswriters who were not familiar with it, but pointed out that Cooperstown was representative of typical American towns that helped develop baseball. Mills' conclusions: "Unless and until new evidence is developed, or a more typical spot is discovered, I'll stand with Cooperstown — and the committee."

Frick amplified the skepticism in his autobiography, *Games, Asterisks and People* (1973): "After all, a battered old baseball, the early memories of an elderly man, and the casual findings of a self-appointed 'ad hoc' committee constitute a pretty tenuous foundation on which to base the origin of a national institution."

Perpetuation of the Myth. The Mills Commission findings were dusted off by the town of Cooperstown for a 1939 baseball centennial celebration. When the plans for the gala were announced and Doubleday was credited with the origins, Bruce Cartwright, Alexander Cartwright's grandson living in Honolulu, wrote a letter mentioning his father's clippings, diary and other documents to set the record straight. The original diary was burned by his father because it contained a number of derogatory references to certain people. Some sources report that Cartwright died a few weeks after sending his letter and a copy of his grandfather's diary. Other more reliable sources report that Cartwright in fact traveled to the mainland with these materials.

Despite the clear implication of his materials, too much money had already been expended by the centennial committee to call off the celebration. As an accommodation, the committee created an Alexander Cartwright Day as part of the festivities.

Sportswriter Fred Lieb visited Cooperstown in 1939 to report on the centennial celebration. He was to do a story for *The Sporting News* on the Abner Doubleday connection, thinking it was legitimate. He found no record of Doubleday's 1839 game and learned that Doubleday was at West Point when the game supposedly took place. Lieb related this to his editor, J.G. Taylor Spink. Spink told him to write the story as if the Doubleday connection were factual because baseball had spent so much time and effort promoting Cooperstown. Lieb then made up an entire story based on the Doubleday myth. In his 1950 book, *The Story of Baseball*, Lieb recounted his trip to Cooperstown but made no reference to the fabrication despite expressing skepticism. He came clean in his 1977 book, *Baseball as I Have Known It*.

The myth was perpetuated by a New York state commission, which in 1937 found "evidence" that Cooperstown was the birthplace of baseball. Even a 1952 Congressional Report, the Celler Report on Baseball (see also **Antitrust**), found that baseball "is a game of American origin."

Typical is a book entitled *The Story of Cooperstown* (see also *Cooperstown*), a general history of the town which devoted an entire chapter to Doubleday's connection to baseball. Though originally written in 1917, it was reprinted through at least 1948, well after publication of authoritative research that discredited the myth.

Books. The most exhaustive early effort to discredit the Doubleday theory was by Robert W. Henderson of the New York Public Library, who wrote *Ball, Bat and Bishop* in 1947. He correctly concluded that baseball was the result of a slow evolution from English games. One of the earliest efforts to counter the Doubleday myth was by Will Irwin in an article in *Collier's* magazine in 1909, "Baseball: Before the Professionals Came."

See also Melvin Adelman, *A Sporting Time: New York City and the Rise of Modern Athletics, 1820–1870* (1986); Warren Goldstein, *Playing for Keeps: A History of Early Baseball* (1990); Irving Leitner, *Baseball: Diamond in the Rough* (1972); Ron McCulloch, *How Baseball Began: The Long Overlooked Truth About the Birth of Baseball* (1995); Harold Peterson, *The Man Who Invented Baseball* (1973); Dean A. Sullivan (ed.), *Early Innings: A Documentary History of Baseball, 1825–1908* (1995).

Jim O'Rourke (1850–1919)

Hall of Fame 1945

"A quiet, gentlemanly Connecticut youth, with Irish blood in his veins, and therefore full of pluck and courage." — Henry Chadwick.

"O'Rourke was one of the first clubhouse lawyers, and his command of the English tongue was astonishing and bizarre." — Lee Allen in "A Letter to Mrs. Gilligan," in *The Hot Stove League* (1955).

O'Rourke had a .310 lifetime average and was one of the stellar outfielders of the 19th century.

A Connecticut native, James Henry "Orator Jim" O'Rourke graduated from Yale Law School and played for Mansfield and Boston in the National Association before the National League was formed for the 1876 season. He had the first National League hit in April 1876 for the Boston Red Stockings.

O'Rourke played 18 seasons in the National League, mostly with Buffalo and then New York in the 1880s. He batted .300 or better 11 times, including a .360 average in 1890 for the Players League club in New York. Primarily an outfielder, he also played every other position, including 209 games at catcher and six at pitcher.

O'Rourke was player-manager for Buffalo from 1881 through 1884 and was player-manager for the Washington Nationals in 1893, his last season as a player. He finished his career with a .310 average, though he later made a cameo appearance at age 52 in 1904 for the Giants. He played catcher and had a hit in a late-season game for manager John McGraw.

After O'Rourke retired in 1893 he umpired in 1894 and managed in the minor leagues until 1908. He became president of the Connecticut League in 1909 and assumed the presidency of the Eastern League for the 1914 season.

Mel Ott (1909–1958)

Hall of Fame 1951

"Love at first sight. That's what happened when grizzled, weather beaten, hard-nosed John McGraw saw apple-cheeked youngster of 16 take first cuts in special batting practice." — Gene Karst and Martin J. Jones, Jr., in *Who's Who in Professional Baseball* (1973)

"A big guy with little legs." — *Sports Illustrated*.

The diminutive Ott retired after 22 seasons with 511 home runs for the Giants.

The 5'9", 170-pound Ott was given a tryout by Giants manager John McGraw at age 16 in 1925 at the urging of the owner of Ott's Louisiana semipro team. The impressed McGraw kept the youngster with the Major League club, though he did not play at all with the Giants in 1925. He appeared in 35 games in 1926, batting .383. He remained with the Giants as a pinch hitter in 1927, batting .282 in 163 at-bats.

Ott became a regular the following season at age 19 and batted .322 in 124 games with 18 home runs. He erupted in 1929 with career highs of 42 home runs and 152 RBIs. From 1929 through 1945 he played regularly in the Giants outfield though he had been a catcher in Louisiana.

He retired after 22 seasons in 1947 as the then–National League home run king with 511. He was second in National League history in games played at 2,734 and first in runs (1,859) and RBIs (1,861). He led the league in home runs six times and drove in 100 or more runs in eight straight seasons. He batted .304 lifetime and had 11 seasons over .300, while hitting 30 or more runs eight times. Ott held the National League home run record until May 4, 1966, when Willie Mays topped him. He played in three World Series for the Giants, all in the 1930s, batting .295 with four home runs.

Ott managed the Giants from 1942 until mid–1948. His best finish was third in his first season at the helm. He then worked with Carl Hubbell in running the Giants' farm system until he left to manage the Oakland Oaks in the Pacific Coast League in 1951 and 1952. He next turned to broadcasting, ultimately calling Tigers games until he was killed in an auto accident in November 1958.

Book. Fred Stein, *Mel Ott: The Little Giant of Baseball* (2004).

Outfielders

"Catching a fly ball is a pleasure, but knowing what to do with it after you catch it is a business." — Yankee outfielder Tommy Henrich.

"Two-thirds of the earth is covered by water; the other one-third is covered by Garry Maddox." — Broadcaster Ralph Kiner on the eight-time Gold Glove Award winner.

"Claudell Washington plays the outfield like he's trying to catch grenades." — Reggie Jackson.

"The phrase 'off with the crack of the bat', while romantic, is really meaningless, since the outfielder should be in motion long before he hears the sound of the ball meeting the bat." — Joe DiMaggio.

"You know, all ballplayers is dumb, but outfielders is the dumbest." — Dodger manager Charlie Dressen, after outfielder Carl Furillo struck out for the third time in a row on the same pitch.

See also **Defensive Gems**, **Fielding and Fielding Percentage** and specific outfield positions.

Longest Together. The Pirates trio of center fielder Bill Virdon, left fielder Bob Skinner and right fielder Roberto Clemente hold the record for consecutive years together. They played as a group for eight seasons from 1956 through 1963.

Best.

"Why there's almost a tangible sense of relief to open Bill James's *Historical Baseball Abstract* and see that under 'Peak Value' Duke Snider is listed as the sixth-best center fielder of all time — behind Mantle, Cobb, Mays, DiMaggio, and Speaker, which is the approximate equivalent of finishing behind Einstein and Newton on your physics final." — Critic David Hinckley in *Cult Baseball Players*, edited by Danny Peary (1990).

Tris Speaker of the Red Sox and Indians is considered by many to be the finest defensive outfielder of the first years of the 20th century. He was known for his shallow outfield play during the dead ball era.

Max Carey was considered the best outfielder in the National League in the late 1910s and 1920s.

Joe DiMaggio is considered the best of the late 1930s and 1940s.

There was an ongoing debate during the 1950s among New York fans as to the best center fielder in town: Willie Mays of the Giants, Mickey Mantle of the Yankees or Duke Snider of the Dodgers. See also Donald Honig, *Mays, Mantle, Snider* (1987).

The defensive star of the 1960s was Roberto Clemente with his rifle arm in right field.

In the 1970s Garry Maddox was often considered the best defensive center fielder.

Jesse Barfield probably had the best arm of the 1980s though the overall best fielder arguably was center fielder Devon White.

The best arm of the 1990s was Raul Mondesi's of the Dodgers, though Larry Walker is a strong candidate. The best overall outfielder probably was Ken Griffey, Jr. By the 2000s, they gave way to Vladimir Guerrero.

Big Day. On April 29, 1997, in a game between the Red Sox and Angels, five of the six outfielders threw out runners. Tim Salmon, Garret Anderson and Orlando Palmeiro did it for the Angels, and Wil Cordero and Troy O'Leary did it for the Red Sox. Only Red Sox center fielder Shane Mack was left out as the Angels won 5–4. The next day, Anderson and Cordero threw out runners again.

Book. Ira L. Smith, *Baseball's Famous Outfielders* (1954).

Outs

"Of all the things we have in this game — hits and runs and stolen bases and home runs — the thing we have the most of is outs." — Manager Bill Rigney.

"It's ridiculous that we are gathered here tonight to honor a man who made more than 7,000 outs." — Bob Prince at Stan Musial's retirement dinner.

"I think about the cosmic snowball theory. A few million years from now the sun will burn out and lose its gravitational pull. The earth will turn into a giant snowball and be hurled through space. When that happens it won't matter if I get this guy out." — Pitcher Bill Lee.

"Ten million years from now, when the sun burns out and the Earth is just a frozen ice ball hurtling through space, nobody's going to care whether or not I got this guy out." — Pitcher Tug McGraw (sounds a lot like the previous quote).

"Since baseball time is measured only in outs, all you have to do is succeed utterly; keep hitting, keep the rally alive, and you have defeated time. You remain forever young." — Roger Angell.

"The only time I really try for a strikeout is when I'm in a jam. If the bases are loaded with none out, for example, then I'll go for a strikeout. But most of the time I try to throw to spots. I try to get them to pop up or ground out. On a strikeout I might have to throw five or six pitches, sometimes more if there are foul-offs. That tires me. So I just try to get outs. That's what counts — outs. You win with outs, not strikeouts." — Sandy Koufax.

Consecutive Retired. Before Harvey Haddix retired a then-record 36 straight during 12⅔ innings of perfect pitching in 1959, Vic Raschi retired 32 straight in 1950 for the Yankees. In 1972 Jim Barr retired 41 batters in a row over two games, breaking Haddix's record.

In May 2004 Randy Johnson retired 39 batters over three starts (including his **Perfect Game**), ending the streak in the 3rd inning of the game following the perfect game.

Extra. On September 9, 1999, the Padres almost got an extra out in their 10–3 win over the Padres. When Reggie Sanders struck out to end the 7th inning, the Expos players didn't leave the field and the umpires didn't notice that it was the third out. Phil Nevin ran the count to 2–1 before someone in the Expos' dugout pointed out the problem to home plate umpire Jerry Layne.

Owners

"The Lords of Baseball."— Sportswriter Dick Young on the Establishment owners of the 1960s; and the name of a 1976 book by former Dodger executive Harold Parrott.

"And even the people that read it will think it is about baseball or some such stupidity as that, for baseball is stupid, Author, and I hope you put it in your book, a game rigged by rich idiots to keep poor idiots from wising up to how poor they are."— Mark Harris in *Bang the Drum Slowly* (1956).

"The speculators from Wall Street … take all the risks; they pay their employees fabulously high salaries and in addition to all that they divide with them the profits of the business half and half…. A shrewd businessman would laugh in their faces at their temerity."— Albert Spalding on the new breed of owners in the 1890 Players League.

"The magnate must be a strong man among strong men, else other club owners in the league will combine in their own interests against him and his interests and by collusion force him out of the game."— Albert Spalding.

"They are strong, independent, successful, bright people … who understandably want to do things their way."— Commissioner Fay Vincent charitably speaking of the contentious owners who eventually dumped him.

"Baseball owners are the toughest set of ignoramuses anyone could ever come up against. Refreshingly dumb fellows. Greedy, shortsighted and stupid."— Commissioner Happy Chandler after he was forced out of office in 1951.

"Welcome to the den of village idiots."— Orioles owner Edward Bennett Williams to Peter Ueberroth when the new commissioner attended his first owners meeting in 1984.

"*No one* but an owner has any real power in baseball, on any guts issue — not the Commissioner, not the league presidents, not the general managers, not the public interest, and not the press (which can manipulate public response). Much flimflam surrounds the exercise of authority by all these people, but it is illusory."— Leonard Koppett in *A Thinking Man's Guide to Baseball* (1967).

"Even from the professional and business angle, the 'Lords of Baseball' are the products of their era — no more money mad, no more piratical, no more ruthless and selfish than their peers in contemporary religion and government, business and communications."— Ford Frick in *Games, Asterisks and People* (1973).

"Catfish Hunter had the distinction of playing for both Charlie Finley and George Steinbrenner, which is enough in itself to put a player in the Hall of Fame."— Peter Ueberroth.

"The owners are so stupid and avaricious, they can't figure out how to share their money with one another. They remind me of 28 little crumb-faced kids, all panting at the one who ate the cookies."— Rick Telander in *Sports Illustrated* during the 1994 player strike.

"Fifty-five, fifty-six million people pay to get into ballparks every year. Not one of them buys a ticket to see an owner."— George Will.

See also *Managers — Owners as Managers* and *Team Sales*.

Cross-Ownership. NFL rules require owners to use independent resources to purchase a team in another sport and independent management in its operation.

Background of Owners.

"It has always been the contention of Comiskey that the only useful owner in baseball has been the one who has been through the mill as a player and manager, and the sentiment has not been in disparagement of that host of sportsmen-capitalists who have had a hand in upbuilding the game."— G.W. Axelson in "*Commy*" (1919).

"Son, all the money I ever earn is earned out of baseball and I can't pay more to my players than I take in. I don't own factories, timberlands, rubber plantations. Baseball is my only source of revenue."— Connie Mack pleading poverty to a ballplayer asking for a raise.

A few team owners have been strictly baseball men who did not have an outside business as another source of income: Walter O'Malley (though he was a lawyer prior to taking over the Dodgers); Clark (a former player) and Calvin Griffith, Bill Veeck, Connie Mack (a former player) and Charles Ebbets (a bookkeeper by trade).

A sampling of other areas of expertise by individual owners:

Entertainment/Communications. Gene Autry (Angels), Danny Kaye (Mariners), Bing Crosby (Pirates), Bob Hope (Indians) and Al Jolson (Cardinals); George Washington Grant (Braves and pioneer movie maker in England); Harry Frazee (Red Sox and Broadway producer); John Fetzer (Red Sox and radio stations); Ted Turner (Braves and Superstation WTBS, CNN and other broadcast and motion picture interests); Powell Crosley (Reds and radio stations); Les Smith (Mariners and radio stations); Tom Werner (Padres and television producer of "The Cosby Show" and "Roseanne"); Wayne Huizenga (Marlins and Blockbuster video, though he made his fortune in the trash hauling business); Rupert Murdoch (Dodgers and television/newspapers); Arturo Moreno (Angels and outdoor advertising).

Oil. Eddie Chiles (Rangers and oil field servicing).

Attorneys. Henry Killilea (Red Sox); William Hepburn Russell (Braves); Judge Emil Fuchs (Braves); Edward Bennett Williams (Orioles); Walter O'Malley (Dodgers); Nick Mileti (Indians); Peter Angelos (Orioles); Eddie Einhorn and Jerry Reinsdorf (White Sox); Fred Saigh (Cardinals).

Construction and Real Estate. Andrew Freedman (Giants); Del Webb (Yankees); David and Richard Jacobs (Indians); Louis Perini (Braves); Arnold Johnson (A's); John Galbreath (Pirates); Arthur Soden (Braves); James Gaffney (Braves); Steve and Ed McKeever (Dodgers); Robert Lurie (Giants); George Argyros (Mariners); Frank McCourt (Dodgers); Steve Schott (A's).

Food. Arnold Johnson (A's and automats); Vern Stouffer (Indians and frozen foods); Charles Weegham (Cubs and cafeterias); William Wrigley (Cubs and chewing gum); Ray Kroc (Padres and McDonald's hamburgers); Tom Monaghan (Tigers and Domino's Pizza); Mike Ilitch (Tigers and Little Caesar's Pizza), Peter Magowan (Giants and Safeway Supermarkets); Drayton McLane (Astros and supermarkets).

Insurance. Morgan Bulkeley (Troy Haymakers and Aetna Insurance); Ellis Ryan (Indians); Charlie Finley (A's and life insurance brokerage).

Publishing. Francis Dale (Reds and *Cincinnati Enquirer*); Nelson Doubleday, Jr. (Mets and Doubleday Books); Charles and John

Taylor (Red Sox and newspaper publishers); Charles Murphy (Cubs and newspaper reporter); Kevin McClatchey (Pirates and newspaper publisher); Horace Fogel (Phillies and newspaper reporter).

Bookkeepers. Charles Ebbets (Dodgers); Frank Navin (Tigers).

Manufacturing. Ewing Kauffman (Royals and pharmaceuticals); Dan Topping (Yankees and tin plating); Walter Briggs (Tigers and auto bodies; Powell Crosley (Reds and auto bodies); Sam Breadon (Cardinals and auto manufacturing); Robert Lee Hedges (Browns and auto manufacturing); Brad Corbett (Rangers and plastic pipe); Robert Carpenter (Phillies and DuPont); Phil Ball (Browns and ice machines and cold storage).

Banking/Finance. Charles Stoneham (Giants and stockbroker); Carl Pohlad (Twins and banking); Don Barnes (Browns and investment banker);

Retail Stores. John Brush (Giants and department stores); Alfred Reach (Phillies and sporting goods), Albert Spalding (Chicago White Stockings and sporting goods).

Transportation/Auto Dealers.

"It was a beautiful thing to behold, with all 36 oars working in unison."—Cardinals broadcaster Jack Buck on George Steinbrenner's new yacht in 1981.

"The Boston Parking Lot Attendant."—The name given to parking garage and Dodger owner Frank McCourt by acerbic *Los Angeles Times* columnist T.J. Simers (one of this author's current favorites).

Jim Dunn (Indians and railroad contractor); Sidney Weil (Reds and auto dealer); Ted Bonda (Indians and parking garages); Bob Short (Senators/Rangers and trucking); George Steinbrenner (Yankees and shipping/shipbuilding); Jerry McMorris (Rockies and trucking); John McMullen (Astros and marine architect); Marge Schott (Reds and auto dealer); Bud Selig (Brewers and auto dealer).

Distilleries/Breweries. Jacob Ruppert (Yankees and Knickerbocker Beer); August A. Busch (Cardinals and Busch Breweries); LaBatt's Brewery (Blue Jays); Jerry Hoffberger (Orioles and National Brewery); Charles Bronfman (Expos and Seagram's); numerous 19th century owners.

Politicians. Boss Tweed (Troy Haymakers and New York City political boss); John Day (Giants and Tammany Hall); Garry Herrmann (Reds and ward boss); Roy Hofheinz (Astros, judge and mayor); Robert Hannegan (Cardinals and Postmaster General); George W. Bush (Rangers, Texas governor and President).

Book. Burton Alan Boxerman and Benita W. Boxerman, *Ebbets to Veeck to Busch: Eight Owners Who Shaped Baseball* (2003); Harold Parrott, *The Lords of Baseball* (1976) (2001 reprint).

"**P** is for Plank,
    The arm of the A's;
    When he tangled with Matty
    Games lasted for days."
—Ogden Nash on Eddie Plank.

Pacific Coast League (1903–)

"Only two seasons into its operation, the PCL displayed many of the characteristics that would underscore its distinctiveness in the world of professional baseball. Most evident were the numbers, individual and team marks of glowing achievement and glaring ineptitude that were a statistician's delight."—Paul J. Zingg and Mark D. Medeiros in *Runs, Hits and an Era: The Pacific Coast League 1903–1958* (1994).

The Pacific Coast League ("PCL") was the successor to the 19th century California League. That league existed sporadically until 1900. The California League and the Pacific Northwest League were both in the National Association when the 1902 season began. After that season the California League decided to expand significantly. When Seattle and Portland left the Pacific Northwest League and joined the California League cities, the Pacific Coast League was formed and competed outside of Organized Baseball in 1903. The league moved into the fold the following season.

Every original Pacific Coast League city now has a Major League franchise except Portland (Seattle, San Francisco, Oakland, Los Angeles and San Diego). In 1996 the PCL clubs were in Vancouver, Salt Lake City, Tacoma, Edmonton, Calgary, Tucson, Colorado Springs, Albuquerque, Las Vegas and Phoenix. In the 2000s the league absorbed the old American Association clubs, creating four divisions. Vancouver and Calgary were replaced by Fresno and Portland, and several American Association locales joined the Central and Eastern divisions of the PCL.

Major League Aspirations. The league had Major League ambitions throughout the 20th century. From 1944 until 1957 the PCL petitioned Organized Baseball to become a third Major League. In 1950 the PCL attempted to form a new league that would include Houston, Dallas, Mexico City and key PCL cities.

From the 1930s well into the 1950s the PCL was the most independent of the minor leagues, in part due to geographic isolation. It retained many of its stars for the balance of their careers, rather than see them snapped up by the Major League clubs.

In his autobiography, Ford Frick reported that after World War II there was a special tour of all PCL cities to determine if the league should be designated as a third Major League. It ended with an executive session in which the PCL owners were presented with detailed figures on the cost of running a Major League operation. Frick contended that the PCL owners themselves rejected the idea because "the plan had no chance of success and could only result in the disruption of a prideful and traditional minor league operation."

Because of its power, in 1952 the PCL received an "Open" classification, which was even higher than the Class AAA designation that it previously carried. The Open classification was in effect recognition of the fact that the PCL was a quasi–Major League. After Major League expansion to the West Coast, the PCL diminished in strength and its clubs became farm teams for Major League clubs. It continues to operate as a Class AAA league with clubs primarily in the Northwest, Southwest and western Canada.

Best Team. The all-time best PCL team may have been the 1934 Los Angeles Angels, which had a record of 137–50 and won the pennant. Some sources consider this club to be the best minor league team of all time.

Books. Bill O'Neal, *The Pacific Coast League: 1903–1988* (1989); R. Scott Mackey, *Barbary Baseball: The Pacific Coast League of the 1920s* (1995); Dennis Snelling, *The Pacific Coast League: A Statistical History, 1903–1957* (1995); Donald R. Wells, *Baseball's Western Front: The Pacific Coast League During World War II* (2004); Paul J. Zingg and Mark D. Medieros, *Runs, Hits and an Era: The Pacific Coast League (1903–1958)* (1994).

Satchel Paige (1906–1982)

Hall of Fame (NLC) 1971

"1. Avoid fried meats which angry up the blood.

2. If your stomach disputes you, lie down and pacify it with your cool thoughts.

3. Keep the juices flowing by jangling around gently as you move.

4. Go very lightly on the vices, such as carrying on in society. The social ramble ain't restful.

5. Avoid running at all times.

6. Don't look back. Something might be gaining on you."—Paige's prescription for a long life.

One of the greatest showmen in baseball history, Paige starred in the Negro Leagues and, though well past his prime, briefly in the Major Leagues in the late 1940s.

Leroy Robert Paige was born in Mobile, Alabama, on July 7, 1906, but in 1948 he claimed to have been born on September 18, 1908. Negro League star Ted Radcliffe claimed that Paige was actually born in 1900.

Paige's first professional pitching job was for the 1925 Chattanooga Lookouts for $50 per month. He later played for the Birmingham Black Barons, Baltimore Black Sox, Chicago American Giants, Pittsburgh Crawfords and even the House of David. In 1934 the Paige All-Stars defeated the Dizzy Dean All-Stars 1–0 in 17 innings. Dean highly respected Paige's pitching ability: "Why, if Satch and I were on the same ballclub we'd have the pennant clinched by the Fourth of July and we could go fishing until the World Series."

Paige had various nicknames for his pitches, including the "hurry up ball" and the "bat dodger pitch." He also threw the "bee ball" (fastball) and hesitation pitch (slow curve). The hesitation pitch eventually was banned by the American League because it included a move that was considered a balk. He often billed himself as the "World's Greatest Pitcher—Guaranteed to Strike Out the First Nine Men."

Paige was at least 42 when he signed with Bell Veeck's Indians in 1948 to become the oldest rookie ever. When he came to the Major Leagues, the only black Major League players were Larry Doby, Roy Campanella and Jackie Robinson. Two years later, Paige was given a rocking chair to use while in the Indians' bullpen.

He made his first Major League start on August 3, 1948, pitching seven innings in a 5–3 victory over the Senators. He threw his first Major League complete game on August 13, 1948, a 5–0 five-hitter against the White Sox. He finished with a 6–1 record that season and helped lead the club to the pennant.

After two years with the Indians he played Negro League ball in 1950. In 1951 he returned to the Major Leagues with the Browns, by then owned by Veeck. He lasted three years before returning to the Monarchs and then to the International League Miami Marlins where he was reunited with Veeck. He made a cameo appearance with the A's in 1965 (see also *Oldest Active Players*). He finished his Major League career with a 28–31 record and 3.29 ERA. Paige was the first Negro League star voted into the Hall of Fame.

Books. Satchel Paige and Hal Lebovitz, *Pitchin' Man* (1948); Satchel Paige and David Lipman, *Maybe I'll Pitch Forever* (1962); Mark Ribowsky, *Don't Look Back: Satchel Paige in the Shadows of Baseball* (1994).

Paint

"Two painters were just beginning work on the fence, and why they did not twist their necks off every time somebody hit the ball is impossible to say. No one who has not tried to paint a fence with a new baseball club opening a new game behind his back can appreciate what those painter men went through ... they still tried to do their duty and daubed away with their paint brushes at the fence,

Legendary Negro League star Satchel Paige delivering a pitch at Yankee Stadium.

and sometimes they painted the boards and sometimes they daubed the air and sometimes they streaked each other."—Game story in the *Chicago Tribune* for the opening game of the White Sox in the new (but still minor) American League on April 21, 1900.

"A practical joker of note, Dean and a teammate once entertained themselves on a rainy day in their Philadelphia hotel by donning overalls and, carrying paint buckets and ladders, invaded the ballroom where a convention was being held. They solemnly announced that the place was to be painted. When the upset conventioneers realized who their tormentor was, a great cheer went up and Dean was invited to make a speech."—Lawrence Ritter and Donald Honig in *The Image of Their Greatness* (1976).

In 1884 the Boston Red Stockings were tired of fans climbing telegraph poles adjacent to the ballpark for a free view of the game. The club solved the "deadhead" problem by painting the poles before games.

In early 1946 the Braves gave a facelift to their ballpark, including a paint job on the seats. When fans in certain sections left the opening game, they noticed green paint stuck to their clothing. Fans complained and the team took out advertisements apologizing and requesting fans to submit cleaning bills. A "paint reimbursement account" was opened at a local bank and more than 18,000 claims were submitted. Only 5,000 apparently legitimate claimants received a total of $6,000.

Jim Palmer (1945–)

Hall of Fame 1990

"I have more fights with Jim Palmer than with my wife. The Chinese tell time by the 'Year of the Horse' or the 'Year of the Dragon.' I tell time by the 'Year of the Back,' the 'Year of the Elbow.' Every time Palmer reads about a new ailment, he seems to get it. This year it's the 'Year of the Ulnar Nerve.' Someone once asked me if I had any physical incapacities of my own. Know what I answered? 'Sure I do,' I said. 'One big one: Jim Palmer.'"— Orioles manager Earl Weaver on the hypochondriac Palmer, quoted in *High Inside: Memories of a Baseball Wife*, by Danielle Gagnon Torrez and Ken Lizotte (1983). Danielle was married to former Orioles pitcher Mike Torrez.

Palmer won 268 games for the Orioles between 1965 and 1985.

Adopted at birth, Palmer rejected a UCLA basketball scholarship in 1963 and signed for a $60,000 bonus ($50,000 in some sources) with the Orioles in 1964, for whom he spent his entire Major League career. After a short stint in the minor leagues he was up with the Orioles in 1965 and won five games. He won 15 in 1966 and beat the Dodgers in the World Series to become at age 19 the youngest pitcher to throw a Series shutout.

By 1967 he was suffering from arm and back problems and spent most of 1967 and all of 1968 in the minor leagues. The scare caused him to work even harder and his physical conditioning kept him pitching for 19 Major League seasons. It did not hurt his endorsements either, as he later signed as the spokesperson for Jockey *Underwear* and became "the underwear guy" (proceeds to the Cystic Fibrosis Foundation).

In 1969 he returned with a flourish and a 16–4 record. He followed that with eight of nine seasons in which he won 20 or more games. He won more games in the 1970s than any other American League pitcher. He finished his career in 1984 with a 268–152 record and a .638 winning percentage. He had 53 shutouts, including 10 in 1975, and won four Gold Glove Awards before entering the broadcast booth for the Orioles. Palmer pitched in six World Series for the Orioles and won four games. He never allowed a *Grand Slam* in the Major Leagues.

He attempted a *Comeback* after he was elected to the Hall of Fame in 1990, but after shredding a hamstring in spring training he abandoned the effort and returned to broadcast for the Orioles, ESPN and ABC, and for a decade was a color commentator for the Little League World Series.

Book. Jim Palmer, *Together We Were Eleven Foot Nine* (1996) (alluding to his up-and-down relationship with diminutive Orioles manager Earl Weaver).

Panama

"Success in the others [sports] is dependent on accidents of birth. To excel at football, you have to be born huge. Basketball requires that you be born tall. And for hockey it is essential that you not be born in Panama."— Art Hill in *I Don't Care If I Never Come Back* (1980).

Origins. The Cubans are credited by some with introducing the game in 1904.

Players.

"What a comfort to know that Omar Moreno loses his mitt between innings, must conduct a recurrent, chagrined, furtive search after all these years for the place he flung it, just as I do in my Sunday morning softball league. Dewy-eyed, pigeon-toed, high-waisted Omar! What a lethargic embodiment of grace! What few fluctuations in Arabian Panamanian temperament! His gloves go astray, but he doesn't. His professionalism is to be found elsewhere."— John Krich in *El Beisbol* (1985).

Rod Carew. The most prominent player from Panama is Carew, who achieved his 3,000th Major League hit on August 4, 1985, and had a lifetime .328 average.

Hector Lopez. The infielder/outfielder played for the A's and Yankees for 12 seasons beginning in 1955.

Roberto Kelly played 14 seasons between 1987 and 2000, mostly in the American League. He batted .290 with 124 home runs.

Orlando Miller played infield mostly for the Astros for four seasons in the mid–1990s.

Sherman Obando played four seasons in the mid–1990s for the Orioles and Expos.

Mariano Rivera is the most dominating postseason reliever of all-time, pitching 10 years for the Yankees through the 2004 season.

Ruben Rivera began in the Major Leagues in 1995 and was still playing in 2004. He is best remembered for stealing Derek Jeter's glove to sell on the memorabilia market and then getting released by the Yankees because of it.

Carlos Lee has played with the White Sox since 1999, hitting 121 home runs through 2003, with a career-high 113 RBIs in 2003.

Allan Lewis. See *Pinch Runners* for A's owner Charlie Finley's use of the pinch running specialist, known as the Panamanian Express.

Professional League. Panama once had a professional league but now competes only on the amateur level controlled by the Panama Baseball Federation.

Parking

"As a nation we are dedicated to keeping physically fit — and parking as close to the stadium as possible."— Sportswriter Bill Vaughan.

"He is one of the Seraphim, the highest order of angels among the California Angels. Or if you prefer, he is a modern-day version of Jude, patron saint of lost causes. He is an all-time all-star at mopping up. He is one of the most spectacular late men ever to toil at Anaheim Stadium."— Bruce Anderson in *Sports Illustrated* on Kevin (I'll find your) Carr, who helped fans find their cars "lost" in the parking lot. This author experienced a similar circumstance in the late 1960s, with his father. Parking early at the game, they came out afterward and were unable to find their car. After 40–50 buses embarked, there was the lone car sitting by itself in the lot.

Parking Problems. As late as 1900 some clubs still allowed cars or carriages to park in the outfield area. By the mid–20th century many minor league teams still sold spaces along the perimeter of the outfield so customers could view the game from their cars.

After World War II, lack of parking spaces was a major problem for many of the older northern parks where subways and streetcars had been the primary mode of transportation to the ballpark. The other major problem was that the older parks were surrounded with close-by residential neighborhoods, making it impossible to build large parking areas. Ebbets Field in Brooklyn had a valet parking system to help alleviate overcrowding.

Newer parks built starting in the 1950s gave considerable

attention to parking spaces. However, older parks still in use have not solved their problems. Yankee Stadium has no significant parking lot and city-owned lots adjacent to the stadium accommodate only 6,900 cars. That's not as bad as Boston's Fenway Park, which has absolutely no parking facility. The surrounding lots are privately owned and operated and the standard charge is usually $10, so public transportation is strongly encouraged. Wrigley Field has only three small parking lots. The rest are privately owned around the residential neighborhood and spaces can cost $15.

In contrast, Dodger Stadium and Anaheim Stadium each accommodate 16,000 cars and parking can be a source of large profits. In 1989 the Dodgers grossed approximately $3.5 million on their parking operation, with a net profit to the club of approximately $2.6 million. Turner Field in Atlanta, built for the 1996 Olympic Games and converted to exclusive baseball use in 1997, has 8,500 parking spaces.

Drive-in. Albuquerque's Sports Stadium, built for the 1969 season, was the first modern park to have drive-in parking. Cars were allowed to park on a bluff overlooking the outfield.

Riverfront Stadium in Cincinnati has a parking garage underneath the ballpark.

Double-Parked. During the Kansas City A's first home opener in 1955, A's players Alex Kellner and Arnie Portocarro had their cars towed away during the game. They each paid $10 to have them removed from the impound yard.

V.I.P. In the 1970s Cuban-born Mike Cuellar was a pitching star for the Orioles. During spring training in Florida the Orioles assigned parking spaces to the local newspapers and provided signs. Cuellar invariably parked his car in the space reserved for the *Cuban Star* newspaper of Miami.

Passed Balls

"It was great. I got to meet a lot of important people. They all sit behind home plate." — Catcher Bob Uecker on all the passed balls he allowed trying to catch Phil Niekro's knuckleball.

"You gotta have a catcher or you're gonna have a lot of passed balls." — Casey Stengel on why the Mets took catcher Hobie Landrith as their first pick in the expansion draft. Landrith was traded early in the season for the immortal Marv Throneberry.

"I want a new catcher. If somebody's going to set a record for passed balls in the World Series, I don't want it to be me." — Giants catcher Wes Westrum during the 1954 World Series, signaling to his manager for a new catcher after dropping a number of Hoyt Wilhelm knuckleballs.

See also *Knuckleballs* and *Wild Pitches*.

Early Rules. In 1889 a passed ball was no longer credited as an error on the catcher. In addition, errors were no longer credited against pitchers for passed balls (nor for wild pitches, balks or hit batters).

Mickey Owen.

"But Mickey Owen missed this strike. The ball rolled far behind,
And Henrich speeded to first base, like Clipper on the wind.
Upon the stricken multitude grim melancholy perched.
"Dark disbelief bowed Hughie's head. It seemed as if he lurched." — A stanza from "Casey in the Box," by Meyer Berger of the *New York Times*.

Dodger catcher Mickey Owen dropped a swinging third strike during the pivotal Game 4 of the 1941 World Series for a passed ball with two outs in the 9th inning and his club leading the Yan-

kees 4–3. The Yankees led the Series 2–1, and a Dodger win would have tied the Series.

Dodger manager Leo Durocher later recalled that the Dodger players were already running on the field in celebration as Yankee batter Tommy Henrich followed through on his swing for the apparent last out. The umpire signaled strike three and fans swarmed on the field, supposedly blocking Owen's path to the ball (not true). One of the regular policemen who covered the game was stationed behind the umpire in the stands. As the police came on the field thinking the game was over, this particular cop (referred to in one source as officer Keystone) tried to kick the ball back to Owen, but he missed. Henrich raced safely to first base and the play ignited a four-run rally that gave the Yankees a 7–4 lead and the win. After Henrich got on, Joe DiMaggio singled and Charlie Keller doubled them home. After Bill Dickey walked, Joe Gordon doubled to score Keller and Dickey.

Dodger pitcher Hugh Casey later supposedly admitted throwing a spitter on the pitch because it dropped wickedly, but at the time it was referred to as a "low curve." Durocher and Henrich believed it was a slider, which moves in a manner similar to a spitball. Durocher claimed that it was not a spitball because Casey had a sinker and did not know how to throw a spitball. Durocher reasoned that Casey would not have thrown a spitball when he had a pitch (sinker) that does substantially the same thing — drop rapidly at the last moment. Some sources reported that only Yankee shortstop Phil Rizzuto thought the ball was a spitter.

Owen's subsequent explanation was even simpler. Casey had two pitches, fastball and curveball. He had two curveballs, one a quick breaking curve and the other a big slower curve. He threw the quick curve all day long until the fateful pitch. Owen's recipe for success in living with the gaffe: "I kept asking myself, 'How did I do it. How did I do it.' Then I made up my mind I'd have to live with it. I've always been able to handle adversity pretty good, and I reasoned that I'd been trying my best. I've been living with it a long time now."

What is often forgotten is that Owen was an All-Star that year and did not deserve the criticism he received. Earlier in the season he tied a record by catching three foul balls in an inning and set a National League record for consecutive errorless chances by a catcher. He was banned from the league from 1946 until 1948 for agreeing to play in the *Mexican League*.

Multiple Passed Balls. On May 12, 1996, Astros back-up catcher Jerry Goff tied the Major League record with six passed balls in a game. Harry Vickers of the 1902 Reds and Geno Petralli of the 1987 Rangers share the record.

On July 28, 1970, catcher Tom Egan used an oversized glove to catch knuckleballer Hoyt Wilhelm of the Angels, but he still gave up five passed balls during the game.

Ray Katt, who played in the 1950s, once allowed four passed balls in one inning.

Streak. Catcher Benito Santiago went 272 games for the Padres without giving up a passed ball. After he signed with the Florida Marlins for the club's inaugural season in 1993, he had 11 — all thrown by knuckleballer Charlie Hough.

Patents See *Balls* — Manufacturers, *Catcher's Equipment*, *Donuts*, *Gloves* and *Inventions*

Payroll See *Salaries* — Team Payrolls

Peak Performance Years See *"Career" Years*

Peanuts See *Concessions*

Pennant Races

"For the lifelong fan, the most abiding pleasure may be cleaving to one club for years and studying it well. Our most engrossing delight comes when that team gets into a tough pennant race. At last all our attention and affection pay off. We sense how every twist of luck or heroism interacts with every wrinkle of providence that has gone before it. In the year when history calls the team to its accounting, we share the club's extremities of joy and anxiety."—Thomas Boswell in *Why Time Begins on Opening Day* (1984).

"All the fret and worry have been wiped from the schedule, and the fanatics may seek some needed repose. The pennant is ours."—Sportswriter Charles Dryden's lead to a 1905 story reporting that the A's had backed into the American League championship.

"I believe there are certain things that cannot be bought. Loyalty, friendship, health, love and an American League pennant."—Orioles owner Edward Bennett Williams.

The Amateur Teams. The New York teams of the early 1860s competed for a "whip pennant."

National League's First Year. The National League decreed that the winner of its first season in 1876 would win a flag to cost no more than $100.

AL and NL Pennant Winners by Club/1901–2004 (not including 1994).

American League	National League
39 Yankees	16 Cardinals
11 Red Sox	15 New York Giants
9 Philadelphia A's	11 Brooklyn Dodgers
9 Tigers	10 Cubs
6 Oakland A's	9 Pirates
6 Orioles	9 Reds
5 White Sox	7 Los Angeles Dodgers
5 Indians	5 Phillies
3 Senators (all before 1961 franchise shift)	5 Atlanta Braves
	4 Mets
3 Twins	3 San Francisco Giants
2 Royals	2 Boston Braves
2 Blue Jays	2 Milwaukee Braves
1 Browns	2 Padres
1 Brewers	2 Marlins
1 Angels	1 Diamondbacks
0 Mariners	0 Rockies
0 Rangers	0 Astros
0 Kansas City A's	0 Milwaukee Brewers
0 Pilots	0 Expos
0 Devil Rays	

Pennant Burial. The Cleveland Indians won the pennant in 1948 but were destined for third place in 1949. When they were mathematically eliminated from the race on September 23, 1949, owner Bill Veeck held a pregame burial of the 1948 pennant. Wearing a top hat, Veeck led a horse-drawn hearse and funeral procession to a grave behind center field. Manager Lou Boudreau and various players were pallbearers. The tombstone read "1948 Champs." Rudie Schaffer, the team's business manager, read the last rites from the "Bible of Baseball," *The Sporting News*.

Earliest Clinched. The 1941 Yankees clinched the American League pennant on September 4, 1941, the earliest ever in either league before the division playoff system. They clinched after 136

of their 154-game schedule, or 88% of their games. The club finished 17 games ahead of the Red Sox.

The earliest clinching during the division play era was the 1998 Yankees, who locked it up on August 29 on their way to 114 wins.

The 1975 Reds clinched the National League West pennant on September 7, the earliest date ever in the National League. On May 20 of that season, the club reached .500 and was 5½ games behind the Dodgers. At that point the Reds moved Pete Rose to third base and over the next 50 games went 41–9, moving ahead of the Dodgers by 12½ games.

The 1955 Dodgers clinched on September 8, the earliest in the National League over a 154-game season. The previous best was in 1953 when the Dodgers clinched on September 12.

In 1995 the Indians clinched the American League Central Division on September 8. They clinched in their 120th game, 83.3% of the scheduled 144 games in the strike-shortened season.

First Pennant Decided on Last Day of Season. The first Major League pennant race decided on the last day of the season was in 1889 in the National League. On October 5 the Giants defeated the Cleveland Spiders while lowly Pittsburgh defeated Boston's highly regarded John Clarkson. At least one source has reported that if Clarkson had won, Boston would have won the pennant. The facts do not support this statement. By 1889 the winner was calculated by percentage, not by total number of wins (see below). Even if Boston had won one more game, its winning percentage would have been slightly below New York's. The Giants won with an 83–43 record and Boston finished at 83–45.

Both Leagues/Last Day of Season. Both the National League and American League had their races decided on the last day in 1908 and 1949. There has never been a year since divisional play began in 1969 when more than two races were decided on the last day.

Best Minor League Race. One source chose the 1920 International League race between Baltimore and Toronto as the best minor league race ever. The teams started September one game apart. Toronto won 20 of 22 but was unable to hold its lead over Baltimore, which won 25 consecutive games.

Comebacks. Sixteen teams have won pennants or division titles after trailing by 10 or more games at the All-Star break. Eight of those teams have done it since the start of division play. In 1964 the Cardinals came back from the largest and latest deficit of all time, when they trailed by 11 games on August 23.

Largest Margin of Victory. The 1902 Pirates won the pennant by 27½ games over the second-place Dodgers in a 140-game schedule. The club had recently obtained the best players from the defunct Louisville club (including Honus Wagner), and survived the American League's raiding far better than other National League clubs.

The 1995 Indians had a 23½ game lead when they clinched. They finished 30 games ahead of the Royals over a 144-game schedule due to the strike-shortened season.

Percentage Winner. In 1879 for the first time the National League pennant winner was determined by calculating winning percentage. Previously, the club with the most number of wins was declared the winner, but this was inequitable because teams often did not play the same scheduled number of games.

Wire-to-Wire. Clubs that have gone wire-to-wire for a pennant or division title since 1901:

1923 Giants
1927 Yankees
1955 Dodgers
1984 Tigers
1990 Reds

1997 Orioles
2001 Mariners
2003 Giants

Exciting 20th Century Pennant Races.

1904.

American League. On October 10 the New York Highlanders met the Boston Pilgrims for a doubleheader on the last day of the season in the Polo Grounds. Boston had 93 wins and New York had 92. New York needed a sweep to clinch because the teams played an uneven number of games due to rainouts that were not rescheduled in those days.

Jack Chesbro was New York's starting pitcher in the first game. The clubs were tied 2–2 in the 9th inning with Chesbro still on the mound. Boston's Freddy Parent reached base and made it to third. Chesbro then threw a wild pitch over the head of catcher Red Kleinow and Boston won 3–2 to clinch the pennant. Chesbro's wife spent the next several years trying to have the **Wild Pitch** ruled a passed ball. See also Benton Stark, *The Year They Called Off the World Series* (1991).

1907.

American League. The A's and Tigers were down to the last nine games of the season and had a three-game head-to-head series. The A's led by one-half game, but Chief Bender lost the first game 5–4 to put the Tigers up by one-half game. The second game was rained out, setting up a doubleheader on Monday, September 30.

The A's took a 7–1 lead in the first game, but the Tigers rallied for four runs in the 7th inning off ace Rube Waddell, who had come on in relief. In the 9th inning the Tigers trailed 8–6, but tied the game when 20-year-old Ty Cobb hit a two-run homer.

Each club scored in the 11th. In the 14th A's first baseman Harry Davis hit an apparent ground-rule double into the outfield crowd, but first base umpire Tom Connolly called him out, ruling that there had been interference from a policeman who lunged for the ball. The A's protested and a fight ensued, but the play stood. The next A's batter hit a single that would have scored Davis, but the rally died.

The game ended in a 9–9 tie in 17 innings, halted by darkness that also wiped out the second game of the doubleheader. The series took the steam out of the A's as the Tigers held their lead over the last six games.

1908. This season saw the two closest races in the same year. See David W. Anderson, *More than Merkle: A History of the Best and Most Exciting Baseball Season in Human History* (2003); G.H. Fleming, *The Unforgettable Season* (1981).

American League. The Indians, Tigers and White Sox went down to the last day of the season in a virtual tie. Detroit was 89–63 at .586, Cleveland 89–64 at .582, and Chicago 88–63 at .579. The highest percentage would win regardless of how many games were played, as rainouts were not made up.

Tigers ace Wild Bill Donovan was scheduled to start against spitballer Ed Walsh of the White Sox, but Donovan had a "rheumatic condition" that had developed in his right arm. He spent the night before being attended to by the trainer with mustard plasters and hot towels. Not only was he able to pitch, he shut out the White Sox on two hits in a 7–0 victory in front of the largest weekday crowd in White Sox history to that point.

The Tigers' victory enabled them to nose out the Indians by one-half game. The Tigers finished 90–63 at .588 and the Indians 90–64 at .584. The White Sox finished third at 88–64 and .579. Because the Tigers' one rainout might have made a difference, the league adopted a rule for 1909 that required teams to play all games that would have an impact on the final standings.

The White Sox lost their second to last game of the season to the Indians on a perfect game by Addie Joss. Chicago's Ed Walsh struck out 15 in eight innings in the 1–0 loss. The run scored on a 3rd inning spitball that the catcher missed for a passed ball.

National League. This was the famous Merkle Boner season (see **Base Running**). A few days before the end of the season, Fred Merkle of the Giants failed to touch second base against the Cubs, turning victory into a tie to be replayed at the end of the season, if needed. After the Merkle game the Giants lost five more games to tighten up the race, with Harry Coveleski of the Phillies beating them three times in the week after the Merkle game (he won only four Major League games that year). The Giants swept the Braves in their last three games to preserve a tie with the Cubs and set up the final make-up game to determine the pennant winner.

The October 8 make-up game created a huge baseball frenzy. Cubs pitcher Three Finger Brown replaced Jack Pfeister after only one-third of an inning and beat the Giants 4–2. If the Giants had lost their last game before the replay and then defeated the Cubs, there would have been a three-way tie with the Pirates.

There was another key incident late in the season involving umpire Hank O'Day, who was also involved in the Merkle incident. The Pirates were losing to the Cubs 2–0 in the 9th inning, but had the bases loaded. Ed Abbaticchio of the Pirates hit an apparent grand slam, but O'Day called it a **Foul Ball**. The Cubs went on to win, with Three Finger Brown getting the victory. Had the Pirates won, they would have won the pennant with a 99–55 record, one better than the Cubs and Giants. Instead, the final standings were:

Chicago	99–55
New York	98–56
Pittsburgh	98–56

1914.

National League.

"Oct. 9, 1914, when the lowly, despised Boston Braves wallowed, humbled, trampled, laughed at the lofty Athletics to the tune of 7 to 1." — Sportswriter Lloyd Lewis during the World Series, which the Braves swept over the heavily favored A's.

The "Miracle Braves" were in last place on July 14. The team got out of the cellar on July 19 with three runs in the 9th inning and never looked back. Boston won 17 of 19 games from September 10 through September 28 and clinched the pennant the next day, finishing the season at 94–59, 10½ ahead of New York. Their record over the final 89 games was a phenomenal 70–19 (.787).

1915.

National League. The Phillies had the all-time lowest winning percentage for a pennant winner before divisional play at .592 (90–62) and the last-place Giants had the best record of any last place club in Major League history. The Phillies won the pennant by seven games over the Dodgers.

Federal League. On the last day of the season the Chicago Whales lost the first game of a doubleheader to Pittsburgh 5–4. Chicago won the second game 4–3. Because St. Louis lost on the last day, Chicago barely finished in first place based on winning percentage:

Chicago Whales	86–66	.5658
St. Louis Terriers	87–67	.5649
Pittsburgh Rebels	86–67	.5621

The Terriers are the only team in Major League history to finish with more wins than the pennant winner; the league did not require rainouts to be made up.

1916.

National League. On the last day of the season the Dodgers won and the Phillies lost two to the Braves, giving the Dodgers the pennant with a 94–60 record. The Phillies finished 91–62.

1920.

American League.

"I slept a real sleep last night for the first time in many a night. When I wasn't lying awake thinking and planning and fighting over that furious pennant race, I was dreaming restless dreams about it."—Smoky Joe Wood, on the Cleveland Indians' 1920 pennant race.

The Indians finished only two games up on the White Sox and three games up on the Yankees.

1921.

American League. Late in the season, the Indians were one game behind the Yankees when the clubs started a four-game series. The Yankees won the first two games and the Indians won the third. A victory by the Yankees would virtually clinch the pennant. Manager Miller Huggins was unsure whether to use Waite Hoyt on two days' rest or the aging Jack Quinn, so he let them choose. Quinn started and was ineffective, but Hoyt replaced him and pitched strongly. In the 9th inning the Yankees were leading 8–7 but the Indians had the bases loaded with two out. On a full count, Steve O'Neill struck out to end the game. The win put the Yankees three games up with only one series to play and they quickly clinched.

National League. In late August the Pirates were up by 7½ games over the Giants when the clubs met for a five-game series. The Giants swept and went on to win the pennant by four games.

1922.

American League. The Yankees won the pennant by one game over the Browns, who swept their last three games but could not catch up.

1924.

American League. The Yankees won 18 of 22 in the stretch run but could not catch the Senators, who took the lead in the last week of August and held on to win by two games.

National League. The Giants had dominated the league over the previous three seasons, but the Dodgers made a run at the flag. On September 22 the Giants were at .601 and the Dodgers at .600, but the Dodgers faded over the next few games and the Giants won by 1½ games.

1925.

American League. In a key late season game, the eventual champion Senators were playing the second-place A's. Late in the game a ball was hit hard up the middle and caromed off the shin of Senators pitcher Win Ballou into a key double play. The Senators won the game and the A's faded badly after that, finishing 8½ games out.

1928.

American League. The Yankees were up by 17 games early in the season, but the A's came back to take the lead on September 8. The next day the Yankees swept the A's in a doubleheader in New York and went on to clinch on September 28, finishing 2½ games ahead.

1930.

National League. The Cardinals were down by 12 games on August 9 to the Dodgers but won the pennant by two games. The Dodgers lost 19 of 27 to fall to fourth place but then won 11 straight games to take a one game lead over the Cardinals with 10 games left. The Cubs were only 1½ games back and the Giants 5½ games back.

The Cardinals won six of their last seven games and the Dodgers faded to fourth as the Cubs finished second. The Cardinals won 39 of their last 49.

1934.

National League.

"Is Brooklyn still in the league?"—Giants manager Bill Terry when asked before the season how he thought Brooklyn would do that season. His club would lose the pennant on the last weekend of the season because of a loss to the Dodgers. According to Lee Allen in *Kings of the Diamond* (1965), Terry had heard nothing out of the Brooklyn front office over the winter, and "he asked the question in order to determine whether the Dodgers were engaged in any activity."

The Cardinals moved into a first-place tie with the Giants going into the last weekend of the season against the Reds. On the Friday night of the last series, Dizzy Dean pitched on two days' rest to win his 29th game, a 4–0 shutout of the Reds. That left the Cardinals in a tie with the Giants, who beat the Dodgers that day.

On Saturday Paul Dean pitched the Cardinals to a 6–1 win over the Reds and the Dodgers defeated the Giants 5–1 to give the Cardinals a one-game lead over the Giants with one game remaining.

On Sunday the Cardinals defeated the Reds 9–0 to clinch. Dizzy Dean pitched on one day's rest for his 30th victory, another complete game. The Giants lost to the Dodgers 8–5 in 10 innings after leading 4–0 in the 1st inning.

Some sources have erroneously suggested that Terry's comments about the Dodgers came closer in time to the last series in which the Dodgers defeated the Giants to end their pennant chances. During that series, visiting Dodger fans carried banners that said, "Yes, we're still in the League!" The Dodger victory prompted the following from writer Dan Daniel in *The Sporting News* of October 4, 1934: "He meant no ill, he meant no offense. He wisecracked, 'Is Brooklyn still in the league?' Well, Brooklyn got sore. It took umbrage. When Brooklyn takes umbrage, it takes it heavier than any other center in baseball."

1935.

National League.

"Hang up the warning signs in the Detroit jungleland. The rampaging Cubs are on their way with leveled sights that seem as if they can't miss. Rising to the crest of baseball greatness and crushing even the mighty Dizzy Dean with a devastating 15-hit barrage, the sensational men of Grimm capped their almost unbelievable drive today by battering the Cardinals 6 to 2 for their 20th straight victory and the National League pennant."—An Associated Press account of the Cubs' streak.

The Cubs were in fourth place at the All-Star break on July 8 with a 40–32 record, 10½ games behind the first place Giants. By September 2 (Labor Day) they were not much better, but the club reeled off 21 straight (with no ties) through the third-to-last game of the season. They won the pennant by four games.

1938.

National League.

"And Big Gabby connected. The North Side idol slammed the ball into the umpteenth row of the left field bleachers in a Frank Merriwell finish that virtually clinched the bunting."—The *Stars and Stripes* military newspaper in September 1945 on Hartnett's "Homer in the Gloamin'."

Going into the second-to-last series of the season, the Pirates held a 1½ game lead over the Cubs. The Pirates had led most of the season, but faltered in the last few weeks. In the first game of the late-season series between the top two clubs, sore-armed Dizzy Dean pitched the Cubs to a 2–1 victory over the Pirates to put the Cubs behind by only one-half game.

In the second game, on September 28, 1938, catcher Gabby Hartnett hit his famous home run at Wrigley Field to give the Cubs a 6–5 win over the Pirates. The home run was off a two-out, 2–2 pitch by Mace Brown in virtual darkness. It broke a 5–5 tie in the 9th inning to give Charlie Root the victory. The umpires had already agreed that this would be the last inning. It was the first time the Cubs had been in the lead since July 12. They hung on through their last four games to win the pennant by two games. The Cubs won 30 of 42 to close the season, while the Pirates were 20–24.

1939.

National League. The Reds defeated the Cardinals 5–3 in the fourth-to-last game of the season, giving the club a 3½ game lead over the Cardinals with three games to play. Paul Derringer won his 25th game that day. See also Lawrence S. Katz, *Baseball in 1939: The Pivotal Season of the National Pastime* (1995).

1940.

American League. The league-leading Tigers arrived in Cleveland to play the second-place Indians needing one win in their last three games to clinch the pennant. Tigers manager Del Baker polled his players for their choice of starting pitchers in the first game of the series. Hank Greenberg and other key players selected Hal Newhouser or Fred Hutchinson. Nevertheless, Baker decided on little-used Floyd Giebell against Bob Feller in the first game to save his best two pitchers for the last two games.

Giebell shut out the Indians and Feller on September 27, 1940. Feller pitched a three-hitter, but Rudy York hit a two-run homer for the Tigers to give the club a 2–0 victory and the pennant. It was one of only three wins in Giebell's Major League career.

1941.

National League. The Dodgers edged out the Cardinals by 2½ games. The Dodgers split a doubleheader on the Sunday before the final two games of the season. The Cardinals won to remain in the race and the Dodgers moved on to face the Braves. The Dodgers swept the short series, and the Cardinals lost their games to give the Dodgers the pennant. See also Robert W. Creamer, *Baseball in 1941* (1991).

1942.

National League. In mid–August the Dodgers were leading the league by 10½ games, but the Cardinals narrowed the lead and then overtook them. On the second-to-last day of the season, the Cardinals led by 1½ games and were scheduled to play a doubleheader. The Cardinals had won nine of 10 and the Dodgers had won seven straight. The Cardinals won their first game 9–2, while the Dodgers won their game 4–3. The Cardinals then won the second game 4–1 to clinch the pennant.

The Cardinals took 43 of their last 51 to win the pennant by two games. They were 21–4 in September while the Dodgers had to settle for second place with a 20–5 record during the month.

1944.

American League. From June 1 to September 4 the Browns led the league, but then the Yankees moved into first place and everyone thought the Browns would fade. Four teams were in contention in mid–September as the Browns, Tigers and Red Sox were all within three games of the Yankees. The Red Sox faded as the World War II draft hurt the team more than others. The Yankees began to fade and were three games out with four to play. This left the Tigers and Browns to fight it out over the last weekend.

The Browns trailed the Tigers by one game and were to play the Yankees in St. Louis. The Tigers hosted the Senators, who had lost 15 of their last 18 against the Tigers.

Thursday's games were all rained out. In Friday's doubleheaders, the Tigers won the opener 5–2 and then Tiger ace pitcher Dizzy Trout was bombed 9–2. The Browns swept the Yankees 4–1 and 1–0 to move into a tie. On Saturday the Tigers won 7–3 behind

MVP pitcher Hal Newhouser. The Browns won 2–0, leaving the clubs in a tie.

On Sunday, Tiger ace Dizzy Trout made his third start in six days (en route to a 27–14 record). Dutch Leonard started for the Senators even though he had not defeated the Tigers in seven starts going back to 1941. He broke the streak with a 4–1 victory, putting the Tigers one-half game back. Detroit fans stayed in the park to listen to inning-by-inning reports from New York.

The Browns clinched by defeating the Yankees 5–2 with pitcher Sig Jakucki on the mound. Jakucki, a notorious drinker who "somewhat" laid off the booze the night before, had retired eight years earlier with an 0–3 record, but came back to post decent numbers in 1944 (13–9) after coming out of the military. He had been recruited in the spring of 1944 from a Texas shipyard team.

The Browns became the last National or American League team to win its first pennant before expansion in the 1960s. They were almost the first team in history to win without a .300 hitter or a 20-game winner, as Mike Kreevich hit only .301 to lead the club.

1945.

American League.

"We're not holding it against you for failing to field that fly ball in Philadelphia, but we expect you to be more consistent next season."— Senators management when it presented Bingo Binks with a $1,000 year-end bonus for his stellar play as a rookie; despite a crucial error in a late-season game.

In a mid–September series between the contending Tigers and Senators, the Tigers won three of four to go ahead by 2½ games. The Senators closed the gap slightly, but a week before the season ended for other clubs, the Senators played their last games. Before the season, owner Clark Griffith assumed his club would be out of the race and rented the stadium to the Washington Redskins for football practice for the entire last week of the baseball season.

For the Senators it came down to a final doubleheader one week early against the A's in Philadelphia. In the first game the Senators were leading 3–0 in the 8th inning, but the A's tied the game after scoring three unearned runs. The crucial error was called by umpire Eddie Rommel on a supposedly dropped fly ball by outfielder Buddy Lewis. Lewis caught the ball and was underhanding it to a nearby infielder when it caught on his baggy pants leg and rolled on the ground. The crowd roared and the umpire turned to see the ball on the ground and called an error. In the 11th inning the sun came out and A's outfielder Sam Chapman called for his sunglasses. In the 12th inning with two outs, A's outfielder Ernie Kish hit a fly ball to Bingo Binks in centerfield, who had neglected to put on sunglasses. He staggered under the ball, dropped it, and George Kell scored the winning run.

The Senators won the second game of the day to finish out their season but had to wait a few days for the Tigers to complete their season. Because the Senators were unable to sweep the A's, the Tigers needed only to win one of two in their final series.

On September 30, 1945, the Tigers played a doubleheader with the Browns after it had rained for three days. One source reported ten days of rain, but this was probably confused with the fact that the Senators had ended their season a week early.

Hank Greenberg, just back from the war, hit a one-out grand slam in the 9th inning to win the first game 6–3, erasing a 3–2 deficit and giving the Tigers the pennant. The unnecessary second game was conveniently rained out after the Tigers batted in the 1st inning.

National League.

"They were dusting off the National League cameras yesterday in anticipation of another of those famous photo finishes after the

Cardinals got through sweeping their three-game series with the tired Cubs…" — The *Stars and Stripes* military newspaper in August 1945.

The Cubs were 1½ games up on the Cardinals with six to play. The Cubs split two at St. Louis and then swept consecutive doubleheaders against the Reds and Pirates. The Cubs clinched the pennant on the arm of reliever Paul Erickson. With two out and two men on and a one-run lead, he threw an 0–1 pitch over the head of Pittsburgh batter Tommy O'Brien. O'Brien ducked and the pitch hit his bat for a foul ball on what otherwise would have been a wild pitch to score the tying run. The next pitch was a curveball for a strikeout and the pennant-clinching win. The Cubs won the pennant by three games over the Cardinals.

1946.

National League. The Cardinals and Dodgers were tied with 73–45 records on August 25, but the Cardinals took the lead on August 28. On September 12, the Dodgers trailed by 1½ games. With three games to play, the Cardinals were up by a game. On September 27 the Cardinals went back into a tie after losing to the Cubs. On September 28 both clubs won as the Dodgers defeated the Braves 7–4, and the Cardinals defeated the Cubs 4–1.

On the last day of the season, the Dodgers lost to the Braves 4–0 and the Cardinals lost to the Cubs 8–3, setting up the first *Play-Off* in National League history. The Cardinals defeated the Dodgers 2–0 in the best-of-three series.

1948.

American League. The Indians were 1½ games up on the Red Sox and Yankees going into the last day of the season. The Indians faced the Tigers and the Yankees and Red Sox met in a doubleheader. The Indians had to lose and either the Yankees or Red Sox needed to sweep to force a play-off. It happened.

Bob Feller and the Indians cooperated by losing 7–1 to Hal Newhouser, who won his 21st. At the same time, the Red Sox swept the Yankees 5–1 and 10–5 to tie the Indians. After a coin toss put the one-game *Play-Off* in Boston, the Indians won the pennant on the following Monday afternoon. See David E. Kaiser, *Epic Season: The 1948 American League Pennant Race* (1998).

1949. This was the first time since 1908 that each league's pennant race was decided on the last day of the season. See also David Halberstam, *Summer of '49* (1989).

American League. In Casey Stengel's first season as Yankee manager, the Red Sox and Yankees entered the final weekend with the Red Sox up by a game. Two games were left to be played in New York. On Saturday the Yankees overcame a 4–0 deficit to win 5–4 on Johnny Lindell's home run. On Sunday New York's Vic Raschi pitched a shutout for eight innings before the Yankees scored four runs in the 8th inning and went on to win 5–3.

National League. The Dodgers trailed the Cardinals by one-half game with four to play, but the Dodgers swept a doubleheader and the Cardinals lost to the Phillies to give the Dodgers a one game lead. Both clubs lost the next day, setting up a final day showdown. The Cardinals did their part by beating the Cubs 13–5, but the Dodgers beat the Phillies 9–7 in 10 innings to clinch (blowing a 5–0 lead in the process). Rookie Jack Banta went the last four innings for the Dodger victory.

1950.

National League. The Phillies had an eight-game lead with 10 days left but were only one game up on the last day when they played the second-place Dodgers. Dick Sisler won the game and the pennant for the Phillies with a three-run homer on a 1–2 pitch in the top of the 10th inning. The Dodgers went out in order in the bottom of the inning to end the game.

The Dodgers should have won the game in the bottom of the 9th inning to set up a play-off. With the game tied, the Dodgers had Cal Abrams on second base with no outs after he walked, and then Pee Wee Reese singled. With Duke Snider at the plate, the Phillies catcher supposedly called for a pick-off throw to second. Reacting to the sign, center fielder Richie Ashburn moved in close behind second base. Pitcher Robin Roberts did not see the sign and pitched to Snider, who singled to center. Ashburn was playing so close in that he was able to throw out Abrams at the plate by five feet, preserving the tie for the moment.

Abrams had hesitated, thinking the second baseman might catch the line drive (described as a ground ball in some sources). Abrams also made a wide turn around third, which added extra steps. Dodger manager Burt Shotten later was criticized for not replacing the slow Abrams with the much faster Eddie Miksis. Perhaps not coincidentally, Shotten and third base coach Milt Stock were fired after the season. According to Abrams, Stock gave a half-hearted and confusing "run" sign to Abrams as he approached third, so Abrams continued around the bag.

Roberts later claimed that there was no pick-off called (he may have missed the sign) and that Ashburn was moving in to back up a throw to second on an anticipated bunt. Ashburn claimed that he was simply playing close in because of a sore arm suffered early in the season.

After the play at the plate and with runners on second and third with only one out, Roberts intentionally walked Jackie Robinson to load the bases. Carl Furillo popped out and Gil Hodges flied to right fielder Del Ennis near the wall. Ennis lost the ball in the sun but caught it against his chest to end the threat.

1951.

National League.

"The Giants is dead." — Supposedly said by Dodger manager Charlie Dressen when his club was up by 13½ games in August. What he may have said after a Dodger victory over the Giants in August: "We knocked them out; they'll never bother us again."

On August 11 the Dodgers led by 13½ games, but the Giants put together a 16-game winning streak that cut the lead by five games. The Dodgers then lost 10 straight games through September 20, but the Giants were still six games out. By September 26 the Giants were one game out as the Dodgers continued to fall apart. Both clubs won that day, but on September 27 the Giants were idle as the Dodgers lost 4–3 to the Phillies. The game was marked by a controversial call that caused Roy Campanella to be thrown out of the game and the Dodger bench to be cleared by the umpires. The Dodgers lost in the 9th inning to the Phillies in the first game of the final series of the season. The Dodgers and Giants were tied at 94–58 with two games to play.

On Saturday Giants pitcher Sal Maglie shut out the Braves 3–0. That night Dodger pitcher Don Newcombe shut out the Phillies to maintain the tie.

On the last day the Giants defeated the Braves 3–2 and then waited for the Dodgers' results against the Phillies. For the third straight year the Dodgers and Phillies played extra innings on the last day of the season to decide the National League pennant.

The Dodgers fell behind 8–5 in the 5th inning but caught up to force the game into extra innings. In the bottom of the 12th inning with the bases loaded, Phillies first baseman Eddie Waitkus hit a line drive up the middle for the apparent game-winner that would give the Giants the pennant. A Western Union operator reportedly thought that the ball had dropped in and the game was over, so he sent a premature message over the wire. However, Dodger second baseman Jackie Robinson snagged the drive barely off the ground to preserve the tie, knocking the wind out of himself as his elbow jammed his midsection. In the top of the 14th inning, he hit a home run off Robin Roberts for a 9–8 victory and a tie with the Giants that set up the famous *Play-Off* series.

When Robinson snagged the liner, Phillies pitcher Robin Roberts was on third base with the potential winning run. He later swore that Robinson trapped the ball; otherwise, he argues, why would Robinson have flipped the ball to second base in an apparent attempt at a force play when his alleged catch was the third out? Frank Graham, Jr., described it differently in *Farewell to Heroes* (1984): "It was one of the most thrilling moments I had experienced in sports, as I watched Robinson lying motionless on the grass, the other players rushing toward him (Reese arriving first), and then the umpires and players rolling him over — and there was the ball, still clutched tightly in his glove."

Much of the Giants' success was attributed to moves by manager Leo Durocher earlier in the season. On May 21 he moved Whitey Lockman to first base and he brought up Willie Mays on May 25. On July 20 he switched Bobby Thomson to third base and Don Mueller took sole possession of right field when a platoon experiment failed. The Giants won 37 of their last 44, 12 of their last 13 and seven in a row.

See also Harvey Rosenfeld, *The Great Chase: The Dodgers–Giants Pennant Race of 1951* (1992); Bobby Thomson with Lee Heiman and Bill Gutman, *The Giants Win the Pennant! The Giants Win the Pennant!* (1991).

1956.

National League. The Braves were one game up over the Dodgers with three to play. The Dodgers were at Pittsburgh for three games and the Braves were at St. Louis. On Friday the Dodgers were rained out and the Braves lost 5–4 to cut their lead to one-half game. On Saturday the Dodgers swept a doubleheader and the Braves lost to the Cardinals 2–1 in 11 innings as Herm Wehmeier got the win for St. Louis. This put the Dodgers up by a game.

The Dodgers clinched on the final day of the season by defeating the Pirates 8–6 to complete a three-game sweep. Don Bessent saved the game for starter Don Newcombe as the Dodgers hit five home runs. The Braves defeated the Cardinals 4–2, but it was too late. The Reds finished only two games back.

1957.

National League. On September 23, the Braves defeated the Cardinals to go up by six games over the Cardinals with five to play. Henry Aaron hit a two-run home run in the 11th inning to clinch the pennant. It was the 109th home run of his career and the one he considered most significant.

1959.

National League. With eight games left the Dodgers and Braves were two games behind the Giants, who were trying to decide whether to open Candlestick Park early or continue using smaller Seals Stadium for the last few games. The Giants began to fade, but on the final Saturday San Francisco's Sad Sam Jones pitched a no-hitter to put the Giants one-half game behind the Dodgers and Braves.

On the last day of the season the Cardinals swept the Giants 2–1 and 14–8 to knock San Francisco out of the race. This left the Dodgers and Braves to fight it out.

The Dodgers played the Cubs in Wrigley Field and Chicago had a number of injured infielders. When Dodger shortstop Don Zimmer rolled a ground ball near second base late in the game, catcher Earl Averill was playing second. The ball rolled between him and the first baseman and the Dodgers took the lead for good, winning

7–1. The Braves kept pace by winning their game a half hour later, defeating the Phillies 5–2. The two clubs then moved to a three-game *Play-Off*, which the Dodgers won in two straight.

1961.

National League. On September 26 the Reds clinched the pennant by defeating the Cubs as the Dodgers were splitting a doubleheader with the Pirates. The Reds ended up four games ahead of the Dodgers.

1962.

National League. The Dodgers had lost 9 of 12 going into the last day of the season. They were still one game up on the Giants, who had gone 6–6. The Dodgers lost to the Cardinals 1–0, the last of four straight losses, and the Giants defeated the Astros 2–1 to earn a tie. This set up a three-game *Play-Off* won by the Giants. See also David Plaut, *Chasing October: The Dodgers-Giants Pennant Race of 1962* (1994).

1963.

National League. The Cardinals won 19 of 20 near the end of the season to move into contention with the Dodgers, but a series in mid–September was crucial. The Cardinals had concluded their streak and had lost the first two games of the series against the Dodgers, including the 11th shutout of the season by Sandy Koufax. The final game of the series was on September 18 and the Cardinals were leading 5–1 with Bob Gibson pitching in the 8th inning. The Dodgers scored three runs and then rookie Dick Nen, in only his second Major League at-bat, homered off Ron Taylor to tie the game at five. The Dodgers won 6–5 in 13 innings and the Cardinals fell four back and lost the pennant by six games. Nen's entire career with the Dodgers lasted seven games and he had only the one hit (see *World Series* — **Player Shares** for Nen's reward).

1964.

American League. The Yankees won the pennant by one game over the White Sox after winning 30 of their last 40. On September 17 the Orioles and White Sox were tied, with the Yankees one-half game back. Both the Orioles and White Sox went into a tailspin and a week later the Yankees were ahead of both clubs by four games. The Yankees finished the season 19–3 and clinched before the final series of the season.

National League.

"I had a commitment to his heart." — Cardinals manager Johnny Keane on why he left in a worn-out Bob Gibson in the late innings of the pennant-clinching game on the last day of the season.

The Phillies were 6½ games up on September 21, but with with 12 games left they lost 10 in a row in one of the most famous collapses in history. Manager Gene Mauch was criticized for using starters Jim Bunning and Chris Short so frequently over the last few games when third starter Dennis Bennett was injured. The Phillies started the losing streak when Reds infielder Chico Ruiz stole home to win the game 1–0. The Reds won two more from the Phillies for a three-game sweep. That was followed by four- and three-game sweeps by the Braves and Cardinals. The awful late September chronology, with dates, scores and Phillies starters noted:

21	Reds	1–0	Mahaffey
22	Reds	9–2	Short
23	Reds	6–4	Bennett
24	Braves	5–3	Bunning
25	Braves	7–5	Short
26	Braves	6–4	Mahaffey
27	Braves	14–8	Bunning
28	Cardinals	5–1	Short
29	Cardinals	4–2	Bennett
30	Cardinals	8–5	Bunning

The losing streak left four teams in contention: the Phillies, Cardinals, Reds and Giants. The Giants were eliminated on the next-to-last day. The Phillies won their next-to-last game against the Reds as Short pitched on three days rest.

On the last day the Cardinals and Reds were tied, with the Phillies one back. The Cardinals defeated the Mets 11–5 and clinched when the Phillies defeated the Reds 10–0. If the Mets had won, there would have been the first three-way tie in history at 92–70. See also David Halberstam, *October, 1964* (1994).

1965.

National League. The Giants were up by 3½ over the Dodgers and Reds with less than two weeks to play. When the Braves snapped the Giants' 14-game winning streak the Giants began to slide and with two games left in the season the Dodgers were up by two games. The Giants defeated the Reds 3–2 but the Dodgers clinched by defeating the Braves 3–1 as Sandy Koufax won his 26th. He pitched a complete game and recorded his then-league record 382nd strikeout of the season.

1966.

National League. On September 11 the Pirates led the Dodgers and Giants by a small margin. The Dodgers then swept a series and the Pirates lost, allowing the Dodgers to move into first place with the Giants right behind them. The race was still undecided on the next-to-last day of the season. The Dodgers were rained out while the Giants swept the Pirates, putting the Giants two games out and eliminating the Pirates. If the Giants won their game on the last day and the Dodgers were swept in their doubleheader, the Giants would be one-half game behind and would play a make-up game on Monday against the Reds.

The Giants did their part by defeating the Pirates 7–3 in 11 innings. Dodger pitcher Don Drysdale lost to the Phillies 4–3 in the first game of the doubleheader on two errors in the 8th inning.

In the second game the Dodgers clinched the pennant when Sandy Koufax, pitching on two days' rest for the first time all year, won 6–3 after giving up three runs in the 9th inning.

1967.

American League.

"The Impossible Dream" — Description of Boston's improbable pennant, as the club started the season at 100–1 odds after finishing ninth the previous year.

On September 2 the Red Sox led by one-half game over the Twins, two over the Tigers and 2½ over the White Sox. The situation became no clearer through the rest of the month.

Going into the the last weekend there was a possible three-way tie between two sets of teams and a possible two-way tie between four sets of teams among the Twins, Tigers, White Sox and Red Sox. After the Friday night games, the Red Sox were tied for second with the Tigers, one game behind the Twins, as the White Sox were eliminated.

The Twins were at Boston and needed to win one of two over the weekend to clinch. The Red Sox defeated the Twins 6–4 in the first game, while the Tigers split a doubleheader with the Angels when Detroit ace Denny McLain gave up six runs in the 8th inning and the Angels won 8–6. This left the Twins and Red Sox tied, with the Tigers one-half game back with a doubleheader on the last day; two clubs could finish tied.

The Twins could have won it outright with a win against the Red Sox. The Twins were leading 2–0 behind Dean Chance, but the Red Sox scored five runs in the 6th inning for a 5–3 victory to eliminate the Twins. The Red Sox would clinch unless the Tigers could sweep a doubleheader against the Angels and finish in a tie.

The Tigers won the first game 6–4 but lost the second game 8–5.

Dick McAuliffe ended the game by grounding into his only double play of the season. The Detroit fans responded by destroying seats and the field. The Red Sox finished one game ahead of both the Twins and Tigers.

Carl Yastrzemski batted .522 over the last two weeks of the season, going 23-for-44 with four doubles, five home runs and 16 RBIs. The *Boston Record* newspaper celebrated the pennant with a full front page picture of two red socks: no headline, caption or story.

1969.

National League East.

"The Miracle Mets"

The Cubs were leading the Mets by 9½ games on August 13. By August 24 the Mets were only five games out as the Cubs had lost eight while the Mets won seven. The Mets then won 10 in a row and had a two-game lead, moving into first place for the first time in franchise history on September 10. The 10-game streak included a win over Steve Carlton in which he struck out a record 19, but lost 4–3 on two Ron Swoboda home runs. The Mets then twice defeated the Pirates 1–0, as pitchers Jerry Koosman and Don Cardwell drove in the winning runs in each game. The Mets eventually pulled away from the Cubs and won the division by eight games.

The Mets were 34–10 to end the season and clinched on September 24. Tom Seaver won his last 10 games and Jerry Koosman eight of nine.

The previous season the Mets had finished only one game out of last place. The Mets won the division despite finishing ninth or worse the previous seven seasons. See also Stanley Cohen, *A Magic Summer* (1988); Rick Talley, *The Cubs of 1969* (1989).

National League West. The Braves won 17 of their last 20, including 10 in row near the end of that streak, clinching on September 30 with a 3–2 over the Reds. The Braves finished three games ahead of the Giants and four games ahead of the Reds.

1971.

National League West.

"The Dodgers can go to hell." — Giants catcher Dick Dietz, taking the on-field microphone after the Giants defeated the Padres to edge the Dodgers by one game on the last day of the season. Going into the last week of the season, the Dodgers trailed the Giants by one game. They still trailed by a game on the last day. The Dodgers beat the Astros 2–1, but it was not enough. The Giants and Juan Marichal beat the Padres 5–1 to clinch. The Giants had led since April 12 but won only eight of their last 24. In the final week, Marichal and Gaylord Perry combined for five wins to hold off the Dodgers.

1972.

American League East. The Red Sox came into Detroit for their final three-game series up by one-half game over the Tigers. The Tigers won the opener 4–1 to go ahead by one-half game and then clinched the division on the next-to-last day with a 3–1 victory over the Red Sox. The Red Sox won on the last day to finish one-half game behind. A brief player strike at the beginning of the season eliminated a few games that were never made up, enabling the Tigers to be the first team in many years to win a pennant based on winning percentage.

1973.

National League West. The Reds were at one point down 11 games to the Dodgers but came back to win by four.

National League East.

"Ya Gotta Believe." — Mets reliever Tug McGraw.

The Mets were in last place on August 30 when McGraw started his "Ya Gotta Believe!" slogan and the Mets caught fire. The slogan supposedly was McGraw's way of mocking a clubhouse speech by owner Donald Grant. Other sources reported that McGraw was having lunch with friends when his confidence level was low and they encouraged him to believe in himself. On the way to the ballpark he began chanting his new mantra all the way into the clubhouse. Regardless of its origin, McGraw went on to record 11 saves and four wins during September.

The Mets were 5½ games out to start the final month and slowly moved up through a tight pack of teams. They were 2½ out and in fourth place on September 12 and reached the .500 mark on September 21 at 77–77. That mediocre record gave the Mets a one-half game lead with one week left.

With five games to go, the Mets had a 1½ game lead on Willie Mays Retirement Night. They lost, enabling the Pirates and Cardinals to move one-half game behind with four to play.

The Mets' last series with the Cubs was to include a Sunday doubleheader. On the previous Thursday, the Pirates lost to fall one game back and the Cardinals were idle to remain one-half game out. The Mets were rained out on Friday and the Pirates lost again to fall 1½ out. The Cardinals lost Friday and Saturday to fall 1½ out in the loss column. The Mets' Saturday doubleheader (make-up for Friday included) was rained out also. This left the Mets with four games to play with only one official day left in the season. A make-up doubleheader would be played on Monday if needed. Their records at that point:

Mets   80–78
Cardinals   80–81

On Sunday the Mets lost the first game of their doubleheader to the Cubs as the Cardinals won 3–1 to finish the season at 81–81 and one-half game behind. The Mets won the second game 9–2 behind Jerry Koosman for a one game lead. The Mets needed to win one of the two Monday make-up games to clinch. It rained during the first game, but Tom Seaver and Tug McGraw combined for a 6–4 win. The Mets finished at 82–79 to win by 1½ games (the second game was not played). The Mets won 20 of their last 28, but their .509 winning percentage was the lowest ever for a championship team.

1974.
American League East. The Orioles won 27 of their last 33 to clinch the pennant. The Red Sox led by eight games in September, but faded badly and finished seven games out. The Yankees came on to finish only two games out.

1978.
American League East.
"Never sell the Yankees short. They played great the last three months. They'll never play that well again as long as they have assholes." — Red Sox coach Johnny Pesky on the Yankees' tremendous finish.

"Our pain isn't as bad as you might think. Dead people don't suffer." — Red Sox pitcher Bill Lee, whose team had blown six games against the Yankees late in the 1978 season.

The Yankees were in turmoil when Bob Lemon took over as manager in late July after George Steinbrenner fired Billy Martin. They were 14 games behind the Red Sox.

The Red Sox began to fade and the Yankees moved into a tie with 20 games to play. The Yankees took over first place in mid–September, but the Red Sox were not dead yet. They came back to win 10 of their last 12. On the last day of the season, the Red Sox were at 98–63 and the Yankees were one game up at 99–62. Luis Tiant and the Red Sox defeated the Blue Jays 5–0 and Rick Waits and the Indians defeated the Yankees 9–2. This created a season-ending tie and forced a one-game *Play-Off* won by the

Yankees 5–4. See Con Chapman, *The Year of the Gerbil: How the Yankees Won (and the Red Sox Lost) the Greatest Pennant Race Ever* (1998).

1979.
National League East. The Expos were in first place on September 24, but faded. The race was decided on the last day of the season when Phillies ace Steve Carlton shut out the Expos 2–0 and the Pirates beat the Cubs 5–3. The Expos were handicapped by eight doubleheaders in September. Even if the Expos had won, they would have had to fly to Atlanta, sweep a doubleheader and then return home for a *Play-Off* game against the Pirates.

1980.
National League East. The Phillies defeated the second-place Expos in the last series of the season to clinch the division title. On Friday night, October 3, Mike Schmidt hit his 47th home run to give the Phillies a 2–1 victory over the Expos. It put the Phillies two games up with two to play. On Saturday night Schmidt hit another home run, his fourth in four days. It allowed the Phillies to clinch the division with a 6–4 win in 11 innings. The Expos won on the last day to finish one game back.

1981. The two-month midseason player strike forced the leagues to create two half-seasons. The teams that were in first place when the strike started in May were retroactively declared the winners of the first half.

American League East (Second Half). The Brewers clinched the second half division crown on the day before the end of the season by defeating the Tigers 2–1.

1982.
National League West. The Braves started the season with 13 straight wins, but needed the Giants to beat the Dodgers on the last day of the season in Candlestick Park to capture the division. San Francisco's Joe Morgan hit an 8th inning home run off Terry Forster to sink the Dodgers. The Braves lost to the Padres to finish one game up on the Dodgers and two up on the Giants.

American League East. The Orioles and Brewers played a four-game series in Baltimore to finish the season. The Brewers were up by three games going in, but blew the lead after a doubleheader sweep by the Orioles on Friday and an 11–3 win by the Orioles on Saturday. Don Sutton and the Brewers recovered to take the last game to capture the division title. American League MVP Robin Yount hit two home runs and a triple in a 10–2 win. Orioles manager Earl Weaver retired after the game. The crowd cheered for a number of minutes after the game, and many of the players came back on the field in response.

1985.
National League East. The Mets were in first place on August 5, but the Cardinals came on strong to lead by a few games near the end of the season. On September 28 and 29, the Mets defeated the Pirates 3–1 and 9–7 in extra innings to remain down three games going into a three-game series against the Cardinals in the next-to-last series of the year.

In the first game Mets pitcher Ron Darling went 11 innings for a 1–0 win. In the second game Dwight Gooden of the Mets defeated Joaquin Andujar 5–2 to move within a game of the Cardinals. In the third game Rick Aguilera of the Mets lost 4–3 to put the Cardinals two games up.

In the first game of the final series of the year, the Mets beat the Expos 9–4, but the Cardinals beat the Cubs to clinch a tie. On Saturday the Cardinals defeated the Cubs 4–2 and the Expos defeated the Mets, clinching the division title for the Cardinals.

American League West. On September 21 the Angels led the Royals by one game and maintained that lead going into the final week. The Angels and Royals then had a showdown in which they split the first two games. In the third game, George Brett hit an inside-the-park three-run homer in the 1st inning to give the Royals a 4–0 lead that they never relinquished. In the fourth game, the Royals won 4–1 to take a one-game lead going into the final weekend.

The Angels went to Texas and the Royals hosted the A's. The Angels lost on Friday night and the Royals won, putting Kansas City up by two games with two to play. On Saturday the Angels kept their hopes alive by winning 3–1, but the Royals won with a run in the bottom of the 10th to beat the A's and clinch the division.

American League East. The Blue Jays held a 5½ game lead over the Yankees going into the final week. They collapsed before recovering to clinch the division. The Tigers swept three from the Blue Jays to reduce their lead to three going into the final weekend showdown between the Blue Jays and Yankees. The Yankees won 4–3 on Friday night on two runs in the 9th inning, but the Blue Jays won 5–1 on Saturday to clinch the division.

1987.

American League East. The Tigers beat out the Blue Jays by two games, with the pivotal game played on Sunday, September 27. Going into the game the Tigers trailed by 4½ games. The Tigers beat the Blue Jays 3–2 with a run in the 13th inning on a single by Kirk Gibson. Gibson had tied the game with a home run in the 9th inning and the Blue Jays could not score in the 11th inning after loading the bases.

The Blue Jays lost two games to start the final week and the Tigers won two. On Wednesday the Tigers and Blue Jays both lost. On Thursday the Orioles beat the Blue Jays to allow the Tigers to draw within one game of idle Toronto. That set up a final weekend showdown.

On Friday night the Tigers beat the Blue Jays to tie. On Saturday the Tigers won 4–3 in 12 innings to lead by a game. In that game, with the infield drawn in and the bases loaded, Tigers shortstop Alan Trammell hit a ground ball through the legs of shortstop Manny Lee. Lee had replaced the injured Tony Fernandez, who had a broken elbow. On the final day Frank Tanana and the Tigers shut out the Blue Jays and Jimmy Key to clinch. The Blue Jays lost seven straight to finish the season.

1988.

American League East. The Red Sox trailed by 9½ games at the All-Star break when they hired manager Joe Morgan. The team went 19–1 when Morgan took over from John McNamara and quickly wiped out the deficit. The Red Sox built a big lead but staggered home with 10 losses in their last 11 games to win the division by one game over the Tigers.

1990.

American League East.

"Like [Kevin] Romine and the rest of his teammates, the Red Sox survived their gut check late in the season and it turned out they had the anatomy of a winner." —1991 *Sporting News Baseball Guide.*

The Red Sox led by 6½ games on Labor Day after 10 straight wins, fell back to second place late in September, and recovered in the final week. With two games to play the Red Sox were two games up on the Blue Jays. The Blue Jays beat the Orioles 2–1 in 10 innings and the White Sox beat the Red Sox 3–2 in 11 innings to put the Blue Jays one game down with one to play. On the last day Red Sox pitcher Mike Boddicker beat the White Sox 3–1 to clinch as the Orioles beat the Blue Jay 3–2 with a run in the bottom of the 9th inning. That gave the Red Sox the division title by

two games. The Red Sox won their game on a throwing error by the White Sox pitcher during a rundown between home and third.

1991.

National League West. The Dodgers led most of the year before the Braves caught them with three weeks left in the season after trailing by 9½ games at the All-Star break. The teams seesawed over the next two weeks and went into the last week of the season with the Dodgers up a game after a miraculous win against the Giants. The Dodgers scored two runs in the 9th inning, with the tying run coming on a ground ball that was struck by a piece of broken bat after the bat glanced off third baseman Matt Williams. Meanwhile, the Braves won in 13 innings.

On October 1 the Braves rebounded from the Reds' six-run 1st inning to win on a David Justice two-run home run in the 9th inning for a 7–6 win.

On October 2 the Braves won again while the Dodgers lost to the Padres 9–3. This left the clubs tied going into the last series of the season.

The Dodgers lost on Friday night to their old nemesis, the Giants, in Candlestick Park. Playing at home, the Braves defeated the Astros to take a one-game lead. On Saturday, the Braves defeated the Astros and three minutes later the Dodgers lost to the Giants to give the Braves their first division title since 1982 — when the Giants knocked the Dodgers out of the race on the last day of the season.

1992.

American League East. The Blue Jays held off the hard-charging Brewers on the second-to-last day of the season. The Brewers were one game out starting the last three-game series of the season. On Friday night, the Blue Jays defeated the Tigers but could not clinch. Brewers center fielder Robin Yount made a diving 9th inning catch that saved the game and led to an extra-inning win in Oakland. The next day the Blue Jays held off the Tigers, and the A's crushed the Brewers to give the Blue Jays the division title.

1993.

National League West.

"Too Young v. Cy Young" — The Giants had led most of the season, were caught by the Braves late in September and then fought back to tie going into the last day. It was the 10th time in the 20th century that two clubs were deadlocked with one game to play. The clubs had won more games than any other pair of tied frontrunners, 103.

On the last day of the season the Giants and Braves were tied for first. Rookie Salomon Torres ("Too Young") started unsuccessfully for the Giants against the Dodgers, and former Cy Young Award winner Tom Glavine ("Cy Young") started successfully for the Braves against the Rockies. The Giants were battered by the Dodgers, and the Braves beat the Rockies for the 12th straight time that season. The Braves went 51–17 from July 31 to the end of the season.

1995.

"Forget the owners, forget the union activists, forget the Baseball Network, whatever that was. Remember that the game, if left alone long enough, can restore itself." — Steve Wulf in *Time* after the disastrous 1994–1995 player strike.

National League West. The Rockies were up by one-half game with a week to play but slipped behind the Dodgers. On Thursday before the final weekend the Rockies lost to the Giants 12–4 to put the Dodgers up by one game. The Rockies still led the Astros by a game for the wild card slot with the Rockies leading by a game. On Friday night both the Dodgers and Rockies lost, but on Saturday the Dodgers clinched with a win when the Rockies lost.

On Sunday the Rockies and Astros were still fighting for the wild card slot. The Astros beat the Cubs 8–7 to remain one-half game behind, but the Rockies came from four down to beat the Giants 10–9 and wrap up the wild card.

American League West. The Mariners were down 13 games on August 4 but rallied to tie the Angels on September 20 after the Angels suffered through two nine-game losing streaks. The clubs finished in a dead heat when the Angels won their last five games. The Mariners and Randy Johnson then beat the Angels in a one-game *Play-Off* for the division title. The Mariners won 17 of their final 22.

1996.

American League East. The Yankees held a commanding lead through most of the season, but Baltimore closed to within four games going into the last two weeks. The Orioles were behind by four games early in the final week when they lost on three home runs by Mo Vaughn of the Red Sox to end their shot at the East Division title. They finished four games out to the Yankees.

American League West. The Rangers were running away with the division title, leading by 10 games with less than three weeks to play. By the second-to-last weekend the lead was down to one game over the Mariners. The Rangers started the final week up by two over the Mariners and slowly pulled away to win by 4½ games.

National League Central. The Astros and Cardinals battled into the final two weeks, but the Astros went into a tailspin, losing 9 of 10 going into the last week. The Cardinals led by five with a week to play and clinched on Tuesday of the final week for their first title since 1987.

National League West. The Dodgers led the Padres by one-half game going into the final 10 games. The two clubs split a four-game series before going into the final week of play to maintain the one-half game spread. After a day off, the Dodgers beat their long-time rivals, the Giants, while the Padres lost at home to the Rockies on a Dante Bichette home run in extra innings. The Dodgers lost their next game to the Giants, putting them two games up with three to play against the Padres. San Diego won the first two games, though both clubs clinched a postseason spot when the Expos lost. On the last day of the season the Padres beat the Dodgers for a three-game sweep and the division title.

1997.

American League East. The Yankees won their last five games but couldn't catch the Orioles, who won the division by two games. The Yankees ended up as the wild card.

National League West. The Giants trailed the Dodgers by two games to start September, but by the 11th they were in first place. They faded to second four days later after a loss to the Braves in which Atlanta scored four in the 9th to beat ace reliever Rod Beck (capped by a two-run homer by Fred McGriff). Then they swept the Dodgers in a two-game showdown, winning 2–1 and 6–5 (in 12 innings) and never looked back.

1998.

National League Wild Card. On Wednesday, September 23, 1998, the Cubs lost 8–7 to the Brewers in a wild game that saw three runs score on a horrendous *Error* with two outs in the 9th. The loss left the Cubs tied with the Mets for the wild card spot and the Giants were close behind. The Mets and Cubs both lost on Friday to remain tied with the Giants. On Saturday the Giants beat the Rockies 8–4 to stay even with the Cubs, who beat the Astros 3–2. Denny Neagle of the Braves shut out the Mets, who fell a game behind.

On Sunday, the Mets lost to fall out of the race. Both the Giants and Cubs lost one-run heartbreakers, the Giants 9–8 to the Rock-ies and the Cubs 4–3 to the Astros in 11 innings, as ace reliever Rod Beck took the loss. This set up a one-game *Play-Off* the next day to determine the wild card winner, won by the Cubs.

1999.

National League Wild Card. The Reds had won six straight through Tuesday of the last week of the season, but lost on Wednesday, September 29, to go 95–64 heading into the weekend. The Mets lost seven straight through Tuesday of the last week. They split their next to games to go into the weekend at 93–66, two behind the Reds.

The Mets swept their series with the Pirates, culminating Sunday with a 2–1 win after a six-hour *Rain Delay* and a wild pitch with the bases loaded on the first pitch after resuming play. The Reds staggered through the weekend, losing two out of three to the Brewers to finish in a tie with the Mets. The Mets won the Monday *Play-Off*, 5–0. The Reds would not experience a *Shutout* again for 208 games until May 24, 2001.

2000.

American League Wild Card. Oakland and Seattle finished the season with 91 wins each, edging out the Indians for a postseason spot by one game. Going into the last three games, the Mariners were 88–71, the A's 88–70, and the Indians 87–72. The Mariners lost on Friday night 9–3 to the Angels, while both the Indians and A's were winners. Another loss by the Mariners and they would have been tied with the Indians. The A's had played one less game, so a loss by them would have forced them to play a make-up game on Monday. All three teams swept their games over the weekend, so the Indians finished a game behind with 90 wins.

National League East. The Mets won eight of their last nine games to finish one game behind the Braves, who had 96 wins. Atlanta staggered home by losing four of their last five. Despite coming in second, the Mets made it to the postseason as the wild card team.

2001.

National League Central. The Cardinals and Astros ended in a tie as Houston slumped in the last week, but the Astros were declared the wild card team and the Cardinals the division champion on the strength of their head-to-head record for the season.

National League West. The race was delayed a week because of the September 11 terrorist attacks. On Tuesday of the last week, the Diamondbacks pulled two games ahead of the Giants. On Friday, Arizona clinched a tie as the Giants lost an 11–10 heartbreaker to the Dodgers despite Barry Bonds' 71st and 72nd home runs in the longest nine inning game, by time, in Major League history. The Diamondbacks clinched on the final Saturday and finished two games up on the Giants.

2003.

National League Wild Card. The Marlins advanced as the wild card over the Phillies by winning 23 of 29 games near the end of the season. The key game was on the Tuesday before the end of the season. The Marlins capped a late five-run rally with a three-run homer by Jeff Conine to beat the Phillies 5–4, and Philadelphia collapsed after that.

National League Central. On September 23, Cubs pitcher Kerry Wood struck out 12 and beat the Reds 6–0 to put the Cubs in first place. It was the latest in a season that they had been in first since 1989, when they won the division title.

On September 26 the Cubs beat the Reds 8–0 and the Astros scored two in the 7th to beat the Giants 2–1 to remain in contention. The Astros then faded in the last few games and the Cubs clinched on the second to last day of the season.

2004.

American League West. The A's and Angels went into a showdown in the second-to-last weekend of the year, with the A's up two games over both the Angels and the surprising Rangers. The A's won on Friday night and Texas lost, putting the A's up by three games, but the Angels won the next two, leaving them a game out to start the final week, and Texas out by two. By Tuesday, the Angels had tied it up and put Texas three games back with an 8–2 win over the Rangers combined with an Oakland loss to the Mariners. Although the Angels took a one-game lead on Wednesday, they squandered it on Thursday, setting up a three-game showdown with the A's over the final weekend.

The Angels blew out the A's 10–0 on Friday night to go one game up. On Saturday the Angels were down 4–2 late in the game, but scored three in the 8th to win 5–4 and clinch the division title. The A's won 3–2 on the last day to finish one game out.

National League West. The Giants and Dodgers faced off on the second to last weekend with the Dodgers up by one-half game after blowing a seven game lead. Eric Gagne walked three in the 9th inning but held on for a 3–2 victory. They split the weekend games and the Dodgers began the final week up by 2½. The biggest blow by the Dodgers came on Tuesday, September 28, when they rallied for five runs in the 9th inning to beat the Rockies 5–4 and stay three games up on the Giants, who also won. On Thursday the Dodgers won in the 12th inning on a home run by struggling catcher David Ross, allowing the club to take a three-game lead into their final weekend series against, of course, the Giants. San Francisco won Friday night's game 4–2, and took a 3–0 lead into the 9th inning on Saturday. The Dodgers rallied for three runs and had the bases loaded when Steve Finley hit a grand slam for a 7–3 win to clinch the division title. The Giants crushed the Dodgers on Sunday to finish one game out.

National League Wild Card. With 12 games left the Giants and Cubs were tied and the Astros were 2½ games back. At the beginning of the final week, the Cubs led the Giants by ½ game, and the Astros were 1½ back. On Tuesday the Giants and Astros won, while the Cubs lost, putting the Giants and Cubs tied, with Houston a half-game back. The Cubs then lost five straight through Saturday of the last weekend to be eliminated. This created a potentially complicated three-way scenario with the Dodgers, Giants and Astros (if the Giants and Astros both swept their weekend series). It didn't happen, as the Dodgers won on Saturday to clinch the division, forcing the Astros and Giants into deciding Sunday games to determine the wild card.

The Astros went into the last day with a one game lead over the Giants, and both clubs had their aces on the mound: Jason Schmidt against the Dodgers and Roger Clemens against the Rockies. Clemens contracted a stomach virus the night before and was a late scratch. Nevertheless, the Astros beat the Rockies 5–3 to clinch the wild card by one game over the Giants.

Books. Dave Anderson, *Pennant Races: Baseball at Its Best* (1994); Phil Berger, *Great Pennant Races* (1989); John Warner Davenport, *Baseball's Pennant Races: A Graphic View* (1981); Frank Graham, *Great Pennant Races of the Major Leagues* (1967); Lowell Reidenbaugh, et al., *The Sporting News Selects Baseball's 25 Greatest Pennant Races* (1987).

Herb Pennock (1894–1948)

Hall of Fame 1948

"Naturally, one left-hander belongs on my [all-time] staff, and I pick my old teammate of Boston and New York days, Herb Pennock. He was a left-handed Mathewson. Though weighing little more than 165 pounds, he had one of the easiest, most graceful deliveries of any pitcher I have ever known. Certainly Rube Waddell and Lefty Grove had more smoke, but they didn't have Pennock's class. He was a real artist on the mound, doing with his artistry what Waddell and Grove did with their superior speed."— Babe Ruth as told to Bob Considine in *The Babe Ruth Story* (1948) (which sportswriter Fred Lieb claimed to have ghostwritten for Considine).

Pennock was an American League pitcher for 22 years beginning in 1912, winning 240 games primarily for the Red Sox and Yankees.

Herbert Jefferis Pennock, "The Knight of Kennett Square (Pennsylvania)," tried out for the A's at age 18 in 1912 and pitched immediately for the club that season. He had an 11–4 record in 1914 but was sold to the Red Sox shortly after beginning the 1915 season. Connie Mack supposedly benched him after he failed to follow directions and Pennock told Mack to trade him if he did not have confidence in his pitching abilities. Mack later admitted poor judgment in making the trade because Pennock eventually blossomed.

Pennock pitched infrequently for the Red Sox until 1919, when he was 16–8. His big break came when he was traded to the Yankees for the 1923 season, in which he was 19–6. He went on to record two 20-game seasons and a career mark of 240–162 over 22 years. He also won five games and had three saves in nine World Series appearances for the Yankees.

The Yankees released him after the 1933 season, and he won his last two games for the Red Sox in 1934. He retired to become a Red Sox coach and then farm system director for two years before becoming Phillies general manager in 1943. He died in January 1948 while attending the National League meetings in New York.

Pension System

"However, unlike most steelworkers their age, the players were *most* concerned about the pension plan. Every player, it seemed, knew of a former big leaguer who was out of the game and out of work, with nothing to show for a career of training, playing ball, and traveling except some memories."— Players Association leader Marvin Miller on his early meetings with the player representatives to decide whether he was the man for the job; recounted in his autobiography, *A Whole Different Ball Game* (1991).

A pension system for professional ballplayers was suggested as early as 1886 in the National League. The idea surfaced again in 1907 though nothing substantial occurred until after World War II.

Modern Origins. Cardinals shortstop Marty Marion is credited with conceiving the idea of a pension in the mid–1940s. He was assisted by long-time Cardinals trainer and osteopath Harrison J. "Doc" Weaver, who held that position from 1927 until his death in 1955. Dick Wakefield, the first Major League **Bonus Baby**, also was active in establishing the pension system. Wakefield claimed that he was blackballed from baseball after 1950 as a result of his pension work.

Marion's pension idea received widespread coverage and support from the Associated Press. The plan called for matching financial contributions from players and ball clubs, with profits coming from a percentage of the broadcast revenue from the All-Star and World Series games, as well as exhibition game receipts between rival city teams during the season. The original goal was a $100-per-month payment at age 50 for 10-year players.

In his autobiography, former Dodgers and Padres general manager Buzzie Bavasi credited Walter O'Malley and George V. Mc-Laughlin of the Brooklyn Trust Company with devising the player pension plan.

First World Series. The 1946 World Series was the first in which pension contributions were made. The receipts were unusually low because of the small seating capacities of Sportsman's Park in St. Louis and Fenway Park in Boston.

The Cardinal players agreed to allocate some of their share of the World Series money to the pension fund. The Red Sox players balked because the shares were so small, but Red Sox owner Tom Yawkey agreed to cover the difference.

First Check. The first Major League pension check was issued to Andy Lotshaw in February 1951. The first player to still be active while eligible for his pension was Hoyt Wilhelm.

Left Out/Lawsuits. In 1996 there were 77 former players still alive who did not qualify for pension benefits because they played before the system was created. That year the group of players from the 1930s and 1940s sued Major League Baseball, claiming that baseball had improperly used their "names, voices, signatures, photographs and/or likeness" without compensation or approval. A California appeals court ruled against them in December 2001.

In October 2003 former 1960s Mets shortstop Al Moran, Ernie Fazio (the first signee of the Houston Astros, who played three seasons in the 1960s), and 1970s White Sox catcher Mike Colbern, sued Major League Baseball on behalf of themselves and another 1,050 players. In their class action suit, they alleged that the vesting requirement for full comprehensive medical benefits for life and full pension benefits were changed after the 1981 players strike. The requirements were reduced to four years, one day for medical benefits, and to four years, 43 days for full pension benefits. Previously, pursuant to the 1968 collective bargaining agreement, the benefits vested after five years, so the change negatively affected players who played before 1980 and were not retroactively included.

Interestingly, the lawsuit also alleged battery, negligence, race discrimination and conspiracy. The battery and negligence claims were related to claims that doctors and trainers from several teams gave players cortisone shots to mask pain and injuries.

The race discrimination arose from Major League Baseball's 1997 decision to grant a $10,000 annual "pension" to black players who played both in the Major Leagues and in the Negro Leagues, even though they never vested under the former requirements.

The conspiracy allegations centered on the owners granting the Negro League players the $10,000, to the exclusion of the white players.

In 2004 the court dismissed the lawsuit. The prevailing argument was that the Negro League players were not receiving a true pension covered by federal ERISA law (it was more of an annual "stipend"), so there was no comparison to the white players who did not qualify for the pension before the rules were liberalized in 1981.

Contributions and Qualifications. Originally each player made a contribution of $2 per day for each day of a season he spent in the Major Leagues, with his club matching that amount. When collective bargaining began in the mid–1960s, the player contributions were eliminated and the money came only from the owners.

Players, coaches and trainers with at least five years of Major League service began accruing pension credits in 1946. Managers were added later, as were players with only four years of service. The 50-year-old threshold for distribution of pension money to a player was later lowered to 45 as the television revenues soared and increased the value of the pension fund.

Efforts in the 1950s by Major League owners to abolish the pension system led to the formation of the Major League Players Association in 1953 (see also **_Unions_**). As a result of the players' unity, in 1954 changes increased the owners' fund contribution from $450,000 to $2 million per year. Also that year the previous operating committee consisting of a four-man group of owners and players, plus the commissioner, was revamped to eliminate the commissioner.

The 1954 changes also called for implementation in 1956 of a plan whereby the pension would receive 60% of the gate receipts and 60% of the radio and television rights from the All-Star Game. The fund already received 60% of the radio and television rights from the World Series.

In February 1969 the players used the threat of a strike to increase pension benefits. The owners agreed to increase their contribution from $4.1 million in 1968 to $5.45 million in each of the next three years. Retirement income at age 50 for a 10-year player was increased from $500 to $600 per month. Players also began to qualify after four years, rather than the previously required five. For service between 11–20 years the monthly increase was between $10 and $20. Payments were allowed at age 45 (instead of 50) and a dental coverage plan was established. Individual life insurance benefits were increased from $25,000 to $50,000.

In 1982 a 50-year-old with five years in the system received $745 per month, compared to the $125 he received in 1966. However, older players do not share equitably in the pension system. Some of today's players will receive up to $100,000 while 1940s player Billy Herman received $3,600 per year in the early 1990s and Dodger shortstop Pee Wee Reese received $7,200. Goose Gossage will receive over $11,000 per month at age 62.

A 1985 player strike was averted when the players agreed that they could seek arbitration only after a third year in the Major Leagues, rather than second. The owners abandoned their insistence on a salary cap and agreed to increase the pension fund contributions so that a 10-year veteran would receive $91,000 per year.

Executives. Larry MacPhail of the Yankees was active in creating a pension system for baseball executive personnel.

Charity Cases. Long-time 19th century sportswriter Henry Chadwick was voted a $600 annual pension by the National League Rules Committee after he fell on hard times in his old age.

When the legendary Cap Anson fell on hard times in the 20th century, he rejected an attempt by a few owners to establish a pension fund for him.

Qualifying Call-Up. In 1968 the Braves signed Satchel Paige just long enough for him to qualify for a pension.

In September 1999 John Cangelosi was toiling in the minor leagues, needing only 12 more days of Major League service to qualify for his 10-year pension benefits. The Rockies called him up and he qualified.

Negro League Players. The Major League Players Association has refused to let Negro League players share in pension benefits, though the MLPA has allowed them into their medical plan.

A 1997 agreement by Major League owners established a form of pension (but not technically so) of between $7,500 and $10,000 for Negro League players who spent at least four years in those leagues and at least one day in the Major Leagues. By 2004 there were at least 120 surviving Negro Leaguers who did not qualify for any type of pension.

In May 2004 more than two dozen Negro League players, all of whom played at least four Negro League seasons after Jackie Robinson broke the color line (but did not play in the Major Leagues), were to receive annual payments from Major League Baseball. The payments would be $10,000 a year for four years ($8833.33 per month), or $375 a month for life. Given their ages, the first option was the likely choice of most.

Strike Problem. In 1994 the owners refused to make their contribution to the player pension fund following the All-Star Game. The owners anticipated the player strike and did not relent until early in the 1995 season.

Replacement Players. Those players who replaced Major Leaguers in spring 1995 and then made it to the Major Leagues are not eligible to receive pension benefits.

Restitution. After Denny McLain was convicted of money laundering, a judge ordered that his pension be used to reimburse his victims. The judge reversed a prior ruling that had allowed McLain's wife to get his pension as part of their divorce settlement.

Pepper Games

"The crowd makes the ballgame. How much pepper do you suppose a player would show if games were played to empty seats?"— Ty Cobb.

George Wright of the original Cincinnati Red Stockings is credited with starting the first pepper game; whereby a few players stand in a small semicircle and pitch the ball at short range to a batter who "peppers" it back to them for reflex development.

The House of David teams were famous for their pepper games, dubbed in their promotional posters "A Most Entertaining Baseball Juggling Act."

Many ballparks have "No Pepper" signs near their backstops to prevent balls from going into the stands and injuring fans.

Tony Perez (1942–)

Hall of Fame 2000

"I doubt that a king at his coronation feels better than me today."— Perez at his Hall of Fame induction ceremony after a nine year wait.

Perez was the third base and first base star of the Reds' 1970s Big Red Machine.

Signed as a 17-year-old Cuban amateur, Antanasio Perez signed with the Reds in 1960 and went on to play 23 Major League seasons. He debuted that year with Geneva to begin a superb minor league career, capped by the Pacific Coast League MVP award in 1964. He would make his first Major League appearance later that summer. Primarily a third baseman in the minors, Perez played first base with the Reds in 1965 and 1966. He moved to third base in 1967 (returning permanently to first in 1972) and hit .290 with 26 home runs and 102 RBIs.

Perez announced himself as an elite run producer in 1969 and 1970. In both seasons he topped 100 RBIs and 100 runs scored. In 1969 he had 37 home runs and 122 RBIs. In 1970 he established career marks with 40 home runs, 129 RBIs and a .317 batting average. His performances helped propel the Reds to pennants in 1970 and 1972. In 1975 the Reds won 108 games with Perez driving in 109 runs. In the World Series versus Boston, Perez managed only five hits but produced three home runs and seven RBIs. His two-run homer in the 6th inning of Game 7 sparked Cincinnati to a 4–3 comeback win and the Series title.

Following the 1976 season and a second title, the Reds, in a curious move, traded Perez to Montreal. In 1977 he drove in 91 runs, the final year in an exceptional run of 11 straight seasons with at least 90 RBIs. He joined the Red Sox in 1980 as a free agent. His first year in the American League he hit .275 with 25 home runs

and 105 RBIs. In 1983, as a part-time player, he won a pennant with Philadelphia. Perez played his final three seasons in Cincinnati, retiring after the 1986 season.

Perez managed briefly with the Reds and Marlins before moving into the coaching ranks. He finished his career with a .279 batting average, 1,272 runs and 1,652 RBIs. He also accumulated 1,867 strikeouts, seventh highest total all-time. His 2,732 career hits include 505 doubles and 379 home runs.

Perfect Games

"Can walk up to guys who have thrown no-hitters and whisper: 'Loser!'"— One of David Letterman's Top 10 Great Things About Throwing a Perfect Game, after Randy Johnson did it in 2004.

"When I start, I try to pitch a perfect game. If I walk a batter, then I still try to pitch a no-hitter. If I allow a hit, I then try to at least pitch a shutout. Failing in that, I still try to win."— Sandy Koufax.

In the 19th and early 20th centuries, perfect games were not considered as big an event as they are today. When the first perfect games were pitched in 1880, the newspapers took almost no note. There have been 20 games of at least nine innings in Major League history which at various times have been characterized as perfect games or in which there were nine perfect innings by a pitcher to start the game. One occurred in the World Series. Three of the 20 have since been disallowed or were never considered perfect games or no-hitters under the rules requiring a complete game of at least nine innings in which no one reaches base. The 17 perfect games (followed by the three near-perfect):

1. John Lee Richmond/1880. Lee Richmond of Worcester pitched the first perfect game in Major League history against Cleveland on June 12, 1880, in front of 700 fans. The left-hander needed only 1 hour and 27 minutes to complete the game and only two balls were hit to the outfield. Richmond had been up all night at college (Brown University) and took the train to meet the team. Rain began in the 8th inning and the infield was covered with sawdust in order to finish the game. Richmond, son of a Baptist minister, took the next day off to graduate with honors from Brown. Richmond's lifetime record was 75–100 over a six-year Major League career that included a record of 32–32 in 1880.

2. John Montgomery Ward/1880. Ward was the youngest player, at age 20 years, three months, to pitch a perfect game. He threw his for Providence five days after Richmond on June 17, 1880. Ward defeated Buffalo 5–0 in 1 hour and 40 minutes in front of 2,000 Buffalo fans. Five balls were hit to the outfield. There was an 11 a.m. start to avoid a conflict with afternoon boat races. The 45-foot pitching distance used that season was changed to 50 feet the next season.

3. Cy Young/1904.

"Funny thing about that one is that there wasn't even one hard chance — until [pitcher Rube] Waddell came up for the final out. He hit a sizzler but it went right at an infielder."— Young.

On May 5, 1904, the Red Sox pitcher defeated the A's 3–0. Young allowed only six fly balls to the outfield and three pop-ups to the infield. A's manager Connie Mack said that Young's effort was the best-pitched game he ever saw.

4. Addie Joss/1908.

"That game was a surprise to both of us for we were sitting on a tarpaulin talking about having some singing in the hotel that night, when Lajoie, he managed Cleveland, and Fielder Jones told us to warm up. A pitcher never knew when he'd work in those days."—Ed Walsh on how he and Addie Joss found out they were pitching against each other on October 8, 1908.

In the heat of a pennant race on the next-to-last day of the season, October 2, 1908, Joss pitched the Indians to a 1–0 victory over the White Sox and Ed Walsh. Walsh gave up only four hits and struck out 15 batters. John Anderson grounded out to end the game in the last at-bat of his 14-year career. White Sox catcher Ossee Schreckengost broke his finger and this turned out to be the last game of his 11-year career. The first perfect game pitcher, John Lee Richmond, taught math to Joss's son in a Toledo, Ohio, high school.

5. Charlie Robertson/1922.

"No-run, no-hit, no-man-reach-first game."—Newspaper description of Robertson's perfect game.

The White Sox pitcher shut down the Tigers 2–0 on April 30, 1922. The game took 1 hour and 46 minutes.

6. Don Larsen/1956 World Series.

"No. Why should I?"—Larsen when asked if he ever got tired of talking about his perfect game.

"The million-to-one shot came in. Hell froze over. A month of Sundays hit the calendar. Don Larsen today pitched a no-hit, no-run, no-man-reach-first game in a World Series."—Sportswriter Shirley Povich.

"Let's all take a deep breath as we go to the most dramatic 9th inning in the history of baseball. I'm going to sit back, light up, and hope I don't chew the cigarette to pieces."—Vin Scully, broadcasting the game for the Dodgers.

"He did it with a tremendous assortment of pitches that seemed to have five forward speeds, including a slow one that ought to have been equipped with backup lights."—Sportswriter Shirley Povich.

Larsen threw 97 pitches during Game 6 of the 1956 World Series on his way to a 2–0 perfect game victory over the Dodgers. The last pitch was a 1–2 called third strike to pinch hitter Dale Mitchell. Mitchell, who only struck out 119 times in 3,984 career at-bats, always maintained that the last pitch was a ball. Yankee center fielder Mickey Mantle also thought the pitch was a ball: "I had a good view from center field, and, if I was under oath, I'd have to say the pitch looked like it was outside."

Larsen struck out seven batters. Shortstop Pee Wee Reese was the only Dodger batter to go to a 3–2 count and he was called out on strikes. The closest the Dodgers came to a hit was a line drive by Gil Hodges to left center field that Mantle ran down and caught; a line drive at third baseman Gil McDougald hit by Jackie Robinson; and a fly ball by Sandy Amoros that would have been a home run but curved foul.

Two weeks before the perfect game, Larsen learned that he had been tipping his pitches by the way he wound up before throwing. He abandoned his wind-up and threw from a stretch the entire game. Casey Stengel said it was the best game he had ever seen, "so far." Larsen reportedly was out until 4 a.m. partying the night before the game. He staggered into the ballpark about 9:30 for a whirlpool and a rubdown before going out to pitch.

According to Larsen and other eyewitnesses, these reports are false. He claimed that he got in by midnight after a late dinner and a "couple of beers." He was not sure that he would be pitching the next day, but said that if he did pitch, "don't be surprised if I throw a no-hitter." Although Casey Stengel apparently had decided on Larsen to start the game, he delayed telling him until the morning of the game so that he would not be nervous the night before. The Yankee ritual for designating the starting pitcher was for coach Frank Crosetti to put a warm-up ball in the shoe of the starter.

Two years earlier Larsen had been 3–21 for the Orioles, the worst record in the Major Leagues from 1939 until the 1990s for pitchers with 20 or more decisions. In 1959 the Yankees traded Larsen to the A's for Roger Maris.

It was the last game ever called behind the plate by Babe Pinelli, who planned to retire after the Series. The 61-year-old sat on a bench in the umpires' locker room and tearfully reminisced about his career and the perfect game, "my greatest thrill in baseball." No one from either team or Major League Baseball came by to congratulate him, and fellow crew member Tom Gorman later called it "a disgrace."

Some contend that Pinelli blew the call to favor Larsen, but Pinelli, whose vision was tested at 20–20 immediately after the Series, claimed otherwise: "Larsen had the greatest pin-point control I've ever seen [and] there was no doubt in my mind. Larsen hit the corner of the plate with a beautiful fast ball [that was] just high enough. It was easy to call—and I called it."

7. Jim Bunning/1964.

"I told 'em to dive for every one."—Bunning on what he told his infielders after sensing that he had a chance for a perfect game.

Bunning pitched a perfect game on Father's Day, June 21, 1964. It was a 6–0 victory over the Mets and was the first perfect game in the National League in 84 years. John Stephenson was the last out of the game. The toughest play was by second baseman Tony Taylor in the 5th inning, when he grabbed a hard ground ball by Jesse Gonder while falling to his knees and threw to first base for the out.

8. Sandy Koufax/1965. Koufax pitched the last of his four no-hitters on September 9, 1965, a 1–0 perfect game against the Cubs. It was the only time in Major League history that only one hit was made in a game and it did not figure in the scoring. Cubs pitcher Bob Hendley gave up a double to Lou Johnson in the 2nd inning. Koufax struck out 14, the most ever in a perfect game.

The Dodgers scored an unearned run in the 5th inning when Johnson walked, went to second on a sacrifice, stole third, and came home on catcher Chris Krug's high throw to third. Former batting champion Harvey Kuenn was the last out on a strikeout. Kuenn also made the last out of Koufax's second no-hitter on May 11, 1963. In Koufax's next start he again faced Hendley, who defeated Koufax and the Dodgers 2–1 on a four-hitter.

9. Jim "Catfish" Hunter/1968. Oakland's Jim Hunter threw a 4–0 perfect game on May 8, 1968, against the Twins in front of 6,000 Oakland fans. Hunter threw 55 strikes and 38 balls, with a total of 107 pitches (including foul balls), using his fastball and slider almost exclusively. Hunter drove in the go-ahead run with a squeeze bunt. Twins first baseman Rich Reese swung and missed a fastball on a full count to end the game. A's owner Charlie Finley gave Hunter an on-the-spot $5,000 raise.

In Hunter's next start, also against the Twins but this time in Minnesota, Twins batter Rod Carew hit a lead-off home run and Tony Oliva hit a three-run homer during a five-run 1st inning.

Hunter was the youngest modern pitcher to throw a perfect game at age 22 years, one month.

10. Len Barker/1981.

"Tell Len I'm very proud of him. I hope he does better next time."—Mrs. Tokie Lockhart after grandson Len pitched a perfect game.

Barker pitched a 3–0 perfect game for the Indians against the Blue Jays on May 15, 1981. On a rainy and cold night in Municipal Stadium, 7,290 fans watched Barker shut out the Blue Jays 3–0 in 47 degree weather. Ernie Whitt made the last out on an easy fly ball. Barker threw 103 pitches, including 75 strikes, and never went to a three-ball count on a batter. He struck out 11, all swinging, and threw 75% curveballs.

11. Mike Witt/1984. Witt pitched a 1–0 perfect game for the Angels against the Rangers on September 30, 1984, the last day of the season. He struck out 10 in front of 8,375 fans during a game that took only 1 hour and 49 minutes.

12. Tom Browning/1988. Browning pitched a perfect game for the Reds against the Dodgers on September 16, 1988. It was the same night as the opening ceremonies of the Olympic Games in Seoul, Korea (September 17 there), requiring frequent channel-changing by this author to follow both events. The 1–0 shutout was delayed 2 hours and 27 minutes due to rain. Browning never went to a three-ball count and threw 72 strikes out of 101 pitches thrown.

13. Dennis Martinez/1991. On July 28, 1991, Martinez of the Expos pitched a 2–0 perfect game against the Dodgers. It was less than 48 hours after Mark Gardner of the Expos pitched nine no-hit innings against the Dodgers, only to lose 1–0 after giving up a lead-off single in the 10th inning.

14. Kenny Rogers/1994. Rogers pitched a perfect game for the Rangers against the Angels on July 28, 1994. Center fielder Rusty Greer made a diving catch of a sinking line drive in the 9th inning to preserve the 4–0 victory. During the game the Rangers players burned Jose Canseco's old pair of cleats. The bonfire in the dugout during the 5th inning brought laughter from everyone on the club except Rogers.

15. David Wells/1998.

"I got here late. What happened?"— Billy Crystal, tongue-in-cheek, to Wells in the clubhouse after the game.

On May 17, 1998, Wells pitched the first regular-season perfect game in Yankees history, beating the Twins. In the 9th inning, he gave up a fly to right, recorded a strikeout and then Pat Meares flied to right to Paul O'Neill. Wells struck out 11 and the game lasted 2 hours 40 minutes. Wells later wrote a book, *Perfect I'm Not! Boomer on Beer, Brawls, Backaches & Baseball* (2003), which was not well-received by almost everyone in baseball. He claimed to be "half-drunk" during the perfect game, and then backed off and said he was only hung over.

In his next start, Wells pitched a four-hit shutout over the Twins. He and Don Larsen went to the same high school, Point Loma in San Diego.

16. David Cone/1999. With Don Larsen sitting behind home plate, the Yankee pitcher beat the Expos 6–0 in an interleague game on July 18, 1999, in front of 41,930 fans. There was a 33-minute rain delay with one out in the bottom of the 3rd, but Cone needed only seven pitches to get through the fourth.

The closest the Expos came to putting a runner on was when Jose Vidro hit a hard grounder up the middle with one out in the eighth. Second baseman Chuck Knoblauch ranged to his right to field the ball, pivoted and made a perfect throw to first baseman Tino Martinez to nip Vidro. It was Cone's first shutout in exactly four years. He did not go to a three-ball count all day and struck out 10. In the 9th, the righthander struck out Chris Widger, then retired pinch hitter Ryan McGuire on a fly to left that Ricky Ledee almost dropped. Pinch hitter Orlando Cabrera worked the count to 1–1, then on Cone's 88th pitch he hit a popup that third baseman Scott Brosius caught in foul territory for the final out. Cone had pitched three one-hitters, but never a no-hitter.

17. Randy Johnson/2004. Johnson became the oldest player to pitch a perfect game, at age 40 years, 8 months, 8 days, on May 18, 2004, in Atlanta. He beat out Cy Young by more than three and a half years as the oldest. Johnson, pitching for the Diamondbacks, struck out 13 Braves in a 2–0 win. He threw 117 pitches and went

to a three-ball count only once: Johnny Estrada in the 2nd inning fouled off three 3–2 pitches, and then struck out swinging on a 98-mph fastball in front of 23,381. It was Johnson's second no-hitter, having pitched one for the Mariners 14 years earlier, the longest span between no-hitters by a pitcher.

In his next game, Johnson was perfect only until the 3rd inning, but got the win against the Marlins. He extended his string of retired batters to 39 over three starts, two short of Jim Barr's record.

Perfect for Nine Innings/No Perfect Game. In 1991 Major League Baseball ruled that 50 nine-inning no-hitters (and perfect games) were dropped from the record books because either they did not go the full nine innings or the opposing team recorded a hit in extra innings (see also **No-Hitters**). The almost perfect:

Harry McIntire/1906. On August 1, 1906, McIntire pitched 10⅔ perfect innings before losing 1–0 in 13 innings. Under the 1991 decision by the rules committee, the game has been stricken from the list of perfect games because he did not pitch a complete perfect game.

Ernie Shore/1917.

"The legal aspects of this one require the services of a Solomon."
— Fred Schwed, Jr., in *How to Watch a Baseball Game* (1957).

"Shore, go in there and stall around until I can get somebody warmed up."— Red Sox manager Jack Barry after Babe Ruth was thrown out of the game after pitching to one batter.

On June 23, 1917, in the first game of a doubleheader at Fenway Park, Babe Ruth walked second baseman Ray Morgan of the Senators on four pitches. Umpire Clarence "Brick" Owens ejected Ruth for arguing the call. Ruth threw a punch that caught Owens on the neck and Shore was called in to replace Ruth. Some sources claim that he threw no warm-up pitches, but a newspaper account described him as throwing warm-up pitches and other sources support this version.

One source reported that Shore picked off the runner. However, Red Sox catcher Pinch Thomas also was ejected with Ruth and he was replaced by catcher Sam Agnew. Agnew threw out the runner on an attempted steal. Shore went on to pitch a 4–0 shutout and retire all 27 batters for what was at the time considered a perfect game.

The closest the Senators came to hits was an attempted bunt caught by second baseman Jack Barry and a great catch in the 9th inning by left fielder Duffy Lewis.

Since Shore was responsible for all 27 outs, he received credit for the perfect game although it was described as a no-hitter in the umpire's report and apparently was treated as a no-hitter for many years. Rule 10.19(f) purportedly was enacted to cover this situation: "No pitcher shall be credited with pitching a shutout unless he pitches a complete game, or unless he enters the game with none out before the opposing team has scored in the first inning, puts out the side without a run scoring and pitches all the rest of the game."

Under this language Shore should not be credited with a perfect game: if he can receive credit for a shutout only if the other team has not scored in the first inning, then what if the other team has a hit before he comes in and then he retires the hitter on an attempted steal; does the other team lose credit for the hit and Shore receive credit for a no-hitter? Similarly, in Shore's situation the other team must be credited with a base on balls in the box score, so how can Shore be credited with a perfect game?

Harvey Haddix/1959.

"The Greatest Game Ever Pitched (and the Braves had his signs)"— Title of an article by Steve Stout in SABR's *The National Pastime*.

Haddix pitched 12 innings of perfect ball for the Pirates against the Braves on May 29, 1959, losing 1–0 in 13 innings. The final score should have been 3–0, but Joe Adcock's game-winning home run in the 13th inning was reduced to a double because of a base-running error.

Don Hoak's throwing error allowed Felix Mantilla to reach base leading off the inning, ending the perfect game. With Mantilla on second and Henry Aaron on first, Joe Adcock hit a ball over the right fight fence to end the game. Aaron thought the ball had not gone over the fence, so he stepped on second (as required to take off the force play), and headed for the dugout believing the game was over on what he thought was Adcock's base hit. When Adcock passed Aaron on the basepaths, Aaron and Adcock retraced their steps, but the umpire said that the hit was a double, Aaron was out, and the final score was to be officially recorded as 2–0. The next day National League president Warren Giles ruled that the final score would be 1–0, with only Mantilla scoring and Adcock being credited with a double. Giles ruled that the base-running mix-up ended the game.

What is overlooked about the game is that Lew Burdette of the Braves pitched a 13-inning, 12-hit shutout. See also **Consecutive Outs** for those pitchers who have retired more than the 36 consecutive batters retired by Haddix. Braves pitcher Bob Buhl admitted in 1993 that the Braves were stealing Haddix's signs from the bullpen and would place a towel in a certain position to signal fastball or breaking ball. Buhl was able to see the signs because catcher Smoky Burgess could not bend over very far when he went into his crouch.

Pedro Martinez/1995. Martinez pitched nine innings of perfect baseball for the Expos against the Mets on May 13, 1995. He gave up a hit in the 10th inning and was lifted for a reliever, who picked up the save in the Expos' 1–0 victory. This game is not an official perfect game.

Shortened Perfect Games. On August 11, 1907, Ed Karger of the Cardinals pitched a seven-inning 4–0 perfect game over the Braves. It was the second game of a doubleheader and had been shortened by agreement.

On October 5, 1907, Rube Vickers of the A's pitched a 4–0 rain-shortened five-inning perfect game against the Senators.

On August 6, 1967, Dean Chance of the Twins pitched a 2–0 rain-shortened five-inning perfect game against the Red Sox.

On April 21, 1984, David Palmer of the Expos pitched a 4–0 rain-shortened five-inning perfect game against the Cardinals.

Odds. One source calculated the odds of pitching a perfect game based on the number of perfect games pitched from 1871 through 1988, when Tom Browning accomplished the feat. A total of 143,972 games were played to that point, and 14 then-official perfect games (not including Harvey Haddix) had been pitched. This made the odds 20,567 to 1 or 5⁄100,000 of 1% (.000002%).

Appearances In. Paul O'Neill of the Yankees is one of only player two players to appear in three Major League perfect games. O'Neill was there for David Cone and David Wells of the Yankees and Tom Browning of the Reds. Alfredo Griffin also played in three perfect games, pitched by Len Barker of the Indians, Tom Browning of the Reds and Dennis Martinez of the Expos. O'Neill was on the winning side all three times, but Griffin's team was the victim each time.

Black Baseball. Dan McClellan pitched a perfect game for the 1903 Cuban X-Giants, the best black team of the era. This is generally credited as the first perfect game in black baseball history.

Japanese Leagues. On May 18, 1994, pitcher Hiromi Makihara of the Yomiuri Giants pitched the 15th perfect game in the 58-year history of Japanese professional baseball. It was a 6–0 victory over the Hiroshima Toyo Carp.

International League. There have been four perfect games in the International League through 2004. On June 1, 2000, Japanese righthander Tomokazu Ohka, pitching for the Pawtucket Red Sox, became the first pitcher in nearly 50 years to throw a nine-inning perfect game in the International League. He beat the Charlotte Knights 2–0. The 24-year-old Ohka needed just 76 pitches for the first nine-inning perfect game in the league since Dick Marlowe did it for Buffalo in 1952.

Close to Perfect. Through 2004 there have been 28 no-hit complete games since 1900 that fell one base runner — by walk, hit batter or error — shy of being a perfect game. A selection of close calls: Hooks Wiltse had a chance for a perfect game while pitching for the Giants on July 4, 1908. He got the first 26 batters in a scoreless game. On a 2–2 pitch to the 27th batter, he hit George McQuillan on the arm. McQuillan was the only Phillies baserunner as the Giants won 1–0 in 10 innings.

On May 12, 1910, Chief Bender of the A's pitched a 4–0 no-hitter against the Indians. The only man he walked was shortstop Terry Turner, who was caught stealing, so Bender faced the minimum 27 batters.

In 1932 Tigers pitcher Tommy Bridges had a perfect game with two out in the 9th inning, a 13–0 lead against the Senators and the pitcher due up. Senators manager Walter Johnson called on his best pinch hitter, Dave Harris, who blooped a single to break up the perfect game.

Carl Erskine's 1952 no-hitter would have been a perfect game except for a walk to the opposing pitcher.

On September 2, 1972, Milt Pappas was pitching a perfect game for the Cubs against the Padres. He was down to a 3–2 count on the last batter in the 9th inning. Umpire Bruce Froemming (who called a Nolan Ryan no-hitter) called a ball on the last pitch and Pappas ended up with a no-hitter. Pappas never stopped sulking about it, but Froemming contended that he had to call it a ball, or he would have had no integrity.

Indians pitcher Dick Bosman lost a perfect game on his own error during his 4–0 no-hitter against the A's on July 19, 1974.

Terry Mulholland of the 1990 Phillies and Jerry Reuss of the 1980 Dodgers both would have had perfect games instead of no-hitters but for errors by infielders.

On June 23, 1994, Bobby Witt of the A's pitched a one-hitter against the Royals. In the 6th inning, Greg Gagne hit an infield roller to first baseman Troy Neel, who threw to Witt covering the bag. It appeared that Witt beat Gagne to the bag, but umpire Gary Cederstrom called Gagne safe. Television replays clearly supported Witt. He did not allow another runner to reach base.

On June 10, 1997, Marlins pitcher Kevin Brown pitched a no-hitter, coming within an inch of a perfect game. He nicked Giants batter Marvin Bernard on the leg in the 8th inning on a 1–2 pitch with two outs.

On May 30, 1997, Mike Mussina of the Orioles retired the first 25 Indian batters before Sandy Alomar singled with one out in the 9th inning. Mussina then struck out the next two batters for a 3–0 shutout. Four years later, on September 2, 2001, Mussina, then pitching for the Yankees, beat the Red Sox 1–0 and came within a strike of pitching a perfect game. Pinch hitter Carl Everett's two-out, two-strike single in the 9th inning ruined Mussina's attempt at a perfect game. It was the third time he had taken a perfect game into the 9th inning. David Cone, the most recent pitcher to throw a perfect game, took the loss.

Close to Perfect/World Series. The closest anyone came to a perfect game in the World Series before Don Larsen was Yankee pitcher Herb Pennock in the 1927 Series. In Game 3 he retired 22 straight Pirates before Pie Traynor singled with one out in the 8th inning. Pennock finished with a three-hitter and won 8–1.

Close to Perfect/Minor Leagues. On July 17, 1993, Spokane pitcher Glenn Dishman retired the first 26 Yakima batters in a Northwest League game. He induced the last batter to ground to the second baseman, who made the easy toss to former Major Leaguer Jason Thompson at first base. Thompson began celebrating early and jumped off the bag, forcing the umpire to call the runner safe. Dishman had to settle for a no-hitter when he retired the next batter.

Fight. Reggie Sanders of the Reds charged the mound against pitcher Pedro Martinez after Martinez threw at him during a game on April 13, 1994. What made Sanders' actions improbable was that Martinez was pitching a perfect game and had an 0–2 count on Sanders late in the game. As he hit Sanders with the pitch, Martinez threw up his arms in disgust before realizing that Sanders was going to charge the mound.

Dumb Luck. Ken High, a partner in this author's law firm, has attended only 13 Major League games over his lifetime, all Dodger games. Two were perfect: Sandy Koufax in 1965 and Dennis Martinez in 1991.

Books. Michael Coffey, *27 Men Out: Baseball's Perfect Games* (2004); Ronald A. Mayer, *Perfect!* (1991).

The Perfect Player

"I suppose there have been some teams in history bad enough to have lost with him anyway. Baseball's not like other sports, you can get eight guys out there bad enough to lose with Jesus Christ Hisself— and make Christ look bad enough so the sportswriters start wondering what's wrong with Him."— Kevin Baker in *Sometimes You See It Coming* (1993).

"Why certainly I'd like to have that fellow who hits a home run every time at bat, who strikes out every opposing batter when he's pitching, who throws strikes to any base or the plate when he's playing outfield and who's always thinking about two innings ahead just what he'll do to baffle the other team. Any manager would want a guy like that playing for him. The only trouble is to get him to put down his cup of beer and come down out of the stands and do those things."— Manager Danny Murtaugh.

"Stanley Frank Musial may qualify as the closest embodiment of all-around perfection baseball has ever seen."— Sportswriter Dick Gordon in 1957.

"Stengel wanted to mold him into that great player. And Mantle resisted. Not openly. Not defiantly…. He was a tremendous competitor, loved to win, but he wasn't obsessed with perfection as some athletes are."— Robert Creamer.

See also *Greatest Players*, *Managers*—The Perfect Manager and *Pitchers*—The Perfect Pitcher.

A subjective combination of various Major League players to create the perfect hitter/fielder:

Pure Hitter/Strike Zone Knowledge. Ted Williams was possibly the best hitter ever, especially when power and average are considered. If he had not lost almost five full seasons to the military, he would have topped virtually all hitting categories. Williams may have walked too much for some, but it was clear evidence of his intimate knowledge of the strike zone. Early baseball men often chose Joe Jackson as the best pure hitter of all time.

Reckless Abandon. Almost every interview of ballplayers from the 1930s and 1940s references Pete Reiser as one of the best ever,

but his playing style did not mesh well with the unpadded brick and cement walls of the era (see also *Injuries and Illness*—Head).

Home Runs. Henry Aaron had the most, but for frequency in an era when home runs were not yet the norm, Babe Ruth is the undisputed king, especially when considering his home run percentage of 8:5. Barry Bonds has to be considered based on his performance from 2001 on.

Base Stealing. Rickey Henderson must get the vote because of his totals in such a short period, plus the added benefit of home run power. Lou Brock or another top base stealer might be the choice on attitude, however (but not Ty Cobb!).

Defensive Ability/Catching the Ball. Willie Mays leads the outfield pack, though Tris Speaker might get the nod from an earlier era. Ozzie Smith may qualify as the best defensive shortstop of all time despite claims that Honus Wagner was the best of his era.

Arm. Right field requires the best outfield arm. Right fielder Roberto Clemente had the best of his era and maybe of all time. Modern observers cite Larry Walker and Raul Mondesi as having the best arms of their era.

Competitiveness. Ty Cobb and Jackie Robinson. This combination would give the perfect player a case of schizophrenia given Cobb's racist attitudes, but there is no denying their competitive fire.

Enthusiasm. Ernie Banks is an easy choice. A small band of Dodger fans might choose Mickey Hatcher.

Personality. Kirby Puckett (before his personal problems surfaced) or, from an earlier era, Luke Appling. Appling was as good-natured as they come, which was required to play over 20 years with the lowly White Sox, though his hypochondria might drop him out of the running. Other choices might be Dale Murphy or Cal Ripken.

Durability. Lou Gehrig and Cal Ripken. Ripken wins on sheer numbers, but shortstop is far more demanding than first base and he should be the choice on that criterion alone. However, Gehrig did not have the advantages of modern medicine or conveniences and must have experienced some of the early symptoms of his disease while the streak continued.

Pure Strength. With a nickname like The Beast and a few legendary home runs, Jimmie Foxx is the choice. Frank Howard's 6'7" and 255-pound frame makes him a close second. It is often forgotten that in three of Howard's last four full seasons he hit 44, 48 and 44 home runs in an era (1962–1975) when only Willie Mays in 1965 hit over 50 home runs. Today's steroid controversy makes it difficult to pick a strongest player in the 2000s.

Switch Hitting. Mickey Mantle and Pete Rose are the clear favorites, though Eddie Murray is a reasonable third choice.

Leadership. By all accounts Pee Wee Reese was the heart, soul, conscience and leader of the Dodgers, so he is the choice over Willie Stargell of the Pirates and Derek Jeter of the Yankees.

Grace.

"Lajoie has been called the most graceful of ball players. But Charley Gehringer surely came close to the big Frenchman in this respect, which isn't a very important matter, after all."— Sportswriter Bob French in the 1943 *Toledo Blade*.

Joe DiMaggio's admirers claim that he made it look easier than anyone; and he was a Yankee, the epitome of class in the 1940s.

Charisma. Babe Ruth had more than anyone, and he personally ushered in a new baseball era.

Clutch Hitting. Lou Gehrig was the greatest RBI man in history. It did not hurt to have Babe Ruth batting ahead of him, but Gehrig still had to produce.

Bunting. Ty Cobb, the master of his era. Maury Wills might be the choice in the recent past. Ichiro Suzuki is easily the top bunter of the past few years (Brett Butler in the 1980s).

Intelligence. He may not be too bright himself, but Pete Rose may be correct when he says that two-time MVP Joe Morgan of the Reds is the smartest baseball man he ever met.

The Perfect Team

"What in theory is the ideal team? Defensive strength down the middle and offensive strength on the corners. A pitching staff with five good starters and five good relievers, all with excellent control."— "The Old Timer" in W.R. Burnett's *The Roar of the Crowd* (1964).

See also Dynasties and Greatest Teams.

Gaylord Perry (1938–)

Hall of Fame 1991

"He should be in the Hall of Fame with a tube of KY jelly attached to his plaque."— Gene Mauch.

"I'd always have [grease] in at least two places, in case the umpires would ask me to wipe off one. I never wanted to be caught out there without anything. It wouldn't be professional."— Perry in *Me and the Spitter*, with Bob Sudyk (1974).

"I reckon I tried everything on the old apple, but salt and pepper and chocolate sauce topping."— Perry.

See also **Spitballs**.

The alleged and later admitted spitball pitcher spent 22 seasons in the Major Leagues while compiling 314 wins.

North Carolina native Gaylord Jackson Perry signed with the Giants for $90,000 in 1958 and spent four years in their farm system in St. Cloud, Corpus Christi, Harlingen and Tacoma. He came up to the Giants in 1962 with a 3–1 record in 13 appearances. He returned to Tacoma in 1963 for one game and then moved up to the parent club for the rest of the season.

In 1966 Perry won 21 games and in 1970 led the league with 23 wins and five shutouts. He was traded to the Indians in 1972 and won 24 games (and 29 complete) to lead the league. He won 21 in 1974 before being traded to the Rangers during the 1975 season. Traded to the Padres in 1978 and deemed "too old," he won 21 games to lead the league in his last excellent season, and then won another 41 over the balance of his career. After 1978 he bounced to various teams in his quest for 300 wins. He finally succeeded with the Mariners in May 1982. He retired in 1983 after a 7–14 record in 30 appearances for the Mariners and Royals.

He and his brother Jim were the second-winningest brother combination in Major leaguer history, second only to the Niekro brothers.

Constantly accused of throwing a spitball, Perry finished his career with a 314–265 record and 3.10 ERA over 22 seasons. He won the Cy Young Award in the American League in 1972 with the Indians (24–16) and in 1978 with the Padres (21–6), becoming the first pitcher to win the award in both leagues. He is eighth all-time in strikeouts (3,534) and sixth all-time in losses (265), but during his career he became only the third pitcher to surpass Walter Johnson's strikeout record of 3,509. He pitched a no-hitter in September 1968, a 1–0 victory over Bob Gibson and the Cardinals. Although he hit six home runs in his career, he batted a paltry .131.

Scott Perry Incident (1918)

Early in 1918 the National League Braves bought Perry from an Atlanta minor league club, but he refused to report. Connie Mack of the American League A's then signed him in March 1918. He won 21 games for the A's, but after the season Boston claimed him based on its preexisting contract.

By a 2–1 vote the National Commission upheld the Braves' claim over the A's. The enormous conflict that ensued caused National League president John Tener to advocate that the National League split from the American League. When the owners did not back him, he resigned and John Heydler took over. This incident led to the further erosion of Ban Johnson's power base and was one more event that led to establishing the position of commissioner of baseball.

Personality

"Just South of comatose."— Blue Jays first baseman John Olerud describing his personality.

"Why is it there are so many nice guys interested in baseball? Not me, I was a real bastard when I played."— Pitcher Burleigh Grimes.

"[Barry Bonds], by all indications a likable fellow away from baseball, is probably the most consistently bitter, arrogant and standoffish player in the Giants' modern history."— Bruce Jenkins of the *San Francisco Chronicle*.

"When I played ball, I didn't play for fun…. It's no pink tea, and mollycoddles had better stay out. It's a contest and everything that implies, a struggle for supremacy, a survival of the fittest."— Ty Cobb.

"People identify with the swashbuckling individuals, not polite little men who field their position well. Sir Galahad had a big following— but I'll bet Lancelot had more."— Bill Veeck.

"He motivates people with his mouth, with his actions, and with his smirk."—1990s Rangers manager Johnny Oates on first baseman Will Clark.

"Dislike him? People got mad at him, but I never heard of anybody who didn't *like* Babe Ruth."— One of Ruth's contemporaries in an interview with Robert W. Creamer.

"A chunky, unshaven hobo who ran the bases like a berserk locomotive, slept in the raw, and swore at pitchers in his sleep."— Lee Allen on Pepper Martin.

"Kirk Gibson could be as nasty as an old goat. He would shout at interns, harass writers, scowl at teammates. When he hobbled to the plate in that ninth inning 15 Octobers ago, there probably wasn't a surlier person in the stadium."— Sportswriter Bill Plaschke in September 2003, lamenting the trade by the Dodgers of the equally surly Gary Sheffield.

"You'd smile too if you hit .340 for 20 years."— Stan Musial to Larry Merchant, HBO boxing commentator and former sports editor of the *Philadelphia Daily News*, on why he was always smiling.

"He's even tempered. He comes to the ballpark mad and stays that way."— Joe Garagiola on Rick Burleson.

"Pete Rose is the most likable arrogant person I've ever met."— Mike Schmidt.

"Hanging out with him sucks because all the women flock to him. Let's see, he's been on the cover of *GQ*, is rich and famous, hits for average and power and is a helluva nice guy."— Tim Raines on Derek Jeter.

"How would I tell the difference?"— Diamondbacks general manager Joe Garagiola, Jr., when told by Randy Johnson's agent, Barry Meister: "If you don't trade him to the Yankees, you're going to have one unhappy player."

"Tim Gladd, Rick Sweet, Gene Good, Alan Kniceley, Chuck Chum, Bob Friend, Ralph Good, Owen Friend, Dave Jolly, Smead

Jolley, Charlie Nice, Mike Goodfellow, Bill Smiley, Happy Felsch, Aloysius Joy, John Smiley"

"Art Quirk, Crazy Schmidt, Bob Grim, Bob Purkey, Dad Meek, Creepy Crespi, Alan Strange, Stuffy McInnis, Tricky Nichols, Tom Letcher, Nick Goulish, Dizzy Dean, Dizzy Nutter, Jeff Twitty, Johnny Sain"

See also *Psychological Problems.*

Mr. Personality. In a 1976 poll of writers by Major League Baseball, Babe Ruth was voted the game's greatest personality, receiving 1,176 votes. Casey Stengel was second with 370 votes and Dizzy Dean was third with 65 votes. Henry Aaron and Mickey Mantle were tied for sixth.

Bad Mask. 1980s outfielder Jeffrey Leonard was known as "Penitentiary Face" for his perpetual scowl (see also *Home Run Trot*).

Enigma.

"Manny Ramirez? The Boston Red Sox star who jumps out of the caldron [sic] of a regular-season series with the New York Yankees because of a sore throat? The guy who refuses to pinch-hit in Philadelphia? The guy who treats fly balls as soaring objects to admire and occasionally chase and who mistakes an extra-inning playoff sprint from second to third for a Sunday stroll on the beach." — Ian O'Connor, who reported that Ramirez's high school coach and Major League managers all said that he was the hardest worker on the team. His high school coach, Steve Mandl, acknowledges some idiosyncrasies: "But people who don't know him call him a cancer in the clubhouse and make it seems like he's hanging out with drug dealers and gun smugglers. It's ridiculous. Manny does get brain-lock, but he's a fun-loving guy."

Ramirez once asked a sportswriter for a $70,000 loan and has cashed six-figure checks.

Philadelphia

"Moved one day by intimations of mortality, that bibulous philosopher, W.C. Fields, looked back on his arid boyhood home and chose his modest alternative to death: 'On the whole, I'd rather be in Philadelphia.'" — Dick Seamon in *Time* magazine in 1956.

Amateur Clubs.

"Parties of a dozen or more used to gather on an afternoon once a week on a field adjoining the upper part of Market Street, near where the Episcopal church now stands, to play the old game; and others again would go over to the Camden fields to enjoy the sport … the players were laughed at in those days for playing ball, the prejudice against wasting time in that way being very prevalent in the Quaker City of that period. The Philadelphians have, however, bravely got over it since then." — Sportswriter Henry Chadwick's description of early baseball in Philadelphia.

Philadelphia had amateur teams during the earliest days of baseball. The Olympic Town Ball Team of Philadelphia was one of the earliest clubs in the city and had switched to the New York Game by 1860 (see also *Amateur Teams*). Another early club was the Minervas, formed in 1857 and which purportedly played its first game on June 11, 1860, against the Equity Club. The Athletics were formed in 1859 and played their first game against a New York club on July 24, 1860. Other early clubs were the Winonas, Uniteds and Benedicts, all formed before the Civil War. By the late 1860s, Philadelphia had five times more clubs than New York City.

Professional Clubs. Some sources report that in the professional National Association of the early and mid–1870s, the Philadelphia entry was known as the Quakers before becoming the Phillies. However, *The Baseball Encyclopedia* reports that the clubs

were named the Athletics (1871–1875), the Centennials (1875) and the Whites (1873–1875).

When the National League organized for the 1876 season, the Athletics were awarded a franchise. When the A's and New York Mutuals were expelled after the first season for failing to complete their schedules, there was no Major League Baseball in Philadelphia for five years.

In 1882 the Athletics were formed as an entry in the new American Association and remained for the duration of the league through the 1891 season.

In 1883 the Worcester franchise in the National League was purchased by Philadelphia sporting goods manufacturer Alfred J. Reach, who transferred the club to Philadelphia, and the Phillies were born (though often known as the Quakers from 1883 through 1889).

Philadelphia had entries in the 1884 Union Association (Keystones) and 1890 Players League (Quakers).

In 1901 the Athletics were charter members of the American League and remained through the 1954 season before shifting to Kansas City.

Despite its size, Philadelphia never hosted a Federal League club.

Philadelphia Athletics

National Association 1871–1875

The Athletics were one of the powerhouses of the league, winning the first league championship in 1871. From 1872 through 1875 the club was led by Cap Anson, who batted at least .318 each season.

Philadelphia Athletics

National League 1876

This original member of the National League finished in seventh place with a 14–45 record. The club featured Levi Meyerle at third base with a .340 average and George Hall with a .366 average and a league-leading five home runs.

After the season the club was expelled from the league for failing to complete its schedule, though gambling may have been the unspoken cause. Owner G.W. Thompson pled injuries and competition from other attractions as the primary reasons for the team's failure. The club suffered financially due to competition from the city's Centennial Exposition held simultaneously that season. The club's season receipts were $11,643, but it had expenses of about $20,000.

After the club was expelled for failing to complete its schedule, the city of Philadelphia had no National League franchise until 1883.

Philadelphia Athletics

American Association 1882–1891

The Athletics were a charter member of the American Association and had some strong teams. Bill Sharsig, Charlie Mason and Lew Simmons owned the club for most of its existence. After finishing second in 1882, the club won the 1883 pennant by one game over the Brown Stockings. Harry Stovey was the club's top player and led the Association with 14 home runs. The A's were mediocre during mid-decade, but improved in 1888 and 1889 with strong winning records as Stovey continued to star. The club struggled in 1890 and disbanded after the season.

The 1891 team was actually the remnants of the 1890 Players League club that had survived the baseball wars of 1890. It finished fourth before the Association dissolved.

Philadelphia Athletics

American League 1901–1954

"Like the little girl with the curl in the middle of her forehead, when the Athletics were good, they were very very good. But when they were bad horrid was hardly the word." — Harry Robert in *The American League*, edited by Ed Fitzgerald (1959).

Origins. When the American League expanded East, Ban Johnson awarded Connie Mack and Benjamin Shibe the new Philadelphia franchise. They shifted their Milwaukee club to Philadelphia.

First Game. The first game played by the Philadelphia A's was postponed by rain, so the club played its inaugural game on Friday, April 26, 1901, losing to the Senators 5–1.

Key Owners.
Connie Mack/1901–1954 and Ben Shibe/1901–1922.
"Don't bet on the A's." — Mack, asked for a tip by a cab driver during a dry spell.

"The last people who went broke in baseball were Roy and Earle Mack, Connie's sons. And I claim they did it on merit." — Red Smith.

"Connie Mack's sons became senile before he did." — Jimmy Isaminger.

Connie Mack was managing Milwaukee in the Western League when Ban Johnson asked him to move the club to Philadelphia as part of the new American League. Mack owned 25% of the club and Ben Shibe held most of the rest. Shibe was induced to accept the franchise on the promise by Johnson that his ball manufacturing company would receive an exclusive contract to supply the new league with balls. Some sources report that when Shibe bought into the A's for the 1901 season, his business partner, Al Reach, was still president of the Phillies. However, Reach apparently sold out in 1899.

Two newspapers also were given 25% of the stock, in part as an inducement to provide favorable coverage of the team. Frank Hough of the *Philadelphia Inquirer* later sold his interest to Mack, who eventually owned the vast majority of the club (not 100% as often reported). Shibe was the club's president, a position he held until his death in 1922. He was in a serious car accident in 1920 and ceased to have much involvement after that.

After successful seasons in 1910–1913, Mack could not afford to keep his stars in the face of competition from the 1914–1915 Federal League. Attendance suffered and salaries increased dramatically and Mack was forced to sell off most of his "$100,000 Infield."

The Depression again made it impossible for Mack to retain many of his stars that had emerged during the club's success of 1929–1931. To raise cash in the early and mid–1930s, he sold catcher Mickey Cochrane to the Tigers for $100,000, slugger Al Simmons and two other players to the White Sox for $150,000; star pitcher Lefty Grove and two others to the Red Sox for $125,000; and Jimmie Foxx to the Red Sox for $150,000. The A's then finished last from 1936 through 1939, setting the pattern for the remainder of the franchise's history.

After Mack sold off his stars during the 1930s, he still needed to borrow $400,000 from Red Sox owner Tom Yawkey to get through the Depression. The A's were always a marginal operation financially, in part because Mack was a baseball man without outside sources of income, the competition from the crosstown Phillies, and the eventually run-down Shibe Park.

After landing in the cellar virtually for good, Mack ran the club with the needed assistance of his sons until he retired at age 87 after the 1950 season. The Mack family continued to own a majority of the club until 1954, when they sold out to Arnold Johnson and he moved the club to Kansas City. Benjamin Shibe MacFarland was the chief minority stockholder at the time of the sale. Mack died in February 1956.

Nickname.
"For ninety-six years, from 1859 to 1955, when the A's fled to Kansas City, there was always a club called the Athletics playing baseball in Philadelphia." — Harold Peterson in *The Man Who Invented Baseball* (1969).

Athletics was a name given to amateur Philadelphia clubs as far back as the 1850s. In 1901 the team had many former National League players, and John McGraw dubbed the players "White Elephants." The A's finished fourth that year and the elephant became the team's permanent symbol. Though abandoned occasionally, the elephant was last revived by the Oakland A's in the late 1980s.

Key Seasons. The A's won nine pennants and five World Series during three distinct eras.

1902. The A's won their first pennant by five games over the Browns. There was no World Series in 1902 because the American and National Leagues were feuding and the event was not created until 1903. Socks Seybold led the league with 16 home runs and Rube Waddell won 24 games.

1905.
"Although bested in the struggle for the supremacy of the world, and parts of New Jersey, the white elephants are not too much cast down. They handed the Giants the best they had, and it was not enough." — *Chicago Tribune* sportswriter Charles Dryden on the Giants' five-game victory over the A's in the World Series.

The A's and White Sox both won 92 games, but the A's lost only 56 to Chicago's 60 and thereby clinched the pennant based on winning percentage. Harry Davis led the league with eight home runs and 83 RBIs and Rube Waddell led the league with 26 wins.

1910. After a second-place finish in 1909, the A's won the pennant with 102 wins, 14½ games ahead of the Yankees. Jack Coombs led the league with 31 wins and the A's beat the Cubs in the World Series for their first championship.

1911. The A's won 101 games and finished far ahead of the Tigers as Jack Coombs again led the league with 28 wins and Frank Baker hit a league-leading 11 home runs. The A's beat the Giants in the World Series for their second consecutive championship.

1913. After slipping to 90 wins and third place in 1912, the A's rebounded with 96 wins and a pennant over the Senators. Frank Baker led the league with 12 home runs and 126 RBIs. The A's again beat the Giants in the World Series, this time in five games.

1914. The A's won the American League crown again with 99 wins but were swept in the World Series by the Miracle Braves. After this four-year run of success, the club's key players were sold off during a cash crunch brought on by the challenge of the Federal League.

1929. The A's were terrible through the 1920s but rebounded just before the Depression began. In 1929 they won 104 games to win the pennant by 18 games. Al Simmons led the league with 157 RBIs, and George Earnshaw led with 24 wins. The A's defeated the Cubs in the World Series in five games.

1930. The club won the American League crown with 102 wins as Al Simmons led the league with a .381 average and Lefty Grove led with 28 wins. They beat the Cardinals in the World Series in six games.

1931. The A's won their third consecutive flag in 1931 with 107 wins as Al Simmons and Lefty Grove again were league leaders in batting average (.390) and wins (31). The club lost the World Series to the Cardinals in seven games.

1932. The A's won 94 games, finishing second to the powerful Yankees, who won 107 games. The glory years ended again as Mack sold off his stars to raise cash during the Depression. The club was terrible for the next two decades through its last season in Philadelphia in 1954.

Key Players.

"Somewhere in Nebraska, there is an aging fan who checks the progress of the Oakland A's every day because, as a boy, he lived in Philadelphia and was bewitched by Jimmy Foxx and Lefty Grove and that bunch. Or, if he's older still, Eddie Collins and Chief Bender and *that* bunch." — Art Hill in *I Don't Care If I Never Come Back* (1980).

Rube Waddell (HF) was an eccentric, but he was an outstanding pitcher for the A's from 1902 through 1907. His peak seasons were between 1902 and 1905, when he won between 21 and 26 games and led the league in strikeouts each year. He had an ERA of less than 2.00 in 1904 and 1905.

Frank "Home Run" Baker (HF) starred for the A's from 1909 through 1914, batting over .300 five times. He also starred in four World Series for the A's from 1910 through 1914, hitting two home runs in 1911 to earn his nickname. He led the league in home runs from 1911 through 1914 (with a high of 12 in 1913) and led in RBIs in 1912 and 1913.

Eddie Collins (HF) led the league in runs scored for three straight seasons starting in 1912. He batted over .300 six straight seasons from 1909 through 1914 and starred at second base. He also hit over .400 twice for the A's in the World Series.

Eddie Plank (HF) pitched from 1901 through 1914 for the A's, winning 20 or more games seven times and throwing 59 shutouts. He won 285 games for the club on his way to 327 wins, 11th all-time.

Chief Bender (HF) pitched for 12 seasons for the A's beginning in 1903. He won 191 games for the club, including seasons of 23 and 21 wins. He won six World Series games for the A's between 1905 and 1914.

Jack Coombs pitched nine seasons for the A's beginning in 1906, with 31 wins in 1910 and 28 wins in 1911. He pitched 13 shutouts in 1910 and won three games for the A's in the World Series that season.

Al Simmons (HF) starred in the A's outfield from 1924 through 1932. He had seasons of .384, .392, .381 and .390. He also drove in more than 100 runs every season and had 200 or more hits five times. He returned to the A's briefly in 1940 and 1941 and also made a four-game appearance for the club in 1944. He starred in three straight World Series for the A's beginning in 1929, batting at least .300 each time.

Mickey Cochrane (HF) was the starting catcher for the A's from his rookie season in 1925 through 1933. He hit over .300 six times, with a high of .357 in 1930 and was considered by many as the best defensive catcher of his era.

Jimmie Foxx (HF) played first base for the A's from 1925 through 1935, hitting over .300 10 times. He led the league in home runs three times for the A's, including 58 in 1932. He won the Triple Crown in 1933 when he hit .356 with 48 home runs and 163 RBIs.

Lefty Grove (HF) was the dominant Major League pitcher of the late 1920s and 1930s. He won 20 or more games in seven straight seasons for the A's beginning in 1927. He peaked with a 31–4 record in 1931, with a 2.06 ERA and four shutouts. He also led the league in strikeouts from 1925, his first season with the A's, through 1931. He won four World Series games for the A's in 1930 and 1931.

Key Manager.

Connie Mack (HF) led a Major League club longer than any other manager, made easier by the fact that he owned the club. By the end of his 50-year run with the club he was in his mid–80s and getting senile. By then he often called on players to pinch-hit who had played for him 20 years earlier.

Star second baseman and later coach Eddie Collins was promised by co-owner Ben Shibe that he could succeed Mack, but it never came to pass and Collins missed out on a number of managing opportunities as a result. He even turned down the Yankee job, offered to him in 1930. When Mack finally retired, he was replaced by Jimmy Dykes.

"Lasts." In the last Philadelphia A's game they defeated the Yankees 8–6 on September 26, 1954. It was pitcher Art Ditmar's first career victory. The Yankees played with three players out of position. Yogi Berra played third base for the only time in his career. Moose Skowron played second base for only the third time (though *The Baseball Encyclopedia* records only two), and Mickey Mantle played shortstop for one of only seven times. Lou Limmer hit the last A's home run on September 25, 1954. It was the last of 19 in his career.

Ballparks. The first A's ballpark was Columbia Park, leased by the club at 29th Street and Columbia Avenue in the Brewerytown section of Philadelphia. The park seated 9,500 and housed the club until **Shibe Park** opened in 1909.

Shibe Park seated 33,000 and generally had dimensions from left to right field of 334–440–331. In 1952 the name was changed to Connie Mack Stadium. The A's played in the ballpark until the franchise shifted to Kansas City for the 1955 season.

Key Broadcasters. Bill Dyer broadcast the first A's game in the 1920s, but the star of Philadelphia radio was Byrum Fred "By" Saam. Saam was the primary A's broadcaster from 1938 until the club departed after the 1954 season. He also broadcast for the Phillies for many years.

Books. The Baseball Padre, *Reflections on a Baseball Team* (1979); David M. Jordan, *The Athletics of Philadelphia: Connie Mack's White Elephants, 1901–1954* (1999); William C. Kashatus, *The Philadelphia Athletics* (2002).

Philadelphia Centennials

National Association 1875
The club played only 14 games in the league, winning two before dropping out.

Philadelphia Keystones

Union Association 1884
The Keystones folded in early August with a record of 21–46. They were replaced by a club in Wilmington that was previously part of the Eastern League. The Wilmington club lasted one month with a dismal 2–16 record before being replaced by Milwaukee from the Northwestern League.

Philadelphia Phillies

National League 1883–
"Baseball is an uncertain game. A Cincinnati pitching staff may

falter. Young Cardinal strong arms may upset the dopesters with their brilliance. Cleveland players may call on Owner Bradley. The Tigers may lose a Hank Greenberg to the Army, and Buck Newsom may lose his fine touch—and I don't mean Mr. Briggs. But in the maze of uncertainties, you always could turn to the Phillies. The Phils would finish last."—J. Roy Stockton in *The Gas House Gang and a couple of other guys* (1945).

"Garland them with timeless lilies!
Although they are a bunch of dillies
Who give honest men the willies.
We still love them for their sillies.
Hail, The Phillies."

—Last stanza of a poem by author James Michener, written upon hearing on an airplane bound for Bangkok that the Phillies had won the 1980 World Series.

Origins. In 1882 the American Association franchise in Philadelphia was doing well. The National League wanted to return to the city after a five-year hiatus and decided to place a team there for the 1883 season. The small-market Worcester club was relocated to Philadelphia and the Phillies were born.

First Game. The Phillies played the Providence Grays to start the 1883 season on May 1, losing 4–3 as Providence scored four runs in the 8th inning. Providence pitcher Charles Radbourn won the first of his 49 games that year, defeating John Coleman for the first of his 48 losses.

Key Owners.

Alfred J. Reach/1883–1899 and John I. Rogers/1883–1903.
"Reach was in business partnership with another man whose name was destined for long lasting connotations in baseball—Benjamin Shibe, one time manufacturer of whips and a connoisseur of leather, who was joined with Reach in turning out baseball gloves."—Donald Honig in *The Philadelphia Phillies* (1992).

"Associated with Reach was Col. John I. Rogers, a lawyer with a flair for Pennsylvania politics. His title was political, as he won his colonelcy by being named to the staff of the Keystone state governor. In the early years of the Reach-Rogers association the colonel was overshadowed by the more glamorous and better-known Reach, but in the 90s Rogers threw his weight around, frequently differed with president Al, and became the more militant member of the partnership."—Fred Lieb and Stan Baumgartner in *The Philadelphia Phillies* (1953).

Reach, a Philadelphia sporting goods manufacturer, purchased the Worcester team and relocated it to Philadelphia and called the club the Phillies. Reach was partners with Colonel John I. Rogers and the two controlled the team together until Reach sold out at the end of the century to concentrate on his sporting goods business (and after a dispute over control of the club). Rogers ran the club until selling out in 1903 after a section of the bleachers collapsed and killed 12 fans watching a fire across the street from the ballpark.

James Potter/1903–1909.
"The club was sold to a syndicate headed by a Philadelphia socialite named James Potter, who it was said knew more about squash and indoor tennis than about baseball. (Then, as now, the chief qualification for owning a big-league baseball team is having a lot of money.)"—Donald Honig in *The Philadelphia Phillies* (1992).

Potter headed a syndicate that bought the club for $200,000 in a sale engineered by Pittsburgh owner Barney Dreyfuss. Potter's group held the club until November 1909.

Horace S. Fogel/1909–1911.
"Horace had a chronic dry whistle, and like most newspaper-men—especially of that era—he lived from one pay day to the next.... Horace, cigar in his mouth, already was sitting there with feet on the president's desk as a sign painter was putting new lettering on the door.... Fogel was an early version of the Larry MacPhail—young Bill Veeck type of a colorful, dynamic club president."—Fred Lieb in *The Philadelphia Phillies* (1953).

In 1909 Potter and his associates sold out for $350,000 to a syndicate headed by Horace S. Fogel. Fogel was the president of the syndicate until 1911. He was also the man who, while managing the Giants, purportedly made Christy Mathewson a first baseman (see also **Players Who Switched Positions**).

The primary investor in the syndicate was Charles P. Taft, who was a minority owner of the Cubs and the brother of U.S. President William Howard Taft. It was clear from the outset that Fogel was merely the front man for Cubs majority-owner Charles Murphy.

Fogel was 48 when he took over, having been a Philadelphia newspaperman who was not wealthy and who had spied for the American League during the interleague wars in the early part of the century. He was forced out of the National League in late 1911 due to fights with league president Thomas Lynch over Fogel's claims that the pennant race was fixed (see also **Barred from Baseball**).

William F. Baker/1911–1930.
"With so much incompetence always on the playing field, Mr. Baker doubtless deeply appreciated the business acumen and skill of the former Miss Mallen, who could add rows of figures forward and backward with equal skill—reading the standings of the clubs backward occasionally must have been a help, in the case of the Phils."—J. Roy Stockton in *The Gashouse Gang and a couple of other guys* (1945), on Baker's secretary, Mae Mallen. She inherited the club's stock after having worked in the Phillies front office for a number of years. She married Gerry Nugent, who later became president of the club. Baker was a former New York police chief (or commissioner) and renowned penny pincher.

Gerry Nugent/1930–1943.
"I went back to Philly to talk contract with Mr. Nugent. My hotel and food cost me more while I was there negotiating than the raise I got."—Pitcher Kirby Higbe in *The High Hard One* (1967).

"Gerry Nugent was a savvy baseball executive, but he had no money and for years had performed feats of financial legerdemain simply to keep the club afloat."—David M. Jordan, Larry R. Gerlach and John P. Rossi.

In 1930 William Baker died and shoe salesman Gerry Nugent took over under unusual circumstances. Nugent was in the leather-goods business when he married Mae Catherine DeSalles Mallen in 1925. She had been William Baker's secretary for many years. Baker left half his estate to Mallen and when Baker's wife died two years later, she also left a sizable amount of stock to her. Nugent entered the Phillies' front office in 1926 to assist Baker and was the business manager when Baker died in 1930. Nugent became president and his wife was named vice-president.

During Nugent's tenure, the club finished seventh four times and last six times. In 1942 Nugent continued to lose money. One local newspaperman calculated that the club owed $330,000. Nugent tried to borrow more money from the league, but was refused. He tried to find a buyer in late 1942, but was unsuccessful. The league met again in February 1943, and essentially sold the club out from under him, though he expressed satisfaction with the deal, which cancelled the debt (owed primarily to the league) and paid the shareholders $10 per share for 2,600 shares. Nugent relied on his baseball income as his sole support, so getting out from under the debt was a priority. A week after the February meeting, the club was sold to a syndicate headed by William D. Cox.

Bill Veeck, Jr., allegedly tried to buy the club in 1943 but was rebuffed when he purportedly went to Judge Landis with a plan to stock the club with a few black players because of the depleted white talent caused by World War II. Landis hated the idea and suddenly the club was no longer available to Veeck. This story is false (see *Integration—Bill Veeck*).

William D. Cox/1943–1944.

"If there's a jerk connected with the Phillies, it's owner Bill Cox. He's the All-American jerk."—Fired manager Bucky Harris after Cox was reported to have accused Harris of calling the Phillies owners "a bunch of jerks."

Cox, president of the family lumber brokerage, headed a syndicate that bought the Phillies out of receivership in early 1943. He was a 36-year-old graduate of Yale and a stamp collector who specialized in stamps with trees. He hired Bucky Harris to manage the club but abruptly fired him on July 28, 1943, and hired Freddie Fitzsimmons. Harris told reporters that Cox had been betting on the Phillies. Judge Landis intervened and forced Cox to sell out his interest and barred him from baseball (see also *Gambling*).

The Carpenter Family/1944–1981.

"I'm going to write a book—*How to Make a Small Fortune in Baseball*—you start with a large fortune…"—Phillies owner Ruly Carpenter.

The Cox interest was purchased for $400,000 by Robert M. Carpenter, Sr., the CEO and chairman of the board of DuPont. He turned the club over to his 28-year-old son, Robert, Jr., who became the powerful owner that guided the club for most of the next four decades. Robert Jr., known as Ruly, was the first baseball owner ever drafted into the military, in 1944, after playing football at Duke. The Carpenters had owned the Wilmington Blue Rocks of the Inter-State League, where the younger Carpenter was club president.

Before he was drafted, Carpenter hired former Yankee pitcher Herb Pennock as general manager and Pennock began to build a respectable club. Pennock died suddenly of a brain hemorrhage during the January 1948 winter meetings.

John Quinn, son of long-time general manager Bob Quinn, was the Phillies general manager from 1959 through 1972. The Carpenter family held the club until 1981 when they sold out to a group headed by Bill Giles for over $30 million. It was a good profit on the $400,000 Bob Carpenter paid in 1944.

Bill Giles/1981–. In 1981 the club was purchased for $30,175,000 by a syndicate headed by Bill Giles. His father, Warren Giles, had been National League president. Bill Giles continued as president of the club into 2004, but general manager Paul Owens died before the 2004 season. There are also five limited partners who have an ownership interest in the club.

Giles is estimated to be worth close to $30 million based on his ownership interest in the club. He owns close to 20% of the club after initially receiving about 10% for putting the ownership group together. He acknowledges that he only had about $50,000 in the bank at the time of the purchase.

Nicknames.

"Since the classic old Philadelphia name of Athletics had already been grabbed by the American Association, Reach called his team simply the Philadelphias, a name eventually to be shortened to Phillies."—Arthur Bartlett in *Baseball and Mr. Spalding* (1951).

The Phillies hold the record for using the same nickname for the longest time, having had the name since joining the National League in 1883. Early accounts sometimes apparently spelled the name "Fillies," which makes no sense considering the gender problem and the fact that the city's name starts with "Phil." The club also was sometimes called the Quakers or Red Quakers in early years due to the Quaker heritage of the state and the club's red uniforms. *The Baseball Encyclopedia* lists the National League Philadelphia club as the Quakers from 1883 through 1889, which is contrary to other sources.

At one point early in the 20th century, owner Horace Fogel tried to change the team's name to "Live Wires." During William Baker's usually dismal reign from 1911 through 1930, the club was sometimes referred to in print is the "Phoolish Phillies."

In 1944 the club had new ownership, which held a contest to rename the team. One of the suggestions was the "Stinkers" and the club had often been called the "Phutile Phillies." After reviewing 5,000 letters with 635 different suggestions, Mrs. John L. Cooks (caretaker of the Oddfellows Grand Lodge in Philadelphia) was awarded a $100 war bond and a season pass to the park for her choice, "Blue Jays": "Mrs. Crooks no doubt made her choice because the team has been getting the bird for several years. If she scrutinized the dictionary, she entered Blue Jays after reading: 'A small, crowlike bird usually of brilliant coloring; also a poor actor, a country bumpkin and a greenhorn.'"—The *Stars and Stripes* military newspaper.

It was later reported that Johns Hopkins University students in Baltimore were upset because the club had misappropriated the school's nickname. The students criticized the club's record, noting that it had finished last 15 times and had lost 100 or more games 12 times. Club president Bob Carpenter, Jr., responded in kind: "Why, they haven't won a ballgame in 20 years, have they? I saw their football team once. Boy what a ragged outfit."

Following all the uproar the club announced that the contest was merely for an "emblem" and "not a name change." The name/emblem survived only one year and was never really used.

Key Seasons.

"That first clunking finish [in 1883] was ominous, because although they were not to have another basement wrapped up until 1904, the Phillies have suffered, through the 1990 season, a National League record 24 last-place finishes."—Donald Honig in *The Philadelphia Phillies* (1992).

"I guess I'm being a tad pessimistic here, but to tell you the truth…. I really don't think that I can say that this team is even capable of putting together a 6-week stretch run…. If we were healthy? Maybe. If someone else were managing? Perhaps. With the current squad of AAA filler, crappy acquisitions and dead weight? Not bloody likely."—From Mark at "I'm Not an Athlete," A Phillies Weblog, on the 2004 squad.

1887. The Phillies finished a strong second, only four games behind Detroit. It was the club's best finish between 1883 and 1913.

1913. The club finished second behind the pitching of Grover Cleveland Alexander, 12½ games behind the Giants. Right fielder Gavvy Cravath led the league with 19 home runs and 128 RBIs.

1915. Manager Pat Moran led the club to its first pennant behind Grover Cleveland Alexander's 31 wins and Gavvy Cravath's league-leading 24 home runs and 115 RBIs. The club lost to the Red Sox in the World Series in five games.

1916. The Phillies finished second by 2½ games to the Dodgers. Grover Cleveland Alexander had 33 wins and a 1.55 ERA.

1917. The Phillies finished second again to the Giants by 10 games. It was the last time they would finish that high until 1950. The club finished last 16 times between 1919 and 1945.

1950. The "Whiz Kids" came from nowhere to edge out the Dodgers on the last day of the season for the pennant. They were led by Robin Roberts with 20 wins and Del Ennis with 31 home runs and a league-leading 126 RBIs. The Phillies were swept by the Yankees in the World Series.

1964. In one of the great collapses in baseball history, the Phillies led by 10 games with only two weeks to play. They lost 10 straight and the pennant race by one game to the Cardinals. See William A. Cook, *A Pennant Lost* (2002); William C. Kashatus, *September Swoon: Richie Allen, the '64 Phillies, and Racial Integration* (2004).

1976. After a second-place finish in 1975, the Phillies won 101 games and the Eastern Division title under manager Danny Ozark. Mike Schmidt led the league with 38 home runs and Steve Carlton won 20 games. The Reds swept the Phillies in the NLCS.

1977. The Phillies again won 101 games and the division title behind another 38 home runs by Mike Schmidt. The club lost the NLCS to the Dodgers in four games.

1978. The Phillies won their third straight division title, but again lost to the Dodgers in the play-offs. Greg Luzinski led the club with 35 home runs and 101 RBIs.

1980.

"*The Team That Wouldn't Die*"—Title of Hal Bodley's book on the 1980 World Champion Phillies.

The club won its third pennant of the 20th century, finishing one game ahead of the Expos for the division title and beating the Astros in a five-game series that included four extra-inning games. The Phillies won the World Series in six games over the Royals. Mike Schmidt led the league with 48 home runs and 121 RBIs. Steve Carlton led the league with 24 wins and Tug McGraw had 20 saves. See also Frank Fitzpatrick, *You Can't Lose 'Em All* (2001).

1981. The Phillies won the first half of the strike-shortened season but lost to the Expos in five games in the division mini-play-off.

1983. After the Phillies finished second in 1982, they won the Eastern Division crown by six games over the Pirates. The Phillies beat the Dodgers in the NLCS in four games before losing to the Orioles in the World Series. Mike Schmidt led the league with 40 home runs and John Denny led the league with 19 wins. Al Holland had 25 saves.

1993.

"We've got all the degenerates from around the league. With 25 degenerates we might generate something."—Phillies pitcher Larry Anderson.

They indeed generated something, as Lenny Dykstra and John Kruk led them to a division title and they beat the Braves in the NLCS. In Game 6 of the World Series, Phillies reliever Mitch Williams gave up a home run to Toronto's Joe Carter in the bottom of the 9th inning to give the Blue Jays the championship. See also *Philadelphia Inquirer* staff, *Worst to First: The Story of the 1993 Phillies* (1994); Rich Westcott, *Phillies '93: An Incredible Season* (1994).

Key Players.

"And if the Phils continue to field a team, [Cleveland owner Alva] Bradley shouldn't fret too much about the drain on his manpower. The Phils, of course, haven't had enough talent to worry about in recent years."—The *Stars and Stripes* military newspaper in 1944.

Grover Cleveland Alexander (HF) played the first seven years of his career with the Phillies, winning 190 games. He led the league in wins five times and won 30 or more games three times while pitching 61 shutouts. He set a Major League record with 16 shutouts in 1916, when he won 33 games with a 1.55 ERA. He was also 0–3 in 1930 for the Phillies in the last year of his career.

Cy Williams played for the Phillies from 1918 through 1930. He hit over .300 seven times and led the league in home runs three times, with a league-leading high of 41 in 1923.

Chuck Klein (HF) had the best start of any player in Major League history. In his first six seasons, all with the Phillies, he never hit less than .337. He led the league four times in home runs, with a high of 43 in 1929. He left for the Cubs in 1934 but returned to the Phillies in 1936 and lasted through part of 1939. He returned again in 1940 to finish out his 17-year career.

Robin Roberts (HF) pitched 14 seasons for the Phillies beginning in 1948. He won 20 or more games six straight seasons, including 28 in 1952. He led the league in strikeouts twice and pitched 35 shutouts for the club.

Steve Carlton (HF) pitched 15 seasons for the Phillies, winning a league high 27 in 1972. He led the league in wins three more times with the Phillies and in strikeouts five times. He won six postseason games for the club, including two in the 1983 World Series when he posted an 0.66 ERA.

Mike Schmidt (HF) played his entire 18-year career for the Phillies from 1972 through mid–1989. He led the league in home runs eight times, including 48 in 1980. He finished with 548 home runs and was one of the best defensive third basemen of his era. He drove in 1,595 runs to go with 1,883 strikeouts.

Curt Schilling pitched almost nine full seasons for the club between 1992 and 2000, when he left for the Diamondbacks. He had win totals of 14, 16, 17, 15, 15 for the club and peaked with 319 strikeouts in 1997.

Scott Rolen began with the club in 1996 and played through most of the 2002 season before being traded to the Cardinals. He routinely hit 25 or more home runs and twice had over 100 RBIs.

Bobby Abreu hit over .300 for the club five times between 1998 and 2003 and had more than 100 RBIs twice.

Key Managers. In the club's first 100 years (1883–1982), it had 37 managers, 31 of whom played Major League Baseball. There was a good mix from each position: seven catchers, six pitchers, nine outfielders, one first baseman, three second baseman, three third baseman and two shortstops.

Harry Wright (HF) managed the Phillies for the longest tenure, 1884 through 1893. His best finish was second place in 1887.

Pat Moran led the club to a first-place finish in 1915 before losing the World Series. After two second-place finishes the club fell to sixth and Moran was fired.

Eddie Sawyer took over the Phillies in mid–1948. He led the club to a pennant in 1950, when the "Whiz Kids" lost to the Yankees in the World Series. The club plummeted in 1951 and he was fired during the 1952 season. He returned to manage the Phillies for part of 1958, all of 1959 and one game in 1960. The club finished last each season.

Gene Mauch managed the club for 8½ years from 1960 to midway through the 1968 season. He guided the club to its famous 1964 collapse at the end of the season when the Phillies finished second.

Danny Ozark.

"Oh, I know we're having troubles, but that's nothing new. Even Napoleon had his *Watergate* [sic]."—Ozark, who managed the club from 1972 until August 1979, with a .538 winning percentage and three straight division titles starting in 1976. Nevertheless, his clubs lost all three of the NLCS.

Dallas Green.

"Talking about Dallas Green's patience is like talking about Dolly Parton's elbows. It's not what he's known for. [He has] built a reputation on intolerance, a demanding nature and an ability to shatter crystal at 20 paces."—Sportswriter Marty Noble.

Green led the club to two first-place finishes in 1980 and 1981, with a World Series victory in 1980 over the Royals. He was fired after losing a division mini-play-off after the strike-shortened 1981 regular season.

Jim Fregosi managed the club for six years between 1991 and 1996, winning one division title and the pennant (1993).

Terry Francona led the club for four uneventful seasons between 1997 and 2000, never finishing above third place.

Larry Bowa was hired for the 2001 season and the Phillies finished second to the Braves. After two third place finishes in 2002 and 2003, he was on the hot seat during the 2004 season, but management indicated that he would be retained through the end of the season despite being intensely disliked by most of his players and the fans. See Barry M. Bloom and Bowa, *I Still Hate to Lose* (2004).

Ballparks.

"An old ballpark has an allure that cannot be dismissed. It evokes warm memories while suggesting another era when baseball was a kinder, gentler game. One cannot simply forget it. It's grip is far too strong."—Rich Westcott, author of *Philadelphia's Old Ballparks* (1996).

Early Ballparks. In 1883 the Phillies played at Recreation Park, built for a minor league club. It was located at Columbia and Ridge Avenues and 24th and 25th Streets. The park was too small and on April 30, 1887, the Huntington Grounds opened.

The Huntington Grounds were built by Al Reach and co-owner John I. Rogers. The ballpark seated 20,000, was double-decked and had dimensions from left to right field of 335–408–272. It had a 60-foot high fence in right field. Center field had club offices and a pool for the players. There was a banked bicycle track in the outfield and the field sloped upward to the outfield walls to accommodate the track. Much of the park burned in 1894, was rebuilt, and then collapsed in 1903, killing 12 of 500 fans who ran to the back wall to watch a fire (fight in some sources) on a nearby street.

Baker Bowl. When the Huntington Grounds burned, the ballpark was rebuilt into what was later called *Baker Bowl* (after owner William F. Baker). The rebuilt facility was the first of the modern parks in the National League.

Shibe Park. The Phillies first played in *Shibe Park* in 1939 as tenants of the A's for night games. They became the sole occupant of the ballpark, later known as Connie Mack Stadium, when the A's left town after the 1954 season. The Phillies then purchased the ballpark and played there through 1970.

Veterans Stadium.

"I stand at the plate in the Vet in Philadelphia and I don't honestly know whether I'm in Pittsburgh, Cincinnati, St. Louis, or Philly. They all look alike."—Richie Hebner.

"It was like a giant concrete dog-food bowl on Philadelphia's back porch, and that's a nice image. Almost everyone likes dogs."—Mark Bowden, just before the Vet was blown up on March 21, 2004, in 58 seconds. It was scrapped to make room for a 5,500-space parking lot.

The "Vet," opened for business on April 10, 1971, after a long effort to get the stadium built. The Phillies had sold Connie Mack Stadium (known earlier as Shibe Park) in 1961, simultaneously signing a three-year lease fully expecting to have a new ballpark by 1964. No progress was made toward a new facility, so the Phillies owners contemplated building a ballpark in New Jersey.

In November 1964 a $25 million bond issue was approved by voters and plans were developed for the ballpark, but a second bond issue was needed before ground was broken on October 2, 1967. The ballpark unexpectedly took 3½ years to build at a cost of $49.5 million.

The park seated 64,538 for baseball and had dimensions from left to right field of 330–371–408–371–330. The Vet covers 14 acres on a site about six miles from the old Connie Mack Stadium in North Philadelphia.

On Opening Day 1971 the club attracted 55,352, the largest attendance figure in Pennsylvania history to that date. Throwing out the ceremonial first pitch in the new ballpark was accomplished by dropping it from a helicopter (bobbled but caught by catcher Mike Ryan). This began a tradition of oddball *Opening Day* first ball throws. To complete the inaugural festivities, a Marine corporal threw out a more traditional first ball from his box seat and then Jim Bunning took over, defeating the Expos 6–1. The ballpark hosted a record 67,064 on October 16, 1983, against the Orioles in the World Series.

The last game was played September 28, 2003, and featured a tribute to reliever Tug McGraw, who died of brain cancer the following January. The Braves beat the Phillies 5–2.

Citizens Bank Park. A new ballpark opened in April 2004, with Citizen's Bank paying $95 million for naming rights. Seating 43,500, the facility initially had 71 luxury suites and cost $458 million. Located on a 21-acre site, it sits on the north side of Pattison Avenue, between 11th and Darien Streets. In December 2000 the Philadelphia City Council approved a $1 billion project for a new sports complex in the area, that would also include a separate facility for the NFL Eagles.

Work began in July 2001, ground was actually broken in January 2002, and the park was ready for Opening Day 2004. The ballpark features 10-foot bronze statues of Phillies greats Mike Schmidt, Richie Ashburn, Robin Roberts and Steve Carlton. The area behind the outfield features retail shops in Ashburn's Alley and BBQ from Bull's, a new eatery using Greg Luzinski's nickname.

The ballparks' dimensions from left to right field are 329–369–401–369–329, though there is an "angle" in left center that juts out to 409 feet. Right field has a 13-foot fence and left field has an eight-foot fence.

In the first game, played April 12, 2004, the Phillies lost to the Reds 4–1 as Paul Wilson got the win in front of 41,626 fans (capacity was 43,500).

Key Broadcasters.

"Hello there Byrom Saam, this is everybody speaking."—Byrum Fred "By" Saam's first words on his first broadcast for the Phillies.

Saam, "the man of a zillion words," first broadcast in 1938 for the Phillies, working simultaneously for the A's and Phillies from 1939 through 1949. He broadcast exclusively for the A's from 1950 through 1954. After the A's left for Kansas City, he went back to the Phillies for 21 years before retiring after the 1975 season because of cataracts. He broadcast 4,935 losing games during his 49 years and never saw a pennant by either team. Ironically, the Phillies won in 1950 when he was exclusively with the A's for the first time. To honor Saam's lifelong contribution to the Phillies, the club brought him out of retirement in 1976 to broadcast the late-season game in which the Phillies clinched the Eastern Division crown.

Former player Richie Ashburn broadcaster for the Phillies beginning in 1963, and lasted through his death following the 1997 season. Andy Musser began broadcasting for the Phillies in 1976 and lasted through 2001. A detached retina forced him out at a bad time; during the 1993 NLCS. He missed the rest of the play-offs and the World Series, but returned to the booth the following season.

Frick Award winner Harry Kalas started with the club in 1971, with his signature call of "Outta here, home run!" begun with Greg Luzinski's long blasts. Kalas began his love for baseball when Senators star Mickey Vernon picked him up during a rainstorm and took him into the dugout. He also is the voice of NFL Films. In 2004 he no longer wanted to work with Chris Wheeler, who had been paired with him since 1977. Former players who broadcast for the club include Kent Tekulve, Larry Anderson, Jay Johnstone, Tim McCarver and Garry Maddox.

Books. Donald Honig, *The Philadelphia Phillies* (1992); David M. Jordan, *Occasional Glory: A History of the Philadelphia Phillies* (2002); Allan Lewis, *The Philadelphia Phillies* (1981); Fred Lieb and Stan Baumgartner, *The Philadelphia Phillies* (1953); Richard Orodenker, *The Phillies Reader* (1996); Chris W. Sehnert, *Philadelphia Phillies* (1997); Rich West-cott and Frank Bilovsky, *The Phillies Encyclopedia* (2004); Fran Zimniuch, *Phillies: Where Have You Gone?* (2004).

Philadelphia Quakers

Players League 1890

The Quakers were owned by two Philadelphia meat packing magnates, the Wagner brothers. The team finished fifth with a record of 68–63. It was one of the financially stronger Players League franchises, and when the rival American Association entry in that city folded, the Players League team took its place for the 1891 season.

Philadelphia Whites (White Stockings)

National Association 1873–1875

This club played the last three seasons of the National Association's existence. The Whites finished second in 1873, four games behind the Boston Red Stockings. In 1874 the club slipped to fourth and in 1875 it finished fifth. It was not the club that composed the first National League club, as that honor went to the rival Philadelphia Athletics, also of the National Association.

Philippines

"Any people who did not take to baseball never will be suited to live under the Stars and Stripes." — Comment by an American writer when the game's popularity in the country faded in the 1920s due to anti–American sentiment.

Origins. Baseball was introduced to this island nation as a result of occupation by American troops during the *Spanish-American War* in 1898. Baseball was again popular after World War II and *Little League Baseball* is now hugely popular in the country.

New Tradition. Ernie Harwell once related a story of Filipino courtship during the time when future U.S. President William Howard Taft was governor of the Philippines. A Filipino man could not marry unless he presented the scalp of his most bitter enemy to his future bride. With the introduction of baseball to the country, the custom was changed. The new tradition required the suitor to hit a home run before getting married: "Americans, acting as muscle-bound cupids, often played simple grounders and easy outs into home runs so their Filipino friends could escape bachelorhood."

Photography

"That picture was taken out of context." — Mets pitcher Jeff Innis complaining that a photograph was not flattering to him.

Early 20th century photographers wait for their chances.

"If we really want to know what these fellows look like (and right now I can't think of any public faces that interest us more; our politicians have never looked so drab, and movie stars tend to be nothing *but* face) we need some baseball portraitists right now — the game's very own Steichens and Avedons, who happen to love and understand this one profession well enough to read their subjects' thoughts and catch their moods on the fly." — Wilfrid Sheed in *The Face of Baseball* (1990), featuring baseball portrait photography by John Weiss.

"A weasel-faced bat boy, probably some executive's nephew, I thought, noticed me staring wide-eyed at the players and the playing field. He curled his lip at me, then stuck out his tongue. He mouthed the words 'Take a picture, it'll last longer,' adding something at the end that I could only assume to be uncomplimentary." — W.P. Kinsella in "How I Got My Nickname" (1984).

"Pop Quiz. What do the photograph and baseball have in common? They both officially were invented in 1839 — though baseball's debut is in fact tougher to pin down — and both stop time, permitting us to retain in our mind's eye what in 'real life' passes before us too quickly." — John Thorn in *The Game for All America* (1988).

"Sliding headfirst is the safest way to get to the next base, I think. And the fastest. You don't lose your momentum ... and there's one more important reason I slide headfirst. It gets my picture in the paper." — Pete Rose.

Early Photographs. The first "action" shot of a baseball game was taken in 1862 or 1863, shot inadvertently at Fort Pulaski, Savannah, Georgia, during the Civil War. The photograph was of troops in the foreground in formation, with a game in progress in the background. *The Sporting News* ran its first photograph in 1902, showing Charles Harper of the Reds signing his 1903 contract.

Photographers on the Field.

"George Moriarity, American League umpire, is regarded as the meanest man by one of the photographers who made shots at the All-Star Game.... Gawge had orders to keep the kodakers off the field and when one did not obey instructions he took, not his picture, but his camera, and put it to the grandstand.... The umpire's next move might have been to transfer the photographer along with it, but the latter did not have to have a lens to see what was going to happen."— *The Sporting News*.

Well into the 20th century, photographers routinely came on the field during plays (but not inside the foul lines) to get close-up photographs. They usually ranged near the on-deck circle, but occasionally a photographer interfered with a runner on the basepaths.

Photographer Charles Conlon caused a rule change in 1910. Photographers apparently were allowed inside the foul lines during play, which caused a controversy involving Giants manager John McGraw. McGraw felt that an umpire had blown a call that Conlon photographed. The next day, McGraw showed a picture of the play to the offending umpire to prove that he blew the call. As a result, National League president Tom Lynch banned photographers from inside the foul lines. Conlon was a pioneering photographer for the *Spalding Guide*. He took pictures of Major League players from 1905 through 1942, over 8,000 shots. His photographs were featured in a 1991 baseball card set issued by *The Sporting News*.

Photographers were first barred from the entire field in the 1930s by the Giants and Cubs because too many photographers were on the field. According to the 1951 *Spink Guide*, the National League formally banned photographers from the field in 1950. Presumably the American League quickly followed suit.

One source reported that an incident in Cincinnati in the 1930s prompted National League president Warren Giles to formally bar photographers from the field: a photographer followed manager Birdie Tebbetts onto the field during an argument with an umpire at second base. The American League reportedly followed quickly with its own ban. Problems with the story include the fact that Tebbets didn't start managing until 1954 and Giles wasn't National League president until 1951.

Informal or formal club bans were delayed, not enforced, or exceptions were made for special events. For example, during the Browns' first night game in May 1940, George McQuinn collided with a photographer rounding third base and went tumbling. He righted himself in time to score, but umpire Bill Summers banned all photographers from the field and kicked the camera into the Browns dugout.

In 1929 it was reported that William Ironson (Old Ironsides) was the first photographer hired by the Major Leagues to attend spring training. The National League hired him to chronicle the spring and he took a brief leave from the International Newsreel Service.

David Blumenthal. Blumenthal was the long-time Yankee official photographer during most of the Dan Topping/Del Webb years (1945–1964). He is responsible for the famous shot of Babe Ruth speaking at the microphone on Babe Ruth Day in Yankee Stadium in June 1948, shortly before Ruth died of throat cancer. Blumenthal first photographed Ruth in 1928 when Blumenthal was 17 years old. His cousin had played catcher on Lou Gehrig's high school baseball team and took Blumenthal into the Yankee clubhouse to introduce him around. When Ruth was informed that Blumenthal was a photographer, Ruth hired him to shoot a picture of Ruth and Yankee clubhouse man Pete Sheehy as a Christmas present for Sheehy.

Blumenthal went on to shoot motion picture footage of professional football teams, including the Packers and Bears. He later invented the zoom lens and claimed to be the first photographer to shoot motion picture footage of pitchers from behind home plate for the benefit of the Yankee hitters.

Camera Day. The first official Camera Day reportedly was held by the Brooklyn Dodgers on August 24, 1957.

Cheesecake Photographer. The Pinnacle baseball card company hired supermodel Christie Brinkley to photograph players during spring training in 1996.

Injury. On July 1, 2003, the Marlins beat the Braves 20–1 in Miami, but the game was marred when a bat slipped from the hands of Atlanta's Darren Bragg and struck a photographer. The photographer was placed on a stretcher and was bleeding profusely. He sustained cuts to his face but never lost consciousness. He was airlifted to a hospital but recovered well.

Books. Thomas Boswell, *Diamond Dreams: Thirty Years of Baseball Through the Lens of Walter Iooss* (1995); Richard Cahan and Mark Jacob (eds.), *The Game That Was: The George Brace Baseball Photo Collection* (1996); Henry Horenstein (photographs) and Bill Littlefield (text), *Baseball Days: From the Sandlots to the Show* (1993); Walter Iooss, Jr., and Dave Anderson, *Classic Baseball: The Photographs of Walter Iooss, Jr.* (2003); Dorling Kindersley Publishing, Major League Baseball Staff, Johnny Bench, *Major League Baseball's Best Shots: The Greatest Baseball Photography of All Time* (2000); Neal and Constance McCabe, *Baseball's Golden Age: The Photos of Charles M. Conlon* (1993); Karen Mullarkey (ed.), *Baseball in America: From Sandlots to Stadiums — A Portrait of Our National Pastime by 50 of Today's Leading Photographers* (1991); David R. Phillips (ed.), *The Old Ball Game* (1975), contains over 250 black and white photos from 1850 through 1930 and features the work of Chicago photographer Francis P. Burke; John Thorn, *The Game for All America* (1988), contains photos from Little League through the Major Leagues across America; John Weiss (photographs), *The Face of Baseball* (1990); Steve Wulf, *Legends of the Field: The Classic Sports Photography of Ozzie Sweet* (1993).

Physics

"A small, but interesting, portion of baseball can be understood on the basis of physical principles. The flight of balls, the liveliness of balls, the structure of bats, and the character of the collision of balls and bats are a natural province of physics and physicists."— Robert K. Adair in *The Physics of Baseball* (1990), which he wrote essentially at the request of then–National League president Bart Giamatti. The book's dedication is poignantly made to Adair's grandfather and son, both of whom were deceased. The book is a technical, but readable, look at the mechanics of throwing, hitting and pitching.

See also **Curveballs**.

Pick-Off Throws

"The best pitchers have the worst moves to first base, probably because they let so few runners get there."—1970 American League stolen base leader Tommy Harper.

"I throw him four wide ones, then I try to pick him off first base."—Pitcher Preacher Roe's strategy for dealing with Stan Musial.

"They got me between taps."—Tigers outfielder Gee Walker was picked off so many times that he was advised to tap his foot on the bag to make sure he was on it. This quote was his explanation after being picked off once again.

"Don't get too far from the bag or the Jew will nip you."—Supposedly said by shortstop Joe Tinker of the Cubs to racist Ty Cobb of the Tigers, who was on second base during the 1907 World Series. Tinker, referring to catcher Johnny Kling, then signaled and as Cobb turned to reply, Kling threw to second baseman Johnny Evers who made the tag for the out. It is an interesting story, except that the only time Cobb was tagged out on the basepaths during the World Series was in Game 5, when he was thrown out attempting to steal third (Kling to Steinfeldt)—and Kling probably wasn't *Jewish*.

"Would you just throw the pitch already. It's muddy over here. Just stop it. Please! I'm not going to steal, OK? I promise."—Rickey Henderson to an opposing pitcher when he was with the Newark Bears in 2003, after the pitcher made him dive back to first nine times in a row before delivering a pitch to the plate.

Good Move. Wilbur Cooper, who pitched principally for the Pirates from 1912 through 1926 with a 216–178 record, picked off seven runners from third base in 1924.

Bob Feller. Feller was notoriously poor at holding runners on base. Opposing players figured out that he only looked at the runner once and never looked again. Feller and his pick-off move were involved in one of the most controversial plays in World Series history.

The Indians were playing the Braves in the 8th inning of a scoreless tie in Game 1 of the 1948 Series. With one out, pinch runner Phil Masi of the Braves was on second base with Feller pitching and good-hitting pitcher Johnny Sain at bat. Feller wheeled and threw to shortstop Lou Boudreau on the pick-off attempt. Umpire Bill Stewart made a bad call and called him safe. After a long and loud argument, Sain lined out. Tommy Holmes then singled home Masi and the Braves won 1–0. Nevertheless, the Indians won the series in six games. Despite photographs clearly to the contrary, Masi claimed later that the tag was on his shoulder (it was) while his hand was already touching the bag (it was not).

Ben Chapman sometimes stole on Feller because he noticed that there was daylight under Feller's right heel when he was going to throw to first base; and no daylight when he was going to throw to the plate.

At age 45 Negro League star Cool Papa Bell played an exhibition game against Feller in Los Angeles. Bell could tell when Feller was not going to throw over because Feller would look hard at the runner for a few moments and then always go home with the pitch.

No Pick-Off Throws.

"There are only so many pitches in this old arm, and I don't believe in wasting them throwing to first base."—Eddie Plank.

Pitcher Sam Jones did not throw to first base for five years. When Jones finally did it, the first baseman dropped the ball.

On May 28, 1990, Roger Clemens of the Red Sox and Charlie Hough of the Rangers combined to throw to first base 51 times in one game.

Rookie Prediction. Art Mahaffey bragged that he would pick off the first baserunner he faced in the Major Leagues. In his first game in 1960, at Busch Stadium in St. Louis, as predicted he picked off Bill White in the 7th inning. He also picked off the second batter after he reached base, Curt Flood (some sources have the order reversed). He also picked off the next baserunner he faced, Jim Marshall, in his next game.

Three in an Inning. On August 24, 1983, the Orioles faced the Blue Jays in Baltimore. After a 9th inning solo homer by Blue Jays designated hitter Cliff Johnson to tie the game, Barry Bonnell singled off Tim Stoddard. Orioles reliever Tippy Martinez came in and picked off Bonnell. Dave Collins walked, but Martinez picked him off. Willie Upshaw singled, but Martinez picked him off to end the inning. Orioles infielder Lenn Sakata hit a three-run home run in the bottom of the 10th inning to win the game 7–4.

In a Daze. After George Brett recorded hit number 3,000 on September 30, 1992, the game resumed after a long celebration. Angels pitcher Tim Fortugno picked off Brett while he was wandering off first base in midsentence with the Angels' first baseman.

On May 13, 1991, Gary Pettis of the Tigers was picked off third base during an intentional walk by the Rangers. No one on either team could recall it occurring before. Pettis apparently did not realize the intentional walk was on and broke for home on an apparent squeeze. One teammate commented that Pettis "had a vapor lock" and that he "does stuff like that all the time."

In 1980 Ron LeFlore of the Expos led the league with 97 stolen bases. When he stole number 62, the Montreal scoreboard noted that the first stolen base had occurred 115 years earlier. LeFlore wandered off second base as he stood mesmerized watching the scoreboard and was promptly tagged out.

Good Throw. In Game 1 of the 2003 World Series, Marlins catcher Ivan Rodriguez picked off Yankee first baseman Nick Johnson in the 3rd inning. Johnson took a big a lead off third base when the game was tied and the play ended the inning. Johnson was left sprawled in the dirt, far short of the bag.

Long Wait. On June 29, 1987, A's reliever Dennis Eckersley picked off Kenny Williams of the White Sox. It was not until May 22, 1991, that Eckersley picked off another runner. The victim: Kenny Williams, who was pinch-running for the Blue Jays.

World Series. In Game 7 of the 1968 World Series, the Cardinals and Tigers were scoreless after five innings. In the bottom of the 6th inning, the most dangerous base stealer of the era, Lou Brock, singled and then took a huge lead off Mickey Lolich. Lolich promptly picked him off. With two outs, Curt Flood singled. Lolich picked him off, though he had never before picked off two runners in an inning. The Tigers scored three runs in the 7th inning to take a 3–0 lead that led to a 4–1 win and the championship.

Pinch Hitters

"I was very calm. What are they going to do if I *don't* get a hit? Bench me?"—Braves catcher Bill Nahorodny on getting a key pinch hit after being benched the entire 1981 season.

"Although perhaps art did not appeal to Comiskey as strongly as a .300 slugger there could be no doubt of his appreciation of its utilitarian advantages. While walking through the National Museum at Naples, Italy, he paused in front of the heroic statue of Hercules. He permitted his eyes to roam admiringly over the massive figure until they rested on the huge club which had done such execution in the Theban and Cretan leagues, and mused: 'What a pinch hitter he would have made!'"—G.W. Axelson in *"Commy"* (1919).

"As an outfielder he is pretty close to his past tense, which may mean that one year from now he will be only a pinch hitter. He has been breaking this news to himself and the customers all year."—Westbrook Pegler of the *Chicago Tribune* on Babe Ruth late in his career.

Early Use. Pinch hitters in non-injury situations were first allowed in 1892 in the 12-team National League (1891 in some sources).

The first pinch hitter most often identified by historians is Jack Doyle of the National League Cleveland Spiders, who singled against the Brooklyn Dodgers on June 7, 1892. Doyle pinch-hit for pitcher George Davies. Another source credits Doyle with playing with the Giants during his pinch hit, probably because he was traded to the Giants that year after 24 games with Cleveland. Doyle was 3-for-5 in his pinch-hitting career.

Some sources credit Charlie Reilly of the Phillies with the first pinch hit on April 29, 1892, replacing Kid Carsey in the 9th inning at Chicago. Reilly's name did not appear in the box scores in the regular weekly baseball publications, but it clearly showed in the daily newspapers covering the game. Connie Mack also had a pinch hit appearance in 1892.

Other sources cite Mickey Welch of the Giants as the first pinch hitter. He struck out pinch hitting for Hank O'Day on September 10, 1889. However, this must have been an injury situation because the pinch-hitting rule was not yet formally in effect. It was not until 1907 that any player pinch-hit more than 20 times in a season.

Substitution Rule. In one 1908 game a pinch hitter for the Phillies was announced. The Pirates countered with a new pitcher and then a new Phillies pinch hitter was sent up to hit. The Phillies manager tried to use the original pinch hitter later in the game. The Pirates protested and the umpires agreed with them. The decision prohibiting reuse of the original pinch hitter was incorporated into the rulebook.

Appearance Rule. Until 1907 in the American League and 1912 in the National League, pinch hitters and other substitutes often were not credited with a game played.

Popularity. After their use began in the 1890s, pinch hitters were used more frequently in the early 1900s, though the practice was still sporadic. The 1902 Pirates used only eight pinch hitters all season.

Dodie Criss of the Browns was the first player to be used frequently as a pinch hitter, leading the American League's pinch hitters with 12 hits in 41 at-bats in 1908. This was more than twice as many pinch hit at-bats as any previous batter. He also led in pinch at-bats and pinch hits for the next three years.

In 1913 Doc Miller had 20 hits in 56 at-bats, the first time a player had 20 pinch hits in a season. Despite the increase in use as the 20th century progressed, the pinch hitter was not a highly popular weapon until the 1950s. Peanuts Lowrey led the 1953 Cardinals with 22 pinch hits. Also successful were Jerry Lynch and Smoky Burgess, who are among the all-time leaders in pinch hits.

Terminology. Giants manager John McGraw is credited by some with the name "pinch" hitter, when he called upon Sammy Strang 14 times in 1905 to bat "in the pinch."

Most/Career. Manny Mota was for several years the all-time pinch hit leader with 150 over a career lasting from 1962 through 1980. He passed Smokey Burgess, who had 145 from 1949 through 1967. Jose Morales finished his career with 123 pinch hits from 1973 through 1984.

In October 2001 Lenny Harris tied and then passed Mota, and was still going strong in 2004 at age 39.

Pitcher Red Lucas had 114 pinch hits, putting him among the all-time leaders. He was also the first pinch hitter to reach 100 pinch hits for his career. He also won 157 games over 15 seasons, mostly for the Reds and Pirates in the 1920s and 1930s.

Most/Season. In 1995 John VanderWal of the Rockies had 28 pinch hits to set a new Major League record.

Jose Morales had 25 pinch hits for the Expos in 1975. Dave Philley is the American League leader with 24 in 1961 for the Orioles. Vic Davalillo of the 1970 Cardinals and Rusty Staub of the 1983 Mets each had 24 pinch hits.

Season Batting Average. Ed Kranepool of the Mets batted .486 in 1974, going 17-for-35.

Lifetime Batting Average.

"What makes a good pinch hitter? I wish to hell I knew!"—Bobby Murcer.

Gordy Coleman is the all-time leader with a .333 average (40-for-120), from 1959 through 1967 (minimum 100 at-bats).

Among more recent players, Rod Carew is fourth all-time with a .323 average (40-for-124). Al Kaline is fifth with a .322 average (37-for-115).

Tommy Davis had a lifetime pinch-hitting average of .320, cited erroneously by many as the highest ever. It is sixth all-time.

Of players with at least 200 pinch hit at-bats, only Bob Fothergill has an average over .300.

Worst Pinch Hitters. Among players with at least 100 pinch hit at-bats, Ivan Murrell is at the bottom with a .117 average (21-for-180) in a career spanning 1963 through 1974.

Hall of Fame. Of all Hall of Famers, only Bill Terry has a pinch hit average over .300 (.301) among players with 100 pinch hit at-bats.

Home Runs.

"I guess I'm in the twilight of a very mediocre career."—Carroll Hardy, more of a *Football* star, who pinch hit 71 times, batting .190 in those at-bats. He hit his first home run while pinch hitting for Roger Maris in May 1958. He also is remembered as the only man to pinch hit for Ted Williams (see below).

Jerry Lynch had 18 career pinch hit home runs and was the Major League leader in that category for many years. In 1984 his mark was surpassed by Cliff Johnson, who hit 20 pinch hit home runs in his career while playing primarily for the Yankees and Blue Jays.

In 1932 Johnny Frederick hit six pinch hit home runs for the Dodgers to establish the then-Major League season record. On September 12, 2000, Dave Hansen of the Dodgers hit his seventh home run of the season to set a new record. The record was tied the following season when Pirates rookie Craig Wilson hit seven.

Doubleheader Home Runs. On June 17, 1943, 37-year-old Red Sox manager Joe Cronin belted pinch-hit home runs in both ends of a doubleheader against the A's in Fenway Park. He had three two-run home runs in four at-bats that day.

His record of two pinch-hit home runs in a doubleheader was tied by Hal Breeden of the Expos on July 13, 1973. Breeden homered in both games against the Braves in Atlanta.

First At-Bat. The first player to hit a pinch hit home run in his first Major League at-bat was Eddie Morgan of the Cardinals on April 14, 1936. The first American Leaguer to do it was Ace Parker for the A's on April 30, 1937.

On April 12, 1955, Chuck Tanner of the Braves became the first pinch hitter to hit the first Major League pitch thrown to him for a home run.

Pinch hitter Gates Brown hit a pinch hit home run in his first Major League at-bat. He hit .472 in 1968 (18-for-39), the second-highest season pinch hit average behind Ed Kranepool's .486. Though Brown's image is as one of the best pinch hitters of all time, other than in 1968 he was lousy at it (with selected seasons of 8-for-39, 10-for-41, 4-for-28, 0-for-4 and 6-for-35).

Consecutive Home Runs. Pitcher Ray Caldwell of the Yankees hit pinch home runs in consecutive games on June 10 and 11, 1915.

Dave Philley of the Phillies had two consecutive pinch hit home runs on September 9, 1958, and April 16, 1959.

Two pinch hitters have hit three consecutive pinch hit home runs in official at-bats: Lee Lacy did it for the 1978 Dodgers, though he walked in between the second and third home runs. Del Unser did so for the 1979 Phillies in three straight plate appearances.

In his book, *Sixty-One*, Tony Kubek recalls that Yankee catcher Johnny Blanchard hit two consecutive pinch hit home runs in 1961. Both were in the 9th inning of games against the Red Sox. The first was a grand slam to win the game and the second was a solo shot that tied the next game. In Blanchard's first at-bat of the next game that he started after the pinch hits (with no intervening appearances), he homered. In his next at-bat he homered again for his fourth home run in four straight at-bats.

Art Shamsky of the Reds hit a pinch hit home run on August 12, 1966. In two subsequent at-bats in the game he also hit home runs.

On June 30, 1999, Willie Greene of the Orioles hit his second pinch hit home run in two at-bats.

Team/Consecutive. The 1995 Red Sox were the last club to tie the record of four consecutive pinch hits in an inning. It was the first time in 55 years that it had been done.

World Series. Yogi Berra hit the first pinch hit home run in World Series history when he connected in Game 3 in 1947.

Dusty Rhodes of the Giants hit two pinch hit home runs in the 1954 World Series. He had six RBIs in the first three games.

Dodger pinch hitter Chuck Essegian hit a pinch home run in both Game 2 and Game 6 in Comiskey Park during the 1959 World Series. He also homered in his first at-bat on Opening Day the next season.

In the 1965 World Series Don Drysdale pinch-hit for Sandy Koufax against Jim Kaat. A pitcher-for-pitcher switch did not occur again until Game 3 of the 1991 World Series between the Twins and Braves. Twins pitcher Rick Aguilera flied out pinch-hitting in the 12th inning against Jim Clancy.

Babe Ruth. The last man to pinch-hit for Babe Ruth was Ben Paschal, after Ruth went 0-for-3 in the 1927 season opener. Paschal had a single to drive in the winning run.

Ted Williams. Only one player ever appeared as a pinch hitter for Williams. Carroll Hardy pinch-hit for him on May 18, 1958, after Williams was injured fouling a pitch off his foot. Hardy hit into a double play.

Henry Aaron. Aaron was lifted for a pinch hitter for the first time on May 21, 1969, when Mike Lum batted for him in the 7th inning of a 15–3 Braves win against the Mets.

Most Used. In a September 1967 game White Sox manager Eddie Stanky used 12 pinch hitters and pinch runners in one-third of an inning.

Strategy. Longtime Orioles manager Earl Weaver sometimes substituted another batter at the start of the game for light-hitting shortstop Mark Belanger; the quintessential "good field, no hit" player. The strategy apparently paid off, as Royle Stillman would lead off the game on the road, and then Belanger would be put into the lineup defensively in the bottom of the inning. Stillman was 4-for-9 using this strategy.

Pinch Runners

"The Panamanian Local" — A's owner Charlie Finley hired Allan Lewis as a full-time pinch runner in the mid–1960s. Finley dubbed him the "Panamanian Express" after he had once stolen 116 bases in a minor league season. Lewis was a bust in the Major Leagues and earned the negative nickname "Panamanian Local" from sportswriter Herb Michelson because he was thrown out at second base so often. Lewis stole 44 Major League bases over six seasons beginning in 1967, while recording only 29 official at-bats.

Herb Washington. In 1974 Finley hired Washington for $40,000 per season to serve exclusively as a pinch runner. Wash-

ington was a world-class sprinter but had not played baseball since high school. He stole 30 bases in his 104-game career in 1974 and 1975. He was thrown out 18 times. He was picked off an inordinate number of times and was criticized for not taking the extra base on balls hit to the outfield.

In the 1974 World Series, Dodger pitcher Mike Marshall picked him off twice. Coincidentally, Washington had taken a physical education class that Marshall had taught at Michigan State University.

Late in Washington's career, manager Alvin Dark asked him if he wanted to pinch-*hit* against Nolan Ryan. He almost did but then thought that his notoriety would end if he ever batted. Washington later successfully invested in a chain of fast-food restaurants in Rochester, New York.

Larry Lintz. Lintz followed in Washington's footsteps for the A's. In 1976 he scored 21 runs and had 31 stolen bases while recording only one official at-bat.

Origins. Pinch runners originally were chosen by the captain of the opposing team. It has been reported that until 1878 pinch runners sometimes stood next to a batter and ran to first on a hit.

Pinch Runner-Turned-Batter. Gene Stephens of the Red Sox was inserted as a pinch runner for Ted Williams in a game in 1959. Stephens was immediately put out on a force play, but the rally continued and he batted. He hit a grand slam in a 13–3 victory over the Yankees.

Hiding Weakness. Outfielder Damon Buford, son of Orioles star Don Buford, pinch ran for the Red Sox in the 9th inning of a game on April 17, 1998. Short on players, the club put him in the infield in the 10th inning and hoped that no one hit him a ball. He started the inning at second base, then switched to third after Cleveland's Manny Ramirez singled. He switched back to second after an out, then switched again after another out. The Indians couldn't score and the Red Sox won 3–2.

Lewis/Lewis. On October 3, 1911, the Red Sox played at New York. In the top of the 2nd inning of the second game of the World Series, Duffy Lewis scored from third while Jack Lewis advanced to second base on a double steal during a strikeout by Hugh Bradley. Jack was shaken up on the play and the umpire let Duffy run for him. The inning ended with no further scoring and Jack took the field.

Pine Tar

"Prior to 1983, I was always ridiculed at ballparks about an ailment [hemorrhoids] I had during the 1980 World Series. Now, since 1983, I'm always known as the Pine Tar Guy. Now what would you rather be known as?"— George Brett.

"Batgate"— New York columnist Ira Berkow's name for the famous George Brett incident.

"Pine Tar Wars"

The most notorious event involving pine tar was the George Brett game of July 24, 1983. Brett's Royals were playing the Yankees in Yankee Stadium. In the top of the 9th inning Brett hit a two-run homer off Goose Gossage to put the Royals ahead 5–4.

Yankee manager Billy Martin immediately protested the bat used by Brett, claiming that there was excessive pine tar on the handle. Umpire Tim McClelland agreed and disallowed the bat, invoking the rule that no substance may be applied to the bat more than 18 inches from the knob. Brett was called out and the home run was disallowed. The Yankees were declared 4–3 winners because Brett was the last out.

Royals outfielder Hal McRae then made the last out in the top of the 9th inning, and reliever Dan Quisenberry got the last three outs against the Yankees to preserve the 5–4 victory. McRae heard Martin screaming to retrieve the bat. Had he reacted quickly, he could have avoided the whole incident by tossing the offending bat in the Royals dugout and mixing it among other bats. Brett later said he didn't mind that McRae didn't get to the bat first: "If Hal had, then I'd only be known for hemorrhoids."

Brett went berserk after the call and had to be restrained as he tried to charge home plate umpire Tim McClelland. McClelland later questioned Brett's wisdom: "I've always said George wasn't a very smart man, because he's charging out at a man who stands 6–6 and weighs 250 pounds. And I had my protective equipment on and I was standing there with a bat in my hand. So I don't know what he was going to do when he got out there."

American League president Lee MacPhail reversed the call and let the home run stand. He further ruled that the game would be completed at a later date if it had bearing on the division standings. Other sources report that the game was ordered finished regardless of the standings, but there were no further games to be played between the clubs. As a result, it was resumed on an off-day, August 18, 1983. Before the game was played, however, two fans sought an injunction in protest over the $2.50 admission price. A lower court granted the injunction, but an appellate court immediately overturned the ruling and the game proceeded.

In the replay, 1,245 fans watched Yankee pitcher Ron Guidry play center field and first baseman Don Mattingly, a left-hander, play second base in the 12-minute affair. The umpires had a notarized letter from the earlier crew stating that the runners had touched the bases on Brett's home run, which they pulled out when Yankee manager Billy Martin protested that Brett had not touched home plate.

Brett's bat was a T-85 Marv Throneberry (!) model, a bat style that he had used for about five years. The bat had no finish or lacquer (Brett did not wear a batting glove), and might have lasted a week had it not been taken out of circulation because of the protest.

Brett did not attend the make-up game, staying on the team's charter plane. Steve Balboni of the Yankees had been sent to the minor leagues, and his replacement was ineligible to play in the game.

On the tenth anniversary of the game during Brett's final season, he hit two home runs. The pine tar incident is recounted in *Pinstripe Pandemonium*, by Geoffrey Stokes (1984), a chronicle of the 1983 Yankee season.

The Rule. In the 1950s Senators owner Clark Griffith advocated the rule prohibiting foreign substances on a bat more than 18 inches from the knob. It has been reported that the parsimonious owner pushed for the rule so that his players would not overuse pine tar. The rule: "Rule 1.10 (b): 'the bat handle, for not more than 18 inches from the end, may be covered or treated with any material (including pine tar) to improve the grip. Any such material, including pine tar, which extends past the 18-inch limitation, in the umpire's judgment, shall be removed from the game."

In the 1990s a new spray-on pine tar was introduced.

Use by Pitchers. Bob Moose of the Pirates was a rookie in August 1968 when he discovered the value of pine tar on a thrown ball. He was getting shelled by the Cardinals. After the inning he rubbed his hand with pine tar and struck out the next four Cardinals.

After Cardinals manager Red Schoendienst called the rule violation to the attention of the umpires, Moose was ordered to the clubhouse to wash off his hand. He was bombed again and a reliever was sent in to mop up the 5–0 loss.

Jay Howell pitched in relief for the Dodgers in Game 3 of the 1988 NLCS against the Mets. On a cold day he rubbed pine tar on his glove to give him a better grip. He was thrown out of the game and suspended for two games of the series.

In August 2004 pitcher Julian Tavares was suspended for 10 days when umpire Joe West determined that the "dirt" on his grimy cap was actually pine tar. Subsequent chemical analysis of the cap showed that the substance was nothing but dirt.

Helmet. Outfielder Vladimir Guerrero abandoned batting gloves in 1999 and began slathering pine tar on his helmet. He would rub his hands in the dirt and then brush then across the tar on his helmet before he batted.

Spray. By the 2000s, a pine tar spray was on the market.

History. The substance has been used for centuries by sailors to preserve wood and rigging. It came originally from Sweden and other northern climates such as Finland and Russia.

Pitch Count/The Count

"You win going 1-and-2, you lose going 2-and-1, and the difference between 1-and-2 and 2-and-1 is a fraction of an inch."— Don Drysdale on the importance of staying ahead in the count.

Less Pitches Thrown. Less pitches in a game were needed in the 19th century because games were much lower-scoring. Also, very few players were long-ball threats so pitchers did not have to bear down on every pitch as they do today. Pitchers in a 19th century game collectively threw about 180 pitches per game, which is not consistent with a game story involving Christy Mathewson in August 1911. The newspaper reported that Mathewson set a record for fewest pitches thrown, with 90 (an average of 10 to an inning and three to a man, noted the newspaper).

Sandy Koufax averaged 155 pitches per game in one season in the early 1960s, not an unusual amount for that era. By 1989 the average for all starting pitchers had dropped to 94, and in 1991 it was approximately 82 pitches per game. This reflected a dramatic drop in complete games rather than total pitch count in a game.

In 1987 there were 106 performances in which a pitcher threw at least 140 pitches in a game. In 1995 there were only 36, and only four performances in 1994 and 1995 of more than 150—two by Randy Johnson.

The protocol by the late 1990s was 120 pitches as the limit to keep a pitcher healthy.

Most Pitches Thrown.

"The pitch count is the addendum to the five man rotation in baseball's quest to keep pitchers healthy."— Tom Verducci in *Sports Illustrated*.

"The way that managers have tested the limits of starting pitchers for the last century is quite a bit like the way they used to test for witches, by pond dunking."— Bill James.

"It obviously ruined his arm because he had to retire 19 years later."— Bill James on Nolan Ryan throwing 235 pitches in a 12-inning game against Luis Tiant and the Red Sox in 1974.

Although pitch counts were not kept with great accuracy until the last few years, Nolan Ryan is known to have thrown 241 pitches in a game for the Angels in the mid–1970s. Ryan believes he averaged between 160–180 pitches per game in the 1974.

When he struck out 21 Orioles in a 16-inning game in 1962, Senators pitcher Tom Cheney threw 228 pitches, including fastballs, knucklers, sliders and curveballs.

An ailing Luis Tiant threw 163 pitches in a complete game 5–4 win by the Red Sox over the Reds in Game 4 of the 1975 World Series. He had just thrown a shutout in Game 1 of the Series and before that pitched a three-hit shutout of the A's to start a sweep of the ALCS.

Fewest Thrown. The fewest number of pitches known to have been thrown by a single pitcher throwing a complete game is 58, by Charley (Red) Barrett of the Braves in a 2–0, nine-inning game against the Reds on August 10, 1944.

In 1915 White Sox spitball pitcher Red Faber threw only 67 pitches in defeating the Senators 4–1. He threw 50 strikes and 17 balls (balls put in play were considered strikes). In two of the innings, each batter hit the first pitch.

On July 22, 1997, Greg Maddux used only 78 pitches to beat the Cubs 4–1 in the first game of a doubleheader. It was the lowest nine-inning complete game pitch count since Bob Tewksbury threw 76 pitches for the Cardinals against the Reds on August 29, 1990.

On May 24, 2001, Cubs starter Jon Lieber needed only 78 pitches to dispatch the Reds in a 3–0 shutout, ending Cincinnati's 208-game streak in which the club scored a run. The Reds managed only one hit.

Most Pitches Thrown To Batter/No Fouls. A batter could see 11 pitches in one at-bat and strike out, with no foul balls. With the count at 2-and-2 (4 pitches)there is a runner on base. On the 3–2 pitch (5) the runner is thrown out trying to steal for the third out of the inning. The same batter starts the next inning with a new count, which he strikes out on 6 pitches (3 balls 3 strikes for a total of 11 pitches).

Intentional Walks. Pitches used to complete an intentional walk are not included in official pitch counts.

Umpire Angst. In July 2001 Major League umpires filed a grievance after the leagues installed cameras to track balls and strikes. They claimed that the leagues were tracking pitch count as a way to determine how well the umpires were managing their strike zones and forcing the umpires to call more strikes. The umpires dropped their grievance a few days later. See also *Umpires —Electronic Umpire.*

Japan. In Japan the count is read with the strikes called first, a full count being 2-and-3.

Pitchers

"All pitchers are liars and crybabies." — Catcher Yogi Berra.

"You don't worry much about a hitter's weakness until you get ahead of him. First you concentrate on getting your good pitches over, to put him in a hole. You don't want to get yourself in a hole by missing a spot and falling behind in a count. So you start by making sure he has to hit your best stuff if he's going to hit you. Then, once you're ahead you can work on his weaknesses." — Don Drysdale quoted in Leonard Koppett's, *A Thinking Man's Guide to Baseball* (1967).

"A good pitcher's main job is not to give up the first run." — Pitcher Sal Maglie.

"The pitcher is the most important player on the field, and on his skills and judgment depends half the battle in a match." —19th century sportswriter Henry Chadwick.

"I never saw a pitcher I didn't feel sorry for." — Rogers Hornsby.

"Next to control, the whole secret of big-league pitching is mixing 'em up. It means inducing a batter to believe that another kind of ball is coming from the one that is really to be delivered, and thus preventing him from getting set to hit it." — Christy Mathewson on the art of pitching.

"After 15 years of facing them, you don't really get over them. They're devious. They're the only players in the game allowed to cheat. They throw illegal pitches, and they sneak foreign substances on the ball. They can inflict pain whenever they wish. And they're the only ones on the diamond who have high ground. That's symbolic. You know what they tell you in war, 'Take the high ground first.'" — Richie Ashburn.

See also *Pitch Count, Pitches* and *Pitching Speeds*

All Teams Beaten. In 1992 Scott Sanderson became the ninth pitcher to defeat all 26 Major League teams then in existence. He joined Nolan Ryan, Tommy John, Don Sutton, Mike Torrez, Rick Wise, Gaylord Perry, Doyle Alexander and Rich Gossage.

Kevin Brown and Randy Johnson had each beaten 29 of 30 teams by 2002, but Johnson needed a win against his own team, the Diamondbacks. Brown had not beaten the Devil Rays, because he had not been in the American League since the club came into existence in 1998 and he had not faced them in interleague play.

On April 30, 2002, Al Leiter became the first pitcher to defeat all 30 Major League teams. Terry Mulholland also did it in 2004.

Appearances. Jesse Orosco is the all-time leader with appearances in 1,252 games, all but four of them as a reliever. He retired after the 2003 season. The other leaders:

1,071 Dennis Eckersley
1,070 Hoyt Wilhelm
1,002 Goose Gossage

Base on Balls. See *Base on Balls*.

Batting Records. For pitchers' batting feats (or lack thereof), see *Batting Averages*, *Hitting* and *Home Runs*.

Best.

"The first time I faced him I watched him take that easy windup — and then something went past me that made me flinch. The thing just hissed with danger. We couldn't touch him ... every one of us knew we'd met the most powerful arm ever turned loose in a ball park." — Ty Cobb on Walter Johnson.

"Any attempt to measure the extent of a pitcher's curve or speed in my judgment, is merely a matter of opinion. I believe [Walter] Johnson excelled in every particular as a twirler, and I would place him at the top of them all." — Eddie Collins, general manager of the Red Sox in 1943, in a letter to Edwin E. Jones of Stockton, California.

"Before you compare me with the great pitchers of all time, let me be around awhile, let me prove what I can do over a long period of time. Don't put me in a class with pitchers like Warren Spahn and Whitey Ford until I've shown I can win games for 10 or 15 years. Spahn has been doing it for 20. That's what it takes to rate as a great ball player, not a couple of good years, but a whole career." — Sandy Koufax in 1964, only two years before his premature retirement at age 30.

Connie Mack chose Rube Waddell as the best pitcher ever. Both Dizzy Dean and Charlie Gehringer picked Satchel Paige. Many early 20th century players picked Walter Johnson as the greatest. Among modern players, Sandy Koufax is often chosen as the best.

Bill James rates Lefty Grove the best all-time pitcher both at the peak of his career and over the entirety of his career. Sandy Koufax was second at the peak of his career and Warren Spahn second over the course of his long career.

Best Fielding Pitchers. See *Gold Glove Awards*.

Best Recent Seasons. Roger Clemens started the 2001 season 20–1, the first time a pitcher had ever achieved that milestone. He finished the year at 20–3.

In 1986 Clemens was 24–4, won the Cy Young Award, struck out 20 in a game, was the All-Star Game winner, won the MVP of the ALCS after winning Game 7, and was the starter of World

Series Game 6 (think Bill Buckner; Clemens was leading when he came out).

In 1995 Greg Maddux was 19–2 for the Braves with an ERA of 1.63.

In 1997 Randy Johnson was 20–4, struck out 19 twice in a game, and missed more than three weeks with a finger injury. He also struck out 291.

In 1999 Pedro Martinez was 23–4 with 313 strikeouts and an ERA of 2.07. In 2002 he was 20–4 with a 2.26 ERA.

"Book." One of the earliest "books" kept by a pitcher on the opposing batters was by Charlie "Crazy" Schmidt in 1893. He even took the book out to the mound with him because, at least according to one source, he had a bad memory. His strategy entry next to Cap Anson's name: "BB" (base on balls). Another source reported that the same entry was next to Honus Wagner's name.

Complete Games. See *Complete Games*.

Conditioning. See *Conditioning*.

Consecutive Years/Same League. Five pitchers worked for at least 22 consecutive seasons in the same league, a Major League record: Sad Sam Jones (1914–1935, American League); Herb Pennock (1912–1934, American League); Early Wynn (1939–1963, American League); Red Ruffing (1924–1947, American League); and Steve Carlton (1965–1986, National League, with two more seasons in the American League at the end of his career).

Consecutive Wins. See *Wins and Winning Streaks*.

Drop in Quality. A number of reasons have been given for the lack of quality among 1980s and 1990s starting pitchers:

1. Video games have taken kids inside during prime outdoor hours;

2. Kids do not do as much physical labor, such as lawn mowing and weed pulling, to help strengthen key muscles;

3. Cable television has been another inducement for kids to stay indoors;

4. Other sports have become more popular over the years and have siphoned off some of the interest previously reserved for baseball;

5. Too much pitching at a young age that wears out the arm. The best example is high school phenom Todd Peters, who won 53 straight games for his Texas high school. At age 20, he had to undergo the tendon transplant operation that Tommy John experienced in the 1970s and flamed out in junior college;

6. Too many trick pitches, rather than simply hard throwing by young pitchers;

7. Expansion from 16 teams in the 1950s to 28 teams in the 1990s, which diluted the talent;

8. Not enough innings pitched to develop durability in the shoulder, elbow, knees and back. In 1980 Steve Carlton was the last pitcher to appear in 300 innings;

9. Too much specialization (starters, middle relievers and closers);

10. High paid relief specialists whom clubs feel obligated to use frequently.

Durability. See also *Complete Games*.

"Pitchers in these times are fragile creatures, most of whom think that nine innings in a day is about enough and that two appearances in the same week are as much as can be expected from the hardiest."—*New York Times* writer after the Dodgers and Braves played to a 26-inning *Tie* in 1920, each using one pitcher.

Nineteenth century Major League pitchers could pitch almost every game and always pitched complete games. Their clubs had more days off during the season and they usually threw with a relatively painless sidearm delivery that traveled only 50 feet. They

also threw fewer pitches. For example, Charles Radbourn started 73 games and won 60 in 1884 with a cricket-style motion and a running start allowed until the early 1890s.

In 1879 Cincinnati's Will White is claimed by one source to be the only pitcher ever to start and win every one of his team's victories. He had 76 starts and 43 wins as the club finished 43–37. Jim Devlin reportedly pitched every inning of every game for Louisville in 1877, so he would have done the same.

Even after the final 1890s changes in the pitching rules (lengthening the distance; adding a pitching rubber), far fewer pitchers were used by teams than in the modern era. For example, the 1904 Red Sox used only five pitchers all season.

Knuckleballer Charlie Hough was the last pitcher to come close to pitching 300 innings in a season when he pitched 285⅓ innings in 1987. The last pitcher to reach 300 innings was Steve Carlton, who threw 304 innings in 1980. Since 1985 only seven pitchers have pitched 275 or more innings, led by Bert Blyleven with 293⅔ in 1985 for the Twins.

The strike zone is now smaller, which means that pitchers generally must throw more pitches per inning. Most clubs use five starters throughout the year and there is a mentality that starters need only pitch 6–7 good innings before the set-up man and the closer are brought in.

Errors. See *Errors*.

Fastest. See *Fastest Pitchers*.

15 Win Seasons. Greg Maddux won 15 games in 17 consecutive seasons through 2004, the only pitcher ever to do so. Only three other pitchers have won 15 or more games at least 12 seasons in a row: Christy Mathewson (1903–14), Gaylord Perry (1966–78) nd Cy Young (1891–1905). When Maddux reached the milestone again in 2004, he said that reaching 200 innings was more important to him, because it showed consistency and quality starts.

Fewest Hits Allowed/Season. In 1972 Nolan Ryan set a record by allowing only 5.26 hits per nine innings, breaking the Major League record of 5.30 by Luis Tiant in 1968.

Hitless Innings. Cy Young holds the record for consecutive hitless innings with 25⅓, set in 1904.

Dennis Eckersley had a string of 22⅓ hitless innings in 1977.

Johnny Vander Meer holds the National League record with 21 straight hitless innings in 1938.

Hits Allowed Per 9 Innings (through mid–2004).

Nolan Ryan	6.555
Pedro Martinez	6.723
Sandy Koufax	6.792
Sid Fernandez	6.851
J.R. Richard	6.876

Hitters Who Pitched. See *Hitters Who Pitched* and *Players Who Switched Positions*.

Home Runs Allowed/Career.

"In the long history of Organized Baseball, I stand unparalleled for putting Christianity into practice."— Robin Roberts on his penchant for giving up home runs. Roberts gave up 502 home runs over a 19-year career, with Willie Stargell hitting the last on September 3, 1966. Bert Blyleven gave up 430 over his 22-year career.

Ed Killian pitched primarily for the Tigers in the early 20th century during the dead ball era. He was the toughest pitcher in Major League history off which to hit a home run. He allowed only nine in 1,598 innings in his career, compiling a 102–78 record.

Home Runs Allowed/Season. Jose Lima of the Astros allowed a National League record 47 home runs in 2000. Bert Blyleven is the American League leader with 50 allowed in 1986. He gave up another 46 the following season.

Home Runs Allowed/Game. George Caster of the 1940 Phillies was the last of five pitchers to give up six home runs in a game until 2004. On August 8, 2004, Tim Wakefield gave up six home runs and still won the game. He gave up the six to the Tigers in an 11–9 victory in Detroit. Before Caster, Philadelphia's Bill Kerksleck gave up six home runs to the Giants on August 13, 1939.

Home Runs Allowed/Inning. Fourteen pitchers, the latest being John Smoltz in 1994, have given up four home runs in an inning.

Illegal Pitches. See *Illegal Pitches*.

Injuries. See *Injuries and Illness*—Pitchers.

Longest Performances. See *Longest Games*.

Losses/Season. In 1883 John Coleman was 12–48 for Philadelphia in the National League. Among modern losers, Hall of Famer Vic Willis was 12–29 in 1904 while losing nine games by one run. Roger Craig was 10–24 for the 1962 Mets.

Most Pitchers Used/Game.

"At least I didn't have to pay for the calls."—A's bullpen coach Art Kusnyer after manager Tony LaRussa used eight pitchers in a game against the Red Sox, including five of them in a span of eight pitches.

"You just listen to the ball and bat come together. They make an awful noise."—Mariners manager Darrell Johnson on when to change pitchers.

On September 11, 2004, the Yankees (8) and Phillies (10) combined to tie the Major League record for most pitchers used in a game. The Phillies tied the National League record and fell one short of the Major League record of 11 used by the Mariners in 1996.

The previous record was set by the Giants and Astros on September 28, 2002, when the clubs combined to use 16 pitchers in a 5–2 San Francisco win.

On September 7, 1999, the Diamondbacks beat the Brewers 11–9 as the teams combined to use a then-Major League record-tying 15 pitchers.

On September 10, 1996, the Expos used nine pitchers in a 10–3 loss to the Cubs, setting a National League mark and tying the Major League mark.

On September 14, 1997, the White Sox used nine pitchers in a 8–3 loss to the Indians. They used five pitchers in the 8th inning, and reliever Keith Foulke came into the game in the 4th inning to intentionally walk a batter after not taking any warm-up pitches.

In 1993 the A's experimented for a few games by intentionally using multiple pitchers in each game, with at least three pitchers going only three innings each.

Most Pitchers Used/Team/Season.

"Every team carries nine or ten pitchers. That's always the wrong number. Either six is too many, or twelve ain't enough."—Earl Weaver.

The 1967 Mets held the Major League record with 27 different pitchers used in a season until the 2002 Padres, who used an astronomical 37 pitchers. Thirty of them had a decision. The Pilots (1969) and Angels (1996) are co-holders of the American League record with 25 different pitchers used in a season.

Most Wins. See also *Three Hundred Wins*. The all-time leaders:

511	Cy Young
416	Walter Johnson
373	Grover Cleveland Alexander
	Christy Mathewson
363	Warren Spahn

Young always insisted that he should be credited with an additional win. In Lee Allen's *The National League Story* (1960), Young

is credited with 510 wins, one less than his official total. However, unofficial SABR research now confirm the 510 figure.

SABR researchers also claim that Walter Johnson had one more win than is customarily attributed to him, making his lifetime total 417 instead of the official 416. Early record books credited Johnson with 414 wins, based on two scoring errors made in 1911. On June 27 of that year he defeated the Yankees 5–3 and on July 9 he beat the Tigers 7–6. He pitched a complete game both times, but Robert McRoy, who was the official statistician that season, listed the victories as defeats.

When Grover Cleveland Alexander won his 373rd game, he thought he had beaten out Christy Mathewson by one game because it had been widely reported that Mathewson had only 372 lifetime wins. Later research indicated that Mathewson had 373 wins. When statisticians discovered the error more than a decade later, poet Stephen Cormany wrote a poem entitled "Big Six and Alexander the Great," in which the last stanza referenced Alexander's response to the change in Mathewson's win total:

"Out on the prairie near St. Paul, Nebraska
Ol' Pete was too drunk to know, or care
Or even differentiate the difference
If anybody had cared to explain it to him."

Most Wins by Decade/1900–1999

1900–1909	236	Christy Mathewson
1910–1919	264	Walter Johnson
1920–1929	190	Burleigh Grimes
1930–1939	199	Lefty Grove
1940–1949	170	Hal Newhouser
1950–1959	199	Robin Roberts
1960–1969	191	Juan Marichal
1970–1979	186	Jim Palmer
1980–1989	162	Jack Morris
1990–1999	176	Greg Maddux

Most Wins/Month. Since 1900, Rube Waddell of the Philadelphia A's won the most games (10) in one month during a Major League season. He piled up those wins in July 1902, while losing one game and also being involved in a tie game during the one-month span.

Ineligible Pitcher. On March 30, 2004, the Orioles optioned pitcher Eric Bedard to Class AAA with the intention of recalling him on April 10 to be their fifth starter that day (which they did). The team thought the 10-day option rule applied, but the commissioner's office fined the club and informed the Orioles that the 10 days can only begin with the first day of the season, which was April 4.

No Wins or Saves/Season. In 1991 Jeff Innis of the Mets became the first pitcher in Major League history to pitch in as many as 60 games in a season and not record a win or a save.

Scott Aldred of the Devil Rays ended a dubious Major League record streak after 50 pitching appearances. On April 11, 1999, he got the win in relief, the first time in 50 appearances that he had a win, loss or save.

No Pitches Thrown for Victory.

"It is possible to dream up a case of a winning pitcher who never threw a pitch at all...*

*I don't know if this ever happened. I am not going to bother to look it up either."—Fred Schwed, Jr., in *How to Watch a Baseball Game* (1957). It happened.

White Sox pitcher Nick Altrock did not throw a pitch when he came into a 1906 game in the 9th inning trailing by two runs with the bases loaded and two outs. The runner was caught stealing before he threw a pitch, and his team won the game in the bottom of the inning.

American League pitcher Dean Stone won the 1954 All-Star Game without throwing a pitch. He came in to the game in the 8th inning with a man on third, two men out and the National League ahead by two runs. The runner on third tried to steal home and Stone threw him out. The American League scored three runs in the bottom of the 8th to take the lead, and Stone was the pitcher of record. Virgil Trucks pitched the 9th inning for the National League to earn the save.

100 Wins in Each League.

"He must be good. He gets them out in both leagues." — Casey Stengel on Jim Bunning.

Cy Young is far and away the winner of this category, winning 289 games in the National League and 222 in the American League. Gaylord Perry is second with 175 National League wins and 139 in the American League. Jim Bunning won 106 in the National League and 118 in the American League. In 1980 Ferguson Jenkins of the Rangers became the fourth pitcher to win more than 100 games in each league, finishing his career with 115 in the American League and 169 in the National League. Nolan Ryan won 100 games in each league, with 135 in the National League and 189 in the American League. Randy Johnson, still active in 2004, won over 100 games in both leagues, primarily for the Mariners and Diamondbacks.

Milt Pappas, one of only a few players to record 200 wins and not win 20 games in a season, came close with 99 National League wins and 110 American League wins.

The Perfect Pitcher.

"What a year Gil went on to have.... Coming into the last game of the year, the rookie had not only tied the record for the most wins in a single season (41), but had broken the record for the most strike-outs (349) set by Rube Waddell in 1904, the record for the most shutouts (16) set by Grover Alexander in 1916, and had only to give up less than six runs to come in below the earned run average of 1.01 set by Dutch Leonard the year he was born. As for the Patriot League records, he had thrown more complete games than any other pitcher in the league's history, and gotten the most strike-outs per nine innings." — Philip Roth in *The Great American Novel* (1973), on mythical pitching phenom Gil Gamesh, who pitched three consecutive no-hitters to end the season (or maybe not — read the book!).

"If the world was perfect, it wouldn't be." — Yogi Berra.

Charisma. Christy Mathewson was the most popular Major League player in the early part of the 20th century and was New York City's first big baseball star.

Clutch Pitcher.

"I was never nervous when I had the ball, but when I let go I was scared to death." — Lefty Gomez.

Whitey Ford was a terrific money pitcher for the Yankees, though Bob Gibson's World Series performances certainly make him a good candidate (and he said he would choose himself). Connie Mack chose Chief Bender as his favorite pitcher in a big game. The author's personal choice: Sandy Koufax.

Competitiveness. Bob Gibson by all accounts was the most ferocious modern pitcher on the mound, though Roger Clemens may approach him among more recent pitchers.

Control. Christy Mathewson, noted for his amazing control, in 1913 went 68 straight innings without giving up a walk. In 1908 he pitched 416 innings and walked only 42 batters. Over his career of 4,781 innings, he walked only 1.56 batters per nine innings. Greg Maddux has surpassed Mathewson in most departments and therefore has to be considered in the top two, if not the best, in this category.

Curveball. Sandy Koufax's curveball was devastating in com-

bination with his legendary fastball. However, many contend that Bert Blyleven had the all-time best curveball.

Delivery. Luis Tiant had more ways to bring the ball to the plate than any other Major League pitcher.

Durability. Nolan Ryan proved his staying power over 27 seasons. Warren Spahn may qualify as most durable left-hander of all time with 363 wins over 21 seasons and a 23–7 record at age 42.

Fastball. Smoky Joe Wood was the fastest Major League pitcher, at least according to candidate Walter Johnson ("ain't no man alive faster than Smoky Joe"). Career minor leaguer Steve Dalkowski of the 1950s and early 1960s might have been the fastest ever (see *Fastest Pitchers*). Mythical **Sidd Finch** does not count. Among recent pitchers, Randy Johnson, Billy Wagner and Jose Mesa have all been clocked several times above 100 mph, though the speed guns vary in their accuracy. Just on intimidation alone at 6'10", Johnson probably would get the nod.

Fielding. Jim Kaat won 16 **Gold Glove Awards** — enough said.

Intelligence. Johnny Sain, particularly after his great years as a **Pitching Coach**, though Greg Maddux might be the choice among recent pitchers.

Meanness. Don Drysdale's favorite pitch was said to be the brushback. Roger Clemens might qualify today.

Physique. Walter Johnson was a big man for his era, standing 6'1" and weighing 200 pounds with huge hands. Randy Johnson at 6'10" is perhaps the modern era's most intimidating figure. C.C. Sabathia of the Indians also cuts a wide swath at 6'7" and 270 pounds.

Pick-off Move. Orioles reliever Tippy Martinez, solely for picking off three runners in an inning.

Pitches. See *Pitches*.

Playing Other Positions. See *Players Who Switched Positions*.

Perfect Month/Season. Whitey Ford had an 8–0 record for the Yankees in June 1961. He went 25–4 that year and almost no one noticed because of the home run heroics of Roger Maris and Mickey Mantle.

In 1937 Johnny Allen of the Indians was 15–0 going into his last start, with a chance to become the first man to go through a season with a perfect record with a minimum number of games. He lost to finish 15–1 (see also **Wins and Winning Streaks**).

Roger Clemens came close in 2001, starting the year 20–1 before losing two to finish the season.

Pitcher an Inning. On the last day of the 1949 season, the Browns used a pitcher an inning against the White Sox in the first game of a doubleheader. The following pitchers took the mound in the 4–3 loss: Ned Garver, Joe Ostrowski, Cliff Fannin, Tom Ferrick, Karl Drews, Bill Kennedy, Al Papai, Red Embree and Dick Starr. In the second game, rookie Eddie Albrecht debuted, having won 29 games for the Browns' Class C team. Albrecht won 5–3 in five innings (called due to darkness), but made only two more appearances in the Major Leagues.

Pitching Triple Crown. Leading the league in wins, strikeouts and earned run average is sometimes referred to as winning the "Pitching Triple Crown." Through 2001 Dwight Gooden was the last to do it in the National League when he led the league in 1985 with 24 wins, 268 strikeouts and an ERA of 1.53. In 2002 Randy Johnson won the mythical National League crown with 24 wins, 334 strikeouts, and an ERA of 2.47.

Prior to 1997, the last American League pitcher to do so was Hal Newhouser in 1945 for the Tigers. In 1997 and 1998 Roger Clemens accomplished the feat and then Pedro Martinez did it in 1999.

It has been accomplished 31 times, with Grover Cleveland Alexander leading all pitchers with four Triple Crowns.

Poor Performances. Louisville's Jack Wadsworth game up 36 hits to the Phillies on August 17, 1894.

Cleveland's Dave Rowe gave up 35 runs to the Chicago White Stockings on July 24, 1882.

On June 21, 1901, Reds pitcher Doc Parker gave up 21 runs to the Dodgers on 26 hits.

In 1932 A's pitcher Eddie Rommel allowed 14 runs on 29 hits in a 17-inning relief appearance but still won 18–17.

Relief Pitchers. See *Relief Pitchers*.

Rookie Records. See *Rookies*.

Saves. See *Relief Pitchers* and *Saves*.

Slow Career Start. Johnny Sain spent four years in Class D ball before his four 20-win seasons over a Major League career that lasted from 1942 through 1955 (with three years lost to World War II).

Pitcher Red Ruffing was only 39–93 over his first five seasons while playing for the Red Sox. He then won 20 games four straight years for the Yankees and finished his career with a 273–225 record.

Starting Pitcher/Consecutive Games. On September 3, 2002, Aaron Myette of the Rangers was ejected from a game against the Orioles, an 8–3 loss in which Myette walked six. He started again the next day, the first time a pitcher had started consecutive games since Steve McCatty in 1980. Five pitchers made back-to-back starts during the 1981 season—the last game before the strike and the first game back. They were Dennis Martinez (Orioles), Bert Blyleven (Indians), Pete Vuckovich (Brewers), Rick Langford (A's) and Juan Eichelberger (Padres).

Starting Pitcher Win/No 5 Innings. On October 3, 1999, Larry Luebbers of the Cubs got the win despite pitching only four innings. This is because Rule 10.19 allows a starting pitcher to receive the win in a shortened game of five innings if the starting pitcher goes at least four complete innings. There are other exceptions to the normal "starting pitcher has to pitch five innings to qualify for the win" rule; exhibition games and other non-championship games like the All-Star Game allows the starter to qualify for the win with less than five innings pitched.

There was also a brief exception in 1990 following the lockout that spring. Because starters were not yet in shape, the players and owners agreed to the following: "Starting pitchers in the regular season's first two weeks could earn a victory by pitching only three or four innings instead of the previously required five, unless the official scorer deemed they did not pitch effectively."

Despite the agreement, research by Jim Storer shows that no starting pitcher received a win during the relevant period (the first week of the season) and pitched less than five innings.

On July 20, 1987 Mike Griffin of the Orioles pitched four innings of a rain-shortened 4–1 win over the White Sox and was credited with the win. Richie Lewis, also of the Orioles, got the win on July 31, 1992 in the same situation. It happened again on June 1, 2001, when Cleveland's C.C. Sabathia got the win when the game was called in the 5th inning due to rain. It had happened only two other times since 1978, according to Retrosheet's David W. Smith.

Starts. If a Major League pitcher is warming up on the mound for his first Major League appearance, but does not throw an official pitch in a game and never appears again, he is nevertheless credited with having appeared in the Major Leagues (see also *Brothers*, for this situation involving Robin Yount's brother). According to the Elias Sports Bureau, however, that same pitcher will not be credited with a start. Orel Hershiser was warming up at the start of a game for the Dodgers in 1993. He had a clause in his contract that paid him $250,000 for every start over 30 that he made in a season. The late-season start would have qualified him for another $250,000, but he injured himself while warming up and did not throw a pitch to a batter. It was ruled that he had not made a start and he did not receive the bonus money.

Starters/No Wins. The 1992 Kansas City A's didn't have a starter win until the 18th game of the season.

Strikeouts. See *Strikeouts*.

Thirty Game Winners. See *Thirty Game Winners*.

Throwing Between Starts. Jim Kaat of the Twins, whose prime pitching years were in the 1960s, was one of the first pitchers, if not the first, to throw regularly between starts.

Toughest to Face. Stan Musial once said on "The Ed Sullivan Show" that Ken Raffensberger was the toughest pitcher he ever faced. Raffensberger, who died in 2002 at age 85, was 119–154 primarily for the Phillies and Reds, winning 18 games in 1949 and leading the league with five shutouts.

Ty Cobb said the toughest pitcher he ever faced was Guy "Doc" White, a graduate of Georgetown University with a degree in dental surgery. White was 18–6 for the Hitless Wonder White Sox of 1906 and led the league with a 1.52 ERA. Cobb batted a lifetime .197 against the lefthander.

Twenty Game Winners and Losers. See *Twenty Game Winners and Losers*.

200 Losses/Less Than 200 Wins. Bob Friend, primarily of the Pirates in the 1950s and 1960s, is the only pitcher to lose 200 games without winning 200.

Winners on Losing Teams. Steve Carlton won 27 games for the 1972 Phillies, the most for a pitcher on a last-place team. Before that, Noodles Hahn won 22 for the 1901 Reds.

Between 1911 and 1917 Grover Cleveland Alexander won 190 games, one-third of the total won by the generally pitiful Phillies.

Winning Percentage/Lifetime. Spud Chandler of the Yankees had a 109–43 career record between 1937 and 1947, giving him a .717 winning percentage, the highest for any player with at least 100 career wins. Among active pitchers, Pedro Martinez had a .712 winning percentage through 2003.

Milt Gaston's .372 winning percentage is the all-time worst among pitchers with 250 or more decisions. He was 97–164 in a career that lasted from 1924 through 1934.

See also *Three Hundred Wins*.

Winning Percentage/Season Leader. In 1900 it was ruled that a pitcher must win at least 15 games, instead of appearing in at least 25 games, to qualify as the league leader in winning percentage. In 1950 there were significant changes to how a pitcher could qualify for a win; they are still in effect. A starter may earn the win only if he pitches at least five innings, his team is leading when he leaves the game, and the relievers never lose the lead. If the starter does not pitch five innings and leaves with a lead that is never given up, the official scorer may credit the win to the relief pitcher whom he believes was most effective.

If the starting pitcher does not get the win, then the relief pitcher who was the pitcher of record when the go-ahead runs are scored (and the lead is maintained) shall receive the win. However, any pitcher who pitches briefly and ineffectively need not receive credit for the win. In that case, the official scorer may credit the win to another relief pitcher.

Winning Streaks. See *Wins and Winning Streaks*.

Worst Inning. Phillies pitcher Hal Kelleher holds the modern record of facing 16 batters in a single inning, in a 21–2 loss to the Cubs on May 5, 1938.

Worst Pitchers. Alan S. Kaufman and James C. Kaufman, *The Worst Pitchers of All Time* (1993).

Books. William Curran, *Strikeout: A Celebration of the Art of Pitching* (1994); Bill James and Rob Neyer, *The Neyer/James Guide* to *Pitchers: An Historical Compendium of Pitching, Pitchers, and Pitches* (2004); Roger Kahn, *The Head Game: Baseball Seen from the Pitcher's Mound* (2001); John Klima, *Pitched Battle: 35 of Baseball's Greatest Duels from the Mound* (2002); Steve Jacobson, *The Pitching Staff* (1975); Pat Jordan, *Suitors of Spring* (1973); John Thorn and John Holway, *The Pitcher* (1987); George Will, *Men at Work* (1990), focusing on Orel Hershiser.

Pitches

> "The fastball
>   that you hope to poke
>   is smoke
> The curveball
>   that you thought was there
>   is air
> The knuckler
>   wobbling up to you
>   can dipsy-do
> The screwball
>   an ironic twist
>   hits your fist
> The sinker
>   comes as some surprise:
>   it dies
> The let-up pitch
>   you can't resist?
>   you missed
> The spitball
>   that by law's forbidden
>   (is hidden)"

—"A Swing and a Miss" by J. Patrick Lewis, first appearing in *Light Quarterly*.

"The whole art is in the wrist. You use the body, the shoulder, and arms in getting power behind the throw but the twist of the wrist determines just what the ball will do." — New York Giants star pitcher Carl Hubbell.

Numerous pitches have been known by different names. The more prominent are covered in separate entries: *Curveballs*, *Eephus Pitch*, *Fastballs*, *Knuckleballs*, *Screwballs* and *Spitballs*. This section contains a general list of pitches and related information.

Calling Your Own. According to catcher Birdie Tebbetts, the Tigers once let Ted Williams call his own pitches because they could not stop him. He went 0-for-5 that day because he could not focus on hitting the ball — he was concentrating on what the Tigers had told him and whether they were on the level.

Change-up.

"It's like being bitten by a stuffed panda." — Lou Piniella after striking out on a change-up by Geoff Zahn.

"My three pitches: my change, my change off my change, and my change off my change off my change." — Preacher Roe.

"Walter's idea of a change-up was to just throw harder." — Ty Cobb on the hard-throwing Walter Johnson.

The change-up was an important part of an early pitcher's repertoire because the pitching distance was only 45–50 feet. Balls had less time to break, so curveballs and other movement pitches were less important and for a time were illegal. The change-up is thrown with the same motion as the fastball but arrives far slower to throw off the hitter's timing. Some have described the motion as if the pitcher were pulling down a window shade at the end of the delivery to take the speed out of the pitch, while still disguising it as a fastball.

The most common modern version is the circle change. The tip of the index finger is pressed against the tip of the thumb, and the grip on the ball is made with the other three finger.

Kid Nichols was an early proponent of the change-up. He was so effective with it in the 1890s that he had seven consecutive 30-win seasons and 361 lifetime wins (sixth all-time). Albert Spalding was also an early user of the change-up.

George Wright referred to his change-up as his "dew-drop" pitch.

Bill "Wee Willie" Sherdel pitched a "slow ball" in the 1920s, which one writer erroneously referred to as the first change-up.

Pete Donohue is credited with "perfecting" the pitch in the 1920s for the Reds, but it is clear that the change-up was used by many pitchers well before that date.

A variation of the straight change-up is the four-seam circle change-up with the index finger and thumb in a circle against the side of the ball and the middle and ring fingers running across the two seams. The off-speed pitch breaks slightly, in contrast to the straight change.

Combination of Pitches. The best curveball/fastball combination pitcher was, according to Connie Mack, the eccentric Rube Waddell. Once he learned to control his pitches, Sandy Koufax may well have had the best fastball/curveball combination because his curveball was almost as fast as his fastball.

Curveball. See *Curveballs*.

Eephus Pitch. See *Eephus Pitch* for Rip Sewell's 20-foot-high lob pitch and later versions of the pitch.

Fadeaway.

"We was talking about the Athaletics [sic] this morning and Callahan says None of you fellows pitch right to Baker. I was talking to Lord and Scott afterward and I says to Scott How do you pitch to Baker? He says I use my fadeaway. I says Why do you call it a fadeaway then? He says Because when I throw it to Baker it fades away over the fence." — Lefty Jack Keefe in the "You Know Me, Al" series by Ring Lardner, which appeared in the *Saturday Evening Post* beginning in 1914.

The fadeaway was Christy Mathewson's version of the *Screwball*.

Fastball. See *Fastballs* and *Fastest Pitchers*.

Fewest Pitches Thrown/Game. See *Pitch Count*.

Forkball.

"I don't, but neither does the batter." — Premier 1950s and 1960s reliever Roy Face on whether he knew which way his forkball would break.

The forkball became more popular when the spitball was outlawed in 1920. Long fingers are required to throw the pitch, as the first two fingers go as far as possible down the sides of the ball.

Dave Keefe of the 1919–1922 A's is credited with developing the forkball. It was a natural pitch for him because he lost the middle finger of his pitching hand in a childhood accident. Though he was only 9–17 in his Major League career, he pitched successfully in the minors until 1932. Broadcaster Ernie Harwell credited the forkball to Bullet Joe Bush in 1920, who pitched for the A's, Yankees, Browns, Red Sox, Senators, Giants and Pirates.

Almost all forkball pitchers had the forkball as their best pitch when they arrived in the Major Leagues. An exception was Bush, who learned it after he had been established in the American League. Bush's curveball would not break, so he learned the forkball while with the Red Sox from 1918 through 1921. He was a steady pitcher in 1921, going 16–9, but he blossomed when he was traded to the Yankees. In his first season with the club in 1922 he had a record of 26–7.

The **Split-Finger Fastball** is similar to the forkball, but the split of the fingers is less severe, making the pitch closer to a fastball, but still dipping at the last moment. Roger Craig, the most prominent advocate of the split-finger, believes that the two pitches are different, though many claim otherwise.

Hesitation Pitch. This pitch was thrown by Satchel Paige in the Negro Leagues but was prohibited in the American League because it was considered a balk.

Illegal Pitches. See *Illegal Pitches* and *Spitballs*.

Kimono Pitch. Tommy Byrne of the Yankees threw this pitch in an exhibition game in Japan in 1955. The pitch was thrown behind his back. Manager Casey Stengel allowed him to throw it in a Miami spring training game against Pee Wee Reese on March 26, 1956. Umpire Larry Napp disallowed the pitch and told Byrne not to throw it again. League umpire chief Cal Hubbard then formally ruled the pitch illegal. Stengel said it was the only new pitch of the half-century.

Knuckleball. See *Knuckleballs*.

Knuckle Curve. This pitch was popularized by Burt Hooton, who won 151 games for the Cubs and Dodgers between 1971 and 1985.

Number of Pitches Thrown. See *Pitch Count*.

Palm Ball. Eddie Plank was an early great palm ball artist with the A's for 14 seasons beginning in 1901.

Pitching Aid. Former pitcher and pitching coach Johnny Sain patented a ball with a pole through its axis to show the spin on the ball in explaining the mechanics of different pitches.

Repertoire.

"A pitcher needs two pitches — one they're looking for and one to cross 'em up." — Warren Spahn.

"Four basic ones — fastball, curve, slider and change-up — plus eight illegal ones." — Tommy John describing the number of pitches he threw.

Murry Dickson was considered to have the largest repertoire of pitches: fastball, curveball, slider, knuckleball, screwball, sinker, and a change-up off each pitch. He pitched primarily in the National League for 18 seasons from 1939 through 1959, compiling a 172–181 record.

Rules. See *Pitching Rules*.

Screwball. See *Screwball*.

Sidearm Delivery.

"Sidearm pitchers don't get many breaks from the umpires. They think we are freaks, that we belong on paddy wagons, with lace wrapped around our faces. They think we should be whipped." — Reliever Dan Quisenberry.

"When I was a semi-pro baseball player of no distinction, I had one weakness in common with most major leaguers. I could not hit a sidearm pitcher. The first time I ever saw Walter Johnson he scared me to death even though I had a position of safety in the bleachers." — Sportswriter Arthur Daley.

Pitcher Silver King pitched primarily for the St. Louis Browns of the 1880s. He is credited by at least one source as the first pitcher to use a sidearm delivery. This seems unlikely considering that pitchers were not allowed to throw above the waist until well after the National League was established.

Sinker.

"Natural grass is a wonderful thing for little bugs and sinker-ball pitchers." — Sinkerballer Dan Quisenberry.

"Oh, yeah? One of them sinkers just splashed me in the eye." — Dodger batter Norm Larker complaining to umpire Frank Secory that alleged sinkerballs were actually spitballs.

Some credit pitcher Tricky Nichols as the earliest to use a sinker,

in 1876. Nat Hudson is credited by others with using it first in the 1860s. Still others credit Albert Spalding in the 1860s with creating this "drop" pitch.

Slider.

"A slider is either a fastball with a very small slow break or a curveball with a very small fast break." — Braves manager Charlie Dressen.

"I can't throw one, so I thought I'd buy one." — Pitcher Curt Schilling on his dog named Slider.

"Probably the best thing about the slider is that it looks like a fastball." — Bob Feller.

"He had a slider that looked like it hung right there and said 'Crush me.'" — Broadcaster Pete Smith.

1920s American League pitcher George Uhle is credited by some with naming the pitch. The pitch is thrown with the "OK" sign made with the thumb and index finger. Unlike a curveball, it requires little or no wrist turn. The first two fingers across a seam apply pressure across the seam as it is released. The elbow is kept above the shoulder and the release is as if passing a football. The pitch is only a few miles slower than the fastball. The ball can be kept low and away from the batter, and the trick is to make it look like a fastball.

The pitch has been cited as a primary reason why modern hitters have lower batting averages than their earlier counterparts. The pitch approaches the plate like a fastball, but will tail to one side at the last moment and usually breaks downward. It is a hard pitch for batters to identify, and Ted Williams claimed that it is the most difficult pitch to hit.

Originally known as the nickel curve, it was thrown by George Blaeholder as early as 1927, and he is credited by some as the originator. A few attribute the pitch to Dave Danforth, an American League reliever and sometime starter from 1911 through 1925. Others credit Bill Lohrman as the first to use the slider, but he did not appear until 1938. Still others simply credit each as part of a group of early proponents.

Bucky Walters said that he learned the pitch from Chief Bender, who supposedly used it in a 1910 no-hitter, but did not call it a slider. Nelson Potter learned the slider in 1943 and had great success with it in leading the Browns to the 1944 pennant.

The slider was more frequently used in the 1950s and especially after expansion in the 1960s to accommodate less-skilled pitchers. It is not difficult to throw and replaced the curveball as the primary "second" pitch after the fastball.

The slider was not used as frequently in the 1980s and 1990s. This is because there are now so many other pitches to augment the basic combination of fastball, curveball and change-up. In the 1980s the **Split-Finger Fastball** was in vogue but began to fade as its negative effect on arms was questioned.

Larry Sherry, a rookie reliever for the Dodgers in 1959, learned to throw a slider over the 1958–1959 winter and had tremendous success with it in the 1959 postseason. He won one of the play-off games against the Braves, won two World Series games and saved two others. Steve Carlton had the top slider of the 1970s and 1980s, winning 329 games.

Slowest Pitches.

"He threw a lot of slow stuff. Then he threw slower than slow stuff. Then he came back with slower stuff." — Coco Crisp, Indians outfielder in 2003, on his club's inability to hit 40-year-old Jamie Moyer's pitches that rarely reached 80 mph.

Spitball. See *Spitballs*.

Split-Finger Fastball.

"A true forkball is jammed far back into the fingers and cannot be thrown hard. But with the split-finger, you spread your fingers as far apart as you want and just throw your fastball. That's what makes it so great. It's the same arm action, and it looks like a fastball, then drops." — Split-finger fastball advocate Roger Craig.

"Roger Craig is the acknowledged maestro of the Split-Finger Fastball." — 1986 *Sports Illustrated* article. Craig taught the pitch to Mike Scott, 1986 Cy Young Award winner in the National League, and to Jack Morris, the winningest Major League pitcher in the 1980s.

In the late 1980s umpires began calling the waist high version of the split-finger pitch a ball (too high), but pitchers could not throw it any lower or it would be on the ground by the time it reached the back of the plate. This has been described as a (sub)conscious attempt by umpires to readjust the delicate balance between pitcher and hitter because the pitch was becoming too difficult to hit.

The pitch is no longer taught in the minor leagues because it is suspected of being hard on the arm and has fallen out of favor in the Major Leagues for the same reason. There have been unsuccessful attempts to find a connection between the pitch and shoulder injuries suffered by a number of pitchers.

Submarine Pitch. Carl Mays, whose low sidearm-style pitch killed shortstop Ray Chapman in 1920, was a classic submariner. He supposedly learned the pitch from black pitcher Dizzy Dismukes while both were overseas during World War I.

Eldon Auker was a submarine pitcher out of necessity, having suffered a shoulder injury playing football at Kansas State. Ted Abernathy of the 1960s Reds was a submarine pitcher of some note, saving 31 games in 1965 and 28 in 1967.

Tipping Pitches. Early in his career, Bob Feller's thumb stuck out when he threw his curveball. At another point in Feller's career, Hal Newhouser noticed that Feller's wrist was stiff on his fastball when he wound up and that Feller went farther back on his wind-up when he was going to use the curveball.

For two years Tommy Henrich of the Yankees could predict whether Feller's fastball or curveball was coming. In Feller's "set" position his arms were separated on the fastball and his glove covered the ball if it was to be a curveball. As Henrich noted, however, it did not matter that he knew what was coming because Feller was so overpowering.

Bob Turley of the Yankees was famous for being able to pick up telltale signs from other players. With 300-game winner Early Wynn, Turley used Wynn's nose as a guidepost. During Wynn's wind-up, if his glove was raised to cover his nose, it meant curveball; if the glove went up only to the tip of the nose, it meant slider; below nose; fastball; chest level meant knuckleball. Turley would call the pitch and then Yankee players on the bench would whistle to alert the batter. Possibly as a result, Wynn was unable to win his 300th game against the Yankees.

Pitching Coaches

"Who? I'm not familiar with that name." — Brien Taylor, the Yankees' 1991 number one **Draft** pick who signed out of high school for $1.5 million, when assigned to pitching instructor and former Yankee star Ron Guidry.

"… sage counselors standing next to the manager, studying the pitcher for signs of fatigue too subtle for the ordinary eye. Obviously they were men of saintly patience, somewhat like the trainers of highly strung racehorses, making countless trips to the box to calm the nerves of unstrung men and boys." — William Zinsser in *Spring Training* (1989).

"When a pitcher is in trouble, he'll stick out his arm and the parrot will fly from the dugout to his arm, tell the pitcher to keep the ball down and then fly back. How long could that take? Parrots work cheap, and they live a hundred years. You wouldn't need a pitching coach for a hundred years." — Pitcher Mike Flanagan on how to eliminate the cliché-filled mound visits by pitching coaches.

"WE WORK FAST, THROW STRIKES, CHANGE SPEEDS." — T-shirt worn by Orioles pitching coach Ray Miller.

Earliest. Mel Harder was one of the earliest coaches to work exclusively as a pitching coach. He coached for the Indians from 1948 through 1969.

Best.

"That man Sain sure puts biscuits in your pan." — Jim Mudcat Grant after Johnny Sain's coaching helped him to a 20-win season for the Twins in 1965. One writer made a case for Sain as the greatest pitching coach of all time. He coached the last 30-game winner (Denny McLain) and 17 20-game winners. Four managers were Manager of the Year with him. Ralph Houk, Mayo Smith and Sam Mele won pennants only with Sain as their pitching coach. In 20 years through 1989 he coached for 12 teams that finished third or better and five that were pennant winners.

Leo Mazzone of the Braves was considered the top coach of the 1990s and 2000s. He helped several journeymen have productive seasons, and kept on track such stars as John Smoltz, Tom Glavine and Greg Maddux.

As Managers. Many pitching coaches have gone on recently to become managers, including Roger Craig, Ray Miller, George Bamberger and Phil Regan.

Pitching Distances

"Youngsters in the amateur ranks and on the sandlots no longer have ambitions to become pitchers. They want to play some other position in which they can get by without being discouraged." — John McGraw after the 1930 season saw a dramatic increase in hitting, apparently due to a livelier ball. McGraw suggested that the pitching rubber be brought in closer to home plate to encourage young pitchers.

The 45-foot distance was the standard from the early amateur days through the 1870s. In 1881 the pitching mound was lengthened to 50 feet. The last significant pre–1900 change in the rules was moving back the pitching distance by another 10 feet to 60'6" for the 1893 season. The distance is measured from the back of home plate to the front of the pitching rubber.

The modern standard of 60'6" is often reported erroneously to have been created by a mistaken measurement. The blueprints for the distance supposedly said 60'0", but a surveyor misread the blueprint to mean 60'6". Robert E. Shipley has pointed out that the increase to 60'6" was a logical increase of five feet rather than a surveyor's error. His conclusion is based on the distances from the *back* of the pitching "box" then in use to the new distance. This was an increase of five feet from 55'6", the "pivot distance" from where pitchers began their delivery at the back of the pitching box (4' × 5'6") and could only take one step forward — rather than an increase of 10'6" from the official point of release of 50 feet at the front of the pitching box. The new distance was adopted at the same time that the **Pitching Rubber** was made mandatory.

The 1893 increase was made primarily due to powerful pitchers such as Amos Rusie. The greater distance in part helped Rusie, as his curveball had a larger break when thrown from the new distance. The change resulted in an increase in the number of .300

hitters from 12 in 1892 to 60 in 1893. In 1891 and 1892 teams combined to score approximately five runs per game, which was considered too low. In 1893 teams combined to score approximately seven runs per game.

It took a few years after 1893 for the pitchers to adjust to the hitters. As a result of the new distance, 1894 had the highest runs per game ever, with three teams that year leading the all-time list. Changes in the pitching distance often forced retirement by a 19th century pitcher who could not adjust to new distances or other changes in the rules.

Pitching Grips

"You spend a good piece of your life gripping a baseball and in the end it turns out that it was the other way around."—Jim Bouton in *Ball Four* (1970).

See also **Pine Tar—Use by Pitchers**.

See also **Pitches** for the grips used on certain pitches.

Whitey Ford used a combination of turpentine, baby oil and rosin to improve his pitching grip on cold days. He kept it in a deodorant can, leading to a **Practical Joke** on Yogi Berra.

Pitching Machines

"Iron Mike"—Generic nickname for mechanical pitching devices; the name may have been used first in *Time* magazine in April 1950.

Crude forms of a pitching machine were used in the 1890s. One type was loaded like a cannon and another was hand-held and shot like a rifle by an exploding cartridge. In 1897 Princeton math professional Charles "Bull" Hinton developed a baseball gun that could change speeds and throw curves. He used gunpowder from a cannon muzzle, which scared batters into not using it. His primary claim to fame was his "Theory of Higher Space" view of the universe, which projected a "fourth dimension."

On June 10, 1897, a mechanical pitcher was used in a game between the Ivy Club and Princeton. The batter stepped on the plate to have a pitch thrown. Mrs. Grover Cleveland, the President's wife, attended the three-inning game.

The *Dickson Baseball Dictionary* reported that the modern version of the machines were not in general use until the Dodgers began using one at Vero Beach shortly after World War II.

In the 1960s, Benny Lefebvre, father of Dodger infielder Jim LeFebvre, marketed his "Silver Arm Pitching Machine" for $279. Benny was fond of the racetrack, and according to neighborhood

Though probably not capable of throwing pitches, this new-fangled pop-up machine is demonstrated during spring training.

friend Dan Reynolds, brother of Dodger batboy Jim Reynolds, Benny often took the boys out of school to visit nearby Hollywood Park racetrack before heading to Dodger Stadium.

In 1970, John Paulson determined what pitching machines were available at the time, but found them deficient. Paulson then purchased a patent covering the use of pneumatic tires to throw baseballs and added some features that he had developed. He named the device the JUGGS Curveball Pitching Machine, from the old-time baseball expression "jug-handled curve." The machine instantly became popular, primarily because of its portability. The machine can throw 600 pitches per hour.

Pitching Mound Conferences

"If a microphone were placed out there, all you'd hear would be a lot of grunts."—Pitching coach Johnny Sain on the utility of mound conferences—usually only to stall for an incoming reliever to make a few more warm-up tosses in the bullpen.

"What do I say when I go out to take the pitcher out? I usually say, 'Hello, darling. How are you this evening?'"—Casey Stengel.

"Those conferences out there on the mound really get me. The pitcher knows he's in a jam. What can they say to him? They just remind him of it, that's all…. All it does is make you even more worried than you already were, which was plenty. There are mighty few pitchers who can survive those conferences on the mound, take it from me."—Pitcher Rube Bressler.

"Not to be outdone, the same night [Tony LaRussa won his 2,500 game as a manager], pitching coach Dave Duncan made his 25,000th needless trip to the mound."—Bill Sceft.

"[H]ere came manager Grady Little, out to hook his ace and pat him on the rump as he left. Little likes to stand below a pitcher,

Jim Lemon of the Senators looks on as a 1960s pitching machine fires 'em in there.

on the downslope of the mound, and here again, looking up at Pedro like a tourist at the Parthenon steps, he said a few words and walked away. This could not be. Martinez had thrown a hundred and fifteen pitches, and given up ringing hits to five of the last seven batters. A Sox-fan friend of mine, Ben, watching in his apartment on West Forty-fifth Street, had gone on his hands and knees, screaming."—Roger Angell, describing Red Sox manager Grady Little's failure to remove a struggling Pedro Martinez from Game 7 of the 2003 ALCS against the Yankees. Martinez had pitched into the 8th inning only five times in his previous 31 starts. Two runs later, the game was tied and the Red Sox lost in extra innings.

Rule. Through the 1950s, managers could make unlimited trips to the mound. Probably as a result of an increase in the use of relief pitchers (which slowed down the game), the rule was modified first in the National League in the 1960s to allow only two trips to the mound before the pitcher had to be removed from the game.

Rule 8.06 now governs mound visits: The second trip by the manager or coach to the mound will cause the pitcher's automatic removal. A manager or coach is prohibited from making the second visit while the same batter is at bat, but he may do so if there is a pinch batter during the at-bat.

Japanese catchers are limited to three trips to the mound during a game in an effort to speed up play.

See **Length of Games** for the effect of catcher Carlton Fisk's trips to the mound.

Mound Conferences. Yankee pitcher Whitey Ford rarely used mound conferences. Catcher Johnny Blanchard recalled that Ford once called him out to the mound and Blanchard thought Ford was hurt. Ford said that he thought Blanchard was tired and might want a break.

White Sox manager Al Lopez once came out to remove pitcher Early Wynn from a game in the 1950s. Wynn was upset at being removed and nailed Lopez in the stomach with the ball. Legend has it that as Lopez retreated to the dugout he mumbled that his star had demonstrated such speed and accuracy that he did not need a relief pitcher.

Right-handed pitcher Bill Donnelly was not the friendliest guy on the mound during the 1940s. When Cardinals manager Eddie Dyer once came to the mound to take him out of a game, Donnelly told him that he would hit him between the eyes with the ball if he took another step. Dyer retreated to the dugout, and Donnelly was quickly traded to the Phillies.

During a spring training game in the 1970s, Dodger manager Tom Lasorda sent comedian Don Rickles to the mound to remove pitcher Burt Hooton.

Personal Conference. Tigers pitcher Mark Fidrych, a **One-Year Wonder**, had animated conversations with himself while on the mound. Once while facing Fidrych, Graig Nettles stepped out of the box and began talking to his bat. After popping out, Nettles noted that his bat was Japanese and did not understand his pep talk in English.

Pitching Mounds

"In 1879, a rule was passed requiring the pitcher to face the batsman. Before that he had much latitude, and could roam around his big pitching box shooting off his delivery whenever the spirit moved him."—Fred Lieb in *The Baseball Story* (1950).

See also **Pitching Mound Conferences**.

Early Circumference. The Knickerbocker Club Rules required the pitching "mound" to be a 4' × 4' unelevated square box. The size was later increased to a 6' × 6' square. Each corner of the area was marked by a flat iron or six-inch square stone fixed in the ground. Between 1876 and 1886 a pitcher could deliver from anywhere in the box and could make a running start from within the box so long as he finished in the box. In 1886 the dimensions were 7' × 4', with the front end 50 feet from home plate.

In 1887 the area was reduced to 5'6" × 4', making the back end of the box 55'6" from the plate. The pitcher was still allowed to take only one step toward the plate and had to plant his foot on the back line of the pitching box. This rectangular area was eliminated in 1893 in favor of the pitching rubber (and perhaps the mound for the first time), which was placed an additional five feet from the plate at 60'6".

Mound Height.

"We, as Americans, can send people to the moon, but Major League Baseball can't get together a crew, or a group of crews, to check every mound to make sure that either they all conform to the 10-inch rule or to some other measurement so at least all the mounds are the same height."—Reds pitching coach Don Gullett in 2004, unhappy about certain mounds being too low.

Pitching mounds were in use well before 1904, the first year in which the mound was formally referred to in the rules. Mounds may have been implemented as early as 1893 when the pitching rubber was first formally adopted in the Major Leagues in place of the pitching "box." The best estimate based on a review of photographs is that the pitching mound began to grow from a minimum of 4 inches to over 20 inches in the late 19th century. It has been speculated that a mound was created because good footing for a pitcher was essential and the slope drained off water more easily and provided a good footing for the pitchers from which to push off. The raised pitching mound has been attributed to John Montgomery Ward, who starred as a pitcher in the 19th century before arm troubles forced him to shortstop. Rule 9 was inserted for the first time in 1904: "The pitcher's plate shall not be more than 15 inches higher than the baselines or home plate."

The exact 15-inch level was made mandatory in 1950. It is likely that pitching mounds were well in excess of 15" at the turn of the century or otherwise a new rule would not have addressed the problem. Deviations in the standard height have been common. For example, in 1941 pitching mounds varied from seven inches in Washington to 15 inches in Boston and Detroit. A's owner Connie Mack had his groundskeeper build the mound up to 20 inches. Christy Mathewson liked working from a flatter mound, and 50-year Giants groundskeeper Henry Fabian kept it at nine inches.

In 1969 the mandatory height was reduced to 10 inches. In 1995 the owners approved the raising of the mound to 12 or 13 inches.

Umpires are required to inspect and measure the mound in each park at least twice each year. This also includes inspection of the bullpen mounds. Some sources report that umpires are required to inspect the mound before each series and they do so using a special measuring device.

Modern Dimensions. The pitching mound is an 18-foot circle, with a 24" × 6" **Pitching Rubber** in the center. The area around the rubber is to be level six inches in front and 18 inches to each side.

Effect on Pitches. Lowering the pitching mound reduces the curve in curveballs and other breaking pitches.

Problems. In stadiums used both for baseball and football, the pitching mound usually is removed and reinstalled on a platform, but this has caused problems. The Oakland Coliseum's mound originally was placed over a steel shell which could be removed for the park's other tenant, a professional soccer team. After each inning of the first game played there, extensive corrective work had to be

undertaken. The steel shell eventually was replaced by a dirt mound that was scraped level for other sports.

Mound to Plate.

"Of course, the ground from the pitcher's position to that of the catcher should be bare of turf, some eight feet in width and laid with hard dry soil."—Henry Chadwick in a *DeWitt's Guide* of the 19th century; but for what purpose? Dirt paths were eliminated by the 1950s, apparently only for aesthetic reasons. A dirt path reappeared at Bank One Ballpark in Phoenix when it opened in 1998.

Pitching Rotations

"Spahn and Sain and Pray for Rain."—The mantra of the 1948 pennant-winning Braves, which did not say much for third and fourth starters Bill Voiselle (13–13) and Vern Bickford (11–5). The phrase came from sportswriter Gerry Hearn. See also **Poetry.**

"What we need is Guidry and three days of rain."—Reliever Sparky Lyle in the late 1970s on the Yankee ace.

"I have given Mike Cuellar more chances than my first wife."—Orioles manager Earl Weaver after he let Mike Cuellar start 13 straight games—he was bombed early each time—before removing him from the rotation.

"The Cubs have more quality arms than [Defense Secretary] Donald Rumsfeld."—Allen St. John in *Playboy* in early 2004.

Early Rotations. Cap Anson is credited with using the first pitching rotation in the 19th century, though many revisionist historians contend that Anson was a braggart who claimed many innovations that were actually begun by others. In 1898 manager Frank Selee of the Boston Red Stockings used the first four-man pitching rotation in the Major Leagues: Kid Nichols (29 wins), Ted Lewis (26), Vic Willis (24) and Bill Klobedanz (19).

Longest Together. The 1949–1955 Indians four-man rotation stayed intact longer than any other: Bob Feller, Bob Lemon, Mike Garcia and Early Wynn. Only 14 pitching rotations of four players have stayed together for at least three seasons.

Modern Rotations.

"It was done for 100 years, and I don't see why it can't be done now. I mean, I don't believe arms are hurt through usage. I think they're hurt by bad mechanics. That's why you see young pitchers coming up hurt and wily veterans like Don Sutton pitching for years."—First year Royals manager Bob Boone in 1995 on his use of a four-man rotation instead of the by-then more common five-man rotation. The Pirates also adopted a four-man rotation for part of the season.

The increase in five-man pitching rotations has decreased the number of starts by pitchers, making it far more difficult for pitchers to achieve some of the season statistical accomplishments of the past, such as strikeouts and wins.

As late as 1973, 37.3% of all starts were made on three days' rest or less, meaning that four-man rotations were still the norm. By 1977 it was 24%, 12% in 1982, 8% in 1987, and under 3% by 1992. A season of 38 starts used to be the modern norm. By the 1990s, 32 starts became a regular workload.

During the 2003 World Series, it was pointed at that pitchers who went on short rest during the postseason between 1999 and 2003 were 7–20, though they include Josh Beckett's Game 6 shutout of the Yankees in 2003 to clinch the championship for the Marlins. He threw on three days' rest.

Overuse.

"He should have been better, pitching on 3,195 days' rest."—Broadcaster Steve Blass on 1995 Pirates strike replacement player Jimmy Boudreau, who last appeared professionally in 1986.

In 1964 Phillies manager Gene Mauch went to a three-man rotation for the last few games of the season (see ***Pennant Races*** for the rotation). Pitching on two days' rest each time, the Phillies pitchers faltered and the club lost 10 straight to blow the pennant to the Cardinals. Mauch was accused of overusing his tired staff and never lived it down.

In 1954 Indians manager Al Lopez did the same thing, using Bob Lemon, Early Wynn and Mike Garcia on two days' rest over most of the last three weeks. The Indians managed to hold off the Yankees, who won 20 of 24 to end the season. However, the exhausted Indians were swept in the World Series by the Giants.

Short Rest Mistake. Hank Borowy was the losing pitcher in the Cubs' last World Series appearance, in 1945. He was sold by the Yankees to the Cubs for $97,500 midway through the 1945 season. He was 11–2 for the Cubs and shut out the Tigers in the Game 1 of the World Series. He lost Game 5 and came back the next day to pitch four innings of relief for the Game 6 win. He asked manager Charlie Grimm to start Game 7 on one day's rest. After getting shelled by the first three batters, he was pulled and the Tigers went on to win 9–3.

Pitching Rubbers

"But in the very first inning the Reds got a couple of bleeders, the miserable fluke hits that break a pitcher's heart, and they made some runs. Just before I was yanked, I kicked angrily at the rubber on the mound. Pitchers always kick the rubber when they're mad. I merely happened to kick it harder than usual." — Pitcher "Mad Monk" Russ Meyer on the broken toe he thought he had suffered. He recovered in three days because the X-rays were showing only an old break.

"Why is safe sex like baseball? If you want to pitch, you need a rubber." — 1990s joke.

Early. The first Major League pitching rubber was installed in 1893 (some sources erroneously report 1883) as a 12" × 4" slab. It replaced the rectangular area known as the pitcher's box that contained no pitching rubber (see also ***Pitching Mounds***). The term "rubber" was used in print as early as 1891, suggesting that the rubber was used in other leagues before being introduced to the National League. If it was used as part of the pitching box before the box was abandoned, then it would have been placed at the back of the box.

Dimensions/Composition. The modern (since 1895) pitching rubber is 24 inches long with four sides, each six inches wide. The black rubber is now hollow and reinforced with aluminum tubing. The four sides often are rotated to the surface for extended wear. The Little League pitching rubber is 18"x4."

Advantage Germany. Pitcher Germany Schmidt sometimes sneaked out to the ballpark the night before he was scheduled to pitch. He supposedly would dig up the pitching rubber and move it a foot closer to the plate.

Ice. Dizzy Dean won his 30th game in 1934, clinching the pennant for the Cardinals. A young boy ran out to the mound and put a four-pound block of ice on the pitching rubber. His explanation, according to Robert Gregory in *Diz* (1992): "Dizzy told me this morning to put it here. He said this slab would be burnin' up and he wasn't foolin'."

Color. In April 1969 it was reported that the National Baseball Congress was going to test a bright orange pitching rubber, foul lines and home plate at its annual tournament. However, none of the ideas was adopted for permanent use.

Distance to First. The distance from the rubber to first base is approximately 63'8½".

Rule. The pitcher must have at least half a foot's length in contact with the rubber during his motion. In early 2004, in a bit of gamesmanship, the Angels claimed that A's pitcher Mark Mulder was violating the rule. No one had ever heard of such a challenge, and the commissioner's office had to make a rule interpretation.

Pitching Rules

"No department in the game of base ball has undergone so many changes since its origin as that of the pitcher. Transitions have been going on and improvements have been made year after year, and the experimental stage, even at this date, has not been passed." — Jacob Morse in *Sphere and Ash* (1888).

"The batsman, on taking his position, must call for either a 'high ball' (above the waist but not higher than the shoulders), a 'low ball' (not lower than within one foot off the ground but not higher than his waist) or a 'fair ball' (between shoulders high and one foot from the ground)." — Pitching rules described in the 1876 *Beadle's Dime Base-Ball Player*. Nonswinging strikes could be called only if a pitcher threw to the desired zone and the batter did not swing.

See also ***Balks***.

Early 19th Century Rules. Early rules were very specific in that a pitcher could not bend his elbow, had to throw from below the waist, and could not snap his wrist on the pitch. According to Jim "Deacon" White, a pitcher was required to "stand flat-footed in the box and swing his arm perpendicular without bending the wrist."

Baseball writer Henry Chadwick covered an 1868 game in which White's pitching motion was ruled illegal, prompting Chadwick to advocate a rule allowing the pitcher to "throw or jerk the ball to the batter with a wrist motion." The then-existing rule effectively prohibited the use of curveballs, but the rule was often circumvented and changes soon were made.

An 1872 rule legalized all types of deliveries except overhand pitching and bowling as in cricket. Release below the waist (some sources say shoulder) was required until 1884, but the rule was ignored well before that.

In 1879 pitchers were required to face the batter immediately before delivering the pitch. Prior to that, pitchers could deliver their pitches from anywhere in the pitching box.

Rules Committee. The first joint rules committee of the National League and American Association met after the 1886 season. There were three key rule changes: 1) base on balls would be recorded as hits; 2) batters could no longer call for a high or low ball; and 3) pitchers were no longer allowed to run up and jump forward when they pitched, in the manner of a cricket bowler's motion. Other sources reported that 1893 (and some, 1888) was the first year that the "running pitch" was eliminated, coinciding with the change in pitching distance and the use of the pitching rubber. By 1893 pitchers were given full freedom to throw the ball in any manner they chose, so long as they faced the batter at the moment of their wind-up and had one foot touching the pitching rubber.

Going to the Mouth.

"Its central provision prohibits the pitcher on the mound from placing his bare hands anywhere near his mouth, even to cover a giggle." — Roger Angell in *The Summer Game* (1972).

See also ***Spitballs***.

A pitcher cannot go to his mouth or lips with his pitching hand while standing on the pitcher's mound. This rule has been modified to give discretion to the umpire in cold weather when pitchers need to blow on their hands to keep them warm. In 1995 the rules committee attempted to speed up the game by deciding that pitchers would be allowed to go their mouths without walking off the mound, provided that they wipe immediately.

Time Limit. Starting in 1957 pitchers were required to pitch within 20 seconds of receiving the ball from the catcher. Bill Veeck installed a "Pitchometer" in Comiskey Park to time pitchers. The rule applied only when the bases were empty. The rule was either abandoned or modified, because during the 1960s baseball again imposed a time limit, this time 30 seconds, in an effort to speed up games. It was rarely enforced.

Pitching Speeds

"Baseball ... is not a game of inches, like you hear people say. It's a game of *hundredths* of inches. Any time you have a bat only that big around, and a ball that small, traveling at such tremendous rates of speed, an inch is way too large a margin for error." — Pitcher Rube Bressler quoted in Lawrence Ritter's *The Glory of Their Times* (1966).

"I can still throw it in the 70s. And I can throw it in the 80s if I don't want to comb my hair for a week." — Bob Feller at age 66 when asked if he could still throw a fastball.

"The man who threw 90 in the '70s and the man who throws 70 in the '90s." — Mets broadcaster Todd Kalas on Frank Tanana, who went from fastball pitcher in the 1970s to junkball pitcher in the 1980s and 1990s due to arm problems.

See also *Fastest Pitchers*.

Early Pitching Speed. In the earliest days of amateur baseball, pitching was almost a lob because of the restrictions placed on throwing the ball to the plate.

Modern Pitching Speed. At a distance of 60'6", a 100-mph fastball arrives at the plate in .41 seconds. An 80-mph curveball arrives in .50 seconds, a 50-mph change-up in .82 seconds, and a 35-mph knuckleball in one second. The distance would be calculated more accurately from the pitcher's release point of approximately 55 feet, making the 100-mph fastball arrive in .38 seconds.

Some sources report that the average Major League fastball is clocked at 90 mph, sliders in the high 70s to low 80s. Curveballs are generally clocked at 68–75 mph. Other sources provide the following average speeds:

85 mph	Fastball
79–80 mph	Slider
75 mph	Curveball
73 mph	Change-up

Pitchouts

"Players watched for years to see if the great Bob Gibson, who terrified both foe and friend, would ever shake off the green [Tim] McCarver.... One day [Davey] Johnson asked Gibson, with McCarver present, if he'd ever shaken off a McCarver sign. McCarver's chest swelled until Gibson said, 'Yeah, I always shook off one sign ... the pitchout. Timmy couldn't throw out anybody.'" — Thomas Boswell in *The Heart of the Order* (1989).

Hits. Reds outfield star Edd Roush is reported to have had seven hits on pitchouts during a single season.

Curveball. Grover Cleveland Alexander may be the only pitcher in Major League history to throw curveballs on pitchouts. His catcher, Bill Killefer, explained that Alexander's fastball was so overpowering that it was easier for Killefer to catch the slower curveball.

Pittsburgh

"Pittsburgh is such a tough town even the canaries sing bass there." — Sportswriter Bugs Baer.

Pittsburgh's first prominent club reportedly was the Enterprise Club, founded by Union soldier Al Pratt. It was followed by the Xanthas and Olympics clubs. Pittsburgh has had the following Major League teams:

American Association Alleghenys 1882–1886
Union Association Stogies 1884
National League Alleghenys 1887–1890
Players League Burghers 1890
National League Pirates 1891–
Federal League Rebels 1914–1915

Pittsburgh also had two prominent Negro League clubs, the Homestead Grays and the Pittsburgh Crawfords.

Pittsburgh Alleghenys

American Association 1882–1886
Owned by "Hustling" Horace Phillips, the club had a 39–39 record in its inaugural season in 1882, followed by horrendous seasons of 31–67 and 30–78. By 1886 the club had moved up to second place and was invited to join the National League for the 1887 season. This was allowed by the enforcers of the National Agreement because of a dispute between the American Association and Organized Baseball over player Sam Barkley. Pittsburgh used the opportunity to jump to the stronger National League.

Pittsburgh Alleghenys

National League 1887–1890
See *Pittsburgh Pirates*.

Pittsburgh Burghers

Players League 1890
Player-manager Ned Hanlon led the club to a sixth-place finish. Jake Beckley hit .324 with 120 RBIs as the team's star. The remnants of the club combined with the National League club to form a stronger National League entry for 1891.

Pittsburgh Crawfords

Negro Leagues
"The Crawfords played everywhere, in every ballpark. And we won, won like we invented the game." — Satchel Paige.

"In 1932 a new figure walked into the Pittsburgh baseball scene: Gus Greenlee, genial tavern owner, numbers king, and sportsman, who already owned an impressive stable of fighters.... Gus wanted a ball club too. He literally bought [Cum] Posey's [Homestead Grays] club right out from under him.... In all, it may have been the best black team in history — Monte Irvin and many others believe it was." — John B. Holway in *Blackball Stars* (1988).

"The Pittsburgh Crawfords may have been the greatest black baseball team of all time. They were certainly the most exciting. The heart of their lineup featured five men destined for Cooperstown's Hall of Fame.... This awesome group, complemented by other stars, powered the Crawfords to the very zenith of black baseball and they did so with marvelous style and grace." — James Bankes in *The Pittsburgh Crawfords* (1991).

Named after a Pittsburgh bathhouse, this Negro League club of the 1930s and 1940s fielded perhaps the strongest Negro League team of all time in 1935. The Crawfords posted a 39–15 record behind Cool Papa Bell, Oscar Charleston, Josh Gibson, Judy Johnson and Satchel Paige. The club disbanded after the 1938 season. A new version of the Crawfords existed in the 1940s, but absent the glory of its predecessor.

Books. James Bankes, *The Pittsburgh Crawfords: The Lives and Times of Black Baseball's Most Exciting Team!* (1991); Rob Ruck, *Sandlot Seasons: Sport in Black Pittsburgh* (1993).

Pittsburgh Pirates

National League 1887–

"This is a free country, including Pittsburgh, even if every hotel-keeper in the place is named Jesse James…. There is something to be merry about in the thought that if the rain had to come it came in Washington instead of Pittsburgh. A week in Pittsburgh at World Series rates would bankrupt organized baseball." — Sportswriter Bill McGeehan during the 1925 World Series between the Senators and Pirates.

Origins. Pittsburgh did not have a National League team until 1887, when the Pittsburgh Alleghenys of the American Association moved over after the 1886 season. The club languished in the second division through the 1880s and continued to be known as the Alleghenys.

The original club lasted until the pressures of the Players League challenge of 1890 forced the team to dissolve after that season. The owners of the defunct Players League club immediately combined with the owners of the National League Allegheny Club to form the Pittsburgh Athletic Company. That entity owned the new Pittsburgh franchise in the National League, known thereafter as the Pirates.

First Game. Pittsburgh's Pud Galvin pitched the club to a 6–2 victory over the White Stockings in Recreation Park on April 30, 1887.

Key Owners.

Harmer Dennis "Denny" McKnight/1887–1890. McKnight had been a stalwart of the American Association and was a principal owner of the club through the 1880s.

J. Palmer O'Neill/1891–1894.

"It is quite true; we have had a meeting and we have resolved to continue in the ring. We have cleared money, and very few people in the baseball business can say that much. We have run our team to meet emergencies, because we have had to deal with untried players. Next year we'll have a team as good as anybody's." — O'Neill in October 1890, after the club reconstituted and combined with the Players League club. This enabled the Pirates to recover a number of players they had lost to the one-season Players League.

William W. Kerr/1894–1900. Kerr was the primary owner of the club through 1897 and president until Louisville owner Barney Dreyfuss bought into the club in 1900. Captain Kerr was a principal in Arbuckle Coffee and is credited by some with recognizing the managerial talents of Connie Mack and putting him in charge.

Barney Dreyfuss/1900–1932. Dreyfuss migrated from Germany to the U.S. at age 17. He had owned the Louisville club in the National League, but that club was eliminated after the 1899 season. Future National League president Harry Pulliam was the club's secretary and loyal to Dreyfuss. The Pirates were not competitive until 1900 when Dreyfuss bought a 50% interest in the team. The other half was owned by William W. Kerr. When Dreyfuss bought into the Pittsburgh club, he and Pulliam brought with them the best players from the defunct Louisville team, including Honus Wagner.

Kerr disliked Pulliam, although the dislike probably went deeper than the following incident reportedly caused. Kerr had an argument with Pulliam after Pulliam agreed to have the team pay for a coat torn by a fan on a nail at the ballpark. Dreyfuss sided with Pulliam and asked Kerr to sell out. Dreyfuss came up with the $75,000 demanded by Kerr and became the sole owner of the team until his death from pneumonia following a prostate operation in 1932.

Bill Benswanger/1932–1946.

"And the Pirate president's liberal and wide awake policies have been equally evident on the playing side of the club. He is his own team's hottest fan and most rabid rooter; a magnate of the rare type who always asked about the score rather than about the attendance." —1943 *Pittsburgh Post-Gazette.*

Bill Benswanger was the son-in-law of Barney Dreyfuss and president of the Pirates during and after the Depression through World War II. He and his future wife Eleanor attended the opening of Forbes Field, although they did not know each other. She was 11 and sat in a special owners box; he was 17 and sat in the bleachers.

Benswanger was born in Pittsburgh and entered the insurance business. He served in World War I before marrying Eleanor. After the death of Samuel Dreyfuss, son of the club's founder, the elder Dreyfuss encouraged Benswanger to become involved with the club. The next year, 1932, Dreyfuss died after prostate surgery and Benswanger took over as president while Dreyfuss's wife continued to hold the stock until her death. Benswanger's grandfather had held stock in the club in 1899. Benswanger sold out after the 1946 season.

The Galbreath Family/1946–1985.

"Pirates owner and real estate baron John Galbraith owned a horse and a ballplayer named 'Roberto,' [Clemente] and the two meant about the same to him." — John Helyar in *Lords of the Realm* (1994).

On August 8, 1946, the club was purchased by Indianapolis banker Frank E. McKinney, Pittsburgh attorney Thomas P. Johnson, and John W. Galbreath, a Columbus, Ohio, realtor and the leader of the group. Bing Crosby spent $250,000 to become a part-owner and held his interest into the 1970s. Crosby purportedly helped sign 162-game winner Vern Law and sometimes worked out with the club at its spring training camp in San Bernardino, California. Galbreath was the club's president until 1969 when his son succeeded him.

Branch Rickey became the general manager in 1952, beginning the club's slow climb to respectability by the end of the 1950s. Joe L. Brown, the son of movie comedian Joe E. Brown, was the general manager from 1955 into the 1970s and the man often credited with the Pirates' success in the 1960s.

Pittsburgh Associates/1986–1995.

"If Vince Sarni [Pirates chairman] bit himself in the arm, he'd die of blood poisoning. The city should tell Sarni and baseball, 'Don't let the door hit you in the [rear end] on the way out of Pittsburgh.'" — Pittsburgh city council president Jim Ferlo on the acrimonious negotiations over renovation of Three Rivers Stadium.

The franchise reached an all-time low after the 1985 season. The club had been rocked by criminal trials in which a number of its players admitted to **Drug** use. Fans had turned increasingly to the powerful football Steelers, and attendance at baseball games in the small-market city had dwindled in light of the club's 57–104 record. The Galbreaths, who had owned the club since 1946, announced that they would have to move the club in order to survive. Local companies came to the rescue and purchased the team, enabling it to stay in the city where it had been for almost 100 years.

In 1986 nine corporations and four individuals each paid $2 million to keep the club in Pittsburgh. The group, known formally as Pittsburgh Associates, included Alcoa, Westinghouse, the Mellon Bank, Carnegie-Mellon University, PPG (Pittsburgh Plate Glass) and USX (U.S. Steel). The city of Pittsburgh helped out by underwriting a $20 million loan, but by the 1990s the club had exhausted a $34 million line of credit. Despite success in the late 1980s and early 1990s the Pirates claimed to be $60 million in debt by 1995 and were expected to lose another $20 million that season.

Kevin McClatchey/1995– .

"The Pittsburgh franchise remains in intensive care."— Bob Nightengale in the *Los Angeles Times* late in the 1995 season when the new ownership structure was unclear.

Kevin McClatchey, a Sacramento newspaper heir, purchased the club in September 1995 for $85 million. He agreed on a lease that would keep the club in Pittsburgh but would allow him to move the club if a new stadium was not in the works by 2000 (it was). McClatchey was to receive $6.5 million in lease concessions and an $8 million loan.

McClatchey's investors included quarterback Dan Marino, who played at Pitt, and Chip Ganassi, who owned an Indy-car team with quarterback Joe Montana. Other investors were developer Dick Means, scrap-metal dealer Bill Snyder, and Fred Anderson, who owned the San Antonio franchise in the CFL and part of the NBA's Sacramento Kings.

Nicknames.

"Its club retained the [Allegheny] name for more than twenty years until — as a result of a freebooting career that saw them buy up most of the Columbus team in 1884, jump the American Association to take over the National League's Kansas City franchise in 1886, and raid the Philadelphia Athletics in 1891— they began being called 'the Pirates' around the league."— Harold Peterson's version of how the club received its nickname in *The Man Who Invented Baseball* (1969). The more accepted version is that during the 1890 off-season, the club was reorganized with ex–Players League members and it "pirated" second baseman Lou Bierbauer from the Philadelphia Athletics of the American Association (which itself was an old Players League team). Pittsburgh club president J. Palmer O'Neill was tagged J. "Pirate" O'Neill as a result of the move and the name stuck.

The team was known originally as the "Pittsburghs" and "Alleghenys," a leftover from the American Association club of the early 1880s. In the mid-1880s, the players wore such outrageously striped uniforms that they were sometimes known as the "Potato Bugs," "Zulus," and "Smoked Italians." When playing poorly from 1888 through 1890 (23–113 in 1890), the team was known as the "Innocents." Because the city historically was dotted with smokestacks from the steel industry, the club was sometimes referred to as the "Stogies."

See also *Uniforms*—Club Names/Nicknames for use of the "h" in Pittsburgh.

Key Seasons.

1901. After second-place finishes only in 1893 and 1900, the Pirates emerged in 1901 with a pennant by seven games over the Phillies. The club was led by recently-acquired Honus Wagner with a .353 average and a league-leading 126 RBIs. Deacon Phillippe and Jack Chesbro each won more than 20 games. There was no World Series because of the continuing feud between the leagues.

1902. The club repeated as National League champions with 103 wins to clinch by 27½ games, the largest margin in Major League history until 1995. The club had the league leader in batting average (Ginger Beaumont at .357), home runs (Tommy Leach with six), RBIs (Honus Wagner with 91), and wins (Jack Chesbro with 28). Due to the continued feud with the American League, there was no World Series.

1903. The Pirates won their third straight pennant as Honus Wagner led the league with a .355 average, Deacon Phillippe won 24 games and Sam Leever won 25. In the first World Series, the Pirates lost to the Red Sox and Cy Young in eight games. Louis P. Masur, *Autumn Glory: Baseball's First World Series* (2003).

1909. After a series of second- and third-place finishes, the Pirates captured the pennant with 110 wins. Honus Wagner led the league with a .339 average and 100 RBIs, and Howie Camnitz won 25 games. The Pirates won their first World Championship when they defeated the Tigers in seven games.

1925.

"In the wettest, weirdest and wildest game that fifty years of baseball have ever seen, the Pirates today proved their right to the mud-horse, twilight and all other championships of the national game."— James R. Harrison in the *New York Times*.

After a series of decent finishes the Pirates won the pennant with 95 wins, 8½ games ahead of the Giants. Pie Traynor and Kiki Cuyler were the club's stars. Traynor batted .320 with 106 RBIs. Cuyler had 220 hits and 102 RBIs to go with his .357 average. The Pirates barely beat the Senators in seven games in the World Series, winning 9–7 in Game 7 with three runs in the bottom of the 8th inning. They were the first team to come back from a 3–1 game deficit.

1927. The Pirates won the pennant by two games over the Cardinals as Paul Waner led the league with a .380 average and 131 RBIs. The club was swept by the Yankees in the World Series.

1938. The club finished in second place, only two games behind the Cubs.

1960. After a number of doormat seasons in the early 1950s, the Pirates and Roberto Clemente finally emerged with a decent team by the end of the decade. In 1960 the club broke through with a pennant by seven games over the Braves. Dick Groat led the league with a .325 average and Vern Law won 20 games. The World Series was wild, as the Yankees overpowered the Pirates in three games and the Pirates barely won four. In Game 7 Bill Mazeroski broke a 9–9 tie with a dramatic home run in the bottom of the 9th inning to give the Pirates their first title since 1925. See also Dick Groat and Bill Surface, *The World Champion Pittsburgh Pirates* (1961); Jim O'Brien, *Maz and the '60 Bucs* (1994).

1970. After a decade of generally strong finishes, the Pirates won a division title by five games over the Cubs. Willie Stargell hit 31 home runs and Roberto Clemente batted .352, but the Reds swept the Pirates in the NLCS.

1971. The Pirates repeated as division winners with 97 victories. Willie Stargell led the league with 48 home runs and Roberto Clemente batted .341. Dave Giusti led the league with 30 saves. The Pirates beat the Giants for the pennant and then Roberto Clemente put on a hitting clinic in the series (.414) as the Pirates won in seven games. See also Greg Spalding, *Sailing the Three Rivers to the Title: Pittsburgh's 1971 Voyage of the Pirate Ship* (1994).

1972. The club won its third straight title behind Willie Stargell's 33 home runs and 112 RBIs. Roberto Clemente hit .312 in his final season and Steve Blass won 19 games. In the NLCS the Reds scored two runs in the bottom of the 9th inning of the deciding Game 5 to beat the Pirates 4–3.

1974. The Pirates won the division title by 1½ games over the Cardinals. They were beaten by the Dodgers in four games in the NLCS. Willie Stargell hit 25 home runs and Richie Zisk drove in 100. The club had four pitchers with between 12 and 16 wins.

1975. The Pirates won their fifth division title in six years. Willie Stargell hit 22 home runs and Dave Parker emerged as a star with 25 home runs and 101 RBIs. The club was swept by the Reds for the pennant.

1979. After three straight second-place finishes, the "We Are Family" Pirates won the division behind Willie Stargell's 32 home runs and Dave Parker's 25 home runs and 94 RBIs. The club swept the Reds for the pennant and then came back from a 3–1 deficit in the World Series to beat the Orioles in seven games.

1990. After a mediocre decade the Pirates returned to the winner's circle with 95 wins to capture the division by four games over the Mets. Barry Bonds led the club with 33 home runs and 114 RBIs and Bobby Bonilla had 32 home runs and 120 RBIs. Doug Drabek led the league with 22 wins. The Pirates lost the NLCS in six games to the Reds.

1991. The Pirates repeated as Eastern Division champions, as John Smiley led the league with 20 wins and Barry Bonds had 25 home runs and 116 RBIs. The Pirates again lost the league championship series, this time to the Braves in seven games.

1992. The club won its third straight division title behind Barry Bonds' 34 home runs and 103 RBIs. The Pirates were leading 2–0 in the bottom of the 9th inning of Game 7 of the championship series against the Braves, but Atlanta scored three runs in the inning to win the pennant.

Key Players.

"You clowns can go on 'What's My Line?' in full uniform and stump the panel." — Pirates manager Billy Meyer during the lean years in the late 1940s and early 1950s.

Honus Wagner (HF) played 18 seasons at shortstop for the Pirates after moving over from the Louisville Colonels. He hit .300 or better in 15 straight seasons and led the league eight times. He stole over 600 bases for the club and led the league in RBIs four times and doubles seven times.

Deacon Phillippe (HF) pitched for 12 seasons in Pittsburgh beginning in 1900. He won 20 or more games for the club five times and a total of 168 for the Pirates.

Pie Traynor (HF) played all of his 17 Major League seasons for the Pirates, beginning in 1920. He batted over .300 ten times while establishing himself as the preeminent third baseman of the era. He hit .320 lifetime and finished with 2,416 hits.

Fred Clarke (HF) moved from Louisville to Pittsburgh in 1900 and played 15 seasons for the Pirates. The outfielder batted over .300 six times for the club.

Paul Waner (HF), "Big Poison" to his brother's "Little Poison," played 15 seasons for the Pirates beginning in 1926. He led the league three times while batting over .300 12 straight times. He scored more than 100 runs nine times and had 200 or more hits eight times.

Lloyd Waner (HF) played 14 full seasons for the Pirates starting in 1927. Alongside his brother in the outfield he hit over .300 ten times and had more than 200 hits in four of his first five seasons in the league.

Roy Face pitched for the Pirates from 1953 through most of 1968 (with the exception of 1954). He was 18–1 in 1959 for the highest winning percentage of all time at .947. He saved 188 games for the club, including a league-leading 28 in 1962.

Roberto Clemente (HF) played 18 seasons for the Pirates beginning in 1955. He hit over .300 13 times, leading the league four times. He had over 200 hits four times and hit 240 home runs for the club. He hit .362 in two World Series, seventh-best all-time, and had exactly 3,000 hits. He died in a plane crash on December 31, 1972, while en route to Nicaragua with earthquake supplies (see also ***Deaths***).

Willie Stargell (HF) played his entire 21-year career for the Pirates beginning in 1962. He hit 475 home runs and led the league in home runs with 48 in 1971 and 44 in 1973. He hit .315 in two World Series for the club, 1971 and 1979, and hit 11 postseason home runs.

Barry Bonds led the club to three straight division titles beginning in 1990 as he established himself as one the dominant players in the game. He hit 176 home runs for the club in seven seasons between 1986 and 1992.

Jason Kendall was one of the few bright spots for the Pirates starting in 1996. He was the club's regular catcher through the 2004 season, and had three consecutive years with at least 20 stolen bases.

Key Managers.

"Managing is a lonely job. Players know you've got the whip and they steer clear." — Pirates manager Bill Virdon.

Fred Clarke (HF) was player-manager for the Pirates from 1900 through 1915 (though his playing career was essentially over after 1911). He won pennants from 1901 through 1903 and in 1909. In the two World Series in which he managed, he lost in 1903 and won in seven games in 1909. His clubs finished in second place four times.

Bill McKechnie (HF) led the club from 1922 through 1926, winning a pennant in 1925 and defeating the Senators in a seven-game World Series. The club finished third in each of the other seasons.

After the 1925 World Series, the Pirates seemed to be a dynasty in the making. Early in the 1926 season, owner Barney Dreyfuss was happy with the situation and left for Europe with his daughters. He left in charge his son, Sam, the club's treasurer. Fred Clarke, a former player and manager, was a small stockholder in the team and often sat on the bench during games.

Clarke became an agitator on the bench, resulting in dissension that soon became public. Son Sam (probably with cabled advice from Barney) took action against certain players loyal to McKechnie. He also released 1909 World Series hero Babe Adams, who was still a decent relief pitcher at 43. He suspended Max Carey, the primary object of Clarke's dissatisfaction, and shipped him to the Dodgers on waivers. He released Carson Bigbee, who had been an outfielder with the club since 1916. At the end of the season, McKechnie was also released, despite an 84–69 record and a third-place finish.

In a surprising turnaround after the season, Clarke sold his stock in the club (probably under pressure from Dreyfuss) and left the team for good. Bob O'Farrell became the manager and McKechnie became a coach for the club. Despite the turmoil, the Pirates finished third in 1926 and then won the 1927 pennant.

Pie Traynor (HF) managed the club from 1934 through 1939, finishing second in 1938.

Frankie Frisch (HF) managed the Pirates from 1940 through 1946, finishing second in 1944.

Danny Murtaugh began managing the Pirates late in the 1957 season and started a 15-season run with the club until his death in December 1976. He missed the 1972 season and part of 1973 due to ill health. The popular manager led the Pirates to World Series wins in 1960 and 1971, and division titles in 1970, 1974 and 1975.

Chuck Tanner.

"It's hard to win a pennant, but it's harder losing one." — Tanner, who took over from Murtaugh and led the club from 1977 through 1985. He won the 1979 World Series after two straight second-place finishes. The club finished second in 1983 before fading under Tanner.

Jim Leyland.

"The main person I will not miss is Jim Leyland. I am simply elated that I will no longer have to watch him biting his fingernails, stroking his moustache, picking his nose and sneaking puffs on his cigarettes."—Pirates fan Arthur J. Brickman, a self-described "old geezer" in his 80s, in a letter to the *Pittsburgh Post-Gazette*.

Leyland became the Pirates manager in 1986 and finished second in 1988. In 1990 he began a string of three straight first-place finishes but could never push the club into the World Series. Though he remained with the club through 1996, the Pirates fell on hard times after their division titles earlier in the decade and finished fifth in three of his last three seasons.

Ballparks.

Recreation Park and Exposition Park. The 1880s Alleghenys played in Recreation Park from 1887 through 1890. The Pirates played in a rebuilt version of Exposition Park from 1891 until midway through 1909 when Forbes Field opened. The 1890 Players League entry also played in the park, as did the 1914–1915 Federal League team. The ballpark seated approximately 16,000 and had dimensions of 400–450–400.

Forbes Field. *Forbes Field* opened on June 30, 1909, and was home to the Pirates until they moved into Three Rivers Stadium in early July 1970. The club played its last game in Forbes Field on June 28, 1970.

Three Rivers Stadium. This ballpark was built on the exact site of the original Exposition Park. It opened on July 16, 1970, two days after the All-Star Game in Cincinnati. The capacity originally was 50,500 but expanded at various times to a high of 58,729 in 1990. Its dimensions from left to right field originally were 340–385–410–385–340 but were reduced slightly in 1975. The ballpark is only a few feet from the Monongahela River (and the Allegheny and the Ohio form the "Three Rivers" trio.

The last game in the ballpark was played on October 1, 2000, after Sister Sledge sang the National Anthem to a season-high crowd of 55,352. The Cubs won 10–9, as Mark Grace had the final putout. On February 11, 2001, the ballpark was imploded in front of thousands of fans.

PNC Park.

"No, not just right. Perfect. This is the perfect blend of location, history, design, comfort and baseball. It's as if the House That Ruth Built had first been designed by Frank Lloyd Wright and then run past Ray Kinsella for final approval."—Jim Caple.

The new ballpark cost $262 million to build and seated 38,000 at the juncture of the Allegheny, Monongahela and Ohio rivers. The first game there was an exhibition game played on March 31, 2001, as the Pirates lost to the Mets 4–3. The first regular season game was played on April 9, 2001, as the Reds beat the Pirates 8–2. Pirates icon Willie Stargell died a few hours before game time after a long illness and the club paid tribute to him with a 90-second visual presentation prior to the game. On July 6, 2002, Daryle Ward of the Astros became the first player to hit a home run into the Allegheny River outside the right field wall.

Key Broadcasters.

"Get upstairs, Aunt Minnie, and raise the window! Here she comes!"—Rosey Rowswell's home run call, followed by his dropping of a tray of silverware to simulate a window breaking.

In 1921 Harold Arlin sat in Forbes Field and conducted the first *Radio* broadcast of a Major League Baseball game. The first regu-lar Pirates broadcast was in 1936, when Albert Kennedy (Rosey) Rowswell began 19 years as the Voice of the team. He retired in 1954 and died at age 71 in 1955.

Hall of Famer Bob Prince, who had dropped out of Harvard Law School, was the club's number two broadcaster from 1948 until Rowswell retired. Prince starred for the next 20 years. He was fired in 1975 when he railed against the involvement of Westinghouse in the purchase of the club. Milo Hamilton left the Braves in 1975 and became the voice of the Pirates. He left following the 1979 season after four difficult years trying to broadcast beyond the shadow of the bitter Prince.

Lanny Frattare started with the Pirates in 1976 and became the number one broadcaster in 1980, a position he held through 2004. Pitcher Jim Rooker retired and began broadcasting for the club in 1980 and remained through 1993. Pitcher Steve Blass joined the crew in 1986 and remained through 2004, and pitcher Bob Walk joined the club in 1994 and was still going in 2004. Greg Brown began in 1994 and also was still with the club in 2004.

Books. David Finoli and Bill Rainer, *The Pittsburgh Pirates Encyclopedia* (2003); Fred Lieb, *The Pittsburgh Pirates* (1948, 1993 reprint); John C. McCollister, *The Bucs! The Story of the Pittsburgh Pirates* (1998); Kip Richeal, *Pittsburgh Pirates: Still Walking Tall* (1993); Chris W. Sehnert, *Pittsburgh Pirates* (1997); Bob Smizik with Gerald Astor, *The Pittsburgh Pirates* (1990); Greg Spalding, *Shine! All-Stars, Shine* (1995); Wayne Stewart, *Pittsburgh Pirates* (2002).

Pittsburgh Rebels

Federal League 1914–1915

The Rebels, also known as the Stogies and the PittsFeds, finished seventh in 1914. Led by player-manager Rebel Oakes for most of 1914 and in 1915, the club finished third in 1915 as Frank Allen won 23 games. The Rebels took over the Pirates' old Exposition Park in Allegheny.

Pittsburgh Stogies

Union Association 1884

During the Union Association's one-year existence in 1884, the Chicago entry moved to Pittsburgh in August. The club lasted until mid–September when it was replaced by St. Paul of the Northwestern League. The Stogies were 7–11 before dropping out of the league.

Eddie Plank (1875–1926)

Hall of Fame 1946

"Plank was not the fastest. He was not the trickiest, and not the possessor of the most stuff, but just the greatest."—Hall of Famer Eddie Collins.

Plank won 327 games and pitched 69 shutouts over a 17-year career primarily for the A's beginning in 1901.

Edward Arthur ["Stewart" in some sources] Plank was born in Gettysburg, Pennsylvania, where he went to college. At age 26 in 1901 he signed with the A's. He was 17–13 in his first season and then won 20 or more games in five of the next six seasons. He won over 20 games again in 1911 and 1912.

Plank played on six pennant-winning A's teams but appeared in only four World Series. In 1902 there was no World Series and in 1910 the A's used only two pitchers to defeat the Cubs in the Series, Chief Bender and Jack Coombs.

Plank left the club after the 1914 season to sign with St. Louis in the Federal League, where he won 21 games in 1915. In 1916 he signed with the Browns, but his Major League career was waning and he won only 16 games. He won five games in 1917 and at age 43 refused to report to the Yankees after a trade in early 1918. After retiring that season, he suffered a stroke in 1926 and died at age 51 later that year.

Plank won 327 games (325 in early sources). He was the winningest left-hander in Major League history until Warren Spahn and Steve Carlton topped him. His 69 shutouts are sixth all-time.

Plate Appearances

Rule. A plate appearance includes all times that a batter comes to the plate, which is different from official *At-Bats*. Plate appearances include unofficial at-bats such as base on balls and hit by pitch. Plate appearances are the key to determining whether a player is eligible to be a *Batting Champion*. Under existing rules, a batter is eligible if he has 3.1 plate appearances for every game played by his team.

Single Season. Pete Rose holds the record for most plate appearances in a season, with 771 in 1974.

Nine-Inning Game. On May 19, 1999, Mike Cameron tied the Major League record of eight plate appearances in a nine inning game when the Reds beat the Rockies 24–12 at Coors Field (see also *Total Bases*).

See *Reaching Base* for reaching base in consecutive plate appearances.

Platooning

"If baseball ever adopted the two platoon system [from football] I'd get $50,000: $25,000 for hitting and $25,000 for sitting."— Gene Green, who played sporadically for the Cardinals and other clubs as an outfielder-catcher in the late 1950s and early 1960s.

"I always use my nine best players — and you're one of them — today."— Manager Roger Craig's favorable view of platooning.

"I don't believe in platooning your hitters. That's a lot of crap to me. If a guy can hit a left-hander, he can hit a right-hander. The pitch has got to come over the same plate. It's got to be a strike. Cobb used to say, 'If you can hit, you can hit from either side.'"— Manager Jimmy Dykes.

Origins/Evolution. The precise origins of platooning are unknown and muddled. Platooning was rare in the 19th century simply because rosters were small and supposedly there were few left-handed pitchers at that time. However, although there were few left-handed pitchers (because there were so few starters overall and virtually no relievers) the left-handers had a larger impact and platooning eventually was recognized as an important strategy.

It is likely that platooning began with catchers who were injury prone because of poor equipment; so each club carried two and usually three catchers. Nineteenth-century managers Cap Anson and Ned Hanlon purportedly were early proponents of platooning. There is evidence that Anson and the Chicago White Stockings platooned at least two players as early as the 1870s.

The first great platooner may have been 1914 Braves manager George Stallings. He may have resorted to platooning out of necessity; his generally mediocre players could not rise to all occasions. According to historian Bill James, it appears that he imported the practice from the American League, where he used it briefly with the Yankees in 1910. Detroit's Hughie Jennings platooned in 1907,

inheriting the practice from Tiger manager Bill Armour, who used it in 1906 with catchers Boss Schmidt and John Warner.

Platooning was commonplace by the 1920s, as clubs often platooned at two or three positions. Tris Speaker of the Indians was the first manager to platoon extensively in the 1920s, doing so at three or four positions.

The practice fell into apparent disfavor through the 1930s and early 1940s, the latter decade primarily because of a lack of quality players with whom to platoon due to the war. Casey Stengel, a successful platoon player in his day, is credited with reviving the practice in the 1950s (though some erroneously report that he was the first great platooner). Stengel acknowledged that he platooned only out of necessity because of the rash of injuries suffered by the Yankees in 1949. Stengel had to deal with injuries primarily to outfielders Joe DiMaggio (heel) and Tommy Henrich (ribs/knee). Stengel later said that he would have gone with a set line-up if the injuries had not forced him to platoon.

Stengel continued the practice through the 1950s. In 1953 only two of the team's regulars played more than 140 games. Reserve outfielder Irv Noren played in as many games as the three starting outfielders. Platooning became a regular feature from the 1950s through the 1990s.

Fired. Former slugger Joe Adcock was fired as the Indians manager in 1967 in large part because the owners were unhappy that he was platooning sluggers Rocky Colavito and Leon Wagner.

Success. The 1979 Orioles platooned Gary Roenicke and John Lowenstein. Lowenstein hit 11 home runs and drove in 34 runs in only 197 at-bats. Roenicke hit 25 home runs with 65 RBIs in 376 at-bats.

Play-Offs

"They say that for great things to happen, the right person has to be in the right place at the right time. On October 3, 1951, Bobby Thomson was that guy. It was one of the most exciting single moments I experienced in all my years in baseball."— Leo Durocher in the foreword to *The Giants Win the Pennant! The Giants Win the Pennant!*," by Bobby Thomson with Lee Heiman and Bill Gutman (1991).

This section covers games played as a result of a season-ending tie for first place or for a wild card in a league or division. There have been seven play-offs in the National League and three in the American League. The Dodgers have been in five of the National League play-offs, winning one and losing four.

The National League used a three-game format until the 1980 one-game play-off between the Dodgers and Astros. The American League has used only a one-game format for its play-offs.

Play-Off Statistics. See *Statistics — Play-Off Statistics*.

National League/1946. Cardinals Defeat Dodgers. In the first play-off in Major League history, the Cardinals swept the Dodgers in two straight games. Ralph Branca lost the first game 4–2 on October 1, 1946. Howie Pollet earned his 21st victory of the season for the Cardinals.

In the second game, in front of 31,437 Dodger fans on October 3, Murry Dickson of the Cardinals gave up 13 hits in an 8–4 victory to sweep the series. The Cardinals were leading 8–1 into the 9th inning, but the Dodgers scored three runs and had the bases loaded when Eddie Stanky and Howie Schultz struck out trying for a grand slam. Enos Slaughter got into a fight with a number of fans at home plate at the end of the game.

American League/1948. Indians Defeat Red Sox. The Indians defeated the Red Sox 8–3 in a one-game play-off. Left-handed

27-year-old rookie Gene Bearden earned his 20th win behind shortstop Lou Boudreau's 4-for-4 and two home runs. If the Red Sox had won, there would have been an all–Boston World Series with the Braves.

National League/1951. Giants Defeat Dodgers.

"The saddest day of my life was October 3, 1951.... It's the only time in my life I seriously considered ending it all. I thought about going to the Brooklyn Bridge and jumping, but I figured the line would be too long."—Broadcaster Larry King, who in 2004 wrote *Why I Love Baseball.*

"The Miracle of Coogan's Bluff"

"The Shot Heard 'Round the World"

The Giants defeated the Dodgers in a best-of-three play-off series. In Game 1 Ralph Branca lost 3–1 by giving up a two-run home run to Bobby Thomson. Both would figure prominently later in the series. The Dodgers won the second game 10–0 on Clem Labine's six-hitter to set up the final game drama.

In Game 3 on October 3, 1951, with 34,230 in attendance at the Polo Grounds (20,000 short of capacity), the Dodgers led 4–1 going into the bottom of the 9th inning. Starter Don Newcombe was still pitching and had allowed the Giants only four hits. Up to that point Thomson was the goat of the game after ending the 2nd inning with a base running mistake when he was picked off going to second base.

Alvin Dark led off the bottom of the 9th inning for the Giants with an infield hit. Don Mueller singled, putting runners at first and third. Monte Irvin popped up for the first out. Whitey Lockman doubled, scoring Dark to make it 4–2. Mueller sprained his ankle sliding into third and had to be carried off the field as Clint Hartung came in to run for him. With runners on second and third, Dodger manager Charlie Dressen called in Branca to pitch, though Dressen later blamed the choice on bullpen coach Clyde Sukeforth.

Sukeforth said that Dressen called down to the bullpen to say that he was sending two more pitchers down to warm up with Branca—Carl Erskine, who had pitched the day before, and Clem Labine. Sukeforth said that Erskine was in no condition to pitch and that Labine could not get ready in time because his ankles were not yet taped and he had his shoes off. Branca was the choice apparently by default. As he walked up to the mound he said to infielders Jackie Robinson and Pee Wee Reese, "anyone have butterflies?"

Branca threw a strike on the first pitch, down the heart of the plate. The next pitch was another fastball, high and inside, not a strike. Branca planned to have Thomson take that fateful pitch to set him up for a curveball low and away; but Thomson did not take the high fastball (identified as a curveball in some sources) and hit a three-run home run to give the Giants a 5–4 victory and a World Series berth. Stan Williams pitched three scoreless innings and Larry Jansen got the win. See *Signs* for recent evidence that the Giants were stealing the Dodgers signals and that Thompson knew what pitch was coming.

Branca later said that it had been a good pitch and noted that the two home runs hit off him by Thomson in the play-offs would not have gone out in Ebbets Field. Branca thus lost three of the National League's first five play-off games. The call by Giants broadcaster Russ Hodges: "Branca throws.... There's a long drive.... It's gonna be.... I believe.... THE GIANTS WIN THE PENNANT! THE GIANTS WIN THE PENNANT! THE GIANTS WIN THE PENNANT! I DON'T BELIEVE IT!.... THE GIANTS WIN THE PENNANT! BOBBY THOMSON HITS INTO THE LOWER DECK OF THE LEFT FIELD STANDS.... THE GIANTS WIN THE PENNANT AND THEY'RE GOING CRAZY.... YAAAHO-O-O!"

Ernie Harwell, broadcasting over the NBC television network, announced immediately that the ball was "gone," and then held his breath as the ball looked like it might fall short and drop onto the field. Thomson hit it just over the 17-foot wall at the 315-foot sign. Willie Mays was on deck when "The Shot Heard 'Round the World" was hit at 3:58 p.m. during the first national postseason television broadcast.

The moment was the theme through Don DeLillo's novel, *Underworld* (1998), and was put on a U.S. **Postage Stamp**.

Author Thomas Kiernan called it the "single most commonly recalled event in the American experience" between the death of Franklin Roosevelt in 1945 and the assassination of John Kennedy in 1963. The game was summed up by Red Smith in the *New York Times*: "Now it is done. Now the story ends. And there is no way to tell it. The art of fiction is dead. Reality has strangled invention. Only the utterly impossible, the inexpressibly fantastic can ever be plausible again."

National League/1959. Dodgers Defeat Braves.

"We go to Chicago!"—Dodger broadcaster Vin Scully after the Dodgers won the play-off series against the Braves and were off to face the White Sox in the World Series.

The Dodgers swept the Braves 2–0 in the best-of-three series. In Game 1 on September 28 at Milwaukee, Dodger rookie Larry Sherry relieved in the 2nd inning and won 3–2, as catcher John Roseboro homered in the 6th inning for the last run of the game. Only 18,000 fans attended the game.

In Game 2 on September 29 at the Los Angeles Coliseum, the clubs went into the 9th inning with Braves pitcher Lew Burdette throwing a five-hitter and holding a 5–2 lead. Wally Moon, Duke Snider and Gil Hodges singled to load the bases for the Dodgers. Don McMahon relieved. Norm Larker followed with a two-run single to make it 5–4 and Warren Spahn came on to pitch. Carl Furillo hit a sacrifice fly to score Gil Hodges to tie the game and Joey Jay came in to retire the last batter of the inning to force the game into extra innings.

In the bottom of the 12th inning, Bob Rush of the Braves walked Gil Hodges. Joe Pignatano followed with a single. Carl Furillo hit a ground ball up the middle that shortstop Felix Mantilla caught up to but threw wildly to first. Hodges scored to give the Dodgers a 6–5 victory and the pennant.

National League/1962. Giants Defeat Dodgers.

"A Flag for San Francisco"—Title of Charles Einstein's chronicle of the 1961 Giants, who fell only a few games short of a pennant. The book was published in 1962, the year the Giants won their first pennant.

"The Dodger team displayed the muscle, the frightfulness, and the total immobility of a woolly mammoth frozen in a glacier; the Giants, finding the beast inert, fell upon it with savage cries and chopped off steak and rump roasts at will, winning 8–0."—Roger Angell describing Game 1 of the 1962 play-off in *The Summer Game* (1972).

The Giants defeated the Dodgers 8–0 in the first game and the Dodgers won the second game 8–7.

In Game 3 Ed Roebuck came in to relieve for the Dodgers in the 6th inning, making his sixth appearance in seven days. The Dodgers led 4–2 and Roebuck held the Giants scoreless until the 9th inning. Roebuck was out of gas in the 8th, but despite coach Leo Durocher's alleged protest, Dodger manager Walter Alston left Roebuck in to pitch the 9th inning.

Giants outfielder Matty Alou led off the top of the 9th with a single but was forced at second by Harvey Kuenn. Willie McCovey and Felipe Alou walked, loading the bases. Willie Mays lined a ball off Roebuck's hand and Kuenn scored to make it 4–3, leaving the bases loaded. Stan Williams came in to pitch for the Dodgers. Orlando Cepeda drove in the tying run with a sacrifice fly for the second out. Ed Bailey was up when Williams threw a wild pitch, allowing Mays to go to second and Alou to third. Bailey was intentionally walked to load the bases to set up a force play. Jim Davenport then walked to score a run and an error led to another run for a 6–4 Giants lead. The Dodgers went out in order in the bottom of the 9th inning and the Giants went to the World Series.

American League/1978. Yankees Defeat Red Sox.

"Bucky Fucking Dent"— Boston fans' nickname for the light-hitting shortstop who broke their hearts.

"In the Boston locker room in 1978, the Red Sox looked as if they had died and were sitting in some anteroom of hell waiting for the barge to take them over into damnation."— Thomas Boswell in *Why Time Begins on Opening Day* (1984).

On October 2, 1978, the Yankees beat the Red Sox 5–4 in a one-game play-off at Fenway Park. Yankee shortstop Bucky Dent hit a three-run 8th inning home run off loser Mike Torrez and Yankee right fielder Lou Piniella made a smart 9th inning defensive play to preserve the New York lead.

Carl Yastrzemski had homered early for a 1–0 Red Sox lead. Yankee pitcher Ron Guidry threw on three days' rest and was behind 2–0 when he left after six innings. The Red Sox held that lead until the 8th inning. In the fateful at-bat by Dent, he noticed after a foul ball that his bat was cracked and Mickey Rivers, next up, handed him his bat. Dent then homered to give the Yankees a 3–2 lead. An injury to Willie Randolph had prevented the Yankees from pinch-hitting for Dent. He had hit only four home runs in 377 at-bats that season and 22 in 1,042 at-bats over his career. Reggie Jackson also homered in the inning to give the Yankees a 5–2 lead going into the bottom of the 8th inning.

What is often overlooked is that the Red Sox came back to score two runs in the 8th to make it 5–4 and threatened in the 9th. With one out, Jerry Remy walked and should have taken third on a single by Rick Burleson, but he held up at second base. Burleson's drive was to right field, which was covered in shadows except for a small pocket of sunlight. The ball headed for the sunlight and outfielder Lou Piniella was momentarily blinded and lost it completely. Piniella decoyed Remy enough (faking a catch) to keep Remy from getting to third and fielded the ball on one bounce. The second out was a deep fly ball by Jim Rice that would have scored Burleson. On a 1–0 count to the last batter, Carl Yastrzemski, reliever Goose Gossage induced him to pop out foul to third baseman Graig Nettles to end the game. Yastrzemski also made the last out of the 1975 World Series.

In 1989 Dent opened a baseball training school which featured a replica of Fenway Park's Green Monster. Mike Torrez appeared for the inaugural game and graciously agreed to replay the home run pitch. Torrez got off the hook in the 1986 World Series when Bill Buckner became the new goat of the Red Sox.

See also Jonathan Schwartz, *A Day of Light and Shadow* (2003).

National League/1980. Astros Defeat Dodgers. After the Dodgers swept the Astros three straight to end the regular season in a tie, the Astros defeated the Dodgers on a Monday afternoon as Dodger pitcher Dave Goltz was bombed early in a 7–4 loss.

American League/1995. Mariners Defeat Angels. On October 2, 1995, the Angels and Mariners faced each other in the Seattle Kingdome in a one-game play-off to determine the American League's Western Division winner. Mariners pitcher Randy John-

son pitched a perfect game early on, and the Mariners exploded for nine runs late in the game for a 9–1 victory over Mark Langston.

National League/1998. Cubs Defeat Giants. The Cubs went ahead 5–0 and held on after the Giants scored three in the 9th to make it close. Cubs closer Rod Beck held on for the save.

National League/1999. Mets Defeat Reds. For the second year in a row the National League wild card was decided by a play-off. On October 4, 1999, Mets pitcher Al Leiter pitched a two-hitter over the Reds to give the Mets the last play-off spot. Mets shortstop Rey Ordonez played his 100th game without an error to set a new record.

Book. Gary R. Parker, *Win or Go Home: Sudden Death Baseball* (2001).

Playboys See *Marriage* and *Sex*

Player Contracts See *Contracts*

Player-Managers See *Managers — Player-Managers*

Player Sales See *Trades and Player Sales*

Players Fraternity (1912–1915)

This attempt at a *Union* was made during the Federal League challenge of 1914–1915.

Players League (1890)

"You may talk of your Wards and your Ewings and of the mighty men who are back of them, but there is one stout, curly-headed man in Philadelphia who made it possible for the Players League to start. That is F.C. Richter, of THE SPORTING LIFE. Had his pen been directed against the new scheme the players would have flocked back to the gold standard like frightened sheep."—*Cincinnati Times Star* article of September 1890.

Origins. When the American Association and National League limited player salaries to $2,000 immediately after the Union Association folded before the 1885 season, the union-like Brotherhood of Professional Baseball Players (the "Brotherhood") became stronger as the decade neared its end. That strength was instrumental in establishing the Players League, which operated for one year in 1890.

Other factors contributed to the formation of the league. In 1889 Jack Rowe and Deacon White were planning to test the reserve clause in court. They had recently bought into the National League's Buffalo club, but both players were sold to Pittsburgh for $7,000 and did not want to play for their new team. In mid–1889 they reluctantly reported to Pittsburgh but were quietly helping to form the new league.

John Montgomery Ward was the first leader of the Brotherhood. While Ward was on tour in 1888 in Australia, John Brush succeeded in establishing a player rating system that fixed *Salaries* at artificially low levels. Ward and other key players attempted to work out a compromise with the owners to void the rigid system. After the compromise efforts were rejected by the owners, the players threatened to strike. The owners did not believe the players would follow through with a strike, but the players began planning for a rival league almost immediately.

Formation. On July 14, 1889, Ward met secretly with Albert Johnson, brother of Cleveland reform mayor Tom L. Johnson.

Johnson was a Cleveland streetcar magnate with influence and money. Ward also met with Brotherhood chapters in other cities to firm up their plans and maintain unity. Each representative was to identify investors to back the plan. The original idea was for the Players League teams to pool their income, but the idea ultimately was rejected and each club stood on its own.

National League Giants owner John B. Day was offered $25,000 to be the league's president and receive 50% of the new New York franchise. Had he joined the group, the National League might have been defeated. He refused, and ironically the baseball war caused him financial ruin.

The Brotherhood planned to build ballparks in all National League cities, and many of the new league's parks were within a few blocks of the competition. The league established teams in all National League cities except Cincinnati. The American Association was already weakening and was an easy target for the new league. The Players League also came at a time when the National League was suffering financially.

Although the story of the new league was broken prematurely in the press by early September, on November 4, 1889, the league formally announced its intent to break from the established leagues and form franchises in Boston (Reds), Chicago (Pirates), Cleveland (Infants), Indianapolis (never formed), New York (Giants), Philadelphia (Quakers), Pittsburgh (Burghers) and Washington (never formed). Before the season began, the Indianapolis and Washington sites were abandoned for Buffalo (Bisons) and Brooklyn (Wonders).

By December 1889 the Players League had signed 71 National League players and 16 American Association players (later increased to 30), and four minor leaguers. In all, 80% of National League players went over to the Players League, including the entire Washington team. A look at the managers of the league's teams gives a good indication of the quality and magnitude of the stars in the league: Mike "King" Kelly in Boston; John Montgomery Ward in Brooklyn; Buck Ewing in New York; Charlie Comiskey in Chicago; Ned Hanlon in Pittsburgh; Patsy Tebeau in Cleveland; Charlie Buffinton in Philadelphia and Jack Rowe in Buffalo.

One writer claims that this was the closest that Major League players ever came to toppling the established leagues. The Players League had signed almost every established star. The only notable exception was Cap Anson, who owned stock in the White Stockings.

Officers. On December 16, 1889, New York real estate tycoon Colonel Edwin A. McAlpin was elected president. Chicago contractor John Addison was elected vice-president. Former sportswriter Frank H. Brunell was elected secretary-treasurer.

The National League's Response. The National League owners created a "War Committee" consisting of Albert Spalding of the White Stockings, John Day of the Giants and John I. Rogers of the Phillies. They filled the newspapers with derogatory comments about the Players League. Leading the way for the National League was *Spalding Guide* editor and long-time sportswriter Henry Chadwick. *The Sporting News* and *Sporting Life* supported the new league and there was tremendous acrimony in the press.

To stop the competition, the National League tried to buy into the Players League clubs and unsuccessfully sought injunctions against the Players League. The National League also tried to retaliate by offering big salaries to its stars. For example, Mike "King" Kelly turned down the astronomical sum of $10,000 offered by Spalding.

The American Association's Response. Although John Montgomery Ward pledged that the Players League would not raid American Association teams, the agreement was never honored and the American Association continued to suffer financially. The weaker American Association met secretly with the Players League representatives in an unsuccessful attempt to merge the two leagues. As a result of the weakness in the Association, its Brooklyn and Cincinnati franchises shifted to the National League for the 1890 season.

Players League Structure. The Players League teams split gate receipts evenly and signed players to three-year contracts at their 1889 salaries, with no reserve clause or classification system. There was also to be no blacklisting of players who moved back to a rival league. Each of these three conditions was part of the problem with the other two leagues. In an attempt at equality and fairness, a governing senate of 16 players was created.

All teams contributed $2,500 toward a $20,000 prize. The first-place club was to receive $7,000. Any team making more than $10,000 profit had to give the excess to the players.

Attendance Problems. The real estate and utility magnates who had backed the Brotherhood lost their enthusiasm as the season progressed and profits were nil. Attendance was low because the product was spread too thin among the three Major Leagues.

The American Association would not report attendance figures, so presumably they were terrible. Estimates for the league's attendance were in the range of 500,000. The National League reported attendance of 813,678, which probably was inflated. A quirk in the statistics (showing their unreliability) is that Philadelphia and Pittsburgh both showed attendance of 16,404. The National League's average attendance in New York was 919, in Cleveland 668 and in Pittsburgh 411.

The Players League had attendance of 980,887, with the highest in pennant-winning Boston at 197,346 and the lowest in Cleveland with 58,430. The *Reach Guide* showed the average attendance in Buffalo as 942 and in Cleveland as 927.

Financial Losses. The National League clubs reportedly lost between $231,000 and $500,000 collectively. The Players League investors lost $340,000, with approximately $215,000 plowed into new ballparks. The true operating deficit thus was approximately $125,000.

Peace. Peace was negotiated primarily by "White-Winged Angel of Peace" Allan W. Thurman, the director of the Columbus club in the American Association. The so-called peace turned out to be a gutting of the Players League and severe crippling of the American Association. The National League had been ready to sue for peace, but the Players League blinked first by attempting a compromise. National League leader Albert Spalding then demanded total surrender and, to his genuine surprise, received it.

The final summit was held in January 1891, when the Players League teams were absorbed or disbanded and the league officially dissolved. Many Players League owners then combined with or sold out to their National League counterparts, causing a rift between the former Players League owners and players. The National League and Players League Pittsburgh clubs were combined, as were the New York clubs. The Players League Chicago players were sold to Spalding's White Stockings for $18,000. The Brooklyn club also was restructured and combined.

Other National League clubs were revamped and the American Association was at a severe disadvantage. The American Association's Philadelphia club could not meet its financial obligations and the Players League entry in that city took its place. American Association founder Al Johnson owned the Cincinnati and Cleveland clubs, but was left out of the realignment negotiations.

Aftermath. After the final disbandment meeting, the Players

League players were supposed to return to the teams they had been with in 1889. Instead, there was a wild scramble to sign players for the 1891 season and payrolls reached an all-time high.

The 1891 season was financially disastrous for many clubs as attendance remained low. The final impact of the Players League and the shortsightedness of the other leagues was finally realized in 1892. The National League expanded to 12 teams by absorbing the four strongest *American Association* clubs, and the Association was negotiated out of existence as a Major League.

Reasons for Failure. The Players League probably failed for three key reasons, as outlined later by the league's secretary. First, each team should have been capitalized for $50,000, not $20,000. The eight best business managers among the Players League teams should have been divided among the eight teams, rather than being concentrated with just a few clubs. Third, the Players League should have raided the National League when the Players League players began defecting back to the National League near the end of the season.

Blacklisting. One source reported that within five years most Players League alumni who returned to the National League were out of baseball. It was attributed to blacklisting, but it is more likely that it was normal attrition.

Players Who Switched Positions

"I did play like Brooks. Mel Brooks." — Andy Van Slyke on the expectations of playing like Brooks Robinson in the minor leagues after being switched to third base.

See also *All Positions Played*.

Henry Aaron. Aaron was a shortstop and second baseman in the minor leagues. He later shifted to the outfield and played only a few games at second base in the Major Leagues and none at shortstop.

Ernie Banks. Banks played nine seasons at shortstop with the Cubs, winning the National League MVP Award two years in a row in the mid–1950s. He played no other position between 1953 and 1960, except 58 games at third base in 1957. In 1961 he played 104 games at shortstop, and another 30 either in the outfield or at first base. In 1962 he switched full-time to the infield, and played another 10 seasons almost exclusively at first base to save his legs. He finished with 1,125 games at shortstop and 1,259 at first base.

Johnny Bench. The Major League catcher was 16–0 as a high school pitcher in Oklahoma.

Moe Berg. Berg broke into the Major Leagues as a shortstop and second baseman. His switch to catcher for the rest of his career may have been distorted in the retelling but is substantially accurate.

One day in 1927 with the White Sox, player-manager and catcher Ray Schalk was desperate for a catcher. Schalk had broken his finger and his second-string catcher broke his finger after only a few innings. Schalk yelled to his road secretary to get a minor league catcher ASAP ("Get me another catcher. Class C, Class D, I don't care, get me a catcher!"). Berg, in his second partial season with the club, said "What do you mean, get a catcher, we have a catcher on this bench." Schalk told him to get in the game, and a catcher was born. Berg later admitted that he actually had in mind first baseman Earl Sheely who had caught a few times in the minors (he never caught in the Major Leagues).

Yogi Berra. Berra started as an outfielder before being converted to catcher. He played often in the outfield later in his career, when Elston Howard and Johnny Blanchard developed as catchers.

Craig Biggio. When Giants second baseman Jeff Kent signed with the Astros for two years and $18.2 million starting in 2003, Biggio agreed to move to center field, where he had previously played before starring at second base. He began his career as a catcher, and played close to 400 games there in his first four seasons for the Astros.

Ken Boyer. The 1960s star third baseman was signed as a pitcher.

Roger Bresnahan. Bresnahan pitched a shutout in his Major League debut at age 18 on August 27, 1897, but later became a prominent catcher.

Jesse Burkett. The outfielder hit .339 over his 16-season career but began professionally as a pitcher. His first appearance in the Major Leagues was as a pitcher for the New York Giants in 1890. After suffering through a 3–10 season, he was sent down to the minors and moved to the outfield. He returned the next year with the Cleveland Spiders for 42 games, batting .269. Two years later he began a streak of nine seasons in which he never hit below .341.

Ben Chapman. The outfielder had a 12-year career primarily for the Yankees and Senators from 1930 through 1941. At age 35 in 1944 he had a 13–6 record as a pitcher in the minor leagues. Late in 1944 as a result of the military's depletion of the Major League pitching ranks, the Dodgers picked him up and he had a 5–3 record while hitting .368 for the club. In 1945 he was 3–3 with a .260 average.

Jimmy Collins. Though considered the greatest third baseman of the turn-of-the-century era, Collins started in the outfield for the Boston Red Stockings before being loaned to the Louisville Colonels during the 1895 season. The story has it that the powerful Baltimore Orioles were bunting repeatedly in a game against the Colonels, and the Louisville third baseman, Walter Preston, asked to be removed from the game. Collins came in from the outfield and took over, establishing himself as the Major League's best third baseman for the next 14 years until Pie Traynor came along in the 1920s.

Joe Ferguson. Manager Tommy Lasorda convinced the slow Dodger outfielder to try catching by telling him that Hall of Fame catcher Gabby Hartnett made the same move. When general manager Al Campanis heard about it, he challenged Lasorda on the veracity of the story about Hartnett. Lasorda's response: "You know that, I know that, and Hartnett knows that, but Joe Ferguson doesn't know that."

Jimmie Foxx. The first baseman began as a catcher and played 109 games at that position over his 20-year career, with a peak of 42 in 1940. Foxx pitched in nine games in 1945.

Kid Gleason. Gleason won 134 games during seven seasons on the mound beginning in 1888. He peaked with a 38–17 record in 1890 and 24–22 in 1891. He then had a solid career as a second baseman for the next 14 seasons.

Chick Hafey. The former college (California Bears) and minor league pitcher left the mound and led the National League in hitting in 1931. He never pitched in the Major Leagues and played exclusively in the outfield for 13 seasons while hitting .317.

Dick Hall. Hall went from a regular spot (102 games) in the Pirates outfield in 1954 to Pittsburgh's pitching rotation (15 games, 13 starts) in 1955, while played three games in the outfield.

Trevor Hoffman. The ace Padres reliever was a hard-hitting infielder when he played junior college baseball in Arizona.

Rogers Hornsby. The Hall of Famer began his career at third base and switched to second base.

Matt Keough. Keough began in the A's chain as a third baseman. After a dismal Class AA season, he converted to pitcher and made the American League All-Star team in his second Major

League season in 1978. After he bombed in 1979 with a 2–17 record (including 14 losses in a row to start the season to tie the Major League record), he was voted 1980 Comeback Player of the Year with a 16–13 record.

Brook Kieschnick. In 2003 Kieschnick tried to make the Brewers as an outfielder and as a pitcher. He had previously played 113 games as an outfielder starting in 1996 for the Cubs. He went on to pitch in 42 games in 2003 for the Brewers, going 1–1, and also batted .300 in 69 games for the club.

In 2004 Kieschnick became the first player to homer as a pitcher, pinch hitter and designated hitter.

Dave Kingman. The enigmatic slugger was a pitcher for USC before being converted to the outfield and first base.

Bob Lemon. The Hall of Famer began in the minor leagues as an infielder and outfielder in 1941–1942, making it up to the Indians for 10 games over those two seasons. He was in the military in 1943–1945 and returned as a pitcher and outfielder in 1946, appearing in 32 games as a pitcher and 12 games as an outfielder. He spent the next 12 years as a pitcher, appearing in only two games as an outfielder in 1947.

Johnny Lindell. Lindell came up to the Major Leagues in 1942 as a knuckleball pitcher, but Yankee manager Joe McCarthy did not like the pitch and switched Lindell to the outfield for seven seasons beginning in 1943. After a dismal 1950 season, Lindell returned to the minor leagues for the 1951 season as a pitcher for the Hollywood Stars. In 1952 he compiled a record of 24–9, batted fourth and was the PCL's MVP. He returned to the Major Leagues as a pitcher in 1953 but threw poorly and was a combined 6–17 for the Pirates and Phillies.

Skip Lockwood. Lockwood was a successful relief pitcher on and off from 1969 through 1980. When he signed a $100,000 bonus contract with the A's in 1964, it was as a third baseman. He appeared briefly in 1965 in the Major Leagues and then was converted to a pitcher in 1968 before playing for the Pilots in 1969.

Mike Marshall. The 1970s relief pitcher began as an infielder in the Phillies system. Chronic back and error problems led to a shift to relief pitching.

Christy Mathewson. Mathewson supposedly played first base much of his very early Major League career and became a full-time pitcher shortly after John McGraw took over as Giants manager. Most sources criticize manager Horace Fogel for a mistake in judgment in using Mathewson at first base. Fogel later defended himself as reported in Fred Lieb's *The Baseball Story* (1950): "I was only a stopgap manager in New York, serving a few weeks between the time George Smith quit in June, 1902, and McGraw came on in middle July. With a tail-end team in a costly [baseball] war year, [Giants owner] Freedman didn't feel he could afford the luxury of much of a bench. So, when my first baseman became incapacitated, I used Mathewson, a hitting pitcher, on first base on such days when he didn't pitch. In that day, hitting pitchers were freely used as first-base substitutes. But I pitched Matty in turn and never thought of him as anything else other than a great pitching prospect."

The Baseball Encyclopedia has no record of Mathewson playing first base.

Danny Murphy. Murphy was a bonus baby with the Cubs in 1960 as an outfielder, but after playing poorly for three seasons he was sent to the minors. He resurrected his Major League career with a spot on the White Sox as a pitcher in 1969. He lasted through 1970 before retiring with a 4–4 record.

Dale Murphy.

"One thing's for sure, Dale. Nobody will be stealing center field on you."—Dale Murphy's father after Murphy threw numerous balls into center field trying to throw out runners from his catching position. At Class AAA Richmond, Murphy once attempted to throw out a runner at second base, only to hit his pitcher in the rear end—while the pitcher was sprawled out on the grass avoiding the throw. The Braves showed great wisdom in placing Murphy in center field, where he won two straight MVP awards.

Stan Musial. Musial began as a pitcher in Class D, and some sources report that he was unsuccessful. Not true. He was 18–5 with Daytona Beach in the Florida State League in 1940 and had a 33–13 minor league record. He also played the outfield when he was not pitching and hurt his shoulder diving for a ball in 1940. His future was in doubt until early the next spring when his hitting impressed management. He played for two Cardinals farm clubs in 1941, hitting .376 and .326. He made it all the way to the Major Leagues late that season and hit .426 in 12 games.

Musial said that he was wild as a minor league pitcher and would not have been that good. In 1946 he shifted from the outfield to first base, a move that helped the Cardinals win the World Series that year.

Dickie Kerr, who was an honest pitcher for the 1919 Black Sox, is credited with converting Musial to the outfield. Musial later showed his gratitude by naming his first-born son after Kerr. When Kerr fell on hard times, Musial quietly bought him a house in Houston.

Lefty O'Doul. On July 7, 1923, the Red Sox pitcher gave up 13 runs in the 6th inning to the Indians, who won 27–3. It was his last of 34 brief appearances as a Major League pitcher (with a 1–1 record). He went down to the minor leagues and did not return until 1928. He returned as an outfielder and hit over .300 in six of his remaining seven Major League seasons. They included league-leading averages of .398 in 1929 and .368 in 1932.

Troy Percival. The Angels reliever switched from catcher to pitcher after his first professional season in 1990.

Mel Queen. Queen played in 32 games as an outfielder for the Reds in 1966 and made seven relief appearances before becoming a regular starter (14–8 with a 2.76 ERA) for the Reds in 1967.

Sam Rice. In 1915 Senators owner Clark Griffith purchased Rice when he was considered his minor league club's best pitcher. After two seasons of pitching mediocrity, Rice became the Senators' right fielder and lead-off batter through 1933. Griffith got only one win out of him in those two early seasons—but 2,889 hits over 19 years.

Frank Robinson. The outfielder played much of 1959 and 1960 at first base due to recurring arm problems.

Pete Rose. Rose is the only Major League player to appear in more than 500 games at five different positions (first base, second base, third base, left field and right field).

Babe Ruth.

"Ruth made a grave mistake when he gave up pitching. Working once a week he might have lasted a long time and become a great star."—Outfielder Tris Speaker, circa 1919.

"I would be the laughingstock of the league if I took the best pitcher in the league and put him in the outfield."—Red Sox manager Ed Barrow to outfielder Harry Hooper, who suggested that Ruth switch because the club had plenty of pitchers but not enough outfielders.

"Certainly Ruth's native ability was prodigious. He might have become the greatest of all—but baseball history would have been inconceivably different."—Leonard Koppett in *A Thinking Man's Guide to Baseball* (1967), in which he noted that Ruth had more victories when he stopped pitching full-time at age 24 than Walter Johnson had at the same age (89 to 82).

"I'm prouder of that record beating Matty's performance [consecutive scoreless World Series innings], and once having struck out Cobb, Crawford and Veach with the bases full, than of any of my home run records."—Babe Ruth to sportswriter Fred Lieb.

Ruth had more wins by a left-handed pitcher before age 23 than any other. By that time he was 67–34, a .663 winning percentage. Ruth was 17–4 against the Yankees before being traded to that club. Ruth once beat Walter Johnson five times in a row, including a 1–0 victory in 13 innings.

By 1919 he was playing much more frequently in right field and pitched only a few times after joining the Yankees in 1920. His lifetime .304 average while a pitcher is the highest for any pitcher with at least 450 lifetime at-bats. He was moderately successful as a hitter after becoming the regular right fielder for the Yankees.

Red Sox outfielder Harry Hooper claims responsibility for pushing 1918–1920 Red Sox manager Ed Barrow (soon to be the Yankee general manager) to move Ruth to the outfield. At least one source reported that Ruth began playing in the outfield due to the shortage of players brought on by World War I. This is perhaps consistent with the statistics, as he played no position except pitcher until 1918 (except for a few pinch hit appearances). In 1918 he played 59 games in the outfield, 13 at first base and 20 at pitcher. In 1919 he played outfield for 111 games, first base in four and pitched in 17. He started the season on the mound but spent eight weeks during midseason as a full-time outfielder-first baseman for the club. He returned to the rotation for the final five weeks of the season and went 7–2.

Ruth made a few brief pitching appearances later in his career, prompting this comment by him in 1933: "I had such a sore arm I had to eat with my right arm for a week."

Ryne Sandberg. Sandberg is the only player to win a Gold Glove Award the year after switching positions. He moved from third base to second base.

George Sisler. The National League hitting star was tried as a pitcher during his rookie season in 1915. He beat Walter Johnson 2–1 in one game and Ty Cobb went 0–5 against him in another. He finished the season with a record of 4–4 in 15 appearances, with eight starts and six complete games. He pitched in another 10 games in his career and finished with a 5–6 record.

"Wonderful" Willie Smith. Smith was an outfielder-pitcher for several teams in the 1960s. He pitched in 11 games for the Tigers in 1963, starting two. His 1964 season with the Los Angeles Angels was his best, when he pitched in 15 games (only once as a starter) while batting .301 as a regular (87 games) in the outfield. He played in the outfield almost exclusively after that season, only pitching in three games for the Indians and Cubs.

Mickey Stanley. See *Strategy* for the switch from center field to shortstop by Tigers center fielder Mickey Stanley during the 1968 World Series.

Bill Terry. The hitting star was the last man to hit over .400 in the National League but was a minor league pitcher before switching to first base.

Ted Williams. One source erroneously reported that Williams began his professional career as a pitcher but failed to note that his pitching was a one-shot situation that was not repeated. In his first professional game with the minor league San Diego Padres in 1936, he volunteered to pitch when the club was down by 10 runs. After getting shelled he moved to his regular spot in the outfield.

Smoky Joe Wood. Wood won 116 games as a pitcher, 57 of them in two years (1911–1912), and then hurt his arm (see also *Injuries and Illness*—Thumb). In 1915 he made a comeback of sorts with a 15–5 record and a 1.49 ERA to lead the league. In 16 starts he pitched 10 complete games, versus his 1912 highs of 38 starts and 35 complete games. Despite the decent record, Wood's arm was gone and he had to find another position in order to remain in the Major Leagues. He moved to the outfield during World War I when teams were in need of decent talent. He played five more seasons (1918–1922) and compiled a lifetime .283 average.

"Coconut Snatchers." This was a term used by Branch Rickey to denote a player who could be switched to a new position and thrive. The phrase came from a story that Rickey liked about monkeys in the jungle. The monkeys had a system for gathering coconuts; some always climbed trees to pick them. They would drop the coconuts to other monkeys, who snatched them in the air and passed them on to other monkeys, who carried them to their villages. A coconut snatcher once became ill and another monkey took his place. The substitute was better at the job, so when the first monkey came back he took a different job—carrying nuts to the village. Rickey's analogy was that a player who could pitch might thrive in the outfield or a pitching prospect might be better as a hitter and base stealer.

Poetry

"Poets are like baseball pitchers. Both have their moments. The intervals are the tough things."—Robert Frost.

"['Casey at the Bat'] has plenty of company, for it is just one of tens of thousands of baseball poems, many of which are housed in the archives of the Baseball Hall of Fame Library in Cooperstown. Some of these efforts are pure doggerel, but others are well-crafted verse from some of our country's best poets..."—Hall of Fame Director of Research Tim Wiles in the *New York Times*.

"B is for Base Ball —
The ball once struck off
Away flies the boy
to the next destined post.
And then home with joy."
—Earliest known baseball poem, in *A Little Pretty Pocket Book*, written in 1744.

"Baseball is to our everyday experience what poetry often is to common speech—a slightly elevated and concentrated form."—Thomas Boswell in *How Life Imitates the World Series* (1982).

"Nothing flatters me more than to have it assumed that I could write prose—unless it be to have it assumed that I once pitched a baseball with distinction."—Robert Frost, who covered the 1956 All-Star game for *Sports Illustrated* (see also *Extra Innings*).

"George Moriarty, Tiger third baseman [was] later a leading American League umpire. Moriarty also wrote poetry, a strange thing for an umpire, who is given little chance to contemplate the lyrical. When he found the muse uncommunicative, George occasionally diverted himself by picking up Cobb, stuffing him in Ty's locker and locking him in, while the 'Georgia Peach' scrambled and clawed like a jaguar."—Sportswriter Tim Cohane.

During a 16-game losing streak by the 1944 Dodgers, *New York Times* writer Roscoe McGowen wrote a poem to which he added another verse for each loss. As part of the streak, the Dodgers lost 27 of 29.

Pulitzer Prize–winning poet Marianne Moore was a Brooklyn Dodger fan until the club left for Los Angeles. She switched her allegiance to the Yankees, for whom she threw out the first ball at the club's 1968 opener.

During a dull Indians game at Minnesota in 1968, broadcaster Mel Allen recited from memory the first 37 lines of "The Song of

Hiawatha," a poem by Henry Wadsworth Longfellow. The setting for the poem was Minnesota's Lake Superior.

In 1994 the Giants showed their support for the public library system by inviting poets to recite their work during pregame ceremonies. The leadoff poet was Allen Ginsberg who, according to the Associated Press, was to "toss out the first stanza on June 1."

Spahn and Sain.

"First we'll use Spahn, then we'll use Sain,

then an off day, followed by rain.

Back will come Spahn, followed by Sain,

And followed, we hope, by two days of rain."— Poem by *Boston Post* sports editor Gerry Hern on September 14, 1948, in the heat of a pennant race involving the Boston Braves and their two key pitchers, Warren Spahn and Johnny Sain. Fans shortened it to "Spahn and Sain and pray for rain," and it stuck. As researcher Dixie Tourangeau noted in 1998: "No one could have guessed how spectacularly the month would unfold or that a thirteen-day string of games and a bit of simple newspaper doggerel would make two members of the Braves mound corps legends forever."

The poem reflected the prior week, when Sain and Spahn dominated, but for the season the club's other starters were also effective. Among the starters, Sain was 24–15, Spahn 15–12, Billy Voiselle 13–13 and Vern Bickford 11–5. Reliever Clyde Shoun was 5–1 in 36 appearances and rookie Bobby Hogue was 8–2 in 40 appearances. The Braves finished at 91–62, 6½ games ahead of the Cardinals.

Books. *The Best of Spitball* is an anthology of the best fiction and poetry from *Spitball*, a baseball literary magazine; *Elysian Fields Quarterly*; Gene Carney, *Romancing the Horsehide* (1993); Tom Clark, *Blue* (for Vida Blue) (1974); Gene Fehler, *Center Field Grasses* (1991); Poet Donald Hall, who wrote *Fathers Playing Catch with Sons* (1985), also authored *The Museum of Clear Ideas* (1992), a book-length poem patterned after the innings of a baseball game — nine-syllable lines, nine lines to a half-inning, etc.; Robert L. Harrison, *Green Fields and White Lines: Baseball Poems* (1995); James Mote, *Everything Baseball* (1989), purports to list every baseball poem; Mark W. Schraf, *Cooperstown Verses: Poems about Each Hall of Famer* (2001); Mike Shannon, *The Day Satchel Paige and the Pittsburgh Crawfords Came to Hertford, N.C.* (1989).

Politics

"A guy who's played one game in the pros is like a former state senator, a big man in most neighborhoods and in any saloon as long as he lives."— Wilfrid Sheed.

"With the growing importance of base ball we observe that our most eminent statesmen are putting themselves in line with sentiment of the day. The late Thomas A. Hendricks was always conspicuous for his interest in the game. Governor Hill is prominent as a citizen interested in our national sport…. Indeed we advise all statesmen of any aspirations for the future to consider that if they have not yet recorded themselves as lovers of our national game or some other sporting interest, they should do so immediately."— August 3, 1889, editorial in the *New York Sun.*

"More than anything, it's a game of innocence. Politicians may come and go, but they always get booed at the ballpark."— Pete Hamill.

"'This is America,' my father used to say to me, 'and in this country, a smart young fellow like you can grow up and do just about anything.' My dad, no doubt, was thinking doctor, lawyer, teacher, scientist or businessman. I was thinking second baseman, New York Yankees."— Senator and 2000 Democratic vice-presidential candidate Joe Lieberman.

"If the World Series runs until election day, the networks will run the first one-half inning and project the winner."— Lindsey Nelson.

"Boston is the perfect city for the Democrats because the Democrats are like the Red Sox. They're optimistic in the spring, concerned in the summer and ready to choke in the fall."— Jay Leno during the 2004 Democratic national convention.

"It is pointed out that the two would make harmonious running mates. Both have won fame as baseball players, and both are popular with the liquor interests. How Rube has distinguished himself at times by acting as a bar tender is a matter of history."— Apparently tongue-in-cheek article in the *Philadelphia North American* in 1910, touting eccentric Rube Waddell as a candidate for Lt. Governor of Pennsylvania to run with gubernatorial candidate and former Major Leaguer John Tener — who won the election and later became National League president.

"Umpires should be natural Republicans — dead to human feelings."— George Will in *Men at Work* (1990).

"A sensational event was changing from the brown suit to the gray contents of his pockets. He was earnest about these objects. They were of eternal importance, like baseball or the Republican Party."— Sinclair Lewis in *Babbitt* (1922).

"Rube Kissinger, Tip O'Neill, Joe McCarthy, Tom Bradley, John Glenn"

See also *Judges*, *Presidents* and *Supreme Court.*

Endorsements. Cap Anson commemorated the 1888 Republican national convention opening in Chicago by dressing his players in black tuxedo coats.

In 1920 Ty Cobb was recruited to endorse James M. Cox for president after the Democratic convention. The Republicans countered by offering an agent $4,000 to recruit Democrat Babe Ruth to endorse Warren Harding's campaign. The deal fell through because Ruth seemed to lose interest, though one source reported that it was because the Black Sox Scandal had broken by the time the appearance was to have been made, and the testimonial of a ballplayer suddenly was not in such demand.

Team Nickname. In late 2003 the owner of a Class AA team in New Hampshire decided not to rename the team the New Hampshire Primaries after the name was rejected by 85% of fans who participated in an Internet poll.

Congress. In 1939 a bill was presented in Congress to designate June 12, 1939, as National Baseball Day, but it never made it out of committee and was never brought up again.

In the annual Roll Call Congressional Baseball Game in 1995, Oklahoma congressman Steve Largent (a former NFL receiver) pitched and hit the Republicans to a 6–0 win over the Democrats. He was still at it in June 2001, when he struck out eight as the Republicans beat the Democrats 9–1. Largent later resigned his position to run for governor, giving the Democrats a chance in the annual game. The Republicans were 26–14 since the Congressional newspaper, *Roll Call*, began sponsoring the game in 1962. Before that it was played sporadically ever since it was organized in 1909 by Republican congressman John Tener, a former Major Leaguer who later became National League president.

Free Tickets. In 2003 the Yankees were fined $75,000 for giving playoff tickets to local politicians in violation of the state's lobbyist laws.

Political Careers.

"Burt [a local ballplayer] was some notches above Albert J. Beveridge and Tom Marshall. After all, they were only political figures, and probably wouldn't know the difference between a curve ball and a change of pace."— Ford Frick in *Games, Asterisks and People* (1973).

"I think so highly of this man's integrity. I can't resist recommending him to the voters of his district." — Ty Cobb's endorsement of Maryland congressional candidate and former pitcher Walter Johnson in 1940. Johnson lost to the incumbent.

A number of former baseball players and baseball executives have had successful or attempted political careers:

Fred H. Brown. Brown, who played in 20 games in the outfield for the 1901–1902 Braves, attended law school in the off-season and became the Democratic governor of New Hampshire in 1922–1924. He was elected to the U.S. Senate in 1933–1939 and was the 1924 Democratic nominee for president. In 1939 he became the Comptroller General of the United States.

Jim Bunning. The former Tigers and Phillies pitcher, who won 224 Major League games, was a long-time member of the Kentucky legislature and in 1986 ran unsuccessfully for governor. He later was elected to the U.S. House of Representatives.

Rico Carty. In 1994 the former outfielder was elected mayor in his hometown of San Pedro de Marcoris in the Dominican Republic. Before he took office, however, a recount revealed that he was not the winner.

Mario Cuomo. The former New York governor loves to tell the story of how he was given a $2,000 bonus to play professional baseball at about the same time that Mickey Mantle received half that amount.

Harry Davis. Davis played for the A's from 1895 through 1917 and was a Philadelphia city councilman during his career.

Carl Furillo. The Dodger outfielder was a county sheriff in Pennsylvania.

Larry Jackson. Jackson had 194 wins in a 14-year career that ended in 1968. He then served in the Idaho state legislature.

Bill Lee. In 1988 the former pitcher was the tongue-in-cheek presidential candidate of the Rhinoceros Party, whose campaign slogan was "no guns, no butter."

Aurelio Lopez. The Tigers relief pitcher, known as Señor Smoke, returned to his native Mexico after his retirement in 1987 and became mayor of his hometown, Tecamachalco. He was killed in a car accident at age 44 in 1992.

Wilmer "Vinegar Bend" Mizell. Mizell pitched primarily for the Cardinals from 1952 through 1962, with a 90–88 record. He later was a Republican member of the House of Representatives from Mississippi and Assistant Secretary of Commerce from 1969 through 1975.

Mickey Owen. The Dodger catcher was a county sheriff in Missouri.

Harry Pulliam. The National League president in the early 20th century later spent two years in the Kentucky State Assembly.

Billy Rogell, the Tigers shortstop notable for knocking out Dizzy Dean during the 1935 World Series, became a city councilman for 40 years.

Pius Schwert. A two-year Yankee backup catcher in 1914–1915, Schwert was a Democratic member of the House of Representatives beginning in 1939. It was the same district later represented by former Buffalo Bills quarterback Jack Kemp.

Luke Sewell. The American League catcher in the 1920s and 1930s was Richard Nixon's Ohio campaign chairman in 1972.

Albert Spalding. The White Stockings/Cubs owner moved to San Diego in the early 20th century and later ran unsuccessfully for a U.S. Senate seat in California.

John Tener. The National League president, who had 25 pitching wins in the 19th century, was a member of the House of Representatives in 1909–1911 and governor of Pennsylvania in 1911–1915.

Polo Grounds (1891–1963)

"Suppose you had a dream it was afternoon at the Polo Grounds in the 1930s (and don't think that people from that time don't have them), you'd have the most beautific smile and your snore would be a purr. It was the happiest place in town. Finally you'd snap awake. No use, those days are gone forever." — Hall of Fame Director Ken Smith in the foreword to *Under Coogan's Bluff*, by Fred Stein (1979).

"The first big-league game I ever saw was at the Polo Grounds. My father took me. I remember it so well — the green grass and the green stands. It was like seeing Oz." — Pitcher John Curtis.

Origins. The Polo Grounds were the home of the Giants from 1891 through 1957 and the New York Mets in 1962 and 1963.

Polo was never played at the Polo Grounds, but the name evolved in a somewhat logical fashion. When National League Troy owner John Day shifted the club to New York in 1883, he arranged for the team to play its games on the polo field of James Gordon Bennett, publisher of the *New York Herald*.

The field was located at 110th Street between Fifth and Sixth Avenues, just north of Central Park. A shoeshine boy supposedly suggested to Day that he use this site. Baseball had been played on the site since September 1880, though some sources reported in error that Day built the first baseball field there when he arrived with his club in 1883. The field had two adjacent diamonds that were used by the National League Giants (then called the Gothams) and American Association Mets.

In early 1889 the city of New York decided to run a road through the old Polo Grounds and evict the Giants. Before finding a new site, the team played most of its games in Jersey City and on Staten Island. Team captain John Montgomery Ward led the Giants to a pennant and defeated American Association champion Brooklyn. One source noted that technically it could be argued that the "World Series" has been played in all five New York boroughs: Queens (Mets), Bronx (Yankees), Manhattan (Giants), Staten Island (Giants), and Brooklyn (Dodgers). However, it is doubtful whether the club played any postseason games in Staten Island because most reliable sources note that the club moved into its new ballpark before the 1889 postseason, on July 8.

The new site was sometimes referred to as Manhattan Field and the Polo Grounds. It was built to hold 15,000 fans at the corner of Eighth Avenue and 155th Street. Just north of the new ballpark was a site used by the 1890 Players League club in New York. Slugger Mike Tiernan supposedly hit a home run from the Giants' ballpark into the Players League ballpark. After the collapse of the Players League, the Giants moved into the Players League ballpark, renaming it the New Polo Grounds. Some sources report that Manhattan Field was the modern Polo Grounds. The Players League site, though often remodeled and expanded, was the home of the Giants through their departure after the 1957 season.

Coogan's Bluff. The Coogan's Bluff name for the left field area of the Polo Grounds evolved from Coogan's Hollow, which was a remnant of a farm granted by the British in the 17th century to John Lion Gardiner. Another source reported that the owner of the property in the early 20th century was Mrs. Harriet Coogan. Mrs. Coogan was married to James J. Coogan, an upholsterer, and she was part of the Gardiner family that originally owned the property and leased it to the Giants. Mr. Coogan was the Manhattan borough president in 1899.

Fire and Renovation. In April 1911, on the night after the second game of the season (after Opening Day in some sources), much of the grandstand at the Polo Grounds burned down and the Giants spent four months as tenants in the Yankees' Highlander Park. The Polo Grounds were enlarged to become the third steel and concrete stadium in baseball (after the ballparks in Philadelphia and Pittsburgh). The new ballpark seated 34,000 by the time the renovations were completed for the World Series at the end of the season. A reported 38,221 fans squeezed in for one series game, though the announced attendance was 50,000. The new structure was to be called Brush Stadium in honor of former owner John Brush, but the name never took hold.

Further Enlargement/Renovation. In 1920 the Polo Grounds were enlarged to seat 46,000 fans. In 1923 the ballpark was enclosed with center field bleachers to bring capacity to 55,000. Few additional changes occurred until the Giants left after the 1957 season. The ballpark was vacant until the New York Mets needed a temporary home while Shea Stadium was under construction. The ballpark received a $250,000 facelift and the Mets occupied the park from 1962 until Shea opened for the 1964 season (Shea had been expected to open in 1963, but wasn't ready). The Mets had planned to play at Yankee Stadium until the Yankees balked.

Dimensions. The ballpark's dimensions were dictated by inner city property dimensions, which generally were rectangular. This created short foul lines and an unusually long center field. The left field foul line was 257 feet and the right field foul line was 279 feet. Left field had an overhang that jutted out for short fly ball home runs, a Dusty Rhodes specialty.

Center field was an astronomical 483 feet, which was reached only three times in the history of the ballpark. Joe Adcock of the Braves was the first player to hit one there off Jim Hearns on April 29, 1953. On June 16, 1962, Henry Aaron did it against the Mets off Al Jackson and the next day Lou Brock did it against Jay Hook.

First Night Game. The first night game in the Polo Grounds was played August 1, 1929, between the Pennsylvania Coal Miners B.B.C. and "Josie Caruso and Her Eight Men." Caruso was a woman semipro player on men's teams between 1929 and 1931.

"Lasts." The last game played by the New York Giants in the Polo Grounds was on September 29, 1957. They lost to the Pirates 9–1 in front of 11,606 fans. The last Mets game in the Polo Grounds was on September 18, 1963. Jim Hickman hit the last Polo Grounds home run for the Mets, during a 5–1 loss to Chris Short of the Phillies. Fittingly, the last outs were on a *Triple Play* hit into by Joe Pignatano.

Demolition.
"At the end of the season they're gonna tear this joint down. The way you're pitching, that right field section will be gone already."— Mets manager Casey Stengel to pitcher Tracy Stallard after Stallard gave up two long home runs to right.

After the Mets vacated the park, it was leveled in 1964 and replaced by 1,700 low-cost housing units known as the Polo Grounds Towers. A plaque to commemorate the Polo Grounds was erected at the approximate site of home plate.

No Polo. Sportswriter Fred Lieb related the early 20th century story of an English couple that he overheard on the L-Train in New York. They were on their way to a polo match on Long Island and asked where the Polo Grounds were. They were directed to the Giants' home field, and Lieb could not resist following them to see their reaction at the baseball game being played. The result was predictable, and they were sent on their way to Long Island.

PONY League Baseball (1950–)

"Protect Our Nation's Youth."— The meaning of the "PONY" acronym, although it first meant, "Protect Our Neighborhood Youth."

This youth league was founded in 1950 in Washington, Pennsylvania, for boys 13–14 years old. Its first games were played in 1951 and its first World Series was held in 1952.

The **Colt League** was founded in 1953 in Martin's Ferry, Ohio, for boys 15–16. The Colt League first merged with other leagues and then in 1959 merged with PONY League to form **Boys' Baseball**, still headquartered in Washington, Pennsylvania.

A division of PONY League Baseball is the Collegiate Summer Baseball Association, founded in 1984. It was created to administer a branch of Pony League Baseball called Thoroughbred, a national program for players 19–22 years old.

By the 2000s there were 28,500 teams in the United States and 12 countries, and over five million youth have played in its leagues, including Major Leaguers Joel Horlen, Wes Parker, Alex Fernandez and Greg Swindell.

Another PONY league existed in Buffalo that was born in 1939, a Class D minor league spread out in small towns in New York and Hamilton, Ontario. Warren Spahn played his first professional season in this league.

Popularity

"Baseball is doomed. It is the inclusive mesh of the TV image, in particular, that spells … the doom of baseball now, but it'll come back. Games go in cycles."— Marshall McLuhan in the 1960s.

"The other sports are just sports. Baseball is a love."— Bryant Gumbel in 1981.

"Call me Un-American; call me Canadian or Swedish, I don't care. I hate baseball…. I have lots of reasons to hate baseball. For one it's dull. Nothing happens. Watching baseball is like going to a lecture by a member of the Slow … Talkers … of… America. It's like turning on the TV— when the cable is out. It's like watching grass— no, Astroturf grow."— Jeff Jarvis in *Entertainment Weekly.*

"With those who don't give a damn about baseball, I can only sympathize. I do not resent them. I am even willing to concede that many of them are physically clean, good to their mothers and in favor of world peace. But while the game is on, I can't think of anything to say to them."— Art Hill.

See also **National Pastime**.

Late 19th Century. The monopolistic National League of the late 1890s experienced declining attendance and popularity, in part due to the rise in violence among ballplayers. The *New York Times* in September 1898 summed up the disenchantment: "Professional baseball, as carried on at the present day, is without power to excite popular enthusiasm…. The attendance has fallen off materially in this city, where squabbles over the rules, the exchange of opprobrious epithets, and fines, and wide and vigorous 'kicking' at the umpire's decisions by the players, are salient features of every game."

The *Times* presented a baseball epitaph on July 25, 1900, an inaccurate prelude to the resurgence of the early 20th century that arrived with the American League: "There was a time when baseball was the National game of this country. It is so now only in name, and chiefly because it is not played in other lands…. Even in the colleges, where the game is played in the highest and most sportsmanlike spirit of rivalry, it has taken a comparatively low position in recent years."

1900–1940s. A number of surveys and studies have chronicled baseball's rises and falls in popularity during these five decades. Before World War II, baseball was the preeminent American sport, evidenced in part by the fact that *The Sporting News* did not cover any other sport until 1942. The falls were marked by the inter-league wars of 1901–1903 and 1914–1915, the Depression of the 1930s and the war-related years of 1918–1919 and 1942–1945. The rises were marked by periods of economic prosperity in the country and particularly the popularity of Babe Ruth during the 1920s.

Post-War Popularity. Some sources contend that baseball experienced its most popular period from postwar 1946 until the early 1960s, in part because of an expanding economy and because television for the first time carried the product to cities that did not have a Major League club. Despite the popularity of Major League Baseball, the minor leagues were dying due to the exposure of Major League Baseball through radio and television in areas that previously saw only minor league baseball.

By the mid–1960s expansion had diluted the product and television began courting football. Baseball began to represent the staid establishment, and its popularity waned in the face of professional football.

Some sources note that the decline began in the 1950s when Major League attendance never reached the late 1940s high of 20 million. This has been attributed to bad ballparks, emergence of other sports, population shifts out of the northeast (where Major League clubs were generally located), the emergence of television as the dominant medium providing exposure to other sports, and a competitive imbalance among Major League teams. For example, between 1947 and 1966 the Yankees and Dodgers won 25 pennants.

1960s–1975. One 1965 survey showed that 38% of sports fans favored baseball and 25% favored football. Only a year earlier, those figures were 45% for baseball and 23% for football. By 1967 the figures were 39–29% in favor of baseball, and in 1968 39–32% in favor of baseball. Among the more affluent, however, football led 52–22% that year. By 1969 football had taken the overall lead at 31–28% and those statistics continued to get worse for baseball: 1970 Football led 30–27% (29–19% in one poll) In 1970 a Sindlinger poll had baseball at 27.1%, football 24.4% and basketball 6.2%.

1972 Football led 28–23%
1974 Football led 23–19%
1975 Football led 24–16%

Mid–1970s Resurgence. Baseball began a renaissance in 1975; the seminal event often has been identified as Game 6 of the 1975 World Series between the Red Sox and the Reds. Boston catcher Carlton Fisk hit a dramatic bottom-of-the-13th-inning home run to force a seventh game.

1980s Strength. After the 1981 strike-shortened season, baseball made a remarkable recovery. This was evidenced in part by the resurgence of the minor leagues. By the end of the decade, however, salary issues dominated the media, and baseball began to fall into disfavor.

1990s Disenchantment.

"So many people who love baseball feel frustrated, just like they do with government. There's a powerlessness brought on by dismay over events that one cannot control. And the feeling is growing. Baseball can't ignore such feelings, because paying customers are the lifeblood of the game." — Baseball Hall of Fame librarian Tom Heitz on fan disenchantment in 1992.

"During the telecast of [an] NBA play-off game between the Houston Rockets and San Antonio Spurs there was a commercial for major league baseball. That's right, the former national pastime was advertising itself on the telecast of a basketball game. Maybe the men who run major league baseball — or run it down — thought they better buy time during a game that is being

watched by a lot of fans in order to plug their sport, which is being played before an alarming number of empty seats." — Sportswriter Ed Schuyler, Jr., in June 1995.

"For football has returned, as it does every August, to knock the books from baseball's arms, steal its lunch money and leave the sport suspended in obscurity — hanging, by its Hanes, from a hook in a locker…. On the surface the two sports have much in common — armored men with Popeye arms playing games that end 17–10. But one's thriving and one's dying. One's cool and one's not. It's the difference between John Wayne and John Wayne Bobbitt." — Steve Rushin.

Financial issues dominated baseball in the 1990s as owners grappled with escalating salaries while television revenues were declining. In 1992 attendance declined at 18 of the 26 Major League parks. Television ratings dropped from an average of 5.1 to 3.4. In one poll only 42% identified themselves as baseball fans, a huge drop from the 60% figure of 1988. The players usually were perceived as the bad guys: in one poll, most baseball fans characterized the players as greedy, while 37% so labeled the owners.

By the 1990s, 54% of the American "sports fan" population called themselves basketball fans and 46% called themselves baseball fans. In 1992 a poll of 600 children ages eight to 12 were asked which sports they "watched a lot" on television. Baseball was chosen among 36% of the kids, 42% said basketball, 43% said football and 45% said wrestling.

In mid–1994, 41% of teenagers named football as their favorite sport to watch. Basketball was second at 22% and baseball was third at 13%. Basketball was identified as the fastest-growing spectator sport.

In late 1994, 39% of all people surveyed said the were baseball fans; 10% were "somewhat" fans and 51% were not fans. In early 1995, during the heat of the strike and talk of replacement players, the percentages changed slightly downward in each category.

In 1995 only 33% of adults surveyed said they followed Major League Baseball, compared with 49% a year earlier. Of those still interested in baseball, 71% said they were less interested than before the strike. Only 16% said they were just as interested as they were, while 12% said they were more interested.

In September 1998, in a nationwide telephone poll of 960 adults conducted in part by the *New York Times* and CBS News, the number of people who said they were at least somewhat interested in Major League Baseball surpassed 60% for the first time since the *Times* and CBS News first asked the question in 1985.

Baseball maintained its stronger popularity ratings into the 2000s, and the 2003–04 postseasons added to baseball's better popularity quotient among fans, though football still led. In a 2004 poll, football was followed by 64.9% of males and 35.7% of females. The Olympics were second with 62.4% of males and 49.7% of females. Baseball was third at 54.0% for males and 33.2% for females. Next was college football at 46.9% and 23.3%.

The Playing Public.

"Although some people may argue that from a spectator standpoint that baseball is no longer the "national pastime," there are no team sports with more participants nor are there any activities more popular among the youth of the United States than baseball [in 2001]. Beyond the 750 major league players, there are approximately 2,100 minor leaguers, 45,000 intercollegiate players, 433,684 high school participants, and nearly two million players in youth leagues." — Stan Conte in *The American Journal of Sports Medicine.*

In 1996 it was estimated that 17 million people over age six played baseball at least once in 1994. The number of those who played at least 52 times increased 24% since 1987. Over 80% of the players were male and two-thirds were 17 or under. The study was conducted by a sporting goods industry association. In 1996 a survey of boys 6–17 showed that almost as many youth, 14.6 million, played basketball as those who played baseball, 8.6 million, and football, 8.1 million, combined.

Player Popularity.

"The romance between intellectuals and the game of baseball is, for the most part, one-sided to the point of absurdity. A large percentage of intelligent Americans evaluate the four hundred men who play major league baseball as awesomely gifted demigods. A large percentage of the muscular four hundred rate intellectuals several notches below umpires."— Roger Kahn in "Intellectuals and Scholars" in *The American Scholar* (1957).

In 1892 a popularity contest was held and the winners were Buck Ewing, Mike Kelly, Cap Anson and Ned Williamson.

In a 1947 national poll, Jackie Robinson was voted the second-most popular American, behind only Bing Crosby.

In a 1990 "likability survey" of 300 athletes from all sports, Nolan Ryan and Bo Jackson were the only baseball players in the top 75.

Postage Stamps and Post Offices

"Writing about Babe Ruth is akin to trying to paint a landscape on a postage stamp."— Sportswriter Arthur Daley.

"Alvin Express Station, Home of Nolan Ryan, Alvin, TX 77511."— During Christmas 1993 Ryan had his own postmark from Alvin, Texas. It depicted him in a pitching stance.

"Wally Post, Rowland Office, Zip Collins, Duster Mails"

First U.S. Baseball Stamp. A United States commemorative postage stamp was issued in 1939 to celebrate what was considered the centennial of the origins of baseball (assuming Abner Doubleday started it in 1839). The stamp was a three-cent purple featuring sandlot players, but only after intense debate over what to put on it.

Early Foreign Stamps. The Philippines was the first country to honor baseball, as part of a 1934 set commemorating the 10th Far Eastern Championship Games in Manila. It was a two-cent brown stamp featuring a catcher in a crouch.

In 1935 Colombia issued an 18-centavos stamp featuring a close play at the plate. The dark violet and buff stamp was issued to honor the Third National Olympic Games of that country.

In 1937 Nicaragua issued a one-centavo stamp featuring a batter ready to swing. The carmine, yellow, blue and green stamp was issued as a tax stamp to defray the cost of the 1937 Central American and Caribbean Games.

In 1938 Panama hosted the Caribbean Games and issued a two-centesimos stamp in green featuring a batter in midswing.

Japan first issued a baseball stamp in 1948, honoring the Third National Games of that country.

In October 1998 the post office of Guyana issued a special edition, 12-stamp set that honored Babe Ruth. Each of the twelve stamps was about four times the size of a regular U.S. postage stamp. They were legal for postage in Guyana and were recognized by every postal authority around the world.

Recent U.S. Stamps. On September 24, 1969, the U.S. Post Office issued a six-cent commemorative stamp to celebrate the 100th anniversary of professional baseball. The new design was essentially that of the logo currently used by Major League Baseball.

A 1982 issue featured Jackie Robinson. A 1983 Babe Ruth 20-cent stamp featured him hitting a home run off Carmen Hill during Game 4 of the 1927 World Series. A 1984 issue featured Roberto Clemente.

On June 10, 1989, to commemorate the 50th anniversary of the Hall of Fame, 2,500 first-day covers were printed to coincide with the introduction of the Lou Gehrig stamp in Cooperstown.

In 1992 the U.S. Postal Service introduced a new baseball stamp to commemorate the addition of baseball as a medal sport for the Olympic Games.

In 2000 the U.S. Postal Service issued a series of stamps commemorating each decade of the 20th century, "Celebrate the Century." For the 1920s, Babe Ruth was on one, issued in 1998. A Jackie Robinson stamp was issued to help illustrate the 1940s. For the 1950s, Ralph Branca's pitch to Bobby Thomson was used, along with "I Love Lucy." [The most popular stamp of all time is the U.S. Bugs Bunny stamp, with over 385 million issued.]

Postmaster General. Postmaster General James A. Farley, who served under President Franklin Roosevelt, was a baseball enthusiast who at times attempted to purchase clubs and was considered as a replacement for Judge Landis in the 1940s. Farley had been a manager of a semipro team in New York in the early 20th century and played first base. Baseball clown Al Schacht once pitched on his club.

Robert Hannegan was a former postmaster general and Democratic senator from Missouri who teamed with Fred Saigh to buy the Cardinals in 1947.

Grenada. In 1988 the island of Grenada issued a nine-stamp commemorative set that was more ambitious than almost every other foreign issue of modern times. The set was authorized by Major League Baseball and featured facial shots and background action shots of an eclectic group of players: Gary Carter, Henry Aaron, Gaylord Perry, Ty Cobb, Andre Dawson, Charlie Hough, Kirby Puckett, Robin Yount and Don Drysdale.

Post Office. In 1955, shortly before Cy Young's death, the post office in Peoli, Ohio, was to be closed permanently. The post office was near Young's farm and when the U.S. congressman from the district learned of the prospective closure, he arranged to have it kept open so that Young could continue receiving his fan mail.

Heavy Mail Bag. During Henry Aaron's 1973–1974 quest to break Babe Ruth's home run record, he was presented with a plaque from the U.S. Postal Service for receiving more pieces of mail— 93,000— than anyone except politicians.

Postponed Games

"The people of Chicago learned with mortification and disgust from the dispatches of yesterday morning that a base ball club claiming to represent this city had been engaging in a public game with another club in Troy during the very hours when the lamented [and mortally wounded President James A.] Garfield was being carried to his grave…. If any or all of them had had a spark of sensibility he or they would have refused absolutely to celebrate the day in a manner so inappropriate."— The *Chicago Tribune* criticizing National League president William Hulbert for failing to postpone a game after President Garfield was shot and later died.

See **Road Games**— Ballpark Problems.

Team officials are empowered to decide whether to begin games. Near the end of the season, however, when tactical considerations might interfere with reasonable decisions, the league president may intervene.

Most Consecutive. The 1903 Phillies suffered through nine straight postponed games. The American League record is seven, held by three teams.

Addie Joss. When the popular pitching died from meningitis in April 1911, the Indians postponed their home opener against the Tigers to attend his funeral.

World War II. On D-Day, June 6, 1944, baseball postponed the two games scheduled that day.

Presidents. When President Warren Harding died in office on August 2, 1923, Major League games were postponed. When Franklin Roosevelt died on April 12, 1945, Major League games of April 14 were postponed.

Martin Luther King. On April 4, 1968, Martin Luther King was assassinated and his funeral was scheduled for April 9. The baseball season was scheduled to open the same day. Commissioner William D. Eckert left it to individual clubs whether to play. Most clubs elected to proceed, but the Mets were among those that delayed their opener until April 10.

Strategic Cancellations. As late as the 1940s, games were often called off so they could be played under better circumstances, usually to generate greater attendance at doubleheaders. An example was the last regular-season series in 1938 between the Tigers and Indians when Hank Greenberg was trying to break Babe Ruth's season home run record (see also *Home Runs*—Assaults on Ruth Before Maris).

On April 26, 1996, the White Sox postponed a game due to cold weather. It was clear to all that the club actually cancelled the game because of a conflict with a Chicago Bulls play-off game that evening that would have impacted White Sox attendance.

Equipment Failure. The Royals game scheduled for June 4, 1999, was postponed a day when an electrical problem knocked out half the lights. While attempting to fix the problem, a small fire started when the equipment exploded.

On July 18, 2001, the Padres game against the Diamondbacks in San Diego was postponed when there was an explosion in the left field light tower. Curt Schilling threw two perfect innings before the postponement. The game was finished the next day, and it allowed Randy Johnson to set a relief record for strikeouts after he started the game.

Football Intrusion. On Saturday, October 2, 2004, the Twins hosted the Indians in a game that would help decide who the Twins would play in the postseason. The game went into the 11th inning before being suspended and completed the next day. The reason: the Minnesota Golden Gophers college football team had a game scheduled that night in the Metrodome and the Twins had gone past their allotted time for baseball.

Construction Crash. On July 15, 1999, the Brewers postponed their game against the Royals after a crane collapsed the day before during construction of their new ballpark, killing three workers.

Train Crash. On July 18, 2001, a train carrying toxic substances derailed in Baltimore, causing the postponement of the second game of the Orioles' day-night doubleheader against the Rangers. Two days later, the toxic substances caused another postponement of Anaheim's game at Baltimore.

September 11. On September 11, 2001, all Major League games were cancelled due to the terrorist attacks. Games did not resume until Monday, September 17, 2001. Some teams were stranded due to the airline shutdown. The Blue Jays took a 12-hour bus ride from Baltimore to Toronto.

As part of a 50-minute pre-game ceremony the night that games resumed, the Yankees placed a special monument in the stadium's Monument Park behind the outfield memorializing those killed. The Orioles wore five-sided patches honoring the victims of the attack on the Pentagon.

Player Death. On June 22, 2002, the body of Cardinals pitchers Darryl Kile was found in his hotel room prior to that Saturday's game (see *Deaths*). The game between the Cubs and Cardinals was postponed.

War. In March 2003 the Yankees and Devil Rays were scheduled to play the first series of the season in Japan, but the U.S. invasion of Iraq forced cancellation of the series. It was played in Tampa instead.

Postseason Play

See also *Championship Series* (19th century), *Divisional Play and Play-Offs*, *League Championship Series*, *Play-Offs* and *World Series*.

Players with the most games played without appearing in the postseason (through 2004):

2,528	Ernie Banks	(1953–1971)
2,422	Luke Appling	(1930–1950)
2,409	Mickey Vernon	(1939–1960)
2,405	Buddy Bell	(1972–1989)
2,243	Ron Santo	(1960–1974)
2,209	Joe Torre	(1960–1977)
2,155	Toby Harrah	(1969–1986)
2,146	Harry Heilmann	(1914–1932)

Pitchers with 200 or more wins without appearing in the postseason:

284	Ferguson Jenkins	(1965–1983)
260	Ted Lyons	(1923–1946)
224	Jim Bunning	(1955–1971)
223	Mel Harder	(1928–1947)
222	Hooks Dauss	(1912–1926)
216	Wilbur Cooper	(1912–1926)

Note that Rod Carew played in the most games (2,469) without appearing in a World Series.

Manager. Jimmy Dykes managed 2,962 games over 21 seasons between 1934 and 1961 without appearing the postseason. Clark Griffith, long-time owner of the Senators, is second with 2,918 games managed over 20 seasons. Griffith's White Sox finished first in 1901, but there was no World Series that season. Bobby Valentine managed for 12 seasons and 1,704 games without reaching the postseason, then finally broke through in 1999 with the Mets.

Longest Team Drought. The Browns went from 1902 to 1944 before playing in the postseason. The Rangers are next on the list with a drought lasting from 1961, when expansion created the new Washington Senators, through 1995. They finally made it in 1996.

Atlanta Braves. In 1997 the Braves set a Major League record with their sixth consecutive postseason appearance. They went on to appear in 13 straight through the 2004 season (except 1994, when the season was cancelled due to the strike).

David Justice. In 2002 when Oakland won the division, David Justice played on his eleventh straight play-off team (though he didn't appear in the 1996 postseason for the Braves due to injury).

Randy Johnson. Despite his regular season brilliance, Johnson lost seven straight postseason games before winning Game 1 of the 2001 NLCS against the Cardinals. He went on to pair with Curt Schilling to surprise the Yankees in the World Series.

Long Time No See. When the Angels faced Roger Clemens in Game 1 of their 2002 division series against the Yankees, it was their first postseason appearance in 16 years, since Game 7 of the 1986 ALCS. The starting pitcher in that game: Roger Clemens.

Power Hitters See *Home Runs*

Practical Jokes and Pranks

"Let's just say I won't be doing it again. That's because I don't want to read my name in the obituaries."—Dodger pitcher Jesse Orosco in spring training 1988 after teammate Kirk Gibson took offense at Orosco's putting shoe polish inside his cap. Gibson's seriousness paid off, as the Dodgers were the surprise World Series champions.

"I couldn't set their shoes on fire, because most of them only had one pair."—Noted hotfoot artist Bert Blyleven on his Class AA Midland teammates during his 1992 comeback from rotator cuff surgery.

"They made him go to the club-house after the key to the batter's box; they wrote him mash notes with fake names signed to them and had him spending half his evenings on some corner, waiting to meet gals that never lived; when he held Florida University to two hits in five innings, they sent him telegrams of congratulations from Coolidge and Al Smith, and he showed the telegrams to everybody in the hotel; they had him report at the ball park at six-thirty one morning for a secret 'pitchers' conference; they told him the Ritz was where all the unmarried ball players on the club lived while we were home.... They was nothing he wouldn't fall for..."—Ring Lardner in *Hurry Kane* (1929).

See also *Sidd Finch*, *Hoax* and *Stunts*.

Bathrobe. On August 30, 1897, Cap Anson of the White Stockings was ejected from a game after protesting a strike call. When the inning ended, it was unclear who would take Anson's place in left field. Left-handed pitcher Dan Friend appeared in a bathrobe and baseball cap as he took his position. After a protest by the Giants manager, Friend was ordered into a uniform.

Easter. On Easter Sunday 1987 catcher B.J. Surhoff of the Brewers reached back with his mitt for a new ball. Umpire Larry McCoy dropped in an egg.

Sharp Dresser. Reliever Roger McDowell once sat in the Mets dugout on national television with his uniform on upside down; including pants over his head and shoes on his hands.

Blood. Outfielder Tom Brunansky was famous for wearing a fake bloody thumb with a large nail stuck in it and showing it to reporters.

Stickum. Yogi Berra was always borrowing Whitey Ford's deodorant. In retaliation, Ford and Mickey Mantle supposedly put stickum in Ford's roll-on deodorant and left it on the shelf for Berra's use. Berra's arms became stuck to his sides and the trainer had to cut off his underarm hair and use alcohol to get the stickum off. The "stickum," which he kept in a deodorant container, was actually Ford's secret formula for making his hands stickier in cold weather.

Cheese. In the late 1950s Sherman Lollar of the White Sox was the team's designated practical joker and glove "fixer." On a hot day he stuffed catcher Clint Courtney's glove with limburger cheese. He also rubbed the stuff on Courtney's uniform. The stench became so strong that the umpire made the catcher change his uniform.

Umpire. In the last game of the season in the 1970s, Jim Colburn of the Brewers dressed up like an umpire and called balls and strikes in the 1st inning. The real home plate umpire cooperated. Colburn threw out Gorman Thomas so that Gorman could get an early start on the off-season.

Bleach. See *Suspensions* for the 1993 incident in which Bret Saberhagen squirted reporters with bleach.

Moo. In 1995 Ken Griffey, Jr., left a pregnant 1,200-pound cow in manager Lou Piniella's office. Griffey owed Piniella a steak din-

ner after being unable to hit a ball off Scott Davidson during batting practice. Piniella's response to the smelly slobber all over his office: "It reminds me a lot of Cincinnati [and Marge Schott's dogs]."

No Nomo. During the mania over Dodger pitcher Hideo Nomo in 1995, a Florida radio station played an interview with a man pretending to be Nomo. The imposter ridiculed Marlin fans, saying that they did not know the difference between sushi and a forkball, and that All-Star outfielder Jeff Conine had no clue against him. No one revealed the hoax and the station was flooded with irate calls.

Presidents

"I don't think changing the president of the United States causes as much commotion as changing the manager of a big league ballclub."—Cubs owner Phil Wrigley.

"I was a nervous wreck out there. Swear to God. I felt like I was in the presence of the president."—Mariners reserve catcher John Marzano, after hitting a double and winding up standing next to Baltimore's Cal Ripken, Jr.

"Like the Presidency its size depends upon the man."—Poet Fred Chappell on the strike zone.

"I really don't like this campaign. The problem is when people take it seriously. One reporter demanded to know my stand on abortion. Come on."—Ken Griffey, Jr., during Nike's 1996 "Griffey for President" shoe campaign.

See also *Politics*.

George Washington.

"He sometimes throws and catches a ball for whole hours with his aide-de-camp."—Washington described at Valley Forge. He was also reported to be an avid rounders player.

John Adams. The second president once wrote that he spent his mornings as a youth playing, among other things, "bat and ball."

Thomas Jefferson.

"Thomas Jefferson, when he wrote the Declaration, made proper provision for baseball when he declared that 'all men are, and of right ought to be, free and equal.' That's what they are at the ball game, banker and bricklayer, lawyer and common laborer."—*Baseball* magazine in the 1920s.

"Games played with the ball, and others of that nature, are too violent for the body and stamp no character on the mind."—Jefferson.

Abraham Lincoln.

"Abe Lincoln? He had a real good cutter."—2003 Marlins manager Jack McKeon, age 72, rumored to have played with Lincoln.

"Gentleman, if any of you should ever take a hand in another match at this game, remember you must have 'a good bat' and strike a 'fair ball' to make a 'clean score' & a 'homerun.'"—Quote about Lincoln in an 1860 Currier & Ives editorial cartoon.

Lincoln is said to have played baseball, or Town Ball, with his grandchildren. There is an apocryphal story that he was playing baseball when he received word that he had been nominated for the presidency. This legend is probably derived from a political cartoon of the era that depicted such a scene. The curator at the Smithsonian says he was playing handball with fellow lawyers in Springfield. There is evidence that while he was president he attended a few amateur games with his son in Washington.

Radio broadcaster Bill Stern aired a story in the 1940s that was typical of the myths he sometimes presented as fact. While Lincoln was on his deathbed he summoned Abner Doubleday, whom he told, "don't let baseball die." To which Art Hill responded in *I*

Don't Care If I Never Get Back (1980): "If Lincoln had spoken at all after being shot, it seems more likely that he would have said, 'Don't let *me* die.'"

Andrew Johnson.

"At about six o'clock, the President, who was prevented from appearing earlier on account of the semi-weekly Cabinet meeting, came on the ground and remained until the close of the game, an apparently interested spectator of the exciting contest." — September 18, 1866, report in the *Washington National Republican* on Johnson's attendance at a game between the Washington Nationals and Brooklyn Excelsiors. The Excelsiors won 33–28.

Johnson reportedly attended a game on August 28, 1865, but though he had promised to do so, he was unable to attend. What is known is that Johnson was the first sitting president to witness an intercity baseball game. He watched a game from a carriage between either the Washington Nationals and Brooklyn Excelsiors or Nationals and Philadelphia Athletics, again depending on the source. It is likely that he witnessed more than one game, thereby explaining the discrepancies.

In August 1867 the Washington Nationals opened their new ballpark and Johnson was the guest of honor. A few weeks earlier he had accepted an honorary membership with the New York Mutuals, a team sponsored by the Tammany Hall political machine.

Ulysses S. Grant.

"The story is often told, too, of General Grant taking time out during the Wilderness campaign to watch and root for a team from an Illinois regiment in a game against a team from Massachusetts." Pure fantasy, of course." — Ford Frick in *Games, Asterisks and People* (1973).

Grant gave the 1869 Cincinnati Red Stockings a private audience and complimented the "Cinderella" club for its skill and winning ways. Some sources report that he saw a game played by the Red Stockings. After leaving office, Grant watched the New York

Gothams play their first game at the original Polo Grounds on May 1, 1883. The Giants defeated the Boston Red Stockings 7–5.

Chester A. Arthur.

"Good ballplayers make good citizens." — Arthur.

Arthur received the Cleveland Spiders at the White House in the spring of 1883.

Benjamin Harrison.

"A great lover of baseball."

Harrison often attended Washington games. He was the first sitting president to watch a Major League game when Cincinnati defeated Washington 7–4 in 11 innings on June 6, 1892. He also saw a game on June 25 that season, as Washington lost to Philadelphia 9–2.

Grover Cleveland.

"What do you [Cap Anson in 1885] imagine the American people would think of me if I wasted my time going to the ball game?" — Alexander.

Cleveland gave the Chicago White Stockings an audience before the team's 1888–1889 World Tour. Pitcher Grover Cleveland Alexander was named after him.

William Henry Harrison.

"If nothing else can draw President Harrison to Louisville, our beautiful base ball pennant should do it. What kind of a national President is it who takes no interest in the national game?" — 1890s Louisville newspaper editorial. One source erroneously reported that in 1893 the Ohio native became the first president to formally attend a National League game; Benjamin Harrison was the first in 1892.

William McKinley.

"M'Kinley On Ball — The President A Lover Of The National Game" — 1897 *Sporting Life* headline.

McKinley was invited to throw out the first National League ball in 1897, but he declined, prompting the following: "President McKinley disappointed the 7,000 spectators at the opening game by failing to appear, and the Senators disappointed them by losing to Brooklyn 5 to 4." — *Washington Star* article.

While governor of Ohio, he was scheduled to throw out the first ball for the Cincinnati Reds at their 1894 Opening Day game. However, the game was rained out and he was unavailable for the next game.

Teddy Roosevelt.

"A mollycoddle game." — Roosevelt's description of baseball.

"O'Reilly closes his left eye as he goes into the wind-up, and sends another blur of horsehide straight down the middle of the plate. Teddy Roosevelt takes an equally vicious swing but does not connect. He turns and looks down and behind him to where Henry Pulvermacher clutches the ball in his warty hand." — W.P. Kinsella in his mystical *The Iowa Baseball Confederacy* (1986).

Franklin D. Roosevelt opens the 1937 season in Washington. Looking on to his left are A's manager Connie Mack and Senators manager Bucky Harris.

"You will find it harder than mauling up the octopus;
It will be a rougher job than a charge up San Juan Hill,
Or a battle with the trusts — it will take a stronger will...
Think of how your pulse will leap when you hear the angry roar...
Chasing mountain lions and such, catching grizzlies will seem tame."

— Excerpt from Grantland Rice's 1908 advice to Teddy Roosevelt after he left the presidency — reportedly to become an umpire.

Though a prominent sportsman, Roosevelt supposedly did not like baseball. Other sources reported that he liked baseball but was a poor player because he had such bad eyesight. He is also quoted as being pleased that his son was a good player: "I like to see Quentin practicing baseball. It gives me hope that one of my boys will not take after his father in this respect, and will prove able to play the national game."

Roosevelt was shot during an assassination attempt in 1912 on the day before the eighth and last game of the World Series that year. He was out of danger by the next day and the game was not postponed.

William Howard Taft.

"The game of baseball is a clean, straight game, and it summons to its presence everybody who enjoys clean, straight athletics." — Taft.

Taft, though later weighing in at over 300 pounds, was an amateur baseball player in Cincinnati. He purportedly was offered a contract with the Washington Nationals of the 1870s National Association, but hurt his arm in a game the day before he was supposed to leave for Washington. Although some sources reported that he had a strong bat and arm, he was slow and was not considered a first-rate player; so it is unlikely that he was offered a contract. Other sources reported that he pitched at Yale and was described as a "stand-out" player while in college.

He attended the American League opener on April 14, 1910 (though some sources report 1911). Some sources incorrectly credit his standing in the 7th inning of the 1910 game as the beginning of the *Seventh Inning Stretch*.

Taft was considered for the position of baseball's first commissioner. This may have been because Taft's brother Charles owned the Cubs and Mrs. Charles Taft owned the Philadelphia ballpark.

Taft saw 14 games while in office, including regular season games in Pittsburgh, Cincinnati, Chicago and St. Louis. He once saw both St. Louis teams play at home on the same day, May 4, 1910. He missed Opening Day in 1912 to attend to the sinking of the *Titanic*, so Vice President Sherman threw out the first pitch.

Taft hated bunts, and after watching the Pirates against the Cubs in June 1909 he told reporters: "Saturday's game was a fine one, but several times when a hit meant a run, the batter was ordered to bunt. I believe they should hit it out. I love the game when there is plenty of slugging."

Woodrow Wilson.

"Wilson would be a good player if he weren't so damned lazy." — The captain of Wilson's Davidson College team.

Wilson organized and played second base for the Light Foot Base Ball Club and was the student-manager of the Princeton college team after transferring from Davidson. Another source makes no reference to his management of the club (a glorified clubhouse boy?), but describes him as the president of the Princeton Baseball Association. Another source reported that a scout had described him as "throwing smoke" while a pitcher at Princeton, though there is no record of his playing there. He is also said to have played semipro ball in Virginia and to have coached at Princeton, the latter probably a mistaken reference to his management duties while in college.

While president, Wilson threw out the first ball three times at American League Opening Day games. He also traveled to Philadelphia in 1915 to become the first sitting president to attend a World Series game (Game 2). He witnessed a total of 11 games during his presidency.

In 1916 Ty Cobb endorsed Wilson for president in an advertisement showing Wilson throwing out the first ball and noting that he "Bats 1000% — They never call a strike on him."

Warren G. Harding.

"I never saw a game without taking sides and never want to see one. There is the soul of the game." — Harding commenting on the beauty of baseball.

"Hot as hell, ain't it Prez?" — Babe Ruth on being introduced to Harding at a game (also described in various sources as a statement he made to Herbert Hoover or Calvin Coolidge).

Harding played baseball in Marion, Ohio, and later owned a minor league franchise there. He was described as the "president of the fans" because of his interest in the game. Babe Ruth was a guest at the White House several times during Harding's administration.

Harding saw three Opening Day Games and one game at Yankee Stadium only a short time after it opened. He saw one other game while President, for a total of five. When he died in office in 1923, Major League games were postponed.

Calvin Coolidge.

"President and Mrs. Calvin [Grace] Coolidge — she knew a lot more about baseball than he did, but so did everybody else — were among the standing room crowd." — Columnist Shirley Povich.

Coolidge attended four Opening Day games, three World Series games, and three more regular season games while President. He attended games during the 1924 World Series involving the Senators, which was more of a political move because of the upcoming November election. However, he and his wife did stay to the end of Game 7, in which Walter Johnson defeated the Giants. After the Series, Coolidge received the Senators at the White House after the club won the World Series.

Though the President was not much of a fan, his wife often stayed to the end of games and kept score. She had been a scorekeeper when she attended Vassar College and became known as the First Lady of Baseball for her fervent rooting for the Senators. In 1930 Coolidge visited Catalina Island off the California coast and posed for pictures with the Cubs at their spring training site.

Herbert Hoover.

"Next to religion, baseball has had a greater impact on the American people than any other institution." — Hoover, who declared himself at age 87 "the oldest living baseball fan."

"Why not? I had a better year than he did." — Babe Ruth, responding to criticism that his $80,000 salary was more than the president's. The response is also reported to have been: "How many home runs did *he* hit last year?"

Hoover was an avid baseball fan — rooting primarily for the Yankees — and once stayed through an entire game despite steady rainfall. When he attended the 1931 World Series, the crowd chanted "We want beer!" in reference to Prohibition. Hoover left early, but supposedly not because of the boos. He cited receipt of two telegrams, one announcing the death of a friend and another announcing that the U.S. was no longer on the gold standard.

Hoover was the Stanford University team manager after failing to make it as a player. Legend has it that he once requested former President Benjamin Harrison to pay the admission price to a Stanford game he had entered without paying.

In 1928 Ruth campaigned for fellow Catholic Al Smith against Hoover. Ruth even formed a political action group on the Yankees to help Smith's campaign. When Hoover visited Yankee Stadium during his campaign, Ruth intentionally stayed in the clubhouse to avoid shaking his hand.

Hoover attended nine games while in office, including four in which he threw out the first pitch during the 1930 and 1931 World Series. He also attended Game 5 of the 1929 World Series.

Franklin Roosevelt.

"Roosevelt enjoys himself at a ball game as much as a kid on Christmas morning."—*Baseball Magazine.*

Roosevelt threw out the first ball of the season eight times while in office and attended a total of 11 games while President. He was once so wild that he hit an umpire (or a photographer) with his throw. He saw one of the 1933 World Series games in Washington, Game 1 of the 1936 Series in the Polo Grounds, and the 1937 All-Star Game in Washington when Dizzy Dean had his toe broken by an Earl Averill line drive.

Roosevelt was unable to make his school team and served as manager instead. One source reported that he was present for the 1932 World Series game between the Yankees and Cubs in which Babe Ruth supposedly "called his shot" on a home run off pitcher Charlie Root.

Roosevelt admitted to betting on the Senators on occasion, an indulgence he claimed was necessary for a president who had to endure the pitiful Senators. A special platform was built at Griffith Stadium so that Roosevelt, who by then had polio, could lift himself directly from his car and pull himself into the special box seats next to the field. The ball he used to start the 1941 season was sold at auction in November 1998 for $17,255.

Roosevelt's famous "Green Light" letter allowed baseball to continue during *World War II.* When he died on April 12, 1945, Major League games scheduled for April 14 were postponed.

Vice president John Nance Garner, who served under Roosevelt, was a baseball fan. His favorite player was Zeke Bonura, and he often asked Senators owner Clark Griffith to trade for him. His wish was granted in 1938 and Bonura, already friends with Garner, went over to Garner's box on Opening Day of the season. Bonura delivered on his promise to hit a home run. He rushed around the bases and ran to Garner's box, giving him a big hug.

Harry Truman.

"I couldn't see well enough to play when I was a boy, so they gave me a special job — they made me an umpire."— Truman.

Truman was ambidextrous; he threw out the first ball of the 1946 season as a left-hander and in 1947 as a right-hander. One of his Opening Day throws was thought to be a spitball and became known as "The Great Expectoration." In both 1950 and 1951 he threw out a ball with each hand.

Truman saw the Senators play 16 times while in office, including every Opening Day. It is the most games attended by a sitting President.

On April 12, 1955, after he was out of office, the Missouri native threw out the first ball of the first game ever played by the Kansas City A's. Truman was a Browns fan, and wife Bess was later a Kansas City A's and Royals fan.

Dwight Eisenhower.

"When I was a small boy in Kansas a friend of mine and I went fishing, and as we sat there in the warmth of a summer afternoon on a riverbank, we talked about what we wanted to do when we grew up. I told him that I wanted to be a real Major League ballplayer, a real professional like Honus Wagner. My friend said that he'd like to be President of the United States. Neither of us got our wish."— Eisenhower.

"The more baseball the better. It is a healthful sport and devel-

ops team play and initiative, plus an independent attitude."— Eisenhower.

Eisenhower once tried to skip a Senators opener to play golf. The game was rained out and Eisenhower received so much criticism that he hurried back to the city for the next day's game.

His apparent apathy about the game contradicts a perhaps fabricated story that he had played minor league ball under the name "Wilson" to protect his college eligibility. He supposedly played 14 games for Junction City in the Central Kansas League (or Kansas State League) in 1908. Though he played well, he quit. Eisenhower reportedly played in the outfield at West Point (he did not make the team, but played a bit on the junior varsity with future general Omar Bradley) and some sources report that he played high school ball and a few games of semipro ball before moving on to college.

According to researcher Evelyn Krache Morris, the rumor of his having played professionally surfaced in June 1945, when he told Giants manager Mel Ott that it was "the one secret of my life." He supposedly played under the assumed name of [manager "Affie"] Wilson. He admitted later to being a center fielder. His secretary, Ann Whitman, once wrote: "DDE did play professional baseball one season to make money, he did make one trip under an assumed name (did not say whether Wilson or not). But, he says not to answer this because it gets 'too complicated.'"

Based on his high school graduation date and entry into West Point, he could only have played in 1910 or during the summer of 1913. He worked a night job in 1910 and the real Affie Wilson played first base, at least according to Kansas State League box scores. Eisenhower suffered a serious knee injury from football in November 1912, so it is unlikely that he played baseball during the short interval that he was home in 1913. The injury almost ended his West Point career. He might have received a little money in semipro games, which was not uncommon in those days (and which still would have been a violation of the NCAA rules and the West Point honor code). Nevertheless, the conclusion appears to be that Eisenhower never played true professional baseball.

Eisenhower saw the Senators play 11 times while in office and attended Game 1 of the 1956 World Series in Brooklyn. He saw a total of 13 games while President. He threw out the first ball at seven Opening Day games. His favorite ballplayer was the Senators' Mickey Vernon, who called him a "real fan."

In 1961 the former president met with Angels manager Bill Rigney during spring training. Rigney asked Eisenhower to manage a few innings of a game with his expansion club, but Eisenhower demurred, claiming he did not know the Angels' signs. Rigney's response: "No problem. Neither do they."

Eisenhower managed the club. Eisenhower's grandson David later covered baseball for a Philadelphia newspaper.

John F. Kennedy.

"A couple of years ago they told me I was too young to be President and you were too old to be playing baseball. But we fooled them."— Kennedy, 45, to Stan Musial, 42, and supposedly Kennedy's favorite player, at the 1962 All-Star Game.

"I'm leaving you in first place. You take it from here."— Kennedy to Senators manager Mickey Vernon after the club won its season opener with Kennedy in attendance.

Kennedy saw four games while in office, including three Opening Day games and the 1962 All-Star Game. Kennedy christened D.C. Stadium on April 9, 1962, as the Senators beat the Tigers 4–1. The ballpark was renamed Robert F. Kennedy Memorial Stadium after the younger Kennedy was assassinated in 1968.

A John Kennedy threw out the first ball for the White Sox in 1961, but it was only a promotional stunt by owner Bill Veeck.

Baseball player John Kennedy, primarily an infielder with the Dodgers in 1962 and 1963, was born on the same date as President John Kennedy, May 29. Infielder Kennedy hit a pinch-home run in his first Major League at-bat on September 5, 1962, for the Senators.

Fifty years before Kennedy threw out the first ball to start the 1962 season in Washington, D.C., Kennedy's grandfather, Boston Mayor John F. "Honey Fitz" Fitzgerald threw out the first pitch at the formal dedication of Fenway Park in 1912.

At the Kennedy memorabilia auction in 1996, Roger Clemens paid $165,000 for the pen that Kennedy used to sign the nuclear test-ban treaty.

Lyndon Johnson.

"A hard-throwing former first baseman who disdained the traditional lob in favor of a fastball." — Sportswriter's description of Johnson's toss, though Johnson did not care for baseball.

"We cheer for the Senators, we pray for the Senators, and we hope that the Supreme Court does not declare that unconstitutional." — Johnson.

Johnson managed to avoid attending all but four games during his presidency (three, in some sources). One game he attended was the first exhibition game played in the Astrodome, out of respect for Astros owner Roy Hofheinz, who had been a campaign manager for Johnson in the 1940s.

Jackie Robinson endorsed Johnson's opponent in the 1964 presidential election, right-wing conservative Barry Goldwater. Robinson endorsed conservative Republican Richard Nixon in 1960 over John Kennedy.

Richard Nixon.

"I don't know a lot about politics, but I do know a lot about baseball." — Nixon.

"He knows his fuckin' football, but not much fuckin' else." — Writer Hunter S. Thompson in 1972.

"If I had my life to live all over again, I'd have ended up as a sportswriter." — Nixon.

Nixon loved baseball and in 1972 he and his son-in-law, David Eisenhower, released a list of their all-time favorite players from both leagues and the reasons for their choices. Nixon updated the choices in July 1992 as part of the opening of a special exhibit at his presidential library in Yorba Linda, California. The exhibit featured the connection between baseball and presidents and included the famous "Green Light" letter written by Franklin Roosevelt to Judge Landis that allowed baseball to continue during World War II.

Vice-President Nixon gave the keynote speech when long-time Senators player Roy Sievers received a "Night" in 1958. Nixon reportedly was offered the commissioner's job after he lost the 1960 presidential election to Kennedy.

While president from early 1969 through August 1974, Nixon attended 11 games, eight of them in Washington. He saw two games in California during 1970 and 1973, the first regular season National League games attended by any president since Taft. He saw a triple play on July 15, 1969, in a game between the Tigers and Senators. He attended the managerial debut of Ted Williams on April 7, 1969, as the Yankees defeated the Senators 8–4.

Gerald Ford.

"I had a life-long ambition to be a professional baseball player, but nobody would sign me." — Ford.

"In baseball when they say you're out, you're out. It's the same way in politics." — Ford.

A college football player (team MVP at center for Michigan), Ford attended two games while in office (three in some sources), a Rangers home opener and the 1976 All-Star Game.

Ford wanted to be associated with sports on a regular basis. His staff maintained a list of at least one sportsperson per week who accomplished something notable: Ford would make contact, usually by telephone, and read from a prepared script about the accomplishment. Al Kaline was one of the first recipients of such a call, on the day he had his 3,000th hit. When flaky Tigers pitcher Mark Fidrych met Ford, he asked the president if his son, Jack, a soap opera star and later a newscaster, would set him up with a date.

Jimmy Carter.

"I heard Jimmy Carter said he had lost control of the U.S. government. That shows you how dumb he is. He thought he had control to begin with." — Pitcher Bill Lee.

Carter, an avid softball player, attended one game while in office, the last game of the 1979 World Series. Carter never threw an Opening Day pitch (the only President since Taft not to do so), but his brother Billy and mother Lillian threw out a few. Carter threw out the first ball twice for the Braves while he was governor of Georgia. He and wife Rosalyn attended most of the Braves postseason games in 1991 and 1992 as the guests of owner Ted Turner. On April 19, 1996, the 70-year-old former president caught a foul ball barehanded while sitting in Turner's field level box in Atlanta.

As a friend of Padres owner John Moores, Carter threw out the first pitch at Petco Park in San Diego in April 2004.

Ronald Reagan.

"I just know it's an ugly rumor that you and I are the only two people left alive who saw Abner Doubleday throw out the first pitch." — Reagan to Gaylord Perry, who at age 43 was about to win his 300th game.

"I was the player that plunked Reagan with a ball between the eyes as he was heading for second." — Peanuts Lowrey on *The Winning Team* (1952) (see **Movies**).

"You know, in a few months I'm going to be out of work and I thought I might as well audition." — Reagan broadcasting an inning during a Cubs game on September 30, 1988.

"I think we ought to nail his (Libyan leader Qadhafi) nuts to that log over there (the Orioles dugout bench) and push him over." — Reagan.

"[Baseball is] our national pastime, that is if you discount political campaigning." — Reagan.

"I never cared for baseball because I was ball-shy at batting [and nearsighted]. When I stood at the plate, the ball appeared out of nowhere about two feet in front of me. I was always the last chosen for a side in any game. Then I discovered football: no little invisible ball — just another guy to grab or knock down." — Reagan.

Reagan attended four games while in office. As governor of California, he attended the inaugural game of the Oakland A's in 1968. In the 1930s Reagan broadcast baseball games, usually re-creations, for radio station WHO in Des Moines, Iowa. During a spring training trip with the Cubs to Los Angeles, Reagan got himself a screen test and the rest is history. He played Grover Cleveland Alexander (who was named after President Grover Cleveland) in the movie *The Winning Team*. He supposedly arranged for his first Hollywood screen test while in California watching the Cubs during spring training.

Reagan played in a Hollywood celebrity fast pitch softball game in June 1949. The charity benefit had Bob Hope pitching, Donald O'Connor playing second base, and Janet Leigh as a cheerleader. William Demarest ("My Three Sons") was the umpire and Reagan had a 2–1 count when he laid down a bunt. He chose to slide into first base, and his leg broke in four places. He was in the hospital for two months.

George Bush.

"The Fall Classic has become a metaphor for America's love with baseball ... for a few golden days every October, each of us becomes a self-anointed expert ... the Fall Classic evokes a continuum of memories. We mark chapters in our lives by the World Series we recall." — Bush.

"There are, however, two famous first basemen who threw left and batted right, Hal Chase and George Bush ... Bush, captain of a fine Yale team that went to the finals of the NCAA tournament, has done an exemplary job recently of throwing out the first ball on opening day." — Robert K. Adair in *The Physics of Baseball* (1990).

"Normally they boo politicians at the ballpark. It kind of goes with the territory." — Bush.

Bush was known as "Spikes" when he played first base on Yale's Eastern Championship clubs in both 1947 and 1948. During his college career he hit .251 with two home runs and 23 RBIs. He played in the first College World Series in 1947, in which the Elis lost two straight to Cal. In one of the games, Elis coach and former Major Leaguer Ethan Allen ordered an intentional walk of a Cal player to get to the pitcher, who happened to be future Major Leaguer Jackie Jensen. Jensen hit a home run to win the game.

In the 1948 College World Series, Yale lost a three-game series to USC and long-time coach Rod Dedeaux. While Bush was team captain that season, he met Babe Ruth at the presentation of various Ruth documents to Yale.

Curt Smith wrote the most exhaustive account of the history of baseball broadcasting, *Voices of the Game* (1987). Smith later was a senior speech writer for Bush while he was in office.

Among the 10 games he appeared at during his presidency, Bush attended the 1991 All-Star Game in Toronto as the guest of Canadian Prime Minister Brian Mulrooney. He christened Baltimore's Oriole Park at Camden Yards with the first pitch on April 6, 1992. Bush appeared at the 1992 All-Star Game in San Diego with the president of Mexico. He kept his Rawlings George McQuinn autograph model Trapper Claw glove from his Yale playing days in his Oval Office desk drawer.

After he lost the 1992 election, Bush threw out the first pitch of an exhibition game between the Astros and Rangers in Houston on April 2, 1993. The game was to honor Nolan Ryan, and the crowd was the largest ever to see a baseball game in Texas. Bush had been a Texas resident and his son, George W. Bush (Now known as Dubya), was one of the owners of the club (and in 1994 was elected governor of Texas).

In August 1997 he attended a Rangers game when the club was still owned by his son. In 2003 Bush attended the Hall of Fame induction ceremonies and he attended Roger Clemens' first game for the Astros in April 2004.

Bill Clinton.

"Clinton likes the White Sox because they play Sax." — *Inside Sports* columnist "The Good Doctor," alluding to Steve Sax and Clinton's love of the saxophone.

"It was like Bush coming back to the Clinton inauguration." — Pirates outfielder Andy Van Slyke on the awkward return to Pittsburgh of former teammate Barry Bonds.

"This may ruin his career. His political career if not his pitching career." — Bill Clinton in August 2003 after posing for a photograph with Mets pitcher Al Leiter, a Republican who discussed entering politics.

On Opening Day in 1994 Clinton attended the first game in Cleveland's new Jacobs Field. He wore a politically correct cap with a "C" rather than the team's Chief Wahoo emblem worn by the players. Clinton left while Randy Johnson was still throwing a no-hitter in the 7th inning. Clinton threw out the first pitch of the championship game of the 1995 National Amateur All-Star Baseball Tournament at Pine Bluff, Arkansas. He threw out the first pitch for the Orioles in 1996. Clinton and Vice-President Al Gore also attended Cal Ripken's record-breaking game.

When he attended the April 15, 1997, ceremony at Shea Stadium with Rachel Robinson to honor Jackie Robinson, he was still in office and on crutches after recent knee surgery. This was Jackie Robinson Night, when the Mets honored Robinson for breaking the color line 50 years earlier by retiring his No. 42; which every other Major League club also did.

On September 27, 1998, when Mark McGwire hit his 70th home run, Clinton telephoned McGwire from his motorcade in San Antonio, Texas, to congratulate him and invite the slugger and his son to the White House.

During the height of the Monica Lewinsky scandal and probe by special investigator Kenneth Starr, a *Sports Illustrated* column noted a coincidence (or *was* it) involving a 1919 pitching start by one Lefty Whitehouse, for the Washington Senators, whose catcher in 1935 was Chick Starr. *Sports Illustrated* described these facts thusly: "The apocalyptic collision of Clinton and Monica Lewinsky was even foretold in an ancient manuscript, encoded in a biblical urtext: *The Baseball Encyclopedia.*"

Clinton attended six games while in office, and he and daughter Chelsea were rained out at a game in San Francisco. Clinton also attended a few Mets games after leaving office.

Former Orioles catcher Jeff Tackett, who appeared in the movie *Dave* to catch a pitch from the imposter President in the movie, had an encounter with Clinton in the mid–1990s. Clinton was at Camden Yard to throw out the first pitch of the season. Well before the game, Tackett was summoned by a Secret Service agent to the ballpark's underground batting cage. Assembled were Clinton and several security people, along with miscellaneous military types and other aides. Clinton wanted to warm up so he wouldn't embarrass himself in front of the crowd. On the first warm-up throw, Clinton bounced the ball to Tackett. Because of the low-hanging netting, Tackett couldn't lob the ball back and had to throw it relatively hard to get it back on the fly to the left-handed Clinton, who was wearing a glove. On the first throw back, Tackett nailed the President of the United States right in the chest. Clinton staggered back a bit, but steadied himself. He was gracious about the incident, but Tackett bounced all ensuing throws. Clinton performed well on the mound in front of the crowd.

George W. Bush.

"Where Mr. [Prime Minister Tony] Blair is an intellectual lawyer with an earnest interest in social responsibility, Mr. Bush is a former oil executive with an earnest interest in baseball statistics." — The *Financial Times*.

"None of my committee members are up for trade. Our [presidential] team is clicking on all cylinders, and I know how trades can turn out. I'm the one who traded Sammy Sosa to the Chicago White Sox." — Bush. As one of the owners of the Texas Rangers, he was responsible for the trade that brought Harold Baines to the Rangers for a young player named Sammy Sosa, whom the Rangers front office thought would be good, but nothing like Juan Gonzalez.

"One of the great things about living here [the White House] is that you don't have to sign up for a baseball fantasy camp to meet your heroes. It turns out, they come here." — Bush.

"Grady Little is the George Bush of managers. Letting Pedro stay in is like George Bush staring into Putin's soul." — Co-worker of writer Roger Angell.

"As an athlete, I peaked in Little League." — Bush, who sort of followed in his father's footsteps at Yale, pitching poorly as a middle reliever during his freshman year. He was the first Little Leaguer elected President.

As a former owner of the ***Texas Rangers***, Bush had an interest in baseball when he took office in 2000 and attended three games in 2001. On April 6, 2001, he threw out the first pitch for the first game played at Milwaukee's new Miller Park. In May 2003 Bush hosted the Angels in honor of the their 2002 championship.

First Ladies. Pat Nixon, Nancy Reagan and Barbara Bush all threw out first balls. Hillary Rodham Clinton also threw out first balls but missed her first scheduled chance due to a death in the family. Hillary threw out the first pitch at the 1994 Cubs home opener. Just before she made her appearance, a plane circled overhead trailing a banner that said "Hillary U Have the Right to Remain Silent," in reference to the Whitewater scandal that was brewing. She sang "Take Me Out to the Ballgame" with broadcaster Harry Caray during the 7th inning stretch.

Ambassadors. After George W. Bush took office in 2000, five current or former Major League owners became ambassadors. All five raised at least $100,000 for Bush's 2000 campaign:

Former Mariners owner George Argyros was ambassador to Spain beginning in 2001;

Cardinals co-owner and former Rangers co-owner Mercer Reynolds III was ambassador to Switzerland between 2001 and 2003;

Cardinals co-owner Stephen Brauer was ambassador to Belgium between 2001 and 2003;

Rangers co-owner Jeffrey Marcus was appointed as ambassador to Belgium in 2003, but never took over the post because of his divorce;

Former Rangers co-owner Craig Stapleton, and the husband of a Bush cousin, was ambassador to the Czech Republic between 2001 and 2003.

Congratulatory Calls/World Series.

"We kind of stunk up the joint tonight." — Cardinals manager Whitey Herzog to President Reagan after the 1985 Game 7 fiasco in which the Royals shut out the Cardinals 11–0 and pitcher Joaquin Andujar was ejected from the game.

Presidential phone calls became passé after Reagan overdid it during the 1980s. Reagan once had the following conversation with Pete Rose after Rose broke Ty Cobb's hit record (erroneously attributed by some sources to 1980 when the Phillies won the World Series — Reagan had not yet been elected):

President: This is the President of the United States... [more likely, this is Ronald Reagan]

Rose: How ya doin'.

President: I'm sorry I couldn't be there.

Rose: Well, you missed a helluva game.

Gold Passes. Presidents routinely receive gold season admission passes from Major League Baseball, though originally they came from individual clubs. Teddy Roosevelt supposedly was the first recipient, but one source identified Clark Griffith as having presented one to William Howard Taft in 1910.

Bodyguard. In early years the home team often assigned one of its bench players to act as a bodyguard for the president to keep errant foul balls from striking him.

Candidate Error. In September 1996 Hideo Nomo pitched a no-hitter for the Dodgers against the Rockies in Colorado. While campaigning in California for the presidency, Republican challenger Bob Dole congratulated Nomo and the "Brooklyn" Dodgers.

All-President's Team. All but nine (indicated by an asterisk) presidents have at least one Major League [sur]namesake:

Claudell Washington	Grover Cleveland Alexander
Bobby Adams	Chuck Harrison
Jesse Jefferson	_____ McKinley*
Dave Madison	_____ Roosevelt*
Zack Monroe	_____ Taft*
Sparky Adams	Willie Wilson
Reggie Jackson	Lou Harding
Deacon Van Buren	_____ Coolidge*
Chuck Harrison	Joe Hoover
Lefty Tyler	_____ Roosevelt*
_____ Polk*	_____ Truman*
Tony Taylor	"Ike" Eisenhower
_____ Fillmore*	John Kennedy
Jack Pierce	Randy Johnson
Jim Buchanan	Russ Nixon
Ezra Lincoln	Dan Ford
Cliff Johnson	Paul Carter
Jim Mudcat Grant	Rip Reagan
Jim Hayes	Guy Bush
Bill Garfield	Jim Clinton
_____ Arthur*	Homer Bush

Book. William B. Mead and Paul Dickson, *The Presidents' Game* (1993), covering the history of the game as it relates to each U.S. president from Teddy Roosevelt to Bill Clinton.

Press Box

"No Cheering in the Press Box." — Unwritten press box rule and the title of sportswriter Jerome Holtzman's 1974 book on 18 veteran sportswriters.

Accommodations for the press were not always made in early ballparks. In the early 20th century, writers in Detroit were forced to climb a ladder to sit on the roof, uncovered, in the snow. The Tigers responded in 1924 with the first press box elevator.

In 1938 the Pirates' management was so sure that there would be a World Series in that city that the club built a press box on the roof to accommodate the anticipated increase in reporters. The club did not made it to the postseason. Three losses to Chicago, including Gabby Hartnett's famous "***Homer in the Gloamin',***" helped knock the Pirates out of the race.

The press box at the Polo Grounds was at ground level in 1921.

Until the early 1950s, the Baseball Writers Association of America technically controlled whether an owner could enter his own press box.

Managing. A's owner Charlie Finley once had manager Joe Gordon manage from the press box. The experiment lasted one game.

Copy Paper. In 1995 Reds owner Marge Schott became upset over the amount of paper the Dodgers were using for their press notes. She was told that the Dodgers, like all visiting teams, use their own paper, but she complained about the wear and tear on her copy machines. The following week she asked her own publicity department to limit their notes to one piece of paper, but the Reds were in first place and information about the club was in demand. She then asked if one set of notes could be made and passed around the press box for everyone to share. In sympathetic response the Reds' public relations director received reams of blank copy paper from his counterparts around the league.

Pressure

"People say baseball players should go out and have fun. No way. To me, baseball is pressure. I always feel it. This is work. The fun is afterwards, when you shake hands." — Dennis Eckersley.

"32 pounds per square inch at sea level." — Pitcher Bill Lee on the pressure he feels during a pennant race.

"I don't feel a damn thing once the game starts. I honestly don't. But before the game, and afterward, the writers and the photographers and the questions. That's pressure. That's hard." — Roger Maris near the end of the 1961 season.

"I told him early on to avoid the pitfalls that plagued me. New York is a place that can swallow you up if you're not able to handle the pressure of success — and of failure. He handles it with class and dignity." — Darryl Strawberry on Derek Jeter.

Profanity　See *Foul Language*

Professionals

"When money comes in at the gate, sport flies out of the window." — Theodore Roosevelt.

"Like bounty hunters and soldiers of fortune, professional baseball players vested their destiny in the personal talents they put on the market each day. Their life was baseball and their accomplishments were greater because they were accomplishments made in the burly ring of the competitive sports jungle." — Ralph Andreano in *No Joy in Mudville* (1965).

See also *The Business of Baseball*.

Jim Creighton reportedly was the first professional baseball player when he pitched for the 1860 Brooklyn Excelsiors (see also *Deaths*). Some sources report that Al Reach (later of the *Reach Guide* and Reach Sporting Goods) was the first with the Brooklyn Eckfords and Philadelphia Athletics in the early 1860s. Reach perpetuated this apparent myth himself, as other records show that Lip Pike of the 1860s Philadelphia A's was an earlier professional.

Another early professional was George Wright, later of Cincinnati Red Stockings fame. He was paid to move from New York to the Washington Nationals in the early 1860s. Officially a government clerk, his working address was listed as a public park on Pennsylvania Avenue.

It has been estimated that 1 in 40,000 amateur baseball players signs a professional contract.

Profits, Losses and Expenses

"It is more profitable for me to have a team that is in contention for most of the season but finishes about fourth. A team like that will draw well enough during the first part of the season to show a profit for the year, and you don't have to give the players raises when they don't win." — Businessman and A's owner Connie Mack.

"If you depend solely on the people who know and love the game of baseball, you'll go broke by Mother's Day." — Entrepreneurial owner Bill Veeck, Jr.

"To figure our own expenses as low as they can possibly be made and I shall spend as little money as possible in running the Cincinnati club." — Philosophy of American Association Cincinnati Red Stockings owner Aaron Stern.

Early Profits.

"… and those games are, as we well know, the source of very great profits; so much so that the business of this association is becoming a very lucrative business productive of immense sums of money annually to those who engage in it." — Judge Ernest Thayer in a December 1885 meeting of the American Association New York Metropolitans.

The 1868 New York Mutuals earned $15,000 in profits, an enormous amount for that period. See *National League* for its early clubs' profit levels.

Albert Spalding admitted to earning over $750,000 in net profits in the late 1880s, though this might have included the profits from his sporting goods business.

1890s. The 1890 Players League caused an escalation of player salaries, but by 1892 both the Players League and American Association had folded. This left the 12-team National League with a Major League monopoly. The league began reeling from its high salaries, as 11 of the 12 teams were unprofitable. By the end of 1894 and after a series of salary cuts, profits were the best since 1889. Eleven of the 12 teams were in the black, with New York and Baltimore the most profitable.

At the end of the 1895 season, the *Reach Guide* reported that for the first time in history all Major League teams recorded a profit for the season. Toward the end of the decade profits began to fall as fan interest in the unwieldy 12-team league faded.

League Fund. In 1886 the National League used gate receipts to create a sinking fund to help run the league. Each club put up $5,000 in $1,000 annual installments drawn from their gate receipts. The same system was adopted by the American Association in 1887. The Major Leagues resurrected a form of the fund to pay off the Federal League clubs after that league folded in late 1915.

Early Income and Expenses. Annual team expenses in 1876 were approximately $20,000. The Cincinnati club's gate receipts at Hartford one day early the first season were $12.75. Cab and bus fare for the team was $12.00 and the team was charged $1.00 for a broken pane of glass: the team lost 25 cents that day.

In 1899 the Cleveland Spiders operated on $45,000. Average clubs incurred expenses of $66,500 each year. At the top, the Red Stockings incurred about $95,000 in expenses. Typical 1898 expenses included $40,000 for salaries for 18 players, $18,000 to the league for administration, $17,500 for groundskeeping, over $13,000 for travel, $4,000 for the manager's salary and $1,000 for insurance.

Early 20th Century. The National League had mixed results with profitability immediately after the 1903 merger with the American League. The New York Giants were the most profitable, while the Cardinals were, as always to that date, the heaviest in debt. By 1904 the National League had finished paying off the teams that were dropped when the league reduced its number from 12 to eight in 1900, allowing more money to go to profit.

The 1940s. *The Sporting News* estimated in 1948 that the total 1947 revenue from all sources in Organized Baseball in 1947 was $100 million. This worked out to the following:

Gate Receipts — $33 million (Majors)
$32 million (minors)
Concessions — $32.5 million
Radio, TV "and — $2.5 million
other privileges"

A profile of the 1945 Yankees provides a broad look at a team's operations in that period:

Income (%)	Expenses (%)
52.3 Home receipts	24.8 Salaries
16.0 Away receipts	23.4 Taxes
11.3 Concessions	18.7 Overhead
8.8 Player sales	9.0 Operating profit

4.4 Stadium rental

3.7 Radio

3.1 Exhibitions

0.4 Miscellaneous

8.8 Stadium operations

4.9 Scouting

4.0 Road expenses

3.7 Depreciation

1.5 Training

0.9 Interest

0.2 Player purchases

0.1 Miscellaneous

1950/1990 Comparison. In 1950 Major League Baseball teams had a combined $765,000 profit, which translates to approximately $3.9 million in 1990 dollars.

In the 1980s, though teams continued to plead poverty, they still appeared to be making money. In 1985 the owners contended that they lost a combined $92 million in 1982 and $66 million in 1983. They also claimed that the last time they made a profit was in 1978 when they collectively earned $4,586. These figures were proven incorrect when the **Collusion** lawsuits of the late 1980s revealed profitability in most markets.

From 1985 through 1989 Major League clubs acknowledged operating at a profit. Clubs showed a pretax profit of $214 million in 1989, an increase of 23% over 1988. Many said that the figures were misleading because the large market teams account for a disproportionately large share of profits.

Profits were down in 1990 because of record expenses primarily through wildly escalating salaries and a less lucrative television contract. Profits declined 33% to $142.9 million, but it was the fifth consecutive year that baseball made money. Total revenues for 1990 were $1,336,530,000 and expenses were $1,193,663,000. Revenue increased 7.7% but expenses increased 16.3%. Salaries were a primary factor, increasing 20.2% to an average of almost $600,000.

The Early 1990s.

"As Selig would confirm, there were decades when the owners wouldn't share handshakes, let alone dollars."— Sportswriter Ross Newhan, noting that Major League clubs' revenue increased from $1.6 billion in 1992, when Selig took over, to $4.1 billion in 2003. Revenue sharing was to increase from $20 million in 1992 to more than $300 million by 2006.

The following are Major League averages of revenue and expenses (note that many clubs have no luxury suite or parking revenue and that broadcast rates fluctuate enormously depending on the size of the market):

Operating Revenue

Regular season gate receipts	$ 20,000,000	34.02%
Spring training gate receipts	500,000	.85
Nat'l broadcasts	13,500,000	22.83
Local broadcasts	11,800,000	20.00
Concessions, net	5,000,000	8.52
Ads/publications	1,400,000	2.42
Parking, net	650,000	1.14
Suite rentals	715,000	1.21
Copyright royalty	500,000	.87
Play-offs/World Series	500,000	.85
National licensing	2,100,000	3.61
Miscellaneous	2,180,000	3.68
	$ 59,000,000	100.00

Operating Expenses

Major League player costs	$ 28,000,000	50.65%
Team operating expenses	4,500,000	8.10
Scouting and player dev.	7,200,000	13.02
Stadium ops.	5,400,000	9.80
Public relations, tickets, mktg.	2,500,000	4.55
General admin.	6,900,000	12.46
Commissioner's office	327,000	.59
Player Relations Committee	188,000	.34
Major League Scouting Bureau	127,000	.23
Umpire development	146,000	.26
	$55,300,000	100.00

Major League profits and losses from 1983 through 1995:

Year	Revenue	Exp.	P/L
1983	$521m	$588m	−$ 67m
1984	$624m	$665m	−$ 41m
1985	$718m	$725m	−$ 7m
1986	$791m	$780m	+ $ 11m
1987	$911m	$808m	+ $103m
1988	$ 1.0b	$886m	+ $122m
1989	$ 1.2b	$ 1.0b	+ $214m
1990	$ 1.3b	$ 1.2b	+ $142m
1991	$ 1.5b	$ 1.4b	+ $ 99m
1992	$ 1.7b	$ 1.6b	+ $ 22m
1993	$ 1.9b	$ 1.8b	+ $ 50m

(reportedly 12 of 28 teams lost money)

1994	$ 1.2b	$634m	− $376m
1995	$ 1.2b	$694m	− $326m

Strike Losses. Major League owners lost $105 million in 1981, not including $47 million in strike insurance reimbursement. As a result of the 1994–1995 player strike, Major League clubs claimed to have lost more than $700 million. The clubs lost $376 million in 1994, $326 million in 1995, and $185 million in 1996. Attendance was still down by 15% in 1996. The strike cost the clubs more than $900 million in revenue and the players about $350 million in salary. Other sources, such as *Financial World*, reported that losses were far less, and even included a profit of $59 million in 1995. Other sources reported that only seven clubs lost money in 1993 and three clubs lost money in 1995.

1995–1999.

"As Deep Throat once told Bob Woodward: 'Follow the money.' Greed has always been baseball's most reliable indicator."— Tim Sullivan in the *Cincinnati Enquirer*.

In July 2000 Major League Baseball published "The Report of the Independent Members of the Commissioner's Blue Ribbon Panel on Baseball Economics." The document stated that the Panel "represent[s] the interests of baseball fans." Note that 12 of the 16 panel members owned or operated Major League teams. The four "independent" members were Yale president Richard C. Levin, who drafted the owners' 1989 salary cap proposal; former Federal Reserve chairman Paul Volcker, who represented the owners on the *last* blue-ribbon economic panel, in 1992; former Senator George Mitchell, often mentioned as a possible commissioner; and columnist George Will, who served on the boards of both the Orioles and the Padres.

The report was based on financial data supplied by the clubs for the 1995–1999 seasons, without independent audit. It claimed that the only the Yankees, Indians and Rockies made any money, that the Braves lost $7 million despite consistent postseason appearances and national cable deals, and that the Dodgers lost $77 million in that span. The report indicated that the industry as a whole lost over $1 billion, or $35 million per team. In contrast, *Financial World* and *Forbes* estimate that Major League clubs collectively earned a net $400 million over this period.

The Panel's figures showed that from 1996 to 1999, gross revenues grew by more than $1 billion, while player salaries rose by only $550 million; yet the report does not account for the other $450 million.

Commentators pointed out that the report used September 1 salary figures, which artificially inflates payroll, as successful clubs take on high-value veterans for the pennant drive; the report did not pro-rate these salaries to account for the percentage of the season salary actually taken on by a club. They also noted that the years chosen for the study made a stronger link between payroll and performance. Although there is certainly a link, many low-payroll clubs have been successful in recent years.

2000s. In 2001 the Brewers were the Major League's most profitable franchise after receiving their portion of revenue sharing income. Without that revenue, the club was the fourth most profitable club. Gate receipts in 2001 were $1.38 billion and broadcast revenue was $571 million. The Yankees led with $98 million in gate receipts and the Red Sox were second at $89 million. The Expos were at the low end at $6.4 million, with the Marlins at $16.7 million. In local broadcast revenue, the Yankees led again with $56.7 million, followed by the Mets at $47.2 million (compared to $74 million in gate receipts). The Expos were last at $536,000 and the Brewers were next-lowest at $5.9 million.

In 2002 the Mariners were baseball's most profitable club with net revenue of $23.3 million. The Yankees were second at $16.1 million and the Giants led the National League at $13.9 million. The Orioles were next in the American League at $12.4 million and the Cubs were at $11.9 million. The Mets followed at $11.6 million. The biggest losers of 2002:

Dodgers	$25 million
Rangers	$24.5 million
Blue Jays	$23.9 million
Diamondbacks	$22.2 million
Marlins	$14.9 million
Angels (World Series winners)	$ 3.5 million.

In 2003, new owner Arte Moreno indicated that the club would lose $7 million that season and an another $14 million in 2004. That didn't stop him from going on a free agent spending spree before that season, coughing up over $172 million for several key free agents, including Bartolo Colon and, most significantly, Vladimir Guerrero.

The 2003 Yankees had revenue of $238 million. Second were the Red Sox at $190 million. Six other clubs had revenue of between $150–$170 million. Nine clubs had revenue under $110 million, including the A's, Royals, Blue Jays, Twins, Devil Rays and Brewers. The Expos were the lowest at $81 million.

Single Player Affecting Profits. Profitability because of a single player is often quantifiable. Fernando Valenzuela in 1981 and Nolan Ryan in 1990 are prime examples of players, usually pitchers, that could increase attendance and revenue by large amounts on days they played. In 1995 Hideo Nomo caused Dodger attendance to increase to 41,000 when he pitched, up from an average of 36,000. Mark McGwire during his 1998 home run season and Barry Bonds throughout the 2000s had a direct impact on road attendance.

Hidden Profits. To help disguise the profitability of Major League Baseball, in the 1910s the *Spalding* and *Reach Guides* stopped printing attendance figures.

More recently, owners simply inflated or decreased the monies paid or earned by interrelated entities to hide profits. For example, Ted Turner can show a lower profit for the Braves by having the club charge itself exorbitantly by Turner Field—which Turner owns. Owners can also pay themselves or family members large salaries to hide profits, which the Brewers were reported to be doing in the 1990s.

Players' Percentage of Revenue. Former Players Association executive director Marvin Miller estimated that in 1966 the players received approximately 12% of the gross revenue earned by Major League teams. By 1982 that percentage was estimated to be 35% and in 1984 it was 40% of baseball's $600 million in revenue. Eight years later they received more than 50% of the $1.6 billion in revenue. In 1996 payroll was $1.120 billion and comprised 63% of the industry's $1.8 billion revenue. In 1997 payroll was $1.2 billion, or 59% of $2.1 billion.

Revenue Sharing. Before the late 1990s, when they were finally adopted, Major League Baseball debated whether to institute a salary cap and profit sharing in a form similar to that used by basketball since 1979. The idea was implemented in 1919 in one minor league (probably as a result of the hard times brought on by World War I) and had no apparent affect on the game.

At the January 1994 meeting, Major League owners fell one vote short of approving a revenue-sharing plan. The plan was blocked by a bloc of large-market teams—Baltimore, Boston, Colorado, Los Angeles, New York (Mets and Yankees), St. Louis and Toronto. The small-market clubs later were able to push the plan through, contingent upon the players approving a salary cap (which later occurred).

In March 1996 the owners agreed to change their revenue sharing agreement on television revenues. This would give some clubs as much as $4 million and cost other clubs as much as $7 million. The vote was 26–1–1, with the Mets voting against it and the Orioles abstaining. The plan was then submitted to the Players Association, which finally agreed in late 1996, and has resulted in significant payments to lower-performing clubs.

In 1997 the top five clubs had to pay a 35% tax on all payroll above $51 million. Any club within $500,000 of the threshold also had to pay. The revenue sharing was phased in at 60% in 1997, 80% in 1998 and was fully implemented in 1999. The checks are mailed monthly from the wealthier teams beginning in April.

The second level of revenue sharing is based on the amount of overall revenue generated by each club. An average is determined, and then the clubs exceeding the average pay into a fund that is distributed to the clubs who fall below the average. In 2003 the Yankees paid in $52.7 million at the top end of the scale, and the Expos received $29.5 million at the bottom end. Teams at the end of the scale shared $169 million in 2002, $220 million in 2003, and approximately $270 million in 2004.

The Yankees paid $80 million in revenue sharing in 2004. This figure is 34% of locally generated revenue (minus ballpark expenses), as called for in the new collective bargaining agreement. This is an increase from the 20% level of the previous agreement. This money is put into a pool and divided among all 30 teams.

Note that revenue sharing is different from the luxury tax (see *Collective Bargaining Agreements*).

Postseason Splits.

The Commissioner's Share. The commissioner's office receives 15% of all World Series receipts, and a set percentage of the League

Championship Series receipts, as agreed upon by the commissioner and the Major League Executive Council.

The Players' Share. 60% of gate receipts from the first three games of each division series.

60% of gate receipts from the first four games of each league championship series.

60% of gate receipts from the first four games of each World Series.

36% to the World Series winner

24% to the World Series loser

24% to the LCS losers (12% to each loser)

12% to the division series losers (3% to each loser)

4% to the four second-place non-wild card teams (1% to each team).

Minor Leagues/1980s– . By the late 1980s and 1990s minor league clubs were realizing a 5–10% profit on gross income, especially if they had a Major League affiliation. Some of the most prosperous clubs were averaging 20% profits.

Debt-To-Value Ratio Rule. See *Team Sales.*

Promotions

"It's not very often we get to see the Lone Ranger and Toronto in the same night." — Rangers manager Bobby Bragan on that night's game against the Toronto Blue Jays and a promotional appearance by Clayton Moore, who played The Lone Ranger on television.

"[Baseball] does not need midgets, exploding scoreboards, fireworks, giveaway programs or any of the other rather pathetic sales gimmicks that have been tried from time to time as a substitute for a good ball team and sound baseball." — "The Old Timer" in W.R. Burnett's *The Roar of the Crowd* (1964).

"This idea might be carried farther. A nine made up of the wild Australian children as the battery, the transparent-headed baby as short stop, Zulus on the bases, and bearded women and living skeletons in the field, would go far toward satisfying even the strongest craving for novelty." — June 9, 1883, article in *Harper's Weekly*, criticizing the "novelty" baseball being played (see also **Amputees**).

"These new Orioles yield to no club in the promotional pennant race. There's Floppy Hat Night, Squeeze Bottle Night, Cooler Bag Night. There's an item called the NationsBank Orioles Batting Helmet Bank, and there's the highly prized Mid-Atlantic Milk Marketing Cal Ripken Growth Poster." — Richard Ben Cramer in *Sports Illustrated.*

See also **Field Days**, **Knothole Gangs**, **Ladies Day**, **Opening Day**, **Practical Jokes and Pranks** and **Stunts.**

Schedules. In 1894 the National League instituted a rule prohibiting a change in scheduled game times by more than one-half hour. This was done primarily because of promotions that were scheduled in conjunction with games, such as a Wild West show in St. Louis.

"Days." In 1915 various teams held a number of "days" in an attempt to boost attendance during the Federal League challenge, including Boosters Day, Flag Day, Newsboys Day and Schoolchildren's Day.

Frank Bancroft.

"Banny's life personified sunshine. He made dark days brighter. He filled life's score with assists of good cheer…. The Great Umpire called him out while his heart was still young. Unafraid to die, he smiled as he crossed eternity's home plate." — Words on a tablet erected at the entrance to Redland Field in May 1921 for Bancroft, known as the "Old Warhorse."

Former field manager Frank Bancroft was a Major League business manager (general manager) from 1892 until his death in 1921. He was the first to heavily use promotions as a regular part of a baseball operation. He staged races, throwing competitions and took teams to Cuba. He also was the first to stage a wedding at home plate. He had the perfect background for the job, having been an advance man on the late 19th century vaudeville circuit.

Bill Veeck, Jr. Veeck pioneered a number of promotions and staged many stunts — such as batting a *Midget* and having fans act as *Managers* during games. He also was the first to install an exploding *Scoreboard*. In Cleveland he once gave away 100 gallons of ice cream and a year's supply of sardines. He staged many promotional nights that he did not advertise in advance, such as putting S & H Green Stamps under selected seats in Cleveland. One of his earliest promotions was a footrace between George Case and track star Jesse Owens.

Veeck once staged "Good Ol' Joe Earley Night," for an auto plant night watchman named Joe Earley. Earley had written a letter to a local newspaper complaining that Veeck never had a special night for the average fan. On September 28, 1948, 60,405 showed up to watch the 26-year-old ex-serviceman and his wife receive a new Ford convertible, a Model T Ford, clothes, luggage, books and appliances. Earley also received a few gag gifts: an outhouse, a swaybacked horse and a circus car complete with backfires. Other fans received livestock that night.

Veeck held a boomerang night in Cleveland and sold 10-cent beer. In the 9th inning when a fly ball tied the game, the fans ran on the field and the game was forfeited to the visitors. On September 28, 1947, Veeck passed out 20,000 orchids worth $30,000 on "Princess Aloha Orchid Night."

Veeck would tape raffle tickets under seats for the winner to cash in on a ton of salt, a barrel of pickles, a truckload of fertilizer, 50,000 nuts and bolts, baby-sitting service for night games, a thousand ice cream bars, or a burro.

He had a player named Jackie Price, who appeared in only seven games for the Indians during his one-year career in 1946. Though lacking on the field, he was a great performer: playing catch while standing on his head, throwing multiple balls simultaneously and accurately. He also wore snakes around his waist through his belt loops.

Veeck once gave away 500 tuxedo rentals to a single fan that all had to be used on the same day. The fan and 499 friends showed up at a game and all sat together in their white tuxedos. Veeck bought the beer for the whole group.

Veeck once had future 300-game winner Early Wynn ride out on a white horse in a black mask and black hat at Comiskey Park. He fell off when the horse spooked and reared.

His most famous promotion after the Gaedel midget novelty was Disco Demolition Night, which was the all-time **Promotion That Backfired** (see below). Because he rejuvenated baseball in Chicago with the White Sox in 1976, the fans staged a Bill Veeck Appreciation Night, but it was rained out.

Mike Veeck.

"The Grand Pooh-Bah of minor league marketing." — Orlando Magic vice president Pat Williams on Mike Veeck, son of legendary promoter Bill Veeck. The son's philosophy is simple: "Make 75% of the crowd laugh, annoy 15%, and who cares about the other 10%?"

Veeck has staged a variety of promotions, including Call in Sick Day (the club faxes excuses to fans' employers), nuns giving massages atop the dugout, Race the Mannequin Night (fan against mannequin from base to base, but the mannequin never moves), and Fan Bobblehead Night (winning fan gets a doll made in his image).

He had a trained pig bring balls to the home plate umpire for the St. Paul Saints, and each year the fans voted on a new name for the mascot: they have included "Kevin Bacon" and "The Notorious P.I.G."). The Viagra drug-makers sponsored a night on which all males over 21 were given inflatable baseball bats.

On Lawyer's Night at Sioux Falls, attorneys were charged double the regular admission to the game and were billed every half inning (proceeds went to Legal Aid). Veeck also promoted Enron Night, which featured paper shredders and attendance figures were continually revised downward during the game.

Charlie Finley. The Kansas City and Oakland A's owner staged a number of promotional stunts. He once had the team's starting line-up delivered to the field by limousine and another time by mule train. He created Harvey the mechanical rabbit that popped out of the ground and presented balls to the umpire; brought sheep and a shepherd to graze behind the rightfield wall; and brought in team mascot "Charlie O.," a mule. Because he was so cheap, Finley was once sued by the Oakland Coliseum commission for $1 million due to his failure to promote the team.

Ray Kroc. The McDonald's hamburger king and Padres owner gave free burgers for Sunday wins upon presentation of a ticket stub at any local McDonald's.

Bat Day. The first bat day was promoted by Rudie Schaffer of the White Sox.

"Ladies" Day. A hybrid of Ladies Day was initiated by Charlie Finley's A's in the early 1970s when the club staged "Hot Pants Day" on which all women in this item of clothing were allowed in free. The team also sponsored a fashion show before the game.

In 1971 the A's held Hot Pants Night. Any woman who paraded on the field would receive two tickets to a future game. The A's expected 500 participants, but the 5,000 women on the field received 10,000 free tickets.

The 1977 Braves showed questionable taste by staging a wet tee shirt contest; the winner's father was a Methodist minister.

Nudity. A Palm Springs minor league club scheduled a nude spectator day, but the overwhelming (positive) response of fans forced the club to cancel the event.

That's Cold. In 2003 the minor league Bisbee-Douglas (Arizona) Copper Kings held a Ted Williams Night, on which the first 500 fans received free Popsicles; homage to Williams' frozen head just down the road in Scottsdale.

Rednecks. In 2003 the independent Fort Worth Cats staged hog-calling and pig's-feet-eating contests to make fun of their opponents, the Jackson (Miss.) Senators.

Shredding It. In 2003 the Portland Beavers gave free admission to anyone named Arthur or Andersen (think accountants); those fans were entitled to shred documents and play "massive debt hide-and-go-seek" for gift certificates to local businesses.

Bobblehead Dolls.

"I don't think she's going to get traded or get a DUI." — Mike Becker, president of bobblehead doll maker Funko, on why his company doesn't make athletes the subject of his dolls and sticks to cartoon characters like Betty Boop.

In 2002 the Devil Rays purchased 15,000 Ryan Dempster bobblehead dolls, but not before trading him to the Reds.

In 2004 the Fort Worth Cats of the Independent Central League held an auction on eBay for the rights to put a fan's head on a bobblehead doll to be given away to 1,500 fans at a 2004 game. The winner was David Spurlin of Richardson, Texas, who paid $5,200. Spurlin, the CEO of Microwave Transmission Systems, asked to put his 19-year-old son's head on the doll. There were 66 total bids from 34 bidders.

Combating Ineptitude. The 2003 Tigers, nearly the losingest team ever, tried to ease the pain by hiring entrepreneur Mike Veeck to handle their promotions, which included Duct Tape Night, Magic Night, Christian concert night, and Baseball Card Blitz, in which the club threw 50,000 packs of baseball cards on the field and let the kids have at them.

Promotions That Backfired.
Balls.

"Giving away baseballs is a bad idea. Why not give them hand grenades?" — Umpire Bruce Froemming after fans pelted players with free baseballs at Candlestick Park. The Dodgers lost a game by *Forfeit* in 1995 when fans threw souvenir baseballs on the field in the 9th inning of a one-run game.

In April 1997 Brewers fans littered the field with giveaway baseballs, causing three injuries and threatening the first forfeit in the club's history. The "Spring Madness" promotion allowed bleacher seats to be purchased for $1. The league offices later directed that similar promotions not give out balls before the games.

Beer.

"The Battle of Little Big Beer." — On June 4, 1974, the Indians held Ten-Cent Beer Night. The 25,000 fans drank 60,000 10-ounce beers. Over 500 fans, some with knives, ran onto the field during a 5–5 tie in the 9th inning and attacked Rangers outfielder Jeff Burroughs, who had refused to give his glove to a fan. Players from both clubs used bats to fend off the fans. The Rangers were awarded a 9–0 forfeit.

Cannon. On June 19, 1975, a U.S. Army unit appeared at a Yankees/Angels game at Shea Stadium (during renovation of Yankee Stadium). In honor of the 200th birthday of the Army, the unit fired off a cannon during the National Anthem. It blew an enormous hole in the center field fence.

Willie Mays. The San Diego Padres held a promotion for Willie Mays' 600th home run. He was scheduled to be in town with the Giants for a 1969 weekend series, already having hit number 599. Padres management had been told that Mays would not play in Friday night's game. In the days preceding the series the Padres promoted the Saturday game by opening their left field bleachers for the first time and announcing that anyone catching Mays' 600th home run would win a new Chevrolet. Unfortunately, Mays pinch-hit in the 9th inning of Friday night's game and hit number 600 into the empty bleachers. The Padres were forced to give Saturday game refunds to whoever wanted them.

This story was related by Padres general manager Buzzie Bavasi in his autobiography. However, the date on which Mays hit number 600, September 22, was a Monday, so it is unclear whether Bavasi's story is a fabrication or he simply had the days wrong.

Disco Demolition. On July 12, 1979, the White Sox held a "Disco Demolition Night" that failed miserably, resulting in one of the more famous forfeits of all time. The evening was sponsored by local radio station 98 WLUP-FM and was the brainchild of deejay Steve Dahl, who wore a military helmet during the detonation. The driving force behind the promotion was owner Bill Veeck's son Mike (identified incorrectly as his son-in-law in some sources), who hated disco music.

More than 50,000 fans showed up for the doubleheader, each paying the 98-cent admission and bringing a disco record. The fans "frisbeed" the records onto the field during the first game, causing delays during a 4–1 Tigers win.

The White Sox burned the records between games. More than 5,000 fans ran onto the field during the bonfire and tore up the grass.

The fans would not return to their seats despite a plea over the public address system by Veeck. The umpires called off the second game and American League president Lee MacPhail later forfeited the game to the Tigers. There were 37 arrests and a 76-minute delay before the forfeit was declared by crew chief Dave Phillips.

Banners.

"Beatles, Schmeatles, We Have the Mets"—Banner at Shea Stadium.

The New York Mets traditionally have sponsored a Banner Day, initiated in the club's first year in 1962.

Turn Ahead the Clock. On July 27, 1999, the "Mercury" Mets hosted the Pirates in the first of Major League Baseball's "Turn Ahead the Clock" nights. Each team wore futuristic uniforms and the scoreboard playfully provided computerized graphics that added extra eyes and pointy ears to player photos, and players were described as playing futuristic positions such as "left quadrant" (left field).

Zero Attendance Promotion. See *Attendance*—Low Attendance.

Pajama Party. On September 11, 1999, the Twins rescheduled a game for 11:05 am to avoid conflict with a University of Minnesota football game later that day at the Metrodome. The club offered free admission to anyone who wore their pajamas. Only 11,222 fans saw Twins pitcher Eric Milton throw a 7–0 no-hitter against the Angels.

Fanny Vote. In June 2002, when players strike talk was rampant, the Independent Northern League Gary Southshore RailCats played the St. Paul Saints, owned by Mike Veeck. The Saints gave away seat cushions featuring the likenesses of Bud Selig and Donald Fehr on opposite sides. During the seventh inning stretch, an informal poll revealed that 90% of the fans were sitting on the Bud-facing side of the cushion.

Sleepover. On June 8, 2002, the Expos beat the White Sox 2–1 and then Chicago hosted its inaugural Fan Sleepover at Comiskey Park, allowing fans to sleep overnight on the field.

Promotions for the Players. Rod Kanehl received 50,000 trading stamps when he hit the first grand slam by a Mets player on July 6, 1962.

The 1962 Mets had circles painted near the foul lines of the Polo Grounds. If one of the club's players hit a ball in the circle, he accumulated points toward winning a boat at the end of the season. Frank Thomas tried to pull so many balls down the foul line that manager Casey Stengel once chastised him, saying: "If you want to be a sailor, join the Navy!"

Richie Ashburn received a boat from the Mets for being its Most Valuable Player. He later said that the boat sank and the salvage operator who bought the remnants bounced his check to him.

See also *Advertising*—Ballpark Fences.

Season Tickets. In 1991 the Buffalo Bisons staged a promotion to commemorate selling one million tickets for their fourth consecutive season. The team offered a $1 million prize to the fan whose name was drawn in the same inning that a player from the home team hit a grand slam. Eddie Zambrano was the only Bison to bat with the bases loaded during the designated inning, and he missed a home run by 25 feet.

In 1992 the Bisons did the same promotion, and Zambrano again was the only player to bat with the bases loaded during the drawing. Unfortunately, Brian Dorsett was picked off second, ending the drama. Zambrano did not hit a three-run homer.

Slow Learners. The Detroit Tigers were one of the last teams to implement promotional days, in part because of conservative long-time owner Walter Briggs, Sr., who died in the mid–1950s.

Cheerleaders.

"We're from Anaheim, couldn't be prouder! None of our players sniff illegal white powder."—Mike Downey of the *Los Angeles Times* after Disney took control of the Angels in 1996; the company added cheerleaders to the club's promotional efforts.

Protective Association of Professional Baseball Players (1900–1903)

This players *Union* was formed in June 1900 amid fighting among the leagues. It lasted for about three years until peace was restored.

Protective Cups

See also *Crotch*.

Catcher Claude Berry is credited with introducing the protective cup to Major League Baseball. He played sporadically from 1904 through 1915. His only regular playing time was for the 1914–1915 Pittsburgh Stogies of the Federal League.

Reds catcher Johnny Bench broke seven protective cups while catching.

Protests

"Wear this and play on our team for awhile."—Casey Stengel offering his uniform to an umpire in protest of a number of bad calls. In 1918 Stengel was fined $50 for taking off his Pirates uniform and giving it to the umpire. According to one source, instead of paying the fine, Stengel enlisted in the Navy. Stengel (and many others) brought out a flashlight in protest when he thought it was too dark to continue play.

On September 22, 1954, the Reds and Braves finished a protested game in Milwaukee in the morning, and later that day the Braves hosted the Cardinals.

Pitcher Lefty Gomez once batted against Bob Feller when darkness was setting in. In protest, Gomez purportedly lit matches at home plate and set them out around the batter's box. The umpire told him that it was not necessary because they could still see Feller. Gomez replied that he was not worried about that, but he wanted to make sure Feller could see *him*.

Rule Change. In 1978 the rules for protested games were changed so that a game need not be replayed from the point of the infraction when a protest is upheld. The game would only be ordered replayed if "in the opinion of the League President the violation adversely affected the protesting team's chances of winning the game" (Rule 4.19). The rule change was designed to protect a team that won a game by a wide margin from being penalized because of a technicality.

Personal Protest. In May 1993 Braves third baseman Terry Pendleton was upset that his pitcher did not hit the first batter of the inning with a pitch in retaliation for a shot taken by teammate Deion Sanders earlier in the game. Pendleton abruptly stormed off the field during the at-bat and was fined by the club.

Providence Grays

National League 1878–1885

"The Grays made it more of a battle the next two seasons [1881 and 1882], but whenever the Providence boys threatened, the White Stockings took a hitch in their blue pants and smacked them down."—Fred Lieb in *The Baseball Story* (1950).

Providence came into the league in 1878 with Milwaukee and Indiana to fill the void left by the departure of Hartford, Louisville and St. Louis.

In 1879 Providence won the pennant behind the pitching of John Montgomery Ward. George Wright became the only manager in history to win a pennant in his only year with a team. The Grays featured Paul Hines, the first National League Triple Crown winner and first repeat batting champion (sort of, see *Batting Champions*). Another key player was future Hall of Fame outfielder Jim O'Rourke.

The club was losing money by 1882 and almost folded during the season, but additional capital contributions by the stockholders gave it a reprieve. The Grays purportedly almost folded again in 1884 when they lost star pitcher Charlie Sweeney to the rival Union Association, but pitcher Old Hoss Radbourn more than made up for the loss. The club won the pennant and defeated the New York Metropolitans of the American Association in the championship series in terrible weather conditions. After the 1885 season, the Boston Red Stockings bought up all the Providence players for $6,600 and the club folded.

The club played its games at the Messer Street Grounds. It was the first ballpark to have a screen behind home plate to guard against foul balls hit into the stands.

Pseudonyms See *College Players* and *Names*

Psychic

"There is legend that he is psychic, that in the wee small hours, eerie, ghostly figures float over his bed whispering magic words of baseball wisdom, which are gratefully received by the docile subject." — Sportswriter Joe Williams on Yankee manager Joe McCarthy.

The founder of the Psychic Friends Network bought Eddie Murray's 500th *Home Run* ball.

Psychological Problems

"Mike Ivie is a $40 million dollar airport with a $30 control tower." — Rick Monday.

"I have no trouble with the 12 inches between my elbow and my palm. It's the seven inches between my ears that's bent." — Wacky 1970's reliever Tug McGraw, who, ironically, died of a brain tumor.

"Some people have a chip on their shoulder. Billy has a whole lumberyard." — Jim Murray on Yankee manager Billy Martin.

"He doesn't want to play in St. Louis. He doesn't want to play on turf. He doesn't want to play when we go into Montreal. He doesn't want to play in the Astrodome. He doesn't want to play in the rain. The other eighty games he's all right." — Cardinals manager Whitey Herzog on temperamental shortstop Garry Templeton.

"Baseball for the Insane. The Remedial Virtues of the National Game Recognized." — Title of an 1891 article promoting baseball as therapy for mental disorders.

"I saw the guy twice and I thought he was crazier than I was." — Reds pitcher Rob Dibble on the psychologist he was ordered to see.

"He's turned his life around. He used to be depressed and miserable. Now he's miserable and depressed." — Harry Kalas on Garry Maddox.

"The last two, three years, I haven't been happy. I think if I'm happy, I wouldn't get hurt at all." — Crybaby A's outfielder Rickey Henderson.

"He's mentally unavailable. Physically, he can play." — A's manager Tony LaRussa on Henderson.

See also *Eccentrics, Personality* and *Suicides*.

Tim Keefe. The 19th century pitching star suffered a nervous breakdown after hitting Boston's Jack Burdock in the temple in 1887. Burdock only missed a few weeks of the season and Keefe could not have missed much time either, as he won 35 games in 56 starts.

Ty Cobb. Much of Cobb's drive to succeed and his vicious attitude toward opponents (and often teammates) has been traced to the fact that his mother blew his father out the window with a shotgun blast in the middle of the night. Cobb apparently never recovered from the trauma.

Jimmy Piersall. The Red Sox outfielder is probably the most famous example of a baseball player who suffered mental problems while playing. The Red Sox sent him down to the minors in 1952 after he suffered a breakdown. The club then suspended him while he was in the minor leagues.

From January 1952 to August 1952, Piersall remembers nothing until he woke up in a mental institution. He was able to come back and complete a 17-year Major League career in 1967. In his first game back he was 6-for-6. Piersall's first autobiography, *Fear Strikes Out*, with Al Hirshberg (1955), led to a 1957 movie of the same name starring Anthony Perkins as Piersall. The choice of Perkins irritated Piersall: "I don't know why they ever picked Anthony Perkins to play me. He threw a baseball like a girl. I hated the movie."

Piersall once yelled to White Sox general manager Frank Lane in the right field pavilion after Lane had criticized second baseman Nellie Fox: "Why don't you jump and get it over with?"

Piersall's second autobiography was *The Truth Hurts*, with Richard Whittingham (1984).

Johnny Evers. Known as the Crab for his rotten disposition, Evers suffered a nervous breakdown during his tenth season, 1911, and played in only 46 games. He returned to play three more solid seasons before slowing down and retiring in 1917 (though he made two cameo appearances in later years).

Josh Hamilton. Hamilton, the Devil Rays' top pick in 1999 and *Baseball America's* top prospect in 2001, rejoined the club's senior minor league affiliate in 2003, after a mysterious six week absence. He had to "address certain non-baseball matters." His mother told the press, "he's fine, he's just taking some personal time like everyone else." In February 2004 he was suspended for violating baseball's drug policy, a follow-up to his missing the entire 2003 season because of drug problems. He was also fined $25,000. A succinct summary of his career at cbs.sportsline's fantasy player news website: "Hamilton's career has been beset by everything from injuries, to car crashes, to depression and now, a drug suspension. The former No. 1 overall pick from 1999 is not worth owning in any Fantasy league."

Alex Johnson.

"Alex Johnson used to position himself in the outfield not according to the hitter, but according to where the shade was." — *Sports Illustrated* writer Ron Fimrite on the eccentricities of the enigmatic 1970s outfielder. Johnson suffered severe psychiatric problems in the early 1970s while with the Angels. He was suspended by the club and ultimately placed on the restricted list by commissioner Bowie Kuhn. The matter went to *Arbitration* over whether a player could be placed on the disabled list for emotional problems as well as physical problems. The arbitrator ruled that Johnson was entitled to be on the disabled list. He recovered sufficiently to play five more relatively solid seasons.

Tony Horton. Horton hit 27 home runs and had 93 RBIs in

1969, but emotional problems put him in the hospital and he was never the same. His career ended the next year at age 25. See also *Eephus Pitch* for Horton's reaction to striking out on a blooper pitch by Steve Hamilton.

Ed Whitson. Whitson was traded to the Yankees for the 1985 season but soon realized that he could not pitch in Yankee Stadium because of the crowd abuse. He was traded to the Padres midway through the 1986 season and had moderate success (with a high of 16 wins in 1989).

Bob Elliott. The infielder was unable to perform well in Pittsburgh in part because of constant booing by fans after a bad day at third base. After he was traded to the Braves, he became the league's Most Valuable Player in 1947.

Kevin Saucier. The pitcher retired at age 26 in 1982 because his fear of hitting batters made it impossible for him to go to the ballpark. He finished with a record of 15–11 and 19 saves over five seasons.

Art Passarella. Pitcher Johnny Sain of the Yankees was called out by umpire Art Passarella in the 10th inning of Game 5 of the 1952 World Series even though he was clearly safe. Passarella was later attacked verbally by commissioner Ford Frick. Because of the pressure Passarella left baseball during the 1953 season.

Willie Horton. See *Eephus Pitch* — **Folly Floater** for the problems experienced by Tiger outfielder Willie Horton.

Pete Harnisch. In early 1997 the Mets starting pitcher was put on the disabled list suffering from depression and insomnia. He had been struggling emotionally since giving up smokeless tobacco three weeks earlier.

Bubba Trammell. In 2004 Trammell settled a grievance with the Yankees that resolved his departure from the club in 2003. The outfielder had left the club on June 30 that season for unspecified reasons. As a result, the Yankees terminated his contract, which had $2.5 million remaining. The union contended that he should not have been placed on the restricted list (and not get paid), rather than the disabled list (getting paid), because he suffered from depression. He signed with the Dodgers in 2004, but was cut at the end of spring training. He then played in the minor leagues with Tampa Bay that season.

Fan Obsession. In 2004 a man was ordered to undergo psychiatric examination after throwing screaming tantrums at Shea Stadium and stalking Mets general manager Steve Phillips.

Psychology

"Half this game is 90% mental." — Phillies manager Danny Ozark.

"To a pitcher, a base hit is the perfect example of negative feedback." — Pilots outfielder Steve Hovley.

"The game had many aspects of interest from a psychoanalyst's point of view. It centers around a father figure, who stands on a raised mound of earth. All around him is lush, green grass. Only the earth on which the father walks is bare. (Is this mound the burial place of his ancestors or only a symbolic burial ground?...)" — Howard L. Katzander in "The Case History of Joey J., Baseball Player" (1958).

"Joe was always into books, anything to get an edge. Sometimes it was like a philosophy class. 'If a tree falls in New York, will Todd Zeile hit the curveball.' Stuff like that." — Expos catcher Darrin Fletcher on former Expos pitching coach Joe Kerrigan, who later coached with the Red Sox.

"The Babe's id appears to have been relatively unimpeded in its quest for satisfaction. Through sex and food, Ruth nurtured the unresolved aspects of his infantile self with abandon." — Psychology professor Adam Cox speaking at a conference honoring the centennial of Ruth's birthday. Buddy Hassett, who played when Ruth was a celebrity coach for the Dodgers briefly in 1938, put it more succinctly: "He had a great digestive tract."

Early Use. In 1938 Cubs owner Phil Wrigley hired University of Illinois psychology professor Coleman Robert Griffith to test the team's reflexes and flexibility.

In 1950 Browns owner Bill Veeck hired psychologist David F. Tracy to help the players. Tracy tried to use psychology and hypnosis to bring the team out of its perennial cellar position. He left the club on May 31, 1950, when the Browns were 8–25 and in last place. Tracy later wrote *The Psychologist at Bat* (1951). Among the stories he related was pitcher Bert Shepard's comeback as a minor league pitcher using hypnosis to help overcome the loss of his right leg (see also **Amputees**).

Hypnotist. Dodger stolen base king Maury Wills hired a hypnotist to help him deal with sore legs and cartilage problems during the 1962 season, in which he stole 104 bases.

In Vogue. The Cardinals hired a part-time psychologist in 1982, the first team to do so since the Browns' ill-fated attempt in 1950. A few clubs in the 1980s and early 1990s used psychologists, including the White Sox, A's, Padres, Dodgers, Orioles and Astros.

The Dodgers hired a team psychiatrist in late 1990, D. Herndon Harding, Jr., the great-great-grandnephew of President Harding.

In May 2003 the Mets fired their psychologist because he was breaking rules by hanging out in the dugout. ESPN Sal Paolantino's response: "Helloooo? If there's any team in baseball that needs a shrink on the bench, it's the [last place] Mets!"

In 2004 Dave Austin, former professional tennis player and college baseball player, rock band promoter/manager, and computer entrepreneur, was hired by the Dodgers to do a one-shot spring training appearance as a consultant to the pitching staff on visualization and the mental preparation for the game. Austin was so popular that the Dodgers hired him for the season for any player that wanted help, and manager Jim Tracy even asked Austin to advise his three sons. Austin also consulted for a Royals catching prospect during the season.

Testing. The Athletic Motivation Inventory (AMI) has been administered since 1969 to minor league prospects. It tries to establish a psychological profile by asking the players to answer a series of multiple choice questions such as "I always do exactly what the coach tells me to do," with "Always," "Never," or "Sometimes." Another source reported, apparently erroneously given the foregoing date, that the first psychological test may have been administered by scout Dick Bogard in 1972 while he was with the Astros. The subject was Dick Ruthven, who went on to pitch for 14 years in the Major Leagues.

Public Address Announcers

"Hearing Bob's voice in the Bronx makes me feel I am in Westminster Abbey." — George Vecsey on public address announcer Bob Sheppard of the Yankees in *A Year in the Sun* (1989). Sheppard spent 43 years announcing for the Yankees.

"Attention, Please! Will the fans along the left field railing please remove their clothing." — Brooklyn Dodgers public address announcer Tex Rickard.

"Let's see ... The Kings are a lockout, the Angels were a walkout and the Rams might move out. Gee, fellas, was it something I said?" — Los Angeles P.A. announcer David Courtney in the fall of 1994.

"One thing I've learned is that if you make a mistake, if you say it with a deep enough voice, you can get away with it." — Cubs P.A. announcer Paul Friedman.

See also *Women in Baseball* — Public Address Announcers.

Early Announcers.

"I always thought that the advent of the public address system in ball parks was Steamer's saddest day." — Sportswriter Freddy Russell on legendary minor league umpire Harry "Steamboat" Johnson, who delighted in bellowing the pregame lineups without a megaphone.

In the early days a megaphoned announcer or the umpire provided line-ups at the beginning of the game by running to each section of the ballpark to call out the information. In 1903 E. Lawrence Phillips reportedly became the first megaphoned public address announcer, for the Washington Senators. He provided lineup information to the spectators and relieved umpires of that duty. He retired in 1928, but not before all other teams copied him.

On-field announcers disappeared by mid-century except at Wrigley Field. Well into the 1960s, restaurant waiter Pat Pieper sat on a camp chair on the field near the screen behind home plate with a hand-microphone until he was forced into the press box. Pieper began as the Cubs P.A. announcer in 1916 and worked for the club until 1974. Pieper was on the field and in a famous photograph of Gabby Hartnett hitting his 1938 "Homer in the Gloamin'."

Bing Devine of the Cardinals was the first general manager to have the public address announcers repeat the line-up throughout the game as players came to bat, instead of only at the start of the game.

First Electronic P.A. Systems. On August 25, 1929, the Giants became the first Major League club to use a full-time electronic public address system. The Giants wired umpire Charlie Rigler for a short time so that the fans could hear his calls.

During the 1922 World Series the radio broadcast was piped in over the public address system to allow the broadcasters and umpires to be heard in the ballpark.

No No-Hitter. Teams routinely withheld information from fans during games, as the public address system was used on a much more limited basis in early years. An example of the problems this created occurred in a game in the early 1930s. The Cubs thought that the first play of the game had been scored as an error and went wild when they thought their pitcher, Guy Bush, had finished the game with a no-hitter. They were wrong, as the official scorer had immediately scored the first play a hit and it was not announced during the game.

Former Ballplayer. Pitcher Rex Barney later became the long-time public address announcer for the Orioles. He was on duty the night Cal Ripken broke Lou Gehrig's consecutive-games-played record. On August 12, 1997, the Orioles played the A's at Camden Yards without a public address announcer. The club was paying tribute to Barney, who was found dead in his home earlier in the day. Barney, 72, had been the Orioles' announcer since 1974.

Longevity. In November 1998 the Brewers' long-time public address announcer, Bob Betts, died at age 70. He announced home games for 23 seasons.

Public Relations

"Who is marketing? The players are the marketing. The reason the Pirates drew two million people wasn't the fireworks or some promotion. It was winning. If the team goes bad, they don't go looking for marketing people." — Padres general manager Jack McKeon.

"I've been told that one has not lived unless one has been to Ebbets Field and has watched the Dodgers play baseball." — General Douglas MacArthur to start a speech at a Dodger game in Brooklyn, shortly after he was relieved of his command in Korea by President Harry S. Truman. Dodger publicist Irving Rudd gave him the line.

See also *Promotions*.

Bob Fishel. Fishel was a popular publicist who started his career in 1946 with the Indians and Bill Veeck. He moved to the Browns with Veeck before working for the Yankees for many years. He finished his career in the American League office and there is now a Robert O. Fishel Award given to the outstanding publicist in the Major Leagues.

Gene Karst. Karst, who died in April 2004 at age 97, was hired by Branch Rickey to write feature articles about the Cardinals in 1931. According to his obituary, the hiring led to the creation of baseball's first press office. One of Karst's projects was the "Cardinal News," a newsletter about the team. He later worked for the Reds and the Montreal Royals before going to work for the State Department in World War II. In 1970, he was a co-writer of *Who's Who in Professional Baseball*.

Good PR. In 2001 Brewers pitcher Curtis Leskanic made a public relations visit to a local school. He was asked to sign the back of a 10-year-old's shirt, which he did, but added the words "KICK ME."

Publicity Stunts See *Opening Day*, *Practical Jokes and Pranks*, *Promotions* and *Stunts*

Kirby Puckett (1961–)

Hall of Fame 2001

"He was Kirby, the baseball icon, and Kirby, the person. Even when he had to leave baseball, people went the extra mile to let him know that they still cared." — Minneapolis mayor (1994–2001) Sharon Sayles Belton.

"In the final analysis, all they really know now in Minnesota is that he was one whale of a baseball player. They'll never be so sure of anyone else again. So, maybe that's a tough lesson well learned." — Frank Deford reporting on the mess Puckett had made of his life.

Puckett was an outfield star for 12 seasons in Minnesota between 1984 and 1995 before glaucoma cut short his career.

Kirby Puckett left a Ford assembly plant to attend college, and then was drafted by the Twins in the first round in 1982. In that same year he led the rookie Appalachian League in batting, hits and runs. From there it was a quick jump to the Majors, making his debut in the spring of 1984.

In his rookie year the center fielder batted .296. As a sophomore he showed flashes of the hitter he would become, and by 1986 he was a star, batting .328 with 223 hits, 119 runs and 31 home runs. He also won the first of six consecutive Gold Gloves. In 1987 he led the league in hits with 207 and the Twins won the World Series over St. Louis, with Puckett batting .357.

In 1988 Puckett had his finest season. He established career highs in batting at .356, hits with 234 and RBIs with 121. He also led the league in hits and total bases. In 1989 he again led the league in hits, topping 200 for the fourth consecutive year. He was also the batting champion at .339. In 1991 the Twins returned to the postseason behind Puckett. He batted .429 and drove in the winning run in Game 5 versus Toronto to clinch the pennant for

Minnesota. In the World Series against Atlanta, the Twins returned to Minnesota for Game 6 down three games to two. Puckett's home run in the bottom of the 11th won it for the Twins and they took the Series the next day.

Puckett had another outstanding individual performance in 1992, again leading the league in hits and total bases. He also scored 104 runs, drove in 110 and batted .329. In 1994 he batted .317 and led the league in RBIs with 112. Following the 1995 season Puckett was forced to retire due to glaucoma and then had a series of personal traumas, including a felony sex offense charge and revelations about his extramarital personal life. He was acquitted of the rape charges involving a woman at a nightclub.

For his 12-year career Puckett hit over .300 eight times. He had five 200 hit seasons and finished as the Twins' all-time leader in hits and runs, batting .318 with 2,304 hits.

Puerto Rico

"Baseball is becoming a great fad here. Most of the American colony are great patrons of the game.... The plan took well with the people and six clubs have been formed from the clerical force of the various Government offices."—1901 *New York Times* article about baseball in Puerto Rico.

Origins and Professional Leagues. Baseball was introduced to Puerto Rico at least as early as the Spanish-American War in 1898. The Puerto Rican Amateur Federation was created in 1940.

The Puerto Rican professional leagues began operating in 1938 and through the 1950s and 1960s were strong winter leagues. They began to decline in the 1970s and were in danger of folding in the late 1980s. The decline occurred because of lack of participation by Major League Puerto Ricans, as high salaries made winter ball less important to these players. The leagues experienced a revival late in the decade and are now financially stable. Despite the periodic problems, the Puerto Rican League is the longest-running winter league in Latin America.

The teams play 54-game schedules from early November through early January. After a round-robin play-off the two best teams stage a championship play-off from which the winner advances to the Caribbean World Series in February.

Clubs may use 10 foreign players if they are needed. Most foreign players are from Class AAA and AA because players may not have more than four years in the Major Leagues, have batted more than 250 times or pitched more than 100 innings in their most recent Major League season. In 1995–1996 the primary Puerto Rican winter league had the following clubs:

Mayaguez Indios (through 2004)

Arecibo Lobos (Wolves) (gone by 2004, replaced by the Carolina Gigantes/Giants)

Santurce Cangrejeros (Crabbers) (through 2004)

Caguas Criollos (Natives) (through 2004)

San Juan Senadores (Senators) (through 2004)

Ponce Leones (Lions) (through 2004)

The owner of the Santurce Crabbers announced that the 2003–2004 season was the club's last because of the encroachment of the Montreal Expos.

Current Popularity. Baseball's popularity has dwindled in Puerto Rico ever since 1989, when the Major Leagues included the island in baseball's annual amateur draft (prompted by large bonuses paid to Juan Gonzalez and Ivan Rodriguez, among others). Baseball hasn't been played in the island's high schools since 1973.

Opening Day. On April 1, 2001, the Rangers and Orioles played their **Opening Day** game in San Juan, Puerto Rico.

Major League Playing Site. In 2003 the Montreal Expos played 22 home games in Puerto Rico's Hi Bithorn Stadium. The games drew very well and the club signed to play an additional 22 games there in 2004, all before July 1 to avoid the intense heat. The small ballpark was a home run mecca: the Expos and their opponents hit 60 home runs in the first 15 games there. Tickets for 2003 games were $10 to $85 for fans whose income is generally one third the average American's.

Key Major League Players.

Hi Bithorn. Born in 1916, Bithorn was the first Puerto Rican star, and one of the first Puerto Ricans to play in the Major Leagues. He played primarily for the Cubs as a pitcher in 1942 and 1943. He won 18 games in 1943 before leaving for World War II. He returned to the Cubs in 1946 and then finished his career with two games for the White Sox in 1947. He died New Year's Eve 1951, allegedly of a self-inflicted gunshot wound at age 35. More reliable sources report that he died under mysterious circumstances in El Mante, Mexico, when he was allegedly shot by a policeman who had stopped him and asked for the car's registration papers, a tourist card, and other documentation. Bithorn was on his way to visit his sister, who years later said an argument ensued between her brother and the policeman before the fatal shot was fired.

Puerto Rico's primary ballpark was named for him in 1962.

Vic Power. Power was known as Victor Pellot in Puerto Rico. In 1955 he became the first Puerto Rican to play in a Major League All-Star Game. He played from 1954 through 1965, finishing with a .284 average and 126 home runs.

Ruben Gomez. Gomez, a San Francisco Giants pitcher, won the first Major League game played on the West Coast and won the first game won by a Puerto Rican in the World Series.

Roberto Clemente. The Hall of Famer was perhaps the greatest and most revered Major League player from Puerto Rico. He hit .317 over 18 seasons for the Pirates from 1955 through 1972.

Orlando Cepeda. After Clemente, Cepeda may have been the greatest Puerto Rican player of all time, hitting 376 home runs during his 17-year career. He finally made it into the Hall of Fame in 1999. He was the first player to be embraced by San Francisco fans, as teammate Willie Mays was viewed as a New York product.

Juan Agosto. Agosto was a left-handed reliever who had a great year in 1984 for the Tigers, but his subsequent poor pitching soon earned him the nickname "Juan Disgusto: the Master of Disaster."

Sandy Alomar. Alomar played 15 Major League seasons at second base beginning in 1964, compiling a .245 average for a number of teams.

Ed Figueroa. In 1978 for the Yankees, Figueroa became the first Puerto Rican to win 20 games in a Major League season.

Jose Cruz. Cruz played almost exclusively for the Houston Astros during his career from 1970 through 1988, batting .289.

Roberto and Sandy Alomar, Jr. Roberto and Sandy followed their father to the Major Leagues. Roberto is considered the best second baseman of the 1990s and one of the most gifted athletes in the Major Leagues before fading in the 2000s. His brother Sandy played catcher for the Indians.

Juan Gonzalez. Gonzalez became one of the most feared hitters in the American League after hitting 43 home runs in 1992, though back problems plagued him through 2004.

Ruben Sierra. Sierra began his Major League career in 1986, and was still at it for the Yankees in 2004. He had appeared in over 2,000 games through 2003 and hit 282 home runs.

Ivan Rodriguez. Rodriguez was the best catcher in the American League in the 1990s and then won a World Series with the Marlins in 2003 before signing with the Tigers for 2004.

Bernie Williams. Williams, an accomplished guitarist, anchored center field for the Yankees in the late 1990s and early 2000s.

Carlos Delgado. Delgado became perhaps the most feared hitter in the American League in the early 2000s.

Book. Thomas E. Van Hyning, *Puerto Rico's Winter League: A History of Major League Baseball's Launching Pad* (1995).

Pull Hitters

"There's no excuse for that [hitting in the .200s]. You know why it happens? They keep trying to pull everything, even low outside sliders. You can't do that. Nobody can. If you're a Major League player, you ought to have pride. Learn to stroke outside pitches to the opposite field. That's part of your job. A Major League hitter is supposed to be a professional."—Stan Musial in an interview with Roger Kahn in the 1970s.

Sportswriters covering the Red Sox tracked the number of foul balls that the chronically pull-hitting Carlton Fisk hit foul, but within three feet of the left field foul line. The exasperated Fisk was kept apprised of the number, which was well over 100 after a few years.

Henry Clay "Harry" Pulliam (1869–1909)

Pulliam was *National League President* from 1903 until 1909, when he committed suicide.

Putouts

See also **Outs**.

Most. Late 19th century first baseman Jake Beckley had 23,721 putouts, the most in Major League history.

Outfielders. In 1946 Dodger Carden Gillenwater tied the Major League record of 12 putouts in a game by an outfielder.

Pitcher. Bob Heffner, pitching for the Red Sox on June 28, 1963, became the second pitcher in Major League history to make three putouts in a single inning.

Unusual. On April 17, 1998, Mets catcher Tim Spehr made an unlikely putout after a bloop single by Reds outfielder Reggie Sanders. Playing first base for the first time, Spehr saw that second base was uncovered as infielders Rey Ordonez and Carlos Baerga had raced to catch the bloop hit to left field. Spehr saw Sanders turn for second and raced with him to the bag as Mets outfielder Bernard Gilkey made the throw. Spehr and Sanders slid in together as Spehr snared the throw and applied the tag. Mets manager Bobby Valentine summed it up: "I'll bet that's his last putout at second base from the outfield in his career. Just call it a hunch."

None by First Baseman. Bud Clancy played primarily for the White Sox from 1924 through 1934. On April 27, 1930, he became one of three first baseman not to record a putout during a game.

"**Q** is Don Quixote
Cornelius Mack;
Neither Yankees nor years
Can halt his attack."
—Ogden Nash on Connie Mack.

Quick Pitch

"Put one in here again—and I'll knock it out of the park for you."—Babe Ruth to Cardinals pitcher Bill Sherdel during the 1928 World Series. The Yankees were up 3–0 in games and 2–1 in the 7th inning of Game 4. Ruth had just taken a called third strike quick pitch from Sherdel. At the time, quick pitches were legal in the National League, but not in the American League. Before the World Series, Judge Landis ruled that the pitch would be illegal for the entire series. Apparently no one told the managers and pitchers.

Ruth argued the call for ten minutes and finally was given another pitch. On a 2–2 pitch he homered for the second time that day. Lou Gehrig followed immediately with another home run. Later in the game, Ruth hit his third home run of the game and the Yankees swept the Series.

See **Hitters Who Pitched** for Rudy York's claim that Ted Williams quick-pitched him to record a strikeout.

Quotes

"I didn't say everything I said."—Yogi Berra.

"Talking to Yogi Berra about baseball is like talking to Homer about the Gods."—A. Bartlett Giamatti.

"I can remember a reporter asking for a quote, and I didn't know what a quote was. I thought it was some kind of soft drink."—Joe DiMaggio.

"It's like what Yogi said. What did Yogi say?"—George Bell.

"What the hell do they need quotes for? They all saw the play?"—Pilots outfielder Tommy Harper on sportswriters.

"Steinbrenner himself was once a walking, unabridged *Bartlett's*. In the 1980s Yankees beat writers privately referred to him as Mr. Tunes because tales and outrageous quotes blasted from his mouth as easily as songs from a jukebox."—Tom Verducci.

"One of the great side benefits of the reporting business is that you get to meet people you'd otherwise never have a chance to be near. But you get spoiled; you meet those folks on such a regular basis that before long they become just sources of quotes for you—you lose sight of the fact that most people would kill for the opportunity to spend time with them."—Bob Greene.

"I don't care if Henderson has an on-base percentage of .000. As long as Rickey's mouth is working, the Dodger season will be fun. They just got one of the best quotes in baseball."—Sportswriter J.A. Adande after the 44-year-old signed with the Dodgers in July 2003.

For John Feinstein's book, *Play Ball: The Life and Troubled Times of Major League Baseball* (1993), Barry Bonds wanted to be paid for any of his quotes that appeared in the book.

When George Hendrick replaced Jack Clark in August 2003 as the Dodgers' hitting coach, he continued a code of silence he had maintained since he claimed to be misquoted in 1973.

Books. More than 50 have been written solely on the subject of baseball quotes, including: Paul Dickson, *Baseball's Greatest Quotations* (1991); Paul Gangi, *Covering the Bases: Quotations on Baseball* (2003); Glenn Liebman, *Grand Slams! The Ultimate Collection of Baseball's Best Quips, Quotes, and Cutting Remarks* (2001); David H. Nathan, *Baseball Quotations: The Wisdom and Wisecracks of Players, Managers, Owners, Umpires, Announcers, Writers and Fans on the Great American Pastime* (1991); David H. Nathan, *The McFarland Baseball Quotations Dictionary* (2000); David Plaut, *Speaking of Baseball* (1983); Louis Decimus Rubin (ed.), *The Quotable Baseball Fanatic* (2004).

"**R** is for Ruth.
To tell you the truth,
There's no more to be said,
Just R is for Ruth."
—Ogden Nash on Babe Ruth.

Racism

"I'm not prejudiced. I hate everybody."— Sign over the locker of Bob Gibson before he won Game 1 of the 1968 World Series against the Tigers.

"Sport free of racism can only exist in a society free of racism."— Richard Lapchick, a white political scientist and civil rights activist, whose father helped integrate the NBA.

"Haughty Caucasions say it's OK to have darkies carry water, but not in the lineup."—19th century white home run star Ned Williamson, citing the hypocrisy of racists in keeping black players out of Organized Baseball.

"You nigger boys are doing all right."— Ty Cobb to Jim "Mudcat" Grant and Vic Power at the 1960 Hall of Fame Game. According to Grant, he had to restrain Power from going after Cobb.

"Robinson will not make the grade in the Major Leagues. He is a thousand-to-one shot at best. The Negro players simply don't have the brains or the skills."— *New York Daily News* sports editor Jimmy Powers; though some sources report that Powers was one of the first to campaign for integration of the Major Leagues.

"[It is disturbing to note that in a] democratic, Catholic, real American Game like Baseball [the] hideous monster of racial or religious prejudice [could exist...]" [except, of course, for the] "Ethiopian."—1920s editorial in *The Sporting News*.

"This is by far my toughest year in baseball. I've been called everything but white."— Bobby Bonds with the Indians in 1979.

See also **Black "Firsts," Ethnicity, Executives, Integration, Jewish Ballplayers, Latin Baseball and Latin Major League Players, Mascots, Mexican Ballplayers, Native Americans** and **Negro Leagues.**

Eliot Asinof. The author of *Eight Men Out* signed a minor league baseball contract with the Phillies and started out in Moultrie, Georgia. Walking down the street of his new home, he stepped aside to allow a black woman and her baby to pass. He was promptly arrested. The next day, after tripling in the game, and after word of his chivalry had circulated through the local black population, he was given an ovation by the "colored" section seated behind third base. He tipped his cap in response. He was fired the next day. He also reported being fired by his next team, in Wausau, Wisconsin, because the club owner's daughter had fallen in love with Asinof, who was Jewish. Aninof later was blacklisted by the House Un-American Activities Committee. Years later he found out that it was because he had signed a petition outside of Yankee Stadium urging the Yankees to sign their first black player.

Cap Anson. Anson has been described as the most prominent racist of 19th century baseball (see also **Integration**). After he retired, he owned and managed a semipro team known as Anson's Colts that played many games against the Leland Giants and other all-black teams without any problems.

Babe Ruth.

"I can't honestly say that I appreciate the way in which he changed baseball ... but he was the most natural and unaffected man I ever knew. No one ever loved life more."— Ty Cobb on Ruth.

There was always some suspicion (however unfounded) that Ruth was of African American descent because of his facial features. There are stories that Ty Cobb particularly disliked Ruth for this reason, although there is strong reason for Cobb to have disliked Ruth simply because Ruth almost single-handedly eliminated Cobb's style of one-run-at-a-time baseball.

One story has it that Cobb once refused to room with Ruth on an exhibition tour, complaining that he had never roomed with a "nigger" and he did not intend to start. Nevertheless, photographs exist of Cobb and Ruth in retirement playing golf together and apparently acting friendly toward each other.

Negro League star Judy Johnson held a similar view of Ruth's racial status, as quoted in Kevin Kerrane's *Dollar Sign on the Muscle* (1984): "Babe Ruth was part black. I can't prove it, but everybody in our league used to talk about it. You could see it in his facial features. And the body build—you know, the thin legs and high rump. I don't want to sound racial, but some things are just the way they are. You can see them. Like it wouldn't be racial to say that Negroes can run, because most of us can. And I've often thought that one reason Mr. Rickey broke the color line is that he was already in love with running. I know that he had a great vision of blacks and whites playing together, but maybe he wouldn't have had that vision unless he looked at the strategy of baseball in a certain way. He even wanted every *white* boy he signed to be able to run like a deer."

Al Campanis.

"Campanis did more in ten minutes than we've done in 20 years. When a black says something, we're radicals, we've got a chip on our shoulder. When a white says something, people have to listen and evaluate and respond ... [Campanis] should have been nominated for the NAACP Man of the Year Award."— Dr. Harry Edwards, black sociologist, on the 1987 "Nightline" television show remarks by Campanis.

"Al Campanis is a good guy. He was very good on integration when it counted."— Jackie Robinson.

On April 6, 1987, Ted Koppel's "Nightline" program featured a 40th anniversary tribute to Jackie Robinson's first year in the Major Leagues. Koppel interviewed Dodger general manager Campanis, then 70, who had been a friend and infield tutor of Robinson's and not considered a racist. Campanis had earned a Master's Degree from New York University.

In response to a question from Koppel as to whether prejudice was a reason for the absence of blacks in executive positions in baseball, Campanis responded: "No, I don't believe it's prejudice. I truly believe that they may not have some of the necessities to be, let's say, a field manager, or perhaps a general manager."

Campanis then mentioned that blacks were not good swimmers because they "lacked buoyancy." In his final remarks, Campanis dug himself in a little deeper: "[Black people] are gifted with great musculature and various other things; they're fleet of foot, and this is why there are a lot of black Major League baseball players. Now, as far as having the background to become club presidents, or presidents of banks, I don't know."

As a result of the furor that arose after the program, the Dodgers fired Campanis. In response to the Campanis remarks, commissioner Peter Ueberroth immediately hired University of California sports sociologist Dr. Harry Edwards to help solve baseball's racial inequality. By the end of that year, there were no minority owners, managers, general managers or managers (one less than at the beginning of the year). As part of the response, in 1987 the Baseball Network, Inc., was founded to assist in affirmative action efforts in the Major Leagues.

Campanis had three photos on his office wall: Jackie Robinson,

Sandy Koufax and Roberto Clemente (an African-American, a Jew and a Puerto Rican).

Don Newcombe was to have been the speaker on "Nightline," but his flight was delayed after another speaking engagement, so the network found Campanis. He had just arrived in Houston, where the Dodgers were opening their season.

After Campanis was fired, popular former Lakers basketball star Tommy Hawkins was brought on as the Vice President of Communications.

Publicist Steve Brenner left the club after 18 years with the Dodgers, apparently a bit of a scapegoat in the incident because he allowed Campanis to appear. Brenner did not learn about the interview until a few minutes before it occurred. He asked Campanis not to go on. Brenner's comment: "I told him I wouldn't recommend it. He was a 70-year-old man who had traveled that day and wound up sitting on a stool behind home plate after the game looking into a camera and the bright lights."

An excuse of sorts was crafted by one of Campanis' sons, George: "As for the buoyancy thing, growing up we always used to hear about my dad's experiences in the Navy in World War II. One of his jobs was to work with the recruits when they had to make a high dive into a tank to simulate falling off an aircraft carrier. My dad would tell us how a lot of the blacks would sink to the bottom and he would have to dive down and pull them up. They were so scared that they would pull and scratch at him. He finally got a pole to pull them up. My dad thought it was because they had a low fat content in their bodies and because a lot of them didn't have their own swimming pool or a place to swim growing up."

Campanis died at age 81 in June 1998.

Barry Bonds. In a 1993 issue of *Playboy* magazine, black Major Leaguer Barry Bonds responded to the question, "What do you think made you such a fine ballplayer?": "Some of it is genetics. Black people in general have the genetics for sports."

Carl Everett. During the Red Sox second workout after the 9/11 tragedy in 2001, the troubled outfielder cursed out manager Jimy Williams (who was soon fired) and called him a racist. Everett was sent home for the season and later traded to the Rangers, one of the six teams he had played for over 11 seasons through 2004.

The 1920s Phillies. The club purportedly was torn by dissension because a number of their players were members of the Ku Klux Klan.

Jake Powell. Powell was an outfielder for the Yankees in 1938 when he responded to a radio interview question about his off-season activities. He said he was a policeman who enjoyed "cracking niggers over the head" for recreation. Soon after, he issued the standard apology: "I have some very good friends among the Negroes of Dayton."

Powell received a 10-day suspension. In his first game back, the crowd booed him and threw bottles (with one writer noting that black groundskeepers picked up the bottles). As a result of the radio faux pas, the Yankees banned all pregame radio interviews. Powell purportedly made amends by going into Harlem by himself. He stopped in every bar he could find, introduced himself, apologized and bought a round of drinks. In 1948 Powell was arrested for passing bad checks and shot himself to death in the police station.

Bob Feller. Feller reportedly claimed prior to 1947 that black players did not have sufficient physical skills to compete in the Major Leagues. He may have said only that Jackie Robinson was too muscle-bound to play at that level.

Joe DiMaggio. Jackie Robinson once roll-blocked Yankee shortstop Phil Rizzuto on a double play. Later in the game, Robinson took a throw at first base on a ground ball hit by Joe DiMag-

gio. Robinson put his foot awkwardly on the bag and DiMaggio had to make an off-balance step on the bag to avoid spiking Robinson. Asked later by a reporter why he did not retaliate against Robinson by spiking him, DiMaggio said: "I thought about it running to first. But Rizzuto and I are Italian, and I didn't want them to think it was the guineas against the niggers. If Phil was black and Robinson white, I guess I would have done the spiking."—Quoted by sportswriter Heywood Hale Broun in *Cult Baseball Players*, edited by Danny Peary (1990).

Jackie Robinson.

"As I write this twenty years later, I cannot stand and sing the anthem. I cannot salute the flag; I know that I am a black man in a white world. In 1972, in 1947, at my birth in 1919, I know that I never had it made."— Last lines of the foreword to Robinson's autobiography, *I Never Had It Made* (1972) (see also **Black "Firsts"** and **Integration**).

Phillies manager Ben Chapman was perhaps the most vocal and abusive against Robinson's appearance with the Dodgers in 1947. New York columnist Walter Winchell turned on Chapman and tried to drive him out of his job. The second time the Dodgers played in Philadelphia, Chapman did an amazing thing. He asked Dodger traveling secretary Harold Parrott if Robinson would agree to shake his hand for the photographers. Chapman thought the gesture might help save his job. Robinson agreed and the two met behind home plate before a game. Chapman smiled broadly and Robinson barely smiled as the two shook hands. Dodger outfielder Dixie Walker, no fan of Robinson's, watched in amazement: "I swear, I never thought I'd see Ol' Ben eat shit like that."

Headhunter.

"[Yankee pitcher Jim] Coates would knock you down whether you were black *or* white."— Whitey Ford when asked about racism on the Yankees. See also **Boxing**, for the story of a racially charged boxing match between Coates and Yankee catcher Elston Howard. Braves pitcher Lew Burdette was renowned for throwing at black players.

Hotel Problems. When Roy Campanella and his family came to Los Angeles in April 1959 for a tribute to the paralyzed catcher, they stayed at the Sheraton Hotel. After his children were denied use of the hotel pool because they were black, Campanella had no success with the hotel manager in ending the policy. Campanella then complained to Walter O'Malley, who reportedly pulled all of his business from the hotel.

Umpires. Puerto Rican power hitter Vic Power claimed that a few umpires unfairly called pitches against black players. He said that pitcher Moe Drabowsky once told him of an umpire who told Drabowsky that he should just pitch the ball because it would be a strike regardless of where it was pitched. This system forced black players to become first ball and **Bad Ball Hitters** to avoid bad calls deep into the count.

Casey Stengel. Stengel liberally used the word "nigger" to taunt opposing black players.

Alvin Dark. Dark got into trouble in the 1960s when he opined that "black people's muscles are built differently than those of whites." The comments cost him at least one managing job in the mid–1960s.

Frank Thomas. Thomas was a utility infielder for the Phillies in the early 1960s who was not friendly with the black players on the club. He had a habit of offering a "soul" handshake to black players and then bending their thumbs back until they cried out in pain. During batting practice on July 3, 1965, Dick Allen and Johnny Callison were riding Thomas for striking out while trying to bunt the previous night. Thomas responded to Allen: "What are you trying to be, another Muhammad Clay [sic], always running your mouth off?"

Allen responded with a left hook to Thomas' jaw. Thomas grabbed a bat and hit Allen on the arm, causing a scuffle that required five players to separate them. Allen was fined $2,500 and told by the club not to say anything. Thomas was released after the game and went public with his railings against Allen. Fans generally sided with Thomas and Allen's image was set. Allen and Thomas shook hands after the incident and apparently were friendly after their careers ended.

Boston.

"Nothing more about poor, old banned Cincinnati owner Marge Schott and her racist ways. (She is probably just Boston Red Sox owner Tom Yawkey with tits.)" — Robert Lipsyte in *Esquire* magazine.

Fair or not, Boston has always been portrayed as a one of the most racist Major League cities. Evidence of that claim is the few blacks historically on the club and the long time it took to integrate the club. However, in 1967 there were six black players on the pennant-winning club, a relatively large number for that era: George Scott, Reggie Smith, Jose Tartabull, Elston Howard, John Wyatt and Joe Foy.

Between 1976 and 1992 the Red Sox failed to sign a single black free agent.

Fans. See *Fans*—*Black Fans.*

Henry Aaron.

"I have to tell the truth, and when people ask me what progress Negroes have made in baseball, I tell them the Negro hasn't made any progress on the field. We haven't made any progress in the Commissioner's office. Even with Monte Irvin in there, I still think it's tokenism. I think we have a lot of Negroes capable of handling front office jobs. We don't have Negro secretaries in some of the Big League offices, and I think it's time that the Major Leagues and baseball in general just took hold of themselves and started hiring some of these capable people." — Aaron in 1970, shortly after his 3,000th hit.

When Aaron was pursuing Babe Ruth's home run record in 1973, he received enormous amounts of hate mail:

"I got orders to do a bad job on you if and when you get 10 from B. Ruth record. A guy in Atlanta and a few in Miami Fla don't seem to care if they have to take care of your family too."

—

"Hey nigger boy,
We at the KKK Staten Island division want you to know that no number of guards can keep you dirty son of a bitch nigger _____ alive."

—

"You are a very good ballplayer, but if you come close to Babe Ruth's 714 homers I have a contract out on you…. If by the all star game you have come within 20 homers of Babe you will be shot on sight by one of my assassins on July 24, 1973."

—

"Dear Nigger Henry,
You are (not) going to break this record established by the great Babe Ruth if I can help it…. Whites are far more superior than jungle bunnies…. My gun is watching your every black move."

—

"Dear Henry Aaron,
How about some sickle cell anemia, Hank?"

Letters arrived from all 50 states and, as Aaron said, the vehemence of the letters "changed me."

When Aaron broke the record, he received only one national endorsement, for Magnavox televisions. The Magnavox spokesman said that "Perhaps most importantly, Henry Aaron is the type of person with whom Magnavox would be proud to associate in its business activities had he never hit a home run." This prompted a retort by Michael Roberts in his book, *Fans!* (1976): "But could anyone name a modestly educated, reticent black man with *no* career home runs who was paid to praise Magnavox products?"

Frank Robinson. In 1988 Robinson and Berry Stainback wrote *Extra Innings*, another Robinson autobiography, but heavily laced with commentary on racism in baseball and the inability of blacks to obtain minor and Major League managing jobs. After he won the Triple Crown in 1966, Robinson made one television appearance and received a total of $1,000 in endorsement money. When Carl Yastrzemski won the Triple Crown in 1967, he received endorsement contracts that paid him approximately $200,000 over the following three years.

Coaches. In 1996 Northeastern University presented its Racial Report Card and awarded baseball an A for its rate of hiring minority coaches. However, it noted that of the 18 minorities coaching the bases in the Major Leagues, only four were third base coaches. These are the coaches who are the conduit from the manager to the runners, and prominent black baseball men Frank Robinson and Willie Randolph both contended that there was a definite bias.

Front Office Personnel.

"I hope I've paved the way. But the scary thing is there's no one in the pipeline of assistant GMs and farm directors. There are no blacks in line. That's where I have a real problem with the system." — Bob Watson.

A June 7, 1987, report noted that 17 of 879 front office personnel in Major League Baseball were minorities. A 1989 survey commissioned by Major League Baseball determined that there were a total of 1,854 front-office positions among all Major League teams. This was up from 1,495 such jobs in 1988. In 1989 there were 273 minorities among those employees, up from 142 in 1988. Of these, 163 were black, 88 Hispanic and 22 Asian. This was 9% of the total employment, up from two percent in 1984. Women held 700 positions in 1989, up from 564 in 1988.

A 1992 study by the commissioner's office showed that 17% of front office personnel were minorities, up one percent from 1991. However, only 21 of 534 executives and department heads were black. In June 1994 Major League Baseball released its Equal Opportunity Committee Report chronicling the level of minority and women hiring in the front office and on the field. From 1987 to 1994 minority employment in front offices rose from 2% to 17%.

Bill Lucas of the Braves became the first black general manager in the 1970s. In early 1993 there were two blacks at high levels of executive team management. Former Astros star Bob Watson was an assistant general manager with the Astros, as was Elaine Steward of the Red Sox. Watson was elevated to general manager after the 1993 season. Watson stepped down due to prostate cancer but accepted the general manager position with the Yankees for the 1996 season when he had successful surgery.

In 1995 there was one minor league general manager who was a person of color, Pete Moore of the Charlotte Knights. By 2001 only Ken Williams of the White Sox was the Major Leagues' sole general manager of color.

In 1996, 9% of front office employees were black, the same as in 1989. Hispanics comprised 7%, up from 5% in 1989. Asian employees remained steady at 2%.

In a 2001 study, it was determined that 764 minorities were among 3,415 people employed by the 30 Major League clubs at midseason. This was 22%, up from 20% in 1997. Black employees actually decreased from 11% to 10%, but Hispanic employees increased from 7% to 9%, and Asians increased from 2% to 3%. Departments heads who were minorities increased from 15% to 16% from 1997. On-field staff— managers, trainers, scouts, coaches and other instructors — increased from 26% to 30%. Overall minority hiring, including in the commissioner's office, increased from 23% to 26%.

The highest ranking person of color in Major League Baseball's business infrastructure in 2003 was African-American Jimmie Lee Solomon, Senior Vice President of Baseball Operations. He has overseen the Scouting Bureau, the Arizona Fall League, and Major League Baseball's domestic and international operations. He was also instrumental in promoting baseball's Youth Baseball Academy.

The CFO of Major League Baseball in 2003 was African-American Jonathan Mariner, 48.

Number of Players. On the 50th anniversary of Jackie Robinson breaking the color line, in April 1997, there were 2% fewer African-American Major Leaguers than there were in 1959, when the Major Leagues were fully integrated for the first time. Much of the decline was attributed to the fact that baseball had all but died in African-American communities.

In 1959 there were 69 African-Americans playing on the 16 Major League teams, representing 17.25% of all players. In 1997 there were 108 on Opening Day rosters (including the disabled list), representing 15.5%.

The number of black players in the Major Leagues declined dramatically between 1995 and 2002, reduced from 19% to 10% of the total Major Leaguers. In 2003 the Angels had three black players on their 40-man roster, the Dodgers six. Of the 50 players drafted by the Angels in June 2003, two were black.

When the Dodgers honored Jackie Robinson in April 1997 (50 years after breaking the color line), the club had only one African-American player, Wayne Kirby. Between 1965 and 1997, the Dodgers had developed only 21 African-American players who made it to the Major Leagues. Only Lee Lacy and Franklin Stubbs had more than 1,000 plate appearances among these players. Ken Howell is the only African-American pitcher drafted by the Dodgers who won more than 10 games in the Major Leagues (18–29) for the Dodgers.

Most of the African-American players drafted by the Dodgers flourished (if at all) after they moved on. The list includes Dave Stewart (multiple 20-game winner for the A's) and Eric Young (strong infielder for the Rockies early in his career after one season with Los Angeles).

In 2003 the Dodgers had two blacks among their 53 scouts. Reggie Smith was the only black coach at the Major League level for the club, and John Shelby, demoted to Class A Savannah in 1997, was the only black minor league coach or manager in the Dodger organization.

In contrast, when **Marge Schott** was suspended for racist remarks in 1996 she had a black assistant general manager and controller and seven black players on the team.

Marge Schott.
"Trying to teach sensitivity to Marge Schott is like trying to teach typing to Schottzie 02." — Columnist Scott Ostler.

"That's what we call a Marge Schott. Just a little to the right." — CBS golf commentator Gary McCord on an errant shot.

Schott created a problem for herself in late 1992 when she was quoted as saying that Hitler may have had the right idea and for having a swastika in her home. She also insulted black people when she noted that she had "niggers" working for her.

In a December 1991 deposition related to a lawsuit filed by a for-

mer employee, Schott acknowledged saying "nigger" in conversation and that it was "possible" that she referred to Martin Luther King, Jr., Day as "Nigger Day." She denied calling Eric Davis and Dave Parker her "million-dollar niggers." Davis later forgave Schott, and shortstop Barry Larkin and Davis said they occasionally called Schott because they remained friends with her.

A former employee of the Oakland A's said that she once heard Schott in an owners' conference call say: "I'd rather have a trained monkey working for me than a nigger."

She was also quoted as saying: "Hitler was good in the beginning, but he went too far."

In a compromise, Major League Baseball sanctioned her for the racial comments but ruled that she could retain her ownership interest in the club and remain as managing general partner. She was fined $25,000, the maximum allowable against an individual (the club as an organization could have been fined $250,000). She was banned from the owners' on-field box and could not be involved in day-to-day operations (nothing about whether Schotzie was banned from the field).

Schott was reinstated to her full duties in November 1993, but she repeated the comments in a May 1996 interview and was in trouble again. As a result she was suspended from day-to-day operation of the club and again was not allowed on the field at least through 1997. During the last controversy Schott passed out business cards bearing the words "No Comment." After selling her interest in the Reds, she died at age 75 in early 2004. See also Mike Bass, *Marge Schott— Unleashed!* (1993).

John Rocker.
"Apple of Our Ire, Foul Mouth of the South, Hate Hurler, Loco Lefty, Boorish Brave, Klu Klux Kloser, Johnny Rotten (and the original Rotten, John Lydon, took exception and labeled Rocker a National Numbskull)." — Rocker nicknames after several of his racist comments surfaced.

In late 1999 during the National League pennant race, Rocker, then a reliever for the Braves, made enemies of virtually all New York Mets fans. The redneck from Georgia was the object of batteries, beer bottles and several other objects when he was on the bullpen bench. He retaliated by throwing fastballs into the bullpen screen, as fans recoiled. Whenever he sprinted to the mound, fans chanted "Asshole! Asshole!"

After Rocker gave up the key hit in Game 4 of the 1999 NLCS against the Mets, a sign appeared in the stands the next day, a tongue-in-cheek reference to the MasterCard ads of the same genre: "Hall of Fame leadoff man: $1.8 million. Best infield in baseball: $15.7 million. No. 1 all-time offensive catcher: $7 million. Wiping that smug look off John Rocker's face: Priceless."

The hate was fueled further by a *Sports Illustrated* article that appeared in December 1999, in which he was quoted as describing the contents of the No. 7 subway train to Shea Stadium: "Looking like you're in Beirut next to some kid with purple hair next to some queer with AIDS right next to some dude who just got out of jail for the fourth time right next to some 20-year-old mom with four kids. It's depressing."

He said that "the biggest thing I don't like about New York are the foreigners. You can walk an entire block in Times Square and not hear anybody speaking English.... How the hell did they get in this country" He also said that he had a black teammate who was a "fat monkey."

Rocker had lived with Braves' star Andruw Jones and other black and Hispanic teammates in a group housing situation. He and his father later met with former U.N. Ambassador Andrew Young, who concluded that "nobody's perfect" and offered the pitcher advice for getting through the next season. Rocker then met with Henry Aaron, who said that Rocker was "convincing." When the article appeared, he was required to submit to psychological evaluation in early 2000 before commissioner Bud Selig decided what punishment was appropriate.

After Rocker was disciplined in early 2000, arbitrator Shyam Das reduced his suspension by half and reduced his fine. Initially, he was suspended for all of spring training and the first 28 days of the regular season, and fined $20,000 (reduced to $5,000). He was also ordered to undergo sensitivity training. He struggled in spring training and was sent down to Class AAA and later fined $5,000 for another confrontation with fans.

At his first game back, on May 1, 2000, a fan ran out of the stands and approached Rocker. The fan dropped his pants, mooning him.

On June 4, 2000, the Yankees beat the Braves in Yankee Stadium. Before the game, Rocker confronted Jeff Pearlman, the reporter who wrote the infamous article about him in *Sports Illustrated*. Rocker reportedly threatened Pearlman, although there was no physical contact between the two. The Braves then sent Rocker to the minors.

On June 9, 2001, Rocker first appeared for the Richmond Braves since being sent down by Atlanta. Prior to the game, he again had words with reporters. Within two weeks the Braves had traded him to the Indians.

On October 9, 2001, during the division playoffs in Seattle, Rocker threw water on some heckling fans. According to Rocker, the fans' reaction is the media's fault: "You guys should see the monster you've helped create. They wouldn't be there if not for the biased coverage, so thank you for making my life on the road hell."

In December 2001 the Indians sent Rocker to the Rangers in exchange for minor league pitcher David Eder. He finished a rocky 2002 season with a hellish 6.66 ERA.

Rocker was released by the Devil Rays in June 2003 while pitching for the Class AA Orlando club. Later that year, radio personality Rush Limbaugh, hosting an ESPN NFL show, made allegedly racist comments about Eagles quarterback Donovan McNabb. Rocker was asked to comment: "All I will say is, people need to stop being so sensitive."

Bruce Froemming. The Major League umpire was scheduled to go to Japan for the start of the 2003 season, between the Yankees and Devil Rays (eventually cancelled due to the U.S. invasion of Iraq and played in Tampa instead). His travel arrangements were apparently fouled up, and he blamed umpiring administrator Cathy Davis. Froemming used an anti-Semitic slur against Davis after he learned of the problem, and was then suspended for 10 days to start the season. He apologized and said "there was no anti-Semitism whatsoever on my part."

The 63-year-old Froemming, with 33 years of service and the senior umpire crew chief, was also banned from the Dodgers' adult fantasy camp that spring, at which he had umpired for the previous 10 seasons.

Bill Singer. In November 2003 the former Dodger pitcher, at the time an executive with the Mets for all of one week, was guilty of uttering insensitive remarks to Dodger vice president and assistant general manager Kim Ng at the postseason general managers meetings. Singer apparently approach Ng at a bar in the hotel and ridiculed her Chinese heritage.

After asking her about her background in a sarcastic tone, Singer began speaking nonsensically in mock Chinese before he departed. Singer later apologized. The substance of the conversation:

Singer: What are you doing here?

Ng: I'm working.

Singer: What are you doing here?

Ng: I'm working. I'm the Dodger assistant general manager.

Singer: Where are you from?

Ng: I was born in Indiana and grew up in New York.

Singer: Where are you from?

Ng: My family's from China.

Singer: (speaking in mock Chinese). What country in China?

Singer was fired a few days later, after a total of 12 days in his new position. Ng was named the 38th most influential minority in *Sports Illustrated's* May 2003 edition and previously had worked as assistant general manager for the Yankees, and had worked for Major League Baseball. She started her career with the White Sox in 1990.

Singer blamed the outburst on his having suffered a chemical imbalance after downing a few beers while otherwise adhering to the protein-rich Atkins Diet (sounds like the infamous Twinkie defense used by Dan White in the killing of San Francisco mayor Harvey Milk). The incident prompted this comment from radio personality Jim Rome: "I heard a lot about the Atkins Diet. I know it seems to work wonders for losing weight. I don't know how safe it is, but I didn't know it could turn you into a bigot."

Affirmative Action. The Marge Schott bigotry incident surfaced before the 1993 season, prompting Jesse Jackson and other minority leaders to call for a boycott of Major League Baseball. As part of the consciousness-raising effort, Jackson and his Rainbow Commission on Fairness in Athletics announced a 10-point plan for Major League Baseball:

1. Plan community development programs and youth leagues to begin in 1994.

2. Add three minority or women members to each team's board.

3. Develop 3-to-5-year affirmative action plans for team and league posts, including umpires and broadcasters.

4. Purchase at least 20% of all goods and services from minority/women-owned vendors.

5. Develop 3–5-year affirmative action plans for manufacturing and merchandising through Major League Properties.

6. Form a committee to seek possible minority team ownership.

7. Include at least two minority candidates for all executive and managerial jobs.

8. Provide personal development and financial management training for players.

9. Provide "diversity and humanities training" for all owners and executives.

10. Appoint a vice president for organization development and diversity.

In response to Jackson, Major League Baseball came up with its own plan:

1. Include minority candidates for jobs throughout their organizations "within a reasonable time frame."

2. Attempt to attract minorities as investors and have "appropriate minority participation" on their boards of directors.

3. Seek minority-owned vendors, including doctors, lawyers and bankers.

4. Insist that non-minority vendors be equal-opportunity employers.

5. Make new efforts to attract minorities as fans.

6. Have their employees undergo sensitivity training "unless clearly unnecessary."

7. Increase community and charitable activities.

Systematic Racism. In a study by Richard Lapchick, director of the Center for the Study of Sport, it was reported that in 1991 there were only 12 black pitchers in the Major Leagues and no black catchers (Lenny Webster of the Twins was the only black catcher in 1992). The study concluded that baseball is no longer a glamour sport for blacks, having been replaced by basketball and, to a lesser extent, football. Major League Baseball attempted to revive interest in baseball by creating "RBI," meaning Revive Baseball in Inner Cities (see also *Youth Baseball*).

New York Mets. When he was released in the mid–1980s, George Foster claimed that the Mets practiced systematic racism. Although the team historically had relatively few black players on the team, the charge as it related to Foster is probably unfounded because he was replaced by Kevin Mitchell, who was black.

Steve Carlton. Carlton may have gone somewhat off the deep end after a career in which he rarely spoke publicly about anything. He was elected to the Hall of Fame in early 1994. In an interview with former pitcher Pat Jordan in a Philadelphia magazine in April 1994, Carlton made some strange comments. Among other things, he said that 12 Jewish bankers in Switzerland controlled the world; that AIDS was created to eliminate blacks and gays; and that PVC pipe was a good way to hide weapons. Carlton later disavowed the statements, but Jordan stood by his story.

Harry Caray.
"If a guy's got a broken arm, he's got a broken arm. If a guy's got slanty eyes, he's got slanty eyes. What's the big deal?"— Caray after being criticized for insulting pitcher Hideo Nomo in 1995.

Drayton McLane. In June 1999 Astros owner Drayton McLane, Jr., made allegedly derogatory remarks about Mexicans and Mexican Americans to the general manager and sales manager of Houston television station KTMD. McLane letter said his remarks were taken out of context and after an investigation there was an apology from Telemundo, owner of the station.

Cito Gaston. In early April 1997, the Toronto Blue Jays manager suggested that three local reporters were racist. He later apologized, though in a much-qualified manner: "I've got one statement that I'm going to say ... and I'm not going to say another word. Whatever has been said, whatever has been written, if it has offended someone and it has unjustly offended them, I apologize. If it hasn't, then I don't apologize."

Gaston admitted that neither he nor his family had experienced racism in Toronto.

Restrooms. In the 1940s, Jackie Robinson and Buck O'Neil, then in the Negro Leagues, developed a policy that if a gas station wouldn't let them use the restroom, then the players refused to allow their large- tank buses to be filled with gas, and they would move to another station. That usually forced open the restrooms.

Spring Training Ban. Jackie Robinson was not allowed to dress with the Dodgers or stay at hotels in Sanford, Florida, during spring training. Sanford was joined by Jacksonville, DeLand and St. Augustine, all of which cancelled games after learning that Robinson was scheduled to play. Exhibition games were also cancelled in Syracuse (New York) and Baltimore.

Weather. In 2003, Giants manager Dusty Baker was criticized for speaking candidly about the ability of black and Latin players to adapt to the heat: "We were brought over here for the heat. Isn't that history? Your skin color is more conducive to heat than it is to the lighter-skinned people. I don't see brothers running around burnt."

Baker stood by the comments and refused to back down when challenged on a claim that his comments were some sort of reverse racism.

Radar Guns See *Fastest Pitchers* and *Speed Guns*

Old Hoss Radbourn (1854–1897)

Hall of Fame 1939

"His showing [in 1884] was all the more remarkable and phenomenal when one knows that this great pitcher suffered untold agony in endeavoring to attain the goal for which he worked so hard and so pluckily. Morning after morning upon arising he would be unable to raise his arm high enough to use his hair brush. Instead of quitting he stuck all the harder to his task, going out to the ball park hours before the rest of the team and beginning to warm up by throwing a few feet and increasing the distance until he could finally throw the ball from the outfield to the home plate."— Radbourn's manager Frank Bancroft in 1897, quoted in *Baseball: Diamond in the Rough*, by Irving A. Leitner (1972).

Radbourn won 311 games in only 11 seasons between 1881 and 1891, including 59 in 1884.

Charles Gardner Radbourn, a native New Yorker, was 27 when he first played in the National League for Providence in 1881. He won 25 games and led the league in winning percentage. Over the next six seasons he won an astounding 221 games. He reached 49 wins in 1883 and in 1884 and had perhaps the most amazing season ever for a pitcher. He was 59–12 for Providence (for many years thought to be 60), starting 73 games (one tie) and completed them all. He also threw in a save for good measure. He pitched 11 shutouts and won 18 straight games at one point during the season. He pitched 678 innings and struck out 441 batters.

Radbourn's arm, always a problem for him, deteriorated badly after that season, and he faded to 28 wins the following season. According to many sources, he was unable to raise his arm in the morning but was ready to go by game time. He moved to the Boston Red Stockings for the 1886 season, winning 20 or more games three times. He played for Boston of the Players League in 1890 and finished out his career with an 11–13 record for Cincinnati in 1891.

He won 311 games over 11 seasons and pitched a no-hitter against Cleveland in 1883. He opened a poolroom after he retired but lost an eye during a hunting accident and became a recluse. He died at age 43 in 1897.

Radio

"Turn the radio on, and you'll hear a friend.... Turn the radio on in your car, in prison, on the beach, in a nursing home, and you will not be alone, you will not be lonely. Newspapers fold, magazines come and go, television self-destructs. Radio remains the trusted common denominator in this nation."— Cardinals broadcaster Jack Buck.

"I like radio better than television because if you make a mistake on radio, they don't know. You can make up anything on the radio."— Phil Rizzuto.

"Broadcasting stories of games as the games go along is the equivalent of a succotash party with neither corn nor beans."—1925 editorial in *The Sporting News* criticizing radio broadcasts. Although an earlier editorial in the publication favored radio, no doubt the editors initially feared competition from the new medium.

"The advent of radio was different. Like Carl Sandburg's fog, radio sneaked in on 'little cat feet' before baseball owners and fans realized what was going on. Yet radio and its buxom offspring, television, have had greater and more revolutionary impact on baseball than any other development in more than a century of the game's history." — Ford Frick in *Games, Asterisks and People* (1973).

"We now pause 10 stations for a minute identification." — Jerry Coleman.

"Hello there, Padre fans! We, uh … we, uh … are we on the air?" — Jerry Coleman.

See also **Broadcasters**, **Re-Creations**, **Television** and Key Broadcasters in each team history.

First Major League Broadcast.

"Our guys at KDKA didn't even think that baseball would last on radio. I did it sort of as a one-shot project, a kind of addendum to the events we'd already done." — Harold Arlin in Curt Smith's *Voices of the Game* (1987), the seminal work on baseball broadcasting.

The first radio broadcast of a Major League game occurred on August 5, 1921. It was heard over KDKA, the first radio station in the country. KDKA went on the air on November 2, 1920, during the presidential elections. It was the first station to broadcast tennis, on August 6, 1921, and football, Pitt versus West Virginia, 63 days later.

The first baseball broadcast emanated from Forbes Field, Pittsburgh. Harold Arlin, 26, a Westinghouse foreman and radio announcer at night, broadcast the game. The Pirates defeated the Phillies 8–5 in 1 hour and 57 minutes. Arlin, who died at 90 in March 1986, sat in a ground level box seat and broadcast the game. One source reported that he sat in the bleachers and at the end of each inning wrote the results on slips of paper and dropped them outside the ballpark fence to a waiting accomplice. The accomplice then called the results into the station and the studio announcer broadcast each inning as a re-creation. This was probably during the 1921 World Series (see **Re-Creations**).

Arlin's grandson Steve had a 34–67 Major League pitching record from 1969 through 1974 with the Padres and Indians.

World Series Broadcasts.

"Hear the crowd roar at the World Series game with radiologist Grantland Rice, famous sports editor of the *New York Tribune*, who will describe every game personally, play by play, direct from the Polo Grounds." — 1922 newspaper advertisement.

"They played two World Series games at the Polo Grounds this afternoon — the one I watched and the one broadcast by Graham McNamee." — Ring Lardner in 1922 on NcNamee's flowery style.

The first World Series broadcast was on October 5, 1921, with Grantland Rice of the *New York Herald Tribune* behind the microphone during a 3–0 Yankee win over the Giants at the Polo Grounds. The broadcast was over WJZ of New Jersey and WBZ of Springfield, Massachusetts, which were linked to KDKA in Pittsburgh.

A year later on October 4, 1922, the radio broadcast was piped into the public address system at the game so the voices of the announcers and umpires could be heard by the crowd. In 1922 the World Series radio audience was approximately five million over a broad area. The 1949 World Series was heard on the radio by 26 million fans. In 1968, 88 million fans listened in and by the 1980s the total was over 100 million.

Early Use by Teams. Fearing a decline in attendance, American League president Ban Johnson prohibited broadcasts from American League ballparks for the 1926 season. Some minor leagues followed his lead and banned radio for a short time in the belief that the medium was cutting into ballpark attendance. After the excitement of the 1926 World Series (Cardinals over Yankees in seven), and the enormous fan interest it generated from the radio broadcast, Johnson allowed radio broadcasts for the 1927 season.

The first authorized radio broadcast in St. Louis was in 1927. Before that the games were pirated from a nearby rooftop. Cubs owner William Wrigley loved radio and first used it in the mid–1920s for a few home games. The club reported a 117% increase in attendance from 1925 through 1931 while broadcasting games, with no substantial increase in the standings. Other teams not using radio saw a 27% rise in attendance in the same time frame.

In 1929 the Reds became the first club to air regular radio broadcasts of all their games. In the early 1930s, WMAQ in Chicago, owned by the *Chicago Daily News*, was the first station to carry all local home games, which included both the Cubs and White Sox. The Browns first allowed a broadcast in 1930, but agreed only to dull play-by-play with no commentary. The response by *The Sporting News*: "This should be mutually satisfactory to both the fans and the magnates, for there are some announcers who prove to wander far from the actual occurrences on the field."

For many years both St. Louis teams and the Pirates banned Sunday and holiday broadcasts. In 1932 baseball debated whether to eliminate radio entirely as it was thought to have contributed to the lower attendance caused primarily by the Depression.

In 1934 only the clubs in Chicago, Boston and Cincinnati had regular radio broadcasts. By 1935 there were 13 clubs with regular radio broadcasts. The primary exceptions were the three New York clubs, who collectively signed a five-year agreement in 1934 prohibiting radio in that city. This ended in 1939 when Larry MacPhail took over as general manager of the Dodgers and refused to renew the agreement. The Dodgers' first radio contract was for $77,000 and the Giants' first contract was for $150,000. The last club to grant broadcast rights were the Yankees in 1939.

There were a few New York broadcasts prior to the creation of the five-year ban in 1934. In mid–1931 four stations broadcast from Ebbets Field. Graham McNamee and future commissioner Ford Frick were two of the broadcasters. There were also broadcasts of the final series of the season. Only after World War II did all teams broadcast their entire schedules.

Powerful Medium. By the 1930s there were approximately 18 million radios available to receive broadcasts (portable and stationary). The power of radio is illustrated by an anecdote recounted by Buzzie Bavasi in his autobiography. During the 1950s the Dodgers staged a split doubleheader at Ebbets Field, meaning that one game would be played in the morning, the stadium would be cleared, and another game would be played in the afternoon. When only 5,000 were in the stands for the start of the morning game, Dodger announcer Red Barber went on the air and said that good seats were still available and that they would hold up the game 15 minutes to allow people to get there. Over 27,000 showed up for the game.

In 1934 Cardinals owner Sam Breadon banned broadcasts of home games. The Cardinals won the pennant, but attendance was down to 334,863, as the Depression heavily affected the figures. When radio returned for 1935, attendance rose to 517,805, despite the fact that the Depression had not yet ended (though a 96–58 record and a second-place finish probably helped).

Early Sponsorship. In the 1920s radio stations did not pay clubs to broadcast games because club owners who favored the medium were happy simply to expose their games to more fans. They reasoned correctly that the increased exposure through radio would bring more fans to the ballpark.

Henry Ford entered into the first major sponsorship deal when he paid $400,000 for four years of World Series games starting in 1934. Other sources report that the first World Series radio sponsor was Mobil Oil, which paid $400,000 for four years beginning in 1934.

The American League clubs' regular season radio revenue was $11,000 in 1933, but skyrocketed to $420,000 in 1939, primarily because the New York teams finally began broadcasting games.

In 1946 Gillette agreed to pay $14 million for 10 years of exclusive radio rights to the World Series and All-Star Games. Until 1965 when the networks took control of the broadcasts, the commissioner and Gillette (which held the exclusive World Series rights for over 20 years) selected the announcers.

Cities with Two Clubs. In cities with two Major League clubs, baseball had special rules for many years. The home team was allowed to broadcast its games, but the team on the road could not because it was thought that broadcasting road games would cut into the home team's attendance.

Car Radios. Car radios were introduced in 1923 by the Springfield Body Corporation.

Portable Radios.

"The eye-ear twin bill."—This was the solution to two games played in New York at the same time; one in Ebbets Field seen in person "using the optic nerve," and "the game across the river [at the Polo Grounds] via the auditory canal" using a portable radio (per *The Sporting News*). "Sidewalk" portable radios proliferated in the 1930s, allowing fans to follow games while they were away from home.

Network Broadcasts. The Mutual Broadcasting System's first sporting event was the first *Night Game* in Major League history, in Cincinnati in 1935. By then there were three networks broadcasting baseball games as re-creations: CBS, NBC and Mutual. Though Mutual had the largest radio network during the 1940s, the Liberty Broadcasting Network of Dallas, run by "The Old Scotchman," Gordon McClendon, dominated the broadcast arena in the 1940s.

Liberty was the first to broadcast Major League Baseball to outlying parts of the country. These were done by Western Union *Re-Creations* over 300 stations by October 1949. Liberty broadcast two games each day. The potential audience was 60–90 million.

All stations within 75 miles (later 50 miles) "from home plate" could not air a network broadcast during a local game as a measure to protect home attendance.

Ford Frick took over as commissioner in September 1951. An ex-sportswriter, he banned Liberty from doing re-creations of games, but Liberty blocked that ban in court. Nevertheless, Liberty was pushed aside by Mutual and by 1953 it was bankrupt. The dominant factor working against Liberty was the loss of its key sponsor, Falstaff Beer, which moved to Mutual.

Liberty's high point was its unpaid-for broadcast of Game 3 of the 1951 play-off between the Dodgers and Giants. No one questioned Liberty's presence at the game, and the network simply carried the game as if it owned the right to do so.

On April 18, 1950, the Yankees played the Red Sox in what was the Mutual Broadcasting System's inaugural "Game of the Day" over a network of 520 stations. It began the longest-running live network radio series in history, as the network did not do re-creations. For the first time a network was paying to broadcast live from inside the ballpark. Mutual worked with baseball by avoiding Sunday and night broadcasts (focusing instead on afternoon games) so that the minor leagues would not be wiped out completely by the Major League coverage that was penetrating outlying areas.

The chief broadcaster for Mutual was Al Helfer, who also broadcast at various times for each of the three New York teams (Giants, Dodgers and Yankees).

Though NBC dominated baseball on television in the late 1960s through the 1980s, CBS controlled the radio side. By 1976 CBS Radio had 267 affiliates, plus stations in Canada, Puerto Rico, the Dominican Republic, Venezuela, Panama and a number of other Latin countries. In 1993 CBS radio signed a new six-year deal with Major League Baseball for $50.5 million per year, replacing a four-year deal at $52 million per year.

Team Networks. By 1964 the Cardinals had 100 radio stations broadcasting their games, the White Sox had 90, and the Reds 60. At the other end of the spectrum the Cubs had one (WGN) and the Senators had 17.

By the 1980s the average team's radio network consisted of 35 stations, which was down from approximately 50 in 1955. By the mid–1990s the Royals had 115 affiliates over nine states and the Cardinals had 135 over 11 states. The Braves led all clubs with 200 stations over eight states. The smallest networks were the Angels (13), Mets (12) and Padres (8).

Language Problems.

"As Duke Ellington once said, the Battle of Waterloo was won on the playing fields of Elkton."—Babe Ruth in a scripted radio interview with Graham McNamee; Ruth's explanation for lousing up the Duke of Wellington and Eton, as told to Grantland Rice: "About that Wellington guy I wouldn't know. Ellington, yes. As for that Eton business—well, I married my first wife in Elkton [Maryland], and I always hated the goddamn place. It musta stuck."

In the very early days of radio, Harold Arlin once conducted a radio interview with Ruth, only to have Ruth freeze up. Arlin continued the interview anyway and many listeners were under the impression that Arlin's voice was Ruth's. The Yankees received a number of letters complimenting Ruth on his voice.

Puerto Rican Vic Power had a tough time with the English language early in his career. During a radio interview he was asked a question about pitchers. His response started with "some of the pitchers," but it sounded exactly like "sons of bitches" and the producer immediately cut off the live feed and ended the interview. The same story has been told using Juan Marichal and Luis Tiant.

Expansion Clubs/Original Broadcasters.

Angels—Don Wells, Bob Kelley and Steve Bailey
Senators—Dan Daniels and John MacLean
Colt 45s—Gene Elston, Loel Passe and Al Helfer
Mets—Lindsey Nelson, Ralph Kiner and Bob Murphy
Royals—Buddy Blattner and Denny Mathews
Pilots—Jimmy Dudley and Bill Schoenely
Expos—Dave Van Horne and Russ Taylor (English); Jean-Paul Sarault (French)
Padres—Frank Sims, Jerry Gross and Duke Snider
Mariners—Dave Niehaus and Ken Wilson
Blue Jays—Tom Cheek and Early Wynn
Rockies—Wayne Hagin and Jeff Kingery
Marlins—Jay Randolph and Gary Carter
Diamondbacks—Greg Schulte, Thom Brennaman and Joe Garagiola
Devil Rays—DeWayne Staats, Paul Olden, Charlie Slowes and Joe Magrane

Books. Ken Reitz, *The Baseball Listener's Guide* (1993), containing then-current radio affiliates of every Major and minor league team; Curt Smith, *Voices of the Game* (1987).

Railroads

"Traveling men, when they learn that they are to ride on a train bearing a ball club, do not take out accident insurance policies for the trip. Railroad passenger agents like to have the patronage of ball clubs, not only for the additional revenue, but because they figure the athletes' presence on the train is an omen that there will not be a disastrous wreck." — Albert Spalding in *America's National Game* (1911).

"For a few fleeting hours yesterday the Dodgers returned to a nostalgic daffy era of the 1930s when anything could — and usually did — happen to Brooklyn as they survived a train wreck.... The hair-raising Dodger experiences began in St. Louis at 1 o'clock yesterday morning when they shuffled aboard day coaches and sat up all night in order to make the scheduled game in Chicago. Coming out of Manhattan, Ill., the train struck a gasoline-laden trailer truck, searing the train in flames. All the players and passengers escaped injury..." — The *Stars and Stripes* military newspaper in 1945.

Rail Stops.
"If he held out his arm, he'd be a railroad crossing." — Joe Garagiola on big Boog Powell.

The 1888 championship St. Louis Browns were rewarded by a local railroad by renaming four of its stops after Browns players: Comiskey, Latham, Foutz and Bushong.

Travel.
"Groundskeepers gathered up the debris around Wrigley Field last night, discovered it was the Cubs baseball team and gently placed it on a train bound for Pittsburgh." — The *Stars and Stripes* military newspaper in 1944.

Some sources reported that teams regularly traveled with two Pullman sleepers, one for the regulars and one for the substitutes and press. Other sources reported that teams used three cars on a train. The rookies and writers traveled in the last car. The prestige location was Lower 7, Car A; the first and steadiest car, a lower birth in the middle of the car.

Joe DiMaggio recalled that those who batted third, fourth and fifth in the order received the center berths on one side, and the starting pitchers received them on the other. Rookies slept over the wheels.

Nickname. In the 19th century, railroad sleeper cars were sometimes known as "Sullivans," after Ted Sullivan, owner of the St. Louis club in the American Association.

Death. Former Major Leaguer Wild Bill Donovan was killed in a train wreck when he was a minor league manager. In the berth above him was future Yankee general manager George Weiss, who was not seriously hurt.

Ballpark. When Enron Field in Houston opened in April 2000 it featured a 27-foot, 24-ton replica of an old west steam train running on a track behind the left field wall.

Rain Checks

"In case rain interrupts the game before three innings are played, this check will admit the bearer to grounds for the next league game only." — 1888 Detroit rain check.

Origins. Abner Powell, who later owned the Atlanta Crackers in the Southern Association, is credited by some with starting rain checks in 1889 in New Orleans. However, Detroit issued rain checks as early as 1888, as evidenced above. Other clubs followed suit and the policy of allowing fans into the next game only, rather than a game farther into the future, continued for years. Powell affirmed his claim in a 1943 article in *The Sporting News* at age 83: "A lot of fellows would climb the fence or get into the park without paying. Then it would rain and they would all get tickets to the next game. We were losing money and had to do something."

Powell claimed that the rain check was introduced in Sportsman's Park in New Orleans. He presented the rain check idea to an Arkansas firm specializing in ticket printing for theaters and ballparks. The firm asked if it could use the idea for other clubs. The tickets were dated so they could not be reused.

Before rain checks, *Tickets* were thin cardboard strips that were often reused. With the advent of the rain check, the new tickets had perforations so that fans could hold the stubs during the game in case a rain check was issued in exchange.

Connie Mack. Connie Mack put his full name on A's rain checks: Cornelius McGilliguddy.

Bill Veeck. Bill Veeck once gave out rain checks at a game which had "gloomy" skies. The game went on anyway and Bobo Holloman pitched a *No-Hitter*. Veeck also offered rain checks, "or a reasonable facsimile," for the next game after the White Sox played horrendously in 40-degree weather against the Blue Jays on Opening Day 1979. The next day only 2,220 fans took advantage of the offer, joining another 1,205 who paid. The "crowd" watched the White Sox blow a 7–2 lead by giving up six runs in the 8th inning.

Rain Delays

"Another thing: if there's a rain delay, I want you loose, but not too loose, understand? No TV. None of that goddamn heebie-jeebie music, neither. Cards is okay. Likewise okay is a little grab-ass in the clubhouse, only don't overdo it. And no thinkin'. I don't put no stock in thinkin'. Any questions?" — The manager to his play-

Rain check from Game 4 of the 1946 World Series between the Red Sox and Cardinals.

ers in David Carkeet's fictional *The Greatest Slump of All Time* (1984).

"I heard that doctors revived a man after being dead for four-and-a-half minutes. When they asked what it was like being dead, he said it was like listening to New York Yankees announcer Phil Rizzuto during a rain delay."— David Letterman in 1982.

"The Human Rain Delay"— Nickname given to Mike Hargrove of the Texas Rangers for his time-consuming batter's box routine after each pitch: stepping out of the box to adjust his helmet, gloves and uniform before getting set for the next pitch. The 2000s version of Hargrove is Nomar Garciaparra, who readjusts wristband, helmet, pants and groin after every pitch.

See also *Rainouts*.

Mound Problems. Game 7 of the 1925 World Series between the Senators and Pirates was marked by steady rain. The home team Pirates pitchers were provided with sawdust when they pitched, allowing them steadier footing on the mound. Senators pitcher Walter Johnson complained, but the umpires did not force the groundskeeper to provide him with the same comforts. Johnson went the distance but the Pirates won the game 9–7 after scoring five runs in the last two innings.

Filler. Former player and long-time broadcaster Waite Hoyt was considered a master at filling dead radio air during rain delays. He later released a record called "The Best of Waite Hoyt in the Rain," containing many of these stories.

Four members of the Cubs were fined $500 each for sliding on the tarp during a rain delay at the first Cubs night game in 1988.

Movies. During rain delays, Atlanta's Fulton County Stadium scoreboard airs baseball movies, presumably from Ted Turner's vast movie library.

Division Decider. On Saturday, October 3, 1999, the Mets were in a tight race with the Reds for the National League wild card spot. They had to finish a game against the Pirates despite intermittent rain. After a six-hour rain delay during a 1–1 tie and the bases loaded, Pirates reliever Brad Clontz bounced his first pitch to allow the winning run to score. The Mets went on to beat the Reds in a one-game play-off for the wild card.

Rainouts

"I can't tell you why this game is stopped, but if you'll stick your head out the window you'll know what I'm talking about."— Broadcaster Dizzy Dean during World War II, when weather information could not be freely disseminated. The 1942 All-Star Game was delayed by 50 minutes because of the "military secret." Weather reports were curtailed significantly during the war because they might have given the enemy an advantage in bombing missions and ship movements.

See also *Postponed Games*, *Rain Checks* and *Rain Delays*.

Pennant Races. Until a few seasons into the 20th century, a rained-out game often was not made up later in the year even when a pennant race depended on it. In 1907 the Tigers finished at 92–58 (.613 over 150 games) and the A's finished at 88–57 (.607 over 145 games). This gave the pennant to the Tigers despite a number of rainouts that might have affected the standings had they been replayed.

In 1908 the Indians finished 90–64 and the Tigers 90–63, one-half game behind. After that season the practice was changed to require rainouts and other canceled games to be played if they had a bearing on the pennant race.

In 1982 the Brewers beat out the Orioles head-to-head on the last day of the season for the Eastern Division title. The game was part of a four-game series the Brewers had to play against the Orioles to end the season. Instead of having already clinched before the final weekend began, the Brewers needed all four games of the series (losing the first three) before clinching.

Earlier in the season the Brewers were leading the Orioles 2–0 late in a game. Brewers catcher Ted Simmons thought John Lowenstein of the Orioles had struck out in an inning. Simmons casually flipped the ball toward the mound while the two runners on base advanced — there was only one out. The next batter singled, driving in two runners instead of one. The game ended in a rained-out 2–2 tie instead of a 2–1 Brewer victory.

Rule. Umpires must wait at least 1 hour and 15 minutes before calling a game due to rain.

Prior to 1980 if a game was called because of rain, the score reverted to the end of the last complete inning. The rule was changed so that visiting teams, who do not control game conditions, were not penalized. Under the new rule, as long as five complete innings are played, all runs will count. A called game ends the moment the umpire terminates it, so it does not revert to the earlier complete inning, except: "if the game is called while an inning is in progress and before it is completed, the game becomes a suspended game in each of the following situations: 1) the visiting team has scored one or more runs to tie the score and the home team has not scored; 2) the visiting team has scored one or more runs to take the lead and the home team has not tied the score or retaken the lead."

On August 13, 1978, the Orioles benefited from the old rainout rule. They were leading the Yankees 3–0 after six innings but the Yankees scored five runs in the top half of the 7th. Heavy rains ended the game in the bottom of the inning and the score reverted to the end of the last completed inning, giving the Orioles the win.

Longest Delay to Cancel.

"Whoever is responsible for this should be slapped."— Rangers outfielder Jack Daugherty.

On August 12, 1990, the White Sox and Rangers had a game scheduled at Comiskey Park for 1:35 p.m. The game was delayed for 7 hours and 23 minutes and finally canceled at 9:05 p.m. The White Sox were in a tight race and they did not want to play a make-up game in Texas and lose their home field advantage (it was the last game in Chicago that year between the two clubs).

More than 30,000 tickets were sold for the game, but only about 200 fans stayed to the end of what is believed to be the longest rain delay in history.

Protest. In 1908 Tigers second baseman Germany Schaefer took the field in high rubber boots, a fisherman's hat, umbrella and raincoat as his commentary on the ability to play baseball on that rainy day. The umpires finally suspended the game.

On July 14, 1925, pitcher Red Faber of the White Sox stole second base, third base and home trying to get thrown out and end a game because of impending rain. The rain never came, but the White Sox still beat the A's 6–4.

A's coach Clete Boyer used an umbrella out on the field in 1983 to protest what he thought should have been a game called because of rain.

Record Washed Out. On June 30, 1934, Lou Gehrig would have tied a Major League record with three triples in a game (in the first four innings), but they were washed out by rain.

Indoor Ballpark. On July 15, 1976, the Astrodome had a game postponed by torrential rains which flooded the access routes and parking area.

In June 1989 the Blue Jays tried to close their retractable roof when it began to rain on a game with the Brewers. The roof stuck

Yankee Stadium groundskeepers hold bases, ready to go, but the game is rained out in July 1964.

just before closing completely, creating a waterfall on home plate. The game had to be canceled. Through 2004 the Skydome has had four rain delays since it opened in 1989.

1911 World Series. This Series was plagued by five days of rainouts. On the fourth day, sportswriter Hugh Fullerton was alone in the hotel suite of American League president Ban Johnson when a call came from Johnson's personal secretary, Robby McCoy. McCoy was calling to inquire whether the game in Philadelphia that day should be canceled because of wet grounds. Fullerton, assuming the role of Johnson, answered "yes" because he had a dinner date in New York already scheduled. Johnson walked in shortly after the conversation and concurred in the decision because he, too, had a dinner date in New York.

Also during the 1911 Series rainouts, Fullerton and fellow sportswriter Bill Phelon killed time by putting an ad in the Philadelphia paper seeking models for a phony pictorial. According to sportswriter Fred Lieb, they spent their idle time taking measurements of the prospective posers.

Clear Skies. On May 20, 1985, the Brewers were rained out in Cleveland. It was the first rainout of the season, the longest stretch in Major League history without a canceled game by any club — 458 games.

The Dodgers once held the team record for most games between rainouts in a non-domed stadium. They went five years between the 1962 opening of Dodger Stadium and 1967. On May 12, 1998, the Padres suffered their first rainout in five years. The 1,184 home game streak was the longest in history for a team without a domed stadium.

On April 11, 1999, the Dodgers had their first rainout since 1988, a streak of 856 games. It was only the 16th rainout in team history.

Not-So-Clear Skies. On May 17, 18 and 19, 1943, every game in the American League was rained out. Between their creation in 1969 and the start of the 2003 season, the Kansas City Royals had 59 home rainouts, 22 in April. The Cardinals had 56 rainouts in Busch Stadium from its opening in 1966 through 2002.

Reach Baseball Guide (1883–1941)

"The Guide contains the full and *complete official* averages of the four Professional Associations of last year, and is the *only* Guide published which *does* contain these details *correct and in full*. As to the truth of this statement, the publishers invite an investigation. That which has long seemed a pressing want among base ball readers is herein found. Namely: a directory of professional clubs and players throughout the country."— Introduction to the 1884 *Reach Guide*.

This annual compilation of facts and figures was first published in 1883 by Alfred James (A.J.) Reach (1840–1928). The *Reach Guide* was the first baseball publication to contain information on low-hit games and game highlights. These features caught on and remained throughout the publication's existence. The *Reach* owners also manufactured early American League balls. The Reach name was left on the balls even after Spalding bought out the ball manufacturing portion of the Reach operation. The publication ceased to exist in the early 1940s after being the official publication of the American League.

A.J. Reach and his sporting goods business partner, Ben Shibe, at times had different rooting interests: In the early 20th century Shibe owned the Philadelphia A's in the American League. Reach had owned the Philadelphia Phillies of the National League in the late 19th century (though it is often reported that he also owned the Phillies in the early 20th century). Shibe joined the Reach Company in 1882 and was worth more than $1 million when he died.

In 1864 Reach received $25 per week to play for the Brooklyn Atlantics, becoming what many believe to be the first professional ballplayer. Reach also managed the 1890 Phillies for 11 games, compiling a 4–7 record.

Reaching Base

"Each base is an obstacle in his path, yet a qualifying of his course: a definition of it, in fact. Home is the vernal equinox, perhaps, and First the Summer solstice. Second base, the keystone, is the Autumn equinox, where we of the City start the year. Third base, most difficult of all, eccentric, chthonic, is the Winter Solstice, where the sun turns round and the runner has his last chance at terra firma before he makes his dash for the goal." — Commentary by a mythic Greek figure in Robert Kelly's "A Pastoral Dialogue on the Game of the Quadrature," contained in *Baseball Diamonds* (1980), an anthology edited by Kevin Kerrane and Richard Grossinger.

See also **On-Base Percentage.**

How to Reach First Base. There are eight ways to reach first base safely:

1. Hit
2. Base on balls
3. Hit by pitch
4. Catcher's interference
5. Error
6. Fielder's choice
7. Passed ball on third strike
8. Wild pitch on third strike

Big Day on Base. One of the greatest single-game on-base performances was by Max Carey of the Pirates. In an 18-inning game against the Giants, Carey had six hits and three walks in nine plate appearances. He also stole three bases, including home.

Consecutive At-Bats. Ted Williams holds the record for consecutive times getting on base with 16. The streak was stopped on September 24, 1957, by Senators pitcher Hal Griggs, a lifetime 6–26 pitcher. During the streak Williams had four home runs, two singles, one hit by pitch and nine walks.

In May 1997, White Sox first baseman Frank Thomas reached based 15 straight times. He ended the streak with a flyout after his fourth at-bat of the day. During the streak he had a home run, three doubles, six singles and five walks.

In early September 1998 Barry Bonds reached base a National League-record 15 straight times. The streak ended with a strikeout in the 1st inning of a game against the Dodgers on September 5, 1998. Bonds was 9-for-9 during the streak, surpassing Pedro Guerrero's record of 14 straight. The feat was overshadowed a bit, as Mark McGwire hit his 60th home run on the day Bonds' streak ended.

Game. On May 19, 1999, Sean Casey of the Reds reached base a record-tying seven times in seven appearances in a 24–12 Reds win over the Rockies at Coors Field.

Inning. On May 21, 1952, Pee Wee Reese became the only National League player in the 20th century to safely reach base three times in one inning.

Season Streak. In 1999 Derek Jeter started the season by reaching base in 53 straight games. The streak ended on the same day that Roger Clemens' 20-game win streak ended. It is believed that Joe DiMaggio reached base in 73 straight games in 1941. Barry Bonds equaled the National League record in 2003 when he reached base in 58 straight games, tying Duke Snider's 1954 record.

Full Season. Lefty O'Doul of the Phillies hit .398 in 1929 and was on base 334 times (254 hits, 76 walks and four hit by pitch), the most in the National League in the 20th century.

Career. During the 2000 season, Rickey Henderson became only the sixth player in Major League history to reach base by either a hit, base on balls, or being hit by a pitch 5,000+ times in his career. He finished with 5,343 in 3,081 games. The others:

Games/Times on Base

Pete Rose	3,562/5,929
Ty Cobb	3,034/5,533
Carl Yastrzemski	3,308/5,313
Stan Musial	3,206/5,282
Henry Aaron	3,298/5,205

Ted Williams had 4,712 (one of 11 players to reach the 4,700 level) and missed five full seasons. Tris Speaker had 4,998 in only 2,789 games.

Streaky. On May 14, 1966, Ron Hunt began a streak for the Mets in which he reached base 18 out of 19 times against the Giants. He singled three times and walked twice. The next day he hit another three singles, reached on a fielder's choice, and struck out. The following week he played in San Francisco. Over the next two games he homered, singled five times, was hit by a two pitches and walked once: 11 singles, one home run, three walks, two hit by pitch, and one fielders choice.

Realignment See **Divisional Play**

Records See **Statistics**

Re-Creations

"At the beginning and the end of each one of those broadcasts, we announced that it was a re-creation, that we were working off of information being transmitted to us over a Western Union ticker. But once we were into it, the fantasy was never interrupted. We would never even hint that we were in a studio in downtown St. Louis while the game was being played [elsewhere]. In fact, people used to argue all the time whether we were recreating a game or doing it live. Even to this day, people aren't sure." — Harry Caray in his autobiography, *Holy Cow!*, with Bob Verdi (1989).

See also **Radio.**

Re-creations were used for many years on radio to enable a station to broadcast a road game without actually having to send a broadcaster on the road to the game. The information about the game was taken off the **Western Union** ticker and re-created in the studio. Western Union charged a fee to hook up ballparks to its system.

First Re-Creation. During the 1921 World Series, radio stations in Newark and Springfield presented the first baseball re-creations from the Polo Grounds. The innings' details were telephoned by a reporter to Tommy Cowan, who did the re-created play-by-play from a shack on top of the Newark Westinghouse Building. The broadcast began at 7:00 p.m. and lasted for 30 minutes, covering the highlights of the day's game in New York. The earliest re-creations were done after the games were completed. Later re-creations were done simultaneously with the live feed from Western Union.

Increase in Re-Creations.

"So there it was. I was happy to have fathomed the mystery, as perhaps no one else in the whole town had done. The Old Scotchman, for all his wondrous expressions, was not only several innings behind every game he described but was no doubt sitting in some

Members of the Atlantic Base Ball Club prepare for a game in Cincinnati during the 2004 SABR convention. The club was established in 1997 and is the official re-creation team of the original Atlantic Base Ball Club of New York.

air-conditioned studio in the hinterland, where he got the happenings of the game by news ticker.... Instead of being disappointed in the Scotchman, I was all the more pleased by his genius, for he made pristine facts more actual than actuality, a valuable lesson when the day finally came that I started reading literature."—Willie Morris in the fictional *North Toward Home* (1967).

The first re-created broadcasts to outlying parts of the country were by Gordon McLendon (The Old Scotchman) over the Liberty Broadcasting System out of Dallas (see also **Radio**—**Network Broadcasts**). Only the Browns would not allow the network to cover its games. By October 1949 the broadcasts were done by Western Union re-creations over 300 stations.

There were two games each day. If both games were rained out then the broadcaster did re-creations of famous old games, including those as far back as the 1869 Cincinnati Red Stockings. McClendon, the acknowledged leader of the business in the 1940s and early 1950s, went out of his way to achieve authenticity. He arranged to have tapes of each of the ballpark's crowd noises and its organist playing the national anthem. The "public address announcer" sat in a nearby men's room to achieve the proper echo for announcing line-up changes. Delays in the Western Union feeds caused broadcasters to make up numerous foul balls or other delays until the feed resumed.

From 1940 through 1953 Marty Glickman broadcast from the Manhattan Western Union station a nightly re-creation of one New York game. Re-creations died out in the late 1950s, though the Los Angeles Dodgers continued to broadcast re-creations in New York until 1962, when the Mets arrived.

"Managed News." Washington sportswriter Shirley Povich once helped save manager Bucky Harris' job with the Senators. During a re-creation Povich was sitting with the Western Union operator who was relaying the particulars back to Washington and broadcaster Arch McDonald. Harris was in trouble with Senators owner Clark Griffith, who undoubtedly would be listening to the game.

The Senators were in the midst of a long losing streak during a game in Cleveland. In the 9th inning the Senators were losing by a run with two Senators runners on base and no outs. Cecil Travis should have bunted, which is what Griffith would have wanted.

Instead, he swung and missed at the first two pitches. To protect Harris, Povich instructed the Western Union operator to report to McDonald that Travis had fouled off both pitches attempting to bunt. Travis tripled in the winning runs and Harris received a reprieve.

Commemorative Record. The Armed Forces Radio Network (AFRN) broadcast a re-creation of Harvey Haddix's near-perfect game in 1959. To commemorate the event, AFRN issued a four-record set of the game with a special dedication to Haddix. The broadcasters were extremely stilted in their delivery, and there was none of the excitement and illusion used by some of the more celebrated re-creation broadcasters.

Pirating. Until 1956 Waite Hoyt did not travel with the Reds and instead did re-creations. He later revealed that Major League officials wanted the broadcasters to make three deliberate mistakes in their calls of the re-creations, so that pirate broadcasts could be identified.

Pee Wee Reese (1918–1999)

Hall of Fame (VC) 1984

"I had only played five games my senior year in high school. I was not large enough. Hell, when I graduated, I was about five foot four and weighed 120 pounds.... I didn't go with the Dodgers until spring training of 1940 ... and I weighed all of 155 pounds soaking wet. Looking like I was sixteen, I guess. When I got there, I didn't know any of the fellas on the team, and I was scared to death.... Wherever they went, they took me with them. Why did they do it? Beats the hell out of me. I was just a scared kid from Kentucky, and these guys had been up in the majors for a while. I guess it was because I was just such a helluva nice kid—if you'll accept that."—Reese quoted in *Bums*, by Peter Golenbock (1984).

Reese played shortstop for the Dodgers from 1941 through 1958.

Harold Henry Reese, a champion marble shooter ("Pee Wees" are marbles), grew up in Kentucky and starred at shortstop for the minor league Louisville Colonels in the late 1930s. Reese was signed by the Red Sox, but they sold him to the Dodgers because Red Sox player-manager Joe Cronin was still solidly handling shortstop in Boston.

After a mediocre 1940 rookie season hampered by injury, Reese became the on-field and spiritual leader of the Dodgers. From 1941 through 1956 he played in at least 140 games every season, except for missing the entire 1943–1945 seasons during World War II. His best year was 1949 when he hit .279 in 155 games, with 132 runs scored and 116 walks. A model of consistency at bat, he was also the top defensive shortstop of the 1940s and early 1950s and was an All-Star from 1947 through 1954. He led the Dodgers to seven National League pennants, finally winning the World Series in 1955.

Reese was extremely popular and captained the Dodgers for many years. It was his attitude both on and off the field that helped teammate Jackie Robinson deal with the pressure of breaking the color line in baseball.

After retiring following the 1958 season, Reese coached and then moved to the broadcast booth with Dizzy Dean. He later became a businessman in Kentucky, at times working for the Louisville Slugger bat company. He died of lung cancer in August 1999.

Book. Gene Schoor, *The Pee Wee Reese Story* (1956).

Reflexes

"This fact—and it is an unyielding fact that the reflex always exists in all humans—is the starting point for the game of baseball, and yet it is the fact least often mentioned by those who write about baseball."—Leonard Koppett in *The New Thinking Man's Guide to Baseball* (1991).

Release

"Lafayette Fresco Thompson and all of his names were released today."—Ballclub's press release announcing shortstop Fresco Thompson's release.

"You were only twelve years old and it couldn't have made much of an impression on you when the mailman delivered my release from the Philadelphia Athletics in January 1949. I wasn't surprised.... Still, it's like death and taxes, and releases. You know they're bound to come, but you don't think about them until they hit you between the eyes."—Rudy York writing to his son, as told to Furman Bisher.

"Whenever I decided to release a guy, I always had his room searched first for a gun. You couldn't take any chances with some of them birds."—Dodger manager Casey Stengel in 1935.

Rule. In the early days of Organized Baseball, players could be released and paid their salary for only the next 10 days. Today, if a player is on a Major League roster for one regular season game and then is released, he must be paid for the entire year.

Retribution. When Tommy Davis was released by the A's a few games into the 1972 season, it was probably because owner Charlie Finley was upset that Davis had recently introduced star pitcher Vida Blue to agent and attorney Robert J. Gerst. The ensuing acrimonious negotiations infuriated Finley.

Guaranteed Contract Woes. In 2003 the Angels cut Kevin Appier, who was owed $15.6 million, the Tigers cut Damion Easley, who was owed $14.3 million, and the Devil Rays cut designated hitter Greg Vaughn, who was owed $9.25 million. These were the largest contractual obligations to released players in the history of baseball. In 2003 Major League teams released six players who had more than $3 million left on their contracts. A total of more than $60 million was wasted in 2003, up from $30.3 million in 2002 and $30.2 million in 2001.

Relief Pitchers

"Why pitch nine innings when you can get just as famous pitching two."—Sparky Lyle.

"It helps to be stupid if you're a relief pitcher. Relievers have to get into a zone of their own. I just hope I'm stupid enough."—Dan Quisenberry.

"A lot of things run through your head when you're going in to relieve in a trouble spot. One of them is, 'should I spike myself.'"—Lefty Gomez.

"Whoever answers the bullpen phone."—Rangers pitching coach Chuck Estrada, on deciding which relief pitcher to bring in.

"Pitchers are generally a twitching bundle of nerve endings to begin with, but relievers are truly in a different league."—Angus G. Garber III in *The Baseball Companion* (1989).

See also *Fireman of the Year Award* and *Saves* (for the save rules).

19th Century. By the late 1870s all teams carried a spare pitcher. However, pitchers were less of a factor in those days because of restrictions on pitching delivery, so a reliever was not necessary.

Early 20th Century.
The National Game (1910) references an early 20th century game in which the St. Louis Browns loaded the bases with no outs against the White Sox. The Chicago leader, Fielder Jones, is credited with bringing in a different pitcher to get out each of the next three batters. The book credits Jones with being the first to do this.

In 1909 there was a sharp increase in relief pitching, as evidenced by 110 Major League saves that year versus 32 in 1901. In 1909 for the first time the National League had only three pitchers with over 300 innings pitched and Three Finger Brown was the only pitcher with more than 30 complete games.

Giants manager John McGraw used pitcher Otis "Doc" Crandall as the first regular relief pitcher from 1908 through 1913. He pitched in up to 42 games per season, mostly in relief. He compiled a lifetime relief record of 37–14, with 21 saves. He led the league in relief wins four times, although his highest save total was only six.

Future Senators owner Clark Griffith occasionally pitched in relief for the Yankees in the early 20th century and later was a manager and owner who strongly believed in relief pitching. He had 26 relief wins and six saves from 1891 through 1914. One source credited him inaccurately with managing the Giants and using relief pitchers when he actually was managing the Yankees/Highlanders.

1920s–1940s. During this era the bullpen was still primarily a haven for former starters who could still pitch, but had physical limitations that made it difficult for them to pitch regularly. However, there were a few notable exceptions.

Fred "Firpo" Marberry pitched for 14 seasons, mainly for the Senators from 1923 through 1932. He compiled a relief record of 53–37, with 101 saves. He had save years of 15, 15, 22, 11 and 13 and led the league in appearances five times.

Perhaps the most valuable reliever of the 1930s was Lefty Grove, who saved 55 games in his career. In 1930 and 1931 he won 49 games as a starter. He also appeared in relief 27 times, winning nine and saving 14. Dizzy Dean had a league-high 11 saves in 1936 to go with his 24 wins.

In 1939 Johnny Murphy of the Yankees set a new club record with 19 saves. In a 13-year career spanning 1932 through 1947 (missing a few World War II years), he was 73–42 with 107 saves. He also had two relief wins and four saves in the World Series.

In 1939 Clint Brown of the White Sox appeared in 61 games, a record at that time. He compiled 11 relief wins and 18 saves that year.

In 1943 Ace Adams appeared in 70 games for the Giants and had other years with appearance totals of 61, 65 and 65. He compiled a relief record of 37–31 with 48 saves in only four years.

Hugh Casey was a top reliever in the 1940s for the Dodgers. Over a nine-year career interrupted by World War II, Casey recorded 55 saves (highs of 18 and 13) and a relief record of 51–21.

A number of quality middle- and late-inning relief specialists emerged shortly after World War II. Joe Page of the Yankees was the first example of a great closer, with a 37–30 career relief record to go with 73 saves. He had a high of 27 saves in 1949. He also had two relief wins and two saves in the World Series.

Bill Bevens is credited with showing Page a new grip on his fastball, which led to Page's stardom with the Yankees. The turning point for Page was May 26, 1947. He had been struggling when he came in to relieve for the Yankees, who were leading the Red Sox 3–0. The bases were loaded with no outs. He got two strikeouts and a fly out to end the inning and went on to pitch six scoreless innings. Had he not retired the first batter after going 3-and-0 in the count, it was clear from those in charge at the time that he would have been lifted and sent back to the minor leagues. According to one report, manager Bucky Harris was on the phone to his bullpen and said: "If it's ball four, he's going to Newark."

Breakthrough Years/1950–1952.

"As I see it, we need another starting pitcher a whole lot more than we do a relief pitcher. You know how I feel about relief pitchers. I don't believe in them. On our club right now, as on most clubs, they are simply necessary evils."— Branch Rickey in a confidential 1949 memo.

Jim Konstanty of the Phillies was the National League MVP in 1950 when he led the club to the pennant with a 16–7 record and 22 saves. He did not start any games in 74 appearances. Nevertheless, he started Game 1 of the World Series, giving up only two hits in a 1–0 loss. He became a starter in 1953, compiling a 14–10 record. See also Frank Yeutter, *Jim Konstanty* (1951).

Former Negro League player Joe Black was a 28-year-old rookie for the Dodgers when he compiled a 15–4 record with 15 saves in 1952. He started only two games in 57 appearances. Hoyt Wilhelm was 29 years old with the Giants that season, appearing in 71 games with a 15–3 record, 11 saves and no starts. Cardinals pitcher Eddie Yuhas was 12–2 with six saves and teammate Alpha Brazle was 12–5 with 16 saves. Between the two, they started only eight games in 110 appearances. From then on, the role of the pure relief pitcher was firmly established, culminating that decade with the performance of Roy Face in 1959. He was 18–1 with 10 saves and made no starts in 57 appearances.

Awards. *The Sporting News* Fireman of the Year Award is awarded separately from the Rolaids Relief Award.

"Fireman." The first "fireman" was labeled as such by Pittsburgh sportswriter Les Biederman in the 1940s. He gave the name to reliever Mace Brown, who posed in a fireman's helmet. Brown doubled as a starter until 1941 and in 1938 was the first reliever named to the All-Star Game.

Most Valuable Player. In 1950 Jim Konstanty of the Phillies became the first relief pitcher to receive an MVP Award.

In 2003 Dodger reliever Eric Gagne received the league's MVP Award after recording 55 saves without blowing one (except, ironically, the All-Star Game). The last relievers to receive the MVP Award before Gagne were Dennis Eckersley of the A's in 1992 and Mark Davis of the Padres in 1989.

First Cy Young Award. In 1974 Mike Marshall of the Dodgers became the first reliever to win the Cy Young Award.

In 1977 Sparky Lyle of the Yankees became the first American League reliever to win the award.

Dual Purpose.

"The Eck, in those skintight frog pants, with his lovelocks flying and his pitching hand lolling, as usual, in mid-windup, ran the count full…"— Roger Angell on Dennis Eckersley in *The New Yorker* magazine. Eckersley made 361 starts between 1975 and early 1987 before saving 390 games (with no starts after two in 1987). He appeared in 1,071 games through 1998.

In 1993 Charlie Hough of the Marlins became the first pitcher to start 400 games and relieve in 400 games. He also became the second player to appear in 400 games in each league, first done by Hoyt Wilhelm.

Effect on Hitting. Hitters often need at least two or three at-bats before they can effectively gauge a pitcher. In today's specialized age, batters rarely see a pitcher more than three times in a game. With more teams, there are less chances per season to see the same pitchers. Even middle relievers are now specialized set-up men and not just pitchers who cannot make it as starters.

Left-Handed. Left-handed relievers became a hot commodity beginning in the 1990s. Elias Sports Bureau determined that the last team to win the World Series without using a left-hander in the postseason was the 1910 Philadelphia A's. In the expansion era only two teams, the 1982 Braves and the 1998 Rangers, have made it to the playoffs without using a left-handed reliever in the postseason. Both of those teams were swept, 3–0, in their series.

Long Relievers.

"A lot of long relievers are ashamed to tell their parents what they do. The only nice thing about it is that you get to wear a uniform like everybody else."— Jim Bouton.

Middle Relievers.

"As the Sox pass through the U.S. customs, the agent will ask if you have anything valuable to declare and the middle relievers can walk right through."— Steve Rosenbloom of the *Chicago Tribune*, describing the White Sox returning from Toronto.

Hall of Fame.

"As a group, we voters of the BBWAA treat them like they're .240-hitting utility infielders. We toss them votes like they're Socialist Party candidates. You'd think it was money out of our pocket, per vote."— Sportswriter Gregg Patton, who advocated in 2003 for Goose Gossage, Bruce Sutter, Lee Smith and Dennis Eckersley. Only Eckersley was elected.

"He's a Hall of Famer. The nicest guy in the world, but he still gets that mean look when I come out to the mound. He just wants the ball."— Lou Piniella on an aging Goose Gossage, who is not in the Hall of Fame.

"Fingers has 35 saves. Rollie has a better record than John the Baptist."— Giants broadcaster Lon Simmons.

In 1985 Hoyt Wilhelm became the first reliever elected to the Hall of Fame, compiling 124 relief wins (out of 143 total wins) and 227 saves. His high was 27 saves in 1964, during an era when complete games were still the norm.

In 1991 Wilhelm was joined by Rollie Fingers, who was elected on the strength of his 341 saves in 17 years. Fingers is often cited as the only Hall of Fame pitcher to have a career losing record (114–118). However, Satchel Paige was 28–31 over his Major League career.

Dennis Eckersley, with 390 saves, was elected in 2003.

Ballpark. Jack Russell Stadium in Clearwater, Florida, the spring training home of the Phillies beginning in 1955, is named for a relief pitcher who compiled a lifetime relief record of 35–40, with 38 saves (high of 13). He played primarily for the Red Sox and

Senators in the 1920s and 1930s before becoming a prominent resident of Clearwater.

Longest Stint. Zip Zabel of the Cubs came in to pitch in the first inning against the Dodgers on June 17, 1915. He pitched 18⅓ innings of relief, giving up nine hits and one walk in a 4–3 victory. Opposing pitcher Jeff Pfeffer gave up 15 hits over 18⅓ innings.

Most Appearances/Season.

"If somebody had come along 15 years ago and told me a guy would some day work 100 games while throwing a fair amount of fastballs, I'd have said it was about as ridiculous as the breaking of Babe Ruth's lifetime home run record."— Hoyt Wilhelm after both numbers were broken in 1974.

"Iron" Mike Marshall of the Dodgers set the all-time appearance record in 1974, pitching in 106 games after appearing in 92 the year before for the Expos. In 1974 Marshall finished 83 of the 106 games he appeared in, winning 15 and saving 21 on his way to the Cy Young and MVP awards. Marshall also holds the American League record with 89 appearances in 1979 for the Twins.

Before Marshall, Wayne Granger of the Reds pitched in 90 games in 1969, and Ted Abernathy of the Reds pitched in 84 games in 1965.

Consecutive Appearances. Mike Marshall appeared in 13 straight games from June 18 to July 3, 1974.

Dale Mohorcic of the Texas Rangers tied Marshall's record by appearing in 13 straight games in 1987. The record is somewhat tainted because in game 13 he was allowed to face one batter when his club had a six-run lead.

Braves manager Billy Cox once forced himself to rest reliever Gene Garber. In 1978 he listed Garber as the center fielder and lead-off hitter and then immediately pinch-hit Rowland Office for him.

First Official Save. The first save earned after the statistic became official was by Bill Singer of the Dodgers against the Reds on April 7, 1969. It was his only save of the season and one of only two in his 14-year career.

Most Saves/Record Progression.

1901	3 (four pitchers)
1904	6 Joe McGinnity, Giants
1905	7 George Ferguson, Giants
1909	8 Frank Arellanes, Red Sox
1911	13 Three Finger Brown, Cubs
1924	15 Firpo Marberry, Senators
1926	22 Firpo Marberry, Senators
1949	27 Joe Page, Yankees
1961	29 Luis Arroyo, Yankees
1965	31 Ted Abernathy, Cubs
1966	32 Jack Aker, Athletics
1970	35 Wayne Granger, Reds
1972	37 Clay Carroll, Reds
1973	38 John Hiller, Tigers
1983	45 Dan Quisenberry, Royals
1986	46 Dave Righetti, Yankees
1990	57 Bobby Thigpen, White Sox

Thigpen was 27 and in his prime when he set the record, but he was out of baseball five years later. During a barnstorming tour in Japan after the record-setting season, he hurt his back (he slipped off a mound) and was never the same. He had only 54 saves over the rest of his career.

John Smoltz had a chance to break Thigpen's season record in 2003, but in September he was put on the disabled list to rest his arm. He returned in the last week of the season to finish with 45 saves, and was strong enough in the division playoff to win one game (blowing the save) and save another. In 2002 Smoltz set the

National League record with 55 saves, breaking the record of 53 held by Randy Myers and Trevor Hoffman. Despite the record, Smoltz had one horrendous outing that season, giving up eight runs in the 9th inning of an 11–2 loss to the Mets.

Eric Gagne of the Dodgers tied the National League record with 55 saves in 2003 after recording 52 in 2002. He slipped to 45 saves in 2004, in part due to overwork that brought on some tendonitis in his shoulder.

Most Saves/Career. Rollie Fingers earned 341 saves in 17 seasons, 1968 through 1985, pitching for the A's, Padres and Brewers. He was the all-time leader until 1992 when Jeff Reardon and then Lee Smith overtook him.

Reardon was the only pitcher to record at least 20 saves in each of the 10 seasons from 1983 through 1992. In 1993 Reardon could not get a job in the Majors. He signed a minor league contract before the season and eventually played briefly with the Reds.

Later in the 1992 season, 35-year-old Lee Smith of the Cardinals broke Reardon's record with his 358th save against the Dodgers. He had a record 478 through his final season in 1997. Through 2003 John Franco was second with 424.

Most Relief Wins/Season. Roy Face won 18 games in relief for the Pirates in 1959. He also set the Major League record for consecutive wins by a reliever, with 22 straight over two seasons between May 1958 to September 1959. He made 98 appearances in that stretch.

The American League record for season wins by a reliever is 17, set by John Hiller for the Tigers in 1974 (after coming back from a heart attack), and tied by Bill Campbell for the Twins in 1976. Hiller broke the American League record of 16 set by Dick Radatz in 1964 for the Red Sox.

Consecutive Season Leader. Through 2004 only three relievers have led the league with at least 40 saves in at least two consecutive seasons. Eric Gagne in 2002–2003 (52, 55), Dan Quisenberry (1982–1985), and Lee Smith (1991–1992).

Most Saves in a Month. In June 1993 Lee Smith of the Cardinals set a Major League record with 15 saves in one month.

Consecutive Saves.

"No one is going to ever even come close again. I think it's the best pitching record out there."— Braves reliever John Smoltz on Eric Gagne's record 84-game save streak.

John Franco of the Mets and Rob Dibble of the Reds held the National League record with 23 consecutive saves without blowing one until Rod Beck broke the record with 24 straight in 1993. In 1992 Dennis Eckersley set the Major League record with 36 and then extended it to 40 into the 1993 season. Jose Mesa of the Indians converted 38 straight save opportunities in 1995, then a record for a single season.

Rod Beck set a new Major League record in 1994 with his 41st consecutive save over three seasons, a record later tied by Padres reliever Trevor Hoffman.

Tom Gordon of the Red Sox recorded 42 straight saves in 1998 and then extended his then-record streak to 54. The streak ended June 5, 1999, against the Braves, who scored two in the top of the 9th to win 5–4. In December 1999 Gordon had ligament reconstruction surgery and missed the 2000 season.

Eric Gagne of the Dodgers, a converted starter, blew everyone away in 2003 with 55 straight converted saves. He also set a record by converting 63 chances in a row dating back to the 2002 season and coming forward through the end of 2003. Gagne's biggest scare during the streak came on September 18, 2003, when two perfect relay throws from the outfield nailed the tying run at the plate in the 8th inning of a 1–0 game. After the Dodgers scored in the bottom of the 8th to make it 2–0, Gagne put runners at 1st and 3rd to start the 9th inning, but again got out of the jam.

Ironically, Gagne blew the save at the 2003 All-Star Game and gave the American League the win and home field advantage in the World Series. The National League looked extremely strong in the bullpen for the game, with Gagne and Smoltz leading the charge. The relief corps prompted this comment from American League manager Mike Scioscia to National League manager Dusty Baker: "I don't want to put any pressure on you Dusty, but I don't know how you're not going to hold a lead with that bullpen."

Gagne added to his streak in early 2004, but on July 5, 2004, his by then unbelievable 84-game save streak came to an end when the Diamondbacks scored two runs in the 9th inning to tie the game. The Dodgers came back to win in the 10th, however. Luis Gonzalez doubled to score a run and Chad Tracy hit an infield ball just out of reach that scored Gonzalez. Both runs scored with one out. Gagne's last blown save was on August 26, 2002, also against the Diamondbacks. After the blown save, he earned a save in his next appearance.

During the streak he entered the game with a one-run lead 31 times, two-run lead 14 times, and a three-run lead 20 times. He entered the game in the 8th inning only 14 times. He struck out 141 in 87⅔ innings, with an ERA of 0.82. Up to the blown save, he had converted 128 of 133 saves in his career. His best pitches were a fastball and a devastating change-up.

Gagne blew his next save attempt on August 18, 2004, against the Marlins. Gagne then blew two more leads during mid-August 2004 and set-up man Darren Dreifort went out for the season due to his frequently damaged knee.

Youngest to 100. Gregg Olson of the Orioles is the youngest player to reach 100 saves in his career. He did it at age 25 in 1992.

Most Prolific. Dennis Eckersley was the first reliever to reach 300 saves within 500 relief appearances (he made 499).

Converted to Starter. In April 2002 Derek Lowe capped his transformation from reliever to starter when he pitched the first Fenway Park no-hitter since 1965. In 2001 he began the season as the Red Sox closer, but eventually became a starter.

On May 9, 1999, Mike Stanton made his first start after a Major League record 552 relief appearances. The previous record for most appearances before starting was held by Giants pitcher Gary Lavelle with 443.

Converted From Starter. Dennis Eckersley is probably the most prominent starter to convert to relief pitching. After starting 359 games between 1975 and 1986, he started two more in 1987 and then never started another game.

John Smoltz was a starter for the Braves between 1988 and 1999. He made his first relief appearance, and got the save, in a 4–3 Atlanta victory over the Mets in the 1999 NLCS. In early 2000 he underwent elbow surgery to repair a torn medial collateral ligament and missed the season, but returned in August 2001 to become one of the premier relievers in the game.

Eric Gagne was a mediocre starter for the Dodgers in the early 2000s (11–14 in 48 starts) before blossoming as one of the league's premier relievers in 2002.

20 Wins/20 Saves. Only five pitchers have won 20 games in a season and saved 20 games in another season: Jim "Mudcat" Grant, Wilbur Wood, Dennis Eckersley, John Smoltz and Derek Lowe. Knuckleballer Wood went from being a reliever to a starter, as did Lowe. In 2002 Lowe, starting for the Red Sox, won his 20th game, becoming the first pitcher in history to win 20 games the season after saving 20. He is also the first to record at least 40 saves and win 20 games in a season. Dennis Eckersley and John Smoltz both did it the other way around.

Longest. On September 3, 2002, three Rangers pitchers threw a combined one-hitter against the Orioles, winning 7–1. Starter Aaron Myette was ejected after two pitches and replaced by Todd Van Poppel for two innings. Joaquin Benoit came in and pitched a scoreless seven innings and received the save. It was the longest stint to earn a save since the statistic was first recorded in 1969.

Older Rookie Relievers. Ellis "Old Folks" Kinder did not pitch in the Major Leagues until 1946 when he was 32. In 1949 he was 23–6 with six shutouts. He became a top reliever in 1951, saving 14 and winning 10, and then set a record with 69 appearances in 1953.

Doug Jones of the Indians was 30 before he pitched more than 18 innings in the Major Leagues. In 1987 he saved eight games, but in 1988 he established himself with 37 saves.

Transport from the Bullpen. See *Bullpen*.

Worst Successful Relief. On July 10, 1932, A's pitcher Eddie Rommel relieved in the 2nd inning while trailing 3–2. After a game that lasted 4 hours and 17 minutes, Rommell had given up 29 hits and 14 runs, but he won 18–17.

Best Successful Relief. Ernie Shore pitched a ***Perfect Game*** after relieving for the ejected Babe Ruth. Amazingly, Shore was credited with a save in his only National League appearance as a rookie in 1902. His team was ahead 21–2 when he went into the game and he left with the team ahead 21–12. One source reported that he had only two other relief appearances in his career, both in 1917. One was the Ruth relief job and another was a six-inning stint in which he was credited with a save. The record books do not confirm this, as he had eight relief wins and five saves in his career (although the 1969 *The Baseball Encyclopedia* credited him with seven relief wins).

Most Appearances/Team/Season. The 1993 Rockies pitchers made 453 relief appearances to set a Major League record.

No Pressure. In 2003 A's reliever Mike Neu earned his first career save by pitching three scoreless innings against the Blue Jays. When he went into the game, his club was up 16–2.

Advice. Then-Padres manager Jack McKeon once phoned a reporter in the press box for his advice before taking out a pitcher.

Books. Bob Cairns, *Pen Men* (1992); Doug Marx, *Relief Pitchers* (1991); Milton Shapiro, *Heroes of the Bullpen* (1967); John Thorn, *The Relief Pitcher* (1979); Paul Votano, *Late and Close: A History of Relief Pitching* (2002).

Religion

"Anyone who thinks that God wins or loses games has to have an awfully weak mind."— NHL owner Harold Ballard. Amen.

"I just think when there is an abundance of [born-again] believers brought together, at times there is going to be a war come out of it. I think sometimes Satan attacks those strong with the Lord."—Brett Butler, ascribing the Giants slow start in 1990 to Satan. Maybe they just weren't very good.

"Baseball is religion without the mischief."— Thomas Boswell.

"I don't think I can get into my deep inner thoughts about hitting. It's like talking about religion."— Mike Schmidt.

"The Red Sox are a religion. Every year we re-enact the agony and the temptation in the Garden. Baseball child's play? Hell, up here in Boston it's a passion play."— George V. Higgins.

"There are three things in my life which I really love: God, my family, and baseball. The only problem — once baseball season starts, I change the order around a bit."— Al Gallagher.

"Never let your head hang down. Never give up and sit down and grieve. Find another way. And don't pray when it rains if you don't pray when the sun shines."— Satchel Paige.

"Many attend, but few understood." — Former catcher Wes Westrum comparing the intricacies of baseball to church.

"I was playing God's own game, under God's own light, on God's own green, green grass." — Line from *Bleacher Bums*, a play about the Cubs and their fans.

"I believe in the Church of Baseball. I've tried all the major religions and most of the minor ones. And the only church that truly feeds the soul, day-in day-out, is the Church of Baseball." — Annie Savoy in *Bull Durham*.

"Baseball is more than a game. It's a religion." — Umpire Bill Klem in a 1949 speech he made during a Day held for him at the Polo Grounds. It has also been reported that he made the comment at a New York Baseball Writers dinner in 1939 when he received their Meritorious Service Award.

"I still maintain that by all the canons of our modern books on comparative religion, baseball is a religion, and the only one that is not sectarian but national." — Philosopher Morris Cohen in 1919.

"There will be no more Acts of God." — Judge Landis after the lights mysteriously shut off as the home team was about to fall behind during a minor league game in Milwaukee.

"Devotion to the New York Giants had been almost as much part and parcel of my family's tradition for three generations as their belief in a righteous and redeeming God. Being the only male issue, I was naturally commissioned to carry on the tradition and pass it on to my own sons." — Author Thomas Kiernan.

"The game is controlled by Satan." — Expos general manager Kevin Malone explaining the ills in professional sports.

"In a broadly 'religious sense,' [Christy] Mathewson epitomized humanity as it was created in the Garden of Eden. He lived and played in a 'garden paradise,' a pure specimen of the ideal ballplayer and created being." — Donald Honig in *Baseball America*.

"God's personal servants, which leaves us wondering why this team ever loses a game." — Marlins ad promoting a game against the Angels (the servants) in 2003.

"God must have some affection for the Marlins. The fish got those people out of a tough jam way back then." — Joe Maddon, citing Jesus feeding the hungry with fish.

"With you as a coach, no wonder your team prayed." — Shortstop Fresco Thompson during an argument with National League umpire Charley Moran. Moran had coached at Centre College, whose teams were known as the "Praying Colonels." Moran's response: "Young man, since you've turned this conversation into religious channels, suppose you go to the clubhouse and baptize yourself with an early shower."

"Charlie Bishop, Conrad Cardinal, Ryan Church, Maurice Archdeacon, Dave Pope, Deacon Jones, Glenn Abbott, Preacher Roe, Johnnie Priest, Johnny Podres, Dixie Parsons, Tiny Chaplin, Howie Nunn, Ed Chaplin, Monk Cline, Charlie Abbey, Bert Abbey, Monk Dubiel, Sam Frock, Wally Moses, Harry Lord, Bris Lord, Luther Roy, Jim Gideon, Pius Schwert, Jesus Figueroa, Jim Gentile, Jesus Alou, Bubba Church, Johnny Temple, Hi Church, Amos Cross, Buddy Bell, Jose Pagan, Brad Havens, Joe Grace, Sam Hope, Tony Faith, Mickey Devine, Fred Rath, Joe Beggs, Jack Dooms"

See also *Jewish Ballplayers* and *Sunday Baseball*.

Baseball Chapel. Yankee second baseman Bobby Richardson, a Baptist, started the first Major League Baseball chapel services before Sunday games in the late 1950s. Baseball Chapel, Inc., was founded in 1973 to promote church services in baseball locker rooms. In April of that season *Detroit News* sportswriter Watson Spolestra began the Sunday services. "Waddy" dedicated himself to the cause after his daughter miraculously recovered from a brain hemorrhage. The organization was later headquartered at Liberty University in Lynchburg, Virginia. Richardson was Liberty's president and baseball coach.

Religious. Long-time relief pitcher Lindy McDaniel was an ordained minister in the Church of Christ. While still active he wrote a monthly newsletter called *Pitching for the Master*.

Seventh Day Adventist Edwin Correa pitched primarily for the Rangers from 1985 through 1987. He would not pitch on Friday nights or Saturday afternoons.

At the 1989 All-Star Game, third baseman Gary Gaetti had a religious slogan taped to his glove, which he held up to the camera during player introductions.

In 1995 many Major and minor league players began a tradition of huddling together before games in the outfield for a brief prayer.

Popes.

"Everyone seemed so surprised that the Pope outdrew the Rockies in Denver. They're forgetting that this is not an expansion Pope." — Columnist Scott Ostler in 1993.

"Well, that kind of puts a damper on even a Yankees win." — Phil Rizzuto on a bulletin announcing the death of Pope Paul VI in 1978.

"If the Pope was an umpire, he'd still have trouble with the Catholics." — Umpire Beans Reardon.

"His Holiness is now walking up the first base line and over to the pitcher's box." — Broadcast description of the Pope's 1965 visit to Yankee Stadium.

"Steve Garvey is not sure whether he wants to be a first baseman or the Pope. He's so good, he goes out behind the barn to chew gum." — Don Rickles.

"He's like the Cal Ripken of the church." — Nicole Valentini explaining to her son Matthew the significance of the arrival in Baltimore of Pope John Paul II.

The 1913 international tour led by Charles Comiskey and John McGraw was received at the Vatican by Pope Pius IX and McGraw received a private audience with the Pope.

Placed among the *Yankee Stadium* baseball monuments are one each for Pope Paul VI and Pope John Paul II, who each performed a mass at the ballpark.

Stan Musial once had dinner with Pope John Paul II and author James Michener, when the two Americans were on vacation in Italy with their families. They also had a private mass with the Pontiff. Michener wrote about the dinner in his 1990 book, *Pilgrimage*. When two young priests kept hounding Musial with baseball questions, he told them that he was "entitled to be here, because I'm also a Cardinal."

In late 1998 Mark McGwire had an audience with the Pope, and *Sports Illustrated* noted that the Pope had the edge in supporting cast: Cardinals and Dominican nuns outshone the St. Louis Cardinals and the Dominican Cub (Sammy Sosa). The magazine also noted that the Pope's "specialty" was "Latin Mass and the Big Guy," while McGwire's was "Muscle mass and the big fly."

In late 2002 Mike Piazza vacationed in Italy and received an audience with the Pope. Piazza was in Europe for three weeks to promote baseball.

Christening.

"One imagines that the Yankees imported the good stuff from Lourdes." — The *New York Times* after Shea Stadium was christened in 1964 with water from the Gowanus Canal in Brooklyn and the Harlem River.

Convert. Speedster Max Carey gave up divinity school for baseball, apparently not putting to good use his ability to read ancient Greek and Latin.

Exorcism.

"Nolan Ryan is baseball's exorcist—he scares the devil out of you."—Dick Sharon.

When the Cubs started the 1997 season 0–13, Francis George, the newly appointed Catholic Archbishop of Chicago and a long-time Cubs fan, volunteered to throw out the first pitch if it would help exorcise the evils of the team's bad start.

Buddhists. In 1974 poet Tom Clark published a verse saluting Willie Davis and Willie Crawford as Buddhist outfielders for the Dodgers.

In 1993 the periodical *Tricycle: The Buddhist Review*, claimed that alleged baseball inventor Abner Doubleday was familiar with Buddhism and infused baseball with mystical numbers when he laid out the first ball field in 1839. The numbers nine, four and three apparently are all important in Buddhism. There is also a seven-card stud poker game known as "baseball" that celebrates the three, four and nine. Threes and nines are wild, and a four dealt face-up entitles a player to an extra card. Another version of the game calls for an extra card when a player receives a four face down—"night baseball."

Misery Loves Company. Ralph Branca, who gave up Bobby Thomson's home run in the 1951 Dodgers-Giants play-off, and Mike Torrez, who gave up Bucky Dent's home run in the 1978 Yankees–Red Sox play-off, at one time lived within a mile of each other in White Plains, New York. They both attended the same church: Our Lady of Sorrows.

Billy Sunday.

"America's most electrifying preacher."—Said of Sunday in the early 20th century.

"Chicago Was That Toddlin' Town That Billy Sunday Could Not Shut Down."—A 19th century lyric.

Sunday was a 19th century ballplayer-turned-minister who presided at pitcher Addie Joss's funeral in 1911. Sunday batted .248 in eight Major League seasons starting in 1883.

Some sources report that he began work with the YMCA when he retired in 1891. Others report that he entered the Moody Bible Institute. He debuted as an evangelist in 1896 and often appeared as a guest umpire for minor league games (but never on Sunday). He became one of the most prominent ministers in the United States and reportedly preached to more than 85 million people.

Priest Abuse. In March 2002 former Major Leaguer Tom Paciorek said that he and three of his brothers were molested when they were children by a priest who was removed from a Michigan church that month. Paciorek said he was attacked by the priest at least 100 times on Detroit's east side, where Paciorek grew up.

Name Change. In 2002 Tampa Bay infielder Russ Johnson, a born-again Christian spent the year attempting to get the club to take the word "Devil" out of its name.

Chaplain. In 2004 the only Major League team that had a full-time chaplain (Gene Pemberton) was the Astros.

Promotion. In 2004 the Class AAA Nashville Sounds used a Christian-based sales program to support their "Faith Night" series in 2004. They passed out Biblical figures Moses, Noah and Sampson. Sampson wore a "God's Gym" t-shirt and Noah carried a closed umbrella on his arm.

Books. Allen E. Hye, *The Great God Baseball* (2004) (religion in modern baseball fiction); Michael O'Connor, *Sermon on the Mound* (2001).

Replacement Players (1995) See ***Strikes and Lockouts***

Reserve Clause (1879–partial death in 1975)

"The Backbone of Baseball"—Long-time tightfisted Senators owner Clark Griffith.

"The Reserve Clause is, on paper, the most unfair and degrading measure … ever passed in a free country. Still … it is necessary for the safety and preservation of the national game."—The *St. Louis Globe-Democrat* in the 19th century.

"A club, by placing the name of a player on a list can reserve exclusive rights to his services from year to year for an unstated and indefinite period in the future. I find this unpersuasive. It is like the claims of some nations that persons once its citizens, wherever they live and regardless of the passage of time and the wearing of other allegiances, are still its own nationals. This 'status' theory is incompatible with the doctrine of policy of freedom of contract in the economic and political society in which we live and of which the professional sport of baseball (the national game) is a part."—Arbitrator Peter Seitz in his ruling of December 23, 1975, effectively abolishing the reserve clause. The opinion can be found in the Labor Arbitration Reports, Dispute Settlements, Volume 66, page 116.

See also ***Antitrust***, ***Arbitration***, ***Collective Bargaining Agreements*** and ***Free Agents***.

The Clause. The essential term of the reserve clause provided that a club had the option to renew its contract with a player for a second year, which evolved into renewal after every season if the club elected to do so. Abuses occurred when teams invoked the clause in perpetuity, preventing players from becoming free agents. Even if a player sat out a full year he was still considered property of the club when he returned, and he still could not freely change teams. This was at the heart of the legal challenges.

Paragraph 10(a) of the basic contract contained the reserve clause and the perpetual option year. The clause, purportedly invoked approximately 100,000 times in Organized Baseball, provided that if a club and a player did not agree on a contract, the club could renew the contract on the prior year's terms.

Origins. The reserve clause grew out of trial and error. The clause originally helped the poorer clubs compete with the wealthy clubs in competition for players by preventing players from selling themselves to the highest bidder. The earliest formal version was put into effect at a meeting of the National League in Buffalo on September 29, 1879, to be used during the 1880 season. The rule provided that a club would not employ another club's player, would not play a team with a player that had violated the reserve clause, and would not allow its park to be used by a club having such a player on its team. It was to be used secretly at first, but it was revealed by the *Cincinnati Enquirer* in October 1879.

The clause supposedly was conceived by William B. Pettit, who owned the Indianapolis franchise in the National League. Indianapolis operated in the National League for only one year in 1878. Other sources credit the origins of the clause to Arthur Soden, owner of the Boston Red Stockings.

In the earliest years of the reserve clause, a player supposedly considered it an honor to be on the reserve list, as it meant that the club wanted him back for the next season. The reserve clause was officially codified for the first time in the historic 1883 National Agreement which governed all of Organized Baseball. The owners thereafter had complete control of player movement because the clause was included in all standard player contracts.

The Wrigley Case. In 1899 George Wrigley played the entire season with Syracuse of the Eastern League. When the minor league season ended, he signed with the National League Giants for 30 days starting on September 15. Four days later Syracuse sold Wrigley's contract to the Dodgers based on a "right of reservation." After Wrigley played four games with the Giants, Dodger manager Ned Hanlon ordered him over to his club. He obeyed and Giants owner Andrew Freedman then appealed to the National Board of Arbitration, a league council.

The league returned Wrigley to the Giants, supporting the novel view that the reserve clause only reserved a player for the following year, but could not bind a player to its club after its season was over and prevent him from playing with another club to finish out the same season.

The reserve clause was clarified a few years later to prevent the Wrigley situation in which a player could play for another club in the same season. The language change was known as the Cincinnati Agreement, which became part of the universal language of the reserve clause: "The Club's right of reservation of the Player, and renewal of this contract as aforesaid, and the promise of the Player not to play otherwise than with the Club or an assignee thereof, have been taken into consideration in determining the salary specified herein and the undertaking by the Club to pay said salary is the consideration for both said reservation, renewal, option and promise, and the Player's service."

Early Union Involvement. The Brotherhood of Professional Baseball Players (see *Unions*) was formed in the 1880s principally to fight the reserve clause. The Brotherhood won court actions in some states in the late 1880s when the clause emerged as the owners' most effective weapon against player freedom. Apparently the decisions were never enforced for fear of blacklisting.

Number of Players Reserved. Originally only five players on a club were reserved, but this was increased to 11 in 1883 by agreement between the National League and American Association (coupled with a minimum $1,000 salary guarantee). The National League total was then increased to 12, and then all 14 players on a roster in 1887. Eventually all 25 players on the expanded rosters, plus an additional 15, were covered.

Negro Leagues. Negro league contracts contained a reserve clause, but generally it was ignored: "If you felt like jumping, you jumped."—Shortstop Bill Yancey.

World War II Effect.

"The system is morally and legally indefensible."—Bill Veeck, Jr., writing to Judge Landis in 1941.

"Somebody once said a little knowledge is a dangerous thing and your letter proves him to be a wizard."—Response by Landis to Veeck quoted in Marvin Miller's autobiography, *A Whole Different Ballgame* (1991).

In 1943 Cubs general manager James T. Gallagher suggested that the leagues pool players and suspend the reserve clause due to the war-induced talent shortage: "That, then, might be the time for a reconstruction of the baseball law which would eliminate the reserve clause."

Cardinals owner Sam Breadon had a direct response: "Unthinkable, unworkable ... an offspring of socialism that has no business in baseball."

Early 1950s/George Toolson Case. Toolson was a minor league outfielder in the Yankee organization when he challenged the reserve clause in court. His effort resulted in the U.S. Supreme Court reaffirming the validity of the reserve clause when it refused to hear the case after the appellate court ruled against him.

1970/Curt Flood Case.

"A well-paid slave is nonetheless a slave."—Flood.

Outfielder Curt Flood challenged the reserve clause in court after he retired following the 1969 season to protest being traded by the Cardinals to the Phillies for Dick (then Richie) Allen and others. His ordeal began with a letter to commissioner Bowie Kuhn: "After 12 years in the major leagues, I do not feel that I am a piece of property to be bought and sold irrespective of my wishes. I believe that any system which produces that result violates my basic rights as a citizen and is inconsistent with the laws of the United States. I feel my services have financially benefited my employers far in excess of the salaries I have earned. I am a man, I live in a democratic society and I believe that I am entitled to participate in our free enterprise system."

Flood sat out the 1970 season and forfeited his $100,000 salary. His salary history:

1961	$12,500	1966	45,000
1962	16,000	1967	50,000
1963	17,000	1968	72,000
1964	23,000	1969	90,000
1965	35,000	1970	100,000 (proposed)

The Major League Players Association advised him not to pursue the lawsuit. Nevertheless, he pushed ahead. The ensuing court case was titled *Flood v. Kuhn*. At the trial, former Major Leaguer and general manager Hank Greenberg predicted chaos if the rules were changed abruptly. Jackie Robinson testified in favor of modification, but not elimination, of the clause. Flood lost at trial, with trial Judge I.B. Cooper writing: "Baseball's status in the life of the nation is so pervasive that it would not strain credulity to say the Court can take judicial notice that baseball is everybody's business. To put it mildly and with restraint, it would be unfortunate indeed if a fine sport and profession, which brings such surcease from daily travail and an escape from the ordinary to most inhabitants of this land, were to suffer in the least because of undue concentration by any one or any group on commercial and profit considerations. The game is on higher ground; it behooves everyone to keep it there."

Flood also lost at the first level of appeal and the case then went to the U. S. Supreme Court (case 407 U.S. 258 (1972)). In June 1972 it held against Flood in a 5–3 opinion that concluded once again that baseball was not subject to the antitrust laws. Justice Harry Blackmun's opinion recited 87 oldtimers' names and made lyrical reference to "Casey at the Bat." Blackmun acknowledged that the reserve clause was an "aberration," but said that 50 years of tradition following the 1922 Supreme Court decision written by Oliver Wendell Holmes could only be changed by Congress (see also *Antitrust*).

Justice Lewis Powell abstained because he owned stock in Anheuser-Busch, which owned the Cardinals. In the dissenting opinion by liberal William O. Douglas, joined by fellow liberals Thurgood Marshall and William J. Brennan, Douglas wrote: "While I joined the Court's opinion in *Toolson* [the 1953 ruling upholding the 1922 decision], I have lived to regret it, and I would now correct what I believe to be its fundamental error.... The unbroken silence of Congress should not prevent us from correcting our own mistakes."

The strain on Flood was immense. He came back to play six weeks in 1971 for the Senators, but his skills had eroded from the long lay-off. He then went to Denmark for a time to get away from the pressure. He eventually recovered sufficiently to have a successful career as an artist, public speaker and baseball instructor. Asked in a 1994 interview whether he would do it again, he replied, "absolutely." He died in 1997 and only three Major League players attended his funeral: Don Baylor, Steve Garvey and Doug DeCinces. See also Curt Flood, *The Way It Was* (1970).

1975/Andy Messersmith and Dave McNally. Though the reserve clause was tested a number of times in court, the owners' stranglehold on players was not broken until late 1975 when arbitrator Peter Seitz ruled that the reserve clause could not last beyond the first option year (see also *Arbitration*). Andy Messersmith and Dave McNally both filed arbitration grievances challenging the option year language, though each came from markedly different situations on the field.

After the 1974 season, McNally refused to sign with the Orioles and he was renewed by the Expos for 1975 with a $10,000 raise to $125,000. He was not producing on the mound, quit in June 1975 and went home with a 3–6 record.

In 1974 Messersmith was 20–6 with the Dodgers. He refused the 1975 contract offered by the club and was automatically renewed at $115,000, a $25,000 raise. He would not sign because the club would not give him a no-trade clause (ironically, he received such a clause when he returned to the Dodgers in 1979). He was 19–14 in his option year of 1975. On October 7, 1975, he filed a grievance to void the automatic renewal clause for 1976. His theory—eventually adopted by Seitz—was that the option contained in the agreement could only be for one year, rather than renewable every year. Because he was automatically renewed after the 1974 season, he claimed that he could not be renewed automatically after the 1975 season. Two days later McNally filed his own grievance.

The players were led by attorney Dick Moss, who was working closely with Players Association executive director Marvin Miller. After an attempt to negotiate away the dispute, the matter was referred to a three-man arbitration panel that included Miller, John Gaherin of the owners' Player Relations Committee and neutral arbitrator Peter Seitz. Gaherin was the former president of the New York City Newspaper Publishers Association.

Seitz cast the tie-breaking vote and wrote the opinion establishing limits to the reserve clause. The panel did not rule that it was illegal; it merely interpreted that the clause was binding for only one year instead of in perpetuity.

The owners were unsuccessful in two court appeals of the arbitration panel's ruling, which was handled for the players by attorney and future players union leader *Donald Fehr*. The decision opened the floodgates for the first truly *Free Agents* in 1976. McNally did not play again, but Messersmith signed a $1.75 million deal with the Braves and had a disappointing 11–11 season (and never regained his earlier form).

Messersmith's contract with the Braves contained a right of first refusal in favor of the Braves. This effectively resurrected the reserve clause in a different form. Marvin Miller forced out the offending clause under the rule that an individual player could not bargain away a right that the union had won through collective bargaining.

In a related but separate matter, Royals owner Ewing Kauffman filed an unsuccessful $6 million injunction to retain the reserve clause and protect his investment. His club's further response shortly after the Seitz decision was to sign all its key players to long-term deals.

New Agreement. After the late 1975 decision favoring the players, a compromise was reached as part of the 1976 *Collective Bargaining Agreement* negotiated between the players and owners. A player could go to arbitration after two years and could request a trade after five years. The player would become a free agent after six years if he was not traded after the request was made. These terms have been modified since they were first incorporated into the basic agreement, but the concept remains. For the effect of subsequent collective bargaining agreements on free agency, see *Free Agents*.

Minor Leagues. The minor league version of the reserve clause is essentially still intact. It has been changed from the Lifetime Minor League contract to a seven-year limitation in 1995. It is actually more restrictive today. In the past, when the season was over, the player could do what he wanted; today, the club can extend the fall season or do anything else to extend the player's time with the club, including preventing him from going to college. He is under contract year-round for seven years. No exceptions.

Restaurants See *Food*

Retired Uniform Numbers

"They're going to retire my uniform with me still in it."— Mediocre A's outfielder Steve Hovley.

"I hope they don't put *me* under glass."— Mets manager Casey Stengel after being told by general manager George Weiss that the team was going to put his uniform under glass.

"The question of what to include in a museum, booklet or whatever more often than not is a matter of opinion. Evidence of this is that the American League *Red Book* for the past several years carried a list of uniform numbers that have been retired, the National League public relations department has not deemed this important enough to include in its *Green Book*. Even my predecessor, the late Lee Allen, apparently did not consider it to be of special significance. At any rate, he did not leave any information in our files."— Hall of Fame director Clifford Kachline in a letter of September 23, 1970.

"As Little Leaguers, we all wanted to wear No. 7 [Mickey Mantle's number]. Once I got to the Yankees, No. 7 didn't seem to be available in the minor leagues.— Buck Showalter.

Jackie Robinson.

"In honor of Jackie, Major League Baseball is taking the unprecedented step of retiring his uniform number in perpetuity. Number 42, from this day forward, will never again be issued by a Major League club. Number 42 belongs to Jackie Robinson for the ages."— Commissioner Bud Selig.

On April 15, 1997, Major League Baseball retired Robinson's No. 42, so it cannot be worn by any player in the Major Leagues. It was the 50th anniversary of Robinson's debut for the Dodgers (see *Integration*).

The players who wore No. 42 at the time, and were allowed to keep it for the remainder of their careers, were Mo Vaughn of the Red Sox, Butch Huskey of the Mets, Mike Jackson of the Twins, Mariano Rivera of the Yankees, Jose Lima of the Royals, Tom Goodwin of the Royals, Buddy Groom of the A's and Marc Sagmoen of the Rangers. Sagmoen had received the jersey earlier that day and made his Major League debut that night.

Multiple Teams. The following individuals have had their numbers retired by more than one club: Henry Aaron, Rod Carew, Rollie Fingers, Carlton Fisk, Reggie Jackson, Frank Robinson, Nolan Ryan and Casey Stengel.

First Retired Numbers. Before 1965 only 12 uniform numbers were retired: Lou Gehrig (1939, Yankees), Carl Hubbell (1944, Giants), Babe Ruth (1948, Yankees), Mel Ott (1949, Giants), Joe DiMaggio (1952, Yankees), Billy Meyer (1954, Pirates), Honus Wagner (1956, Pirates), Bob Feller (1956, Indians), Ted Williams (1960, Red Sox), Robin Roberts (1962, Phillies), Stan Musial (1963, Cardinals) and Jim Umbricht (1964, Astros). A team-by-team breakdown of retired numbers (through 2004):

Anaheim Angels

11—Jim Fregosi (1998)

26—Gene Autry (1982) He controlled the club from its creation in 1961 through late 1995, never winning a pennant. The club retired number 26 in honor of Autry's role as the "26th man" on a 25-man roster.

29—Rod Carew (1991)

30—Nolan Ryan (1992) His number was retired while he was still active with the Rangers (for whom he wore number 34).

50—Jimmie Reese (1995) He coached for the club into his 90s.

Arizona Diamondbacks

None

Atlanta Braves

3—Dale Murphy (1994)

35—Phil Niekro (1984) Niekro returned to pitch one game for the club in 1987.

41—Eddie Mathews (1969) His number was reactivated in 1970 when he managed and coached the team. He also played for both the Boston and Milwaukee Braves.

44—Henry Aaron (1977) The Brewers had already retired his number in 1976, making him the first player to have his number retired by two different clubs.

See also **Milwaukee Braves**

Baltimore Orioles

4—Earl Weaver (1982) He managed the club from 1968 through 1982 and then in 1985 and 1986.

5—Brooks Robinson (1977)

8—Cal Ripken (2001)

20—Frank Robinson (1972) His number was retired just before he played the 1972 season for the Dodgers.

22—Jim Palmer (1985)

33—Eddie Murray (1989) His number was retired while he was still active, having been traded to the Dodgers (erroneously 1993 in some sources). His number was re-retired by the Orioles in 1998.

Boston Braves

All numbers were retired after the club moved to Milwaukee.

Boston Red Sox

1—Bobby Doerr (1988)

4—Joe Cronin (1984)

8—Carl Yastrzemski (1989)

9—Ted Williams (1960) His number was retired before the start of his dramatic last game.

27—Carlton Fisk (2000)

Brooklyn Dodgers

All numbers were retired after the club moved to Los Angeles.

Chicago Cubs

10—Ron Santo (2003)

14—Ernie Banks (1982) His number is embroidered on a flag atop the left field foul pole at Wrigley Field.

23—Ryne Sandberg (1995) He came out of retirement for the 1996 season and apparently his number was "unretired" temporarily.

26—Billy Williams (1987) His number is embroidered on a flag atop the right field foul pole.

Chicago White Sox

2—Nellie Fox (1976)

3—Harold Baines (1989) A fan favorite, his number was retired after he was traded to the Rangers.

4—Luke Appling (1975)

9—Minnie Minoso (1983)

11—Luis Aparicio (1984)

16—Ted Lyons (1987)

19—Billy Pierce (1987)

72—Carlton Fisk (1997) The 72 is the reverse of his retired number with the Red Sox, 27. Fisk was still bitter over his 1993 release and not being allowed into the locker room during the play-offs that season, Fisk requested that the ceremony not be attended by White Sox owner Jerry Reinsdorf and general manager Ron Schueler.

Cincinnati Reds

1—Fred Hutchinson (1965) He resigned as Reds manager in mid–1965 when his cancer began progressing rapidly. He died shortly before his number was retired.

5—Johnny Bench (1984)

8—Joe Morgan (1998)

18—Ted Kluszewski (1998)

20—Frank Robinson (1998)

24—Tony Perez (2000)

Cleveland Indians

3—Earl Averill (1975)

5—Lou Boudreau (1970)

14—Larry Doby (1994)

18—Mel Harder (1990)

19—Bob Feller (1956)

21—Bob Lemon (1998)

Colorado Rockies

None

Detroit Tigers

2—Charlie Gehringer (1983)

5—Hank Greenberg (1983)

6—Al Kaline (1980)

16—Hal Newhouser (1997)

23—Willie Horton (2000)

Some sources report that Charlie Dressen's number 7 was retired by the club and that a clubhouse man later gave the number by mistake to new outfielder Cesar Gutierrez. The Tigers' media relations department denied that Dressen's number was ever retired. The department also reported in 1996 that none of the numbers were officially retired until 1995, though the club did not issue any of the numbers after the years indicated.

Florida Marlins

5—Carl Barger (1993) He was a popular club executive who died shortly after the Marlins were created in late 1992.

Houston Astros

25—Jose Cruz (1992)

32—Jim Umbricht (1964) He died of cancer at age 34 at the start of the season and the club immediately retired his number.

33—Mike Scott (1992)

34—Nolan Ryan (1996) He became the first player to have his number retired by three clubs (Astros, Rangers and Angels).

40—Don Wilson (1975)

49—Larry Dierker (2002)

Kansas City Royals (note: all honored again in 1997)

5—George Brett (1994)

10—Dick Howser (1987) A respected manager of the club, his number was retired shortly after he died of brain cancer.

20—Frank White (1995)

Los Angeles Dodgers

The club has retired the numbers of players who played exclusively for Brooklyn and players (and a manager) who were with both clubs.

1—Pee Wee Reese (1984) He played only for Brooklyn.

2—Tommy Lasorda (1997)

4—Duke Snider (1980) He played only for Brooklyn.

19—Jim Gilliam (1978) He suffered a brain hemorrhage just before the start of the 1978 World Series and died during the Series. His number was retired during the Series.

20—Don Sutton (1998)

24—Walter Alston (1977)

32—Sandy Koufax (1972)

39—Roy Campanella (1972) He played only for Brooklyn.

42—Jackie Robinson (1972) He played only for Brooklyn.

52—Tim Crews (1993) He was killed in spring training of 1993 while playing for the Indians but had played the previous six years with the Dodgers and had been very popular. Most Internet sites don't recognize this number as being officially retired, and the Dodgers report now that he was merely "honored," and that the number was not retired (though at the time it certainly seemed so).

53—Don Drysdale (1984)

Milwaukee Braves

21—Warren Spahn (1965) He played in Boston and Milwaukee and was the only Braves player whose number was retired before the club moved to Atlanta in 1966.

Milwaukee Brewers

4—Paul Molitor (1999)

19—Robin Yount (1994)

34—Rollie Fingers (1992)

44—Henry Aaron (1976) His number was retired also in 1977 by the Atlanta Braves.

Minnesota Twins

3—Harmon Killebrew (1975)

6—Tony Oliva (1991)

14—Kent Hrbek (1995)

29—Rod Carew (1987)

34—Kirby Puckett (1997) The ceremony took 1½ hours.

47—Sherry Robertson (1970) In 1995 the Twins public relations office reported that the number was only "unofficially" retired. Robertson was the farm director for the Senators and the brother of long-time owner Calvin Griffith.

In the early 2000s the club unofficially retired a jersey in honor of long-time announcer Bob Casey.

Montreal Expos

8—Gary Carter (1993)

10—Rusty Staub (1993)

10—Andre Dawson (1997)

42—Jackie Robinson (1996) The Expos retired Robinson's No. 42, which was worn by him when he played for the Montreal Royals in 1946.

New York Giants

4—Mel Ott (1949)

11—Carl Hubbell (1944)

John McGraw, Christy Mathewson and Bill Terry had jersies retired by the San Francisco Giants.

New York Mets

14—Gil Hodges (1972) He managed the Mets to their first championship (1969) and his number was retired after his death from a heart attack at age 47 in 1970 while he still managed the club.

37—Casey Stengel (1965) His number was retired also by the Yankees.

41—Tom Seaver (1988)

New York Yankees

1—Billy Martin (1986)

3—Babe Ruth (1948) Many sources report that this was the second time any player had his number retired (Gehrig was first). However, Carl Hubbell's number was retired in 1944, four years before Ruth's. Cliff Mapes wore Ruth's number before it was retired. At Ruth's farewell address at Yankee Stadium on June 13, 1948, shortly before he died of throat cancer, Mapes wore Ruth's No. 3. The number was retired a few weeks later. Mapes then became the first Yankee player to wear No. 13 and later wore No. 7, which would be worn by Mickey Mantle. Mapes subsequently wore number 5 for the Tigers, later to be retired as Hank Greenberg's number.

4—Lou Gehrig (1939) His was the first retired number.

5—Joe DiMaggio (1952)

7—Mickey Mantle (1969)

8—Bill Dickey/Yogi Berra (1972) Dickey did not wear this number at the beginning of his career when it was worn by Benny Bengough. Nor did he wear it at the end of his career, when Berra had taken it over.

9—Roger Maris (1984)

10—Phil Rizzuto (1985)

15—Thurman Munson (1979) Munson's number was retired shortly after his death in 1979.

16—Whitey Ford (1974)

23—Don Mattingly (1997)

32—Elston Howard (1984)

37—Casey Stengel (1970) His number was retired also by the Mets.

44—Reggie Jackson (1993) Retired No. 9 by the A's in 2004.

49—Ron Guidry (2003)

Oakland A's

9—Reggie Jackson (2004) Retired No. 44 by the Yankees in 1993.

27—Jim "Catfish" Hunter (1990)

34—Rollie Fingers (1993) The number was worn by Dave Stewart, who was miffed that his number was retired for Fingers after Stewart had won 20 games four straight times.

Philadelphia Phillies

1—Richie Ashburn (1979)

14—Jim Bunning (2001)

20—Mike Schmidt (1990)

32—Steve Carlton (1989)

36—Robin Roberts (1962)

*****—(No number) Grover Cleveland Alexander (2001)

*****—(No number) Chuck Klein (2001)

Pittsburgh Pirates

1—Billy Meyer (1954)

4—Ralph Kiner (1987)

8—Willie Stargell (1982)

9—Bill Mazeroski (1987)

20—Pie Traynor (1972)

21—Roberto Clemente (1973)

33—Honus Wagner (1956) This was the number Wagner wore only as a coach. He never wore a number as a player.

40—Danny Murtaugh (1977)

St. Louis Cardinals

1—Ozzie Smith (1997)

2—Red Schoendienst (1996)

6—Stan Musial (1963)

9—Enos Slaughter (1996)

14—Ken Boyer (1984)

17—Dizzy Dean (1974)

20—Lou Brock (1979)

45—Bob Gibson (1975)

85—August Busch, Jr. (1984)

*****—(No number) Rogers Hornsby (2001)

San Diego Padres
6— Steve Garvey (1989)
19— Tony Gwynn (2002)
31— Dave Winfield (2001)
35— Randy Jones (1997)
San Francisco Giants (See New York Giants)
* (No Number) John McGraw (1988)
* (No Number) Christy Mathewson (1988)
3— Bill Terry (1985)
24— Willie Mays (1972) He was still active with the Mets when his number was retired.
27— Juan Marichal (1975)
30— Orlando Cepeda (1999)
44— Willie McCovey (1975) He was still active with the Padres when his number was retired. McCovey then returned to the Giants to finish out his career and his number was reactivated.

Seattle Mariners None
Tampa Bay Devil Rays
12— Wade Boggs (2000) Boggs was a hometown hero, thereby justifying the retirement after he played only two seasons with the club.

Texas Rangers
34— Nolan Ryan (1996) His No. 30 was retired by the Angels in 1992.

Toronto Blue Jays
The Blue Jays have not retired any numbers, but in 1995 the club "honored" Dave Stieb's number 37 and George Bell's number 11 by emblazoning their numbers on the SkyDome facade. The public relations department made a point of indicating that this was not a "retirement" of numbers.

Umpires. In May 1995 the uniforms of umpires Jocko Conlan, Bill Klem and Al Barlick were retired at Wrigley Field.

Minor Leagues. Peninsula of the Carolina League retired Johnny Bench's number when he was 18 years old in 1966.

In 1991 Tim McCarver had his number retired by the Memphis Chicks of the Southern League. McCarver played for the club only in 1960, but was part-owner of the Chicks when the number was retired and the stadium had already been renamed in his honor.

The Durham Bulls of the Class A Carolina League retired second baseman Joe Morgan's number in 1993, 30 years after he played for three months with the club. The Bulls retired number 18, but a typewritten roster for the club found by a fan revealed that he wore number 8, the same number he wore with the Reds.

No Respect. In late 1992 Barry Bonds signed with the Giants for $43.75 million. He was criticized for requesting that the No. 24 worn by Willie Mays be brought out of retirement to accommodate him. He relented and took 25, the number worn by his father, though Mays had said it was fine with him if his number was worn by Bonds.

Retirement

"A ballplayer should quit when it starts to feel as if all the baselines run uphill."— Babe Ruth.

"You start chasing a ball and your brain immediately commands your body to 'Run Forward! Bend! Scoop Up the Ball! Peg It to the Infield.' Then your body says, 'Who! Me!'"— Joe DiMaggio on when to retire.

"The manager's toughest job is not calling the right play with the bases full and the score tied in an extra inning game. It's telling a ballplayer that he's through, done, finished."— Jimmy Dykes.

"I'll never make the mistake of being 70 again."— Casey Stengel on being forced to retire by the Yankees after the 1960 World Series.

"Hey, Mantle, these golden years suck, don't they!"— Duke Snider to Mickey Mantle during a 1990s baseball card show and perpetual autograph session. Mantle said he was enjoying himself. This was just before he entered an alcohol rehabilitation clinic.

"I guess this is one of the few times when you get to see your own last rites."— Pitcher Steve Stone at his retirement.

"You are George Brett and all the cheering has about stopped. The music is muted, the hour is late and they will be taking the banners down and emptying your locker any minute now. As the late Jimmy Cannon would say it, all your bats are broken."— Jim Murray near the end of Brett's last season in 1993.

See also *Last At-Bat and Last Game of Career*.

Premature Retirement.

Ted Williams. Williams suffered a broken collarbone during spring training in 1954 and contracted pneumonia during the season. Though he batted .344 in 112 games, after the season he announced his retirement in a bylined magazine article for which he reportedly was paid $60,000. He returned the next spring, saying he needed the money, which probably superseded his quest for better career statistics. However, Williams also was motivated by a statistics guru, Ed Mifflin, who contacted him about all the career goals he could achieve by playing longer (see also *Statistics* — Ted Williams).

Dick Allen. When Allen "retired" one month before the end of the 1974 season, he gave no reason and still led the American League in home runs. He returned to play three more seasons.

Roger Clemens. Everyone thought that Clemens pitched his last game during the 2003 World Series. Yet he was persuaded by buddy Andy Pettitte to sign with the Astros, for whom Clemens was quite successful in 2004 (while Pettitte was lost for the season with a torn elbow ligament), winning the Cy Young Award for the seventh time.

In April 2004 Clemens debuted for the Astros and pitched seven scoreless innings in a 10–1 win over the Giants. Looking on were Nolan Ryan and former president George Bush. Clemens lived 20 minutes from the ballpark. He also had a hit-and-run single in his first at-bat and kept the ball as a a souvenir. When Barry Bonds came to the plate, it was the first time that a 300-game winner had faced a batter with 600 home runs. Clemens was the top pitcher in the National League that season and finished with 18 wins and an ERA under 3.00. Although teammate Roy Oswalt finished with 20 wins, Clemens was the superior pitcher and had several no-decisions and only four losses.

Jackie Robinson. When Robinson retired under strained circumstances with the Dodgers, he sold his retirement story to *Look* magazine for a sizable sum. Before publicly announcing his retirement, however, he was sold by the Dodgers to the Giants, but would not report. Robinson publicly stated that the trade caused him to retire, but in fact he did not want to back out of the retirement because of the sale to *Look*. Dodger owner Walter O'Malley apparently was insulted by Robinson's refusal to play for the Giants, and some sources report that they never spoke again. It might be more accurate to say that Robinson and O'Malley never got along; Robinson was aligned with Branch Rickey, who was O'Malley's arch rival.

Former Dodger general manager Buzzie Bavasi said in his autobiography that the Giants might not have moved because their attendance would have improved with Robinson on the team. This is highly unlikely in light of the overall economic factors involved in the move to the West Coast and the pressure by the Dodgers on the Giants to move with them.

Lifestyle Decision. Relief pitcher Tim Burke retired before the 1993 season when he decided that he needed to spend more time with his family. By the time of his retirement, he and his wife had adopted four children from around the world, all of whom had significant disabilities.

His five-year-old daughter was a Korean-born infant who was born prematurely and had residual problems. His five-year-old son came from Guatemala with a thyroid condition and possible retardation. Burke left the 1989 All-Star Game in Anaheim shortly after the final pitch to fly to Central America to pick up the boy. His two-year-old daughter, also Korean, was born without a right hand and had a serious heart condition. She also suffered up to 40 seizures a day. Burke was once traded to the Mets and had to leave for the club only an hour after she had undergone open heart surgery. At the time of his retirement, he was scheduled to pick up child number four, a two-year-old from Vietnam who had a club foot. See also Tim and Christine Burke with Gregg Lewis, *Major League Dad* (1994).

Abrupt Decision. Ryne Sandberg retired early in the 1994 season, walking away from about $15 million due him over the remainder of 1994 and 1995. He worked out a deal with the Cubs that would pay him about $2 million for personal services. Nevertheless, he returned to the field for the 1996 season.

Rockies coach and long-time former manager Don Zimmer retired simply by leaving the dugout during the 5th inning of a game against the Cardinals in June 1995. He reportedly was depressed over the deaths of long-time friends Don Drysdale and Bob Miller. He returned as a bench coach for several years thereafter.

John Kruk retired during a game in mid–1995 at age 34. He cited bad knees as the main reason.

See *Phil Rizzuto* for his 1995 midseason decision to retire from the broadcast booth after regretting his decision not to attend Mickey Mantle's funeral.

Age of Retirement. In the 1880s the average age of retirement from professional baseball was 29.6 years.

Book. Lee Heiman, Dave Weiner and Bill Gutman, *When the Cheering Stops* (1990).

Revenue Sharing See *Profits, Losses and Expenses*—Revenue Sharing

Reviving Inner City Baseball ("RBI") See *Youth Baseball*

Sam Rice (1890–1974)

Hall of Fame (VC) 1963

"In personality, Rice is a great deal like Charlie Gehringer, steady, quiet, durable and consistent. A left-handed batter, he stood very close to the plate and never jawed at the umpires. He murdered fastball pitchers, and his particular target was Lefty Grove. The pitchers who were apt to stop him were the change-of-pace boys…"—Lee Allen and Tom Meany in *Kings of the Diamond* (1965).

Rice starred in the Senators' outfield primarily during the 1920.

Born in Indiana, Edgar Charles "Sam" Rice (see **Names**) joined the Navy at age 23 in 1913 and became a minor league pitcher at age 25. He was discovered by Clark Griffith of the Senators. Although never discussed by Rice, his first wife and their children were wiped out in a tornado while he was away trying out for a minor league club in 1912.

Because he was a good pinch hitter, he shifted to right field in 1915. Rice was purchased for $800 by the Senators and played four games for the club in 1915 and 58 in 1916. He established himself in 1917 with a .302 average in 155 games but missed most of the 1918 season due to military service during World War I. He returned in 1919 to post a .321 average and continued with the Senators through the 1933 season. He recorded over 200 hits six times and had a 31-game hitting streak in 1924, when he led the American League with 216 hits.

He finished his career with one season for the Indians in 1934, ending with a .322 lifetime average and only 13 hits shy of 3,000 (see also *Three Thousand Hits*—**Short of 3,000**).

His most famous moment came during the 1925 World Series when he dove into the bleachers to make a tremendous catch at a crucial moment in Game 3. There was great controversy over whether he made the catch. He wrote a famous letter that was opened at his death in which he confirmed making the catch (see also *World Series*—**Controversial Calls**). After his retirement, he raised chickens in Maryland.

Richmond Virginians

American Association 1884

"There was considerable excitement at one time owing to what the spectators considered a wrong decision by the umpire, expressing their disapprobation by a general outburst of indignant protest. The umpire very foolishly faced the whole crowd and singled out one individual upon whom to vent his anger by attempting to have him put out of the grounds, instead of not heeding the protest and attending to his duties."—Game account in the *Richmond Dispatch* of 1884, a few months before the club joined the American Association.

The club operated as part of the Eastern League in 1884. Near the end of the season the Washington franchise in the American Association failed. To maintain a full schedule in the Association, Richmond was invited to join. The Virginians did not do well, finishing 12–30, and when the Association reduced its number of teams after the season Richmond was dropped. Richmond would not have another shot at Major League Baseball until the ill-fated United States League of April 1912.

Francis Richter (1854–1926)

"With Mr. Richter, the game of baseball is a very serious matter, and his editorial opinions are in wide respect. The motto at the head of his editorial column is 'Devoted To Base Ball Men and Measures, With Malice Toward None And Charity For All,' sums up his character, and accounts for his strength in Base Ball."—Richter's obituary in the 1926 *Reach Guide*.

Richter was a sports chronicler around the turn of the century as editor of the weekly *Sporting Life* (founded in 1883) and then the *Reach Baseball Guide* when it began publication in the 1880s. He helped organize the American Association and its Philadelphia Athletics in the 1880s and then helped form the Phillies of the National League. He turned down the National League presidency in 1907.

Richter is credited with proposing an amendment to the National Agreement in the 1880s to allow minor league teams to reserve 14 players from raiding by Major League clubs. This fostered protection of the minor leagues and also led to creation of the "Millennium Plan," which was the first formal *Draft* allowing Major League teams to pick annually from among minor league players.

Branch Rickey (1881–1965)

Hall of Fame (VC) 1967

"Nobody ever could match his talent for putting a dollar sign on a muscle." — Dodger traveling secretary Harold Parrott on Rickey's ability to evaluate young talent.

"Imagine, a man trained for law devoting his entire life to something so cosmically unimportant as a game. This symbol [holding ball]. Is it worth a man's whole life?" — Rickey on his career choice.

"There but for the grace of God, goes God." — Mercurial baseball executive Larry MacPhail, paraphrasing Winston Churchill about the egotistical Rickey. The phrase could have applied just as easily to MacPhail.

"Next to Abraham Lincoln, the biggest white benefactor of the Negro has been Branch Rickey." — Grantland Rice.

After a brief Major League catching career, Rickey was a longtime front office executive in the National League who established the first modern farm system.

Wesley Branch Rickey was raised in Lucasville in Southeastern Ohio. He attended Ohio Wesleyan, playing on the school's football and baseball teams. He signed as a catcher with the Reds organization in 1903 and made the Major Leagues in 1905, but the devout Methodist would not play baseball on Sundays. He was released by manager Joe Kelley primarily because of poor play.

He came up again with the Browns (1905–1906) and Yankees (1907), batting .239 in 343 total at-bats, but tuberculosis forced him out and back to practicing law in Idaho. He returned to baseball in 1913 with the Browns at the request of owner Robert Lee Hedges. Rickey started as an administrative assistant and then took over as manager from George Stovall very late in the season. He also made two cameo appearances on the field in 1914. He remained as manager through the 1915 season, finishing in the second division each season before moving into the Browns front office for three years.

He became manager of the Cardinals in 1919, remaining in that position until 1925. His best finish was third in 1921 and 1922. While with the Cardinals, Rickey was responsible for implementing an early **Farm System**, in which he would place Cardinal players on minor league clubs where they could be controlled and trained. He remained in the Cardinals organization until after the 1942 World Series, enjoying enormous success with the club.

Rickey left the Cardinals for the Dodgers to replace general manager Larry MacPhail, who had joined the Army. Rickey remained with the Dodgers through the 1940s. His Cardinal and Dodger legacies were nine National League pennants and six world championships.

Rickey took credit for bringing Jackie Robinson to the Major Leagues. However, Rickey was no saint regarding black players and simply saw tremendous potential for new fans after the heavy influx of black workers and families into northern cities during World War II. Black groups were pushing for integration and professional football had already integrated.

Rickey was notoriously cheap and his venture into Brooklyn Dodgers **Football** in the late 1940s was a flop.

In 1950 Rickey and Dodger co-owner Walter O'Malley finally had enough of each other and O'Malley bought him out. Rickey moved to the Pirates from 1951 through 1956. He later was to become commissioner of the fledgling Continental League that was attempting to become a third Major League in 1960. When that effort failed, Rickey was not formally affiliated with a club until 1963, when he became a special consultant to Cardinals president August Busch.

Brooklyn Dodgers general manager Branch Rickey interviewed in his office after suspending manager Leo Durocher for the 1947 season.

On November 13, 1965, Rickey suffered a heart attack while giving a speech during his induction into the Missouri Hall of Fame. He never recovered and died a month later at age 83. Rickey was known as the "Mahatma" for supposedly having the personality of Indian Hindu spiritual leader Mohandas K. Gandhi. See also **Sunday Baseball**, for Rickey's refusal to play or manage on Sunday.

Books. Harvey Frommer, *Rickey and Robinson: The Men Who Broke Baseball's Color Barrier* (1984); David Lipman, *Mr. Baseball* (1966); MacMillan (ed.), *Branch Rickey's Little Blue Book: Wit and Strategy from Baseball's Last Wise Man* (1995); Arthur Mann, *Branch Rickey* (1957); Andrew O'Toole, *Branch Rickey in Pittsburgh: Baseball's Trailblazing General Manager for the Pirates, 1950–1955* (2000); Murray Polner, *Branch Rickey* (1982); Branch Rickey and Robert Riger, *The American Diamond* (1965).

Right Fielders

"Thus it is almost mandatory that the right fielder, whatever his arm strength, have a keen sense of strategy, since a variety of important plays can develop from the deep field. From the time of Babe Ruth, right field has been a glamour position. Showstoppers play there, those who *know* how to display the merchandise." — David Falkner in *Nine Sides of the Diamond* (1990).

"[Right field] is the position that the poorest player of the nine — if there be any such — should occupy; not that the position does not require as good a player to occupy it as the others, but that it is only occasionally, in comparison to other portions of the field, that balls are sent in this direction." — 1865 *Beadle's Dime Base-Ball Player*.

"I never thought I'd ever say that somebody could throw better than [right fielders] Carl Furillo or Roberto Clemente, but this guy can." — Vin Scully on Dodger rookie Raul Mondesi.

For a starting line-up on an all-time all-star team, Babe Ruth must be in right field. However, Henry Aaron is a reasonable second choice and for purely defensive purposes Roberto Clemente should be the pick. Casey Stengel said that Clemente was the best right fielder he had ever seen. Clemente is regarded as having the all-time best arm in right field (see also **Defensive Gems**). Among recent players, Larry Walker and Raul Mondesi lead the pack of best arms in right field.

Riots

"Baseball is very big with my people. It figures. It's the only time we can get to shake a bat at a white man without starting a riot." — Black comedian Dick Gregory.

After an 1896 game in Louisville, every player on the Cleveland Spiders was arrested for inciting a riot.

On the Dodgers' Opening Day in 1912, 20,000 fans crowded into their 15,000-seat ballpark to watch them play the Giants. The Giants were leading 18–3 in the sixth inning when hundreds of angry fans stormed onto the field and sat behind the catcher. For the safety of the Giants, the game was called in the sixth "due to darkness" even though there was plenty of light left. A riot started and some of the players were beaten though they used their bats for protection.

On June 23, 1943, Detroit was suffering through terrible race riots and armed troops were used to guard Briggs Stadium. This was unprecedented in baseball's history.

After the Pirates' 1971 World Series victory, 40,000 fans rioted and 100 were injured. Rioting after a pennant or World Series championship game occurred occasionally in other cities after that season.

The Dodgers had to reschedule four games in 1992 because of rioting that followed the verdict in the Rodney King beating case in May of that year. One of the games was to be replayed against the Expos on the day before the July 14 All-Star Game, traditionally an off-day. No one consulted with the Expo players, who voted against using the off-day. As a result, the game was replayed as part of three doubleheaders in three days that the clubs played in early July in Los Angeles before the All-Star break. It resulted in a 22-game home stand for the Dodgers.

Rivalries

Cubs/White Sox.

"Yuppie Scum Go Back to Wrigley" — Sign at Southside Chicago's Comiskey Park during a period of success for the White Sox in which Cub fans bought many Comiskey Park tickets. The Northside Cubs are considered the team of the elite while the White Sox have historically been the team of the Southside working class. The Cubs and White Sox staged their first postseason "City Series" in 1903. The 15-game series ended in a 7–7 tie with one rainout.

"It's like the slug calling the worm a crawler." — Chicago radio producer Tom Serritella on White Sox and Cubs fans verbally attacking each other.

"I'd rather have a sister in a whorehouse than be a White Sox fan." — Wrigley Field tour guide extraordinaire Brian Bernardoni.

"It used to be that by raising their children to be White Sox or Cub fans, parents unwittingly were producing kids suited for just one career: crime scene photographer…. People witnessed some horrifically bad baseball in this city, and the only thing that made it palatable was the knowledge, built on bravado, self-medication and other coping techniques, that their pathetic team was better than the pathetic team on the other side of town. This was like being smug about having heart disease instead of lung disease." — Rick Morrissey of the *Chicago Tribune*.

"If a man tells you he's a fan of both the White Sox and the Cubs, check your wallet, make sure your watch is still on your wrist, and lock your car doors. It doesn't work that way in Chicago." — Jay Johnstone in *Temporary Insanity* (1985).

Chicago columnist Mike Royko once took an oath on Sox owner Bill Veeck's wooden leg that he was switching allegiance to the White Sox after a lifetime of support for the Cubs. Said Royko: "I always believed that being a Cubs fan built strong character. It taught a person that if you try hard enough and long enough, you'll still lose. And that's the story of life."

Long-time Chicago sportswriter Bill Gleason focuses on the religious differences, in that the Cubs started with Protestant fans on the North Side, and the White Sox courted the South Side Irish Catholics. Others focus on race, as some of the black players on the Cubs couldn't get housing on the North Side and most black fans supported the White Sox.

Because of interleague play, the Cubs and White Sox were able to face off in 1997 for the first time officially since the 1906 World Series. On June 16, 1997, at Comiskey Park, the Cubs won 8–3 as both teams donned vintage uniforms. Fittingly, Illinois native Kevin Foster got the win. The White Sox had their two largest crowds ever during the three-game series, 44,249 and 44,204.

See also **Feuds**.

Giants/Dodgers.

"Historians of New York baseball do not exaggerate. Never in the history of the game has there been a rivalry to equal the interborough clash between the Giants and the Dodgers — for intensity, for color, romance and pure baseball entertainment. The much-heralded feud between the Yankees and the Red Sox was by comparison a ladies' club contretemps." — William Curran in *The National Pastime*.

The Giants and Dodgers were archrivals through the 1950s and 1960s, as evidenced by the fact that from 1956 until 1968 no trades were made between the clubs. In 1968 the Giants traded catcher Tom Haller to the Dodgers for Nate Oliver and Ron Hunt.

The rivalry can be traced to October 18, 1889, when the National League champion Giants played a championship series against the American Association Brooklyn Dodgers at the old Polo Grounds. The Dodgers won the first game (and three of the first four), but the Giants won the last four to clinch the championship.

In 1955 the Giants drew 25% of their attendance from home games with the Dodgers. The Dodgers drew 42% of their crowds to Giants games.

The Giants knocked the Dodgers out of the pennant race in the last game or two in 1951, 1962, 1971, 1982 and 1991. The Dodgers finally reciprocated in 1993, knocking the Giants out on the last day of the season with a 12–1 rout to give the Braves the Western Division title.

The Dodgers beat the Giants with a wild 9th inning comeback in the second-to-last game of the 2004 season to clinch the Western Division title and also help eliminate the Giants from the wild card race when Houston won on Sunday.

Yankees/Red Sox.

"When the Red Sox come to New York, the I.Q. level in Yankee Stadium goes up an average of 10 points." — Columnist George Vecsey on the number of Red Sox fans living in New York.

When Fenway Park opened in 1912, the Red Sox beat the Yankees 7–6 in 11 innings: "Unfortunately for the Red Sox, the victory did not establish a trend."—Larry Stewart.

The Yankees and Red Sox have battled for the flag in the late 1930s, 1940s, 1970s and 2000s. The rivalry peaked in 1978 with a one-game play-off for the American League Eastern Division title, and then renewed again in the 2003 ALCS, when the Yankees won Game 7 in extra innings. The Red Sox have almost always come out second-best (but see, 2004!). See also Harvey Frommer, *Baseball's Greatest Rivalry* (1982) and Harvey Frommer and Frederic J. Frommer, *Red Sox vs. Yankees: The Great Rivalry* (2004).

Northern/Southern California. For the first time, in 2004 both the Dodgers and Angels clinched postseason berths in the same season. They did it within one half hour of each other on the Saturday before the end of the season; and they each did it against their Northern California rivals, the Giants and A's. The Angels rallied for three runs in the 8th to beat the A's and clinch the American League West. Twenty-nine minutes later Steve Finley of the Dodgers capped a seven-run 9th inning rally with a grand slam to beat the Giants 7–3 and clinch the National League West for the Dodgers.

Eppa Rixey (1891–1963)

Hall of Fame (VC) 1963

"How dumb can the hitters in this league get? I've been doing this for fifteen years! When they're batting with the count two balls and no strikes, or three and one, they're always looking for the fastball. And they never get it."—Rixey.

"They're really scraping the bottom of the barrel, aren't they?"—Rixey, joking about learning of his election to the Hall of Fame.

Rixey won 266 games over 21 National League seasons beginning in 1912.

Eppa Jeptha Rixey was the winningest left-hander in National League history until Warren Spahn came along. Rixey played for the Reds and Phillies from 1912 through 1933, usually for second-division teams. He nevertheless won 266 games over his 21 Major League seasons. During his last few years he pitched almost exclusively against the Pirates until he retired at age 43.

Born in Virginia, he attended the University of Virginia and planned to become a chemist (earning his degree) until former umpire Charlie Rigler saw him pitch. Rigler was a coach at the school.

Rixey won 20 games four times, including a high of 25 in 1922, two years after being traded to the Reds from the Phillies. After his retirement, he joined his father-in-law's successful insurance business in Cincinnati, and the current Eppa Rixey Insurance Agency has a motto of "Hall of Fame Performance for Your Insurance Needs." In 1969 he was voted the all-time left-handed pitcher in Cincinnati history.

Phil Rizzuto (1917–)

Hall of Fame (VC) 1994

"Holy Cow!"—Rizzuto's famous broadcast refrain.

"My best pitch is anything the batter grounds, lines or pops in the direction of Rizzuto."—Yankee pitcher Vic Raschi.

Rizzuto played 13 seasons at shortstop for the Yankees between 1941 and 1956.

Fiero Francis Rizzuto (Phil sounded more American) dropped out of high school to pursue pro baseball. A native Brooklynite and Dodger fan, he had a failed tryout with the Dodgers and Casey Stengel (managing at the time). He then signed with the Yankees and was the 1940 Minor League Player of the Year in Kansas City. He made it to the Major Leagues in 1941 and immediately became the club's regular shortstop. Known as Scooter, the diminutive (5'6", 150 pounds) Rizzuto was the starting Yankee shortstop during 11 of his 13 Major League seasons. He batted .307 in 133 games in 1941 and had another solid season in 1942 before he was swept into the military by World War II.

During the war Rizzuto served as a chief petty officer in the Navy's athletic program. He served three years overseas and organized baseball programs. He also played military baseball for much of his three-year stint, sometimes playing third base alongside Pee Wee Reese.

After the war, Rizzuto returned to his regular shortstop position with the Yankees. He was runner-up to Ted Williams for MVP in 1949 and in 1950 was named MVP with a career-high .324 batting average, 200 hits and 125 runs scored. In 1951 he was the World Series MVP after batting .320. His last full season was 1954 when he hit only .195. He played two more seasons for the Yankees and then retired.

Rizzuto batted .273 lifetime and played in nine World Series for the Yankees. He is sixth all-time in World Series games played and had a .246 average. He was the Yankee lead-off batter for most of his career and was considered one of the top shortstops in the American League. He led the league in various fielding categories 11 times and led in sacrifice hits five years in a row. He once went 289 games without an error, then an American League record.

Shortly after his retirement he moved into the broadcast booth, where he remained from 1957 until August 1995. He retired abruptly after regretting his decision not to attend Mickey Mantle's funeral. He left the booth after five innings, too distraught to continue. He was just short of his 78th birthday: "The New York Yankees' play-by-play gabbler apparently retired last week after 39 years of digressions about traffic, cannoli, movies, electric storms, golf, worms, snakes, possums, phobias, people, birthdays, hospitals and people having birthdays in hospitals."—*Sports Illustrated.*

He returned to broadcast more than 30 games for the club in 1996 and then retired permanently. In 2004 Phil Rizzuto Park opened in Union, New Jersey. It had zero baseball diamonds; rather, it featured a single large soccer field.

Book. Dan Hirshberg, *Phil Rizzuto: A Yankee Tradition* (1994); Hart Seely and Tom Peyer (eds.), *O Holy Cow!: The Selected Verse of Phil Rizzuto* (1994); Joe Trimble, *Phil Rizzuto* (1951).

Road Games

"Schopenhauer once said, 'Life is a useless interruption of an otherwise peaceful non-existence.' So is a road trip. On the other hand, it's also a non-existence."—Jim Murray.

"Take those fellows over to that other diamond. I want to see if they can play on the road."—Casey Stengel at a Mets spring training camp.

"All of the Mets' road wins against L.A. this year have been at Dodger Stadium."—Ralph Kiner.

See also **Home Teams** and **Scheduling**.

19th Century Cost/Distance. In 1877 the Chicago White Stockings calculated the cost of a typical road trip at $4,866. The cost was helped considerably by discounts provided by the railroads.

Road Trips.

"I really love baseball. The guys and the game, and I love the challenge of describing things. The only thing I hate—and I know you have to be realistic and pay the bills in this life — is the loneliness on the road." — Vin Scully.

In 1946 the Red Sox had eight home stands and eight road trips, typical of the league. The club averaged 9.8 games for each. The shortest home stand was five games and the longest was 20 games. The shortest road trip was three games and the longest was 17 games.

By the 1960s and expansion, the Red Sox had 14 home stands and 14 road trips. The average was 5.9 games, the home stands from two to 19 games and road trips from two to 15 games.

1990s Cost. In 1994 the Angels went on a three-city Midwest road trip. They spent $95,218 on air fare, $27,000 on lodging, $22,800 on meal money, $3,000 on buses, $1,500 on trucks and $1,500 on incidentals, for a total of $151,000.

Bad Planning. The Yankees were to host the Red Sox in their second-to-last series of the 1904 season. The Yankees had to shift the series to Boston because Yankee owner Frank Farrell had leased the stadium to Columbia University for a football game. Boston ended up winning the flag over the Yankees by 1½ games.

Sick Call. During one season in the 1950s, New Orleans played all its games on the road due to an outbreak of yellow fever in the city.

Contract Clause. When Roger Clemens signed his 2004 deal with the Astros, he was allowed to skip any road games in which he was not pitching.

Long Trip.

"I was hoping, when I was 50 or 60 years old, to take a trip around the U.S. to see the country. I didn't plan on it happening when I was still playing." — Astros infielder Casey Candaele on the Astros' extended 1992 road trip caused by the Republican National Convention occupying the Astrodome for most of August. Players received the following perks for the 28-day, 26-game, eight-city tour: a first-class round-trip ticket for wife or guest from Houston to Chicago, when the team made its sixth stop; waiving of the club rule requiring suits or sports jackets on travel days; a laundry allowance in addition to the $59-per-day meal money called for in the collective bargaining agreement. The Astros traveled 9,196 miles and had a record of 12–14 on the trip.

Due to the 1996 Olympic Games, the Braves went on a 17-game road trip to five cities.

The Expos played 22 home games in San Juan, Puerto Rico, in 2003, and then embarked on a brutal extended road trip from San Juan to Seattle. The team played 22 games in 25 days, covering 11,310 miles. They finished the trip with a six game losing streak, but won the last game. The trip lasted from May 25 to June 20 and followed this route: Miami, Philadelphia, San Juan, Seattle, Oakland and Pittsburgh.

Ballpark Problems.

A's.

"Las Vegas would like to have a major league team on a permanent basis, but that will happen right after Marge Schott makes the cover of *Vogue*." — Gerry Callahan in *Sports Illustrated* after the A's were forced to play their first six home games of 1996 in Las Vegas. Their ballpark's $100 million refurbishments were not yet complete. The club went 2–4.

Giants. The 1889 Giants played on Staten Island because their stadium was being razed.

Expos. In 1991 the Expos had an unplanned 26-game road trip because the club's stadium was defective. Steel support beams were unstable and the ballpark was abandoned for the remainder of the season. The club was 13–13 on the trip.

Mariners. In August 1994 the Mariners had problems with their *Indoor Ballpark* roof, which forced them to play their home games out of town. Had the player strike not intervened, they would have traveled 14,228 miles on a 30-game road trip covering 32 days.

Yankees. On April 13, 1998, a 500-pound beam fell at Yankee Stadium prior to a game against the Angels. There were no fans inside the ballpark when the beam fell from the underside of the upper deck into the mezzanine section and landed on seats between third base and left field. The game was cancelled and plans were made to move games to Shea Stadium.

Over 1,600 Yankee parking passes were honored at Shea. The Yankees used the visitors locker room (with permission from the Chicago Cubs, the Mets' opponents in a three-game series played at the same time). The Angels used the old Jets locker room and the first-base dugout. Bob Sheppard, the voice of Yankee Stadium, was the public address announcer. The Yankees outdrew the Mets in their own ballpark. The Yankees had 30,000 advance ticket sales for a game that was heavily promoted with reduced ticket prices in honor of the 75th anniversary of Yankee Stadium. The Mets for the game against the Cubs had advance ticket sales of 14,000. When the Yankees and Mets played on the same day in the same stadium, it was the first time teams from the National and American Leagues hosted games in the same park on the same day.

The American League asked Tigers' owner Mike Ilitch to switch the series with the Yankees to Detroit, while the inspection and repairs to Yankee Stadium continue. George Steinbrenner said: "It's been reported that I made insensitive comments regarding the difficulties incurred by the Tigers' organization and their fans to accommodate the unavoidable switch of this series to Tiger Stadium. I would never say that such a gracious act is no big deal. It is a 'big Deal!'"

World War II. Due to wartime travel restrictions in 1943, each club's total road trips were reduced to 28, down from a norm of 38.

Unwanted. The pitiful 1899 Cleveland Spiders traveled from July 3 until August 23, playing 50 games in 52 days.

Expansion. See *Expansion* — Effect on Travel.

Road Winning Streaks. See *Wins and Winning Streaks* — Road Wins.

Road Losing Streaks. See *Losing Streaks*.

Roberto Clemente Award (1971–)

"To the player best exemplifying humanitarian service to the community."

This award is presented annually by Major League Baseball. Some sources reported that it was created to recognize Clemente's public service efforts, which included the 1972 mercy flight to Nicaraguan earthquake victims that crashed with Clemente on board. However, the award was initially known as the Humanitarian Award when it was created in 1971, and the name was changed after Clemente's death. The two winners before Clemente's death were Willie Mays in 1971 and Brooks Robinson in 1972. The award is also presented locally to community members outside of Major League Baseball who exhibit the same qualities.

In the mid–1990s True Value Hardware attached its corporate name to the award and since then donates $28,000 to Clemente's foundation each season. Another $25,000 goes to the winner's designated charity.

Robin Roberts (1926–)

Hall of Fame 1976

"I never slept when I lost. I'd see the sun come up without ever having closed my eyes. I'd see those base hits over and over and they'd drive me crazy." — Roberts.

Roberts won 286 games primarily for the Phillies over 19 seasons beginning in 1948.

Robin Evan Roberts was a baseball and basketball star at Michigan State (among 37 Major Leaguers from that school), before signing a minor league contract in 1948. He was called up by the Phillies midseason and won seven games. After winning 15 games in 1949, he posted six straight 20-win seasons, with a high of 28 in 1952. He led the Phillies to the 1950 National League pennant, only their second since 1883. He won the pennant-clincher on the last day of the season, defeating Don Newcombe and the Dodgers 4–1 in extra innings.

Shoulder problems turned him into a finesse pitcher after the 1956 season, when he won less than 20 games for the first time since 1949. After going 1–10 through mid–1961, the Phillies released him. He signed with the Yankees, was released without pitching for them, and was picked up by the Orioles. He won 42 games for the Orioles from 1962 through most of the 1965 season before being released. He signed with the Astros and won eight games over parts of two seasons. After finishing out the 1966 season at age 40, he went down briefly to the minor leagues before retiring. His lifetime Major League record was 286–245, with 45 shutouts and 2,357 strikeouts.

After he retired, he was head baseball coach at the University of South Florida and worked in the Phillies organization as a pitching instructor.

Brooks Robinson (1937–)

Hall of Fame 1983

"The decision on who was the best is easy, easier than for any other position. I can never be convinced that anyone in this millennium has played third better than Brooks Robinson. Needless to say, I don't hold this opinion in isolation. In a brilliant sixteen-year career [actually 23], Brooks simply rewrote the book on third-base play. He wasn't fast, he didn't have a cannon arm; but he may have had the finest 'nose' for the ball of any infielder in history, and his hands were as soft as a safecracker's. I can't believe that we will see his like again." — William Curran in *Mitts* (1985).

"I'd like to be like Brooks. The guys who never said no to nobody, the ones that everybody loves because they deserve to be loved … those are my heroes." — Orioles manager Earl Weaver quoted in Thomas Boswell's *How Life Imitates the World Series* (1982).

"I'm a guy who just wanted to see his name in the lineup everyday. To me, baseball was a passion to the point of obsession." — Robinson.

"There's not a man who knows him who wouldn't swear for his integrity and honesty and give testimony to his consideration of others. He's an extraordinary human being, which is important, and the world's greatest third baseman of all time, which is incidental." — John Steadman of *The News American*.

Robinson was perhaps the best defensive third baseman of all time for the Orioles between 1955 and 1977.

Discovered in a Little Rock church league after playing no high school ball, the 18-year-old Robinson signed for $4,000 in early 1955 and played with the Orioles later that season. He slowly

became a replacement for Hall of Famer George Kell and finally made it into the starting line-up in 1958, playing in 145 games and batting .238.

Robinson was the American League MVP in 1964 with a .317 average, 28 home runs and 118 RBIs. He was the MVP of the 1970 World Series, when he made a series of *Defensive Gems* against the Reds. He was also the starting American League third baseman in 15 straight All-Star Games. He has the all-time best fielding percentage for third basemen at .971 and dominates in most other important fielding categories. He led all third baseman 11 times in fielding percentage. He batted .267 with 268 home runs and 1,357 RBIs.

Robinson is considered by many to be the greatest defensive third baseman in history. Over 23 years with the Orioles he won the Gold Glove Award 16 times, the most by any player at any position.

A series of bad investments left him with financial problems near the end of his career, and the Orioles voluntarily left him on the roster for at least a year after his ability had badly deteriorated. After his retirement, Robinson became president of the Major League Baseball Players Alumni Association and broadcast for the Orioles from 1978 through 1993. By the mid–1990s Robinson was working for a petroleum company and a player representation agency.

Book. Rick Wolff, *Brooks Robinson* (1991).

Frank Robinson (1935–)

Hall of Fame 1982

"Thy only regret I have in my heart today is that I didn't speak out a whole lot more about baseball's injustices to blacks. If I and others had been hollering in the 1970s that blacks were being systematically excluded from positions of authority in the game, probably we would not have to holler so often now." — Robinson.

"Frank Robinson might have reached for a zip gun or a switchblade knife. He might have followed the well-worn trail that led from the tough West Side of Oakland, California, to reform school or the penitentiary … but young Frank found another one. He followed it to a playground, and someone put a baseball bat in his hands. It was love at first sight." — Sportswriter John M. Ross.

Robinson hit 586 home runs over 21 seasons beginning in 1956 and was the first black manager in Major League history.

Frank Robinson grew up in Oakland and was playing American Legion ball when he signed for $3,000 with the Reds in the early 1950s. He made it to the Major League club for the 1956 season, winning Rookie of the Year honors with a .290 average, 38 home runs and 83 RBIs.

He won three straight slugging titles starting in 1960 but had to switch to first base for most of the 1960 and 1961 seasons because of recurring arm problems. Nevertheless, he led the Reds to the 1961 World Series and was the National League MVP. He was traded to the Orioles for the 1966 season and led the club to a world championship while winning the Triple Crown. He hit .316 with 49 home runs and 122 RBIs and became the only man to win the MVP Award in both leagues.

He led the club to the World Series three straight years from 1969 through 1971 (winning in 1970) before being traded to the Dodgers in 1972. He moved back to the American League with the Angels in 1973 and 1974 before being traded to the Indians late in the season. He became player-manager of the club in 1975, the first black manager in Major League history (see also ***Black***

"Firsts"). He finished his playing career with a .224 average in 36 games for the Indians in 1976.

Robinson batted over .300 nine times over his 21-year career and hit 586 home runs, fourth all-time when he retired. He hit eight home runs in five World Series. He managed the Indians to an 81–78 record in 1976 but was fired midway through the 1977 season when the club was 26–31. He managed the Giants from 1981 through most of 1984, finishing third twice. He took over as the Orioles manager in early 1988 (midway through a horrible losing streak) and led the club to a second-place finish in 1989 before being fired 37 games into the 1991 season. He moved into the Orioles front office and remained there through the 1994 season.

He later became the discipline czar for Major League Baseball and then was tapped to manage the Montreal Expos beginning in 2002.

Books. Larry Reston, *Frank Robinson* (1974); Frank Robinson with Dave Anderson, *Frank: The First Year* (1976); Frank Robinson with Al Silverman, *My Life Is Baseball* (1968); Frank Robinson with Berry Stainback, *Extra Innings* (1988); Russell J. Schneider, *The Making of a Manager* (1976).

Jackie Robinson (1919–1972)

Hall of Fame 1962

"Yes, I know that [the Dodgers profited enormously by my presence on the club]. But I also know what a big gamble [Branch Rickey] took. A bond developed between us that lasted long after I had left the game. In a way I feel I was the son he had lost and he was the father I had lost." — Robinson on his relationship with Rickey in *I Never Had It Made*, by Robinson with Alfred Duckett (1972).

"The Jackie Robinson story is to Americans what the Passover story is to Jews: It must be told to every generation so that we never forget." — Historian Jules Tygiel.

"He was an intelligent man, sensitive and understanding to what was going on around him at all times, and that made his task some much more difficult. He was aware of what he was there to do. He was aware of the tremendous load he carried. Think about it. Imagine being *the* Black man in Baseball. Imagine having to think every day, 'What would it mean to my people if I'm a bust?'" — Vin Scully.

Robinson was the first black player to play officially in the Major Leagues in the 20th century (see **Integration**).

Jack Roosevelt Robinson was a star track man at UCLA and briefly professional football. He enlisted in the Army during World War II, coming out as a lieutenant. He went on to play shortstop for the Kansas City Monarchs of the Negro Leagues. He signed with the Dodger organization on August 28, 1945, and led the International League in batting while playing for the Montreal Royals.

He began his Major League career with the Dodgers at age 26 as a first baseman in 1947, winning Rookie of the Year honors (the award was later renamed for him). He was fifth in the MVP voting that year and was runner-up to Bing Crosby in a 1947 national popularity poll.

He replaced Eddie Stanky at second base the next year and won the MVP award in 1949, the first black player to do so. He played 10 full seasons for the Dodgers, retiring after the 1956 season with a .311 lifetime average and a .234 average in six World Series.

After retirement he held a number of business positions. After a second heart attack and only two weeks after being honored at the 1972 World Series, he died at age 53.

Books. Maury Allen, *A Life Remembered* (1987); David Falkner, *Great Time Coming: The Life of Jackie Robinson from Baseball to Birmingham* (1995); Harvey Frommer, *Rickey and Robinson: The Men Who Broke Baseball's Color Barrier* (1984); Jackie Robinson with Alfred Duckett, *I Never Had It Made* (1972); Jackie Robinson and Carl T. Rowan, *...Wait 'Til Next Year* (1960).

Wilbert Robinson (1863–1934)

Hall of Fame (VC) 1945

"He was bumbling, very profane, and very fat." — Harold Seymour recalling his three seasons as a Dodger batboy in *Baseball: The Golden Age* (1971).

"Gimme good hitting and long hitting and let the rest of them managers get just as smart as they want." — Robinson.

Robinson was a catcher for the 1890s Baltimore Orioles and managed the Dodgers from 1914 through 1931.

A native of Massachusetts, Wilbert Robinson began his professional career in 1885 and joined the Philadelphia Athletics of the American Association in 1886. Always a catcher, he was a regular on the club until he was traded near the end of the 1890 season to Baltimore of the American Association. He remained with the Orioles when they moved into the National League and became a powerhouse of the 1890s. He was the club's first string catcher until he was traded to the Cardinals for the 1900 season. He went back to Baltimore in 1901, this time with the Orioles of the American League where he finished his career in 1902.

Robinson batted .273 and stole 163 bases over his 17-year career, but his greatest influence was behind the plate. Following his retirement he remained John McGraw's close friend, business partner and coach with the Giants until the two reputedly had a falling out during the 1913 World Series.

By then known as "Uncle Robbie," Robinson left the Giants to manage the Dodgers, winning a pennant in 1916 and the World Series in 1920. He managed the club from 1914 through 1931, winning 1,375 games and finishing with an even .500 record. After club ownership shifted, he fell into disfavor and was fired after the 1931 season. Robinson spent his last years primarily at his winter home in Georgia where he was president of the Atlanta minor league club.

Rochester Broncos

American Association 1890

The club had a 63–63 record in its one season of Major League play.

Rockford Forest Citys

National Association 1871

The club had a 4–21 record and finished last in the nine-team league.

Bullet Joe Rogan (1894–1967)

Hall of Fame (VC) 1998

"Yeah, I pitched against Bullet Joe. Rogans was one of the world's greatest pitchers. I never did see him in his prime if you want me to tell you the truth. I came up from Birmingham to Kansas City. He beat me 1–0 in the 11th inning. Yeah, he was the onliest pitcher I ever knew, I ever heard of in my life, was pitching and hitting in the cleanup place. He was a chunky little guy, but he could throw hard. He could throw hard as Smokey Joe Williams —yeah. Oh yes, he was a number-one pitcher, wasn't any maybe so."—Satchel Paige, quoted in John B. Holway's *Voices From the Great Black Baseball Leagues* (1993).

Rogan was a Negro League pitching and hitting star for 22 years, beginning with the Kansas City Colored Giants in 1917.

Born in Oklahoma in 1894 (not 1890 as many sources report), Wilbert Joe Rogan played semipro ball in Kansas City with Fred Palace's Colts in 1908 and the Kansas City Giants in 1909. In 1911 Rogan joined the military. He played on various Army teams, most notably in Hawaii and Arizona. It was in Arizona that he was allegedly discovered by a barnstorming Casey Stengel. Rogan's teammates included Dobie Moore, Heavy Johnson and Lem Hawkins. All four players would later star for the fine Kansas City Monarch teams of the 1920's.

Rogan's own tenure with the Monarchs began in 1920. Over the first half of his career he was perhaps the finest all-around player in the Negro Leagues and author Phil Dixon makes a case for Rogan as, along with Babe Ruth, the greatest two-way threats of all-time.

An elite pitcher, he was noted for a dizzying array of pitches and excellent defense. He led the Negro National League in wins in 1924 and 1925 and was regularly among league leaders in strikeouts. At the plate Rogan was equally effective, though only 5'6". Frequently hitting from the clean-up spot, he batted over .300 eight consecutive years between 1922 and 1929. In 1922 he hit 16 home runs, sharing the league lead with Oscar Charleston.

Between 1923 and 1926 Rogan helped Kansas City to four consecutive pennants. In their successful 1924 Negro World Series versus the Philadelphia Hilldales, Rogan won two games on the mound and was the team's second leading hitter. The following year Rogan dominated the playoff with the St. Louis Stars. In the nine-game series Rogan won all four of his starts, including two shutouts, and led the team in hitting. A freak accident prevented him from again opposing the Hilldales in the series, a Philadelphia triumph.

Rogan performed as a player/manager for the Monarchs through the 1930's. He pitched less as he got older but continued to play well past age 45. John Holway credits Rogan with 155 Negro League wins, tied with Satchel Paige. In 1937 at the age of 48 he was a productive bench player for the fifth pennant-winning team of his career. Rogan retired from playing and managing in 1938. He was an umpire in the Negro American League through 1946. He passed away in Kansas City in 1967.

Rookie Leagues

"It is a summer of truth, a gathering of fastballs and fast feet. The Appalachian League, one of baseball's rookie leagues, is a place for major league bodies and high school minds. For some it also is the place for homesickness and loneliness, for finding out that a lifelong dream is a delusion, for bus rides and boredom and fast food three times a day. For others, 'God's Country' begins to look like heaven as they find out they actually may be among the elect."— Thomas Boswell in *How Life Imitates the World Series* (1982).

Rookie of the Year Award (1947–)

"Our Phenoms aren't Phenomenatin'."—Angels manager Lefty Phillips on the poor results from his highly-touted rookies.

"I declined the position. I wasn't sure which year the gentlemen had in mind."—Satchel Paige sarcastically commenting on his belated entry into the Major Leagues; referring to his not receiving the 1948 Rookie of the Year Award.

See also *Rookies*.

Origins. In 1947 the Baseball Writers Association (BBWAA) began presenting the current version of the Rookie of the Year Award. The first recipient was Jackie Robinson, for whom the award was later named. He was selected on September 12, two weeks before the season ended. Various baseball publications and organizations, most prominently *The Sporting News*, already had been presenting a Rookie of the Year award. For two seasons the BBWAA named a single winner for the Major Leagues. Beginning in 1949, a winner from each league was selected.

In 1948 Alvin Dark would have been a favorite to win the award, but was ineligible because of 15 games and 13 at-bats he had in 1946. *The Sporting News* had already selected Richie Ashburn, but the BBWAA president and treasurers, Edward Burns and Ken Smith, met to change the rules to allow rookies with less than 25 games to be eligible in another year. When the change was made, Dark was selected with 27 votes (Cleveland's Gene Bearden had 8 and Ashburn had 7).

The Sporting News. In 1946 *The Sporting News* presented a rookie award. For the first three seasons a single winner was chosen for the entire Major Leagues. In 1949 each league had a winner, but in 1950 *The Sporting News* reverted to a single selection. Beginning in 1951 two winners again were chosen.

In 1957 *The Sporting News* began selecting a rookie pitcher and a rookie player in each league, although no pitcher was chosen in the American League that season. In 1959 and 1960 the magazine chose only a single player in each league but returned to picking both a pitcher and a player in 1961. After flip-flopping again in 1962, *The Sporting News* finally settled on the dual selection system for each league beginning in 1963.

Qualifying. The original BBWAA qualifying rules required a player to be on a Major League roster for less than 90 days in any prior season, play in less than 30 games in a season or pitch in less than 60 innings in a season.

In 1971 the definition of a rookie was changed by Major League Baseball at the request of the BBWAA. To qualify as a rookie, a player now must not have more than 150 at-bats (referred to erroneously as 130 at-bats in one source), or 50 innings pitched in the Major Leagues during any previous season, or more than 45 days on a Major League roster during the 25-player limit period from the start of the season through August 31 (after which rosters are expanded to 40 players for the remainder of the season). Excluded from the calculation is any time in the military while a player is officially on a team's roster.

Brothers. Carlos May in 1969 and Lee May in 1967 are the only brothers to win the award.

Close. In 1968 Johnny Bench won the award by one point over Jerry Koosman to become the first catcher to win the award.

Consecutive. The Dodgers had four straight Rookies of the Year from 1979 through 1982: Rick Sutcliffe, Steve Howe, Fernando Valenzuela and Steve Sax. They had another five straight with Eric Karros in 1992, Mike Piazza in 1993, Raul Mondesi in 1994, Hideo Nomo in 1995 and Todd Hollandsworth in 1996. A broken thumb in August 1995 kept Hollandsworth eligible for 1996.

Injury. Scott Rolen of the Phillies was the 1997 Rookie of the Year, but barely qualified based on what happened in 1996. That season he had 130 at-bats before a broken wrist on September 7 ended his season. Had he had one more plate appearance, he would have had too many at-bats to qualify as a rookie in 1997.

Japanese League Players. In 2003 Hideki Matsui of the Yankees was probably the best new player in the Major Leagues. Nevertheless, two voters for Rookie of the Year left him off the ballot in protest over his several seasons in the Japanese major leagues. Angel Berroa of the Royals finished with 88 points on 12 firsts, seven seconds and seven thirds. Matsui finished second with 84 points on 10 firsts, nine seconds, and seven thirds.

Most Valuable Player. In 1975 Fred Lynn of the Red Sox became the first player to win the Rookie of the Year Award and Most Valuable Player Award in the same season.

In 2001 outfielder Ichiro Suzuki of the Mariners matched Lynn's record after coming over from the Japanese leagues.

Oldest. In 2000 Mariners reliever Kazuhiro Sasaki won the American League Rookie of the Year Award. He was the second-oldest winner ever at age 32. Former Negro League player Sam Jethroe was a month older when he won the award with the Braves in 1950.

Oldest/Minor Leagues. When Negro League star Ray Dandridge finally made it to Organized Baseball at age 40 with the Minneapolis Millers of the American Association, he was voted Rookie of the Year. He was the MVP the next year at 41. He never made it to the Major Leagues, in large part because he was the biggest drawing card for the minor league club.

Relief Pitcher. Joe Black of the Dodgers was the first relief pitcher to win the award. In 1952 he was 15–4 with 15 saves on the pennant-winning club.

Short Season. Willie McCovey won the 1959 award after playing in only 52 games. He hit .354 with 13 home runs and 38 RBIs.

Books. David Craft, *Rookies of the Year: New Kids Who Took the Field* (1995); Donald Honig, *American League Rookies of the Year* (1989); Donald Honig, *National League Rookies of the Year* (1989).

Rookies

"The removal of the straight-arm pitching restriction, by the amendment of the rules in 1884, was responsible for the evolution of the 'Phenom.' He came into the game from Keokuk, Kankakee, Kokomo and Kalamazoo. He was heralded always as a 'discovery.' His achievements were '*simply phenomenal.*' Once in a great while he 'made good.' Usually he proved to be a flat and unmitigated failure. The trying-out of these wonders became a very frequent occurrence, and the appearance of one for that purpose was sure to call out the ejaculation, 'Hello, here's another phenom. Wonder how long he'll last?'"— Al Spalding in *Baseball—America's National Game* (1911).

"Always be cautious about rookie performances in September. They don't indicate what'll happen in April."— Rangers general manager Tom Grieve on the advice given to him by long-time general manager Paul Richards.

"Baseball is the sport that cackles back at can't-miss kids. Baseball humbles every player sooner or later. Baseball confers greatness stingily, in its own sweet time…. At least that's what the bow-tied essayists and sandlot scouts solemnly tell us…"— Johnette Howard in *Sports Illustrated*.

See also **Rookie of the Year Award** for the criteria to qualify as a rookie.

Terminology. The term "rookie" is said to come from the chess piece, the rook, which is usually the last piece to be moved into the game.

All-Rookie Line-Up. On September 27, 1963, the Houston Astros fielded an all-rookie line-up that lost 10–3 to the New York Mets. The line-up contained a few future stars: Jimmy Wynn, Rusty Staub, Joe Morgan and Jerry Grote. Jay Dahl started the game and went 2⅔ innings in his only Major League appearance.

The 17-year-old was back in the minors in 1964 and early 1965, but was killed in a June 1965 car accident before he made it up to the Major Leagues again.

Oldest.

"I've been to every baseball park in America except those in the American League and National League."— Rich Amaral, 30-year-old rookie shortstop for the Mariners, after spending nine seasons in the minor leagues.

"NINE INNINGS. FOUR HITS. FIVE STRIKEOUTS. WINNING PITCHER PAIGE. DEFINITELY IN LINE FOR THE SPORTING NEWS AWARD AS ROOKIE OF THE YEAR"— Bill Veeck's telegram to J.G. Taylor Spink of *The Sporting News*, after Spink severely criticized Veeck for bringing up 42-year-old Satchel Paige in August 1948. Spink's response was to congratulate Paige but to lament the poor quality of baseball that allowed him to pitch in the Major Leagues.

Paige was the oldest Major League rookie at age 42 for the Indians. On August 13, 1948, in his 12th appearance and second start, he pitched a complete game 5–0 victory against the White Sox at Comiskey Park in front of 51,013 fans. His second straight shutout was a 1–0 three-hitter against the White Sox on August 20, 1948, in front of a record night game crowd of 78,382. That year he pitched in 73 innings over 21 games, with a 6–1 record and 2.48 earned run average.

Paige almost did not make it to the Major Leagues. In 1948 Cool Papa Bell was managing the Kansas City Monarchs "B" team of mostly promising young players. Paige was playing with the team but had a sore arm because of a long winter ball campaign. Indians manager Lou Boudreau called Bell to ask if he had any good young pitchers. Bell recommended Paige, but Boudreau was concerned that he was too old. Nevertheless, Veeck and Boudreau took a chance.

Chuck Hostetler played his first Major League game in 1944 for the Tigers. He was almost 41 years old during the wartime season. He is best remembered for falling down rounding third base with what would have been the winning run in Game 6 of the 1945 World Series. The Tigers survived the mishap by winning Game 7.

Heinie Groh's brother Lew played in two games for the A's in 1919 at age 36, with one game at third base and one pinch at-bat, but no hits in four attempts.

Lou Fette and Jim Turner were over 30 when they each won 20 games for the Braves as rookies in 1937.

Bob Keegan was a pitcher for the White Sox in the mid–1950s, making his debut as a 32-year-old rookie in 1953. In 1954 he was 12–3 at midseason and made the American League All-Star team.

Diomedes Olivo pitched for the Pirates in 1960 at age 40.

Doug Jones was a 30-year-old rookie reliever for the 1987 Indians.

Jim Miller (see below) relieved for the Devil Rays in 1999 at age 36.

Tampa Bay pitcher Alan Newman made his Major League debut after over 11 seasons in the minor leagues. He was 30 when he debuted on May 14, 1999. He balked home a run before he threw his first pitch.

On May 11, 2000, Joe Strong relieved for the Marlins at age 37.

Thirty-year-old Giants rookie Brian Dallimore made his first Major League start on April 30, 2004, after eight years in the minor leagues. He dazzled his family and friends with a grand slam in his first at-bat and then reached base four more times and scored two more runs. The Marlins and Giants were tied 9–9 after two innings, and the Giants went on to win 12–9.

Best Rookie Story. Jim Miller was a Texas high school baseball coach and science teacher who made a deal with his players in 1999: "Make the playoffs and I'll try out for the Major Leagues." They did, and he did. He was a 36-year-old ex-pitcher who had been firing fastballs during batting practice to his team. He had been drafted by the Brewers in the first round of the secondary phase of the 1983 draft, fourth overall. He hurt his arm shortly after being drafted and had a short minor league career before moving to the classroom.

Apparently, the years of batting practice throwing had re-strengthened his arm and allowed him to throw a fastball in the mid–90s. He went to an open tryout by the Devil Rays and shocked the scouts with his velocity. Within four months he made his debut with Tampa Bay. On September 18, 1999, the Rangers defeated the Devil Rays 6–1, but Morris fanned Royce Clayton in the 8th inning. At 36, he became the oldest rookie pitcher since Diomedes Olivo (age 40) with Pittsburgh in 1960. Miller appeared in 21 games over the 1999 and 2000 seasons for the Devil Rays, with a 4.80 ERA over 15 innings, striking out 13. He then got homesick and headed back to Texas.

Miller's story was quickly made into a successful *Movie*, *The Rookie*, starring Dennis Quaid.

Rookie Batting Records.

"There is no major league record held by a rookie. It's revealing to see just how far the rookie marks are below the single season marks. This is a testament to how difficult the game is to learn and to play." — Luke Salisbury in *The Answer Is Baseball* (1989).

No Major League season records are held by a rookie. As for rookie season records, Ted Williams holds the RBI record with 145 in 1939 and Mark McGwire holds the home run record with 49 in 1987. McGwire's slugging average of .618 that year topped the previous record of .609 set by Williams. Williams still holds the record of 107 base on balls by a rookie. Albert Pujols broke the National League rookie record in 2001 when he drove in 130 to break Wally Berger's record of 119, set in 1930.

Joe Jackson is the only rookie to bat over .400 when he hit .408 in 1911 for the Indians. He had 233 hits.

Max Carey stole 51 bases in 1923 as a rookie. Some sources report that "rookie" Maury Wills had 50 in 1960, the first to reach 50 since Carey. However, Wills had 242 at-bats in 1959 and that is considered his rookie season. Tim "Rock" Raines of the Expos now holds the rookie record with 71 steals in 88 games in 1981.

Fred Lynn had 47 doubles in 1975 for the American League rookie record. Johnny Frederick had 52 in 1929 for the Dodgers to set the Major League record. In 2001 Albert Pujols broke Frederick's rookie record of 82 extra base hits when he recorded 88.

Catcher Benito Santiago holds the rookie record for hitting streaks, with 34 straight games for the Padres in 1987.

Pitching Performances. Grover Cleveland Alexander won 28 games as a rookie in 1911, a modern record.

Bob Feller struck out 15 in his first start at age 17 in 1936. He struck out 17 three weeks later.

Alex Kellner was a rookie for the A's in 1949 when he went 20–12, but lost 20 the next year and never won more than 12 after that.

Rookie Gene Bearden of the Indians recorded his 20th win during the 1948 American League play-off against the Red Sox. He never again won more than eight games in a season.

Rookie Bob Grim of the Yankees won 20 games in 1954. He never again won more than 12 in a season.

Rookie Tom Browning of the Reds won 20 games in 1985. The closest he came again was 18 in 1988.

Rookie Babe Adams of the Pirates pitched three complete game wins in the 1909 World Series.

Marlins pitcher Dontrelle Willis started fast in 2003 with a 10–1 record and eight straights wins on his way to an appearance in the All-Star Game. He slowed considerably late in the season and was not particularly effective in the postseason.

Hazing. In keeping with the annual ritual of hazing rookies, in September 2004 the Yankees dressed several of their rookies in Elvis outfits, complete with wigs and sunglasses, while classic Elvis tunes played over the loudspeaker.

Books. Doug Marx, *Rookies* (1991); David Nemec and Dave Zeman, *The Baseball Rookies Encyclopedia* (2004).

Roommates

"I get the bed and you get the dresser drawer." — 6'2", 240-pound Ted Kluszewski to his 5'5", 140-pound Angels roommate, Albie Pearson. After a night of drinking, Kluszewski supposedly came in and tried to prove that Pearson fit in the drawer.

"Everybody who roomed with Mickey said he took five years off their career." — Whitey Ford on Mickey Mantle.

"In my time, I have roomed with a lot of crazy rookies, a situation that probably was more my fault than theirs. They got thrown in with me because I was kind of the elder statesman on the Barons; and whenever you have a big-league baseball team that has a coach who's been around a long time, you almost always room some wild busher with him. The idea is it is a restraining influence. It calms the kid down." — Charles Einstein in "The Sleeper."

No Roommate.

"We never saw much of him, just on the field. On the road, he roomed by himself." — Yankee shortstop Mark Koenig on Babe Ruth (see also *Curfews*).

After Yankee reliever Joe Page came in drunk one night, roommate Joe DiMaggio requested and received permission to room alone for the remainder of his career. He paid the difference in the room rate.

Ted Williams was allowed to room alone beginning in 1953.

Mickey Mantle and Whitey Ford were the only Yankee players of the 1950s to room alone on the road. Single rooms became common in the late 1970s.

Longest Together. Sam Rice and Joe Judge roomed together throughout the 1920s, claimed by at least one source to be the longest pairing in Major League history.

Walter Johnson and center fielder Clyde Milan were signed by the Senators on the same scouting trip. They were roommates with the club for the next 15 years.

Name Problem. The 1962 Mets had left-handed pitcher Bob Miller and right-handed pitcher Bob Miller. The traveling secretary solved the identity problem by having them room together: "That way, anybody phoning Bob Miller won't disturb anybody else if he gets the wrong number."

Competing Managers. In 1944 Cardinals manager Billy Southworth and Browns manager Luke Sewell shared an apartment together in St. Louis. One of them was always on the road, and that helped alleviate the housing shortage during World War II. During the 1944 World Series, in which each manager's team participated, they took separate apartments.

Segregation Problem. When Jackie Robinson went on the road during his first season with the Dodgers in 1947, his roommate was black sportswriter Wendell Smith (see also *Black "Firsts"*—Roommates).

Rosin Bag

"I just figured if the rosin bag is out there, you're supposed to use it." — Gaylord Perry on his "puffball," thrown loaded with rosin.

"He has one other talisman whose significance is somewhat obscure. This is what seems to be a small white sack that lies on the bare earth behind him. From time to time he reaches down, lifts it from the earth with his bare hand and quickly drops it as though there was something repulsive about the feel of it." — Howard L. Katzander in "Case History of Joey J., Baseball Player" (1958).

The pitcher's rosin bag was introduced in 1925.

A rule change occurred as a result of a maneuver by Yankee pitcher Whitey Ford. If the ball was wet, Ford would put it in his throwing hand and pick up the rosin bag with it at the same time. The rosin would stick to the moisture, allowing Ford to "load up" the ball with rosin and make it behave erratically. The rule change prohibited picking up the rosin bag using the hand holding the ball.

Rosters

"The vines were still dead now and the crowd was small and the wind blew off the lake, but this time I did not mind the loneliness. I was not only on the roster. I was in the lineup." — Outfielder Bill Bailey in "Voo and Doo," by Hoke Norris (1968).

1880s. In 1881 rosters were set at 11 players. By the mid–1880s, rosters were set at 14 players.

1890s. In 1892 teams started the year with 15 players, but because the National League had a monopoly on Major League ballplayers and wanted to save money, rosters were reduced in June to 13 players and some salaries were reduced by 40%.

1900–1918. To tie up more players during its 1901 war with the National League, the American League supposedly expanded its rosters to 18. However, the 18-player limit was allowed only until May of that season, when clubs were required to reduce their rosters to 14, the level until 1906.

By 1908 rosters in both leagues were set at 17 players and stayed at that level through 1912. After the 1912 season the National Agreement was revised to restrict a team to 35 players under its control. Between May 15 and August 20, 25 players could be on the active list. Within two years the Major League roster limit was expanded to 25 for the entire season, in part to allow American and National League teams to restrict the number of quality players accessible to the new Federal League. In 1915 rosters were reduced to 21 players to help save money during the Federal League challenge because all leagues were suffering from low attendance and increased salaries being paid to keep quality players from jumping leagues. World War I followed soon after the end of the Federal League and low attendance and government restrictions combined to ensure that rosters would remain lower than in the past.

1919–1940. After World War I ended in 1918, the leagues increased the roster limit to 25 for the 1919 season. That number was reduced to 23 during the Depression but was increased to 25 by the late 1930s. During the Depression, teams sometimes were allowed to carry 21 and even 20 players as an economy measure.

World War II. During the war there was doubt that Major League Baseball could continue to operate unless clubs could maintain a minimum of 18 players on their rosters. Nevertheless, the 25-player limit was not reduced during the war. Just after the war rosters were expanded to 30 to accommodate returning serviceman. The protected lists also were expanded, from 40 to 48.

1950– . Major League rosters continued to be set at 25 until the 1980s, when the number was reduced to 24 as a cost-saving measure. In 1990 teams were given the option of going with a 24- or 25-man roster, and most opted for 25 and virtually all continue to do so except in exceptional circumstances on a temporary basis. For example, in May 1996 the Padres opted to go with 24 players instead of putting Ken Caminiti on the disabled list for a brief period.

Beginning in 1961 because of expansion, American League teams were allowed to keep 28 players on their rosters for 30 days, rather than the traditional 25 players. This gave teams further opportunities to look at marginal players before making cuts. This practice continued into the 1970s. In 1995 as a result of the player strike, the season began in late April and teams were allowed to keep 28 players through May 15.

Minor Leagues. In 1902 the minor leagues adopted set rosters depending on the team's classification. For example, Class D league clubs had 14 players on their rosters, while Class A clubs were allowed 18 (Class AAA and Class AA did not yet exist).

By the 1990s Class AAA clubs were allowed 23 players through August 10 and then could increase to 25; Class AA had a limit of 23 and increased to 24 on August 10; Class A had a 25-player limit and Rookie leagues allowed 30.

Negro Leagues. The Negro Leagues ultimately allowed 16 players on a roster, but 14 was the limit for a number of years.

40-Man Roster. Any player promoted from the minor leagues to a Major League club must first be placed on the 40-man roster.

Roster Composition. In the early 1880s, when 11 players were on a roster, there were typically eight regulars, two pitchers and one substitute. A typical 1906 team roster consisted of seven pitchers (up from a 1900 average of 4–5), four infielders, three outfielders and three catchers. By the middle of the second decade, teams were carrying as many as nine pitchers, as the value of relief pitching began to be recognized.

Today the typical roster includes 10 or 11 pitchers (up from 9 or 10 in the 1950s and 1960s), six or seven infielders, five or six outfielders and two or three catchers.

Most Roster Moves. The 1915 A's used a then-Major League record 56 players, as did the 2000 Padres. The 1967 Mets used a National League record 27 pitchers and 27 position players. In 1969 the Pilots used 53 players. The 2002 Padres and Indians set the Major League record with 59 players and the 2003 Reds used 54 players to tie the National League record.

Most Players Used/Game. See *Substitutions*.

Postseason Roster. September 1 has been the traditional deadline for setting a team's postseason roster.

In 1923 Wally Pipp of the Yankees was injured just before the World Series. The Yankees asked for permission to substitute newcomer Lou Gehrig on its World Series roster. Judge Landis agreed, but opposing Giants manager John McGraw refused the request.

Lower-Paid Players. Underscoring the trend to lower-paid players filling out rosters, a record 66 non-roster spring training invitees made it onto Major League clubs in April 2004.

Books. S.C. Thompson, *All Time Rosters of Major League Baseball Clubs* (1967, 1973), contains year-by-year rosters from 1882 through 1972; John Thorn and Peter Palmer (eds.), *Total Baseball* (1992 and updates), contains complete team rosters for all Major League clubs.

Rotisserie League Baseball See *Fantasy League Baseball*

Rounders

"… baseball, *the* game in the United States, although undoubtedly originating in our old game of rounders, has been so built up and improved that the Americans are justified, perhaps, in claiming it as an invention of the New World…. Than baseball there is no more exact and scientific game. The Americans have a genius for taking a thing, examining its every part, and developing each part to the utmost. This they have done with our game of rounders, and, from a clumsy, primitive pastime, have so tightened its joints and put such a fine finish on its points that it stands forth a complicated machine of infinite exactitude."— Angus Evan Abbott in *The Sports of the World* (1904).

"Rounders with a stick."— One British writer's description of the 1914 baseball exhibition in his country.

"You remember baseball? A sort of razzamatazz rounders, played by rowdy roughnecks, wielding oversized clubs and oversized tennis balls."— Robert Steen.

Edd Roush (1893–1988)

Hall of Fame (VC) 1962

"I didn't expect to make it all the way to the big leagues, but I didn't care. I just had to get away from them damn cows."— Roush.

Roush was a stellar outfielder primarily for the Reds from 1917 through the 1920s, batting .323 lifetime.

Indiana native Edd J (no period, no meaning) Walsh was with Evansville in 1912 when he was signed by the White Sox. He played nine games for Chicago in 1913 before jumping to the Federal League for two seasons. In 1916 he played for both the Giants (39 games) and Reds (69 games). Legend has it that Giants manager John McGraw did not recognize Roush's potential and got rid of him after he was batting only .188. McGraw only traded him, however, because he had made a bigger financial investment in Federal League star Benny Kauff, and one of the outfielders had to go (one source reported a clash over the use of a particular bat).

Roush blossomed with the Reds, leading the league with a .341 average in 1917 and .321 in 1919, two of his 11 straight seasons over .300. He was Cincinnati's star through the 1920s, with a career high .352 average in both 1921 and 1922, and .351 in 1923. He had 27-game hitting streaks in 1920 and 1924.

He was traded to the Giants in 1927, where he hit .304 that season, but began to slide after tearing stomach muscles in 1928 in the middle of a three-year contract. Notorious for being a *Hold-Out* many springs, Roush sat out the entire 1930 season in a contract dispute with the Giants. In 1931 he was back in Cincinnati for his final season. He finished his career with a .323 average and 2,376 hits and later coached briefly for the Reds. After his retirement he made frequent appearances at spring training and his shrewd investing made him enough money not to have to work following his retirement from the game.

Rover

Box scores of the 1860s showed a tenth player, sometimes designated as "right shortstop," who played in short right center field. This practice lasted for about 10 years.

A tenth player, or rover, was used for only one season in 1874 in the National Association, two years before the formation of the National League in 1876. Most sources point out that the "rover" was actually a fifth infielder rather than a fourth outfielder. Other sources are more specific in noting that the rover was used only as an additional infielder between first and second base or as an additional catcher.

Henry Chadwick suggested in 1874 that 10 men be used to diminish large gaps in the infield. From 1874 through 1882 either the *DeWitt's Guide* or the *Beadle's Dime Base-Ball Player* (both edited by Chadwick) suggested use of a tenth man on the field.

Royalty

"Nice to meet you, king."— Yogi Berra upon meeting King George of England.

"I've just been informed that the fat lady is the Queen of Holland."— Dizzy Dean on the air after asking who the fat woman was below the broadcast booth. When told it was the Queen of the Netherlands (Holland), he asked on the air where that was.

"A king may be a king because his father was, but a ballplayer is a Major Leaguer only so long as his average shows he is."— Jim Murray.

"Royal Shaw, Gary Gentry, Ray Noble, Harvey Gentry, Marv Breeding, Slick Castleman, Ed Buckingham, Don Castle, Count Campon, Prince Oana, Harry Lord, Ray Knight, Hal King, Bill Marquis, Duke Carmel, Mel Queen, Walter Prince, Duke Sims, Howard Earl, King Cole, Lady Baldwin, Don Prince, Bris Lord, Mike Squires"

During their 1888–1889 international tour, Albert Spalding of the White Sox sat with the Prince of Wales during a game in England. Spalding made headlines in England when, after an outstanding fielding play, he good-naturedly poked the Prince. Spalding's response to the uproar: "It wasn't any more offensive than a game of tag, and I wouldn't have done it if he hadn't first slapped me on the leg."

Before World War I, King George V of England hired former Major Leaguer Arlie Latham as his personal baseball instructor. When John McGraw was on his world tour in 1912–1913 with the Giants and White Sox he was given a personal introduction to King George V.

On July 4, 1918, during World War I in England, the King and Queen watched a baseball game and were apparently puzzled by the arguing with the umpire, at least according to a British journalist. That writer had the following comment: "If the Yanks are not bothered by the overwhelming dignity and autocratic authority of the umpire, they would have no trouble with the Germans."

Lord Louis Mountbatten, Grand Admiral of the British Fleet and cousin of the Prince of Wales, attended Game 1 of the 1922 World Series in New York.

Queen Elizabeth II of England attended an Orioles game on May 15, 1990. She left in the 3rd inning of a game that featured seven walks, one wild pitch and three errors, prompting pitcher Mike Flanagan to note: "Everyone else left in the 5th. Maybe she's more accustomed to baseball than we knew."

Red Ruffing (1904–1986)

Hall of Fame 1967

"But what was a little pain to a man who had come out of the coal mines near Nokomis, Illinois? Red Ruffing had lost four toes in the mines, nearly lost his left foot, and had narrowly missed decapitation. He had seen his father emerge from the mines with a broken back, his brother's kneecap and fingers smashed, and the death of his twenty-year-old cousin. Now he was pitching for the New York Yankees in a World Series — another story of 'Pluck and Luck.'"— Richard C. Crepeau in *Baseball: America's Diamond Mind—1919–1941* (1980).

Ruffing won 273 games over 22 seasons beginning in 1924, with his best years for the Yankees.

Charles Herbert Ruffing played for his father on a mining team in Illinois before moving on to the minor leagues. He had been an outfielder when a mining accident cost him four toes on his left foot. He converted to pitching and made his way to the Red Sox in 1924 at age 19.

Ruffing was a mediocre pitcher with the club through 1929, leading the league in losses with 25 and 22 in 1928 and 1929. The Yankees traded for him in 1930, and he became a star with the powerful club. After winning from 15 to 19 games in all but one year between 1930 and 1935, he won 20 or more games four straight seasons beginning in 1936. After three more seasons of 14 or 15 wins he entered the military in 1943 and missed more than two seasons. He returned in 1945 but his career was effectively over. He played in 1946 for the Yankees and 1947 for the White Sox before retiring.

Ruffing finished his 22-year career with a 273–225 record and 48 shutouts to go with a 3.80 ERA. He won seven games over seven World Series with the Yankees. Ruffing was one of the best hitting pitchers of all time, batting .269 with 36 home runs and reaching .300 eight times. He stole only one base in his career due to severe pain in his foot and no speed on the basepaths.

Ruffing later scouted for the White Sox and Indians and managed a few minor league clubs before becoming the first pitching coach for the Mets in 1962. He was elected to the Hall of Fame in 1967, his last year of eligibility.

Rule V Draft See Drafts

Rules

"I try not to break the rules but merely to test their elasticity." — Bill Veeck, Jr.

"In spite of their importance we fear there are sections of the Official Rules that are somewhat less than exhilarating. So don't bother your pretty wits about them; simply race through the few pages assembled here and we guarantee that you'll end up knowing more about baseball than any man worth looking at." — A Housewife's Guide to Baseball (1958).

"In fact, most of the arguments male baseball fans engage in have little or nothing to do with the rules. Usually these tiffs are inspired by the sort of my-team-can-lick-your-team emotional blatherings that men love to wallow in when the sweet spring air is scented with the pungent smell of horsehide." — More from A Housewife's Guide to Baseball (1958).

See also Base on Balls, Hits, Origins of Baseball, Pitching, Stolen Bases and Strikeouts.

Uniformity. The National League rules were completely rewritten before the 1880 season. Even though the National Agreement of 1883 helped codify the rules of Organized Baseball, there were still differences in the rules between the National League and American Association. In November 1886 a joint rules committee was appointed to develop uniformity among all National Agreement teams.

Recodification. Major League Baseball's rules were completely recodified in 1950 with numerous minor changes. For example, the home team was now required to bat last; before that the home team could elect whether to bat first.

Ignoring Old Rules. The Special Records Committee of 1968 overturned a number of decisions of past years. Prominent among them was the overturning of the 1887 rule scoring Base on Balls as hits. There has been controversy over applying these modern

views to 19th century standards: "One can only urge baseball historians to unite in common cause to right these wrongs. To this end, historians should chant each day at their breakfast tables this exorcism of wrongheaded revisionists: 'Don't meddle with past official records.' The lamentable urge to change past records to square with the present is a familiar totalitarian practice. It is anathema to the search for truth and to the integrity of American baseball history." — David Quentin Voigt in The National Pastime.

Books. Rich Marazzi, The Rules and Lore of Baseball (1980); David Nemec, The Rules of Baseball (1994).

Rundown See Base Running

Running Bases Backwards See Base Running

Runs

"Just as the A's were about to get the last out and retire to the clubhouse to admire themselves in the dressing room mirror, the Senators came up with four runs." — Red Smith.

First Run. Tim McGinley of the National League Boston Red Stockings is credited with scoring the first Major League run on April 22, 1876.

One Millionth Run. The one millionth run in the history of Major League Baseball (American and National Leagues only) was scored by Astros first baseman Bob Watson at 12:32 p.m. on May 4, 1975, during a Sunday game against the Giants. His shoes and home plate from the game are in the Hall of Fame. The race to score the milestone run was closely monitored by an elaborate electrical hookup among all stadiums that day, anchored in the broadcast booth by Ralph Branca and Mel Allen in New York.

In the 2nd inning at Candlestick Park after a base on balls, Watson was on second and Jose Cruz on first. On a home run by Milt May off John Montefusco, Watson raced home knowing it was close. Cruz and May almost crossed paths, which would have nullified the run. Watson scored only three seconds before a home run dash was completed by Reds shortstop Dave Concepcion, and only seven seconds before a run scored in Milwaukee.

Bad Seasons. The 1930 Phillies gave up 1,199 runs in tiny Baker Bowl, including 19 runs four times. The club's pitchers had a combined ERA of 6.71.

The 1899 Cleveland Spiders scored 529 runs, while their opponents scored 1,252.

Last Inning Rallies.

"The Padres need one run to tie and two to win. So, going into the 9th the score is San Francisco one, the Yankees [sic] nothing." — Jerry Coleman.

The most runs scored in the 9th inning of a game to take the lead is nine. In May 1901 Cleveland was down 13–5 to Washington in the 9th inning. With two out and none on, the Indians scored nine runs to win 14–13. Two weeks later, Boston was up 4–2 on Milwaukee with two outs and none on in the top of the 9th inning, but Milwaukee scored nine runs to take the lead and win.

During a 1929 game the Indians scored nine runs in the 9th inning to defeat the Yankees.

Until 1990 the National League record for 9th inning rallies was seven runs when the Cubs trailed the Reds 8–2 in a 1952 game. On August 21, 1990, the Phillies scored nine runs in the 9th inning to defeat the Dodgers 12–11.

On August 29, 1986, the Angels trailed the Tigers 12–5 entering the 9th inning. Light-hitting shortstop Dick Schofield hit an

0–2 pitch for a grand slam to cap the Angels' 13–12 comeback victory.

No Runs Scored/Most Hits. It is possible to have six hits in an inning, but no runs scored. After three base hits two runners are picked off base, and then two more singles are recorded without a runner scoring, again loading the bases. The third out is a runner hit by a batted ball, which is automatically scored as a single for the sixth hit.

Most Runs/19th Century Season. Philadelphia's Billy Hamilton scored 196 times in 1894 and had 166 runs the next. In the same season Joe Kelley of the Orioles hit .393 and scored 165 runs (167 in older sources), the third best total in National League history.

Most Runs/20th Century Season. Babe Ruth holds the 20th century Major League record, scoring 177 runs in 1921.

Most Runs Scored/Career. On October 4, 2001, Rickey Henderson homered to become baseball's all-time run-scoring leader, with 2,247, passing Ty Cobb. Henderson finished his Major League career in 2003 with 2,295. Henry Aaron and Babe Ruth are tied for third at 2,174 and Pete Rose is fifth at 2,165. Through 2004 Barry Bonds had 2,070 good for sixth place.

Most Runs/Single Inning.

"The last time I saw anything like this I was playing for Tastee Freeze in Little League." — Houston Astros pitcher Dave Smith, after his team fell behind the Cincinnati Reds by 14 runs — in the 1st inning.

On June 18, 1953, in front of 3,108 fans, the Red Sox scored 17 runs in the 7th inning against the Tigers. Gene Stephens had three hits in the inning and Sammy White scored three times, a Major League record for one inning. The Red Sox batted for 48 minutes, sending 23 men to the plate, knocking out 14 hits and breaking all single-inning records except the 18 runs scored by the Chicago White Stockings on September 6, 1883. Tommy Burns and Ned Williamson scored three times in that inning. The day before the big inning, the Red Sox won 17–1.

Steve Gromek was on the mound when the onslaught started and gave up nine of the runs. After the 23–3 final, Gromek started four days later and shut out the Athletics.

On April 19, 1996, the Rangers scored 16 runs on eight hits and eight walks in the 8th inning against the Orioles. The final score was 26–8.

The Indians hold the American League record for scoring in the 1st inning with 14 on June 18, 1950 in a 21–2 win over the A's.

The Dodgers scored 15 runs at Ebbets Field in the 1st inning against the Reds on May 21, 1952. The Dodgers scored 12 runs after two outs against four Reds pitchers on their way to a 19–1 win. Three Dodgers made three plate appearances in the inning.

On April 23, 1894, the Boston Red Stockings pitchers gave up 14 runs in the 9th inning to the Orioles, a last-inning record that has never been broken.

Most Runs/9th Inning. On August 8, 2001, the Tigers scored 13 runs in the 9th inning for a 19–6 win over the Rangers. It set a modern Major League record for most runs in that inning. On April 24, 1894, the Baltimore Orioles of the National League scored 14 in the 9th inning against Boston.

Most Runs Before One Out.

"It was miserable. It was embarrassing." — Marlins third baseman Mike Lowell.

On June 27, 2003, the Red Sox scored 14 runs in the 1st inning of an interleague game against the Marlins, including a record 10 before the Marlins could record an out. Marlins manager Jack McKeon accused the Red Sox of running up the score in the 25–8

victory. The 1st inning took 50 minutes and included 91 pitches by three Marlins pitchers. The Red Sox tied a team record with 28 hits. The previous record for runs before an out was nine, by the Phillies against the Giants on August 13, 1948. The Red Sox equaled the American League mark for runs scored in an inning, one less than the 15 scored by the Dodgers in 1952.

Johnny Damon tied a record with three **Hits** in an inning, but the game was marred by a line drive off the bat of Boston's Todd Walker that smashed into the skull of pitcher Kevin Olsen (see *Injuries and Illness*—Head).

Most Runs/Both Teams.

"When the wind is favorable in the Windy City, rare things happen — as they happened yesterday in Wrigley Field. The Phillies and Cubs went right down to the wire in a sort of pitchers' duel (the pitchers vied with each other to see which could remain alive longest)…" — Art Hill in *I Don't Care If I Never Come Back* (1980). On May 17, 1979, the Phillies defeated the Cubs 23–22 at Wrigley Field in the highest scoring game in 57 years.

The highest scoring game ever was on August 25, 1922, when the Cubs defeated the Phillies 26–23 at Wrigley Field. The Cubs scored 10 in the 2nd inning and 14 in the 4th for a 25–6 lead. The Phillies came close with eight in the 8th inning and six in the 9th, but left the bases loaded to end the game. Despite all the scoring, the game lasted only 3 hours and 1 minute. The teams to combine to leave 25 runners on base.

Prior to 1922 the highest scoring Major League game was played on July 12, 1890, when Brooklyn and Buffalo of the Players League combined to score 44 runs.

On May 19, 1999, the Reds beat the Rockies 24–12 for the third highest combined run total in the 20th century.

Must Runs/One Team. On June 8, 1869, at Buffalo, New York, the Niagaras defeated Columbia 209–10. The game only took three hours. The Columbia pitcher, a Mr. Mack, had a good 4th inning when he shut out the Niagaras. The line score:

	1	2	3	4	5	6	7	8	9	
Niagara	40	20	9	0	18	19	26	58	19	209
Columbia	2	3	1	0	1	3	0	0	0	10

The score prompted some tortured logic by the local newspaper, the *Buffalo Courier and Republic*: "We are somewhat inclined, in baseball matters, to reason logically. For instance, the Red Stockings beat the Niagaras by a score of 42–6, or 7–1. The fair inference is, if the Cincinnatians had played the Columbias, the score would have been 1,463 to 1 or 2; that is, multiplying the score of the Niagaras by 7 and dividing that of the Columbias by the same number. 'Logic is logic.'"

On June 29, 1897, the Chicago White Stockings defeated Louisville 36–7 for the all-time Major League one-team scoring record.

On June 8, 1950, the Red Sox defeated the Browns 29–4 to set the American League record. The record was tied by the White Sox against the A's on April 23, 1955.

On July 6, 1929, the Cardinals scored 10 runs in both the 1st and 5th innings on their way to a 28–6 win over the Phillies in the second game of a doubleheader. The Cardinals set a modern National League record with the 28 runs.

On April 30, 1944, the Giants defeated the Dodgers 26–8. The Dodgers gave up 18 hits and 17 walks, including five straight walks to Mel Ott.

On August 18, 1995, the Cubs beat the Rockies in Denver 26–7. The game included an almost three-hour rain delay.

On September 9, 2004, the Royals beat the Tigers 26–5, to score the fifth-most runs in the 20th century. Joe Randa became the first American League player to have six hits and score six runs in a game. The Tigers then shut out the Royals in the nightcap of the doubleheader. The last time that number of runs was scored was by the Rangers, who beat Baltimore 26–7 on April 19, 1996.

Scoring in Every Inning. Since 1900 only three teams have scored in every inning of a nine-inning game. On June 1, 1923, the Giants defeated the Phillies 22–8. On September 13, 1964, the Cardinals defeated the Cubs 15–2. Both winning teams won the pennant and beat the Yankees in the World Series. On May 5, 1999, the Rockies scored in every inning of their 13–6 victory over the Cubs.

On June 30, 1996, the Rockies came close, scoring in all but the 1st inning of a 16–15 comeback win over the Dodgers.

On September 14, 1998, the Royals scored in all 8 innings in which they batted in a 16–6 victory over visiting Oakland.

Most Runs/Two Teams/Inning. On August 25, 1922, the Phillies and Cubs scored 15 in the 4th inning (14 by the Cubs) on the way to a 26–23 Cubs win.

Doubleheader. On August 14, 1937, the Tigers scored 36 runs against the Browns in a doubleheader to set a Major League record.

20-Run Games.

"CARNAGE. JUST PLAIN SLAUGHTER. BROOKLYN POUNDS STIMMEL TO THE BENCH."— Headline after the Dodgers beat the Reds 25–6 on September 23, 1901.

The 1900 Phillies, the 1939 Yankees and 1950 Red Sox each scored 20 or more runs in a game three times in a season. The Tigers had two such games early in the 1993 season but did not reach the mark again that year.

In 1950 there were five teams that scored 20 or more runs in a game. In 1996 there were six such games.

Comebacks.

"The sooner you fall behind, the more time you have to catch up."— Sam Ogden in *Time* magazine in 1979.

The record for biggest comeback is 12 runs, done three times in the American League. The A's rallied from a 15–3 deficit to beat the Indians 17–15 on June 15, 1925. The Tigers came back from a 13–1 deficit to defeat the White Sox 16–15 on June 18, 1911. On August 5, 2001, the Indians beat the Mariners 15–14 in 11 innings after being down 12–0 and 14–2. Cleveland scored three runs in the 7th inning, four in the 8th, and five in the 9th. Omar Vizquel hit a bases-loaded triple in the 9th off All-Star reliever Kazuhiro Sasaki.

In the National League the record is 11 runs. On June 15, 1962, the Cardinals rallied from 11–0 to beat the Mets 14–12.

The Phillies were down 12–1 to the Cubs on April 17, 1976, but rallied for an 18–16 win.

On July 18, 1994, the Astros trailed the Cardinals 11–0 after three innings but came back to win 15–11. The rally came four days after the Astros blew an 8–0 lead and lost 11–8 to the Pirates.

On September 30, 1894, the Cleveland Spiders came back from a 15-run deficit to tie Cincinnati before the game was called because of darkness.

Opening Day. On April 1, 1997, the Padres scored 11 runs in the 6th inning of a 12–5 win over the Mets. The 11 runs in an inning was a National League Opening Day record for the 20th century. The inning featured three straight home runs by Chris Gomez, Rickey Henderson and Quilvio Veras. The Major League record is 14, set by the 1894 Baltimore Orioles in the 9th inning after trailing 3–1 on April 24, 1894.

Postseason/One Team. On October 10, 1999, the Red Sox set a postseason record when they scored 23 runs against the Indians. The 23–7 win tied the five-game series at 2–2 and the Red Sox won the deciding fifth game 12–8.

World Series Game. On October 20, 1993, the Blue Jays ral-

lied for a 15–14 win over the Phillies to take a 3–1 lead in the World Series. The 29 runs broke the Series record of 22, set in Game 2 in 1935, when the Yankees beat the New York Giants 18–4. The Blue Jays scored six runs in the 8th inning to take the lead after the Phillies had led 14–9. The nine-inning game took 4 hours and 14 minutes, the longest ever for the World Series.

World Series Comeback.

"It remained for our beloved Cubs to furnish the greatest debacle, the most terrific flop, in the history of the World Series and one of the worst in the history of major league baseball games of all kinds."— Sportswriter Edward Burns in the lead to his story of the A's comeback against the Cubs on October 12, 1929, in Game 4 of the World Series. The A's scored 10 runs in the 7th inning to erase an 8–0 lead. The A's won the game and then clinched the series in Game 5. What is generally forgotten is that in Game 5 the A's again staged a dramatic comeback. They were down 2–0 going into the bottom of the 9th inning. A two-run homer and two doubles gave them a 3–2 win and the championship.

Most Players Scoring. On October 3, 1999, the Braves beat the Marlins 18–0. The Braves had 21 hits and a Major League record 15 players scored runs.

On September 30, 2000, the A's beat the Rangers 23–2, as 14 Oakland players scored to set a new American League record.

More Runs than Games/Career. Three players have scored more runs in their careers than the number of games in which they played: 19th century stars George Gore, Harry Stovey and Billy Hamilton. One source reported erroneously that the record was more runs than *at-bats*.

Scoring Runs/Consecutive Games. The 20th century record was held solely for many years by Red Rolfe, who scored in 18 straight games for the Yankees in August 1939. He scored 30 runs during the streak on his way to a league-leading 139. In August and September 2000, Indians outfielder Kenny Lofton scored in 18 straight games. In the last game of the streak, on September 3, 2000, he stole five bases and hit a walk-off home run in the 13th inning to win the game.

Ted Kluszewski of the Reds scored in 17 straight games from August 27 through September 13, 1954. Prior to 1900, sliding Billy Hamilton scored in 23 straight games for Philadelphia.

In July 1994 Mike Stanley of the Yankees scored in 14 straight games.

Most Runs/One Player/One Game. Pitcher Guy Hecker of the Louisville Colonels scored seven runs in an American Association game in 1886. He went 6-for-7, a record for pitchers. He is erroneously identified as "Becker" in at least two sources.

Division Winner. The 1987 Twins were the first championship team to score fewer runs than their opponents over an entire season.

Scoring Trends. Average runs scored by one club over nine-inning games since 1930:

1930	5.5 (supposedly livelier ball)
1931	4.8 (definitely deader ball)
1933	4.4
1943	3.9 (war year; first time below 4.0 since 1918)
1949	4.7
1952	4.2
1962	4.5 (lousy expansion pitchers)
1963	3.9 (reduced strike zone)
1968	3.4 (the "Year of the Pitcher")
1978	4.1 (post–Designated Hitter)
1988	4.1
1990	3.95

1992   4.12
2000   5.15
2003   4.75

Most Runs/College. On April 3, 1996, Robert Morris College played the College of St. Francis. St. Francis had finished fifth in the NAIA tournament in 1995 and Robert Morris had started its baseball program only two years earlier. The final score was 71–1, as St. Francis set an NCAA record for runs scored. The game lasted only four innings after Robert Morris coach Gerald McNamara ended the carnage.

The Division 1 record is Cornell's 43–4 victory over Coppin State.

Runs Batted In ("RBIs")

"There is no greater pleasure in the world than walking up to the plate with men on base and knowing that you are feared."— Cardinals catcher Ted Simmons.

"[We're] about to the point where we'd embrace a telemarketer if he'd drive in a few runs."— Chicago columnist Rick Morrissey, after the White Sox traded for umpire attackers Roberto Alomar (spitting) and Carl Everett (bumping).

"[Before that,] I couldn't drive home Miss Daisy."— Boston outfielder Lee Tinsley, who finally recorded his first three RBIs of the season.

See also *Game Winning RBIs* and *Rookies*.

Old School. Note that this author prefers "RBIs" to the modern usage "RBI" popularized on ESPN. The latter simply doesn't roll off the tongue properly.

Recognized Statistic.

"The *Chicago Tribune* proudly presented the "Runs Batted In" record of the Chicago players for the season, showing Anson and Kelly in the lead. Readers were unimpressed. Objections were that the men who led off, Dalrymple and Gore, did not have the same opportunities to knock in runs. The paper actually wound up almost apologizing for the computation."— Preston D. Orem in *Baseball (1845–1881) from the Newspaper Accounts* (1961, 1966– 1967).

Some sources report that the first RBI totals were compiled by Buffalo in 1879. Others report that the RBI was introduced in 1880 by the *Chicago Tribune* but did not catch on for some time and was not reported by newspapers and other sources until 1907.

Nineteenth century sportswriter and National League Rules Committee member Henry Chadwick suggested that the RBI be recognized in the official records and box scores, but in 1891 the rules committee rejected the change. As one newspaper account of the day noted, the committee "humiliated and crushed the father of baseball" in his attempt at recognition for the RBI. There were no official RBI records kept until 1920, and most newspaper box scores did not show RBIs for another 10 years.

Rules. The 1930 official scorekeeper rules provided that the number of RBIs should be totaled for each batter, but the rules provided no clue for unusual situations. This was rectified at a December 1930 meeting when specific rules were adopted. For example, "with less than two out, if an error is made on a play on which a runner from third would ordinarily score, credit the batsman with a Run Batted In."

Double Play Rule. In 1939 it was ruled that a batter would no longer receive credit for an RBI if he grounded into a double play while a runner scored.

Most/One Inning. On May 3, 1951, rookie Gil McDougald of the Yankees drove in six runs in one inning to tie the Major League record. He had a two-run triple and a grand slam in the 11-run inning that led to a 17–3 win over the Browns at Sportsman's Park.

On July 5, 1996, Matt Stairs of the A's became the 12th player to drive in six runs in an inning. The A's scored 13 runs in the 1st inning against the Angels as Stairs hit a grand slam and a two-run single. Carlos Quintana of the Red Sox had been the last to do so in 1991.

Matt Williams tied the record on August 27, 1997, when he drove in six runs in the 4th inning of a 10–4 victory over the Angels. He had a three-run double and a three-run homer.

Most/Game. Jim Bottomley set the Major League record of 12 RBIs in a game. He went 6-for-6 for the Cardinals against the Dodgers at Ebbets Field on September 16, 1924. He broke Wilbert Robinson's record of 11 RBIs (set June 18, 1892, when Robinson had seven *Hits*). Robinson was the Dodger manager when Bottomley surpassed him. Bottomley had a two-run single in the 1st inning, one-run double in the 2nd, grand slam in the 4th, two-run homer in the 6th, two-run single in the 7th, and a one-run single in the 9th inning.

On September 7, 1993, Mark Whiten of the Cardinals tied Bottomley's record when he drove in 12 runs on four *Home Runs* against the Reds.

Most/Two Games. Tony Lazzeri of the Yankees once had 15 RBIs in two consecutive games.

Most/Doubleheader. Nate Colbert of the Padres had 13 RBIs while hitting five *Home Runs* during a doubleheader on August 1, 1972. The Padres defeated the Braves in Atlanta 9–0 and 11–7.

Most in One Game/Entire Career. On July 19, 1955, Babe Birrer drove in six runs with a pair of three-run home runs. They were the only RBIs of his career, despite pitching in 56 games and batting 27 times over his four years in the Major Leagues.

Most/Month. Hack Wilson of the Cubs drove in a Major League record 53 runs in August 1930 on his way to a record 191 (previously thought to be 190— see below).

Rudy York of the Tigers drove in 49 runs during August 1937 for the American League record.

Lou Gehrig drove in 48 runs in August 1935.

In 1994 Joe Carter of the Blue Jays set a record for April with 30. Andres Galarraga of the Rockies tied the record later in the same month. In April 1997 Tino Martinez had 34 RBIs. He had 40 in his first 30 games, the first player to do so since Roy Campanella in 1953 (44). Martinez's April record fell the next season when Juan Gonzalez had 35 RBIs in April 1998 for the Rangers.

Most Through July. Chuck Klein had 116 RBIs through July 1930 and he finished with 170. Jeff Bagwell of the Astros had 107 through July 1994, but a broken wrist and the player strike ended his season.

Most Through All-Star Break. Hank Greenberg had 103 RBIs at the 1937 All-Star break but could not continue on a pace to 200, finishing the season with 183.

Juan Gonzalez of the Rangers had 101 RBIs by the break in 1998, but injuries slowed him and he finished with 157.

Carlos Delgado had over 100 RBIs for the Blue Jays by the break in 2003, but finished with only 145.

Most/Season. For many years it was thought that Hack Wilson of the Cubs drove in 190 runs in 1930 for the Major League record. SABR researchers established that he drove in 191, but the higher number was not recognized by Major League Baseball in 1977 when historian Clifford Kachline first presented findings to the Baseball Records Committee.

In 1996 the issue resurfaced when Kachline discussed it at a SABR convention and made a formal presentation on the subject in 1997. The research determined that there were eight mistakes in the box score for the game in which Wilson should have been credited with another RBI. Through a laborious process of checking and re-checking by SABR and other members of the baseball fraternity, including Seymour Siwoff of Elias and Dave Smith at Retrosheet, it appeared clear that the 191 figure was correct and verifiable. Heavy media coverage of the subject occurred because of midseason assaults on the record by Juan Gonzalez and then Manny Ramirez. In June 1999 the new figure was accepted, at the same time that six walks were added to Babe Ruth's total (Rickey Henderson was fast-approaching Ruth's all-time record, so the issue of updating records to be accurate was hot). Bud Selig's comment at the time: "I am sensitive to the historical significance that accompanies the correction of such a prestigious record, especially after so many years have passed, but it is important to get it right."

The entire inquiry started in 1977 when Kachline, at the time the historian of the Baseball Hall of Fame, received a letter from one James Braswell of Chicago, who made reference to a game in which Wilson (he thought) had an RBI. Baseball's records said otherwise, and the chase was on. The game in question was played on July 28, 1930, when Charlie Grimm was credited with two RBIs and Wilson with none. They each had one.

Not a bad controversy for a 5'6" alcoholic who wore a size 5½ shoe (Wilson, not Kachline). He did have an 18-inch neck and huge forearms on his 190-pound body.

In 1927 much attention was given to Lou Gehrig's attempt to drive in 200 RBIs. Babe Ruth stole the show with 17 home runs in September to finish with 60. Gehrig faded badly as he worried about his mother's illness, finishing with 175. He had 184 in 1931, but it was the result of a strong finish and he never had a legitimate chance for 200.

Averaging One RBI a Game. George Brett had 118 RBIs in 117 games in 1980, the year he batted .390. The last player before Brett to average more than an RBI per game was Walt Dropo in 1950 for the Red Sox. He had 144 RBIs in 136 games.

Clutch Hitters. Babe Ruth had an RBI every 3.79 at-bats, the all-time record. Lou Gehrig is second at 4.02 at-bats.

Two Teams/Season/League Leader. Gus Zernial is the only man to lead the league in RBIs while playing for two teams (and second to lead in *Home Runs*). He had 129 RBIs and 33 home runs while playing for the 1951 White Sox and A's.

Home Run Efficiency. According to Bill James, of the top 10 home run hitters of all time, Jimmie Foxx got the most mileage out of them. He had 944 RBIs on 534 home runs—1.76 per home run. Willie Mays had the least until Barry Bonds, with 1,039 RBIs on 660 home runs, or 1.57 per home run. Through 2003 Bonds had 1,013 RBIs on 658 home runs, or a 1.54 ratio.

Home Run/RBI. During his 70-homer season in 1998, Mark McGwire went two months in June through August 7 when he never drove in a run without a home run.

In 2001 Barry Bonds hit 73 home runs with only 137 RBIs to become only the second player not to double his home run total with RBIs. Kevin Maas had 21 home runs and 41 RBIs in 1991. In 2003 Bonds had 45 home runs and 90 RBIs, to cut it close.

Most/First Two Seasons. Joe DiMaggio holds the record with 292 RBIs in his first two Major League seasons. Dale Alexander is second at 272. Ted Williams is third at 258 and Albert Pujols had 257 in his first two seasons.

Four Seasons. In 2001 Sammy Sosa had 160 RBIs, the highest total in the National League since Chuck Klein's 170 in 1930. Sosa's four year total broke Klein's record, set in 1929–1932.

In 2004 Albert Pujols became the fourth player to drive in over 100 RBIs in each of his first four seasons. The others: Ted Williams, Joe DiMaggio and Al Simmons.

Consecutive Games. The Major League record for RBIs in consecutive games is held by Ray Grimes of the 1922 Cubs. He had RBIs in 17 straight games, but the streak was over a longer string of games because Grimes suffered injuries during the streak and did not play.

Taffy Wright of the White Sox had RBIs in 13 consecutive games in 1941 for the American League record. In six of the games, he did not have a hit. Mike Sweeney of the Royals tied the record with 13 in 1999.

One Batter Driving in All Runs/Game. On September 2, 1996, Mike Greenwell of the Red Sox drove in nine runs in a 9–8 victory over the Mariners. By driving in all his team's runs, Greenwell broke the record of eight shared by George Kelly of the 1924 Giants and Bob Johnson of the 1938 A's.

RBIs/No Hits. On September 20, 2000, Colorado's Ben Petrick had four RBIs without benefit of a hit. He had a sacrifice fly, bases loaded walk, and two ground outs. Nevertheless, the Padres beat the Rockies 15–11 after leading 15–4.

Heavy Hitters. The pennant-winning 1920 Indians were the first team with three men with 100 or more RBIs in a season: Elmer Smith (103), Larry Gardner (118) and Tris Speaker (107).

More Hits than RBIs. In 1999 Mark McGwire became the only player ever to record more RBIs than hits in a season (100 hits minimum). He had 147 RBIs and 145 hits. The next-closest player was Jay Buhner in 1995, who had 121 RBIs and 123 hits.

Consistency. In 1995 Eddie Murray recorded his 19th straight season of 75 or more RBIs, tying the record set by Henry Aaron.

Fast Career Start. Chuck Klein is the only man to drive in 120 or more runs in each of his first five years in the Major Leagues. Albert Pujols has done the same through the first four years of his career through 2004.

Worst RBI Season. Enzo Hernandez of the 1971 Padres had 12 RBIs in 549 at-bats, the worst season record of any batter with 500 or more at-bats.

For players with at least 500 at-bats, the highest average and fewest RBIs is held by Luis Castillo of the Marlins, who had 17 RBIs in 2000 and batted .334. Lloyd Waner and Matty Alou each had 27 RBIs in a season, Waner batting .355 in 1927 and Alou batting .342 in 1966 (and Alou batted .338 with 28 RBIs the following season).

Minor League Leader.

"Lynn Parson, the hip black outfielder from Berkeley, California, started telling Eddie about 'making his hundred.' Poor in English and worse in slang, Eddie groped for the meaning, so Joey came over to explain. One hundred R.B.I.s is an achievement even in 162 major-league games; in A-ball's short season of 140 it is a rare accomplishment indeed. 'You gotta make your hundred,' Lynn crooned and Eddie got the idea. 'Ninety-nine,' the black player sang, 'and a half won't do.'"—Jerry Klinkowitz in *Short Season and Other Stories* (1988).

In 1948 Bob Crues of Amarillo in the Class C West Texas–New Mexico League, drove in 254 runs in 140 games. He batted .404 and hit 69 home runs.

Amos Rusie (1871–1942)

Hall of Fame (VC) 1977

"Amos Rusie was the first genuine sports idol of New York City. Actress Lillian Russell asked to be introduced to him. Comedians [Joseph M.] Weber and [Lew M.] Fields wrote a skit in his honor.

A hotel bar concocted a cocktail that bore his name, and small boys everywhere saved their pennies — 25 of them — so they could buy a paperback titled 'Secrets of Amos Rusie, the World's Greatest Pitcher, How He Obtained His Incredible Speed on the Ball.'"— Lowell Reidenbaugh in *Cooperstown* (1986).

Rusie won 246 games primarily for the New York Giants over only nine full seasons beginning in 1889.

"The Hoosier Thunderbolt," Amos Wilson Rusie was the fastest and best pitcher of the 1890s and is credited as the inspiration for lengthening the distance between the plate and mound. By age 18 in 1889 he was in the Major Leagues with Indianapolis of the National League. The 6'1", 200-pound right-hander moved over to the Giants for the 1890 season and immediately established himself with 29 wins, though he led the league with 34 losses.

He won 32 or more games from 1891 through 1894, with a high of 36 in 1894. He also led the league in strikeouts in four of those seasons. He won 23 games in 1895 but sat out the 1896 season when universally despised Giants owner Andrew Freedman refused to pay him what he wanted. Rusie filed suit and challenged the reserve clause, but the other owners kicked in the money to get Rusie back in uniform because they feared the challenge to the system.

Rusie won 28 games in 1897 and another 20 through part of the 1898 season before tearing shoulder muscles on a pickoff throw. After sitting out five weeks he attempted to throw but was unable to do so without severe pain. His career was over at only 27 years old, though he pitched in one game for the Reds in 1901.

He finished with 246 wins in only nine seasons (not counting 1901) and had an ERA of 3.07. He finished with 30 shutouts, 1,934 strikeouts and 1,704 walks.

After working as a steamfitter in Seattle, he returned to the Giants in the 1920s to become superintendent of the Polo Grounds under John McGraw for eight years. He returned to the Northwest and bought a farm, but a 1934 car accident handicapped him until his death in 1942 at age 71.

Russia

"There are more Americans interested in Soviet baseball than Soviets interested in Soviet baseball."— Russian axiom.

"What a town. They boo Willie Mays and cheer Khrushchev."— Writer Frank Coniff on San Francisco.

"*A Pennant for the Kremlin*"—1964 book by Paul Molloy about Soviets who take over a Major League Baseball team.

In the spring of 1988 two Soviet coaches received a special spring training tour of U.S. baseball facilities, including the Dodgers' camp at Vero Beach. The U.S. Baseball Federation sponsored the tour for Alexander Ardatov and Guela Chikhradze, which helped trigger an upsurge in amateur baseball in Russia.

Russia fielded a baseball team at the 1990 Goodwill Games. The team's first coaches were from Cuba and Nicaragua. The Russians also had an instructional arrangement with the Eastern League in the United States and Dodger owner Peter O'Malley promised equipment and a few coaches.

Japan contributed over $3 million to finance the artificial-turf stadium built at Moscow University.

The top team in Russia for many years has been the Moscow Red Devils.

Some Russians contend that *lapta*, a Russian folk game with a bat and ball, was the inspiration for American baseball. This may explain why the February 4, 1962, issue of the Soviet state newspaper, *Izvestia*, reported categorically that baseball was Russian in origin. A similar claim was made in a 1925 edition of the Russian magazine *Smena*: "It is well known that in Russian villages they played lapta, of which beizbol is an imitation. It was played in Russian villages when the United States was not even marked on the maps."

Another Russian game, known as *Svinka*, was imported from Germany in the 18th century and is considered a form of baseball.

In 1992 after the break-up of the Soviet Union, the Angels signed three Unified Countries players to rookie league contracts.

In 1992 a Major Leaguer born in Russia was called up for the first time since 1921. Leningrad native Victor Cole had a record of 0–2 in eight appearances for the Pirates. Cole had lived in Russia until he was four.

Russian pitcher Victor Starfin is a member of the Japanese Hall of Fame. Born in Russia, he pitched for the Yomiuri Giants after coming to Japan as a child following World War I. He was the all-time leader in wins until 1960, with 301.

Book. John Leo, *How the Russians Invented Baseball and Other Essays of Enlightenment* (1989).

Babe Ruth (1895–1948)

Hall of Fame 1936

"The Ruth Is Mighty and Shall Prevail."— Sportswriter Heywood Broun in the lead to his story describing Ruth's heroics in the 1923 World Series: a .368 average and three home runs against John McGraw's Giants.

"All the lies about him are true."— Joe Dugan.

"Wives of ballplayers, when they teach their children their prayers, should instruct them how to say: 'God bless Mommy, God bless Daddy, God bless Babe Ruth. Babe Ruth has upped Daddy's paycheck by fifteen to forty percent.'"— Waite Hoyt.

"To understand him you had to understand this: he wasn't human. No human could have done the things he did and lived the way he lived and been a ball player. Cobb? Could he pitch? Speaker? The rest? I saw them. I was there. There was never anybody close. When you figure the things he did and the way he lived and the way he played, you got to figure he was more than animal even. There was never anyone like him. He was a god."— Joe Dugan.

"Yet there was buried in Ruth a humanitarianism beyond belief, an intelligence he was never given credit for, a childish desire to be over-virile, living up to credits given his home-run power — and yet a need for intimate affection and respect."— Pitcher Waite Hoyt in a letter about his teammate.

"He was the most uninhibited human being I have ever known. He just did things."— John Drebinger.

"He would not have known how to deal with an enemy for the simple reason that he never had one."—Frank Graham.

"He was a parade all by himself, a burst of dazzle and jingle, Santa Claus drinking his whiskey straight and groaning with a bellyache.... Babe Ruth made the music that his joyous years danced to in a continuous party.... What Babe Ruth is comes down, one generation handing it down to the next, as a national heirloom."— Jimmy Cannon.

"Ruth was head and shoulders over everyone, a behemoth, outsize, out of sight. And he did what he did with panache, with brio, with élan, all those words that mean he was fun to watch."— Robert W. Creamer.

Ruth hit 714 home runs and won 94 games over a 22-year career in which he established himself as the greatest ballplayer of all time.

George Herman "Babe" Ruth (see *Nicknames*) was born in Baltimore and spent much of his youth at the St. Mary's Industrial

Home for Boys where he was a left-handed catcher. Ruth signed a minor league contract in 1914 and began pitching for Jack Dunn's Baltimore Orioles in the International League. He was in the Major Leagues with the Red Sox later that season and became a starter the following season, compiling an 18–8 record. He won over 20 games in 1916 and 1917, with 15 shutouts over those two seasons and was considered the best left-hander in the league.

In 1918 he appeared as a pitcher in only 20 games as he began the transition to full-time outfielder (see also *Players Who Switched Positions*). He pitched in only 17 games in 1919 before moving full-time to the outfield following a trade to the Yankees before the 1920 season.

He had an incredible 1920 season, hitting .376 with 54 home runs and 137 RBIs with an all-time high slugging average of .847 until Barry Bonds in 2001. Amazingly, he improved in 1921 to a .378 average with 59 home runs and 171 RBIs though his slugging average dropped a point to .846. During his 15 full seasons in the outfield he led the league in slugging average 12 times (and twice before that while still pitching), in home runs 10 times (and twice before that while still pitching), RBIs six times, batting average once, runs scored eight times and base on balls 11 times (including a then-record 170 in 1923). He never struck out more than 93 times in a season. He also had 123 stolen bases, with a high of 17 in 1923. He hit 60 home runs in 1927 and topped 50 or more home runs in a season four times.

Ruth played in 10 World Series, batting .326 with 15 home runs. He led the Red Sox to three World Championships (1915, 1916 and 1918) and the Yankees to four (1923, 1927, 1928 and 1932).

He was released by the Yankees after the 1934 season and signed with the Braves with the hope of managing the club. He appeared in 28 games before retiring with a flurry of three home runs in a game against the Pirates shortly before his last game. He finished his career with a .342 average, .690 slugging average (first all-time), 714 *Home Runs* and 2,211 RBIs (both second all-time behind Henry Aaron).

After his playing career ended he was never able to secure a position as a *Manager* with any club, though he coached briefly for the Dodgers as a publicity stunt. He died of throat cancer in 1948.

Last Yankee Stadium Game. Ruth's last player appearance in Yankee Stadium was on Monday, September 24, 1934, in front of a small crowd.

Famous Firsts. Ruth hit a home run in his first game of his first full season for the Red Sox (some sources report it as the first game ever for the club, but he played in five games for Boston in 1914, with no home runs). He hit the first home run by any player in Yankee Stadium. He hit the first home run in the All-Star Game.

Effect on Kids.

"Somewhere there may be a trivia buff with a list of the expiring young lives pulled back from the brink by the fulfilled promise of a personalized Ruthian home run; going by stories handed down, the teenage population of the 1930s would have been greatly reduced if not for the baseball-healing of the previous decade."—Michael Roberts in *Fans!* (1976).

In October 1926, 11-year-old Johnny D. Sylvester of Essex Falls, New Jersey, was suffering from blood poisoning. He listened to the World Series game that day, in which Ruth hit three home runs. The boy's father and his doctor attributed an immediate temperature break to words of encouragement he had received from Ruth before the game.

Books. Robert W. Creamer, *Babe: The Legend Comes to Life* (1974); Dan Daniel, *The Real Babe Ruth* (1963); Brother Gilbert,

Babe Ruth, at age 26, watches the action from the Yankee dugout during the 1921 season.

C.F.X., *Young Babe Ruth: His Early Life and Baseball Career, from the Memoirs of A Xaverian Brother* (2004); Tom Meany, *Babe Ruth* (1947); Dorothy Ruth Pirone with Chris Martens, *My Dad, the Babe* (1988); Jim Reisler, *Launching the Legend* (2004); Lawrence S. Ritter and Mark Rucker, *The Babe: A Life in Pictures* (1988); Babe Ruth and Bob Considine (claimed to be ghostwritten by Fred Lieb), *The Babe Ruth Story* (1948); Babe Ruth, *Babe Ruth's Own Book of Baseball* (ghostwritten in 1928); Marshall Smelser, *The Life That Ruth Built* (1975); Kal Wagenheim, *Babe Ruth: His Life and Legend* (1974).

Nolan Ryan (1947–)

Hall of Fame (1999)

"Nolan Ryan is the only guy who put fear in me. Not because he could get me out, but because he could kill me.... You just hoped to mix in a walk so you could have a good night and go 0 for 3."—Reggie Jackson.

"When he walked off the mound, I realized, That's it, Nolie's done. No more of his no-hitters. No more of his strut or his grunt—all that makes Nolan what Nolan is."—Rangers infielder Jeff Huson after Ryan injured his pitching elbow in his last game (see also *Injuries and Illness*—Elbow).

"One of the beautiful things about baseball is that every once in a while you come into a situation where you want to, and where you have to, reach down and prove something."—Ryan.

Ryan played 27 seasons in the Major Leagues, winning 324 games, striking out a record 5,714 batters and pitching a record seven no-hitters.

Texas native Lynn Nolan Ryan was drafted in the 12th round by the Mets in 1965 and the following year at Greenville of the Carolina League he was 17–2 with 272 strikeouts. Ryan made his Major League debut in two games with the Mets in September 1966. In Game 3 of the 1969 NLCS, Ryan pitched seven innings in relief, getting the win against Atlanta as the Mets clinched the pennant. He contributed 2⅓ innings of scoreless relief in Game 3 of the World Series. Ryan won 29 games as a Met before he was traded to the California Angels for the 1972 season.

It was in California where Ryan established himself as the top strikeout pitcher in baseball. In 1972 he went 19–16 with a 2.28 ERA and a league-leading nine shutouts. His 329 strikeouts led the league, as did his 157 walks. It would be the first of six times Ryan would lead the league in strikeouts and walks in the same season. In 1973 Ryan won 21 games, pitched two no-hitters and broke Sandy Koufax's record for strikeouts in a season with 383. In 1974 Ryan won 22 games and threw another no-hitter. With his league-leading 367 strikeouts he became the first pitcher to post three consecutive 300 strikeout seasons. Ryan's 1975 season was cut short by elbow surgery, but not before he tossed his fourth no-hitter. Ryan swept four consecutive strikeout titles from 1976–1979. In his only postseason appearance for California, Ryan received no decision in Game 1 of an eventual ALCS loss to Baltimore in 1979.

Ryan signed with the Houston Astros for the 1980 season. He would reach several career milestones while with Houston, including his 3,000th strikeout in 1980, an unprecedented fifth no-hitter in 1981, and passing Walter Johnson in 1983 as the career strikeout leader. On July 11, 1985 Ryan reached 4,000 strikeouts. He appeared in two postseasons with the Astros, but Houston failed to advance in both 1980 and 1986.

In 1987 Ryan led the league in strikeouts and ERA at 2.67. His .199 batting average against was also the league best. He finished with an 8–16 record on a weak-hitting club and his career seemed to be waning. Ryan moved back to the American League with the Rangers and added two more strikeout titles in 1989 and 1990 and no-hitter Nos. 6 and 7 in 1990 and 1991. On July 30, 1990 Ryan won his 300th game. He had records of 13–9 and 12–6 in 1990 and 1991, his last two productive seasons. He was 10–14 over his last two seasons, 1992 and 1993. Fittingly, he blew out his arm on the last pitch of his career in 1993 and walked off into retirement.

His 27 years of service is the longest in baseball. He finished with a record of 324–292, 12th in wins and 3rd in losses all-time. He holds numerous **Strikeout** records, including the all-time mark of 5,714. Ryan is also the career **Base On Balls** leader with 2,795. He leads both these categories by wide margins. To his seven **No-Hitters**, Ryan added 12 one-hitters and holds the record for lowest opponent batting average all-time at .204.

Ryan was elected to the Hall of Fame in 1999, his first year of eligibility, winning 98.79% of the vote. He had heart bypass surgery in the late 1990s and has remained a Texas businessman since his retirement.

Books. Nolan Ryan and Harvey Frommer, *Throwing Heat* (1988); Nolan Ryan with Jerry Jenkins, *Miracle Man: Nolan Ryan* (1992), Nolan Ryan, Skip Bayless and Tom House, *Nolan Ryan's Pitching Bible* (1991); Ellyn Sanna, *Nolan Ryan* (2003).

"**S** is for Speaker,
Swift center-field tender;
When the ball saw him coming,
It yelled, 'I surrender.'"
—Ogden Nash on Tris Speaker.

Sabermetrics See *Society for American Baseball Research* and *Statistics and Statisticians*

Sacrifices

"It was just stupid, a gastric disturbance in the brain area."—John Kruk after forgetting how many outs there were and letting a run score on a sacrifice fly.

"To sacrifice, or not to sacrifice, that is the question.
Whether 'tis better in the average to suffer
the absence and lack of base hits,
Or take chances against a lot of fielders.
And by the slugging make them....
to find—to fan—
To Fan! perchance to touch—ay, there's the rub."
—1893 *Reach Guide* parody of Shakespeare.

Rules. Sacrifices became common in the 1880s. The new rule of 1908 (used today) credited a batter with no time at bat if the runner on third base scored on the batter's fly ball. The sacrifice fly was liberalized in 1926 to award a sacrifice when any runner moved up on a fly ball. It was eliminated entirely in 1931 in response to extremely high batting averages. In 1939 it was restored for one year for all runners and in 1954 the 1908 rule was reinstated to allow credit only for run-scoring sacrifice flies.

Two/Inning. Tiger pitcher Al Benton is the only player to record two sacrifice bunts in the same inning. He did it in the Tigers' 11-run 3rd inning against the Indians on August 6, 1941.

Most/Game. The most sacrifice flies in a game by a single player is three, a record held by nine players through 2004.

St. Louis

"'A very charming little city,' Mr. G. H. B. Ruth remarked graciously as he eased his avoirdupois [heaviness] from the Pullman, 'very charming indeed. St. Louis, if memory serves, is the home of short right-field fences and receptive right-field seats. I have business here.'"—Red Smith on Babe Ruth and the Yankees arriving in St. Louis.

"The list of ball tossers who have played in this neck of the woods would make a scroll yards long—and there is still more sandlot and semi-pro ball played here than anywhere else. Yes, this was a great baseball town long before the Redbirds started to scream and champions are nothing new."—*New York Herald Tribune* sportswriter Harry Cross.

"St. Louis is just a little better than any other city on the face of the earth. Its women were the most beautiful, its soil more fertile than the Nile."—Bill Borst in *Still Last in the American League* (1992).

The first reported formal game played in St. Louis was on July 9, 1860. The Empires were the class team of St. Louis in the late 1860s, having been organized by fire chief Henry Sexton. They were the city's representative chosen to play (and lose to) the Cincinnati Red Stockings during that club's historic 1869 tour. The Empires later changed their name to Brown Stockings (or Browns) and played in the National Association. The club was the National League entry from that city in 1876.

St. Louis had a broad mix of Major League teams during the 19th century, starting with the Brown Stockings in the National League in 1876 and 1877. There was no Major League team in St. Louis until an 1882 American Association entry, also known as the Brown Stockings. That club was the remnants of the National League entry but had operated as an independent in the interim.

Interest in 19th century baseball in St. Louis was fanned by sportswriter Alfred H. Spink, who founded *The Sporting News* in 1886. It was his efforts that helped lead to the formation of the American Association in 1882.

The Union Association had a team in St. Louis in 1884, the Maroons, and that club moved into the National League for the 1885–1886 seasons.

After the Players League of 1890 helped weaken the established leagues, the American Association's St. Louis entry moved into the National League for the 1892 season. That franchise lasted through the 1898 season when it was bought by the owners of the Cleveland Spiders. The best Cleveland players moved into St. Louis and the club soon changed its name to Cardinals.

The American League put a team in St. Louis in the league's second year in 1902, where the new Browns remained until they departed for Baltimore after the 1953 season. A total of 70 Major Leaguers played for both the Cardinals and Browns.

The 1914–1915 Federal League included the St. Louis Terriers. The full list of Major League teams in St. Louis:

National League Brown Stockings (1876–1877)
American Association Brown Stockings (1882–1891)
Union Association Maroons (1884)
National League Maroons (1885–1886)
National League Cardinals (1892–)
American League Browns (1901–1953)
Federal League Terriers (1914–1915)

In 2000 *Sports Illustrated* named St. Louis the best baseball town in America.

St. Louis Brown Stockings

National Association 1875
This club was the remnants of the part-amateur/part-professional Empires of earlier in the decade. The club finished fourth with a 39–29 record in its only year in the National Association. This club is not to be confused with the St. Louis Red Stockings, who appeared briefly in the National Association in 1875. The Brown Stockings were members of the National League in 1876.

St. Louis Brown Stockings

American Association 1882–1891
"THE BROWNS ARE HERE! The Hardest Hitters, the Finest Fielders, the Best Base-Runners, the Coming Champions."— Advertisement for the club.

Origins. When the National League Brown Stockings left the league following the 1877 season, the club became a prominent independent club. In 1882 it became part of the new six-club American Association.

Key Owners. Christopher Von der Ahe bought into the club in 1880, along with W.W. Judy and newspaperman Al Spink. Von der Ahe owned a saloon and boarding house adjacent to the local ballpark and had bought the beer concession at the park. After buying

the club, the flamboyant owner purportedly took out full page ads calling himself "der boss president of der Browns." Von der Ahe owned the club throughout its affiliation with the American Association and continued on during its move over to the National League in 1892 when the American Association folded.

Key Seasons. The Brown Stockings won consecutive American Association pennants from 1885 through 1888, with Charles Comiskey as the manager.

1885. The club won the pennant by two games over the Cincinnati Red Stockings. Bobby Caruthers won a league-leading 40 games, and first baseman Charles Comiskey batted .340. In the championship series between the National League and American Association pennant winners, the Brown Stockings defeated the Chicago White Stockings in a controversial series that some call a tie.

1886. The team won the pennant by 12 games over Pittsburgh and they were led by Bobby Caruthers, who was 30–14 on the mound and batted .342. In postseason play, the Brown Stockings again defeated the White Stockings, this time in six games.

1887. The Brown Stockings won the pennant by 14 games but lost the postseason series to the Detroit Wolverines in a drawnout and boring 15-game series that saw Detroit clinch after 11 games. Tip O'Neill led the league with a .435 average and 14 home runs.

1888. St. Louis won the pennant by 6½ games over Brooklyn as Tip O'Neill again led the league in hitting at .335 and Silver King led with 45 wins. The Brown Stockings lost the championship series to the New York Giants.

Nickname. The club was known as the Brown Stockings in 1882. From 1883 through 1891 the club was known primarily as the Browns.

Ballpark. The club played its games in the original Sportsman's Park, which seated 12,000 fans by 1886. The dimensions in that era from left to right field were 350–400–460–330–285.

Book. Jon David Cash, *Before They Were Cardinals; Major League Baseball in 19th Century St. Louis* (2002); Thomas Hetrick, *Chris Von Der Ahe and the St. Louis Browns* (2000).

St. Louis Brown Stockings

National League 1876–1877
"The newly formed National League of Professional Baseball Clubs played its first game in this city today when the local St. Louis entry engaged the Chicago nine. The efforts of the local team were rewarded with a 1–0 victory. Bradley, the St. Louis pitcher, gave up two hits and also made two of the seven hits St. Louis collected against the Chicago pitcher, Spalding."— Game summary of May 5, 1876.

Origins. The Brown Stockings were a charter member of the National League in 1876, having moved over from the National Association.

First Game. The first National League game in St. Louis was played on May 5, 1876, at the Grand Avenue Grounds in front of 3,000 fans. St. Louis won 1–0 as George Bradley gave up only two hits to the Chicago White Stockings and Al Spalding. On July 15 that year, Bradley pitched the first no-hitter in National League history, defeating Hartford 2–0.

Key Owner. The club's owner was John R. Lucas, whose son Henry was instrumental in financing the 1884 Union Association. After the 1877 season, the Louisville club folded because of a scandal involving certain players on that team (see also *Gambling and Fixed Games*). Lucas then absorbed some of the Louisville players onto his St. Louis team (including some of those involved in the scandal. When he was accused of knowing about the scandal, he turned his franchise back to the league and the league did not place a new franchise in the city until 1885.

The Brown Stockings were not disbanded, however, and continued as an independent club until 1882, when they joined the newly formed American Association.

Key Season. The Brown Stockings finished the 1876 season with a 45–19 record, good for second place behind the White Stockings.

St. Louis Browns

American League 1902–1953
"First in booze, first in shoes and last in the American League."
— The Browns' counterpart to the Senators' chant.

"In 1951, in a moment of madness, I became owner and operator of a collection of old rags and tags known to baseball historians as the St. Louis Browns. The Browns, according to reputable anthropologists, rank in the annals of baseball a step or two ahead of Cro-Magnon man."— The opening lines of *Veeck — As in Wreck*, by Bill Veeck and Ed Linn (1962).

"A charitable organization formed to provide work for the otherwise unemployable."— Veeck.

Origins. The Browns were created when Milwaukee of the Western Association transplanted to St. Louis for the American League's second season in 1902.

First Game. On April 23, 1902, the Browns defeated Cleveland 5–2 in Sportsman's Park.

Key Owners.

Robert Lee Hedges/1903–1915. A club from Milwaukee was to move into St. Louis for the 1901 American League season, but brewer Zachary Tinker failed to back the club any longer. Instead, Ban Johnson found the money himself and controlled the club in Milwaukee for a year before he found Robert Lee Hedges and others to take over from Matt and Tim Killilea. Hedges owned a company that manufactured Banner Buggies, an early automobile. He had known Johnson in Cincinnati when Johnson was a reporter in the 1880s. The primary contribution to baseball made by Hedges was to lure Branch Rickey back into baseball from his law practice.

Phil Ball and Heirs/1915–1936.
"Ball had been born during the Civil War. His father wanted him christened Ap Catesby in honor of the famous Welshman. Mrs. Ball had other plans for her son and he was named Philip Decatesby Ball. His youth was a hardening and adventurous experience that shaped his Horatio Alger demeanor. He had been a promising catcher with a minor league team in Shreveport, Louisiana. A knife fight during a barroom brawl nearly cost him the permanent use of his left hand. His baseball career at end, Ball worked as a cowboy and later on a railroad for $50 a month."— Bill Borst in *The St. Louis Browns — An Informal History* (1978).

Philip deCatesby Ball was the wealthy owner of the Federal League's St. Louis entry. He was an ice machine and cold storage manufacturer, and his partner in the Federal League club was brewer Otto Seifel. After the 1915 season, Ball and Seifel purchased the Browns from an ailing Robert Hedges for $750,000 ($425,000 in some sources). Ball controlled the club until he died in 1933, having lost $300,000 over the 15 years of his ownership. The only year he made any profit was 1922, when the Browns fell one game short of the pennant.

Ball's 87% interest in the club was left to his widow and two

children. His lawyer, Louis B. Von Weise, controlled the club for the next three years until a buyer could be found.

Bill DeWitt and Don Barnes/1936–1945.
"After the war, the Browns were in good financial shape. Had no bills — when the DeWitts took over, they were known as some of the best paying people because you got a discount for paying cash and they usually took advantage of this…. They needed that little edge."— *The Brown Stockings Fan Club Book*, edited by Bill Borst (1985).

When Ball died, Louis B. Von Wiese, as trustee of Ball's estate, took control of the club. He knew nothing about the game and neither did any of Ball's relatives. Von Wiese tried to interest Branch Rickey of the Cardinals. He declined but helped find a buyer. Bill DeWitt, who had risen from vendor in the park to Rickey's assistant vice-president, arranged to buy the club in partnership with his wealthy father-in-law, investment banker Don Barnes. Barnes had turned a $25,000 investment into a finance company worth $250 million in the 1930s.

The deal closed in November 1936 for $375,000 ($325,000 in some sources) and the price included San Antonio of the Texas League. Barnes arranged for a public offering of $100,000 at $5 per share for some of the purchase price. The additional purchase money came from Barnes ($150,000), Al Curtis ($25,000), Bill DeWitt ($25,000) and International Shoe ($25,000). The American League loaned the club an additional $50,000 for the purchase price or for operating expenses. Barnes held the controlling interest in the club until he sold out in 1945. Some of the public investors owned their shares until 1981 (by then the Orioles), when new owner Edward Bennett Williams bought them out.

Richard Muckerman/1945–1949.
"Muckerman, heir to the St. Louis City Ice & Fuel Company fortune, later was to take over the team and run it down as skillfully as had the previous ice millionaire, Phil Ball."— William B. Mead in *Even the Browns* (1978).

Muckerman, a prominent St. Louis businessman, invested $300,000 in the club as part of a February 1942 stock offering. In 1945 Don Barnes sold his 56% interest of 50,000 shares for $200,000 to Muckerman. Muckerman spent considerable sums to improve the ballpark, but nothing on player development. By 1949 Muckerman was unable to continue subsidizing the club, and he sold out to Bill DeWitt and his brother. They in turn sold the club to Bill Veeck in 1951.

Bill Veeck/1951–1953.
"Many critics were surprised to know that the Browns could be bought because they didn't know the Browns were owned."— Writer John Larcher on Bill Veeck's maverick ownership style.

Veeck bought the club in 1951 and lost a reported $396,000 the first season. He tried to move the club to Milwaukee, which was subsequently occupied by the Boston Braves. In 1953 Veeck was forced to sell for financial reasons, and on September 29 the American League approved both the sale (for $2,475,000) and a move to Baltimore. The *Franchise Shift* ended American League baseball in St. Louis.

Nickname. The Browns name continued the Brown Stockings tradition. When the National League Cardinals abandoned the Brown Stockings name late in the 19th century, the new American League entry adopted the shortened version of the name.

Key Seasons.
"The Mets achieved total incompetence in a single year, while the Browns worked industriously for almost a decade to gain equal proficiency."— Bill Veeck.

The Browns were the most inept team of the first half of the 20th century. With two brief exceptions, the club never challenged for anything but the cellar.

1922. The 1920s began well for the Browns, who fought for the 1922 pennant, finishing only one game behind the Yankees. See also Roger A. Godin, *The 1922 St. Louis Browns* (1991). The club faded to fifth in 1923 and returned only briefly to the first division in 1928 and 1929.

1944.

"When the St. Louis Browns started the 1944 season with nine straight victories, even their best friends laughed. People are like that. These well-wishers only knew that the Browns never had won a pennant in the long life of the American League. They figured that the inevitable descent of the Browns, a time-honored feature of the league season, would be farther and harder than usual. But after all, it was fun while it lasted, so they laughed."—J. Roy Stockton in *The Gashouse Gang and a couple of other guys* (1947).

"EVEN THE BROWNS"—Headline in a 1944 preseason edition of the *St. Louis Globe-Democrat*, with a subheading containing a quote from American League president Will Harridge: "Every club in our league has a chance at the pennant." This was also the title of William Mead's 1978 chronicle of World War II baseball, with focus on the Browns.

The Browns won their only pennant in 1944, a year in which the Major Leagues were decimated due to World War II. The club's winning percentage of .578 was the lowest of any pennant winner to that time. The pennant may have been won because the entire Browns infield was classified 4-F for the war. Vern Stephens led the league with 109 RBIs and Nelson Potter had 19 wins. The Browns lost the World Series to the Cardinals in six games. See also Bill Borst, *The Best of Seasons: The Celebration of the 1944 St. Louis Cardinals and St. Louis Browns* (1994).

"Lasts." The last game was played on September 27, 1953, as the White Sox and Billy Pierce defeated Duane Pillette 2–1 in 11 innings. The last Browns home run was by Billy Hunter on September 26, 1953.

The last active Major Leaguer who played for the Browns was pitcher Don Larsen. He retired in 1967 after last playing for the Browns in 1953, when he had a 7–12 record.

Key Players.

Bobby Wallace (HF) was one of the best shortstops of his era, playing for the Browns from 1902 through 1916. He was player-manager of the club in 1911 and 1912.

Ken Williams was the second-best power hitter in the American League in the early 1920s, with seasons of 24, 39, 29 and 25 home runs before a beaning diminished his skills.

George Sisler (HF) played the first 12 years of career with the Browns, from 1915 through 1927. He batted over .400 twice, including a 20th century record .420 in 1922.

Urban Shocker pitched for the Browns from 1918 through 1924, winning 20 or more games four straight seasons beginning in 1920. He led the league with 27 wins in 1921.

Key Managers.

Jim McAleer was the club's first manager. He led the Browns to a second-place finish in their first season in the league, the high water mark of his eight-year tenure. His easy disposition and the fact that the club was a money-maker for owner Robert Hedges allowed him to last despite a series of poor finishes.

Branch Rickey (HF) had his first Major League managerial experience with the Browns. He took over in late 1913 (remaining in eighth place) and over the next two full seasons finished fifth and sixth.

Lee Fohl took the Browns to their only moment of glory in the

first 40 years of their existence. The club challenged for the 1922 pennant and finished a strong second. Fohl also managed in 1921 and 1923 before giving way to player-manager George Sisler.

Rogers Hornsby (HF) managed the club from 1933 through 1937, never finishing above sixth place. He returned briefly to manage the club for 51 games in 1952 with poor results.

Luke Sewell took over the Browns in 1941 and managed the club well into the 1946 season. He led the Browns to a pennant in 1944 and a third-place finish in 1945 before the club faded back to mediocrity and worse.

Ballparks. The club occupied *Sportsman's Park* throughout its existence.

Key Broadcasters.

"I worked with Bud Blattner on Brownies' TV. Looking back, I'm not sure I was ready for the big leagues yet. 'Course, I had a lot of company—neither were the Browns."—Milo Hamilton quoted in *Voices of the Game*, by Curt Smith (1987).

The first radio broadcast from Sportsman's Park was in 1927 by Garnett Marks. France Laux began an 18-year stint for the Cardinals and Browns in 1929. He broadcast the World Series from 1933 through 1938 and every All-Star Game from 1934 through 1941. The dull Laux was taken off Cardinals broadcasts after the 1946 World Series but did a few Browns games over the next few years when the regular broadcasters were unavailable. He retired when the Browns left town after the 1953 season. Dizzy Dean broadcast for the Browns from 1947 through 1949.

Books. Bill Borst (ed.), *The Brown Stockings Fan Club Book* (1985); Bill Borst, *Still Last in the American League* (1992); *Ables to Zoldak* (Vol. I–III 1988–1990), from the St. Louis Browns fan club, covers every Browns player; Bill Borst and Erv Fischer, *A Jockstrap Full of Nails* (1992); William B. Mead, *Even the Browns* (1978); Fred Nichols, *The Final Season: The 1953 St. Louis Browns* (1991); Steve Steinberg, *Baseball in St. Louis, 1900–1925* (2004).

St. Louis Cardinals

National League 1892–

"It seems most unlikely that the St. Louis Cardinals were really named in 1900 by an unknown lady who saw the red-trimmed gray uniforms and gushed, 'Isn't that the loveliest shade of cardinal!'"—Tristram P. Coffin in *The Old Ball Game* (1971).

Origins. The American Association Brown Stockings suffered financially as a result of the 1890 Players League challenge. After the battle ended, the American Association weakened and then dissolved after the 1891 season. The Browns, later to be known as the Cardinals, remained intact and were absorbed into the National League for the 1892 season.

The Cardinals were the westernmost and almost southernmost team in the modern leagues and became the first truly regional team in the Major Leagues.

Key Owners.

Christopher Von der Ahe/1892–1898.

"Der Boss Owner"

Long-time Brown Stockings owner Christopher Von der Ahe tried to duplicate his excesses of the American Association 1880s when his team was a champion, but the club played poorly after it entered the National League and revenues fell off. Von der Ahe lost a huge amount of money from too much high living and lavish spending.

To raise money, Von der Ahe began using his ballpark as an amusement park and short course racetrack. In 1895 his mistress began spreading gossip in the papers and his wife divorced him. His son sued him in a property dispute and Von der Ahe was jailed in Pennsylvania. By 1896 his real estate holdings were heavily mortgaged. To pay his creditors, he sold off his star players and was unable to replace them with good ballplayers.

In the late 1890s the National League owners stripped Von der Ahe of his ownership through "more or less legal means" because he was heavily in debt. Von der Ahe eventually was jailed due to his indebtedness, and the park was sold from the courthouse steps. Some sources reported that he sold his interest after the 1898 season for $35,000. More accurately, he tried to sell, but his many creditors forced the appointment of a receiver. The club was auctioned off, but its charter was suspended by the league for nonpayment of minor league players so that the league could control who owned it.

Frank and Stanley Robison/1899–1911. The Browns had a succession of very short-term owners until early 1899 when Frank and Stanley Robison, the Cleveland Spiders owners, bought the club. The Robisons wanted out of Cleveland and switched their best Cleveland players, including Cy Young, to St. Louis. The Robisons controlled the club into the 20th century. Frank Robison died in 1905 and Stanley continued to run the team on his own until he died of blood poisoning at age 54 in 1911.

Helene Schuyler Britton/1911–1917. In 1905 Frank Robison's estate was distributed to his 32-year-old daughter, Helene Schuyler Britton. When Stanley died, Britton's husband, Schuyler Parsons Britton, became the nominal president under her ownership. Britton was a suffragette who first openly held the title of club president in 1916. She sold the club in 1917 for $375,000 ($350,000 in some sources).

James C. Jones/1917–1922. Jones was an attorney who put together a syndicate that sold stock in the club. The most important task completed by the syndicate was to hire Branch Rickey. Future owner Sam Breadon was one of the stock purchasers. Singer Al Jolson owned shares in the club starting in 1917. Jones is credited by some with starting the ***Knothole Gang***.

Sam Breadon/1922–1947. In 1917 the club held a public stock offering to raise operating capital. Future majority owner Sam Breadon paid $2,000 for 80 shares of the stock to please his automobile manufacturing and dealership partner. Breadon slowly increased his holdings until 1922, when he acquired control with another 1,048 shares from J.C. Jones and named himself president. Breadon had come from a poor New York background, moving from a bank clerk position in New York to wealth and prominence in St. Louis.

Branch Rickey was a long-time front office executive with the Cardinals and until 1926 owned a minority interest in the club. When Breadon replaced him as Cardinals manager in 1925 (though he remained as general manager), Rickey's interest was sold to new manager Rogers Hornsby. The club was strong and stable through most of the 1930s, but late in the decade a rift had widened between Rickey and Breadon.

Rumors were spreading that Breadon was unhappy with Rickey, and at the end of the 1942 season Breadon did not renew Rickey's five-year general manager contract. Breadon claimed that he got rid of Rickey because he could not afford Rickey's $75,000 salary ($80,000 in some sources), the highest of any executive in baseball. Rickey moved on to the Dodgers to replace Dodger general manager Larry MacPhail, who went into the military.

Breadon sold out in 1947, but before doing so he unloaded much of his talent to the Braves to raise cash. The 1948 Cardinals were derisively called the "Cape Cod Cardinals" in reference to the number of Boston Braves who had been traded to the Cardinals the year before.

Fred M. Saigh, Jr., and Robert E. Hannegan/1947–1953. Sam Breadon had set aside almost $5 million in capital to build a new ballpark, which he was required to do within five years or declare the cash as ordinary income and pay taxes. Fred Saigh, a tax-law specialist who was aware of Breadon's predicament, offered to buy the club to avoid Breadon's tax liability. To give Breadon some comfort that he was a viable purchaser, Saigh brought in Bob Hannegan. Hannegan had been postmaster general, a Democratic senator from Missouri, and a director of the IRS. The ill Breadon sold out in November 1947.

Hannegan paid $10,000 for his share of the Cardinals and a year later cashed out for $1 million. Saigh apparently was not the tax genius he thought he was, as he had serious tax problems and spent 15 months in jail for tax fraud.

August Busch and Busch Brewery/1953–1996.

"His fiefdom was run from his 281-acre estate, Grant's Farm, on the edge of the city where Ulysses S. Grant once resided before Lincoln chose him as his general. There Busch and his family lived in a thirty-four-room French Renaissance manor house set in a park stocked with exotic animals and through which the lord often passed on coach-and-fours, landaus, phaetons, or Russian sleighs. The question was: If Busch knew everything that there was to know about the beer business, what in fact did he know about baseball?"— Murray Polner in *Branch Rickey* (1982).

Commissioner Ford Frick forced Fred Saigh to sell the club after his tax problems surfaced. Saigh complied by selling out to local brewer August Busch, owner of Anheuser-Busch Brewery. This was not the first time a Busch had been involved in St. Louis baseball. Adolphus Busch was an investor in the 1884 Union Association team in St. Louis. Groups in Milwaukee and Houston were interested in buying and moving the club. Busch bought the club primarily to ensure that the team would stay in St. Louis in the face of competing bids.

Busch paid $3.75 million and was president of the club from 1953 until his death at age 90 in 1990. His family continued to own the club following his death, but the heirs were not interested in baseball and put the club up for sale in 1995. The asking price was approximately $200 million.

Bill DeWitt, Jr., Andrew Baur, Fred Hanser, et al./1996– .

"There was a certain sadness, but the DeWitt group is a remarkable group. He comes from a great baseball background."— Acting commissioner Bud Selig on the end of the Busch era and new owner Bill DeWitt's family history in Major League Baseball (his father owned the Browns in the 1930s and 1940s).

A group led by Cincinnati baseball man Bill DeWitt, Jr., bought the club for $150 million. The price included the ballpark and parking garages. Among the 15 significant shareholders, DeWitt holds a BA from Yale and a Harvard MBA. Other high-profile members of the ownership group include long-time St. Louis fans Fred Hanser and Andrew Baur. Hanser is a prominent business attorney in the city and Baur is a successful homegrown businessman and banker. Hanser, 56 at the time of the purchase, and DeWitt have known each other since they were children and Hanser says Bauer is his best friend.

Walt Jocketty was named general manager and helped shape the team into the mid–2000s. According to one source, all of the 15 owners are significant Republican contributors and some received federal appointments as a result of their connections to the George W. Bush administration.

Nicknames. There are conflicting stories about how the Cardinals name was chosen to replace Brown Stockings. *The Baseball Encyclopedia* reports that the club was known as the Perfectos in 1899.

One version is that in 1898 the Brown Stockings switched to red socks and sportswriter William McHale of the *St. Louis Republican* starting calling them the Cardinals. Another version has it that McHale adopted the name after hearing the name used by a woman who liked the cardinal red trim. The color became a bird many years later when Branch Rickey went to a luncheon where a woman doing the decorations had turned the color into a red bird perched on a bat. The Cardinals were known as the "Gas House Gang" in the 1930s and early 1940s (see also *Uniforms*—Cardinals).

Key Seasons.

"Dad, they stink! All of the kids are going to make fun of me."— Twelve-year-old son of new club president Mark Lamping in the mid–1990s.

1892–1899. The club was mediocre to terrible during the 1890s and never finished in the first division until a fourth-place finish in 1899.

1926.

"Armistice Day Recalled by Wild Orgy; Thousands Abandon Selves to Saturnalia of Celebration in Heavy Downpours of Rain." — Headline in the *St. Louis Globe-Democrat* on the day the Cardinals clinched the pennant.

Under player-manager Rogers Hornsby the club won the pennant by two games over the Reds and then defeated the Yankees in seven games in the World Series. Grover Cleveland Alexander came in to strike out Tony Lazzeri with the bases loaded in Game 7 and went two more innings to preserve the victory. Jim Bottomley led the league with 120 RBIs, and Flint Rhem led with 20 wins.

1928. With Bill McKechnie managing the club, Jim Bottomley led the league in home runs and batting average and the Cardinals won the pennant by two games over the Giants. They were swept by the Yankees in the World Series.

1930. Gabby Street managed the club to a 92–62 record, two games in front of the second-place Cubs. Every regular batted over .300 in the Year of the Hitter and five pitchers had over 12 wins. The A's defeated the Cardinals in the World Series in six games.

1931. The Cardinals ran away with the pennant with 101 wins, led by batting champion Chick Hafey. The Cardinals beat the A's in the World Series in seven games.

1934. After two mediocre seasons, the *Gas House Gang* was born (though the name did not originate until 1935). Led by player manager Frankie Frisch, the Cardinals won the pennant by two games over the Giants. Dizzy Dean and Paul Dean combined for 49 wins, and the Cardinals went on to defeat the Tigers in the World Series in seven games (winning the last game 11–0). See also G.H. Fleming, *The Dizziest Season (1934)* (1984).

1942. In 1941 the Cardinals finished second to the Dodgers despite winning 97 games. In 1942 manager Billy Southworth led them to 106 wins to beat out the Dodgers by two games. Mort Cooper led the league with 22 wins and 10 shutouts. The Cardinals won the World Series against the Yankees in five games.

1943. The Cardinals ran away with the pennant with 105 wins. Stan Musial led the league with a .357 average and Mort Cooper led with 21 wins. The club lost to the Yankees in the World Series 4–1.

1944. The Cardinals again ran away with the pennant with another 105 wins. They again were led by Stan Musial's .347 average and Mort Cooper's 22 wins, though neither led the league. This time the Cardinals faced the crosstown Browns in the World Series and won in six games. See also Bill Borst, *The Best of Seasons: The Celebration of the 1944 St. Louis Cardinals and St. Louis Browns* (1994).

1946. After barely losing out to the Cubs in 1945, the Cardi-

nals returned to the World Series in 1946 after defeating the Dodgers by two games for the pennant. Stan Musial led the league with a .365 average, and Enos Slaughter led with 130 RBIs. Howie Pollet led the league with 21 wins and a 2.10 ERA. The Cardinals won Game 7 of the series against the Red Sox when Enos Slaughter dashed home from first in the 8th inning (see *Base Running*). The Cardinals finished a strong second in 1947 and 1948 and continued to be a contender until the mid–1950s.

1964. After finishing second in 1963, the Cardinals broke through for the first time since 1946 and won the pennant by one game over the Reds. In the World Series the Cardinals defeated the Yankees in seven games behind Bob Gibson's outstanding pitching. MVP Ken Boyer led the league with 119 RBIs and Ray Sadecki had 20 wins.

1967. After two mediocre seasons, the Cardinals won the pennant by 10½ games over the Giants and faced the Red Sox in the World Series. In a dramatic seven-game series, the Cardinals won on the strong right arm of Bob Gibson. The club had five pitchers with 10 or more wins and Orlando Cepeda led the league with 111 RBIs.

1968. The Cardinals repeated as National League champions, this time by nine games over the Giants. In the World Series, the Tigers came back from a 3–1 deficit and defeated the Cardinals in seven games. Bob Gibson won 22 games and Joe Hoerner saved 17 games.

1981. Despite the best overall record in the National League East, the Cardinals were deprived of a division crown because of the strike-shortened split season. They were unable to win either half of the hybrid season. In the first half they finished 1½ games behind the Phillies; in the second half they finished one-half game behind the Expos.

1982. The Cardinals erased the frustration of the 1981 season by winning the National League East by three games over the Phillies and then defeating the Braves for the pennant. In the World Series, the Cardinals defeated the Brewers in seven games. Bruce Sutter led the league with 36 saves and George Hendrick drove in 104 runs.

1985. After two mediocre seasons, the Cardinals won the National League East crown by three games over the Mets. No Cardinal player had more than 70 RBIs or 14 wins. Nevertheless, they beat the Dodgers in six games for the pennant. The club lost the World Series in seven games to cross-state rival Kansas City after a controversial Game 6 call that led to a Royals win. Game 7 was a disaster for the Cardinals as starter John Tudor was bombed and reliever Joaquin Andujar was thrown out of the game in an 11–0 loss. See Doug Feldmann, *Fleeter Than Birds* (2002).

1987. The Cardinals returned to the World Series after winning the division by three games over the Mets and then beating the Giants in seven games for the pennant. They lost in seven games to the Twins in the first World Series played entirely on artificial turf. Jack Clark had 35 home runs and 106 RBIs. Willie McGee drove in 105 runs.

1996. The Cardinals won their first division title since 1987 by six games over the Astros. After sweeping the Padres in the division play-offs, the Cardinals blew a 3–1 series lead against the Braves and lost the pennant in seven games. Ron Gant hit 30 home runs, Dennis Eckersley saved 30 games and Andy Benes won 18 games.

2000. The club won the division by 10 games over the Reds, winning 95 games. After sweeping the Braves in the division play-off, they lost to the Mets in five games in the NLCS. Jim Edmonds led the club with 42 home runs and 108 RBIs, and Mark McGwire had 32 home runs. Darryl Kile was 20–9, Pat Hentgen was 15–12, Garrett Stephenson was 16–9, and Dave Veres saved 29 games.

2001. The Cardinals tied the Astros for first place in the Central Division with a 93–69 record and were the wild card team that season. In the division play-offs, they lost to the eventual champion Diamondbacks in the deciding fifth game. Mark McGwire, Jim Edmonds and J.D. Drew each had between 27 and 30 home runs, and Edmonds had a .304 average and 110 RBIs. Matt Morris was 22–8, Darryl Kile was 16–11, and Dustin Hermanson was 14–13.

2002. The club was 97–65 en route to the Central Division title by 13 games over the Astros. They swept the defending champion Diamondbacks in the division series and then lost to the Giants in five games in the NLCS. Sophomore Albert Pujols had 34 home runs and 127 RBIs, and Jim Edmonds and Tino Martinez each hit 21 or more home runs. Matt Morris was 17–9 and Jason Isringhausen had 32 saves.

2004. The Cardinals were back in the postseason after winning the National League Central Division with a record of 105–57, 13 games ahead of the Astros (who also made the play-offs as the wild card). Albert Pujols had another amazing season, with a .331 average along with 46 home runs and 123 RBIs. Jim Edmonds had 42 home runs and 111 RBIs, and Scott Rolen, though injured some of the second half, had 34 home runs and 124 RBIs. Jeff Suppan was 16–9, and Jason Marquis, Chris Carpenter and Matt Morris each won 15 games. Jason Isringhausen had 47 saves. The Cardinals beat the Dodgers in the division series and then faced the Astros in the NLCS. After falling behind 3–2, the Cardinals returned home and beat the Astros in Game 6 with a 9th inning home run and then beat Roger Clemens in Game 7. In the World Series, a reprise of the 1967 Cardinals/Red Sox Series, St. Louis failed to show up. The hot Red Sox swept the Series after a wild 11–9 Game 1 that the Cardinals could have won. The torrid Cardinal bats disappeared after that, as the Red Sox starters did not give up an earned run over the final three games.

Key Players.

Dizzy Dean (HF). In seven seasons for the Cardinals, Dean won 20 or more games four times, with a high of 30 in 1934. He led the league in strikeouts four times and shutouts twice.

Frankie Frisch (HF) played the last 11 years of his 19-year career with the Cardinals, five of them as player-manager. He batted .300 or better seven times and was a stellar second baseman. He played in four World Series for the club.

Marty Marion played shortstop for 11 years with the Cardinals, helping lead them to four World Series appearances in the 1940s.

Stan Musial (HF) spent his entire 22-year career with the Cardinals. He batted .331 and led the league in batting seven times and hit 475 home runs.

Lou Brock (HF) was the all-time base stealing king with 938 until Rickey Henderson. After being traded to the Cardinals in 1964, he batted over .300 eight times and led the league in stolen bases eight times.

Bob Gibson (HF) spent his entire 17-year career with the Cardinals, winning 251 games overall and 20 games or more in a season five times. His peak year was 1968 when he won 22 games and had 13 shutouts while posting an ERA of 1.12.

Ozzie Smith (HF) was traded to the Cardinals for the 1982 season. He began a string of 15 straight seasons at shortstop for the club and established himself as the all-time greatest defensive player at that position. He played in three World Series for St. Louis and then retired after the 1996 season.

Mark McGwire spent his last 4½ seasons with the Cardinals and set his then-single season record for home runs with 70 in 1988. He hit 220 of his 583 home runs with the club, with other highs

of 65 in 1999 and a total (with the A's after a midseason trade) of 58 in 1997. He retired after the 2001 season.

Albert Pujols had one of the fastest starts in Major League history after being drafted in the 13th round by the Cardinals in 1999. In his first four seasons beginning in 2001, he had 159 home runs and 497 RBIs while batting .331.

Key Managers.

"In St. Louis it was Rickey's custom to change managers as casually as he changed his shirt."— Sportswriter Bill Corum.

Branch Rickey (HF) left the Browns to join the Cardinals in 1917 as president and he took over as manager in 1919. He managed the club from 1919 until mid–1925, with mediocre results. His best finishes were third place in 1921 and 1922

Rogers Hornsby (HF) was player-manager for the Cardinals when they won the 1926 World Series. Owner Sam Breadon had been talking to Cubs manager Bill Killefer about replacing the difficult Hornsby. They again discussed the deal on the victory train back to St. Louis after the World Series. The news leaked and Breadon was vilified in the press. Apparently, the reason that Hornsby was fired was because he had sworn at Breadon over the scheduling of an exhibition game during the season. Sportswriter J. Roy Stockton reported that in telling off Breadon in very foul language, Hornsby suggested "an utterly impossible disposition of the game."

Breadon was in no mood to pay Hornsby $50,000 per year for three years, so he traded him to the Giants in December 1926. Hornsby wanted $120,000 for his 1,000 shares of stock in the Cardinals, for which he had paid $45,000 to Rickey when he succeeded Rickey as manager in mid–1925. When Breadon offered only $80,000 Judge Landis intervened and persuaded the other National League owners to pay $5,000 each to make up the difference.

Bill McKechnie (HF) was hired for 1928 and won the pennant but lost the World Series to the Yankees. Despite the success he was ousted before the 1929 season, but came back to manage the club for the last 63 games of the season.

Frankie Frisch (HF) managed the ball club from 1933 through most of 1938. During that span he won the World Series in 1934 and finished second in 1935 and 1936. After a fourth-place finish in 1937, the Cardinals were in sixth place in 1938 when he was fired.

Billy Southworth was hired for the 1929 season and lasted 90 games. He returned in 1940 to manage the club through World War II, leading it to a second-place finish in 1941 and the World Series in 1942 through 1944. After a second-place finish in 1945 he moved on to the Braves.

Johnny Keane.

"Johnny Keane, you're a gosh-dang good manager."— Cardinals "special consultant" Branch Rickey after the club clinched the 1964 National League pennant.

Keane managed the Cardinals starting in mid–1961, leading them to a second-place finish in 1963 and the pennant in 1964. During the 1964 season Cardinals owner August Busch was planning to fire Keane, but the situation became awkward when the Cardinals put on a late-season surge and won the pennant. When Keane was asked to stay, he thumbed his nose at the club and took over as manager of the Yankees, whom the Cardinals had just defeated in the World Series.

Red Schoendienst (HF).

"In difficult circumstances, Red Schoendienst, the reluctant manager, made Gussie [Busch] look good. And for that he has been rewarded. Today [1989], as a coach under Whitey Herzog, he has the job he always wanted and the security he always craved; Gussie has made sure he can stay as long as he cares to." — Harry Caray in *Holy Cow!* (1989), alluding to Schoendienst stepping in to manage the Cardinals to two National League pennants in 1967 and 1968.

Schoendienst had a successful career as an infielder before taking over the Cardinals in 1965, beginning 14 years at the helm. He won consecutive pennants in 1967–1968 and finished second three more times before moving into the front office after the 1976 season. He returned to manage the club briefly in 1980 and 1990.

Whitey Herzog.

"I've been thinking about baseball almost as long as I've been thinking." — Herzog, who took over the Cardinals midway through the 1980 season and managed the club for 12 years. He led them to pennants in 1982, 1985 and 1987, winning the World Series in 1982. See also Whitey Herzog and Kevin Horrigan, *White Rat* (1987).

Tony LaRussa. After 19 generally successful seasons with the White Sox and A's, LaRussa took over the Cardinals in 1986 and led them to three division titles through 2004. He was named 2002 Manager of the Year.

Ballparks.

Robison Field. The Cardinals occupied what was to become known as Robison Field from 1893 through mid–1920. The name was changed from Sportsman's Park when the Robison brothers bought the club in 1899. The 351-foot left field fence was so deep, especially in the dead ball era, that it was not until 1919 that Rogers Hornsby hit the first ball over the left field wall.

Sportsman's Park. In 1920 Cardinals owner Sam Breadon sold the land under the old park for $300,000 and used it as working capital for the Cardinals. From that point until 1954, the Cardinals were tenants of the rival Browns in *Sportsman's Park*. The Cardinals bought the ballpark in 1954 when the Browns left town after the 1953 season. The club remained in Sportsman's Park until Busch Stadium was ready for occupancy in 1966.

Busch Memorial Stadium. The current home of the Cardinals opened in 1966. It has been reported that the private developer got into financial trouble and August Busch stepped in with $3 million to bail him out. In return, the stadium was named after Busch. Artificial turf was installed in 1970 and the dirt infield was replaced by dirt cutouts at the bases in 1974.

The original dimensions from left to right field were 330–386–414–386–330. The power alleys and center field were reduced slightly in subsequent years. The ballpark originally seated 49,275, but that number was increased to 54,727 in 1988, with standing room of 1,500 allowed in 1990 for a total of 56,227. In 1997 the club removed several thousand seats and installed a hand-operated scoreboard.

In April 2000 the Cardinals announced plans for a new $370 (or $386) million ballpark to open as early as 2004, just south of the current facility, but it did not materialize by that year. It was later on schedule for 2006, and the club intended to keep the Busch name after the brewery announced a 20-year extension to the marketing rights on the ballpark name. The club contributed $90 million and over $200 million was financed by bonds. The ballpark was slated to seat 46,000.

Key Broadcasters.

"Holy Cow!" — Signature line of 25-year Cardinals broadcaster Harry Caray.

"Mike's always been pretty brutal to listen to. Admittedly, he knows a lot about baseball, but sometimes he has a difficult time articulating it. The Cardinals gave him the job originally, I recall, because he was very sick and couldn't play anymore. I don't think they dreamed he would live this long. He's grown on me over the

years, but it can be painful to wade through the talk to glean the baseball gems." — Internet posting by "FredBird" on broadcaster and former player Mike Shannon.

France Laux broadcast in a lackluster style for the Cardinals from 1929 through 1947, when ailing owner Sam Breadon decided to give an exclusive sponsorship contract to Griesedieck Brewery and Laux was forced out. *Harry Caray* became the exclusive number one broadcaster after being the number two man since 1944, and remained with the club for more than a quarter century. He received the Frick Award in 1989. Dizzy Dean also broadcast for the club between 1941 and 1946.

Caray was paired with former catcher Gabby Street until Street's death at age 68 in early 1951. Caray was then paired with former catcher Gus Mancuso until 1954, when Jack Buck and Milo Hamilton (the latter for one season) joined Caray after Busch Brewery bought the club. Joe Garagiola also joined the Cardinals broadcast booth that season and stayed through 1962. He then went on to a successful career with NBC, the "Today" show, Yankee telecasts in the 1960s, and numerous All-Star Game and World Series assignments.

Buck got his start broadcasting Ohio State football games and then broadcast International League games in Columbus and Rochester before Cardinals executive Bing Devine discovered him and brought him to St. Louis in 1954 as the color man. When Harry Caray left for Oakland after the 1969 season, Buck took over as the leading radio broadcaster. Buck also broadcast several Super Bowls (1970, 1978–1984) and received the Frick Award in 1990. He ended his career in 2001 when he succumbed to disease (he died in June 2002). His son Joe carried on the family tradition when he broadcast for the club from 1991 through 2002. Joe broadcast for Fox Sports beginning in 1996 and went national full-time after the 2002 season.

After a nine-year playing career ending in 1970, Mike Shannon, considered a bland announcer by many, joined the booth in 1972, where he has remained ever since. Long-time broadcaster Wayne Hagin (A's, Giants, White Sox and Rockies since 1981) joined the club in 2003.

Books. Bob Broeg, *Redbirds: A Century of Cardinals Baseball* (1981); David Craft and Tom Owens, *Red Birds Revisited: Great Memories and Stories from the St. Louis Cardinals* (1990); Donald Honig, *St. Louis Cardinals: An Illustrated History* (1991); Fred Lieb, *The St. Louis Cardinals* (1946); Rob Rains, *The St. Louis Cardinals: The Official 100th Anniversary History* (1992); Steve Steinberg, *Baseball in St. Louis, 1900–1925* (2004); Tina Wright (ed), *Cardinal Memories: Recollections from Baseball's Greatest Fans* (1985).

St. Louis Maroons

Union Association 1884

Key Owners. This Union Association entry was owned by millionaire realtor Henry Lucas, whose uncle James H. "John" Lucas sponsored an early professional club in St. Louis. Investors in the Maroons with Lucas included Ellis Wainwright and Adolphus Busch of Busch Brewery fame. Busch's grandson, August A. Busch, bought the St. Louis Cardinals in 1953. Henry Lucas was an amateur player who built a field at his large estate, which was used as the site for his club's games. His grandfather was an early St. Louis settler and had bought a tremendous amount of land in the city.

Some sources claim that Henry Lucas lost his fortune in the Maroons, which is unlikely. In 1873 he and his six siblings had each inherited $1 million from their father. Nevertheless, Lucas admitted losing $17,000 in the Union Association. He eventually succeeded in losing his fortune due primarily to other equally risky ventures. He later worked for the Vandalia railroad, managing the ticket office.

The Season. The club breezed to the pennant with a 91–16 record and .850 winning percentage. Second-place Cincinnati finished 21 games out with a 68–35 record. Fred Dunlap led the league with a .412 average and 13 home runs.

Ballpark. The Maroons built a ballpark at Cass Avenue and West 25th Street that was easily reached by street car lines. It was known as The Palace Park of America and seated 10,000 fans. It was later known as Robison Field (after the late 1890s owners) and then League Park, home of the St. Louis Cardinals until 1920.

Postseason Activity. Some sources report that the Maroons were unable to compete effectively with the American Association St. Louis Brown Stockings. This apparently was not true because after the Union Association's single season, the strong Maroons were accepted into the National League to compete against the Browns.

This move would have been a violation of the National Agreement, which had reserved St. Louis for the American Association. A compromise was reached (probably with cash to Browns owner Von der Ahe), and the Maroons remained in the National League for two seasons in 1885 and 1886.

St. Louis Maroons

National League 1885–1886

"Oddly, too, for two years there was a Union Association and National League club called the St. Louis Maroons, owned by a nephew of John Lucas. Probably the Maroons, who later moved to Indianapolis, gave a St. Louis newspaper writer the idea, in 1899, of brightening up the Browns' drab image with a more colorful nickname [Cardinals]."—Harold Peterson in *The Man Who Invented Baseball* (1969).

The National League did not have a franchise in St. Louis from 1878 until 1885. After the 1884 Union Association disbanded, its St. Louis Maroons were absorbed into the National League as part of the overall compromise reached with the other remaining Major League, the American Association. The team remained as the Maroons during its two-year stay in the league. Henry Lucas owned the club during both National League seasons. The club finished in the cellar in 1885 and sixth in 1886.

St. Louis Red Stockings

National Association 1875

"The Reds of St. Louis were alive only in that they had not officially disbanded."—William J. Ryczek on the dismal showing of the club in *Blackguards and Red Stockings* (1992).

The Red Stockings are not to be confused with the Brown Stockings, as two St. Louis clubs operated for one National Association season in 1875. The Brown Stockings were the National League entry the following season. The Red Stockings played only 18 National Association games before disbanding, finishing with a 4–14 record under manager Charlie Sweasy.

St. Louis Terriers

Federal League 1914–1915

"The Junkyard."—Local newspaper's sarcastic reference to the club's ballpark (It was still under construction at the time).

Otto Steifel was a brewer and bank director who owned the club along with Philip deCatesby Ball. Ball owned a string of ice manufacturing plants and bought the St. Louis Browns after the Federal League folded.

The Terriers finished last in 1914 under managers Three Finger Brown and Fielder Jones. Under Jones in 1915 the Terriers improved to second place, only percentage points behind the Chicago Whales (87–67 to 86–66 for Chicago). Babe Borton led the club with 83 RBIs in 1915 and three pitchers won at least 20 games: Eddie Plank, Doc Crandall and Dave Davenport.

St. Paul Saints

Union Association 1884

"Other clubs struggled against mounting deficits. As the season advanced, new Union clubs came into the fray for longer or shorter terms of existence—mostly shorter. St. Paul played exactly eight games before giving up the ghost."—Arthur Bartlett in *Baseball and Mr. Spalding* (1951).

The Saints had a 2–6 record before leaving the league.

Salaries

"Whenever a guy says, 'It's not about the money,' the one thing we know for sure is, it's about the money."—Jeff Bagwell.

"People think we make $3 million and $4 million a year. They don't realize that most of us only make $500,000."—Former Rangers outfielder Pete Incaviglia in the 1980s.

"I can say for myself that my only thought [as a player] was to win ballgames. Salary was a secondary consideration. And that was the attitude of most of the old-timers."—Yankee manager Miller Huggins during the 1920s.

See also *Managers*—Salaries.

1860s and early 1870s. The earliest professionals were usually paid by the game. In 1873 the National Association Boston Red Stockings paid their players a total of approximately $16,000. Boston pitcher Albert Spalding was the highest paid player in the league at $1,800 per season. Instead of paying salaries, some early clubs acted as cooperatives and split the receipts among the players.

Salaries in the early days of professional baseball were sometimes quoted by position according to the following schedule:

Catcher	$2,000
Pitcher	2,000
First Baseman	1,500
Second Baseman	2,500
Third Baseman	3,000 (frequent bunting required a top fielder at this position)
Shortstop	2,000
Outfielder	1,500

Sportswriter Henry Chadwick wrote after the 1876 National League season that the league needed to lower admission from 50 cents to 25 cents and also lower salaries. He said $1,000 annually was enough even for pitchers and catchers, and others should get $100 per month for the seven-month season.

1880s.

"It is ridiculous to pay ballplayers $2,000 a year, especially when the $800 boys often do just as well."—William Hulbert in 1880.

"Salaries must come down or the interest of the public must be increased in some way. If one or the other does not happen, bankruptcy stares every team in the face."—Albert Spalding in 1882.

The Providence Grays players earned a total of $13,175 in 1881. Competition from the American Association (starting in 1882) and the Union Association (1884 only) generated a rise in salaries through the decade. The unofficial minimum salary was $1,000, and preeminent players such as catcher Buck Ewing earned $5,000 in 1889. Salaries averaged approximately $2,000 during the decade, with a high average of $2,600 by 1889.

1890s. Salaries in 1890 and 1891 were in many cases almost double previous years because of the fallout from the 1890 Players League. By the end of 1892, when both the Players League and American Association were gone, the National League's monopoly allowed it to make across-the-board salary cuts. Salaries continued to move downward through most of the decade.

The Phillies are an example of the effect of the monopoly. In 1889 the club's salaries ranged from $1,400 to $2,500. At the start of 1892, salaries were $3,000–3,500 as a result of the bidding war between the leagues. Two weeks before the end of the season all club owners terminated their player contracts and renegotiated for 1893. In 1893 each of the Phillies players earned approximately $1,800.

As a result of the downsizing of salaries, the official salary limit through much of the 1890s was $2,400. Consistent with this scale, rookies usually earned close to $1,500. Teams often circumvented the limit by paying "bonuses." Established Major Leaguers usually earned $3,000. Outstanding players earned $4,000–5,000, and superstars after several years earned $6,000–10,000. The average wage earner in the 1890s made approximately $12–15 per week.

1900–1910. Salaries ranged from $1,000 to $12,000 by the end of the first decade of the 20th century, with an average of about $2,500. In 1906 the highest salary in the American League was the $6,500 paid to Bobby Wallace of the Browns, who had moved over from the Cardinals in a bidding war. The contract was for $32,000 over five years and had a no-trade clause. Christy Mathewson earned approximately $8,000 per year before 1910. Honus Wagner peaked at $10,000 in 1909 and remained at that level for the remainder of his career.

1910–1920/Federal League.

"[The Federal League's] promoters originated the perambulating bank which consisted of a satchel crammed with $1,000 bills. It was carried around the country.... Whenever a draft on major league talent was made the satchel would be opened and the contents would be dumped in the center of the table. If this did not make an impression on the player the promoters took the next train."—G.W. Axelson in *"Commy"* (1919).

Salaries escalated after 1910 due in part to a stronger economy and because of the challenge from the Federal League starting in 1914. In 1913, 20 key Major League players were paid $76,350, averaging $3,817.50. In 1915 those same players were paid $146,550, a $7,327.50 average and 92% increase. Hal Chase earned $6,000 in 1911, 1912 and 1913. Ty Cobb earned $9,000 in each of 1910–1912, $12,000 in 1914 and $20,000 in 1915.

A's owner Connie Mack could not afford to pay Eddie Collins, arguably the best player in the American League in 1914. Rather than lose Collins to the Federal League, American League president Ban Johnson engineered a sale of Collins to the White Sox for $50,000 and a $15,000 salary.

Walter Johnson made $10,000 (or $12,000) in 1914. Chicago of the Federal League offered him $16,000 plus a $10,000 bonus. Griffith matched the salary and convinced White Sox owner Charlie Comiskey to pay the $10,000 bonus (or loaned it to Comiskey) so that Johnson would not compete against the White Sox for the Federal League club in that city.

Salaries were inflated from 1914 through 1916 because of the Federal League challenge, but the combination of that league's failure and World War I deflated salaries through the end of the

decade. Some sources report that after World War I, Major League owners secretly agreed to lower salaries to recoup some of their losses caused by the shortened schedule.

1920s.

"I played baseball because I could make more money doing that than I could doing anything else."—Bill Terry.

The average salary during the 1920s was between $5,000 and $7,500. In 1922 Babe Ruth began a five-year contract that earned him a Major League–high $52,000 annually. The second-highest paid Yankee was Frank "Home Run" Baker at $16,000. By 1927 Ruth was making $70,000, with Herb Pennock second on the team at $17,500. Lou Gehrig earned $8,000 that year. Second-lowest on the team was Wilcy Moore at $2,500. Manager Miller Huggins earned $37,000. Ruth peaked at $80,000 in 1930 and 1931.

Ty Cobb went from $1,800 in his third season in 1906 (some sources say first season) to $70,000 his last season in 1928, with a purported high of $85,000 in 1927. Eddie Collins made $40,000 in 1926.

Lefty O'Doul hit .398 with 32 home runs and 122 RBIs when he earned $8,000 in 1929. He held out unsuccessfully for $17,000 in 1930. Dazzy Vance of the Dodgers was the highest paid pitcher in 1926 at $25,000. Shortstop Dave Bancroft of the 1928 Dodgers received $40,000, believed to be the highest Dodger salary through at least 1945.

Negro League Salaries. See *Negro Leagues*.

1930s/The Depression.

"You will never hear of another ballplayer getting that kind of money. I'm sure there will never be another one on *this* ballclub."—Yankee general manager Ed Barrow on Babe Ruth's 1930 hold-out for $85,000; he received $80,000.

Salaries in 1930 averaged $7,000, but were down to $6,000 by 1933 as a result of the Depression. In 1932 and 1933, Dizzy Dean earned $3,000. In 1934 Paul Dean earned $3,000, Dizzy $7,500 and Leo Durocher $6,500. Player-manager Frankie Frisch earned $18,500 but had earlier made $28,000.

In 1934 Babe Ruth made $35,000, Bill Terry, $30,000; Al Simmons, $27,500; and Lou Gehrig was at $23,000. Chuck Klein made $22,000, Mickey Cochrane $20,000, and Jimmie Foxx supposedly $20,000. Foxx later said that he did not make that much.

By 1935 Dizzy Dean was earning $18,500, based on his 30-win season the year before. After winning 28 games in 1935, he earned $27,500 in 1936 and 1937.

Branch Rickey earned a $50,000 base salary and 20% of the profits on player sales in the late 1930s. In 1941 he earned $88,000, the highest salary in baseball.

1941–1945/World War II.

"Accept this, and I'll take care of you."—Branch Rickey to Cardinals shortstop Marty Marion.

"Give me what I want and I'll take care of myself."—Marion's response.

The average Major League salary was $7,000 in 1940, the same as in 1930. However, there were serious inequities among clubs. The highest paid player on the 1941 Phillies received only $7,500. When general manager Branch Rickey left the Cardinals in 1942, he was earning $80,000. The highest paid player on the team made $15,000. Joe DiMaggio earned $37,500 in 1941 and Ted Williams earned $20,000.

In 1943 the government imposed salary freezes in most industries, including entertainment, to prevent an inflationary spiral during wartime. Players, like other civilians, could earn no more than they were paid in 1942 and no less than the lowest paid player the year before (this was before the official minimum salary in Major League Baseball). The average salary in 1942 was $6,400, a few hundred dollars below 1940. This number remained relatively constant during the war years, even dropping somewhat as quality (and thus more highly paid) players went into the military.

1946–1950s.

"There was an unwritten code not to talk or write about salaries, and the writers honored that code. They wouldn't betray your confidence. We didn't want anybody to know how little we were making."—Eddie Lopat.

"I'm glad to sign this contract [from $100,000 to $80,000] because a couple of times in the past the Cardinals have had me sign for more than we agreed upon orally. This year I thought I'd be kind to them."—Stan Musial at age 39 in late 1959.

Salaries began a steady escalation after the war. The average salary in 1949 was $15,000 and through the 1950s about 75% of the players earned between $10,000 and $25,000. Tiger pitcher Hal Newhouser earned $60,000 in 1946, the second highest salary in club history behind Hank Greenberg.

For the first time, a select few players began making $100,000 or more. They included Hank Greenberg, Stan Musial, Joe DiMaggio, Bob Feller and Ted Williams (See also **First $100,000 Players**). Williams earned $125,000 in 1950, DiMaggio $100,000, Ralph Kiner $65,000, Lou Boudreau $65,000, Jackie Robinson $35,000 and Pee Wee Reese $35,000. Kiner earned $90,000 in 1954. The $125,000 earned by Williams in 1950 can be adjusted for inflation to $643,125 in 1990 dollars, still substantially lower than stars of the 1990s.

Yankee shortstop Phil Rizzuto's highest salary was $50,000, the third-highest Yankee salary in history until 1961. Joe DiMaggio earned a total of $704,769 during his 13-year career. Roy Campanella's top salary was $36,000. Jackie Robinson peaked at $39,000, Gil Hodges at $40,000 and Duke Snider at $38,000. Ned Garver was the all-time highest paid Browns player when he earned $25,000 in 1952.

1960s.

"Guys like Willie Mays, Catfish Hunter and Juan Marichal, all Hall of Famers, must look at today's salaries like Frank Sinatra looks at rap music."—1980s Giants first baseman Will Clark.

Salaries averaged $18,000 by the mid–1960s and rose to $29,000 in 1969. When Roger Maris hit 61 home runs in 1961, he earned $42,500. He was offered $60,000 by the Yankees for the 1962 season. He asked for $90,000 but received $72,500 plus $5,000 for living expenses. In 1961 Mickey Mantle made $75,000 and then received a raise to $100,000, his highest salary. One source reported that when Warren Spahn earned $85,000 from the Braves in 1964, he was the highest paid pitcher in the Major Leagues. Spahn's highest salary was $87,500.

In 1966 Willie Mays earned $125,000 as the highest paid player in the game. Sandy Koufax earned $120,000 and Don Drysdale earned $110,000 after their joint **Hold-Out**. Henry Aaron earned his first $100,000 salary in 1967. Mays' top salary supposedly was $125,000 in 1966, but one of his autobiographies reported that he made $160,000 in 1971 and negotiated a two-year deal with the Mets totaling $360,000.

1970s.

"I was the most loyal player money could buy."—Pitcher Don Sutton.

"I believe salaries are at their peak, not just in baseball, but all sports. It's quite possible some owners will trade away, or even drop entirely, players who expect $200,000 salaries. There's a superstar born every year…. But still there is no way clubs can continue to

increase salaries to the level some players are talking about."—Dodger owner Peter O'Malley in 1971.

The averages in the 1970s rose dramatically from $31,000 in 1972, $52,000 in 1975, $76,000 in 1977 (free agency had begun), $99,000 in 1978 and $113,000 in 1979.

In the early 1970s, Dick Allen was the highest paid player in the game at $225,000. By 1972, 20 players were earning $100,000 or more. Bobby Murcer became the all-time highest paid Yankee player in 1974 when he signed for $120,000. In 1975, the last year before free agency exploded and the average salary was $52,000, the highest paid players were the following:

$250,000	Dick Allen
240,000	Henry Aaron
190,000	Johnny Bench
185,000	Lou Brock
181,000	Willie Stargell
175,000	Ferguson Jenkins
170,000	Tom Seaver
160,000	Luis Tiant
	Gaylord Perry
155,000	Steve Carlton
	Don Sutton

Following the 1975 season, free agency started and salaries began escalating rapidly. See also **Free Agents** for a discussion of the first free agents and their salaries. Reggie Jackson led the group, receiving $4.293 million over five years starting in 1977.

In 1978 Larry Hisle of the Brewers increased his salary from $47,200 in 1977 to $525,000 per year for six years. In late 1978, Dave Parker signed the first contract calling for $1 million annually over five years. Other sources report that Nolan Ryan signed the first $1 million contract, when he signed with the Astros.

In 1979 Rod Carew signed a contract calling for $4 million over five years and Jim Rice signed for $700,000 for one year.

Between 1978 and 1981, 43 players signed contracts for $1 million or more per season. They were led by Dave Winfield, who received a $13 million deal from the Yankees that would escalate to almost $20 million with subsequent cost-of-living increases.

Pete Rose barnstormed the country in 1979 at age 37 trying to cut a deal with a new team. He signed with the Phillies for a four-year deal worth $3.225 million. He had been receiving $375,000 per year from the Reds.

1980s.

"That's like Al Capone speaking out for gun control."—Sportswriter Blackie Sherrod on Ted Turner, noted signer of undeserving free agents for outrageous sums (e.g., Claudell Washington), who was then pleading for other owners to be rational in their salary negotiations.

During the 1980s the average salary escalated from $143,000 at the start of the decade to almost $500,000 by the end of the decade. After the 1981 season, George Foster signed the largest contract to that date, a guaranteed deal calling for $1.45 million in 1982, $1.8 million in 1983 and a $1 million bonus. It also had two option years that the Mets never exercised because Foster was a bust.

In 1983 Ozzie Smith signed a three-year deal worth $3.2 million. In 1985, 36 players were earning between $1 million and $2 million. Players earning $2 million or more were Ozzie Smith, Mike Schmidt, Jim Rice, Eddie Murray and George Foster.

1990s Frenzy.

"For 100 years we've been trying to find a way to destroy this game, and we finally found the key."—Giants general manager Al Rosen.

"These owners can't spend their money fast enough." — Anonymous player agent.

"A prune pit of a pitcher." —*Sports Illustrated* in 1992 after lifetime 67–104 pitcher Mike Morgan signed a four-year contract with the Cubs worth $12.5 million.

After the 1990 season Major League Baseball teams went crazy buying up free agents. The Giants spent $33 million on three: Willie McGee signed for $13 million and Bud Black and Dave Righetti signed for $10 million each. At the winter meetings that year teams spent $122 million on 20 free agents during a six-day frenzy. The worst deal may have been the $6.35 million three-year contract signed by Matt Young. Young had a .395 career winning percentage, third-lowest of all active pitchers with 50 or more decisions. The biggest winner was Darryl Strawberry, who signed a five-year $20.3 million deal with the Dodgers.

1992. Ryne Sandberg led the pack of new contracts by quietly signing a $28.4 million contract over four years, averaging $7.1 million per year. One sportswriter noted that if Felix Fermin's $950,000 salary was removed from the Indians' 1992 payroll, the club's total payroll would have been the same as the $7.16 million that the Cubs were to pay Sandberg once his new contract took effect. He retired unexpectedly early in the 1994 season, walking away from a substantial portion of his contract. However, he returned in 1996.

The big excitement in 1992 was the quest by Bobby Bonilla for a $5 million-plus per year contract. He got what he was after from his hometown Mets: a guaranteed package worth $29 million. He received a $1.5 million signing bonus and an average of $5.8 million over five years. After losing salary arbitration with the Pirates the year before, Bonilla had made $2.4 million before signing the multi-year pact. In 1992 a total of 270 players made over $1 million annually, 68 over $3 million and 22 over $4 million.

1993.

"Matt Young is to [Red Sox general manager] Lou Gorman what Al Capone's vault is to Geraldo Rivera." — Dan Shaughnessy of the *Boston Globe* after the Red Sox released pitcher Matt Young after paying him $6.35 million over three years to win three games. Rivera did a live show uncovering the secret Capone vaults. In the dramatic finale he opened the vaults — to find them empty.

Cecil Fielder signed a five-year, $36 million contract, including a record $10 million signing bonus. The bonus was just over the $9 million bonus that David Cone received from the Royals when he signed shortly after the 1992 season. The contract would pay Fielder $7.2 million over each of the last three years of the contract.

Ruben Sierra and Mark McGwire each signed with the A's for $28 million over four years. Bret Saberhagen signed a $27.75 million contract that would pay him through the year 2028. He was guaranteed $20.15 million, making him the highest paid pitcher in baseball at an average yearly salary of $6.72 million.

When Gary Sheffield earned $3.11 million in 1993, he was the 86th-highest paid player.

1994. Frank Thomas signed quickly after the 1993 season for $30.5 million over five years. Rafael Palmeiro left the Rangers to sign with the Orioles for five years and $27.5 million.

In 1994 the Yankees had by far the highest average salaries at $1,760,974. The second-highest average was the Tigers, who paid $1,594,700 per man. The lowest payroll was in San Diego at $515,231 per man. Second-lowest were the Angels at $750,268 each.

1993–1994 Top Paid.

$7,291,667   Barry Bonds
$7,250,000   Frank Thomas

$7,237,500   Cecil Fielder
$7,100,000   Ryne Sandberg
$6,500,000   Joe Carter
$6,500,000   Cal Ripken
$6,225,000   Lenny Dykstra
$6,150,000   Matt Williams
$6,070,000   Rafael Palmeiro
$6,000,000   Will Clark
$6,000,000   David Cone
$6,000,000   Ken Griffey, Jr.
$6,000,000   Kirby Puckett
$5,800,000   Bobby Bonilla
$5,430,000   Jack Morris
$5,380,000   Roger Clemens
$5,150,000   Dwight Gooden
$5,120,000   Barry Larkin
$5,100,000   Danny Tartabull
$5,000,000   Doug Drabek

Other sources report the figures differently, as the following highest paid by position demonstrates (based on salary plus prorated signing bonus):

P	$5,300,000	Jack McDowell
C	$3,800,000	Benito Santiago
1B	$5,469,479	Rafael Palmeiro
2B	$6,299,966	Ryne Sandberg
SS	$5,665,822	Cal Ripken, Jr.
3B	$6,300,000	Bobby Bonilla
OF	$5,500,000	Joe Carter
OF	$5,200,000	Kirby Puckett
OF	$5,166,667	Barry Bonds

1995. Very few new contracts were made at high levels because of the financial instability and uncertainty caused by the player strike. Jay Buhner received a three-year deal from the Mariners worth $15.5 million. Barry Bonds reportedly earned over $8 million. A number of players took extreme pay cuts in their new contracts at the start of the 1995 season. A sampling (figures in millions):

Name	Team	1995	1994
Bobby Witt	Marlins	$1.80	$3.25
Terry Pendleton	Marlins	1.50	2.95
Orel Hershiser	Indians	1.45	3.00
Terry Mulholland	Giants	1.25	3.35
Dave Stewart	A's	1.00	3.50
Mike Devereaux	White Sox	0.80	3.38
Kirk McCaskill	White Sox	0.75	2.00
Paul Assenmacher	Indians	0.70	2.25
Bud Black	Indians	0.35	3.00
Pat Borders	Royals	0.31	2.50
Tom Browning	Royals	0.30	3.50
Danny Darwin	Blue Jays	0.30	2.40
Teddy Higuera	Padres	0.27	2.97
Bob Welch	A's	0.23	2.90

1996.

"If it comes down to taking care of my mother in her old age and taking care of my centerfielder in his young age, I hope she understands." — Mariners owner Jeff Smulyan on Ken Griffey Jr.'s new contract.

The highlight of the winter signings was Ken Griffey's deal with the Mariners worth $34 million over four years, an average of $8.5 million per season. David Cone signed with the Yankees for $16.5 million over three years. Catcher Ron Karkovice signed with the White Sox for $3.6 million over two seasons despite hitting .217

and throwing out less than a third of the baserunners he faced. Ramon Martinez became the highest paid Dodger pitcher of all time when he signed a three-year deal for $15 million.

The top salaries by position:

C	$4,200,000	Terry Steinbach
1B	$9,237,500	Cecil Fielder
2B	$4,958,333	Robby Thompson
3B	$6,550,000	Matt Williams
SS	$6,877,521	Barry Larkin
OF	$8,416,667	Barry Bonds
OF	$8,500,000	Ken Griffey, Jr.
OF	$6,500,000	Joe Carter
P	$6,500,000	Greg Maddux

1997.

"They haven't negotiated his salary yet. That's a bribe to keep his mouth shut." — A's General Manager Sandy Alderson on Barry Bonds' 1997 $22.9 million contract extension with the Giants.

Albert Belle led with $11 million ($10 million in some sources), followed by Cecil Fielder at $9.237 million, Barry Bonds at $8.7 million, Roger Clemens at $8.4 million (three years at $24.75 million with the Blue Jays), and Jeff Bagwell at $8.04 million. Catchers Ivan Rodriguez received $6.825 million from the Rangers ($42 million over five years) and Mike Piazza $7 million from the Mets ($91 million over seven years). Mark McGwire received $7.15 million from the Cardinals. Cal Ripken received $6.85 million from the Orioles. During the season Greg Maddux signed a new contract worth $57.5 million over five years, making him the highest paid player in the game, if ever so briefly. In comparison, the Pirates' total payroll in 1997 was $9,071,667.

Alex Rodriguez received a four-year, $10.4 million contract to begin the 1997 season. Derek Jeter's 1997 contract was $525,000 after he was Rookie of the Year in 1996.

In 1997 Gary Sheffield signed a $61 million contract with the Marlins, a six-year extension that was the largest deal ever at that time. The contract was to run from 1998 through 2003. It surpassed the $55 million five-year contract that Albert Belle signed for the 1997 season and the $43.75 million six-year contract that Barry Bonds had signed. Sheffield's analysis: "Am I worth it? All I can say is, I think the Marlins think so. I can't hold myself accountable for the way baseball's economics are."

1998. The top earners:

Albert Belle $10 million from the Orioles
Gary Sheffield $10 million from the Marlins
Greg Maddux $9.6 million from the Braves
Barry Bonds $8.9 million from the Giants
Mark McGwire $8.34 million from the Cardinals
Roger Clemens $8.25 million from the Blue Jays
Bernie Williams $8.25 million from the Yankees
Andres Galarraga $8 million from the Braves
Mike Piazza $8 million from the Dodgers
Sammy Sosa $8 million from the Cubs
Ken Griffey, Jr., $7.98 million from the Mariners
Jeff Bagwell $7.945 million from the Astros

1999. Albert Belle signed with the Orioles for $65 million over five years ($13 million per season), but after the season Randy Johnson signed a four-year deal with the Diamondbacks worth $52.4 million, making him the highest paid pitcher in baseball, and number two player overall, behind Mo Vaughn. Vaughn signed with the Angels for $80 million, about $13.3 million annually, and was out most of the season with injuries. That contract followed the then-largest total contract in history, when Mike Piazza signed with the Mets for $91 million and Bernie Williams received $87.5 million

from the Yankees. The Dodgers then signed a new largest contract in history, giving $105 million to pitcher Kevin Brown, who rewarded the club by going on the disabled list five times over the next four seasons. His contract averaged out at $15 million per season and the Dodgers traded him to the Yankees after the 2003 season (and he was on the disabled list again in 2004).

2000. The Dodgers signed Shawn Green for $14 million a year. The Padres signed Trevor Hoffman to a four-year $32 million deal, with a fifth year option, making him the highest paid reliever in history. He then had arm troubles and missed a significant portion of the 2002 and 2003 seasons.

Ken Griffey, Jr., signed a nine-year, $116.5 million contract with the Reds.

2001. Alex Rodriguez signed his mega-deal for $252 million over 10 years, far eclipsing any other total or annualized deal in history. Two days later the Red Sox signed Manny Ramirez to an eight-year $160 million deal. Yankees owner George Steinbrenner immediately signed shortstop Derek Jeter to a 10-year, $189 million contract.

Mike Hampton had earlier signed an eight-year contract with the Rockies for $121 million, at the time the largest contract in history. Sammy Sosa made $12 million that season for the Cubs and Carlos Delgado received $12.2 million from the Blue Jays (though the contract averaged out to much more).

Roger Clemens signed for $15.45 million for each of 2001 and 2002. Next was Hampton at $15.125 million for 2001–2008, followed by Kevin Brown at $15 million for 1999–2005, and Mike Mussina at $14.75 million for 2001–2006 ($88.5 million total). Mussina said the deciding factor was a call from manager Joe Torre.

Perhaps the best of the group was Randy Johnson at $13.1 million for each of 1999–2002 and Pedro Martinez at $12.5 million for each of 1998–2003. Mariano Rivera was the highest paid reliever for a single season at $9.15 million.

Albert Belle made over $12 million, but was forced to retire before the season started with an arthritic hip. David Wells signed with the White Sox for $9.925 million, but sat out most of the season with a bad back (5–7 in 16 games). Wilson Alvarez made over $9 million from the Devil Rays while sitting out the season with a bad arm.

2002. Jason Giambi left the A's to sign with the Yankees for seven years and $120 million. It was a slow year for winter signings, however, as clubs began to pull back. Only $188.5 million was paid to six players, despite their being 154 free agents. The year before $739.2 million was paid to 25 players.

Chan Ho Park signed with the Rangers for an average of over $13 million per season, sixth among pitchers (Rogers Clemens was the high at $15.45 million and Randy Johnson was the low at $13.1 million).

2003. Jim Thome signed for $72 million for six years with the Phillies and Tom Glavine received $32 million over three years from the Mets. Catcher Ivan Rodriguez signed for $10 million for one season with the Marlins. It worked. They won the World Series. Jeff Kent signed for two years and $18.2 million with the Astros for the 2003–2004 seasons.

After Alex Rodriguez, the highest paid players for the season:

Carlos Delgado $18.2 million
Manny Ramirez $17.2 million
Mo Vaughn $17.2 million
Sammy Sosa $16.9 million

2004.

"After the year I had last year, it's a little disappointing come the 1st and 15th [paydays], but I'm going to keep on ticking." —

Frank Thomas in early 2004 while making $6 million a year. He must have felt great when he stunk up the joint a couple of years earlier while earning substantially more.

A's shortstop Miguel Tejada signed a six-year, $72 million deal with the Orioles. The Angels signed Kevin Escobar for $18.75 million over three years. Rod Beck signed with the Padres for 2004 after making a comeback in 2003. His salary for 2004 was $1.85 million.

The Expos offered Vladimir Guerrero $75 million over five years and then withdrew the offer. He then signed with the Angels for $70 million over five years after rejecting an offer by the Orioles for $78 million over six years. The Dodgers had a deal all set with Guerrero, but couldn't pull the trigger because of the uncertainty over the ownership situation until Frank McCourt finalized his purchase in late January 2004. In the meantime, the Yankees signed Javier Vasquez, the Expos ace, for approximately $11.5 million per season over four years. See *Trades* for the Yankees' signing of Alex Rodriguez.

In the last year of his contract with the Blue Jays, Carlos Delgado earned $18.5 million. Roy Halladay signed with the Blue Jays for $42 million over four years after going 22–7 in 2003.

The Marlins re-signed Mike Lowell for $32 million over four years and Luis Castillo for $16 million over three years. To reward World Series pitching hero Josh Beckett, the Marlins *cut* his pay by 12.5%. It was the most they could reduce it under the collective bargaining agreement. He was not eligible for arbitration.

Randy Johnson earned $16.5 million from the Diamondbacks in both 2004 and 2005. Pedro Martinez was unable to come to terms on a multi-year deal with the Boston, so he played for $17.5 million, highest for any Major League pitcher.

Andy Pettitte signed with the Astros for $31.5 million for three years. The Yankees had offered $26 million over two years, and another $13 million for 2006 if he wasn't on the disabled list for much of 2005. Pettitte was a native Texan and wanted to play at home. He also indicated he was going to try to lure Roger Clemens out of retirement to join him, which is exactly what he did. Clemens signed with the Astros for $5 million and attendance incentive clauses.

In March 2004 Albert Pujols signed a $100 million seven-year deal with the Cardinals that could bring him as much as $111 million if the Cardinals exercise an option for an eighth year. He was the ninth player to receive a $100 million contract.

Squeezing the Mid-level Players.

"It isn't really the stars that are expensive. It's the high cost of mediocrity."— Bill Veeck, Jr.

One of the by-products of the inflationary spiral of the 1990s was that long-time midlevel performers were being pushed out of the game. Teams unwittingly developed a caste system of highly compensated players alongside low-priced players at or near the minimum. Players on their way down in their careers were finding it difficult to get work because teams could not (or would not) pay salaries in the $1–2 million range for such players.

An example was Jeff Reardon, who set the all-time save record in 1992 but was unable to find a team after being released by the Braves after the season. He signed a non-guaranteed contract that could have left him in Class AAA. Notwithstanding the disparity, 265 players were paid at least $1 million in 1993, an average of nine per team. It was estimated that 13% of the players earned 50% of the Major League payroll.

The squeeze was reflected in the 1995 *median* salaries—an equal number of players making above and below a specific amount. This figure dropped 39% in 1995 to $275,000, down from $450,000.

The median salary was $350,000 in 1996, up from $300,000 in 1995. However, 13% of the players (the top 100) earned 53% of the payroll.

In 2001 the 100th ranked player, by salary, earned $6 million. The 200th ranked player earned $3.4 million, and 425 players made at least $1 million, leaving 325 players making far less.

Highest Salary/Milestones.

"With the money I'm making, I should be playing two positions."— Pete Rose in 1979.

"Last year the highest paid player made $8 million. So, the White Sox jumped Belle to $11 million. Can't they count? What happened to nine and 10?"— Orioles Assistant General Manager Kevin Malone after Albert Belle moved from $8 million to $11 million, making him the highest paid player in history to that point.

1922	$ 50,000	Babe Ruth
1927	$ 70,000	Babe Ruth (or Cobb's reported $85,000 in 1926)
1947	$ 100,000	Hank Greenberg
1950	$ 125,000	Ted Williams
1972	$ 225,000	Dick Allen
1975	$ 250,000	Dick Allen
1975	$ 578,000	Catfish Hunter
1979	$1,000,000	Dave Winfield
1979	$1,300,000	Nolan Ryan
1981	$1,450,000	George Foster
1981	$2,200,000	Dave Winfield
1989	$3,000,000	Kirby Puckett (three years later Puckett was No. 64 on the list of highest paid players)
1990	$ 4,700,000	Jose Canseco
1991	$ 5,380,000	Roger Clemens
1991	$ 5,800,000	Bobby Bonilla
1992	$ 7,100,000	Ryne Sandberg
1993	$ 7,200,000	Cecil Fielder
1995	$ 8,000,000	Barry Bonds
1995	$ 8,000,000	David Cone
1995	$ 9,237,500	Cecil Fielder
1997	$11,000,000	Albert Belle
1997	$11,500,000	Greg Maddux
1999	$13,000,000	Albert Belle
1999	$13,300,000	Mo Vaughn
1999	$15,000,000	Kevin Brown
2000	$15,450,000	Roger Clemens (or Kevin Brown at $15.7 million)
2001	$17,000,000	Carlos Delgado
2002	$21,000,000	Alex Rodriguez (signed for $252 million over 10 years)
2003	$22,000,000	Alex Rodriguez

Note that figures differ depending on how signing bonuses are factored in. For example, one source reported that Barry Bonds was the highest paid in 1995 at $7.29 million. Others report that in 1996 Bonds became the first player to formally receive $8 million in a season.

Average Salaries.

1878 $1,730 (Boston's average, which was probably representative of the league, though possibly slightly higher)

1879 $1,430 (Boston's average)

1880 $1,300

1882 $1,447 (Providence's average—American Association competition begins). $2,000 was the overall average for the 1880s.

1889 $2,670 (The average American industrial worker earned $440 per year)

1890 $3,000 (Players League boosted competition for players)
1910 $2,500 ($1,000 to $12,000 was the range)
1911 $4,000
1922 $5,000
1929 $7,500
1930 $7,000
1933 $6,000
1940 $7,000
1942–1944 $6,400 (wartime wage freeze)
1949 $15,000 (The average American was earning $3,000.)
1950s 75% of the players earned between $10,000 and $25,000. The overall increase was due in part to fewer players because the minor leagues were thinning out. In addition, there was increased competition from other emerging professional sports such as football and basketball.
1967 $19,000
1969 $25,000
1971 $31,543
1972 $34,092 (Over 20 players were earning at least $100,000.)
1973 $36,566
1974 $40,839
1975 $44,676 (other sources reported that pitchers averaged $51,000 and position players averaged $55,000.)
1976 $51,501 ($52,300 in some sources)
1977 $76,000–$95,000 (UPI reported that the average salary was $95,149, due essentially to the increase in free agents over the previous year. Another usually accurate source reported that average salaries were $76,066, which is considered the more correct range.)
1978 $99,876
1979 $113,558
1980 $143,756
1981 $185,651
1982 $241,497
1984 $329,408
1985 $371,571
1986 $412,520
1987 $431,521 (the Players Association reported $414,454)
1988 $438,729
1989 $497,254
1990 $597,537
1991 $851,492
1992 $1,043,156 (or $1,028,667)
1993 $1,116,353 (or $1,076,089) (This was the smallest increase since the collusion season of 1987.)
1994 $1,188,679 or $1,153,118 ($1,168,263 by the union, which factors in signing bonuses differently).
1995 $1,173,498. This was for the top 25 on each team and did not include the bottom three players on the expanded 28-man roster (due to the strike). If all players were included, the average was $1,073,582, a 9.7% drop. Other sources reported $1,110,766.
1996 $1,172,000 (the Players Association reported $1,119,981)
1997 $1,336,609 (or $1,370,000)
1998 $1,398,831
1999 $1,720,050 ($1,611,000 in other sources)
2000 $1,895,650
2001 $2,198,312 ($2,138,896 in other sources)
2002 $2,380,106
2003 $2,555,000
2004 $2,490,000 (3% drop; first time since the 1995 strike)
Major League Minimum Salaries.
"I was only in the Majors two months before I got a raise. The minimum went up."—Bob Uecker.

There was no formal guaranteed minimum salary in the 20th century until after World War II when the players forced the issue. In 1944, without the minimum and during a shortage of players during that peak war year, many Latin players, particularly Cubans, were signed onto Major League clubs for lower than the "going rate" minimum salary. The official minimums:

1947 $ 5,000
1954 $ 6,000
1957 $ 7,000 (with some exceptions)
1969 $ 10,000
1970 $ 12,000
1972 $ 13,500
1979 $ 21,000
1986 $ 60,000
1988 $ 72,000
1990 $108,000
1993 $109,000 There were 49 players who made the minimum. In contrast, in 1991 there were 100 players at the minimum level, nine of whom were with the Astros who only had three players at the $1 million level.
1997 $150,000
1998 $170,000
1999 $200,000
2002 $300,000
Minor League Salaries/Minimums. See *Minor Leagues*.
First $100,000 Players.

"Later Rose would remark that one of his ambitions was to become the first $100,000-a-year singles hitter. The phrase was catchy.... It summoned up contracts with other $100,000 players: Ted Williams, Stan Musial, Joe DiMaggio. All were masters of the long ball."—Pete Rose and Roger Kahn in *Pete Rose: My Story* (1989).

At least one source cited Joe DiMaggio as the first $100,000 player when he signed for that amount on February 7, 1949. He had the option of accepting $90,000 and having an attendance bonus clause instead of a flat $100,000. Restaurant owner Toots Shor told him to turn down the bonus, which he did.

Other sources question whether DiMaggio was actually the first $100,000 player, focusing instead on Bob Feller. In 1947 Feller made $80,000 and was probably the highest paid postwar player that year. He had incentives built into his contract tied to attendance figures that probably put him over $100,000 that year and most certainly in 1948 when the Indians won the pennant.

One source reported that Ted Williams confirmed Feller's numbers but noted that Williams was making $100,000 in 1950 and possibly was the first player to actually have $100,000 written into his contract without any bonus or incentive clauses. In the late 1940s, Williams turned down $300,000 for three years to play in the *Mexican League* for the Pascual brothers.

One source reported that Stan Musial was the first National Leaguer to earn $100,000, although it was originally to be $91,000. Cardinals owner August Busch supposedly thought it would be beneficial to make Musial the first $100,000 player in the league. Busch did not buy the club until 1953, so Musial probably was not the first to reach that level.

Another source reported that Hank Greenberg was the first National League player to earn $100,000 when he signed with the Pirates for that amount in 1947. His complicated contract called for him to receive between $100,000 and $145,000, depending on certain incentives.

Miscellaneous $100,000 Milestones. Tom Seaver of the Mets was the youngest $100,000 pitcher of his era. In 1974 he became the highest paid pitcher in history to that point when he was paid $172,500.

Randy Hundley was the first $100,000 Major League catcher, for the Cubs in the 1960s.

Frank Robinson received his first $100,000 salary after his Triple Crown season for the Orioles in 1966.

Catfish Hunter was the first $100,000 player on the A's. He signed before the start of the 1974 season, followed shortly by Reggie Jackson at $135,000.

Denny McLain became the first $100,000 Tigers player when he signed a new contract after his 31-win season in 1968.

$200,000 Contracts. Before free agency in early 1976, only Henry Aaron and Dick Allen ever earned over $200,000 in a season.

Millionaires.

"Man, if I made $1 million, I would come in at six in the morning, sweep the stands, wash the uniforms, clean out the offices, manage the team and play the games." — Duke Snider in 1980.

"I coined the phrase Lords of Baseball when owners were absolute. Now, we have millionaires masquerading as proletariat, the Limousine Laborers." — Columnist Dick Young in 1981.

Between 1978 and 1981 there were 43 millionaires in the Major Leagues. The figure was 36 in 1985 alone, 58 in 1988, 225 in 1991 and almost 270 in 1992. There were 265 (or 262) in 1994, but only 189 on Opening Day in 1995 because of the squeeze on the midlevel players. The number of players making $200,000 or less in 1995 was 321, up from 248 in 1994.

There were 239 millionaires on the Opening Day rosters in 1996. There were 385 players in 2000 who made $1 million or more, 413 in 2001 and 425 in 2002.

Matching Offers. By the 1990s the free agent process required clubs to make their players offers at 110% of their prior year's salary in order for the club to be entitled to match any offer made by another club to that player.

Sponsorship.

"Say we want to get a pitcher for the stretch, and company X is willing to pay his salary. We'd get the guy and say company X is sponsoring him. We could provide advertising, and every time his name came on the scoreboard, we'd remind people that he was acquired because of his sponsor." — Reds general manager Jim Bowden, announcing in July 1995 that he was considering finding a sponsor to pay for the salary of a prominent player.

Manager Salaries. See *Managers* — Salaries.

Comparison to Other Sports. In 2003 when Major League players averaged $2.555 million, other major sports were higher and lower:

NHL $1.64 million
NFL $1.25 million
NBA $4.54 million

Comparison to Average Worker.

"The most overcompensated player is one who signs an eternal contract in his late twenties or early thirties. Suddenly he is further into his thirties, falling out of shape, becoming more injury-prone, playing like dog meat, but still drawing the salary of a stud in his twenties." — Michael D. McDermott; perhaps Ken Griffey, Jr., is the best example?

"Jimmy Connors plays two tennis matches and winds up with $850,000, and Muhammad Ali fights for one bout and winds up with five million bucks. Me, I play 190 games — if you count exhibitions — and I'm overpaid!" — 1970s catcher Johnny Bench.

In 1869 a good professional baseball player earned seven times the salary of the average American worker. That ratio was similar

in 1976 at eight times. By 1994 the average baseball player earned almost 50 times the average American worker.

Today's Dollars. Miscellaneous 1990s equivalent salaries:

Babe Ruth $700,000 in 1930
Ted Williams $630,000 in 1959
Joe DiMaggio $620,000 in 1949
Willie Mays $580,000 in 1969
Ty Cobb $155,000 in 1911

Long-term Contracts. See *Contracts* — Long-Term Contracts.

Release of Player/Eating Contract. See *Release*.

Percentage of Revenue/Expenses. See *Profits, Losses and Expenses*.

Team Payrolls.

"George Steinbrenner, sensing another chance to fuel Red Sox paranoia, will henceforth refer to the Yankees' burgeoning $185-million payroll as the Green Monster." — Dwight Perry in the *Seattle Times*.

In the 1870s and early 1880s team payrolls averaged $15,000. In 1911 the average payroll was $40,000–50,000.

In 1950 the Yankees had the highest team payroll at $488,500. The Browns had the lowest payroll at $192,000. Total payroll in the Major Leagues was $5.3 million. In 1962 the expansion Mets had a team payroll of $600,000, higher than the league average.

In 1969 the Cardinals had a $1 million payroll, the highest in either league after coming off two World Series appearances. The 1973 champion A's had a payroll of $773,000 among its eight starters and four key pitchers.

Payrolls skyrocketed after baseball's free agency ruling in 1976. Total Major League payrolls went from $31,380,000 in 1976 to $268,944,000 in 1986 ($283 million in some sources).

In 1977 the Phillies had the top salaries, totaling $3,497,900, a $139,916 average. In 1977 the Cardinals were twelfth with $1,782,675. In 1985 the Cardinals had an almost $6 million payroll, nineteenth in the Major Leagues.

In recent years the typical payroll is measured by the 40-man roster.

The A's payroll in 1990 was $21.7 million, primarily as a result of their World Series appearances the previous two years. In 1993 their payroll had risen to $39.6 million. The Mets payroll was almost $46 million in 1992; they became the second club, along with the 1986 Braves, to finish last and lead the league in payroll. Such records have been kept officially since 1978.

The Mets had the highest team payroll in 1992 at $44,464,002, averaging $1.7 million per player. The lowest was the Astros at $13,352,000, though other sources later reported that the Indians were at $9.2 million. Teams paid a total of $772,978,936 in 1992.

The Blue Jays had the highest team payroll in 1993 with an average of $1,707,963 per man for a total of $42.7 million. The average team payroll was $30 million. During the 1993 season the Padres shaved their payroll from over $29 million to $11.3 million. The Rockies had a 1993 Opening Day payroll of $8,767,500, lowest in the Major Leagues.

In 1994 the Braves had the largest payroll at $52.1 million. The Padres were at the bottom at $15.5 million. Other sources report that the top 1994 payroll was the $56.8 million paid by the Tigers and the $53.9 million paid by the Braves. The lowest payrolls were the $20.3 million paid by the Padres and the $24.3 million paid by the Expos.

In 1995 the Blue Jays started the season with the top payroll at $49,853,500, and the Brewers had the lowest at $15,273,600. The Yankees finished with a record $58.1 million. They were followed by the Orioles at $48.7 million. The world champion Braves were fourth at $46.4 million. The Mets finished with a payroll of $13 million, down from $25.9 million on Opening Day.

In 1996 the total Major League Opening Day payroll was $901,464,368, down from between $905 million and $923,000 million the previous three seasons. In 1996 the Yankees led the Major Leagues with $52 million. The Expos were at the bottom at $15 million, which went even lower in 1998 at $9.2 million.

In 1997 the Yankees had the highest payroll at $58.5 million ($61 million in some sources). The Pirates were at $9,071,667.

In 2001 the Yankees led with $109,791,893 on Opening Day, followed by the Red Sox at $109,558,908 and the Dodgers at $108,980,852. The lowest were the Twins at $24,350,000, followed by the A's, Expos and Marlins, all between $33.8 million and $35.5 million.

In 2002 the Yankees exploded with a payroll of $163,442,745, followed by the Rangers at $120,794,791 and the Dodgers a distant third at $111,449,515. At the low end were Montreal at $35,346,09 and Tampa Bay at $35,339,505. Total Major League payroll was $2,236,873,706. Including performance and award bonuses, as well as benefits, the total cost for players was $2,506,485,506. The Yankees led at $175,327,055 and the Expos trailed at $43,549,061. The World Series-winning Angels had salaries of $69,274,444 and total player expenses of $77,183,754.

The Yankees' 2003 Opening Day payroll was over $150 million ($180.3 million for the 40-man roster, including benefits). The Mets were next at $116.9 million, the Dodgers at $109.2 million, the Rangers at $106.3 million, and the Red Sox at $104.9 million.

To illustrate the chronic disparity, during a game in July 2003, the Yankees' starting lineup was paid $82.8 million for the season, while the Indians' starting lineup was paid $2.75 million. The Yankees completed a four-game sweep.

In 2003 Alex Rodriguez earned $22 million, more than the entire Tampa Bay Opening Day roster of $19.6 million. Seventeen of the club's 25 players were making the minimum $300,000. Two others made $305,000 and $325,000.

In 2004 the Yankees were by far the leader with a payroll of $183 million after adding Alex Rodriguez's $21.7 million (or at least some of it, as the Rangers picked up some of the tab). Boston was second at $125 million and the Angels were third at $101 million, followed by the Mets at $100 million and the Phillies at $93 million.

Protest. On April 30, 1999, the Royals defeat the Yankees, 13–6, as 2,500 Kansas City fans protested the disparity in team payrolls by turning their backs during Yankee at-bats, and walking out early.

Revenue Sharing. See *Profits, Losses and Expenses*—Revenue Sharing.

Contracts/Performance. A study by economists at Northern Illinois University concluded that Major League players do not perform as well after receiving big contracts — no surprise to Major League general managers and Fantasy League owners.

Strategic Signings in the Early 1990s. The Indians signed several players at low prices when they were young, enabling them to lock up several talented players early in their careers. They used their salary strategy to get into the 1997 World Series. They wrapped up the nucleus of Albert Belle, Kenny Lofton, Jim Thome, Sandy Alomar, Carlos Baerga, Jose Mesa, Charles Nagy, Manny Ramirez, Omar Vizquel and Julian Tavares. Shortly after the Series, however, Belle, Baerga and Lofton either left or were traded.

Fast Action. In December 2002 the Yankees simultaneously offered the same two-year, $4.6 million contract to three left-handed relievers — Mike Stanton, Mark Guthrie and Chris Hammond. Each was given 15 minutes to decide whether to take the offer. Hammond signed for $4.8 million, but Stanton went to the Mets a week later.

Salaries Too Low. In the late 1980s, despite skyrocketing salaries, two economists studied the salary structure and concluded that, based on the income generated for their clubs, players generally were still not paid enough. Presumably that was rectified with the wild escalation of the early 1990s.

Early Attempts at Salary Caps. Salary caps have been imposed in professional basketball and football. Baseball owners have pushed unsuccessfully for caps during labor negotiations during the 1980s and 1990s. Attempts at salary caps are nothing new, though the proposed 19th century versions were crude and unfair.

In 1885 the Major Leagues approved a Limitation Agreement to reduce player salaries to $2,000 and prohibit salary advances during the winter. There were numerous ways around the salary cap. When Mike "King" Kelly was traded to Boston in 1887, he was paid $5,000: $2,000 in salary and $3,000 "for use of his picture."

An 1888 Classification Plan was created by National League Indianapolis owner John Brush to reduce player salaries. It helped lead to the formation of the 1890 Players League by forcing players to rebel against the artificial cap. The Plan called for players to be slotted into salary levels according to ability. "A" players were rated highest:

A	$2,500
B	2,250
C	2,000
D	1,750
E	1,500

A form of the plan had been considered in 1882 and 1884, but the formation of rival leagues in those years created competition for players that inhibited implementation of the rigid structure. Ratings were based on conduct and effort, but owners were not required to pay if the player was injured. A different rating system was proposed in 1894 in an article in the *Detroit Journal*, but the salary structure was related directly to production by hitters and fielders:

This ridiculous system would have resulted in John McGraw earning the following:

156 runs at $50	=	$ 7,800
143 putouts at $40	=	5,720
265 assists at $30	=	7,950
141 singles at $10	=	1,410
18 doubles at $20	=	350
14 triples at $30	=	420
1 home run at $40	=	40
TOTAL		$ 23,690*

*not including sacrifices

In 1903 *The Sporting News* proposed a salary cap for all Major League players with from one to three years' experience depending on the minor league level at which a player last played. See also *Strikes and Lockouts* and *Unions* for recent salary cap proposals.

Payment Plan. Some players get paid evenly throughout the year. Others are paid every two weeks during the season.

Until the late 1970s, minor league players did not receive their first paychecks until May 1. Because they received no pay during spring training, they would not receive a paycheck for six weeks once spring training began in mid–April.

Small Bills. A's owner Connie Mack once paid eccentric pitcher Rube Waddell his $2,200 salary in $1 bills to make it go farther. The Browns did the same thing to 1912–1916 pitcher George Baumgardner.

Tall Tale. After the 1916 season in which the Dodgers won the pennant, outfielder Hy Myers wanted more money and wrote to owner Charles Ebbets on the subject. Myers said that his breeding stock farm was too prosperous for him to leave if he could not make more money than offered by Ebbets. Ebbets supposedly wrote back to say that he would visit Myers to see the operation. Myers panicked because his venture was in name only. He frantically rounded up cattle from all of his neighbors to temporarily stock his ranch. Ebbets allegedly fell for the ruse and gave Myers a raise.

Late Payment. Chief Bender pitched for the A's in the early 20th century. In his first professional game in 1901, he was promised $5 to pitch for the Dillsburg club, a few miles from his alma mater, the Carlisle Institute. Though he struck out 21 and hit a grand slam into a cabbage patch, the manager paid him only $3.20 and told him he would be paid the rest at a later date.

In 1942 Bender related the incident in a Philadelphia newspaper article. A few days later he received a bag containing various 19th century coins that added up to $1.80 and the following letter:

"Mr. Chief Bender

Philadelphia, PA

Dear Sir:

In going over our records we have an outstanding account due you from the summer of 1901. Owing to government regulations under the New Deal all outstanding accounts should be liquidated at once. Not knowing your whereabouts nor having seen you for all these years, we were unable to remit.

The cabbages were harvested and sold later that year, giving us a little surplus. We are enclosing the money reserved for you. We have had good and some bad years. We are not enclosing any interest as we felt we were overcharged but we want to settle the account. Owing to a good friend of ours from Philadelphia we were able to locate your whereabouts.

Yours Truly,

DILLSBURG BASEBALL CLUB

Dillsburg, Pa."

Casey Stengel purportedly had a similar experience. When the Kankakee club disbanded, he was owed half a month's salary of $67.50. In 1956, 46 years later, he was making a speech in Kansas City when a local bank presented him with a check for $483.05, the principal amount plus interest. Stengel then presented the check to the local Little League.

Oops.

"Bank error in your favor. Do not pass go!"

In 2004 the Cubs, owned by the Chicago Tribune, owed reliever Mark Guthrie $301,000. By mistake, they deposited it into the bank account of *Chicago Tribune* newspaper carrier Mark Guthrie. Five weeks later the club realized its mistake and got back $275,000 before Guthrie froze his account in order to sort things out.

Websites. Baseball-reference.com and retrosheet.com contain salary histories for all recent Major League players.

Sales See *Team Sales* and *Trades and Player Sales*

Saliva

"There was so much spit flying around, I thought about putting on a raincoat. But I figured I'd be a man and sit back and enjoy it." — Donna Greenwald on sitting in the Yankee Stadium dugout before she sang the National Anthem, during her 1990s quest to sing in every Major League ballpark.

See also *Illegal Substances*.

San Diego Padres

National League 1969–

"I have some good news and some bad news. The good news is that we've outdrawn the Dodgers. The bad news is that I've never seen such stupid ballplaying in my life." — McDonald's founder and Padres owner Ray Kroc, speaking on the ballpark public address system after the Padres' Opening Day loss in Kroc's first season as an owner. After his tirade, Kroc grew even more irate as a streaker bolted onto the fielder as security guards chased him.

"The good news is that we may stay in San Diego. The bad news, I guess, is the same thing." — Club president Buzzie Bavasi in the 1970s amid rumors of a move.

Origins. On May 28, 1968, San Diego was granted a Major League franchise and the Padres were added as an *Expansion* team for the 1969 season. The minor league team of the same name had operated successfully in the Pacific Coast League since 1936.

First Game. The Padres played their first game on April 8, 1969, beating the Astros 2–1 in front of 23,370 fans at San Diego Stadium (later Jack Murphy Stadium). Ed Spiezio hit the team's first home run and also had the first hit. The club swept the opening series, but was 49–110 the rest of the season.

Key Owners.

C. Arnholdt Smith/1969–1974. The original principal owner of the club was C. Arnholdt Smith, majority shareholder of the United States National Bank and the owner of the local minor league franchise. Smith immediately brought in Dodger general manager Buzzie Bavasi, who had been with the Dodgers since 1938. Bavasi later claimed that he was to receive a 32% ownership interest in the Padres if he was successful.

Smith's ownership became precarious when his banking empire collapsed, the largest bank failure in history up to that point. Bavasi's claimed 32% ownership interest in the club was sold for taxes when Smith was convicted of tax evasion and forced to pay $26,753,420.42. Smith was offered $12.5 million for the franchise by grocery store magnate Joe Danzansky, who planned to move the club to Washington, D.C., and hire Minnie Minoso to be the manager. The deal was accepted by Smith and would have been approved by the league except that the club was unable to get out of its stadium lease in San Diego.

Hollywood Park racetrack owner Marje Everett made a $12.5 million offer with songwriter Burt Bacharach and others who planned to leave the club in San Diego. She also suggested that Willie McCovey be traded for to boost attendance. This deal fell through, though McCovey did sign with the Padres.

Ray Kroc/1974–1984.

"I'm not buying the Padres to make money. I'm buying the Padres because I love baseball. The Padres will be my hobby." — Kroc on January 25, 1974.

The McDonald's hamburger magnate bought the club in 1974 for $12.5 million. Kroc created an irrevocable trust before the 1976 season, leaving 60% to his wife, Joan Kroc, 5% to general manager Ballard Smith, and 15% to McDonald's chairman Fred Miller. Another 20% went to Buzzie (15%) and Peter (5%) Bavasi. Kroc controlled the club for 10 years until his death in early 1984.

Joan Kroc/1984–1990.

"She's poisoning the world with her cheeseburgers." — Reliever Goose Gossage.

When Ray Kroc died early in 1984, his wife Joan took control. She was not particularly interested in running the club, but it was another six years before she sold out. In March 1987 she announced the sale of the club to future Mariners owner George Argyros for between $45 million and $50 million. She called off the deal two months later and then sold out in 1990. She died in 2003 of brain cancer at age 75, but left $200 million to National Public Radio and over $1 billion to the Salvation Army to build service centers around the country.

Tom Werner/1990–1994.

"San Diego Swap Meet."—Nickname given to the club when Werner began an austerity program after the 1992 season. The club cut its payroll from about $30 million to $11.4 million by trading high-priced stars such as Gary Sheffield and Fred McGriff for a number of relatively unknown players. The club was criticized for the moves, often unjustly, as they received in return such key future players as Trevor Hoffman, Andy Ashby, Brad Ausmus, Tim Worrell and Joey Hamilton.

In 1990 two groups vied for purchase of the club. The first was a San Diego–based syndicate and the other was a group headed by Tom Werner, producer of the Bill Cosby and Roseanne Barr television shows. At the time, Werner's net worth was estimated at a reported $175 million, all of which he had earned in less than eight years primarily from the two shows. The two groups, whose estimated net worth was over $500 million, combined forces and paid $75 million for the team in the summer of 1990. The Los Angeles group included Los Angeles labor law attorney Michael W. Monk, Werner's Harvard College roommate and a good friend of the author — the author's three-year-old twin girls saw their first Major League game in the owner's box at Jack Murphy Stadium and spilled drinks on an owner worth perhaps $300 million). The Los Angeles group held a 50% interest and the partnership agreement provided that the club could not be moved from San Diego without a 75% vote.

Caught in the swirling escalation of player salaries in the early 1990s, Werner attempted to tailor the club's payroll to match their typically small-market revenues. It did not work. The Werner group (including the San Diego faction) sold their controlling interest during the 1994 player strike, prompting additional unfair parting shots: "Tom Werner's reign as majority owner, filled with more errors than hits, has ended..."—*Baseball Weekly*.

John Moores/1994– .

"I believe there comes a time when we all have to look in the mirror and say, 'Hey, I'm the most ordinary person in the world, and that's OK.' I've been described as a pudgy computer nerd. I think two of three are correct."—Moores.

John Moores purchased a 90% interest in the franchise. Former Orioles executive Larry Lucchino teamed with Moores, who would later buy the remaining 10% from Werner and his partners (upon payment of a loan made by Werner and his group). Moores, age 50 at the time of the purchase, turned a $1,000 investment in 1980 in his own software company into $330 million by the mid–1990s. He has been a philanthropist in recent years, giving more than $70 million to his alma mater, the University of Houston.

Nickname. The nickname came from the long-time minor league franchise in the area. The minor league club took the name from the trail of Spanish missions along the California coast and the Catholic padres who organized and controlled them during the 18th century.

Key Seasons.

1969. The expansion Padres finished in last place with a 52–110 record in the new divisional alignment.

1984. The Padres won their first division title and then lost the first two games of the championship series to the Cubs. They won Game 4 in dramatic fashion: Steve Garvey's uniform is painted on the outfield wall where he hit a last-inning home run to set up the deciding fifth game. The Padres won to move on to the World Series, which they lost in five games to the Tigers. Tony Gwynn led the league with a .351 average and Goose Gossage saved 25 games.

1989. The club finished only three games behind division-leading San Francisco. The Padres featured Jack Clark's 26 home runs and Tony Gwynn's league-leading .336 average.

1996. The Padres swept a three-game series from the Dodgers to win the National League West title before being swept in the division play-offs by the Cardinals. Ken Caminiti had 40 home runs and 130 RBIs and Trevor Hoffman had 42 saves.

1998. The Padres won 98 games to finish first in the National League West. They beat the Astros in four games in the division play-off and then beat the Braves in five games for the pennant. The Yankees then blew them out in a four-game sweep in the World Series. Greg Vaughn had 50 home runs and 119 RBIs and Tony Gwynn batted .321. Kevin Brown won 18 games and Andy Ashby 17, while ace reliever Trevor Hoffman had 53 saves.

A highlight for this author was sitting two rows from Mark McGwire and one seat away from actor Tom Cruise while watching the deciding Game 4 of the World Series with former Padres minority owner Michael Monk.

Key Players.

Nate Colbert.

"Tradition here [in St. Louis] is Stan Musial coming into the clubhouse and making the rounds. Tradition in San Diego is Nate Colbert coming into the clubhouse and trying to sell you a used car."—Former Padres pitcher Bob Shirley.

Colbert had five seasons for the Padres between 1969 and 1974 in which he hit more than 20 home runs, including five in a doubleheader.

Dave Winfield played the first eight seasons of his career with the Padres beginning in 1973. He hit 20 or more home runs five times for the club and led the league with 118 RBIs in 1979.

Randy Jones pitched for the Padres from 1973 through 1980. After losing 22 games in 1974, he won 20 games in 1975 and peaked in 1976 with a league-leading 22 wins and 25 complete games to capture the Cy Young Award.

Tony Gwynn.

"I just wonder sometimes if people really realize and appreciate how hard it is to do what I've done, but I don't think we'll get a handle on that until I've been retired for a while and we have an opportunity to see if anyone comes along to do what I've done."—Gwynn in 1995.

Gwynn is the all-time Padre, playing for the club from 1982 through 2001 at age 41. He led the league six times in batting and approached .400 in 1994 before the player strike shut down the season. He had more than 200 hits four times and had a lifetime average of .338.

Trevor Hoffman. Traded from the Marlins to the Padres in mid–1993, Hoffman went on to record 347 saves over the next nine full seasons. He was injured in early 2003 and did not pitch again until 2004.

Key Managers.

"Padres Ex-Communicate Non-Communicator."—*The Sporting News* headline when Alvin Dark was fired after 113 games in 1977. He left with a 48–65 record and the club in fifth place.

Dick Williams.

"Dick Williams is the best manager I've ever played for ... but as soon as he gets out of baseball, I'm going to run him over with my car."—Former Padres infielder Tim Flannery.

Williams managed the club from 1982 through 1985. The Padres won their first division crown in 1984 under Williams, who led them into the World Series. He finished third in 1985 before being fired.

Bruce Bochy. After Williams, five managers spent less than three years each with the club, none finishing higher than third (with the exception of Jack McKeon's second in 1989). Bochy took over in 1995 and won a division title in 1996 before being swept by the Cardinals. He was named National League Manager of the Year that season. After a drop in 1997, he was back in 1998 with a National League pennant before being swept by the Yankees in the World Series. The club fell apart after that season, finishing no better than fourth after that through 2003. In 2004 the Padres rebounded in conjunction with their new ballpark, finishing a strong third at 87–75; they weren't eliminated from the wild card race until the last week of the season.

Ballpark.

Qualcomm/Jack Murphy Stadium.

"Qualcomm is nice, but it's not the kind of place I'll be telling my grandkids about decades from now."—Landscaper James Jenkins.

Jack Murphy Stadium was the home of the Padres from their arrival in the league in 1969 through the 2003 season. In 1971 San Diego Stadium was renamed for Murphy, a local sportswriter who figured prominently in bringing the club to San Diego. The stadium was completed in late 1967 for $27.75 million and the NFL Chargers have played in the park since it opened. It lies on 166 acres in Mission Valley, north of downtown San Diego.

Its capacity in 1969 was 50,000 but later was increased to over 59,000. The original dimensions were 330–375–420–375–330 but were reduced slightly in 1982. The last game was played in the stadium in 2003, and Petco Park opened for the 2004 season.

Jack Murphy's bust is displayed at the stadium next to that of former Padres owner Ray Kroc. A *Sports Illustrated* writer doing a feature on West Coast baseball noted "the half dollar-sized dollop of pigeon pudding on Kroc's forehead," which made him look alarmingly like former Soviet premier Mikhail Gorbachev.

When John Moores took over the club, Qualcomm paid $18 million for naming rights.

Petco Park.

"It's so nice, guys have said they feel guilty spitting in the dugout."—Manager Bruce Bochy.

Petco Park was built at a cost of $458 million on 18 acres near the San Diego waterfront and the famous downtown Gaslight district. Petco obtained the naming rights for $60 million over 22 years. Season ticket sales immediately increased from 11,000 to 20,000 in 2004, and revenue increased from $85 million to about $150 million.

The ballpark opened on April 8, 2004, with former President Jimmy Carter throwing out the first pitch along with Bud Selig. The Padres won 4–3 in 10 innings after Trevor Hoffman blew the save. David Wells, a San Diego native, pitched seven scoreless innings in front of 41,400 fans. Capacity is 42,000 and the dimensions from left to right field are 334–367–396–411–322, as the facility has emerged as a pitcher's park.

Broadcasters.

"In San Diego you have the Pacific Ocean to the West, Mexico to the South, the desert to the East, and Vin Scully to the North."—Pirates broadcaster Bob Prince on the undesirability of broadcasting for the Padres.

"Hi folks, I'm Jerry Gross."—Broadcaster Jerry Coleman, former infielder and some-time manager who broadcast for the club from 1972 through 1979, and then again from 1981 through the 2004 season. Coleman's trademark (in addition to malapropisms) is to wave a gold star when a great play is made.

Former Dodger slugger Duke Snider broadcast from 1969 through 1971.

Ted Leitner, often very funny during the dark cellar days of the club, started in 1981 and remained through the 2004 season. Rick Monday broadcast for the club between 1979 and 1982, and former players Rick Sutcliffe and Mark Grant started in 1997.

Books. Joe Naiman and David Porter, *San Diego Padres Encyclopedia* (2002); Nelson Papucci, *San Diego Padres: 1969–2002 a Complete History* (2002); Chris W. Sehnert and Paul Joseph, *San Diego Padres* (1997).

San Francisco

"For years San Franciscans have read headlines about their boys making major league history back East. JOE [DiMaggio] HITS ONE! TONY [Lazzeri] POOSHES ANOTHER! Now somebody seems to have latched onto a good idea. Why leave home to play in the big leagues? Why not do it in the back yard? San Franciscans, sophisticated and critical, but hospitable and simpatico too, will decide how they like the idea. It may be fun."—Joe King in *The San Francisco Giants* (1958).

"Some of our guys don't know what to do with the free time. I suggested they go to San Francisco. They said, 'What is there to do there?'"—A's pitcher Brian Kingman.

In 1859 the Eagle Baseball Club became the first organized club in San Francisco and played its first game on November 4. It had no formal rival until the next year when the club played the Red Rovers.

The sport languished in the Bay Area until after the Civil War when fire engine companies around the city formed clubs. This led to the formation of the Pacific Coast Baseball Convention, and the clubs capitalized on the arrival of the Cincinnati Red Stockings in 1869. The first ballpark was at 25th and Folsom, opening November 26, 1868, for a game between the Eagles and the Wide Awakes.

The San Francisco clubs were part of either the California Baseball League or the California State League in the 1880s and 1890s. San Francisco was a stalwart of the Pacific Coast League from 1903 (when the California League changed its name to the PCL) until the San Francisco Seals were abandoned in favor of the National League Giants in 1958. By 1954 the Seals were bankrupt and the Oaks had fled to Canada. The Bay Area was once home to three Pacific Coast League teams: the Seals, the Mission Reds and the Oakland Oaks.

The Bay Area was home to a number of Major League players, including Hall of Famers Joe DiMaggio, Harry Hooper, George (Highpockets) Kelly, Harry Heilmann, Joe Cronin, Chick Hafey, Tony Lazzeri, Ernie Lombardi, Lefty Gomez, Billy Martin, Frank Robinson and Joe Morgan.

Book. Dick Dobbins and Jon Twichell, *Nuggets on the Diamond: Baseball in the Bay Area from the Gold Rush to the Present* (1994).

San Francisco Giants

National League 1958–

"Giant fans are famous front-runners. Made wary over the years by the Giants' obligatory June swoon and patented furious, insufficient September rush, which have kept the team habitually in second place, the fans have stayed away from Candlestick Park in notable numbers."—Roger Angell in *The Summer Game* (1972).

McCovey Cove behind the right field wall at SBC Park in San Francisco. Note the boardwalk next to the field that has viewing portholes allowing fans to watch the game; ushers rotate out the fans every few innings.

Origins.

"That's why the pioneering push of the Giants all the way up and over the Continental Divide dumped grandpop out of the rocking chair. He thought it could never happen. The major leagues had voted a straight Eastern ticket for more than fifty years, although Geronimo, Sitting Bull, and free silver had sagged as Western issues since the Super Chief." — Joe King in *The San Francisco Giants* (1958).

Brooklyn Dodgers owner Walter O'Malley prevailed upon Giants owner Horace Stoneham to move his club to the West Coast with the Dodgers. When the Giants moved from New York to San Francisco after the 1957 season, it was the first time since 1882 that the National League did not have a franchise in New York (see also *Franchise Shifts* and *New York Giants*).

First Game.

"A sportswriter always gets wholesome satisfaction by being present when history is being made. That made attendance compulsory for the first major league game on the Pacific Coast..." — Sportswriter Arthur Daley.

On April 15, 1958, at Seals Stadium in San Francisco in front of 23,448 fans, the Giants defeated the Dodgers 8–0 in the first Major League game played on the West Coast.

Key Owners.

Horace Stoneham/1958–1976.

"The years have sped by since Horace Stoneham announced the death of the New York Giants, ordered all the old stationery thrown away, and changed the letters on the team's shirt fronts to 'San Francisco.'" — Art Rosenbaum and Bob Stevens in *The Giants of San Francisco* (1963).

"Like other owners, Horace Stoneham, who, when sober, was more than average..." — Curt Smith in *Voices of the Game* (1987).

Stoneham, son of longtime Giants owner Charles Stoneham, owned the club when he moved it from New York to San Francisco for the 1958 season. Unlike most modern owners, baseball was his sole source of income. He sold out in 1976 after mixed success in San Francisco and died in 1991 at age 86.

Robert Lurie/1976–1992.

"Bob Lurie, the visible half of the Giants, is a guy who makes Pollyanna look like a grump. He smiles a lot, talks like the ultimate optimist, and will even shake hands with sportswriters who can be critical." — Sportswriter Art Spander.

Lurie's father was colorful real estate tycoon Louis R. Lurie and one of San Francisco's best-known figures. Bob Lurie, reportedly worth $350 to $480 million from the family fortune, bought the club for $8 million in 1976 and saved it from being sold to a Toronto group. In 1976 Lurie owned 51% of the stock and Bud Herseth owned the rest. Herseth was an Arizona meat packer who bought in with a promise that the team would conduct spring training in Phoenix. That kept Lurie involved longer and avoided a sale to a Toronto group and subsequently a Florida group. Lurie first advertised the club for sale at $35 million in 1985 and finally sold in 1992 for over $100 million (see also *Franchise Shifts*). Herseth was part of the group that bought the 1998 expansion club in Phoenix.

Peter Magowan/1992– .

In late 1992 the club was finally sold to a San Francisco–based group led by Safeway supermarket magnate Peter Magowan, who had been a member of the club's board of directors for 10 years. The club's season ticket sales immediately rose by $2 million.

Magowan at present owns less than 10% of the club along with a group of Bay Area investors. A New York native, Magowan began as a Safeway grocery store manager in 1968 and became CEO in

1980 at age 37 (his father owned the company). It is estimated that he is worth $60 million.

Key Seasons.

"… the Giants, who have frequently been favored to win the pennant in their five-year residence here but have staged a series of exaggerated pratfalls, sometimes in the final week of the season."—Roger Angell in *The Summer Game* (1972).

1958. The Giants finished third in their first season in San Francisco, 12 games behind first-place Milwaukee. See Steve Bitker, *The Original San Francisco Giants: The Giants of '58* (1998).

1962. The club won its first West Coast pennant after winning a play-off against the Dodgers. Willie Mays had 141 RBIs and a league-leading 49 home runs. Jack Sanford won 24 games and Stu Miller saved 19. In the World Series against the Yankees, Willie McCovey lined out to end Game 7 with the tying and winning runs on base. See *The Giants of San Francisco*, by Art Rosenbaum and Bob Stevens (1963).

1965–1969. The Giants finished second in each of these seasons.

1971. The Giants finally broke through with a division title, winning 90 games to edge out the Dodgers by one game. Bobby Bonds led the club with 33 home runs and 102 RBIs. The Giants lost to the Pirates in four games in the NLCS.

1987. The club won the division with 90 wins as Will Clark established himself with 35 home runs and 91 RBIs. The Cardinals beat the Giants in seven games for the pennant as St. Louis pitchers threw shutouts in Games 6 and 7.

1989. San Francisco had 92 wins to edge out the Padres by three games. Kevin Mitchell led the league with 47 home runs and 125 RBIs. The Giants beat the Cubs in five games for the pennant and then were swept by the A's in a World Series that was interrupted for a full week after an *Earthquake* shattered the Bay Area.

1993. In manager Dusty Baker's first season at the helm, the club led the Western Division for most of the season before falling behind the Braves. The Giants caught up during the last week, and the clubs were tied going into the last day of the season. The Braves won while the Giants lost to the Dodgers, finishing one game out.

1997. The Giants won the National League West with a 90–72 record and then lost the first two games of the division series against the Marlins, each time in the bottom of the 9th inning. The Marlins swept the third game to bounce the Giants out of the postseason. Barry Bonds led the club with 40 home runs and he, J.T. Snow and Jeff Kent each had at least 101 RBIs. Shawn Estes led the club with 19 wins and Rod Beck had 37 saves.

2002. The Giants were the wild card team in the National League with a record of 95–66. They beat the Braves in the division series with a 3–1 victory in Game 5. In the NLCS the club beat the Cardinals in five games with two one-run victories to close out the series. The Giants were five outs from winning the World Series when the Angels rallied for five runs in Game 6 and then won Game 7. Barry Bonds had 46 home runs and 110 RBIs, and Jeff Kent had 37 home runs and 108 RBIs. Seven pitchers won between six and 14 games and Robb Nen had 43 saves.

2003. The Giants won their division by 15½ games over the Dodgers with a record of 100–61. The eventual champion Marlins beat them in the division playoffs in four games. They were led by Barry Bonds with 45 home runs and 90 RBIs. Jason Schmidt was 17–5 and Tim Worrell had 38 saves.

Key Players.

Willie Mays (HF) starred for San Francisco from 1958 until his departure for the Mets early in the 1972 season. Mays hit over .300 seven times and led the league in home runs in 1962, 1964 and 1965. He drove in more than 100 runs eight straight times for the club.

Willie McCovey (HF) is the most popular Giants player of all time. He began his career in 1959 and remained with the club through 1973. He returned in 1977 for four more seasons. He led the league in home runs three times and drove in more than 100 runs four times.

Juan Marichal (HF) was one of the best pitchers of the 1960s. He had six seasons of more than 20 wins, and he pitched 52 shutouts for the Giants between 1960 and 1973. He finished his career with 238 wins for the club.

Orlando Cepeda (HF) played slightly more than eight seasons for the Giants. He hit over .300 six times and led the league with 46 home runs in 1961.

Bobby Bonds played seven seasons for the Giants while being touted as the successor to Willie Mays. He hit over 30 home runs four times for the club though he set a Major League record with 189 strikeouts in 1970.

Barry Bonds arrived from Pittsburgh in 1993 and through 2004 had 537 of his 703 home runs, including 73 in 2001. He never hit more than 49 before or after that year.

Key Managers.

"I'm very unhappy about the Giants. I didn't think Bill Rigney knew very much, but I don't think Tom Sheehan knows anything at all."— Last words of convicted murderer Richard T. Cooper on his way to the California gas chamber in 1960.

Bill Rigney was the first manager in San Francisco, leading the club to two third-place finishes before being fired while the club was in second place in 1960 (they finished fifth).

Alvin Dark led the club for four seasons starting in 1961 and guided the Giants to their first pennant in 1962.

Herman Franks.

"Franks is famed for his obscenities when asked any question at all, as he walked around the clubhouse with a minimum of clothing covering his unlovely body."— Glenn Dickey in *The Jock Empire* (1974).

Franks led the club to four straight second-place finishes between 1965 and 1968.

Charlie Fox managed the Giants for five seasons beginning in 1970 and led the club to a division title in 1971.

Roger Craig took over the club in 1986 and led the Giants to division titles in 1987 and 1989 before being fired after the 1992 season. The Giants won the pennant in 1989 but were swept by the A's in the World Series.

Dusty Baker. Johnnie B. Baker, Jr., led the Giants for 10 years before signing with the Cubs for the 2003 season. His last year was 2002, when the club made it to Game 7 of the World Series before losing to the Angels. He led the Giants to two division titles and six second place finishes and was Manager of the Year three times.

Ballparks.

Seals Stadium. The Giants originally played in Seals Stadium, built in 1931 by Charles Graham. It was located at 16th and Bryan Streets, had a seating capacity of 18,600 (later 23,000) and dimensions from left to right field of 340–400–385.

Candlestick Park/3Com Park. *Candlestick Park* opened on April 12, 1960, and was home to the Giants through 1998. In 1995 the park was renamed 3Com Park when the new corporate sponsor paid for the name change.

PacBell Park/SBC Park. In 1996 plans were made for a new ballpark on another site in the city. China Basin is a few miles north of Candlestick in one of the warmest and sunniest areas of the city known as Fisherman's Wharf. Construction began in 1997 and it was originally thought the occupancy would be in 2000. Tight construction schedules brought it up for use in 1999.

Pacific Bell Ballpark ("PacBell") opened in 1999 with a capacity of 40,800. Although it was on the same peninsula as Candlestick Park on the east side of San Francisco, its location and configuration minimized the effect of wind and cold; making it a much more pleasant experience. It was also within walking distance of downtown San Francisco, which made it a much more attractive and accessible venue. Originally budgeted at $255 million, the new facility eventually cost $319 million. PacBell bought the naming rights for $50 million and then changed its company name to SBC, thus changing the name of the park. After selling premium boxes and permanent seat rights, along with $15 million from local government, the Giants borrowed the remaining $170 million. One proponent of the ballpark said that "it's closer to a classic urban park than any other ballfield constructed in the past 75 years."

Right field is 307 feet, but the fence juts out dramatically to 420 in right center. Portholes at the chain link fence in right field allow fans to stand and watch the game on the walkway adjacent to the bay (15 feet away). The Giants acknowledged that they can meet their $20 million annual debt service simply from the in-stadium advertising that is everywhere.

The first game was played April 11, 2000, as the Giants lost to the Dodgers 6–5 in front of 40,930 fans. The first pitch was a ball thrown by Kirk Reuter to Devon White, who singled for the first hit. The first Giants batter was Marvin Bernard, who flied out. Although light-hitting Kevin Elster of the Dodgers hit the first home run in the park in the 3rd inning (and two more in the game), Barry Bonds fittingly hit the first Giants home run, in the bottom of the same inning. Bonds' first home run into McCovey Cove (over the right field fence) was on May 1, 2000. He was the first batter to do so. It took the Giants a record six games to record their first win in the new ballpark.

Key Broadcasters.

"I don't mind hate mail, but when a letter comes to the station addressed 'Jerk, KSFO, San Francisco,' and I get it, then I start to worry."— Giants broadcaster Lon Simmons in 1978.

Home-grown Lon Simmons broadcast for the Giants from their first West Coast game in 1958 through 1978. Longtime New York Giants broadcaster **Russ Hodges** first worked the 1958 season with Simmons over a 14-station network. He stopped broadcasting for the club in 1979 and 1980 when his wife died. He then moved to the A's when KSFO had a dispute with Giants owner Bob Lurie and lost its broadcast rights. Simmons returned in 1996 and broadcast through 2002, when he retired to Hawaii at age 78. He received the Frick Award in 2004.

Al Michaels broadcast for the club between 1974 and 1976. Lindsey Nelson arrived from the Mets and broadcast from 1979 through 1981. Ron Fairly broadcast for the club from 1987 through 1992.

Hank Greenwald was the Voice of the Giants from 1979 through 1986 before departing for two years with the Yankees. He returned in 1989 and remained with the club through 1996. Jon Miller came over from the Orioles in 1997 and remained with the club through 2004.

Duane Kuiper started in the booth in 1987 and, with the exception of 1993, he remained with the club through the 2004 season. Former pitcher Mike Krukow started in 1991 and remained with the club through 2004. Second baseman Tito Fuentes broadcast in Spanish for 10 years primarily in the 1980s.

Books. Charles Einstein, *A Flag for San Francisco* (1962); Joe King, *The San Francisco Giants* (1958); Mike Mandel, *The San Francisco Giants: An Oral History* (1979); Nick Peters, *San Francisco Giants Almanac: 30 Years of Baseball by the Bay* (1988); David Pietrusza, *San Francisco Giants Baseball Team* (2002); Tom Schott and Nick Peters, *The Giants Encyclopedia* (2003); Chris W. Sehnert, *San Francisco Giants* (1997); Fred Stein, *A Century of Giants Baseball in New York and San Francisco* (1987).

Saves

"I shake hands like a demon now. I've shaked hands thirty-seven times so far this year! Walking off! That's like thirty-seven complete-game wins! But the other side of it — losing! Brutal."— Former starter and then reliever Dennis Eckersley quoted in *Baseball Lives*, by Mike Bryan (1989).

See also **Fireman of the Year** and **Relief Pitchers** (for all save statistics).

Rules.

"All of his saves have come during relief appearances."— Ralph Kiner on Steve Bedrosian.

The original save rules were first suggested by Lou Boudreau when he was a Cubs announcer. In 1959 or 1960, depending on the source, Boudreau was approached by Chicago sportswriter Jerome Holtzman to outline their vision of the rules. They received support and cooperation from J.G. Taylor Spink of *The Sporting News* in promoting the rule with Organized Baseball. The save finally became an official statistic in 1969. On April 7, 1969, against the Reds, Bill Singer of the Dodgers recorded the first official Major League save.

In 1973 Major League Baseball refined the save rules. A relief pitcher entering the game was entitled to a save if the potential tying run was on base or at the plate; or the reliever pitched at least three effective innings and in either case preserved the lead. If more than one pitcher qualified for the save, the scorer could credit the save to the most effective pitcher. It was also not mandatory to credit a save. The exception for pitchers who may not have finished a game is so infrequent that for all games before 1969, statisticians have retroactively awarded saves only to pitchers who completed games.

In 1975 the save rules were amended again, and the revisions are in effect today. A relief pitcher must finish the game and then qualify under one of three criteria: he enters the game with a lead of no more than three runs and pitches for at least one inning; he enters the game with the potential tying run either on base, at bat, or on deck; or he pitches effectively for at least three innings regardless of his team's lead.

Holds. Recent teams have instituted the "hold," an unofficial method of determining if a relief pitcher has maintained a lead even though he did not qualify for a save.

Rainout. According to Elias Sports, if a reliever is on the mound, but has not yet thrown a pitch, he will receive credit for a save (assuming a save situation) if rain forces a rainout before he throws a pitch.

Ray Schalk (1892–1970)

Hall of Fame (VC) 1955

"Schalk appeared on the Sox field towards the end of the [1912] season. His first job was to warm up Ed Walsh in pitching practice. [Walsh] sized up the youngster behind the plate and felt compassion in his soul.... It was tradition that Walsh's neck assumed a carmine tint in proportion to his physical effort. He never left the box with a more ruddy sunset above his collar than he did after that warm-up. High and low, in and out, they came, spitter, curve and straight. All looked alike to the pigmy [sic] back stop, who acted as if he was suffering from ennui." — G.W. Axelson in "*Commy*" (1919).

Schalk was considered the premier defensive catcher in the Major Leagues during the late 1910s and early 1920s.

After playing in the Illinois-Missouri League, Ray William Schalk signed with the White Sox and started his first game the day before his 20th birthday in 1912. After 23 games that season he played another 16 years with Chicago, 14 of them as the starting catcher.

Over his career Schalk set then–Major League catching records for most games and putouts and still holds the record for double plays and the American League record for assists. He is credited with innovations such as running to first base to back up the first baseman on infield throws. Though a weak hitter with a .253 lifetime average and 12 home runs, he hit for the cycle in 1922 and also hit .304 as one of the clean Black Sox of the 1919 World Series. He also caught four no-hitters, including a perfect game by Charlie Robertson in 1922.

Schalk managed the White Sox in his last two playing seasons, 1927–1928, but after refusing a pay cut to remain as a player, he moved over to the Giants as a player for the 1929 season. He managed minor league clubs from 1932 through 1940 and in 1950. He also scouted for the Cubs, but his primary occupation was bowling alley owner in Chicago. He also was an assistant baseball coach at Purdue.

Scheduling

"The guys who made up this schedule must have been in a room with a bottle of Wild Turkey and 40 straws." — Tigers infielder Dave Bergman on a schedule that had his club hopping all over the country.

See also *Game Starting Time*.

First All-Professional Team. The first all-professional team, the Cincinnati Red Stockings, barnstormed the country from April to mid–November, generally following the seasonal schedule used today.

First Professional League. The National Association of 1871–1875 did not have a formal schedule. Each team was required to play all other teams in the league in five series consisting of three games each. The team with the most wins after all the series were played was declared the winner based on best winning percentage. However, not all clubs completed the schedule each season.

The National League's First Season. In 1876 eight teams were to play 10 games against every other team for a total of 70 games each. Three games were to be played each week. Of the 280 games scheduled, 20 were never played and there were three ties. The season ran from April 22 through October 21 and games were often terminated by darkness. New York and Philadelphia were expelled from the league after failing to complete their schedules.

Uniform scheduling was maintained from 1877 on, which was important because fans would always know when future games would be played and this helped sustain fan interest and loyalty. The first year in which all scheduled National League games were played was 1878 (except rainouts).

Complete Major League Scheduling History.
National League
1876 — 8 teams to play 10 times/70 games.
1877–1878 — 6 teams to play 12 times/60 games.
1879–1883 — 8 teams to play 12 times/84 games.
1884–1885 — 8 teams to play 16 times/112 games.
1886–1887 — 8 teams to play 18 times/126 games.

1888–1891 — 8 teams to play 20 times/140 games (note: varying numbers of teams in these years)

American Association
1882 — 8 teams to play 12 times/84 games.
1883 — 8 teams to play 14 times/98 games.
1884 — 12 teams to play 10 times/110 games.
1885 — 8 teams to play 16 times/112 games.
1886–1891 — 8 teams to play 20 times/140 games. This began two years before the National League instituted the 140-game schedule in 1888.

Union Association
1884 — 8 teams to play 16 times/112 games (though the pennant-winning St. Louis Maroons managed to play 113 games).

Players League
1890 — 8 teams to play 20 times/140 games.

National League
1892 — 12 teams to play 14 times/154 games. First and second half schedules were set up for the only time in history, except for the strike-shortened 1981 season.

1893–1897 — 12 teams to play 12 times/132 games. Clubs were not drawing well, and it was decided to reduce the number of games.

1898–1899 — 12 teams to play 14 times/154 games. This was a return to the number of games in 1892 but without the split-season format.

1900 — 8 teams to play 20 times/140 games.

National League and American League
1901–1903 — 8 teams to play 20 times/140 games.

1904–1960 — 8 teams to play 22 times/154 games. This was the format for every year except the *World War I*–related years of 1918 (approximately 125 games) and 1919 (140).

Federal League
1914–1916 — 8 teams to play 22 times/154 games, the same as the National and American Leagues.

American League
1961 — 10 teams to play 18 times/162 games, reflecting the two-team expansion. The National League stayed at 154 games because it had not expanded.

National League and American League
1962–1968 — 10 teams to play 18 times/162 games. The owners briefly considered a 153-game schedule in which each team would play 17 games against every other team.

1969–1976 (and through 1992 in the National League) — 12 teams with two divisions created a 162-game schedule in which a team would play 18 games against its divisional rivals and 12 against the six teams in the other division. The National League opposed this schedule and wanted 165 games with 15 games against each of the 11 other teams. This was due in part to a number of teams not wanting to lose lucrative dates with teams that would be put into the other division (see also *Divisional Play*). The American League wanted a 156-game schedule that still would have resulted in different numbers of games being played inside and outside a division.

American League
1977–1978 — The American League expanded from 12 to 14 teams, with seven teams in each division. This created a scheduling nightmare because one team from each division always had to be playing outside its division. The American League had each team play 15 games against other teams in its division and 10 against the other seven teams. This created two extra games that had to be dispersed randomly among the teams each year (see **Swing Team**).

1979–1992 — The 1977–1978 scheduling format was abandoned

when the Western Division teams wanted more lucrative games with the Yankees and Red Sox. The American League switched to a format whereby each team played 13 games against its division rivals and 12 against the other seven clubs.

National League

1993 — In addition to working the two expansion clubs into the schedule for the 1993 season, the National League unsuccessfully attempted to realign its divisions on orders from commissioner Fay Vincent (see also *Divisional Play*). This left the league with the same dilemma faced by the American League a few years earlier: how much interdivision play should be allowed. Though Vincent's divisional plan was abandoned, the National League still had a scheduling problem caused by expansion.

The National League eventually opted for the same balance as in the American League: each club played 13 games against clubs within its division and 12 games against the other clubs. The Atlanta Braves and others favored a system that allowed 20 games against intra-division clubs and only six games against clubs outside the division.

National and American Leagues

1994, 1996 — Each league was realigned into three divisions; each 14-team league had one division with four clubs and two with five. Each club played 13 games against its division rivals and either 13 or 12 games against the other clubs in the league.

1995 — An aberration was created because of the player strike that cut into the first three weeks of the regular season. The leagues rearranged their schedules and created a 144-game schedule among the 28 franchises.

1997 — *Interleague Play* was scheduled for the first time, with a limited number of interleague games by each club.

1998 — Expanded interleague play was scheduled to accommodate the two expansion franchises in Florida and Arizona. The expected odd number of clubs in each league mandated interleague play — otherwise, one club in each league would always be idle. Matters were simplified significantly, however, when the Brewers moved from the American League to the National League to create a 16-team National League and a 14-team American League. Interleague play thus would not be required every day.

The National League played an unbalanced schedule in 1998. It included 12 games against each division rival and nine games against each team in the other two divisions.

2001 — Both leagues created an unbalanced schedule, in which teams play division rivals more often than others, for the first time since 1992 in the National League and 1976 in the American League. Division rivals were to play each other 18 or 19 times during the season.

Union. The players union must approve the schedule each season.

Bad Team. The Browns of the early 1940s were so bad that the American League reportedly made sure that all holiday games and other key games that traditionally drew large crowds would not be scheduled in St. Louis.

Canceled Games. See *Postponed Games.*

Day Games/Businessman's Specials.

"A baseball game is twice as much fun if you're seeing it on company time." — William Feather in *The Business of Life* (1968).

"Occasionally, like maybe once a season, they still played baseball on a weekday afternoon. This way, they don't have to throw the word 'hooky' out of the dictionary and baseball can still call itself family entertainment. These always seem to be the most beautiful days of summer, maybe because they are so rare." — Jane Leavy in *Squeeze Play* (1990).

"To the business or professional man nothing affords more pleasure than a ballgame. Here he can throw off all cares and troubles. He forgets to think about them in the relaxation he enjoys in the excitement of a close contest, and he goes to his home feeling all the better for the few hours spent in the air." — Jacob Morse in *Sphere and Ash* (1888, reprinted in 1984).

"Be with us for the return of the two–Martinez business lunch." — Expos publicist Richard Griffin promoting an afternoon game featuring pitchers Ramon Martinez of the Dodgers and Dennis Martinez of the Expos.

Days Off Comparison. In 1946 teams averaged about 38 days off over a 167-day season, including the All-Star break. In 1961 American League teams had approximately 32 days off over a 174-day season, based on a 162-game schedule and scheduled doubleheaders.

In 1969 teams averaged only 30 days off even though the schedule was four days longer at 178 days. Fewer scheduled doubleheaders reduced the number of days off. In 1989 teams averaged only 20 days off as scheduled doubleheaders were almost entirely eliminated.

Illustrative of the decrease in days off are the Mets. In 1969 the club had 29 days off between May and September (six per month), but in 1989 the team had only 15 days off in the same period (three per month). The reason is obvious: there were 14 scheduled doubleheaders in 1969 and none in 1989.

On Monday, June 29, 1998, there were no games scheduled. It was the first scheduled open date in the Major Leagues since April 30, 1973.

Days of the Week. The National League originally scheduled games on Tuesdays, Thursdays and Saturdays. Non-league games were scheduled on the other days but had to include league balls, league rules and league umpires. In 1878 and 1883 teams could waive these requirements (see also *Sunday Baseball*).

Delayed Schedule. Almost a week was added to the 2001 schedule in October because of the postponements caused by the September 11 terrorist attacks.

Doubleheaders. See *Doubleheaders.*

Holidays. Holiday dates are no longer a popular day for baseball games. On Memorial Day 2003, only 18 teams were scheduled for the Monday. In the past, all teams would have scheduled doubleheaders.

Interleague Play. See *Interleague Play.*

Minor Leagues/Split Season. The minor leagues generally play a split season beginning in mid–April and ending by September 1 when Major League rosters are expanded.

Night Games. In 1940 there were 70 night games scheduled. By 1946 there were 260 night games; 138 in the National League and 122 in the American League. The Cardinals and Browns led their leagues with 54 and 53 night games. In 1950 the Phillies played 55 night games. In 1961 the Red Sox played 45% of their games under lights. By 1969 more than half the club's games were under lights (75 day games and 87 night games).

In 1966 there were 1,620 games played in the Major Leagues: 861 at night and 759 during the day. By 1972 virtually all Major League non-weekend games were played at night. The exceptions were the Cubs, with no lights, a number of day games in San Francisco because of the cold, and the occasional Businessman's Special on weekdays (usually Thursdays).

In 1977 the Phillies were 71–39 in 110 night games. In 1980 they were 66–46 in night games; this number of night games was typical for most teams through the 1980s. In the 1990s the trend reversed somewhat with a few clubs as they found benefit in scheduling more day games. Though 11 teams were scheduling less than 20 games during the day, the A's scheduled 38 in one recent season: "Our attendance revival in the early 1980s can be directly traced to more day games."—A's vice-president of business operations Andy Dolich.

Pacific Coast League/Long Schedules. Late in 1910 Charles Ebbets of Brooklyn pushed for a 168-game schedule. After studying weather patterns, he suggested starting and ending the season later to avoid early-season rainouts.

In August 1946 Larry MacPhail of the Yankees advocated a 168-game season. His rationale was that the game's postwar popularity would generate more attendance, and additional revenues were needed to pay for the newly agreed-upon pension plan for the players. Red Sox owner Tom Yawkey is credited with leading the successful opposition to MacPhail's scheduling plan.

In 1904 the Pacific Coast League played 225 games and George Van Haltren had 941 at-bats. In the 1930s and 1940s the PCL routinely scheduled 198 games. The PCL usually played a 168-game schedule through the 1950s because of good weather in the region. The large number of games was conducive to a split-season schedule until 1932. That year the league decided to have a single schedule. The powerhouse Los Angeles Angels were 66–18 and led the league by 19½ games when the rest of the clubs decided to reinstate the split-season. Starting over did not help the other clubs, as the Angels were 71–32 over the second half, 12 games ahead of the nearest competition. To cut down on travel during the regular season, the PCL usually scheduled a seven-game week-long series culminating in a Sunday doubleheader, with Monday as a travel day.

Poor Planning. During the 1945 season the Senators might have made it to a play-off with the Tigers if the Tigers had lost a doubleheader on the last day of the season. The Senators had not played in a week, however, as owner Clark Griffith — never dreaming his club would be in a pennant race — rescheduled his home games that week to dates earlier in the year so that the stadium could be prepared for Redskins professional football.

The Expos suffered through a nightmare schedule in 2003, at one point crossing five time zones during one long road trip that went through Puerto Rico (see *Road Trips*).

Rivalry. In 2003 the Red Sox and Yankees played 26 times, the most ever by two clubs in a season. They broke the record of 25, held by seven other opponents, most recently the 1953 Tigers and A's.

Schedule-Makers. In the early 20th century, league executives prepared tentative schedules, which were then given to traveling secretaries to provide additional input and changes. After the 1903 merger of the National and American Leagues and the formation of the National Commission, teams still had disputes over scheduling, particularly in cities with teams from both leagues. In response, the commission set up a joint scheduling committee controlled by the two league presidents.

In 1982 scheduling was entrusted to Henry and Holly Stephenson. They used a computer for about 85% of the schedule, then completed the task by hand. Working out of their home on Staten Island, they also scheduled for the NBA and pro soccer. They were replaced after the 2004 season.

The schedule for the following season is required to be finalized by September 1 the prior year.

Various factors considered by modern schedule-makers:

1) scheduling around concerts and other conflicting events in a ballpark;

2) same-city teams in opposite leagues: New York, Chicago, San Francisco–Oakland and Los Angeles–Anaheim.

3) Basic Agreement Terms: No team can play for more than 20 consecutive days and no team can have more than two consecutive days off in a seven-day period. Teams traveling from the Pacific time zone to the Eastern time zone must have an off-day before the first game in the East. A day game cannot follow a night game unless the games are played within a 90-minute flight of each other.

4) Individual team needs: for example, the Red Sox require a home game on Patriot's Day, which is the third Monday in April and the same day as the Boston Marathon. The Twins want to be out of town when Walleye fishing season opens in May. The Orioles choose to be on the road during the Preakness horse race in May. The Mariners want to be out of town during the Water Festival. The Indians want to be home on July 4th and other clubs do not. The Blue Jays want to be home on Canadian holidays.

5) Weather: In the Stephensons' first season of scheduling baseball in 1982, on Opening Day they had two domed-stadium teams playing each other (Seattle and Minnesota) and the Angels and A's squaring off in the West. The blizzard of 1982 hit and wiped out a week's worth of games in the Eastern and Midwestern cities. The schedule-makers learned their lesson and began scheduling early-season games as much as possible in warm-weather and domed-stadium cities.

For the 1997 season, schedulers attempted to set early season games in warm weather ballparks and domed stadiums to avoid the early season postponements that dominated the 1996 season. Nevertheless, several 1997 games were postponed due to extremely cold weather.

Split-Seasons.

1892. The National League was faced with a 12-team league and the potential for a number of teams to be out of the race early on. The league responded by creating two half-seasons. Boston won the first half and Cleveland won the second half. The split season was unpopular, and the league abandoned it after that one season.

1981. The player strike forced a split-season. The Reds and Cardinals had the best records in baseball but did not win either half of the season. The Reds lost out to the Dodgers in the first half by one game and finished behind the Astros by 1½ games in the second half. The Cardinals missed by 1½ games to the Phillies in the first half and the Expos by one-half game in the second half.

Sunday Baseball. See *Sunday Baseball*.

Superstition. Old-timers supposedly disliked starting a trip on a Friday, so the schedule makers avoided this as much as possible. Even today, perhaps coincidentally, most trips begin and end on Sundays; though this is more likely because Sunday games are almost exclusively played during the day and allow for teams to make plane connections.

Swing Team. The American League had 14 teams starting in 1977, creating a scheduling problem. With the odd number of teams in the two divisions, exclusively intradivisional play could never exist at any given time. The American League dealt with this situation by having one of the seven teams in each division finish the last few weeks of the season against teams exclusively from the other division. The system was unpopular and turned into a nightmare when a division race involved a swing team; there were no opportunities for key head-to-head games with the other pennant contenders.

In 1988 the Brewers suffered with this problem, finishing the season with 22 straight games against Western Division clubs. They were never able to make up ground in head-to-head games against the other contenders and finished third, two games back. The change to a three-division format in 1994 did not end the problem for the five-team divisions.

Switching Schedules. When the Boston Braves moved to Milwaukee for the 1953 season only three weeks before it was to begin, Milwaukee took over Pittsburgh's schedule as the "western" team, and Pittsburgh took over Boston's as the new "eastern" team.

In October 1998 Major League Baseball approved a schedule swap engineered by Reds executive John Allen. He traded the Cubs a three-game series with the White Sox in exchange for a three game series against the Indians, so all four teams could play intrastate rivals in 1999 during interleague play.

Total Number of Games/Season. The 154-game schedule generated 1,232 games. The 162-game schedule when there were 20 teams (1962–1968) generated 1,620 games. The 1969–1976 total of 24 teams playing 162-game schedules totaled 1,944 games. The 26 Major League teams of 1977–1992 played 2,106 games each season. Beginning in 1993 the 28 Major League teams played 2,260 games each season. In 1998 and beyond the 30 teams played 2,430 games per season.

Unfair Treatment. The Orioles felt that their 1996 schedule was created to treat them unfairly because they had refused to field a team during the 1995 strike. The did not visit Oakland, Anaheim and Seattle consecutively, forcing them to take four round trips to the West Coast. In contrast, the Yankees only had to make two such trips.

World War I. The 1918 season ended 27 days early on September 2 by order of the Secretary of War. As a result, approximately 125 games were played by each Major League team. In 1919, anticipating poor attendance as a carry-over from the previous year (even though World War I had ended the previous November), the owners reduced the schedule to 140 games.

World War II. Wartime workers had odd shifts and many minor league games were scheduled virtually around the clock with morning, twilight, and twi-night doubleheader games (see also *Night Games—World War II Restrictions*). A number of Major League owners wanted to shorten the season to 140 games because of anticipated poor attendance, but they were voted down.

In 1943 the World Series schedule was rearranged to cut down on travel. The first three games were played in New York and the next four, if needed, were played in St. Louis. The Cardinals only won Game 2 as the Yankees won the series in five games.

Mike Schmidt (1949–)

Hall of Fame 1995

"Mike Schmidt is the best player in the National League today. There's no question about that. He honestly doesn't realize how much ability he has. All he has to do is get the most out of those abilities on a daily basis because, believe me, he can play. He can do it all and he's just starting to want to more and more."— Pete Rose in 1980.

"If you could equate the amount of time and effort put in mentally and physically into succeeding on the baseball field and measured it by the dirt on your uniform … mine would have been black."— Schmidt at his election to the Hall of Fame.

Schmidt hit 548 home runs in an 18-year career at third base for the Phillies between 1972 and 1989.

Considered the best third baseman of all time combining offense and defense, Mike Schmidt played college ball at Ohio University and was drafted by the Phillies in the second round in 1971. He made it to the Major Leagues in late 1972. In his first full season for the Phillies in 1973 he batted .196 but hit 18 home runs.

After winter ball in Puerto Rico he returned to establish himself as the premier third baseman in the game. In 1974 he hit 36

home runs and had a .546 slugging average to lead the league in both categories. He led in home runs in 1975 and 1976 to become a legitimate home run king.

Over his 18 seasons with the Phillies he led the league in home runs eight times, with a high of 48 in 1980. He also led in RBIs four times and finished his career with 548 home runs and 1,595 RBIs. His home run total is ninth all-time and he places sixth in strikeouts with 1,883.

Schmidt played in five NLCS, batting .241, and hit .220 in his two World Series — though the figure is somewhat skewed because he starred in the 1980 Series with a .381 average and two home runs. He also won three MVP Awards. He was pathetic in the 1983 Series with an .050 average — one hit in 20 at-bats.

After a serious rotator cuff injury in 1988 he retired in May 1989. Nevertheless, he was selected by the fans to start in the All-Star Game that season (though he declined to play). Schmidt retired to Florida to become a businessman and tournament golfer. In 1995 he became the 31st player elected to the Hall of Fame on the first ballot, with 96.52% of the vote. Schmidt retired after one year of managing in the minor leagues in 2004, for the Class A Clearwater club in Florida, a Phillies affiliate. He said he needed to be out earning more money.

Books. Mike Herbert, *Mike Schmidt: Baseball's King of Swing* (1983); William C. Kashatus, *Mike Schmidt* (1999); Mike Schmidt and Barbara Walder, *Always on the Offense* (1982) (mostly instructional); Jim Wright, *Mike Schmidt— Baseball's Young Lion* (1979).

Red Schoendienst (1923–)

Hall of Fame (VC) 1989

"Run everything out and be in by twelve."— Schoendienst's managerial creed.

"The supermodel's name was Uvula, a towering brunette raised on a wombat ranch in Australia…. In truth, her birthplace was Ashtabula, Ohio, and her real name was Nora Schoendienst. By sweet coincidence she was distantly related to Red himself, the great St. Louis Cardinals infielder and, later, manager. There was, I am relieved to report, no physical resemblance whatsoever."— Writer Carl Hiaasen in a fictional account for the 2003 *Sports Illustrated* swimsuit issue.

Schoendienst was an outstanding second baseman primarily for the Cardinals from 1945 through 1963 and then had a successful managerial career for the club.

Red-headed Albert Fred Schoendienst began his minor league career during World War II and was the International League MVP in 1943. He spent 1944 in the Army and played most of 1945 with the Cardinals despite shoulder and eye injuries suffered while in the military. He played 118 of his 137 games that season in the outfield.

Schoendienst became the starting second baseman for the Cardinals in 1946 and remained in that slot through the 1955 season. His best season was 1953 when he hit .342 with 15 home runs. With the exception of Jackie Robinson, he was considered the premier second baseman in the National League.

He was traded to the Giants for parts of the 1956 and 1957 seasons before moving over to the Braves to aid them in their 1957 pennant drive. He finished the season with 200 hits and helped lead them to a World Series win over the Yankees. In 1958 he again helped the Braves into the World Series, batting .300 in the postseason.

Schoendienst appeared in only five games in 1959 after contracting tuberculosis, but returned in 1960. He was traded to the Cardinals in 1961, appearing primarily as a pinch hitter. In 1962 he led the league in pinch hits while batting .301. He finished his career in 1963, batting .289 over 19 seasons with 1,834 games played at second base.

After coaching from 1962 through 1964, he took over as manager of the Cardinals in 1965 and remained on the job until 1976. He led the club to pennants in 1967 and 1968, with a World Championship in 1967. After coaching for the A's for three years starting in 1977, he returned to manage the Cardinals briefly in 1980 before moving into the St. Louis front office.

Book. Al Hirshberg, *The Man Who Fought Back: Red Schoendienst* (1961); Red Schoendienst, *The Red Schoendienst Story* (1961).

Schools

See also **Instructional Schools**.

A number of elementary and secondary schools have renamed themselves after Major League ballplayers. There are at least seven Roberto Clemente Schools in the United States and numerous more in Puerto Rico. A sampling of other namesakes: Jackie Robinson, Gil Hodges, Lou Gehrig, Steve Garvey and Walter Johnson.

Scoreboards

"The [DiamondVision] board would not be a prompter, but a mirror. The game must always be the dominant feature, with nothing else even a close second. The board will never interfere with the game or question an umpire. The board does not belong at second base. Show a replay, but be modest. Between the innings, go wild. Be a TV set. But during the game, mute yourself. It may bring the fan in the upper deck closer to the field by way of showing a close-up of the batter, but the board shouldn't be active when someone is batting at the plate. That's a sacred rule at Memorial Stadium." — Baltimore scoreboard operator Charles A. Steinberg, who ran his dental practice around Orioles games, quoted in *Baseball Lives*, by Mike Bryan (1989).

Off-Site Scoreboards. In 1905 Madison Square Garden had a mechanical scoreboard. Giants owner John Brush sometimes rented it out to let fans follow road game play-by-play fed in by Western Union. In 1908 the *Chicago Tribune* sponsored a baseball scoreboard at a local theatre.

In 1911 a 16' by 7' electronic scoreboard in Times Square in New York was connected directly to the Polo Grounds and recorded the results for a large crowd of fans. The electronic scoreboard recorded balls, strikes and outs. Innings and score were still recorded manually. The outdoor board began to disappear in the 1920s as radio began to dominate.

Ballpark Scoreboards.

"Since 1946, the Cubs have had two problems: They put too few runs on the scoreboard and the other guys put too many. So what is the new management improving? The scoreboard." — George Will of the *Washington Post*.

In 1908 George A. Baird of Chicago invented the first electronic scoreboard though such scoreboards did not appear in Major League ballparks until the 1930s.

Ted Kennedy (apparently no relation to the political Kennedy

The inner workings of the hand-operated Wrigley Field scoreboard.

family) was a well-known electronic scoreboard designer and former ballplayer who also designed and manufactured gloves.

Clubs initially were against scoreboards because they felt that they would cut into scorecard sales. The first scoreboards were hand-operated, as electronic scoreboards did not appear until the 1930s.

In 1910 the Boston teams used a new scoreboard and Shibe Park in Philadelphia had a board listing names of the players and batting order.

Most early scoreboards only had enough room to list the other three games in the league and the teams playing, with update information coming from the Western Union ticker.

Future owner Bill Veeck, Jr., is credited with supervising the construction of the Cubs' hand-operated scoreboard in 1935 while his father was an executive with the club. It was the largest hand-operated scoreboard at that time.

When the Kansas City A's remodeled their ballpark in 1955 to accommodate the transplanted franchise from Philadelphia, owner Arnold Johnson paid $100,000 to buy and install the scoreboard from old Braves Field in Boston.

By the late 1980s only the Cubs and Red Sox had manual scoreboards. In 1990 A's owner Roy Eisenhardt installed a hand-set manual scoreboard in his ballpark and The Ballpark in Texas opened in 1994 with a hand-operated scoreboard. This started a trend toward such scoreboards at new fields in the 1990s and 2000s.

Remote Control. William McCloskey built baseball's first remote control scoreboard, using it in Little League games. McCloskey also played music between innings and scored 1,327 Little League games. He often noted important events in his official scorebook, such as "game called in third inning due to Truman announced Japanese surrender."

Sportswriter. Nineteenth century sportswriter Tom Rice of the *Brooklyn Eagle* campaigned to identify lineup changes and use numbers on the scoreboard. League rules soon required that such information be disseminated and special announcers did it using megaphones.

Career Move. Commissioner Bowie Kuhn was a scoreboard operator for the Senators while growing up in Washington.

Facial. On April 26, 2004, Richie Sexson of the Diamondbacks hit a home run measuring 503 feet that smacked off the BankOne Ballpark centerfield scoreboard, which at the time bore a huge image of Sexson.

Message Board.

"Moreover, the possibilities of message board hypnosis are frightening. Imagine one flashing, 'Buy a beer, buy a beer.' You might get trampled in the aisles. Or, at the Oakland Coliseum, they may yet flash a sign, 'You will love Charlie Finley.' That's going too far." — Glenn Dickey in *The Jock Empire* (1974).

The first message board was installed by the Yankees in 1959. It was eight lines high and eight spaces wide.

In early 1996 Marge Schott ordered her club to stop flashing score updates from other games on the scoreboard during games. It was part of a cost-cutting effort by the Reds — the service that supplied the information cost $350 per month. Schott denied knowing anything about the cancellation.

Exploding Scoreboards. The earliest exploding scoreboard was built at Comiskey Park in 1960 by entrepreneurial owner Bill Veeck. He supposedly got the idea for the scoreboard from a flashing pinball that exploded at the end of a William Saroyan play, "The Time of Your Life." Veeck's scoreboard featured fireworks, aerial bombs and 30 seconds of 35 different noises. Mortars flew out of the top of the scoreboard each time a White Sox player hit a home run.

The Yankees were not fans of the new scoreboard. When Mickey Mantle hit a home run in Comiskey Park shortly after the scoreboard was installed, the Yankees lit sparklers in the dugout in celebration. Occasionally eccentric outfielder Jimmy Piersall was so irritated by the scoreboard that he threw a ball at it.

Instant Replay Boards. The first *Instant Replay* boards were installed in Yankee Stadium and Fenway Park in 1976.

Largest. The scoreboard in Toronto's SkyDome is 110 feet wide, at the time of installation in 1989 three times larger than any other in the world.

Modern Technology. Mitsubishi introduced DiamondVision to Major League Baseball at Dodger Stadium at the 1980 All-Star Game. Installed at a cost of $3 million, it was the first large-screen video display. The board had a 20,000-hour lifespan. By 1992, of the 23 video display screens in Major League ballparks, 19 were made by Japanese companies, three by Swiss companies, and one by an American company that later went out of business.

Scorecards

"You can't tell the players without a score-card." — Concessionaire Harry M. Stevens.

"… my totals indicated six singles, one homer, four walks, one hit batsman, one sacrifice bunt, four disheartened pitchers, and one bollixed scorecard." — Roger Angell in *The Summer Game* (1972), describing the Tigers' 10-run 2nd inning during Game 6 of the 1968 World Series.

"I remember one game I got five hits and stole five bases, but none of it was written down because they forgot to bring the scorebook to the game that day." — James "Cool Papa" Bell of the Negro League Homestead Grays.

See also *Concessions*, *Official Scorers* and *Scorekeepers*.

Earliest Known. There was a scorecard for the alleged first recorded game in 1846 involving the New York Knickerbockers. Possibly the earliest formal scorecard produced for a baseball game was at the October 11, 1866, game between the Brooklyn Atlantics and the Philadelphia Athletics.

Earliest Distributors. Englishman Harry M. Stevens, the "King of the Scorecard Sellers," developed an extraordinary concession empire that began simply with scorecards.

"Scorecard boys" were used in the late 1890s to deliver oversized scorecards to paying clients such as taverns and retail stores. They contained the day's scores and league standings and were posted in windows and above bars for the convenience of customers.

Ladies Day. In 1913 the Cardinals, under the ownership of the first woman owner, Helene Schuyler Britton, handed out free scorecards and flowers to women patrons to encourage their attendance.

Prizes. Lottery numbers on scorecards were

The scorecard from Mark McGwire's 62nd home run on September 8, 1998.

used as early as 1917, the prize usually being tickets to another game.

Scorekeepers

"One whose gentlemanly conduct will render him acceptable to all who are liable to make inquiries of him relative to the score of the game." — Early description of an appropriate scorekeeper.

"That play went 5–4–3 if you're scoring at home — or even if you're watching by yourself." — Keith Olberman on ESPN's "SportsCenter."

"In the days of the Knickerbocker club they tallied much in the same manner Rip Van Winkle tallied his drinks on the inn door." — The *New York Evening World* newspaper in 1923.

"Any person claiming to be a baseball fan who does not also claim to have invented the quickest, simplest and most complete method of keeping score probably is a fraud." — Thomas Boswell.

See also **Official Scorers**.

According to *The Sporting News* of June 12, 1965, the letter "K" to indicate a strikeout was first used by M. J. Kelly in 1861. See also **Strikes and Strikeouts**. Kelly was a sportswriter for the *New York Herald* and editor of the *DeWitt's Guide* for 1868. The first explanation of symbols for how to score appears to have been in the 1861 *Beadle's Dime Base-Ball Player*, edited by Henry Chadwick, in which K was used to denote strikeout. It indicates that "K" is the last letter of struck. Chadwick confirmed this in an 1868 publication.

KS designates a swinging strikeout; KC is sometimes used to identify a called third strike. The designations are sometimes simply "K" for called strike and a backward "K" for a swinging strike. "K 2–3" signifies a dropped third strike and a force out at first base on the batter.

When former slugger Ralph Kiner moved into the broadcast booth, he did not know how to score a game, so broadcaster Bob Prince taught him.

Phil Rizzuto is credited by some with the scorebook notation "WW": Wasn't Watching.

Hazardous Duty. *Sporting Life* reported in November 1902 that fan Stanton Walker was keeping score of a game in Morristown, Ohio, when he asked a companion for a knife to sharpen his pencil. Just as he grasped the knife, a foul ball flew into the stands and struck Walker's hand, forcing the blade into his heart. He died instantly.

Book. Paul Dickson, *The Joys of Keeping Score: All About Box Scores, Official Scorers, and the Fine Art of Tending a Scorecard* (1995).

Scoreless Innings

"Gamesh was seen to shed a tear only once in his career: when his seventh major league start was rained out.... Gil announced afterward that had he been able to work in his regular rotation that afternoon, he would have extended his shutout streak through those nine innings *and on to the very end of the season*. An outrageous claim, on the face of it, and yet there were those in the newsrooms, living rooms, and barrooms around this nation who believed him." — Philip Roth in the fictional *The Great American Novel* (1973).

See also **Shutouts**.

Pitching Streaks.

Walter Johnson. The Senators pitcher had a scoreless string of 55⅔ innings from the 5th inning of Opening Day on April 10, 1913, to the 4th inning of a game on May 14, 1913. He finally gave up a run to the Browns while leading 6–0. For many years he was officially credited with 56 innings.

The previous American League record of 53 innings was held by Jack Coombs of the Athletics, whose streak ended September 25, 1910 (he was 31–9 that season). When Johnson's streak began, however, it was generally thought that the record was 45 innings by White Sox pitcher Doc White in 1904.

Don Drysdale. The Dodger pitcher recorded six straight shutouts on his way to a then-record 58⅔ scoreless innings during 1968, the "Year of the Pitcher." He began the streak on May 14 with a shutout of the Cubs. It ended in the 5th inning of a 5–3 win over the Phillies on June 8, 1968. Phillies outfielder Howie Bedell hit a sacrifice fly to score Tony Taylor to end the streak [during a game attended by this author for classmate Bill Spelman's birthday party]. Drysdale retired a year later with a rotator cuff tear in his pitching shoulder.

The night that Drysdale's streak ended was the same night that Robert Kennedy was assassinated, and Kennedy had congratulated Drysdale in a speech earlier in the evening. The streak almost ended prematurely with a hit batter with the bases loaded against the Giants. In the 9th inning of a game at Candlestick Park, Giants catcher Dick Dietz was hit by a Drysdale pitch. He had told his teammates that he would try to be hit by a pitch, as long as it was not a fastball. Umpire Harry Wendelstedt ruled that Dietz had made no effort to avoid the pitch and under the rules required him to continue batting. Dietz then flied out for the second out. Jack Hiatt popped up for the last out and the streak was preserved.

Orel Hershiser.

"It's hard to gaze at the sun, or Orel Hershiser, for too long. Everybody is looking at him. But how many can see him through the blaze of his brilliance?" — Thomas Boswell in *The Heart of the Order* (1989), after Hershiser's 67 consecutive scoreless innings that included part of the 1988 postseason.

"There really is a Big Dodger in the Sky and I think he has come down and taken over Hershiser's body." — Dodger manager Tommy Lasorda after Hershiser had pitched his eighth game in 10 starts without giving up a run in 1988.

Hershiser broke Don Drysdale's record in 1988 when he recorded five shutouts on his way to a record 59 straight regular season scoreless innings. The streak began on August 30 and continued through his last start of the regular season. Like Drysdale, Hershiser was helped by an umpire's call. On a double play ground ball with a man on third, Dodger second baseman Steve Sax was upended by the runner going to second and threw wildly to first. This allowed the runner on third to score on what should have been the third out. Umpire Paul Runge ruled that the runner going to second had illegally gone out of the baseline and therefore the double play was allowed to stand and the inning ended, nullifying the run.

When it appeared that Hershiser might reach Drysdale's record, there was debate whether Drysdale's record should include the partial two-thirds of an inning. Major League Baseball finally ruled that it did not and rounded it to 58 innings. Either way, Hershiser broke the record in a game against the Padres in San Diego in his last start of the season. He pitched 10 scoreless innings to break the record by one inning. A double shutout was the only way that Hershiser could have broken the record that night, as a nine-inning complete game would have only tied him with Drysdale. He left after the 10th inning and the Dodgers eventually lost the game.

Hershiser's accomplishment is even more astounding given other pressure he was under that month. On September 15 his second son,

Jordan, was born and immediately spent the first week of his life in intensive care.

Hershiser added another eight innings to the streak against the Mets in Game 1 of the 1988 National League Championship Series. He took a 2–0 lead into the 9th inning but faltered and was replaced. The Mets went on to win 3–2 but lost the series when Hershiser pitched a shutout in Game 7 of the NLCS. Hershiser also pitched a shutout in Game 2 of the World Series against the A's and won the deciding Game 5.

By the end of 1989 Hershiser was experiencing pain in his shoulder and early in the 1990 season he underwent major reconstructive surgery. He returned to pitch in mid–1991 with moderate success for a few months but was hurt again by the end of the season. He pitched with moderate success again starting in 1992, but in 1995 he pitched well for the Indians and helped lead them into the World Series. See also Orel Hershiser and Jerry Jenkins, *Out of the Blue*, covering the Dodgers' improbable 1988 championship season and Hershiser's performance.

Greg Maddux. Maddux had the best scoreless inning streak since Orel Hershiser when he pitched 39⅓ scoreless innings in late August and early September 2000.

Postseason Play. Babe Ruth for many years held the record for scoreless postseason innings with 29⅔. His record was broken by Whitey Ford, who had 33 scoreless innings in the late 1950s. His postseason (but not World Series) record was broken by Yankees reliever Mariano Rivera, who had 33 consecutive postseason scoreless innings in the late 1990s and 2000.

Nearly Perfect. In 1968 Bob Gibson came close to perfection. His 1.12 ERA was supported by a streak of 92 innings in which he gave up only two runs. One was on a wild pitch and the other was on a full-count double that landed on the foul line.

Scoreless Innings from Start of Season. Fernando Valenzuela pitched 41 consecutive innings without giving up an earned run at the start of the 1981 season that featured Fernandomania.

Scoreless from Start of Career. George McQuillan pitched in his first Major League game for the Phillies on May 8, 1907. He did not give up any runs but still was sent back to the minor leagues. He came back up in September for parts of five more games and completed 25 innings before giving up a run. He pitched a total of 41 innings that season over five starts and one relief appearance, going 4–0 with an 0.66 ERA. He won 23 games the next season and had a career record of 85–89 over 10 years.

Minor League Record. The minor league record for consecutive scoreless innings is 78, set by Wilmington's Jack Faulkner in 1903.

Team Futility. The 1968 Cubs and 1906 A's each went 48 innings without scoring a run.

Scoreless Innings/Single Game. On September 11, 1946, the Dodgers and Reds played 19 innings of scoreless ball, the longest non-scoring tie on record. The futility might have continued except that the rules at the time prohibited the lights from being turned on. Johnny Vander Meer of the Reds pitched 15 shutout innings and struck out 14.

Scoring in Every Inning See *Runs*—Scoring in Every Inning

Scouting

"Ivory Hunters"—Early term used to describe scouts; "Ebony Hunters" was used to describe late 1940s scouts who were primarily assigned to find talent among Negro League players.

"Oh, in Hong Kong the millionaires scout all through the country. All over China. It was just like the Brooklyn Dodgers baseball team looking for ballplayers. As soon as a beautiful girl was located in any town or village their agents bought her and she was shipped in and trained and groomed and cared for."—Ernest Hemingway in *Islands In The Stream*.

"Good Field. No Hit."—Mike Gonzalez's classic succinct assessment of catcher Moe Berg. The telegrammed report was prepared in 1924 for Minneapolis Millers owner Mike Kelley and actually said "This player, she's good field, no hit."

"It wasn't possible that there was still a ballplayer—a *real* ballplayer—out there anywhere who hadn't already been discovered, inspected, and signed or rejected by Ellsworth Pippin's scientific scouting machine. Not in the jungles of Venezuela, or the dirt-road sugar-cutting towns of the Dominican Republic, or even the rice paddies of Japan. Certainly not any white kid who had gone to high school and played organized ball anywhere in the United States."—Kevin Baker in *Sometimes You See It Coming* (1993).

"The Employee pledges to maintain the confidentiality of all scouting information which he acquires hereunder, and to preserve such information for the exclusive benefit of the Club. Disclosure by the Employee of any such information to any unauthorized organization or personnel will, in addition to providing grounds for termination of this contract, subject the Employee to disciplinary action."—Clause 3(b) of the National League's Uniform Scout's Contract.

First Scout. Some sources report that the first scout was Harry Wright, who traveled to California to scout for the Athletics. He found Jim Fogarty and Tom Brown, who later became Major League stars.

Early "Scouting."

"Old-time ball players, watching sandlot games in their communities, would contact their favorite clubs with a tip on a likely prospect. Bartenders and grocers vied with school teachers and bankers in combing the countryside. All wanted to find that young man who could either 'hit the ball a country mile' or 'knock a squirrel from a tree with a stone three times out of five, at twenty paces.'"—Ford Frick in *Games, Asterisks and People* (1973).

Before scouting became more organized, many clubs learned of prospects through letters from interested fans or players themselves. In the 19th century scouts and managers frequently held open try-outs. For example, Giants team captain John Montgomery Ward often held morning tryouts before the regular afternoon game.

In the late 19th century *The Sporting News* allowed advertisements for clubs and player services, and Albert Spalding started a Baseball Bureau in Chicago, New York and Denver to assist players in finding jobs.

There were no full-time Major League scouts until 1909, so the normal practice prior to that was for players to be signed by local clubs and be seen by other baseball people. Most teams had commissioned "bird dogs" who sent information to clubs hoping that a club would sign one of their "finds." John McGraw is said to have had the most extensive network of bird dogs and others who provided him with player information.

Branch Rickey predicted incorrectly in 1937 that the modern farm system would put an end to scouting as a means of locating talent. The greatest blow suffered by scouts was the advent of the amateur draft in 1965; in part because scouts could no longer sign talent on the spot.

Umpires As Scouts. Pitcher Eppa Rixey signed early in the 20th century on the recommendation of Cy Rigler, prompting other clubs to join together in an effort to ban scouting by umpires.

First Full-Time Scouts.

"I've been combing the baseball bushes for forty years — forty years of rotten meals in hick hotels; of making connections at three o'clock in the morning for Moose Jaw or Cowtail, or missing them and sleeping in the station; of thinking up good rejoinders when the club president wires and asks if your brains are made of mush because you recommended a fellow that looked good in his home town." — Larry Sutton of the Dodgers, who may have been the first full-time scout. He discovered 11 of the Dodgers who later played on the 1916 pennant-winning club. He is credited with discovering Dazzy Vance, Jimmy Ring, Jake Daubert, Howard Ehmke, Zack Wheat, Nick Altrock, Casey Stengel and Hy Myers.

Another early scout was Charlie Barrett with the Cardinals, who was once described by Cardinals executive Branch Rickey as able to "assay the gold content in a handful of ore." Barrett is credited as instrumental in expanding and perfecting the Cardinals' farm system. Bob Connery was a long-time scout for the Yankees after discovering Rogers Hornsby in 1915 for the Cardinals.

Paul Krichell was one of the all-time greats, working for the Yankees from 1920 until 1957. He is credited with signing Lou Gehrig for the Yankees. He even put Gehrig's coach, Andy Coakley, on the Yankee payroll as a commissioned scout to encourage Coakley to talk Gehrig into signing with the Yankees. Krichell also signed Tony Lazzeri, Red Rolfe, Charlie Keller, Mark Koenig, Phil Rizzuto and Whitey Ford. Notwithstanding all these greats, Krichell's highlight was witnessing a long home run by Gehrig as a college player in 1922: "I knew then that I'd never have another moment like it the rest of my life."

Note that a few sources have confused Krichell's contribution with that of Tom Greenwade, who discovered Mickey Mantle. Greenwade worked closely with Branch Rickey of the Dodgers in evaluating Negro League talent such as Jackie Robinson. He had pursued both Robinson and Roy Campanella before the Yankees hired him in 1948. He signed Elston Howard and then Mantle, his crowning achievement: "Then I looked again at Mickey, and he pulled a line-shot to left for a double, and it all came together. Finally I could see that seventeen-year-old body, how it worked like a damn baseball *machine*, and how it was gonna fill out. I understood how he'd been blessed. And I was blessed too."

One of the first full-time scouts was "Sinister" Dick Kinsella, who was signed by the Giants. His greatest discovery was Carl Hubbell, whom he saw while taking a break as a delegate to the 1928 Democratic National Convention.

Joe Devine scouted for the Pirates (signing Joe Cronin and the Waner brothers) before scouting for the Yankees from 1931 through 1951. He is credited with signing Joe DiMaggio and over 20 other Major Leaguers.

Another early scout was Cy Slapnicka of the Indians, who later became general manager of the club. He is credited with signing Bob Feller and later was instrumental in signing Herb Score.

It is commonly reported that scout Don Curtis discovered Dizzy Dean, but apparently Dean was first discovered by a train conductor who wrote to Branch Rickey of the Cardinals. Rickey then sent Curtis to scout him.

A salesman tipped Pittsburgh owner Barney Dreyfuss about Walter Johnson, but Dreyfuss concluded that the hype was so great that Johnson could not be nearly as good as advertised, and Dreyfuss refused to send any bonus money. Johnson then signed with the Senators.

World War II. Most clubs fired their scouts to save money during World War II, as virtually all players worth scouting were in the military. The Dodgers and Cardinals were among the few clubs that did not make wholesale cuts in their scouting corps. This foresight was reflected in the two teams' success immediately following World War II.

Postwar Scouts. Joe Cambria was a famous Senators scout, mining talent in Cuba. He signed over 400 players in 10 years and was instrumental in bringing Pedro Ramos, Camilo Pascual and Zoilo Versalles to the Senators. He twice rejected Fidel Castro at tryout camps and became such a fixture in Cuba that a cigar was named after him (Papa Joe). He had previously signed Early Wynn, Mickey Vernon and Eddie Yost.

Negro League star Judy Johnson scouted for the A's after World War II but was unable to persuade Connie Mack to sign future stars such as Henry Aaron. He later moved to the Phillies and helped sign Richie (Dick) Allen for $60,000.

Joe Mathes, "The Old Hustler," scouted for the Cardinals from 1936 through 1958 and 1964 through 1976, with stints in between for the Tigers, Mets and Giants. He is most well known for recommending the conversion of Stan Musial from pitcher to outfielder (see also *Players Who Switched Positions*).

Clyde King of the Yankees developed a reputation as a super-scout, as did Jim Russo of the Orioles and Howie Haak of the Pirates in the 1960s. Haak scouted from 1943 until 1979 when he ended the incessant travel that marks the life of a scout. Haak cultivated the Caribbean after general manager Branch Rickey signed Roberto Clemente out of the Dodger organization. Clemente had originally been discovered and signed by future Dodger general manager Al Campanis, who also signed Sandy Koufax.

By 1990 Phillies scout Tony Lucadello had signed 49 players who eventually made it to the Major Leagues. That number was believed to be a record for one scout. His most famous signee is Mike Schmidt, though he also signed Ferguson Jenkins and reliever Mike Marshall.

1960s Scouting Systems. By the 1960s each club had at least 20 full-time scouts, as well as a network of part-time and commission scouts who were paid only if one of their players signed.

Major League Scouting Bureau. This scouting combine was formed in late 1974 to provide player information to a number of subscribing Major League clubs. Originally only 17 clubs who put up $120,000 each were part of the combine. By 1981 there were 65 scouts in the combine and by the 1990s each club was contributing $170,000 to the bureau. In 1993 after 19 years, the Bureau cut 55 scouts, about 50% of its staff, to avoid increased contributions from each club.

Number Used/Salaries. The average scouting salary in 1985 was $23,000. By the 1990s most clubs employed between 15 and 20 scouts.

Modern Scouting Technique. Today's scouting is not so much discovering talent, but making the most accurate assessment of talent of which everyone is already aware. Every player is under a microscope in both high school and college, and very few talented players escape notice. The trick is to predict who has reached his potential and who has not.

Advance Scouts. Some sources attribute the first advance scouts to the Yankees in the 1950s under Casey Stengel.

Hall of Fame.

"A scout knows he has retired when they throw dirt on his face." — Scout Gary Johnson of the Royals.

There are no scouts in the Hall of Fame. In the 1990s the Hall polled 30 executives to recognize six prominent scouts at a special exhibit. Six more scouts would be recognized every few years, but there were no plans to induct any scouts into the Hall of Fame.

Long-time player, manager and scout Bobby Mattick is in the

Canadian Baseball Hall of Fame because of his contributions to Canadian baseball. He played for the Reds and Cubs and later managed the Blue Jays before going into the club's front office, where he remained through age 87. He was inducted in 1999 at age 83, and is credited with discovering Major League players Frank Robinson, Curt Flood, Vada Pinson, Rusty Staub, Don Baylor, Tommy Harper, Bobby Grich and Dave Stieb.

Assistance. The Professional Baseball Scouts Foundation raises money to help down-and-out former scouts.

Criteria. Scouts look for five key factors: the abilities to run, throw, field, hit, and hit with power.

Books. Charles Chapman and Henry Severeid, *Play Ball* (1941), includes a summary of what scouts looked for and how contracts were prepared and signed; David V. Hanneman, *Diamond in the Rough* (1989), about legendary scout Tony Lucadello; Stan Hart, *Scouting Reports* (1995), contains the actual scouting reports on many Major League players; Kevin Kerrane, *Dollar Sign on the Muscle* (1984), is an in-depth look at scouting; Mark Winegardner, *Prophet of the Sandlot* (1990), is a look at the life of a scout.

Screens

"The proximity of the short left-field fence to home plate left me open-mouthed. So I couldn't wait to see the reactions of the ballplayers themselves to O'Malley's Alley and the new sport which was immediately dubbed 'Screeno.'" — Sportswriter Tim Cohane on the Los Angeles Coliseum's short left field screen (250 feet away, as opposed to the cavernous right field fence that followed the football field's length, at an unreachable 440 feet.

See also *Batting Practice*.

The first safety screen in any section of a ballpark was put up in 1879 by the Providence Grays. The area screened off was referred to as the "slaughter pen."

According to one source, the first protective screen behind home plate was installed at Fenway Park. The screen over the Green Monster in left field was installed in 1936, to cut down on the balls flying out of the park and hitting Landsdown Street.

In the 1950s the Yankees installed a green screen in center field. The screen was raised to make hitting easier for the Yankees on days when the Yankee pitcher was not particularly effective; it was lowered when a strong Yankee pitcher was on the mound.

Riverfront Stadium in Cincinnati was to be built with a plexiglass screen behind home plate. However, general manager Bob Howsam rejected the plan after seeing how it blocked out the sound of the game at San Francisco's Seals Stadium.

Screwballs

"It was a cross between a changeup and a screwball. It was a screw-up." — Cubs pitcher Bob Patterson.

"It kills my arm; so I save it for the pinches." — Christy Mathewson, who called the screwball his "reserve pitch" and threw it only 10–12 times each game (although other generally reliable sources report that he threw it three of every five pitches).

The screwball was first known as the fadeaway. Charlie Sweeney is known to have thrown it as early as 1880 even though future Senators owner Clark Griffith claimed in the 1930s to have thrown it first in 1891 when he developed a sore arm.

Some sources attribute its first use to Christy Mathewson. He supposedly "invented" the pitch in 1908 during an exhibition game in Columbus, Ohio, calling it a "dry spitter." Mathewson did not invent the pitch, but he had it in his repertoire as early as 1905. He was taught the pitch by Ned Garvin of the Dodgers, a mediocre Major League pitcher at the turn of the century. It could be said that Mathewson was the first pitcher to really master its delivery and be effective with it in the Major Leagues.

Negro League pitcher Rube Foster was a 20th-century screwball star who taught the pitch to selected white players, and some say he taught Mathewson the pitch. It is known that he worked with Mathewson.

Only Carl Hubbell and Fernando Valenzuela had long-term success throwing the pitch regularly. Hubbell discovered the screwball in 1925 while in spring training with an Oklahoma City minor league club. He was trying to develop a sidearm sinker but found that if he put pressure on the ball with his middle finger and turned his wrist inward, it would break like a screwball. He used three different speeds and also used it as a change-up. The pitch had a devastating effect on Hubbell's arm, which was twisted grotesquely inward. Nevertheless, Hubbell won 253 games in 16 years, including five straight 20-win seasons in the 1930s.

Hubbell said that Valenzuela's screwball was the best he had seen in 40 years because he threw it with an overhand motion, like his fastball. Valenzuela burst into the Major Leagues in 1981 after a 2–0 record late in the 1980 season. He immediately generated a phenomenon known as Fernandomania and won the Rookie of the Year and Cy Young Awards with a 13–7 record and eight shutouts during the strike-shortened season. Valenzuela burned out with the Dodgers by the end of the 1980s. He made a few attempts to return to the Major Leagues and then pitched in the Mexican Leagues. He reappeared with the Orioles and Phillies in 1994 and the Padres from 1995 through 1997.

As Warren Spahn got older and needed another pitch, he learned to throw the screwball.

Vin Scully (1927–)

Hall of Fame (Frick Award) 1982

"After even a brief wisp of Scully, my first thought was that hearing him exceeded being at the game." — Curt Smith in *Voices of the Game* (1987).

Referred to in print as "Vince" as late as 1971, Scully played some center field and varsity basketball for Fordham University in the late 1940s, but his fame came in the broadcast booth. He joined Red Barber and the Dodgers at age 22 in 1950 and was the club's number one announcer by 1954. He became enormously popular when the club moved to Los Angeles; when the club announced a fan vote in 1976 of the Most Memorable Dodger personality, Scully was the choice.

Scully is renowned for *not* being a "homer," never referring to the club as the collective "we," in contrast to such renowned cheerleaders as Harry Caray of the Cubs. Scully joined CBS part-time in 1975 for a few seasons and worked a few less weekend games for the Dodgers. In 1983 he returned to working national baseball broadcasts for the NBC "Game of the Week," though his primary affiliation has always been with the Dodgers. He continued with the club through the 2004 season.

Sculpture   See *Statues and Sculpture*

Season Tickets   See *Tickets*

Seasons

"[Baseball] breaks your heart. It is designed to break your heart. The game begins in the spring, when everything else begins again, and it blossoms in the summer, filling the afternoons and evenings, and then as soon as the chill rains come, it stops and leaves you to face the fall alone."—A. Bartlett Giamatti in his essay, "The Green Fields of the Mind," appearing in the *Yale Alumni Review* (1977).

"Carl Summer, Jack Spring, Jerry Augustine, June Barnes, Dave May, June Green, George Winter, Matt Winters"

A full season is calculated to be 172 days for purposes of determining cut-offs for players' eligibility for pension benefits and arbitration.

Seating Capacity See *Ballparks*

Seats

"Our marketing department's exhaustive research has concluded that our low attendance figures may be due in large part to uncomfortable seating. Please remember to fold the seat down. Thank you."—The Pirates' tongue-in-cheek advertising during their dismal 1995 season.

"If the [Fenway Park] bleacherites weren't the most knowledgeable fans, they were close to it, and they were certainly the most faithful. I suspect I was exposed to more genuine baseball lore, more understandings of the subtleties and stratagems of the game, and perhaps most importantly, more sheer love for the sport by sitting exclusively in the bleachers from boyhood through my early twenties than I've encountered in any reserved seat press box since."—George Kimball in "Opening Day at Fenway" (1973).

Theatre-type seats made of cast-iron, aluminum or plastic are the seats of choice in modern ballparks. The American Seating Company, in business since the 1920s, is the primary supplier of seats to Major League ballparks. A seat costs approximately $70-$80 installed.

In the mid–1970s the Red Sox still allowed standing-room-only crowds at Fenway Park, a practice discontinued when the fire marshal outlawed it. The extra fans had raised capacity to 47,000 from approximately 34,000. St. Louis has had standing room only for several years.

Memorabilia. In 1973 seats from refurbished Yankee Stadium sold for $7.50 and five empty boxes of Winston cigarettes. In 1987 the Tigers sold their original seats for $5 and in 1988 the Cubs sold many of their original seats for $15. Two years later, the White Sox sold Comiskey Park seats for $250 each.

Lawsuit. In February 2003, former Reds owner Marge Schott sued the club over what she believed were inferior seats at the club's new ballpark. She contended that she was entitled to premium seats as part of her 1999 sale of the club. She had use of 21 seats in the first two rows of a private box at Cinergy Field. The new deal provided her with somewhat less desirable seats, but the club said it was reasonable given her 1/13th ownership interest in the club at the time she sold. The case eventually settled.

Protection. The Red Sox occasionally closed off a few rows of seats nearest to Ted Williams, so that he would not have to hear as much abuse from the fans.

Bleacher Bum. In April 1996 actor Charlie Sheen bought 5,000 bleacher seats in Anaheim Stadium and sat there with two of his friends—guaranteeing that he would catch a home run ball—except that no balls were hit to the bleachers that night.

Dodger broadcaster Vin Scully (left) receives the 1960 Eveready Broadcaster of the Year Award from the Southern California Broadcasters Association. Presenting the award is Robert M. Light, the Association president and father of the author.

Seattle

"My feeling is that Seattle is the kind of cosmopolitan city that may never be good for baseball. People *are* interested in cultural events. They're interested in boating. They're interested in a great variety of outdoor sports. I don't think they're very interested in sitting and watching a baseball game. I guess to really like baseball as a fan you've got to have some Richard Nixon in you."—Jim Bouton in *Ball Four* (1970).

The first professional team in Seattle was formed in 1890. The Seattle Reds played in the Class A Pacific Northwest League in 1901 and 1902. Seattle was a charter member of the Pacific Coast League in 1903. The Pacific Coast League folded the next season and Seattle was independent from the PCL between 1906 and 1917, playing in the Northwest League. Seattle rejoined the PCL in 1919 as the Indians and remained in the league through 1968.

Public approval for a ballpark was obtained in 1967, paving the way for Major League expansion with the Pilots in 1969 for one ill-fated season, after which the club moved to Milwaukee. Seattle had an entry in the Class A Northwest League between 1972 and 1976, before the Mariners arrived in 1977.

Seattle Mariners

American League 1977–

"What a place to start from.... Here I was in Seattle, the city of April showers throughout the year, of empty seats at baseball games, of Seahawk fans in a Seahawk town, about to drop their second baseball franchise in 20 years, due at least in part to that hideous concrete monstrosity — the Kingdome. At least things would only get better." — Bob Wood beginning his trek across America to every Major League ballpark, in his book *Dodger Dogs to Fenway Franks* (1988).

Origins. Seattle experienced what passed for Major League Baseball with the Pilots in 1969. After the club left town, the city filed a $90 million lawsuit against Major League Baseball trying to force it to award the city another franchise. As a result, the Mariners *Expansion* franchise was awarded to Seattle for the 1977 season.

First Game. On April 6, 1977, Angels pitcher Frank Tanana shut out the Mariners 7–0 in Seattle. Diego Segui was the losing pitcher. Senator Henry "Scoop" Jackson threw out the first ball, as he did when the Pilots played their first home game in 1969.

Key Owners.

Les Smith and Danny Kaye, et. al/1977–1981.

"The Baseball Dream of Walter Mitty" — Headline in the *Christian Science Monitor* referring to the purchase by entertainer Danny Kaye; Kaye had played Walter Mitty in the movies and was one of the original seven equal partners in the Mariners. He had tried to buy the White Sox and considered the Giants before buying into the Mariners. The managing partner was Smith, who owned radio stations and other interests in the Northwest with Kaye.

George Argyros/1981–1989.

"We purchased this club because we think it holds out great promise for the future. We think it won't be long before we have a contender — that's our aim. We want to make Seattle a showcase for Major League Baseball, not only for the Mariners, but also for great teams like the Yankees, Red Sox, Royals and Angels." — Argyros.

"George Argyros is a mighty schmuck ... he traded Jeffrey Leonard for a pregnant gnome." — Lyrics from a 1989 song parody about the ineffective Mariners owner. The song was played repeatedly by a local radio station, prompting the club to pull several thousand dollars of advertising.

Although successful as a Southern California real estate and airline entrepreneur, Argyros failed miserably as a baseball owner. Argyros (pronounced ARR-jurr-iss) bought a controlling interest in the club in January 1981. Four of the original Mariners owners remained as minority owners at 5% each: Stan Golub, Walter Schoenberg, Les Smith and Danny Kaye. Argyros turned down a $37 million offer in 1987, but in 1989 he sold out to Jeff Smulyan for $76 million, making about $40 million in the deal.

Jeff Smulyan/1989–1992. Under Smulyan the team enjoyed some minor success, finishing over .500 for the first time and developing superstar Ken Griffey, Jr. Nevertheless, the club had perennial financial problems because it operated in such a small market. Its payroll went from $8 million in 1989 to $17 million in 1991, and the club's gross revenue was lower than the payroll of three other clubs.

Though Smulyan lived in Indianapolis, he made it to every Mariners home game in 1991. He lost $10 million that year and was looking to sell the club, which he did in 1992.

Nintendo/1992– .

"I don't think I would change my statement because what I said was there is a policy or set of principles, and in light of those principles, it would be my judgment that a transaction of a sort which has been presented would not be approved." — Commissioner Fay Vincent, who reversed his doublespeak a few weeks later and spoke favorably of Japanese ownership of a Major League club.

"I don't see why we don't get them in. The Japanese aren't any dumber than we are." — Astros owner John McMullen on all the fuss over Nintendo's majority-interest purchase of the Mariners.

"It was an absolute miracle when Mr. Yamauchi came in at the 11th hour to help keep the club in Seattle, but I don't know where the next Santa Claus is." — Mariners chairman John Ellis.

In 1991 Nintendo president Hiroshi Yamauchi offered to finance $75 million of the $125 million needed to buy the club. The company had a strong local presence in Seattle, but there was initial opposition to foreign ownership of clubs. There was precedent for Japanese ownership of American ballclubs, however, as the Suntory Distillery of Japan bought the Birmingham Barons in 1990. Japanese owners also controlled minor league clubs in Salinas, Vancouver and Visalia. The first game that Yamauchi saw the Mariners play was on Opening Day, March 25, 2004, when he was 75. Of course, the game was played in the Tokyo Dome.

Jeff Smulyen had paid $76 million for the club in 1989 and was to receive $106 million for his interest, with the balance of the $125 million purchase price going to club operations. The sale was finally approved by Major League owners on June 11, 1992, on a 25–1 vote. Only Indians co-owner Richard Jacobs objected. Nintendo put up $75 million of the $125 million price but agreed to own less than 50% of the voting stock.

Nintendo explained that it felt a civic duty to invest in the club and profit motive was not the most important factor. That was a good thing, considering that the small-market club lost $12 million in 1992 and averaged only 21,000 fans per game. The franchise lost at least $67 million from the time the new owners took over in 1992 through 1995.

Key Seasons.

"The Seattle Mariners tried a novel promotional gimmick Saturday night — winning." — E.M. Swift in *Sports Illustrated*.

"Seattle has a pitcher named [J.J.] Putz, appropriate considering the kind of season the Mariners are having." — Bud Geracie of the *San Jose Mercury News*.

1977. The Mariners finished with a 64–98 record in their first season, one-half game ahead of the last-place A's.

1991. The only year until 1995 that approximated a "key season" for the Mariners is the year they first finished over .500. Manager Jim Lefebvre led the club to an 83–79 record behind Randy Johnson's 13 victories, Jay Buhner's 27 home runs and Ken Griffey, Jr.'s 22 home runs, 100 RBIs and .327 average.

1995. The Mariners were down 13 games to the Angels on August 4 but rallied to tie on September 20 and the clubs finished in a dead heat. The Mariners won the one-game play-off behind Randy Johnson and then beat the Yankees in the division play-off. They lost to the Indians in the ALCS. Jay Buhner hit 40 home runs, Edgar Martinez hit .356 with 29 home runs and Randy Johnson was 18–2 and won the Cy Young Award.

1997. The Mariners won the American League West after taking over first place in June. They finished with a 90–72 record and then lost the division series to the Orioles in four games. Ken Griffey, Jr., was the American League MVP with 56 home runs and 147 RBIs. Jay Buhner had 40 home runs and 109 RBIs. Jeff Fassero (16 wins), Jamie Moyer (17) and Randy Johnson (20) led the pitching staff.

Key Players.

Alvin Davis played eight seasons for the Mariners starting in 1984. He hit over 20 home runs three times for the club and drove in 100 or more runs twice.

Ken Griffey, Jr., began with the Mariners in 1989 and emerged as a superstar. He hit 398 home runs for the club, peaking with 56 homes in both 1997 and 1998. He batted over .300 and was named to Major League Baseball's All-Century Team. He left after the 1999 season, landing in Cincinnati where a series of injuries plagued him.

Randy Johnson emerged as the leading pitcher in the American League by the mid–1990s after moving to the Mariners in mid–1989. He was 19–8 in 1993, 13–6 in strike-shortened 1994 and 18–2 in 1995. He peaked in 1997 with a 20–4 record and 2.28 ERA before leaving for the Astros in mid–1998.

Jay Buhner joined the Mariners in 1989 and was a steady home run hitter until he exploded with 40 home runs and 121 RBIs in 1995. He hit another 84 over the next two seasons before injuries slowed him. He finished his career in 2001 with 310 home runs and 965 RBIs.

Edgar Martinez began with the Mariners in 1987, batting over .300 in each of his six full seasons with the club. He was the American League batting champion in 1992 with a .343 average and finally retired after the 2004 season. He finished his career with 2,242 hits, 309 home runs and 1,259 RBIs.

Ichiro Suzuki, known simply as Ichiro, joined the club from Japan, where he was a perennial All-Star. In his first season he was the American League Rookie of the Year and the MVP. He averaged .339 and scored 450 runs over his first four seasons with the Mariners and set a new Major League season record with 262 hits in 2004.

Key Manager.

"Being named manager of the Seattle Mariners is like becoming head chef at McDonald's."—Columnist Charles Bricker.

Lou Piniella.

"I was glad to see him get the Devil Rays job … because he wanted the Mets job."—Jeff Cirillo, Mariners third baseman, on former Mariners skipper Lou Piniella.

Piniella was the first successful manager of the Mariners. He joined the club in 1993 and led it to its second winning season in history. After fading in 1994, the Mariners were 79–66 in 1995 and won the American League West title in a play-off over the Angels. The club finished first in 1997 and 2001, but couldn't make it into the World Series. Piniella was Manager of the Year in 1995 and 2001, and then left the Mariners after the 2002 season (finishing third in his farewell season).

Ballpark.

Kingdome.

"I would apologize to an Edsel. We have a building here that was never well designed, that was never well built and was poorly maintained from day one. Plus, it's downright homely. It was outdated at the time it was built."—Mariners club president Ken Behring after calling the Kingdome an Edsel.

The Seattle Kingdome was built primarily for football for the 1977 season at a cost of $60 million. It took 16 hours to convert the ballpark from a baseball facility to football. Other names considered for the Kingdome: Aquadome, Majordomo, Sports Port, Fan Colony, Crowd Capsule and Seattle Sports Support System.

The indoor ballpark was called the ugliest in the Major Leagues and had serious structural problems in 1994 when tiles fell from the roof and forced its closure for the remainder of the strike-shortened season (see also ***Indoor Ballparks***).

The Kingdome seated approximately 58,000, and its original dimensions from left to right field were 315–375–405–375–315. These dimensions were reduced slightly over the years.

The last game at the Kingdome was played on Sunday, June 27, 1999, and Ken Griffey, Jr., fittingly hit the last home run there. Safeco Field opened on July 15 after the All-Star break.

The 110,000-ton Kingdome was leveled on March 26, 2000, but not before over 70,000 tons of the facility were removed first. It was to be replaced with a football field for the Seahawks.

Safeco Field.

"In lieu of flowers, a 'Yes' vote on the new baseball stadium would be appreciated."—Obituary of Mariners fan Thomas E. Fallihee. In 1995 voters barely approved $325 million for a stadium aimed at keeping the ballclub in Seattle.

"Citizens for More Important Things"—Name of the group opposing the new ballpark in Seattle.

In 1995 a $325 million financing package was approved for a new ballpark. It was to be called New Century Park and seat 45,960, with a soft retractable roof on two 450-foot tracks. The club later sold the naming rights to Safeco for $40 million over 20 years, even though the Mariners didn't own those rights—the ballpark is owned by a government agency. The referendum approving public financing was narrowly defeated 50.1% to 49.9% in early September, but late in the season the Mariners caught fire and caught the Angels and the public's imagination, then beat the Yankees in a five-game play-off. After a special legislative session called for by the governor, they were able to hammer out a financing plan.

Safeco Field was dedicated on July 15, 1999, six months late after a cost of $517 million—more than $232 million over the original budget. One commentator noted that, at that price, the club now couldn't afford a pitching staff. Some seats are farther from the action than in the Kingdome. The Mariners keep all revenue from luxury boxes, advertising, parking and non-baseball events; good thing, as they are responsible for approximately $100 million of the overrun.

In the first game at Safeco, the Padres scored two runs in the 9th for a 3–2 win in front of a sellout crowd of 44,607.

Key Broadcasters. Dave Niehaus was the first Seattle Mariners play-by-play announcer, arriving from Anaheim and the Angels. He was still at the helm in 2004, having missed only 70 games since he began. He has been nominated for the Frick Award and was named one of the *Seattle Times'* 10 most influential people of the century in Seattle. He is also a member of the club's Hall of Fame.

Ron Fairly broadcast for the club beginning in 1993 and was still going in 2004. Rick Rizzs started on television with the club in 1983 and then left after the 1991 season to broadcast for the Tigers for three years. He returned in 1995 and was still with the club in 2004. Other former players who have broadcast for the club include Bill Freehan (1980), Wes Stock (1982–193), Nelson Briles (1984–1985), Ken Brett (1986), Dave Henderson (1998–), Dave Valle (1998–), Tom Paciorek (2001), Jay Buhner (2002–) and Julio Cruz (2003– Spanish).

Books. Paul Joseph, *Seattle Mariners* (1997); Art Thiel, *Out of Left Field: How the Mariners Made Baseball Fly in Seattle* (2003).

Seattle Pilots

American League 1969

"We'd lose nine out of seven [sic] on mental errors, physical errors, and just plain old lack of ability, and [manager] Joe Schultz would call a team meeting to chew us out. He'd holler for a while and then he'd look around the room at all those forlorn faces belonging to nobody and you could see him start to feel sorry for us. He wanted to motivate us, but he didn't want to break our spirit. So at the end of his lecture—or maybe you'd call it harangue—he'd pause, then finish with 'Aww, shitfuck, we're not that bad. What the hell, we're as good as anybody. Fuckshit, we're better than anybody.'"—Jim Bouton in "*I Managed Good, But Boy Did They Play Bad,*" with Neil Offen (1973), quoting manager Joe Schultz, whom Bouton reports said "shitfuck" 211 times during the 1969 season. Schultz was nicknamed "Ol' Shitfuck" by the Tiger players, for whom he coached later in his career.

Origins. Seattle was awarded an American League franchise for the 1969 season for a $6 million franchise fee. See also *Expansion*.

Owners. The president of the Pilots was the former president of the Pacific Coast League, Dewey Soriano. The owner of the club was Pacific Northwest Sports, Inc., a group Soriano headed. Soriano and his family owned about 30% of the stock. William R. Daley, former chairman of the Indians, owned 25% of the club and was chairman of the Pilots' board of directors. His brother Max was also active with the club. Eventually the Daley brothers owned 47% of the stock and two other Cleveland investors had ownership interests that brought the Cleveland interest to over 60%. The balance of the shares was owned by Seattle-based investors.

The franchise was so shaky that the American League had to loan the club $650,000 to stay afloat during the season. Board chairman Daley repeatedly tried to sell the club that year but was unsuccessful. After the season the American League gave the city until November 9, 1969, to fulfill three conditions for keeping the franchise:

1) expand the small stadium by 75%;
2) break ground on a new facility; and
3) find local buyers for the club.

The city was unable to meet the conditions and the club moved to Milwaukee for the 1970 season (see also *Franchise Shifts*).

First Game. The Pilots played their first game on April 11, 1969, as Gary Bell beat the White Sox 7–0 at Sicks Stadium.

Nickname. One source reported that the Pilots nickname came from the local aircraft industry, but another attributes it to minority owner Dewey Soriano, a former Coast Guard ship pilot who chose the nautical theme.

The Season. The Pilots finished last with a 64–98 record. Attendance during the club's one year was 677,944, 200,000 less

Manager Joe Schultz of the 1969 Pilots; known affectionately by his players as "Ol' Shitfuck."

than anticipated. Part of the reason for low attendance (other than having a terrible team) was that the club had the highest ticket prices in the American League and played in a ballpark that seated less than 25,000.

Last Game. The Pilots' last game was on October 2, 1969, a 3–1 loss to the A's. Steve Barber was the losing pitcher and Jim Roland the winner for Oakland.

Key Players. The team employed 53 players over the season. Only Diego Segui played for both the Pilots and the Mariners. Four players spent their entire Major League careers with the Pilots: Dick Bates (one game as a pitcher), Miguel Fuentes (eight games as a pitcher), Gary Timberlake (two games as a pitcher), and Billy Williams (four games as a pinch hitter and outfielder).

Tommy Harper was the closest the club had to a star as he led the league with 73 stolen bases. It was the only positive statistical category led by a Pilots player.

Manager.

Joe Schultz, one of the more profane managers of all time (see also *Foul Language*), led the club to a 64–98 record. He managed again, briefly: 28 games for the Tigers at the end of the 1973 season.

Ballpark.

"The holidays passed without a start on renovation. Now, time, as they say, is of the essence. Not only has the time shrunk, it has been known to rain here in the winter, which would cut the toil and increase the trouble." — *The Sporting News* in January 1969.

The Pilots played in Sicks Stadium, named after local brewery owner Emile Sicks. The ballpark was truly dilapidated. The club had promised that the park would be enlarged and upgraded before Opening Day, but the renovation began only three months before the start of the season. With three weeks left, only 7,500 seats were ready for occupancy. Only 18,000 of the promised 25,000 seats were ready at the start of the season.

Plumbing was another major problem. With the increased attendance, water pressure was next to nothing. Toilets backed up and showers for the players did not work. It took a few innings for the water pressure to build, so the reporters in the press box started a tradition called the "7th Inning Flush."

Broadcasters. Jimmy Dudley, voice of the Indians for 20 years until 1967, was the Pilots' primary broadcaster for the season.

Book. Jim Bouton with Leonard Schechter, *Ball Four* (1970) (see also *Books*); Carson Van Lindt, *The Seattle Pilots Story* (1993).

Tom Seaver (1944–)

Hall of Fame 1992

"Blind people come to the park just to listen to him pitch." — Reggie Jackson.

"And maybe the funniest guy up there was Seaver, because most fans wouldn't expect him to be the type who performs in nightclubs. But Tom does everything well. He's the kind of man you'd want your kid to grow up to be like. Tom's a studious player, devoted to his profession, a loyal cat, trustworthy — everything a Boy Scout's supposed to be. In fact, we call him 'Boy Scout.' But with all that, Tom's not stiff. He's a fun-loving guy, and he's the first guy to kid himself. Someone walked up to him in Vegas and started reeling off all the records he'd set, and Tom looked back at him and said, 'Yeah, but you forgot one thing: I'm the only pitcher in the history of the Mets who's lost a ball game in the World Series.'" — Cleon Jones in *Cleon*, with Ed Hershey (1970), on the Mets players' postseason appearance in Las Vegas as a lounge act.

"My idea of managing is giving the ball to Tom Seaver and sitting down and watching him work." — Sparky Anderson.

Seaver won 311 games and pitched 61 shutouts over a career lasting from 1967 through 1986.

George Thomas Seaver played at USC before being offered a $40,000 bonus by the Braves. The contract was voided and the Mets obtained him in a lottery as a ***Free Agent***. He won his first Major League game on April 20, 1967, defeating the Cubs 6–1. Seaver won 16 games during his first season and made the All-Star team. In 1968 he began a record streak of nine straight seasons in which he struck out 200 or more batters. He exploded for 25 wins in 1969 and won 20 or more games for the Mets in 1971, 1972 and 1975. He led the Mets to their first World Series in 1969, and they were back again in 1973.

Seaver was traded to the Reds during 1977, winning a combined 21 games for the two clubs. He remained with the Reds through 1982. He led the league with 14 wins during the strike-shortened 1981 season. He returned to the Mets for one year and then ended his career with the White Sox and Red Sox. He retired in 1986 with 311 victories over 20 seasons. He finished with 3,640 strikeouts, now sixth all-time, and 61 shutouts, seventh all-time.

In 1970 Seaver struck out 19 Padres, including a record 10 in a row to end the game. He pitched his only no-hitter on June 16, 1978, a 4–0 win over the Cardinals. He played in two World Series, winning one game for the 1969 Mets. He won his 300th game in 1985, a 4–1 win over the Yankees.

Seaver worked as a broadcaster as early as the 1975 postseason. After his retirement due to injury, he broadcast for NBC, ABC and CBS radio into the 1980s and broadcast for the Yankees in the 1990s before moving over to the Mets broadcast booth in 1999.

Books. Joe Cohen (ed.), *Inside Corner* (1974); Gene Schoor, *Seaver: A Biography* (1986); Tom Seaver with Lee Lowenfish, *The Art of Pitching* (1994); George Sullivan, *Tom Seaver of the Mets* (1971).

Second Basemen

"Second base is the prettiest position to play of the entire infield. In the number of chances offered it is next to first base, and in the character of the work to be done and the opportunities for brilliant play and the exercise of judgment, it is unsurpassed."— John Montgomery Ward in 1889.

"They're very much alike in a lot of similarities."— Casey Stengel comparing 1950s second basemen Billy Martin and Nellie Fox.

"Sports Classics — Dogs on the Field: The long, detailed history of every second baseman who has ever played for the Colorado Rockies."— Bernie Lincicome on proposed Christmas DVD gifts.

Greatest.

"To my way of thinking no contest at second base, Hornsby couldn't catch a pop fly, much less go in the outfield after them, could not come in on a slow hit, Lajoie could not go out, nor come in, and did not cover too much ground to his right or left. [Eddie] Collins could do it all, besides being a great base stealer and base runner. Career average of .330-odd, I think. Also another manager on the field…"— Ty Cobb in a 1945 letter to Ernest Lanigan of the Hall of Fame. The top second basemen of the early 20th century were Rogers Hornsby, Eddie Collins, and Nap Lajoie.

Often referred to as the best second baseman of the 19th century is Bid McPhee, who led the American Association and National League in putouts eight times, double plays 11 times, assists six times and fielding percentage nine times between 1882 and 1899.

Hall of Famer Rogers Hornsby is considered by many as the greatest second baseman of all time, and certainly the best right-handed hitter of all time. He had a .358 lifetime average, second-highest ever, but was considered only a decent fielder and had a rotten personality.

Prior to Hornsby, Eddie Collins was considered by many to be the outstanding second baseman of all time. He was a starter for 20 of his 25 Major League seasons for the A's and White Sox from 1906 through 1930. He batted .333 lifetime, with 19 seasons over .300 and 743 stolen bases.

Nap Lajoie has also been called the greatest second baseman of all time. He was elected to the Hall of Fame in 1937, the sixth player chosen. He was a lifetime .338 hitter with 1,599 RBIs over a career from 1896 through 1916.

The best of the late 1920s and 1930s was Charlie Gehringer of the Tigers, who batted .320 over a 19-year career.

In the 1930s and 1940s Billy Herman may have been the best, playing for the Cubs from 1931 until 1947 and batting over .300 eight times. Leo Durocher considered him to be the greatest of that

Yankee second baseman Billy Martin demonstrates how to avoid getting spiked during a double play.

era. Joe Gordon of the Yankees played in six World Series for the Yankees and Indians in the 1930s and 1940s and was regarded by many as the best defensive second baseman of the era.

In the 1950s Nellie Fox of the White Sox may have been the best and had come excruciatingly close to making the Hall of Fame. He finally made it in 1997 (see *Hall of Fame*—**Belated Entry**).

Glenn Beckert of the Cubs may have been the best of the 1960s, though many believe that Ken Hubbs of the Cubs would have been had he not been killed in a plane crash in 1965 after two stellar seasons.

Hall of Famer Joe Morgan is the consensus best of the 1970s, winning consecutive MVP awards for the powerhouse Cincinnati Reds.

Ryne Sandberg/Roberto Alomar.

"Sandberg's sudden departure should not keep him out of the Hall of Fame. He is one of the best second basemen ever — Rogers Hornsby, Joe Morgan and Eddie Collins are the only ones with a clear claim to being better. And defensively he was indisputably No. 1: His .990 fielding percentage ranks as the best in history at his position."—*Sports Illustrated* after Sandberg retired abruptly early in the 1994, season though he returned for the 1996 season. In early 1997. Sandberg broke Joe Morgan's home run record for second baseman and went on to hit a total of 282 for his career.

In the 1980s Sandberg emerged as the dominant second baseman, a role he maintained into the early 1990s, though Roberto Alomar of the Blue Jays assumed the top spot by 1992, as confirmed by Phillies scout Jimmy Stewart in 1993: "There are no peers. He's the best I've ever seen, and probably the best we'll ever see."

Unfortunately, however, Alomar faded badly later in his career and there is doubt whether he will be elected to the Hall of Fame.

Weak Power. In 1989 Mariners second baseman Harold Reynolds hit no home runs.

Security Guards

"The most miserable thing in the world is to walk around with somebody having to monitor everything you do."— Henry Aaron in *Baseball Weekly* on having a security guard during the 1973–1974 seasons. Police officer Calvin Wardlaw was assigned to guard Aaron.

Major League Baseball has an executive director of security, who oversees the Resident Security Agent program. The program requires that each club have a local police officer who works part-time as its personal security consultant. Resident agents are required to attend 40 home games each season. They determine that everyone on the field and in the clubhouse is authorized to be there. They also stay on the alert for suspicious people or activities.

Segregation See *Black "Firsts," Integration, Negro Leagues* and *Racism*

Frank Selee (1859–1909)

Hall of Fame (VC) 1999

"To tell the truth I would not have any one on a team who was not congenial. If I make things pleasant for the players, they reciprocate."—Selee on his managing philosophy.

Selee was a Major League manager for 16 seasons in the 1890s and 1900s, winning five National League pennants.

Frank Selee's professional managerial career began in 1886 with Haverhill, Massachusetts, of the New England League. He would close the first phase of his minor league career in 1889, winning a Western Association title with Omaha.

Selee took over the Boston Beaneaters in 1890, finishing fifth. 1891 was the first of three consecutive first place finishes, followed by two more titles in 1897 and 1898. Although overshadowed by the famous Oriole teams of the decade, Boston in fact enjoyed more success. Selee's Beaneaters had the most first place finishes, five (Baltimore had 3, 1894–1896), and the best winning percentage of the decade.

Selee moved to Chicago in 1902 to take over a 6th place team. By 1904 the Cubs were winners of 93 games and finished second. An excellent talent evaluator, Selee is credited with molding the Joe Tinker, Johnny Evers, Frank Chance infield combination.

In December of 1903 Sele traded for Three Finger Brown to anchor his rotation. All the pieces were in place for the 1905 season when Selee contracted tuberculosis and Frank Chance took over at midseason. The Selee-built, Chance-managed Cubs would go on to win four of the next five National League pennants.

Selee would manage briefly with Class A Pueblo of the Western League in 1906 and 1907 before retiring permanently due to ill health. He died only two years later in Denver.

Selee finished his Major League managerial career with a 1284–862 won-lost record. His .598 winning percentage is fourth best all time.

Senior Professional Baseball Association (1989–1990)

"I wish I had the ice-machine concession for this league."— Hal McRae on the frequency of sore muscles suffered by the over–40 players in the league.

"I like playing on this team. We actually been doin' real good. Got a different mix here. Most important thing is you gotta keep pickin' up in paces. That's why we're playing contentious play. We got top names, guys can still hit in the majors, guys been out of the game hittin' the ball, shockin' it. Don't have no old, old guys. Not sayin' they don't get a good job done. Fact is, they've been vice versa. So that's incentive right there. It's been a plus."— Mickey Rivers' nonsensical comments on his teammates in the SPBL in 1989.

Origins. The league was the brainchild of 33-year-old real estate developer Jim Morley. He sent 1,250 postcards to former Major League players and received 700 favorable replies. In addition to signing a number of former stars to play, he hired Curt Flood as commissioner of the league. Play started over the 1989–1990 winter season and restarted for a second season before shutting down in December 1990 due to financial problems.

Schedule. The league had a 72-game schedule and each owner contemplated spending $1 million the first year to keep it afloat.

The Clubs. West Palm Beach Tropics, Winter Haven Super Sox, Fort Myers Sun Sox, Gold Coast Suns (Miami and Pompano Beach), St. Petersburg Pelicans, Orlando Juice, Bradenton Explorers (Explos) and St. Lucie Legends.

Key Players. Dave Kingman, Bernie Carbo, Bill Madlock, Jon Matlack, Ferguson Jenkins, Bert Campaneris, Graig Nettles, Cecil Cooper, Mike Cuellar and Juan Eichelberger.

First Pitch. The ceremonial first pitch was thrown out by Connie Mack, Jr. (the legendary Mack's grandson), then a Florida senator and proponent of baseball in Florida (see also *Antitrust*).

MVPs. *Sports Illustrated* created the tongue-in-cheek Cy Old Award and Most Valuable Patriarch.

Too Serious. Former Orioles manager Earl Weaver was up to his usual standards as a Senior League manager — getting thrown out of a game after berating an umpire. In an uncharacteristic move, however, he apologized the next day.

Salaries. The highest monthly player salary the first year was $15,000, with an average of $7,000 per month. The maximum monthly salary during the short-lived second season was $10,000.

Attendance. Clubs needed to average 2,000 fans per game to break even, but actual attendance was more in the range of 1,200.

Player Eligibility. Players were required to be over 35, except catchers, who could be as young as 32.

Fantasy Fulfilled. One of the best stories about the league was Don Mincberg, the only player signed to a Senior League contract who did not have previous professional baseball experience. He played baseball briefly in college before finishing his education. He was a 41-year-old South Florida criminal lawyer who made the team managed by the less-than-congenial Dick Williams. Mincberg started one game at first base and for the season was 1-for-11 for the West Palm Beach Tropics.

Books. Peter Golenbock, *The Forever Boys* (1991), covering the St. Petersburg Pelicans; David Whitford, *Extra Innings* (1991).

Series Sweep

"The hordes of invading Yankee fans even took to taunting the Sox in their own lair. In the tunnel under the Fenway stands, Yankee fans set up a cheer each night as they passed the doors of the Boston locker room. 'Three, three, three … two, two, two … one, one, one … ZERO, ZERO, ZERO,' they counted down the dwindling Boston margin each night as the Yankees swept the famous 4-game series that will live in lore as The Boston Massacre."— Thomas Boswell in *How Life Imitates the World Series* (1982), describing the Red Sox collapse and the Yankee surge during the 1978 pennant race.

"I sure hope you're staying alive for the upcoming Dodgers series."— Padres broadcaster Jerry Coleman.

"They say anything can happen in a short series. I just didn't expect it to be that short."— Al Lopez.

Season Series Sweep. In 1993 the Braves swept their 13-game series with the Rockies, outscoring them 106–50. It was the first time since 1899 that a National League team swept a season series.

The 1994 Expos swept the Padres in their 12 games that season. In the American League four teams have done so: the 1996 Indians over the Tigers (12–0); the 1990 A's over the Yankees (12–0); the 1988 Royals over the Orioles (12–0) and the 1978 Orioles over the A's (11–0).

1998 Tigers. On May 7, 1998, the Tigers completed their first series sweep of the Oakland A's, *ever*. The last time the Tigers swept the A's was when the club was in Kansas City, in 1965. The Tigers won both games played in the 1998 series, and luckily the third game was rained out.

1998 Yankees. In June 1998 the Yankees tied the record for most consecutive times not losing a series, with 24, tying the 1912 Red Sox and 1970 Reds.

2001 Mariners. In 2001 the Mariners won 116 games and won the season series against all 18 opponents they faced (including interleague play): 13 American League teams and five National League teams. The last team to win every season series was the 1968 Tigers against nine American League teams. Researcher Walt Wilson determined that the Mariners broke the record of the 1899 Brooklyn Dodgers, who won series against 11 National League teams.

Consecutive Road Series Wins. The 2001 Mariners won 29 straight road series. The old record was 26, by the 1906 Chicago Cubs.

Seventh Inning Stretch

"The [Cincinnati] spectators all arise between halves of the seventh inning, extend their legs and arms, and sometimes walk about. In so doing they enjoy the relief afforded by relaxation from a long posture upon hard benches."— Harry Wright in a letter home about the 1869 Cincinnati Red Stockings fans and their version of the 7th inning stretch. His brother George, also with the Red Stockings at the time, is said to have reported that Cincinnati fans would rise spontaneously in the 7th inning to cheer.

See also "***Take Me Out to the Ball Game.***"

In June 1869 the *New York Herald* reported on a game between the Red Stockings and the Brooklyn Eagles: "At the close of the long second inning, the laughable stand up and stretch was indulged in all around the field."

Another story in the *Cincinnati Commercial-Gazette* reported on a West Coast game between the Red Stockings and the Eagle Club of San Francisco: "One thing noticeable in this game was a ten minutes' intermission at the end of the sixth inning—a dodge to advertise and have the crowd patronize the bar."

The most popular, though inaccurate, story about the origin of the 7th inning stretch relates to President William Howard Taft on Opening Day 1910 in Washington, D.C. Taft stood up and stretched his 6-foot, 300-pound frame, and the crowd joined him.

The first widely reported 7th inning stretch was on May 31, 1882, when Manhattan College (now in the Bronx) played the New York Metropolitans at the Polo Grounds. On a warm Sunday afternoon, Brother Jasper, the school's athletic director and coach, told the student fans to stretch and move around; it just happened to be in the 7th inning.

The Metropolitans defeated Manhattan 6–0 in a game that lasted 1 hour and 45 minutes. Some sources reported that the New York Giants (previously the Metropolitans) adopted the stretch from the annual Manhattan College games.

The 1876 National League Louisville club is said to have employed a stretch in the 5th inning.

From the 1870s through at least World War I, the 7th inning was known as the "Lucky Seventh."

Modern treatment of the 7th Inning Stretch. Cubs announcer Harry Caray performed probably the best-known 7th inning rendition of "Take Me Out to the Ball Game." He rose with the microphone, head out the window of the broadcast booth and led the Wrigley faithful in the tune. Caray first began the practice with the White Sox in 1976.

In Milwaukee the club plays the Andrew Sisters' version of "Take Me Out to the Ballgame." The club also plays "Roll Out the Barrel."

In the early 1970s the Orioles played the "Mexican Hat Dance" and from 1975 through 1986, "Thank God I'm a Country Boy," by John Denver. He performed the song live at the 1983 World Series.

The Blue Jays have used 8–10 students leading the crowd in exercises to "O.K., Blue Jays."

The Rangers have featured "Cotton Eye Joe."

The Cardinals played "Here Comes the King," a Budweiser theme song, with pictures of the Clydesdales rolling across the giant screen television. The club played "Take Me Out to the Ballgame" during the 8th inning "stretch."

For a few weeks in 1984 the Angels suffered an outbreak of 7th inning "tortilla tossing" in their bleachers. Fans flung round corn tortillas about the stands like frisbees until the situation was brought under control.

Since September 11, 2001, "God Bless America" has been sung during the 7th inning stretch at all Yankee home games.

The ill-fated **Global League** planned to have an intermission and entertainment at the end of the 5th inning.

Joe Sewell (1898–1990)

Hall of Fame (VC) 1977

"There are a *few* good players today—you can count them on the fingers of one hand. But generally they're just out there going through the motions, just playing for the money. I get a kick out of ... they have to get ready 'mentally' for the ball game. Shucks, when I crawled out of bed in the morning, I was ready to play. Nobody had to pamper me around."—Sewell quoted in *Voices from Cooperstown*, by Anthony J. Connor (1982).

Sewell played shortstop and is best known for his few strikeouts over a career lasting from 1920 through 1933 primarily with the Indians.

Joseph Wheeler Sewell had the dubious distinction of replacing Ray Chapman of the Indians after Chapman was killed by a pitch from Carl Mays. Sewell was in his first professional season when he was called up in August 1920 to replace the injured Harry Lunte, who had been the first to replace Chapman. Although Sewell batted .329 in the final 22 games of the season, he batted only .174 in the World Series and had six errors.

Sewell played another 10 seasons with the Indians, batting over .300 in eight of those years. He never struck out more than 20 times in a season, and in nine of his 13 seasons he struck out less than 10 times. He was traded to the Yankees in 1931 and played three full seasons for the club before retiring after the 1933 season. He finished with a .312 average and also had a streak of 1,103 consecutive games played for the Indians from late 1922 through early 1930. His 114 career strikeouts are by far the lowest of any modern player with comparable at-bats.

He retired to become a coach with the Yankees and then scouted for the Indians. He later coached for the Mets and was the baseball coach at the University of Alabama for six years in the 1960s. He left baseball and became a representative for a dairy. Sewell died in Alabama in March 1990 at age 91.

Sex

"Barry Bonds is such a dickhead that when he takes Viagra, he gets taller."—Robert Ostrove.

"Steve Garvey is not my Padre."—1980s bumper sticker after revelations that the Padres first baseman fathered two illegitimate children by different women.

"I saw Gomez undressed in the clubhouse, and anybody who's got a prick as big as he's got can't pitch winning ball in the Major Leagues."—Scout Cy Slapnicka's reasoning in not signing future Yankee pitcher Lefty Gomez to a contract after watching him pitch for the San Francisco Seals.

"It would take some of the lust [sic] off the All-Star Game."—Pete Rose on the effect of interleague play on the Major Leagues.

"The Red Sox brass were always telling Sparky Lyle that if he kept screwing around he would lose his fastball. They claimed it would float right out of his dick. Later he told me they were right, but that they forgot to mention how it would add all sorts of movement to his slider and carry him to the Cy Young Award."—Bill Lee in *The Wrong Stuff*, with Dick Lally (1984).

"The incidence of immorality among itinerant workers is highest."—Sportswriter Harold Rosenthal in 1952; Rosenthal then translated: "What that means is that the road'll make a bum outa the best of 'em."—Quoted in Leonard Koppett's *A Thinking Man's Guide to Baseball* (1967).

"Men, I'm just going to say one thing. I just want to remind every one of you that you're only this far away from big-league pussy [holding his thumb and forefinger about an inch apart]."—Best minor league manager's pep talk, by Don Hoak, according to Jim Bouton in "*I Managed Good, But Boy Did They Play Bad,*" by Bouton with Neil Offen (1973).

"The American League has more smut magazines in the clubhouses."—Bob Uecker on the difference between the two leagues.

"The game, the game!
To our women one and all,
We will see you in the fall,
But for now we've got to stall
Every Dame!
And think about the game!"
—Last lines from "The Game," a song from the Broadway musical *Damn Yankees*.

"When describing female encounters, males of my generation sought to know what 'pitch' to use. A 'change of pace' might serve, especially if she 'threw' me a 'curve.' 'Getting to first base' or 'hitting in the clutch' or 'going into extra innings' all indicated a kissing relationship which if foregone could earn a player the coveted title of 'ace'! But being 'caught off base' or 'caught stealing' or 'thrown out' described ardor rebuffed, while 'striking out' described abject failure."—David Quentin Voigt in the *Journal of Popular Culture*.

"Sex is okay, but it'll never take the place of night baseball!"—Alleged baseball axiom (started by whom?).

"From the start it is easy for the athlete to get laid. It is no trouble at all. It comes with the deal, is issued with the high school letter sweater. The athlete needn't reapply for sex as he would a passport or a driver's license; the lay is for the duration—career permanence."—Herb Michelson in *Sportin' Ladies* (1975).

"Having said that, I wish I could explain *my* lifelong obsession with baseball. But it is like trying to explain sex to a precocious six-year-old. Not that I have ever done this, but I assume the child would say something like 'Okay, I understand the procedure. But *why?*' There is no answer for that. You have to be there."—Art Hill in *I Don't Care If I Never Come Back* (1980).

"Baseball without fans is like Jayne Mansfield without a sweater. Hang on, that can be taken two ways."—Richard Nixon.

"Girls are therapeutic. The ballplayer uses them medicinally, like an apple a day."—Curt Flood in *The Way It Was* (1971).

"I'd never sleep with a player hitting under .250 unless he had a lot of RBIs or was a great glove man up the middle. A woman's got to have her standards."—Annie, in *Bull Durham*.

"He's a hunk, and I don't even like that word. Women like guys who have a big presence but sort of play it down. It's very appealing."—Actress Kim Basinger on Derek Jeter.

"That's interesting. He's kissing her on the strikes, and she's kissing him on the balls."—Broadcaster Mel Allen describing an amorous couple in the stands, to which his partner, Phil Rizzuto, responded: "Mel, this is just not your day."

"Hickey Hoffman, Hickie Wilson, Ed Hug, Stubby Clapp, Gene Brabender, Herb Score, Jim Hickey, Phil Bedgood, Cuddles Marshall"

See also **Marriage**.

Babe Ruth.

"His phallus and home-run bat were his prize possessions, in that order."—Sportswriter Fred Lieb.

Lieb, in his book, *Baseball as I Have Known It* (1977), related some of the legendary sex escapades of Babe Ruth, including the night on a road trip that Bill Dickey watched roommate Ruth match seven cigars with the same number of "trips to the plate" with a young woman in his suite.

During the 1926 World Series, a fan came up to Cardinals owner Sam Breadon and told him that Ruth would not do well that day because he had been with five women the night before. Ruth hit three home runs. At least one source placed this anecdote at the 1932 World Series.

Modern sources have reported that Ruth's "stomachache heard 'round the world" was a coverup for an outbreak of syphilis.

In 1980, 32 years after Ruth died, Dorothy Pirone discovered that she was the natural daughter of Ruth. Ruth and his first wife, Helen (who died in a fire after they were divorced), raised Dorothy as an adopted daughter. The natural mother, Juanita Jennings Ellias, had an affair with Ruth in 1920 in California. Ellias posed as a close family friend for years. She only revealed the secret to Dorothy on her death bed in 1980. There is no other known natural offspring of Ruth.

It has been reported that the boy who was responsible for sorting through Babe Ruth's mail was ordered to throw away everything except checks and "letters from broads." Ruth generally received 200 letters per day.

Christy Mathewson. Mathewson had a public persona of the straight arrow, but in a letter from historian Lee Allen to another historian, Tom Shea, Allen recounted the following: "Even more amusing than the Carry [sic] Nation cause of death [paresis, a brain disorder caused by untreated syphilis], however, is the 'image' that Christy Mathewson has. Never smoked or drank, but he could handle the women. Tom Swope, the retired Cincinnati baseball writer, has always disliked Mathewson because he (Swope) saw Matty coming out of a whorehouse on Christmas Eve."

Trade. Broadcaster Shelby Whitfield reported in *Kiss It Goodbye* (1973) that Senators catcher Paul Casanova once traded sportswriter Tom Quinn three joints of marijuana for a dildo.

Managerial Problems. The inability to halt extracurricular activities by the Yankee players in the spring of 1946 supposedly contributed to the resignation of manager Joe McCarthy (though his *Alcoholism* did not help). Manager Billy Southworth supposedly resigned under pressure from the Cardinals in 1949 for the same reason.

In 1955 White Sox manager Marty Marion caught and fined four White Sox players for sexual escapades, which caused dissent among the players. Marion's comment: "Dames wrecked more teams than bad liquor, big bonuses or all the sore arms."

Indecent Exposure. Ed Bouchee, who played first base primarily for the Phillies in the late 1950s, was suspended from baseball after pleading guilty to indecent exposure in Spokane, Washington.

Former Mets general manager Joe McIlvaine, a Minnesota assistant general manager in April 1999, was arrested for public nudity on a beach.

Romance. After winning 19 straight games in 1912, Rube Marquard went on the vaudeville circuit, where he performed with Blossom Seeley, a well-known burlesque performer. They fell in love and were married after Seeley divorced her husband (after Marquard settled a lawsuit with him for loss of consortium). Five months later she bore Marquard's son.

During the Blue Jays' 1993 World Series parade, Pitcher Todd Stottlemyre gave a speech to the large Toronto crowd that ended with an announcement that he was going home to have sex with his wife. As noted by one commentator, in Calvinist Toronto this didn't go over very well.

On the Prowl.

"For most athletes, the sexual chase is nothing but a game, and they never progress beyond the little-boy-peeping-into-the-bedroom stage in their relationships with women. Thus the popularity of 'shooting beaver' among baseball players." — Glenn Dickey in *The Jock Empire* (1974). In *Ball Four* (1970), Jim Bouton described the sophisticated practice of "beaver hunting" from the dugout, looking up the skirts of female fans in the stands.

"One percent of ballplayers are leaders of men. The other 99% are followers of women." — John McGraw.

"Being with a woman all night never hurt no professional ballplayer. It's staying up all night looking for a woman that does him in." — Casey Stengel.

In the 1920s pitcher Phil Douglas (later ***Barred from Baseball***), before games threw baseballs bearing his name and telephone number to women in the stands.

Playboys.

"I've got to find out whether he is the lousiest lay in the world or the cheapest son of a bitch in baseball. Why else wouldn't a girl date him twice?" — White Sox manager Al Lopez on Bob Shaw's reputation as a playboy.

"[Starlet] Mamie Van Doren is here to serve as my physical fitness director." — Pitcher Bo Belinsky on bringing his girlfriend and future wife to training camp in 1965 (see also ***Marriage***).

"I only go out with girls when I'm horny." — Mark Fidrych.

Protection. "Champ" prophylactics were marketed in the 1950s bearing a likeness of Ted Williams. A set of the Williams-endorsed condoms bearing his picture sold for $165 at auction in December 1993. According to reliable sources they were not game-used.

League. The Arizona Mining League existed early in the 20th century and its clubs were owned by brothels.

Baseball Annies.

"Today's players don't even womanize as much as yesterday's. They don't have to … the women *manize*." — Charles Einstein in *Willie's Time* (1979).

A number of nicknames have been used to describe women in various cities who hang around attempting to meet and sleep with ballplayers: for example, the Pirate Pair; the Varsity Four (Milwaukee); and the Dayton Fliers. An early term was "Daisies," used to describe women who dated the opposing team's pitcher on the night before he was to pitch.

Chicago Shirley was a big-time Baseball Annie who, according to Jim Bouton in *Ball Four* (1970), "says that Chicago is a great place to live because teams in both leagues come through there. She doesn't like to miss anybody." *Sportin' Ladies*, by Herb Michelson (1975), chronicles the sexual relationships of a number of women and famous (but unnamed) professional athletes.

Dodger Stadium. When the Dodgers moved West, they considered moving into Gilmore Field, home of the Hollywood Stars. Legend has it that the club decided to go to the Los Angeles Coliseum because owner Walter O'Malley was offended by the brothel across the street from Gilmore. In reality, there was not enough parking spaces at the field.

Wade Boggs. Perhaps the most publicized recent sexual escapades by a player involved Wade Boggs and Margo Adams, who later posed nude for *Penthouse* magazine. Boggs was married, but on the road he stayed with Adams for over four years before the affair was revealed beyond the club's players.

Dysfunction? Rafael Palmeiro may have had some sexual dysfunction, as he was a Viagra spokesman in the 2000s.

Extramarital. In late 1998 it was announced that Mets general manager Steve Phelps would take a paid leave of absence while sexual harassment charges were resolved against him. He acknowledged having an extramarital affair with the woman, but denied any harassment. A week later he was reinstated and the parties settled out of court.

***Penthouse* Pet.** Mets pitcher Kris Benson married a *Penthouse* centerfold. His wife, Anna, started a cosmetics line in addition to having three kids with Benson. One of her goals was to have sex in every city in which Kris pitches: "We have a ways to go, but that's what we want to do."

Population Control.

"We'd hoped to give away a vasectomy. Complications arose and the idea got snipped." — Minor league owner Mike Veeck, on an aborted promotion scheduled by his club.

In 2003 the Charleston RiverDogs proposed Vasectomy Night, but scrapped the idea ("nipped in the bud," according to *Sports Illustrated*) after a public outcry.

It's a Wonderful Life.

"Me and my dog, sitting around watching porn." — Former pitcher Rob Dibble describing his home life to radio announcer Dan Patrick.

Lost Bet? In Game 3 of the 1951 play-off game between the Dodgers and Giants, New York's Bobby Thomson hit his famous home run in the 9th inning to defeat the Dodgers. Fans went crazy after the game and many ran onto the field in jubilation. A number of people reported seeing a woman performing oral sex on a man lying in the dirt next to the first base box seats. Newspaper photographers were observed recording the event, but their work was never published. At least one source reported that the event occurred *in* the box seats.

Ladies? Pitcher Dave Stewart suffered an embarrassing moment when he was arrested for soliciting prostitution, compounded when it was determined that he had received oral sex from a transvestite. The transvestite's name was Lucille. Shortly after the incident an opposing club's organist reportedly played "Lucille" when he came to bat.

Minnie Minoso once danced all night at a New Orleans club with a woman over six feet tall. Minoso kept bragging to teammate Vic Power about her — until the lights went on at 4 a.m. and, according to Power, they discovered that she was a he.

Porn Stars/Strippers.

"That's not Morganna, that's Bea Arthur." — Overheard at a Senior Professional Association Game (per David Letterman).

Morganna Roberts, the Kissing Bandit, the extraordinarily buxom part-owner of a minor league club in the 1980s, "bounced" her way onto Major League fields numerous times to kiss ballplayers during games. She usually appeared in Cincinnati in the on-deck circle. Early in her "career" on August 31, 1969, she accosted Clete Boyer, who was mired in a 1-for-17 slump. After the kiss he had an RBI single and went on an 8-for-15 binge. Morganna made her American League debut in April 1970 during the presidential opener at RFK Stadium in Washington when she climbed over the third base railing and gave Frank Howard a kiss at home plate.

One night she chased Dodger infielder Wes Parker across the field from first base into the arms of the third baseman, who held him for her. Morganna signed all photographs, "Your Breast Friend, Morganna."

Reports surfaced in the late 1980s that a number of players on the Twins had sex with porn star Seka.

When Roger Maris and Mickey Mantle were chasing Babe Ruth's record in 1961, a stripper adopted the name Mickey Maris.

Lulu Devine was the 1990s version of Morganna, getting herself arrested a number of times trying to kiss players on the field. She often attended Blue Jays games in 1992.

SkyDome. Toronto's SkyDome was built with an adjoining restaurant and hotel above the outfield, with windows facing down onto the field. During a game soon after the ballpark opened, many in the crowd witnessed the sexual activities of an amorous pair through the couple's hotel window. They forgot to close the curtains and now all who stay in one of the outfield rooms are cautioned to keep the curtains closed.

Doll. In 1991 Red Sox fans were admonished for periodically passing through the stands a nude and anatomically correct inflatable female doll.

Fertility Problems. In 1991 Dave Righetti's triplets were born to Righetti's sister-in-law. As teenagers, Righetti's wife and her sister agreed that the sister would bear her children because she would be unable to do so. Righetti's sperm was used in an in-vitro fertilization of his wife's egg and then implanted into the sister's uterus.

Albert Spalding. Baseball patriarch Albert Spalding had a longtime mistress named Elizabeth Mayer Churchill, a childhood friend. Spalding's wife died in 1899, and he married Churchill two years later. The two had long before produced a son named Spalding Brown Spalding, who had lived with Spalding's sister. When they married, Spalding formally recognized the boy as his son and renamed him Albert Goodwill Spalding, Jr.

Paternity Problems.

"Boy, I'd like to bang her again." — Dodger player in court, to his team-appointed lawyer, eyeing the plaintiff in a paternity suit against him.

To avoid service of paternity suits, 19th century teams sometimes allowed their players to avoid playing in certain states.

Fan Club. During the 19th century it was common for brothels to sponsor lavish Saturday night parties for players.

The Philadelphia Athletics of the 1880s had a "women's auxiliary" known as "The Big Bosom Girls." Wilbert Robinson, later the manager of the Dodgers, purportedly was the official measurer.

Fast Exit. Pitcher Van Lingle Mungo once had to be smuggled out of Cuba during spring training to avoid the knife-wielding husband of a nightclub dancer with whom he had shared a bed.

Poser. Outfielder "Disco" Dan Ford of the Angels and Orioles once posed nude for *Playgirl* magazine.

New Bullpen Use. In 1991 Mets pitcher David Cone was accused by three women of harassing them and masturbating in front of them in the Mets bullpen. The day after the charges were made public, the last day of the season, Cone struck out 19 batters.

Heidi Fleiss. Fleiss became an infamous celebrity in 1993 when she was accused of running a sex-for-hire service that catered to the rich and famous among Hollywood's movie crowd. Cincinnati Reds players were accused of having some of the Fleiss girls delivered to them while on road trips in Los Angeles.

Platonic? In 2003 the daughter of Hall of Famer Don Sutton, by then a Braves broadcaster, was dating reliever John Rocker, infamous for some of his insensitive racial and homosexual remarks.

Mistaken Identity. In 2003 this author received a call from one of his clients asking if he had published a new book. "No," replied the author. "Then you might want to check out Barnes & Noble's website." Listed under the author's titles was *The Art of Porn*, by Jonathan Light (not the author!). Turned out to be *another* Jonathan Light (not Jonathan Fraser Light), who had self-published his book under Lighthouse Publications in Santa Barbara (less than 30 miles from the author's office).

Books. In *The Long Season*, by Jim Brosnan (1961), the Reds pitcher delicately described the sexual escapades of his teammates. He was far more discrete than Jim Bouton in *Ball Four* (1970) though much of that book might be considered tame by today's standards (see also *Books*); Herb Michelson, *Sportin' Ladies* (1975).

Shibe Park (1909–1970)

"On April 12, 1909, baseball entered a new era, and it happened in the Swampoodle section of north Philadelphia. Some said the new stadium — the first ever made of concrete and steel — was too big and too far from the center of the city. But it was built by a pair of dreamers, Athletics owners Ben Shibe and Connie Mack — who also managed the team. In baseball, dreamers are right more often than skeptics."— William B. Mead in *Baseball in the Depression, 1930–1939* (1990).

Philadelphia's Shibe Park was home to the Philadelphia A's from its completion in 1909 until the A's left for Kansas City after the 1954 season. It was also home to the Phillies starting in mid–1938 when the club abandoned tiny **Baker Bowl**. The Phillies occupied Shibe Park through the end of the 1970 season, when Veterans Stadium was completed for 1971.

Shibe Park was the first triple-decked ballpark and the site took up the largest area of any park built to that point. Built over an old brickyard, it covered 252,200 square feet in the vicinity of Lehigh and 21st Street. The park cost $500,000 and was the first steel and concrete ballpark. It was designed in the French Renaissance style and was considered the most beautiful park of its day.

Its first major renovation was in 1913 when a grandstand roof and left-field stands were added. A second deck was added in 1925 along the right field foul line, and additional seating was added in 1929 and 1930.

In 1934 owners of adjacent apartment buildings rented out bleacher seats on the roof to watch games. A's owner Connie Mack tried unsuccessfully to block this activity in court. After his court defeat, he succeeded in blocking their view by raising the right field wall from 12 feet to 50 feet for the 1935 season.

The ballpark was sold to the Phillies for $2 million when the A's left for Kansas City before the 1955 season. In 1961 the Phillies sold the park to a realty company and signed a series of leases until the club moved to Veterans Stadium.

First A's Game. The first game was played on Monday, April 12, 1909, in front of 30,162 fans. The A's defeated the Red Sox 8–1.

First Phillies Game. The Phillies played their first game in the ballpark on July 4, 1938, losing 10–5 to the Braves.

Dimensions. The original dimensions from left to right field were 360–393–420–393–360. By the late 1960s the dimensions were 334–387–410–390–329.

Capacity. The ballpark held 33,233 at its closure in 1970, which was the approximate capacity throughout its history.

No-Hitters. The ballpark was the site of nine no-hitters.

Name. The ballpark was named after club owner Benjamin Shibe. In 1952 Shibe Park was renamed Connie Mack Stadium by a vote of the A's board of directors (against the wishes of Mack).

First Night Game. Shibe Park was the site of the first American League **Night Game** on May 16, 1939, as the A's lost to the Indians 8–3.

Last Game. The last game in Connie Mack Stadium/Shibe Park was October 1, 1970, as the Phillies and Dick Selma defeated the Expos 2–1 in 10 innings. To help prevent vandalism, fans at the game were presented with a souvenir seat slat as they entered the park. The slats were used as weapons at the end of the game, and

the park was decimated by fans immediately after the game. One fan ran on to the field during a play, preventing left fielder Ron Stone from making a catch.

Destruction. A 1971 fire set in the press box by two teenagers destroyed most of the abandoned park, and it was completely demolished in 1976. By 1990 the site was empty except for weeds and trash, though a housing development had been planned for the site when it was abandoned in 1970 and purchased by a real estate company for $1 million. The Deliverance Evangelistic Church now stands on a portion of the site.

Book. Bruce Kuklick, *To Everything a Season* (1991).

Shifts See *Strategy — Williams Shift*

Shinguards See *Catcher's Equipment*

Shoe Polish

"He can step on your shoes, but he doesn't mess up your shine."— Joe Morgan on the managing style of Frank Robinson.

"SHOE SHINE, 10 Cents. Giant fans, 15 cents."— Sign outside Ebbets Field.

"Listen kid, you better go and get yourself a shoeshine box. That is the only way you'll make a living."— Then-Brooklyn Dodger manager Casey Stengel to Phil Rizzuto at a high school tryout. Rizzuto later signed with the Yankees and Stengel took over the club in 1949.

See also *Shoes and Spikes*.

World Series Controversy. In Game 4 of the 1957 World Series, the Braves and Yankees were tied 4–4 after Yankee catcher Elston Howard hit a three-run homer in the top of the 9th inning. In the 10th inning the Yankees went ahead 5–4.

In the bottom of the 10th, Braves pinch hitter Nippy Jones led off, and the first pitch from Tommy Byrne was in the dirt. Jones argued that he had been hit by the pitch by pointing to the shoe polish on the ball. Umpire Augie Donatelli agreed and awarded him first base. Pinch runner Felix Mantilla scored on a double by Johnny Logan and then Eddie Mathews homered to win the game. With the 7–5 victory, the Braves tied the Series at two games each and went on to win in seven games. Jones never again appeared in a Major League game after Game 4.

Cleon Jones of the Mets had a similar experience during the 1969 World Series. In the deciding Game 5, Jones led off the 6th inning against pitcher Dave McNally of the Orioles. Jones claimed he had been hit on the shoe by the pitch and Mets manager Gil Hodges retrieved the ball to point out the shoe polish to umpire Lou DiMuro. DiMuro reversed his call and awarded Jones first base. The Mets then rallied on a Donn Clendenon home run to turn a 3–2 deficit into a 5–3 victory and the World Championship. In the top of the inning, DiMuro made a controversial call in which he ruled that a ball had hit Frank Robinson's bat for a foul before it hit him in the thigh.

Shine. The Astrodome had a shoe shine stand in the tunnel area behind home plate.

Shoelaces See *Shoes and Spikes*

Shoes and Spikes

"My feet are killing me."— Catcher Yogi Berra to Stan Musial in the bottom of the 12th inning of the 1955 All-Star Game in Milwaukee. Musial told Berra to relax and that he would "get him out of there in a hurry." Musial homered to end the game.

See also *Shoe Polish*.

Early Shoes. High top shoes were prominent in the early days of Organized Baseball. Spikes were widely used by the 1880s. In 1877 Harvard changed from canvas to leather shoes with ankle laces. In 1890 heel and toe plates were added by many players. By 1910 shoes were still hand-made calfskin or kangaroo with riveted spikes.

Modern Shoes. Baseball shoes come in four primary styles. Infielders and outfielders wear tops made of cowhide or kangaroo hide. Soles are plastic. While the soles are still soft at the factory, galvanized steel or cleats are embedded (see also **Spikes**).

Base stealers' shoes are sometimes all-nylon and are more lightweight than other shoes. Pitchers' shoes are similar to those for fielders, but the toe is built up with plastic so it does not wear out from pushing off the pitching rubber.

"Shoeless" Joe Jackson. Jackson despised his nickname because it made him sound like a hick, so he made a point of wearing expensive alligator and patent leather shoes.

High Tops Revisited. Because of his weak ankles, Bill Buckner reintroduced hightops to baseball in 1986. They later became fashionable, worn by stars including Joe Carter, Jack Clark, Tom Brunansky, Eric Davis and Mike Greenwell.

Synthetic Surfaces. Shoes for use on synthetic surfaces do not have metal cleats. They usually have 150 or more vulcanized rubber nubs.

Colors. For many years shoes were black, but now they come in the color of a team's uniform. Modern colored shoes were introduced in 1967 when Adidas came out with a Kangaroo leather dyed white for the A's. In the late 1960s the A's brought in three Kangaroos and named them after three local sportswriters who made fun of the Kangaroo skin shoes.

That same year Indians manager Joe Adcock protested a game with the A's because their white shoes "imitated the ball" in violation of Rule 1.11(e). The protest was rejected. A's owner Charlie Finley also had white skates for his San Francisco Seals hockey team.

In the 1970s Reds general manager Bob Howsam ordered that all shoes be black and that white stripes be rubbed out with polish. He contended that white shoes looked like clown shoes and distracted from the ball. His Cincinnati Reds were the first club in the late 1960s to match shoes other than white to uniform color (red). However, pitchers Jim Maloney and Tony Cloninger could not (or would not) pitch in the colored shoes so they switched to black. Howsam ordered that if two players wore black shoes, all had to wear black shoes. The club stayed with the black shoes until well into the 1980s.

Smallest Feet. Myril Hoag played 13 years in the American League from 1931 through 1945, batting .271. Despite being 5'11" and weighing 170 pounds, he reportedly wore size four shoes. Phil Rizzuto wore a size 5½ shoe.

Socks. See also *Uniforms—Socks and Stirrups*.

Shoeless Joe Jackson supposedly once played in his socks due to tight shoes.

Manufacturers. By the 1990s the largest baseball shoe manufacturers were Nike, Reebok, Mizuno, Apex and Converse, the last of which had dominated the market in earlier years.

Wrong Size. In August 1999 Juan Guzman started a game for his new club, the Reds, but had to come out of the game in the 7th inning because his shoes were too small. After he was traded by the Orioles, he arrived with the Reds carrying his size 10½ orange and black Orioles shoes. Puma shipped Guzman some Reds-colored

shoes, but they were size 9½ and Guzman developed blisters during the game and had to come out. The Reds won 9–2 despite the discomfort by their starter.

Dr. Scholl Take Note.

"They make me too high and I'm hitting over the ball."—Cardinals shortstop Pepper Martin on why he took out the inner soles from his baseball shoes.

According to Mrs. John McGraw, the Orioles used thin pieces of beef as innersoles for their shoes.

Lost Shoes. Pitcher Ray Kremer pitched for the Pirates from 1924 through 1933. He drank heavily and was known to tear up Pullman cars and throw his teammates' shoes out the train windows on road trips.

Performance Art. In 1993 residents of Santa Fe, New Mexico, began noticing shoes appearing on one of the main routes into the city. The phenomenon made the front page of the local newspaper: "Is it art, litter or just ... shoes?" The apparent conceptual art piece was completed in June 1994 when the following ad appeared in the local paper: "LOST SHOES. Frequently. Vicinity Old Pecos Trail. Please call Joe Jackson, Chicago."

Shoelaces.

"We have been handicapped by our inability to secure the quality of shoestrings to which we have been accustomed for the past five years. The Eastern clubs, knowing how largely we have depended upon this peculiar brand of lacing, formed a pool and purchased all the shoestrings of that manufacturer in the market. Such action was unfair and unprofessional, and it completely unnerved every member of the team."—Cap Anson's facetious explanation in May 1884 for Chicago's poor early-season performance.

In certain seasons in the 19th century the Boston Red Stockings purportedly issued their players one pair of shoestrings for the season. If the shoestrings lasted two years, the players received free trolley fare to and from the ballpark.

On April 17, 1945, Frankie Zak of the Pirates cost the team a game when a home run was disallowed after he had called time while standing on first base. His shoe was untied, and as he bent over to tie it he called time. The home plate umpire did not hear him, and teammate Jim Russell hit a home run to put the Pirates ahead. After the first base umpire ruled that time had been called, the home run was disallowed and Russell was forced to bat again. He failed to get on base and the Pirates lost. The next day manager Frankie Frisch presented Zak with buckled shoes to prevent further problems.

During the celebration on the field after the Red Sox clinched the 1967 pennant, a fan stole pitcher Jim Lonborg's shoelaces, but not his shoes.

Spikes. In the 1860s players began using clip-on spikes. Spikes were widely used by the 1880s, and in the 1890s the Cleveland Spiders under Patsy Tebeau were known to file their spikes. By the 1890s aggressive play led to calls for banning spiked shoes: "... those spikes cut like knives.... You might as well arm a man with a pitchfork."—Player quoted in the *New York Clipper* in 1895.

At one time spikes were overused to hurt opposing players, reportedly resulting in a ban for a few years in the late 19th century. In 1891 Pittsburgh fined Pete Browning for not wearing spikes, which were mandatory by that year. Golf spikes are specifically prohibited and no attachments may be added to shoes.

For modern shoes, usually six spikes 3/8th inches in length are put at the front and back of the heel. Although Ty Cobb denied ever filing his spikes, a number of players (including teammate Charlie Gehringer) recalled that Cobb would sit on the bench in the dugout and file them. Cobb claimed that it was a myth started by writer Bugs Baer.

Casey Stengel had a standard story about spikes from his managerial days in 1939 with the Braves. He sent rookie Otto Huber in to pinch run. Huber rounded third with the winning run but fell on his face and the game ended in a tie. The next day Stengel looked at Huber's shoes and noticed that his spikes were worn down to nothing, but Huber had a new pair in his locker. Huber acknowledged to Stengel that he had not used his best equipment, but that the new shoes hurt his feet and he had not expected Stengel to use him. Stengel then supposedly made a practice of looking at his players' spikes before sending them into a game to pinch run.

On July 2, 1939, the Giants and Dodgers squared off for a doubleheader amid the New York World's Fair, as players wore the Fair emblem, the trylon and the perisphere, on their uniform sleeves. A huge crowd of 51,000 came to the Polo Grounds, and in the second game rookie Giants manager Leo Durocher, playing shortstop, grounded into a double play in the 4th inning of a close game. He deliberately spiked big Dodger first baseman Zeke Bonura, who turned and fired the ball at Durocher and chased him down the right field line and put him in a headlock while he pounded away. Both were ejected from the game. Durocher later contended that he spiked Bonura because Dodger pitcher Hal Schumacher was throwing at the Giants. The Giants squeaked out a 6–4 victory for a split of the doubleheader.

Toots Shor (1903–1977)

"During the 1930s and 1940s, Toots Shor's restaurant in midtown Manhattan was the Giants' unofficial headquarters for the show business and sporting crowd."— Fred Stein in *Under Coogan's Bluff* (1978).

"Through booze I met two Chief Justices, 50 World Champs, Six Presidents, and DiMaggio and Babe Ruth."— Shor.

"Shor is a friend of the world at large, barring all communists and hypocrites."— Grantland Rice.

"The original site of Toots Shor's restaurant where the 'crumb bums' who played sports and the 'crumb bums' who wrote about them got together with those who rooted for them and read them, especially Toots."— Plaque laid down in 1977 on the sidewalk in front of the original site of the restaurant at 51 West 51st Street.

Toots Shor owned a famous New York City watering hole frequented by the great Yankee teams of the 1940s and 1950s and earlier by the 1930s Giants. He took over the tavern in the mid–1930s after the death of owner Billy Lahiff. As it became more popular with the common folk, Yogi Berra remarked: "It's so crowded, nobody goes there anymore."

Judge Landis once visited the restaurant in an effort to curtail Shor's gambling habits. The restaurant was closed in 1971 due to tax liens imposed by the IRS.

Shor vehemently denied being on the field in jubilation after Bobby Thomson's home run in the 1951 play-off against the Dodgers. Many eyewitnesses, including commissioner Ford Frick, saw Shor on the field with tears streaming down his face as he embraced the players.

It was at Shor's restaurant that Casey Stengel fell and broke his hip, ending his managerial career.

Shortest Careers See At-Bats and One-Game Career

Shortest Games See Fastest Games

Shortest Players See Smallest Players

Shortstops

"The position of shortstop was not considered important by the early professional teams until Dickey Pearce of the Atlantics commenced playing that position. Then it was that the business in that portion of the field was brought into the limelight for the first time."— Alfred H. Spink in 1910.

"Good stockbrokers are a dime a dozen, but good shortstops are hard to find."— A's owner Charlie Finley.

"If I had a shortstop with a 25-foot wingspan, who could leap 25 feet in the air, all my problems would be solved."— Pitcher Jerry Reuss.

Early Shortstops. George Wright, shortstop with the Cincinnati Red Stockings of 1869, was at age 29 one of the premier shortstops at the inception of the National League in 1876. He helped revolutionize the shortstop position by playing deeper, rather than in the baseline, and he was also able to throw with either hand.

Dickey Pearce of the St. Louis Browns was a shortstop who made innovations in shortstop play before Wright. He moved closer to the infield, whereas before the shortstop often played as a short fielder (the opposite of Wright's positioning).

Bobby Wallace played for 25 years starting in 1894, primarily with the Browns. He was the first American League shortstop to be elected to the Hall of Fame. He changed fielding, as other early shortstops fielded the ball and then straightened up for the throw. He started scooping the ball on the run and tossing while off balance. This may have been made easier because of the evolution of gloves during this period.

Greatest Shortstops.

"Perhaps the greatest pair of hands baseball has ever seen dangled at the end of the long arms of Hans Wagner. They, indeed, were more like twin steam shovels than human hands, literally ploughing under National League infields. The Flying Dutchman of the Pirates never fielded the ball alone. He would blithely scoop a handful of dirt too and ball and dirt would go flying over to first base impartially. It left Old Honus hidden behind a smoke screen of his own raising."— *Baseball* magazine on Honus Wagner in August 1943. Wagner is considered by many as the best shortstop of all time. He batted .327 over 21 seasons (1897–1917) with 3,418 hits. He was known for his large hands and graceful moves on the field despite being big and gangly (5'11" and 200 pounds).

"The experts will rave about Joe Cronin as a hitting shortstop, Phil Rizzuto as a fielder, Travis Jackson as a thrower and so on. But Wagner, eight times the batting champion of the National League, was a better hitter than Cronin. Old-timers will tell you he was a better thrower than Jackson, a better fielder than Rizzuto and, on top of all that, he was the base-stealing champion of the league for five seasons."— Arthur Daley on Wagner.

"Cal [Ripken] is a bridge, maybe the last bridge, back to the way the game was played. Hitting home runs and all that other good stuff is not enough. It's how you handle yourself in all the good times and bad times that matters. That's what Cal showed us. Being a star is not enough. He showed us how to be more."— Joe Torre.

The best of the 1930s was Joe Cronin, who hit .301 with 1,424 RBIs and was a player-manager for most of his career.

Manager Miller Huggins of the 1920s Yankees described shortstop Leo Durocher as the best infielder he had ever seen. Durocher needed those skills because his bat was weak; Babe Ruth dubbed him "The All-American Out."

Arky Vaughan was an excellent-hitting National League short-stop in the 1930s and early 1940s, with a .318 lifetime average. However, he had as many as 52 errors in a season and was not known for his defensive play for the Pirates and Dodgers.

Pee Wee Reese was probably the best defensive shortstop of the 1940s and early 1950s though Phil Rizzuto, Lou Boudreau and Marty Marion also stood out in those decades.

Luis Aparicio revolutionized base stealing and was a terrific defensive shortstop in the 1950s and 1960s.

The best of the 1970s include Larry Bowa, Freddie Patek and Mark Belanger, but Dave Concepcion was probably the best defensive shortstop of the group.

For pure athleticism and grace at the position, Ozzie Smith will probably rank as the best ever, and his hitting improved dramatically during his career. His average rose steadily from a low of .211 in 1979 to a high of .303 in 1987.

Ernie Banks hit many of his 512 home runs while playing first base for the Cubs later in his career. Banks is highly rated because he hit over 40 home runs and had over 100 RBIs five times in his eight full seasons at shortstop, 1954 through 1961.

Another all-time shortstop is Cal Ripken, Jr. His consecutive game streak speaks for itself, and his fielding has been near-flawless (see also *Errors—Shortstops*).

Barry Larkin of the Reds and Omar Vizquel of the Indians have been considered the best shortstops of the 1990s. In 1995 Larkin was the National League MVP and Visquel led his club into the World Series.

Alex Rodriguez is the class of the 2000s. Rodriguez moved over to third base when he joined the Yankees, in deference to Derek Jeter (though Rodriguez was considered the better fielder).

Home Runs. In 1991 Barry Larkin became the first shortstop in history to hit five home runs over two consecutive games.

On July 12, 1992, Braves shortstop Jeff Blauser hit three home runs in a game against the Cubs at Wrigley Field. He joined Ernie Banks, Larkin and 5'4" Freddie Patek (!) as the only shortstops to hit three home runs in a game through that season. John Valentin did it for the Red Sox in 1995.

Cal Ripken had 343 home runs while a shortstop through the 1996 season (his last as a shortstop), the most at the position until 2003, and finished with 431. He played third base for the rest of his career after 1996. The most before Ripken was the 277 hit by Ernie Banks while he played the position between 1953 and 1961. Alex Rodriguez holds the record with 57 home runs in a single season by a shortstop, in 2001. He had 345 through the 2003 season for the Mariners and Rangers, but when he signed with the Yankees for the 2004 season he moved to third base.

Shutouts

"Allen S. Sothoron pitched his initials off yesterday."—Bugs Baer, after the journeyman pitcher threw a shutout.

"Either it was the best he's ever thrown against us or the worst we've ever swung."—Bill Madlock of the Pirates on a Mike LaCoss shutout.

"Goose eggs are becoming as staple an item of Father Penn's diet as scrapple."—*New York Sun* reporter on the Giants' several shutouts of the Philadelphia Athletics in the 1905 World Series.

"He is the only man I've ever seen pitch a shutout on a day when he had absolutely nothing. Pitchers have those days … [Sal] Maglie got by on meanness."—Alvin Dark in his autobiography, *When in Doubt, Fire the Manager* (1980).

First. Jacob Morse reported in *Sphere and Ash* (1888) that the first shutout (which were rare in the early days of baseball), was on November 8, 1860. The Brooklyn Excelsiors and pitcher Jim Creighton beat the St. George's Cricket Club.

Chicagoed.
"For the Glory of Its Base-Ball Representatives Has Departed. And Their Proud Championship Banner Is Plastered with Whitewash.
A Liberal Coat of Which Was Administered Yesterday
  by the Erratic Chicagos."
— Headline of June 1876 when the Chicago White Stockings shut out the Boston Red Stockings 2–0.

In the early days of the National League the White Stockings were so dominant that to be "Chicagoed" or "Whitewashed" was synonymous with a shutout. In 1876 the team won 52 games, many of them by shutout, on its way to the National League pennant.

The BaseballLibrary.com website, relying on the Retrosheet researchers for statistics, has one researcher fond of using the term "calcimine" to describe a shutout ("The Dodgers calcimined the Padres"). Calcimine is a white liquid.

Most/Career. Walter Johnson pitched 110 shutouts in his career. For years he was credited with 113 shutouts, but the total was reduced when it was determined that three of them were not complete games. Johnson pitched in 64 1–0 games, winning 38 of them for the usually mediocre Senators. Three of the losses were to Babe Ruth and the Red Sox. Second all-time is Grover Cleveland Alexander, with 90. Among more recent pitchers, the leaders are Warren Spahn with 63, Nolan Ryan and Tom Seaver with 61, and Bert Blyleven with 60.

Most/Season. Grover Cleveland Alexander pitched 16 shutouts in 1916 for the Phillies, up from 12 in 1915. He had another eight in 1917 for a total of 36 in three years. He had 90 over his 20-year career, though 81 were in his first 11 seasons. Bob Gibson is second in National League history with 13 shutouts for the Cardinals in 1968.

One source reported that Lefty Gomez holds the American League record with 11 shutouts in 1941. Gomez only had two that year and the most he had in any year was six, in 1934 and 1937. The American League record is 13 by Jack Coombs of the A's in 1911.

Two in One Day. On September 26, 1908, Ed Ruelbach of the Cubs pitched the only pair of shutouts in one day by the same pitcher. He shut out the Dodgers 5–0 and 3–0.

Three in Four Days. Walter Johnson is famous for a three game run over four days: he pitched a 3–0 shutout against the Highlanders (Yankees) on a Friday. On Saturday he beat them 6–0. On Monday (there was no Sunday ball) he beat them 4–0.

What is not readily recalled, as discovered by Lyle Spatz, is that Jimmy Dygert pitched three shutouts in four days during the heat of a pennant race the year before Johnson's feat. The Athletics were (unsuccessfully) trying to catch the Tigers, and with only a few games before the end of the season, Dygert threw shutouts against Cleveland on Saturday, October 1, and Monday, October 3, 1907, and then shut out Washington on October 4. He allowed 12 hits and three walks, while striking out 24 batters. Johnson struck out only 12 during his streak. Dygert finished the year with a 21–8 record.

See **World Series Shutouts** below for Christy Mathewson's three shutouts in a single series, but not over four days.

Team Avoidance. Until 2000, the 1932 Yankees were the only team to avoid a shutout through an entire season. This was part of a streak of 211 games that began on August 5, 1931, when the Red Sox defeated the Yankees. The 1927 Yankees were shut out only one time.

In Frank Graham's 1940s history of the Yankees, he erroneously reported that the Yankees went 308 straight games without suffering a shutout, with the streak purportedly ending on August 3, 1933, when Lefty Grove shut them out.

In 1993 the Phillies broke the National League record held by the Pirates, who were not shut out over 150 games in 1924–1925. The Phillies went 174 games without suffering a shutout until September 30, 1993. That record was broken by the Cincinnati Reds over three seasons. On October 4, 1999, the Reds were shut out 5-to-0 by the Mets in a one-game playoff that cost them a postseason berth. The Reds were not shut out again, for a National League record 208 games, until May 24, 2001, when the Cubs beat them 3–0. Cubs pitcher Jon Lieber needed only 78 pitches. On the day that the Reds broke the Phillies' record, there were a record 11 games decided by one run, breaking a daily record set in 1967.

The Colorado Rockies hold the record for most home games not being shut out, 353, a record streak that ended in late August 2003.

Major League Trend. During the 1968 season there were 150 shutouts in the first 810 games, which contributed to rule changes favoring hitters following the season. The Major Leagues experienced a record 339 shutouts that year, along with 82 1–0 games.

Lopsided.

"If you told every hitter each pitch would be a fastball down the middle, you wouldn't get a score like that."—Derek Jeter after the Indians pounded the Yankees 22–0 on August 31, 2004. It was the worst defeat in their history, as Cleveland shortstop Omar Vizquel had six hits.

The most lopsided shutout in Major League history was a 28–0 victory by Providence over the Philadelphia Phillies on August 21, 1883.

On September 16, 1975, the Pirates defeated the Cubs 22–0. This was the same game in which Rennie Stennett had seven *Hits* in seven at-bats, including two in the same inning. At least two sources have reported the score as 18–0. Pittsburgh beat up on Cubs starter Rick Reuschel, scoring nine runs in the 1st inning. Despite all the hitting, the game was played in two hours and 35 minutes. The Pirates collected 24 hits, including three by Willie Stargell and Frank Taveras, in addition to Stennett's seven.

Next in line are the 21–0 wins by the Tigers over the Indians on September 15, 1901, and by the Yankees over the Philadelphia A's on August 13, 1939.

On June 10, 1944, the Reds lost to the Cardinals 18–0, and Joe Nuxhall became the *Youngest Player* in Major League history when he debuted in the 9th inning for the Reds. Despite the score, the game lasted only 2 hours and 23 minutes.

Other 18-run shutouts in the first half of the 20th century found the Phillies on the short end. They lost by that score three times, in 1910, 1930 and 1934.

On August 3, 1961, the Pirates scored a 19–0 victory over the Cardinals for the largest shutout score in a National League night game. On May 10, 2002, the Angels beat the White Sox 19–0, becoming the 11th team in the 20th century to win by shutout and score at least 19 runs.

On April 16, 1990, the Brewers beat the Red Sox 18–0 in Fenway Park. Amazingly, the Brewers did it without hitting a home run or knocking any of their nine doubles off the Green Monster.

Consecutive by Pitcher. Don Drysdale had six consecutive shutouts on his way to a then-record 58⅔ *Scoreless Innings* streak. The innings record was broken in 1988 by Orel Hershiser, who recorded six shutouts on his way to 59 consecutive scoreless innings. This included 10 shutout innings against the Padres in his last start of the season, but the Dodgers could not score and he was lifted before the 11th inning began.

Bob Gibson pitched five straight shutouts in 1968, only a few weeks after Drysdale set his scoreless innings record while pitching six straight shutouts. Gibson was asked after the fifth shutout if he felt pressure to break Drysdale's record: "I face more pressure every day just being a Negro."

The most pitchers to combine on a shutout is six. Until 1994 it had happened only once in the National League. Within two days in May of that year, the Marlins and Cardinals each had six pitchers combine to throw a shutout. The Marlins also did it on June 4, 2002, the last club to do so.

Brothers. Paul and Rick Reuschel are the only brothers ever to combine on a shutout. Paul started and went 2⅔ innings and Rick finished the game, a 7–0 shutout against the Dodgers on August 21, 1975.

Consecutive by Team. The 1995 Orioles finished the season with five straight shutouts, including a four- and two-hitter by Mike Mussina. Two were against the Blue Jays and three were against the Tigers. The shutouts tied the club and American League record.

Before the Tigers in 1995, the 1991 Indians were the last of a number of teams that have been shut out in three consecutive games.

World Series Shutouts. Christy Mathewson of the Giants pitched three shutouts in six days during the 1905 World Series against the A's. He gave up 14 hits in 27 innings, struck out 18 and allowed one walk. Every game of the five-game series was a shutout.

Extra Inning. Late in the 2003 season, Blue Jays pitcher Roy Halladay (who won the Cy Young Award that season) pitched a 10-inning 1–0 shutout over the Tigers, making him the first pitcher to throw an extra-inning shutout since Twins pitcher Jack Morris beat the Braves in Game 7 of the 1991 World Series.

One of the most famous games of the 19th century was played on August 17, 1882. After 17 innings neither John Montgomery Ward of Providence nor George Weidman of Detroit had given up a run. Providence's Old Hoss Radbourn, normally a pitching star, hit a home run in the 18th inning for a 1–0 victory. The Detroit outfielder attempted to retrieve Radbourn's drive and make a play on him, but he had difficulty getting underneath the horses and carriages that occupied the open outfield area where the ball landed.

On July 2, 1963, Giants pitcher Juan Marichal threw 16 innings to shut out the Braves 1–0. Forty-two-year-old Warren Spahn went the distance for the Braves. Willie Mays connected for a home run off Spahn in the bottom of the 16th inning for the win.

On June 2, 1998, when 43-year-old Braves pitcher Dennis Martinez tied Juan Marichal for most victories by a Latin pitcher (243), he shut out the Brewers 9–0 and gave up 12 hits.

Shutout/No Complete Game. In 1988 Yankee pitcher Neil Allen came into the game in the 1st inning with a man on first. He picked him off and finished the game for the victory. The official scorer credited him with a shutout, but he was not credited with a complete game.

25 Wins/No Shutouts. Joe Bush is the only pitcher in modern history to win at least 25 games and not pitch a shutout. He was 26–7 in 1922 with the Yankees.

Rookie Debut. On September 3, 2002, Andy Van Hekken became the first American League pitcher to throw a complete game shutout in his debut since Mike Norris in 1975, and the first Tiger pitcher since Schoolboy Rowe in 1933. Van Hekken beat Cleveland 4–0. He only appeared in five games that year and had not returned to the Major Leagues by September 2004.

No One Shot Wonder. Yankee pitcher Russ Van Atta threw a shutout in his first Major League game, a five-hitter against the Senators on April 25, 1933. He also went 4-for-4. One source reported that he never pitched another shutout in seven years of Major League pitching and 76 starts. However, *The Baseball Encyclopedia* credits him with two more shutouts, including a second in 1933.

Dominating One Team. In 1966 Larry Jaster was 11–5 for the Cardinals and spent part of the year optioned to Tulsa. He pitched five shutouts against the Dodgers; none against the other teams in the league.

Grover Cleveland Alexander pitched five of his 16 shutouts in 1916 against the Reds.

Tough Ballpark. It took the Astros 132 games before the home team shut out an opponent in Enron Field (now Sunkist Field), which opened on April 7, 2000. The old record for a new facility was 103 games, set by the Rockies after moving into Coors Field in 1995. On June 12, 1996, the Rockies recorded only their third home game shutout in franchise history.

In 2000 the Astros only threw two shutouts, both on the road.

Most Hits Allowed. On September 14, 1913, Larry Cheney of the Cubs pitched a 14-hit shutout against the Giants. This was one of three straight 20-win seasons for him that included 12 shutouts.

Christy Mathewson is also credited with a 14-hit shutout. He gave up hits to the first two batters in each of the first seven innings. He bore down and retired the side in the 8th and 9th innings.

In July 1993 Steve Avery and Mark Wohlers of the Braves combined on a 13-hit shutout.

Most Shutout Losses/Season. Jim Bunning of the Phillies set a Major League record when he lost five shutouts in 1967. All were by scores of 1–0.

Oldest to Pitch. Phil Niekro holds the record for oldest to pitch a shutout at age 46 years six months. On the last day of the 1985 season he shut out the Blue Jays 8–0. The Blue Jays had just clinched the pennant and fielded a team primarily consisting of rookies and bench players.

Charlie Hough is the second-oldest at 46 years five months. Satchel Paige is third at 46 years two months.

Two Shutouts/First Two Starts. In 1981 Fernando Valenzuela joined a group of nine other pitchers who pitched shutouts in their first two Major League starts: Tom Phoebus (1966), Karl Spooner (1954), Al Worthington (1953), Dave "Boo" Ferriss (1945), Johnny Marcum (1933), Joe Doyle (1906), Jim Hughes (1898) and John Montgomery Ward (1878).

Fast Start/Slow Finish. Earl Caldwell pitched a shutout in his Major League debut in 1928 for the Phillies and then did not pitch again in the Major Leagues for seven years.

Delayed Gratification. Jason Schmidt of the Giants started 163 games before throwing his first shutout, the longest streak of its kind since 1900. The second-longest streak belonged to Angels starter Jarrod Washburn, who lasted 145 games before throwing a shutout.

Percentage of Games Started. Shutouts are pitched an average of about 6–7% of the time. The total was higher in the early 20th century (over 9% until 1920) and was lowest in the power eras of the 1920s and 1930s (over 5%). The best pitcher was Big Ed Walsh, who pitched a shutout in over 18% of his career starts. Walter Johnson, the all-time leader with 110 shutouts, pitched one over 16% of the time. One of the best of the modern era, Sandy Koufax, pitched a shutout almost 13% of the time. Babe Ruth had 17 shutouts (18 in older sources) among his 94 wins and 148 starts (11.5%).

Scoreless Innings/World Series. Whitey Ford had 33 shutout innings in the 1960, 1961 and 1962 World Series, breaking Babe Ruth's record of 29⅓ innings.

Book. Joe MacKay, *Great Shutout Pitchers: Twenty Profiles of a Vanishing Breed* (2003).

Siblings

See also **Brothers** and **Twins**, for players whose brothers played Major League Baseball.

Lou Gehrig's sister Adeline was the American Women's Foil Champion from 1920 through 1923.

Pitcher Randy Moffitt's sister is tennis star Billie Jean King.

Signing Bonuses See **Bonus Babies**

Signs

"Sometimes it looks like five guys trying to bring a jet onto an aircraft carrier. Some are signs, some are decoys, and it's fascinating to sit there and watch the stuff flying all over the place."—Pitching coach Ray Miller.

"I have no clue what any of this means. For all I know, we don't even have signs."—Angels reliever Troy Percival, who didn't understand any of third base coach Rick Burleson's signs when asked to go to the plate for his first career at-bat.

"The game is getting so scientific that the catchers are going to need fluorescent manicures."—Broadcaster Al Michaels during the 1995 World Series on how difficult it sometimes is for a pitcher to read all the catcher's signs.

Origins. By the 1890s catchers were routinely signaling for pitches. At least three versions of the origins of pitcher/catcher signs credit players on the early 1880s Chicago White Stockings with beginning the practice.

One source reported that 1880s White Stockings pitcher Larry Corcoran is considered one of the first to give signs to his catcher. He supposedly did it by shifting the tobacco chaw in his mouth.

Another source reported that White Stockings catcher Mike "King" Kelly was the first to use finger signals with pitchers. A third source credits both Corcoran and Kelly as jointly devising the signaling system along with catcher Silver Flint of that team. The "signal" for Flint was his tobacco chaw, which he (not Corcoran) shifted in his mouth.

Hall of Famer Tommy McCarthy of the 1890s Boston Red Stockings is credited by some with developing the practice of signaling to batters and runners while managing from the bench. However, he managed only during the 1890 season. Nineteenth-century manager Bill McGunnigle signaled his fielders by using a whistle. Signs flourished in the early 20th century when the hit-and-run and other strategies were in vogue during the last years of the dead ball era.

Indicator. The standard protocol is for the sign giver to have an "indicator" sign. Until the indicator sign is given, all the signs before it are meaningless. The sign given immediately after the indicator is the key sign for the batter or baserunner.

Mascot. Former Padres general manager Jack McKeon was once ejected from a minor league game but returned to the field dressed in the mascot's outfit to give his signs.

Second Base. Nineteenth century barehanded shortstop Jack Glasscock is credited as the first infielder to signal the catcher whether the shortstop or the second baseman was going to cover second base on a steal attempt.

Ted Williams. Lou Boudreau's hitting was wearing out the Red Sox, and Williams was disgusted with the pitches being called by his club's catcher, Birdie Tebbetts. Williams thought he could call the pitches better than Tebbetts and signaled in from left field by touching his body. Tebbetts reluctantly followed Williams' signals and then blamed Williams when Boudreau kept hitting. Williams claimed that Tebbetts called exactly the opposite of what he called from the outfield.

Eye in the Sky. In 1990 the American League outlawed the system by which coaches sat in the press box and positioned the defense by phone to the dugout. The ban stemmed from a claim by the Orioles that the White Sox had their "eye" at ground level to help steal signs. The National League continued to allow the eye in the sky.

Manager Leo Durocher was once ejected from a game. He sneaked into the press box and whispered instructions to writer Barney Kremenko, who signaled the information to the players on the field.

Special Relationship.

"If you believe your catcher is intelligent and you know that he has considerable experience, it is a good thing to leave the game almost entirely in his hands." — Bob Feller.

In 1933 shortstop Joe Cronin was managing the Senators at the tender age of 27. He confidentially told his catcher, Luke Sewell, that he knew little about pitching. He asked Sewell to help him decide when to warm up a reliever and bring in a new pitcher. Depending on which direction Sewell threw dirt from behind the plate, Cronin would know what to do. Only Sewell and Cronin knew about the sign for the entire season.

Nose. John McGraw later revealed that his favorite signal was to blow his nose.

Wired. In Fred Lieb's *Philadelphia Phillies* (1953), he recounted a story of stolen signs. Tommy Corcoran of the Reds was coaching third base in 1898. He found a metal wire in the coaching box and traced it across the field to the Phillies locker room. There he found Morgan Murphy, a reserve catcher, sitting with a telegraph instrument by an open window with a form of binoculars. He was stealing the signals and sending them by buzzer to the coach, who relayed them to the batter.

The Phillies initially claimed that the wiring in the coaching box was left over from a carnival lighting system. It was also determined that this devious practice had been encouraged by owner John I. Rogers.

In 1901 the A's stole signs by relaying information from beyond the center field fence by positioning a weather vane just before each pitch.

Mirrors. Yankee manager George Stallings rented an apartment beyond right field and hired someone to steal pitches and relay signs by mirror.

Secret System. The 1951 Giants supposedly had an elaborate sign-stealing network that helped them in the miracle September pennant race and National League play-off against the Dodgers. The rumors about it finally came to light in a 2001 article by *Wall Street Journal* writer Josh Prager.

Members of the New York Giants finally admitted that they set up an elaborate sign-stealing system at the Polo Grounds. Giants catcher Sal Yvars sat in the Giants clubhouse, located behind the center field bleachers, and used binoculars (a telescope in an earlier source) to read the catcher's signs (an earlier source commenting on the rumors reported that it was coach Herman Franks). He then set off a bell or buzzer in the Giants bullpen that would identify the pitch, and a bullpen pitcher would relay the signal in to

the hitter. Bobby Thomson indicated that he didn't steal the sign for the pitch that he drove into the bleachers, but prior to that he waffled on the question with, "I'd have to say more no than yes." Yvars later said "yes" when asked if it happened. Mueller said "as for my home runs and the sign stealing, this has been much talked about and I would prefer not to comment."

Ralph Branca was more pointed on the subject after the report came out: "It would have tarnished Bobby's accomplishment, and I didn't want to do that. He still hit the ball. He still hit a home run. I don't want to be a crybaby. I don't want to cry over spilt milk. I don't want to be a sore loser. But now that it's come out, it's loosened my tongue so that I can talk about it. If you watch the replay, he's in a crouch. He steps into the bucket a little bit, and he attacks the ball. He's like a lion jumping on top of a wounded antelope. He says, no, he didn't have the sign, and I say he did. So we disagree on that. I blame Giant management. It was immoral. There was no law against it, because nobody thought anybody would be so despicable as to conceive of that system. I mean they really worked it out. They had a buzzer system they sent to the bullpen and to the dugout. They had a telescope where you could see a fly on a chimney from 300 feet away. We had no clue they were calling the signs. But he told me, at that moment, he didn't take the sign. He's said he was proud of that swing. The sign was given. Whether he took it or not, I can't get into his head."

Electronic Communication.

"Great, dial-a-pitch. Now [Jim] Palmer can blame you instead of me." — Orioles catcher Rick Dempsey to manager Earl Weaver on the new electronic gadget that allowed catcher and pitcher to communicate without using fingers. Weaver's response: "I just hope that you don't electrocute yourself."

In 1992 the Orioles accused the White Sox of stealing their pitches from the stands and sending them to the bench through a walkie-talkie. American League president Bobby Brown banned all electronic communication to and from the dugout. Television monitors are also a problem because they are in the clubhouse and usually have a center field camera peering in to see the catcher's sign.

In 1974 Billy Martin was managing the Rangers. He tried using a transistor hook-up to his coaches to relay signals. The transmission was faulty one day and the frustrated Martin could not get the suicide squeeze information to coach Frank Lucchesi after screaming repeatedly into the microphone. Red Sox pitcher Luis Tiant finally stepped off the mound and yelled: "Frank, Billy said he wants the suicide squeeze."

Martin abandoned the microphone.

Tipping Pitchers/Fielder's Position. In a "Game of the Week" telecast in 1978, Tony Kubek called many of the Red Sox pitches because of shortstop Rick Burleson's movements just before the pitch.

Peeking. Pitchers and catchers have a way of dealing with a batter who peeks a look at the catcher's sign. Royals outfielder Al Cowens had his jaw shattered in 1980 when he peeked at a call for a curveball. The pitch was a fastball high and tight thrown by Ed Farmer.

Double standard.

"Bootling information to the batter through a hidden observer equipped with field glasses is a dastardly deed. But the coach who can stand on the third base line and, using only his own eyes and intelligence, tap the enemy's line of communication, is justly admired for his acuteness." — Sportswriter Red Smith in 1950.

Novel Ideas. In 1962 Charlie Metro was part of the Chicago *College of Coaches* revolving manager experiment. To gain an edge, he hired two Chicago ventriloquists to help him learn how to throw his voice while on the field. He couldn't get the hang of it. He also hired a handwriting expert to analyze the signatures of the other National League managers (see *Autographs*).

Dumb Players. Zeke Bonura was a first baseman for the White Sox in the 1930s. He was so poor at receiving signs that manager Jimmy Dykes would simply yell, "Bunt, you meathead." A few years later, after Bonura had been traded to the Senators, he was on third base when White Sox manager Dykes was shooing flies with a towel—which was Dykes' sign for a steal. Bonura broke for home and bowled over the catcher and was safe. He said later that he saw Dykes give the steal sign and took off, but "I forgot I wasn't on his team anymore."

Rudy Law of the Dodgers was so poor at remembering signs that teammate Rick Monday started using a large arrow from the dugout to signal Law when the Dodgers wanted him to steal.

Teeth. Braves manager George Stallings had a dark complexion, so he used his bright white teeth to signal from the bench.

Scoreboard Manipulation. Around 1905 the Yankees had a man with binoculars behind the fence near an advertisement for hats. As soon as he had stolen the pitch called for, he would manipulate the h in "hatter" to let the batter know whether a fastball was coming. This incident may be related to a 1909 discovery by Detroit trainer Harry Tuthill. He found that the "o" in a sign on the Yankees' outfield wall had a shutter that allowed a sign stealer to observe the field.

The Giants used a player sitting in front of the center field Polo Grounds clubhouse to hold up a bottle for a curveball, no bottle for a fastball.

The 1950s White Sox were known to manipulate their scoreboard to tip pitches.

The Astros turned a light on in their scoreboard to tip their batters.

Top Sign Stealers. In 1957 *The Sporting News* solicited opinions as to the best sign stealers since World War I. The list included Del Baker, Eddie Collins, Frank Crosetti, Charlie Dressen, Leo Durocher, Freddie Fitzsimmons, Art Fletcher, Mike Gonzalez, Billy Herman, John McGraw, Merv Shea and Rudy York.

Former outfielder and White Sox coach Joe Nossek was considered by some to be the best at stealing signs, which many believe can add up to four or five wins a year.

Charlie Dressen was such a good sign stealer that he told the 1953 National League All-Stars that they would not need a set of signs for the game. He would simply give each player the signs used by his own team. Dressen was crossed up by signs at least once, however, when he managed the Dodgers in the 1953 World Series. Billy Martin of the Yankees intercepted the squeeze bunt sign because Dressen used the same sign that he had used years earlier when he managed Martin in the Pacific Coast League.

When Harvey Haddix pitched 12⅔ innings of a **Perfect Game** in 1959 against Milwaukee, the Braves apparently had figured out the signals and knew what Haddix was going to throw.

Hard to Decipher. A's owner Charlie Finley once insisted that manager Alvin Dark show him all the signs the club used. Dark spent over an hour detailing the signs in slow motion. When he finished, Finley asked him to flash the signs the way he would do it in a game. Finley could not identify a single sign.

Umpire Signals. See *Umpires—Hand Signals*.

Book. Harold Southworth, *The Complete Book of Baseball Signs* (1993).

Silver Slugger Award (1946–)

This award was given annually beginning in 1946 by *The Sporting News* to the player at each position in each league with the best batting average. The first winners were Stan Musial and Mickey Vernon, but eventually the award was discontinued. Bat manufacturer Hillerich & Bradsby began its own version of the award in 1980. Managers and coaches now vote (but not for their own players) based on a combination of batting average, slugging percentage and on-base percentage. More recently, Mike Piazza won 10 in a row between 1993 and 2002. Shortstop Cal Ripken won eight over his career and Alex Rodriguez won six straight through 2003.

Al Simmons (1902–1956)

Hall of Fame 1953

"If I could only have nine players named Simmons."—Connie Mack.

"A swaggering man and a savage hitter, Simmons hated all pitchers and his batting averages showed it."—Lawrence Ritter and Donald Honig in *The Image of Their Greatness* (1976).

"Al Simmons arrived in 1924 with his foot in the bucket and his bat in the groove."—Murray Olderman in *Nelson's 20th Century Encyclopedia of Baseball* (1963).

Simmons starred primarily for the A's beginning in 1924, hitting .334 over 20 seasons.

Born Aloys Szymanski in Milwaukee, Simmons began his Major League career in the outfield as an immediate starter with the A's in 1924, where he enjoyed his greatest success. Despite a nickname of "Bucketfoot Al" for his unorthodox hitting style, he hit over .300 in each of his first 11 seasons. They included league-leading averages of .381 in 1930 and .390 in 1931. He drove in over 100 runs in 11 straight seasons and had 200 or more hits six times.

He was traded by Connie Mack after the 1932 season and spent three years with the White Sox. After hitting .331 and .344 in 1933 and 1934, he began to fade due to a career of hard drinking. After bouncing around various clubs he returned to the A's in 1940 for 37 games. He played parts of three more seasons and retired after four games in 1944.

Simmons finished with a .334 average and 2,927 hits. He hit .329 in four World Series and his .658 slugging average is in the top ten all-time. He was a player-coach for the A's from 1940 through 1942 and then coached for the club from 1945 through 1949. After coaching for the Indians in 1950, he retired to Milwaukee.

Singers

"Playing the Field"—When outfielder Tony Conigliaro made it to the Red Sox in 1964, he recorded this song. On the flip side of the "45" record was "Little Red Scooter." He also recorded a duet with singer Dionne Warwick.

"It's like I'm Elvis. I walked into a Burger King and got a standing ovation."—Josh Beckett of the Marlins after his 2–0 shutout of the Yankees in Game 6 of the 2003 World Series won the championship.

"Eddie Fisher, King Cole, Charlie Daniels, Jim Morrison"

See also *Musicians, National Anthem* and *Songs*.

Al Mamaux. The Pirates pitcher had back-to-back 21-win seasons in 1914 and 1915 and was dubbed the "New Christy Mathewson." He fell apart after that, but throughout his baseball career and later he was a vaudeville singer known as "The Golden-Voiced Tenor."

Red Sox. Marty McHale ("The Baseball Caruso"), Buck O'Brien, Hugh Bradley and Bill Lyons formed the "Red Sox Quartette" that played vaudeville together for three years in the 1910s.

Cohen and Hogan. In the 1920s second baseman Andy Cohen and catcher Shanty Hogan performed a vaudeville act called "Cohen and Hogan." When they hit Boston (in Hogan's home state), the billing was always changed to "Hogan and Cohen."

Waite Hoyt. The Yankee pitcher earned $1,500 a week in the late 1920s as a vaudeville performer.

Mickey McDermott. The 1950s Red Sox pitcher was a colorful player who sang in Boston nightclubs. He also sang with crooner Eddie Fisher in the Catskills resort hotels.

Charlie Pride. The future country-western singer was the first player cut in the Angels' first spring training camp in 1961.

Beatles. The last public concert by the Fab Four was held on August 29, 1966, at Candlestick Park.

Mudcat Grant. Pitcher Jim "Mudcat" Grant of the 1960s Indians and Twins was the lead singer in a group known as Mudcat & the Kittens.

Lee May. Outfielder Lee May, primarily of the 1960s Reds and Orioles, was the lead singer in Andrew Lee May and the Crowns and occasionally sang with The Platters. One source identified the group as "Arthur Lee Maye..." May's most successful song was "Halfway Out of Love," which sold 500,000 copies in 1964.

Mets. After the 1969 World Series, seven of the World Champion Mets appeared in a Las Vegas lounge act with comedian Phil Foster. Each player was paid $10,000 for the two-week engagement.

Umpire. National League umpire Joe West is a singer and songwriter who has performed at the Grand Ole Opry.

Deion Sanders. Sanders recorded a CD, "Prime Time," that was on the R&B charts for several months and one of the songs, "Must Be the Money," was in the top 10.

Bruce Hornsby. In the 1990s the singer once pinch-ran for the Angels during an exhibition game.

Garth Brooks. The country music star appeared in a 1999 spring training game at age 37 for the Padres, pinch running for Wally Joyner in an exhibition game against the Cubs. He joined the club for two days of workouts, taking batting practice, shagging balls and planning to watch games from a luxury box. He made it safely back to first on a pick-off attempt (on a generous call by umpire Ed Montague), and then was out at second base on a double play. He also had spring training stints with the Padres in 1998 and with the Mets in 2000. He was 1-for-39 in the preseason. In 2004 he was back, this time with the Royals, to again raise awareness and money for his foundation, Teammates for Kids Foundation.

Rock Star. In 2003 the Red Sox began airing a between-innings video clip (bootlegged to the club by a friend) of first baseman Kevin Millar as a teenager lip-synching Bruce Springsteen's "Born in the U.S.A." Millar's response: "I was rolling ground balls when I heard the song come on. It didn't dawn on me at first, and then I looked up and saw the biggest dork I'd ever seen. I looked over at the Oakland dugout and saw [pitcher Tim] Hudson laughing so hard he actually fell off the water cooler."

Tour. In 2004 singers Bob Dylan and Willie Nelson embarked on a 22-town stop throughout the country, focusing on small venues at minor league ballparks to entertain fans. The opening show of the "WillieBob" tour was in early August in Cooperstown at Doubleday Field. They tried to book the "Field of Dreams" in Iowa, but the owners declined.

Vendor. In 2004 Comerica Park vendor Charley Marcuse began singing opera while peddling hot dogs in the stands. The club barred his arias until fans rose up and complained—even creating a website in support of Marcuse. The club relented, but was still peeved that Marcuse berated fans over using ketchup, and sometimes refused to provide the condiment.

Singles

"If I had played my career hitting singles like Pete, I'd wear a dress."—Mickey Mantle on Pete Rose in *The Mick*, with Herb Gluck (1985).

"The Chicago Cubs are like Rush Street—a lot of singles, but no action."—Joe Garagiola

See also ***Hits***.

On August 17, 1894, Jack Wadsworth of Louisville gave up a 19th century-record 28 singles to the Philadelphia A's.

On April 28, 1901, Indians pitcher Bock Baker gave up a modern-record 23 singles to the White Sox, who won 13–1.

Pirates outfielder Lloyd Waner had a record 198 singles in 1927, his rookie year. He had 223 hits for a .355 average. In the American League, Wade Boggs of the Red Sox in 1985 and Ichiro Suzuki with the Mariners in 2001 each hit a then-record 187 singles. Suzuki did it in his rookie season (though after several years in the Japanese leagues). In 2004 Suzuki (by then known simply as Ichiro) shattered the record with 225 singles among his record 262 hits (24 doubles, 5 triples and 8 home runs).

On June 6, 1934, Myril Hoag of the Yankees hit a Major League record six singles in a 15–3 defeat of the Red Sox.

On May 20, 1947, the Pirates beat the Braves 4–3 in a game that produced 22 hits—all singles.

On May 20, 1951, Richie Ashburn hit eight singles in a doubleheader. This epitomized his career, as he hit only 29 home runs in 15 seasons.

In 1996 Mark McGwire hit 39 home runs and set a record for most home runs by a player with more home runs than singles (he had 35). He broke the record set by Don Drysdale in 1958, who had seven home runs and six singles.

George Sisler (1893–1973)

Hall of Fame 1939

"I'd say that he was the smartest hitter that ever lived. He was a professional with that bat in his hand. He never stopped thinking. Like Stan Musial today, he was a menace every time he stepped to the plate. You could feel the ripple of anticipation in the crowd as he moved up there. And he seldom failed to provide the excitement they expected. On the bases he ran with the judgment of Pee Wee Reese and with vastly greater speed. In the field, he was a picture player, the acme of grace and fluency."—Branch Rickey.

Sisler was a stellar first baseman primarily for the Browns between 1915 and 1930, batting .340.

George Harold Sisler was a star pitcher at the University of Michigan under coach Branch Rickey. His pitching gave way to outstanding hitting when he began his Major League career with the Browns in 1915 (see also ***Players Who Switched Positions***). He hit over .300 from 1916 through 1925, including league-leading averages of .407 in 1920 and .420 in 1922. He set a Major League record with 257 hits in 1920. He led the league in stolen bases four times and assists seven times and is considered one of the best first basemen of all time.

Sisler might have become the best hitter ever but for a serious sinus condition that affected his eyes. The severity of the problem forced him to sit out the 1923 season. He returned for several more strong seasons, including a .345 average and 224 hits in 1925.

In 1928 he moved to the Senators and then the Braves, for whom

Members of the Reds practice their slides during spring training.

he hit a collective .331 that season. He finished his career with two more seasons for the Braves, hitting .326 and .309. His lifetime average was .340, and he had 2,812 hits to go with 375 stolen bases and 425 doubles. He had a 41-game hitting streak in 1922.

Sisler managed the Browns from 1924 through 1926 and managed in the minor leagues in 1932. He scouted for the Dodgers in the 1940s and the Pirates for most of the 1950s and 1960s before retiring in 1972.

Slander See *Defamation*

Enos Slaughter (1916–2002)

Hall of Fame (VC) 1985

"On the ball field he is perpetual motion itself. He would run through a brick wall, if necessary, to make a catch, or slide into a pit of ground glass to score a run." — Sportswriter Arthur Daley.

"If you haven't got that competitive fire, you may stay in the big leagues for a few years, but you're not going too far. That competitive spirit means the difference between great and mediocre. I'll give you two examples. Pete Rose and Enos Slaughter. There are plenty of players around with more ability who'll be forgotten long before those two fellows. They're both bear-down guys. Rose'll make the Hall of Fame, and I sincerely hope Slaughter does. Any young player could take those two as models." — Catcher Bill Dickey quoted in *Voices from Cooperstown*, by Anthony J. Connor (1982).

Slaughter hit an even .300 over a 19-year career primarily for the Cardinals and Yankees beginning in 1938.

Enos Bradsher "Country" Slaughter of North Carolina began his professional career in the mid–1930s before making it with the Cardinals in 1938. The Pete Rose of his day always hustled on the ballfield and batted .300 or better 10 times in his 19-year career. He spent the first 13 seasons with the Cardinals, playing outfield and leading the league in various fielding categories during a number of stellar seasons.

In his fifth season with the Cardinals he led the club to the 1942 World Championship before leaving for three years during World War II. He returned in 1946 to help lead the club to another pennant. His dash from first base to home in Game 7 on a bloop hit beat the Red Sox for the World Championship (see also *Base Running*). He once spiked Jackie Robinson at first base to show his displeasure at integration.

In 1954 he moved over to the Yankees and then the A's, returning to the Yankees from 1956 through 1958 and helping them reach the World Series in each of those seasons. He ended his career in 1959, splitting time with the Yankees and Braves before retiring.

Slaughter finished his career batting an even .300, with 2,383 hits and 1,304 RBIs. Like Rose, he had 169 home runs (Rose had 160). Slaughter batted .291 in five World Series (Rose batted .269). He managed in the minor leagues in 1960 and 1961 and then retired to his tobacco farm and helped coach the Duke baseball team.

Book. Enos Slaughter with Kevin Reid, *Country Hardball* (1991).

Sliding

"With the salary I get here, I'm so hollow and starving I'm liable to explode like a lightbulb if I hit the ground too hard." — Outfielder Casey Stengel's 1918 rationale for not sliding.

Early Sliding.

"It was risky to slide in the early days of the game on any except the best kept diamonds. Feet first and it might mean a broken leg or a twisted ankle. Head first and it was 'raw meat' from the shoulders to the hips. With [Charles] Comiskey it was the latter and many give him the credit for originating the trick."—G.W. Axelson in "*Commy*" (1919).

"The feat fairly astonished the natives, who at first roared with laughter … and they woke up to the fact that a large, new, and valuable 'wrinkle' had been handed out to them."—1859 newspaper account of a slide during a game in Portland, Maine.

Sliding occurred at least by 1857, though Robert Addy is credited by some with stealing the first base by sliding in 1866. Addy is also credited with the first head first slide. Eddie Cuthbert also employed sliding in the 1860s, and at least one source credited him with the first slide in 1865.

One source credited Mike "King" Kelly as the father of the slide, but his career postdates most of the earlier-credited players and it may be more due to the "Slide, Kelly, Slide!" chant popularized during his playing days in the 1880s.

Headfirst Slide.

"Nearly everyone else slid into bases feetfirst. Charlie Hustle dove headfirst and belly flopped into the bag like a torpedo connecting with its battleship target. It was exhilarating to watch. It looked fun to do. And no one else, in the whole century-long history of baseball, had ever slid quite like that."—Michael Y. Sokolove in *Hustle: The Myth, Life, and Lies of Pete Rose* (1990).

Hook Slide.

"As I hooked the bag I was sure I had beaten the tag, but when I looked up, there was Rowland waving me out and all the time he was grinning and saying, 'It's a shame to have to call that close one after that slide. You're out, Babe, but I never saw a better hook slide. It was perfect.'"—Babe Ruth about umpire Clarence Rowland as quoted in Ford Frick's autobiography, *Games, Asterisks and People* (1973).

William Stryker Gummere, captain of the 1869 Princeton University team, is credited by some with inventing the hook slide. Mike "King" Kelly supposedly popularized it: "He would jump into the air 10 feet from the sack, dive directly for it, dig one of his spiked shoes into the bag and then swerve clear over on his side. Few second basemen had the nerve to block his hurricane dives."—Teammate Joe Quinn.

"Yeah, but my fantasy's different. I'm ninety-some years old, see, and I'm in Florida, playing in one of those Geriatric Softball Leagues they have down there … it's a tie game, last of the last, and I tear around third with the winning run. Halfway down the line the old ticker starts to stop. But on sheer effing will power alone I stagger six more steps and collapse into a perfect hook slide. Notice that I don't go straight into the catcher as some softballers have been known to do."—Kevin Kerrane in "Season Openers" (1977).

Sliding Practice. Branch Rickey is credited with first using sliding pits as a spring training practice aid.

One 1886 writer recommended that indoor spring practice include sliding, by spreading sand on the floor or by nailing down carpeting to simulate the sliding surface.

Sliding Pads

"They bunch when they're sweaty and slow me down."—Maury Wills on why he abandoned sliding pads.

Early Use. Sliding pads were used routinely by the 1880s. Harry Stovey, an 1880s Philadelphia star, is credited by some with using the first pads. Sam Morton of Spalding Sporting Goods is credited by others with introducing sliding pads to baseball. Players also put strips of felt inside their pants for greater protection. Rawlings sold a 19th century uniform with sliding pads already sewn in. By 1912 pads were sold separately from uniform pants.

Improvements. Long-time Cardinals trainer Harrison J. "Doc" Weaver devised a better woolen underwear for sliding pads. Weaver also patented a device for hay fever sufferers, called the "nasal filter."

Modern Pads. Modern sliding pads weigh approximately six ounces and are worn in slots at the rear of the pants.

Sliding Gloves. These were popular in the 19th century and came up to the elbows to allow safer head first slides. See also *Batting Gloves*.

Slippery Elm See *Illegal Pitches*

Slowest Runners

"The wind always seems to blow against catchers when they are running."—Joe Garagiola.

"His knees were too low to the ground, and his center of gravity was four feet behind him, so that he was never endowed by nature with adequate speed. As he got

Fay Dancer of the All-American Girls Professional Baseball League executes a perfect hook slide past the tag of third baseman Marge Wenzell. Notice Dancer's left hand holding her cap high and out of harm's way.

older he slowed down, becoming surely the slowest player ever to play major league baseball well. The slowest player today is probably [catcher] Butch Wynegar, and my guess is that if they raced three times around the bases Butch would lap him." — Bill James on catcher Ernie Lombardi in *The Bill James Historical Baseball Abstract* (1988). Lombardi stole eight bases in 17 years and Wynegar stole 10 bases in 13 years. Lombardi still managed 27 triples in his career, including nine in his first full season, 1932. Wynegar managed 15 triples.

"[Doggie Miller] covered about as much ground as a woodshed, and threw to first like a drunkard with a cork leg." — Len Washburn on the 19th century catcher/infielder.

"That's another example of the lack of the speed the Giants have — or don't have." — Ron Fairly.

"If he raced his pregnant wife he'd finish third." — Los Angeles Dodgers manager Tommy Lasorda, on catcher Mike Scioscia, although Lasorda is credited with saying the same thing about catcher Bruce Benedict.

"Let's go Mo Vaughn on that one." — Expression supposedly used in the slo-mo truck by Fox Sports when it wanted to use its super slo-motion replay camera; named after the huge and superslow ex-first baseman who was plagued with injuries at the end of his career.

See also **Stolen Bases — Fewest Steals.**

Slugging Average

"Man, you picked one helluva year to go from being a .245 hitter to doing your Babe Ruth imitation." — Orioles teammate to John Lowenstein, who in 1982 hit .320 with 24 home runs and a league-leading .602 slugging average in only 322 at-bats.

See also **Silver Slugger Award.**

Slugging average, also known as "slugging percentage," is calculated by dividing total official at-bats by total bases, the latter calculated by adding singles, doubles, triples and home runs.

The highest slugging average of all time is Babe Ruth's lifetime .690. For many years he held the record for highest single-season slugging average at .847 in 1920, until Barry Bonds broke his record with .877 in 2001.

Slumps

"A batting slump is baseball's version of the common cold. Sooner or later every hitter gets one, it can keep him up at night, and there is no known cure, though that does not prevent everyone and his doorman from passing on homemade remedies and get-well wishes." — Tom Verducci.

"I'm the only man in the history of the game who began his career in a slump and stayed in it." — Rocky Bridges.

"When you're going like this, it looks like even the umpires have gloves." — Pete Rose.

"Slumps are like a soft bed. They're easy to get into and hard to get out of." — Johnny Bench.

"What a ballplayer needs most when in a deep slump is a string of good alibis." — Yankee manager Miller Huggins.

"When you're in a slump, thank God for the invention of the water cooler." — Lou Piniella.

"Right now I'd have to say one through nine." — Pitcher Joe Magrane on which hitters he was having trouble with during a slump.

The English language term "slump" comes from the Norwegian word *slumpa* ("to fall").

Rabbit Maranville was mired in a slump when he appeared at the plate against Dazzy Vance carrying a tennis racquet.

In 1977 Reds shortstop Dave Concepcion tried to snap out of a slump in a unique way. He tried to get "hot" by climbing into a clothes dryer and having pitcher Pat Zachry push the spin button. He was slightly burned on the arms, and his hair was singed. Despite the injuries he produced three hits against the Cubs that day.

After going 1-for-April in 1978, Angels outfielder Lyman Bostock volunteered to forfeit his first month's salary, but owner Gene Autry refused the gesture. Bostock improved as the season progressed but was **Murdered** late in the season.

Smallest Players

"I'd rather be the shortest player in the Majors than the tallest player in the minors." — 1970s shortstop Freddie Patek. Patek was officially listed at 5'5" (he later admitted to 5'4") and 148 pounds but once hit three home runs in a game (with a high of six in a season). He led American League shortstops in double plays in four of his 14 seasons and was the starting shortstop in the 1978 All-Star Game.

"4'8". I used to be 4'10", but I shrunk." — Mamie Moberly, sister of Babe Ruth, who survived into her 90s and lived 40 years beyond her famous brother, when asked how tall she was.

"Don't give me that stuff. You can't even play first for a midget team." — A Yankee Stadium guard to diminutive New York Yankee infielder and Hall of Famer Phil Rizzuto, who was late for a game on October 3, 1947, and could not get in the ballpark. Rizzuto was 5'7" (5'6" in some sources) and 156 pounds as the Yankee shortstop in the late 1940s and early 1950s. He was rejected in a tryout with the Dodgers because then–Dodger manager Casey Stengel thought he was too small.

"Jeff Little, Jack Little, Ray Short, Shorty Desjardien, Slim Love, Tiny Graham, Jim Small, Skinny Graham, Slim Salee"

Pete Burg was 5'1" (but 150 pounds), the shortest Major Leaguer in history. He played 13 games, all but one at second base, for the 1910 Boston Braves.

Dan Sweeney is listed as 5'5" in *Total Baseball*, but local papers in 1895 in Louisville listed him as 4'10". In San Francisco, where he played in 1890, the local paper listed him as 4'8".

The second-smallest Major League player of all time supposedly was Nin Alexander, listed in some sources as a 5'2" member of the 1884 Kansas City Unions and American Association Brown Stockings. However, *The Baseball Encyclopedia* lists him at 5'4½".

Kid Keenan may have been the lightweight champion, supposedly weighing in at 95 pounds while pitching one game that he lost for the 1891 Cincinnati Kellys of the American Association. *The Baseball Encyclopedia* does not list a height or weight for the Kid.

Dickey Pearce, a regular in the National Association, was 5'3½" when he played shortstop for two years for the National League's St. Louis club, batting .198.

Mel Ott was only 5'9", but he managed to hit 511 home runs, though 63% of them were at the Polo Grounds. Hack Wilson, only 5'6", hit 56 home runs in 1930.

Less than 2% of all players in Major League history have been shorter than 5'6½".

The last year that non-pitchers averaged under 5'9" was 1875. By 1907 non-pitchers averaged 5'10" and broke the 6-foot barrier in 1954. By 1912 the average pitcher was already over six feet. See also **Tallest Players** for average player heights over the years.

In 1991 a total of 45 Major League players out of 1,018 were 5'9" or under. Ricky Otero of the 1996 Phillies stood 5'5" as the shortest recent Major League player.

Deaf mute Dummy Hoy was only 5'4" and 148 pounds as an outfielder in the 1890s. He hit .288 and stole 597 bases over his 14-year career.

Larry McClure, who had one at-bat for the Yankees in 1910, had only 130 pounds on his 5'6" frame.

Outfielder Wee Willie Keeler was only 5'4½" and 135–140 pounds, but he played for 19 years at the turn of the century, primarily with Baltimore, Brooklyn and the New York Highlanders. He hit .345 lifetime with a high of .424 in 1897.

When 118-pound Johnny Evers arrived with the Cubs in 1906, the veterans made him ride on the roof of the bus that carried the players to the ballpark.

Rabbit Maranville is a Hall of Famer who played 23 years in the National League, primarily with the Boston Braves. He appeared in 2,670 games (2,154 at shortstop) while only 5'6" (5'5" in some sources), but weighing 155 pounds.

Pitcher Bobby Shantz was 5'6" but managed a record of 119–99 over 16 years. He also won eight straight Gold Glove Awards beginning in 1957 (the award's first year).

Shortstop Harry Chappas of the late 1970s White Sox was only 5'3".

Two-time National League MVP and 1990 Hall of Famer Joe Morgan was only 5'7" and 145 pounds.

The all-time number of players at smaller heights, putting Nin Alexander in the 5'4" group:

5'1"—1
5'2"—0
5'3"—11
5'4"—23
5'5"—44
5'6"—155

Smartest Players

"Out of what? A thousand?"—Mickey Rivers, when told that Yankee teammate Reggie Jackson, who was known to quote poet Robert Frost, had an IQ of 160.

"He didn't sound like a baseball player. He said things like 'Nevertheless' and 'if, in fact.'"—Dan Quisenberry on Ted Simmons.

"Joe Morgan is the smartest baseball man I ever met."—Pete Rose.

"Henry Sage, Rick Wise, Casey Wise, Harry Bright, Elmer Ponder, Jennings Poindexter, Mike Witt"

Hilton Smith (1912–1983)

Hall of Fame (VC) 2001

"In the end, while Hilton Smith may not have had the name appeal of many of his contemporaries, he was one of the great pitchers of the Negro Leagues…. He should not be remembered as a second hand talent scout for Branch Rickey or as a faceless reliever who came to the mound when Satchel's arm tired, but as one of the best pitchers of his time."—David Marasco.

Smith was a vital presence with the Kansas City Monarch teams that dominated the Negro American League in the 1930s and 1940s.

Born in 1912 in Giddings, Texas, as the son of a teacher, Hilton Smith attended Prairie View A&M College, where he played baseball. He began his professional career in 1931 with an Austin semipro team. In 1932 Smith, age 20, faced Negro Major League talent while pitching for the Monroe, Louisiana, Monarchs of the

Negro Southern League (NSL). The NSL had Negro Major League status that year due to the demise of the Negro National League. He later played for numerous teams of lesser caliber before joining the barnstorming Kansas City Monarchs in 1936.

In 1937 the Monarchs became a charter member of the Negro American League, where Smith quickly established himself. That season he earned six victories, pitched a no-hitter on May 15 and won two games in the pennant-clinching series versus the Chicago American Giants. Over the next five seasons Smith posted a composite 39–9 record, leading the NAL in victories in each season, including a perfect 10–0 in 1941. He pitched in the East-West All-Star game six consecutive seasons from 1937–1942, starting two.

In 1942 the Monarchs appeared in the first black World Series versus the NNL champion Homestead Grays. Kansas City swept four games, with Smith pitching shutout ball to earn the win in Game 1. An arm injury rendered Smith a diminished but still highly effective pitcher from 1943–1945. He is credited with recommending in 1945 a fellow Army officer to Kansas City Monarchs owner J.L. Wilkinson, Jackie Robinson.

In 1946 Smith returned to prior form with an 8–3 mark, helping Kansas City to another pennant. In their series loss to the Newark Eagles Smith earned a victory, 5–1 in Game 5.

A wonderful all-around player, Smith commanded a variety of pitches, including an excellent fastball and what was generally credited as the finest curve in black baseball. He was also a fine utility player, primarily at first base and in the outfield, with good hitting skills.

Smith capped his career in 1947. In March he faced the New York Yankees while pitching for the Vargas club of Venezuela. At the age of 35 he faced a team featuring Yogi Berra, Phil Rizzuto and Tommy Henrich. He pitched five innings of one-hit ball in Vargas' 4–3 win. In the NAL season to follow, Smith earned seven victories (with some sources crediting him with a perfect 7–0 mark). He played one more season in 1948, had one win against two losses and retired. At least one source credits him with a 161–32 record in Negro League games.

After his playing career Smith worked in education as a teacher and served as a scout for the Chicago Cubs. He died in Kansas City in 1983.

Ozzie Smith (1954–)

Hall of Fame 2002

"Instead of '1' his number should be '8,' but turned sideways because the possibilities he brings to his position are almost infinite."—Thomas Boswell of the *Washington Post*.

"He plays like he's on a mini-trampoline or wearing helium kangaroo shorts."—Andy Van Slyke.

"Ozzie Sucks! He is the worst shortstop of all time. The only reason he will be remembered in history is his fucking backflips.(cheerleaders do that too)."—Email to Nathan Hill's website tribute to Smith, whose Opening Day trademark was to do a *front* flip as he ran out to his position for the 1st inning of the season.

Smith was the premier National League shortstop of the 1980's and perhaps one of the finest defensive players ever to play the game.

Undrafted out of high school (where he played with Eddie Murray), Osborn Earl Smith received an academic scholarship to Cal Poly San Luis Obispo, where he was a walk-on to the baseball team. After completing his senior year he was drafted fourth overall and played a single season in the minors before beginning his Major League career in San Diego in 1978.

Smith played four seasons in San Diego and established himself as a classic good-field/no-hit shortstop. Although he batted .258 in his rookie year he managed just 24 extra base hits and subsequently did not average higher than .230 in his last three years with the Padres. Fortunately, his defense was a different matter. In 1980 he won a Gold Glove and set a single-season Major League record for assists by a shortstop. In 1981 he won a second Gold Glove, led National League shortstops in fielding and was named to his first All-Star team. Following the 1981 season Smith was traded to the Cardinals for fellow shortstop Garry Templeton.

St. Louis is where Smith became a star. He played 15 seasons in St. Louis, helping the Cardinals to three National League pennants and one World Series championship. He won 11 straight Gold Gloves and led National League shortstops in fielding seven times as a Cardinal.

Although Smith brought his glove from San Diego, he apparently left his bats behind, for it was also in St. Louis that his hitting skills flourished. Smith arrived in 1982 with a .231 batting average. He would hit .272 as a Cardinal and develop into a versatile offensive threat. His best season was 1987. The switch hitter batted .303 with 40 doubles and 75 RBIs, scored 104 runs and stole 43 bases. He was the MVP of the NLCS in 1985 with a game-winning 9th inning home run in Game 6.

Though solid enough, his offense would always be overshadowed by his peerless defense. His fielding marks are numerous. Smith played every game of his career at shortstop, 2,511, most for a National League shortstop. He holds the Major League marks for both assists and double plays at the position. He led the league in fielding average and assists eight times each. Offensively, he finished with 2,460 hits, 580 stolen bases and a .262 batting average. After he retired, he moved to broadcasting, where, among other things, he hosted "*This Week In Baseball.*"

Red Smith (1905–1982)

Hall of Fame (Spink Award) 1976
"Baseball is dull only to those with dull minds."
"Writing is easy, I just open up a vein and bleed." — Smith.
"I was a good speller in school." — Smith on how he became an encyclopedia and dictionary consultant.

Walter Wellesley Smith was probably the best-known and most respected sports columnist of all time. He began his career with the *Milwaukee Sentinel* in 1927 and wrote his last column for the *New York Times* five days before his death in 1982.

From Milwaukee he moved on to St. Louis and Philadelphia before settling in New York. He wrote for the *New York Herald Tribune* from 1945 through 1966 when the paper folded. He then drifted for a few years after the death of his first wife. He was primarily a columnist for *Women's Wear Daily* magazine but made a comeback in the 1970s. From 1971 until his death he wrote a "Sports of the Times/Red Smith" column for the *New York Times*. In 1976 he won a Pulitzer Prize for Distinguished Commentary.

Book. Ira Berkow, *Red* (1986). Berkow later developed a Broadway play based on Smith's work (see *Theatre*).

Smoking See *Tobacco*

Duke Snider (1926–)

Hall of Fame 1980
"For those of you who were not treated to the special skills of 'The Duke of Flatbush,' ... Duke Snider was the perfect player for

his time and place.... 'The Dook,' as he was called in Brooklyn, was the royalty which gave Brooklyn respectability. No player contributed more to our team both offensively and defensively. No player agonized more when he didn't perform well. Could he have been better? Some say yes. I say they didn't know him the way I did." — Carl Erskine in the introduction to *The Duke of Flatbush*, by Snider with Bill Gilbert (1988).

Snider starred primarily for the Dodgers in center field from 1947 through the early 1960s, hitting 407 home runs over 18 seasons.

Los Angeles native Edwin Donald Snider arrived in the Major Leagues with the Dodgers in 1947, the same season as Jackie Robinson. Snider quickly established himself as one of the three dominant center fielders of the 1950s, along with Mickey Mantle and Willie Mays. He was the top home run hitter of the 1950s with 326.

He hit 40 or more home runs for five straight seasons beginning in 1953 and drove in more than 100 runs six times. He batted over .300 seven times. The move from Ebbets Field to the huge Los Angeles Coliseum in 1958 cost the left-handed Snider many home runs. He moved to the Mets for one season in 1963 and the Giants in 1964. He retired after 18 seasons with 407 home runs and 1,333 RBIs. He batted .286 in six World Series and is fourth all-time with 11 World Series home runs.

Following retirement, he scouted for the Dodgers and managed in the minor leagues through 1968. He became a Padres broadcaster and batting instructor until 1971. In 1973 he joined the Expos as a broadcaster where he remained into the 1980s.

Book. *The Duke of Flatbush*, by Snider and Bill Gilbert (1988).

Snow See *Weather*

Society for American Baseball Research ("SABR") (1971–)

"This book is dedicated to the man who has done more for baseball research than anyone else living — L. Robert Davids" — Bill James in *The Bill James Historical Baseball Abstract* (1988).

"To foster the study of baseball as a significant American social and athletic institution." — SABR's mission statement.

Origins/Membership. This baseball research organization, known as SABR, was founded on August 10, 1971, by L. Robert Davids, who had been a regular contributor to *The Sporting News*. He and nine others met in Cooperstown, New York, to formalize American baseball research from that point forward. SABR membership passed 5,000 in October 1984 and had over 6,000 members by the early 1990s. Davids died in 2002 at the age of 76.

Publications. SABR publishes the *Baseball Research Journal* and *The National Pastime*, as well as at least nine other newsletters, covering such topics as ballparks, Latin Leagues, Negro Leagues, minor leagues, 19th century teams, players and statistics.

Awards. For more than two decades, SABR has recognized outstanding baseball scholarship with annual and discretionary awards funded by the society (Seymour Medal, Lee Allen Award, Jack Kavanagh Award, Bob Davids Award Citation) or in collaboration with leading baseball publishers (the McFarland-SABR, *Sporting News*-SABR, *Sports Weekly*, and Jerry Malloy awards).

"Sabermetrics." This term was coined by statistician and baseball historian Bill James to refer to the unique statistical analyses developed by various SABR members to look at baseball from a different historical perspective.

Socks See *Uniforms — Socks and Stirrups*

Softball

"This is baseball. Softball, that's like Methadone. Time enough for that stuff when we get older…. If we do." — Rock and roll star George Thorogood, whose sandlot baseball team and his band were known as the Destroyers.

"They have stubble on their chins, tattoos on their arms and look a little bit like a slo-pitch softball team in town for a state championship tournament." — Houston sportswriter Neil Hohlfeld on the 1993 pennant-winning Phillies.

Origins. Softball appeared around 1900 and by 1908 was formally promoted as an "indoor baseball" alternative. Its precursor was an *Indoor Baseball* game invented in 1887 in Chicago by George Hancock.

The first national softball championships were held in 1933. The governing Amateur Softball Association of America (ASA) first met in 1933 as part of the Century of Progress Exhibition in Chicago and eventually was headquartered in Oklahoma.

Major Leaguers. Long-time Major League shortstop Bud Harrelson was released in 1977 and started playing amateur softball. The Phillies picked him up later that year, and he played with the club through their 1980 World Championship season.

Pitcher Kevin Hickey was signed off a softball team after an open tryout by the White Sox in the 1980s. He appeared in 175 Major League games, compiling a 7–11 record over four seasons (1981–1983 and 1989).

Olympic Games. Softball was first played in the Olympic Games in 1996 in Atlanta. The Americans won gold in Sydney in 2000 and then in Greece in 2004, when the team won by a combined 51–1. They didn't give up a run until the finals, when Australia scored a late run in a 5–1 loss to the U.S.

The King. Eddie Feigner is the most famous softball player of all time. He led "The King and His Court" four-man team. Playing fast-pitch exhibitions from 1946 into 2003 (at age 80), with a 104 mph pitch, Feigner once struck out, in order, Willie Mays, Willie McCovey, Brooks Robinson, Maury Wills, Roberto Clemente and Harmon Killebrew. After his Major League career, Astros catcher John Bateman played with Feigner and his club.

Jennie Finch. The softball pitcher, formerly of the University of Arizona, was voted the "Hottest Female Athlete" on ESPN.com in 2003, beating out tennis player Anna Kournikova. Finch became a member of the "This Week In Baseball" broadcast team and taped a segment during spring training in which she struck out Major Leaguers Scott Spiezio, Paul Lo Duca, Larry Walker and Mike Cameron. The 6'1" pitcher threw over 70 mph from 43 feet, equivalent to a baseball thrown in the mid–90s from 60'6".

Finch was scheduled to pitch against Barry Bonds, who engaged her with some good-natured trash-talking at the 2003 All-Star Game. Alex Rodriguez watched her pitch from the batter's box, but without a bat. He promised to face her if the U.S. won the softball gold medal at the 2004 Olympics (they won). The U.S. also won the 1996 and 2000 gold medals. At the time of the Major League face-offs, Finch was engaged to Arizona Diamondbacks minor leaguer Casey Daigle. Asked if Daigle can hit her riseball, Finch said, "he won't even try." They married in late 2004.

Slo-Pitch Hall of Fame. The Slo-Pitch Hall of Fame is located in Petersburg, Virginia.

Songs

"The entire social history of America begins to emerge from such songs — the nation's exuberance after the grim years of the Civil War, the emphasis on baseball as a form of healthy exercise for sedentary types, the response of the old puritan work ethic to men who abandon jobs for play, and the chauvinism (national and male) that early on found a home in baseball. No wonder that baseball quickly caught the fancy of American music composers and enjoyers." — Joel Zoss and John Bowman in *Diamonds in the Rough* (1989).

See also *Musicians*, *National Anthem*, *Singers* and "*Take Me Out to the Ball Game.*"

Number of Baseball Songs. There have been at least 50,000 baseball songs, the number amassed in a collection owned by J. Francis Driscoll of Massachusetts. The Newberry Library in Chicago contains the Driscoll Collection of baseball sheet music and songsheets. By the 1980s, approximately 300 baseball songs had been published. Baseball broadcaster Warner Fusselle has amassed a significant collection of baseball recordings.

Earliest Baseball Recordings. "The Baseball Polka" by J. Randolph Blodget was published in either 1858 or 1860, depending on the source, and was written for the Niagara Base Ball Club of Buffalo.

The first wax recording of a baseball song was made in 1893 when "Slide, Kelly, Slide" was recorded. The first disc recording was of the 1906 ditty, "Jimmy and Maggie at a Base Ball Game."

Miscellany. In the 1860s and 1870s, teams developed their own songs and traditionally rode carriages to the ballpark singing the songs.

Writer Ring Lardner suspected early on that the Chicago White Sox were throwing the 1919 World Series. During the series he walked through the club's railroad car singing "I'm Forever Blowing Ballgames," a short verse he wrote to the tune of a popular song of the day called "I'm Forever Blowing Bubbles."

Before he became a front office executive with the Cubs, Bill Veeck, Sr., wrote for the *Chicago Evening American* newspaper under the name Bill Bailey. The song of the same name ("Won't You Come Home, Bill Bailey?") was written after he switched papers during a contract dispute.

There are at least 10 songs written about Babe Ruth, including 1919's "Batterin' Babe" and Irving Berlin's 1925 "Along Came Babe."

"Joltin' Joe DiMaggio" was written as a tribute to DiMaggio's 56-game hitting streak in 1941. The song was written by Allan Courtney and Benjamin Homer and became the number one swing tune that year. It was performed by Les Brown's Big Band, with 14-year-old Betty Bonney on vocals.

A popular World War II song was "You're Gonna Win the Ballgame, Uncle Sam," written by umpire (and former manager and Tigers third baseman) George Moriarty.

When Larry Doby broke the color line in the American League in 1947, a fan wrote "The Doby Boogie."

In the 1950s, Yankees Tommy Henrich and Phil Rizzuto, along with Dodgers Roy Campanella and Ralph Branca, recorded a children's song, "The Umpire."

Willie Mays and Mickey Mantle have sung back-up on songs.

When Simon & Garfunkel performed "Mrs. Robinson," Joe DiMaggio was annoyed at the lyric, "Where have you gone, Joe DiMaggio?," because he didn't understand it.

In 1969 some of the Mets players recorded an album of songs titled "The Amazing Mets."

Angels owner Gene Autry, the "Singing Cowboy," recorded "Rudolph, the Red-Nosed Reindeer" and holds the copyrights to the song, which has sold more than 50 million copies.

Tigers broadcaster Ernie Harwell has published a number of songs, including, "Move over Babe, Here Comes Henry," when

Aaron was closing in on Ruth's home run record. Harwell wrote the words and Tigers pitcher Bill Slayback wrote the music.

"Go, Go Joe Charboneau" was written in 1980 to honor the sensational *One-Year Wonder*.

Theme Songs. The Red Sox Royal Rooters sang "Tessie" at Game 3 of the 1903 World Series in Pittsburgh. The song remained at various levels of popularity among Red Sox fans for almost 50 years. It was not related to baseball but somehow became the battle song of the club.

Long-time Brooklyn Dodgers *Organist* Gladys Gooding wrote the Dodger fight song.

The Phillies have used "Go, Go Phillies."

The White Sox have used "Let's Go White Sox," based on the club's informal "Go Go Sox" nickname of the late 1950s.

The Blue Jays have used "Hang on Blue Jays."

The Expos have used "Les Bus Squad."

The Mets have used "Let's Go Mets" since the early 1960s.

The Cubs have used "Go Cubs Go."

The 1979 Pirates adopted the song "We Are Family," by Sly and the Family Stone, on their way to a World Series victory in seven games over the Orioles.

The 1980s White Sox adopted a song by Steam: "Nah Na Hey, Kiss Him Good Bye."

The 1964 World Champion Cardinals used "Pass the Biscuits, Miranda," which had been adopted by the 1946 Cardinals, who also won the World Series that year.

Modern Songwriters. Probably the best-known modern baseball songwriter is Terry Cashman. He has recorded the "Talkin' Baseball" songs for almost every Major League team. For years he held out and did not record one for Seattle.

Dave Frisberg recorded "Van Lingle Mungo," a musical recitation of a number of old-time ballplayers' names.

Warren Zevon wrote "The Ballad of Bill Lee" in honor of the former Major League pitcher.

John Fogerty, formerly of Creedence Clearwater Revival, wrote "Centerfield," now played by many clubs during games.

Songbook. Addison Lovejoy, *Baseball Songbook* (1971); James Mote, *Everything Baseball* (1989), lists almost all published baseball songs to the date of publication.

Warren Spahn (1921–2003)

Hall of Fame 1973

"The difference between winning 19 games and winning 20 for a pitcher is bigger than anyone out of baseball realizes. It's the same for hitters. Someone who hits .300 looks back on the guy who batted .295 and says 'Tough luck, buddy.' Twenty games is the magic figure for pitchers; .300 is the magic figure for batters. It pays off in salary and reputation. And those are the two things that keep a ballplayer in business."— Spahn, who won 20 or more games 13 times, including six straight seasons beginning at age 35.

Spahn won 363 games, the most by a left-handed pitcher, in a career spanning 1942 through 1965.

Warren Edward Spahn started his career in Buffalo, his hometown, playing first base while his father played third on a semipro team, the Buffalo Lake City Athletic Club. He wanted to play first base in high school, but another player already starred there, so Spahn switched to pitching. He signed with the Braves in 1940 for $80 a month, but had arm trouble twice in Class D.

Spahn appeared in four games for the 1942 Braves before World War II interrupted his career and he saw combat. He did not return to the Major Leagues until 1946 when he won eight games for the Braves. Over the next 20 years he became the winningest left-hander in Major League history.

Spahn won 21 games in 1947 and led the league with a 2.33 ERA and seven shutouts. Between 1949 and 1963 he won 20 or more games in 12 of 15 seasons. He was the league leader in wins eight times and four times in shutouts and strikeouts. Even as he reached his late 30s and early 40s he was a workhorse, leading the league in complete games seven straight times from 1957 through 1963. He appeared in 14 All-Star Games.

In 1965 he moved on to the Mets and Giants, ending his career that season with seven wins to finish with 363, fifth all-time. He also pitched 63 shutouts, sixth all-time. He won four games for the Braves in three World Series. He was also one of the better-hitting pitchers of all time, with 35 home runs, 4th all-time for pitchers. He pitched a no-hitter in 1960 and another in 1961 a few days after turning 40. After leaving the Major Leagues in 1965, Spahn pitched briefly in Mexico and the minor leagues until 1967. He later managed in the minor leagues and coached for the Indians in the 1970s.

Albert Goodwill Spalding (1850–1915)

Hall of Fame 1939

"*Historic Facts Concerning the Beginning, Evolution, Development and Popularity of Base Ball With Personal Reminiscences of Its Vicissitudes, Its Victories, and Its Votaries.*"— Ponderous subtitle of Spalding's 1911 book, *Base Ball—America's National Game.*

Spalding was a premier pitcher of the 1860s and early 1870s and later established himself as the owner of the Chicago White Stockings and Spalding Sporting Goods.

Legend has it that Spalding learned the game at age 12 from returning Civil War veterans. He became the star pitcher for the Rockford Forest Citys in the 1860s and then played on four consecutive championship teams for the Boston Red Stockings of the National Association. He was 207–56 as the league's leading pitcher from 1871 through 1875. In 1875 he was 57–5 with his underhand delivery. He adapted well to the new National League in 1876, winning 47 games for the Chicago White Stockings.

After Spalding's playing career ended with brief appearances in 1877 and 1878, he continued in an ownership and management capacity with the White Stockings (see also *Chicago Cubs*). He took over a controlling interest in the club in 1882 and purportedly sold it in 1891 when *Spalding Sporting Goods* was expanding so rapidly that he had no time for the club. However, he merely gave up the presidency title and remained firmly in control of the club through the end of the century.

Spalding early on obtained the right to publish the official National League guide, *The Spalding Guide*. He continued to be a leader of the National League through the end of the century. He lost a United States Senate race in California late in his life and died there in 1915. See also *Origins of Baseball*.

Books. Peter Levine, *A.G. Spalding and the Rise of Baseball* (1985); Albert Spalding, *Base Ball—America's National Game* (1911).

The Spalding Guide (1877–1941)

"We have paid the National League Association liberally for the exclusive privilege of publishing the official Book of the League, containing the Constitution, playing rules, players averages etc., and we hereby warn all parties that the book is copyrighted, and the removal of the cover for the substitution of another, or the publication of any extracts from it, in book form, will be followed by a prosecution to the fullest extent of the law."—1877 *Spalding Guide*.

When the National League began play in 1876, Albert Spalding was granted the exclusive right to publish the league's official guide. The *Guide* was first published in 1877 and edited by Lewis Meacham. It was then edited for 27 years by pioneer sportswriter Henry Chadwick. It was discontinued in 1941 and replaced as the National League's official publication in 1942 by the *Baseball Guide*, published by *The Sporting News*.

Spalding Sporting Goods (1876–)

"… a large emporium in Chicago where he will sell all kinds of baseball goods and turn his place into the headquarters for the western ball clubs." — The *Chicago Tribune* on the new store that Albert Spalding opened when he jumped from Boston in the National Association to the National League's Chicago White Stockings.

Known initially as the A.G. Spalding & Bros. Sporting Goods Company, the enterprise was capitalized with $800 in 1876 by Spalding and his brother J. Walter. By 1892 the company stock was worth $4 million. Along the way, Spalding bought out competitors Reach, Peck & Snyder, and Wright & Ditson. On April 1, 1885, Spalding opened his first New York store.

In 1876 the fledgling sporting goods mogul received the right to manufacture the National League's **Ball** and official guide. Over the next few decades Spalding not only dominated ball manufacturing, but also controlled the bicycle manufacturing trust into the 20th century.

Spanish-American War (1898)

"It seems a mere Gettysburg guide is futile stacked up against a real war hero. Mr. Owen fought at San Juan Hill with Mr. Roosevelt and he is therefore a warrior of prowess and renown." — Sportswriter Charles Dryden on Frank Owen's heroics in a key 1905 game between the A's and White Sox.

"'I have been umpiring in the Patriot League since Dewey took Manila,' Mike the Mouth liked to tell them on the annual banquet circuit, after the World Series was over." — Philip Roth in *The Great American Novel* (1973).

This brief conflict just prior to 1900 hurt the game for several months as many teams lost money because of poor attendance. During the war the government levied a special tax on "exhibitions of base ball playing." The war's greatest effect on baseball was to spread the game to the *Philippines*, where *Little League Baseball* eventually became popular.

Tris Speaker (1888–1958)

Hall of Fame 1937

"He basically reinvented center field play, challenging the traditional idea that a center fielder should play deep and keep the ball in front of him. He made, in essence, exactly the same decision in center field that Graig Nettles made at third base … to risk an occasional double or triple to cut down on the number of singles falling in front of him." — Bill James in *The Bill James Historical Baseball Abstract* (1988).

Speaker is considered the greatest center fielder of the early 20th century and batted .345, fifth all-time.

Tristram E (no middle name) Speaker, born in Hubbard, Texas, began his Major League career with the Red Sox in 1907. He established himself in center field in 1909 and became the premier center fielder of his day. His shallow playing style enabled him to lead

in assists in a number of seasons and set a Major League record in that category.

Speaker led the Red Sox to the 1912 World Series and won the Chalmers Award, equivalent to the MVP Award. In 1915 he batted .322 and led the Red Sox to another World Series. He became disenchanted with the Red Sox after a salary dispute and was traded to the Indians for the 1916 season. He responded to the perceived insult by batting a league-leading .386 with 211 hits.

He took over the Indians as player-manager in 1919 and remained in that position until 1926. During that span he led the league in doubles four straight seasons and consistently batted around .375.

A 1926 *Gambling* charge against him and Ty Cobb resulted in his banishment from the Indians. He played one more season each for the Senators and A's before retiring. He never again managed in the Major Leagues, apparently as a result of the charges. He finished his 22-year career with 792 doubles, first all-time, and 223 triples, third all-time. He batted over .300 18 times and finished his career with a .345 average, fifth all-time. He batted .306 in his three World Series appearances.

Following retirement as a player, he managed in the minor leagues for two seasons and later became a broadcaster.

Speakers See *Indoor Ballparks*

Speed Guns

"I'd save that much in bonus money by not signing some guy who couldn't throw. This thing measures throwing speed factually, without trusting to guesswork." — Earl Weaver in 1975 on why he would spend $1,200 on the gun.

See also *Fastest Pitchers*.

In 1939 the *Cleveland Plain Dealer* reported that electrical engineer Rex D. McDill had built a pitching machine meter and made it available for such tests. The device, produced by the Pitching Speed Meter Company, was to be manufactured for commercial purposes. It was eight feet long, four feet high and six feet wide. The device operated on photoelectric cells and "other ingenious circuits," setting up a span across which the ball flew, clocking intervals.

In a test on June 6, 1939, Jimmie Foxx threw a ball at 122 feet per second (only 83 mph). Pitchers were not officially clocked, but Bob Feller threw a ball from a distance of 20 feet and recorded a top speed of 119 feet per second (only 81 mph). Teammate Johnny Humphreys registered a throw of 127 feet per second (87 mph).

In 1946 Feller became the first pitcher clocked by a form of speed gun while pitching on a mound. Clark Griffith and the Senators borrowed a photoelectric cell device from an Aberdeen, Maryland, Army ordinance plant. The device had been used to determine the speed of projectiles; a baseball certainly qualifies.

An extra 20,000 fans attended the game due to Griffith's heavy advertising of the stunt, but Griffith had not told Feller about it. Feller demanded and received $700 to go along with the promotion. He was clocked at 98.6 mph.

Modern Speed Guns. Modern speed guns appeared in the Major Leagues for the first time in 1975 and were used fairly regularly by at least three clubs. Former Major Leaguer Danny Litwhiler showed up with one of the guns at the Orioles spring training camp that season. In an October 1990 letter to the Hall of Fame, Litwhiler offered to provide the Hall with the first radar gun used to time a thrown baseball.

Litwhiler claimed that he got the idea for the gun in 1973 when he was the head baseball coach at Michigan State. In 1974 he experimented with a campus police radar gun and then contacted the manufacturer, John Paulson, president of Jo-Paul Industries, about making a prototype. Litwhiler gave the prototype to managers Earl Weaver and Red Schoendienst to try with their pitchers. Paulson then put the gun on the market as the JUGGS gun.

In 1989 JUGGS developed a gun that could give readouts at two points in the throw; one closer to the pitcher and one closer to the batter. According to Litwhiler, scouts prefer to have readouts within 5–15 degree angles from the release point.

The JUGGS gun and the Decatur Electronics devices both cost approximately $1,200–1,300 in the early 1990s. Decatur's RAGUN was considered the "slow gun" because it measured speed 10 feet from the plate when most pitches have lost four mph. The JUGGS is the "fast gun" because its older models measured speed four feet from the pitcher's release point. Its newer model can measure 10 feet from the plate. Some earlier models of the JUGGS gun could not measure speed beyond 101 mph leaving the hand and 96–97 mph at the plate. The AMTECH radar gun costs over $800 and can measure speeds from 10 to 200 miles per hour.

In October 1980 the manufacturer of the JUGGS gun filed a lawsuit against NBC television, claiming that the gun was libeled as to its accuracy in comments made by broadcasters during the World Series. The case eventually settled.

Spikes See *Shoes and Spikes*

Spink Award (1962–)

"Nothing on earth is more depressing than an old baseball writer."—Ring Lardner, an old baseball writer and Spink Award recipient.

See also *Sportswriters*.

The Spink Award was created in 1962 and is named after the primary 20th-century publisher of *The Sporting News*, J.G. Taylor Spink. The award honors a baseball writer for "meritorious contributions to baseball writing" and is presented at the Hall of Fame induction ceremony by that year's BBWAA president. Nominees are recommended by a BBWAA screening committee and voting takes place at the preceding year's World Series or winter meetings. Eligible writers must have at least 10 years of covering Major League Baseball, and then there is a nomination and evaluation process before entry is allowed. Internet writers are not allowed into the organization. Spink himself was the first recipient. The winners, their sportswriting cities and year of admittance to the BBWAA:

1962 J.G. Taylor Spink (St. Louis, 1912)
1963 Ring Lardner (New York, 1910)
1964 Hugh Fullerton (New York, 1908)
1965 Charles Dryden (Chicago, 1909)
1966 Grantland Rice (New York, 1912)
1967 Damon Runyon (New York, 1911)
1968 Harry G. Salsinger (Detroit, 1909)
1969 Sid Mercer (New York, 1909)
1970 Heywood C. Broun (New York, 1911)
1971 Frank Graham (New York, 1915)
1972 Dan Daniel (New York, 1913)
Fred Lieb (New York, 1911)
J. Roy Stockton (St. Louis, 1922)
1973 Warren Brown (Chicago, 1922)
John Drebinger (New York, 1923)
John F. Kieran (New York, 1922)

1974 John Carmichael (Chicago, 1932)
James Isaminger (Philadelphia, 1908)
1975 Tom Meany (New York, 1924)
Shirley Povich (Washington, 1925)
1976 Harold Kaese (Boston, 1934)
Red Smith (New York, 1929)
1977 Gordon Cobbledick (Cleveland, 1928)
Edgar Munzel (Chicago, 1929)
1978 Tim Murnane (Boston, 1908)
Dick Young (New York, 1943)
1979 Bob Broeg (St. Louis, 1942)
Tommy Holmes (Brooklyn, 1923)
1980 Joe Reichler (New York, 1944)
Milton Richman (New York, 1946)
1981 Allen Lewis (Philadelphia, 1950)
Bob Addie (Washington, 1942)
1982 Si Burick (Dayton, Ohio, 1946; the first recipient from a non–Major League city)
1983 Ken Smith (New York, 1927)
1984 Joe McGuff (Kansas City, 1955)
1985 Earl Lawson (Cincinnati, 1949)
1986 Jack Lang (Brooklyn, 1946)
1987 Jim Murray (Los Angeles, 1961)
1988 Bob Hunter (Los Angeles, 1958)
Ray Kelly (Philadelphia, 1946)
1989 Jerome Holtzman (Chicago, 1957)
1990 Phil Collier (San Diego, 1962)
1991 Ritter Collett (Dayton, Ohio, 1947)
1992 Leonard Koppett (New York, 1951)
Bus Saidt (Philadelphia, 1967)
1993 Wendell Smith (Pittsburgh, 1948)—the first black recipient
1994 None
1995 Joseph Durso (New York, 1964)
1996 Charles Feeney (New York, Pittsburgh, 1946)
1997 Sam Lacy (Baltimore, 1934)—the second black recipient and still active as a writer into his 90s
1998 Bob Stevens (San Francisco, 1940)
1999 Hal Lebovitz (Cleveland, 1946)
2000 Ross Newhan (Los Angeles, 1961)
2001 Joe Falls (Detroit, 1945)
2002 Hal McCoy (Dayton, Ohio, 1961)
2003 Murray Chass (New York, 1962)

Spitballs

"An unsavory curiosity"—Branch Rickey.

"Wins, Losses and Relative Humidity."—Red Smith on the pitching categories maintained for Lew Burdette, who was thought to throw the spitter.

"Not intentionally, but I sweat easily."—Pitcher Lefty Gomez when asked if he threw a spitball.

"They were starting to hit the dry side of the ball."—Lew Burdette, on when he knew it was time to retire.

Rules. See *Illegal Pitches*.

How to Throw.

"I don't throw a spitter, but I can teach you how to throw once since you asked."—Lew Burdette.

The spitball is thrown by wetting the tips of the fingers so that there is no friction at the contact point between finger and ball. This reduces the spin on the ball and makes it drop sharply. There should be moisture on only one side of the ball to make it drop properly.

Most old-time legal spitball pitchers chewed slippery elm to maintain saliva.

Origins. Some sources credit Bobby Mathews with throwing the first spitball in 1867 or 1868 as a 16-year-old. He was the starting pitcher in the first professional league game in the National Association in 1871. He supposedly dried one side of the ball and then wet his fingertips to touch the other side, causing the ball to drop and curve. Some sources report that Bill Hart learned the pitch in 1896 from Baltimore catcher Frank Bowerman.

The most prominent and generally accepted story for the origin of the spitball involves pitcher Elmer Stricklett and minor league player and future American League umpire George Hildebrand. However, there are a number of versions of their collaboration.

Hildebrand said that he got the idea for the spitball from pitcher Frank Corriden in 1902 after Corriden had a pitch drop significantly after it lay on wet grass in a minor league park. Hildebrand claims that he taught Stricklett the pitch in the Sacramento minor leagues.

Another version has it that Corriden taught Stricklett while both played for Newark in the minors. Still another version has Hildebrand as an outfielder in 1902 for Providence. He was throwing with rookie pitcher Frank Corriden and noticed Corriden warm up by wetting his finger. The result produced a no-spin change-up. As a joke, Hildebrand loaded up the ball with spit and threw it. It made a peculiar drop. He showed what he had done to Corriden, who used it in an exhibition against Pittsburgh. He struck out nine batters in five innings and then could not raise his arm.

One other story has Hildebrand finishing his playing career in the Pacific Coast League, where he met Stricklett. Stricklett had a sore arm until Hildebrand showed him the spitball. Stricklett then won 11 in a row after practicing the pitch for four days. He spent two more years with Sacramento in the Pacific Coast League and then two years in the Major Leagues. Stricklett later corroborated this version. Hildebrand retired in 1913 and umpired in the American League until 1934.

Spitball Outlawed/Grandfathered Pitchers. In 1920 baseball outlawed the spitball and other substance-abuse pitches but grandfathered in a number of spitball pitchers for the duration of their careers. Pitchers who specialized in other illegal pitches were not grandfathered in.

The recognized spitballers were Yancey "Doc" Ayers of the Tigers; Ray Caldwell and Stan Coveleski of the Indians; Bill Doak of the Cardinals; Phil Douglas of the Giants; Urban "Red" Faber of the White Sox; Dana Fillingim of the Braves; Ray Fisher of the Reds; Marvin Goodwin of the Cardinals; Burleigh Grimes and Clarence Mitchell of the Dodgers; Dutch Leonard of the Tigers; Jack Quinn of the Yankees; Dick Rudolph of the Braves; Allen Russell of the Red Sox; and Urban Shocker and Allen Sothoron of the Browns.

Teams submitted names of their spitballers for inclusion on the exempt list. The White Sox reportedly forgot to put Frank Shellenbach on the list, and he was forced to go to the Pacific Coast League for two decades, where he won 296 games. He was 1–3 for the White Sox in 1919, so it is unlikely that he was the focus of much controversy. It also appears that he was back in the minor leagues by the time the rule was enacted.

One-Year Grandfathering. The grandfather clause for spitballers originally was for only one year, but near the end of the 1921 season, the few designated spitballers were allowed to use the pitch for the rest of their careers.

Writer Gary Eller in "Say It Ain't So, Hod" (an essay in *The Ol'*

Ball Game (1990)), advances the proposition that other illegal pitch hurlers were not grandfathered in because of the connection between the shine ball and the Black Sox scandal. Black Sox conspirator Eddie Cicotte and Reds pitcher Hod Eller both threw the shineball — Eller beat the White Sox twice in the 1919 World Series and reportedly was offered a $5,000 bribe to throw the last game. Though Eller was innocent, the notoriety of the pitch in the context of the scandal may have influenced the decision to ban the shineball and its ilk without grandfathering in any pitchers known to throw those pitches.

Last Legal Spitballer. Burleigh Grimes was the last of the great (and legal) spitball pitchers. He made his last appearance for the Pirates against the Dodgers on September 20, 1934. He pitched the 8th inning, striking out one.

Balk Call.

"See to it that they do not moisten the ball in an ostentatious and objectionable manner such as holding it a foot or so from the mouth with one hand and licking the fingers of the other hand preparatory to rubbing them on the ball." — National League president Harry Pulliam's 1905 instruction to umpires on how pitchers should load up the ball. Otherwise, a balk was to be called. Spitballer Jack Chesbro apparently heeded this directive, as "the King of the Spitballers" at that time is said to have applied saliva in a "genteel" manner so that fans could not see it.

Concealment. In 1941 Tigers catcher Birdie Tebbetts of Detroit was behind the plate for alleged spitballer Tommy Bridges. Yankee manager Joe McCarthy asked to see a ball that had dropped into the dirt and rolled away. Yankee batter Joe Gordon and Tebbetts raced to grab the loose ball. Tebbetts got it and "inadvertently" threw it into the outfield where three fielders touched it before throwing it back into the infield.

Efforts to Deter. The Phillies were playing 1910s spitballer Jeff Tesreau of the Giants. The Phillies' trainer had capsicum salve, which he applied liberally to the game balls. The salve is a tissue irritant and Tesreau's lips swelled up and he had to come out of the game in the 3rd inning.

There is a similar story involving the Phillies around the same time. In 1912, Pirates first baseman Fred Ludurus figured out a way to deter Phillies star spitball pitcher Marty O'Toole. Pirates manager Red Dooin authorized his clubhouse man to put liniment on all the balls, not for the purpose of making the pitchers tongue hurt (sure!), but, as Dooin put it: "That ball may be carrying the germs of any one of many contagious diseases. So we put disinfectant on it whenever we face a spitball pitcher. I do not deny it, and I'm not afraid to say that we are going to continue to do so. I do not see how we can be refused the privilege of protecting ourselves."

An early 20th century Texas League manager put a creosote derivative on the ball that caused swelling and stinging to those pitchers who attempted to throw spitballs. It required the Texas A & M chemistry department to identify the substance.

The 1950s Reds put a camera on Lew Burdette to determine how he concealed the pitch. Even though he later said he threw 60% spitballs, the club was unable to figure out how he did it.

Health. Some early 20th century doctors spoke out against the spitball because it was believed that the spit promoted tuberculosis.

Injury Problems. In the early 20th century a rumor circulated that throwing the spitball would injure a pitcher's arm. It apparently turned out that the rumor was spread by Elmer Stricklett and Jack Chesbro, two early proponents of the pitch. They supposedly spread the tale to scare off other pitchers from using the effective pitch. Apparently the rumor was largely ignored, as a number of pitchers continued to employ the pitch.

Moisturizing Choice. Most pitchers used slippery elm to wet the ball, but Hall of Famer Red Faber used tobacco. He thought that the elm created too much saliva and made the ball hard to control. Like many ballplayers, he chewed tobacco only on the field. Faber lasted 20 years throwing the pitch while winning 254 games for the White Sox.

Spitball Tip-off. Big Ed Walsh learned the pitch from Jack Chesbro, who learned it from Stricklett. Though Walsh was considered the greatest of the spitball pitchers, he had a "tell" whereby some players (apparently on the A's, against whom he had his worst outings) could predict what he would throw. Walsh was one of the few pitchers who relied heavily on the spitball, rather than often faking the pitch to cross up hitters. It was determined that when he brought his glove up to cover his face while applying saliva, his cap moved only if he actually applied the material. It stayed still if he faked the application.

Burleigh Grimes threw a spitball while with the Dodgers in the 1920s. He had a tight cap and it did not move when he was not going to throw the spitter. When he needed saliva to put on the ball, his jaw would move with enough force to loosen the cap, tipping the fact that a spitball was the next pitch.

During the 1920 World Series against the Dodgers, Indians coach Jack McAllister noticed that second baseman Pete Kilduff would throw dirt in his glove to counter the effects of a wet ball, tipping that Grimes was about to throw a spitter.

Efforts to Legalize. After the spitball was banned in 1920, periodic efforts were made to legalize it again. In 1949 National League president Ford Frick, who favored legalization, called for a vote, but the owners refused. The next time he tried was in 1955 when he was the commissioner. In a poll conducted by *The Sporting News* that spring, 64 baseball people said yes to legalization, 36 said no, and 20 were not sure. Nevertheless, no action was taken.

In 1959 American League president Joe Cronin pushed for legalization, but only former umpire and Tigers general manager Billy Evans voted yes. Cronin wanted to: "heed the cries of the hurlers in their desert of dire need by letting them use the spitter."

Long-time spitballer Burleigh Grimes was one of the pitchers allowed to continue throwing the pitch after the 1920 ban. After he retired, he continued to campaign for its legalization: "It is a perfectly safe pitch, easier to control than the knuckleball."

Casey Stengel wanted to see it legalized: "Let them revive the spitter and help the pitchers make a living."

Branch Rickey was against it: "Give the pitchers the right to apply saliva to the ball and you might give them the impression that they would be winked at if they again laved the ball with tobacco juice, anointed it with oils, powdered it with talcum, or even stuck phonograph needles in it."

Ejections. The first spitball ejection was on July 20, 1944, by umpire Cal Hubbard against pitcher Nelson Potter of the Browns. Hubbard favored legalizing the spitball and said that he ejected Potter not because of anything he found on the ball but because of Potter's "cantankerous attitude" and "huffing" on the ball. Another version has it that Potter had a habit of licking his fingers but did not throw a spitball. His manager, Luke Sewell, complained about opposing pitcher Hank Borowy of the Yankees, which forced umpire Hubbard to warn both pitchers. Borowy complied, but Potter began an exaggerated licking motion that ultimately forced Hubbard to eject him.

Potter claimed that he never threw the spitball, but that he needed moisture on his fingers on the cool, dry night. He was sus-

pended for 10 days and went home; his wife gave birth ninth months later. After Potter was ejected, the new pitcher came in and got out of a jam, prompting broadcaster Dizzy Dean to compliment the "pitching change" by umpire Cal Hubbard: "It looks like ol' Hub changed pitchers just at the right time."

The next ejection was on May 1, 1968, when National League umpire Ed Vargo tossed Phillies pitcher John Boozer at Shea Stadium.

Gaylord Perry.

"SPITTER" — Perry's personalized license plate.

"Gaylord Perry is a very honorable man. He only calls for the spitter when he needs it." — Indians president Gabe Paul.

"I licked my fingers, faked a wipe and let her go as hard as I could…. She dipped into the dirt like a shot quail." — Perry on his first spitball, thrown on May 31, 1964.

One well-researched source identified Perry as the only pitcher to be ejected for throwing a spitter since Nelson Potter (which would negate the Boozer ejection). On August 23, 1982, Perry was pitching for the Mariners against the Red Sox. Respected umpire Dave Phillips warned Perry. On a later pitch that dropped significantly, Phillips called it a strike, then changed his call to a ball and ejected Perry based on the "flight of the ball." This was at the umpire's discretion under the rules then in effect. Perry received a $250 fine and a 10-day suspension.

At the Hall of Fame ceremony for Perry in 1991, it was noted that when Rod Carew was inducted, Panamanian flags flew; when Ferguson Jenkins was inducted, Canadian flags flew; and when Perry was inducted, it began to rain. When he reached **Three Hundred Wins**, Perry revealed that he was wearing a tee-shirt that said: "Winning 300 Games Is Nothing to Spit At."

Preacher Roe. Long after he retired in 1954 with a 127–84 record in 12 seasons, Roe admitted that his "money pitch" was the spitball.

Split Season See *Scheduling — Split Seasons*

Sporting Life (1883–1917)

"But, though '*Sporting Life*' appears in new garb, which is but as the covering to the man, it will still be, in contents, in policy, in scope, the good old '*Sporting Life*'; ever fair, honest, trustworthy, sincere, impartial, clean and high-toned in its presentation of the news and consideration of sporting affairs, men and measures. Withal it will be even more enterprising and progressive than heretofore, which is saying much." — The February 16, 1895, edition of *Sporting Life* on its new format.

"The best and cheapest sporting paper in America." — The *Sporting Life* masthead.

Sporting Life magazine was published in Philadelphia by Francis Richter in the 19th and early 20th centuries. Its first issue was published in 1883, three years before *The Sporting News* went into print.

Sporting Life supported the 1914–1915 Federal League and for that and other reasons folded in 1917 shortly after the Federal League's demise. Richter, who supposedly hated *The Sporting News*, then went to work reporting for his long-time rival.

The Sporting News (1886–)

"The Bible of Baseball" — The newspaper's self-styled title.

"You go through *The Sporting News* for the last 100 years and you will find two things are always true. You never have enough pitching, and nobody ever made money." — Players Association president Donald Fehr.

First Edition. The weekly paper's first edition was distributed on St. Patrick's Day 1886, three years after rival *Sporting Life* first appeared.

Coverage. The newspaper was devoted to baseball and other sports until J.G. Taylor Spink took over in 1914 after the death of his father, C.C. Spink. The publication covered baseball exclusively until 1942 when low circulation caused by World War II forced the publication to expand its coverage to other sports.

Ownership.

"If I hadn't, Spink would have fired me for the 41st time." — Sportswriter Dan Daniel on why he arrived early at J.G. Taylor Spink's funeral.

The Spink family owned and operated the St. Louis–based newspaper for approximately 90 years after migrating from Canada following the Civil War. Alfred H. Spink and his brother Charles Claude (C.C.) Spink were the original owners. Al Spink had been with the *St. Louis Dispatch* newspaper and was an early supporter of Ban Johnson's Western League.

Over the balance of the 19th century a rift developed between the Spink brothers, culminating in 1914 when Charles died and his son, J.G. (John George) Taylor Spink, took over as editor at age 26. He became the paper's driving force over the next 48 years. Al Spink died at age 74 in 1928. O.P. Caylor, who had been involved with the American Association, was an early editor for *The Sporting News*.

J.G. was eccentric about punctuality and had a knack for locating his writers anywhere. He was abrasive and often fired his writers many times over. In the early days of his stewardship, Spink earned money from minor league teams and leagues under an agreement whereby *The Sporting News* published every box score from every minor league game.

Spink feuded with Judge Landis and continued the family tradition of supporting American League president Ban Johnson, as the newspaper was often a mouthpiece for the views espoused by Johnson. Spink even named his only son after Johnson. He also published the *Spink Baseball Guide* and the *Baseball Register*. Spink and his publications were powerful forces in baseball through the 1950s. In addition to helping shape baseball policy the paper sponsored a number of **Awards**.

J.G. died at age 74 in 1962 and his son, Charles C. (C.C.) Spink, was named president that year at age 46. C.C. had no children and no successor, so to maintain continuity he sold the paper in January 1977 for $18 million to the Times-Mirror Company, owner of the *Los Angeles Times* and other properties. The sale allowed Spink to remain as editor for five years and consultant for another five years.

Official Status. Judge Landis designated *The Sporting News* as the first official baseball record book, but Landis revoked that status after supposedly becoming upset that J.G. Taylor Spink was referred to by many as "Mr. Baseball." Spink openly supported Ban Johnson while Johnson was still in power, and Landis was unhappy about that relationship. Happy Chandler reinstated the designation when he took office in 1945.

Subscription Price. The newspaper cost five cents until 1918, when the price was raised to seven cents for two weeks and then raised to 10 cents. It increased to 15 cents in the 1940s, 20 cents in 1946, 25 cents in 1951, 35 cents in 1966, 50 cents in 1969, 60 cents in 1970, and reached $1.00 in 1977. It rose to $1.25 in 1979, $1.50 in 1980, $1.75 in 1984, $1.95 in 1985, $2.50 by the mid–1990s, and $4 by 2004. In 1916 a year's subscription cost $2.75, and the subscriber received a bonus of 75 baseball pictures.

Circulation. Circulation was 3,000 in 1886 when the paper began as a weekly. By 1888 weekly circulation had jumped to 6,000.

During World War I, circulation dropped to 5,000 per week, but the paper was rescued when Spink's close friend Ban Johnson arranged for the American League to buy 150,000 copies and ship them to soldiers in Europe. Circulation was 50,000 in 1920 and increased to 90,000 by 1924.

During World War II, 400,000 copies were sent overseas every week. By 1985 weekly circulation was almost 700,000. In the mid–1990s, circulation was guaranteed to advertisers at 515,000, which meant that it could be significantly higher. In 2003 it was 708,000.

Minor League Coverage. *The Sporting News* was legendary for its coverage of minor league baseball, but eventually it eliminated inclusion of all minor league box scores. A newer publication, *Baseball Weekly* (distributed by the publishers of *USA Today*), has taken over most of the minor league coverage.

Other Publications. *The Sporting News* has a publishing group that annually puts out a number of books and statistical compilations.

Sports Illustrated (1954–)

"Do baseball and boxing fans mingle with fox hunters in pink coats? A hard book to sell ad space for with the audience all over the lot…. Looks like a sure money loser." — Advertiser on the prospective new sports magazine.

First Cover Boy. In 1954 Eddie Mathews became the first person to appear on the cover of *Sports Illustrated*.

Top Cover Boys. In the first 50 years of *Sports Illustrated* (*SI*), Pete Rose was the all-time *SI* baseball cover boy with 15, followed by Mickey Mantle with 13, and Willie Mays and Mark McGwire with nine each. The top four in any sport were Michael Jordan (49), Muhammad Ali (37), and tied at 22 were Kareem Abdul-Jabbar and Magic Johnson. Football had the most covers, with 511, followed by baseball with 502 and pro basketball with 295. The Yankees had the most team covers, with 59, followed by the Lakers with 57 and Cowboys with 45.

Late Choice. In 1956 Johnny Podres was hastily chosen the *SI* Sportsman of the Year only after original choice Bill Woodward, Jr., was accidentally killed by his wife.

Best Seller. The magazine's all-time best-selling cover was an unprecedented midweek add-on that featured Mark McGwire's 62nd home run.

Sports Pages See Newspapers

Sportsman's Park (1876–1966)

"You should have been in the old St. Louis ballpark. It was a rat hole, that's what it was. You couldn't leave your shoes or gloves on the floor because rats would come up and chew them up. They had no shower stalls, one pipe in the middle of the room, hot and cold water, but it never got real cold because it was beastly hot in St. Louis." — Senators infielder Ossie Bluege.

"Baseball virtually became a side line at Sportsman's Park under the [1940s] Barnes regime as loud-speaker plugs for the park-owned fried-fish concession and a brand of cigarettes filled in the quiet moments between cracks of the bat." — Dan Parker in a 1945 *Saturday Evening Post* article.

This St. Louis ballpark — actually three different versions on the same site — was home to the American Association Brown Stockings from 1882 through 1891, the National League Browns in 1892, National League Cardinals from 1920 through 1966, and the American League Browns from 1902 through 1953.

19th Century. Sportsman's Park consisted of nine acres that supposedly were traded to resolve a dispute over a strip of land only nine inches wide.

St. Louis was an original National League entry in 1876 that performed in an enclosed wooden grandstand at Grand and Dodier that some sources report being known as Sportsman's Park since 1874. After two seasons, the team left the league and for a few years the park was used for exhibition games promoted by Al Spink, future founder of *The Sporting News*. Other sources, most notably *Green Cathedrals*, report that the early park was known as Grand Avenue Park and was different from the site known as Sportsman's Park.

In 1882 St. Louis again had another Major League team, this time in the rival American Association. Owner Christopher Von der Ahe ran a beer garden one block from Sportsman's Park and began using it for his Browns.

The Browns were the American Association pennant winners from 1885 through 1888, but fell on hard times when the team merged into the National League for the 1892 season. As a result, Von der Ahe converted the park into "The Coney Island of the West" in an attempt to raise money beyond the diminishing baseball revenue. Visitors watched boating, Wild West shows, boxing matches, horse racing and an all-girl cornet band.

The ballpark suffered six fires in 10 years, which strained Von der Ahe's resources. Coupled with a poor team, the expense of the fires forced him to sell off his better players, and ultimately he lost the team in the late 1890s. The Robison brothers of Cleveland took over ownership of the club, changed its name to Cardinals, and began using a different ballpark, Robison Field. Sportsman's Park was not used from 1899 through 1901.

20th Century. In 1902 the American League Milwaukee franchise was shifted to St. Louis to become the Browns. The new club occupied a rebuilt Sportsman's Park. Additional improvements were made in 1909 when a second deck was constructed to raise seating capacity to over 18,000. The Cardinals became tenants of Sportsman's Park in 1920, staying in the facility until they abandoned it during the 1966 season for new Busch Stadium.

In 1925 Browns owner Phil Ball added another deck to the grandstands at a cost of $500,000, raising the capacity to 30,000. In 1938 the original scoreboard was replaced and in 1940 lights were installed and the first **Night Game** in the park was played on May 24 that season.

Dimensions. The modern dimensions in 1909 from left to right field were 360–393–502–400–393. The ballpark configurations were changed infrequently, and the last dimensions were significantly shorter at 334–387–410–400–390.

Leases and Sales. When Phil Ball died in 1933, his family retained title to the ballpark and leased it to both the Browns and Cardinals. In 1947 Browns owner Robert Hedges purchased the ballpark from the estate of owner Phil Ball and modernized it considerably.

By 1953 the more prosperous Cardinals wanted to make improvements to the ballpark but not while the Browns still owned the site and the Cardinals were merely tenants. Browns owner Bill Veeck was strapped for cash after trying to move the franchise to Milwaukee. On April 9, 1953, Veeck sold the park to Cardinals owner August A. Busch, Jr., president of the Anheuser-Busch Brewery. The name of the facility was then changed to Busch Stadium. Busch paid $800,000 for the park and poured in another $400,000 (or $1.5 million depending on the source).

The name was originally to be changed to Budweiser Stadium, but that was abandoned at the last minute in favor of Busch Stadium because baseball wanted to avoid the strictly beer-oriented name.

Reconfiguration. When Babe Ruth hit 60 home runs in 1927, he hit four into an open area in right field that extended to center field. In 1930 the club decided that home runs to this part of the park were too cheap and put up a screen. In 1932 when Jimmie Foxx of Philadelphia hit 58 home runs, he supposedly hit 12 drives that were stopped by the screen (but more recent research suggests a lower number; see also **Home Runs—Assaults on Ruth Before Maris**). In 1955 the screen was removed to accommodate a predominately left-handed lineup. One year later the screen was restored when it became clear that the Cardinal batters were not the only ones benefiting from the change.

Last Game.

"Busch Stadium—a seamed, rusty, steep-sided box … reminded me of an old down-on-her-luck dowager who has been given a surprise party by the local settlement house; she was startled by the occasion but still able to accept it as no less than her due."—Roger Angell in *The Summer Game* (1972) describing the renamed Sportsman's Park as it hosted the 1964 World Series.

The last game played at Sportsman's Park was on May 8, 1966, when the Giants defeated the Cardinals 10–5. The band played "Auld Lang Syne" while 17,803 fans sang and groundskeeper Bill Stocksick pried up home plate and placed it aboard a helicopter to bring it to new Busch Memorial Stadium. The park was demolished later that year and became the site of the Herbert Hoover Boys' Club.

Sportswriters

"The baseball writer has it tough. He is many things: part psychiatrist, part stool pigeon, part house detective, part doctor, certainly part friend and enemy."—Jimmy Cannon.

"Sportswriters have as much gift for reasoning as a giraffe would have to play a flute in the dark."—Editorial in the 19th century *St. Louis Union* newspaper.

"Interviewing this guy is like trying to mine coal with a nail file and a pair of scissors."—A sportswriter's lament about tight-lipped Tony Lazzeri of the Yankees.

"This passion for language and the telling detail is what makes baseball the writer's game."—Thomas Boswell in *How Life Imitates the World Series* (1982).

"Astronomers delight in discovering new stars in the firmament. So do baseball writers."—Sportswriter Arthur Daley.

"I never had any problem with radio or TV people. It was always something written that wasn't right. I was always being misquoted or the guy writing didn't know a damn thing about baseball."—Ted Williams in 1997.

See also **Baseball Reporters Association of America, Baseball Writers Association of America, Newspapers** and **Spink Award**.

Early Sportswriters.

"To Henry B. Chadwick, who created the profession of baseball writer a century ago, and to Suzanne, Katherine and David, who must put up with it now."—Dedication by Leonard Koppett in *The New York Mets—The Whole Story* (1970).

"Keep your mouth shut, your ears open, your pants buttoned, your feet on the ground, and keep one eye on the clock."—*Brooklyn Eagle* editor Jimmy Murphy to new baseball writers.

"In the earlier days a lot of us were often broke or next to it. But one thing about The Greatest Profession, a little thing like money or the lack of it never gave us much concern." — Grantland Rice in *The Tumult and the Shouting* (1954).

"What smug sycophants were most of those old-timey baseball writers, patronizing the ballplayers, sucking around the owners, protecting their own soft lives. It was the stories they *didn't* write that hurt us more than the clunky paeans they tapped out on fingers that sometimes wore World Series rings they thought they had helped win." — Robert Lipsyte in *Esquire* magazine.

"Never mind all that cuff spewed by those ignorant and disdainful of anything that happened before they were born about the 'good old days' having been a gentler, kinder, less critical era in regard to media treatment of baseball players and athletes in general. Anyone who professes to believe that the so-called 'gee whiz' and hero-worshipping school of sports writing prevailed universally until 'tell it like it is' reporting took over in the past two or three decades is flying in the face of printed evidence to the contrary. The published record is clear, ugly, and often terribly unfair." — George Vass.

"A little fellow who dripped acid, spleen extract, and venom from his pen." — Fred Lieb on 19th century sportswriter O.P. Caylor. Caylor has also been described as a "monkey-faced cur," "mongrel skeleton," and "cucumber-head." Oliver Perry Caylor helped form the **American Association** of the 1880s and reportedly had been an attorney before becoming involved with the Association. Caylor managed the American Association Cincinnati Red Stockings in 1885 and 1886 and the New York Metropolitans for part of 1887. He edited the **Reach Guide** and was the baseball editor of the *Cincinnati Enquirer* for 20 years until his death in 1897 at age 48.

The first writers to travel with teams did so just after the Civil War when traveling club teams emerged. Clubs paid for the writers to travel with them. Harry Miller was the only sportswriter to travel with the 1869 Cincinnati Red Stockings during their undefeated cross-country tour.

Early sportswriter Charles Peverelly wrote one of the first histories of the game. The most famous of the early sportswriters was **Henry Chadwick**, a New York writer who promoted baseball from the 1850s to the early 20th century.

When the National League was formed, the *Chicago Tribune* sent a sportswriter to cover the meeting. The writer knocked eastern establishment sportswriter Henry Chadwick as "the Old Man of the Sea … a dead weight on the neck of the game." Chadwick, sometimes also known as baseball's "Chief Justice," responded by chiding the National League for forming in secret and causing the breakup of the Eastern-based National Association.

Sportswriters Finley Peter Dunne of the *Chicago News* and Charles Seymour of the *Chicago Herald* are credited with an early writing style of focusing on the more dramatic moments of the game, rather than bland fact reporting, which evolved into the modern style of sportswriting.

One of the most influential but least-known sportswriters of the 19th century was Len Washburn, whose humorous style was a benchmark in baseball reporting. He wrote for Chicago's *Inter Ocean* newspaper in the late 1880s until 1891 when he was killed in a train crash.

Sportswriters eventually became baseball's watchdogs, especially when newspaper popularity peaked in the early 1920s before radio entered the arena.

Player/Sportswriter.

"I guess this means I have to put on 30 pounds, smoke smelly cigars, and wear clothes that don't match." — Former player Garth Iorg in 1985 after agreeing to cover the play-offs for the *Toronto Star*.

"Can't do it. Don't know 200 words." — Alleged response of a ballplayer when his sports editor friend wired him the following spring training telegram: "Send me 200 words on the game."

In 1877 reporter John Haldeman of the *Louisville Courier-Journal* reported on and was the scorer of games for the National League Louisville club. He was also the son of the club's owner. He was asked to play second base in one game, going 0-for-4 and committing three errors.

Haldeman was one of the eyewitnesses who accused the Louisville players of throwing games. The scandal resulted in the league expelling the offending players for life and then rescinding the club's franchise (see also **Gambling and Fixed Games** and **Louisville Colonels**).

Tim Murnane played in the Major Leagues briefly in the 1870s National League and 1884 Union Association. He was later a prominent sportswriter and sports editor at the *Boston Globe*.

Sam Crane was a Major Leaguer in the 1880s and early 1890s before becoming a sportswriter for the *New York Journal*. Ford Frick reported in his autobiography that Crane was the first writer to publicly urge Organized Baseball to create a shrine honoring the great players of the game.

In 1911 Rube Marquard and Christy Mathewson, both pitching for the Giants, wrote World Series columns for rival newspapers. When Marquard gave up a home run to A's third baseman Frank Baker (dubbed "Home Run" Baker after the Series), Mathewson criticized Marquard's pitch selection in his column. When Baker hit his second home run off Mathewson, Marquard had the last word in his own column. Jack Wheeler ghostwrote Mathewson's column. After complaints by other sportswriters, the National Agreement in 1913 banned ghostwriting by players on a team participating in the World Series.

Pitcher Early Wynn wrote a column for the *Cleveland News* during the 1950s until he was traded after blasting management for trying to trade him. His writing career ended with the trade to the White Sox after the 1957 season.

Pitcher John Curtis of the Giants wrote a column for the *San Francisco Examiner* while still an active player.

Mets pitcher David Cone wrote a column at the start of the 1988 NLCS against the Dodgers. He wrote that Orel Hershiser, who had just set a scoreless innings streak record, was lucky, and that pitcher Jay Howell was a "high school pitcher." Cone received so much criticism that he quickly abandoned the column. Dodger manager Tommy Lasorda posted the column to inspire his club. It must have helped, as the Dodgers were the surprise winners in seven games.

All-Time Greats.

"Sportswriting, like any writing, is equal parts hard work, long observation and lively imagination." — Jim Murray, who was named national Sportswriter of the Year 14 times. Rick Reilly of *Sports Illustrated* won the award nine times through 2003. The winner receives a personalized Louisville Slugger bat.

"Quietly, perhaps without ever knowing it, he brought about a revolution in the approach to, and technique of, writing a sports column in this country. Gradually editorial opinion gave way to reporting, to conversation pieces and interviews and 'mood' pieces that strove to capture for the reader the color and flavor and texture of the event. No other sportswriter in Frank's lifetime exerted such effect on his own business. None was imitated so widely, or so unsuccessfully." — Red Smith on *New York Sun* columnist Frank Graham.

"Roger Angell, by contrast, comes from the magazine writer's school of sportswriting: calm, meditative, not deadline driven or space cramped, free to follow the fast-and-slow, squeeze-and-relax rhythms of the game." — Lev Grossman in *Time*.

Some of the greatest sportswriters of all time began their New York writing careers in 1911. Fred Lieb started that year with the *New York Press*. Damon Runyon started at the *New York American* and Heywood Broun at the *Morning Telegraph*. Grantland Rice started with the *New York Evening Mail*. Rice had worked at the *Atlanta Journal* as sports editor in 1902 at age 22. He coined the Notre Dame football "Four Horsemen" phrase and wrote a well-known sequel to "*Casey at the Bat.*" After playing shortstop at Vanderbilt, Rice was a semipro baseball player in Atlanta when he struck out four times against pitcher Fred Rucker. He then recommended Rucker, whom he nicknamed "Nap," to the Dodgers. Rucker signed with the Dodgers and began a 10-year Major League career in 1907.

Shirley Povich.

"The first thing you say is that Shirley Povich was why people bought the paper. You got the *Post* for Shirley and the sports section. He was the sports section. For a lot of years, he carried the paper, and that's no exaggeration." — Ben Bradlee, retired executive editor of the *Washington Post*.

"I take it one decade at a time." — Povich's secret to longevity. The *Post* writer was still going strong at his desk at age 90 in 1995 and died in June 1998 at age 92, two days after submitting his last column from home (he had been feeling poorly for about a month and had a heart condition after collapsing at an Orioles' postseason game in 1997). In 1947 he published a 15-part series on racism in baseball entitled "No More Shutouts." He was listed in the inaugural edition of *Who's Who of American Women*, where it was reported that he was the wife of Ethyl.

Fred Lieb. The Spink Award winner saw his first Major League game in 1904 and started covering games in 1911 as a newspaperman for the *New York Press*. As a chronicler of the New York teams in baseball's Golden Age of the 1920s through the 1950s he had a bird's eye view of most of baseball's great moments. He retired to St. Petersburg in 1948 but continued to be active in the game. At age 86 he was still writing a column for the *St. Petersburg Times* in Florida.

Lieb wrote *Baseball as I Have Known It* (1977), a detailed account of his observations of the game from before 1900 through the 1960s. He also wrote a series of histories of various Major League teams. Lieb, who spoke German, is credited with persuading Lou Gehrig's mother to attend Gehrig's wedding.

See also *Ernest Hemingway*, *Ring Lardner* and *Red Smith*.

Lee Allen.

"Fans look for and receive everything from baseball; thrills that border on ecstasy, intense excitement, and inevitably, glum disappointment. But seldom are they bored, and through the winters that interrupt their passion they remember all the victories and even the lost causes of the deep purple past with sweet nostalgia that will never be forgotten." — Allen in the preface to his *100 Years of Baseball* (1950).

Well known in the 1950s and 1960s, Allen was the official chronicler of the National League in the early 1960s. He was a Cincinnati native and sportswriter before moving into the Reds' publicity department in the 1940s. In 1948 he became the team's publicist and wrote a history of the club. He was also a staff writer for *The Sporting News* and a feature writer for the *Cincinnati Enquirer*.

By 1961 Allen considered himself "probably the only person in the United States devoting full time to baseball research." Allen played a key role in the preparation of MacMillan's *The Baseball Encyclopedia*, but died shortly before it was first published in 1969.

His books include *The National League Story* (1961), *The American League Story* (1962), *The Dodgers and the Giants* (1964), *Cooperstown Corner: Columns from The Sporting News, 1967–1969* (1990).

Hall of Fame/Spink Award. The Hall of Fame has admitted several writers to a special wing named after the long-time publisher of *The Sporting News*, J.G. Taylor Spink. Winners have been presented the **Spink Award** since 1962. Spink himself was the first recipient.

Henry Chadwick is the only sportswriter elected directly into the Hall, as opposed to the writer's wing.

The National Sportscasters and Sportswriters Hall of Fame is located in Salisbury, North Carolina.

Rivalry with Electronic Media.

"I flinch whenever I see the word literature used in the same sentence with my name. I'm just a bum trying to make a living running a typewriter." — Red Smith.

Sportswriters have a technique for dealing with radio and television interviewers who interrupt print journalists — they curse into the microphone to ruin the interview.

Pulitzer Prize. New York writer Arthur Daley was the first sports columnist to win a Pulitzer Prize. He was followed by Red Smith and Dave Anderson. All three were writers for the *New York Times*. *Los Angeles Times*–based Jim Murray also won a Pulitzer Prize.

Walt Whitman. The quintessential 19th century American poet spent some time as a sportswriter for the *Brooklyn Eagle*, often using a very stilted prose: "Mr. John S. struck the ball well in the seventh inning," though at times he also wrote a bit more flowery. After a Brooklyn Excelsiors loss, he wrote that they "have always reflected credit upon the manly and healthful game they practice." Whitman was friends with 19th century baseball great Harry Wright and Wright sometimes visited Whitman late in Whitman's life and talked baseball for many hours.

Bill Stern.

"In the old radio days, Bill Stern (the Colgate Shave Cream man) had a weekly sports show on which he related little-known true stories of incidents in the lives of famous people. Every story had to have a sports angle, and it had to be 'inspirational.' Since there are only about five such stories (all of them duller than Buffalo), he soon ran out of material — and that's when the anecdotes began to get interesting. Once we realized he was making them up out of thin air (apparently assisted by someone with a really bizarre imagination), we could hardly wait for them." — Art Hill in *I Don't Care If I Never Come Back* (1980); see for example *Presidents* — **Abraham Lincoln.**

By-Line. John Kieran received the Spink Award in 1973 after a newspaper and radio career that began in 1915. The *New York Times* gave him the first by-lined sports column in 1927, and later he was an expert on the "Information, Please" radio program. Kieran and concessionaire Harry Stevens were close friends and according to Ford Frick often spent afternoons trying to stump each other with obscure quotations from Shakespeare.

Feud.

"When Ted Williams was inducted into the Hall thirty-seven years ago he said he must have earned it because he certainly didn't win it because of his friendship with the writers. I guess in that way I'm proud to be in his company." — Eddie Murray at his Hall of Fame induction ceremony in 2003.

Chicago Daily News sports editor Lloyd Lewis once ran a midseason column asking fans to vote for a new manager. Owner Phil Wrigley almost ran an ad asking for a vote on a new sports editor for the paper.

Hal McCoy, the 2002 Spink Award recipient, was banned from the media dining room four times while covering the Reds after writing unflattering stories about owner Marge Schott. Schott papered her office floor with his columns so Schotzie would know exactly where to leave his droppings. Eric Davis sent pizza to the press box when Schott banned McCoy from the media dining room. It also prompted a canned food drive that was delivered to his seat in the press box.

He was nearly blind from a stroke in his eye when he received the award. In spring training 2002 he suffered a stroke in the other eye, so with 75% of his eyesight lost, he was nevertheless back on the road (with some help).

Other Positions Held. In the 19th century, sportswriters often became executives with clubs or leagues. American League president Ban Johnson is the prime example, moving from a newspaper to head of the Western League in the 1890s. In the 20th century a number of sportswriters entered baseball in executive capacities. Ford Frick was a ghostwriter for Babe Ruth in the 1930s before moving into the National League office, becoming National League president and commissioner. In the 1940s sportswriter Lee Allen went into the Reds front office. In the 1960s sportswriter Arthur Richman became the Public Relations Director of the Mets and Maury Allen went to the Reds. Sportswriter Ken Smith became Executive Director of the Hall of Fame.

Early Salaries. The best baseball reporters of the 19th century earned $15 per week, less than the police beat writers and $25 less than the general assignment writers.

Black Sportswriters.
"They [the Black writers] too were victims of Jim Crow ... Segregation hid their considerable skills from the larger white audience and severely restricted their income earning potential. Yet they rarely mentioned their own plight. Indeed, the barriers for Black journalists lasted long after those for athletes disappeared."—Jules Tygiel in *Baseball's Great Experiment* (1983).

"I've always felt that there was nothing special about me. And I know how this may sound. But any person with a little vision, a little curiosity, a little nerve could have done what I did."—Sam Lacy, who died in 2003 at age 99, five years after being inducted into the Writer's Wing of the Hall of Fame.

In the early 1930s a group of black sports editors from the major black papers around the country formed the National Negro Newspaper All-American Association of Sports Editors. The NNNAA named All-Americans and elected their own all-star teams. The work of NNNAA to publicize the outstanding play of Negro Leaguers helped speed integration of the Major Leagues.

Sam Lacy of the *Baltimore Afro American* (for over 50 years) was a black sportswriter instrumental in pushing for and then chronicling the integration of baseball during the 1940s. He was still active as a sportswriter and editor into the 1990s, and finally made it in to the Writers wing in 1998 while still active as a sportswriter in his 90s. Lacy was inducted into the Maryland Media Hall of Fame in 1984 and the Black Athletes Hall of Fame in Las Vegas in 1985. He was on the President's Council on Physical Fitness and the Hall of Fame's Negro League Selection Committee. However, Wendell Smith of the *Pittsburgh Courier* was the first black recipient of the Spink Award in 1993. Lacy was Jackie Robinson's road roommate during the 1947 season. See Sam Lacy with Moses Newson, *Fighting For Fairness: The Life Story of Hall of Fame Sportswriter Sam Lacy* (1998).

In 1946 Lacy was barred from the New Orleans press box during an exhibition game. A number of sympathetic white writers joined him on the roof to cover the game. On the other hand, Tom Swope, chairman of the Cincinnati chapter of the BBWAA, barred Lacy from the Crosley Field press box during the 1947 season. Other prominent black sportswriter of the 1940s, all of whom agitated for integration of Organized Baseball, were Joe Bostic of *The People's Voice* in Harlem and Fay Young of the *Chicago Defender*.

See also Jim Reisler, *Black Writers/Black Baseball: An Anthology of Articles from Black Sportswriters Who Covered the Negro Leagues* (1994); Dick Clark and Larry Lester (eds.), *The Negro Leagues Book* (1994), contains a brief but informative section on black sportswriters and newspapers that covered baseball (primarily the Negro Leagues).

Player/Manager Relations.
"Pour hot water over a sportswriter and you'll get instant shit."—Ted Williams.

"Meusel began to say hello when it was time to say good-bye."—Sportswriter Frank Graham on uncooperative Bob Meusel, who began to court reporters when his career was in decline.

"I thought it was uncalled for. But when you've got a five-year-old mind, what do you do?"—Anonymous Cubs official after slugger Dave Kingman presented a rat to a woman sportswriter. In a similar vein, Bill Terry referred to sportswriters as "a bunch of rats."

"By and large, baseball writers and baseball managers get along like husband and wife. They respect each other, but not much."—Jim Murray.

"Baseball players are, by consensus, the rudest, crudest, prickliest interviews in the business. There are several exceptions, but for the most part, the rule for a reporter is simple. You are invisible. You may make peeping noises to attract attention, but there is always the chance you will annoy the great man and he will have to curse or shout at you."—Sportswriter C.W. Nevius of the *San Francisco Chronicle*.

"The year I hit 58 [home runs in 1938], the fans got pretty rough. Drunks called me Jew bastard and kike, and I'd come in and sound off about the fans. Then the next day I'd meet a kid, all pop-eyed to be shaking my hand, and I'd know I'd been wrong. But the writers protected me then. Why aren't the writers protecting Maris now?"—Hank Greenberg on the writers' reporting of a minor *faux pas* by Roger Maris during the pressure-packed 1961 season.

Ty Cobb had a "son of a bitch list" of writers and others.

Dizzy Dean took his spiked shoes over the head of writer Jack Miley of the *New York Daily News*, whom he called "a big man now, especially between the ears," who made "tie salesman pay."

New York sportswriter Dan Daniel was a member of the Baseball Writers Association (BBWAA) beginning in 1913 and was one of the first to use a typewriter in New York. Daniel, like most writers of his day, was much closer to the players than in more recent seasons. Daniel claimed that he persuaded Babe Ruth to sign for $80,000 one year after a hold-out, after Daniel arranged for Ruth and club owner Jacob Ruppert to meet secretly to work out their differences.

Daniel also claimed to have intervened with Ruppert for pitcher Red Ruffing when it was reported that Ruffing would not sign unless he was paid an additional $5,000 for pinch hitting duties. Ruffing told Daniel that he never said this, and Daniel was able to bring Ruppert and Ruffing together.

Daniel said that he talked 1950s catcher Ralph Houk into going back to Kansas City to manage at the request of Yankees general manager George Weiss. Weiss had promised Houk that he would be back with the big club, but Houk was going to quit rather than report to Kansas City. Houk reported and came back to manage the Yankees in 1961, the first of his three pennant-winning years for the club.

In 1916 Zack Wheat was a hold-out with the Dodgers. Reporter Abe Yager sent a telegram to Wheat implying that the terms of his contract demands would be met, but not identifying the sender of the wire. Wheat reported and he and Dodger owner Charles Ebbets came to terms. Yager confessed to the ploy only during midseason.

In August 1964 playboy pitcher Bo Belinsky was suspended for knocking out 64-year-old *Los Angeles Times* reporter Braven Dyer.

Steve Carlton did not speak to the media from 1976 until his retirement in the late 1980s, prompting broadcaster Ernie Johnson to say in 1982: "The two best pitchers in the National League don't speak English — Fernando Valenzuela and Steve Carlton."

Women Sportswriters. See also **Women in Baseball**.

In the 1960s Judge Roy Hofheinz of the Astros created a press box for women society-page writers. The "Hen Coop" produced stories on such important topics as whether is was proper for a man to wear his cowboy hat indoors in the Astrodome.

Replacement Columnist. In early 1995 during the player strike, Leigh Montville wrote a tongue-in-cheek column in *Sports Illustrated* to introduce a "replacement columnist": "HELLO. I are the replacement kolumnist. It is just about the greatest honner I can think of. The magazine called me just out of the blue (!!!!) and asked if I could write this major league column while replacement players played major league baseball. Quick as a wink, I said I could!!!! This were something beyond my wildest dreams."

Lost in Translation. A minor controversy broke out in June 2003 when the Associated Press quoted Dominican Sammy Sosa in his grammatically incorrect English the night of his corked bat incident. In response, the Players Association sent a memo urging foreign players to speak in their native tongues: "Let the AP [Associated Press] worry about the translation."

Live. In 2003 a *Sacramento Bee* sportswriter, with 34 years on the job, was fired after it was revealed that he had covered a Pirates-Giants game "live" off a television from an undisclosed location (perhaps his BarcaLounger?).

Father/Son. *Los Angeles Times* Hall of Fame sportswriter Ross Newhan's son, David, made it to the Major Leagues briefly in 1999 for 32 games with the Padres, and then made it into 32 games over the next two seasons. He missed all of 2001–2002 before returning with the Orioles in 2004 after several injuries, including a severe shoulder injury that required two surgeries. He was spectacular in the weeks after his return, including a home run in his first at-bat the day he was called up. Ross Newhan wrote poignantly about covering his son objectively for the *Times*, and then being strictly a fan in the stands when David returned to the Majors.

Books. Bob Broeg, *Bob Broeg: A Hall of Famer's Look at Sports in the 20th Century* (1995); Arthur Daley, *Times at Bat* (1950) (reprinted as *Inside Baseball* in 1971), a 50-year history of classic stories, most of which appeared in his column, "Sports of the Times"); Jerome Holtzman (ed.), *No Cheering in the Press Box* (1974); Roger Kahn, *Memories of Summer: When Baseball Was an Art, and Writing About it was a Game* (2004); Fred Lieb, *Baseball as I Have Known It* (1977); Tom Meany, *Mostly Baseball* (collection of 20 years of mostly baseball articles by Meany) (1958).

Spring Training

"Spring training. Even the sound of it has attracted me for more than forty years of my life.... I wanted to experience spring training myself, precisely because what I knew about it existed exclusively in my imagination — and my imagination, it turned out, was driven not so much by anything so complex as the problem of putting a multimillion-dollar organization into winning gear as of trying to be faithful to old childhood memories." — David Falkner in *The Short Season* (1986), subtitled *The Hard Work and High Times of Baseball in the Spring.*

"That's the true harbinger of spring, not crocuses or swallows returning to Capistrano, but the sound of a bat on the ball." — Bill Veeck in 1976.

"These days baseball is different. You come to spring training, you get your legs ready, you arms loose, your agents ready, your lawyer lined up." — Dave Winfield.

"Men are from Mars, Women are from Venus, and, starting next spring, the Cardinals are from Jupiter." — Dan O'Neill of the *St. Louis Post-Dispatch* after the Cardinals moved to Jupiter, Florida, for their 1998 spring training.

"Watching a spring training game is as exciting as watching a tree form its annual ring." — Jerry Izenberg [author's note: Izenberg seems to have missed the point of spring training.]

"Spring is the time of year a baseball writer comes down with an occupational disease known as superlativitis." — Sportswriter Jack Orr in a 1953 edition of *Sport* magazine.

19th Century Origins. Clubs originally trained at their home parks for one or two weeks before the season. If it rained or snowed, the clubs practiced under the stands or indoors.

Cap Anson is credited by some with conducting the first Southern spring training by a Major League club, for the Chicago White Stockings in 1886 (1885 and 1887 in some sources) in Hot Springs, Arkansas. The Washington club, with catcher Connie Mack, is credited by some as the first to go to Florida (Jacksonville) for the first time in 1888. The Boston Red Stockings trained in New Orleans in 1884.

In 1877 Indianapolis of the League Alliance may have been the first team to hold spring training in the South. Still another source credits Jimmy Wood, Chicago White Stockings second baseman, with leading the 1870 club to New Orleans for spring training, and the New York Mutuals are credited with going to New Orleans in 1869. New Orleans was a popular spot for a number of clubs in the 1870s, as was Shreveport.

In 1886 Louisville, Pittsburgh and Detroit went to Savannah, while Philadelphia went to Charleston, South Carolina. The Cleveland Spiders held their spring training in 1893 in Gainesville, Florida.

Early 20th Century. Early 20th century spring training camps were held in Texas, Louisiana, the Carolinas, Alabama and Georgia. John McGraw took his team to California for the first time in 1906 only to encounter rainstorms, so he moved the club to San Antonio. Florida did not emerge as a popular training site until 1911

Opposite Top: Manager John McGraw and his New York Giants on the bench during a spring training game in the 1920s. ***Opposite Bottom:*** Arkansas was once a popular spring training destination for Major League teams, but now is home to the Class AA Arkansas Travelers. The 1986 Texas League Travelers played their home games in Little Rock across the street from the city's zoo. Hence the team photograph in front of the giraffes, who generally ignored the intrusion. Photograph provided by pitcher and future high school coach Ernie Carrasco, fourth from left, middle row (who played in the Little League World Series [losing to Taiwan] and also played two years of defensive end for the University of Utah before signing with the Cardinals for $30,000). To his left is future Cardinals pitcher Joe Magrane. Future Major Leaguer Lance Johnson is third from right, top row, and manager Jim Riggleman (later to manage the Padres and Cubs) is top row, tenth from left. Future Cardinals infielder Rod Booker is middle row, far left.

Arkansas Travelers
1986 Texas League

when Al Lang of Pittsburgh moved his training to St. Petersburg. He tried to encourage other teams to move with him to set up convenient exhibition games.

Local towns often provided subsidies to clubs who trained there. Spring training was generally profitable for the clubs even though the spring rite cost anywhere from $2,000 to $6,000 in the early days.

New Orleans became popular in the 1920s. The Tigers cashed in on player-manager Ty Cobb's fame by training in his home state at Augusta, Georgia. In 1905 White Sox owner Charles Comiskey chartered a houseboat down the Mississippi River.

The Yankees were the first club to leave the U.S. during spring training when they traveled to Bermuda in 1911 (reported as 1913 in some sources).

Illness. Cozy Dolan's death from typhoid in the spring of 1907 prompted cancellation of the Boston Braves' spring training camp. Perhaps it would have helped, as the club finished seventh with a 58–90 record.

First Permanent Site. The 1908 Giants are credited as the first club to establish a permanent spring training site, at Marlin Springs, Texas. The second permanent National League site was by the Cubs on Catalina Island off the coast of California in the early 1920s. William Wrigley owned the entire island, except the town of Avalon, for which he paid $3 million in 1919. See Jim Vitti, *The Cubs on Catalina* (2003).

In 1914 the St. Louis Browns and Branch Rickey began training in St. Petersburg (specifically, Coffee Pot Bayou). The Browns are credited by some with the first permanent training site in Florida. Rickey also began the first mass training camp involving minor leaguers and Major Leaguers, with the Dodgers in 1949 at Vero Beach.

Early Objections. Some early professionals objected to training in the warmer climates and then moving back north for the season. As a result, some players simply stayed home in the earliest days of spring training in the 19th century. However, as the ritual became more formalized, few players missed spring training.

Hot Springs, Arkansas. This resort was the preeminent spring training mecca from 1886 until it faded in the 1920s. Cap Anson's White Stockings began the tradition. After winning the National League pennant, the White Stockings returned to Hot Springs in 1887 and this cemented the town's popularity with a number of Major League clubs. They were followed in 1890 by Pittsburgh, Brooklyn and Cleveland. The resort's popularity peaked in 1910 when four clubs trained there regularly.

By 1914 the resort began to decline as a Major League destination. A fire swept through much of the area in September 1913, just as Florida was becoming a popular training destination. Bad weather was sometimes a problem and helped in part encourage teams to move their training sites to Florida. The Springs' popularity itself was a problem, as there were too many fans and players in the area during the spring.

By 1923 only the Pirates and Red Sox were still training in Arkansas. However, bad weather forced the Red Sox to San Antonio and the Pirates to Paso Robles, California. Teams still went occasionally to Hot Springs in the 1920s, but eventually it ceased to host any Major League clubs.

Federal League. The Federal League spring training sites:
1914
Baltimore — Southern Pines, North Carolina
Brooklyn — Columbia, South Carolina
Buffalo — Danville, Virginia
Chicago — Shreveport, Louisiana
Indianapolis — Wichita Falls, Texas

Kansas City — Marshall, Texas
Pittsburgh — Lynchburg, Virginia
St. Louis — Monroe, Louisiana
1915
Baltimore — Fayetteville, North Carolina
Brooklyn — Brownswell, Mississippi
Buffalo — Athens, Georgia
Chicago — Shreveport, Louisiana
Kansas City — Wichita Falls, Texas
Newark — Valdosta, Georgia
Pittsburgh — Augusta, Georgia
St. Louis — Havana, Cuba

Spring Games. Until the mid–1920s Major League clubs generally played their spring games against local minor league clubs. In the 1920s the leagues stopped discouraging games between clubs in the same league, and regular exhibition games among Major League teams became the norm.

1920s Florida Boom/Bust/Boom Again.
"The Grapefruit League" — Reference to the Florida spring training sites and the surrounding citrus orchards.

"No class of people is so infected by the Florida land boom as Major League Baseball players." — *The Sporting News*.

"A word about Florida. It's as flat as a barber shop quartet after midnight. It's surrounded by salt water and covered by fresh air. It's a great place if you're a mosquito. An *old* mosquito." — Jim Murray.

Al Lang, a Pittsburgh laundry owner and Florida real estate investor, put Florida on the map as a legitimate spring training site after moving there in 1911. In 1925 the former Pirates minority owner was the mayor of St. Petersburg when he persuaded the Yankees to come for spring training that season. This was three years after the Braves had made the town their home.

In the 1920s a speculators' land boom caused a few players to quit and become real estate brokers. Among them were Bill Doak (of *Glove* fame), Milt Stock and Jack Fournier. New York Giants manager John McGraw was swept up in the craze, investing heavily and appearing in advertisements to encourage others to invest. A 1926 hurricane ended the boom when the Florida coast was devastated. McGraw purportedly paid back all who invested based on his urging (a self-serving statement by his wife many years later?).

World War II.
"The Long Underwear League" — Cardinals trainer Doc Weaver about the cold-weather World War II spring training sites required because of wartime travel restrictions.

"If you can see your breath when you walk out of the hotel in the morning, don't go to the field. Go to the high school gym. We'll play basketball instead of baseball." — Pirates manager Frankie Frisch at the club's cold weather training camp at Muncie, Indiana.

During World War II from spring 1942 through spring 1945, government-imposed travel restrictions forced all teams except the Cardinals to train north of the Ohio and Potomac Rivers and east of the Mississippi River. This made for some very cold March spring training sites. These boundaries became known as the Landis-Eastman Line (spoofing the Mason-Dixon Line) because they were enforced by Judge Landis and the head of the Office of Defense Transportation, Joseph B. Eastman.

In the National League, the Braves switched from Sanford, Florida, to Wallingford, Connecticut. The Dodgers switched from Havana and Daytona Beach to Bear Mountain, New York. This site was only five miles from the Army's military academy at West Point, so the Dodgers were housed there and manager Leo Durocher helped coach the West Point club.

The Cubs moved from Avalon on Catalina Island in California to French Lick, Indiana (later home to basketball's Larry Bird). The Reds moved from Tampa to Bloomington, Indiana. The Giants moved from Miami to Lakewood, New Jersey. Philadelphia moved from Miami Beach to Hershey, Pennsylvania. Pittsburgh moved from San Bernardino, California, to Muncie, Indiana. The Cardinals moved from St. Petersburg to Cairo, Illinois.

Most Spring Games. In 1941 the Dodgers played 50 spring training games from Havana to Ft. Worth, the most ever by a club during the preseason.

Jack Russell Stadium. The ballpark opened in 1955 as the spring training site of the Phillies, which they used through 2003. The last game was played by the Phillies' minor league affiliate in August 2003, exactly 10 years after the last double no-hitter in professional baseball. Clearwater beat Winter Haven 1–0 on two walks and two bunts in the bottom of the 9th inning. The ballpark was the backdrop for the film *Long Gone* (1987) and was the site of the first U.S. concert by The Rolling Stones in 1965.

Cactus League. The Cleveland Indians moved to Tucson, Arizona, in 1947 to establish the state's first permanent spring training site. The Giants were second with a permanent site in Phoenix in the early 1950s, enabling the clubs to continue their long tradition of spring training barnstorming together. The tradition began in 1934 and after 50 years the clubs had played close to 500 games in 27 states. The Giants and Indians eventually played each other 537 times as Cactus League rivals. Their last game was on April 1, 1992. The Giants won 4–3 to improve their record in the series to 279–249 (with nine ties). Though exhibitions had been played before in Arizona, the first exhibition game between clubs training officially in Arizona was on March 8, 1947. The Indians beat the Giants in front of 4,934 fans, a 3–1 win for pitcher Bob Lemon.

The Cubs became the third Arizona club in 1952 when they arrived in Mesa for the next 14 springs. The Orioles opened their first spring training in 1954 in Yuma, Arizona. With the arrival of the fourth club, the "Cactus League" was formed. The criticism of the Arizona sites is that the heat is too dry and the players can't work up a sweat (tell that to the players when it's 95 degrees—it's the same argument that year-round residents of Las Vegas give for saying its livable in the summer, "but it's a *dry* heat").

In the 1980s the Arizona Cactus League had eight clubs:
California Angels: Yuma (and Palm Springs)
Seattle Mariners: Tempe
Milwaukee Brewers: Sun City
San Francisco Giants: Scottsdale
Cleveland Indians: Tucson
Chicago Cubs: Mesa
Oakland A's: Phoenix
San Diego Padres: Yuma

By the mid–1990s the Cactus League still had eight clubs, but the Rockies had replaced the Indians in Tucson, the Angels had moved to Tempe, the Mariners had moved to Peoria, and the Brewers were in Chandler.

By the late 1980s and early 1990s, it appeared that the Cactus League would die, as Florida cities were waving cash and new facilities at Arizona-based clubs. With the 1997 opening of Ho Ho Kam Park in Mesa, seating 12,500 for the Cubs, the Cactus League began to stabilize. In 1998 the White Sox moved from Florida to share a new complex with the Diamondbacks in Tucson. The Brewers moved from Chandler, Arizona, to a new facility closer to central Phoenix.

In a 1993 report, it was determined that the Cactus League poured $265.8 million into Maricopa County, with tourists spending 93% of that amount.

Las Vegas. In 1996 the Rangers, Royals, Reds and Astros were approached to train in Las Vegas, but no commitments were made.

Attendance. In 1978 spring training games drew 1,147,000 fans; 955,000 at regular spring training sites and another 191,000 at off-site games in foreign countries and other U.S. cities. By the 1980s and 1990s total attendance had climbed to 1.5 million, and the traditional intimacy of spring training had almost disappeared. The Cactus League accounted for 662,000 fans in 1992 and 812,000 fans in 1994. The league drew a record 1.25 million in 2004. Spring attendance is fueled by 500,000 out-of-state fans. Fears that the Diamondbacks' presence in Arizona would hurt spring attendance never materialized.

In 2004 the Cubs set a spring training attendance record of 189,692, breaking the Yankees' 1996 record of 173,254.

California. Among early clubs, the Cubs, Pirates, White Sox and Browns all had prominent training camps in California.

Latin Sites. Major League teams have held extended training camps in Mexico City, Havana, Ciudad Trujillo (Dominican Republic), and Panama City.

Reporting Dates. In 1946 it was ruled that clubs could not begin their 1947 spring training before February 15 and subsequent spring trainings before March 1. This rule later was relaxed to allowed certain players to report on the earlier date. The beginning of March is still the first date on which teams may require players to report to spring training. Most clubs bring in pitchers, catchers and injured players by February 15.

Regular Players. There is an informal guideline that each club must field at least five regulars during any spring training game.

Sportswriter Freebie. By 1957 the Dodgers were the only club to still pay for its beat writers to go to Florida for spring training.

Primary Spring Training Sites/1901– (Note that teams that switched regular-season cities or their team names are listed together by the name of the first-identified name of the team).

Anaheim Angels. See **Los Angeles.**

Arizona Diamondbacks. Tucson AZ (1998–).

Boston, Milwaukee and Atlanta Braves (franchise shifts in 1953 and 1966). Norfolk VA (1901), Thomasville GA (1902–1904), Charleston SC (1905), Jacksonville FLA (1906), Thomasville GA (1907), Augusta GA (1908–1912), Athens GA (1913), Macon GA (1914–1915), Miami FLA (1916–1918), Columbus GA (1919–1920), Galveston TEX (1921), St. Petersburg FLA (1922–1937), Bradenton FLA (1938–1940), San Antonio TEX (1941), Sanford FLA (1942), Wallingford CT (1943–1944), Washington D.C. (1945), Ft. Lauderdale FLA (1946–1947), Bradenton FLA (1948–1961), Palmetto FLA (1962), West Palm Beach FLA (1963– 1996); Orlando FLA (1997–).

Boston Red Sox. Charlottesville VA (1901), Augusta GA (1902), Macon GA (1903–1906), Little Rock ARK (1907–1908), Hot Springs ARK (1909–1910), Redondo Beach CA (1911), Hot Springs ARK (1912–1918), Tampa FLA (1919), Hot Springs ARK (1920–1923), San Antonio TEX (1924), New Orleans LA (1925–1927), Bradenton FLA (1928–1929), Pensacola FLA (1930–1931), Savannah GA (1932), Sarasota FLA (1933–1942), Medford MA (1943), Baltimore MD (1944), Pleasanton NJ (1945), Sarasota FLA (1946–1958), Scottsdale AZ (1959–1965), Winter Haven FLA (1966–1992), Ft. Myers FLA (1993–).

Brooklyn and Los Angeles Dodgers (franchise shift in 1958). Charlotte NC (1901), Columbia SC (1902–1906), Jacksonville FLA (1907–1909), Hot Springs ARK (1910–1912), Augusta GA (1913–1914), Daytona Beach FLA (1915–1916), Hot Springs ARK (1917–1918), Jacksonville FLA (1919–1920), New Orleans LA (1921), Jacksonville FLA (1922), Clearwater FLA (1923–1932), Miami FLA

(1933), Orlando FLA (1934– 1935), Clearwater FLA (1936–1940), Havana, Cuba (1941–1942), Bear Mountain NY (1943–1945), Daytona Beach FLA (1946), Havana, Cuba (1947), Ciudad Trujillo, Dominican Republic (1948), Vero Beach FLA (1949–).

Chicago Cubs. Champaign ILL (1901–1902), Los Angeles CA (1903–1904), Santa Monica CA (1905), West Baden IND (1906–1908), Shreveport LA (1909), West Baden IND (1910–1911), New Orleans LA (1912), Tampa FLA (1913–1916), Pasadena CA (1917–1920), Catalina CA (1921–1941), French Lick IND (1942– 1944), Catalina CA (1945–1951), Mesa AZ (1952–1965), Long Beach CA (1966), Scottsdale AZ (1967–1978), Mesa AZ (1979–).

Chicago White Sox. Excelsior Springs MO (1901–1902), Mobile AL (1903), Marlin Springs TEX (1904), New Orleans LA (1905–1906), Mexico City, Mexico (1907), Los Angeles CA (1908), San Francisco CA (1909–1910), Mineral Wells TEX (1911), Waco TEX (1912), Paso Robles CA (1913–1915), Mineral Wells TEX (1916–1920), Waxahachie TEX (1921), Seguin TEX (1922–1923), Winter Haven FLA (1924), Shreveport LA (1925–1928), Dallas TEX (1929), San Antonio TEX (1930–1932), Pasadena CA (1933–1942), French Lick IND (1943–1944), Terre Haute IND (1945), Pasadena CA (1946–1950), Pasadena and Palm Springs CA (1951), El Centro and Pasadena CA (1952), El Centro CA (1953), Tampa FLA (1954–1959), Sarasota FLA (1960–1997); Tucson AZ (1998–).

Cincinnati Reds. Cincinnati OH (1901–1902), Augusta GA (1903), Dallas TEX (1904), Jacksonville FLA (1905), San Antonio TEX (1906), Marlin TEX (1907), St. Augustine FLA (1908), Atlanta GA (1909), Hot Springs ARK (1910–1911), Columbus GA (1912), Mobile ALA (1913), Alexandria VA (1914–1915), Shreveport LA (1916–1917), Montgomery ALA (1918), Waxahachie TEX (1919), Miami FLA (1920), Cisco TEX (1921), Mineral Wells TEX (1922), Orlando FLA (1923–1930), Tampa FLA (1931–1935), San Juan, Puerto Rico/Tampa FLA (1936), Tampa FLA (1937–1942), Bloomington IND (1943–1945), Tampa FLA (1946–1987), Plant City FLA (1988–1997); Sarasota (1998–).

Cleveland Indians. None in 1901, New Orleans LA (1902–1903), San Antonio TEX (1904), New Orleans LA (1905–1906), Macon GA (1907–1909), Alexandria LA (1910–1911), New Orleans LA (1912), Pensacola FLA (1913), Athens GA (1914), San Antonio TEX (1915), New Orleans LA (1916–1920), Dallas TEX (1921–1922), Lakeland FLA (1923–1927), New Orleans LA (1928–1939), Ft. Meyers FLA (1940–1942), Lafayette IND (1943–1945), Clearwater FLA (1946), Tucson AZ (1947–1992), Homestead FLA (1993), Winter Haven FLA (1994–) [In 2004 the Indians notified Winter Haven officials that they would be leaving, although a 2005 move was unlikely.]

Colorado Rockies. Tucson AZ (1993–).

Detroit Tigers. Detroit MI (1901), Ypsilanti MI (1902), Shreveport LA (1903–1904), Augusta GA (1905–1907), Hot Springs ARK (1908), San Antonio TEX (1909–1910), Monroe LA (1911–1912), Gulfport MISS (1913–1915), Waxahachie TEX (1916–1918), Macon GA (1919–1920), San Antonio TEX (1921), Augusta GA (1922–1926), San Antonio TEX (1927–1928), Phoenix AZ (1929), Tampa FLA (1930), Sacramento CA (1931), Palo Alto CA (1932), San Antonio TEX (1933), Lakeland FLA (1934–1943), Evansville IND (1944–1945), Lakeland FLA (1946–).

Florida Marlins. Melbourne FLA (1993–1994), Cocoa FLA (1995), Melbourne, FLA (1996–2002); Jupiter, FLA (2003 —; shares with Cardinals).

Houston Colt 45s/Astros. Apache Junction AZ (1962–1963), Cocoa Beach FLA (1964–1984), Kissimmee FLA (1985–).

Kansas City Royals. Ft. Meyers FLA (1969–1987), Baseball City, Davenport FLA (1988–2002); Phoenix/Surprise AZ (2003–).

Los Angeles/California/Anaheim Angels (miscellaneous name changes). Palm Springs CA (1961–1964), Holtville AZ/Palm Springs CA (1965–1979), Palm Springs CA (1980–1981), Palm Springs CA/Casa Grande AZ (sharing with the Giants, except in 1984 when they split between Palm Springs and Mesa AZ (1982–1991), Palm Springs CA (1992), Tempe AZ (1993–). The Angels announced that they would be moving in 2005 to Goodyear, Arizona, 18 miles west of Phoenix.

Montreal Expos. West Palm Beach FLA (1969–1972), Daytona Beach FLA (1973–1980), West Palm Beach FLA (1981–1997); Melbourne FLA (1998 — 2002); Jupiter FLA (2003 —).

New York and San Francisco Giants (franchise shift in 1958). New York (1901–1902), Savannah GA (1903–1905), Memphis TN (1906), Los Angeles CA (1907), Marlin Springs TEX (1908–1918) (first permanent spring training site), Gainesville FLA (1919), San Antonio TEX (1920–1923), Sarasota FLA (1924–1927), Augusta GA (1928), San Antonio TEX (1929–1931), Los Angeles CA (1932–1933), Miami FLA (1934–1935), Pensacola FLA (1936), Havana Cuba (1937), Baton Rouge LA (1938–1939), Winter Haven FLA (1940), Miami FLA (1941–1942), Lakewood NJ (1943–1945), Miami FLA (1946), Phoenix AZ (1947–1950), St. Petersburg FLA (1951), Phoenix AZ (1952–1981), Scottsdale AZ (1982–).

New York Mets. St. Petersburg FLA (1962–1987), Port St. Lucie (1988–).

New York Yankees. Atlanta GA (1903–1904), Montgomery ALA (1905), Birmingham ALA (1906), Atlanta GA (1907–1908), Macon GA (1909), Athens GA (1910–1911), Atlanta GA (1912), Hamilton, Bermuda (1913), Houston TEX (1914), Savannah GA (1915), Macon GA (1916–1918), Jacksonville FLA (1919–20), Shreveport LA (1921), New Orleans LA (1922–1924), St. Petersburg (1925–1942), Asbury Park NJ (1943), Atlantic City NJ (1944–1945), St. Petersburg FLA (1946–1950), Phoenix AZ (1951) (switched with Giants), St. Petersburg FLA (1952–1957), Scottsdale AZ 1956–1958), St. Petersburg FLA (1959–1961), Ft. Lauderdale FLA (1962–1995), Tampa FLA (1996–).

Philadelphia, Kansas City and Oakland Athletics (franchise shifts in 1955 and 1968). Philadelphia PA (1901), Charlotte NC (1902), Jacksonville FLA (1903), Spartanburg SC (1904), Shreveport LA (1905), Montgomery ALA (1906), Dallas TEX (1907), New Orleans LA (1908–1909), Atlanta GA (1910), Savannah GA (1911), San Antonio TEX (1912–1913), Jacksonville FLA (1914–1918), Philadelphia PA (1919), Lake Charles LA (1920–1921), Eagle Pass TEX (1922), Montgomery ALA (1923–1924), Ft. Myers FLA (1925–1936), Mexico City, Mexico (1937), Lake Charles LA (1938–1939), Anaheim CA (1940–1942), Wilmington DE (1943), College Park MD (1944–1945), West Palm Beach FLA (1946–1962), Bradenton FLA (1963–1968), Mesa AZ (1969–1978), Scottsdale AZ (1979–1983), Phoenix AZ (1984–).

Philadelphia Phillies. Philadelphia PA (1901), Washington D.C. (1902), Richmond VA (1903), Savannah GA (1904), Augusta GA (1905), Savannah GA (1906–1908), Southern Pines NC (1909–1910), Birmingham ALA (1911), Hot Springs ARK (1912), Southern Pines NC (1913), Wilmington NC (1914), St. Petersburg FLA (1915–1918), Charlotte NC (1919), Birmingham ALA (1920), Gainesville FLA (1921), Leesburg FLA (1922–1924), Bradenton FLA (1925–1927), Winter Haven FLA (1928–1937), Biloxi MISS (1938), New Braunfels TEX (1939), Miami FLA (1940–1942), Hershey PA (1943), Wilmington DEL (1944–1945), Miami FLA (1946), Clearwater FLA (1947–).

Pittsburgh Pirates. Hot Springs ARK (1901–1914), Dawson Springs KY (1915–1917), Jacksonville FLA (1918), Birmingham ALA (1919), Hot Springs ARK (1920–1923), Paso Robles CA

(1924–1934), San Bernardino CA (1935), San Antonio TEX (1936), San Bernardino CA (1937–1942), Muncie IND (1943–1945), San Bernardino CA (1946), Miami FLA (1947), Hollywood CA (1948), San Bernardino CA (1949–1952), Havana, Cuba (1953), Ft. Pierce FLA (1954), Ft. Meyers FLA (1955–1968), Bradenton FLA (1969–).

St. Louis Browns/Baltimore Orioles (franchise shift in 1954). French Lick IND (1902), Baton Rouge LA (1903), Corsicana TEX (1904), Dallas TEX (1905–1906), San Antonio TEX (1907), Shreveport LA (1908), Houston TEX (1909–1910), Hot Springs ARK (1911), Montgomery ALA (1912), Waco TEX (1913), St. Petersburg FLA (1914), Houston TEX (1915), Palestine TEX (1916–1917), Shreveport LA (1918), San Antonio TEX (1919), Taylor ALA (1920), Bogalusa LA (1921), Mobile ALA (1922–1924), Tarpin Springs FLA (1925), West Palm Beach FLA (1926–1936), San Antonio TEX (1937–1941), Deland FLA (1942), Cape Girardeau MO (1943–1945), Anaheim CA (1946), Miami FLA (1947), San Bernardino CA (1948), Burbank CA (1949–1952), San Bernardino CA (1953), Yuma AZ (1954), Daytona FLA (1955), Scottsdale AZ (1956–1958), Miami FLA (1959–1990), Sarasota FLA (1991) (sharing with the White Sox), St. Petersburg FLA (1992–1995) (sharing with the Cardinals), Fort Lauderdale FLA (1996–).

St. Louis Cardinals. St. Louis MO (1901–1902), Dallas TEX (1903), Houston TEX (1904), Marlin Springs TEX (1905), Houston TEX (1906–1908), Little Rock ARK (1909–1910), West Baden IND (1911), Jackson MISS (1912), Columbus GA (1913), St. Augustine FLA (1914), Hot Wells TEX (1915–1917), San Antonio TEX (1918), St. Louis MO (1919), Brownsville TEX (1920), Orange TEX (1921–1922), Bradenton FLA (1923–1924), Stockton CA (1925), San Antonio TEX (1926), Avon Park FLA (1927–1929), Bradenton FLA (1930–1936), Daytona Beach FLA (1937), St. Petersburg FLA (1938–1942), Cairo ILL (1943–1945), St. Petersburg FLA (1946–1997), Jupiter FLA (1998–).

San Diego Padres. Yuma AZ (1969–1993), Peoria AZ (1994–).

Seattle Mariners. Tempe AZ (1977–1992), Peoria AZ (1993–) (considered a "road club" in 1993 — no permanent home site established that season).

Seattle Pilots/Milwaukee Brewers (franchise shift in 1970). Tempe AZ (1969–1972), Sun City AZ (1973–1985), Chandler AZ (1986–1993), Peoria AZ (1994), Chandler AZ (1995–1996), West Phoenix AZ (1997–).

Tampa Bay Devil Rays. St. Petersburg FLA (1998–).

Toronto Blue Jays. Dunedin FLA (1977–).

(old) Washington Senators/Minnesota Twins (Franchise shift in 1961). Phebus VA (1901), Washington D.C. (1902–1904), Hampton VA (1905), Charlottesville VA (1906), Galveston TEX (1907–1909), Norfolk VA (1910), Atlanta GA (1911), Charlottesville VA (1912–1916), Atlanta GA (1917), Augusta GA (1918–1919), Tampa FLA (1920–1929), Biloxi MISS (1930–1935), Orlando FLA (1936–1942), College Park MD (1943–1945), Orlando FLA (1946–1990), Ft. Myers FLA (1991–).

(new) Washington Senators/Texas Rangers (New franchise in Washington in 1961 when old franchise moved to Minnesota; franchise shift to Texas in 1972). Pompano Beach FLA (1961–1986), Port Charlotte FLA (1987–2002); Phoenix/Surprise AZ (2003–).

Books. Ken Coleman and Dan Valenti, *Grapefruit League Road Trip* (1989); David Falkner, *The Short Season* (1986); William Zinsser, *Spring Training* (1989).

Spy

"The strangest fella I ever met." — Casey Stengel on Moe Berg.

"I'd rather be a ballplayer than a justice of the United States Supreme Court." — Berg.

"I understand, Moe, that you are in counterintelligence, which, I assume, means you are against intelligence." — Red Smith.

"Berg often visited *Boston Globe* sports columnist Arthur Seigel, whose book-filled apartment was a haven for Boston newspapermen who shared Seigel's insomnia. Seigel once asked: 'Moe, do I detect second thoughts in you? Was that damn ball game and all the mystery stuff worth it? Wasn't Mr. Chips a better bet?' 'Arthur,' replied Berg, 'I seek no other man's shoes. If I've misdirected my priorities, and I'm confident that this is not so, I've had a pretty fair time in lost country. There are no regrets. I loved every day on the ball field and the gentlemen who played it in my time. Even grandmothers should experience the pure excitement of covering home plate with an ape charging home, cleats flying high.'" — Louis Kaufman on Berg.

Moe Berg graduated from Princeton in 1923 and passed the bar exam in New York while a Major League ballplayer, but played baseball for 13 more seasons. He was primarily a catcher who hit .243 over a 15-year career from 1923 through 1939. He was a genius who spoke and read Sanskrit and 12 to 17 other languages (depending on the source), but was not a particularly adept hitter — prompting this comment: "He can speak 12 languages, but he can't hit in any of them."

In 1934 Berg traveled with Babe Ruth as part of an American All-Star tour of Japan. During the tour Berg delivered a speech in Japanese. When the other players went home, Berg stayed and took military-sensitive photographs of Tokyo and other Japanese cities. He wore a ceremonial kimono up to the rooftop of a building and then pulled out a camera that he had strapped to his hip. The information proved valuable when World War II broke out and military installations needed to be identified for bombing raids. Berg was a member of the OSS (Office of Strategic Services), the predecessor of the CIA, and spent some of his active duty time in Latin America on covert operations for the United States.

During World War II, Berg was instructed to assassinate Nazi nuclear scientist Werner Heisenberg at a 1944 meeting in Switzerland. Berg changed his mind when he realized from Heisenberg that the Nazis were not close to developing their own nuclear capability.

Later in his life Berg was told that he was a likely recipient of the Medal of Freedom. He asked permission to tell people what he had done to merit it but was told that the information was classified. He then refused the medal, but after he died his sister claimed the award and it is now at the Baseball Hall of Fame.

Book. Nicholas Dawidoff, *The Catcher Was a Spy* (1994); Lewis Kaufman, et al., *Moe Berg: Athlete, Scholar, Spy* (1974).

Squeeze Play

"A squeeze play? No, let's score in an honorable way." — Alleged response of Braves owner and inept one-year manager Judge Emil Fuchs after he asked his players what strategy they thought he should follow.

The 1890s Baltimore Orioles are said to have originated the squeeze play. It has been written that the play was invented by mistake: Pitcher Jack Chesbro broke for home plate thinking the steal sign was on and batter Wee Willie Keeler bunted to protect him. It makes for a good story, but the two players were never teammates until 1903, well after the play was used in the Major Leagues.

The suicide squeeze is executed by having the runner on third break for home and continue on regardless of whether the batter makes contact for the bunt. If the batter fails, then the runner is usually out at the plate, a victim of his own "suicide."

Stadiums See *Ballparks* and *Indoor Ballparks*

Star Spangled Banner See *National Anthem*

Willie Stargell (1940–2001)

Hall of Fame 1987

"People like us are afraid to leave ball. What else is there to do?…. When baseball has been your whole life, you can't think about a future without it, so you hang on as long as you can … you've got to prove to yourself beyond a doubt that you can't play anymore. If your teammates and the fans find it sad, at least you can say to yourself, 'I'm through.' So what if everybody else decided that long before?"—Stargell.

"The most admired and admirable player of his time."—Roger Angell.

Stargell was the on-field leader of the Pirates in the late 1960s and 1970s.

Oklahoma native Wilver Dornel Stargell began his Major League career in 1962 with the Pirates, for whom he played 21 seasons. He established himself in 1964 with 21 home runs, the first of 13 straight seasons of 20 or more home runs. He led the league in home runs with 48 in 1971 and 44 in 1973. He helped lead the Pirates to the 1971 World Series, but batted only .208 in the Series. He hit .253 in six NLCS appearances between 1970 and 1979. He was voted National League co–MVP in 1979 when he led the Pirates to the World Championship.

The outfielder moved to first base in 1972 after suffering a knee injury. He became the leader of the club following the death of Roberto Clemente after the 1972 season. "Pops" finished his career with 475 home runs and 1,540 RBIs, having hit more home runs in the 1970s than any other player. His 1,936 strikeouts are fifth all-time. Following a series of injuries he retired after the 1982 season and became a coach with the Pirates and Braves. He died at age 61 in Pittsburgh.

Books. Bill Libby, *Willie Stargell* (1973); Willie Stargell and Tom Bird, *Willie Stargell—An Autobiography* (1984).

Starting Time See *Game Starting Time*

Statistics and Statisticians

"A passion for statistics is the earmark of a literate people."—Paul Fisher.

"I didn't take that at school."—Marlins manager Jack McKeon on his disdain for the fashionable statistical analysis.

"We put our faith in a handheld calculator. *On a pace to …* is our mantra. Big mistake. In baseball you cannot count on Texas Instruments any more than you can on Texas Rangers. Emboldened by mathematics, we ignore physics. The weight and spin of 162 games exerts a gravitational pull on the hottest of hitters and pitchers."—Tom Verducci in a 1994 *Sports Illustrated* article about hot early-season players who were chasing milestones such as 61 home runs and .400 batting averages.

"Statistics are about as interesting as first base coaches."—Jim Bouton.

"They both show a lot, but not everything."—Rangers infielder Toby Harrah comparing statistics to bikinis.

"Baseball's Kilimanjaro of repeated legend and legerdemain."—Bill James' description of baseball's conventional wisdom.

"A baseball fan has the digestive apparatus of a billy goat. He can—and does—devour any set of statistics with insatiable appetite and then nuzzles hungrily for more."—Sportswriter Arthur Daley.

"Who says there's an unemployment problem in this country? Just take the five percent unemployed and give them a baseball stat to follow."—Pirates center fielder Andy Van Slyke.

"Baseball isn't statistics—baseball is DiMaggio rounding second."—Jimmy Cannon.

"Baseball fans love numbers. They love to swirl them around their mouths like Bordeaux wine."—Author Pat Conroy.

"I don't know whether you know it, but baseball's appeal is decimal points. No other sport relies as totally on continuity, statistics, orderliness of these. Baseball fans pay more attention to numbers than CPAs."—Jim Murray.

"Statistics are used much like a drunk uses a lamp post: for support, not illumination."—Vin Scully, who could have been talking about his broadcast partner, the stat-obsessed Ross Porter (but we mean that in a good way, sort of).

"Statistics are the lifeblood of baseball. In no other sport are so many available, and studied so assiduously by participants and fans. Much of the game's appeal, as a conversation piece, lies in the opportunity the fan gets to back up opinions and arguments with convincing figures, and it is entirely possible that more American boys have mastered long division by dealing with batting averages than in any other way."—Leonard Koppett in *A Thinking Man's Guide to Baseball* (1967), subtitled, "*Being an account and perceptible evaluation of the techniques, customs, style, strategies, finances, working conditions, living habits, personalities, myths, and realities of America's most publicized spectator sport.*" Koppett made a persuasive argument that statistics do not have much relative worth.

See also *Oldest Statistical Leaders*.

Early Statistics.

"[Nap] Lajoie was perhaps the first player to attract nation-wide attention because of his batting average. Prior to his time the fans were only mildly interested in statistics."—Bob French in the *Toledo Blade.*

The scorebook of the New York Knickerbockers contains the earliest recorded information about player performance. See *Libraries—New York* for the story of its theft.

In 1876 newspapers carried "hits per game" and "errors per game" averages. In midseason, Chicago's Ross Barnes was the top hitter with 2.1 hits per game. Dave Eggler of the Athletics was the leading fielder with .19 errors per game.

National Association. The official statistics for the 1871–1875 National Association burned in a fire.

Early Statistician.

"Anybody with a pencil could be a statistician back then."—Seymour Siwoff of the **Elias Sports Bureau** on 19th century statisticians.

One of the earliest acclaimed statisticians was Clarence Dow, an 1890s writer from Boston. The National League's official statistician doubled originally as the league's secretary. The first was Nicholas Young, later National League president. Young was often extremely liberal with his record-keeping and was known to add a few hits to the statistics of his favorite players.

In 1879 Young credited Cap Anson with 90 hits in 221 at-bats for a .407 batting average. It was later determined that Anson was only 72 for 227, a .317 average. Using the earlier statistics, the Hall of Fame upon his induction credited Anson with 90 hits in 227 at-bats that season.

In 1896 Young at first credited Bug Holliday with 57 stolen bases, when in fact he had stolen only one. Young's 1896 official averages, published a few weeks after the season, were accompanied by a note: "A careful perusal of the tables shows that the figures, in several instances, differ from those published last fall. In one case the records give Holliday a credit of fifty-seven stolen bases, whereas he stole only a single base."

Official Statistics.

"This book is dedicated to those men whose devotion to the decimal point and rabid research for records in the past hundred years accumulated the baseball statistics which have come to be recognized as the lifeblood of the game.

"Their friends and families often refer to these unsung archaeologists of our national pastime, either in amusement or exasperation, as 'nuts.' We won't. After all, we would like to be considered their kindred spirits." — Dedication to the Jubilee Edition of *The Official Encyclopedia of Baseball*, by Hy Turkin and S.C. Thompson (1951).

"Baseball fans are junkies, and their heroin is the *statistic*." — Robert S. Wieder in *In Praise of the Second Season* (1981).

The National League did not maintain official daily statistics until 1903. The American League followed in 1905. In the modern era, the official statistics were maintained at the league offices, but were compiled by outside services. In 1912 the American League hired Irwin M. Howe and his Howe News Bureau, which produced the leagues statistics until 1972. Sports Information Center purchased Howe in 1972 and handled the leagues figures through 1986.

The National League hired Al Munro Elias and his Elias Sports Bureau in 1923 and Elias handled the National League ever since. Elias became the American League's official statistician in 1987.

Elias receives a play-by-play and official scorer's report of each game by fax shortly after the final out. These are cross-checked before being entered into the computer.

Newspapers. Home runs were not recorded in the newspapers until the 1920s, but sacrifices and stolen bases were included. Most cities had several daily newspapers in the early part of the 20th century, and this often resulted in multiple sources — often conflicting, for all games.

Baseball Records Committee. In the 1960s a Special Baseball Records Committee was created to consider special circumstances created by the erratic record-keeping prior to 1920. The committee members met twice in 1968 to consider each situation and then to evaluate the effect of their decisions on the records. Much of the work was done in connection with the preparation of MacMillan's *The Baseball Encyclopedia*.

In 1975 the Baseball Records Committee was founded in Milwaukee during the All-Star Game break. It was formed to analyze discrepancies between the Elias Bureau's *Book of Baseball Records* and *The Sporting News's Baseball Record Book*, along with several mistakes discovered in the official records over the years.

Joseph Reichler was authorized by the commissioner and the two league presidents to formally create the committee, which consisted of 10 members at its inception and later was expanded to 15 members. It included representations from the commissioner's office, the two league publicists, three from the Baseball Writers' Association, the head of Elias, and representatives of the Hall of Fame and *The Sporting News*.

Rectifying Errors.

"Baseball statistics are approximations ... close approximations, but they're only approximations." — ESPN's Rob Neyer in 2002,

responding to news that SABR researchers had discovered two missing walks for Ted Williams during the 1941 season.

Statistics before 1950 are notoriously spotty, in part because of somewhat sloppy record-keeping and in part because of the lack of available cross-checking sources. In the famous dispute over Hack Wilson's 1930 **Runs Batted In** total, researchers located eight errors in the box scores for his games. In another game played between the Yankees and Red Sox on September 25, 1929 (the day Yankees manager Miller Huggins died), there were 22 mistakes involving 10 players, including an erroneous entry that the Yankees had completed a triple play (nice trick with one out). In June 1999 Major League Baseball officially recognized changes to Hack Wilson's 1930 **Runs Batted In** total and Babe Ruth's career **Base on Balls** total.

The committee included Hall of Fame historian Lee Allen and Joseph Reichler, the director of public relations for the commissioner's office.

John Tattersall was a statistical devotee who specialized in compiling home run information. He came to prominence in the early 1950s when he correctly determined Nap Lajoie's batting average for the 1901 season. Lajoie was credited originally with a .422 average, but in 1918 a statistician determined that 220 hits in 532 at-bats produced only a .405 average. In 1953 Tattersall reviewed all the A's box scores for the season and determined that the original mistake was in the number of hits; Lajoie had 229 instead of the reported 220. Tattersall was one of the creators of the Tattersall-McConnell **Home Run** log of every home run ever hit in the Major Leagues.

A number of statistics changed in the 8th edition (1990) of *The Baseball Encyclopedia*. Although commissioner Bart Giamatti had formed a Committee on Historical and Statistical Accuracy, apparently the committee was not consulted by the publisher, Macmillan, and the book's new editor, Rick Wolff, before MacMillan made the changes. An example was Cap Anson's hit total. He lost 41 hits in the new edition, to an even 3,000. Honus Wagner lost 12 hits. Wolff explained the changes by noting that MacMillan was simply correcting editing errors perpetuated after the first edition came out in 1969. Nevertheless, Giamatti's committee was unhappy that it had not been consulted.

SABR Executive Director Frederick Ivor-Campbell discovered that 19th century pitcher Old Hoss Radbourn actually had 59 wins, not 60.

Hall of Fame.

"Some of these numbers acquire a kind of a poetry to them. When somebody takes them away or changes them and says we've improved baseball record-keeping, it's someone else's loss." — Hall of Fame Director of Research Tim Wiles on whether the Hall would change the numbers engraved on its plaques after researchers determined that some of the figures were inaccurate.

Baseball researchers have determined periodically that errors existed in older "official" statistics. However, Major League Baseball has declined on a number of occasions to change some of the statistics. The Hall of Fame has made no changes on any plaques, deciding to stay with the statistics as they were recognized at the time the player was inducted. All of the Hall of Fame's plaques and other information now carry a blanket disclaimer that the statistics used are those recognized as official at the time the player was inducted.

Black Sox. One of the first official moves by Judge Landis when he took over as commissioner in 1920 was to eliminate from the record books the statistics of the Black Sox players. Nevertheless, they are included in the official encyclopedias, first *The Baseball Encyclopedia* and now *Total Baseball*.

Daily Statistics. The National Baseball Library storage facility houses all of baseball's official records, known as "day-by-days."

A group of 1990s statisticians formed **Retrosheet**, which is dedicated to creating a play-by-play for every Major League game.

Protested Game. On August 1, 1932, the Yankees and Tigers played a game that ended with a protest by the Yankees. Tony Lazzeri usually batted fifth for the Yankees and Ben Chapman batted sixth. On this day they were on the line-up card in reverse order. In the 2nd inning, Lazzeri came up as the fifth batter and questioned the umpire about the order. When told of the mistake, Yankee manager Joe McCarthy came out to ask umpire Dick Nallin if they could reverse the order and correct the mistake. Nallin okayed the move. When Lazzeri singled, Tiger manager Bucky Harris protested the game. The protest was upheld and the game was replayed. The replay ended in a 7–7 tie due to darkness, but the Tigers won the next day's replay of the replay.

The incident created a problem with lifetime statistics for the players who appeared in the protested game. Statisticians for the 1932 season correctly tallied the individual player statistics from the protested game but failed to include the game in the total games played by each player that season. For example, this left Lou Gehrig with one less game, which reduced his consecutive game streak by one. The mistake was corrected in 1937, but even *The Baseball Encyclopedia*'s first edition (and some subsequent editions) had the number of games wrong for a few of the players who appeared in the game.

Play-Off Statistics. Play-off statistics created when teams end the regular season in a tie (nonchampionship series) are included in overall regular season statistics.

In 1959 Milwaukee's Eddie Mathews hit a home run in a play-off against the Dodgers. His 46th home run enabled him to win the home run crown over Chicago's Ernie Banks, who finished with 45.

This rule cost Frank Robinson the 1962 batting title and the top spot in total bases. During the play-off that season between the Giants and Dodgers, Tommy Davis of the Dodgers surpassed him in the batting race and Willie Mays increased his total bases to lead the league.

Statistics Services.

"Baseball is probably the world's best documented sport." — Ford Frick in *Games, Asterisks and People* (1973).

The **Elias Sports Bureau** in New York City, for many years run by Seymour Siwoff, became the preeminent statistical resource for Major League Baseball, as well as the NBA and NFL, in the early 1960s. Elias is now recognized as the official statistical service for Major League Baseball (see also **Official Statistics**). The Bureau originally was the official statistician for only the National League, while the Chicago-based **Howe News Bureau** covered the American League and the minor leagues. The **Heilbroner Baseball Bureau** was founded in 1905 and began publishing the *Baseball Blue Book*, a version of which is still published.

The advent of computers has caused a boom in statistics and statistical services to compete with the old-line companies such as Elias. Stats, Inc. is among the more recent editions to the field, keeping track of such oddities as most pick-off throws. Major League clubs and Fantasy League team owners have come to rely heavily on statistics, thus encouraging the dramatic increase in available statistics, now primarily accessed on the Internet.

Modern Gurus.

"Perhaps the club's most significant personnel move was the signing, to a one-year contract, of a big, lumbering fifty-three-year-old right-hander from Kansas (six feet four, and well over two hundred pounds) who spends far more time on the Little League diamond..." — Ben McGrath in *The New Yorker*, on the Red Sox' 2003 signing of statistician Bill James, a former boiler room attendant.

"What do you have in there, Lenny? Decimal points?" — Sportswriter Jimmy Cannon to statistics-minded writer Leonard Koppett, as Koppett entered the press box with a large briefcase. Koppett died in 2003, having been one of the first writers to focus on the statistical analysis of baseball. He was also very gracious to this author on the phone in 1996.

Bill James has become the most prominent of modern statisticians, with his *Bill James Abstracts*. James was first noticed, though barely, when he placed a one-inch ad in *The Sporting News* in 1977 for a $3 copy of his "Baseball Abstract: Featuring 18 Categories of Statistical Information That You Just Can't Find Anywhere Else." It was 68 pages, photocopied and stapled, and he sold 75 copies (one each to writer Norman Mailer and screenwriter William Goldman). Before signing on with the Red Sox, James had surreptitiously worked for three Major League teams, but was not allowed to acknowledge the work.

A seminal moment in Sabrmetrics history arrived in late 2002, when the Red Sox announced that they had hired James to provide statistical information to them. The *Society for American Baseball Research* ("SABR") is the preeminent collective research authority on historical statistics and has developed novel ways of interpreting and arranging baseball statistics, known as "SABR-METRICS." Other prominent recent statistically-oriented writers are John Thorn and L. Robert Davids. The latter, who was the founder of SABR, passed away in the 2000s.

Bill James was not the first stat guru hired by the Red Sox. Michael Gimbel used to write books for fantasy baseball fans. He was listed in 1997 as a team consultant for statistical evaluation for the Red Sox. He once declared a preference for Rob Deer over Ken Griffey, Jr. Six alligators, five turtles and an iguana were once discovered in his Brooklyn apartment. General manager Dan Duquette said that Gimbel "was not entirely unlike Boo Radley from *To Kill a Mockingbird*" (the character played by Robert Duvall in his first movie role).

Gimbel was a full-time employee of New York City's Bureau of Water Supply, and Duquette was criticized for letting a Rotisserie League devotee influence his personnel decisions. It was an embarrassment to the club and more fodder for the unhappy players.

Retrosheet. David Smith is the leader of Retrosheet, an effort by several baseball historians to record the play-by-play for every Major League game. Smith, a mid–50s biology professor at the University of Delaware, has worked on the project since 1989, and his group has collected over 100,000 play-by-play accounts, including multiple version of the same games. See retrosheet.com.

Smith asked every Major League club to let him copy their scoresheets. Most clubs ignored him and most didn't have the records. Finally, every team cooperated and about 20 retired reporters and broadcasters let him copy their records. Smith expected to come up about 25,000 games short of a full record, with full scoresheets that he has copies of dating back to 1963 for the American League and 1974 for the National League.

They have completed close to 100% of the games played from 1901, the start of the modern era, through 1983, when complete records already existed. Their task was made more difficult by the fact that the leagues discarded their game summaries once the statistics were entered into the league records. Unfortunately, those records contain a multitude errors discovered by Smith and his researchers. The project found over 1,000 mistakes in Major League

Baseball's official records. Included is an extra RBI for Roger Maris in 1961. The researchers usually have found between 50 and 60 mistakes per season, but the peak was 120 for 1975.

The Baseball Index. The Baseball Index, sponsored by SABR, has over 180,000 records loaded onto a database for access by any researcher.

Ernest J. Lanigan.

"I really don't care much about baseball, or looking at ball games, major or minor. All my interest in baseball is in its statistics."

Known as "Figure Filbert" by writer Damon Runyon, Lanigan was the nephew of the Spink brothers of *The Sporting News*. He worked as a reporter, league representative, club executive, and in 1946 he was named curator of the Hall of Fame and later served as its historian. He was a moving force in the formation of the Baseball Writers Association and was an early publisher of a baseball statistics book, *The Baseball Cyclopedia* (1922).

Earnshaw Cook. Cook, a mechanical engineer, was one of the first statisticians to make a dent in the general truisms of baseball strategy, in his book *Percentage Baseball* (1964). He was largely ignored at the time, except that novelist Philip Roth patterned a character after him; Isaac Ellis, the boy genius who coaches the Ruppoert Mundys in *The Great American Novel*.

Allan Roth. Roth has often been acknowledged as the first full-time sports statistician. He began charting the National Hockey League in the 1940s. In 1947 he was hired by Dodger general manager Branch Rickey to chart batting averages against specific pitchers, a novelty at the time. He left the Dodgers in 1964 to move to NBC as the "Game of the Week" statistician and later went to ABC. He died at age 74 in 1992.

Ted Williams. In his book *My Turn at Bat* (1969), Williams claimed that he "un"retired after the 1954 season. He had broken his collarbone in the spring and missed winning the batting title even though his .345 average was better than the .341 by **Batting Champion** Bobby Avila; Williams did not have enough at-bats to qualify (386 of the needed 400).

Williams was planning to retire until he met statistics nut Ed Mifflin. Mifflin told him of the many lifetime goals that he could reach if he stayed in the game a few years longer. Williams reconsidered, and Mifflin provided him steady encouragement with phone calls and notes pointing out Williams' milestones as they were achieved. Williams went on to win the next two batting titles and hit 155 home runs over the next six years.

Statues and Sculpture

"Here stands baseball's perfect warrior. Here stands baseball's perfect knight."—Inscription on the statue of Stan Musial outside Busch Memorial Stadium in St. Louis. Musial did not like the statue because his torso looked too thick and his shoulders were too broad.

"I like it. It's 10 feet tall, weighs 1,500 pounds and is home to every pigeon in Cleveland."—Bob Feller on his new statue at the entrance to Cleveland's Jacobs Field. It shows him in his pitching motion.

"I think that was his playing weight during his last season."—David Letterman on Babe Ruth's new nine-foot, 800-pound statue in Baltimore, unveiled in 1995. Though the creators had painstakingly researched all of the details of the Babe's uniform, they put a right-hander's glove on the left-hander's belt.

"Swing the bat, for Christ's sake. You're not a statue until you have pigeon shit on your shoulders."—Pitcher Bill Lee.

Statue of Willie Mays in front of SBC Park in San Francisco.

Yankee Stadium. See *Yankee Stadium*— **Monuments** for a list of the statues in the outfield area.

Chicago. A Chicago statue of Civil War general Philip Sheridan on horseback was the subject of a National League tradition that began in the 1970s. The statue is on the route from the hotels to Wrigley Field. Some clubs, notably the San Francisco Giants, stopped and painted the horse's testicles bright colors.

Casey. There are at least 15 "Casey at the Bat" statues around the country, all financed by the same group from Nebraska.

Glove. Claes Oldenberg sculpted a 12-foot high 5,800-pound lead and wood first baseman's glove.

Harry Caray. The only statue at Wrigley Field is of long-time announcer Harry Caray, holding out a microphone while singing during the 7th inning stretch.

Roberto Clemente. At the 1994 All-Star Game in Pittsburgh, the club unveiled a statue of Clemente done by Susan Wagner.

Ty Cobb, Henry Aaron and Phil Niekro. Outside Atlanta's Fulton County Stadium are statutes of Georgia native Ty Cobb and Braves stars Henry Aaron and Phil Niekro.

Charles Comiskey.

"I'm trying to give him a 'he-man' look to capture his stature.

I just finished his face, and now I'm reworking his hips. His face is noble. He had a hook nose and sleepy eyes."—Sculptor Jerry McKenna in 2003, after the White Sox announced that they had commissioned an 800-pound life-size bronze statue of "The Old Roman."

Bob Gibson. In April 1998 the Cardinals unveiled a bronze statute of the Hall of Fame pitcher outside of Busch Stadium.

Connie Mack. Outside Philadelphia's Veterans Stadium is a statue of Connie Mack and one of a runner sliding into a base.

Mickey Mantle. Shortly after Mantle died, a former Yankee Stadium security guard was arrested for offering on the Internet a stolen bronze bust commemorating Mantle's 500th home run. The bust had been pulled from a pillar behind the right field wall during the stadium renovation in the mid–1970s.

Jackie Robinson. Montreal's Olympic Stadium features a plaque and statute dedicated to Robinson, who played for the Montreal Royals in 1946.

Nolan Ryan. In 1991 the Alvin, Texas, city council voted to erect a $52,000 life-size bronze statue of Ryan.

Frank Robinson. The Reds erected a statue of Robinson at their new facility, Great American Ball Park.

Babe Ruth and Ted Williams. Armand LaMontagne is one of the best-known baseball sculptors. His works include lifesize sculptures of Ruth and Williams that stand inside the entrance to the Hall of Fame and reportedly are the most photographed items in Cooperstown.

Honus Wagner. A Wagner statue that stood in front of Pittsburgh's Forbes Field was moved to the front offices of Three Rivers Stadium.

Cy Young. A 1,000-pound bronze statue of Young was dedicated in 1994 at Northeastern University.

Book. James Mote, *Everything Baseball* (1989), purports to list all reasonably well-known baseball sculpture to that date.

Turkey Stearnes (1901–1979)

Hall of Fame (VC) 2000

"You expected Turkey to take off and fly when he was running"—Buck O'Neil.

"If they don't put Turkey Stearnes in the Hall of Fame, they shouldn't put anybody in."—Cool Papa Bell.

"One of the greatest hitters we ever had. He was as good as anybody ever played ball."—Satchel Paige.

Stearnes was an outfield star in the Negro Leagues in the 1920s and 1930s.

Born Norman Thomas Stearnes in Nashville, Turkey's career spanned three decades in the Negro Leagues. Nicknamed for his unusual running style, Stearnes was a sleak, left-handed centerfielder who paired excellent speed with exceptional power to become one of the outstanding players of the 1920s and 1930s.

Stearnes played three seasons in the Negro Southern League before making it in 1923 with the Detroit Stars of the Negro National League. In his rookie year he hit .365 with 17 home runs and a league-leading 15 triples. He led the league in home runs in both 1924 and 1925. In 1926 he batted .375 with 20 home runs. He followed that with another 20 home runs in 1927 and led the league in doubles and triples. He won his third home run title in 1928, hitting 24. Stearnes' extra base production, especially when considering the relatively short (generally less than 100 official league games) NNL season, was indeed superb.

Stearnes stayed in Detroit through 1931 while also appearing with the New York Lincoln Giants in 1930 and the Kansas City Monarchs in 1931. He moved to the Chicago American Giants in 1932. From 1933 to 1935 he teamed with fellow slugger Mule Suttles for an impressive power combination, with Stearnes frequently batting lead-off to take advantage of his speed. In 1933 he appeared in the inaugural East-West All Star Game, getting two hits for the victorious West squad. In 1935 he batted .430 to lead the NNL.

Stearnes then played single seasons in Philadelphia and Detroit in 1936 and 1937. Stearnes' final three seasons, 1938–1940, were spent with the Kansas City Monarchs. He retired with a .359 career batting average.

After leaving baseball Stearnes eventually returned to Detroit, where he worked for the Ford Motor Company for 25 years.

Casey Stengel (1890–1975)

Hall of Fame (VC) 1966

"It was as though the State Department had borrowed Emmett Kelly from Ringling Brothers and introduced him as the government's new Chief of Protocol."—Joseph Durso in *Baseball and the American Dream* (1986).

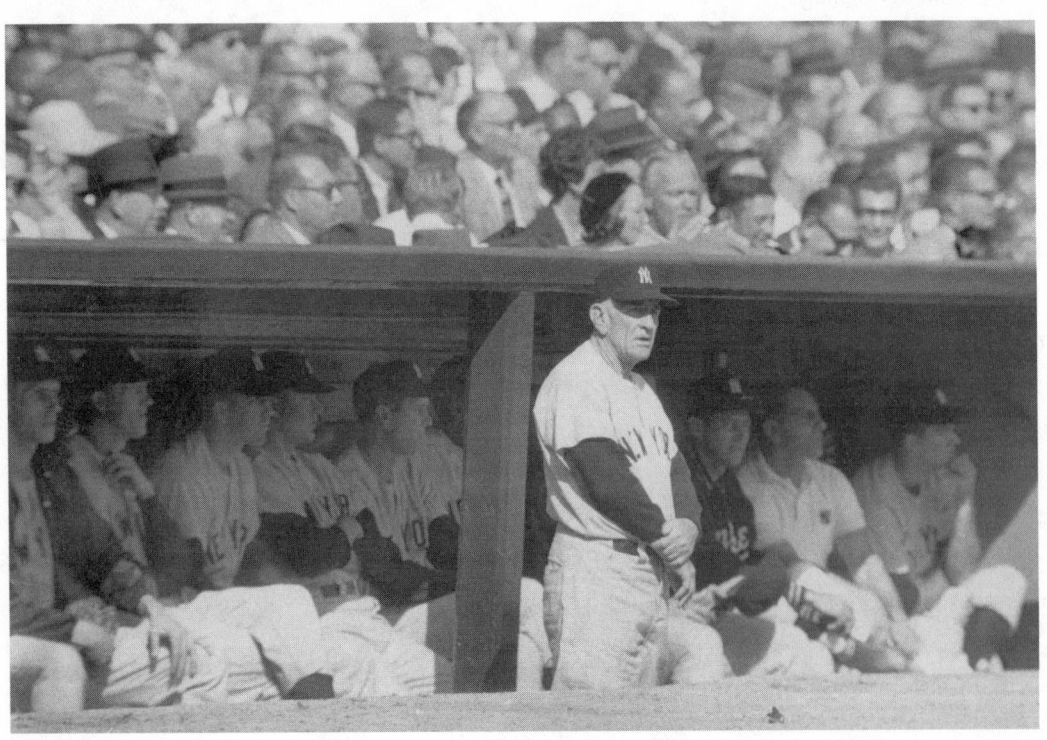

The Ol' Perfessor, Casey Stengel, managing the Yankees in the late 1950s.

"Don't rush me."— Stengel to sports editor Shirley Povich after Povich reminded him that he had not answered the question after an hour-long response.

"More words, probably, have been written about Casey Stengel than about any other sports personage, anytime, anyplace, from Achilles through Y.A. Tittle."— Leonard Koppett in *A Thinking Man's Guide to Baseball* (1967).

"Good hands, good power, runs exceptionally well, nice glove, left-handed line drive hitter. Good throwing arm. May be too damn aggressive, bad temper."— Larry Sutton's 1911 scouting report on Stengel.

"You look at Casey Stengel and you have to resist the temptation to ask him what ever became of Snow White."— Jim Murray.

Stengel played primarily in the 1910s and 1920s but made his most lasting mark as a Major League manager with the Yankees and Mets between 1949 and 1965.

A native of Kansas City ("Casey"), Charles Dillon Stengel was slated to be a *Dentist* when he signed a professional baseball contract. He eventually gave up dental school after two winters of it while in the minor leagues. He then played for five National League clubs from 1912 through 1925. An outfielder, he had a lifetime .284 average with 60 home runs. He also hit two home runs in the 1923 World Series for the Yankees.

Stengel's first job as a manager (and club president) was with Worcester of the Eastern League in 1926. It was also his initial contact with future Yankee general manager George Weiss, who at the time was Hartford's general manager.

Stengel managed in the minor leagues for the next seven years before beginning his Major League managing career in 1934 with lowly Brooklyn. In three years with the Dodgers he never cracked the first division and moved on to the Braves. In six years with that club he never finished higher than fifth. He returned to the minor leagues in the 1940s, spending five successful years as manager of the Oakland Oaks of the powerful Pacific Coast League.

"The Old Perfessor" was the surprise choice to manage the Yankees in 1949, but in the next 12 years his clubs won seven World Series, 10 pennants and finished second once (1954) and third once (1959). He was forced into *Retirement* by the Yankees after the 1960 World Series loss in seven games to the Pirates. He was then hired to manage the expansion New York Mets in 1962 where he stayed until he broke his hip on July 25, 1965, five days short of his 75th birthday.

Stengelese.

"Casey Stengel is a white American male with a speech pattern that ranges somewhere between the sounds a porpoise makes underwater and an Abyssinian rug merchant."— Jim Murray.

"Charles Dillon Stengel should be interviewed only by a plumber, the one artisan skilled enough to turn off the faucet. Ordinary sports writers find themselves engulfed by a torrent of words. Then, just as they are being drowned by the cascade and are going down for the third time, they discover to their dismay that they haven't learned a doggone thing."— Arthur Daley.

"I always understood everything Casey Stengel said, which sometimes worried me."— Long-time USC baseball coach Rod Dedeaux.

Stengel's odd speech pattern was coined "Stengelese" by sportswriter Ernie Havemann. See *Antitrust* for part of Stengel's rambling speech to a Congressional committee investigating baseball's antitrust exemption.

In the early 1940s a poll of 151 sportswriters found that Stengel was the "funniest" manager in the Major Leagues — even though he was managing in the Pacific Coast League at the time (many considered the PCL a third Major League).

Books. Maury Allen, *You Could Look It Up* (1979); Ira Berkow and Jim Kaplan, *The Gospel According to Casey* (1992); David Cataneo, *Casey Stengel: Baseball's "Old Perfessor"* (2004); Robert Creamer, *Stengel: His Life and Times* (1984); Joseph Durso, *Casey* (1967); Frank Graham, Jr., *Casey Stengel* (1958); Norman MacLean, *Casey Stengel* (1976); Fred McMame, *Quotable Casey* (2002); Casey Stengel with Harry T. Paxton, *Casey at the Bat* (1962).

Stirrups See *Uniforms*—Socks and Stirrups

Stolen Bases

"His head was full of larceny, but his feet were honest."— Sportswriter Arthur "Bugs" Baer describing Ping Bodie thrown out by several yards in 1917.

"The thing I looked for was how [the pitcher] released the ball."— Lou Brock on his base stealing technique.

See also *Fastest Runners*, because the fastest runners are not necessarily the best base stealers, *Sliding* and *Pinch Runners*.

First Stolen Base. Robert Addy is credited by one source with the first stolen base by sliding in an 1866 game. Another source credited Eddie Cuthbert in an 1865 game between his Philadelphia Keystones and the Brooklyn Atlantics. It is likely that neither was the first and they are credited today only because a newspaper account of each game made note of the novelty; or the players later took credit for the feat and the mythology mill of baseball accepted the claims as true.

Rules. Stolen base records prior to 1898 are distinguished from later records because between 1886 and 1898 stolen bases were credited whenever a runner advanced an extra base on a hit or an out. Also in 1898 it was ruled that the catcher would not be charged with an error trying to throw out a base runner on a stolen base attempt unless the throw was so wild it gave the runner an additional base.

In 1909 for the first time a runner on an attempted double steal was not credited with a stolen base if either runner was thrown out.

In 1920 it was ruled that a runner would not receive credit for a stolen base if no effort was made to throw him out. This change was in response to those situations late in a game when runners were allowed to run unchallenged because the other team had given up. The rule eventually was rescinded.

By 1950 if a foul tip hit directly into the glove was caught for an out, the runner stealing was not required to return to the previous base.

19th Century. Stolen bases were thought to have little value in the very early days of baseball. Even master strategist and manager George Wright of the early Cincinnati Red Stockings admitted that he saw no value. By the late 19th century, however, stolen bases were in vogue and continued to be so into the 1920s. The best of the 19th century were sliding Billy Hamilton with 915 stolen bases between 1888 and 1901 and Bill Lange with 399 in only seven seasons in the 1890s.

1900–1930. Ty Cobb was the consummate base stealer of the era, with a high of 96 in 1915 and a total of 892 for his career. Another top base stealer at the time was Clyde Milan of the Senators, who had a high of 88 in 1912 and finished his career with 495.

Stolen bases became a lost art after the home run era began in 1920, as even Ty Cobb cut down dramatically on stolen bases (in part due to advancing age). He stole 96 in 1915, but from 1919 on he never stole more than 28 and had less than 15 in six of those seasons. Eddie Collins was probably the unrivaled base stealer of the early 1920s, twice leading the league with over 40 steals. He finished his career with 743.

1930–1950.

"… Pepper Martin for St. Louis in 1931 against the Athletics — that was the year Pepper stole everything in sight and was generally hotter than an acetylene hot foot…" — The *Stars and Stripes* military newspaper.

"Today thirty [stolen bases] will get you in the Hall of Fame and a player is considered a terrific runner if he doesn't get thrown out at first on a base on balls." — Sportswriter Bugs Baer in the 1930s when the number of stolen bases declined dramatically because of an increase in the reliance on home runs.

The only notable exception to the home run binge of the 1930s and 1940s was George Case, who led the American League in stolen bases five straight years starting in 1939. He had a high of 61 in 1943 and finished his 11-year career with 349 steals.

Stolen bases remained absent from the offense after World War II, as teams still relied heavily on the long ball. In 1950 Dom DiMaggio led the American League with an all-time low of 15 steals. Teams rarely, if ever, stole when they were behind.

1950s. The trend began to shift in favor of stolen bases with the "Go Go" White Sox of the 1950s. The Sox went from last in the league in 1950 to second in 1957, winning a pennant with their matchless speed in 1959. White Sox shortstop Luis Aparicio led the American League in stolen bases nine straight years beginning in 1956 and finished his career with 506. He led a resurrection of the stolen base in the early 1960s, passing the torch first to Maury Wills and then to Lou Brock.

1960–1980.

"Cobb's record of ninety-six stolen bases in a season probably never will be broken, because modern ball has virtually eliminated the steal as a method of progression." — Arthur Daley in a 1945 *New York Times* column.

Maury Wills stole 104 bases in 1962 to break Cobb's season record of 96 (see below). Wills played shortstop for the Dodgers and won six straight stolen base crowns from 1960 through 1965. He almost did his running for the Tigers. In the late 1950s he was conditionally sold to the Tigers when the Dodgers believed that he was expendable because Don Zimmer had emerged as the heir-apparent to long-time shortstop Pee Wee Reese. Zimmer then broke his toe and the deal was canceled. See also Maury Wills with Mike Celizic, *On the Run* (1991); Maury Wills with Don Freeman, *How to Steal a Pennant* (1976); Maury Wills and Steve Gardner, *It Pays to Steal* (1963).

Negro League star Cool Papa Bell told Wills that if his teammates would stand far back in the batter's box, he would have a better chance of stealing bases. The catcher would have to move farther back and would add another foot or two on the distance of the catcher's throw to second base.

Lou Brock was the foremost base stealer of the mid–1960s and 1970s, winning eight stolen base crowns in nine years, with a high of 118 in 1974 (see below). He finished his career in 1979 with 938 steals and was elected to the Hall of Fame in 1985.

In 1973 there were over 2,000 stolen bases in the Major Leagues for the first time since the lively ball became permanent in the 1920s.

By the late 1970s teams were using a balanced combination of speed and power, which remained the norm into the 1990s. Some teams were overbalanced one way or the other, sometimes to accommodate their ballpark. For example, the Cardinals focused on speed and had few home runs because of artificial turf and large field dimensions.

1980– . The 1980s were dominated by Vince Coleman of the Cardinals, Tim Raines of the Expos and all-time base-stealing leader Rickey Henderson. Coleman started fast in 1985, winning stolen base crowns for the Cardinals in each of his first six seasons, including more than 100 steals in each of his first three.

Raines won four National League crowns in his first four full seasons starting in 1981 (with 71 steals in only 88 games in that strike-shortened season). He retired after a few cameo appearances during the 2002 season, finishing with 808 stolen bases in 2,502 games, 5th all-time.

Henderson led the American League in 11 of his first 12 full seasons starting in 1980, with a record 130 in 1982 (see below). Harold Reynolds of the Mariners interrupted the streak in 1987, with 60. Henderson was hurt and only played in 95 games, with 41 stolen bases. Henderson continued to be among the elite base stealers through 2000 (leading in 1998 with 66), and hung on through the 2002 season at age 43. He hooked up with an independent minor league team in 2003 at age 44, and then signed with the Dodgers for a few games that season (see also ***Longest Careers***).

Juan Pierre of the Rockies and Marlins, and Luis Castillo of the Marlins, dominated the 2000s in the National League, with between 46 and 65 RBIs per season as league leaders.

(Un)Balanced Attack.

"We are living in a very special time in the Live Ball era. This is the first time in baseball history that speed and power have flourished at the same time … the modern base-stealer has a much higher success rate than in past eras — it is in the game's interest to protect that success rate and perhaps even to raise it." — Craig R. Wright in *The Diamond Appraised* (1989).

The Major League stolen base and home run totals in selected seasons show the trend from stolen base domination (1909–1919), to home run domination (1939–1959), to parity between the two disciplines (1969–1989), to home run domination (1999–2003):

Year	SB	HR
1909	3,052	259
1919	2,077	447
1929	1,328	1,349
1939	957	1,445
1949	730	1,704
1959	853	2,250
1969	1,850	3,119
1979	2,983	3,433
1989	3,116	3,083
1999	3,421	5,528
2003	2,573	5,207

Most Steals/Career. On August 29, 1977, Lou Brock stole No. 893, breaking Ty Cobb's career record of 892. Rickey Henderson, who wore number 24 in honor of Willie Mays, broke Brock's record of 938 steals on May 1, 1991. Henderson's feat was overshadowed by Nolan Ryan's seventh no-hitter that night. Henderson was Ryan's 5,000th strikeout victim and was the second-to-last out of Ryan's sixth no-hitter.

Henderson started the 1991 season only two steals behind Brock. Henderson immediately went on the disabled list with a thigh injury after being caught stealing in two out of three attempts. In his first time on base after returning, he was picked off, but then stole one base to tie. The next time he was on base he stole third base. After sliding in head first, wearing wraparound dark glasses on a sunny day, he pulled the base from its anchor and held it aloft for the crowd. Brock had followed Henderson from game to game for days anticipating the record-breaker so that he would be there for it.

When Henderson passed Ty Cobb in 1990, he needed only 1,511 games to reach Cobb's 892 stolen bases. Cobb had needed 3,033 in amassing his total. Henderson had 1,406 through 2003. See also Rickey Henderson and John Shea, *Off Base: Confessions of a Thief* (1992).

Most Steals/Season.
"You don't think Hemingway or Michelangelo would have been delighted to see their achievements surpassed, do you?"— Maury Wills after Lou Brock broke his single-season stolen base record in 1974. When Wills stole 104 in 1962 to break Ty Cobb's record of 96, he also broke Bob Bescher's National League record of 81, set in 1911 (see also **Asterisks**).

Rickey Henderson stole his 119th base on August 27, 1982, breaking Lou Brock's 1974 season record of 118. Henderson finished the season with 130 stolen bases.

Most Steals/Season/Minor Leagues. Vince Coleman stole 145 bases for Macon in 1983, the all-time professional mark.

Most Rookie Steals/Season. Tim Raines of the Montreal Expos stole 71 bases in 1981, but that record was shattered in 1985 when Vince Coleman stole 110 bases for the Cardinals in his rookie season. Ironically, Coleman's leg was caught in the Cardinals' automatic tarp roller just before the start of Game 1 of the National League Championship Series and he had to watch as his club won the World Championship without him.

100+ Steals/Season.
"If you aim to steal thirty to forty bases a year, you do it by surprising the other side. But if your goal is fifty to one hundred bases, the element of surprise doesn't matter. You go even though they know you're going to go. Then each steal becomes a contest, matching your skills against theirs."— Lou Brock.

Players who have stolen 100 or more bases in a season are Rickey Henderson (1980, 1982, 1983), Maury Wills (the first to do so in 1962), Lou Brock (1974) and Vince Coleman (1985, 1986 and 1987; his first three seasons in the National League).

For many years, 1890s outfielder Bill Lange was credited with being the last player before Wills to steal 100 bases in a season. Later research determined that his best was 84 in 1896. He also led the league with 73 steals in 1897.

Consecutive Seasons/20 or More/Shortstop. Since 1900 only Honus Wagner and Ozzie Smith among shortstops have had 16 consecutive 20-steal seasons.

Percentage Leaders/Season. Max Carey is the all-time season leader for successful stolen base attempts. In 1922 he was thrown out only twice in 53 tries. The second most successful percentage is held by Jerry Mumphrey of the Padres in 1980, who stole 52 bases and was caught twice.

The 1975 Reds had a success rate of 82%, the best team percentage of all time.

Percentage/Worst. The worst career stolen base percentage (minimum 300 attempts) is held by Pete Rose, at 57%.

Most Team Steals/Season. The 1976 A's stole 334 bases for the American League record, led by Billy North with 75, Bert Campaneris with 54 and Don Baylor with 52.

The 1911 Giants stole 340 bases for the National League and Major League record. They were led by Joss DeVore with 61, Fred Snodgrass with 51, Fred Merkle with 49 and Red Murray with 48.

Most Steals/Game. George Gore of the Chicago White Stockings stole seven bases on June 25, 1881. Sliding Billy Hamilton also stole seven in a game in the 19th century, but both were during an era when taking the extra base on a hit credited a runner with a stolen base.

The modern record of six was last tied on June 16, 1991, by Otis Nixon of the Braves. Eddie Collins of the A's stole six bases in a game twice in September 1912 (September 11 and 22).

Most Steals/Inning. Giants outfielder Josh Devore stole four bases in one inning in 1912. Devore stole second and third base twice each after coming to bat twice.

All Bases Stolen in a Single At-Bat. Ty Cobb holds the record for having three times stolen second, third and home in the same at-bat. Ten National League players and 20 American League players have accomplished the feat at least once. Dave Nelson of the Rangers did it in the 1st inning against the Indians on August 30, 1974, the last to do it before 1996.

On May 12, 1996, Royals rookie Chris Stynes became the last player to record three stolen bases in an inning to tie the Major League record.

Senators catcher Eddie Ainsmith stole all three bases on June 26, 1913, in a lopsided game against A's pitcher Chief Bender, who simply was not paying attention because of the lopsided score. It was not a total fluke, however, as Ainsmith had 17 stolen bases for the season — not bad for a catcher who appeared in only 79 games.

Triple Steal. On July 25, 1930, the A's performed a triple steal twice in a game against the Indians. It is the only time that the feat has occurred twice in a Major League game.

By Catchers.
"[Choo Choo Coleman] is quick on the base paths, but this is an attribute that is about as essential for catchers as neat handwriting."— Roger Angell in *The Summer Game* (1972).

John Wathan of the Royals holds the record for most steals by a catcher with 36 in 1982. Ray Schalk stole 30 in 1916 for the White Sox and Roger Bresnahan stole 34 in 1903 for the Giants. In 1998 Pirates catcher Jason Kendall stole 26 bases to break John Stearns' National League season record for catchers, 25, set in 1978.

40/40 Club.
"If I'd known it was going to be such a big deal, I'd have done it a long time ago."— Mickey Mantle, who never really came close to the milestone with a high of 21 stolen bases in 1959. In 1965 Willie Mays supposedly could easily have done 50–50. He had 52 home runs, but according to coach and later manager Charlie Fox, the club asked him not to steal so much so he wouldn't risk injury. Odd, considering Mays only had nine steals that season and had not stolen more than 30 since 1958 (reaching 40 only in 1956).

In 1989 Jose Canseco became the first player to steal at least 40 bases and hit 40 home runs in a single season.

Bobby Bonds just missed when he had 39 home runs and 43 stolen bases in 1973. He lost one home run in a rainout. Bobby's son, Barry, joined the club in 1996 for the only time in his career.

In 1998 Alex Rodriguez became the third 40/40 player while with the Mariners.

30/30 Club. Reaching 30 home runs and 30 steals in a single season was a relatively rare event until the mid–1990s.

The earliest to achieve it were Ken Williams in 1922 (39 HR and 37 SB) and Willie Mays twice in the 1950s. In the 1960s only Bobby Bonds in 1969 and Henry Aaron in 1963 did it. In the 1970s Tommy Harper reached it once and Bonds made it four times.

It occurred seven times in the 1980s, by Dale Murphy, Eric Davis, Howard Johnson (twice), Darryl Strawberry, Joe Carter and Jose Canseco (40–40).

From 1990 through 1996 it was done by Barry Bonds (three times), Ron Gant (twice), Howard Johnson and Sammy Sosa (twice), Barry Larkin, Dante Bichette and Ellis Burks. At least 20 players have done it after that, including Alex Rodriguez in 1998 (the sixth American Leaguer).

20/50 Club. Rickey Henderson is one of three players to hit 20 or more home runs and steal at least 50 bases in the same season. He did it four times. Eric Davis did it twice early in his career (80 stolen bases in 1986) and Barry Bonds did it once, when he stole 52 bases and hit 33 home runs in 1990.

200/500 Club. In 1978 Joe Morgan became the first player to steal 500 bases and hit 200 home runs in his career. His record was matched by Rickey Henderson on his first home run of 1993.

200/300/3,000 Club. Four players have 200 stolen bases, hit 300 home runs and had 3,000 hits: Willie Mays, Henry Aaron, Dave Winfield and George Brett.

300/300 Club. Four players have stolen 300 bases and hit 300 home runs: Willie Mays, Bobby Bonds, Andre Dawson and Barry Bonds.

500/500.

"This is nothing. I've got nine writers standing here. McGwire had 200 writers when he had 30 home runs." — Barry Bonds on being the first player to hit 400 home runs and steal 400 bases. He then reached the 500/500 mark in June 2003.

200 Hits/50 Steals. In 2001 Ichiro Suzuki became only the 15th player since 1900 to collect 200 hits and steal 50 bases in a season.

Consecutive Steals.

"One night a puzzler about consecutive steals has the especially active group of fans down in box 28 sending up dozens of unlikely answers, the wackier of which Bill reads to the crowd — [comedienne] 'Imogene Coca' is his favorite." — Jerry Klinkowitz in *Short Season and Other Stories* (1988).

Vince Coleman stole 50 consecutive bases between September 1988 and July 1989. He then was thrown out by Montreal's Nelson Santovenia attempting to steal second base. The previous record was held by Davey Lopes, who stole 38 consecutive bases in 1975. The Lopes streak ended August 24, 1975, when Gary Carter threw him out in the 12th inning. Lopes broke Max Carey's 1922 season record of 31.

Until 1995 the American League record was 32 straight, held by Willie Wilson and Julio Cruz. Brady Anderson of the Orioles had a short-lived record of 36 straight stolen bases between May 1994 and July 1995. He was caught attempting to steal third base. In mid–1995 Tim Raines of the White Sox broke Anderson's record with 40 straight steals between July 23, 1993, and August 4, 1995.

Oldest Season Leader. Eddie Collins of the White Sox stole 42 bases in 1924 to lead the league at age 37. Lou Brock was 35 when he led the league and set a National League record of 118 steals in 1974.

Fewest Steals.

"I thought they'd stop the game and give me second base." — Catcher Milt May after stealing his first base in six years. He finished 15 seasons with four stolen bases.

"I could hear him coming. I was dumbfounded. I didn't know how to act." — Umpire Tim Tschida on Cecil Fielder's first steal. American League catcher Russ Nixon held the no-steal record with 906 games played without a steal from 1957 through 1968. Tigers first baseman Cecil Fielder broke his record when he became the first player to play in 1,000 games without stealing a base. He had five attempted steals through the 1995 season and 1,096 games. In his second game of 1996 he stole his first base. Fielder's comment: "I've been working on my jumps for nine years."

The new leader was Expos catcher Darrin Fletcher, who had played in 487 games without a steal.

Catcher Ernie Lombardi may have been the slowest player of all time, stealing eight bases in 1,853 games. Incredibly, Lombardi is the only catcher to win two batting titles, obviously without any "leg" hits to boost his average.

Red Sox outfielder Dom DiMaggio led the American League in 1950 with 15 steals, the lowest all-time season-leading total.

The 1957 Senators had 13 steals, led by Julio Becquer with three.

League Leader/Steals and Home Runs. Chuck Klein of the A's is the last man to lead a league in stolen bases (20) and home runs (38) in the same season. The only other was Ty Cobb, who in 1909 led the league with nine home runs and 76 stolen bases.

Led Both Leagues. Ron LeFlore is the only man to lead both leagues in stolen bases. He led the American League with 68 stolen bases in 1978 for the Tigers. In 1980 he led the National League with 97 steals for the Expos.

500 Stolen Bases/3,000 Hits. Six players have reached this milestone: Ty Cobb, Eddie Collins, Honus Wagner, Lou Brock, Rickey Henderson and Paul Molitor.

Stealing Home.

"Gomez, it took you ten years to get to third base and now you want to louse it up. Stay there." — Yankees third base coach Art Fowler when weak-hitting pitcher Lefty Gomez wanted to steal home.

"Me, I'm not running into somebody with pads on. I think that's insane. If you're going to steal home, most of the time it's in double-steal situations. That's when it happens." — Barry Bonds.

Up through the early part of the 20th century, when runs were harder to come by, attempted steals of home were far more common. For example, the 1902 Giants attempted 40 steals of home, with 11 successes. In contrast, in 2003, of the 2,923 stolen bases in the Major Leagues, 18 were of home plate.

Ty Cobb is the career leader with 54 steals of home (some sources credit him with 35 and one source put his total at 50). In 1991 SABR researchers confirmed that Cobb stole home eight times in 1912. Prior to that, all sources credited the leaders as Pete Reiser in 1946 and Rod Carew in 1969 with seven. Reiser always contended that he stole eight that season, but umpire George Magerkurth called him out and immediately realized his mistake: "Goddamn, did I blow that one. Called you out, kid. Sorry."

Carew stole home six times in 1969 long before midseason. It took him another month to reach seven, but he missed number eight twice. He was cut down on September 10 on a throw by Tommy John, ending his streak of nine straight (after two in exhibition games and seven during the season). On September 26 he again attempted to steal home, knocking umpire Jim Honochick off his feet. When Honochick regained his balance he called Carew out for not touching the plate although it appeared from his slide mark that Carew clipped the plate.

All of Carew's steals were straight steals, while at least six of Cobb's eight were on the back end of a double steal. Carew finished his career with 17 steals of home. Carew's view of the feat: "After I got into it, I really enjoyed doing it because I wasn't just stealing home for the sake of stealing home. I'd put us up by a run, tie a game, or put us up by two runs which was important if we had a one-run lead. I only did it at opportune times when I felt it was important for the team."

Ty Cobb, Vic Power, Shoeless Joe Jackson and eight others have stolen home twice in one game. Power succeeded at it in 1958, once to tie a game at 8–8 and once to win it 9–8. Ironically, he stole only one other base all season. On June 28, 1910, Joe Tinker of the Cubs became the first player to do it twice in a game.

Max Carey is second all-time with 33 steals of home.

Jackie Robinson stole home 19 times during his career, including three times during his 1947 rookie season. He accomplished the feat at least once each year for 10 seasons except 1953. Robinson was caught stealing home 12 times.

Pitchers have stolen home 30 times in the 20th century.

In 1931 it was ruled that a pitcher would not be credited with an assist on runners thrown out while trying to steal home on a pitch.

Lou Gehrig's first steal in a Major League game was a steal of home.

Steals of home were more likely in earlier times, as pitchers were encouraged to use a full wind-up with a runner on third so as not to disrupt their pitching motion (according to former Twins pitcher Jim Kaat).

World Series Steals of Home. Lou Brock of the Cardinals stole seven bases in a World Series and three in a single series game in both 1967 and 1968.

Perhaps the most famous steal of home during the World Series was Jackie Robinson's effort against catcher Yogi Berra and the Yankees during Game 1 in 1955. Almost 50 years later, Berra stilled claimed that he made a successful tag: "He was out. No question." Yankee shortstop Phil Rizzuto thought from his vantage point that Robinson was safe.

Giants outfielder Monte Irvin, who was on the Giants when Bobby Thomson hit his famous play-off home run, said his greatest baseball thrill was stealing home during the 1951 World Series off pitcher Allie Reynolds The last steal of home before that was by Hank Greenberg in 1934.

Research by Eric Hallett reveals that of the 14 steals of home through the 2002 World Series (when Brad Fullmer did it), only three were not the back end of a double steal. Monte Irvin did it on October 4, 1951, for the Giants against the Yankees. Ty Cobb was the first, on October 9, 1909, for the Tigers against the Pirates. When Fullmer did it during the 2002 Series for the Angels, the man in the booth calling the play for Fox Sports was former catcher Tim McCarver, the last man to be credited with a steal of home in the World Series. He did it on the back end of a double steal (like Fullmer) on October 15, 1964, for the Cardinals against the Yankees.

Stealing First Base. See *Base Running— Stealing First Base.*
Caught Stealing.

"They have been thrown out only one less time than the last place team has been thrown out the most."— Broadcaster Ralph Kiner attempting to explain how bad the Expos were at stealing bases in the late 1980s.

"The only dumb play I saw Ruth make."— Yankee general manager Ed Barrow on Babe Ruth's attempted steal that resulted in the last out of Game 7 of the 1926 World Series. With two outs in the 9th inning and the Cardinals leading 3–2, Ruth walked and then was thrown out by catcher Bob O'Farrell on an attempted steal. Ruth explained later that he thought pitcher Grover Cleveland Alexander had forgotten he was there and that the way Alexander was pitching, the Yankees were not going to score anyway.

During the 1921 World Series, John McGraw's Giants walked Ruth whenever possible and rarely threw him a strike. In one game, after singling in a run, Ruth walked three times in a row. After the last one, he bolted for second and stole the base standing up. He then stole third for good measure. Many forget that Ruth stole 123 bases despite his girth, more than DiMaggio (30), Gehrig (102) and Ted Williams (24).

Caught stealing statistics were not regularly kept by the American League until 1928 and the National League until 1951.

In 1982 Rickey Henderson set a record with 42 times caught stealing, while successful a record 130 times. The next worst efforts (caught/successful):

Ty Cobb	38/96	1915	Tigers
Miller Huggins	32/36	1914	Cardinals

Catchers Throwing Out Baserunners. See *Catchers—Throwing Out Runners.*

Feller's Move to First Base. Ben Chapman stole on Bob Feller because he noticed that there was daylight under Feller's right heel when he was going to throw to first base; and no daylight when he was going to throw to the plate.

Cool Papa Bell, playing in an exhibition game in Los Angeles against Feller, could tell when Feller would not throw over because Feller would look hard at the runner for a few moments and then always went home with the pitch.

Umpire Silence. In 1906 Pirates outfielder Fred Clarke was on third base with the bases loaded on a 3–1 pitch. There was no call by the umpire on the pitch, and Clarke assumed it was a ball and strolled home. The umpire then yelled "strike two" and said that he had a frog in his throat and could not speak. The run counted as a stolen base.

Unnecessary Steals.

"My game is running and I have to do it at every opportunity, both to keep myself sharp and to keep the opposition on edge. Besides, when can you have too many home runs. Is a home run hitter criticized for hitting a home run after the score is 10–1?"— Maury Wills.

In July 2001 Brewers manager Davey Lopes was suspended for two games for threatening to order his pitchers to hit Rickey Henderson. Lopes was upset when Henderson stole second base in the 7th inning of the Padres' 12–5 win.

Double Steal Rules. Earlier in the 20th century, if a runner was thrown out on a double steal, the other runner got credit for a stolen base.

Four Decades. In the second game of 2000, played in the Tokyo Dome in Japan, Rickey Henderson of the Mets stole a base to join Ted Williams as the only players at the time to steal bases in four decades. Tim Raines joined them in September 2001.

Book. Renardo Barton, *Base Stealers* (1991); Steve Fiffer, *Speed* (1990).

Strategy

"Don't throw him anything good enough to hit, but don't walk him."— Generic advice to a pitcher with the bases loaded and the other team's best hitter coming up.

"I never play by the book because I never met the guy that wrote it."— Manager Dick Williams.

"We go over positioning for relays and bunt plays. Then we play hangman."— Mets bullpen coach Dave LaRoche, on why the club had a blackboard in the clubhouse.

See also *Cliches, Fielding and Fielding Averages, Hit and Run* and *Switch Hitters.*

Outfield Positioning. See *Fielding and Fielding Averages.*
Right-Handers/Left-Handers.

"[T]here is almost an unwritten tradition among baseball managers ... that the left *vs* left, and right *vs* right offers the best chance for any game strategy to succeed. Baseball thrives on oral tradition and legend and this particular one is a modern creation and will no doubt continue to remain as an important part of managerial strategy in the future, the work of the 'scientific statisticians' to the contrary."— Ralph Andreano in *No Joy in Mudville* (1965), citing statistical evidence that the percentage baseball involved in creating left vs. right and right vs. left batter/pitcher situations is not statistically sound.

Because of his own hitting difficulties, manager Ned Hanlon of the 1890s Orioles is credited with introducing the use of right-handed pitchers versus left-handed batters and vice versa.

Ted Williams Shift.

"You can't hit 'em where they ain't when there ain't no place where they ain't." — Ted Williams on a slump brought on in part by the shift employed against him. The shift was first used against him in 1946 by Indians player-manager Lou Boudreau. The entire Indians infield and two outfielders were deployed to the right side, leaving only left fielder George Case in his regular position, though much shallower than usual.

Boudreau later recalled that Williams had hit three home runs in the first game of a doubleheader (the same game in which Boudreau had five extra base hits in a nine-inning game to tie a record). Boudreau was mad and had thought for weeks about shifting against Williams. When he yelled "Yo!" everyone switched. The first time he saw it, Williams lined a one-hopper into short right field — to the second baseman — and he was thrown out.

Williams claimed that the shift cost 20–30 points off his lifetime batting average of .344. One bit of revenge by Williams: On September 13, 1946, he hit the only inside-the-park home run of his career (to the opposite field) against the Indians in a pennant-clinching 1–0 game.

Other Shifts.

"Gentile is the stubborn right field pull hitter of all time. He plays with the rest of us, but he has his private set of arcs and azimuths. Everyone stands in right field, even the third baseman. The catcher would too if they'd let him. It's more than the Williams shift. It's the Gentile shift." — Richard Grossinger in "Berkeley Softball" (1979); the Gentile referred to was one of the sons of Major Leaguer Jim Gentile of the Orioles.

Before Williams, other hitters experienced shifts put on exclusively for them. In the 1920s Ken Williams of the Browns and Cy Williams of the Phillies both forced opponents to employ shifts identical to the shift used against Ted Williams. It was also tried most recently against Darryl Strawberry.

Indians player-manager Tris Speaker tried a shift on Babe Ruth, but without success.

White Sox shortstop Luke Appling dealt successfully with a Yankee shift against him.

The Cubs employed a shift against Wally Berger of the Giants in 1937. The plan backfired in a crucial late-season game when weak-armed Cubs second baseman Billy Herman was shifted to shortstop. He was unable to make the throw to first on key plays and the Giants came back from a 7–2 deficit to knock the Cubs out of the pennant race.

In the 1995 World Series the Indians at times used a Ted Williams Shift against Fred McGriff of the Braves.

World Series Position Shift.

During the 1968 season (pre-designated hitter), future Hall of Fame outfielder Al Kaline had been the heart and soul of the Tigers. He was injured late in the season, however, and when he returned there was no place to put him.

For the World Series, manager Mayo Smith wanted Kaline in the line-up because of his leadership. To do it, he moved Jim Northrup to center field and Kaline to right field in place of Northrup. Most critically, he moved center fielder Mickey Stanley to shortstop where he had rarely played. He replaced the weak-hitting Ray Oyler, who had hit only .138 in 111 games.

Stanley prepared for the role by playing shortstop the last six games of the season (among a total of nine all year). The switch to shortstop was suggested by Norm Cash, who along with his teammates considered Stanley the best athlete on the team.

The first ball of the series was a ground ball to Stanley by base-stealing king Lou Brock. Stanley made the play and went on to make only two errors in 29 chances, neither of which hurt the Tigers on their way to the championship. Stanley believed that Brock hit the ball to him intentionally, because Brock took a half swing and seemed to direct the ball in his direction.

Stanley became the starting shortstop in 1969 when Oyler was drafted by the Seattle Pilots. He hurt his arm on the first ground ball of spring training and was never the same again. See Donald Hall's essay, "October Shortstop," in *The Ol' Ball Game* (1990).

Surprise Pitchers.

Curly Ogden. Senators manager Bucky Harris came up with a novel strategy for Game 7 of the 1924 World Series against the Giants. Surprisingly, he started right-hander Curly Ogden, which forced Giants manager John McGraw to use Bill Terry at first base, rather than George Kelly. Ogden faced one batter, whom he struck out, and then walked the next batter. As planned, Ogden was immediately lifted for left-hander George Mogridge, who had been warming up under the stands. Terry stayed in the game until the 6th inning when he was replaced by Kelly. Though the strategy kept the Senators in the game, they still trailed 3–1 in the 8th inning.

This was the famous game in which Senators pitcher Walter Johnson, having already lost two games in the series, was brought into the game in the 9th inning after the Senators had tied it in the 8th. Johnson pitched into the 12th inning and the Senators won the series when they scored in the bottom of the 12th. The winning run scored after Giants catcher Hank Gowdy stepped in his mask and dropped a foul pop fly (batter Muddy Ruel then doubled) and a *Bad Hop* ground ball skipped over Fred Lindstrom's head to score Ruel and give the Senators a 4–3 victory.

Ralph Branca. The Dodgers employed the same pitching strategy in a key game during the 1946 pennant race with the Cardinals, with a slight twist. On September 14, 1946, the Dodgers planned to start sore-armed Ralph Branca to pitch to one batter, then lift him and put in a left-handed pitcher to foul up the Cardinals batting order. Branca got the first man out, so manager Leo Durocher let him pitch to the next batter. He got the side out and went on to pitch a three-hit shutout.

Howard Ehmke. The A's faced the Cubs in the 1929 World Series. In Game 1, A's manager Connie Mack went with surprise starter Howard Ehmke on the mound. Ehmke was 35 years old and had pitched only 55 innings that year. He was 7–2 but had not been with the club in the last few weeks of the season, as he had been scouting the Cubs. Even some of the A's players were openly critical of Mack's decision. Nevertheless, Ehmke established a new Series record with 13 strikeouts and pitched eight innings of shutout ball before the Cubs scored a run in the 3–1 A's victory.

Near the end of the season, Mack supposedly called Ehmke into his office to release him, but Ehmke said that he always wanted to pitch in a World Series and that he had one great game left in his arm. Mack apparently bought the hype because he implemented his secret plan and later said that it was his most satisfying moment in baseball. Ehmke pitched three more innings in the Series and appeared in only three more games in his career.

Red Smith once had a conversation with Ring Lardner in which Lardner reported on a conversation he had with Cubs manager Joe McCarthy in the summer before the World Series. McCarthy was well aware that he might face Ehmke in the Series: "We're not worried about Grove and Earnshaw. We can hit speed. But there's one guy on the club…. He's a shit pitcher. That's Howard Ehmke, and he's the guy we're going to see in the Series." — Reported by Ira Berkow in his biography of Smith, *Red* (1986).

Gary Waslewski. In Game 6 of the 1967 World Series, with his club down 3–2 in games, Red Sox manager Dick Williams called on little-used pitcher Gary Waslewski as his starter. He had spent most of the season in the minors, had not started a game for the Red Sox since July 29 and had never completed a game in the Major Leagues. Nevertheless, he held back the Cardinals into the 6th inning, which was enough to preserve a Red Sox victory and force a seventh game.

Four Outfielders. During the 1969 Miracle Mets season, manager Gil Hodges used four outfielders to defend against San Francisco's Willie McCovey during the Mets' pennant drive. The ploy worked, as Cleon Jones caught a deep drive to left center field above the fence in the 13th inning of a scoreless tie. Tommy Agee won the game in the 14th inning with a home run. Hodges used the same strategy in the World Series against Frank Robinson of the Orioles. It apparently worked, as Robinson batted only .188 (3-for-16).

In 1954 Birdie Tebbetts of the Reds used four outfielders against Stan Musial.

Bad Move. It has been reported that Casey Stengel might never have become the Yankee manager in 1949, but for a strategy move by Yankee manager Bucky Harris in the 1947 World Series. Yankee pitcher Bill Bevens was pitching a no-hitter into the 9th inning of Game 4. In the top of the inning, Harris ordered Bevens to walk Pete Reiser with Al Gionfriddo on second. Bevens had already walked a number of batters that day. Cookie Lavagetto then doubled to break up the no-hitter, and the Dodgers went on to win the game.

Though the Yankees eventually won the Series, it has been written that the Yankee management, in particular the volatile Larry MacPhail, was furious over the decision to walk Reiser and the anger remained the following season. Harris was fired after the 1948 season when he finished third. However, MacPhail had left before the season, leading to the conclusion that the 1947 World Series decision may not have been the catalyst for the dismissal of Harris by MacPhail's successor, George Weiss.

Fake-Out. Charlie Gehringer once hit a fly ball to deep left field in Detroit. Left fielder Babe Ruth pretended that the ball was a home run; Gehringer relaxed and slowed down as he headed to second base. Ruth took the ball off the wall and threw him out at second.

Play-Off Game. In the 9th inning of the third 1951 play-off game between the Giants and Dodgers in which Bobby Thomson hit his miracle home run, Dodger manager Charlie Dressen had first base open when he opted to let Ralph Branca pitch to Thomson. Although it would have put the potential winning run on first base, Branca would have faced rookie Willie Mays.

Championship Series. Dodger manager Tommy Lasorda was criticized severely for allowing Tom Niedenfuer to pitch to the Cardinals' Jack Clark in the top of the 9th inning of Game 6 of the 1985 National League Championship Series. With first base open and his club down 5–4, Clark drilled a pitch into the left field bleachers for a three-run homer to give the Cardinals the pennant.

Switching Pitchers. 1950s and 1960s manager and general manager Paul Richards is credited with the strategy of putting a pitcher at a different position, rather than removing him from the game, to bring in another pitcher to face a single batter in a crucial situation. After the at-bat, the first pitcher is brought back in to pitch. Richards supposedly first tried it in 1951 when he moved pitcher Harry Dorish to third base to bring in Billy Pierce to pitch to Ted Williams. After Williams popped out, Dorish went back to the mound and Pierce came out of the game.

Richards is also credited with walking the opposing pitcher to prevent the next batter, slugger Sam Jethroe, from moving freely on the basepaths if he got on. It supposedly happened at least once on May 25, 1949, according to such usually reliable sources as Jules

Tygiel's *Baseball's Great Experiment* (1983). Careful research and interviewing by Joseph Overfield in the 1980s determined that the story is pure myth.

Distraction. Jimmy Piersall was once thrown out of a game for running back and forth in the outfield to distract Ted Williams while he was batting.

Street Names

"If, perchance, the council cannot agree on Comiskey Road … may we suggest Seventh Place?"— Sarcastic Chicago sportswriter in a 1936 article during efforts to name the road to Comiskey Park in honor of the recently deceased Charles Comiskey.

"How come we drive on parkways and park on driveways?"— Pitcher Larry Anderson.

"Jerry Lane, Boardwalk Brown, Bob Way, Alex Main, Charlie Metro, Gabby Street, Jack Urban, Urban Shocker, Dusty Rhodes, Gene Alley, Hunter Lane, Luke Urban"

Spring Training. Many clubs use the names of former stars to grace the streets of their spring training sites. For example, Hank Aaron Drive is the address for the Atlanta Braves spring training site in West Palm Beach, Florida. Many of the interior streets of Dodgertown in Vero Beach are named after former Dodgers such as Roy Campanella and Sandy Koufax. After Tommy Lasorda was elected to the Hall of Fame, the Dodgers named the main street that leads into their training camp at Vero Beach Tommy Lasorda Lane.

Harry Agganis. In November 1995, Gaffney Street, near the former site of Braves Field in Boston, was renamed Harry Agganis Way, after the former Boston University and Red Sox star who died during the 1955 season. James Gaffney was an owner of the Boston Braves in the early 20th century who died in 1932.

Lou Boudreau. When Boudreau's number was retired by the Indians, the street bordering Municipal Stadium was renamed Boudreau Boulevard.

Roberto Clemente. There are numerous Calle Roberto Clementes in Puerto Rico.

Al Kaline and Mickey Cochrane. Kaline Drive in Detroit was formally Cherry Street, adjacent to Tiger Stadium. Nearby National, a narrow street behind the ballpark, was later renamed Cochrane Street.

Jackie Robinson. As part of Baseball's celebration of the 50th anniversary of Jackie Robinson's entry into the Major Leagues, in April 1997 New York's Interboro Parkway was renamed Jackie Robinson Parkway.

Billy Rogell. William G. (Billy) Rogell Drive is adjacent to Detroit's Metro Airport.

Pete Rose. Cincinnati has Pete Rose Way, the major thoroughfare from Interstate 75 to Riverfront Stadium. Some consideration was given to changing the name when Rose was implicated in a gambling scandal, but the proposal was dropped quickly.

Nolan Ryan. In 1992 the Nolan Ryan Expressway was dedicated in Texas.

George Steinbrenner. The Yankees' spring training site in Port St. Lucie is located on Steinbrenner Drive.

Bill Veeck. Bill Veeck Drive leads to both old and New Comiskey Park.

Ted Williams. When the San Diego Padres hosted the 1992 All-Star Game, the city rededicated a highway as Ted Williams Parkway in honor of the hometown hero.

Hack Wilson. Hack Wilson Drive is located in Ellwood City, Pennsylvania.

Tom Yawkey. Yawkey Way, adjacent to Fenway Park in Boston, was formerly known as Jersey Street.

Streetcars

"There has not been such a slaughter of innocents in Brooklyn since the day that trolley cars were first run and knocked every other man down." — Lead to a game story for a 21–3 Dodger home win over the Reds in 1901.

See also *Transportation*.

Early ballparks were built in areas that were easily accessible by streetcar, the primary mode of urban transportation around 1900. Streetcar owners were sometimes baseball club owners, including Henry V. Lucas in St. Louis and the Robison brothers in Cleveland. Brooklyn's "Trolley Dodgers" name derived from the many streetcar lines that ended at Washington Park in the 1890s. Sportsman's Park in St. Louis had streetcar lines within 200 feet of the entrance.

Strike Zone

"Young man, when you pitch a strike, Mr. Hornsby will let you know." — Umpire Bill Klem to young pitcher Johnny Sain after three close pitches. It must have occurred in spring training because Sain never faced Hornsby in a regular-season game.

"I didn't get over 1,300 walks without knowing the strike zone." — Wade Boggs, on being ejected for the first time in his 17-year career for arguing a called third strike.

"Two!"

"Two What?!"

"Too low — much too low!" — Purported 1965 exchange between rookie umpire Marty Springstead and 6'7" slugger Frank Howard, after Springstead called a knee-high strike on the enraged Howard.

"It's between the top and the bottom of the belt buckle." — Old-time pitcher Boo Ferriss lamenting the unofficially smaller strike zone of the 1980s.

"Maybe it's because we see so much of it. There are 275 to 300 pitches in your standard Major League game, sometimes more, sometimes less. Take away the pitches that hitters swing at, the ones that bounce a foot in front of the plate, and the ones that come precariously close to hitting the backstop, and you're still left with a good 25 questionable pitches a game. That's 25 chances to debate whether the umpire is second only to St. Peter among the universe's great arbiters, or whether he needs to make a quick pit stop at his friendly, neighborhood LensCrafters." — Jim Armstrong.

"The Strike Zone is that area over home plate the upper limit of which is a horizontal line at the midpoint between the top of the shoulders and the top of the uniform pants, and the lower level is a line at the hollow beneath the kneecap. The Strike Zone shall be determined from the batter's stance as the batter is prepared to swing at a pitched ball." — The official description of the strike zone as of 2001.

Rule. Although some sources reported that before 1900 there was no formal strike zone, 1887 batters were no longer allowed to call for a high or low pitch and the strike zone was defined as the area between the top of the shoulder and the bottom of the knees.

In 1950 the zone was reduced to include the area from the batter's armpits to the top of his knee. In 1963 it was expanded to include the top of the shoulders.

After the 1968 season, in response to pitcher dominance (symbolized by the 1–0 All-Star Game, in which the sole run scored on a double play), the zone was reduced to include from the top of the armpits to the top of the knees.

In 1987 the strike zone was formally redefined with a diagram in the official rules: "A horizontal line at the midpoint between the top of the shoulder and the top of the uniform pants ... [the lower level] is "a line at the top of the knees."

It was also ruled in 1987 that the strike zone shall be determined from the batter's stance as the batter is prepared to swing at the ball. This prevented a player from crouching before the pitch to reduce his strike zone.

In late 1994 the Rules Committee required umpires to begin calling the "high strike" in 1995 to conform more closely with the official rules. Umpires had been calling a ball on almost every pitch above the belt buckle.

In 1999 the commissioner's office issued an order that umpires call strikes on pitches two inches above the belt. That is still lower than what is called for in the official rules. Again in 2001 the commissioner's office, through Sandy Alderson (the man in charge of enforcing the strike zone rule), directed umpires to call strikes more in accordance with the strike zone by calling the high strike. This was done in an effort to give pitchers more of an edge against the power hitters throughout the leagues.

Japanese Strike Zone. The Japanese strike zone is wider on each side of the plate by the width of a baseball.

The Cleveland Indians arrive by trolley car for a day of practice during spring training in New Orleans, their spring home intermittently between 1901 and 1939.

Uniform. The 1970s uniform of the Reds was cut below the knee, intentionally providing a well-defined reference point and making low strikes more likely (Query: why would this have benefited the Reds batters?). Reds general manager Bob Howsam once experimented with his Denver minor league club with a uniform that was color-coded to reflect the zone.

Experiment. In 1950 Branch Rickey asked General Electric engineers to design a machine of three mirrors and electric eyes. If a pitch came through the strike zone, the mirrors saw it in 1–2–3 order and electric impulses lit a lamp-indicating a strike. Otherwise, it was a ball.

Strikes and Lockouts

"Baseball? Rather like rounders, isn't it? Never saw the game myself. But I suppose the underwriters never actually saw the Titanic, either."—David Larner, Lloyds of London insurance underwriter, after Lloyds was required to pay out $50 million to Major League Baseball owners on their 1981 strike insurance policy.

"The Cubs' striking is about as significant as the buggy whip manufacturers going on strike. What difference does it make."— *Chicago Sun-Times* columnist Mike Royko on the 1981 player strike that included the anemic Cubs.

"Cheap billionaires fighting with whiny millionaires."—Former commissioner Fay Vincent during the 1994–1995 strike.

See also *Arbitration*, *Collective Bargaining Agreements*, *Free Agents*, *Reserve Clause* and *Unions*.

1889 Strike. The first player strike may have been in 1889, when six American Association Louisville players refused to take the field after owner Mordecai Davidson fined them for errors and sloppy play. They failed to show for the June 14 game, which was rained out after two innings. They missed two games before returning to the field.

On July 4, 1889, the Brotherhood of Professional Base Ball Players planned a strike, but it failed due to lack of player unity. Their discontent led directly to the formation of the 1890 Players League.

1912/First Strike. The generally-recognized first strike by Major League ballplayers occurred in 1912 when members of the Tigers refused to play because of the American League's suspension of teammate Ty Cobb. Cobb had gone into the stands to beat up a crippled heckler (he had no hands) for calling him a "half-nigger."

American League president Ban Johnson threatened Tigers owner Frank Navin with a $5,000 fine for every game in which his team failed to take the field. The Tigers played the first game of a three-game series against the A's before striking (Cobb later remembered inaccurately that no game was played).

The second game was a sham as rookie Herb Pennock pitched for the A's. The Tigers hired college players for $10 each; except the pitcher, who received $25 if he pitched a complete game (he did).

Al Travers, who later became a Jesuit priest, lost 24–2 in front of 15,000 fans. The next game was called off by agreement of the teams. The Tigers moved on to Philadelphia, and Johnson threatened the striking players with a lifetime expulsion. They played. This incident supposedly led to the formation of the Players Fraternity, a quasi–*Union*, but that action was in the works well before this incident.

1913–1918/Threatened Strikes. The first threatened general strike by Major League players occurred in 1913 (1914 in some sources) when the leagues failed to abide by the agreement they had entered into with the Players Fraternity. A strike was averted when the players backed down.

In 1918 the players threatened to strike when the owners cut their salaries as a result of World War I. This was a threatened one-day strike that never occurred.

1919 Phillies. A 1943 newspaper account reported that, when Phillies manager Gavvy Cravath was fired in mid–1919, his players sat down in the stands in a show of support for Cravath. They refused to play until owner William Baker threatened to forfeit the game and make the players pay the $1,000 fine to be imposed against the club by the league. The strike ended immediately. The problem with the story is that Cravath was hired in mid–1919 and was not fired until after the 1920 season.

1946/Strike Vote. In May 1946 the Pirates came close to striking when the players, in a narrow vote, took to the field instead of striking in favor of forming a union.

1947/Cardinals. It has been reported that the Cardinals threatened to strike if Jackie Robinson took the field against them, but this incident has been reported inaccurately. The players never threatened to strike at that time (see also *Integration*).

1969/Threatened Strike. During spring training 1969, new commissioner Bowie Kuhn inherited a problem with the Major League Players Association, which was upset with pension contributions. The union called for its membership not to sign their new contracts and not to report to spring camps.

On February 25, 1969, the dispute was resolved and the players received concessions from the owners on the pension issue. The Players Association gained somewhat more credibility in the eyes of both owners and players, but its bargaining position was solidified far more in 1972.

1972/First General Strike.

"We're not going to give them another *goddamn* cent! If they want to strike — let them strike."— Cardinals owner Gussie Busch before the 1972 strike.

At the start of the 1972 season, the players struck for 14 days from April 1 to April 13, the first general strike in Major League Baseball history. It was important for the Major League Baseball Players Association to establish credibility with the owners, who were represented by John Gaherin, the former president of the New York Newspaper Association. This was difficult, however, because a number of name players were unwilling to support strong-willed Marvin Miller, executive director of the association.

The players were in part trying to make the owners increase their contribution to the *Pension Plan* by 17% to make up for the 17% increase in the cost of living over the previous four years. The owners were already paying in $5.4 million per year, but the players succeeded in having that increased by $500,000. The owners also increased their contribution to the health care fund by $400,000. The strike hurt attendance, as demonstrated by the Mets' delayed Opening Day crowd of only 16,000.

Ten game days were lost, and there was no agreement between the players and owners to replay the 86 total games that were lost (see also *Scheduling*). The Tigers won the American League East title by one-half game over the Red Sox due to the uneven scheduling. The last active player from this strike year was Goose Gossage, who played into the 1994 strike season.

1973/Spring Training Lockout. On February 8, in the absence of a collective bargaining agreement, the owners locked out the players from spring training. On February 25 they agreed on a new three-year deal that established salary arbitration for players with two or more years of Major League service.

1976/Spring Training Lockout. On December 23, 1975, Dave McNally and Andy Messersmith were declared free agents after an arbitration panel ruled that the reserve clause was valid for only one option year. The owners then declared that baseball had to reach an agreement on the issue of free agency no later than the start of spring training in 1976. When no agreement was reached, the owners made good on their threat to lock out the players. They announced their decision on February 13 and the lockout began on March 1, 1976.

Because their position seemed weaker as long as they kept practicing on their own, the players stopped working out on March 12. On March 17 the 22 player representatives voted 17–5 to reject the owners' final offer, which provided that players with at least eight years of service who did not sign their contracts could become free agents. Bowie Kuhn stepped in that day and ended the lockout although some claim that the Players Association was cracking and after a few more days would have given in to the owners.

The lockout ended and a new collective bargaining agreement was signed on July 12 during the All-Star break. The two sides agreed to a new four-year deal which established free agency rules. Players with at least six years service could become free agents, but players were required to wait five years before becoming free agents again. Players with two years service were eligible for arbitration.

1980/Spring Training Walkout. The collective bargaining agreement expired December 31, 1979, and the players rejected a key bargaining point advanced by the owners: that a club losing a free agent was allowed to choose a player from the club that signed the free agent. In the final week of spring training 1980, the players walked out and threatened to strike on May 23. The vote by the players was 967–1 in favor of a strike (all players on the 40-man roster are eligible to vote). The only player to vote against the strike was Royals player representative Jerry Terrell. A total of 92 exhibition games were lost in 1980.

Just before the threatened strike, both sides agreed to set up a committee to study the situation. The two sides reached a new four-year agreement, but which allowed free agency issues to be reopened during the following season. They established a deadline of January 31, 1981, to explore the key issue. That deadline passed with nothing resolved and a strike was averted only until June 1981.

1981/50-Day Strike.

"This strike wouldn't have happened if Bowie Kuhn were alive today."— Red Smith's sarcastic remark about the commissioner's lack of action to end the strike.

On June 12, 1981, the players began a 50-day strike that was not settled until July 31. The strike caused the loss of 712 games: 328 in the National League and 384 in the American League. The second half split-season schedule began with the All-Star Game in Cleveland in front of an All-Star Game record 72,086 fans. The Reds and Cardinals had the best overall records in the National League but did not win either half of the season and did not participate in postseason play.

As a result of the strike, a rule was instituted whereby a team losing a player to free agency was entitled to a replacement player. This format was abandoned later. Many owners were disgruntled with the way in which Bowie Kuhn handled the situation, and much of his support among the owners was eroded permanently.

The 650 Major League players lost $28 million in salary during the strike, led by Dave Winfield, who lost $7,770 each day. The 26 teams lost $116 million in revenue but received $50 million back on their strike insurance. There was fear that the strike would cause a drop in attendance the following year. Not so, as reflected in the Dodgers' new attendance record in 1982 of 3.6 million.

Pete Rose tied Stan Musial's National League hit record in the last game of the first half of the season. He passed Musial in the first game after the strike ended.

1985/Two-Day Strike. Major League Baseball experienced a two-day strike starting August 6. The owners wanted a salary cap similar to the format used in basketball, but this would have cut the heart out of the players' bargaining wins over the previous years. As a result the players refused to accept the owners' proposal. New commissioner Peter Ueberroth was active in avoiding a lengthier confrontation.

The strike was averted after the players union agreed that a player could seek arbitration only after his third year, rather than second. The owners abandoned their salary cap proposal and agreed to increase the pension fund contributions so that a 10-year veteran would receive $91,000 per year. The two sides agreed on a new five-year deal.

1990/Spring Training Lockout. The owners staged a spring training lockout in an attempt to impose new contract terms. The lockout lasted from February 15 through March 28, all during spring training. The first week's regular season games were canceled and rescheduled for later dates during the season. The season was extended by three days to accommodate the completion of the full schedule.

1993/Strike Threat. During midseason discussions (usually in the press), the players threatened to strike on September 1, but nothing came of it.

1994/Lost Season and World Series.

"They're like a guy driving around lost but congratulating himself that he's making good time."— Bob Costas on the owners during the 1994 strike.

"Both owners and players are broadly disdained by fans increasingly disinclined to regard baseball as oxygen — essential. But fans, at first marginally partial to the owners' side, increasingly understand that the owners, or a controlling cabal of them, are the aggressors, demanding large changes in the status quo of baseball's compensation system and that the players struck defensively to avoid unilateral imposition of changes by ownership."— Columnist George Will.

"This has all the elements of a Greek tragedy, but the fans have to remember that the owners didn't go out on strike and didn't force the players to go out."— Owners' representative Richard Ravitch, who received less than 5% of the vote when he ran for mayor of New York in 1989.

The players went on strike for 52 days starting on August 12, 1994. The season and the World Series were canceled on September 14, resulting in the loss of 669 regular season games and the postseason. It was estimated by the union that the owners lost gross revenue of $600–$800 million; or $400–$500 million after deducting for player salaries.

The 1994–1995 Dispute in a Nutshell.

"We try every way we can to kill the game, but for some reason nothing nobody does never hurts it."— Tigers manager Sparky Anderson. Columnist George Will said later that "Sparky spoke too soon."

The owners wanted a salary cap that would split industry revenues evenly between owners and players and guarantee a minimum of $1 billion yearly for player salaries. The owners wanted to establish an "average" payroll; half the earnings of the teams divided by 28. After four years, individual club payrolls would have to be between 84% and 110% of the average. The owners also hoped to reduce free-agency eligibility from six years to four and eliminate salary arbitration.

The players initially wanted to return salary arbitration eligibility from three years to two; increase the minimum salary from $109,000 to $175,000–$200,000; require the owners to pay $7.8

million into the pension fund, which the owners withheld during the strike; add additional income for the play-offs and World Series; alter the termination pay for players cut in spring training; and other minor free agency rule changes.

The owners made their first serious proposal on June 14, 1994. They had several months within which to present it, and it was thought that the late presentation was intentional — the owners were trying to force a strike and break the union. The players met June 16, but no strike vote was taken. They voted later to strike after the games of August 11 and followed through with that decision, ending the season.

On November 17 both sides reconvened for negotiations, but the players broke off negotiations to study a new 102-page plan presented by the owners. They reconvened in late November as the December deadline for unilateral action by the owners loomed. By December 1994 the players and owners stood as follows:

Payroll Tax: The players proposed a flat payroll tax to generate $35 million for revenue sharing, which would have amounted to 5.02% in 1994.

The owners proposed a tiered tax plan that was not much different, except that the tax would be calculated on those franchises whose payrolls exceeded 112% of the industry average.

Salary Arbitration: The players proposed no change, with players with three or more seasons but less than six eligible, along with the top 17% by service time among those with between two and three years.

The owners wanted to create an escalating salary structure: $115,000 for first-year players; $175,000 for second-year players; $275,000 for third-year players and $500,000 for third-year players.

Revenue Sharing: The players proposed that visiting teams receive 25% of base price ticket money, up from 20% in the American League and about 5% in the National League. The total shared in 1994 would have been $57.5 million.

The owners proposed that the revenue (approximately $35 million under their system) would be shared by the nine teams from small markets.

Free Agency: Players proposed eligibility at six years.

The owners proposed eligibility for players with four or more seasons, but less than six, to become restricted free agents, with their current clubs given 10 days to match an offer. There would be no change in the system for players with six or more seasons in the league.

Under the owners' proposal, projected player salary growth was between 7% and 14% by 2001 depending on revenue growth: from $1.2 billion in 1994 to a minimum of $1.635 billion in 2001 (7%) to $2.607 billion (14%).

Last Play of 1994.

"Baseball games are won and lost because of errors — and this will go down as the biggest 'E' of all. 1994 — the season that struck itself out." — Former commissioner Peter Ueberroth.

A's pinch hitter Ernie Young struck out against Randy Johnson of the Mariners to end the season late on August 11.

Cancellation.

"In order to protect the integrity of the Championship Season, the Division Series, the League Championship Series and the World Series, the 28 Clubs have concluded with enormous regret that the remainder of the 1994 season ... must be cancelled and that the Clubs will explore all avenues to achieve a meaningful, structural reform of baseball's player compensation system in an effort to ensure that the 1995 and future Championship Seasons can occur as scheduled and uninterrupted." — Part of the owners'

resolution of September 14, 1994, canceling the remainder of the season.

Foreign Players. The Players Association approached the U.S. Labor Department to force the Immigration and Naturalization Service (INS) to refrain from issuing visas for foreign players. When the Department of Labor certified the strike on December 8, 1994, it prevented any foreign players from being strike-breakers. The move had no effect on players from Puerto Rico and the U.S. Virgin Islands (which had one player in the Major Leagues in 1994, Midre Cummings of the Pirates).

Federal Mediator. William J. Usery was appointed by the White House on October 15, 1994, to mediate the dispute. He was 71 and a former union organizer and labor secretary under Gerald Ford. Usury was paid $60,000 per *month* for his unsuccessful efforts.

Unfair Labor Practice. On October 31, 1994, the owners filed an unfair labor practice grievance with the National Labor Relations Board (NLRB). They claimed that players Bobby Bonilla, John Franco and Scott Kamieniecki made threats of violence against anyone who crossed a picket line to play ball.

Unemployment Benefits. New York and Rhode Island (the latter with no Major League team) are the only two states to provide unemployment benefits to striking workers, so only the Yankees and Mets players were able to collect.

Lawsuit. In March 17, 1995, New York radio station WABC filed a lawsuit against the Yankees, seeking $10 million in damages for the club's breach of contract for using unknown and unskilled **Replacement Players.** The suit was dropped on April 6, 1995.

Rules. Players received no salary during the strike, even if they were on the disabled list. They also did not receive credit for Major League service during the work stoppage, but such credit is usually negotiated in favor of the players when a strike ends. In this instance the end of the strike did not result in a new collective bargaining agreement, so this was not resolved when the players came back (it was later, in their favor).

Special privileges such as automobiles and personal gear end during a strike. Performance bonuses are prorated if earned. Bonuses contained in contracts for winning an award must be paid. Greg Maddux received $50,000 for winning a third straight Cy Young Award in 1994.

Managers and Coaches. Managers and coaches continued to be paid during the strike because they were under league contracts, even though they fell under the pension and benefit plan and are members of the union.

Strike Fund. The players created their $200 million strike fund ($175 million in some sources) by stockpiling their earnings from licensing royalties generated from merchandise sales coordinated by Major League Baseball. The players earned almost $100 million in 1993 alone. Each Major League player was scheduled to receive $100,000 from the licensing fund in the absence of a strike, but because of the potential strike it was decided by the union to pay only $5,000. It was estimated that each player would have received close to $200,000 for the 1994 sales. The first checks were mailed to the players in September 1994.

Lost Wages. A player making the Major League average of $1.2 million lost $355,776 in salary during the 1994 portion of the strike ($6,976 per day).

Fan Poll.

"Long live organized labor. It's time the players were freed from the yokes that bind them to multimillion-dollar contracts, eight-month work years, mansions and Mercedes. Free them from having to work in beautiful stadiums, from per diems, lucrative endorsements, paid medical and retirement benefits and, of course, from celebrity status. We cannot tolerate an employer who insists that his employees labor in such unjust conditions. Oppressed workers struggled so that ballplayers could ascend from lowly millionaires to struggling multimillionaires."—Ted Duffy in a letter to *Sports Illustrated* during the strike.

In a poll in August 1994 when the strike began, 39% of fans backed the owners and 32% backed the players. By January 1995 the owners were at 50% and the players had dropped to 28%. Eighteen percent of fans said "neither" and 2% said both.

Replacement Players. Teams began holding tryouts for replacement players in early January 1995. On January 13 Major League clubs released a set of rules to cover those players. Replacement players were to receive the proposed Major League minimum salary of $115,000 and receive $5,000 signing bonuses, payable April 16. Three players on each club could sign for a maximum of $275,000 each, provided they had three years of Major League service. If they made an Opening Day roster, they were to receive another $5,000, payable May 1. Players were to receive $20,000 in termination pay if they were released when the strike ended or if replaced by a union player. None of the contracts were to be guaranteed, and none could contain award or performance bonuses.

In early 1995 polls, fans were generally willing to attend Major League games featuring replacement players. Each team was allowed to carry 32 replacement players and could pick 25 to be used in any game. There would be no disabled list. Players could be traded, sent to the minor leagues or assigned to the commissioner's office "talent pool," all without clearing waivers.

Replacement players were on Major League rosters and played exhibition games through the last Saturday of spring training. The Orioles refused to field a replacement club, in part because owner Peter Angelos wanted to preserve Cal Ripken's consecutive game streak. After a federal judge ruled that the owners had violated federal law by their negotiating tactics, the owners immediately terminated the replacement player contracts and the regular players opened spring training for three weeks without a contract.

The only severance the replacement players were entitled to was the original $5,000 bonus they received for signing contracts and their spring training expense money. Had they played even one regular season game, the replacements were guaranteed at least another $25,000 in bonuses and the Major League minimum salary of $668.61 a day.

The Cardinals paid the $25,000 anyway and other clubs paid from $2,000 to $5,000 per man. In contrast, the Expos gave their players a travel bag and a game jersey. The Reds gave their players garbage bags to haul away their equipment, but 30 of the 32 received minor league assignments.

After the strike ended, many replacement players were signed to minor league contracts. On occasion during the 1995 season a replacement player was brought up to the Major Leagues, which created a prickly situation among the players who had been out on strike. The first replacement player in a Major League game was 23-year-old Red Sox outfielder Ron Mahay. He debuted on May 21, 1995, and apparently was not ostracized by his teammates. In contrast, the Padres players voted not to allow a replacement player onto their roster and the club complied. The presence of Joel Chimelis with the Giants caused so much disruption that he was sent down to Class AAA the next day.

Eighteen replacement players appeared on Major League rosters in 1995. In early 1996 the Players Association refused to allow the players to join the union and share in the licensing royalties. Reliever Brendan Donnelly was a member of the Angels' 2002

championship team, but he was unable to share in any of the licensing fees earned by the Players Association because he was barred from the union. He, like other non-union players, is also barred from participating in the pension plan. In response, in 2003 a San Diego fan took up a petition and obtained 798 signatures urging the union to accept Donnelly. The union rejected the petition.

Donnelly capped his career by getting the win for the American League in the 2003 All-Star Game. He received more votes from players, coaches and managers than any other reliever except Eddie Guardado of the Twins.

Two years after being a replacement player, Matt Herges was still shunned by his teammates.

In spring 1997 the Yankees announced that three replacement players who made the roster would receive 1996 World Series shares of $25,000 each and World Series commemorative rings. The decision by owner George Steinbrenner was criticized by the Yankee players who went out on strike. The replacement players were Dale Polley, Dave Pavlas and Matt Howard.

As of May 2000 the following replacement players were on Major League rosters: Benny Agbayani and Rick Reed, Mets; Trenidad Hubbard, Kerry Ligtenberg, Keith Lockhart, Braves; Cory Lidle and Damian Miller, Diamondbacks; Keith Osik and Rich Loiselle, Pirates; Matt Herges, Dodgers; Joe Slusarski, Astros; Shane Spencer, Yankees; Jeff Tam, A's; Donne Wall, Padres.

NLRB Ruling. On March 31, 1995, the National Labor Relations Board ruled that the owners had violated federal labor laws in carrying out their bargaining. The NLRB issued an injunction against the owners, something the players were unsuccessful in obtaining in 1981. As a result, the earlier collective bargaining agreement was reinstated pending further negotiations and the players voted to resume play. However, the owners had the option of continuing the impasse by ordering a lockout. At least 21 of the 28 owners had to vote for a lock-out for it to be put into effect. They did not exercise that right.

Owner/Player Differences. By the time the strike ended, the issues were pared to a few, but they were significant. The owners wanted a 50% tax on payrolls above $44 million. The players wanted the threshold to be $50 million but left the tax rate at 25%. Based on the 1994 payrolls, the players' plan would have required six teams to pay $4.7 million each in taxes ($28.2 million). The owners' plan would have caused 11 teams teams to pay a total of $33 million.

Post-Strike.

"So that's it. Guilt over the 232-day baseball strike. Players. Owners. They're trying to get back on our good side. Two hundred and eighty-six million letters of apology, one for every Canadian and U.S. citizen, might have been a start, but the players and owners have decided to make peace in their own way. Owners roll back prices to 1958 levels and invite Little Leaguers to throw out the ceremonial first pitch. Players discover the things kids wave under their noses are pens, not switchblades, so they are pausing to sign something other than seven-figure contracts."—Sportswriter Michael Farber.

In mid–1995 Randy L. Levine was appointed the new head negotiator for the owners. Levine had been the chief negotiator for the State of New York. In late 1996 a new ***Collective Bargaining Agreement*** was finally signed.

Financial Losses. See ***Profits, Losses and Expenses***.

2002 Negotiations. In 2002 another season was threatened by a proposed strike that had been the primary subject of Major League Baseball for the entire season, and on August 16, 2002, the Players Association announced a tentative strike date of August 30 if an agreement could not be reached with the club owners. Two weeks later, on August 30, 2002, the players and owners agreed to a contract that prevents the players from going out on strike (see *Collective Bargaining Agreements*).

During the acrimonious labor negotiations that year, Reds general manager Jim Bowden compared union boss Donald Fehr to the September 11 terrorists, prompting outrage from many corners, and Bowden apologized profusely.

Umpire Strikes. See *Umpires—Strikes*.

Personal Strike.

"They keep saying we're all supposed to be a family here. If you're a family, you don't send your children to Cleveland."— Red Sox pitcher Bill Lee staged a one-day strike in 1978 over teammate Bernie Carbo's trade to the Indians. He was fined $533, equal to one day's pay. He then asked them to triple the fine and give him the weekend off.

In 1990 Red Sox outfielder/first baseman Mike Marshall staged a one-day strike to protest the club's failure to pay his wife's traffic ticket that she received outside the stadium.

During spring training 2002, Derek Bell of the Pirates staged "Operation Shutdown," when he determined that manager Lloyd McClendon was not treating him fairly and that he should not have to compete for one of the outfield slots. The club shut Bell down by cutting him. He left baseball and focused on running his nightclub in Florida; which then added strippers as part of the menu.

When Nomar Garciaparra took over at shortstop for the Red Sox, an unhappy John Valentin staged a one-day work stoppage and demanded to be traded.

Japanese League. See *Japan—Strike*.

Strikes and Strikeouts

"Few who know [Steve Carlton] doubt that, barring accidental injury or onslaught of disease, Carlton will be striking out batters long after Nolan Ryan, his rival in total strikeouts, has called it quits."— The opinion of one sportswriter who wrote off Ryan a bit too soon. Ryan lasted five years longer than Carlton and struck out 1,578 more batters.

"He got him looking for something he wasn't looking for."— Berra-esque broadcaster Rex Hudler on a called third strike against Scot Shields.

Early Rules.

"[T]he so-called three strikes allotted the batter are a great snare and delusion. In point of fact it is only two strikes, for he is allowed to miss the ball only twice, but nobody but the batter ever thinks of that. The third time he misses it he is out."— Paul Gallico splitting hairs in *Farewell to Sports* (1938).

In very early games batters received four strikes. After the third strike, the umpire gave a warning of "good ball," meaning that the batter must swing at the next strike.

Called Strike.

"Rudy didn't care; he kept pitching them in to Guerra, and the Rockhill batters kept walking back to their dugout, shrugging their shoulders and saying nothing…. He had not only pitched a *perfect* game, but he had struck out twenty-seven consecutive batters. Not once during the entire game did a Rockhill player even swing at one of his pitches."—"Naked to the Invisible Eye," by George Effinger (1973), about a pitcher whose mind power could force batters not to swing at his pitches.

By 1859 or 1860 new rules required umpires to call strikes, even if a player did not swing. This prevented pitchers from tiring out after throwing so many pitches.

Hidden Count. In 1893 manager Harry Wright suggested that umpires keep the ball-strike count secret. He reasoned that this would increase offense by forcing batters to swing at more pitches.

Strike/Foul Tip. In 1895 a strike was assessed on a foul *tip*, but not on a foul ball. The difference between a tip and a foul ball was within the umpire's discretion.

Strikes/Foul Balls. In 1901 the National League first ruled that any foul ball hit prior to two strikes would be a strike. The rule was adopted by the American League in 1903. This change was made in part because of the ability of Roy Thomas to foul off balls indefinitely. The Philadelphia Phillies outfielder led the league in base on balls seven out of eight years in the prime of his career from 1900 through 1907.

The new foul ball/strike rule changed batting averages dramatically, from .280 in 1902 to .240–.250 from 1903 through 1909. Not surprising, strikeouts increased by 50%.

Third Strike Rule. In the late 1860s a dropped third strike required a runner to run to first base, which often caused double plays. The rule was modified to require the runner to go to first only if the base was unoccupied. This rule still exists.

Scorebook Designation. In 1872 M.J. Kelly, editor of the *DeWitt Base Ball Guide*, chose the letter "K" to designate a strikeout in his scorebook. His reasoning was that the last letter of the word "struck" was a "K." KS is a swinging strikeout; KC is sometimes used to identify a called third strike. The designations are sometimes simply "K" for called strike and a backwards "K" for a swinging strike. "K 2–3" signifies a dropped third strike and a forceout at first base on the batter. See also *Scorecard*.

Catchers' Rules. Until 1880 catchers were not required to catch the third strike on the fly to record a strikeout. The new rule forced catchers to move up behind the plate to catch the third strike before it bounced.

Assist. Pitchers were given an assist on all strikeouts for one year in 1885.

Official Statistic. In the 1890s the New England League became the first league to count a hitter's strikeouts as an official statistic, 20 years before Major League Baseball.

Frequency. Strikeouts decreased by 50% between the 1892 and 1893 seasons, principally because the pitching mound was extended to its present 60'6". Strikeouts were less frequent prior to the 1930s because players choked up on the bat more often with two strikes and used thicker bats. By the 1940s and early 1950s, despite the presence of many power hitters, batters did not strike out nearly as frequently as their successors of the 1960s and later. For example, in 1950 only two players struck out more than 100 times, Roy Smalley, Jr. (not a home run hitter), and Gus Zernial. In 1990 there were 42 players who struck out 100 or more times. By 2000 there were 58.

Strikeout/Walk Ratio.

"Throw strikes. Home plate don't move."— Satchel Paige.

From 1920, when the lively ball was introduced permanently, until 1951, the ratio of strikeouts to walks were within 10% of each other virtually every season. However, a gradual increase in strikeouts began during the 1950s. By the 1990s, there were almost 70% more strikeouts than base on balls each season.

The best all-time ratio among hitters belongs to Elmer Valo of the 1952 A's, who had 101 walks and 16 strikeouts. The worst was by John Bateman, a catcher for the Astros in the 1960s. He struck out 103 times while drawing only 13 walks. See also *Base on Balls*.

Team/Pitcher Strikeouts. The 2001 Cubs (1,246) and 2001 Yankees (1,266) set league records for most strikeouts recorded in a season by a team's pitching staff.

Most Strikeouts by Pitcher/Career.

"I was just in the right place at the right time." — Cesar Geronimo, who was the 3,000th strikeout victim of both Bob Gibson in 1974 and Nolan Ryan in 1981.

"He just blew it by me. But it's an honor. I'll have another paragraph in all the baseball books. I'm already in the books three or four times." — Rickey Henderson on being Nolan Ryan's 5,000th victim.

Nolan Ryan ended his career near the end of the 1993 season when he suffered a torn ligament in his pitching elbow. He finished with 5,714 strikeouts and had 11 strikeout titles. Ryan's most frequent victims were Claudell Washington with 36 and Freddie Patek with 31.

Ryan struck out Danny Heep of the Mets on three pitches in the 6th inning of a game on July 11, 1985, for his 4,000th strikeout. He struck out Rickey Henderson on August 22, 1989, for his 5,000th strikeout. Steve Carlton ended his career in 1988 in second place (later passed) with 4,136 strikeouts. Ryan also holds the record of 22 seasons with 100 or more strikeouts, breaking Don Sutton's record of 21 years. Ryan had more strikeouts after age 35 than Hall of Famers Lefty Grove, Sandy Koufax, Juan Marichal and Jim Palmer each had in their careers.

In 2003 Roger Clemens became only the third pitcher to reach 4,000 strikeouts, in the same game as he won his 300th. He struck out Edgar Renteria on June 13, 2003. On July 5, 1998, Clemens struck out Randy Winn of the Devil Rays for No. 3,000. Clemens moved into second place on May 5, 2004, with his 4,138th strikeout to pass Carlton. He did it while moving to 6–0 with the Astros after coming out of a short-lived retirement.

Randy Johnson struck out his 3,000th batter on September 10, 2000 and passed Steve Carlton in September 2004. Johnson struck out batter No. 4,000 on June 29, 2004. He struck out eight in the game, including Jeff Cirillo of the Padres for the milestone whiff. Johnson reached 4,000 faster than any other pitcher in history, with a strikeouts-per-nine-innings ratio of 11.12 over 17 seasons. Ryan was at 9.55 over 27 seasons.

George Brunet struck out 3,175 minor league batters to go along with 921 Major League strikeout victims.

Fastest to 500. Reds Reliever Rob Dibble reached 500 strikeouts in only 368 innings, the fastest in history. He flamed out with a sore arm in late 1993 after five strong seasons and never pitched effectively again.

Fastest to 1,000. Cubs pitcher Kerry Wood reached 1,000 strikeouts in 134 games, the fastest of any pitcher in Major League history.

Most Strikeouts by Pitcher/Season.

"It cut the middle of the plate.
You missed because you swung too late.
You'll have to learn before you're older.
You can't hit the ball with the bat on your shoulder."
— Third strike call by Bill Byron, known as the singing umpire during his National League career between 1913 and 1919.

Nolan Ryan holds the record for most strikeouts in a season, with 383 for the Angels in 1973. He struck out Twins first baseman Rich Reese on the last pitch of the season on September 27, 1973, to break a tie with Sandy Koufax. Koufax struck out 382 for the Dodgers in 1964. Ryan struck out at least 300 batters in six different seasons. Randy Johnson had season totals of 364 in 1999 and 372 in 2001.

For many years prior to Koufax, it was thought that Bob Feller held the season strikeout record of 348, set in 1946 for the Indians. A close check of the statistics at a later date revealed that in 1904 A's pitcher Rube Waddell set the record at 349. Waddell's record was known in 1946, but the number was thought to be lower. A 1946 newspaper article about Feller's record made reference to the "official record" of 343 by Waddell, but noted that the "unofficial record" of 349 was derived from "recent records." The discrepancy arises from the box scores for Waddell's 46 games in 1904. Of that total, 38 are in agreement as to the number of strikeouts. In the other games, various box scores create differences giving totals of 352, 349, 348 and 347. He is now credited with 349.

In 1999 Pedro Martinez of the Red Sox struck out over 300 batters to join Randy Johnson as the only pitchers to strike out 300 hitters in each league.

300/Consecutive Seasons. Randy Johnson struck out over 300 batters five seasons in a row beginning in 1998.

In 1998 Curt Schilling of the Phillies became only the fifth pitcher to strike out 300 batters in consecutive seasons.

Double Digits. Randy Johnson struck out 10 batters in a game for the 200th time in mid-2004, the second player to reach that milestone. Nolan Ryan had 215 such games.

Teammates. In 2002 Diamondbacks pitchers Randy Johnson and Curt Schilling became the first teammates to strike out 300 batters in the same season.

Cubs fireballer Kerry Wood shows off the form that resulted in 20 strikeouts in a game on May 6, 1998, in only the sixth start of his career.

Strikeouts per Game/Average. In 1995 Randy Johnson set a new Major League record when he averaged 12.3 strikeouts per nine innings by a pitcher who qualified for the ERA title (usually that would exclude relievers). Johnson's average is over 11.00 through 2003. That record was broken by Kerry Wood in 1998, with an average of 12.58. Other top pitchers:

9.55 Nolan Ryan
9.28 Sandy Koufax
8.86 Sam McDowell
8.67 Roger Clemens
8.37 J.R. Richard

Reliever Strikeout Ratio. In 1999 Astros reliever Billy Wagner set the record of 14.95 strikeouts per nine innings for pitchers with at least 50 innings pitched. After the season he signed a $10.5 million, three-year deal with the Astros. Reliever Eric Gagne of the Dodgers raised the bar in 2003 when he averaged 14.98 strikeouts per nine innings (see also **Relief Pitchers**). Wagner set an all-division college record with 19.1 strikeouts per nine innings for Ferrum College in 1992.

Most Strikeouts/Season/Rookie Pitcher. Herb Score struck out 235 batters in his rookie season, breaking the record of 227 set by Grover Cleveland Alexander in 1911. Dwight Gooden set a new record in 1984 when he struck out 276 during his rookie season. Kerry Wood of the Cubs struck out 233 during his 1998 rookie season.

Most Strikeouts by Pitcher/Game.

"I always thought that record would be broken. Records like that are easier to break than the endurance type. All it takes is one phenomenal outing against a certain type of ballclub — a free-swinging team, not a bunch of contact hitters. Will someone break Clemens's record [of 20 in a 9-inning game]? It's a possibility, but it might also stand for fifty years." — Nolan Ryan quoted in Stanley Cohen's *A Magic Summer — The '69 Mets* (1988).

In 1933 Dizzy Dean raised the modern Major League strikeout record when he struck out 17 Cubs on July 30. He increased the record from 16, held by Noodles Hahn, Christy Mathewson, Rube Waddell and Nap Rucker. Dean's record of 17 was broken by various pitchers over the next 50 years. The 20th century progression of strikeout records for nine-inning games after Dean:

18	October 2, 1938	Bob Feller
19	September 15, 1969	Steve Carlton
20	April 29, 1986	Roger Clemens

Both Feller and Carlton lost their games.

21 Strikeouts. Senators pitcher Tom Cheney struck out 21 Orioles in 16 innings on September 12, 1962. He had 12 strikeouts after nine innings. He fanned every Baltimore starting player except first baseman Boog Powell, and struck out five other batters three times each.

20 Strikeouts. Red Sox pitcher Roger Clemens first set the current Major League record for a nine-inning game, striking out 20 Mariners on April 29, 1986. The *Boston Globe* noted that it had not been done in the previous 150,000 games in Major League history.

Clemens matched his record on September 18, 1996, striking out 20 Tigers in a 4–0 win that required 156 pitches.

Cubs phenom Kerry Wood, later sidelined by an elbow problem, struck out 20 batters in his sixth Major League start, on May 6, 1998. He gave up only one hit, an infield single by Ricky Gutierrez in the 3rd inning that may well have been scored as an error if it had occurred later in the game. Wood became only the second pitcher to strike out the number of his age (Bob Feller was 17 when he struck out 17). Wood struck out the first five batters of the game and later struck out seven in a row. When he went down with the injury, he had struck out 233 batters in 166⅔ innings.

On May 8, 2001, Diamondbacks pitcher Randy Johnson struck out 20 Reds in Arizona's 4–3 win over Cincinnati in 11 innings. Johnson recorded all 20 in his nine innings of work, but did not get credit for tying Clemens and Woods because the game went into extra innings. The Reds scored two in the top of the 11th, but the Diamondbacks scored three in the bottom of the inning, culminating in a bases-loaded walk given up by reliever Danny Graves.

19 Strikeouts.

"We'll be right back to wrap things up and talk about David Cone's 19 strikeout performance, after this word from Bud Black [sic]." — Mets broadcaster Ralph Kiner, who meant Bud *Beer*, not the pitcher, after Cone got the last out of the last game of the 1991 season for the New York Mets (see below).

Twenty-one-year-old Charles Sweeney of the Providence Grays struck out 19 Boston Red Stockings on June 7, 1884. Boston recorded a triple play in the 5th inning but lost the game 2–1. Sweeney might have struck out many more but for the rules then in effect. For example, foul tips caught on the first strike were recorded as outs.

Sweeney's record was tied one month later by Hugh "One Arm" Daily of Chicago in the Union Association. On July 7, 1884, he beat the Boston Unions 5–0. Under modern rules, Daily would have been credited with 20 strikeouts — his catcher dropped a third strike and the runner made it to first base.

Luis Tiant struck out 19 for the Indians against the Twins in 10 innings on July 3, 1968. In the 10th inning with runners on first and third with no outs, he struck out the side. Cleveland scored in the bottom of the inning for the 1–0 victory.

Steve Carlton of the Cardinals struck out 19 Mets on September 15, 1969, but lost 4–3 as Ron Swoboda hit two two-run homers, in the 4th and 8th innings. Carlton struck out the side four times in the game, including the 9th inning. Both of the home run pitches to Swoboda came on two strikes, and Carlton later acknowledged that he was challenging the hitters in order to get the strikeout record.

Tom Seaver of the Mets struck out 19 Padres on April 22, 1970, including 10 straight. Al Ferrara was the first and last victim (to end the game). Seaver won 2–1 and pitched a two-hitter. It was his 13th straight win over two seasons and his third straight that year.

Nolan Ryan of the Angels struck out 19 batters three times during the 1974 season. On June 15, 1974, he struck out 19 Red Sox in 15 innings as the Angels won 4–3. Cecil Cooper struck out six times. Ryan struck out 19 Red Sox on August 12, 1974, in a 4–2 win. When he struck out No. 19, a woman ran on the field and gave him a hug. On August 20, 1974, Ryan struck out 19 in a 1–0, 11-inning loss to the Tigers.

On the last day of the 1991 season, David Cone of the Mets struck out 19 Phillies in a 7–0 win. He struck out the first six batters of the game. The last Phillies batter, Dale Murphy, reached out and poked a weak ground ball to the shortstop to prevent Cone from tying the Major League record. The day before Cone had been publicly accused of sexual misconduct (see also **Sex**).

On June 24, 1997, Randy Johnson of the Mariners struck out 19 A's at the Kingdome, but lost 4–1. Mark McGwire hit a homer off Johnson that reportedly traveled 538 feet. On August 8, 1997, Johnson pitched a five-hit shutout in a 5–0 victory over the White Sox. He again struck out 19 to become the first pitcher ever to record 19 strikeouts twice in a season.

18 Strikeouts. Bob Feller struck out 18 Tigers in a losing effort on October 2, 1938, at age 19. The Indians lost 4–1 as the Tigers got seven hits.

On June 14, 1952, Warren Spahn of the Braves struck out 18 Cubs in a 3–1, 15-inning loss.

On August 31, 1959, Sandy Koufax set a new National League record for nine innings with 18 strikeouts against the Giants in a 5–2 win. He also struck out 18 Cubs in a 10–2 victory on April 24, 1962.

Jim Maloney struck out 18 Mets in the first of his two no-hitters, on Father's Day, June 14, 1965, but lost 1–0 in 11 innings. This game is no longer considered a no-hitter because Maloney gave up a lead-off home run to Johnny Lewis in the 11th inning.

Don Wilson of the Astros struck out 18 Reds on July 14, 1968. He won 5–4 in 10 innings and struck out eight in a row during one stretch.

Ron Guidry of the Yankees struck out 18 on June 17, 1978, in a 4–0 win over the Angels. He struck out 15 in the first six innings.

Bill Gullickson, who later became a junkball pitcher when his arm gave out, set a rookie strikeout record when he fanned 18 on September 10, 1980, as the Expos defeated the Cubs 4–2.

Ramon Martinez of the Dodgers struck out 18 Braves in a three-hit, 6–0 shutout on June 4, 1990.

Randy Johnson of the Mariners struck out 18 Rangers in a 3–2 win on September 27, 1992. Johnson had thrown 160 pitches and was exhausted when he asked not to pitch the 9th inning.

On August 25, 1998, Roger Clemens struck out 18 in a 3–0 win over the Royals. He allowed three hits and no walks while pitching for the Blue Jays.

Strikeouts/Consecutive Games. On May 11, 1998, Kerry Wood set a new Major League record when he struck out 13 batters. Those strikeouts, combined with the 20 he had in his previous outing, gave him 33 over two games to set the record.

On May 14, 2001, Randy Johnson of the Diamondbacks struck out 12 to tie Luis Tiant's American League record with 32 strikeouts over two games, though he did not do it in conjunction with one of his 20-strikeout games. Others to strike out 32 over two games are Nolan Ryan in 1974 and Dwight Gooden in 1984.

Japanese Leagues. In 1995 Koji Noda, pitching for the Orix BlueWave of the Pacific League (managed by Bobby Valentine), struck out 19 Chiba Lotte Marines but gave up the tying run in the bottom of the 9th inning and did not get the win. He broke the record of 17.

Negro Leagues. On August 7, 1930, at Kansas City versus the Monarchs, Negro Leaguer Smokey Joe Williams of the Homestead Grays hooked up with Chet Brewer in a legendary duel. In 12 innings Brewer gave up just four hits while striking out 19. Incredibly, Smokey Joe was even better, striking out 27 while allowing just a single hit. Oscar Charleston scored the lone run in the 12th, giving Homestead and Williams the 1–0 victory.

College. While playing for Columbia College in New York, Lou Gehrig struck out 17 and lost 5–1 against Williams College on April 18, 1923.

Relief Pitcher. On July 19, 2001, the Diamondbacks beat the Padres 3–0 in a game suspended the day before because of a light tower malfunction. Randy Johnson struck out 16 batters in seven innings of relief of starter Curt Schilling. That number broke Walter Johnson's Major League relief record, set on July 25, 1913. Johnson struck out seven straight during the game.

Strikeouts/Pitching Debut. Bob Feller struck out a then–Major League rookie record 15 batters in his Major League debut at age 17 in 1936. He struck out 17 in a game three weeks later.

Dodger pitcher Karl Spooner struck out 15 in his debut during the last week of the 1954 season. He also struck out six in a row during the game, a two-hit shutout against the Giants. He pitched a 1–0, five-hit shutout in his next game, striking out 12. During spring training the following year, he hurt his arm and lost his

fastball. He finished the season with an 8–6 record and never again pitched in the Major Leagues.

On September 5, 1971, Astros pitcher J.R. Richard struck out 15 Giants in his Major League debut, a 5–3 complete game win.

In his first Major League game on April 12, 1962, Pete Richert of the Dodgers struck out four Reds in one inning as catcher John Roseboro dropped a third strike.

In his debut for the Orioles on September 1, 1978, Sammy Stewart struck out seven consecutive batters.

Most Strikeouts Professionally/Game.

"Well, what happened was more incredible than that. The first twenty-six Tycoons he faced went down on strikes: seventy-eight strikes in a row. There had not even been a foul tip—either the strike was called, or in desperation they swung at the ozone. Then, two out in the ninth and two strikes on the batter.... Strike-out number twenty-seven."—Philip Roth on mythical pitcher Gil Gamesh in *The Great American Novel* (1973).

On May 5, 1952, Ron Necciai of the Bristol Twins threw a no-hitter and struck out 27 batters in a 7–0 victory over the Welch Miners in the Class D Appalachian League. One strikeout victim reached base on a passed ball. Necciai had a 1–6 record for the Pirates in 1952, his only Major League season.

In 1948 in a 15-inning game in the Class C Canadian-American League, Schenectady Blue Jays pitcher Tommy Lasorda struck out 25 Amsterdam Rugmakers, a since-broken professional record.

According to the 1909 *Reach Guide*, on July 25, 1908, Corry and Falconer battled 23 innings before Falconer won 3–1. Winning pitcher and future Major Leaguer Hugh Bedient struck out 42 of the 69 men he faced.

Most Strikeouts/World Series Game. Bob Gibson struck out 16 Tigers in Game 1 of the 1968 World Series. Opposing pitcher Denny McLain called it the best pitching performance he had ever seen.

All-Star Heroics. In the 1934 All-Star Game Giants pitcher Carl Hubbell struck out, in order, Babe Ruth, Lou Gehrig, Jimmie Foxx, Al Simmons and Joe Cronin.

Season Consistency. In 1946 Bob Feller struck out every batter at least once who qualified for the batting title.

Consecutive Strikeouts.

"There's an old baseball superstition about jinxing a pitcher in a situation like this, but I might mention that Ramirez has struck out the first six men to face him. The record for consecutive strikeouts is eleven, held by Gaylord Perry of the old Cleveland Indians. That mark was set the last year the Indians played in Cleveland, before their move to New Orleans."—"Naked to the Invisible Eye," fiction by George Effinger (1973).

Tom Seaver struck out 10 straight Padres on April 22, 1970, with Al Ferrara the last victim. Seaver broke the modern record of eight, held by a number of players. Before the game, Seaver received the Cy Young Award from the previous season.

On May 4, 1981, Yankee reliever Ron Davis struck out eight against the A's.

On June 17, 2001, Royals pitcher Blake Stein struck out eight straight Brewers, and 11 in 5⅔ innings, but the Brewers beat Kansas City 5–2. The only other American Leaguers to strike out eight in a row are Nolan Ryan (twice) and Roger Clemens.

Ron Davis' reliever record was approached by Diamondbacks pitcher Randy Johnson, who struck out seven straight for the National League record during a seven-inning relief effort on July 19, 2001.

Sandy Koufax had a high of five straight. In Kerry Wood's 20-

strikeout performance in May 1998, he had strings of five and seven straight batters struck out.

Mickey Welch of Troy in the 19th century National League is reported to be the first pitcher to strike out the first nine batters in a game played August 28, 1884.

On June 23, 2004, Luis Ramirez of Class A Aberdeen (Md.) struck out 12 consecutive batters, a professional record.

Strikeouts/Start of Game. On September 23, 1986, Jim De-Shaies of the Astros struck out eight straight Dodgers to start the game, the modern Major League record. On May 28, 1986 Joe Cowley of the White Sox struck out seven straight Rangers to start the game, to set the American League record.

Consecutive Strikeouts/World Series. In Game 5 of the 1919 World Series, Hod Eller of the Reds struck out six straight White Sox, none of whom were among the infamous Black Sox.

Most Strikeouts/Inning/4. In 1926 it was ruled that a pitcher would not be credited with a strikeout if the batter reached base on a wild pitch on the third strike. The rule was later changed, creating the possibility of four strikeouts in an inning.

Over 30 pitchers have struck out four batters in an inning because a catcher has dropped a third strike and allowed the batter to reach first base.

On September 16, 1998, rookie Kirt Ojala of the Marlins struck out four batters in the 4th inning of a 3–2 loss to the Expos. He became the fourth pitcher to strike out four consecutive batters in an inning. He gave up a passed ball to the second victim, Vladimir Guerrero.

On August 15, 1999, Chuck Finley of the Angels became the first player to strike out four batters in a game on two occasions. He did it on May 12, 1999, and both times it was in the 1st inning. He also did it for a third time on April 16, 2000.

On September 2, 2002, Kerry Wood had four strikeouts in the 4th inning against the Brewers.

Pitcher/Five Strikeouts/Inning. No pitcher has recorded five strikeouts in an inning in a Major League game. Joe Niekro and his knuckleball gave catcher Cliff Johnson fits in a 1977 exhibition game in which Niekro had five strikeouts in an inning.

In the minor leagues, Beloit Brewers pitcher Kelly Wunsch struck out five batters in an inning on April 15, 1994. Ron Necciai fanned five in an inning when he struck out 27 on May 5, 1952. John Perkovitsh of the Wisconsin Rapids accomplished it against Oshkosh in a Class D Wisconsin State League game on May 17, 1946. Scott Gardner of the Fayetteville Generals did it in 1995.

In July 2004 Class A Lancaster (Calif.) JetHawks pitcher Mike Schutz struck out five batters in the 7th inning after two batters reached first on third-strike wild pitches (Schutz allowed five runs in the inning).

Fewest Strikeouts/Doubleheader. On August 28, 1926, Emil Levsen of the Indians pitched two complete-game victories over the Red Sox, 6–1 and 5–1. He did not strike out a batter in either game.

Nine Pitches/Three Strikeouts.

"He could throw a lamb chop past a wolf."—Writer Bugs Baer after Lefty Grove struck out Babe Ruth, Lou Gehrig and Bob Meusel on nine pitches.

"They were all fastballs right down the middle. I couldn't understand why he didn't hit every one ten miles. But he didn't. So I kept throwing 'em."—Scott McGregor after striking out Reggie Jackson in three straight at-bats on nine pitches.

Striking out the side on nine pitches has been accomplished over 35 times in the Major Leagues, with Pedro Martinez becoming the 35th in the 1st inning on May 18, 2002.

Sandy Koufax is the only National League pitcher to do it twice.

Bob Feller did it twice for the Indians in the American League. Nolan Ryan was the first pitcher to do it in both leagues.

The last American League pitcher before Martinez to do it was Jeff Montgomery on April 29, 1990. He was the first pitcher to do it in relief since Jim Bunning in 1959. The last National Leaguer to do it was Urgueth Urbina on April 4, 2000, for the Expos in a 10–4 loss to the Dodgers.

The only rookies to strike out the side on nine pitches are Hod Eller (1917), Sloppy Thurston (1923), Nolan Ryan (1968) and Alan Ashby (1991).

Rube Waddell struck out three batters in an inning on nine pitches in his first American League game for the A's in 1902. He defeated Baltimore 2–0 and gave up two hits while striking out 13. Legend has it that Waddell once called in his outfielders in a Major League game and then struck out the side; the fact is that he did it a few times only in exhibitions. Another source reported that in 1902 Waddell pitched in all six games in a series against Detroit. In the last inning of the last game he called in his outfielders and struck out the side.

Dropped Third Strike. Eddie Collins quit the A's at age 44 but stayed with the team as captain and coach. His experience came in handy when he was coaching at third base during the 1931 World Series against the Cardinals.

Jimmie Foxx of the A's walked, which was followed by a fly out, strikeout and another base on balls. This left men on first and second. With two strikes on Jimmy Moore, Foxx broke for third on the pitch. The ball was in the dirt, but the batter swung for strike three. Catcher Jimmie Wilson caught the ball and threw to third base to get Foxx. The game was thought to be over because of the swinging strike; but Collins ran out and yelled to the runners to stay on their bases and for the batter to run to first. This was the correct response because the rule at the time provided that if a ball bounced in the dirt a batter had to be tagged out or the ball thrown to first for the force play. Even though Collins was alert on the play, the pitcher got out of the jam and the Cardinals won the game.

See **_Passed Balls_** for the story of Mickey Owen's dropped third strike in the 1941 World Series.

Fewest by Hitter. Joe Sewell replaced Ray Chapman at shortstop for the Indians after Chapman was killed by a pitch to the head in 1920. Sewell struck out only 114 times in 14 years while hitting .312. This was an average of slightly over eight times per year and only once every 62 at-bats, an .016 percentage. Others who rarely struck out were Wee Willie Keeler at .019 and Lloyd Waner at .022.

Ted Williams struck out an average of only 41 times during his 17 relatively complete seasons. Yogi Berra was even better, striking out an average of only 25 times while hitting 358 home runs. In five of his 25-or-more home run seasons (1950, 1951, 1952, 1955 and 1956), Berra had fewer strikeouts than homers, and during those years he totaled 142 home runs with just 105 strikeouts.

Most by Hitter/Season.

"Strike three! San Jose, California. The garden spot of America."—Strikeout call of umpire Jack Sheridan.

Adam Dunn set a new Major League record with 195 strikeouts for the Reds in 2004. He was still productive, as he batted .266 with 46 home runs and 102 RBIs. Until Dunn, Giants outfielder Bobby Bonds held the Major League record with 189 strikeouts in 1970 (and 187 the year before). He still managed to bat .302 with 26 home runs and 77 base on balls. Rob Deer came close to the record in 1987 when he struck out 186 times for the Brewers. He hit .238 with 28 home runs. Mo Vaughn struck out 181 times in 2000 for the Angels, while hitting 36 home runs. Preston Wilson struck out 187 times in 2000 for the Marlins, hitting 31 home runs.

Brewers shortstop Jose Hernandez struck out 188 times in 2002 while hitting only 24 home runs. Manager Jerry Royster benched him for the club's final four home games so he would only be humiliated on the road. Milwaukee fans had cheered derisively and held aloft "K" signs. He struck out 185 times the year before, with only 24 home runs.

Most By Hitter/Game. Sam Horn struck out six straight times on July 17, 1991. Cecil Cooper struck out six times against Nolan Ryan during Ryan's 19-strikeout performance on June 15, 1974. Cooper managed a double in the 15th inning. Horn and Cooper tied the record set in 1913 by Browns pitcher Carl Weilman. On September 9, 1998, Toronto's Alex Gonzalez struck out six times in 13 innings. Several players have struck out five times in a game.

Most By Hitter/Two Games. In July 1997, Jose Canseco of the A's tied the Major League record, held by many, with eight strikeouts in two consecutive games against the Brewers and A's.

Postseason Futility. In 2003 Yankee second baseman Alfonso Soriano set a postseason record with 26 strikeouts.

Most/Team/Game. On June 8, 2004, the Brewers struck out 26 times in 17 innings against the Angels, tying the Major League record.

Most/Two Teams/Game. On July 12, 1997, the Blue Jays and Red Sox combined to strike out 29 times in nine innings, one short of the Major League record. Toronto's Roger Clemens struck out 16 of his former teammates in a 3–1 win by the Blue Jays. The next day, on July 13, 1997, the Mariners and Rangers combined for 31 strikeouts to break the record of 30, set by the Mariners and A's on April 30, 1986. Randy Johnson of the Mariners had 14 strikeouts in seven innings as his club lost 4–2 to the Rangers.

In 1964 the Mets and Giants combined for 36 strikeouts in a 23-inning game, the National League record.

Pitchers' Batting Futility. Jerry Koosman struck out 62 times in 91 at-bats his rookie season, the most by a National League pitcher since 1900.

Future evangelist Billy Sunday supposedly struck out the first 14 times he batted in the Major Leagues in May 1883.

Cubs pitcher Bill Hands set the modern Major League record when he struck out in 14 straight official at-bats in 1968. Hands finished his career with a batting average of .078.

Cardinals pitcher Jose DeLeon tied the record when he struck out 14 straight times in 1991.

Senators pitcher Jim Hannan holds the American League record with 13 straight strikeouts on his way to a lifetime .091 batting average during the 1960s. Hannan later wrote his master's thesis on the Major League Baseball pension system.

Career Futility. Lefty Grove struck out 593 times in his career, most by a pitcher.

Reggie Jackson is the all-time futility leader, with 2,597 strikeouts over his 21-year career. Somewhat surprisingly, Andres Galarraga was second at 2,000 through 2003. Sammy Sosa was third going into the 2004 season, at 1,977, and passed Galarraga early in the year.

Home Run Champion. New York Giants slugger Johnny Mize hit 51 home runs in 1947 to lead the league. He struck out only 42 times, the least by any home run champion with more than 40 home runs.

Most Strikeouts/No Home Runs. In 1991 shortstop Manny Lee of the Blue Jays became the first player in Major League history to strike out over 100 times and not hit a home run.

World Series/Alexander and Lazzeri.

"In the twilight of this gloomy and dripping Sunday afternoon 38,000 hard-boiled New Yorkers tumbled down out of the stands in the Yankee Stadium bawling the name of Grover Alexander, the ball player who won't behave because he doesn't have to, because old Aleck had just done something that would have brought a lump as big as an egg into the neck of a police captain."—*Chicago Tribune* sportswriter Westbrook Pegler after Alexander struck out Tony Lazzeri to save Game 7 of the 1926 World Series against the Yankees.

"Hell, I'd rather him pitch a crucial game for me drunk than anyone I've ever known sober. He was that good."—Cardinals manager Rogers Hornsby on Alexander.

Probably the most famous strikeout in baseball history was Tony Lazzeri's strikeout on a pitch by Grover Cleveland Alexander in the 7th inning of Game 7 of the 1926 World Series. With two out and the bases loaded, Alexander came in to preserve the Cardinals lead and held on for the save.

Alexander was a legendary drinker whose problem may have been exacerbated by his epilepsy (or vice versa). In the 1926 World Series, Alexander won Game 6 for the Cardinals and supposedly drank heavily that night in celebration, knowing that he would not pitch the next day in Game 7. Nevertheless, Cardinals manager Rogers Hornsby called for Alexander to pitch to the Yankee second baseman in the crucial situation.

Hornsby supposedly went out to the bullpen to look into Alexander's eyes before he called him into the game. Passing the test, Alexander came in to strike out Lazzeri with the bases loaded and pitched two more innings to save a 3–2 win. The strikeout pitch was a low-breaking curve ball on the outside corner of the plate. Back-up catcher Bob O'Farrell swore that Alexander was asleep in the bullpen when he got the signal for Alexander to warm up.

Team/Hitter Futility. The 1991 Tigers set a then-team season record with 1,149 strikeouts, breaking the 1986 record set by the Mariners. The big four for the Tigers in strikeouts and home runs were Rob Deer (175/25), Cecil Fielder (151/49), Mickey Tettleton (131/31) and Travis Fryman (149/21). Deer recorded his 1,000th strikeout in only 868 games, the fastest pace ever. He surpassed Dave Kingman, who reached 1,000 in 950 games.

The 1996 Tigers raised the bar with 1,268 strikeouts, and then the 2001 Reds' hitters broke the record with 1,272.

The 2002 Cubs ended the season leading the Major Leagues in both strikeouts by their pitchers of opposing batters (1,333) and by the club's batters (1,269). It was the first time this had been accomplished by a team since Boston of the Union Association in 1884.

Bet. Dizzy Dean once bet that he could strike out Vince DiMaggio four times in a game. After the first three strikeouts, his catcher obliged his request to drop a pop foul. Dean then struck out DiMaggio for number four and $80. Joe DiMaggio recalled the incident differently; the catcher caught the foul ball.

Soft Touch. Tigers infielder Harry Heilmann recalled that when he reported to the club, Walter Johnson was known to ease up on rookies in the late innings of games he was leading. Sure enough, Johnson let the first two rookies hit singles off him, then Heilmann approached the plate. According to Heilmann, Johnson said, "sorry kid, but you're the tying run." Heilmann looked at three fastballs and the game was over.

Consistency. Yogi Berra holds the Major League record by not striking out in 105 straight plate appearances.

Strikeout Humor.

"A man has no right to be sillier than God intended him to be."—Dodger manager Wilbert Robinson in 1931, putting an end to pitcher Clyde "Pea Ridge" Day's habit of celebrating an inning-ending strikeout by flapping his arms and screaming out a piercing hog call.

In April 1994 Marlins reliever Yorkis Perez struck out Barry Bonds. He was so excited that he pumped his fist in the air and ran to the dugout. It was only the first out of the inning, prompting teammate Orestes Destrade to comment: "I was dumbfounded. I guess he figured striking out Barry Bonds is worth three outs."

See also *Eephus Pitch* for a few silly strikeouts.

Strongest Players

"Hank Bauer was the strongest player I ever saw. He had muscles in his breath." — Mickey Mantle.

"Watching Frank Howard come out of the Dodger dugout to start a game is like watching the opening scene of a horror movie. You know the bit: There's an explosion under a polar ice cap some place, the earth rumbles and opens up, and out of it comes this Thing." — Jim Murray. Howard was 6'7" and at least 255 pounds and was known as "Hondo" or "The Capital Punisher" (the latter while with the Senators).

"Mantle and Jimmie Foxx hit it hard, but you're the strongest guy I've ever seen play this game. I'd have hit a thousand home runs if I'd been as strong as you." — Ted Williams to Frank Howard.

"Harmon Killebrew has enough power to hit home runs in any park — including Yellowstone." — Orioles General Manager Paul Richards.

"No man in the history of baseball had as much power as Mickey Mantle. No man. You're not talking about ordinary power. Dave Kingman has power. Willie Mays had power. Then when you're talking about Mickey Mantle — it's an altogether different level. Separates the men from the boys." — New York Yankees manager Billy Martin.

"He has muscles in his hair." — Lefty Gomez on 6-foot, 195-pound slugger Jimmie Foxx.

"He has the body of a Greek goddess [sic]." — Sparky Anderson on Jose Canseco.

Ted Kluszewski. Kluszewski, who wore trademark sleeveless jerseys with the Reds, was 6'2" and 225 pounds and was one of the strongest players of the 1950s.

Brian Downing. One of the strongest players, pound-for-pound, may have been Downing of the White Sox, Angels and Rangers. The gym rat beefed up his 5'10", 170-pound frame to become a decent power hitter; he hit 20 or more home runs six times between 1982 and 1988.

Bo Jackson. The *Football* star packed 222 pounds of muscle on his 6'1" frame.

Mo Vaughn. Vaughn may have been the strongest player of the 1990s, though Jose Canseco was in the running (steroid enhanced, perhaps; as were several others).

Stunts

"It's in my contract. I'm not allowed to jump over cars anymore. Can't jump fences, either." — Devil Rays outfielder prospect Joey Gathright, who agreed to eliminate one of his favorite pastimes, leaping over cars in a single bound.

"This spud's for you. Bres." — Dave Bresnahan, grandnephew of catcher Roger Bresnahan, who was catching in August 1987 for the Class AA Eastern League Williamsport Bills, an Indians farm team. He told the home plate umpire he had a problem with his glove and ran to the dugout. After he came back behind the plate and the game resumed, he tried to pick off the runner on third base.

He threw the "ball," which actually was a peeled potato, into left field and then tagged the runner coming home with the real ball. The umpire was extremely upset by the ploy and called the runner safe.

Bresnahan was fined $50 by the no-nonsense club and released immediately. A sense of humor by the Bills management might have been appropriate: The team was in seventh place, 26 games out of first place with only four games remaining. In his fourth year in the minor leagues, the 25-year-old Bresnahan was batting .149 in 52 games during what was to be his last season.

The day after the stunt, Bresnahan brought 50 potatoes to his manager, saying in a note that he could not pay the fine, but invoking the quote above. The team warmed up to the stunt a few nights later — after receiving national publicity — and staged a Potato Night at which fans were admitted free if they brought a potato.

Horse Races. See *Fastest Runners* for descriptions of races around the bases between players and horses.

Bill Veeck. See *Midgets — Eddie Gaedel*, *Opening Day*, *Practical Jokes and Pranks* and *Promotions*.

Washington Monument.

"No figure, not even that of [Ted] Williams, was as dominant on those Senator teams as the Washington Monument." — Thomas Boswell about Frank Howard in *How Life Imitates the World Series* (1982).

The real Washington Monument opened in December 1884 (erroneously 1886 in many sources) and thereafter became a source of contention as to whether a ballplayer could catch a ball dropped from the 540-foot observation deck (504 feet in some sources — transposed numbers no doubt; and 555 in other sources, but that's to the tip, above the observation deck).

Shortly after the monument opened, a hotel clerk named H.P. Burney tried to convince ballplayers that they could catch a ball thrown from the top. It was a number of years, however, before any ballplayer attempted it.

Cap Anson of the Chicago White Stockings thought that catcher William F. (Pop) Schriver could do it, and Schriver obliged in August 1894. Pitcher Clark Griffith was chosen to drop the ball. After a practice drop to see how hard the ball was coming, Schriver caught one on his first attempt.

Catcher Gabby Street was reputed to be able to "catch anything" because he handled fastball pitcher Walter Johnson with the Senators for "many" years (except that he had caught Johnson for less than a year when he performed his Monument stunt). Street's greatest fan was Pres Gibson, a Washington newspaperman and drama critic. Gibson thought that Street could catch a ball dropped from the top of the Monument.

On August 21, 1908, Gibson went to the top of the Monument with 13 baseballs and dropped them to Street one by one. After figuring out the wind currents and the proper place to drop from, Street finally caught the last ball dropped. Some sources reported incorrectly that Street was the first to do it.

On August 24, 1910, White Sox catcher Billy Sullivan caught three of 23 balls dropped from the Monument by teammates Ed Walsh and Doc White.

One source noted that it was not the speed of the ball that made it difficult to catch. The ball was coming at 140 feet per second, slower than a fastball. Instead, the knuckling effect caused by a physics principle increased the difficulty.

Grapefruit. There are variations on this story involving former catcher Wilbert Robinson of the Dodgers. During a 1920s spring training at Daytona Beach, Florida, Robinson, then the Dodger manager, attempted to catch what he thought was a ball dropped from an airplane. The pilot and dropper was one of the foremost women pilots of her time, Ruth Law. She claimed that she intended to drop a baseball but that she forgot the ball as she climbed into the cockpit. An obliging workman at the airport gave her a grapefruit out of his lunch pail. The grapefruit landed on Robinson, and he thought he was bleeding when it splattered on him. Robinson always suspected that Casey Stengel was behind the stunt, but Stengel denied any involvement.

Another version of this incident attributes it to co-conspirators Stengel and Dodger trainer Frank Kelly. In this version, Stengel allegedly provided the grapefruit to Kelly, who dropped it on Robinson from an altitude of 400 feet while a passenger with an unidentified pilot (Ruth Law?).

Dropped Balls. On August 20, 1938, Indians third baseman Ken Keltner attempted unsuccessfully to catch a ball dropped from the 675-foot Cleveland Terminal Tower. Another version places the height at 700 feet and gives credit to Indians catcher Hank Helf, who supposedly caught the ball.

On August 3, 1939, former Indians catcher Joe Sprinz tried to catch a ball on San Francisco's Treasure Island dropped 800 (or 1,000) feet from a blimp. On the fifth attempt he caught the ball, but the impact broke his jaw.

Golf Balls. See *Golf*.

Lone Ranger. Bill Veeck once disguised White Sox pitcher Early Wynn as the Lone Ranger and had him ride onto the Comiskey Park infield on horseback to execute rope tricks for the crowd.

Atlanta Embarrassments. In the 1970s the Braves staged ostrich racing and a contest in which owner Ted Turner and Phillies pitcher Tug McGraw pushed baseballs down the baseline with their noses. Promotions man Bob Hope (no relation to the comedian) staged these fiascos, as well as the wet T-shirt contest that inspired two women to remove their tops for the crowd.

Outfield Relief. Rick Bosetti reached his goal of relieving himself in the outfield of every Major League ballpark in which he played.

Flying Walenda. Tightrope walker Karl Walenda once walked a 640-foot span across steel cables at Veterans Stadium in Philadelphia.

Long Walk Home. In 1989 former Pirates pitcher and then-broadcaster Jim Rooker commented idly during a game that if the club lost to the Phillies after leading 10–0 that he would walk back to Pittsburgh. The Pirates lost 15–11. After the season he completed the 315-mile trek in a 12-day fundraising effort dubbed "Rook's Unintentional Walk."

Parachute. During Game 6 of the 1986 World Series between the Mets and Red Sox (the Bill Buckner game), a parachutist landed on the field during the game. The perpetrator was Mike Sergio, a "bandit" skydiver who once jumped illegally off the World Trade Center. He and his cohort who piloted the plane dodged air traffic controllers in order to position themselves over Shea Stadium for the drop. He landed down the third base line to the roar of the crowd. He received a standing ovation while being led off the field, and Mets starting pitcher Ron Darling gave him a high five.

Silver Dollar. Strong-armed pitcher Walter Johnson once threw a silver dollar across the Rappahannock River in a reprise of the stunt performed by George Washington.

Good Aim. 1970s pitcher Pedro Borbon often showed off his ability to throw strikes to the plate from the center field warning track.

Throwing Out the First Pitch. See *Throwing Out the First Pitch*.

Submarine Pitches See *Pitches*

Substitutions

See also *Pinch Hitters*, *Pinch Runners* and *Relief Pitchers*.

Rules. Through the early 1870s player substitutions were not allowed. When they were finally allowed, the rule had to be refined so that a new player could come into the game only when the ball was dead. The rule purportedly was instituted in part because Mike "King" Kelly once came off the bench as a substitute for catcher Charlie Ganzel while the ball was in play in order to catch a foul ball.

For the National League's first season in 1876, substitutions were allowed only after the 4th inning and a substitute runner was allowed only if chosen by the opposing team. In 1880 no substitutions were allowed after the 8th inning.

In 1884 substitutions were allowed only with the consent of the opponent. In 1888 no substitutions were allowed. In 1889 one replacement was allowed at any time with the approval of the other team. In 1890 two substitutions were allowed with approval.

In 1891 the rules were modified to allow substitutions consistent with modern rules. Until 1907 in the American League and 1912 in the National League, pinch hitters, pinch runners and other substitutes often were not credited with a game played.

No Return Rule. Throughout all the rule changes, a player who left the game was not allowed back in. An exception occurred in 1952. Cubs manager Phil Cavarretta agreed to allow Pirates catcher Ed Fitzsimmons to reenter the game after he had pinch-hit for catcher Clyde McCullough. McCullough was injured late in the game and the Pirates had no other player capable of playing the position.

In 1958 Major League Baseball carried on a debate over allowing repeat substitutions of a player once he had been removed from a game, but nothing came of it.

None Used. During the 1910 and 1913 World Series, the A's never used a substitution of any kind.

Most Players Used.

The Mariners and Rangers set a Major League record on September 25, 1992, by using a combined total of 54 players after the rosters were expanded for the last month of the season. The Mariners used 11 pitchers (tying the Major League record) and the Rangers used five. The Mariners won 4–3 in 16 innings.

On September 2, 1986, the Cubs and Astros used 53 players in an 18-inning game for the National League record.

On September 29, 2002, the Mets and Braves used 45 players in a nine-inning game, tying the Major League record set by the Cubs and Expos on September 5, 1978.

On September 21, 2003, the A's and Mariners used an American League record 44 players in a nine-inning game.

On September 16, 2000, the Tigers beat the Red Sox 7–6. The two teams combined to use a then-American League record-tying 42 players.

Subway Series

The first known written reference to this term is in a 1941 Willard Mullin cartoon. The regular season subway series ended when the Giants and Dodgers moved west in 1958. It resumed with interleague play between the Mets and Yankees, and then a Subway World Series occurred in 2000 when the Mets and Yankees squared off.

Suicide

"Your desperate attempt to commit suicide is deeply lamented." — Frankie Frisch in a telegram to Casey Stengel after Stengel was hit by a cab while managing the Braves. The mock feud continued for years.

"Don't cut my throat. I may want to do that myself later." — Casey Stengel at the barber for a shave while managing the Yankees during a bad stretch of games.

"This isn't a psychiatric ward. Nobody's going to commit suicide. Nobody's beating their wives. It's not as drastic as people make it out to be." — Tigers outfielder Dmitri Young on the 2003 club's 37–105 record at the time.

Harry Pulliam. The *National League President* committed suicide on July 28, 1909, after coming under pressure from National League owners and suffering from some form of depression. He shot himself through the right eye, and the bullet passed completely through his skull. He did not die immediately, and he was even able to knock the telephone receiver off its cradle. After being put under arrest for attempted suicide, he told an arriving coroner that he had not been shot. He then slumped over and died.

Major League Players and Managers. There have been 8–10 suicides per decade of current or former professional ballplayers and managers, although there have been fewer after the 1960s. Gunshot has been the primary method of choice, with razor number two. A sampling:

Edgar McNabb. McNabb was a pitcher for Baltimore in 1893 with an 8–7 record. On February 28, 1894, he committed suicide after shooting his girlfriend. She was married to the president of the Pacific and Northwest Leagues and died shortly after the shooting.

Frank S. "Terry" Larkin. Larkin pitched principally in the National League in the late 1870s, with three good years of 29, 29 and 31 wins. He was struck in the head by a batting practice line drive by Cap Anson late in the 1879 season. As a result of the accident he became mentally deranged. After failing in a comeback attempt (0–5 with Troy in 1880), he spent most of the rest of his life in and out of asylums. After a number of unsuccessful attempts, he committed suicide in a Brooklyn mental hospital by slashing his throat on September 16, 1894.

Marty Bergen. On January 19, 1900, National League Boston Red Stockings catcher axed his family to death and, depending on the source, committed suicide either by slitting his throat or slashing his wrists.

Win Mercer. Mercer was primarily a pitcher at the turn of the century. On January 12, 1903, after pitching for the Tigers in 1902, he committed suicide by gas in San Francisco a few days after he was appointed manager of the team at age 28. He left a note warning of the evils of women and gambling.

Bob Lankswert. Lankswert played one game for the Louisville Colonels in 1899 but had a 15-year minor league career in the South and Midwest. While warming up in the mid–1890s he was struck in the temple by a ball thrown by teammate Pat Daniels. Lankswert suffered severe hearing loss and exhibited strange behavior at times over the rest of his career. On January 10, 1907, he swallowed carbolic acid and died at the age of 41.

Chick Stahl. The Red Sox player-manager committed suicide at age 34 by ingesting carbolic acid at the club's training camp in Indiana on March 28, 1907. He had taken over as manager the previous year, guiding the team to a last-place finish. He resigned as manager only three weeks before the suicide, remaining only as team captain. Stahl died under what was described as "mysterious" circumstances, and his wife died 18 months later. It has been sur-

mised that he and his wife were drug addicts, though it appears he was also manic depressive and friends were not surprised at the suicide. On his deathbed Stahl said: "Boys, I couldn't help it. It [drugs] drove me to it."

Ed Strickland. On January 2, 1909, the minor league pitcher shot himself and his girlfriend.

Dan McGann. The former National League first baseman shot himself on December 13, 1910. It was two years after he last played in the Major Leagues, but he had been playing minor league ball and was scheduled to play for Louisville in 1911. He was shot through the heart, but foul play was not suspected. His brother had committed suicide earlier in the year.

Eddie Hohnhorst. Hohnhorst played in 1910 and 1912 for the Indians, but his professional career ended after the 1913 season. He became a policeman and was involved in a shootout in 1915 in which he killed a suspect. On March 27, 1916, he quit his job and shot himself on a street corner at age 31.

Patsy Tebeau. The former National League infielder and manager killed himself on May 15, 1918, at age 53.

Benny Frey. Frey was sent down to the minor leagues by the Reds in 1937 at age 31. He refused to report and committed suicide the following November.

Willard Hershberger. The Reds catcher cut his throat and died in his hotel bathroom after he had substituted for Ernie Lombardi at catcher on August 3, 1940. He was 30 years old. Baseball lore has it that Hershberger thought his bad pitch selection had cost the Reds the pennant (it did not), as they were leading 4–3 with two outs in the bottom of the 9th inning and lost on a home run. His death in early August was far too early in the season to have had an effect on the race.

It appears that this game was the final event that drove him over the edge after years of depression and hypochondria. Shortly before his death he revealed part of his problems to manager Bill McKechnie, who swore never to tell anyone. True to his word, McKechnie died in 1965 without revealing the secret.

Investigators found a number of uncashed paychecks in Hershberger's pocket, and it was speculated that there had been a murder. More recent accounts make it reasonably clear that there was no foul play. The Reds won the World Series that season and voted Hershberger's mother a full share of over $5,000.

Hershberger's father had committed suicide, as did two of the father's cousins. The man who discovered Hershberger in the hotel, a local friend, committed suicide in 1961. Even the team's other starting catcher, Ernie Lombardi, unsuccessfully tried to commit suicide in 1953 by slashing his throat with a razor. Lombardi lived until 1977 and was elected to the Hall of Fame in 1986.

Charlie Hollocher. In 1918 the rookie star repeatedly complained of stomach ailments, but x-rays and other examinations revealed no problem. He played over the next few years with sometimes excellent results (lifetime .304 hitter) but repeatedly missed games. In 1924 he went home early in the season to "recuperate" — as he had done the year before. He never returned despite announcing a comeback repeatedly over the next few years. He committed suicide in August 1940 at age 44.

Johnny Mostil. One source reported that the White Sox outfielder attempted suicide with a razor and then died of neuritis on March 9, 1927. He must have returned from the dead, because he returned to the White Sox late that season and played two more years. He did try to commit suicide on that date but he lived until 1970. It was rumored that he was having an affair with the wife of teammate Red Faber. Mostil tried suicide after Faber found out and threatened to kill him.

Hugh Casey. The Dodger pitcher committed suicide in 1951, two years after he retired following a nine-year Major League career (see also *Boxing* for his relationship with another suicide victim, *Ernest Hemingway*).

Don Wilson. The Astros pitcher, who pitched two no-hitters in the 1960s, committed suicide by carbon monoxide poisoning on January 5, 1975, at age 30. He had posted an 11–13 record the previous year and had been expected to return to the Astros for another season.

Donnie Moore. Moore was a relatively successful relief pitcher in the 1980s and signed a multi-million dollar contract with the Angels. His career was overshadowed, however, by one pitch he made in the 1986 ALCS. The Angels were leading the Red Sox in the series 3 games to 1.

In the top of the 9th inning of Game 5, the Angels were leading and a victory would have put them in the World Series for the first time. On a two-strike pitch, Dave Henderson of the Red Sox homered off Moore and the Red Sox went on to win the game in extra innings. The Red Sox then swept the last two games in Boston for the pennant.

Moore's career quickly deteriorated due to arm injuries, and he left the Major Leagues in 1988. Shortly after he was cut by a minor league club and despondent over family problems, he shot himself in July 1989.

College Player. In the 1960s a USC pitcher hurt his arm shortly after being drafted. He walked out to the school's Bovard Field and shot himself on the mound.

Umpire. In January 1995 umpire-turned-author and broadcaster Ron Luciano committed suicide by carbon monoxide poisoning. He had umpired for 11 years in the American League until his retirement in 1980.

Bad Thoughts. In the mid–1990s Jose Canseco received counseling for his thoughts of suicide during his divorce.

Minor Leagues. On June 11, 1950, at Buff Stadium in Houston, an unemployed laundry route manager took a seat in the television booth during a Houston Buffalos game. He pulled out a pistol and shot himself in the right temple.

Japanese Baseball. Katsutoshi Miwata of the Japanese Pacific League's Orix Bluewave had been unable to persuade 18-year-old pitcher Nagisa Arakaki, the team's No. 1 draft pick, to sign. Miwata, 53, jumped to his death from an 11th floor apartment in Okinawa's capital of Naha. Miwata had been under pressure to rebuild the team after losing the Japan Series in 1997 and then suffering through a nightmare season in 1998. Miwata had been a top high school baseball player. He was drafted in the first round by the Hankyu Braves in 1970 and played professional baseball in Japan until 1973.

Good Planning. In 1938 a Cincinnati woman left a suicide note providing for the distribution of her All-Star Game tickets that she had not yet received.

Nagging Wife. An Atlanta cab driver shot himself to death after his wife told him to turn off the television and go to work. He did, just missing Henry Aaron's 715th home run.

Sullivan Award (1930–)

"Based on the qualities of leadership, character, sportsmanship, and the ideals of amateurism, the AAU Sullivan Award goes far beyond athletic accomplishments and honors those who have shown strong moral character." — The Sullivan Award website.

The Sullivan Award is presented annually to the amateur athlete of the year. The award is named after James E. Sullivan (1862–1914), founder of the Amateur Athletic Union (AAU). Sullivan was the head of Albert Spalding's publishing business, American Sports Publications Company, and a member of the 1907 Mills Commission that looked into the *Origins of Baseball*. He also is credited with developing the modern children's playground and organized recreation. He was on the New York Board of Education between 1908 and 1912 after he and others opened the first public playground in New York City in 1906. He was commissioner of athletics for the 1904 St. Louis Exposition and a director of the 1904 Olympic Games, and was commissioner of three other Olympic Games.

Pitcher Jim Abbott is the only baseball player to win the award. He won it in 1988 after leading the Americans to a gold medal in the *Olympic Games*.

Sun

"I found myself looking into the sun and I couldn't see anything. You know how it is." — Pitcher Billy Loes on how he lost a batted ball in the sun in a Dodger-Yankee World Series game. He must not have touched it, because he was never charged with an error in four World Series appearances.

"Turner pulls into second with a sun-blown double." — Broadcaster Jerry Coleman.

"The sun has moved." — During a 1950s World Series, Yankee infielder Gil McDougald claimed that the sun was not setting in the same place as in prior years and was causing glare problems. McDougald was right because the end of daylight savings time had been moved to late October instead of late September, and the sun was one hour lower in the sky.

See also *Glasses* — **Sunglasses**.

Ballpark Construction. Modern ballparks must be constructed so that the sun sets behind third base and so that the "sun field" is right field, the field least likely to receive fly balls (because there are fewer left-handed hitters). At Toronto's old Exhibition Stadium, which was also used for football, the sun set at the left field foul pole.

In 1920 Babe Ruth played right field for the Yankees in the Polo Grounds (before Yankee Stadium was built) and left field in other ballparks. He did not particularly like the sun field (right field) and did not want to adjust to the other ballparks during his first full year in that position. When Yankee Stadium opened in 1923, Ruth moved to right field because left field was the sun field in that ballpark.

Lost Ball. During Game 4 of the 1929 World Series, the Cubs led 8–0 before the A's scored 10 runs in the 7th inning and went on to win the game. The key to the inning was a three-run homer by Mule Haas over the head of center fielder Hack Wilson, who lost the ball in the sun.

Solar Eclipse. A total eclipse of the sun once forced cancellation of a game in Ventura, California.

Sunday Baseball

"I have seen Morris-dancing, cudgel-playing, baseball and crickets, and many other sports on the Lord's Day." — Complaint by the Reverend Thomas Wilson of Maidstone, in Kent, upset over ungodly Sunday activities in the 17th century.

"Sunday baseball is deplorably wrong in principle. But it must be admitted that this year the Sunday games have broken up the Sunday beer picnics. The breaking up of those picnics has materially lessened the number of crimes for the September Criminal

Court. Besides this, it must be recognized that young people can attend ball games on Sunday afternoon and still be able to attend church services in the evening with a clear mind, if not a clear conscience. But those who are out on drunken carousals are totally unfit for attendance at public worship. If it comes to a choice of the two evils, baseball is certainly the lesser." — Pennsylvania clergyman's 1907 pronouncement.

"Sunday has been a day of hypocrisy, pretense and falsehood. But no longer should it be a day of sorrow and restless idleness. There is no reason why, in the afternoon, the people should live under this black, bitter cloud of restraint." — A 1925 editorial in *The Sporting News* advocating Sunday baseball.

Ancient Prohibition. In 1553 at the Easter sessions of the court in Surrey, five men were indicted for playing stoolball on Sunday.

General Prohibition. Baseball on the "Continental Sabbath" was frowned upon during the 19th century and well into the 1920s in many locales.

The *Commercial Advertiser* of New York City carried a complaint on February 4, 1824: "A correspondent of ours calls the attention of the proper officers to the numerous boys who collect on the Sabbath, in the Park. They were last Sabbath quietly permitted to 'play ball,' and to amuse themselves in other exercises, without any interposition of the city authorities."

Given how cold it was at the time and how much ice there was in the city, according to local papers, it is unlikely that the boys were playing anything resembling true baseball.

National League. In 1876 the National League ruled that no league games were to be played on Sundays. In 1878 the league informally ruled that teams would be expelled for violating the prohibition against Sunday baseball, regardless of whether it was a league game being played.

In 1880 the National League formally voted to outlaw Sunday baseball of any kind in response to the Cincinnati club's having scheduled Sunday games in the past. As a result of the club's refusal to comply, it was expelled from the league.

St. Louis dropped out of the league after the 1886 season in protest of the Sunday ban, even though a local court ruled that Sunday baseball was not against the law.

In 1892 the National League finally began allowing teams to schedule Sunday games after it absorbed the American Association clubs. It was done during the split-season arrangement which tried to accommodate the unwieldy new 12-team league and stimulate fan interest. The league had absorbed the few remaining strong American Association teams and Sunday baseball was made a local option with the approval of the visiting team. The first Sunday game that season was on April 17, 1892, as home team Cincinnati defeated St. Louis 5–1.

The American League. The American League never had a formal prohibition against Sunday baseball. Restrictions were based solely on state or local prohibitions.

19th and Early 20th Century Problems. In the 1880s ministers affiliated with the "Good Citizen's League" went to ballparks and wrote down the names of spectators who frequented Sunday games. The ministers supposedly were tossed out of the parks.

On May 28, 1885, Joseph Andrews Sommers was arrested for playing Sunday baseball in Cleveland. He was convicted of the offense by a jury. The defense argued that the game had been played on Sundays for years without enforcing local laws. On appeal, the defense argued unsuccessfully that they were "playing" baseball, and that the players had a right to their "avocation."

The Ministers' Association and the Liquor League, "an unholy alliance," worked together to ban Sunday baseball in certain cities.

Ministers disapproved of Sunday ball because it conflicted with worship services; the Liquor League did so because it believed that Sunday baseball fans could go to bars and taverns instead. As a result of the alliance's efforts, the entire Cleveland and Washington teams were arrested in Cleveland on a Sunday in May 1897. Cleveland Spiders player Jack Powell was fined $5 and ordered to pay $153 in court costs. On June 19, 1898, a group of Cleveland Spiders players were arrested again while playing Sunday ball in Collinwood, Ohio.

In March 1897 in New York City, the Raines Law was passed, which formally prohibited Sunday baseball. This new Blue Law was part of the effort to absorb Brooklyn into greater New York as of January 1, 1898.

In 1900 a Presbyterian minister told his congregation that the Lord had assumed control of Pittsburgh and crippled its players for playing Sunday ball. A Baltimore Catholic priest approved of Sunday baseball in 1895, and a prominent Baltimore attorney publicly attacked the issue on the ground of separation of church and state.

In April 1909 the Yankees played a Sunday exhibition against Eastern League Jersey City in Jersey City, New Jersey. The clubs passed out cards asking the crowd to be quiet and not to cheer during the Yankees' 6–3 victory. The 1,000 fans in attendance complied with the request, but the Yankees took no chances and used a reserve player as the lead-off batter in case he was arrested by local police. The club also apparently did not charge admission, but rather had "donation boxes" placed at entrances.

For a few games early in the 20th century, to get around the prohibition against charging admission on the Sabbath, the Dodgers staged Sunday games in which they did not charge admission but sold scorecards for the same price as admission. Scorecards usually were five cents, but on Sunday the club charged from 25 cents to $1, depending on seat selection. The first game was played on April 17, 1904. There were four more such games in 1904 and five in 1905. The police did not intervene, but eventually the practice was challenged in court. Dodger owner Charles Ebbets won the first round and continued the practice for a few more Sundays until he lost on appeal.

On July 1, 1917, the Dodgers hosted another unsanctioned Sunday game against the Phillies. The club staged a benefit concert beforehand and charged admission. To get around the Blue Laws, no admission was charged for the late afternoon game against the Phillies. Owner Charles Ebbets and manager Wilbert Robinson were arrested and fined $250 for staging a Sunday game.

The Giants held their first nonlegal Sunday game on August 19, 1917, with no problems. In 1918 the Giants held an outdoor concert before a game, ostensibly to raise money for the war effort. Managers Christy Mathewson and John McGraw were arrested. One source reported that after magistrate Francis X. McQuade became a club official in 1919, he dismissed the charges.

The Yankees staged their first nonlegal Sunday game on June 17, 1917.

First Legal Sunday Games.

"I defy anyone to say that the morals of New York have been lowered since Sunday baseball was given to the people." — New York City mayor Jimmy Walker.

Each city handled Sunday baseball in its own way. It was a problem largely in the northeastern cities, as the less sanctimonious midwestern cities generally allowed Sunday ball. When Sunday baseball became the norm in virtually all cities, it was seen as a victory for the blue collar worker.

New York and Brooklyn. Among the last holdouts was New York City, which first formally allowed Sunday baseball in 1919.

Finally, New York state senator and former mayor Jimmy Walker introduced a Sunday baseball bill, which passed in time for the 1919 season (1920 in one source). The first legal Sunday game was played at Ebbets Field on May 4, 1919 (erroneously April 4 in many sources). The Dodgers defeated the Braves 6–2. The Giants also played their first Sunday game on that date, losing to the Phillies 4–3 in front of 35,000 fans. The Yankees played their first legal Sunday game on May 11, 1919, a 0–0 12-inning tie against the Senators.

Boston.

"Bostonians are known for the ability to endure the trials and tribulations associated with their local ball clubs and politicians. Local residents and fans can attest to one overriding parallel between the two institutions, and that is a consistent record of futility, disappointment, and illogical behavior demonstrated at the expense of the emotional well-being of Bostonians."— William E. Brown, Jr., in *The National Pastime*, on Sunday baseball in Boston.

The Braves played their first sanctioned Sunday home game on May 5, 1929. The first Sunday game played by the Red Sox at Fenway Park was on July 3, 1932. The Red Sox had played Sunday games at Braves Field as early as April 28, 1929 (and through June 1932) because Fenway Park was deemed too close to a church.

Pittsburgh and Philadelphia. The last state to allow Sunday baseball was Pennsylvania, which did so only after voters approved a public referendum in 1933. The first officially sanctioned Sunday game in Philadelphia was on April 29, 1934. The Dodgers defeated the Phillies 8–7. In 1903 the Phillies first agreed to play road games on Sundays.

Pirates owner Barney Dreyfuss claimed that Sunday games hurt Saturday attendance and consequently the Pirates were one of the last teams to schedule Sunday home games. The Pirates played their first Sunday game on the same date as the Phillies, April 29, 1934.

The A's played their first Sunday game on April 22, 1934. However, on August 22, 1926, the A's played one Sunday game when they obtained a temporary injunction prohibiting enforcement of the state law.

St. Louis, Cincinnati and Chicago. These cities allowed Sunday play in the 1880s or earlier, and all three clubs began league play on Sundays immediately after the National League lifted the ban in 1892. The St. Louis Brown Stockings hosted their first Sunday game on April 17, 1892. The Cincinnati Reds played their first officially sanctioned Sunday game on April 24, 1892. The Chicago White Stockings played their first Sunday game on May 14, 1893. The American League White Sox played their first Sunday game on April 22, 1900. Once the American League was recognized as a Major League, their first Sunday game was on April 28, 1901.

The American League Browns played their first Sunday game on April 27, 1902.

Cleveland. Cleveland prohibited Sunday baseball until 1911. The Indians played their first Sunday game on May 14 that season.

Detroit. It has been reported that the Tigers hosted their first Sunday games in 1910. However, their first Sunday game was played on April 28, 1901 (erroneously reported in some sources as August 18, 1907).

Washington. The Senators introduced Sunday baseball during World War I to accommodate government workers. Their first Sunday game was played May 19, 1918.

Zane Grey. In one of *Zane Grey's* early baseball novels, *The Shortstop* (1909), the Sunday baseball controversy was resolved by having businesses shut down on Saturday afternoons to allow laborers to attend games on that day.

Refusal to Play or Manage. Christy Mathewson and Leroy Pfund, who pitched one season in 1945, reportedly refused to play on Sundays (but Mathewson was arrested for it in 1917).

Much has been written about Branch Rickey's refusal to play ball on Sundays. He did not promise his mother that he would not play on Sundays, as widely reported. Rather, Rickey simply did not play on Sundays or even go to the park on that day as a show of love and respect for his mother's Methodist faith. He would have Jimmy Austin and a succession of others, including Burt Shotten, manage for him. Ironically, both his Cardinal and Dodger clubs of the 1930s and 1940s were the hardest-drinking and most boisterous in either league. Rickey apparently made one exception to his Sunday rule in April 1943, when the U.S. Treasury Department held a ceremony at a game to honor the Dodgers' war bond effort.

Radio. The Cardinals and Browns banned Sunday radio broadcasts in the early years of broadcasting.

Out of Town. Because of the prohibition against Sunday baseball, a number of teams scheduled home games outside their home city. For example, in 1898 the New York Giants played their first Sunday home game in Weehauken, New Jersey, to avoid the prohibition (see also *Home Teams*).

Sunday Night Game. The first Sunday night game was played on June 9, 1963. The Houston Colt 45's hosted the Giants.

Home Run Sunday. On June 20, 1948, Ralph Kiner hit a home run for the eighth straight Sunday.

Charlie Maxwell hit 40 of his 148 home runs on Sunday during his 14 years in the American League beginning in 1950.

Sunday Draw. Ted Lyons pitched 21 years for the White Sox. Late in his career he developed a knuckleball to save his ailing arm. Manager Jimmy Dykes began using Lyons only on heavily attended Sundays to save the arm and because of Lyons' popularity with the fans. This pattern continued for four years from 1939 through 1942 when Lyons entered the military.

Charlie Bevis, *Sunday Baseball: The Major Leagues' Struggle to Play Baseball on the Lord's Day, 1876–1934* (2003).

Sunglasses *See Glasses*

Superstition

"Superstitious people don't discuss their superstitions."— Rusty Staub.

"I only have one superstition. I make sure to touch all the bases when I hit a home run."— Babe Ruth.

"For five years in the minor leagues, I wore the same underwear and still hit .250, so no, I don't believe in that stuff."— Dusty Baker on superstitions.

"Superstition is good for a ballplayer. It has psychological effects. It keeps a player's mind revolving around baseball."— Lefty O'Doul, who often wore green suits for luck.

See also *Luck*.

Albino.

"'Don't try none of that on us. You're an albino and that's all there is to that,' says O'Reilly. 'You're gonna sit on the bench with us and we're gonna rub your head for luck. Albinos are luckier than hunchbacks; everyone knows that.'"— W.P. Kinsella in *The Iowa Baseball Confederacy* (1986).

Astrology. Pitcher Wes Ferrell was an astrology buff who always wanted his starting assignments to coincide with the proper alignment of the stars.

Bats. Ty Cobb brought a black bat to games in 1907 but never used it. It was there only for luck.

Nineteenth century catching star Buck Ewing had the batboy spit on his bat before each at-bat, which may or may not have contributed to a .311 lifetime average.

Orlando Cepeda supposedly only used a bat for as long as it produced hits. Once he made an out, it was time for a new bat.

Before the game in which he hit his 62nd home run to break Roger Maris's record, Mark McGwire held the bat that Maris used to hit his 61st and rubbed it against his chest.

On August 4, 1999, Angels batting coach Rod Carew decided to have every player in the lineup use the same bat as a way of loosening up the struggling team. Orlando Palmeiro struck out to start the game and he left the bat at the plate. Umpire Tim Tschida thought that Palmeiro was trying to show him up after the strikeout, so he ejected the leadoff hitter. Angels manager Terry Collins finally convinced Tschida that Palmeiro was only following Carew's plan, so Tschida changed his mind and reinstated Palmeiro. The Angels won, 4–3.

Black Cat.

"Rhubarb [a cat], enthroned in the owner's box, seemed to be fully aware of what was going on and what was expected of him. His tail jerked at regular intervals and his little elevator went up and down and up and down so the players could touch him. They touched him and went out and stole bases that were burglar proof; they bunted when bunting was insane and got away with it, and they swung when they should have bunted and knocked the ball out of radar range. Lardhead Lloyd, the astute Philadelphia manager, was fit to be tied."—H. Allen Smith in *Rhubarb* (1946), about a cat who owns a Major League baseball team and becomes a lucky charm by allowing the players to touch him.

"Don't worry, that cat ain't gonna get nobody out."—Cubs pitching coach Billy Connors after a fan threw a black cat on the field at Shea Stadium in 1984.

The Chicago White Stockings of the early National League deified a black cat named "Champion."

For a few weeks in 1955 the Red Sox used a plastic black cat as a good luck charm, but it had no effect. The players then buried it in their bullpen (complete with headstone) and then lost to the Indians 19–0.

A black cat walked across the dugout roof of the Cubs at the start of their 1969 collapse to the "Miracle" Mets.

Boston Red Sox Curse.

"This was, after all, the postseason from hell, what with all the talk about the ghosts in New York, the curse in Boston and the dead goat in Chicago. Forget a scorecard. You needed a cauldron and a clove of garlic to follow these playoffs."—Tom Verducci in 2003, when the Red Sox were beaten by the Yankees in seven games.

Dan Shaughnessy argued in *The Curse of the Bambino* (1990) that the retired numbers on the outfield wall of Fenway Park highlight the sorry history of the Red Sox. They have not won a World Series since 9/4/18 (or close enough to the last game on September 11). These are the same numbers retired to Fenway's walls — Ted Williams (9), Joe Cronin (4), Bobby Doerr (1), and Carl Yastrzemski (8).

Many fans believe that the reason the Red Sox have not won a World Series since 1918 ("The Curse of the Bambino"—when Ruth won two World Series games), is because the players on the 1918 championship club never received their World Series mementos. World Series rings were not issued to all winning players until 1922, but a diamond stick pin would have been awarded. A campaign began in 1993 to urge Major League Baseball to award the pins posthumously. The pins were finally awarded in 1993 to family members of the players.

In 1975 when the Red Sox were about to face the Orioles in the ALCS, a Baltimore radio station sent a reporter to Kenya to find a witch doctor to cast a spell on the Red Sox. Boston retaliated by finding a Salem woman purporting to be a witch to cast a spell on the Orioles. She declined, citing a lack of dignity in the proceedings.

In an effort to exorcise the Curse, a fan carried a 1918 photograph of Babe Ruth to the top of Mount Everest.

On August 31, 2004, Manny Ramirez hit a foul ball at Fenway Park that knocked out two teeth of fan Lee Gavin, 16. Gavin lived at 558 Dutton Road in Sudbury, better known as The House That Ruth Bought. Babe Ruth lived there between 1916 and 1926, and many hoped that this encounter would help break the curse; the Red Sox won that night 10–7, and the Indians beat up the Yankees in their worst defeat ever, 22–0.

Brooms. For many years umpires used long-handled brooms to sweep home plate. Many players were superstitious about what position the brooms lay on the ground. Honus Wagner supposedly once quarreled with a player over the position of a broom, believing that the direction it faced dictated whether the next pitch would be a ball or strike.

Buttons. It was considered bad luck to go back and fasten a missed buttonhole on a uniform.

Caps. In July 1999 the Dodgers had a ritual cap-burning in their bullpen. They discarded all of the new uniform pieces that were white, a new addition for the 1999 season. It didn't help, as the Dodgers lost their sixth straight and finished third with a 77–85 record.

Cigarettes. Cubs owner Phil Wrigley supposedly would never light a cigarette until the Cubs came to bat in an inning. He would smoke the same cigarette until the inning ended, no matter how far down the butt burned.

Clothes.

"The second day [of the 1945 World Series] proceedings put a crimp in Cub Coach Red Smith's 'Superstition Club.' He made the Cubs do everything exactly as they did the day before, even to the extent of wearing the same shirts and ties. Recalling the line drive that hit Roy Johnson, his coaching colleague, the first day, Red tried to arrange a similar mishap yesterday. But Johnson wouldn't go for the idea as he gingerly rubbed his aching shin."—The *Stars and Stripes* military newspaper.

A number of baseball people have refused to wear different clothes during a hot streak. One manager at least had the good sense to wash the clothes during the streak. During the 1914 World Series, Braves manager George Stallings refused to change his suit or underwear. Each day he arranged for his son to take the clothes to the local cleaners and wait while they were cleaned. His son then took the clothes to the clubhouse and locked them in a closet for the next game. It might have helped, as the Braves swept the Series from the A's.

During the 1940s Dodger manager Leo Durocher once went three weeks in the same shoes, gray slacks, blue coat and blue knitted tie.

Elvis. In June 1996 the Reds players demanded that broadcaster Marty Brennaman remove a shrine to Elvis Presley in the booth.

Eyes. An early superstition was that players avoided looking at someone with an artificial eye, one eye or crossed eyes.

Cubs owner Phil Wrigley once hired an "Evil Eye" to jinx opposing batters. According to Bill Veeck, Wrigley paid the person $5,000 and guaranteed him $25,000 if the Cubs won the pennant.

Family. Pitcher Bobo Holloman scratched the initials of his wife and son in the dirt by the foul line before each game he started.

Food. Manager Charlie Metro once ate cantaloupe for breakfast 15 days in a row during a winning streak. He also used ventriloquism on the field and graphology to help his club. He studied the handwriting of opposing managers to obtain insights into their managing styles. See also *Food*.

Fortune Teller. The 1913 A's had a fortune teller in their dugout before the World Series. He accurately predicted that the A's would defeat the Giants in five games.

Foul Lines.

"It didn't hurt me or help me. I just didn't want to take any chances." — Ralph Kiner on why he always avoided stepping on the foul lines.

Gloves. Baseball clown Al Schacht reported in his autobiography that his teammate, pitcher Alvin "General" Crowder, was the most superstitious ballplayer he had ever known. Crowder once borrowed Schacht's glove for a game and pitched well. He then borrowed Schacht's glove for the next 12 games. In game 13 he started to go in to pitch and realized he did not have Schacht's glove. He refused to enter the game and sat on the bench until the glove was found in the clubhouse. The Senators almost forfeited the game because of the delay. Crowder was bombed, and for the next inning he used his own glove.

It was considered bad luck for any player other than a catcher to use the catcher's mitt.

During the years when ballplayers routinely left their gloves on the field, various superstitions developed. Players often left their gloves with the fingers pointing in a particular direction. Others would not let their gloves be handed to them; they had to pick them up from the ground. Others would touch their opposing position player's glove (left on the field) before picking up their own.

Lefty O'Doul tossed his glove in the field after each inning. If the glove landed pointing to right field, O'Doul purportedly would get a hit.

Goats. In 1945 Chicago tavern owner William Sianis went everywhere with his billy goat. The tavern naturally was called "Billy Goat's." Sianis tried to attend Game 4 of the World Series with the goat, named Sonovia, but the Cubs allegedly would not issue a ticket to the goat. More accurately, Sianis got to his seat with the goat, but ushers escorted him out because of the smell. The owner vowed that the Cubs would never win another World Series and supposedly placed a hex on the club. He also purportedly sent a telegram to Cubs owner Phil Wrigley after the World Series, which read "Who Smells Now?"

On July 4, 1973, Sianis's nephew Sam brought another goat to a Cubs game, draped in a shawl reading ALL IS FORGIVEN. Security turned them away, and the Cubs finished 5th.

In May 1996 the curse was removed on the "Tonight Show" while Jay Leno was broadcasting in Chicago. Cubs first baseman Mark Grace was the special guest while most of the team sat in the audience.

During the 1993 All-Star break, pitcher Jose Rijo returned to his native Dominican Republic to change his luck — he had been winless in 10 starts since May 22. He sacrificed two goats at a family feast. He would have sacrificed only one, but he "wanted to make sure." He won his first game after the break.

"Goofer" Dust. Tap Dancer Bill "Bojangles" Robinson was a rabid Yankee fan. He always carried a vial of "goofer" dust to each game. Before important games he did a little dance and scattered the goofer dust on Yankee bats and gloves.

Hairpins. Finding a hairpin meant that a player would get a hit. In *Baseball Wit and Wisdom*, by Frank Graham and Dick Hyman (1962), the authors contributed the following rather racist (and no doubt apocryphal) anecdote: "Jake Powell, once of the Yankees and Senators, believed that every time he found a hairpin he'd get a hit. He found 208 in one season, his last in the minors, and got 208 hits that year. One day while in a slump, he followed a stout Negro lady for three miles. Waiting for one of those big bone hairpins to fall out of her hair. It finally fell. Jake grabbed it, raced to the ball park, and broke his slump with a triple the first time up."

Given that Powell once remarked in a radio interview that he spent the winter "cracking niggers over the head" (see also *Racism*), it is possible that Powell knocked the hairpin out of her hair.

Hat. Slugger Al Simmons of the A's once was mired in a slump. He took his postgame shower and then stood dejectedly in the raw in front of his locker trying to figure out the cause of his misfortune. He put on his hat, which caused uproarious laughter in the clubhouse. He then dressed quickly and stomped out. The next day he banged out four hits and continued the same ritual of wearing his hat in the nude. The habit supposedly was adopted by some of his teammates and other players around the league.

Horrors. On April 25, 2002, horror author Stephen King attended the Devil Rays' home game, and the club then went on to lose 15 straight. Players thought the writer had cursed the team, so they stuck pins in a photo of him.

Hunchbacks. See *Mascots*.

Managers. Manager George Stallings of the 1914 Braves would not move from his position in the dugout when his team got a hit. He once suffered back spasms after holding the same position during a long rally and then stooping to pick up a peanut shell.

Marriage. It was considered bad luck to marry during the season, and Leo Durocher was criticized for getting married shortly before the 1934 World Series when he played shortstop for the Cardinals (see also *Marriage*).

Mascot. The Braves were in the thick of a pennant race in August 1982 when they decided to take out the large tepee of their mascot, Chief Noc-a-Homa, to make room for 235 more seats. They promptly lost 15 of 16 games and fell out of first place. They reinstated the chief in September and won the pennant on the last day of the season.

The club repeated the seat changes in August 1983, again resulting in a losing streak that ended when the chief's tepee was put back in September. This time, however, the club lost the pennant to the Dodgers by three games.

Midgets. See *Mascots* and *Midgets*.

Mothers-in-Law. One source reported that ballplayers are supposedly so superstitious that they do not carry pictures of their mothers-in-law. Who does?

No-Hitters. During the 1947 World Series, Bill Bevens went into the last inning with a no-hitter, only to lose. Broadcaster Mel Allen, following time-honored tradition, made no reference to the no-hitter through the first 4½ innings of his portion of the broadcast. Red Barber, however, discussed it frequently during the second half of the game when he was the primary broadcaster.

When Nolan Ryan threw his seventh no-hitter, umpire Tim Tschida had a ritual throughout the game. Whenever he had to put a new ball into play, he made sure that he, and not Rangers catcher Mike Stanley, threw the new ball back to Ryan. In the 9th inning when Tschida flipped a new ball to Stanley to throw to Ryan, Stanley threw it back to Tschida; Tschida threw it to Ryan, who completed the no-hitter.

Number 13. For a short time, teams were allowed to carry a maximum of 13 players, which was considered bad luck.

Dodger pitcher Ralph Branca was issued uniform number 13 as a rookie in 1944 because it was the only uniform his size. He wore number 13 throughout his career and posed for photographers with a black cat on Friday, April 13, 1951. He reportedly had 13 kids in his family. He gave up Bobby Thomson's famous play-off home run in October 1951, and generally it was understood that Branca purposely stopped wearing number 13 in 1952 after the disastrous home run.

Branca claimed that he was not superstitious at the beginning of the 1952 season and that a clubhouse man simply gave him number 12 instead. Branca was irritated and refused to take it until team captain Pee Wee Reese urged him to change numbers. Branca hurt his back wearing number 12 and returned to number 13 the following year.

Reds shortstop Dave Concepcion and Dodger catcher Joe Ferguson are among the recent ballplayers who have worn number 13.

When Mets pitcher Roger Craig lost his 18th straight game during the club's first season in 1962, he changed his uniform number to 13 to end the streak. It worked, but he still lost 24 games for the year and another 22 the next year.

The Expos had a bad time with the number 13 and its multiples in a game on Friday, May 13, 1977. The Expos lost 5–3 to even their record at 13–13. The winning Cubs had 13 hits and left 13 men on base. Larry Biittner, number 26, had the game-winning RBI. The losing pitcher was Dan Warthen, number 39.

Frank Chance only slept in lower berth number 13 on all train trips. If there was no 13, he would write number 13 on the outside of the stateroom door.

Paper. Pitcher Bobo Newsom hated to have any scraps of paper on the pitching mound, and was forever picking them up. Opposing players picked up on this and often deposited bits of paper on the mound. Newsom also took a drink from the water fountain the same way after each inning in which he got the side out in order.

Photographs.

"I'm not superstitious, I just happen to think it's unlucky."— Cubs pitcher Lon Warneke, refusing to have his picture taken on the day he was to pitch in Game 2 of the 1932 World Series. It did not help, as he lost 5–2.

Cubs manager Frank Chance refused to allow his 1908 club to be photographed before the end of the season. It must have worked because the Cubs won the pennant over the Giants during the famous Merkle Boner season.

Dodger pitcher Hugh Casey hated to be photographed before games that he started.

Pitcher. Orioles pitcher Mike Cuellar had a full set of peculiarities. He wore lucky blue clothes and special medallions when he flew. He did not sign autographs on days he pitched and always ate his pregame meal with his catcher. He smoked one cigarette each inning, sitting in the same seat every time. He always had to pick up the ball to start the inning; if a teammate threw it to him he would dodge it and let it roll dead. He always had to take the infield throw from his shortstop after an out. For unexplained reasons, many of these idiosyncracies disappeared when he pitched in Puerto Rico after his Major League career ended.

Rabbit. The Phillies once ceremoniously buried a plastic rabbit, which they believed brought them luck when they faced Dizzy Dean.

On June 4, 1951, the Indians distributed 15,000 rabbits' feet to fans at a game against the Yankees to end the jinx against their club by Yankee pitcher Eddie Lopat. He had a career 30–6 record against the Indians. In the 1st inning, a black cat purportedly ran out to Lopat on the mound (rather, a fan ran on the field at the start of the game and threw a grey kitten at him). The Indians scored five runs in the inning and one in the 2nd to knock Lopat out of the

game. The Indians went on to win 8–2. They also beat Lopat 8–0 in their next meeting.

Shoelaces. If a player breaks a shoelace during a game, he is supposed to tie the ends together rather than replace it with a new shoelace.

Pitcher Bobo Newsom would never tie his own shoelaces on the days he pitched. He would stand in the middle of the clubhouse until one of his teammates came over and tied them for him.

Shutouts. Long-time Senators owner Clark Griffith, who won 240 games in the 19th century, reportedly said it was bad luck to pitch a shutout. This may explain why he did not do it until six years and almost 175 starts into his career. He pitched his first shutout on August 13, 1897, during his fourth straight 20-win season.

According to Frank Chance, when he made his Chicago White Stockings debut on April 29, 1898, Griffith ordered him to botch a couple of routine pop-ups and let a few runs score to avoid a shutout. As a result, the Cubs won the game 16–2 instead of 16–0. Ironically, Griffith pitched the longest shutout in Cubs history, 14 innings on June 19, 1900. The Cubs won 1–0 against Rube Waddell when Griffith knocked in the game-winner in the bottom of the 14th inning. Griffith finished his career with 23 shutouts, leading the league in 1900 and 1901.

Somersaults. At least one 19th century player always did somersaults when he ran on the field, a tradition resurrected by Ozzie Smith at the start of each season when he performed a front flip while running out to his position for the first time.

Sophomore Jinx.

"I got the sophomore jinx out of the way and I think I'll have my best year ever next year. There's no junior jinx, is there?"— Joe Charboneau.

***Sports Illustrated* Jinx.** A superstition developed that a team or player featured on the cover of *Sports Illustrated* immediately suffered misfortune. One victim was Matt Williams of the Giants. In early June 1995 Williams was the magazine's cover boy. Three days later he fouled a ball off his foot and went on the disabled list with a broken bone.

The magazine guaranteed Cubs and Red Sox losses in the 2003 postseason after featuring both clubs on its cover during the same week — different covers for different regions of the country. Then Pedro Martinez and Kerry Wood, who each appeared in the covers, started the fateful Game 7 of each series. The covers, and the results, prompted fan Justin Z. Schroeder of Indiana to write to *SI*: "I can only hope that next year you find it in your hearts to put the Yankees on the cover as much as possible." It worked.

Sportswriter. A 19th century superstition was that any team picked to win by famed sportswriter Henry Chadwick was doomed to failure (an early version of the *Sports Illustrated* jinx?).

Time. Red Sox third baseman Wade Boggs always ran wind sprints at 7:17 p.m. before all 7:30 games. He also drew a Hebrew letter in the batter's box before each at-bat.

Tinker to Evers to Chance. The trio supposedly had various superstitions. Tinker would walk directly to the plate to bat if he had reached base in the previous at-bat. If he made an out, next time up he would circle home plate before entering the batter's box.

Evers 'saved' his luck by sitting down if he began hitting well during batting practice — to save the hits for the game.

Before games Frank Chance wandered around first base looking for lucky four-leaf clovers from the nearby grass.

Touching Bases. Babe Ruth and Willie Mays, like many ballplayers, always touched second base coming in from the outfield.

Uniforms. Giants manager John McGraw had his team wear black uniforms in the 1905 World Series. As a result of the team's victory, the club wore black uniforms again in the 1911 Series. It did not work, as the A's defeated the Giants in six games in a rematch of the 1905 Series.

Eccentric Rube Waddell sometimes went into the stands after two innings of pitching and had a fan cut off two inches of his shirt-sleeve.

Voodoo. Urban Shocker and Bobo Newsom reportedly practiced voodoo before games in which they pitched. It is unclear what type of voodoo they practiced.

In May 2001 Julio Zuleta borrowed from a scene in the movie *Major League* and used a voodoo stick on the Cubs' bats to bring on the hits. It was a successful effort.

White Horses/Barrels. White horses were considered good luck and in 1904 Giants manager John McGraw arranged to have a team of white horses pass by the Polo Grounds each day for a week as the team arrived at the park. The team hit well and kept remarking on the presence of the horses. A similar story regarding the 1905 World Series substituted empty barrels for the horses. It was considered good luck to have a wagonload of empty barrels pass by.

White Pigeon. When the Boston Red Stockings of the early National League lost, the players looked all over for a white pigeon to bring them luck.

Witch Hunt.

"George Stallings, a well-educated man, was as superstitious as a Haitian witch doctor." — *The Sporting News* in 1964.

During a 10-game Red Sox losing streak in 1976, a Boston television news crew accompanied a witch to a road game in Cleveland to cast a positive spell over the team. The players were not amused.

"X" Marks the Spot. Pete Reiser and Al Rosen are among the players who made an "X" in the batter's box before each at-bat.

Book. Mike Blake, *The Incomplete Book of Baseball Superstitions, Rituals and Oddities* (1991); Steve Gatto, *Da Curse of the Billy Goat: The Chicago Cubs, Pennant Races, and Curses* (2004).

Supreme Court

"Kranepool flies to right. Agnew resigns." — Note passed to Supreme Court Justice Potter Stewart while hearing oral argument during a 1973 postseason game between the Mets and Reds.

"I always turn to the sports section first. The sports page records people's accomplishments; the front page has nothing but man's failures." — Chief Justice Earl Warren shortly after the assassination of Robert Kennedy in 1968.

See also *Antitrust*, *Judges* and *Reserve Clause*.

During the 1912 World Series, the court was hearing the Bathtub Trust case and received inning-by-inning bulletins of the game. The bulletins were passed in notes down the bench during oral argument.

Suspended Games   See *Postponed Games*

Suspensions

"I'm 43 years old and I'm married to a five year old." — Anita Piniella, whose husband Lou was suspended by commissioner Bart Giamatti from his Reds managerial duties after bumping an umpire.

See also *Barred from Baseball*, *Ejections*, *Fights*, *Fines*, *Gambling and Fixed Games*, *Horse Racing* and *Spitballs*.

The Baseball Encyclopedia's inaugural 1969 edition listed all known suspensions. The feature was dropped in subsequent editions.

Early Rules. By the 1890s umpires were authorized by the league to eject players from a game. The Fleischmann Resolution of 1902 and the Brush Amendment of 1904 made it mandatory to fine players $10 if they were ejected. If a league president suspended the player after that, another $10 fine was levied. Players were also fined an additional $10 for each day of a suspension. However, the owners undermined this effort at discipline by paying the fines for the players.

Tony Mullane. In 1885 pitcher Tony Mullane was suspended for one year for trying to sell his services to the highest bidder after signing a contract with the St. Louis Browns. This has also been reported as one of the earliest *Hold-Outs*.

Cleveland Spiders. In 1896 the entire Cleveland Spiders team was arrested after a game in Louisville for starting a riot after protesting an umpire's call. Manager Patsy Tebeau was fined $200 by the National League and told that he was suspended until the fine was paid. Cleveland owner Stanley Robison obtained an injunction preventing the league from interfering with Tebeau's managing and the league backed down.

Babe Ruth. In 1922 Ruth was suspended by Judge Landis for defying an order not to go on a 1921 postseason barnstorming tour. Ruth was suspended until May of the new season. In the first game after his return he was called out at second base. In frustration at what he thought was a bad call, he threw dirt in the face of the umpire. The crowd booed him, and he went into the stands after abusive fans. He was suspended again and stripped of his position as team captain.

In 1925 Ruth was sick early in the season and the Yankees continued to flounder even after he returned to the club. He was late for a warm-up in St. Louis, and matters came to a head. Manager Miller Huggins suspended him indefinitely and fined him $5,000. Ruth was forced to apologize in order to be reinstated, but the season was a washout for the Yankees and Ruth was considered over the hill at age 30 — an opinion he shattered in the next few years.

Bill Dickey. In 1932 the Yankee catcher was suspended for breaking the jaw of Washington's Carl Reynolds after Reynolds knocked the ball out of Dickey's mitt. Dickey received a 30-day suspension and a $1,000 fine during the heat of a pennant race. American League president Will Harridge later said that the disciplinary action against Dickey was his most difficult moment in the job. It did not have much of an effect on the outcome of the race, as the Yankees won by 13 games over the A's.

Wes Ferrell. In 1932 the Indians pitcher, a six-time 20-game winner, was fined and suspended by manager Roger Peckinpaugh after refusing to leave a game. He still managed to start 38 games and compile a record of 23–13.

Dizzy Dean. In 1937 Dean was suspended by National League president Ford Frick for a fight with the Giants.

Zeke Bonura of the White Sox, who played chiefly in the 1930s, was suspended when he went out on the town dancing. He had been out of the line-up with a bad back but still went to the Chez Paree club and did the Cha Cha to the sounds of bandleader Xavier Cugat (who discovered and later married entertainer Charro).

Leo Durocher. Durocher was once suspended for five days and fined $100 by Ford Frick for "inciting riots and fights."

On June 8, 1945, Durocher punched fan John Christian, who had been extremely abusive to him. Christian's civil suit was settled by the Dodgers for $6,500, and later Durocher was acquitted of the criminal charges.

In late 1946, while Durocher was still the Dodger manager, club president Branch Rickey asked Durocher to meet with commissioner Happy Chandler about his behavior. Chandler warned Durocher about associating with certain undesirable people, including actor George Raft (who had numerous mob connections) and known mobsters Bugsy Siegel and Lucky Luciano. Durocher was just about to marry actress Laraine Day, who was having trouble getting a divorce. Other indiscretions were noted when Durocher's phone was tapped and he received a call from racketeer Joe Adonis.

As a result of the mob issues and Durocher's known gambling on horse races, Chandler decided to suspend Durocher after an unfortunate set of circumstances during spring training in Havana, Cuba, in 1947. This came on the heels of a boycott started by the Brooklyn Catholic Youth Organization, which claimed that Durocher was "undermining the moral training of Brooklyn's Roman Catholic Youth."

In Havana, volatile Yankee general manager Larry MacPhail had hosted well-known gamblers in his private stadium boxes. Rickey pointed this out to the press and a feud between MacPhail and Rickey caught Durocher in the middle because of his own mob friends. Durocher attended hearings with Chandler and was confident that nothing would come of the charges against him. Nevertheless, on April 9, 1947, Chandler, trying to impress the owners with his toughness, suspended Durocher for the entire season. MacPhail, apologetic for involving Durocher after Durocher received such a stiff sentence, received a small fine of $2,000. The Dodgers also were fined $2,000 for their handling of the situation. In 1951 Arthur Mann wrote *Baseball Confidential*, the "secret history" of the feud among Happy Chandler, Leo Durocher, Larry MacPhail and Branch Rickey.

In the early 1970s, Durocher, then managing the Astros, was again the subject of scrutiny over gambling allegations. Commissioner Bowie Kuhn was embarrassed over the handling of the investigation, which turned up nothing.

Dewey Williams. In 1948 the Reds catcher was suspended for touching an umpire. He served his suspension in uniform in the clubhouse because the Reds were short of catchers. The Reds' number one catcher, Ray Mueller, was on the disabled list and Ray Lamanno was the only catcher available. The Reds received permission to have Williams available if Lamanno was hurt. Williams would serve an additional day of suspension for any day in which he played. He never had to play.

Dick Allen. In 1969 Allen received a 28-day suspension and $500 per day fine for disobeying team rules. He was then traded to the Phillies for Curt Flood and others, but Flood refused to report and then unsuccessfully tested the *Reserve Clause* in his famous court case. Absent Allen's suspension, Flood might never have been forced to test baseball's most restrictive rule.

Bert Campaneris. The A's infielder was suspended for the first seven games of 1973 for throwing a bat in Game 2 of the 1972 ALCS against Detroit. Campaneris threw the bat only after he was hit on the ankle after going 3-for-3 against Lerrin LaGrow. Campaneris was also suspended for the remainder of the championship series against the Tigers, but not for the World Series.

George Steinbrenner. See *Barred from Baseball* for Steinbrenner's two suspensions.

Ted Turner. See *Barred from Baseball*.

Reggie Jackson. In mid–1978 the Yankees were in extra innings with a man on first and Jackson at the plate. Manager Billy Martin flashed the bunt sign for Jackson to advance the runner. Jackson, already feuding with Martin, was upset that he was not allowed to hit away. After Jackson missed on the bunt attempt, Martin signaled for Jackson to hit away. Peeved, Jackson ignored the sign and continued to bunt (unsuccessfully). After the at-bat, Martin suspended Jackson for five days and fined him. This led to Martin's firing and dramatic rehiring by George Steinbrenner during the Yankees' Oldtimers Day that year (see also *Managers—Firings*).

Fights with Umpires. See *Umpires—Attacks*.

Goose Gossage. In August 1986 Gossage was suspended for 20 days without pay by the Padres for insubordination after repeated criticism of owner Ray Kroc and team president Ballard Smith.

Jim Rice. The Red Sox suspended Rice for three days after he attacked manager Joe Morgan after Morgan sent up light-hitting Spike Owen to pinch hit for him.

Pete Rose. In April 1988 the Reds manager was suspended for 30 days after shoving umpire Dave Pallone. Pallone was having his own difficulties controlling his temper and later was fired by the National League. He later revealed that he was a *Homosexual*.

Roger Clemens. During Game 4 of the 1990 ALCS, the Red Sox pitcher exploded in the 2nd inning of the deciding game. As a result of his tirade against the home plate umpire, he was suspended for five games at the start of the 1991 season and assessed a $10,000 fine.

Bret Saberhagen. On July 27, 1993, the Mets pitcher sprayed bleach at a group of reporters. As part of his punishment he agreed to donate one day of pay—$15,384.62—to a charity designated by the New York chapter of the Baseball Writers Association of America. He denied spraying the reporters intentionally, saying that the bleach was shot out of a squirt gun and accidentally hit the reporters. He lied about the incident initially, prompting a number of sportswriters to note that his initials are B.S.

Albert Belle. See *Fines*.

Pedro Martinez. Martinez, then with Montreal, was suspended for one game at the end of the 1996 season and for the first seven games of the 1997 season after participating in a bench-clearing brawl in Philadelphia in September 1996.

Randy Johnson. In April 1998 Johnson, pitching for the Mariners, was suspended for three games for twice throwing at Indians outfielder Kenny Lofton. Johnson threw at Lofton's head, inciting a bench-clearing confrontation. Sandy Alomar jumped between batter and pitcher and the situation de-escalated until Mariners manager Lou Piniella started screaming and going after Lofton. After order was restored, Johnson buzzed Lofton's head again, and the players again gathered on the field for a fight/dance. As reported in the *New York Times*: "The tense ballgame included an inside-the park homer, the ejection of three All-Stars, two injured pitchers and malfunctioning bullpen phones."

Roberto Alomar. See *Umpires—Attacks*.

Carl Everett. On July 20, 2000, the volatile Red Sox outfielder received a 10-game suspension for twice bumping an umpire during a game against the Mets. Everett blamed the media for the suspension.

Jose Guillen. On September 27, 2004, Guillen was suspended by the Angels for the rest of the season, including the postseason (if any), because of a series of incidents. The culmination was when he publicly objected to being lifted for a pinch runner late in a game against the A's in the middle of a pennant race. Guillen was known to be temperamental and volatile, evidenced by his playing for five teams in four seasons. Earlier in the season he had criticized the Angels pitchers for not retaliating sufficiently after he was hit in the ribs by a pitch. There were other problems, but the team only said that there had been "a series of incidents" that led to the suspension. At the time, he was second on the team in home runs (27) and RBIs (104), so it was a blow to the team.

Guillen appealed the suspension immediately and attempted to recoup his salary.

Manager. Managers are not allowed to appeal suspensions.

Minor League Manager. In 2002 former National League MVP Kevin Mitchell was managing the Class A Sonoma County Crushers. He was suspended by the Western Baseball League for throwing a punch at Solano Steelhead third base coach Larry Olenberger after Mitchell concluded that Olenberger was stealing signs.

Spring Training. In spring training 1993 Hal Morris of the Reds and Jose Mesa of the Indians were suspended for three regular season games and fined for their part in a brawl during an exhibition game. It was the first time since 1985 that penalties imposed in spring training carried over into the regular season. In 1985 Lonnie Smith of the Cardinals was suspended for three days after using abusive language to an umpire during a spring training game. Morris paid even more heavily for the brawl; he separated his shoulder and was out of action for several weeks.

In 2003 Mike Piazza was suspended for four regular season games after charging the mound during a spring training at-bat in which he took offense to a pitch that hit him.

Postseason. During the 1999 postseason, Mets coach Cookie Rojas was suspended five games for pushing umpire Charlie Williams.

Record Number Suspended. On April 22, 2000, the White Sox beat the Tigers 14–6 in a game that featured two fights and 11 ejections. Major League Baseball quickly announced what was believed to be a record number of suspensions, 16, for a total of 82 games. Managers Phil Garner and Jerry Manuel were suspended for eight games each, Detroit coach Juan Samuel for 15 games and Tigers third baseman Dean Palmer for eight games.

Don Sutton (1945–)

Hall of Fame 1998

"Don Sutton, who is [at the time] 11th on the all-time list in games won ... still won't get voted in the Hall of Fame. It must be something he said, because it can't be something he hasn't done."— Jim Murray in 1997. Sutton finally made it on his fifth try, with 81.6% of the vote.

Sutton was a right-handed pitcher who recorded 324 wins over 23 seasons from 1966 through 1988.

An Alabama native originally signed by the Los Angeles Dodgers in 1964, Donald Howard Sutton began his professional career in 1965 with Santa Barbara of the California League. He appeared in 10 games before being promoted to Albuquerque of the Texas League. Sutton excelled at both stops, winning 23 games collectively, and then went to the Major Leagues with the Dodgers in 1966. Sutton's outstanding rookie season would see him post a 12–12 record with a 2.99 ERA and 209 strikeouts.

Sutton pitched unevenly over the next four seasons, collecting 54 wins during a deep slide by the Dodgers. Sutton began to establish himself as an elite starter in 1971, winning 17 games and finishing fifth in the National League in ERA and strikeouts. In 1972 Sutton went 19–9 with a 2.08 ERA. His nine shutouts led the league. Sutton won 18 more games in 1973 and again was among the league leaders in ERA (2.42) and strikeouts (200). He won Game 1 and the series-clinching Game 4 of the NLCS against the Pirates, allowing just seven hits and one earned run in 17 innings pitched. In the World Series the Dodgers were defeated by the Oakland A's in five games, with Sutton getting the only Dodger win in Game 2.

Sutton had the only 20-win season of his career in 1976, going 21–10. He closed out the Los Angeles portion of his career in 1980, winning the National League ERA title. He left Los Angeles with 233 wins, the Dodger club record.

Sutton signed as a free agent with the Houston Astros for the 1981 season and was traded to the American League Brewers late in the 1982 season.

On June 18, 1986, Sutton defeated the Rangers 3–1 to win his 300th career game. He closed out his career back with the Dodgers in 1988, going 3–6 in 16 appearances. He finished his 23-year career with a 324–256 mark, 12th all-time in wins (tied with Nolan Ryan). His 5,282.1 innings pitched and 3,574 strikeouts are both 7th on the career list. Sutton had 58 career shutouts, 10th all-time. He was a four time All-Star. He retired to the Braves' broadcast booth, where he remained through the mid–2000s.

Switch Hitters

"Don't worry about hitting from that side. I've got that side taken care of."— Right-handed Cliff Johnson, A's designated hitter, trying to intimidate a switch-hitting rookie teammate.

"But it is Murray's attitude toward switch hitting itself that is most revealing. He obviously did not polish this part of his game overnight. It was something that took time and, as nothing else, showed just how he approached his work.... From it, he learned a great deal about himself—and others—as hitters. To hit from the opposite side, Murray discovered, 'you had to be hit by a pitched ball before you knew how to move. It was something entirely different.'"— David Falkner in *The Short Season* (1986).

See also *Ambidextrous*.

Purpose. A switch hitter is valuable because of the purported advantage that a left-handed batter has over a right-handed pitcher. The converse is also true, but right-handed batters have fewer opportunities to bat against left-handers. The theory is that a right-handed batter does not pick up the ball as quickly against a right-handed pitcher (and vice versa). This is in part because the ball is coming at the batter from the same side as he is standing and appears to be thrown at him. See also *Strategy* for the logical claim that these advantages are illusory.

Early Switch-Hitters. Bob "Death to Flying Things" Ferguson is considered one of the earliest switch hitters in a career that spanned the 1860s, the National Association of 1871–1875, the National League from 1876 through 1883, and the American Association in 1884. One source identified him as the first player to reach 1,000 hits in the Major Leagues, but he only had 625 in the Major Leagues and another 287 in the National Association.

John Montgomery Ward taught himself to switch-hit, though *The Baseball Encyclopedia* reports that he switch-hit only in 1888. He batted .251 that season, compared to his career average of .275.

Two other notable early switch-hitters were Will White, who played from 1877 through 1886, and Tommy Tucker, American Association batting champion in 1889. The practice of switch-hitting expanded greatly in the 1890s.

Most Switch-Hits. George Davis played 20 years beginning in 1890. He was the first Major League switch-hitter to reach 2,000 hits. He finished with 2,667, down from 2,688 in earlier sources. It was the most by a switch-hitter until Pete Rose broke his record with 4,256. Switch-hitter Eddie Murray reached 3,000 hits in mid–1995 and finished with 3,255.

Best.

"If that kid only hit right-handed, he'd be tree-mendous. If he only hit left-handed, he'd be tree-mendous. But since he does his hittin' both ways, he's…. He's just tree-mendous."—Casey Stengel on Mickey Mantle as reported by Arthur Daley.

The Society for American Baseball Research (SABR) once held a vote to identify the all-time switch-hitting team by position:

First Base. Rip Collins had a .296 average over nine seasons. He would likely be replaced today by Eddie Murray. Murray became a switch-hitter in 1975 while in the minor leagues, only two years before he arrived in the Major Leagues.

Second Base. Frankie Frisch hit .316 over 19 seasons.

Third Base. Pete Rose hit .303 over 24 seasons and had 4,256 hits.

Shortstop. Maury Wills set a then–Major League stolen base record with 104 in 1962. He led the league in that category from 1960 through 1965.

Catcher. Ted Simmons hit .285 with 248 home runs over 21 years.

Pitcher. Early Wynn won 300 games while hitting .214 with 17 home runs over 23 seasons between 1939 and 1963. Wynn batted right-handed exclusively from 1939 through 1944 (1941–1944 in *The Baseball Encyclopedia*).

Outfielder. Mickey Mantle hit 536 home runs over 18 years.

Outfielder. Max Carey hit .285 with 738 stolen bases over 20 years. He led the league in stolen bases 10 times.

Outfielder. Reggie Smith hit .287 with 314 home runs over 17 seasons. Another source, Ken Lombardi, put Ken Singleton and Tim Raines in the top five with Mantle, Murray and Reggie Smith, with Pete Rose sixth.

Long-Running Quartet. The most famous all-switch-hitter infield is the 1960s Dodger infield of Maury Wills at shortstop, Jim Gilliam at third base, Jim Lefebvre at second base and Wes Parker at first base. The light-hitting Lefebvre homered from both sides of the plate on May 7, 1966.

Switch-Hit Home Runs. Mickey Mantle hit 373 home runs left-handed and 163 right-handed.

The first switch-hitter to hit home runs from both sides of the plate in the same game was Wally Schang of the A's on September 8, 1916, at Shibe Park in Philadelphia. He did it off pitchers Slim Love and Allen Russell. Some sources reported erroneously that the first American Leaguer was Johnny Lucadello of the Browns, who followed Schang on September 16, 1940.

The first National Leaguer to do it was Augie Galan for the Cubs in June 1937. He did it despite having a deformed arm.

Jim Russell of the Braves in 1948 and Dodgers in 1950 hit home runs from both sides of the plate in the same game. He was the first player to do it twice.

In May 1987 Eddie Murray became the first man to hit home runs from both sides of the plate in two consecutive games. On September 16–17, 1995, Ken Caminiti of the Astros became the first National League player to hit home runs from both sides of the plate in consecutive games.

On April 21, 1994, Murray, then with the Indians, hit home runs from both sides of the plate in the same game for the eleventh time to set a Major League record. He had shared the record of 10 with Mickey Mantle. Chili Davis also hit home runs from both sides of the plate in 11 games.

On April 23, 2000, Bernie Williams and Jorge Posada of the Yankees each hit home runs from both sides of the plate in a 10–7 win over the Blue Jays. It was the first time that teammates had accomplished the feat in the same game. In late March 2004 the Yankees and Devil Rays opened the season in Japan's Tokyo Dome. In the second game of the series, Posada did it again, with three-run homers from both sides of the plate.

Two Home Runs/Same Inning. On April 8, 1993, Carlos Baerga of the Indians made Major League history by hitting home runs from both sides of the plate in the same inning. He batted right-handed when he hit a home run off Steve Howe of the Yankees with no outs in the 7th inning. With two outs he hit a solo home run batting left-handed against Steve Farr.

At least two minor leaguers have done it: in 1961 by Ellis Burton of Class AAA Toronto of the International League; and on April 30, 1979, by Gary Pellant of Class A Alexandria of the independent Lone Star League. Both did it in the 7th inning, as did Baerga.

Dept. of Obscurity. The 1992 Mets were the first team with eight switch-hitters with at least one home run each.

First Home Runs. On August 2, 1991, Expos infielder Bret Barberie hit his first two Major League home runs in the same game, batting from both sides of the plate.

Experiment. Orioles catcher Rick Dempsey tried to become a switch-hitter during spring training 1982. He was 0-for-19 during the spring but manager Earl Weaver let him bat left-handed on Opening Day to get it out of his system. Dempsey hit a pop fly single and kept flailing away whenever he had the chance during the rest of April. He then abandoned the project permanently.

100 Hits/Both Sides. In 1979 shortstop Garry Templeton of the Cardinals became the first player to reach 100 hits from both sides of the plate in one season. Royals outfielder Willie Wilson duplicated the feat the next year.

Most Home Runs/Season. Mickey Mantle had the most home runs in a season by a switch-hitter, with 54 in 1961.

Batting Champions. Mickey Mantle was the first switch-hitter to win a batting title, as part of his 1956 Triple Crown.

In 1968 Pete Rose became the first National League switch-hitting batting champion.

All-Time Leaders.
Home Runs — Mickey Mantle 536
RBIs — Eddie Murray 1,917
Batting Avg. — Frankie Frisch .316
Hits — Pete Rose 4,256
Stolen Bases — Max Carey 738

Symbols *See* *Logos*

Syndicate Ball *See* *Cross-Ownership*

Syracuse Stars

National League 1879
The Stars were admitted into the National League in 1879 even though the city's population did not meet the minimum 75,000 required by the league. The club finished the year in seventh place with a 22–48 record, 30 games out of first place.

Syracuse Stars

American Association 1890
The club finished in seventh place with a 55–72 record, 30½ games out of first place.

"T is for Terry
The Giant from Memphis
Whose 400 average
You can't overemphis."
—Ogden Nash on Bill Terry.

Tabletop Games

"Uncle Bud arrived at Christmas with a baseball board-game. I was about seven. At first I wanted nothing to do with it, but Uncle Bud, showing great patience, coaxed me into trying it…. The game was played with dice, a board in the shape of a baseball field, and two teams of markers, one yellow, one green, to use as baseball players. The players were placed on the field, the batting player rolled the dice and moved his men around the bases according to 12-single, 7-double, 2-homerun, 3-walk, 6-strike out, all the rest of the numbers were outs…. Within a day we had made up a league of real and imagined teams…"— W.P. Kinsella in "Bud and Tom" (1984).

"Does this guy have a *Clue*? That tantrum … really got him in *Trouble*. It was no *Trivial Pursuit* either…. Clearly he was not *Sorry* … Bradley is having a tough time in *The Game of Life*…. With his unusual temperament, Bradley is putting himself at *Risk* when he's on the field."— Bob Raissman in the *New York Daily News*, after new Dodger Milton Bradley exploded and dumped a bag of balls onto the field in protest of an umpire's bad decision in May 2004. Bradley received a four-game suspension and has often appeared to be a bit disturbed: "If you don't know me and I don't know you, don't approach me and I won't approach you. Don't insult me and I won't insult you, because you don't know what I will or won't do."

Bradley was pretty much universally despised. One of his team-mates put a sign next to his locker that said, "SHUT UP AND PLAY." Bradley taped a photograph of a ball clearly off the plate that was called for a third strike by umpire Ed Rapuano.

Strat-o-Matic.

"The only time was in Strat-o-Matic, against my brother."— Phillies pitcher Roger McDowell when asked if he had ever seen a rally as big as his club's nine runs in the 9th inning to defeat the Dodgers 12–11 on August 21, 1990.

This dice board game is the long-standing king of tabletop baseball games. The precise statistical tendencies of a player during a particular season are translated into a pitcher or hitter card that produces a result with each throw of the dice. Given enough rolls of the dice, pitchers should issue strikeouts, doubles, walks, etc., at the same rate they did in real life. Similarly, hitters in theory should produce home runs, groundouts, fly outs, and even become injured, at the same rate they did in that particular season. The cards even reflect the statistical tendencies of a player against right-handed or left-handed hitting or pitching opponents.

The game was invented by Hal Richman at age 11 in Great Neck, New York. He came up with the idea after rolling dice thousands of times to see what the probabilities might be. He developed the game a week before summer camp, and at first it had no fielding or pitching, just hitting cards. His bunkmates at camp formed leagues and the game was a success. Later, at age 15, Richman's game was banned at camp because it was used as the basis for a parallel dice sex league. To avoid at least some of the moral problem, he changed the game to use cards but reverted to dice at age 22. After three years of marketing starting in 1961, the game took off and made him wealthy. It is the all-time largest selling tabletop baseball game.

Most hardcore baseball fanatics have replaced Strat-o-Matic with Rotisserie or **Fantasy League Baseball**, which are based on actual performances of Major League players as they occur.

Beat Generation writer Jack Kerouac created a game similar to Strat-o-Matic when he was 13 years old. The game featured six teams, named after automobiles, such as the St. Louis Cadillacs and Washington Chryslers. Kerouac apparently played the game throughout his life, and the remnants of the board game were later displayed at the New York Public Library. In 2003 the Class A Lowell (Massachusetts) Spinners presented a bobblehead figure of Kerouac holding a pen and notebook and standing on a copy of his definitive work, *On the Road*. Kerouac had been a beat writer (before being a Beat writer) for *The Lowell Sun* in 1942 and was an avid sports fan. The event was sponsored in part by the English department at the University of Massachusetts at Lowell.

Predecessors to Strat-o-Matic. The original quasi-tabletop game was Parlor Base-Ball, designed by Francis C. Sebring, a pitcher for the Empire Base Ball Club of New York in the 1860s. In 1868 he received a patent for the game, which resembled a pinball machine. Another pinball-like game was patented in 1867 by William Buckley of New York.

Strat-o-Matic Baseball had 20th century predecessors that were patented as early as 1925. Clifford A. Van Beek patented a game that was not marketed until 1931, using statistics from the 1930 season. Another predecessor was a 1932 version by J.

The most simple of tabletop baseball games, 1885.

Yogi Berra of the Yankees tags out runner Jim Landis of the White Sox, as umpire John Stevens makes the call.

Richard Seitz, the American Professional Baseball Association (commonly referred to as APBA). By 1967 APBA had its own journal circulating to its large following of players.

All-Star Baseball.

"Even as a young child, I knew, from my cousins, about Monopoly, Parcheesi, Clue and The Great Game of Sorry, but my board game was All-Star Baseball. It was a simple affair. The board consisted of some glossy printing and two mounted spinners. The players consisted of round disks marked off in numbered sections. The numbers stood for various kinds of hits and outs. The game consisted of placing the disks over the spinners and awaiting fate's control of the spin."—Howard Senzel in *Baseball and the Cold War* (1977) (the author's chosen tabletop game).

Major Leaguer Ethan Allen worked with Cadaco to develop All-Star Baseball, a board game that was first marketed in 1941. It contained pie charts on discs that use spinners to determine the outcome of an at-bat. Cadaco has sold over 1 million of the games. Allen coached future U.S. President George Bush and Yale to a postwar appearance in the first College World Series in 1947.

Strike Season. During the 1981 player strike, radio station WITS in Boston used play-by-play announcers Jon Miller of the Orioles and Ken Coleman of the Red Sox to re-create Strat-o-Matic games over the air.

Computer Games. Computer games began to supplant tabletop games in the 1980s, as APBA and Strat-o-Matic went to computerized versions by the 1990s.

Retro Games. In 2002 Old Century Baseball company introduced a truly retro game, a pinball-style wooden board, that sold more than 50,000 units by the end of the year and was a finalist for *FamilyFun* magazine's Toy of the Year.

Books.

"He wiped his eyes with the beery towel, stared down at the game on the table. That was what did it, it was just a little too much, one idea too many, and it wrecked the whole league. He stood, turned his back on it, feeling old and wasted. Should he keep it around, or...? NO, better to burn it, once and for all, records, rules, books, everything.... He saw the dice, still reading 2–6–6, and—almost instinctively—reached forward and tipped the two over to a third six. Gave York and Wilson back-to-back homers and moved the game over to the Extraordinary Occurrences Chart. Easy as that."—Robert Coover's 1968 novel, *The Universal Baseball Association, Inc., J. Henry Waugh, Prop.*, is a fascinating dark psychological study of a man obsessed with the statistical dice baseball game he created, which he alone plays. His consciousness drifts back and forth between reality and the fantasy world of baseball games that the dice produce. His imagination attributes personalities, physical characteristics, crowd interaction, sweat and dust to each development in his imaginary game. Even more than the modern day Fantasy League Baseball aficionado, his day-to-day happiness and personality are affected by, and intertwined with, the success or failure of his make-believe heroes.

See also Mark Cooper with Douglas Congdon-Martin, *Baseball Games* (1995).

Tag

"Edwards missed getting Stearns at third base by an eyeball."—Jerry Coleman.

"You could see it all happening in the same twilight instant—the ball coming in a deadly line, and Allison's desperate, skidding slide, and the tag, and the umpire's arm shooting up, and the game and the season saved." —Roger Angell in *The Summer Game* (1972), describing Carl Yastrzemski's throw to second base to nail Bob Allison of the Twins in the last game of the 1967 season. The tag saved a run and preserved a Red Sox victory. The Tigers' loss later in the day of the second game of its doubleheader assured the pennant for the Red Sox.

See also *Home Plate Collisions*.

Larry Doyle. In Game 5 of the 1911 World Series, the Giants were down 3–1 in games to the Phillies. In the bottom of the 10th inning, Giants first baseman Fred Merkle hit a long fly ball to score Larry Doyle from third base for the game-winning run. However, Doyle failed to touch home plate and umpire Bill Klem stood by waiting to make the call. No Phillie tagged Doyle before he reached the clubhouse, and the play stood. Nevertheless, the Phillies closed out the series when Chief Bender won Game 6.

Luke Sewell. In a 1933 game, the Senators catcher made a double tag at home plate in the 9th inning against the Yankees. Lou Gehrig hesitated on a drive to the outfield and rookie Dixie Walker was right behind him on the basepaths. Outfielder Goose Goslin relayed to shortstop Joe Cronin, who wheeled and threw to Sewell at the plate. He tagged the sliding Gehrig and spun around just in time to tag Walker. One play later the game was over and the Senators had a 6–3 win on their way to finishing seven games ahead of the Yankees.

Elrod Hendricks. In the 1970 World Series, the Orioles catcher became entangled with umpire Ken Burkhart as Hendricks was attempting to tag Bernie Carbo of the Reds. Burkhart called Carbo out even though the replay made it clear that Hendricks made the tag with his glove while the ball was in his other hand.

Ron Gant. During Game 2 of the 1991 World Series, Twins first baseman Kent Hrbek pulled Braves runner Ron Gant off the bag and then tagged him out in front of the oblivious umpire.

Tagging Up

The tag-up rule was modified in the 1890s to allow a runner to advance after the ball was first touched, rather than actually caught. The change was made as a result of a ploy, attributed to outfielder Tommy McCarthy, which prevented runners from tagging up. On fly balls to him in the outfield, he would tap the ball in the air without catching it as he ran back into the infield.

Third baseman John McGraw is "credited" with holding the back of the belt of runners trying to tag up from third base.

Taiwan

"If you think Central Park in New York is scary, you ain't seen nothing yet. On Aug. 2, 1996, four players from the Brother Elephants were abducted and held in a hotel room in the city of Taichung. Second baseman Fu-lien Wu was reportedly roughed up and pitcher Yi-hsin 'Knife Thrower' Chen had a pistol barrel shoved in his mouth. According to prosecutors, the kidnappers were from a syndicate that had lost $125,000 on an Elephants game. They believed the players had intentionally thrown it after being paid off by a rival gang." —Andrew Wong at BaseballGuru.com.

Baseball Origins. Baseball was introduced to Taiwan by the Japanese, who occupied the island for 50 years beginning in 1895.

Amateur Association. The Chinese Taipei Amateur Baseball Association was formed in 1949, and its national team became one of the top teams in the world. The amateur association later became known as the National Baseball Commission.

Little League Baseball. The island's baseball tradition was strengthened enormously in 1968 when a group of Taiwanese aborigine children from the town of Red Leaf defeated the Japanese world champion *Little League Baseball* team. The next season Taiwan's team advanced to the Little League World Series in Williamsport. Still composed largely of aboriginal players, the club returned with the championship. Baseball in Taiwan exploded after that milestone. The father of the Taiwanese Little League is Hsieh Kuocheng and Taiwan's teams have won 17 Little League championships.

Olympic Games. Taiwan's baseball team won a bronze medal in the 1984 *Olympic Games*. Taiwan fared poorly at the 1988 Olympics, losing all three of its games in the eight-team field. In 1992 Taiwan won the silver medal behind Cuba and ahead of Japan.

Taiwanese Players Abroad.

"Welcome to 'The Show!' No commercials. No director. No money. Just the simple complexity of America's favorite past time sport, presented in an intelligent fashion. Enjoy!!!" —Taiwanese-Heroes.com.

The best of the Taiwanese players have played in Japan's lower-level professional leagues, and one player made it to the U.S before the 1990s. Pitcher Tan Shin-ming was loaned to the Class A Fresno (California) Giants for the 1974 season. He had an 8–4 record in his only pro season. Later he managed one of the Taiwanese professional teams of the 1990s.

In January 1999 the Dodgers signed Taiwanese outfielder Chin-Feng Chen for a bonus of $680,000. He was a rightfielder on the 1990 Taiwanese Little League World Series champions and made his Major League debut in September 2002, the first Taiwanese player to do so. The first Taiwanese pitcher to make his debut in the Major Leagues was Chin-Hui Tsao, on July 25, 2003, for the Rockies. He had been signed in October 1999.

Professional League. Taiwanese businessmen formed a professional league for the 1991 season, called the Chinese Professional Baseball Association (CTPA). The original four teams (later eight) of 25 players were the Wei-Chuan Dragons, President Lions, Brother Elephants and Mercuries Tigers.

Eighty of the original players had played in the Taiwanese Little Leagues and nine had been to the Little League World Series. Each of the four pro teams could carry five foreign players because of the shortage of native players. In 1992 the league had 11 Americans, including Darrell Brown, who had played for the Minnesota Twins. Former Tiger pitcher Kevin Wickander played in the league in 1994 and Padres pitcher Mark Grant played there in 1995.

All players must be at least 24 years old, so that the national team is not depleted for international competition. The league has a 90-game schedule from March through October. Attendance in the first year was 800,000 and reached close to 1.2 million in 1992. By 2003 teams were averaging between 1,000 and 5,000 fans per game.

A player who hits a home run in the league receives a stuffed replica of the team's mascot from a young girl as the player crosses home plate. A similar tradition exists in Japan.

The "Black Eagles" gambling scandal rocked the league in 1997, leading to the banishment of three players and the dismantling of their club, the China Times Eagles. As a result of the scandal, the four-team Taiwan Major Leagues was formed that season, but it merged with the CTPA prior to the 2003 season.

By 2003 the average ticket price was U.S.$6 and the average Taiwanese player earned U.S. $58,000. Their American counterparts in Taiwan earned U.S.$96,000. The six professional teams in 2003: President Lions; China Trust Whales; Brother Elephants; Makoto Gida; First Securities Agan; and Sinon Bulls. Teams play 50 games a season and usually have a week off after a three-game series (teams previously played upwards of 100 games per season). Teams do not have home ballparks, and instead rotate around the country.

Take Me Out to the Ballgame (1908)

"Take me out to the Ballgame,
Take me out to the crowd.
"Buy me some peanuts and Cracker Jack,
I don't care if I never get back.
Let me root, root, root for the home team,
If they don't win it's a shame.
For it's 1, 2, 3 strikes you're out
At the old ball game."
— Chorus of the famous song, without the little-known first stanza.

"A friend of mine, Harry Williams, wrote 'In the Shade of the Old Apple Tree' and he never saw an apple tree." — Jack Norworth defending his ability to write the song without ever attending a baseball game.

"Take Me Out to the Corporate Sponsored Megaplex" — David Letterman's take on an updated version of the song.

See also *Seventh Inning Stretch*.

Jack Norworth was a top vaudeville performer when he wrote the song in 1908, among 2,500 he wrote over his career. He submitted the lyric to Albert Von Tilzer, who put music to it. It was published by the York Music Company and became an instant hit as the top song of 1908.

Norworth was inspired by a subway advertisement for a Giants game: "BASEBALL TODAY—POLO GROUNDS." Yet Norworth did not see a Major League game until 32 years after he wrote the lyric when the Dodgers staged a day for him on June 27, 1940. Von Tilzer waited only 20 years to see his first game.

Norworth performed the song regularly at the Folies Bergère with his wife, Nora Bayes. The song was performed by Anne Sheridan and Dennis Morgan in the 1944 movie, *Shine on Harvest Moon*, and in 1949 by Gene Kelly, Esther Williams (who swam to it) and Frank Sinatra in a movie of the same name. Norworth and Bayes also wrote "Shine on Harvest Moon," as well as the lesser known "Let's Get the Umpire's Goat." Norworth's version:

"Katie Casey was baseball mad,
Had the fever and had it bad;
Just to root for the hometown crew,
Every Sou [French coin, spelled "Soo" in Norworth's original] Katie blew,
On a Saturday, her young beau,
Called to see if she'd like to go,
To see a show, but Miss Kate said, 'No,'
I'll tell you what you can do."

The *Whole Baseball Catalog*, by Dan Schlossberg (1983), contains a version that is patterned on the Norworth version:

"Katie Casey was born mad,
Had the fever and had it bad;
Just to root for the hometown crew,
Ev'ry son, Katie knew.
On a Saturday, her young beau,
Called to see if she'd like to go,
To see a show but Miss Kate said, 'No,'
I'll tell you what you can do."
[Chorus]

There have been more than 100 recordings of the song, including a 1950 rendition by Ralph Branca, Phil Rizzuto and Tommy Henrich with Mitch Miller and the Sandpipers, and a 1978 version by Cubs announcer Harry Caray. Ken Griffey, Jr., and Sammy Sosa recorded a rap version of the song with LL Cool J.

The lyric sung during the 7th inning stretch is only the chorus. Another version is about Nelly Kelly, who may have been the first Baseball Annie:

"Nelly Kelly loved baseball games,
Knew the players, knew all their names.
You could see her there every day,
Shout 'Hurray' — when they'd play —
Said to Coney Isle, dear, let's go,
Then Nelly started to fret and pout,
And to him I heard her shout:
[Chorus: Take Me Out to the Ballgame...]
"Nelly Kelly was sure some fan,
She would root just like any man.
Told the umpire he was wrong,
All along — good and strong —
When the score was just two to two,
Nelly Kelly knew what to do,
Just to cheer up the boys she knew.
Sure made the gang sing this song":
[Chorus]

Harpo Marx. Nontalker Harpo Marx once played a classical version of the tune on his harp during an "I Love Lucy" episode.

No Fan. Relief pitcher Larry Anderson took a dim view of the baseball classic: "In the seventh inning, [the fans] all get up and sing, 'Take Me Out to the Ball Game,' and they're already there. It's really a stupid thing to say. And I don't know who made 'em sing it. Why would somebody that's there get up and sing, 'Take Me Out to the Ball Game?' The first person to do it must have been a moron."

Harry Caray. Caray was in the habit of singing "Take Me Out to the Ballgame" during the 7th inning stretch but did it to no one in particular and without a microphone. On Opening Day in 1976 White Sox owner Bill Veeck noticed that a few fans looked up at the broadcast booth and started singing when Caray started in. Veeck arranged the next day for a secret microphone to broadcast Caray to the crowd. It was a success, and the tradition continued through 1997 while Caray was with the Cubs (he died in February 1998). Veeck's rationale: "Harry, anybody in the ballpark hearing you sing 'Take Me Out to the Ball Game' knows that he can sing as well as you can. Probably *better* than you can. So he or she sings along. Hell, if you had a good singing voice, you'd intimidate them, and *nobody* would join in."

Caray sang it on the "Tonight Show" with Jay Leno on May 2, 1996, while the show was broadcasting in Chicago.

In the 14th inning of a game at Wrigley Field, fans looked expectantly at the broadcast booth, waiting for Caray to belt out a second "Take Me Out to the Ballgame." Alas, Harry was nowhere to be found, but the fans nevertheless spontaneously broke into song without him.

At the 2003 Hall of Fame induction ceremony, Johnny Bench donned oversized black-rimmed glasses *à la* Caray and sang a credible version of the song.

Ken Burns. Filmmaker Ken Burns recorded 250 versions of the song for his 1994 baseball documentary (see also *Television Shows*).

Ozzy Osbourne. In mid-August 2003 rocker Ozzy Osbourne butchered the song at Wrigley Field. After Osbourne slopped his way through the song, the *Chicago Tribune* headlined the story with "Dysfunctional fun at the old ballpark" and called Osbourne the "world's most notorious mumbler" and said his performance "is yet another reason why this once quaint tradition needs to be stuffed in a trunk and sent to the bottom of Lake Michigan."

TAKE ME OUT TO THE BALL GAME
BY JACK NORWORTH

KATIE CASEY WAS BASE BALL MAD
HAD THE FEVER AND HAD IT BAD,
JUST TO ROOT FOR THE HOME ~~TEAM~~ TOWN CREW
EVERY SUE — KATIE BLEW
ON A SATURDAY, HER ~~XXXX~~ YOUNG BEAU
CALLED TO SEE IF SHE'D LIKE TO GO
TO SEE A SHOW BUT MISS ~~XXXX~~ KATE SAID NO,
I'LL TELL YOU WHAT YOU CAN DO —

TAKE ME OUT TO THE BALL GAME
TAKE ME OUT ~~TO~~ WITH THE ~~XXXX~~ CROWD
BUY ME SOME PEANUTS AND CRACKERJACK
I DON'T CARE IF I NEVER GET BACK
LET ME ROOT, ROOT, ROOT FOR THE HOME TEA
IF THEY DON'T WIN ITS A SHAME,
FOR ITS ONE, TWO, THREE STRIKES, YOUR OUT
AT THE OLD BALL GAME

Original notes for the lyric written by Jack Norworth.

In an Internet vote of fans, the Osbourne version was voted the worst by 63.2% of the voters. Mike Ditka was second with 24.8%; Ditka sped through the song in record time.

Sacked. On August 7, 2001, during the 7th inning stretch of the Cubs' 5–4 win over the Rockies, former Chicago Bears lineman Steve McMichael led the crowd in the song. Just before starting, McMichael, upset at a call that went against the Cubs in the 6th inning, yelled to the crowd, "Don't worry, I'll have some speaks with that home plate umpire after the game." Umpire Angel Hernandez threw McMichael out of the game, which required him to leave the stands. The Cubs won in the 9th inning when Ricky Gutierrez slid under a tag at home.

Bad Timing. During Kirby Puckett's assault trial in 2003, a phone rang in the courtroom during expert witness testimony. The tone, of course, was "Take Me Out To the Ballgame," which caused a titter of laughter during the otherwise solemn proceedings.

Tallest Players

"Howard Schultz, first baseman for whom the Dodgers gave St. Paul $40,000 and players, is still six-feet seven inches tall, his draft board learned today, after measuring him for the second time." — World War II newspaper report.

"Winfield is on first base, and he's always a threat to grow." — Jerry Coleman on 6'6" Dave Winfield.

"Maybe Cal might get shortstop changed to bigstop." — Giants manager Dusty Baker on 6'4" Cal Ripken.

"I fouled off one of his 2-and-2 sliders, and when I looked up, he was standing 10 feet away, giving me this frightening serial killer stare, and I said to myself, 'My God, what is he going to throw me now?' I ain't seen nothing that big on a pitching mound." — Reds first baseman Sean Casey, on facing 6'10" Randy Johnson.

"No. The ball is too big, and there's no chance of a rainout." — 6'10" pitcher Eric Hillman on why he never played basketball. Hillman made his debut in 1992 as a pitcher for the Mets (pitching in 49 games over three seasons). Hillman and Mariners pitcher Randy Johnson were, until 2002, the all-time tallest Major League players at 6'10". Hillman must have been quite a curiosity when he pitched for the Chiba Lotte Marines in the Japanese leagues in 1996. In June 2002 the Mariners drafted 6'10" high school pitcher Ryan Anderson from Michigan, nicknamed "Big Unit II." He was the 19th pick overall and was still in the minor leagues through 2004.

In spring 2002, 6'11" pitcher Jon Rauch made the White Sox roster and was 2–1 in eight appearances for the club, but did not make it back in 2003.

Yankee pitcher Mark Hendrickson stood 6'9" when he pitched for the club in 2003.

Before them was 6'9" Johnny Gee, who won seven Major League games during the 1940s.

Gene Conley was a 6'8" pitcher who appeared in 91 Major League games in the 1950s and 1960s. Conley also played for the Boston Celtics championship **Basketball** teams.

In 1944 the Tigers gave a tryout to pitcher Ralph Siewert, who stood 6'11" and was classified 4-F during World War II. He did not make it. Nor did 6'9" James Stewart, who was given a tryout by the Phillies. Siewert had the privilege of wearing the practice pants of pitcher Schoolboy Rowe, who was 6'4½" and by then in the Navy.

The 1992 Orioles may have had the all-time tallest starting rotation, averaging almost 6'5". Ben McDonald and Rick Sutcliffe were 6'7", Storm Davis and Bob Milacki were 6'4" and Mike Mussina was 6'2". Dennis Rasmussen, who stood 6'7", attempted to break into the rotation early in spring training. Mussina's comment about the five: "I'm the point guard — I move the ball around."

Tall Offer. After midget Eddie Gaedel appeared in a game for the Browns in 1951, an English circus giant named Ted Evans offered his services to Browns owner Bill Veeck. He claimed to be 9'3½" and according to George Plimpton in *Out of My League* (1961), "would have had a truly splendid strike zone."

Tampa Bay Devil Rays

American League 1998–

"The Best Practical Joke. Tell a teammate he's been trade to the Devil Rays." — Roger Clemens doing a David Letterman "Top 10 Things Baseball Has Taught Me."

Origins. Tampa/St. Petersburg was threatening Major League Baseball with antitrust litigation after local investors were rebuffed in their efforts to obtain the Giants. The Major League owners agreed on March 9, 1995, to award the city an *Expansion* franchise for 1998.

First Game. The team's first game was played March 31, 1998, as the Devil Rays lost to the Tigers 11–6. Wilson Alvarez was the loser and Wade Boggs hit the club's first home run.

Owners. The ownership group was headed by Vince Naimoli, a New Jersey native, Tampa resident and graduate of Notre Dame and Harvard Business School. Naimoli made his millions in various manufacturing businesses. Other investors include the Home Shopping Network and various individuals with a net worth of over $3 billion.

In May 2004 a group headed by New York investor Stuart Sternberg bought 48% of the Devil Rays. Vince Naimoli continued as managing general partner running the day-to-day operations.

Nickname.

"Martha Rays, Stevie Rays, Fay Rays or Billy Rays." — One fan's alternatives to the already unpopular Devil Rays.

The club sponsored a "name that team" contest for which it received 7,000 name entries. The largest percentage included the word "Ray," so the club decided to use some form of that word. Two local fans spent $87 to obtain trademark rights to "Thunder," "Thunderbolts," and "Tarpons," hoping to sell their rights to the club owners at a large profit, but lead owner Vince Naimoli refused to negotiate. The club also considered "Stingrays," but the Hawaiian League entry refused to give up its name.

The club settled on Devil Ray, which is something like a manta ray, a warm-sea fish with a flat body, expanded fins and a long, thin tail. There were immediate complaints about the club's nickname, in part because Ray spelled backward is "Yar," the name of a satanic dog. In late 2002 Tampa Bay infielder Russ Johnson requested that the team drop the "devil" from its name. After suffering from depression he returned midseason as a born-again Christian and said, "there's no use honoring that part of the spirit."

Key Seasons.

"Tampa Bay Double A's" — Steve Rushin's nickname for the 2003 club.

1998. The club hasn't had anything resembling a "key season," other than perhaps the inaugural season. They were 63–99 under manager Larry Rothchild.

2004. The Devil Rays set a record by coming back from 18 games under .500 to go back over that mark, but faded later in the season and finished 70–91; still a franchise record, however.

Key Ballplayers.

Roberto Hernandez. The reliever had three stellar seasons for the crummy club, with save totals of 26, 43 and 32 beginning in 1998.

Fred McGriff hit 99 home runs for the club during 3½ seasons before leaving for the Cubs in late 2001.

Key Managers.

Larry Rothchild, former Marlins pitching coach, was the club's first manager and finished last each full season he was at the helm from 1998 through 2000. He was fired 14 games into the 2001 season.

Lou Piniella took over the club in 2003 and led the Devil Rays to a last-place finish. They started poorly again in 2004, but came from 18 games below .500 to even, but then faded to 70–91 with a poor second half. Nevertheless, it was a franchise-record number of wins.

Ballpark.

"Tropicana Field is a useful civics lesson in how to build a lousy ballpark in a terrible location." — W. Blake Gray.

"Putting a baseball face on the faceless ThunderDome wasn't easy." — Joel Poiley in *Baseball Weekly*.

Tropicana Field is located in downtown St. Petersburg and seats 43,000. It was renamed in 1993 after first being called the Florida Suncoast Dome and later the Thunderdome when the NHL Tampa Bay Lightning played there. Construction of the indoor ballpark began in 1986 and opened in 1990 at a cost of $138 million. In 1995 it was determined that it was already terribly outdated and required another $47 million for upgrades. In 1998 the upgrades had cost $70 million to its owner, the city of St. Petersburg.

When the Devil Rays began play on March 31, 1998, the ballpark featured the shortest left-field line in baseball at 315 feet. It had the second-deepest center field at 416 (Joe Robbie Stadium has a 434-foot center field fence; later reduced to 404 feet). Right center was 370 feet and right field was 322 feet. It has artificial turf and had an original capacity of 45,000. The Teflon-coated fiberglass roof is 225 feet high and glows orange at night.

Key Broadcasters. The four original broadcasters, all still with the club in 2004, were former pitcher Joe Magrane, Paul Olden, Charlie Slowes and DeWayne Staats.

Books. (Why bother?) John Nichols, *The History of the Tampa Bay Devil Rays* (2000).

Tampering with the Ball See *Illegal Pitches* and *Spitballs*

Tarpaulins

"Covers the Field" — Big bold letters on the new tarpaulin unveiled in 1990 by the White Sox.

Evolution. Before the use of tarps, teams poured gasoline and burned the fields to dry them out. New Orleans owner Abner Powell is credited with using the first form of infield tarpaulin in 1889. In 1943 in *The Sporting News*, Powell claimed that he used a tarp on the field during a spring training visit to New Orleans by the Cincinnati Red Stockings and that the club took the idea north.

Early tarps were made of heavy canvas and required drying out after each use. Some clubs tried using giant sponges to soak up water in the infield. Prior to the 1915 season, the Reds spent $1,800 on an army duck cover 160 feet square to cover the infield. That was the same year in which the National League first required all clubs to have such covers. The next innovation was by the Indians in the 1940s, who used a lightweight nonabsorbent spun-glass tarp.

In the 1960s teams began using tarps with plastic-coated nylon,

a form of which is the standard tarp of today. The foremost maker of modern tarpaulins is Putterman & Co. of Chicago. Most manufacturers now use polyethylene to make the 160' × 160' covers. The covers cost approximately $10,000 and weigh one-half ton.

Worn Out. The Indians once claimed that Bill Veeck's Browns were using a sieve to cover their infield; the Browns' tarp was so old and had so many holes in it that it was useless.

Injuries. Vince Coleman was "attacked" by the Cardinals' automatic tarpaulin roller prior to Game 1 of the 1985 World Series and was unable to play because of a leg injury.

Mickey Klutts was on the disabled list at least 10 times and once put himself out of action after running into a tarp.

Forfeit. The Blue Jays have played one forfeit game, a 9–0 decision against Baltimore on September 15, 1977. In that game Jim Clancy had held the Orioles to two-hits over five innings before Earl Weaver pulled his club off the field. His reason was that the tarps on the Blue Jays bullpen created a hazard for his players.

Assist. In a 7–7 tie during Game 7 of the 1925 World Series between the Pirates and Senators, Kiki Cuyler batted against Senators pitcher Walter Johnson. With two outs in the 8th inning and the bases loaded, Kuyler hit an apparent inside-the-park grand slam that rolled into a tarpaulin. The umpires ruled it a ground rule double instead and the Pirates had to settle for only two runs as the next batter popped out to end the inning. The Pirates won anyway 9–7.

Tattoos

"I've got some tribal symbols, a few skulls, there's a dragon on one of my arms … you might say I've got issues." — Jason Giambi, explaining his tattoos in *Spin* magazine.

"It hurts worse than a tattoo." — Pitcher Arthur Rhodes on shock-wave therapy for his injured back.

"If I got a tattoo of a grapefruit when I was your age, Rob, it would look like a raisin now." — Broadcaster Ernie Harwell talking to his co-host, former pitcher Rob Dibble, who has 15 tattoos.

In 1993 the Blue Jays won the World Series and September call-up Mike Maksudian, a catcher who played a total of three games with the Jays, was the darling of the fans after his speech at the club's celebration in downtown Toronto. The press had reported that he had eaten a huge insect he had found crawling around right field. This earned him the nickname "Bugsy" and put him on the local news for a week. Upon receiving his ring, Maksudian announced that he was going to live up to a commitment to get a Blue Jay tattooed on his rear end if the team won. It was unclear with whom this deal had been struck. Two weeks later Bugsy was released by the organization, and he played a few games the following year as a Cub.

Taxes

"The fur-coated millionaire who goes to the Yale Bowl in his Rolls Royce and thermos bottle of hot scotch within reach doesn't have to pay a 10% tax, but some poor boob who washes dishes in an all-night restaurant has to come across with the tax; just the same. Where's the consistency?" — Editorial after the 1918 war tax was dropped from college football tickets, but not professional baseball.

"Good news from the IRS if you're a Cubs fan. They say if you're a Cubs fan, you can deduct the entire year now as a total loss." — Jay Leno in 1997 after the Cubs started the year 0–14.

"They hate when you pick up the money, so I always do. I

declare the $1.50 a season on my income tax."—Twins outfielder Torii Hunter after picking up coins thrown at him by A's fans.

See **Collective Bargaining Agreements—2002** for a discussion of Major League Baseball's luxury tax on more prosperous teams.

Team Ownership. Bill Veeck revolutionized the purchase of Major League Baseball teams by the way he structured his purchase of the Indians in 1946. Prior to that a buyer paid for the value of the club. Veeck did not do this because of the adverse tax consequences. He paid $50,000 for title to the club and the remainder for the players. By doing this he could depreciate the value of the players over five to 10 years, like any piece of equipment in a company.

This method made team ownership much more attractive to a businessman who had another business. He could use the write-offs from the sports team against profits from his other enterprise. Because of the abuse of this approach, the IRS limits to 50% (60% for many years) the amount of the purchase price that may be allocated to the players. The basic tax issues involved in buying a ballclub were explained succinctly by Veeck in his autobiography, *Veeck—As in Wreck*, with Ed Linn (1962).

One of the first cases that future White Sox owner Jerry Reinsdorf handled as a tax lawyer for the IRS involved tax delinquencies by the White Sox and Veeck.

Canada. Players who play for Canadian Major League teams suffer the greatest hardship because of taxes, sometimes paying 30% more than their U.S.-based counterparts.

World War II. During the war an entertainment tax of 10% was levied on baseball's gate receipts. In 1944 the tax was increased to 20%, but was eliminated after the war.

City Tax. In 1992 the city of Philadelphia began collecting a 4.3% city wage tax on visiting workers, including professional athletes, for money earned there.

Nice Try. Maury Wills once tried to exclude from his gross income the value of awards he had received by claiming they were awards for "artistic achievement." A federal tax court disallowed the claim in 1969.

Memorabilia Sales Abuse.

"A lot of us would like to see Darryl Strawberry wearing stripes—just not the same ones that Joe DiMaggio and Mickey Mantle wore."—Sportswriter Todd Phipers when Strawberry signed with the Yankees after finishing a drug suspension and serving a sentence for tax evasion.

By the 1980s the sale of autographs and other memorabilia by players was rampant. Many players were paid in cash for their services and failed to declare the income for tax purposes. Pete Rose was a prime target in the 1980s (see also **Gambling**). In 1994 Darryl Strawberry and his agent, Eric Goldschmidt, were indicted for covering up $500,000 in income that Strawberry earned from promotional appearances and autographs. Later he pleaded guilty but served no jail time.

In July 1995 Duke Snider and Willie McCovey pleaded guilty to tax evasion after failing to declare income from memorabilia shows. Snider admitted not reporting $100,000 in cash and McCovey admitted to receiving $41,800 in 1989 and a total of $69,800 between 1988 and 1990. They were the first in a series of players who were indicted for tax fraud arising from a 1989 memorabilia show.

The IRS said that Pete Rose owed $151,689 in federal taxes from 1998, according to a lien filed on a Rose home near Los Angeles. He later pleaded guilty to tax evasion. In 2004 the IRS filed another lien against Rose for unpaid back taxes of $973,693.28 between 1997 and 2002.

Salary Deduction Limitation. In 1995 there was a bill that moved through Congress that would have limited the business deduction for sports franchise owners on player salaries. Salaries were entirely deductible before the bill, but it proposed that all salaries in excess of $1 million would not be deductible. Based on 1995 professional salaries, the change would have generated an additional $800 million in tax revenue. The bill died in committee.

Team Captain

"The leader of each team must be listened to by his team members."—1796 description of a German form of baseball called *das deutsche Ballspiel*, "the Germanball Game."

"The kid who was lucky enough to come up with a real league ball, or a 'store-bought' bat, automatically became team captain."—Ford Frick in *Games, Asterisks and People* (1973).

19th Century.

"The chief duty of team captains was to try to keep at least some of the players sober."—Glenn Dickey on early captains, in *The History of National League Baseball* (1979).

Nineteenth century team captains were what would today be described as the team managers. The original "managers" were more like the general managers and business managers of the modern era. In the late 19th century, captains gradually became less important as the club manager began concentrating more on field activities rather than the business end of the club. This resulted in the creation of the business manager position, which later evolved into the general manager position.

The 19th century team captain had additional duties. For example, Hugh Duffy of the 1890s Red Stockings was required to make sure that all bats and balls were returned to the clubhouse after the game. He received a raise of $12.50 per month for his troubles.

Bob Ferguson of the 1876–1877 National League Hartford Dark Blues and a former National Association president, wore a white belt printed with "I Am Captain."

In the early part of the 20th century, Kid Gleason was captain of the Phillies. He kept a leather belt in his locker that he used on young players who "misbehaved."

Yankees. The Yankees had no team captains between Lou Gehrig in the 1930s and Thurman Munson in the 1970s, both of whom died tragically. Gehrig remained captain through his death, despite not playing for the last three years of his tenure. Babe Ruth was the Yankee captain in 1922 for six days in May, but lost the job after a fight with a fan.

Ron Guidry and Willie Randolph were named co-captains in 1986. Randolph believed that he should have been named captain two years earlier but that racism was a factor in the delay. Don Mattingly captained the club from 1991 through 1995. In June 2003, despite making negative remarks about Derek Jeter during spring training, owner George Steinbrenner named Jeter captain of the team.

Hal Chase was the first Yankee captain, in 1912, followed by Roger Peckinpaugh from 1914 to 1921. Between Ruth and Gehrig was Everett Scott from 1922 through mid-May 1925. Graig Nettles followed Munson in 1982 through 1984.

Cubs. Third baseman Ron Santo was the youngest Cubs captain at age 25 in 1965.

Red Sox. In 1967 Dick Williams took over as manager of the Red Sox, who had finished ninth the previous season. One of his first acts was to strip Carl Yastrzemski of his role as team captain. William said that he was the boss and the club did not need a captain. Yastrzemski was not upset because it freed him to concentrate on his own game. It must have helped because he won the Triple Crown and led the team to the World Series against the Cardinals.

Black Team Captain. See *Black "Firsts."*

Rough Cut. On July 5, 1923, the second-division Phillies cut their team captain, Goldie Rapp. It may be the only time in Major League history that a club's team captain was sent down to the minor leagues.

Team Physicians See *Doctors* and *Trainers*

Team Sales

"It is hard to lose money selling a baseball team, in part because there are probably more major Van Gogh paintings floating around than available big league franchises." — Walter Shapiro in *Time* magazine.

Approval. By the 1990s a sale required approved of three quarters of the league's clubs and a majority of the other league's clubs.

Evolution of Sales Price/20th Century.

1902. Reds sold for $125,000.

1903. Phillies sold for $200,000.

Yankees, a new franchise, sold for $18,000.

1904. Tigers sold for $50,000.

1909. Phillies sold for $350,000.

1915. Browns sold for $750,000.

1917. Red Sox sold for $400,000.

1923. Red Sox sold for $1.5 million.

1927. Indians sold for $1 million.

1934. Reds sold for a Depression-era $450,000.

1944. Phillies sold for $400,000 during World War II.

1945. Yankees sold for $2.8 million, a post–World War II–deflated price (after being valued at $7 million in 1939).

1946. Indians sold for a postwar deflated price of $1.6 million.

1947. Cardinals sold for $4 million.

1949. Indians sold for $2.5 million.

1953. Browns sold for almost $2.5 million and moved to Baltimore.

Cardinals sold for $4.5 million ($3.75 million in some sources).

1955. A's sold for $3.5 million and moved to Kansas City.

1956. Tigers sold for $5.5 million.

1964. Yankees sold for $11.2 million.

1969. Senators sold for $10 million.

1970. Brewers sold for $10.8 million.

1973. Yankees sold for $10 million.

1976. Braves sold for $12 million.

1979. Astros sold for $19 million.

Orioles sold for $10.5 million.

1980. Mets sold for $21.1 million.

A's sold for $12.7 million.

1981. Phillies sold for $30.2 ($31.7 million in some sources).

Cubs sold for $20.5 million.

White Sox sold for $20 million.

Mariners sold for $13 million.

1983. Tigers sold for almost $50 million ($53 million in some sources).

1984. Twins sold for $43 million ($36 million and $38 million in some sources).

Reds sold for $24 million.

1985. Pirates sold for $22 million ($26 million in some sources).

1986. Mets sold for $95 million ($80.75 million in some sources).

Indians sold for $35 million.

1987. Red Sox sold for $150 million, including the ballpark.

1988. Orioles sold for $70 million.

1989. 57.5% of the Rangers sold for $46 million, and the club was valued at $80 million.

Mariners sold for $76 million.

1990. Padres sold for $75 million.

Expos sold for $86 million ($80 million in some sources).

Giants sold for $100 million.

Astros sold for $95 million ($100 million and $116 million in some sources).

Tigers sold for $85 million.

Mariners sold for $90 million ($106 million and $125 million in some sources).

Marlins and Rockies sold for $95 million as expansion franchises.

1993. Orioles sold for $173 million.

1994. Padres sold for $83.5 million, with $30 million going to pay off debt.

One-third of Red Sox sold for $33 million.

1995. A's sold for $85 million.

Pirates sold for $85 million.

1996. Cardinals sold for $150 million.

1998. Dodgers sold for $311 million, the highest price paid for an American sports franchise.

1999. Indians sold for $320 million ($323 million in some sources)

2001. Red Sox sold for $660 million, but the price included a cable network and related properties.

2003. Angels sold for $184 million

Dodgers sold for $430 million (including real estate)

Franchise Values/1990s. In 1994 *Baseball Weekly* printed estimates of value for each Major League franchise. The estimates were developed from *Financial World* and *Sports Inc.* magazines, with assistance from economics professor Robert Baade at Lake Forest (Ill.) College. The 1996 values from the same source are in parentheses:

New York Yankees	$160 million ($209m)
Toronto Blue Jays	$155 ($152)
New York Mets	$145 ($131)
Baltimore Orioles	$140 ($168)
Boston Red Sox	$136 ($143)
Los Angeles Dodgers	$135 ($147)
Oakland Athletics	$124 ($ 97)
Chicago White Sox	$123 ($144)
Colorado Rockies	$120 ($133)
Florida Marlins	$115 ($ 98)
Kansas City Royals	$111 ($ 80)
Texas Rangers	$106 ($138)
California Angels	$105 ($ 90)
San Francisco Giants	$103 ($122)
Cincinnati Reds	$103 ($ 99)
San Diego Padres	$103 ($ 67)
Chicago Cubs	$101 ($140)
St. Louis Cardinals	$ 98 ($112)
Detroit Tigers	$ 97 ($106)
Philadelphia Phillies	$ 96 ($103)
Pittsburgh Pirates	$ 95 ($ 62)
Minnesota Twins	$ 95 ($ 74)
Atlanta Braves	$ 88 ($163)
Houston Astros	$ 87 ($ 97)
Montreal Expos	$ 86 ($ 68)

Milwaukee Brewers $ 86 ($ 71)
Seattle Mariners $ 86 ($ 92)
Cleveland Indians $ 81 ($125)

In 2000 the Yankees were worth $540 million, according to *Forbes*. In 2003 the values had increased dramatically for several teams, according to *Forbes*:

New York Yankees $849 million
New York Mets $498
Boston Red Sox $488
Los Angeles Dodgers $449
Atlanta Braves $423

The Angels were 20th at $225 million and the Devil Rays were at the bottom at $113 million.

60/40 Debt-to-Value Rule. In the 1960s the American League's Long Range Planning Committee instituted a rule that required all prospective purchasers to have 60% of the purchase price in cash or the equivalent. Only 40% could be borrowed. This rule was used to temporarily block Bill Veeck's purchase of the White Sox in 1975. It eventually was adopted also by the National League. In 2002 Commissioner Bud Selig announced that he was going to enforce the rule for future purchases, prompting this comment from baseball finance expert Doug Pappas (a prominent SABR member who died in 2004 at age 47 from heat prostration while camping): "At best, this is one more example of Bud's arbitrary and selective enforcement of MLB's rules, retroactively punishing owners who've spent more on players than Bud would like. At worst, it's yet another grotesque case of Selig, he of the permanent conflict of interest, twisting the rules for his own benefit. In 1995, his Milwaukee Brewers were so far in debt they couldn't borrow money to contribute to the construction of their new park. *Forbes* estimated that as of the 1997 season, the Brewers' debt had risen to an incredible 97% of franchise value. Selig said nothing about the 60/40 rule. But the Brewers' new park opened in 2001. The first-year attendance spike sent club revenues to a record $113 million. Isn't it amazing how the Commissioner suddenly decided to enforce the rule just when his own club could finally meet the standard?"

It also became an issue in 2003 when Frank McCourt was in the process of buying the Dodgers in a highly leveraged sale. The deal eventually concluded in January 2004 when the seller, Rupert Murdoch's News Corporation, agreed to retain a 20% interest that would be paid off over time.

In 2003 *Forbes* magazine prepared an estimate of the debt-to-value ratios of all clubs (including stadium construction financing), and several did not meet the 60% test supposedly enforced by Major League Baseball, including the Diamondbacks (debt of 109% of value), Dodgers (105%), Phillies (64%), Tigers (85%), Brewers (63%) and Expos (83%).

Teammates

"When I got to the big leagues, there was a man, Eddie Murray, who showed me how to play this game day-in and day-out. I thank him for his example and for his friendship." — Cal Ripken at the ceremony following his record-breaking game.

"Roger [Clemens] is a great teammate. But on the mound? He's a badass mother." — Jason Giambi.

"He solidified the club. We became a great team when he came to know us and how much he could do for all of us." — Brooks Robinson on Frank Robinson's impact with the Orioles.

"Yes sir, they were fairly amazing in several respects, and that's the damn truth." — Casey Stengel on Mickey Mantle and Whitey Ford at their 1974 Hall of Fame inductions.

"I thought I'd be a catcher. And I'm sure Bags [Jeff Bagwell] thought he'd be in a Red Sox uniform, playing at Fenway Park. Next thing you know, you're two guys from New York and Connecticut living in Texas for the rest of your life." — Craig Biggio in 2003, when only six individual players had been on the same team (forget teammates) during the same period: John Franco (Mets), Barry Larkin (Reds), Edgar Martinez (Mariners), John Smoltz (Braves), Frank Thomas (White Sox) and Bernie Williams (Yankees). All were with their same clubs in 2004 also. Biggio and Bagwell had been teammates since 1991, when Bagwell joined the Astros (Biggio had been there since 1988).

Teams

See individual team entries and ***Major Leagues***.

For most teams played for, see ***Trades***.

For most years with one team, see ***Longest Careers*** — **Most Seasons With One Club**.

Books. Peter Filichia, *Professional Baseball Franchises* (1993), a complete club directory that includes teams in the Negro Leagues and minor leagues; Michael LeBlanc, *Professional Sports Team Histories* (1994).

Teeth

"Dave Kingman was like a cavity that made your whole mouth sore." — Cubs pitcher Bill Caudill.

See also ***Dentists***.

Dentures. Ty Cobb's dentures sold for $7,475 at a 2003 auction.

Mouthpiece. Roger Clemens went through about four mouthpieces a season while pitching. He found early in his career that he was having jaw problems and headaches because he clenched his teeth so tightly during games.

His Dentist Would Be Proud. Cubs pitcher Turk Wendell, a snuff and tobacco chewer, brushed his teeth between innings.

Toothpick. Tom Seaver's toothpick sold for $440 at an auction.

Teenagers

See ***High School Players***, ***Youngest Players*** and entries for various youth leagues such as ***Little League Baseball*** and ***Pony League***.

Telegraph and Telegrams

"Well, I see in the game in Minnesota that Terry Felton has relieved himself on the mound in the second inning." — Royals broadcaster Fred White noticing an error on the Western Union ticker describing Felton as coming in to relieve after he had started the game.

"PLEASE TELL US ONLY WHEN METS WIN" — Telegram from Mets owner Joan Payson, vacationing in Greece, to the club during its first season in 1962. She was frustrated after repeated negative news from New York. Payson noted that it "was about the last I heard from America that summer." Payson did not witness her first Mets victory until July 6, 1962, a game in which Rod Kanehl hit the club's first grand slam.

"You sacrificed a World's Championship for the American League to maudlin sentiment." — Telegram from Ban Johnson to Senators manager Bucky Harris after 37-year-old Walter Johnson blew two leads in Game 7 of the 1925 World Series. The Senators led 6–3 after four innings and 7–6 until the bottom of the 8th inning when they gave up three runs for a 9–7 loss. Johnson pitched a complete game, giving up five runs in the last two innings. The telegram ignored the eight errors in the series by shortstop Roger Peckinpaugh.

See **Re-Creations** for Western Union's role in the broadcast of radio re-creations.

Nineteenth Century. In 1886 the Cincinnati Red Stockings received $100 and free telegram service from Western Union in return for the right to carry game information over the wires. In 1897 the National League entered into a contract with Western Union whereby each club received $300 worth of telegram service in return for the telegraph concession for baseball. In the late 19th century, Western Union capitalized on the investment by installing private wires into pool rooms and other business establishments so they could obtain game information and post scores on blackboards. Western Union offices also posted inning-by-inning scores in their windows in pre-radio days.

Dodgers. In the early part of the 20th century, the Dodgers were less prosperous than their New York counterparts. While the Yankees and Giants paid for writers to cover them in spring training, the Dodgers paid the local Western Union operator to send information back to New York, a practice common to many teams at that time. Copywriters turned the wire reports into newspaper stories.

Western Union Contracts. For many years the telegraph operators in each city had separate contracts with the leagues and teams. In 1913 all teams asked their leagues to negotiate a single contract. As a result, Western Union paid $18,000 each year to each league, with an additional $1,000 to the National Commission.

In the 1950s and 1960s, Western Union charged a flat rate of $27.50 for play-by-play to be transmitted (for re-creations or otherwise), so long as the home team did not object. In the 1980s, Western Union still had exclusive rights to supply game reports to local stations.

Operators Barred. Around 1900 Charlie Comiskey barred telegraph operators from his ballpark because he claimed that they were cutting down on attendance by allowing fans to follow the game in progress without being there.

Motivation. In 1933 Giants shortstop Blondy Ryan had been hurt and was about to rejoin his pennant-contending team in St. Louis. He sent a telegram reading: "AM ON MY WAY! THEY CAN'T BEAT US." This turned into the rallying cry for the club, and the Giants won the pennant by five games.

Code. When Branch Rickey was looking for a suitable black player to be the one to integrate Organized Baseball, he sent a scout to the Caribbean. Tom Greenwade would wire back his reports with code letters at the beginning to let Rickey know the status of the ballplayer being reviewed: N–Z would start the report if it was a white Latin American player; A–M if it was a black player.

Initials. The initials of long-time Red Sox owners Tom Yawkey and Jean Yawkey are spelled out in Morse Code on the Fenway Park scoreboard. Above the Yawkey name is an enormous billboard that spells out "Red Sox Nation" in Morse Code.

Protest. In 1941 Dixie Walker of the Dodgers held out during spring training and 5,000 Brooklyn fans signed a telegram to manager Leo Durocher in Havana, Cuba: "Put Walker back in right field or we will boycott Dodgers."

Big Load. When Henry Aaron broke Babe Ruth's home run record, he received 20,000 congratulatory telegrams.

Hoax. Lou Proctor purportedly played in one game for the Browns in 1912. In the 1970s it was discovered that "Proctor" was a Western Union telegrapher who inserted his name into a box score for posterity. His statistics in *The Baseball Encyclopedia* showed him with one base on balls and no appearance in the field. After the truth was discovered, his name was removed from the official records.

Telephones

"'We'll practice for the play-offs at my house,' said the [Little League] coach. 'If you can't come, call me. Does everybody know my phone number?' Without a cue, the team chanted the correct phone number in unison. How come Billy Martin couldn't get the Yankees to do that?"—Thomas Boswell in *How Life Imitates the World Series* (1982).

"To reach most old ballplayers, even millionaire old ballplayers like Hank Greenberg, you simply call their homes around dinner time. A pleased, remembered voice comes through the phone."—Roger Kahn.

900 Number. In 1991 at the height of his popularity, Oakland A's slugger Jose Canseco had a 900 telephone number that fans could call for the latest scoop. In one of the recordings, he described his wife Esther's body (maybe one of the reasons why they were divorced).

Perk. Rick Reichardt negotiated a contract with the Angels that allowed him free phone calls totaling $7,500 per season.

In 1992 to lure downtown businessmen to the ballpark for afternoon games, the minor league Buffalo Bisons began offering free cellular phone and fax service. Haircuts and shoeshines were also offered.

Easy to Remember. The telephone number for Cubs announcer Harry Caray's sports bar in Chicago was 312-HOLY-COW.

Assault. During the 1945 World Series between the Tigers and Cubs, Yankee general manager Larry MacPhail was arrested on assault and battery charges growing out of his inability to place a long-distance call during a telephone strike near his estate in Maryland. MacPhail stormed into the local telephone office, insulted an operator and struck the manager in the face.

Billy Martin. In 1981 Martin was suspended as manager of the Yankees but still telephoned instructions to the dugout during games. Umpire Ken Kaiser realized what was happening and took the phone from a player, yelled to Martin, "You're disconnected, Billy!" and ripped the phone from the wall.

Phone Assault. When Dodger reliever Eric Gagne ripped a phone out of the wall in the visitor's clubhouse in San Francisco, the Giants charged him $600. He responded that it was only a wire, and that he had a $5 phone at home the club could have.

Television

"So many sports organizations have built their entire budgets around television that if we ever withdrew the money, the whole structure would collapse."—Television executive Roone Arledge.

"Football is to baseball as blackjack is to bridge. One is the quick jolt. The other the deliberate, slow-paced game of skill, but never was a sport more ideally suited to television than baseball. It's all there in front of you. It's theatre, really. The star is the spotlight on the mound, the supporting cast fanned out around him, the mathematical precision of the game moving with the kind of inevitability of Greek tragedy. With the Greek chorus in the bleachers!"—Vin Scully in the *Los Angeles Times* in 1976.

"Back in the middle 1940's a cloud no larger than a small man's hand suddenly appeared above the fields of sport. It was known as

Television or TV. Within a few short years this cloud was a raging storm, spear-headed by a wrecking cyclone. It struck two of the country's most popular sports — baseball and football — with a devastating crash." — Grantland Rice in *The Tumult and the Shouting* (1954).

See also **Television Shows** (not involving televised baseball games).

Baseball's First Televised Event. A's manager Connie Mack was interviewed on February 11, 1937, by television manufacturer Philco at the Philco plant. The interview was broadcast to the local cricket club where an audience of 200 journalists watched.

First Televised Game.

"Good afternoon ladies and gentlemen. Welcome to the first telecast of a sporting event. I'm not sure what it is we're doing here, but I certainly hope it turns out well for you people who are watching." — Broadcaster Bill Stern of station W2XBS in New York, at the first televised baseball game. The broadcast was over NBC on May 17, 1939, and featured Columbia and Princeton at Manhattan's Baker Field.

First Major League Telecast.

"It's difficult to see how this sort of thing can catch the public fancy." — Anonymous *New York Times* critic on televised baseball.

On August 26, 1939, NBC televised a Major League game over station W2XBS. The Reds played the Dodgers in a doubleheader at Ebbets Field. The first batter was Reds third baseman Billy Werber.

Almost no homes had television and fewer than 400 sets were in existence. Most of them were at companies interested in the technology. Two cameras were used for the first game, but viewers could not see the ball on the small kinescope screen. One camera was placed behind home plate, and the other was in the second deck. Broadcaster Red Barber did the talking for NBC, and before the game Reds pitcher Bucky Walters demonstrated how he gripped his curveball.

The game was broadcast to the Dodger club offices and press room, the Broadway Theater and the television building at the New York World's Fair. *The Sporting News* reported that the response was "instantaneous and amazing."

World Series Telecast. The first national World Series broadcast occurred in 1951, although the National League play-off which preceded that Series is actually the first national postseason broadcast.

Color. The first color broadcast was on August 11, 1951, for a Dodger home game doubleheader against the Braves carried on NBC television.

First Television Rights Sold. The Yankees were the first team to sell television rights, to DuMont in 1946 for $75,000. The sale is ironic considering that the Yankees were the last club to allow radio broadcasts.

Regular Telecasts. The first regularly televised Major League games were announced by Jack Brickhouse and Harry Creighton in 1948 over WGN for the Cubs.

On June 15, 1948, for the first time in Boston, a Major League club televised one of its games. The Braves were to go into first place that night, and it was caught live by WBZ-TV. It was a 6–3 win over the Cubs as regular radio announcers Jim Britt and Tom Hussey took turns doing radio and television.

Network Telecasts/"Game of the Week."

"I don't know how our folks come off callin' this the 'Game of

A fan and her portable television at the 1959 All-Star game in Los Angeles Memorial Coliseum.

the Week.' There's a much better game — Dodgers and Giants — *over on NBC.*" — Dizzy Dean broadcasting on CBS.

ABC aired the first weekly network telecasts in 1953 and 1954, but local blackouts were required. Commissioner Ford Frick opposed the games and only three teams agreed to allow them (A's, Indians and White Sox). The first "Game of the Week" aired June 6, 1953, with Falstaff Beer as the sponsor.

In 1955 the "Game of the Week" moved to CBS with Dizzy Dean working with Buddy Blattner through 1959. In 1957 CBS added a Sunday "Game of the Week." Blattner had started radio "Game of the Week" broadcasts in 1950 and left Dean after the 1959 National League play-off over a dispute with the network involving Dean's inability to broadcast that play-off. Dean thought Blattner had sided with the network when Blattner went ahead and broadcast without him. Blattner was forced out by Dean's behind-the-scenes maneuvering and Blattner went to the Cardinals (1960–1961), Angels (1962–1968) and Royals (1969–1975).

Former Dodger shortstop Pee Wee Reese succeeded Blattner as Dean's partner from 1960 through 1965 when Reese moved over to NBC to broadcast with Curt Gowdy in 1966–1968.

In 1957 NBC added its own "Game of the Week," but Dean on CBS was enormously popular and drowned NBC in the ratings. NBC's "Game" featured Lindsey Nelson, who teamed with Leo

Durocher in 1957–1959, Fred Haney in 1960, and Joe Garagiola in 1961.

In 1989 the "Game of the Week" was dropped as a regularly scheduled weekly show, prompting this comment from broadcaster Vin Scully after the last game, on October 9, 1989: "It's a passing of a great American tradition. It is sad. I really and truly feel that. It will leave a vast window, to use a Washington word, where people will not get Major League Baseball and I think that's a tragedy."

The "Game of the Week" was still broadcast through 1992, but irregular scheduling killed the ratings. Ratings reached 6.3 in 1981 and 6.5 in 1985. They then began a steady decline. CBS's ratings for the show dropped from 5.1 to 3.4 in the first two years of its last contract (1990–1992), and then to 3.1 in the third year. The 1993 ABC-NBC baseball deal eliminated the "Game of the Week." Under the new package that was in place for the 1994–1995 seasons, the networks were obligated to televise only 16 regular-season games, none before the All-Star break.

Ratings dropped significantly in the early 1990s for regular-season network telecasts (Reg.), League Championship Series (LCS), World Series (W.S.), and ESPN regular-season games (ESPN):

Year	Reg.	LCS	W.S.	ESPN
1990	4.7	11.6	20.8	2.1
1991	4.0	11.9	24.0	2.0
1992	3.4	10.5	20.2	1.5

"Ratings" are a measure of the percentage of television sets in the country (whether turned on or not) tuned to the program. A "share" is the percentage of television sets which are turned on *and* which are tuned to the program.

Fox Sports saw a tremendous increase in 1998, the largest burst in 32 years. Fox's ratings increased 15%, from 2.7 to 3.1. Because of the home run chase by Mark McGwire and Sammy Sosa, broadcasts during the final nine weeks of the season average 3.4 rating, up 31 percent from the 2.5 rating during the final nine weeks the previous year.

In 2003 Fox's regular season ratings were up 8%, a 2.7 rating compared to 2.5 in 2002, its best numbers since 1999.

Mutual Broadcasting. Expansion hurt the 1950s Mutual Broadcasting System, which reached many regional and local television markets that had no direct access to Major League Baseball. Prior to expansion in the early 1960s, 55% of the country had no Major League coverage. Starting in 1960, network television broadcast an astounding 123 games over the 25-week season. The combination of ABC, CBS and NBC effectively cut out the heart of Mutual's market, mirroring its losses on radio.

First Baseball Network Package/1965 Season. As early as 1951 owner Bill Veeck of the small-market Browns wanted to pool television revenues evenly among Major League clubs, but the successful Yankees and other large-market teams opposed the idea. The Yankees were often featured and the lowly Browns were not.

In 1964 NFL commissioner Pete Rozelle spearheaded the drive to have Congress eliminate the antitrust implications and allow professional sports leagues to bargain with the networks on behalf of all teams. This led to the equal share for each team concept that soon was adopted by baseball.

The first Major League Baseball network pact was announced on December 15, 1964. The one-year agreement with ABC did not include the Phillies, whose local contract barred it from participating. It also did not include the Yankees, whose contract with CBS had one more year to run. The agreement was between baseball and ABC for $5.4 million and included Saturday and holiday broadcasts.

ABC's "Game of the Week" featured broadcaster Merle Har-

mon. It was the first time that a broadcaster in the booth was connected to a production truck. ABC did not renew its option after that first season, not only because of low ratings, but because the network needed the cash for its purchase of college football games.

ABC's telecasts were killed by CBS's few regional and local games featuring Dizzy Dean. In addition, there were no restrictions on local broadcasts at the same time as the network show, which cut into ABC's ratings.

NBC Begins its Domination.

"I think the game lost a little of its integrity that year [1969], but there's no getting away from the idea that television eyes did light up. Television has very little stake in integrity. Ratings are its Holy Grail."—Jim Murray on the new League Championship Series.

On October 19, 1965, the Major League owners signed an exclusive three-year agreement with NBC, which was renewed in different forms through the 1980s and allowed NBC to dominate baseball on television. The first contract called for NBC to broadcast 28 regular season games, the All-Star Game and the World Series. Ted Williams was set to be the color man on the broadcast with Curt Gowdy, but because of a sponsorship problem, Pee Wee Reese was chosen. Williams had been affiliated with another product that conflicted with the sponsor for the NBC games.

Despite the wealth and stability brought on by a single network contract, baseball suffered from underexposure. The exclusive contract that NBC negotiated reduced the number of games from a high of 123 regular-season games on three networks to 28 games on one. To protect the network broadcast, no team could broadcast its own local game during the national telecast.

From 1966 through 1975, Curt Gowdy broadcast NBC's "Game of the Week." Gowdy also called every World Series and All-Star Game in that stretch. NBC's domination ended after the 1989 season, when CBS bought the "Game of the Week" rights. However, unlike NBC, CBS did not air regular season games every Saturday and haphazard scheduling caused the show's demise.

Value of Network Deals/1965–1993.

"This broadcast is intended for the exclusive use of our audience and any rebroadcast, retransmission or other use of this program is expressly prohibited by Major League Baseball."—Standard copyright notice.

After the one-year, nonexclusive ABC deal for 1965, the first multiyear exclusive network package was the NBC three-year pact negotiated in late 1965, worth $5.4 million for 1966–1968.

The 1969–1971 network contract was worth $16.5 million. The 1976–1978 package was worth $50 million. The 1982–1984 pact was worth $53.4 million (or $65 million) *annually* for weekly national telecasts, the All-Star Game, league championship games and the World Series. In 1985 baseball's new six-year contract was worth $1.125 billion, or $188 million annually.

In 1990 CBS paid $1.06 billion (or $1.125 billion or $1.48 billion depending on the source and method of calculation) over four years for 16 regular-season games per year (over a 26-week season), the All-Star Game, and all postseason play. The disparity in value appears to be based on CBS's obligation to pay at least $1.06 billion, which could escalate to the higher figures depending on the ratings.

The 1990 season turned out to be a huge loser for CBS—$100 million (or $275 million depending on the source)—primarily because the American League play-offs and the World Series resulted in four-game sweeps and low ratings. CBS wrote off $500 million in losses after the 1992 World Series.

ESPN lost an average of $40 million over the first three years of its 1990s Major League Baseball contract and a total of approximately $240–250 million over four years. ESPN announced that it would not extend the contract beyond 1993, paying $14 million to buy out of the contract and negotiate a new deal (see below).

1994 Television Deal. In recognition of the huge losses suffered by CBS as a result of a 15% decline in television ratings, a new package contained a different structure entirely. In addition, the agreement for the first time was made with separate but cooperating networks, ABC and NBC. In June 1993 Major League owners approved a six-year deal with ABC and NBC starting in 1994 that contemplated a new round of play-off games and league championship series games that would only be shown regionally. Only the Mets and Red Sox opposed the deal (with the Yankees abstaining). CBS made a late counter-offer, but it was rejected almost before it was presented.

Under the new format there would be no televised network baseball until after the All-Star Game, and only 12 weekly games broadcast by the networks, all at night. There had been 16 in 1993, 43 in 1987 and 41 in 1980. ESPN had broadcast 175 games in 1988.

There would be no postseason day games under the new plan, and the networks would bounce around among simultaneous games in the manner that the networks broadcast the NCAA men's basketball tournament. Baseball executives claimed that the switch was necessary because the ratings for the league championship series declined from an average of 15.6 in 1985 to an average of 10.2 in 1992.

The key to the deal was that there were no up-front television rights fees. Baseball would sell the commercial time and produce the telecasts in association with ABC and NBC, and the three partners would share the profits. Baseball was to receive 85% of the first $140 million. Baseball and the networks would split the next $30 million, and baseball would keep 80% of all additional revenue.

The body that governed the joint venture was a 13-person board of directors, consisting of four representatives from each of the networks and five from baseball. It was estimated that television revenues would be cut in half.

The new formula was never fully tested in 1994 because of the player strike. The two networks each contributed $10 million in start-up costs and posted solid ratings before the strike ended the season. The All-Star Game posted a 15.7 rating, its highest in three years. ABC's four regular-season, prime-time telecasts before the strike featured regional coverage and averaged 7.1, up from the 3.5 CBS had averaged for regular season telecasts the previous year.

Major League Baseball also negotiated a new cable deal with ESPN. The cable network went from a $175 million deal in 1993 to a $75 million deal in 1994 that was part of a six-year agreement worth $255 million.

ABC and NBC asked the baseball owners to start the six-year deal again because the 1994 season was wiped out. When the owners refused in June 1995, both networks canceled the deal and vowed not to bid on baseball again through the end of the century.

Late 1990s-2000s. The 1996 television contract was a five-year deal calling for $1.7 billion to be paid by four broadcast entities: Fox Network, NBC (backing down from its threat not to bid), ESPN and Prime Liberty Media Cable. The money would be paid in equal installments of $340 million. The breakdown: Fox reportedly would pay $575 million, ESPN $440 million, NBC $400 million and Prime Liberty $172 million. The deal guaranteed each Major League club $11 million per season.

The deal called for the return of the "Game of the Week" and coast-to-coast airing of all postseason games. The "Game" would recommence on Memorial Day and consist of four games each week.

In the late 1990s Fox paid $2.5 billion for six years worth of telecasts. To illustrate the poor ratings baseball received at night, Fox Television did not broadcast a regular season prime time game between late 1998 and April 16, 2004. The 1998 broadcast was when Mark McGwire broke Roger Maris' home run record. The 2004 game was between the Yankees and Red Sox, as a follow-on to the dramatic 2003 postseason series between the two clubs.

Networks generally assign 90% of their revenue figures to postseason games.

ESPN.

"If you're a fan, what you'll see in the next minutes, hours and days to follow may convince you you've gone to sports heaven."— The first words on the first ESPN telecast, spoken by "SportsCenter" anchor Lee Leonard.

"Callahan's views do not represent the opinion of ESPN. ESPN thinks all sports are wonderful and would never ever make jokes about them. Never."— Caption under an ESPN cartoon ad featuring a piano player singing "Don't Ya Come Back Nomo Nomo Nomo Nomo...."

"Kids used to dream of becoming astronauts or ballplayers; now they dream of sitting next to Bobby Valentine on 'Baseball Tonight.'"— Norman Chad on the new tryouts and "American Idol"-style contests for jobs on ESPN and College Sports Television.

The ponderously-named Entertainment and Sports Programming Network debuted on September 7, 1979. The superstar of the program has always been 6'5", 250-pound Chris Berman, who debuted with the show in its first season. ESPN became profitable as it matured, reaching $80 million in the black by 1992. The broadcast center is located in Bristol, Connecticut. In 1992 ESPN broadcast 162 Major League games but declined to renew its television contract because, like CBS, it was losing heavily on the contract.

In December 1999, Major League Baseball and ESPN agreed to settle their lawsuit by signing a new six-year, $800 million deal. The suit involved ESPN's decision to give NFL football games priority over late-season Sunday night baseball games on its main channel.

ESPN2.

"Good evening, and welcome to the end of our careers."— Broadcaster Keith Olbermann's debut line to open the first show of ESPN2. In late 1993 ESPN2 debuted with a "hipper" version of ESPN. It had poor ratings, but managed to improve sufficiently to stay on the air and celebrate its tenth anniversary in 2003.

ESPN-Crazy. In the 2000s at least three couples named their sons after versions of ESPN, including "Espn" and "Espen." Fittingly, ESPN planned to run a special on the three toddlers, prompting this from Greg Cote of the *Miami Herald*: "Not sure what the show will be called, but I would suggest, 'My Parents are Idiots.'"

Local Team Telecasts/1955-1964.

"It would be uncharitable to say what your typical [1950s] baseball owner was at the time, but it rhymed with Frick: If you wanted to *see* a ball game, went their shortsighted thinking, you would simply have to buy a ticket to the ballpark."—*Sports Illustrated.*

By 1955 only four teams were without television: the A's, Indians, Braves and Pirates. The Dodgers, Giants, Cubs and Yankees broadcast every game. The Cardinals broadcast every road game. The Tigers broadcast 42 games and the Senators and Red Sox broadcast only a few games. The Orioles broadcast 65 selected home and road games. The Reds broadcast all weekday afternoon games and the Phillies broadcast 29 home and 27 road games.

In 1958, 13 of 16 teams televised games, with only the Giants, A's and Braves blacked out. The 13 teams aired 781 telecasts. There were 883 telecasts in 1957, but the Giants, who had telecast in New York, moved West before the 1958 season and did not televise games that year.

The total number of telecasts in 1959 was even lower at 669. There were no home games broadcast in Los Angeles, Milwaukee, Pittsburgh, St. Louis, San Francisco and Kansas City. The A's began televising games in 1959, with 10 road games. Totals were up in 1960, as the American League had 411, with the Yankees leading with 123. The National League televised 276 games.

In 1964 the Mets and Yankees aired 126 and 124 games. The Dodgers and Astros aired only nine and 12 away games. For the seventh year in a row, the Giants had no television.

In contrast to the early years, most teams telecast far in excess of 100 games by the 1990s. In 2004 the Angels had an American League-low 90 telecasts.

1950s Effect on Attendance. Some claimed that broadcasting home games cut down on home attendance. The Dodgers' 1949 attendance was 1,633,747 when the club finished first. By 1952, also a pennant-winning year, the Dodgers broadcast all home games and barely drew 1 million. For the Yankees from 1949 through 1953, all winning years, attendance fell by 500,000 in a period when the club televised all home games. However, these drops in attendance were also attributed to the glut of teams in New York and the lack of competition outside of New York. Among all teams home attendance fell by 6,287,798 from 1948 through 1952.

Miscellaneous Revenue Figures. In 1939 approximately 7% of Major League revenue came from broadcast rights (none from television). By 1950 the figure was 10.5%, and it rose to more than 30% in the mid–1970s. As for television, the percentage of revenue was 3% in 1946, 16.8% in 1956, and was more than 50% by the 1990s. In 1993 broadcast revenue from all sources (local and network) was $350 million.

Year Network Broadcast Fee/Amount Received Per Team
1976 $ 23.2 million/$900,000
1980   47.5 million/$1.8 million
1984   187.5 million/$7.2 million
1990   365 million/$14 million
1994   180 million/$6.4 million
2004   500 million/$16.6 million

Local TV Revenues/a Sampling.
"The best show on television is Red Sox baseball. Everything else sucks."—Novelist Stephen King.

In 1959 the Senators received $150,000 for television rights while the Giants received $125,000. For both radio and television, the Yankees received $875,000, and the Phillies received $600,000. Revenue then rose steadily in parallel to the network package.

In 1960 baseball derived $12.4 million from the sale of radio and television rights, with $6.2 million from regional/local sales. The Yankees received $900,000 for their rights and the Dodgers, who televised no home games, received $600,000. In the mid–1960s the Yankees received over $1 million for their television rights, and the Dodgers received slightly under $1 million. At the low end of the scale, the Senators and Pirates each received less than $300,000 for their rights.

Revenues in the 1990s and beyond were highly unequal among markets. For example, the Yankees' 1990 television package was worth in excess of $50 million, while the small-market Mariners anticipated a package worth only $2 million (some sources cite $42

million for the Yankees and $1.5 million for Mariners). In 1993 the Yankees were at the high end of local revenue with $40.5 million, followed by the Red Sox at $21 million. The Royals ($3.5 million) and Twins ($3.3 million) were at the bottom. By 1998 the Yankees generated $60 million per year in local broadcast revenue and then increased that figure to $250 million in 2002. Their 1998 deal was with Fox Sports, making them one of 22 teams with deals with that network. It ended a 49-year affiliation by the Yankees with Channel 11 in New York. The cable deal money did not flow directly to George Steinbrenner, but he was paid a flat fee per game by the cable network, which amounted to $54.25 million in 1999, or $361,555 per game.

24-Hour Network. Major League Baseball hoped to establish a 24-hour network for the 2005 season, just before its national television contracts with Fox and ESPN expired.

Sunday Baseball. The first network telecast on a Sunday under the NBC Network package was the last game of the 1967 season between the Red Sox and Twins. The Red Sox won 5–3 to clinch the pennant. Before the network deals, CBS added a Sunday "Game of the Week" in 1957.

In the 1990s, ESPN's "Sunday Night Baseball" became a fixture, though the games were moved to ESPN2 when football season started and ESPN televised NFL games instead.

Camera Coverage. Harry Coyle of NBC is considered the father of television baseball production. The center field camera has been the standard angle for pitcher/hitter matchups since 1951. In the 1957 World Series, Coyle began shooting from over the catcher and focusing on the infielders.

In 1966 NBC first began using at least five color cameras and instant replay for all games. Slow-motion instant replay is claimed to have been used first in 1964 by CBS during an Army-Navy college football game on New Year's Eve.

On August 2, 1997, Astros catcher Brad Ausmus became the first catcher to wear the Fox Sports Catcher-Cam, a small camera on top of his mask, during a 6–0 win over the Mets.

All-Star Game. The first All-Star Game telecast was over NBC in 1950. The highest rated games:
1. 1970 Cincinnati (NBC) 28.5
2. 1976 Philadelphia (ABC) 27.1
3. 1971 Detroit (NBC) 27.0
4. 1980 Los Angeles (ABC) 26.8
5. 1978 San Diego (ABC) 26.1
6. 1968 Houston (NBC) 25.9
7. 1967 Anaheim (NBC) 25.6
8. 1982 Montreal (ABC) 25.0
9. 1979 Seattle (NBC) 24.4

The 1995 game was the least watched in history up to that time. It received a 13.9 rating and a 25 share. To boost ratings, Fox hyped the 2003 game because of the format change that determined the World Series home field advantage for the All-Star Game winner. Nevertheless, the 9.5 rating was the lowest in history, but had a 9.8 rating in Japan despite the 9:30 a.m. start time.

World Series. For the 1947 World Series, the Bell Telephone System started a small television network that included New York, Philadelphia, Baltimore and Washington. The series was broadcast over the NBC network from Ebbets Field in Brooklyn and Yankee Stadium in New York. The 1947 radio rights sold for $175,000 and the television rights for $65,000.

In the 1940s Judge Landis first ruled that the principal announcer for each team during the season had to be on the World Series broadcast (a ruling later applied to television). In 1950 NBC paid $1 million per year for three years of World Series telecasts. It was the first million-dollar deal for a sporting event. In 1953 the agreement called for $2.5 million per year, and in 1958 the price was $6 million.

World Series Ratings.

"No, I'm not watching. Given the choice between watching Darth Vader and his minions add another trophy to their pile of treasure with a yawn and a snicker or the 4 die hard Marlins fans celebrate, I've chosen to pursue other hobbies." — Paul of the Red Sox Rag Internet site on the 2003 World Series.

Game 7 of the 1975 World Series was viewed by 75 million people, the most up to that time. Game 7 of the 1986 World Series between the Mets and Red Sox was watched by 81 million, a new record.

The 1978 Dodger/Yankee World Series received a 32.8 rating, the highest of all time. In contrast, the 1993 Series had a poor 17.3 rating and a 30 share. The only lower rated series was the 1989 *Earthquake* Series between the Giants and A's, when the Giants swept after a one-week mid–Series delay.

The 1998 World Series received the lowest Nielson rating for a televised Series to that date. The Yankees' four game sweep produced a 14.1 average rating, 14 percent lower than the previous low, a 16.4, for the 1989 earthquake delayed Series between the Giants and Athletics. The 14.1 rating was down 2% from NBC's rating after four games the previous year. However, since the 1997 Series went seven games, the ratings went up to 16.7, overall. The lack of a fifth game in 1998 for Fox meant the loss of $115 million in gross advertising sales. Generally, carrying five games means breaking even on a Series, and six games creates a profit.

Game 7 of the 2001 Series between the Diamondbacks and Yankees was the highest rated Series game in 10 years, with 39.1 million viewers, and at least 72 million people watching at least some of the game.

Because it was the Marlins against the Yankees in the 2003 World Series, the least-desired of the possible match-ups, that World Series was the third-lowest rated of all-time with a rating of 12.8 and a 22 share for Fox Sports. The only two lower-rated Series were 2000, when the Yankees beat the Mets in five games (12.4/21) and the 2002 Series when the Angels beat the Giants in seven games (11.9/20).

The overall 2003 postseason ratings were 45% higher than 2002, and one of the Monday night games for the first time received a higher rating than "Monday Night Football."

League Championship Series. Major League Baseball hurt itself by not having national network coverage of the league championship series games from their inception in 1969 through 1976. The format was changed for 1977 so that all games were broadcast nationally in their entirety. In 1995 the format reverted so that most of the early play-off games (both division and league championship series) were not broadcast nationally in their entirety. Games were broadcast simultaneously and the networks shifted back and forth to catch the action. The 1996 format returned to national telecasts of all games.

Near the end of Game 1 of the Arizona/St. Louis 2002 division series, the ABC Family Channel mistakenly left the game with two outs in the 9th inning to air parts of a "Growing Pains" re-run. The cable channel caught its error and returned to the game before the last out.

The 2003 league championship series games were highly rated because of the presence of the Cubs and Red Sox, finishing with ratings that forced the other networks to postpone the season debut of some key shows. Game 7 of the ALCS between the Yankees and Red Sox drew a 17.1 rating and 28 share, making it the highest-rated

non–World Series game since 1993, when Game 6 of the NLCS between the Phillies and Braves posted a 17.4/28 rating/share. Over 27.5 million viewers watched the Yankees beat the Red Sox in Game 7. The night before, the Cubs/Marlins Game 7 drew 26.5 million viewers on a Wednesday night, the largest audience for a league championship game since Game 7 of the 1991 NLCS between the Phillies and Braves, which drew 28.3 million viewers. The Cubs/Marlins game had a 16.9 rating and a 27 share.

International Broadcasts.

"Why would I do that? It only gets Spanish stations." — Phillies outfielder Jeff Stone when asked if he would bring his television back with him after playing winter ball in Venezuela.

An international broadcast of a Major League Baseball game first occurred in 1961. The new Telstar satellite became operative, and technicians broadcast to Europe a two-minute segment of a Cubs/ Phillies game during an NBC news broadcast with David Brinkley. The broadcast broke into what was to be a presidential news conference.

Game Tapes. Experts believe that there are only five regular-season games televised prior to 1965 that have been retained on videotape. Games required at least five reels of tape, and through 1974 there are few games which were fully retained.

Pay Television/Cable. A predecessor to cable television, pay television, was instituted in Los Angeles in 1964. Games were aired over home television for a fee. Frank Sims and former Major League shortstop Fresco Thompson were hired to do play-by-play. Theater owners banded together to fight this concept, and it was declared unconstitutional. A new version of pay television emerged with the advent of cable and pay-per-view in the late 1970s and 1980s.

Satellite Dish. ESPN and SportsChannel New York were the first companies to scramble their signals and charge their satellite users a nominal fee for the year.

Books. Benjamin R. Rader, *In Its Own Image: How Television Has Transformed Sports* (1984); Curt Smith, *Voices of the Game* (1987).

Television Shows

"He said he wanted to go home and watch 'The Andy Griffith Show.'" — Red Sox pitcher Aaron Sele when asked what manager Butch Hobson told him during a late-inning trip to the mound.

"Lem's sort of like an Andy Griffith character. You know, take it easy, don't panic, we'll think of something. You need an Andy Griffith on this team. We've got a lot of guys like Don Knotts." — Yankee outfielder Jay Johnstone on mild-mannered manager Bob Lemon, who managed in the Major Leagues in the 1970s and early 1980s.

"The shortstop looked like a man who had just seen his wife in the sack with Don Knotts." — Steve Rushin on Yankee shortstop Derek Jeter just after the Marlins won the 2003 World Series over Jeter's club.

What? Yankee infielder Phil Rizzuto was the first mystery guest on the television program "What's My Line" when the show premiered February 2, 1950.

Tommy Lasorda. In the 1950s when a live television audience watched comedian Red Skelton being pelted with baseballs by a pitcher at a mock carnival, it was a young Tommy Lasorda doing the throwing.

Don Drysdale. Drysdale made appearances in "The Lawman" and "The Brady Bunch."

Wes Parker. The Dodger first baseman appeared on "The Brady Bunch."

Mud Hens. On "M*A*S*H*," Corporal Max Klinger wore the uniform of his beloved hometown Toledo Mud Hens.

Johnny Berardino.

"His experience with the Browns may have helped Beradino express the pathos and tragedy that Dr. Hardy so often encounters during the daily dramas." — William B. Mead in *Even the Browns* (1978), about daytime soap opera star and former Browns infielder Johnny Berardino. Berardino changed his name to Beradino and became an actor. During Berardino's playing days with the Browns, owner Bill Veeck took out a $1 million insurance policy on his face as a gimmick.

For 25 years Berardino starred as Dr. Steve Hardy on the popular soap opera "General Hospital." He was also a child actor who played in a few *Our Gang* comedies and was also featured in *The Kid from Cleveland*, a 1949 short film featuring the championship Indians.

Chuck Connors.

"When I was hitting home runs in the sandlot in Brooklyn somewhere, nobody would have called me to MGM. But that's how I made the transition. Thank goodness the Cubs had a [minor league] team in L.A. If I had been playing in Boston, they'd have sent me to Louisville and they don't make movies in Louisville." — Chuck Connors, who played television's "The Rifleman" after his baseball career ended. He played in one game for his hometown Dodgers in 1949 and 66 games for the Cubs in 1951. The 6'5" actor batted .238 with two home runs in his career. Connors (Kevin Joseph Aloysius Connors) annually recited "Casey at the Bat" at the Vero Beach minor league spring training camp with the Dodgers. After the 1952 season, in which he played in the Pacific Coast League, Connors had a bit part in the Spencer Tracy/Katharine Hepburn movie, *Pat and Mike*.

Dodger center fielder Duke Snider once appeared on "The Rifleman": "Duke Snider had it coming to him. He was an ornery varmint who deserved to be gunned down without mercy. He'd tormented the good guy in his bullying way, riding into town with four other killers just to pick a fight." — Sportswriter Arthur Daley.

Warren Spahn. The pitcher was a fan of the television show "Combat." When the Braves were in Los Angeles for a game in the early 1960s, a team publicist called ABC publicity to see if Spahn could come to the set at MGM. The producers offered Spahn the role of a German machine gunner. The publicist was worried because Spahn was pitching that night. No problem: he pitched a one-hitter and there was a full-page photo of him in a German helmet that ran in *Life* magazine.

Jim Bouton. Pitcher Jim Bouton co-wrote and appeared in a short-lived television series based on his book, *Ball Four* (1970).

Bob Uecker. The catcher was a regular on television talk shows before getting his own sitcom, "Mr. Belvedere." He made over 80 appearances on the "Tonight Show" with Johnny Carson. Though Uecker's style was self-deprecating because of his .200 lifetime average, he hit .400 against Sandy Koufax, including two of his 14 home runs.

Reggie Jackson. Jackson appeared in a 1979 episode of "The Love Boat" entitled "The Designated Lover." The plot has Jackson, playing himself, falling in love with an obsessed fan played by Telma Hopkins.

John Forsythe. The long-time actor of "Dynasty" fame was the public address announcer briefly for the Dodgers during the 1940s. He once announced Mickey Owen's race around the bases against a horse.

Cheers. The television series "Cheers" included the Boston Red Sox seven times, including one featuring Wade Boggs and another with bartender and former Red Sox relief pitcher Sam Malone's unsuccessful comeback attempt. On the day of the last "Cheers" episode on May 19, 1993, John Ratzenberger, who played letter carrier Cliff Clavin, threw out the first ball of the Red Sox game against the Blue Jays at Fenway Park. It had been rumored that Ted Danson would appear, but no deal was ever made and Ratzenberger came down at the last minute from his home in Bridgeport, Connecticut.

The Simpsons. On February 20, 1992, an episode of "The Simpsons" featured animated cameo voiceovers by Darryl Strawberry, Jose Canseco, Ken Griffey, Jr., Roger Clemens, Mike Scioscia, Don Mattingly, Steve Sax, Ozzie Smith and Wade Boggs. Each player stopped in during the season at the studio in Los Angeles to record his lines. Homer Simpson recruited them for the Springfield Nuclear Plant softball team.

Soap. On July 8, 1992, David Justice of the Braves appeared in an episode of the soap opera, "The Young and the Restless."

Marlins. In the opening episode of the 1993 television series "SeaQuest DSV," set in the year 2018, a crew member wore a Florida Marlins jersey with "World Series Champions 2010" on the back (should have been more optimistic).

Spanish. In 1993 shortstop Ozzie Guillen of the White Sox starred in the Spanish-language "La Raya de Cal" ("Foul Line"), a three-hour miniseries about a teenager who dumps his girlfriend to date the daughter of a professional baseball club owner.

Jim Abbott. In 1994 pitcher Jim Abbott appeared as himself on the Suzanne Somers show, "Step by Step."

Barry Bonds. In 1994 Barry Bonds appeared as a golfer in "Melrose Place."

Not Married. In 1994 Mike Piazza, Frank Thomas, David Winfield, Danny Tartabull, Bret Saberhagen and Joe Morgan appeared as themselves on "Married ... With Children."

Seinfeld. The fictional character George Costanza on "Seinfeld" went to work for the Yankees and George Steinbrenner in 1994. Steinbrenner terminated Costanza in the season finale in May 1996.

Failed Series. In 1995 Fox Television premiered "Hardball," a sitcom with a Marge Schott–type owner played by Rose Marie from the "Dick Van Dyke Show."

ER. In 1995 Angels first baseman J.T. Snow made a cameo appearance on "ER."

Deion Sanders. Sanders hosted "Saturday Night Live" in early 1995.

Talk Show. Roy Campanella was the first guest on Edward R. Murrow's, "Person to Person." The live show first aired on October 2, 1953, on the night of Game 2 of the World Series between the Dodgers and Yankees. Earlier that day Campanella had homered in the 8th inning to give the Dodgers a 3–2 victory.

Early in his career, Red Sox slugger Tony Conigliaro appeared on Merv Griffin's talk show.

During the 1973 season when Henry Aaron was chasing Babe Ruth's home run record, Aaron appeared on the "The Flip Wilson Show," "Hollywood Squares" and did some cooking on Dinah Shore's show.

On May 2, 1996, the entire Cubs roster appeared on the "Tonight Show" with Jay Leno, which was broadcasting from Chicago that week. On July 23, 2003, several Hall of Famers presented David Letterman's Top 10 list, including Lou Brock, Gary Carter, Bob Feller, Rollie Fingers, Bob Gibson, Harmon Killebrew, Phil Niekro, Ozzie Smith and Brooks Robinson.

Game Shows. Royals first baseman Pete LaCock is the son of former "Hollywood Squares" host Peter Marshall.

In January 1967 Red Sox manager Dick Williams was on "Hollywood Squares." He was the show's first Grand Champion, winning $2,500, a stereo, car, motorcycle and trips to Las Vegas and Paris. It must have been his lucky year, as the 100-to-1 shot Red Sox won the American League pennant and extended the Cardinals to seven games in the World Series.

Spitball pitcher Gaylord Perry once appeared on a television show called "Lie Detector," in which he passed the test after being asked if he doctored the ball.

Ed Sullivan.

"He moves like a sleepwalker; his smile is that of a man sucking a lemon; his speech is frequently lost in a thicket of syntax; his eyes pop from their sockets or sink so deep in their bags that they seem to be peering up at the camera from the bottom of twin wells." — *Time* magazine in October 1955 on Sullivan.

In 1960 Willie Mays appeared on "The Ed Sullivan Show." Members of the World Champion 1969 Mets, including Nolan Ryan, sang on the show.

Payment. When Ken Griffey, Jr., read a Letterman "Top 10" list in 2004, he was paid $800.

Canadian Debut. Roger Clemens' first game for the Toronto Blue Jays was televised in Canada. With two outs in the 9th inning the network cut away to a more important event, women's curling.

Emmy Award. Yankee broadcaster Phil Rizzuto was nominated for an Emmy Award in 1982.

In 1992 Dodger broadcaster Vin Scully received a special television Emmy Award for television broadcast excellence.

Joe Charboneau received a local Cleveland television Emmy Award in 1994 for "The Joe Charboneau Show," a humorous look at the world of sports.

Ken Burns and "Baseball."

"If he [Burns] treats this [a Lewis & Clark film] as badly as his *Baseball* film, they'll wind up in Miami!" — Broadcaster Jack Brickhouse.

Burns, who produced the epic series on the Civil War for public television, scored again in 1994 with a nine-part series on baseball. The 18-hour epic, divided into nine two-hour "innings," was a critical success despite a few factual errors. It was shown during the baseball strike in September 1994 to favorable reviews despite its length. More than 43 million people watched at least a portion of the series. It was the largest cumulative audience in the 25-year history of PBS. The innings:

1st: 1840s to 1900, "Our Game."

2nd: 1900s, "The Look of Eagles," featuring Ty Cobb, Walter Johnson and John McGraw.

3rd: 1910s, "The Faith of Fifty Million People," featuring the Black Sox Scandal and Christy Mathewson.

4th: 1920s, "A National Heirloom," featuring Babe Ruth.

5th: 1930s, "Shadow Ball," featuring the Depression and the Negro Leagues.

6th: 1940s, "The National Pastime," featuring the 1941 season and 1940s integration.

7th: 1950s, "The Capital of Baseball," featuring New York City.

8th: 1960s, "A Whole New Ball Game," featuring the threat of football and stars such as Sandy Koufax.

9th: 1970–present: "Home," focusing most prominently on the seminal Game 6 of the 1975 Series, as well as the future of baseball.

Book. James Mote, *Everything Baseball* (1989), lists all baseball television shows and appearances by players.

Temple Cup (1894–1897)

"This convinces me that the whole Temple Cup business has been a farce, and I shall offer a resolution … that the trophy be refunded to Mr. Temple with thanks." — Baltimore Orioles owner Harry Von der Horst after learning that the players on the two clubs competing for the Temple Cup agreed secretly to split their winnings evenly.

See also *Championship Series*.

William Chase Temple's National League Pittsburgh Pirates finished second in 1893. He wanted a chance for future second-place clubs to challenge the first-place winner of the 12-team league in a postseason series. At that time there was no championship series because the rival American Association had disbanded and the National League had no Major League competition. Early in 1894 Temple proposed that the winner of the championship series between the league's first- and second-place finishers receive a victory cup (one source described this incorrectly as occurring in the American Association). The winner of the series received the Temple Cup, and any team that won three championships would keep the trophy permanently.

The 1894 Temple Cup revenue was to be split 65–35 between the winning and losing players. However, before the series, five players from each team agreed to split the money 50/50, and then the same five winning Giants refused to pay the losing five Orioles their equal shares. The dispute became public and Temple and others were upset. The irritated Temple sold his Pittsburgh stock and left baseball. The Temple Cup continued without him, as Baltimore won it in 1895 and 1896, and finished second in 1897.

By 1896 interest in the Temple Cup was fading, especially so after the Cleveland Spiders were four days late to play the series in Baltimore after a train crash and after the two teams had been rivals all year. In addition, the teams played exhibition games against other clubs in between the series games and only 1,600 paid to see each of the last two games. The winning Baltimore players received $200 each and the Cleveland players each received $117. After the 1897 series, won by Boston over Baltimore, the Temple Cup competition was abandoned.

Through the efforts of *The Sporting News*, the cup was located in 1939 through correspondence with Mrs. Dorothea Temple Mason, who then resided in Florida. It was displayed at the New York World's Fair that summer. She later offered the cup to the Hall of Fame for a price, but director Bob Quinn's written response was succinct: "I haven't any idea what it is worth and for that reason I would not want to make an offer. If, however, you wish to make a proposition, I will submit it. It is rather a sentimental thing and I am not very good where sentiment comes in."

The Hall eventually paid $750 for it. An old trademark book identified the Temple Cup as having been made by George W. Shiebler & Co. of New York City.

Book. John Phillips, *The Fall Classics of the 1890s: The Temple Cup of 1894–1897 and the Championship Series of 1892* (1989).

Tennis

"I always felt the pitcher had the advantage. It's like serving in tennis." — Yankee pitcher Allie Reynolds.

"The true fan is not only violently partisan, but very noisy.... I used to amuse myself with wondering what would happen if a group of fans of this order would turn up at a tennis match or a golf meet." — W.R. Burnett.

"Take his tennis game, for example, a sport he plays with great joy and enthusiasm, without threatening the memory of Bill Tilden. He runs and flails and chatters away in sheer happiness at competition. He *works* at baseball. He *plays* tennis. There is none of the heavy cathedral silence of professional tennis on a court with Rose, no barking at line calls, no tantrums." — Roger Kahn in *Pete Rose: My Story*, by Rose and Kahn (1989).

"If there has to be a reason, baseball is still my favorite sport because it was my first unforgettable love." — Tennis legend Alice Marble quoted in 1955 in *The New Yorker* magazine. She was the official mascot of the San Francisco Seals in the 1920s at age 13. She was allowed to shag flies with the players and was described as "The Little Queen of Swat." In May 1941 Marble was a spectator at a game between the Tigers and Indians in Detroit. Despite being hit in the back by a foul ball during batting practice, she was well enough to broadcast an inning in place of Jack Graney.

English tennis star Fred Perry attended his first baseball game with a reporter. When the pitcher was shelled and taken out of the game, he began walking off the field. When told the pitcher was going "to the showers," Perry reportedly responded: "It's a hot day. I imagine he will feel famously when he comes back." — Related by sportswriter Charles Einstein in Fred Schwed's *How to Watch a Baseball Game* (1957).

Tennis maven Billie Jean King is the sister of pitcher Randy Moffitt.

Tennis pro Pam Shriver was a minority owner in the group that purchased the Orioles in 1993.

Pro tennis player Mary Pierce, often troubled in her career and with a meddlesome father, was engaged for a time to second baseman Roberto Alomar until she called it off.

Terminology

"Baseball needs a Webster and a standing–Revision Board to keep the dictionary of the game up to date. The sport is building its own language so steadily that, unless some step soon is taken to check the inventive young men who coin the words that attach themselves to the pastime, interpreters will have to be maintained in every grand stand to translate for the benefit of those who merely love the game and do not care to master it thoroughly." — Hugh S. Fullerton in *The American* magazine of June 1912, quoted in the introduction to Paul Dickson's *The Dickson Baseball Dictionary* (1989). Dickson's work contains over 5,000 baseball terms and has a bibliography of sources for the origins and first printed usage of baseball terms.

"The bases were drunk, and I painted the black with my best yakker. But blue squeezed me, and I went full. I came back with my heater, but the stick flares one the other way and chalk flies for two bases. Three earnies! Next thing I know, skipper hooks me and I'm sipping suds with the clubby." — Ed Lynch. Loose translation: The bases were loaded, and I threw my best curveball on the corner of the plate. But the umpire called it a ball and I went to a full count. I threw my best fastball, but the batter hit a soft liner that hit the foul line for a double and three earned runs scored. Then the manager took me out of the game and I was drinking a beer with the clubhouse attendant.

Bill Terry (1896–1989)

Hall of Fame 1954

"He was in his prime as a first baseman, the best in the league at that position. As a batter he received no particular help from the short foul lines at the Polo Grounds as he was a slashing hitter, with his power to left center and right center. There were few better hitters in the game." — Lee Allen in *The Giants and the Dodgers* (1964).

"Weighing 200 pounds and standing an inch and a half above six feet, he had all the physique and strength to be a pull-hitting producer of home runs. He preferred, however, to get the most out of his batting by hitting to all fields.... Terry's great batting tended to overshadow his talents as a fielder.... Determination, tenacity, intelligence and imaginativeness are among the traits of character which enabled Terry to gain baseball fame." — Ira L. Smith in *Baseball's Famous First Basemen* (1956).

"Could be that he's a nice guy when you get to know him, but why bother?" — Dizzy Dean on the disliked first baseman.

Terry batted .341 as a first baseman for the Giants in the 1920s and 1930s.

William Harold Terry is a classic example of a late bloomer who switched positions to establish himself in the Major Leagues. He pitched in the Georgia-Florida League in 1915 but was too wild. He quit professional baseball after the 1917 season in Shreveport, moving to the oil fields and playing semipro ball. He rejoined the professional ranks and was sold for $750 to John McGraw's Giants sight unseen. He reported to Toledo in 1922 at age 26 and pitched decently, but hit so well that he was moved to first base.

In 1923 he moved up to the Giants and established himself as the best defensive first baseman of the decade and one of the best hitters of all time. He peaked with a .401 average in 1930 and had three other seasons over .350 during his 14-year Major League career. He had a lifetime .341 average and a slugging average of .506.

Terry was the Giants' player-manager for the last five seasons of his career and for four seasons after that. He won pennants in 1933, 1936 and 1937 after taking over the club from John McGraw.

Disliked by the media for his coldness and impatience, he was elected to the Hall of Fame 18 years after his retirement; despite being the last man in the National League to hit over .400.

After ending his managerial career in 1941, Terry stayed briefly in the Giants' front office before moving to Florida to run his car dealership full-time (though cotton is the subject below): "Bill Terry bowed out of baseball forever recently, and on his leaving made a speech that blasted the national sport all over the lot. He said the game had become too cheap, that players and managers weren't paid enough and that there was nothing more in the game for him. Bill said that he was buying into a cotton manufacturing concern. What he didn't say was that the dough he was going to use was part of the half million dollars he got out of baseball." — The *Stars and Stripes* military newspaper in February 1944.

Texas Rangers

American League 1972–

"We need just two players to be a contender. Babe Ruth and Sandy Koufax." — Manager Whitey Herzog in 1973 (and in the 2000s, not even A.Rod could help).

Origins. Bob Short was the owner of the Washington Senators in the late 1960s when he arranged for the Rangers to move to Texas (see also *Franchise Shifts*). In moving to Arlington, Short was required to pay each of the six Texas League clubs $40,000 because he was invading their territory. He also agreed to have his team meet a team of Texas League All-Stars in an annual game.

First Game. There were 20,105 fans at the club's first home game, played on April 21, 1972. Frank Howard hit the first home run in the ballpark for the Rangers in a 7–6 victory over the Angels.

Key Owners.
Bob Short/1972–1974.
"Bob Short should be named Minor League Executive of the Year."—Sportswriter Russ White on the Major League owner who was criticized for his ownership techniques.

Short owned the club when it was the Washington Senators before shifting to Texas. He held the club briefly before selling out in 1974. Short received $7.5 million when he arrived in exchange for 10 years of broadcast rights. It was correctly predicted that he would sell after his five-year tax depreciation schedule ran out in 1973.

Bradford G. Corbett/1974–1980.
"Baseball is a tremendous business for men with big egos. But ego can only take you so far. After that, it has to be a good business proposition."—Corbett.

Corbett parlayed a $360,000 loan from the Small Business Administration in 1967 into $55 million in industrial and commercial plastic pipe sales in 1973. At age 36 he took over as the majority owner of the Rangers with a group of Dallas–Ft. Worth businessmen. Bob Short retained a 10% interest. Corbett committed $4–5 million of his own money. Other stockholders were Amon Carter, Jr., who had recently sold the *Ft. Worth Star-Telegram* newspaper, and various real estate and life insurance brokers.

Eddie Chiles/1980–1989.
"Our problem, I hate to say this, and I hope no other owners are listening, but I think we've got a worse problem with some of our owners than we do with Marvin Miller. If I get shot at sunrise, I'll blame you for it."—Chiles to a talk show host during the 1981 player strike.

Chiles was a limited partner in the 1970s and then became the principal owner of the Rangers at age 69 on April 29, 1980. He owned the world's largest oil field servicing company, but his business began to slip during the 1980s.

Edward Gaylord, an Oklahoma broadcasting and publishing magnate, purchased a 30% interest in late 1985 to infuse cash into the operation. Gaylord also took a right of first refusal if Chiles attempted to sell the club. Chiles sold out in mid–1989 to a new group headed by future Texas governor and U.S. President George W. Bush. Gaylord approved the purchase and retained his interest. He had previously vetoed a sale to a Tampa group.

Chiles was credited with streamlining the Rangers' front office and turning it into a profitable organization. When he died at age 83 in 1993, the players wore his initials on their sleeves for the duration of the season.

George W. Bush and Edward W. Rose III/1989–1998.
"The Mortician"—Nickname of Edward Rose, who made a fortune in the stock market betting on companies losing value.

Future U.S. President George W. Bush and Edward Rose led a group that bought the club from Chiles for $46 million in March 1989. Rose was a stock trader who made over $100 million by short-selling stocks. Bush paid $600,000 for 2% of the club, for which he was named managing partner. The two largest interests were held by Edward Gaylord (10%) and Bush's Yale classmate, Roland Betts (10.9%).

When the group sold in 1998, Bush received $14.9 million for his holdings. Most of this appreciation is attributable to the value of The Ballpark in Arlington.

Tom Hicks/1998– .
"He kicked me in the shins and called me a turd."—Hicks, on his high school football coach, after Hicks dropped a pass in a 1963 play-off that cost his team the game.

Hicks was chairman and CEO of Hicks, Muse, Tate & Furst, Inc., a leveraged-buyout firm, formed in 1989. He has other ties to sports, having bought the NHL Dallas Stars and watching them win four consecutive division championships and a Stanley Cup. He also arranged a $500 million television deal for Stars and Rangers broadcasts. *Forbes* magazine put his net worth at $750 million, making him among the 400 wealthiest Americans.

In May 1999 Tom Schieffer resigned as the president of the Rangers in order to spend more time developing real estate around The Ballpark in Arlington. He also helped then-Texas governor George W. Bush run for the White House.

Nickname. The name Rangers was the choice of the 1950s general manager of the minor league Dallas club. The Rangers name was formally adopted by the new Major League club on November 23, 1971, shortly after it was announced that the team was moving to Texas.

Key Seasons.
1972. In the club's first season in Texas, the Rangers finished last in the Western Division with a record of 54–100 under manager Ted Williams.

1977. The Rangers finished a strong second for the first time with 94 wins behind Doyle Alexander's 17 wins and Toby Harrah's 27 home runs.

1986. The club finished second for the fourth time in its history. Charlie Hough won 17 games and Pete Incaviglia hit 30 home runs.

1994. In the strike-shortened season the Rangers were in first place when the season ended prematurely in August; though with a losing record of 52–62 and having lost eight of their last 10.

1996. The Rangers won their first division title even after blowing a 10-game lead over the Mariners, but lost in the first round of the play-offs to the Yankees. Juan Gonzalez hit 47 home runs and had 144 RBIs and Dean Palmer hit 38 home runs.

1998. The Rangers won the American League West with an 88–74 record and then were blown out by the Yankees in the division series. Juan Gonzalez had a career-year with 45 home runs and 157 RBIs and Will Clark contributed 23 home runs and 102 RBIs. Catcher Ivan Rodriguez was the team leader with stellar defensive play, a .321 average, 21 home runs and 91 RBIs. Rick Helling was 20–7 and Aaron Sele was 19–11, and reliever John Wetteland had 42 saves.

Key Players.
Toby Harrah was the club's first power hitter, with at least 20 home runs three times in his seven seasons for the club.

Pete Incaviglia played five seasons for the club, hitting 30 home runs his rookie season and at least 21 each year.

Charlie Hough pitched 10 seasons for the club from 1981 through 1990, winning 137 games.

Ruben Sierra played six seasons for the Rangers starting in 1986, hitting over .300 twice with over 20 home runs three times. He returned in 2000 and also played for the club in 2001 and part of 2003.

Nolan Ryan played the last five years of his career with the Rangers, winning 51 games and pitching his final two no-hitters.

Kevin Brown pitched the first eight seasons of his career for Texas, arriving as a regular starter in 1989 and peaking with 21 wins in 1992.

Juan Gonzalez.
"The ball is smaller, the planets are in line, the hole in the ozone layer is bigger, and so is Juan Gonzalez."—Pitcher Terry Mulholland, on the increase in home runs.

Gonzalez arrived in 1989 and established himself with 43 home runs in 1992 and 46 home runs in 1993. Though back problems plagued him somewhat, he continued to power the ball for the Rangers through the 1996 season, with 47 that year. He was traded to the Tigers after the 1999 season and then return to the Rangers for the 2002 season. He had 340 home runs for the Rangers though 1999, but he was injured for much of the 2002 and 2003 seasons.

Ivan Rodriguez played 12 seasons for the club beginning in 1989 and was elected to the All-Star Game from 1992 through 2001 and was a Gold Glove Award winner in each of those seasons. He was the American League MVP in 1999 when he hit 35 home runs and drove in 113 runs. He left after an injury-plagued 2002 season for the Florida Marlins.

Alex Rodriguez played three seasons for the Rangers beginning in 2001 after signing the richest *Contract* in Major League history. He had home run totals of 52, 57 and 47 before being traded to the Yankees.

Key Managers.
Ted Williams (HF) moved with the club from Washington and stayed at the helm for one season in 1972. The club finished last with a 54–100 record.

Billy Martin.
"Billy must be pretty insecure about his chances of being rehired [by the Yankees]. But if he loses that job I'll rehire him — to sell pipe." — Disenchanted Rangers owner Brad Corbett in late May 1976, when Yankee manager Martin was having trouble with the Yankees' front office. Corbett had fired Martin in mid–1985 after a series of disruptions by Martin. Between 1973 and 1975 Martin brought the team from last to second in one season, and then finished third before wearing out his welcome.

Bobby Valentine managed the club for almost eight seasons beginning in 1985. His best finish was second place in 1986. After two third-place finishes, he was fired during mid–1992 when the club was in third place with a 45–41 record.

Johnny Oates took over in 1995 and lasted through 28 games of the 2001 season. He was the 1996 Manager of the Year and the club finished first three times under the popular manager, but could never get past the division playoffs. He was diagnosed with brain cancer in October 2001 and was still battling the disease in early 2004 after the tumor reappeared and surgery was not considered an option. In the meantime in 2003 he was inducted into the Rangers' Hall of Fame. He died in late 2004.

Ballparks.
Arlington Stadium.
"If it hadn't been for Nolan Ryan, it would be hard to name five great moments in the Texas Rangers' 22-year history at Arlington Stadium. 'I know two: the day it opened and the day it closed,' says former Ranger coach Rich Donnelly. 'The father-son-daughter game in 1983 was pretty good too.'" — Tim Kurkjian in *Sports Illustrated*.

"The real legacy of the old place, which gives way to the new Ballpark in Arlington this season: Warm beer, cold nachos and bad baseball. Bring on the bulldozers." — Bill Sullivan of the *Houston Chronicle*.

Arlington Stadium was known as Turnpike Stadium during the city's minor league days in the 1960s until the Rangers moved in for the 1972 season. The ballpark opened in April 1965 at a cost of $1.5 million and had dimensions from left to right field of 325–400–325.

The park originally held only 10,000 fans but was expanded to seat 20,000 in 1970 (22,000 in some sources). It was expanded again in 1971 following the announcement that the Senators were moving to Texas. On Opening Day 1972 the park had a capacity of over 35,000. Subsequent expansions created a capacity of 43,508.

The park's last dimensions from left to right field were 330–380–400–380–330, with minor variations in the power alleys over the years.

The first sellout in the ballpark's history was on June 27, 1973, when **High School** phenom David Clyde made his debut against the Twins.

One source reported that the name "Turnpike" was changed to Vandergriff Stadium in honor of mayor Tommy Vandergriff, who was instrumental in bringing the club to Arlington. Other sources point out that Vandergriff rejected the name and chose Arlington Stadium. Vandergriff threw out the first ball at the original Opening Day of the Rangers on April 21, 1972, flanked by American League president Joe Cronin and Rangers owner Bob Short.

Before the last game in the ballpark on October 3, 1993, Nolan Ryan and George Brett exchanged line-up cards in front of a sellout crowd of 41,039, as the Royals won 4–1. The ballpark was torn down in mid–1994.

The Ballpark. The club's new stadium, known as "The Ballpark," opened in April 1994 at a cost of $165 million. Its original dimensions from left to right field were 334–388–400–375–330 and its capacity is 49,292. The first home run was hit by Australian native Dave Nilsson. It became apparent that although the left field fence was only a few feet deeper than Arlington Stadium's, right-handed batters were having trouble reaching it because of prevailing winds. Each of the 67 private boxes is named for a Hall of Famer.

Key Broadcasters. Frank Glieber was with the club in the late 1970s. In 1972 Don Drysdale broadcast television for the club and Jimmy Piersall was with the club in 1974. Jon Miller broadcast in 1978 and 1979 and then Mel Proctor took over as the leader play-by-play man for two seasons.

Merle Harmon was with the club in the early 1980s. Mark Holtz broadcast from the early 1980s through the mid–1990s. Eric Nadel started in 1979 and was still in the booth through 2004. Pitcher Steve Busby began with the club in 1986 and remained through 1995. Catcher Jim Sundberg began in the booth in 1990 and lasted three seasons. Tom Grieve began with the club in 1995 and was still broadcasting for the Rangers in 2004. Curt Gowdy, Jr., was with the club as a broadcast executive briefly in the early 1980s.

Book. Aaron Frisch, *The History of the Texas Rangers* (2002); Eric Nadel, *The Texas Rangers: The Authorized History* (1997); *Phil Rogers, The Impossible Takes a Little Longer* (1990), covers the club's first five years.

Theater

"I understand people who boo us. It's like going to a Broadway show. You pay for your tickets and expect to be entertained. When you're not, you have a right to complain." — Manager Sparky Anderson.

"Going to the theater [to a ballplayer] means lying in an unmade hotel bed and slurping a can of Lite Beer, while he watches 'As the World Turns.'" — Columnist Lowell Cohn of the *San Francisco Chronicle*.

"But I don't know nearly as much about baseball as [stage actress] Ethel Barrymore. Ethel is a real fan, can give you batting averages, the test of the infield fly rule, and comment on an umpire's vision." — Actress and baseball fan Tallulah Bankhead.

"It's the first role I've ever played in a foreign language." — Actor Charles Durning on portraying Casey Stengel on the stage.

"It is the best of all games for me. It frequently escapes from the pattern of sport and assumes the form of a virile ballet.... The movement is natural and unrehearsed and controlled only by the unexpected flight of the ball." — Jimmy Cannon.

"Baseball is an allegorical play about America, a poetic, complex, and subtle play of courage, fear, good luck, mistakes, patience about fate, and sober self-esteem." — Saul Steinberg.

Damn Yankees.

"One long ball hitter, that's what we need. I'd sell my soul for one long ball hitter — hey, where did you come from?" — Robert Shafer, Senators manager, meeting the devil in *Damn Yankees*. This 1950s movie was adapted from a theater production of the same name and a Douglas Wallop book entitled *The Year the Yankees Lost the Pennant*. An aging Washington Senators fan named Joe Boyd sells his soul to the Devil (aka Mr. Applegate) to become slugger Joe Hardy and lead the Senators to a pennant over the hated Yankees.

Damn Yankees debuted on Broadway in May 1955, one month before librettist George Abbott turned 68. When the musical reprised on Broadway in late 1994, Abbott was still at it: At age 106 he was making changes to the libretto by fax machine. He died early the following year at age 107. Joe Namath performed in the Joe Hardy role in a 1981 stage version.

Jackie Robinson. After his death, Jackie Robinson was the subject of a Broadway musical, *The First*.

Bleacher Bums. In the early 1970s, Chicago's Organic Theater debuted *Bleacher Bums*, a play about the 1969 season between the Cubs and Miracle Mets. Theatregoers sat in stadium-type seats and ate popcorn and peanuts during the production, which had nine innings instead of acts. The setting was a Cubs-Cardinals game at Wrigley Field. Actor Joe Mantegna co-authored the play and later wrote the Tony Award- winning *Glengarry Glen Ross*. A fanatical Cubs fan, Mantegna wore a Cubs cap during a curtain call on the night in 1984 when the Cubs lost the pennant to the Padres.

Cap Anson. Anson played a bit part in a play called *A Parlor Match*, in which he appeared in the last scene as a Chicago White Stockings player (then known as the Colts). His part called for him to slide in safe at home on an inside-the-park home run — except on the night that famous umpire Tim Hurst made a cameo appearance as the umpire in the scene and called him out.

Rube Waddell. The eccentric pitcher once played a small part in a play called *The Stain of Guilt*. His job was to beat up the villain. He purportedly lost the job the night he inflicted too realistic a beating on the other actor.

Rube is a play about Waddell that debuted in 2003. It was reprised in 2004 on the theory that the Cubs did well in 2003.

Christy Mathewson. In 1910 Mathewson co-wrote a Broadway play that had a 20-night run, a comedy entitled *The Girl and the Pennant*.

John McGraw. In 1912 McGraw was the highest paid act in vaudeville, getting $3,000 a week to tell baseball stories.

Babe Ruth. In April 2001, the musical *The Curse of the Bambino* opened in Boston. Written by David Kruh with music and lyrics by Stephen Bergman, the comedy was staged as a Greek tragedy complete with a Greek chorus composed of four fans.

Homosexual Theme. In 2003 the Broadway play *Take Me Out*, about an openly gay Major Leaguer, won three Tony Awards, including best play.

Seeing Red. In 2004 a play about columnist Red Smith debuted in New York: *The Shakespeare of the Press Box: The Life and Times of Red Smith*, written by *New York Times* sports columnist Ira Berkow. Actor Eli Wallach, 87, did the one-man play in New York City.

It Ain't Over...

"But he's not Oscar Wilde. He didn't sit home thinking about those things. But when he talked baseball nobody was smarter." — Actor Ben Gazzara in *The New Yorker* on Yogi Berra's malapropisms. In 2003 Gazzara took on the role of Berra in a one-man show called *Nobody Don't Like Yogi*, written by Thomas Lysaght.

In the early 1960s, shooting of the movie *Convicts 4* had to be delayed while Gazzara's broken leg healed. He shattered it sliding into home unnecessarily while playing a pick-up game of baseball wearing metal cleats. His teammates were, according to Gazzara, "a terrible team of football jocks, gamblers, writers, actors and mainly losers."

Theme Songs See *Songs*

Third Basemen

"You have to have extra-big ones to stand at third base, 85 feet from the batter when you're playing in on the grass, risking a whistling line-drive at your body or a one-hopper at 120 miles per hour that you have to dive into the dust to stab." — Peter Golenbock in *The Forever Boys* (1991).

"Anything a third baseman don't get they call it a base hit. A third baseman ought to pay to get into the park." — Ring Lardner.

"He's either the greatest rotten third baseman in baseball or the rottenest great third baseman. But he's never in between." — Branch Rickey on the erratic Frenchy Bordagaray.

Type of Player. The position evolved over the years from requiring a defensive specialist good at fielding bunts to a power hitter anchoring the batting line-up.

Fielding style.

"There's nothing tough about playing third. All a guy needs is a strong arm and a strong chest." — Frankie Frisch.

Jimmy Collins of the turn-of-the-century Red Sox and Braves is credited as the first to play third base off the bag and the first to play shallow and charge the ball.

Hall of Famers. The following Major League third basemen have been inducted into the Hall of Fame: Frank "Home Run" Baker, Jimmy Collins, Fred Lindstrom, Pie Traynor, George Kell, Eddie Mathews, Brooks Robinson and Mike Schmidt. Collins is the only pre–1900 third baseman who made it into the Hall. Also admitted are Negro League third base stars Ray Dandridge and Judy Johnson.

Best.

"Black veterans who saw him agree: Squat, bow-legged Ray Dandridge played third base like Brooks Robinson and hit like Pie Traynor, a combination that would make Ray, along with Mike Schmidt, the greatest third baseman of all time, black or white." — John B. Holway in *Blackball Stars* (1988).

"That ain't a third baseman. That's a fucking acrobat." — Casey Stengel on Dodger third baseman Billy Cox, considered by many as the best defensive third baseman prior to Brooks Robinson. Stengel also said that Cox had the best arm among third basemen. Stengel believed that Pie Traynor was the best overall third baseman, with Brooks Robinson a close second. Traynor spent 17 years in the Major Leagues, all with the Pirates, compiling a .320 lifetime average. Traynor was thought by some to be a better player than Jimmy Collins. Bill McKechnie offered a comparison: "I never saw Collins, but Tommy Leach did, and he told me that Collins couldn't carry Traynor's glove."

Brooks Robinson spent 23 years with the Orioles, compiling only a .267 batting average, but was the preeminent defensive third baseman of the 1960s and early 1970s. He also batted .348 in five World Series. Let it be noted, however, that Robinson had three errors in one inning on July 28, 1971, against the A's. He played in a record 2,870 games at third base.

Mike Schmidt led the league eight times in home runs, spending his entire career with the Phillies.

Revolving Door. A number of clubs have had difficulty finding long-term players at third base. A few examples:

The Padres used 72 third basemen from their creation in 1969 through 1991.

The Mets used 89 third basemen from 1962 through 1991.

After Ron Santo retired in 1973, the Cubs employed 69 third basemen through mid–1995.

The Yankees used 30 third basemen from the retirement of Graig Nettles after the 1983 season through 1991.

Thirty Game Winners

"GOING FOR WIN NO. 12" — Sign taped on the back of Chuck Dobson, the pitcher who faced Denny McLain during McLain's quest for season win No. 30 on September 14, 1968. The Tigers scored two runs in the bottom of the 9th inning to defeat the A's 5–4 on a Saturday NBC "Game of the Week" telecast. Al Kaline pinch-hit for McLain to lead off the 9th inning. Dick McAuliffe popped out, but Mickey Stanley singled, sending Kaline to third. Jim Northrup bounced to Danny Cater at first base, who threw home too late to get Kaline with the tying run. Willie Horton then hit a single over the head of drawn-in outfielder Jim Gosger to score Stanley with the winning run and give McLain his 30th win. He finished with 31 wins for the year.

McLain should have won 32 games, but manager Mayo Smith pulled him out of a 1–0 game after seven innings. McLain was furious for being pulled from a potential victory, and Don McMahon came in and blew the lead. See **Gambling** for the rest of McLain's life story.

"Maestro on the Mound" — Song written in celebration of Dizzy Dean's 30th win on the last day of the 1934 season. Dean won 9–0 over the Giants on one day's rest as the Cardinals clinched the pennant.

Pitchers have won 30 games in a season 21 times in the 20th century, but only twice after 1933.

In 1920 Jim Bagby was the last right-hander to win 30 games in the American League until Denny McLain won 31 games in 1968 for the Tigers.

Walter Johnson won 32 and 38 games in 1912 and 1913, averaging 26 wins per year over the prime 10 years of his 21-year career.

Lefty Grove won 31 games for the A's in 1931, winning exactly 300 games in his career. Grove and Dizzy Dean each won four games in relief when they won 30 games.

Close to 30. Hal Newhouser won 29 games in 1944 for the Tigers, the closest anyone has come to 30 and not made it since Eddie Cicotte won 29 for the Black Sox in 1919. Newhouser won his last nine starts and pitched on the second-to-last day of the season, so he had no chance at 30. Robin Roberts won 28 for the Phillies in 1952 and Dizzy Dean won 28 in 1935.

Bob Welch of the A's won 27 games in 1990, the most since 1968. Steve Carlton won 27 for the Phillies in 1972. Sandy Koufax won 27 for the Dodgers in 1966 and Don Newcombe won 27 for the club in 1956.

"This Week in Baseball"

"I've never been fired from any job, but I think I've signed my last contract. If AT&T and the municipal bonds don't fall flat, I'll be retired by '83.

"Then, when 'This Week in Baseball' comes on TV, I'll be on the golf course and couldn't care less. And a year after that, nobody will remember Earl Weaver." — Orioles manager Earl Weaver quoted in Thomas Boswell's *How Life Imitates the World Series* (1982).

"TWIB" — The show's nickname.

"This Week in Baseball" debuted in June 1977 as a production of the Major League Promotions Corporation. At around the same time, Sony introduced the mass-produced ¾-inch videotape, making it possible to record each day's full schedule of games in production trucks around the Major Leagues. In the early years the ¾-inch tapes had to be transferred to 2-inch tapes in order to be edited.

Mel Allen was the long-time voice of TWIB and Juan Vena broadcast the shows in Spanish. By the early 1990s, TWIB broadcast to 29 of the top 30 American markets. As cable television expanded and more games and summaries were broadcast throughout the week (especially on ESPN), TWIB changed its format to have fewer weekly summaries and more features and highlights.

Ozzie Smith took over as host when Allen died in 1996. He continued the updated magazine style format. After a one-year hiatus in 1999, the show returned in May 2000 with a rotating group of hosts, led off by Derek Jeter. It was the lead-in for Fox's national game of the week on Saturdays. The 2003 segments featured star **Softball** pitcher Jennie Finch pitching to several Major Leaguers, who had no success against her.

Sam Thompson (1860–1922)

Hall of Fame (VC) 1974

"Sam Thompson, with a wallop in his bat like the kick of a Missouri mule." — Fred Lieb in *The Baseball Story* (1950).

"Thompson belongs to that rutting class of slugging batsmen who think of nothing else when they go to the bat but that of gaining the applause of the 'groundlings' by the novice's hit to the outfield of a 'homer', one of the least difficult hits known to batting in baseball, as it needs only muscle and not brains to make it." — 1896 *Spalding Guide*.

Thompson batted .331 between 1885 and 1898 as a National League outfielder.

Born in Indiana, Samuel Luther Thompson began his professional career in 1884 and broke into the Major Leagues with Detroit in 1885. He was a large player for the era at 6'2" and 207 pounds and was one of the few home run threats in the dead ball era. One source reported that his 128 home runs (129 in older sources) were the Major League record until Babe Ruth arrived; except that Roger Connor had 136 between 1880 and 1897 (though some sources might not have included the 13 Connor hit in the 1890 Players League).

Thompson starred with the Phillies from 1889 until 1896 when a bad back curtailed his playing time over the 1897 and 1898 seasons (a total of 17 games over those two years). The injury forced his retirement early in the 1898 season.

He batted a lifetime .331, including .404 in 1894 and .392 in 1895. He drove in over 100 runs eight times and had the highest season RBI total in the 19th century when he drove in 166 runs in 1887. He also played eight games for the 1906 Tigers, batting .226 at age 46 when the Tigers were desperate for players due to injuries.

Three Hundred (.300) Hitters

"But goddamn, to think you're a .300 hitter and end up at .237 in your last season, then find yourself looking at a lifetime .298 average—it made me want to cry."—Mickey Mantle in *The Mick*, with Herb Gluck (1985).

"The only way I can't hit .300 is if there's something physically wrong with me.—Pete Rose.

"He could have hit .300 with a fountain pen."—Joe Garagiola on Stan Musial.

"We're going down. We're going down and I have a .300 lifetime average to take with me. Do you?"—Pete Rose, to his airplane seatmate Hal King, during a rough flight.

"Do you know what the difference between hitting .250 and .300 is? It's 25 hits. Twenty-five hits in 500 at-bats is 50 points, okay? There's six months in a season. That's about 25 weeks. That means if you get just one extra flare a week, just one, a gork, you get a ground ball, you get a grounder with eyes, you get a dying quail … just one more dying quail a week, and you're in Yankee Stadium."—Kevin Costner's character, Crash Davis, in *Bull Durham* (1988).

See also **Batting Champions** and **Four Hundred Hitters**.

Consecutive Seasons. Ty Cobb batted .300 23 times in the Major Leagues. Tony Gwynn batted over .300 for 19 straight seasons through the end of his career in 2001. In March 2000, Gwynn would have had to go 0 for 1,165 to fall below .300. Stan Musial was the last to reach 10 straight when he had 16 straight from 1942 through 1958 (missing 1945 due to the war and not counting the .426 he hit in 12 games in 1941). Pete Rose would have had 15 straight seasons had he not hit .284 in 1974. Dan Brouthers hit .300 16 straight times in the 19th century. Players with multiple .300 seasons:

23 Ty Cobb
19 Tony Gwynn
17 Honus Wagner
16 Stan Musial
16 Pete Rose
15 Ted Williams
15 Rod Carew
15 Wade Boggs
14 Dan Brouthers
14 Willie Keeler

200 Hits/Under .300 Hitter. Buddy Bell is the only American Leaguer with 200 hits in a season who did not hit .300. He had 200 hits in 670 at-bats for a .29851 (.299) batting average. Five National Leaguers have accomplished this dubious feat:

Joe Moore (1935 NY) 201 hits .295
Maury Wills (1962 LA) 208 hits .29928 (.299)
Lou Brock (1967 StL) 206 hits .29898 (.299)
Matty Alou (1970 Pitt) 201 hits .29690 (.297)
Ralph Garr (1973 Atl) 200 hits .29940 (.299)

Garr's total of 200 hits in 668 at-bats is the fewest number of at-bats that can occur and still achieve 200 hits without a .300 average.

Exacting. John Kruk finished his career with exactly a .300 average, exactly 1,200 games played, and exactly 100 home runs.

Three Hundred Wins

"300 Wins Is Nothing to Spit At."—On a T-shirt worn by noted spitballer Gaylord Perry after winning his 300th game.

"I don't want to win my 300th game while he's still there. He'd take credit for it."—Jim Palmer on Orioles manager Earl Weaver. Palmer need not have worried; Weaver left before Palmer and Palmer won only 268 games.

The 22 members of the 300-win club in chronological order:

1. Pud Galvin became the first 300-game winner on October 5, 1888. He is sixth all-time with 361 wins.

2. Tim Keefe won his 300th game while pitching for the Giants on June 4, 1890. He is eighth all-time with 342 wins.

3. Mickey Welch won his 300th game on July 28, 1890. He is nineteenth all-time with 307 wins.

4. Old Hoss Radbourn won his 300th game on June 2, 1891. He is eighteenth all-time with 309 wins (originally thought to be 311).

5. John Clarkson won his 300th game on September 21, 1892. He is eleventh all-time with 328 wins.

6. Kid Nichols won his 300th game on July 7, 1900, an 11–7 victory over the Cubs. At age 31, he was the youngest ever to reach 300. He is fifth all-time with 364, though he was for many years thought to be at 361 and tied with Pud Galvin.

7. Cy Young won his 300th game on July 12, 1901, a 5–3 win for the Red Sox over the A's. He is first all-time with 511 wins.

8. Christy Mathewson won his 300th game on June 13, 1912, for the Giants. He is tied for third all-time with Grover Alexander with 373 wins.

9. Eddie Plank won his 300th game on August 28, 1915, for the St. Louis Terriers of the Federal League. He is eleventh all-time with 326 wins (earlier thought to be 327).

10. Walter Johnson won his 300th game on May 14, 1920, a 9–8 win over the Tigers. He is second all-time with 416 wins.

11. Grover Cleveland Alexander won his 300th game on September 20, 1924. He is tied for third all-time with Christy Mathewson with 373 wins.

12. Lefty Grove.

"When I got to 275, I said 'by gosh, I'm gonna win three hundred or bust.' And when I got number 300 in Boston in 1941—I beat Cleveland 10–5—then that was all. Never won another game. I knew it was time to go. You know how your old body feels. I just couldn't do it anymore."—Grove, who took three tries for the Red Sox, succeeding on July 25, 1941, with a 10–6 (not 5) win over the Indians. Ted Williams homered and Jimmie Foxx tripled to break a late-inning tie. Grove is tied for twenty-first all-time with Early Wynn; both won exactly 300 games.

13. Warren Spahn succeeded on his first try at age 40 with a 2–1, six-hit win over the Cubs at Milwaukee on August 11, 1961. Spahn became the third left-hander to reach the 300 mark. His catcher that night was future Yankees manager Joe Torre. He finished his career with 363 wins, fifth all-time, and probably would have won more than 400 games had he not lost over three seasons to World War II. He did not win his first game in the Major Leagues until age 26.

Spahn missed the 1943 through 1945 seasons and all but four starts in 1942. Had he won even 15 games in those seasons he would have won more than Walter Johnson's 416 lifetime wins, putting him second all-time.

14. Early Wynn

"Somebody will have to come out and take the uniform off me, and the guy who comes after it better bring help."—Wynn during his laborious quest for number 300. He needed eight tries and nine months over two seasons to reach the milestone. His first attempt was a 1–0 loss as Bill Momboquette pitched a no-hitter. He finally made it after 23 seasons on July 13, 1963. He pitched the first five innings of a 7–4 win by the Indians over the A's in Kansas City.

Despite his lack of success in reaching 300 wins, he was pitching well. For the 23 innings prior to July 13, his ERA was 1.96. Wynn was pitching about once a week during his quest for 300. He had one more decision, a loss, after the 300th win. He is tied for twenty-first all-time with Lefty Grove.

15. Gaylord Perry was released by the Braves with 297 wins after the 1981 season. In the spring of 1982 the spitball pitcher signed with the Mariners, convincing them that his quest for 300 would be a good gate attraction for the club. He started 32 games that year and won 10, including number 300 on the first try on May 6, 1982, a 7–3 win over the Yankees. Perry supposedly wore a different uniform each inning in order to sell them on the memorabilia market. Perry is sixteenth all-time with 314 wins.

16. Steve Carlton won his first attempt at 300 on September 23, 1983, with a 6–2 win over the Cardinals. He is ninth all-time with 329 wins.

17. Tom Seaver won four of five games for the White Sox to reach 300 on August 4, 1985. He defeated the Yankees 4–1 on a six-hitter (all singles). The Yankees staged Phil Rizzuto Day, and it was the same day that Rod Carew had his 3,000th hit. Seaver did it at age 40 after 19 Major League seasons. He is seventeenth all-time with 311 wins.

18. Phil Niekro was released in 1983 with 268 wins at age 43. The Yankees signed him and he won 16 games in 1984 and 15 games by September 1985 to put him at 299. On September 8, 1985, he made his first attempt at 300 and lost. He needed all five of his remaining September starts to reach 300. On the last day of the season he became the oldest pitcher to throw a shutout at age 46 by defeating the Blue Jays 8–0. Although known for the knuckleball, he threw only two all game, including the last pitch of the game to strike out Jeff Burroughs. Another source reported that he threw no knuckleballs until the last batter, whom he supposedly struck out on three knuckleballs. Niekro pitched against a number of rookies that day, because the Blue Jays had clinched the pennant the day before.

Niekro's father was dying of lung cancer and the pitcher's inability to concentrate and win over those last few starts supposedly contributed to the Yankees' failure to win the division over the Blue Jays. Niekro pitched two more seasons and finished fifteenth all-time with 318 wins.

19. Don Sutton, playing for the Angels, won his 300th game on June 18, 1986, a 5–1 victory over the Rangers. He was 41 years old. He is thirteenth all-time with 324 wins, tied with Nolan Ryan.

20. Nolan Ryan won his 300th game on his second try on July 31, 1990, while with the Rangers. He lasted into the 8th inning of an 11–3 win over the Brewers. He is tied with Don Sutton with 324 wins, thirteenth all-time.

21. Roger Clemens won his 300th on June 13, 2003, in Yankee Stadium against the Cardinals. He pitched 6⅔ innings of the 5–2 win. He also recorded his 4,000th *Strikeout* that night. He finished the season 17–9 with a lifetime record of 310–160, a .660 winning percentage. On May 21, 2003, Clemens won No. 299. Then he had two losses. On June 7, 2003, against Kerry Wood of the Cubs in an interleague game, Clemens went for his 300th win for the first time. Clemens carried a 1–0 lead into the 7th, but after a walk and a hit he was lifted and reliever Juan Acevado gave up a home run on the first pitch he threw to Eric Karros.

In his first game after 300, Clemens threw a no-hitter for 7⅓ innings, but had a no-decision in a 1–0 loss that lasted 12 innings. Clemens noted that he had not thrown a no-hitter since he began pitching at age 7. When Clemens won his 200th game in May 1997 for the Blue Jays over the Yankees, he was the 94th pitcher to reach that plateau.

By the end of 2004, Clemens had won 328 games, tied for 10th all-time.

22. Greg Maddux, pitching for the Cubs, had his first try at 300 in early August 2004, but didn't win No. 300 until his next start, on August 7, 2004. He was 38 years old. The Cubs rallied from three runs down to beat the Giants 8–4. Maddux left in the 6th inning with a 6–3 lead after throwing 82 pitches. He improved his record to 300–170. It was the first time a pitcher won his 300th game against a pitcher making his Major League debut since Cy Young won No. 300 against John McPherson in 1901. By the end of 2004 Maddux had 305 wins, good for 20th all-time.

Complete Game. Early Wynn, Steve Carlton, Nolan Ryan, Roger Clemens and Greg Maddux did not complete their 300th wins.

300-Game Winner v. 300-Game Winner. Pud Galvin and Tim Keefe hooked up four times between 1890 and 1892 in battles of eventual 300-game winners. The next time 300-game winners faced each other after winning 300 games was in 1986 between Don Sutton and Phil Niekro. Neither pitcher had a decision in the game as the Angels scored six runs in the 8th inning to win 8–3. After that, Sutton faced Tom Seaver later in the 1986 season, Niekro again in June 1987 and Steve Carlton in August 1987.

World Series. In 2003 Roger Clemens became the first 300-game winner not to win a game in the World Series since Grover Cleveland Alexander in 1926. Steve Carlton was the only other 300-game winner to appear in the World Series in that span, for the Phillies in 1983.

Minor Leagues. Ramon Arano is the only 300-game winner in one minor league (Mexican League).

400 wins. Cy Young reached the 400-win mark on August 22, 1904. Walter Johnson did it on May 12, 1926.

500 Wins. On July 19, 1910, Cy Young achieved his 500th career victory as the Cleveland Indians defeated the Senators 5–4 in 11 innings.

Winning Percentage. Through 2003, Roger Clemens' .660 winning percentage was higher than all but two 300-game winners, Christy Mathewson (.665) and Lefty Grove (.680).

Three Thousand Hits

"I was probably as big a fan of the event as anyone else there. After all, I'd never seen anybody get three thousands hits, either."— Lou Brock on his 3,000th hit, quoted in *Late Seasons*, by Roger Angell (1982).

"The three-thousand hitting thing was the first time I let individual pressure get to me. I was uptight about it. When I saw the hit going through, I had a sigh of relief more than anything."— Carl Yastrzemski.

See also **Hits**.

The 24 members of the 3,000 Hit Club in chronological order (It is now only 24 because Cap Anson is now officially below 3,000 according to *Total Baseball*):

(Honorable Mention). Cap Anson was originally credited with 3,041 hits. That total was adjusted downward in subsequent editions of *The Baseball Encyclopedia*, in part due to errors in transcription from the first edition to later editions. Anson was credited later by most sources with exactly 3,000 hits. He achieved the milestone on October 3, 1897. In the late 1990s the editors of *Total Baseball*, now the official Major League publication and the one recognized by the Hall of Fame, reported that Anson had only 2,995 hits.

1. Honus Wagner recorded his 3,000th hit on June 9, 1914, and newspaper accounts noted the accomplishment. He finished his career with 3,418 (adjusted down from 3,430), seventh on the all-time list.

2. Nap Lajoie did it on September 27, 1914, on his way to a total of 3,251, tenth on the all-time list.

3. Ty Cobb recorded his 3,000th hit on August 19, 1921, against Elmer Myers of the Red Sox. At age 34, Cobb was the youngest ever to reach the milestone (see also *Four Thousand Hits*).

4. Tris Speaker did it on May 17, 1925, against Senators pitcher Tom Zachary on his way to 3,515.

5. Eddie Collins hit number 3,000 on June 3, 1925, while managing the White Sox against the Tigers. He finished with 3,311 (adjusted from 3,310 in earlier sources).

6. Paul Waner was playing for the Braves when he singled off *Eephus* pitcher Rip Sewell of the Pirates (Waner's long-time team). He did it on June 19, 1942, in a 7–6 Braves win.

Waner had 2,999 hits before the game of June 17. On a hit-and-run play with Waner at bat, shortstop Eddie Joost moved to cover second base. Waner bounced a ball to the spot abandoned by Joost. Joost reversed his course and got his glove on the ball but could not throw it. As umpire Beans Reardon came over to Waner to present him with the ball, Waner shook his head at the press box and the official scorer obliged by scoring it as an error, so he could reach No. 3,000 on a more dignified hit. He finished with 3,152 hits, the last being his only hit for the Yankees.

7. Stan Musial.

"Going for his 3,000th hit, Musial neglected to concentrate and took his stride too early. But he kept his bat back, as all great hitters do. On sheer reflex, he slugged a double to left."—Roger Kahn in *A Season in the Sun* (1977).

Musial recorded his 3,000th hit, a pinch hit double, against Moe Drabowsky of the Cubs at Wrigley Field on May 13, 1958. It had been 16 years since a player had reached 3,000, and it was to be another 12 years before it happened again.

8. Henry Aaron's 3,000th hit was an infield base hit in the 1st inning of the second game of a doubleheader against the Reds on May 17, 1970. He also hit his 570th home run that day (hit number 3,001) to become the first player to reach 500 home runs and 3,000 hits. Stan Musial presented him with the ball as the only living member of the 3,000 Hit Club.

9. Willie Mays.

"Willie swings … ground ball … base hit … hit number 3,000 for Willie Mays. A single to left field. They are stopping the game and the ball is being flipped over to Willie. Now here come National League president Chub Feeney, Willie's former boss, and Stan Musial, the other member of the 3,000-hit club [*sic*, see Aaron above], here today to congratulate Willie."—Broadcaster Russ Hodges.

Mays hit number 3,000 on July 18, 1970, against the Expos. It was a 2nd inning single through the infield off pitcher Mike Wegener.

10. Roberto Clemente.

"I have to get that hit this year. I might die."—Clemente.

Clemente started the 1972 season needing 118 hits to reach 3,000. He was having severe ankle tendon problems and missed 50 games during the season. With 26 games remaining he needed 25 hits, but he missed a few more games because of the tendon problem.

With two games left in the season, he had 2,999 (the last of these off Steve Carlton). In the second-to-last game he hit a ball off Tom Seaver's glove that second baseman Ken Boswell bobbled. The "hit" sign was flashed on the screen, but the official scorer ruled it an error. Later in the game he hit a hard line drive down the right field line, only to have it caught by Rusty Staub. Staub said that he normally did not play that close to the line for Clemente but wandered over by mistake. Some sources incorrectly report the Boswell error as being in the same game as hit number 3,000.

This set up the last game heroics on September 1 in a 5–0 Pirates win over the Mets and pitcher Jon Matlack. Matlack gave up a long double to left-center field for Clemente's 3,000th hit. It was his last hit of the season and his career. He was killed in a plane crash that winter while delivering supplies to earthquake-stricken Managua, Nicaragua (see also *Deaths*).

11. Al Kaline, who finished with 3,007 hits, had number 3,000 on September 24, 1974. It was a double off Orioles pitcher Dave McNally in the 4th inning. More than a month earlier Kaline had a dream in which he recorded his 3,000th hit off McNally. McNally had helped Kaline obtain a Ford dealership through Ford president Lee Iacocca. Kaline was the first American Leaguer to reach 3,000 since Eddie Collins in 1925.

12. Pete Rose hit number 3,000 on May 5, 1978, at Riverfront Stadium for the Reds against Steve Rogers of the Expos. It was a 5th inning single, appropriate given that Rose had more singles than any player in Major League history. Rose was the youngest National League player to reach the mark, having turned 37 on April 14 that season (see also *Four Thousand Hits*).

13. Lou Brock

"I guess I'd better send my fingers to Cooperstown."—Pitcher Dennis Lamp of the Cubs after Brock singled off his hand for hit number 3,000 on August 13, 1979.

14. Carl Yastrzemski hit number 3,000 on September 12, 1979, a single off Jim Beattie of the Yankees. He later became the first American Leaguer to reach 3,000 hits and 400 home runs.

15. Rod Carew recorded his 3,000th hit on the same day that Tom Seaver won his 300th game, August 4, 1985. Carew, playing for the Angels, singled off Frank Viola, who was pitching for Carew's former team, the Twins. Carew finished with 3,053 hits.

16. Robin Yount hit number 3,000 on September 8, 1992, a single against Jack Armstrong of the Indians. Yount also had hits number 1,000 and 2,000 against the Indians. He finished with 3,142 hits.

17. George Brett.

"If I stay healthy, I have a chance to become the first player ever to collect three thousand hits and one thousand errors."—Brett after a particularly bad day at third base.

Brett was injured during much of the last week of the 1992 season while the Royals were on the road. He returned to the line-up for the club's last road game before heading home to finish the season. Against the Angels in Anaheim on September 30, 1992, he began the game four hits shy of 3,000. He had three hits early in the game to put him at 2,999 when he faced Tim Fortugno in the 7th inning. He lined a single for number 3,000. After the ovation died down and the game resumed, Brett was picked off first base. He finished his career with 3,154 hits and 292 errors.

18. Dave Winfield. On September 16, 1993, Winfield was playing for the Twins when he hit a single for number 2,999 in his third at-bat of the night. In the 9th inning against reliever Dennis Eckersley of the A's, he hit a single for an RBI and hit number 3,000. Only 14,654 fans attended the game in Minnesota.

19. Eddie Murray.

"I hope things get back to normal. It'll be a lot better once I'm done playing. I never set 3,000 as a goal. I know there were people out there happier than I was. It's not what I was focused on."—Murray.

On June 30, 1995, Murray hit number 3,000 off Mike Trombley of the Twins in the Metrodome. He singled in the 6th inning for the Indians during a 4–1 victory. Murray and Dave Winfield became the first teammates with 3,000 hits since Ty Cobb, Tris Speaker and Eddie Collins played for the 1928 Philadelphia A's. When Murray reached 3,000, the next most hits by an active player were the 2,723 by Andre Dawson. Murray was only the second switch hitter, after Pete Rose, to break 3,000. Murray broke three ribs in a home plate collision a few days later and went on the disabled list.

20. Paul Molitor. On September 16, 1996, the 40-year-old Molitor of the Twins hit a triple off Royals pitcher Jose Rosado in Kansas City for his 3,000th hit. He became the first player to record 200 hits in the same season in which he reached 3,000 hits (he finished with 225 that season). He finished his career with 3,319 hits.

21. Tony Gwynn. On August 6, 1999, his mother's birthday, Gwynn went 4-for-5 in a 12–10 Padres win over the Expos to reach 3,000. He was the first National Leaguer to do it in 20 years, with a single (of course) in the 1st inning off Dan Smith in Montreal.

22. Wade Boggs. On August 7, 1999, the day after Tony Gwynn reached the milestone (and two days after Mark McGwire reached 500 home runs — it was a big week), Boggs hit a 6th inning home run off Indians pitcher Chris Haney. It was the first time a player hit a home run for No. 3,000, and it was only the second home run by Boggs that season. Boggs went 3-for-4 in the Devil Rays' 15–10 loss.

23. Cal Ripken. On April 15, 2000, Ripken lined a 7th inning single off Twins pitcher Hector Carrasco. The first person to congratulate him was first base coach Eddie Murray, also a member of the 3,000-hit club. Ripken finished with 3,184 hits.

24. Rickey Henderson. On October 7, 2001, the last game of the season, Henderson hit a leadoff bloop double off John Thomson, as the Padres lost to the Rockies, 14–5. Henderson left the game after the hit. Coincidentally, it was Tony Gwynn's *Last Game* of his career. Henderson had 3,055 hits through 2003, apparently his last year in the Major Leagues.

Criticism of Recent Hall of Fame Admittees.

"Let's be blunt. The three thousand-hit club has always been one of baseball's premiere frauds. Now that Carl Yastrzemski, career average .288, and Lou Brock (.292) have joined Al Kaline (.297) in the three thousand-hit circle, all that remains is for Rusty Staub, .278 hitter, to reach membership in 1983, for the club to be totally devalued.... No one mentions that, in the case of both forty-year-olds, the three thousand mark is entirely a by-product of longevity. As a nation, we tend to forget to ask whether our hamburgers or our stars are truly prime or just choice." — Sportswriter Thomas Boswell.

Short of 3,000.

"At that time not much attention was paid to records. The truth of the matter is I did not even know how many hits I had. A couple of years after I quit, Clark Griffith told me about it, and asked me if I'd care to have a comeback with the Senators and pick up those thirteen hits. But I was out of shape, and didn't want to go through all that would have been necessary to make the effort. Nowadays, with radio and television announcers spouting records every time a player comes to bat, I would have known about my hits and probably would have stayed to make three thousand of them." — Sam Rice quoted in *Kings of the Diamonds*, by Lee Allen and Tom Meany (1965).

Rice had 2,987 hits and Sam Crawford had 2,964. Rice hit .293 in 1934 in his one year with the Indians (after 19 seasons with the Senators) and probably could have come back for one more year.

Crawford hit only .173 in 61 games in 1917, mostly as a pinch hitter, though he still might have played a few games in 1918. Nevertheless, Crawford made the Hall of Fame in 1957 after a 19-year career primarily for the Tigers.

Others who were close to 3,000 are Wee Willie Keeler (2,947), Frank Robinson (2,943), Jake Beckley (2,931), Rogers Hornsby (2,930), and Al Simmons (2,927).

Book. Fred McMame, *The 3000-Hit Club* (2004).

Threes

"The field, the literal plot of the game, consists of a square whose four sides are ninety feet long.... Not quite in the middle of the square, sixty feet, six inches from home plate, is a circle, with a radius of nine feet, at whose center (we are on the pitcher's mound) is a 'rectangular slab of whitened rubber, 24 inches by six inches.' So far, all the dimensions are multiples of three." — A. Bartlett Giamatti in *Take Time for Paradise* (1989).

Baseball multiples of three: three strikes and three outs; nine innings; nine players to a side; basepaths are 360 feet, the number of degrees in a circle; three thousand hits, a .300 average and 300 wins are all significant milestones; The 30/30 club of home runs and stolen bases is an often-cited milestone; 30 wins is the magical milestone for a pitcher in a season and an ERA under 3.00 for a season is considered excellent; 162 games in a season, 81 home and 81 road games; the three-game series is the norm in scheduling.

Throwing Objects at the Ball

If a fielder throws his glove at the ball, the batter is entitled to three bases. If a fielder throws his cap, shoe or other uniform part at the ball, the batter is entitled to two bases. There is no historical or logical explanation for the difference.

Throwing a glove at a fair ball has always been illegal, but a 1954 rule change allowed a glove to be thrown at a foul ball.

On July 27, 1947, Red Sox first baseman Jake Jones was credited with a triple after pitcher Fred Sanford threw his glove at the ball.

Throwing Out the First Pitch

"[Massachusetts] governor Leverett Saltonstall showed up at the State House today with his left arm in a sling. The reason? He threw his arm out Tuesday when he tossed in the first ball at the Boston Red Sox opener!" — The *Stars and Stripes* military newspaper during World War II.

"I don't know why they took me out after one pitch." — Former Dodger manager Tommy Lasorda, after throwing out the first pitch at Dodger Stadium on April 1, 1997 (he had retired during the 1996 season). He was still frustrated at not making his mark as a Major Leagues pitcher in the 1950s (0–4).

"For Walter Johnson, with the hope that he may continue to be as formidable as in yesterday's game." — Inscription on a baseball by President William Howard Taft after he witnessed Walter Johnson's Opening Day victory over the A's on April 14, 1910. Johnson pitched a 3–0 shutout that included only one hit, a windblown double by Frank "Home Run" Baker. Before the game Taft started the presidential tradition of throwing out the first ball to start the season. Umpire Billy Evans suggested that the president throw out the first ball, a privilege usually reserved for a District of Columbia commissioner. His throw as described by one newspaper: "He did it with his good, trusty right arm, and the virgin sphere scudded across the diamond, true as a die to the pitcher's box, where Walter Johnson gathered it in."

Forgotten Man. In 1913 in the first game at Ebbets Field, the Dodger pitcher struck out the first batter, but everyone quickly realized that the mayor had not thrown out the ceremonial first ball. The clubs disregarded the first out, completed the ceremony and started the game over again.

During the Dodgers' Opening Day ceremony on April 17, 1934, borough president Raymond Ingersoll was the forgotten man. After the first pitch by Van Lingle Mungo, time was called and Ingersoll was trotted out to make the throw. The strike by Mungo was disregarded and the game was restarted. The day began inauspiciously for other reasons when a grandstand flag caught fire and fell onto the field, a fan threw firecrackers at the players during their pregame parade around the field and another fan threw a huge lemon on the field just before the game restarted.

World War II. In 1943 at the height of the war, U.S. manpower commissioner Paul V. McNutt threw out the first ball of the season in lieu of the traditional presidential toss.

New Tradition. The Phillies have made a practice of starting the season with an odd way of throwing out the first ball. Phillies president Bill Giles christened Veterans Stadium in Philadelphia by having a helicopter drop a ball to catcher Mike Ryan at second base. Ryan could not immediately see the ball and then realized it was headed for the seats. He made the catch just in front of the dugout on the dead run. It bounced out of his glove and he caught it in the air.

Another time the Phillies had the ball delivered by a human cannonball. In another they had it dropped from the roof of the stadium. They have also had Parachute Man and a motorcycle rider on a high wire with a woman suspended underneath him on a trapeze. For a short time National League president Bart Giamatti banned these wild Opening Day stunts.

On Opening Day 1972 in Philadelphia, a stuntman known as Kiteman was supposed to fly off a ramp in the outfield stands in his hang glider to deliver the ball. The season was delayed a week by a player strike and Kiteman had a prior commitment that conflicted with the scheduling change. A substitute was found, but he froze on the ramp. When he finally took off, he veered backward and crashed into the bleachers. The next season, with a wider ramp, Kiteman crashed in center field. In 1980, the third time a hang glider was used, the new man made it.

In 1938 the president of the Eastern League flew over the ballpark in Binghamton, New York, and dropped the Opening Day ball from the plane.

Feud. In the 1970s A's owner Charlie Finley feuded repeatedly with the mayor of Oakland. For one Opening Day he snubbed the mayor by inviting the mayor of nearby San Jose to throw out the first ball.

World Series Restrictions.

"All first-ball throwers are subject to final approval of the commissioner. Recommendations are solicited from the participating clubs, but no commitments should be made until approval has been made. The use of politicians, movie stars etc. will not be approved except in rare or unusual circumstances." — World Series Manual Section 7.13.

In 1979 Baltimore owner Jerry Hoffberger was fined $2,500 for breaking the rule that prevented movie stars and politicians from throwing out the first ball at the World Series. Maryland governor Harry Hughes threw out the first pitch of Game 2.

Staying In Shape. After age 60 Bob Feller kept planks on a tree

in his yard to practice his throwing so that he did not embarrass himself when he was asked to throw out the first ball.

Strike Year. When the 1981 season resumed after a two-month player strike, U.S. Labor Secretary Ray Donovan threw out the first pitch of the second season at Yankee Stadium after helping to settle the strike.

Active Player. Henry Aaron was the first active player to throw out the first ball at a World Series. He did it at Game 1 of the 1973 Series, shortly after he had hit home run number 713 and was poised to break Babe Ruth's record the next season. His comment: "As bad as my arm is, they ought to let me hit it out."

Cal Ripken threw out the first pitch of the 1995 World Series.

Tight Straps. At the 1978 opener for the Tucson club in the Rangers' farm system, a nude skydiver dropped the first pitch onto the field.

Funny Guy. In keeping with his persona, Jimmy Piersall intentionally threw the first pitch of the 1974 Babe Ruth World Series over the backstop and into the parking lot.

Good Aim. In 1940 a *Washington Post* photographer asked President Franklin Roosevelt to throw out a second ball so that he could get another shot in. The noted scatter-armed Roosevelt nailed the photographer's camera and broke the lens.

In 1953 President Eisenhower was asked to throw a second ball. Umpire Bill McKinley was not paying attention and "was dusted off by a Presidential blooper to the seat of the pants."

According to *The Sporting News*, in May 1965 mayor Tom Johnson of Thomasville, North Carolina, threw out the first ball of the season. He struck Miss North Carolina in the head and almost knocked her out.

Wrong Sport. When Chicago Bears coach Mike Ditka threw out the first pitch of one Cubs season in the 1980s, Cubs catcher Joe Girardi threw back a football that he had hidden behind his back. Ditka caught it.

Stealing the Spotlight. Basketball star Michael Jordan threw out the first pitch of the 1993 ALCS. During the game, played in Chicago, rumors began circulating that Jordan would retire from the NBA Chicago Bulls. The rumor was confirmed by Jordan at a press conference the next morning. White Sox owner Jerry Reinsdorf was devastated, as he owned both the Sox (who lost that night) and the Bulls.

Jordan played professional baseball for a season and then returned to the Bulls near the end of the 1994–1995 basketball regular season (see also **Basketball**).

Relief Needed. In August 2003 Roger Clemens made his 600th start and gave up nine runs in a 13–2 loss to the White Sox. His mother had thrown out the ceremonial first pitch after missing his 300th win due to complications with emphysema. Clemens' comment after the game: "It was great. They should have let her stay on the mound. She had better stuff than I had."

Luis Tiant. On August 26, 1975, the Cuban pitcher's father, a 69-year-old former player, had been granted travel papers by Fidel Castro to see his son pitch. He threw out the first pitch of the game at Fenway Park, a low and outside fastball to catcher Tim Blackwell. Disgusted, the senior Tiant asked for the ball back and threw a fastball across the plate as the crowd erupted. Son Luis later related that as he left the field, his father "told me he was ready to go four or five."

Dueling Candidates. On July 25, 2004, presidential candidate John Kerry threw wildly from the grass in front of the mound before a Red Sox/Yankees game. In contrast, George W. Bush threw a strike from the mound before Game 3 of the 2001 World Series.

Thrown Balls

See *Defensive Gems* and *Longest Throws*.
Rule. Until 1910, if a ball was thrown in the stands, it was still in play.

Thrown Out of the Game See *Ejections*

Ticket Takers

"The average woman is more honest than the average man; the men may nearly always be counted upon to hold out overchange." — An 1896 advocate for women ticket takers and sellers.

"God love them — the familiar faces, the grizzled, toothless, cabbage-eared mugs of guys and gals who have been working the ballpark for years. Program sellers, ticket-takers, ushers, counter ladies, the whole crew. Not pretty, but as real as corn on the cob." — From *Murder in Wrigley Field*, by Crabbe Evers (1991).

"A ticket seller before a big ball game is like St. Peter standing at the portals of paradise, holding in his or her hands the word on an applicant's fate. There *is* one pair of seats behind home plate. Heaven lies just past the turnstiles." — John Thorn in *The Game for All America* (1988).

See also *Tickets, Turnstiles* and *Ushers*.

Nineteenth Century. Early utility players often were used as ticket takers. Future Senators owner Clark Griffith performed this task with the St. Louis Browns in 1891.

Eccentric and despised owner Andrew Freedman of the New York Giants fined rookie pitcher Cy Seymour $10 for sneaking a peek at the game while taking tickets.

Ticket Machines. In 1992 the Twins began using automated teller machines in supermarkets to sell tickets.

Tickets

"It is well worth 50 cents to see a good game of baseball and when the public refuses to pay that; then good bye to baseball. They do not object to paying 75 cents to $1.50 to go to the theater and numbers prefer baseball to theatricals. We must make the games worth witnessing and there will be no fault found with the price of admission. A good game is worth 50 cents, a poor one is dear at 25 cents." — 19th century sportswriter Henry Chadwick.

See also *Gate Receipts, Rain Checks, Ticket Takers* and *Turnstiles*.

Early Ticket Prices. The first known admission, 50 cents, was charged for an 1858 game between the New York and Brooklyn clubs at Fashion Race Course. Harry Wright and his New York club defeated Brooklyn 22–18. This was an all-star contest that drew considerable interest and therefore a premium ticket price. At least one source reported that the first ticket price was actually paid in 1857.

The ticket price in the early 1860s for regular season games was often 10 cents. In 1866 at the championship match between Philadelphia and Washington, 8,000 tickets were sold at 25 cents each and scalped for $5. Ticket prices for the third game of the series were raised to $1.

Early National League and American Association Prices. Early National League admissions started at 50 cents, but admission was only 10 cents after the 3rd inning (some sources reference the 1st inning).

Although the National League formally imposed the 50-cent minimum, during hard times in 1883 Philadelphia was allowed to reduce its admission price to 25 cents. It was a poor club that drew few fans, and the price reduction helped improve attendance. The 25-cent price ended in 1884 but was reinstituted in 1886 and expanded to other poor-drawing cities. Some teams instituted a 3-for-a-$1 plan. By 1888 all reductions were banned by the National League, and the 50-cent minimum was made mandatory.

American Association clubs of the 1880s generally charged 25 cents for admission. In the 1880s Baltimore at times tried to boost attendance by charging five-cent admissions and 25 cents for a Sunday doubleheader. The American Association experimented unsuccessfully with 50-cent ticket prices in 1888.

During the National League's 1891 war with the American Association, the National League lowered its ticket price to 25 cents. The American Association disbanded after the season and the National League immediately returned to the 50-cent minimum.

By the end of the 1890s the glut of 12 National League teams without competition from other leagues created poorly financed non-contenders at the bottom of the league. To boost attendance many of these teams reduced admission to 25 cents.

Early 20th Century. The average cost of tickets in the first twenty years of the 20th century: bleacher seats 25 cents; grandstand seats 50 cents; pavilion seats 75 cents; box seats $1.00. By 1920, 50 cents was the minimum ticket price for the cheapest seats.

At the 1905 World Series bleacher seats were 50 cents and grandstand seats were $1. At the 1923 World Series, seats were $1.10 for the bleachers, $3.30 for the upper stand, $5.50 for the lower stand and $6.60 for box seats.

Mid–20th Century. Clubs raised ticket prices during World War II when the federal government imposed taxes on entertainment events such as baseball. In 1944 the Phillies raised box seats to $2, grandstand seats to $1.25 and bleacher prices to 65 cents. The three New York clubs all had the same prices for games: $2.40 for box seats, $1.80 for reserved seats, $1.20 for grandstand seats and 60 cents for bleachers.

At the 1944 World Series tickets in the reserved section were $37.50 for six. In 1945 a World Series ticket cost $6.

1970s. In 1977 average ticket prices were $4.88 for box seats, $3.61 for reserved and $2.07 for general admission, for a $3.75 average. The Dodgers did not raise their ticket prices during their first 18 years in Los Angeles. Until 1975 the top price was $3.50, but the club raised that ticket to $4.00 for the 1976 season.

The Cubs historically had the cheapest seats in baseball, $1 for bleacher seats until the mid–1970s, and held back 17,000 tickets for walk-up sales each game.

1990s. The average ticket price in 1994 was $10.45, up from $9.60 in 1993. The average price for a family of four to attend a game, including parking, concessions and souvenirs, was $95.80. The highest average prices were charged by the Red Sox, at $13.51 per ticket. The low was in Colorado at $7.90.

The average price in 1997 rose 7.1% to $11.98, the highest increase in six years. The Red Sox had the highest prices at $17.69. The National League high was the Cardinals at $12.36, a 24.7% increase. The Expos were the lowest at $6.81 (in U.S. currency). The average ticket price rose 38.7% between 1991 and 1997, when it was $8.64. NFL ticket prices rose 41.8% to $35.74. NBA prices rose 41.6% to $34.08. It cost a family of four an average of $106 to attend a Major League Baseball game, $214 to see an NBA team, $222 to attend an NFL game and $229 in the NHL.

The fan cost index rose 3.5% to $106.20 for 1997, which included the price of four average tickets, four small drinks, two small beers, four hot dogs, parking for one family, two programs and two ball-caps. The Braves were the highest at $129.16 and the Expos were the lowest at $80.42.

2000s. In 2003 the Red Sox had the highest average ticket price, at $42.34. In 2004 average ticket prices in the Major Leagues were $19.82.

Club Allotments. In 1915 the American League adopted a policy allowing each player to receive two passes to all games. However, free passes to other than players became a severe problem because it was skewing the gate receipts and profits to both clubs. In response, the National League adopted a rule in 1920 that passes could not exceed 6% of a team's season attendance.

Under the most recent rules, visiting teams are entitled to a block of 500 tickets for each regular season game; each player may buy five tickets; league and other clubs' officials also have the right to purchase tickets to games (100 are set aside for other Major League clubs' personnel).

Strike Prices. In late 1994 and 1995 many clubs began making preparations to sell tickets at rolled-back prices to accommodate the possibility of replacement players of lesser quality than the regular Major League players. For example, the Dodgers were prepared to roll back prices to 1958, their first season in Los Angeles. The Angels charged only one dollar per ticket for Opening Day 1995 after the strike ended.

Raising Price. In the early 20th century, Charles Comiskey and the White Sox raised the admission price along the foul lines to 50 cents, reasoning that 25-cent fans would throw bottles. They were relegated to the bleachers where "they can throw their arms off and bother no one," according to Comiskey.

Forgeries. Tickets were forged for the 1911 World Series.

Eighty-one fake tickets were confiscated before Game 1 of the 1995 World Series. Most fans paid $150 for the bogus tickets.

World Series Tickets. The 1935 Cubs won every game from Labor Day until the third from last day of the season to clinch the pennant. Because the club forgot to print World Series tickets, the Series began in Detroit.

During the 1994 player strike the White Sox mailed out four World Series tickets to each of their season ticket holders to remind them what might have been. It is common for contenders to preprint tickets in early August so that they are not caught short late in the season.

In New York for the 1998 World Series, tickets were $150 for a box seat, $100 for reserved seats and $40 for the bleachers, compared with $70, $45, and $25 for the 1996 Series.

Free Tickets. For a late September 1946 Indians game featuring Bob Feller on the mound, owner Bill Veeck let all fans in free as a "thank you" for their support during the season. The Astros did the same thing for a game early in the 1995 season after the player strike ended.

Negro League stars generally were not required to pay to attend Major League games. The exception was St. Louis, where they not only paid, but were relegated to the Jim Crow section of right field.

Tickets that were pre-punched to show they were complimentary were known as Annie Oaklies, in honor of the famous sharpshooter's ability to shoot out the suit designations on playing cards.

Military. At the 1945 World Series, many wounded veterans were brought to Game 1 in Detroit, but there were no tickets available. An appeal for tickets was made outside the ballpark and 716 fans gave up their seats.

In 2003 the Marlins set up a program to allow military families free access to ballgames in light of the war with Iraq.

Scalping. According to one source, ticket scalping may have cost the Dodgers the 1920 World Series. In the best-of-nine series,

the Indians were up four games to two over the Dodgers. Dodger pitcher Rube Marquard was scheduled to start Game 7, but he was arrested as a ticket scalper after trying to sell a set of box seats for $350. Though Marquard did not go to jail, Dodger manager Wilbert Robinson did not start him and Dodger ace Burleigh Grimes pitched instead on one day's rest. The Dodgers lost 3–0 and the Indians won their first World Series.

Marquard was convicted of scalping but was fined only $1. Nevertheless, the Dodgers punished him by unloading him to the Reds. The league even considered banning him for life for the transgression.

During a 1940 Reds doubleheader that was expected to break attendance records, a scalper was arrested for selling 60-cent bleacher seats for $1.50.

In 1995 the Orioles addressed the scarcity of their tickets and problems with scalping. They designated an area outside of their ballpark for fans to sell tickets legally to other fans on game days. Those entering the "Bird's Nest Scalp-Free Zone" were allowed to sell tickets for face value two hours before each home game.

People lined up overnight in Atlanta to get tickets for the Braves' 1995 play-off games against the Rockies. Most of the overnighters appeared to be homeless and were paid $50 to stand in line. As soon as they bought their tickets they walked across the street and delivered them to waiting ticket scalpers or brokers.

Rangers pitcher Ed Vosberg was caught scalping his All-Star Game tickets outside the ballpark before the game in July 1995.

Season Tickets.

"Giants fans were the businessmen. They were there at the Polo Grounds with their shirts and ties in the same box seats game after game. Tickets were passed down generation after generation, just like the team."—Harvey Frommer in *New York City Baseball* (1985).

Season ticket packages were established by the early 1870s and were part of at least some clubs' sales in the National League's inaugural season in 1876. Hartford is one of the clubs sometimes identified with selling season tickets.

Cleveland of the 1871 National Association offered an unusual season ticket package. Tickets were $6 for the season, but if a woman accompanied a male fan, the package was $10 for the couple and included parking of their horse carriage behind first or third base.

The 1884 National League Providence club charged $15 for season tickets if purchased before March 15 and $20 if purchased before April 15. The Boston Red Stockings charged $15, but only $10 if the tickets were purchased by a woman.

According to at least one source, modern season ticket plans were first instituted by the 1934 Reds.

1990s Selected Season Ticket Levels. In 1992 the clubs with the highest number of season ticket sales were the Dodgers (27,000), Blue Jays (26,000) and Orioles (24,400). In contrast, the Giants have never sold more than 10,000 season tickets until the club's new ballpark opened in the late 1990s.

In their first season in 1993 the Rockies sold 28,250 season tickets and presold 2.8 million tickets on their way to a new Major League attendance record.

The Braves went from 5,000 season ticket holders in 1991 to 17,000 in 1992 after winning the National League pennant.

In the Indians' last season in cavernous Municipal Stadium in 1993, the club sold only 2,800 season tickets. Sales immediately increased to 21,000 for 1994 in Jacobs Field. On December 2, 1995, the Indians sold out for the 1996 season. After selling out 25,000 season tickets, the club put another 1.3 million single-game tickets on sale November 24, 1995. They sold out in nine days. Only 41,000 SRO tickets and a few single-game tickets were available for sale beginning in January 1996. The sales guaranteed attendance of at least 3.3 million in 1996. In 1997 the Indians sold out every home game in nine days for the second year in a row. The Indians peaked at 25,000 in 1998, but fell to 21,000 in 2002 and 15,000 in 2003. On April 4, 2001, the Indians staged their first non-sell-out in six years at Jacobs Field, ending the longest consecutive game sellout streak in Major League history at 455 games.

After their player housecleaning in 1993, the Padres sold only 3,000 season tickets in 1994.

Tampa Bay, which was not scheduled to start play until 1998, sold 32,079 season tickets before the end of 1995.

In 1993 the White Sox offered a "Hip Season Ticket Plan," using Bo Jackson and his rehabilitating hip as the promotional gimmick.

In 1999 the Giants became only the second club, after the 1996 Indians, to sell out all available season tickets (29,000) before Opening Day.

Late Rally. On September 29, 2002, the last day of the season, the Marlins had their second–largest crowd of the year, 28,599, due to the purchase of 18,000 tickets by an unnamed fan. The Marlins ended the season with attendance of 813,118 just ahead of the Expos at 812,545.

Thinking Ahead. Securities trader Michael Mahan spent about $36,000 for 6,458 tickets ($6 face value) to buy out the right field bleachers at Dodger Stadium for games of October 1 and 3, 2004. He calculated that Barry Bonds would be shooting for his 700th home run at that point. He missed by about two weeks, as Bonds hit No. 700 on September 17, 2004, at SBC Park. Mahan donated about 400 to charity and gave about 300 to family and friends. The others he sold for $15 per ticket, and buyers had to sign a contract promising to give the ball to Mahan and they would split the proceeds of sale.

Child's Play. The Cubs were the first club to offer tickets at lower prices for children.

Tie Games

"If a tie is like kissing your sister, losing is like kissing your grandmother with her teeth out." — George Brett.

Rules. Tie games must be replayed as soon as possible on the same field if scheduling permits.

Before 1885 players' individual statistics were not counted in tie games. Starting that season, individual statistics counted for all tie games of five or more innings.

First Major League Tie. The first tie in Major League history was on May 25, 1876, when the Philadelphia Athletics and Louisville Grays played a 14-inning 2–2 tie.

Longest. See *Longest Games* for the 26-inning tie between the Dodgers and Braves in 1920.

On July 21, 1945, the Tigers and A's played a 24-inning tie. Les Mueller pitched 19⅔ innings for the Tigers in the 1–1 game.

Opening Day. On April 3, 2000, the Reds and Brewers tied 3–3 in a game called in the 6th inning because of rain. It was Ken Griffey, Jr.'s, debut with the Reds and was the first tie game on Opening Day in 35 years.

Coincidence. In an August 13, 1910, tie between the Dodgers and Pirates, *each team* had eight runs, 38 at-bats, 13 hits, 12 assists, two errors, five strikeouts, three walks, one hit batter and one passed ball. Each team used 10 players. The two second baseman had the same number of hits and runs, and the shortstops had the same number of hits. The game was called because of darkness.

World Series. There have been three ties in World Series history, one each in 1907, 1912 and 1922; all because of darkness. See also *World Series*—Player Shares.

Tiger Stadium (1912–1999)

"For 87 years the Detroit Tigers have played baseball at the corner of Michigan and Trumbull. During that time, the stadiums they've played in have been renovated, expanded, renamed, belatedly lit and even wheeled around 90 degrees, but rarely have hitters complained." — John Holway in *The Sluggers* (1989).

Tiger Stadium was known originally as Bennett Park, then Navin Field and later Briggs Stadium.

Bennett Park. Bennett Park opened on April 28, 1896, as home to the Detroit Wolverines of the Western League. Detroit defeated the Columbus Senators that day 17–2. The ballpark was named after 19th-century catcher Charlie Bennett, who had lost his legs in a railroad accident (see also *Amputees*).

The original ballpark was the site of an old haymarket where farmers brought their hay for weight and sale. The site was paved with cobblestones, which sometimes were found in the infield. It was also the site of the city's first zoo.

Navin Field. The ballpark was rebuilt for the 1901 American League season. It was rebuilt again for the 1912 season, and the field was turned 90 degrees to change the angle of the sun to favor the hitters. The new single-decked, concrete park replaced Bennett Field and was renamed Navin Field after owner Frank Navin.

In 1924 the area behind home plate from first base to third base was double-decked to increase seating capacity. The club also installed an elaborate press box on the roof.

Briggs Stadium. After the 1936 championship season, the Tigers double-decked the right-field pavilion and the bleachers. After Navin's death in late 1936, the park was renamed Briggs Stadium after new owner Walter O. Briggs. Lights were installed in 1948, and the first night game was played on June 15, 1948.

Tiger Stadium. John Fetzer bought the club in 1960 and changed the name to Tiger Stadium on January 1, 1961. The cost to change the name on the ballpark's facade was $20,000 although the I, G and R from Briggs were used in the new Tiger Stadium name.

In 1977 Fetzer sold the site to the city for one dollar and took a 30-year lease to avoid property taxes. The ballpark is now registered with the U.S. Department of the Interior on the National Register of Historic Sites. Federal funds were used for a major renovation for two years beginning in 1980, strengthening the foundation and steel beams.

New Ballpark. Though the club has obligated itself to play in Tiger Stadium through 2008, efforts were underway to build a new ballpark. In the late 1980s after the Tigers announced their intention to build a new ballpark, the Tiger Stadium Fan Club commissioned the American Institute of Architects (AIA) to study the feasibility of saving the ballpark. The AIA's report indicated a number of structural problems with the facility and concluded that it could not be saved.

In 1995 there were pledges by local government to help finance a new ballpark although architectural drawings were not yet available. That year the city and the club agreed to plans to build a $235 million stadium in downtown Detroit. The club was to finance most of the project, with money also coming from the state and through local bond measures. The club was scheduled to move into a new park in 1998 or 1999, but until 1996 plans were moving slowly because of financing concerns.

Tenants. The ballpark was home to various Negro League clubs in the 1920s and 1930s.

Seating Capacity. The original Bennett Park contained 8,500 seats, with additional seating on the rooftops of adjacent streets. As part of the 1911–1912 renovation, capacity was increased to 14,000. In 1913 capacity was increased to 23,000 as the old ballpark was rebuilt almost from the ground up. Adding a double-decked area behind home plate increased capacity to 29,000 in 1924. Additional double-decking increased capacity to 36,000 in 1936. Final double-decking in 1938 increased capacity to 58,000. It was reduced to around 53,000 during subsequent remodelings and to 47,051 for the 1996 season.

Dimensions. The dimensions from left to right field originally were 345–467–370. Always a hitter's park, Tiger Stadium's dimensions remained the same in the 1920s. The dimensions have been adjusted downward over the years, with the most recent configuration from left to right field at 340–365–440– 375–325.

Home Runs. In June 1997 Bobby Bonilla became the 33rd and last player to clear the roof since the second deck was built in 1938. Of the 33, only Harmon Killebrew (1962), Frank Howard (1968), Cecil Fielder (1990) and Mark McGwire (1997) cleared the left-field roof. Tiger Stadium is the first ballpark in which 10,000 home runs have been hit.

Last Game. On September 27, 1999, the Tigers played their last game in the ballpark. Each starter wore the uniform number of a past great at the position (Gabe Kapler wore no number to honor Ty Cobb), and Robert Fick's grand slam in the 8th inning propelled the Tigers to an 8–2 win. Brian Moehler got the win over Jeff Suppan of the Royals. Former Tigers shortstop Billy Rogell threw out the first pitch.

Books. Michael Betzold and Ethan Casey, *Queen of Diamonds* (1992); Richard J. Moss, *Tiger Stadium* (1976); Tom Stanton, *The Final Season: Fathers, Sons, and One Last Season in a Classic American Ballpark* (2002).

Time Zones

See also **Scheduling.**

The Colorado Rockies were the only Major League club in the mountain time zone until the Arizona Diamondbacks joined them

Joe Tinker (1880–1948)

Hall of Fame (VC) 1946

"Though not quite as good as Johnny Evers, Joe Tinker was a quality offensive and defensive player for a sustained period of years.... He was recognized as an outstanding defensive player— Adams' poem was setting down something that was in the air, not creating a myth from whole cloth..."— Bill James in *The Bill James Historical Baseball Abstract* (1988).

See also **Tinker to Evers to Chance**

Tinker played shortstop in the Major Leagues from 1902 through 1916, batting .263.

Joseph Bert Tinker grew up in northeastern Kansas and played at Coffeyville in 1899. He was discovered during a game in which the opposing manager was Bill Hulen, the last left-handed shortstop in the Major Leagues. Tinker moved through the minor leagues and landed with the Cubs in 1902.

He spent 11 years at shortstop for the Cubs, leaving in 1913 for the Reds. During those 12 seasons he made 601 errors and batted over .300 only once (.317 with the Reds). He batted .235 in four World Series for the Cubs.

Tinker moved to the Chicago Whales in the Federal League as player-manager for the 1914–1915 seasons. He returned to the Cubs in 1916, but played in only seven games before moving down to the minor leagues for a brief period and then retiring.

He was among the Major League leaders in fielding categories consistently throughout his career and batted a respectable .263. He was often contentious about his salary and sat out briefly during the 1909 season.

After his playing days he moved on to Columbus in the American Association and Orlando of the Florida State League where he was both the owner and manager. He made a fortune in the Florida land boom of the 1920s but lost it all after a hurricane devastated the coastline.

Tinker suffered from diabetes later in life and lost a leg as a result. He died on his birthday in 1948 at age 68.

Tinker to Evers to Chance (1910)

"These are the saddest of possible words;
'Tinker to Evers to Chance.'
Trio of Bear Cubs and fleeter than birds,
Tinker to Evers to Chance.
Thoughtlessly pricking our gonfalon* bubble,
Making a Giant hit into a double—
Words that are weighty with nothing but trouble:
Tinker to Evers to Chance."
  *pennant (from the medieval Italian for an army's flag)
— Titled "Baseball's Sad Lexicon."

This ode to Cubs shortstop Joe Tinker, second baseman Johnny Evers and first baseman Frank Chance (originally a catcher), was written in 1910 by Franklin P. Adams (1881–1960). As a Cubs fan and sportswriter for the *New York Evening Mail*, Adams supposedly wrote the poem on the way to a game at the Polo Grounds after he was told that his newspaper column for the day was too short. The poem first appeared in print on July 10, 1910, but Adams thought the lines "weren't much good." Adams later appeared as a panelist on the radio show, "Information, Please."

The three infielders first played together on September 16, 1902, and made their first double play two days later in front of 260 fans, with one umpire in a game that took 2 hours and five minutes to play. They had a team-record low of 76 double plays in 1908. Nevertheless, they helped the Cubs win four pennants and two World Series. Chance only played 31 games for the club in 1911 and two in 1912 as player-manager, so the double-play combination was effectively broken up by the end of 1910.

The trio was not a top double play threat or the best infield unit of the era. Only Chance was a top offensive player. Third baseman Harry Steinfeldt was probably the best of the group, but he was overlooked and is the answer to one of the most-asked trivia questions.

Tinker and Evers did not get along and rarely, if ever, spoke off the field. Sources conflict over the basis for the feud and later reconciliation. Some report that the dispute arose over an argument over cab fare, which escalated into a brief fight between them during an exhibition game on September 13, 1905. They fought again the next day.

Another source reported that Tinker later said that they stopped speaking after Evers took his own cab, leaving his teammates stranded after an exhibition game in 1908 or 1909. Evers remembered the feud differently. He claimed that in early 1907 Tinker threw a ball at him as hard as he could from only 10 feet away that broke Evers' finger.

They did not talk for more than two years and declined to shake hands until they appeared together on a radio show in 1938 for the dedication of the Cubs Hall of Fame many years after they retired. Some sources report that, unknown to each other, they were both invited to broadcast the 1938 World Series in Chicago. Evers was in a wheelchair and Tinker had lost a leg. They saw each other and came forward to embrace as both wept.

Evers, known as "The Crab" for his sour disposition, was the difficult one of the three. Tinker recollected: "Evers was a great player, a wonderful pivot man. But boy, how he could ride! Chance used to say he wished Evers was an outfielder so he couldn't hear him."

After Ralph Kiner recited the poem on the air while broadcasting a Mets game, he received a letter from Evers' niece, indicating hat her uncle's name was pronounced "Eevers" (rhymes with Tom Seaver).

See also *Superstition*—Tinker to Evers to Chance.

Book. Gil Bogen, *Tinker, Evers, and Chance: A Triple Biography* (2004).

Tobacco

"Way to 'snuff out' that rally, Sammy."—Orioles teammate to reliever Sammy Stewart after he swallowed his snuff by mistake just before coming into the game and ending a threat.

"Keep away from tobacco ... until you have attained full growth."—One of Babe Ruth's "Ten Commandments for Boys," in Dan Daniel's *Babe Ruth—Idol of the American Boy* (1930).

"Steroids are no worse than cigarettes."—Noted "scientist" Gene Orza, a Players Association executive. To which Richard Corliss in *Time* responded: "To which some major leaguers must have thought, Show me a cigarette that can help me hit 73 homers a season, and I'll buy a carton."

See also *Chew*.

Early Use.

"You'll find cigarette stubs ... on the path to baseball oblivion."—Giants manager John McGraw.

Chewing tobacco has been part of baseball since at least the 1840s. By 1909 Bull Durham tobacco advertisements adorned over 150 Major and minor league ballpark fences.

Cigars were the choice of ballplayers until the 1920s because for many years cigarettes were considered effeminate and linked to slumps and bad eyesight. A 1920 Liggett & Myers Tobacco Company advertisement billed its product as the "home run" cigarette because of its "cool taste." Around this time, smokeless tobacco replaced chewing tobacco because spitting became less socially acceptable, having been linked to tuberculosis and other diseases.

According to Robert Smith in *Baseball* (1970), Tris Speaker would have been in the Major Leagues sooner except that Pittsburgh owner Barney Dreyfuss refused to purchase him when he learned that Speaker smoked the unmanly cigarettes. Smith's comments on cigarettes: "[A ballplayer] was meant to smoke, of course, unless he felt the call of the church, but if he lent himself to the consumption of little white paper rolls of tobacco, he might as well have worn soft collars for all the standing he would have had among his fellows."

Most Prolific Chewers/Smokers.

"Generally regarded as the champion tobacco-chewer in baseball (i.e., the world), [Pirate scout Howie] Haak has averaged between one and two packs of Red Man a day since 1928. He even has a spittoon in his Cadillac, hooked up with a brass ring so it won't tip over when he puts on the brakes."—Kevin Kerrane in *Dollar Sign on the Muscle* (1984).

"I couldn't. I carry my cigars in my back pocket and I was afraid I'd break them."—Long-time White Sox manager and former player Jimmy Dykes on why he did not slide. He smoked between 20 and 40 cigars a day.

"A stumpy pixie full of gags and good humor. He loved cigars and people—not necessarily in that order."—Ernie Harwell on Dykes in *Diamond Gems* (1991).

Astros owner Roy Hofheinz smoked 25 cigars a day.

In 1998 Dr. John C. Greene, an oral cancer specialist, estimated that as many as 300 of the 750 players in the Major Leagues chewed tobacco. Studies show that using spit tobacco for 30 minutes provides the same amount of nicotine as four cigarettes.

Ban. A 1987 survey of professional ballplayers revealed that more than 50% used some form of smokeless tobacco. That figure dropped steadily as the decade progressed. In the early 1990s, colleges and four professional leagues banned smokeless tobacco by players, coaches, managers, umpires and team personnel. The four leagues were the Appalachian, Gulf Coast, Northwest and Pioneer.

As of June 15, 1993, minor league players were banned from smoking and chewing tobacco at minor league ballparks. Players were to be fined $300 for violating the rule. Minor league officials could implement the ban unilaterally, but at the Major League level a ban would be the subject of the collective bargaining agreement between the players and owners. No action was taken.

Knoxville Smokies pitcher Travis Baptist became the first player ejected and fined when he was caught with snuff on June 26, 1993. The Phoenix Firebirds protested the ban for a week by not speaking to the media, refusing to sign autographs or making public appearances.

In 1988 the American Dental Association determined that chewing tobacco does not improve play. Researchers studied 158 players on seven Major League clubs in 1988. The chewers batted .238, compared to .248 for the non-chewers. The non-chewers also had a higher fielding average, .978 to .968.

Charity. During World War II, fans brought cigarettes to Reds games for distribution to servicemen overseas.

Cigar Factory Owner.

"A good cigar is like a beautiful chick with a great body who also knows the American League box scores."—Corporal Max Klinger in an episode of "M*A*S*H*."

"He [Pedro Bello] called and said he wanted to do this because of what El Duque represents, which is a Cuban who risked his life for freedom."—Rene Guim, a spokesman for the agent Joe Cubas, who represents pitcher Orlando Hernandez. Bello, the owner of Havana Sunrise, a Miami-area cigar manufacturer, decided to donate to a charity of Hernandez's choice, a box of his most expensive cigars, which sell for $500, for each San Diego batter Hernandez struck out in Game 2 of the World Series. On October 18th, 1998, Hernandez struck out 7 batters.

Babe Ruth owned a cigar factory in Boston, turning out five-cent cigars in 1919. Ruth's movie debut in 1927's *Babe Comes Home* is about his quitting tobacco chewing at the request of his girlfriend. He falls into a terrible slump, but she gives him a big plug of tobacco in the 9th inning of the big game, which allows him to hit the game-winning home run. They live happily ever after.

Smooth Chew. Outfielder Enos Slaughter chewed tobacco and gum together to keep the chaw smooth.

Fire. Halsey Hall broadcast for the Twins from 1961 through 1967. During a broadcast his coat caught fire from his cigar ashes. He did not miss a play while he put out the fire. Fans responded by sending him asbestos jackets.

Tobacco Stains.

"I thought I was going to get foot cancer." — Pirates outfielder Andy Van Slyke after sharing center field with Lenny Dykstra of the Phillies, a notorious tobacco chewer and spitter.

In 1988 the Astros bought a $23,000 machine guaranteed to remove tobacco juice stains from artificial turf.

No Smoking. In 1991 the A's became the first ballclub to ban smoking in ballpark seats. In 1993 the Dodgers and Orioles joined the Tigers, Padres and A's in banning smoking in an open-air ballpark. Smoking is banned in each of the indoor ballparks.

When the city of Cincinnati banned smoking in public places in the 1990s, Reds owner Marge Schott lit up defiantly through four games at Riverfront Stadium at the start of the season. She began complying with the ban after city officials warned her to stop. In reporting the incident, *Time* magazine called the ballpark River-*boat* Stadium.

Dugout Smoking. Smoking by players is allowed in the tunnels, but not in the dugout.

Advertising. George Case was the acknowledged fastest runner and top base stealer of the 1940s. Camel cigarettes did an advertising campaign showing him sliding into a bag. Indignant parents and fans wrote letters to American League president Will Harridge demanding that the campaign be stopped because it encouraged children to smoke. Harridge met with Case, and they agreed that Case (and all other ballplayers) would not do any cigarette advertising while in uniform. Case did new ads in street clothes, and he is probably the last ballplayer to wear an official Major League uniform while advertising cigarettes.

Before the 1993 season the Astros banned tobacco ads in the Astrodome. Because the club was unable to find a new advertiser for its huge center field billboard, the club put a giant black plastic bag over the Marlboro sign.

The Mariners banned tobacco ads for the 1994 season, and the Red Sox ended such ads in Fenway Park in 1995.

In the 1990s Philip Morris paid the Mets about $250,000 per season to place a large Marlboro sign in the ballpark.

Combatting Tobacco.

"Cancer is not a tradition." — Joe Garagiola during his 1995 campaign to encourage players not to use tobacco products.

"It cost him his cheekbone, his appearance, his teeth, his taste-buds, his appetite and part of his hearing, but not his dignity nor his desire to help others." — *Baseball Weekly* in April 1996 when Joe Garagiola, chairman of the National Spit Tobacco Education Program, accompanied 66-year-old former Major Leaguer Bill Tuttle to spring training sites to encourage players to stop using tobacco products. Tuttle had lost most of one side of his face to cancer caused by four decades of chewing tobacco.

Nolan Ryan, whose father was a heavy smoker and died of lung cancer, headed a group called Athletes Through with Chew in an attempt to deter young players from following the chewing tradition.

Umpire Doug Harvey worked 31 years while chewing tobacco. After 60 radiation treatments and feeding himself through a straw-sized hole in his breast bone, he began speaking engagements to high school kids.

Stunt. Joe Charboneau once ate six cigarettes to win a $5 bet.

Ashtray. White Sox owner Bill Veeck had an ashtray carved into his wooden leg.

Trying To Quit. In April 1997 Angels reliever Troy Percival was averaging 94 mph on his pitches, much lower than his usual high 90s. He scoffed at the notion that cutting out chewing tobacco and coffee had affected his velocity. He was right, as later he underwent shoulder surgery.

Toledo Blue Stockings

American Association 1884

The Blue Stockings had a record of 46–58 and finished seventh. The club featured pitcher Tony Mullane, who won 37 games.

Toledo Maumees

American Association 1890

The Maumees had a 68–64 record under manager Charlie Morton, good for fourth place in the league. Key players were White Wings Tebeau and Frank Scheibeck. It appears that the term "Maumee" derives from "Maumet," meaning an idol.

Tombstones See *Burial and Cemeteries*

Toronto

"Toronto is not only the provincial capital of Ontario, but the seat of provincial baseball loyalties which range across the continent. There is a large brotherhood of Yankee fans here. There are Dodger fans, Red Sox fans, virtually every kind of fan, including probably at least one Cleveland fan. Toronto, you see, has been a good baseball town for almost as long as Detroit and New York. The old Maple Leafs of the International League had a long and glorious history…" — Art Hill in *I Don't Care If I Never Come Back* (1980).

Attempts at Major League Status. There was a rumor that the Senators would move to Toronto in 1915. Yankee executive Ed Barrow proposed Toronto as a Major League franchise as early as the 1920s, when the Maple Leafs minor league club was a strong force in the International League. Future Los Angeles Lakers and Washington Redskins owner Jack Kent Cooke ran the minor league franchise for a time. Cooke tried to buy the Detroit Tigers in the mid–1950s and move them to Canada, but he lost out to a lower bidder. Toronto had no professional baseball between the departure of the Class AAA Maple Leafs in 1967 and the arrival of the American League Blue Jays in 1977.

In 1976 Toronto almost obtained the San Francisco Giants franchise, but the conditional deal with Giants owner Horace Stoneham was canceled when Bob Lurie and Bud Herseth bought the team and kept it in the Bay Area.

Toronto Blue Jays

American League 1977–

"It had been only a tiny past. The blink of an eye in cosmic terms. But for the Toronto Blue Jays it hung heavy on their souls, a great weight of opportunities squandered and roads not taken, of dead ends and detours and the cul-de-sac where also-rans resided. The Blue Jays pined to move up in the world, way up, all the way to the high-rent district of the World Series." — Rosie DiManno in *Glory Days: Canada's World Series Champions* (1993).

Origins. After attempting to move the San Francisco Giants to *Toronto* in 1976, the club was created that year for the 1977 season and paid a franchise fee of $7 million. It was the second Major League club to be placed in Canada (see also *Expansion* and *Expansion Drafts*).

A 30-year-old North York alderman named Paul Godfrey, a chemical engineer by training, who later was CEO of a prominent Toronto newspaper, became the driving force for bringing a team to Toronto. His group beat out several other groups for purchase of the San Francisco Giants, but at the last minute the San Francisco mayor arranged for local interests to purchase the team. After lobbying hard with National League owners to take over the Giants, Godfrey and his group had to change focus on the American League. The work paid off, as the American League voted to expand, adding two teams in 1977, one in Seattle and the other in Toronto.

First Game. On April 7, 1969, the Blue Jays defeated the White Sox 9–5 on a field covered with snow for most of the game and a wind chill temperature of –10 degrees at the start. Al Woods of the Blue Jays became the 11th pinch hitter to hit a home run in his first at-bat.

Key Owners.

LaBatt's Brewery, et al./1977–2000. The John LaBatt's Brewery, which also held dairy and entertainment interests and two other institutional investors, bought the new franchise in 1976. LaBatt's controlled 45% of the stock, Imperial Trust, Ltd., controlled another 45%, and the Canadian Imperial Bank of Commerce controlled the remaining 10%. The Imperial Trust is the outgrowth of the fortune of R. Howard Webster. Labatt's also owned the Toronto Argonauts of the Canadian Football League. Paul Godfrey was installed as the president of the club, and he remained in that role into the 2000s. Peter Bavasi was appointed as the first general manager.

In 1991 the Trust sold its interest to LaBatt's and until mid–1995 LaBatt's continued to hold 90% of the club. In June 1995 the brewery was bought by a Belgian brewer, Interbrew, for $2.9 billion. The purchase brought a comment from new owner Gerald Fauchey of Interbrew: "Baseball is a very obscure sport in our country."

Interbrew was looking for a buyer for the club in 1996. One possible choice was Zoetrope Studios, once owned by director Francis Ford Coppola.

Sam Pollock was the senior chairman of the Blue Jays between 1995 and 2000. He had been the vice-president and general manager of the Montreal Canadiens hockey team from 1964–1978, winning the Stanley Cup nine times under his leadership, and he was later elected to the NHL's Hall of Fame.

Rogers Communications/2000– . Canadian ownership of the club returned in September 2000, when one of the world's largest cable television companies bought 80% of the Blue Jays. The Labatt's/Interbrew interest remained at a lower 20% and the Canadian Imperial Bank of Commerce gave up its 10% stake. In January 2004 Rogers bought out Labatt's and then held 100% of the ownership interest. The club has not made money during a slump on the field and in the Toronto economy, and the cable company has also been posting huge losses in its core business.

Nickname. The "Blue Jays" name was chosen in a fan poll and it is often shortened to "Jays." The board of directors selected the name from over 4,000 names and 30,000 entries in a "Name the Team" contest. It has been reported that the name was chosen because LaBatt's had a beer brand called "Blue," and the owners hoped that sportswriters would shorten the name to "Blues," instead of "Jays."

Key Seasons.

1977. The Blue Jays were 54–107 in their inaugural season behind Ron Fairly's 19 home runs and 64 RBIs.

1983. The club broke through with its first winning season at 89–73, only nine games off the pace.

After a second-place finish in 1984 the Blue Jays won the Eastern Division by two games over the Yankees. Doyle Alexander won 17 games and George Bell hit 28 home runs with 95 RBIs. The Blue Jays lost the pennant to the Royals in seven games after leading 3–1 in the series.

1987. The Blue Jays fell apart in the last week of the season and lost the Eastern Division title to the Tigers by two games. George Bell had a career year with 47 home runs and 134 RBIs. Tom Henke led the league in saves with 34.

1988. In a tight race the Blue Jays fell only two games short of the Red Sox and tied for third.

1989. The Blue Jays won the division by two games over the Orioles as Fred McGriff led the league with 36 home runs. The club lost the League Championship Series in five games to the A's.

1990. In another tight race, the Blue Jays again fell only two games short of the division title, this time to the Red Sox.

1991. The Blue Jays won the division title with 91 wins as Joe Carter hit 33 home runs. Once again the Blue Jays fell short in the League Championship Series, this time in five games to the Twins.

1992. The club won the division with 96 victories as Jack Morris led the league with 21 wins and Joe Carter hit 34 home runs. After beating the A's in six games for the pennant, the Blue Jays beat the Braves in six games for their first World Series victory. See also Rosie DiManno, *Glory Days: Canada's World Series Champions* (1993).

1993. The Blue Jays won the pennant for the second year in a row, this time beating the White Sox. They went on to defeat the Phillies in the World Series on a dramatic Game 6 home run in the bottom of the 9th inning by Joe Carter. The Blue Jays were the first repeat champions since the 1977–1978 Yankees.

Key Players.

George Bell played the first nine seasons of his career with the Blue Jays. He hit more than 20 home runs six times, including 47 in 1987. He drove in more than 100 runs three times and batted over .300 twice.

Dave Stieb has the most wins by a Blue Jays pitcher. In a career that began in 1979, he won 14 or more games seven times, including 18 in 1990. He also pitched a no-hitter and 30 shutouts.

Jesse Barfield played eight full seasons for the Blue Jays, hitting over 175 home runs. He hit a league-leading 40 home runs in 1986.

Tom Henke was one of the premier relievers in the American League until injuries slowed him. Between 1986 and 1992 he saved at least 20 games each season, including a league-high 34 in 1987.

Tony Fernandez played eight straight seasons for the Blue Jays at the start of his career in 1983, and then played parts of four others with the club. He starred at shortstop for the club and regularly drove in 50–70 runs.

Carlos Delgado signed out of Puerto Rico in 1988 and made it to the Major Leagues in 1993, when he played briefly that year and in 1994–1995. He became a star in 1996 and hit over 40 home runs three times through 2003. He was the American League's second highest-paid player in 2001 and 2002, and third in 2003.

Roy Halladay put together two stellar seasons in 2002 and 2003, with records of 19–7 and 22–7, but injuries plagued him before and after those two meteoric years.

Key Managers.

Jimy Williams lasted four seasons with the club from 1986 through part of 1989. He led the club to its 1987 collapse in which the Blue Jays finished second after leading going into the final week.

Cito Gaston is the only manager to achieve significant success with the club. He took over early in the 1989 season when the Blue Jays were in sixth and led them to a division title. After a second-place finish in 1990 he led the club to four consecutive division titles. The club finally made it to the World Series in 1992 and beat the Braves. Gaston led them to a repeat in 1993 over the Phillies, but the club slipped in 1994 before the player strike ended the season. He was fired in September 1997 when the club was in last place. He finished his career with the club with a record of 683–636 and a winning percentage of .518.

Ballparks.

"A season in the sun and the wind and the rain. But mostly in the hermetically sealed comfort of the SkyDome in Toronto, the most vainglorious playpen ever built by man, with the synthetic carpet underfoot and the steel-strutted carapace overhead. A roof shunted open like the aperture of a camera, letting in light and air, but only at the whim of timid custodians, a kind of wussy weather synod that convened prior to every home game. It was a futuristic RoboDome for a team that was trying to bury its past."— Rosie DiManno, in *Glory Jays* (1993), on the SkyDome.

Exhibition Field. The first ballpark used by a Major League club in Toronto was the old Canadian National Exhibition Grandstand. It was built in 1959 for football and was known as Exhibition Field. After receiving a minor facelift for the 1977 Major League season, its seating capacity for baseball was 38,500 (increased to 43,700 for 1978). Its dimensions from left to right field were 330–375–400– 375–330.

Skydome. The Toronto SkyDome was built for $583 million (including a $100 million roof), which included a hotel/restaurant complex (see also *Sex*). The club's first game in the SkyDome was on June 5, 1989, when the Blue Jays lost to the Brewers 5–3. The club leased its skyboxes for $35 million in 1991, and there have been a few problems with the roof (see also *Indoor Ballparks*). The Skydome seats over 50,000, and its original dimensions from left to right field were 328–375–400–375–328.

Key Broadcasters. Tom Cheek was the club's primary broadcaster from its inception through mid–2004. He broadcast 4,347 consecutive games from 1977 through June 2, 2004, when he missed a game due to the death of his father. While he was out, Cheek was diagnosed with a brain tumor and had to have it removed, further delaying his return to the booth.

Don Chevrier broadcast for the club from 1977 through 1996, and then again in 2001. Jerry Howarth has done radio broadcasts for the club since 1981. Chevrier did play-by-play for the Athens Olympics, covering badminton and synchronized swimming, prompting this from Bob Costas: "My hat's off to Don Chevrier. I've got a feeling that badminton and synchronized swimming are not covered at sportscasters' camp."

Major League players who have broadcast for the club include Early Wynn (1977–1981), Tony Kubek (1977–1989), Buck Martinez (1987–2000), Tommy Hutton (1990–1996), Gary Matthews (2000–2001) and Joe Carter (1999–2000).

Books. Rob Bradford, *Chasing Steinbrenner: Pursuing the Pennant in Boston and Toronto* (2004); Michael Goodman, *The History of the Toronto Blue Jays* (2002); Peter Bjarkman, *The Toronto Blue Jays* (1990); Stephen Knight, *Diamond Dreams: 20 Years of Blue Jays Baseball* (1996).

Total Baseball

"To me that's the equivalent of saying that if we disinterred Napoleon and found that contrary to all written reports he was not 5'2" but 6'2" we should keep this a secret."— *Total Baseball* editor John Thorn responding to criticism that his book had changed certain time-honored statistics in favor of historical accuracy.

This baseball tome was first published by Viking Press in 1989. The fourth edition came out in 1995 and for the first time received the official endorsement of Major League Baseball. Previously, Major League Baseball had endorsed Macmillan's *The Baseball Encyclopedia*, which eventually ceased publication (and then returned several years later). *Total Baseball* took a revisionist approach to many statistics, revising Ty Cobb's hit totals and reducing Cap Anson's total from 3,000 to 2,995. The 8th edition was published in 2004, with Barry Bonds on the cover gesturing to God after hitting his final home run of the 2001 season.

Lost Bet. In 2004 physicist Stephen Hawking, stricken for many years with Lou Gehrig's Disease, lost a bet to particle physicist John Preskill. In 1997 Hawking bet an encyclopedia "from which information could be recovered at will" that "information swallowed by a black hole is forever hidden from the outside universe." Hawking admitted that his theory was wrong and bought Preskill a copy of *Total Baseball*.

Total Bases

Origins. Total bases was introduced as a statistic in 1883. Total bases is the sum of all hits (one for a single, two for a double, etc.) and base on balls.

Most/Game. On May 23, 2002, Dodger outfielder Shawn Green hit four **Home Runs**, a double and a single for 19 total bases to set a new Major League record. Green had a home run and two singles in his next game to reach a record-tying 25 total bases in two games.

Before Green's big day, Joe Adcock of the Milwaukee Braves had held the Major League record with 18 total bases in one game. He hit four **Home Runs** and a double for the Braves on July 31, 1954.

Six players have reached 17 total bases and several players have matched the American League record of 16 total bases in a game, including Lou Gehrig, Rocky Colavito and Fred Lynn. Gehrig and Colavito did it while hitting four **Home Runs** in a game. Ty Cobb went 6-for-6 with three home runs, a double and two singles for the Tigers against the Browns on May 5, 1925.

Team Total. On June 8, 1950, the Red Sox defeated the Browns 29–4. The Red Sox had 28 hits and 60 total bases. The National League record is 55 by the Reds.

Most/Game/Two Teams. On May 19, 1999, the Rockies and Reds had 81 total bases in a 24–12 Reds victory at Coors Field. The runs were the third-highest total in the 20th century and several other National League or team records were set or tied.

Season Total. Babe Ruth had 457 total bases in 1921, the best all-time. The National League record is held by Rogers Hornsby, who had 450 total bases in 1922. The only player between 1948 and 2000 to reach 400 total bases was Jim Rice, who had 406 in 1978.

In 2001 Sammy Sosa had 425 total bases, the seventh best all-time. Todd Helton had back-to-back seasons of at least 400 total bases, ending with 405 in 2001.

Career Total. Henry Aaron had a Major League record 6,856 total bases during his career.

Lead-Off Hitter. Davey Lopes of the Dodgers had three home runs, a double and a single for 15 total bases leading off for the club on August 20, 1974.

Town Ball

"In any review of baseball history, one comes inevitably upon versions of the game known as 'town ball' and 'old-cat'…. The evidence shows that 'town ball' was merely another name, a New England name, for rounders (baseball) and hence new — and American — in name only." — Douglas Wallop in *Baseball — An Informal History* (1969).

Town Ball was an early version of baseball played originally in the 1830s primarily in Boston and then Philadelphia. This evolved into the **Massachusetts Game** that differed somewhat from the more prevalent and ultimately dominant **New York Game** of baseball.

A key feature of Townball was that fielders could "soak" runners by throwing the ball at them on the basepaths to record an out. Each team used 11 to 16 players.

Trades and Player Sales

"Being traded is like celebrating your hundredth birthday. It might not be the happiest occasion in the world, but consider the alternatives."— Joe Garagiola.

"He's in the twilight of his career."— Red Sox general manager Dan Duquette after Roger Clemens left the Red Sox as a free agent after the 1996 season; this was before Clemens won two more Cy Young Awards.

"The Giants are looking for a trade but I don't think Atlanta wants to *depart* with a quality player."— Ron Fairly.

"I've got a special feeling for Sidney, and I will in 20 years — unless he blows up my house or something."— Orioles manager Mike Hargrove after pitcher Sidney Ponson was traded to the Giants in mid–2003.

"Trade talk is just about the cheapest thing in baseball. There will always be outlandish trade rumors. Some are planted by clubs themselves to shake up certain personnel. Some people in baseball like to keep everyone loose. Some trade rumors are started by writers because they need a story. Many trade rumors are legitimate, even though they may later be denied by officials simply because the club was not successful in making the deal."— Shelby Whitfield in *Kiss It Goodbye* (1973).

"I got a sore throat and a cough just from spending two weeks on the phone talking to those clowns [other general managers]. I think when it comes to trading, the American League is 98 percent air and about two percent balloon."— Yankee general manager Syd Thrift in 1989.

"Well, Al old pal I suppose you seen in the paper where I been sold to the White Sox. Believe me Al it comes as a supprise [sic] to me and I bet it did to all you good old pals down home. You could of knocked me over with a feather when the old man come up to me and says Jack I've sold you to the Chicago Americans."— Lefty Jack Keefe in the opening lines of Ring Lardner's "A Busher's Letters Home" (the "You Known Me, Al" series) as they appeared in the *Saturday Evening Post* starting in 1914.

"The economics in baseball stink. The economics stink, and if this isn't a clear enough signal to the doubters and naysayers, to be forced to trade an 18–game winner to your arch enemy ... the economics stink."— Braves general manager John Schuerholz in December 2002.

"When Allen was traded to Cleveland the press-box criticism roasted McCarthy's ears to a crusty brown veneer."— Joe Williams on Joe McCarthy's trade of pitcher Johnny Allen from the Yankees to the Indians in the 1930s.

"Tony Taylor was one of the first acquisitions that the Phillies made when they reconstructed their team. They got him from Philadelphia."— Jerry Coleman.

"Whenever the Giants call to talk about trades, I bet more than one general manager has had to hold a pillow over his face to keep from laughing into the phone."— Lowell Cohn.

"Vince Coleman for Kevin McReynolds raises the question: 'Is there *deja vu* in hell?'"— Sportswriter Ray Ratto of the *San Francisco Examiner* on the two difficult players.

"Here's to all the buccos,
May we never, ever disagree.
But in case we do,
The hell with all of you,
And here's to me!"

— Dave Parker, anticipating a trade from the Pirates, toasting his teammates in the locker room.

Intraleague Trading Deadline. The in-season intraleague trading deadline was established as June 15 in the 1920s by Judge Landis. The deadline was extended in 1986 to August 31. Landis supposedly instituted the deadline for clubs in the same league after the Yankees traded for Joe Dugan of the Red Sox in July 1922. The Cardinals protested a similar trade by the Giants and Braves (both teams were attempting to beef up their ranks for the World Series).

In 1939 Senators owner Clark Griffith offered a rule change that was approved by the American League: The previous year's pennant winner was not allowed to make any intraleague trades the following year. The move was aimed at the Yankees, who had just won their fourth straight pennant. The Yankees did not win the pennant in 1940, and the rule was repealed after one year.

Interleague Trading Deadline.

"They Need Bat Man, Get Robin"— Headline in the *Los Angeles Times* after the anemic-hitting Dodgers acquired Robin Ventura on the last day of interleague trading in 2003.

An off-season interleague trading window did not exist until a three-week period was created on November 21, 1959. Before that date, the leagues had a waiver rule allowing all teams in the league to pass on a player before he could be traded out to the other Major League. Now, waivers are not required during the trading windows.

Soon after the three-week window was created, the interleague trading period was expanded to include from five days after the World Series to the end of the winter baseball meetings (usually in December). In 1977 a spring interleague trading period was added from February 15 to March 15. Later, an in-season trading deadline of July 31 was established. Trades could be made after that date through August 31, but during August the players must clear waivers out of the league before the deal can be consummated.

10-Day Return Rule. If a team discovers that a player is injured, it may return the player to the other club within 10 days from the date the trade was made.

In July 2003 the Pirates traded for reliever Brandon Lyon of the Red Sox, after being assured that Lyon's elbow was okay. After Lyon sat out a couple of games, the Pirates learned that he had a frayed ligament in his elbow, thereby entitling them to void the trade and pick another player from the Red Sox.

Veto Power. In 1973 a new rule was added to the collective bargaining agreement. It allowed a 10-year player who had five years with the same team to veto a trade. Ron Santo was the first player to exercise this right when he refused a trade to the Angels on December 4, 1973. He later approved a trade to the White Sox.

19th Century "Big" Trades/Sales.

"Boston is in mourning. Like Rachel weeping for her children, she refuses to be comforted because the famous baseball nine, the perennial champion, the city's most cherished possession, has been captured by Chicago."— *Worcester Spy* newspaper on July 24, 1875, reporting on the move to the Chicago White Stockings by Albert Spalding and three other key Red Stocking players.

In the very earliest days of professional baseball, before professional leagues were formed, player sales were uncommon and the few sales often were done in secret. In addition, because the reserve clause was not created until 1879, players could sell their services to the highest bidder. By 1885, however, all pretenses were dropped and sales from one club to another were common.

In February 1887 Mike "King" Kelly was sold by the Chicago White Stockings to the Boston Red Stockings for $10,000. The price was so incredible that the Red Stockings publicized the contract to prove the price. White Stockings owner Al Spalding was said to have unloaded Kelly because he was unhappy that his club had not won a winner-take-all championship series with the American Association Browns in 1886. Chicago had won five of the seven previous championship series and then did not win another for 20 years. Late in 1887 Spalding sold pitcher John Clarkson to the Boston Red Stockings for $10,000. Clarkson peaked two years later with 49 wins.

Yankees/Red Sox Trades. Probably the most famous sales and trades were those in which the Yankees received players from the Red Sox in the late 1910s and early 1920s, including one involving Babe Ruth. In 1919 Red Sox owner Harry Frazee received $525,000 for Ruth, which included a $400,000 loan ($350,000 in some sources) by the Yankees, secured in part by Boston's Fenway Park. The loan secured by the ballpark was not revealed until many years later.

In 1923 seven of the top 13 Yankees were ex–Red Sox players while the Red Sox received only one regular player, Norm McMillan. Frazee sold 15 players to the Yankees in five years, contributing to eight out of nine last-place finishes for the Red Sox starting in 1922.

Yankees/Red Sox Rivalry Continues.

"And after a century of watching the Yankees club America's small-market teams like baby seals and tigers and red sox, you have to suffer during the off-season too. In the biggest moral affront yet to your sense of fairness, last week the Yankees — already the richest, best team in baseball — traded for Alex Rodriguez (a-Rod) — the richest, best player in baseball." — Joel Stein in *Time*.

"A-Rod a sure thing? Remember the Alomar." — Headline in the *New York Post*, reminding fans of the busted trade the Mets made for perennial All-Star Roberto Alomar, whose performance sank to new lows. In 2004 Alomar signed for $1 million with the Diamondbacks after earning $8 million in 2003 (when he played for the White Sox after the Mets unloaded him).

In late 2003 a blockbuster deal was attempted with Alex Rodriguez going to the Red Sox. The complicated restructuring of his enormous contract ended the trade talks, however, as the Players Association vetoed changes to his contract. The proposed changes were for a reduction of $28-$30 million of the $252 million deal. Manny Ramirez, the only other $20 million player, would have gone to Texas. The union would only approve a change of $12 million.

Less than a month after the negotiations collapsed, in February 2004 the Yankees announced that *they* were picking up Rodriguez, in exchange for second baseman Alfonso Soriano and a minor leaguer. The trade never would have happened but for Yankee third baseman Aaron Boone's season-ending injury on January 16, 2004, when he tore up his knee playing basketball (he was only owed $5 million in termination pay for violating the no-basketball clause in his contract). The Yankees did the deal in 72 hours, considerably less time it took the Red Sox to blow a deal for Rodriguez and alienate incumbent shortstop Nomar Garciaparra.

The Rangers agreed to absorb an astounding $67 million of the remaining $179 million (over seven years) on Rodriguez's contract, making Rodriguez a relative bargain for the Yankees at $16 million per season. The Rangers saved about $120 million (with interest), freeing up money to invest in pitchers. The Players Association

quickly approved the deal and Rodriguez agreed to move to third base alongside regular Yankee shortstop Derek Jeter. Also in the powerhouse line-up were Jason Giambi (with a surgically repaired knee) and Gary Sheffield, who had signed as a free agent.

If Rodriguez had come to the Red Sox, there was talk of Nomar Garciaparra going to the Angels in exchange for Troy Glaus, who was scheduled to earn $9.55 million in 2004. Garciaparra was to be paid $11.5 million in 2004. He was traded to the Cubs in July 2004.

Connie Mack's Fire Sales. The 1914 Federal League challenge put a financial strain on many clubs. A's owner Connie Mack unloaded his stars after the 1914 season to raise cash. He received $50,000 from the White Sox for Eddie Collins and later sold off the other members of his famous "$100,000 Infield."

Mack staged another fire sale in December 1933 as a result of the Depression. He received $900,000 for his star players, including Jimmie Foxx.

One source contended that Mack sold ace pitcher Rube Waddell after the 1907 season because Waddell had blown a lead in a crucial game with the Tigers, the eventual pennant winners.

Lost Bet. John I. Taylor was the owner of the poorly run Red Sox in late 1908. In the off-season he purportedly lost a drinking match with Cleveland owner Charles Somers, who persuaded Taylor to part with the extraordinarily popular Cy Young (though aging at 41) for only $12,500 and two ineffective pitchers. Young had one more good season in him, going 19–15 for the Indians before fading to 7–10 and 7–9.

Ty Cobb/Tris Speaker. In 1914 it was widely rumored that Cobb was to be traded for Tris Speaker of the Red Sox. The trade was arranged because of Cobb's constant attempts to be paid more than Speaker by the parsimonious Tigers. When the Federal League challenge caused a dramatic rise in salaries, Cobb held out and threatened to jump to the new league. The Tigers relented and made him the highest-paid player in the game (see *Salaries*). In 1916 the Indians paid $50,000 to the Red Sox for Speaker.

Feud. By 1918 the deteriorating relationship between American League powers Charles Comiskey and president Ban Johnson broke down completely over a dispute involving pitcher Jack Quinn. Quinn pitched in the Pacific Coast League in 1918 until that league shut down temporarily late in the year due to World War I. Comiskey's White Sox signed him on the assumption that the disbanded Pacific Coast League club had no further contractual rights over him. He had a 5–1 record for the White Sox over the remainder of the 1918 season. After the season the Yankees formally bought Quinn from the PCL club, and the National Commission had to decide whether the White Sox or Yankees were entitled to him. The Yankees prevailed and from that point forward Comiskey opposed Johnson openly.

See also *Carl Mays Incident*.

Cardinals. When Branch Rickey paid $10,000 for knuckleball specialist Jesse Haines in 1919, it was the last player purchase by the Cardinals for over 25 years (as a result of their *Farm System*).

Minor League Sales. Before International League Baltimore Orioles owner Jack Dunn sold Babe Ruth and Ernie Shore to the Red Sox, he tried to sell them to Connie Mack and the A's. Dunn received $100,000 for Ruth. A few years later, Mack paid Dunn $100,600 for pitcher Lefty Grove (Lefty *Gomez* in one source).

In late 1922 the Giants paid $75,000 for Jimmy O'Connell, at the time a National League record for a minor league player. He hit a respectable .250 in 1923 and .317 in 1924 before he was *Barred from Baseball* for life because of a bribery comment to another player.

In 1923 the White Sox paid $100,000 for Willie Kamm, at the time the highest price ever paid for a minor leaguer. He became an immediate starter at third base for 12 seasons with the White Sox and Indians.

In 1927 the Pirates sold minor leaguer Bill Cissell for $123,000. He hit .267 as an infielder primarily for the White Sox.

Big 1920s Trades. The December 1926 trade between the Cardinals and Giants was considered the biggest of the decade because of the stature of future Hall of Famers Frankie Frisch and Rogers Hornsby. The Cardinals traded Jimmy Ring along with Frisch. Sportswriters considered there to be $500,000 in talent in what was described as "the biggest trade in modern baseball history." The disagreeable Hornsby moved frequently; in late 1928 the Braves sold him to the Cubs for $200,000 and five players.

Tom Yawkey/Big Spender. Millionaire Tom Yawkey bought the Red Sox in 1932. In 1934 he paid $250,000 for Joe Cronin, who was sold by his uncle-in-law, Senators owner Clark Griffith. Another source put the figure at $150,000 and still another source reported it as $225,000. So long as the number was in the $200,000 range, it was the highest amount paid for a player up to that time. Yawkey also spent lavishly on other players in the 1930s, including slugger Jimmie Foxx. By 1936 during the Depression he had spent $3.5 million to improve the club:

$1 million to buy the club
$1.5 million to rebuild Fenway Park
$125,000 to the A's for Lefty Grove
$250,000 to the Senators for Joe Cronin
$35,000 to the Yankees for Lyn Lary
$25,000 to Baltimore of the International League for Moose Solters
$60,000 to the Yankees for Bill Werber and George Pipgras
$55,000 to the Browns for Rick Ferrell and Lloyd Brown
$25,000 to the Browns for Carl Reynolds
$25,000 to the Indians for Wes Ferrell
$350,000 to the A's for Jimmie Foxx and three others
$100,000 for miscellaneous other players

The effort was futile, as the Red Sox won American League pennants under Yawkey only in 1947, 1967 and 1975, never winning a World Series in those years.

In the 1950s Yawkey unsuccessfully offered $1 million for pitcher Herb Score.

Dizzy Dean. Dean developed a sore arm from altering his pitching motion due to a broken toe suffered in the 1937 All-Star Game. In 1938 he was traded to the Cubs for $185,000 and three players. He won seven of eight decisions with 75 innings pitched, helping to lead the Cubs into the World Series (though he lost his only decision in the series).

World War II. The war inhibited trading because clubs were never sure of the status of players who might be subject to the military draft.

Willie Mays Goes Home. Long-time New York matriarch Joan Payson, who owned a small part of the Giants and later all of the Mets, tried to bring Willie Mays home to New York with a $1 million offer to the Giants in the mid–1960s. Though Mays was never thoroughly embraced by San Francisco fans (instead, they loved home-grown Orlando Cepeda and Willie McCovey), the Giants knew that it would be a public relations disaster to sell Mays while he was still productive.

Payson finally succeeded in obtaining Mays in the twilight of his career in 1972 with a $50,000 payment and a player. In his first series with the Mets they played the Giants in Shea Stadium. Mays did not play in the first two games of the series, but he led off the game on Mother's Day. He walked his first time up, struck out in the 3rd inning, and then broke a 4–4 tie with his 647th home run off Don Carrithers.

Recent Big Trades.
"I was tired of reading about who the next 10 millionaire would be. So we thought we'd give everybody a good old baseball trade."— Padres general manager Joe McIlvaine on his club's trade with the Blue Jays before the 1991 season. Free agency stifled trading because of the complexity of recent player contracts and the increase in no-trade and player approval clauses. The Padres traded outfielder Joe Carter and second baseman Roberto Alomar to the Blue Jays for shortstop Tony Fernandez and first baseman Fred McGriff. The trade took 24 hours to complete and was a success for both clubs. Alomar had wanted to play shortstop, but he established himself as the premier second baseman of the 1990s.

On August 31, 1992, Jose Canseco of the A's was traded to the Rangers for Ruben Sierra and Jeff Russell. Canseco was called back from the on-deck circle at the start of the game that night to be informed of the trade.

On July 31, 1997, the A's traded Mark McGwire to the Cardinals for three pitchers—minor leaguers Eric Ludwick and Blake Stein, along with Major League pitcher T.J. Mathews. McGwire was to become a free agent after the season and the A's knew they wouldn't be able to sign him. McGwire then signed a three-year deal with the Cardinals worth $28.5 million.

On May 15, 1998, the Dodgers and Marlins completed one of the biggest trades of the modern era. The Dodgers, giving up on their acrimonious salary negotiations with catcher Mike Piazza, sent him to the Marlins, along with third baseman Todd Zeile. In return they received slugger Gary Sheffield, outfielder Jim Eisenreich, catcher Charles Johnson, third baseman Bobby Bonilla and pitcher Manuel Barrios. The Marlins were housecleaning after their World Series win the previous season, and a week after the trade they sent Piazza to the Mets to unload his salary. In return they received outfielder Preston Wilson, pitcher Ed Yarnell and a player to be named later.

In July 1998, after rumors of trades to the Yankees or Indians, Randy Johnson went from the Mariners to the Astros in exchange for infielder Carlos Guillen, pitcher Freddy Garcia and a player to be named later.

In February 1999 the Yankees traded David Wells and two other players to the Blue Jays for Cy Young Award winner Roger Clemens.

The big trade of mid–2004 was the Dodgers' trade of star catcher Paul LoDuca, considered the heart and soul of the first place team, along with key set-up man Guillermo Mota, to the Marlins for pitcher Brad Penny and first baseman Hee Seop Choi. The ultimate Dodger goal apparently was to obtain Diamondback pitcher Randy Johnson, but that trade never materialized. After throwing eight innings of shutout ball in his first start, Penny hurt his arm in his second start. First year Dodger general manager Paul DePodesta was skewered for the trade (especially after new set-up man Darren Dreifort blew his first chance and then went out for the year), but initially it appeared to be a good one for the Dodgers. The trade really looked bad when Choi did nothing and Penny tried to pitch one more time and was lost for the year with a biceps strain.

Two weeks earlier the Dodgers said they weren't interested in trading Mota or DeLuca. They also said that Milton Bradley would never be asked to move from center field. When the club signed center fielder Steve Finley, Bradley moved to right field.

Creative. A strange trade occured late in 2002 involving Rockies pitcher Mike Hampton. Colorado signed him to multi-year deal worth approximately $10 million per year, the largest for a pitcher at that time. As Hampton's predecessors discovered, Colorado is not friendly to pitchers, and Hampton wanted out. The Rockies traded him to the Marlins, who immediately sent him to the Braves in a three-way negotiation specially approved by the commissioner's office. What made the deal strange was the fact that the Rockies still had to pay Hampton $6.5 million over three seasons to pitch for the Braves in 2003, Florida was to pay him $23.5 million, and the Braves only had to pay him $5.5 million over the same time frame.

Hall of Famers.

"Among all the men who play baseball there is, occasionally, a man of such qualities of heart and mind and body that he transcends even the great and glorious game, and that such a man is to be cherished, not sold."—Bart Giamatti on Tom Seaver's sale by the Mets.

"Congratulations. For years I've been looking for a manager who had the nerve to do that."—Cubs owner William Wrigley in a telegram to manager Joe McCarthy after the manager had traded star pitcher Grover Cleveland Alexander, who lacked leadership and interest in the team's success.

More than two-thirds of all Hall of Fame players were traded at some point in their careers, dispelling the notion that player movement was less frequent in the pre-free agency era. See also *Free Agents* for a discussion of the effect of free agency on player trades.

Playing for Two Teams/Same Day. On May 30, 1922, Cliff Heathcoate of the Cubs and Max Flack of the Cardinals were traded for each other between games of a doubleheader between their clubs. They each played in both games for a different club. Each had a hit in the first game, and neither had a hit in the second game.

Joel Youngblood had hits for two Major League clubs on the same day. On August 4, 1982, playing for the Mets, he singled against Ferguson Jenkins of the Cubs. He was removed from the game and told that he had been traded to the Expos. He immediately left to join the club in Philadelphia. When he arrived, he replaced Jerry White in the 6th inning and singled off Steve Carlton. With the hit, he can also claim a hit off two Hall of Famers and 3,000-strikeout pitchers on the same day.

Even Split. In April 1999 the Tigers traded Brian Hunter to the Mariners during a series between the two clubs. The teams split the four-game series, and Hunter was on the winning side all four times.

Most Players/One Trade. On November 18, 1954, Orioles general manager Paul Richards and Yankee general manager George Weiss put together a trade involving 18 players. It took two weeks to finish all aspects of the deal. The key players in the deal were pitchers Don Larsen and Bob Turley, who went to the Yankees.

After the strike-shortened 1994 season, the Padres and Astros traded 12 players, each club swapping six. The trade was negotiated between Houston president Tal Smith and his son, Padres general manager Randy Smith. The key players in the swap were Derek Bell to Houston and Ken Caminiti to the Padres. Both clubs benefited from the deal, as the two players did well for their new clubs.

Houston's Bad Trades. The Astros had a 1960s history of bad trades. In 1963 the club traded Rusty Staub. Jerry Grote was sent to the Mets in 1965, Dave Giusti to the Cardinals in 1969 and Joe Morgan to the Reds in 1971. The club also got rid of future stars Cesar Geronimo, Jack Billingham, John Mayberry and Mike Cuellar.

Most Teams in a Deal. On December 8, 1977, the Mets, Braves, Pirates and Rangers were involved in a complicated four-team deal:

The Braves traded first baseman Willie Montanez, the key to the deal, to the Rangers. The Braves received pitcher Adrian Devine, Tommy Boggs and outfielder Eddie Miller from the Rangers. The Rangers sent Montanez and outfielders Tom Grieve and Ken Henderson to the Mets for Jon Matlack. The Rangers sent Bert Blyleven to the Pirates for Al Oliver and shortstop Nelson Norman. The Mets sent John Milner to the Pirates.

Another four-team deal occurred in February 1953. The Phillies sent Russ Meyer and cash to the Braves for Earl Torgeson. The Braves sent Meyer to the Dodgers for infielder Rocky Bridges. The Braves sent Bridges and a player to be named later to the Reds for slugging first baseman Joe Adcock.

League Leaders.

"It was like trading hamburger for steak."—Indians general manager Frank Lane in late 1959 after he traded popular 1959 home run champion Rocky Colavito to the Tigers for 1959 batting champion Harvey Kuenn. In the first game of 1960 the Tigers played the Indians. Colavito went 0-for-6 and Kuenn went 2-for-7 as the Tigers won 4–2 in 15 innings. The next day Colavito hit a three-run home run as the Tigers won 6–4. Kuenn did not play because of a pulled muscle.

In the most talked-about trade of the era, Kuenn turned out to be a bust for the Indians and was traded the next year to the Giants. Colavito was a hit, averaging almost 40 home runs over the next few years. Tigers general manager Bill DeWitt was pleased with the deal: "I like hamburger."

Fast Work. On May 15, 1960, Pete Whisenat was traded by the Indians to the Senators. Only 35 minutes after the trade, he was almost used as a pinch hitter by the Indians against the Cubs (although he did not actually bat because a new pitcher was brought in and another pinch hitter replaced Whisenat at the plate).

Argument. In 1943 Dodger manager Leo Durocher and pitcher Bobo Newsom argued repeatedly. Durocher finally suspended Newsom even though he was his best pitcher. The players threatened to strike after the suspension, but only Arky Vaughan made good on his threat and missed one game. Durocher quickly arranged a trade that sent Newsom to the Browns on July 15, 1943.

Bad Reaction. Red Sox outfielder Bernie Carbo learned of his 1976 trade to the Brewers while preparing to leave the Fenway Park parking lot. His reaction was to run his four-wheel-drive vehicle into a hot dog wagon, scattering food and customers. After the season, the Brewers, realized that Carbo was somewhat of an eccentric and required the Red Sox to take him back as part of another trade.

Even Statistics. After the 1946 season, Yankee second baseman Joe Gordon was traded to the Indians. He had played in exactly 1,000 games with 1,000 hits. The ratio changed slightly after that, as he retired with 1,530 hits in 1,566 games after another four years in the Major Leagues.

Managers/Coaches Trade. In June 1916 the Reds traded player/manager Buck Herzog to the Giants for players Bill McKechnie, Edd Roush and Christy Mathewson (who became the manager and pitched in only one more game.

In 1929 Cardinals outfielder Billy Southworth was traded out of the Major Leagues for minor league Red Wings manager Bill McKechnie.

During the 1960 season manager Joe Gordon of the Indians was traded for manager Jimmy Dykes and coach Luke Appling of the Tigers. General managers Frank Lane of the Indians and Bill DeWitt of the Tigers wanted to revive interest in their clubs through the trade and attendant publicity.

In 1963 Giants catcher Wes Westrum was sent to the Mets for coach Cookie Lavagetto. The move was orchestrated because Casey Stengel thought that Westrum might become his successor (he did).

In 1967 manager Gil Hodges was traded by the Senators to the Mets for pitcher Bill Denehy. Hodges managed the Mets to their 1969 "miracle" World Series win.

After the 1976 season Charlie Finley of the A's traded manager Chuck Tanner and $100,000 to Pittsburgh for catcher Manny Sanguillen. One year later Finley traded Sanguillen back to the Pirates for "prospects" that included Elias Sosa, Miguel Dilone and Mike Edwards.

Trading Family Members. In 1934 Senators owner Clark Griffith traded for his nephew-in-law, Joe Cronin. He also traded for son-in-law Joe Haynes in 1948.

Dodger general manager Al Campanis traded son Jim to the Royals in 1968.

The daughter of Padres general manager Trader Jack McKeon married Padres pitcher Greg Booker. Booker played with the club from 1983 through 1988 but was considered an embarrassment because of his mediocre performances (5–6 with one save in six seasons). Nevertheless, McKeon did not want to upset his daughter by trading him. Fans booed Booker unrelentingly and in 1989 McKeon finally arranged a trade with the Twins, who unloaded their own disaster, pitcher Fred Toliver. Toliver's final season was 1989 and Booker lasted through two appearances in 1990 for the Giants.

Good Deal? In 1987 Tigers General Manager Bill Lajoie (yes, related to Nap) traded John Smoltz for Doyle Alexander. Alexander went 9–0 down the stretch with a 1.53 ERA, and the Tigers won the American League East by two games. Smoltz was only 20 at the time and of course became a long-time member of the Braves' rotation, helping the club to more than a dozen division championships.

Most Teams Played For.

"People ask me where I live and I tell them: 'In escrow.'" — Pitcher Mike Krukow after being traded three times in three years.

"I definitely lead the league in teammates." — Pitcher Dave LaPoint on the number of times he had been traded.

"I'll tell you what, I'm getting good at packing" — Pitcher Bruce Chen in 2003 after hooking up with his fifth team in 14 months.

"After joining my eighth team in three years, don't buy a Toronto apartment. Don't rent a Toronto apartment. Don't even exchange 20 bucks at the airport." — New Year's resolution in 2004 for Bruce Chen, proposed by Alan Schwartz.

"Senators owner Clark Griffith liked him as a bridge partner." — Detroit News columnist Joe Falls on why Griffith signed pitcher Bobo Newsom five different times. Newsom was part of 16 trades to 17 clubs in 20 years, pitching five times for the Senators, twice for the Dodgers, three times for the Browns, twice for the A's and once each for the White Sox, Red Sox, Tigers, Yankees and Giants.

George Case recalled a story from one of Newsom's trades. Newsom drew all his money out of the bank and asked for a $10,000 bill. Then he went among his teammates asking for change.

Pitcher Dick Littlefield was traded 10 times between 1950 and 1958. Pitcher Bob Miller played for 10 different clubs (some more than once) between 1962 and 1973, covering eight trades and 16 uniform changes.

Tommy Davis and Ken Brett each played for 10 different clubs (not including repeats).

In April 1998 Mike Morgan pitched for his tenth team, tying the Major League record held also by Bob Miller and Ken Brett.

Versatile Juan Beniquez holds the American League record for having played with eight different American League clubs between 1971 and 1988.

Nineteenth-century catcher Deacon McGuire played for 14 clubs over a 26-year career. Jack Doyle and Joe Quinn each played for 12 clubs.

Most Played for/Consecutive Seasons. Paul Revere "Shorty" Radford played for eight teams in eight consecutive seasons from 1885 to 1892. Reggie Sanders played for seven teams in seven seasons in the late 1990s and early 2000s.

Yankees/A's Connection. During the 1950s the Kansas City A's acted as a form of farm club for the Yankees. For the most part this was because of the close business relationship between A's owner Arnold Johnson and Yankee owners Del Webb and Dan Topping. Between 1955 and Johnson's death in 1960, the clubs made 16 trades (see also Kansas City Athletics).

DiMaggio/Williams. In April 1947 in *Toots Shor*'s restaurant, Yankee owner Dan Topping (or general manager Larry MacPhail, depending on the source) and Red Sox owner Tom Yawkey talked over a possible swap of Joe DiMaggio and Ted Williams. Each player was more suited to the other's ballpark. The deal apparently was made, but Yawkey wanted to sleep on it. The next morning he changed his mind and also wanted "the little left fielder," who happened to be a young Yogi Berra. His reasoning was that the Boston fans thought Williams was the better player and that a second player was needed to complete the trade. Topping declined to add Berra because he would not be able to justify the deal to New York fans if it was not a one-for-one exchange.

Most Trades/Season.

"I've had more numbers on my back than a bingo board." — Rocky Bridges on the frequency of his trades.

A number of players have been traded three times in a season and have played for four different clubs. One source reported that in 1904 Frank Huelsman played for five clubs. However, he played only for four (unless one minor league club is included): the White Sox (four games), Tigers (four games), Browns (20 games) and Senators (84 games).

George Strief played for four Major League clubs in three leagues in 1884; St. Louis (American Association), Kansas City (Union Association), Chicago/Pittsburgh (Union Association) and Cleveland (National League). All the travel must have affected him because he batted a collective .189.

Tex Westerzil was traded three times in the Federal League in 1915: playing in Brooklyn, Chicago, St. Louis and back to Chicago.

Wes Covington played for the 1961 Braves, White Sox, A's and Phillies. At least nine other players have played for four clubs in a season, including Frank Fernandez in 1971 and Mike Kilkenny in 1972.

All Divisions/One Season. Dave Kingman achieved notoriety in 1977 when he played with the Mets, Padres, Angels and Yankees to become the only player to play on clubs in each of the four divisions in the same season.

Repeat Performance. Bobo Newsom made five separate appearances with the Washington Senators, the last in 1952. Only Rickey Henderson (A's) and Tony Fernandez (Blue Jays) have played for four teams.

Oops. On June 15, 2002, while playing in San Diego, the Mariners released veteran outfielder Eugene Kingsdale. The Padres immediately picked him up, but no one told the Mariners players or coaches. After the Mariners took the field for warm-ups, several players ran back to the clubhouse to tell the coaching staff that

Kingsale was in a Padres uniform. Kingsdale pinch-hit in the 5th inning and flew out in a 6–3 Mariners win.

Worst Trades.

"End of an Error"—*New York Post* headline after Roberto Alomar was traded in 2003 after a miserable 1½ seasons with the club.

Various writers have dubbed the following as the worst trades of all time: In 1900 Christy Mathewson was 20–2 for Norfolk of the Virginia League. The Giants purchased him for $1,500 but returned him and canceled the deal when he lost his first three decisions. The Reds drafted him for $100 and traded him to the Giants for sore-armed Amos Rusie, who had not pitched for two years. Historian Lee Allen in *The National League Story* (1961) cites this trade as evidence of his theory that Reds owner John Brush knew he would be buying the Giants shortly and let Mathewson go to the Giants for that reason.

In 1960 the Indians traded Norm Cash to the Tigers for Steve Demeter. Cash played 15 seasons for the Tigers and had 373 home runs after the trade. Demeter played four games for the Indians and had no hits before being sent down to the minor leagues.

In 1964 the Cubs traded Lou Brock to the Cardinals for Ernie Broglio. Brock went on to become the all-time leading base stealer (until Rickey Henderson), while Broglio won only seven games for the Cubs over the next three seasons. The trade prompted this headline to an article written by young reporter (and future broadcaster) Brent Musberger: "Cubs Get Greatest Steal Ever"

In 1966 the Astros traded catcher Jerry Grote to the Mets for Tom Parsons, who had a 1–10 record with the Mets in 1965. Grote became one of the leading defensive catchers of the era, but Parsons never returned to the Major Leagues.

In 1982 Ryne Sandberg was traded to the Cubs by the Phillies (along with an aging Larry Bowa) for Ivan DeJesus.

In 1987 Dennis Eckersley, on the verge of reliever superstardom, was traded to the A's by the Cubs for Dave Wilder, Brian Guinn and Mark Leonette.

In March 1987 the Royals traded Ed Hearn to the Mets for pitcher David Cone. Hearn batted in 13 games in two seasons for Kansas City and his career was over. Cone pitched 16 more seasons, and though he was mediocre in 1987, he won 21 games in 1988 among his career 194 wins.

Padres general manager Kevin Towers admitted in 2003 that his August 2001 trade of pitcher Woody Williams for $10-million bust Ray Lankford was the worst move he has made in almost nine years in the job. Williams left for the Cardinals in early August 2001, and went 28–8 through the 2003 All-Star Game and the Cardinals were 33–14 in his starts. In the last two months of 2001 Lankford hit four homers, and in 2002 he hit six homers with 26 RBIs in 81 games.

Rules Restricting. In the 1970s, in response to A's owner Charlie Finley's attempts at numerous player sales, commissioner Bowie Kuhn set $400,000 as an arbitrary cash limit for a straight player sale. Kuhn's prohibition of Finley's sales was upheld in a federal court action. By the 1980s the limit was $1 million.

Giving Up. On July 1, 1997, the White Sox were only 3½ games behind the Indians in the American League Central race. Nevertheless, the Indians traded eight players with a combined 92 years of Major League experience, including starting pitchers Wilson Alvarez, Danny Darwin and Roberto Hernandez. Third baseman Robin Ventura was not happy: "We didn't realize August 1 was the end of the season."

Traded for Themselves.

"I went through life as the 'player to be named later.'"—Joe Garagiola.

The trade for a "player to be named later" has resulted in a player being traded for himself. This has happened to Clint Courtney, Harry Chiti and Jose Gonzales, who later adopted the name Uribe. Because of the structure of the deals, none of the "trades" appears in the "Trades" section of *The Baseball Encyclopedia*.

On April 25, 1962, the Indians traded Chiti to the last-place expansion Mets for a player to be named later. On June 15 the deal was completed when Chiti returned to the Indians. The New York media reported tongue-in-cheek that the Mets were fleeced in the deal.

Players Traded for Goods. Pitcher Joe Martina of New Orleans was traded for a sack of oysters.

San Francisco of the Pacific Coast League received Jack Fenton for a sack of prunes.

In 1931 Chattanooga shortstop Johnny Jones was traded to Charlotte in exchange for turkeys so the team could have turkey dinners.

Cy Young was traded by his minor league club for, among other things, a new suit.

The minor league Nashville owner traded golf clubs for Charlie "Greek" George.

The minor league Omaha owner traded two players for an airplane.

Rookie Buddy Frye was traded to Montgomery by the Browns when the club could not pay for its 1931 spring training site at Montgomery's home field. The Tigers did the same thing in Augusta in 1905, trading future Black Sox pitcher Eddie Cicotte to the local minor league club.

Pitcher Lefty Grove was picked up by Baltimore owner Jack Dunn when Dunn paid another team's bill for a new outfield fence at a minor league ballpark.

In 1983 the A's traded Keith Comstock to the Tigers for $100 and a bag of balls which Comstock had to deliver to the Tigers' spring training camp in Florida.

In the 1990s pitcher Tim Fortugno was traded for a gross of baseballs.

In July 1998, Kenny Krahenbuhl was traded to the Greenville Bluesmen of the Texas-Louisiana League for a 10-pound catfish and two players to be named later ("players" in this situation is often a euphemism so as not to hurt the traded player's feelings). The deal was with the Oxnard (California) Pacific Suns [the author was on the Suns board of directors and had a front-row seat as the club imploded financially. The Suns got off to a bad start when their home opener was cancelled after the 4th inning when the lights wouldn't go on and fans were freezing; the ballpark was located only five miles from the ocean].

Krahenbuhl had a *Planes, Trains and Automobiles* experience joining the Bluesmen, but the ordeal didn't seem to affect him. In his first game, against the top hitting club in the league and its best pitcher, with lightning thunder and rain during the last two innings, he pitched a perfect game.

Trade Expenses. When a player is traded, he is entitled to between $600 and $1,200 from his old team, depending on the distance of the new team's home city. Players are also entitled to a moving allowance.

Big Finish. Reds second baseman Joe Morgan believes that the 1976 World Series saved Johnny Bench from being traded. Bench had a subpar regular season, hitting .234 with 16 home runs. He batted .533 in the World Series, including two home runs in the last game to sweep the Yankees. His World Series performance confirmed that he could still play after serious lung surgery a few years earlier.

Broadcaster. Long-time Tigers broadcaster Ernie Harwell was broadcasting for the Atlanta Crackers in 1948. He was traded to the Dodgers for catcher Cliff Draper of Brooklyn's Montreal farm club. Draper took over as manager of the Crackers, and Harwell began his Major League broadcasting career.

Books. *Total Baseball* and *The Baseball Encyclopedia* contain a complete list of all Major League trades since 1900; Joseph Reichler, former editor of the *Encyclopedia*, published *The Baseball Trade Register* (1984), which chronicles the same subject in a somewhat different format; Richard Kubik, *Baseball Trades and Acquisitions* (1981), covers all trades from 1950 through 1979.

Websites. Baseball-reference.com has a comprehensive list of trades, sorted by player.

Trainers

"That's what separates the good trainers from the great ones. The greats save the patient and the bug."—A clubhouse visitor after Astros trainer Dave Labossiere extracted a moth that had flown into the right ear of Astro outfielder Mike Simms. Labossiere used a pair of tweezers to dislodge the moth intact.

"A bonus guy is a prospect, and the trainers rub his arms with a secret salve from India. A suspect—a guy like me—got his arm rubbed with Three-in-One oil."—Bo Belinsky in 1980.

See also *Conditioning* and *Medical Treatment*.

Early Years.

"In the early days, a trainer was some old friend of the manager, with a gift of gab and a collection of patent medicines, with some secret-formula liniment in his secondhand doctor's bag, and as much alcohol on his breath as in the bag. His education was strictly haphazard and based only on experience, often someone else's experience imperfectly understood."—Leonard Koppett in *A Thinking Man's Guide to Baseball* (1967).

Trainers originally were called "rubbers" and their primary duty was to rub down pitchers.

Bonesetter Reese. John D. "Bonesetter" Reese was a popular early trainer. He had no medical training but was good at manipulation and massage during the first three decades of the 20th century. Reese first treated Jimmy McAleer, an outfielder for the Cleveland Spiders. McAleer later became the manager of the St. Louis Browns and spread the word about Reese's talents. As a result, Reese was hired in 1903 by the Pittsburgh Pirates as full-time team physician.

Reese opined that injury to the elbow usually meant fastball pitcher; injury to the shoulder, curveball specialist. Several players claimed that he saved their careers, and his prowess extended beyond the ballfield. He also treated Theodore Roosevelt, Chief Justice Charles Evans Hughes, and former British Prime Minister David Lloyd George, evangelist and player Billy Sunday (during both careers), and Will Rogers. Reese died of heart failure at 76 in 1931.

Ejections. In 1957 Braves trainer Joe Taylor was ejected from the bench after engaging in a fight in center field.

Dodgers trainer Charlie Strasser once was once ejected from a ball game for excessive bench jockeying and use of profanity.

Manager. Phillies trainer Dusty Cooke was named interim manager for 13 games in 1948, finishing with a 6–6–1 record (only 11 games in some sources).

Membership. Major League trainers are members of the Professional Baseball Athletic Trainers Society (PBATS). The organization was created to enhance the image of professional trainers and to disseminate information.

Certification. The National Athletic Trainers Association (NATA) is based in Greenville, North Carolina, and certifies Major League trainers and others. Founded in 1950, it certifies approximately 700 new trainers each year.

Training See *Conditioning*

Trains See *Railroads*

Transportation

"To appreciate the importance of Baseball as a Business, one has but to visit Dexter Park in Chicago, or the Capitoline grounds at Brooklyn, on the occasion of an important match game. Say it is Dexter Park. Two or three extra trains are run on each of the two railroads leading from the city to the Park. Each train is packed like a train of cattle-cars. Besides this, the street cars and every accessible buggy and barouche in town are brought into requisition, and the thoroughfares leading to the Park are the scene of a continuous caravan of vehicles and dust."—1870s article in *The Western Monthly* quoted in *Baseball: Diamond in the Rough*, by Irving A. Leitner (1972).

"Subways, elevated trains, buses, street-cars, private automobiles and taxicabs were loaded with eager hopeful fans making their way to the Blues Field to see Old Pop Clark's Royal Blues of New York play their first game of the season in the United League."—Opening lines of what is considered to be the first baseball mystery, *Death on the Diamond*, by Cortland Fitzsimmons (1934).

See also *Airline Travel*, *Automobiles*, *Buses*, *Parking*, *Railroads* and *Streetcars*.

In the late 19th century fans in many cities used streetcars and subways to travel to games. Some cities had special rail cars for transport to out-of-town sites. In the 19th and early 20th centuries, players already in uniform were carried to and from ballparks in carriages and were subjected to jeers, trash and fruit missiles. As a result, in 1909 the National League banned carriage parades.

Pie Traynor (1899–1972)

Hall of Fame 1948

"The greatest team player in the game."—John McGraw on the Pirates third baseman.

"Pie was a great ballplayer. I think the greatest third baseman who ever lived. A terrific hitter and a great fielder. Gosh, how he could dive for those line drives down the third base line and knock the ball down and throw the man out at first! It was remarkable.... In addition to his hitting and fielding he was a good base runner, too. Most people don't remember that."—Teammate Paul Waner quoted in *The Glory of Their Times*, by Lawrence S. Ritter (1966).

"Young Mr. Traynor is from the rock-ribbed, rock-headed coast of Massachusetts. He wanted to play baseball; consequently he used to haunt Fenway Park at practice time. He would worm himself into the practice infield and work himself into large gobs of perspiration."—Sportswriter Bill McGeehan in 1925.

Traynor starred at third base and batted .320 for the Pirates over 17 seasons beginning in 1920.

A native of Massachusetts, Harold Joseph "Pie" Traynor began his career with Portsmouth of the Virginia League before the Pirates purchased his contract for $10,000. He played a few games with the Pirates in 1920 before moving down to Louisville for the 1921 season. Though originally a shortstop, he shifted to third base in his first full season with the Pirates in 1922.

Traynor batted over .300 10 times and drove in over 100 runs seven times. Over his 17-year Major League career, Traynor batted .320, with a high of .366 in 1930. He led the league with 19 triples in 1923 and had 164 over his career. He was considered one of the best defensive third baseman of the early 20th century. Many regarded him as the best third baseman of all time, and he was voted onto the all-time team when professional baseball celebrated its centennial in 1969.

Beginning in 1934, his last full season as a player, he managed the Pirates for six seasons, leading the club to a best finish of second place in 1938. After sliding to sixth in 1939, he resigned under pressure. Following his managerial career, he was a broadcaster in Pittsburgh and remained part of the Pirates organization as a scout until his death.

Trick Plays

"I've always said the bat girl was the key to that play. We always tell our runners, 'never go for the extra base until you've checked to see what the bat girl does.'" — Miami Hurricanes coach Ron Fraser. On a pick-off attempt during the College World Series, his entire infield, outfield and bullpen on the sideline were faking as if the ball had gone past the first baseman and down the right field line. Even the ball girl got into the act, pretending to point at the ball. The runner got up and ran to second but was out by several feet on a throw by the pitcher.

See also **Hidden Ball Trick.**

In 1915 during the 7th inning of a tie game with a man on third, Cardinals manager and third base coach Miller Huggins asked Dodger rookie pitcher Ed Appleton for the ball. Appleton obliged and threw it to him: Huggins let it roll away and the runner scored. The umpires allowed the run, as time had not been called.

On April 21, 1994, Steve Sax was cut by the White Sox. A day later he was picked up by the A's. In his first game back he got caught in a rundown and ended up on second base with teammate Stan Javier. Yankee second baseman Mike Gallego tagged both runners, but only Javier was out because Sax was the lead runner and entitled to the base. Gallego told Sax, "You're out, Saxy." Sax believed him and walked off the bag. Gallego tagged him to complete the double play.

Triple Crown

"TRIPLE CROWN WINNER EUTHANIZED" — 2001 Associated Press headline describing the death of *horseracing* Triple Crown winner *Affirmed.*

"Because he's an old 30." — Reds president Bill DeWitt explaining in late 1965 why he traded Frank Robinson to the Orioles. Robinson responded by winning the Triple Crown and leading the Orioles to a World Championship.

"And if I have my choice between a pennant and a Triple Crown, I'll take the pennant every time." — Carl Yastrzemski.

"I can remember winning the pennant on the last day of the season and not knowing I won the Triple Crown until I read it in the paper the next day. I was just so focused on the face." — Yastrzemski.

See also, **Pitchers — Pitching Triple Crown.**

Terminology. Paul Dickson's *The Dickson Baseball Dictionary* (1989) does not attribute a date of earliest usage for the term "Triple Crown," but presumably it was not in vogue until the 20th century because RBI statistics were not kept regularly before then.

Criteria. A player wins the Triple Crown by leading his league in batting average, home runs and RBIs.

Winners Since 1901.

	YEAR	AVG	HR	RBIs
Nap Lajoie (A's)	1901	.422	14	125
Ty Cobb (Tigers)	1909	.377	9	115
H. Zimmerman (Cubs)	1912	.372	14	98
R. Hornsby (Cards)	1922	.401	42	152
R. Hornsby (Cards)	1925	.403	39	143
Jimmie Foxx (A's)	1933	.356	48	163
Chuck Klein (Phillies)	1933	.368	28	120
Lou Gehrig (Yankees)	1934	.363	49	165
Joe Medwick (StL NL)	1937	.374	31	154
(Tied With Mel Ott for home run title)				
Ted Williams (Red Sox)	1942	.356	36	114
Ted Williams (Red Sox)	1947	.343	32	130
Mickey Mantle (Yankees)	1956	.353	52	130
Frank Robinson (Orioles)	1966	.316	49	122
Carl Yastrzemski (Red Sox)	1967	.326	44	121

Pre–1900 Winners. The Triple Crown was not recognized until the 20th century, in part because RBI statistics were not kept regularly until at least the 1890s. Modern statisticians have gone back and calculated RBI totals based on available data. The reconstructed data revealed that there were two Triple Crown winners during the 1876–1900 era, Paul Hines and Hugh Duffy.

In 1878 Hines hit four home runs, batted .358 and drove in 50 runs in 62 games for Providence of the National League to lead in each category. Even if the Triple Crown had existed in the 19th century, Hines' accomplishment would not have been official until many years later, when his statistics from two unrecorded tie games increased his totals to give him the milestone.

In 1894, for the first time with a 60'6" pitching distance, Duffy hit .438 with 18 home runs and 145 RBIs for the Boston Red Stockings.

Major League Triple Crown. Five players have led both leagues in the three Triple Crown categories in the same season:

1909	Ty Cobb
1925	Rogers Hornsby
1934	Lou Gehrig
1942	Ted Williams
1956	Mickey Mantle

Just Missed a Triple Crown. Ted Williams came the closest to winning three Triple Crowns. In 1949 he was the American League's top home and RBI man but lost the batting title by two-tenths of a percentage point to George Kell.

In 1953 Al Rosen just missed when he was unable to beat out a ground ball in his last at-bat of the season. He lost the batting title with a .336 average to .337 for Mickey Vernon of the Senators.

Babe Ruth won two legs of the Triple Crown seven times but never led in all three categories. No other player has done it more than three times. Ruth had the most trouble with batting average: In 1923 he led in home runs and RBIs but lost the batting title even though he hit .393. Harry Heilmann of the Tigers hit .403.

Ruth did win a batting title in 1924 but had only a second-place 121 RBIs to go with his league-leading 46 home runs. Goose Goslin of the Senators led the league with 129 RBIs. It was the only time Goslin led the league in that category though he regularly had 100 or more RBIs.

Frank Robinson suffered an injury before the 1967 All-Star break that probably cost him a shot at back-to-back Triple Crowns.

Trade. Chuck Klein of the A's won the Triple Crown in 1933 and then was traded on November 21 of that year by cash-poor Connie Mack. Klein was sent to the Cubs for three players and $65,000 as Mack conducted another fire sale of top players.

The Reds traded Frank Robinson to the Orioles after the 1965 season, and he went on to win the Triple Crown in 1966.

Most Recent Attempts/Degree of Difficulty.

"Winning the Triple Crown is so difficult that perhaps there should be an award each season for the player who simply comes closest to doing so." — Tim Kurkjian in *Sports Illustrated*.

In 1992 Gary Sheffield of the Padres led the National League in all three categories as late as September 3. A hamstring injury slowed him down over the last month and he broke a finger to end his season five days early. He still led the league in batting average at .330, was third in home runs with 33 (two behind the leader), and was fifth in RBIs with 100 (nine behind the leader).

The most difficult leg is the batting title, because only a few recent players have chosen to cut down on power and go for average (such as Wade Boggs and Rod Carew). Since Carl Yastrzemski won the Triple Crown in 1967, only Joe Torre in 1971 and Al Oliver in 1982 have won the batting title and another leg of the Triple Crown. Both fell at least 15 home runs shy of the league leader in home runs.

Barry Bonds won the home run and RBI titles in 1993 and 2001, but fell short on batting average. In 1993 he was fourth at .336, behind Andres Galarraga at .370. In 2001 he was seventh at .328, behind Larry Walker at .350. Bonds won a batting title in 2002, hitting .370, but he was second in home runs and sixth in RBIs.

Ken Griffey, Jr., led the league in 1997 in home runs (56) and RBIs (147), but hit only .304 and has never won a batting title.

Alex Rodriguez won the home run and RBI titles in 2002, but batted only .300. In 1996 he won a batting title at .358, but his 36 home runs and 123 RBIs were well behind the leaders.

There was talk of a Triple Crown for Albert Pujols of the Cardinals in 2003. He won the batting title with a .359 average, and was fourth in both home runs (43) and RBIs (124). The leaders had 47 home runs (Jim Thome) and 141 RBIs (Preston Wilson).

Triple Plays

"We got to work on our defense against the triple play." — Casey Stengel of the Mets when asked if there was anything special he wanted his players to learn.

"A bad biorhythm day." — Chili Davis's explanation for hitting into a triple play and a double play in a game on June 17, 1999.

"What we need is a second-base coach." — Yankee third baseman Graig Nettles after the club ran itself into a triple play.

Earliest. Early professional Jim Creighton (who died shortly after an at-bat), is credited with one of the first triple plays. In a game between the Brooklyn Excelsiors and Lord Baltimores on July 22, 1860, Creighton was playing left field and made a one-handed catch for one out with men on second and third. Both men were too far off the bag to return safely. They were thrown out to complete the triple play.

First Professional Unassisted. The first unassisted triple play in a professional game was made by first baseman Hal O'Hagan of the International League Rochester Broncos against Jersey City on August 18, 1902.

World Series/Triple Plays.

Bill Wambsganss/1920.

"You'd think I was born the day before and died the day after." — Indians second baseman Bill Wambsganss. Despite a 13-year Major League career, he has been remembered almost exclusively for making an unassisted triple play in the 5th inning of Game 5 of the 1920 World Series.

Wambsganss caught a line drive by Dodger pitcher Clarence

Mitchell, stepped on second to retire Pete Kilduff, then tagged Otto Miller coming from first base. Mitchell, who grounded into a double play in his next at-bat, was one of the few left-handed legal spitballers, and he filled in occasionally at first base because of his .252 lifetime average.

Blue Jays/1992.

"I thought I was correct at first, but then I saw the pictures, and I had to admit I probably missed it." — Umpire Bob Davidson after blowing a call that would have given the 1992 Blue Jays the first triple play in the World Series since 1920.

In the top of the 4th inning of Game 3 the Braves had men on first and second with nobody out. Blue Jays center fielder Devon White made a sensational catch against the wall and relayed the ball to the infield. Terry Pendleton, running from first base, passed Deion Sanders near second and was called out for the second out. The Blue Jays then relayed the ball unnecessarily to first base to double off Pendleton. In the meantime, Sanders tagged up at second and headed for third in the confusion. Blue Jays first baseman John Olerud threw to third baseman Kelly Gruber, who ran Sanders back to second while making a diving tag on his foot. What should have been a triple play was only a double play because second base umpire Bob Davidson did not see the tag and called Sanders safe.

Regular Season Unassisted Triple Plays. There have been 11 regular season unassisted triple plays:

Neal Ball/1909. On July 19, 1909, in the first game of a doubleheader, the Indians shortstop recorded the first Major League unassisted triple play in the top of the 2nd inning against the Red Sox. He caught Amby McConnell's liner, touched second to retire Heinie Wagner, who was running to third base, and then tagged Jake Stahl as he approached second. In the bottom of the inning, he hit an inside-the-park home run to become the only person until 1994 to hit a home run in the same inning in which he executed a triple play. Ball had made 81 errors during the previous season.

George Burns/1923. The Red Sox first baseman accomplished the feat on September 14, 1923, in the 2nd inning against the Indians. Burns caught Frank Brower's liner, tagged Rube Lutzke off first and then beat Riggs Stephenson back to second base for the third out.

Ernie Padgett/1923. The rookie shortstop did it for the Braves against the Phillies on October 6, 1923 during the last game of the year. It happened in the 4th inning of the second game of a doubleheader. The Braves won 4–1. Padgett caught Walter Holke's liner, stepped on second to retire Cotton Tierney, then tagged Cliff Lee running from first.

Glenn Wright/1925. The Pirates shortstop recorded his triple play in the 9th inning of a game against the Cardinals on May 7, 1925. Jimmy Cooney was caught off second base on the play on a ball hit by Jim Bottomley, and then Wright tagged Rogers Hornsby on his way to second base. When Cooney made his own unassisted triple play two years later, he became the only player involved in two unassisted triple plays.

Jimmy Cooney/1927. The triple play by the Cubs shortstop occurred in the 4th inning of a game on May 30, 1927. Pirates outfielder Paul Waner hit a line drive while his brother Lloyd moved off second base headed for third. Cooney stabbed the line drive and doubled Waner off second. The runner on first, Clyde Barnhart, thought the ball had gone over Cooney so he slid into second base and Cooney's waiting glove. The Cubs won 7–6 in 10 innings.

Johnny Neun/1927. On May, 31, 1927, the day after Cooney's triple play, Tigers first baseman Johnny Neun had an unassisted triple play that ended the game in the 9th inning. It saved a 1–0 shutout for Rip Collins, his only one of the season. Neun caught Homer Summa's liner, ran over and tagged Charlie Jamieson between first and second and then touched second base before Glenn Myatt could return.

Ron Hansen/1968. The Senators shortstop did it on July 30, 1968, snaring a line drive with men on first and second. During the game, Hansen struck out four times against Sam McDowell. The next day he struck out two more times against Denny McLain. The day after that he hit a grand slam. The day after that he was traded to the White Sox and started that night against the Senators.

Mickey Morandini/1992. On September 20, 1992, the Phillies second baseman turned the first unassisted triple play in the National League in 65 years. Morandini snagged a line drive by Pirates third baseman Jeff King, stepped on second to double off Andy Van Slyke and tagged Barry Bonds coming from first base. The runners had been going on a 3–2 pitch. Morandini did not realize the play's significance immediately, as he flipped the ball onto the mound as he trotted to the bench. The ball was put in play and hit foul the next inning.

Morandini became the first second baseman to execute the play in a regular season game. There had been only four unassisted triple plays in the National League, and Pittsburgh's stadium announcer, Art McKennan, age 84 in 1992, witnessed three of them.

John Valentin/1994. On July 8, 1994, the Red Sox shortstop made an unassisted triple play against the Mariners. With the Mariners runners moving from first and second base in the top of the 6th, Valentin caught a line drive by Marc Newfield. He stepped on second to double off Mike Blowers and then tagged Keith Mitchell. Valentin led off the bottom of the inning with a home run.

Randy Velarde/2000. On May 29, 2000, against the Yankees, A's second baseman Randy Velarde became the 11th player to execute a regular season unassisted triple play. In the 6th inning, he caught a line drive from Shane Spencer, tagged Jorge Posada off first and stepped on second to retire Tino Martinez. Despite Velarde's heroics, Andy Pettitte of the Yankees pitched a two-hitter and won 4–1. In 1995, while with the Yankees, Velarde turned an unassisted triple play against the Dodgers in spring training following the strike.

Rafael Furcal. On August 10, 2003, the Braves shortstop had an unassisted triple play in the 5th inning against the Cardinals. Batter Woody Williams lined a ball to Furcal as the runners were going on the 1–1 pitch. Furcal stepped on second to double up Mike Matheny and tagged Orlando Palmeiro as he tried to turn back to first. The situation was set up when Furcal made an error earlier in the inning. The Cardinals still won the game when Albert Pujols homered offered reliever John Smoltz late in the game.

Unassisted Triple Play by an Outfielder. All Major League unassisted triple plays have occurred with runners on first and second and all have been by infielders. There is at least one instance of a minor league unassisted triple play by an outfielder. On July 19, 1911, outfielder Walter Carlisle of Vernon in the Pacific Coast League executed an unassisted triple play. He caught a fly ball off his shoetops, fell into second base, got up and jogged to first base.

The closest Major League effort may have been by Paul Hines of the Providence Grays against Boston on May 8, 1878. With runners on first and third, Hines caught a short fly ball in center field. He ran to third to double up the runner going home and purportedly then ran to second base as both runners had rounded third before the catch. Some participants claim that he merely had two putouts and an assist because he threw to second for the third out. A November 15, 1922, *Milwaukee Journal* account of the arrest for

pickpocketing of outfielder Paul A. Hines, 69 at the time, cited him as the first to accomplish an unassisted outfield triple play.

Many years after the play, sportswriter Fred Lieb spoke with one of the players, who confirmed that Hines caught the ball, ran to third base and then threw to second baseman Charlie Sweasy to complete the assisted triple play.

Two Triple Plays in One Season by an Outfielder. In 1928 Charlie Jamieson of the Indians became the only outfielder to be involved in two triple plays in one season.

Turned in a Season/Team. The 1965 Cubs and 1964 Phillies each turned three triple plays. Cubs pitcher Bill Faul was on the mound during each of his club's three.

Two in One Game. On July 17, 1990, the Red Sox became the first team to hit into two triple plays in one game, although they still won. They did so against the Twins, whose Gary Gaetti started both plays by picking up ground balls and stepping on third base. The next day the Red Sox and Twins set another record by combining on 10 *Double Plays*, a Major League record.

History. Between 1901 and May 1999, there were 237 triple plays in the National League.

Most Hit Into/Career. George Sisler and Brooks Robinson each hit into three triple plays.

Unusual. On May 21, 1950, the Phillies had two men on and Eddie Waitkus at the plate against the Cardinals. On a strikeout by Waitkus, catcher Joe Garagiola threw to third base, trapping Richie Ashburn between second and third. Shortstop Marty Marion tagged him out and then threw to first baseman Stan Musial to pick off back-tracking Granny Hamner to complete the triple play.

Wind-Aided. On May 10, 1997, the Cubs pulled off a strange triple play against the Giants. With two on, Stan Javier hit a popup to short center field that the wind played tricks with. Umpire Bob Davidson was slow to call an infield fly (but did) because of the tricky wind, and the ball dropped off of Brian McRae's glove for the first out as three Cubs reached for it. Runner Kirk Rueter tried to reach third, but was thrown out by McRae. Darryl Hamilton tried for second, but third baseman Jose Hernandez threw him out on a tag by Ryne Sandberg. The Giants still won the game 4–2.

Using His Head. With the bases loaded and nobody out in the 9th inning of a 1935 game, Red Sox player-manager Joe Cronin hit a line drive through the glove of Indians third baseman Odell Hale. It hit him in the forehead and caromed to shortstop Bill Knickerbocker, who caught it for the first out. He threw to second baseman Roy Hughes for out number two, and Hughes threw to Hal Trosky at first base to end the inning.

Last At-Bat. Joe Pignatano ended an undistinguished career in grand fashion by hitting into a triple play against the Cubs on September 30, 1962. They have been reported as the last three outs in Polo Grounds history, but the Mets also played the 1963 season in that ballpark.

Good Hitter. Despite being a stellar hitter, Tony Gwynn was the first batter in the 1990s to hit into a triple play.

Good/Bad. On August 3, 2002, Scott Hatteberg of the Red Sox hit a grand slam and lined into a triple play in the same game — a feat never before accomplished.

Bad Year. On April 14, 2002, Seattle Mariners rookie designated hitter Ron Wright debuted and went 0-for-3. He accounted for six outs with a strikeout, double play and triple play to become the second player since 1950 to hit into a triple play in his first game (Leo Foster for the Braves in 1971 was the other). It was Wright's only appearance of the season and he never again appeared in a Major League game.

Hit Into Most/Player/Career.

"He always looks like his team has just hit into a game-ending triple play." — Leonard Koppett on manager Fred Hutchinson.

Brooks Robinson of the Orioles is credited with the most times hitting into a triple play, with four.

Leo Durocher. In 1955 in Durocher's last game as Giants manager, Willie Mays hit his 51st home run of the year. However, a 9th inning rally with the bases loaded ended with a triple play and a 5–2 loss.

Drought. In June 1996 the Dodgers recorded their first triple play since 1949. Chipper Jones of the Braves hit into the triple play after doing the same thing in spring training against the Dodgers.

Quadruple Play. A game in Cuba once almost yielded a legitimate four-out play. The bases were loaded with none out in a tie game. The right fielder caught a long fly in right center field and relayed the ball to second and then it went to first to double off two runners. The runner on third tagged up and had crossed the plate before the third out at first base. Because the final out (at first base) was not a force out, the run counted.

The opposing manager appealed the runner tagging at third, claiming he left too early. One of the umpires signaled that the runner on third was out, creating a *fourth* out, but the other umpires upheld the run; a triple play and a run scored.

Tripleheaders

"Kansas City and Cleveland, a doubleheader, was postponed because of rain. They'll play four tomorrow." — Giants broadcaster Hank Greenwald misreporting in 1981; the most in the Major Leagues has been a tripleheader.

19th Century. On Labor Day, September 1, 1890, Brooklyn and Pittsburgh of the National League played a single morning game followed by an afternoon doubleheader and charged two separate admissions. The first game started at 10:30 a.m. and attendance was 915. Pittsburgh won 10–9 despite Brooklyn scoring nine runs in the 9th inning. Brooklyn won the second game 3–2 and the third 8–4. There was speculation that the tripleheader was staged to compete with a rival Players League game in the same town that day.

On Labor Day, September 7, 1896, Baltimore and Louisville of the National League played a tripleheader. Baltimore swept the games by scores of 4–3, 9–1 and 12–1. The third game went only eight innings. Orioles catcher Wilbert Robinson played all three games without an error.

20th Century. The only 20th century tripleheader was played between the Pirates and the Reds on October 2, 1920. Third place was at stake for both clubs, which had become important only recently because the third-place finisher began to share World Series money.

The Friday game had been rained out and the teams already had a doubleheader scheduled for Saturday. No games were allowed on Sunday in Pittsburgh that year. National League president John Heydler approved owner Barney Dreyfuss' request to play all three games on the same day, and a single admission was charged.

The first game began at noon and was completed in 2 hours and 3 minutes as the Reds won 13–4. The second game was completed in 1 hour and 56 minutes, as the Reds won again 7–3. The third game lasted six innings before being called for darkness after 1 hour and 1 minute with the Pirates leading 6–0. The teams played 24 innings in exactly five hours. The results left the Reds with third place money and the Pirates in fourth with nothing.

Pirates third baseman Clyde Barnhart was the only player to get a hit in all three games. The only other players to appear in all three games were Pat Duncan and Morrie Rath of the Reds and Fred Nicholson and Cotton Tierney of the Pirates.

Minor Leagues. The Charlotte Knights and Pawtucket Red Sox played a tripleheader in June 1996, finishing a suspended game before playing a doubleheader.

Triples

"The most exciting 12 seconds in sports" — Many.

"A triple is like meeting a woman who excites you, spending the evening talking and getting more excited, then taking her home. It drags on and on, never sure how it's going to turn out." — Slugger George Foster, who had 47 triples in his career.

"The sad truth is that this era's emphasis on the long ball is shoving the triple into a corner of the game's dusty archives, next to woolen uniforms, doubleheaders and World Series day games. Triples are on baseball's endangered species list. Over the years, they have been disappearing from box scores like northern spotted owls from Oregon's forests." — Michael Knisley in *The Sporting News*.

"I never thought home runs were all that exciting. I still think the triple is the most exciting thing in baseball. To me, a triple is like a guy taking the ball on his 1-yard line and running 99 yards for a touchdown." — Henry Aaron.

"I can't tell a lie, Angela. There just ain't nothin' like it." — Ballplayer Luke Gofannon in Philip Roth's *The Great American Novel* (1973). He professes to love his girlfriend, Angela Whittling Trust, more than a stolen base, a shoestring catch, a letter-high fastball and a home run, but only after admitting that he does not put her above his beloved triple, which he describes thusly: "Well … smackin' it, first off. Off the wall, up the alley, down the line, however it goes, it goes with that there crack. Then runnin' like blazes…. Two hunerd and seventy feet of runnin' behind ya, and with all that there momentum…. Over he goes. Legs. Arms. Dust. Hell, ya might be in a tornado, Angela. Then ya hear the ump, 'safe!'…. Only that ain't all…. The best part, in a way. Standin' up. Dustin' off y'r breeches and standin' up there on that bag."

Demise. In the first 20 years of the 20th century, when balls were deader and outfields were bigger, one out of every 18 hits was a triple. By the mid–1980s, that number was down to one out of every 43 hits. By 2001 the figure was once every 47.5 hits. Evidence comes from Rickey Henderson, the most prolific base stealer ever, who hit only 65 triples over his career, and never more than seven in a season. Tony Gwynn had 85 triples.

Percentage of Hits. A triple by the 2000s was only 2.1% of hits, compared to 11.8% for home runs.

Most/Inning. In 1882 Joseph Hornung of the Boston Red Stockings had two triples in one inning, the first of a handful of players to do so. The club had four triples in the inning, a total never exceeded.

On May 15, 1997, three Cubs tripled in the same inning against the Padres in an 8–2 Cubs win. Sammy Sosa, Brian McRae and Doug Glanville all tripled in the 7th inning off pitcher Tim Scott.

Most/Game. The Major League record is four in a game, by Bill Joyce of the Giants on May 18, 1897.

The American League record is three, last tied by Lance Johnson of the White Sox in September 1995. The last player before Johnson to do it was Ken Landreaux of the Twins on July 3, 1980. The first player to hit three triples in an American League game was Elmer Flick, who did so on July 6, 1902. The last three National Leaguers to hit three in a game were Rafael Furcal on April 21, 2002, Herm Winningham on August 14, 1990, and Shawon Dunston on July 28, 1990.

Twice in 1900 Dodger shortstop Bill Dahlen had three triples in a game, including two in an inning.

Most/Season. Owen Wilson had 36 triples for the Pirates in 1912. The record is amazing because the most he had in any other season was 13. More confounding is that no other player at any level of Organized Baseball in either century has had more than 26. It is not surprising that the season record was set in spacious Forbes Field, famous for yielding triples. Adding to the Forbes Field "triples mystic" was an umpiring decision in the 1903 World Series. For games played in Pittsburgh, the umpires created a "ground rule triple" because of overflow crowds. With 17 triples in four games in the park, it became known as "Triple Paradise." There were 25 triples in the eight-game series.

None/Season. In 2002 A's shortstop Miguel Tejada set a record when he had 662 at-bats without hitting a single triple. He was the American League MVP that season. The previous record for at-bats without a triple was set by Sammy Sosa in 1998, who was the National League MVP that season.

Strong Finish. Lance Johnson led the American League in triples four years in a row between 1991 and 1994. In 1995 he was leading the league going into the last two games of the season. However, Indians outfielder Kenny Lofton hit three triples to tie Johnson and then on the last day Lofton hit another to clinch the league lead.

Famous. In Game 7 of the 1968 World Series, Jim Northrup of the Tigers hit a two-run triple over the head of Cardinals left fielder Curt Flood to drive in the go-ahead run. Flood had misjudged the ball and momentarily froze.

Catchers.

"Players, through the years, have been in the habit of standing around, looking at the ball. The triple mostly comes from running hard right out of the box." — Former catcher and broadcaster Tim McCarver.

In 1966 Tim McCarver became the only catcher to lead the Major Leagues in triples, with 13 for the Cardinals. In 1972 catcher Carlton Fisk of the Red Sox led the American League with nine triples. The next year, he had no triples; possibly the only time in history that a player led in a category one season and then had none in that category the following season.

Infield Triple. In 1947 Jake Jones of the Red Sox was awarded an infield triple after Browns pitcher Fred Sanford tossed his glove at a ground ball.

Tripped Up. In Game 2 of the 1916 World Series, Boston's Chester "Pinch" Thomas drove a ball deep to left centerfield. As he rounded second and head for third, Dodgers shortstop Ivy Olson tripped him. Instead of getting up and running to third, Thomas stayed and brawled with Olson. The umpire broke up the fight and awarded Thomas third base.

First (and only) Game. Ed Irvin had a record two triples in his Major League debut, his only game. It occurred on May 18, 1912, when he substituted along with others for the Tigers' players who were on *Strike*. Irvin also surfaced earlier in the season in answer to an ad by Phillies manager Red Dooin (looking for a catcher), but Irvin wouldn't go down to the minor leagues and therefore didn't sign with the club.

More than Home Runs. The 1979 Astros were the last team to have more triples (52) than home runs (49).

Trivia

"Trying to understand baseball's history through mastery of trivia is like trying to understand the American Civil War through Mrs. Lincoln's dress size." — John Thorn and Bob Carroll in *The Whole Baseball Catalogue* (1990).

"The various details about baseball, according to the last census, amount to 10,051. I do not know all of them and this is fortunate for all concerned." — Fred Schwed, Jr., in *How to Watch a Baseball Game* (1957).

Best Book. Doug Lyons and Jeffrey Lyons, *Out of Left Field* (multiple editions).

Troy Haymakers

National Association 1871–1872

The Troy Haymakers were a notorious amateur team of the late 1860s known for fixing games through their New York gambler owners. Among the owners was congressman John Morrissey, who had been the heavyweight boxing champion in 1858. The club moved into the professional National Association for two seasons beginning in 1871. The first season the club was 13–15 and finished sixth. In 1872 the club was 15–10 and finished fifth.

Troy Trojans

National League 1879–1882

Troy was admitted to the National League in 1879 despite a population below the 75,000 minimum required by the league. Albany was a close natural rival of Troy, and Troy's application to the league was rejected initially when it would not stop playing nonleague rival Albany. Troy was rejected repeatedly by the league in its efforts to admit Albany into the league.

Troy finished last in 1879 with a 19–59 record. It finished much stronger the following season, with a 41–42 record and a fourth-place finish. Mediocrity continued the following two seasons with second-division finishes. Key players over the four seasons were Dan Brouthers, Tim Keefe, Mickey Welch and Bob Ferguson.

The club was weak financially and the league revoked its charter after the 1882 season, when it had to finish the season with cash infusions from other clubs. After the season the franchise moved to New York to become the Giants.

Tryout

"Another source of player supply in the case of the Phillies was an open-door policy. If a young man — he didn't have to be too young — knocked at the door, he was invited to come in and try. He could get into an early game, if he had any talent at all. One or a dozen defeats, what difference? You never knew what the open door might bring — some day a Sisler or a Ruth or a DiMaggio might knock. None knocked at the Phillies' door." — J. Roy Stockton in *The Gas House Gang and a couple of other guys* (1945).

Origins. The Cardinals are credited by some with holding the first Major League tryout camp in 1919 at Robison Field in St. Louis. Tryouts were held routinely in the 19th century, but the Cardinals' efforts may have been the first time that mass tryouts were held in an attempt to find raw talent that could be developed. The top discovery of the Cardinals' first effort was Ray Blades, who was converted from a pitcher to a solid outfielder and had a 10-year career with the club beginning in 1922.

World War II. During the war the Cardinals held a number of tryouts and signed many young players. This was contrary to the policy of most clubs, which were trying to cut costs because of poor wartime attendance. The Cardinals' strategy paid off, as they were one of the strongest teams during and shortly after the war.

Scouting Bureau. All clubs now use the Major League Scouting Bureau for mass tryout camps (see also *Scouts*). The MLSB conducts over 50 tryouts each year around the country for players who are between the ages of 16 and 25. Until the late 1980s, a number of teams still conducted tryouts on their own, including the Braves, Orioles, Cubs, Reds, Tigers, Brewers, Phillies, Mariners and Cardinals.

Pete Rose's Gofer. Pete Rose's long-time gambling buddy and gofer, Tommy Gioiosa, received a tryout with the Orioles in 1981. Rose had arranged the tryout, and Gioiosa received a contract. He was not totally out of his element, as he had played second base and batted over .300 for the University of Cincinnati. At 24, however, he was old for a prospect and was released after spring training in 1982. With nothing else in his life, Gioiosa returned to Cincinnati and continued his relationship with Rose (see *Barred from Baseball*).

Cross-over Sport? Jan Zelezny is a three-time Olympic gold medal winner in the javelin for the Czech Republic. In 1996 he was given a pitching tryout by the Braves on the strength of his amazing arm strength.

Turnstile

"If it gets any smaller, they'll have to put fractions on the turnstiles." — *New York Globe* columnist Mark Roth on the poor attendance of the 1908 Yankees.

"The inventor of the turnstile, that remarkable mechanical device which records admissions to ball parks and other places of commercial amusement, has not yet been honored with a hallowed niche at the Cooperstown shrine, an enormous oversight on the part of the type of baseball magnate that confines his interest in the pastime to the turnstile's merry click." — Lee Allen in *100 Years of Baseball* (1950).

"Jackie's nimble,
Jackie's quick,
Jackie's making the turnstiles click."
— Sportswriter Wendell Smith on Jackie Robinson's effect on Major League attendance.

See also *Ticket Takers*.

Turnstiles were patented in 1876 as Bright's Turnstile. The first ballpark turnstiles appeared in New York and Providence in 1878 and were able to count to 10,000. The early turnstiles were free spinning, so ticket takers had to make sure that one customer came through on each turn and that they received a ticket on each turn. Otherwise, the ticket taker was responsible for the extra customers and had to pay the difference.

To help with the count, the turnstile operators hired "stile boys" at 75 cents per day to help regulate the turnstiles. By the early 1880s turnstiles were mandatory in the National League to calculate *Gate Receipts*, but were not required immediately in the American Association when it began play in 1882.

Twenty-Game Winners and Losers.

"Now let's take the twenty-game winner. He's always given the accolade, no matter what his earned-run average is or how many games he's lost. All right, let's say he's won twenty and lost eighteen. He's two over par. And the only thing you can say about him, if his earned-run average is good, is that he's a fine but vastly overworked pitcher with a bad ball team. Now how about the pitcher who wins fourteen and loses five. Do you ever hear about him? Maybe. Casually. But since he didn't reach the magic number of twenty — though his record is far more helpful to a team — he's passed over. This is stupid. It's the result of 'thinking' without using your brain. Baseball is full of it, and sportswriting is made up largely of it. Let's call it the superstition of the twenty-game winner." — "The Old Timer" in W.R. Burnett's *The Roar of the Crowd* (1964).

"It's the damnedest thing. All my life I've been trying to win 20. This year I win 24, and all anybody asks me about is home runs." — Yankee pitcher Whitey Ford in 1961 when Roger Maris and Mickey Mantle staged their assault on Babe Ruth's home run record.

"They do have the damnedest ideas. 'If you only come up with three twenty-game winners, you'll be all right.' Well, who the hell wouldn't." — Cubs owner Phil Wrigley on fan phone calls that he picked up himself; quoted by William Furlong in the *Saturday Evening Post*.

Team/Four Pitchers. The 1920 White Sox had four 20-game winners: Red Faber, Eddie Cicotte, Lefty Williams and Dickie Kerr. Near the end of the 1921 season Cicotte and Williams were implicated in the Black Sox scandal.

The 1971 Baltimore Orioles had four 20-game winners: Jim Palmer, Dave McNally, Mike Cuellar and Pat Dobson. All but Dobson had won 20 or more for the Orioles the year before; Dobson had won 14 with the lowly Padres before being traded.

15 Wins. Although perhaps not quite as impressive as 20-game winners, the 1998 Braves had five 15-game winners: John Smoltz, Greg Maddux, Denny Neagle, Kevin Millwood and Tom Glavine. The last team with five was the 1930 Washington Senators.

25-Game Winners. The last time that either league had more than one 25-game winner was 1946: Boo Ferriss of the Red Sox (25), Bob Feller of the Indians (26) and Hal Newhouser of the Tigers (26).

200 Wins/No 20-Win Seasons. Five pitchers have won over 200 games in their careers but never won 20 games in a season. The list, (with highest season win total):

245	Dennis Martinez	(16)
240	Frank Tanana	(19)
220	Jerry Reuss	(18)
216	Charlie Hough	(18)
209	Milt Pappas	(17)
200	Chuck Finley	(18)

Last-Place Club. Ned Garver and Steve Carlton are the only players to win 20 games for a last-place club. Carlton won 27 games for the 1972 Phillies. Garver won 20 for the 1951 Browns, winning his last four starts of the season.

Irv Young won 20 games for the 1905 Boston Beaneaters (Braves), who came in seventh despite losing 103 games.

Least Innings/Twenty Wins. Rookie Bob Grim of the 1954 Yankees is the only pitcher to win 20 games with less than 200 innings pitched. He had eight relief wins over his 199 innings. Grim had calcium deposits on his elbow which limited his effectiveness.

20 Wins/Two Teams. In 1984 Rick Sutcliffe became the first pitcher since Hank Borowy in 1945 to win 20 games while pitching for two different clubs in the same season. Sutcliffe, 20–6, played for the Indians (4) and Cubs (16), and Borowy, 21–7, played for the Yankees (10) and Cubs (11). In 2002 Bartolo Colon won 10 games each for the Expos and Indians.

Fewest Appearances. Ernie Bonham pitched for the 1942 Yankees. He won 22 games in only 28 appearances, the fewest ever for a pitcher who won at least 20. He made 27 starts while leading the league in shutouts (six), winning percentage (.808) and complete games (22).

Youngest. Bob Feller was 20 years, 10 months when he won his

20th game for the Indians in 1939. Dwight "Doc" Gooden won his 20th for the Mets in 1985 when he was 20 years, nine months to break Feller's record (Gooden won 24 for the season).

Most Years In Between. In 1998 David Cone won 20 games for the Yankees, 10 years after he did it in 1988 for the Mets. He broke the record held by Jim Kaat, who went nine years between 20-win seasons; 1966 for the Twins and 1975 for the White Sox. Kaat was a Yankee broadcaster when Cone broke his record.

19th Century Rookies. There were 37 players in the 19th century who won 20 or more games in their rookie seasons.

Three Decades. Roger Clemens, Tom Seaver and Warren Spahn are the only three pitchers to win 20 games in each of three decades.

Oldest First-Timer. In 2001 the Mariners won their 116th game of the season to set a new American League record. In the process, Jamie Moyer became the oldest first-time 20-game winner, at age 38.

Twenty Game Losers.

"I'm having fun with it now. But when I was doing it, it was a nightmare. My dream as a kid was to get to the big leagues. I guess I wasn't specific enough. I should have said my dream was to get to the big leagues and be successful."— Former A's pitcher Brian Kingman, who lost 20 games in 1980, the first pitcher to do so since 1922. Kingman was also that first pitcher since 1922 to lose 20 games with a winning team. After two more dismal seasons (7–18 collectively), he pitched eight innings in the Major Leagues in 1983, pitched in the minors in 1984, and then retired to a successful real estate and business career. One of his friends later created a website to honor his achievement, 20gamelosers.com. Kingman managed to maintain some notoriety over the years despite a 23–45 record over five Major League seasons.

Jim Abbott came close in 1996 when he was 2–18. When Omar Daal was 3–19 in 2000 for the Phillies and had two starts left, Kingman flew in to see both games — one win and a no-decision. Kingman rooted for wins in both games. His rationale: "Right now I'm the answer to a trivia question. But whenever anyone loses 19, I'm on trivia death row."

He had another scare in 2001 when Albie Lopez lost a total of 19 games for the Devil Rays (5–12) and Diamondbacks (3–7). Lopez threw a three-hit shutout on October 5, 2001, to clinch the Western Division title for Arizona and avoid his 20th loss. Kingman had created a group of voodoo dolls to scare off potential losers.

It all came crashing down in 2003, when the futile Tigers had two players approach the magic mark. Mike Maroth and Jeremy Bonderman both had lost 15 games when Kingman began to take interest. Maroth finally broke through with his 20th loss in September, but Bonderman was held out at the end of the season to avoid the dubious distinction. Kingman followed Maroth around to his starts, hoping to see him avoid the magic number as Kingman enjoyed his celebrity status as the last to reach the mark. Maroth finished the season with 21 losses (but won his first start of 2004), but became a father in October. Ever the optimist, he named his son Nolan. Kingman's melancholy rationale: "I wish I had been the first to lose 20 games, because then they could never take it away from me."

Missed. See *Ejections*—Touching Umpire for the story of Dave Wickersham's ejection from a game that would have been his 20th win of the season.

Twins

"No other left-hander gave me so much trouble. When I think about how many points in Earl Averill's lifetime batting average came off Gomez deliveries, I thank the good Lord he wasn't twins.

One more like him would probably have kept me out of the Hall of Fame."— Lefty Gomez quoted in the *National Hall of Fame and Museum Yearbook 50th Anniversary*, edited by Bill Guilfoile (1989).

"'Twins,' the wizard proclaimed proudly, pressing the newly taut skin on Fernadella's belly. 'Twin sons.' The inside of the wizard's tent was stifling and smelled of fruit rinds and stale clothing…. 'Twin sons who will be great, no, not just great, but two of the greatest baseball players ever to originate in the Dominican Republic,' … "—W.P. Kinsella in "The Battery" (1984).

Major League Twins. According to one source, until Jose and Ozzie Canseco in the late 1980s, there was only one other known instance of twins playing in the Major Leagues: Ray and Roy Grimes in the 1920s. This is in error, as at least six other sets of twins played in the Major Leagues: John and Phil Reccius played for the Louisville Eclipse club of the 1882–1883 American Association. Their older brother Bill briefly managed the club.

Bill Hunter played outfield in 16 games for the Indians in 1912, and George Hunter played 45 games for the Dodgers in 1909–1910.

Joe and Red Shannon played together in 1915 for the Boston Braves, and Red went on to play another 11 seasons in the Major Leagues.

Bubber Jonnard batted .230 in 103 games in the 1920s and twin brother Claude was 14–12 as a pitcher that same decade.

Johnny and Eddie O'Brien played second base and shortstop for the 1953 Pirates and both later pitched for the club. There final pitching statistics were a mirror image of each other. Johnny gave up 61 hits in 61 innings and Eddie gave up 16 hits in 16 innings.

Mike and Marshall Edwards were another pair; their younger brother Dave also played in the Major Leagues. Mike batted .250 as an infielder for the A's and Pirates between 1977 and 1980. Marshall played for the Brewers and was among the players featured in the classic *Nine Innings*, by Daniel Okrent (1985).

Stan and Stew Cliburn played for the Angels in the early 1980s.

Tiger infielder Tom Brookens came close to being part of this group, as his twin brother made it to the high minor leagues.

Mirror Image Twins. Eric and Derek Spielhagen were identical twins who in 1992 played on the baseball team at Woodberry Forest (Va.) School. The seniors each batted .486 with 17 hits in 35 at-bats.

Two Sets. In March 1993 Virginia Military Institute (VMI) faced Duke in an intercollegiate baseball game. In the 9th inning both clubs had a battery consisting of identical twins: Merlin and Marlin Ikenberry for VMI and Phil and Matt Harrell for Duke.

Battery. This author's identical twin daughters, Katherine and Elena, were the battery for their 8-under softball team (coached by the author), but ballet swept away Elena two years later.

Two Hundred Hits   See *Hits*

Two-Sport Players   See *Basketball*, *Bowling*, *Boxing*, *Football*, *Golf* and *Hockey*

"U would be Ubbell
If Carl were a cockney;
We say Hubbell and baseball
Like football and Rockne."
—Ogden Nash on Carl Hubbell.

Ugly Ballplayers

"So What? Ya don't hit the ball with your face." — Yogi Berra to Mike Ryba after being described as having the "ugliest face in baseball."

"I don't know if we'll be the oldest, but we'll certainly be the ugliest." — Forty-year-old Yogi Berra when he came out of retirement briefly to catch for 44-year-old Warren Spahn for the 1965 Mets.

"He's got the kind of face, if he came into your home with your daughter, you'd disown them both." — Sportswriter Bob Verdi on Gorman Thomas.

"You scare people — you could be anything in the jungle but the hunter." — Luis Tiant to Gorman Thomas.

"I do know one thing for sure. He's got a chance to be a member of the all-ugly club." — Scout Grady Hatton on Fernando Valenzuela's potential.

"He's so ugly. When you walked by him, your pants wrinkle. He made fly balls curve foul." — Mickey Rivers on teammate Danny Napoleon's looks.

"He is so ugly he should have to wear an oxygen mask." — Mickey Rivers on teammate Cliff Johnson's looks.

Umpires

"Ideally, the umpire should combine the integrity of a Supreme Court judge, the physical agility of an acrobat, the endurance of Job and the imperturbability of Buddha." — "The Villains in Blue," in a 1961 *Time* magazine article.

"It's the only occupation where a man has to be perfect on

Long-time Orioles catcher Andy Etchebarren, who sometimes made various "Ugly Ballplayers" lists. Not a bad looking guy, actually, despite the "unibrow." "All-hairy" team perhaps.

Opening Day and improve as the season goes on." — Variations of this quote have been attributed to many umpires and others.

"They're submerged in the history of baseball like idiot children in a family album." — Sportswriter Furman Bisher.

"Umpire's Heaven is a place where he works third base every game. Home is where the heartache is." — Ron Luciano.

"Many fans look upon an umpire as a sort of necessary evil to the luxury of baseball, like the odor that follows an automobile." — Christy Mathewson.

"Umpiring is best described as the profession of standing between two seven-year-olds with one ice-cream cone." — Umpire Ron Luciano.

First-Known Umpire. Many sources have reported incorrectly that Alexander Cartwright of the New York Knickerbockers was the first umpire in 1846. He apparently was an umpire on occasion, but the Knickerbocker scorebook does not identify him as the umpire of the alleged "first game" of June 19, 1846 (see also *Origins of Baseball*).

The same scorebook reflects an earlier game of October 6, 1845, in which attorney William R. Wheaton is identified as alternating between player and umpire. Wheaton also sat on the club's by-laws committee.

Early Amateur Umpires.

"The average umpire is a worthless loafer." — 1880 editorial in the *Chicago Tribune*.

In 1850s games between amateur teams, one umpire stood on the first base side while advocates for each team sat together on the third base side. They would argue their respective positions and the neutral arbiter would have the final say. This practice was abandoned by 1858 pursuant to the amateur National Association rules.

19th Century Professional Umpires.

"To secure the presence of intelligent, honest, unprejudiced, quick witted, courageous umpires at all contests in scheduled games has been one of the most vexatious problems confronting those in control of our national sport." — Albert Spalding.

William McLean was considered one of the first, if not the first, professional umpire. He received $5 per game and was paid to travel from city to city to umpire games.

In the 1871–1875 National Association the home club chose the umpire from among five names submitted by the visiting team. This practice was carried forward into the National League until 1879 when the league created a list of 20 umpires, and clubs could choose from among them.

National League president William Hulbert purportedly was sympathetic to the umpires, who were low paid and usually had little education. In early 1882 he ruled that no umpire could work in his home city or live in a league town. Hulbert also ended the practice of allowing the team captains to agree upon an umpire from the list, and he formed a staff of trained umpires who were assigned to games by the league. In 1882 umpires were told to stop soliciting the opinions of players and fans.

The American Association, organized in 1882, was more formalized in its treatment of umpires. Four regular umpires were paid $140 each month, or about $1,000 for the season. Association umpires were required to wear coats and caps and were given $3 per day expense money. They were required to take an oath of honesty and could not umpire in the city in which they lived. An umpire could be removed from the ranks if five clubs voted against him, if two clubs testified against him, if he was drunk or if he broke various other rules. The National League soon copied these rules and many of its umpires went to the Nick Young **Umpire School** in Washington.

A much trimmer-looking umpire crew meets at home plate with managers Bobby Cox of the Braves and Rene Lachemann of the Marlins.

Early 20th Century Umpires. From its start in 1901 the American League had a stable group of umpires that did not change frequently (continuing a tradition begun by Ban Johnson during the 1890s Western League prior to the league's name change). In contrast, prior to World War I the National League annually hired several new and inexperienced umpires who often would be released at the end of the season.

Appeals. See *Appeals.*

Arguments.

"I wouldn't umpire a baseball game for the world; it requires too much judicial and temperamental balance."—Judge Landis more than 10 years before he became commissioner.

"Call me anything, call me motherfucker, but don't call me Durocher. A Durocher is the lowest form of living matter."—Umpire Harry Wendelstedt shortly after Leo Durocher became an unmellowed 69 years old.

"The thing that has surprised me most in baseball is the amount of integrity that most umpires have. It actually took me a while to believe what a good game they'd give you the next night after a blowup."—Earl Weaver.

"President Heydler of the National League is said to have told his umpires to reduce the upper lip extensions (gab to you) of the players, this being the reason for so many expulsions."—*The Sporting News* in 1934.

Bill Klem was the first umpire to "draw the line" in the dirt and dare players and managers to cross it. Klem was a rookie umpire in 1905 when he ejected Giants manager John McGraw the first time they met. Klem was reversed on baseball decisions by the league office only two times in his career, once each in 1911 and 1934.

During an argument with umpire Beans Reardon, Casey Stengel lay down on the ground to continue his ranting. Reardon promptly lay down next to him and fired back, prompting Stengel

to say later: "When I peeked out of one eye and saw Reardon on the ground, too, I knew I was licked."

In 1949 Andy Pafko argued strenuously with umpire Al Barlick that he had caught a ball, rather than trapped it as Barlick had ruled. While the argument raged, batter Rocky Nelson rounded the bases for a 220-foot home run.

In 1956 Reds outfielder Frank Robinson was called out on strikes during an argument with umpire Larry Goetz, after Goetz ordered pitcher Steve Ridzick of the Giants to continue pitching while Robinson continued arguing.

Mets pitcher David Cone once argued so fiercely on a call at first base that he neglected to notice that two runners scored while he held the ball during the tirade.

In Game 2 of the ALCS against the Indians in 1998, Yankee second baseman Chuck Knoblauch was responsible for the loss in the 12th inning of the 4–1 Indians victory. With Enrique Wilson on first and none out, Travis Fryman laid down a bunt that Yankee first baseman Tino Martinez fielded inside the line. Martinez's throw to Knoblauch covering first hit Fryman in the back and caromed 20 feet away. Instead of grabbing the ball, Knoblauch ignored it to argue with umpire Ted Hendry, claiming interference by Fryman. During the debate, Wilson rounded the bases to score the tiebreaking run. The Indians went on to score two more runs to seal the victory and even the series.

Attacks.

"Mother, May I slug the Umpire, May I Slug him right away?
So he cannot be here, mother, when the clubs begin to play?
Let me clasp his throat, dear mother,
In a dear, delightful grip with one hand, and with the other Bat him several in the lip.
Let me climb his frame, dear mother, While the happy people shout;

I'll not kill him, dearest mother, I will only knock him out.
Let men mop the ground up, mother, with his person, dearest, do;

If the ground can stand it, mother, I don't see why you can't too.
Mother, may I slug the umpire, slug him right between the eyes?
If you let me do it, mother, You shall have the champion prize."
—1886 poem.

"During the excitement between the umpires and the players, someone hit [umpire Bill] Dineen with a bag of peanuts. Wasteful extravagance." — Colorful sportswriting in the *New York Times* in 1920.

"I've been mobbed, cussed, booed, kicked in the ass, punched in the face, hit with mud balls and whiskey bottles; and had everything from shoes to fruit thrown at me … an umpire should hate humanity." — Umpire Joe Rice.

"They shot the wrong McKinley!" — Yelled at American League umpire Bill McKinley, namesake of the assassinated president.

"If plunking down his silver piece entitled a fan to make tin gods of baseball heroes, the same act qualified him to make devils of others. But why they chose to add umpires to the company of the damned requires more consideration." — David Quentin Voigt in *American Baseball* (1966).

See also **Deaths**.

In 1884 the Baltimore franchise installed a barbed wire fence to protect the umpires, and police escorts often were necessary.

In 1899 Jimmy Sheckard of the Orioles attacked an umpire.

A crowd of 200 attacked an umpire at the Polo Grounds in 1884.

Umpire Hank O'Day, a former player, was beaten by a crowd in St. Louis until he was rescued by players and police.

Umpire Tom Lynch recalled that during the 1890s, two mastiffs were sometimes chained to the wall in distant center field during games at one ballpark. After one hotly contested game, the mastiffs were let loose to attack Lynch.

Tom Connolly was hit in the mouth with a bottle after calling out Ty Cobb for stepping out of the batter's box.

Clarence "Brick" Owens earned his nickname by having one thrown at him.

When ex-umpire Nick Young took over as National League president in the late 19th century, wrangling with umpires by ballplayers was a key problem. It was hoped that his background in the profession could help alleviate this.

In 1887 Young told his umpires to give "the closest call and most doubtful decisions to the home club" to keep order. An umpire who quit in the 1880s needed more protection: "Some defensive armor for protecting the umpire against bad language and beer glasses is imperatively called for."

In 1898 Reds owner John Brush proposed a series of rules, known as the Brush Resolution, designed to protect umpires. The 21-point plan adopted by the National League barred "villainously foul language" and created a disciplinary board. The board never worked and no grievances ever made it to the board, but players, managers and to some degree fans reportedly became more respectful.

Umpire Tom Connolly umpired the first American League game on April 24, 1901, though he almost did not make it. The year before in Albany he was almost killed by a mob of angry fans. He escaped by boat across the Hudson, enabling him to continue his 58 years in Organized Baseball.

In a single week during 1901 the Giants refused to play with umpire William Nash, who was dismissed; Umpire Elmer Cunningham was mobbed by fans in Pittsburgh and knocked down by a player in Cincinnati; and umpire John Sheridan was assaulted by players in Detroit.

All-American Girls Professional Baseball League batter Pat Keagle gives umpire Gadget Ward an earful as catcher Dottie Naum tries to avoid the tirade.

Umpire Bill Summers once was knocked out with a whiskey bottle in Detroit.

On August 21, 1901, pitcher Big Jack Katoll (6'4", 200 lbs.) threw a baseball at umpire Jack Haskell. The toss started a brawl resulting in a split lip for Haskell from shortstop Frank Shugart. Katoll and Shugart were arrested and then suspended.

In 1907 umpire Billy Evans was nearly killed by a bottle thrown at his head, and in 1921 he was beaten by Ty Cobb.

Sherry Magee/Bill Finneran.

"There was that episode, not forgotten by any means, when Magee suffered a lengthy vacation for mussing up an umpire."— Ed M'Grath of the *Boston Sunday Post*.

On July 10, 1911, Sherry Magee of the Phillies, perhaps an epileptic and certainly the 1910 National League batting champion, was called out on strikes and according to some sources "inadvertently tossed his bat." Rather, he was called out on a high third strike by rookie umpire Bill Finneran, and Magee protested by throwing his bat high in the air. Finneran threw him out of the game and an enraged (and apparently hung over) Magee smashed Finneran in the mouth. Bleeding profusely, Finneran fell back, apparently unconscious. St. Louis catcher Roger Bresnahan and the other umpire, Cy Rigler, grabbed Magee and pushed him into the dugout. When Finneran came to, he ran to the Phillies dugout, but he was blocked by Phillies players and the police. Earlier in the game Magee had protested vehemently over being called out on an attempted steal.

Finneran had established himself as a hothead and allegedly had bragged during the season that he was an excellent fighter. Manager Red Dooin said that Magee had served as a peacemaker earlier in the season when Finneran offered to fight Dooin under the stands.

National League president Tom Lynch fined Magee $200 and suspended him for the season. Due to injuries to a number of Phillies and the impending pennant race, the club appealed for Lynch to lift the suspension. He initially refused, but after the Phillies dropped in the standings, Lynch allowed Magee to return early, on August 16.

Ironically, Magee later was a well-respected umpire in the National League, but died of pneumonia in 1929 after only one year in the position.

John McGraw/Lord Byron. In 1917 the Giants manager split the lip of umpire Bill "Lord" Byron. McGraw received a 16-day suspension and a $500 fine.

Cold Move. Hothead Cubs pitcher Dolf Luque once went after umpire Babe Pinelli with an icepick.

Fans.

"If anybody comes on the field, jumps on a player or one of our umpires, the gloves are off. There is not a security guard that's going to stop me."—Umpire Laz Barrera after an April 2003 on-field attack by a fan during a game between the White Sox and Royals. Eric Dybas later pleaded not guilty to felony aggravated battery and one count of misdemeanor criminal trespass.

After a series of 1920s attacks on umpires, *The Sporting News* blamed them on a certain type of fan: "born of foreign parents and high-pitched emotionally."

See *Fans—Attack on Umpires.*

New Rules. In 1927 Judge Landis issued an edict throughout Organized Baseball requiring a 90-day suspension without pay for any ballplayer who attacked an umpire. By the 1940s players were suspended a full year for such an attack.

George Moriarty. On Memorial Day 1932 the umpire enraged the White Sox players in a 12–11 loss to the Indians. In a dugout runway after the game, Moriarty challenged the entire Chicago

team to a fight. In the brawl, Moriarty suffered bruises, a broken hand and spike wounds. Three White Sox players and manager Lew Fonseca were fined a total of $1,350. Pitcher Milt Gaston was suspended for 10 days and the others were suspended for lesser terms, while Moriarty was given a reprimand. Catcher Charlie Berry, who later became an umpire, was involved in the fight.

Moriarty was no stranger to brawls, having been a rough-and-tumble Tigers player and manager. During the heat of the 1915 pennant race in a game against the Red Sox in Detroit, Moriarty belted catcher Bill Carrigan after Carrigan spat tobacco juice in his face. A mob of Tiger fans gathered outside the Red Sox dressing room to attack Carrigan, but a maintenance man disguised him and he was able to slip out to a waiting train.

George Magerkurth. On September 16, 1940, Dodger fans were fired up after the Dodgers feuded with umpire George Magerkurth during the entire game. At the end of the game, a large fan attacked the 6'3", 240-pound umpire before he left the field, knocking him to the ground. The attacker was pulled off by umpire Bill Stewart. The fan was taken to jail and identified as a parole violator. Magerkurth's run-ins with Leo Durocher were legendary, and there is evidence this particular incident was simply a diversion so the fan's pickpocket partner could work the stands.

Ben Chapman. On September 16, 1942, the former Major Leaguer slugged umpire I. H. Case. At the time, Chapman was player-manager of Richmond of the Piedmont League. He received a one-year suspension in 1943 but returned to the Major Leagues in 1944 as a pitcher after a 12-year career as an outfielder. He was 8–6 in 25 wartime appearances.

Johnny Allen. In 1943 the Dodger pitcher was suspended after charging and shaking umpire George Barr because of a balk call. Manager Leo Durocher tackled Allen and broke up the fight. Allen later was traded to the Giants.

Mickey Mantle. Although Mantle did not physically attack an umpire, he was thrown out of a game for playing "umpire dodge-ball" with umpire Bill Valentine. Mantle and some of the other Yankees did not like Valentine. Mantle began taking ground balls in center field and throwing them back to Tony Kubek at shortstop; except that Kubek would intentionally line himself up directly behind Valentine, who would routinely venture into short center field to follow the ball to Mantle. Valentine had to hit the ground twice while ducking throws before throwing Mantle out of the game.

Bill Madlock. In May 1980 National League president Chub Feeney suspended Madlock for 15 days and fined him $5,000 for shoving his glove in the face of home plate umpire Jerry Crawford.

Mike Reilly. In a 1981 ALCS game between the Brewers and Yankees, umpire Mike Reilly was attacked by a fan in the 7th inning.

Earl Weaver. The Orioles manager was suspended in 1982 and fined $2,000 for trying to punch umpire Terry Cooney.

Steve Palermo. See *Murder* for the 1991 parking lot shooting of umpire Steve Palermo that left him disabled.

Julian Tavares. In early June 1996 the Indians pitcher was in the middle of a brawl in Milwaukee when he was grabbed from behind. He reacted by throwing his attacker to the ground. Though Tavarez did not realize that it was umpire Joe Brinkman who grabbed him, Tavarez was suspended for three games.

Roberto Alomar. Alomar became the most reviled man in baseball after a run-in with umpire John Hirschbeck on September 27, 1996. After a disputed call, Alomar exchanged words with Hirschbeck and then spit in his face. A day later he hit a home run that clinched the wild card for the Orioles.

Alomar aggravated matters when he noted that Hirschbeck had become bitter since the 1993 death of his seven-year-old son from a disease known as adrenoleukodystrophy (ALD). Another of Hirschbeck's children suffered from the same disease. Although umpires threatened to strike and many called for Alomar to be suspended for at least part of the postseason, Alomar received a five-game suspension to be served at the start of the 1997 season. At the beginning of the 1997 season, umpires were still furious that Alomar wasn't suspended during the previous season's play-offs. Particularly upset was Bruce Froemming, who said that umpires would be less tolerant of arguing.

Alomar attempted to make amends by donating $50,000 to a foundation that conducted research into the disease suffered by Hirschbeck's sons (see *Charity*). The Orioles matched that amount. Alomar also issued an apology and Hirschbeck later said that he had forgiven Alomar.

Jorge Posada. In 2001 Yankee catcher Jorge Posada was called out on strikes in a game in Toronto. He turned to curse, spit on and bump umpire Andy Fletcher, who Posada mistook for umpire Justin Klemm; Klemm had called Posada out on strikes a month earlier.

Japanese Leagues. On May 6, 2000, in a Japanese league game at the Nagoya Dome against the Yokohama BayStars, home plate umpire Atsushi Kittaka called a third strike on Dragons infielder Kazuyoshi Tatsunami. Tatsunami argued the call, and his teammates rushed from the dugout, surrounding and wrestling with the umpire. Kittaka's uniform was left with spike marks and his ribs were fractured. Three years earlier, Major League umpire Mike DiMuro quit the Japanese leagues after being pushed in the chest by a batter.

Back-Up Umpires. The league offices use a beeper system to alert Class AAA umpires when they are needed to fill in for a Major League game.

Bad Calls.

"Well, I blew it the way I saw it." — Minor league umpire Ralph DeLeonardis.

"I never called one wrong ... from down here [while lightly punching his heart]." — Umpire Bill Klem, although the latter part of the statement was added after he retired.

"You called one right and she fainted." — Nick Altrock to umpire Bill McGowan when McGowan asked him what happened to the woman who was being carried from her seat on a stretcher.

"It was a tough night sleeping last night. Sure, I would have liked another whack at it. It was a close play, and I understand the situation. But every day you turn a new page. You have to." — 21-year umpiring veteran Tim Welke in 2003, after he admitted that replays showed he blew a game-ending call that prevented the Rockies from scoring the tying run.

See also *World Series* — Controversial Calls.

Yankee manager Lou Piniella once disputed a strike call with umpire Steve Palermo by asking "Where was that pitch at?" Palermo replied that a manager in Yankee Stadium, with the long history of the Yankees, should know better than to end a sentence with a preposition. Piniella rephrased the question: "Where was that pitch at, asshole?"

Bending Over.

"He brushed home plate 'with the flurry of a fox terrier digging out a mole.'" — Description of the technique by minor league umpire Harry "Steamboat" Johnson.

Umpires are required to face the crowd when they bend over to clean home plate, for reasons that should be obvious given the girth of many umpires.

Benefits. See **Salaries and Benefits**.
Black Umpires. See *Black "Firsts"* — Umpires.
Brothers. See *Brothers* — Umpires.
Burial. See *Burial and Cemeteries*.
Chest Protectors. See **Equipment**.
Chief Umpire. In 1895 Harry Wright of Boston Red Stockings fame was appointed as the first chief umpire in the Major Leagues. The title was honorary and awarded to provide him with a pension for his long service to baseball.

The ceremonial position was filled again in 1900 by former Giants owner John B. Day to provide him with a stipend. Day did some work by going out to investigate and report to the National League president, but he had no real authority. Other former umpires have held the title, including Bill Klem, though by the mid–20th century the job had a legitimate purpose. The modern Coordinator of Umpires worked out of each league office (until consolidation of the leagues) and the crew chief is the senior umpire in a regular group of four.

Clothing.

"He wore gray checked trousers, a horrid mustard-colored tweed coat with a plaid check overlay in red and green. His shirt was a gray-and-brown awning stripe worn with an orange necktie. From his pocket peered a dreadful Paisley handkerchief of red and yellow. On his head he wore a broad flat steamer cap of Kelly green with a white button in the center.... This sartorial catastrophe stalked to the plate ... and against a gasping roar that shook the girders of the field dedicated to Charlie Ebbets, called 'Play ball! Anybody makes any cracks is out of the game!'" — "The Umpire's Revolt," by Paul Gallico (1954).

Umpires in the 1850s and 1860s often wore top hat and tails and were seated at a table along the baseline. In the 1930s National League umpires wore white pants on Sundays and holidays. In the 1950s National League president Warren Giles allowed his umpires to shed their coats and ties on hot days. Also during the 1950s small uniform numbers were added to National League umpire uniforms, a feature absent in the American League until the early 1970s.

Until the 1960s, American League umpires were required to wear full suit and tie regardless of the weather, but the National League allowed a bit more flexibility. In July 1936 a heat wave persuaded National League president Ford Frick to allow them to work in shirtsleeves. In the early 1950s, the National League provided umpires with blue tropical shirts for July and August.

In 1913 American League president Ban Johnson announced that his umpires would wear fashionable white flannels on special days. In 1926 the league tried light brown khaki suits for summer games. In 1927 they wore blue blazers and gray slacks, but the crowds ridiculed them and they reverted to blue suits until the 1960s. The National League went to white pants for a brief period in the late 1930s, but players spit tobacco juice on them and the dirt was horrendous. In 1952 umpires were outfitted in jumpsuits and photos at the Hall of Fame show them looking like "garage mechanics," according to researcher Beth Martin.

In 1968 the American League became the first to issue blue coats and gray pants to its umpires. The league then switched to royal blue blazers, then burgundy blazers with black pants, blue shirt and red cap. In 1976 American League umpires again wore gray pants, which the National League umpires had already worn for many years. American League umpires added a few new colors to their wardrobes in 1996 and wore turtlenecks and tee shirts in red for special occasions. They continued to wear blue for regular games, as the National League continued to do at all times.

With the melding of much of the two leagues' umpiring rules and styles in 1980, league emblems were worn on the jacket pocket and on the cap (AL or NL). In 1988 they wore numbers on their right sleeves.

Coaching. Joe Cronin once pinch-hit in a meaningless late-season game. He asked umpire Cal Hubbard what he could expect from the pitcher. Hubbard told him that based on past performance, Cronin would see a curveball on the first pitch and that he should swing because he would see nothing but knuckleballs after that. He got a hit on the first pitch, a curveball.

Consecutive Games/Longest Careers. In the American League, Tom Connolly umpired for 31 Major League seasons from 1901 through 1931 and worked eight World Series. He preceded that with seven seasons in the minor leagues.

Bob Emslie worked 39 professional seasons, including 36 in the National League between 1889 and 1924.

Bill Klem worked 37 years in the National League beginning in 1905 and worked 18 World Series. He had three more seasons in the minor leagues for a total of 40 professional seasons.

Bill McGowan worked 38 professional seasons, including 32 American League seasons between 1925 and 1956.

Harry "Steamboat" Johnson worked 37 professional seasons, 1910–1946. They included 5,700 games, 54 of which were in the National League and the rest in the minor leagues. He was reported as having worked 4,400 straight games over 27 seasons in the Southern Association.

American League umpire Bill McGowan umpired 2,541 consecutive games between 1925 and 1954, covering over 16½ years (with time out for World War II).

George Hildebrand claimed to have umpired in 3,510 straight games between 1912 and 1934.

Babe Pinelli umpired from 1935 through 1956 and his last game behind home plate was Don Larsen's perfect game during the 1956 World Series. He was a base umpire for the last two games of the Series, though most sources report erroneously that the perfect game was his last game anywhere on a Major League field. In 1979 he wrote a letter to the Society for American Baseball Research to announce that he never missed a game in 22 years. After he retired, the Reds hired him as a West Coast scout.

Consistency Between Leagues. In 1978 Major League officials made several changes to foster consistency between the leagues on uniformity in procedure, position, hand signals, rules interpretation, and dress. The 1979 umpire strike delay implementation, but the 1980s was a time of blending between the two leagues.

Deaths.
"Please do not shoot the umpire; he's doing the best he can."— 1886 Kansas City ballpark sign.

See also *Burial and Cemeteries*

At least two 19th century minor league umpires were killed by players wielding bats. The umpires were Samuel White in Alabama in 1889 (or 1899, depending on the source) and Ora Jennings in Indiana in 1901.

A Carson City, Nevada, prisoner named Casey was allowed to umpire a full game on prison grounds as a last request. He was then put to death.

American League umpire Cal Drummond died as a result of a blow to his mask on June 10, 1969, in a game between the Orioles and the Angels. He wore the standard bar mask that had very little cushion. He finished the game but later had to be taken to the hospital. He was diagnosed with a blood clot and spent considerable time in intensive care. He recovered sufficiently to umpire in the minor leagues in early 1970, but four hours after a May 1970

game in Iowa, and complaining of dizziness, he died. Ironically, he was to be called back up to the American League on the day he died. He had worked 10 Major League seasons, two All-Star games and two World Series.

Nick Bremigan and Dick Stello both died of heart problems while active umpires.

Lou DiMuro died after being hit by a car following a 1982 White Sox–Rangers game in Texas.

Lee Weyer died of a heart attack in 1988 after umpiring a game in San Francisco.

John McSherry, age 53 (though listed as 51) and 6'2" and 328 pounds, died of a heart attack on the field during a 1996 Opening Day game between the Reds and Expos in Cincinnati. McSherry had been scheduled to undergo tests the next morning for an irregular heartbeat. He had been removed from games before for dehydration and exhaustion and in the past had been ordered to lose weight. When the game was immediately postponed, Reds owner Marge Schott said she felt "cheated" out of her Opening Day festivities.

Delayed Calls.
"Have him fax the call up to the booth."— Bob Costas on the slow calls by umpire Joe Brinkman during Game 6 of the 1995 World Series. The broadcasters also criticized Brinkman because he was standing at least three feet behind the catcher.

Discipline. In mid–2002 Major League Baseball filed suit in New York, asking the court to issue an injunction allowing it to discipline umpire John Hirschbeck for telling a member of his umpiring crew, Mark Carlson, not to warn pitcher Gabe White for intentionally throwing at batter Barry Bonds. Baseball had already issued a warning letter to Hirschbeck on May 10, 2002, accusing him of misconduct during a game on April 28 of that season. The umpire's union attempted to file a grievance regarding the matter, but baseball rejected the request and indicated that arbitration did not cover the subject. When the union indicated that Hirschbeck would not appear at a meeting with Sandy Alderson, Executive Vice Pesident of Baseball Operations, the commissioner's office filed the lawsuit. Eventually it was dismissed.

See also *Fines*—Umpires.

Dishonesty. See *Gambling*—Umpires.

Dressing Rooms. Dressing rooms for umpires were not supplied until 1895. Until then umpires often dressed with or near the players.

Electronic Umpire.
"The suits who run the major leagues.... They've come up with the outlandish idea that — get this — pitches thrown over the plate should be strikes and those that are not should be balls. Whoa."— Tom Verducci in *Sports Illustrated* in 2003 after Major League Baseball began installing QuesTec cameras to measure umpires' accuracy in calling balls and strikes.

The system of rating umpires by using the cameras immediately came under attack, as umpires received grades based on an electronic strike zone established by QuesTec. The "Umpire Information System" was accurate to within half an inch, using technology developed by the military. The goal was to have at least 90% of the calls match the machine. The umpires filed a grievance, alleging that the system wasn't a "reasonable means to assess" their performance. The measurement was generated by several cameras stationed around various stadiums.

Baseball had signed a five-year deal in 2001 with the QuesTec manufacturer to use it as a training aid for umpires. In 2003 only 10 ballparks had the system in place. Operators of the monitors are hired by QuesTec for $100 on a game-by-game basis. Their qualifications: "live within 50 miles of an MLB ballpark, have solid baseball knowledge and be computer literate."

In mid–2003 pitcher Curt Schilling was fined $15,000 for destroying one of the new $5,000 cameras that judged the umpires' accuracy in calling balls and strikes. He and others were complaining that the umpires were calling the pitches far too tightly in order to avoid a reprimand from the league because their calls deviated too significantly from the cameras' determinations.

Tom Glavine was one of the other pitchers especially critical of the system, as he felt that it unfairly squeezed his strike zone. Shea Stadium had the cameras, and Glavine's record early in the season clearly indicated that he was more effective on the road. Umpires were calling more balls, because they wanted to ensure that their often too generous strike zones were cut down to remain in conformance with the regulation strike zone established by the QuesTec cameras.

During one spring training in the 1970s, General Electric installed an experimental electronic device that called balls and strikes.

Equipment. Until the late 1970s umpires were required to pay for their own equipment purchases and upkeep.

Ball and Strike Indicator. Ball and strike indicators record balls, strikes and outs. A crude version was first introduced in the 1880s at 50 cents apiece. The "Umpire's Assistant" was a patented black walnut hand-held indicator with thumb screws to record information.

Umpire Tony Benzon could not hold an indicator in his right hand, as all other umpires did, because he did not have a thumb.

If there is a discrepancy between the scoreboard and the umpire's indicator, the indicator governs.

Ball Bag. Umpires could stuff balls into the pockets of their large jackets, but by the 1960s, when the leagues relaxed their rules about wearing jackets, another means of holding balls had to be developed. The two ball bags kept on the home plate umpire's belt each hold six balls. This method had been used for many years by amateur umpires, so this wasn't a dramatic change.

Broom/Brush. Some sources reported that in the 1890s National League umpires were the first to use small whisk brooms to dust off home plate. American League umpires initially used full-length brooms. After a catcher stepped on a broom, American League president Ban Johnson ordered that the field be clear of brooms. For safety reasons, their long-handled brooms were replaced with pocket-sized brooms in 1904 (or 1910, depending on the source).

Another source reported that an early 20th century player with the Cubs hurt his ankle rounding third when he tripped over a full-size broom. As a result, National League president Harry Pulliam was the first to ban full-sized brooms and require that whisk brooms be carried in the umpire's pocket. Within two years the American League followed suit.

In the 1970s A's owner Charlie Finley supplied umpires with the "Little Blowhard," a battery-powered hand blower used to clean off the plate.

In 2002 umpire John Shulock refused to brush off home plate after Mariners manager Lou Piniella buried it in dirt to protest some alleged bad calls. Mariners catcher Dan Wilson had to borrow the umpire's broom so that his pitcher could see the plate.

Cap. The field umpires wore the "university" style of longer-billed cap. The home plate umpire wore the shorter-billed "Boston style" that would fit under his mask.

Chest Protector.

"My advice to young umpires is to use the old-fashioned rubber-inflated protector at first until you get some experience. The new fiber protector that is worn under the coat is likely to cause you some discomfort and interfere with your movements when you are new to the business. After you have been working for a few months, you can try out one of the light fiber protectors successfully."—Harry "Steamboat" Johnson in his autobiography, *Standing the Gaff* (1935).

"Good, I guess I won't need this."—Umpire Bill Klem while letting the air out of his chest protector after pitcher Al Schacht told him he had already thrown his best fastball 10 times in warm-ups.

"National League umpires wear inside chest *protesters.*"—Jerry Coleman.

Bill Klem is credited by some with inventing the inside chest protector, worn inside the umpire's coat. Klem indicated that American League umpire (1901–1914) Jack Sheridan invented the inside protector after suffering numerous injuries. The heavy cardboard and leather shield, fashioned from a hotel ledger, was worn inside the coat and was about 20 inches by 10 inches.

Klem claimed that the inside protector gave him a better view of the ball. Before that umpires used a "balloon," the name for the outside protector because it had an inflatable bladder that deflated for travel and was worn outside the coat. This protector was advertised by A.J. Reach Co. as early as 1906, with a 1903 patent, offered at $12. The outside protector evolved in design to where it could not be deflated. Therefore, two outside protectors were kept at each ballpark so that umpires did not have to travel with them.

Klem was the dean of the National League umpires in the 20th century (1905–1941), so the inside protector eventually was made mandatory for all National League umpires. The only exception was Jocko Conlan, who was given a five-year reprieve. Conlan had a throat problem and was allowed to continue wearing the outside protector because it afforded greater protection. The American League stayed with the larger outside protector for most of the 20th century. Conlan developed the "mattress" protector, made by the Wilson Sporting Goods Company in 1950.

By the mid–1960s the American League office was quietly encouraging its umpires to use the inside protector, in part, some speculated, to look better on television. In 1975 American League president Lee MacPhail made it optional to wear either an inside or outside protector. For the 1977 season, the inside protector was made mandatory for all new American League umpires. The last umpire to wear an outside chest protector was Jerry Neudecker in 1985.

The different protectors had an effect on how the umpires in each league viewed and called balls and strikes. With the less cumbersome inside protector, National League umpires were able to squat lower and peer from the side of the catcher and thus called more low strikes. American League umpires looked more over the shoulder of catchers and called more high strikes.

Face Mask. Nineteenth century umpire Dick Higham, later barred from baseball for **Gambling**, is credited as the first umpire to wear a face mask. They adopted the basic catcher's mask on the market in the 1880s. In 1918 Sears, Roebuck offered a neck-protecting mask for $3.

Twentieth century umpire Jack Sheridan wore only a mask, disdaining shin guards or a chest protector. The modern umpire's face mask is heavier than the catcher's flip-off mask. Umpires pay for their own masks.

Shinguards. Shinguards were in standard use by umpires by 1911, worn under their pants. Umpire Jocko Conlan once was saved from some nasty bruises by his shinguards. Manager Leo Durocher made the mistake of getting into a shin kicking contest with Conlan in 1961. An umpire's shinguards are not as big as a catcher's because they are worn under the pants.

Shoes. By 1906 umpires could buy a kit to screw in spiked plates to prevent slipping on the field. An umpire's shoes are now fitted with a steel toe, which has been available at least since the late 1930s for $22.50. The Major League Umpires Association has its own shoe endorsement.

Evaluation System. In 1995 the first group of Major League umpire evaluators were chosen by the league presidents. The American League's choices were former Major Leaguers John Roseboro and Billy Sample, as well as Phil Janssen, the coordinator of umpire supervision for the American League since 1992. The National League chose former umpires Doug Harvey and Steve Palermo.

See also, **Electronic Umpire.**

Expenses. See **Salaries and Benefits.**

Fan Appreciation.

"Burnham had a little watch;
Its face was white as snow,
And everywhere that Burnham went
The watch was sure to go." — First line of an 1883 poem about umpire George Burnham. It was inspired by his scheme to have himself presented with a watch by the fans in Baltimore. In July 1883 Burnham was abused by fans in Chicago, so he arranged secretly to be presented with a watch by Baltimore fans "in appreciation of his umpiring skills." Word leaked out that he had orchestrated the gift, and he was known forever after as Watch Burnham.

On July 9, 1911, in Tacoma, Washington, the teams staged an Umpire Day. The umpires were presented with flowers and the teams agreed not to engage in any arguing with the umpires.

Father and Son Umpires. See *Fathers and Sons*—Umpires.

Feuds. See *Feuds*—Umpires.

See *Ejections* for the long-time feud between Orioles manager Earl Weaver and umpire Ron Luciano.

Fielding. Between innings of a game in 1969 a Major League umpire took the first baseman's glove sitting on the field (the first baseman had run into the dugout) and threw ground balls to warm up the other infielders.

Fights. See *Fights*—Fights Started by Umpires.

Fines/Ejections. See *Ejections* and *Fines*—Umpires.

Former Major League Players. Outfielder Bob "Death to Flying Things" Ferguson became an umpire in the 1890s.

Lip Pike, the first well-known Jewish Major Leaguer of the 19th century, umpired in the National League in 1890.

Honest John Kelly played in the National League in 1879, batting .155 as a catcher. He then turned to managing and umpiring. He umpired throughout the 1880s and briefly in the 1890s before becoming a boxing referee.

Outstanding 19th century pitcher Tim Keefe umpired for two years in the 1890s and then went into the real estate business.

Wahoo Sam Crawford umpired in the Pacific Coast League for four years after he retired from Major League Baseball in 1917.

Bob Emslie was the first former Major Leaguer to have an extensive 20th century umpiring career. He pitched for Baltimore of the American Association in the 1880s before joining the National League umpiring crew in 1889. He umpired in the league until 1924.

Ex-Yankees Bill Kunkel and Dale Long (the last out of Don Larsen's perfect game) became umpires after finishing as active players. Kunkel umpired in the American League from 1968 through 1984, the last former player to do so in either league. Long quit before making it to the Major Leagues because the travel schedule was too hard on his family. Kunkel was also a college basketball referee for 20 years.

George Hildebrand was an early spitball pitcher who became an American League umpire after his minor league playing career ended.

Former Yankee pitcher George Pipgras was part of Lou Gehrig Day in 1939 and then umpired the game. One source reported incorrectly that he was the player Gehrig replaced to start his consecutive games streak (apparently confusing Pipgras with Wally Pipp).

Eddie Rommel, the first full-time knuckleball artist who won 27 games one year, was an American League umpire from 1938 through 1959.

Frank Secory played a few games in the Major Leagues during and after World War II before beginning a 19-year umpiring career in the National League ending in 1970.

Early 20th century pitching star Big Ed Walsh hated umpiring and quit after two months on the job in 1922 in the American League.

George Moriarty played and managed early in the 20th century before turning to umpiring (see also *Fights*). In 13 seasons he hit .251 with 248 stolen bases, including 11 steals of home.

Jocko Conlan became an umpire by accident. He played outfield for the White Sox in 1934 and 1935, hitting .264. While a reserve for the club in 1935, he umpired a game after one of the regular umpires passed out from the heat. He began his formal Major League umpiring career in 1941 and retired in 1965.

Firpo "Fred" Marberry, who won 147 games in the Major Leagues, quit in the middle of the 1936 season with the Tigers to take an umpiring job with the American League. He was never assigned to the pennant-winning Tigers that season.

A total of 36 Major League players have gone on to serve formally as Major League umpires. *The Baseball Almanac* reported that there have been over 300 instances in which players were called upon to serve as umpires during games.

Future League Presidents. John Heydler and Tom Lynch both umpired in the 1890s and later became National League presidents. Both said that they often had nightmares of their umpiring days.

Gambling. See *Gambling*—Umpires.

Game Statistics. Umpires call 280–300 balls and strikes per game and call 65–70 runners safe or out on the bases. Over the course of a season they work about 1,400 innings over 180 days and 162 games. In recent years, in-season vacations have been allowed.

Guns. See *Guns*—Umpires.

Hall of Fame. The following eight umpires have been inducted into the Hall of Fame: Al Barlick, John "Jocko" Conlan, Nestor Chylak, Tom Connolly, Billy Evans, Cal Hubbard, Bill Klem and Bill McGowan.

Hand Signals. According to long-time Tigers outfielder Sam Crawford, deaf mute outfielder Dummy Hoy is responsible for the use of hand signals by umpires to call balls and strikes. Hoy played primarily in the National League from 1888 through 1902. This is probably a myth, however.

Some sources credit long-time umpire Cy Rigler (1905–1922 and 1924–1935) as the first Major League umpire to use his right hand to signify strikes. He first did it in approximately 1904 in Evansville, Indiana, the year before he moved to the National League. In 1929 Rigler experimented with a microphone and speaker in his mask, but it never caught on. The equipment included wires in his shoes and an underground amplifier to pick up the sound.

Another reason for the use of hand signals by umpires early in the 20th century was because fans and players could not hear the umpires' calls. The *Spalding Guide* once reported that umpires were against the use of the signs. Bill Klem is credited by some with the first "fair" and "foul" signs.

Injuries/Pitched Ball. In a game on May 31, 2002, between the Devil Rays and A's, home plate umpire Steve Rippley was forced to leave the game after being hit in the head by a pitch from Tampa Bay's Lee Gardner. The ball hit batter Adam Piatt and deflected off catcher John Flaherty before hitting Rippley. He suffered a small fracture between his left temple and cheekbone but never lost consciousness while being removed on a stretcher.

On July 13, 2003, umpire Marty Foster sustained a concussion and had to be removed from the field on a stretcher when he was hit on the mask by a pitch from the Expos' Britt Reames.

Instant Replay. See *Instant Replay*.

Judgment Calls.

"He ain't nothin' till I say so." — Umpire Bill Guthrie.

"If you don't think you're out, read the morning paper." — Umpire Bill McGowan after a close call at first base.

Players and managers were not allowed to *Appeal* a judgment call even in the very earliest days of amateur baseball. This was codified in the 1871 National Association rules. In 1882 the National League issued a rule prohibiting umpires from soliciting scoring opinions from fans.

"King of the Umpires."

"Never change a decision, never stop to talk to a player — make 'em play ball and keep their mouths shut and never fear but the people will be on your side and you'll be King of the Umpires." — Former 19th century player and umpire Bob Ferguson.

An early "King of the Umpires" was Billy McLean, an ex-prize fighter who worked in the National Association in the early 1870s. He umpired in the National League through 1884.

Doug Haney was known as the "Lord of the Umpires" in the late 19th century.

James "Honest John" Gaffney was one of the first to be known as "King of Umpires." Gaffney umpired in the 1880s and 1890s and later became part-owner of the Boston Braves.

Tom Connolly umpired in the National League from 1898 through 1900 and in the American League from 1901 through 1931. He worked in eight World Series. When he retired from field duty at age 60 in 1931, he became the Umpire-in-Chief. He remained in the position through age 83. In 1953 he and Bill Klem became the first two umpires elected to the Hall of Fame.

"The Old Arbiter" was umpire Bill Klem, the most famous 20th century umpire. In 1949 the Giants honored him at the Polo Grounds. In his speech Klem said: "Baseball is more than a game. It's a religion to me."

Major League Baseball Umpire Development Program. This organization was created in 1964 to help standardize umpire training by the two primary schools. Most of its members were former National League staff members who urged young umpires to use the inside chest protector.

This is now a 10-person group that supervises and employs all minor league umpires. Its reports are reviewed by the Major League umpire supervisors to find the best of the group for promotion. The 10 earned about $35,000 each in the early 1990s and travel upwards of 35,000 miles each year to evaluate all the umpires in the minor league system.

Managers/General Managers. Umpire Honest John Kelly, already a celebrity at age 30 in the 1880s, managed the Louisville Eclipse of the American Association in 1887. He led the club to a 76–60 record and fourth place.

American League umpire Billy Evans became general manager of the Tigers after working originally as a sportswriter.

Movie. *Kill the Umpire* was a 1950 comedy starring William Bendix about the lifestyle of an umpire. Bendix played Babe Ruth in the 1948 movie of Ruth's life story.

Negro Leagues. Usually there was only an umpire for home plate. The home team would then select a base umpire.

Number of Umpires Used on the Field.

"The double umpires system should be restored, and that speedily in both leagues … reason should tell them that the innovation would prove a good investment. The satisfaction accruing among the patrons of the sport from the change would be sufficient to provide the revenue necessary for the increased expense, in addition to the crowds attending the games. The magnates of the National League used a fine-toothed comb to find an excuse for the abolition of the double umpire system, with which to go before the public, and could only ascribe their change to the burden of the extra expense." — *The Sporting News* in June 1901.

"How the hell can you play 'Four Blind Mice.'" — Dodger Sym-Phoney Band member Lou Soriano in 1952 after the National League began using four umpires in all regular season games. Ebbets Field organist Gladys Gooding first played "Three Blind Mice" as the umpires took the field on May 9, 1942, her second day on the job. "Three Blind Mice" was published on October 12, 1901, reportedly the first secular song to be published in the U.S.

"I would also be pleased to test in a game the plan of having two umpires, one stationed behind the plate to pass judgment on balls and strikes, the other near second base to decide all putouts made on the bases and in the field." — Detroit Wolverines owner Frederick Stearns advocating use of two umpires for the 1887 National League and American Association championship series.

In 1879 the National League chose one umpire for each game among a pool of 20 men. The 1887 postseason marked the first time that two umpires were used throughout a championship series between the National League and American Association winners. The American Association was more progressive, as it used two and three umpires per game at times in 1888. The National League rejected this approach because of the added cost.

In the 1886 postseason championship between the St. Louis Browns and Chicago White Stockings, one umpire was used in Games 1 and 3. In Games 2 and 4, one umpire was chosen by each team, with a third "neutral" umpire, Honest John Kelly, to resolve disagreements.

In 1890 the Players Association, with the best players and umpires, used two umpires (as *Total Baseball* said, "Leave it to the players to understand the importance of having at least two umpires on the field of play.")

In the mid–1890s National League umpire James Gaffney called for two umpires because of more hitting in the league; it was now tougher to follow the base runners and keep up with all the action. The mound had been moved farther away and the increase in offense made it more difficult for the umpires. One source noted that in 1893 the two-umpire system was abolished, suggesting that two umpires had been used more frequently than generally assumed. The 12-team National League of the 1890s had seven umpires to cover six games (one in relief), and occasionally used two per game.

In 1897 the use of two umpires was again debated seriously in the National League, though even three umpires per game had been proposed in the 1880s by Albert Spalding after the American Association's one-year trial in 1888.

In 1895 it was agreed that when two umpires were used, one would stay behind home plate and the other would only assist on the bases as needed. In 1898 the National League formally sanctioned the use of two umpires. This was rescinded for 1900 and re-adopted in 1901. For a time the second umpire was known as the assistant umpire.

In 1906 the American League hired a fifth umpire for its staff, Billy Evans, who had attended Cornell University. One umpire worked each game, with the fifth held in reserve. In 1908 there were still only six umpires on each league staff, with one among them acting as alternate. Each day three of the umpires worked alone and two worked together in the fourth game. In 1909 the National League moved up to seven umpires, and the American League had eight.

In 1910 the National League went to two umpires and never reduced the number again, while the American League went back to seven umpires covering four games. In 1911 they both had eight.

By 1912 two umpires were required to cover each game in both leagues. They gradually increased to three for certain games until 1933, when three-man crews were required for the first time during the regular season. In 1952 four-man crews became standard.

In 1961 the National League used five-man umpire crews (one not on the field) to train new umpires in anticipation of the need for another full crew during the 1962 expansion season. By the mid–1990s there were 64 full-time Major League umpires, with seven reserves per league.

Number Used/World Series. Through 1907 only two umpires were used during a World Series. The 1908 Series had four umpires available, but only two were used at one time. Jack Sheridan and Hank O'Day umpired the first game and Tommy Connolly and Bill Klem the second. One source noted that Klem experienced his second year in a row in which there was a ground rule double controversy, so umpire Billy Evans suggested using all four umpires at the same time. However, Klem did not umpire in the 1907 Series and only two umpires were used in each game of the 1908 Series. Based on the following, it appears that the controversy occurred during the 1909 World Series.

In Game 3 of the 1909 Series between the Tigers and Pirates, for the first time four umpires were used at the same time (one source reported it as Game 2). The decision to use four umpires in this game came about as a result of an incident in Game 2 (reported by some as Game 1), when only two umpires were used. In the first inning, Pirates left-hander Dots Miller hit a line drive to right field (reported by some as left field). Neither of the two umpires saw where the ball landed. Home plate umpire Billy Evans asked the fans where it landed. They pointed, saying that it was a home run, but he nevertheless ruled it a ground rule double. To avoid further controversy, four umpires were used in each of the remaining games and the number stayed at four for the next 38 years.

Cy Rigler called for the use of six umpires in the World Series after the 1925 fiasco involving Sam Rice's alleged outfield catch (see *World Series*—**Controversial Calls**), but nothing changed for another 22 years. In 1940 one reserve umpire was added to the World Series squad of four in case of injury. In 1947 six umpires were used on the field for the first time. The two extras were placed down the foul lines in the outfield but did not rotate with the other four. They were used not because of any controversy over fair or foul calls, but because it was an honor to be in the World Series and the leagues wanted to allow more umpires to participate. The first two foul line umpires were George Magerkurth and Jim Boyer. Beginning in 1964 all six umpires rotated positions during the Series.

Minor Leagues. In the minor leagues, two umpires are used in Rookie and Class A games; three work Class AA and Class AAA games.

Other Career. Umpire Ken Kaiser was a former bouncer and pro wrestler. He wore a black hood, carried an ax and was known as "The Hatchet Man" (as a wrestler, not an umpire).

Position on the Field. In 1888 John Gaffney became the first umpire to move behind the plate to call pitches when there was no runner on base. As late as 1904 most umpires were still stationed by the pitcher when only one umpire was used and runners were on base.

When the use of three umpires was standardized in the 1930s, the leagues differed initially in how base umpires rotated around the infield. In the American League, with a man on first, umpires were stationed at second and third base. The National League put umpires at first and second. Both now use the National League's format when an umpire is unavailable.

In 1973 one of the last differences in field positioning between the leagues was worked out. Before that the American League had the second base umpire stand behind the bag, while the National league umpire stood in front. Both leagues then adopted the National League approach.

Until recently American League base umpires stood in foul ground at the corners, while National League umpires straddled the foul line. Now both leagues have the umpires stand in foul territory.

Pregame Duties. The third-base umpire is required to monitor pregame activities to ensure no fraternization among players. This technically requires him to sit in the stands to watch batting practice. The umpires are also required to rub down balls with a special *Mud* that removes the gloss. Until 1906 umpires were not required to take control of the balls before the game.

Rating.

"It will never happen, because when you do that you've taken away all the alibis. Who can the manager blame losses on? Who can pitcher and hitters blame their troubles on? Believe me, the umpire will always be with us."—Umpire Beans Reardon in 1969, 20 years after he retired. He was friends with Mae West and appeared in a few of her movies. He also had a successful beer distributorship, which he sold to Frank Sinatra for $1 million. He was honored on the "This Is Your Life" television program; representing the fans was Hilda Chester, the "Brooklyn cowbell lady."

The two league offices graded umpires with statistics to see if any were far outside the norm in terms of strike and ball calls.

In March 1999 the Players Association released a survey of the quality of Major League umpires. Tim McClelland (American League) and Jerry Crawford (National League) were rated the highest. Ken Kaiser (American League) and Charlie Williams (National League) were rated the lowest.

Retaliation by Umpires. Umpire Tim Hurst once threw a beer mug at a crowd, hurting a fireman. He was tried and fined $200. Tom Lynch once struck a player, and Billy McLean once threw a bat into the crowd and was arrested.

Umpire Tom Gorman admitted that he called Johnny Bench out on strikes intentionally after Bench refused to autograph a baseball for him.

Retirement. Ed Hurley, home plate umpire when *Midget* Eddie Gaedel came to bat in 1951, sued the American League when it forced his retirement in 1965. The league prevailed.

Umpire Bill Klem retired immediately after a game during the 1941 season when he realized that he was not positive whether a runner had been tagged out. It was his cue that it was time to get out of the game after 37 seasons.

For the Padres' final spring training game in 1993, they asked the league if umpire Doug Harvey could umpire behind the plate.

Harvey had retired after the 1992 season and was to work only that game. However, the league office denied the request because of insurance problems.

Robbery. In 1993 umpire Terry Tata was drugged and robbed by a woman who went to his room with a bottle of wine. He lost his watch, a gold bracelet, two World Series rings and $500 in cash.

Rotation. Four-man umpire crews rotate from home plate backward around the diamond from one game to the next. Umpire Bill Klem refused to work anywhere except home plate for the first 16 years of his National League career. One source reported that it was his superiority in calling balls and strikes that allowed him to stay behind the plate for such a long period.

Rulebooks.

"Keep your eye everlastingly on the ball while it is in play."—Instruction in an early umpire's rulebook.

The "Special Instructions to Umpires" that accompanies the standard Major League rule book is now available to anyone. One source reported that umpiring handbooks existed in 1875. Another source found evidence of handbooks as early as the 1860s.

Former Major League umpires Joe Brinkman and Charlie Euchner wrote the most complete guide to umpiring baseball (and softball), *The Umpire's Handbook* (1987).

19th Century Conduct. In the 1880s under American Association rules, umpires could not enter a poolroom or saloon while in uniform. In the 1890s in the National League, umpires had to be addressed as "Mr. Umpire."

Salaries and Benefits.

"The pay is good and you can't beat the hours — 3 to 5."—1890s umpire Tim Hurst.

"If a player was making $20,000 a year, I would have minded my own business. But I figured out that Jim Rice was making $582 for every strike I called and I was making seven cents. *Seven cents.* There's no way I'm going to keep my place for seven cents."—Outspoken umpire Ron Luciano, who committed suicide in 1995.

19th Century. In 1878 the National League paid $5 for each game. In 1882 the American Association paid its umpires $140 per month and $3 per day for meals, lodging and transportation.

In 1883 the National League appointed four umpires at $1,000 each for the season. Complaints by any team against an umpire were grounds for dismissal of that umpire. Only one National League umpire survived the entire season.

The 1883 *Reach Guide* listed allowable umpire expenses: hotel/travel, meals, tickets and $3 per day maximum for hotel bills. By the 1980s umpires no longer had to pay to drag 75–80 pounds of equipment from city to city. The leagues pay for this now. In the 1990s a Major League umpire received over $150 per day in meal money and flew first class. John Gaffney's salary in 1888 was $2,500 plus expenses, more than many players, which made him the highest paid umpire of the era.

20th Century. In 1944 Bill McGowan was the highest paid umpire in the American League. After 21 years he earned $9,000. Two other strong umpires, George Pipgras and Eddie Rommel, were paid $6,000 each. By 1950 umpires were earning a maximum of $10,000 for the six-month season. In 1945 Ernie Stewart was the youngest umpire in the American League at age 35 and had been in the league for five years. He talked to Happy Chandler about raising umpire salaries and promptly was fired by American League president Will Harridge.

In 1972 the minimum pay was $11,500, plus an increase from $3,000 to $7,500 and then $8,000 per man for working the World Series ($4,000 for the league championship series). In 1975 the minimum was $14,500 and the high was $36,000 for a 20-year man, plus a pension plan and $9,500 for the World Series. There was a $52 per diem expense allowance.

The minimum salaries were $17,500 in 1980 and $26,000 in 1983. The high was $70,000 for senior umpires, with per diem expenses of $77. Umpires received $10,000 for working a league championship series and $15,000 for the World Series. In 1988 the maximum salary was $105,000. Umpires drew a pension at the rate of $1,000 per year for every year of Major League service. They received an in-season two-week paid vacation.

By the late 1980s minor league umpires earned starting monthly salaries of approximately $1,800 in rookie leagues, $1,900 in Class A, $2,000 in Class AA and $2,400 in Class AAA. In the early 1990s the 212 minor league umpires earned $1,700 to $3,100 per month during the season. A Class AAA crew chief earned $3,300 per month, plus an $18 per diem. Rookie Major League umpires earned $65,000, plus $206.50 per diem.

The umpires went on strike during spring training in 1995. They settled in early May, a week after the striking players began the delayed regular season. The umpires received pay raises ranging from 25% to 37.5% over the five-year life of the contract. Rookie umpires were guaranteed $100,000 in salary and bonuses, up from $75,000. Thirty-year veterans could make $282,500, up from $206,000. All umpires who worked the postseason would receive a bonus of $20,000; previously, younger umpires received $10,000 and more senior umpires received $20,000. Crew chiefs receive $7,500 extra, up from $6,000. All-Star bonuses rose to $5,000, up from $2,500. Umpires working the new round of division play-offs received $12,500. Umpires in the league championship series received $15,000, up from $5,000. Umpires in the World Series received $17,500, up from $5,000.

The per diem, out of which umpires still must pay all expenses except air fare, rose from $206.50 to $220. Severance pay rose to $375,000 during the first three years of the contract and to $400,000 during the final two. Under the old agreement, umpires received $100,000 in severance pay and $200,000 in early retirement pay. A salary comparison to other sports in 1995:

	Baseball	*Football*	*Basketball*	*Hockey*
Min.	$100,000	$21,200	$ 68,000	$ 70,000
Max.	$282,500	$78,400	$177,000	$190,000

Substitute Umpires. In July 2004 three college umpires worked the first inning and a half of a game between the Phillies and the Cubs after bad weather forced three members of the regular umpiring crew to change their travel plans. A plane from Cleveland carrying Joe West, Paul Emmel and Mike DiMuro was diverted to Baltimore due to rainy weather in Philadelphia. They finally arrived in the bottom of the second inning as regular umpire Darren Spagnardi, replacing a vacationing Terry Craft, arrived on time and worked the plate. Former replacement umpire Scott Graham, and Frank Sylvester and John McArdle, started the game.

Suspension. In 1948 umpire Bill McGowan was suspended for ten days without salary. He was charged with having thrown a baseball and his ball-strike indicator at Washington Senators players and also with having used offensive language. He was suspended again in 1952 after ejecting a player from a game in St. Louis. Reporters asked him to identify the player; he refused, and a protest was lodged with the league office. League president Will Harridge then suspended McGowan for his action.

In 1990 National League president Bill White was going to suspend umpire Joe West for slamming Phillies pitcher Dennis Cook to the ground, but Commissioner Faye Vincent intervened and no discipline was imposed.

In July 1999 umpire Tom Hallion was suspended for three games based on his conduct during a game on June 26, 1999. He had an argument with Rockies catcher Jeff Reed and pitching coach Milt May after telling Rockies pitcher Mike DeJean to get in the dugout after complaining about a check-swing. It was apparently the first in-season suspension of a Major League umpire.

For umpire Al Clark's problems with memorabilia fraud, see *Memorabilia*—Umpire Fraud.

Umpire Schools.

"We were given lots of abuse to show us what we were getting into. Some kids folded when they were called obscene names but for me it was just like being back in the ghetto."—Black umpire Eric Gregg on umpire school.

Before he became National League president, 19th century umpire Nick Young ran an umpire school in Washington, D.C. Modern umpiring schools have existed since 1935 when George Barr established his program. Hall of Famer Bill McGowan began his school in 1941.

Former umpire Joe Brinkman owned an umpiring school for many years, until he sold out. More recently the Al Somers Umpire School in Florida and the Bill Kinnamon Umpire Schools in California and Florida opened for business. The New York School of Umpiring is also a successful facility. Long-time American League umpire Jim Evans began his umpiring school in the late 1980s.

The Harry Wendelstedt and Brinkman schools have been the premier schools. In 1988, of the 195 umpires working in the minor leagues, 103 came from Brinkman's school and 90 from Wendelstedt's. By 2004 Wendelstedt's school, which had been called the Al Somers School, boasted that it had trained more Major League umpires than all the others combined. Wendelstedt was the chief instructor at the Somers school for 17 years. He was also voted the best umpire in the National League at least four times.

Brinkman's school is located at the old Houston Astros training facility in Cocoa, Florida. Wendelstedt's school is located in Ormand Beach, Florida. Among the 400 new umpiring candidates each year, approximately 10% make it to the low minor leagues. Less than one percent of all Class AAA umpires will ever umpire in the Major Leagues. It usually takes about 7–10 years for an umpire to prove his abilities and make it to the Major Leagues.

Strikes. See **Unions and Strikes.**

Uniforms. Umpire uniforms changed very little over the years until the 1980s, and often reflected the style of the league president or dean of the umpires. Some umpires wore street suits rather than an official blue suit sold by a few manufacturers to this small segment of the market.

Unions and Strikes.

"The way we have been playing I might tell my players not to cross the picket line."—Royals manager Whitey Herzog during an umpire strike.

1968. This was the first year in which umpires made a serious effort to unionize. The Major League Umpires Association was formed on September 29, 1968, with umpire Augie Donatelli instrumental in that effort.

Soon after forming their union, the umpires threatened a general strike unless umpires Al Salerno and Bill Valentine were reinstated by American League president Joe Cronin. Cronin claimed that the two were relieved for "incompetence." The umpires filed an unfair labor practice, claiming that they were fired for trying to organize the union. A strike was avoided through bargaining, and the dismissed umpires pursued their lawsuits independent of a strike by their peers. Though their claims were pursued to the U.S. Supreme Court, they were dismissed for lack of evidence. Valen-

tine was the umpire behind the plate in 1967 when Tony Conigliaro was hit in the face by a pitch.

1970.

"Bush-league bluecoats."—Rogell Angell in *The Summer Game* (1972), describing the replacement umpires used for one game during the 1970 League Championship Series.

On October 3, 1970, Major League umpires staged a one-day walkout from the National League championship series. Umpire Bill Deegan crossed the picket line and the strike was settled the next day. The strike also prompted a reopening of contract negotiations. The resulting agreement increased wages for senior umpires along with new pension benefits and pay raises for postseason games.

1978. On August 25, 1978, umpires went on strike over the $52 daily allowance that had to cover hotel, meals and in-town travel. A federal judge ordered them to work the next day and they complied.

1979. The umpires were on strike from the start of the season until May 19 when they signed a new contract. This led to the hiring of a number of scab umpires, two of whom stayed in the Major Leagues after the strike was settled. Dan Morrison had turned down a scab contract and was hired when Lou DiMuro was injured. The eight new umpires, including Dave Pallone, Fred Brocklander and Darryl Cousins, were ostracized severely by the other umpires throughout the remainder of their careers. Pallone had emotional problems during his career and later revealed that he was a ***Homosexual***. The two former scabs prompted the following comment from umpire Billy Williams, who resented them but worked with them: "Nobody tells me who I have to eat, sleep, or drink with, but when the blue suit goes on, it's a different story."

Pallone was 27 at the time. He once found a padlock on his mask, his cap mangled and his shinguard straps cut. It appeared to many that another umpire had done the damage.

1984. On the day before the league championship series began, the umpires struck over pay for postseason games and job security. All American League championship series games and four of the National League games had to use minor league and college umpires. New commissioner Peter Ueberroth stepped in and settled the dispute before the World Series began.

1987. As a result of another brief late-season strike, senior umpires were to earn as much as $100,000 in 1988.

1991. The umpires struck on Opening Day of the season, but the dispute was quickly resolved.

1994–1995.

"Just do what you always do. Boo the umpires—only do it a little louder."—National League umpire Eric Gregg on what the regular umpires told fans before games umpired by the replacement umpires.

The umpires had a contract clause that allowed them to be paid for the first 75 days of a player strike, which they exercised during the 1994 player strike. The umpires went on their own strike during spring training in 1995. The strike was hardly noticed during the preseason because of the concurrent player strike and the use of replacement players. When the regular players ended their strike, the umpire strike continued into the regular season. Replacement umpires were used for the preseason and the first week of the regular season. A few managers were ejected for arguing what appeared to be obvious mistakes by the umpires.

In April 1995 the Ontario Labor Relations Board of Canada ruled that replacement umpires would be barred from officiating games in Toronto after the Blue Jays' first home stand. The board ruled that the owners had illegally locked out the umpires because neither the teams nor the umpires triggered Ontario's compulsory conciliation process. The strike ended after a week into the regular season, and the umpires received salary and benefit concessions (see **Salaries and Benefits**).

1999–2002. In July 1999 umpire union chief Richie Phillips set in motion a disastrous series of events when he announced that 57 Major League umpires would resign on September 2 if certain demands were not met. The leagues called their bluff by immediately accepting the resignations.

On July 26, 1999, the umpires filed a lawsuit in federal district court seeking to withdraw their mass resignations, but dismissed it on August 10. The American League had already accepted nine of the 14 umpires' attempts to withdraw their resignations. Of the 56 umpires who resigned, 47 were still in limbo at that time. On July 29, 13 of the National League umpires' resignations were accepted by the league.

On August 3, 1999, the umpires filed a grievance with the National Labor Relations Board seeking to block the leagues from using replacement umpires from the minor leagues. A few days later, Phillips announced that he would seek an injunction prohibiting the Major Leagues from firing 22 umpires on September 2. In late August the umpires threatened to go on strike to protest Major League Baseball's failure to accept rescissions of all the resignations. The league presidents warned the umpires that they would be fired if they were to strike.

On September 3, 1999, in a lawsuit filed by the Major Leagues, a federal district court upheld the 22 umpire resignations that the leagues refused to reinstate. After the ruling, several dissident umpires opposed to Phillips announced their intent to form a rival union and seek certification to represent all umpires.

In January 2000 a federal court refused to overturn the November election which ousted Phillips and created a new union to represent the umpires. Of the 93 eligible umpires, 57 voted to form a new organization (one vote was voided because the umpire signed his name).

In February 2000 the National Labor Relations Board certified the election and designated the new World Umpires Association as the new bargaining unit in place of the Major League Umpires Association. About 50 of the 71 umpires joined the new union and Phillips ended 21 years as the head of the Major League Umpires Association. American League umpire John Hirschbeck was elected as the first president of the World Umpires Association.

On July 20, 2000, Major League Baseball offered to rehire 10 of the 22 umpires who were in limbo. The offer was conditioned upon signing a new labor contract, and only if the old union agreed to settle its grievance with baseball. This deal eventually was accepted.

On December 14, 2001, a federal judge upheld an arbitrator's May 2001 decision that ordered Major League Baseball to rehire nine of the 22 umpires who lost their jobs. On February 28, 2002, Major League Baseball announced that it had rehired five of those nine — Gary Darling, Bill Hohn, Larry Poncino, Larry Vanover, and Joe West. The other four — Drew Coble, Greg Kosc, Terry Tata, and Frank Pulli — were allowed to retire. Three more were allowed back in August 2002 — Paul Nauert, Bruce Dreckman and Sam Holbrook. That left 10 still trying to regain their jobs, but the ruling effectively ended the dispute. The 10 who were not reinstated as of late 2004: Bob Davison, Tom Hallion, Jim Evans, Dale Ford, Richie Garcia, Eric Gregg, Ed Hickox, Mark Johnson, Ken Kaiser and Larry McCoy.

Weight Problem.

"Let's not overdo this. I'm an umpire, remember? I only have to call the bases, I don't have to steal them." — Eric Gregg to a trainer helping him to lose some of his more than 300 pounds. At one point Gregg weighed 357 pounds and went on a diet to lose 106. He dropped down to 280 but ballooned up again in 1988. He was required to go to a fat farm in 1989 to lose some of his excess weight. As a result of John McSherry's **Death** in early 1996, the 44-year-old Gregg took a leave of absence to lose 60 pounds. He returned in mid–July.

"One of the misguided, unwritten rules of Major League Baseball says that an umpire shall be a man of considerable bulk. If someone is lacking in substantial height and weight, he at least must stand six feet or over and tip the scales at or beyond the 200 pound mark." — Ed Rumill in *The Sporting News*.

Umpires have been notorious for their weight problems. In 1971 John McSherry was accepted as a National League umpire on the condition that he lose 50 pounds before the season started. He did, but his weight contributed to his heart problems that led to his on-field death.

Umpire Stan Landes was the first president of the Umpires Association. Though he was fired in 1972 after 17 years in the Major Leagues for what some thought were union-related reasons, his weight was the real cause of his problems. He ballooned to 360 pounds before losing 75 in a crash diet. He was also heavily in debt, which made him a potential target of gamblers.

Women Umpires. See *Women — Umpires*.

World Series/Selection. For many years umpires were selected for the World Series based on the quality of their work. There may have been a quiet shift in that attitude by the leagues and key umpires in the 1970s. In 1975 after being chosen for the World Series, Shag Crawford refused to appear because he claimed that the umpires and leagues secretly had worked out a strict rotation system for selecting umpires to the World Series and he believed that the selections should be based solely on quality.

As a result of the umpires' 1987 labor action, umpires again officially rotated on the All-Star Game and all-postseason play. That decision was reversed in 1990 when baseball reverted to a merit system. However, merit was not the sole criterion: American League executive director for umpiring Marty Springstead admitted in 1992 that they selected on the basis of merit among those umpires who had not worked a World Series in some time. The 1992 Series crew was indicative of the problem: three were working their first Series, three had one Series behind them, and none was a crew chief.

Books.

"An umpire actually has lots of time available for literary effort.... It is a wonder so few of them ever have taken time to jot down the stirring events of which they have been the center. Their view of the melodramatic spectacle that is baseball is far different from that of the fan in the bleachers, the players on the field or the sports writers in the press box." — Ed Danforth in the foreword to *Standing the Gaff*, the autobiography of minor league umpire Harry "Steamboat" Johnson (1935, reprinted in 1994). It was the first autobiography by an umpire. The first commercially published umpire's autobiography was by Babe Pinelli in 1953, with sportswriter Joe King, *Mr. Ump*.

See also Eliot Asinof and Jim Bouton, *Strike Zone* (1994) (fiction); Jocko Conlan and Robert Creamer, *Jocko* (1967); Billy Evans, *Umpiring from the Inside* (1947); Larry Gerlach, *Men in Blue* (1980); Tom Gorman as told to Jerome Holtzman, *Three and Two!* (1979); Eric Gregg and Marty Appel, *Working the Plate: The Eric Gregg Story* (1990); Lee Gutkind, *The Best Seat in Baseball, but You Have to Stand* (1975); John Hough, Jr., *Conduct of the Game* (1986) (fiction); James Kahn, *The Umpire's Story* (1953); Ken Kaiser, *Planet of the Umps: A Baseball Life from Behind the Plate* (2003); Durwood Merrill, *You're Out and You're Ugly, Too!* (1998); Ron Luciano and David Fisher, *Fall of the Roman Umpire* (1986), *Remembrance of Swings Past* (1988), *Strike Two* (1984) and *The Umpire Strikes Back* (1982; Dave Phillips with Rob Rains, *Center Field on Fire* (2004).

Underwear

"They're not all alike. Gary wears dirty underwear." — Expos pitcher Steve Rogers comparing clean-cut Gary Carter with squeaky clean-cut Steve Garvey, whose image later was tarnished (see *Sex*).

"Bill Buckner had a nineteen-game hitting streak going and always wore the same underwear. Of course, he didn't have any friends." — Mariners infielder Lenny Randle.

See also *Crotch* and *Jockstraps*.

Babe Ruth. Ruth endorsed a line of underwear even though for much of his career he did not wear underwear. Ruth was criticized early on for wearing the same sweaty underwear both during and after the game. In response he simply stopped wearing underwear for a few years. In 1994 a mint box of Babe Ruth Juniors Underwear sold at auction for $1,523. A single pair once sold for $531.46.

Jim Palmer.

"Cakes [Jim Palmer] has won 240 games, but it took a picture of him standing in his underwear to get nationally known." — Mike Flanagan.

"It's not fair. She ain't seen me in *my* underwear." — Pitcher Sammy Stewart on meeting rock and roll star Joan Jett at a game, only to learn that she was there to meet teammate Jim Palmer.

Palmer was the 1980s glamour boy of the underwear set with his endorsement of Jockey brand underwear.

Bowie Kuhn. For Game 2 of the 1976 World Series on a Sunday during football season, NBC asked to switch the game to the evening. Though it was under 50 degrees in Boston that night, commissioner Bowie Kuhn refused to wear an overcoat to show that baseball was appropriate for late October night play. Unknown to the public, however, he wore long underwear.

Uniforms

"A century of baseball uniform research and design, trial and error, innovation and experimentation, and you get a uniform that looks like it was painted by Earl Scheib." — Columnist Scott Ostler on the uniforms of the expansion Florida Marlins.

"I wrote to him: 'Dear Mr. [Brooks] Robinson: If your uniform isn't doing anything near the end of October would you consider letting me borrow it for Halloween? I'll take really good care of it and send it right back' — you know, the whole thing. I got this letter from him, in his handwriting, a week or two later, saying he thought it was a great idea but the uniform belonged to the Orioles, and I should write to Jack Dunn and tell him Brooks said it was okay. I showed it to an Oakland A's fan and he said, 'Wow! That's like getting a letter from God!' I wrote the next letter and then I received this package with Brooks Robinson's home uniform.... You could tell it was real because there was a button missing and the leg was worn from sliding.... I was on cloud nine." — Stephanie Vardavas, a lawyer in the commissioner's office, on a letter she wrote as a young girl to Brooks Robinson, as described in a SABR publication.

Early Uniforms.

"1. Double-shrunk virgin wool flannel

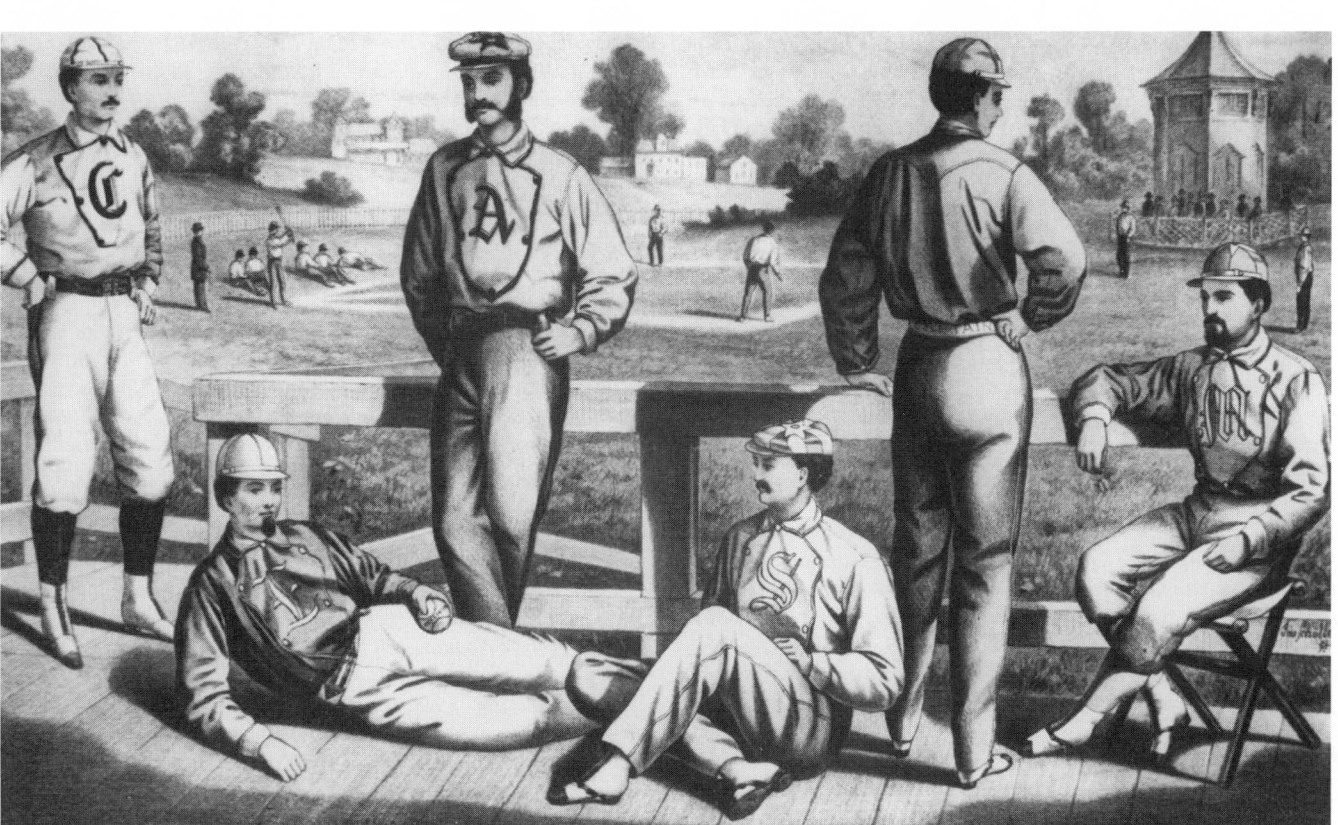

Uniform styles of the 1870s.

2. Triple-stitched seams

3. Ventilated crotch and armpits

4. Tailored to individual measure. Plenty of roominess

5. Choice of heavy leather or elastic belt

6. Pure worsted ribbed hose made any color or style, with feet or footless

7. Fully trimmed and lettered in any style and color"— Early advertisement for Goldsmith uniforms.

The earliest known formal uniforms appeared on the Knickerbockers sometime between 1849 and 1851, depending on the source. They played a Washington nine while wearing long blue trousers, white shirts and straw hats. The hats, which were flat-topped mohair caps like those worn by cricket players, were abandoned in 1855.

Another early uniform was worn by the Charter Oaks club of Brooklyn, whose players donned white pants with pink stripes, pink shirts and white stars, white caps with a blue peak and black belts with Charter Oaks written on it.

By the 1850s most club teams wore long dark pants and light shirts with bow ties. The 1864 New York Mutuals wore all-white with blue belts.

Until 1867 players wore long white or dark cricket pants. George Allard, who had played with the Cincinnati Red Stockings as an amateur, suggested that new uniforms be designed for the professional Red Stockings of 1869. He placed an order with Bertha Bertram's tailor shop. She created knee length pants with white flannel shirts and bright red stockings. They became known as knickers. The term "Knickerbocker" came from the name for Dutch settlers in New York. In contrast to knickers, the "New York Style" of uniforms in 1875 had pants worn to the ankles. The Red Stockings initially received jeers for the new fashion statement.

Accessories. Metal, glass and other foreign materials were not formally barred from Major League uniforms until 1931.

Belts. A fight between Cap Anson and Mike "King" Kelly supposedly led to the revolutionizing of the belt loop style. Kelly grabbed Anson to prevent him from running. Anson asked the maker of the uniform to thread the belt through much wider fabric loops to prevent grabbing.

Caps. See *Caps.*

Cardinals. *The Sporting News* reported that the Cardinals began using two birds on their uniforms in 1921 because of Mrs. Clarence L. Keaton, née Miss Allie May Schmidt. She was a member of the Presbyterian Church in St. Louis County and was in charge of decorations at a meeting of the Men's Fellowship organization, at which Branch Rickey was to speak. She was unsure what to do for decorations until she looked out the snow-covered window and saw two red birds perched in a tree. She decided to use red birds, and Rickey adopted the emblem for the Cardinals' uniforms. See also *St. Louis Cardinals*—Nickname.

Changes.

"The Padres win the Calvin Klein Award for excellence in baseball uniform design. The Padres' original road uniforms were a unique shade of beige that some people mistook for pink and others thought were just dirty. They eventually migrated to a brown and yellow scheme that resembled a Hershey bar with mustard. They have now thrown in the towel on the traditional brown and yellow altogether, and borrowed ideas from half the other major league franchises to create a blue and orange ensemble."— Diamondfans.com.

There have been approximately 3,000 different uniform styles worn by Major League ballplayers.

The White Sox changed their uniform style 57 times between 1900 and the early 1990s.

Colors.

"Instead of looking like the American flag, I look like a taco."— Steve Garvey on the Padres uniform he received after leaving the Dodgers. In 1991 the new Padres uniforms eliminated the brown trim and went with a more classic dark blue and orange.

"The Red Sox were being humiliated by the lowly Kansas City Athletics (commonly referred to at the time as the 'Kansas City Faggots,' since they wore bright gold suits with green trim, long before mod uniforms became fashionable)…"— George Kimball in "Opening Day at Fenway" (1973).

"And then there was the unfortunate psychedelic period when the Oakland Athletics wore a gruesome gold and green combination in the 1970s. The Houston Astros took the field in a hideous orange conflagration and the San Diego Padres developed a uniform whose primary color was brown."— Angus G. Garber III in *The Baseball Companion* (1989).

In 1881 the National League tried to implement color-coded uniforms, but the players threatened rebellion. One source reported that this fashion statement ended in June 1882 when the silk jerseys became too hot. The color scheme:

pitchers — light blue
catchers — scarlet
first basemen — scarlet/white
second basemen — orange/black
shortstops — maroon
third basemen — gray/white
left fielders — white
center fielders — red/white
right fielders — gray
substitutes — green or brown

In 1882, as a result of the rash of outlandish uniforms, the National League ruled that teams no longer were allowed to freely choose the types of uniforms and restricted each team to certain designated colors. National League founder William Hulbert is credited with this change:

Boston — red
Cleveland — navy blue
Chicago — white
Providence — light blue
Buffalo — gray
Troy — green
Detroit — old gold
Worcester — brown

After the 1882 season the National League required white for belts, stockings, pants and ties. By the next year, however, the restrictions were eliminated except for stockings.

Tim Keefe, a right-handed pitcher for five years with the Giants in the 1880s, designed the clubs' all-black uniforms with white lettering.

The Dodgers under manager Wilbert Robinson were the first — and hopefully last — team to wear checkered uniforms.

The 1901 Orioles wore pink caps and black and yellow shirts with pearl buttons.

In 1963 the A's were given permission to wear colors other than white as the dominant color on their home uniforms.

On St. Patrick's Day 1978 the Reds wore green uniforms for the first time during a spring training game. Other teams have since participated in the St. Patrick's Day spirit. The Mets once changed their blue and orange to green and orange for the game. The Tigers used green trim on their home uniforms for the game. When they switched uniforms for the game, every player wore number 30. Team owner Tom Monaghan's Domino's Pizza at the time promised delivery in "30 minutes or less" (until the company lost a lawsuit arising out of a traffic accident caused by one of its speeding delivery people).

Cost. In the 1890s an entire Major League uniform cost $12.50 ($4 in some sources and $56 for a flannel version in still other sources). By 1912 uniforms reportedly cost $30 and Major League players still were required to buy their own. In the early 1920s Major League clubs reportedly paid $25 for a complete uniform, including cap, shirt, pants, belt and stockings.

By the 1980s uniforms cost $100–125, not including socks, cap or shoes. It now costs approximately $1,300 for a team to outfit a single player for the season, depending on how hard he is on his uniform. Players used to have one home and one road uniform. Today they have two sets of each, and catchers usually have four because they perspire so much.

Desecration. In 2003, baseball card company Donruss announced that it was cutting up a Babe Ruth jersey to insert swatches into baseball card packs. Donruss previously put sliced-up jerseys of Ruth's road flannels and of football legends Doak Walker, Red Grange and Jim Brown. Only three game-worn Ruth jerseys remained after Donruss cut up the uniform in 2003.

Diplomatic. In 1962 the owners of the expansion Mets created their uniforms by combining elements of the three original New York teams: the pinstripe of the Yankees with the blue of the Dodgers and orange of the Giants.

Fielders. Only players in uniform may take a defensive position or bat. This rule has been in effect since the 19th century.

Game Day. Roger Clemens wore one jersey on the days he pitched and then put it away for safekeeping until his next start.

Honoring the Dead. One of the first attempts to honor a fallen player was by the 1881 Worcester Ruby Legs, who wore black crepe on their sleeves in memory of Chub Sullivan, who had died of tuberculosis.

The Pirates wore a sleeve patch with No. 21 in 1973 to honor Roberto Clemente.

Padres owner Ray Kroc died shortly before the club began its pennant-winning 1984 season. His initials, RAC, were on the Padres uniforms for the entire season.

The Braves wore JWM during their 1991 National League championship season. John Wildred McHale was the vice president and assistant general manager when he died in the spring of 1991 after 31 years with the club.

The 1976 and 1992 Red Sox wore the initials of Tom (1976) and Jean (1992) Yawkey in the year in which each died.

The Angels wore "DJ" on their sleeves during the 1992 season to honor batting coach Deron Johnson, who died of cancer that year at age 53.

The Royals placed the initials "EMK" on their uniforms when long-time owner Ewing Kauffman died in July 1993.

When Mets founder William Shea died in October 1991, the Mets wore a black "S" on their sleeves.

In 1995 after Mickey Mantle died, the Yankees wore black armbands and Mantle's number 7 on their sleeves.

When Darryl Kile died in 2002, the Cardinals wore a sleeve patch featuring his uniform number and initials.

When reliever Tug McGraw died of brain cancer in 2004, the Mets embroidered his rallying cry, "Ya Gotta Believe," on their right sleeves. The Phillies wore a sleeve patch shamrock inscribed with "Tug." The Phillies patch included a small red ribbon imprinted with "Pope," to honor long-time executive Paul "The Pope" Owens.

In 2004 the Twins wore an "Eloise" patch to honor owner Carl

Pohlad's wife. The Braves wore a home plate-shaped sleeve patch with No. 21 to honor pitcher Warren Spahn.

After the 2002 season, Major League teams passed a rule prohibiting the placement of individual tributes on their uniforms or caps, such as was done for Cardinals pitcher Darryl Kile, who died during the 2002 season.

See also Internet site "Uniwatch.com" by Paul Lukas.

Knickers. See **Pants.**

Material.

"It's no coincidence that female interest in the sport of baseball has increased greatly since the ballplayers swapped those wonderful old-time baggy flannel uniforms for leotards."—Mike Royko on the new stretch material popular in the 1970s.

Early uniform material usually consisted of lightweight wool flannel. Silk was used occasionally but was too hot. Quilted knickers were used to keep warm during cold weather. A blended flannel or orlon and wool was common by the mid–20th century. The last two clubs to discard the traditional orlon-wool-blend were the Yankees and Giants in 1973.

Some sources reported that in 1972 the Reds became the first team to wear double-knits. However, the Pirates wore double-knits for the first time on the first day they played in Three Rivers Stadium, on July 16, 1970. The new uniforms were easier to clean, were brighter, and allowed for greater movement than the traditional flannels.

In late 2002 Major League Baseball and the Players Union agreed to several new uniform standards. No more extremely loose fitting uniforms, because they could interfere with a pitch; as happened to Manny Ramirez when his uniform (described in *Sports Illustrated* as "mumulike") was struck by a pitch. Uniforms could not be so long that they tucked into the wearer's shoes. Also banned were written messages on caps.

Memorabilia. See *Memorabilia.*

Names on Uniforms.

"Last year we had so many people coming in and out they didn't bother to sew their names on the backs of the uniforms. They just put them there with Velcro."—Andy Van Slyke of the pitiful Pirates.

"The difference between the old ballplayer and the new ballplayer is the jersey. The old ballplayer cared about the name on the front. The new ballplayer cares about the name on the back."—Steve Garvey.

Early teams embroidered the players' names on the uniform sleeves to keep track of them, as numbers were not yet in vogue. In 1960 White Sox owner Bill Veeck became the first Major League owner to add names to his players' uniforms. General manager Bing Devine of the Cardinals followed suit almost immediately. Veeck put slugger Ted Kluszewski's nickname on his jersey as a publicity gimmick: "Klu." Veeck sometimes used Klu's full name and reversed the "z." Note that the Negro Leagues put player names on uniforms at least as early as the 1940s.

Rule 1.11(i) requires the last name of a player to appear on the back of the jersey. The Mariners had to obtain permission from the commissioner's office to allow Ichiro Suzuki to wear his first name on the back of his uniform. Suzuki is a common name in Japan, and when Ichiro began playing in Japan, there were three other players on his team with the same last name. To avoid confusion, the manager allowed Ichiro and the other Suzukis to be identified by their first names.

Club Names/Nicknames. The 1908 Cubs were the first club to put their nickname on their uniforms. By 1915 the A's, Cubs, White Sox, Red Sox and Pirates had nicknames on their uniforms.

Until about 1915 the Pirates did not use the "h" in Pittsburgh on their uniforms. From 1758 through 1889, the "h" was used by the local population. In 1890 the U.S. Board on Geographic Names attempted to establish some consistency by ordering all towns and cities ending in "burgh" to drop the h. In 1911 the city officially restored the "h" and the club later returned it to its uniforms.

In 1901 the White Sox of the new American League had a bitter rivalry with the National League Cubs. Cubs owner James A. Hart pushed through city amendments prohibiting the White Sox from using "Chicago" on their uniforms. He relented for the 1903 season, probably as part of the overall peace established between the leagues.

On July 14, 1994, Joe Carter arrived on the field wearing his game uniform with a spelling of "Torotno" on the front, courtesy of Wilson Sporting Goods.

Adam Riggs joined the Angels in late 2003 and was given his new uniform. When he came onto the field, fans noticed that his jersey was spelled "ANGEES."

Numbers on Uniforms.

"I wear 37, but prefer 337. If you turn that upside down, it spells LEE. Then I could stand upside down and people would know me right away." — Bill Lee.

See also *Retired Uniform Numbers*.

Numbers on uniforms were promoted unsuccessfully by scorecard makers in the 1880s. In 1883 the American Association Cincinnati Red Stockings had their players wear numbers on their sleeves, but they protested. The players thought they looked like prisoners and fans thought the players were being ranked according to ability.

The 1907 Reading Roses are credited by some as the first to experiment with numbers.

The Indians, at the urging of general manager Bob McRoy, briefly wore numbers on their sleeves in 1916 (not on their backs as is sometimes reported). Jack Graney led off the 1st inning for the Indians on June 26, 1916, thereby becoming the first Major League player in the 20th century to wear a number (he was also the first to bat against Babe Ruth in the Major Leagues and the first former player to enter the broadcast booth).

The Sporting News campaigned for numbers in the 1920s, noting that both basketball and football used numbers on uniforms. In 1923 the Browns wore numbers on their backs, but the fans started calling them convicts, and the players asked to have them taken off.

In 1924 and 1925 the Cardinals and White Sox put numbers on their sleeves, but the practice ended quickly until later in the decade. One source reported that Jim Bottomley of the Cardinals wore a small number 5 on his sleeve in 1923.

At the start of the 1929 season the Indians became the first Major League club to wear numbers permanently on at least their home uniforms. The Yankees also began wearing numbers that season. According to sportswriter Fred Lieb, Tommy Rice of the *Brooklyn Eagle* was the first modern sportswriter to tout the use of numbers on uniforms. Rice and Lieb encouraged Jake Ruppert of the Yankees to begin using them.

The Yankees were the first team to have permanent home and away uniform numbers. The numbers were issued based on the batting order: center fielder Earle Combs wore number 1, shortstop Mark Koenig number 2, right fielder Babe Ruth number 3 and first baseman Lou Gehrig number 4. Pitchers and substitutes were given numbers based on seniority. The Yankees first appeared in their numbered road uniforms on April 23, 1929.

The first time that Major League clubs wore numbers in the same game was when the Indians played the Yankees at Yankee Stadium on May 13, 1929. The last club to add numbers were the 1937 Philadelphia A's, but only after the American League made them mandatory for road uniforms in 1931. The National League followed suit in 1933, but all clubs had already complied.

In 1952 the Dodgers became the first club to put numbers on the front of a Major League uniform.

On September 27, 1999, the Tigers honored their former greats by having their present-day players wear the uniform numbers of the all-time greats at their positions. Gabe Kapler in right field wore no number to honor Ty Cobb. It was the last game played at *Tiger Stadium*.

Best Players by Number.

0 Al Oliver (who was the first "0" in 1978; after he was traded he said he was "starting over again")

00 Jeffrey Leonard (The first "00" was Paul Dade of the Indians in 1977); Junior Ortiz

1 Ozzie Smith, Bobby Doerr, Pee Wee Reese (and Sadaharu Oh)

2 Charlie Gehringer, Leo Durocher, Derek Jeter

3 Babe Ruth, Jimmie Foxx, Alex Rodriguez

4 Lou Gehrig, Mel Ott, Duke Snider

5 Joe DiMaggio, Johnny Bench, Hank Greenberg, Brooks Robinson

6 Stan Musial, Al Kaline, Tony Lazzeri, Tony Oliva, Steve Garvey

7 Mickey Mantle, Al Simmons, Ivan Rodriguez

8 Carl Yastrzemski, Yogi Berra, Cal Ripken, Joe Morgan

9 Ted Williams, Reggie Jackson

10 Lefty Grove, Johnny Mize, Chipper Jones

11 Carl Hubbell, Luis Aparicio, Barry Larkin

12 Bill White, Tommy Davis, Roberto Alomar

13 Dave Concepcion, Ralph Branca

14 Pete Rose, Ernie Banks, Jim Bunning

15 Thurman Munson, Red Ruffing, Shawn Green

16 Whitey Ford, Hal Newhouser, Dwight Gooden

17 Dizzy Dean, James "Cool Papa" Bell, Denny McLain

18 Red Faber, Mel Harder, Eppa Rixey, Darryl Strawberry, Don Larsen

19 Bob Feller, Tony Gwynn, Robin Yount, Waite Hoyt

20 Frank Robinson, Lou Brock, Josh Gibson, Mike Schmidt

21 Roberto Clemente, Roger Clemens, Warren Spahn, Dazzy Vance, Sammy Sosa (25 with the White Sox)

22 Jim Palmer, Max Carey, Will Clark

23 Ryne Sandberg, Don Mattingly, Luis Tiant, Kirk Gibson

24 Willie Mays, Early Wynn, Ken Griffey, Jr., Rickey Henderson

25 Tommy John, Mark McGwire, Barry Bonds, Jim Thome, Jose Cruz, Rafael Palmeiro

26 Billy Williams, Wade Boggs, Boog Powell

27 Catfish Hunter, Juan Marichal, Fred McGriff, Carlton Fisk, Vladimir Guerrero

28 Bert Blyleven, Sparky Lyle

29 Satchel Paige (he also briefly wore 22 and 49 during 1951), Rod Carew, Mickey Lolich, John Smoltz

30 Nolan Ryan (with Mets and Angels; 34 with Astros and Rangers), Orlando Cepeda, Maury Wills, Tim Raines

31 Ferguson Jenkins, Dave Winfield, Greg Maddux, Mike Piazza

32 Sandy Koufax, Steve Carlton

33 Honus Wagner (coach only), Eddie Murray

34 Rollie Fingers, Kirby Puckett, Nolan Ryan (at times during his career)

35 Frankie Frisch, Phil Niekro, Frank Thomas, Mike Mussina
36 Gaylord Perry, Robin Roberts, Jim Kaat
37 Casey Stengel
38 Rocky Colavito, Curt Schilling
39 Roy Campanella, Dave Parker
40 Ken Harrelson, Rick Sutcliffe
41 Eddie Mathews, Tom Seaver, Glenn Davis
42 Jackie Robinson, Al Lopez, Mariano Rivera
43 Dennis Eckersley
44 Henry Aaron, Willie McCovey, Reggie Jackson
45 Bob Gibson, Pedro Martinez
46 Lee Smith, Andy Pettitte, Mike Flanagan, Jim Maloney
47 Jack Morris, Tom Glavine, Jesse Orosco, Rod Beck
48 Sam McDowell, Ramon Martinez, Randy Myers
49 Ron Guidry, Hoyt Wilhelm, Armando Benitez, Charlie Hough
50 Bucky Harris, Jamie Moyer, Sid Fernandez
51 Randy Johnson, Ichiro Suzuki, Bernie Williams, Trevor Hoffman
52 Jim Abbott
53 Don Drysdale
54 Goose Gossage
55 Orel Hershiser, Hideki Matsui
56 Jim Bouton
57 Johnny Vander Meer, Darryl Kile
61 Chan Ho Park, Livan Hernandez
65 Bill McKechnie
67 Edd Roush
72 Carlton Fisk
75 Barry Zito
77 Joe Medwick, Jack Armstrong
87 Smoky Burgess
88 Rene Gonzalez
96 Bill Voiselle
99 Mitch Williams, Turk Wendell

The definitive book on uniform numbers is *Baseball By the Numbers*, by Mark Stang and Linda Harkness (1996).

Number Change. Joe DiMaggio began his Major League career wearing number 9 but switched to the more familiar number 5.

Henry Aaron was given number 5 but wanted a double-digit number, which ultimately was 44. Braves executive Donald Davidson tried to dissuade him, pointing out that the game's stars usually wore single-digit numbers.

Mickey Mantle was number 6 in 1951 before wearing number 7.

Roberto Clemente wore number 13 in 1955 before switching to number 21.

Yankee shortstop Tony Kubek thought he was going to receive number 34 from long-time Yankee clubhouse man Pete Sheehy. However, Mickey Mantle stepped up and told Sheehy to issue Kubek a lower number because he was "going to be here awhile." Kubek received number 10 and stayed nine years until a neck injury forced him to retire.

In 1991 Pirates third baseman Bobby Bonilla switched from number 25 to 23 in honor of pitching coach Milt May's son, Scott, who was in a coma as a result of a car accident. He made a miraculous recovery.

When Benito Santiago joined the Florida Marlins for the 1993 season, he wore number "09."

Omar Oliveras switched to "00" because it contains his initials.

Hometown/State. Bill Voiselle wore 96 for his hometown of Ninety Six, North Carolina. Voiselle came up to the Majors in

1942 and won 21 games in 1944. Mel Ott purportedly fined him $500 in 1945 for making an 0–2 pitch that resulted in a triple. The fine was rescinded, but Voiselle supposedly was never the same again. It is more likely that the quality players returning from World War II made it tougher on Voiselle, who still managed to play five more years, with high win years of 14 in 1945 and 13 in 1948. One source placed the town of Ninety Six in South Carolina.

Pitcher Sid Fernandez wore number 50 to honor his home state of Hawaii.

Free Advertising. When Andy Messersmith signed with the Braves as an early free agent in 1976, owner Ted Turner gave him number 17 and the word "Channel" was stenciled where Messersmith's name otherwise would be. This signified Turner's Channel 17, superstation WTBS, the cornerstone of his broadcast empire. National League president Chub Feeney disallowed the uniform.

Wrong Way Perez. After getting lost on the freeway on his way to the ballpark, Atlanta Braves pitcher Pascual Perez wore I-285 on his warm-up jacket.

Number Trade.

"I don't care how much money he makes. He can have my locker, I'll take him to all the best restaurants in New York. He can even have my wife. But he can't have my number, no way."—Number 16 Dwight Gooden after number 16 Frank Viola arrived with the Mets in 1989.

Rickey Henderson reportedly paid Turner Ward $25,000 for his number 24 when Henderson joined the Blue Jays from the A's. Before receiving the number, Henderson started off 3-for-24 for the Blue Jays. After the payment, Henderson commented facetiously (we hope) that he was not happy with Ward:

"I told him he was garbage. I told him he was tight and should be honored to wear my number. Oh well, at least I got it."

In fact, Henderson paid Ward for the number with only a pair of cowboy boots and a few bats.

When Mitch Williams joined the Phillies in 1993, he wanted number 28. John Kruk already had the number but gave it up in return for a case of beer. Williams later switched to 99.

Number 13. See *Superstitions*.

Pants. At the 2002 winter meetings, Major League general managers approved new rules prohibiting players from tucking their pants into their shoes.

Patriotism. During World War I, Minneapolis of the American Association adopted khaki uniforms with an American Flag embroidered across the shirt, and red, white and blue stripes on the caps and stockings. Starting in 1942 the Dodgers' kelly green trim was changed to royal blue and white to assume a more patriotic look during World War II.

Pinstripes.

"The Yankees are the only team that teaches the true story of our country—that might mixed with class, talent and hard work often breeds success. Also, that pinstripes have a slimming effect. Except on David Wells."—Joel Stein in *Time*.

The Cubs were the first club to wear pinstripes, during the 1907 World Series.

The Yankee pinstripes are perhaps the most famous uniform additions in history. Some historians claim that the reason the Yankees adopted the pinstripes was the enormous girth of Babe Ruth. When Ruth ballooned from 215 pounds in 1923 to 260 in 1925, Jake Ruppert commented that Ruth looked "like a load of hay out there." Ruth supposedly looked thinner wearing pinstripes. Actually, by 1911 the Yankees had received permission to use pinstripes. According to Frank Graham, Jr., in the 1930s the pinstripes were not black but actually a dark purple.

Road Uniforms. By the early 20th century a few Major League clubs had different home and road uniforms. The Giants and Phillies were the first clubs to wear generally white uniforms at home and generally darker uniforms on the road. Other sources credit Connie Mack of the A's with using gray uniforms on the road. This protocol became mandatory in 1911 to make it easier to distinguish players from opposing clubs.

Shirts.

"There were no red sleeves for Klu. His naked pneumatic arm muscles rippled in the sunshine, visible from the farthest reaches of Crosley Field. With typical modesty, Ted let it be known that he found the tight sleeves too confining, constricting his bearlike swing. But he wasn't fooling me. I knew deep down, he was showing off. There was a hidden strain of arrogant barbarity under that fey demeanor." — Actor John Lithgow in *Cult Baseball Players*, edited by Danny Peary (1990). In 1941 the Cubs became the first Major League club to wear sleeveless jerseys. The experiment lasted three years. The Reds debuted their sleeveless shirts in 1956, modeled most memorably by Kluszewski. The Pirates and Indians experimented briefly with this fashion statement.

Early uniform jerseys had high collars, which eventually gave way to lower necklines. John McGraw's 1906 Giants are credited as the first team to wear collarless jerseys. They also had "Champions of the World" lettered on their shirts.

Detachable long sleeves were worn in the 19th century. An early Harvard team wore short sleeve shirts, a novelty at the time.

In 1986 players began wearing pregame pullover jerseys to keep their game jerseys clean. Charlie Finley's A's started wearing colored jerseys, and he is credited with first issuing pullover jersies to his players in the 1970s.

The modern snug polyester uniforms reduce the weight of the shirt from 8–9 ounces to one-half that amount.

No frayed shirtsleeves are allowed because they are a distraction to the batter. Sleeves must be of similar length among players. Since 1931 no polished metal or glass buttons have been allowed on the uniform.

On June 7, 1938, Indians pitcher Johnny Allen walked off the mound in the 2nd inning and did not return after umpire Bill McGowan ordered him to cut his torn sweatshirt sleeve because it was distracting the Red Sox hitters. Allen was fined $250 by manager Ossie Vitt, and the shirt was sent to the Hall of Fame.

In April 1997 Reds outfielder Deion Sanders tried to honor Jackie Robinson by cutting off the sleeves of his road jersey, similar to the style worn by Robinson and other players of the era. Sanders was reprimanded by the league for violating Rule 1.11(a)(1) which requires that "sleeve lengths may vary for individual players, but the sleeves of each individual player shall be approximately the same length." The Reds then decided to have all the players wear their sleeves in this style, thereby avoiding league sanction.

Shorts.

"I'm going to retire. No way will I wear those damn hotpants." — Bobby Bonds on Bill Veeck's White Sox uniforms that featured short pants in the mid–1970s.

The Chicago White Sox first wore shorts for a season during the early 1950s. Also in the early 1950s the Hollywood Stars of the Pacific Coast League and Ft. Worth of the Texas League played in Bermuda shorts and rayon shirts. These two Pirates farm clubs, controlled by Branch Rickey, returned to regular uniforms after two seasons.

Size.

"If I look bitchin', it adds 20 points to my average." — Dick Stuart, who hit 30 home runs in each league in the 1960s, on why

he wore his uniform too small, to shore off his muscles. Clubs generally issued flannel uniforms one size too large to allow for shrinkage during the season.

The Sporting Life complained that the 1888 White Stocking pants were so tight they were "positively indecent."

The first form-fitting uniform may have been worn by Willie Mays, in 1960, after he had a tailor eliminate the loose material.

Slump.

"Tomorrow, we're gonna try mix-and-match. Half the guys are gonna wear red shirts. Half are gonna wear gray shirts. And the guys who don't look good in shirts are gonna go out there naked." — Phillies first baseman John Kruk explaining how the Phillies were going to try to break out of a 1993 slump.

Toronto's Damaso Garcia once burned his uniform after a bad game.

Socks and Stirrups.

"Later in the season … 'Commy' [Charles Comiskey] sent his secretary, Harry Grabiner, to the Forest City with instructions to buy [Joe] Jackson, to fame known as 'sockless Joe,' and one of the leading hitters in the league." — G.W. Axelson in "*Commy*" (1919), on Joe Jackson, known more commonly as "Shoeless."

"Custom-made stockings can bring the cutouts halfway up the shin and calf, giving the wearer's legs the unmistakable look of whitewall tires." — Roger Angell in *The Summer Game* (1972).

Stirrups were popularized in the 1910s as a result of scares about blood poisoning. The dyes used in colored baseball socks were capable of causing blood poisoning if they seeped into an open cut from spiking. As a result, to maintain the tradition of colored uniform stockings while reducing the poisoning risk, clubs resorted to colored cut-outs (stirrups) over white socks. The socks were dubbed "sanitaries" in the 1920s after being manufactured in a relatively sterile environment to protect against infection.

In 1961 baseball executives tried to limit the length of the cutouts on stirrups. Frank Robinson started the trend of extremely high stirrups, of which baseball's hierarchy did not approve. Some sources claim that George Hendrick also was an early proponent of high stirrups, but he did not reach the Major Leagues until 1971, well after Robinson. Some sources credit Ken Harrelson and Tito Fuentes with wearing high stirrups in the mid–1960s. Willie McCovey had the highest stirrups in the National League in 1968. In 1991 the style began to revert to an earlier period, with pant legs worn extremely low over the ankle to block out almost all of the stirrup and sock.

Warm-Up Jackets. In the 1920s players wore woolen sweaters instead of warm-up jackets.

Pitchers Larry Anderson and Neil Walk once went up to bat wearing their warm-up jackets by mistake.

Books. Bill James, *The Bill James Historical Baseball Abstract* (1988), contains an informal survey of uniform evolution; Marc Okkonen, *Baseball Uniforms of the 20th Century: The Official Major League Baseball Guide* (1994).

Union Association (1884)

"It isn't so long ago that a great American President, Abraham Lincoln, freed Negro slaves. Now we have leagues which practice a reserve clause which holds athletic young men in perpetual bondage." — Henry Lucas, who disliked the reserve clause and did not allow its use in the Union Association.

Origins. The Union Association, also known as the Union League, was formed September 12, 1883, and operated only during the 1884 season. The driving force behind the league was Henry

V. Lucas, a wealthy young St. Louis landowner whose father had sponsored the National League's St. Louis team in 1876. Lucas planned for the Union Association players to receive better financial treatment and hoped to eliminate the reserve clause. Lucas was the primary president of the association, though he was preceded for a short time by Henry B. Bennett.

Clubs. The Union Association initially included the St. Louis Maroons, Cincinnati Outlaw Reds, Boston Reds, Chicago Browns, Baltimore Monumentals, Philadelphia Keystones, Washington Nationals and Altoona Mountain Citys.

Altoona was the first casualty early in the season and was replaced by the Kansas City Unions. Philadelphia disbanded early in August and was replaced by the Wilmington Quicksteps of the Eastern League. That club was replaced after a month by the Milwaukee Cream Citys. Chicago moved to Pittsburgh in August and became the Stogies, but the club folded in September and the spot was filled by the St. Paul Saints. Only five of the teams were functioning at the end of the season.

The St. Louis Maroons, owned by Lucas, won the pennant by 21 games with a 91–16 record.

Owners. A.H. Henderson, a Baltimore mattress manufacturer, invested in the Baltimore and Chicago clubs. Brewers Ellis Wainwright and Adolphus Busch (grandfather of future Cardinals owner August A. Busch of Busch Brewery) also invested in the league. The Pennsylvania Railroad invested in the Altoona club. George Wright headed the Boston club and his sporting goods company, Wright & Ditson, supplied the league with its official ball.

Rival Leagues. The National League and American Association derisively called the Association players "Onions" (a play on "Unions") and Lucas "St. Lucas." With the addition of the Union Association teams, there were 34 clubs operating at the Major League level in 1884. There were two in each of eight cities and three in Philadelphia. Five were in Ohio and four in New York.

Leagues that were part of the National Agreement that governed Organized Baseball banned play by their teams with Union Association teams. This was enforced by barring from Organized Baseball any league that had a club in a city where a National Agreement team already had a club.

The clubs covered by the National Agreement created "reserve teams" of younger professional and semipro teams and supplied umpires. This was done to siphon off players and fans from the rival Union Association.

Players. Hugh "One Arm" Daily, Fred Dunlap, Jack Glasscock, Tommy Bond, Charlie Sweeney and George "Orator" Shaffer were the top National League players who jumped to the Union Association. The top American Association players who jumped were Jack Gleason, Tony Mullane and George Bradley. A total of 27 American Association and National League players jumped to the Union Association. Those players were allowed back at the end of the Union Association's one season but reportedly were allowed back into the National League only if they paid a $1,000 fine (unlikely given that this amount was about half their salaries).

Thirty Union Association players had not had prior National League or American Association experience, but they were good enough to play later in one or both of the established leagues.

The greatest effect of the Union Association was to wreck the National League's Cleveland franchise after a number of key players jumped to Cincinnati of the Union Association. They included shortstop Jack Glasscock and pitcher Jim McCormick.

Disintegration of the Association.

"It has enacted no new laws, brought out no valuable players, and leaves not one piece of healthy legislation on its annals. It has

caused several players to be cast out of the ranks of reputable professionals and has given a few others a chance to show the treachery that was in them…. The result has been predicted in these columns and its coming so soon is gratifying. All reputable players and managers are to be congratulated on it."—The *Cleveland Herald* in January 1885.

The Union Association clubs collectively lost about $250,000. Lack of balance among the clubs hurt the league, as fans became disinterested when the Maroons finished 21 games ahead of the pack. St. Louis was one of the strongest clubs in the country, which led to the team's invitation to join the National League after the season.

At the association's winter meetings, only the five remaining active clubs showed up. Two of them, Washington and Cincinnati, were surreptitiously seeking entry into the American Association. By the December 18 meeting, Henry Lucas was already arranging for his St. Louis club to join the National League. Only Kansas City and Milwaukee showed up at the second meeting on January 15, 1885. With no show of support from other clubs, the remaining two voted to disband. After the Union Association folded and St. Louis went to the National League, the remnants of the association formed a new Eastern League for the 1885 season.

Unions

"Over the years, major league baseball had been plagued by futile attempts to start a players' union…. With the expanded minor leagues, these old problems were again raising their heads [in 1946]. Players' fears of being buried in the bushes was only one area to be addressed. Certainly the players would be looking for bigger paychecks and more individual rights. The whole baseball picture was ripe for the proper organizer to step in. Standardized pay, insurance, continued salary in the case of the injured, better equipment, meal and transportation allowances, laundry, transportation, etc…, would become the issues."—Ed Walton in *The Rookies* (1982).

"Players were not only ignorant about unions, they were positively hostile to the idea: They didn't know what a union was, but they knew they didn't want one. There was a reason for this attitude. From time immemorial, the baseball powers-that-be forcefed the players propaganda: The commissioner (although appointed and paid by the owners) represented the players; players were privileged to be paid to play a kid's game; and (the biggest fairy tale of all) baseball was not a business and, in any case, was unprofitable for the owners."—Players Association leader Marvin Miller, who many believe is a legitimate candidate for the Hall of Fame, in his autobiography, *A Whole Different Ball Game* (1991).

See also *Strikes and Lockouts*.

National Brotherhood of Professional Base Ball Players/1885–1891.

"To protect and benefit ourselves collectively and individually. To promote a high standard of professional conduct. To foster and encourage the interests of … baseball."—Preamble to the Brotherhood's constitution.

"We ask that a man who has fulfilled his contract with a club for a term of years shall be at liberty to make another contract where and with whom he sees fit, and without restraint; that it shall not be in the power of any club to say to a man; we are going to release you to such and such a club, and you will play there or nowhere else."—Brotherhood spokesman Arthur Irwin of the Philadelphia Athletics.

Historian Lee Allen wrote about the brotherhood with antiunion sentiment: "It resulted in the impoverishment of several club owners, caused the death of the American Association, forced a decline in attendance and almost wrecked the National League."

The brotherhood was formed in the minor leagues in June 1885 by William H. "Billy" Voltz, a baseball writer in Cleveland and Philadelphia and a minor league manager. The original idea was to start a fund for ill or indigent players to enable them to survive the winter. Voltz was not well known by Major Leaguers, but on October 22, 1885, nine players on the National League's New York Giants joined the Brotherhood, including stars Tim Keefe, Roger Connor and Buck Ewing. Eventually close to 200 Major League players enrolled in 1885, with each contributing $5 to help fund a pool for sick or indigent players. Other sources reported that only 107 players had enrolled by 1886. Some sources reported that the brotherhood was the closest the players came to controlling the game until free agency in the 1970s.

John Montgomery Ward was a founder and first president of the brotherhood at the Major League level. *The Sporting News* dubbed him "St. George of Baseball, for he has slain the dragon of oppression." During 1886 Ward began to organize chapters publicly in other National League cities, starting in Detroit. Charles Comiskey was involved with the brotherhood while he played for Cincinnati. To counter the brotherhood, team owners bribed newspapermen to discredit union players as "hot-headed anarchists."

Ward, Ned Hanlon and Dan Brouthers formed a committee to attend the National League owners meeting in 1887. Al Spalding, a former player and by then the dominant National League owner, supposedly persuaded the other owners to at least listen to the players. The primary motivation of the brotherhood was to abolish the reserve clause. Although the owners asked the brotherhood to come up with an alternative to the reserve clause, Ward apparently admitted that there was no better system.

By 1887 it was clear that a rift existed between players and owners, and some effort was made at compromise (though at least one source reported that the nonsensical "compromise" was that Ward "succeeded in having the reserve clause formally included in all player contracts"). The chief problem by 1888 was that the National League had instituted a cap on salaries known as the Limitation Rule. When the American Association and National League limited player salaries to $2,000, the brotherhood was instrumental in establishing the *Players League*.

The brotherhood's strength peaked with the formation of the Players League for the 1890 season. When the league died after one year and the American Association disbanded after the 1891 season, the brotherhood was dealing with a group of National League owners who could now monopolize Major League Baseball. As a result, the brotherhood faded almost immediately.

Protective Association of Professional Baseball Players/ 1900–1903. When the war between the National and American Leagues began escalating around 1900, a number of Major League players formed the Protective Association of Professional Baseball Players. It was also known as the League Protective Players Association. As with the earlier brotherhood, it died with the end of the baseball wars in 1903.

The Protective Association was formed June 10, 1900, in response to abuses by the National League. Three players from each team met and formed the association, electing Pittsburgh's Chief Zimmer as president. Boston catcher Bill Clarke was elected treasurer, and Hughie Jennings was elected secretary. The identification of the players who participated in the initial meeting was kept secret until the names were leaked. Also active was Clark Griffith, who organized a strike to force the unofficial minimum salary to be raised to $3,000 and for teams to pay for uniforms.

The American Federation of Labor sent a delegate to the players' initial meeting. The players rejected the overture from the union in fear of even stronger retaliation by the owners. Harry Taylor, a Buffalo attorney and ex-ballplayer, addressed the approximately 100 players who attended the initial meeting. The group formed a grievance committee and required a $5 initiation fee and monthly dues of $2.

The National League needed to cooperate somewhat with the Protective Association because of the threat of competition from the American League and slowly reviving American Association. The National League met with the players in December 1900. The owners complained of rowdyism while the players presented the usual demands for better conditions, more expense money and overall better treatment. In return for a few concessions, the players agreed not to jump to the American League, but many did eventually, based on contract technicalities. When peace between the leagues was established in 1903, the Protective Association lost its leverage and died out quickly.

Players Fraternity/1912–1917.

"In the end, the owners remained triumphant. It is easy to see in retrospect that the call for a strike was a disaster that lost the Fraternity support from fans, the press, and some of its own members. The Fraternity was crushed. The best that can be said for it is that it laid down a gauntlet that would be successfully picked up many years later." — Historian David Q. Voigt.

On September 6, 1912, in New York, attorney David L. Fultz, a former A's and Yankees outfielder (and graduate of Brown University in 1895), organized the Baseball Players Fraternity. Fultz was elected president and Ty Cobb and Christy Mathewson were elected vice-presidents. Also on the board were Sam Crawford, Johnny Evers, Miller Huggins and catcher John Henry. Henry was so supportive of the Fraternity that Ban Johnson later threatened to bar him from Organized Baseball because of his union activities.

By 1913 over 700 players had signed up and the union was successful in receiving some attention from the owners. Fultz was also somewhat of a player agent, as he advised players behind the scenes in their contract negotiations. Even though many owners despised him, he later became president of the International League.

It has often been reported that the impetus for the fraternity was a one-day *Strike* by the Tigers following the fine and suspension of Ty Cobb in 1912. However, Fultz was approached to lead the players as early as 1910, but it took until 1912 to raise enough support and formally begin the organization.

Annual dues were $18 and the fraternity initially had 300 members. At its peak it had 1,200 players in the Major Leagues and high minor leagues. The fraternity sought support from the American Federation of Labor and its leader, Samuel Gompers, but reportedly (and illogically) the union rejected the players' overture (possibly because the players had rejected the union a decade earlier).

National Commission members Ban Johnson and Garry Herrmann purportedly professed acceptance of the fraternity so long as no attorneys met with them. As of 1913 no major changes had been implemented, although 17 "demands" and 17 "requests" presented to the National Commission resulted in improved salaries and rights. Yet most of the concessions were either minor or, more likely, as a result of the coming competition from the new Federal League.

At a meeting in January 1914 the National Commission acceded to many demands by the fraternity, including limitations on the reserve clause: a 10-year player waived out of the league was free to make a deal with any club; a player with 15 years combined service of Major League and top level minor league experience could deal with any club. The leagues agreed also that no player could be sent to a lower classified team without first having to be bid on by a team of a higher classification. The union attempted unsuccessfully to obtain a portion of the revenues derived from the motion picture documentaries of the World Series.

The first time a *Strike* of an entire league was threatened was in 1913, when the owners failed to honor the new agreement with the Fraternity. With some "quick negotiations" (more likely threats by the owners), a strike was avoided.

The union recognized the Federal League as a Major League, but the union's existence may have hurt the Federal League because the two established leagues provided certain minor concessions to the players to help prevent player defections to the rival league. The Players Fraternity was a voice for the players at least through 1915, bringing grievances to the National Commission and recovering money for players. The fraternity faded after the Federal League folded and World War I began to negatively affect Major League Baseball. Most sources dismiss the fraternity as ineffective after the Federal League died, but historian Harold Seymour noted that by the end of 1916 the fraternity still had 1,215 members. He also reported that the fraternity focused primarily on reforms in the minor leagues, where most of its membership was based.

Fultz left for Europe to become an aviator in the U.S. Army. Ironically, he returned to be offered the position of president of the International League, where he stayed for two years.

National Baseball Players Association of the United States/ 1922. Ray Cannon was a Milwaukee attorney who represented several of the Black Sox players in 1922 when they unsuccessfully sought reinstatement to Major League Baseball. He also tried to obtain back pay for the Black Sox and attempted a congressional investigation into baseball's management practices.

Cannon began leading the National Baseball Players Association that year, but his representation of the Black Sox players gave the union a bad image. In 1923 the organization claimed 225 members among the Major and minor leagues. It then issued an unsuccessful demand for a vote on the governing structure of Organized Baseball. Within a year most of the members had lost interest, and the group quickly collapsed. The climate for unions was poor during the prosperous 1920s, and it was not until the 1930s that unions were looked on more favorably. Nevertheless, a baseball union received little public support until after World War II. The delay in recognizing the value of a baseball players union was due primarily to four factors:

1. A union implied a wage scale, which was an unworkable system for baseball;

2. A union generally involved a standard work week with a set number of hours, while players worked only 2–3 hours per day (other than practice time);

3. A strike of baseball players was thought to be unconscionable;

4. There was little public sympathy because of the relatively high salaries paid to baseball players.

American Baseball Guild/1946.

"Guilds have no place in baseball. I was in the big leagues for 20 years and never once figured I was being underpaid or mistreated. Baseball is very generous and has kept quite a number of fellows from pushing plows for a living."—Pirates outfielder Paul Waner reflecting the attitude of many players that historically had led to the failure of efforts to form a strong players union.

In May 1946 Boston lawyer Robert Murphy, a former National Labor Relations Board examiner, tried to form a baseball union

known as the American Baseball Guild. The Pirates just missed voting in favor of the union against the wishes of owner Bill Benswanger. They reluctantly took the field after a pregame "no" vote.

Though the effort failed, club owners were pressured into better working conditions and asked the players to submit suggestions for improvements. The initial suggestions were relatively innocuous, as the players demanded and received: 1) more meal money; 2) a $5,000 minimum salary, and 3) buses to the park, rather than cabs paid for by the players. It has been argued that the more mature postwar players were more militant because many players returning from the military were fighting to regain their old jobs and salaries.

The owners later offered a few more concessions: eliminating the 10-day release clause; restricting salary cuts to 25% of the previous year's salary; $25 spring training meal allowances, paid in advance. Players also won the right to negotiate through player representatives, though few (if any, until the 1960s) risked the wrath of the owners by actually engaging an agent to handle negotiations.

Major League Baseball Players Association/1956– .

"I think that a union sounds like a very good thing. But don't get me wrong. I don't think ballplayers should or ever would strike. We love the game too much. But if we stick together in a union, we'll get more benefits. And we may find a way to help the minor leagues get stronger."— Braves slugger Eddie Mathews in 1957.

"Ballplayers have never envisioned their representatives as a trade union. When Allie Reynolds and Ralph Kiner first came to me for legal help, they both insisted that a union wouldn't satisfy the needs of the players. They didn't want to think about strikes or anything like strikes.... I prefer to think of it as a corporation.... With the 400 big league players as the stockholders, the 16 representatives as members of the board of directors and with the league representatives, now Bob Feller and Robin Roberts, as president and chairman of the board."— Players union leader and New York attorney J. Norman Lewis in April 1955.

See also *Strikes and Lockouts*.

In 1953 attorney J. Norman Lewis was hired to fight the owners' attempt to abandon the *Pension* plan negotiated shortly after World War II. These efforts led eventually to the formation of the Major League Baseball Players Association (MLBPA) in late 1956.

Player representatives from each team were chosen and a panel created to oversee administration of the pension plan. The first player representatives to the administrative panel were Johnny Murphy of the Yankees and Dixie Walker of the Dodgers.

Lewis was pushed aside in the late 1950s and the players hired Robert C. Cannon, who was a municipal judge in Milwaukee. The ballclubs actually paid his salary and he did very little to advance the players' cause. He was the son of Raymond Cannon, a militant players' advocate during the 1920s and 1930s who had tried to organize a union in the 1920s (see above).

In 1965 the players formed a search committee to find a new director. The committee consisted of Jim Bunning, Robin Roberts and Harvey Kuenn. Cannon was about to sign for $50,000 per year, but he balked over some minor compensation issues and eventually he walked away from the deal. The players then went to their second chose, *Marvin Miller*.

The Players Association added significant clout when Miller was named executive director at age 48 in 1966. He was a former assistant to the president of the United Steelworkers. After Miller's appointment the labor climate in Major League Baseball changed forever. The first collective bargaining agreement was negotiated in 1967. Miller then guided the players through the 1970s free agency battles against the reserve clause and secured the organization's position through the strikes and lockout years into the 1980s.

Miller retired on December 31, 1982, and was succeeded by Ken Moffett until November of that year, when Miller took over again briefly. He retired for good shortly thereafter, and his assistant, **Donald Fehr**, was appointed. Fehr chose as his assistant former Orioles shortstop Mark Belanger. In 2004 Gene Orza was promoted to Chief Operating Office of the union, a name change for the No. 2 man in the organization. He had been with the Players Association since 1984.

Each team has two player representatives. Roberto Clemente was the first non-white player to serve as a player representative on the union's executive board. Players for several years paid $20 in union dues for each day of the regular season, approximately 180 days. That figure is now $40 per day.

Books. Lee Lowenfish and Tony Lupien, *The Imperfect Diamond* (1980). Lupien had been a first baseman with the Phillies when he was discharged from the Navy after World War II at age 28. The Phillies sold him to the Hollywood Stars, but Lupien unsuccessfully challenged the sale by invoking the new veteran's rights law which guaranteed a veteran a year's employment with his former employer. See also James B. Dworkin, *Owners Versus Players: Baseball and Collective Bargaining* (1981); Paul D. Staudohar, *Diamond Minds: Baseball and Labor* (2000).

United States Baseball League

"What you may not know is that the latest proposal for a third major league has been in the works for more than five years. By 1989 the proposed United States Baseball League had landed owners for eight teams, including Donald Trump, and scheduled a 1990 debut. But when baseball's collusion problems were solved and players began signing long-term contracts, the idea went back into hiding." — Bill Gallo.

During the 1994–1995 player strike this league was proposed to begin play in 1996. The league was formed in November 1994 by former congressmen John Bryant and Robert Mrazek, sports agent Dick Moss and economist Andrew Zimbalist, who had written an analysis of *The Business of Baseball*.

The league was to begin with 10–12 teams, including franchises in Mexico, Venezuela, Puerto Rico and Canada. The ownership structure by late 1995 was developer Clay Parker in Los Angeles, banker Churchill Carey in Puerto Rico, Mike Casey in New Orleans, Howard Milstein in Washington D.C., Samuel Thaler in Central Florida, and banker Alan Altschuler in Long Island, New York. Casey was the only one with any baseball experience, having been the Mets' minor league executive of the year in 1989.

The league then was to have eight clubs and a 154-game season. If successful, it was to expand to Asia within two years. American sites considered were Orlando, Charlotte, Sacramento, San Bernardino– Riverside and Washington, D.C. However, in late 1995 the league announced the delay of its inaugural season until at least 1997 (and were still at it a couple of years after that) while organizers looked for more playing sites. The plans eventually were abandoned.

United States League (1912, 1913)

"There can be no such thing as too much good baseball." — Motto of William Abbott Witman, the mayor of Reading, Pennsylvania, and first president of the United States League. He had owned a club in the Pennsylvania State League.

"IS BUILDING ON SAND! The President of the United States League Announces a Policy as Regards Contracts With, and Reservations of, Players Which Foredooms the Organization to Utter Fail." — 1913 banner headline in *Sporting Life*.

A meeting was held on January 20, 1912, at which it was announced that the new league's initial seven clubs would be located in New York, Brooklyn, Reading, Cincinnati, Pittsburgh, Richmond and Washington. National League leader Garry Herrmann of the Reds at first looked upon the new league (as well as the upstart **Columbian League**) with benign amusement: "The two leagues are not outlaws, they are independent bodies within their rights and not trespassing on ours."

The next day National League president Thomas Lynch took a stronger stand: "You can take it from me, these new leagues are outlaws and know they will get no recognition from us."

Cleveland was named as the eighth club and the league set a 126-game schedule. It was announced that the New York club would play Sunday ball, an illegal novelty at the time in New York until 1919.

The league lasted for three games in 1912 in the eight eastern cities (a "few weeks" in some sources). The league attempted a resurrection in 1913, but the opening day game was forfeited and the league never got off the ground that season. This was the second attempt in two years to establish a new major league without the blessing of the National Association of Professional Baseball Leagues. The other was the **Columbian League**, which lasted a few days in 1912. Some of the United States League's owners became Federal League owners in 1913.

United States League (1945)

In 1945 Dodger general manager Branch Rickey announced the formation of the United States League. Rickey's club was to be the Brooklyn Brown Dodgers. The league was to warehouse Negro League players to ease the transition of black players into the Major Leagues. Most sources that reference the league are quite vague. Some report that the team and the league lasted only a few months with little fanfare, as black players began to move into the minor leagues in 1946. However, it does not appear that the club or the league ever played any games.

Rickey intentionally was vague about the league because he was using it as an excuse for his scouts to get a jump on the rest of the Major Leagues and begin scouting black talent. All the Dodger scouts reportedly believed that they were looking for future Brown Dodgers, but scout Tom Greenwade claimed later that he was aware of the real purpose for their scouting efforts. Speculation is that Rickey would have confided in scout George Sisler if he was going to tell anyone the truth about the proposed league. Sisler later denied knowing anything about the plan, suggesting that Greenwade also was unaware.

The Brown Dodgers were to play in Ebbets Field. One source reported that the new league failed quickly, going out of business in a matter of months. Bill Veeck claimed that Rickey decided to bring Robinson to Organized Baseball only after the Brown Dodgers failed.

Rickey admitted later that the Brown Dodgers were used as a front so that he could scout black players who would eventually play in the Major Leagues. Jackie Robinson agreed with that assessment. Negro League star Oscar Charleston supposedly managed (or was supposed to manage) the Brown Dodgers.

Members of Pittsburgh's Forbes Field usher crew.

Ushers

"We're a select group chosen to break heads. Last week I wrestled a guy down and hit him in the mouth with the best punch I ever nailed a fan … don't get me wrong, he was wearing a Yankee hat."—Fenway Park bleachers usher quoted in Thomas Boswell's *How Life Imitates the World Series* (1982).

See also *Ticket Takers*.

Ushers apparently were first used in 1912 to police the stands after Ty Cobb created problems when he went into the stands to attack a fan.

Utility Players

"You just got caught in a position where you have no position."—Manager Sparky Anderson, explaining why he was forced to cut a utility player.

"I don't mind taking it from the lions and tigers, but I ain't about to take it from the gnits and gnats."—Umpire Al Barlick to utilityman Johnny Temple after Temple complained that the star players were not treated the same by umpires.

"Having one Dykes is like having five or six players and only one to feed, clothe and pay."—A's manager Connie Mack about versatile Jimmy Dykes. At various times from 1918 through 1932 for the A's, the mostly-infielder played every position except catcher.

"Maybe they ought to change our name to the Cleveland Utility Company. We don't have anything but utility men."—Indians infielder Lou Camilli in 1971.

"… Stengel looked into his closet of spare parts, which is far less well stocked than his old Yankee cornucopia."—Roger Angell on Stengel's Mets in *The Summer Game* (1972).

"Today I told my little girl, 'I'm going to the ballpark,' and she asked 'What for?'"—Dave Anderson of the Dodgers, commenting on his lack of playing time.

"In fact, he is the *most* utility infielder in history. He spent two years as Cal Ripken's backup in Baltimore."—Bob Costas describing Rene Gonzalez, who spent over 15 years as a utility player for several clubs.

"**V** is for Vance
The Dodgers' own Dazzy;
None of his rivals
Could throw as fast as he."
—Ogden Nash on Dazzy Vance.

Dazzy Vance (1891–1961)

Hall of Fame 1955

"Since the beginning, baseball in Brooklyn has been a peculiar sport…. A scout sent to the Southern Association with definite instructions to buy a young catcher, bought an old pitcher instead. The young catcher never was heard of again, but the old pitcher was Dazzy Vance."—Tom Meany and Bill McCullough in a 1937 article in the *Saturday Evening Post*.

"Dazzy Vance was a big, ambling, friendly man who was fond of good times and had little use for training…. But when he cut loose his hard pitch with that tattered underwear flapping behind it, the ball whistled into the plate so fast that batters sometimes hadn't even time to blink."—Robert Smith in *Baseball* (1970).

Vance was a late-blooming strikeout pitcher for the Dodgers in the 1920s.

Clarence Arthur Vance began in the Major Leagues later than any other Hall of Famer except Satchel Paige. Vance spent over 12 years bouncing around the minor leagues and being rejected by Major League teams. He appeared in nine games for the Pirates and Yankees in 1915 at age 24, losing four games. He reappeared in two games for the Yankees in 1918 but did not return for good to the Major Leagues until 1922 at age 31 with the Dodgers. Arm trouble delayed his reentry, but surgery and a 21–11 season in 1921 in the Southern League gave him his break.

For the next 11 years he was one of the top strikeout pitchers in the National League, leading seven straight seasons in that category. He won 28 games for the Dodgers in 1924, 25 in 1925 and 22 in 1928. He finally appeared in a World Series in 1934 at age 43, striking out three for the Cardinals in 1⅓ innings.

Vance won 197 games over his 16 years in the Major Leagues, but only 12 of those years were productive. He also pitched 30 shutouts (32 in older sources) and struck out 100 or more batters in 11 straight seasons.

After he retired, he operated a fishing camp at Homosassa Springs, Florida. He developed heart trouble and suffered a fatal heart attack in 1961, two weeks before his 70th birthday.

Arky Vaughan (1912–1952)

Hall of Fame (VC) 1985

"I'd say he was as good a man at short as I ever saw. He could do it all. And he was a good hitter. He could hit for power, and he could hit for average. And could he ever fly around those bases! I never saw anybody who could go from first to third or from second to home faster than Vaughan. Like we used to say, when he went around second his hip pocket was dipping sand. That's how sharp he cut those corners." — Rip Sewell of the Pirates quoted in

the *National Baseball Hall of Fame and Museum Yearbook*, edited by Bill Guilfoile (1989).

Vaughan played shortstop primarily for the Pirates in the 1930s, batting .318 over 14 seasons.

Born in Arkansas, Joseph Floyd Vaughan began his Major League career in 1932 with the Pirates. He started immediately for the club at shortstop and batted .318 in 129 games. Over the next nine seasons he batted .300 or better every year and led the league in 1935 with a .385 batting average and .607 slugging average. He was named *The Sporting News* MVP that season, though the BBWAA only voted him third.

Vaughan led the league in batting, runs scored and base on balls three times each during his 10 years with the Pirates. He was recognized as the premier-hitting shortstop in the National League during the 1930s and was considered a decent defensive shortstop.

The Dodgers traded for Vaughan after he batted .316 in 1941. He hit only .277 in 1942 and then was back to .305 in 1943. After that season his differences with manager Leo Durocher caused him to leave the club and return to his farm in California where he remained through the end of World War II. He returned to the Dodgers in 1947 for 64 games when Durocher was suspended for the season, batting .325 in a pinch-hitting role. He finished his 14-year career in 1948, batting .244 in 63 games.

Vaughan hit .300 or better 12 times for a .318 lifetime average and was elected to the All-Star team nine straight seasons. After he retired, he returned to California where he died in a boating accident at age 40.

Bill Veeck, Jr. (1914–1987)

Hall of Fame (VC) 1991

"The P.T. Barnum of Baseball" — Veeck's showman nickname.

"Whatever I've said over the years, the owners have looked at me as though I were a little boy trying to run fast so the propeller on my beanie would spin." — Veeck.

"With all the enemies he keeps making, baseball will let Veeck back in the day the Klan decides to welcome Jackie Robinson." — Anonymous 1965 remark about Veeck's chances of owning a Major League team again, which he did in 1975.

"I was fortunate enough to have a fine man to work for: Bill Veeck was probably the nicest and the greatest man that I ever met. Even at that particular time he never showed any prejudice or bigotry or racism within himself. He fought for the little man, the underdog. Bill Veeck didn't look at me as a black man but as an individual who could play baseball and who could possibly help his team win some games." — Larry Doby quoted in *For the Love of the Game*, by Cynthia J. Wilber (1992).

Veeck was one of the most innovative owners of all time during a baseball career lasting from the 1930s through 1981.

Veeck was the son of Chicago sportswriter Bill Veeck, Sr., who became president of the Cubs in 1919. Veeck, Sr., was the inspiration for the song, "Won't You Come Home, Bill Bailey?" Bailey was Veeck's pen name, and the song was inspired when Veeck went to work for a rival Chicago newspaper.

Veeck, Jr., has been called the most influential owner ever, in part because of his maverick attitude, innovative promotions and charisma. His method of depreciating players revolutionized the manner in which Major League owners paid **Taxes** on their clubs.

Veeck got his start with the Cubs, for whom his father served as an executive until his death in 1933. Veeck stayed with the club in promotions until 1941, when at age 26 he bought the Milwaukee club in the American Association. Upon returning from mili-

Bill Veeck, Jr., legendary owner, promoter and raconteur, circa 1977. He owned the White Sox, for the second time, between 1975 and 1981.

tary duty, he bought the American League Indians at age 31 in mid–1946. He was forced to sell the club in 1949 because of financial difficulties, but the club drew 2,620,627 fans during the pennant-winning 1948 season; a record that stood until the 1970s. He bought the Browns for the 1951 season but was forced to sell out in 1953 and the club moved to Baltimore.

Veeck bought the White Sox in 1959 (they went to the World Series), but sold out in 1961 due to poor health. After a long sabbatical from Major League Baseball (enforced by the other owners, who regarded him as a nuisance and a flake), he bought the White Sox again in December 1975. He made it a practice to sit in the Comiskey Park stands with the fans for the duration of his ownership, which ended in 1981.

Veeck was involved heavily in the effort to integrate Major League Baseball, bringing the first black player to the American League: Larry Doby to the Indians in 1947. He brought venerable Satchel Paige to the Indians in 1948. Veeck was unsuccessful in one of his early attempts to buy a Major League club when it was rumored that he intended to stock the club with black players (see also **Integration**, showing this to be a fabrication). See **Midgets** and **Promotions** for Veeck's sometimes wild efforts to put fans in the seats.

Veeck had a number of health problems after a World War II leg injury that resulted in amputation. Complications from that plagued him throughout his life and he underwent 31 operations as a result.

Books. Gerald Eskenazi, *Bill Veeck: A Baseball Legend* (1988); Bill Veeck with Ed Linn, *The Hustler's Handbook* (1965); Bill Veeck with Ed Linn, *Thirty Tons a Day* (1972), about Veeck's ownership of a horse racing track; Bill Veeck and Ed Linn, *Veeck—As in Wreck* (1962).

Vendors See *Concessions and Concessionaires*

Venezuela

"The fans [Satchel] Paige remembers best lived in the wild country of northwestern Venezuela. These fans were short, dark, fierce fellows who ran about the forest in G strings, shooting poisoned arrows at birds and occasional oil-line workers. Every so often, some of them sneaked into the Maracaibo ball park and had to be run out to keep them from scaring the customers and stealing baseballs."—Sportswriter Richard Collier in a 1953 *Collier's* magazine article. Apparently it was a toss-up for Paige between being shot with a blow dart or being saluted by the natives. After they presented Paige with a baseball, he joined the locals for a meal of pig, roots and bugs.

Origins. The Cubans are credited by some with introducing the game to Venezuela in 1895, and a Venezuelan baseball league supposedly was established that season (according to some sources). Others report that, as with other Latin American countries, baseball was introduced by students returning from the U.S. during the 1890s. The Venezuelan Federation of Amateur Baseball was formed in 1927 and baseball is now the national sport.

Professional League. Venezuela has a six-team professional league that plays a 60-game winter schedule. The league began in 1946 with four teams. Today, teams may use seven foreign players, though the strong Caracas club is allowed only six foreigners. The league requires that at least four Venezuelan players be on the field at all times.

The winter league teams in 1995 were the Leones del Caracas, Caribes de Oriente, Navegantes del Magallanes, Tiburones de la Guaira, Aguilas del Zulia, Cardenales de Lara, Tigres de Aragua and Pastora de Occidente.

In support of a national strike, in December 2002 the Venezuelan professional league suspended its games. Many of the eight teams in the league were owned by members of the news media, who were opposed to President Hugo Chavez. The league canceled its season on January 13.

By 2004 there were two divisions with four teams. The Western Division (in English): Zulia Eagles, Lara Cardinals, Aragua Tigers, Los Llanos Pastora; the Eastern Division: Caracas Lions, Magallanes Navigators, La Guaira Sharks, Eastern Caribbeans.

Hostages. In 1971 the White Sox and Yankees scheduled an exhibition game in Venezuela because Red Sox shortstop Luis Aparicio was a Venezuelan icon. After the series the two clubs were bussed to the airport for the flight back to the U.S. The Venezuelans refused to let the clubs leave until taxes on the gate receipts were paid. The clubs were unable to make good immediately, so each club left a hostage so the others could depart. Yankee publicist Bob Fishel and White Sox traveling secretary Don Unferth were left behind. Mickey Mantle stood at the base of the airplane and took up a collection for Fishel. Yankee president Lee MacPhail gave Fishel a blank check to cover expenses. The taxes were paid the next day, and Fishel and Unferth were released.

Major League Players. A number of Venezuelans have starred in the Major Leagues. There were 17 Venezuelan Major Leaguers in 1993, led by Andres Galarraga of the Rockies. Between 1939 and 1996 there were over 70 Venezuelan Major Leaguers and over 150 minor leaguers. The country is the second-largest Latin supplier of Major League talent, behind only the Dominican Republic.

Chico Carrascuel. Carrascuel played for 10 years in the American League, batting .258 while starting at shortstop. During the early 1950s the only Venezuelan Major Leaguers were Carrasquel, Yo-Yo Davalillo (Vic's brother) and Ray Monzant. Only Carrasquel made more than a brief appearance.

Luis Aparicio. Aparicio was elected to the Hall of Fame in 1984 after playing shortstop for 18 years beginning in 1956. He led the American League in stolen bases nine straight seasons.

Cesar Tovar. Tovar batted .278 over a 12-year career primarily with the Twins in the 1960s and early 1970s.

Dave Concepcion. Concepcion made the All-Star team at shortstop for the Reds in 1973 and 1975 through 1982, winning Gold Glove Awards in 1974, 1977 and 1979.

Vic Davalillo. Davalillo played for 16 years in the Major Leagues, batting .279 despite being only 5'7" and 150 pounds.

Tony Armas. Armas hit more home runs than any other American League player over the six years from 1980 through 1985.

Andres Galarraga. Galarraga starred for the Expos in the late 1980s and 1990s before being traded to the Cardinals. After two dismal seasons, he signed with the Rockies for the club's first season and won a batting title after flirting with .400 most of the year.

2000s. Some of the Venezuelan players of the 2000s include Edgardo Alfonzo, Wilson Alvarez, Tony Castillo, Roger Cedeno, Ramon Garcia, Ozzie Guillen, Carlos Guillen, Freddy Garcia, Carlos Hernandez, Magglio Ordonez, Robert Perez, Edgar Ramos, Luis Sojo and, perhaps the best of the group, Omar Vizquel.

Perhaps the biggest surprise was the emergence of pitcher Johan Santana for the Twins, who blossomed in 2004 as one of the top pitchers in the American League.

2002/2003 Postseason Stars. The 2002 and 2003 postseasons featured two 20-year-old Venezuelans. Relief pitcher Francisco Rodriguez was terrific for the Angels in the 2002 postseason, after being added to the roster at the last minute. He won his first Major

League game in the postseason and a total of three that year as the Angels won the World Series. He had a postseason ERA of 1.93 in 11 appearances.

In 2003, 20-year-old Miguel Cabrera of the Marlins, a Class AA third baseman in June of that season, batted clean-up for the Marlins in the postseason. He hit a home run off the Cubs' Kerry Wood in Game 7 of the NLCS and hit another home run off Roger Clemens in Game 4 of the World Series. He set rookie records for postseason home runs and RBIs.

Managers. In mid-2004 Al Pedrique replaced Bob Brenley as manager of the Diamondbacks, joining Ozzie Guillen of the White Sox as the only Venezuelan managers in the Major Leagues.

Museum. The Venezuela Baseball Museum opened in 2004 in Sambil Center in Valencia.

Vietnam War

"If the Mets can win the World Series, the United States can get out of Vietnam."—Tom Seaver in 1969.

"It's a weird scene. You win a few baseball games and all of a sudden you're surrounded by reporters and TV men with cameras asking you about Vietnam and race relations."—Vida Blue in 1971.

Major League Veterans. Few Major League careers were impacted by the Vietnam War, as most players had National Guard commitments or reserve programs that allowed them to miss only a few games. None of the five Major Leaguers who served in the war were killed, but two minor league players lost their lives.

One of the Major Leaguers impacted was Jim Holt, a Vietnam veteran who played for the Twins and A's from 1968 through 1976, with a .265 average. He led the American League in pinch hits in 1975.

Phil Hennigan won 17 games for the Indians and Mets between 1969 and 1973. His career was delayed a year because of a military commitment in Vietnam.

Pitcher Larry Dierker had his Major League career interrupted by military duty in 1967 (not in Vietnam), but he returned to play into the mid-1970s and pitched a no-hitter on July 9, 1976.

Outfielder Bobby Jones was almost deaf as a result of 14 months of combat in Vietnam. He signed with the Senators in 1967 but did not make it to the Major Leagues until 1974. He lasted nine years before playing in Japan.

Al Bumbry, who played from 1972 through 1984 for the Orioles and was the American League Rookie of the Year in 1973, received a Bronze Star in Vietnam.

Troop Visits. Joe DiMaggio and Pete Rose were among the ballplayers who visited troops in Vietnam.

Roy Gleason.

"I'm glad I'm on this wall, instead of the other wall."—Vietnam veteran Roy Gleason, who had one hit for the Dodgers before being drafted, but who is on the club's private Dodger Stadium wall containing the club's all-time roster.

On September 28, 1963, the 6'4" Gleason had his only Major League at-bat. He had pinch-run seven times earlier in the month, but in a 12–3 loss to the Phillies he had a double and scored a run. During spring training in 1964 he was drafted into the Army and shipped to Vietnam. He had thought he could not be drafted because he was the sole supporter of his mother and sister, but before a year-long paperwork struggle ended, he had already been wounded while an infantry point-man on patrol in the jungle (for which he received a Purple Heart). His 1963 World Series ring disappeared at a base camp while he was out on patrol. His skills diminished from the wounds and he was unable to make the club two years later when he returned.

Forty years after his one at-bat, someone learned of his story and arranged for the Dodgers to let him throw out the first pitch and to receive a replica of his original World Series ring.

False Information. In March 1999 Blue Jays manager Tim Johnson was fired after he admitted lying about being a Vietnam veteran.

Virgin Islands

"The best place on earth."—Former Major Leaguer Valmy Thomas, who ran unsuccessfully for the Virgin Islands senate. He is usually listed as being Puerto Rican, because he was born there. His mother simply wanted better medical attention during the birth, so she took a boat over to Puerto Rico and then returned home to the Virgin Islands after the birth. He spent five seasons playing catcher for four different clubs, from 1957 through 1961.

Elrod Hendricks is the most prominent Major League player from the Virgin Islands. He played catcher for the Orioles from 1968 through 1979.

Second baseman Jerry Browne of the Rangers was the 1987 Rookie of the Year in the American League.

Infielder Horace Clarke averaged .256 for the Yankees from 1965 through early 1974.

Midre Cummings had a nine-year Major League career beginning in 1993, mostly for the Pirates as an outfielder.

"**W**, Wagner,
The bowlegged beauty;
Short was closed to all traffic
With Honus on duty."
—Ogden Nash on Honus Wagner.

Rube Waddell (1876–1914)

Hall of Fame 1946

"One of those characters, at once the most enviable and the saddest in the world, who are too great at heart for the civilization in which they live."—*Literary Digest* at Waddell's death.

Waddell played 13 seasons in the Major Leagues, winning 191 games between 1897 and 1910.

George Edward Waddell was a legendary *Eccentric* that made him an immortal of baseball. His childlike demeanor and strange habits caused him to wear out his welcome frequently, though A's owner Connie Mack put up with him simply because he was the best pitcher Mack ever had. Mack also credited Waddell with the finest curveball he ever saw.

Waddell joined the A's midway through the 1902 season at age 24 but still won 24 games for the club in 33 appearances. It was the first of four straight 20-win seasons for the A's through 1905. His top season was 1905 when he won 26 games, had an ERA of 1.48 and pitched eight shutouts. He also led the league in strikeouts, something he accomplished seven times in his career. In 1904 he struck out 349 batters, a record that was first surpassed by Sandy Koufax and twice by Nolan Ryan. It was widely believed for many years that Waddell's *Strikeout* record was lower and had been broken by Bob Feller with 348 in 1946.

Waddell won 19 games for the Browns in 1908, but he faded badly in 1909 and was out of Major League Baseball after 10 appearances in 1910. He finished with a 191–145 record and the sixth lowest ERA of all time at 2.16. He played for various minor league teams before contracting tuberculosis in St. Louis. He moved to San

Legendary shortstop Honus Wagner, considered by some as the greatest player of the first 20 years of the 20th century.

Antonio, Texas, where he died in a sanitarium on April Fool's Day 1914.

Waddell was a heavy drinker, but that was not the direct cause of his death. His last health problems stemmed from being immersed for hours in cold water when a levee broke where he was living. He never truly recovered and died less than two years later (see also **Burial and Cemeteries**).

Honus Wagner (1874–1955)

Hall of Fame 1936

"There ain't much to being a ballplayer, if you're a ballplayer."—Wagner.

"It is hoped that Louisville didn't throw away very much money on the Wagner deal, as times are hard and Wagner won't set the world afire as a third baseman. He is a better outfielder than infielder."—*Sporting Life* on July 24, 1897.

"You can have your Cobbs, your Lajoies, your Chases, your Bakers but I'll take Wagner as my pick of the greatest. He is not only a marvelous mechanical player, but he has the quickest baseball brain I have ever observed."—John McGraw.

Wagner primarily played shortstop for Louisville and Pittsburgh from 1897 through 1917, batting .327.

John Peter Wagner was considered the greatest player ever by Giants manager John McGraw, Branch Rickey and Yankee general manager Ed Barrow. Barrow discovered Wagner in a Pennsylvania railroad yard in February 1896 while scouting Wagner's older brother, Butts Wagner. Wagner's first Major League game was for Louisville in 1897, for whom he batted .338 in 61 games. He did not play shortstop until 1901, and then only because the regular shortstop, Bones Ely, was caught trying to sign players to American League contracts.

Wagner hit .381 in 1900 when Louisville's best players were brought to Pittsburgh by owner Barney Dreyfuss. Over the next 13 seasons he never hit less than .324. Between 1900 and 1911 he led the league in hitting eight times, slugging average six times, doubles seven times, triples three times and RBIs four times.

With his huge hands and quick moves he was considered the premier shortstop of the era and probably the best of all time given the size of the gloves and playing surfaces. He also led the league in stolen bases five times, finishing with 722, tenth all-time.

Over 21 seasons Wagner hit .327 with 101 home runs, 1,732 RBIs and 3,418 hits. A versatile player, in addition to 1,888 games at shortstop, he played the outfield 372 times, first base 248 times, third base 209 times, second base 57 times and pitched in two games.

He managed the Pirates for five games in mid–1917, but the easygoing player-manager did not like the job and purportedly declined to return for the 1918 season (though he probably was simply an interim manager between Nixey Callahan and Hugo Bezdek — the latter returned for the 1918 season). For a short time after he retired following the 1917 season he managed a sporting goods store in Pittsburgh and played semipro ball for seven years. He became a Pirates coach in 1933, a position he held into the 1950s.

In sportswriter Fred Lieb's, *Baseball as I Have Known It* (1977), Lieb recounted how he resurrected Wagner from poverty during the Depression. Based on a letter from a woman in Pittsburgh in 1933, Lieb began a series of columns about Wagner in which Lieb chastised the Pirates for letting Wagner slip into obscurity. The Pirates responded by putting him on the payroll permanently and paying off his debts.

Book. Arthur D. Hittner, *Honus Wagner: The Life of Baseball's Flying Dutchman* (2004).

Waivers

"A waiver means that your arm is in the ragbag and the old clothes man is singing his twilight song to the little birdies in the trees." — Nick Altrock.

"Enclosed is one dollar. Please send me my Yogi bear to the following address…" — Letter to the Mets after Yogi Berra was put on waivers and could be claimed for $1.

"I'm sure we'll be able to work out a fair price for your services, based on the fact that you are unemployed." — Comic writer Marvin Kitman claiming Dick Stuart for the $1 waiver price in 1968, quoted in *Voices of Baseball*, by Bob Chieger (1983).

"Now somewhere in this favored land the sun is shining bright.
The band is playing somewhere, and somewhere hearts are light.
And somewhere men are laughing, but here the money's saved
For justice has hit Mudville — Moody Casey has been waived." — Last stanza of a parody by Mike Dwornicki.

Origin/Early Rules. The waiver rule was designed to allow all other teams in a league the opportunity to sign a player cut by another club. Prior to that if a player was cut by a club, he was free to be signed by any other team in any other league. Under the waiver rules, the player could not sign with a club outside of the league until every other club had passed on him.

The rule has its origins in an 1882 meeting among three American Association teams and the Northwestern League in an effort to establish order and harmony: the primary purpose was for each club to respect each other's players. The rule was embodied in the 1885 National Agreement, which was amended due to the abuses of the 10-day waiting period by signing players for 10 days only. It also allowed players to negotiate with other teams in the league after that period was over.

In 1905 all teams in a league had to pass on a player for him to be waived out of the league. This was more important in an era when many players continued their careers in the minor leagues.

The lowest team in the league's standings had first choice for claiming a player on waivers. If claimed, the player could be withdrawn by the club that put him on waivers.

Lawsuit. During the Federal League challenge in 1914, Hal Chase gave the White Sox 10 days' notice that he was departing for Buffalo of the outlaw league. The New York Supreme Court upheld Chase's right, holding that the 10-day notice provision, used exclusively by clubs to cut players, was reciprocal.

Armando Marsans was the first prominent Cuban player in the Major Leagues. He was an early challenger of baseball's standard player contract, giving Cincinnati 10 days' notice in 1914 and then jumping to the Federal League. An injunction barring him from playing for St. Louis in the Federal League eventually was dismissed.

The Modern Rule.

"A permission granted for the assignment of a Major League Player contract to either another Major League Club or National Association Club. Such permission is granted for a specific period … and only after each Major League Club has been given an opportunity to accept the assignment of that player contract and none has filed a claim accepting assignment of that contract." — Rule 10(A).

The waiver rules are contained in the Professional Baseball Agreement and National Association Agreement of the National Association of Professional Baseball Leagues (minor leagues).

The early waiver rules have remained largely intact. Before June 15 a player may be traded to any club in his own league during the season without clearing waivers. He may be traded out of the league before that date only if he clears waivers (see also *Trades and Player Sales*). After June 15 he may not be traded to any club in either league without clearing waivers. A club that claims a player must have room on its roster. The waiver rule still works according to the reverse order of the league standings, so that the worst clubs have priority in claiming a player from the waiver list.

If a player is released, then a club may invoke the $1 waiver price but must assume the player's contract. Clubs often negotiate to determine how much the releasing club might pay of the player's contract in order to move him to another club through the waiver system.

A player cannot be put on waivers and then withdrawn more than twice in any one season. If he is waived a third time by the same team, the waiver is irrevocable.

Waivers may not be requested on players whose status is voluntarily retired, in the military, suspended, disqualified or on the ineligible list. He must be an active list player. Certain restrictions apply to players on the disabled list, but they can be waived.

From August 1 through November 10, a player on the 40-man roster of a club must clear league waivers before a club can trade him. If a club makes a claim to a player, the club that placed him on waivers has 48 hours to decide whether to let him go, try to trade him to the club that claimed him, or simply withdraw his name. If the player is withdrawn, he cannot be placed on waivers again for 30 days. If a player is placed on waivers a second time during a single waiver period and is claimed, the claiming team must put him on its 25-man roster and pay his former team a $25,000 waiver fee. If two or more teams claim a player, a trade cannot be made, but the player can still be sent to the team that is lowest in the standings who claims him for the waiver fee. Waivers cannot be requested between October 10 and November 10, which traditionally was the 30-day period during and after postseason play.

Number of Waivers. The waiver wire often has as many as 210 players on it, as each team may put up to a maximum of seven players on at a time.

Waiver Price.

1909	$ 1,800
1944	7,500
1964	20,000
1969	25,000
1990	20,000

Most Players Waivable. After his club lost the 1941 World Series, Dodger general manager Larry MacPhail purportedly put his entire club on waivers for the purpose of selling then en masse to the Browns. The deal allegedly fell through when the financing failed to materialize for Browns owner Don Barnes. A club now cannot request waivers on more than seven players in a day.

Bobby Wallace (1873–1960)

Hall of Fame (VC) 1953

"The best player in the American League, the only man I would get if I could, plays on a tail-end team, and few people pay any attention to him. I mean Bobby Wallace of St. Louis. There's a boy who can play any position and hit. I wish I had him." — Pirates owner Barney Dreyfuss, describing Wallace in 1902 at the height of the war between the American and National Leagues. Wallace was then with the Browns and was the highest paid player in baseball.

Wallace played 25 seasons in the Major Leagues between 1894 and 1918, batting .266 while playing primarily at shortstop.

Rhoderick John Wallace was born within three months of and near the same town as Honus Wagner and played in Wagner's shadow throughout most of his 25-year career. Wallace began as a pitcher in 1894 with the Cleveland Spiders, but three years later played exclusively in the infield. He moved to the Cardinals in 1899 and established himself as one of the dominant shortstops in the league.

Wallace signed with the crosstown rival Browns in 1902 and remained with the club through the 1916 season though he primarily *umpired* in the American League during 1915 and 1916. He finished his playing career with the Cardinals in 1917 and 1918 at age 44. He managed the Browns in 1911 and 1912 and also the Reds in 1937. He scouted for the Reds until his death in 1960.

Known primarily for his defensive play, Wallace batted over .300 three times and had a .266 lifetime average. He stole 201 bases and hit 153 triples.

Ed Walsh (1881–1959)

Hall of Fame 1946

"This being regarded as a Star Pitcher is a harder job than being a coal miner." — Walsh.

"Coal mining around Plains, Pennsylvania, in his early days had failed to stunt his physique, and 'Apollo' proved no misnomer. When, however, he came to carry out the role of the Grecian divinity aside from music and oratory, Walsh fell afoul of the 'Old Roman' [Comiskey]. Posing had never been an attribute of 'Commy.' It was an art with Walsh. On the point of delivering the ball he sometimes would stand for a minute or more, with arms poised on high, shoulders thrown back, one foot a step in front of the other and all the time never moving a muscle." — G.W. Axelson in *"Commy"* (1919).

"Great big, strong, good-looking fellow. He threw a spitball — I think that ball disintegrated on the way to the plate and the catcher put it back together again. I swear, when it went past the plate it was just the spit went by." — Sam Crawford in *The Glory of Their Times*.

Walsh won 195 games over 14 seasons from 1904 through 1917.

Edward Augustine "Big Ed" Walsh of Pennsylvania became the greatest *Spitball* pitcher of all time, although he had only four stellar seasons. He began his Major League career in 1904 with the White Sox, winning six games. After a 17–13 record in 1906 he won two games in the World Series. He won 24 games in 1907 with a 1.88 ERA and 10 shutouts to establish himself as one of the best pitchers in the game.

Walsh exploded for 40 wins in 1908 for the White Sox and pitched 464 innings (most ever in the American League) in 66 games (49 starts). He also had six saves and five relief wins among the 40. He won 27 games in both 1911 and 1912 and then his arm wore out. More specifically, his career came to a halt after hurting his shoulder throwing a medicine ball during spring training in California in 1913. He won eight games in 1913 and pitched in only 17 games over the next five seasons. He finished his career with four appearances in 1917 for the Braves but added no wins to his career total of 195. He has the all-time lowest lifetime ERA at 1.82.

During World War I he worked in a munitions factory and after the war he umpired in the American League in 1922. He then retired to private life though he did some scouting around New England.

Lloyd Waner (1906–1982)

Hall of Fame (VC) 1967

"The Pirates took Lloyd along to spring training in 1927, mostly just to look at him a little closer. They never thought he could possibly make the team, 'cause Lloyd only weighed about 130 pounds then. He was only twenty years old, and was even smaller than me." — Paul Waner quoted in *The Glory of Their Times*, by Lawrence S. Ritter (1984).

Waner batted .316 over 18 seasons principally with the Pirates beginning in 1927.

Waner, known as "Little Poison" to his brother Paul's "Big Poison" (though they were almost exactly the same height and weight) began his Major League career in the Pirates outfield in 1927, one year after his older brother arrived. He batted .355 in 150 games with a rookie-record 223 hits and a league-leading 133 runs scored. He went on to hit over .300 six straight times before two off-seasons in 1933 and 1934.

Waner hit .309 in 1935 for the Pirates and then hit .313 or better through 1938. He began to fade after that and was traded in 1941. He bounced around to various National League teams, retired briefly in 1943 and returned to the Pirates for a few games in 1944 and 1945. He retired permanently in 1945 after 18 seasons, batting .316 lifetime with 2,459 hits. He hit .400 in the 1927 World Series for the Pirates as a rookie. He played side-by-side in the outfield with his brother Paul for 14 seasons: Lloyd in center field and Paul in right. After his retirement he scouted for the Pirates until 1949 and then scouted briefly for the Orioles in 1955.

Book. Clifton Blue Parker, *Big and Little Poison: Paul and Lloyd Waner* (2002).

Paul Waner (1903–1965)

Hall of Fame 1952

"He could drink pretty good. That's no secret. But he could also sober himself up in a hurry. He would do backflips. He had remarkable agility, like an acrobat. Fifteen or twenty minutes of backflips and he was cold sober, ready to go out to the ball park and get his three hits." — Buddy Hassett quoted in *Baseball Between the Lines*, by Donald Honig (1976).

Waner batted .333 over 20 seasons primarily with the Pirates beginning in 1926.

As the better-hitting Waner brother, "Big Poison" Paul starred in the Pacific Coast League in the mid–1920s before signing with the Pirates in 1926, one year earlier than Lloyd. He started immediately in the outfield and hit .336 in 144 games. He led the league in hitting in 1927 with a .380 average and never hit below .300 through 1937. He was the National League MVP in 1927 and led the league in hitting in 1934 (.362) and 1936 (.373). He remained with the Pirates through 1940 when he hit .290 in 89 games.

A notorious drinker, he began to fade in 1941 while playing for the Dodgers and Braves, though he bounced back to hit .311 in 82 games for the Dodgers in 1943. He finished his career with a few games for the Yankees in late 1944 and one game in 1945. Over his 20-year career he batted .333 with 603 doubles and 190 triples. He had 3,152 hits and batted .333 in his one World Series for the Pirates in 1927.

Waner managed in the minor leagues in 1946 and later became a hitting coach for the Braves, Cardinals and Phillies, but his alcoholism prevented him from managing again.

War

"I have observed that baseball is not unlike war, and when you get right down to it, we batters are the heavy artillery." — Ty Cobb.

See *Civil War*, *Korean War*, *Spanish-American War*, *Vietnam War*, *World War I* and *World War II*.

John Montgomery Ward (1860–1925)

Hall of Fame (VC) 1964

"One was hard-working John Montgomery Ward, now the front-line pitcher, who was destined to become one of the great personalities in nineteenth-century baseball. A close student of the game, he continually practiced playing other positions, and in time his prowess rested on his ability as a shortstop. But in 1879, he pitched Providence to the pennant." — David Quentin Voigt in *American Baseball* (1966).

Ward generally pitched and played shortstop during his 17-year Major League career that began in 1878.

John Montgomery Ward, known as Monte or Johnny, won 165 games in seven years with Providence and New York from 1878 through 1884, with a high of 47 wins in 1879 to lead the league. He pitched a perfect game in 1880. He played a number of games in the outfield through 1884 and when his pitching arm wore out he switched to shortstop for the 1885 season.

Ward remained in the infield for the remainder of his career, first playing for the Giants through the 1889 season. He moved over to Brooklyn of the Players League in 1890 and then back to the National League Dodgers in 1891 and 1892. He finished his career back with the Giants for the 1893 and 1894 seasons, retiring after 17 years with a .275 batting average. He led the National League in stolen bases with 111 in 1887 and 88 in 1892, finishing his career with 504 (although no records exist for seasons prior to 1887). Ward was a player-manager in 1880, 1884 and for the last five years of his career through 1894.

Ward purportedly entered Penn State University at age 13. He received a law degree from Columbia University in 1885 and spoke five languages. He was an attorney during his playing days and was instrumental in the formation of the 1890 Players League. At the height of his managerial career, Ward quit baseball and began practicing law. He was an accomplished attorney who for a time was the chief counsel to the National League.

In 1909 he was touted for the position of National League president to succeed Harry Pulliam. He was not selected, in part because of the controversy surrounding his prior representation of players against individual owners and the league. In 1911 he became a part-owner of the Boston Braves and later was an executive with the Brooklyn club in the Federal League.

Ward was wealthy and married for a short time to a well-known New York actress (see also *Dauvrey Cup*), so he had no need to pursue a baseball job following his playing days. He was a distant cousin of Aaron Ward, who founded the Montgomery Ward department store. He was a leading amateur golfer and supposedly died shortly after playing in the 1925 Masters Tournament in Augusta, Georgia. However, the Masters did not exist until 1934 and was not called the Masters until four years later. Other sources report that he died of pneumonia while on a hunting trip in Georgia.

Book. Bryan Di Salvatore, *Clever Base-Ballist: The Life and Times of John Montgomery Ward* (1999); David Stevens, *Baseball's Radical for All Seasons* (1998); John Montgomery Ward, *Base-Ball: How to Become a Player* (1888) (reprinted in 1994 by SABR).

Nineteenth century New York Giants shortstop (and attorney) John Montgomery Ward.

Warm-Up Pitches

"Ryne Duren was a one-pitch pitcher. His one pitch was a wild warm-up." — Jim Bouton in *Ball Four*, with Leonard Schechter (1970). The bottle glasses-wearing pitcher made a habit of scaring opposing batters by intentionally hitting the backstop with one of his warm-up pitches.

"I figured the old arm had just so many throws in it and there wasn't any use wasting them. Like, for instance, I never warmed up ten, fifteen minutes before a game like most pitchers do. I'd loosen up for maybe three, four minutes. Five at the outside. And I never went to the bullpen. Oh, I'd relieve all right, plenty of times [90], but I went right from the bench to the box and I'd take a few warm-up pitches there and I'd be ready." — Cy Young in *The Immortals*, by Lee Allen and Tom Meany (1965).

Rule. Nineteenth century pitchers sometimes threw warm-up pitches after a putout. In 1911 Ban Johnson decreed that there would be no warm-up pitches before an inning. Prior to that, five warm-up pitches were allowed. It was believed that Johnson issued the decree to speed up games that had been lengthened as a result of the introduction of the lively ball the previous year (which caused more time-consuming scoring).

One source reported that if Johnson's rule was broken, it would result in an inside-the-park home run. This erroneous statement was made apparently because of an incident arising from the new rule.

Fast Start. On June 27, 1911, at Fenway Park, Red Sox pitcher Ed Karger, noting that his outfielders were not in position, began to throw warm-up pitches. On the second warm-up throw, A's batter Stuffy McInnis drove a single to right-center field but continued circling the bases for a home run as outfielder Tris Speaker failed to chase the ball. Umpire Ben Egan allowed the home run because of the rule. Johnson rejected the Red Sox protest, which was based on the claim that not all the A's outfielders had left the field before the hit.

Grover Cleveland Alexander. Alexander was noted for his pinpoint control. During the 1926 World Series he came into the game in the 7th inning with the bases load, two out and Tony Lazzeri at the plate. Some sources report that he took no warm-up pitches, partly because he was so hung over from celebrating his previous day's victory. He then struck out Lazzeri and went on to save the game. More reliable sources include warm-up pitches in their descriptions.

Still another source reported that Alexander supposedly walked onto the mound to the waiting Hornsby, who asked him how he was feeling. Alexander said he felt fine but did not want to throw any warm-up pitches that would give away that fact.

One source reported that Alexander often warmed up before a game with a 12-pound shot for a few throws so that the ball would seem light in comparison.

Injury. A player other than a pitcher who comes into the game for an injured player is allowed five warm-up throws.

Assault. On April 23, 1999, Wichita State University pitcher Ben Christensen hit Evanston's lead-off batter with a warm-up pitch, even though the batter was standing in the on-deck circle 30 feet from the batter's box. Batter Anthony Molina took 30 stitches to close the gash. Christensen said that Molina was trying to time his pitches and that pitching coach Brent Kemnitz told him to brush back anyone who stood too close to the plate during his warm-ups. Christensen and Kemnitz were suspended for the season by the conference. Molina filed assault charges that resulted in a 2002 settlement.

Warning Tracks

"It's a different color."— Architect's inadequate response when asked how outfielders would know they were on the artificial turf warning track of Kansas City's new Royals Stadium. After Willie Horton was hurt running into the outfield wall, the Major League Players Association successfully fought to have the warning track surface changed to dirt.

"I once scouted a pitcher who was so bad that when he came into a game the ground crew dragged the warning track."— Scout Ellis Clary.

"Grubb goes back, back … he's *under* the warning track, and he makes the play."— Jerry Coleman.

"I was at Dodger Stadium last year and I was confused because I don't know why a stadium that cost so much money, they can't spend enough money to have the grass go all the way to the wall!"— Actor Garry Shandling.

Early Days.

"They taught me how to climb up the damn hill, but not how to come down."— Frustrated 1910s outfielder Smead Jolley on the rising outfield terrace at Fenway Park known as "Duffy's Cliff," named after outfielder Duffy Lewis.

Crosley Field in Cincinnati had a rising terrace that created a four-foot slope to the wall. This was the usual way of giving warning to players that the wall was nearby. It was not until the 1920s that dirt warning tracks were used (but not in the Major Leagues), a practice sometimes attributed to Branch Rickey.

Modern Warning Tracks. In 1948 the Dodgers installed the first dirt warning track in the Major Leagues because outfielder Pete Reiser kept running into the wall (see also *Injuries and Illness*—Head).

Ocean Motif. The warning track at minor league Jack Russell Stadium, used by the Phillies for many years as their spring training site, was composed of crushed sea shells.

Washington, D.C.

"It was during this tense period [1859] that the Game of Base Ball—thus it was called, with capital letters—first made its appearance in the parks of Washington. In the summer of '59, government clerks, fascinated by newspaper accounts of the Game of Base Ball in other cities, formed a team called the Potomacs."— Columnist Shirley Povich.

"Washington is the only city in America to have lost its baseball team twice: the original Senators moved to Minnesota (to become the Twins) in the nineteen-sixties, and the expansion Senators moved to Texas (to become the Rangers) in the seventies. Its crime rate is high, its culture is iffy, and its weather is so oppressive that, in the years before air-conditioning, some diplomats got hardship pay."— Jeffrey Frank in *The New Yorker*.

Early Amateur Baseball. Baseball was popular in the capital before the Civil War. The game existed in the city since at least 1859, when a group of government clerks formed the Potomacs/Nationals. By 1865 the National Athletic Club drew upwards of 6,000 fans to the Ellipse behind the White House, where President Andrew Johnson was among the spectators. The first extended road trip of an American club was by the Washington Nationals in 1867, who travelled 3,000 miles to play nine games.

Professional Clubs. Professional baseball existed in Washington through the 1870s, as the Olympics were part of the 1871–1875 National Association. In 1872 the Washington Nationals were also admitted to the association though neither club fared well. The Olympics lasted only the first two seasons; the Nationals were in the league in 1872 and 1875. The Major League clubs:

Union Association Nationals (1884)
American Association Nationals (1884)
American Association Statesmen (1891)
National League Statesmen (1886–1889)
National League Senators (1892–1899)
American League Senators (1901–1971)
National League Nationals (2005–)

Washington Monument

See *Stunts* for efforts by ballplayers to catch balls dropped from the top of the Washington Monument.

Washington Nationals (Amateur)

"Washington also caught the baseball bug. Government clerks formed the Potomac Club there in the summer of 1859, and that November a second team, the Nationals, composed mainly of government clerks, joined them. These teams practiced and played each other in the backyard of the White House."— Harold Seymour in *Baseball: The Early Years* (1960).

Formed in November 1859 and one of the top 1860s amateur teams, the exploits of the Nationals underscore the heated East/West rivalry in baseball. The team toured the West in 1867 (including Columbus, Cincinnati, Louisville, Indianapolis and St. Louis) and beat all teams except Rockford (who had 17-year-old Al Spalding on the mound), to whom they lost 29–23 at Dexter Park in Chicago. The Washington team then offered a letter acknowledging that they were no longer the "National Champions." The team's 53–10 defeat of the amateur Cincinnati Red Stockings on this tour was part of the impetus for the Red Stockings to reorganize into baseball's first all-professional team for the 1869 season.

Washington Nationals

National Association 1872, 1875

The club made an inauspicious debut in the National Association with an 0–11 record early in the 1872 season before dropping out of the league. The Nationals returned to the league in 1875, completing only part of the season with a 4–23 record (but what was to be expected from a club led by a manager named Holly Hollingshead).

The first fenced ballpark in Washington was built in 1870 by Mike Scanlon, a pillar of Washington baseball in that decade. He built the park at 17th and S Streets N.W., put up 500 seats and charged a 25-cent admission. This was the home of the Washington Olympics in 1871 and the Olympics and Nationals in 1872.

Washington Nationals

Union Association 1884

Long-time Washington baseball man Mike Scanlon owned and managed the club to a seventh-place finish in the 12-team league with a record of 47–65.

Washington Nationals

American Association 1884

The Nationals were admitted to the American Association in response to the 1884 Union Association threat. The club disbanded after finishing last with a 12–51 record.

Washington Nationals

National League 2005–

Origins. The *Montreal Expos* moved to Washington for the start of the 2005 season while still owned collectively by Major League owners. Frank Robinson remained the manager.

Washington Olympics

National Association 1871–1872

The Olympics were 15–15 in the league's first season and in 1872 played only nine games before dropping out with a 2–7 record.

Washington Senators

National League 1892–1899

See *Washington Statesmen/Senators*.

Washington Senators

American League 1901–1971

"First in War, First in Peace, and Last in the American League."
— Sportswriter Charles Dryden in 1909; but as one pundit noted

during the Vietnam War, Washington was "Last in War, Last in Peace, and still last in the American League."

"I nearly went to the Senators, but there is a federal law which forbids them to win." — Author John Steinbeck on which team was his favorite.

Origins. The National League abandoned second-division Washington after the 1899 season. In December 1900 Kansas City of the newly named American League moved to Washington.

First Game. The Senators played their first game on April 26, 1901, after two rainouts. They beat the Phillies 5–1 in Philadelphia as Bill ("Can't Win") Carrick won. The club's first home game was on April 29, 1901, a 5–2 win over the Orioles.

Key Owners.

Ban Johnson and Fred Postal/1901–1903. Tom Manning, owner and manager of the Kansas City club, was to take over the new club. However, over the winter it was revealed that Manning would merely be the manager, and American League president Ban Johnson would control 51% of the club. The president of the club was to be Detroit hotel owner Fred Postal. Johnson controlled the club secretly until August 1903 when he announced that the league had bought out Postal for $15,000.

Early in 1904 the new owners included the owner of the *Washington Star* newspaper, Thomas C. Noyes. It also included attorney Wilton J. Lambert and former sportswriter William Dwyer.

Clark Griffith (HF)/1912–1955.

"For many years, Griff was pictured as a pinchpenny owner — canny in all his deals, hard-boiled in his baseball philosophy, and niggardly in his treatment of players. Clark was tough. He had to be. Griff was not a wealthy man, and the financial demands of keeping the Washington franchise alive were enough to challenge the patience of a saint, or cause the most confirmed optimist to cry in his beer." — Ford Frick in *Games, Asterisks and People* (1973).

Hall of Famer *Clark Griffith* bought 10% of the club for $27,000 in 1912 when he arrived to manage. Some sources reported that between 1912 and 1920 he bought up blocks of stock in the club; others reported that he bought all of the stock. What appears to be most accurate is that after the 1919 season when the club finished seventh, the stockholders refused to give Griffith a freer hand with club finances. Griffith then bought control of the club for the first time, using an investor brought to him by Connie Mack of the A's. William Richardson, an exporter from Philadelphia, and Griffith each paid $145,000 for 40% of the club, for a controlling 80% interest. Griffith received an $85,000 loan to make the deal.

Griffith ran the operation through the 1940s, with occasional success, but in 1950 he lost some control of the club. Richardson had died and his estate had no interest in baseball. Before the 1950 season the estate sold out its 40% interest to John Jachym of Jamestown, New York, who wanted an active role in the operation. Griffith managed to persuade the other shareholders to continue with him in control of the club and he did so until his death in October 1955. His adopted son Calvin (who was his nephew) took over the club, but the franchise was suffering from mediocrity and fan disinterest.

Calvin Griffith/1955–1960.

"He's the perfect businessman. He likes to get the most for the least. And he likes the least part best." — Pitcher Dave Goltz.

"Calvin Griffith returned from the fishing season opener with his limit of walleyes. Calvin immediately took the walleyes to a grocery store and traded them for a package of Mrs. Paul's frozen fish sticks and ten dollars in cash." — Sportswriter Charley Walters on the poor quality of Griffith's trades.

Calvin and his sister were adopted by Clark Griffith in 1922 when Calvin was 10 years old. He became a batboy for the Senators when they moved to Washington. As an adult he returned to the Senators after managing in Chattanooga and North Carolina. After Clark's death, Calvin became the leader of the club and held a controlling interest with his sister, Thelma Griffith Haynes. By the late 1950s, they each owned 26% of the stock.

During the 1958 All-Star break, reports first surfaced that the club had agreed to move to Minneapolis and its new ballpark. Despite congressional threats of antitrust action if the club moved, the city of Minneapolis continued its public overtures to the Senators. The deal was consummated as part of the American League's **Expansion** for the 1961 season (see also **Franchise Shifts**). See also Jon Kerr, *Calvin: Baseball's Last Dinosaur* (1990).

The club departed for Minnesota on October 26, 1960, and new owners took over an expansion franchise in Washington for the 1961 season.

New Franchise Owners.

James M. Johnston and James Lemon/1961–1968. Johnston was the chairman of the board in the 1960s until his death. Lemon succeeded him and quietly put the franchise up for sale in early 1968. Lemon gave comedian Bob Hope a verbal option to buy the club, but Hope eventually bowed out.

Bob Short/1968–1971.

"There are plenty of people who wonder why there are boobs like me who would buy this team, which right now looks like a license to lose money. The team now probably isn't worth what I paid for it, but nobody ever lost money selling a big-league baseball franchise."—Short.

Short was in Washington in October 1968 raising money for Hubert Humphrey's presidential campaign when he learned that the Senators were for sale. Short had sold the NBA Lakers three years earlier and had tried to buy the Senators at that time. He had been active in Democratic politics since he was a 21-year-old delegate to the 1940 convention that nominated Franklin Roosevelt to a third term. By the mid–1960s he was the Democratic National Committee Treasurer. In 1967 his trucking empire grossed $40 million and he was thought to be worth $10 million in the late 1960s. He paid approximately $9 million for the Senators. Short moved the club to Texas to become the Rangers for the 1972 season, and Washington has not had a Major League club since that **Franchise Shift**.

Nickname. Washington clubs have been called the Senators or Nationals almost since their beginning. In 1905 the club was doing so poorly that a newspaper called a meeting to come up with a new name. Nationals was recommended to permanently replace Senators, but also considered were Rough Riders, Teddyites, Has Beens and Tailenders. The club stayed with Senators.

Key Seasons.

"… you were just short of twenty-five at the time they last won, and now you're fifty. Did it ever occur to you that you may even die before you see them win the pennant again? For that matter you may die before any team other than the Yankees wins it. There's something rather tragic about that, something very sad."—Mr. Applegate (the Devil) to Joe Boyd in *The Year the Yankees Lost the Pennant*, by Douglas Wallop (1954), better known by its stage play name of *Damn Yankees* (see also **Theater**).

The Senators averaged 22 games behind first place in their 71 seasons.

1924.

"Dreams came true in the twelfth—Washington's dream and Walter Johnson's—and when the red September sun dropped down behind the dome of the Capitol the Senators were the baseball champions of the world."—Sportswriter Bill Corum.

The Senators won the pennant by 3½ games over the Yankees and won the World Series in seven games over the Giants for their only championship. Walter Johnson won Game 7 on a **Bad Hop** single over Giants third baseman Fred Lindstrom. Johnson led the league with 23 wins and Goose Goslin hit .344 with a league-leading 129 RBIs. See Mark Gauvreau Judge, *Damn Senators* (2003).

1925. The club repeated as American League champions but blew a 3–1 Series lead to the Pirates, and Walter Johnson lost Game 7 in the rain in Pittsburgh. Stan Coveleski and Johnson each won 20 games and Fred Marberry was the league's save leader for the second straight season.

1933. The Senators won the pennant with 99 wins under player-manager Joe Cronin. The club lost the World Series to the Giants in five games. General Crowder led the league with 24 wins and Cronin drove in 118 runs.

1944. The usually pitiful Senators came in second in 1943 due to the dilution of talent around the league. This set the stage for the exciting 1944 pennant race in which the Senators lost on the last day of the season—due in part to the failure of outfielder George "Bingo" Binks to wear his dark **Glasses** in the bright sun.

Key Players.

Walter Johnson (HF) is arguably the greatest pitcher of all time. He won 416 games over his 21-year career with the Senators from 1907 through 1927. He is first all-time with 110 shutouts and seventh with a 2.17 ERA. He won 20 games or more 12 times and over 30 games twice.

Sam Rice (HF) played 19 of his 20 seasons for the Senators from 1915 through 1933. He batted over .320 lifetime and had over 200 hits in a season six times for the Senators. He just missed 3,000 hits, finishing with 2,987 (2,889 with the Senators).

Goose Goslin (HF) played for the Senators for 12 seasons, 10 of them from 1921 through 1930. During that stretch he batted a high of .379 to lead the league in 1928. He also helped the club to three World Series appearances in 1924, 1925 and 1933.

Joe Cronin (HF) played seven seasons for the Senators from 1928 through 1934, batting over .300 four times and leading the club to the World Series in 1933 when he was player-manager.

Mickey Vernon played first base for the Senators for the first eight seasons of his career beginning in 1939 (with two years lost to World War II). He batted .353 in 1946 to lead the league. He returned to the club in 1950 for another six seasons and led the league in 1953 with a .337 average.

Key Managers.

Clark Griffith (HF) managed the club from 1912 through 1920, finishing second in 1912 and 1913.

Bucky Harris (HF), the "Boy Wonder" player-manager, took over the club in 1924 at age 28. He guided the club to the World Series and a victory in Game 7. He repeated the first-place finish in 1925 but lost the Series in seven games. He left after the 1928 season but returned in 1935 to manage for eight seasons, never finishing higher than fourth. He returned again in 1950 for five straight second division finishes through 1954.

Walter Johnson (HF).

"As much as I admired and liked Johnson, I also had my doubts about him as manager. It looked like the old story: you can take the boy out of the country, but you can't always take the country out of the boy…. Walter never changed; he was always the big, good-natured hick, yet with a streak of stubbornness that could hurt him when he had to direct a bunch of hard-bitten pros. I was afraid the players might take advantage of him…. That's just what happened the following season."—Al Schacht in his autobiography, *My Own Particular Screwball* (1955). Johnson managed the club for four seasons beginning in 1929, finishing second in 1930. He then became the general manager of the club.

Joe Cronin (HF) managed the club for only two seasons, but as player-manager of the club in 1933 he led the Senators to a pennant.

Cookie Lavagetto was the last Senators manager before the club left for Minnesota. He managed from May 7, 1957, until 74 games into the 1961 season with the Twins. His best finish was fifth place in 1960.

Ted Williams (HF).

"All managers are losers; they are the most expendable pieces of furniture on earth." — Williams just before taking over as manager of the Senators in 1968. He was the last Senators manager before the club moved to Texas. He led the club to a fourth-place finish in 1969 and then finished sixth and fifth before the club departed to become the Rangers.

"Lasts" for the First Franchise. The last home run for the team was by Bob Allison on September 28, 1960. The club's last game was played October 2, 1960, a 2–1 loss to the Orioles as Milt Pappas defeated Pedro Ramos.

"Lasts" for the Second Franchise. On September 30, 1971, the Senators played their last game. The club was leading the Yankees 7–5 with two out in the top of the 9th inning when fans ran onto the field and tore it up. Unable to restore order, the umpires forfeited the game to the Yankees. Neither pitcher's record was affected by the forfeit, so the official last decision for the Senators was by Jim Shellenback, a 6–3 loss to Mel Stottlemyre of the Yankees in the previous game. Frank Howard hit the club's last home run in that game.

Played for Both Franchises. Only three players were on both Washington franchises. Pitcher Hector Maestri appeared in two games for each club. Rudy Hernandez and Hal Woodeshick also played for both. All three played on the 1960 and 1961 clubs.

Last Active Player. Jim Kaat, who played 25 seasons over four decades, was the last active Senators player. Though the Senators disappeared after the 1971 season, Kaat did not retire until after the 1983 season.

Ballparks.

American League Park. When the American League arrived in 1901 the National League still held the lease on National Park, the only decent ballpark in Washington. That park had housed the National League entry during the 1890s and was the eventual site of Griffith Stadium.

The new American League club was forced to play its games at 14th Street and Bladensburg Road N.E., which was known as American League Park. The first Senators game played there was on April 29, 1901, in front of over 10,000 fans. The crowd included Admiral Dewey, the hero of Manila Bay during the Spanish-American War.

Washington Park/Griffith Stadium.

"Where losing clubs and vacant seats were perpetually bound…" — Curt Smith in *Voices of the Game* (1987).

After peace was established between the leagues in 1903, the club switched to National Park on Florida Avenue, and it became known as Washington Park (also known as American League Park and Boundary Field). On March 17, 1911 (erroneously 1913 in one source), the ballpark burned down before the season with the exception of a small section of the bleachers. It was rebuilt sufficiently in 18 days to host Opening Day. It had no box seats initially, except for a presidential box, and had no roof over the single-deck stands behind home plate. By 1920 Clark Griffith was entrenched as the club president and had renamed the park Griffith Stadium. It remained the club's home through the 1961 season (a year after the original club had already departed for Minnesota).

Griffith Stadium was a cavernous ballpark with early dimensions from left to right field of 408–391–421–378–328. It had seating capacity of 32,000 in 1911. Capacity fluctuated from a high of 35,000 in 1952 to 27,550 when the new Senators began play in 1961. Light standards were added in 1941 and night games were played that season. Washington shortened the massive dimensions in 1956 only after Calvin Griffith took over the presidency from his deceased father. Dimensions from left to right field were reduced to 386–372–421– 373–320.

Griffith Stadium was abandoned after the 1961 season, with the last game played September 21, 1961. Only 1,498 attended as the Senators lost 6–3. The game was played between the old Senators, by then the Minnesota Twins, and the expansion Senators born just that year. The ballpark was demolished in 1965 and the Howard University Hospital now occupies the site.

On September 10, 1950, Joe DiMaggio became the first player to hit three home runs in a game at the ballpark. Only Josh Gibson and Mickey Mantle hit balls over the left field bleachers.

D.C. Stadium/Robert F. Kennedy Memorial Stadium. In 1962 the Senators played in District of Columbia Stadium, on which construction had begun in 1960. The stadium was built on the banks of the Potomac and seated 43,500 (45,000 by 1971). The ballpark's dimensions from left to right field generally were 335–385–410–385– 335.

President John F. Kennedy attended the first game and threw out the first ball as the Senators defeated the Tigers 4–1. The ballpark was later renamed Robert F. Kennedy Memorial Stadium after he was assassinated in 1968. RFK Stadium was home to the Senators until they departed for Texas after the 1971 season.

Key Broadcasters.

"Nothing could kill your interest in baseball faster than three years of the Senators." — Vin Scully on his first broadcasting job, in Washington, D.C., quoted in *Voices of Sports*, edited by Maury Allen (1971).

Arch McDonald broadcast for 22 years for the Senators starting in 1934 over WJSV and later WTOP. When McDonald moved over to the Yankees for one year in 1939 (with Mel Allen as his assistant), former pitching great Walter Johnson replaced him. McDonald returned immediately after a change in beer sponsorship in New York (in an era when sponsors had control over the choice of broadcasters). McDonald broadcast re-creations of Senators road games from a drug store in which he installed bleachers for fans to liven up the atmosphere. He left four years before the original Senators departed and died in 1960 at age 59.

Bob Wolf broadcast for the Senators from 1947 through their departure after the 1960 season. The new era Senators had Dan Daniels and John McLean broadcasting their games during the 1960s until Bob Short bought the club in late 1968. Short hired Shelby Whitfield, who had broadcast for years on Armed Forces Radio. Whitfield broadcast for the club until its move to Texas after the 1971 season. Warner Wolf did the television broadcasts and radio color late in the 1960s.

Books. Morris Bealle, *Washington Senators* (1947); Shirley Povich, *The Washington Senators* (1954); Shelby Whitfield, *Kiss It Good-Bye* (1968), covering the Senators' last three years in Washington before moving to Texas; Mark Rucker, Frank Ceresi and Carol McMains, *Baseball in Washington, D.C.* (2002).

Washington Statesmen

American Association 1891

After the Players League revolt of 1890, Washington received a franchise for the 1891 American Association season. The club finished last with a 44–91 record, 49 games behind the leader. The Association disbanded after the season and the Washington franchise was purchased by the owners of the American Association Philadelphia A's, the Wagner brothers. The club was admitted to the National League for the 1892 season (see also *Washington Statesmen/Senators*).

Washington Statesmen/Senators

National League 1886–1889, 1892–1899

Statesmen/1886–1889. The team first played in the National League in 1886 under the ownership of brothers Robert and Walter Hewitt. The Statesmen were managed by Mike Scanlon, who had been involved in the city's National Association entry. The team finished last with a 28–92 record. The brothers constructed 6,000-seat Capitol Park on Capitol Avenue between F and G Streets. They changed the team's name to Senators and brought up catcher Cornelius McGillicuddy, better known as Connie Mack. The Hewitts owned the club until it folded after the 1889 season.

Senators/1892–1899. When the National League expanded to 12 teams in 1892, brothers George and Jacob Earl Wagner of Philadelphia acquired the new Washington franchise. They owned it until its ouster from the league after the 1899 season. The Wagners were highly unpopular among other owners, in part because of their 1893 effort to schedule a number of home games in the opposing club's ballpark to capitalize on higher attendance. The league quickly passed a rule prohibiting such scheduling changes.

The Wagners built 6,500-seat National Park at The Boundary, at the intersection of 7th Street N.W. and Florida Avenue, the eventual site of Griffith Stadium.

The team floundered throughout the 1890s, never finishing higher than a tie for sixth. After the Senators finished ninth in 1899 the National League bought out the Wagners for $46,500 and reduced the league to eight clubs. This marked the end of the National League's presence in the city.

Weather

"The only way I'd worry about the weather is if it snows on our side of the field and not on theirs."—Dodger manager Tommy Lasorda on the frigid weather in Montreal during the 1981 NLCS.

"[Baseball is] really a part of the whole weather of our lives."—Writer Thomas Wolfe.

"Carl Sandburg called Chicago the 'city with broad shoulders.' He didn't tell you you'd need to bring an overcoat to put over those broad shoulders."—Vin Scully during an early April broadcast from Wrigley Field when the wind chill made the temperature 12 degrees.

"He came into spring training as a hurricane and left as a gentle breeze."—Sportswriter Jimmy Cannon on Luke Hamlin, who started fast and finished slow. Hamlin did manage to win 20 games for the Dodgers in 1939.

"I was brought up in Florida, so there isn't much difference between playing there and playing here. The climax are about the same."—Mickey Rivers on playing in Texas.

"Cyclone Miller, Ernie Gust, Roy Weatherly, Windy McCally, Dewey Williams, Mark Clear, Cyclone Ryan, Ribs Rainey, Foghorn Bradley, Nippy Jones, Icehouse Wilson, Frosty Thomas, Curt Flood, Bill McCool, Jack Freeze, Icebox Chamberlain, Icicle Reeder, Rich Gale, Dave Frost"

See also *Altitude*, *Artificial Turf*, *Candlestick Park*, *Floods* and *Wind*.

Heat Stroke and Humidity.

"It's like breathing through mud."—Braves third baseman Chipper Jones describing the humidity in Atlanta.

There was once a belief that the Washington, Cincinnati and St. Louis teams had to be 25% better than the other teams due to the harsh summer weather that sapped the strength of the players.

Some commentators have opined that the "heavy air" caused by humidity slows down the ball and has a strong effect on curveballs. Apparently, however, while thin dry air (e.g., in Colorado) affects the flight of the ball and a pitched ball, humidity (e.g., in St. Louis) has only a slight affect. Water molecules are less dense than air molecules (clouds!), so that humidity should have little effect on a ball because the air is less dense as the humidity goes up. One commentator said that Darryl Kile was terrible in Colorado because the altitude flattened out his curveball, but that the humidity in St. Louis brought the pitch back to life and enabled Kile to win 20 games.

See also *Balls— Storage* on how teams have stored their balls to decrease the affect of humidity.

Snow. In 1982 a huge snowstorm over the northeastern United States wiped out much of the entire first week's schedule and many clubs went south to practice. Openers were canceled in New York, Detroit, Chicago, Milwaukee, Cleveland, Philadelphia and Pittsburgh.

The Brewers worked out in Houston, while the Red Sox returned to Florida. The Blue Jays and White Sox played an exhibition game in Minnesota's new indoor ballpark, and the Yankees worked out at the West Point Field House in New York. The Rangers practiced under the stands at Shea Stadium, and the Indians used an indoor facility at Cleveland State University.

As a result of the postponement nightmare, *Schedules* were altered to put more early season games in warm-weather cities or cities with domed ballparks. The plan must have changed by the mid–1990s. At the Yankee home opener in 1996 snow flurries escalated into blinding conditions as wind blew through Yankee Stadium in the late afternoon. Third base umpire Ken Kaiser and some of the players wore ski masks. A number of games across the northeast were snowed out and the Dodgers and Cubs played in 30 degree weather in Chicago.

Low Pressure System. The lively ball phenomenon of 1983 was attributed by some to a low pressure system that hovered over much of the country that season.

Fog. On May 20, 1960, the Cubs were playing at Milwaukee when the scoreless game was called in the 5th inning because of fog. A Cubs game at Brooklyn also was "fogged out" in 1956.

On April 30, 1991, the game at Shea Stadium between the Mets and Padres was fogged out after six innings.

On June 18, 1997, the Blue Jays had to delay their game in the 4th inning for 14 minutes because of fog. Once the retractable roof was closed, the fog dissipated and the game resumed against the Braves.

Hurricane. On September 21, 1938, the Boston Braves were at home against the Cardinals. Umpire Beans Reardon called the game when balls hit to center field were blowing back behind home plate and caught by catcher Al Lopez.

In September 2004 a hurricane blasted the Florida coast, making it impossible for the Devil Rays to get out of town on time for a doubleheader in New York (scheduled after the previous day's game was cancelled because the club couldn't leave town). The Yankees protested Tampa Bay's absence and asked for a forfeit to be declared. The protest was denied and the games were rescheduled.

On September 13–14, 2004, the Marlins hosted the Expos at Chicago's U.S. Cellular Field. Hurricane Ivan had driven the Marlins out of Miami and a third of the $15 ticket price went toward hurricane relief.

Even though the Devil Rays play in a domed stadium, they cancelled their game of September 26, 2004, because of another in a series of hurricanes that threatened the area.

Lightning.

"There's a little thunder to be heard now, but no lightning. However, where there's thunder, there's bound to be lightning. Or so they tell me. The only lightning seen around here though was that homer li'l ole Mickey blasted in the second." — Red Barber quoted by sportswriter Tom O'Reilly of the *New York Morning Telegraph* in the 1950s.

In 1892 a fire caused by lightning forced the cancellation of a game between the Chicago White Stockings and Cleveland Spiders.

On July 17, 1914, Giants outfielder Red Murray was knocked unconscious by lightning as he caught the game-ending fly ball in the 21st inning of a 3–1 win against the Pirates. He was not injured.

Ray Caldwell was struck by lightning in Cleveland while pitching for the Yankees in the 9th inning on August 8, 1919. He was leading 2–1 with two outs when he was knocked down. He recovered immediately and finished the game.

On August 7, 1949, in the Miami (Ohio) Valley League, first baseman Harold Jensen was killed by lightning and five others, including two umpires, were injured.

Bobo Holloman once stopped pitching with an approaching rainstorm and lightning in the distance. What he did not tell his minor league manager was that his brother had been struck and killed by lightning. Ironically, he made history when he pitched a no-hitter in his first Major League start while pitching in a light rain.

Orioles outfielder Willie Tasby once played barefoot during an approaching storm, not wanting to wear metal spikes on the wet grass for fear of being struck by lightning.

Cold Weather.

"On a cold night you have to hit the ball 25 feet farther. So in other words, if the fence is 338 feet and you hit the ball 338 feet, you'll be 25 feet short." — Broadcaster Ralph Kiner trying to explain the effect of cold weather on the flight of the ball.

See *Underwear* for Bowie Kuhn's fashion statement at the World Series.

Tornado. On June 15, 1982, pitcher Lynn McGlothlin thought he saw a tornado coming toward the Columbus Clippers ballpark and he dashed off the mound. Virtually at the same time there was national focus on Columbus because a prank call had caused a wire service to report that a tornado had struck the ballpark and killed a number of players and fans.

Earl Weaver (1930–)

Hall of Fame (VC) 1996

"Earl Weaver was a strong proponent of baseball megatonnage. A manager's best friend, he said, is the three-run home run." — George Will in *Men at Work* (1990).

"Earl Weaver totally got it. He didn't have the mathematical proof, I don't think, to back up a lot of what he was saying, but his intuition was phenomenal. Without doing the math, he understood how the game worked." — Dodger general manager Paul DePodesta.

"This man's a genius at finding situations where an average player — like me — can look like a star because a lot of subtle fac-

tors are working in your favor. He has a passion for finding the perfect player for the perfect spot." — John Lowenstein.

Weaver managed the Orioles for 17 seasons, winning six division titles and one World Series.

Earl Sidney Weaver played 13 minor league seasons at second base in the Cardinals and Pirates organizations between 1948 and 1957. Although he never played Major League Baseball, he was the MVP of three minor leagues. He became a player-manager in the Orioles organization in 1958 and remained in the minors through mid–1968. He took over the Orioles midway through the 1968 season and in 1969 he began a string of 14 straight full seasons managing the club.

The Orioles won three straight division titles between 1969 and 1971 and swept the ALCS each season. Weaver won his only World Series in 1970. He won two more division titles in 1973 and 1974, but lost to the A's each season for the pennant. Between 1975 and 1982 his clubs finished second six times (including half of 1981) and first in 1979, losing the World Series to the Pirates after being up 3–1 in games.

Weaver retired after the 1982 season, in which the Orioles lost the division title on the last day. He came out of retirement for part of 1985 and all of 1986, but his clubs finished fourth and last — the latter was the first time he had ever suffered a losing season. He retired to Florida for good with a 1480–1060 record and a .583 winning percentage, tenth all-time.

Weaver was known for his hot temper and umpire-baiting. He was thrown out of games almost 100 times and suspended four times. His long-running feud with umpire Ron Luciano is legendary (see also *Ejections*). He was once tossed from both games of a doubleheader.

Book. Earl Weaver with Berry Stainback, *It's What You Learn After You Know It All That Counts* (1982).

Weightlifting See *Conditioning* and *Strongest Players*

George Weiss (1895–1972)

Hall of Fame (VC) 1971

"I never made a single deal with him. He was too smart." — General manager "Trader" Frank Lane.

"Bismarckian and austere in a pudgy sort of way, George Weiss … was both smart and lucky." — Harold Rosenthal in *The 10 Best Years of Baseball* (1979).

Weiss was the general manager of the Yankees from 1947 through 1960.

George M. Weiss started in baseball as a "gofer" with the 1912 New Haven High School team. In 1917 he worked at Yale and ran the New Haven semipro team, the Colonials. His club started beating the local professional teams and he began scheduling Sunday games against barnstorming Major Leaguers, including Ty Cobb and Babe Ruth.

In 1919 Weiss bought the New Haven club and worked in the minor leagues through most of the 1920s. In 1929 he became general manager of the Baltimore Orioles in the International League. He succeeded long-time owner Jack Dunn, who had died as the result of falling off a horse.

In 1932 Weiss was hired by Yankees owner Jake Ruppert as farm director to build the club's farm system. He moved up the ranks to secretary, general manager and president. Weiss was the general manager from 1947 through 1960, during which the club won 10 pennants and seven World Series. When Casey Stengel was let go after the 1960 World Series, Weiss was forced out with him.

Weiss became the first president of the Mets from 1961 until he voluntarily retired in 1966 at age 72, tracking Stengel's career with the club. He remained associated with the Mets until his death in 1972. Weiss was named Major League Executive of the Year at least 10 times by various wire services and magazines.

Mickey Welch (1859–1941)

Hall of Fame (VC) 1973

"Smiling Mickey's pay check never exceeded $4,000 a year and he earned the money. Manager Jim Mutrie had him playing center field on the days he wasn't pitching and he also had to be at the park an hour ahead of time to watch the turnstile."— Welch's 1941 obituary.

Welch won 308 games in only 13 seasons beginning in 1880.

Brooklyn native Michael Francis "Smiling Mickey" Welch played two seasons in the minor leagues before joining Troy in the National League in 1880 as a right-handed pitcher. He won 34 games in his rookie year and then slipped to 21- and 14-win seasons. The club moved to New York for the 1883 season and Welch began a string of seven stellar seasons. He peaked in 1885 with a record of 44–11 and pitched 492 innings. His high was 557.1 innings in 1884 when he won 39 games in 65 starts. He attributed his enormous success to drinking beer, although pitching from distances of 45 and 50 feet probably helped.

In 1890 he slipped to 17 wins and then faded to six wins in 1891 for the Giants. He was demoted to the minor leagues in 1892 and appeared in only one game for the Giants that season. He finished his 13-year career with a 308–209 record and is fifth all-time with 525 complete games. He pitched 40 shutouts.

After his retirement he left New York for Massachusetts. He returned to the Giants in 1912 when he was offered a job as an usher at the Polo Grounds.

Willie Wells (1906–1989)

Hall of Fame (VC) 1997

"Intense. That's what I was. I just wanted to be the best. I never wanted to lose."— Wells.

Wells was one of the two greatest Negro League shortstops of all-time over a career that spanned the 1920s through 1940s.

Austin, Texas, native Willie James Wells, Sr., joined the Negro National League in 1924 with the St. Louis Stars, the first of nine teams he played for in the Negro Leagues. In the eight years he was with the Stars, the club won three pennants with Wells hitting over .300 five times, including .404 in 1930. The old Negro National League dissolved after the 1931 season and Wells bounced among several clubs in 1932. He settled with the Chicago American Giants in 1933, winning the first pennant of the new Negro National League.

Wells moved to the Newark Eagles in 1936, hitting over .300 three times in four years while teaming with Mule Suttles, Dick Seay and Ray Dandridge in Newark's "One Million Dollar Infield."

Beginning in 1940 Wells spent four of the next five years in Latin American leagues in Mexico, Cuba and Puerto Rico, where he was dubbed "El Diablo (the Devil)" for his defensive prowess at shortstop. He returned to Newark as the Eagle's player-manager in 1942. For the remainder of the 1940's Wells bounced between several Negro League clubs, continuing to play stellar shortstop and hitting .328 in 1948 at the age of 40.

An eight-time All-Star, Wells is credited with a .331 average and leading the Negro Leagues in career doubles. He is third all-time in steals and fifth in triples and home runs, and batted over .300 10 times. Wells hit .410 in exhibition games against white Major League teams. He was the 14th Negro League entry into the Hall of Fame, and the second shortstop, joining the great Pop Lloyd.

Considered an excellent mentor, Wells was a player-manager in the early 1950s in Canada, returning to the States in 1954 to manage the Birmingham Black Barons. After retiring from baseball Wells lived and worked in New York City until 1973, when he returned to his hometown of Austin, Texas. Wells passed away there in 1989, at the age of 83 (though some sources report his birth year as 1905, rather than 1906).

Western League (1892–1899)

"Although unsuccessful, the [1900] attempt to resurrect the American Association concealed the activities of more resolute interlopers. While league men worried about this threat, Ban Johnson quietly launched an attempt to win major-league status for his Western League. Boldly blackmailing the league barons, he demanded and received, as the price for his loyalty, the right to rename his circuit the American League and to plant franchises in Chicago and Cleveland. As a result Reach's Official Base Ball Guide predicted 'a new and probably highly promising career for the American League.'"— David Quentin Voigt in American Baseball (1966).

The Western League was the forerunner of the American League. It began operation in 1879 and folded in the early 1890s, but was revived in 1892 after two previous attempts. At various stages of its development the league was composed of remnants of other leagues, including the Northwestern League and the 1884 Union Association.

The 1892 Western League cities were Minneapolis, Milwaukee, Toledo, Kansas City, Detroit, Sioux City, Grand Rapids, and Indianapolis. The league was stronger in part because it was able to absorb some of the National League and American Association cast-offs who did not survive the early 1890s reorganization that resulted in a single 12-team National League.

After the 1893 season, the presidency of the league opened up and owner Charles Comiskey recommended that Cincinnati sportswriter Ban Johnson take over. Johnson was 28 years old when representatives of each city met and elected him their president on November 20, 1893.

In 1895 Comiskey bought the Sioux City franchise and moved it to St. Paul. Connie Mack took over the Milwaukee franchise. By 1896 the Western League was extremely successful and Johnson wanted to expand into key National League cities including Chicago, Cleveland and St. Louis. Johnson and Comiskey were aided by supportive news reports by the Spink family, owners of The Sporting News.

The Western League remained intact until October 1899, when Johnson implemented his plan to elevate the league into a legitimate rival of the long-established National League. He renamed it the American League for the 1900 season and shifted a number of franchises into larger cities, including existing National League cities. Notwithstanding the name change, the newly named league was not recognized as a Major League during 1900. This was probably Johnson's strategy, as the National League would view the American League clubs in National League cities as less of a threat if the American League was considered only a minor league. The last Western League/American League champions before the league was treated as a Major League were the 1900 Chicago White Sox.

Statistics. Organized Baseball initially ruled that players coming from the Western League who entered the National League or new American League would be credited with hits made in the Western League for their lifetime statistics. Nevertheless, later official bodies have not included the Western League among recognized Major Leagues and the players' statistics through 1900 have not counted in their lifetime Major League totals.

Western Union See *Re-Creations* and *Telegraph and Telegrams*

Zack Wheat (1888–1972)

Hall of Fame (VC) 1959

"He was the most graceful left-handed hitter I ever saw. With the dead ball, many of his line drives were caught, but they were just shot out of a cannon almost every time up." — Casey Stengel.

Wheat batted .317 with 2,884 hits over 19 seasons almost exclusively for the Dodgers beginning in 1909.

Missouri native Zachary Davis Wheat and his brother McKinley "Mack" Davis were Major Leaguers early in the 20th century. Zack signed with the Dodgers in 1909 and hit .304 in 26 games. He became the starting left fielder in 1910 and hit .284 in 156 games. He established himself in 1912 with a .305 average and hit over .300 in all but two of the next 13 seasons. He became the most popular player in New York by 1920, and according to sportswriters even the presence of Babe Ruth did not diminish his popularity.

He led the Dodgers to the 1916 World Series though he batted only .211 in postseason play. He batted .328 in 1920 when the club again made it to the World Series, and this time he batted .333 in seven games.

He held out in 1923 but returned midseason to bat .375 in 98 games. He batted .375 in 1924 and .359 in 1925, his best all-around season. His legs began to go in 1926, and he once was the subject of one of the "longest" home runs in history when he pulled muscles in both legs reaching second base before the ball cleared the fence for a home run. It was estimated that it took him five minutes to reach home plate to complete the trip.

The Dodgers released him after the season and he played his final 88 games with the A's in 1927, batting .324. He finished his Major League career with a .317 average and 2,884 hits that included 172 triples and 132 home runs. He played in the American Association in 1928 before retiring permanently. He returned to Missouri and ran a bowling alley for many years and was briefly a member of the Kansas City police force. He later owned a hunting and fishing lodge and almost died in a car accident, but recovered in time to see himself elected to the Hall of Fame.

"Who's on First?"

The famous William "Bud" Abbott and Lou Costello routine, which they essentially took from another vaudeville pair, featured the following players:

1B	Who
2B	What
3B	I don't know
SS	I don't give a darn
LF	Why
CF	Because
C	Today
P	Tomorrow

Right field was never identified. In the routine, Abbott played Dexter Broadhurt, manager of the mythical St. Louis Wolves. Costello played peanut vendor Sebastian Dinwiddie, who asked all the questions.

The routine first appeared in the movies in 1945 in Universal Pictures' *The Naughty Nineties*. Abbott and Costello became famous as regulars on the 1930s "Kate Smith Hour," a CBS radio show. In their first appearance on the live show, as they approached the microphones to begin the routine, they began to argue heatedly and both threw their scripts into the wings of the theater. The audience of over 400 gasped, and the producer and director in the booth almost had heart attacks. Kate Smith stifled a scream. It was not generally known that the pair had performed the routine dozens of times in night clubs and on vaudeville stages. This author's father was on the show that night and reported this anecdote.

Trivia books often ask "who are the only two members of the Hall of Fame who had nothing to do with baseball?" The answer supposedly is Abbott and Costello, but this is false. They are not enshrined in the Hall, but rather they are only featured at the Hall.

The routine was translated into over 30 languages, some of them performed by the famous duo in languages they didn't understand. The full dialogue:

Abbott: Alright, now whaddya want?

Costello: Now look, I'm the head of the sports department. I gotta know the baseball players' names. Do you know the guys' names?

Abbott: Oh sure.

Costello: So you go ahead and tell me some of their names.

Abbott: Well, I'll introduce you to the boys. You know sometimes nowadays they give ballplayers peculiar names.

Costello: You mean funny names.

Abbott: Nicknames, pet names, like Dizzy Dean

Costello: His brother Daffy

Abbott: Daffy Dean

Costello: And their cousin!

Abbott: Who's that?

Costello: Goofy!

Abbott: Goofy, huh? Now let's see. We have on the bags — we have Who's on first, What's on second, I Don't Know's on third.

Costello: That's what I wanna find out.

Abbott: I say Who's on first, What's on second, I Don't Know's on third

Costello: You know the fellows' names?

Abbott: Certainly!

Costello: Well then who's on first?

Abbott: Yes!

Costello: I mean the fellow's name!

Abbott: Who!

Costello: The guy on first!

Abbott: Who!

Costello: The first baseman!

Abbott: Who!

Costello: The guy playing first!

Abbott: Who is on first!

Costello: Now whaddya askin' me for?

Abbott: I'm telling you Who is on first.

Costello: Well, I'm asking YOU who's on first!

Abbott: That's the man's name.

Costello: That's who's name?

Abbott: Yes.

Costello: Well go ahead and tell me.

Abbott: Who.

Bud Abbott and Lou Costello perform their fabled routine, "Who's on First?"

Costello: The guy on first.
Abbott: Who!
Costello: The first baseman.
Abbott: Who is on first!
Costello: Have you got a contract with the first baseman?
Abbott: Absolutely.
Costello: Who signs the contract?
Abbott: Well, naturally!
Costello: When you pay off the first baseman every month, who gets the money?
Abbott: Every dollar. Why not? The man's entitled to it.
Costello: Who is?
Abbott: Yes. Sometimes his wife comes down and collects it.
Costello: Who's wife?
Abbott: Yes.
Costello: All I'm tryin' to find out is what's the guy's name on first base.
Abbott: Oh, no — wait a minute, don't switch 'em around. What is on second base.
Costello: I'm not askin' you who's on second.
Abbott: Who is on first.
Costello: I don't know.
Abbott: He's on third — now we're not talkin' 'bout him.
Costello: Now, how did I get on third base?
Abbott: You mentioned his name!

Costello: If I mentioned the third baseman's name, who did I say is playing third?
Abbott: No — Who's playing first.
Costello: Never mind first — I wanna know what's the guy's name on third.
Abbott: No — What's on second.
Costello: I'm not askin' you who's on second.
Abbott: Who's on first.
Costello: I don't know.
Abbott: He's on third.
Costello: Aaah! Would you please stay on third base and don't go off it?
Abbott: What was it you wanted?
Costello: Now who's playin' third base?
Abbott: Now why do you insist on putting Who on third base?
Costello: Why? Who am I putting over there?
Abbott: Yes. But we don't want him there.
Costello: What's the guy's name on third base?
Abbott: What belongs on second.
Costello: I'm not askin' you who's on second.
Abbott: Who's on first.
Costello: I don't know.
Abbott & Costello: THIRD BASE!
Costello: You got an outfield?
Abbott: Oh yes!

Costello: The left fielder's name?

Abbott: Why.

Costello: I don't know, I just thought I'd ask you.

Abbott: Well, I just thought I'd tell you.

Costello: Alright, then tell me who's playin' left field.

Abbott: Who is playing fir—

Costello: STAY OUTTA THE INFIELD! I wanna know what's the left fielder's name.

Abbott: What's on second.

Costello: I'm not askin' you who's on second.

Abbott: Who's on first.

Costello: I don't know.

Abbott & Costello: THIRD BASE!

Costello: The left fielder's name?

Abbott: Why.

Costello: Because!

Abbott: Oh, he's center field.

Costello: Look, you gotta pitcher on this team?

Abbott: Now wouldn't this be a fine team without a pitcher.

Costello: The pitcher's name.

Abbott: Tomorrow.

Costello: You don't wanna tell me today?

Abbott: I'm tellin' you now.

Costello: Then go ahead.

Abbott: Tomorrow.

Costello: What time?

Abbott: What time what?

Costello: What time tomorrow are you going to tell me who's pitching?

Abbott: Now listen. Who is not pitching. Who is on fir—

Costello: I'll break your arm if you say Who's on first. I wanna know what's the pitcher's name.

Abbott: What's on second.

Costello: I don't know.

Abbott & Costello: THIRD BASE!

Costello: You got a catcher?

Abbott: Oh, absolutely.

Costello: The catcher's name.

Abbott: Today.

Costello: Today. And Tomorrow's pitching.

Abbott: Now you've got it.

Costello: All we've got is a couple of days on the team.

Abbott: Well, I can't help that.

Costello: Well, I'm a catcher too.

Abbott: I know that.

Costello: Now suppose that I'm catching, Tomorrow's pitching on my team and their heavy hitter gets up.

Abbott: Yes.

Costello: Tomorrow throws the ball. The batter bunts the ball. When he bunts the ball, me being a good catcher, I wanna throw the guy out at first base. So I pick up the ball and throw it to who?

Abbott: Now that's the first thing you've said right.

Costello: I don't even know what I'm talkin' about!

Abbott: Well, that's all you have to do.

Costello: Is to throw the ball to first base.

Abbott: Yes.

Costello: Now who's got it?

Abbott: Naturally!

Costello: If I throw the ball to first base, somebody's gotta catch it. Now who caught it?

Abbott: Naturally!

Costello: Who caught it?

Abbott: Naturally.

Costello: Who?

Abbott: Naturally!

Costello: Naturally.

Abbott: Yes.

Costello: So I pick up the ball and I throw it to Naturally.

Abbott: NO, NO, NO! You throw the ball to first base and Who gets it?

Costello: Naturally.

Abbott: That's right. There we go.

Costello: So I pick up the ball and I throw it to Naturally.

Abbott: You don't!

Costello: I throw it to who?

Abbott: Naturally.

Costello: THAT'S WHAT I'M SAYING!

Abbott: You're not saying it that way.

Costello: I said I throw the ball to Naturally.

Abbott: You don't — you throw the ball to Who?

Costello: Naturally!

Abbott: Well, say that!

Costello: THAT'S WHAT I'M SAYING! I throw the ball to who?

Abbott: Naturally.

Costello: Ask me.

Abbott: You throw the ball to Who?

Costello: Naturally.

Abbott: That's it.

Costello: SAME AS YOU!! I throw the ball to first base and who gets it?

Abbott: Naturally!

Costello: Who has it?

Abbott: Naturally!

Costello: HE BETTER HAVE IT! I throw the ball to first base. Whoever it is grabs the ball, so the guy runs to second. Who picks up the ball and throws it to What, What throws it to I Don't Know, I Don't Know throws it back to Tomorrow — triple play.

Abbott: Yes.

Costello: Another guy gets up — it's a long fly ball to Because. Why? I don't know. He's on third and I don't give a darn!

Abbott: What was that?

Costello: I said I don't give a darn!

Abbott: Oh, that's our shortstop.

Wild Card See *Divisional Play and Play-Offs*

Wild Pitches

"Make a wild pitch as a doctor and they bury you." — Braves owner Ted Turner comparing the two professions.

"As pitches go, this one was the wildest of the wild. He uncorked one Saturday against the Padres that a catcher could have tracked only on a Global Positioning System could have tracked." — Tom Fitzgerald of the *San Francisco Chronicle* on a 2003 pitch by Hideo Nomo. The pitch landed well up the screen behind home plate.

"Rex Barney would be the league's best pitcher if the plate were high and outside." — Bob Cook on Barney's legendary wildness.

"If they think I'd stand there in that sun and pitch another nine innings waiting for our bums to make another run, they're crazy." — A's pitcher Jack Nabors after wild-pitching in the winning run to break a 1–1 tie in the 9th inning of a 1916 game.

Statistic. The wild pitch was added as a statistic in 1883. Wild pitches and base on balls originally were part of the pitcher's fielding statistics. The wild pitch was scored as an error for the pitcher until 1889.

Key Games. Jack Chesbro set a modern Major League record by winning 41 games for the Highlanders in 1904, but his season ended on a sour note. The Highlanders and Red Sox went into the last day of the season with the Red Sox up by a game and the Highlanders needing a sweep of their doubleheader. Chesbro pitched the first game. With the score tied in the top of the 9th inning, he wild-pitched home the winning run and the Red Sox won the pennant. Catcher Red Leinow was criticized by some for failing to catch the 1–2 pitch, though it was well over his head: "The only way Kleinow could have caught that ball would have been while standing on top of a stepladder."—Giants shortstop Kid Elberfeld.

In the bottom of the 9th with two outs and the tying run on second for the Highlanders, Patsy Dougherty struck out on a 3–2 pitch to end the game. Chesbro's widow spent much of the rest of her life trying to change the scoring of the wild pitch to a passed ball. One source reported erroneously that Chesbro loaded up a spitball that broke four feet (upward?).

In the deciding game 5 of the 1972 NLCS, a wild pitch by Pirates pitcher Bob Moose allowed Reds outfielder George Foster to score the winning run in the bottom of the 9th inning. The Pirates had gone into the inning up 3–2, but Johnny Bench tied the game with a home run. Two more singles and the wild pitch ended the game. It was Roberto Clemente's last game.

Wild Coincidence. Tim McCarver, while broadcasting for the Mets with his partner, Ralph Kiner, related how pitcher Ryne Duren was so wild that he once hit an on-deck batter. Kiner replied, "That was me."

Most/Inning. In October 2000 Rick Ankiel, spiraling down due to a loss of control, became the first pitcher in 110 years to throw five wild pitches in a single inning. It was the first game of the National League division series against the Braves, but St. Louis overcame Ankiel's wildness for a 7–5 win.

Dodger manager Tommy Lasorda once tied the modern Major League record with three wild pitches in an inning.

In 1991 Phillies pitcher Jason Grimsley tied Jaime Cocanower's 1986 Major League record by throwing a wild pitch in nine consecutive games.

Most/Game. On April 10, 1982, Bill Gullickson tied a Major League record with six wild pitches in one game.

Most/Season. Red Ames holds the modern Major League season record with 30 wild pitches for the Giants in 1905.

Nolan Ryan, Walter Johnson and Earl Wilson once held the American League record with 21 wild pitches in a season. That record was increased to 24 by Jack Morris in 1987 and 26 by Juan Guzman in 1993.

Most/Career. Phil Niekro threw 217 wild pitches during his long career, due almost entirely to the difficulty in handling his knuckleball.

Fewest/Career. Robin Roberts had such good control that he threw only 33 wild pitches in 19 seasons.

Hoyt Wilhelm (1923–2002)

Hall of Fame 1985

"He had the best damn knuckleball I've ever seen."—Teammate Tom McCraw.

"Wilhelm never earned high wages. While with the Giants he lived in a tiny five-room house in Westchester, about half an hour by parkway from the Polo Grounds. Here he enjoyed the quiet life of a small-salaried commuter. A few disgruntled batters who grew

tired of trying to straighten out his half-speed knuckle ball said he threw like one too."—Robert Smith in *Baseball* (1970).

"But if I had to pick myself one guy that I wouldn't want to hit against when he was right, it would be Hoyt Wilhelm. It was a battle just to get the bat on that knuckleball. You know good and well, how in the hell is a man going to hit a ball that the catcher can't even catch?"—Billy Goodman quoted in *Baseball Between the Lines*, by Donald Honig (1976).

Wilhelm won 143 games and saved 227 over a 21-year career that began in 1952.

James Hoyt Wilhelm's early professional career was interrupted by World War II, in which he was awarded a Purple Heart after being wounded during the Battle of the Bulge. The knuckleballer pitched in the North Carolina State League before signing with the Giants in 1948. He spent another four years in the minor leagues before moving into the Giants bullpen at age 28 in 1952. He was an immediate sensation, but not for his pitching. He homered and tripled in his first two at-bats; he never did either again in over 21 seasons.

Wilhelm was outstanding his first season, winning 15 games in 71 relief appearances and compiling 11 saves. His 2.43 ERA was the lowest in the league. He had 15 saves in 1953 and 12 relief wins in 1954. After two mediocre seasons he was traded to the Cardinals and then to the Indians, both in 1957.

Wilhelm was traded to the Orioles midway through the 1958 season and was converted to a starter. He pitched a no-hitter in September that year. He started 27 games in 1959 and was 15–11 while leading the league with a 2.19 ERA. The starter role continued for part of 1960, but he returned to the bullpen that season and remained there for the rest of his career, with the exception of three starts in 1963 for the White Sox. He remained with the White Sox through the 1968 season, saving 98 games and winning 46 in relief. They lost him in late 1968 in the expansion draft, although he was traded immediately to the Angels. From 1969 through 1972 he bounced around to various teams, with a high of 14 saves for the Angels and Braves in 1969.

He finished his 21-year career in 1972 at age 48 with 124 relief wins, first all-time, out of a total of 143. He also had 227 saves, a record at the time. He appeared in 1,070 games, an all-time record for many years. Despite his first at-bat heroics, his lifetime batting average was .088. He died in Florida in 2002 at age 80.

Billy Williams (1938–)

Hall of Fame 1987

"The Rajah [Rogers Hornsby] watched the sweet-swinger take his stance at the plate. He noticed the quick hands, the whiplash wrists. As the ball reached the plate Hornsby took note of Williams uncoiling like a cobra striking or a steel trap suddenly snapping shut."—Eddie Gold and Art Ahrens in *The New Era Cubs* (1985).

Williams starred primarily for the Cubs between 1959 and 1976, batting .290 and hitting 426 home runs.

During minor league seasons with Houston in the American Association, Billy Leo Williams had brief trials with the Cubs in 1959 and 1960 before moving full-time to the Chicago outfield in 1961. Over his 18-year career he was an even quieter (though less productive) version of the consistent Henry Aaron.

Williams hit around .300 for most of his career, with his first .300 season coming in 1964. He batted over .300 five times, with a league-leading .333 in 1972. He hit with power, with 20 or more home runs in 13 straight seasons and a high of 42 in 1970. He also had over 200 hits three times.

Williams was consistently in the line-up with a then–National League record 1,117 **Consecutive Games** played from September 1963 to September 1970. After the 1974 season he was traded to the A's for two seasons. He hit 23 home runs in 1975 but his skills were diminishing and he retired after hitting .211 in 1976.

Williams finished his career with a .290 average, 2,711 hits and 426 home runs. His only postseason play consisted of appearances in three games for the A's in the 1975 ALCS. After his retirement he became a coach and batting instructor for the Cubs and then moved to Oakland in 1983 for three years in the same role. He returned to the Cubs and began working in the front office.

Smokey Joe Williams (1886–1946)

Hall of Fame (VC) 1999

"During the first half of its existence, Smokey Joe Williams was to black baseball what Satchel Paige was to the latter half. Old-timers who saw him play remember him as Satchel's equal, if not his superior." — Blackbaseball.com.

"Imagine the Major Leagues without Ken Griffey, Jr." — Historian John Thorn.

Williams was one of the most dominant pitchers of the early Negro Leagues.

Smokey Joe was born Joseph Williams in 1886, at Seguin, Texas, just east of San Antonio. At 6'4", Williams was an imposing physical presence. In photos from the period he towers over teammates and rivals. A hard-throwing righthander, Williams dominated early competition in Texas, compiling gaudy win totals primarily for the San Antonio Black Broncos.

His first year in the Black Major Leagues was 1910 with the Chicago Giants. In 1912 he began a 12 year association with the New York Lincoln Giants. With the Giants, Williams would team with Cannonball Dick Redding for five years, creating surely one of the most fearsome pitching tandems in the history of the game. Williams also pitched extensively against white Major Leaguers in exhibition games. In 1915 against a team of primarily Philadelphia Phillies, the National League champions, Smokey Joe threw a 3-hit shutout with 10 strikeouts, winning 1–0.

After a single season with the Brooklyn Royal Giants, Williams joined the Homestead Grays in 1925. In 1930 while pitching for the Grays he had perhaps his most dominant performance, striking out 27 in 12 innings (see **Strikeouts**). Although statistics are difficult to corroborate, all sources indicate Williams was one of the premier pitchers of the era, in any league, black or white. He is rivaled perhaps only by Satchel Paige as the greatest pitcher in the history of the Negro Leagues. Williams passed away in New York in 1946.

Ted Williams (1918–2002)

Hall of Fame 1966

"Williams is the classic ballplayer of the game on a hot August weekday, before a small crowd, when the only thing at stake is the tissue-thin difference between a thing done well and a thing done ill." — John Updike.

"Ted worked unsparingly to fulfill his dream of becoming the greatest hitter who ever lived. But the times he lived in, the wars, the accidents, and Fenway Park with its long reaches in right field all worked against him. Despite it all, the records prove that in the power era he was second as a batter and slugger only to Babe Ruth, and not by much." — Sportswriter Tim Cohane.

"I predict that when Ted Williams comes back he will smash Babe Ruth's record of 60 homers in one year. Ted is about the most powerful snap-hitter I have ever seen. He is just as natural as Ruth, but his build makes him lighter on his feet. He has speed and power — what a combination." — Former pitcher Ed Walsh during World War II.

"Ted Williams is a really, really great guy.
He really likes kids, but he hates wearing ties;
He won two Triple Crowns and was the MVP twice,
He feuded with sportswriters, but to kids he was nice.
521 homers, he's in the Hall of Fame,
He's The Kid, The Thumper, and Teddy Ballgame.
He would do anything for the Jimmy Fund,
And I'd like to say thank you for all that he's done." — Ten-year-old Kate Shaughnessy, daughter of Boston columnist Dan Shaughnessy, who had leukemia when she wrote this ode to Williams as part of a thank you to the Boston-based cancer fighting organization, The Jimmy Fund.

Williams may be the premier hitter of all time, hitting 521 home runs and batting .344 over 19 war-interrupted seasons beginning in 1939.

San Diego native Theodore Samuel Williams began his professional career with the minor league San Diego Padres at age 17 in 1935 and starred with Minnesota of the American Association in 1938. He made it to the Red Sox as their left fielder in 1939, playing in 149 games and batting .327. He led the league with 145 RBIs.

Williams tore up the league in 1941 with a .406 average and a league-leading 37 home runs but was overshadowed by Joe DiMaggio's 56-game hitting streak. Williams won the Triple Crown in 1942 before entering World War II as a fighter pilot in the Pacific Theater. After a three-year layoff during the war he barely broke stride when he returned to hit .342 in 1946 and won another Triple Crown in 1947.

Among his best seasons was 1949, when he hit .343 and led in each of the following categories: .650 slugging average, 39 doubles, 43 home runs, 150 runs scored, 159 RBIs and 162 base on balls. Despite a number of incredible seasons, he won the MVP Award only in 1946 and 1949.

Williams suffered a badly broken elbow during the 1950 All-Star Game and his career came close to ending. He returned for a strong 1951 season before losing virtually all of 1952 and 1953 to the Korean War. He again flew fighter missions on bombing raids, completing a total of over 40 missions in two wars. Though his career was thought to be in its twilight following his return from Korea, he hit no less than .345 over the next three seasons through 1956 despite a series of injuries.

In 1957 at age 39 he hit a league-leading .388 with 38 home runs and followed up with another batting title in 1958 at age 40. He tapered off in 1959 due to a pinched nerve in his neck but returned to hit .316 in 1960. He finished his career that season with a dramatic **Last At-Bat** home run in Fenway Park.

Williams finished with a .344 lifetime average, sixth all-time, a .634 slugging average, second all-time, and 521 home runs. He lost almost five full prime years to the military, meaning that an average of 30 home runs in those years would have put him around 700 for his career and the increase in his RBI total of 1,839 (now 13th all-time) probably would have put him first. His only weakness was in the field, where he was considered no more than better-than-average.

Williams retired to fishing and boating but returned to manage the Senators from 1969 through 1971 and then the Rangers in 1972 after the franchise left Washington. His clubs never finished higher than fourth in division play. He died on July 5, 2002, touching off a furor over the handling of his body, which was cryogenically frozen and his head severed for final preservation (see **Deaths**).

Books.

"It's the first biography since the New Testament in which the subject dies and his status is still in doubt."—Leigh Montville on his 2004 book, *Ted Williams: Biography of an American Hero.*

Lawrence Baldassaro (ed.), *The Ted Williams Reader* (1991); Lawrence Baldassaro (ed.), *Ted Williams: Reflections on a Splendid Life* (2004); Richard Ben Cramer, *Ted Williams: The Season of the Kid* (1991); David Halberstam, *The Teammates* (2003); Dick Johnson and Glenn Stout, *Ted Williams: A Portrait in Words and Pictures* (1991); Ed Linn, *Hitter: The Life and Turmoil of Ted Williams* (1993); Bill Nowlin and Jim Prime, *Ted Williams: The Pursuit of Perfection* (2002); Edwin Pope, *Ted Williams: The Golden Year 1957* (1970); Michael Seidel, *Ted Williams: A Baseball Life* (1991); Ted Williams, *My Turn at Bat* (1969) (his ex-wife Delores proposed her own book title: *My Turn at Bat Was No Ball*).

Williams Shift   See *Strategy*—Williams Shift

Vic Willis (1876–1947)

Hall of Fame (VC) 1995

"A curve-ball wizard who acquired control by throwing at a target built for him by Jack Ryan, old Boston catcher…"—Ed Fitzgerald in *The National League* (1959).

Willis won 248 National League games between 1898 and 1910.

Victor Gazaway Willis was born in Maryland (Delaware in earlier sources) and was an immediate sensation with the Boston Red Stockings in 1898 when he won 25 games as a 22-year-old rookie. He won 20 or more games for Boston three more times through 1905. He also lost a league-leading 25 games in 1904 and a 20th century record 29 games in 1905. He was traded to the Pirates for the 1906 season and began four straight seasons of 22 or 23 wins. He finished his career in 1910 for the Cardinals, winning nine games.

Willis had a record of 248–204 over 13 seasons, using a great curveball to go with a decent fastball. He threw a no-hitter in 1899 and pitched 50 shutouts. He lost his only World Series start, for the Pirates in 1909.

Wilmington Quicksteps

Union Association 1884

The Quicksteps were not. They played only part of the season, finishing with a 2–16 record.

Hack Wilson (1900–1948)

Hall of Fame (VC) 1979

"I've never played drunk. Hung over, yes, but never drunk."—Wilson.

Wilson hit 244 home runs and batted .307 over 12 National League seasons starting in 1923.

Lewis Robert Wilson packed over 195 pounds on his 5'6" frame and might have had a much more productive career but for a serious drinking problem. He appeared briefly with the Giants in 1923 but played most of the season in the minor leagues. He came up for 107 games with the club in 1924, batting .295 while playing well in the outfield.

After 62 games with the Giants in 1925, Wilson was sent down to the minor leagues and the Cubs picked him up in the minor league draft. He starred for the Cubs from 1926 through 1931, hitting over .300 in all but 1931. He led the league in home runs four times and had one of the greatest seasons of all time in 1930. He hit a National League–record 56 home runs and drove in a Major League–record 190 runs while batting .356.

Alcohol began to take its toll and he hit only .261 with 13 home runs in 1931. The Cubs traded him to the Dodgers after the season, and he rebounded somewhat to hit 23 home runs. He fell apart in 1933 with only nine home runs, and after 67 games in 1934 the Dodgers unloaded him to the Phillies. He played seven more games and retired at age 34 with 244 home runs and a .307 average in 12 seasons. He hit .319 in two World Series, one each for the Giants and Cubs. He died of alcoholism at age 48.

Book. Robert S. Boone, *Hack* (1978).

Wind

"This wouldn't be such a bad place to play if it wasn't for that wind. I guess that's like saying hell wouldn't be such a bad place if it wasn't so hot."—Pitcher Jerry Reuss on Candlestick Park.

"The wind at Candlestick tonight is blowing with great propensity."—Broadcaster Ron Fairly.

"The first thing you do when you get out to center field is put up your finger and check the wind-chill factor."—Mickey Rivers.

See also **Candlestick Park** and **Weather**.

Certain ballparks have a reputation for high winds. The most notorious was Candlestick Park in San Francisco, but Cleveland's Municipal Stadium is another strong candidate. Strong winds blowing in off Lake Erie made it a difficult park in which to play. Wrigley Field is also strongly affected by wind but more in the category of high-scoring games rather than extremely cold weather.

In 1891 Pittsburgh's Exposition Park had its pavilion roof ripped off by high winds.

In designing Chicago's New Comiskey Park, experts used wind-tunnel tests to determine the effect of Chicago's famous wind currents on batted balls. As a result, home plate in the new park was situated at the northwest corner. It was located in the southwest corner in the old park.

In a game in April 1994 at The Ballpark in Texas, high winds blew winning pitcher Rick Helling off the mound. The wind forced fans to be moved from the upper deck and caused a 45-minute delay. *Sports Illustrated* wondered whether, if the game had been called off, it would have been recorded as a "blowout."

On April 30, 1984, the game between the Blue Jays and Rangers was called due to a 35-mph wind. The Rangers had scratched pitcher Frank Tanana and went with 250-pound Jim Bibby so that he would not blow around on the mound.

Wind-Up

"Many a pitcher uses an elaborate wind-up, and I have been repeatedly asked to adopt one. I have persistently refused. I don't approve of it because it interferes with the control of the ball. It's a useless exertion on the arm, and as far as confusing the batter is concerned, it doesn't always work."—Kid Nichols, star pitcher for the Boston Red Stockings in the 1890s, who did not use a wind-up.

"Get him out of his wind-up, then get him out of the game."—Baseball axiom meaning that getting men on base (and thus unable to use a wind-up) will ultimately force a pitcher to be replaced.

"The pitcher is happiest with his arm idle. He prefers to dawdle in the present, knowing that as soon as he gets on the mound and starts his windup, he delivers himself to the uncertainty of the future." — George Plimpton.

Don Larsen abandoned his wind-up a few games before pitching a **Perfect Game** in the 1956 World Series.

During the 1995 ALCS, Ken Griffey, Jr., stepped out of the batter's box at the last moment before Dennis Martinez of the Indians threw his pitch. Martinez was forced to abort his delivery just as he was about to release the ball. Martinez was not to be shown up; on the next pitch he went into an elaborate wind-up and threw toward home but held on to the ball.

Dave Winfield (1951–)

Hall of Fame 2001

"I never had to cheat, I get them with what I got." — Dave Winfield.

Winfield was an outfield star for 22 seasons beginning in 1973, appearing with six teams while batting .283 with 465 home runs.

Winfield went directly from the University of Minnesota to the San Diego Padres in 1973. As a pitching and outfield star at Minnesota, he led the Gophers to the College World Series in 1973 and was named tournament MVP. He debuted in San Diego's outfield later that summer.

At 6'6" Winfield was an exceptional athlete, possessing a strong throwing arm and a long, lethal right-handed batting stroke. In his rookie season of 1974 he hit 20 home runs. His finest of eight seasons in San Diego was 1979. He batted .308 with 34 home runs and a league-leading 118 RBIs. He also led the league in total bases and won his first Gold Glove.

Compelled by the smell of George Steinbrenner's money and the Padres' losing ways, Winfield signed as a free agent with the Yankees in 1981. Although he played exceedingly well, the Yankees never won a World Series during his tenure and he gained a reputation, unfairly or not, as a player who did not deliver at crucial times. The antics of the Steinbrenner did not help (see **Barred From Baseball**). Winfield did play on his first pennant winner in 1981. In the World Series, a six-game loss to the Dodgers, he managed just one hit.

In the following years Winfield would have some of his best seasons statistically. In 1982 he had a career best 37 home runs with 106 RBIs. In 1984 he hit a career high .340. In both 1984 and 1985 he topped both 100 RBIs and 100 runs scored. He was awarded Gold Gloves in four consecutive seasons, 1982–1985, and again in 1987.

Winfield missed the entire 1989 season to back surgery and was traded to California in 1990. He spent two seasons with the Angels before signing with Toronto as a free agent in 1992. The Blue Jays won the pennant that year with the 40-year-old Winfield contributing 108 RBIs. Winfield had the winning 11th inning double in the deciding Game 6 World Series win over the Braves.

Winfield moved to the Twins for the 1993 and 1994 seasons and then appeared briefly with Cleveland in 1995 before retiring. He was a two-time Glove Glove Award winner. While with Minnesota he gained his 3,000th hit in 1993 and finished his career with 3,110 hits and 1,833 RBIs.

Winners

"A winner never quits and a quitter never wins. Watkins is a winner." — Catcher Gabby Street, apparently the first to use this phrase, defending the use of George Watkins over a better hitter. Watkins hit .288 over seven National League seasons in the 1930s.

"Always root for the winner. That way you won't be disappointed." — Tug McGraw.

See also **Dynasties**.

Frank Crosetti of the Yankees holds the all-time record for playing only on winning teams. He played shortstop for the club from 1932 through 1948.

Pete Rose holds the record for playing the most games on a winning team — 1,952.

Winners to Losers

"In part, that's why the transformation of a perennial loser into a winner, or the deterioration of a winner into a loser, is usually so gradual. It takes years to assemble all the hidden people in a club's chain of command, and then it takes years to tear that infrastructure down." — Thomas Boswell in *Why Time Begins on Opening Day* (1984).

See also **Losers to Winners**.

The 1915 A's won the pennant and then became the first team in history to follow up a pennant year by finishing last. This dubious feat was achieved because owner Connie Mack decimated his team by getting rid of a number of high salaried players in the face of declining revenues caused by competition from the Federal League.

The 1986 Angels finished first and then tied for last in 1987. The 1991 and 1992 Dodgers came close to duplicating the feat, finishing only one game out of first in 1991 and then finishing a distant last in 1992.

The 1993 A's finished last after winning the division title in 1992.

The 1998 Marlins, depleted by free agent losses in an attempt to shed salaries, finished last with a 54–108 record after winning the World Series in 1997. They set the record for most losses after winning the previous year, breaking the record of 88 set by the 1991 Reds (who were 9–0 against the Marlins in 1998).

Wins and Winning Streaks

"The secret to keeping winning streaks going is to maximize the victories while at the same time minimizing the defeats." — Deep thinker and outfielder John Lowenstein.

"Everything looks better when you win. The girls are prettier. The cigars taste better. The trees are greener." — Billy Martin.

"The main idea is to win." — John McGraw.

"Around here winning is second to breathing." — Yankees owner George Steinbrenner in September 2003, shortly before the Yankees lost the World Series to the Marlins. They must have had some bad air (which might also explain the mediocre Yankees teams of the mid–1980s through the early 1990s).

This section covers most wins by teams and winning streaks by both teams and pitchers. All other pitching records, such as 300 wins, are covered elsewhere (see, e.g., **Pitchers**).

"Jimmy Wynn, Early Wynn, Win Kellum"

Most Wins/Team. The Indians won 111 games in 1954 to set the American League record before the 1998 Yankees broke it with 112. Then the 2001 Mariners won 116 after the fastest start in history with a record 20 wins in April (breaking the 1997 Braves' record of 19).

The Cubs won 116 games in 1906 to set the Major League record. Ironically, the 2001 Mariners never made it to the World Series and the Cubs lost the World Series in their record seasons. The 1998 Yankees swept the World Series from the Padres and the 1954 Indians lost to the Giants. The Yankees' 125 wins in 1998 (including postseason) was the most ever for a Major League club.

The 1906 Cubs were 19–3–1 against the Phillies and their worst record was 15–7–1 against the Giants. Some sources contend that two of the Cubs' games were never completed and the club should be credited with two less wins. On June 9, 1906, the Cubs were ahead 2–0 when the Dodgers came to bat in the bottom of the 9th inning. With two outs, Dodger third baseman Doc Casey hit a ground ball to second baseman Johnny Evers for an easy putout at first base. However, Evers' throw to first base drew first baseman Frank Chance's foot off the bag.

Umpire Jimmie Johnstone apparently called the runner safe without making a gesture. The fans thought he was out and swarmed out of the stands. The *Chicago Tribune* reported that "before the protest could be made the game was over."

On September 16, 1906, almost the same situation occurred. This time shortstop Joe Tinker's throw pulled Chance off the bag. Chance rushed for the clubhouse and, with the crowd on the field, the umpire took no action and the Cubs' victory stood.

100 Wins/No Pennant.

"All I can say is that it's a helluva state of affairs if a manager can win one hundred four games [actually 103] like us and not win a pennant. As for the Giants, they're not a great team; we would have murdered them." — Yankee manager Casey Stengel, whose 1954 club won 103 games, after the Indians won 111 games but were swept by the Giants in the World Series.

The 1909 Cubs won 104 games but finished second to the Pirates.

The 1942 Dodgers won 104 games but finished second to the Cardinals.

The 1993 Giants won 103 games but finished second to the Braves.

The 2001 A's won 102 games and finished 13 games behind the Mariners, who won 116 games.

Consecutive 100 Win Seasons. Only four franchises have had three consecutive 100-win seasons: the 2002–2004 Yankees, the 1997–1999 Braves, the 1969–1971 Orioles, and the 1929–1931 Athletics.

Consecutive Wins/Team. The 1916 New York Giants won 26 consecutive games from September 7 through September 30. The club nevertheless finished in fourth place, seven games out of first. The Giants also had a 17-game winning streak that season. The two streaks combined were half the club's total of 86 wins. Some sources report that the 26 wins were all against weaker western clubs. However, only half the games were against weaker clubs.

The 2002 A's set the American League record with 20 straight wins, in August and September that season. They did it in wild fashion in game 20, blowing an 11–0 lead and then coming back in the bottom of the 9th inning to win 12–11 over the Royals. They were shut out 6–0 by the Twins in their next game.

The Cubs won 21 straight games in September 1935, moving into first place on September 15 and finishing four games up.

The 1906 White Sox won 19 straight games from August 2 through August 23.

The 1951 Yankees won 19 straight games until July 18.

The 1951 Giants won 16 straight games.

In 1875 the Boston Red Stockings dominated the league with 71 wins and ended the season with 24 straight wins (or 26) and a tie.

Consecutive Wins/Minor Leagues. Corsicana, Texas, won a then-record 27 straight games in 1902. That record was broken in 1987 when the Salt Lake City Trappers won 29 straight games.

Consecutive Wins/Start of Season. The 1982 Braves started the season with 13 straight wins, finally losing 2–1 on April 22. On April 20 the Braves won their 12th straight game, a 4–2 win over the Reds in Atlanta. That win broke the then-modern Major League record of 11 set a year earlier by the A's. The Braves went on to win the pennant by one game over the Dodgers after squandering their lead late in the season.

On April 19, 1987, the Brewers scored five runs in the 9th inning to beat the Rangers 6–4 to set an American League record with 12 straight wins to start the season.

The 1955 Dodgers won 10 straight to start the season.

In 1933 the Yankees won seven straight to set the American League record at the time. It was broken by the Browns in 1944 with nine straight.

The 1884 New York Giants won their first 12 games.

The 1884 St. Louis Maroons of the Union Association started the season with 20 straight wins, an all-time record.

Consecutive Wins/One Team v. Another. The Orioles beat the Royals 23 straight times over the 1969–1970 seasons.

The Senators were 0–18 in their 1907 season series with the Tigers. In game 19, the Senators scored five quick runs to take a 5–1 lead. Manager Joe Cantillon was celebrating a bit too early as a storm washed out the game before it became official.

Consecutive Home Wins. In 1988 the Red Sox won 24 straight at home over a span of two managers. John McNamara was fired after road losses, but a five-game home winning streak was intact. He was replaced by long-time coach Joe Morgan (not the former Cincinnati second baseman), and the team responded with 19 more wins at home. The team started 19–1 under Morgan.

The 2001–2002 A's won 20 straight home games over two seasons. They were beaten on April 4, 2002, after going undefeated at home since August 24, 2001.

The 1994 Indians won 18 straight home games in their new ballpark, Jacobs Field.

Consecutive Wins/One Season/20th Century Pitchers.
19/Rube Marquard/1912.
"Who 'put it over' 19 straight?
Marquard.
Who seems the Baseball pet of Fate?
Marquard.
Who walks alone on Manhattan's streets
with cheers from every man he meets?
Marquard.
Who drove the knockers from the seats?
Marquard.
Who'll lose a game some day, perhaps?
Marquard.
Who, when the scroll is rolled up tight,
when players never more shall fight,
Will get the praise that is his right?
Marquard."
— Poem written by William F. Kirk to honor Rube Marquard's 19 straight wins in 1912 for the Giants. He began his streak on April 11, 1912, with an 18–3 victory over the Dodgers.

Marquard is credited with 19 straight wins, though he should have been credited with 20. Early in the streak, he came in to relieve for what would have been his 20th win, but the old scoring rules did not credit him with the victory. In the old days, the win was given to a starter if he pitched strongly over most of the game even if the go-ahead run was not scored while he was the pitcher of record.

In that game at the Polo Grounds on April 20, 1912 (1937 in one source!), Giants pitcher Jeff Tesreau was leading 2–0 going into the 9th inning, but blew the lead. Marquard came in to relieve him after the Dodgers went ahead 3–2. The Giants scored two runs in the bottom of the 9th to win 4–3 on a home run by Art Wilson. The Dodgers claimed vehemently that Wilson's home run was foul and manager Bill Dahlen was so vocal that the umpire hit him in the face. They had a fist fight which was broken up by Wilbert Robinson. Regular Giants manager John McGraw was not around because he was serving a five-day suspension. Tesreau was credited with the win, and Marquard was deprived of what would have been his third straight win.

Marquard's streak ended July 8, 1912, in a 7–2 loss to the Cubs in Chicago. He was only 7–11 the rest of the season. During the streak he beat every club in the league, with the Braves and Phillies at the short end four times each.

One source related an odd story in connection with the loss that ended the streak. A woman supposedly climbed a tree just outside the fence and began waving a shawl and screaming insults at Marquard. By the 6th inning Marquard apparently had lost his concentration and control and had to be replaced. She continued shrieking until the game was over. The fire department arrived to get her down and took her to the hospital. A Chicago newspaper reporting the event apparently quoted Marquard after the game: "That poor woman certainly put the jinx on me. Her shrill voice affected me so deeply that I just simply could not do a good job of pitching."

It has been reported that because of the pressure during the streak, Marquard had nightmares, could not sleep, and was sometimes dazed out on the mound.

17/Roy Face/1959. Face was a reliever for the Pirates in 1959 when he won 17 straight, mixing in 10 saves with his 18 total wins. All the wins were in relief. His only loss that season came on September 11, 1959, a 5–4 defeat by the Dodgers.

16/Walter Johnson/1912. Johnson's 16-game streak in 1912 (in which he averaged two days of rest between starts) ended in a game that under today's rules he would not have lost. He was beaten in St. Louis when he came in to relieve in the 7th inning with the score tied 2–2. With two out and men on first and second, he gave up a single that scored the go-ahead run. League president Ban Johnson ruled that Johnson was the losing pitcher even though pitcher Tom Hughes had put the runners on base. Despite attempts to reverse the decision, Johnson remained the losing pitcher and the streak ended.

In retrospect, the decision by Ban Johnson was out of character. He normally would have done anything that he could to show up the National League: having his star pitcher produce a long winning streak accomplished that purpose. A few years later he allowed some questionable hits to remain in the record books so that an American League batter could reach the .400 mark.

In 1913 Walter Johnson had winning streaks of 14, 11 and 10 games on his way to a 36–7 record.

16/Smoky Joe Wood/1912. Wood had a 16-game winning streak in 1912, the year he was 34–5. He had reached 13 straight and Walter Johnson's 16-game streak had ended when the two met in a heavily publicized showdown at Fenway Park. Wood continued his streak with a 1–0 win.

16/Lefty Grove/1931. On August 23, 1931, the A's pitcher was on his way to a season record of 31–4, with a 16-game winning streak. That day he went after number 17 against the Browns in St. Louis, but A's outfielder Jimmy Moore was substituting in left field for starter Al Simmons. Moore dropped a routine fly ball and the only run of the game scored. Grove destroyed the locker room after

the game. His anger was directed not at Moore but at his team's lack of hitting and the absence of Simmons because of a doctor's appointment.

16/Schoolboy Rowe/1934. Rowe's 16-game winning streak for the Tigers ended on August 29, 1934, when the A's beat him 13–5.

16/Carl Hubbell/1936. Hubbell won 16 straight games for the Giants in 1936 and continued with another eight straight wins in 1937, for a total of 24 straight over two seasons (see below).

16/Ewell Blackwell/1947. The Reds pitcher won 16 straight games and pitched five shutouts during his streak. The streak ended after he was leading the Giants 4–3 in the 9th inning. Willard Marshall then tied the game with a one-out homer and Blackwell lost 5–4 in the 10th inning.

16/Jack Sanford/1962. Sanford won 16 straight for the Giants during his streak, which ended in a 5–1 loss to the Pirates on September 15, 1962. Willie Mays had collapsed a few days earlier during the pennant race and was unable to play.

15/Bob Gibson/1968. The Cardinals ace won 15 straight in 1968. The last was a two-hit shutout of the Phillies, his 18th win and 10th shutout of the season. He lost his next start 6–2 to the Pirates on unearned runs in the 9th inning. Gibson struck out 15 in the game.

15/Dave McNally/1969. McNally's 15-game streak for the Orioles in 1969 ended when the Twins' Rich Reese hit a grand slam for a 5–2 Twins victory on August 3. McNally won 17 straight over two seasons.

15/Steve Carlton/1972. The Phillies pitcher won 15 straight in 1972, with three no-decisions mixed in. The streak ended when he lost 2–1 in 11 innings to Phil Niekro of the Braves. Carlton pitched 14 complete games during the streak. He did not finish the first game because of a muscle pull in the 7th inning.

15/Gaylord Perry/1974. The Indians pitcher won 15 straight games from the start of the season. He spent the next six weeks trying for number 16 and finished the season with a record of 21–13.

15/Roger Clemens/1998. Clemens won 15 straight for the Blue Jays in 1998, on his way to 20 straight wins over two seasons (see below). He also won 11 straight for the club to start the 1997 season.

15/Roy Halladay/2003. The Blue Jays starter began the season at 0–2 and then reeled off 15 straight wins. Pitching on three days rest for the third time that season, he had his last win of the streak on July 27, 2003, a 10–1 win over the Orioles. He had five no-decisions during the streak and fell one short of the American League record when he lost 5–0 to the Angels on August 1, 2003. It was his first loss in 21 starts, but he came back to win his next game and went on to win 22 games and the Cy Young Award.

Consecutive Wins/19th Century Pitchers.

19/Tim Keefe/1888. The New York Giants pitcher had 19 straight wins in 1888 on his way to 35 wins and 51 complete games. Keefe is not credited by some with one of the wins because he left after two innings with a 9–0 lead on July 16. Rules for qualifying for a win were rather loose in those days. Under current rules he would not receive credit for the win because he did not complete five innings.

18/Old Hoss Radbourn/1884. The Providence Grays pitcher won 18 straight games during the 1884 season. His streak lasted from August 7 through September 6 and included 14 wins during August. He won 60 games that season and had 73 complete games.

17/Mickey Welch/1885. Welch won 17 straight for the New York Giants.

17/John Luby/1890. Luby won 17 straight for the Chicago White Stockings.

16/Jim McCormick/1886. McCormick won 16 straight for the Chicago White Stockings.

Consecutive Wins over Two Seasons.

24/Carl Hubbell/1936–1937. The Giants pitcher won 24 straight from July 17, 1936, through May 27, 1937. Hubbell's streak ended on May 31, 1937, when he lost 10–3 to the Dodgers. His last defeat had been on July 13, 1936, a 1–0 loss to the Cubs. He won 16 of the games in 1936 and eight in 1937. The screwball pitcher had elbow surgery in 1938 and won only 11 games in each season from 1939 through 1942.

22/Roy Face/1958–1959. The Pirates pitcher was 18–1 during the 1959 season. His first loss ended a 22-game winning streak over two seasons and 98 appearances starting May 30, 1958. The streak ended on September 11, 1959, with a 5–4 loss to the Dodgers, who scored two runs in the bottom of the 9th inning.

20/Roger Clemens/1998–1999. Clemens won 15 straight at the end of the 1998 season for the Blue Jays and then five more in 1999. On June 1, 1999, he won his 20th consecutive decision with an 11–5 win over the Indians. The streak ended five days later in a 7–2 loss to the Mets. The streak started on June 3, 1998, with a 1–0 shutout of the Tigers.

17/Johnny Allen/1936–1937. Allen won 17 over two seasons for the Orioles.

17/Dave McNally/1968–1969. The Orioles pitcher won 17 straight over two seasons, going 15–0 to start 1969 and pitching to a 29–2 record starting from the 1968 All-Star break.

16/Randy Johnson/1995–1997. Johnson's streak began in August 1995 and ended on May 8, 1997 (two seasons later), against the Orioles in a 13–3 loss. He struck out 10 in six innings, but gave up five runs on six hits and two walks. Johnson's last loss was on August 1, 1995. When he won his first game in April 1997, it was his first pitching performance since May 12, 1996. He won the 1996 game, but shortly thereafter went on the disabled list with back problems. He was almost unbeatable in 1997, with a seven game winning streak after the loss. That streak ended with a 19-strikeout performance against the A's that he lost 4–1.

15/Wilson Alvarez/1993–1994. The White Sox pitcher won 15 straight over two seasons until May 27, 1994.

Consecutive Wins/Start of Career. George "Hooks" Wiltse began his career on May 29, 1904. He won 12 straight through September 15 and finished with a 13–3 record. He won 139 games over his 12-year career.

Butch Metzger began his career with 12 straight wins, although it took him three years to do it. He won one game in 1974 for the Giants, one game in 1975 for the Padres, and 10 games to start the 1976 season for the Padres. He finished the year 11–4 and was Rookie of the Year. He won only six more games in his Major League career.

It has been reported that Lefty Krause of the A's started his career with 10 straight wins in 1909, including six shutouts. However, he was 1–1 in 1908 for the club and pitched only four shutouts in 1909, when he was 18–8.

Kirk Reuter of the Expos won 10 straight at the start of his career in 1993.

Yankee pitcher Whitey Ford won nine straight at the start of his career in 1950.

Fernando Valenzuela won nine straight for the Dodgers from the end of 1980 (two wins) through early 1981, when Fernandomania gripped baseball fans.

Consecutive Home Wins/Pitcher. Ray Kremer of the Pirates won 22 straight home games during the 1926–1927 seasons. Lefty Grove won 20 straight at home for the Red Sox over four seasons

(1938–1941). Modern pitchers Kenny Rogers and Frank Viola each won 19 straight at home. Rogers did it for four clubs during his streak, the Yankees, Mets, Rangers and A's.

Consecutive Road Wins/Pitcher. On August 26, 1995, Greg Maddux pitched his 16th consecutive road victory to tie the modern Major League record held by Denny McLain (1968), Cal McLish (1958–1959) and Richard Dotson (1983–1984). On September 16, 1995, Maddux pitched his 17th consecutive road win in the Braves' 6–1 victory over the Reds. His streak ended at 18 on April 11, 1996, when the Padres beat him 2–1. He had not lost on the road since losing 7–2 to the Expos on June 27, 1994.

Minor League Streak. Rube Parnham was an eccentric pitcher for the minor league Baltimore Orioles in 1923. He finished the year with a 33–7 record and 20 straight wins. He had 18 straight when he jumped the club with a week to play. He reappeared on the last day of the season and won both ends of a doubleheader.

In 1904 Baxter Sparks of Yazoo City in the Delta League (later the Cotton States League), won 21 in a row.

Most Wins/No Losses. Tom Zachary, who delivered the pitch for Babe Ruth's 60th home run in 1927, won 12 games without a loss for the Yankees in 1929, appearing in 26 games. He was 186–191 over his 19-year career.

Howie Krist went 10–0 for the Cardinals in 1941, which was his first full season. He was 37–11 over a six-year career interrupted by World War II.

Most Appearances/No Wins. Ed Olwine made 80 appearances for the Braves from 1986 through 1988, finishing his career with an 0–1 record. He had three saves.

Tigers left-hander Buddy Groom came close to Olwine's record, appearing in 77 games over parts of four seasons, but he finally won a game the day after his son was born in 1995.

Wins Versus One Team/Pitcher. The National and Major League record is held by Grover Cleveland Alexander, who was 70–24 against the Reds. Christy Mathewson was 64–18 against the Reds. Perhaps the best record was Carl Mays' 35–3 record against the A's when he pitched first for the Red Sox and then the Yankees. Juan Marichal of the Giants was 37–18 against the Dodgers.

Senators pitcher Walter Johnson beat the Tigers 66 times (and lost 42), by far a record against one team by an American League pitcher.

Pete Donohue of the 1920s Reds won 20 straight games against the Phillies.

Christy Mathewson had a record 24 straight wins over the Cardinals.

Book. Allen Lewis, *Baseball's Greatest Streaks: The Highs and Lows of Teams, Pitchers and Hitters in the Modern Major Leagues* (1992).

Winter League Baseball

"Amazin'. But I don't think we can catch the Dodgers — unless we play winter ball." — Casey Stengel after the Mets put together a two-game winning streak in August 1962.

Instructional Leagues. Casey Stengel is credited by some with the idea of the winter instructional leagues that were created in 1958. Typically 14 teams have played in Florida and another four in Arizona for approximately two months late in the year.

Foreign and Non-Instructional Winter Leagues. By the 1990s there were winter leagues in Arizona, Australia, Hawaii, and the traditional Latin locales of Cuba, Mexico, Venezuela, Puerto Rico and the Dominican Republic. The leagues begin play in either late October or November. See also separate entries by country or state.

Winter Meetings

"Mr. Frick called the joint meeting to order.... Holding a typewritten sheet in front of him, he began going over the points at issue, one at a time. He read the first, then looked up. Joe Cronin, the American League president, rose and said, 'the American League votes yes.' Then he sat down. Warren Giles, the National League president, rose and said, 'the National League votes yes.' Then *he* sat down. 'Passed,' said the commissioner. Then he read the next point. Again Cronin rose and said, 'the American League votes yes,' and again he sat down. And again Giles rose and said, 'the National League votes yes,' and again he sat down.... This went on until Frick had covered all the points on the agenda.... Not once did they disagree. And nobody else except the commissioner uttered a word. The meeting lasted exactly seven minutes. Frick announced this fact with great pride. I was amazed. We weren't sheep. We were presumably successful men with substantial financial interests who kept a close watch on our affairs which we ran with prudence. We made decisions only after careful discussion and exchange of ideas with associates and subordinates." — White Sox owner Arthur Allyn in the early 1960s after attending his first midwinter owners' meeting. The owners traditionally meet for a week during early December of each year. Now they meet two times per year, once in the off-season and once during the season.

"Oh, did we vote on you yet?" — A befuddled Gene Autry to new Padres owner Tom Werner out in the hall a few minutes after the owners had voted to approve Werner's ownership group; Werner was thanking Autry for his support.

The winter meetings were attended by the clubs' general managers from 1901 through 1992. However, after a buying frenzy that saw $280 million in contracts committed in four days in December 1992, acting commissioner Bud Selig ended the December sessions for general managers. They were to attend only the "minimeetings" held in mid–January to cut down on face-to-face meetings that might foster more expensive trades.

Wives *See Marriage*

Women in Baseball

"When women enter Baseball
They'll shake a batter's nerves;
I never knew a player
Who could catch on their curves.
When Women enter Baseball
The time to take your heed
is when by chance you tackle those
who have both curves and speed."
— July 1919 poem in *The Sporting News*; "Quite So," responded the paper.

"Ken Burns calls baseball a metaphor for democracy. He's wrong. It is a metaphor for sexism. The great theme is that it's a boy's game; women have been shut out again and again." — Susan J. Berkson.

See also ***All-American Professional Girls Baseball League.***
Baseball Wives. See *Marriage* and *Sex.*
19th Century Women Players.
"The female has no place in Baseball, except to the degradation of the game. For two seasons ... [people] have been nauseated by the spectacle of these tramps." —1880s newspaper account of women's baseball exhibitions.

"Apart from Lizzie Arlington and a handful of other female play-

ers, women's baseball in the nineteenth century caricatured the game, but for young women with a yen for adventure, women's baseball teams presented a novel opportunity, provided they had the courage to disregard the stuffed-shirt and starched-blouse guardians of propriety and endure the derision of male spectators and the gibes of the press. In so doing, they constituted one segment, however minor, of the women's movement and did their bit to weaken prejudice against them." — Harold Seymour in *Baseball: The People's Game* (1990).

"The second half of the 1800s set the stage for an unlikely convergence. A small group of Victorian ladies left their parlor couches, their smelling salts, and their feminine frailty behind to participate in the new national pastime of baseball, both as spectators and as players." — Gai Ingham Berlage in *Women in Baseball: The Forgotten History* (1994).

Women played baseball at Vassar College as early as 1866 and first appeared in a baseball exhibition in 1875 in Illinois. The "Blondes" and "Brunettes" played a series of games in Springfield and Decatur.

In the 1880s Harry S. Freeman attempted unsuccessfully to form the first organized women's baseball club. The first successful effort was in 1890, when W.S. Franklin organized a women's league in New York. The players' abbreviated costumes created a stir when they played an exhibition game against the Giants. Pitcher May Howard was "showing all the curves," according to the *Police Gazette* report of the game. During the 1890s women players were called "fair base ballists."

The Young Ladies Baseball Club was the best team of 1890–1891, traveling to various cities and playing exhibitions against men and among themselves. There was some question as to whether all the players were women. The team attracted crowds and press, but there was some censure because it was an activity "not proper for Victorian young ladies."

Elizabeth Stroud.
"She went about it like a professional even down to expectorating on her hands and wiping her hands on her uniform." — The *Reading Eagle* on Stroud's play in a minor league game.

On July 5, 1898, Stroud, also known as Lizzie Arlington, pitched for Ed Barrow's team in the Atlantic League. Barrow was later the general manager of the Yankees. Stroud gave up no runs, two hits and one walk in one inning of work. Barrow later said that she appeared a few times around the league, but there is no record of any other appearances.

Bloomer Girls.
"Miss Conry has no equal as a pitcher among any of the girl players around Boston, and there are few men who can twirl a faster ball or furnish a better assortment of curves." — August 1903 description in the *Boston Herald.*

The Bloomer Girls were women's teams that began play in the 1890s and barnstormed either nationally or regionally. The term was used generically by a number of clubs in cities throughout the East and Midwest. The term supposedly came not from baggy pants called bloomers but from suffragist Adelaide Jenks Bloomer.

Men were sometimes recruited for key positions such as pitcher, catcher or shortstop, and they donned skirts and wigs. Future stars such as Rogers Hornsby and Smoky Joe Wood played on Bloomer Girl clubs before making it in Organized Baseball. According to newspaper accounts of the era, the women's clubs often had excellent results against men's teams.

The Bloomer Girls have almost disappeared by the end of the 1920s. Mae Arbaugh played in over 4,000 games for the Bloomer Girls over 33 years. Another prominent women's team of the era was the Philadelphia Bobbies.

Lizzie Murphy. On August 14, 1922, the Red Sox played a benefit game against a team of American League all-stars. Lizzie Murphy played one inning at first base for the all-stars (some sources report incorrectly that she played for the Red Sox). She had one putout in the effort to raise money for the family of former Major Leaguer Tommy McCarthy, who had died at age 59 the previous week. She also played semipro ball on men's teams from 1918 through 1935.

Slapsie Maxie. In the late 1930s "Slapsie Maxie's Curvaceous Cuties" played exhibition games around the country. Slapsie Maxie Rosenbloom was a fighter of some renown in the 1920s and 1930s, and then retired to go into the entertainment business, primarily radio and movies.

Babe Didrikson. Didrikson, considered by many as the greatest female athlete of the 20th century, pitched for the A's against the Dodgers and for the Cardinals against the Braves in exhibition games during 1934. The Olympian and professional golfer once played in an exhibition game in New Orleans against the Indians. She also barnstormed successfully with a House of David team.

Jackie Mitchell.

"It takes curves to pitch baseball, and Miss Mitchell's aren't that kind." — *The Sporting News*, which also noted the "bawdy publicity" for the exhibition game in which Mitchell faced members of the Yankees.

On April 2, 1931, Jackie Mitchell (aka Virne Beatrice Mitchell) pitched for the Class AA Chattanooga Lookouts of the Southern Association in a preseason exhibition against the Yankees. The 17-year-old struck out Babe Ruth looking on a 1–2 count and Lou Gehrig on three straight pitches. After walking Tony Lazzeri, she was removed from the game. The 5'8" left-hander had only high school and semipro experience. After the game, Judge Landis voided her minor league contract.

Sonny Dunlap. The last woman to play in Organized Baseball until 1994 was Frances "Sonny" Dunlap, who played right field on September 7, 1936, for the Class D Fayetteville Bears in Arkansas. She went hitless but connected each time up.

Dorothy Kamenshek. The 1940s softball star was offered a contract by Class B Ft. Lauderdale, but her softball league would not release her from her contract. She later played in the All-American Girls Professional Baseball League.

Eleanor Engle. During the summer of 1952, the 24-year-old Engle was about to sign to play shortstop for the Harrisburg Senators of the Class B Inter-State League. The league president stepped in and blocked the deal. Organized Baseball then instituted a rule barring women from signing pro contracts, a rule which technically was still in effect until the 1990s. *The Sporting News* noted at the time that even innovative Bill Veeck, Jr., was against using women: "Even President Bill Veeck of the Browns, who presented a Midget in a game last year and tried many bizarre stunts, declared it was going too far."

Modern College Players.

Julie Croteau. In March 1989 Croteau debuted at first base for St. Mary's College of Maryland, handling six chances at first base and going hitless in three at-bats. After playing three seasons and hitting .171, she quit the team because of harassment by team members, including the reading of pornographic magazines on road trips. The school said that she was merely reacting to isolated instances. Prior to her college experience, Croteau played semipro ball briefly in the Virginia Baseball League. She later played for the professional **Colorado Silver Bullets** and the Maui Stingrays in the Hawaiian Winter Baseball League. In 1996 she began work as an assistant baseball coach at the University of Massachusetts.

Jodi Haller. Haller was the first woman to pitch in a college baseball game. In 1990 she pitched during her freshman year for NAIA St. Vincent's College of Latrobe, Pennsylvania. In 1995 Haller pitched for Meiji University in the Tokyo Six University Baseball League, Japan's oldest and most competitive college league.

Ila Borders. Borders, a 5'11" (or 5'10"), 175-pound (or 165) left-hander, pitched as a freshman on partial scholarship (the first woman to receive one for baseball) in 1994 for NAIA Southern California College in Costa Mesa, California. On February 15 that season she beat Claremont-Mudd 12–1 (the first ever complete game by a woman) and finished with a 2–4 record and 2.92 ERA. She was 1–7 with a 7.20 ERA in her sophomore season. She appeared primarily in relief in 1996 as a junior, with mediocre results. She had an 82-mph fastball to go with a curve and screwball/changeup.

On July 9, 1998, Borders became the first woman to start a minor league game, when she took the mound for the Duluth-Superior Dukes in an 8–3 loss to the Sioux Falls Canaries in the Northern League. She gave up five hits and three runs in five innings, striking out two and walking two. She was credited with the loss.

On July 24, 1998, she became the first woman to win a men's regular season professional game, for the Dukes again against the Canaries. Borders played three full seasons of men's professional baseball between 1997 and 1999, primarily in the Northern League, and then retired in June 2000. She finished her career with the Zion Pioneerzz of the Western Baseball League.

Minor Leagues/Pamela Davis. On June 4, 1996, Pamela Davis pitched one inning of scoreless relief for the Jacksonville Suns, a Class AA affiliate of the Tigers. She shut out the Australian Olympic team as part of a 7–2 win for the Suns. She was believed to be the first woman to pitch for a Major League farm club under the current minor league structure.

Draft Pick. The first woman drafted by a Major League club was Karey Schueler, daughter of White Sox general manager Ron Schueler. She was selected as the club's 43rd pick (out of 49) in 1993.

Colorado Silver Bullets. This all-women's baseball team was formed in 1994 to play against professional men's teams. Coached by former Major Leaguer Phil Niekro, the club was scheduled to play almost 30 exhibition games against minor league teams.

Financed by Coors Brewery, the club was recognized officially by the National Association of Minor Leagues in December 1993. Players had to be at least 21 years old and were guaranteed a minimum salary of $20,000. Some of the pitchers threw underhand in the manner of fast-pitch softball.

In their first game the Silver Bullets lost 19–0 to a group of Northern League All-Stars on Mother's Day, May 8, 1994. They were outhit 21–2 and committed six errors. More than 8,100 fans and 50 media representatives were on hand to witness the game. On the Northern League roster were former Major Leaguers Dennis "Oil Can" Boyd, Leon Durham and Carl Nichols. Underhand pitcher Lisa Martinez was able to strike out Darius Gash, who played in the Padres' farm system a year earlier.

The team included Gina Satriano, daughter of former Major Leaguer Tom Satriano and reportedly the first female to play Little League Baseball in California. Also playing was Julie Croteau, who sued to play on her high school team and played college baseball. Players received $4,000 a month in salary and had contracts with Mizuno, Bike, Hillerich & Bradsby and Starter.

Two weeks later the Silver Bullets announced that they would play no more games against male professionals. They still scheduled semipro teams and teams of over–30 men's players.

The Silver Bullets won their first game on May 27, 1994, a 7–2 defeat of the Richfield Rockets, a 35-and-over men's amateur team in St. Paul, Minnesota. Lee Anne Ketcham struck out 14, including the side in the 7th to end the game. The win brought their record to 1–6.

They finished with six wins as Ketcham recorded five of the victories. The other win was a no-hitter that pitcher Lisa Martinez threw on July 8 against the Summerville Yankees in Charleston, South Carolina.

The club drew 300,000 fans, including 33,179 to a game in Denver, for an average of 7,000. Their record of 6–37 was caused primarily by a team batting average of .140 and a team ERA of over 7.00.

Women who did not make it in tryouts with the club in 1995 were scheduled to play in a new Mediterranean League in Spain and southern France.

Leagues. The first formal women's professional baseball league was the *All-American Girls Professional Baseball League*. It was formed in 1943 and lasted through 1954.

The next all-women's baseball league was formed in 1987 when Darlene Mehrer founded the American Women's Baseball Association in Glenview, Illinois. The league featured a 50-foot pitching distance and 80-foot bases. *Basewoman* magazine originally was edited by the founder of the Glenview league and covered women in professional and amateur baseball, both on the field and in the front office.

In July 1998, the Ladies Professional Baseball League suspended play because of low attendance. The final game was a 7–0 shutout by the San Jose Spitfires over the Long Beach Aces.

By 2000 there were approximately 2,000 women playing organized baseball in an amateur league know as the Women's National Adult Baseball Association.

World Amateur Competition. Three teams played in the 2003 third annual women's round-robin baseball world series in Australia. Japan beat Australia, as the U.S. came in third.

Little League and Babe Ruth Leagues. There are almost 8,000 girls playing *Little League Baseball* today, approximately 28 out of every 10,000 players (out of over 2.5 million).

In the next age group, Babe Ruth Baseball, there are less than 1,000 girls among over 450,000 players. There are a few women every year who play American Legion Baseball (16–18-year-olds), but by age 16 the disparity is usually too great.

Kitty Burke. On July 31, 1935, singer Kitty Burke attended the sixth night game at Cincinnati's Crosley Field. After being teased by Joe Medwick, Burke insisted that she could hit a pitched ball. There was one out in the 8th inning and the Cardinals were leading 2–1. Sammy Byrd was on first. Burke grabbed a bat from Babe Adams and batted against Paul Dean of the Cardinals. Dean threw a hard pitch, which she missed, and then tossed one underhand, which she grounded out to him.

Ball Girls. The first foul line ball girls were used in 1971 by the A's. Debbie Fields was the first, hired by A's owner Charlie Finley. She often made cookies for the players and umpires, and Finley was so impressed with the taste that he financed her business start-up that later became the highly successful "Mrs. Fields Cookies."

Black Sox Scandal. *The Sporting News* noted that there were two women sitting on the grand jury that would help decide the fate of the Black Sox players. The newspaper applauded this fact, noting that although the "deadlier sex" tended to lie about age, the "high ideals of the woman fan" would be a positive factor in the case.

Broadcaster. The first regularly scheduled woman broadcaster was Mary Shane with the 1977 White Sox.

Executives. Phyllis Collins became the highest ranking woman in baseball as the vice president of the National League in the late 1980s. She was considered for the top spot in the league when Bart Giamatti was named commissioner. She began her baseball career in 1968 as an executive secretary for the Braves. She moved to the National League staff in 1978 as an administrative assistant to the president.

Rawlings Sporting Goods sponsors a Woman Executive of the Year in the minor leagues.

A 1989 survey commissioned by Major League Baseball determined that there were 1,854 front-office positions among all Major League teams. This was up from 1,495 such jobs in 1988. Women held 700 of the 1989 positions, up from 564 in 1988. In 1996 women comprised 35% of front office staff (though mostly secretarial), a steady decline from 40% in 1992 and 38% in 1994.

Commissioner of Baseball.

"I seriously doubt that a female would be chosen. More than likely a woman will have to be elected president of the good ol' USA before we have a lady czar." — Bill Bartholomay, chairman of the commissioner's search committee in 1993.

Hall of Fame. The National Women's Baseball Hall of Fame was created in 1998 in Chevy Chase, Maryland. Winners have included current managers and players, as well as famous "previous players" from the past. Winners include Mildred "Babe" Didrikson (2001) as an infielder/pitcher for the barnstorming House of David teams and Claire Schillace, a centerfielder for the Racine Belles of the All-American Girls Professional Baseball League.

Negro Leagues.

"A woman has her dreams, too. When you finish high school, they tell a boy to go out and see the world. What do they tell a girl? They tell her to go next door and marry the boy that their family's picked out for her. It wasn't right." — Toni Stone to New Orleans Creoles teammate Al Lombardi.

No women played in the Negro Leagues until the leagues began to fade in the 1950s. At that point, at least three women played on Negro League teams. The most prominent and successful was Marcenia Lyle Alberga, who played as Stone, a lifetime .243 hitter who signed with the Indianapolis Clowns in 1953 and played two seasons with the Clowns and Kansas City Monarchs. She once got a hit off of Satchel Paige and she also played for three minor league teams.

Nineteen-year-old Connie Morgan played in 1954 and 1955 for the Indianapolis Clowns, replacing Toni Stone at second base. Before that, she played for five years with the North Philadelphia Honey Drippers, an all-girl baseball team.

A utility player and pitcher, Mamie "Peanut" Johnson (nicknamed for her small size) played one season for the Clowns in 1954. She studied medicine and engineering at New York University before signing with the Clowns and was the last woman to play on a Negro League team. She also pitched on a Police Athletic League team in the 1940s, the only black player and the only female. She was turned down for a spot in the All-American Girls Professional Baseball League because she was black. See Michelle Y. Green, *A Strong Right Arm: The Story of Mamie Peanut Johnson* (2002).

Major League Owners.

"There's no good reason why a woman cannot run a ball club as well as a man.... In fact there are apt to be things that we on the feminine side can see in connection with a team, that the male of the species might overlook. Certainly, the woman belongs — just as much as she does in other sports." — Mrs. Bob Seeds, pre–World

War II co-owner of the Amarillo club of the West Texas–New Mexico League.

Helene Britton owned the Cardinals from 1911, when her husband died, until 1916 when she sold out.

Joan Whitney Payson was the principal stockholder of the Mets during the 1960s and early 1970s.

Jean Yawkey controlled a majority interest in the Red Sox after husband Tom Yawkey died in 1976 (though not without a protracted trust estate fight).

Grace Comiskey controlled the White Sox from 1939, when her husband Lou died (son of patriarch Charles), until 1958 when she and her daughter sold out to Bill Veeck.

Marge Schott became the majority owner of the Reds when her husband died in the 1970s.

Joan Kroc owned the Padres for six years after her husband Ray died before the 1984 pennant-winning season.

Public Address Announcers. The first full-time female public address announcer was hired by the Giants for the 1993 season. Legal secretary Sherry Davis was hired after she proved that she could keep score by producing her scorebook that she had maintained since 1987.

Joy Hawkins McCabe, an aspiring actress and daughter of a Senators' public relations director, announced one game in 1966. She filled in for Phil Hochberg, who was away at Army basic training. Television reporter Kelly Saunders filled in for one Orioles game in 1992 when the regular announcer was ill.

Scout. In the 1920s Bessie Langer scouted Texas sandlots with her husband, discovering such future stars as Smead Jolley and Luke Appling.

Edith Houghton has been described by at least one source as the first and possibly last woman to be a Major League scout. She was hired in 1946 by Bob Carpenter of the Phillies. None of the players she signed over her few years with the club made it to the Major Leagues.

Sportswriters.

"No Dogs or Women."—Common sign on the door of press boxes around the Major Leagues in the 1940s and later.

"What will happen to the women reporters on the road? Most of the women writers I've seen are girls I wouldn't cross the street to ask for a date."—Sportswriter Maury Allen.

"Sure, women sportswriters look when they're in the clubhouse. Read their stories. How else do you explain a capital letter in the middle of a word?"—Bob Uecker.

The earliest women sportswriters appeared in the 19th century. According to Gai Ingham Berlage in *Women in Baseball: The Forgotten History* (1994), two of the first were Ella Black, who wrote for *Sporting Life*, and Sallie Van Pelt, the baseball editor of the *Dubuque Times*.

Jeane Hofmann of the *New York Journal-American* was a sportswriter in the 1940s who experienced varying degrees of discrimination while covering baseball.

Dave Kingman once sent a shoebox gift-wrapped with a pink ribbon to Susan Fornoff of the *Sacramento Bee* newspaper. Inside was a dead rat. Fornoff later wrote *Lady in the Locker Room* (1993), chronicling her difficulties as a beat writer covering Major League Baseball.

The first woman sportscaster to enter a Major League locker room was Anita Martini. In 1974 at age 35, she made history by entering the Dodgers' locker room after a game at the Houston Astrodome.

In 1978 when the Yankees first reluctantly allowed female reporters in their locker room, the women were greeted with a large cake commissioned by one of the players. The two-foot-long cake was in the form of a penis. Chocolate shavings served as pubic hair around the portion shaped like testicles.

In 1979 commissioner Bowie Kuhn ordered clubhouses opened to women sportswriters, though he actively fought the discrimination lawsuit over the same issue filed by *Sports Illustrated* writer Melissa Ludtke. Some sportswriters, including Red Smith, did not support women writers in their efforts to gain access to locker rooms.

At the 1984 NLCS, there was an incident in the Padres locker room. *Hartford Courant* writer Claire Smith was the subject of vicious remarks by certain players, who called on club officials to toss her out of the locker room. Major League Baseball officials ignored her complaints until commissioner Peter Ueberroth stepped in and sided with the reporter.

Alison Gordon wrote *Foul Ball* (1984), about her years as a beat writer covering the Blue Jays.

Umpires.

"There will never be a woman student in my school; it's just not a job for a woman."—Umpire school owner Al Somers.

"This is not an occupation a woman should be in. In God's society, woman was created in a role of submission to the husband. It's not that woman is inferior, but I don't believe women should be in a leadership role."—Pitcher Bob Knepper on Pam Postema umpiring in the spring of 1988.

"In a way an umpire is like a woman. He makes quick decisions, never reverses them, and doesn't think you're safe when you're out."—Umpire Larry Goetz in 1955.

Early Umpires. The first woman umpire may have been Dolly Frerer, who signed the Knickerbocker scorebook as the umpire for a game on June 12, 1846. It has been noted that the numerous corrections and handwriting style suggest that a woman scored the game but did not umpire it.

The first-known woman umpire in Organized Baseball was Amanda Clement, who umpired semipro games in South Dakota and northern Iowa in 1905 and 1906 before quitting; though other sources report that she umpired through 1911 to pay for her schooling.

An 1897 editorial suggested that women be umpires to curb rowdyism and physical violence.

Bernice Gera.

"Within the space of a week man got to the moon and a woman became an umpire…. You win one and you lose one. I don't know which event is more significant, but I notice that the moon is still going strong. I doubt if we'll be able to say the same for baseball now that milady has got her tootsies in the door."—Tim Hogan of Boston's *Sunday Herald Traveler* on Gera's signing with the New York–Pennsylvania League.

Gera was the first woman to pursue professional umpiring in the modern era. In the 1960s she umpired amateur and semipro games while a housewife in New York. At 5'2" and 130 pounds, she was the first woman to graduate from the Florida Baseball School. She then went to court and won the right to umpire professional games after she was denied a contract on the ground that she was too short.

On June 24, 1972, at age 41, Gera umpired second base during a game between the Geneva Rangers and Auburn Phillies of the Class A New York–Pennsylvania League. Her calls were protested repeatedly and she even reversed a call. Reduced to tears, she quit umpiring immediately after the game.

Christine Wren. Wren umpired in the minor leagues from 1975 through 1977 and then retired.

Pam Postema.

"There has been a longstanding prejudice against women and an agreement and understanding … generally tacit, but often expressly stated, that women should not be employed as umpires."—Contentions in Postema's discrimination lawsuit against Major League Baseball.

Postema progressed the farthest in professional umpiring, making it through a few years in Class AAA ball during a career that began in 1979. She finished number 17 in a class of 130 in a 1977 umpire school and was assigned to the Gulf Coast Rookie League. She first worked as a crew chief in 1988 and worked home plate at the Class AAA All-Star Game that season.

Postema called a few Major League spring training games from 1983 through 1985 in the American League and in 1988 in the National League but never got the call for the regular season. In 1990 she was released after failing to make it to the Major Leagues, and she went to work for Federal Express.

In late 1991 at age 37, Postema filed a sex discrimination lawsuit based on her failure to make it to the Major Leagues. The case later settled. Interviewed when the lawsuit was filed, she noted that: "I'm in real good shape. A lot better shape than those umpires I see in the Majors. They don't miss many meals."

Postema wrote a book on her experience, *You've Got to Have Balls to Make It in This League*, with Gene Wojciechowski (1992).

Theresa Cox. In 1989 Cox graduated from the Harry Wendelstedt School for Umpires and started work in the Arizona Rookie League.

Books. Gorman Bechard, *Balls* (1995) (fiction); Gai Ingham Berlage, *Women in Baseball—The Forgotten History* (1994); Barbara Gregorich, *Women at Play* (1993); Susan E. Johnson, *When Women Played Hardball* (1994); Dave Kindred, *The Colorado Silver Bullets: The Women Who Go Toe-to-Toe with the Men* (1995); Elinor Nauen (ed.), *Diamonds Are a Girl's Best Friend: Women Writers on Baseball* (1994).

Worcester Ruby Legs

National League 1880–1882

"Worcester was the biggest complainer among the National League teams and insisted that the Reds discontinue their 'distasteful practice.' The entire city of 'Old Zinzinnati' was outraged at the antibeer stand, and a Cincy newspaper reflected the militant mood: 'Puritanical Worcester' is not liberal Cincinnati by a jugful and what is sauce for Worcester is wind for the Queen City.'"—Harvey Frommer in *Primitive Baseball* (1988).

The Ruby Legs replaced Syracuse in the National League in 1880 even though the city did not have the required minimum population of 75,000. Troy threatened to veto the inclusion of Worcester because it wanted its natural rival, Albany, in first. A unanimous vote on Worcester's entry into the league was required because of the failure of the city to meet the minimum population requirement. The league supposedly circumvented the problem by including population within a four-mile (40?) radius of Worcester.

The Massachusetts club lasted only three seasons, but in 1880 pitcher John Montgomery Ward pitched the second perfect game in National League history. After two last-place finishes, the club moved to Philadelphia and became the Phillies for the 1883 season.

World Baseball Association

This was an aborted 1974 effort to create a league with teams in Jersey City, Tampa–St. Petersburg, Mexico City, Birmingham, Columbus and Memphis.

World Cup (2006–)

In 2004 a Major League Baseball committee was working on a proposed World Cup tournament for mid–March 2005, involving Major League players from different countries. It was anticipated that 16 teams would play, including teams from Cuba and China.

The players accepted an Olympics-style drug testing system. In mid–2004 Japanese baseball officials opposed the set-up and there was talk of delaying the game for another year. The Japanese believed that the International Baseball Federation should organize the game, and not Major League officials and the Players' Union. As a result of various complications, the tournament was delayed until at least 2006.

World Series (1903–)

"The time has come for the National League and American League to organize a World Series. It is my belief that if our clubs played a series on a best-out-of-nine basis, we would create great interest in baseball, in our leagues, and in our players. I also believe it would be a financial success."—A letter from Pirates owner Barney Dreyfuss to Red Sox owner Henry Killilea.

"'Daddy, why is it called the World Series?' I could tell him. I could recount the bitter corporate rivalry between the greedy American and National Leagues that produced these fall games as a kind of peace treaty."—John Krich in *The Temple of Baseball*, edited by Richard Grossinger (1985).

See **Championship Games** for championship series prior to the first World Series in 1903.

First World Series. In 1903 the American League Boston Pilgrims beat the National League Pirates 5–3 in a scheduled nine-game Series. See Roger I. Abrams, *The First World Series and the Baseball Fanatics of 1903* (2003).

Attendance. The highest attendance for a single World Series game was 92,706 for Game 3 at the Los Angeles Coliseum in 1959 between the Dodgers and White Sox.

Broadcasting. See **Radio** and **Television**.

Controversial Calls.

1912 World Series. In Game 3 (after one tie), the Giants beat the Red Sox 2–1 as Rube Marquard picked up the victory. In the bottom of the 9th inning with two out, Forrest Cady of the Red Sox hit a long drive with two men on. Giants outfielder Josh Devore dove for the ball and apparently made the catch in the near-darkness. He then kept running to the clubhouse. Many thought the ball went past him and that he faked the catch; if it had dropped, the Red Sox would have scored two runs for a 3–2 win. In one recent definitive book containing every play of every World Series game, no mention is made of the dive except to describe the out as a "line drive to Devore in right center."

The Giants went on to win the Series in eight games (one tie), 4–3–1.

1925 World Series. In Game 3 the Senators led the Pirates 4–3 in the top of the 8th inning. Pirates catcher Oil Smith lined a ball toward the right field stands. Right fielder Sam Rice leaned over the fence and reached into the stands with his glove. After a few seconds, Rice withdrew his arm from the stands and showed the ball to umpire Cy Rigler. Rigler ruled that the ball was caught and the Senators held on for the win; though the Pirates loaded the bases with one out but failed to score. Unnoticed by the Pirates was that the Senators batted out of order in the bottom of the 8th inning. The Senators took a 2–1 series lead, but the Pirates came back from a 3–1 deficit to sweep the last three games and clinch the Series.

The controversy over the alleged catch escalated when a Pittsburgh businessman wrote a letter to Judge Landis: "I learned from a number of people who sat very near … that Rice did not catch the ball. It touched his glove and fell into the stand where it was retrieved by a colored man who handed it to Rice."

Rice never admitted anything and in 1965 while at a Hall of Fame induction ceremony wrote a letter explaining the event. The letter was to be opened at his death. Dated July 26, 1965, on the stationery of the National Baseball Hall of Fame and Museum, the letter was read publicly on November 4, 1974, after his death on October 13 that year. Written in long-hand, it read: "It was a cold and windy day—the rightfield bleachers were crowded with people in overcoats and wrapped in blankets, the ball was a line drive headed for the bleachers towards right center. I turned slightly to my right and had the ball in view all the way, going at top speed and about 15 feet from bleachers jumped as high as I could and back handed and the ball hit the center of pocket in glove (I had a death grip on it). I hit the ground about 5 feet from a barrier about 4 feet high in front of bleachers with all the brakes on but couldn't stop so I tried to jump it to land in the crowd but my feet hit the barrier about a foot from top and I toppled over on my stomach into first row of bleachers. I hit my adams apple on something which sort of knocked me out for a few seconds but [Senators outfielder Earl] McNeely around about that time grabbed me by the shirt and picked me out. I remember trotting back towards the infield still carrying the ball for about half way and then tossed it towards the pitchers mound. (How I have wished many times I had kept it.)

At no time did I lose possession of the ball.

'Sam' Rice"

He wrote a postscript at the bottom of the letter: "P.S. After this was announced at the dinner last night I approached Bill McKechnie (one of the finest men I have ever known in Baseball) and I said Bill you were the mgr of Pittsburgh at that time, what do you think will be in the letter. His answer was, Sam there was never any doubt in my mind but what you caught the ball: I thanked him as much to say, You were right — S. Rice"

Third baseman Ossie Bluege stated that in 1972 Rice told him that he never caught the ball. Among Rice's papers at the Hall of

Scorecard from the 1903 World Series, won by the Boston Pilgrims (Red Sox) over the Pittsburgh Pirates in eight games (scheduled nine-game series).

Fame is a letter written by Maryland resident Norman Budesheim, who Rice crashed into while trying to catch the ball. The letter reports that Rice had the ball when he left the field, but "definitely dropped" it when he hit Budesheim and a friend. All three scrambled for the ball, but Rice got it first. Budesheim's final comment: "When Sam says 'at no time did I lose possession of the ball,' he is generally and literally correct."

1948 World Series. See *Pick-Off Throws* for Bob Feller's unsuccessful Game 1 pick-off attempt of Boston Braves runner Phil Masi.

1969 World Series. See *Base Running* for the Game 4 controversy surrounding a throw from Orioles pitcher Pete Richert on a bunt that hit Mets runner J.C. Martin on the wrist.

During Game 1 of the 1921 World Series, Yankee outfielder Elmer Miller lines a single to left center off Giants pitcher Phil Douglas, and later scores on a single by Babe Ruth. The Yankees won the game 3–0 behind Carl Mays on the mound, but the Giants came back to win the Series in eight games.

1975 World Series. See *Interference* for the Game 3 controversy surrounding Reds hitter Ed Armbrister's interference with Red Sox catcher Carlton Fisk.

1985 World Series. In the bottom of the 9th inning of Game 6 between the Royals and Cardinals, the Cardinals were leading 1–0 and about to clinch the Series. Controversy erupted when first base umpire Don Denkinger called Royals runner Jorge Orta safe on what replays made clear was an obvious out. What is often forgotten is that on the next play, Cardinals first baseman Jack Clark dropped a foul ball hit by Steve Balboni. Given a second chance, Balboni singled. A passed ball, intentional walk and a two-run pinch-single by Dane Iorg gave the Royals a 2–1 victory.

The Royals went on to destroy the Cardinals in Game 7, as Cardinals pitcher Joaquin Andujar was ejected from the 11–0 blowout. Denkinger received a good deal of hate mail and a Kansas City entrepreneur distributed a poster featuring the incorrect call.

Crosstown World Series. In addition to the Yankees playing the Giants and Dodgers many times in the World Series when all three clubs were in New York, there have been four other crosstown World Series:

1906 White Sox/Cubs
1944 Browns/Cardinals
1989 A's/Giants
2000 Yankees/Mets

World Series Winner Down 2–0.

"THIS ISN'T FUNNY, FELLOWS" — Headline in the *Brooklyn Eagle* after the 1955 Dodgers lost the first two games of the Series to the Yankees before winning in seven games for the first championship in club history.

The 1921 World Series was the first in which a team lost the first two games and came back to win. The Giants defeated the Yankees in eight games, 5–3 (one tie).

In 1956 the Yankees lost the first two games of the Series before beating the Dodgers in seven games.

In 1958 the Braves won the first two games before the Yankees came back to win the Series in seven games.

The 1965 Dodgers lost the first two games of the Series to the Twins before rallying to win the Series in seven games.

The 1971 Pirates lost the first two games to the Orioles before the Pirates rallied to win the Series in seven games.

In 1978 the Dodgers won the first two games over the Yankees before the Yankees rallied to win in six games.

The 1981 Dodgers lost the first two games of the Series to the Yankees before winning four straight for the title.

The 1986 Mets lost the first two games of the Series to the Red Sox before the Curse took over and the Mets rallied for a seven-game miracle championship.

World Series Winner Down 3–1.

"The best possible thing in baseball is winning the World Series. The second best thing is losing the World Series." — Tommy Lasorda (not unlike Pirate manager Chuck Tanner in 1985: "The greatest feeling in the world is to win a Major League game. The second-greatest feeling is to lose a Major League game").

"The seventh game of the World Series. Say it aloud — it's got a *sound* to it, doesn't it?" — Enos Slaughter.

In 1925 the Pirates were down 3–1 in the Series to the Senators before winning the last three games for the title.

The 1968 Tigers were down 3–1 in games before rallying to beat the Cardinals in seven games.

The 1979 Pirates were down 3–1 to the Orioles before winning the final three games of the Series.

The 1985 Royals were down 3–1 to the Cardinals before rallying for a World Series win.

Eligibility. Players must be on their team's roster as of September 1 to be eligible for the World Series. This rule has been in effect since the first World Series in 1903.

Famous Firsts/Single Game. The game of October 10, 1920, produced three memorable firsts: the first unassisted *Triple Play* in Series history, by Bill Wambsganss; the first *Grand Slam* in World Series play, by Elmer Smith; and the first home run by a pitcher in the World Series, by Jim Bagby.

Federal League. The 1914–1915 Federal League tried to arrange a three-way World Series with the National and American Leagues, but this overture was rejected by the established leagues.

Series Wins on Final Pitch.

"The romance of baseball … is in its capacity for stirring fantasy. We are never too old or too bothered to see ourselves wrapping up a World Series victory with a homer in the final inning of the seventh game." — Ron Fimrite in *Way to Go* (1979).

Nine World Series have ended with the winning team scoring a run in the bottom of the last inning of the final game:

1912. This Series was the first in which the game ended when the team at bat scored in the bottom of the last inning to win. This was the famous Fred Snodgrass World Series (see also *Errors*). In Game 8 (after one tie), the Giants scored in the top of the 10th inning for a 2–1 lead. In the bottom of the 10th inning Snodgrass dropped a fly ball that somewhat contributed to two runs for the Red Sox and a 3–2 victory.

1924. In Game 7 Earl McNeely of the Senators hit a *Bad Hop* single over third baseman Fred Lindstrom of the Giants with one out in the 12th inning. The hit scored Muddy Ruel from second and gave the Senators a 4–3 victory and the Series.

1927. In Game 4 the Yankees had the bases loaded with no outs in the 9th inning of a tie game against pitcher Johnny Miljus of the Pirates. Miljus struck out Lou Gehrig and Bob Meusel but then threw a wild pitch (his second of the inning) past catcher Johnny Gooch to give the Yankees a 4–3 victory and a Series sweep.

1929. In Game 5 the Cubs led 2–0 going into the bottom of the 9th inning. The A's tied the game on a two-run homer by Mule Haas. Al Simmons doubled with two outs and Jimmie Foxx was walked intentionally. Bing Miller then doubled off Pat Malone and Simmons scored for the third run of the inning to give the A's the game and the Series.

1935. In Game 6 the score was tied at three between the Tigers and Cubs going into the 9th inning. Stan Hack of the Cubs led off the top of the inning with a triple. Tigers pitcher Tommy Bridges then retired the side, stranding Hack at third base.

In the bottom of the 9th, Mickey Cochrane reached second base for the Tigers and with two outs Goose Goslin singled him home off Larry French for a 4–3 win and the Tigers' first World Series title.

1953. In Game 6 the Dodgers scored two runs in the top of the 9th inning to tie the Yankees. In the bottom of the 9th, Yankee second baseman Billy Martin singled off Clem Labine with one out to score Hank Bauer from second base. It gave the Yankees a 4–3 win and their fifth consecutive World Series title.

1960. Bill Mazeroski's lead-off home run in the bottom of the 9th inning of Game 7 was on October 13. The hit came off Ralph Terry and gave the Pirates a 10–9 win. The Pirates won the Series despite being outscored by 28 runs (55 to 27) and outhit by 31. The Yankees won three games by scores of 16–3, 10–0 and 12–0.

The Pirates took a 4–0 lead in Game 7, but the Yankees scored one in the 5th inning and four in the 6th to go ahead. The Yankees led 7–4 in the top of the 8th inning. In the bottom of the 8th, Pirates outfielder Bill Virdon hit a *Bad Hop* ground ball to Yankee shortstop Tony Kubek that hit him in the throat. Dick Groat singled and Bob Skinner sacrificed them to second and third. Gene Nelson then flied out to score a run. With two outs, Roberto Clemente hit a ground ball to the right of the mound that should have been the third out. No one covered first base and the runners were safe at first and third. The next batter, former Yankee prospect Hal Smith, hit a three-run homer for a 9–7 Pirate lead.

In the top of the 9th, the Yankees scored two runs to tie the game. Bobby Richardson and Dale Long singled to chase pitcher Bob Friend. Game 5 winner Harvey Haddix came in and got Roger Maris to foul out; but Mickey Mantle singled to score Richardson, Long taking third. Yogi Berra grounded into an infield out, but Long scored. Moose Skowron fouled out to end the inning in a 9–9 tie. Mazeroski then led off with a home run off Bill Terry in the bottom of the inning to win the Series.

Terry redeemed himself by pitching a 1–0 shutout in Game 7 of the 1962 World Series against the Giants, avoiding disaster when he induced Willie McCovey to line out to Yankee second baseman Bobby Richardson with two on and two out in the 9th inning to end the game and the Series.

1991. In Game 7 the Twins and Braves were scoreless until the bottom of the 10th inning. Dan Gladden led off for the Twins with a double and was bunted to third. After two intentional walks, Barry Larkin hit a pitch from Alejandro Pena over the drawn-in outfielders to win the game and the Series. Jack Morris pitched a 10-inning complete-game shutout for the Twins.

1993. Flamboyant early 1990s reliever Mitch Williams was the goat of the 1993 Series. Pitching for the Phillies, he blew a lead in Game 5 to give the Blue Jays a 15–14 victory in one of the wildest games in World Series history. In Game 6 he appeared in the 9th inning trying to preserve a 6–5 lead for the Phillies, who needed a win to even the Series. Instead, he walked a batter and then gave up a two-run homer to Joe Carter to give the Blue Jays an 8–6 victory and the championship.

Williams was shipped to the Astros in the off-season, but he pitched poorly in early 1994 and the club cut him a few weeks into the season. He retired to his Texas ranch but signed for 1995 with the Angels. He continued to pitch poorly and was cut in June. See also *Base on Balls* — **More Walks Than Hits.**

1997. In Game 7 of the 1997 World Series in Florida, the Marlins were down by a run in the 9th inning against the Indians, but Craig Counsell tied the game on a sacrifice fly and Edgar Renteria won the game in the 11th, driving home Counsell with a single to left for a 3–2 win.

2001. The Diamondbacks and Yankees went down to Game 7 at Bank One Ballpark in Phoenix after wild finishes in two of the previous games. In Games 4 and 5 the Yankees came back to win after Diamondbacks reliever Byung-Hyun Kim failed to protect two-run 9th inning leads, giving up home runs in both games. Tino Martinez hit a two-run homer in Game 4 to tie and Derek Jeter won it with a homer in the 10th. Scott Brosius hit a two-run homer in the 9th inning of Game 5 and the Yankees won it in the 12th inning on a single by Alfonso Soriano. On September 18 that season, the same thing happened. The Rockies came back from a 6–0 deficit, but Arizona went into the bottom of the 9th up by a run. After back-to-back home runs by the Rockies off Kim, the Diamondbacks were losers in the middle of a pennant race.

In the 9th inning of Game 7, the Yankees led 2–1 with star

reliever Mariano Rivera in the game to finish out the Series. He had already shut down the Diamondbacks in the 8th inning, striking out the side. Mark Grace led off the 9th with a single up the middle that Rivera just missed. With David Dellucci on first as a pinch-runner for Grace, Damian Miller laid down a bunt that Rivera fielded cleanly, but threw the ball into center field attempting to force Dellucci at second. Rivera said later that he didn't have a good grip on the ball. The error put runners on first and second. Rivera then got Dellucci on a force at third on Jay Bell's bunt. Tony Womack then doubled down the right field line, scoring pinch-runner Midre Cummings from second to tie the game. With runners on second and third, Rivera hit Craig Counsell on the hand to load the bases and bring up Luis Gonzalez. Gonzalez had struck out in the 8th inning against Rivera. With the Yankee infielders drawn in for a potential play at the plate, he choked up on the bat and drove a single over the shortstop to score the winning run.

First Loser. Cy Young was the first pitcher to lose a World Series game when he lost Game 1 of the 1903 Series.

Home Runs. Gene Tenace of the A's is the only player to hit a home run in his first two World Series at-bats. In Game 1 of the 1972 World Series, he hit one in both the 2nd and 5th innings off Reds pitcher Gary Nolan for a 3–2 A's victory.

Light-hitting shortstop Jim Mason (lowest average in the 1970s with at least 1,500 at-bats) is the only player in World Series history to hit a home run in his only Series at-bat. He did it in Game 3 of the 1976 Series for the Yankees.

Home Team. Under the original World Series rules proposed by Giants owner John Brush, the host of the first and last game would be determined by a coin toss, but that idea was never implemented.

The format for the early years was that if the teams were in close proximity, games would alternate. If not, then they would be played in groups of two. For example, in 1923 the Yankees and Giants alternated between the Polo Grounds and newly opened Yankee Stadium (in 1922 all games were played at the Polo Grounds and the Yankees and Giants switched home team designation each game).

In the early years, a coin toss determined the Game 7 location, done after Game 6. After the 1924 Series, it was decided that Game 7 would be fixed prior to the start of the Series and would be at the same site as Game 6. This 2–3–2 format was formalized for the 1925 World Series, except for some travel restriction issues that affected scheduling during 1943 and 1945 (1944 was an all-St. Louis affair); a 3–4 format was used.

Before 1925, a coin toss generally was also used to determine the site of the first game of the Series. Also, Landis created the system whereby the American League had the home field advantage in even years, the National League in odd. This worked until 1935, when scheduling conflicts (a large convention in St. Louis and a tight National League pennant race) caused him to move the opening game to Detroit. This caused the odd/even designations to switch, which worked until the 1995 Series was cancelled; this forced the original Landis rule (American League in even years) to be re-adopted.

Before 1957 games were usually scheduled on consecutive days so that the Series could be concluded in seven days. This deviated only if games could not be played on Sunday in a host city, or lengthy travel was required.

In 1935 the Cubs won 21 straight near the end of the season but were unprepared to host the Series as scheduled; they failed to print tickets in time. They waived their right to host the first two games and the Series started in Detroit.

In 1944 the Cardinals and Browns became the last two teams to play the World Series in a shared ballpark.

In 1945, because of wartime travel restrictions, the first three World Series games were scheduled in Detroit and the final four were scheduled in Chicago.

Latest October Finish. The 1981 Series ended with Game 5 on October 28 because of an extra five-game division Series resulting from the split season created by the players strike.

The 1989 Series between the Giants and A's ended on October 28 with a four-game A's sweep after a one-week delay due to the San Francisco *Earthquake*.

The 1911 Series ended with Game 6 on October 26 because there was a week of rain delays before Game 4.

Most Series Losses by Pitchers. George Frazier and Claude "Lefty" Williams each lost three games in one World Series. Frazier lost his three for the 1981 Yankees and Williams lost his for the 1919 Black Sox.

Most Valuable Player. The Series MVP Award is named after Babe Ruth and was first presented in 1955 to pitcher Johnny Podres of the Dodgers. There were three winners from the Dodgers in 1981, Pedro Guerrero, Steve Yeager and Ron Cey. The 2001 Diamondbacks had two winners, Randy Johnson and Curt Schilling.

Name. There was a long-time baseball myth that the World Series was named for the *New York World* newspaper, which supposedly sponsored the early matches. This was not true, despite repeated references to this alleged fact in some baseball literature. The postseason series between the league champions was originally known as the "Championship of the World" or "World's Championship Series." That was shortened through usage to "World's Series" and finally to "World Series." The best source for this lineage is the annual baseball guides. The *Reach Guide* used "World's Championship Series in its 1904 edition, but by 1912 it used the term "World's Series," with an apostrophe. *The Sporting News Guide,* first published in 1942, used the term with an apostrophe through 1963, and then switched to "World Series" in 1964.

Never Played in World Series. See *Postseason Play*.

Never Played Again. Yankee pitcher Bill Bevens took a no-hitter into the 9th inning of Game 4 of the 1947 World Series. He lost the game after the no-hitter was broken up by Cookie Lavagetto. Neither ever played another Major League game.

Never Won Again. At age 35, A's pitcher Howard Ehmke won the 1929 World Series opener as the club's surprise starter (see also *Strategy*). He never won another Major League game. He had a 7–2 record in 1929 but pitched in only three games in 1930, losing one with two no-decisions.

Night Games. The first pitcher to throw under the lights in a World Series game was Paul Minner. In the last inning of the 1949 Series at Ebbets Field, the lights were turned on because of darkness. It was Minner's only World Series inning.

The first officially scheduled night game was Game 4 of the 1971 Series, played on October 13. The Pirates beat the Orioles 4–3.

No World Series.

"There is nothing in the constitution or playing rules of the National League which requires its victorious club to submit its championship honors to a contest with a victorious club in a minor league.

"Neither the players nor the manager of the Giants nor myself desires any greater glory than to win the pennant in the National League. That is the greatest honor that can be obtained in baseball." — Giants owner John Brush on why he would not allow his club to participate in the 1904 World Series. Brush refused to play because of the "inferior" quality of the American League. National

League president Pulliam said that playing in the Series was in the discretion of each club. Shortly after Brush refused to allow his club to play, the National League clubs voted to require the pennant winner to play in the Series.

Many sources report that Giants manager John McGraw supported Brush's refusal enthusiastically, but others report that McGraw wanted to play the Series. Ironically, Brush quickly proposed new rules for the World Series and his club played in the 1905 Series. Ninety years later the 1994 Series was canceled because of the player strike.

Number of Games per Series. The clubs played a best-of-nine format in the first World Series in 1903. The seven-game format began in 1905 (no Series in 1904) and continued through the 1918 Series. The Series expanded to nine games from 1919 through 1921. The best-of-seven format was restored after Judge Landis supposedly decided that the longer format was boring to fans. Some early Series had eight games because of ties that were not completed because of darkness.

The nine-game format seems to have occurred because the regular season schedule was shorter in 1919 (140 v. 154 games) and there was some sentiment among owners that a longer Series would give fans more opportunities to see at least one game (not to mention the financial rewards of gate receipts). After three years, perhaps tainted by the Black Sox Series in 1919, Judge Landis pushed for a reversion to the seven-game format for the 1922 Series, which was approved by the owners late in 1921. Part of the reason was Landis's apparent belief that the large gate receipts from the longer Series would perhaps cause a public backlash.

Pitching Starts. Bob Gibson is the only pitcher to start three Game 7's, losing in 1964 to the Yankees and Tigers 1968, and winning against the Red Sox in 1967.

Player Shares.

"When we played, World Series checks meant something. Now all they do is screw up your taxes." — Don Drysdale.

According to Major League rules, players on the 25-man roster for the entire period between June 1 and August 31 receive full shares, as does the manager. All other shares are discretionary.

In the first World Series in 1903 the winning players each received $1,182. The winners were to receive 75% of the player proceeds, but actually the losing Pirates received more money because owner Barney Dreyfuss kicked in his share of the proceeds for his team. The players each received $1,316. Red Sox owner Henry Killilea had to pay two more weeks salary to his players plus a share of the gate because their contracts expired October 1.

In 1907 Ban Johnson announced that players would share in gate receipts for tie games, so naturally the first game was a 3–3 tie. Tiger catcher Boss Schmidt let the ball get away with two outs and two strikes in the bottom of the 9th inning. The error allowed the Cubs to score two runs and create a tie that was not broken before darkness ended the game after 12 innings. It appeared to some that Schmidt made the error intentionally to preserve the tie and increase the players' share. As a result, Johnson ruled before Game 2 that all player shares would be based on the first four games only, which continued the original format and is still in effect.

In 1910 the winning share was $2,068, and the losers each received $1,375. In 1917 the shares were $3,669 for the winners and $2,442 for the losers.

Under the 1905 Brush Plan, 60% of the gate receipts from the first four games went to the players, with a 75/25% split between the winners and losers. The remainder of the receipts were split by the two owners and a small amount went to the National Commission.

In 1918 a new World Series gate receipt plan lowered the player shares. National League president John Tener induced the leagues to allow the second- through fourth-place clubs in each league to share. The players on the two World Series clubs were not consulted on this, which reduced their share of gate receipts. That year the Series donated 10% of the receipts to the Red Cross for use in connection with World War I. Ticket prices were no higher because fan interest was down due to the war.

The 1918 player minimums were to be $2,000 for the winners and $1,400 for the losers, but this was reduced to $1,200 and $800. As a result, the players threatened to strike. The players wanted a flat $1,500, and before Game 5 they would not take the field. They agreed to play after Ban Johnson and the National Commission threatened them with disciplinary action. Tener was not around to justify his new gate receipt plan to the players because he had resigned on August 6, 1918.

The 1918 first place share of $1,102.51 was the lowest ever and the $671.09 loser's share was the second lowest ever. Another source placed the winner's share at $890 and the loser's at $535.

Normalcy was restored in 1919 when the winners received $5,207 and the losers received $3,254. For the most part, this was the average payout throughout the 1920s and 1930s.

Prior to 1920 the rules prohibited a player traded during the season from receiving a World Series share from his old team. This arose from a 1909 incident when the Pirates traded a player to the Cardinals and announced immediately that the player would still receive a World Series share.

During World War II players received a percentage of their shares in War bonds. In 1946 the players received the lowest shares in 30 years, dividing only $212,000. The winning Cardinals each received $3,742. The losing Red Sox each received only $2,141, less than the umpires. The next year, with the pension fund in place, the owners agreed to a minimum Series share of $250,000 for the players, which translated to a guaranteed $5,000 per player.

Phil Rizzuto of the Yankees said that twice he made more in World Series money than his season salary was worth.

In 1954 for the first time the winner's share was over $10,000, at $11,118 per player. Each losing player received $6,713. It took another five years for a winning player to receive over $10,000. The winning share fluctuated around $10,000 throughout the 1960s.

In 1969 the winning players each received $18,338, including their share of the league championship series money. Losers received $14,904 ($9,350 of which was from the World Series).

In 1972 for the first time a winner's share was above $20,000 at $20,705. Losers each received $15,080. The shares increased dramatically in the 1980s and 1990s. In 1985 a full winning share was $76,341, as the clubs split $7.8 million. In 1986 the winning Mets received full shares of $86,254 and the losing Red Sox each took $74,985.

The 1990 player share was worth $114,252.11 to the winners and $83,529.26 to the losers. The winners received more than the minimum salary for some of the players.

The 1993 winners' shares were worth $127,920. The losing Phillies received $91,227. Shares for the division champions who did not make it to the World Series (Braves and White Sox) were worth $40,000. Second-place finishers in each division received from $9,000 to $11,000 each, while third-place shares were worth $1,600 to $3,500.

The 1998 Series ticket prices were doubled, so the winning Yankees took home more than $100,000 than previous Series winners, $312,137.33. The players' pool increased to $39.3 million, up from $23.4 million in 1997. The Yankees received $14.2 million of that amount. The previous record was set by the 1996 Yankees, who received $216,870 each.

In 1963 Dodger batboy Jim Reynolds received a $900 World Series share. Infielder Dick Nen, who played only a few games for the Dodgers but hit a crucial late-season home run for the club (see **Pennant Races**), received $1,000. The $100 difference prompted some good-natured but snide remarks by *Los Angeles Times* sportswriter Sid Ziff, implying that Nen couldn't do much better than a lowly batboy. Reynolds' parents wrote a mild rebuke to Ziff, who responded as follows:

"Dear Mr. and Mrs. Reynolds:

I feel very badly about my smart-alecky remark. I wish to apologize to you and your son, Jim.

Now I hate myself."

Player Shares Not Received.

"Hey, Mark, who are those cheapskates you're with." — Babe Ruth to former teammate Mark Koenig at the 1932 World Series between the Yankees and Cubs. Koenig's new team, the Cubs, voted him only a half share though he was instrumental in the club's pennant drive for the last 33 games of the season.

"If you were only around in the first half, by September, well, out of sight, out of mind. A lot of guys will say, 'To hell with him.'" — Giants catcher Bob Brenley on voting shares to partial-season players.

In 1932 unpopular player-manager Rogers Hornsby received nothing from the Cubs players after their World Series victory. He appealed to Judge Landis, but the commissioner refused to intervene.

Coach Jesse "The Crab" Burkett was so rotten that the 1921 Giants players refused to allocate him a share. Manager John McGraw gave him a share of his.

Ted Williams supposedly gave his 1946 losers share to the clubhouse boy as a tip.

In 1985 the division-winning Dodgers considered not voting a share to suspended cocaine-addicted pitcher Steve Howe. They decided to vote him a one-eighth share, but only if they could give the money directly to his wife. They could not.

World Series Program. Until 1974 each Major League team prepared its own program for the World Series. With expansion and the division playoffs, there were situations when several clubs would spend time and money preparing programs that were never used because they didn't make it to the World Series. The program was consolidated into a single effort in 1974, with the commissioner's office controlling production.

World Series Rings. See *Jewelry*.

Sweep.

"We Came, We Saw, We Went Home." — Slogan of the 1938 New York Yankees, who swept the Cubs in the World Series.

One source reported that the 1914 Miracle Boston Braves were the first club to sweep a World Series. However, the Cubs swept the Tigers in 1907. There have been 18 Series sweeps through 2004, though the 1907 and 1922 Series each featured a tie.

Tie Game. The first game of the 1907 Series was called after 12 innings with the score 3–3 and Game Two of the 1922 Series was called after 10 innings with the score also 3–3, both because of darkness.

Wild Card. The 2002 Angels, the 2003 Marlins and the 2004 Red Sox are the only wild card teams to win a World Series.

Books. Lee Allen, *The World Series* (1969); Richard Cohen and David Neft, *The World Series* (1986, 1990); John Devaney and Burt Goldblatt, *The World Series* (1972); John Durant, *Highlights of the World Series* (1973); Eric Enders, *100 Years of the World Series*

(2004); Donald Honig, *World Series: An Illustrated History from 1903 to the Present* (1986); Barry Levenson, *The Seventh Game* (2004); Ken Leiker, *An American Classic: The World Series at 100* (2003); Fred Lieb, *The Story of the World Series* (1965); Bill Littlefield and Richard Johnson, *Fall Classics: The Best Writing about the World Series' First Hundred Years* (2003); Louis P. Masur, *Autumn Glory* (2003); Don Schiffer, *World Series Encyclopedia* (1961); Gene Schoor, *The History of the World Series* (1990); Robert Smith, *World Series* (1967); *The Sporting News* (ed.), *The Series: An Illustrated History of Baseball's Postseason Showcase* (1988).

World War I

"Up in Beantown, the owner of the Boston Red Sox accuses major-league players of misjudging the "solidarity" of the owners: Had the players waited for the end of the 1994 season to strike, he insists, everything might have been different. Sure, and if someone hadn't plugged the archduke, World War I would never have started." — Bill Gallo.

"This is a war of democracy against bureaucracy. And I tell you that baseball is the very watchword of democracy. There is no other sport or business or anything under heaven which exerts the leveling influence that baseball does. Neither the public school nor the church can approach it. Baseball is unique. England is a democratic country, but it lacks the finishing touch of baseball." — National League president John K. Tener in May 1918, trying to turn public opinion in favor of keeping baseball operating during the war. The proclamation and other actions by the owners provoked criticism: "With an astonishing disregard for the new proprieties and new decencies ... the so-called 'magnates' of baseball have proclaimed in both 'leagues' their unswerving adherence to the wretched fallacy of 'business as usual.'" — The *New York Times*.

World War I hurt Major League Baseball, but fan interest had already been dwindling due to a poor economy, other leisure time diversions and the Federal League challenge. World War I had an impact, but it probably would not have been as severe had it not been for the other factors which existed prior to the onset of the war.

Although war was declared by the United States on April 6, 1917, it had no significant impact on baseball that year. Lower attendance and the military draft did not start until July, and few players were drafted. Nevertheless, by early 1918 it was clear that baseball was going to suffer. At baseball's winter meetings, Ban Johnson flip-flopped repeatedly on his position. At first he proposed asking the government to exempt ballplayers from the draft, but the owners voted down the idea. The leagues cut their schedules from 154 to 140 games after heavy media criticism that leisure time activities should not interfere with the war effort.

Early Enlistees. Braves catcher Hank Gowdy was the first player to enlist. His last game until 1919 was on June 26, 1917. He enlisted the next day. After the war he was offered $1,500 per week to tell war stories in theaters and other gatherings. Gowdy also enlisted in the military during World War II at age 53.

"Wake Up America Day" was sponsored by Major League Baseball to promote enlistments at ballparks.

The Draft/Player Losses. It was estimated that 200 Major League players were eligible for the draft. By March 1918 all teams had at least one player in the war, but married men and those with dependents were exempt.

Pitcher Alvin "General" Crowder, who began his Major League career in 1926, was nicknamed for General Enoch Crowder, Provost Marshal of the Army in charge of the draft during the war.

Babe Ruth was a reservist in 1918 and an honorary National Guard member in 1924. Detroit outfielder Harry Heilmann was in the Navy during the war and served on a submarine.

See also **Players Killed** and **Players Injured**.

1918/Government Intervention. On May 23, 1918, the government issued a "work or fight" order, making it mandatory for men to get into "essential" work by July 1, 1918, or risk induction. Baseball was declared a "nonessential" industry, and this order caused the loss of 124 American League and 103 National League players (a total of 247 in one source). Many players went into cushy jobs at industrial sites such as steel mills and shipyards. Major League clubs replaced them with young and over-the-hill minor leaguers.

The War Department never tried to shut down baseball. Instead it issued an edict on July 27, 1918, stating that it "saw no reason to stopping or curtailing the baseball schedule." Clark Griffith appealed the drafting of catcher Eddie Ainsmith based on three claims: 1) baseball was a business and its activities were not convertible to another industry; 2) baseball players did not have skills to work in other industries to make as much money; 3) baseball was the national sport and suspension would inflict social harm.

Secretary of War Newton D. Baker refused to change the ruling, which had ramifications for many other players. Ban Johnson's patriotic fervor caused him to advocate ending the season immediately and closing "every theater, ball park, and place of recreation in the country." Under pressure from the owners, Johnson reversed his position one month later, pointing out that baseball was essential because it was delivering $300,000 to the government through the new entertainment tax. He also noted that baseball purchased $8 million in liberty war bonds. The war tax supposedly applied also to rooftop and treetop spectators, but it is unclear how the tax was administered.

The secretary allowed a two-month extension on the work-or-fight order to enable the season to end in relatively normal fashion. The clubs played through Labor Day (September 2), ending the season one month early. The secretary then allowed a two-week extension for the two World Series teams.

The owners released all players from their contracts for the remainder of the season, saving $200,000. Players technically were free agents as a result, but the owners agreed not to hire another club's players. Jake Daubert of the Dodgers sued on this issue and ultimately settled, though he was traded to the Reds in the process. Senators outfielder Burt Shotten sued for the remainder of his $1,400 salary and was waived out of the league, signing with the Cardinals.

Effect on Minor Leagues. The war had a devastating effect on the minor leagues. For example, the usually strong Pacific Coast League disbanded in 1918 because of poor attendance and lack of quality players. In 1918 only the International League survived the season out of the 10 that started it. None of the others lasted beyond July 22.

Summons. During World War I, Judge Landis, at the time a sitting federal court judge, issued a summons for the appearance of Kaiser Wilhelm to his courtroom to answer for the sinking of the *Lusitania*. In another decision during the war, later overturned by the U.S. Supreme Court, he wrote about German Americans, "their hearts are reeking with disloyalty."

Fundraising. The Major Leagues established a "Bat and Ball Fund" and raised close to $100,000 for equipment to be sent overseas (see also ***Benefit Games***). In 1918 clubs donated a percentage of each week's profits to the Red Cross.

At the outset of the war in 1914, but before the U.S.'s entry, the National League held a Red Cross Day and presented the organization with a percentage of the gate receipts. The American League fans responded to Ban Johnson's appeal by sending baseball equipment to Europe.

Clark Griffith raised money to send 3,100 baseball kits to military bases in Europe. The $30 kits contained catcher's equipment, a first baseman's glove, three bats, three bases, 12 balls, 125 scorecards and a rule book.

Military Drills. During the 1917 season, the National Commission ordered all clubs to perform one hour of military drill daily. The Dodger players refused to do it, and the drills were dropped that season by both leagues. When the war fever increased in 1918, the drills were reinstated. Teams began marching in military formation before games, sometimes carrying bats instead of rifles. American League president Ban Johnson offered $500 to the "best drilled team in close formation." It was won by the Browns.

1919. Shortly after the 1918 season was completed, it was assumed by some that there would be no baseball in 1919 because of the effects of the war. As an example, Ebbets Field and the Federal League park in Brooklyn were to be used as warehouses for war supplies. As reported in one newspaper, the "action was taken to indicate Brooklyn [Dodgers] officers do not contemplate Baseball in 1919."

The war ended in November 1918, and the owners tried to recoup their losses by limiting 1919 salaries and lowering rosters from 25 to 21. They assumed that 1919 would be a bad year again, so they retained the shortened 140-game season, not realizing that the first year after the war would be a big hit with the fans. Major League ***Attendance*** increased to over 6.5 million, more than twice the 1918 figure of only 3,080,126 (lowest since 1902).

Best World War I Story. Larry MacPhail, later the general manager of the Reds, Dodgers and Yankees, was in the military during World War I. Near the end of the war he and a few comrades decided to kidnap Kaiser Wilhelm, leader of the German forces. The group secretly entered a castle at Amerongen, Holland, owned by Count von Bentinck and known to house the Kaiser. They disarmed a guard but were soon driven back by other guards. For his trouble, MacPhail stole an ashtray bearing the Kaiser's crest, which he displayed proudly on his desk in later years.

Players Killed. Three current or former Major League players were known to have been killed in the war. The first casualty was Marcus Milligan, a minor league pitcher under contract to the Pirates, who was killed in an air crash. Another unnamed professional is known to have been killed, as was former Major Leaguer (Captain) Eddie Grant. Grant was a Harvard graduate who was out of baseball when he enlisted, though it has often been implied that he was an active player at the time. The confusion may have arisen because reportedly he was on the New York Giants reserve list at the time.

Grant played third base for the Phillies, Reds and Giants from 1907 through 1915. He retired and began practicing law in New York before enlisting. He was killed one month before the end of the war in 1918 at age 35. He had been leading troops to save the famous Lost Battalion in the Argonne Forest. A statue in his honor was erected in center field at the Polo Grounds; its inscription: "Soldier, scholar, athlete — erected by friends in Baseball, Journalism and the Service."

Players Injured. Grover Cleveland Alexander, whose epilepsy reportedly was discovered during a military induction examination (then why was he drafted?), was wounded seriously during the war (see also ***Injuries and Illness***—Epilepsy).

Christy Mathewson eventually died from what was diagnosed

as tuberculosis brought on by his exposure to mustard gas in France. Mathewson joined the Army Chemical Warfare Division as a captain inspecting trenches after World War I. A pocket of poison gas erupted near him and he suffered severe coughing spells, later diagnosed as tuberculosis. Other sources report that he suffered repeated exposure to the gas because he was a gas mask instructor; and one reported that Ty Cobb was with him during the fateful drill. Others who volunteered for the Chemical Warfare unit were Branch Rickey, Ty Cobb and George Sisler.

World War II

"To Hell with Babe Ruth!"—Epithet yelled by Japanese soldiers to Americans during attacks.

"It's like apples and oranges, you can't compare it. It was just a matter of playing anyone who was breathing."—Broadcaster Red Barber on baseball before and during World War II.

"I honestly feel it would be best for the country to keep baseball going. There will be fewer people unemployed and everybody will work longer hours and harder than ever before. Here is another way of looking at it—if 300 teams use 5,000 or 6,000 players, their players are a definite recreational asset to at least 20 million of their fellow citizens—and that, in my judgment, is thoroughly worthwhile."—President Franklin Roosevelt's "Green Light" letter to Judge Landis, written January 15, 1942. Landis had written Roosevelt for guidance in a January 14, 1942 letter: "Baseball is about to adopt schedules, sign players, make vast commitments, go to training camps. What do you want it to do?"

Landis listed several options, from shutting down entirely to changing nothing. Landis was credited with persuading Roosevelt to write the letter, but it was originally Senators owner Clark Griffith who provided the impetus. Landis was virulently anti–Roosevelt and was outspoken in his opposition to the U.S. entering the war.

See also **Military Baseball** for baseball played by service teams.
Early Enlistees/Draftees.

"I might have got hit with a line drive if I spent six more months with the Phillies."—Hugh Mulcahy of the Phillies, who was the first Major League player drafted, entered the military on March 8, 1941. One source noted facetiously that Mulcahy was probably in a hurry to get drafted considering that he had lost 76 games for the Phillies over the previous four years. He did not pitch again until late 1945, in part because he was too weak from a tropical disease he had contracted in the Pacific. He returned for 16 games in 1946 and two games in 1947, but with little success.

Eugene Stackowiack (aka Gene Stack), a White Sox rookie, was the first player on a Major League roster to enter the military. Stack enlisted in January 1941 and died on June 27, 1942. He suffered heart trouble after pitching for an Army team in Michigan. Some sources reported that he was killed in action.

Hank Greenberg had a very high draft number and assumed that he would be drafted early, so he went ahead and enlisted. He was a sergeant early in 1941 and was released two days before the bombing of Pearl Harbor (December 7), as were 28 other players who had enlisted. He made headlines when he reenlisted immediately after the bombing. Greenberg saw duty as an officer in charge of a bomber squadron command center in the China-Burma-India theater. He received the Presidential Unit Citation and four battle stars.

Greenberg's fabulous baseball career seemingly was over at that point. In the four seasons immediately preceding his enlistment, he averaged 43 home runs and 148 RBIs. He played only 2½ years

after the war but hit .311 in 1945 and then hit a league-leading 44 home runs in 1946 before retiring after the 1947 season.

The only other Major Leaguer to be drafted in 1941 was Dodger outfielder Joe Gallagher.

Bob Feller enlisted while on national radio and lost four years of his career. He may have seen more active combat than any other Major Leaguer. For three years he commanded a 24-man anti-aircraft crew aboard the USS *Alabama* with the Third Fleet. He received five campaign ribbons and eight Navy battle stars while fighting at Tarawa, Iwo Jima and the Marshall Islands. He also served on convoy duty in the North Atlantic but still had time to pitch for a service team (see also **Military Baseball**). Feller's most memorable day was in June 1944, when the Third Fleet shot down 474 Japanese planes in one day protecting the Marine Corps assault on Saipan beaches. A half-century later it was still known as the "Great Turkey Shoot." The Marines were led by General "Howlin' Mad" Smith.

Criticism. Indians owner Alva Bradley advocated shutting down baseball near the end of the war. He was criticized by other owners, including Reds general manager Warren Giles: "We plan to operate and not with any low form of comedy. If that's all Cleveland can offer, they should quit."

Joe DiMaggio was criticized for not enlisting in the military after rival Ted Williams had done so. In response, DiMaggio enlisted in the Army in February 1943 and refused a furlough.

Medical Deferments.

"The Leaning Tower of Flatbush"—Nickname by *The Sporting News* for Dodger first baseman Howie Schultz, who received a deferment because he was 6'6½".

"As a Giant, he doesn't like being called a Dodger, particularly a Draft Dodger."—The *New York Daily News*.

"We have a good chance to win the pennant."—Formal reason given by Cubs pitcher Harry Weaver for seeking a deferment from the draft.

"That's just your trouble. You've got 1-A ears and 4-F eyes. You hear everything everybody has to say but you don't see half the things you're supposed to see."—Dodger executive Fresco Thompson to Chuck Solodare, who never played in the Major Leagues.

"But the mainstay of the big leagues was the reservoir of 4-Fs—males of draft age who had been rejected on physical grounds by the Armed Forces. Not since harem attendants had gone out of style were men's physical deficiencies so highly prized. Ulcers, hearing defects, and torn cartilages were coveted by team owners."—Frank Graham, Jr., in *Farewell to Heroes* (1981).

Baseball's official line was that there would be no attempt at deferments and no other special treatment sought.

Outfielder Bingo Binks had a hearing problem, as did second baseman Eddie Stanky, who had suffered three beanings and was deaf in his left ear.

Shortstop Lou Boudreau avoided World War II with an arthritic ankle that had been aggravated by having been broken three times. He was criticized for being slow, but he was able to play only because he taped the ankle heavily.

Pitcher Al Javery, who pitched from 1940 through 1946, was not drafted because of varicose veins.

Outfielder George Case had a bad shoulder from six outfield collisions and also was color blind.

Two-time MVP pitcher Hal Newhouser wanted to be sworn into the Army Air Corps on the Briggs Stadium pitching mound but was rejected four times because of a heart problem.

Pitcher Dizzy Trout was rejected because of poor eyesight.

One-armed Pete Gray shows off his batting form during a 1943 Memphis Chicks game, a season in which he earned MVP honors and a stint with the St. Louis Browns in 1944, when the player ranks were decimated by World War II.

Outfielder Andy Pafko had high blood pressure.

Third basemen George Kell had bad knees.

Bob Elliott had suffered head injuries.

Outfielder Morrie Arnovich was rejected for bad teeth, but was criticized for allegedly attempting to avoid the draft as a "slacker." He called a press conference to show his bad teeth and his rejection papers. He took out his bridges to impress the gathered media.

Pitcher Tex Shirley had a hernia.

Third baseman Whitey Kurowski had osteomyelitis.

Shortstop Marty Marion had broken his leg severely as a kid and always had problems with it.

The only two bachelors on the 1943 Yankees were Snuffy Stirnweiss, who had ulcers, and Atley McDonald, who had back and eye problems.

First baseman Phil Cavarretta had an inner ear problem caused by a childhood bout with spinal meningitis.

Dizzy Dean was rejected due to a punctured eardrum.

The 1944 Browns won the pennant with 18 players who were categorized as 4-F (medical deferment) at the start of the season. By the end of the season, 13 of the team's players were 4-F, and there were 200 players in the Major Leagues classified 4-F.

Married Players. Players who were married and had children born before Pearl Harbor Day (December 7, 1941), had priority over other categories of married men with children.

Johnny Sturm was the first married player to be drafted, shortly after the 1941 season (his only one in the Major Leagues).

The Age Factor. In 1942 only 10 Major League players were over 38 or younger than 18. By 1944, of the 157 Major League players who received deferments, 10 were over 38 years old, six were Latin American citizens, and the rest were classified 4-F.

Pittsburgh's youngest pitcher in 1945 was 26 year old Ken Gables.

Nellie Fox was in the Boy Scouts at age 16 when he went to the 1944 A's training camp (see also *Youngest Players*).

Career Interrupted.

"Mr. Tojo will wake up some night with the feeling he got into this thing with two strikes against him, and Feller having one hell of a day. Nuts to the Nippons." — Casey Stengel.

Barney McCoskey was an outstanding lead-off hitter in 1939 and 1940 for the Tigers. He hit well the next two seasons but lost the 1943–1945 seasons to the war. When he returned to the Tigers in 1946, he hit poorly (under .200) and was traded early in the season. He rebounded and had two more .300 seasons before fading.

Benny McCoy was declared a free agent by Judge Landis in 1939 after Detroit was accused of improperly handling its minor league players. He played for the A's in 1940 and 1941, entered the Navy, and never played again.

Warren Spahn pitched in four games for the Braves and Casey Stengel in 1939 before returning to the minor leagues. He missed three seasons because of the war but returned to the Major Leagues in 1946 to pitch in 24 games and compile an 8–5 record. He exploded after that, recording 20 or more wins in 13 of his next 17 seasons for the Braves. Spahn went into the Army in 1943 and served in Europe. He was wounded and decorated for bravery with a Bronze Star and Purple Heart after being awarded a battlefield commission. He served at the Battle of the Bulge and the battle for the bridge at Remagen, in which several of his comrades were killed.

Ted Williams missed three full seasons, 1943 through 1945, while serving as a fighter pilot flying Corsairs (he flew jet fighters during the Korean War). He led the league in hitting the two seasons before entering World War II. When he returned, he hit .342 in 1946 and then led the league the next two seasons. He also missed almost two full seasons during the Korean War.

Infielder Jerry Coleman of the Yankees flew 120 combat missions as a Marine pilot in World War II and Korea and earned two Distinguished Flying Crosses.

Bob Feller missed almost three full seasons starting in 1942, coming back for nine appearances in 1945. In the three seasons immediately before he entered the military and the two full seasons immediately after, he led the league in wins, strikeouts and innings pitched.

Enos Slaughter lost three full seasons, 1943 through 1945, but returned in 1946 to hit .300 and lead the league with 130 RBIs.

Joe DiMaggio lost three full seasons to the war, 1943 through 1945. He returned to bat .290 in 1946 and then increased his average in each of the next three seasons.

Dom DiMaggio lost three full seasons, 1943 through 1945, after playing three Major League seasons starting in 1940. He returned in 1946 to hit .316. The third and oldest DiMaggio brother, Vince, was not drafted.

Stan Musial was luckier that most Major League stars. He was healthy, 23 years old and had a son born after Pearl Harbor Day. In the off-season he worked in a war plant and managed to avoid the draft until after the 1944 season. He lost the 1945 season to the war, but returned to win another batting title in 1946.

Ralph Kiner had his Major League career delayed until 1946 though he was only 24 when he finally reached the Pirates that season.

Zeke Bonura, a big first baseman for the Dodgers, spent five years in the military during the war and had his career cut short. He was called up before December 7, 1941, and set up leagues and laid out diamonds in North Africa. He had 44 service teams playing on the continent and staged the African World Series. He also organized baseball teams for Italian and French children in their countries.

Vic Wertz served as an athletic director during World War II and was in charge of a Navy team on Anguar in the Palau Islands in 1944.

See also Rick Van Blair, *Dugout to Foxhole: Interviews with Baseball Players Whose Careers Were Affected by World War II* (1994).

Hall of Fame. Through 2004, 29 people who had fought in World War II were inducted into the Hall of Fame: Luke Appling, Al Barlick, Yogi Berra, Leon Day, Bill Dickey, Joe DiMaggio, Bobby Doerr, Bob Feller, Charlie Gehringer, Hank Greenberg, Billy Herman, Monte Irvin, Ralph Kiner, Bob Lemon, Ted Lyons, Larry MacPhail, Johnny Mize, Stan Musial, Pee Wee Reese, Phil Rizzuto, Jackie Robinson, Red Ruffing, Enos Slaughter, Duke Snider, Warren Spahn, Bill Veeck, Hoyt Wilhelm, Ted Williams and Early Wynn.

Players Injured in the War. See *Amputees* for Bert Shepard's story of pitching in one Major League game on an artificial leg.

Lou Brissie's legs were badly injured from shelling in Italy, which wiped out almost his entire unit on December 7, 1944. He suffered through 23 operations but was able to play in 1948 with the A's, pitching to a 14–10 record. He continued to wear a leg brace and won 19 games in 1949.

One source reported that he wore a catcher's shinguard for protection and that Ted Williams once lined a ball off the metal plate in his leg, causing a loud clanging sound but no injury.

Future Indians pitcher Gene Bearden was on a cruiser in the Pacific in 1943 when it was hit by a Japanese torpedo. He spent several days in a life raft without medication, suffering from skull and knee injuries. He recovered sufficiently to win 20 games for the Indians in 1948.

Johnny Beazley ruined his arm pitching in a military game after winning 21 Major Leagues games in 1942. Once source reported that he never pitched in the Major Leagues again, but he returned in 1946 and won a total of nine games over the next four years.

Creepy Crespi, a top second baseman in 1941 and 1942 for the Cardinals, broke his leg in a tank training accident in Kansas and then broke it again crashing it into a wall during a wheelchair race. A nurse then misread directions for an acid wash on his leg, applying a 10% solution instead of 1%; the solution ate right down to the bone. He never played in the Major Leagues again and missed his pension by 50 days.

Cecil Travis hit .359 in 1941 as an infielder for the Senators and led the league with 218 hits (after seven out of eight seasons in which he hit over .300). He suffered frostbite to his feet during the Battle of the Bulge and never hit above .252 when he returned to the Major Leagues for three seasons starting in 1945.

Catcher Frank Mancuso was hurt in a parachute accident in which he hurt his back and broke a leg. He was discharged from the Army and he signed with the St. Louis Browns in 1944. He was unable to look up and back for pop fouls but managed to hang on for three years (and was a starter in 1945).

Tommy Warren, a Creek Indian, was the first wounded veteran of World War II to return and play for a Major League club. He was 1–4 for the Dodgers in 1944.

Players Killed in the War. A total of 292,131 American servicemen were killed in the war. The first professional baseball player killed after the war started was Lt. Gordon Houston of the Army Air Corp. He was killed in a Washington air crash on February 10 (or 12), 1942. He had played for Texarkana of the Class C East Texas League in 1940. More than 40 minor leaguers were killed during the war.

The first professional player killed in combat was William Herbert Merced of the California League. He died on October 30, 1942, from injuries sustained on Guadalcanal.

Two Major League players were killed while serving in the military. Elmer Gedeon played five games for the Senators in 1939 as an outfielder. He was killed at age 27 in France on April 20, 1944, in air action over St. Pol, France while piloting a B-26 bomber. He had been an outstanding track (hurdles), football and baseball star at the University of Michigan. Before he was commissioned as a lieutenant in the Army Air Corps and before being sent overseas, he received a medal for rescuing one of his crew trapped in the wreckage of a burning bomber that had crashed in Raleigh, N.C.

Harry O'Neill caught one game for the A's in 1939 and was killed at age 27 on Iwo Jima on March 6, 1945.

The *Stars and Stripes* military newspaper estimated that 800 American sports stars were killed during World War II. The newspaper reported erroneously on August 29, 1945, that Ardys Keller, Forrest Brewer and Franklin Schultz were all Major League players killed during the war. None had been in the Major Leagues. Keller had been a catcher for Toledo and "Lefty" Brewer had been a pitcher for Charlotte. Other minor leaguers killed in Europe were Elmer Wright, who pitched for San Antonio, and Ordway Cisgen, who pitched for Utica.

Japanese pitcher Eiji Sawamura was killed in the war. During a

1934 exhibition he struck out in order Charlie Gehringer, Babe Ruth, Lou Gehrig and Jimmie Foxx.

Attendance. Major League *Attendance* slumped in 1942 and 1943, as many stars were still in the military. In 1944 and 1945 attendance was even worse, at levels not seen since the early Depression year of 1930. The lack of players and attendance forced a number of minor leagues to shut down for the duration. For example, the Texas League shut down for three seasons.

Wartime Jobs.

"It's all very strange. I work eight hours a day — and no [Johnny] Murphy to relieve me."—Yankee starting pitcher Lefty Gomez on his wartime factory job.

Donations/Benefit Games. Using a format devised by Paul A. Smith, a Columbia University mathematics professor, the Giants, Dodgers and Yankees played a three-sided *Benefit Game* to sell war bonds. It was attended by 50,000 fans.

The owners were at their winter meetings when the Japanese bombed Pearl Harbor. Judge Landis immediately pledged $25,000 for baseball equipment for servicemen. Another $25,000 was donated to the same fund in 1942. Baseball donated proceeds to the USO from the gate receipts of the 1942 World Series.

Latin Connection. Cuban players arrived in the United States during World War II with entertainment visas good for six months. They were required to register for the draft within 90 days of arrival to determine their draft status, but mandatory appeals strung out the process until after the end of the season — by that time the players were back in Cuba and could restart the process the following season.

In 1944 the Senators had 10 players on their roster who were from Latin America.

Manager Drafted. The first manager drafted into the military was 34-year-old Mel Ott, who was leading the Giants in April 1944 when he was called up.

Number of Players in the Military. By 1942 there were 119 Major League players in the service. By 1943 the total was 219. Another source reported that as of March 1943, 144 Major League players were in the military, the same as in all of World War I.

There are conflicting figures for all professional ballplayers in the service in 1944. One source reported that by late 1944 there were over 4,000 Major and minor league players in the service. Another reported that by April 1944 there were 340 Major Leaguers and 3,000 minor league players in the military. Another reported that of the 5,800 professional ballplayers in 1941, 5,400 were in the military in 1944. Another reported that by 1944 there were 4,076 minor league players in the service.

The effect on most teams was devastating. For example, in the 1943 World Series the Cardinals had four starters returning from the 1942 team and the Yankees had three. By 1944 the Yankees had lost all of their 1942 starters.

By the end of the war in 1945, there were 384 active or retired Major League players in the service. Discharges were processed rapidly, and only 22 were still in the service by 1946. One source reported that a total of 428 Major Leaguers served in the U.S. Armed Forces during World War II. Still other sources report that the total for the entire war was the 384 figure reported above.

No Charge. Servicemen usually were admitted free to ballgames. The Browns admitted 39,000 without charge in 1942 alone.

Prisoners of War.

"Italian war prisoners were treated to a look at baseball here [Ft. Meade, Md.] yesterday as the Philadelphia Athletics whipped Buffalo.... The Ities raked the field before the game, then sat along the sidelines with 10,000 GIs and enjoyed the contest."—The *Stars and Stripes* military newspaper.

Umpire Augie Donatelli was a POW, umpired softball after the war, and then began a 24-year National League umpiring career in 1958.

Phil Marchildon had been a pitcher for the A's before the war. The Canadian was a gunner in the Royal Canadian Air Force and was shot down on his 26th mission in 1944. He lost almost 40 pounds while living for 10 months on the typical rations for a POW in Germany — three slices of black bread a day. He returned to baseball in June 1945 for three appearances but was too weak to continue that year. His first appearance drew 35,000 fans and he pitched three innings and was awarded a $1,000 war bond. He returned to pitch regularly in 1946.

Talent Pool.

"All I can say is that we will have a large number of human beings at the training camp."—Dodger general manager Branch Rickey on the quality of the players in early 1944.

"Any resemblance between the Brooklyn Dodgers and a major league ball team seemed a case of myopia as the bums dropped two tilts to the Chicago Cubs…"—The *Stars and Stripes* military newspaper.

"The fat men against the tall men at the office picnic."—Sportswriter Frank Graham's description of the 1945 wartime World Series between the Tigers and Cubs.

"With most of the good players in the service, a collection of old men and children and men with one arm and seven dependents gathered regularly and battered around a dull spheroid, and this was called 'major league baseball' for four years."—Bill James in *The Bill James Historical Baseball Abstract* (1988).

One writer suggested that the pool of talent during the war was not as bad as assumed. Otherwise, he claims, why didn't the few stars who played through that era dominate the league: Mel Ott, Stan Hack, Joe Medwick and Lou Boudreau. Ott hit only .234 in 1943 and was well past his prime though only 34 years old.

Major League Baseball owners briefly considered pooling their players over concerns in 1944 that "there may not be enough 4-Fs and 17-year-olds to make for balanced leagues."

Bill James estimated that 40% of the Major Leaguers during the war years were qualified to be at that level of play. He bases the statistic on an analysis of how many wartime players lasted beyond the end of the war as compared to a later, non-war year.

One sign of the poor quality of play was a significant increase in the number of errors. Also, power numbers were down. For example, Nick Etten's 22 home runs for the Yankees in 1944 led the league. It was the lowest total since Babe Ruth tied Tilly Walker for the 1918 title with 11.

Another indicator was the performances of Johnny Dickshot and Tony Cuccinello. Even though they each hit over .300 in 1945, they were released after the season. Batting king Snuffy Stirnweiss hit .309 with 10 home runs in 1945, but never hit over .261 after that season.

Eddie Boland was a New York City sanitation worker who spent the summer of 1944 playing 19 games in the Senators outfield. He returned to his sanitation job because he did not want to jeopardize his pension.

Part-Time Players. In 1944 Denny Galehouse pitched almost exclusively on Sundays for the Browns when they were at home. He returned to his wartime factory job in another city the rest of the week.

Players Who Came Out of Retirement. Estel Crabtree had one kidney and was classified as 4-F. He had played from 1931 through 1933 before returning to the Major League to play for the Reds from 1941 through 1944.

Babe Herman was 42 when he played for the Dodgers in 1945, eight years after his retirement. He fell rounding first after singling in his first at-bat but managed to hit .265 in 37 games.

Ben Chapman had been an outfielder with the Yankees in the 1930s. He returned to go 5–3 as a pitcher with the Dodgers in 1944 and 3–3 with the Dodgers and Phillies in 1945.

After retiring in 1942, Jimmie Foxx returned to baseball for 15 games with the Cubs in 1944 and 89 games with the Phillies in 1945. He also pitched in nine games for the Phillies and won one (he had pitched in one game for the Red Sox in 1939).

Hod Lisenbee was 47 when he signed with the Reds and pitched in 31 games. He had not seen Major League action in nine years.

Umpire.

"Ex A.L. Umpire Finds Ball Field One Place He Need Not Take Orders."— *The Sporting News* on umpire Art Passarella, who was the first Major League umpire to go into the military during the war. He continued to umpire military games during his tour.

War Bonds. In addition to numerous wartime benefit games, baseball-related war bond drives were staged throughout the country. On June 8, 1943, the New York and Brooklyn chapters of the Baseball Writers Association staged an auction that raised $123,850,000 in war bond pledges. Each pledging organization was required to pledge consistent with the players' performance that season: $2,500 for each single, $5,000 per double, $7,500 for a triple and $10,000 per home run. Pitchers contributed with wins priced at $35,000 and shutouts at $50,000.

During some of the war years ballplayers and officials took 10% of their pay in war bonds.

All-Star Game Cancellation. Even though the war in Europe was over in May 1945, that season's All-Star Game was canceled because of heavy travel by troops returning home (or moving cross-country to join the Pacific front against Japan) that clogged the rail lines. Some sources reported that the lack of stars in the game at that time encouraged the owners to cancel the game, but that had not deterred them in prior years.

Military World Series. In 1945 the military World Series took place at about the same time as the Cubs/Tigers World Series in the States. Over 50,000 GIs filled Nurenberg Stadium in Germany to watch former National League pitcher Sam Nahem and Negro League star Leon Day lead the Overseas Invasion Service Expedition (OISE) all-stars to a five game victory over the 71st Infantry Division.

Star Tours. Major League players did not tour military sites until the 1944–1945 seasons. A few exhibition games were scheduled for 1943, but morale was still low because the war had not completely shifted in favor of the Allies. It was thought that the servicemen would resent the ballplayers, so the appearances were canceled. Another reason given was that the locations were still volatile and not safe for ballplayers. When the Major Leaguers began to tour, they went in groups to Europe, the Mediterranean, the Middle East, the Pacific, China, Burma and India.

Grantland Rice found that resentment of ballplayers by servicemen was not prevalent. He compared the attitude of servicemen in World War II versus World War I. In the earlier war there was significant resentment by servicemen, and Rice reported that as a result the sports section of the military newspaper was canceled. Not so in World War II: "There is no longer any resentment against those left behind, deferred for family or physical reasons. Our servicemen want baseball and football particularly carried on for their own interest, entertainment and relaxation. This not only goes for home consumption, but also for those overseas."

Returning Servicemen. Returning servicemen who had been Major League ballplayers when they left were entitled to at least 30 days on the club if it was during spring training and 15 days if it was during the season.

Exhibition. The Hall of Fame created an exhibit highlighting baseball's contribution to the war effort during World War II. The exhibition was on display from mid–1995 through 1996.

Books. Gary L. Bloomfield, *Duty, Honor, Victory: America's Athletes in World War II* (2004); Steven R. Bullock, *Playing for Their Nation* (2004); Craig Allen Cleve, *Hardball on the Home Front: Major League Replacement Players of World War II* (2004); Bill Gilbert, *They Also Served* (1992); Richard Goldstein, *Spartan Seasons* (1980); William B. Mead, *Even the Browns* (1978) (later republished as *Baseball Goes to War*).

Worst Teams See *Losing Teams*

George Wright (1847–1937)

Hall of Fame 1937

"I'd rather be Wright than President."— Wright.

Wright played professional baseball primarily as a shortstop from the 1860s through the early 1880s.

Wright was the brother of the more famous Harry Wright and was the key member of the 1869 ***Cincinnati Red Stockings***. He is credited with a number of innovations at shortstop where he played in the National Association for the Boston Red Stockings from 1871 through 1875. He led the club to four pennants in five seasons.

Wright was the first batter in the history of the National League in 1876. He batted .299 for the Boston Red Stockings that season and played two more years for the club before moving on to Providence in 1879. He batted .276 in 85 games while managing the club to a pennant. He was back with the Red Stockings in 1880 and 1881 but played only eight games. In 1882 he concluded his playing career with 46 games for Providence, batting .162. He finished with a lifetime National League average of .256.

Wright left baseball to devote full attention to his Wright & Ditson Sporting Goods Company and branched out into other sports. His son became a Davis Cup tennis star, which helped increase business. Wright was one of the first players elected to the Hall of Fame when he was selected by a special committee on 19th century stars in 1937. He was also a member of the tongue-in-cheek Mills Commission set up by Albert Spalding in 1907 to determine the ***Origins of Baseball***. He died in Boston in 1937.

Harry Wright (1835–1895)

Hall of Fame (VC) 1953

"Every magnate in the country is indebted to this man for the establishment of base ball as a business, and every patron for furnishing him with a systematic recreation. Every player is indebted to him for inaugurating an occupation by which he gains a livelihood, and the country at large for adding one more industry (for industry it is in one respect) to furnish employment."— *Sporting Life* in 1894 shortly before Wright's death.

"It was Harry Wright who truly dramatized the business potential of baseball by lifting the game from the shaded area of pseudo-professionalism at the close of the Civil War and elevating it to a commercial venture providing a high quality product played by professionals."— Ralph Andreano in *No Joy in Mudville* (1965).

"As a trainer and captain of a baseball nine … his high character, honesty of purpose, and aptitude in governing his men with kindness making him very successful."— Henry Chadwick.

Wright was a prominent player and manager from 1858 through 1893.

Harry Wright was born in England, and his father had been a famous English cricket player. Wright joined the New York Knickerbockers in 1858 before moving on to Cincinnati to live and work in and outside baseball.

He became a Cincinnati cricket teacher in 1866, but there was far less interest in the British sport after the war. He began focusing exclusively on baseball and helped form the professional Cincinnati Red Stockings, pitching, playing center field and managing the club. Wright hired East Coast players to fill out the Red Stockings roster, including his brother George from the Washington Nationals. After Cincinnati had enormous success in 1869 and 1870, Wright moved over to the Boston Red Stockings and managed the club for each of its five seasons in the National Association. The club won the pennant from 1872 through 1875. Wright batted .263 over those five seasons and played primarily in the outfield.

Wright managed the National League Boston Red Stockings from 1876 through 1880, and then moved over to manage Providence for two seasons. He led the Red Stockings to pennants in 1877 and 1878 and a second-place finish in 1879. Providence finished second and third under his leadership. He made one appearance as a player in both 1876 and 1877. He moved to the Phillies in 1884, where he remained as manager through the 1893 season, though he gave up the reins temporarily in 1890 when he lost his sight for a period of time. He died two years later. He managed for 18 Major League seasons, twice winning pennants.

When he died, the National League held a Harry Wright Day to raise funds for a monument and contributed additional monies when bad weather lowered the expected gate receipts. Despite his reputation as a *Father of Baseball*, Wright was not among those voted into the Baseball Hall of Fame at its inception in 1939.

Book. Christopher Devine, *Harry Wright: The Father of Professional Base Ball* (2004).

Wrigley Field (1914–)

"At a place like Wrigley Field, you quickly learn what baseball is all about. It is a comfortable place, built for baseball and nothing else, with the stands so close to the field that it seems fans are almost in the batting box … the creature comforts aren't always what they are in the new parks. Indeed, at Wrigley Field, the players claim there are rats running through the passageway they take to get to the field." — Glenn Dickey in *The Jock Empire* (1974).

Only the players change, as Wrigley Field's entrance sign has been the same almost since the ballpark opened.

"By all accounts, Wrigley Field was the most beautiful ballpark in the country. It was the last of the old National League stadiums not yet condemned to the wrecker's ball and the only one whose roof was unadorned by floodlights. Located in the heart of Chicago's North Side, it offered the feel of rustic serenity banked against the hard-muscled pull of the working-class streets. Its red brick walls were covered with ivy in the outfield, and in dead center field were steeply sloped tiers of old-fashioned bleachers." — Stanley Cohen in *A Magic Summer—The '69 Mets* (1988).

"Wrigley Field is the Peter Pan of ball parks; it has never grown up and it has never grown old." — E.M. Swift.

"I would play for half my salary if I could hit in this dump all the time." — Babe Ruth.

Origins. Wrigley Field was built originally to house the Chicago Whales of the 1914–1915 Federal League. Wrigley was designed by Zachary Taylor Davis, who patterned the park after New York's Polo Grounds. Davis previously had most of his experience building apartment buildings, but had designed and built Comiskey park four years earlier.

Value. In a 2002 study, the National Sports Law Institute of Marquette University School of Law estimated that Wrigley Field was worth $287 million.

Names. The ballpark was first known as North Side Ball Park when it opened in 1914 but soon after was called Weegham Park for Federal League Whales owner Charles Weegham. It was known as Whales Park in 1915. When the Federal League folded in 1916, part of the settlement included a sale of the National League Cubs to Weegham. The ballpark was known as Cubs Park from 1916 through 1925 but was sometimes referred to as Wrigley Field after William Wrigley, Jr., who bought a controlling interest in the club in 1918. During the mid–1920s it became known exclusively as Wrigley Field. For a short time later it was known as Wrigley's Seminary, in recognition of the site having once been used as a seminary. It was sometimes referred to as Wrigley's Dollhouse.

The smiling face of long-time broadcaster Harry Caray gazes across Waveland Avenue at Wrigley Field. Note the apartment roof seats to the right, overlooking the field.

First Whales Game. The Whales played their first game in the park on April 23, 1914, defeating Cincinnati 7–6 in 11 innings.

First Cubs Game. The Cubs played their first game in the park on April 20, 1916, defeating the Reds 7–6 in 11 innings.

World Series. It should be noted that when the Cubs last won the World Series, in 1918, they didn't win it in Wrigley Field. Because Comiskey Field was much larger, the Cubs played their World Series home games in the White Sox' home park.

Flags. After home games the club has long flown a blue flag with a white "W" for wins in center field above the scoreboard, or one with a blue "L" against a white background for losses.

Ivy.

"Oh sure, it's not historic Wrigley Field without the ivy growing on the walls. This is actually a sign of poor maintenance, but it causes baseball writers, who spend their entire lives in dingy press boxes where the only green organic thing they ever see is relish — to spurt little prose orgasms. Wow! Wall vegetation!"— Dave Barry.

The famous ivy on the outfield wall was planted in 1937 by Bill Veeck. He started with 350 Japanese bittersweet plants and 200 Boston ivy plants.

Bill Buckner once hit a ball that stuck in the ivy, and he was able to circle the bases for a home run. That would now be ruled a ground rule double unless the ball fell out.

Late in his career Ralph Kiner attempted to make a catch as he ran into the ivy. He leaped and stuck to the wall as if held by Velcro.

Capacity. Capacity originally was 14,000, but expanded to 18,000 for the 1915 season, 20,000 in 1923, and 38,396 in 1927. It fluctuated around that total into the 1990s, when its capacity was 38,710.

Dimensions. The park's dimensions from left to right field originally were 345–368–440–363–356. The most recent dimensions are 355–368–400–363–353.

Other Uses.

"Sgt. Torger Tokle won the Norge Ski Club jump in Chicago with a leap of only 89 feet. The slide was built into the second deck of the Wrigley Field ball park and wasn't long enough for the usual distance." — The *Stars and Stripes* military newspaper in 1944.

The NFL Chicago Bears, who played in the ballpark from 1921 (as the Staley's) through 1970, barely fit into the ballpark, as the corner of one end zone ended in one of the dugouts and the other was only 18 inches from the stands. The Chicago Cardinals and the Chicago Tigers also played in the ballpark.

Lights.

"Putting lights in Wrigley Field is like putting aluminum siding on the Sistine Chapel." — Columnist Roger Simon.

Lights for *Night Games* were to be installed in 1942, but World War II compelled the Wrigley family to donate the steel towers and lights to the government for the war effort. As a result, day games at Wrigley became sacred and lights were not installed until 1988. The first night game was played on August 9, 1988, after a rainout the night before.

The All-American Girls Professional Baseball League All-Star Game was played at night in July 1943 using temporary lights.

Scoreboard. The hand-operated scoreboard, the largest ever, was constructed in 1935 under the supervision of Bill Veeck. Veeck was a young executive with the club during an era when his father, Bill Veeck, Sr., ran the club. The scoreboard is 27 feet high and 75 feet wide. In 1982 an electronic message board was installed under the scoreboard in center field.

Damage. In July 2004 chunks of old concrete fell from the rafters, endangering fans. The first time it happened, a fist-sized chunk fell right next to a five-year-old fan. The club was ordered by the city to install netting that might catch the falling pieces. The club complied, but building inspectors were not satisfied, and they ordered a total overhaul following the season after almost shutting down the ballpark midseason.

Apartment View. In April 2002 the Cubs erected a green tennis wind screen on the left field fence to prevent rooftop viewing of the game from adjacent apartment buildings. One owner was selling 22 tickets at $113 apiece on Waveland Avenue and sued the Cubs. The combatants finally settled their lawsuit by the rooftop owners agreeing to pay a license fee to the Cubs for a set number of years.

Book. William Hartel, *A Day at the Park: In Celebration of Wrigley Field* (1994) (photographic essay); Mark Jacob, Stephen Green and Ernie Banks, *Wrigley Field: A Celebration of the Friendly Confines* (2002).

Though not a book, one of the most thorough recitations of Wrigley's history is found in the Wrigley Field Tour Narrative, provided to the author by Brian A. Bernardoni; who said that although he authored the notes, they are based on tour guide extraordinaire Ed Hartig, "who knows more about Cubs Baseball History and Wrigley Field than any human being should be allowed to."

Wrist Bands

Ken "Hawk" Harrelson is credited with popularizing wrist bands in the mid–1960s.

Writers See *Books* and *Sportswriters*

Early Wynn (1920–1999)

Hall of Fame 1972

"The space between the white lines: that's my office. That's where I conduct my business."— Wynn

Wynn pitched for 23 American League seasons between 1939 and 1963, winning exactly 300 games.

Born Early (NMI) "Gus" Wynn, Jr., signed a professional contract at 17 and pitched in three games for the Senators in 1939 at age 19. He was back up to stay in late 1941 and in 1943 he had his first good season, winning 18. After playing eight seasons for the mediocre Senators, Wynn was picked up by the Indians and owner Bill Veeck in 1949 and had his greatest success.

Pitching for the much stronger Indians of the 1950s, Wynn won 20 or more games four times for the club through 1957. In 1954 he led the league in wins and helped the Indians into the World Series against the Giants, but lost the one game he started.

After a mediocre season in 1957 he was traded to the White Sox. After another middling season in 1958, he led the league with 22 wins in 1959 as the White Sox won the pennant. In the World Series against the Dodgers he was 1–1 in the three games he started. He began to fade immediately, winning only 13 games in 1960 and eight in 1961. As 300 wins became a probability, he hung on long past his prime. He was cut in 1962 by the White Sox with 299 wins. He signed with the Indians in 1963 and won number 300 on July 13, 1963. He finished out the season with a total of 20 appearances (1–2 for the season) and retired.

Wynn had a 300–244 record over 23 seasons. He pitched 49 shutout and had 2,334 strikeouts to go with a 3.54 ERA. He was a good hitting pitcher with a .214 average, 17 home runs and 90 pinch hit appearances. He became a coach with the Indians and then the Twins before managing in the Minnesota farm system. He died in Florida in April 1999.

"**X** is the first
Of two x's in Foxx
Who was right behind Ruth
With his powerful soxx."
— Ogden Nash on Jimmie Foxx.

X-Rays

"I've had so many X-rays that my pitches might take on a subtle glow."— Pitcher Jim Palmer.

"I've been X-rayed so often I glow in the dark."— Dodger infielder Billy Grabarkewitz.

"I've had so many X-rays that my pitches might take on a subtle glow. It will be tough to pick up my ball. It will look like an opaque-type fog."— Pitcher Joe Magrane.

"The X-rays came back negative? All X-rays are negative."— A's broadcaster Lon Simmons.

"The doctors X-rayed my head and found nothing."— Supposedly said by Dizzy Dean after Tigers shortstop Billy Rogell hit him in the head with a thrown ball at second base during the 1934 World Series (see also *Injuries and Illness*—Head); though the actual headline in the newspaper was: "X-Ray Dean's Head; Find Nothing"

The first reported use of X-rays on a ballplayer occurred in 1896, to locate the source of a wrist problem of Louisville Colonels first baseman Peter Cassidy. It was determined that he had a bone fragment that was subsequently removed.

After Sammy Sosa was caught using a corked bat in early 2003, the Hall of Fame X-rayed every bat of his that it had. The bats passed inspection.

"**Y** is for Young
The Magnificent Cy;
People batted against him,
But I never knew why."
— Ogden Nash on Cy Young.

Yankee Stadium

"The House That Ruth Built"— Sportswriter Fred Lieb coined the phrase in 1923, the ballpark's first year of operation.

Origins. In 1913 Yankees owner Frank Farrell signed a lease for the club to occupy the Polo Grounds as tenants of the Giants. The Yankees' home, Hilltop Park, located at Amsterdam Avenue and 168th Street, had become too run down.

The Yankees contemplated building a new stadium as early as 1915 when Jacob Ruppert and Cap Huston took control of the team. They were uncomfortable with a year-to-year lease with the Giants due to the possibility of a high rent increase. Ruppert offered to take over a 50% ownership interest in the Polo Grounds, but when the Giants did not respond, he commissioned plans for Yankee Stadium. Some sources reported that the Giants no longer wanted the Yankees as tenants when they outdrew the Giants by over 350,000 fans in 1921. Giants manager John McGraw purportedly demanded that owner Horace Stoneham evict the Yankees even though the lease by then had two more years to run.

Bill Veeck, Jr., later discovered a diary at Comiskey Park indicating that Ban Johnson tried to persuade the Giants to cancel the lease. He wanted to assume the lease himself in the name of the American League so that he could force out Ruppert and Huston. Ruppert was Johnson's leading opponent due to player ownership disputes. In return, Johnson would have let the Giants pick a new third member of the National Commission.

On February 5, 1921, Ruppert announced that he had purchased 10 acres across from the Harlem River. The site was at 161st Street and River Avenue in the Bronx, less than one mile from the Polo Grounds. The Yankees bought the land for approximately $600,000 from the Astor estate, owned by William Waldorf.

The ballpark was designed by the Osborn Engineering Company, the foremost ballpark engineers of the era. Ruppert consulted with the company on designing a short right field fence to accommodate his new slugger, Babe Ruth.

The ballpark was built in 185 working days (or 284 days in some sources) at a cost of $2.5 million ($3.2 million in other sources). The Yankees became the last then-existing team to build a modern concrete and steel stadium. It was the first triple-decked facility and was the largest in baseball at the time, seating approximately 65,000 (67,224 in some sources). As a result it was the first to be called a "stadium." It was built with 950,000 board feet of Pacific Coast Fir brought to New York through the Panama Canal. It was the last privately built ballpark until Dodger Stadium was completed in 1962.

First Game.

"I'd give a year of my life if I can hit a home run in the first game in this new park."—Babe Ruth.

John Philip Sousa's Seventh Regiment Band led the Opening Day ceremonies for the first game in Yankee Stadium on April 18, 1923. Governor Al Smith threw out the first ball and Babe Ruth hit the first home run in the ballpark. The ball was sold at auction in November 1998 for $126,500. Marc Scala found the ball in the attic of his grandmother's house, and after authentication the bid was $110,000 (the auction house commission made the price higher).

Although the announced attendance was 74,217, the Yankees later admitted that they had 60,000 in the ballpark. New York beat Boston 4–1, as Ruth hit three home runs.

Capacity. Yankee Stadium's original capacity was 58,000 (65,000 and 67,545 in other sources). The park's largest crowd was on September 9, 1928, when 85,265 (many SRO) watched the Yankees play the A's. Other sources report that it was 86,533 for a doubleheader against the Red Sox on May 30, 1938.

The first game after the renovation was on April 15, 1976, with an announced capacity attendance of 57,545 during a 4–1 win over the Twins. One source reported the largest attendance under the new configuration was 56,821 on October 14, 1976, against the Royals.

The largest crowd in Yankee Stadium for any type of event was the 123,707 that attended a Jehovah's Witness convention in 1958.

Dimensions. The original dimensions from left to right field were 280–460–295. The famous 296-foot figure for right field did not exist until 1930, at least according to Philip J. Lowry in *Green Cathedrals* (1992). After a remodeling in 1974–1975, the ballpark's dimensions from left to right field were adjusted to 312–417–310.

Home Runs. See *Home Runs—Longest.*

Anniversary. The Yankees celebrated their silver anniversary in Yankee Stadium on June 13, 1948, which featured Babe Ruth's farewell in front of 49,641 fans. Ruth died two months later on August 16, 1948.

Milestone. When the Marlins beat the Yankees in Game 6 of the 2003 World Series, it was the 100th World Series game played at Yankee Stadium.

Land. Owner Dan Topping sold the land underneath the stadium to the nonprofit Knights of Columbus so he would not be required to pay property taxes. The Knights then leased the ground and stadium back to the Yankees, but the City of New York bought the land in 1971 and entered into a new lease with the club.

Monuments. Lou Gehrig's center field plaque was installed on July 6, 1941. He had died four days earlier during Joe DiMaggio's 56-game hitting streak. The three original monuments featured Gehrig, Babe Ruth and Miller Huggins. The full list of baseball people with monuments or plaques (doesn't include Pope John Paul II):

Miller Huggins	Joe McCarthy
Casey Stengel	Lefty Gomez
Thurman Munson	Whitey Ford
Jacob Ruppert	Elston Howard
Lou Gehrig	Bill Dickey
Roger Maris	Phil Rizzuto
Babe Ruth	Yogi Berra
Ed Barrow	Billy Martin
Joe DiMaggio	Allie Reynolds
Mickey Mantle	

The Maris plaque reported that he was a "courageous" [sic] player and that Howard was a true "gentleman" [sic]. They were replaced at the engraver's expense. Placed among the baseball monuments are one each for Pope Paul VI and Pope John Paul II, both of whom performed a mass at the ballpark.

Until the 1970s renovation, the monuments were in play in the outfield.

Most Home Runs. Mickey Mantle hit 266 home runs in Yankee Stadium. Babe Ruth hit 259 at the ballpark and another 69 at the Polo Grounds, which was his home park from 1920 through 1922.

First Negro League Game. The first Negro League game played at Yankee Stadium was on July 10, 1930.

Tenant. The New York Giants football team of the NFL became a tenant in 1956.

Remodeling. In 1946 the ballpark underwent a $600,000 facelift that included arc lights. The first *Night Game* was played on May 28, 1946.

In 1971 the City purchased the land from the Knights of Columbus and the stadium from Rice University in Texas, and then negotiated a 30-year lease with the Yankees. John William Cox, a Chicago banker who bought Yankee Stadium in 1957, had sold

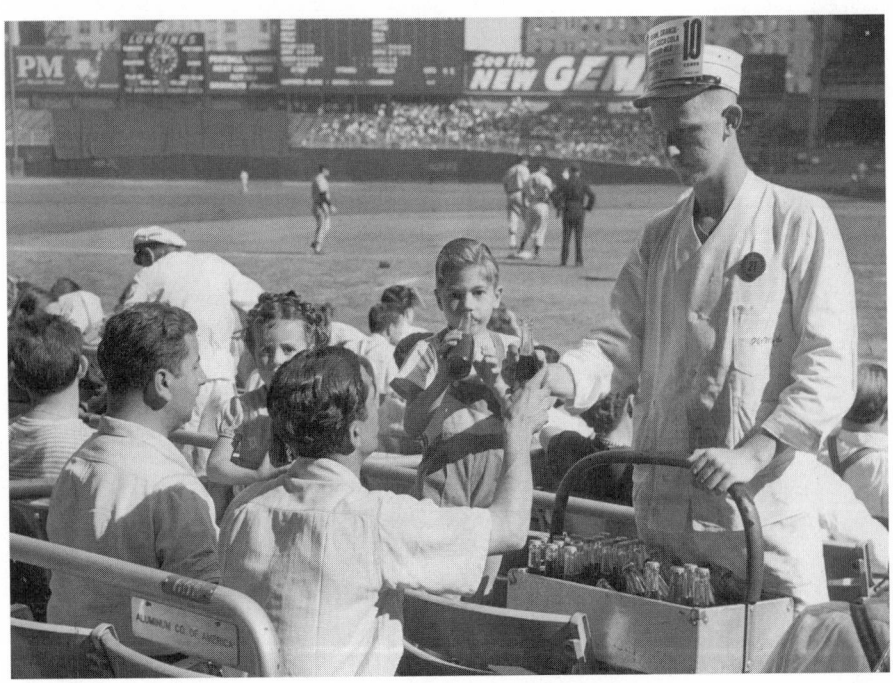

A Coca-Cola vendor at Yankee Stadium in 1956.

the land to the Knights of Columbus and made the stadium a gift to Rice on March 2, 1971,

In 1972 the club threatened to move to New Jersey for its games if the city would not pay for refurbishment. In response, a 1974–1975 remodeling was budgeted to cost $24 million but ended up costing the city $100 million ($110 million in some sources). When the city voted to spend the money, on the same day the New York City Board of Education voted to cancel contracts with 3,500 teachers for lack of funding.

The frieze façade along the roof— the signature element of the old Yankee Stadium — was made of copper and turned green as it aged. The grandstand seats were also green. In 1961 the Yankees painted the frieze and exterior of the stadium white and the seats blue, a color pattern maintained in the 1973 renovation.

September 30, 1973, was the date of the last game in the ball-park before the two-year remodeling. The day was marked by the postgame resignation of Ralph Houk. The game was preceded by a ceremony in which Claire (Mrs. Babe) Ruth received home plate and Mrs. Lou Gehrig received first base. The Yankees played in Shea Stadium during the remodeling, returning to Yankee Stadium on April 15, 1976. The featured guest at the game was Bob Shawkey, who had pitched the first game for the Yankees in the ballpark 53 years earlier. The Yankees beat the Twins 11–4 in front of a capacity crowd of 57,545.

In 1995 the Yankees lost a lawsuit against an architectural firm that was never paid for its 1984 blueprints for luxury boxes in Yankee Stadium that were not built. Eighteen luxury boxes eventually were built.

In April 1998 a 500-pound beam fell before a game against the Angels, forcing postponement of a few games (See *Postponed Games*).

New Ballpark.

"Tradition is great. History is important. The monuments are neat. But more folks would go to see the Yankees, and enjoy them, if they played somewhere else. Almost anywhere else. It probably is time now for the traditionalists and historians to realize that this game is just about over. Progress has won out again."— John Heyman of *Newsday*.

The Yankee Stadium lease expired in 2002 and the Yankees announced in the mid–1990s that they were looking into the possibility of a new stadium. There were discussions regarding a domed, multi-sport stadium on the West Side of Manhattan that would cost $1 billion. Also considered was a $770 million refurbishment of Yankee Stadium. Despite all the discussions, the lease was renegotiated and the Yankees remained there through 2004.

The Yankees indicated in mid–2004 that they wanted to build a $750 million stadium across the street from Yankee Stadium.

Book. Joseph Durso, *Fifty Years of Drama* (1974); Ray Robinson, Christopher Jennison, Chris Jennison, *Yankee Stadium: Drama, Glamour, and Glory* (2004); Neil J. Sullivan, *The Diamond in the Bronx* (2001).

Carl Yastrzemski (1939–)

Hall of Fame 1989

"He has lasted so long because he has a small center of gravity. He's compact, not real vulnerable. It could be the scotch, too. It numbs the pain."— Bill Lee in *The Wrong Stuff*, with Dick Lally (1984).

"I love the game. I love the competition. But I never had any fun. I never enjoyed it. All hard work all the time."— Yastrzemski reflecting on his career during his last season.

Yastrzemski played 23 seasons for the Red Sox between 1961 and 1983, batting .285 and hitting 452 home runs.

New York-born Carl Michael Yastrzemski signed with the Red Sox for $100,000 in 1959 after playing shortstop at Notre Dame University. He arrived in the Major Leagues in 1961 and immediately became the club's new left fielder, replacing the retired Ted Williams. The Red Sox were a poor club in 1963, but "Yaz" led the league in hitting with a .321 average.

In 1966 the club finished ninth and Yastrzemski had a mediocre season. In 1967 the Red Sox won the pennant, and Yastrzemski won the Triple Crown and the MVP Award with a .326 average, 44 home runs and 121 RBIs. He batted .400 in the World Series and hit three home runs, but the Red Sox lost in seven games to the Cardinals.

He repeated as batting champion in 1968, though with the lowest winning average ever at .301. He hit 40 home runs in both 1969 and 1970, but then his production began to slip. Nevertheless, he remained a steady performer throughout the decade. By 1974 he was the club's primary first baseman, and in 1975 [world series season]. He returned to the outfield for a full season in 1977 and batted .296 with 28 home runs. In 1978 he hit a key home run off Ron Guidry in the one-game play-off won by the Yankees.

Yastrzemski was mainly a designated hitter in 1979 as he reached age 40. He played full seasons as a designated hitter with occasional play at first base and the outfield until his retirement after the 1983 season. He finished with a lifetime .285 average, second all-time in games played, third in at-bats, ninth in RBIs, sixth in doubles, and sixth in hits with 3,419. Known for his defensive play off the Green Monster in Fenway Park, Yastrzemski won seven Gold Glove Awards and led the league in outfield assists during each of his 12 full seasons in left field.

After he retired, he worked briefly as a sportscaster, tried to become a minority owner of the Red Sox, and bought a share of Ann's Boston Brownie Company and became a spokesman for Kahn's meat products.

Books. Carl Yastrzemski and Gerald Eskenazi, *Baseball, The Wall, and Me* (1990); Carl Yastrzemski and Al Hirshberg, *Yaz* (1968).

Tom Yawkey (1903–1976)

Hall of Fame (VC) 1980

"I want to own the Red Sox until the day I die; then I'll decide what to do with them."— Yawkey on suggestions that he make provisions for an orderly succession of ownership of the team before he died.

Yawkey was the long-time owner of the Boston Red Sox.

Thomas Yawkey came from a wealthy background as the nephew and foster son of the former owner of the Detroit Tigers. After attending Yale, Yawkey inherited several million dollars at age 30 and bought the *Boston Red Sox* in 1933. Yawkey hired his long-time friend, Hall of Famer Eddie Collins, to be the general manager and bring respectability to the club. Yawkey spent lavishly but always had mixed results. He bought stars Joe Cronin, Lefty Grove and Jimmie Foxx, paid his players well (see also *Trades and Player Sales*), and spent heavily to refurbish *Fenway Park*.

Despite the perennial spending spree, the Red Sox won only three pennants for Yawkey, in 1946, 1967 and 1975. Each time they lost in the World Series in heartbreaking fashion. His wife Jean took over the club at his death in 1976, and he was elected to the Hall of Fame in 1980 on the strength of his popularity rather than his baseball acumen.

Cy Young (1867–1955)

Hall of Fame 1937

"1. Pitchers like poets are born, not made.

2. Cultivate good habits: Let liquor severely alone, fight shy of cigarettes, and be moderate in indulgence of tobacco, coffee, and tea…. A player should try to get along without any stimulants at all: Water, pure cool water is good enough for any man.

3. A man who is not willing to work from dewy morn until weary eve should not think about becoming a pitcher.

4. Learn to be patient and cool. These traits can be cultivated.

5. Take the slumps that come your way, ride over them, and look forward.

6. Until you can put the ball over the plan whenever you choose, you have not acquired the command necessary to make a first-class pitcher. Therefore, start in to acquire command."—Young's 1908 "Rules for Pitching Success."

Young won an astounding 511 games for five different clubs over 22 seasons from 1890 through 1911.

Denton True "Cy" Young was born in eastern Ohio and made his Major League debut in 1890 for the Cleveland Spiders. In his last game before being sold to the Spiders, he pitched a no-hitter and struck out 18 for Canton against McKeesport, Pennsylvania.

Young spent the first nine years of his Major League career with Cleveland before the club was transferred in its entirety to St. Louis in 1899. In 1901 he signed with the Boston Puritans (Red Sox) of the new American League, where he played for eight seasons before being traded to the Indians in 1909. In 1911 he pitched in seven games for the Indians early in the season and then spent his last few games with the Braves in the National League.

According to one source, he retired after 22 seasons not because his arm went bad, but because his big gut would not let him field bunts. He returned to his farm in Peoli, Ohio, where he worked until his death.

Young won a record 511 games, including 20 or more almost for 14 straight seasons (19–19 in 1900). He also won more than 200 games in each league. He won 30 or more games five times and pitched 76 shutouts, fourth all-time. He had three no-hitters, one of which was a perfect game. He completed 750 games and pitched 7,356 innings, both Major League records. His best season was 1892, when he won 36 games, had a winning percentage of .750 and an ERA of 1.93.

He was honored in 1948 on his 80th birthday when Indians owner Bill Veeck staged a celebration at which Young received a new car. He died of a heart attack in 1955 at age 88.

Book. Ralph Romig, *Cy Young: Baseball's Legendary Giant* (1964).

Nicholas Young (1840–1916)

Young was *National League President* from 1884 through 1902.

Youngest Players

"Well, son, I think you've had enough."—Reds manager Bill McKechnie to pitcher Joe Nuxhall after his Major League debut in which he gave up two hits and five walks in two-thirds of an inning. Nuxhall was a 6'2" junior high school student on June 10, 1944, when he pitched for the Reds at age 15 years, 316 days. He became the youngest player in Major League history after signing a contract with the club in April of that year.

Even though Nuxhall began inauspiciously, he was the South-ern Association MVP in 1944 and returned to the Major Leagues in 1952 to resume his 16-year Major League career. His one-game experience is recounted in Bob Fulton's essay, "Trip to the Big Leagues," in *The Ol' Ball Game* (1990).

According to many sources, Mel Ott was 16 years old when he first played for the New York Giants. However, he was born in March 1909 and played his first season in 1926, which made him 17. He sat on the bench with manager John McGraw while still 16.

On September 6, 1943, Carl A. Scheib set the American League record when he pitched for the A's at 16 years, 248 days. He allowed two hits in two-thirds of an inning. He made five more relief appearances that year and was 45–65 over 11 seasons through 1954.

Cass Michaels appeared in two games for the White Sox at third base in August 1943 at age 17. He lasted until 1954, compiling over 500 RBIs and a .262 lifetime average in 1,288 games.

Since 1900 the youngest pitcher to start a game was Jim Derrington, a White Sox bonus baby. He started on the last day of the 1956 season, losing 7–6. He was 16 years, 10 months. He singled, becoming the youngest player to get a hit in the American League.

Johnny Lush was the youngest everyday player of the early 20th century when he played first base and pitched at age 18 in 1904 for the Phillies. He batted .276 in 369 at-bats and compiled an 0–6 record as a pitcher.

Tommy Brown was a Dodger infielder during World War II at 16 years, 8 months. He debuted on August 3, 1944. He fielded his first ball and threw it 20 feet over the 6'6" first baseman and into the stands. He was a regular in the lineup for the balance of the season, hitting .146. He is the youngest player ever to hit a home run, doing so the next year at age 17 against the Pirates.

Ed Kirkpatrick made his Major League debut at 17 in 1962 for the Angels. He lasted 15 years with a lifetime .238 average.

Lew Krausse of the A's was two weeks out of high school when he shut out the Angels 4–0 on a three-hitter in his first start on June 16, 1961. He was signed by his father, an A's scout, for $125,000 earlier that month. He was sent down to the minors after 12 games but made it back for a few games the following season. Though he bounced back to the minor leagues a few times, he lasted in the Major Leagues through 1974.

Ed Kranepool signed with the Mets for $85,000 straight out of high school at age 17. He did not play much during his first season in 1962, prompting Casey Stengel to respond sarcastically to critics: "Listen. He's only 17 and he runs like he's 30."

On June 23, 1978, 18-year-old Blue Jays catcher Brian Milner started and went 1-for-4, becoming the youngest American Leaguer since Kirkpatrick. Alex Rodriguez was the next, at age 19 (19 days shy of 20) when he debuted on July 8, 1994.

Pitching Match-Up. On September 13, 1936, Bob Feller of the Indians faced Randy Gumpert of the A's. Both were 18, making it the youngest pitching match-up in Major League history.

Minor Leagues. In 1943, 15-year-old Bill Sarni played sporadically for the Los Angeles Angels in the Pacific Coast League.

On July 19, 1952, 12-year-old Joe Louis Reliford of Georgia became the youngest professional baseball player. The batboy pinch-hit for the Class D Fitzgerald (Ga.) Pioneers. He hit a sharp line drive and was barely thrown out at first base.

In August 1993 four-year-old Kyle Carnaroli, age 4, was set to play right field for at least an inning for the Pocatello Posse of the Pioneer League. The 3'6", 50-pounder had won a contest, but at the last minute the National Association of Professional Baseball Leagues ruled that he was ineligible.

Batting Leader. Al Kaline was the youngest batting leader when he hit .340 for the Tigers in 1955. He was 20 years, 280 days. In

1941 Dodger Pete Reiser led the National League with a .343 average at age 22 years, 114 days.

Pitching Leaders. There have been no 20th century 20-game winners among pitchers who have not reached their 20th birthday. The closest: Wally Bunker, who won 19 games at age 19 in 1964; Bob Feller, who won 17 games at age 19 in 1939; and Dwight Gooden, who won 17 games at age 19 in 1984 (Gooden was 24–4 with a 1.53 ERA at age 20 in 1985).

In 1890 Amos Rusie won 29 games for the Giants at age 18.

Willie McGill won 20 games for the Brown Stockings in 1891 at age 17.

Shutouts/Youngest Pitcher. On June 3, 1891, 17-year-old Willie McGill pitched an 11–0 shutout for St. Louis against Baltimore in the American Association.

World Series. Fred Lindstrom became the youngest player to appear in a World Series game when he played for the Giants in 1924 at age 18 years, 10 months, 13 days.

Most Games Played. Rusty Staub played in 150 games at age 19, the most by a teenager in a season.

Prodigy. Joe Cronin was a Most Valuable Player at age 24, manager at 27, general manager at 42 and president of the American League at 53.

Modern Signing Age. Players are now eligible to sign professional contracts only after turning 17.

Ross Youngs (1897–1927)

Hall of Fame (VC) 1972

"He was the hardest-running, devil-may-care guy I ever saw—the best at throwing those savage cross-blocks to break up a double play."—Frankie Frisch.

"We're not playing for marbles."—Youngs after sliding hard into Babe Pinelli.

"It was Ross Youngs, the man John McGraw called the best outfielder the Giants ever had."—Negro League star pitcher Smokey Joe Williams, recalling Youngs in a game Williams pitched against the Giants in 1917.

Young starred in right field in the 1920s for the Giants before suffering a fatal kidney disease.

A native Texan, the diminutive (5'8", 162 lbs.) right fielder was a star for the Giants from 1918 through 1925. He batted a lifetime .322, with highs of .351 in 1920 and .356 in 1924. He was one of the top outfielders in the National League, and manager John McGraw called him his best outfielder ever.

Youngs was accused of knowing about an attempt to fix a 1924 game but denied the charges and was acquitted. In 1925 he hit only .264 and was diagnosed with Bright's Disease the following spring. He struggled through the 1926 season with the progressive kidney disease, hitting .306 in 95 games. He died in October of the following year at age 30.

Robin Yount (1955–)

Hall of Fame 1999

"How did a lanky, baby-faced kid from California transform himself from exuberant batboy to a major-leaguer and, ultimately, a Hall of Fame hero? The people who knew him as a child believe it was a combination of things: environment; family support; solid coaching; the important influence of older brother Larry, who played professionally with the Houston organization; a burning desire to succeed; and, perhaps more than anything else, incredible natural ability."—Drew Olson of the *Milwaukee Journal Sentinel.*

Yount was one of the Major League's most versatile infielders and outfielders over his 20-year career, all with the Brewers, between 1974 and 1993.

Drafted in the first round out of Taft High School in Los Angeles by the Brewers in 1973, Robin R (no middle name) Yount was an everyday Major League shortstop by the age of 18, making his debut Opening Day 1974 after playing 64 games in the New York-Penn League the previous fall. In his second year Yount hinted at his offensive potential, hitting .267 with 28 doubles. By 1977 he had raised his average to .288. In 1980 he led the league with 49 doubles, scored 121 runs and hit .293. In 1981, a split season due to the players strike, the Brewers won the second half division title but lost in the playoffs to the Yankees. For the short season, Yount led league shortstops in fielding.

Yount had the most successful year of his career in 1982. The Brewers won the pennant and Yount was named MVP. In one of the finest seasons ever by an American League shortstop, Yount scored 129 runs with 210 hits, 29 home runs and 114 RBIs, all career best marks. He led the league in hits, doubles, total bases and slugging. He lost the batting title by a fraction, hitting .3307 to Willie Wilson's .3316.

In a seven-game World Series loss to the Cardinals, Yount hit .417 with two four-hit games. It was his last postseason performance, as the Brewers were generally mediocre for the rest of his career. Yount's performance, however, did not waver. In 1983 he hit .308 with 42 doubles and a league-leading 10 triples. In 1985 he moved to centerfield. Beginning in 1986 he hit over .300 four consecutive seasons. In 1989 Yount won his second MVP, becoming the only player to win the award at both shortstop and centerfield. For the season he hit .318 with 21 home runs, 103 RBI and 101 runs. On September 9, 1992, Yount recorded his 3,000th hit against the Indians.

Yount retired after the 1993 season with a .285 lifetime average, 3,142 hits, 1,632 runs scored and 1,406 RBIs. He is 13th all time with 583 doubles. Yount was elected to the Hall of Fame in 1999, his first year of eligibility. In 2002 he joined the Diamondbacks as a batting coach.

Book. S. Cameron, *Robin Yount* (1994).

Youth Baseball

"It appearing that a play at present much practised by the smaller boys among the students and by the grammar Scholars with balls and sticks in the back common of the College is in itself low and unbecoming gentlemen Students, and in as much as it is an exercise attended with great danger to the health by sudden and alternate heats and colds and as it tends by accidents almost unavoidable in that play to disfiguring and maiming those who are engaged in it for whose health and safety as well as improvement in Study as far as depends on our exertion we are accountable to their Parents and liable to be severely blamed by them.... Therefore the faculty think it incumbent on them to prohibit both the Students & grammar Scholars from using the play aforesaid."—A college administrator's 1787 warning against baseball for younger players.

"In me younger days 't was not considered rayspictasble f'r to be an athlete. An athlete was always a man that was not sthrong enough f'r wurruk. Franctions dhruv him fr'm school an' th' vagrancy laws dhruv him to baseball."—Finley Peter Dunne in *Mr. Dooley's Opinions* (1910).

"He's hitting .450. Of course, everybody is hitting .450."

Braves center fielder Marquis Grissom on his son D'Monte, who was playing T-ball at the age of 4.

See *Little League Baseball* and other youth leagues (including *Babe Ruth League* and *Pony League*).

Return to Baseball. Inner-city black youth began abandoning baseball for other sports in the 1980s. Major League Baseball responded in 1990 by supporting the RBI Program—"Reviving Baseball in the Inner Cities" (also called "Return Baseball to..."). The program began in South-Central Los Angeles, then New York and Houston, and then spread quickly to St. Louis and Atlanta. It provides equipment and playing areas to stimulate interest in baseball. The program was conceived by Florida Marlins scout and former Cubs scout John Young with the help of Major League Baseball and the Los Angeles Sports Council.

In 1993 the RBI World Series, sponsored by Major League Baseball and the Sporting Goods Manufacturers Association, featured teams from Atlanta, Boston, Cleveland, Kansas City, Los Angeles, St. Louis, Miami, Newark, New York, Richmond, Philadelphia and San Juan, Puerto Rico.

By 1995 there were 10,000 players in 47 cities. RBI's third annual World Series was held in 1995, with teams from the U.S., Puerto Rico, Taiwan and Czechoslovakia. The 1995 tournament also featured a girls' softball division for the first time.

By 1997 the program was active in almost 70 cities involving 300,000 boys and girls between the ages of 13 and 18. Gary Sheffield contributed over $25,000 to the RBI program based on the number of his doubles, triples and home runs. By 2003 apparently the numbers had dropped, as the organization announced that it had 120,000 players in 185 cities worldwide.

Former Major League pitcher Jim "Mudcat" Grant established a foundation to promote baseball among inner city youth, using his book, *The Twelve Black Aces*, as a springboard for his work. The books covers the best dozen African-American pitchers in Major League history.

Book. A realistic portrayal of an inner-city effort to reestablish youth baseball in Chicago is Daniel Coyle's *Hard Ball: A Season in the Projects* (1994).

Members of the 2004 Laguna Niguel (CA) Little League 11-year-old All-Star team perform some extracurricular activities after being eliminated from the District 55 All-Star Tournament. Apparently, kids take a loss less seriously than adults! Bottom, from left: Matt McCreadie, Collin Gallagher, Christian Knauer, Nick Stavert, Brandon Voss; second row, from left: Ryan Richards, Nick Ahrold, Mark Wilson, Eric Hsieh; third row: Clay Williamson, Nick O'Brien; top: Tyler Craft.

"Z is for Zenith,
The summit of fame.
These men are up there,
These men are the game."
— Ogden Nash.

Index

The index contains references to every person, place, team and topic identified in the text, including every author or other person mentioned in quotations and in book lists. It includes every magazine, newspaper and most books identified in the main text, except those in book lists. The speakers of quotations cited in the text are indexed but not the sources in which the quotations originally appeared.

The index entries for many of the key figures in baseball history, as well as other key topics, have subentries. Entries under team names refer only to the main history of that team and 19th century references to it. Narrow-topic references involving teams are provided three ways: by finding a person's name linked to that team; by finding a topic in the index which is known to relate to that team; or by using the alphabetical arrangement of the main text for a particular topic (e.g., looking at **Base on Balls** records will yield the Boston Red Sox for most received in a season by a team).

For a large topic with many subheadings (e.g., **World Series**), the first page numbers given in the index are for the primary entry on that topic. Topics that appear as subentries in the text (e.g., **Broken Bats** under **Bats**) do not generally appear as index entries.

Numbers in boldface refer to pages with photographs.